(S., S. & W.) Commercial Law, 4th Ed. ACB—1

American Casebook Series
Hornbook Series and Basic Legal Texts
Nutshell Series

of

WEST PUBLISHING COMPANY
P.O. Box 64526
St. Paul, Minnesota 55164–0526

ACCOUNTING

Faris' Accounting and Law in a Nutshell, 377 pages, 1984 (Text)

Fiflis, Kripke and Foster's Teaching Materials on Accounting for Business Lawyers, 3rd Ed., 838 pages, 1984 (Casebook)

Siegel and Siegel's Accounting and Financial Disclosure: A Guide to Basic Concepts, 259 pages, 1983 (Text)

ADMINISTRATIVE LAW

Davis' Cases, Text and Problems on Administrative Law, 6th Ed., 683 pages, 1977 (Casebook)

Gellhorn and Boyer's Administrative Law and Process in a Nutshell, 2nd Ed., 445 pages, 1981 (Text)

Mashaw and Merrill's Cases and Materials on Administrative Law–The American Public Law System, 2nd Ed., 976 pages, 1985 (Casebook)

Robinson, Gellhorn and Bruff's The Administrative Process, 3rd Ed., 978 pages, 1986 (Casebook)

ADMIRALTY

Healy and Sharpe's Cases and Materials on Admiralty, 2nd Ed., 876 pages, 1986 (Casebook)

Maraist's Admiralty in a Nutshell, 390 pages, 1983 (Text)

Schoenbaum's Hornbook on Admiralty and Maritime Law, Student Ed., about 675 pages, 1987 (Text)

Sohn and Gustafson's Law of the Sea in a Nutshell, 264 pages, 1984 (Text)

AGENCY—PARTNERSHIP

Fessler's Alternatives to Incorporation for Persons in Quest of Profit, 2nd Ed., 326 pages, 1986 (Casebook)

AGENCY—PARTNERSHIP—Cont'd

Henn's Cases and Materials on Agency, Partnership and Other Unincorporated Business Enterprises, 2nd Ed., 733 pages, 1985 (Casebook)

Reuschlein and Gregory's Hornbook on the Law of Agency and Partnership, 625 pages, 1979, with 1981 pocket part (Text)

Selected Corporation and Partnership Statutes and Forms, about 550 pages, 1987

Steffen and Kerr's Cases and Materials on Agency-Partnership, 4th Ed., 859 pages, 1980 (Casebook)

Steffen's Agency-Partnership in a Nutshell, 364 pages, 1977 (Text)

AGRICULTURAL LAW

Meyer, Pedersen, Thorson and Davidson's Agricultural Law: Cases and Materials, 931 pages, 1985 (Casebook)

ALTERNATIVE DISPUTE RESOLUTION

Kanowitz' Cases and Materials on Alternative Dispute Resolution, 1024 pages, 1986 (Casebook)

Riskin and Westbrook's Dispute Resolution and Lawyers, about 525 pages, 1987 (Coursebook)

Teple and Moberly's Arbitration and Conflict Resolution, (The Labor Law Group), 614 pages, 1979 (Casebook)

AMERICAN INDIAN LAW

Canby's American Indian Law in a Nutshell, 288 pages, 1981 (Text)

Getches and Wilkinson's Cases on Federal Indian Law, 2nd Ed., 880 pages, 1986 (Casebook)

ANTITRUST LAW

Gellhorn's Antitrust Law and Economics in a Nutshell, 3rd Ed., 472 pages, 1986 (Text)

List current as of June, 1987

ANTITRUST LAW—Cont'd

Gifford and Raskind's Cases and Materials on Antitrust, 694 pages, 1983 with 1985 Supplement (Casebook)

Hovenkamp's Hornbook on Economics and Federal Antitrust Law, Student Ed., 414 pages, 1985 (Text)

Oppenheim, Weston and McCarthy's Cases and Comments on Federal Antitrust Laws, 4th Ed., 1168 pages, 1981 with 1985 Supplement (Casebook)

Posner and Easterbrook's Cases and Economic Notes on Antitrust, 2nd Ed., 1077 pages, 1981, with 1984–85 Supplement (Casebook)

Sullivan's Hornbook of the Law of Antitrust, 886 pages, 1977 (Text)

See also Regulated Industries, Trade Regulation

ART LAW

DuBoff's Art Law in a Nutshell, 335 pages, 1984 (Text)

BANKING LAW

Lovett's Banking and Financial Institutions in a Nutshell, 409 pages, 1984 (Text)

Symons and White's Teaching Materials on Banking Law, 2nd Ed., 993 pages, 1984, with 1987 Supplement (Casebook)

BUSINESS PLANNING

Painter's Problems and Materials in Business Planning, 2nd Ed., 1008 pages, 1984 with 1987 Supplement (Casebook)

Selected Securities and Business Planning Statutes, Rules and Forms, about 475 pages, 1987

CIVIL PROCEDURE

Casad's Res Judicata in a Nutshell, 310 pages, 1976 (text)

Cound, Friedenthal, Miller and Sexton's Cases and Materials on Civil Procedure, 4th Ed., 1202 pages, 1985 with 1987 Supplement (Casebook)

Ehrenzweig, Louisell and Hazard's Jurisdiction in a Nutshell, 4th Ed., 232 pages, 1980 (Text)

Federal Rules of Civil-Appellate Procedure—West Law School Edition, about 600 pages, 1987

Friedenthal, Kane and Miller's Hornbook on Civil Procedure, 876 pages, 1985 (Text)

Kane's Civil Procedure in a Nutshell, 2nd Ed., 306 pages, 1986 (Text)

Koffler and Reppy's Hornbook on Common Law Pleading, 663 pages, 1969 (Text)

Marcus and Sherman's Complex Litigation–Cases and Materials on Advanced Civil Procedure, 846 pages, 1985 (Casebook)

Park's Computer-Aided Exercises on Civil Procedure, 2nd Ed., 167 pages, 1983 (Coursebook)

CIVIL PROCEDURE—Cont'd

Siegel's Hornbook on New York Practice, 1011 pages, 1978 with 1987 Pocket Part (Text)

See also Federal Jurisdiction and Procedure

CIVIL RIGHTS

Abernathy's Cases and Materials on Civil Rights, 660 pages, 1980 (Casebook)

Cohen's Cases on the Law of Deprivation of Liberty: A Study in Social Control, 755 pages, 1980 (Casebook)

Lockhart, Kamisar, Choper and Shiffrin's Cases on Constitutional Rights and Liberties, 6th Ed., 1266 pages, 1986 with 1987 Supplement (Casebook)—reprint from Lockhart, et al. Cases on Constitutional Law, 6th Ed., 1986

Vieira's Civil Rights in a Nutshell, 279 pages, 1978 (Text)

COMMERCIAL LAW

Bailey's Secured Transactions in a Nutshell, 2nd Ed., 391 pages, 1981 (Text)

Epstein and Martin's Basic Uniform Commercial Code Teaching Materials, 2nd Ed., 667 pages, 1983 (Casebook)

Henson's Hornbook on Secured Transactions Under the U.C.C., 2nd Ed., 504 pages, 1979 with 1979 P.P. (Text)

Murray's Commercial Law, Problems and Materials, 366 pages, 1975 (Coursebook)

Nickles, Matheson and Dolan's Materials for Understanding Credit and Payment Systems, 923 pages, 1987 (Casebook)

Nordstrom and Clovis' Problems and Materials on Commercial Paper, 458 pages, 1972 (Casebook)

Nordstrom, Murray and Clovis' Problems and Materials on Sales, 515 pages, 1982 (Casebook)

Nordstrom, Murray and Clovis' Problems and Materials on Secured Transactions, 594 pages, 1987 (Casebook)

Selected Commercial Statutes, about 1500 pages, 1987

Speidel, Summers and White's Teaching Materials on Commercial Law, 4th Ed., about 1400 pages, 1987 (Casebook)

Speidel, Summers and White's Commercial Paper: Teaching Materials, 4th Ed., about 565 pages, 1987 (Casebook)—reprint from Speidel, et al. Commercial Law, 4th Ed.

Speidel, Summers and White's Sales: Teaching Materials, 4th Ed., about 756 pages, 1987 (Casebook)—reprint from Speidel, et al. Commercial Law, 4th Ed.

Speidel, Summers and White's Secured Transactions—Teaching Materials, 4th Ed., about 463 pages, 1987 (Casebook)—reprint from Speidel, et al. Commercial Law, 4th Ed.

COMMERCIAL LAW—Cont'd

Stockton's Sales in a Nutshell, 2nd Ed., 370 pages, 1981 (Text)
Stone's Uniform Commercial Code in a Nutshell, 2nd Ed., 516 pages, 1984 (Text)
Uniform Commercial Code, Official Text with Comments, 994 pages, 1978
UCC Article 9, Reprint from 1962 Code, 128 pages, 1976
UCC Article 9, 1972 Amendments, 304 pages, 1978
Weber and Speidel's Commercial Paper in a Nutshell, 3rd Ed., 404 pages, 1982 (Text)
White and Summers' Hornbook on the Uniform Commercial Code, 2nd Ed., 1250 pages, 1980 (Text)

COMMUNITY PROPERTY

Mennell's Community Property in a Nutshell, 447 pages, 1982 (Text)
Verrall and Bird's Cases and Materials on California Community Property, 4th Ed., 549 pages, 1983 (Casebook)

COMPARATIVE LAW

Barton, Gibbs, Li and Merryman's Law in Radically Different Cultures, 960 pages, 1983 (Casebook)
Glendon, Gordon and Osakive's Comparative Legal Traditions: Text, Materials and Cases on the Civil Law, Common Law, and Socialist Law Traditions, 1091 pages, 1985 (Casebook)
Glendon, Gordon, and Osakwe's Comparative Legal Traditions in a Nutshell, 402 pages, 1982 (Text)
Langbein's Comparative Criminal Procedure: Germany, 172 pages, 1977 (Casebook)

COMPUTERS AND LAW

Maggs and Sprowl's Computer Applications in the Law, 316 pages, 1987 (Coursebook)
Mason's An Introduction to the Use of Computers in Law, 223 pages, 1984 (Text)

CONFLICT OF LAWS

Cramton, Currie and Kay's Cases-Comments-Questions on Conflict of Laws, 4th Ed., about 925 pages, 1987 (Casebook)
Scoles and Hay's Hornbook on Conflict of Laws, Student Ed., 1085 pages, 1982 with 1986 P.P. (Text)
Scoles and Weintraub's Cases and Materials on Conflict of Laws, 2nd Ed., 966 pages, 1972, with 1978 Supplement (Casebook)
Siegel's Conflicts in a Nutshell, 469 pages, 1982 (Text)

CONSTITUTIONAL LAW

Barron and Dienes' Constitutional Law in a Nutshell, 389 pages, 1986 (Text)

CONSTITUTIONAL LAW—Cont'd

Engdahl's Constitutional Federalism in a Nutshell, 2nd Ed., 411 pages, 1987 (Text)
Lockhart, Kamisar, Choper and Shiffrin's Cases-Comments-Questions on Constitutional Law, 6th Ed., 1601 pages, 1986 with 1987 Supplement (Casebook)
Lockhart, Kamisar, Choper and Shiffrin's Cases-Comments-Questions on the American Constitution, 6th Ed., 1260 pages, 1986 with 1987 Supplement (Casebook)—abridgment of Lockhart, et al. Cases on Constitutional Law, 6th Ed., 1986
Manning's The Law of Church-State Relations in a Nutshell, 305 pages, 1981 (Text)
Miller's Presidential Power in a Nutshell, 328 pages, 1977 (Text)
Nowak, Rotunda and Young's Hornbook on Constitutional Law, 3rd Ed., Student Ed., 1191 pages, 1986 (Text)
Rotunda's Modern Constitutional Law: Cases and Notes, 2nd Ed., 1004 pages, 1985, with 1987 Supplement (Casebook)
Williams' Constitutional Analysis in a Nutshell, 388 pages, 1979 (Text)
See also Civil Rights

CONSUMER LAW

Epstein and Nickles' Consumer Law in a Nutshell, 2nd Ed., 418 pages, 1981 (Text)
Selected Commercial Statutes, about 1500 pages, 1987
Spanogle and Rohner's Cases and Materials on Consumer Law, 693 pages, 1979, with 1982 Supplement (Casebook)
See also Commercial Law

CONTRACTS

Calamari & Perillo's Cases and Problems on Contracts, 1061 pages, 1978 (Casebook)
Calamari and Perillo's Hornbook on Contracts, 3rd Ed., 904 pages, 1987 (Text)
Corbin's Text on Contracts, One Volume Student Edition, 1224 pages, 1952 (Text)
Fessler and Loiseaux's Cases and Materials on Contracts, 837 pages, 1982 (Casebook)
Friedman's Contract Remedies in a Nutshell, 323 pages, 1981 (Text)
Fuller and Eisenberg's Cases on Basic Contract Law, 4th Ed., 1203 pages, 1981 (Casebook)
Hamilton, Rau and Weintraub's Cases and Materials on Contracts, 830 pages, 1984 (Casebook)
Jackson and Bollinger's Cases on Contract Law in Modern Society, 2nd Ed., 1329 pages, 1980 (Casebook)
Keyes' Government Contracts in a Nutshell, 423 pages, 1979 (Text)
Schaber and Rohwer's Contracts in a Nutshell, 2nd Ed., 425 pages, 1984 (Text)

CONTRACTS—Cont'd

Summers and Hillman's Contract and Related Obligation: Theory, Doctrine and Practice, 1074 pages, 1987 (Casebook)

COPYRIGHT

See Patent and Copyright Law

CORPORATIONS

Hamilton's Cases on Corporations—Including Partnerships and Limited Partnerships, 3rd Ed., 1213 pages, 1986 with 1986 Statutory Supplement (Casebook)

Hamilton's Law of Corporations in a Nutshell, 2nd Ed., 515 pages, 1987 (Text)

Henn's Teaching Materials on Corporations, 2nd Ed., 1204 pages, 1986 (Casebook)

Henn and Alexander's Hornbook on Corporations, 3rd Ed., Student Ed., 1371 pages, 1983 with 1986 P.P. (Text)

Jennings and Buxbaum's Cases and Materials on Corporations, 5th Ed., 1180 pages, 1979 (Casebook)

Selected Corporation and Partnership Statutes, Regulations and Forms, about 550 pages, 1987

Solomon, Stevenson and Schwartz' Materials and Problems on Corporations: Law and Policy, 1172 pages, 1982 with 1986 Supplement (Casebook)

CORPORATE FINANCE

Hamilton's Cases and Materials on Corporate Finance, 895 pages, 1984 with 1986 Supplement (Casebook)

CORRECTIONS

Krantz's Cases and Materials on the Law of Corrections and Prisoners' Rights, 3rd Ed., 855 pages, 1986 (Casebook)

Krantz's Law of Corrections and Prisoners' Rights in a Nutshell, 2nd Ed., 386 pages, 1983 (Text)

Popper's Post-Conviction Remedies in a Nutshell, 360 pages, 1978 (Text)

Robbins' Cases and Materials on Post Conviction Remedies, 506 pages, 1982 (Casebook)

CREDITOR'S RIGHTS

Bankruptcy Code, Rules and Forms, Law School Ed., about 835 pages, 1988

Epstein's Debtor-Creditor Law in a Nutshell, 3rd Ed., 383 pages, 1986 (Text)

Epstein, Landers and Nickles' Debtors and Creditors: Cases and Materials, 3rd Ed., about 1175 pages, 1987 (Casebook)

LoPucki's Player's Manual for the Debtor-Creditor Game, 123 pages, 1985 (Coursebook)

Riesenfeld's Cases and Materials on Creditors' Remedies and Debtors' Protection, 4th Ed., 914 pages, 1987 (Casebook)

CREDITOR'S RIGHTS—Cont'd

White's Bankruptcy and Creditor's Rights: Cases and Materials, 812 pages, 1985, with 1987 Supplement (Casebook)

CRIMINAL LAW AND CRIMINAL PROCEDURE

Abrams', Federal Criminal Law and its Enforcement, 882 pages, 1986 (Casebook)

Carlson's Adjudication of Criminal Justice, Problems and References, 130 pages, 1986 (Casebook)

Dix and Sharlot's Cases and Materials on Criminal Law, 3rd Ed., 846 pages, 1987 (Casebook)

Federal Rules of Criminal Procedure—West Law School Edition, about 475 pages, 1987

Grano's Problems in Criminal Procedure, 2nd Ed., 176 pages, 1981 (Problem book)

Israel and LaFave's Criminal Procedure in a Nutshell, 3rd Ed., 438 pages, 1980 (Text)

Johnson's Cases, Materials and Text on Criminal Law, 3rd Ed., 783 pages, 1985 (Casebook)

Johnson's Cases on Criminal Procedure, about 790 pages, 1987 (Casebook)

Kamisar, LaFave and Israel's Cases, Comments and Questions on Modern Criminal Procedure, 6th Ed., 1558 pages, 1986 with 1987 Supplement (Casebook)

Kamisar, LaFave and Israel's Cases, Comments and Questions on Basic Criminal Procedure, 6th Ed., 860 pages, 1986 with 1987 Supplement (Casebook)—reprint from Kamisar, et al. Modern Criminal Procedure, 6th ed., 1986

LaFave's Modern Criminal Law: Cases, Comments and Questions, 789 pages, 1978 (Casebook)

LaFave and Israel's Hornbook on Criminal Procedure, Student Ed., 1142 pages, 1985 with 1986 P.P. (Text)

LaFave and Scott's Hornbook on Criminal Law, 2nd Ed., Student Ed., 918 pages, 1986 (Text)

Langbein's Comparative Criminal Procedure: Germany, 172 pages, 1977 (Casebook)

Loewy's Criminal Law in a Nutshell, 2nd Ed., about 350 pages, 1987 (Text)

Saltzburg's American Criminal Procedure, Cases and Commentary, 2nd Ed., 1193 pages, 1985 with 1987 Supplement (Casebook)

Uviller's The Processes of Criminal Justice: Investigation and Adjudication, 2nd Ed., 1384 pages, 1979 with 1979 Statutory Supplement and 1986 Update (Casebook)

CRIMINAL LAW AND CRIMINAL PROCEDURE—Cont'd

Uviller's The Processes of Criminal Justice: Adjudication, 2nd Ed., 730 pages, 1979. Soft-cover reprint from Uviller's The Processes of Criminal Justice: Investigation and Adjudication, 2nd Ed. (Casebook)

Uviller's The Processes of Criminal Justice: Investigation, 2nd Ed., 655 pages, 1979. Soft-cover reprint from Uviller's The Processes of Criminal Justice: Investigation and Adjudication, 2nd Ed. (Casebook)

Vorenberg's Cases on Criminal Law and Procedure, 2nd Ed., 1088 pages, 1981 with 1985 Supplement (Casebook)

See also Corrections, Juvenile Justice

DECEDENTS ESTATES

See Trusts and Estates

DOMESTIC RELATIONS

Clark's Cases and Problems on Domestic Relations, 3rd Ed., 1153 pages, 1980 (Casebook)

Clark's Hornbook on Domestic Relations, 754 pages, 1968 (Text)

Krause's Cases and Materials on Family Law, 2nd Ed., 1221 pages, 1983 with 1986 Supplement (Casebook)

Krause's Family Law in a Nutshell, 2nd Ed., 444 pages, 1986 (Text)

Krauskopf's Cases on Property Division at Marriage Dissolution, 250 pages, 1984 (Casebook)

ECONOMICS, LAW AND

Goetz' Cases and Materials on Law and Economics, 547 pages, 1984 (Casebook)

See also Antitrust, Regulated Industries

EDUCATION LAW

Alexander and Alexander's The Law of Schools, Students and Teachers in a Nutshell, 409 pages, 1984 (Text)

Morris' The Constitution and American Education, 2nd Ed., 992 pages, 1980 (Casebook)

EMPLOYMENT DISCRIMINATION

Jones, Murphy and Belton's Cases on Discrimination in Employment, 1116 pages, 1987 (Casebook)

Player's Cases and Materials on Employment Discrimination Law, 2nd Ed., 782 pages, 1984 (Casebook)

Player's Federal Law of Employment Discrimination in a Nutshell, 2nd Ed., 402 pages, 1981 (Text)

Player's Hornbook on the Law of Employment Discrimination, about 575 pages, 1987 (Text)

See also Women and the Law

ENERGY AND NATURAL RESOURCES LAW

Laitos' Cases and Materials on Natural Resources Law, 938 pages, 1985 (Casebook)

Rodgers' Cases and Materials on Energy and Natural Resources Law, 2nd Ed., 877 pages, 1983 (Casebook)

Selected Environmental Law Statutes, about 800 pages, 1987

Tomain's Energy Law in a Nutshell, 338 pages, 1981 (Text)

See also Environmental Law, Oil and Gas, Water Law

ENVIRONMENTAL LAW

Bonine and McGarity's Cases and Materials on the Law of Environment and Pollution, 1076 pages, 1984 (Casebook)

Findley and Farber's Cases and Materials on Environmental Law, 2nd Ed., 813 pages, 1985 (Casebook)

Findley and Farber's Environmental Law in a Nutshell, 343 pages, 1983 (Text)

Rodgers' Hornbook on Environmental Law, 956 pages, 1977 with 1984 pocket part (Text)

Selected Environmental Law Statutes, about 800 pages, 1987

See also Energy Law, Natural Resources Law, Water Law

EQUITY

See Remedies

ESTATES

See Trusts and Estates

ESTATE PLANNING

Kurtz' Cases, Materials and Problems on Family Estate Planning, 853 pages, 1983 (Casebook)

Lynn's Introduction to Estate Planning, in a Nutshell, 3rd Ed., 370 pages, 1983 (Text)

See also Taxation

EVIDENCE

Broun and Meisenholder's Problems in Evidence, 2nd Ed., 304 pages, 1981 (Problem book)

Cleary and Strong's Cases, Materials and Problems on Evidence, 3rd Ed., 1143 pages, 1981 (Casebook)

Federal Rules of Evidence for United States Courts and Magistrates, about 330 pages, 1987

Graham's Federal Rules of Evidence in a Nutshell, 2nd Ed., 473 pages, 1987 (Text)

Kimball's Programmed Materials on Problems in Evidence, 380 pages, 1978 (Problem book)

EVIDENCE—Cont'd

Lempert and Saltzburg's A Modern Approach to Evidence: Text, Problems, Transcripts and Cases, 2nd Ed., 1232 pages, 1983 (Casebook)

Lilly's Introduction to the Law of Evidence, 2nd Ed., about 600 pages, 1987 (Text)

McCormick, Sutton and Wellborn's Cases and Materials on Evidence, 6th Ed., 1067 pages, 1987 (Casebook)

McCormick's Hornbook on Evidence, 3rd Ed., Student Ed., 1156 pages, 1984 with 1987 P.P. (Text)

Rothstein's Evidence, State and Federal Rules in a Nutshell, 2nd Ed., 514 pages, 1981 (Text)

Saltzburg's Evidence Supplement: Rules, Statutes, Commentary, 245 pages, 1980 (Casebook Supplement)

FEDERAL JURISDICTION AND PROCEDURE

Currie's Cases and Materials on Federal Courts, 3rd Ed., 1042 pages, 1982 with 1985 Supplement (Casebook)

Currie's Federal Jurisdiction in a Nutshell, 2nd Ed., 258 pages, 1981 (Text)

Federal Rules of Civil-Appellate Procedure—West Law School Edition, about 600 pages, 1987

Forrester and Moye's Cases and Materials on Federal Jurisdiction and Procedure, 3rd Ed., 917 pages, 1977 with 1985 Supplement (Casebook)

Redish's Cases, Comments and Questions on Federal Courts, 878 pages, 1983 with 1986 Supplement (Casebook)

Vetri and Merrill's Federal Courts, Problems and Materials, 2nd Ed., 232 pages, 1984 (Problem Book)

Wright's Hornbook on Federal Courts, 4th Ed., Student Ed., 870 pages, 1983 (Text)

FUTURE INTERESTS

See Trusts and Estates

HEALTH LAW

See Medicine, Law and

IMMIGRATION LAW

Aleinikoff and Martin's Immigration Process and Policy, 1042 pages, 1985, with 1987 Supplement (Casebook)

Weissbrodt's Immigration Law and Procedure in a Nutshell, 345 pages, 1984 (Text)

INDIAN LAW

See American Indian Law

INSURANCE

Dobbyn's Insurance Law in a Nutshell, 281 pages, 1981 (Text)

INSURANCE—Cont'd

Keeton's Cases on Basic Insurance Law, 2nd Ed., 1086 pages, 1977

Keeton's Basic Text on Insurance Law, 712 pages, 1971 (Text)

Keeton's Case Supplement to Keeton's Basic Text on Insurance Law, 334 pages, 1978 (Casebook)

York and Whelan's Cases, Materials and Problems on Insurance Law, 715 pages, 1982, with 1985 Supplement (Casebook)

INTERNATIONAL LAW

Buergenthal and Maier's Public International Law in a Nutshell, 262 pages, 1985 (Text)

Folsom, Gordon and Spanogle's International Business Transactions – a Problem-Oriented Coursebook, 1160 pages, 1986, with Documents Supplement (Casebook)

Frank and Glennon's United States Foreign Relations Law: Cases, Materials and Simulations, about 875 pages, 1987 (Casebook)

Henkin, Pugh, Schachter and Smit's Cases and Materials on International Law, 2nd Ed., 1517 pages, 1987 with Documents Supplement (Casebook)

Jackson and Davey's Legal Problems of International Economic Relations, 2nd Ed., 1269 pages, 1986, with Documents Supplement (Casebook)

Kirgis' International Organizations in Their Legal Setting, 1016 pages, 1977, with 1981 Supplement (Casebook)

Weston, Falk and D'Amato's International Law and World Order—A Problem Oriented Coursebook, 1195 pages, 1980, with Documents Supplement (Casebook)

Wilson's International Business Transactions in a Nutshell, 2nd Ed., 476 pages, 1984 (Text)

INTERVIEWING AND COUNSELING

Binder and Price's Interviewing and Counseling, 232 pages, 1977 (Text)

Shaffer and Elkins' Interviewing and Counseling in a Nutshell, 2nd Ed., 487 pages, 1987 (Text)

INTRODUCTION TO LAW STUDY

Dobbyn's So You Want to go to Law School, Revised First Edition, 206 pages, 1976 (Text)

Hegland's Introduction to the Study and Practice of Law in a Nutshell, 418 pages, 1983 (Text)

Kinyon's Introduction to Law Study and Law Examinations in a Nutshell, 389 pages, 1971 (Text)

See also Legal Method and Legal System

LAW SCHOOL PUBLICATIONS—Continued

JUDICIAL ADMINISTRATION

Nelson's Cases and Materials on Judicial Administration and the Administration of Justice, 1032 pages, 1974 (Casebook)

JURISPRUDENCE

Christie's Text and Readings on Jurisprudence—The Philosophy of Law, 1056 pages, 1973 (Casebook)

JUVENILE JUSTICE

Fox's Cases and Materials on Modern Juvenile Justice, 2nd Ed., 960 pages, 1981 (Casebook)

Fox's Juvenile Courts in a Nutshell, 3rd Ed., 291 pages, 1984 (Text)

LABOR LAW

Atleson, Rabin, Schatzki, Sherman and Silverstein's Collective Bargaining in Private Employment, 2nd Ed., (The Labor Law Group), 856 pages, 1984 (Casebook)

Gorman's Basic Text on Labor Law—Unionization and Collective Bargaining, 914 pages, 1976 (Text)

Grodin, Wollett and Alleyne's Collective Bargaining in Public Employment, 3rd Ed., (the Labor Law Group), 430 pages, 1979 (Casebook)

Leslie's Labor Law in a Nutshell, 2nd Ed., 397 pages, 1986 (Text)

Nolan's Labor Arbitration Law and Practice in a Nutshell, 358 pages, 1979 (Text)

Oberer, Hanslowe, Andersen and Heinsz' Cases and Materials on Labor Law—Collective Bargaining in a Free Society, 3rd Ed., 1163 pages, 1986 with Statutory Supplement (Casebook)

See also Employment Discrimination, Social Legislation

LAND FINANCE

See Real Estate Transactions

LAND USE

Callies and Freilich's Cases and Materials on Land Use, 1233 pages, 1986 (Casebook)

Hagman's Cases on Public Planning and Control of Urban and Land Development, 2nd Ed., 1301 pages, 1980 (Casebook)

Hagman and Juergensmeyer's Hornbook on Urban Planning and Land Development Control Law, 2nd Ed., Student Edition, 680 pages, 1986 (Text)

Wright and Gitelman's Cases and Materials on Land Use, 3rd Ed., 1300 pages, 1982, with 1987 Supplement (Casebook)

Wright and Wright's Land Use in a Nutshell, 2nd Ed., 356 pages, 1985 (Text)

LEGAL HISTORY

Presser and Zainaldin's Cases on Law and American History, 855 pages, 1980 (Casebook)

See also Legal Method and Legal System

LEGAL METHOD AND LEGAL SYSTEM

Aldisert's Readings, Materials and Cases in the Judicial Process, 948 pages, 1976 (Casebook)

Berch and Berch's Introduction to Legal Method and Process, 550 pages, 1985 (Casebook)

Bodenheimer, Oakley and Love's Readings and Cases on an Introduction to the Anglo-American Legal System, 161 pages, 1980 (Casebook)

Davies and Lawry's Institutions and Methods of the Law—Introductory Teaching Materials, 547 pages, 1982 (Casebook)

Dvorkin, Himmelstein and Lesnick's Becoming a Lawyer: A Humanistic Perspective on Legal Education and Professionalism, 211 pages, 1981 (Text)

Greenberg's Judicial Process and Social Change, 666 pages, 1977 (Casebook)

Kelso and Kelso's Studying Law: An Introduction, 587 pages, 1984 (Coursebook)

Kempin's Historical Introduction to Anglo-American Law in a Nutshell, 2nd Ed., 280 pages, 1973 (Text)

Kimball's Historical Introduction to the Legal System, 610 pages, 1966 (Casebook)

Murphy's Cases and Materials on Introduction to Law—Legal Process and Procedure, 772 pages, 1977 (Casebook)

Reynolds' Judicial Process in a Nutshell, 292 pages, 1980 (Text)

See also Legal Research and Writing

LEGAL PROFESSION

Aronson, Devine and Fisch's Problems, Cases and Materials on Professional Responsibility, 745 pages, 1985 (Casebook)

Aronson and Weckstein's Professional Responsibility in a Nutshell, 399 pages, 1980 (Text)

Mellinkoff's The Conscience of a Lawyer, 304 pages, 1973 (Text)

Mellinkoff's Lawyers and the System of Justice, 983 pages, 1976 (Casebook)

Pirsig and Kirwin's Cases and Materials on Professional Responsibility, 4th Ed., 603 pages, 1984 (Casebook)

Schwartz and Wydick's Problems in Legal Ethics, 285 pages, 1983 (Casebook)

Selected Statutes, Rules and Standards on the Legal Profession, about 300 pages, 1987

Smith's Preventing Legal Malpractice, 142 pages, 1981 (Text)

Wolfram's Hornbook on Modern Legal Ethics, Student Edition, 1120 pages, 1986 (Text)

LEGAL RESEARCH AND WRITING

Cohen's Legal Research in a Nutshell, 4th Ed., 450 pages, 1985 (Text)
Cohen and Berring's How to Find the Law, 8th Ed., 790 pages, 1983. Problem book by Foster, Johnson and Kelly available (Casebook)
Cohen and Berring's Finding the Law, 8th Ed., Abridged Ed., 556 pages, 1984 (Casebook)
Dickerson's Materials on Legal Drafting, 425 pages, 1981 (Casebook)
Felsenfeld and Siegel's Writing Contracts in Plain English, 290 pages, 1981 (Text)
Gopen's Writing From a Legal Perspective, 225 pages, 1981 (Text)
Mellinkoff's Legal Writing—Sense and Nonsense, 242 pages, 1982 (Text)
Ray and Ramsfield's Legal Writing: Getting It Right and Getting It Written, 250 pages, 1987 (Text)
Rombauer's Legal Problem Solving—Analysis, Research and Writing, 4th Ed., 424 pages, 1983 (Coursebook)
Squires and Rombauer's Legal Writing in a Nutshell, 294 pages, 1982 (Text)
Statsky's Legal Research and Writing, 3rd Ed., 257 pages, 1986 (Coursebook)
Statsky and Wernet's Case Analysis and Fundamentals of Legal Writing, 2nd Ed., 441 pages, 1984 (Text)
Teply's Programmed Materials on Legal Research and Citation, 2nd Ed., 358 pages, 1986. Student Library Exercises available (Coursebook)
Weihofen's Legal Writing Style, 2nd Ed., 332 pages, 1980 (Text)

LEGISLATION

Davies' Legislative Law and Process in a Nutshell, 2nd Ed., 346 pages, 1986 (Text)
Eskridge and Frickey's Cases on Legislation, about 930 pages, 1987 (Casebook)
Nutting and Dickerson's Cases and Materials on Legislation, 5th Ed., 744 pages, 1978 (Casebook)
Statsky's Legislative Analysis and Drafting, 2nd Ed., 217 pages, 1984 (Text)

LOCAL GOVERNMENT

McCarthy's Local Government Law in a Nutshell, 2nd Ed., 404 pages, 1983 (Text)
Reynolds' Hornbook on Local Government Law, 860 pages, 1982, with 1987 pocket part (Text)
Valente's Cases and Materials on Local Government Law, 3rd Ed., 1010 pages, 1987 (Casebook)

MASS COMMUNICATION LAW

Gillmor and Barron's Cases and Comment on Mass Communication Law, 4th Ed., 1076 pages, 1984 (Casebook)

MASS COMMUNICATION LAW—Cont'd

Ginsburg's Regulation of Broadcasting: Law and Policy Towards Radio, Television and Cable Communications, 741 pages, 1979, with 1983 Supplement (Casebook)
Zuckman and Gayne's Mass Communications Law in a Nutshell, 2nd Ed., 473 pages, 1983 (Text)

MEDICINE, LAW AND

Furrow, Johnson, Jost and Schwartz' Health Law: Cases, Materials and Problems, 1005 pages, 1987 (Casebook)
King's The Law of Medical Malpractice in a Nutshell, 2nd Ed., 342 pages, 1986 (Text)
Shapiro and Spece's Problems, Cases and Materials on Bioethics and Law, 892 pages, 1981 (Casebook)
Sharpe, Fiscina and Head's Cases on Law and Medicine, 882 pages, 1978 (Casebook)

MILITARY LAW

Shanor and Terrell's Military Law in a Nutshell, 378 pages, 1980 (Text)

MORTGAGES

See Real Estate Transactions

NATURAL RESOURCES LAW

See Energy and Natural Resources Law

NEGOTIATION

Edwards and White's Problems, Readings and Materials on the Lawyer as a Negotiator, 484 pages, 1977 (Casebook)
Peck's Cases and Materials on Negotiation, 2nd Ed., (The Labor Law Group), 280 pages, 1980 (Casebook)
Williams' Legal Negotiation and Settlement, 207 pages, 1983 (Coursebook)

OFFICE PRACTICE

Hegland's Trial and Practice Skills in a Nutshell, 346 pages, 1978 (Text)
Strong and Clark's Law Office Management, 424 pages, 1974 (Casebook)
See also Computers and Law, Interviewing and Counseling, Negotiation

OIL AND GAS

Hemingway's Hornbook on Oil and Gas, 2nd Ed., Student Ed., 543 pages, 1983 with 1986 P.P. (Text)
Kuntz, Lowe, Anderson and Smith's Cases and Materials on Oil and Gas Law, 857 pages, 1986, with Forms Manual (Casebook)
Lowe's Oil and Gas Law in a Nutshell, 443 pages, 1983 (Text)
See also Energy and Natural Resources Law

PARTNERSHIP

See Agency—Partnership

LAW SCHOOL PUBLICATIONS—Continued

PATENT AND COPYRIGHT LAW

Choate, Francis and Collins' Cases and Materials on Patent Law, 3rd Ed., about 1050 pages, 1987 (Casebook)

Miller and Davis' Intellectual Property—Patents, Trademarks and Copyright in a Nutshell, 428 pages, 1983 (Text)

Nimmer's Cases on Copyright and Other Aspects of Entertainment Litigation, 3rd Ed., 1025 pages, 1985 (Casebook)

PRODUCTS LIABILITY

Noel and Phillips' Cases on Products Liability, 2nd Ed., 821 pages, 1982 (Casebook)

Noel and Phillips' Products Liability in a Nutshell, 2nd Ed., 341 pages, 1981 (Text)

PROPERTY

Bernhardt's Real Property in a Nutshell, 2nd Ed., 448 pages, 1981 (Text)

Boyer's Survey of the Law of Property, 766 pages, 1981 (Text)

Browder, Cunningham and Smith's Cases on Basic Property Law, 4th Ed., 1431 pages, 1984 (Casebook)

Bruce, Ely and Bostick's Cases and Materials on Modern Property Law, 1004 pages, 1984 (Casebook)

Burke's Personal Property in a Nutshell, 322 pages, 1983 (Text)

Cunningham, Stoebuck and Whitman's Hornbook on the Law of Property, Student Ed., 916 pages, 1984, with 1987 P.P. (Text)

Donahue, Kauper and Martin's Cases on Property, 2nd Ed., 1362 pages, 1983 (Casebook)

Hill's Landlord and Tenant Law in a Nutshell, 2nd Ed., 311 pages, 1986 (Text)

Kurtz and Hovenkamp's Cases and Materials on American Property Law, 1296 pages, 1987 (Casebook)

Moynihan's Introduction to Real Property, 2n Ed., about 250 pages, 1987 (Text)

Uniform Land Transactions Act, Uniform Simplification of Land Transfers Act, Uniform Condominium Act, 1977 Official Text with Comments, 462 pages, 1978

See also Real Estate Transactions, Land Use

PSYCHIATRY, LAW AND

Reisner's Law and the Mental Health System, Civil and Criminal Aspects, 696 pages, 1985, with 1987 Supplement (Casebooks)

REAL ESTATE TRANSACTIONS

Bruce's Real Estate Finance in a Nutshell, 2nd Ed., 262 pages, 1985 (Text)

Maxwell, Riesenfeld, Hetland and Warren's Cases on California Security Transactions in Land, 3rd Ed., 728 pages, 1984 (Casebook)

REAL ESTATE TRANSACTIONS—Cont'd

Nelson and Whitman's Cases on Real Estate Transfer, Finance and Development, 3rd Ed., about 1184 pages, 1987 (Casebook)

Nelson and Whitman's Hornbook on Real Estate Finance Law, 2nd Ed., Student Ed., 941 pages, 1985 (Text)

Osborne's Cases and Materials on Secured Transactions, 559 pages, 1967 (Casebook)

REGULATED INDUSTRIES

Gellhorn and Pierce's Regulated Industries in a Nutshell, 2nd Ed., 389 pages, 1987 (Text)

Morgan, Harrison and Verkuil's Cases and Materials on Economic Regulation of Business, 2nd Ed., 666 pages, 1985 (Casebook)

See also Mass Communication Law, Banking Law

REMEDIES

Dobbs' Hornbook on Remedies, 1067 pages, 1973 (Text)

Dobbs' Problems in Remedies, 137 pages, 1974 (Problem book)

Dobbyn's Injunctions in a Nutshell, 264 pages, 1974 (Text)

Friedman's Contract Remedies in a Nutshell, 323 pages, 1981 (Text)

Leavell, Love and Nelson's Cases and Materials on Equitable Remedies and Restitution, 4th Ed., 1111 pages, 1986 (Casebook)

McCormick's Hornbook on Damages, 811 pages, 1935 (Text)

O'Connell's Remedies in a Nutshell, 2nd Ed., 320 pages, 1985 (Text)

York, Bauman and Rendleman's Cases and Materials on Remedies, 4th Ed., 1029 pages, 1985 (Casebook)

REVIEW MATERIALS

Ballantine's Problems

Black Letter Series

Smith's Review Series

West's Review Covering Multistate Subjects

SECURITIES REGULATION

Hazen's Hornbook on The Law of Securities Regulation, Student Ed., 739 pages, 1985, with 1987 P.P. (Text)

Ratner's Securities Regulation: Materials for a Basic Course, 3rd Ed., 1000 pages, 1986 (Casebook)

Ratner's Securities Regulation in a Nutshell, 2nd Ed., 322 pages, 1982 (Text)

Selected Securities and Business Planning Statutes, Rules and Forms, about 470 pages, 1987

SOCIAL LEGISLATION

Hood and Hardy's Workers' Compensation and Employee Protection Laws in a Nutshell, 274 pages, 1984 (Text)

LaFrance's Welfare Law: Structure and Entitlement in a Nutshell, 455 pages, 1979 (Text)

Malone, Plant and Little's Cases on Workers' Compensation and Employment Rights, 2nd Ed., 951 pages, 1980 (Casebook)

SPORTS LAW

Schubert, Smith and Trentadue's Sports Law, 395 pages, 1986 (Text)

TAXATION

Dodge's Cases and Materials on Federal Income Taxation, 820 pages, 1985 (Casebook)

Dodge's Federal Taxation of Estates, Trusts and Gifts: Principles and Planning, 771 pages, 1981 with 1982 Supplement (Casebook)

Garbis, Struntz and Rubin's Cases and Materials on Tax Procedure and Tax Fraud, 2nd Ed., 687 pages, 1987 (Casebook)

Gelfand and Salsich's State and Local Taxation and Finance in a Nutshell, 309 pages, 1986 (Text)

Gunn's Cases and Materials on Federal Income Taxation of Individuals, 785 pages, 1981 with 1985 Supplement (Casebook)

Hellerstein and Hellerstein's Cases on State and Local Taxation, 4th Ed., 1041 pages, 1978 with 1982 Supplement (Casebook)

Kahn and Gann's Corporate Taxation and Taxation of Partnerships and Partners, 2nd Ed., 1204 pages, 1985 (Casebook)

Kragen and McNulty's Cases and Materials on Federal Income Taxation: Individuals, Corporations, Partnerships, 4th Ed., 1287 pages, 1985 (Casebook)

McNulty's Federal Estate and Gift Taxation in a Nutshell, 3rd Ed., 509 pages, 1983 (Text)

McNulty's Federal Income Taxation of Individuals in a Nutshell, 3rd Ed., 487 pages, 1983 (Text)

Pennell's Cases and Materials on Income Taxation of Trusts, Estates, Grantors and Beneficiaries, about 400 pages, 1987 (Casebook)

Posin's Hornbook on Federal Income Taxation of Individuals, Student Ed., 491 pages, 1983 with 1987 pocket part (Text)

Selected Federal Taxation Statutes and Regulations, 1576 pages, 1987

Solomon and Hesch's Cases on Federal Income Taxation of Individuals, 1068 pages, 1987 (Casebook)

TAXATION—Cont'd

Sobeloff and Weidenbruch's Federal Income Taxation of Corporations and Stockholders in a Nutshell, 362 pages, 1981 (Text)

TORTS

Christie's Cases and Materials on the Law of Torts, 1264 pages, 1983 (Casebook)

Dobbs' Torts and Compensation—Personal Accountability and Social Responsibility for Injury, 955 pages, 1985 (Casebook)

Green, Pedrick, Rahl, Thode, Hawkins, Smith, and Treece's Advanced Torts: Injuries to Business, Political and Family Interests, 2nd Ed., 544 pages, 1977 (Casebook)

Keeton, Keeton, Sargentich and Steiner's Cases and Materials on Torts, and Accident Law, 1360 pages, 1983 (Casebook)

Kionka's Torts in a Nutshell: Injuries to Persons and Property, 434 pages, 1977 (Text)

Malone's Torts in a Nutshell: Injuries to Family, Social and Trade Relations, 358 pages, 1979 (Text)

Prosser and Keeton's Hornbook on Torts, 5th Ed., Student Ed., 1286 pages, 1984, with 1987 pocket part (Text)

See also Products Liability

TRADE REGULATION

McManis' Unfair Trade Practices in a Nutshell, 444 pages, 1982 (Text)

Oppenheim, Weston, Maggs and Schechter's Cases and Materials on Unfair Trade Practices and Consumer Protection, 4th Ed., 1038 pages, 1983 with 1986 Supplement (Casebook)

See also Antitrust, Regulated Industries

TRIAL AND APPELLATE ADVOCACY

Appellate Advocacy, Handbook of, 2nd Ed., 182 pages, 1986 (Text)

Bergman's Trial Advocacy in a Nutshell, 402 pages, 1979 (Text)

Binder and Bergman's Fact Investigation: From Hypothesis to Proof, 354 pages, 1984 (Coursebook)

Goldberg's The First Trial (Where Do I Sit?, What Do I Say?) in a Nutshell, 396 pages, 1982 (Text)

Haydock, Herr and Stempel's, Fundamentals of Pre-Trial Litigation, 768 pages, 1985 (Casebook)

Hegland's Trial and Practice Skills in a Nutshell, 346 pages, 1978 (Text)

Hornstein's Appellate Advocacy in a Nutshell, 325 pages, 1984 (Text)

Jeans' Handbook on Trial Advocacy, Student Ed., 473 pages, 1975 (Text)

Martineau's Cases and Materials on Appellate Practice and Procedure, about 550 pages, 1987 (Casebook)

TRIAL AND APPELLATE ADVOCACY—Cont'd

McElhaney's Effective Litigation, 457 pages, 1974 (Casebook)

Nolan's Cases and Materials on Trial Practice, 518 pages, 1981 (Casebook)

Parnell and Shellhaas' Cases, Exercises and Problems for Trial Advocacy, 171 pages, 1982 (Coursebook)

Sonsteng, Haydock and Boyd's The Trialbook: A Total System for Preparation and Presentation of a Case, Student Ed., 404 pages, 1984 (Coursebook)

TRUSTS AND ESTATES

Atkinson's Hornbook on Wills, 2nd Ed., 975 pages, 1953 (Text)

Averill's Uniform Probate Code in a Nutshell, 2nd Ed., 454 pages, 1987 (Text)

Bogert's Hornbook on Trusts, 6th Ed., Student Ed., about 800 pages, 1987 (Text)

Clark, Lusky and Murphy's Cases and Materials on Gratuitous Transfers, 3rd Ed., 970 pages, 1985 (Casebook)

Gulliver's Cases and Materials on Future Interests, 624 pages, 1959 (Casebook)

Gulliver's Introduction to the Law of Future Interests, 87 pages, 1959 (Casebook)—reprint from Gulliver's Cases and Materials on Future Interests, 1959

McGovern's Cases and Materials on Wills, Trusts and Future Interests: An Introduction to Estate Planning, 750 pages, 1983 (Casebook)

Mennell's Wills and Trusts in a Nutshell, 392 pages, 1979 (Text)

Simes' Hornbook on Future Interests, 2nd Ed., 355 pages, 1966 (Text)

TRUSTS AND ESTATES—Cont'd

Turano and Radigan's Hornbook on New York Estate Administration, 676 pages, 1986 (Text)

Uniform Probate Code, 5th Ed., Official Text With Comments, 384 pages, 1977

Waggoner's Future Interests in a Nutshell, 361 pages, 1981 (Text)

Waterbury's Materials on Trusts and Estates, 1039 pages, 1986 (Casebook)

WATER LAW

Getches' Water Law in a Nutshell, 439 pages, 1984 (Text)

Sax and Abram's Cases and Materials on Legal Control of Water Resources in the United States, 941 pages, 1986 (Casebook)

Trelease and Gould's Cases and Materials on Water Law, 4th Ed., 816 pages, 1986 (Casebook)

See also Energy and Natural Resources Law, Environmental Law

WILLS

See Trusts and Estates

WOMEN AND THE LAW

Kay's Text, Cases and Materials on Sex-Based Discrimination, 2nd Ed., 1045 pages, 1981, with 1986 Supplement (Casebook)

Thomas' Sex Discrimination in a Nutshell, 399 pages, 1982 (Text)

See also Employment Discrimination

WORKERS' COMPENSATION

See Social Legislation

COMMERCIAL LAW
TEACHING MATERIALS
Fourth Edition

By

Richard E. Speidel
Professor of Law
Northwestern University School of Law

Robert S. Summers
McRoberts Research Professor of Law
Cornell University School of Law

James J. White
Robert A. Sullivan Professor of Law
University of Michigan School of Law

AMERICAN CASEBOOK SERIES

WEST PUBLISHING CO.
ST. PAUL, MINN., 1987

50 West Kellogg Boulevard
P.O. Box 64526
St. Paul, Minnesota 55164–0526

Library of Congress Cataloging-in-Publication Data

Speidel, Richard E.
Commercial law: teaching materials.

(American casebook series)
Rev. ed. of: Teaching materials on commercial and consumer law. 3rd ed. 1981.
Includes index.
1. Commercial law—United States—Cases.
2. Consumer protection—Law and legislation—United States—Cases. I. Summers, Robert S. II. White, James J., 1934– . III. Speidel, Richard E. Teaching materials on commercial and consumer law. IV. Title. V. Series.

KF888.S58 1987 346.73'07 87–10612
347.3067

ISBN 0–314–40504–6

(S., S. & W.) Commercial Law, 4th Ed. ACB

Preface

In its third reincarnation, published in 1981, this book was a little tired. Some of our ideas that made the first edition novel had been adopted by others, and were, in any case, no longer new. A few problems and cases had found their way into the book without having earned their right to be there. Here and there an old case or problem sagged like flesh around an aging matron's eyes. Topics such as bankruptcy attached themselves to the work a bit like cancerous ganglia rather than as synchronic elements of a coherent whole. By 1985 it was clear that we either had to give the book a decent burial or completely redo it. Whether because of an unbecoming attachment to royalty checks, an inability to resist one more chance to reform the world, or a simple desire to have congenial materials to teach, we have chosen to do a fourth edition.

But "fourth edition" is something of a misnomer. This is essentially a new book. For example, we have abandoned the old organization in Article 9 where we dealt functionally and separately with equipment, inventory, farm products and other types of collateral. In our new book, we have substituted analytical and historical modes of organization. We have also reexamined every problem and case—have asked which should be included and which not. As a result, more than two-thirds of the materials are new. We have beefed-up the check and letter of credit material with new cases and problems that raise the issues now current in such commercial transactions (including commercial fraud). We have brought all topics up to date as of the end of 1986.

Because the trend toward a single integrated UCC course has now stopped and perhaps even reversed itself, we also publish this book in four versions. The large book can be used for a completely integrated course (and we continue to teach such courses ourselves). In the smaller versions, the various books can be used alternatively for an Article 3, 4, 5 course or for an Article 9, or Article 2 course. Although we have always agreed that an integrated course seemed the best idea, none of the three of us has ever in fact taught a course that completely covered the Code from one end to the other.

The book remains for us a labor of love, a joy to construct and a delight to teach. We can hardly ask others to find such pleasure in its use, but we have selected materials with the hope of stimulating not just the teacher, but also the students, including some of the back row. Surely there could have been more humor in the book, but we are now less confident of general receptivity to Summers' own brand of wit and to White's scatological instincts. Summers and White now find themselves less capable of convincing a skeptical Speidel that their jokes should be included and less certain of the appeal of these jokes to generations now younger than their own children. Besides, hard cases, demanding problems, and sophisticated materials generally are easier to assemble and prepare than good (and widely acceptable) humor. Nevertheless we hope this edition, like the earlier ones, is a bit of a gas.

R.E.S.
R.S.S.
J.J.W.

Acknowledgments

The editors wish to thank the following students for assistance in the review of the proofs: John Held, Candace Ridgeway, and Jay Smith, all Cornell Law School Class of 1987, and Harry Davis, Kathryn Moore, Alan Pasternak and Douglas Perry, Cornell Law School Class of 1988; Kevin Recchia, Michael Turner, and Edward Shakin, University of Michigan Class of 1986; and Perry Pappas and Christopher Murdock, University of Michigan Class of 1987.

In addition the editors wish to thank Anna Tileston and Kathryn West for various forms of valuable assistance in preparation of the manuscript.

We acknowledge and thank the many publishers and authors who graciously consented to the reprinting of extracts from copyrighted articles and books in earlier editions of this Casebook. Some of this material has been retained in the Fourth Edition, and the permissions are duly noted.

We are especially grateful for the permission to reprint copyrighted material for the first time in the Fourth Edition. When requested, these permissions have been duly noted at the end of the extract. A complete list of those to whom we are indebted and the copyrighted materials extracted follows, with the page where the material can be found:

The American Bar Association and Mr. Donald J. Rapson;

Rapson, *U.C.C. Article 6: Should It Be Revised or "Deep-Sixed?"*, 38 Bus.Lawyer 1753 (1983) at page 956.

The Arizona State Law Journal and Professor Joan E. Vogel;

Vogel, *Squeezing Consumers: Lemon Laws, Consumer Warranties, And A Proposal for Reform,* 1985 Ariz.St.L.J. 589 at page 894.

Duke University School of Law, Professor Ronald J. Allen and Professor Robert Hillman;

Allen & Hillman, *Evidentiary Problems In—And Solutions For—The Uniform Commerical Code,* 1984 Duke L.J. 92 at page 515.

The Georgetown Law Journal and Professor Ingrid M. Hillinger;

Hillinger, *The Article Two Merchant Rules: Karl Llewellyn's Attempt to Achieve the Good, the True, the Beautiful In Commercial Law,* 73 Geo.L.J. 1141 (1985), at page 428.

The George Washington Law Review and Professor Jay L. Westbrook;

Westbrook, *Glitch: Section 9–402(7) and the UCC Revision Process,* 53 Geo.Wash.L.Rev. 408 (1984) at page 123.

The Hastings Law Journal and Professor Emma Coleman Jordan;

Jordan, *Ending the Floating Check Game: The Policy Arguments for Delayed Availability Reform,* 36 Hastings L.J. 515 (1985) at pages 1147 and 1264.

Rutgers Computer and Technical Law Journal;

Prtuzman, *Chips and the Proposed Uniform Payments Code,* 10 Rutgers Computer & Tech. L.J. 1 (1984) at page 1313.

The SouthWestern Law Journal;

Mann & Phillips, *The Reclaiming Cash Seller and the Bankruptcy Code,* 39 S.W.L.J. 603 (1985) at page 946.

The Syracuse Law Review;

Wechsler, *Delayed Funds Availability,* 35 Syracuse L.Rev. 1117 (1984) at page 1265.

The Wall Street Journal ©;

Cony & Penn, *Check Kiting,* Vol. LXVII, No. 210, August 11, 1986.

Warren, Gorham & Lamont, Inc.:

Shanker, *A Proposal For A Simplified All-Embracing Security Interest,* 14 U.C.C.L.J. 23 (1981), at page 84;

N. Penney & D. Baker, The Law of Electronic Fund Transfer Systems 9–12 (1980 & Supp.1984) at page 1307;

J. Dolan, The Law of Letters of Credit: Commercial and Standby Credits (1986) at page 1386.

West Publishing Company;

J. White & R. Summers, Handbook Of The Law Under The Uniform Commercial Code 27–31 (2d Ed. 1980) *passim.*

The Wisconsin Law Review;

Goldberg, *Price Adjustment in Long-Term Contracts,* 1985 Wis.L.Rev. 527 at pages 548 and 560.

RES
RSS
JJW

Summary of Contents

BOOK TWO: SALES

PART ONE. INTRODUCTORY MATERIALS

PART TWO. THE AGREEMENT STAGE

PART SIX. DISPUTES AMONG CREDITORS OVER POSSESSION OF GOODS SOLD

BOOK THREE: COMMERCIAL PAPER

*

Table of Contents

BOOK TWO: SALES

PART ONE. INTRODUCTORY MATERIALS

PART TWO. THE AGREEMENT STAGE

PART FOUR. THE STAGE OF GETTING THE GOODS OR DOCUMENTS TO THE BUYER

PART FIVE. THE RECEIPT–INSPECTION STAGE

PART SIX. DISPUTES AMONG CREDITORS OVER POSSESSION OF GOODS SOLD

BOOK THREE: COMMERCIAL PAPER

Table of Cases

The principal cases are in bold type. Cases cited or discussed in the text are roman type. References are to pages. Cases cited in principal cases and within other quoted materials are not included.

Table of Statutes

UNIFORM COMMERCIAL CODE

UNIFORM COMMERCIAL CODE

UNIFORM COMMERCIAL CODE

UNIFORM COMMERCIAL CODE

UNIFORM COMMERCIAL CODE

UNIFORM COMMERCIAL CODE

UNIFORM COMMERCIAL CODE

UNIFORM COMMERCIAL CODE

UNIFORM COMMERCIAL CODE

UNIFORM COMMERCIAL CODE

UNIFORM COMMERCIAL CODE

UNIFORM COMMERCIAL CODE

UNIFORM COMMERCIAL CODE

U.C.C. Sec.	This Work Page
2–725(1) (Cont'd)	828
2–725(2)	713
	760
	792
3–102(1)(e)	51
	1023
3–103	8
3–104	51
	52
	409
	676
	1023
	1024
	1025
	1026
	1060
3–104(1)	971
	996
	1026
	1028
3–104(1)(b)	994
	1023
	1025
	1026
	1030
3–104(1)(d)	1026
3–104(2)	970
	994
3–104(2)(b)	971
3–104, Comment 4	994
3–105	52
	994
	1024
	1026
	1028
	1030
3–108	974
3–110	1035
	1089
3–111	994
	1034
	1089
3–112	52
	996
	1026
	1028
3–112(1)(b)	52
3–112(1)(c)	1026
3–115	980
	994
3–115(1)	995
3–118(f)	1002
3–120	1024
3–122(1)	974
3–201	1022
	1045
3–202	1003
	1034
	1035
3–202(1)	995
	1035
3–202(2)	1034
3–203	1110

UNIFORM COMMERCIAL CODE

U.C.C. Sec.	This Work Page
3–204	994
3–204(2)	1089
3–206(3)	1073
3–301	1145
3–302	50
	202
	410
	978
	1022
	1023
	1040
3–302(1)	1022
	1044
	1045
3–302(2)	1044
3–302(4)	1145
3–302, Comment 2	1044
3–303	1035
	1044
3–304	1047
3–304(3)(c)	986
3–305	50
	202
	409
	410
	978
	1035
3–305(1)	1022
	1035
3–305(2)	999
	1035
	1044
	1051
	1052
	1053
3–305(2)(c)	1052
3–306	1064
	1068
3–306(d)	999
	1064
3–307	978
	1022
3–307(2)	1023
3–401	409
	971
	1013
3–401(1)	978
	1013
3–402	974
3–403	13
	974
3–403(1)	1012
3–403(2)(a)	1013
3–403(2)(b)	1013
3–403, Comment 1	1012
3–404	13
	1136
3–405	1069
	1071
	1118
	1119
	1134
	1136

UNIFORM COMMERCIAL CODE

UNIFORM COMMERCIAL CODE

UNIFORM COMMERCIAL CODE

UNIFORM COMMERCIAL CODE

U.C.C. Sec.	This Work Page
4-401 (Cont'd)	1243
	1268
4-401(1)	1072
	1268
	1269
4-401(2)	1268
	1269
4-402	1268
	1279
	1280
4-402, Comment 2	1279
4-402, Comment 3	1279
4-402, Comment 5	1280
4-403	1270
4-403(1)	1270
	1273
	1286
4-403(2)	1270
4-403(3)	1274
4-403, Comment 2	1270
4-406	1069
	1071
	1072
	1073
	1118
	1129
	1134
	1269
	1330
4-406(1)	7
4-406(4)	1130
4-406(5)	1079
4-407	1269
	1274
4-501	410
	1220
4-501 through 4-504	1219
4-502	410
4-503	410
5-102	1353
	1354
5-102(1)(a)	714
5-102(3)	1353
5-102(4)	1354
5-103(1)	714
5-106(2)	714
5-109	1355
5-111	1356
	1383
	1384
5-113	1356
5-114	1022
	1355
	1409
5-114(1)	714
	1355
5-114(2)	1355
	1385
5-114(2)(a)	1409
5-114(2)(b)	1385
5-114(3)	1410
5-116	1383
5-116(3)	1347

UNIFORM COMMERCIAL CODE

U.C.C. Sec.	This Work Page
6-101, Comment 2	950
6-102	950
	956
6-103	950
	956
6-103(3)	955
6-104	956
6-105	950
	956
6-106	956
	960
6-107	956
6-108	956
6-109	956
6-111	956
7-102(1)(a)	654
7-102(1)(b)	658
7-103	659
	684
7-104	692
7-104(1)	654
7-203	700
7-204(1)	654
7-205	693
7-210	237
7-301	407
	700
7-301(4)	406
7-303	700
7-303(1)	697
7-306	407
7-309	406
	659
7-309(1)	659
7-309(2)	659
7-402	685
7-403	689
	690
	707
7-403(1)	706
7-403(3)	706
7-403(4)	658
7-404	693
	707
7-501	407
	693
	696
7-501 et seq.	202
7-502	407
	691
	693
	696
	700
7-502(1)	693
7-503	407
	693
	696
	707
7-504	700
	707
7-601	407
7-602	693
8-102	994

UNIFORM COMMERCIAL CODE

UNIFORM COMMERCIAL CODE

UNIFORM COMMERCIAL CODE

UNIFORM COMMERCIAL CODE

UNIFORM CONSUMER CREDIT CODE

U.C.C.C. Sec.	This Work Page
2.407	85

UNITED STATES

UNITED STATES CODE ANNOTATED

7 U.S.C.A.—Agriculture

U.S.C.A. Sec.	This Work Page
499a–499r	684
499b	739
499n	739
1551	871
1631	201
	202
1631(b)(3)	202
1631(c)(2)	201
1631(d)	201
	202
1631(e)	201
1631(e)(1)	201
1631(h)	202

9 U.S.C.A.—Arbitration

U.S.C.A. Sec.	This Work Page
1–14	579

11 U.S.C.A.—Bankruptcy

U.S.C.A. Sec.	This Work Page
12	396
101(45)	375
101(48)	352
	363
Ch. 3, Subch. 1	351
361	46
	386
	387
	396
361(1)	395
361(2)	395
361(3)	395
362	45
	46
	354
	384
	386
362(a)	352
362(a)(5)	352
363	386
	397
364	386
	400
	401
365	281
502(b)(2)	395
506	352
506(b)	386
	387

UNITED STATES CODE ANNOTATED

11 U.S.C.A.—Bankruptcy

U.S.C.A. Sec.	This Work Page
506(b) (Cont'd)	395
507	352
522(d)	355
	380
	384
522(d)(2)	384
522(f)	142
	179
	353
	354
	380
	384
522(f)(2)(B)	384
524(c)	401
541(a)(1)	352
541(d)	309
542	352
544	39
	44
	46
	97
	309
	353
	354
	356
544 through 553	46
544(a)	22
	36
	302
	354
	356
	359
	371
	941
544(a)(3)	320
544(b)	353
	354
	356
	359
545	375
	941
546	941
546(b)	302
546(c)	302
	941
547	45
	46
	353
	354
	356
	359
	360
	361
	362
	364
	365
	366
	372
	941
547(b)	361
	362
	363

UNITED STATES CODE ANNOTATED

11 U.S.C.A.—Bankruptcy

15 U.S.C.A.—Commerce and Trade

18 U.S.C.A.—Crimes and Criminal Procedure

UNITED STATES CODE ANNOTATED

26 U.S.C.A.—Internal Revenue Code

28 U.S.C.A.—Judiciary and Judicial Procedure

46 U.S.C.A.—Shipping

49 U.S.C.A.—Transportation

STATUTES AT LARGE

POPULAR NAME ACTS

BANKRUPTCY ACT

FEDERAL BILLS OF LADING ACT

INTERSTATE COMMERCE ACT

NEW–CAR BUYER PROTECTION ACT

PERISHABLE AGRICULTURAL COMMODITIES ACT

STATE STATUTES

ALABAMA CODE

COLORADO REVISED STATUTES

MASSACHUSETTS UNIFORM COMMERCIAL CODE

MINNESOTA STATUTES ANNOTATED

NEW YORK MCKINNEY'S PENAL LAW

CODE OF FEDERAL REGULATIONS

FEDERAL REGISTER

COMMERCIAL LAW

TEACHING MATERIALS

Fourth Edition

*

CHAPTER ONE

THE NATURE AND SOURCES OF COMMERCIAL LAW

SECTION 1. A BRIEF CURRICULAR NOTE TO THE STUDENT

A glance back at the table of contents will show that these materials are divided into three "books," one each on security, sales, and commercial paper. But the student must not think of these as three wholly separate subjects. They are closely related, functionally, analytically, and historically, and we have sought to integrate them here. Instructors differ, however, on modes of integration and we have arranged the materials to facilitate varied approaches.

The materials have this in common, too: They may be viewed, in part, as a kind of advanced course in contracts. Contract necessarily undergirds nearly the whole of the law school curriculum; we do not apologize for its reappearance here. Indeed, our own classroom experience tells us that a great many students would profit from an exact repetition of their first year contracts course! (And two of us teach first year contracts regularly.) But the materials we offer here will duplicate few of your first year experiences. These materials will treat a few contracts topics to which you were exposed in your first year, but generally in greater depth or from a quite different angle. Further, we will take you into new and distinctive areas of advanced contracts including security, credit, documents of title, and commercial paper. In addition, here you will encounter far more regulatory law than is true in first year contracts courses. As we shall see, in some branches of our subject, freedom of contract is dramatically waning and regulatory law is rapidly supplanting it. Finally, and perhaps most important of all, the materials that follow afford students opportunities to develop skills in working with complex statutory schemes far beyond anything possible in the first year contracts course. We are now in the Age of the Statute.

SECTION 2. ORIGINS OF NEEDS FOR COMMERCIAL LAW

Millions of "deals" occur each day in the United States. Many are between businessmen and many are between businessmen and consumers. These deals and their performance are the stuff of commercial and consumer life to which these materials will be addressed.

The deals involved vary greatly. Many involve sales of goods or intangibles, and the like. Many consist of leasing arrangements. Many involve loans or extensions of credit, with or without "security interests" (interests that give a creditor priority rights in a specific asset of the debtor). Many involve the rendition of services by insurers, carriers, storers and the like. Many involve the use of notes, checks and other "negotiable instruments." The overwhelming majority of these deals go through without incident. But when something does go wrong, there may be occasion to resort to law and to legal processes. What kinds of law? What kinds of processes? The answers to these questions turn on the nature of the real world problems which generate the needs for laws and legal processes in the first place.

Suppose, for example, that one party to an alleged deal simply denies that a deal was ever made. He, in effect, says that under the law no binding relationship came into being. To determine whether he is correct, resort to what might be called *rules of validation* is required. These rules specify the requisites of a valid contract of sale, or of a valid security interest, and so on. The legal need is for *such rules,* and for them to be clear, definite, accessible, and ascertainable, in advance of deals. Rules specifying *how* to "make it legal" are fundamental. Without them, private ordering under law could not exist. One of the primary functions of bodies of commercial and consumer law is to facilitate and sanction private ordering and private autonomy. In our system there is, we think, positive value in affording individuals extensive power to give their deals the force of law. *How* they must do this is the province of rules of validation.

Parties to a transaction may have sought, in writing, to specify their wants and expectations in Durer-like detail, only to find, at a later point, that they disagree over the interpretation or construction of some part of their agreement. Here the specific legal need is for rational and just *rules of interpretation and construction.* Such rules guide courts; they facilitate counseling; they may also lead parties to settle their differences without resort to courts.

Assume the parties have not planned out their deal in detail. At some later stage, something goes wrong or some question arises on which their written agreement or their general understanding, as the case may be, is wholly silent. For example, goods contracted for are destroyed by fire while in transit. Or a pledgee of goods pledged to secure a loan decides he would like to repledge these same goods to a third party. Or a borrower wants to know if he has the right to pay back a loan without penalty. Here the legal need is for substantive *suppletive rules,* rules which presuppose and supplement the incomplete private transaction with specific "terms." To be generally fair and just, such rules should be based upon the likely commercial or consumer understanding of such matters. For, insofar as there is a standard understanding, it is not unreasonable to feed it into the skeletal deal.

A variation on the immediately preceding problem is this: The reality of many deals is that parties typically do not specify their expected performances in detail. Here the legal need is for rationally conceived suppletive rules which specify the substance of the deal. In modern law, "implied warranties" are perhaps the best example. In many simple sales nothing is ever said at the time of the deal about the standard to which the goods must conform. Such warranty or warranties are left to be supplied by law. The very existence of such suppletive law gives rise to a further distinctive kind of legal need: the need for *rules of disclaimer,* rules which specify *how* the parties can modify or exclude altogether what the suppletive law would otherwise supply. That such rules should generally be clear, definite, and ascertainable in advance requires no argument.

People being what they are, and society being what it is, some parties will try to take advantage of others and some sometimes will not know what is in their own best interest. For example, a consumer may enter an entirely lopsided and unfair deal. The "real" world thus generates the problem of whether or not the terms of such deals are to be enforced. And the law must then face another specific kind of legal need—a need for what might be called *regulatory policing rules.* It has been suggested that the "core task" of commercial and consumer law is "to determine the relatively few rules which are not subject to change by agreement, the rules which are designed to stake out the necessary minimum area of protection for parties whose bargaining power is inferior." See Schlesinger, *The Uniform Commercial Code in the Light of Comparative Law,* 1 Inter-Am.L.Rev. 11, 33 (1959). Extensive needs for policing rules to regulate exchanges have only recently been recognized in our system. Such rules plainly invade the province of private autonomy and limit freedom of contract. That, so far as possible, parties should know in advance what they cannot enforceably agree to seems obvious.

Akin to regulatory policing rules are rules which may be designated as *third party protection rules.* Many consumer and commercial transactions, occurrences, and events impinge directly or indirectly on the interests of third parties not privy to the transaction at hand. Some occur fraudulently, as where a seller of goods in his possession sells these same goods successively to two different parties and then absconds. But other such transactions are not necessarily dishonest, as where a creditor establishes a preferred position *vis a vis* other creditors of the same debtor. Here the specific legal need is for rules which protect, as far as possible, the interests of all concerned. For example, in the creditor situation, the law might require that any creditor seeking such a preferred position must in some way give public notice of this fact so that interested third parties may act accordingly. Like policing rules, third party protection rules limit freedom of contract, for to be effective they must not be subject to variation by agreement of the parties.

Within the world of commerce, the activities of selling and buying and of lending and borrowing are ubiquitous. And they are often intertwined. Buyer-debtors are actually more common than general debtors. Seldom is a debtor a debtor of only one person. Moreover, in a typical year, a significant minority of debtors fall into financial difficulty. Assuming that such a debtor does not have enough assets to pay all of his debts, which creditors are to receive what? The specific legal need generated by such problems is for *rules of priority,* rules which, in circumstances of scarcity, determine who gets what. Prospective lenders, as well as sellers selling on credit, would often want to know in advance the bearing such rules could have on their situations.

Failure to pay a debt when due is but one kind and perhaps the simplest kind of failure of promised performance known to the law. Among others are non-delivery or nonconforming delivery of, goods; failure of a carrier or a bank to obey agreed instructions from the seller or the buyer; misconduct of a warehouseman, and so forth. Here, the specific legal need is for *suppletive remedial rules and procedures.* Of course, the parties themselves might agree in advance on remedies and on the steps to be taken to perfect rights to such remedies. But in most transactions, remedies and remedial procedures are left to be supplied by the law. "Remedies" is used here in an appropriately broad sense to include all of the permissible responses to breach of a deal: abandonment, specific relief, and damages. "Procedures" is used here to include the various hoops to be jumped through in order to perfect rights to particular remedies. Thus the law might, with reason, require a disgruntled buyer to notify his seller immediately of any specific defects in goods he wishes to reject for nonconformity. Similarly, the law might specify a whole series of steps that a creditor should take in order to walk off with some asset of a debtor against the protests of other similarly unpaid creditors. The law must provide remedial rules and procedures if "making a deal legal" is to have any meaning at all in that vast majority of transactions in which the parties, assuming business will go forward as usual, say nothing of such matters in their agreement. To be fair, and in order to further one of the fundamental purposes of our law, such rules and procedures must, over the mine-run of conflict situations, provide remedies that protect the general expectations of parties similarly situated in deals of that kind. What such expectations are is a fact to be approximated, if not ascertained, and then embodied in the relevant legal doctrines.

Rules of validation, rules of interpretation and construction, substantive suppletive rules, rules of disclaimer, policing rules, third party protection rules, priority rules, and remedial suppletive rules and procedures: these, and others, are the kinds of rules that a legal system must introduce, through code law or case law, to meet legal needs arising out of commercial and consumer activities. One or more of these kinds of rules, in turn, furthers one or more of the varied general aims of such law, whether it be statutory or judge-made: to minimize the occasions for disputes in the course of commercial and consumer dealings; to facilitate *private* ordering of human relations; to protect justified expectations; to protect individuals from various forms of over-reaching and from their own improvidence; to safeguard the interests of third parties; and more.

There is one further type of legal need that the stuff of consumer and commercial life generates, one which cuts across most of the others identified here. This is the need for rules, principles, and processes capable of accommodating and governing the *ever changing varieties* of transaction patterns that occur in the real world of commerce and business. Change and variety are now, have been, and certainly will continue to be distinctively dominant themes in this field.

SECTION 3. THE UNIFORM COMMERCIAL CODE AND ITS ANTECEDENTS—CODIFICATION OF COMMERCIAL LAW

The foremost champion of codification in the entire history of the Common Law was the 19th Century British jurist Jeremy Bentham. His pupil, John Austin, favored codification, but was cautious about it.

AUSTIN, 2 LECTURES ON JURISPRUDENCE 132–133 (Campbell ed. 1869).

"Whoever has considered the difficulty of making a good statute, will not think lightly of the difficulty of making a code. To conceive distinctly the general purpose of a statute, and the subordinate provisions through which that must be accomplished, and to express both in adequate and unambiguous language, is a task of extreme delicacy and difficulty. It is far easier to conceive justly what would be useful law, than so to construct that same law that it may accomplish the design of the lawgiver. Accordingly, statutes made with great deliberation, and by learned and judicious lawyers, have been expressed so obscurely, or constructed so unaptly, that decisions interpreting or supplementing their provisions, have been of necessity heaped upon them by the Courts of Justice. Such is notably the case with the celebrated Statute of Frauds.

"It follows that the question of Codification is a question of time and place. Speaking in abstract, or without reference to the circumstances of a given community, there can be no doubt that a complete code is better than a body of judiciary law; or is better than a body of law partly consisting of judiciary law, and partly of statute law stuck patchwise on a body of judiciary.

"But taking the question in concrete, or with a view to the expediency of codification in this or that community, a doubt may arise. For here we must contrast the existing law—not with the beau idéal of possible codes, but—with that particular code which an attempt to codify would then and there engender. And that particular and practical question, as Herr von Savigny has rightly judged, will turn mainly on the answer that must be given to another: namely, Are there men, then and there, competent to the difficult task of successful codification? of producing a code, which, on the whole, would more than compensate the evil that must necessarily attend the change?

"The vast difficulty of successful codification, no rational advocate of codification will deny or doubt. Its impossibility none of its rational opponents will venture to affirm."

Bentham, had he heard them, might have been offended by these remarks, for he considered himself competent to codify any law, anywhere, any time. Bentham died in 1832 without having much impact on the codification of English law during his lifetime. But partly as a result of his posthumous influence, a codification movement in England and in America began within fifty years of his death. Interestingly enough, some of these early efforts at codification were in fields of commercial law. The British Bills of Exchange Act of 1882 was the first successful attempt to codify a major branch of English commercial law. This Act was followed in 1893 by the British Sale of Goods Act. M.D. Chalmers, the principal draftsman of these two Codes, was invited to address the convention of the American Bar Association in 1902 on the desirability of codifying commercial law. He closed his speech with these remarks:

CHALMERS, CODIFICATION OF MERCANTILE LAW, 19 L.Q.Rev. 10, 17–18 (1903).

"In the United States, the case for codifying mercantile law is stronger than in England. I am told that an American lawyer who wishes to keep abreast of the current of judicial decision has to take in some fifty-eight volumes of Law Reports every year. In America, there is no choice between common law on the one hand and statute law on the other. Each state is independent in matters of legislation and judicature. The American lawyer, therefore, has to deal not with one but with forty streams of common law, each of which is liable to be disturbed by the action of an independent Legislature. But Commerce knows nothing of State boundaries, and it seems intolerable that if a man in Chicago makes a contract with a man in New York, his rights and duties cannot be determined without an elaborate investigation into the conflict of laws. The only possible remedy that I can see for this state of affairs is codification."

At the time Chalmers spoke, the movement to codify particular branches of commercial law in the United States was already underway. In the 1890's the National Conference of Commissioners on Uniform State Laws had been formed, with representatives from each state many of whom were dedicated to the cause of uniform codification. In 1896, the Conference promulgated the Negotiable Instruments Law, a Code governing the rights and liabilities of parties to checks, promissory notes, and other kinds of commercial paper. Ultimately, the "NIL" was adopted by all state legislatures. In 1906, the Conference presented the Uniform Sales Act for adoption and more than two-thirds of the states enacted it. With this Act, American law professors entered the codification arena, and have been central figures there ever since. Professor Samuel Williston of the Harvard Law School drafted the Uniform Sales Act on behalf of the Conference, and also the Uniform Warehouse Receipts Act, promulgated in 1906, and the Uniform Bills of Lading Act promulgated in 1909 both of which became law in all states. Later, Professor Karl Llewellyn of the Columbia Law School drafted the Uniform Trust Receipts Act, which the Conference promulgated in 1933.

Thirty-two states adopted it. Another uniform commercial act, dealing with "conditional" sales, was drafted by Professor Bogert, but it met with success in only ten state legislatures.

In 1940, the idea of a single comprehensive commercial code covering all the foregoing branches of commercial law was conceived and proposed to the Conference of Commissioners on Uniform State Laws. The foregoing uniform acts had become outdated in two ways: changes had occurred in the patterns of commercial activity extant when these laws were enacted, and wholly new patterns had emerged giving rise to new kinds of legal needs. Moreover, even with the Uniform Acts most widely enacted, uniformity no longer existed, for the various state legislatures and judiciaries had added their own distinctive amendments and glosses.

The American Law Institute joined with the National Conference of Commissioners to co-sponsor the "Uniform Commercial Code" project. Professor Karl Llewellyn, then still at Columbia Law School, became chief architect, and his wife, Ms. Soia Mentschikoff, his principal assistant (designated, respectively, "Chief Reporter" and "Associate Chief Reporter"). Ms. Mentschikoff described the drafting process, in Mentschikoff, *The Uniform Commercial Code: An Experiment in Democracy in Drafting,* 36 A.B.A.J. 419 (1950). The drafting process is also discussed extensively in a recent symposium to which five drafters contributed. See *Symposium, Origins and Evolution: Drafters Reflect Upon the Uniform Commercial Code,* 43 Ohio St.L.J. 537–642 (1982).

In 1951, the sponsors promulgated the Uniform Commercial Code, and, with minor revisions, it was enacted in Pennsylvania in 1953, effective July 1, 1954. Between 1953 and 1955, the New York Law Revision Commission dropped all other work and made a thorough study of the Code, recommending many changes in the official text. During the hearings there were, from time to time, rather sharp conflicts between academicians defending the Code and practitioners attacking it.

In 1956, the Editorial Board of the Code made recommendations for revision of the 1952 Official Text, many of which were based on criticisms made at the New York Law Revision Commission Hearings. In 1957 a revised Official Text was promulgated incorporating recommended changes. Further Official Texts, with minor changes, were promulgated in 1958 and 1962.

By 1968, the Uniform Commercial Code had been enacted by all but one state in the United States. A "Permanent Editorial Board" was established by the sponsoring organizations primarily to consider the wisdom of proposed amendments to the Code. (The idea for such a Board was set forth in Schlesinger, *The Uniform Commercial Code in the Light of Comparative Law,* 1 N.Y. Law Revision Commission 87 (1955). This Board has made various reports.

The Code's sponsors and its Permanent Editorial Board have not left it alone. In 1972, the new "1972" Official Text of the Code was promulgated. That Text left nearly all of the 1962 Official Text intact except in the field of personal property security governed by Article 9. Article 9 was given a good overhaul in the 1972 Official Text, though its basic theory, structure, and scope remains the same. As of 1987, the 1972 text of Article Nine was in force in forty five states. There is now also a new "1978" Official Text, which in 1987 had been adopted by 19 states. This version includes changes in Article Eight, Investment Securities.

The Code is divided into nine substantive articles. The first is a general article bearing on various aspects of the entire Code. The remaining eight articles are broken down first into "Parts" and the "Parts" are in turn subdivided into sections. Some brief remarks on each article are in order:

Article 2: Sales

Article 2 applies to "transactions in goods" and supersedes the Uniform Sales Act. Major innovations in Article 2 include de-emphasis of the title concept in settling sales controversies, several novel provisions governing formation of the sales contract, and different standards of conduct applicable to merchants and to nonmerchants in discharging their contract obligations.

Article 3: Commercial Paper

Article 3 is a revision of the Uniform Negotiable Instruments Law. It includes fewer innovations than any other major Article of the Code. Unlike the Uniform Negotiable Instruments Law, Article 3 does not apply to bank deposits and collections, letters of credit, or corporate securities. Articles 4, 5, and 8, respectively, deal with these subjects.

Consolidation was a chief aim of the draftsmen of Article 3. While the Uniform Negotiable Instruments Law had 198 provisions, Article 3 has only 80. The most dramatic instance of consolidation in the entire Code appears in Article 3: The Code takes only 11 sections to deal with presentment, notice of dishonor, and protest, while the Uniform Negotiable Instruments Law took 67 sections to deal with these subjects.

Article 4: Bank Deposits and Collections

Article 4 replaces statutes governing bank deposits and collections. There was no prior uniform act in this field. Article 4 therefore fills an important void. Article 4 includes basic provisions settling such old questions as: When does a depository bank buy an item rather than take it for collection only? UCC 4–201, 4–213. And, as of what point in time does a bank pay an item? UCC 4–213. Among the novel provisions of Article 4 are those requiring depositors to exercise due care in discovering forgeries, UCC 4–406(1), and a provision granting bank and depositor full freedom to govern their relations by contract, "except that no agreement can disclaim a bank's responsibility for its own lack of good faith or failure to exercise ordinary care * * *." UCC 4–103(1).

Article 5: Letters of Credit

Article 5 governs a subject that in most states has been governed almost entirely by case law. In the typical letter of credit transaction, a bank, at the buyer's request, issues a "letter" to the seller, providing that the bank will, under certain conditions, honor drafts drawn by the seller on the buyer for payment of the purchase price of goods.

Article 6: Bulk Transfers

Article 6 deals with bulk transfers and, as such, emphasizes protection of the transferor's creditors.

Article 7: Documents of Title

Article 7 applies both to warehouse receipts and to bills of lading, two types of documents of title formerly governed separately by the Uniform Warehouse Receipts Act and the Uniform Bills of Lading Act.

Article 8: Investment Securities

Article 8 replaces the Uniform Stock Transfer Act and related statutes, including several provisions of the Uniform Negotiable Instruments Law. Article 8 is often called a "negotiable instruments" law for investment securities. It endows certain bonds, stocks, and other securities with attributes of negotiability and defines the rights and liabilities of issuers, transferors, and transferees. Article 8 does not supersede regulatory laws governing issuance of securities.

Article 9: Secured Transactions

Article 9 is the most novel division in the Code. It is designed to provide a simple and unified structure within which the immense variety of present-day secured financing transactions can be effected with less cost and greater certainty. The most radical innovation in Article 9 is its substitution of a unitary security device for the plethora of security devices previously in use. Terms such as "mortgagee," "pledgee," "conditional sale," and "trust receipt" do not appear in Article 9. Instead, its unitary security device is formulated in terms of four basic concepts: "secured party," "debtor," "collateral," and "security interest."

The foregoing, then, represents the general structure of the Code and demonstrates that its scope is broad. Chronologically, the Code applies to transactions "entered into" after its effective date. See UCC 10–102(2). In terms of territorial application, it applies to transactions "bearing an appropriate relation" to the enacting state. In terms of subject-matter, it applies to a wide-range of transactions. There is not, in the Code, a single "scope" provision which defines the *subject-matter* to which the *entire* Code applies. Instead, the Code is divided into ten "articles," eight of which purport to govern aspects of basic types of commercial transactions. The precise scope of each such article must usually be determined by examining not merely a specific "scope" provision within the article (if there be one) but other provisions as well, some of which are definitional in nature. The student should, at this point, become familiar with the basic "scope" provisions of Articles 9, 2, and 3.

There is no general "de-minimus" limitation on the Code's application. Thus, for example, Article 2 could apply to the sale of a fifteen-cent hamburger. See UCC 2–314.

While many of the articles of the Code can, in relation to some kinds of transactions, apply separately and alone, frequently provisions from more than one article will be applicable to the transaction at hand.

The Code recognizes the possibilities of conflict between Articles, and includes provisions governing such possibilities. See, e.g., UCC 2–102, 9–113, 3–103, 4–102(1), 8–102(1)(c), and 9–102.

SECTION 4. WHAT KIND OF A CODE IS THE UNIFORM COMMERCIAL CODE?

One of the Code drafters had this to say:

GILMORE, ARTICLE 9: WHAT IT DOES FOR THE PAST, 26 La.L.Rev. 285, 286 (1966).

"Surely the principal function of a Code is to abolish the past. At least a common lawyer assumes that that was the theory on which the great civil law codes were based. From the date of the Code's enactment, the pre-Code law is no longer available as a source of law. The gaps, the ambiguities, the unforeseen situations cannot be referred for decision to the accumulated wisdom of the past. There is a fresh start, a new universe of legal discourse, in which the only permissible way of solving a problem is to find (or pretend to find) the answer in the undefiled, the unconstrued, the uncontaminated text of the Code itself. How well the theory worked in practice, or whether it worked at all, you, as civilians, are much better equipped to say than I.

"The Uniform Commercial Code, so-called, is not that sort of Code—even in theory. It derives from the common law, not the civil law, tradition. We shall do better to think of it as a big statute—or a collection of statutes bound together in the same book—which goes as far as it goes and no further. It assumes the continuing existence of a large body of pre-Code and non-Code law on which it rests for support, which it displaces to the least possible extent, and without which it could not survive. The solid stuff of pre-Code law will furnish the rationale of decision quite as often as the Code's own gossamer substance."

A useful general discussion of the jurisprudence of the Uniform Commercial Code, primarily Article 2, appears in Danzig, *A Comment on the Jurisprudence of the Uniform Commercial Code,* 27 Stan.L.Rev. 621 (1975).

SECTION 5. THE SPECIAL PITFALLS IN USING THE UNIFORM COMMERCIAL CODE (AND SIMILAR CODES)

These pitfalls are numerous. First, the Code includes more than the usual quota of definitions. Consider, for example, the first *line* of UCC 2–205. How many of the fourteen words in that line are defined in other provisions of the Code? Where is "offer" defined? How is the researcher to know what words are defined and what ones are not? Are the "Definitional Cross References" in the Comments always exhaustive? They purport to be, but, as will be seen, they are not.

Once all defined terms have been looked up, it is still not possible to be sure that the Code answer has been found. It is essential that the researcher also check the bearing of any related provisions in the Code. The Code is an "integrated" and "interrelated" body of law. This poses a special pitfall, for it means that it often compels research beyond what seems on the surface to be the controlling provision. Check, for example, the bearing of UCC 2–508 and 2–609 on 2–601. How is one to know of such related provisions? There are "Cross References" in the Comments, but it should not be assumed that they are exhaustive.

The "legislative history" relevant to interpreting the Code is of several kinds, each posing its own special problems. The four types of such history are: (1) Official Comments, (2) Prior versions of the Code, (3) Legislative hearings and reports made prior to enactment in specific states, and (4) Books and articles by Code draftsmen. See generally, Braucher, *Legislative History of the Uniform Commercial Code,* 58 Colum.L.Rev. 798 (1958). An extensive treatment of the major research sources on the Uniform Commercial Code is Kavass, *Uniform Commercial Code Research: A Brief Guide to the Sources,* 88 Commercial L.J. 547 (1983). See also, Kelly, *Uniform Commercial Code Drafts* (1984), Vols. I & II.

As promulgated by the American Law Institute and the Conference of Commissioners on Uniform State Laws, the Official Text of the Code appears with comments on each section. As enacted by state legislators, however, only the Official Text (with whatever amendments were made) appears on the statute books. In many states the Code with comments (and local annotations) is available to the bar through private publishing houses. A lawyer must, however, bear in mind that the Official Comments are not authoritative and further that they do not cover a state's changes in the Official Text.

The Comment to each section usually contains five parts. In the first, entitled "Prior Uniform Statutory Provisions," there appears a list of references to provisions of prior Uniform Acts displaced by the section. In the second part, designated "Changes," the difference, if any, between the superseded law and the Official Text are indicated in a general way. In the third part of the Comments, called "Purposes of Changes" or "Purposes of Changes and New Matter," the purposes of the particular Official Text Code section are explained, and, in some instances, illustrated. In the fourth part, "Cross References," there is a list of related Code provisions. In the last part there appears a list of definitional cross references.

It should not be assumed that for purposes of interpretation and construction, the Official Comments stand in the same relation to the Official Text as true legislative history typically stands to the language of ordinary statutes. The Comments, or some of them, differ from such history in several ways. They were not always laid before the enacting legislators at the time of Code adoption. Some of the present Comments were not even in existence when the sections commented on were enacted into law in some states. Some of the existing Comments appear to have been addressed to earlier drafts of sections of the Code different from the later sections enacted into law. In some important parts of the Code, the draftsman of the Comments was not the draftsman of the section commented on. See generally Skilton, *Some Comments on the Comments to the Uniform Commercial Code,* 1966 Wis.L.Rev. 597.

Still, the Comments have influenced many judicial decisions and will certainly continue to do so. That they are not entitled to exactly the same weight as true legislative history may, therefore, be unimportant. But it is important to appreciate the special hazards and pitfalls in the use of the Comments. A detailed appreciation of these must await immersion in the processes of problem solving that lie ahead in this book. For now, a general survey of the most common hazards and pitfalls must do.

Perhaps the principal hazard in using the Comments (apart from the inexhaustiveness of their cross references) is that they not uncommonly add to or vary the Code language. Some insight into why this is so is revealed in the following passage from a speech made by the chief draftsman of the Code, Karl N. Llewellyn:

LLEWELLYN, WHY A COMMERCIAL CODE? 22 Tenn.L.Rev. 779, 784, 794, 782 (1953).

"I am ashamed of it in some ways; there are so many places that I could make a little better, there are so many beautiful ideas I tried to get in that would have been good for the law, but I was voted down * * * when we weren't allowed to put in where we wanted to go * * *, we at least got the thing set up so that we are allowed to state in accompanying comments where the particular sections are trying to go."

The Comments are both expansive and restrictive in nature. Their expansiveness frequently takes the form of explicit rejection of negative implications from the text of the section. In view of such Comments, the maxim *expressio unius exclusio alterius est* (the expression of one thing is the exclusion of the other) loses some of its force. (See, for an example, the Comments to UCC 2–318.) On the restrictiveness of Comments, it has been remarked that, "it would not be difficult to cite examples where the draftsman has wisely left a breathing space, so to say, in the text to allow a free case-law development and then come back to the comment to nail the coffin lid down tightly." Gilmore, *On the Difficulties of Codifying Commercial Law,* 57 Yale L.J. 1341, 1355 (1948). Of course, if the Comments are not *law* then perhaps the lid is not so tight as all that.

It has been said that the definitional and sectional "cross references" in the Comments cannot be relied on as exhaustive. As an example, note that the definitional cross references to UCC 2–316 fail to mention the crucial fact that "conspicuous" is defined in UCC 1–201(10). And there are still other sources of frustration. Comments often blithely assume that the reader is familiar with the details of prior law. Some Comments deal with sections other than the one they are addressed to. (See, e.g., Comment 2 to UCC 2–312 dealing with UCC 2–607). Comments vary greatly in quality. Some are overly long, others not long enough. Some offer insight. Some confuse.

We turn, now, to earlier versions of the Code as a distinctive source of guidance and misguidance in resolving problems of interpretation and construction. The lawyer should know of the existence of such earlier drafts. The main prior drafts are:

1945 Drafts and Redrafts of Parts of the Proposed Code (Unpublished).

1949 Proposed Draft with Comments.

1950 Proposed Final Draft with Comments.

1951 Final Text with Comments.
Amendments in May, 1951.
Amendments in September, 1951.

1952 Official Text with Comments.

1953 Changes Recommended by a Meeting of the Enlarged Editorial Board. Part A, Part B.

1956 Recommendations of the Editorial Board.

1957 Official Text with Comments.
Supplement to the 1957 Official Edition of the Code.

1958 Official Text with Comments.

1962 Amendments to the Uniform Commercial Code, Permanent Editorial Board for the U.C.C., Report 1.

1962 Official Text with Comments.

1965 Report No. 2 of the Permanent Editorial Board for the Uniform Commercial Code.

1966 Report No. 3 of the Permanent Editorial Board for the Uniform Commercial Code.

1971 Review Committee for Article Nine, Final Report.

1972 Official Text with Comments.

1978 Official Text with Comments.

Inferences based on changes in the language of successive revisions of Code sections are inherently unreliable. They are all the more unreliable because "frequently matters have been omitted as being implicit without statement and language has been changed or added solely for clarity." This quote comes from the comment to a section in the 1952 text of the Code which read: "Prior drafts of text and comments may not be used to ascertain legislative intent." This section itself was eventually deleted from the Official Text of the Code. It should have been left in. It will have to be left to the Supreme Court of the United States to rule out the use of prior versions of sections and comments as an unconstitutional form of cruel and inhuman punishment of fellow lawyers. Or perhaps the decisive argument will be that because of their scarcity (only a few libraries have them) their use denies equal protection of the laws.

Another basic type of material that is of relevance in resolving problems of Code interpretation and construction consists of legislative hearings and official reports made by agencies of enacting states. These form the more immediate background of Code enactment. Their status is somewhat uncertain in regard to the Code, for it includes its own "legislative" history in the form of comments. In the face of conflict, which is to control? And there are other problems.

A further type of material that has figured in Code interpretation and construction consists of books and articles and memoranda written by persons who participated in the drafting of the Code. The outstanding instance to appear to date is a two volume treatise: Gilmore, Security Interests in Personal Property (1965). In a footnote at p. 289 of the first volume of this treatise, Professor Gilmore confesses that he had a large hand in the drafting of Article 9 of the Code. And his treatise has been justly acclaimed in reviews.

John Locke might have said that Professor Gilmore's treatise has a natural and inalienable right to be quoted and cited on any and all Article 9 problems. Actually such is not without parallel. After the Uniform Sales Act, promulgated in 1906, was widely enacted, its draftsman, Professor Samuel Williston, published a treatise, *Williston on Sales,* which explained what the Act was all about. It would startle no one to find that Williston's treatise influenced the law. Similarly, Gilmore's has influenced the law.

An exceptionally fine article on methods of interpreting the Uniform Commercial Code is: McDonnell, *Purposive Interpretation of the Uniform Commercial Code: Some Implications for Jurisprudence,* 126 U.Pa.L.Rev. 795 (1978). Modesty forbids two of us from calling attention to another book that lawyers and judges regularly resort to: J. White and R. Summers, The Uniform Commercial Code (2d ed. 1980). In moments of levity we will refer to it as the "Crutch." Otherwise, it is known as "White and Summers."

SECTION 6. COMMERCIAL LAW NOT IN THE UNIFORM COMMERCIAL CODE

Despite its seemingly wide sweep, the Code is far from comprehensive. There are some transactions it does not govern at all, and there are many aspects of many transactions to which its provisions might apply but will not, for various reasons.

First and at the fore, the parties can generally make their own "law." As one authority has put it, "We are within that area of law where—to use an old-fashioned, pre-positivistic phrase—businessmen are free to make their own law. They do so expressly through contract, implicitly through a course of dealing, collectively through custom and resultant business understanding." By their own agreement, then, the parties to a commercial deal can vary most of the provisions of the Code.

Second, the Code itself, by its own terms, does not purport to control many important types of transactions that can fairly be called commercial. For example, it does not apply to sales of commercial realty nor to security interests therein. It does not apply to the formation, performance, and enforcement of insurance contracts. It does not apply to suretyship transactions (except where a surety is a party to a negotiable instrument). It does not encompass the law of bankruptcy. It does not govern legal tender.

Third, the Code does not even purport to govern exhaustively all aspects of all transactions to which its provisions do apply. Many of its provisions obviously can come into play only by virtue of some key event, e.g., "default," which may be defined by the terms of the agreement between the parties. See, e.g., UCC 9–501(1). Furthermore, resort to supplemental principles of law outside the Code will often be necessary. See generally, UCC 1–103. Consider the following three examples. To apply the provisions on authorized and unauthorized signatures in Article 3 (UCC 3–403 and 3–404), local agency principles must be considered. To determine what title a "transferor" has under UCC 2–403, it is essential to refer to non-Code law. The "grounds" of impossibility and frustration as a defense to the breach of a contract of sale are not exhaustively stated in the Code. See UCC 2–613, 2–614, and 2–615. Presumably additional grounds recognized in "general contract law" can be invoked. In addition, the Code has its own "gaps"—situations arising within the framework of the Code on specific aspects of which the Code is altogether silent.

Fourth, there are state statutes, most of which are regulatory in nature, which either supplement or supersede Code provisions altogether. See, e.g., UCC 2–102, 9–201, and 9–203(4) for references to the possible existence of such statutes. Usury laws and so-called "Retail Installment Sales Acts" are outstanding examples. It is appropriate at this point to emphasize that the Code does *not,* in terms, concern itself with the general problems of the *consumer* as consumer.

Fifth, the Uniform Commercial Code is *state* law. This means that any valid and conflicting federal commercial law supersedes it. Thus, for example, there are the Federal Consumer Protection Act and the Magnuson-Moss Warranty Act. The Federal Bills of Lading Act (sometimes called the Pomerene Act) 49 U.S.C.A. §§ 81–124 (1982), rather than Article 7 of the Code, applies to all interstate bills of lading transactions.

Sixth, there is a growing body of federal regulatory law that supplements commercial law at many points. For example, the federal Food and Drug Act imposes controls on the quality of goods sold and on the ways they are marketed. The Robinson-Patman Act operates to regulate the price of some goods. Federal statutes govern the creation of security interests in some types of collateral. See, e.g., the Ship Mortgage Act, 1920, referred to in UCC 9–104 Comment 1.

Seventh, this survey of non-Code sources of commercial law would not be complete without some reference to procedural law. Generally, commercial claims are litigated in accordance with the procedures applicable in any ordinary case. There are, however, a few procedural doctrines that have a distinctively commercial flavor. Some of these are incorporated in the Code, although it generally does not purport to cover procedural law. See, e.g., the "vouching in" provisions of UCC 2–607(5).

Finally, there are practices and attitudes of legal officials and of men of commerce which cannot really be captured in the language of any Code but which, nonetheless, have an inevitable impact on legal evolution. Professor Edwin W. Patterson has said of these that they seem "to be a part of the societal matrix, a kind of semantic and narrative substratum of law and other articulate forms of social control." 1 N.Y. Law Revision Commission Report 56 (1955) (footnote omitted).

BOOK ONE

SECURITY INTERESTS IN PERSONALTY

CHAPTER TWO

AN INTRODUCTION TO PERSONAL PROPERTY SECURITY

SECTION 1. WHAT IS A SECURITY INTEREST AND WHY DOES IT MATTER?

According to section 1–201(37) "Security interest means an interest in personal property or fixtures which secures payment or performance of an obligation." The section goes on to embellish the definition in various ways not relevant for our introductory purposes. The following examples illustrate common types of security interests:

(1) Edgar Jarvis bought a dump truck from Hellas Trucking Company pursuant to an agreement whereby Edgar paid $5,000 down and agreed to pay $500 a month for five years. Edgar signed a promissory note for the unpaid balance, naming the trucking company as payee. Edgar also signed a piece of paper headed "security agreement." This piece of paper included a clause whereby the Trucking Company retained a "security interest" in the truck sold to Edgar as security for the unpaid balance.

(2) Irene Watson owned a bookstore. She sold large batches of books to public schools in the area on open account pursuant to arrangements whereby she was paid by the public school system involved once every sixty days. Irene wished to enlarge her store. She borrowed $20,000 from Ready Bank, signed a promissory note in that amount and a security agreement giving the Bank a "security interest" in her book inventory and in her accounts receivable as security for the repayment of the $20,000 (in $1,000 monthly installments).

(3) Fred Wirtz was a tomato grower. Canwell Company was a major tomato canning company in the area, and usually bought Fred's tomatoes. To finance Fred's planting, cultivating, and harvesting, for the upcoming crop, Canwell lent Fred $50,000 pursuant to a promissory note and a security agreement which gave Canwell a "security interest" in the growing crops and provided in effect that Wirtz was obligated to sell his tomato crop to Canwell.

In all three of these transactions, the parties entered into a *contract* that provided for a "security interest." The legal consequences of so agreeing to a "security interest" are crucial, and we turn to these in the next paragraph. Although many persons (especially consumers) who agree to a "security interest" probably do not fully understand these consequences, they are nonetheless taken to have *agreed* thereto. The theory and much of the reality is that security interests under Article 9 are consensual. This does not mean there are no limits on freedom of contract here. We will see that there are some major ones. The security interest in each of the above cases was in some species of *personal property:* a truck, books, accounts receivable, and crops. The security interest in each instance also secured the *repayment or performance of an obligation.* For now, read UCC 1–201(3) and (11), 9–203(1), 9–105(1)(*l*).

What if the debtor in the above examples failed to repay or perform? That is, what if the debtor defaulted? In that event, the secured creditor would be entitled under Article 9, Part 5, of the Code to have the collateral sold and the proceeds applied on the debt, or, in some cases, to take the collateral in satisfaction of the debt. These rights are called rights to "foreclose." Thus, the idea of a *conditional property right* is the conceptual key to understanding what a security interest is. A creditor can fall back on this right and exercise it *if* his debtor fails to pay (or perform) as promised. An extensive set of Article 9 rules governs how a security interest is created, how it may be made as effective as possible against third parties (often debtors deal with other creditors and still other third parties who will have their just claims as well), who has priority in the property subject to the creditor's security interest when two or more parties claim it, what rights the creditor has against the property on default, and so on.

Some creditors take security interests not in "personal property or fixtures" to which Article 9 applies, but in real estate. These interests are governed by a vast, ancient and complex body of law dealing with mortgages, land sale contracts, and the like, a body of law studied in other courses, but on which we will draw from time to time by way of historical background and analogy.

A great many creditors are unsecured. That is, they do not take security interests in personalty or in realty, even though they lend money or extend credit. They therefore do not have the conditional property rights that secured creditors do. This frequently puts them at a real disadvantage. If the debtor defaults, they cannot simply take specific property of the debtor and dispose of it to pay off their claims. They have no right of foreclosure against particular assets of the debtor (as above). They must first file a law suit, reduce their claims to judgment, and proceed from there. Also, certain other creditors (and many purchasers) who do have security interests in the debtor's property will usually take *priority* over the claims of unsecured creditors.

It is easy to see, then, why creditors take security interests when they lend or extend credit. This gives them a right to foreclose and certain priority rights against third persons, in the event the debtor defaults. But why would anyone who lends or extends credit *not* take security? Another basic question is this: Is the legal recognition and enforcement of security interests a good thing for society on the whole? Some scholars have recently expressed doubt. An example is Schwartz, *Security Interests and Bankruptcy Priorities: A Review of Current Theories,* 10 J. Legal Stud. 1 (1981). A more recent analysis of the competing theories can be found in Scott, *A Relational Theory of Secured Financing,* 86 Colum.L.Rev. 901 (1986). We will return to this question in due course.

Of course the debtor who defaults may also be a debtor who "files for bankruptcy." We will shortly see that bankruptcy can operate to eliminate or to limit drastically the advantage that the secured creditor has over the unsecured creditor.

Problem 2–1

Sam Seller sells a used car to Ben Buyer for $2500 with Ben paying $500 down and signing a promissory note for the balance, which is to be repaid monthly. One month later, unknown to Sam, Ben borrows $2000 from Ace Finance Company pursuant to a valid security agreement duly created and perfected (by a notation on the certificate of title). The agreement gives Ace a security interest in Ben's car. Ben defaults on his obligation to Sam. He also defaults on his debt to Ace. Sam goes to Ben's house where he sees the car parked in the street (Ben having gone on vacation). Can Sam lawfully drive it off (assuming he has a key)? Can Ace, who arrives at the same time? See UCC 9–503. If Sam takes the car, will he be liable for the tort of conversion? Can Ace sell the car and apply the proceeds to its loan? See UCC 9–504. Suppose both Sam and Ace claim the proceeds of the foreclosure sale ($1000), who wins? See UCC 9–201.

SECTION 2. PRE-ARTICLE 9 LAW ON PERSONAL PROPERTY SECURITY INTERESTS: SOME HISTORY AND SOME FUNDAMENTALS OF THEORY

In the next section, we provide a detailed roadmap and introduction to Article 9 of the Uniform Commercial Code on secured transactions. Article 9 is a single integrated body of rules governing the creation and effect of consensual security interests in personal property (of nearly all kinds). This body of law was drafted in the late 1940's and early 1950's. It is widely heralded as one of the great statutory advances in modern times. You are not yet fully in a position to understand why this is so, but here we will identify the main explanations so that you can bear them in mind as we proceed.

First, Article 9 gathered up not only some statutory but also the vast case law on personal property security, modernized it, and put all of its essential elements into statutory form. Since the law of security interests is largely planner's law, the more accessible and certain statutory form represents a major improvement. Second, in place of the plethora of pre-Code personal property security devices to which we will turn immediately, i.e., the pledge, the chattel mortgage, the conditional sale, the trust receipt, the factor's lien (and more), Article 9 substituted *one* basic security device and one body of law. This represents the most significant single unification effort in the history of modern American private law. At one fell swoop, the Many became the One, with corresponding elimination of excess concepts, needless boundary disputes, and much else. Third, Article 9 extended and rationalized beyond any body of law before it one of the most basic policies in the field, namely, that in general a party with a security interest in personal property should not prevail over most competing claimants unless that party has in effect given the world notice or potential notice of that interest either by taking possession of the collateral or by making a public filing of the interest in a publicly accessible filing office where third parties can go to learn of it or of its possible existence.

Before the magnitude of all these changes can be grasped, it is essential to consider some historical background. We will also see that this background can be useful in still other important ways.

The document (called a "security agreement" in the Uniform Commercial Code) that creates a security interest then is both a contract and a conveyance which finds its roots not only in contract but also in property. As we will see below, the typical commercial security agreement will run to tens of (and perhaps many more) pages. It will be full of promises, mostly made by the debtor, but also some by the creditor. Of course, the most basic promise of the debtor will simply be a promise to pay off the indebtedness owed the secured party. Unlike the typical deed, the agreement is not necessarily formal; as long as it contains a few fundamental terms, it can contain most others that the parties might wish. Typically the creditor agrees to lend money and the debtor promises to pay it back according to explicit terms, perhaps to operate his business in a specific way, to make reports to the creditors and to limit his behavior in other ways.

Invariably the document is also a conveyance of some property interest of the debtor to the creditor. This is the creditor's "security interest." Such an interest is a conditional property right—the right to repossess an asset of the debtor on default, and (within limits) to take an asset ahead of others.

Absent overreaching or some other unusual and egregious event, the agreement controls the rights of the debtor and the secured creditor. That is not necessarily true of the rights of the secured creditor versus third parties who have also dealt with the debtor such as purchasers, secured and unsecured creditors, and the debtor's trustee in bankruptcy (if there be one). The presence of such persons presents different questions. Recall the real property recording statutes that you have studied in your first-year property course. For example, those statutes modify what would otherwise be legal rights of various parties to land based on conventional common law doctrines such as *nemo dat quod non habaet* (he who hath not cannot give.) If A transfers his real estate to B, presumably A has no title left and cannot transfer anything to C, yet that is not the outcome if B fails to record. Here if B fails to record C may take ahead of B if C is a bona fide purchaser. You learned that real property recording statutes in effect undo our conventional views about conveyance of property and in some cases grant title to a party later in time (C above) who, according to conventional common law doctrine, would be thought to have received no title, since the seller had already conveyed it to another.

The very same idea has also emerged in the field of personal property security. In the early days, the courts faced essentially the same problems in personal property security as they faced in structuring fair and appropriate rules with respect to real estate conveyances. The basic question is: To what extent should a court be allowed to disregard the rights contractually established between the parties when those rights are challenged by a third person? In pre-industrial society the possessor of personal property was generally expected to be the owner or his agent. Indeed it was thought to be fraudulent and misleading to keep possession of that very property while at the same time creating a security interest in it in favor of a creditor. In fact, giving such a creditor possession was generally deemed to put others on notice of the creditor's interest. But suppose the debtor retains possession of his personalty while giving a security interest in it. Or suppose the debtor buys property on credit, takes possession of it, yet grants the seller a security interest. In such cases, should the courts recognize the secured creditor's interest ahead of claims by other creditors? Should not these other creditors prevail on the ground that they were misled by the debtor's possession and "ostensible ownership"? See, generally, Baird, *Notice Filing and the Problem of Ostensible Ownership,* 12 J. Legal Studies 53 (1983).

Consider the cases that follow with the foregoing questions in mind. Here we see earlier courts wrestling with such questions. The cases involve pre-Uniform Commercial Code security arrangements called "conditional sales contracts" under which, in the jurisdictions at hand, title remained with the seller of goods until the condition was met, namely payment of the full price. If that condition was not met, title never went to the buyer; it follows, too, that on conventional property analysis the buyer did not have the power to convey it to, or to create a security interest in it on behalf of, third parties. Of course, this was contrary to the principle of ostensible ownership according to which the possessor has such rights. Moreover, there was no recording statute in the jurisdiction providing that the secured creditor could file notice of a security interest and thus give public notice that the possessor-debtor was not the sole owner. The student should also keep these cases in mind when reading the materials that follow on the history of personal property in the United States. Of course, today, Article 9 of the UCC generally requires that the secured creditor either take possession or file to maximize rights against third parties. The notion that a creditor-seller of goods could effectively provide by agreement for the retention of "good title" (until payment) against third parties to goods that had been sold and delivered to a debtor-buyer under a conditional sale contract without public notice to such third parties now seems laughable. The modern student of Article 9 would cut quickly through the language and would recognize this agreement, in conditional sale terms, to be no more than an "unperfected security interest," and would decide against the secured creditor. Earlier, the problem was not so easy.

MCINTOSH & BEGAN v. HILL

Supreme Court of Arkansas, 1886.
1 S.W. 680.

COCKRILL, C.J. This is replevin for the possession of a mule. The facts, as taken from the abstract, are as follows: "In March, 1884, S.S. Wann contracted to sell to one Overton the mule in controversy, for $90, due in the fall. Until the purchase money was paid the mule was to be and remain the property of Wann, and, upon failure to pay in the fall, Overton was to deliver the mule to Wann, and pay for its *use.* Soon after the purchase, Overton mortgaged the mule, with the crop to be raised by him, to the appellants, for supplies for the year 1884; and at the time told the appellants that he had bought the mule on a credit. Overton died soon after the mortgage. The mule was used to make the crop, a part of which was paid on the mortgage. The parties, not being able to pay for the mule in the fall, returned it to Wann, and settled for the use of it. Wann then sold the mule to the appellee, from whom it was replevied by the appellants under their mortgage. The value of the mule was fifty or sixty dollars. The mortgage was duly acknowledged and recorded while the mule was in Overton's possession, and the sum of about $40 was still due on it." The judgment of the court was against the right of the mortgagees.

The question presented, put in the best light for them, is whether the title of a vendor parting with the possession of a chattel, upon the condition that the title shall not pass until the purchase money is paid, shall prevail against a *bona fide* purchaser for value from the vendee in possession, before the condition is complied with, without notice of the original seller's claim of ownership, or of the condition upon which the delivery was made.

In *Carroll v. Wiggins,* 30 Ark. 402, it was decided that a sale and delivery of personal property, on condition that the title is not to pass until payment of the purchase price, does not vest the title in the vendee until the condition is performed, and the rule was enforced against a purchaser from the vendee with notice of the condition.

In *Andrews v. Cox,* 42 Ark. 473, the question as to the attitude of a purchaser, without notice from a vendee holding subject to a like condition, was discussed by the court in considering a kindred question, and, though this question is not expressly ruled, the intimation is very strong that the title of the original vendor must prevail.

The hardship that is sometimes discovered when the condition is to be enforced against a *bona fide* purchaser has induced some of the courts to come to the conclusion that, as against him, possession is *per se* a badge of fraud; and that the doctrine that, where one of two innocent parties must suffer, the loss should fall on the one who caused the dilemma, protects the *bona fide* purchaser. But possession alone gives no right to transfer title, and one who has no title (and the conditional vendee before performance of the condition has none, according to *Carroll v. Wiggins, supra*) can confer none. Possession of personal property is only *prima facie* evidence of title, and the doctrine of *caveat emptor* prevails, notwithstanding the possession. The *prima facie* title must yield to the actual title, when it is asserted, and the buyer who trusts to appearances must suffer the loss, if they prove delusive. If the vendor is estopped from reclaiming his property from an innocent purchaser, there is no principle, as was said in *Andrews v. Cox,* upon which we could stop short of holding that one who had borrowed or hired any personal property might divest the true owner of his title simply by assuming the power to sell. We think that reason and the overwhelming weight of authority pronounce in favor of the right of the original vendor. The leading case on the subject is that of *Coggill v. Hartford, etc., R.R.,* 3 Gray, 545. See, too, *Ketchum v. Brennan,* 53 Miss. 596; *Fairbanks v. Eureka Co.,* 67 Ala. 109; *Blackwell v. Walker,* 5 Fed.Rep. 419; cases cited in note to *Stadtfield v. Huntsman,* 37 Amer.Rep. 661, 662; Schouler, Pers.Prop. § 300.

Affirmed.

IN RE CRAIG LUMBER CO.

Circuit Court of Appeals, Ninth Circuit, 1921.
269 Fed. 755.

[In the court below, in a bankruptcy proceeding, the appellees filed their petition to reclaim certain machinery and fittings which they had placed in the bankrupt's sawmill in accordance with a contract performed before the bankruptcy. The court below upon the pleadings and the evidence found the facts to be substantially as follows:

That on October 31, 1917, the appellees and the bankrupt entered into a contract whereby the appellees agreed to furnish all machinery, fittings, etc., necessary to equip the bankrupt's sawmill at Craig, Alaska, in accordance with specifications, and agreed to install said machinery and erect necessary buildings therefor. The contract provided that the cost of the sawmill complete should not exceed the estimate of $32,125. It contained a provision that the title to the "apparatus and material herein agreed to be sold" should not pass from the appellees until fully paid for in cash, that upon defaults in payments the appellees might retake the property "agreed to be sold," and in that event it was agreed that the money theretofore paid to the appellees on the contract should be presumed to be the amount of their liquidated damages to be retained by them for breach of the agreement; that the contract further bound the bankrupt to pay the appellees the actual cost of labor and machinery, equipment, and building material, cost of insurance charges, of material and men from Seattle, Wash., to Craig, Alaska, plus 10 per cent., and the bankrupt agreed to pay the appellees in installments, the last of which to be due 30 days from completion of contract; that the appellees fulfilled their contract on or about May 1, 1918; that there remained due them the sum of $12,980.36 on the contract; that before the trial of the cause the trustee in bankruptcy and the Bank of Alaska entered into a stipulation with the appellees whereby the bank took possession of the property described in the contract, and stipulated with the appellees that, if the court should find the contract to be a conditional sale contract, it should make a further finding as to the amount due the appellees under the contract, which sum, if so found, the bank undertook to pay; that the sawmill is constructed on piles on tidelands in a forest reservation, title to which is in the government, and that all the machinery, etc., were so attached to the building as to be easily removable therefrom without damaging the same; that the Bank of Alaska, a party to the suit, holds a mortgage upon the mill and the machinery, but at the time of the execution of said mortgage the bank had notice of the conditional sale contract, and that the appellees had not been fully paid for the machinery; that the material, etc., furnished under the contract by the appellees, together with the work performed thereunder, and the percentages agreed upon in the contract, amount to the sum of $32,539.74, and that in addition thereto the appellees also furnished and delivered to the bankrupt other material, machinery, etc., not included in the contract, amounting to $5,958.79; that after allowing the total credits for payments made there remained a balance due the appellees under the contract of $9,827.39, and the court entered judgment for the appellees for that sum.]

Before GILBERT, ROSS, and HUNT, CIRCUIT JUDGES.

GILBERT, CIRCUIT JUDGE (after stating the facts as above). The appellants contend that it was error to hold that the contract was an agreement for a conditional sale, and they argue that at the time when it was made the appellees had nothing to sell, that the lumber company was merely employing them to build and equip their mill according to plans and specifications at a cost not to exceed a specified sum, that in buying the machinery and fulfilling the contract the appellees were merely agents or employés, and that in paying for the same out of their own funds they but advanced the purchase money as agents for their principal. It has been held that conditional contracts of sale are not favored in the law, and where it is doubtful upon the face of the instrument whether the contract is a conditional sale or a mortgage, it should generally be treated as a mortgage. But here the terms of the instrument leave no room to doubt that a conditional sale was provided for. The appellees were to buy and pay for the machinery and to take title thereto in the first instance in their own name. The purchase price therefor was to be paid by them, not with funds advanced by the lumber company, but with their own money. There is nothing in the instrument to give color to the suggestion that they were agents for the lumber company. On the contrary, it appears that they were contractors, who bound themselves to furnish machinery which the contract provided was thereafter to be sold to the lumber company. There is nothing in the instrument to rebut the intention, expressed in clear terms, that the sale is conditional and that—

"Title to the apparatus and material herein agreed to be sold shall not pass from the company until all payments hereinunder shall have been fully paid in cash. Upon default in any such payments, the company may retake the property agreed to be sold."

It is not rebutted by the fact that the contract provided that the title should not pass until the payment of, not only the cost of the machinery and material, but also the expense of erecting buildings and installing the machinery. All of these sums were reckoned together as constituting the cost of that which was agreed to be conditionally sold. But whether or not the appellees could retain title to the machinery until all these sums were paid is immaterial here.

Under the appropriation of payments which the court below made, the unpaid balance is solely for the purchase price of the machinery and apparatus. In Harkness v. Russell, 118 U.S. 663, 7 Sup.Ct. 51, 30 L.Ed. 285, Mr. Justice Bradley said:

"Such contracts are well known in the law and often recognized, and when free from any fraudulent intent are not repugnant to any principle of justice or equity, even though possession of the property be given to the proposed purchaser."

* * *

We find no merit in the contention that the trustee is, as to the mill and the machinery, in the position of an attaching creditor with rights superior to those of the appellees. Under the amendment of 1910 (section 47a of the Bankruptcy Act [Comp.St. § 9631]), the trustee may attack the validity of any lien or other claims against the bankrupt's property which a creditor holding a lien by legal or equitable proceedings might have attacked. * * * But it does not appear that creditors holding such liens could have successfully attacked the appellees' title.

The appellants cite Washburn v. Inter-Mountain Min. Co., 56 Or. 578, 109 Pac. 382, Ann.Cas. 1912C, 357, a case in which a stamp mill, title to which was reserved by the seller, was with his consent permanently affixed to the freehold; the conditional agreement not being recorded. The court affirmed the rule that an agreement for the conditional sale of a chattel is valid, as well against third parties as against parties to the transaction, but held that the rule relates to parties dealing for the property as a chattel, and does not apply to third parties without notice of the condition, where the character of the property has been changed to realty by being affixed to the soil. In the present case there is no realty and no freehold estate, and the machinery never became a fixture. * * *

"If a person owns a building, and has no property in the land, and may remove the structure when and where he pleases, it is a chattel." 11 R.C.L. 1081; Curry v. Commonwealth Ins. Co., 10 Pick. (Mass.) 535, 20 Am.Dec. 547.

The sawmill was constructed on piles on the tideland, within a forest reservation, to which no one had any title, except the government of the United States.

The decree is affirmed.

Notes

1. This case is a classic priority case. One competitor is the appellee, seller of the goods, who claims to have title because he sold goods under a conditional sales contract whose condition was never met. A second potential competitor was the Bank of Alaska who had a mortgage on the real estate and on the goods but who apparently conceded that it was subordinate to the seller's claim because, according to the court, it had "notice of the conditional sale contract." The third competitor is the trustee in bankruptcy who then, as today, asserts the rights of a hypothetical lien creditor (the rights that would have been those of a creditor under state law had he procured a lien on the date the bankruptcy petition was filed). Today, the trustee prevails under UCC 9–301(1)(b) and section 544(a) of the Bankruptcy Code. But to a lawyer steeped in the logic of real property conveyancing who views the world from the perspective of 1920 and before, the court's logic is unassailable: "Because the debtor never complied with the condition he never received the title and therefore his successors could do no better than he. Therefore appellee (conditional seller) must prevail over mortgagee and trustee."

In using the court's logic, would you come to a different conclusion if the appellee's document was not a conditional sale contract but a mortgage?

The case demonstrates the inevitable conflict between recognition of conveyancing ideas and the policy that one should not be entitled to priority unless he has given publicity to his interest sufficient to put third parties on notice of it. The fact that the outcome might be different if the lawyer had used a mortgage form instead of a conditional sale form and even though the underlying commercial transaction was the same, should also make one question the holding. Rights of third parties, those by definition not party to the contract, should vary according to commercial realities, not according to the boilerplate used by the lawyer, not so? Put more bluntly, if public policy demands public notice to third parties for one to have priority, the law should not allow lawyers to escape that policy by choice of a different form to which the aggrieved party is not a signatory.

2. In Chapter Seven we will discover that we should not be so confident of our superiority over the early courts. Even under the Uniform Commercial Code we will

find difficulty in deciding who should take goods allegedly belonging to one that are in the possession of another under a form titled a "lease" or a "consignment" or a "contract for processing." Do you suppose that the answers to those questions that now trouble American courts will be as obvious to our successors as the answers to *Craig Lumber* are to us? That is a terrible thought.

SECTION 3. PRE CODE PERSONAL PROPERTY SECURITY LAW IN THE UNITED STATES

The Pledge

Security in some form has existed at least since the time of Hammurabi. In primitive society, and even in rather well developed ancient societies, personal property security typically took the form of the pledge. We will see the modern version of the pledge in UCC 9–305. Its identifying characteristic is that the creditor takes possession of the debtor's personal property. This not only prevents the debtor from squandering the property, but also puts all others on notice of the creditor's interest. The mortgage on real property is also a time honored security device. The mortgage is the transfer of a conditional interest in the debtor's realty to the creditor to secure the debt. In some settings this transfer took the form of an absolute conveyance with the understanding, oral or written, that the creditor will reconvey the real estate upon the debtor's payment. In its modern form there is no such absolute deed but rather a document variously described as a mortgage, a deed of trust, or something of the kind that can be recorded in the real estate records and that discloses certain of the terms of the agreement between the parties. In effect it clouds the debtor's title and precludes him from conveying good title to a third party.

For several quite obvious reasons the pledge cannot be widely used as a security device in a modern society. In the first place, certain intangible rights are not "pledgeable." That is, there is no talisman that identifies the right that can be passed from hand to hand and will put others on notice. Thus, it would be impossible to do an effective "pledge" of an account receivable or of a right to a royalty. Equally important, most debtors need to enjoy the use of their personal property in their business or personal life and are unwilling to part with possession while paying the debt. While pledges of certain passive assets such as stock certificates or bonds still take place, pledges are obviously unsuitable with respect to industrial equipment, inventory, or even a consumer's car.

The Chattel Mortgage

With the coming of industrial society in the nineteenth century and the increase in wealth represented by personal property in the form of goods and intangibles, creditors and debtors sought alternatives to the pledge and to the real estate mortgage. A first and most obvious step was to apply real estate mortgage rules to personal property; so in the 1820's the "chattel mortgage," in which the debtor retained possession of the property, came into being. This child of the real estate mortgage inhabiting the household of the pledge suffered from grossly debilitating genetic difficulties. The courts had become accustomed to the pledge as the exclusive type of personal property security. The courts were also influenced by early cases such as *Twyne's case*, 76 Eng.Rep. 809, 3 Cone 80 (Star Ch. 1601) in which it was held that allowing a debtor possession of collateral was in and of itself a form of fraud. It is therefore hardly surprising that the courts at first were most hostile to the chattel mortgage. Although the chattel mortgage was usually authorized by statute, some courts found it still to be a jury question whether allowing the debtor's possession of the collateral was itself fraudulent. They conceded to the legislature only the fact that such possession was no longer fraudulent as a matter of law and allowed the creditor to get to the jury because of the statute that apparently authorized the chattel mortgage. That judicial response to the chattel mortgage statute shows how deeply entrenched was the idea that possession was critical to an effective security interest in personal property.

The chattel mortgage also suffered from its real estate mortgage lineage. The real estate cases brought with them a nearly fanatical insistence upon accurate description of the collateral and slavish attention to detail in the execution of the instrument and in compliance with the statutory requirements. Thus many chattel mortgages were struck down as invalid because they described property plainly known to all as subject to the chattel mortgage in a way that was insignificantly deviant from an accurate description, as for example, the transposition of two numbers in a thirteen digit motor number in an automobile.

When the parties attempted to apply the chattel mortgage to inventory, they met yet further obstacles. For example, some courts held that the idea of a creditor's security interest in a debtor's inventory was fundamentally inconsistent with the idea that the debtor could convey good title to that inventory to third-party ordinary course purchasers. Furthermore the courts were unwilling to accept the proposition that a chattel mortgage could attach to after-acquired property. Again, real estate conveyance ideas were influential: The courts decided that one could not make a valid present transfer of property to be acquired in the future. Finally, the chattel mortgage did not cover intangibles. Here the courts were doubtless correct in concluding that certain intangibles such as negotiable notes should not and could not be property covered by a chattel mortgage statute without seriously interfering with the free transferability of such assets or with the expectations of those who took them expecting to get good title by possession.

Because the chattel mortgage statutes, again following real estate law, required that a chattel mortgage be executed with respect to each particular piece of property and that the mortgage itself be recorded, the taking of such mortgages in property that was likely to depreciate or be exchanged for other property was exceedingly expensive and cumbersome. Moreover, the courts' incorporation of real estate foreclosure procedures, procedures with a long and tedious history designed to protect debtors, imposed heavy burdens on a creditor who sought to repossess and resell.

Thus—because retention of possession by the debtor had traditionally been thought to be a sign of fraud, because of the excessively formal rules for creating security, because of the difficulties of adaptation to a changing body of goods such as inventory, and because of inapplicability to intangibles—the chattel mortgage was only marginally better than the pledge.

Professor Gilmore has described the process of escaping from the idea that debtors' possession is equivalent to fraud as follows: "That process, however, took the best part of a century, during which the law of personal property security transactions came to resemble the obscure wood in which Dante once discovered the gates of hell." [1 Gilmore, *Security Interests in Personal Property,* 27 (1965).] Professor Gilmore describes the courts' reaction to the chattel mortgage statutes as follows:

> "Anyone could give a chattel mortgage on any of his property (except his stock in trade) to anyone to secure any sort of obligation. However, chattel mortgage law more than made up for the relative simplicity of its theoretical structure by a fastidious, cranky, at times almost insane insistence on documentary formalities

> * * * The description requirement was sometimes treated as a sort of statute of frauds, so that failure to describe the mortgaged property in terms which suited the court's arbitrary whim voided the mortgage and could not be cured even by uncontroverted and uncontrovertible proof of what was covered by the mortgage. A typical case of this sort would set aside a mortgage of machinery, described in the mortgage in such a way that there could be no possible doubt what machinery was meant, because the serial numbers of the machines were missing.
>
> Id. at 52–53.
>
> "Nineteenth century cases of this sort can be explained on the grounds that the real estate mortgage analogy was more compelling seventy-five years ago than it is today and that the period was one of generalized judicial hostility to all chattel security transactions with the borrower remaining in possession. If it is assumed that the only good mortgage is a dead mortgage, it must be a laudable act to do a mortgage to death with any weapon that comes to hand (footnotes omitted)."

Of course, today Article Nine allows the creation of perfected non-possessory security interests. See UCC 9–303(1).

The Conditional Sale

A third personal property security device, one with attributes superior not only to the pledge but also to the chattel mortgage is the "conditional sales contract." In the eighteenth century a clever English lawyer proposed and Lord Mansfield adopted at common law the idea that a seller of goods could make passage of title to his buyer "conditional" on payment. In this transaction the seller would provide that he would retain title until all paid off. If the buyer failed to make the payments, the seller who had retained title had a right to the goods. Because the buyer had breached the contract, typically he had no right to the return of the payments that he had made. In certain obvious respects this device was far superior to the chattel mortgage. In the first place, it found its roots in the law governing sale of goods. That law did not encourage the judges to require that the parties execute any documents, let alone execute them with great formality and obsessive attention to detail. Thus, a clerical error in the preparation of the document did not mean instant death to the security interest. If the debtor was willing to give up the goods upon his default, no judicial or other foreclosure proceeding was necessary because title had always remained with the seller and nothing was necessary to return it to him. Presumably, even if the debtor was unwilling, the procedure in sales for the return of property owned by the seller was quicker and less cumbersome than the comparable procedure might have been had it been the foreclosure of a chattel mortgage. Finally, the conditional sale did not necessarily require any recording of a document. Thus, one possibility for error was omitted at least until statutes were passed that required recording.

Nevertheless the conditional sale contract had its limitations. It applied only to sellers of goods. Banks or other financing agencies wishing to finance a debtor's personal property could not invoke the device. The device contemplated the sale of individual goods and their use by the buyer and retention of title by the seller. Thus, it was not adaptable to inventory which by definition would be passed on to third parties. Of course, the device also did not apply to intangibles, accounts receivable, and such. Thus, the conditional sale contract found its principal use in the sale by sellers of industrial equipment for use in plants and of consumer hard goods. Even today one will find occasional reference in the cases to the "conditional sale" of a television to a consumer. In

Article 9 itself, particularly in the area of purchase money security interests in consumer goods, UCC 9–302(1)(d), one sees the residue of the classical conditional sale contract, the purchase money security interest perfected without filing.

The Trust Receipt

A fourth security device, developed early in the twentieth century, was the trust receipt. This device originated initially with the grain trade and was developed to finance buyer's purchase of imported goods. In the classical common-law trust receipt, an east coast bank would finance a buyer's purchase of goods from Europe. The bank would take possession of the bill of lading or other document, pay the seller of the goods, and retain a claim against the goods in the hands of the buyer until paid. The buyer was thought to be a "trustee" holding the goods in trust for the bank. At common law the bank's claim was held to be superior to the claims of the other creditors of the "trustee" and that was so despite the fact that when the trust receipt first developed, the bank was not required to give any public notice.

For a time after 1930 it looked as though the trust receipt would become the dominant form of personal property security at least in the commercial context. The Uniform Trust Receipts Act was widely adopted and that act validated and elaborated upon the common law trust receipt transaction. It found its most common use in domestic transactions in bank financing of the purchase of autos by dealers. In that setting the bank would pay the price of the automobile to the manufacturer. It would give possession of the automobile to the car dealer who was the trustee. The debtor-dealer would make out a trust receipt with respect to the automobile and the bank gave notice of its interest by filing a general and singular public notice. Note that this was the first deviation from the idea of *recording* of the operative document. Unlike the chattel mortgage where the document itself had to be recorded, here the secured creditor merely filed a notice that dealt with all of the transactions to be undertaken with the debtor.

The Uniform Trust Receipts Act was thus a large step beyond the chattel mortgage law, for it did not require the same fanatical insistence upon detail; it did not require a recording of each document. Moreover it allowed the automatic transfer of the secured creditor's claim from the automobile to the proceeds upon its sale.

Yet this act too had its limitations. First, it was designed for, and largely limited to, purchase money loans against goods. It was doubtful whether it could be adapted to securing an existing unsecured debt against existing collateral or to serving as a loan against existing and presently owned collateral that would not be purchased with the loan proceeds. Moreover, it was apparently limited to lenders and did not apply to sellers in most circumstances. It did not provide for a continuing or "floating" lien that would float over all of the debtor's assets without respect to individual trust receipts on a particular asset. Nor did it permit a general loan against intangibles. While it apparently worked well on import transactions and with purchase money security interests in large-item collateral such as automobiles, it was not readily adaptable to inventory lending as a general matter.

So it was with tangible personal property on the eve of the UCC's birth. The nineteenth and twentieth centuries saw a similar haphazard common law and legislative development of a body of law to permit secured lending against intangibles. Of course to the extent an intangible was pledgeable, as was a note, there had always been a mode of financing against an intangible. But many intangibles such as accounts receivable, were thought not to be pledgeable and did not fit under any of the other obvious security devices.

The Factor's Lien

One device, originally specific to the textile trade (a large part of its history) is the factor's lien. Originally factors were persons who took the output of textile mills on commission, had a common law lien with respect to the goods in their possession, and sold them to third parties for a commission. If that sale was on credit, the payment was presumably to be made directly to the factor and served as security for any amount owed him by the textile manufacturer. In time the factor ceased selling the goods and became nothing more or less than a lender to the textile manufacturer. The factor would claim a lien on the inventory of the mill owner to whom he had made a loan. Since the factor was not in possession of the inventory, there was no public notice of his interest, and that raised a serious question about the validity of this lien. The principal value of the collateral was the receivables produced on sale of the inventory. The factor became a "buyer" of these accounts. That is to say, the factor took the credit risk inherent in the account and if the account debtor failed to pay, it was his loss, not the loss of the textile manufacturer. Moreover, typically the factor gave notice of the sale of the account to the account debtor and required that the account debtor make payments directly to him, not to the debtor (textile manufacturer). Often the term "factor" is used in this sense today, but not invariably so. Usually one who refers to a "factor" today refers to a party who buys accounts, i.e., who takes them and assumes the credit risk, not one who lends against them with full recourse against his assignor-debtor.

Ultimately factoring was blessed by section 45 of the Personal Property Law, enacted in 1911 in New York. This section was applied many times by the courts, was amended, and ultimately copied in other states. Whether the factor's lien could be used as a device for a long-term loan secured by a "floating lien" on the revolving inventory and accounts was unclear—that was not the normal mode of financing and apparently the issue was not tested. Likewise, section 45 was not designed and apparently not used for a loan secured only by accounts receivable without regard to inventory and there were questions whether it authorized non-notification financing (taking security in accounts without notifying the account debtor). In any event the factors' lien laws did not constitute a wholesale indorsement of accounts receivable lending. Even in the later stages, factoring acts lending was limited mostly to the textile industry and expanded only in a hesitating way under the newly enacted statutes to other areas. It was doubtful under most of the factors lien acts whether one could engage in what would now be regarded as traditional, non-notification accounts receivable financing not accompanied by a prior security interest in the inventory.

The Assignments of Accounts

At common law there was a development parallel to the New York factor's lien law that permitted accounts receivable financing. This was to treat an assignment of an account receivable for the purpose of security like any other assignment and to grant priority to the assignee over other parties claiming the account either on the basis of the time of assignment or on the basis of the time of notification to the account debtor. If one analyzed the problem merely as a question of "assignment" and "ownership," there was no requirement of a public filing nor any doubt about the superior ownership of the first assignee.

The decision in Corn Exchange National Bank and Trust Co. v. Klauder, 318 U.S. 434, 63 S.Ct. 679, 87 L.Ed. 884 (1943), disrupted the comfortable relationship of the bank and others, who being first assignees, were thought to be true owners. It held that, at least in a jurisdiction where priority dated from the time of notification to the account debtor, a creditor who had taken an assignment was subordinate to the debtor's bankruptcy trustee unless the notification had been given more than four months before the debtor's bankruptcy. That decision called into question the lender's claim in accounts in states that followed the notification rules at least where there had not been notification. Following in its wake, most states passed accounts receivable statutes that validated lenders' interests. Some of these did not require notification as a condition of perfection, but ultimately most of them were amended to require public notification. Many of the statutes covered all assignments of accounts and so included in their scope many assignments that were not intended for security. Moreover they wrestled with the question how to define an account, whether it was to include rights represented by negotiable instruments or certain non-negotiable instruments (such as security agreements). Some of the Article 9 distinctions among different forms of Article 9 collateral, "chattel paper," "accounts," "instruments" and "general intangibles," grow out of the learning under the accounts receivable statutes.

The Field Warehouse

The field warehouse is a final pre-Code personal property security device that merits a word. This was a device under which the debtor put his goods out of his possession and into the hands of a "field warehouse." It was said to be a "field" warehouse because the warehouse was located on the debtor's own premises. Typically such a warehouse would be set off from the debtor's own inventory by a chicken wire or other fence, or consisted of a locked room to which the debtor theoretically did not have access. A person in the employ of the warehouse company (but often a former employee of the debtor) was assigned to oversee the goods, to issue receipts to the lender covering them, and to deliver them only upon direction from the holder of the warehouse receipt, the lender. By limiting the debtor's physical possession and use of the asset and by holding the warehouseman's net worth available for claim in case the warehouse was not properly run, this device protected not only against the claims of third party creditors and trustees in bankruptcy, but also against certain fraudulent behavior of the debtor himself. With the passage of the Uniform Commercial Code and the appearance of an easy method of perfecting a security interest in a shifting mass of inventory, the field warehouse has doubtless declined in importance. Yet even today it persists. Although it is more expensive than a conventional inventory loan, it protects against serious risks (i.e., the debtor's own fraud) that a conventional security interest does not touch.

Although we will not return to the history of personal property security as such, the student should not dismiss it as unimportant. A knowledge of this history will help the student both to understand some of the provisions of Article 9 of the Uniform Commercial Code and to appreciate the significance of some decisions under the Code. The roots of personal property security in real estate mortgage law explain the nineteenth century judicial insistence that secured creditors dot their i's and cross their t's. The occasional recurrence of such cases, despite Article 9's instruction that the courts should interpret the filing and notice requirements in a less formal way may, too, be the product of a real estate mentality. Conceivably historic skepticism about the propriety of non-possessory security in personal property also stems from this mentality. We believe that such skepticism forms the basis for an occasional modern decision in which the court strikes down a secured creditor's claim on grounds that seem inappropriate under Article 9.

Our review of the varied forms of pre-Code personal property security suggests how radical, even heretical, was the idea that a single statute could embody a single form of security device that would cover all personal property security. The entire pre-Code history of American personal property law reveals a crazy quilt evolution of various security devices designed to solve particular problems. The very idea of a single, unitary security device to cover all of these must have seemed bizarre in the extreme when it was first proposed after World War II.

The study of Article 9 will reveal, however, some residual traces of various pre-Code personal property security devices. A security interest in certain collateral can be perfected only by possession (see UCC 9–304(1)): a security interest in other forms of collateral can be perfected only by acts excluding possession (see UCC 9–302). Here we can detect pre-Code notions of what could be pledged and what not. The Code recognizes automatic perfection without either possession by the creditor or the filing of a financing statement in some situations. These are the natural descendents of the conditional sale contract (and to a lesser extent of the common law accounts receivable lien). Thus to say we today have but one security device is not to say there is only one mode of perfection or to say that all of the legal rules apply to every transaction irrespective of the type of collateral.

Finally, history should tell us something of the future, at least if we read it with care. In the nineteenth century we saw how a major personal property security device, the chattel mortgage, grew out of real estate mortgage law and carried with it the burdens of that law. Later we saw clever lawyers and judges adapting and developing ideas from sales law, such as the conditional sale, and from trust law, such as the trust receipt. Like the chattel mortgage, these devices have the genetic imprint of their predecessors and not surprisingly courts respond to that imprint. On the other hand, the drafters of Article 9 forgot to insulate that body of law from "outside" influence. For example, they recognized that the rules that might be appropriate and fair for a two-party sales contract ought not necessarily be carried over to a security transaction where the interests of third-party creditors were often at stake. But as we will see, the drafters were not completely successful in stifling the imaginations of lawyers and judges. Some of the most interesting questions under Article 9 have to do with the scope and coverage of present day transactions designed to function as security but also to escape some of the Article 9 requirements. For example, the courts have been faced with the recurring question: Is this document a lease to be analyzed under the common law of bailments or is it a security agreement to be governed by Article 9 of the Uniform Commercial Code? They have struggled at length with the question whether one taking an interest in a real estate mortgagee's right was governed by Article 9 or by some other law. We will deal with these and other scope questions in Chapter Seven, and they may fairly be regarded as reminiscent of earlier developments that brought us the conditional sale contract, the trust receipt and other security devices. Time and experience foretell that the drafters' attempt to bring all conceivable personal property security devices and quasi security devices entirely under Article 9's tent was doomed from the start. No drafters' pen can be equal to the ingenuity and imagination of creditors and their lawyers.

SECTION 4. STRUCTURE OF ARTICLE 9, A ROADMAP

A. Scope

In Chapter Seven we will deal with some subtle and difficult scope problems. For the time being, however, the student should understand what kinds of transactions in general are covered and what are excluded. The basic scope provision is UCC 9–102; that provision is supplemented by UCC 9–104, titled Transactions Excluded from Article. Consistent with the idea that there is but a single security interest and security agreement, that substance is everything, and that form is very little, section 9–102(1) provides that the article applies "to any transaction (regardless of its form) which is intended to create a security interest in personal property * * *." Thus, Article 9 would cover transactions that were formerly chattel mortgages, conditional sales, liens on accounts receivable under statute or at common law, and uniform trust receipt lending. Section 9–102(2) contains a laundry list making it clear that a security agreement "regardless of its form" is to be included. Section 9–102(1)(b) includes certain "sales" and 9–102(3) extends it to security in security interests outside the article, e.g., security interests in notes and mortgages.

Section 9–104 has 12 exclusions from Article 9. Most of those apply to transactions that either are only marginally related to financing and already have a separate body of statutory or common law that govern them or that are almost completely unrelated to commercial financing. An example of the former would be UCC 9–104(i) excluding from Article 9 coverage "any right of set-off." An example of the latter would be 9–104(k) that excludes from Article 9 the transfer of an interest in a tort claim. Despite the breadth of 9–102 and the specificity of 9–104, Chapter Seven reveals that there remain many complicated scope issues, issues that will dog the courts and scholars as long as Article 9 survives.

The student should appreciate that there are several basic types of scope questions. For example, there is the question of the *geographic scope* of Article 9 as it is enacted in any particular state. Put in its most common form: Does A perfect a security interest by filing in State Y or State Z? Section 9–103 answers that question in most circumstances.

There is also a scope *conflict with federal law.* The most common such conflict arises between Article 9 and the federal Bankruptcy Code, but there is a variety of other arguably relevant federal laws such as those dealing with copyrights, patents, filing of liens on aircraft, ship mortgages, etc. There is also the federal common law that applies to the United States government in its capacity as a lender and there is the potential for conflict with other state statutory law. For example every state has a statute that confers liens, sometimes referred to as mechanics liens, on those who do certain work on real or personal property and improve its value. For the most part, the rights of such claimants and their priority are governed by these specialized statutes and are entirely outside of Article 9. Ironically, therefore, one of the most interesting and difficult lawyer questions has nothing whatever to do with the substance of Article 9 but with the question: does Article 9 govern this transaction at all?

Problem 2–2

Alfredo is a contractor who builds houses and small buildings. Typically he sells the building at the end of its construction to the owner and takes back a land-sale contract or a mortgage and note. The bank asks you if it must comply with Article 9 if it wishes to enjoy the economic value in the mortgagee's interest in the note or the vendor's interest in the land-sale contract. These are the intangible assets that the contractor Alfredo has offered to transfer to the bank. See UCC 9–102 and 9–104.

Problem 2–3

Edgar has a savings account with First Bank. If he wishes to borrow from the University Credit Union, giving a security interest in his account, will it be sufficient for the Credit Union to comply with Article 9 rules on the creation and perfection of the security interest?

Problem 2–4

Irene bought a heavy plastic swimming pool from Ajax Cc. on credit. She plans to have a large hole dug in her back yard, where she will install the pool. She also plans to construct firm wooden walkways around the edge of the pool. If Ajax wants to perfect a security interest in the pool, does Article 9 apply?

B. Creation of the Security Interest

At the outset we have seen that Article 9 visualizes a security interest that arises when the events under UCC 9–203 have occurred. Section 9–203, like UCC 9–102, contemplates a single document called a security agreement as the typical means of creating a security interest. While a security agreement to give a security interest in accounts receivable might be quite unlike a security agreement giving a security interest in an automobile, each would be titled "Security Agreement" and each would be tested by the same rules under UCC 9–203. Under that provision a security interest arises and becomes enforceable between the parties and third parties when there is an appropriate writing (or when the creditor has possession pursuant to agreement) and has given value (usually making the loan), see UCC 1–201(44), and when the debtor has "rights in the collateral" (usually title). Note the absence of any formal requirement other than a signature. There is no requirement of notarization or of witnesses to the signature; there is no requirement that the description of the collateral be specific and, indeed, UCC 9–110 provides that it need only be such as would "reasonably identify" what is described. There is no particular form; it may be written on the back of an envelope or on a plain sheet of paper.

As we have indicated above, section 9–203 rejects the formalism of much pre-Code law. In each of the following cases a security interest would be enforceable and "attached," would it not?

(1) Johnny, a close friend of Robert in a northern Alabama hill town, has agreed to lend Robert $3,000 for one year. In return Robert has agreed to give Johnny a lien on his 1983 F–100 pickup. Robert writes out the following statement on the back of an envelope and gives it to Johnny:

> I give Johnny title to my pickup until I pay him off. Robert.

Johnny gives the $3,000 to Robert and later when Robert fails to repay it, Johnny has a valid and enforceable security interest against Robert's pick-up. Certainly value has been given (the loan). The debtor has rights in the collateral (presumably Robert had title to the pickup). Is the document they signed a "security agreement" which contains a "description of the collateral"? We would argue that it is, and we would argue that the description is adequate. What do you think?

(2) In a more formal way Robert might choose to borrow $9,000 to purchase his pickup from his local credit union. As a part of that transaction he is likely to sign a document similar to the following. It too would be an adequate security agreement and the credit union, like Johnny, would have a valid and enforceable agreement once the loan had been made and the document had been signed.

DATE

SECURITY AGREEMENT

CREDIT UNION COPY

(hereinafter called "Debtor"; said term "Debtor" to be read as if in the plural where more than one debtor is a party hereto), for valuable consideration, receipt whereof is hereby acknowledged, hereby grants to

THE UNIVERSITY OF MICHIGAN CREDIT UNION
333 WILLIAM STREET • ANN ARBOR, MICHIGAN 48107
(Hereinafter called secured party)

ACCOUNT NUMBER

a security interest in the property described below, in any accessions thereto, in proceeds of such property or accessions, and, if farm crops, in the products thereof growing, or to be grown, on the premises indicated below (hereinafter called the "Collateral")

COLLATERAL

TITLED PROPERTY ▶	MAKE	YEAR	MODEL	BODY STYLE	IDENTIFICATION NUMBER

All Household Goods, Furniture, and Appliances of Debtor(s) now located in or about the residence of the first named Debtor including, but not limited to, the items described in Schedule B attached hereto and made a part hereof.

(APPLICABLE ONLY WHEN CHECKED)

I/We, the undersigned, hereby jointly and severally pledge all paid shares and deposits and payments on shares and deposits which I/we now have or hereafter may have in this credit union, except shares or deposits which may be held pursuant to any "Individual Retirement Trust" or "Keogh Plan" or as an All-Savers Certificate, as security for (1) principal and interest of the loan evidenced by the Note of even date herewith and of any refinancing of all or any part thereof and (2) any other sums which may become due under the Security Agreement and/or real estate mortgage securing such obligations. Shares, deposits and payments thereon are only pledged to an amount equal to the unpaid balance of such indebtedness.

I/We hereby authorize the credit union in the event of default to apply any or all such paid shares and deposits and payments on same to the repayment of any such indebtedness.

However, Borrower may withdraw shares or deposits in excess of $ if loan payments are up to date.

as security for (1) principal and interest of the loan evidenced by the Note of even date herewith and of any refinancing of all or any part thereof and (2) any other sums which may become due under any real estate mortgage securing said Note or under this Security Agreement.

Any Debtor who has joined herein solely for the purpose of supplying Collateral, and is not a party of the Note, shall not be liable for the debt, or for any deficiency after resale of the Collateral.

Authority is hereby given the Secured Party to complete this Security Agreement in any necessary respect in the event that it is executed while still incomplete.

DEBTOR HEREBY WARRANTS AND COVENANTS THAT:

(A) The collateral is bought or used primarily for

☐ Personal, family, or household purposes ☐ Farming operations use ☐ Business use and, if checked here ▶ ☐ is being acquired with

the proceeds of the note or notes, the check for which secured party may make payable to the debtor and seller, or may disburse directly to the seller of the collateral.

(B) The Collateral will be kept at the address shown at the beginning of this Security Agreement or at any other place in the State of Michigan if Debtor notifies Secured Party of such location. Debtor shall not remove such Collateral from the State of Michigan without the consent of Secured Party.

(C) If the collateral is bought or used primarily for business use, debtor's principal place of business in said state (if any) is that shown at the beginning of this agreement; and all other places of business in said state outside of the town or city mentioned in the previous clause are located as follows:

→

→

(D) The following is the legal description of real estate on which farm crops are growing or to be grown, or to which collateral is to be attached.

→

→

and the name and address of the record owner is

→

(E) Debtor represents that Debtor's residence (place of business) is that shown opposite Debtor's name above, and agrees that all notices required to be sent or received shall be sent to or received at said address or any subsequent address of which Debtor gives written notice to Secured Party.

This Security Agreement is subject to and includes the additional provisions set forth on the reverse side hereof, the same being incorporated herein by reference. The word "herein" shall refer to and include the provisions of both sides hereof.

Debtor hereby acknowledges receipt of a duplicate original of this Security Agreement

DEBTOR ☒	DEBTOR ☒
DEBTOR ☒	DEBTOR ☒
DEBTOR ☒	DEBTOR ☒

(Where the Collateral is Household Goods, Furniture, and Appliances, the instrument must be signed by both husband and wife)

[E1224]

ADDITIONAL PROVISIONS

FURTHER WARRANTIES AND COVENANTS OF DEBTOR. Debtor hereby warrants, covenants and agrees that:

1. (a) Except for the security interest granted hereby, Debtor is the owner of the Collateral free from any adverse lien, security interest or encumbrance; and Debtor will defend the Collateral against all claims and demands of all persons at any time claiming the same or any interest therein.
(b) There is no unpaid balance of principal or interest owing on the purchase price of the Collateral or for money loaned for the acquisition of the Collateral or any unpaid charges in connection therewith.
(c) No financing statement covering any of the Collateral is on file in any public office other than contemplated by this Security Agreement.

2. (a) Debtor will join with the Secured Party in executing one or more financing statements in form satisfactory to the Secured Party.
(b) Debtor will join with the Secured Party in executing one or more amendments to the financing statement when same may be necessary to correct any errors in the financing statement.

3. Debtor will not sell or otherwise transfer any part or all of the Collateral or any interest therein without the written consent of Secured Party.

4. (a) Debtor shall maintain in force at Debtor's expense at all times theft, fire and extended coverage and, for motor vehicle collateral, physical damage insurance on all of the Collateral now or hereafter subject to the terms of this Security Agreement in such amounts as approved by the Secured Party. Such insurance shall be payable to Secured Party and Debtor as their interests shall appear, and shall require not less than 10 days written notice of cancellation to the Secured Party.
(b) If the Debtor does not maintain the insurance as required, the Secured Party may procure same and pay the premiums thereon. The amount of premiums so paid shall be due and payable forthwith by the Debtor to the Secured Party and shall be secured by the Collateral hereunder pursuant to the terms of this Security Agreement. Such action by the Secured Party shall not constitute a waiver of the Debtor's default.

5. Debtor shall at all times keep the Collateral:
(a) Free from any adverse liens, encumbrances or other security interests.
(b) In good order and repair and in as good condition as the Collateral now is, reasonable wear and tear excepted.
(c) Available for examination and inspection by the Secured Party at the address of the Debtor.
(d) If the Debtor does not comply with "5(a)" above, the Secured Party may discharge the liens, security interests or encumbrances. If the Debtor does not maintain the Collateral as required by "5(b)" above, the Secured Party may procure and pay for the maintenance or repair. In such events the amounts paid by the Secured Party shall be due and payable forthwith by the Debtor to the Secured Party and shall be secured by the Collateral hereunder pursuant to the terms of this Security Agreement. Such action by the Secured Party shall not constitute a waiver of the Debtor's default.

6. Debtor shall not use the Collateral in violation of any statute or ordinance.

7. (a) Debtor shall pay when due all taxes and assessments upon the Collateral or in connection with its use or operation or upon this Security Agreement or upon any Note or Notes secured by this Security Agreement.
(b) Upon failure to make such payments when due, same may be made by Secured Party. Amounts so paid by the Secured Party shall be due and payable forthwith by the Debtor to the Secured Party and shall be secured by the Collateral hereunder pursuant to the terms of this Security Agreement. Such payment by the Secured Party shall not constitute a waiver of Debtor's default.

DEBTOR: READ CAREFULLY

8. Debtor shall forthwith cause the security interest of the Secured Party in the Collateral to be noted or endorsed upon a certificate of title, or application therefor, where required to perfect that interest.

MUTUAL COVENANTS. The parties hereto agree that:

9. This Security Agreement, any financing statement or amendments thereof, any continuation statement, termination statement, statement of release of collateral, and statement of assignment may be produced in as many counterparts through carbon impression or imprintation or other methods, and may be executed through signature of the top document and through carbon or other simultaneous impressions or imprintation of the succeeding duplicates thereof. Each of such documents so prepared and executed shall be deemed fully executed duplicate originals.

10. From time to time additional or substituted collateral may be made subject to the terms of this Security Agreement by the execution of an amendment to the financing statement setting forth such additional collateral. This Security Agreement shall be deemed so amended upon the execution of such amended financing statement or statements.

11. Secured Party shall have authority to complete any financing statement or amendment thereof in any necessary respect in the event same shall be executed while still incomplete.

12. If Debtor does not reimburse Secured Party for any amount advanced by Secured Party pursuant to paragraphs 4(b), 5(d) or 7(b) hereof, Secured Party may add the unreimbursed amounts to the principal balance of the loan secured by this Security Agreement.

EVENTS OF DEFAULT. The Debtor shall be in default under the terms of this Security Agreement:

13. Upon default in whole or in part of any payment or payments due under any Note or indebtedness secured by the terms of this Security Agreement.

14. If any warranty, representation or statement made or furnished to Secured Party by or on behalf of the Debtor proves to have been false in any material respect when made or furnished.

15. Upon the loss, theft, substantial damage, destruction, sale or encumbrance to or of any of the Collateral, or the making of any levy, seizure or attachment thereof or thereon.

16. Upon the insolvency of the Debtor, or the appointment of a receiver over any of Debtor's property, or upon the institution of any proceeding for the liquidation of the debts of the Debtor in any State or Federal Court.

17. Upon removal of the Collateral by Debtor from the place of keeping herein designated, except as permitted by paragraph (B) on the reverse hereof.

18. In the event of the falsity or upon the breach of any of the warranties or covenants set forth in paragraphs one through eight inclusive above.

19. When funds are loaned for the acquisition of specified Collateral, failure of the Debtor to acquire the specified Collateral with the loan proceeds.

REMEDIES.

20. In the event of a default listed in paragraphs 13 through 19 above and at any time thereafter Secured Party may declare all obligations secured hereby immediately due and payable and Secured Party shall have the right to take possession of the Collateral wherever located without judicial process if such taking can be made without breach of the peace but otherwise by use of judicial process. In the event of such taking possession, the parties hereto shall have the rights and duties with respect to such Collateral, and otherwise, as prescribed by law.

21. Secured Party may require Debtor to assemble the Collateral and make it available to Secured Party at a place to be designated by Secured Party which is reasonably convenient to both parties.

22. Unless the Collateral is perishable or threatens to decline speedily in value or is of a type customarily sold on a recognized market, Secured Party will give Debtor reasonable notice of the time and place of any public sale thereof or of the time after which any private sale or any other intended disposition thereof is to be made. The requirements of reasonable notice shall be met if such notice is mailed, postage prepaid, to the address of Debtor specified in paragraph (E) on the reverse hereof at least five days before the time of the sale or disposition.

23. Expenses of retaking, holding, preparing for sale, selling or the like shall include such reasonable attorney fees and expenses as may be legally permitted, and if paid by Secured Party shall be secured by the Collateral hereunder pursuant to the terms of this Security Agreement.

24. Debtor agrees that Secured Party or its agents in taking possession of any vehicle after default may also take possession of any personal property therein. If during said repossession, personal property within the vehicle is seized, such property shall be held by the Secured Party or its agents for a period of 5 days after such seizure and if the Debtor does not within that time deliver to the Secured Party a written request for said property, same shall be deemed abandoned by the Debtor.

GENERAL.

25. No waiver by Secured Party of any other default shall operate as a waiver of any other default or of the same default on a future occasion.

26. All rights of Secured Party hereunder shall inure to the benefit of its successors and assigns; and all obligations of Debtor shall bind Debtor's heirs, executors, administrators, successors or assigns.

27. If there be more than one Debtor, their obligations hereunder shall be joint and several. [E1225]

(3) In large commercial transactions the security agreement is likely to look quite different from the document set out above. In that transaction lawyers on both sides will have been involved and while some of the terms will be boilerplate, others may be specifically drawn for the particular transaction. For an example of such a security agreement, see page 87 (Chapter Three).

In Chapter Three we will deal with some of the more intricate questions involved in UCC 9–203 and with the law's application to the imperfect attempts by creditors and debtors to comply with UCC 9–203. Occasionally, for example, a creditor is embarrassed to find that he has no security agreement at all because it was lost or never signed even though the parties agreed on security and executed many other documents that indicate they intended such. All of these complications together with questions involving subsequent advances, after-acquired property, and various description issues, we will confront in the next chapter.

Problem 2–5

Fritz owned a racehorse which was kept by Richard at his farm. Fritz sold the horse on January 1 to Jean for $7,500, Jean to pay $1,500 down on January 10 and the balance on March 1. Fritz told Jean: "I'll keep title until you pay me" and Jean said: "O.K." Does Fritz have an enforceable security interest?

C. Perfection of the Security Interest

(1) Is Filing Required?

Section 9–203 describes "attachment and enforceability." To say that a security agreement is valid between the creditor and the debtor is important, but a question of equal or greater importance deals with its enforceability against third parties. When a third party gets a lien on the asset or the debtor grants a security interest to a third party, is that person's claim superior to or subordinate to the secured creditor's claim? When the debtor goes into bankruptcy, can the secured creditor take the asset in preference to the trustee? These questions relate to "priority," which typically depends upon "perfection." See UCC 9–303(1). To say that a security interest is "perfected" is to say that the secured creditor has complied with UCC 9–302 and, usually, that his interest will therefore be superior to others whose claims against the property arise later. Attachment produces enforceability against the debtor; perfection gives rise to enforceability against third parties. (As we will see, in some situations, attachment constitutes perfection.)

An unperfected security interest is not worthless, but section 9–301 tells us that it may be nearly so. That section 9–301(1)(b), says that an unperfected security interest is subordinated to the interests of a lien creditor. Technically, a lien creditor is a party who has acquired a lien on the debtor's property by attachment, levy, or the like. But the archetype lien creditor is the trustee in bankruptcy. The combination of UCC 9–301(1)(b) and section 544(a) of the Bankruptcy Code (giving the trustee the rights of a lien creditor) means that the trustee will be entitled to assets in which there is a secured but unperfected interest. Generally the opposite will be true if the interest has been perfected prior to bankruptcy. Thus, one may assume that no secured creditor in his right mind intentionally remains unperfected. He finds himself so because he has failed to file in the proper place or failed to file at all or because he has stumbled in some other way along the road to perfection. Rarely, if ever, will he have consciously adopted the position of an unperfected secured creditor.

Section 9–302 may be read as an inventory of the ways in which one becomes perfected. It is important to read part 3 of Article 9 together with the definitional sections, 9–105, 9–106, 9–107, and 9–109. Those sections distinguish accounts from general intangibles and from chattel paper. They identify which goods are consumer goods, which are equipment and which are farm products, and they add some other definitions as well. The definitions find their principal use in instructing the lawyer which mode of perfection is permitted and which may be necessary. For example, UCC 9–302(1)(a) defines possession as provided in 9–305 as a mode of perfection. However, reading UCC 9–305, one discovers that only certain assets "may be perfected" by the creditor's possession. These of course include goods. They also include certain intangibles appropriately represented, e.g., a negotiable instrument. The comments to 9–305 make it clear that they exclude things such as general intangibles and accounts receivable for which there is no such representative embodiment.

If we have followed a single strand through UCC 9–102 and 9–203, it now breaks into individual threads in 9–302 and to some extent leads along individual paths through the remainder of Article 9. The student who has read the history above can now see the reappearance of some of the threads that come from that history. For example, 9–302(1)(d) provides for the automatic perfection (i.e., without filing or taking possession or any other act) of a "purchase money security interest in consumer goods." Here we encounter descendants of the conditional sale.

Return now to UCC 9–302(1). In a kind of back-handed way it states the general proposition of Article 9: "A financing statement must be filed to perfect all security interests except the following." Thus, filing is the normal mode of perfection under Article 9. Putting aside for the moment the consumer goods exception, filing must outstrip all other modes of perfection by a factor of thousands to one.

By now it should be obvious that the usual function of "perfection" is to provide a notice or a warning to later creditors that tells them of the earlier creditor's interest. The penalty for not giving notice to such third parties in the prescribed form is usually to be subordinated to them whether they be the trustee in bankruptcy or a later secured creditor. The student should read through Part 3 of Article 9, and bear in mind that filing is the norm and that the events described in UCC 9–304 and 9–305 deal with a small minority of all the transactions. Most of the learning about perfection as to proceeds of collateral can wait, but it is not too soon to look at 9–306, a provision that both authorizes a security interest in "identifiable" proceeds (e.g., a check which is received on the sale of inventory collateral), and also specifies in 9–306(3) the rules for perfecting a security interest in proceeds.

The bank in our last example above would be perfected by filing a document like the one set out below, would it not?

Financing Statement—Form UCC-1

UNIFORM COMMERCIAL CODE FINANCING STATEMENT
(Approved by the Secretary of State and Michigan Association of Registers of Deeds)

INSTRUCTIONS:

1. TYPE OR PRINT All information required on this Form.
2. If dual filing is made, send the WHITE copies to the Secretary of State, Lansing, Michigan. Send the YELLOW copies to the local register of deeds. Retain PINK copies for files of the secured party and debtor.
3. Enclose filing fee.
4. IF ADDITIONAL SPACE IS NEEDED for any items on this Form, continue the items on separate sheets of paper (5" × 8"). One copy of these additional sheets should accompany the WHITE Forms, and one copy should accompany the YELLOW Forms. USE PAPER CLIPS to attach these sheets to the Forms (DO NOT USE STAPLES, GLUE, TAPE, ETC.) and indicate in Item 1 the number of additional sheets attached.
5. At the time of filing, the filing officer will return acknowledgement. At a later time, the secured party may date and sign the termination legend and use acknowledgement copy as a termination statement.
6. Both the WHITE and YELLOW Filing Officer copies must have original signatures. Only the debtor must sign the financing statement, and the signature of the secured party is not necessary, except that the secured party alone may sign the financing statement in the following 4 instances. Please specify action in Item 7 below.
   (1) Where the collateral which is subject to the security interest in another state is brought into Michigan or the location of the debtor is changed to Michigan.
   (2) "For proceeds if the security interest in the original collateral was perfected."
   (3) The previous filing has lapsed.
   (4) For collateral acquired after a change of debtor name, and a filing is required under MCLA 440.9402 (2) and (7); MSA 19.9402 (2) and (7).

1. No. of additional sheets	Liber	Page	For Filing Officer (Date, Time, Number, and Filing Office)
2. Debtor(s) (Last Name First) and address(es)	3. Secured Party(ies) and address(es)		
4. Name and address(es) of assignee(s) (if any)	CHECK ☒ if applicable 5. ☐ Products of collateral are also covered. 6. ☐ Collateral was brought into this state subject to a security interest in another jurisdiction.		

7. This financing statement covers the following types (or items) of property:

________________ Signature(s) of Debtor(s)   by ________________ (Signature of Secured Party or Assignee of Record)

(1) Filing Officer Copy [C206]

Compare the UCC–1 form set out above with the requirements specified in 9–402. Think for a moment about the ways in which Murphy's Law could apply to the preparation of a UCC–1. For example, the signature might not correspond to the name of the debtor. The debtor's name might be abbreviated in a variety of ways and, of course, it is always possible that the description of the collateral will be found to be too broad to be meaningful or will be so narrow that it excludes some of the assets. In the chapter that follows we will deal with the question whether the financing statement need describe after-acquired property or proceeds.

Problem 2–6

Bank will lend against debtor's inventory and accounts receivable. Assume in turn that the debtor and the debtor's assets are located in a state that has UCC 9–401 alternative 1, alternative 2 and alternative 3. In each case a filing at the Secretary of State's office would be necessary. Would it be sufficient in all cases?

Return now to the transactions involving Johnny and Robert, described on page 31. How should the secured parties perfect?

The credit union would be perfected without filing anything. That would be because of UCC 9–302(1)(d). Can you see why we tolerate perfection without filing in the 9–302(1)(d) case and why that non-filing rule is *not* extended to purchase money security interest in motor vehicles? Note that the credit union can be a purchase money lender under UCC 9–107(b) even though it is not the seller of the commodity.

Johnny would perfect his security interest in Robert's pickup truck neither automatically nor by filing a UCC–1 form. To see why that is so, read UCC 9–302(3). The interrelationship between the certificate of title legislation and Article 9 is one that we will explore again. In almost all states today the effect of UCC 9–302(3) is to defer to the perfection rules laid down in certificate of title legislation. For some transactions in a few states, a certificate of title listing may still be an optional, rather than a required, mode of perfection.

(2) Where to File the Financing Statement

Section 9–302 and its allies are interesting and perhaps even fun to play with but part 4 of Article 9 is where the battles are fought—where the secured creditor is vanquished, or where he defeats the trustee and subsequent parties. More frequent than any other Article 9 claim is the allegation on behalf of a trustee in bankruptcy (or occasionally a subsequent creditor) that our classical secured creditor has not filed the right document, has not filed it in the right place, or has omitted some relevant information. Finding that the creditor has not complied with part 4 of Article 9 typically leaves him unperfected under UCC 9–302 and naked to the priority attack of most third parties, including the trustee under § 544 of the Bankruptcy Code and UCC 9–301(1)(b). Thus, the legal issues in such a law suit have not to do with UCC 9–302 or 9–301, or even with any provision of the Bankruptcy Code. They are all fought out on the battleground of UCC 9–401, 9–402 and, to a lesser extent, the remaining sections of part 4 in Article 9.

Section 9–401(1) defines the "where" of intrastate filing. Note the three alternatives and bear in mind that when one is practicing law, it is not enough to look merely at the uniform version of the UCC. Lawyers must examine their own state's law to see which of these variants has been adopted. Each requires marginally different filing; the first alternative has the most central filing, the third alternative requires more local filing than the others.

Problem 2–7

Assume that debtor is located in Lansing, Michigan, or alternatively, in Syracuse, New York. Michigan has the second alternative of UCC 9–401; New York has the third. If secured creditor were going to perfect a security interest by filing on a piece of industrial equipment in the possession of debtor in Lansing or Syracuse, where would he file? Michigan would not require a local filing, would it? New York might require a local filing. From the facts given, can one be sure?

One should read UCC 9–401 together with 9–103, the provision which directs one to a particular state or another in the case of collateral with actual or possible multi-state contacts. A filing in Albany is no good if New York's version of 9–103 directs one to file in Columbia, South Carolina, because that is the debtor's residence. Why did the drafters suggest three alternatives? Would it not have been simpler to have had a single filing place for all financing statements in the world located at The Hague or, if one wished to think less globally, in St. Louis (where the Cardinals are)? Why, in this day of rapid data transmission and of instantaneous computer conversation, should we require a Dallas creditor to file in Amarillo?

Part 4 of Article 9 contains more mysteries than may be apparent to the unstudied eye. If, for example, the county recorder of deeds has separate indices for personal property and for real property, should a financing statement be filed in one or in the other with respect to fixtures? What if a financing statement is passed across the counter, the fee paid, but it is then left in a shoe box for a month and other later-presented documents are ultimately filed before it? Recorders and their employees are fallible, and a student dealing with 9–401 should appreciate that.

Even more than UCC 9–401, section 9–402 is the battleground between trustees and secured creditors. Note that it provides for a financing statement that "indicates the types or describes the items of collateral." Because it provides that the financing statement need only indicate "the types," it is clear that this is the kind of filing that was contemplated, for example, by the Uniform Trust Receipts Act, not the kind contemplated by the chattel mortgage statutes. It is not the operative document, the security agreement (the big, fat agreement in a commercial transaction) that is filed. Rather, it s a single-page document describing the collateral in quite general terms, in many cases (all automobiles and other inventory of debtor). On reading the financing statement, one finds little more than whom to pursue for more information. The required public filing will not reveal the amount of the debt or even if there is one. It will not indicate whether there is one or many cars subject to the security agreement, what the interest rate or the term of the loan is or any of the other provisions. Section 9–402 adopts the "notice" filing rule and rejects the idea that the operative document should be "recorded."

Section 9–402(8) is an explicit direction to courts to abandon the kind of fanatical insistence upon detail that characterized judicial behavior with respect to chattel mortgages, at least in the nineteenth century. Even though a financing statement contains "minor errors which are not seriously misleading," it is a valid financing statement. Thus, transposition of motor numbers, description of a blue car as a red one, mistakes in the debtor's or creditor's address, possibly even in the debtor's name, all may be overlooked if they are not seriously misleading.

What do you suppose is the most important thing on the financing statement that is described in UCC 9–402(1) and (3)? The debtor's name or the debtor's address? Is the address of the secured party more important than that of the debtor? Undoubtedly the debtor's name is the single most important factor on the financing statement. Do you see why? The remainder of part 4 of Article 9 contains a series of relatively straightforward and infrequently used provisions. Read them; someday they may be important to you.

Problem 2–8

Assume that the bank had decided to go ahead and make the loan to Alfredo in Problem 2–2. The Bank is going to take security in his interest in the note and mortgage, and in his interest in the land-sale contract. If you decide that the transaction will be governed by Article 9, how would you suggest the bank create a security interest? Perfect it? Note that perfection in this case turns on the definition of the type of collateral. The note is surely an instrument. What if it were not negotiable? What about the vendor's interest in the land-sale contract? Is it critical for the purpose of perfection to determine the identity and classification of the collateral? YES!.

D. Priority of the Security Interest

In addition to Sections 9–201 and 9–301, and commencing with UCC 9–306(5), the remaining sections in part 3 of Article 9 are priority sections. They neither describe the mode of attachment nor the mode of perfection but in general establish the relative status of a perfected secured creditor, vis a vis another party, whether that party be a purchaser, a subsequent secured creditor, or a lien holder.

It is not too soon to understand that even a perfected security interest is not perfect. Section 9–307(1) tells us that a retail purchaser takes free of a perfected security interest in the retailer's inventory. When one buys a washing machine from the local department store, he does not expect to have to search the files and to make arrangements to get it free from the department store's bank; the law does not expect one to do that either. Even if the security agreement provides otherwise, the buyer in the ordinary course of business takes free under 9–307(1). Less important are the priority provisions in UCC 9–308, 9–309 and 9–310.

The most basic priority provisions are UCC 9–201 and 9–312. Read both. Section 9–312 is unhappily complex. The student should focus particularly on 9–312(5) under which most cases are resolved.

Every first-year student encounters the priority rules in real estate recording statutes. These typically provide "first in time, first in right," but that statement itself, as we shall see, is wildly ambiguous. The common real estate statute is a "notice-race" statute. It gives priority to a transferee of the debtor who is second in time only if this transferee takes without notice (no "notice") and files first (wins the "race" to the courthouse filing). Actually, such statutes might better be called "no notice-race winner" statutes. Section 9–312 is *not* such a statute. It is a "pure race" statute; knowledge of another's security interest does not subordinate the claim to that interest. (Recall how the Bank of Alaska, in *In Re Craig Lumber Co.,* supra at p. 20, apparently conceded that it was inferior to the conditional seller's rights because of its notice of the conditional sale. Under UCC 9–312 the bank's knowledge of the security interest would not have subordinated it; it presumably would have pursued its rights more vigorously.) Read UCC 9–312 carefully and see if you can extract that conclusion. The section is complicated and is filled with references that resolve some of the problems of the nineteenth century discussed earlier. For example, 9–312 explicitly addresses priority questions with respect to future advances, after-acquired property, and the rights of a purchase-money lender who comes second in time but who provides financing for specific assets.

Section 9–313 on fixtures is also unhappily complex, and we will deal with it at length. Sections 9–314 and 9–315 are at least superficially easy to understand. Section 9–318 is an old friend from the contracts course that has some, but limited, relevance to security interests.

Again, to conclude that a security interest is perfected is not necessarily to say that it has "priority." That should be obvious, first of all, because two parties presumably could have perfected security interests in the same collateral, yet one would enjoy priority over the other under UCC 9–312(5), for example. A large share of all Article 9 lawsuits ultimately involve the relative priority of competing third parties, and many of these involve two secured creditors. Few lawsuits are between the debtor and the creditor.

If one assumes that one competitor is a secured creditor under Article 9, the initial question to be asked in determining relative priority is the identity of the other competitor. If the other competitor is a lien creditor, the proper rule of priority is to be found in UCC 9–201 and 9–301. If the other competitor is a perfected secured creditor, the rule normally is to be found in UCC 9–312 or, with respect to fixtures, UCC 9–313, or occasionally with respect to proceeds in UCC 9–306. If the competitor is a buyer of goods, one should look to UCC 9–301, 9–306(2), and 9–307. If the competitor is a purchaser of notes or chattel paper, or the like, UCC 9–308 and 9–309 contain the rules of priority. So initially the question should be: Who is the competitor, unsecured creditor, secured creditor, purchaser, assignee, trustee, lien creditor?

An examination of the sections cited above that deal with priority tells one that the most commonly applicable priority rule in Article 9 is first in time, first in right. Now we come to the ambiguities in this seemingly simple principle. First what? One could give priority to the person who takes the "first conveyance" from the debtor. Alternatively one might look to the first public notice or to the first public notice by one who is himself without knowledge of any prior transfer, or possibly to the time when the first loan was made irrespective of when the conveyance occurred or of when the financing statement was filed. In the history of American commercial law and, indeed, in current commercial law, one can find precedents for each of the proposed first-in-time rules—conveyance, public notification, public notification by one ignorant of prior conveyances, or the time the loan is made.

Moreover, a first-in-time rule may be subject to significant exceptions. For example, the purchase money loan provisions of UCC 9–312(3) and (4) give priority to a party second in time. The same is true of certain provisions protecting the interest of the buyer in ordinary course under UCC 9–307.

Of course the basic and most commonly applicable rule, that embodied in UCC 9–312(5) is that the person who first files (or in case of other forms of perfection, perfects) has priority over later parties irrespective of the time of signing the security agreement, the time the first loan is made, or the time the debtor acquires rights in the collateral. As we have indicated above, this is a "pure race," not a "notice race" statute. Consider Example 1 from Comment 5 to UCC 9–312:

> "A files against X (debtor) on February 1. B files against X on March 1. B makes a non-purchase money advance against certain collateral on April 1. A makes an advance against the same collateral on May 1. A has priority even though B's advance was made earlier and was perfected when made. It makes no difference whether or not A knew of B's interest when he made his advance."

Note, however, that Article 9 makes a minor bow to notice in UCC 9–401(2) (seeing an improperly filed financing statement will likely subordinate one).

The student should start giving some thought to the question why the drafters of the Article 9 priority rules picked any one particular event as opposed to another for determining priority: for example, filing first regardless of notice vs. filing first without notice of a prior interest? Similarly, why do some parties who are second in time, such as buyers in the ordinary course under 9–307 and purchase money lenders under UCC 9–312(3) and (4), enjoy priority even over prior perfected security interests? Surely the general answer to the former question is that the law here should favor certainty even at the cost of fairness. Here the legislature is really enacting traffic rules among relatively sophisticated commercial parties. Better to let the first filer with notice prevail and thus the ignorant second filer suffer than to take up the court's time determining whether or not a particular party's knowledge of specific facts was knowledge of the security agreement which subordinated him. It seems equally obvious why 9–307 should protect the second in time interest at least of the consumer buyer over the bank with an inventory security interest who buys out of the retailer's inventory. Here the law is doing no more than recognizing common expectations, expectations that the law has little power to change. It would be unfair to allow the secured creditor to repossess the refrigerator that Mr. Jones had purchased from the floor of his local appliance dealer. Less obvious are the reasons for recognizing purchase money security interests as superior to prior perfected security interests. We will deal with that question later.

It is not too early to note two areas where there are additional complexities in the priority rules. The first is with respect to fixtures where 9–313 contemplates separate rules of priority with respect to real property claimants and to personal property claimants. Some filings may protect against both, some only as to one but not the other. (Recall in the *Craig* case at p. 20 the court was careful to state that the equipment at issue had not been affixed to the realty in such a way as to become a fixture. Had that happened, the bank with the mortgage on the realty might well have prevailed over the conditional seller. Who is to prevail when one properly files in the real estate records and another properly files in the personal property records as to an item which was once goods, but which has now become quasi real estate in the form of a fixture? Section 9–313 answers most of those questions.) More important is the priority between the secured creditor, on the one hand, and the trustee in bankruptcy on the other. Most such priority disputes are resolved under 9–301, but we will see that the trustee in bankruptcy has a series of rights conferred by federal law, namely the Bankruptcy Code. In Chapter Eight we will give special attention to the trustee in bankruptcy.

Problem 2–9

Edith bought a boat from George, a retail boat dealer. George had bought the boat from Ajax, a wholesale boat dealer. Ajax had granted a security interest in the boat to TIA Finance Company, which TIA perfected by filing. Ajax has not paid TIA, which now seeks to repossess the boat from Edith. Who wins?

Problem 2–10

Jean wanted to borrow $10,000 from Ready Bank. At the start of the negotiations, July 2, Ready Bank filed a financing statement naming Jean as debtor and describing the collateral as "equipment." Meanwhile, Jean, on July 20, borrowed $5,000 from Ideal Finance Company, giving Ideal a security interest in her equipment, which was perfected by filing on the same day. On July 30, Ready Bank lent Jean $10,000 under an enforceable security agreement. Jean defaulted on both loans and both Ready Bank and Ideal claim the equipment. Who wins?

Problem 2–11

Credit Union had a perfected security interest in furniture owned by Tenant. Tenant was in default on the loan to Credit Union and three months in arrears on the rent. Both Credit Union and Landlord claim the furniture. Who wins?

SECTION 5. TRUSTEE IN BANKRUPTCY

By far the most important type of priority conflict in the life of the typical secured creditor is that with the trustee in bankruptcy. While one may be captivated by the intricacies of UCC 9–312, 9–308, and 9–313 on relative priorities among creditors, one must not assume that these conflicts are the most common daily fare. For every competing secured creditor or actual creditor with a judicial lien, there are hundreds, perhaps thousands, of bankruptcies and bankruptcy trustees. For that reason alone, the rights of the trustee—some derived from Article 9 and some from the bankruptcy law—are of much greater practical significance than the rights, for example, of a mechanics' lienor or of another secured creditor or even of a buyer. It has been said many times and correctly that survival despite bankruptcy is the acid test of a security interest.

There are several kinds of bankruptcy proceedings. For our purposes it is sufficient if the student knows Chapter 11 and Chapter 7. Chapter 7 of the Bankruptcy Code provides for the liquidation of the debtor's assets. Typically in a Chapter 7 proceeding, a trustee is appointed who will collect and liquidate the debtor's property. This independent party can be expected to challenge defective security interests in order to bring that property into the estate for distribution to the unsecured creditors. Note, incidentally, most increases in the value of the estate increase the trustee's fee. In Chapter 11 the trustee's role is played by, and powers are held by, a person called the "debtor-in-possession." The debtor-in-possession is in fact the same person who was the debtor the day before the petition was filed. Chapter 11 contemplates continuation of the business during its reorganization. Invariably in Chapter 11 the business continues for a time although it often winds up in liquidation. One reading a Chapter 11 opinion will find the court speaking of the "debtor-in-possession" sometimes shortened to DIP. For our purposes, the trustee encompasses both the trustee in Chapter 7 and the debtor-in-possession in Chapter 11.

In theory a perfected security interest prevails over the trustee in bankruptcy. In theory, the perfected secured creditor has a right to his collateral or its value and, if he is fully secured, cannot lose anything by his debtor's bankruptcy. In general, this theory does not conform to reality, and this is one of the worst kept secrets of modern commercial law. In the first place, when the debtor goes bankrupt, the trustee is treated as though he has a lien on all of the debtor's assets acquired by judicial process. Section 544 of the Bankruptcy Act gives the trustee that right and section 9–301 of Article 9 specifically recognizes the trustee as a lien creditor.

The upshot of this unequivocal grant of lien creditor status to the trustee in bankruptcy is that there are no complex or interesting legal issues associated with that power. The interesting questions in the cases in which the trustee is asserting his 544 right have to do with the perfection or not of the security interest. In those cases one encounters the complicated perfection questions under Article 9 of the UCC. The other side of the 544(a) coin is that the trustee can never invoke this section to defeat a security interest that is perfected before the bankruptcy petition is filed. Like others, the trustee is subordinated to the perfected security interest (to the extent he is a lien creditor) by 9–201 and by the negative implication from 9–301(1)(b).

OMIT *Problem 2–12*

Assume that our bank in Problem 2–2 filed a financing statement covering all "notes, mortgages, land-sale contracts, and other accounts receivable" of Alfredo. Because these are real estate transactions the bank filed its financing statement with the local register of deeds office in a state with the second alternative to 9–401. You have been employed as the lawyer for the trustee in bankruptcy in Alfredo's Chapter 11.

1. Can you attack the bank's security interest, and if so, how?
2. Be careful to articulate the trustee's argument in detail.
3. If *In re Craig Lumber* now arose (see page 20), and you represented the trustee in bankruptcy in that case, explain how you would defeat the "conditional seller's" interest.

One should not assume, however, that the trustee is without weapons against even a perfected secured creditor. Section 547 on voidable preferences can sometimes be used to require the creditor to disgorge payments that have been made to him and in other cases to overturn a security interest that was perfected within 90 days, or in some instances within one year of the filing of the petition. Section 547 is designed to prohibit "secret liens" and thus, in effect, it allows the trustee to set aside virtually every security interest where there is a gap between the making of the loan, on the one hand, and/or the giving of the security interest and its perfection where the perfection occurs within 90 days of the bankruptcy, on the other. Thus, if a secured creditor takes a security interest in 1983 but fails to perfect it until the eve of bankruptcy, the "transfer" will be deemed to have occurred within 90 days of the bankruptcy and the trustee will be able to upset it under section 547. In that context the section is designed to prohibit collusion between the debtor and a particularly friendly creditor to enable the former to mislead other creditors by keeping the security interest secret. The rules under section 547 are complex and important; we will devote substantial time to them in Chapter 8.

Other sections from 548 through 553 give the trustee the power to challenge secured creditors, sometimes perfected secured creditors, and we will deal in passing with many of those. They are much less significant than section 544, on the trustee's rights as a lien creditor, and section 547, on the trustee's power to invalidate preferential transfers by the debtor to others. For the time being, the student should proceed with the assumption that a security interest perfected within 10 days of making a loan, or perfected before 90 days prior to the petition is valid against the trustee in bankruptcy.

The theory of the supremacy of the perfected security interest falls not only to direct attack via section 547 on preferences or the other avoidance powers of the trustee under Bankruptcy Code that allow for explicit and complete subordination of the perfected secured creditor; that theory falls also in the light of the more subtle provisions of the Bankruptcy Code: the "automatic stay" under section 362 and the "cramdown" rules of Chapters 11 and 13 of the Bankruptcy Act. To lose to the trustee under section 547 is to be struck dead by lightning. To lose to the trustee because of section 362 (the automatic stay) and attendant provisions, or because of the cramdown rules is to suffer a lingering illness which may, nonetheless, prove fatal. Section 362 simply says that the status quo is preserved upon filing of the petition. This is the section that stops the creditor lawsuits and Article 9 foreclosure proceedings the moment the debtor files bankruptcy; this is the section that prohibits a secured creditor from repossessing when the debtor files bankruptcy; this is the section that prohibits an unsecured creditor from engaging in any self help collection activity. In general, the "cramdown" rules in Chapters 11 and 13 and the rules having to do with lifting the stay and adequate protection under section 362 and section 361 give the trustee the right to keep the collateral, perhaps indefinitely, if he can convince the court that he can give the secured creditor assurances that are roughly equivalent to it. Equivalence in the mind of the bankruptcy judge may differ substantially from equivalence in the mind of the secured creditor.

Inevitably therefore the filing of a bankruptcy petition burdens the secured creditor. Almost without exception it means the secured creditor will suffer a loss of interest on the money lent for a time and perhaps suffer certain other opportunity costs, and at least in some cases it means that he will be crammed down, i.e., that he will be made to take something which he does not regard as equivalent to his collateral, but which the court finds to be so. The operation of section 362 and of the general cramdown provisions are to a considerable extent hidden in the mists of the bankruptcy court and in the negotiations that surround a classic Chapter 11 case. For those reasons they are more subtle, harder to see, and more difficult to grasp. Yet, they are often no less significant than the more obvious and crude powers under sections 544 and 547.

The trustee in bankruptcy may thus be regarded as a particularly powerful and important competitor to the secured creditor. The student should now read sections 544 through 553. We will return to all of these and to sections 361 and 362 in Chapter 8.

SECTION 6. DEFAULT, REPOSSESSION AND FORECLOSURE

Part 5 of Article 9 deals with default. When the debtor who owes $1,000,000 and who has granted a security interest in his grain in a grain elevator defaults on the loan, the grain is not turned into money instantaneously. Part 5 of Article 9 governs the process by which the creditor himself or through others transforms the collateral in the debtor's hands into cash in his own. We use foreclosure here as a generic word to refer to the process by which a secured creditor ultimately liquidates collateral, whether that collateral be an automobile, a farm, or an account receivable.

The foreclosure laws, as they deal with real estate (to which Article 9 does not apply), have been a major scene of battles between creditors and debtors throughout the history of the United States. We will pause now to explore some of these battles, as general background. In times of economic stress, such as farmers are suffering as this is written in 1986, debtors have frequently turned to the state legislatures and to the Congress for help. There debtors argue that foreclosure proceedings invariably fail to bring fair prices for collateral sold and fail to give the honest debtor a fair opportunity to get back on his feet once he has stumbled. With respect to farmland, the debtors occasionally make another argument, namely that the creditors are about to destroy an important part of the American heritage by driving the small farmer off his land and replacing him with a corporation or worse, a foreigner.

The creditors respond to such an argument by pointing out that they must comply with a specific set of foreclosure laws and by arguing that these laws necessarily do not bring the highest price because they inevitably conclude in a forced auction. Moreover, the creditors will suggest that the very failure of the debtor is evidence that the collateral cannot produce the kind of income that would support the high price that the debtor assigns to it. The creditors will argue that adding additional burdens to the foreclosure process will merely reduce the ranks of creditors willing to lend and will therefore increase the cost of borrowing to the detriment of all.

In one way or another nearly every legislature has, at one or more times, responded to the debtor's argument and, one suspects, thousands of different courts have responded in individual cases to those arguments. In the real estate arena the legislative response has taken several forms. The first and almost universal response is to enact a rigid, lengthy and formal procedure which the creditor must follow in order to sell the land and realize on his collateral. Typically such statutes will require publication over a long period in a local newspaper, demand that the sale be at a specified place and conducted in a specified way. Some states have other and more novel ways of encouraging that the largest possible amount be bid in at the sale. For example, some states have "upset" prices under which the sale is upset unless a price equal to a specified percentage of the fair market value of the land (as found by a third party) is bid in at the sale. All of these devices are designed to protect the debtor's interest by realizing the fair value of the collateral on sale. One perceives that most of them are not effective to achieve the debtor's desire. In many cases that is because the debtor's desire is unattainable. In fact the property does not have as high a value as the debtor would assign to it.

Many states also add a "redemption" period. During the redemption period the debtor and certain junior creditors have the right to repurchase the property sold at foreclosure for the amount bid at the time of the sale. Typically the debtor also has the right to continued possession of the land during the redemption period which may be six months or a year.

We now turn to Article 9. A quick reading of the basic foreclosure provision of Article 9, section 9–504, will show that the drafters were skeptical of the capacity of formal devices to produce the highest prices. The core of the foreclosure rules in part 5 of Article 9 is found in section 9–504(3) which provides that "disposition of the collateral may be by public or private proceedings and may be made by way of one or more contracts. Sale or other disposition may be as a unit or in parcels or at any time and place and on any terms, but every aspect of the disposition, including the method, manner, time, place, and terms must be commercially reasonable." Not only does the section reject a formal approach, it encourages the use of any method, however informal, that will produce the best price. It explicitly authorizes private sale and is careful to include not just sales, but also "other dispositions." Comment 1 to UCC 9–504 makes the point as follows:

> "Although public sale is recognized, it is hoped that private sale will be encouraged where, as is frequently the case, private sale through commercial channels will result in higher realization on collateral for the benefit of all parties. The only restriction placed on the secured party's method of disposition is that it must be commercially reasonable."

In effect, section 9–504 may be read as inviting the creditor to deal with the goods as though they were his own. Mr. Banker if this were your car, how would you dispose of it? If at a private sale, then presumably the private sale is appropriate. If at a dealer auction, then presumably a dealer auction is appropriate. Note, too, that there is no post-sale redemption period (UCC 9–505), that the creditor need not go to court for a court order to seize the property (if he can get it without breach of the peace, UCC 9–503), nor to authorize or approve the sale (UCC 9–504). The entire process often is carried out without any party ever setting foot in court.

That is not to say there are no legal issues associated with part 5 of Article 9. Exactly what constitutes a breach of the peace is a much litigated issue under UCC 9–503. What is and is not commercially reasonable is often disputed under UCC 9–504. Harking back to the earlier times, debtors often beseech the court to read the procedural requirements of notice under UCC 9–504(3) narrowly and to find that the creditor failed to comply with them.

Part 5 of Article 9 does not articulate all of the debtor's remedies for the creditor's violation of that part. Certain rights are explicitly granted under UCC 9–507, including the right to punitive damages under certain circumstances, but the courts have not found UCC 9–507 to be exclusive. Many courts have held that one who does not comply with UCC 9–504 loses his right to a deficiency judgment (a deficiency in this case is equal to the amount of the debt less the amount realized on sale of the collateral). Other courts have found creditors guilty of conversion or of other torts in the process of repossessing. Of course, section 9–507 invites the court to grant the debtor actual damages suffered from a violation of that part.

In general, however, the legal issues in part 5 of Article 9 are not as difficult and complex as in other parts of Article 9.

SECTION 7. NON-UNIFORMITY IN A UNIFORM STATUTE

A principal aim of the Uniform Commercial Code was that of having commercial law that would be uniform throughout the United States. Of course, it was obvious from the outset that perfect uniformity could not be achieved and one sees many optional, and necessarily non-uniform, provisions sprinkled throughout the Code. Some of these were initially inserted to meet the concerns of those who would otherwise have been powerful opponents of the Code. In other cases these were inserted in recognition that differing conditions called for different outcomes.

The principal non-uniformity in the Code, however, comes not from these optional provisions. Rather, in Article 9 it comes from the fact that the drafters themselves found many faults with the Code as originally enacted in most states, and proposed a set of uniform amendments in 1972. Those amendments have now been enacted in 44 states. Thus when one refers to the uniform version of Article 9, typically one is referring to the 1972 version. Nevertheless, one should be aware that a few states still have the 1962 version and that almost all UCC states had it for a time, and that many cases were decided thereunder. In some circumstances a case decided under the 1962 version is not good precedent under the 1972 version.

A second substantial source of non-uniformity arises within the states themselves. For example, many states have chafed at the rule embodied in 9–307 that allows a perfected security interest to carry over against a bona fide purchaser of farm products. As we will see, the courts have restricted that rule by a variety of forms of judicial manipulation. More recently the legislatures have also come to the aid of buyers and have modified 9–307 to allow many buyers to take free of perfected security interests even in farm products. For example, Tennessee now has an extensive non-uniform version of 9–307; California never adopted the farm products limitation in 9–307. Furthermore, with the Food Security Act of 1985, Congress enacted legislation which grants purchasers of farm products federal protection. Farm products legislation is further discussed in Chapter 5.

The supreme nonconformist jurisdiction in Article 9 matters, California, adopted a large set of non-uniform provisions when it passed the Code originally, and this non-uniformity has grown with time. Doubtless the drafters will have to confront this piecemeal enactment of non-uniform versions. For the time being, the student should understand that while the Uniform Commercial Code is highly uniform, it has never been completely so, and it is becoming less so with the passage of time.

SECTION 8. THE UNDERLYING OBLIGATION OF THE DEBTOR AND THE SPECIAL BODIES OF LAW DEALING WITH THE NEGOTIABLE NOTE

It is easy to be misled by the intense and detailed study which we will devote to the security interest, to all of its intricacies and legal attributes, for the security is not the all important thing. The debt owed by the debtor to the creditor is the all important thing. The collateral, the security interest, and all of the attendant trappings are no more than parasites that have found a home in the debt transaction. In the final chapters of this book we will deal at length with Articles 3 and 4 of the Uniform Commercial Code. Those articles govern commercial paper and set out rules for the presentation and collection of debts evidenced by checks and other commercial paper. For now, however, it is important for the student to understand how the underlying obligation arises and to appreciate some of the attributes of the negotiable note embodying this obligation, an instrument often also signed by the debtor at the time the loan transaction takes place.

Our review in Section 2 of the history of personal property security in the United States provides the student with some taste of the variety of transactions in which security interests arise. Among them is the conventional contract obligation found under Article 2 of the UCC in which a buyer agrees to pay a certain amount "on time" to the seller for the purchase of goods. Another is a loan from either the seller or the bank to purchase a piece of equipment. Another is an outright loan of a specified amount from the bank secured by assets already owned.

The standard debt might involve a single transaction in which the entire amount is advanced by the creditor either in the form of money or in the form of goods sold in which the debtor makes periodic payment or in some cases a single repayment. A form of debt frequently found in modern transactions is one with no fixed amount. An example would be a bank granting a line of credit to a debtor with the expectation that the debtor would make periodic draws and periodic payments but that the amount of debt would fluctuate and would not be paid to zero for an indefinite period. Such arrangements are familiar to the consumer in the form of credit card advances and checking account overdraft protection. These are merely consumer lines of credit, and they contemplate a wide variety of uses to which the credit may be put.

The nature of the liability secured presents only a few problems. Most of those we will deal with in the next chapter. One recurring issue is whether a provision in a security agreement that purports to cover "all indebtedness of the debtor" in fact is intended to cover not only debts of the kind incurred at the time the agreement was made but also debts that might arise out of another business or even out of a consumer transaction by the business debtor.

The other issues relate to the negotiable note. One is more likely to find a negotiable note in the single-shot transaction described above than in a line of credit. In the standard deal, the debtor signs a note at the time he signs the mortgage or security agreement. Thereafter, he makes either a single payment or periodic repayments on the note. In Chapter 24, Section 2, we will deal extensively with the requirements of negotiability and with the intricacies of Article 3 that relate to negotiability. For now the student should understand some of the rules and some of the consequences of negotiability. The idea of negotiability is defended principally as a mode of enabling one creditor to sell his debt to another and thus to allow money to flow from places where there is excess to places where there is too little. Thus, for example, a local bank in Osage, Iowa might make a loan to farmer for the purchase of a $100,000 combine. The farmer may sign a negotiable note for $100,000 plus interest, and sign a security agreement. Wishing further money to lend to others, Osage then might assign that note to a New York bank who might pay face value. It would be uneconomical for the New York bank to lend directly to the farmer in Osage. It might not be uneconomical for it to buy a negotiable note from the Osage bank, particularly if the Osage bank agreed to repurchase it on default, and that is more likely true if the note is negotiable.

By saying that the note is negotiable, a lawyer typically means that one who takes it for value and in good faith takes it free of the defenses that the farmer in Osage might be able to raise on the underlying contract against the seller of the combine (should it, for example, be defective) or under the note itself against the Osage bank. By being a "holder in due course" (roughly, a "bona fide purchaser") of the negotiable note, the New York bank limits its risk to the credit risk; it becomes merely a lender who can insist upon its money irrespective of hanky panky in the underlying transaction, of disputes between the underlying parties, or of setoffs the parties may have arising out of other transactions. These rights are summarized in a very basic provision of Article 3—section 3–305; the student should read that section now.

Fifty years ago the importance of negotiability would have gone unquestioned. Whether it is critical in today's credit market is subject to much dispute. In the area of consumer paper, the Federal Trade Commission has effectively wiped out holder in due course status. There the doctrine of negotiability disappeared without a measurable impact upon that market. Whether the same would be true in the non-consumer market is uncertain.

It is clear that every commercial lawyer needs to know something about negotiability and that it will often be in the interest of a plaintiff to be able to maintain that he is a holder in due course. To that end let us paint the requirements of negotiability with a relatively broad brush through Article 3 of the UCC. We have already started with the operative provision which allows a holder in due course to take free of most defenses of the underlying maker. Proceeding backwards from UCC 3–305, one sees the definition of a holder in due course in UCC 3–302 as a person who takes (1) an instrument, (2) for value, (3) in good faith, (4) without notice that it is overdue, has been dishonored, or of a defense. Section 3–305 defines taking for value and, to the surprise of some, includes one who takes an instrument in payment of or as security for an antecedent debt. Section 3–305 tells us who is to be regarded as having notice of a claim or defense and who has not. For example, one who takes a domestic check more than 30 days after its issuance is presumed to be on notice that it is "overdue."

A more troublesome and subtle requirement for the holder in due course status, is that the holder be a holder of a negotiable instrument. Note that in Article 3 the word "instrument" means "negotiable instrument" (see UCC 3–102(1)(e)). Section 3–104 defines the form of negotiable instruments; note how restrictive the definition is. Note particularly under UCC 3–104(1)(b) that the instrument must "contain an unconditional promise or order to pay a sum certain in money and no other promise, order, obligation or power * * *." Thus, the typical sales contract which surely includes a promise to pay cannot be a negotiable instrument, at least because it will include many other promises. By the same token, a promise that is construed to be "conditional" cannot be a negotiable instrument, nor can one that is to be payable to a specific person, as opposed to "order or bearer," or is payable at an uncertain time. What is the purpose of these rigid rules? Why does the Code, an enlightened and modern document, take a position that seems so formal, and thus so inconsistent with the looseness of Article 2 and Article 9? Part of the answer is to put those on notice who deal with negotiable instruments. Presumably not only the maker but also the payee and most of all the indorsee or assignee wish to be certain that they are dealing with a negotiable instrument when that is so. Conceivably some of the limitations have been imposed by the powerful buyers of these instruments to free them from the need to examine closely maverick instruments to decide whether the conditions are important or not, and to minimize the transaction costs of the transfer of such documents.

One authority has explained the rationale for each of these requisites in the following terms:

HAWKLAND, COMMERCIAL PAPER 5, 11, 14, 19 (1959).

"* * * The Promise or Order Must be Unconditional—3–105.

"One function of negotiable instruments is to supplement the supply of currency. Another function is to represent the future payment of money. These currency and credit functions would be defeated by conditional promises, for costly and time-consuming investigations would be made necessary by such promises, and circulation, therefore, would be impeded. Risks would be great and discount rates high. Substitutes for money must be capable of rapid circulation at minimum risks, and credit documents are feasible only when low discounting prevails. Obviously, then, negotiable instruments must be unconditional to serve the purposes for which they were created. * * *

"The Instrument Must Be Payable in Money and the Sum of Money Must Be Certain—3–106 and 3–107.

"In order for an instrument to be negotiable at common law and under the N.I.L. [Uniform Negotiable Instruments Law] it is essential that it be payable in money and that its sum be certain. These formal requisites of negotiability are designed to promote certainty in ascertaining the present value of the instrument, and they have been long regarded as indispensible to the concept of negotiability. Consequently, it is not surprising to note that these requisites have been retained, with little change, by sections 3–106 and 3–107 of the Commercial Code. A few changes have been made by these Code sections in the interests of clarification and completeness. * * *

"The Instrument Must Be Payable at a Time Certain—3–108 and 3–109.

"The N.I.L. requires that a negotiable instrument either be payable on demand or at a fixed or determinable time. This requirement, like the other formal requisites of negotiability, is designed to promote certainty in ascertaining the present value of a negotiable instrument. In determining the value of an instrument, it is necessary to know when the obligor can be compelled to pay, when the obligations of secondary parties will arise, and when the statute of limitations will start to run. Without this information, interest and discount rates, which vary according to the duration of the obligation, cannot be fixed. Nor can credit risks be properly assessed. In short, the present value of the instrument cannot be rationally determined.

"Because 'time certain' is important to the concept of negotiability, it has been retained by the Commercial Code. * * *

"The Instrument Must Contain Words of Negotiability—3–104(1)(d).

"The formal requisites of negotiability were formulated to bring about certainty, and the use in instruments of words of negotiability is one of the most clear indications that the parties have intended the paper to be negotiable. The N.I.L., accordingly, requires negotiable instruments to contain words of negotiability. The Code (3–104(1)(d)) continues this requirement with little or no change. * * *"

The rigidity of section UCC 3–104 is alleviated somewhat by UCC 3–105, 3–112, and by some of the other provisions in part 1 of Article 3. The student should read those sections and should note, for example, that UCC 3–112(1)(b) would permit a statement on the note that collateral has been given to secure it.

Problem 2–13

Do you think the note set out below is negotiable?

DATE OF NOTE

NOTE

For value received, I/WE, jointly and severally promise to pay to the order of

ACCOUNT NUMBER

THE UNIVERSITY OF MICHIGAN CREDIT UNION, A MICHIGAN CORPORATION AT 333 WILLIAM STREET, ANN ARBOR, MICHIGAN, the sum of

.... dollars and .... cents $..............

WITH INTEREST ON UNPAID BALANCES AT THE RATE OF	PAYABLE IN	INSTALLMENTS OF	THE FIRST PAYMENT TO BE MADE ON	AND A LIKE AMOUNT	PLUS AN IRREGULAR OR FINAL PAYMENT
per cent per year		$ inclusive of Principal and Interest			OF............ DUE ON ....

COLLATERAL

TITLED PROPERTY ▶	MAKE	YEAR	MODEL	BODY STYLE	IDENTIFICATION NUMBER

☐ (APPLICABLE ONLY WHEN CHECKED) HOUSEHOLD GOODS, FURNITURE, AND APPLIANCES AS DESCRIBED IN SECURITY AGREEMENT

I/We, the undersigned, hereby jointly and severally pledge all paid shares and deposits and payments on shares and deposits which I/we now have or hereafter may have in this credit union, except shares or deposits which may be held pursuant to any "Individual Retirement Trust" or "Keogh Plan" or as an All-Savers Certificate, as security for (1) principal and interest of the loan evidenced by this Note and of any refinancing of all or any part thereof and (2) any other sums which may become due under the Security Agreement and/or real estate mortgage securing such obligations. Shares, deposits and payments thereon are only pledged to an amount equal to the unpaid balance of such indebtedness. I/We hereby authorize the credit union in the event of default to apply any or all such paid shares and deposits and payments on same to the repayment of any such indebtedness.

However, Borrower may withdraw shares or deposits in excess of $ if loan payments are up to date.

INSURANCE ADVANCES

The Credit Union hereby agrees to loan the Borrower(s) an amount equal to the Total Premium indicated below, plus any increase thereof resulting from Borrower(s) not making payments on time, in a series of monthly advances for the term of this loan or until the Borrower's insurance is terminated. Borrower(s) hereby agree(s) to the monthly addition of such insurance premiums to the outstanding principal balance owing hereunder. Credit Union shall not be obligated to extend credit for premiums that cause the outstanding principal balance to exceed legal limits. The amount of the insurance premium to be added to the loan is based on the rates now in use by the insurance company as determined by the original term of the loan as applied on the same day of each month to the outstanding principal balance.

INSURANCE PREMIUMS (CHECK IF APPLICABLE) ▶	☐ GROUP CREDIT LIFE	$

Credit Union wavies any and all security for the indebtedness evidenced by this Note or for any refinancing of all or any part thereof or for any other sums which may become due under the Security Agreement and/or real estate mortgage securing such obligations other than security granted by such Security Agreement and/or real estate mortgage by the foregoing pledge of shares and/or deposits, or provided by statute. Fines or charges may be imposed for late payments as provided in the Credit Union's bylaws.

In the event any payment on this loan account is not made when due, or if an "event of default" occurs under any Security Agreement given by the member(s), then the entire unpaid balance of this loan account plus accrued interest shall become immediately due and payable, without notice at the option of the Credit Union. The undersigned further agrees to pay all usual and customary costs of collection including reasonable attorney fees and all taxable court costs permitted by law. Each party to this Note, whether as maker, comaker, indorser or guarantor, severally wavies presentment for payment, demand, protest or notice of protest and dishonor of same.

Authority is hereby given the Credit Union to complete this Note in any necessary respect in the event it is executed while still incomplete. This Note is secured by a Security Agreement and/or real estate mortgage of even date herewith.

SIGNATURE OF MAKER	SIGNATURE OF COMAKER
X (SEAL)	X (SEAL)
SIGNATURE OF MAKER	SIGNATURE OF COMAKER
X (SEAL)	X (SEAL)

CHAPTER THREE

CREATION OF THE SECURITY INTEREST

SECTION 1. INTRODUCTION

In Chapter Two we outlined the history of personal property security in the United States. There we noted a frequent insistence on or fanatical attention to detail in the documents creating a security interest. For example, judges struck down chattel mortgages because of very minor errors in the description of the collateral. This formalistic attitude derived partly from a similar approach to real estate mortgages; indeed one still encounters it in the formalities required for the execution of deeds and other such documents (e.g., witnessing, notarization, affidavits, etc.).

An examination of UCC 9–203, the principal section that governs the creation of an enforceable Article 9 security interest, reveals none of this. Moreover, UCC 9–203 purports to cover all personal property security transactions regardless of form and rejects pre-Code rules requiring one to label certain documents "conditional sales contracts", others "chattel mortgages," and still others, "factor's liens."

The student should now examine UCC 9–203, 9–204 and the comments to each section. Although we have labeled this chapter the "creation" of a security interest, the Code in the title to UCC 9–203 and the cases sometimes refer to "attachment." Under the 1972 version of Article 9, the terms are interchangeable: Both refer to the enforceability of the security interest. Both of these terms, however, are to be distinguished from perfection, an event considered in the next chapter. Note that UCC 9–204 deals explicitly with after-acquired property and future advances, including "optional" advances.

The general thrust of UCC 9–203 and UCC 9–204 is to make the granting of security easy and inexpensive. Presumably this reflects the drafters' belief that no rigid formalities are necessary here to impress the debtor with the importance of the transaction or to attempt to protect against ignorant or fraudulent behavior. That thrust is strengthened by UCC 9–110 which instructs the courts to adopt a liberal rule for the description of property covered by the security agreement.

Despite the simplicity of the requirements of UCC 9–203 and 9–204 and the ease with which one may acquire a security agreement, there remain a variety of ways to go wrong. For example, a debtor (1) might forget to sign the security agreement, or (2) might materially misdescribe the collateral, or (3) a series of loans might be made at different times and the debtor might argue that some were intended to be covered and others not, or (4) a dispute might arise over the debtor's rights in the underlying collateral and thus about the capacity of the debtor to pass those rights on to the secured creditor. We will deal with all these problems.

Note that UCC 9–203 (1)(a) does not require a writing if "the collateral is in the possession of the secured party pursuant to agreement * * *". Presumably possession by the secured creditor sufficiently meets the statute of frauds concern about the likely existence of an agreement. Otherwise why would the secured creditor have possession of the debtor's assets? Possession—the pledge—is now an uncommon means of creating and perfecting a security interest. We will discuss some of the problems with it in the next chapter. Presently it is largely limited to pawn shop loans, loans against certificated securities and some other relatively uncommon and unusual transactions.

SECTION 2. THE REQUIREMENTS OF UCC 9–203

A. *Rights in the Collateral*

Recall that under pre-Code law, it was often the case that some security interests could not be created in property acquired by the debtor after the loan was made, and could secure only the debt that existed at the time the agreement was signed and not future advances. The Code blesses both after acquired property and future advance clauses. See UCC 9–204. Some serious issues remain.

IN RE SAMUELS & CO.

United States Court of Appeals, Fifth Circuit, 1976.
526 F.2d 1238, *cert. denied* 429 U.S. 834.

[Owners of cattle sold them to Samuels, a packing house. Samuels had previously given a perfected security interest in its inventory (pursuant to an after-acquired property clause) and in other property to CIT. Samuels had paid the sellers for the cattle by checks that ultimately were dishonored. Samuels in turn sold the carcasses to third parties. Both the sellers and CIT, the secured creditor, claimed the proceeds of the sale when Samuels defaulted and went bankrupt. One issue was whether and to what extent CIT's security interest had attached to the cattle when they became a part of Samuels' inventory. The sellers' principal arguments were based on various provisions of Article 2, which give the seller a limited right to reclaim the goods from a buyer. In one way or another all of the sellers' Article 2 arguments sought to undermine the secured creditors' claim that the debtor had adequate "rights in the collateral" pursuant to UCC 9–203(1)(c).

[The Referee in Bankruptcy held for the unpaid sellers over C.I.T. The district court reversed, holding for the secured party. The Court of Appeals reversed the district court and held for the unpaid sellers, Judge Godbold dissenting. The gist of the decision was that the sellers had priority under the Packers and Stockyard Act. 483 F.2d 557 (5th Cir.1973). The Supreme Court reversed, holding that the Packers and Stockyards Act did not determine priorities between the competing parties and remanded the case for that determination under state law. Mahon v. Stowers, 416 U.S. 100, 94 S.Ct. 1626, 40 L.Ed.2d 79 (1974). On remand, the court of appeals held that the Texas Uniform Commercial Code dictated that the sellers prevail. 510 F.2d 139 (5th Cir.1975). Judge Godbold again dissented. The decision of the panel was then reversed *per curiam* by the court en banc, the judgment of the district court was affirmed and the dissent of Judge Godbold, reprinted in part below, was adopted by the majority. Five judges dissented from the majority opinion.]

* * *

GODBOLD, CIRCUIT JUDGE.

This case raises one primary question: under the Uniform Commercial Code as adopted in Texas, is the interest of an unpaid cash seller in goods already delivered to a buyer superior or subordinate to the interest of a holder of a perfected security interest in those same goods? In my opinion, under Article Nine, the perfected security interest is unquestionably superior to the interest of the seller. Moreover, the perfected lender is protected from the seller's claims by two independent and theoretically distinct Article Two provisions. My result is not the product of revealed truth, but rather of a meticulous and dispassionate reading of Articles Two and Nine and an understanding that the Code is an integrated statute whose Articles and Sections overlap and flow into one another in an effort to encourage specific types of commercial behavior. The Code's overall plan, which typically favors good faith purchasers, and which encourages notice filing of nonpossessory security interests in personalty through the imposition of stringent penalties for nonfiling, compels a finding that the perfected secured party here should prevail.

My brothers have not concealed that their orientation in the case before us is to somehow reach a result in favor of the sellers of cattle, assumed by them to be "little fellows," and against a large corporate lender, because it seems the "fair" thing to do. We do not sit as federal chancellors confecting ways to escape the state law of commercial transactions when that law produces a result not to our tastes. Doing what seems fair is heady stuff. But the next seller may be a tremendous corporate conglomerate engaged in the cattle feeding business, and the next lender a small town Texas bank. Today's heady draught may give the majority a euphoric feeling, but it can produce tomorrow's hangover.

I. RIGHTS UNDER § 2.403

My analysis begins with an examination of the relative rights of seller and secured party under § 2.403(a).

Section 2.403 gives certain transferors power to pass greater title than they can themselves claim. Section 2.403(a) gives good faith purchasers of even fraudulent buyers-transferors greater rights than the defrauded seller can assert. This harsh rule is designed to promote the greatest range of freedom possible to commercial vendors and purchasers.

The provision anticipates a situation where (1) a cash seller has delivered goods to a buyer who has paid by a check which is subsequently dishonored, § 2.403(a)(2), (3), and where (2) the defaulting buyer transfers title to a Code-defined "good faith purchaser." The interest of the good faith purchaser is protected pro tanto against the claims of the aggrieved seller. §§ 2.403(a); 2.403, Comment 1. The Code expressly recognizes the power of the defaulting buyer to transfer good title to such a purchaser even though the transfer is wrongful as against the seller. The buyer is granted the *power* to transfer good title despite the fact that under § 2.507 he lacks the *right* to do so.

The Code definition of "purchaser" is broad, and includes not only one taking by sale but also covers persons taking by gift or by voluntary mortgage, pledge or lien. § 1.201(32), (33). It is therefore broad enough to include an Article Nine secured party. §§ 1.201(37); 9.101, Comment; 9.102(a), (b). Thus, if C.I.T. holds a valid Article Nine security interest, it is by virtue of that status *also* a purchaser under § 2.403(a) * * *.

While I shall discuss in detail infra, the implications of C.I.T.'s security interest under Article Nine and under other Article Two provisions, I here note that C.I.T. is the holder of a perfected Article Nine interest which extends to the goods claimed by the seller Stowers.

Attachment of an Article Nine interest takes place when (1) there is agreement that the interest attach to the collateral; (2) the secured party has given value; and (3) the debtor has rights in the collateral sufficient to permit attachment. § 9.204(a).

(1) The agreement: In 1963, Samuels initially authorized C.I.T.'s lien in its after-acquired inventory. The agreement between these parties remained in effect throughout the period of delivery of Stowers' cattle to Samuels.

(2) Value: At the time of Stowers' delivery, Samuels' indebtedness to C.I.T. exceeded $1.8 million. This pre-existing indebtedness to the lender constituted "value" under the Code. § 1.201(44).

(3) Rights in the collateral: Finally, upon delivery, Samuels acquired rights in the cattle sufficient to allow attachment of C.I.T.'s lien. The fact that the holder of a voluntary lien—including an Article Nine interest—is a "purchaser" under the Code is of great significance to a proper understanding and resolution of this case under Article Two and Article Nine. The Code establishes that purchasers can take from a defaulting cash buyer, § 2.403(a). Lien creditors are included in the definition of purchasers, § 1.201(32), (33). A lien is an Article Nine interest, §§ 9.101, Comment; 9.102(b); 9.102, Comment. The existence of an Article Nine interest presupposes the debtor's having rights in the collateral sufficient to permit attachment, § 9.204(a). Therefore, since a defaulting cash buyer has the power to transfer a security interest to a lien creditor, including an Article Nine secured party, the buyer's rights in the property, however marginal, must be sufficient to allow attachment of a lien. And this is true even if, arguendo, I were to agree that the cash seller is granted reclamation rights under Article Two * * *.

If the Article Nine secured party acted in good faith, it is prior under § 2.403(a) to an aggrieved seller. Under the facts before us, I think that C.I.T. acted in good faith. The Code good faith provision requires "honesty in fact", § 1.201(19), which, for Article Two purposes, is "expressly defined as * * * reasonable commercial standards of fair dealing." §§ 1.201, Comment 19; 2.103(a)(2). There is no evidence that C.I.T. acted in bad faith in its dealings with Samuels, or that Stowers' loss resulted from any breach of obligation by C.I.T. There is no claim that the 1963 security agreement was the product of bad faith. The lender's interest had been perfected and was of record for six years when Stowers' delivery to Samuels occurred. There is no suggestion that the $1.8 million debt owing from Samuels to C.I.T. was the result of bad faith or of a desire to defeat Stowers' $50,000 claim. There is no claim that C.I.T. exercised or was able to exercise control over Samuels' business operations. There is no evidence that C.I.T. authorized or ordered or suggested that Samuels dishonor Stowers' check. There is no contention that C.I.T.'s refusal to extend credit on May 23, the date Samuels filed a voluntary petition on bankruptcy at a time when it owed C.I.T. more than $1.8 million, was violative of an obligatory future advances clause. The Code's good faith provision requires "honesty in fact", § 1.201(19); it hardly requires a secured party to continue financing a doomed business enterprise.

The majority deny that C.I.T. acted in good faith because, they claim, the lender had "intimate" knowledge of Samuels' business operations. The majority's source of information on the scope of C.I.T.'s knowledge is a little puzzling. The Referee in Bankruptcy found only that "C.I.T. knew or should have known of the manner by which the bankrupt bought livestock * * * on a grade and yield basis." In the Matter of Samuels & Co., Inc., No. BK 3–1314 (N.D.Tex., order of Jan. 19, 1972). This factual finding was affirmed by the District Court which reversed the Referee and upheld C.I.T.'s priority over Stowers. Id., orders of Nov. 24, 1972, and Jan. 16, 1973. Neither the Referee nor the District Court found, nor have the parties alleged, that C.I.T.'s knowledge of Samuels' business extended to knowledge of the debtor's obligations to third party creditors.

However, even if evidence had established that C.I.T. knew of Samuels' nonpayment and of Stowers' claim, C.I.T.'s status as an Article Two good faith purchaser would be unaffected. Lack of knowledge of outstanding claims is necessary to the common law BFP, and is similarly expressly required in many Code BFP and priority provisions. See e.g., §§ 3.302; 6.110; 8.301, 8.302; 9.301(a)(2). But the Code's definition of an Article Two good faith purchaser does not expressly or impliedly include lack of knowledge of third-party claims as an element. The detailed definition of the Article's counterpart of the common law BFP requires only honesty in fact, reasonable commercial behavior, fair dealing. And this describes precisely C.I.T.'s dealings with Samuels: during the period May 13–22—the time when the bulk of Stowers' cattle were delivered and the time of the issuance of the NSF checks—C.I.T.'s advances to Samuels totalled $1 million. The advances were curtailed on May 23 because of Samuels' taking voluntary bankruptcy at a time when its indebtedness to C.I.T. was enormous. The decision to terminate further funding was clearly reasonable. It was also fair, and honest, and, as the majority have failed to grasp, was not the cause of Stowers' suffering. As I note infra in my analysis of rights under Article Nine, the sellers' loss was avoidable through perfection of their security interests in the cattle. If they had perfected, they would not only have been prior to C.I.T. as an Article Nine lender, § 9.312, but also protected against C.I.T. as an Article Two purchaser, § 9.201. As it happens, Stowers did not perfect. I believe the sellers cannot now be permitted to force an innocent, if prosperous, secured creditor to shoulder their loss for them.

II. Rights Under § 2.507

The majority opinion devotes much of its concentration and energy to an analysis of the sellers' "reclamation right" under § 2.507 and § 2.702. Relying on an expansive reading of these Sections, the opinion concludes that a cash seller whose right to payment is frustrated through a check ultimately dishonored can "reclaim" proceeds of goods delivered to the buyer despite an interim third-party interest, and despite a year-long delay in seeking reclamation. I am unable to accept this reading of Code policy and requirements.

Although the Code expressly grants a credit seller the right and power to reclaim goods from a breaching buyer, the right is triggered only by specific and limited circumstances; it can be asserted only if an exacting procedure is followed; and the right can never be asserted to defeat the interests of certain third parties who have dealt with the defaulting buyer. § 2.702(b), (c). There is no Code Section expressly granting a similar reclamation right to a cash seller.

The seller's remedies upon breach are enumerated in § 2.703. These provisions do not include or suggest a right or power in a cash seller to recover goods already delivered to a breaching buyer. Nevertheless the courts have read a reclamation right into the Code. It is this judicially-confected right to reclaim goods in which the majority's reclamation analysis is grounded. However, the majority take the reclamation right beyond anything intimated by the Code or heretofore permitted by courts recognizing a cash seller's reclamation right.

The cash seller's right to reclaim has been drawn from the language of § 2.507(b) and § 2.507, Comment 3. I note, first, that the remedy granted by § 2.507(b) is one of seller against buyer, see In re Helms Veneer Corp., 287

F.Supp. 840 (W.D.Va., 1968). It does not concern rights of seller against third parties. Section 2.507, Comment 3 explains that the seller's rights under § 2.507 must "conform with the policy set forth in the bona fide purchase section of this Article," i.e., with § 2.403. As I have noted above, under this provision the rights of an aggrieved cash seller are subordinated to those of the buyer's good-faith purchasers, including Article Nine lenders such as C.I.T. Thus, the Code provisions supporting a cash seller's reclamation right expressly precluded recovery by Stowers as against C.I.T. See §§ 2.507(b); 2.507, Comment 3; 2.702(b), (c) * * *.

Moreover, those courts which have permitted reclamation under § 2.507 have invariably adhered to § 2.507, Comment 3's express requirement that demand for return be made within ten days after receipt by the buyer or else be lost.

* * *

In the instant case, demand was not made within ten days or ten weeks; it came a full year after delivery to Samuels. The majority excuse this gross noncompliance by finding that the sellers' failure was the product of innocent error, and, in any event, was not required since the "purpose" of the demand rule—protection of purchasers of the delivered goods—was served through C.I.T.'s alleged intimate knowledge of Samuels' business operations.

The Code's ten-day provision is an absolute requirement. There is no exception in the Code Sections or Comments, express or implied, to the statutory period. I would be hesitant to read any extension into a statute of limitations clear and unambiguous on its face, and particularly unwilling to allow an extension some 36 times greater than the statutory maximum. My reluctance is all the greater where the right at issue is not granted by the Code but is rather the product of judicial interpretation of a Comment which, whatever grant of power it may suggest, expressly limits that right to a ten-day life.

The spirit in which the rule was broken seems to me irrelevant. Even conceding that Stowers' noncompliance occurred in absolute good faith, it was nonetheless noncompliance. Mistake of law does not constitute excuse of mistake.

C.I.T.'s apocryphal intimate knowledge of Samuels' business operations is, I believe, also irrelevant to a determination of the validity of Stowers' claim. The majority find the purpose of the ten-day rule to be one of notice to third parties that a claim exists. I have somewhat greater difficulty than my brothers in pinpointing the purpose of the ten-day rule. But I am convinced that the goal is not one of protection or notice to third-party purchasers, for their rights are secure under the Code as against the aggrieved seller even if demand is timely made. §§ 2.507, Comment 3; 2.702(c). The Code does not condition the purchasers' rights on a lack of knowledge of the seller's interest. With or without knowledge, the purchaser rests secure. I am therefore forced to conclude that the ten-day rule serves some function other than notifying third-party takers, and, consequently, that even if C.I.T. knew of Stowers' claim, the sellers' obligation under the ten-day rule would not have been excused. And even if knowledge by the purchaser suspended the sellers' duty to make a timely demand, the record in this case is devoid of any hint that C.I.T. knew of Samuels' breach and Stowers' reclamation right.

Moreover, § 2.507 and § 2.702 speak of a right to reclaim goods. Neither provision grants a right to go after proceeds of those goods. Where a right or interest in proceeds is recognized by the Code it is recognized expressly. See e.g.,

§ 9.306. The right granted by § 2.507 is narrowly defined. I am unwilling to imply an extension to such a short-lived and precisely drawn remedy.

Finally, even if there were a right to reclaim proceeds, even if the right had been timely exercised, and even if it could have been exercised despite the transfer of interest to C.I.T., Stowers would have taken subject to C.I.T.'s perfected Article Nine interest. See §§ 9.201, 9.301, 9.306, 9.312. See also my discussion of C.I.T.'s rights and interest under Article Nine, infra.

III. Rights Under § 2.511

The majority opinion states that C.I.T.'s interest cannot be found superior to Stowers' because such a finding would violate § 2.511's prohibition on penalizing a seller for accepting as payment a check which is ultimately dishonored. I believe the majority have misconstrued the scope and significance of § 2.511.

Like § 2.507, § 2.511 concerns claims of the seller as against the buyer. See § 2.511(c), § 2.511, Comment 4. On its face it does not affect the rights of third parties taking from the defaulting buyer. Moreover, and more important, the seller is not here "penalized" for taking an N.S.F. check. Such loss as Stowers suffered is the direct result of his failure to comply with Code provisions which, once followed—and regardless of Stowers' acceptance of Samuels' check—would have made his interest invulnerable to claims by C.I.T. See, e.g., §§ 9.107; 9.201; 9.312(c), (d).

IV. Rights Under Article Nine

I am also unable to agree with the majority's conclusion that, under the Code, Stowers' interest is different from and greater than a security interest. Similarly, I disagree with the theory that by virtue of Stowers' power under Article Two, C.I.T.'s security interest is subject to defeat since it (1) could not attach because the debtor's rights in the collateral were too slight to permit attachment and (2) was subject to defeat even if it attached because a security interest collapses if the debtor's right to the property is extinguished. The majority's result is achieved only by ignoring or circumventing the plain meaning of Article Nine and Article Two.

Prior to the enactment of the Uniform Commercial Code, seller and buyer could agree that, despite buyer's possession, title to goods sold was to remain in the seller until he was paid. Such a reservation of title under the "cash sale" doctrine would defeat not only a claim to the goods by the defaulting buyer, but also the claims of lien creditors of the buyer, for the buyer's naked possession could give rise to no interest to which a lien could attach.

However, the UCC specifically limits the seller's ability to reserve title once he has voluntarily surrendered possession to the buyer: "Any retention or reservation by the seller of the title (property) in goods shipped or delivered to the buyer is limited in effect to a reservation of a security interest." § 2.401(a). See also § 1.201(37). The drafters noted the theory behind this provision: "Article [Two] deals with the issues between seller and buyer in terms of step by step performance or non-performance under the contract for sale and not in terms of whether or not 'title' to the goods has passed." § 2.401, Comment 1.

The majority opinion interprets § 2.401(a) as applying only to "credit" sales, and of no effect where the parties have contracted a "cash" sale. However, the Code provision speaks of "any reservation of title." It does not on its face apply solely to credit sales. There is no authority under the Code for the majority's restrictive interpretation. Numerous courts have, in fact, applied § 2.401 to cash sales.

* * * I have been unable to find even one case suggesting that § 2.401 applies only to credit sales.

If the majority were correct, the section would be merely definitional, for a credit sale is but a sales transaction in which the seller reserves a security interest. However, § 2.401 is not definitional. It is operational and concerns the effect of transfer of possession under a sales contract upon any reservation of title. Neither law nor logic leads me to believe that § 2.401 is correctly interpreted to exclude cash sales.

The majority also suggest that Stowers' interest cannot be characterized as a security interest subject to Article Nine requirements and priorities since, the majority conclude, such interests must be "consensual". While it is true that many interests governed by Article Nine are consensual, §§ 9.102; 9.102, Comment, the Code clearly subjects Article Two security interests arising not by consent but by operation of law to Article Nine. See §§ 2.401(a); 9.113; 9.113, Comment 2. See also §§ 2.326; 9.114; 9.102, Comment 1.

Since Stowers' interest upon delivery of the cattle to Samuels was limited to a security interest subject to Article Nine, §§ 2.401(a); 9.113, the validity of C.I.T.'s Article Nine interest becomes crucial. If C.I.T. is the holder of a perfected Article Nine interest in the collateral claimed by Stowers through its unperfected § 2.401 interest, C.I.T.'s interest will prevail over Stowers, § 9.312(e).

The majority assert that C.I.T. cannot claim an interest in the cattle because Samuels' interest was too slight to permit attachment. See § 9.204(a). As I noted in my discussion of rights under § 2.403, this argument ignores the significance of § 2.403(a) and § 1.201(32), (33). The Code anticipates a situation where the interest of an unpaid cash seller who has delivered goods to a breaching buyer is subordinated to the interest of "purchasers" of the buyer. Lien creditors are included in the definition of "purchasers"; in order that there *be* lien creditors, the buyer's interest must be great enough to allow attachment. Therefore, however Samuels' interest upon delivery of the cattle is defined, and however slight or tenuous or marginal it was, it was necessarily great enough to permit attachment of a lien, including C.I.T.'s Article Nine interest.

The majority find that even if attachment occurred, C.I.T.'s interest would be defeated by Stowers' reclamation. The theory behind this argument is that the rights of the Article Nine secured party are at best coextensive with the rights of the debtor; if the debtor loses his rights, the security interest too is lost.

Upon nonpayment Samuels lost the right to retain or dispose of the property, but the Code recognizes that the breaching buyer had the power to encumber, despite nonpayment, so long as he retained possession. §§ 2.403(a); 1.201(32), (33). In the instant case, this power arose as a result of Stowers' delivery, and it did not terminate while the goods remained in Samuels' hands. The whole point of Article Nine is the continuity of perfected security interests *once they have properly attached,* despite subsequent loss of control or possession of the collateral by the debtor. § 9.201. Article Nine does not except an unpaid cash seller from this overall plan. In fact it specifically provides a means for him to perfect and become prior to previous perfected security interests. § 9.312(c), (d).

To hold that a reclaiming seller is given the power to sweep away a security interest which was able to attach only as a direct and Code-approved result of his voluntary act of delivery to the buyer would require ignoring the meaning and interplay of Article Two and Article Nine. Article Two recognizes the continuous vitality and priority of an Article Nine interest over the rights of an aggrieved seller. See §§ 2.403(a); 2.507, Comment 3; 2.702(c). It would be error to believe that a proper analysis of Article Nine could require the extinction of an identical Article Nine interest in the very circumstances specified by Article Two as triggering the priority of lienor over seller. See §§ 2.403(a); 2.507(b); 2.507, Comment 3; 2.702(b), (c); 9.102; 9.107(1); 9.312(c), (d).

Any seeming unfairness to Stowers resulting from the Code's operation is illusory, for the sellers could have protected their interests, even as against C.I.T.'s prior perfected interest, if they had merely complied with the UCC's purchase-money provisions. §§ 9.107, 9.312(c), (d). The Code favors purchase-money financing, and encourages it by granting to a seller of goods the power to defeat prior liens. The seller at most need only (1) file a financing statement and (2) notify the prior secured party of its interest before delivery of the new inventory. The procedure is not unduly complex or cumbersome. But whether cumbersome or not, a lender who chooses to ignore its provisions takes a calculated risk that a loss will result.

In the instant case Stowers did not utilize § 9.312's purchase-money provision. The sellers never perfected. Thus, in a competition with a perfected secured party they are subordinated, and, in this case, lose the whole of their interests. See §§ 9.201, 9.301, 9.312(e). * * *

Note: "Rights in the Collateral"

One of the principal issues in the *Samuels* case concerns the nature of "rights in the collateral" held by Samuels, the debtor. Presumably the seller's theory was that CIT, the secured creditor, derived its title—here a security interest—from the title held by Samuels. If Samuels did not get title or sufficient title from the sellers of the cattle it would be incapable of passing title or greater rights on to a third party, namely, the secured creditor. This is the basic property rule *nemo dat quod non habet.* (He who hath not cannot give.) In *Samuels* that argument failed and essentially the court found that title had passed from the sellers to Samuels, the debtor, and that C.I.T.'s interest attached free of the claimed reclamation rights. Note that initially the question of the title of the debtor is to be determined by Article 2 and the common law. As a general rule one can start with the proposition that the debtor cannot convey greater rights to a secured creditor than he himself has, but as we saw in Chapter Two, clearly such a rule cannot govern all transactions. See UCC 2–401(1).

If we were to say that a debtor can never convey greater rights in collateral than he himself has, we would be reverting to rules of the kind we encountered in *In re Craig Lumber,* supra at p. 20, rules of the nineteenth century. Under such rules the owner of property could put the property in the hands of a third party under a conditional sale contract, for example, and retain a completely secret and private interest. Article 9 in many respects rejects such outcomes and at least in some cases establishes rules of substantive law that allow a third party to achieve greater rights than the debtor himself had. See, e.g., UCC 9–307(1). The starting point in each case, however, should be to examine the debtor's title under non-Article 9 law. Does the debtor have good title under Article 2? Does the debtor have good title under rules of common law dealing with leases, bailments, and other relevant areas? If the secured creditor who has been granted a security interest or a third party who has a claim against the debtor's property now asserts *greater* rights than have been conveyed to the debtor himself, that person must find a rule of substantive law somewhere that endows him with those rights. In *Samuels* ultimately the court finds that the debtor procured title to the carcasses from the seller despite the fact that the sellers were unpaid. Thus CIT was not claiming greater rights than Samuels had acquired. But in some settings the relevant substantive law will give greater title to those buyers because they are in effect bona fide purchasers. That can be the outcome under UCC 2–702(3), the section also applied in *Samuels.* Suppose that Samuels had defrauded the sellers and the sellers had a good claim *against Samuels* under UCC 2–702(2). CIT would still prevail under UCC 2–702(3), thereby taking greater rights than the sellers had conveyed to Samuels.

If the secured creditor cannot find a rule of law outside of Article 9 that grants him greater rights than his debtor had, we believe that the rule of *nemo dat* should be applied and that he should be limited to the rights of his debtor. For that reason, in the problem that follows we would decide that the lessor gets the Electra without paying any part of the fixed base operator's bill. Examine this problem to see why.

Problem 3–1

Lessor was the owner of a Lockheed Electra for which it no longer had any use. Lessor entered into a ten-year lease for a specified payment with an air freight service, Freight Service, that was located in Sacramento, California. Freight Service granted a security interest in the aircraft to a local fixed-base operator for $100,000 worth of unpaid work done on the aircraft. The Operator perfected its security interest on the aircraft by an appropriate filing under the federal law. If Freight Service defaults on its lease obligation to Lessor, must the Lessor pay off the entire $100,000 debt to Operator to get the Electra or is the airplane to be returned to the Lessor simply because the Freight Service is in default? Clearly the lessee had some possessory "rights in the collateral" and thus was capable of granting a security interest. Is it equally clear that UCC 9–203 states that Operator has greater rights than Lessor? If not, Operator could achieve priority over the Lessor only if the court made a mistake (as the court in fact did in a similar case) or if the secured creditor could find some rule of common law dealing with bailment that would say that those who lease items of this kind lose their rights to bona fide purchasers. This, however, would not be a rule found in Article 9. See, e.g., UCC 2–403(2). Could Operator go outside of Article 9, via UCC 1–103 for such a rule?

OMIT *Problem 3–2*

Debtor One has given a perfected security interest in a large and expensive piece of industrial machinery to Bank One. Debtor One then sold the machine to Debtor Two whose bill of sale explicitly provided that Debtor Two took subject to Bank One's security interest. Debtor Two then went to Bank Two, represented that he (Debtor Two) owned the machine free and clear and procured a $200,000 loan against it. Bank Two checked the files under Debtor Two's name and, finding nothing, perfected its security interest by a filing. When the scheme was discovered, both Bank One and Bank Two claimed the asset. Assume that there was a defect in Bank One's financing statement that caused it to be unperfected. Bank Two argues that it is a perfected secured creditor and as such has priority over Bank One's interest because of UCC 9–201 and UCC 9–312.

Can you see an argument that you would make on behalf of Bank One? Who prevails?

B. Scope of the Security Agreement

As secured transactions have become more complex, collateral more diverse, and the Code has expanded the capacity of the parties to cover not only existing loans but new loans and not only existing collateral but subsequently acquired collateral, courts have had to deal with a variety of new circumstances. Repeatedly courts are asked to determine whether security agreement covers a *new loan* or a loan made after the original one in an apparently unrelated transaction. Even more frequently, with poorly drafted clauses, courts are asked to decide whether the security agreement covers *after-acquired collateral* of the same type as the original collateral. In general the Code treats these matters as simply matters of contract between the debtor and creditor. If the security agreement is carefully drafted, seldom will a problem arise. However, an examination of the cases shows that many security agreements are not carefully drafted or, when so drafted, are later distorted by the interpretation of one party or another. Only UCC 9–110 deals with this question at all. It requires only that a description of the property "reasonably identify" the collateral or other property.

Two questions must be separated. The first question is whether the security agreement covers this loan and this collateral. If not, the security interest is not enforceable. The second is whether the financing statement that was filed is adequate to perfect a security interest in this collateral or as to this loan. As to the second question, section 9–402(8) says that "minor errors that are not seriously misleading" do not invalidate the perfection. There is no comparable provision with respect to the security agreement. Our focus in this chapter is on the first question. The second is taken up in the next chapter.

In some cases one may be able to infer from the general description of the property such as "inventory" or "accounts receivable" that the parties intend to cover not only existing but after-acquired accounts. Otherwise, given that the collateral "turns over," the creditor would soon be entirely unsecured. In other cases, such as where a security agreement covers "all indebtedness of debtor now or hereafter incurred," the issue of interpretation is much more problematic. Here, the court may find that the agreement does not reach certain debt, as for example, when the original indebtedness was a $1,000,000 business debt and one later sought to be included was a $5,000 debt for the purchase of a personal car. To the extent that these questions deal with the creation of a security interest and depend upon private documents not subject to public scrutiny, namely the security agreement, these are presumably contract interpretation questions. To the extent that they affect third parties who lend or act in reliance upon the public record, a rather different question arises. With this background consider *Idaho Bank and Trust v. Cargill.* It deals at length with just these questions.

IDAHO BANK & TRUST CO. v. CARGILL, INC.

Court of Appeals, Idaho, 1983.
105 Idaho 83, 665 P.2d 1093.

SWANSTROM, J. Idaho Bank & Trust Co. made a series of loans to Floyd Idle, a grain dealer at Rupert, Idaho. Some of the loans had not been repaid when Idle declared bankruptcy in 1977. The bank sought payment of the unpaid loans from Cargill, Inc., under the theory that Cargill was an "account debtor" who had wrongfully made several payments to Idle on grain contracts, the proceeds of which Idle had assigned to the bank as security. When Cargill refused to accept liability for the bank's losses, the bank brought this suit. Following trial, the district court held that the bank did not have a security interest in the disputed contracts and entered judgment for Cargill. We affirm.

Broadly phrased, the issue is whether Cargill, having paid Idle on certain grain contracts, should be compelled to pay again—this time to the bank—for failing to honor the assignment. The answer to this question depends on whether Cargill was an "account debtor" with respect to the disputed contracts. To decide this question, we must address two legal issues. Did Idle and the bank have a written security agreement meeting the minimum requirements of IC § 28–9–203? Did the parties' security agreement apply to "future advances" and "after-acquired collateral"?

* * * Idle's business consisted of purchasing grain from farmers and reselling it to large, west coast grain concerns, such as Cargill, Inc. Early in 1974, Idle had obtained a $50,000 line of credit with the bank. His line of credit was unsecured, and the bank was unwilling to increase the credit limits without collateral for the loans.

The bank agreed to loan Idle 80% of the face value of the grain contracts he made with Cargill in exchange for an assignment of contract proceeds, as security for the loans. The only document the bank and Idle used to evidence this arrangement was entitled an "Assignment" prepared by the bank and signed by Idle. It reads as follows:

> KNOW ALL MEN BY THESE PRESENTS: That I, Floyd Idle dba Idle Warehouse the undersigned, of Minidoka County, Idaho, for value received, do hereby set over, assign and transfer all monies now due or to become due under certain Grain Contracts held in your Warehouse. All checks are to be made payable to Idle Warehouse and Idaho Bank & Trust Company. Mail all checks to Box 604, Rupert, Idaho, 83350.
>
> Floyd E. Idle
>
> Floyd E. Idle dba Idle Warehouse

In November of 1974, the bank sent a copy of the assignment to Cargill. Accompanying the document was a letter giving notice that Idle had assigned to the bank "all funds due him from the sale of grain to your Corporation" and requesting that the bank be listed as a joint payee on all future checks. On December 2 Cargill acknowledged receipt and acceptance of the assignment. This was the last communication between the bank and Cargill until the end of April, 1977.

At Idle's direction Cargill placed the bank's name and Idle's name on each grain contract that Idle made with Cargill. Idle would bring these contracts to the bank and obtain advances from the bank of up to 80% of the cash value of each contract, by executing a promissory note for the amount of each advance. In all, the bank made short term loans on approximately two hundred contracts. When paying the contracts on which the bank's name appeared Cargill placed the bank's name as a joint payee on the checks. Cargill mailed these checks to Idle who took them to the bank. The bank routinely endorsed the checks for deposit to Idle's account and computed the amount of any loan then due. Idle wrote his check to the bank for the amount then due on his loans.

* * * Trouble began in early 1977 when the bank cut off Idle's line of credit. In response, Idle temporarily stopped performing the contracts on which he had received advances from the bank. Instead, he entered into a new series of grain contracts with Cargill. Idle directed Cargill not to put the bank's name

on these contracts and Idle did not use them to obtain loans. In payment of these contracts, Cargill issued checks to Idle in his name alone. After performing seven of these contracts, Idle resumed performance of the contracts on which the bank had loaned money. However, he directed Cargill to scratch the bank's name off these remaining contracts and to issue checks without the bank's name as a co-payee. In all, Cargill issued checks to Idle for $77,667.34 on which the bank's name did not appear. These checks were issued in payment of five grain contracts on which the bank had loaned money to Idle in 1977.

In the spring of 1977, Idle went bankrupt. Idle defaulted in repayment of five promissory notes leaving him approximately $56,000 in debt to the bank. The bank sued Cargill on the theory that Cargill was an "account debtor" as that term is used in the Uniform Commercial Code. The bank contends that as an account debtor Cargill should be held liable for the losses the bank sustained when Cargill, in disregard of the notice sent by the bank, paid the proceeds of the grain contracts to Idle. The bank claimed that if Cargill had obeyed the assignment the bank would have received sufficient funds to cover Idle's $56,000 debt. This likewise is the theory of liability the bank advances on appeal.

It is obvious the bank intended Idle's assignment would provide security for loans the bank made to Idle. Accordingly, IC § 28–9–102(1)(a) provides that Chapter 9—"Secured Transactions" of our Uniform Commercial Code—shall apply. * * *

The basic premise on which the bank stakes its claim against Cargill is * * * as follows:

> "Section 9–318(3) [of the UCC] clearly delineates the legal relationship between the account debtor and the assignee once the account debtor receives adequate notification of an assignment. The account debtor, upon receipt of said notification, is duty-bound to pay the assignee and not the assignor. Payment to an assignor, after notification of assignment, does not relieve the account debtor of his obligation to pay the assignee unless the assignee consents to such a collection process. (See official comment # 3, 9–318.) The account debtor's failure to pay the assignee after receiving due notification gives rise to an assignee's claim for wrongful payment."

The dispute in this case focuses upon whether Cargill was an account debtor in respect to certain contracts coming into existence after the assignment was given. The district court determined that the assignment contained neither a "future advances" clause nor an "after-acquired property" clause. The court concluded as a matter of law that the assignment did not contain a description of the collateral sufficient to create a security interest in the proceeds of contracts which did not come into existence until 1977. The court also held the assignment did not protect the bank with respect to advances made by the bank in 1977.

Underlying the court's reasoning is the assumption that the relationship of assignee to account debtor does not come into existence unless the assignee has a security interest in the subject of the assignment. In other words, where, as here, the assignment is used as a security device, the mere fact of assignment, even coupled with notice, does not suffice to create the relationship of assignee to account debtor. There must be an underlying security interest. This conclusion of the trial court is supported by the language of the code.

Former IC § 28–9–105(1)(a) defined "Account debtor" as "the person who is obligated on an account, chattel paper, contract right or general intangible." Official Comment No. 2 to that section stated in part: "Where the *collateral* is an account, contract right, chattel paper or general intangible the original obligor is called the 'account debtor' * * *." [Emphasis added.] "Collateral" was defined in former IC § 28–9–105(1)(c) as "the property subject to a *security interest,* and includes accounts, contract rights and chattel paper which have been sold." [Emphasis added.] It is implicit from these definitions and comments that an obligor's legal status as an "account debtor" comes into being only when the assigned "contract rights" are collateral subject to a security interest. The code extends no protection to an assignee if a security interest has not attached to the assigned contract rights.

* * * What concerns us here is whether the assignment given by Idle to the bank met the code's requirement for a written security agreement. We must also determine whether the language in the assignment was adequate to secure future advances with after-acquired collateral.

Courts have often repeated that no magic words are necessary to create a security interest and that the agreement itself need not even contain the term "security interest." This is in keeping with the policy of the code that form should not prevail over substance and that, whenever possible, effect should be given to the parties' intent. For example, former § 28–9–102 provided in part as follows:

> "[T]his chapter applies * * * to any transaction (regardless of its form) which is intended to create a security interest in personal property or fixtures including . . . contract rights; * * *
>
> "This chapter applies to security interests created by contract including pledge, assignment * * * or consignment intended as security * * *."

One court noted "there must be language * * * in the instrument which when read and construed leads to the logical conclusion that it was the intention of the parties that a security interest be created." * * *

We conclude that the document satisfied the requirement of IC § 28–9–203(1) that there be a written security agreement.

Former IC § 28–9–203(1)(b) also required that the security agreement contain a description of the collateral. To satisfy this requirement, "any description of personal property * * * is sufficient whether or not it is specific if it reasonably identifies what is described. * * *" IC § 28–9–110. The official comment to this section makes it clear that the policy of the code with regard to this provision is quite liberal. The comment urges courts to reject the view contained in older chattel mortgage cases that descriptions of collateral are "insufficient unless they are of the most exact and detailed nature." In this case the assignment describes the collateral as "all monies now due or to become due under certain Grain Contracts held in your Warehouse." We believe that this description minimally meets the requirements of IC § 28–9–110 as to any grain contracts existing between Idle and Cargill at the time Cargill received notice of the assignment. As the comment to that section notes, "the test of sufficiency of a description laid down by this section is that the description do the job assigned to it—that it make possible the identification of the thing described."

The question remains, does the assignment give the bank a security interest in "after-acquired collateral," that is, proceeds of contracts entered into by Idle and Cargill subsequent to the assignment? Under former IC § 28–9–106 the collateral, which the bank claims in this case, was defined as a "Contract right," meaning "any right to payment under a contract not yet earned by performance and not evidenced by an instrument or chattel paper." Former IC § 28–9–204(3) stated that "a security agreement may provide that collateral, whenever acquired, shall secure all obligations covered by the security agreement."[2] The comments to this section make it clear that a security interest arising by virtue of an after-acquired property clause is no longer a disfavored arrangement. As specified in this section a security interest will attach in such collateral when value has been given and when the contract has been made. * * *

Section 28–9–110 of the code provides in part: "For the purposes of this chapter any description of personal property * * * is sufficient whether or not it is specific if it reasonably identifies what is described. * * *"

The official comment to this section notes:

> "The test of sufficiency of a description laid down by this section is that the description do the job assigned to it—that it make possible the identification of the thing described. Under this rule courts should refuse to follow the holdings, often found in the older chattel mortgage cases, that descriptions are insufficient unless they are of the most exact and detailed nature, the so-called 'serial number' test. * * *"

In the present case the bank argues that the language used in the assignment gave the bank a security interest in the proceeds of all contracts on which it loaned money to Idle during the course of their two-year relationship. Moreover, the bank contends that provisions of the assignment, coupled with the course of dealing between Idle and the bank, make it obvious that the assignment was also intended to apply to future as well as present loans made by the bank.

We are not persuaded by the bank's argument. Whatever the parties may have intended, their intent is not clearly expressed by the assignment. The phrase "all monies now due or to become due under certain Grain Contracts held in your Warehouse" hardly encompasses the collateral to which the bank lays claim—the proceeds of five contracts entered into by Cargill and Idle in early 1977. The quoted language could reasonably be construed to mean monies due and coming due on *existing* contracts, at the time of the assignment in 1974. Moreover, this construction of the language is consistent with provisions of the UCC as it existed at the time of these transactions. An example of this is the comment to the official text under former § 9–106. It states that " 'Contract right' is a right to be earned by future performance under an *existing contract.*" [Emphasis added.] See also Comment No. 2 to § 28–9–318. We agree with the trial court that the assignment did not reasonably identify or describe the after-acquired collateral, that is, Idle-Cargill contracts not then in existence. But compare Valley National Bank of Arizona v. Flagstaff Dairy, 570 P.2d 200 (Ariz. App.1977) ("all monies due or to become due debtor from the sale of milk" held sufficient to include accounts receivable earned after the date of the security agreement).

The assignment was similarly inadequate in providing security for future advances. There is absolutely no mention in the assignment of future advances. Under former IC § 28–9–204(5) "obligations covered by a security agreement may include future advances." Official Comment No. 8 to this section stated that in pre-code law there was a "vaguely articulated prejudice against future advance agreements." The comment goes on to observe, however, that § 9–204

2. Former § 28–9–204 was repealed in 1980, and was replaced by a new section. Now, § 28–9–204(1) provides: "Except as provided in subsection (2), a security agreement may provide that any or all obligations covered by the security agreement are to be secured by after-acquired collateral."

"validates the future advance interest, *provided only that the obligation be covered by the security agreement.*" [Emphasis added.] This comment has been interpreted to mean that "to cover future advances, the security agreement must clearly specify that the security interest in the collateral is meant to secure future advances." Texas Kenworth Co. v. First National Bank of Bethany, 564 P.2d 222, 225 (Okla.1977). We agree with this interpretation. Absent a clause in the security agreement which clearly covers future advances, such advances do not fall within the scope of the agreement. * * *

The bank argues that the "course of dealing" and "course of performance" of the parties should be considered in construing the scope and meaning of the assignment. Indeed, the code provides that a course of dealing between parties may "give particular meaning to and supplement or qualify terms of an agreement." IC § 28–1–205(3). Likewise, § 28–2–208(1) provides that where a "contract for sale involves repeated occasions for performances by either party with knowledge of the nature of the performance and opportunity for objection to it by the other, any course of performance accepted or acquiesced in without objection shall be relevant to determine the meaning of the agreement." See also IC § 28–1–201(3).

We have already related the course of conduct which occurred during the two years after notice of the assignment was given. There was no communication between the bank and Cargill. Idle alone dealt with Cargill and all of Cargill's checks were mailed to Idle.

As mentioned earlier, in late 1976 the bank suspended its loan commitment, while it pondered whether a renewed commitment would be made. At the bank's request Idle reduced his loan balance to zero around December 1. The bank nevertheless made several additional loans to Idle upon contracts that Idle brought to the bank between December 6, 1976, and February 16, 1977. On February 16 Idle learned the bank would make no more loans. Idle then stopped having Cargill place the bank's name on his contracts. Idle even instructed Cargill to strike the bank's name from some contracts previously entered into, but which neither Idle nor Cargill had then performed. When Idle did deliver grain on these contracts, Cargill made payment to Idle. These are the payments the bank seeks to recover from Cargill.

The bank argues that, by reason of Cargill's conduct in providing joint payment checks over a long period of time, we should construe the assignment to cover future advances and we should hold that Cargill had notice of the true nature of the security agreement between Idle and the bank. However, Cargill was not a party to the assignment and played no part in selecting the language employed by the bank to create its security interest in the Idle-Cargill contracts. Idaho Code § 8–9–201 provides in part that "except as otherwise provided in this act, a security agreement is effective according to its terms between the parties, against purchasers of the collateral and against creditors." In addition, subsection (3) of § 9–318 provided:

> "The account debtor is authorized to pay the assignor until the account debtor receives notification that the account has been assigned and that payment is to be made to the assignee. A notification which does not reasonably identify the rights assigned is ineffective. If requested by the account debtor, the assignee must seasonably furnish reasonable proof that the assignment has been made and unless he does so the account debtor may pay the assignor."

Cargill, as much as anyone, had a right to rely on the assignment language, in determining whether it could safely follow Idle's request to discontinue

issuing joint payment checks after the bank terminated Idle's former line of credit. Nothing in the 1974 assignment indicated it was to cover future advances made by the bank. We are therefore not persuaded that any legal or equitable principles require us to construe the assignment so as to cover loans made by the bank after the date of the assignment. To do so would not, in our view, be consistent with the stated policies of the UCC "to simplify, clarify and modernize the law governing commercial transactions." IC § 28–1–102.
* * *

In summary, we hold that the assignment was adequate to create a security interest in existing contracts. However, after-acquired collateral was not reasonably identified or described. The assignment created no security interest in the after-acquired collateral and it did not cover future advances. An examination of the course of performance by the parties does not reveal legal or equitable reasons to construe the language against Cargill. We conclude that Cargill was not an account debtor with respect to the proceeds in question. Thus, Cargill cannot be held liable to the bank under IC § 28–9–318(3) for breaching the assignment by paying the proceeds of these contracts to Idle rather than to the bank. * * *

WALTERS, C.J., concurs.

Problem 3–3

The bank could have cured its problem by a modest change in its security agreement. Draft the change.

Problem 3–4

Assume that the granting clause in the security agreement contains the following language:

1. Debtor hereby grants a security interest to creditor in its inventory.
2. Debtor hereby grants a security interest to creditor in its machinery.
3. Debtor hereby grants a security interest to creditor in its crops.

Do any of the grants include after-acquired property? How might one justifiably distinguish among them? Do any of the grants include proceeds?

We will return to questions of the proper description in our consideration of perfection by filing under Article 9 in the next chapter. For now the student should ask whether the policy should be different with respect to the security agreement description on the one hand and the financing statement description on the other. Compare UCC 9–110 with UCC 9–402(1).

C. Value

We have given little consideration to the requirement of value, because that is seldom at issue. Section 1–201(44) contains an expansive definition of value. Under it, for example, a creditor who agreed to make a loan, would have given value even before the money was advanced. In most cases the making of the loan itself, the advance of the money, will be value; thus there will be no issue about that.

D. Requirement of a Signed Writing

A common defect "in" the security agreement is its nonexistence. In a surprising number of cases the parties prepare all the necessary documents, but when trouble strikes, the creditor has no security agreement in the file or the one in the file has never been signed. It then falls to the creditor to argue that the note, the financing statement, and any other scraps of paper that may have been signed by the debtor can be pasted together to constitute a security agreement. Courts approaching this question as a "statute of frauds" issue have sometimes concluded that UCC 9–203 can be satisfied by other documents if the parties intended a security agreement although it was never signed. Other courts, more deeply influenced by the relatively formalistic history of real and personal property security, have taken the position that the creditor is in control and is required to cross his t's and dot his i's. The latter conclude that the absence of a "granting" clause or the presence of a defect in the description of the collateral renders the secured creditor unsecured. The case that follows is among the former group. Is its reasoning persuasive?

IN RE BOLLINGER

United States Court of Appeals, Third Circuit, 1980.
614 F.2d 924.

ROSENN, CIRCUIT JUDGE. This appeal from a district court review of an order in bankruptcy presents a question that has troubled courts since the enactment of Article Nine of the Uniform Commercial Code (UCC) governing secured transactions. Can a creditor assert a secured claim against the debtor when no formal security agreement was ever signed, but where various documents executed in connection with a loan evince an intent to create a security interest? The district court answered this question in the affirmative and permitted the creditor, Zimmerman & Jansen, to assert a secured claim against the debtor, bankrupt Bollinger Corporation, in the amount of $150,000. We affirm.

I.

Industrial Credit Corporation (ICC) made a loan to Bollinger Corporation (Bollinger) on January 13, 1972, in the amount of $150,000. As evidence of the loan, Bollinger executed a promissory note in the sum of $150,000 and signed a security agreement with ICC giving it a security interest in certain machinery and equipment. ICC in due course perfected its security interest in the collateral by filing a financing statement. * * *

Bollinger faithfully met its obligations under the note and by December 4, 1974, had repaid $85,000 of the loan, leaving $65,000 in unpaid principal. Bollinger, however, required additional capital and on December 5, 1974, entered into a loan agreement with Zimmerman & Jansen, Inc. (Z & J), by which Z & J agreed to lend Bollinger $150,000. Z & J undertook as part of this transaction to pay off the $65,000 still owed to ICC in return for an assignment by ICC to Z & J of the original note and security agreement between Bollinger and ICC. Bollinger executed a promissory note to Z & J, evidencing the agreement containing the following provision:

> "Security. This promissory note is secured by security interests in a certain security agreement between Bollinger and Industrial Credit Company * * * and in a financing statement filed by [ICC] * * *, and is further secured by security interests in certain security agreement to be delivered by Bollinger to Z and J with this promissory note covering the identical machinery and equipment

as identified in the ICC security agreement and with identical schedule attached in the principal amount of Eighty-Five Thousand Dollars ($85,000)."

No formal security agreement was ever executed between Bollinger and Z & J. Z & J did, however, in connection with the promissory note, record a new financing statement signed by Bollinger containing a detailed list of the machinery and equipment originally taken as collateral by ICC for its loan to Bollinger.

Bollinger filed a petition for an arrangement under Chapter XI of the Bankruptcy Act in March, 1975 and was adjudicated bankrupt one year later. In administrating the bankrupt's estate, the receiver sold some of Bollinger's equipment but agreed that Z & J would receive a $10,000 credit on its secured claim.

Z & J asserted a secured claim against the bankrupt in the amount of $150,000, arguing that although it never signed a security agreement with Bollinger, the parties had intended that a security interest in the sum of $150,000 be created to protect the loan. The trustee in bankruptcy conceded that the assignment to Z & J of ICC's original security agreement with Bollinger gave Z & J a secured claim in the amount of $65,000, the balance owed by Bollinger to ICC at the time of the assignment. The trustee, however, refused to recognize Z & J's asserted claim of an additional secured claim of $85,000 because of the absence of a security agreement between Bollinger and Z & J. The bankruptcy court agreed and entered judgment for Z & J in the amount of $55,000, representing a secured claim in the amount of $65,000 less $10,000 credit received by Z & J.

Z & J appealed to the United States District Court for the Western District of Pennsylvania, which reversed the bankruptcy court and entered judgment for Z & J in the full amount of the asserted $150,000 secured claim. The trustee in bankruptcy appeals.

II.

* * * The requirements of § 9–203(1)(b) further two basic policies. First, an evidentiary function is served by requiring a signed security agreement and second, a written agreement also obviates any Statute of Frauds problems with the debtor-creditor relationship. Id. Comments 3, 5.

* * * The financing statement serves the purpose of giving public notice to other creditors that a security interest is claimed in the debtor's collateral.

Despite the minimal formal requirements set forth in § 9–203 for the creation of a security agreement, the commercial world has frequently neglected to comply with this simple Code provision. Soon after Article Nine's enactment, creditors who had failed to obtain formal security agreements, but who nevertheless had obtained and filed financing statements, sought to enforce secured claims. Under § 9–402, a security agreement may serve as a financing statement if it is signed by both parties. The question arises whether the converse is true: Can a signed financing statement operate as a security agreement? The earliest case to consider this question was American Card Company v. H.M.H. Co., 196 A.2d 150, 152 (R.I. 1963) which held that a financing statement could *not* operate as a security agreement because there was no language *granting* a security interest to a creditor. Although § 9–203(1)(b) makes no mention of such a grant language requirement, the court in American Card thought that implicit in the definition of "security agreement" under § 9–105(1)(h) was such a requirement; some grant language was necessary to "create or provide security."

* * *

The Ninth Circuit in In Re Amex-Protein Development Corporation, 504 F.2d 1056 (9th Cir.1975), echoed criticism by commentators of the American Card rule. The court wrote: "There is no support in legislative history or grammatical logic for the substitution of the word grant for the phrase creates or provides for." Id. at 1059. It concluded that as long as the financing statement contains a description of the collateral signed by the debtor, the financing statement may serve as the security agreement and the formal requirements of § 9–203(1)(b) are met. The tack pursued by the Ninth Circuit is supported by legal commentary on the issue. See G. Gilmore, Security Interests in Personal Property, § 11.4 at 347–48 (1965).

Some courts have declined to follow the Ninth Circuit's liberal rule allowing the financing statement alone to stand as the security agreement, but have permitted the financing statement, when read in conjunction with other documents executed by the parties, to satisfy the requirements of § 9–203(1)(b). The court in In re Numeric Corp., 485 F.2d 1328 (1st Cir.1973) held that a financing statement coupled with a board of directors' resolution revealing an intent to create a security interest were sufficient to act as a security agreement. The court concluded from its reading of the Code that there appears no need to insist upon a separate document entitled "security agreement" as a prerequisite for an otherwise valid security interest.

> "A writing or writings, regardless of label, which adequately describes the collateral, carries the signature of the debtor, and establishes that in fact a security interest was agreed upon, would satisfy both the formal requirements of the statute and the policies behind it."

Id. at 1331. The court went on to hold that "although a standard form financing statement by itself cannot be considered a security agreement, an adequate agreement can be found when a financing statement is considered together with other documents." Id. at 1332.

More recently, the Supreme Court of Maine in Casco Bank & Trust Co. v. Cloutier, 398 A.2d 1224, 1231–32 (Me.1979) considered the question of whether composite documents were sufficient to create a security interest within the terms of the Code. Writing for the court, Justice Wernick allowed a financing statement to be joined with a promissory note for purposes of determining whether the note contained an adequate description of the collateral to create a security agreement. The court indicated that the evidentiary and Statute of Frauds policies behind § 9–203(1)(b) were satisfied by reading the note and financing statement together as the security agreement.

In the case before us, the district court went a step further and held that the promissory note executed by Bollinger in favor of Z & J, standing alone, was sufficient to act as the security agreement between the parties. In so doing, the court implicitly rejected the American Card rule requiring grant language before a security agreement arises under § 9–203(1)(b). But although we agree that no formal grant of a security interest need exist before a security agreement arises, we do not think that the promissory note standing alone would be sufficient under Pennsylvania law to act as the security agreement. We believe, however, that the promissory note, read in conjunction with the financing statement duly filed and supported, as it is here, by correspondence during the course of the transaction between the parties, would be sufficient under Pennsylvania law to establish a valid security agreement.

III.

When the parties have neglected to sign a separate security agreement, it would appear that the better and more practical view is to look at the transaction as a whole in order to determine if there is a writing, or writings, signed by the debtor describing the collateral which demonstrates an intent to create a security interest in the collateral. In connection with Z & J's loan of $150,000 to Bollinger, the relevant writings to be considered are: (1) the promissory note; (2) the financing statement; (3) a group of letters constituting the course of dealing between the parties. The district court focused solely on the promissory note finding it sufficient to constitute the security agreement. Reference, however, to the language in the note reveals that the note standing alone cannot serve as the security agreement. The note recites that along with the assigned 1972 security agreement between Bollinger and ICC, the Z & J loan is "further secured by security interests in a certain Security Agreement *to be delivered* by Bollinger to Z & J with this Promissory Note, * * *" (Emphasis added.) The bankruptcy judge correctly reasoned that "[t]he intention to create a separate security agreement negates any inference that the debtor intended that the promissory note constitute the security agreement." At best, the note is some evidence that a security agreement was contemplated by the parties, but by its own terms, plainly indicates that it is not the security agreement.

Looking beyond the promissory note, Z & J did file a financing statement signed by Bollinger containing a detailed list of all the collateral intended to secure the $150,000 loan to Bollinger. The financing statement alone meets the basic § 9–203(1)(b) requirements of a writing, signed by the debtor, describing the collateral. However, the financing statement provides only an inferential basis for concluding that the parties intended a security agreement. There would be little reason to file such a detailed financing statement unless the parties intended to create a security interest. The intention of the parties to create a security interest may be gleaned from the expression of future intent to create one in the promissory note and the intention of the parties as expressed in letters constituting their course of dealing.

The promissory note was executed by Bollinger in favor of Z & J in December 1974. Prior to the consummation of the loan, Z & J sent a letter to Bollinger on May 30, 1974, indicating that the loan would be made "provided" Bollinger secured the loan by a mortgage on its machinery and equipment. Bollinger sent a letter to Z & J on September 19, 1974, indicating:

> "With your [Z & J's] stated desire to obtain security for material and funds advanced, it would appear that the use of the note would answer both our problems. Since the draft forwarded to you offers full collateralization for the funds to be advanced under it and bears normal interest during its term, it should offer you maximum security."

Subsequent to the execution of the promissory note, Bollinger sent to Z & J a list of the equipment and machinery intended as collateral under the security agreement which was to be, but never was, delivered to Z & J. In November 1975, the parties exchanged letters clarifying whether Bollinger could substitute or replace equipment in the ordinary course of business without Z & J's consent. Such a clarification would not have been necessary had a security interest not been intended by the parties. Finally, a letter of November 18, 1975, from Bollinger to Z & J indicated that "any attempted impairment of the collateral would constitute an event of default."

From the course of dealing between Z & J and Bollinger, we conclude there is sufficient evidence that the parties intended a security agreement to be created separate from the assigned ICC agreement with Bollinger. All the evidence points towards the intended creation of such an agreement and since the financing statement contains a detailed list of the collateral, signed by Bollinger, we hold that a valid Article Nine security agreement existed under Pennsylvania law between the parties which secured Z & J in the full amount of the loan to Bollinger.

* * *

Affirmed. [Footnotes omitted.]

Notes

As we have seen, UCC 9–203(1)(a) is said to be in the nature of a statute of frauds. *In re Bollinger* and other cases like it show how critical the framing of the issue can be. The statute of frauds is a much despised statute that has fallen into disrepute in the United States, is the laughing stock of Article 2, and has been repealed in England. Section 2–201 of Article 2 is so full of holes today that only a lawyer totally devoid of imagination will fail to find some plausible argument to sustain an oral contract of sale. There are the standard exceptions such as part performance, special manufacture and such. Also, arguments have been upheld that there is fraud, that the contract was admitted by the defendant, and on and on. Moreover, it is today thought to be "good" to strike down barriers to recognition of true intent and to enforce oral contracts notwithstanding the absence of a writing.

On the other hand, one finds a long history of judicial hostility to secured creditors, and an insistence that they comply with the law in exacting detail. This, too, is said to be a "good" thing, for many believe that secured creditors are oppressors, that they manipulate the legislatures and thus that they should be required to toe the line before getting what the law allows.

With the two opposing general attitudes, then if the lawyer can get the court to adopt one as opposed to the other, one suspects that the case itself is over. In cases such as *Bollinger* there is rarely any doubt that the debtor and the creditor intended a security interest, intended that the debt be paid off with specific interest and on a particular schedule. There has been performance and there is evidence in the form of cancelled checks, a financing statement, letters or other documents, usually undenied by the debtor, that show the intention to create a security interest. These are not merely statute of frauds cases; they are easy statute of frauds cases.

If, on the other hand, one approaches the case with a deep suspicion of secured creditors, and harbors true concern about their overreaching, it is equally easy to conclude that they should be made to comply strictly with the laws that so obviously favor them. Having so concluded, it is easy to throw out a security interest that does not comply with the simple rules of UCC 9–203.

Problem 3–5

Assume that you represent the trustee in bankruptcy in each of the following cases. How would you challenge the security agreement? Do you think you would be successful?

A. Joseph Corsi bought an automobile for his wife Mary. He gave the car to her and she procured a certificate of title listing herself as the owner and Ford Motor Credit as the first lien holder. Joseph signed a security agreement that granted a security interest to Stewart who assigned it to Ford Motor Credit. Mary's name did not appear on the security agreement. When Mary went into bankruptcy both the trustee and Ford Motor Credit claimed the car. Would it matter whether Joseph signed the security agreement before or after he made the gift to Mary?

In discussing the rights of the secured creditors here, the court held as follows:

> "The fallacy with Stewart's position is that it concludes that the application for a certificate of title containing the name and address of the lienholder perfects a security interest in a vehicle. Stewart presumes the existence of such a security interest when in fact none exists. A security agreement was in fact executed on November 28, 1975 between Stewart and Joseph D. Corsi, husband of Mary W. Corsi, to whom he made a gift of the vehicle. The certificate of title issued by the Vermont Department of Motor Vehicles shows the owner as Mary W. Corsi and Ford Motor Cr. Co. as first lienholder. There was never any security agreement by and between the owner of the vehicle, Mary W. Corsi, and Stewart or Ford Motor Credit Co., its purported assignee.
>
> "Under the UCC as adopted in Vermont a security interest cannot attach until there is agreement that it attach and value is given and the debtor has rights in the collateral. It attaches as soon as all of the events in the preceding sentence have taken place unless explicit agreement postpones the time of attaching. 9A VSA sec. 9–204(1).
>
> "In the instant case, there was no agreement between the owner of the vehicle, Mary W. Corsi, and Stewart at the time that the application for a certificate of title was made by her showing Ford Motor Credit Co. as lienholder."

The case is wrong if the security agreement was granted prior to the making of the gift. True? The court quotes from a Connecticut case involving a similar matter in which the court made the following statement:

> "[A] bank listed as first lienor on a certificate of title issued in the name of a wife acquired no security interest in two vehicles since the wife never signed the retail installment contracts covering them and purchased by the husband and wife. Nor did the bank acquire an enforceable security interest in the vehicles through the husband who had signed the security agreements since the husband had not acquired title to the automobiles and had no rights in them to which a security interest could attach."

Can a husband who signs a security agreement prior to the purchase of an automobile, then make a gift of that automobile (before he buys it) to his wife in such a way that title never passes through his hands and the security agreement never attaches?

B. On his bankruptcy, debtor owned a 1980 and a 1981 Yamaha motorcycle, a 1980 Jeep Wagoneer, and three cash registers that he used in his business. The Jeep was worth more than $6,000 and the remaining balance on the debt originally incurred to Bank for the Jeep was under $2,000. The value of the other collateral was in each case less than the amount of the outstanding debt. Bank claimed the right to realize the debt existing on the other three items out of the proceeds of sale of the Wagoneer.

On page one of the Bank's Security Agreement form, "1980 Jeep Wagoneer SN# JOE15NN048763" was typed in the space for collateral. In small typed letters the form stated:

> "To secure payment of the indebtedness evidenced by *a* certain promissory note of even date herewith, in the amount of *$7494.84*
>
> ( ) and any other indebtedness, present or future, of the debtor, payable to the secured party or order.

(x) payable to the Secured Party, or order, repayable as follows: $209 monthly for 36 months."

The first box is *not* checked.

On page two of the security agreement the following appeared:

"In addition, I give the Bank a security interest in my *1980 Jeep Wagoneer SN# JOE15NN048763* and have executed a security agreement on this date that fully describes this property. The security agreement secures not only this, but any other debt which I owe the Bank, including future debts, and covers property (subject to the limitation of the UCC) which I might not now have, but may acquire in the future."

Can the bank use the proceeds from sale of the Wagoneer to satisfy the other debts (a) if it checks the first block; (b) if it does not check the first block? See UCC 9–203, 9–204 & 9–306.

C. Assume that both the security agreement and the financing statement filed in the register of deeds office contains the following description:

"Crops growing or to be grown on the following real estate:

Farm(s) or Other Real Estate Owner	Appx. No. of Acres	County & State	Appx. Distance and Direction From a Named Town or Other Description
Faye McMannis	160	Pratt	From Iuka: 2 N 2¼ W
McMannis Heirs	1100	Pratt	4¼ W
Helena Thompson	80	Pratt	4 W ½ N
Orvalene Becker	160	Pratt	½ N

Would the security agreement cover a herd of sheep maintained on the same McMannis land?

D. On a loan application Debtor asked for a $500,000 loan and specified that the collateral would include a security interest in "all accounts receivable and inventory" of the debtor. When the security agreement was signed, it contained a form with a series of blocks to identify the kind of collateral claimed. As executed, the security agreement contained check marks next to the blocks marked "all equipment and machinery, furniture and fixtures" but there was none beside the block for inventory and none next to the block for accounts receivable. A financing statement was filed that described the collateral as "inventory and accounts receivable." On bankruptcy, does the trustee in bankruptcy or the secured creditor take the inventory and accounts? Is the debtor's testimony that the parties intended to cover inventory and accounts receivable admissible?

SECTION 3. THE CREATION OF SECURITY INTERESTS IN PROCEEDS

Under the 1972 version of Article 9, assume the creditor has an automatic security interest in proceeds of collateral even if the security agreement is silent on the question. Section 9–203(3) specifies: "unless otherwise agreed, the security agreement gives the secured party the rights to proceeds provided by section 9–306." That sentence in turn leads to UCC 9–306's definition of proceeds and to its description of the reach of the proceeds claim. Note in UCC 9–306(1) that proceeds include "whatever is received upon the sale, exchange, collection or other disposition of collateral or proceeds." Section 9–306(2) provides, however, that the security interest continues only in "any *identifiable* proceeds." It is obvious, is it not, that a secured creditor who has a perfected security interest in a dealer's inventory of automobiles, has a proceeds interest in the note and security interest given by a consumer when buying a specific automobile out of the dealer-debtor's inventory? That note and security interest i.e., chattel paper, UCC 9–105(1), is identifiable proceeds received in exchange for the collateral pursuant to 9–306(1) and (2); it can be tied to a particular transaction and to a particular automobile that was sold. So far, so good.

But one need not travel far down the proceeds road before the path becomes indistinct and the way less clear. Assume, for example, that our debtor-dealer sells a car for cash and that he deposits the cash in his general bank account that includes revenues from a variety of sources as well as some of his own personal funds. Clearly, the cash received was proceeds at the outset, but does it still remain "identifiable proceeds"?

Or consider the case in which the debtor is involved in an accident with the automobile and procures a tort recovery from the person at fault in the accident. Is that tort recovery "received upon the sale, exchange, collection or other disposition of the collateral"? If so, it is proceeds and covered by UCC 9–306; if not, the creditor has no secured claim in the tort recovery.

IN RE SAN JUAN PACKERS

United States Court of Appeals, Ninth Circuit (1983).
696 F.2d 707.

PER CURIAM. This is a dispute between a secured creditor of a bankrupt food processor and a secured creditor of farmers from whom the food processor bought vegetables. The food processor, San Juan Packers, Inc., bought cans on credit from a can manufacturer, National Can Corporation, and granted the can manufacturer a floating lien on all of its inventory. In late summer, 1976, the food processor bought vegetables from many farmers, including the three involved in this litigation. These three farmers had obtained financing from Peoples State Bank and had granted the bank a security interest in their crops and the "proceeds" thereof.

The food processor filed a petition in bankruptcy after it had received the farmers' vegetables and processed and sold a portion of them, but before it had finished paying all purchase price installments due the farmers. Not having been paid by the food processor, the farmers did not pay the bank. The bank brought this adversary proceeding in bankruptcy court against all of the food processor's secured creditors to establish the priority of the bank's security interest in the farmers' vegetables and in the cash proceeds thereof. The parties agreed to the sale of all vegetables in the food processor's possession and creation of a fund from the proceeds to satisfy any judgment that might arise from this action.

The bankruptcy court found for the bank, and the can manufacturer appealed to the district court, which affirmed. The can manufacturer appeals to this court, advancing three contentions.

I.

The can manufacturer first contends that money received by the food processor for the farmers' vegetables are not "proceeds" to which the bank's security interest attached under its security agreements with the farmers.

The Uniform Commercial Code (UCC) provides that "[p]roceeds includes whatever is received when collateral or proceeds is sold, exchanged, collected or otherwise disposed of." Section 9–306(1). Under this definition, the money the food processor received for the farmers' vegetables is "proceeds" unless the vegetables ceased to be collateral when purchased by the food processor.

> " 'Collateral' means the property subject to a security interest. * * *" Section 9–105(1)(c). "Except where * * * Article [9] otherwise provides, a security interest continues in collateral notwithstanding sale * * * by the debtor unless his action was authorized by the secured party * * *." Section 9–306(2). Since the can manufacturer does not dispute the bankruptcy court's finding that the bank did not authorize the sale free of its security interest, and Article 9 does not otherwise provide, it would appear that the bank's security interest continued in the vegetables after their sale to the food processor, that the vegetables remained "collateral," and that whatever was received by the food processor when the vegetables were sold is "proceeds."

The can manufacturer points out that § 9–306(2) provides that a security interest continues, "notwithstanding sale * * * *by the debtor* and * * * in any identifiable proceeds including collections *received by the debtor*" (emphasis supplied), and argues that the bank's security interest was not saved by § 9–306(2) when the vegetables were sold and cash received by the food processor rather than by the farmers because the farmers and not the food processor were the "debtors." But under § 9–105(1)(d), the food processor *is* the "debtor":

> "(1) In this article, unless the context otherwise requires:
>
> "(d) 'Debtor' means the person who owes payment or other performance of the obligation secured, whether or not he owns or has rights in the collateral * * *. *Where the debtor and the owner of the collateral are not the same person, the term 'debtor' means the owner of the collateral in any provision of the Article dealing with the collateral,* the obligor in any provision dealing with the obligation, and may include both where the context so requires." (emphasis supplied).

Official Comment 2 to § 9–105 makes it clear that an owner of the collateral is a "debtor" whether he acquired his rights in the collateral at the time the security interest was created or at a later date:

> "In all but a few cases the person who owes the debt and the person whose property secures the debt will be the same. Occasionally, one person furnishes security for another's debt, *and sometimes property is transferred subject to a secured debt of the transferor which the transferee does not assume;* in such cases, under the second sentence of the definition, the term 'debtor' may, depending on the context, include either or both such persons." (emphasis supplied).

The can manufacturer protests that under this view the bank could follow these vegetables into the hands of the ultimate consumer.
But this is precisely what the plain language of the UCC requires.

* * *

II.

The can manufacturer's second argument is that by the terms of § 9–306(2) the bank's security interest continued only in "identifiable proceeds" and was lost because the food processor mixed together vegetables purchased from various farmers making it impossible to identify vegetables, or proceeds from the sale of vegetables remaining in the food processor's possession, as attributable to any particular farmer.

Section 9–315 of the UCC requires rejection of this argument. The bank had a perfected security interest in the farmers' vegetables, and those vegetables became part of a mass of vegetables in the hands of the food processor, so commingled that their identity became lost in the mass. By the express terms of § 9–315(1), where collateral loses its identity by commingling or processing, the security interest continues in the mass or product—and it is not disputed that the proceeds in the fund established in this case can be traced to commingled vegetables in the hands of the food processor.

* * *

III.

Finally, the can manufacturer argues that if § 9–315 is applied, the can manufacturer was entitled to share in the fund since the can manufacturer had a security interest in the vegetables in the food processor's possession grown by farmers other than the three in whose crops the bank had a security interest, and by the terms of § 9–315 each party whose collateral is commingled in the mass is entitled to a ratable share of the proceeds of the sale of the mass.

The bank resists application of § 9–315 on the ground, relied upon by the district court, that § 9–315(1) "requires the attachment of two security interests to the product or mass." The attachment of two security interests to the product or mass is an explicit condition only to the operation of § 9–315(2), not § 9–315(1). Moreover, this condition to the application of § 9–315(2) was satisfied because both the bank's interest in the vegetables of the three farmers with whom the bank had its security arrangement and the can manufacturer's security interest in the other vegetables in the food processor's inventory attached to the mass of each variety of vegetables when the vegetables of the same variety purchased from various farmers were commingled.

The bank contends further that § 9–315 does not apply because the vegetables were not sufficiently processed. The statute, however, refers to processing *and* commingling, both in the caption of the section and in § 9–315(1)(a). "Commingled" is not a term of art in this context; it simply means "to mix together," Webster's Third New International Dictionary 457 (1961), or "[t]o put together in one mass." Black's Law Dictionary 246 (5th ed 1979). As the bank points out, Official Comment 3 to § 9–315 refers to commingling flour, sugar and eggs into cake mix, a process involving more than mere mixing, but there is no indication that the drafters meant to exclude simple mixing of fungible goods.

IV.

Application of § 9–315(2) does not, however, completely resolve this case. It is not clear from the record whether vegetables of the bank's three farmers were sold between the time these vegetables were delivered to the food processor and the time the food processor filed a bankruptcy petition. If such sales occurred and proceeds were not dissipated before bankruptcy, they are available to the secured parties subject to the provisions of § 9–306(4). Proceeds of sales made under the supervision of the bankruptcy court are, of course, not subject to § 9–306(4). Furthermore, there may be more than one § 9–315(2) ratio for each mass of vegetables because additional deliveries from farmers other than the three having security arrangements with the bank were subject to the can manufacturer's security interest; when such deliveries were added to the various masses of corn, peas, and carrots, the proportion of the security interest in each mass to which the can manufacturer was entitled increased.

The judgment appealed from is therefore vacated, and the case is remanded.

* * *

Notes

1. How does the court sort out the commingled proceeds? In light of the foregoing opinion, can you think of any examples of proceeds that would not be "identifiable" in which a creditor accordingly would not have a proceeds interest?

2. Does UCC 9–306, when read in its entirety, contemplate that proceeds placed in a commingled bank account (that is, in which there are also placed funds not classified as proceeds) be regarded as identifiable? What clues do you get from § 9–306(2) and (4)?

McLEMORE, TRUSTEE v. MID–SOUTH AGRI-CHEMICAL CORP.

United States Bankruptcy Court, M.D. Tennessee. (1984).
41 B.R. 369.

KEITH M. LUNDIN, BANKRUPTCY JUDGE.

The trustee's complaint seeks to recover Payment-in-Kind ("PIK") certificates of entitlement owing to the debtors. The issues are: (1) whether PIK payments constitute crop "proceeds;" and (2) whether the debtors' assignment of PIK wheat payments to one of the defendants constitutes a preferential transfer. After consideration of the briefs, arguments and stipulations, the court holds that PIK entitlements are "proceeds," and the assignment of wheat PIK to Mid-South Agri-Chemical Corporation ("Mid-South") constituted a preferential transfer. However, Mid-South holds a properly perfected security interest in the debtors' corn PIK, the Farmers Home Administration ("FmHA") holds a perfected security interest in PIK for the debtors' wheat crop, and these security interests are enforceable post-bankruptcy.

* * *

I.

* * * On April 27, 1983, William Earl and Glenda F. Judkins ("debtors") filed a voluntary Chapter 11 petition. Prior to the filing, the debtors farmed several parcels of leased property in DeKalb County, Tennessee.

Mid-South is a creditor holding a security interest in the debtors' corn crop. Mid-South's security interest was perfected June 2, 1982 and extends to "proceeds" of the corn crop.

FmHA is a creditor holding a security interest in "all crops, annual and perennial, and other plant products now planted, growing or grown, or which are hereafter planted or otherwise become growing crops or other plant products" of the debtors. The FmHA perfected its security interest on June 23, 1982 and June 24, 1982. The financing statements covered all "proceeds" from the debtors' crops.

On January 28, 1983, the debtors executed a "Contract to Participate in the 1983 PIK Diversion Program" with the Commodity Credit Corporation ("CCC") covering four of their leased farms. A contract for the fifth farm was executed March 10, 1983. The contracts were approved March 18, 1983 and the debtors became entitled to deficiency and diversion payments.

On March 25, 1983, the debtors filed a "Payment-in-Kind Assignment and Power of Attorney" with the CCC designating Mid-South as their assignee for diversion payments, including payments due for the nonproduction of wheat.

The debtors also compromised the outstanding balance of an earlier promissory note by executing a demand note to Mid-South.

The debtors thereafter received several installments under the PIK program. The remaining PIK certificates were delivered to the trustee to be sold. The trustee liquidated 7,657 bushels of corn for $25,153.24 and 829 bushels of wheat for $2,677.67.

II.

If PIK entitlements constitute "proceeds" to which a creditor's security interest in crops attaches although the crops are never planted then the creditors prevail over the trustee in this proceeding. Although the issue of whether PIK payments are "proceeds" is one of first impression in this district, other courts have held that crop subsidy and crop entitlement payments do constitute "proceeds" of the crops involved. In the leading case, *Pombo v. Ulrich (In re Munger),* 495 F.2d 511 (9th Cir.1974), the United States Court of Appeals for the Ninth Circuit explained that federal sugar beet abandonment payments were "proceeds" subject to security agreements covering the crops they replaced:

> Although resembling insurance payments, these subsidy payments flow not from private contract between the debtor and a third party, but rather from a government program designed to protect both the United States * * * and [farmers] * * * Abandonment payments, like the subsidy payments, * * * are an integral part of the * * * farming business and, when received, are within a broad reading of "proceeds." *Not to include such payments within the term "proceeds" would be to raise distinctions of form over the realities underlying this financing transaction, a result contrary to the intent of the Uniform Commercial Code.* (emphasis added).

Id. at 513. Other decisions, including several dealing directly with PIK entitlements, are in unanimous accord. * * *

Because any corn grown on the debtors' farm would have been covered by security interest, the crop substitute—benefits under the PIK program—should be treated the same; *In re Preisser,* 33 B.R. 65, 67 (Bankr.D.Colo.1983) (government benefits the debtor receives for the nonproduction of grain is a substitute for what would have been produced); *In re Nivens,* 22 B.R. 287, 291 (Bankr.N.D. Tex.1982) (subsidy payments are a substitute for crops and are "proceeds;" therefore, the creditor's security interest continues in deficiency and disaster payments).

This court agrees that PIK entitlements constitute "proceeds" of crop collateral, even if the crop was never planted.[2] Tenn.Code Ann. § 47–9–306(1) provides that: [quoting]

The definition of "proceeds" should be given a flexible and broad interpretation. * * * Under federal agricultural regulations PIK entitlements are considered substitutes for the crops that otherwise would have been planted:

2. The court in *Kruse* made a distinction between subsidy payments to abandon or destroy crops and subsidy payments not to plant particular crops. This court does not share the application of such a distinction. The phrase "other disposition" is extremely broad and encompasses any type of disposition, actual or constructive. *In re Nivens,* 22 B.R. at 291 n. 4. The term "other disposition" is sufficiently broad to cover PIK payments received in lieu of the originally crop collateral. When a debtor contracts for PIK payments, the debtor precludes the creation of the corresponding crop collateral. Participation in the PIK program "disposes" of the debtor's crops by precluding their cultivation. This issue is irrelevant with regard to the PIK entitlements allocable to wheat in the instant case because a wheat crop was originally planted, but mowed under when the debtors contracted to participate in the PIK program.

> Payments in kind are intended to compensate producers who have reduced their arrearages which would have otherwise been planted to the 1983 crops * * * Accordingly, quantities of these commodities which were made available as payment-in-kind are considered to be 1983 production.

48 Fed.Reg. 9, 233 (1983). The contract rights created when participation in the PIK program is approved are "substituted" for the crops that would have been harvested, but for participation in the program. The PIK payments are traceable to the crops subject to the defendants' security interests. The PIK entitlements are for specific crops, on specific acreage, and for specific production. Such a nexus between the entitlements and the original collateral indicates that participation in the PIK program was a substitute for the planting of the crop collateral.

A liberal construction of "proceeds" is necessary to avoid unintended interference with the objectives of federal agricultural subsidy programs. The trustee's interpretation would impair the effectiveness of the subsidy programs because encumbered crops would disqualify participation in federal subsidy programs or produce the anomalous result that the government would eviscerate its own security interest (and the interests of other "crop" financers) in crop collateral by approving a debtor's participation in subsidy programs.

> It would create an unconscionable means by which a farmer could defeat a creditor's security. If PIK payments were not proceeds, a farmer could abandon all farming activities in favor of program participation, thereby allowing him to dissipate the proceeds of the programs without any regard for their creditor's interests. Such a result cannot be permitted.

Wapakometa Production Credit v. Cupp, 38 B.R. at 956. Certainly this result was not intended and should not be judicially imposed. A flexible interpretation of the concept of "proceeds" promotes responsible management of farming operations by allowing alternatives to growing crops while simultaneously protecting creditors' security interests.

The defendants' security interests in crop "proceeds" survives the filing of the bankruptcy petition. 11 U.S.C.A. § 552 (West 1979) provides in relevant part:

> (b) Except as provided in sections 363, 506(c), 544, 545, 547, and 548 of this title, if the debtor and a secured party enter into a security agreement before the commencement of the case and *if the security interest created by such security agreement extends to property of the debtor acquired before the commencement of the case and to proceeds,* product, offspring, rents, or profits of such property, *then such security interest extends to such proceeds,* product, offspring, rents, or profits *acquired by the estate after the commencement of the case to the extent provided by such security agreement* and by applicable nonbankruptcy law, except to the extent that the court, after notice and a hearing and based on the equities of the case, orders otherwise. (emphasis added).

The trustee has not alleged any defects in the security agreements or financing statements that would nullify the defendants' security interests. FmHA, therefore, has a continuing security interest in all of the debtors' crops and crop proceeds. Mid-South, however, has a first priority in the debtors' corn crop and corn proceeds by virtue of its prior perfected security interest. * * *.

[Some footnotes omitted.]

Notes

1. The trustee must have been a really low-down skunk to make the argument he did in this case. Not so?

2. Not all government subsidy programs are alike. Some are payments for crops destroyed. Some are payments for crops planted and then abandoned, and some are payments for leaving certain acreage fallow that previously had been devoted to the particular crop. Does the court conclude that the last version are proceeds of the crop? How can that be?

3. If one wished to take a direct security interest in the right to the payments in kind (PIK), how does he do that? Is the Payment In Kind a general intangible, an account or something else? Review UCC 9–105(1) & 9–106.

4. Assume that creditor had a perfected security interest in debtor's existing stock of "cows and proceeds." If the cows had calves, would they be subject to the security interest as proceeds? Review UCC 9–109(3). How would you modify the security agreement in order to make the answer to that question clear?

5. Ajax lent $50,000 to Happy Vending Co. (HV). HV gave a perfected security interest in "all game machines owned by debtor." When HV became bankrupt, the vending machines had $14,000 in them. Who gets the money, Ajax or HV's trustee?

Problem 3–6

Auto Dealer floor plans his cars with GMAC. Dealer sells a car out of inventory to Consumer for cash. He deposits the cash in his general bank account and later uses money from that account to purchase another car for his inventory. Assume that GMAC now asserts a claim in the second car as proceeds. Does GMAC have a good claim? See especially UCC 9–306(3).

Assume alternatively that the total funds in the bank account between the time of the deposit of the proceeds and the time of the challenge (a) stayed approximately the same; (b) declined to zero and returned to a positive amount. Do these call for different outcomes? GMAC is likely to have an alternative claim to the automobile and thus not to depend upon its proceeds claim, not so?

SECTION 4. DESCRIPTIONS IN THE SECURITY AGREEMENT—A PROPOSED REFORM

Evaluate the proposal set forth below.

SHANKER, A PROPOSAL FOR A SIMPLIFIED ALL–EMBRACING SECURITY INTEREST 14 U.C.C.L.J. 23, 25–29 (1981).

* * * Secured parties who wish a security interest in *all* of the debtor's personal property (and that includes most institutional lenders) now have a fairly sure way of obtaining it. Until now, the courts have refused to uphold a description stating "all personal property." Nevertheless, the secured parties' desire for an all-embracing lien can be accomplished merely by copying *all* of the collateral categories listed in Article 9. And the list is not that long. If I have counted correctly, it includes ten or eleven items, namely: consumer goods, equipment, farm products, inventory, fixtures, accounts, chattel paper, documents, instruments, and general intangibles. And, for good measure, it might not be a bad idea to add deposit accounts and cash to this list. One suspects that it will not be long before well-counseled secured parties will have learned this lesson. And, since they have learned it, this Article 9 list of collateral categories will soon become a standard boiler plate on most security documents.

If the law intends that security over all of the debtor's assets can be obtained (and, indeed, is now often being obtained) by simply copying from a boiler-plate list of words found in Article 9, then why even require it? At best, continuing to require this boiler-plate list can serve only as a trap for those who, by reason of inadvertence or lack of proper advice, fail to copy it precisely. And that seems a poor reason to penalize these unfortunate souls. Why not, then, remove the trap and, instead, simplify the process by amending Article 9 to declare that identification of collateral is no longer needed? Instead, the mere execution of a security agreement and financing statement (even though containing no collateral description whatsoever) would have the legal effect of giving to the secured party an all-embracing lien, that is, a security interest on all of the debtor's personal property. That is what most secured parties want, and that is what most of them are now getting.

This proposal is not nearly as startling as it may first sound. It follows the lead already taken by our Canadian neighbors who have adopted Article 9–type legislation. More important, the proposal simply recognizes that the law ought not require a lot of useless motion or formalistic ceremony in order to achieve a permissible objective.

There are important limitations on this proposal to obtain an all-embracing lien. First, the proposal will still require most nonpossessory security interests to be filed in order to achieve perfection. Thus, even though the precise category of collateral will not even be listed on the financing statement, knowledge by the secured party of the specific kind of collateral involved will be required to assure that he files it in the appropriate office. Further, this proposal will not prohibit the parties from limiting the collateral to something less than all of the debtor's personal property, if they conscientiously choose to do so. (Conditional sellers of a particular piece of equipment and banks financing only the inventory and accounts of the debtor are examples where such a choice might be made.) But, absent a deliberate decision to limit the collateral, the presumption would be, consistent with what is probably the fact, that all of the debtor's personal property is covered; and all third parties finding a financing statement on file would be charged with that knowledge.

Of course, the law itself will continue to put some limits on the extent to which all of the debtor's collateral would be swept into an all-embracing lien. For example, Section 9–204(2) of the Code will continue to limit the scope of an after-acquired property clause where consumer goods are involved, whereas Section [2.407 of the UCCC] * * * will continue to limit the collateral of sellers of consumer goods only to the goods which have been sold. But, absent such a limiting arrangement worked out by the parties themselves or by some rule of law, the rule would be that the secured party intended to obtain and legally would obtain a security interest that embraces all of the debtor's personal property; this would be so without the present necessity of typing onto his security documents the boiler-plate list of categories of collateral now found in Article 9. Thus, validity and priority of security interests will no longer depend on these endless (and largely useless) battles over the description found on the security documents—descriptions that are now becoming matters of boiler plate. Rather, these questions essentially would be determined simply by the order of perfection.

Social Policy Considerations

This is not to suggest that giving to secured parties this easy way of obtaining an all-embracing security interest is necessarily the wisest social policy. This proposal simply recognizes that the wisdom of this policy has already been accepted by Article 9. It urges only that this already accepted policy be implemented without the necessity of going through the useless motions now required—that is, mechanically copying the list of collateral now found in Article 9. And, an incidental advantage of the proposal is that it will save our judicial system a great deal of time, energy, and cost which is now being expended to litigate questions of whether collateral description is sufficient.

This kind of thinking is exactly what moved the UCC drafters to authorize the floating lien in the first place. They, in fact, recognized that the argument against even enacting a floating lien has much to be recommended.

> *This Article [9] decisively rejects it not on the ground that it was wrong in policy but on the ground that it was not effective.* In pre-code law there was a multiplication of security devices designed to avoid the policy; field warehousing, trust receipts, factors lien acts, and so on. * * *
>
> In almost every state it was possible before the code for the borrower to give a lien on everything he held or would have. There has no doubt been sufficient economic reasons for the change. *This Article in expressly authorizing the floating charge merely recognizes an existing state of things.* [Emphasis added.]

If that kind of thinking made sense when the floating lien was first authorized in the early 1950s, then it seems that the time has now come to take the next step—that is, to permit an all-embracing lien to be obtained without going through all the trouble, cost, and energy presently required to accomplish it. No effort has been made in this article to work out all of the details of this proposal or the specific statutory language needed to implement it. Rather, this article is presented to determine whether there is agreement that the basic idea makes sense. If there is marked disagreement with it, then, hopefully, this paper will stimulate a dialogue on what purpose is being served by the present approach. In particular, just what purpose continues to be served by requiring the boiler plating on security documents of a readily available list of words to achieve an objective which most want, which many already are obtaining, and which seems fully permissible under Article 9—namely, an all-embracing lien? [Footnotes omitted.] [Reprinted with permission from: Uniform Commercial Code Law Journal, Summer 1981, Vol. 14, No. 1. Copyright © 1981, Warren, Gorham & Lamont, Inc., 210 South Street, Boston, MA 02111. All Rights Reserved.]

SECTION 5. THE SECURITY AGREEMENT: DOING IT RIGHT

At least in law school, the study of law tends to become the examination of other people's errors. Law practice on the other hand is much more prophylactic. Your job is to do it right so there is no cataclysm. The security agreement that we have set out below is a well-drafted document. It was prepared by a skilled lawyer on behalf of a large regional bank. To get a better understanding of how one might avoid the pitfalls demonstrated in the cases in Sections 1 through 3 of this chapter, consider the various provisions in the security agreement. (Needless to say, the document set out below was designed for the creditor and was aimed at protecting its, and not the debtor's, interest.)

Note first the breadth of the debt described in the first paragraph. This security agreement covers not just the specific loan made on the date the security agreement is signed, but also loans of different kinds, those arising later and even those arising out of the issuance of letters of credit (to be studied in

Chapter 29). Can you think of a debt that might not be covered by this security agreement?

Somewhat less comprehensive is the description of the collateral. In some cases, one might quibble with the drafters' use of the word "inventory," as, for example, where chickens might in some person's eyes be inventory and in others', farm products. Presumably the use of the word "continuing" together with the word "inventory" makes it clear that the parties intend to include after-acquired property. Does the security agreement make it even more clear in other ways?

The document shows that the creditor is interested in much more than just the collateral. Read over the warranties and promises made by the debtor. Why do you suppose the creditor is interested in the prohibition against other encumbrances in 2.5? Will the provision concerning legal fees in 2.9 be effective?

Note that default can be caused by many events in addition to the failure by the debtor to pay money. Do you think 4.1(vi) is valid under the Uniform Commercial Code? What about the anti-waiver clause contained in 4.5, can it too be waived? Note the use of the limited power of attorney in 4.6 as an aid to conveying title to a buyer at a foreclosure sale.

Presumably the agreement contemplates a line of credit or a series of periodic loans and repayments between the creditor and the debtor. What is the creditor obliged to lend under the agreement? What will determine the interest rate that the debtor is obliged to pay?

Think of three ways in which you would change this agreement if it were to cover equipment and not inventory.

Problem 3–7

Answer the following questions by reference to the security agreement below.

1. Occasionally third parties, as in *Samuels,* assert that the debtor did not have good title to collateral. By hypothesis such parties are not signatories to the security agreement and thus cannot be directly bound by it. How might a security agreement deal with this problem? How does this security agreement address it? See 2.2 through 2.5.

2. In the immediately preceding section we have dealt with the question of the identifiability of proceeds and their commingling. How does the security agreement address that problem? See 3.1.

3. In Chapter Six we will come to foreclosure. There we will deal with a series of thorny questions about the proper procedure one is to follow on repossession and resale: whether secured creditor has conducted a "commercially reasonable resale" is often the subject of litigation. Debtor will frequently claim that the creditor failed to give him adequate notice of the sale, failed to advertise the sale, etc. How does the security agreement deal with those problems? See 5.6 and 5.7. Will both of those sections stand up in court?

SECURITY AGREEMENT

(Inventory)

For value received, the undersigned, herein called "Debtor", hereby grants to ______ (the "Secured Party"), whose principal office is located at ______ ______, a continuing security interest in (i) Debtor's Inventory, (ii) Debtor's Property in Possession of Secured Party, and (iii) the proceeds and products of all of the foregoing, to secure payment of any and all indebtedness and liabilities whatsoever of Debtor to Secured Party, whether direct or indirect, absolute or contingent, due or to become due, now existing or hereafter arising and howsoever evidenced, including obligations arising from applications or agreements for the issuance of letters of credit or otherwise (herein collectively called the "Indebtedness").

1. DEFINITIONS. As used herein:

1.1 "Inventory" or "Debtor's Inventory" means all goods, wherever located, now owned or hereafter acquired by Debtor, which are held for sale or lease or furnished or to be furnished under any contract of service (including, but not limited to, any such goods which are returned to or repossessed by Debtor), or are raw materials, work in process or materials used or consumed in Debtor's business, including, but not limited to, those items of inventory hereinafter described and/or described in Schedule A (if any) attached hereto and made a part hereof.

1.2 The phrase "Debtor's Property in Possession of Secured Party" means and includes goods, instruments, documents, policies and certificates of insurance, deposits, money or other property now owned or hereafter acquired by Debtor or in which Debtor now has or hereafter acquires an interest and which are now or hereafter in possession of Secured Party, or as to which Secured Party now or hereafter controls possession by documents or otherwise.

1.3 "Collateral" means and includes any and all property of Debtor in which Secured Party now has or by this Agreement now or hereafter acquires a security interest, including without limitation, Debtor's Inventory and Property in Possession of Secured Party.

1.4 The phrase "Uniform Commercial Code" means Act No. 174 of the Michigan Public Acts of 1962, as amended.

1.5 Except as otherwise herein provided, the terms used herein shall have the meanings assigned to them in Article 9 (or, absent definition in Article 9, in any other Article) of the Uniform Commercial Code.

2. WARRANTIES, COVENANTS AND AGREEMENTS. Debtor warrants, covenants and agrees as follows:

2.1 Secured Party at its option may disburse loan proceeds directly to the seller of any Collateral to be acquired by Debtor with proceeds of loans from Secured Party.

2.2 Debtor shall (i) furnish to Secured Party, in such form and at such intervals as Secured Party may request, information adequate to identify the Inventory, its cost and location, and reports with respect to the acquisition and sale of Inventory; (ii) keep adequate records of the Collateral and such other records as Secured Party shall determine to be necessary; and (iii) allow Secured Party to examine, inspect and make abstracts from, or copy any of Debtor's books and records (relating to the Collateral or otherwise and whether printed or in magnetic or other machine readable form).

2.3 Debtor shall at the request of Secured Party deliver to it all accounting and other records pertaining to, and all writings evidencing, the Collateral or any portion thereof, together with all books, records and documents of the Debtor related thereto in whatever form kept by Debtor, whether printed, on magnetic tape or discs, or in other machine readable form, and all forms, programs, software and other materials and instructions necessary or useful to Secured Party in connection with such accounting and other records.

2.4 At the time any Collateral becomes subject to a security interest in favor of Secured Party, Debtor shall be deemed to have warranted that (i) Debtor is the lawful owner of such Collateral and has the right and authority to subject the same to a security interest in Secured Party; (ii) none of the Collateral is subject to any security interest other than that in favor of Secured Party and there are no financing statements on file, other than in favor of Secured Party; and (iii) Debtor acquired its rights in the Collateral in the ordinary course of its business.

2.5 Debtor will keep the Collateral free at all times from any and all liens, security interests and encumbrances other than those in favor of Secured Party. Debtor will not, without the prior written consent of Secured Party, sell or lease, or permit or suffer to be sold, or leased, all or any part of the Collateral, except in the ordinary course of its business. Secured party or its agents or attorneys may at any and all reasonable times inspect the Collateral and may enter upon any and all premises where the same is kept or might be located.

2.6 Debtor will do all acts and things, and will execute all writings requested by Secured Party to establish, maintain and continue the perfected and first security interest of Secured Party in the Collateral, and will promptly on demand pay all costs and expenses of filing and recording, including the costs of any searches deemed necessary by Secured Party to establish and determine the validity and the priority of Secured Party's security interest.

2.7 Debtor will pay promptly and within the time that they can be paid without interest or penalty all taxes, assessments and similar imposts and charges which are now, or hereafter during the effective period of this Agreement may become, a lien, charge or encumbrance upon any of the Collateral except to the extent contested in good faith and bonded in a manner satisfactory to Secured Party. If Debtor fails to pay any such taxes, assessments or other charges as they become due, Secured Party shall have the option to do so and Debtor agrees to repay all amounts so expended by Secured Party immediately upon demand, together with interest at the highest rate charged by Secured Party to Debtor on the Indebtedness or any part thereof.

2.8 Debtor will keep the Inventory in good condition and shall safeguard and protect the same from loss, damage or deterioration from any cause whatsoever, Debtor has and will maintain at all times during the effective period of this Agreement with respect to the Inventory, insurance against fire and other risks customarily insured against by persons engaged in similar business to that of Debtor, in such amounts, containing such terms, in such form, for such purposes and written by such companies as may be satisfactory to Secured Party, payable to Secured Party as its interests may appear, and Debtor will deliver to Secured Party evidence satisfactory to Secured Party that such insurance has been so procured and made payable to Secured Party. If Debtor fails to maintain satisfactory insurance, Secured Party shall have the option to do so and Debtor agrees to repay all amounts so expended by Secured Party immediately upon demand, together with interest at the highest rate charged by Secured Party to Debtor on the Indebtedness or any part thereof.

2.9 Debtor will reimburse Secured Party for all expenses, including reasonable attorney fees and legal expenses, incurred by Secured Party in seeking to collect the Indebtedness or any part thereof, in defending the priority of Secured Party's security interest or in pursuing any of its rights or remedies hereunder.

3. COLLECTION OF PROCEEDS

3.1 Subject in any event to the last sentence of this Section 3.1, Debtor agrees to hold in trust for Secured Party all payments received on accounts receivable and from the sale of any Inventory, all rights by way of suretyship or guaranty which Debtor now has or may hereafter acquire to enforce payment of accounts receivable, and all rights in the nature of a mortgage, lien or security interest whereby Debtor may satisfy any account receivable out of property. Debtor agrees to collect and enforce payment of all accounts receivable until Secured

Party shall direct Debtor to the contrary and, from and after such direction, Debtor agrees to fully and promptly cooperate and assist Secured Party (or any other person as Secured Party shall designate) in the collection and enforcement of all accounts receivable. Immediately upon notice to such effect to Debtor by Secured Party and at all times thereafter, Debtor agrees to (i) indorse to Secured Party and forthwith deliver to Secured Party all payments received by Debtor on accounts receivable or from the sale of any Inventory or arising from any other rights or interests of Debtor therein, in the form received by Debtor without commingling with any funds belonging to Debtor, and (ii) forthwith deliver to Secured Party all property in Debtor's possession or hereafter coming into Debtor's possession through enforcement of any such rights or interests.

3.2 Debtor authorizes Secured Party or any employee or agent thereof to indorse the name of Debtor upon any checks or other items which are received in payment for any Inventory, and to do any and all things necessary in order to reduce the same to money.

3.3 Secured Party shall have no duty as to the collection or protection of Collateral or the proceeds thereof, nor as to the preservation of any rights pertaining thereto, beyond the use of reasonable care in the custody and preservation of Collateral in the possession of Secured Party. Debtor agrees to take all steps necessary to preserve rights against prior parties with respect to Debtor's Property in Possession of Secured Party.

3.4 For the purpose of calculating interest on the Indebtedness, Debtor understands that Secured Party imposes a standard one business day delay in crediting payments received by Secured Party on accounts receivable against the Indebtedness to allow time for collection (or that Secured Party may, at Secured Party's option, make such credits when such payments are actually collected by Secured Party in immediately available funds). For the purpose of calculating the principal amounts available for borrowing by Debtor under any borrowing arrangements with Secured Party, Debtor understands that Secured Party may, at Secured Party's option, use a method different from that used for the purpose of calculating interest, and such methods may include either of the options hereinabove described or Secured Party may, at Secured Party's option and solely for the purposes described in this sentence, elect to credit payments received by Secured Party on accounts receivable on the date of receipt.

4. DEFAULTS, ENFORCEMENT AND APPLICATION OF PROCEEDS

4.1 Upon the occurrence of any of the following events (herein sometimes called an "Event of Default"), Debtor shall be in default under this Agreement:

(i) Any failure or neglect to comply with, or breach of, any of the terms, provisions, warranties or covenants of this Agreement, or any other agreement or commitment between Debtor or any guarantor and Secured Party; or

(ii) Any failure to pay the Indebtedness when due, or such portion thereof as may be due, by acceleration or otherwise; or

(iii) Any warranty, representation, financial statement or other information made, given or furnished to Secured Party by or on behalf of Debtor or any guarantor shall be, or shall prove to have been, false or materially misleading when so made, given or furnished; or

(iv) Any loss, theft, substantial damage or destruction to or of any of the Collateral, or the issuance or filing of any attachment, levy, garnishment or the commencement of any proceeding in connection therewith or of any other judicial process of, upon or in respect of Debtor or any guarantor or any of the Collateral; or

(v) Sale or other disposition by Debtor of any substantial portion of its assets or property; or death, dissolution, termination of existence, insolvency, business failure or assignment for the benefit of creditors of or by Debtor or any guarantor; or commencement of any proceedings under any state or Federal bankruptcy or insolvency laws or laws for the relief of debtors by or against Debtor or any guarantor; or the appointment of a receiver, trustee, court appointee, sequestrator or otherwise, for all or any part of the property of Debtor or any guarantor; or

(vi) Secured Party deems the margin of Collateral insufficient or itself insecure, in good faith believing that the prospect of payment of the Indebtedness or performance of this Agreement is impaired or shall fear deterioration, removal or waste of the Collateral.

4.2 Upon the occurrence of any Event of Default, Secured Party may at its discretion and without prior notice to Debtor declare any or all of the Indebtedness to be immediately due and payable, and shall have and may exercise any one or more of the following rights and remedies:

(i) exercise all the rights and remedies upon default, in foreclosure and otherwise, available to secured parties under the provisions of the Uniform Commercial Code and other applicable law;

(ii) institute legal proceedings to foreclose upon and against the lien and security interest granted by this Agreement, to recover judgment for all amounts then due and owing as Indebtedness secured hereby, and to collect the same out of any of the Collateral or the proceeds of any sale thereof;

(iii) institute legal proceedings for the sale, under the judgment or decree of any court of competent jurisdiction, of any or all of the Collateral;

(iv) personally or by agents or attorneys, enter upon any premises where the Collateral or any part thereof may then be located, and take possession of all or any part thereof and/or render it unusable; and, without being responsible for loss or damage to such Collateral,

(a) hold, store, and keep idle, or lease, operate, remove or otherwise use or permit the use of the Collateral or any part thereof, for such time and upon such terms as Secured Party may in its sole and complete discretion deem to be in its own best interest, and demand, collect and retain all hire, earnings and other sums due and to become due in respect of the same from any party whomsoever, accounting only for net earnings, if any (unless the Collateral is retained in satisfaction of the Indebtedness, in which case no accounting will be necessary), arising from such use (which net earnings may be applied against the Indebtedness) and charging against all receipts from the use of the same or from the sale thereof, by court proceedings or pursuant to subparagraph (b) below, all other costs, expenses, charges, damages and other losses resulting from such use; or

(b) sell, lease, dispose of, or cause to be sold, leased or disposed of, all or any part of the Collateral at one or more public or private sales, leasings or other dispositions, at such places and times and on such terms and conditions as Secured Party may deem fit, without any previous demand or advertisement but with reasonable notification to Debtor of any such sale, lease or other disposal; and except as herein provided, all notice of sale, lease or other disposition, and advertisement, and other notice or demand, any right or equity of redemption, and any obligation of a prospective purchaser or lessee to inquire as to the power and authority of Secured Party to sell, lease or otherwise dispose of the Collateral or as to the application by Secured Party of the proceeds of sale or otherwise, which would otherwise be required by, or available to Debtor under, applicable law are hereby expressly waived by Debtor to the fullest extent permitted by such law.

At any sale pursuant to this Paragraph 4.2, whether under the power of sale or by virtue of judicial proceedings, it shall not be necessary for Secured Party or a public officer under order of a court to have present physical or constructive possession of the Collateral to be sold. The recitals contained in any conveyances and receipts made and given by Secured Party or such public officer to any purchaser at any sale made pursuant to this Agreement shall, to the extent permitted by applicable law, conclusively establish the truth and accuracy of the matters therein stated (including, without limiting the generality of the foregoing, the amounts of the principal of and interest on the Indebtedness, the accrual and nonpayment thereof and advertisement and conduct of such sale in the manner provided herein and by applicable law); and all prerequisites to such sale shall be presumed to have been satisfied and performed. Upon any sale hereunder of any of the Collateral or any interest therein, the receipt of the officer making such sale under judicial proceedings or of Secured Party shall be sufficient discharge to the purchaser for the purchase money, and such purchaser shall not be obligated to see to the application thereof. Any sale hereunder of any of the Collateral or any interest therein shall forever be a perpetual bar against Debtor with respect to such Collateral.

4.3 The proceeds of any sale or other disposition of Collateral authorized by this Agreement shall be applied by Secured Party first upon all expenses authorized by the Uniform Commercial Code and all reasonable attorney fees and legal expenses incurred by Secured Party; the balance of the proceeds of such sale or other disposition shall be applied in the payment of the Indebtedness, first to interest, then to principal; and the surplus, if any, shall be paid over to Debtor or to such other person or persons as may be entitled thereto under applicable law. Debtor shall remain liable for any deficiency which it shall pay to Secured Party immediately upon demand.

4.4 Nothing herein contained is intended, nor should it be construed, to preclude Secured Party from pursuing any other remedy provided by law for the collection of the Indebtedness or any portion thereof, or for the recovery of any other sum to which Secured Party may be or become entitled for the breach of this Agreement by Debtor, nor shall anything contained herein reduce in any way any rights of Secured Party contained in any existing agreement between Debtor and Secured Party.

4.5 No waiver of default shall be effective unless in writing signed by an officer of Secured Party, and no waiver of any default or forbearance on the part of Secured Party in enforcing any of its rights under this Agreement shall operate as a waiver of any other default or of the same default on a future occasion or of any such right.

4.6 Debtor hereby irrevocably appoints Secured Party (which appointment is coupled with an interest) the true and lawful attorney of Debtor (with full power of substitution) in the name, place and stead of, and at the expense of, Debtor:

(i) to make all necessary transfers of all or any part of the Collateral in connection with any sale, lease or other disposition made pursuant hereto;

(ii) to execute and deliver for value all necessary or appropriate bills of sale, assignments and other instruments in connection with any such sale, lease or other disposition, Debtor hereby ratifying and confirming all that its said attorney (or any substitute) shall lawfully do hereunder and pursuant hereto. Nevertheless, if so requested by Secured Party or a purchaser or lessee, Debtor shall ratify and confirm any sale, lease or other disposition by executing and delivering to Secured Party or such purchaser or lessee all proper bills of sale, assignments, releases, leases and other instruments as may be designated in any such request;

(iii) to execute and file in the name of and on behalf of Debtor all financing statements or other filings deemed necessary or desirable by Secured Party to evidence or perfect the security interests herein granted.

4.7 Upon the occurrence of an Event of Default, Debtor also agrees, upon request of Secured Party, to assemble the Collateral and make it available to Secured Party at any place designated by Secured Party which is reasonably convenient to Secured Party and Debtor.

5. MISCELLANEOUS

5.1 This Agreement shall in all respects be governed by and construed in accordance with the internal laws of the State of Michigan.

5.2 This Agreement shall be terminated only by the filing of a Termination Statement in accordance with the applicable provisions of the Uniform Commercial Code. Until terminated, the security interest hereby created shall continue in full force and effect and shall secure and be applicable to all advances now or hereafter made by Secured Party to Debtor whether or not Debtor is indebted to Secured Party immediately prior to the time of any such advance.

5.3 This Agreement and all the rights and remedies of Secured Party herein shall inure to the benefit of Secured Party's successors and assigns and to any other holder who derives from Secured Party title to or an interest in the Indebtedness or any portion thereof, and shall bind Debtor and the heirs, legal representatives, successors and assigns of Debtor.

5.4 If there is more than one Debtor, all undertakings, warranties and covenants made by Debtor and all rights, powers and authorities given to or conferred upon Secured Party shall be made or given jointly and severally.

5.5 Notwithstanding the security interest described herein, any indebtedness owing from Secured Party to Debtor can be set off and applied by Secured Party on any Indebtedness at any time and from time to time either before or after maturity or demand upon or notice to anyone.

5.6 In the event that any mandatory requirement of applicable law shall obligate Secured Party to give prior notice to Debtor of any action to be taken hereunder, Debtor hereby agrees that a written notice given to it at least five (5) days before the date of any such act, shall be deemed to be reasonable notice of such act and, specifically, reasonable notification of the time after which any private sale, lease or other disposition intended to be made hereunder is to be made. A notice shall be deemed to be given when delivered to Debtor or when placed in an envelope addressed to Debtor and deposited, with postage thereon prepaid, in a post office or official depository under the exclusive care and custody of the United States Postal Service. The mailing shall be registered, certified or first class mail.

5.7 Debtor and Secured Party hereby irrevocably waive the right to trial by jury with respect to any and all actions or proceedings at any time in which Debtor and Secured Party are parties whether such actions or proceedings arise out of this Agreement or otherwise.

5.8 A carbon, photographic or other reproduction of this Agreement shall be sufficient as a financing statement under the Uniform Commercial Code and may be filed by Secured Party as such in any filing office.

6. STATEMENT OF BUSINESS NAME, RESIDENCE AND LOCATION OF COLLATERAL

Debtor warrants, covenants and agrees as follows:

6.1 Debtor's principal place of business is located in the County of ______, State of ______. The mailing address is: ______________________________.

6.2 If Debtor is an individual or sole proprietor, Debtor's residence (if any) is located in the County of ______, State of ______. The mailing address is: ______________________________.

6.3 If not already indicated above, any other places of business and/or residences of Debtor are indicated below: ______________________________.

6.4 Until Secured Party is advised in writing by Debtor to the contrary, all notices, requests and demands required hereunder or by law shall be given to, or made upon Debtor at the address indicated in Paragraph 6.1.

6.5 The Collateral will be kept at the address of Debtor shown in Paragraph 6.1 and/or at such other address as is indicated below: ______________________________.

6.6 Debtor will give Secured Party prompt written notice of any change in Debtor's name, identity or corporate existence and/or any of the above addresses.

IN WITNESS WHEREOF, the undersigned have signed this Agreement on the ______ day of ______, 19__.

In the presence of:

____

____

____
Debtor

By ______________________________

Its ______________________________

By ______________________________

Its ______________________________

SECTION 6. CREATING A SECURITY INTEREST IN STOCKS AND BONDS

It is commonplace to borrow against stocks and bonds. Customers borrow from their brokers; brokers borrow from banks, and it is important to have an inexpensive and certain mode of creating a valid security interest in stocks and bonds. Prior to the official 1977 amendments to Article 8 (and in the large majority of states that have not yet enacted the 1977 amendments to Article 8), the classical security interest in stocks and bonds was created under UCC 9–203 by the debtor giving the creditor possession of the certificates. This satisfied the creation requisites of 9–203; it also satisfied the requirement of perfection under 9–305.

With the 1977 amendments to Article 8, UCC 9–305 has been modified to *exclude* "certificated securities" from its provisions. When those amendments apply to a transaction, one must proceed to 8–321 which treats "enforceability, attachment, perfection, and termination of security interests." One seeking to understand the mode of perfection under Article 8 is then led through a dizzying set of cross references to 8–313 and elsewhere. We will deal with problems associated with those in the next chapter. At this point, however, the student should understand why Article 8 was modified in 1977. In a sense, shares of stock are going through one full cycle from being completely intangible, to having tangible form, and now traveling back to complete intangibility. Initially, a shareholder's interest in a corporation was evidenced only by his name on the books of the corporation as the owner of a specific number of shares. Later it became useful to have certificates that evidenced those shares and the certificates were passed back and forth among shareholders, creditors (as pledgees), and others. The certificate was treated as representing the ownership in the share in the same way as a certificate of title represents ownership in a car or a note represents ownership of a debt.

As transactions multiplied and much transmission of data was done electronically, people began to realize that the certificates sometimes inhibited effective transfer of rights and imposed significant costs on the system. Thus, for example, it is common for a brokerage house customer to permit the brokerage house to keep all of the certificates representing his shares of stock in the broker's name and for the owner to hold no certificates. This enables the customer to direct the broker to make trades over the phone without the necessity of going to the safety deposit box, getting out the certificates, and assigning them to the broker in each case. If one is able to protect his computer memory better than he can protect certificates, he may also minimize theft losses by having only electronic or written records of stock ownership and doing away with certificates which must be safely kept. For all of these reasons, the next ten to fifteen years may witness the "decertification" of shares of stock. Already ownership rights to securities have become more "intangible."

This development, in turn, presents the question, how can one perfect a security interest in a share of stock that is not represented by a certificate or is represented by a certificate in the name of a trustee? If it is merely represented by the shareholder's name on the books of the corporation, presumably the right is something like a general intangible, not an instrument, as a certificated security would be. If it is a general intangible, perfection would call for a filing, yet those in the securities industry are not accustomed to searching UCC files and thus such a filing seems an inappropriate way to perfect a security interest. Because of that and for other reasons we now have a newly modified Article 8. At this writing Article 8 has been enacted in California, Colorado, Connecticut, Delaware, Minnesota, Montana, New York, Texas, and West Virginia. We will give the students some exercise in its use in the next chapter.

In many cases the same act constitutes creation and perfection of a security interest under Article 8. Section 8–321(1) states that a security interest "is enforceable and can attach" only if it is transferred pursuant to 8–313(1). Section 8–313(1) contains ten separate subsections defining the acts necessary for a "transfer" and thus for the creation of a security interest. The nature of these acts depend upon whether there is a certificate outstanding, whether the certificate is held by a financial intermediary or by some other person, etc. For example, subsection 8–313(1)(a) provides that a transfer occurs with respect to a certificated security at the time when the person designated as a transferee (creditor, in our case) acquires possession. On the other hand, under subsection 8–313(1)(d), a transfer would occur at a time when a financial intermediary sends a person "confirmation of the purchase * * * [and] identifies [the security] as belonging to the purchaser * * *." There is not space here to examine the various circumstances under which securities may be held or to consider which of the particular subsections of UCC 8–313(1) fit with a particular form of ownership.

CHAPTER FOUR

PERFECTION OF THE SECURITY INTEREST

SECTION 1. INTRODUCTION

The word "perfection" is a classic term of art. It appears in Article 9 as a noun (perfection) and as a verb (to perfect), and the verb form in turn appears as an adjective (perfected). This terminology (which itself had some antecedents in commercial law) has now been widely adopted for limited purposes by the Bankruptcy Code, by the Internal Revenue Code, and in the future one can expect to see it robustly applied also to real property security devices.

By far the most important consequence of having a "perfected" as opposed to an "unperfected" security interest can be understood by examining UCC 9–301. That section subordinates unperfected security interests to the rights of lien creditors under the law. (Section 9–301(3) defines a lien creditor as a "creditor who has acquired a lien on the property involved by attachment, levy or the like.") Section 544 of the Bankruptcy Code gives each trustee in bankruptcy the rights of such a lien creditor at the date that a petition in bankruptcy is filed. Thus, the combination of those two sections means that virtually every unperfected secured creditor will be forced to give up his security interest to the trustee in bankruptcy and will be made to appear before the bar of justice as an unsecured creditor, a low form of life. If, on the other hand, a creditor is perfected, neither the lien creditor nor the trustee can use UCC 9–301 to defeat him and, in general, he prevails against such parties because of the broad protection given by UCC 9–201 and the absence of any overriding priority rule in Part Three. Of course, it is also important (though less so) that the perfected secured creditor generally prevails against other secured creditors and against certain subsequent purchasers. In sum, the importance of perfection is that it maximizes the protection that the secured creditor gets under Article 9 rules on what constitutes perfection set forth in Parts Three and Four of Article 9 and other law including the federal Bankruptcy Code. Although we have just alluded to a number of these priority rules, we will not study them in depth until the next chapter.

To state the consequences of perfection is to deal with the simplest part. The interesting questions in "perfection" cases between secured creditors and trustees in bankruptcy do not deal with such "no contest" clashes under sections 544 and 9–301. The creditor will typically stipulate that he loses to the trustee if he is found to be unperfected. The sport, and the subject of this chapter, revolves around the basic question: What must a secured creditor who has jumped through the hoops studied in the preceding chapter, and has thus created a security interest, do to become perfected?

One should begin with UCC 9–302. Although it does not say so in so many words, we believe that it might be paraphrased as follows: "The normal method of perfecting a security interest is by filing a financing statement. One who has filed a proper financing statement in the proper place is perfected, and except in the following cases, one who has not so filed is unperfected." Thus, the student should understand that filing a financing statement is the norm and that the provisions (a) through (g) in UCC 9–302(1) are exceptions to that general rule.

Reading UCC 9–302(1) will disclose that there are three basic methods of perfecting a security interest. The first is to file an appropriate financing statement. The second is to take possession of the collateral, i.e., set up a "pledge" (9–305). The third is to have "automatic perfection," i.e., to be perfected without having done any specific perfecting act. See if you can determine which of the sections of 9–302 provides for automatic perfection and which transaction is likely to be the most significant of those providing for automatic perfection.

After one has digested UCC 9–302 he should turn to the remaining perfection sections in Part Three, namely, UCC 9–303, 304, 305, and 306. We will study all of these in this chapter. Of greater significance and worthy of yet more study are all of the sections in Part Four of Article 9. These spell out what must be filed to perfect by filing, what must be contained in what must be filed and where the filing must be made. We will dig deeply into each of these sections in this chapter. Of particular interest are UCC 9–401 and 9–402.

Finally the student must consider UCC 9–105, 9–106 and 9–109 on the classification of various kinds of collateral. A quick examination of the sections in Part Three and Part Four reveals that a mode of perfection that may be sufficient and even necessary for one kind of collateral may be neither necessary nor sufficient for another. For example, filing or possession will perfect a security interest in goods, yet filing is wholly insufficient to perfect an interest in money, and possession will not perfect a security interest in accounts receivable. We will see why.

Having learned the general meaning and significance of perfection and having considered, however briefly, that one perfects, normally, by filing, sometimes by possession, and in certain special cases "automatically," the student should now ask why such acts are required of the secured creditor? Do they have anything to do with the creditor's rights against the debtor? It is true that a secured creditor earns no additional rights against his debtor after he has complied with UCC 9–203 by jumping through the other hoops under UCC 9–302, 9–401, etc. The function of perfection, of course, is to put third parties on notice of a possible security interest claimed by the creditor. By filing a public document (the financing statement) or by withholding possession of the debtor's assets from him, the perfecting creditor gives at least diligent third parties the opportunity to discover that security interest and take it into account in dealing with the debtor. The penalty the secured creditor pays for failing to give others the chance to discover his interest is that these other parties or their representative (the trustee in bankruptcy) acquire priority over an unperfected security interest, even a prior one. This raises the question of how one explains the various sections in UCC 9–302(1) that permit perfection automatically without notice. As to these, no such public notice or shift in possession to the creditor takes place. We will return to this puzzle.

In the sections that follow we will deal first with the most important mode of perfection, filing. Then we will cover legal issues raised by perfection, by possession, and by the automatic perfection rules. Throughout the chapter and at the end we will deal with a variety of related, but somewhat different, issues. For example, we must consider the question of choice of law in multistate transactions, and the special problems presented by securities, by proceeds, and by fixtures.

SECTION 2. CLASSIFYING THE COLLATERAL: A SUBSET OF PERFECTION ISSUES

UCC 9–105, 9–106, 9–107 and 9–109 all contain important definitions. Whether perfection of a security interest in consumer goods is automatic depends on its character as a purchase money security interest; that term is defined in UCC 9–107. In like fashion it is essential to consult the Code scheme of definitions of various kinds of collateral, UCC 9–105(1)(c), chattel paper, 9–105(1)(b), deposit account, 9–105(e), instrument, 9–105(i), account and general intangibles, 9–106, consumer goods, 9–109(1), equipment, 9–109(2), farm products, 9–109(3), and inventory, 9–109(4), etc. The requirements of perfection sometimes vary depending on the nature of the collateral.

To the unstudied eye, an account is apt to look much like chattel paper and only by examining the definitions can one be sure whether a particular security interest in such collateral is perfected or not under UCC 9–305. The same is true of the division between instruments and general intangibles. For most purposes the latter can never be perfected by possession and the former can be perfected only by possession. (Find the sections that say this.) Yet certain things (a vendor's interest in a land-sale contract, for example) might appear to some to be general intangibles and to others to be an instrument.

Note finally the particular definitions of kinds of goods in UCC 9–109. Do you see why the same refrigerator at different times during its life might be classified as inventory, consumer goods, or, possibly, as equipment? Note that those definitions do not arise from the attributes of the commodity, but from the use to which their owner, the "debtor," puts them. The same washing machine which is consumer goods in the hands of a private homeowner is inventory in the hands of the retailer and equipment in the hands of a commercial laundry.

Thus, the definitions are critical to perfection and the mode of perfection. Not only do they affect the way in which one perfects, they also affect the place where one might file a financing statement, and they might render a particular description (e.g., as inventory or equipment) to be appropriate or invalid. Consider the definitional problems posed by the following case and problem. A handy index to the definitions is to be found in Comment 5 to UCC 9–102.

IN RE K.L. SMITH ENTERPRISES, LTD.

United States Bankruptcy Court, District Colorado (1980).
2 B.R. 280.

GLEN E. KELLER, JR., BANKRUPTCY JUDGE.

The facts are in large measure undisputed. The principal officer of the plaintiff over a number of years pioneered a method of housing laying hens and collecting eggs which is, by all accounts, unique in the industry. The chickens are housed in "egg production units," which are large, circular structures containing four concentric circles of caged hens, 10 tiers high. The circles revolve through the building, passing stations for feeding, watering, egg collection, and manure removal. The chickens pass a collection station, which consists of an elevator which the operator rides up and down among the tiers, hand collecting the eggs. After the eggs are collected, they are cooled and then processed by washing, spraying with a light oil to seal the shell, and "candling."

The candling operation is nothing more than passing the eggs in a rotating fashion over a light to detect cracks or other defects which render the egg nonmarketable to the consumer trade. The eggs are then sized by weight and packaged in cartons. Where appropriate, the cartons of the customer, which have been preprinted, are used, and on other occasions, the eggs are packaged in 30-dozen cartons, where they are separated by layers of fiberboard. On some occasions, the Debtor does not put the eggs through the entire process of candling, washing, and oiling and sells the eggs as "nest run eggs," which puts the processing burden upon the purchaser.

The United Bank of Denver loaned the total principal sum of $2,400,000.00 to the Debtor on November 5, 1976. Four separate security agreements were executed in connection with this loan, two of which have specific application here. The first grants to the Bank a security interest in all inventory, accounts and contract rights of the Debtor, plus the proceeds therefrom. The second gives the Bank a security interest in all equipment and machinery of the Debtor. Appropriate financing statements were filed in the requisite offices to perfect the security interest in all of the described collateral.

The Bank became concerned about the Debtor's financial condition in the spring of 1979. Its concern became progressively more pronounced until, on September 21, 1979, the Bank forced the resignation of Kenneth L. Smith as the president and executive officer of the Debtor. The Bank then arranged for Mr. Norman Bell to serve as the Debtor's chief operating officer. Thereafter, and until November 23, 1979, Mr. Smith was not active in the operations of the Debtor's business and was without authority. The petition herein was filed November 23, 1979, and Mr. Smith thereupon resumed active operation of the Debtor's business.

The Debtor's primary customer for a number of years had been Safeway Stores, Inc. Safeway and the Debtor had a written contract, pursuant to which all of the Debtor's egg production meeting minimum standards was sold to Safeway. On September 24, 1979, Safeway Stores gave notice of its cancellation of the contract effective 30 days later in accordance with the termination clause in the contract. Safeway did continue to buy eggs, however, by sending inspectors to the egg facility and selecting eggs which would be purchased from time to time. On November 19, 1979, Safeway took delivery of an egg shipment which was not invoiced until November 24, 1979, pursuant to the routine billing practices of the Debtor. In addition to the receivable for the eggs shipped on November 19th, the Debtor had at the close of business on November 22nd other accounts receivable, which totaled, together with the Safeway account, a stipulated $40,192.50.

On November 24, 1979, an occasional customer of the Debtor, Mr. Gonzales, picked up a shipment of "nest run eggs" for resale in Mexico and paid the sum of $11,205.00 cash for such eggs. Mr. Gonzales, through his agent and interpreter, had spoken to the production foreman of the Debtor prior to November 16th to determine whether eggs might be available for his needs around the 16th of November. He was instructed that it was possible such delivery could be made. Due to travel difficulties and a storm, Mr. Gonzales did not arrive until the 24th of November. The arrangement with Mr. Gonzales had always been that he could purchase such "nest run eggs" as were available when he arrived to pick up delivery, and while he liked to obtain a full truckload, on a number of occasions, he had not been able to purchase a full truckload and had filled his truck with other merchandise, such as television sets or onions provided by other suppliers in the area.

After the filing of the petition herein, the Debtor delivered several shipments of eggs to Safeway, the last of which occurred on December 1, 1979. In December, as well, three flocks of chickens, totaling some 120,000 birds, were sold to the Campbell Soup Company. These hens had passed the age of prime laying capacity and no longer had utility in the production of eggs.

The Bank contends that the eggs are inventory within the meaning of its security instruments and that the chickens may be inventory or may in fact be equipment. It asserts that it, therefore, had a valid security interest in chickens and eggs. Notwithstanding the status of the chickens and eggs, it asserts a security interest in all of the sales to Safeway, which it claims to have been pursuant to contract; the sale to Mr. Gonzales, likewise asserted to have been pursuant to contract; and the sale of the chickens to Campbell Soup Company, which the Bank suggests may have been pursuant to contract as well. The Bank further claims a security interest in the accounts receivable as of the date of the filing of the petition, thus concluding that all of the cash in the Debtor's possession is "cash collateral," to which the Bank's security interest extends. The Debtor asserts that the chickens and eggs are "farm products" as that term is used in the Colorado version of the Uniform Commercial Code. 1973 CRS § 4–9–109. That section describes farm products as:

> " * * * crops or livestock or supplies used or produced in farming operations or if they are products of crops or livestock in their unmanufactured states (such as ginned cotton, wool-clip, maple syrup, milk, and eggs), and if they are in the possession of a debtor engaged in raising, fattening, grazing, or other farming operations. If goods are farm products they are neither equipment nor inventory."

It would thus seem that if eggs are products of "livestock," the hens themselves must be "livestock" within the meaning of that section. There does at least seem to be a biological connection. Official Comment to UCC § 9–109; United States v. Pete Brown Enterprises, Inc., 328 F.Supp. 600 (ND Miss 1971). The Bank has not disavowed the biological connection but asserts that in an operation such as this, where the sole business is the production of eggs, the eggs lose their characteristic as farm products and instead become inventory in the operation of a business. Great emphasis is placed by the Bank on the fact that there are no residents on the property of the Debtor and that while certain wheat was grown on adjacent land owned by the Debtor, it was not harvested. The Official Comment to UCC § 9–109 states:

> "Products of crops or livestock, even though they remain in the possession of a person engaged in farming operations, lose their status as farm products if they are subjected to a manufacturing process. What is and what is not a manufacturing operation is not determined by this Article. At one end of the scale some processes are so closely connected with farming—such as pasteurizing milk or boiling sap to produce maple syrup or maple sugar—that they would not rank as manufacturing. On the other hand an extensive canning operation would be manufacturing. The line is one for the courts to draw. After farm products have been subjected to a manufacturing operation, they become inventory if held for sale."

The pasteurization of milk or the boiling of sap seem to the court to be even more significant treatment of raw product than does the washing, candling, and spraying with oil of eggs. At the very least, they are in the same category, and the internal structure of the egg is not changed. The packaging of eggs in cartons does not seem to this court to be analogous to the "extensive canning operations" characterized by the Official Comment. Nearly all farm products must be packaged in some way for delivery to the farmer's customer. The facts that the packaging is done in the customer's package to eliminate a step in handling or that the operation is highly mechanized, do not seem to this court to disqualify the operation from the normal farm category. The language of the Code seems reasonably specific in its determination of what are farm products and does not appear to distinguish between the methods of producing the same product. The Bank's refreshing view that only conventional farming techniques which are unmechanized, unsophisticated, and labor intensive can produce farm products is unpersuasive. It is somewhat interesting to note that the loan at the Bank was made through its agricultural loan department.

The cases have uniformly found cattle feeding operations to be "farms" for the purposes of UCC § 9–109, although they are not farms in the traditional sense. See, for example, In re Charolais Breeding Ranches, Inc., 20 UCC Rep 193 (E.D.Wis.1976), where the court held that a tax shelter cattle feeding operation produced farm products, saying: "Although the bankrupt was not a farmer in the conventional sense, its business consisted of raising, breeding, and maintaining cattle." See also, Swift & Co. v. Jamestown National Bank, 426 F.2d 1099 (8th Cir. 1970).

* * * Similarly, in Mountain Credit v. Michiana Lumber & Supply, 31 Colo.App. 112, 498 P.2d 967 (1972), the court determined that a logging operation was not a "farming operation" within the meaning of 1973 C.R.S. § 4–9–401(1)(a). It was noted that trees could be farmed in a nursery setting, however. The construction of this statute, however, compels the conclusion that chickens are livestock and eggs are products of livestock. The statutory language is simply too clear. More importantly, the purposes of the Code could be badly abused. The Code was designed to provide a simple public explanation of claimed security interests so that the public might know under what conditions they were dealing with a debtor. To strain the statutory construction as sought by the Bank would seriously impair the public notice features which are the hallmark of the Uniform Commercial Code.

The court must conclude that the Bank has no security interest in the proceeds of either chickens or eggs, except to the extent such proceeds generated a prepetition "account" as defined in 1973 C.R.S. § 4–9–106 (1978 Supp). * * *

Problem 4–1

In each of the following cases a definitional section is critical in determining whether or not a secured creditor is perfected. Identify the section and identify the issue in that section which is relevant.

1. Debtor speaks to his banker about the purchase of an expensive stereo system that will cost approximately $1,200. Upon assurance that he will receive the loan, he buys the set and pays for it with $1,200 that belongs to his friend. Three days later he goes to the bank, signs a security agreement, gets the promised loan, and repays his friend. The bank does not file or take possession. Is it perfected?

2. Debtor goes to bank to borrow a large sum of money. Debtor offers as collateral four real estate mortgages covering a total indebtedness of $1,000,000 on which she is the creditor-mortgagee. She signs a proper security agreement and

gives bank possession of the mortgages. (Assume there are no notes.) Is the bank perfected?

3. Instead of mortgages, in 2. above, assume that the borrower was holder of several notes representing total obligations of $100,000 and also the lessor under several leases of automobiles. She gives possession of these items to the bank in return for a loan. Is the bank perfected?

SECTION 3. PERFECTION BY FILING—WHERE TO FILE

The normal mode of filing under the UCC is to execute what is commonly known as a UCC–1; a standard form of what is meant by a UCC–1 is set out below. See UCC 9–402(1).

UNIFORM COMMERCIAL CODE FINANCING STATEMENT
(Approved by the Secretary of State and Michigan Association of Registers of Deeds)

INSTRUCTIONS:

1. **TYPE OR PRINT All information required on this Form.**
2. **If dual filing is made, send the WHITE copies to the Secretary of State, Lansing, Michigan. Send the YELLOW copies to the local register of deeds. Retain PINK copies for files of the secured party and debtor.**
3. **Enclose filing fee.**
4. **IF ADDITIONAL SPACE IS NEEDED for any items on this Form, continue the items on separate sheets of paper (5" × 8"). One copy of these additional sheets should accompany the WHITE Forms, and one copy should accompany the YELLOW Forms. USE PAPER CLIPS to attach these sheets to the Forms (DO NOT USE STAPLES, GLUE, TAPE, ETC.) and indicate in Item 1 the number of additional sheets attached.**
5. **At the time of filing, the filing officer will return acknowledgement. At a later time, the secured party may date and sign the termination legend and use acknowledgement copy as a termination statement.**
6. **Both the WHITE and YELLOW Filing Officer copies must have original signatures. Only the debtor must sign the financing statement, and the signature of the secured party is not necessary, except that the secured party alone may sign the financing statement in the following 4 instances: Please specify action in Item 7 below.**
   (1) Where the collateral which is subject to the security interest in another state is brought into Michigan or the location of the debtor is changed to Michigan.
   (2) "For proceeds if the security interest in the original collateral was perfected."
   (3) The previous filing has lapsed.
   (4) For collateral acquired after a change of debtor name, and a filing is required under MCLA 440.9402 (2) and (7); MSA 19.9402 (2) and (7).

1. No. of additional sheets	Liber	Page	For Filing Officer (Date, Time, Number, and Filing Office)
2. Debtor(s) (Last Name First) and address(es)	3. Secured Party(ies) and address(es)		
4. Name and address(es) of assignee(s) (if any)	CHECK ☒ if applicable 5. ☐ Products of collateral are also covered. 6. ☐ Collateral was brought into this state subject to a security interest in another jurisdiction.		
7. This financing statement covers the following types (or items) of property:			

____________________ by ____________________
Signature(s) of Debtor(s) (Signature of Secured Party or Assignee of Record)

What information is available from the financing statement? Can one tell the interest rate? The principal amount of the loan? The terms of repayment? The duration? Can one be sure from the financing statement that there is any loan at all? The answer to these questions is "no," and the lesson to be learned is that the UCC calls *only* for "notice filing," that is for filing which merely puts third parties "on notice" that they may have to look further. The secured creditor is not required to file the security agreement (or loan application, etc.). This is to be contrasted with the *recording* of real estate mortgages where the operative document itself (the entire mortgage) is put on record and can be examined by any member of the public.

The question where to file divides into at least two questions. The first is in what state? The second, where within the state? The first question is answered largely by UCC 9–103, a provision we deal with in Section 7 infra. Here we are concerned mostly with where within the state one files. That is answered by UCC 9–401. Looking not at just one state, but at the various states, the issue is complicated by the fact that there are three alternatives to UCC 9–401. The student should read each of the alternatives with care and should note how they differ. Alternatives one to three progressively calls for more local filing. Only the third alternative calls for filing in more than one place, although a prudent creditor may, even under the first and second alternatives, choose to do more than one filing. Even a quick examination of 9–401 reaffirms the importance of definitions. For the purposes of the second and third alternative, farm products call for a local filing, but inventory does not. Fixture filings are local, but equipment filings are not. Note the third alternative does, however, call for a local filing in many cases in which the second alternative would call only for a state-wide filing. How does one explain these differences, and how does one explain the fact that the local filing is called for only in the case in which the debtor has but a single place of business in the state?

The notice filing provisions afford scope for overreaching on the part of the creditor. By filing a financing statement that covers "all farm products" the creditor can in effect cast a shadow over a given debtor's title to all of his significant personal property. To minimize that problem, section 9–208 gives the debtor a right to demand a more specific statement from his creditor concerning the amount of the debt and the identity of the collateral claimed by the creditor.

To test your understanding of UCC 9–401, consider the following problem.

Problem 4–2

(Assume that the second alternative to UCC 9–401 is in force except where the problem states otherwise.)

1. Debtor is a nurseryman who grows a substantial number of the shrubs, flowers and bushes that he sells at his nursery. He has a 100 acre plot on which he grows these items and has two greenhouses. In the front of one of the greenhouses he has a sales office and display room and outside of one of them during the summer months he sells various plants. Secured creditor filed a financing statement at the county seat of DeKalb County where the debtor's residence and the greenhouses and farm are located. He described in his financing statement the collateral as follows: "All nursery stock, all tractors, all farm equipment, all nursery equipment, one 530 Case backhoe, one tractor plow, one 24 disk." The nurseryman has now gone into bankruptcy and the trustee asks whether he can successfully challenge the security interest as it applies to the nursery stock. He estimates the value of the nursery stock to be in excess of $300,000. Some is maintained in pots in the greenhouses and on display; some in a holding area; and all of it is growing. At any given time the nurseryman reports that he has certain mature plants and others in various stages of development from one to seven years.

2. Debtor owned a ranch in central Kansas. He farmed that ranch and maintained both crops and a significant number of cattle on the ranch. From time to time he fattened cattle and sold them and at other times he purchased cattle and resold them without ever bringing them to his ranch. Bank's security agreement covered all "farm products, crops and farm implements."

The security agreement also contained the following clauses: "If marked here [X] debtor grants a security interest in all similar property owned by debtor during the period when the obligations are outstanding although such property may have been acquired or be natural increase after the date hereof.

"If marked here [X] the security interest will attach to all products and proceeds of the collateral but secured party does not hereby consent to the sale of collateral. * * *

"Debtor warrants that unless marked otherwise the collateral is used or being sought primarily for family or household purposes; but if marked here

[X] for farming operations;
[ ] for business operations; and
[ ] the collateral is being acquired with proceeds of the note * * *"

Bank filed a financing statement at the county seat where debtor's ranch was located. On debtor's bankruptcy he had 400 head of cattle on his ranch and was the owner of another 300 head that had been purchased the week prior to the bankruptcy and were being held at a local stockyard awaiting a sale that was to occur on the date following the day when the petition was filed. The trustee has asserted a claim to all of the cattle. If you were his counsel and he asked whether he would be successful, how would you advise him?

3. Assume that the debtor does business in a state with the third alternative to UCC 9–401. At the Secretary of State's office, Creditor filed a financing statement covering a large "International Td Dozer" worth more than $20,000. Creditor made no local filing. Trustee now argues that the creditor is unperfected. Is that so? The Dozer belonged to Yale Mining Corporation which did all of its mining in Lee County, Virginia, and in Harlan County, Kentucky. It leased equipment to other mining operators in other Virginia counties. The security agreement and the financing statement were signed and contained as an address of the debtor an address in Pennington Gap, Lee County, and it appears that shortly before the agreement was signed debtor had closed an office it had in Wise County and moved to Lee County. Debtor still retained a Post Office Box in Wise County and its registered agent for the purpose of service and a business bank account were at a bank in Wise County. On these facts, who gets the Dozer?

4. Bank takes a security interest in debtor's five race horses that are kept at Arlington Park in Illinois. Bank files a financing statement covering "horses" with the Secretary of State's office in Springfield, but does not do a local filing. Assuming that Illinois has the second alternative to UCC 9–401, is the bank perfected?

SECTION 4. PERFECTION BY FILING: WHAT TO FILE

An examination of UCC 9–402 and a consideration of the UCC–1 set out above show how little information needs to be included on a financing statement. It must have the names of the two parties, be signed by the debtor, give an address of the secured party and of the debtor, and contain a statement indicating the "types or describing the items of collateral." The security agreement can operate as the financing statement, but, except in consumer cases with very simple security agreements, that will not often be feasible. There is so little to be done, yet there are so many ways to go wrong. One cannot begin to imagine the ways in which a financing statement can be filled out incorrectly without reading some of the vast volume of cases that have now arisen under these sections. No person's imagination extends that far.

First, the creditor may omit something entirely. For example, the creditor may fail to get the debtor's signature or may omit the address itself. The description can and will be challenged if it is too narrow or too broad, but the most certain source of trouble for the creditor is the debtor's name. Is the name correct? Is it misspelled? Has the creditor used the corporate instead of the individual name or vice versa? Any one of these factors can render a financing statement invalid and cause the secured creditor to lose to a trustee in bankruptcy or other third party.

By far the most important requirement in UCC 9–402 involves the name of the debtor. The student should understand why that is so. It is only through indexing of the debtor's name that subsequent parties will find a financing statement. If others cannot find the financing statement, it is worthless. Thus, one can expect the trustee to examine the debtor's name with care and for the court to treat a trustee's complaint about errors in the debtor's name with real seriousness.

In fact name questions are likely to be much more complex than one can imagine at first blush. The first sentence of UCC 9–402(7) specifies the correct way to file where the debtor might plausibly be identified by either of two names, as for example, a partnership and a partner, a corporation run exclusively by one person, or any business organization that does business under another name. Note the apparent conflict between that sentence in UCC 9–402(7) and the first paragraph in Comment 7 to UCC 9–402. The statute seems to say what is sufficient, but not necessary; the Comment appears to say that compliance with the statute is both necessary and sufficient.

Yet more troublesome are the cases in which the debtor changes his, her or its name. In the consumer context a woman with an outstanding debt may assume her husband's name upon marriage or may take her original name upon divorce. Must the creditor file an amended financing statement? Business entities occasionally change their names. Must the creditor amend?

There is also the possibility of more fundamental business reorganization as when a sole proprietorship becomes a corporation. Of course, in the latter case one must worry not just about the proper mode of perfection, but about the efficacy of the underlying security agreement which by hypothesis has not been signed by a representative of the new organization.

In general UCC 9–402(7) and (8) are a bit of statutory leavening for the strict constructionists' judicial loaf. Many courts have been sticklers for absolute and strict compliance with the law regarding documents filed to give notice to third parties. In some cases this requirement has been carried to unseemly extremes and used to avoid financing statements that could not possibly mislead anyone. One suspects there is a deeper meaning to such judicial hostility to modestly defective filings. In several ways section 9–402(7) can serve as a shield against such hostility. In the first place it provides by implication that a financing statement filed in the old name continues effective even as to new collateral where the name change is not "seriously misleading." Even where the name change renders the old filing seriously misleading, section 9–402(7) provides that the filing remains effective as to collateral existing at the time of the name change and for that acquired within four months thereafter. Most important of all is the instruction in UCC 9–402(8), "a financing statement substantially complying with the requirements of this section is effective even though it contains minor errors which are not seriously misleading." That, presumably, is a direction from the legislature to the court to abandon fanatical insistence upon detail. After all, Article 9 was designed to "deformalize" the pre-Code law in these very respects.

IN RE LINTZ WEST SIDE LUMBER, INC.

United States Court of Appeals, Seventh Circuit, 1981.
655 F.2d 786.

CUDAHY, CIRCUIT JUDGE.

The Farmers & Merchants Bank of Fort Branch, Indiana seeks review of an order entered October 10, 1980, by the Honorable Gene E. Brooks, a United States District Judge, acting as a Judge of the Bankruptcy Court. This order granted the petition of J. Robert Duvall, trustee in bankruptcy for the estate of Lintz West Side Lumber, Inc., to set aside an earlier order entered by Judge Brooks, which authorized the abandonment of certain assets of the bankrupt. We affirm.

I.

Lintz West Side Lumber, Inc. ("Lintz Lumber" or the "bankrupt") was indebted to the Farmers & Merchants Bank (the "Bank") on two promissory notes totalling $90,000. To secure the indebtedness, the Bank obtained a security interest in the bankrupt's inventory and accounts receivable. The parties executed a security agreement to this effect, and the Bank prepared a financing statement which listed the debtor as:

Lintz, John Richard

Lintz, Mayella

2 Red Bank Road

Fort Branch, Indiana

The Bank filed the financing statement at the office of the Indiana Secretary of State and at the office of the Recorder of Gibson County, Indiana. * * *

On May 7, 1979, Lintz Lumber filed a voluntary petition in bankruptcy. * * * [In attacking the financing statement] the trustee argued that the statement, filed under the names of John and Mayella Lintz, rather than Lintz West Side Lumber, Inc., was insufficient to perfect the Bank's security interest because the difference in names would seriously mislead other creditors. * * *

[After the trial court decided against it,] the Bank subsequently instituted this appeal. * * * The Bank argues that the Uniform Commercial Code's system of "notice filing" was designed to assure that minor errors in the information provided on the financing statement would not defeat the perfection of a security interest. Since the bankrupt here is a close corporation located in a small town, the bank contends that a filing under the name of John and Mayella Lintz, the principal owners, directors and officers of the corporation, was sufficient to provide notice of the Bank's security interest to other creditors in the community.

Judge Brooks concluded, however, that the Bank's failure to include the correct name of the debtor corporation in the financing statement was seriously misleading because subsequent creditors had to depend upon a government official to search state records for the financing statement. *See* Anderson, *Uniform Commercial Code,* § 9–402:28 (1971); Ind.Adm.Rules and Reg. §§ 26-1-9-407-1 to 9. As a duly constituted corporation, Lintz West Side Lumber, Inc., is a legal entity separate and distinct from John and Mayella Lintz (whose names appear on the financing statement). A creditor would ordinarily, and could reasonably, assume that *corporate* assets would not be encumbered by a security interest filed under the names of these individuals despite the similarity in the names. Unless a creditor requested a search for the security interests held by others in the Lintz' personal property, the Bank's security interest would not be found. Under these circumstances, we cannot say that the names of the debtors were sufficiently similar to provide a creditor or official searching the records on behalf of a creditor with reasonable notice of the Bank's security interest.[7]

The Bank's argument that the security agreement was entered in good faith and without intent to defraud creditors does not alter this result. The bank's good faith is not at issue here. Moreover, good faith is only a necessary, not a sufficient, condition for perfection under the Uniform Commercial Code.

The Bank's allegation that no creditor in this case was actually mislead [sic] is similarly without merit. The district court noted that "Section 70(c) of the Bankruptcy Act clothes the trustee with the 'status of an ideal, imaginary creditor, irreproachable and without notice, and arms him with every conceivable right and power which under the applicable state law would be available to the most favored creditor who might have acquired a lien on the bankrupt's properties by legal or equitable proceedings.' Collier Bankruptcy Manual, *Trustees and Receivers in Bankruptcy Handbook,* § 13.001; J. White and R. Summers, *Handbook of Law Under the Uniform Commercial Code,* § 24–3 page 867 (1972)." *In re Lintz West Side Lumber,* No. EV 79–205–B (Bankr.Ct. Oct. 10, 1980). The district judge, an expert in bankruptcy matters and presumably in the mechanics of perfection of security interests in personal property in Indiana, found that the trustee, as an ideal, hypothetical creditor of the bankrupt, can be considered to have been prejudiced by the Bank's seriously misleading financing statement. See *In re Thrift Shoe Co., Inc.,* 502 F.2d 1211 (9th Cir. 1974). After reviewing the record in this case, we are not persuaded that this finding is clearly erroneous. * * *

[Some footnotes omitted.]

Note

How do you suppose that the trustee learned that a secured creditor had filed an inadequate financing statement?

IN RE GLASCO, INC.

United States Court of Appeals, Fifth Circuit (1981).
642 F.2d 793.

RONEY, CIRCUIT JUDGE. The sole issue on appeal is whether a financing statement, filed with the Florida Secretary of State by a creditor, perfected a security interest in certain property of the bankrupt debtor. The bankruptcy court held the financing statement to be inadequate because it listed the debtor by the name in which it did business rather than its legal corporate name. The

7. Both *In re Platt,* 257 F.Supp. 478 (E.D. Pa.1966) and *In re Hatfield Construction Company,* 10 UCC RS 907 (M.D.Ga.1971) are thus distinguishable from the instant case. In *Platt,* the court held that a financing statement filed under the name, Platt Fur Company, would not seriously mislead creditors of the true debtor, Henry Platt. Platt Fur Company, however, was an unregistered trade name for the business of Henry Platt and not a licensed corporate entity. In *Hatfield,* the financing statement securing assets of Hatfield Construction Company, a licensed corporation, was filed under the name of Wayne L. Hatfield. Although the court found that the financing statement was not seriously misleading, there is no indication that a government official was required to perform the search in that case. In addition, in both *Platt* and *Hatfield,* the court *affirmed* the determination of the bankruptcy judge.

district court affirmed. Holding the debtor's name used in the financing statement was not seriously misleading, we reverse. * * *

Prior to its bankruptcy, the debtor engaged in the manufacture and sale of boats in Florida. Although its legal corporate name was "Glasco, Inc.," the debtor operated its business solely under the name, "Elite Boats, Division of Glasco, Inc."

Appellant, the Citizens Bank of Perry ("the bank"), was "floor planning" marine engines for the debtor. In 1977, in connection with this financing, the debtor executed promissory notes and a security agreement in the name of "Elite Boats, Division of Glasco, Inc." The bank, to perfect its security interest in the marine engines, timely filed a standard form UCC–1 financing statement with the Florida Secretary of State, as required by Florida law. The bank listed the debtor on the form as "Elite Boats, Division of Glasco, Inc." The form was signed at the bottom by an officer of the debtor, without any designation as to office, capacity or affiliation. A filing clerk in the Secretary of State's office indexed this financing statement under the name listed, but did not cross-index it under "Glasco, Inc."

Later in 1977, the debtor filed for bankruptcy. The trustee in bankruptcy, appellee here, inquired of the Secretary of State whether any financing statements had been filed under "Glasco, Inc." Since the trustee did not request a search under "Elite Boats" or "Elite Boats, Division of Glasco, Inc." as well, the bank's financing statement was not disclosed. With permission of the bankruptcy court and without notice to the bank, the trustee then sold the marine engines. The bank commenced this action against the trustee for the sale proceeds.

In granting the trustee's motion for summary judgment, the bankruptcy court held the financing statement to be improper because it did not list the debtor by its legal name, "Glasco, Inc." The court further held the Secretary of State had no duty to cross-index the financing statement under the debtor's legal name, and the trustee was not bound by its actual knowledge that the debtor did business as "Elite Boats, Division of Glasco, Inc." The district court affirmed. On appeal, the bank contends that (1) listing the debtor as "Elite Boats, Division of Glasco, Inc." was sufficient because it was not seriously misleading to future creditors; and (2) in any event, the Secretary of State should have cross-indexed under "Glasco, Inc."

To perfect a security interest in collateral, a creditor must file a financing statement which complies with the filing requirements of the Uniform Commercial Code, as adopted in Florida. Fla.Stat.Ann. §§ 679.9–401 et seq. (1966). The purpose of the filing system is to give notice to creditors and other interested parties that a security interest exists in property of the debtor. * * * Perfect accuracy, however, is not required as long as the financing statement contains sufficient information to "put any searcher on inquiry." * * * The emphasis of the Uniform Commercial Code is thus on commercial realities rather than on corporate technicalities. * * * Section 9–402(5) reflects this emphasis by providing: "A financing statement substantially complying with the requirements of this section is effective even though it contains minor errors which are not seriously misleading." * * *

The effect of errors in the listing of the debtor's name has been the subject of extensive litigation. * * * The decisions appear generally to turn on the particular factual circumstances involved. The case here, then, must be judged on its own facts, with the focus on whether potential creditors would have been misled as a result of the name the debtor was listed by in the bank's financing statement.

It is undisputed the debtor held itself out to the community and to creditors as "Elite Boats, Division of Glasco, Inc." Its checks, stationery, and bank account all bore the latter name. Apparently the same name was used in its bills, contracts and telephone listing, because there is no indication in the record the debtor ever used the name of just "Glasco, Inc.," or any other name. Thus, listing the debtor by the sole name in which it did business was not misleading, because any reasonably prudent creditor would have requested the Secretary of State to search under "Elite Boats" in addition to "Glasco, Inc." Of course, the trustee in bankruptcy is considered to be in the position of a hypothetical but prudent creditor. * * *

Siljeg v. National Bank of Commerce, 509 F.2d 1009 (9th Cir. 1975), is analogous. Siljeg involved a security interest in property of a corporate debtor which later merged into another company. The parties disputed whether the "true name" of the debtor was the pre-merger or post-merger name, for the purpose of determining the accuracy of the financing statement. In rejecting this focus of inquiry, the court held:

> "The issue to be determined is not the true name of the entity, but whether the filing was misleading. Filing under an assumed trade name is effective unless it is misleading * * * It is likely that the * * * corporation did business under only one name and it may well be that a filing under that name was not seriously misleading." 509 F.2d at 1012–13.

The court then remanded the case for consideration under this standard.

The trustee relies on several cases each involving an individual who is engaged in business under an assumed trade name. These cases generally hold that a financing statement listing only the trade name as the debtor will be insufficient to perfect a security interest effective against the individual. * * * There is a crucial distinction, however, between these cases and the case here. In the former, a single debtor is necessarily held out to the credit community under two names, that of the individual and of the business. The individual's credit for personal needs is unrelated to the business. A personal creditor would not necessarily be aware of the business or trade name, and thus may not discover security interests filed solely under the business name. In the present case, where the company does business only under one name, the opportunity for creditors to be misled is substantially reduced, even though that name is not the company's "true name." See Siljeg, supra, 509 F.2d at 1012.

We hold the listing of the debtor as "Elite Boats, Division of Glasco, Inc." rather than as "Glasco, Inc." was not seriously misleading. The financing statement was therefore in substantial compliance with the filing requirements under Florida law and was sufficient to perfect the bank's security interest.

Because of our holding on the first issue presented by the bank, we need not decide whether the Secretary of State had a duty to cross-index the financing statement under "Glasco, Inc." A creditor who has complied with the filing requirements does not bear the risk of improper indexing by the Secretary of State. * * *

Thus, the bank would have a perfected security interest whether or not the Secretary of State had breached a duty to cross-index.

Reversed.

TUTTLE, CIRCUIT JUDGE, dissenting. With deference, I dissent. The majority opinion treats this case as presenting a group of narrow issues arising under the filing provisions for perfection of security interests under the Uniform Commercial Code, Fla.Stat.Ann. § 679.9–401. The majority eschews technicality to reach what might be considered to be a common sense solution in finding a perfected security interest despite an irregularity in the filing. Because this superficially appealing result contains the seeds for future mischief I cannot concur.

The filing system under the Code revolves around the concept of "notice filing," where a filing is to " 'give the minimum information necessary to put any searcher on inquiry.' " In re Excel Stores, 341 F.2d 961, 963 (2d Cir. 1965); see UCC § 9–402, comment 2. To effectuate the Code's spirit of liberality and disdain for rigid technicality the drafters included the provision, now relied upon by the majority, that a financing statement is effective even if "it contains minor errors which are not seriously misleading." Fla.Stat. § 679.9–402(5). This provision clearly was designed to accomplish substantial justice and "to discourage the fanatical and impossibly refined reading of such statutory requirements in which courts have occasionally indulged themselves." UCC § 9–402, comment 8.

This provision of liberality, however, was never intended to vitiate the beneficial effects of having a single filing system for the benefit of both existing creditors and searchers of the files. In its decision which protects the rights of the bank-appellant, the majority has unfairly burdened the other persons who must rely upon the filing system. A variety of different types of errors may cause the name on the financing statement to be erroneous and result in an incorrect filing of the statement. In deciding whether an error is "seriously misleading" a court must apply an "appropriate sensitivity to the relevant factors." J. White & R. Summers, Handbook of the Law Under the Uniform Commercial Code § 23–16, 958 (2d ed. 1980). In this regard the Court of Appeals for the Second Circuit has held that a subsequent creditor might never search the filings under the trade name of "Landman Dry Cleaners" where the debtor's name was "Leichter." In re Leichter, 471 F.2d 785, 787 (2d Cir. 1972). On the other hand, a filing under a trade name may be so similar to the debtor's real name that a searcher would be put on notice despite the technical error.

> The Referee found that a search of the public records under the name of Henry Platt would not have disclosed F.C.A.'s interest. Platt Fur Co. was an unregistered fictitious name for the business of Henry Platt. He also used Kenwell Fur Novelty Co. as a fictitious name.
>
> "The use of Kenwell as the debtor would clearly have left F.C.A. without a perfected security interest. However, the name Platt Fur Co. is sufficiently related to the name of the debtor, Henry Platt, to require those who search the records to make further investigation. Furthermore, the Referee found that the name was 'not seriously misleading,' the criterion for effectiveness under § 9–402(5)."

In re Platt, 257 F. Supp. 478, 482 (E.D. Pa. 1966).[1] The majority distinguishes cases such as Leichter as cases where the credit records of an individu-

1. The Florida law, amended subsequent to the beginning of this case, provides that: "A financing statement sufficiently shows the name of the debtor if it gives the individual partnership, or corporate names of the debtor, whether or not it adds other trade names or names of partners." Fla. Stat. Ann. § 679.9–402(6) (West. Supp. 1980). Leading commentators have inferred that this provision would alter the result of Platt: "With this provision on the books, the wise lawyer would advise Henry Platt and his creditors to use 'Henry

al's business should be distinguished from the credit records of the individual. The majority reasons that: "A personal creditor would not necessarily be aware of the business or trade name, and thus may not discover security interests filed solely under the business name. In the present case, where the company does business only under one name, the opportunity for creditors to be misled is substantially reduced, even though that name is not the company's 'true name.'" At 796. This distinction will not support the majority's result. The majority points to indications that the debtor always did business under the name "Elite Boats, Division of Glasco, Inc." and concludes that therefore any potential creditor would know to check under that non-legal name. But we are reviewing a case that was disposed of on a motion for summary judgment. Given this state of the record there may have existed creditors who would have perceived the debtor as simply "Glasco, Inc.," the legally proper title which, of course, it was. Surely the trustee could be taken to stand in the shoes of such an ideal creditor who had no notice. And in searching for "Glasco, Inc." one would not normally come across an item filed under the title of "Elite Boats." This is simply not a case where a searcher looking for the actual name would be put on notice by a filing under a similar trade name. A filing under the trade name in this case would not be filed near the actual name. Moreover, even if such creditors knew the trade name, they would still be justified to search only under the debtor's *legal* name. The terms of UCC § 9–402 require no more. Searching under a trade name would be completely unnecessary but for the majority's opinion. From now on in this Circuit, potential creditors must undertake to discover trade names and to conduct additional searches in order to avoid a judicial determination that they lacked diligence. And even if they follow such precautions they might yet overlook one trade name and face potentially expensive litigation over whether they should have known about that trade name.

Of course, the majority's conclusion may yet be saved if the Secretary of State wrongly failed to carry out a duty to cross index the financing statement. A creditor who complies with the filing requirements may not bear the risk of errors by the filing officer. See UCC § 9–407, comment 1. This rule holds true because under the Code "Presentation for filing of a financing statement * * * constitutes filing under this chapter." Fla. Stat. § 679.9–403(1). See In re Royal Electrotype Corp., 485 F.2d 394, 395–96 (3d Cir. 1973); In re Fowler, 407 F. Supp. 799 (W.D. Okla. 1975). But those authorities do not aid the bank in the present case. The error lay in the bank's submission of the debtor's name as "Elite Boats, Division of Glasco, Inc." The filing officer dutifully filed the statement under precisely this name. The bank may argue that the filing officers usually cross index under all names given. For example, a financing statement using a "doing business as" listing of a debtor would be indexed under the legal name and the trade name. This argument by the bank differs from the position that the bank will not bear the risks of the filing officer's mistakes; rather this argument holds that the filing officer must correct the bank's errors. If the bank had clearly indicated two names separated by a notation such as "d.b.a.", its position would be stronger. But the fact remains that the bank's submission could very easily be taken to be *one* name especially by a clerk untrained in legal

Platt' as the name on the financing statement." White & Summers, supra, at 958. Although not the law in any state, the official comment to the revision behind this new Florida provision provides some insight on this situation: "Trade names are deemed to be too uncertain and likely not to be known to be the basis for a filing system." UCC § 9–402, comment 7.

subtleties.[4] "A secured party does not bear the risk of improper filing or indexing *as long as his conduct does not lead to the error on the part of the filing officer.*" In re Fowler, 407 F.Supp. at 803 (emphasis added.)

Courts may have the opportunity to view a situation with perfect hindsight which is unavailable to participants in daily activities. The bank had the opportunity to submit the correct name of the debtor and failed to do so. A searcher versed in the operation of the UCC would know that the filing should be under the debtor's legal name. He would have no reason to look under a trade name, even if he is aware of the trade name's existence, because he should be able to rely on the bank to submit the legal name and not a trade name. Future creditors must now anticipate mistakes by would-be secured creditors in order not to be ensnared in the hindsight of courts. The trustee should prevail against the bank which is responsible for any confusion in this case.

I would affirm the district court's judgment. [Some footnotes omitted.]

Notes

1. Can you square *Lintz* and *Glasco?*

2. Should a court be willing to accept a less precise financing statement in a thinly populated rural area than it would accept in Los Angeles County?

3. Should the capacity of a subsequent search to turn up the financing statement be determinative of proper filing? What, for example, of the particularly diligent clerk who finds one that is improperly filed or of the inadequate computer cross-index that misses even those that would be obvious to a human searcher, such as one that omitted a period or a space?

4. Currently much searching is sometimes done by computer. In the future we can expect that nearly all UCC filing records will be maintained on computer memory and will be searched by computer. Note that the use of the computer as a searching device may restrict the search if the computer is programmed narrowly, but modern and developing computer technology may enhance the capacity of the searcher to find a misfiled or defective statement. For example, a computer can now be programmed to search not just under Christiansen, but also under names that sound the same, i.e., Christianson, Cristensen, Christenson etc. If collateral is also entered on the computer memory, the computer can do a cross indexing between the names and the kind of collateral and come up with a variety of alternatives.

5. Assume that you are a trustee in a case like *Glasco* and that you are contemplating the possibility of challenging a secured creditor's interest. What might be a first step in determining whether to proceed or not?

IN RE ALEXANDER

United States Bankruptcy Court, District North Dakota, 1984.
39 B.R. 110.

WILLIAM A. HILL, BANKRUPTCY JUDGE. Phillip D. Armstrong, Trustee of the estates of Larry Alexander and John and Norma Alexander, requests that his interest in various of the Debtors' personal property be found superior to that of the Defendant, Farmers Home Administration. The Debtors filed petitions for relief under Chapter 7 of the Bankruptcy Code and were discharged in their bankruptcy proceedings on January 10, 1983. * * *

4. The bank's argument that the filing officer should have recognized that there were two names on the form actually cuts against the bank. If it is so easy to see that "Elite Boats" is not a legal name then there is no reason or excuse for the bank's failure to submit the debtor's name as simply "Glasco, Inc."

John Alexander testified at the hearing held February 9, 1983, that he had refinanced his farming operation in 1978 through the Farmers Home Administration. The Farmers Home Administration required, however, that John Alexander execute a partnership agreement with his son, Larry, before it would enter into the refinancing arrangement. Although the partnership agreement was drawn up by the Farmers Home Administration and signed at its request, John Alexander testified that he and his son actually maintained separate farming operations. Each of the Alexanders had his own machinery, had his own seed, paid his own operating expenses, and filed his own tax returns.

The Farmers Home Administration filed a financing statement with the Register of Deed's office in Benson County, North Dakota, on February 6, 1979. The Debtors named in the financing statement were listed, as follows:

ALEXANDER DEBTOR(S) FARMS	SECURED PARTY	For Filing Officer
John J. Alexander Norma L. Alexander (Name) Larry J. Alexander (Name)	UNITED STATES OF AMERICA acting through FARMERS HOME ADMINISTRATION	File No: 251129 Date: 2/6/79 Time: 3:15 PM
Leeds, North Dakota 58346 (Mailing Address)	Box 207, Minnewaukan, N. D. (County Office Address) 58351	Filing Officer: RJF, pd3.00

The financing statement indicated that the Farmers Home Administration was claiming the following property as collateral for their loans:

> "Livestock, supplies, inventory, farm and other equipment and other farm products except growing and unharvested crops."

Armstrong contends that the financing statement filed by the Farmers Home Administration does not meet the requirements of NDCC § 41–09–41(1) and therefore is ineffective to perfect a security interest in the Debtors' property.

Section 41–09–41(1) of the North Dakota Century Code provides, in part:

> "A financing statement is sufficient if it gives the names of the debtor and the secured party, is signed by the debtor, gives an address of the secured party from which information concerning the security interest may be obtained, gives a mailing address of the debtor, and contains a statement indicating the types, or describing the items, of collateral."

Section 41–09–41 of the North Dakota Century Code codified section 9–402 of the Uniform Commercial Code. * * * The Eighth Circuit Court of Appeals, in a case involving the Minnesota statute codifying UCC § 9–402, stated that "a financing statement covers the collateral in question if it merely makes it reasonable for a subsequent creditor interested in the collateral to make further inquiries." Thorp Commercial Corp. v. Northgate Industries, Inc., 654 F.2d 1245, 1252 (8th Cir. 1981). A financing statement, therefore, must reasonably notify a creditor of prior interests in the Debtors' property.

In this instance, the financing statement filed by the Farmers Home Administration is sufficient to perfect a security agreement in machinery owned separately by the two Debtors, John and Larry Alexander. Although the financing statement was indexed under the name Alexander Farms, the court believes it reasonable that a creditor interested in the property of John and Larry Alexander within the largely rural county of Benson County, North Dakota, would examine all financing statements filed under the name Alexander. Further, the collateral listed in the financing statement of the Farmers Home Administration is not specified in overly broad terms. The term "farm and other equipment" is a reasonable notification that there may be a security interest claimed by FHA in the Debtors' farm machinery.

For the reasons stated,

It is ordered that the financing statement of the Farmers Home Administration is sufficient notice to perfect any security interest it may claim in the property of the Debtors.

Problem 4–3

Debtor, Smokee-Linc, Inc., a sausage manufacturer, executed a security interest in its accounts, equipment and inventory to secure a working capital loan from Centerville National Bank (CNB). CNB filed a financing statement covering the property at the Secretary of State's office. The UCC–1 filed by CNB listed "Smokee-Linc, Inc." as the debtor.

One month after CNB filed the UCC–1, Debtor filed for a corporate name change as required under the Corporation Code. The corporation name was changed to "Smokey Link, Inc." CNB was not notified of the change of corporate name.

Six months after CNB filed its UCC–1, Debtor filed in Chapter 11.

1. Assume that the Secretary of State files its UCC–1's in a central computing system. Whenever a filing search is requested, the computer searches for the debtor's name. Once this name is found, the computer prints out all filings under that name. The computer also prints out the filings under the three names alphabetically prior to and the three names alphabetically consecutive from the spot where the requested name should appear. On the date of the filing of the petition in bankruptcy, the trustee requested a filing search of "Smokey Link, Inc." and received the following names on the computer print out:

Smoker Heaven, Inc.

Smokers Anonymous, Inc.

Smoker's Nook, Inc.

Smokey Mountain Trails, Ltd.

Smoothee-Cream Ice Creams, Inc.

Smothers, Richard

Smothers, Thomas

The trustee argues that CNB is not perfected because the change in the debtor's name did not appear on the search and that the filing is therefore seriously misleading. Is she correct?

2. Assume that the Secretary of State does not have a computerized filing system. All filing searches are performed by those lower grade phenomena known as humans. Is it clear that CNB would not be perfected if a search requested by the trustee did not uncover the filing under "Smokee-Linc, Inc."?

Problem 4–4

1. Debtor had been doing business as and was incorporated as Mountainaire Chevrolet Inc. Bank filed a financing statement that appeared as follows:

The **FINANCING STATEMENT** is presented to a Filing Officer for filing pursuant to the Uniform Commercial Code

CREDIT UNION ACCOUNT NUMBER	1. MATURITY DATE (IF ANY)	2. NUMBER OF ADDITIONAL SHEETS PRESENTED (IF ANY). (SEE INSTRUCTION 3)	FOR FILING OFFICER (DATE, TIME, NUMBER, AND FILING OFFICE)
39495A-1			

3. DEBTOR(S) (LAST NAME FIRST) AND ADDRESS(ES):
Mountainaire Chevrolet, Inc.
1452 Crestlane Avenue
Glasgow, Kentucky

4. SECURED PARTY (IES) AND ADDRESS (ES):
Second NATIONAL BANK of Glasgow
631 North Vermont
Glasgow, Kentucky

(APPLICABLE ONLY WHEN CHECKED)
All household goods, furniture, and appliances belonging to the debtor or debtors now at the address stated above.

9. THIS FINANCING STATEMENT COVERS THE FOLLOWING TYPES (OR ITEMS) OF PROPERTY:

All inventory and Equipment

MCUL 421 (REV. 4/81)

SIGNATURE(S) OF SECURED PARTY(IES)	Second Nat'l BANK of Glasgow	BY: Miles Lord, Loan Officer
SIGNATURE(S) OF DEBTOR(S)	X Mountainaire Chevrolet, Inc.	X Harry Reed, President
	X	X

(4) FILE COPY - DEBTOR(S)

Subsequently the debtor changed its corporate name to Bud Long Chevrolet, Inc. by a proper filing with the commissioner of corporations in its state of incorporation. It thereafter went bankrupt. Assume that some of the assets in which the bank has a security interest (the equipment) had been purchased while the debtor was doing business as Mountainaire, but that all of the inventory of cars and parts had completely turned over in the year since the name change. Who takes the assets—the trustee in bankruptcy or the bank?

2. In the foregoing case assume that the principals of Mountainaire had sold their stock to a third party who had merged the Mountainaire Chevrolet into a pre-existing corporation by the name of Bud Long Chevrolet, Inc. Assume further that the bank continued to make loans to Bud Long Chevrolet, but as in the previous case it never filed a new financing statement, nor did it ever execute a new security agreement. Upon the dealer's bankruptcy, the bank is owed $1,000,000 and the collateral is worth $1,500,000. Who gets the collateral?

Note: Inadequacy of Filing

Your editors start with considerable skepticism about the arguments made by many who challenge financing statements. The most common competitor is the trustee in bankruptcy. The trustee is representing either himself and the unsecured creditors (in a Chapter 11) or the unsecured creditors (in a Chapter 7). We believe that very few of the persons represented by such trustees have been misled to their injury by defective filings. A few may have checked the files; a few more may have discovered what is in the files by reviewing a Dun and Bradstreet report on the debtor, but most would have extended credit to the debtor in blissful disregard of any public filings. Some will have done so with knowledge of the creditor's loan that is now being challenged. Others will have done so without any concern as to whether the debtor borrowed from the creditor in question. In short we suspect that most of those who challenge financing statements as defective have not been injured by reliance upon a defective filing. To the extent that we listen to their challenges and enrich them by avoiding the secured creditors' interests, we do so out of a latent hostility for secured creditors or, more rationally, as a prophylactic measure to encourage secured creditors to file accurately, thus to protect the few who do check the files.

Given this skepticism about the reliance of the challengers (and their representatives, such as the trustee), we would be relatively generous in accepting as valid financing statements that contain marked deviations from perfection requirements. Moreover, we think it appropriate for the court to consider the setting in which the case is to be found in analyzing whether security interests should be avoided or not. It is not too much to ask the secured creditor to determine how searches are made in the particular filing system in which he is filing, and to exercise particular care to insure that his financing statement conforms in those critical respects. Thus, if a search is done by computer and if the computer program is shorted out by periods or spaces in the name, we would expect the secured creditor to be particularly careful about spaces and periods in the name. Moreover, we would apply still different standards in different settings. If the filing is in a rural county in Nebraska where there are a handful of filings each year, and the total number of filings number only in the hundreds, we would accept more slovenly filings by comparison to those we would accept in Los Angeles County that run to hundreds every day and tens of thousands during a year's time. We are also taken with the common-sense approach in the *Glasco* case. If everyone is put on notice by a filing though it is not exemplary, shouldn't that be enough?

Most who study from this casebook will live to see all of the filing records computerized. Once the records are computerized, it will be possible to improve searches merely by modifying the searching program. Currently programs are in existence that will search under the name given by the searcher and by a variety of other spellings of the same name, and by phonetic spellings of it. Doubtless we have not seen the last of such program enhancement. As these search programs become more sophisticated and more likely to uncover even defective filings, such filings should be accepted as fulfilling their function.

One should not overlook the sections located further in the bowels of part 4 of Article 9, namely UCC 9–403 through 9–408. Particularly important is UCC 9–403. It tells, among other things, that a financing statement is good for a period of five years, and that debtor's insolvency proceedings in effect continue a filing. Moreover it has some intricate rules about continuation statements and their effect. Other sections provide for termination (9–404), assignment (9–405), and there is even a provision that alleviates the anxiety of one who really thinks he has a lease but files nevertheless (9–408). To get some understanding of the problems that untimeliness can cause consider the following case.

IN RE HAYS

United States Bankruptcy Court, Northern District, Ohio, 1985.
47 B.R. 546.

Memorandum Opinion and Order

Richard L. Speer, Bankruptcy Judge.

This cause comes before the Court upon the Motion for Relief From Stay filed by the Defiance Production Credit Association (hereinafter PCA). The Court has conducted a hearing on this motion and has heard all the evidence offered on this issue.

At the conclusion of that Hearing, the parties agreed that the only issue to be decided by this Court is whether PCA or the Farmers Home Administration (hereinafter FHA) has a superior lien on the proceeds of certain crops. * * * The Court finds that FHA has a superior lien on the proceeds in question.

Facts

The Debtors-In-Possession in each of these two cases are a husband and wife engaged in a farming operation. The Debtor Eugene Hayes and the Debtor Joseph Hayes are father and son, respectively. Their farming operations are situated in two locations, one in Williams County, Ohio, and one in Steuben County, Indiana. The property which comprises the estates in each of these two cases is the same property. * * *

At the time the Motion for Relief From Stay was filed, the Debtors-In-Possession owed to PCA approximately Two Hundred Seventy-two [Thousand] Nine Hundred Thirty-two and 02/100 Dollars ($272,932.02) by virtue of two promissory notes in favor of PCA. These notes and the accompanying security agreements are part of an ongoing financial arrangement between the parties which began about 1976. On March 25 of that year, PCA filed a financing statement in the Williams County Recorders Office which reflected that PCA had taken a security interest in all the Debtors' growing crops, harvested crops, farm machinery, livestock, and equipment. Attached to that financing statement was an extension sheet which purported to describe the real estate on which the crops were located. This description was made by reference to a county road and the number of miles a particular parcel is located from a town that lies on that road.

On March 17, 1981, PCA filed a second financing statement in Williams County which indicated that PCA had a lien on the same collateral covered by its first filing. There is no evidence that a continuation statement was ever filed, nor is there any evidence that new value was given at the time of this second filing. On May 3, 1982, FHA filed a financing statement in Williams County which covered the same property as was covered in PCA's filings. The description of real estate in FHA's filing is made by reference to township and section numbers. It is unclear whether the real estate described in PCA's statement is the same as described in FHA's. However, to the extent it can be ascertained from the documents, it appears to be the same land. The parties have agreed that all of the Williams County filings were either actually made in or indexed to the real estate section of the Recorder's records.

On April 21, 1978, PCA filed a financing statement in the Recorder's Office of Steuben County, Indiana. This financing statement contained a description of the same collateral that was covered in its statement filed in Williams County. There was only one entry on this statement as to the location of the real estate. The description of that land was given in relation to a highway and a town.

On May 5, 1980, FHA filed a financing statement in Steuben County that gave notice of its security interest in the same collateral covered by PCA's Indiana filing. On this statement there were listed four parcels of land, with the description of real estate made by reference to section and township number. On March 18, 1981, PCA filed a second financing statement in Steuben County covering the same collateral as was covered in their first statement. However, on this second statement, the real estate was described by a general reference to section and township number. Reference to the specific locations within the individual sections was not included. Again, it is unclear whether the land described in FHA's statement is the same as described in the statement filed by PCA; however, it appears to be. On March 31, 1982, PCA filed a continuation statement in Steuben County which referred to the financing statement filed on April 21, 1978.

Subsequent to these filings, the Debtors-In-Possession harvested certain crops from the real estate described in these financing statements. They have subsequently sold these crops as well as a portion of their livestock. As a result of an agreement between themselves and PCA, the Debtors have sequestered the proceeds generated by these activities pending the outcome of the Motion presently before the Court.

The Debtors-In-Possession have offered into evidence a copy of a letter dated April 19, 1982, wherein PCA indicated to FHA that it would agree to subordinate its liens on the Debtors' property to those of FHA. This letter does not reflect which county's crops were contemplated in this agreement. The Debtors have also offered a copy of a subordination agreement dated May 3, 1982, which is signed by PCA and which purports to grant to FHA a superior position with respect to the 1982 Steuben County crops. Although these documents were admitted into evidence without objection, there was virtually no testimony offered by either party which further explained their contents.

LAW

As previously indicated, the only issue to be decided by the Court is whether or not PCA has, as to FHA, a superior lien on any of the proceeds in question. However, before the Court can begin a discussion of this case, it should be pointed out that even in view of this limited issue, a review of the evidence is made most difficult by the fact that it has been presented in less than the best of organized fashions. It is also made more difficult by the fact that the Court is unable to definitively ascertain, based upon the minimal descriptions in the financing statements, what real estate is covered by each of those statements. Had full legal descriptions been used, this problem would not have occurred. * * * Nevertheless, the Court has been able to find sufficient information so as to be able to determine the priority of liens as between PCA and FHA.

The priority of creditors that have a perfected security interest in the same collateral is addressed by the provisions of Ohio Revised Code § 1309.31(E) which state in pertinent part:

> "(E) * * * priority between conflicting security interests in the same collateral shall be determined as follows:
>
> (1) in the order of filing if both are perfected by filing, regardless of which security interest attached first under division (A) of section 1309.15 of the Revised Code and whether it attached before or after filing."

In Indiana, the issue of priority is addressed by Indiana Statutes Annotated § 26–1–9–312(5), the provisions of which are identical to the Ohio statute. Under these statutes, a creditor's priority is established by the order in which its security interests are perfected. Perfection of a lien on equipment, livestock, *see,* Ohio Revised Code § 1309.07(C), Indiana Statutes Annotated § 26–1–9–109(3), or crops is perfected by the filing of a financing statement in the recorder's office of the county in which the collateral is located. *See,* Ohio Revised Code § 1309.38, Indiana Statutes Annotated § 26–1–9–401. If the filings involve crops, the statements must contain a description of the land on which they are located. *See* * * * 9–402(3). In addition, financing statements filed in Ohio that cover crops must be indexed to the real estate records of the recorder's office. * * * It appears that in the present case, the financing statements are properly filed, thereby giving both PCA and FHA a *prima facia* position as perfected secured creditors. However, it must also be determined whether or not these filings effectively perfect the creditors security interest.

I

A review of the facts finds that as to the Williams County property, PCA filed their first statement on March 25, 1976. Ohio Revised Code § 1309.40 states in pertinent part:

> "(B)(1) * * * Any * * * filed financing statement is effective for a period of five years from the date of filing * * *"

By virtue of this expiration period, PCA's perfection would lapse on March 24, 1981, if not continued. On March 17, 1981, PCA filed a second financing statement which listed the same collateral as was covered by their first filing. It did not make any reference to PCA's first financing statement and did not reflect PCA's earlier interest.

In order to constitute a filing which effectively continues the perfection afforded by a financing statement, the filing:

> "* * * must be signed by the secured party, identifying the original statement by file number and state that the original statement is still effective * * *"

Ohio Revised Code § 1309.40(C). Financing statements and continuation statements serve a distinct and different purpose, and are not interchangeable within the meaning of Ohio Revised Code § 1309.40. PCA's second financing statement fails to include essential statutory elements of a continuation statement. Such disregard of a positive legislative enactment prescribing the conditions necessary for the preservation of a statutory lien cannot be overlooked. The filing of a new financing statement cannot be viewed as a substantial compliance with the statute. * * * Therefore, it appearing that the filing of a second financing statement does not preserve PCA's first priority, and that PCA's perfection expired on March 24, 1981, it must be concluded that FHA, by virtue of their currently perfected security interest, has superior rights to that portion of the proceeds derived from the Ohio farm.

II

With regard to the farm in Indiana, PCA's first financing statement was filed on April 21, 1978, thereby giving it an expiration date of April 20, 1983. * * *

As has already been shown, the filing of a second financing statement is insufficient to preserve the perfection of a security interest. Accordingly, PCA's second financing statement that was filed on March 18, 1981, is without effect. However, on March 31, 1982, PCA filed a continuation statement under the provisions of Indiana Statutes Annotated § 26–1–9–403(3). That section states in pertinent part:

> "(3) A continuation statement may be filed by the secured party * * * within six (6) months prior to the expiration of the five (5) year period specified in subsection (2)." * * * This section of the Uniform Commercial Code

* * * does not permit continuation statements to be filed prior to the beginning of the six month period which precedes the expiration of a financing statement.

The provisions of Section 26–1–9–403(3) explicitly state that effectiveness of the original filing is made contingent upon the "timely filing of a continuation statement." Timely filing, as the term is used in that statute, clearly means filing within the time provided therein. A continuation filed prior to the six month period is not timely filed and cannot have the effect of continuing the original statement. In the present case, it appears that PCA's continuation statement was filed more than six months prior to the expiration of their original statement. In view of the untimely filing of that statement, it must be concluded that PCA's perfection has lapsed, despite the existence of the second financing statement. It must also be concluded the FHA, having properly perfected its security interest in the Indiana property, has the first interest in that property.

It should be noted that the Court is cognizant of the provisions of Ohio Revised Code § 1309.31(B) and Indiana Statutes Annotated § 26–1–9–312(2) which provide a first lien to any creditor that extends, within three months from the planting of crops, new value which enables the debtor to produce those crops in that year. Although there is some indication that these statutes may apply in this case, the fragmentary nature of the evidence does not allow the Court to make such a finding. As previously indicated, the evidence presently before the Court does not illustrate [indicate?] whether the proceeds from prior years were used to finance the crops now under dispute, or whether they were financed by new value. Without such evidence, it must be concluded that any party asserting a lien based upon the operation of those statutes has failed to sufficiently demonstrate the existence of that interest.

The Court also notes that with regard to the subordination agreement, if it were to be held to be effective as between PCA and FHA, FHA would have a superior interest in the proceeds. However, because it is unclear as to the origin of these proceeds, this Court cannot find that FHA should prevail based upon this purported agreement. Even if it were clear as to what property was covered by that document, a photocopy of an agreement along with a letter referring to the agreement are, by themselves, of questionable value in assessing the intent of the parties to subordinate their liens. Had the Debtors-In-Possession been able to produce original documents or had they supplied testimony supporting these copies, the Court would be able to weigh more seriously the ramifications of these documents. Nevertheless, without such supporting evidence, the Court must conclude that FHA does not prevail on the basis of an agreement to subordinate.

CONCLUSION

Based upon the foregoing analysis, the Court finds that FHA has the first priority to the proceeds under dispute. As the result of PCA's failure to properly continue the perfection of its security interest in the Williams County property, FHA has succeeded to the first lien position. Similarly, the untimely filing of PCA's continuation statement has caused a lapse in its perfection of its security interest in the Indiana property. FHA, having a currently perfected security interest, possesses the first priority to the Indiana property. Therefore, it must be concluded that FHA has * * * prevailed in both Ohio and Indiana and is entitled to the proceeds.

In reaching these conclusions the Court has considered all the evidence and arguments of counsel, regardless of whether or not they are specifically referred to in this Opinion.

It is ordered that the Farmers Home Association be deemed to have the first and best lien on the proceeds being held in escrow by the parties pending the outcome of this litigation.

Notes

1. How detailed must the description of the land be in order to have a perfected security interest in crops? See UCC 9–402(1), 9–110. Note that the party in the *Hays* case seems in some cases to have used traditional legal descriptions in some settings, and descriptions in relation to a "highway and a town" in others.

2. If a creditor could prove that his agent presented a proper financing statement together with the correct fee even though it was never entered in the index, would you treat it as though he had filed properly or as though he had never filed? How should one conduct his business in order to be able to prove other than by the index that one has made a filing and paid the fee?

Note: Post Filing Changes

After the creditor has filed a financing statement, many events can occur that will arguably render the financing statement invalid as a perfecting device. A common problem that the students confront in Problem 4–4 is for the debtor's name to change or for the debtor to be reorganized. UCC 9–402(7) deals extensively but not exhaustively with that question. As precisely as possible, that subsection defines the consequence of the name change. It appears to contemplate events even more significant than name changes when it speaks of changes in the "corporate structure." If the debtor's underlying form of organization changes, as for example from a partnership to a corporation, or from one corporation to another by merger or acquisition, the creditor has a second problem, namely, whether the security agreement itself is still valid. The student should consider both of those in connection with Problem 4–4.

A second common post perfection change is for the goods to move from one state to another or for the debtor's chief executive office to move from one state to another or for either to move simply within the state. In Section 8 below we will examine UCC 9–103 in detail. That section and the cases under it give a detailed body of rules for the interstate movement questions. To a lesser extent, UCC 9–401(3) deals with intrastate movement of headquarters or collateral.

A third problem, dealt with in Problem 4–2, and considered in detail in Section three with respect to proceeds, arises when the collateral itself changes form. At least one court has held that growing plants are farm products, but that when they are moved to the same debtor's retail spot for sale, they become inventory. In any case, collateral is goods when purchased and become fixtures when attached at some later time. These problems we deal with in Section Five. In a sense, UCC 9–306 on proceeds is a codification of the rules concerning perfection in the most common form of collateral change.

WESTBROOK, GLITCH: SECTION 9–402(7) AND THE U.C.C. REVISION PROCESS, 53 Geo.Wash.L.Rev. 408, 408–11 (1984).

Consider subsection 402(7) of Article 9 of the Uniform Commercial Code, that obscure detail buried amidst the banalities of Article 9, Part 4, which is devoted to the mechanics of filing financing statements. The little that has been written about this provision suggests no cause for alarm. Yet, every commercial lawyer or law teacher whom I have forced to read subsection 402(7) carefully has been startled and bemused.

Suppose that in 1974 an Amarillo, Texas company named Pierce-Arrow, Inc. procures a loan, secured by its present and after-acquired inventory and equipment. In 1975, Pierce-Arrow moves its principal plant to Houston and changes its name to General Motors. In 1978, it seeks and obtains a loan from the Enormous State Bank of Houston. The second loan is secured by the same types of collateral. Each bank obtains proper security agreements and files appropriate financing statements under the debtor's name at the time of that transaction. The Enormous Bank carefully searches the files in the Secretary of State's office and determines that no other financing statement is on file. In 1979 the debtor goes bankrupt. What result and why?

Now suppose the same facts, except Pierce-Arrow transfers all of its assets to a Houston company named General Motors, which obtains the second financing.

In both situations, the Amarillo Bank has the first claim on the equipment and the Houston bank has the first claim on the inventory. If Pierce-Arrow buys a drill press in 1975, three months after its move, Amarillo has a prior lien on that as well. If Pierce-Arrow buys a second drill press in early 1976, Houston will have the priority.

Why the difference between equipment and inventory? Why the difference between property the debtor obtained within four months of the name change or transfer and subsequently acquired property? Above all, the Enormous Bank of Houston might ask in anguish, whatever happened to the rule against secret liens? Why do we have an elaborate filing system for security interests in personal property and then permit the maintenance of liens that a reasonably diligent creditor cannot discover without going entirely outside the filing system, if then?

Note that a first-secured lender has a superior lien on all the debtor's pre-existing property even though it *knows* of the name change or transfer. So if Larsene E. Whipsnade walks into the Amarillo bank seeking a loan on business equipment, the bank can safely file a financing statement naming Whipsnade Co. even though it is told that the company will shortly be called ABC Widgets. Its security interest will be safe notwithstanding the name change or transfer. If Whipsnade mentions, with a grin, that there will be no need to file a new financing statement under the new name, the bank is presumably free to grin back and oblige. If Whipsnade later seeks a second loan on the equipment from a bank in another town, the second bank will not find the Amarillo bank's financing statement under ABC Widgets.

Thus, Whipsnade could borrow seventy-five percent of the value of the equipment from each of two banks and walk away with one hundred-fifty percent of the value, a fifty percent profit. If he is greedy, he could do it three times, more than doubling his investment. In each case, the Amarillo bank will receive its money; later lenders get only an expensive education.

While the fraud possibilities are endless, subsection 9–402(7) can work its magic absent fraud as well. Imagine a debtor manufacturing company that has acquired equipment from other companies that had given blanket liens on their equipment. In a period of cash flow difficulty, it seeks additional financing, offering its equipment as security. After a file check, the bank makes the loan. Several of the companies in the industry, including the debtor and some of its equipment vendors, then go bankrupt, and subsequent checking by various lenders reveals the transfers. The lenders to the other companies claim a significant part of the equipment, and the debtor's lender ends up seriously undersecured.

Surely, then, subsection 9–402(7) is the classic "glitch," a slip of the drafter's pen, a multi-word typo. In fact, it is perfectly clear from the Official Comments to subsection 9–402(7) that it was meant to achieve precisely the results described above.

* * *

[Footnotes omitted.] [Reprinted with the permission of Jay L. Westbrook and the George Washington Law Review © 1984.]

SECTION 5. PERFECTION IN FIXTURES

To understand the rules concerning perfection by filing with respect to fixtures, one must read UCC 9–313 together with UCC 9–401 and 9–402. Perhaps a small bit of history will help explain what will otherwise seem like a highly confusing set of rules. Under the 1962 version of Article 9, one first had to determine whether goods had become fixtures or not. If they had become fixtures, one filed a financing statement in the local office where a real mortgage on the property to which the fixtures were attached would have been filed. If he guessed wrong and the goods proved to be equipment and thus called for a statewide filing, the secured creditor was unperfected. The theory of the local filing was to include that filing in the real estate records and thus to alert parties who dealt with the real estate subsequent to the attachment of the fixture claim.

Unfortunately, nothing in the 1962 Code explicitly stated that this filing as to fixtures should be indexed *in the real estate records* to enable the real estate searcher to find it. Apparently, in some filing offices it was so indexed, and in others it was not. Moreover, if the creditor guessed wrong about the status of an item as a fixture or not, he was wholly unperfected if he filed in the wrong spot. Filing at the state capital was totally ineffective as to an item that later proved to be a fixture, and a local filing was totally ineffective as to an item that proved to be equipment.

In the 1972 version of Article 9, the drafters addressed these problems. First, they concluded that a secured creditor with an interest in a fixture should be offered two levels of protection. If he chose to be protected against subsequent *personal property* lenders, he could file as though the fixture were personal property (an ordinary Article 9 filing) and the Code would grant him protection. In the next chapter we will see how UCC 9–313(4) together with the other provisions of UCC 9–313 and 9–401 produced that result. If he also sought protection against subsequent *real estate* claimants such as purchasers and mortgagees, he was required to do a "fixture" filing. Fixture filing was defined in UCC 9–313 and provided for in UCC 9–401 and 9–402. The Code provides for the indexing of such a filing in the real estate records to enable a subsequent real estate searcher to find the fixture filing.

Those ignorant of this history, and even some who know of it, can easily read UCC 9–313, 9–401 and 9–402 to mean that one must do a fixture filing or be totally unperfected as to a fixture. That is not correct. Read UCC 9–401 with care. Note section 9–401(1)(b) (second alternative) provides for a local filing when "the collateral is timber to be cut or is minerals * * * or when the financing statement is filed *as a fixture filing.*" Note it provides always for local filing as to timber and minerals, but for a local filing as to fixtures only when there is "fixture filing," not in every case when the collateral is "fixtures." Thus it contemplates, and indeed permits, a filing as to fixtures under (1)(c) "in all other cases." If one wishes to have a perfected security interest (for protection against a subsequent trustee in bankruptcy under UCC 9–313(4)(d)), he may file as though the goods were equipment or consumer goods or whatever else they are if not fixtures (an ordinary Article 9 filing), and so have an interest with limited perfection, and limited protection, namely, protection against non-real estate payments. If all of that is not clear, read UCC 9–313 and 9–401 again.

What is a fixture? Section 9–313(1)(a) states that goods are fixtures "when they become so related to the particular real estate that an interest in them arises under the real estate law * * *." To one ignorant of the real estate law of a particular jurisdiction, that definition is useless. Even for one who has read the cases in Arkansas or New York or Florida, the definition is not likely to be helpful because the cases are likely to be in disarray. Only a foolish lawyer thinks he knows a fixture "when he sees one." While it is true that the size, weight, mode of attachment and degree of difficulty in removing a good attached in some way to the real estate are all likely to have an impact on a court's judgment whether a particular item has become a fixture or not, in thirty minutes in the library one can turn up cases that would call swimming pools goods, not fixtures, and define entirely mobile business machines as fixtures. The lesson for the planner is clear: the planner should never concern himself with trying to classify collateral as a fixture or not as a fixture! If there is some possibility that a good is a fixture, one should file as if it were *and* as if it were not.

After the fact (when *someone else* has not followed the advice given above) lawyers and judges must decide whether something is a fixture. Cases often state that the "intention of the parties determines whether something is a fixture." That test leaves a good deal to be desired, for the intention expressed at trial will invariably be self serving. Intentions expressed prior to the dispute are likely to be in a private document, not available for the observation of third parties who are asserting rights based upon the status of the collateral.

A few states follow the so called "institutional" doctrine for classifying collateral as fixtures. According to that doctrine, the proper test is to determine whether the item in question is somehow integral to the operation of something built on the real estate irrespective of its ease of movement. For example, a modest sized but critical machine important to the operation of a manufacturing or processing facility would be a fixture. Because UCC 9–313(1)(a) essentially incorporates the state common law defining fixture for the purpose of Article 9, one will have to look at the cases in the state in which the item is located to decide whether something is or is not a fixture. Unfortunately few courts have adopted the proposal of White and Summers which would have at least the virtue of certainty, if nothing else: "Anything that cannot be moved by one man in one hour armed with a crescent wrench is a fixture." The ensuing case grapples with the question how one determines whether an item is a fixture.

CUMMINGS, INC. v. BEARDSLEY

Supreme Court of Arkansas, 1980.
271 Ark. 596, 609 S.W.2d 66.

JOHN F. STROUD, JUSTICE. This is a suit filed in chancery court to foreclose the lien securing the balance of the purchase price and installation charge for two large illuminated motel and restaurant signs. Appellees filed a Motion for Summary Judgment which was granted by the trial court. We affirm the Chancellor as we agree that he properly granted the motion resulting in a dismissal of appellant's complaint.

In 1973, appellant contracted with Erect-O-Therm Structures, Inc., to fabricate and install two large signs on certain premises owned by Erect-O-Therm in Prescott, Arkansas. The signs were to advertise the location of the Stockholm Restaurant and Check Inn Motel. To secure the unpaid balance of the purchase price, Erect-O-Therm granted appellant a security interest in the signs by the execution of a security agreement describing them. A financing statement was filed with the Secretary of State of Arkansas in 1974. The security agreement between appellant and Erect-O-Therm also provided that the signs were not to be so affixed or related to realty as to become a part of the realty. The larger of the two signs was hung some 80 feet from the ground on steel poles anchored in a concrete foundation four feet deep by 16 feet wide by 20 feet long. The smaller sign is supported by steel poles which rise 12 feet from their concrete foundation.

Subsequently, Erect-O-Therm experienced financial difficulties and apparently lost the motel and restaurant property, including the two signs, to Union Planters Bank of Memphis by virtue of the bank's foreclosure of a mortgage on that realty. Appellees Conrad and Lillemore Beardsley then acquired the property from Union Planters. On January 31, 1979, appellant brought this foreclosure suit against appellees for the unpaid balance of the purchase price in the amount of $20,355.35, plus 10% of that amount as attorney's fees, possession of the signs and a deficiency judgment against appellees for any deficit remaining after the proceeds of a resale of the signs are applied to the indebtedness. Appellees denied the material allegations of appellant's complaint by specifically alleging that they had not purchased the signs from appellant nor entered into any agreement with appellant, that they had no knowledge of any indebtedness for the signs nor had they assumed any such debt, and that the financing statement was filed in the wrong place. Appellees also filed a third party complaint against Union Planters, not involved in this appeal, where they allege that they should have judgment over against the bank for any damages they suffer in this suit inasmuch as the bank represented to them that the property was free of liens and encumbrances. Some nine months thereafter, appellees filed a motion for summary judgment which was submitted on the pleadings, deposition of an officer of the appellant company, deposition of appellee Conrad Beardsley, and briefs. From a granting of the motion appellants bring this appeal, urging that the court erred in granting the motion for summary judgment.

It is well-settled that summary judgment should be granted only when a review of the pleadings, depositions and other filings reveals that there is no genuine issue as to any material fact and the moving party is entitled to judgment as a matter of law. Rule 56, Arkansas Rules of Civil Procedure. In the present case, in its order of January 24, 1980, the trial court found as follows:

> 1. The Defendants, Conrad Beardsley and Lillemore Beardsley, did not purchase the signs and related property referred to in the complaint from the Plaintiff, and there is no genuine issue as to this fact.
>
> 2. The Defendants, Conrad Beardsley and Lillemore Beardsley, are not personally liable to the Plaintiff under the security agreement referred to in the complaint since these Defendants were not a party thereto and have not assumed the indebtedness referred to in said security agreement, and there is no genuine issue as to this fact.
>
> 3. As between the Plaintiff and Erect-O-Therm Structures, Inc., those parties agreed that the signs in question were not, and would not become fixtures, and so as between them the signs are not fixtures, but as between the Plaintiff and the Defendants, the signs, which include the supporting pipes, are fixtures. The Defendants were entitled to rely on the filings in the Nevada County Circuit Clerk's office at the time they purchased property on which the signs are located on September 28, 1976. Ark.Stat.Ann. § 85–9–401 (addendum 1961) is the applicable statutory section since the filings involved in this case were made prior to the effective date of the 1973 amendment to Article 9 of the Uniform Commercial Code, and thereunder the proper place to file a security instrument in order to perfect securing interest was in the office where a mortgage on the real estate concerned would be filed or recorded. The Plaintiff filed its financing statement with the Secretary of State and not in the office of the Circuit Clerk of Nevada County, Arkansas, being the County where the real estate is located, and thus did not properly perfect its security interest in the signs as between it and the Defendants.
>
> 4. There are no genuine issues as to any material fact as between the Plaintiff and the Defendants, Conrad Beardsley and Lillemore Beardsley, d/b/a Check Inn and Check Inn; consequently, these Defendants are entitled to a judgment as a matter of law.

As to the trial court's first and second rulings, we agree there clearly is no genuine issue as to those matters. The copy of the security agreement attached to appellant's complaint reflects that the signs were purchased by Erect-O-Therm, not appellees, and that appellees were not a party to the agreement. There is nothing in the record to indicate, not even as an allegation, that appellees knew of or assumed the indebtedness when they purchased the motel and restaurant. The third ruling of the trial court, pertaining to the characterization of the signs as fixtures, is the only holding which appellant disputes. The trial court ruled that as between appellant and Erect-O-Therm the signs were not fixtures because of the provision in the security agreement which stated the signs would not be considered part of the realty. However, the trial court further held that, inasmuch as it was undisputed that appellees were not parties to the security agreement and were without knowledge of the aforementioned provision, the signs were fixtures as between appellant and appellees and there is no genuine issue as to that fact. These large signs anchored deep in concrete were so clearly fixtures, appellees had the right to rely on the records in the office of the Circuit Clerk of Nevada County, where filings covering fixtures are to be made, to determine if a lien was in existence at the time of their purchase. A good faith filing made in the wrong place (in this case the office of the Secretary of State) was not constructive notice to appellees as it is notice only to "any person who has knowledge of the contents of such financing statement." Ark.Stat.Ann. § 85–9–401(2) (addendum 1961).

* * * As noted previously, it was undisputed in the record that appellees were not in any way involved with the purchase of the signs from appellant; that they had not assumed the indebtedness referred to in the security agreement; that they had no knowledge of the agreement between appellant and Erect-O-Therm; and that appellant had not filed the financing statement in the Nevada County Circuit Clerk's office prior to appellees' purchase. As appellant failed to file the financing statement in Nevada County, as the security agreement was not determinative of the rights [and] obligations of appellees, and as the security agreement was the only proof offered by appellant to support his contention that summary judgment should not lie, we cannot say that there was a genuine issue as to any material fact or that the trial court erred in granting appellees' Motion for Summary Judgment.

Affirmed. [Dissent omitted.]

Problem 4–5

1. Client plans to sell a radio transmission tower (pursuant to a "lease," in fact a security agreement), attached to the ground by guy wires covering eight acres and put on a concrete base that measures 10′ by 10′ and was 8′ deep. Would the radio tower be a fixture? Would you give your written opinion that it is?

2. In many cases courts state that if an item is found to be a fixture, the creditor will have to do a fixture filing in order to perfect its security interest to any degree. That statement is not correct. Consider the following examples by reading UCC 9–313 and 9–402 and determine in which cases the creditor is perfected and those in which he is not.

(a) Assume the court finds that the radio tower is a fixture and that the creditor has filed a UCC–1 with the Secretary of State's office. Debtor goes into bankruptcy. Does the trustee take the radio tower?

(b) Assume that the creditor does a fixture filing, the debtor goes bankrupt and the radio tower is found to be a fixture. Who wins now?

(c) Assume that the creditor does a fixture filing, but the radio tower is found not to be a fixture and that the debtor goes into bankruptcy. Who wins now?

What do you take to be the moral of this story? This is a wonderful case for the operation of Peskind's Law, not so? (This law says: "File everywhere possibly required.")

SECTION 6. PERFECTION BY POSSESSION

A. *What is Possession?*

Section 9–305 authorizes perfection as to certain assets by the creditor's possession. These are letters of credit, goods, instruments, money, negotiable documents, and chattel paper. UCC 9–304(1) requires possession in certain circumstances. The Code does not define what is "satisfactory possession," but that issue is seldom presented. For example, in a field warehouse setting in which perfection depends upon possession by the field warehouseman and where the debtor's employees are permitted access to the warehouse goods, substantial questions about possession can easily arise. However, in modern practice a wise creditor will not rely solely upon the field warehouseman's possession for perfection. The creditor will have filed a financing statement as well. Whether the creditor's possession suffices is rarely a serious issue. In the most common pledge cases, the creditor bank plainly has possession of a certificate of deposit or other instrument. In other cases, the creditor locks up the debtor's airplane or the pawn shop has stuck the watch in a safe.

In at least one area, however, issues of possession may be significant. What, for example, of the case of an escrow agent who has possession of money or instruments on behalf of both parties. Is that possession adequate to perfect a security interest? Or what of the case in which two secured creditors claim an interest in a note and only one of them has possession? Unless the first acknowledges that he has possession on behalf of both of them, this can be troublesome. In the escrow case the courts have held the possession requirement has not been met in circumstances where the escrow agent is not the exclusive agent of the secured creditor, but is the agent of both the creditor and the debtor. Consider the following questions that might arise with respect to possession.

Problem 4–6

Secured creditors #1 and #2 both have security interests in debtor's certificate of deposit.

1. If the three execute an agreement stating that the debtor will hold possession "on behalf of secured creditors #1 and #2," will the security interest be perfected?

2. As an alternative, secured creditor #1 proposes simply that he hold possession and suggests that his possession will perfect the interest of both parties. How would you advise secured creditor #2?

The student should ask why certain forms of collateral are pledgeable and others are not. That clearly is the outcome under UCC 9–305, but why? Consider the following case.

M.M. LANDY, INC. v. NICHOLAS

United States Court of Appeals, Fifth Circuit, 1955.
221 F.2d 923.

[M.M. Landy, Inc. advanced money to Continental Charterers, Inc. and, as security, took an assignment of accounts receivable due Continental from the U.S. government. Also as security, Landy took possession of certain "warrants"—non-negotiable orders on the U.S. Treasury—payable to Continental which were to be in satisfaction of the government's debt. Continental became bankrupt and its trustee attacked Landy's security. The Referee in bankruptcy held that because certain filing requirements had not been met under the applicable federal and (pre-Code) state law, Landy's security was not perfected. Hence Continental's trustee prevailed. The Court of Appeals reversed, holding that filing was not necessary for perfection because Landy had taken possession of the warrants (a pledge); the case was remanded for further proof on an ancillary point. In the course of the opinion, the court discussed the concept of pledgeability.]

TUTTLE, CIRCUIT JUDGE.

* * *

Effectiveness of the Transaction as a Pledge.—Certain kinds of instruments represent obligations sufficiently that a delivery of them pledges the obligations. This was true of the common law specialty or sealed instrument; it is true of the commercial specialty or negotiable instrument. The idea of negotiability has now been extended to documents of title such as warehouse receipts and order bills of lading, and at the same time the idea of embodiment of a right to money has been and is being extended to certain non-negotiable choses. Stock certificates, insurance policies, and savings bank books may be the subject of pledges by delivery alone. Of course, not all written instruments embody the obligation; the delivery of an ordinary written contract, even if it is a memorandum necessary under the Statute of Frauds, is not a pledge of the obligation.

Williston proposed a rational distinction between the non-negotiable instruments which embody obligations and those which do not:

> "Certain contractual rights are embodied in instruments that are more than mere evidence of a claim and are popularly referred to and regarded as if they were themselves the obligations. To some extent the law has sanctioned this popular view, and there is a sound basis for it where by contract or custom, enforcement of a right is conditional on the surrender of the document evidencing the right. * * * The delivery of the document with donative intent transfers a right * * *. This is true of the gift of a policy of insurance, a savings bank book, a non-negotiable or unindorsed bill or note of a third person, a non-negotiable bond, a certificate of stock, or lottery ticket."

This distinction has been received with favor by all the leading text authorities. Brown, Personal Property § 59; 4 Collier, Bankruptcy (14th Ed.) ¶ 70.86; 2 Glenn, Fraudulent Conveyances and Preferences (Rev.Ed.) § 526. The Restatement of Contracts § 173(b)(iv) extends this concept of embodiment still further, to any "tangible token or writing, surrender of which is required by the obligor's contract for its enforcement." The Restatement of Security is more conservative, in that it would give this quality only to "indispensable instruments," which are defined in § 1, Comment *e*, as follows:

> "An indispensable instrument as used in the Restatement of this Subject means the formal written evidence of an interest in intangibles, so representing the intangible that the enjoyment, transfer or enforcement of the intangible depends upon possession of the instrument. If the instrument cannot be produced, the interest which it represents can be effectively asserted only by accounting for the absence of the instrument and obtaining as a substitute for it, either a duplicate or some form of court decree. Indispensable instruments include not only negotiable instruments such as promissory notes and bills of exchange, but also share certificates, bonds, interim certificates, savings bank books and insurance policies. Where the instrument is not an indispensable one, for example, a written assignment of

a list of book accounts as security, the interest obtained by the assignee in the accounts is not a pledge."

Section 2, Comment *b,* and Illustration 7, recognize that non-negotiable indispensable instruments are not restricted to any special categories, and also recognizes [sic] a pledge interest even in a paper which might have value as evidence of a right, but is *not* indispensable to enforcing the right. In such a case the pledgee has a pledge interest in the paper, but not in the intangible right; such an interest is said to be in the nature of a "worrying asset." Section 8, Comment *a* points out that under the Uniform Warehouse Receipts Act, § 42, the Uniform Bills of Lading Act, § 33, and 49 U.S.C.A. § 112, a pledge of goods in the possession of a carrier or warehouseman may be created by delivery of a non-negotiable warehouse receipt or straight bill of lading to the pledgee, upon notification of the carrier or warehouseman. See also Restatement, Trusts, § 163; Restatement, Restitution, § 126, Comment *f.*

There are a considerable number of cases which support these principles contended for by the texts and Restatements. In Herman v. Connecticut Mutual Life Ins. Co., 218 Mass. 181, 105 N.E. 450, Ann.Cas. 1916A, 822, the assignee of an insurance policy who left the policy in the hands of an assignor, in reliance on fraudulent representations of the assignor, was held to have a claim inferior to that of a subsequent pledgee. In Talty v. Freedman's Savings & Trust Co., 93 U.S. 321, 23 L.Ed. 886, the security for a loan was a warrant of the City of Washington, D.C., certifying approval of the borrower's claim against the city. The Supreme Court recognized the lender's interest in this paper, presumably quite similar to the warrants in the present case, as a pledge. The case of Citizens State Bank v. O'Leary, 140 Tex. 345, 353, 167 S.W.2d 719, noted 21 Texas L.Rev. 642, involved the pledge of a "Certificate of Membership" in an unincorporated association, which entitled the member to certain income and $3,000 upon his retirement or death and the surrender and cancellation of the certificate. The certificate also provided that any assignment without the consent of the association would be void. The court held that a pledgee without the consent of the association has a valid security interest which cut off a prior assignment and unrecorded instrument called a mortgage. * * * [Footnotes omitted.]

Note

To return to our issue above, how should a secured creditor perfect a security interest in his debtor's (a mortgagee's) note and mortgage?

Problem 4–7

Bank (client) has inquired as to its rights with respect to a debtor who has recently filed in bankruptcy. Debtor had a savings account in an out-of-state bank containing $15,000. As security for a loan by bank, debtor gave possession of the passbook in the out-of-state bank that represented the account with the $15,000. Debtor's trustee in bankruptcy has asserted a right to the $15,000. Does bank have a perfected security interest? (Assume that Bank will defeat the trustee if that is so.) The case would be changed if the savings deposit were not in an out-of-state bank but were held in your client's bank. Why so? Do not overlook UCC 9–104. -(l)

B. *Rights and Duties of Parties to a Pledge*

In the case of possessory security, it is the secured party who has control of the collateral. In the absence of relevant contract provisions in the security agreement, to what degree must the secured party care for the pledged collateral? What freedom does he have to use and dispose of it? See UCC 9–207.

COOKE v. HADDON

Nisi Prius, 1862.
176 Eng.Rep. 103.

Trover, for four cases of champagne.

Pleas: not guilty and not possessed, and also a plea of lien.

Laxton and Eyre Lloyd for the plaintiff.

Barnard for the defendant.

The action was in trover for the recovery of four cases of champagne, deposited with defendant, a money-lender, by way of collateral security for a loan of money, for which, also, a bill of 25£ was given by the plaintiff. The sum actually received by the plaintiff was 18£, 19*s.*, and in respect of the bill several payments were, from time to time, made for interest, renewal, and in liquidation of the principal sum; but eventually a judgment was obtained against the present plaintiff, and execution was put into his premises in Farringdon street, where he kept a refreshment-room, for the balance, under which 11£, 7*s.* was realized. Plaintiff then called on defendant and demanded the champagne, and was by him referred to a person named Staff, in whose possession the wine was alleged by the defendant to be. Upon application to Staff, plaintiff was informed by that person that the return of the wine was impossible, as part of it had been drunk.

For the defence it was contended that the right of lien still subsisted, inasmuch as the full amount due upon the bill had not been realized under the execution, owing to a mistake of the defendant's attorney, by whom credit had been given in respect of a sum of 5£ twice over.

The learned Judge, in summing up, told the jury that when a deposit of goods was made by way of security for * * * a debt, it was the undoubted duty of the pledgee neither to use nor in any way to dispose of the goods so deposited, and that by so doing he would forfeit his lien. Here, therefore, the wine having been drunk, the plaintiff, independent of any question as to the amounts paid on account of the bill, was entitled to recover the value of the pledge. The other question for their determination was, as to damage, whether the payments which had at different times been made (the account between the parties being somewhat complicated) sufficed to discharge the debt.

The jury found a verdict upon both issues in favour of the plaintiff, assessing the value of the wine at 20£.

Notes

1. We sometimes hear of the borrower who is a credit drunk. Here it is the reverse. Would the case have come out the same way under UCC 9–207? Suppose the parties had signed a security agreement in which the pledgor had waived "all rights to the collateral." What result then? See Article 9 and Seasongood, *Drastic Pledge Agreements,* 29 Harv.L.Rev. 277 (1915). Would it be unprofessional to draft such a clause?

2. Suppose the wine had been destroyed by fire and that while the pledgor did not have insurance, the pledgee did. Assume that the pledgee's insuror paid the pledgee the full value of the wine, which proved to be equivalent to the amount that

the pledgor owed the pledgee. Would the secured party still be entitled to collect the debt from the pledgor? Would the pledgee's insuror be entitled, via subrogation, to reimbursement from the pledgor? See UCC 9–207(2)(b). What result would occur if the following clause appeared in the security agreement between the pledgor and pledgee? "Pledgor hereby agrees that if he shall fail to procure insurance as agreed, the secured party's insuror shall be entitled to collect from pledgor any indebtedness of pledgor to pledgee to the extent that insuror has paid insurance proceeds therefor to secured party."

What is the duty, if any, of a pledgee to convert debentures he holds as security? This question has arisen in several recent cases applying section 9–207 of the Code. One commentator has posed the problem in these terms:

> "The hybrid nature of a convertible debenture may require special treatment when this type of security is pledged as collateral. Like a debt, a debenture represents an obligation of the corporation to pay a sum certain at a future date, together with periodic interest. Thus, a debenture is similar to a bond having a minimum value and providing a fixed return on an investment. At the same time, a debenture grants the holder the option of converting the bond into common stock of the corporation at a fixed price prior to a predetermined redemption date. If debentures are called by a corporation prior to their redemption date, the question arises whether a pledgee-bank has a duty to the pledgor to convert the securities." [Footnote omitted.] Note, *Reasonable Care Under the U.C.C.: The Pledgee's Duty to Preserve Value of Convertible Debentures,* 59 Georgetown L.J. 240, 240–241 (1970).

The answer in one court, at least, was yes under UCC 9–207(1) and that damages under UCC 9–207(3) should be measured from the date that the debtor had a right to possession of the collateral rather than the date that the secured party should have converted. Traverse v. Liberty Bank & Trust Co., 5 UCC Rep.Serv. 535 (Mass.Sup.Ct.1967). But see Reed v. Central Nat'l Bank of Alva, 421 F.2d 113, 118 (10th Cir.1970), holding that damages should be measured by the difference in value just before and just after the negligent failure to convert.

CAPOS v. MID–AMERICA NATIONAL BANK OF CHICAGO

United States Court of Appeals, Seventh Circuit 1978.
581 F.2d 676.

PELL, CIRCUIT JUDGE. Dr. Nicholas J. Capos brought this action against the Mid-America National Bank of Chicago (Mid-America) invoking at trial section 7 of the Securities Exchange Act of 1934, 15 U.S.C. § 78g, and Regulation U promulgated thereunder by the Federal Reserve Board, 12 C.F.R. § 221.1 et seq., and a common law theory that a bank holding stock as collateral for a loan has not only a right but a duty to foreclose on the collateral if its value should fall to the vicinity of the amount owed. After considering an extensive factual and documentary stipulation, deposition and live testimony of Capos and live testimony of a Mid-America official, the district court entered judgment against Capos on his complaint and for Mid-America on its counterclaim for principal and interest due. This appeal followed.

The salient facts are not complicated. In 1966 Capos purchased 5000 shares of stock in Diversified Metals Corporation (Diversified),[3] on the advice of his broker. Later that year, on further advice, he purchased 5000 additional shares with funds borrowed from the Michigan Avenue National Bank. The first 5000 shares were used as collateral, and Regulation U was explained to Capos at that time. In 1968, when the bank told Capos it wanted to sell the shares because their value was declining, Capos moved the loan to Mid-America. The April 10 Mid-America loan provided $50,591.83 to pay the loan at the Michigan Avenue National Bank, along with nearly $60,000 to pay income taxes. An earlier $10,000 working capital loan was consolidated therewith, and the entire $120,000 loan was secured by 6000 shares of Diversified, worth at the time about $360,000. No suggestion is made here that this transaction was other than in complete compliance with Regulation U.

In April 1969, Mid-America loaned Capos an additional $25,000 to pay income taxes, the loan being consolidated with the $120,000 previously owed. The Diversified stock then secured the entire loan, in compliance with Regulation U.

On July 25, 1969, Capos borrowed an additional $22,000 from Mid-America, secured by 4000 additional shares of Diversified stock with a value between $84,000 and $87,000. Capos and Mid-America executed a Form U–1 at the time, as required by 12 C.F.R. § 221.3(a), which stated that the proceeds were to be used for the "purchase of stock (regulated)." If, as the district court found, the purpose of the loan was to purchase margin stock, the loan violated Regulation U because the maximum loan value of the securing stock would have been $17,400. The premise of Capos' Regulation U theory is thus that Mid-America lent him $4600 more than it should have.

While the collateral originally was adequate, the situation changed dramatically in time. The value of Diversified stock fell from $60 per share on April 10, 1968, to approximately $21 per share on July 25, 1969. Unfortunately for all concerned, the slide continued. Although Mid-America at all pertinent times had the right to sell the collateral, it did not do so. Indeed, it was not until May 1972, when the value of the collateral had fallen to approximately $88,000, or $8.80 per share originally pledged[5] (the outstanding indebtedness being $147,000 at the time), that Mid-America proposed to sell the stock. Because Capos expressed optimism in Diversified and began a regular principal repayment plan, the stock was not sold. It eventually became worth $3.20 per share originally pledged, if indeed there was a market for the stock even at this price. The district court found, on ample evidence from Capos himself, that Capos had actual knowledge, at least on a week-to-week basis, of the price of the stock during the pertinent period.

* * *

II.

With regard to the common law theory, the district court thought that there was a duty on Mid-America to exercise reasonable care in preserving the value of the Diversified stock collateral, but concluded that the bank had not breached

3. The firm later changed its name to Diversified Industries, Inc. For convenience our reference to the firm will be simply as Diversified.

5. At some point, Diversified stock split, so the actual value per share may have been somewhat lower in May 1972. The figure per share originally tendered is useful for comparison.

its duty, and that Capos' contributory negligence barred recovery in any event. We would have no difficulty affirming the court's judgment on the ground of contributory negligence if the underlying duty were that found by the district court to exist. Clearly Capos had equal opportunity with Mid-America to stay apprised of the declining value of the stock, and the district court's finding that Capos in fact did so, at least weekly, is fully supported by the evidence. At any point prior to the stock's value becoming less than the amount owed, Capos could have instructed the bank to sell the stock and liquidate the debt. Thereafter, he could have acquiesced in Mid-America's suggestion that the stock be sold. The loss in the stock's value was, quite simply, an investment loss, the investment was Capos', not Mid-America's, and any negligence in not cutting the losses was *at least* equally his.

Mid-America urges us to affirm the district court judgment on the alternative ground that a bank has no duty to its borrower to sell collateral stock of declining value. We think it appropriate to do so. It is the borrower who makes the investment decision to purchase stock. A lender in these situations merely accepts the stock as collateral, and does not thereby itself invest in the issuing firm. Nor, unless otherwise agreed, does the lender undertake to act as an investment adviser, although imposing a duty on the lender to sell the stock at the "reasonable" time would foist that role upon it. Not surprisingly, Illinois common law did not impose a duty on a pledgee to sell shares of stock at any time or liability for depreciation of the shares' value while in his possession. Rozet v. McClellan, 48 Ill. 345, 348 (1868).

The Uniform Commercial Code, which now governs these situations, provides:

> "A secured party must use reasonable care in the custody and preservation of collateral in his possession. In the case of an instrument or chattel paper reasonable care includes taking necessary steps to preserve rights against prior parties unless otherwise agreed."

Ill.Rev.Stat.1975, ch 26 § 9–207(1). The Illinois Comments on this provision make it clear that the first sentence adopts the standard of care of the Restatement of Security, § 17 (1941), and that the second sentence adopts the standard of Restatement § 18. Restatement § 17 is in language quite similar to that used in § 9–207(1), but Official Comment a. is dispositive evidence that the duty imposed is not that urged by Capos:

> "The rule of reasonable care expressed in this Section is *confined to the physical care of the chattel,* whether an object such as a horse or piece of jewelry, or a negotiable instrument or document of title." (Emphasis added.)

The language of Restatement § 18 is much like that of the second sentence of § 9–207(1), and neither would appear to have any pertinence to the mere diminution in market value of securities. If there can be any doubt, Official Comment a. to the Restatement provision ends it: "The pledgee is not liable for a decline in the value of pledged instruments, even if timely action could have prevented such decline."

We see no warrant in Illinois law for engrafting a new and significantly burdensome duty onto § 9–207(1). Although the district court's opinion referred to "harsh" results not in keeping with present day commercial realities if the statute's language is given its natural and apparently intended meaning, we see nothing harsh or unrealistic about requiring a borrower/investor to contract for investment advice if he wishes to receive it. As for the authorities relied upon by Capos and the district court,[9] they are readily distinguishable, as they involved failures to exercise rights to convert debentures into stock and a failure to present a note for payment (thus releasing a solvent indorser). Either situation falls within the second sentence of § 9–207(1), see Illinois Code Comment 2, whereas this case, as we have said, does not.

For the reasons set out herein, the judgment of the district court is affirmed. [Some footnotes omitted.]

Notes

1. Assume that the securities in *Capos* were convertible debentures. During the term of the loan and at a time when the debtor was on an extended vacation in Europe the debentures with a value of $100,000 (because the underlying stock was worth $100,000) were called. Being ignorant of the call, the bank did not tender the debentures. After the call date, the debentures were worth only $20,000 (that being the value of the debenture as a debt security only without the conversion feature). On debtor's return from Europe, she comes to you and asks whether she has a cause of action against the bank for failing to convert. At all times after the conversion feature ends, assume the debentures as dead instruments are worth $20,000. Assume that the stock into which it could have been converted was worth $100,000 on the conversion date, and $200,000 six months later when the loan became due, and $75,000 at the time of trial.

2. If Debtor can make a case under UCC 9–207, what are her damages?

3. If Debtor pledges stock to her stockbroker, can the stockbroker repledge them in a commingled pot with other securities to a bank? (See UCC 9–207(2)(e).)

C. Pledges of and Other Security Interests in Securities: The 1977 Amendment to Article 8

Securities present a special case for perfection by possession. For most of the twentieth century, rights in shares of stocks and in bonds have been represented by stock certificates and by pieces of paper called bonds. In the most common case, a stock certificate would be registered in the name of the true owner and his name would appear on the face of the stock certificate as the owner. That, of course, was not true of bearer bonds where the principal attribute of ownership was possession. In such cases, the debtor-owner whose name appeared on the stock certificate could grant a perfected security interest by an agreement, written or oral, with his creditor and by transferring possession of the certificate to the creditor. In initial versions of Article 9 and Article 8 this transaction fits comfortably within UCC 9–203 and 9–305. Indeed, it probably represents the most frequent form of perfection by possession.

Increasingly since World War II, but particularly in response to the massive increase in the number of transactions since 1960, those who deal with securities and bonds have looked for ways to minimize the paperwork associated with the issuance and transfer of ownership rights in stocks and bonds. Ultimately this trend may cause the abolition of stock certificates entirely. Sometime in the 21st century we may find that stock certificates are merely a thought from a remote past and that ownership in corporations is indicated by identification on

9. Reed v. Central National Bank of Alva, 421 F.2d 113 (10th Cir. 1970) (conversion rights); Grace v. Sterling, Grace & Co., 30 App.Div.2d 61, 289 N.Y.S.2d 632 (1968) (conversion rights); State Bank of Clinton v. Parkhurst, 155 Ill.App. 101 (1910) (presenting note for payment).

the books of the corporation, by notations in a computer memory somewhere, but not by pieces of paper with the owners' names specified on them.

As an intermediate step toward that conclusion it is now common for corporations to issue certificates in the "street name," that is in the name of a stockbroker with the understanding by all that the stockbroker is merely a nominee for the true owners, the customers of the brokerage house. Thus, for example, all of the shareholders of Merrill Lynch might own millions of shares of IBM, yet there might be only a few certificates outstanding, each for large amounts and each showing Merrill Lynch or its nominee as the apparent owner. In such cases the shareholder's interest in IBM is reflected exclusively by a Merrill Lynch computer memory and by the monthly statements and confirmations of purchase that he receives from Merrill Lynch. Both that case and the one that we foresee on the horizon where there is no certificate at all outstanding raise the question: How does one perfect a security interest in the customer-debtor's right in stock?

For the creditor the simplest method is to ask the debtor to procure a certificate in his name and to give the certificate to the creditor. This would today be a perfected interest under Articles 8 and 9. But if that is not done, the question arises: What is the debtor's interest and how is the creditor to perfect its security interest in the debtor's rights? If the certificate were in existence with the debtor's name on it, debtor's interest would be in the "instrument" under UCC 9–105. If his interest is properly portrayed as merely a claim against his stockbroker, it may well be no more than a general intangible.

In response to all of these problems the drafters of the Uniform Commercial Code have proposed the 1977 amendments to Article 8. These amendments remove the entire perfection process with respect to securities from Article 9 and place it in Article 8. Moreover, they provide an intricate set of rules to deal with the various permutations described above in which the debtor is not in possession of a certificate bearing his name. The new Article 8 has thus far been enacted by New York and California and by several other states. With the two leading commercial states in the fold, it seems likely that the new version of Article 8 will eventually be adopted by all of the states and will become the law of the future. That means one must understand how Article 8 works. It also means that one must decide which cases involve securities and are therefore under Article 8 and which remain under Article 9.

Consider the definition of a certificated security in UCC 8–102(1).

(1) In this Article, unless the context otherwise requires:

(a) A "certificated security" is a share, participation, or other interest in property of or an enterprise of the issuer or an obligation of the issuer which is

(i) represented by an instrument issued in bearer or registered form;

(ii) of a type commonly dealt in on securities exchanges or markets or commonly recognized in any area in which it is issued or dealt in as a medium for investment; and

(iii) either one of a class or series or by its terms divisible into a class or series of shares, participations, interests, or obligations.

Problem 4–8

In which of the following cases is the asset involved a certificated or an uncertificated security subject to Article 8 and therefore not subject to Article 9?

1. The rights represented by a security held by Johnny in a closely held corporation. All of the other shares in the corporation are held by Lucille and Robert, Johnny's parents. These shares are not traded over the counter or on any exchange.

2. If in the foregoing case there is no certificate outstanding but Johnny is simply listed as the owner of a one-third interest in the corporation, is his interest now a security or not?

3. Chloe comes to the Bank with a document that shows her to be the owner of a $5,000 "limited partnership unit" in a Florida apartment development. The Bank is willing to make a loan, but would like a perfected security interest in that "unit." Is the right an Article 8 security or an interest outside of Article 8 and governed by Article 9?

Read the comments to 8–102 with care.

GENERAL ELECTRIC CO. v. TRACEY SERVICE CO., INC.

United States Court of Appeals, Third Circuit, 1984.
38 UCC Rep. 330.

GIBBONS, CIRCUIT JUDGE. General Electric Company obtained a judgment against Tracey Service Company, Inc. and attempted to satisfy that judgment by levying a writ of execution on stock owned by the judgment debtor in its subsidiary, Tracey Mechanical, Inc. No certificates of stock could be found, and General Electric proceeded under FedRCivP 69 for supplementary relief requiring that Tracey Service Company, Inc. cause its subsidiary to issue a certificate evidencing ownership. The trial court directed Tracey Service Company, Inc. to execute a lost certificate affidavit, and on March 20, 1981 Tracey Mechanical, Inc. issued a certificate of stock in the name of the parent corporation. Counsel for General Electric Company obtained possession of the certificate and requested from the court an order directing the United States Marshal to seize it.

At this point Continental Bank intervened, making a claim of property. Continental's claim is predicated upon a security agreement executed by Tracey Service Company, Inc. on September 7, 1976, and on a Uniform Commercial Code financing statement filed on September 10, 1976. The security agreement grants Continental "a security interest in all accounts receivable * * * all Borrower's rights, powers and privileges with respect to any merchandise * * * and all general intangibles now owned or hereafter acquired, which means all personal property (including things in action) other than goods, accounts, contract rights, chattel paper, documents, and instruments, including but not limited to, records, ledgers, books, journals, check books, print-outs, blue prints, designs, computer programs, computer tapes, punch cards and other computer software, formulae, drawings, patents, trademarks, trade names and copyrights." The financing statement covers "[a]ll accounts receivable, contracts and contract rights, chattel paper, instruments, documents, all returned or rejected merchandise, and all general intangibles, all of the foregoing whether now owned or hereafter acquired and all cash and non-cash proceeds of the foregoing." Continental contends that the security agreement and financing statement give it a perfected security interest in Tracey Service Company, Inc.'s stock in its subsidiary, prior in time to the General Electric Company levy. Continental relies on the reference to "general intangibles" in both documents. It contends, further, that the stock certificate evidencing the Tracey Service Company, Inc. ownership of its subsidiary, issued on March 20, 1981, represents "proceeds" of a general intangible interest in the subsidiary within the meaning of the financing statement.

The trial court accepted the General Electric Company argument that although the financing statement includes proceeds of general intangibles, the security agreement does not cover such proceeds. Thus, the court reasoned, Continental's interest in the stock of Tracey Mechanical, Inc. depended on the reference in the security agreement to "instruments." As to these, the court held that the filing of the financing statement did not perfect Continental's security interest against third parties.

The financing statement covered proceeds, and 13 Pa. Cons. Stat.Ann. § 9306(c)(1) (Purdon 1983) provides that a security interest in proceeds becomes unperfected ten days after a debtor's receipt of proceeds unless:

> "(1) a filed financing statement covers the original collateral and the proceeds are collateral in which a security interest may be perfected by filing in the office or offices where the financing statement has been filed and, if the proceeds are acquired with cash proceeds, the description of the collateral in the financing statement indicates the type of property constituting the proceeds."

Continental's filed financing statement would seem to be within § 9306(c)(1) since it covers general intangibles, a security interest in which may be perfected by filing, and it contains a description of the proceeds as "instruments." The trial court reasoned, however, that 13 Pa. Cons. Stat.Ann. § 9203(a)(1) governed. That section provides that a security interest is not enforceable against the debtor or third parties unless:

> "(1) the collateral is in the possession of the secured party pursuant to agreement, or the debtor has signed a security agreement which contains a description of the collateral * * *."

While the financing statement covered proceeds of general intangibles, the court concluded that the security agreement did not. Thus Continental's interest in Tracey Mechanical, Inc. terminated when the parent corporation's interest in it was converted from unissued stock—a general intangible—to issued stock, an instrument.

Perfection of a security interest in instruments requires that the secured party take possession. 13 Pa. Cons. Stat.Ann. § 9304(a). There is an exception in § 9304(a) for instruments which are proceeds of secured interests which may be perfected by filing, and a cross-reference to 13 Pa. Cons. Stat.Ann. § 9306(c). The latter section provides that proceeds become unperfected ten days after receipt by the debtor unless "the security interest in the proceeds is perfected before the expiration of the ten-day period." 13 Pa. Cons. Stat.Ann. § 9306(c)(3). Continental did not obtain possession of the stock certificate issued by Tracey Mechanical, Inc. within ten days, or indeed prior to the General Electric levy.

The judgment appealed from will, therefore, be affirmed.

BECKER, CIRCUIT JUDGE, concurring. While I concur in the judgment of the court, I would affirm on different grounds than the majority. Contrary to Judge Gibbons, I believe that Tracey Service's interest in Tracey Mechanical was at the time the security agreement was entered into an *instrument* under the Pennsylvania Uniform Commercial Code and not a general intangible, and that appellant therefore never had a security interest, perfected or otherwise, in the Mechanical stock,[1] but only a perfected security interest in general intangibles.[2] The problem with Continental's claim to the stock certificates is not so much that they represent unperfected proceeds of an earlier perfected security interest, but that Continental lacked a perfected security interest in the stock certificates in the first place.

The threshold question is whether Tracey's interest in Tracey Mechanical was represented by a stock certificate, and was, in UCC terms, an "instrument." Section 9–105(a) of the Uniform Commercial Code defines an instrument as a "negotiable instrument (defined in § 3–104), or a security (defined in § 8–102) or any other writing which evidences a right to the payment of money and is not itself a security agreement or lease and is of a type which is in ordinary course of business transferred by delivery with any necessary indorsement or assignment." Section 8–102, in turn, defines a security as "an instrument which: (i) is issued in bearer or registered form * * * and (iv) evidences a share, participation or other interest in property or in an enterprise or evidences an obligation of the issuer." Subsequent parts of § 8–102 make reasonably clear that a security is conceived of as being represented by some form of writing.

Because of these definitional provisions, there can be little doubt that under ordinary circumstances Continental Bank would not even have a colorable claim in Tracey's stock certificates: Continental's security agreement claimed general intangibles and specifically disclaimed instruments.[3] The question arises as to whether a different result obtains here because the stock in Tracey Mechanical was not generally negotiable and the stock in Tracey Mechanical was eventually lost. I consider these matters in turn.

In In re Weber, 29 UCC RepServ 690 (Bankr. W.D. N.Y.1980), the court dealt with the issue of whether "Milk Certificates" issued by a dairy cooperative as evidence that the bearer had a claim against a reserve fund established by the cooperative were instruments under § 9–105(a) of the UCC. The court held that, despite the fact that the certificate was retirable at the sole discretion of the cooperative and that it was transferable only on the books of the corporation (i.e., that it was a registered security), it was an instrument nonetheless.

In Citizens National Bank of Orlando v. Bornstein, 374 So.2d 6 (Fla.1979), the Florida Supreme Court dealt with the question of whether a non-negotiable certificate of deposit, ownership of which could be changed only by transfer on the books of the bank, was an instrument under the UCC. The court held that it was. "If the code drafters had intended to exclude non-negotiable instruments from coverage under section [9–105], they would not have added [the last clause] but would have limited it to include only 'negotiable instruments' as was done in article 3." The court also cited First National Bank in Grand Prairie v. Lone

1. Under 13 Pa. Cons. Stat.Ann. § 9203 (Purdon 1983), "a security interest is not enforceable against the debtor * * * with respect to the collateral and does not attach unless: (1) the collateral is in the possession of the secured party pursuant to agreement, or the debtor has signed a security agreement which contains a description of the collateral * * *." Since there can be absolutely no contention that Continental satisfies the first of these prerequisites, I examine its claim to the stock certificates based on a security agreement describing the collateral.

2. Were this a case where physical stock certificates were *never* issued by the corporation (rather than issued and lost), a creditor's claim to general intangibles would likely cover a debtor's equity interest in such a corporation.

3. The fact that Continental's financing statement claimed instruments is, of course, irrelevant. See Pa. Cons. Stat.Ann. § 9–203(a)(1).

Star Life Ins. Co., 524 S.W.2d 525 (Tex.Civ.App.1975), as further authority for its holding. I find these cases persuasive and see no reason to believe that the Pennsylvania courts would decide the issue differently.

A second factor that might be offered to except this case from the ordinary rule, i.e., that the creditor must assert a claim to instruments where the debtor's equity interest in another corporation is represented by stock certificates, is that these certificates were lost. The problem with this argument, however, is that there is no evidence whatsoever that anyone knew the certificates were lost (or that the certificates were indeed lost) in 1976 when the security agreement was signed. If the creditor bank genuinely thought the certificates were lost, it did not take any steps that would be consistent with such a belief, such as requesting the debtor to obtain new stock certificates.

In sum, I would hold that where a corporation issues physical stock certificates, a creditor, in order to claim a security interest in a debtor stockholder's equity interest in that corporation, must follow the UCC procedures for instruments. I also conclude that the fact that stock in Tracey Mechanical was not negotiable, and that it was lost, does not alter the conclusion that Continental lacked a security interest in these certificates.

Problem 4–9

Rebecca has a large stock portfolio at E.F. Hutton. All of the shares are in the street name and she holds no certificates in her own name. Assume:

(a) That the state of Rebecca's residence has not enacted the 1977 version of Article 8. How should the bank perfect a security interest in her stock portfolio?

(b) That the state has enacted the 1977 version of Article 8. How then does the bank perfect?

Problem 4–10

Kelly Green is the registered owner and Commercial Credit the registered pledgee of the stock of Shamrock, Inc., all the stock of which is uncertificated. If Green wishes to use his interest in Shamrock as collateral for a loan from Manufacturer's Bank, and if Manufacturer's is willing to make the loan, how can Manufacturer's "perfect" an interest in Green's uncertificated shares? If Commercial later releases its security interest, what happens to Manufacturer's "perfection."?

Problem 4–11

[Note: For purposes of this problem, assume that Ohio has and Michigan has not enacted the 1977 amendments to Article 8.]

Noah, a resident of Ohio, created Arkcraft, Inc. under the laws of Michigan. Arkcraft made and marketed boats for a national market. Arkcraft's chief executive offices were in Toledo, Ohio.

Waterfront Bank and Trust made a personal loan to Noah of $100,000, taking a "pledge" of 10% of Noah's stock in Arkcraft. Arkcraft's stock was uncertificated, and so Waterfront perfected its interest under Ohio's UCC 8–321, 8–313(1)(b) by becoming a registered pledgee of the uncertificated shares.

Six months later Noah filed for bankruptcy in the Northern District of Ohio, still owing Waterfront $100,000. The trustee seeks to set aside Waterfront's security interest as unperfected. The trustee argues that under section 8–106 in Ohio, the laws of Michigan (the state of incorporation) govern the case. Since Michigan treats uncertificated securities as general intangibles, requiring an Article 9 filing for perfection, Waterfront is unperfected.

Waterfront responds by arguing that the laws of Ohio, the location of the debtor's chief executive offices, govern the case. Since Ohio treats uncertificated securities under Article 8, and since Waterfront complied with Article 8 perfection rules, Waterfront asserts that it is properly perfected. As Judge, how do you rule?

SECTION 7. AUTOMATIC PERFECTION

UCC 9–302(1) contemplates at least six situations in which there will be automatic perfection. In most of those cases automatic perfection is granted because there is no significant prospect of a third party, and the parties very likely do not think of the transaction as a financing transaction. However two of them, namely the purchase money security interest in consumer goods under (1)(d) and the specialized security interest in (1)(b) (that incorporates UCC 9–304), do involve financing transactions and do have substantial significance.

Here for the first time the student meets the purchase money security interest. The automatic perfection in UCC 9–302(1)(d) depends on purchase money status. Purchase money status entitles a creditor to favored treatment in at least three separate settings. Under UCC 9–302(1)(d) the purchase money secured creditor is automatically perfected as to consumer goods without any filing or other act. Under UCC 9–312(3) and (4) the purchase money secured creditor enjoys priority over others who have filed prior to his filing. Under section 522(f) of the Bankruptcy Code, a purchase money secured creditor is immune from the attack that the trustee can otherwise make on certain perfected security interests.

The reasons for each of these three forms of special treatment are not necessarily identical. However, each in effect recognizes that the purchase money secured creditor is somehow superior to a conventional secured creditor. In the chapter on priority we will return to the question why should a purchase money secured creditor enjoy priority over others. Now it is enough to ask the question why such a creditor is given special treatment under UCC 9–302(1)(d) by way of automatic perfection status. Part of the basis for UCC 9–301(1)(d) is the reliance of the purchase money secured creditor. By taking a security interest in the assets sold or specifically financed by him, the creditor has in effect said, "I would not have made this loan, sold this commodity to the debtor without having a first security interest in it." In that sense he is unlike the conventional creditor who may have made an unsecured loan, and who, as times grew more perilous insisted upon a security interest as an afterthought. To some extent UCC 9–302(1)(d) may merely be a modern day equivalent of the conditional sale contract in consumer goods; it doubtless builds upon that history.

Moreover one can question the need for a filing in the case of security interests in consumer goods. Typically such goods depreciate rapidly; it would be uncommon for a *second* creditor to lend in reliance upon the value of a consumer's equity in most such items. The dollar amounts are frequently quite small. Furthermore, it would not be economic to require such secured creditors to perfect by filing. Why clutter the files at the county seats and in the state capital with such filings?

The student should read UCC 9–107 with care (the definition of a purchase money security interest). In all three areas where purchase money status is relevant the courts have had difficulty in determining how to distinguish purchase money from non-purchase money loans particularly in the setting in which the creditor takes a security interest in several assets of the debtor or makes several loans to the debtor or both. Note that UCC 9–107 requires that the purchase money lender made the loan "to enable" the debtor to acquire the asset. Can you think of settings in which the creditor might have difficulty in showing his loan enabled the debtor to acquire the asset? For one example consider the following case, a case whose facts have recurred in many jurisdictions with varying outcomes. As you read the case, consider the other alternatives that were open to the judge.

IN RE MANUEL

United States Court of Appeals, Fifth Circuit, 1975.
507 F.2d 990.

NICHOLS, ASSOCIATE JUDGE:

This case originated in the bankruptcy of James Lucius Manuel. On December 7, 1972, he purchased certain household furniture from appellant Roberts Furniture Co. On February 13, 1973, he purchased a television set, also from appellant. The purchase money security agreement he then signed referred to an unpaid balance of $573.32 from the first purchase, deducted $116.03 for refunds, leaving a prior unpaid balance of $457.29 which was added to the unpaid balance on the TV set, $174.07, making a total balance owed of $631.36. This agreement was never filed for perfection as Georgia law required, nor was perfection obtained by retaining possession. The agreement also failed to indicate the order in which purchases were paid off, and the amounts still due on each item and secured by the paid-up items. The apparent purpose of Roberts Furniture was to ensure that title to nothing passed until title to all passed. The February 13 purchase money agreement provided:

> "It is agreed that the contracts, whether one or more, heretofore entered into between Seller and Buyer, having an unpaid balance of $573.32 referred to as "prior balance" shall remain in full force and effect, that Seller's security interest in the goods sold thereunder shall remain perfected, until full payment for said goods has been made, and that the contract evidenced by this instrument shall have no effect on the above mentioned existing contract except to modify the terms of payment thereof.
>
> It is further agreed, however, that for the purposes of the payment of the said prior balance and total of payments on the contract evidenced by this instrument, that Buyer shall make one payment in the amount and for the period set forth below until the total of payments as set forth has been paid. Upon a default in the contract evidenced by this instrument the said existing contract shall also be deemed to be in default. Until all installment payments and all other amounts due hereunder, have been paid, Seller shall retain a security interest in the Goods and any and all equipment, parts, accessories, attachments, additions and other goods, and all replacements thereof, now or hereafter installed in, affixed to or used in connection with said Goods and, if Buyer sells or otherwise disposes of the Goods in violation of the terms of this agreement, in the proceeds of such sale or disposition. *Goods may secure all present and future liabilities, debts and obligations of whatever nature of BUYER to SELLER or its assigns."* (Emphasis supplied.)

Manuel filed a voluntary bankruptcy petition on May 3, 1973. Roberts Furniture claimed reclamation in bankruptcy on the basis of priority of their "Purchase Money Security Interest." The bankruptcy judge found that except for the TV set Roberts failed to acquire a Purchase Money Security Interest as defined by Georgia Code § 109A–9–107; that Roberts failed to perfect the security interest in any other manner provided by the Georgia and Uniform Commercial Codes; and that Section 70(c) of the Bankruptcy Act, 11 U.S.C. § 110, and Georgia Code § 109A–9–301(3) gave the bankruptcy trustee preference over Roberts' unperfected security interests.

The District Judge would have denied reclamation for the TV set also, except that the point was not preserved by cross appeal. Appellee now stipulates, contrary to the impression of the court below, that the combined value of all the involved merchandise is not equal to the debt owed Roberts Furniture Co. Nevertheless, we affirm.

I

* * *

The issue here is whether Georgia law would allow the arrangement below to be considered a Purchase Money Security Interest, which requires no filing for perfection. Georgia has enacted the Uniform Commercial Code. Georgia Code § 109A–9–107 defines a Purchase Money Security Interest: [court quotes 9–107] Georgia Code § 109A–9–302 provides the exceptions where filing is not required for perfection. One of the exceptions is:

* * *

(d) a purchase money security interest in consumer goods; * * *

There are other exceptions to the filing requirement, not here relevant. Otherwise, if not perfected by filing, under Georgia Code § 109A–9–301, the unperfected security interest is subordinate to the rights of "(1)(b) * * * a lien creditor * * *;" which term includes "(3) * * * a trustee in bankruptcy * * *;" unless all the creditors had actual knowledge of the security interest, which is not contended here.

Roberts Furniture claims the exception for consumer goods. As the judges below noted, citing Allen v. Lokey, 307 F.2d 353 (5th Cir.1962), and National Silver Co. v. Nichols, 205 F.2d 52 (5th Cir.1953), the burden of proof to establish a security interest is upon the party seeking reclamation, and Roberts has not met that burden. The problem here begins with the fact that the security agreement filed with the court shows about $150 paid on about a $900 total debt, for 7 pieces of furniture and a TV set, with no clues as to what items are paid for and which are not, nor does any rule of first-bought, first-paid for appear.

A plain reading of the statutory requirements would indicate that they require the purchase money security interest to be in the item purchased, and that, as the judges below noted, the purchase money security interest cannot exceed the price of what is purchased in the transaction wherein the security interest is created, if the vendor is to be protected despite the absence of filing. Except as to the TV set, if at all, the interest here is not a "purchase money security interest" because it is not taken or retained by the seller of the collateral solely to secure all or part of *its* (emphasis supplied) price. Roberts attempted to make collateral secure debt other than its own price. The statutory exception does not reach the case.

The judges below drew their conclusion on the statutory language and on authority other than Georgia cases. Appellee has collected and cited to us a number of Georgia cases, which we have examined. We have no doubt that the Georgia courts will henceforward observe the express command of their legislature, but we find it unnecessary to analyze in detail cases which show no more than that they have hitherto done so, with respect to parts of the enactment here involved, other than those to be construed here. The District Judge refers to In re Simpson, 4 U.C.C.Rep. 243 (D.C.W.D.Mich.1966). This referee in bankruptcy's opinion is well thought out, and documented with references to the Official Code Comment # 2, and to secondary authority. It was a case stronger for the vendor, than the one here, in that the farm machinery item in dispute was sold under the agreement which failed, in the referee's view, to create a purchase money security interest without filing, only because it included a clause making the item security, not only for its own price, but also for future advances. The entire discussion may be regarded as dictum since the referee ends up by holding that the vendor saved its security interest after all by recovering possession before the bankruptcy, without fraud on the creditors. In view of the wide circulation of the referee's opinion by the U.C.C. Reporting Service, the absence of contrary case authority, and its inherent reasonableness, we think our District Judge properly gave much weight to it.

The error of the belief below, that the value of the intended collateral exceeded the debt, is not fatal to the conclusion reached, though it does impair some of the reasoning, and prevents us from adopting the opinion below as our own.

We express no view as to whether a valid purchase money security interest was created with respect to the TV set. Nothing we say is to be taken as a holding as to that.

Affirmed.

Notes

1. How is the TV set distinguished from the other assets?

2. If the security agreement had contained a fifo clause, would that have cured the problem (that is, the first payments would first go to pay off the first item until it was free of the security interest; later payments for the next item, and so on, so that with the end payment for a particular item it would be freed from the security interest)?

Problem 4–12

Your client, Bank One, buys paper from a variety of consumer lenders. Often each document covers several items sold as in the *Manuel* case. The client has said that it is economically infeasible to write separate security agreements on each transaction, and asks whether the problem can be dealt with in some other way. What do you suggest?

Problem 4–13

Bank writes a letter of credit for its customer, Local Purchaser. The beneficiary is Swedish seller. In accordance with the agreement with customer, Bank has a security interest in the document and goods that are to be delivered under the letter of credit in return for its promise to pay against those documents. After the bank pays, it gives its customer the bills of lading to enable the customer to get possession of the goods. Unfortunately, a week after it has given the bills of lading to the customer and before the goods have arrived, the customer files a petition in Chapter 11. Does the bank have a right to the goods when they arrive or do the goods go into the bankruptcy estate, leaving the bank as an unperfected secured creditor?

What if the bank failed to take any action for three weeks after the bankruptcy petition had been filed?

SECTION 8. MULTIPLE STATE TRANSACTIONS, INCLUDING THE SPECIAL CASE OF THE AUTOMOBILE

When collateral is located in more than one state, or when the debtor has some association with more than one state, or when the collateral is moved or to be moved, the creditor must think of the law of several states to determine how to perfect a security interest. UCC 9–103 answers most of these questions. Note that it calls for perfection at the place where the goods are located for the most part, but it then gives a grace period if the goods are moved to another state. In certain circumstances (where the goods have no fixed situs), UCC 9–103 calls for perfection at the "location" of the debtor, itself sometimes uncertain.

IN RE KEN GARDNER FORD SALES, INC.

United States Bankruptcy Court, Eastern District Tennessee 1984.
41 B.R. 105.

RALPH H. KELLEY, BANKRUPTCY JUDGE.

The plaintiffs sued American National Bank and the bankruptcy trustee for Ken Gardner Ford Sales to recover damages for conversion. The plaintiffs alleged that they had a security interest in car parts and used cars owned by a Ford dealership in South Carolina, that the parts and used cars were transferred to the debtor, Ken Gardner Ford Sales, that the plaintiffs' security interest continued and was perfected at the time of the debtor's bankruptcy, and that the trustee abandoned the collateral to another secured creditor, American National Bank, which sold the collateral.

* * *

The question before the court is whether the plaintiffs had a valid, first priority security interest in the parts. The plaintiffs introduced security agreements as proof that they had a security interest in the inventory, including car parts, belonging to the South Carolina dealership. The security interest was perfected by the filing of a financing statement in South Carolina on May 14, 1979.

The car parts in question were transferred to the debtor in Tennessee during February and March, 1980. The debtor filed its petition in bankruptcy on March 28, 1980.

American National Bank had a security interest in the debtor's inventory, including car parts. The security interest was perfected in the parts in question when the debtor acquired them.

The plaintiffs contend that their security interest in the parts was perfected in Tennessee at the time of the debtor's bankruptcy and was superior to the rights of the trustee and the bank. The plaintiffs rely on Uniform Commercial Code (UCC) § 9–103(3), as enacted in Tennessee. Tenn Code Ann § 47–9–103. The relevant part provides:

> "If the security interest was already perfected under the law of the jurisdiction where the property was when the security interest attached and before being brought into this state, the security interest continues perfected in this state for four (4) months and also thereafter if within the four-month period it is perfected in this state. The security interest may also be perfected after expiration of the four-month period; in such case perfection dates from the time of perfection in this state."

For collateral such as car parts, Tennessee law requires filing of a financing statement to perfect security interest in Tennessee. The problem is determining whether the "automatic" perfection during the four months after arrival of the collateral is conditional on perfecting in Tennessee during the four months.

The early decisions heavily favored *absolute* perfection during the four months. Under the absolute perfection rule, the security interest is treated as perfected forever as to any interest acquired in the four months. The later decisions have split, with some favoring *conditional* perfection. Under the conditional perfection rule, the security interest becomes unperfected during the four months if not re-perfected during that time in the state to which the collateral was moved. J. White & R. Summers, Handbook of the Law Under the Uniform Commercial Code § 23–18 at 975 (2d ed. 1980).

Consider application of the different rules to the facts of this case. Under the absolute perfection rule, it would make no difference that the plaintiffs did not perfect their security interest in Tennessee by filing a financing statement during the four months after the collateral came into Tennessee. The plaintiffs' security interest would be automatically perfected for four months and would have priority over the defendants' interests, since they were acquired during the four months. Under the conditional perfection rule, the plaintiffs' security interest would be treated as unperfected in Tennessee during the four-month grace period because the plaintiffs failed to file a financing statement during the four months.

The language of the statute appears to establish the absolute perfection rule, but Official Comment 7 explains the statute as providing for conditional perfection during the four months.

> "The four month period is long enough for a secured party to discover in most cases that the collateral has been removed and to file in this state; thereafter, if he has not done so, his interest, although originally perfected in the state where it attached, is subject to defeat by those persons who take priority over an unperfected security interest * * *. Under § 9–312(5) the holder of a perfected security interest is such a person even though during the four month period the conflicting interest was junior. Compare the situation arising under § 9–403(2) when a filing lapses."

Not surprisingly, § 9–403(2) also appears to adopt an absolute perfection rule but Official Comment 3 says that it provides only for conditional perfection.

Despite the apparent inconsistency, the court is of the opinion that a careful analysis of § 9–103(3) supports the rule that automatic perfection is conditional on perfection in Tennessee during the four month grace period.

The statute provides that if the security interest is not perfected in Tennessee until after the four months then perfection in Tennessee dates from the time of perfection. This obviously means that the security interest was not previously perfected in Tennessee, even during the "automatic" perfection period of four months. For example, if a financing statement is filed after the four months, then perfection dates from the time of filing and not earlier. This leads to the conclusion that automatic perfection during the four months is dependent on perfection in Tennessee by filing during the four months.

The other alternative is the nonsensical conclusion that a secured creditor who perfects in Tennessee after the four months will lose perfection against an interest arising during the four months but a secured creditor who never perfects in Tennessee will prevail.

The effect of perfection after the four months has also been explained in terms of whether perfection relates back to an earlier time. The problem is with rights acquired in the gap after the collateral arrives in Tennessee and before the security interest is perfected by performing any additional acts, such as filing, required for perfection in Tennessee. It has been said that perfection after the four months does not relate back to arrival of the goods and therefore does not protect the security interest from other interests arising in the gap. This again leads to the conclusion that filing during the four months is required so that perfection will relate back to the arrival of the collateral in Tennessee.

Moreover, the wording of the statute makes more sense if it provides for conditional perfection during the four months. When filing in Tennessee is required for perfection, the problem is with rights acquired in the gap between arrival of the collateral and filing. There is no problem with rights acquired after filing. Nevertheless the absolute perfection rule treats perfection during the four months as a condition only to perfection thereafter. G. Gilmore, Security Interests in Personal Property § 22.8 at 626–627 (1965). The statute is read as follows:

> "The security interest continues perfected in this state for four (4) months without filing and continues perfected after filing during the four months."

Of course the security interest continues perfected after perfection by filing during the four months. This is so obvious that the statute need not have said it. The statute makes more sense if read as follows:

> "[T]he security interest continues perfected in this state for four (4) months * * * if within the four-month period it is perfected in this state."

Thus, perfection within the four months is not only a condition to the obvious—perfection after perfection—but also a condition to perfection in the gap after removal of the goods and before perfection.

The well-known commentators on the UCC have disagreed on the issue of whether § 9–103(3) establishes conditional or absolute perfection for the four months after removal of the collateral to another state. G. Gilmore, Security Interests in Personal Property § 22.8 at 626–627; J. White & R. Summers, Handbook of the Law Under the Uniform Commercial Code § 23–18 at 848–850 (1st ed. 1972). The court agrees with Professors White and Summers, who favored the conditional perfection rule.

The 1972 version of the UCC has not been adopted in Tennessee, but the changes in § 9–103 indicate what the drafters intended in the version of § 9–103(3) in question. The 1972 version of § 9–103 adopts a conditional perfection rule as to "purchasers" during the four month period. UCC § 1–201(32) & (33). In a situation like this, the bank as a purchaser could prevail but not the trustee as a judgment lien creditor. J. White and R. Summers, Handbook of the Law Under the Uniform Commercial Code § 23–18 at 974–976 (2d ed. 1980).

* * *

More troubling is a decision by the Tennessee Court of Appeals. First Bristol County National Bank v. Shirley, 11 UCC Rep.Serv. 378 (Tenn.App.1972). The court treated the case as one in which the collateral, a car, was moved from Rhode Island to Tennessee without the secured party's consent. The court then ruled in the secured party's favor, apparently on the ground that the collateral had been brought to Tennessee without the secured party's consent.

Despite the court's reasoning that consent controlled, the court discussed the operation of § 9–103(3). The court said:

> "In at least two other states (New Jersey and Connecticut) the appellate courts have held that where an automobile subject to a conditional sale contract

made in one state and properly recorded therein, was moved to another state, the party who bought such automobile from the conditional buyer within four months of its removal took title subject to the interest of the conditional seller even though the seller did not file such conditional sale contract within the four month period in the state to which the automobile was removed without the seller's consent." 11 UCC Rep.Serv. 381.

The court thus seems to have reached the conclusion that a security interest is absolutely perfected in Tennessee for four months. The court of appeals decision is doubtful authority since it was not officially reported. It is a good indicator of what the law is in Tennessee but is not precedent binding on a federal court applying Tennessee law. Wright, Miller & Cooper, Federal Practice & Procedure, Jurisdiction § 4507 (1982).

The Tennessee Supreme Court has also ruled in favor of a secured party who did not consent to removal of its collateral to Tennessee. Ford Motor Credit Co. v. Quality Motors, 541 S.W.2d 119 (Tenn.1976). In that case, the debtor bought the car in Arkansas, a certificate of title state. A title certificate was issued showing the plaintiff as the first lienholder. The debtor took the car to Alabama, a non-title state, and obtained a receipt showing no liens. The debtor then sold the car to the defendant in Tennessee. The court held that the defendant took the car subject to the plaintiff's lien because the plaintiff had not consented to removal of the car from Arkansas.

The court could have reached the same conclusion under UCC § 9–103(4), without regard to whether the plaintiff consented to removal of the car from Arkansas.

The court, however, only mentioned the UCC. After summarizing the consent rule, the court said, "We find nothing in the Uniform Commercial Code that changes this rule of law." 541 S.W.2d 121.

It is hard to believe the court had the four-month rule of § 9–103(3) in mind when it said this. Section 9–103(3) does not make the four-month rule applicable only when the secured party consents to removal of the goods. Indeed, the four-month rule does not entirely make sense if it applies only when the secured party consents to removal of the goods. Why should the secured party who knows the goods are being moved to another state and consents to the move be given four months to perfect in the new state? This is especially troublesome if the four months is four months of absolute perfection. The official comment, quoted earlier, also implies that the secured party's consent is irrelevant. The comment says that the secured party is given four months to "discover" the removal of the collateral and take whatever additional steps are required for perfection in the new location. Professor Gilmore pointed out that consent or notice were meant to be irrelevant under § 9–103(3).

> "Section 9–103(3) establishes a four-month period, after which, unless there has been reperfection, a perfected out-of-state interest becomes unperfected. This rule applies whether the removal was with the secured party's consent or was unauthorized; it applies whether the secured party has notice of the removal or does not have notice (departing in this respect from the policy of § 14 of the Uniform Conditional Sales Act)." G. Gilmore, Security Interests in Personal Property § 22.8 at 626 (1965).

Section 9–103(3) says when a security interest in incoming goods becomes unperfected. The court does not see how a security interest unperfected under the statute can be treated as perfected because the secured party did not consent to removal of the goods to Tennessee, at least in cases where no actual fraud was involved in removal of the goods.

* * *

The court thinks that the plaintiffs had plenty of time from February and March, 1980, until the trustee disposed of the parts in September, 1980 to discover the removal of the parts to Tennessee and assert their interest. The plaintiffs knew that the Tennessee dealership was a related corporation to the South Carolina dealership. In the summer of 1980 Mr. Williams knew the Tennessee dealership was in bankruptcy but seems never to have inquired specifically whether it had received the inventory from the closed South Carolina dealership.

The official comments to § 9–103 are not part of the statute but are probably consistent in their use of UCC terminology. In this respect, the use of "discover" in the official comment was probably intentional. "Discover" means to acquire actual knowledge of fact, as distinguished from "reason to know," which means learning other facts that should lead to the conclusion that the fact in question exists. Tenn.Code Ann. 47–1–201(25).

* * *

The court has already concluded that statutory construction favors the conditional perfection interpretation of § 9–103(3). It should also be adopted for practical reasons.

Consider the common situation in which goods are brought into Tennessee and Tennessee law requires some additional step, such as filing, to perfect a security interest in the goods. Under either the absolute perfection rule or the conditional perfection rule, there is a four-month danger period. Any interest acquired in the four months may be subordinate to a security interest perfected in another state. Under the conditional perfection rule, this danger ceases after four months if the security interest has not been perfected in Tennessee. This may seem unfair if the debtor brings the goods into Tennessee, waits four months, and then sells them. The debtor can deprive the secured party of its collateral against its will. The secured party, however, has four months to discover that the debtor has moved the collateral and to perfect in the new state or to repossess if moving the collateral was a default. Four months is ample time especially since § 9–103(3) is meant to apply to many other situations. The debtor may not have brought the goods into Tennessee. The debtor may have transferred the goods to a third party who brought them into Tennessee. The goods may have been transferred several times within the four months. See Arrow Ford, Inc. v. Western Landscape Construction Co., 23 Ariz.App. 281, 582 P.2d 553 (1975). The question is how long should the security interest be perfected against intervening parties without notice when perfection is required as a means of giving notice. The court is of the opinion that, in the absence of adoption of the 1972 version of § 9–103, the conditional perfection rule better serves the interests of fairness and commerce and would be adopted by the Tennessee Supreme Court as the better rule.

Since the plaintiffs failed to file a financing statement in Tennessee during the four months, their security interest became unperfected as to the trustee and the bank, unless their rights against the plaintiffs were somehow frozen at the time of bankruptcy.

The general rule is that the rights of the parties in the debtor's property are determined as of the time of bankruptcy. 4 Collier on Bankruptcy ¶ 541.04 (15th ed. 1983). The statutes, however, allow a security interest in the debtor's property to be perfected after bankruptcy when state law allows such perfection to relate back to an earlier date so that the security interest will be treated as perfected at the time of the debtor's bankruptcy. 11 U.S.C. §§ 547(b) & 362(b)(3). This obviously means that perfection of a security interest is not fixed at the time of bankruptcy if perfection is conditional on performing some later action to make the perfection relate back.

The result is that the plaintiffs' security interest became unperfected against the trustee because of the plaintiffs' failure to file a financing statement within four months after the parts arrived in Tennessee.

The plaintiffs also failed to assert their security interest against the trustee during the four months. It is not sufficient that the trustee could have or may have discovered the security interest during the four months.

The trustee abandoned the bankruptcy estate's interest in the parts and the debtor allowed the bank to repossess. The bank took the parts and sold them at auction. However, under an agreement with the trustee, the bank returned the proceeds of the sale after it later collected the proceeds of life insurance on Ken Gardner, Sr.

The trustee's rights in the parts and the proceeds from their sale were superior to the plaintiffs' unperfected security interest. 11 U.S.C. § 544; Tenn. Code Ann. § 47–9–301(1)(b). The trustee was entitled to keep the parts and all the sale proceeds for the benefit of the bankruptcy estate to the exclusion of the plaintiffs' rights. 11 U.S.C. § 550. Since this was the ultimate outcome, the plaintiffs were not harmed by the disposition of the parts and cannot recover.

Apparently the bank's security interest also became superior to the plaintiffs' security interest. Thus, the bank and the trustee both had rights superior to the plaintiffs' security interest. If the bank had been allowed to foreclose and the sale proceeds had exceeded its secured debt, the trustee, not the plaintiffs, would have been entitled to the excess. Thus, no matter how the facts are viewed, the plaintiffs cannot recover.

* * *

Accordingly, the court will enter judgment for the defendants.

This memorandum constitutes findings of fact and conclusions of law. Bankruptcy Rule 7052.

Note

Had the 1972 version of Article 9 been in effect in Tennessee, would the South Carolina creditor have won? Consider not just UCC 9–103, but also Part 4 of Article 9. Is a judicial lien creditor a "purchaser" as that term is used in UCC 1–201(33) and (32)?

Problem 4–14

The Dandy Printing Company has its principal place of business in New Mexico. First Bank loaned Dandy $100,000 for general expansion and, among other things, created and perfected (in New Mexico) a security interest in equipment, existing and after-acquired. Thereafter, Dandy entered into two transactions. First, Dandy contracted to purchase a book binding machine from a manufacturer in California for $50,000. When the machine was ready, Dandy sent its truck to California and brought the machine directly back to New Mexico. Five days after the machine was installed in Dandy's plant (you may assume that it is not a fixture), the manufacturer perfected a purchase money security interest in the machine by an appropriate filing in California. A month later the manufacturer filed a financing statement in Santa Fe. Second, Dandy purchased for cash in New Mexico ten aluminum containers for the shipment of books. Thereafter, the containers were transported to a branch office in Colorado where inventory was stockpiled to be shipped all over the country. Shortly thereafter Dandy borrowed $25,000 from Second Bank in Colorado for general purposes and, among other things, permitted Second Bank to create and perfect a security interest in the containers. It is now six months later and no further action has been taken by any of the parties to these transactions. Are either of these security interests effective?

Note: Motor Vehicles, A Special Case

The certificate of title laws that now exist in all of the states in some form provide a mode of perfection that was in use in many states at the time of enactment of the Code, and which is entirely separate from the Code system of perfection. The drafters of Article 9 bowed to the certificate of title mode of perfection by adopting section UCC 9–302(3). That subsection in effect removes perfection as to most motor vehicles from the Article 9 filing system. In many states it was formerly possible and in some states, it may still be possible, to perfect certain security interests in titled vehicles under the UCC. Certificate of title legislation that allowed for optional perfection in certain cases under the UCC was known as an "incomplete" act whereas those that required certificate of title perfection were referred to as "complete" certificate of title acts. The trend has been toward complete title acts and away from incomplete ones.

This removal from Article 9 has left a few jagged edges. For example, it was not always clear whether a creditor could perfect a security interest in automobiles held by a dealer in inventory by a UCC filing or whether it was necessary to procure a certificate of title and get one's name on that certificate. That was particularly true in the case of used cars where a certificate would be outstanding (typically none would be outstanding with respect to a new car until its first sale). In section 9–302(3) the 1972 Code made it clear that an inventory financer of autos must perfect pursuant to Article 9 and nothing is required of such a party under certificate of title perfection rules.

Yet more clearly within Article 9 are the rules concerning the state of perfection and the continuation or not of perfection when an automobile is moved from one state to another or when the residence of the debtor changes. At least with respect to the continued perfection of the security interest section 9–103(2) gives most, if not all, of the answers. One should first read section 9–103(2) and *In re Nunley* with care and then answer the problems that follow.

IN RE NUNLEY

United States Bankruptcy Court, Eastern District Tennessee, 1982.
21 B.R. 826.

CLIVE W. BARE, BANKRUPTCY JUDGE.

I

The dispute in this case between the plaintiff, Associates Commercial Corporation, and the defendants, the debtors [1] and their trustee, involves a 1979 Freightliner tractor truck. The plaintiff contends that it is the holder of a perfected security interest against the vehicle in question, whereas the trustee alleges that the security interest of the plaintiff is unperfected. The issue is

1. A default judgment has been entered against the debtors.

whether or not the trustee may defeat the security interest of the plaintiff on the basis that: (i) the vehicle was *registered* in a jurisdiction other than the jurisdiction which *issued* the certificate of title for the vehicle; (ii) no action was taken by the plaintiff secured creditor within the four-month period following removal, subsequent to the change of residence by the debtors from one jurisdiction to another and the concomitant removal of the vehicle into the jurisdiction of the debtor's new residence. See Va Code § 8.9–103(2), infra.

The parties are in agreement as to the following facts:

Earl Franklin Nunley purchased a 1979 Freightliner tractor truck, serial number CA213HL171013, on July 30, 1980, from Atlanta Freightliner Truck Sales and Service, Inc., Atlanta, Ga. A security agreement was executed by Nunley and assigned to Associates Commercial Corporation. Nunley had knowledge of this assignment as evidenced by the fact that he submitted monthly installment payments to Associates through their Georgia offices for a period of more than one year beginning in September of 1980. Associates forwarded the necessary documentation to the appropriate office in the Commonwealth of Virginia, which was the state of Nunley's residence when the tractor truck was purchased, for the purpose of obtaining a certificate of title reflecting the existence of Associate's first lien. (Nunley is a truck driver who leases his services to various carriers. His work requires that he drive his truck through many of the contiguous states.) A Virginia title certificate was issued on September 5, 1980, but the title certificate contained an erroneous serial number. (The serial number which appears on the certificate of title is CA21*4*HL171013. The correct serial number is CA21*3*HL171013.)

When Nunley purchased the vehicle in question, he was employed by Watkins Motor Lines, which informed him that he would have to register the tractor truck in either Florida or Georgia. A Florida Vehicle Registration Certificate bearing the correct serial number of the truck was issued on November 10, 1980. This registration expired on June 30, 1981.

In February of 1981, Nunley entered into a contract for the lease of his tractor truck and services with the Interstate Contract Carrier Corporation. His new employer informed him that he would be required to register his truck in either Illinois, Oklahoma or Utah. The debtor chose Oklahoma, and an Oklahoma registration was issued on May 11, 1981. The tractor truck was proportionally registered between the state of Oklahoma and 25 other states, including Tennessee and Virginia.

The debtors were residents of Virginia until August 5, 1981, when they moved to Tennessee. Associates was directly informed by Nunley of his change of residence. The debtors filed their chapter 7 bankruptcy petition on December 14, 1981, which was more than 120 days after their change of residence from Virginia to Tennessee.

The only action taken by Associates to perfect its security interest was the procurement of the Virginia certificate of title reflecting its first lien claim. Neither Associates nor Nunley sought issuance of a new title from any state in which the vehicle was reregistered and no state other than Virginia has issued a certificate of title covering the vehicle.

II

The plaintiff filed a complaint seeking relief from the automatic stay of 11 U.S.C.A. § 362 on February 9, 1982. The plaintiff alleged that: (1) the debtor had monetarily defaulted on a conditional sales contract assigned to the plaintiff;

(2) plaintiff has a validly perfected security interest in a Freightliner tractor truck, the fair market value of which was less than the unpaid secured debt; (3) physical damage insurance on the security vehicle had been cancelled and the vehicle had been abandoned.

In his answer, the trustee denied that the plaintiff had a validly perfected security interest. The trustee alleged that the title certificate was ineffective since there was a variance between the actual serial number of the vehicle and the serial number reflected on the title certificate.[2] Additionally, the trustee alleged that "the subject vehicle was subsequently reregistered in the states of Florida and Oklahoma so as to require the proper notation in the respective states by the plaintiff in order to maintain the claim of a perfected security interest." [3]

The trustee takes the position that Virginia law is applicable in determining the outcome of this case. The trustee further believes that the outcome is to be determined by application of Va.Code § 8.9–103(2), which provides in apposite part:

> "(2) Certificate of title.
>
> "(a) This subsection applies to goods covered by a certificate of title issued under a statute of this state or of another jurisdiction under the law of which indication of a security interest on the certificate is required as a condition of perfection.
>
> "(b) Except as otherwise provided in this subsection, perfection and the effect of perfection or non-perfection of the security interest are governed by the law (including the conflict of laws rules) of the jurisdiction issuing the certificate until four months after the goods are removed from that jurisdiction and *thereafter until* the goods are *registered in another jurisdiction,* but in any event not beyond surrender of the certificate. After the expiration of that period, the goods are not covered by the certificate of title within the meaning of this section." (Emphasis added.)

The defendant trustee asserts that the reregistration in Florida and Oklahoma, which *preceded* the debtor's change of residence, coupled with the passage of more than 120 days from the date on which the debtors moved from Virginia to Tennessee and the accompanying removal of the collateral, cut off the perfected lien of the plaintiff, absent the issuance of a new title certificate in Tennessee within the four-month statutory period.

The plaintiff-lender, Associates, presents a tripartite argument. Initially, the plaintiff takes the position that the Virginia certificate of title serves to perfect its security interest and that "the debtors' multiple, nonresident registration of the truck" and subsequent move to Tennessee are inconsequential with regard to the perfection of the plaintiff's security interest in the tractor truck. Secondly, the plaintiff argues that Va.Code § 8.9–103(2) is inapplicable to the instant facts since: (a) the motor vehicle in question was removed from as opposed to being brought into Virginia; (b) Va.Code § 8.9–302(4) provides that duration of a perfected security interest is governed by Va.Code § 46.1–68

2. In their briefs, the parties did not address the issue of the mistake in the serial number shown in the certificate of title. However, a single digit error in a financing statement, absent prejudice, is harmless.

* * *

3. By agreement of the parties, the vehicle has been sold by the trustee for $29,000.00, which was the highest bid at an advertised sale. The bid price, less expenses, has been paid by the plaintiff and deposited in an escrow account of the trustee pursuant to an order of the court.

through § 46.1–98.1. Finally, the plaintiff asserts that the perfection of its security interest in the tractor truck is continued even if Va.Code § 8.9–103(2) is controlling.

III

The starting point to resolve this conflict is T.C.A. § 47–9–103. Subsection (2) thereof provides in part:

"(2) If the chief place of business of a debtor is in this state, this chapter governs the validity and perfection of a security interest and the possibility and effect of proper filing with regard to general intangibles or with regard to goods of a type which are normally used in more than one (1) jurisdiction (such as automotive equipment, rolling stock, airplanes, road building equipment, commercial harvesting equipment, construction machinery and the like) if such goods are classified as equipment or classified as inventory by reason of their being leased by the debtor to others. Otherwise, the law (including the conflict of laws rules) of the jurisdiction where such chief place of business is located shall govern. If the chief place of business is located in a jurisdiction which does not provide for perfection of the security interest by filing or recording in that jurisdiction, then the security interest may be perfected by filing in this state."

The chief place of business of the secured debtor is in Tennessee. Consequently, the provisions of T.C.A. § 47–9–101 et seq. are apposite.

T.C.A. § 47–9–103(4) provides that:

"Notwithstanding subsections (2) and (3), if personal property is covered by a certificate of title issued under a statute of this state or any other jurisdiction which requires indication on a certificate of title of any security interest in the property as a condition of perfection, then the perfection is governed by the law of the jurisdiction which *issued* the certificate." (Emphasis added.)

Consequently, since Virginia does require indication on a certificate of title of any security interest in a motor vehicle, the laws of the Commonwealth of Virginia are applicable in this case. (The parties do not dispute this conclusion.)

Va.Code § 8.9–302 provides in pertinent part:

"(3) The filing of a financing statement otherwise required by this Article is not necessary or effective to perfect a security interest in property subject to

* * *

"(b) the following statutes of this state; §§ 46.1–68 through 46.1–98.1.

* * *

"(4) Compliance with a statute or treaty described in subsection (3) is equivalent to the filing of a financing statement under this title, and a security interest in property subject to the statute or treaty can be perfected only by compliance therewith except as provided in section 8.9–103 on multiple state transactions. *Duration and renewal of perfection of a security interest perfected by compliance with the statute or treaty are governed by the provisions of the statute* or treaty; in other respects the security interest is subject to this title." (Emphasis added.)

The continuity and duration of the perfection of the security interest of Associates against the tractor truck is governed by Va Code § 46.1–68 et seq., unless Va Code § 8.9–103 is applicable.

The facts in the instant case are similar but not identical to the facts in a recent Sixth Circuit Court of Appeals decision. Uhle v. Parts and Trucks (In re Paige), 679 F.2d 601 (6th Cir. May 26, 1982) involved a debtor, a Michigan resident, who purchased a truck tractor in Indiana. A purchase money security agreement executed by the debtor was assigned to Associates Commercial

Corporation, who is also the assignee of the security agreement involved in the subject dispute. The debtor drove as an interstate hauler for a company whose terminal was in Indiana and whose home office was in Minnesota. However, the debtor's employer also had a business office in Illinois. An agent of debtor's employer prepared an application for an Illinois certificate of title, which was subsequently issued. The certificate of title reflected the security interest of Associates. No financing statement was filed and no other certificate of title had been sought when Paige, the debtor, filed bankruptcy.

The Bankruptcy Court (Judge Nims) held that the security interest of Associates, although noted on the Illinois title certificate, was unperfected under Michigan law and invalid vis-à-vis the bankruptcy trustee. In re Paige, 3 B.R. 115 (Bankr. W.D.Mich.1980). The district court affirmed Judge Nims' holding in an unpublished order.

The court of appeals noted that the issue was simply whether or not the notation of the lien on the Illinois certificate of title served to perfect the security interest under Michigan law. The court of appeals concluded that Judge Nims erred in his interpretation of Mich.Stat.Ann. § 19.9103(4); M.C.L.A. § 440.9103(4), which is identical to T.C.A. § 47–9–103(4), quoted heretofore. The court of appeals based its conclusion on a literal reading of UCC § 9–103(4), which clearly provides that perfection is to be governed by the law of the certificating state if that state requires notation of a security interest on a certificate of title as a condition of perfection. The court noted that Illinois does require such a notation on a certificate of title and found Illinois law applicable, which meant that the security interest of Associates was properly perfected *vis-à-vis* the trustee.

In Paige, as in the instant case, the certificating state had adopted the 1972 version of the UCC. The respective destination states, Michigan and Tennessee, each have the 1962 version of the UCC as the source of law for commercial transactions. The only distinguishing fact which may be material is that there is no report of any registration in any state other than Illinois in the Paige case, whereas there were multiple registrations in the instant case, all of which *preceded* the removal of the vehicle from Virginia to Tennessee. This factor does not, in this court's opinion, preclude the application of the Paige decision to determine the outcome of the instant case.

The trustee cites Patti v. Barnett Bank (In re Hartberg), (Bankr. E.D.Wis. 1979), in support of his position that the Associates' security interest is unperfected in the subject case. The debtors in Hartberg had purchased a vehicle in November of 1976, while residing in Florida. A security agreement was executed by the debtors in favor of Barnett Bank, and a Florida certificate of title was issued on December 10, 1976. The certificate of title, which reflected the security interest of the bank, was retained by Barnett Bank. In September of 1977, the debtors established a residence in Wisconsin, where the security automobile was registered on December 3, 1977. No certificate of title was issued by the State of Wisconsin. The debtors filed bankruptcy on July 3, 1978, which was 3 months after the debtors stopped making payments to Barnett Bank.

The bankruptcy trustee contended that the lien was never perfected in Wisconsin. Judge Hilgendorf agreed with the bankruptcy trustee. The holding of the case is that a secured creditor whose interest is noted on a certificate of title must take action within 4 months from the date of removal to continue the perfection of his interest in a motor vehicle which is removed from the certificating jurisdiction and *registered* in another jurisdiction.

The plaintiff does note in its brief, based on the following quotation from Hartberg, that the decision might have been different if the case had been decided under the provisions of the 1962 Code:

> "The original 1962 version of the Uniform Commercial Code relating to motor vehicles was substantially different from the 1972 official text which was adopted in Wisconsin in 1973. The 1962 Code was interpreted by most courts to grant priority to a lien holder whose lien was perfected by indication on the certificate of title regardless of where the automobile may have been taken and regardless of the period of time it remained in another jurisdiction." Hartberg, 25 UCC Rep.Serv. at 1432.

It is arguable that the decision in Hartberg is incorrect. The district court in the case of Strick Corp. v. Eldo-Craft Boat Co., Inc., 479 F.Supp. 720 (W.D.Ark. 1979) interpreted "registered," as that term is employed in UCC § 9–103(2), to require the procurement of a certificate of title. The court noted:

> It is the opinion of this court that the section just quoted (UCC § 9–103(2)) continues in force the perfection of a security interest noted on a foreign certificate of title until a certificate has been issued by another jurisdiction." Strick, 479 F.Supp. at 725.

A more "customary" interpretation of registration is found in the district court's opinion in the case of In re Howard, 9 B.R. 957 (N.D.N.Y.1981). The bankrupt had purchased a truck in November of 1978 from a Massachusetts dealer. The security interest of GMAC was duly noted on the Massachusetts title certificate. In January of 1979, the bankrupt moved from Massachusetts to New York. The security vehicle was registered in New York in July of 1979, but no title certificate was issued in conjunction with the registration. In a contest between GMAC, the secured creditor, and the bankruptcy trustee, the district court affirmed the decision of the bankruptcy court that the GMAC security interest was unperfected. The decision was based on the "plain language" of UCC § 9–103(2)(b) and the fact that the debtor's truck was reregistered in New York more than 4 months after its removal from Massachusetts.

This court's decision is governed by the Sixth Circuit's decision in Paige. The holding in Paige is that the perfection of a security interest in a motor vehicle which is brought into a jurisdiction which has adopted the 1962 version of the Uniform Commercial Code continues if the certificating state requires indication of the security interest on the certificate of title as a condition of perfection and the security interest is perfected in the jurisdiction which issued the certificate of title. Applying the holding of Paige to the instant facts, the court finds that the security interest of Associates is perfected by virtue of the Virginia certificate of title and that the interest is not unperfected as a result of the removal of the vehicle from Virginia to Tennessee. The statute under scrutiny herein, Va.Code § 8.9–103(2)(b) provides that:

> "[p]erfection and the effect of perfection or non-perfection of the security interest are governed by the law * * * of the jurisdiction issuing the certificate until four months after the goods are removed from that jurisdiction *and thereafter until the goods are registered in another jurisdiction.* * * *" (Emphasis added.)

There was in fact no registration of the vehicle in another jurisdiction *after* removal from Virginia to Tennessee. If there had been, the court would have been confronted with a different question. Since perfection of the interest of

Associates is governed by the law of Virginia, the certificating state, that interest remains perfected because the Virginia certificate of title is valid and unsurrendered.

This Memorandum constitutes findings of fact and conclusions of law, Bankruptcy Rule 752.

Submit judgment. [One footnote omitted.]

Notes

1. What did the drafters intend with respect to a truck that was "registered" in many states?

2. The first sentence in UCC 9–103(2)(b) is one of the most complex in the entire Uniform Commercial Code. Read it with care. Both the *Nunley* case and the problem that follows should give the student some understanding of its meaning.

Problem 4–15

In which of the following cases has the creditor become unsecured?

1. Debtor procures a certificate of title in Ohio, and lists secured creditor's name on it. Debtor moves to Pennsylvania and resides there for two years. Debtor retains his Ohio registration and certificate. At the end of two years, is debtor still perfected?

2. Assume in the foregoing example that the debtor procured a new certificate of title and relinquished his old one in Pennsylvania one week after he arrived there. Creditor discovers this and seeks to repossess the car 30 days after it has been removed from Ohio. Is the creditor unperfected?

3. Debtor buys a Porsche 928 for $45,000. Debtor pays $20,000 down and borrows $25,000 from Bank One in Columbus. Bank One properly perfects by getting its name noted on the certificate of title. Shortly after the car is purchased it is stolen off the street one night in Columbus. Five months later the car turns up in Birmingham, Alabama in the hands of a local doctor who claims to be a bona fide purchaser. The doctor displays an apparently clean Alabama certificate of title which was issued to him after he purchased the car from a used car dealer in Birmingham. It appears that the thief somehow procured a false or fraudulent clean certificate of title in Alabama and then sold the automobile under that title to the used car dealer. Assume that the car is now worth $27,000, that Bank One's debt still stands at $24,000 and that the Birmingham bona fide purchaser paid $30,000 for the car. Who gets what parts of the car among the Ohio owner, the Ohio Bank, and the Alabama purchaser? Is only a part of the answer provided by UCC 9–103? Assume that Bank One still has possession of the Ohio certificate of title.

Problem 4–16

Boscoe purchased a new car for $35,000 from Slick Motors. A certificate of title, duly noting Slick's security interest, was issued by State A where Boscoe resided. Six months later the car was stolen, taken to State B and, after some skillful fraud by the thief, a "clean" certificate of title was issued by State B. Shortly thereafter, the thief sold the car to Hume, a BFP, and delivered the clean certificate of title.

1. Assuming that State B has both the Uniform Act and the 1972 Official Text, what is the effect of this last transaction on the title of Boscoe and the security interest of Slick?

2. What provisions and procedures in the Uniform Act are designed to prevent the issuance of fraudulent certificates? If the state has in fact issued the fraudulent,

but "clean" certificate, why shouldn't those who rely in good faith and pay value receive full protection?

SECTION 9. PERFECTION IN PROCEEDS

In the previous chapter we considered the nature of proceeds, how and in what circumstances a security interest attaches to proceeds and what "identifiable" proceeds are. Once one has resolved those issues, the questions of perfection are relatively clear, if somewhat complex. Here the student must read UCC 9–306(3) with care. Beware, it is easy to misread that subsection, particularly (3)(a). Consider the following problem.

Problem 4–17

In which of the following cases will Bank have a perfected security interest in the proceeds? In which cases will additional acts be required in order to continue its perfection?

1. Bank makes a secured loan to local corporation and files a financing statement covering inventory. It mentions neither "proceeds" nor any of the items such as accounts or chattel paper. When inventory is sold, it produces cash, accounts receivable, and in some cases, chattel paper.

2. Assume that debtor retail merchant is a division of a larger corporation whose chief executive office is in another state. Now the Bank will be unperfected as to the accounts and chattel paper. True?

3. Assume now that the debtor uses some of the cash to purchase new inventory and some to purchase equipment. Assume further that the cash was deposited in a commingled bank account before it was drawn out to pay for that inventory and equipment. Ignoring the effect of any after-acquired property clause and relying exclusively on its proceeds claim, will the bank have a perfected proceeds interest now?

Problem 4–18

Assume that debtor sells collateral and takes his buyer's note. The note, of course, is proceeds and identifiable as such, and thus the security interest that formerly attached to the collateral attaches to the identifiable proceeds (buyer's note). Debtor goes into bankruptcy a month after he procures the buyer's note. Who takes the note: the trustee in bankruptcy or the secured creditor with the proceeds claim?

CITICORP (USA) v. DAVIDSON LUMBER CO.

United States Court of Appeals, Eleventh Circuit, 1983.
718 F.2d 1030.

Before GODBOLD, CHIEF JUDGE, RONEY and TJOFLAT, CIRCUIT JUDGES.

GODBOLD, CHIEF JUDGE:

Florida Steel Corp., a petitioning creditor of Davidson Lumber Co. and Davidson Timber Co., the "debtors," appeals from the judgment of the district court. That court held that a certificate of deposit (CD) constituted cash proceeds under Fla.Stat.Ann. Sec. 679.306(1) (West Supp.1983), and that therefore the appellees, Citicorp and Southeast Bank, had a continuing perfected security interest in the CD at issue, even though they were not in possession of the instrument. The district court's decision reversed the holding of the bankruptcy court, 19 Bankr. 871 (Bankr.S.B.Fla.1982), that the banks' security interest was unperfected. We reverse.

The banks shared a perfected security interest in various of the debtors' assets, including general intangibles, as collateral for the debtors' indebtedness of approximately $3 million. Shortly before various of the debtors' creditors filed an involuntary petition under chapter 7 of the Bankruptcy Code, the debtors received a federal tax refund of approximately $1.3 million. The banks had been aware that the debtors would receive this money, although the banks did not know exactly when. Without the knowledge of the banks the debtors used this refund to purchase a CD of which the banks did not take possession.

In Florida security interests are governed by the Uniform Commercial Code. Under Florida law a perfected security interest in collateral continues in the proceeds generated by disposition of that collateral for at least 10 days. Fla.Stat. Ann. Sec. 679.306(3) (West Supp.1983). Continuation beyond the tenth day depends in part on how those proceeds are classified under Sec. 679.306. Section 679.306 provides in relevant part:

> (1) "Proceeds" includes whatever is received upon the sale, exchange, collection or other disposition of collateral or proceeds. Insurance payable by reason of loss or damage to the collateral is proceeds, except to the extent that it is payable to a person other than a party to the security agreement. Money, checks, deposit accounts, and the like are "cash proceeds." All other proceeds are "non-cash proceeds."
>
> (2) Except where this chapter otherwise provides, a security interest continues in collateral notwithstanding sale, exchange, or other disposition thereof unless the disposition was authorized by the secured party in the security agreement or otherwise, and also continues in any identifiable proceeds including collections received by the debtor.
>
> (3) The security interest in proceeds is a continuously perfected security interest if the interest in the original collateral was perfected, but it ceases to be a perfected security interest and becomes unperfected 10 days after receipt of the proceeds by the debtor unless:
>
> (a) A filed financing statement covers the original collateral and the proceeds are collateral in which a security interest may be perfected by filing in the office or offices where the financing statement has been filed and, if the proceeds are acquired with cash proceeds, the description of collateral in the financing statement indicates the types of property constituting the proceeds; or
>
> (b) A filed financing statement covers the original collateral and the proceeds are identifiable cash proceeds; or
>
> (c) The security interest in the proceeds is perfected before expiration of the 10-day period.
>
> Except as provided in this section, a security interest in proceeds can be perfected only by the methods or under the circumstances permitted in this chapter for original collateral of the same type.

The district court held that CD's are cash proceeds within the meaning of Sec. 679.306(1), and that therefore the banks' security interest in the CD remained perfected under Sec. 679.306(3)(b). Because the court's decision was based on its interpretation of Florida law, we have the fullest scope of review; the district court's interpretation of the Florida statute is not shielded by any presumption of correctness. *See Universal Minerals, Inc. v. C.A. Hughes & Co.,*

669 F.2d 98, 102 (3d Cir.1981); *see also International Horizons, Inc. v. Committee of Unsecured Creditors (In re International Horizons, Inc.),* 689 F.2d 996, 1002–05 (11th Cir.1982) (engaging in de novo review of district court's decision on choice of law on review of bankruptcy court).

Applying Sec. 679.306 to the present case, we find the banks had a temporarily perfected security interest in the CD for 10 days after it was acquired by the debtors. For that perfected security interest to continue, however, the banks had to fall within one of the three subsections of Fla.Stat.Ann.Sec. 679.306(3). The banks did not.

Neither of the parties argues that the banks' security interest continued to be perfected under Sec. 679.306(3)(a) or (c). Rather the issue presented is whether the CD constituted "identifiable cash proceeds" within the protection of Sec. 679.306(3)(b).

Cash proceeds are defined in Sec. 679.306(1):

> Money, checks, deposit accounts, and the like are "cash proceeds."

A CD is not a check or money. Likewise, a 1979 amendment to Fla.Stat.Ann. Sec. 679.105(1)(e) (West Supp.1983) explicitly provides that the term "deposit account" does not include CD's.

> "Deposit account" means [something] other than an account evidenced by a certificate of deposit. * * *

The 1979 amendment is particularly pertinent in the present case because the Sponsors' Notes to the amendment state:

> A definition of "deposit account" has been added to facilitate references to such accounts *in the section on proceeds* (s. 679.306).

(emphasis added). The narrow question we must decide is whether, as the banks argue, CD's fall within the "and the like" language of Sec. 679.306(1). It defies common sense, however, to suggest that the Florida legislature added the amendment excluding CD's from the definition of deposit accounts (one of the specified types of cash proceeds), and referred the reader to the section on cash proceeds, only to intend that CD's be treated as cash proceeds in the catch-all clause "and the like." The obvious legislative intent behind the amendment is that CD's are not cash proceeds.

The banks rely on *Citizens National Bank v. Bornstein,* 374 So.2d 6 (Fla. 1979), in support of their argument that CD's are "like" checks and therefore are cash proceeds. This reads too much into the *Bornstein* opinion. It held that a CD is an "instrument." While checks may be instruments, so are promissory notes and bills of exchange, Fla.Stat.Ann. Sec. 673.104(2) (West 1966 & Supp. 1983), neither of which is listed under Sec. 679.306(1) as identifiable cash proceeds.[1] *Bornstein* did not compare CD's to checks as the banks imply.

1. Generally, to perfect a security interest in an instrument the secured party must take possession of it. *See* Fla.Stat.Ann. Sec. 679.304 (West 1966 & Supp.1983). The banks admit that they did not take possession of the CD.

Under Sec. 679.306, checks represent a narrow departure from the general requirement of possession of instruments. That section provides that checks may be the object of a perfected security interest without possession when they are identifiable cash proceeds. Far from being "like" checks, however, CD's are similar to promissory notes. *Maxwell v. Agnew,* 21 Fla. 154 (1884). In *Southview Corp. v. Kleberg First Nat'l Bank,* 512 S.W.2d 817 (Tex. Civ.App.1974), the court explained:

> The promissory note theory of certificate of deposit has been incorporated into the Code as illustrated by the definition of a certificate of deposit: "[A] receipt of money with an engagement to repay it." * * * Following this definition of certificate of deposit, the Code makes such definition ap-

The banks argue that the result reached here would be "preposterous," because it "provides an opportunity for a debtor to conceal proceeds of collateral from a secured creditor, to secretly convert that collateral into another form which requires perfection by taking possession, and then to effectively extinguish the right of that secured creditor by consciously withholding that collateral or keeping its existence a secret. * * *" Brief for Appellees at 18–19. This argument is misconceived. The Code gives secured creditors many methods of policing their debtors. By contractual agreement lenders may require their debtors to permit on-premises inspections of their books or they may insist that payments owed to the debtor by third parties must be sent directly to the lender. Fla.Stat.Ann. Sec. 679.502 (West Supp.1983). As Florida Steel points out, the banks might also have availed themselves of the Federal Assignment of Claims Act, 31 U.S.C. Sec. 203 (1976), *amended by* 31 U.S.C.A. Sec. 3727 (West 1983), which permits creditors to obtain directly from the government sums of money, such as tax refunds, which are liquidated claims owed by the government to the debtor. *See, e.g., King v. Gilbert,* 569 F.2d 398 (5th Cir.1978) (per curiam).

Because the district court misconstrued Sec. 679.306, we reverse its judgment and remand to the district court with instructions to affirm the judgment of the bankruptcy court.

Reversed and remanded.

SECTION 10. SECURING AN INTEREST WHEN THE COLLATERAL IS MULTIPLE ASSETS, I.E., CHATTEL PAPER

Whenever a secured creditor takes a security interest in chattel paper or "realty paper," the creditor will wish to be secured not only with respect to the stream of payments that come from the account debtor, but also with respect to the underlying collateral, whether that collateral be an automobile, stereo or a piece of real estate. It is easy for creditors to overlook the fact that they must concern themselves with two sets of competing creditors in such cases. In one class are those parties who are creditors of the debtor (the assignor of the chattel paper and the secured creditor on the chattel paper). Still another class consists of those parties who are creditors of the account debtor (the original buyer of automobile or stereo, or the mortgagor on the real estate). Think for a moment about the methods by which one would perfect a security interest in such cases.

Before dealing with the problem below, one should consider several UCC sections. Section 9–105(1)(b) defines chattel paper as follows:

> "Chattel paper" means a writing or writings which evidence both a monetary obligation and a security interest in or a lease of specific goods, but a charter or other contract involving the use or hire of a vessel is not chattel paper. When a transaction is evidenced both by such a security agreement or a lease and by an instrument or a series of instruments, the group of writings taken together constitutes chattel paper[.]"

Note that chattel paper includes security agreements and leases of goods; it does not include a note standing alone or a mere contractual promise to pay. One purchasing chattel paper should always be concerned with the question whether

plicable to other chapters which would necessarily include Chapter 9. * * * In its usual and ordinary form, a certificate of deposit contains the elements of a promissory note, rather than of a mere receipt, and in general has that legal effect.

Id. at 819–20 (citations omitted). For this reason as well, the banks' argument that CD's are like checks must fail.

the chattel paper is itself a security interest and, if so, whether that security interest is itself perfected. If the original secured creditor perfected the security interest in the underlying collateral now covered by the chattel paper, the assignee need not file again with respect to the underlying debtor (the account debtor) because of 9–302(2) which states:

> "If a secured party assigns a perfected security interest, no filing under this Article is required in order to continue the perfected status of the security interest against creditors of and transferees from the original debtor."

Possession is a common mode of perfection as to chattel paper. The creditor's possession of another's chattel paper would put some, but not all, of the relevant parties on notice. Do you see which parties would not be put on notice? The issues are illustrated by the problem that follows and occur in a particularly exquisite and subtle form in *In re Leasing,* the case that follows the problem.

Problem 4–19

Retail merchant sells a $1500 stereo system for use in Buyer's home. Buyer signs a security agreement granting a security interest to merchant. Merchant then transfers its rights in the chattel paper to Bank. Assume that Bank neither takes possession nor files a financing statement with respect to the chattel paper. Are the following propositions true?

a. If consumer-debtor goes into bankruptcy, Bank will have a perfected security interest in the stereo that will be superior to the claim of the consumer's trustee in bankruptcy and of his other creditors.

b. If merchant goes into bankruptcy, Bank's claim to the chattel paper sold to it will be superior to the claim of merchant's trustee.

c. If Bank had a perfected security interest in merchant's "inventory," it would fare better (1) in a; (2) in b.

IN RE LEASING CONSULTANTS, INC.

United States Court of Appeals, Second Circuit, 1973.
486 F.2d 367.

Before FRIENDLY and HAYS, CIRCUIT JUDGES, and JAMESON, DISTRICT JUDGE.

JAMESON, DISTRICT JUDGE:

Respondent-Appellant, First National City Bank (Bank), appeals from an order of the district court affirming, on a petition for review, the order of a referee in bankruptcy directing the Bank to turn over to the Petitioner-Appellee, George Feldman, Trustee in Bankruptcy (Trustee) of Leasing Consultants, Incorporated, (Leasing) the proceeds from the sale of equipment which had been leased by Leasing, located in New York, to Plastimetrix Corporation, located in New Jersey. The leases covering the equipment had been assigned to the Bank as security for a loan to Leasing.

The district court held, 351 F.Supp. 1390, on the basis of stipulated facts, that the perfection by the Bank by filing and possession in New York of its security interest in the lease/chattel paper was not a perfection of the Bank's security interest in Leasing's reversionary interest in the leased property, located in New Jersey. Consequently, the Trustee's lien was held superior to the Bank's unperfected security interest in the leased equipment.

SUMMARY OF FACTS

In March and June of 1969 Leasing entered into eight leases with Plastimetrix covering heavy equipment. The leased equipment was at all relevant times located in New Jersey. Leasing filed financing statements with the Secretary of State of the State of New Jersey covering each transaction, each statement bearing the legend: "THIS FILING IS FOR INFORMATIONAL PURPOSES ONLY AS THIS IS A LEASE TRANSACTION."

On December 15, 1969 Leasing entered into a "Loan and Security Agreement" with the Bank for the financing of its business of purchasing and leasing equipment. The agreement provided in part for the assignment of "a continuing security interest in the lease(s) and the property leased" as collateral security for advances and loans not to exceed 80% of aggregate unpaid rentals.

Pursuant to the security agreement Leasing borrowed money from the Bank in December, 1969 and February, 1970 and assigned as collateral security the eight Plastimetrix leases, each assignment covering all moneys due or to become due under the lease and the "relative equipment" described in the lease. The lease documents were delivered to the Bank.

On December 30 and 31, 1969 the Bank filed financing statements against Leasing with the Secretary of State of the State of New York and the Registrar of the City of New York, Queens County, where Leasing had its principal place of business.[1] No financing statements were filed by the Bank in New Jersey; nor did the Bank take possession of the leased equipment.

On October 14, 1970 Leasing was adjudicated bankrupt by the United States District Court for the Eastern District of New York. On October 30, 1970 Plastimetrix filed a petition under Chapter XI of the Bankruptcy Act in the United States District Court for the District of New Jersey.

The leases were in default and an offer was made to purchase the Bank's interest in the property for $60,000. On May 21, 1971 the Trustee, the Bank, and the purchaser entered into a stipulation providing for acceptance of the offer and execution of bills of sale by the Trustee and Bank covering all "right, title and interest" in the property, and that the sum of $60,000 "be substituted for the Property" and the "respective rights of the Trustee and of the Bank * * * be impressed upon and relegated to said fund of $60,000 with the same priority and to the same extent as they now have against the Property."

The Trustee petitioned the Referee in Bankruptcy for an order directing the Bank to turn over to the Trustee the sum of $60,000. Under stipulated facts the Trustee and Bank agreed that the question presented was solely one of law—involving the construction of Article 9 of the Uniform Commercial Code—and that the precise issue was:

> "Was the Bank required to file a financing statement against the Bankrupt with the Secretary of State of New Jersey in order to perfect a security interest in the leases assigned to it and the equipment leased thereunder by the Bankrupt to Plastimetrix?"

The Referee answered in the affirmative and ordered the Bank to turn over the $60,000, with interest, to the Trustee. On review the district court affirmed.

1. The financing statement covered "continuing security interest in leases and any and all rents due and to become due thereunder, including all related equipment described therein, chattel paper represented thereby, accounts receivable therewith and proceeds arising therefrom."

DECISION OF DISTRICT COURT

As the district court recognized, the aim of Article 9 of the Uniform Commercial Code, relating to "Secured Transactions", is "to provide a simple and unified structure within which the immense variety of present-day secured financing transactions can go forward with less cost and with greater certainty". Uniform Commercial Code, § 9–101, Official Comment. The drafters of this article eliminated many distinctions among security devices based on form alone. On the other hand, distinctions based on the type of property constituting the collateral were retained. Id.

Based on the stipulation of counsel, the court assumed that the agreements between Leasing and Plastimetrix were "true leases" and not "conditional sales agreements" or devices intended to create only a security interest.[2] Accordingly the court found that the Bank acquired "a security interest in both the right to receive rental payments under the lease and in the reversionary interest in the underlying equipment."

The court held, and the parties agree, that the leases themselves were "chattel papers" (U.C.C. § 9–105(1)(b)) and that the Bank's security interest in the chattel paper was perfected by filing financing statements in New York and taking possession of the leases. U.C.C. § 9–304(1), 9–305, and 9–102(1).

The court held further: "By contrast, the machines themselves constituted 'equipment' located in New Jersey and hence, for perfection purposes, came within the scope of the New Jersey requirements." The Bank having failed to perfect its interest in the reversion in New Jersey, the court concluded that the Trustee "—a lien creditor within the meaning of Uniform Commercial Code § 9–301(3)—has priority over an unperfected security interest under § 9–301(1)(b)."

Emphasizing the distinction between rights under the chattel paper and the reversionary interest in the equipment, the court quoted from Professor Levie as follows:

> "In one situation the purchaser of a security agreement may have an advantage over the purchaser of a lease. Where [he] purchases equipment leases, he takes only an assignor's interest in the equipment lease itself. If [he] wishes to be secured by an interest in the goods as well, he must obtain a security interest * * * [in the goods] and perfect it." Levie, Security Interests in Chattel Paper, 78 Yale L.J. 935, 940 (1969).[3]

2. Where a lease is intended as a security device the lessee usually becomes the owner or has the option to become the owner of the property at the end of the lease term. U.C.C. § 1–201(37). The lessor holds merely a security interest and has no reversionary right in the leased property.

3. The court continued:

"Practical considerations support this conclusion. The property leased was heavy manufacturing equipment. A potential creditor observing these complicated and non-portable machines should be entitled to believe that he could discover all non-possessory interests by consulting the files in the state where the equipment is located. The equipment was obviously of great value; the New Jersey files revealed only that the lessee held it under a lease. Since the lease agreement required each piece of equipment to have a plate affixed indicating that it was the 'property' of the lessor, judgment creditors of the lessor might assume that its reversionary interest in the equipment was of substantial value. Not being alerted to the diminution of value which would be effected by the creditor's security interest, they might then, for example, attach the lessor's interest, relying on an apparently unencumbered and valuable reversionary interest."

The district court concluded:

"The distinction between the rights represented by the lease and those represented by the reversionary interest in the equipment is a real one, supported by logic and precedent. To ignore the distinction contributes neither to clarity nor uniformity under the Uniform Commercial Code. Moreover, it may mislead third party creditors. The simple solution for a bank in the situation of petitioner is to file notices as to its interest in the reversion in accordance with the law of the state where the equipment is located."

CONTENTIONS OF APPELLANT

Appellant Bank contends that (1) whether the leases be considered "true leases" or security devices, the filing of the security interest in New York (where lessor and the chattel paper were located) covered all of the lessor's rights in the rentals and related equipment wherever located, without a separate filing against the equipment; or (2) alternatively, if a distinction is recognized between a "true lease" and a security device, appellant is entitled to an evidentiary hearing to determine whether the instruments were "true leases" or security interests in the equipment through the device of a lease; and (3) in any event, Leasing in fact had no "reversionary" interest in the property leased to Plastimetrix.

FAILURE TO FILE FINANCING STATEMENT IN NEW JERSEY

In contending that the filing and physical possession of the lease instruments in New York were sufficient to cover the leased equipment located in New Jersey, appellant argues that the "reversionary interest" of Leasing is "an intangible interest, sited at Leasing's domicile in New York, and not in New Jersey." If the reversionary interest in the equipment were characterized as a "general intangible", the Bank's security interest in the equipment would have been perfected when it filed with the New York Department of State and in the county in which Leasing had a place of business. N.Y.U.C.C. §§ 9–103(2), 9–401(1)(c) (McKinney 1964).

The policies of the Code, however, militate against such an interpretation. We agree with the district court that the reversionary interest is an interest in "goods" rather than an interest in intangibles, and that to perfect the security interest in the reversionary interest in the equipment it was necessary to file a financing statement in New Jersey where the equipment was located. N.J.Stat. Anno. 12A:9–102(1) (1962), 9–302, 9–401(1)(c) (Supp.1972).

Obviously the leased property itself is "goods". We conclude, as did the district court, that the future reversionary interest is likewise an interest in goods, whether it represents "equipment" or "inventory" collateral. The drafters of the Code classified collateral mainly according to the nature or use of the underlying entity, rather than the character of its ownership at any given time. Significantly, the examples of "general intangibles" given in the Official Comment to § 9–106 are all types of property that are inherently intangible. And several Code sections and comments suggest that a collateral interest in "goods" remains such even when the goods are leased. See §§ 9–103(2); 9–109(4) and Official Comment 3; 9–304(3); N.Y.U.C.C. 9–109, Practice Commentary 2 (McKinney 1964) (Kripke).

We conclude accordingly that if the instruments were "true leases", the security interest in the leased equipment was not perfected because of the failure of the Bank to file financing statements in New Jersey.[4]

[The court concluded that the case should be remanded to determine whether the lease instrument was a "true lease" or intended as security. If the district court determined that the agreements were "true" leases, then it will also be necessary to consider the effect of stipulations by the parties and whether the $60,000 fund "represents the sale of the leasehold as well as the sale of the reversionary interest in the equipment." The case was then remanded for determination of these and other matters. Hays, Circuit Judge, dissented. Some footnotes omitted.]

Notes

1. If you were to handle this transaction again on behalf of Citibank, what would you include in your security agreement and how would you perfect your security interest?

2. Did the lawyers, who apparently entered into a stipulation without appreciating its ramifications, commit malpractice?

3. If you knew that your opponent did not appreciate the significance of the stipulation about whether the security agreements were true leases or were not true leases and you nevertheless induced him to agree to the stipulation, would you have engaged in unethical conduct?

4. Appellant alternatively contends that since "Leasing had assigned all of its interest in the machinery and equipment to the Bank" it had preferential rights to the equipment under "the law of bailment leases" regardless of the Code provisions. The assignment of the equipment from Leasing to the Bank, however, was expressly made "as security for any and all obligations of [Leasing] to the Bank under and pursuant to the Loan and Security Agreement * * *." This assignment clearly created a security interest in the Bank and made the requirements of Article 9 applicable to the Bank's interest in the equipment. U.C.C. § 9–102(1)(a).

CHAPTER FIVE

PRIORITIES

SECTION 1. INTRODUCTION

Perfection generally affords the secured creditor the maximum protection, i.e., priority, that the law allows. Yet as we noted earlier, and as will become clear in this chapter, the law does not always accord priority even to the prior perfected secured creditor. In this chapter we will consider the priorities between a perfected secured creditor on the one hand and a variety of challengers on the other. We will briefly consider the rights of the unperfected secured creditor as well.

Although the rules of priority to be learned here may sometimes apply elsewhere by analogy, students should not assume that they understand all, once they have studied these rules. It is possible, for example, to have a priority conflict between a real estate mortgagee and a mechanic's lienor, between two mechanic's lienors, between a tax lienor and a seller, and on and on. We will address none of the rules governing such conflicts in this chapter. Here, for the most part, we consider the priority rights of the perfected secured creditor under Article 9 against the world (gegen der Welt!).

The secured creditor, even the unperfected secured creditor, starts out from a general position of priority granted him by UCC 9–201. A secured creditor has the rights that his contract grants him not just against the debtor but against *everyone* * * * "except as otherwise provided by this act * * *." Most of what we will study in this chapter consists of the "other provisions" that in one way or another subordinate the secured creditor. Although UCC 9–201 will seldom be the end point of a lawyer's analysis, it should always be the beginning.

Next in importance is probably section 9–301. Its main effect is to subordinate an unperfected secured creditor to the rights of lien creditors and certain buyers. Third among the basic provisions is section 9–307 which subordinates even a perfected secured creditor to the rights of a buyer in the ordinary course in certain circumstances, and in some cases to others who do not even rise to the level of buyers in the ordinary course. Here is the first rude shock: even a perfected secured creditor may be subordinate to some buyers even though they know of the secured creditor's interest! Finally, among the basic provisions is UCC 9–312; it determines priority among secured creditors whose interests are in the same collateral. It is doubtless less important than UCC 9–301, but it is much more interesting and much more challenging intellectually. It is, however, somewhat like a house with many rooms, an attic filled with obscure relics.

The aforementioned four sections, 9–201, 9–301, 9–307 and 9–312 express some of the most fundamental ideas embodied in Article 9. First, those sections give bite to the perfection requirements (as for example by subordinating an unperfected secured creditor to the trustee in bankruptcy). Second, they carry out the general policy of Article 9 that a secured creditor who has checked the files only once, and has done a notice filing will then enjoy maximum priority allowed by law against other creditors and purchasers, including even as to after-acquired property and future advances (those rules are set out mostly in UCC 9–312(5)). It should be noted how by virtue of UCC 9–201's provisions granting general priority over purchasers, and by virtue of the modest concessions in 9–301(1)(c) to non-ordinary course buyers and in UCC 9–307(1) to ordinary course buyers, the sections together sustain the superiority of the perfected secured creditor over all but the most exceptional buyers and subsequent purchasers. Of course, section 9–312 recognizes that certain purchase money buyers should have priority even though they are second in time. Our study of UCC 9–312(3) and (4) will show how the statute meets various policies associated with purchase money lenders, and how the statute deals with them and their rights in proceeds in a detailed and intricate way.

Problem 5–1

A. Bank # 1 lends Debtor $50,000 and, on July 1, creates an enforceable security interest under UCC 9–203(1) in Debtor's factory equipment, UCC 9–109(2), "existing and after-acquired." See UCC 9–204(1). On July 15, C, an unsecured creditor, lends Debtor $25,000. On August 1, Bank # 1 perfected the security interest by filing a financing statement in the proper place. Read, again, UCC 9–302(1), 9–401(1) and 9–303(1). On October 1, D defaults to C, who sues, gets a judgment and, on December 1, obtains a judicial lien through execution upon the equipment. Bank # 1, declaring default, claimed priority over C in the equipment, which is worth $40,000. Who should prevail? See UCC 9–201 & 9–301(1).

B. On August 15, Bank # 2 lent D $25,000 and perfected a security interest by filing on the same date. On December 1, D defaulted on obligations to both banks and both claim priority in the equipment. Who has priority? See UCC 9–312(5).

C. On September 1, S sold D new factory equipment on credit for $25,000 and retained an enforceable security interest. The equipment was delivered to D on September 15. What must S do to obtain priority over Bank # 1 and Bank # 2? See UCC 9–107 & 9–312(4).

D. On October 1, D sold all of the equipment to B, another factory owner, for $50,000. B purchased in good faith and without knowledge of any outstanding security interests. B's check for $50,000 was placed in a safe in D's office. The sale of collateral without approval by the secured party was prohibited and constituted a default under the security agreement. Can Bank # 1 and Bank # 2 enforce their security interests in equipment against B? What about claims to the check? See UCC 9–306 & 9–307.

SECTION 2. PRIORITY AMONG COMPETING SECURITY INTERESTS IN THE SAME COLLATERAL, UCC 9–312

A. Introduction—Future Advances

The most important rule in UCC 9–312 is that embodied in 9–312(5). Basically it tells us that the Code priority is limited by the time of filing or, in some cases, the time of perfection. (Can you identify a case in which the time of filing is *not* the time of priority?) In effect, UCC 9–312 rejects the time the security interest *attaches,* the time a particular loan is *made,* and the time the debtor *acquired* an interest in the property as the operative event determining priority. Having filed, the secured creditor need not run back to check the files every time he makes an advance or every time the debtor acquires a new piece of property subject to the creditor's after-acquired property clause.

Moreover, there is no reference to being without notice when one wins the race to the place of filing. This tells us that our statute is a pure race statute.

Sometimes students confuse future advances (new loans) with after-acquired property (new assets). In most cases the rules as to both will be the same under UCC 9–312, but that is not true in all cases, and it is probably desirable to distinguish them. Consider the following examples which are chosen from comments 5 and 7 to UCC 9–312. As you read them, go back and read the statute and see whether you can make it say the things that the examples purport to disclose. If you cannot, you are not reading the statute correctly.

> Example 1. A files against X (debtor) on February 1. B files against X on March 1. B makes a non-purchase money advance against certain collateral on April 1. A makes an advance against the same collateral on May 1. A has priority even though B's advance was made earlier and was perfected when made. It makes no difference whether or not A knew of B's interest when he made his advance.
>
> The problem stated in the example is peculiar to a notice filing system under which filing may be made before the security interest attaches (see Section 9–402). The Uniform Trust Receipts Act, which first introduced such a filing system, contained no hint of a solution and case law under it was unpredictable. This Article follows several of the accounts receivable statutes in determining priority by order of filing. The justification for the rule lies in the necessity of protecting the filing system—that is, of allowing the secured party who has first filed to make subsequent advances without each time having, as a condition of protection, to check for filings later than his. Note, however, that his protection is not absolute: if, in the example, B's advance creates a purchase money security interest, he has priority under subsection (4), or, in the case of inventory, under subsection (3) provided he has properly notified A. * * *
>
> Example 2. A and B make non-purchase money advances against the same collateral. The collateral is in the debtor's possession and neither interest is perfected when the second advance is made. Whichever secured party first perfects his interest (by taking possession of the collateral or by filing) takes priority and it makes no difference whether or not he knows of the other interest at the time he perfects his own.

At common law in some cases one's priority dated not from the time of perfection but from the time the loan was made. In those jurisdictions the courts often distinguished between cases in which there was an "obligatory advance" (one in which the creditor was contractually bound to make) and those which were non-obligatory (where the creditor was free not to make the loan on the date he made it). Not surprisingly, in the former the courts sometimes dated the priority from the time the agreement had been made.

> Example 5. On February 1 A makes an advance against machinery in the debtor's possession and files his financing statement. On March 1 B makes an advance against the same machinery and files his financing statement. On April 1 A makes a further advance, under the original security agreement, against the same machinery (which is covered by the original financing statement and thus perfected when made). A has priority over B both as to the February 1 and as to the April 1 advance and it makes no difference whether or not A knows of B's intervening advance when he makes his second advance.
>
> A wins, as to the April 1 advance, because he first filed even though B's interest attached, and indeed was perfected, before the April 1 advance. The same rule would apply if either A or B had perfected through posses-

sion. Section 9–204(3) and the Comment thereto should be consulted for the validation of future advances.

The same result would be reached even though A's April 1 advance was not under the original security agreement, but was under a new security agreement under A's same financing statement or during the continuation of A's possession.

Problem 5–2

Answer each of the hypothetical questions below under the 1972 official text.

Ajax Sisters, a famous private banking concern, had filed a financing statement covering "accounts existing and after-acquired" of Neiman Marcus. You are counsel for Ajax and they ask you the following questions and pose to you the following cases:

1. If we file on January 15 with respect to accounts, as above, but neither lend nor make any agreement to lend at the time, and on January 20 a second creditor files and lends on the same account, will that lender have priority over us if we lend some money on January 30?

2. If in the foregoing example we make a series of non-obligatory advances to Nieman Marcus, will we continue to have priority over the intervening creditor or after we have knowledge of his loan, or will we be subordinated to the extent of our subsequent non-obligatory advances?

3. We are contemplating a loan to a large Atlanta department store to enable that store to purchase several new lines of appliances. We know that an Atlanta bank has already filed a financing statement that covers all of the inventory and accounts of that department store. Is there any way in which we can make a loan and set up a security arrangement so that we will have priority over the previously perfected Atlanta bank?

4. We contemplate lending as purchase money lenders on $50,000 of equipment that American Airlines will use as part of its fixed base operation in Dallas. We have two questions with respect to this equipment:

a. What steps must we take to ensure that we have priority over prior parties who have filed blanket financing statements covering existing and after-acquired equipment?

b. To the extent that this equipment is ultimately sold, will we have priority with respect to the accounts that it produces or will the prior filed general financier?

B. Purchase Money Priority

1. Purchase Money Security

In Chapter Four we already met the purchase money security interest when we considered the problem of the secured creditor who takes a "cross collateral clause" under which items purchased from the same seller at different times "cross collateralize" the prices of each other. *In re Manuel*, supra at p. 143 is such a case. Here we see the purchase money secured creditor in a different context, not as one asserting merely that he has perfected without filing, but asserting that he has priority over someone whose perfection pre-dates his. Section 9–312(3) and (4) are important purchase money provisions that grant priority to the purchase money lender with prior perfected security interests.

Why should one grant priority to a creditor that is later in time than the one whose interest is subordinated? There are at least two reasons for granting such priority, one historical and doctrinal, the other arising out of the policy to protect a debtor from creditor overreaching. The purchase money security interest has long been recognized in the sale of real estate where, for example, a seller would retain a mortgage when he sold his real estate to a buyer. Buyer would then grant a mortgage to a bank or a third party who would record the mortgage. In the priority dispute between the seller's prior but unrecorded mortgage and the bank's later and recorded mortgage, seller would often win. The rationale for this victory was that the seller's entire interest had not passed to the buyer and thus could never pass to the bank, for under the rule of *nemo dat qui non habet* (he who hath not cannot give), the bank could only get as good a title as its debtor had. That may have been a satisfactory explanation in the days when traditional conveyance law reigned; it is clearly not adequate to explain UCC 9–312(3) and (4).

A more modern justification for purchase money priority may be found in a desire to protect the *debtor* from the initial secured creditor's overreaching. If the security agreement with the first creditor contained a blanket description of the debtor's assets, including after-acquired collateral and a broad definition of debt, the debtor would become virtually indentured to the initial secured creditor. If that creditor refused to lend more money and also refused to grant a subordination agreement, the debtor would be unable to borrow to finance the purchase of a new asset from a second creditor willing to lend only against a security interest in that very asset having priority over the first creditor. The purchase money priority rule in effect frees the debtor from the reach of the first security agreement. By complying with UCC 9–312(3) or (4), the debtor can promise a subsequent purchase money lender that he will have priority over the first creditor as to the items newly purchased.

The issues for the lawyer under UCC 9–312(3) and (4) are similar to those seen above in *In re Manuel* and include some others as well. Here, as in *Manuel,* one must determine whether the loan by the creditor enabled the debtor to procure the asset. Here too one must determine the rights of the competing parties to the proceeds of the purchase money loan. The student should read UCC 9–312(3) and (4) with care. Note that the former grants priority only as to "identifiable cash proceeds" whereas the latter grants priority to "its proceeds." As part of the 1972 amendments to Article 9, these phrases were carefully chosen. What is the difference between them? Can you illustrate this difference?

Note finally that there is a notice requirement with respect to inventory in UCC 9–312(3) but no such requirement under UCC 9–312(4). The need for notice presumably arises out of the nature of inventory and accounts receivable loans. Typically these loans are "revolving loans" that involve continuous and periodic advances by the creditor as well as continuous and periodic payments by the debtor. Because these revolving loans contemplate such advances, there is a likelihood that a dishonest debtor might mislead his original creditor into making new advances based on another party's purchase money collateral. Hence the purchase money lender must notify the revolving loan financer of inventory to get priority. But because such advances are not usual with respect to non-inventory financing under UCC 9–312(4), the drafters saw no need for such notice.

Assume that you represent a creditor who has a perfected security interest in a retailer's inventory. Your client receives a notice that another party is going to claim a purchase money security interest in a new line of inventory. What action should your client take in order to protect its interest?

IN RE SMITH

United States Bankruptcy Court, Western District Missouri, 1983.
29 B.R. 690.

PELOFSKY, BANKRUPTCY JUDGE.

* * * In this petition the Bank sought a determination of priorities as between it and FmHA as to certain collateral and for other relief. The Bank also filed Count II to a complaint, precisely which of the three then pending being unknown, again naming debtors and FmHA as defendants, seeking a determination of priorities and asking that the proceeds of the sale of cattle repossessed by FmHA be used to satisfy the Bank's debt.

* * *

The evidence shows that debtor Lloyd Smith was borrowing money from the Bank's predecessor in 1970. In August of 1976 the Bank took a security interest in "All livestock now owned and after acquired". No significant amount of money was advanced to debtors at this time. There is no evidence that debtors had any livestock in August of 1976. In March of 1979 debtors borrowed money from FmHA and executed a security agreement in favor of FmHA identifying cattle and hogs as collateral. Just prior to the advance a financing statement was filed and designated as security, inter alia, " * * * proceeds and products thereof: (a) * * * livestock * * * ". Debtors deposited the funds in their account at the Bank and purchased the cattle and hogs called for in the security agreement.

During the period June 1981 through January 1982 debtors borrowed $20,222.59 from the Bank. During the period from April 17, 1981 through January 1982 debtors gave the Bank four financial statements. Debtors gave a statement in September of 1980 but this, the court finds, is too remote in time to be of probative value except that it also, as do the others, omits any reference to the FmHA debt. On August 24, 1981 the Bank filed a continuation statement of its 1976 UCC filing.

According to an affidavit filed by FmHA, an agent searched the UCC filings in Pulaski County on September 1, 1981 and found no continuation filing by the Bank. In late September 1981, debtors executed a security agreement in favor of FmHA identifying cattle and hogs as collateral. No financing statement was filed in connection with this security agreement. In March of 1982 FmHA foreclosed its security interest in the cattle and sold them, applying the proceeds against the loan. Debtors filed for relief under Chapter 7 of the Code on March 18, 1982, after the foreclosure. This adversary was filed shortly thereafter.

Section 400.9–312, R.S.Mo.1969, deals with "[p]riorities among conflicting security interests in the same collateral". The section provides, in part, that * * * [quoting 9–312(3) and (4)]

Section 400.9–109(3) R.S.Mo.1969 classifies goods as "[f]arm products" if they are " * * * livestock * * * used * * * in farming operations * * * If goods are farm products they are neither equipment nor inventory." The statutory comment notes that

> "4. Goods are 'farm products' only if they are in the possession of a debtor engaged in farming operations. Animals in a herd of livestock are covered whether they are acquired by purchase or result from natural increase."

The evidence shows that FmHA filed its financing statement prior to the funds being paid to debtor. Debtor used a substantial part of the money to purchase pigs and cattle. The purchases were made within two months of the advance. The purchase money security interest therefore was perfected when debtors received the collateral.

Debtors were engaged in farming at all times herein set out and § 400.9–109(3) excludes, therefore, these animals from the definition of inventory. The question of priority of creditors consequently is determined by reference to § 400.9–312(4). That section does not require notice to a creditor holding a prior filing in the same product with an after acquired clause and allows the creditor making a purchase money advance to have priority over the creditor holding "after acquired" rights. Thus, in May of 1979, FmHA had a priority in the purchased cattle over the claim of the Bank.

In its brief the Bank concedes that FmHA had a purchase money security interest in the collateral until September 27, 1981. The Bank argues that the security agreement dated September 28, 1981, destroyed that status and gave FmHA a security interest for an antecedent debt, thus restoring the Bank to its first filed priority status. There is no evidence that FmHA released its first security agreement or UCC filing or advanced new funds in return for execution of this September, 1981 security agreement. No financing statement was filed in connection with the 1981 security agreement.

There was no testimony explaining the 1981 agreement. It would appear that it was taken after the FmHA agent ran a lien search and discovered, or so it seemed, that the Bank lien had expired. The 1981 agreement may have been taken to identify the then existing security.

There are a number of reasons why execution of the 1981 security agreement is immaterial. The Bank had filed a continuation statement and the court so finds. The Bank is not charged with FmHA's failure to discover such a filing or the apparent failure of the Recorder to index or file. The Bank continued to occupy a secured position in some respects. Nonetheless, as to the purchased cattle, FmHA's purchase money position was a priority without regard to the prior Bank filing and needed no subsequent action to maintain that priority even if the Bank's filing had lapsed.

The court concludes that execution of the 1981 security agreement, without more, is of no significance. The 1979 agreement was perfected and not altered by the subsequent agreement. Section 400.9–108 does not apply. In this instance the secured party made no advance, incurred no obligation, released no specific security interest and gave no value when the 1981 agreement was executed. [Citations omitted.]

The Bank also contends that the FmHA security agreement loses its purchase money character and priority as to cattle produced from those purchased. Calves which are bred are not purchased. They are "after acquired" in a general sense. The FmHA security agreement also covers all increases. The question then is whether cattle bred from security for a purchase money security interest are themselves purchase money security.

Section 400.9–107, R.S.Mo.1969, defines a purchase money security interest as one "taken by a person who by making advances . . . gives value to enable the debtor to acquire rights in or the use of collateral if such value is in fact so used." Here there is no question that debtors used the FmHA advance to purchase cattle which they used for their benefit. The advance ultimately, through a natural process, also enabled debtors to have the use of calves, i.e., the products of the purchase money collateral.

The Uniform Commercial Code enables a security interest to follow collateral even if it is transformed. See § 400.9–314, R.S.Mo.1969, as to rules concerning accessions and § 400.9–315, R.S.Mo.1969, as to rules concerning commingled or processed goods. But these statutes, while preserving a security interest, do not resolve the issue as to whether the interest retains its purchase money character but there are clear suggestions that the character remains unchanged. See, for example, § 400.9–315(1)(b) which provides that a financing statement covering goods "also covers the product into which the goods have been manufactured, processed or assembled." See also Holzman v. L.H.J. Enterprises, Inc., 476 F.2d 949 (9th Cir. 1973) where the court held that inventory purchased from the sale of inventory subject to a purchase money security interest retained the character of purchase money security.

The purchase money security interest as an exception to the rules of priority of filing allows the creditor to have a security interest in identified collateral which it enabled the debtor to obtain. While such collateral may be transformed, as through manufacturing, it does not expand through its own effort. Cattle do (ignoring the biological act). The purchase money security interest is maintained by keeping the collateral intact or tracing the proceeds. Cattle as collateral expand by natural process.

In a case styled In re Ingram, 11 UCC Reporting Service 605 [468 F.2d 564] (5th Cir. 1972) the court held a security interest in progeny of leased cattle was not a purchase money security interest because the creditor only enabled the debtor to acquire "rights in and use of the breeder stock" and not the progeny. The suggestion in § 400.9–204, R.S.Mo.1969 is that since the debtor had no rights in unconceived progeny at the time the security agreement was executed, no security interest could attach and therefore the creditor acquired no rights in such unconceived animals.

The purchase money security interest priority is an exception to the general rule and should be construed narrowly even though the application to a cattle situation is inexact. Compare Index Store Fixture Co. v. Farmers' Trust Co., 536 S.W.2d 902 (Mo.App.1976). It must be remembered, in support of a narrow reading, that even the natural process of herd growth does not proceed without assistance not provided by the purchase money creditor. The result could be different if the evidence showed that some part of the purchase money collateral was sold and new animals purchased, but that is not the case here. Similarly this could be a variation if the calves only replaced cattle that had died. Again, while the herd has diminished here, there is no evidence that diminution occurred from the aging process.

The court concludes, therefore, that the purchase money security interest does not apply to the calves. FmHA is entitled to the proceeds of the sale of those cattle which retained purchase money character at the time of foreclosure but the Bank is entitled to the proceeds from the sale of any others.

The evidence shows that debtors purchased 19 cows and 20 pigs with the FmHA loan. FmHA sold 13 cows and 7 calves. Debtors owned no pigs at the time of the foreclosure. There is no evidence as to disposition of the other cows. The sale price was not allocated among the animals, although it appears that all of the cows could have been part of the purchase money herd. The parties are directed to confer and to advise the court whether a further hearing would be necessary to resolve the issue of allocation.

The court also reserves the question of the nondischargeability of the debt to the Bank until the issue of allocation is resolved. Further evidence may be necessary on that question.

Notes

1. The foregoing case was decided under the 1962 Code. Under UCC 9–312(4) of the 1972 Code, would it have come out differently? Are calves "proceeds"? In security agreements dealing with livestock one frequently sees reference to all livestock including "products." The reference to all livestock including "products" is presumably there because the secured creditor is uncertain whether calves, milk, and such fit the definition in 9–306(1). What do you think? What of PIK payments? Term agreements to purchase milk?

2. Assume that a creditor files a financing statement that covers all of the debtor's inventory. Over a period of time the inventory loan goes up and down and ultimately is paid off. A year later a new security agreement is executed between the parties and a new loan is made. Does this loan date to the earlier financing statement and achieve priority over an intervening loan?

3. Assume in 2 that the new loan had covered not just inventory, but also accounts receivable and in connection with the second security agreement an amendment to the original financing statement was filed to cover "accounts receivable and inventory." What would be the date of priority as to accounts?

Problem 5–3

Your client Finance Company does a great deal of purchase money lending. Some of that consists of lending to farmers as in *In Re Smith,* in which the Company lends money for the acquisition of cattle and hogs and takes a security interest in those animals and in proceeds and products thereof. In other cases your client lends to retail merchants, takes a perfected security interest in their inventory, accounts receivable and proceeds. In most of these cases there is a prior perfected security interest that includes an after-acquired property clause, and it is critical to your client's interest to maintain priority over the earlier creditor. Having achieved purchase money status by complying with UCC 9–107, having given notice in compliance with UCC 9–312(3), and having filed in compliance with UCC 9–312(3) and (4), can you assure your client of priority, not only as to the original collateral but also to the proceeds in both cases? If not (and the answer should be no), how do you advise your client to conduct its business in order to minimize its risk?

JOHN DEERE CO. v. PRODUCTION CREDIT ASSN. OF MURFREESBORO

Court of Appeals of Tennessee, Western Section, 1984.
686 S.W.2d 904.

NEARN, P.J. This appeal involves a dispute between two commercial lenders, John Deere Company and Production Credit Association (P.C.A.), over their interests in the proceeds from the sale of a piece of farm equipment purchased by James Willis. The Chancellor held that neither had priority over the other under Article 9 of the UCC (T.C.A. § 47–9–101, et seq.), and that their rights in the proceeds were pro rata, according to the amount each loaned to Willis.

The facts are not disputed. In a transaction prior to the one in question here, P.C.A. acquired a security interest in "all farm machinery and equipment, including but not limited to all tractors, tilling and harvesting equipment" owned by Willis and in all such property acquired in the future. The financing statement was properly filed on December 10, 1980. At that time, Willis owned a John Deere 6600 combine.

In September, 1981, this combine burned. The insurance proceeds on the combine were turned over to P.C.A. and applied to Willis' debt. Shortly thereafter, Willis borrowed $17,859.03 from P.C.A. to be used as a down payment on the purchase of a new combine and flex head from General Equipment Company (hereinafter "General").

To provide these funds, a sight draft made payable to General, drawn on a P.C.A. account and signed by Willis, was given to Willis by P.C.A. The face of the draft contained wording that it was to be used for the purchase of a John Deere 6620 combine, with a specific serial number. At the time of the issuance of this draft, P.C.A. did not obtain a new security agreement from Willis, nor was a new financing statement filed. However, the P.C.A. financing statement filed on December 10, 1980, contained both a future advances clause and an after-acquired property clause.

The same day that the sight draft was issued by P.C.A.—October 14, 1981—Willis signed a retail installment contract for the purchase of a new John Deere 6620 combine and a new John Deere 215 flex head from General for $59,000.00 less a down payment of $17,800.00. At the same time, he also signed a security agreement and financing statement in favor of General, which was properly filed on October 23, 1981. General accepted the draft of P.C.A. as down payment on the combine. Shortly after the transaction was completed between Willis and General, General assigned the security agreement and financing statement to the John Deere Company. John Deere accepted the assignment from General on October 29, 1981.

Subsequently, Willis defaulted on both the debts to P.C.A. and to John Deere. He voluntarily released the combine and flex head to P.C.A.. At the time of the default, the balance owed to Deere was $52,216.28 and the balance owed to P.C.A. was $17,859.03. Deere filed suit against Willis and P.C.A., seeking possession and sale of the combine, that the proceeds be paid into the court for a determination of the interests of P.C.A. and Deere and that a judgment for any deficiency be entered against Willis. P.C.A. surrendered the collateral with a reservation of its rights in the proceeds and filed a cross-claim against Willis and John Deere claiming a purchase money security interest in the combine in the amount loaned to Willis by P.C.A. for the down payment, $17,859.03. P.C.A. based its claim upon the draft dated September 14, 1981, issued by it to General and upon its original financing statement and security agreement filed in December, 1980. * * *

John Deere Company . . . insists that P.C.A. could not have a purchase money security interest in the collateral based on the filing of their financing statement of December 1980 that contained an after-acquired property clause. We hold that P.C.A. does have a purchase money security interest in the collateral and because their financing statement was filed prior to Deere's, they also have priority over Deere's interest. We therefore must affirm in part and reverse in part.

* * * In order to perfect a security interest in farm equipment to insure that it will be superior to interests of third parties, the secured party must file a financing statement in the county of the debtor's residence. See T.C.A. § 47-9-401(1). If the value given is used by the debtor to purchase the collateral, then the secured party has a purchase money security interest in the collateral, which normally would give him priority over any other security interest in the same

collateral, as long as he perfected his interest by filing a financing statement within twenty days of the debtor receiving possession of the collateral. See T.C.A. §§ 47–9–107(b) and 47–9–312(4).

In this case we have two secured parties fighting over the same collateral, now converted to money. It is undisputed that Deere has a perfected purchase money security interest in the collateral. It is also undisputed that P.C.A. gave the debtor money to purchase the collateral. The problem is that the security agreement and financing statement that P.C.A. is relying on were filed earlier, in another loan transaction. However, both of these instruments include an after-acquired property clause that we believe is sufficient to accomplish the purpose of giving P.C.A. a purchase money security interest in the combine. This is especially true in this case because the recorded financing statement specifically describes farm equipment. The purpose of the financing statement is to put third parties who check the filings on notice. We believe the financing statement P.C.A. had on file would have alerted Deere to the possibility that P.C.A. had an interest in the collateral. After thus being notified, it was incumbent upon Deere to look into the matter further if they wanted to make sure that they had the highest priority interest in the collateral. That is the purpose of notice filing. The burden is upon the party seeking a purchase money security interest to check recorded filings. Such task certainly should be performed when the credit advanced is substantially less than the purchase price of the collateral. Such fact clearly opens up the distinct possibility that someone else has advanced the debtor funds and will therefore be claiming a purchase money security interest in that collateral. * * * As far as we can determine from record, P.C.A. had a security agreement and a prior recorded financing statement and based thereon advanced to the debtor $17,859.03. The draft for $17,859.03 was given to the debtor, who in turn gave it to Deere, who applied it as a down payment for the new collateral. The undisputed testimony of P.C.A. was that no payments were made on the new loan. There is no difficulty in determining what portion of the loan was represented by the purchase money.

Additionally, P.C.A. is not claiming a purchase money security interest in the collateral any greater than the purchase money it loaned. They are claiming a purchase money security interest to the extent of the present consideration they advanced for the purchase of the combine, not for any prior loans they made. If they were, different results might be reached. See T.C.A. § 47–9–107, comment 2.

Therefore, we hold that P.C.A. has a purchase money security interest in the combine only up to the amount of the value they gave that was used for the purchase, that is, for $17,859.03. It is not our view that in all cases where a financing statement is filed and the lender has an after-acquired property clause in the financing statement that a *purchase money* security interest is retained in whatever the borrower purchases. A security interest yes, but the type will depend upon the circumstances. Where the funds are delivered by the lender for the specific purpose of purchasing specific equipment that is specifically covered by the prior financing statement of the parties, that security interest is a purchase money security interest when the funds are so used. Such are the provisions of T.C.A. § 47–9–107(b).

Deere asserts that a new financing statement had to be filed for P.C.A. to obtain a purchase money security interest in the combine. We see no reason for a second filing of a financing statement by P.C.A. to insure a purchase money security interest. The first filing was notice to the world of a security interest in farm equipment and after-acquired property, and any further notice filing would be, in our opinion, supererogation.

Since we hold that both parties have a perfected purchase money security interest in the combine, it must be determined which has priority.

Both interests attached at the same time, that is, when the debtor acquired rights in the collateral. P.C.A. had, in essence, a pre-filing and Deere's filing related back to the day the debtor obtained possession under T.C.A. § 47–9–312(4). Since this section does not assist us in determining which party has priority, we must look to the "clean up" section, § 47–9–312(5). Since both parties perfected by filing, the first to file has priority. See T.C.A. § 47–9–312(5)(a). Therefore, P.C.A.'s purchase money security interest is superior to Deere's.

Accordingly, P.C.A. is entitled to $17,859.03 of the disputed fund and John Deere is entitled to the balance.

The result is that the holding of the Chancellor that both P.C.A. and Deere possess purchase money security interest in the collateral is affirmed. However, his holding that the interests are held equally on a pro rata basis is reversed. Costs below are as there adjudged. Since the assessment of costs of appeal are not governed by the UCC, we adopt in principle the policy of the Chancellor and assess them on an equal, pro rata basis of one-half to each.

TOMLIN and HIGHERS, JJ. concur.

Problem 5–4

Consumer debtor has purchased ten items of hard goods from your client, Retail Appliance Mart. In each case the debtor executed a security agreement with your client; each was for the purchase price of the item sold. However, as the items mounted, the secured creditor was interested in having a security interest in the items previously purchased to support the amounts owed on items subsequently purchased and vice versa. Thus, each of the security agreements contain "cross-collateral clauses" in which the debt for one was secured by the asset purchased earlier and by assets purchased later. Moreover, the payments were consolidated because the debtor would have been hopelessly confused if each month he had to make a series of five or six different payments. Debtor is now threatening bankruptcy; his total outstanding balance is almost $12,000. His lawyer has made an offer. He has asked that the debt be written down to something under $10,000 in return for the debtor not going into bankruptcy. Debtor's lawyer makes two arguments against the retail seller's position. First, he argues that the bank no longer has a perfected security interest because perfection depends upon automatic perfection under UCC 9–302(1)(d). He argues that bank is not a purchase money lender because its cross-collateral clause keeps it from complying with UCC 9–107 inasmuch as the interest is not taken or retained by the seller, in the words of UCC 9–107 to secure all or part of "its" price.

For the same reason he argues that the debtor in bankruptcy will be able to shuck even a perfected security interest under Section 522(f) of the Bankruptcy Code because the security interest will no longer be a purchase money interest and it will be in items of household goods as to which the debtor would otherwise have an exemption.

Evaluate these arguments and determine whether you will advise your client to accept the offer. Advise your client how such problems might be avoided in the future.

Problem 5–5

United Bank of Littleton granted a secured loan to Drug Fair Inc., a retail drug store and pharmacy. The bank's security agreement and financing statement covered "all inventory, furniture, fixtures, equipment, accounts receivable, and machinery now owned or hereafter acquired." A year later Davis Brothers, a sales supplier of Drug Fair loaned $62,822 to Drug Fair, took a security interest in and filed a financing statement covering the following, "all drug and sundry inventory of debtor which debtor has purchased or may purchase from secured party and in which secured party has taken or will take a security interest." The security agreement and financing statement also covered "all prescription records." Davis gave no notice to United Bank of Littleton. Two years after Davis had filed its financing statement, a representative of United Bank discovered the financing statement by happenstance in connection with another search. Upon Drug Fair's bankruptcy, the trial court awarded Davis the inventory and the prescription records. United Bank has come to you to ask whether it has any basis for appeal. What do you think? (In the course of your analysis compare the 1962 version of UCC 9–312(3)(b) with the 1972 version of UCC 9–312(3)(b).)

C. Monitoring Against Collateral Risks

It is easy for a lawyer or even a law student to acquire an exaggerated opinion of the importance of his work. The fear of subordination to another secured creditor because of failure to file is far down in the hierarchy of creditor concerns. More likely the creditor will be disappointed because the debtor commits fraud, the collateral declines in value or the documents are never executed at all. Some of those problems are considered in the discussion that follows.

Accounts

Accounts are mere rights to payment. Indeed, they are not even embodied in any unique piece of paper. That is, there is no such piece of paper that is the unique embodiment or exclusive representation of a specific account. We have already seen that for this reason an account cannot be the subject of a possessory security arrangement. All this foretells that an alleged account may not even exist, although the debtor may wave a sheet of paper around and proclaim its existence with Bishop-like solemnity. Assuming that the lender has satisfied himself that the *initial* accounts existed, he must be sure that subsequent advances under a floating lien are similarly secured. An occasional lender has been duped into lending against wholly fictitious accounts. See, e.g., Firestone Tire & Rubber Co. v. Central Nat'l Bank, 159 Ohio St. 423, 112 N.E.2d 636 (1953).

Even though it is real, an account is no more valuable than the account obligor's ability to pay. And in this world many an account obligor has become insolvent or very "slow pay". There is a story told along the banks of the Upper Mississippi of an accounts lender who lent large sums to his borrower (against the accounts) only to find that 111 of the 112 account obligors had taken bankruptcy in the preceding month prior to default. (The 112th owed an account only for $6.13.) Then, too, there are places where all the credit customers (or nearly all) of a given dealer are employed by the same employer. If that employer were to shut down, many of the employees would not be able to pay their bills and the collateral would be rendered worthless. If there is any risk of shut down, perhaps a lender should not lend to a dealer against such accounts.

Even if the account is real and the account obligor solvent, risks remain. For example, the obligor may have or acquire a defense against the obligee-assignor. As every first year law student of contracts learns, the account obligor can set up most such defenses not only against the obligee-assignor, but against the assignee-secured party as well. (On this, more later.)

How can a party with a floating lien in accounts protect against such risks? Review the material below:

KRIPKE et al., BUSINESS FRAUDS, THEIR PERPETRATION, DETECTION AND REDRESS, 20 Bus.Law. 83, 105, 106, 107–08, 109, 111–12 (1964).

"The third reason that I use this topic as an example of the problem of fraud on lenders is that accounts receivable financing is peculiarly susceptible to fraud unless expertly administered. Unlike the case where you discount promissory notes or trade acceptances or lend against them, the security in the accounts receivable field is an invoice—a unilateral piece of paper not signed by the account debtor whom you hope to charge, but prepared by the seller, his creditor. Moreover, the copy of the invoice which is submitted by the seller to the lender may not coincide at all with the copy of the invoice that the debtor himself receives. The lender may be deceived as to whether there is a solid agreement to pay or whether there is on the side a consignment arrangement or a sale-or-return arrangement or the like. Similarly, the invoice does not prove that the goods have been shipped and received; again, the opportunity for fraud is there. Finally, most accounts receivable financing is done on a non-notification basis, where the lender who is the assignee of the account has no direct contact with the account debtor. The assignor, the original seller, collects the account and is supposed to account for the collection to the lender. Because of that lack of direct contact, the possibility and the opportunity for a completely fabricated system of assignments of collateral—a Ponzi scheme—is there, and there is real potentiality for fraud.

* * *

"What can the financial community do in this potentially dangerous field to provide the financing that is so important to the economy, and at the same time, not get badly burned? The first recommendation is similar to the recommendation I made in the case of internal fraud—demand from your debtor certified reports of its financing condition by independent public accountants, because there is the first measure of protection. But, be sure that they are certified! One of the evils which the leaders of the accounting profession have been fighting against is the practice of some auditing firms of lending their name and their stationery to the publication of reports which are, in fact, not certified. * * *

* * *

"Suppose you have gotten accountants' certified statements, and you discover, nevertheless, that the statements were false, and you didn't have a fair picture of the financial condition of the borrower. Can you as a third-party lender, in this case, hold the public accountants responsible for their false statement of the condition of the company they examined? They didn't, of course, enter into any agreement with the lender—the question is whether they are liable to third parties for failure to perform their audit of the borrower properly.

* * *

"There will be very few cases in which the lender can make the showing necessary to put his loss back on the shoulders of the accountant. I go further than that. I was involved in one group of litigations against accountants arising out of fraudulent borrowing—and it is perhaps the only case in the history of a very honorable profession in which the contention made against the accountants was not merely that they had made a mistake in judgment or even that they had passed the shadowy line between negligence and gross negligence, but it was that they had deliberately and consciously failed to disclose the desperate financial condition of a dishonest debtor. I walked the streets of New York for weeks trying to find an accountant witness who would support that allegation. I could find plenty of accountants who would tell me that the conduct of the certifying accountants in that case was outrageous, but they would tell me so only privately. When it came to doing so in court, the profession closed ranks against the outsider like the medical profession does, and one could not find a witness. Thus, the remedy against accountants for the lender's loss is a very unlikely one.

"Let us now turn, as we did before on the subject of internal fraud, to the possibility that you can have insurance against this loss. There has been recently much litigation and much controversy on the question whether the type of surety bond which all bankers and all finance companies carry, namely, the banker's blanket bond, or the modified form of broker's blanket bond for finance companies, gives the lender coverage against fraudulent loss in this accounts receivable field. * * *

* * *

"This leaves the accounts receivable finance business, both as practiced by banks and as practiced by the specialized finance companies and factors, back to its own operating capabilities, without being able to put the loss on the accountants' shoulders or on a surety company. What have they done to protect themselves against these risks and how successfully have they done so? You may argue to me that it is obvious that they haven't been successful, or the surety companies wouldn't be withdrawing from the risk. This does not necessarily follow. There is a gray area here. For every *Estes* case or *Salad Oil* case that makes the newspapers, every experienced administrator of accounts receivable financing can cite you ten cases where his outside staff or his inside staff detected a fraud at the early stages. These finance companies have groups of what they call auditors. Perhaps they should not be called auditors, to avoid confusion with the independent public accountants. They might perhaps more properly be called inspectors. These staffs pay surprise visits to the financing clients, at intervals as frequent as 30 to 60 days. They are trained in accounting, but start with an attitude somewhat different from that of the public accountant, who is entitled to assume in the first instance, that his client is honorable. They are supposed to start with a quizzical or skeptical or even a suspicious attitude and to look for fraud, knowing that these frauds start not with someone who is known to be a bad moral risk but someone who, because of financial pressure, takes a little bit and converts himself into a bad moral risk. Thus, these inspectors employed by the lender make investigations that approximate the kind of detailed audit of all transactions which the public accountants have always said that they did not perform. These fellows check the books, check the delivery receipts, check the shipping receipts, reconcile the borrower's books with the lender's—all of this in a detailed fashion going far beyond that which time permits for the public accountant under the terms of his engagement. When they see something irregular—when they don't understand why the payables are so high in view of the fact that it is the purpose of accounts receivable financing to give a fellow a jump on his cash so that he will be current on his payables—when they see an inconsistency between the borrower's and the lender's books—when they see invoices that are created outside the regular numbering system, or typed on a different typewriter or written longhand—when they find the shipping clerk in possession of a pad of blank receipts signed by a trucker—when they see suspiciously large accounts—when they see a large receivable in the name of a company that looks like it simulates the name of a leading corporation—when they see their own loan checks with curiously irregular endorsements, *e.g.*, where the check didn't go through a bank account, but through a professional check cashier—all of these and many more red flags that are set forth on check lists six, eight or ten pages long of points to be checked, all of these become indications of fraud that the external auditing staff and the internal operating staff of a finance company are trained to watch. Even without the benefit of surety bond protection, these specialized techniques enable them to keep the losses down to manageable proportions. They have similar techniques for lending against inventory under warehouse receipts and it is of some interest that in the big *Salad Oil* fraud, only one finance company is involved in those hundreds of millions of dollars of loss and that one is involved not because it was directly deceived but because it lent money to someone else who was deceived.

"A question is forming as the demands for accounts receivable financing grow increasingly with the pressures on the working capital of small business, and the banks enter increasingly into this field—what are the banks going to do to overcome this peculiar susceptibility for fraud? One choice would be to set up their own auditing staffs with this special skill that I have just attempted to describe, but this is expensive and it necessitates a rate of charge somewhat in excess of that which banks are accustomed to charge. Or the banks can say, 'We'll deal only with the finest credits and not worry about fraud,' and then perhaps they may suffer the experience that this West Coast bank is now suffering with a million dollar accounts receivable fraud, from a good moral risk that turned sour.

"Finally, some of the banks are, in effect, buying the extra skills of the finance companies by entering into this field on a participation basis. The field is too new yet for anyone to determine just in which way the banks will finally resolve the problem of how they enter the field. It will be an interesting development. Above all, the message has to be that accounts receivable financing can only be successfully handled against this threat of fraud by building up techniques which go beyond the auditing of the independent public accountant and approach almost the detailed audit of individual transactions."

Inventory

The debtor can squander, damage, lose, secrete, etc., items of inventory. Or he may fail to care for it. And it may burn up, etc. If the inventory can be readily insured at economic rates, the secured creditor may want to insist on insurance. But insurance is either not available or too expensive for coverage of some risks. The possibilities are legion and the variations numerous. Consider, for example, the risk that a car dealer will borrow against an inventory that he represents to include cars that it in fact does not include. This is a pervasive risk. Below is one way one lender seeks to protect against this type of risk:

BIBOROSCH, FLOOR PLAN FINANCING, 77 Banking L.J. 725, 736–40 (1960).

"Except in the case of a sale, merchandise cannot be removed from the dealer's place of business for demonstration purposes without the bank's authorization. Merchandise on floor plan should be so stored as to allow reasonable accessibility for purposes of inspection. The agreement should include a provision that the bank's representative be permitted to inspect the dealer's inventory periodically at the bank's discretion. Seeking additional floor plan accommodation from another bank or finance company without prior discussion constitutes sufficient reason for discontinuing the floor plan arrangement.

"There are a number of different thoughts relating to the extent and frequency of checking dealer floor plan, but in the final analysis the procedure and manner of handling is a decision that rests with management. A collateral check is necessary for the bank's protection. This should be scheduled to keep the bank's exposure to a minimum, at the same time keeping in mind the effect that too frequent checking would have on dealer goodwill in relation to the risk involved (as well as the costs of a stepped up program). Common sense should weigh the benefits to be gained or lost by a plan that is economically unsound.

"In our bank an inspector calls on the dealer and obtains permission to make a physical inspection of the inventory listed on his floor plan checking report. He must personally see the serial or motor numbers on the merchandise and is not permitted to accept the 'say-so' of any other person who may volunteer to call the numbers to him. If for any reason the checking of the dealer's inventory is delayed by the dealer, the inspector must note this fact, together with the dealer's reasons in the 'remarks' section of the inspection report.

"In the case of automobiles, notations are made describing license plates on the cars. If the car or tires show any evidence of usage, this fact is also stated, and in all cases a record of the mileage is entered on the inspector's report. If a missing car is reported by the dealer as on hand at the dealer's branch location or off the floor or lot for any reason, full particulars must be given. When a car is sold and therefore not in the dealer's possession, a notation to this effect is also made for verification covering the period of delay in remitting payment. However, in nearly all instances the inspector will obtain a check from the dealer to be returned with his signed and dated report. This report should be studied and appropriate action taken with regard to the exceptions. When these have been cleared the report is filed and held available for future review of the dealer's performance record in the event exceptions become too frequent.

"Floor plan inspectors should never be assigned to call on the same dealer twice in succession because of the possibility of collusion. Furthermore, an excellent test check on an inspector's accurate or perfunctory performance is made possible by deliberately transposing or rearranging the last several numbers on his floor plan checking report covering a few of the items listed. Inspectors are also required to report new locations where merchandise is being stored in order to obtain a landlord's waiver. Reference should be made concerning potential fire or theft hazards. Comments by the dealer's employees concerning unethical sales practices or other important information should also be reported.

"It is customary to check floor plan once a month, but naturally not always on the same day. We follow this policy for every dealer. If, in our opinion, a dealer is not remitting proceeds as promptly as he should, we will check him again in four, five, or ten days. Some companies check dealers monthly until a favorable experience has been developed. If the circumstances warrant, the dealer may be moved up to a bimonthly basis, then to 90 days, and ultimately to a four, five, or six month basis for dealers of outstanding financial, moral, and operating stability.

"Other companies permit the use of stickers, written in ink and placed on windshields, to facilitate inspection of large inventories. Another policy, for desirable dealers, is the spot check system covering a certain percentage of the dealer's wholesale. If the inspection is in order, the balance of inventory is not checked.

"Checking appliance floor plan may pose a problem if the merchandise is in cartons stored on top of one another. In 1950 we ran into a situation where we found ourselves financing some empty containers. Many manufacturers place serial numbers on their cartons, either stenciled or in crayon, and some are tagged. We accept these figures after taking reasonable precautions that the cartons are sealed and we spot check several units in areas that are partially hidden or covered.

"In checking the floor plan of automobile dealers where there is an extremely large amount of wholesale outstanding, we have learned that a considerable amount of time can be saved by having the inspectors check the dealer's entire inventory in the order of accessibility, and then comparing this list with his floor plan checking report. By this means the inspectors do not have to peruse 20 to 40 sheets of serial numbers for every car inspected. This method has also disclosed some instances where factories have shipped cars to dealers but we had not paid for these automobiles. This enabled the dealer to sell from such shipments and withhold prompt remittance on the assumption that his inventory would not be checked for another 30 days.

"The consumer credit division records should be checked by the auditors each month to ascertain that there is an inspector's wholesale checking report on file for each dealer and that the same inspectors have not checked the same dealers on consecutive inspections.

"The auditors should make an independent physical inspection on a non-notification basis of all floor plan at least once a year on the dealer's premises. The list of floor plan, covering the account in question, should be prepared on the regular wholesale floor plan check reports assembled from the consumer credit department's ledger records, and the auditors should follow the same procedure as outlined for the regular inspectors.

"All wholesale floor plan accounts should be verified annually by direct confirmation with the dealers and, at that time, the following duties should be performed by the auditors.

"1. A trial balance of the ledger cards should be run by the dealer and verification of the total should be made with the dealer control cards and the general ledger control.

"2. Preparation of confirmation forms from information on the ledger records showing the dealer's name and address and loan balance as of the confirmation date. It is not necessary to confirm serial numbers in this case.

"3. It is impractical to run a trial balance of the floor plan notes because these are filed in loan folders together with other supporting papers, but a test check of the notes should be made against the ledger record from which a trial balance was taken.

"4. A test check of serial numbers should be made of merchandise on floor plan from the standpoint of the ledger records against trust receipts to ascertain that a trust receipt or other security agreement is on file and that merchandise represented by the serial numbers shown on the ledger records are recorded on the executed trust receipts.

"5. Dealer files should be checked to ascertain that proper filing has been made at the inception of the line of credit to show that we have a lien on any products floor planned for our dealer.

"6. Dealer files should be examined to establish that the bank has power of attorney to execute trust receipts, security agreements, chattel mortgages, and other documents in connection with the floor plan program, if that is company policy.

"7. A test check of the interest records should be made to ascertain that floor plan interest is billed properly and payment received. It is a customary practice to bill dealers for interest on a daily average balance basis.

"Inasmuch as wholesale credit is normally extended to dealers in order to obtain retail paper, it is recommended that precise records for every individual dealer covering wholesale collections be kept, and that these be related to the amount of retail paper received from the account. This particularly applies to automobile floor plan. By this means an average is established by totaling collections for the entire operation and total new car financing contracts submitted for discount. If a dealer's offerings are slightly below average, the account is still considered satisfactory or profitable if the deficiency in new retail volume is more than offset by used car installment contracts.

"In our analyses we maintain individual records for each dealer covering the amount of business received, the number of units discounted, the average amount of new car as well as used car deals, the number of repossessions and the total amount of losses per dealer, the number of rejections for each dealer account, and the number of contracts approved for each dealer but never submitted to us for discount. In connection with the latter, it is not uncommon for some dealers to call in two deals—one being an excellent piece of paper and the second a borderline deal. We like to reassure ourselves that the good credit is not used for window dressing to sell the marginal risk.

"This same procedure can be used as a practical approach if the bank floor plans heavy construction and road building equipment and boats. This system is not too realistic when applied to appliance financing because considerable merchandise is purchased on open account or by trade acceptances. It is good to note the average unpaid balance of appliance installment sale contracts to determine whether or not these balances are large enough to cover the cost of handling and to allow a reasonable profit."

SECTION 3. BUYERS OF GOODS, UCC 9–307(1) AND (2), 9–301

Read UCC 9–307(1) and 9–307(2). Read them twice. Now, which cases are governed by subsection (1) and which by subsection (2)? In fact, the provisions are mutually exclusive, but that certainly does not appear from a casual reading. In its early form section 9–307(1) started out with a prepositional phrase "In the case of inventory * * *." In effect the drafters were saying that if the goods were inventory in the hands of the *seller,* the buyer's rights were governed by subsection (1). If, on the other hand, the goods were consumer goods in the hands of the *seller,* the rights of a buyer were governed by subsection (2).

Presumably, if the goods were equipment, they were governed by neither and the buyer was left to his meager fare in UCC 9–201 and 9–301(1)(c).

An academic critic of the Code pointed out that the reference to inventory in 9–307(1) was redundant because the idea that the seller had to have the goods in inventory was inherent in the idea of the "buyer in the ordinary course." Section 1–201(9) defines the buyer in the ordinary course as a person who buys from one "in the business of selling goods of that kind," i.e., from one who holds them as inventory. The criticism was correct, yet the redundancy in the former provision made it easier to understand.

It is easy to identify the standard buyer under each subsection. Mrs. Jones who purchases a television set from her local appliance or department store falls in subsection (1). Whether she buys for credit or with cash, she is buying in the ordinary course. She expects, the seller's secured creditor expects her, and the seller expects her to take free of the security interest that exists in favor of the secured creditor financing the store inventory. To say that Mrs. Jones should check the financing statements would be laughable. Given these expectations, it would be doubly mad to say that the security interest could carry over into the TV set in her hands. Thus the consumer retail buyer is the standard buyer covered by UCC 9–307(1). Not surprisingly, published cases arising under UCC 9–307 do not involve Mrs. Jones, but others whose status is not so clear.

Read carefully, section 9–307(2) represents a breach in the secured creditor's armour so narrow as to be insignificant. In the words of Professor Gilmore, it involves only sales "by amateurs to amateurs," and not all of those sales are covered by UCC 9–307(2), for if the security interest in seller's goods is perfected by a filed financing statement, even an amateur-to-amateur sale does not allow the buyer to take free of a security interest. The standard case here is the second hand sale by Mrs. Jones of her used television set to her neighbor. In that case the appliance store will have perfected its security interest in the television set automatically under UCC 9–302(1)(d), for it will be a purchase money security interest in consumer goods. Thus, in the words of the beginning prepositional phrase, the goods are "consumer goods" in the hands of the seller. They must also be consumer goods in the buyer's hands ("for his own personal, family or household purposes") and the security interest must have been perfected other than by filing.

Consider our amateur-to-amateur case of Jones and her neighbor Smith. Smith buys the television from Jones. Even if Smith had thought to check the files he would have found nothing because there was automatic perfection (of the retailer's security interest) without a filing. In such circumstances no one would seriously argue that Smith should be subordinate to the appliance store's security interest. Note how narrow the exception is, however. Goods must be consumer goods on both sides of the sale. If they are equipment in the hands of the seller, the initial prepositional phrase knocks them out of subsection (2). If the secured creditor has filed a financing statement, the buyer is deprived of the protection of the subsection.

Before we turn to the cases, the student should understand two additional limitations in UCC 9–307(1). Note first that one takes free only of a security interest "created by his seller." Thus, if the seller was not the debtor whose signature on the security agreement created the security interest, the buyer in the ordinary course does not take free of the security interest. Can you think of a case where that would be so?

Second, and most important, note the exception in the sentence for farm products, "other than a person buying farm products from a person engaged in farming operations * * *." The farm products exception in UCC 9–307(1) has been a festering sore. The case set out below is a representative example of a court tussel over that exception. Increasingly it has been drawn into question in the legislatures and in the courts. Some states (e.g., Tennessee) have abolished the exception. In one way or another the courts have avoided the exception in circumstances where it seemed appropriate to do so, even in cases in which the drafters might have thought otherwise. Recently even the Congress of the United States has become involved. A new federal law now will have the effect of overriding the farm products exception in some cases. We consider it below. But UCC 9–307(1) presents some highly relevant and hotly contested issues.

CHRYSLER CORP. v. ADAMATIC, INC.

Supreme Court of Wisconsin, 1973.
59 Wis.2d 219, 208 N.W.2d 97.

This action was commenced on October 21, 1970, by Appellant Chrysler Corporation, seeking to replevin certain goods which it had contracted to purchase from Defendant Adamatic, Inc. Respondent Lakeshore Commercial Finance Corporation was subsequently permitted to intervene on the basis that it claimed a perfected security interest in the goods in question. During the pendency of this action, Adamatic went into receivership and, consequently, Adamatic's receiver, Russell A. Eisenberg, was also permitted to intervene. On February 9, 1972, judgment was entered giving Chrysler possession of the goods but requiring it to pay certain sums to Lakeshore. Chrysler, Lakeshore, and the receiver have all appealed.

The facts of this lawsuit are largely undisputed.

Chrysler owns and operates a plant in Indianapolis, Indiana, where it manufactures alternators and other electrical components for the motor vehicles it assembles elsewhere. Construction of the alternators requires a "stator winder," a highly specialized machine which can wind copper wire around a component part known as the "stator." For several years Chrysler had been purchasing this equipment from an Ohio manufacturer but had been seeking to find a more efficient winding machine. Chrysler engineers discovered that Adamatic was producing an advanced machine at its Milwaukee plant which, while designed for a different purpose, potentially could be converted for use as a stator winder in the Chrysler plant. Chrysler's interest in utilizing the Adamatic machine led to the transactions forming the basis of this lawsuit.

In 1967, Adamatic had entered into various security agreements with Lakeshore, whereby the latter agreed to finance Adamatic's operations and in return took a security interest in Adamatic's inventory and various other assets. The security agreements were duly filed, and it is undisputed that Lakeshore had a valid security interest in Adamatic's inventory at all relevant times.

Chrysler's first transaction with Adamatic, in March 1969, involved a contract calling for Adamatic to produce a prototype six-coil stator winder. Although the proposed machine was based on designs already formulated by Adamatic, it was to be custom built to Chrysler's specifications. The contract also required Adamatic to manufacture a "cell inserter," a separate machine, which was to be used in conjunction with the winder. The original purchase order quoted a price of $77,150 for the two units, but the price was later increased by $4,000 to cover an additional accessory for the cell inserter.

The agreement required Chrysler to make progress payments as the work neared completion. By the time the machines had been completed for shipment, Chrysler had paid 90 percent of the original purchase price. The remaining 10 percent was to be withheld until the goods were delivered and made to perform satisfactorily. Adamatic has never requested payment of this retainage, and it has not been paid.

On February 9, 1970, the completed winder and cell inserter were delivered to the Chrysler plant in Indianapolis. Although the cell inserter evidently performed to contract specifications, the six-coil winder failed to function well enough for production-line use. Over the next few months, Adamatic employees were in almost constant attendance at Chrysler's plant assisting Chrysler engineers in trying to get the winder working. Their attempts were unsuccessful, and on June 9, 1970, Chrysler sent a telegram to Adamatic threatening to cancel the second contract, executed in April 1970, between the parties if the winder could not be made to perform.

Finally, upon Adamatic's suggestion, it was decided to ship the units back to Milwaukee for additional work by Adamatic. By this time, Chrysler had decided that the six-coil winder should be converted for twelve-coil operation. On August 12, 1970, the cell inserter and six-coil winder were shipped back to Adamatic under a non-negotiable bill of lading. On August 20, 1970, Adamatic sent a quotation giving an additional price of $22,410 for the conversion. The quotation was accepted by Chrysler on a change order dated September 11, 1970. Subsequently, the parties executed a "Consigned Material Receipt Agreement," drafted by Chrysler, in which Chrysler purported to retain title to the goods.

Previously, in February, Chrysler had decided to enter into a second transaction with Adamatic involving additional machines of the same type. During that month, personnel from Lakeshore and Adamatic met with Chrysler in Detroit to discuss the financing of the second transaction. At that time, Chrysler was informed of Adamatic's shaky financial condition and the fact that Lakeshore held a security interest in Adamatic's inventory. Lakeshore told Chrysler that it was prepared to lend up to $300,000 to Adamatic if Chrysler would make progress payments on the proposed, second contract.

Chrysler's second contract with Adamatic was entered into in April 1970. A Chrysler purchase order requested Adamatic to produce three twelve-coil stator winders at a price of $83,646.43 per unit. The order, which was accepted by Adamatic, specified that the first machine was to be delivered on September 7, 1970, with the second and third twelve-coil winders to follow at thirty-day intervals. Chrysler agreed to make progress payments after the work was 25 percent complete, in an amount up to 80 percent of the value of the labor and materials put into the machines at that time.

In August 1970, Adamatic requested the first progress payment on the second contract. Chrysler sent an engineer to Milwaukee, who checked the work done and approved a progress payment of $105,761.55, representing 80 percent of the value which had been put into the machines. A payment in that amount was subsequently given to Adamatic, which immediately turned the money over to Lakeshore.

The six-coil winder had been returned in August, and by mid-September, 1970, the three twelve-coil winders were in various stages of construction. Adamatic's financial condition had long been shaky; by September, it had reached a perilous point. Its current balance sheet indicated a net deficit of $135,624.95. In addition, Adamatic had been delinquent for several months in making federal withholding tax payments to the Internal Revenue Service, and the I.R.S. was threatening Adamatic with a tax lien. Moreover, Adamatic was no longer able to pay its suppliers for parts going into the Chrysler machines, and construction was being slowed by suppliers who were withholding delivery. It appears that Adamatic was still operating only because Lakeshore was continuing to make cash advances sufficient to meet Adamatic's payroll.

On September 15, 1970, Lakeshore and Adamatic personnel met to discuss Adamatic's progress on the Chrysler contracts and the company's general financial prospects. At this time, Lakeshore advised Adamatic that it was in default and that unless it found some other source of financing, Lakeshore would be forced to liquidate its loan. Nevertheless, Lakeshore advanced an additional $30,000 to $50,000 to Adamatic, and by October 15, 1970, the loan balance was approximately $340,000. By the time of trial, however, Lakeshore had foreclosed on other secured assets still in Adamatic's possession, and Adamatic presently owes Lakeshore more than $200,000. It was stipulated that Adamatic was in default under its security agreements when this action commenced.

On October 12, 1970, Chrysler sent one of its engineers to Milwaukee in an attempt to expedite delivery of the twelve-coil winders, since the delivery dates for the first two machines had passed. He was told to return at the end of the week, when he could expect to receive the first machine. He returned on Friday, October 16th, and the following day the first twelve-coil winder was given a test run at the Adamatic plant. The machine was intended to handle two stators at once, but the tooling for one phase of the operation did not function. Moreover, the machine lacked a paint job and safety guards. Nevertheless, the engineer indicated that he would accept delivery and directed Adamatic to prepare the machine for shipment. Chrysler had arranged for a common carrier truck to be present that day, and the cell inserter was loaded on. Adamatic employees continued to work on the first twelve-coil winder during Saturday, October 17th, and on Sunday, the 18th, it operated properly. On Monday, October 19th, the truck returned, and the winder was skidded to the Adamatic dock for loading.

At this point, Lakeshore learned that Chrysler was trying to take delivery of the first twelve-coil winder. By telephone, Lakeshore's president directed Adamatic not to ship the machines. Accordingly, Adamatic personnel removed the cell inserter from the truck and moved the winder back into the plant.

Chrysler sought legal advice, and a meeting was held between the attorneys and representatives of Lakeshore and Chrysler on October 20, 1970. The participants in this meeting differ as to what transpired. According to Chrysler's witnesses, Lakeshore demanded that Chrysler renegotiate the price if it wanted delivery of the machines. Lakeshore's president testified, however, that he told Chrysler that Lakeshore had a perfected, security interest in the machines and was asserting its rights to possession.

Chrysler then commenced this replevin action to obtain possession of the machines. On October 21st, the sheriff seized the three twelve-coil winders and the cell inserter. At the time of the seizure, the first of the twelve-coil winders was substantially completed. The second was only about half finished, and the third was little more than a naked frame. The sheriff also seized the original six-coil winder, which had been completely stripped of usable parts after its return to Adamatic. In its original complaint, Chrysler declared the value of the goods to be $190,000 and put up a surety bond in twice that amount. Lakeshore immediately sought, and was granted, leave to intervene. Nevertheless, Lakeshore failed to file a sufficient redelivery bond, and the goods were turned over to Chrysler and removed to Indianapolis on or about October 27, 1950.

Adamatic, which had been insolvent for some time before the replevin, shortly thereafter went into receivership.

The trial of this action was held before a jury from November 16 to 23, 1971, and questions were submitted on a special verdict. The jury found that, as to the second contract for the twelve-coil winders, Chrysler had been a buyer in ordinary course of business. The jury further found that Lakeshore wrongfully caused Adamatic to detain the property involved in both transactions and that Chrysler's damages as a result of the detention were $40,000. It also found that Adamatic had been insolvent on the date this action commenced. The parties stipulated that issues regarding the first transaction (six-coil winder and cell inserter) were to be decided by trial judge, who determined that Chrysler had the right to possession of these machines.

The jury further found that the total value of the three twelve-coil winders was $220,000. It valued the cell inserter at $20,350, and the six-coil winder at $27,900. The trial judge changed the jury's answer with respect to the six-coil winder to $8,300 and reduced the finding of damages to Chrysler from $40,000 to $4,800.

Judgment was entered accordingly. The judgment essentially provided that Chrysler is entitled to all the goods involved in the action but denied Chrysler damages for the retention. For reasons not readily apparent, however, the trial judge ordered that Chrysler pay to Lakeshore (by way of the receiver) the value of the machines less the amounts which Chrysler had already paid Adamatic. In effect, he found that Chrysler held the goods subject to Lakeshore's security interest, despite the fact that he found Chrysler to be a buyer in ordinary course of business.

* * *

HEFFERNAN, JUSTICE.

It should be emphasized that the cause of action is for replevin. The action was brought by Chrysler to gain possession of the machines and for damages against Lakeshore for their wrongful detention. Although there is evidence in the record indicating a breach of contract by the manufacturer, Adamatic, no relief is sought for that. Lakeshore, on the other hand, asserts ownership of the machines because of its prior perfected security agreement with Adamatic. The receiver, representing the general creditors, bases its claim upon Lakeshore's rights as a secured creditor, but in addition asks for an accounting by Lakeshore for any excess which Lakeshore may receive from Chrysler. As an alternative only, the receiver argues that Chrysler's taking of the goods was an avoidable preference as against the unsecured creditors. No claim is asserted by either creditor against Chrysler for amounts unpaid on the contract price.

The legal issues fall into the natural division between the first contract involving the six-coil winder and the subsequent contract concerned with the three machines that are designated as twelve-coil winders.

THE FIRST CONTRACT—SIX-COIL WINDER

As recited in the statement of facts, the six-coil winder and the cell inserter were returned to Adamatic for alterations on August 12, 1970. Chrysler asserts, in respect to the six-coil winder, that it had title and possessory rights to the machine from the time it was first delivered to the Chrysler plant in February 1970. It asserts that the machine was returned to Adamatic on a bailment, by which Adamatic was to hold the winder for repair and alteration. Both creditors, Lakeshore and the receiver, assert that the return of the machine revested the title in Adamatic and made it subject to their claims.

Under sec. 402.401(1), Stats., subject to the provisions of ch. 409 and other limitations not applicable here, "title to goods passes from the seller to the buyer in any manner and on any conditions explicitly agreed on by the parties." The contract between Chrysler and Adamatic explicitly agreed that title to the six-coil winder and the cell inserter would vest in Chrysler upon the completion of manufacture and shipment to the Chrysler plant. Chrysler, therefore, obtained title to this machine when it was shipped from the Adamatic plant in early February 1970. At that time, under the terms of sec. 402.106(1), Stats., there was a completed sale. It is undisputed that this sale was in good faith and in the ordinary course of business. There is no claim that the original sale was in violation of Lakeshore's security interest or constituted a preference against the unsecured creditors.

In accordance with the provisions of sec. 409.307(1), Stats., Chrysler took the machines free of Lakeshore's security interest. The creditors, however, assert that Chrysler never "accepted" the goods or, if there were an initial acceptance, such acceptance was subsequently revoked. They rely upon sec. 402.401(4) for the proposition:

> "A rejection or other refusal by the buyer to receive or retain the goods, whether or not justified, or a justified revocation of acceptance revests title to the goods in the seller. Such revesting occurs by operation of law and is not a 'sale.'"

This question was fully litigated, and the trial judge made the finding that Chrysler had title to the six-coil winder and the cell inserter at all times after their initial delivery to Chrysler. A review of the record reveals that this finding is fully supported by the applicable law and the evidence adduced at trial.

The fact that title passed when the goods were first delivered, however, does not ipso facto evince Chrysler's acceptance of them. A sale of goods does not necessarily imply the buyer's acceptance. White & Summers, Uniform Commercial Code, p. 249, sec. 8–2. While the delivery of the goods completed the sale, whether Chrysler accepted the machine depends on Chrysler's conduct after the delivery. Sec. 402.606, Stats., delineates conduct that constitutes the acceptance of goods. A buyer accepts goods if he notifies the seller that he accepts them, if he fails to make an effective rejection, or does an act inconsistent with the seller's ownership. There is no evidence that Chrysler expressly notified Adamatic that it was accepting the goods. On the other hand, Chrysler retained the six-coil winder for over six months without rejecting it. Under sec. 402.602, the rejection of goods must be made within a reasonable time after delivery and rejection will be ineffective unless the buyer seasonably notifies the seller.

No notification was ever given of the rejection of the six-coil winder. While there was evidence that Chrysler was displeased with the performance of the initial winder, there was no intimation that the winder was being rejected, although a letter from Chrysler to Adamatic carried the suggestion that, if the six-coil winder did not operate satisfactorily, the second contract—the contract for the three twelve-coil winders—would be cancelled. Chrysler in fact retained the six-coil winder for at least two months following the threat to cancel the other contract.

There was also evidence that Chrysler, during the period of possession, treated the six-coil winder as its own. It tagged the machine with a brass plate, giving it a Chrysler inventory serial number. Such conduct alone has been found to be evidence of acceptance. Julian C. Cohen Salvage Corp. v. Eastern Electric Sales Co. (1965), 205 Pa.Super. 26, 206 Atl.2d 331, 2 U.C.C.Rep. 432. The cell inserter was completely acceptable to Chrysler, but it, too, was returned to Adamatic. There is no contention that the mere return of the cell inserter constituted a rejection; rather, it was needed by Adamatic to run tests on other winders that were being manufactured. The documents that passed between Chrysler and Adamatic at about the time of the return of the six-coil winder and cell inserter show that Chrysler wished to retain title and possession of the machine and was returning it merely for adjustment and modification.

The questions of acceptance or rejection of goods are questions to be resolved by the finder of fact and depend upon the ascertainment of the intent of the parties. * * *

* * *

There is sufficient evidence to show that Chrysler acquired full title in the six-coil winder and cell inserter at the time of their initial delivery, and that Lakeshore's security interest could not re-attach to the goods in absence of a rejection by Chrysler. The rights acquired by Adamatic were those of a bailee, who had possessory interest for a limited purpose, but did not amount to "rights in the collateral." Sec. 409.204(1), Stats.; Cain v. Country Club Delicatessen of Saybrook, Inc. (1964), 25 Conn.Sup. 327, 203 Atl.2d 441, 2 U.C.C.Rep. 247. See, also, 1 Gilmore, Security Interests in Personal Property (1965), p. 353, sec. 11–5; 4 Anderson, Uniform Commercial Code (2d ed.), p. 179, sec. 9–204:7.

* * *

We hold that Chrysler, under the applicable law, was entitled to replevin of the six-coil winder and cell inserter. * * *

* * *

THE SECOND CONTRACT—TWELVE-COIL WINDERS

The situation in respect to the three twelve-coil winders is markedly different from that of the six-coil winder and the cell inserter. In respect to the twelve-coil winders, although there had been a contract entered into at an earlier time, the delivery of the goods was occasioned only by the replevin seizure itself. In the absence of Chrysler's claim, Lakeshore's right to the possession of the twelve-coil winders would be unquestioned.

It was conceded that Lakeshore had loaned substantial sums to Adamatic and, under ch. 409, Stats., had perfected a valid security interest in Adamatic's inventory. It was stipulated by the parties that, prior to the replevin, the twelve-coil winders were a part of that inventory. Had Chrysler not seized the machines under its claim of right, upon Adamatic's default Lakeshore could have taken possession of the machines under sec. 409.503 and sold them under the provisions of sec. 409.504 to satisfy, in part at least, Adamatic's obligations.

The mere physical transfer of the machines from Adamatic to Chrysler does not defeat Lakeshore's right to foreclose on the collateral. A perfected security interest gives the secured creditor rights in the goods themselves, and under the rule of sec. 409.201, Stats., those rights follow the collateral into the hands of subsequent owners.

Applying the principles of the Uniform Commercial Code, it is apparent that Chrysler took physical possession of the machines at a time when Lakeshore would ordinarily be entitled to their possession. Chrysler's possession of the goods is, therefore, subject to Lakeshore's security interest unless some other provision of the Code is sufficient to supersede the rights of Lakeshore.

Chrysler relies upon sec. 409.307(1), Stats., as an exception to the general rule that a purchaser is subject to an outstanding security interest. * * *

Chrysler claims to be "a buyer in ordinary course of business." That term is defined by sec. 401.201(9), Stats. * * *

Chrysler claims that it became a buyer in ordinary course of business at the time it originally contracted to purchase the twelve-coil winders. It further argues that Lakeshore's security interest was cut off at the time of entering into the contract and, at the time it took possession of the machines by replevin, its possession was free and clear of any claims of the secured creditor. Lakeshore and the receiver for the general creditors are united in disputing this claim. They argue that nothing less than a bona fide transfer of the goods could cut off the security interest, and that a replevin cannot constitute a transaction in ordinary course.

The initial question posed is whether one can become a buyer in ordinary course before a sale has occurred. While it is apparent that the contract was a contract to sell, only the position of the creditors can be reconciled with the language of the Uniform Commercial Code.

Under sec. 401.201(9), Stats., "buying" includes receiving goods under a pre-existing contract for sale. The statute is silent on the question of whether "buying" encompasses a situation where there has been a nonreceipt of the goods; but the enumeration in the statute, when reasonably construed, limits buying in ordinary course of business to those situations where a "sale," defined by sec. 402.106(1) as "the passing of title from the seller to the buyer for a price," has occurred. There is no contention that title passed to Chrysler prior to the physical transfer occasioned by the replevin, but, under sec. 401.201(9), the buyer in ordinary course must buy without knowledge that the sale is in violation of the rights of a third party. In the instant case Chrysler, at the time of the replevin, had full knowledge of the perfected security interest of Lakeshore.

The commentators who have written on sec. 401.201(9), Stats., shed but confused elucidation on whether one can become a buyer in ordinary course merely by entering into a contract to buy. Professor Gilmore notes that the Uniform Commercial Code, unlike prior uniform acts, does not require that a buyer actually take delivery to attain the status of buyer in ordinary course of business. 2 Gilmore, Security Interests in Personal Property, p. 696, sec. 26.6. * * *

It seems clear that, if there is a sale and the buyer has obtained title to the goods, his status as a buyer in ordinary course will not be defeated merely because he has not taken possession. Such is not our situation here, where Chrysler buttresses its claim as a buyer in ordinary course by asserting the replevin action was a part of the process by which title passed. Moreover, in the contract between the parties, delivery was envisaged as an integral part of the title-passing process.

Although both parties have treated all three twelve-coil winders as being "identified to the contract," the state of the record reveals grave doubt that this is really the fact. Only one machine was in a deliverable state. The other two, at the most, were but incompletely assembled component parts. While the Commercial Code, as pointed out above, does not require that in all cases the buyer actually take delivery in order to have a buyer in ordinary course of business status, sound policy considerations in the instant situation would seem to dictate that the rights of a secured creditor ought not be impaired in the absence of a physical transfer or assignment of the goods. We agree generally with the position submitted by the National Commercial Finance Conference as amicus curiae. It points out that the Code generally gives preference to property interests which are evidenced either by recording or possession and that, to adopt the view of Chrysler, the financier of an inventory would no longer be able to rely on recorded interests and the status of his debtor's inventory. We recognize that this policy argument has been criticized by writers who contend that the commercial reality is that lenders rely not upon inventories or recorded instruments but rather upon the credit ratings of prospective debtors. * * *

* * *

This court, in Columbia International Corp. v. Kempler, *supra,* p. 559 of 46 Wis.2d, p. 469 of 175 N.W.2d, took a different position, stressing the policy of this jurisdiction—to place major reliance upon "apparent or ostensible ownership: People should be able to deal with a debtor upon the assumption that all property in his possession is unencumbered, unless the contrary is indicated by their own knowledge or by public records."

Thus, if Chrysler is to be afforded a status as a buyer in ordinary course of business, we conclude that such status must be determined as of the time he actually took possession of the goods.

The remedy of replevin is an unusual and drastic mode of recourse to secure the rights of a purchaser; and, from the viewpoint of common knowledge, it is almost absurd to argue that the acquisition of possession by replevin is in the ordinary course of business. It is certainly so in the instant case when we consider sec. 402.402, Stats. (the buyer's right of replevin) and sec. 402.716. Sec. 402.402(3)(a) provides:

> "Nothing in this chapter shall be deemed to impair the rights of creditors of the seller:
>
> "(a) Under the provisions of ch. 409 * * *."

The Commercial Code itself specifically negatives Chrysler's contention that the replevin alone can in any way affect the rights of a prior secured creditor. Even if it be argued that these three machines were identified to the contract, sec. 401.201(37), Stats., states:

> " * * * the special property interest of a buyer of goods on identification of such goods to a contract for sale under s. 402.401 is not a 'security interest' * * *."

Chrysler thus makes the anomalous and unacceptable claim that its buyer's interest gives it a right superior to the holder of an antecedent perfected security interest.

Chrysler is not a buyer in ordinary course of business and holds the machines subject to the security interest of Lakeshore. From the viewpoint of equity, this is an unsatisfactory result, for the record shows that, prior to the replevin, Chrysler had substantially paid the contract price for all the goods involved. Our conclusion, however, is supported by the writings of distinguished commentators, who have pointed out that the Code itself affords but little protection for the prepaying buyer. The Code, however, gives broad latitude whereby a prepaying buyer, acting timely, can enter into suitable arrangements for his own protection.

In the instant case Chrysler was fully aware of the fact that it was not only a buyer but was financing the manufacturing process. It was for that reason it made progress payments on the basis of the work and materials as the manufacturing progressed. By proper negotiations with the other creditors, it might well have protected itself by obtaining a security interest in the goods it had contracted to buy. Lakeshore as a substantial creditor, interested in the well being of Adamatic, might well have been amenable to a Chrysler proposal that Lakeshore in part subordinate its security interest. In view of the size of this contract in proportion to the limited assets of the manufacturer, it was almost foolhardy for Chrysler to proceed in the face of the perfected security interest of Lakeshore.

Numerous law review articles discuss the problems posed for the prepaying buyer by the Code and various methods that may be used to obviate the very situation which resulted here. * * * The taking of the machines by Chrysler under the circumstances was unlawful. Lakeshore, not Chrysler, was entitled to possession of the twelve-coil winders.

Problem 5–6

Each of the following problems is based on the facts of a reported decision. How do you think the cases came out and how should they have come out?

1. Winnetka Motors agrees to buy two new automobiles from Birmingham Auto House, a dealer in an adjoining county. Winnetka pays for the cars at once and the parties agree that Auto House will hold them for a couple of weeks until Winnetka is ready for them. In the intervening two weeks Commercial Credit, the secured lender of Birmingham, does an inventory and finds that Birmingham has been selling automobiles and has not been remitting the proceeds and is thus in default. Commercial then repossesses all of Auto House's cars, including the two that have been sold to Winnetka. Winnetka sues Commercial for conversion and argues essentially that it had acquired prior rights because of UCC 9–307(1). How would you respond as Commercial's counsel?

2. Tanbro Fabrics Corp. is a textile manufacturer who purchases textiles from a mill and finishes them into dyed and patterned fabrics. In this case, Deering Milliken produced goods manufactured for Mill Fabrics. Under the agreement between Deering and Mill Fabrics, Deering was entitled to hold the goods and to retain a security interest in them until Mill Fabrics paid. Mill Fabrics resold the goods while they were still in Deering's warehouse to Tanbro. Tanbro paid Mill Fabrics and a month later demanded the delivery of the goods still in Deering's possession to it. Mill Fabrics in the meantime went bankrupt and accordingly Deering refused to deliver the goods. It asserted that it has a prior right in them to secure the debt owed by Mill Fabrics to it. Who gets the goods, Deering or Tanbro? If Deering is the winner, how would you advise Tanbro in the future? If Tanbro is the winner, how would you advise Deering?

Problem 5–7

Daisy Bank and Trust has a security interest in refrigerators, stoves, appliances and all other hard goods of Marie Louise, Inc., a department store. Assume that the security agreement purports to continue the security interest in the goods even after they have been sold. Now consider the following transactions in goods covered by the perfected security interest.

1. Wilbur buys a washing machine for cash. Wilbur takes free of Daisy's security interest. True or false?

2. Wilbur buys a washing machine on credit and signs a security agreement giving Marie Louise a security interest in the machine. Wilbur takes free of Daisy's security interest. True or false?

3. Wilbur buys a refrigerator on credit from Marie Louise and signs a security agreement. A month later Wilbur sells the refrigerator to his next-door neighbor, Charlotte. Identify the correct statement or statements:

a. Charlotte takes free of the security interests of both Daisy and Marie Louise;

b. Charlotte takes free of Daisy's security interest because she qualifies under UCC 9–307(1);

c. Charlotte takes free of Marie Louise's security interest because of the application of UCC 9–307(1);

d. Charlotte does not qualify for the protection of UCC 9–307(1), nevertheless she takes free of both security interests.

LISBON BANK & TRUST CO. v. MURRAY

Supreme Court of Iowa, 1973.
206 N.W.2d 96.

McCormick, J. This appeal involves a problem under the Uniform Commercial Code arising out of a sale of cattle. Plaintiff Lisbon Bank and Trust Company loaned defendants to cross-petition (Glenn Meier and Joan Meier) $6620.00 on January 15, 1969, to purchase 48 Holstein heifers and received a duly perfected security interest in the cattle. On March 25, 1969, Glenn Meier sold 12 of the heifers to defendant Richard Murray for $2428.80. Subsequently the Meiers defaulted on their note and filed bankruptcy. The bank seeks in this action to collect $2428.80 from Murray on the theory he purchased the cattle subject to the bank's lien. Trial court found the sale was made free of the lien and dismissed the bank's petition. We affirm.

The determinative issue is whether the sale was authorized by the bank. Section 554.9306(2). The Code, provides:

> "Except where this Article otherwise provides, a security interest continues in collateral notwithstanding sale * * * by the debtor unless his action was authorized by the secured party in the security agreement or otherwise, and also continues in any identifiable proceeds including collections received by the debtor."

The Iowa Code commentators state this section was adopted from § 9–306 of the 1962 official text of the Uniform Commercial Code and compare this subsection with previous Iowa law:

> "Prior Iowa law was in accord that the lien of the secured party continued in the collateral after a sale thereof, Waters v. Cass County Bank, 65 Iowa 234, 21 N.W. 582 (1884), although the mortgagee could waive his lien by agreeing to the sale, Livingston v. Heck, 122 Iowa 74, 94 NW 1098 (1903)." 35B Iowa Code Annotated at 414.

The commentators add that the statute departs from former law by imposing a continuing lien on sale proceeds. However, as explained in the comment, where the lienholder authorizes the sale he waives his lien on the collateral under the Uniform Commercial Code just as under prior law.

We will assume the purchase in this case was by "a person buying farm products subject to a perfected security interest from a person engaged in farming operations" within the meaning of Code § 554.9307, under which other buyers in the ordinary course of business take free of a security interest even where the sale is unauthorized. See Uniform Commercial Code Comment, Iowa Code Annotated, at 431.

Trial court made a finding of fact that Glenn Meier had authority to sell the cattle. * * *

Sale may be authorized by the secured party "in the security agreement or otherwise." § 554.9306(2), The Code. The security agreement in this case did not authorize sale and therefore the bank cannot be held to have waived its security interest in the collateral unless it "otherwise" consented to the sale.

There was evidence the Meiers lived on a 33 acre tract near Lisbon where they bred sows, farrowed feeder pigs, grew hay and grazed livestock. The bank started loaning Glenn Meier money on his livestock operation in January 1968. Several loans covered by security agreements were made prior to January 15, 1969. At trial the bank acknowledged a general course of dealing, notwithstanding the security agreements, permitting him to sell collateral and apply the proceeds either to substitutions or on the notes. The bank admitted Meier accordingly sold hogs and horses on several prior occasions but denied he was authorized to sell cattle. There had been only one earlier cattle loan and those cattle had evidently not been sold at the time of the loan involved in this case. There was no evidence of any communication from the bank to Glenn Meier making any distinction as to cattle.

Glenn Meier told the bank at the time of the January 15, 1969, loan some of the cattle being purchased were bred, the others would be bred, and he intended to pasture them for six to 12 months on land owned by his father in Clinton County, selling them just before they calved. He hoped to pay the loan through enhancement in their value. The bank asserted it did not learn of the March 25, 1969, sale of 12 of the heifers to Murray until after the Meiers filed bankruptcy in May 1970.

However, it was undisputed that Glenn Meier took Murray's $2428.80 check to the bank the day after the sale. His version is that he told the bank's loan officer he sold some of the cattle and was permitted to deposit the money in his checking account rather than have it applied on the note. He said he spent the money on sows which became substitute collateral. The bank records show the check was deposited in his checking account. The bank loan officer denied Meier told him of the sale and said if he had the money would have been applied on the cattle loan. It was trial court's prerogative to pass on the credibility of the witnesses.

Both Glenn Meier and Murray testified Meier told Murray of the bank's security agreement on the cattle at the time of sale and Meier assured Murray he would take care of it.

Evidence of a course of dealing has relevance in interpreting agreements under the Uniform Commercial Code. Section 554.1205(1), The Code, defines course of dealing as "a sequence of previous conduct between the parties * * * which is fairly to be regarded as establishing a common basis of understanding for interpreting their expressions and other conduct." It may give particular meaning to and supplement or qualify terms of an agreement. § 554.1205(3), The Code.

A leading case on establishment of authority to sell secured farm products under the Uniform Commercial Code is Clovis National Bank v. Thomas, 77 N.M. 554, 425 P.2d 726 (1967). There the security agreement expressly prohibited sale of the collateral without the prior written consent of the secured party. The court found the secured party had nevertheless as a matter of common practice permitted the debtor to make such sales without prior written consent. The secured party was held to have waived the requirement of written consent and its security interest. Clovis has been criticized for recognizing course of dealing as a basis for waiver of the requirement of written consent to sale. This is because the Uniform Commercial Code provides where express terms of an agreement and a course of dealing are inconsistent the express terms control. § 554.1205(4), The Code. See, generally, 47 Tex.L.Rev. 309, 313–314.

A different result was reached by the Nebraska Supreme Court in Garden City Production Credit Assn. v. Lannan, 186 Neb. 668, 186 N.W.2d 99 (1971). That case also involved a security agreement containing an express prohibition against sale without prior written consent. The Nebraska trial court had found waiver based on the secured party's failure despite knowledge of the sale to object to it until after the purchaser's check failed to clear.

We are not here confronted with a security agreement with a provision requiring written consent prior to sale, and we have a course of dealing which raises a question of fact as to the debtor's authority to sell. Clovis and Garden City each recognize, in accordance with the general rule, that a finding of authority to sell may be implied from a prior course of dealing at least in the absence of a security agreement prohibition against sale without written consent. * * *

This principle is unaffected by a finding such as was made here that the authority to sell was conditioned upon the debtor's agreement to apply the proceeds to the debt:

> "Where the sale of mortgaged property is made with the consent of a person authorized to give such consent, any failure of the mortgagor to live up to an agreement he made relating to accounting for the proceeds does not affect the waiver of the lien." United States v. Hansen, 311 F.2d 477, 480 (8 Cir. 1963).

* * *

If the authority had been conditioned on the purchaser making payment to the secured party, it appears the lien would not have been lost. * * * Waiver substitutes the personal obligation of the debtor for the collateral. * * * It was not so conditioned. And we are not here confronted with a situation where the purchaser had notice of any condition.

The fact the purchaser had actual notice of the security interest and was unaware it was waived does not alter the result. Waiver was between the bank and the Meiers. It was not necessary that it be communicated to the purchaser. Where sale is authorized the lien is divested and the purchaser takes the property free of it. * * *

In the present case there is substantial evidence from which the trier of fact could find the bank gave general authority to Glenn Meier to sell collateral subject to his duty to account for the proceeds. The bank acknowledges no complaint would have been made here had the proceeds been applied against the note. The bank lost because it trusted Glenn Meier to do what he had done before when he sold collateral. Murray trusted his assurance the sale was free of lien. As between the bank and Murray, the law imposes the risk of loss in these circumstances on the bank.

There is substantial evidence to support trial court's finding the bank consented to the sale. The case is affirmed.

Affirmed.

Problem 5–8

Assume that Rural Bank, having read the Lisbon Bank case, instructs its lawyer to draft a security agreement that will "solve the problem." Lawyer presents a security agreement with the following clauses:

1. *Debtor may not sell.* Debtor is expressly forbidden from selling the collateral under this security agreement without the prior written consent of the Bank. Upon any sale that is authorized by the Bank, Debtor shall procure payment directly to the Bank or jointly to the Bank and Debtor.

2. *No Waiver.* None of the provisions of this security agreement may be waived except in writing by an authorized officer of the Bank. No waiver or trade practice or course of performance in any past case will operate as a waiver in any future case. Thus, the fact that the Bank permits debtor to sell cattle or other products and keep the proceeds shall not be regarded as a grant of authority to do that in the future.

Assume that Debtor sells cattle and remits the proceeds on several occasions. On none of these occasions did he seek or get approval of the Bank. On the final occasion he sells all of his cattle for $220,000, departs to Las Vegas, where over the period of two weeks he loses the entire amount at the gaming tables. Bank is able to locate most of the livestock in the hands of purchasers. Will it be able to sue them for conversion, or replevy the livestock?

Problem 5–9

Assume that you are general counsel for a large Minneapolis bank. The bank comes to you with the following problem. A rather slovenly loan officer has managed to lend $1,000,000 to a large cattle dealer in the southern part of Minnesota. The loan officer from the bank was taken around various cattle yards to observe the cattle at the time of the loan and was informed that various of the cattle totalling in excess of 6,000 head were owned by the debtor. Loan officer did not check the brands nor make any other effort to confirm the actual number or the ownership of the debtor. It now appears that at the time the large loan was made, the debtor owned fewer than 100 head of cattle. Some of the property which he claimed to have under "oral lease" in fact was property of others not leased to him, and all of the cattle shown to the loan officer belonged to third parties.

During the six months when the loan was outstanding the farmer acquired a few hundred head of his own. In addition, he owned for a short period as many as 7,000 head which went through a very active cattle auction barn that he ran on his property. In the typical case he actually held title to these cattle for a short period of time and then sold them to third parties. Through his records all of the third parties can be identified and the total value of the cattle sold to them is approximately $800,000. Bank would like to pursue each of those buyers for conversion on the ground that its security interest attached to the cattle owned, however briefly, by the Debtor under the after-acquired property clause, and on the theory that these buyers did not take free under UCC 9–307. Note that there is no prior experience (as there was in *Lisbon*) and that the security agreement does not authorize the Debtor to sell cattle.

Bank would like your opinion about the probability of success in that lawsuit. Your junior associate has come up with the following tentative analysis:

"The security agreement specifically attaches to after-acquired property and such terms are explicitly authorized by UCC 9–201, 9–203, and 9–204. It is conceded by all that the bank's debtor held title to these cattle for a period of time. When they were sold, those parties did not take free because of the exception in UCC 9–307 for farm products (sale was prior to 1987). It follows therefore the security interest traveled with the cattle into the hands of the third party and that the bank has a right to pursue those cattle. There is some chance that facts that are not now available to us may suggest that the bank gave the debtor authority to sell. Absent such facts, the security interest would continue in the cattle."

Would you act on this analysis?

Note: Federal Limitation on UCC 9–307(1)

By 1985 legislation, Congress has provided a mechanism which can override the "farm products" exception of UCC 9–307(1). Enacted within the Food Security Act of 1985, 7 U.S.C. § 1631 (Supp.1985), the statute grants federal protection to purchasers of farm products. In relevant part the statute provides:

> (d) Except as provided in subsection (e) and notwithstanding any other provision of Federal, State, or local law, a buyer who in the ordinary course of business buys a farm product from a seller engaged in farming operations shall take free of a security interest created by the seller, even though the security interest is perfected; and the buyer knows of the existence of such interest.

This general prohibition against lien enforcement is relatively straightforward. However, lengthy and complex exceptions may swallow the rule. The most important exceptions to the protection of purchasers of farm products are found in section 1631(e).

The first exception concerns buyers in the ordinary course with "actual knowledge" of the security interest. The general rule protects buyers with mere knowledge of the existence of a prior security interest. On the other hand, 1631(e)(1) provides that a buyer will take the purchased farm products subject to the existing security interest if the buyer receives written notice from the seller or secured party of the security interest within one year of sale and the buyer defaults on his obligation to pay for his purchase. At first blush the traditional notice system seems to have been turned on its head. No longer can a secured party depend on a centralized filing system for protection; if the secured party desires priority, he must send notice of his security interest to all potential purchasers of farm products from his debtor.

Of greater interest are the provisions creating a *second* filing system which permits the secured party to gain priority over purchasers of farm products. The second and third exceptions to 1631(d) concern the operations of a new creature called a "central filing system." Defined in 1631(c)(2), a central filing system is a centralized information system which registers secured creditors, debtors and purchasers of farm products. The central filing system is to be administered by the Secretary of State of each state, and each system is to be certified by the United States Department of Agriculture. Under the central filing system the Secretary of State periodically distributes all registered financing information to all registered buyers. If a state adopts a central filing system into its zoo of regulatory animals, an ordinary course purchaser of farm products will lose the general protections of 1631(d) if he is either not registered in the system or if he has received notice of a prior security interest from the Secretary of State. Thus, a state's enactment of a central filing system can return to the farm products exception originally contained in UCC 9–307(1).

Finally, a secured party in a non-central filing system jurisdiction may reduce the number of potential purchasers which he must notify if he requires his debtor to identify specifically all potential purchasers of the debtor's farm products. See 7 U.S.C. § 1631(h) (Supp.1985). If the debtor sells to a party not listed on the "accredited" purchaser list and neither gives prior notice to the secured creditor of the potential sale nor forwards the proceeds of the sale to the secured party, section 1631(b)(3) subjects the debtor to a fine of the greater of $5,000 or 15 percent of the proceeds of the sale. Note, however, that the *purchaser* will still receive the protection of 1631(d).

The basic effect of section 1631 is to shift the burden of informing. The purchaser's burden to seek out information regarding prior security interests is shifted either to the secured party (to notify all potential purchasers in non-central filing system states) or to the Secretary of State (to notify all registered purchasers in central filing system states).

Time will tell whether adoption of section 1631 was worth the effort. All states may effectively opt out of the 1631(d) protections by implementing a complex farm products filing system. Because of the cost and complexity of establishing an entirely new filing system, it seems more likely that most states will not enact a central system. Note that the central filing system puts a burden on the Secretary of State affirmatively to notify certain parties. That is a burden that a harried and understaffed Secretary of State will staunchly resist. Of course, the bankers may yet get Congress to modify the rule. At this writing only Mississippi has adopted a qualifying central filing system.

SECTION 4. PRIORITY AMONG BUYERS OF INTANGIBLES, UCC 9–306, 9–308, 9–309, 8–302

A. Chattel Paper, Instruments and the Like

The most renowned bona fide purchaser of intangible rights is barely mentioned in Article 9; he is the holder in due course of a negotiable instrument. We will meet that person in Chapter Twenty-Four, but it is not too soon to examine UCC 3–302 defining a holder in due course or UCC 3–305 specifying the rights of a holder in due course. Note that section 9–309 bows to those rights and to the rights of other lesser known bona fide purchasers such as the "due negotiatee" of a negotiable document of title under UCC 7–501 et seq., and the bona fide purchaser of a security under UCC 8–302. In addition, UCC 9–308 deals explicitly with competing claims to chattel paper and UCC 9–306(5) unravels priorities upon repossession of the underlying collateral.

Upon examination of UCC 3–302, 9–308, and the other sections, the student should be prepared to generalize from those sections and to ask why the law allows such a buyer necessarily second in time to have priority over someone who preceded him. Is the explanation no more than that this is the expectation of the parties that arises out of possession by the seller? Traditionally it has been thought desirable to allow a holder in due course to take free of other claims if the holder does nothing more than give new value to one who appears from the face of the instrument to be the owner. By such a method credit is easily and quickly extended and money was thought to flow readily from one place to another. In today's world where money is much more likely to pass over a wire than from hand to hand in response to a negotiable instrument, one might question the need for holder-in-due-course status.

Sections 9–308 and 8–302 rest on more specific commercial underpinnings. People do buy and sell chattel paper, and section 9–308 represents the drafters' judgment about the reasonable expectations of the various parties in that narrow setting. The same can be said about UCC 8–302, though a skeptic might argue that the section really represents only the buyer bank's interest and not that of customers on the selling end of the transaction.

Students should keep these questions in mind when they examine the cases and problems that follow. At minimum one needs to be able to answer the technical question: When will one lose to a subsequent party who may qualify under UCC 9–308 or 8–302? A good advocate will need also to address the policy question: when should such a person win, and why?

REX FINANCIAL CORP. v. GREAT WESTERN BANK & TRUST

Court of Appeals of Arizona, 1975.
23 Ariz.App. 286, 532 P.2d 558.

DONOFRIO, JUDGE.

This is an appeal from a judgment in favor of the appellee, Great Western Bank & Trust, on a motion to dismiss which was treated by the trial court as a motion for summary judgment under Rule 56 of the Arizona Rules of Civil Procedure, 16 A.R.S. The trial court considered all of the pleadings, affidavits, other matters of record, and the oral arguments of counsel and determined that there was no genuine issue of material fact, in reaching its judgment. For the reasons given below we affirm the judgment of the trial court.

* * * In December of 1971 appellant entered into an agreement with Liberty Mobile Home Centers, Inc., a dealer in mobile homes, under which appellant agreed to finance this dealer's inventory of mobile homes. The dealer delivered to appellant certain manufacturer's certificates of origin on mobile homes to secure repayment of the loans, and gave appellant a security interest in the vehicles by way of a security agreement between the parties. This appeal concerns four of those mobile homes. The four mobile homes were sold by the dealer in the regular course of his business to certain individuals on security agreement contracts. These four security agreement contracts were then sold and assigned to the appellee, Great Western, in the ordinary course of its business for a certain sum which was paid to the dealer. Unfortunately, the dealer did not use these funds to pay off its outstanding loans owed to the appellant.

The basis for attacking a Rule 56 summary judgment ruling is that there were material factual issues disputed by the parties. All facts considered by the trial court appear in the pleadings, affidavits, depositions, and of course, oral arguments of the parties. On reviewing the record we are compelled to agree with the trial court that there were no material issues of fact, and that this was a question of law concerning the construction and application of A.R.S. § 44–3129 (UCC § 9–308) concerning the priority between certain secured creditors and purchasers of chattel paper.

A.R.S. § 44–3129 states:

> "A purchaser of chattel paper or a non-negotiable instrument who gives new value and takes possession of it in the ordinary course of his business and without knowledge that the specific paper or instrument is subject to a security interest has priority over a security interest which is perfected under § 44–3125 (permissive filing and temporary perfection). *A purchaser of chattel paper who gives new value and takes possession of it in the ordinary course of his business has priority over a security interest in chattel paper which is claimed merely as*

proceeds of inventory subject to a security interest (§ 44–3127), even though he knows that the specific paper is subject to the security interest. Added Laws 1967, Ch. 3, § 5." (Emphasis added)

Since it was established that Great Western Bank had knowledge of the security interest claimed by Rex Financial Corporation in the four mobile homes, the second sentence of the foregoing section is the critical one for our purposes.

Appellant's first argument concerns the definition of "chattel paper" used in the above-mentioned sentence of A.R.S. § 44–3129. Appellant argues that the manufacturer's certificates of origin, which remained in its possession, were a part of the chattel paper and were necessary ingredients along with the security agreements purchased by Great Western to make up the "chattel paper" which must be possessed by the purchaser. We do not agree. A.R.S. § 44–3105(A)(2) defines "chattel paper" as: * * *. [quoting 9–105(1)(b)]

Appellant asserts that A.R.S. § 42–643 and § 28–325 of the Motor Vehicle Code contemplate that a manufacturer's certificate of origin is a part of the "transaction" where chattel paper is purchased as in A.R.S. § 44–3105(A)(2) above. We do not think that such comparison is relevant here. "Chattel paper" clearly must evidence "both a monetary obligation and a security interest in or a lease of specific goods." The manufacturer's certificates of origin do not meet this definition, and the trial court's construction of A.R.S. § 44–3105(A)(2) was correct in the application to this factual situation. It was undisputed that Great Western gave "new value" for the four security agreements it purchased from the dealer, all in accordance with § 44–3129.

The next requirement of § 44–3129 which is attacked by appellant is the requirement that the purchase of the chattel paper be "in the ordinary course of *his* business." (emphasis added) Appellant maintains that this refers to a practice which "should have been followed" and not to the practice of this particular purchaser of chattel paper. Again we do not agree. The plain language of the statute refers to *"his business"* (meaning the purchaser of the chattel paper). It is undisputed that this purchase was the normal means used at Great Western to obtain this type of chattel paper. As was stated in the deposition of Mr. McFadden, a representative of Great Western, he expected the *dealer* to disburse funds to appellant to pay off the loans for the "floor plan" financing that the dealer had obtained from appellant. The term "buyer in the ordinary course of business" with its requirements of good faith, as used elsewhere in the Uniform Commercial Code, is to be distinguished from the use here of "buyer in the ordinary course of *his* business." In fact, § 44–3129 (second sentence) allows the purchaser of the chattel paper to have priority even if he has knowledge of a prior security interest in the collateral. As noticed by White and Summers in their Treatise on the Uniform Commercial Code, " * * * the later party is favored on the assumption that chattel paper is his main course but merely the frosting on the cake for the mere proceeds claimant." White and Summers, Uniform Commercial Code, Sec. 25–17, p 951 (1972 Edition).

This brings us to the final issue raised by appellant: the fourth requirement of the second sentence of § 44–3129, that the security interest claimed by appellant is claimed "merely as proceeds of inventory subject to a security interest." We find Comment 2 to this section of the UCC (as found in the Final Report of the Permanent Editorial Board for the Uniform Commercial Code, Review Committee for Article 9, April 25, 1971) instructive on this issue. There it is stated:

> "Clause (b) of the section deals with the case where the security interest in the chattel paper is claimed merely as proceeds—i.e., on behalf of an inventory financer who has not by some new transaction with the debtor acquired a specific interest in the chattel paper. In that case a purchaser, even though he knows of the inventory financer's proceeds interest, takes priority provided he gives new value and takes possession of the paper in the ordinary course of his business."

We take this language to mean that the drafters of the Code contemplated a situation such as the instant one where the inventory financer, Rex Financial Corp., had a security interest in the collateral (mobile homes) and the proceeds upon sale. The record before us does not indicate that Rex entered into any new transaction with the debtor/dealer. The trial court had before it the security agreement between Rex and the dealer as well as the affidavit of Rex's president, and found that Rex's claim was merely to the proceeds of the inventory when sold. We do not find error in this construction and application of the term "mere proceeds of inventory" by the trial court. We think it is a reasonable interpretation of the record that the appellant, Rex, did not place a substantial reliance on the chattel paper in making the loan, but rather relied on the collateral (mobile homes) and the proceeds when the collateral was sold. The proceeds of the sale of these four mobile homes included the chattel paper sold by the dealer to Great Western. Rex could have protected itself by requiring all security agreements executed on sale of the mobile homes to be turned over immediately to Rex, or if sold, that all payments for the security agreements (chattel paper) be made to itself.

A case that aptly illustrates the operation of UCC § 9–308 (A.R.S. § 44–3129) is Associates Discount Corporation v. Old Freeport Bank, 421 Pa. 609, 220 Atl.2d 621 (1966). In that case a finance company which purchased chattel paper from an auto dealer (in a factual situation somewhat similar to ours) prevailed over a bank which had "floor planned" the inventory of the dealer. The court found that the bank's claim was a mere proceeds claim to the chattel paper and that UCC § 9–308 (second sentence) would operate to give priority to the purchaser of the chattel paper. The inventory financer's interest in the "proceeds" of the sale of the inventory had been shifted to the money paid by the purchaser of the chattel paper to the dealer. * * *

* * *

In any case, the construction and application of A.R.S. § 44–3129 (UCC § 9–308) to undisputed facts is a question of law for the trial court which was reasonably determined in the instant case.

Affirmed.

OGG, P.J. * * * and STEVENS, J. concur.

Notes

1. Assume that you are the inventory lender in a *Rex Financial* case and that you would like to have priority as to the chattel paper as well. How do you arrange that?

2. Assume a case like *Rex Financial,* but one in which the original secured creditor filed a financing statement listing "inventory and chattel paper." Assume further that its security agreement recited specifically that the creditor "relied upon" the chattel paper in making the loan. At trial the secured creditor argues two bases for a finding that it is not "merely" a proceeds claimant. First it points to the security agreement that specifies her reliance. Second it says that only a person without a financing statement representing chattel paper can be a "mere" proceeds

claimant. If you represent the purchaser of the chattel paper, how do you respond to those arguments?

Problem 5–10

Bank has a perfected security interest in retailer's supply of mobile homes. It has a $500,000 loan outstanding that is secured by 20 mobile homes, each with a value of $25,000. Retailer's business does not go well and ultimately he declares bankruptcy. Upon his bankruptcy all concede that the 15 remaining new mobile homes go to the Bank with a perfected security interest in inventory. However, there are three additional mobile homes that have been repossessed and returned to the dealer's lot. As to these, there is chattel paper outstanding which was sold to a bona fide purchaser, Local Loan (for this purpose assume Local Loan had priority under UCC 9–308). Bank now argues that when the mobile homes were returned to the lot its security interest reattached and, as the first to file, it has priority. Local Loan argues that Bank's security interest was cut off under UCC 9–308 and that it does not reattach. Each of the two cites different portions of UCC 9–306(5) to support its case. What are those portions and who should win?

B. Repledged Collateral

A variety of priority conflicts can arise if the pledgee of stock or other collateral repledges the collateral to secure his own loan, sells it or otherwise gives an interest in the collateral to some third party. The pledgee's right to repledge collateral is explicitly recognized by UCC 9–207(2)(e) in the circumstances in which the repledge will be on terms "which do not impair the debtor's right to redeem it." The most common example of a case in which the repledge does not impair the debtor's right to redeem is the case in which the collateral is pledged for a loan of the same or lesser amount and of the same or lesser duration than the original loan. Presumably in such circumstances the repledgee will be willing to give up the collateral to the original pledgor upon the pledgor's payment of the second debt. The pledgor's payment of the pledgee's debt to the repledgee would presumably extinguish the obligation between them or reduce it pro tanto.

In the securities market it is commonplace for a customer of a stockbroker to pledge stock to secure margin borrowing from the broker. It is also common for the customer to authorize the stockbroker to repledge the stock to a bank or other financing institution and so to finance the stockbroker's operation. When the stockbroker goes broke and the bank appropriates the collateral to satisfy its debt, where is the customer? On this question, consider the following problems.

Problem 5–11

1. Mr. Barron was a customer of Ira Haupt and Co. He was a wheeler-dealer in the stock market and purchased "on the margin"—that is, he would sometimes put up $5,000 or $7,000 and Haupt would buy stock with a fair market value of $10,000. In effect, of course, Haupt was lending money to Barron and was in turn borrowing money from banks in order to make loans to his customers. In order to secure each loan with the other banks, Haupt put up Barron's stock as security for a longer term than pledged by Barron to Haupt. This stock was carried in the name of Haupt's nominee (street name) and it was endorsed to the bank at the time it was put up. Haupt now goes bankrupt as a result of the famous DeAngelis affair. Who gets the stock—Barron or the bank? You may assume that Barron signed an agreement with Haupt which contained terms essentially like the following:

"This agreement covers all securities and other property whatsoever which you may at any time be carrying for the undersigned (either individually or jointly with others), or which may at any time be in your possession for any purpose including safekeeping, or to be held by you as security for all liabilities of the undersigned to you with the right on your part to transfer money or securities from any one of my accounts (other than from Regulated Commodity Accounts) to another when in your judgment such transfer may be necessary. You are hereby authorized, without notice to the undersigned, and without regard to whether you have in your possession or subject to your control at the time thereof either separately or together with securities and other property of other customers, either for the amount due you from the undersigned or for a greater sum."

See UCC 9–309, 8–301 et seq.

2. If the Barron/Haupt bank transaction had been undertaken with uncertificated securities, how would it come out? Assume that Barron borrowed from Haupt to buy the stock but did not explicitly authorize Haupt to repledge the stock to a third party. Assume nevertheless that Haupt did so and that all the parties took the steps necessary under the new Article 8 to perfect their interests. On Haupt's bankruptcy who gets the stock, Barron or the bank?

SECTION 5. PRIORITY WITH RESPECT TO FIXTURES, UCC 9–313

We might have dealt with the fixture issues in Chapter Seven on the ground that fixtures questions are essentially scope questions. Fixtures, of course, are items that started out their existence as personal property but that were then attached to personal property in such a way that they acquired some of the attributes of real estate while retaining some of those of personal property. They did not go through a complete metamorphosis in the way normal building materials might. Presumably normal building materials incorporated in the structure are neither personal property nor fixtures. For almost all purposes they have become real estate, will pass with a deed, be subject to a claim of a traditional mortgagee, and will for almost all purposes be treated like the dirt upon which they sit.

Fixtures, on the other hand, are things such as air conditioners, furnaces and the like. These are not so incorporated in the real estate that they are unquestionably a part of it; they still have a separate existence and, in most cases, could be detached and used elsewhere. Of course, the courts and the legislatures have long recognized the potential conflict between the claim of the real estate secured creditor (or purchaser) with regard to the fixture and the claim of a personal property secured lender to the fixture. Section 9–313 was incorporated in the Code to determine the priorities between personal property claimants on the one hand and real estate claimants on the other. Rarely does one see a competition between two real estate claimants to a fixture or between two personal property claimants to a fixture. The first of such conflict is probably not governed by UCC 9–313, but by the law of real estate, or in the case of two personal property claimants, by UCC 9–312.

For now we focus on UCC 9–313. Initially the student should read the section with care. It is quite complex, but the student should see parallels to section 9–312. Having studied the distinction between a "fixture filing" and a filing that is not a fixture filing but nevertheless perfects a security interest in a fixture, the student should now understand that UCC 9–313(4) requires in effect a real estate filing (a fixture filing) for one to enjoy the priority given under subsections (4)(a) and (b), but requires only a personal property filing to give the fixture claimant the priority specified in subsections (4)(c) and (d). The student should also see how 9–313 has dealt with the issue of fixtures owned by a lessee (subsection (5)) and with a construction mortgage (subsection (6)).

IN RE FINK

United States Bankruptcy Court, Western District of New York, 1980
4 B.R. 741.

EDWARD D. HAYES, BANKRUPTCY JUDGE.

This is an action by the Trustee to avoid a security interest in a mobile house claimed by defendant, Endicott Trust Company of New York hereinafter referred to as "Endicott" and to preserve that lien pursuant to Bankruptcy Rule 611 as to defendant Wemco Corp. hereinafter referred to as "Wemco."

The facts appear to be as follows. The bankrupt, Pauline Fink, purchased a mobile home from Palmer Mobile Homes, Inc. on or about August 20, 1977. She entered into a retail installment contract. The security interest was transferred by assignment to Endicott on or about August 20, 1977. Endicott filed a financing statement which described the collateral as 24 × 52 1977 Bendix. Thereafter, the mobile home was delivered to Route 415 in the Town of Campbell which the bankrupt was leasing from Wemco. On August 24, 1977, the bankrupt contracted to purchase the real property on which the mobile home was placed from Wemco for $24,000. The realty consisted of about four acres and the only structure thereon was a store. The realty was transferred on December 1, 1977 by Wemco to the bankrupt and the bankrupt gave back to Wemco a purchase money mortgage for the full purchase price of $24,000.

The mobile home or modular home, which ever it may be, was delivered by Palmer Mobile Homes, Inc. and was placed on a foundation of concrete footers, concrete blocks and steel and wooden beams running the width and length of the building.

The details of construction follow. A foundation was evacuated. A septic tank was installed. Concrete footers were installed around the edge of the crawl space and at least one pillar of concrete blocks was erected in the center of the crawl space. Concrete blocks were installed and cemented to the footers. After this was done, the house was delivered to the lot in two sections (12′ × 52′) on steel cradles. The sections with cradles were then placed on the cement blocks. The house sections were bolted together. A roof cap was put on over the place in the roof where the sections were joined together and it was cemented and nailed down. Siding was put on the two ends of the house and nailed over the spot where the joinder of the section occurred to give the appearance of a continuous wall. The septic system was hooked up. Water lines were connected. An electrical line was connected to the store's system and the store's electrical system and capacity were increased. At this point, the top course of cinder blocks were placed in but not cemented to the course immediately below. No tie downs were used in the construction. The house even has an open fireplace, although this hangs on the side of the house. From the pictures in evidence, the house appears to be a normal ranch home without front or back steps.

Additional facts which were developed at the trial follow. Palmer, who installed the mobile home on the foundation, testified that he could remove and transport the home for about $500 by removing the roof cap and the siding and shingles from the end, disconnect water lines, electric septic tank and unbolt the sections of the house and transport it on the cradle of steel beams which support each section.

The officer of Wemco said that the house was constructed in the same fashion as any construction and that the attachment to realty was the same as in any stick built house.

Additionally, when Wemco transferred the property to the bankrupt, Fink, in December, 1977, the attorney for Wemco had the abstract redated. There was nothing on the abstract that gave Wemco any notice of an interest by Endicott in the house. Wemco, when it transferred the property to Mrs. Fink, took back a purchase money mortgage for $24,000.

The facts stated above raise the issue as to whether or not the home in question is a chattel that requires perfection by filing pursuant to New York State UCC 9–302(1)(d) or a fixture attached to real property that requires filing in accordance with New York State UCC 9–313(1)(a). Section 9–302(1)(d) of the Uniform Commercial Code holds that a financing statement must be filed to perfect a security interest in a motor vehicle. This section has been held to govern mobile homes * * *. UCC 9–313 requires a special filing where the item is a fixture. The filing must be in the office where a mortgage on real estate is filed and it must conform to the requirements of UCC 9–402(5) which requires that a financing statement filed as a fixture must show that it covers this type of collateral, must recite that it is to be indexed in the real estate records and the financing statement must contain a description of the real estate sufficient for its identification and it must show the name of the record owner.

If the home in question is considered to have ceased to be personalty and become a fixture by annexation to the real property, the filing made by Endicott was improper. The case turns upon whether the home is personalty or a fixture.

UCC § 9–313 states in part that "(1)(a) 'goods' are fixtures when they become so related to particular real estate that an interest in them arises under real estate law." The official comments which accompany this section say in part, "in cases where mobile homes or prefabricated steel buildings are erected by a person having an ownership interest in the land, the question into which category the buildings fall is one determined by local law." The definition of fixture is not an exact one. Recent law review article on the subject of fixtures under the UCC defines the term as follows:

> "A fixture is a former chattel which, because of its annexation to and association with realty, has become part and parcel thereof but which has not lost its separate physical identity. A fixture is neither personalty nor realty within a strict definition of those terms. Rather, it partakes of the characteristics of each, since prior to annexation it is movable and not associated with realty, but after annexation it loses its character as personalty and is deemed realty. Various definitions of fixture have been utilized, all of which emphasize the former chattel aspect and the annexation to realty." [1]

23 N.Y.Jur. Fixtures § 2 (1962) says as follows:

> "As a general rule, the true criterion of a fixture is based on the united application of three requisites: (1) actual annexation to the real property or something appurtenant thereto; (2) application to the use or purpose to which that part of the realty with which it is connected is appropriated; and (3) the

1. Trade Fixture-Secured Transactions Under New York's Uniform Commercial Code, 44 Alb.L.Rev. 165, (1979).

intention of the party making the annexation to make a permanent accession to the freehold * * *".

In re Lido Beach Sewage Collection Dist., 40 Misc.2d 384, (County Ct. 1963), said at page 385:

"Ordinarily for an article to become a fixture the following requisites must be met: Firstly, there must be annexation to the realty. Secondly, there must be adaptability of the article affixed to the use of the freehold. Thirdly, the intention of the party creating the annexation is to make the article a permanent accession to the freehold."

The two cases which have dealt with mobile homes in the context of UCC 9–313 are In re Foskett, 7 UCC Rep.Serv. 267 (W.D.Wisc.1970) and George v. Commercial Credit Corp., 440 F.2d 551 (7th Cir. 1971). They seem to follow the New York State tests set forth above. A recent 1979 Vermont Supreme Court case, Hartford Nat'l Bank & Trust Co. v. Godin, 398 Atl.2d 286, 26 UCC Rep. Serv. 221 (Vt.Sup.Ct.1979), also held a mobile home a fixture based on the same three tests set forth above.

Applying these principles to the case at bar, we find that the bankrupt contracted to purchase the mobile home at about the same time she entered into a contract to purchase the realty. She had a crawl space dug. She had footings installed and she had cinder block cemented to the footings to hold the home. The bankrupt installed a septic tank system, ran water and electric into the home. The bankrupt lived in the home.

Looking at the house, in the pictures that were taken of the house, it looks at least to the uninitiated eye like any other ranch house you might see erected in the country. There would be nothing to warn anyone that this was in fact a trailer or a motor vehicle. If it was a trailer, it came certainly in two parts and had to be separated into two parts to be moved along the road. Should someone wish to move the house, they would have to dismantle it, separate it into two parts, remove part of the roofing and remove five to six feet of the center strips of shingles at either end of the home. The house in the manner in which it was annexed to real property certainly meets the test set forth in the cases cited above. Therefore, this court finds that Endicott is an unsecured creditor and that their filing should have been under UCC § 9–313 rather than under UCC § 9–302(1)(d).

With regard to Wemco's interest, it is paramount to the trustee because Wemco had a filed mortgage agreement which is a lien upon the real property.

This Memorandum and Decision shall constitute Findings of Fact and Conclusions of Law in accordance with Rule 752 of the Rules of Bankruptcy Procedure.

Notes

1. The 1972 revisions to Article 9 did not become effective in New York until July 2, 1978. Why does the court apply the 1972 version of 9–313 to this case?

2. Assume that the value of the mobile home and real estate was more than enough to satisfy the mortgagee's claim. If there were $10,000 of value left over, how would that be divided between the trustee and Endicott?

a. under the 1972 version?

b. under the 1962 version? (Assuming that Endicott filed the UCC–1 form in the proper place for a personal property perfection, where would that be?)

Problem 5-12

1. Assume that Bank had financed the purchase of a washer, dryer and stereo, and that each was installed in debtor's house in such a way that under state law it would have become a fixture. Bank filed a financing statement covering these items in the personal property records, but not in the real estate records in the county where the debtor lived. Does Bank or the mortgagee have a better right in these?

2. Assume bank had taken a security interest only in debtor's mobile home. Bank inserted its name on the certificate of title and also filed in the personal property records in the county where the debtor resided at the time the mobile home was purchased. Debtor ultimately placed the mobile home in another county and moved into it. Subsequently Debtor went into bankruptcy and trustee now claims the mobile home. Who has priority?

Problem 5-13

Larry buys a farm from Moe in January by advancing a down payment of $80,000 and agreeing to pay off the remainder of $250,000 over 5 years. In February, Larry borrows $54,000 from Curly to pay for the installation of an irrigation well and pump. Curly receives a security interest in "all farming and irrigation equipment." Assume the security interest attaches to the pump before it is installed. In July, Larry is having trouble making his payments to Moe. They reach an agreement whereby Larry pays half of the July payment and the loan is rescheduled over 10 years. In November, Larry gives up farming and delivers a quitclaim deed to Moe in exchange for release from the debt.

1. Can Moe forbid Curly from removing the pump because he filed only in the personal property records in the county clerk's office?

2. If the 1962 version of Article 9 applies and assuming that Curly has priority over Moe under UCC 9–313(2), would the rescheduling agreement constitute a subsequent advance for the purpose of UCC 9–313(4)(c)? Would the delivery of the quitclaim deed in exchange for forgiveness of the loan make Moe a subsequent purchaser under UCC 9–313(4)(a)?

SECTION 6. SECURITY INTERESTS ARISING BY LABOR, ACCESSION, OR COMMINGLING, UCC 9–310, 9–314, 9–315

The sections cited above are in one sense analogous to the fixture rules. In the fixture cases typically one takes a security interest in an asset which then becomes a fixture and so becomes subject to a mortgage and to other real estate interests. Of course, the same thing can happen when a motor is installed in an automobile subject to an existing security interest, when a mechanic repairs an automobile or equipment and asserts a mechanic's lien for his work, or when goods are commingled or processed with other goods and two parties have security interests in different parts of the goods. UCC 9–314 on accession is closely analogous to UCC 9–313 and, in fact, bears a striking resemblance to UCC 9–313 as it existed in its 1962 incarnation. Section 9–315 in effect grants a prorata security interest in commingled goods. Section 9–310 governs a very small slice of mechanic's lien law. Note that section 9–310 grants priority over a prior perfected security interest but only to goods "in the possession" of the mechanic and only if the relevant mechanic's lien law does not expressly provide otherwise. Beware, for the law in some states explicitly states that the mechanic's lien is subordinate to an existing perfected security interest. The rule does not apply to all statutory lienors who might exist, but only to those who provide "services or materials" in the ordinary course of business.

A question not answered by UCC 9–314 or 9–315, but one that may be critical to the ultimate decision is the question whether the original secured creditor's security interest attaches to the accession or the commingled goods. Assume, for example, that a creditor has a security interest in a truck. After the security interest is granted the debtor causes the truck to be modified for logging operations by the addition of a new third axle, a loader, and a "jake brake." Unless the original security agreement covered accessions, it would not be clear that the original creditor even claimed an interest in those parts. In most cases, presumably, a well drafted security agreement will cover accessions and in the case of commingling will cover the end product either explicitly or by reference to proceeds or products. In *In re Lyford,* 34 U.C.C.Rep.Serv. 754 (Bkrtcy.D.Me.1982), the court concluded that such additions to a truck were accessions and were covered by the original security agreement. The court goes through an analysis not unlike that a court might use in determining whether goods attached to realty had become fixtures. Implicit in the court's analysis is the assumption that if the goods were not accessions, they would not have been covered by the original security agreement. That judgment, of course, would depend upon the language of the particular agreement.

Note that it will not always be obvious whether UCC 9–314 or 9–315 applies or, indeed, whether either of them does. Nor will it always be clear how to apply the applicable rule of priority. Consider the case that follows.

FIRST NATIONAL BANK OF BRUSH v. BOSTRON

Court of Appeals of Colorado, 1977.
564 P.2d 964.

STERNBERG, JUDGE.

The issues presented by this appeal are whether, under the Uniform Commercial Code, a perfected security interest in feed survives after consumption of the feed by cattle in which the secured party has no interest, and if so, whether the secured party is entitled to any of the proceeds from the sale of these cattle. We answer these questions in the negative and therefore affirm the judgment of the trial court.

One Eldon Weiss owned a ranch on which he raised cattle and feed crops. As a separate and distinct part of this operation Weiss entered into a joint venture with the defendant, Reinhold Bostron, under which Bostron was to supply the money and Weiss the labor necessary to raise Holstein heifers. The heifers were purchased by Bostron and Weiss with money borrowed from the plaintiff, First National Bank of Brush, which retained a perfected purchase money security interest in the animals. The Bostron-Weiss joint venture cattle were segregated from other cattle on the Weiss ranch. Feed for all the cattle, however, was commingled and fed to the animals Weiss owned individually and to those owned by the Bostron-Weiss joint venture. Intervenor, Colorado High Plains Agricultural Credit Corporation, held a perfected security interest given by Weiss, individually, in, among other things, "all feed now owned or hereafter acquired, all crops now growing or to be grown, proceeds and products of collateral."

The cattle raised by the joint venture were eventually sold at a loss, and consequently, even after paying most of the proceeds from the sale to First National Bank of Brush, there was a deficiency owing that bank. None of the proceeds from the sale of the Bostron-Weiss cattle were paid to the intervenor.

Plaintiff bank sued Weiss and Bostron to recover the remaining balance of the loan, and Colorado High Plains intervened claiming an interest in any recovery which the bank might obtain against Bostron. Weiss was adjudicated a bankrupt and proceedings against him in this action were stayed. Since the intervenor's security interest attached only to the feed owned by Weiss, its right of recovery, if any, from Bostron must be premised on the benefit which Bostron individually received from the joint venture as a result of the Weiss feed being fed to the joint venture cattle.

The provisions of the Uniform Commercial Code—Secured Transactions, § 4–9–101, et seq., C.R.S.1973, govern this case. Section 4–9–315, C.R.S.1973, provides:

> "(1) If a security interest in goods [1] was perfected and subsequently the goods or a part thereof have become part of a product or mass, the security interest continues in the product or mass if:
>
> "(a) The goods are so manufactured, processed, assembled, or commingled that their identity is lost in the product or mass; or
>
> "(b) A financing statement covering the original goods also covers the product into which the goods have been manufactured, processed or assembled."

In light of the wording of this section, we conclude that cattle are neither a "product" nor a "mass" as these terms are used in the statute. The reference in subsection (a) to "manufactured, processed, assembled, or commingled" precludes any other interpretation. The feed which the cattle ate did not undergo any of these transformations, that is, it was not manufactured, processed, assembled or commingled with the cattle. Cattle consume food as motor vehicles do gasoline. Once eaten the feed not only loses its identity, but in essence it ceases to exist and thus does not become part of the mass in the sense that the code uses the phrase. Section 4–9–315, C.R.S.1973 (Comment 3), makes this evident:

> "This section applies not only to cases where flour, sugar and eggs are commingled into cake mix or cake, but also to cases where components are assembled into a machine."

Feed as consumed by cattle is distinguishable from this notion of accession which the code's drafters visualized.

Moreover, since the financing statement did not specifically cover the product "into which the goods have been manufactured, processed or assembled" the language of § 4–9–315(1)(b), C.R.S.1973, does not support intervenor's claim.

Relying on § 4–9–306, C.R.S.1973, intervenor next contends that the cattle are proceeds of the feed as that term is defined in that portion of the code. The pertinent part of that statute states:

> "(1) 'Proceeds' include whatever is *received* when collateral or proceeds is sold, exchanged, collected, or otherwise disposed of * * *
>
> "(2) Except where this article otherwise provides, a security interest continues in collateral notwithstanding sale, exchange, or other disposition thereof by the debtor unless his action was authorized by the secured party in the security

1. There is no question but that the reference to goods in this section applies to the feed in question here. Section 4–9–105(f), C.R.S. 1973, provides:

" 'Goods' includes all things which are movable at the time the security interest attaches * * * 'Goods' also include the unborn young of animals and growing crops." See also § 4–2–105, C.R.S.1973.

agreement or otherwise, and also continues in any identifiable proceeds * * *" (emphasis supplied)

This contention also is unavailing for several reasons. First, the trial court found that the intervenor lost its interest in the proceeds because it authorized the disposition of its collateral, i.e., the feed, by Weiss to the Bostron-Weiss joint venture. See Farmers National Bank v. Ceres Land Co., 32 Colo.App. 290, 512 P. 2d 1174 (1973). This finding is supported by evidence in the record and therefore is dispositive. However, we also conclude that even if the intervenor had not authorized the use of the feed subject to its security interest by the joint venture, nevertheless intervenor's interest still would not have survived its consumption by the cattle.

Weiss *received* nothing when he disposed of the collateral by feeding it to the joint venture cattle. As noted in our discussion of § 4–9–315, C.R.S.1973, the collateral was consumed, and there are no traceable proceeds to which the security interest may be said to have attached. To interpret § 4–9–306, C.R.S.1973, as intervenor urges would extend the security interest of one in the position of the intervenor to the parts of the butchered animal, into the supermarket, and ultimately into the hands of the consumers. We cannot attribute such legislative intent to the General Assembly when it adopted this section of the UCC.

Intervenor's final contention is that by § 4–9–307(1), C.R.S. 1973, it had an interest in the cattle which ate the feed. That section of the code provides:

> "A buyer in ordinary course of business * * * *other than a person buying farm products from a person engaged in farming operations* takes free of a security interest created by his seller even though the security interest is perfected and even though the buyer knows of its existence." (emphasis supplied)

Assuming, without deciding, that the joint venture was a buyer in the ordinary course of business from Weiss, a cursory reading of this portion of the code would suggest, as intervenor asserts, that its security interest continues into the cattle. However, the joint venture did not sell the feed; rather, it sold the cattle to which it was fed. As previously noted, in our analysis of § 4–9–315, C.R.S.1973, the collateral in which the security interest was initially taken is, after having been fed to the cattle, non-existent, and thus buyers of the cattle cannot reasonably be equated with buyers of the feed in which there exists a security interest.

In summary then, we hold that a security interest in feed does not in and of itself extend to the cattle which eat that feed by application of § 4–9–315, C.R.S.1973, nor do cattle which eat the feed constitute proceeds of the collateral by application of § 4–9–306, C.R.S.1973. We hold further that under the facts here, § 4–9–307(1), C.R.S.1973 does not extend the security interest in the feed after its ingestion by the cattle.

Judgment affirmed.

COYTE and ENOCH, JJ., concur.

Note

Assume that the manure produced in the debtor's feeding operation has considerable value and was routinely sold to others as fertilizer. Would the creditor with the security interest in the feed, have an interest in the proceeds or other interest in the manure?

Problem 5–14

Consider the following problems under UCC 9–310, 9–314, 9–315 as appropriate.

1. Assume that secured creditor One had a perfected security interest in debtor's 100 head of Brangus cattle. Secured creditor Two had a perfected security interest in debtor's 100 head of Hereford cattle, including two Hereford bulls. Upon debtor's bankruptcy, the inventory disclosed 30 Brangus, 25 Hereford, including the 2 bulls and 80 calves. At trial the testimony was conflicting, but it seems likely that at least 10 of the calves were offspring of the Hereford bulls mating with the Brangus cows and one witness testified that the flop ear which is an identifying characteristic of Brahman line descendents, including Brangus cattle, carry forward to the 1/32nd degree. Another testified, "When you've got a half-Brahman-cow-to-a-one-quarter-Brahman-cow cross with an Angus cow and then you put a Hereford bull in there with them, you're going to breed the ear off." Of the remaining calves it seemed that some were the offspring of Brangus cows who had been artificially inseminated and some were offspring of the Hereford who had been inseminated by the Hereford bulls. Assume that both secured creditors had a perfected security interest that included not only specific livestock originally covered, but also products and proceeds; that the party doing the artificial insemination has not been paid and asserts a lien under local law. How will the calves, cows and bulls be divided?

2. Bank has a perfected security interest in all of computer manufacturer's inventory, accounts receivable, present and after acquired. Seller of microchips also has a perfected security interest in the items sold by it to manufacturer including products and proceeds. Assume that the microchips are assembled in the computer in such a way that they are clearly identifiable, but cannot be removed without destroying the computer. The debt owed the microchip seller is $500,000. The value of the existing computers is $600,000. The bank has an unpaid debt of $3,000,000. Microchip seller asserts a first priority under UCC 9–314. Who will prevail? (Assume that the computers were sold under a stipulation that a security interest would attach to the proceeds in the same way as they would attach to the original items.)

3. Lessor obtained a security interest in a drilling rig leased to debtors Fred and Barbara Yost. Whayne Supply Company performed $2500 of repairs on the rig's Caterpillar engine, and properly perfected its material and service lien under Kentucky law. Several months after the repairs, the drilling rig was heavily damaged by fire and $75,000 of insurance proceeds were paid to and are now held by the lessor. Kentucky provides that one repairing machinery shall have a claim, but that the "lien shall not take precedence over a mortgage or bona fide sale and delivery." If you represented the lessor, how would you argue in this case? What responses might be made on behalf of Whayne?

SECTION 7. PRIORITY IN REPOSSESSED GOODS: A REPRISE

When Bank creates a security interest in Dealer's inventory, there is a substantial risk that it will be cut off by a sale to a buyer in the ordinary course of business. UCC 9–307(1). Dealer, however, may perfect a security interest in the goods sold to secure Buyer's obligation to Dealer. If Dealer receives chattel paper from Buyer, i.e., "non-cash" proceeds, UCC 9–306(1), Bank will undoubtedly claim a perfected security interest in the chattel paper to secure Dealer's obligation to Bank. UCC 9–306(3). But remember, the chattel paper evidences Buyer's obligation to Dealer and a security interest to secure that obligation.

Suppose Buyer defaults and Dealer repossesses the goods. If Bank has been paid, there is no problem: Dealer will simply enforce the security interest in the goods to satisfy Buyer's obligation. But suppose Bank has not been paid. What are Bank's rights upon repossession? The answer to this and other questions is contained in UCC 9–306(5). Read it carefully and work the following problems. Review also Problem 5–10.

Problem 5–15

In the situation described above, what are Bank's claims, if any, to the repossessed collateral? Would they have priority over Dealer's interest?

Problem 5–16

Suppose that after Dealer sold the goods to B, a buyer in the ordinary course of business, but before they were repossessed, Finance Company perfected a security interest in the goods. Upon repossession, Bank, Dealer and Finance Company claim a perfected security interest in the goods. Is that claim correct? If so, which party has priority?

Problem 5–17

Suppose that Dealer, without Bank's consent, assigned the security interest and negotiated the note to Bank # 2 in the ordinary course of its business. Bank #2 knew of Bank's security interest. Upon Buyer's default, Bank # 2 repossessed the goods from Buyer. Which party has a perfected security interest with priority in the chattel paper? Which party has a perfected security interest with priority in the goods?

Problem 5–18

The facts are the same as in Problem 5–16 except that Dealer grants Bank # 2 a written security interest in the chattel paper and retains possession and Bank # 2 perfects the security interest by filing. Upon Buyer's default, Dealer repossessed the goods from Buyer. Which party has a perfected security interest with priority in the chattel paper? Which party has a perfected security interest with priority in the goods?

Bank will argue that under UCC 9–306(5), Bank # 2 must perfect a security interest in the repossessed goods to have priority. Do you agree?

CHAPTER SIX

DEFAULT AND FORECLOSURE

SECTION 1. INTRODUCTION

In this chapter we will explore default and its consequences. We will survey the problems involved in determining the nature and extent of any default and the various alternatives that may be open to the secured creditor when default does occur. The most important of these alternatives—so-called "foreclosure by sale"—is subjected to intensive analysis.

In the first several sections of this chapter, we will treat problems that arise in determining whether default has occurred. We will then survey the various remedies of the secured creditor on default. Most of these remedies are set forth in Part Five of Article 9 and include:

(1) negotiation and readjustment,

(2) creditor's right to judgment and execution,

(3) creditor's remedies under applicable real estate law,

(4) creditor's right to collect on intangibles and to repossess tangibles,

(5) strict foreclosure with respect to tangibles,

(6) foreclosure by sale with respect to tangibles, and right to any deficiency,

(7) suit on any negotiable paper.

See generally, White & Summers, Chapter 26.

SECTION 2. DEFAULT AND ACCELERATION

Default triggers the secured creditor's rights under Part 5 of Article 9. Despite that fact, one looks in vain for a definition of default in Article 9; instead the Article leaves this definition to the parties and to any bits of common law that may be available. However, UCC 1–208 deals with acceleration upon default and legislation in various states does restrict the creditor's power to declare default and to cause acceleration of indebtedness where the debtor is a consumer. When the debtor is not a consumer, the law generally permits the parties to establish the terms for acceleration and to define default by their agreement.

Invariably, security agreements contain acceleration clauses and lengthy, carefully drafted clauses to define default. Non-payment of the indebtedness is the first step in defining default in such clauses. A typical default clause will also take into account the possibility that the debtor will declare bankruptcy, will make an assignment for the benefit of creditors, will move the collateral or permit it to be damaged or destroyed. To sharpen your consideration of the problems presented to the creditor in defining default and acceleration, consider the following problems and consider particularly the clause (which we believe to be well drafted) included in the problem.

Problem 6–1

Polypol, Inc. is manufacturer of a variety of adult and children's toys. It manufactures a variety of dolls. Polypol purchases all of its raw materials on credit from Heathcliff, Inc., a wholesaler of metal, plastic, and wood products. Typically, Polypol will owe Heathcliff between $75,000 and $150,000 at any one time for materials delivered in the previous sixty days. Polypol has agreed to make payments every other month on the 10th for all purchases made up to thirty days preceding. To secure all indebtedness, Polypol has signed a security agreement with Heathcliff; the security agreement contains the following default and acceleration clause:

> Section 7. Events of Default; Acceleration. Any or all liabilities shall, at the option of Creditor and notwithstanding any time or credit allowed by any instrument evidencing any Liability, become immediately due and payable without notice or demand upon the occurrence of any of the following events of default: (a) default in the payment, when due and payable, of any amount due and payable hereunder or default in the payment or performances of any of the Liabilities; (b) default in the performance of any obligation or covenant contained or referred to herein; (c) any warranty, representation or statement made or furnished to Creditor by or on behalf of Debtor proves to have been false in any material respect when made or furnished; (d) failure of Debtor, after request by Creditor, to furnish financial information or to permit the inspection of its books and records; (e) any event which results in the acceleration of the maturity of the indebtedness of Debtor to others under any indenture, agreement or undertaking; (f) loss, theft, damage, destruction, sale or encumbrance to or of any of the Inventory, or the making of any levy, seizure or attachment thereof or thereon, or the entry of any judgment against Debtor; (g) death, dissolution, termination of existence, insolvency, business failure, appointment of a receiver of any part of the property of, assignment for the benefit of creditors by, or the commencement of any proceeding under any bankruptcy or insolvency laws by or against, Debtor or any guarantor or surety for any of the Liabilities of which, in the good faith opinion of Creditor, impairs Creditor's security or increases its risk.

How would you answer each of the following questions if you were counsel for Heathcliff? In answering the questions, one should consider not only the default clause and security agreement but also UCC 1–208 and 9–506 set forth below and the case that follows.

1. If Polypol were simply an assumed name of Hareton Earnshaw, sole proprietor doing business as Polypol, and Earnshaw died, would that be a default? (Some cases hold that the death of the debtor is not a default if no payments are due at the time of death and the security agreement is silent.)

2. The president of Heathcliff calls in a panic. He tells you that two large unsecured creditors of Polypol have levied on certain of Polypol's goods and will probably dispose of those goods within the next two or three days. He tells you that Polypol has not failed to make any payments but that Polypol will surely default when its next payment comes due in 60 days if the goods allegedly seized by the other creditors are not available for its operation. He asks two questions:

   (a) Is the levy by the other creditors a default?

   (b) If it is not a default, are there any problems in the way of getting some use out of the goods so seized by levying creditors (assuming we have a prior security interest in the goods) between now and the time when Polypol defaults 60 days from now?

3. Earnshaw, the president of Polypol, and Linton, the president of Heathcliff, have a violent oral dispute about the quality of certain goods delivered by Heathcliff to Polypol. Linton calls to tell you of the fight and states that he wishes to commence legal proceedings for the collection of the entire indebtedness ($148,000) at once. He tells you that Polypol is not now in default (the next payment is due in 30 days) but that Earnshaw drove Linton off his place under threat of the use of force and will surely refuse to make any more payments. If you assume that the goods delivered by Heathcliff to Polypol were not defective, is Polypol now in default?

UCC § 1–208. Option to Accelerate at Will

A term providing that one party or his successor in interest may accelerate payment or performance or require collateral or additional collateral "at will" or "when he deems himself insecure" or in words of similar import shall be construed to mean that he shall have power to do so only if he in good faith believes that the prospect of payment or performance is impaired. The burden of establishing lack of good faith is on the party against whom the power has been exercised.

UCC § 9–506. Debtor's Right to Redeem Collateral

At any time before the secured party has disposed of collateral or entered into a contract for its disposition under Section 9–504 or before the obligation has been discharged under Section 9–505(2) the debtor or any other secured party may unless otherwise agreed in writing after default redeem the collateral by tendering fulfillment of all obligations secured by the collateral as well as the expenses reasonably incurred by the secured party in retaking, holding, and preparing the collateral for disposition, in arranging for the sale, and to the extent provided in the agreement and not prohibited by law, his reasonable attorney's fees and legal expenses.

KARNER v. WILLIS

Supreme Court of Kansas, 1985.
238 Kan. 246, 710 P.2d 21.

PRAGER, J.

This is a dispute between two judgment creditors and a garnishee bank over funds held by the bank in the defendant Lloyd's bank account. In answer to the garnishment, the garnishee bank responded that it had no funds of the defendant because it had exercised its right of setoff against the defendant's account. The plaintiff creditors contended that the setoff was wrongful. The district court held in favor of the bank. The plaintiffs then appealed, and the court of appeals affirmed in a published opinion in Karner v. Willis, 10 Kan.App.2d 432, 700 P.2d 582 (1985). The supreme court granted the plaintiffs' petition for review.

The facts in the case were undisputed and essentially were as follows: On March 15, 1983, the plaintiffs, Herbert and Ruth Karner, obtained a judgment against the defendants, Willis and Lloyd, in the sum of $58,352.40 in the State of Oklahoma. Judgment was filed in the district court of Ellsworth County. On April 4, 1983, a duly authenticated copy of the Oklahoma judgment was filed in the district court of Ellsworth County. On August 3, 1983, an order of garnishment was issued by the district court of Ellsworth County directed to the Citizens State Bank of Ellsworth and the Kanopolis State Bank. Dale E. Hoosier, vice-president of Kanopolis State Bank, who received the garnishment, called the Ellsworth County sheriff's department and notified them that he had been served with a garnishment directed to the Citizens State Bank. The dispatcher of the sheriff's department notified the deputy of the mistake, and he immediately returned to the Kanopolis State Bank and exchanged the Citizens State Bank garnishment for the garnishment directed to the Kanopolis State Bank.

During the interim period, Dale E. Hoosier, acting on behalf of the Kanopolis State Bank, exercised a setoff against the account of the defendant debtor, Lloyd. In the court of appeals opinion, the Kansas statutes which control the right of a creditor bank to accelerate the maturity of a debt and to exercise a right of setoff against the debtor's account are discussed. Simply stated, K.S.A. 84–1–208 states that a contractual term providing that a party may accelerate payments or performance "when he deems himself insecure" or in words of similar import shall be construed to mean that he shall have the power to do so only if he *in good faith* believes that the prospect of payment of performance is impaired.

In the present case, the defendant debtor was indebted to the bank on a note which contained a provision which permitted the bank to accelerate the maturity of the debt if it deemed itself insecure. The trial court, in effect, found that the garnishee bank had acted in good faith in accelerating the debt and in setting off the note against the debtor's bank account.

The court of appeals viewed the basic issue on appeal to be whether there was substantial competent evidence in the record to support the findings of the trial court that, at the time the bank executed the setoff, it in good faith believed that the prospect of payment of the note was impaired. The court of appeals affirmed on the basis that "good faith" was a fact issue which the trial court resolved in the bank's favor, and found there was substantial competent evidence to support the trial court's findings.

When the trial court has made findings of fact and conclusions of law, the scope of appellate review is for this court to determine whether the trial court's findings are supported by substantial competent evidence. Woods v. Midwest Conveyor Co., 236 Kan. 734, Syl. ¶ 2, 697 P.2d 52 (1985). The appellate court will not weigh the evidence or pass upon the credibility of the witnesses. The reviewing court must review the evidence in the light most favorable to the party prevailing below. Marcotte Realty & Auction, Inc. v. Schumacher, 229 Kan. 252, 254, 624 P.2d 420 (1981).

At the hearing of this case, the only witness who testified was Dale E. Hoosier, the vice-president of the garnishee, Kanopolis State Bank. Hoosier testified that the day before the garnishment was served, the bookkeeper for the debtor depositor had been to the bank and requested signature cards to change the account name and signatures. Hoosier was aware of the Oklahoma judgment filed in Ellsworth County against the debtor earlier that year. At the time he made the setoff, he did not actually know whether the debtor was insolvent or not. The debtor had not been delinquent on any payments and was current on August 3, 1983, when the setoff was made. Mr. Hoosier testified that he deemed the bank was impaired in its security because the garnishment would have resulted in the sum of $40,000 being taken from the debtor's operating account as a farm implement dealer and, as a result, "he would have had no liquidity to operate." The bank records showed that on August 16, 1983, 13 days after the setoff, the bank loaned the debtor an additional $50,000, but in the interim period the debtor had paid $99,000 on the loan and pledged his used farm equipment as additional collateral.

In its opinion, the court of appeals recognized that there certainly was evidence presented that, viewed objectively, the bank was not insecure, but that the test of good faith dictated by K.S.A. 84–1–208 is subjective and requires only honesty in fact. Iola State Bank v. Bolan, 235 Kan. 175, 183, 679 P.2d 720 (1984); and K.S.A. 84–1–201(19). The court of appeals then applied the subjective test required by the statute and concluded that the trial court's finding of good faith was supported by substantial competent evidence. The majority of this court has concluded from the record that the court of appeals correctly determined the issue.

The judgment of the district court is affirmed. The judgment of the court of appeals is affirmed.

HERD, J., dissenting: I disagree with the majority holding that Kanopolis State Bank was acting in good faith when it deemed itself insecure on Ronald F. Lloyd's note and exercised its right of setoff against his checking and reserve accounts.

The evidence in this case consists of the testimony of Dale E. Hoosier, bank vice-president, the Lloyd note and the bank ledger.

Mr. Hoosier acknowledged that the bank officials knew an Oklahoma judgment in the amount of $58,352.40 had been properly filed of record in Ellsworth County against Mr. Lloyd. He testified the judgment did not make the bank deem itself insecure. He further testified that Mr. Lloyd's note with his bank was secured by a first mortgage on Ellsworth County real estate and did not mature until more than four months after the August 3 setoff. Hoosier also testified Lloyd was not delinquent in any note payments when the setoff was made. The bank ledger sheet shows that thirteen days after the setoff of $39,178.20 from Lloyd's account was applied on his note, and the bank loaned Lloyd an additional $50,000. Mr. Hoosier testified the reason he deemed the bank insecure with regard to Lloyd was because he knew a garnishment summons was going to be served on the bank to aid in satisfying the foreign judgment against Lloyd.

The bank argues the garnishment of Lloyd's bank accounts would have destroyed his liquidity and thus justifies its deeming itself insecure. This argument ignores the nature of the secured note. Neither the garnishment nor the foreign judgment affect the bank's security. As testified to, the bank was satisfied with the security for the Lloyd debt. The garnishment was seeking payment from Lloyd's unmortgaged assets. The bank's lending Lloyd an additional $50,000 thirteen days after the setoff is clear evidence it did not, in good faith, deem itself insecure.

A creditor has the power to accelerate debt payments when he deems himself insecure only if he in good faith believes the prospect of payment of the debt is impaired. K.S.A. 84–1–208. "Good faith" is defined at K.S.A. 84–1–201(19) as "honesty in fact in the conduct or transaction concerned."

While it is true, as the majority points out, that the test of good faith is a subjective one which must be considered from the viewpoint of the creditor, that does not mean a creditor can accelerate a note to maturity at its whim. As stated by the Utah Supreme Court in Clayton v. Crossroads Equipment Co., 655 P.2d 1125, 1128 (Utah 1982), "The obvious purpose of requiring that a secured party act in good faith is to impose the basic obligation of fair dealing, and to protect the purchaser from the mere whim or caprice of the secured party." If the good faith requirement of K.S.A. 84–1–208 is to have any meaning or purpose, we cannot allow the bank to use its acceleration and setoff authority to defeat a creditor's rights under the garnishment statute as Kanopolis State bank did here. This was the determination reached by the Indiana Court of Appeals in Universal C.I.T. Credit Corp. v. Shepler, 164 Ind.App. 516, 520–21, 329 N.E.2d 620 (1975). There, the Indiana court held that if the good faith provisions of Indiana Code Annotated §§ 26–1–1–208 and 26–1–1–201[19] * * * were to have any real effect, they must be modified to include a more objective standard, i.e., what would a "reasonable man" do under the same set of facts and circumstances. See also Williamson v. Wanlass, 545 P.2d 1145, 1149 (Utah 1976), where the Supreme Court of Utah recognized that acceleration is a harsh remedy which should be allowed only if there is some reasonable justification for doing so, such as a good faith belief that the prospect of payment is impaired as expressly provided in the U.C.C.

I would hold, as have courts of other jurisdictions, that in considering whether a creditor acted in good faith in deeming itself insecure, a secured party must show compelling facts of insecurity because the secured creditor is in a less precarious position than is an unsecured creditor. McKay v. Farmers & Stockmens Bank of Clayton, 92 N.M. 181, 183, 585 P.2d 325 (1978); Van Horn v. Van De Wol, Inc., 6 Wash.App. 959, 497 P.2d 252 (1972), 61 A.L.R.3d 241.

Here, the debtor's note with the bank was secured by a first mortgage on real estate. There is no evidence the collateral was impaired in any way. Nor is there any evidence the debtor was delinquent in payments on the note or that the prospect of payment was impaired. There is no evidence, compelling or otherwise, to support the bank's contention its setoff was in good faith. To be in good faith, the bank's action must have been in response to a bona fide belief, based on evidence, that its prospect of payment from Lloyd was impaired.

Finally, we find the reasoning of the Utah Supreme Court in Williamson v. Wanlass, 545 P.2d 1145, instructive. In *Williamson,* the debtor's promissory note was secured by a second mortgage on farm property which the debtors had purchased for $111,000. The court found that the holders of the promissory note failed to show a good faith belief that prospect of payment was impaired, justifying acceleration of the note under Utah Code Ann. 70A–1–208 (1980). The court made this finding notwithstanding the fact that the defendants were frequently late in making monthly installment payments on the note. The key factor was the fact that the plaintiffs had a second mortgage on extensive property and there was little doubt the note would be paid, principal and interest.

As in *Williamson,* here there is no evidence indicating an inability of the debtor to pay off the note, especially in light of the bank's first mortgage on Lloyd's Ellsworth County real estate. The debtor here was not delinquent in any payments, in contrast to the debtor in Williamson.

Under the construction given K.S.A. 84–1–208 by the majority opinion, any debtor who signs a standard note is vulnerable to acceleration of his note and setoff of his bank account upon the unsubstantiated statement of a bank that it deems itself insecure. In Iola State Bank v. Bolan, 235 Kan. 175, Syl. ¶ 8, 679 P.2d 720 (1984), we construed the good faith rule:

> "Where a bank knows sums deposited in the account of one of its depositors belong to a third party, it does not act in good faith when it applies such funds of the third party against the depositor's debts to the bank. Under such circumstances the third party has an action directly

against the bank for conversion of the third party's funds from the debtor's accounts."

In Iola State Bank, the bank knew of outstanding checks from its delinquent borrower to various farmers for the purchase of grain but nevertheless set off the borrower's account, dishonoring his outstanding checks. We held the bank's action was not in good faith. Here, the bank knew of the judgment against its borrower and that a garnishment summons was en route to seize the bank account for application on the judgment. With this information, Kanopolis State Bank accelerated Lloyd's note and set off his bank account before the impending garnishment attached, even though the Lloyd note was not delinquent. This case is analogous to Iola State Bank, but stronger, because here the borrower's note was not delinquent. Thus, according to our own precedent, the Kanopolis State Bank lacked good faith in its set off of Lloyd's account.

I would reverse

HOLMES, J., joins the foregoing dissenting opinion.

SECTION 3. NEGOTIATION AND READJUSTMENT ON DEFAULT

It should not be assumed that, on default, all secured creditors always automatically and immediately seek payment in full by any available legal means. Realization on the collateral is, of course, one such means, and the secured creditor has contracted precisely for it. Even so, many a secured creditor will first try to work out some plan of voluntary repayment before resorting to his rights as a secured creditor. Indeed, he may excuse the default altogether. In the case of a default that signifies true difficulty in making payment, the secured creditor may be willing to reduce the amount of payments due, or extend time to the debtor. All this can be readily accomplished by modification of the basic security agreement.

Sometimes the debtor will be in difficulty with several creditors at the same time, who may then join together with the debtor to help him work out a satisfactory overall readjustment of his obligations.

SECTION 4. CREDITOR'S RIGHTS ON DEFAULT TO SEEK JUDGMENT AND EXECUTION

This remedy is the prime remedy of the *unsecured* creditor. It therefore may seem oddly out of place here. Yet UCC 9–501(1) expressly authorizes a secured creditor to "reduce his claim to judgment" as one way of proceeding, and UCC 9–501(5) states in full:

> "When a secured party has reduced his claim to judgment the lien of any levy which may be made upon his collateral by virtue of any execution based upon the judgment shall relate back to the date of the perfection of the security interest in such collateral. A judicial sale, pursuant to such execution, is a foreclosure of the security interest by judicial procedure within the meaning of this section, and the secured party may purchase at the sale and thereafter hold the collateral free of any other requirement of this Article."

Comment 6 to this section adds that a judicial sale pursuant to judgment and execution, though one of the methods of realizing contemplated by Article 9, is "governed by other law and not by this Article and the restrictions which this Article imposes on the right of a secured party to buy in the collateral at a sale under Section 9–504 do not apply."

The Code does not say what the creditor must do to obtain judgment and execution on the debt; state statutes and common law of ancient vintage specify these steps, and they vary somewhat from state to state. Generally, the creditor must first commence suit and obtain a judgment for the debt owed. After judgment the clerk of the court will, on request, issue a "writ of execution" (or the like). This writ recites that a judgment has been obtained and directs the sheriff or other appropriate officer to seize the property of the debtor and sell it to satisfy the judgment debt. With the writ in hand, the officer will levy against the debtor's property at his home or place of business (i.e., exercise dominion over it such that it is safely preserved for satisfaction of the debt). Finally, after giving public notice, the officer will sell the property at a public auction to the highest bidder and then turn proceeds necessary to satisfy the debt over to the creditor. The surplus, if any, goes to the debtor.

Given that Article 9 contemplates that even a *secured* creditor might choose judgment and execution over enforcement of his security interest, we should explain why he might so choose. First, this route allows the creditor to reach assets of the debtor in addition to the collateral (which may have declined in value). Second, by immediately procuring judgment and execution, the creditor eliminates the two step process of first selling the collateral and then suing for a deficiency (under UCC 9–504). Third, this route generally requires only that the creditor prove the debt and the default, whereas proceeding under Article 9 may give rise to other disputed issues. Fourth, the statute of limitations may, in an unusual case, dictate judgment and execution as a first step, for a deficiency proceeding might come too late. Cf. Associates Discount Corp. v. Palmer, 47 N.J. 183, 219 A.2d 858 (1966). Fifth, the creditor might want to get the collateral quickly, yet under Article 9 be forbidden to act because the contemplated repossession would involve a breach of the peace. In such case, by filing a complaint and procuring a writ of attachment or by rapidly procuring judgment and execution, the creditor might be able to reach the collateral more quickly. Sixth, since officers of the court administer judgment and attachment or execution, the creditor eliminates the risk of incurring liability for improper foreclosure under UCC 9–504 and 9–507. Finally, UCC 9–501(5) allows the creditor to purchase the collateral at the sheriff's sale, something he usually cannot do at a private sale under UCC 9–504(3).

Despite the foregoing advantages, it is unusual for the secured creditor to pursue the judgment and execution route. Of course, if he does, he need not comply with Part Five of Article Nine. An illustrative example is C & T Recreation, Inc. v. Connon Minnesota Corp., 367 N.W.2d 591 (Minn.Ct.App. 1985).

SECTION 5. INTANGIBLES AS COLLATERAL—CREDITOR'S RIGHT TO MAKE COLLECTIONS ON DEFAULT

We have seen such intangibles as accounts, contract rights, instruments and certain proceeds may be used as collateral. If so and the debtor defaults, may the secured creditor then look directly to the *debtor's obligor* for payment as and when the payment falls due? Sections UCC 9–502(1) and (2) are addressed to this general problem, and provide:

§ 9–502. Collection Rights of Secured Party

(1) When so agreed and in any event on default the secured party is entitled to notify an account debtor or the obligor on an instrument to make

payment to him whether or not the assignor was theretofore making collections on the collateral, and also to take control of any proceeds to which he is entitled under Section 9–306.

(2) A secured party who by agreement is entitled to charge back uncollected collateral or otherwise to full or limited recourse against the debtor and who undertakes to collect from the account debtors or obligors must proceed in a commercially reasonable manner and may deduct his reasonable expenses of realization from the collections. If the security agreement secures an indebtedness, the secured party must account to the debtor for any surplus, and unless otherwise agreed, the debtor is liable for any deficiency. But, if the underlying transaction was a sale of accounts or chattel paper, the debtor is entitled to any surplus or is liable for any deficiency only if the security agreement so provides.

Note that the last sentence of UCC 9–502(2) provides an exception to the usual rule that a secured party must account to the debtor for any surplus after the collateral is disposed of and the proceeds applied to expenses and the outstanding debt. See UCC 9–504(2). Although Article Nine applies, in general, to "any sale of accounts or chattel paper," UCC 9–102(1)(b), a "sale" in the disposition context has different consequences. How does one determine whether the debtor has "sold" the collateral or simply granted a security interest in it? The answer depends upon the amount of risk the secured party assumes if the accounts do not in fact exist (fraud) or the account debtor is unable to pay. If the secured party assumes all of the risk, the transaction is clearly a sale. If the secured party has "recourse" against the debtor, the transaction may be treated as intended for security if the debtor agreed, through warranties or otherwise, to assume substantially all of the risk. Whether risk allocation is intended as a sale or security turns on the facts of each case—a complex inquiry for which Article 9 provides little guidance. See Major's Furniture Mart, Inc. v. Castle Credit Corp., 602 F.2d 538 (3d Cir.1979) (transaction a "sale" where debtor assumes risk of both existence and collectibility of debt).

Problem 6–2

1. Bank has a perfected security interest in debtor's accounts receivable. It understands that it has the right to notify the account debtors and to make collections. However it is fearful that if it undertakes the collection process on its own, the debtor will go into bankruptcy during that process and the automatic stay will stop its collection activity and it will be forced to turn over the remaining accounts to the bankruptcy estate. Accordingly creditor would like to give notice to the debtor that it intends to take the accounts in full satisfaction of the debt under UCC 9–505, and to cut off the debtor's entire interest 21 days after the notice is given.

2. How would you respond to the argument that one with a perfected security interest in accounts was obliged to sell those accounts under UCC 9–504 and could not simply collect them under UCC 9–502?

Problem 6–3

Your client, Commercial Credit, has loaned $500,000 to debtor and has taken a perfected security interest in debtor's inventory and accounts receivable. Debtor is now in default on the loan and you estimate the value of the accounts and inventory to be somewhere between $1,600,000 and $2,100,000. Bank has a perfected security interest securing a loan of $1,500,000 which has priority over your client's security interest.

1. If the loan to the Bank is not in default (and accordingly Bank is not proceeding to collect), what are the rights of your client, Commercial Credit?

2. If debtor defaults on Bank's loan and Bank commences proceedings under UCC 9-504 with respect to the inventory and UCC 9-502 with respect to the accounts, what are your client's rights and how does your client protect them?

The problems become devilishly difficult when the collateral is chattel paper (UCC 9-105(1)(b)). Recall that chattel paper usually gives the creditor some interest in two kinds of collateral. In the first place it gives him a claim upon the account debtor's obligation to pay and in the second place it gives him some form of claim to the underlying collateral—at least in certain circumstances. Moreover, it is not always clear whether the transfer of the chattel paper carries with it any right in a reversionary interest that might exist in the debtor after the account debtor had ceased to pay on a lease or other non-purchase arrangement. In this connection, review *In re Leasing Consultants, Inc.,* Chapter 4, Section 10, supra.

SECTION 6. TANGIBLES—CREDITOR'S RIGHT TO REPOSSESSION ON DEFAULT EITHER FOR SETTLEMENT LEVERAGE OR AS A STEP IN FORECLOSURE

UCC 9-503 does not give the debtor a right to notice and a hearing prior to any repossession. That section provides:

> **§ 9-503. Secured Party's Right to Take Possession After Default**
>
> Unless otherwise agreed a secured party has on default the right to take possession of the collateral. In taking possession a secured party may proceed without judicial process if this can be done without breach of the peace or may proceed by action. If the security agreement so provides the secured party may require the debtor to assemble the collateral and make it available to the secured party at a place to be designated by the secured party which is reasonably convenient to both parties. * * *

Note, though, that the secured creditor may utilize self-help to repossess only "if this can be done without breach of the peace." Otherwise, he must resort to "judicial process"—replevin, a claim and delivery statute, or the like. Moreover, if the debtor has gone into bankruptcy, the secured creditor loses all rights of repossession.

STONE MACHINERY CO. v. KESSLER

Court of Appeals of Washington, 1970.
1 Wash.App. 750, 463 P.2d 651.

EVANS, CHIEF JUDGE.

Plaintiff Stone Machinery brought this action in Asotin County to repossess a D-9 Caterpillar Tractor which plaintiff had sold to defendant Frank Kessler under conditional sales contract. Service of process was not made on the defendant but plaintiff located the tractor in Oregon and repossessed it. The defendant then filed an answer and cross-complaint in the Asotin County replevin action, alleging that the plaintiff wrongfully and maliciously repossessed the tractor, and sought compensatory and punitive damages under Oregon law. Trial was to the court without a jury and the court awarded defendant compensatory damages in the sum of $18,586.20, and punitive damages in the sum of $12,000 on defendant's cross-complaint.

The operative facts are not in serious dispute. Defendant Kessler purchased, by conditional sales contract, a used D–9 Caterpillar Tractor from the plaintiff Stone Machinery for the sum of $23,500. The unpaid balance of $17,500 was to be paid in monthly installments, with skip payments. The defendant's payment record was erratic and several payments were made late. However, payments of $3600 on March 29, 1966, and $1800 on July 18, 1966, put the contract payments on a current basis. The payment due on August 10, 1966 was not made and, on September 7, 1966, plaintiff's credit manager, Richard Kazanis, went to the defendant's ranch in Garfield, Washington, and demanded payment of the balance due on the contract or immediate possession of the tractor. At this time defendant had made payments on the purchase price totaling $17,200, including the trade-in. The defendant was unable to make full payment, or any payment at that time, and informed Mr. Kazanis that he would not relinquish possession of the tractor to him at that time, or at any time in the future, in the absence of proper judicial proceedings showing his right to repossess, and that "someone would get hurt" if an attempt was made to repossess without "proper papers." At that time the defendant informed Mr. Kazanis that he, the defendant, expected to be awarded a contract by the U.S. Bureau of Fisheries to do some work with the D–9 at their installation on the Grande Ronde River near Troy, Oregon, and that he would then be able to pay on the tractor.

On September 13, 1966, the plaintiff instituted this action in Asotin County, Washington, but the sheriff was unable to locate the tractor in that county. Thereafter, the plaintiff instituted another action in Garfield County, but the sheriff was unable to locate the tractor in that county. The evidence indicates that on September 24 Kessler took the tractor to Oregon to work the bureau of fisheries job.

On September 27, 1966, Mr. Kazanis, by use of an airplane, located the tractor on the Grande Ronde River, west of Troy, Wallowa County, Oregon. He then contacted the sheriff of Wallowa County and requested him to accompany them in the repossession of the tractor to prevent any violence by the defendant. The sheriff agreed to meet with Mr. Kazanis at Troy, Oregon, and on September 27, 1966, Mr. Kazanis in his private car, plaintiff's mechanic in a company pickup, and the plaintiff's truck driver in the company lo-boy truck, left Walla Walla, and the following morning met the Wallowa County Sheriff at Troy, where the sheriff was shown a copy of the conditional sales contract. The sheriff confirmed previous legal advice plaintiff had received that the plaintiff had the right to repossess the tractor (although not by the use of force) and thereupon the sheriff, in his official sheriff's car, followed by Mr. Kazanis in his private car, the mechanic in the pickup, and the truck driver in the lo-boy, proceeded to the scene where the defendant was operating the D–9 tractor in the Grande Ronde River approximately 7 miles west of Troy, pursuant to contract with the U.S. Bureau of Fisheries.

Upon arriving at the scene the sheriff, accompanied by Mr. Kazanis, walked to the edge of the river and motioned the defendant, who was working with the tractor in the river, to bring the tractor to shore. The sheriff was in uniform and wearing his badge and sidearms. The sheriff informed the defendant that the plaintiff Stone Machinery had a right to repossess the tractor, and stated, "We come to pick up the tractor." The defendant asked the sheriff if he had proper papers to take the tractor and the sheriff replied, "No." The defendant Kessler protested and objected to the taking of the tractor but offered no physical resistance because, as he testified, "he didn't think he had to disregard an order of the sheriff." The plaintiff's employee then loaded the tractor on the lo-boy and left for Walla Walla, Washington.

Within a few days the tractor was sold to a road contractor at Milton-Freewater, Oregon, for the sum of $7,447.80 cash, on an "as is" basis. The sale price represented the balance due on the contract, plus the plaintiff's charges for repossession.

Plaintiff's first assignments of error are directed to the following findings of the trial court:

XII

> That the plaintiffs actions in repossessing the defendant's tractor on September 28, 1966, and the actions of the Wallowa County Sheriff, in aid of the plaintiffs, amounted to constructive force, intimidation and oppression, constituting a breach of the peace and conversion of defendant's tractor.

XIV

> That the plaintiffs failed to show just cause or excuse for the wrongful act of repossession of the defendant's tractor on September 28, 1966.

XV

> That the wrongful act of repossession, done intentionally on September 28, 1966, was malicious and was so wanton and reckless as to show disregard for the rights of the defendant, Frank Kessler.

* * *

Retaking possession of a chattel by a conditional seller, upon the default of the buyer, is governed by O.R.S. 79.5030 (U.C.C. 9–503):

> Secured party's right to take possession after default. Unless otherwise agreed a secured party has on default the right to take possession of the collateral. In taking possession a secured party may proceed without judicial process *if this can be done without breach of the peace* or may proceed by action. (Italics ours.)

Defendant Kessler was admittedly in default for nonpayment of the August and September contract installments. By the terms of the above statute Stone Machinery had the right to take possession of the tractor without judicial process, but only if this could be done without a breach of the peace. The question is whether the method by which they proceeded constituted a breach of the peace.

No Oregon cases have been cited which define the term "breach of peace" so we must look to other authority. In Restatement of Torts 2d, § 116 (1965), the term is defined as follows:

> A breach of the peace is a public offense done by violence, or one causing or likely to cause an immediate disturbance of public order.

In the case of McKee v. State, 75 Okl.Cr. 390, 132 P.2d 173 (1942), breach of peace is defined (headnote 9, 132 P.2d 173), as follows:

> To constitute a "breach of the peace" it is not necessary that the peace be actually broken, and if what is done is unjustifiable and unlawful tending, with sufficient directness to break the peace, no more is required, nor is actual personal violence an essential element of the offense.

* * *

In the instant case it was the sheriff who said that he had no legal papers but that "We come over to pick up this tractor." Whereupon, the defendant Kessler stated, "I told him I was resisting this; there was an action started and I wanted to have a few days to get money together to pay them off." At this point defendant Kessler had a right to obstruct, by all lawful and reasonable means, any attempt by plaintiff to forceably repossess the tractor. Burgin v. Universal Credit Co., 2 Wash.2d 364, 98 P.2d 291 (1940). Had the defendant offered any physical resistance, there existed upon both the sheriff and plaintiff's agents a duty to retreat. See Westerman v. Oregon Auto. Credit Corp., 168 Or. 216, 122 P.2d 435 (1942). However, confronted by the sheriff, who announced his intention to participate in the repossession, it was not necessary for Kessler to either threaten violence or offer physical resistance. As stated by the court in Roberts v. Speck, 169 Wash. 613, at 616, 14 P.2d 33 at 34 (1932), citing from Jones on Chattel Mortgages § 705: (4th ed.)

> "The mortgagee becomes a trespasser by going upon the premises of the mortgagor, accompanied by a deputy sheriff who has no legal process, but claims to act *colore officii,* and taking possession without the active resistance of the mortgagor. To obtain possession under such a show and pretence of authority is to trifle with the obedience of citizens to the law and its officers."

Acts done by an officer which are such a nature that the office gives him no authority to do them are "*colore officii.*" See 7A Words & Phrases at 296 (Perm. Ed.), * * *.

In the instant case, when the sheriff of Wallowa County, having no authority to do so, told the defendant Kessler, "We come over to pick up this tractor", he was acting *colore officii* and became a participant in the repossession, regardless of the fact that he did not physically take part in the retaking. Plaintiff contends that its sole purpose in having the sheriff present was to prevent anticipated violence. The effect, however, was to prevent the defendant Kessler from exercising his right to resist by all lawful and reasonable means a nonjudicial take-over. To put the stamp of approval upon this method of repossession would be to completely circumvent the purpose and intent of the statute.

We hold there is substantial evidence to support the trial court's finding that the unauthorized actions of the sheriff in aid of the plaintiff amounted to constructive force, intimidation and oppression constituting a breach of the peace and conversion of the defendant's tractor.

* * *

Defendant Kessler was in default of his contract and had announced his intention to resist any attempted nonjudicial repossession. The words used in announcing his intention, namely, "someone would get hurt", were of such a nature as to justify the presence of a sheriff during any attempt at peaceable repossession although, as we have already held, this did not justify participation by the sheriff in the process of repossession. However, the fact that the sheriff did undertake to act *colore officii* in the repossession was not, under the circumstances, sufficient to support a finding that the plaintiff thereby displayed a particularly aggravated disregard for the rights of Kessler, within the meaning of Douglas v. Humble Oil & Refining Co., supra.

Judgment for compensatory damages is affirmed. Judgment for punitive damages is reversed.

Notes

1. Is this decision sound?
2. Can you explain how the damages were computed?

BLOOMQUIST v. FIRST NATIONAL BANK OF ELK RIVER

Court of Appeals, Minnesota, 1985.
378 N.W.2d 81.

FOLEY, J.

Debtor, Martin Bloomquist, appeals from a summary judgment and a deficiency judgment for creditor, First National Bank of Elk River. Debtor sued the bank asserting, inter alia, that the bank committed a breach of the peace when it repossessed collateral from the debtor's locked business without his consent. Debtor was unsuccessful in obtaining an injunction to enjoin the bank's sale of the collateral and the sale occurred before an appeal could be heard. The bank moved for summary judgment on the debtor's claims and sought a deficiency judgment on the notes arguing it had a right to "self-help" repossession. The trial court granted the bank summary judgment dismissing the debtor's claims and entered a deficiency judgment against the debtor. We reverse the summary judgment, vacate the deficiency judgment and remand for trial on the issue of damages for the conversion.

FACTS

Appellant, Martin Bloomquist (debtor) owned and operated an automobile repair service in Elk River, Minnesota. In the course of his business, debtor borrowed money from respondent First National Bank of Elk River (bank). Two notes are at issue here: (1) a promissory note dated July 14, 1983 in the amount of $11,540.20, which renewed a November 27, 1981 note for which all of debtor's business tools and equipment were given as security under a November 27, 1981 agreement, and (2) a promissory note in the amount of $3,505 dated November 23, 1982 for which a jeep with a snowplow was given as security.

On June 15, 1984 the bank sent debtor a letter demanding all note obligations be brought current by the end of June or "we will have to start action." The letter noted delinquencies of $1,405.00 on the equipment note and $1,790.68 on the jeep note.

Debtor paid the bank $470 on June 20, 1984. Mr. Wheaton, the bank's vice president, stated that in the next few weeks he visited debtor at his place of business, "informing him that unless the accounts were brought to date, repossession must take place." Debtor responded, "That will put me out of business." Wheaton replied, "I realize that." On one occasion Wheaton inventoried some of the equipment.

Debtor's version of the events is that Wheaton repeatedly threatened, "I will have to send in the boys and close you down." Debtor stated that he told Wheaton he would not give the bank his tools and that he was working on raising the money.

On about August 10, 1984, debtor offered the bank $600.00 but it was refused as inadequate. On August 20, 1984 the bank sent debtor a letter, noting the defaults, accelerating payment, demanding full payment, and concluding: "If payment is not made within the next three days the Bank will take possession of the secured goods. * * * "

On Saturday August 25, 1984, when debtor's business was closed, the bank's agents repossessed debtor's business tools and equipment. One of the bank's agents removed a cracked window pane, that was taped shut, to enter debtor's closed business. He then climbed through the window and opened the overhead garage door which had been secured with a deadbolt lock. The bank's agents, including the bank's vice president, the bank's attorney, an off-duty highway patrol officer and his son, then removed debtor's tools and equipment.

During the repossession, some of debtor's business tenants complained to bank agents that they could not just break and enter into debtor's business and remove his goods. Affidavits of these tenants indicate they protested the actions and were upset by what they observed. One tenant called the police after observing what she thought was a crime.

Debtor did not learn of the repossession until he arrived at his business on Monday morning and observed a repossession notice on a vehicle he was repairing. He denied consenting to the repossession and protested the bank's right to repossess. Within a few days, he commenced this suit claiming, inter alia, unlawful repossession and conversion, and seeking general, special and punitive damages.

During November 1984, debtor redeemed his jeep with snowplow. On January 5, 1985 the bank auctioned off the repossessed business tools and equipment for a total of $4,850. Debtor had sought to enjoin the sale, but the injunction was denied. An appeal to this court followed, but the sale occurred before the appeal could be heard.

Following the sale, debtor sought to amend his complaint disputing the method of sale and asserting other claims for damages. The bank moved for summary judgment on the issue of unlawful repossession and on its counterclaim for the balance due on the notes plus attorney's fees. The court granted the bank summary judgment—dismissing debtor's claims, and entered a deficiency judgment of $10,866.11, plus interest and attorney's fees against debtor. The court also granted the bank possession of debtor's "remaining shop equipment." Debtor appeals from the adverse judgments.

ISSUES

1. Did the bank commit a breach of the peace in repossessing collateral when its agents, without debtor's consent, entered debtor's locked business by removing a window pane?

2. Did the bank's sale of the repossessed goods constitute conversion as a matter of law?

ANALYSIS

Standard of review:

The function of a court reviewing summary judgment is to determine whether there are any genuine issues of material fact for trial, and whether the trial court erred in its application of the law. Betlach v. Wayzata Condominium, 281 N.W.2d 328, 330 (Minn.1979).

Trial court decision:

The trial court ruled as a matter of law that debtor's cause of action failed to state a claim for which relief might be granted based on its findings:

"That because of Plaintiff's breach of the notes and security agreements with Defendant, Defendant had an absolute right to take possession of the tools and equipment which it repossessed on August 25, 1984.

"That the First National Bank of Elk River did repossess the tools and equipment made the subject matter of this action in good faith in order to enforce its rights under the notes and security agreements given to it by Plaintiff Martin Bloomquist. That the repossession was by self help without Breach of Peace."

Statute at issue:

Minn.Stat. § 336.9–503 states:

"Unless otherwise agreed a secured party has on default the right to take possession of the collateral. In taking possession a secured party may proceed without judicial process if this can be done *without breach of the peace* or may proceed by action * * *."

Wrongful repossession?

Debtor claims that creditor wrongfully repossessed his tools and equipment. Debtor claims that because he specifically told the bank he would not willingly give up his tools and equipment and since he never consented to the bank's entry into his business in any way, including in the security agreement, the bank had no authority to repossess and should have sought judicial relief. Moreover, the bank committed a breach of the peace when it repossessed by breaking and entering into the debtor's locked and closed business.

Creditor argues and the trial court agreed, that self-help repossession was appropriate because the debtor was in default. Therefore, debtor's breach of the notes gave creditor "an absolute right to take possession" of debtor's tools and equipment. Creditor notes that Minn.Stat. § 336.9–503 (1984) authorized self-help repossession if there is no breach of peace and the security agreement signed by debtor granted creditor the right to inspect the collateral. Creditor admits the agreement did not specifically authorize entry into debtor's business to repossess collateral.

We agree with debtor. Self-help repossession is not lawful where it requires or constitutes a breach of the peace. See Minn.Stat. § 336.9–503. Minnesota has not specifically delineated a test to determine whether a breach of the peace has occurred. However, we are guided by Minn.Stat. § 645.22 (1984) in construing this phrase.

"Laws uniform with those of other states shall be interpreted and construed to effect their general purpose to make uniform the laws of those states which enact them." Id. * * *

State courts in Florida and Pennsylvania enunciate the following test or guidelines as helpful in determining whether a "breach of the peace" has occurred during the repossession of collateral:

(1) Whether there was entry by creditor upon debtor's premises, and

(2) whether the debtor or one acting in his behalf consented to the entry and repossession.

Quest v. Barnett Bank of Pensacola, 397 So.2d 1020, 1023 (Fla.App.1981) (quoting White & Summers, Uniform Commercial Code 966 (1972)); see Walker v. Walthall, 121 Ariz. 121, 122, 588 P.2d 863, 864 (1978). In Quest, the Florida court explained that the debtor's express consent for creditor to enter an enclosed area must be freely and voluntarily given, and that implied consent only covers those activities that are within a fair and reasonable interpretation of the terms of the grant. The Arizona court, in Walker, noted that generally the facts of each case must be evaluated to determine if a breach of the peace has occurred.

Here, debtor repeatedly told the bank's vice president that he would not consent to a repossession. When a debtor has not consented to repossession and in fact, has specifically revoked any implied right to such repossession, a creditor is not entitled to the self-help remedy but must pursue a judicial remedy. Quest, 397 So.2d at 1023, see Walker, 121 Ariz. at 122, 588 P.2d at 864. Self-help repossession denies to the objecting debtor an opportunity to assert a defense to the repossession such as whether the parties' course of conduct has varied the agreements. See Cobb v. Midwest Recovery Bureau Co., 295 N.W.2d 232 (Minn. 1980).

The case of Laurel Coal Co. v. Walter E. Heller & Co., Inc., 539 F.Supp. 1006 (W.D.Penn.1982) is nearly analogous to the instant case. In Laurel, the debtor's note was secured by a bulldozer. Upon the debtor's alleged default and failure to tender full payment as demanded, creditor repossessed the bulldozer by cutting a chain that secured a fence surrounding the debtor's business premises. The debtor sued, alleging that the self-help repossession was unlawful because it constituted a breach of the peace. The Pennsylvania court held "that the actual breaking of a lock or fastener securing property, even commercial property, constitutes a 'breach of the peace' * * *." Id. at 1007. The court also noted that, "even non-forceful repossessions may be found unlawful." Id. at 1008.

In the *Laurel* opinion, the Pennsylvania court cited with approval the earlier case of Stewart v. North, 65 Pa.Super. 195 (1916), which is factually similar to the instant case. In *Stewart,* the court held that breaking a window to unlock a door to a residence in order to repossess a piano was a breach of the peace constituting an unlawful repossession. See Laurel at 1007.

The case of Kimble v. Universal TV Rental, Inc., 65 Ohio Misc. 17, 417 N.E.2d 597 (1980) also supports our decision here. In *Kimble,* the Ohio court found that even though creditor and debtor had entered into an agreement providing for peaceable entry to recover goods, breaking into debtor's locked apartment and taking a rental TV set, without express or implied consent to do so, amounted to criminal acts and constituted a "breach of the peace" within the meaning of the Uniform Commercial Code. The Ohio court defined breach of the peace as a "violation of the public order, a disturbance of public tranquility, by an act or conduct inciting to violence or tending to provoke or excite others to breach the peace [*including*] *any violation of any law enacted to preserve peace and good order.*" Id. at 22, 417 N.E.2d at 602 (quoting 2 Anderson, Wharton's Criminal Law and Procedure, § 802 (1957)) (emphasis added).

Other cases supporting our holding include Thompson v. Ford Motor Credit Co., 324 F.Supp. 108 (D.S.C.1971) (no element of violence is needed in order for repossession of collateral to constitute a breach of the peace); Quest v. Barnett Bank of Pensacola, 397 So.2d 1020 (Fla.App.1981) (a breach of peace can occur if creditor damages debtor's property during the repossession); Dixon v. Ford Motor Credit Co., 29 Ill.Dec. 230, 72 Ill.App.3d 983, 391 N.E.2d 493 (1979) (a creditor's repossession in disregard of debtor's unequivocal oral protest may be found to be a breach of the peace); General Electric Credit Corp. v. Timbrook, 291 S.E.2d 383 (W.Va.1982) (an unauthorized entry into a debtor's dwelling to repossess collateral constituted a breach of the peace within the meaning of the UCC).

We note that the bank asks us to consider a number of cases where a breach of the peace is not found. See C.F. Adams Co. v. Sanders, 66 S.W. 815 (Ky.1902); Wirth v. Heavey, 508 S.W.2d 263 (Mo.App.1974); Global Casting Industries, Inc., v. Daley-Hodkin Corp., 105 Misc.2d 517, 432 N.Y.S.2d 453 (1980); Cherno v. Bank of Bablyon, 54 Misc.2d 277, 282 N.Y.S.2d 114 (Sup.Ct.Nassau Co. of 1967) aff'd 29 A.D.2d 767, 288 N.Y.S.2d 862 [4 UCC Rep 1185] (2d Dept.1968); North v. Williams, 120 Pa. 109, 13 A. 723 (1888); Harris Truck & Trailer Sales v. Foote, 58 Tenn.App. 710, 436 S.W.2d 460 (1968); Robertson v. Union Planters National Bank of Memphis, Tennessee, 561 S.W.2d 901 (Tex.Civ.App.1981). These cases do not control the instant case. All of these cases base their holding on the fact that the creditor entered the debtor's premises to repossess collateral, or repossess a motor vehicle, with debtor's express or implied consent.

The bank asserts that many of these same cases hold that there is no breach of the peace when the repossession occurs without violence or threat of violence. See e.g., *Harris Truck; Global Casting* (a breach of the peace is "a disturbance of public order by an act of violence, or by an act likely to produce violence. * * *" Id. 432 N.Y.S.2d at 455). The requirement of violence apparently represents a minority view. See, e.g., 6 Uniform Laws Annotated § 9–503, n. 15 (West 1981). This does not seem consistent with the commercial practices encouraged by the Minnesota Supreme Court and this court. See, e.g., Cobb, 295 N.W.2d, at 237–38; Steichen v. First Bank Grand, 372 N.W.2d 768 (Minn.Ct.App. 1985). We believe the better view, expressed in the cases we have relied on, holds that no violence or threat of violence need occur before a breach of the peace may be found. See *Quest; Laurel: Thompson.* The Minnesota Supreme Court has already adopted the view in Berg v. Wiley, 264 N.W.2d 145, 150 (Minn. 1978), that a non-violent, forcible entry to retake possession of a tenant's premises constitutes a breach of the peace.

Here it is uncontested that the bank's agents and their attorney entered debtor's closed and locked business without his consent. We are appalled at the course of conduct in this matter by the bank's officers and the bank attorney, their position is indefensible, and their actions in breaking and entering appellant's business premises were totally inappropriate since judicial process was readily available to enforce any claimed rights. The bank's breaking and entering debtor's business to repossess collateral constitutes a breach of the peace within the meaning of Minn.Stat. § 336.9–503, as a matter of law. See *Berg* (self-help repossession of premises was non-peaceable and wrongful as a matter of law where landlord retook possession in tenant's absence by picking the locks and locking her out).

CONVERSION

Our holding here requires a finding that the bank's sale of the unlawfully repossessed tools and equipment constitutes a conversion. See Kloos v. Gatz, 97 Minn. 167, 169–70, 105 N.W. 639, 640–41 (1906); see also Molm v. Barton, 27 Minn. 530, 8 N.W. 765 (1881).

> "To constitute conversion, there must be an execution of dominion over the goods which is inconsistent with and in repudiation of the owner's right to the goods or some act done which destroys or changes their character or deprives the owner of possession permanently or for an indefinite length of time."

Hildegarde, Inc. v. Wright, 244 Minn. 410, 413, 70 N.W.2d 257, 259 (1955).

We remand for trial on the issue of debtor's damages. The measure of damages for conversion is the fair market value of the repossessed goods at the time of the conversion, plus interest from that date. McLeod-Nash Motors, Inc. v. Commercial Credit Trust, 187 Minn. 452, 460, 246 N.W. 17, 20 (1932). Debtor also pled special damages and punitive damages. Debtor may be entitled to special damages including lost profits if he is able to prove the loss with reasonable certainty. See Cushing v. Seymour, Sabin & Co., 30 Minn. 301, 304–05, 15 N.W. 249, 250 (1883). Punitive damages are appropriately recovered in a wrongful repossession case. *Cobb* at 237–38; Steichen v. First Bank Grand, 372 N.W.2d 768, 772 (Minn.Ct.App.1985), pet. for rev. denied, (Minn. October 18, 1985). "Punitive damages, where permitted by law, should be used as a deterrent against future unlawful conduct and as a warning that unlawful self-help repossession will not be condoned." *Steichen* at 773. These damage claims should be assessed by a jury at trial.

DECISION

The bank's repossession of collateral from debtor was unlawful because the bank committed a breach of the peace when its agents entered debtor's business without permission by removing a window pane to unlock the garage door. The subsequent sale of debtor's tools and equipment was therefore unauthorized and constitutes conversion as a matter of law.

We reversed the summary judgment, vacate the deficiency judgment, and remand for trial on the issue of damages for conversion, including a determination whether the bank is entitled to offset for the notes from compensatory damages and whether debtor is entitled to punitive and other damages.

Reversed and remanded for trial with deficiency judgment vacated.

Problem 6–4

Defendant Chrysler Credit Corporation appeals from a judgment entered against it and in favor of the plaintiffs in the amount of $20,000.

In July 1980, Jimmy McKinney bought a Dodge Mirada from Countywide Dodge for his wife's use. He negotiated and executed on behalf of McKinney Ceramic Tile Co., Inc., of which he was president and majority stockholder, a retail installment contract financing the automobile with Chrysler Credit Corporation. McKinney made only two payments pursuant to this agreement, because Countywide Dodge failed to repair the car to his satisfaction.

McKinney returned the car to Countywide Dodge on numerous occasions for repairs. The dealership successfully repaired most of the defects, but never succeeded in repairing a leak in the roof of the automobile. This leak was so bad that at times, after a rainshower, two inches of water was left standing in the front floor. Because of this repeated leaking, the car's interior had an offensive odor, and the leather interior was damaged.

Mr. McKinney visited the dealership time after time and, at one point in September, explained the problem to the owner of Countywide Dodge, who assured him it would be repaired. It was not. He then wrote letters to the dealership, Chrysler Corporation, and Chrysler Credit Corporation, notifying them that he would make no more payments on the vehicle until the leak was repaired. He received no response to these letters. Chrysler Credit later telephoned him about his failure to make the payments on the vehicle. Once again, he discussed the leak in the roof and was assured that it would be repaired. Soon thereafter, James Smith, a repossession agent of Chrysler Credit, contacted Mrs. McKinney about the car and the McKinneys' failure to make the payments on the note. Mrs. McKinney met Smith at a restaurant to discuss the matter. After a conversation, wherein Mrs. McKinney detailed to Smith the problem with the car, she and Smith reached an agreement. Mrs. McKinney testified as follows concerning the agreement:

> "He [Smith] told me that everything was fine, that all he had to do was to get me to take the car into the lot and it would be fixed. You know, they would fix the leak in it. And, if they fixed the leak in it, then we would bring up the payment, which I agreed to."

Mrs. McKinney called their attorney from the restaurant. He spoke with Smith and confirmed the agreement not to repossess the car unless and until the McKinneys failed to bring the payments up to date following the repair of the vehicle's roof.

Mrs. McKinney and Smith then left the restaurant and drove to the dealership, where Mrs. McKinney surrendered the automobile to the dealership for repairs. The owner of the dealership confirmed the agreement to catch up the past due payments when the car was repaired.

A few days later, Chrysler Credit sent repossession notices to the McKinneys, advising them that the automobile had been repossessed and would be sold within five days after the receipt of those notices. The attorney for the McKinneys corresponded with Chrysler Credit, informing them of the agreement that repossession would not occur unless the repairs were made and the payments were not then brought up to date. Chrysler Credit did not respond to this letter.

The day after the repossession took place, Chrysler Credit called upon Countywide Dodge to pay off the McKinney account, pursuant to its recourse agreement, which it did.

Following these events, Countywide again made numerous attempts to repair the leaking roof in the car. Several times Mr. McKinney went in to the dealership and, each time, the roof leaked when tested. Later, Mr. McKinney was told to remove his personal belongings from the vehicle because it was no longer his car and was being sold. Thereupon Mr. McKinney filed suit against Chrysler Credit, Chrysler Corporation, and Countywide Dodge.

The trial court granted Countywide's motion for directed verdict at the close of the plaintiffs' case. The jury returned a verdict against Chrysler Corporation and in favor of the plaintiffs for breach of warranty. That verdict is not at issue in this appeal. The jury also returned a verdict against Chrysler Credit Corporation for $20,000.00 on a conversion claim.

1) On Appeal, what are the strongest arguments for both sides?

2) How would you decide the appeal?

Note: Other Legal Controls Upon Repossession

Upon default by a debtor, the secured party may seek to repossess the collateral through state statutory procedures granting replevin or detinue. These procedures are invoked before a judgment has been entered and customarily involve the issuance, upon an affidavit from the secured party, of a writ by a clerk of court to the sheriff to seize described property. Frequently, the secured party must post a bond. These statutory pre-judgment procedures pass muster under the Fourteenth Amendment to the United States Constitution if the debtor is entitled to a hearing on the merits within a reasonable time after repossession and before the collateral is sold. See, e.g., North Georgia Finishing, Inc. v. Di-Chem, Inc., 419 U.S. 601, 95 S.Ct. 719, 42 L.Ed.2d 751 (1975); Mitchell v. W.T. Grant Co., 416 U.S. 600, 94 S.Ct. 1895, 40 L.Ed. 2d 406 (1974).

If self-help is exercised in a manner that breaches the peace, however, the debtor, as a practical matter, will not have a hearing on the merits until the secured party has sued for a deficiency judgment. By that time the collateral will have been sold and considerable costs incurred. Put differently, unless the debtor is able to enjoin the repossession, see UCC 9–507(1), the debtor's day in court, if available at all, comes after the alleged dirty work has been done.

The federal courts have held that in self-help cases the debtor is not protected by the Fourteenth Amendment: There is no "state action" that justifies granting the debtor procedural due process before the repossession. See, e.g., Flagg Brothers, Inc. v. Brooks, 436 U.S. 149, 98 S.Ct. 1729, 56 L.Ed.2d 185 (1978), holding that a warehouseman's proposed sale of goods entrusted to him for storage to enforce a statutory lien granted by the New York enactment of UCC 7–210 was not state action. See also, Adams v. Southern California First National Bank, 492 F.2d 324 (9th Cir.1973), cert. denied, 419 U.S. 1006, 95 S.Ct. 325, 42 L.Ed.2d 282 (1974) (self-help repossession under UCC 9–503 not subject to constitutional control).

What about additional protection under state law? You should check the constitution and statutes of the state where you intend to practice to determine whether any other controls are imposed upon self-help repossessions. If so, what are they? Do they apply to both commercial and consumer debtors? What remedies are available if the limitations are ignored by the secured party?

If there are no state constitutional or legislative limitations, the debtor may, in a proper case, be able to recover punitive damages for a "wrongful and outrageous" repossession. See, e.g., Mitchell v. Ford Motor Credit Co., 688 P.2d 42 (Okl.1984); Alaska Statebank v. Fairco, 674 P.2d 288 (Alaska 1983). But see Betterton v. First Interstate Bank of Arizona, N.A., 800 F.2d 732 (8th Cir.1986) (bad faith repossession not a tort under Arizona law).

SECTION 7. CREDITOR'S RIGHT TO RETAIN COLLATERAL IN SATISFACTION OF DEBT—"STRICT FORECLOSURE"

This option is, of course, not one that the secured creditor would generally want to elect unless the value of the collateral was equal to or greater than the amount of the outstanding indebtedness. It is an option that was recognized early in the law of real property security where it was called, and continues to be called "strict foreclosure." In this field, it had the effect of cutting off, by judicial decree, any right that the debtor might have to reacquire the realty. Such an interest was and is today called the debtor's "equity of redemption." Obviously, collateral would have highly uncertain value to a secured party taking it in satisfaction of the debt if the debtor might, *at any time thereafter,* require it by paying the indebtedness due. Hence, the law recognized the device of "strict foreclosure" whereby the secured party could go to court and, in effect, get an order cutting off the debtor's right to redeem should he not exercise it by a specified date. Observe that this device not only cut off the debtor's "equity of redemption"; it also cut off his "ownership equity"—the proportion of the property that was truly his. Thus the device did not certainly protect debtors against *forfeitures.* At the same time, it did not allow a creditor any deficiency, should the realty prove to be worth less than the outstanding indebtedness.

Section 9–505 provides:

Compulsory Disposition of Collateral; Acceptance of the Collateral as Discharge of Obligation

(1) If the debtor has paid sixty per cent of the cash price in the case of a purchase money security interest in consumer goods or sixty per cent of the loan in the case of another security interest in consumer goods, and has not

signed after default a statement renouncing or modifying his rights under this Part a secured party who has taken possession of collateral must dispose of it under Section 9–504 and if he fails to do so within ninety days after he takes possession the debtor at his option may recover in conversion or under Section 9–507(1) on secured party's liability.

(2) In any other case involving consumer goods or any other collateral a secured party in possession may, after default, propose to retain the collateral in satisfaction of the obligation. Written notice of such proposal shall be sent to the debtor if he has not signed after default a statement renouncing or modifying his rights under this subsection. In the case of consumer goods no other notice need be given. In other cases notice shall be sent to any other secured party from whom the secured party has received (before sending his notice to the debtor or before the debtor's renunciation of his rights) written notice of a claim of an interest in the collateral. If the secured party receives objection in writing from a person entitled to receive notification within twenty-one days after the notice was sent, the secured party must dispose of the collateral under Section 9–504. In the absence of such written objection the secured party may retain the collateral in satisfaction of the debtor's obligation.

On all this, White and Summers have still more to say:

WHITE & SUMMERS, HANDBOOK OF THE LAW UNDER THE UNIFORM COMMERCIAL CODE 1104–08 (2d ed. 1980).

"Upon default and repossession, the secured creditor may wish to avoid the headache of resale and therefore accept the collateral in complete satisfaction of the debt under 9–505(2). By so doing he forgoes any right to a deficiency. This alternative of 'strict foreclosure' was known to the common law and was available under the Uniform Conditional Sales Act. Sometimes the secured creditor will find strict foreclosure an attractive alternative to sale and suit for a deficiency. Presumably, when the value of the collateral is roughly equivalent to the amount of the outstanding debt, the secured creditor will choose strict foreclosure. Strict foreclosure has certain advantages over resale of the collateral or an action on the debt. In the first place, it may be accomplished with a modicum of effort on the part of the secured party. More important the secured creditor who strictly forecloses knows that the debtor or other parties cannot later plague him about the fairness of a resale price under 9–504. Section 9–505(2) authorizes strict foreclosure.

* * *

"Thus, section 9–505(2) presents an uncomplicated blueprint for strict foreclosure on default. First, the secured creditor must take possession of the collateral after default. Secondly, he is required to send a written notice to the debtor stating his intention to retain the collateral in satisfaction of the debtor's obligation, unless the debtor renounces his right to such notice after default. If the collateral is consumer goods, the foreclosing secured creditor must await the passage of twenty-one days without an objection from the debtor. If the collateral is consumer goods and the debtor has renounced his right to notice, the secured creditor may keep the goods, without ever having contacted any other creditor of the debtor claiming an interest in the collateral. However, if the collateral is not consumer goods, the secured creditor must send notice of intent to foreclose strictly to any other creditor of the debtor who has previously sent him written notice of a claim of an interest in the collateral. Then, if the unrenounced debtor or one of the other interested parties enters a written objection during the twenty-one days after the notice was sent, the secured party must dispose of the collateral under 9–504.

"Furthermore, when the collateral is consumer goods and the debtor has paid 60 percent of the price, 9–505(1) provides that the secured creditor may not use strict foreclosure unless the debtor *after default* signs a statement renouncing his right to require the collateral resold in compliance with section 9–504. This provision is based upon the supposition that a debtor who has paid 60 percent of the purchase price has built up equity in the goods, and that resale would result in a surplus. Hence in this situation the secured creditor may not strictly foreclose unless the debtor expressly renounces his right to demand resale.

"Another potential problem for the secured party lies in the duration of the period when another party is entitled to object to strict foreclosure. Section 9–505 stipulates that the parties entitled to notice have twenty-one days 'after the notice was sent' to object; thereafter the right of redemption and other rights are cut off. A wise secured party will give notice by registered or certified mail so that he can prove the time of sending.

"Failure to give notice renders strict foreclosure invalid at least as to those entitled to receive notice who did not receive it. *In re Sports Autos Inc.* involved a secured party who was also the president and sole shareholder of the debtor corporation. Without giving notice to the corporation or other secured creditors, he repossessed collateral worth approximately $90,000 more than the debt it secured and then set up essentially the same business under a different name. When the debtor's other creditors filed a petition for an involuntary declaration of bankruptcy, the Referee concluded that the secured party's failure to give notice deprived him of his right to retain the property.

"In some cases debtors have attempted to force strict foreclosure upon an unwilling secured creditor. * * *"

SCHMODE'S INC. v. WILKINSON

Supreme Court of Nebraska 1985.
219 Neb. 209, 361 N.W.2d 557.

CAPORALE, J.

Defendants-appellants, Mary and Ronald Wilkinson, doing business as M & R Trucking, challenge the deficiency judgment entered against them, jointly and severally, under Neb U.C.C. art. 9 (Reissue 1980), in favor of the plaintiff-appellee, Schmode's Inc., a Nebraska corporation. Among the Wilkinsons' assignments of error is the failure of the trial court to find that Schmode's elected to retain the collateral in satisfaction of the Wilkinsons' obligation. The record sustains that assignment, making it unnecessary that we address the remaining assignments. We reverse, remand, and direct that the cause be dismissed.

We note at the outset that this is an action at law. * * * The findings and disposition of the trial court therefore, the cause having been tried without a jury, have the effect of a jury verdict and will not be disturbed unless clearly wrong. * * *

Reviewed in accordance with that standard, the relevant facts are as follows.

Schmode's entered into a business transaction with Harco Leasing Company, Inc., whereby Schmode's sold to Harco a 1978 International tractor truck and a 1978 Hobbs trailer. Harco and the Wilkinsons then, on April 27, 1978, executed a conditional sales agreement, entitled "LEASING AGREEMENT," with respect to the truck, which obligated the Wilkinsons to pay Harco a principal amount, plus amortized interest and other charges, in 60 equal monthly installments and a larger 61st payment representing the truck's "residual value." On May 19, 1978, Harco and the Wilkinsons entered into a similar agreement with respect to the trailer, obligating the Wilkinsons to pay Harco a principal amount, plus amortized interest and other charges, in 60 equal monthly installments and a larger 61st payment representing the trailer's "residual value." Schmode's guaranteed Harco that if the Wilkinsons defaulted on their obligation such as to result in Harco's reclaiming the truck and trailer from the Wilkinsons, Schmode's would repurchase them from Harco.

The Wilkinsons defaulted, and on December 19, 1979, they delivered possession of the truck and trailer, collectively the collateral, to Schmode's.

The collateral was in need of repair and Schmode's restored it to sound mechanical condition, the restoration work being completed by May 3, 1980. The collateral was then placed on Schmode's lot in an attempt to sell it. As the collateral did not sell, Schmode's used it by leasing it to others through about mid-April of 1983, during which time it was operated a minimum of 204,000 miles.

Schmode's honored its agreement with Harco and paid the sums due Harco from the Wilkinsons. The parties do not dispute that Schmode's had a security interest in the collateral.

The collateral was publicly sold on April 28, 1983, pursuant to the trial judge's order. At the trial on the merits the trial judge found that the April 28 sale had not been commercially reasonable "because of the lapse of nearly three years and the use of said vehicles before the sale." The trial judge accordingly ruled that the Wilkinsons were entitled to setoffs for the damages they suffered due to the commercially unreasonable sale.

The Wilkinsons argue that Schmode's elected to retain the collateral in satisfaction of the obligation by keeping and leasing it for a period of almost 3 years after restoration and causing it to be operated for at least 204,000 miles, and therefore cannot obtain a deficiency judgment.

Neb U.C.C. § 9–505(2) (Reissue 1980) provides in relevant part:

> "In any other case involving consumer goods or any other collateral a secured party in possession may, after default, propose to retain the collateral in satisfaction of the obligation. Written notice of such proposal shall be sent to the debtor if he has not signed after default a statement renouncing or modifying his rights under this subsection."

Although we have not had occasion to deal with whether acts by a secured party other than the sending of notice may result in a § 9–505(2) election, other states with statutes virtually identical to ours have. There appear to be three different approaches.

One approach holds that an election under § 9–505(2) is impossible absent the service of notice on the debtor of the secured party's intent to retain the collateral in payment of the debt. Flickinger v. Genesee Corp., 71 A.D.2d 382, 423 N.Y.S.2d 73 (1979), typifies this view which seems to be premised on the notion that since the code provides a specific method for indicating that the secured party has elected to retain the collateral to satisfy the obligation, such an election cannot be implied from conduct not specified by the code. We reject this view on the ground that a secured party ought not be allowed to penalize a debtor by asserting the secured party's own failure to give the notice contemplated by § 9–505(2).

A second approach is that an election can be implied from an unreasonably prolonged retention of the collateral by the secured party and that the determination of what constitutes an unreasonable period of time is a question for the trier of fact. Service Chevrolet v. Sparks, 99 Wash.2d 199, 660 P.2d 760 (1983); Shultz v. Delaware Trust Co., 360 A.2d 576 (Del.Super.1976). This view appears to rest on the theory that to allow the secured party to retain the collateral for an unreasonably long time and then elect to sue the debtor on the underlying obligation would be unfair to the debtor.

The third approach requires that the secured party manifest an intent to accept the collateral in satisfaction of the obligation by some conduct other than an undue delay in disposing of the collateral. Nelson v. Armstrong, 99 Idaho 422, 582 P.2d 1100 (1978) (retaining farm equipment for 4½ months did not constitute an election); Jones v. Morgan, 58 Mich.App. 455, 228 N.W.2d 419 (1975) (keeping automobile for almost 2 years did not constitute an election); Tanenbaum v. Economics Laboratory, Inc., 628 S.W.2d 769 (Tex.1982) (taking back collateral at request of debtor that such be done in satisfaction of debt constituted election). This view rests, at least in part, on the notion that since the debtor is protected by other provisions in the code and because, at common law, the analogous concept of accord and satisfaction requires proof of the creditor's assent, in the absence of notice a clear manifestation of an election on the part of the creditor is required.

Under the circumstances of this case we need not choose at this time between the second and third approaches. Although we consider the question to be one of fact, we hold that in this case there is but one reasonable conclusion, and, therefore, as a matter of law, Schmode's, by using the collateral for a period of nearly 3 years after restoration by leasing and causing it to be operated for at least 204,000 miles, elected to retain the collateral in satisfaction of the Wilkinsons' obligation. The trial court was clearly wrong in not so holding.

We leave to another day and another case the question of whether under some circumstances the mere retention of collateral for an unreasonably long time may in and of itself imply a § 9–505(2) election.

The judgment is reversed and the cause remanded with directions to dismiss.

Reversed and remanded with directions to dismiss.

SECTION 8. CREDITOR'S RIGHT TO RESELL OR OTHERWISE DISPOSE OF THE COLLATERAL ON DEFAULT—"FORECLOSURE BY SALE"

Section 9–504 provides for foreclosure by sale. The jargon "foreclosure by sale," like "strict foreclosure" also derives from the law of real property. Foreclosure by sale may be explained as a legal invention designed to protect any ownership equity of the debtor from forfeiture, even though it, too, cuts off the debtor's "equity of redemption" (UCC 9–506). Of course, foreclosure by sale is a double-edged sword. Except as modified by regulatory law, if the UCC 9–504 foreclosure sale yields less than necessary to satisfy the debt, the debtor remains liable for the deficiency. See UCC 9–504(2).

We saw that in the land law, the "equity of redemption" was supposed to protect the debtor's "ownership equity" from forfeiture. But "strict foreclosure" evolved to protect the foreclosing secured party from the possibility that the debtor would later redeem. This protection for the secured creditor (the right of "strict" foreclosure) largely nullified the protection of the debtor's ownership equity given by his right to redeem. In a particular case, strict foreclosure might be invoked to cut off a quite substantial ownership equity of the debtor. This should seem doubly bad, for it not only deprived the debtor of his property, but gave the secured party a windfall as well. Hence, in came foreclosure by sale, which, among other things, was supposed to protect the debtor's ownership equity by (a) tending to assure a greater return from the collateral than just the amount of the debt due (a "surplus" representing debtor's "ownership equity") and (b) imposing a duty on the secured party to account to the debtor for such "surplus." Cf. UCC 9–504(2).

But, from the debtor's viewpoint, foreclosure by sale was and is a double-edged sword. Strict foreclosure, as such, left the secured party with no recourse if his collateral turned out to be worth less than the debt. Foreclosure by sale, on the other hand, brought with it the deficiency judgment, and foreclosure by sale could not, in and of itself, *assure* a return sufficient even to discharge the debt due, let alone provide a surplus representing any ownership equity of the debtor. As Professor Gilmore remarked:

> "Sad experience has taught us that a power of sale, coupled with a right to a deficiency judgment can be harder on the debtor than strict foreclosure ever was. The surplus to be returned to the debtor after the sale is a glittering mirage; the deficiency judgment is the grim reality. Furthermore the person who buys at the sale today, nine times out of ten, is not our hero, the good faith purchaser for value, but the holder of the security interest who pays not in cash but by a credit against the debt."

2 GILMORE, SECURITY INTERESTS IN PERSONAL PROPERTY 1188–89 (1965).

From the creditor's point of view, what is at stake in any "realization" process is obvious enough: It is simply whether he is to be paid his due. But from the debtor's viewpoint, much more may be at risk, as Professor Gilmore indicates.

SECTION 9. SECTION 9–504(3): REQUIREMENTS OF COMMERCIAL REASONABLENESS AND THE EFFECTS OF NONCOMPLIANCE

Section 9–504(3) authorizes one who has repossessed collateral to resell it by public or private sale but it requires that "every aspect of the disposition including the method, manner, time, place and terms must be commercially reasonable." The Section goes on to require notice to the debtor (and certain others) in most circumstances. It is not surprising that UCC 9–504(3) has produced a great deal of litigation. Debtors have argued that sales are commercially unreasonable for the following reasons, among many others:

1. The price realized at the sale was too low.

2. The creditor waited too long to conduct the sale.

3. The creditor sold the goods in the wrong market (e.g. wholesale not retail).

4. The creditor failed to give the appropriate notice.

5. The creditor failed to do an adequate job of drumming up bidders at the sale, or to advertise properly the forthcoming sale.

In many circumstances the judgment of whether the sale was commercially reasonable was rather a subjective one, but the cases that follow will give the student a taste of the kinds of considerations that may be relevant. (See also White & Summers §§ 26–9 through 26–12.)

In reading the cases, the student should be mindful of these basic questions: Who is attacking the validity of the sale? On what grounds? And with what desired effect? Note that sometimes the party attacking the sale will be seeking affirmative recovery on a conversion theory or the like. At other times this party will merely be resisting a deficiency judgment. And there are still other possibilities.

A. Public or Private Proceedings?

UNITED STATES v. WILLIS

United States Court of Appeals, Sixth Circuit, 1979.
593 F.2d 247.

KEITH, CIRCUIT JUDGE.

The Small Business Administration (SBA), an agency of the United States government, appeals from a judgment of the district court denying its claims against Duane G. Willis and Mary J. Willis. Plaintiff commenced this action on December 22, 1975, alleging that the defendants were liable to it pursuant to a guaranty executed in conjunction with an SBA loan. The guaranty was assigned to the SBA upon default of the primary debtor performance by SBA pursuant to its own guaranty. Jurisdiction was invoked pursuant to 28 U.S.C. § 1345. The district court held that the SBA was not entitled to any monetary recovery because it had failed to dispose of collateral securing the loan in a commercially reasonable manner. We affirm Judge Robert B. Krupansky's decision,

FACTS

The facts are relatively straightforward. On March 22, 1972, Opticron, Inc., a Delaware corporation, together with Opticron International, Inc., and Opticron of Pennsylvania, Inc., (hereinafter collectively referred to as Opticron) executed a $325,000 promissory note in favor of the Union Commerce Bank of Cleveland, Ohio (UCB). The note was guaranteed up to 90 percent by the SBA. In conjunction with Opticron's execution of the note and as an inducement for the extension of credit, defendants Duane G. and Mary Jayne Willis signed a separate instrument in favor of the UCB and its successor and assigns unconditionally guaranteeing the prompt payment when due of the principal and interest owed on the note. That same day, all of the corporate signatories to the promissory note executed security agreements in favor of the UCB, collateralizing the $325,000 loan with all assets of the several corporations, except cash.

Opticron defaulted on the note. SBA loan officer Gordon Miller met on February 1, 1973, with representatives of Opticron, UCB and other interested parties regarding the financial position of Opticron. On February 7, 1973 the UCB requested payment from the SBA of 90 percent of the $325,000 loan pursuant to the SBA guaranty agreement.

The SBA subsequently took possession of the assets and operations of Opticron and placed a notice in the Business Opportunity Section of the Sunday Cleveland Plain Dealer, February 18, 1973, advertising a summary public auction sale to be held on Thursday, February 22, 1973, at the offices of Opticron. The notice contained a minimum bid requirement of $150,000.

On February 21, 1973, the SBA paid to the UCB the sum of $296,530, being payment in full of 90 percent of the $325,000 loan, plus 90 percent of the interest due on the loan. The February 22, 1973 auction did not take place as advertised. Apparently, questions were raised as to the legal sufficiency of the notice and so none of the parties present would place a bid. On March 13 and 14, and April 12, 1973, however, the public auction sales were held, and $47,456.63 was realized from the sale of Opticron's assets. Deductions from gross sales for rent, expenses and auctioneers' fees resulted in net proceeds of $41,115.47 from all auction sales.

In the meantime, Opticron had received two firm private offers to purchase its assets. On January 30, 1973, an offer from Will Ross, Inc. (Will Ross) to purchase all of the assets of Opticron as reflected on the latter's November 30, 1972 balance sheet for the sum of $200,000 cash was communicated by letter to Opticron's Board of Directors. On January 31, 1973, a prior offer from Marcrum Optical of Florida, Inc. (Marcrum) to purchase all assets as reflected on the January 30, 1973 balance sheet of Opticron for $210,000 was confirmed by letter. Marcrum offered to pay $100,000 in cash with the remaining $110,000 to be paid over a period of 10 years.

At the above-mentioned meeting on February 1, 1973, defendant Duane Willis communicated these two offers to the interested parties then present, viz., Gordon Miller of the SBA and a representative of the UCB. With the apparent concurrence of all present, a telegram dated February 2, 1973, was sent to Will Ross accepting its offer subject to the final agreement and concurrence of UCB.

Subsequent to the February 1, 1973 meeting, Miller informed Willis that a public sale was *necessary* to dispose of the assets collateralizing the promissory note. Thereafter, the aforementioned advertisement of the summary public auction ran in the Cleveland Plain Dealer on February 18, 1973.

Notwithstanding the receipt of $41,115.47 from the auction sales, the SBA seeks by this action to recover from defendant guarantors the full amount of the loan principal outstanding plus accrued interest; a total of $297,174.66 plus daily interest of $43.9071 from December 27, 1974. At trial, defendants asserted that the sale of Opticron's assets was not conducted in a commercially reasonable manner and that plaintiff had the burden of establishing the commercial reasonableness of the sales. The plaintiff countered by asserting that the defense of commercial reasonableness was not available to the defendants and that, in any case, the burden of proof on that issue rested with the defense. The district court found that the defense was available to the defendants and that once it had been raised, the burden of establishing the commercial reasonableness of the sales in question rested with the plaintiff. Additionally, the court found that the Government had failed to carry its burden.

The Government presents four issues for decision on appeal: 1) whether unconditional guarantors can avail themselves of the defense of commercial reasonableness to defeat its alleged federal right of recovery; 2) assuming the defense is available to unconditional guarantors, whether the defendants are estopped to assert it; 3) whether defendants proved at the trial below that the sale of Opticron's assets was commercially unreasonable; and, 4) whether the district court erred in denying SBA any monetary recovery. These issues will be addressed in the order in which they have been set out above.

[The court held that the guarantors could avail themselves of the "defense of commercial reasonableness," and that they were not estopped to assert it.]

* * *

II.

Commercial Reasonableness of the Sale

A. Effect of Raising the Defense

As noted above, the defense of commercial reasonableness is available in this case and was raised by the defendants at the trial below. While courts differ as to the effect of asserting this defense, it appears that the great weight of authority holds that it has the effect of shifting the burden of proof on this issue to the secured party. 59 A.L.R.3d, p. 369 (1974); Vic Hansen & Sons, Inc. v. Crowley, 57 Wis.2d 106, 203 N.W.2d 728 (1973); Dynalectron Corp. v. Jack Richards Aircraft, supra, [337 F.Supp. 659 (W.D.Okla.1972)] 69 Am.Jur.2d, Secured Transactions, § 623, pp. 520–531 (1966). This also appears to be the position taken by the courts of Ohio. See In re Frye, 9 U.C.C.Rep.Ser. 913, 921 (S.D.Ohio 1970). We see no reason not to follow this authority as did the district court below.

The district judge made it clear to the Government at the outset of the trial below that it had the burden of proof on this issue. Yet, despite this notice, the Government's only proof regarding this issue at trial focused upon the reasonableness of the public sale which it conducted. Even in its briefs filed in connection with its appeal to this court, the Government still restricts its arguments to the proposition that the auction was properly conducted. The entire thrust of the Government's proof and argument appears to be that proof that the collateral was properly sold in a recognized market by means of an accepted method of disposition, i.e. an auction sale, is also proof that the sale was commercially reasonable.

This court cannot accept the Government's argument because it rests on the assumption that a properly conducted public sale is inherently reasonable, a premise which is clearly false. In Old Colony Trust Co. v. Penrose Industries Corp., 280 F.Supp. 698 (E.D.Pa.1965), the court stated:

> "Although the words of § 9–504(3) seem to grant the secured parties an absolute option of whether to have a public or private sale, it seems unwise to take such words literally. To begin with, the second sentence of § 9–504(3) would at least seem to include within the words 'method, manner, time, place and terms' the fundamental choice of public versus private sale, and thus the secured parties must choose between a private or public sale according to which, if either, is the more 'commercially reasonable.'"

280 F.Supp. at 712. At a later point, the court notes:

> "Commentary on Article 9 has convincingly pointed out that '[t]he policy of Article 9 is to provide a simple, efficient, and flexible tool to produce the maximum amount from the disposition of the collateral.' To effectuate this, § 9–504 'attempts to chart a path in the narrow area between two policy positions—one a desire to impede dishonest dispositions, and the other, a reluctance to strangle honest transactions with red tape.'"

280 F.Supp. at 714–715 (footnote omitted). Finally, the court notes, and we agree:

> "The relevant test is thus whether every aspect of the sale is commercial reasonable. It is commercially reasonable if the party (1) acts in good faith, (2) avoids loss, and (3) makes an effective realization. Furthermore, the party may obtain court approval if he (4) sells in the usual manner in a recognized market, or (5) sells at the current price in a recognized market, or

(6) sells in conformity with reasonable commercial practices among dealers in the type of property."

280 F.Supp. at 715. In light of the above, we think it is clear that the Government did not have absolute discretion in choosing between a public and a private sale. Whatever discretion it had in choosing the method of sale was limited by its good faith duty to maximize the proceeds upon sale of the collateral. If the original choice of method was unreasonable, we think it matters little, if at all, that this unreasonable choice was executed in a reasonable and proper fashion.

Moreover, we are of the opinion that the Government's choice of a public sale as opposed to a private sale in the circumstances of this case was unreasonable. The evidence establishes that at the time the Government decided on the public sale, it had firm and outstanding offers of $200,000 and $210,000, respectively. The Government knew of these two offers at least 2½ months prior to its own sale and the $200,000 offer had been tentatively accepted with its apparent approval. Yet, despite the fact that the auctioneer hired to conduct the sale provided an estimate—although concededly only a guesstimate—of $45,000 for the assets upon public sale, the Government, without explanation or apparent good cause, announced and proceeded with the public sale.

And while price is not determinative, UCC § 9–507(2), the fact that the offers were five times greater than the proceeds realized upon the sale is at least probative on the question of commercial reasonableness. See *Mercantile Financial Corp.*, [292 F.Supp. 797 (E.D.Pa.1968)] at 801:

> "Although § 9–507(2) clearly provides that a discrepancy between a price received by a creditor disposing of assets pursuant to § 9–504 and an isolated price later shown to have been obtainable, is not alone sufficient to grant a debtor affirmative relief under § 9–507(1), certainly such a discrepancy, if substantial, is relevant to a determination of whether a challenged sale was 'commercially reasonable.' "

In light of these facts, we conclude that the Government failed to carry its burden and that the trial court was correct in holding that the sale was commercially unreasonable.

B. Effect of Breach

Having determined that the Government failed to carry out the duty imposed upon it by § 9–504(3), there still remains the question of the effect of this breach. The courts have differed. Some have held that failure to comply with the requirements of § 9–504(3) absolutely precludes recovery by the secured party in a subsequent action against the debtor for a deficiency. * * * Other courts have held that failure to meet the requirements of § 9–504(3) creates a presumption that the value of the collateral equalled the indebtedness secured, thereby extinguishing the indebtedness unless the secured party rebuts the presumption * * *.

In circumstances such as presented in this case, divergence in the law provides substance for federal choice. As noted already, Ohio courts appear to follow the first approach set out above. * * * While we are not required to follow the approach taken by the Ohio courts, we do so out of our belief that the rebuttable presumption rule is the more enlightened and equitable.

Applying the rule to the facts of this case, we agree with the trial court that the Government cannot recover because it failed in its duty to rebut the presumption. The fact that two offers five times greater than the proceeds were made and that the Government's own original minimum bid requirement was $150,000 is sufficient to establish that, in all probability the assets' fair market value exceeded the price received upon actual sale. Yet, a review of the record of the trial below reveals that the Government failed to adduce any evidence tending to show that the fair market value of these assets was less than the indebtedness secured and if so, by what amount. Its entire presentation of testimonial evidence focused on establishing that the auction was properly conducted and the sale was commercially reasonable by virtue of this fact alone.[2]

The Government correctly notes that even a secured party who fails to dispose of collateral in a commercially reasonable manner has often been held entitled to recover the difference between the outstanding debt and the fair market value of collateral. But the Government would ignore that part of the rule followed in this case that before recovery is permitted, the secured party must 1) establish the fair market value of the collateral and, thereby, 2) rebut the presumption that the value of the collateral equalled the indebtedness secured. The Government failed to do either here and thus, we agree with the trial court that it was not entitled to any recovery.

As its final argument, the Government maintains that it is entitled to a judgment for $96,530, the difference between the $296,530 outstanding debt and $200,000. It argues that since the basis of the trial court's determination that the sale was commercially unreasonable was the fact that two private offers of $200,000 and $210,000, respectively, were made by prospective purchasers prior to the public sale and that since defendants offered no evidence to show that the collateral was worth more than $200,000 it is entitled to this amount at a minimum.

This court cannot agree. The $200,000 figure which appellant would not select to represent the fair market value of the assets was introduced at trial not to establish fair market value per se, but rather, to show that the amount received upon the actual sale was substantially less than what might have been obtained in a sale conducted in a commercially reasonable manner. The introduction of this figure to suggest the inadequacy of the price actually obtained is not proof of the assets' actual value.[3]

In essence, the Government argues that an amount which no one contended at trial to be the fair market value of the assets should now be adopted by this court as the fair market value of the assets. The Government surely did not contend at trial that this figure was the fair market value for it would then have

2. Presumably, the Government's proof on this point also encompassed the fairness—measured by fair market value—of the price actually obtained. Otherwise, the Government would have been in the anomalous position of arguing that, while the assets' fair market value greatly exceeded the price obtained, the price actually obtained was still a fair one.

3. The evidence presented at trial as to the fair market value of Opticron's assets at the time of sale was conflicting at best. Ken Miller, the auctioneer retained by the Government to conduct the sale, testified that he appraised the assets at $45,000 before conducting the sale. Upon inquiry by the district court, Miller confided that even this appraisal was a "gut reaction," a mere "guess" or "guesstimate." In the notice placed in the Business Opportunity Section of the Sunday Cleveland Plain Dealer on February 18, 1973, advertising a summary public auction sale of the assets to be held on Tuesday, February 22, 1973, five days later, appellant included a minimum bid requirement of $150,000. Plaintiff, on its behalf, adduced evidence at trial of two firm private offers to purchase the assets for $200,000 and $210,000, respectively. Mr. Willis' testimony suggested a market value of the assets of up to $240,000. [Footnotes omitted and renumbered.]

been in the anomalous position of arguing that $47,456.63 was a reasonable price for the assets despite their fair market value of at least $200,000.

We have adopted as the rule in this case that where the secured party has disposed of the collateral in a commercially unreasonable manner, it rests with him to carry the burden of proof in rebutting the presumption that the fair market value of the assets equalled the indebtedness secured. Had sufficient evidence been adduced at trial, whether by appellant or defendants, to establish the fair market value of the assets in question, this court would not hesitate to permit appellant any benefit that it could derive therefrom. However, the fair market value of these assets was not established by the evidence of either party at trial.

For the foregoing reasons, the judgment of the district court is affirmed, the parties to bear their own costs.

Note: Private v. Public Sales

According to the *Willis* case, the failure to hold a private rather than a public sale may itself be commercially unreasonable. Article Nine does not define public and private sales. It is evident, though, that the Code drafters viewed a public sale as a sale open to the general public (or a segment thereof) and which is so advertised. By contrast, a private sale is not open to the general public and does not call for general advertisement. The Code explicitly attaches several consequences to the private-public sale distinction. First, UCC 9–504(3) provides that notice to the debtor and others in the case of a private sale need only provide reasonable notice of the time after which any private sale is to be made, but such notice in the case of a public sale must give reasonable notice of the time and place thereof. Second, section 9–504(4) says that the rights of a purchaser at a public sale may be somewhat greater than the rights of a purchaser at private sale. Third, section 9–504(3) allows the secured creditor to buy at a public sale but not at a private sale (except in special circumstances).

Comment 6 to 9–504 makes clear that "the policy adopted * * * [is] to encourage disposition by private sale through regular commercial channels." Doubtless such disposition does occur. But it is also now evident that very frequently secured creditors will first hold public sales at which they themselves buy in at or below the amount of the outstanding debt, after which they *then* resell "through regular commercial channels." Why might a secured creditor prefer this route rather than that of going directly to the private outlet in the first place? Should courts be careful to scrutinize such a process of public sale purchase and private resale on the part of the secured creditor?

B. *Was "Notice * * * Sent by the Secured Party to the Debtor"?*

Read UCC 9–504(3) again. Unless excused (under what circumstances?) or renounced by the debtor (how?), a notice "shall be sent by the secured party to the debtor * * *" When other than consumer goods are involved, the notice requirement may also include another secured party.

There are at least four problems lurking here: (1) Who is entitled to notice; (2) What should be the content of the notice; (3) When is the notice "sent;" and (4) What consequences flow from the failure to give a required notice?

Problem 6–5

On July 1, Bank lent Dobbs, the owner of a small business, $10,000 and perfected a security interest in equipment. Before the loan was made, however, Bank insisted that Alice, Dobb's wealthy sister, sign the note as a guarantor. At that time, Alice signed a writing renouncing any right to notice under UCC 9–504(3) should Dobbs default and Bank enforce the security interest. At no time did Alice have any interest in Dobb's business.

On August 1, Finance Company lent Dobbs $5,000 and perfected a security interest in the equipment. On September 1, Dobbs defaulted and Bank repossessed the equipment. On September 5, Finance Company sent Bank a written notice that it claimed an interest in the collateral. Bank proposes to dispose of the equipment at a private sale. To whom should it send notice?

LEASING ASSOCIATES INC. v. SLAUGHTER & SON, INC.

United States Court of Appeals, Eighth Circuit, 1971.
450 F.2d 174.

MATTHES, CHIEF JUDGE.

Negotiations between Leasing Associates, Inc., a Texas corporation, hereinafter referred to as plaintiff, and Slaughter & Son, Inc., an Arkansas corporation, and F.E. Slaughter, as guarantor, hereinafter sometimes referred to as defendants, culminated in the execution of a leasing agreement dated May 10, 1967. Under the terms of the lease, Slaughter obligated itself to make certain payments to plaintiff and F.E. Slaughter guaranteed payment of all sums due under the instrument. Slaughter, as lessee under the agreement, took possession of a 1967 Chevrolet truck and a 1964 GMC Barco Log Loader.

A controversy developed between plaintiff and defendants over the fitness of the Chevrolet truck. Defendants repeatedly complained that the truck was defective and not fit for its intended use in hauling logs. Eventually, they discontinued making payments due under the lease. They returned the truck to plaintiff and thereafter, pursuant to proper notice from plaintiff to the defendants, the truck was sold by plaintiff.

The complaint in this action was filed on October 21, 1968 in the United States District Court for the Western District of Arkansas. Plaintiff sought a judgment for $10,001.42, representing the accrued and unpaid rent due on the truck, the amount expended by plaintiff for repairs, and the deficiency after giving credit for proceeds of sale. Defendants, on October 10, 1969, answered and counterclaimed for damages allegedly sustained because of the unfitness of the truck.

Defendants also defaulted in payments due on the log loader. In June, 1969, possession of that equipment was taken from defendants in a replevin proceeding filed in an Arkansas state court. The plaintiff obtained possession of the log loader on June 11, 1969. Pursuant to a notice to the defendants, the reasonableness of which is an issue on appeal, the log loader was sold for $500 on or about October 16, 1969.

On August 31, 1970, nearly two years after the filing of the original complaint, plaintiff filed its first amended complaint to recover, in addition to the amount allegedly due on the truck transaction, the amount it claimed to be due on the log loader transaction.

A jury trial resulted in a verdict in favor of plaintiff and against both defendants for $18,508.73, being the full amount prayed for.

Two issues are presented for our determination.

* * *

II

Defendants' second point relates to that part of the judgment for $8,507.31, the amount due on the Barco log loader. Specifically, defendants' contention is that the court erred in admitting into evidence over their objection an exhibit purported to be a copy of a letter dated October 6, 1969, claimed to have been sent by plaintiff's credit manager to "Mr. F.E. Slaughter, F.E. Slaughter & Sons., Inc., Junction City, Arkansas." The argument is advanced that the proper foundation was not laid for admission of the exhibit, i.e., that evidence was insufficient to support a finding that the original of the letter had been sent to the above-named addressee via the United States mails.

Before we review the factual foundation bearing upon this question, we turn to the applicable provisions of the Uniform Commercial Code, as adopted in Arkansas, and case law pertinent to the issue. * * *

* * *

The sanction which makes the foregoing requirement [commercial reasonableness] viable is a rebuttable presumption that the value of any collateral sold without notice is equal to the debt. Therefore, as a prerequisite to the recovery of a deficiency judgment in Arkansas, the secured party has the burden of proving either the actual value of the collateral at the time of its sale after repossession, or proving that reasonable notice was sent (receipt need not be proven). * * *

In the present case, however, the plaintiff offered no proof that the $500 realized from the sale of the log loader was the fair and reasonable market value of that equipment. Therefore, if plaintiff failed to discharge its burden of proving that it gave reasonable notice as required it would be precluded from recovering the deficiency under attack.

There are two prongs to the notice question: (1) whether the mailing of a notice through regular mail channels will suffice to support a finding that reasonable notice was sent to the debtor; (2) whether the evidence here was sufficient to show as implicitly found by the jury that the letter of October 6 was in fact mailed.

Turning to the first of these, the Arkansas Supreme Court has been confronted with the identical question, that is, whether a notice in the form of a letter sent by regular United States mail was "reasonable notification," as required by Ark.Stat.Ann. § 85–9–504, supra. In reversing the trial judge, who had ruled that the letter constituted reasonable notice as a matter of law, the Supreme Court held that the evidence was sufficient to present a question of fact for the jury to resolve. Baber v. Williams Ford Co., 239 Ark. 1054, 396 S.W.2d 302 (1965). Thus, it appears that the *Baber* case definitely resolves the first phase of the notice issue in favor of the plaintiff.

We turn then to the more troublesome problem of whether the evidence was sufficient to say that the letter of October 6, 1969 was sent by placing the same in the mails. On this question, the evidence is sketchy and far from satisfactory.

The notice issue first entered the case near the end of the trial. Larry Slaughter, son of F.E. Slaughter, when asked on cross-examination by plaintiff's counsel whether he had received the letter of October 9, replied:

"Not that I can remember.

"Q. You have any knowledge of anyone in your company receiving this letter?

"A. Well, I don't know it if they did."

The foregoing is the only evidence pertaining to the receipt of the letter. F.E. Slaughter, to whom the letter was addressed, and who testified, was not interrogated as to receipt by him of the notice.

Following Larry Slaughter's testimony, plaintiff's counsel, apparently realizing plaintiff had the burden of proving that the notice had been sent, called Ernest M. Dillinger as a rebuttal witness.

The substance of this witness' testimony was that Exhibit 11 was a copy of the letter which he had written to Slaughter & Son, and that it was sent by regular mail. On cross-examination, Dillinger stated that he dictated the letter to his secretary, "she gave it to me for my signature and it went out in the normal course of business in my office as all mail does each day."

"Q. You assumed, then, that it went out? A. Yes, I assumed that it went out * * * I cannot prove it ever got inside the mailbox. All I can say is that it went out of our office in the normal course of business.

"Q. You assumed that it did? A. That's right.

"Q. You don't know whether it ever got past your secretary's desk, do you? A. Yes, it came back for my signature, I put it in my out box for the mail clerk to pick up and mail."

Whether the foregoing meager statements were of such qualitative nature as to provide an adequate foundation for admission into evidence of the carbon copy and the implicit finding by the jury that the original of the letter was actually mailed is, of course, governed by Arkansas law. The question brings into play reliance upon office custom or practice in mailing to show "reasonable notification." Our attention has not been directed to any Arkansas case and independent research has disclosed none that has specifically decided the circumstances in which such custom and practice can support a finding that a particular letter was mailed.

The most analogous Arkansas case is Dengler v. Dengler, 196 Ark. 913, 120 S.W.2d 340 (1938). There the evidentiary problem was whether defendant's testimony that she personally mailed a particular letter was sufficiently precise to warrant a presumption that the letter was received. Of importance here is the fact that the tenor of the Arkansas court's approach to the problem was cautiously to require clear proof of all the facts of a proper mailing, i.e., proper stamping, addressing and posting. Moreover, the Arkansas court's view of this type of evidence is clearly matched by its zealous protection of the debtor under Ark.Stat. § 85–9–504(3) in *Barker* and *Norton,* supra. We therefore are constrained to approach this question with the narrow view of *Dengler,* that "the technicalities that make for justice may not be casually disregarded." 120 S.W.2d at 345.

As shown by *Annotations,* 25 A.L.R. 9, 13, supplemented at 85 A.L.R. 541, 544, and 30 Am.Jur.2d Evidence § 1119, the weight of authority holds the evidence here presented to be insufficient due to the failure to call the mailclerk to verify either that he mailed this particular letter or at least that it was his custom to mail such letters. Thus if Arkansas were to adopt the "majority rule," reversal would here be required. Conversely, it may be that the Arkansas court would share, as we do, Professor McCormick's view that testimony of the mailclerk would only be cumulative since, considering the modern volume of corporate correspondence, he could not be expected to remember posting a particular letter or emptying the mail tray on a particular day and probably could only reiterate the executive's description of the office practice. McCormick on Evidence, § 162, p. 343 n. 13 (1954). However, even if Arkansas law were in accord with the "minority view," a jury finding that clerical personnel performed their duties in properly posting the mail would be permissible only if there were clear testimony by the executive as to the customary practice in his office and his actions in compliance therewith. The problem in this case, however, is that plaintiff's sole witness on this point, Dillinger, proffered no description of the office practice from which a jury properly could determine whether his actions were in accord with it. He gave no indication as to who customarily did such basic acts as addressing, sealing, and stamping the envelopes and whether he could verify that he and his secretary had done such of those as was their customary duty before he signed the letter and placed it in the tray on his desk. His conclusory statement that "it went out in the normal course of business in my office as all mail does each day" is simply not enough. "The essential elementary facts may be shown by course of business properly proved, but an offer of [such] proof * * * must be directed to facts and not mere conclusions * * *." * * * While the plaintiff may "show the essential facts constituting transmission by mail by showing the course of business, it failed because there is no evidence in the record as to what this office routine may have been." * * * "That may be rather technical but the appellee relies upon a presumption which does not arise, unless the evidence itself discloses" the basic facts underlying it. * * *

Accordingly, whichever view Arkansas might be deemed to follow, we are constrained to hold that the evidence was not adequate to support the requisite jury finding that notification was placed in the United States mail.

In summary, we affirm the judgment of $10,001.42 as the deficiency due on the truck transaction. The remainder of the judgment, $8,507.31, is vacated and the claim for the balance due on the Barco Log Loader is remanded to the district court for another trial. One-half of the costs of printing the appendix and briefs shall be taxed against the plaintiff and one-half against the defendants.

STEPHENSON, CIRCUIT JUDGE concurring, with whom CHIEF JUDGE MATTHES and JUDGE BRIGHT join.

In concurring I add the comment that the issue here, which has occupied the busy time of the trial court and this court, should have been disposed of by the parties prior to trial through routine discovery and at the very latest during pretrial. [Footnotes omitted.]

Notes

The foregoing case illustrates a problem too often overlooked in law school, namely how does one prove his case in court; what specifically must he introduce into evidence; what questions must he ask of a witness, and what must the witness say? The creditor can fail to prove his case for a variety of reasons. In the first place, the secured party may have done everything correctly yet be unable to prove that because he has kept incomplete records or has destroyed the records. Secondly, even if the records are available, counsel for the secured party can bungle their introduction and so lose the case.

Each student should ask the following questions:

1. What pieces of documentary evidence should I introduce into evidence? (Security agreement? Notice? Copy of notice? Bill of Sale?)

2. What foundation must I lay for the documentary evidence and what witnesses can provide that foundation? (Will the credit manager be able to handle the entire thing or must I call the office manager?)

3. What witnesses must say what things to prove the necessary elements? (Need I call the repossessor? Or the Credit Manager?)

MALLICOAT v. VOLUNTEER FINANCE & LOAN CORP.

Tennessee Court of Appeals, 1966.
57 Tenn.App. 106, 415 S.W.2d 347.

McAMIS, P.J. [What follows is merely an extract from the opinion.] After providing generally that the method, manner, time, place and terms of disposing of the collateral shall be 'commercially reasonable' the Act expressly requires that reasonable notification of the time and place of any public sale or reasonable notification of the time after which any private sale or other intended disposition is to be made shall be sent by the secured party to the debtor.

The requirement that the property be disposed of in a "commercially reasonable" manner seems to us to signify that the disposition shall be made in keeping with prevailing trade practices among reputable and responsible business and commercial enterprises engaged in the same or a similar business. It is general in scope and effect and is not mutually exclusive of the express requirement that notice of the intended disposition, whether by public or private sale, be sent to the debtor. The purpose of this notice, without doubt, is to enable the debtor to protect his interest in the property by paying the debt, finding a buyer or being present at the sale to bid on the property or have others do so, to the end that it be not sacrificed by a sale at less than its true value. Compare Range Motor Co. v. Tipton, 161 Tenn. 427, 33 S.W.2d 75, a suit under the Conditional Sales Statute.

In view of the undisputed proof in this case that the debtor did not receive the notice and that the secured creditor was aware that he had not received it, it is our opinion the creditor not only failed to show a compliance with the Act but that the record affirmatively shows a lack of compliance and a conscious disregard of the debtor's right to notice. The property was not perishable. The debtor lived in Knoxville where the creditor had its place of business and sold the property. In addition, the creditor had information as to where the debtor was employed and where his parents lived. Yet, the sale was allowed to proceed without any further effort to comply with the notice requirement.

In commenting on this provision of the Commercial Code, it is said at p. 788, 15 Am.Jur.2d, Commercial Code, Section 84:

> "Unless collateral is perishable or threatens to decline speedily in value or is of a type customarily sold on a recognized market, reasonable notification of the time and place of any public sale or reasonable notification of the time after which any private or other intended disposition is to be made shall be sent to the debtor. * * *"

The Act, T.C.A. § 47-1-201(26) reads:

> "A person 'notifies' or 'gives' a notice or notification to another by taking such steps as may be reasonably required to inform the other in

ordinary course whether or not such other actually comes to know of it. * * *"

Under this provision of the Act, the Supreme Court of Arkansas held in Hudspeth Motors, Inc. v. Wilkinson, 382 S.W.2d 191 that a public sale of the property would not be invalidated because the debtor failed to receive the notice sent by mail until after the sale. This case is urged upon us in this case as supporting the judgment. We consider it inapposite, however, since the creditor in that case was unaware of the failure of the debtor to receive the notice in time. If interpreted as holding valid a sale where the creditor proceeds to sell the property knowing the debtor had never received the notice we would not be disposed to follow it.

The requirement of notice is for the benefit and protection of the debtor. This provision of the Act should be construed and applied in a manner to effectuate this salutary purpose and in the light of Tennessee law.

In Burden v. Burden, 44 Tenn.App. 312, 313 S.W.2d 566, it was said:

> "Notice which is a mere gesture is not notice. The means employed must be such as one desirous of actually informing the absent party might reasonably adopt. Mullane v. Central Hanover Bank & Trust Co., 339 U.S. 306, 70 S.Ct. 652, 94 L.Ed. 865."

* * *

Note: Effect of Secured Party's Failure to Comply With Article 9, Part 5 on Right to Deficiency

Assume that, after default, Secured Party has repossessed and disposed of the collateral. Secured Party applies the proceeds as directed in UCC 9–504(1) and brings suit to recover a deficiency as authorized by UCC 9–504(2). Debtor claims and is able to establish that the disposition was defective under UCC 9–504(3). No notice was sent and the manner of the resale was commercially unreasonable. It is probable that if the disposition had been proper, the amount of deficiency would have been reduced by 25%. Debtor, however, argues that compliance with UCC 9–504(3) should be a condition precedent to Secured Party's right to a deficiency. He asserts that the failure to give notice deprived Debtor of an opportunity to redeem the collateral under UCC 9–506 and that the commercially unreasonable resale so complicates the proof issue on damages that it would be unfair to require Debtor to prove loss under UCC 9–507(1). How should this argument be treated in commercial default cases?

Three views have emerged in the cases. The first, a pro-creditor position, follows the literal language of UCC 9–507(1): The secured party may recover the deficiency subject to a setoff for damages caused by the defective resale. The burden is on the Debtor to prove these damages. The second, a pro-debtor position, concludes that compliance with UCC 9–504(3) is a condition precedent to recovering a deficiency. This result is most likely to be reached when the defect is a failure of notice. The third, a compromise, holds that if a defective disposition has been established by Debtor, the value of the collateral is presumed to equal the outstanding debt unless Secured Party proves otherwise. This proof-shifting device forces Secured Party to show that the defect did not reduce the proceeds that could have been obtained if UCC 9–504(3) has been followed.

The cases prior to 1980 are discussed in White and Summers § 26–15. Recent cases illustrating the judicial disagreement include, Farmers State Bank of Leeds v. Thompson, 372 N.W.2d 862 (N.D.1985); First Galesburg National Bank & Trust Co. v. Joannides, 103 Ill.2d 294, 82 Ill.Dec. 646, 469 N.E.2d 180 (1984) (rebuttable presumption adopted) and Stockdale, Inc. v. Baker, 364 N.W.2d 240 (Ia.1985); Havelock Bank

v. McArthur, 220 Neb. 364, 370 N.W.2d 116 (1985); Bank of Sheridan v. Devers, ___ Mont. ___, 702 P.2d 1388 (1985) (absolute bar).

Should the outcome in these cases turn on whether the debtor is only a guarantor or a co-maker of the obligation? Suppose the guarantor is a compensated surety?

C. Was the Public Disposition Commercially Reasonable?

Assuming that the secured party's decision to conduct a public sale was commercially reasonable, when is the method by which that sale is conducted commercially reasonable?

SAVAGE CONSTRUCTION, INC. v. CHALLENGE-COOK BROS., INC.

Supreme Court of Nevada, 1986.
714 P.2d 573.

PER CURIAM:

FACTUAL AND PROCEDURAL BACKGROUND

In the spring of 1979, Challenge-Cook Bros., Inc. (Challenge-Cook) entered into negotiations with Savage Construction, Inc. (Savage) and John Tom Ross (Ross) for the purchase and sale of four cement mixers. These negotiations led to the contract purchase, by Savage, of the cement mixers. The installment contract provided that it should be interpreted under California law, which brings the contract under the California version of the Uniform Commercial Code. After the installment payments became delinquent, Challenge-Cook peacefully repossessed the equipment in September of 1981. Challenge-Cook then caused the publication of notice of a public sale, to be held October 15, 1981, in San Leandro, California, in three publications; October 4th, 11th and 14th in the Nevada Appeal, once on October 5th in the Inter-City Express and once October 9th in the Daily Pacific Builder. Challenge-Cook, the only bidder at the public sale, purchased the equipment for the amount of their own in-house appraisal of $39,500 per cement mixer. Within two weeks after the auction, Challenge-Cook sold two of the cement mixers for a combined cash price of $99,000, plus tax, and the other two cement mixers for a total of $94,000, plus tax, on a conditional sales contract. The record indicates that the source of at least one of these purchases was negotiating with Challenge-Cook before the auction regarding a retail purchase of the equipment; however, Challenge-Cook did not notify that potential purchase of the upcoming auction.

Challenge-Cook filed suit to recover a deficiency judgment. The case was tried to the court, which found Savage and Ross liable for the deficiency but, nevertheless, credited Savage and Ross with the price received by Challenge-Cook in its retail sale of the equipment.

Subsequent to the judgment, Savage and Ross filed a motion to retax and settle costs. This motion was denied. Challenge-Cook also filed a motion to alter or amend judgment. This motion as also denied. This appeal, seeking to set aside the deficiency judgment, followed. The cross appeal by Challenge-Cook requests the recomputation of the amount of the deficiency judgment.

THE APPEAL

Initially, we note that because the parties intended that California law govern this matter, we have deferred to the law of that jurisdiction.

Appellants first contend that the public auction that occurred after the repossession of the equipment was not "commercially reasonable." We agree. They point to a number of factors that support this position: the quality of the publicity, the price obtained at the auction, the price obtained at a subsequent retail sale that took place within two weeks of the auction, the number of bidders in attendance at the auction, and the respondent's failure to advise known potential purchasers of the scheduled auction. We will examine each of the factors individually.

The law is clear that "[t]he fact that a better price could have been obtained by a sale at a different time or in a different method from that selected by a secured party is not of itself sufficient to establish that the sale was not made in a commercially reasonable manner." Clark Equipment Co. v. Mastelotto, Inc., 87 Cal.App.3d 88, 96, 150 Cal.Rptr. 797 (1978). However, the conditions of the sale must be reasonably calculated to bring the fair market price that is equitable to both the debtor and the secured party. General Elec. Credit Corp. v. Bo-Mar Construction Co., 72 Cal.App.3d 887, 889, 140 Cal.Rptr. 417 (1977). Since a secured creditor is generally in the best position to influence the circumstances of sale, it is reasonable that the creditor has an enhanced responsibility to promote fairness.

The Quality of Publicity

Section 9504(3) of the California Commercial Code requires that "Notice of the time and place of a public sale shall also be given *at least five days before the date of sale* by publication once in a *newspaper of general circulation published in the county in which the sale is to be held.*" (Emphasis added.) In order to meet the requirements of Section 9504(3), Challenge-Cook was required to advertise the sale:

1. at least five days before the sale;
2. in a paper of general circulation; and
3. in a paper published in the county in which the sale is to take place.

The sale in the instant case took place in San Leandro, California. The publications used to meet the legal requirements were the Nevada Appeal, the Inter-City Express and the Daily Pacific Builder. There is no question that the advertisements used were timely. The Nevada Appeal, however, is not published in the county where the sale took place. The record shows that the other two papers were used without knowledge of circulation of readership.

Publicity is intended to encourage competitive bidding. The sources of advertising utilized by Challenge-Cook were notably inefficacious in light of the fact that Challenge-Cook was the only bidder at the auction.

The Price Obtained at the Auction and the Subsequent Retail Sale

A public auction need not bring in the highest possible price. See Clark Equipment Co., supra, 87 Cal.App.3d at 96, 150 Cal.Rptr. 797. However, the conditions of sale must be reasonably calculated to facilitate a sale at fair market value, whether wholesale or retail. See Bo-Mar, supra, 72 Cal.App.3d at 889, 140 Cal.Rptr. 417. So, in the instant case, the price received at the subsequent retail sale, held within two weeks of the auction sale, is an indicator of fair market value of the equipment. See Kobuk Engineering & Contracting Services, Inc. v. Superior Tank & Constr. Co-Alask, Inc., 568 P.2d 1007 (Alaska 1977).

Using the price received at the subsequent retail sales as an indicator of fair price, it is difficult for this court to justify the actions of the district court in computing Ross' and Savage's deficiency judgment. The district court held that the public auction was commercially reasonable. Yet appellants were given credit based on the subsequent retail sale. We find no basis for this in the law. If the public auction was commercially reasonable, it follows that the price received at the earlier sale should have been credited to appellants' remaining indebtedness. If the public auction was not commercially reasonable then, under California law, no deficiency judgment is allowed. See Atlas Thrift Co. v. Horan, 27 Cal.App.3d 999, 104 Cal.Rptr. 315 (1972).

The Number of Bidders in Attendance at the Auction

It is important to advertise a public sale properly in order to provide public notice to a potential buying audience, but the actual goal is to have bidders attend the auction. When no one attends the auction, there are many inferences that may be drawn. The lack of attendance and the purchase of collateral by a secured party does not necessarily indicate improper notice. In fact, the California Commercial Code permits a secured creditor, following repossession, to purchase collateral for himself "provided he acts in a good faith and commercially reasonable manner." Bo-Mar, supra, 72 Cal.App.3d at 889, 140 Cal.Rptr. 417. However, the fact that the same advertising efforts are used for many years and never produced anyone other than the secured party may indicate either a lack of good faith or inadequate and ineffective publication on the part of the secured party.

The Respondent's Failure to Advise Potential Buyers of the Auction

When a sale is being advertised to an open but unknown market, then the normal minimum legal requirements for commercial reasonableness of an auction may be sufficient. But when, as in the instant case, potential buyers are identified and not advised of the auction, then there is a breach of duty by the secured party. See Connex Press, Inc. v. International Airmotive, Inc., 436 F.Supp. 51 (D.C.Dist.Cal.1977).

Conclusion

We have carefully considered all the factors involved in Challenge-Cook's public auction. We have also considered the approach taken by the district court in determining the deficiency assessed against appellants. We conclude that the district court erred when it determined that the auction was commercially reasonable, but that appellants should be credited with the price received by Challenge-Cook from the subsequent retail sale. We also conclude that the respondent's public sale was not commercially reasonable for the reasons previously specified, and in particular, because potential buyers had been identified but were not advised of the upcoming auction sale. Therefore, the judgment of the district court is reversed and the case is remanded to the trial court for entry of judgment in favor of the appellants and a determination of costs and attorney's fees, if any.

Due to our disposition of this appeal, it is unnecessary to address the issue regarding appellant Ross' execution of a personal guaranty. Likewise, there is no need to consider those issues raised on cross-appeal and we make no decision with regard to them.

Notes

1. For another case holding that a public disposition was commercially unreasonable, see Smith v. Daniels, 634 S.W.2d 276, 278–79 (Tenn.App.1982). The court stated:

> Although the Code is careful to point out that a creditor's failure to procure the maximum possible price for collateral does not in and of itself make a sale commercially unreasonable, a sufficient resale price *is* the logical focus of the protection given debtors by these sections. See White & Summers, Uniform Commercial Code, § 26–11, p. 1115 (2d Ed.1980). This court's duty, then, is to determine from all the evidence contained in the record, presuming the chancellor's conclusions to be correct, whether the facts preponderate that appellee took all steps reasonably necessary to insure that the sale of the collateral would bring appellant a fair price.
>
> There are several factors which, taken together, caused this sale to be commercially unreasonable. First, no list was made of the equipment collateral that was repossessed. As a result, no definitive list was available at sale. We feel that it should be a bare minimum in repossession proceedings to keep a detailed and accurate list of exactly what has been reclaimed. Failure to do so creates the potential for all manner of abuses in the repossession process. With no clear record of what was available at sale, potential purchasers were handicapped in making their decisions. For the same reason, it is impossible for this court to adequately review the record and assess commercial reasonableness when we have no way of knowing for sure what was sold. Appellee erred in not making a list, for a simple lack of information directly affected the commercial reasonableness of the sale in this case.
>
> A second factor which materially affected the reasonableness of this sale was the manner in which it was advertised. In Mallicoat v. Volunteer Finance & Loan Corp., 57 Tenn.App. 106, 415 S.W.2d 347 (1966), this court stated that "[t]he requirement that the property be disposed of in a 'commercially reasonable' manner [signifies] that the disposition shall be made in keeping with prevailing trade practices among reputable and responsible business and commercial enterprises engaged in the same or a similar business."
>
> In this case, there is a conflict in testimony concerning the standard practices for sales of amusement equipment between appellee's witness, who is an employee of the general auction company that conducted this sale, and appellant's witness, who is one of the leading dealers in amusement equipment in the state of Tennessee. Appellee's witness has participated in several sales of amusement equipment in his two years with Action Auction Company. This witness did not consider himself an expert in amusement equipment, was not personally familiar with individual types of the equipment, but felt that he could give a fair opinion as to what it was worth.
>
> Appellant's witness is a regular and successful dealer in amusement equipment in the East Tennessee area, is personally familiar with individual types of amusement equipment, and considers himself an expert in the field. Under the authority of Mallicoat, we feel that more weight should be given to the testimony of appellant's witness because he is clearly better able to give information relevant to the prevailing trade practices in this type of business.
>
> Appellant witness' testimony indicates with certainty that this sale was conducted in a commercially unreasonable manner. The sale was advertised twice in the Sevier County News five days and three days before the date of the sale, respectively. Notice was posted at the Sevier County Courthouse. Telephone calls were also made to amusement equipment dealers listed in the

Knoxville "yellow pages." Appellant's expert testified that it was the standard practice in sales of this type to advertise in newspapers in each of the states major cities, to advertise in trade magazines, and to circulate flyers to dealers. We do not today specifically endorse or require that these steps be taken. It does, however, appear from this testimony that the specific advertising efforts made for this sale were inadequate to reach persons interested in the sale of this type of equipment and to assure that a reasonable price would be attained at sale. Appellee made inadequate advertising efforts in this case to protect the debtor's interests.

Other factors were present at this sale which contributed to its unreasonableness. The equipment was stored in such a way as to make individual inspection difficult and individual testing impossible. The warehouses had no electric lights or electricity, and the machines were stacked together in such a way that easy access was impossible. Finally, the equipment in this case was sold in bulk rather than individually. Appellant's expert testified that the standard method of sale was by the individual unit. We make no absolute requirement today that such equipment be sold individually, but compounded by the fact that no list of the merchandise was available and inspection was unduly hampered, we must hold that this sale was not commercially reasonable, and reverse the chancellor's finding as being against the preponderance of evidence.

Because appellee failed to conduct a commercially reasonable sale and a deficiency resulted, we must presume that a commercially reasonable sale would have satisfied appellant's debt. Commercial Credit Corp. v. Holt, 17 U.C.C. 316 (Middle Section, Court of Appeals, April 25, 1975). Appellee did not prove at trial before the chancellor by a preponderance of the evidence that the value of the resold collateral was less than the amount due on the note. Therefore, the chancellor's award of the deficiency judgment is reversed. Let all costs be taxed to appellee.

But see In re Zsa Zsa Limited, 352 F.Supp. 665, 671, 672 (S.D.N.Y.1972), affirmed 475 F.2d 1393 (2d Cir.1973), where the district court, in affirming the Referee's order confirming a public sale, stated that "the language of Section 9–507 reveals that the primary focus of commercial reasonableness is not the proceeds received from the sale but rather the procedures employed for the sale. * * *." In addition:

Close scrutiny satisfies the court that the instant sale meets the requirement of commercial reasonableness, as that standard has developed for sales of collateral under the UCC. The sale herein had the benefit of judicial guidance. While the sale was not made pursuant to a detailed plan of the referee, the hearing before the referee did pass the plans through a judicial filter. When there has been such a hearing all interests have an opportunity to comment upon the arrangement for disposition of the collateral, and this should raise the presumption that the sale is commercially reasonable. Cf. § 9–507(2). Moreover, the conditions of the sale, as modified, were reasonable in terms of notice, manner, place, time, method and terms of sale. The code requires reasonableness; it does not make the secured party an insurer of a hypothetical expected return.

D. *Was the Private Disposition Commercially Reasonable?*

ATLAS CONSTRUCTION CO. v. DRAVO-DOYLE CO.

Court of Common Pleas, Pennsylvania, 1965.
3 UCC Rep.Serv. 124.

McKENNA, J.

This case is before us on defendant's motion for judgment n.o.v., or, in the alternative, for a new trial. Also before the court is plaintiff's motion to mold the verdict.

The litigation arose out of a Security Agreement entered into on May 4, 1960, for the sale of a truck crane by defendant, a dealer in construction equipment and machinery, to plaintiff, a construction contractor. Plaintiff instituted suit to recover damages in the amount of $11,993.79 due to defendant's wrongful repossession and resale of the machinery after plaintiff defaulted on the payment of installments under the Security Agreement.

Defendant filed a counterclaim for $3,752.44, the deficiency due after applying the proceeds of the resale of the collateral to the unpaid balance of the Security Agreement.

The case came to trial on October 9, 1964. On October 13, 1964, the jury returned a verdict in favor of plaintiff, Atlas Construction Company in the amount of $10,333.79, and also found in Atlas' favor on the counterclaim.

FACTS

As this matter is before us on defendant's motion for judgment n.o.v., the facts as hereinafter set forth appear in a light most favorable to plaintiff, the verdict winner.

On January 25, 1960, the parties entered into a rental contract for one 1959 Model 375 B.T. American Truck Crane. Under the Rental Agreement, plaintiff, lessee, had an option to purchase. On May 4, 1960 plaintiff exercised its option to buy and at that time a Security Agreement was signed. The Agreement called for a total contract price of $39,119.60. A sum of $7,400.00, which had been received as rent, was credited to the purchase price, and a cash down payment of $650.00 was made. The deferred balance, $31,069.60, was payable in twenty equal monthly installments of $1,553.48.

Atlas Construction Company maintained its offices in New Castle, Pennsylvania, and was primarily engaged in steel erection work. It used the truck crane for lifting and moving steel beams and arches. The machine was eleven feet high, weighed approximately 25 tons, and had a 95-foot boom. Though the crane was mounted on a truck and could be driven on the highway, the machine was not licensed as a motor vehicle, and a special state permit was required before it could be moved.

In the fall of 1961, plaintiff construction company, experiencing financial difficulties, defaulted on its payments on the crane. Defendant repossessed and moved it to Pittsburgh. On that occasion, however, the parties were able to agree upon an arrangement for the payment of installments, and the crane was returned to plaintiff.

Atlas again fell behind in its payments, and on February 25, 1962, agents of Dravo-Doyle repossessed the crane a second time. It was moved from Atlas' yard in New Castle to the property of one T. Bruce Campbell in West Middlesex, Pennsylvania, a distance of about ten miles. Plaintiff's President, Eugene

Natale, was notified of this action, and was told that the equipment would be stored on Campbell's lot (T 10–11). On the same day a registered letter was sent by Dravo-Doyle to Natale, advising him that the repossessed crane would be disposed of by private sale after March 3, 1962. The registered letter bore the following address:

"Atlas Construction Company
Box 306
1025 Ryan Avenue
New Castle, Pennsylvania." (T 169)

Neither Natale, nor anyone else connected with Atlas received this letter, and on March 7, 1962, it was returned unclaimed to defendant's plant in Pittsburgh. On the same day defendant sent a second notice, by regular mail, to plaintiff. This was addressed to "Atlas Construction Company, 1025 Ryan Avenue, New Castle, Pennsylvania," and was received by Eugene Natale on March 8th. A copy of the registered letter of February 23rd was enclosed, along with a statement that Dravo-Doyle considered this earlier communication to be valid notification of the private sale of the repossessed equipment.

Subsequent to the repossession, defendant sold the crane to T. Bruce Sales Company, West Middlesex, Pennsylvania, a competitor of Atlas. Bruce Campbell, with whom the equipment was stored after repossession, was a principal of T. Bruce Sales Company. The resale price was $19,500.00.

The testimony conflicted as to the date of resale. Defendant produced a formal bill of sale for the crane, dated March 15, 1962. Plaintiff produced several records from defendant's files, however, which indicated that the sale to T. Bruce Sales Company was consummated on March 3rd (T 55, 75–76). Plaintiff also introduced a notation from a record in defendant's files, dated February 23, 1962, which stated that "Bruce Campbell will pay $2,000 down on a rental purchase option." (T 57).

Thomas Natale is the older brother of Eugene, and in 1962 was Vice President of Atlas Construction Company. This witness testified that within two days after the repossession, he contacted one Andrew Marapese, a general contractor, and told him that due to the repossession, Atlas would be willing to sell the truck crane. Marapese replied that he would be interested in buying, and said that he would discuss the matter with his partner, Walter P. Perman. On the afternoon of February 26th or 27th Marapese, Perman and Thomas Natale went to Campbell's lot in West Middlesex for the purpose of inspecting the equipment. When they arrived the crane was not present at the lot (T 39). Other testimony on behalf of the plaintiff indicated that the crane was absent from Campbell's premises at least three times during the period immediately following the repossession (T 106).

Both Marapese and Perman testified at the trial as to the price they were willing to pay for the crane. Marapese stated that they would have paid between $25,000.00 and $28,000.00 for the equipment (T 107), while Perman stated that they were prepared to pay "in the twenty bracket." (T 111).

Thomas Natale testified that he had several conversations with the President of Dravo-Doyle, Charles Hollingsworth, in the period immediately following the repossession. Natale stated that when he told Hollingsworth that he had a prospective purchaser for the crane, the latter replied:

"* * * all right, Tom, you go ahead and make the preparation on it." (T 36).

As of the date of repossession, plaintiff had paid a total of $22,663.30 on the crane, including the down payment of $8,050.00. The unpaid balance at that time was $16,456.21. Atlas' account had also been charged with a sum of $1,050.06, representing interest on past installments which had not been paid when due. After repossessing the equipment, defendant charged plaintiff's account with an additional $1,996.17, as expenses of repossession. Thus, the total amount shown on defendant's books as owing by plaintiff was $19,502.44.

Plaintiff filed the complaint in assumpsit on July 9, 1963, alleging that Dravo-Doyle's sale of the crane to Campbell violated the applicable provisions of the Uniform Commercial Code (Act of April 6, 1953, P.L. 3, § 9–101 et seq. as amended; 12A P.S. § 9–101 et seq.). As a result of the improper resale, plaintiff contended that it was deprived of the opportunity to protect its equity in the equipment by selling it to Marapese and Perman.

Plaintiff sought as damages the difference between $16,456.21, the unpaid balance on the contract, and $28,000.00, the amount which it is alleged that Marapese and Perman would have paid for the crane, a sum of $11,543.79. It is also claimed that when Dravo-Doyle repossessed the crane, it took a pick-up truck valued at $450.00, which had not been sold pursuant to the Security Agreement. Thus, Atlas claimed damages of $11,543.79, plus $450.00, or a total sum of $11,993.79.

Dravo-Doyle filed a counterclaim for damages in the amount of $3,752.44. Defendant alleged that when it repossessed the crane, it was unable to regain possession of four boom sections which had been sold pursuant to the Security Agreement. Consequently, when it resold to T. Bruce Sales, it was obliged to replace these boom sections from its own stock. The value of these boom sections, $3,750.00, was thus deducted from the resale price of $19,500.00, and plaintiff was given credit for the difference of $15,750.00. As noted above, the amount shown as owing on Atlas' account with Dravo-Doyle was $19,502.44. Defendant's counterclaim for $3,752.44 was based on the difference between this amount and the $15,750.00 credit from the resale.

Discussion

1. *Defendant's Motion for Judgment n.o.v.*

Part 5 of Article 9 of the Uniform Commercial Code (12A P.S. § 9–501 et seq.) governs the rights and liabilities of the parties to this case. While recognizing that Dravo-Doyle was entitled to take possession of and to resell the crane upon default, plaintiff asserts that defendant failed to comply with the provisions of Section 9–504(3) of the Code, setting forth the obligations of a secured party in disposing of repossessed collateral. Briefly stated, this section requires that every aspect of the disposition of collateral be "commercially reasonable." This also provides that reasonable notification of the time after which a private sale is to take place must be sent by the secured party to the debtor.

Plaintiff's claim for damages is based upon Section 9–507(1) of the Code, which provides that the debtor has a right to recover from the secured party "any loss caused by a failure to comply with the provisions of this Part."

* * *

[The court held that the secured party had "sent" a proper notice even though it was not received by the debtor.]

Plaintiff also relies upon Section 9–504(3) of the Code and contends that considering all aspects of the disposition to Campbell, the jury could find that it was not carried out in a commercially reasonable manner. Emphasis is placed upon the fact that the resale price of $19,500.00 was substantially lower than the price of between $25,000.00 and $28,000.00 which Mr. Marapese was willing to pay for the crane. From this, it is argued that the resale price was unreasonably low.

In support of this contention, plaintiff introduced a publication known as the Green Guide Handbook, a loose-leaf book containing lists of average prices for new and used construction equipment, and published by the Equipment Guide-book Company (T 30). This book revealed that as of February, 1962, the average sale price for a 1959 Model 375 American Truck Crane was $23,200.00, plus $2,110.00 for booms and equipment, a total value of $25,310.00 (T 95–98).

The average prices listed in this book are competent evidence of value. Plaintiff's President stated (T 30) that the Green Guide is the recognized authority for market values. Charles Hollingsworth, the President of Dravo-Doyle, testified that his company keeps a copy of this book (T 90), and one of its salesmen admitted that he uses it on occasion as an indicator of equipment values (T 131).

In Family Finance Corp. v. Scott, 24 D. & C.2d 587 (1961), Judge Van der Voort of this court held that since the resale price of a repossessed automobile was substantially lower than its "Blue Book" value, a question was presented whether the sale upon repossession was commercially reasonable. The Green Book for construction equipment is comparable to the Blue Book for automobiles, and should be equally probative of market values.

It is true that Section 9–507(2) of the Code provides that:

"The fact that a better price could have been obtained by a sale at a different method than that selected by the secured party is not of itself sufficient to establish that the sale was not made in a commercially reasonable manner."

In the present case, however, there are factors in addition to the inadequate price, from which the jury could conclude that Dravo-Doyle's disposition of the crane was not commercially reasonable. George Hickson is a salesman for Dravo-Doyle, in charge of the promotion and sale of cranes (T 112). Hickson testified at the hearing that although his territory covered parts of Pennsylvania, Ohio, Maryland and West Virginia, he made no effort to contact a purchaser for the crane other than Campbell (T 140).

From the fact that the price received by Dravo-Doyle was substantially lower than the value of the equipment, as evidenced by Marapese's testimony and the Green Guide quotation, and from the fact that Dravo-Doyle contacted only one purchaser, the jury could conclude that defendant failed to take adequate steps to ensure that a fair price was received. Therefore the jury was justified in concluding that the sale was not "commercially reasonable."

The motion for judgment non obstante veredicto must be refused.

2. Defendant's Motion for a New Trial

It is contended that the court erred in excluding the testimony of one John H. Combs, Jr., who had been called to testify on behalf of defendant. Mr. Combs is employed by the Anderson Equipment Company, a competitor of Dravo-Doyle. He is presently the Treasurer of Anderson, and had previously served as Assistant Treasurer and Credit Manager of that Corporation.

Counsel for plaintiff requested an offer of proof as to the witness, whereupon the following conversation took place at sidebar (T 153–154):

"Mr. Wolfe: I propose to show by this witness that he is engaged in the same work as Dravo-Doyle Company, that he is familiar with the problems of the repossession of equipment, that he is familiar furthermore with the legal requirements concerned with respect to resale of repossessed equipment, and that in his experience notification on one-week's time of a private sale is reasonable and practiced in the trade.

"Mr. Libenson: I object to all of this witness' testimony.

"The Court: I think it is for the jury.

"Mr. Libenson: This is strictly for the jury.

"The Court: I will let in as to the notice. The rest is for the law and the jury.

"Mr. Libenson: If you let that in as to notice, this is extremely prejudicial. The Act says, 'Reasonable.' It is the jury's question. He has nothing to do with the sale or anything. If he testifies as to what prior practice was, it is extremely prejudicial because the jury will think it is accepted practice. There is no accepted practice. It is extremely prejudicial. I will move for withdrawal of a juror.

"Mr. Wolfe: You have to give the jury something to go on. * * *

* * *

* * * [Interest] should have been included in the verdict. We must, therefore, mold the jury's verdict to include interest, at six percent (6%), from February 23, 1962, until October 13, 1964, a period of thirty-two (32) months. The jury's verdict was $10,333.79, and interest thereon for thirty-two (32) months, totals $1,653.40. The verdict, as amended, will consequently total $11,987.19.

ORDER OF COURT

And now, June 7, 1965, upon consideration of the Motions for Judgment n.o.v. and for a New Trial filed by the defendant herein, it is ordered that the same be and they are hereby refused.

It is further ordered that Plaintiff's Motion to Mold the Verdict be granted and the verdict is hereby molded so as to include interest, in the sum of $1,653.40. The jury's verdict, as molded, will therefore be in the amount of $11,987.19.

Judgment to be entered on payment of the verdict fee.

SCHOOL SUPPLY CO., INC. v. FIRST NATIONAL BANK OF LOUISVILLE

Court of Appeal, Kentucky, 1984.
685 S.W.2d 200.

McDONALD, J. This is an appeal wherein the appellants claim that the trial court erred in granting appellee First National Bank of Louisville a summary judgment. The appellants contend that because an issue of fact is involved a summary judgment is precluded from consideration.

Appellants' sole claim of error is stated thus: The trial court erred in granting the in rem judgment and order of sale since the question of the commercial reasonableness of the disposition of the inventory collateral by the First National Bank is a question of fact and not one of law.

The background for the actions taken shows that appellant School Supply Company, Inc., on December 11, 1979, borrowed $240,000 from the appellee bank. The note contained a payment schedule with 12% interest and was signed by appellant James J. Gormley, Jr., President. By a separate transaction a guaranty agreement was signed by James J. Gormley, Jr., as an individual. Additional collateral securing the loan and the guaranty agreement were mortgages signed by James J. Gormley, Jr., and Elizabeth S. Gormley, his wife, securing for the bank two lake lots and a house with lot in Lexington.

In addition to the real estate mortgages the bank held a security interest in all accounts receivable, all inventory, all machinery and equipment, all office furniture and fixtures, and certain described vehicles.

There is no question that the appellants defaulted on the notes causing the appellee to file suit demanding the following:

1. Acceleration of payments on the note and judgment in the sum of $233,088.21, plus accrued interest in the sum of $18,541.64:

2. To be adjudged first mortgage lien on the real properties;

3. That real properties be sold by the court; and

4. That all nonreal property of School Supply Company, Inc. be repossessed, sold, and the proceeds applied to the court costs, attorneys fees and the debt; further, that the bank have judgment for any deficiency after the proceeds of sale are applied to the loan.

With the help of the Fayette County Sheriff, and armed with an order of court, the bank took possession of the premises and inventory of the defaulting company. The sheriff made a return on the writ of possession by filing an inventory list. Next, the appellee moved the court for an order of sale of the collateral repossessed but the court denied the motion.

The appellee then proceeded on its own to sell the collateral without the approval of the court. Attempts were made to dispose of the collateral through sales to dealers and wholesalers, but to no avail. The bank then sought the services of Vernon Hatton, a liquidator and auctioneer in Lexington. A decision was made to conduct a private sale on the premises of the supply company, and then auction the large and other remaining items. Notices were mailed to all concerned and advertisements were circulated.

The appellants contend that the private sale of February 25 and 26, and the auction of February 27 and March 6, 1982, were not only unapproved by the court but expressly refused by the court when approval was sought. The events were glorified garage sales which were contrary to accepted methods of liquidation of instructional materials and school supplies, and as such constituted a "commercially unreasonable" method of disposing of such collateral. Appellants' brief stated, "Never has so much been sold for so little with so much effort."

Argument is made that by simply looking at the mathematics of the disposition of the property, where $163,194.40 of assets were sold for a net liquidation sum of $20,564.14, these facts alone make it facially a commercially unreasonable disposition.

The appellee counters that argument by stating that out of the gross liquidated amount of $38,613.41, $18,045.27 had to be paid in expenses, i.e., $9,050 in lease and back rent payments.

In opposition to the motion for summary judgment, the appellant filed an affidavit of counsel which they believed created a factual issue sufficient to overcome summary disposition of the case. Counsel's affidavit revealed a potential expert witness. Larry Singer, of Winwood, Pennsylvania. Mr. Singer was formerly marketing director of Instructo-McGraw Hill Publishers. He began and operated two companies dealing in school supplies and instructional materials. Mr. Singer proffered, through counsel's affidavit, that it was not normal practice in the trade for dealers in inventories of instructional materials and school supplies of distressed businesses to sell the property at public auction because this results in excessive loss. Mr. Singer was of the opinion that the property should have been sold in bulk through an organization such as the National School and Equipment Association. Notwithstanding the affidavit filed, the court nevertheless granted summary judgment.

Our statutory guidance is found in KRS 355.9–504(3), Secured Party's Rights To Dispose of Collateral after Default—Effect of Disposition. "* * * Disposition of the collateral may be by public or private proceedings * * * but every aspect of the disposition including the method, manner, time, place and terms must be *commercially reasonable.*" (Emphasis added.)

It is necessary for us to determine whether "commercially reasonable" is a question of law for the court to decide or a question of fact for a jury to consider. In review, the following are undisputed facts. Prior to the disposition the appellee: 1) employed a qualified and experienced auctioneer, Vernon Hatton, to advise the appellee and conduct the liquidation of the collateral; 2) advertised prominently the sale in 21 separate publications in the area's largest newspapers; 3) advertised the sale in the largest professional journal for educators; 4) sent individual notices to 58 private and parochial schools; and 5) put up signs on the premises of the defaulting company and circulars were distributed in the area's shopping centers. This effort resulted in the following: 1) 200–300 bidders attending the proceedings; 2) 116 successful bidders were accounted for on the two days of the auction; and 3) bidders came from as far away as Cincinnati, Ohio.

Unquestionably the appellants were on notice of the method of disposition of the collateral as the case progressed. We agree with the appellants that the secured party (appellee) rather than the debtor (appellants) has the burden to prove commercial reasonableness. See Bank Josephine v. Conn, Ky.App., 599 S.W.2d 733 [28 U.C.C.Rep. 1226] (1980), and Central Bank and Trust Company v. Metcalf, Ky.App., 663 S.W.2d 957 [87 U.C.C.Rep. 1796] (1984).

The phrase "commercially reasonable" under the statutory scheme is the ultimate or conclusory fact which becomes the conclusion of law for the court to determine. However, KRS 355.9–504(3) is explicit in requiring even the evidentiary facts to be commercially reasonable, including method, manner, time, place and terms of the disposition. If there is a dispute concerning the evidentiary facts, i.e., one party contending notices of the sale were mailed and the other party denying it, then an evidentiary fact issue is created which must be resolved by the fact finder. However, whether or not notice by regular mail is "commercially reasonable" is an issue of law for the court to decide. With the great disproportionate difference between the value of the property and what ultimately was realized from the sales and auctions, the trial court had a duty to scrutinize the proof. We are impressed that he did. Keep in mind that under KRS 355.9–507(2) the fact that a better price could have been obtained by a sale at a different time or in a different method is not of itself sufficient to establish that the sale was not made in a commercially reasonable manner. This principle falls within the general theme found in Sizemore v. Bennett, 408 S.W. 2d 449 (Ky.1966). There it was said that mere inadequacy of price alone is not ground for setting aside a judicial sale. We do believe that the great disproportionate difference between the value of the property and what was realized by sale created a presumption of "commercial unreasonableness" which had to be overcome.

That presumption was overcome by the trial court concluding, as a matter of law, that appellee's disposition proceedings were commercially reasonable. It is also significant to note the fact that the appellants made no effort to stop the sale and auction.

It is our opinion that the trial court was under a duty to enter the summary judgment as it did under the authority of Bennett v. Southern Bell Telephone and Telegraph Company, 407 S.W.2d 403 (Ky.1966), because there was no genuine issue as to any material fact.

MILLER, J., concurs.

GUDGEL, J., concurs in result.

Note: Planning for Commercial Reasonableness of the Resale

The secured creditor may get advanced court approval of the procedures and terms of a 9–504 resale. This approval will bind all parties. See 9–507(2). Moreover, courts have upheld clauses in the security agreement that purport to govern some or all aspects of a 9–504 disposition. Aetna Finance v. Culpepper, 171 Ga.App. 315, 320 S.E.2d 228 (1984) (nature of notice to debtor agreed to); Ford Motor Credit Co. v. DeValk Lincoln-Mercury, Inc., 600 F.Supp. 1547 (N.D.Ill.1985) (entire mode of disposition agreed to). Of course, if the debtor agrees, after default, to a mode of disposition, that will generally be conclusive. Sections 9–501 and 9–504 so provide. Becknell v. First National Bank in Little Rock, 740 F.2d 609 (8th Cir.1984).

E. Valuation of Collateral Where Disposition Unreasonable

CONTRAIL LEASING PARTNERS LTD. v. CONSOLIDATED AIRWAYS

OMIT

United States Court of Appeals, Seventh Circuit, 1984.
742 F.2d 1095.

Appeals from the United States District Court for the Northern District of Indiana. Before POSNER and COFFEY, CIRCUIT JUDGES, and KELLAM, SENIOR DISTRICT JUDGE.

POSNER, CIRCUIT JUDGE. This diversity suit, which the parties agree is governed by the Uniform Commercial Code as codified in Indiana, raises a number of questions regarding a secured creditor's right to repossess and sell his collateral on the debtor's account.

In 1976 Consolidated Airways, Inc. sold a Grumman Gulf Stream commercial aircraft to Contrail Leasing Partners, Ltd. for $575,000—$60,000 down and the rest to be paid in monthly installments. Consolidated took back a chattel mortgage on the plane. Beginning with a missed payment in May 1978 Contrail defaulted, and in July Consolidated repossessed the plane and began trying to sell it to realize the unpaid balance on the mortgage. Consolidated made a deal to sell the plane to Emerald Airlines for $675,000, and on August 31 it sent Contrail a telegram notifying it that the sale would take place on or about September 5. Even though it had referred Emerald to Consolidated in the first place, Contrail notified Emerald that it objected to the sale; and fearing that the sale would become entangled in legal proceedings, Emerald backed out. Later the plane required substantial maintenance work which included rebuilding its propellers to comply with the Federal Aviation Administration's safety requirements. The work cost Consolidated a little more than $26,000. When the work was completed Consolidated notified Contrail (on March 23, 1979) that it planned to sell the plane at a public auction in two and a half weeks (April 9). Contrail brought this suit on March 26, before the sale, and moved for a preliminary injunction to prevent the sale. The motion was denied, and on April 6 Contrail filed a notice of lis pendens (litigation pending) with the FAA. At the sale, held as scheduled on April 9, Consolidated was the only bidder. It bid $515,000 for the plane, and became the owner. Contrail got nothing from the sale, because the sale proceeds were less than the sum of the unpaid balance of the mortgage plus various expenses that Consolidated claimed.

Contrail's case came on for trial. Fifteen months after the two-day trial ended, the district judge issued his opinion. In it he found that the sale had been commercially unreasonable and that the plane had been worth $625,000 on the day of the sale (to which had to be added the $38,000 that Consolidated had earned from leasing the plane during the period of repossession), and he concluded that Contrail was entitled to the difference between (1) the sum of these figures ($663,000) and (2) the amount owed to Consolidated on its mortgage plus the expenses Consolidated had incurred in the sale. The difference, as the judge calculated it, was $133,000, and he entered judgment for Contrail for that amount. Consolidated has appealed on the ground that $133,000 is too much, and Contrail has cross-appealed on the ground that it is too little because the plane was worth more than $625,000 on the date of the sale.

A creditor who, having repossessed the debtor's goods, sells them to satisfy his debt is entitled to retain so much of the proceeds of the sale as is necessary to pay off the debt. See UCC § 9–504, Ind.Code § 26–1–9–504. If he has incurred reasonable expenses in preparation for the sale he is entitled to deduct those as well. See UCC § 9–504(1)(a), Ind.Code § 26–1–9–504(1)(*l*). The district judge recognized this principle and therefore allowed Consolidated to deduct various expenses, but he misapplied the principle in two respects:

1. He did not allow Consolidated to deduct the interest that had accrued on the note secured by the chattel mortgage between the date of default, May 17, 1978, and the date of sale, April 9, 1979. The unpaid principal on May 17, 1978, was $403,056.90, and the note called for interest at the rate of one percent a month. The district judge did not explain why he had not credited Consolidated with this interest. Contrail conjectures that he meant to penalize Consolidated for its improper conduct regarding the sale, of which more presently. But there is no indication that this was what was in the judge's mind. Contrail had argued that Consolidated's behavior was so egregious as to entitle Contrail to punitive damages, and there is support in Indiana law for awarding punitive damages "where the debtor can clearly show that the secured party is intentionally and maliciously violating the rights of the debtor." Hall v. Owen County State Bank, 175 Ind.App. 150, 160 n. 10, 370 N.E.2d 918, 927 n. 10 (1977). But Contrail's request for punitive damages was turned down because the judge could find no malice or willfulness or other circumstances of aggravation in Consolidated's behavior. His opinion offers no ground for lopping off part of Consolidated's claim. His action is made more difficult to understand by the fact that he (quite properly) credited Contrail with the $38,000 that Consolidated had

earned from leasing the plane during the period of repossession. Consolidated was able to generate that income for the debtor only because it had possession of the plane, and one of the costs of possession to Consolidated was going without the $403,000 that the debtor owed it. It was an opportunity cost, which is a real cost in law as in economics. See, e.g., Simmons v. United States, 698 F.2d 888, 898 (7th Cir.1983). Consolidated is entitled to recover that opportunity cost by charging interest for the period of repossession.

There is no suggestion that one percent a month for the 10 months of the repossession was an unreasonable charge for Consolidated's money; and it is not clear that it would make a difference if it were (provided it was not usurious). Though we have treated the interest as an expense of the creditor, it is more appropriately regarded as a part of the underlying debt (but it makes no difference which it is). The debt was unpaid principal plus one percent interest for every month the principal was unpaid; and it was the principal plus accrued interest that Consolidated was entitled to keep along with expenses when it sold the plane on August 9, 1979. Alternatively, the one percent a month can be viewed as prejudgment interest to which Consolidated was entitled under well settled principles illustrated by Indiana Telephone Corp. v. Indiana Bell Telephone Co., 171 Ind.App. 616, 634–35, 358 N.E.2d 218, 229 (1976), modified, 171 Ind.App. 638, 360 N.E.2d 610 (1977), since the principal was a definite amount and Contrail does not deny that one percent was the reasonable rate of interest in the circumstances.

2. Another cost incurred by Consolidated during the period of repossession was the money that it spent to rebuild the propellers. Some of the language in the district judge's opinion makes it appear that he intended to allow Consolidated that expense, but we are unable to find such an allowance in his final computation. The question is not, as Contrail would have it, whether the expense was necessary to keep the plane from being grounded, though there is much evidence that it was; the question is whether it was prudent. See UCC § 9–504(1)(a), Ind.Code § 26–1–9–504(1)(a). A prudent expenditure could be expected to be reflected in the value of the plane at the date of sale. The plane the district judge valued at $625,000 as of April 9, 1979, was a plane with rebuilt propellers; and it is not suggested that Consolidated paid more to rebuild them than was necessary. Since Contrail was the beneficiary of the expenditure, Consolidated was entitled to deduct it from the proceeds that it paid over to Contrail.

If, pursuant to the parties' stipulation which was erroneously copied by the district court, we correct the principal amount on the date of the default to $403,056.90, and if we then add: $43,395.65, which is interest at one percent a month during the repossession period; $26,143.77, for the propeller work (on which interest is not sought); and finally the expenses (including a prior lien) allowed by the judge, which came to $122,649.67, then the grand total of what Consolidated should have been allowed to keep from the sale is $595,245.99—not, as the judge thought, $529,514.87. From this should be deducted the $38,000 in lease income that Consolidated earned on Contrail's account during the repossession period, for a net due Consolidated of $557,245.99.

Further adjustments to this figure, relating to the issue of brokerage expense, will be considered later; but accepting its accuracy for the moment, one can see that if the sale was commercially reasonable, then since it yielded proceeds ($515,000) smaller than the amount due Consolidated, Contrail is entitled to nothing and Consolidated is entitled to the deficiency judgment it sought in a counterclaim that the district judge dismissed. But if the sale was commercially unreasonable, it becomes necessary to calculate the fair market value of the plane on April 9, 1979, and if that fair market value was more than what is due Consolidated, Contrail is entitled to the excess, plus (it is undisputed) interest since April 9, 1979.

* * *

[The court held that the disposition was commercially unreasonable.]

Although the sale was unreasonable, and Contrail was therefore entitled to the fair market value of the plane on the day of sale (minus whatever was due Consolidated), we do not think the district court's valuation of $625,000 can be sustained. True, there was some basis for this figure, even though in arriving at it the district court applied a pretty stiff discount of the $675,000 price for which Consolidated had agreed to sell the plane to Emerald Airlines ten months earlier—a price agreed on, moreover, before the extensive repair work that Consolidated undertook. But the testimony showed that the market for used Grumman Gulf Stream commercial aircraft is rather thin, and the fact that Emerald was willing to pay a high price in 1978 doesn't prove that anyone would have been willing to pay as high a price a year later—in 1982 Consolidated sold the plane for only $616,000. There was also testimony that similar Grumman Gulf Stream aircraft were sold during the late 1970's in the $400,000's, though these planes were not in such good condition as this one.

Although $625,000 may seem a fair if rough average of the various figures, it has three problems:

1. We cannot ignore Consolidated's argument that the relevant value is that of a plane against which a lis pendens has been filed, although the judge ignored the argument in his opinion. (The fact that the opinion was written so long after the trial may explain why several issues were not discussed.) Contrail cannot walk away from the consequences of having filed a notice of lis pendens on the eve of sale. It had no valid reason to try to block the sale. It had an adequate remedy at law against Consolidated—the remedy it is pursuing in this case—if Consolidated failed to sell the plane in a commercially reasonable manner; for there is no suggestion that Consolidated is not good for any money it may owe Contrail. The only effect of filing the lis pendens was to make it less likely that a sale would command a good price. But it is not true, as Consolidated suggests, that the filing of the lis pendens drove the value of the plane to zero because no one but a creditor would pay for a plane so marked. When three years after the sale to itself Consolidated sold the plane for $616,000 the lis pendens was still on file—as it was when this case was argued. But on remand the district judge must make findings on the effect of the lis pendens on the plane's fair market value on the date of sale.

2. The judge did not explain why he gave no weight to two $750,000 offers for the plane made to Consolidated in or around March 1979. Although the complete terms of these offers are not in the record, the existence of the offers required the judge to explain why he chose the figure of $625,000, which was considerably lower. He may have a good explanation—the lis pendens perhaps, for it is unclear whether the offerors knew about it.

3. A point that cuts in the opposite direction—that suggests that $625,000 may have been too high an estimate—is that the judge did not (so far as appears anyway) allow for brokerage expense, which would have reduced the net proceeds of the sale to Contrail. In the aborted sale to Emerald Airlines, Consolidated had agreed to pay Emerald's broker a $35,000 commission, which works

out to a shade over five percent. If Consolidated had found a buyer on April 9 at a price of $625,000, it might have had to pay a similar commission to the buyer's broker. The net proceeds from the sale would therefore have been less than $625,000. It makes no difference whether we say that the relevant market value was 95 percent of $625,000 (assuming a commission of five percent), or that it was $625,000 but that Consolidated is entitled to deduct a five percent brokerage commission as an expense of a commercially reasonable sale. In either event an additional adjustment is necessary. But we do not know what the adjustment should be.

Errors 2 and 3 could be offsetting. If the proper brokerage fee is five percent, and if the judge by disregarding the offers that Consolidated received in March 1979 undervalued the plane by five percent, then his estimate of $625,000 would be unchanged. But these are guesses. We do not know either percentage—or the bearing of the lis pendens. We do not even know whether the judge's valuation was net of brokerage—which leads to a further complication:

4. Consolidated may have been permitted to deduct certain expenses incurred in its sale to itself that it would not have incurred had it used a broker, in which event there would be double counting if it were allowed to deduct brokerage expense as well. Official Comment 2 to UCC § 9–507 states that the secured creditor is not required to resell the collateral at retail rather than wholesale. Although it is true that Indiana has not enacted the official comments, as some states have, see, e.g., Piper Acceptance Corp. v. Yarbrough, 702 F.2d 733, 735 (8th Cir.1983) (Arkansas), no negative inference can be drawn; and even without the comment, it is pretty clear that § 9–507 does not require sale in a retail market. It provides that if the creditor "sells the collateral in the usual manner *in any recognized market therefor* * * * he has sold in a commercially reasonable manner." § 9–507(2), Ind.Code § 26–1–9–507(2) (emphasis added). Wholesale markets are recognized markets for most goods, including aircraft, as we know from the *Piper* case; and an ironclad rule against selling collateral at wholesale rather than retail would make no sense. Although retail prices tend to be higher than wholesale prices, this is because it costs more to sell at retail. Not only can there be, therefore, no presumption that the net gains to the seller are different at the two levels, but economic theory implies that returns at the two levels will tend toward equality, since until they are equalized dealers will have incentives to enter at the level where the higher returns are being earned and by entering will bid those returns down.

So the important thing is to match expenses with estimated value correctly. If the judge estimates a retail price, there should be a deduction for brokerage if retail sales of airplanes normally are made through brokers but not a deduction for expenses of a sale at wholesale; but if he estimates a wholesale price, then only the expenses associated with wholesale sales should be deducted.

To sum up, a remand is necessary to permit the district judge to clarify his findings. He must on remand reestimate the value of the plane (with the lis pendens) on April 9, 1979; specify whether that is a retail or a wholesale price; subtract from that price all pertinent expenses of sale, which we said earlier amount to $557,245.99—but the figure may have to be adjusted if the judge estimates a retail rather than a wholesale price; and award Contrail what is left after the subtraction, plus interest from April 9, 1979.

No costs will be awarded in this court, and Circuit Rule 18 shall not apply on remand.

Affirmed in part, reversed in part, and remanded with directions.

SECTION 10. RIGHTS OF THIRD PARTIES BEFORE AND AFTER THE DISPOSITION OF COLLATERAL

We have examined the rights of the debtor as the secured party declares default, repossesses and either retains or disposes of the collateral. What are the rights, if any, of third parties, i.e., creditors of or purchasers from the debtor, in the process?

Consider the following problems.

Problem 6–6

First Bank lent Debtor $25,000 and, on July 1, perfected a security interest in Debtor's equipment. The equipment's value was estimated to be $30,000. On August 1, Second Bank lent Debtor $10,000 and perfected a security interest in the equipment. First Bank learned of Second Bank's interest from Debtor, but did not declare a default under the security agreement. Six months later, Debtor defaulted on its obligation to First Bank, who peacefully repossessed the equipment. At that time, Debtor owed First Bank $20,000 and the collateral was valued at $25,000. Debtor then signed a written statement renouncing his right to object to any proposal by First Bank to retain the equipment under UCC 9–505(2) in full satisfaction of the obligation.

1. May First Bank retain the collateral in full satisfaction of Debtor's obligation without any obligation to account to Second Bank for any surplus? See UCC 9–505(2) & 9–507(1). See Blackhawk Production Credit Association v. Meridian Implement Co., 82 Ill.App.3d 93, 37 Ill.Dec. 387, 402 N.E.2d 277 (1980), suggesting that Second Bank has a potential claim under UCC 9–507(1).

2. Suppose, instead, that First Bank disposed of the collateral for $20,000 and settled with Debtor for an additional $500. Second Bank believes that the disposition was commercially unreasonable. Does Second Bank have any standing to complain? See Louis Zahn Drug Co. v. Bank of Oak Brook Terrace, 95 Ill.App.3d 435, 50 Ill.Dec. 959, 420 N.E.2d 276 (1981), holding that Second Bank has a potential claim under UCC 9–507(1).

3. What change did the 1972 revisions in UCC 9–505 and 9–504 make in the obligation of First Bank to give notice? What reasons were offered by the Permanent Editorial Board to justify the major shift in the burden of giving notice?

Problem 6–7

Suppose, in Problem 6–6, First Bank repossessed and disposed of the equipment in a commercially reasonable manner for $30,000. After application of the proceeds under UCC 9–504(1), a surplus of $7,500 was realized.

1. To whom should the surplus be paid, Debtor or Second Bank? See UCC 9–504(1)(c) & 9–504(2). What should Second Bank do to insure payment?

2. Suppose that First Bank paid the $7,500 to Debtor. What are Second Bank's rights against Debtor? Against First Bank? Does UCC 9–507(1) protect Second Bank here?

Problem 6–8

Assume, in Problem 6–6, that Debtor defaulted in its obligation to Second Bank but not First Bank. Second Bank, without actual knowledge of First Bank's security interest, peacefully repossessed the equipment and sold it in a commercially reasonable manner to Buyer for $20,000. After applying the proceeds, Second Bank paid a surplus of $7,500 to Debtor. Shortly thereafter, First Bank learned of this activity. What rights, if any, does First Bank have against Buyer? UCC 9–504(4)? Against Debtor? Against Second Bank?

CHAPTER SEVEN

SPECIAL PROBLEMS OF SCOPE

SECTION 1. INTRODUCTION

Section 9–102 contains an expansive definition of the transactions to which Article 9 applies. It applies not only to transactions that have relation to real property, but also to transactions that take the form of an absolute sale, and even to some that appear as leases or bailments. Moreover, the article governs aspects of analogous transactions such as consignments, and specifically treats real estate transactions involving fixtures. The process of defining the border between transactions within and those without Article 9 has been a continuous and difficult one for the courts. For example, the issue of "true lease" vs. security agreement has arisen in hundreds of courts in thousands of cases. To cite a second example, when is a bailment really a security interest? Then, too, the courts have recently begun to face the issue whether security in a mortgagee's interest and in rights under a land-sale contract are within Article 9. Numerous other scope issues have arisen, including the extent of the exclusions under UCC 9–104, and the federal government's obligation as a creditor to comply with the terms of Article 9. We will begin this chapter with the conventional lease versus security agreement issue. For reasons we will explain below, the new Bankruptcy Code has rekindled general interest in that question.

Next we will examine the status of the bailment and quasi-bailment and its relation to Article 9. When one puts goods in the hands of another for sale to third parties, that transaction looks much like and is in many ways the economic equivalent of an inventory loan. It has distinctive legal qualities, but it functions like a bank loan. The same might be said when one "bails" seed to a farmer for the production of a crop. By the same token some suggest that a purchaser of goods who has left them in the hands of his seller or an owner of goods who has given them to another for processing should be regarded merely as a creditor.

The borderline between real estate transactions and those under Article 9 has now been the scene of a host of new and troublesome problems. What law governs when a mortgagee (who holds a mortgage and the note of his debtor, mortgagor) comes to the bank and seeks to borrow against those? Is he to be treated like the holder of chattel paper or is this transaction exclusively under the real property law of a particular state? Section 9–102(3) and Comment 4 to 9–102, tell us that to some extent it is within Article 9. But to what extent?

Next we see competition between a bank asserting rights of setoff and others asserting security interests in bank accounts or in certificates of deposit. While it is clear from the exclusions in Article 9 that banks need not file a financing statement or take other Article 9 action to "perfect" a right to setoff, Article 9 still might establish the priority between setoff and another claim.

Finally we will consider some issues involving the federal government. Of course the federal government is not governed by state law but by its own law. Federal law determines the rights of Uncle Sam when he is the lender. Although the Supreme Court has chosen to apply Article 9 in many situations, the lower courts have been slow to follow the Supreme Court's direction and have been hesitant to treat the federal government as merely another lender. In the arena where the United States holds a tax lien, federal law clearly governs priority disputes with perfected security interests.

Scope issues often raise complex and sophisticated problems that presuppose an overall grasp of Article 9 if they are to be resolved satisfactorily. It is for this reason that we have postponed consideration of them until this point. Define the scope issue in the following problem.

Problem 7–1

Creditor, General Electric Credit Corporation, had a perfected security interest in a truck. The truck broke down and was taken for repairs to the shop of Great Lakes Energy Systems. Great Lakes installed a new motor in the truck but was never paid by the debtor. While the truck was still in the possession of Great Lakes, debtor filed a voluntary petition in bankruptcy. Thereupon Great Lakes removed the new motor from the truck and installed the old one. With the new motor, the truck is worth $26,000; without it, it is worth between $10,000 and $13,000. Must Great Lakes reinstall the motor and, if so, who gets the truck with the motor in it, General Electric, Great Lakes, or the trustee in bankruptcy?

SECTION 2. LEASES—SECURITY AGREEMENTS

IN RE MARHOEFER PACKING CO., INC.

United States Court of Appeals, Seventh Circuit, 1982.
674 F.2d 1139.

PELL, CIRCUIT JUDGE.

This appeal involves a dispute between the trustee of the bankrupt Marhoefer Packing Company, Inc., ("Marhoefer") and Robert Reiser & Company, Inc., ("Reiser") over certain equipment held by Marhoefer at the time of bankruptcy. The issue presented is whether the written agreement between Marhoefer and Reiser covering the equipment is a true lease under which Reiser is entitled to reclaim its property from the bankrupt estate, or whether it is actually a lease intended as security in which case Reiser's failure to file a financing statement to perfect its interest renders it subordinate to the trustee.

I

In December of 1976, Marhoefer Packing Co., Inc., of Muncie, Indiana, entered into negotiations with Reiser, a Massachusetts based corporation engaged in the business of selling and leasing food processing equipment, for the acquisition of one or possibly two Vemag Model 3007–1 Continuous Sausage Stuffers. Reiser informed Marhoefer that the units could be acquired by outright purchase, conditional sale contract or lease. Marhoefer ultimately acquired two sausage stuffers from Reiser. It purchased one under a conditional sale contract. Pursuant to the contract, Reiser retained a security interest in the machine, which it subsequently perfected by filing a financing statement with the Indiana Secretary of State. Title to that stuffer is not here in dispute. The other stuffer was delivered to Marhoefer under a written "Lease Agreement."

The Lease Agreement provided for monthly payments of $665.00 over a term of 48 months. The last nine months payments, totaling $5,985.00, were payable upon execution of the lease. If at the end of the lease term the machine was to be returned, it was to be shipped prepaid to Boston or similar destination "in the same condition as when received, reasonable wear and tear resulting from proper use alone excepted, and fully crated." The remaining terms and conditions of the agreement were as follows:

1. Any State or local taxes and/or excises are for the account of the Buyer.
2. The equipment shall at all times be located at

   Marhoefer Packing Co., Inc.
   1500 North Elm & 13th Street
   Muncie, Indiana

   and shall not be removed from said location without the written consent of Robert Reiser & Co. The equipment can only be used in conjunction with the manufacture of meat or similar products unless written consent is given by Robert Reiser & Co.
3. The equipment will carry a ninety-day guarantee for workmanship and materials and shall be maintained and operated safely and carefully in conformity with the instructions issued by our operators and the maintenance manual. Service and repairs of the equipment after the ninety-day period will be subject to a reasonable and fair charge.
4. If, after due warning, our maintenance instructions should be violated repeatedly, Robert Reiser & Co. will have the right to cancel the lease contract on seven days notice and remove the said equipment. In that case, lease fees would be refunded pro rata.
5. It is mutually agreed that in case of lessee, Marhoefer Packing Co., Inc., violating any of the above conditions, or shall default in the payment of any lease charge hereunder, or shall become bankrupt, make or execute any assignment or become party to any instrument or proceedings for the benefit of its creditors, Robert Reiser & Co. shall have the right at any time without trespass, to enter upon the premises and remove the aforesaid equipment, and if removed, lessee agrees to pay Robert Reiser & Co. the total lease fees, including all installments due or to become due for the full unexpired term of this lease agreement and including the cost for removal of the equipment and counsel fees incurred in collecting sums due hereunder.
6. It is agreed that the equipment shall remain personal property of Robert Reiser & Co. and retain its character as such no matter in what manner affixed or attached to the premises.

In a letter accompanying the lease, Reiser added two option provisions to the agreement. The first provided that at the end of the four-year term, Marhoefer could purchase the stuffer for $9,968.00. In the alternative, it could elect to renew the lease for an additional four years at an annual rate of $2,990.00, payable in advance. At the conclusion of the second four-year term, Marhoefer would be allowed to purchase the stuffer for one dollar.

Marhoefer never exercised either option. Approximately one year after the Vemag stuffer was delivered to its plant, it ceased all payments under the lease and shortly thereafter filed a voluntary petition in bankruptcy. On July 12, 1978, the trustee of the bankrupt corporation applied to the bankruptcy court for leave to sell the stuffer free and clear of all liens on the ground that the "Lease Agreement" was in fact a lease intended as security within the meaning of the Uniform Commercial Code ("Code") and that Reiser's failure to perfect its interest as required by Article 9 of the Code rendered it subordinate to that of the trustee. Reiser responded with an answer and counterclaim in which it alleged that the agreement was in fact a true lease, Marhoefer was in default under the lease, and its equipment should therefore be returned.

Following a trial on this issue, the bankruptcy court concluded that the agreement between Marhoefer and Reiser was in fact a true lease and ordered the trustee to return the Vemag stuffer to Reiser. The trustee appealed to the district court, which reversed on the ground that the bankruptcy court had erred as a matter of law in finding the agreement to be a true lease. We now reverse the judgment of the district court.

II

The dispute in this case centers on section 1–201(37) of the Uniform Commercial Code, I.C. 26–1–1–201. In applying this section, the bankruptcy court concluded that "the presence of the option to renew the lease for an additional four years and to acquire the Vemag stuffer at the conclusion of the second four-year term by the payment of One Dollar ($1.00) did not, in and of itself, make the lease one intended for security."

The district court disagreed. It held that the presence of an option to purchase the stuffer for one dollar gave rise to a conclusive presumption under clause (b) of section 1–201(37) that the lease was intended as security. Although it acknowledged that the option to purchase the stuffer for only one dollar would not have come into play unless Marhoefer chose to renew the lease for an additional four-year term, the district court concluded that this fact did not require a different result. "It would be anomalous," said the court, "to rule that the lease was a genuine lease for four years after its creation but was one intended for security eight years after its creation."

Reiser, relying on Peter F. Coogan's detailed analysis of section 1–201(37), Coogan, Hogan & Vagts, Secured Transactions Under the Uniform Commercial Code, ch. 4A, (1981) (hereinafter "Secured Transactions Under U.C.C."), argues that the district court erred in construing clause (b) of that section as creating a conclusive presumption that a lease is intended as security where the lease contains an option for the lessee to become the owner of the leased property for no additional consideration or for only nominal consideration. It contends that by interpreting clause (b) in this way, the district court totally ignored the first part of that sentence which states that "[w]hether a lease is intended as security is to be determined by the facts of each case." Reiser claims that because the totality of facts surrounding the transaction indicate that the lease was not intended as security, notwithstanding the presence of the option to purchase the stuffer for one dollar, the district court erred in reversing the bankruptcy court's determination.

We agree that the district court erred in concluding that because the Lease Agreement contained an option for Marhoefer to purchase the Vemag stuffer at the end of a second four-year term, it was conclusively presumed to be a lease intended as security. However, in our view, the district court's error lies not in its reading of clause (b) of section 1–201(37) as giving rise to such a presumption,[2] but rather in its conclusion that clause (b) applies under the facts of this case.

2. This reading of section 1–201(37) is not without support in the reported cases. In Peco v. Hartbauer Tool & Die Co., 262 Or. 573, 500 P.2d 708 (1972), for example, the court noted that

[a]t first glance the provisions of * * * section [1–201(37)] may be somewhat confusing, probably because they are stated in the inverse order of importance. However, upon a careful reading of the entire section

The primary issue to be decided in determining whether a lease is "intended as security" is whether it is in effect a conditional sale in which the "lessor" retains an interest in the "leased" goods as security for the purchase price. 1C Secured Transactions Under U.C.C. § 29A.05[1][C], p. 2939. By defining the term "security interest" to include a lease intended as security, the drafters of the Code intended such disguised security interests to be governed by the same rules that apply to other security interests. *See* U.C.C., Art. 9. In this respect, section 1–201(37) represents the drafter's refusal to recognize form over substance.

Clearly, where a lease is structured so that the lessee is contractually bound to pay rent over a set period of time at the conclusion of which he automatically or for only nominal consideration becomes the owner of the leased goods, the transaction is in substance a conditional sale and should be treated as such. It is to this type of lease that clause (b) properly applies. Here, however, Marhoefer was under no contractual obligation to pay rent until such time as the option to purchase the Vemag stuffer for one dollar was to arise. In fact, in order to acquire that option, Marhoefer would have had to exercise its earlier option to renew the lease for a second four-year term and pay Reiser an additional $11,960 in "rent." In effect, Marhoefer was given a right to terminate the agreement after the first four years and cease making payments without that option ever becoming operative.

Despite this fact, the district court concluded as a matter of law that the lease was intended as security. It held that, under clause (b) of section 1–201(37), a lease containing an option for the lessee to purchase the leased goods for nominal consideration is conclusively presumed to be one intended as security. This presumption applies, the court concluded, regardless of any other options the lease may contain.

We think the district court's reading of clause (b) is in error. In our view, the conclusive presumption provided under clause (b) applies only where the option to purchase for nominal consideration necessarily arises upon compliance with the lease. *See* 1C Secured Transactions Under U.C.C. § 29.05[2][b] pp. 2947–49. It does not apply where the lessee has the right to terminate the lease before that option arises with no further obligation to continue paying rent. But see In re Royers Bakery, Inc., 1 U.C.C.Rep. 342 (Bankr.E.D.Pa.1963). For where the lessee has the right to terminate the transaction, it is not a conditional sale.[3]

Moreover, to hold that a lease containing such an option is intended as security, even though the lessee has no contractual obligation to pay the full amount contemplated by the agreement, would lead to clearly erroneous results

it is clear that the first question to be answered is that posed by clause (b)—whether the lessee may obtain the property for no additional consideration or for a nominal consideration. If so, the lease is intended for security. If not, it is then necessary to determine "by the facts of each case" whether * * * the fact that the lease contains an option to purchase "does not (of itself) make the lease one intended for security." Id. at 575, 500 P.2d at 709–10, quoting Ore.Rev.Stat. § 71–2010(37) (1969).

3. See S. Williston, The Law Governing Sales of Goods at Common Law and Under the Uniform Sales Act § 336, p. 528 (1909):

It is, however, essential in order to make a conditional sale, in the sense in which that term is used ordinarily in statutes or elsewhere, that the buyer should be bound to take title of the property, or at least to pay the price for it. Therefore, a lease which provides for a certain rent in installments is not a conditional sale if the buyer can terminate the transaction at any time by returning the property, even though the lease also provides that if rent is paid for a certain period, the lessee shall thereupon become the owner of the property.

under other provisions of the Code. Under section 9–506 of the Code, for example, a debtor in default on his obligation to a secured party has a right to redeem the collateral by tendering full payment of that obligation.[4] The same right is also enjoyed by a lessee under a lease intended as security. A lessee who defaults on a lease intended as security is entitled to purchase the leased goods by paying the full amount of his obligation under the lease. But if the lessee has the right to terminate the lease at any time during the lease term, his obligation under the lease may be only a small part of the total purchase price of the goods leased. To afford the lessee a right of redemption under such circumstances would clearly be wrong. There is no evidence that the drafters of the Code intended such a result.

We therefore hold that while section 1–201(37)(b) does provide a conclusive test of when a lease is intended as security, that test does not apply in every case in which the disputed lease contains an option to purchase for nominal or no consideration. An option of this type makes a lease one intended as security only when it necessarily arises upon compliance with the terms of the lease.[5]

Applying section 1–201(37), so construed, to the facts of this case, it is clear that the district court erred in concluding that the possibility of Marhoefer's purchasing the stuffer for one dollar at the conclusion of a second four-year term was determinative. Because Marhoefer could have fully complied with the lease without that option ever arising, the district court was mistaken in thinking that the existence of that option alone made the lease a conditional sale. Certainly, if Marhoefer had elected to renew the lease for another term, in which case the nominal purchase option would necessarily have arisen, then the clause (b) test would apply. But that is not the case we are faced with here. Marhoefer was not required to make any payments beyond the first four years. The fact that, at the conclusion of that term, it could have elected to renew the lease and obtain an option to purchase the stuffer for one dollar at the end of the second term does not transform the original transaction into a conditional sale.

This fact does not end our inquiry under clause (b), however, for the trustee also argues that, even if the district court erred in considering the one dollar purchase option as determinative, the lease should nevertheless be considered a conditional sale because the initial option price of $9,968 is also nominal when all of the operative facts are properly considered. We agree that if the clause (b) test is to apply at all in this case, this is the option that must be considered. For this is the option that was to arise automatically upon Marhoefer's compliance with the lease. We do not agree, however, that under the circumstances presented here the $9,968 option price can properly be considered nominal.

It is true that an option price may be more than a few dollars and still be considered nominal within the meaning of section 1–201(37). Because clause (b)

4. Section 9–506 of the Code states:

Debtor's Right to Redeem Collateral

At any time before the secured party has disposed of collateral or entered into a contract for its disposition under Section 9–504 or before the obligation has been discharged under Section 9–505(2) the debtor or any other secured party may unless otherwise agreed in writing after default redeem the collateral by tendering fulfillment of all obligations secured by the collateral as well as the expenses reasonably incurred by the secured party in retaking, holding and preparing the collateral for disposition, in arranging for the sale, and to the extent provided in the agreement and not prohibited by law, his reasonable attorneys' fees and legal expenses.

5. This reading of clause (b) is in no way inconsistent with the plain language of that provision since, by its terms, it does not refer to the situation where there are alternate ways of complying with a lease, only one of which results in the nominal purchase option arising.

speaks of nominal "consideration" and not a nominal "sum" or "amount," it has been held to apply not only where the option price is very small in absolute terms, but also where the price is insubstantial in relation to the fair market value of the leased goods at the time the option arises.[7]

Here, however, the evidence revealed that the initial option price of $9,968 was not nominal even under this standard. George Vetie, Reiser's treasurer and the person chiefly responsible for the terms of the lease, testified at trial that the purchase price for the Vemag stuffer at the time the parties entered into the transaction was $33,225. He testified that the initial option price of $9,968 was arrived at by taking thirty percent of the purchase price, which was what he felt a four-year-old Vemag stuffer would be worth based on Reiser's past experience.

The trustee, relying on the testimony of its expert appraiser, argues that in fact the stuffer would have been worth between eighteen and twenty thousand dollars at the end of the first four-year term. Because the initial option price is substantially less than this amount, he claims that it is nominal within the meaning of clause (b) and the lease is therefore one intended as security.

Even assuming this appraisal to be accurate, an issue on which the bankruptcy court made no finding, we would not find the initial option price of $9,968 so small by comparison that the clause (b) presumption would apply. While it is difficult to state any bright line percentage test for determining when an option price could properly be considered nominal as compared to the fair market value of the leased goods, an option price of almost ten thousand dollars, which amounts to fifty percent of the fair market value, is not nominal by any standard.

Furthermore, in determining whether an option price is nominal, the proper figure to compare it with is not the actual fair market value of the leased goods at the time the option arises, but their fair market value at that time as anticipated by the parties when the lease is signed. 1C Secured Transactions Under U.C.C. § 29A.05[2][b], p. 2953. Here, for example, Vetie testified that his estimate of the fair market value of a four-year-old Vemag stuffer was based on records from a period of time in which the economy was relatively stable. Since that time, a high rate of inflation has caused the machines to lose their value more slowly. As a result, the actual fair market value of a machine may turn out to be significantly more than the parties anticipated it would be several years earlier. When this occurs, the lessee's option to purchase the leased goods may be much more favorable than either party intended, but it does not change the true character of the transaction.

We conclude, therefore, that neither option to purchase contained in the lease between Marhoefer and Reiser gives rise to a conclusive presumption under section 1–201(37)(b) that the lease is one intended as security. This being so, we now turn to the other facts surrounding the transaction.

III

Although section 1–201(37) states that "[w]hether a lease is intended as security is to be determined by the facts of each case," it is completely silent as to what facts, other than the option to purchase, are to be considered in making that determination. Facts that the courts have found relevant include the total

7. The trustee argues that the determination of whether the option price is nominal is to be made by comparing it to the fair market value of the equipment at the time the parties enter into the lease, instead of the date the option arises. Although some courts have applied such a test, the better approach is to compare the option price with the fair market value of the goods at the time the option was to be exercised.

amount of rent the lessee is required to pay under the lease, whether the lessee acquires any equity in the leased property, the useful life of the leased goods, the nature of the lessor's business, and the payment of taxes, insurance and other charges normally imposed on ownership. Consideration of the facts of this case in light of these factors leads us to conclude that the lease in question was not intended as security.

First, Marhoefer was under no obligation to pay the full purchase price for the stuffer. Over the first four-year term, its payments under the lease were to have amounted to $31,920. Although this amount may not be substantially less than the original purchase price of $33,225 in absolute terms, it becomes so when one factors in the interest rate over four years that would have been charged had Marhoefer elected to purchase the machine under a conditional sale contract.[8] The fact that the total amount of rent Marhoefer was to pay under the lease was substantially less than that amount shows that a sale was not intended.

It is also significant that the useful life of the Vemag stuffer exceeded the term of the lease. An essential characteristic of a true lease is that there be something of value to return to the lessor after the term. Where the term of the lease is substantially equal to the life of the leased property such that there will be nothing of value to return at the end of the lease, the transaction is in essence a sale. Here, the evidence revealed that the useful life of a Vemag stuffer was eight to ten years.

Finally, the bankruptcy court specifically found that "there was no express or implied provision in the lease agreement dated February 28, 1977, which gave Marhoefer any equity interest in the leased Vemag stuffer." This fact clearly reveals the agreement between Marhoefer and Reiser to be a true lease. See Hawkland, The Impact of the Uniform Commercial Code on Equipment Leasing, 1972 Ill.L.Forum 446, 453 ("The difference between a true lease and a security transaction lies in whether the lessee acquires an equity of ownership through his rent payments.") Had Marhoefer remained solvent and elected not to exercise its option to renew its lease with Reiser, it would have received nothing for its previous lease payments. And in order to exercise that option, Marhoefer would have had to pay what Reiser anticipated would then be the machine's fair market value. An option of this kind is not the mark of a lease intended as security.

Although Marhoefer was required to pay state and local taxes and the cost of repairs, this fact does not require a contrary result. Costs such as taxes, insurance and repairs are necessarily borne by one party or the other. They reflect less the true character of the transaction than the strength of the parties' respective bargaining positions.

IV

We conclude from the foregoing that the district court erred in its application of section 1–201(37) of the Uniform Commercial Code to the facts of this case. Neither the option to purchase the Vemag stuffer for one dollar at the conclusion of a second four-year term, nor the initial option to purchase it for $9,968 after the first four years, gives rise to a conclusive presumption under clause (b) of section 1–201(37) that the lease is intended as security. From all of

8. The bankruptcy court found that Reiser was originally willing to sell Marhoefer the stuffer under a conditional sale contract the terms of which would have been $7,225 down and monthly installments of $1,224 over a twenty-four month period. The total payments under such an agreement would have amounted to $36,601, substantially more than the amount Marhoefer was required to pay over four years under the lease.

the facts surrounding the transaction, we conclude that the agreement between Marhoefer and Reiser is a true lease. The judgment of the district court is therefore reversed. [Some footnotes omitted.]

Notes

1. If a court chooses to use the option price as a test of whether a lease is truly a lease or is merely a security agreement, should the court determine this price at the outset of the lease (and irrespective of the ultimate value of the property) or at the end of the lease (when the court knows the actual value of the property)?

2. Would any of the following factors be relevant in determining whether an arrangement should be treated as a lease or as a security agreement?

a. Who received the investment tax credit.

b. Whether any warranties were given by the lessor to the lessee.

c. Who bore the responsibility for maintenance of the leased product.

3. In doing what the court calls "first tier" analysis, one must impute an interest or discount rate. How should a court do that?

Note: The Lease in Bankruptcy

The differential treatment accorded a "lease" on the one hand (under section 365 in bankruptcy) and a security agreement on the other (under 1129 and other sections in bankruptcy) means that the lease/security agreement controversy will continue and even intensify in bankruptcy cases under the 1978 Code.

Under sections 1129 and 1322, a plan can be imposed by the court on a secured creditor, even though the plan pays the secured creditor much less than his loan agreement calls for. This is the so-called "cramdown." Under a cramdown, however, the creditor is assured of payments equal to the present value of his collateral ("adequate protection"). Assume, for example, that an arrangement constituted a security agreement rather than a true lease, with the creditor having a security interest in a piece of equipment worth $50,000 which secured a $100,000 debt. Here, the secured creditor could be made to take payments with a present value of $50,000 and the remaining $50,000 could be treated as unsecured debt to be paid, perhaps, only a few cents on the dollar.

On the other hand, if the agreement were found to be a "lease," it would be governed by section 365 and the debtor would be faced with the choice of either returning the asset to the creditor or of complying explicitly with every term of the lease. Thus, in such a case, the debtor would presumably either return the equipment or, if it were particularly valuable, would be obliged to pay the full $100,000 in order to keep it. In effect, under a lease arrangement the lessor is entitled to realize the unique value of the lease to this particular debtor even though that value greatly exceeds the market value of the asset to others. If, in our hypothetical case, the value to the particular debtor of the collateral in question is only $50,000, obviously he would exercise his power under the Bankruptcy Code to reject the lease and procure similar equipment elsewhere for much less than $100,000. Thus, in In re Witowski, 37 B.R. 352 (Bkrtcy.D.N.D.1984), the court found that a "lease" was in fact a security agreement and thus concluded that the debtor farmer could keep his 120 head mini-swine nursery if he paid only its market value, even though that value was substantially less than the value of the remaining lease payments and even though the farmer may have valued the nursery much more highly.

SECTION 3. THE BORDER BETWEEN BAILMENT AND ARTICLES TWO AND NINE

Almost all of the conflicts between Article 2 and Article 9 deal in some way with the legal consequences arising from possession of goods by a given party. Some of these questions have grown up as discrete and well-recognized issues in the law of sales. For example, under a consignment the owner places goods in the hands of another for resale to third parties. This is an ancient practice, designed in some cases to allow the seller to maintain price control over the resale price. In other cases, the consignment is used as a device in effect to finance the retailer's business or to encourage the retailer to sell the consignor's goods by minimizing the retailer's risk. Because the consignor's interest is closely akin to a purchase-money seller's security interest, one might ask whether the creditors of the retailer should have rights prior to the consignor's interest, at least when the consignor has not put third parties on notice in any way. It is not surprising to find that section 2–326 of Article 2 which, when combined with UCC 9–114, treats the consignor for many purposes like a seller who retains a purchase money security interest.

Equally well recognized and developed is the doctrine set out in sections 2–702, 2–507 and 2–511 giving a defrauded seller the right to the return of his goods despite the fact that he has transferred possession to a buyer. The fraud in such cases is the buyer's receiving goods on credit while insolvent or after a representation of solvency. Yet here, too, one must ask whether the creditors of the buyer should have rights prior to the defrauded seller. Others such as the buyer's secured creditor with a floating lien, lien creditors, trustees in bankruptcy, and buyers in the ordinary course will certainly be ready to challenge the seller's right to the return of his goods.

The bailment cases give rise to a third well-recognized point of abrasion. Parties claiming as bailors may actually finance part of a debtor's operations. But should one who owns seed and "bails it" to a farmer be entitled to the crop produced (to repay the seed and harvesting loan) or should the crop go to a lender who has taken a specific security interest in the crop?

Finally, the courts have encountered a series of less well defined questions that partake partly of one and partly of another of the transactions described above. We will call one the "quasi consignment." Here an owner of goods puts them in the hands of a third party for processing and alternatively for their return or possibly for sale. Is this merely a bailment? A consignment? Something else? A similar case is one in which a purchaser buys goods and yet leaves them in the hands of the seller. This problem is governed in part by UCC 2–502, but some courts have used UCC 9–307 to deal with it. It resembles in some sense an ancient fraudulent conveyance in which it is argued that a buyer has allowed his seller to defraud subsequent creditors by permitting the seller to retain possession and thus apparent ownership of the property.

Because the typical transaction will often have attributes of more than one of the arrangements described above, each case is dependent to some extent on its own facts and each will form a basis for one party to argue for one of the doctrines described above and for another to argue a second and conflicting one. Thus, it is not uncommon to see a set of cases dealing with the problem, for example, under UCC 2–502 co-existing with cases that would appear to be in direct conflict, but decided under UCC 9–307. Each set fails to mention the other.

At the outset a student should examine the relevant Article 2 sections: UCC 2–326, 2–401, 2–402, 2–403, 2–502, 2–507, 2–511, 2–702, 2–711(3). The most directly relevant Article 9 sections should also be considered: UCC 9–102, 9–113, 9–114, 9–307. Having taken a quick look at those sections, the student is prepared to begin work on the problem and cases that follow.

Problem 7–2

Analyze the following problem under UCC 2–326.

Assume that General Electric sold a series of lamps, bulbs, and other electrical equipment to a retailer, Pettingale Electric. Most of these goods were on a "sale or return" basis. If they were not sold within 30 or 60 days, Pettingale had the right to return them to General Electric and get a refund of the money paid. General Electric did not file a financing statement under Article 9 and when Pettingale went into bankruptcy the trustee claimed the assets. In which of the following cases would General Electric win in competition with the trustee:

1. If General Electric had filed a financing statement six months prior to the filing of a petition.

2. If Pettingale did business under the name of "General Electric Supply Company."

3. If General Electric proved that a competing bank, who itself had lent more than half of the entire debt to Pettingale knew of General Electric's claim.

4. If General Electric introduced persuasive evidence that the purpose of its consignment was not to finance Pettingale, but to control the resale price and also to minimize tax liability.

SIMMONS FIRST NATIONAL BANK v. WELLS

Supreme Court of Arkansas, 1983.
279 Ark. 204, 650 S.W.2d 236.

HAYS, JUSTICE.

This suit presents the issue of whether the interest of a secured creditor in the inventory of a grain dealer is superior to that of a rice grower who subsequently deposits his rice with that dealer.

On May 1, 1980, Simmons First National Bank made a loan of $520,000 to Western Rice Mills, Inc., for which Western granted Simmons a security interest in all of its real and personal property, including all inventory and after acquired property. Western defaulted and in September of 1981, a receiver was appointed. Shortly thereafter, Harold Wells intervened, claiming ownership of certain rice and proceeds from the sale of rice, pursuant to a previous agreement with Western.

Wells had dealt with Western for a number of years, the standard arrangement being that Western would buy the rice outright from Wells, would mill it and then sell it. In April and May of 1981, because of financial difficulties, Western could not buy the rice outright from Wells. Wells and Western orally agreed instead that Western would mill the rice for a certain price and then market the rice at an agreed minimum price for Wells. The charge for milling would be deducted when Western sold the rice, and the remaining proceeds would go to Wells. In the interim, the rice was stored with Western.

The trial court, relying on the rationale of *In Re Sitkin Smelting and Refining, Inc.*, 639 F.2d 1213 (5th Cir.1981), [infra p. 288] found the arrangement between Wells and Western to constitute a bailment and found Ark.Stat.Ann.

§ 85–2–326 (Add.1961) inapplicable. Under this finding, the inventory lien of the bank did not extend to the rice or to the proceeds claimed by Wells.

Simmons argues for reversal that the Chancellor erred in finding that § 85–2–326 was inapplicable to the facts of this case. We agree and find that § 85-2-326 *is* applicable and we reverse as to those grounds.

The Chancellor mistakenly relied on *Sitkin,* whereby he found the arrangement to be a bailment and, apparently, found that that precluded the possibility of finding a consignment and § 85–2–326 applicable. We see two flaws in this analysis: first, the *Sitkin* case is factually distinguishable, the main issue there being whether the arrangement was a sale or a bailment. Second, even if a particular arrangement is found to constitute a bailment as opposed to a sale, that does not preclude a finding that there is also a consignment arrangement and, hence, § 85–2–326 is applicable.

In *Sitkin,* the issue was whether the bankruptcy court had erred in determining that possession of film entrusted to a bankrupt metal refiner, Sitkin, should be given to a secured creditor of the refiner rather than to the film manufacturer, Kodak, which had entrusted it to Sitkin. The arrangement between Sitkin and Kodak was basically that Sitkin would retain possession of film waste delivered to it by Kodak. But for Kodak's business purposes, not until the film had been reduced and destroyed and the silver content removed by Sitkin, would Kodak's ownership cease, and at that time a "settlement" would be made as to the amount owned by Sitkin. The court looked at a number of factors surrounding the transaction and found it to be a bailment and not a sale. The court also determined that the transaction was not a "sale or return" within the meaning of § 85–2–326 since the goods were not delivered for resale with an option to return. Although we are not convinced that the court was correct in finding a bailment and not a sale in *Sitkin,* that is irrelevant here.

Whether the arrangement in this case was a bailment or a sale is not determinative of the rights of the parties. Even if under the analysis of *Sitkin,* the trial court found a bailment and not a sale, the question of whether § 85–2–326 is applicable must still be answered. Western could have been a bailee for Wells and at the same time been a consignee under § 85–2–326. We emphasize the following language of § 85–2–326(3) which we find applicable to this fact situation: [quoting]

> The comment to this section reinforces the policy indicated by the language of this section:
>
> 2. Pursuant to the general policies of this Act which require good faith not only between the parties to the sales contract, but as against interested third parties, subsection (3) *resolves all reasonable doubts as to the nature of the transaction in favor of the general creditors of the buyer.* * * * (our italics).

Here, Wells delivered his goods, the rice, to Western for sale and Western maintained a place of business where it dealt in goods of that kind, under a name other than the name of the person making the delivery, Wells. With regard to the rights of creditors, it is irrelevant whether the transaction between the two parties was a bailment or a sale if the provisions of § 85–2–326(3) are also satisfied.

We find *In Re KLP, Inc. Finance Co. of America v. Morris,* 7 B.R. 256 (Bkrtcy.N.D.Ga.1980) more analogous to our case and it provides a more appropriate and clearer application of § 85–2–326. In *KLP,* the plaintiff had leased space from the debtor to store two organs. The organs were delivered to the debtor's warehouse where the debtor had traditionally dealt in organs and related goods. At the time of delivery, the agreement was modified to allow the debtor to secure offers for the purchase of the organs, subject to the debtor obtaining prior approval of the offers and sale by the plaintiff. When the debtor filed for bankruptcy, the plaintiff filed to recover the organs. The court ruled in favor of the Trustee whose status under the Bankruptcy Code is that of a hypothetical lien creditor who would have priority over a consignment seller who failed to comply with the requirements of UCC § 2–326. The following passage states the policy and reasoning behind UCC § 2–326:

> The applicable UCC provision, § 2–326, is not only one of the more important UCC sections, but is also one of the most unique provisions in the UCC article which governs the sale of goods. The uniqueness of the section lies primarily in the fact that the section applies to transactions which are not true sales at all, since the section governs agreements which somehow provide that "delivered goods may be returned by the buyer even though they conform to the contract." The section's importance lies primarily in the role it plays, along with the notice provisions of article nine, in giving disclosed claims to property priority over secret claims. To encourage disclosure of in rem claims is a central feature of any well-reasoned system of commercial law.
>
> Of particular importance to the instant case is the fact that certain types of transactions are "deemed" by § 2–326(3) to constitute "consignment sales." The statute so characterizes a transaction when the following three circumstances are present:
>
> (1) when goods are delivered for sale,
>
> (2) when the "consignment buyer" maintains a place of business at which he deals in goods of the kind so delivered, and
>
> (3) when the business name of the "consignment seller" is different than the business name of the consignment buyer.
>
> If a transaction is so deemed to constitute a consignment sale, the consignment seller may obtain priority over the consignment buyer's creditors only by complying with the notice requirements of UCC § 2–326(3).

The facts of this case require us to examine § 85–2–326 for its applicability. The language of the statute and the commentary convince us that the reasoning of the court in *KLP* is sound. * * * Therefore, because we think the theory on which the case was tried would bring it within § 85–2–326, and since there was no evidence or argument that Wells complied with any of the requirements of § 85–2–326(3) so as to remove him from the provisions of that section, the priority of Simmons' interest would prevail on that issue.

* * *

FIRST STATE BANK OF WIGGINS v. SIMMONS

Supreme Court of Colorado, 1932.
91 Colo. 160, 13 P.2d 259.

CAMPBELL, J.

A full statement of the material facts in this case will not only shorten the discussion, but it is the best way to dispose of the controversy.

The Associated Seed Growers, a corporation, entered into a contract with M.L. Miller by the terms of which it delivered to him certain seeds and Miller agreed to act as bailee thereof for the purpose of raising a crop or crop of seeds therefrom which was to be redelivered to the seed company. Miller was to prepare the ground or soil for planting and was to plant approximately fifteen acres. The land on which the seed was planted belonged to a third party. Miller agreed to cultivate and care for the crop and harvest the same so as to secure the greatest possible return of seed suitable for seedmen's use and to sack all such seed that was grown and deliver the same to the seed company at Masters, Colorado. The parties in their agreement referred to this contract as a bailment. It expressly provides that the seed which was furnished by the seed company to Miller, and the entire seed crop produced therefrom, were at all times to be the property of the seed company and it had the right of possession of the same at any time, or, at its option, to harvest the crop or to cultivate the ground and deduct the cost of such cultivation from the compensation agreed to be paid to Miller for his services in planting and caring for the crop. The contract further provides that Miller shall have no right at any time to sell or dispose of the said stock seed furnished to him or the seed crop produced therefrom. As compensation for his services Miller was entitled to receive, and the seed company was required to pay him, at the rate of 7 cents per pound for the crop grown.

After this seed contract was made the defendant in error, here, Simmons, brought an action against Miller to recover on the latter's debt to him, and served a writ of garnishment upon the Associated Seed Company. The seed company made answer that there was owing to Miller under this seed contract the sum of $108.30. The plaintiff in error, the First State Bank of Wiggins, Colorado, intervened in this action and claimed the money which the seed company admitted it owed to Miller and based its claim upon a chattel mortgage given to it by Miller upon the crop produced.

The question for decision upon this review is whether the beans grown by Miller under the contract with the seed company are subject to the mortgage of the bank. Perhaps a better statement of the question is, did Miller have the right and power under his contract with the seed company to give a valid chattel mortgage on the prospective bean crop to the Wiggins Bank as against the claim and right which the seed company had thereto under its seed contract? We think Simmons' rights under his judgment against Miller are superior to that of the bank under its mortgage from Miller. Not only did the seed company and Miller designate the bean contract as a bailment, but a reading of the same makes it entirely clear that the transaction between the seed company and Miller was of that character. No property right in the crop to be grown passed under the contract from the seed company to Miller. It expressly provides that his interest under the contract is only the right to receive for his services to the seed company in caring for the crop a certain sum of money but it gave him no right whatever to the crop to be grown. In Morsch v. Lessig, 45 Colo. 168, 100 P. 431, we held that an owner is not affected by an unauthorized pledge of his goods by an agent to whom he has entrusted them. This contract between the Associated Seed Company and Miller was unquestionably a bailment. In Clay, Robinson & Co. v. Martinez, 74 Colo. 10, 218 P. 903, we held that the owner of bailed property is not estopped to deny the ownership of the bailee because he permits the latter to enter into contracts with third parties concerning the same. We also held in that case that every one deals with a bailee at his peril and, in the absence of special legislation to the contrary, one who deals with the bailee concerning the bailed property not only does so at his peril but is charged with notice of its real ownership. See, generally, 6 C.J. p. 1084 et seq.; 1 Bouv.Law Dict. p. 313 et seq.; 3 R.C.L. p. 71 et seq., §§ 35, 66.

Applying this recognized doctrine of bailment to the present case, we say that even though there might have been an equitable lien or assignment by Miller to the bank if the contract between the seed company and Miller was not a bailment, that doctrine is wholly inapplicable to the facts of this case, because the contract between the seed company and Miller constituted a bailment. Since no property right in and to the crop that was grown under this contract was ever acquired by Miller, he had no right or power, as against the rights of the seed company or its assignee, to give a chattel mortgage on the crop to the bank which was his creditor. The judgment is, therefore, affirmed.

Affirmed.

ADAMS, C.J., and ALTER, J., concur.

Notes

1. How would this case come out under the Code? In relation to a similar case, it has been said that: "The result seems pretty plainly contrary to the philosophy of the Commercial Code, but seems not to be overruled directly by any of its specific provisions." Bunn, *Financing Farmers,* 1954 Wis.L.Rev. 357, 363. Do you agree?

2. If the bailment device will not work under the Code, how might the financing buyer protect himself? Consider the following problem.

Problem 7–3

Farmer raises grapefruit. Nearby cannery cans grapefruit. F needs funds at the beginning and at the end of the growing season to pay for the care of his trees and for harvesting. C needs assurance that at the end of the growing season C will have enough harvested grapefruit to make the best possible use of C's canning facilities. Accordingly, in return for F's commitment to sell his crop to C, C is willing to advance funds to F to be used by F in growing and harvesting his crop, such money to be applied on the purchase price of the grapefruit when delivered to C. Assume that C has come to you "to set this thing up." First of all, what are the risks to C in such a venture? If we assume that C advances, say, $10,000 to F, what risks can materialize between the time of such advance and the date harvested grapefruit are to be delivered to C? The crop could fail for lack of care, or because of weather conditions. F could repudiate. F could harvest but wrongfully resell to a third party. An unsecured creditor of F could levy on the growing crop or on it as it is harvested. A secured creditor of F could foreclose. F could go bankrupt.

How might C maximize its protection against some or all of the foregoing hazards? What C most wants is as much legal assurance as is possible that C will actually get the grapefruit when harvested. As a buyer of goods under Article 2, C would potentially have rights under UCC 2–502(1) and UCC 2–716 to possession of the grapefruit *as against* F. But are these rights adequate, even as against F? As against third parties? Do these provisions give C sufficient rights against third parties? UCC 2–402(1) favors C as against unsecured creditors of F. But UCC 2–402(2) qualifies this, and UCC 2–402(3)(a) makes it plain that secured creditors are not affected by UCC 2–402(1). Moreover, C may lose to purchasers from F under UCC 2–403(2). What would you recommend?

Omit

IN RE SITKIN SMELTING & REFINING, INC.

United States Court of Appeals, Fifth Circuit, 1981.
639 F.2d 1213.

RONEY, CIRCUIT JUDGE. This case raises a single issue: whether the Bankruptcy Court erred in determining that possession of film entrusted to a now bankrupt metal refiner should be given to a secured creditor of the refiner rather than to the film manufacturer that entrusted it to the refiner. Holding that the bankrupt did not gain sufficient rights under the contract with the manufacturer to give its creditor a security interest in the film, we reverse.

The background of the transaction between plaintiff and the bankrupt company, as well as the terms of the contract, are somewhat unique. Prior to its bankruptcy, Sitkin Smelting and Refining Company was in the business of processing industrial waste for the recovery of precious and base metals. On January 19, 1978, Sitkin entered into an agreement with plaintiff, Eastman Kodak Company, in which it agreed to process a minimum of 500,000 pounds of print film waste and purchase the silver content recovered upon processing. This film waste consisted of film manufactured by Kodak which had been rejected as inferior by its quality control department. Its silver content is recovered by a controlled burning process which leaves an ash containing the metal.

The contract provided that it would run on a trial basis for at least two months. The waste would be picked up by Sitkin at Kodak Park in Rochester, New York, in lots of 36,000 pounds each. Responsibility for the waste transferred to Sitkin upon leaving Kodak Park.

Kodak would not sell outright the unprocessed film waste for two reasons: first, since the film was inferior, Kodak was concerned that it not find its way into the possession of persons who would use it as film; and second, collateral litigation made it important that the film not fall into the hands of Polaroid, for whom Sitkin had also been disposing of film waste. Therefore, under the contract, Kodak's ownership of the film waste would cease only upon its "destruction or change of identity." Either party had the right to cancel the contract with two days' notice. Upon cancellation, the film waste in Sitkin's possession would, at Kodak's option, be returned to Kodak or processed. In no event could Sitkin do anything with the film but destroy it.

The contract called for a "settlement," which was a determination of the amount owed by Sitkin after it processed each lot. A settlement would be calculated by multiplying the troy ounces of silver recovered in a lot by a percentage of a published price quote for silver. A settlement would take place thirty days after receipt of each lot, with payment due sixty days after receipt.

On March 13, 1978, within the two-month period of the contract, Sitkin filed for protection under Chapter 11 of the Bankruptcy Act, and was adjudicated bankrupt shortly thereafter. At that time, Sitkin had in its possession over 382,000 pounds of Kodak film waste.

On August 30, 1978, Kodak filed suit to reclaim the unprocessed film waste, which is stored in the original Kodak cartons in two Alabama warehouses. The defendants are the Trustee in Bankruptcy and the C.I.T. Corporation, a secured creditor of Sitkin. Although an additional quantity of film had already been processed and Kodak has not been paid for the recovered silver, it does not seek payment for the silver in this action.

* * *

Kodak's claim is based on the general rule that a bailor may reclaim property it entrusts to a bailee who subsequently files for bankruptcy. See, e.g., Sandack v. Tamme, 182 F.2d 759 (10th Cir.1950). See generally 4A Collier on Bankruptcy ¶ 70.18[4] (1978). C.I.T., as a secured creditor, claims all property in the possession of Sitkin to which its security interest "attaches." Under Alabama law, a security interest attaches to property in which the bankrupt has "rights," provided that the property falls within the security agreement and the secured creditor has given value. Ala.Code tit. 7, § 9–204 (1975). C.I.T. contends that its security interest attaches to the film waste and that Kodak has only an unperfected security interest in the property.

In resolving the conflicting claims, the Bankruptcy Court found that the agreement between Kodak and Sitkin contemplated both a bailment and a sale: Sitkin held the unprocessed waste as bailee for Kodak; a sale arose only after Sitkin processed the waste and became obligated to purchase the recovered silver content. The court went on to hold, however, that Sitkin's possession of the unprocessed waste, even though only a bailment, was a sufficient "right" in the waste under Alabama law so that C.I.T.'s security interest attached and was superior to Kodak's interest. Ala.Code tit. 7, § 2–403 (1975). In so holding, the court relied on this court's decision in In re Samuels & Co., 526 F.2d 1238 (5th Cir.1976) (en banc).

Section 2–403, identical to its counterpart in the Uniform Commercial Code, permits transferors of property to pass greater title in certain circumstances than they can themselves claim. Section 2–403(1) provides that a buyer of goods who holds only voidable title has the power to transfer good title to a "good faith purchaser." The purpose of this rule is to "promote the greatest range of freedom possible to commercial vendors and purchasers." In re Samuels & Co., 526 F.2d at 1242.

In Samuels, this court held that a secured creditor may be a "good faith purchaser" within the meaning of § 2–403(1), and may thus take good title to property to which its security interest attaches. Concluding that a creditor's security interest in inventory attached to goods in the possession of a bankrupt, we denied the petition to reclaim by the unpaid sellers of those goods.

Samuels, however, involved a bankrupt who was a purchaser from the claimant. In the present case, the Bankruptcy Court erroneously extended Samuels to bailments. The section involved in Samuels was § 2–403(1), which applies where the bankrupt was a *purchaser* of the goods in question. With a security interest that gave it the position of a "good faith purchaser" from a bankrupt who was itself a purchaser, C.I.T. would take title as against a seller to the bankrupt.

Section 2–403(2), however, is the provision which applies where the bankrupt holds the goods as a *bailee*, instead of as a purchaser. That section provides that a merchant who is entrusted with goods has power to transfer good title only to a "buyer in ordinary course of business." Although C.I.T. may be a good faith purchaser, it is specifically excluded from being a buyer in ordinary course of business under Alabama law. Ala.Code tit. 7, § 1–201(9) (1975). Section 1–201(9), which defines a buyer in ordinary course, states that "buying" does not encompass a transfer "as security for * * * a money debt." This language has been consistently interpreted to exclude holders of security interests from the coverage of § 2–403(2). * * *

The less inclusive "buyer in ordinary course" term was used for bailments because the "older loose concept of good faith and wide definition of value combined to create apparent good faith purchasers in many situations in which the result outraged common sense." Official Comment to § 2–403, Ala.Code tit. 7, § 2–403 (1975). By restricting the category of protected buyers, § 2–403(2) serves to provide greater protection for a bailor of goods than for a seller. See R. Duesenberg & L. King, 3A Sales and Bulk Transfers under the UCC § 10.06[2] (1980). These commentators state:

> "It should be noted that the test of Subsection (2) is not that of good-faith purchase, but a purchase in the ordinary course. This is an important distinction * * * [T]he categories of sheltered parties under Subsection (1) of Section 2–403 is considerably more expansive than under the entrustment subsections, for 'buyer in the ordinary course of business,' while it does include a secured or unsecured transaction, does not include a taking 'as security for or in total or partial satisfaction of a money debt.' Comparing the two criteria, it follows, for example, that an owner defrauded by a buyer giving a bad check would lose against a creditor of the buyer who took a security interest in the goods; but would not lose against such a creditor if in place of a fraudulent purchase, the owner had entrusted the goods to a merchant who without authority pledged them as security for a debt." Id. (footnotes omitted).

In light of its finding of a bailment of the unprocessed film waste, the Bankruptcy Court erred in applying § 2–403(1) rather than § 2–403(2). Because C.I.T. is not a buyer in ordinary course within the meaning of the latter provision, it cannot divest Kodak of title in the film waste.

C.I.T. disputes on appeal the Bankruptcy Court's finding that Sitkin's possession of the unprocessed film waste was a bailment. It contends that the agreement between Kodak and Sitkin was under Alabama law a contract for sale of goods at a future time. While the question is a close one, we conclude that the Bankruptcy Court did not err in finding a bailment.

NYTCO Services, Inc. v. Wilson, 351 So.2d 875 (Ala.1977), is the controlling Alabama case. There, the Supreme Court of Alabama in finding a bailment rather than a sale between farmers and a grain company, cited two principal factors: the option of the farmers to require the return of their grain or to direct its sale, and evidence indicating the grain was being stored on the farmers' behalf. 351 So.2d at 879.

Both factors are present here. First, Kodak clearly retained the option under the contract to have the film waste returned or processed. Processing, of course, would result in the sale of the silver content to Sitkin. That Sitkin also had the right to bring about a sale by processing the waste makes no difference. A bailment may still exist where the bailee has a continuing option to purchase or to sell. * * *

Second, as the Bankruptcy Court noted, several aspects of the arrangement indicated a bailment. Responsibility for the waste transferred to Sitkin upon leaving Kodak Park, which is consistent with a bailee's duty of care. The film was clearly imprinted with Kodak's name, tagged identifying it as Kodak property, stored in the original Kodak cartons, and kept in separate warehouses apart from similar material to be processed. Finally, in their bookkeeping, Kodak did not show the waste as a receivable; Sitkin did not carry it as inventory.

The First Circuit case of In re Medomak Canning Co., 25 U.C.C.Rep.Serv. 437, is an analogous case finding a bailment. In that case a large food retailer agreed to supply Medomak with certain ingredients for processing, and to then purchase the finished product. When Medomak filed for bankruptcy, the retailer sought possession of the ingredients. As here, the case turned upon whether the transaction between the two companies was a bailment or a sale.

In finding that Medomak held the ingredients as a bailment, the Bankruptcy Court looked into the intentions and circumstances of the parties rather than to a provision in the contract designating the transaction a "purchase" by Medomak. In particular, the court found that no purchase price was agreed upon as to the ingredients prior to processing. A price was instead fixed only for the finished product. In addition, the court held that the parties did not intend for the retailer to part with any interest in the ingredients furnished to Medomak until they were processed.

As in Medomak, the agreement between Kodak and Sitkin did not set a purchase price for the film waste prior to its processing. Although the contract estimated the silver content of the waste, the exact amount of silver as well as the purchase price became certain only after the waste had been processed. Moreover, as the Bankruptcy Court held, Kodak and Sitkin clearly showed an intention to avoid any rights in Sitkin until the destruction of the film waste.

C.I.T.'s final argument, rejected by the Bankruptcy Court, is that the waste was delivered to Sitkin on a "sale or return" basis. Ala.Code tit. 7, § 2–326 (1975). Under § 2–326, goods in the possession of a buyer which were delivered on a sale or return basis are subject to the claims of the buyer's creditors.

The type of sale or return contemplated in § 2–326 is a consignment, where a buyer "purchases" goods with the understanding that the seller will accept their return in lieu of payment if they fail to be resold. The Official Comment to § 2–326 states that this type of transaction is "so strongly delineated in practice and in general understanding that every presumption runs against a delivery to a consumer being a 'sale or return.'" Official Comment to § 2–326, Ala.Code tit. 7, § 2–326 (1975).

The transaction between Kodak and Sitkin is not a sale or return within the meaning of § 2–326, since the goods were not delivered for resale with an option to return. C.I.T., then, fails to overcome the presumption against the application of § 2–326.

The Bankruptcy Court properly concluded that the agreement between Kodak and Sitkin provided for a bailment of the unprocessed waste. Since under Alabama law the bailed goods are not subject to C.I.T.'s security interest in the inventory of the bankrupt, Kodak is entitled to reclaim possession.

Reversed.

THOMAS A. CLARK, CIRCUIT JUDGE, dissenting. I respectfully dissent. This court has recognized that "[i]n distinguishing bailments from sales, the test of a bailment is that the identical thing is to be returned in the same or in some altered form; if another thing of equal value is to be returned, the transaction is a sale." Guidry v. Continental Oil Co., 350 F.2d 342, 345 n. 10 (5th Cir.1965). Consideration of the contract at issue and the authority relied on by the majority leads me to the conclusion that this transaction was a contract to sell goods at a future time and not a bailment. Since this type of agreement amounts to a "contract for sale" under § 2–106(1) of the Uniform Commercial Code, Ala.Code § 7–2–106(1), this court's holding in In re Samuels & Co., 526 F.2d 1238 (5th Cir. 1976) (en banc), gives the C.I.T. Corporation sufficient right in the film waste under Alabama law so that its security interest attached and was superior to

Eastman Kodak's unperfected interest in the goods. Therefore, I would affirm the district court's judgment for the C.I.T. Corporation on the ground that the transaction at issue here was a sale, and accordingly Samuels controls our disposition of this appeal.

With one important exception, I agree with the majority's statement of facts in this case. The majority states that in the contract between Eastman Kodak, (hereinafter referred to as "Kodak") and Sitkin, the latter "agreed to process a minimum of 500,000 pounds of print film waste *and purchase the silver content recovered upon processing.*" Ante, at 1214 (emphasis added). I disagree. While the silver content in the film waste was without question the sole reason these companies entered into this agreement, I think the majority has incorrectly identified the goods being sold. The goods to be sold by Kodak to Sitkin were the 500,000 pounds of film waste which contained recoverable silver. There was no sale or purchase of just the silver content in the film waste. The silver content in the film waste, which could only be salvaged upon processing, was to serve only as a pricing mechanism for the sale of the 500,000 pounds of film waste. This is readily apparent from the contract itself which, because of its importance to an understanding of this case, I set forth in its entirety:

SITKIN SMELTING & REFINING, INC.
Brass, Bronze & Aluminum Ingots
Gold, Silver & Nobel Metals
P.O. Box 708 – R.D. #3
Lewistown, Pa. 17044
Phone: (717) 543–5631

No. MP 6147

EASTMAN KODAK COMPANY
KODAK PARK DIVISION
BUILDING 211
ROCHESTER, NY 14650
Attn: Mr. Dennis Zink
Sales Supervisor
Surplus Materials

Page 1 of 2

Date January 19, 1978

Sitkin Smelting & Refining, Inc. Agrees To Purchase From The Above

QUANTITY — MATERIAL

PERIOD: Two-month minimum trial contract.

MATERIAL: Loose PR–10 print film waste containing approximately 173 T.O. of silver per net ton of film waste.

VOLUME: Minimum 500,000 pounds.

LOT SIZE: Trailerload – minimum 36,000 pounds net weight.

SETTLEMENT: To be effected 30 days after receipt for each lot (trailerload).
The net dollar value for each lot payable to Kodak will be calculated by using 50% of the calculated average Handy & Harman quote for silver during the 30-day settlement period, multiplied by the agreed upon troy ounces of silver content per lot. The values quoted are minimal values only. If higher values are realized during the two-month trial contract period, those values will be automatically passed on to Kodak.

PAYMENT: 60 days after receipt.

F.O.B. Our trailers at Kodak Park, Rochester, NY

Ship on or before:

Terms See page 2.

Remarks

(1) HYDRAULICALLY BRICKED OR BRIQUETTED MATERIAL NOT ACCEPTABLE.

(2) ANY MATERIAL OVER 15 INCHES IN MORE THAN TWO DIMENSIONS WILL BE SUBJECT TO A PREPARATION CHARGE.

(3) VARIATION OF PLUS OR MINUS 5% FROM THE AGREED–UPON AMOUNT IS ALLOWABLE.

KINDLY SIGN THE ORIGINAL COPY AND RETURN IT TO US FOR OUR FILES, RETAINING THE OTHER COPY FOR YOUR FILES.

Sitkin Smelting & Refining, Inc.

Accepted ____________________

By ____________________

Date ____________________

By: /S/ David Cohen
David Cohen

Above subject to attached condition sheets

SITKIN SMELTING & REFINING, INC.
Brass, Bronze & Aluminum Ingots
Gold, Silver & Nobel Metals
P. O. Box 708 – R. D. #3
Lewistown, Pa. 17044
Phone: (717) 543–5631

No. MP 6148

EASTMAN KODAK COMPANY

Page 2 of 2

Date January 19, 1978

SITKIN SMELTING & REFINING, INC. AGREES TO PURCHASE FROM THE ABOVE

QUANTITY	MATERIAL

REMARKS: Responsibility for the material will be transferred to Sitkin upon leaving Kodak Park. Ownership or claim to the material ceases upon destruction or change of identity.

Sitkin will furnish a destruction warranty for each shipment at the time of settlement. Sitkin will furnish a secrecy agreement if deemed necessary by Kodak.

This trial contract may be terminated by either party by written notification within two (2) days of cancellation. All materials delivered to the date of cancellation will, at Kodak [sic] option, either be returned to Kodak freight collect or be processed under the contract terms.

F.O.B.

Terms

Remarks

(1) HYDRAULICALLY BRICKED OR BRIQUETTED MATERIAL NOT ACCEPTABLE.

(2) ANY MATERIAL OVER 15 INCHES IN MORE THAN TWO DIMENSIONS WILL BE SUBJECT TO A PREPARATION CHARGE.

(3) VARIATION OF PLUS OR MINUS 5% FROM THE AGREED-UPON AMOUNT IS ALLOWABLE ______

KINDLY SIGN THE ORIGINAL COPY AND RETURN IT TO US FOR OUR FILES, RETAINING THE OTHER COPY FOR YOUR FILES.

Sitkin Smelting & Refining, Inc.

Accepted Eastman Kodak Company – Kodak Park Division
W. H. Gabruk –

By /S/ W. H. Gabruk Director of Purchasing

Date January 25, 1978

By: /S/ David Cohen
David Cohen

Above subject to attached condition sheets

From its reading of the contract above and consideration of the circumstances surrounding this transaction, the majority concludes that, although it is a "close question," Sitkin's possession of the unprocessed film waste was a bailment under Alabama law. In so holding, the majority relies primarily on NYTCO Services, Inc. v. Wilson, 351 So.2d 875 (Ala.1977), and In re Medomak Canning Co., 25 U.C.C.Rep.Serv. 437 (D.Me.1978). I have reviewed the Kodak-Sitkin contract in light of those two cases. Unlike the majority, however, my conclusion is that NYTCO and Medomak require a holding here that the film waste was not being held by Sitkin as a bailee.

In NYTCO Services, Inc. v. Wilson, the Supreme Court of Alabama considered the bailment or sale question in the context of soybeans that were being stored in a grain warehouse. NYTCO Services was a New York warehousing firm that was engaged in the business of storing farmers' agricultural products in storage bins. As part of its business, NYTCO leased the Covington Grain storage facilities in Andalusia, Alabama. During the 1974 harvest season, local farmers had delivered soybeans to the Covington grain storage facility under a type of agreement which provided "for a price to be agreed upon later." 351 So. 2d at 877. Under the agreement the farmer,

> "after delivering his soybeans to Covington Grain, could purchase an equivalent quantity of soybeans with a five cents per bushel handling charge plus a one and a half cent per bushel per month storage charge. The receipts most farmers received for their deliveries were various Covington Grain weight tickets; however, some received Covington Grain statement sheets. The weight tickets had the words 'Bought of' printed on them together with the name of the farmer and some had the word 'Hold' written on them. A number of the statement sheets had the words 'Store,' 'Stored,' or 'On Storage' written on them together with the name of the farmer." Id.

The majority reasons that in NYTCO the Supreme Court of Alabama found a bailment instead of a sale for two principal reasons: (1) the farmers had the option to require the grain storage company to either return the grain or sell it; and, (2) the evidence indicated that the soybeans were being stored by the company on the farmers' behalf.

Unlike the majority, I do not find either element present in the Kodak-Sitkin transaction. My brothers suggest that Kodak had "the option under the contract to have the film waste returned or processed." Ante, at 1217. However, as the contract itself reveals, Kodak only had such an "option" if the contract were terminated by either Kodak or Sitkin. Any right Kodak may have had to cancel the contract was extinguished when the waste was processed. The majority suggests this "makes no difference" because "[a] bailment may still exist where the bailee has a continuing option to purchase or to sell." Id., at 1217. However, under the terms of the contract, Sitkin as the purported bailee was given no "continuing option to purchase or to sell." Sitkin was required by the contract to purchase the film waste, process it, and pay Kodak. Sitkin certainly had no option to decide whether to process the waste and it was not given the liberty to sell the waste without processing it first.

Examining the second factor in NYTCO the majority concludes that several aspects of the Kodak-Sitkin arrangement evidenced a bailment instead of a sale. First the majority finds support for a bailment in Sitkin's agreement to assume responsibility for the waste by picking it up at Kodak's facility in New York and transporting it to warehouses in Alabama that Sitkin had leased. I fail to see how this aspect of the transaction indicates a bailment. The film waste apparently had little if any value to Kodak due to its inferior quality. Sitkin approached Kodak and offered to turn what was to Kodak a virtually worthless commodity into a saleable commodity from which both parties could benefit financially. Sitkin was in the business of purchasing industrial waste, transporting the waste to its own processing facilities and salvaging valuable metals from what was unusable, unmarketable junk to the sellers. Sitkin's acceptance of the goods in New York is just as consistent with a sales transaction as it may be with a bailment.

The majority also notes that the film waste had Kodak's name on it, was tagged as Kodak property, and was stored in Sitkin's warehouses in the original Kodak shipping cartons. To me these facts do not support a finding of bailment. Certainly it was more practical for Sitkin to transport and store the inferior film in its original packaging and shipping cartons. There would be no reason for Sitkin to assume the added expense and trouble of removing the film from its cartons and crossing out Kodak's brand name before the company began the salvaging process.

Furthermore, the company's accounting treatment for this transaction is totally consistent with a future sale of the film waste. For the reasons that the film waste was of no value to either party in its unprocessed state and that the sales price could only be determined by the pricing formula once the waste was processed, Kodak probably could not legally carry the waste on its books as a receivable.

In re Medomak Canning Co., supra, is considered by the majority to be "an analogous case finding a bailment." Ante, at 1217. In the Medomak case, a large food concern, William Underwood Co., did not want to produce baked beans itself. Underwood wanted to acquire finished pork and bean products from other sources. The Food company entered an agreement with Medomak under which Medomak essentially would process and package the pork and beans. Underwood would purchase the food ingredients and the packaging and shipping supplies and then have them delivered to Medomak. Medomak would process the food, can it, and then ship the finished product to locations designated by Underwood. In the court's words, it considered itself presented with "an entrusting of possession of goods to be transformed by processing or manufacture *for return to the entruster or its consignees.*" 25 U.C.C.Rep.Serv. at 445 (emphasis added). The court concluded that "the parties contemplated merely that Medomak would process the goods entrusted to it by Underwood for later sale *by Underwood* to its own customers." Id. at 448 (emphasis in original).

The holding of the court in In re Medomak Canning that the processing transaction was a bailment is perfectly reasonable. The parties there clearly intended that Medomak simply receive the goods which were bought and owned by Underwood, process them, and return them to Underwood. But those circumstances which support a finding of bailment are just not present in this case. Neither Kodak nor Sitkin intended that Sitkin process the film waste and return either it or the silver content to Kodak. The only item Kodak wanted to receive from Sitkin was cash. The intent of the transaction was that the goods would be destroyed by Sitkin. There was no resale of the film waste envisioned by either Sitkin or Kodak.

Noting the Medomak court's emphasis on the fact that the parties there intended a bailment because "no purchase price was ever agreed upon in respect to those ingredients and other materials which were *never processed,*" 25 U.C.C. Rep.Serv. at 447 (emphasis in original), the majority suggests that the Kodak-Sitkin contract reproduced above "did not set a purchase price for the film waste prior to its processing." Ante, at 1217. While Kodak and Sitkin did not specify an exact dollar amount at the time of contracting, the parties did agree to a reasonable and enforceable price calculating formula based on two factors: (1) the quantity of silver recovered from the film waste; and, (2) the market value of silver during the thirty day settlement period. There is no requirement in Article 2 of the Code that a certain dollar price be stated in the contract in order for there to be a sale. Clearly, this is not a contract in which the parties failed to agree on a price for their goods. Such an "open price" situation would be governed by Ala.Code §§ 7–2–204 and 7–2–305. Kodak and Sitkin clearly agreed to a specific price setting formula. Thus, I consider the majority's reliance on the decision in Medomak to be misplaced.

Therefore, I conclude that the transaction at issue amounted to a contract for sale of the film waste. I acknowledge that in the contract Kodak sought to reserve title to the goods by providing that "[o]wnership or claim to the material ceases upon destruction or change of identity." In my view this provision evidenced the parties' intent to engage in a future sale of the goods. Kodak argues that the parties really intended two transactions from their one contract. First, Kodak contends that they agreed to a bailment. Second, according to Kodak, they also agreed to a future sale of future goods. Kodak convinced the majority that the goods being sold here were the silver ash "which had not yet come into existence" at the time of contracting. (Appellant's reply brief at 12.) This is belied by the contract. As noted at the outset, the goods being sold here were the 500,000 pounds of film waste. Ala.Code § 7–2–105 specifies that "[g]oods which are not both existing and identified are 'future' goods." Obviously, the film waste was "existing" at the time of contracting and clearly, as the film waste already had been delivered to Sitkin, the goods had been identified to the contract within the meaning of U.C.C. § 2–501, Ala.Code § 7–2–501. Whether we choose to consider the contract for sale to be a present sale or a future sale is not important, however. Under Article 2 of the Code, both types of sales are permissible and are treated similarly.

Ala.Code § 7–2–106 provides in pertinent part:

> " 'Contract for sale' includes both a present sale of goods and a contract to sell goods at a future time. A 'sale' consists in the passing of title from the seller to the buyer for a price (section 7–2–401)."

Furthermore, as Official Comment 1 to § 2–106 explains, "the rights of the parties do not vary according to whether the transaction is a present sale or a contract to sell unless the Article expressly so provides." Under Ala.Code § 7–2–103(1)(d), a seller is defined as "a person who sells or contracts to sell goods." Kodak's role in this transaction falls within this definition.

Thus, Eastman Kodak as a seller of the goods sought to reserve title to the goods until such time as they underwent the silver salvaging process. U.C.C. § 2–401 speaks directly to an effort by a seller to reserve title to goods:

> "(1) Title to goods cannot pass under a contract for sale prior to their identification to the contract (section 7–2–501), and unless otherwise explicitly agreed the buyer acquires by their identification a special property as limited by this title. *Any retention or reservation by the seller of the title (property) in goods shipped or delivered to the buyer is limited in effect to a reservation of a security interest.*"

Ala.Code § 7–2–401(1) (emphasis added). Therefore, under the logically related provisions of the Code, Kodak as a seller had only a security interest in the goods which it admittedly failed to perfect.

Because the majority has decided to view this contract as a bailment-sale hybrid transaction, my brothers chose to apply Ala.Code § 7–2–403(2) to this case. However, since I consider this transaction to be an Article 2 contract for sale, I submit that instead we should apply subsection (1) of § 2–403 to this case. Ala.Code § 7–2–403 provides in pertinent part: [quoting]

* * *

It is undisputed that at all times during the Kodak-Sitkin transaction C.I.T. had a perfected security interest in all of Sitkin's inventory, including after-acquired inventory. As the majority acknowledges, this court, sitting en banc, held in In re Samuels & Co., 526 F.2d 1238 (5th Cir.1976), that a secured creditor such as C.I.T. may be a good faith purchaser within the meaning of § 2–403(1), and thus its perfected security interest would be superior to the unperfected security interest of the original seller of the goods. The majority here states that § 2–403(1) applies only "where the bankrupt was a *purchaser* of the goods in question." Ante, at 1215. Because I consider Sitkin a "purchaser" of the film waste from Kodak, I would hold that under Samuels, C.I.T. is a good faith purchaser within the meaning of § 2–403(1) and its perfected security interest would give it title to the film waste as against Kodak, the unperfected seller of the goods to the bankrupt Sitkin.

For these reasons, I would affirm the district court's judgment for the C.I.T. Corporation.

Notes

In a subsequent case also titled *In re Sitkin Smelting and Refining,* and set out at 648 F.2d 252 (5th Cir.1981), Judge Roney passed on yet another question. He describes the issue as follows:

> Prior to its bankruptcy, Sitkin Smelting and Refining was in the business of processing industrial waste for the recovery of precious and base metals. Sitkin had an agreement with plaintiff WESGO Division of GTE Products Corporation to process certain scrap material. At WESGO's option, Sitkin agreed to either purchase the precious metals recovered upon processing or return metals of like kind and quality less a processing fee. The metals actually recovered from WESGO's scrap could not be returned, because during the refining process the metals from one client's scrap were commingled with those from other scrap.
>
> When Sitkin was adjudicated bankrupt, it had in its possession thirty-five drums of scrap material that had been delivered by WESGO. WESGO filed this suit to reclaim the unprocessed scrap.

How do you think the Fifth Circuit came out in the second *Sitkin* case?

Problem 7–4

1. United Steel Products was deeply in debt to Hoesch America, Inc. Ultimately they worked out their differences and an agreement was reached in which Hoesch would cancel its entire debt of $1,800,000 in return for U.S.P.'s transfer to it of its entire inventory. After that transfer had occurred and Hoesch had sold the steel, Maremont Corporation made a claim against Hoesch for approximately $400,000 of steel. Maremont claimed that it had purchased that steel from U.S.P. but in the downturn of the auto industry in 1983 had allowed the steel to remain in the possession of U.S.P. for more than a year. Maremont produced invoices that show that the steel formerly owned by U.S.P. had been "delivered" to it and had been paid for. In fact the steel remained in U.S.P.'s inventory and was not marked in any particular way as separate from its inventory. Is Hoesch liable to Maremont on a conversion theory (or any other theory) for the value of the steel?

2. You are counsel for First Bank. It is contemplating the possibility of being the general financer of a clock manufacturer. As such it would take perfected security principally in inventory and accounts receivable of the manufacturer. An examination of the prospective debtor's operation discloses the following: frequently and in accordance with the practice in the clock trade, buyers prepay for clocks. Typically the clocks are manufactured and put in boxes. They often sit in inventory for weeks, and in some cases, months. The bank wishes to know whether it will have a right in the clocks superior or subordinate to the rights of the buyers. The clocks are generic, that is, they are not marked with any particular buyer's name nor are any specifically designed for particular buyers. However, the boxes in which the clocks are contained will typically be marked with the buyer's name. If the Bank insists upon a prior right in order to make the loan, what do you suggest?

For one of your editors' (White) view about how these cases might be put together, consider the following:

Note: Ostensible Ownership and the Integrity of Article 9

We have already confronted the transaction in which one party signs a document entitled a "lease" which obliges him to make certain payments and gives him the option to purchase at the end of the term for a nominal consideration. The parties may frame their transaction so for a variety of reasons; never mind what they are for the time being. In UCC 9–102(1) and 1–201(37) the Code makes plain that substance is to govern form in such a transaction. A document masquerading as a lease is a security agreement. This is but one example of the function of UCC 9–102, which provides that Article 9 covers "any transaction (regardless of its form) which is intended to create a security interest in personal property * * *" Its purpose is to avoid the dismal history under which legislatures drafted laws to govern security arrangements and clever lawyers routinely escaped the grasp of such laws by devising ingenious documents that suited their clients' needs but did not fit the statutory definitions.

Many skirmishes have been fought over whether a lease was a "true lease" or a security agreement. It has always been implicit in such decisions that if one could convince the court that his document was a "true lease", he need not file a financing statement to recover the goods upon the lessee's bankruptcy. At least in the bona fide lease, the law has disregarded the fact that the debtor has possession; it has not required that the lessor make a public filing in order to protect his rights against third party claimants who might be misled by the lessee's possession.

Consider 9–102's application in a case once removed from the lease. In In re Medomak Canning Co., 25 UCC Rep.Serv. 437 (D.Me.1977), Underwood, a large New England food company, entered into an agreement with a smaller company, Medomak Canning, under which the larger would supply ingredients, packaging and shipping material for the canning and packaging of certain foodstuffs and would pay a fixed fee for the canned goods when they were shipped at its direction to third parties. The exact nature of the transaction between the parties is unclear, for the large manufacturer was apparently attempting to set up the transaction as a sale and repurchase agreement whereas Medomak would have preferred to characterize the transaction as one in which it was simply processing Underwood's goods. With very little analysis of 9–102 the court assumed that upon Medomak's bankruptcy Underwood would have the right to the return of the approximately $100,000 of canned goods, raw materials and supplies if the contract were held to be one for processing and not for purchase and resale. Under UCC 9–102 that is far from clear. It is obvious from the opinion that at least Medomak's interest in the transaction was to achieve financing, for the court points out "it lacked the necessary capital to acquire approximately $100,000 worth of ingredients and packaging and shipping materials. * * *" Conceding that the transaction was in fact not a sale, Medomak's secured creditors who were competing with Underwood might have argued that they had superior rights nevertheless because the transaction was in effect one "intended to create a security interest in personal property", thus subject to Article 9 and no more than an unperfected security interest.

Before we analyze *Medomak* consider a third case, twice removed from the lease. In Chrysler Corp. v. Adamatic Inc., 59 Wis.2d 219, 208 N.W.2d 97 (1973), reprinted supra at 188, Chrysler had been financing the manufacture of certain equipment by a Milwaukee company that went bankrupt. At the time of the bankruptcy some of the machines were complete; others were in various states of manufacture. Two of the machines in Adamatic's possession had been previously delivered to Chrysler and been returned to Adamatic for further work. Chrysler argued that it was the "owner" not only of the delivered machines but of the others as well and thus could take the assets free of the after-acquired claim of the secured lender. Chrysler won only as to two machines which had been delivered and returned. As to the rest it was simply an unsecured creditor.

How does one square the cases? Bear in mind that in the first we have a true lease of equipment to be used in the lessee's business. In the second, we have the provision of inventory to be processed by another party and then either returned to the person furnishing the inventory or sent to a third party. Thirdly we have the purchase money financer who has neither possession nor a perfected security interest but simply argues that on completion, the title passes to him because of his prior payment.

At the outset we must reject the easiest answer. It would be easiest to say that all true owners who are not in possession must file public documents to show their ownership if they are to defeat competing creditors. Such a rule is so foreign to our general ideas of ownership that no one would agree to it. No one would say that a person must file a financing statement with respect to his own automobile in the repair shop to protect himself against the claims of the repairman's creditors. For that and other reasons we reject that result as outrageous.

Perhaps we should opt for the second easiest outcome, namely to say that the debtor's possession has no significance. Thus for example we would say that if Chrysler's contract with Adamatic provided for title to pass to Chrysler upon completion of the equipment, Chrysler would *ipso facto* enjoy superior rights. The fact that Adamatic retained possession and that the goods thus remain the inventory of Adamatic would not give competing creditors any interest superior to Chrysler's. Surely we cannot tolerate that rule. We cannot tolerate it, for it would rip a huge gash in the fabric of Article 9. It would undermine the whole idea that a secured creditor can take a security interest in the debtor's inventory and, by checking the files and filing, make himself superior to almost all other claimants. So the second easiest result is also unacceptable.

Where then do we draw the line between the pure lease where we allow the lessor to retake the goods against even secured creditors notwithstanding the lessee's possession and the failure of the lessor to give public notice of his interest, and Chrysler's case on the other hand where, notwithstanding the underlying contract, we allow the other secured creditors to claim the machine in preference to Chrysler's claim that title passed to it upon completion? *Medomak* lies in this gray area and so does the consignment.

Consider some factors that one might weigh. First we might ask whether the transaction has attributes *known in the trade* (other than filing) which put competing creditors on notice of the owner's interest. Equipment leases are now widespread; surely no sensible creditor relies upon any person's possession of equipment without at least rudimentary inquiry into his rights in the goods. Exactly the same must be true of the many cars sitting in a repairman's shop and of the used clocks and watches in a jeweler's place of business. The other creditors' knowledge of the possessor's business puts them on notice of third party claims in various of those goods. A second telling factor may be the acts that the possessor expects to take with respect to the goods when he is finished with them. If he is to return them to the owner and that is known in the trade, it looks much less like a sale than if he is to pass them to third parties. Conceivably one might also be put on notice by the nature of the function to be performed. If for example large and expensive furnaces were in the plant of a person known to manufacture and install only small electric motors, that alone might be enough notice to other creditors to tell them that he was not the owner of the furnaces which were placed there for the installation of the motor and which were to be returned to the owner.

One might also look to analogous provisions of the Code to guide his judgment. Section 2–401 indicates that retention of title by a "seller" is nothing more than a security interest but that section is really not helpful, for it assumes the question, namely that there is a "buyer" and a "seller". More to the point is the idea of ostensible ownership, an idea grown in the common law and embodied in UCC 2–402(2). That doctrine tells that a creditor who is misled by a seller's continued possession after sale will have rights superior to those of the buyer. By the same token we let buyers override others' title interests in UCC 2–403 and security interests in UCC 9–307 in circumstances where the buyer is purchasing from inventory and would reasonably expect to receive clear title. UCC 2–326 draws a distinction between goods that are out "on approval" versus those that are "on sale or return". In the latter case the creditors of the possessor are likely to prevail, in the former they do not. Finally in Article 6 we find unsecured creditors with rights superior to those of a bulk purchaser in many cases. What are the unarticulated premises of these sections and how can they help in resolving the borderline secured transaction? First, they recognize what we have suggested above, namely that there are different expectations aroused by a debtor's possession of items that appear as his *inventory* than are aroused by his possession of *equipment*. Second, they reveal assumptions about the importance of the relative sophistication of the competing claimants. We find that the code subordinates relatively sophisticated persons such as bulk purchasers and buyers from farmers notwithstanding possession, but other less sophisticated claimants such as buyers in the ordinary course are given good title by the Code. We would suggest that these sections are no more than an explicit recognition and direct application of some of the general ideas and factors described above. They may serve as fruitful analogues, but neither they nor the factors described above are likely to provide certain answers.

Where does *Medomak* fall in all of this? It appears to us that it falls on the *Adamatic* side of the line. Financing the debtor was a clear purpose of the transaction. The collateral was inventory not equipment which could be expected to be returned to the original owner. The completed goods were to be shipped not back to Underwood but to various places at Underwood's direction. Moreover Underwood conceived of the transaction as a sale and repurchase and not simply as a lending for processing. Thus we think the case is wrong.

We are uncertain about the size of the gray area that lies between the true lease and the *Adamatic* case. However we are confident that this area is sizeable and that no certain answer can be given for the cases that fall within it. Consideration of the factors described above should assist a court in protecting the integrity of Article 9 and should tell it when it can safely uphold the owner, non-possessor's interest in the absence of compliance with Article 9 and without frustrating the expectations of other creditors. Nevertheless, *Medomak* illustrates that there will be hard cases on which reasonable persons will differ.

SECTION 4. THE RECLAIMING SELLER, UCC 2–702, ETC.

The Uniform Commercial Code, the Uniform Sales Act, and before that, the common law, have recognized the right of a limited class of unpaid sellers to the return of their goods in limited circumstances. This right of an unpaid seller contributes an exception to the general rule that a seller who does not specifically retain a security interest is no better off than an unsecured creditor of the buyer. That limited right of the unpaid seller to reclaim is set out principally in section 2–702 of the UCC:

> (1) Where the seller discovers the buyer to be insolvent he may refuse delivery except for cash including payment for all goods theretofore delivered under the contract, and stop delivery under this Article (Section 2–705).

(2) Where the seller discovers that the buyer has received goods on credit while insolvent he may reclaim the goods upon demand made within ten days after the receipt, but if misrepresentation of solvency has been made to the particular seller in writing within three months before delivery the ten day limitation does not apply. Except as provided in this subsection the seller may not base a right to reclaim goods on the buyer's fraudulent or innocent misrepresentation of solvency or of intent to pay.

(3) The seller's right to reclaim under subsection (2) is subject to the rights of a buyer in ordinary course or other good faith purchaser under this Article (Section 2–403). Successful reclamation of goods excludes all other remedies with respect to them.

The student should also read UCC 2–507 and 2–511, sections that have been construed to give cash sellers and sellers who receive checks on delivery rights similar to those enjoyed by credit sellers under UCC 2–702.

On their face, sections 2–702, 2–507 and 2–511 raise a series of technical, interpretative questions. What, for example, is necessary to constitute a written misrepresentation of solvency? Must the demand for return be made in writing or is an oral demand adequate to perfect the unpaid seller's rights under UCC 2–702? Does the ten day limitation embodied in UCC 2–702 also apply to UCC 2–507? What about the right to proceeds? We need not answer all of these questions here, but the student should be sensitive to them. Prior to enactment of the Bankruptcy Code in 1978, a series of cases had arisen concerning the rights of the trustee in bankruptcy vis a vis a seller reclaiming under 2–702. Routinely the trustee had argued that he was superior to the reclaiming seller either on the ground that he had a lien under 70c (now 544(a)) or that the UCC 2–702 right was, in fact, a form of statutory lien or a lien that first arose upon bankruptcy and so could be struck down under section 67 (now 546(b)). Congress sought to resolve these disputes by enacting 546(c). It reads in full as follows:

Except as provided in subsection (d) of this section, the rights and powers of a trustee under sections 544(a), 545, 547, and 549 of this title are subject to any statutory or common-law right of a seller of goods that has sold goods to the debtor, in the ordinary course of such seller's business, to reclaim such goods if the debtor has received such goods while insolvent, but—

(1) such a seller may not reclaim any such goods unless such seller demands in writing reclamation of such goods before ten days after receipt of such goods by the debtor; and

(2) the court may deny reclamation to a seller with such a right of reclamation that has made such a demand only if the court—

(A) grants the claim of such a seller priority as a claim of a kind specified in section 503(b) of this title; or

(B) secures such claim by a lien.

Do you see how Congress has left threads hanging? Compare UCC 2–702 with § 546(c). Presumably the former was the template for the latter, but the template was substantially bent before it was used!

UNITED STATES v. WEST SIDE BANK

United States Court of Appeals, Twelfth Circuit, 1984.
732 F.2d 1258.

JOHN R. BROWN, CIRCUIT JUDGE:

This statutory interpleader brought pursuant to 28 U.S.C. § 1335 was filed by the Small Business Administration (SBA) to determine the proper distribution of proceeds from a foreclosure sale. The fund represents the remaining assets of Texas Electronics Mart, Inc. (TEMI). In distributing the fund, the District Court determined that Westside Bank of San Antonio (Westside) held the only priority claim. The Court thus denied the priority status asserted by O'Sullivan Industries, Inc. (O'Sullivan) based on its right to reclaim the proceeds from the sale of goods it delivered to TEMI just prior to the foreclosure. O'Sullivan duly perfected this appeal. We hold that a seller of goods (here, O'Sullivan) retains a priority status to the extent of traceable proceeds from the sale of those goods where he has complied with all the requirements of Texas Business and Commerce Code Annotated § 2.702 (Vernon 1968) (the Texas UCC), and diligently pursued the right of reclamation created under that section. We therefore affirm in part, reverse in part, and remand for a determination of whether O'Sullivan diligently pursued its right to reclamation.

FACTUAL BACKGROUND

In April of 1976 TEMI executed a promissory note and security agreement in favor of Westside for the sum of $99,500. The note was guaranteed by the SBA. TEMI granted Westside a security interest in "all machinery, and equipment, fixtures, inventory and accounts receivable now owned, to be purchased with loan proceeds and hereafter acquired." The agreement included a future advance clause, a clause securing any legal fees incurred in enforcing the agreement, and a clause securing the interest due. Westside duly perfected its security interest.

In September of 1979, TEMI executed a second promissory note to Westside for the sum of $16,000. The note was collateralized with the 1976 security agreement through the future advance clause. At the time of trial, Westside asserted an outstanding claim on this note in the amount of $12,471.52.

Pursuant to the SBA guarantee, Westside assigned its rights under the first note to the SBA sometime in December, 1979.[3] The SBA declared the note delinquent and accelerated its maturity on December 14, 1979. In accordance with the security agreement, the SBA conducted a foreclosure sale of all TEMI's assets on January 21, 1980. After deducting the loan balance and expenses of the sale, the SBA deposited the remaining proceeds ($50,750.95) with the District Court for proper distribution among TEMI's creditors.

The District Court awarded Westside the sum of $17,666.60, representing its claim on the second note plus interest and attorney's fees. The Court, however, denied the priority right of reclamation asserted by O'Sullivan under Texas UCC

3. When a debtor defaults on a loan that the SBA has guaranteed, the lender may avoid the time, expense, and potential liability of foreclosure by assigning its rights under the loan to the SBA. The SBA then pays the lender the full amount of the loan and becomes subrogated to the rights of the lender, including any security interest or priority status the lender had attained. The UCC recognizes the utility of this practice and provides for it in § 9.504(c). Thus, when Westside assigned its rights under the first note to the SBA, both the SBA and Westside had a perfected security interest in TEMI's assets pursuant to the security agreement executed in April of 1976.

§ 2.702. The Court reasoned that any right of reclamation would be cut short by a prior secured lender's foreclosure. Because in this case the SBA had foreclosed, the Court found that O'Sullivan had no right to the proceeds from the sale of the goods. In disposing of the case on this basis, the District Court deemed it unnecessary to reach the issue whether O'Sullivan had complied with the statutory requirements for reclamation under § 2.702. The Court therefore distributed the remaining funds pro rata among O'Sullivan and TEMI's other general unsecured creditors.

THE RECLAMATION RIGHT

The right of reclamation is specifically created in favor of a credit seller by Texas UCC § 2.702. This right exists only in "specific and limited circumstances; it can be asserted only if an exacting procedure is followed; and the right can never be asserted to defeat the interest of certain third parties who have dealt with the defaulting buyer." *Matter of Samuels & Co., Inc.,* 526 F.2d 1238 (5th Cir.1976) (en banc), *cert. denied,* 429 U.S. 834, 97 S.Ct. 98, 50 L.Ed.2d 99 (1976).

In order for the right to arise, certain conditions must be met. First, the buyer must have received the goods on credit. There is no dispute that TEMI received the goods shipped by O'Sullivan on credit. Second, the buyer must receive the goods while insolvent. The District Court made no finding as to when TEMI became insolvent, but it did find that O'Sullivan did not know of TEMI's insolvency when it shipped the goods. Finally, the seller must learn of the buyer's insolvency and make demand for return of the goods within ten days from the date of delivery. The District Court found that O'Sullivan shipped furniture accessories valued at $36,756.94 on November 19 and 21, 1979, and that the shipments were received by TEMI on November 21 and 23, respectively. The Court determined that O'Sullivan learned of TEMI's insolvency sometime between November 21 and November 30. It also found that O'Sullivan made written demand for payment of the entire amount of TEMI's open account ($50,727.07) on November 30.

In addition to the demand made upon TEMI, O'Sullivan also made written demand upon Westside[6] through O'Sullivan's parent corporation, Conroy, Inc. The letter from Conroy also demanded payment for the full amount of TEMI's open account. This letter, however, also specified that it was a demand pursuant to § 2.702 of the Texas UCC. The goods were not returned, nor was payment made to O'Sullivan.

O'Sullivan filed suit against TEMI in state court on January 18, 1980 to enforce its right of reclamation. However, on January 21 the SBA foreclosure sale was conducted, and TEMI ceased to exist for all practical purposes as a business entity. This effectively terminated the state court litigation. In order to further protect the reclamation right it was asserting, O'Sullivan repurchased

6. The record implies that O'Sullivan was unable to locate TEMI's principal officers. The issue presented is whether by November 30 Westside had assumed control of TEMI so as to become its fiduciary representative. If so, then written demand on Westside would be equivalent to written demand on TEMI. We find however, that there are insufficient facts in the record to determine this issue. Therefore, we remand for the limited purpose of resolving whether O'Sullivan's demands on Westside were tantamount to proper demand upon TEMI. *See* note 21, *infra. See also U.S. v. Terrey,* 554 F.2d 685 (5th Cir.1977) (where a creditor decides to liquidate collateral, he must act as the debtor's fiduciary in disposing of assets); *Tackett v. Mid-Continent Refrigerator Co.,* 579 S.W.2d 545 (Tex.Civ.App.1979) (secured party who repossesses property has duty to make commercially reasonable disposition on account for proceeds).

797 of the 1,000 pieces of furniture from the November shipment at the foreclosure sale for a price of $27,500. On appeal, O'Sullivan continues to urge its priority status as to the full sales proceeds of $36,756.94. Alternatively, it urges priority status as to $27,500—the traceable proceeds from the goods O'Sullivan has sought to reclaim.

In determining that O'Sullivan's right to reclaim was terminated by the SBA foreclosure and therefore could not attach to proceeds, the District Court relied on *Matter of Samuels, supra.* We believe the Court's reliance was misplaced.

Distinguishing Samuels

In *Samuels,* a divided *en banc* Court adopted Judge Godbold's dissent from the panel opinion, which held that an unpaid *cash* seller's right of reclamation is subordinate to a preexisting perfected security interest in the buyer's after acquired property. *Id.* at 1245. In so holding, the Court emphasized several important factors which are not present in the case before us. At the outset, the Court recognized that the reclaiming seller was a *cash* seller. *Id.* at 1244. Furthermore, he had not made a demand under § 2.702 until a full year after the delivery. The Court refused to find that his reclamation right had been timely exercised. *Id.* at 1245. Disturbed by the fact that in recognizing the cash seller's right to reclaim courts had extended the § 2.702 remedy, the Court refused to further extend the time within which the right could be exercised.

* * * [T]he meticulous analysis provided by *Samuels* regarding the interplay between Articles Two and Nine of the UCC is fully consistent with a finding in favor of O'Sullivan in the instant case. Turning first to the Texas UCC, § 2.401(a), the *Samuels* Court determined that the seller's interest was in the nature of a security interest. *Samuels, supra,* 526 F.2d at 1246. The Court went on to recognize that the UCC makes security interests that arise by operation of law under Article Two (such as the right of reclamation) subject to Article Nine. *Samuels, supra,* 526 F.2d at 1247. The Court found this crucial to the final outcome. It is not inconsistent with this reasoning for us to hold now that the express language of § 9.504, which makes the power of foreclosure "subject to Article Two," creates a duty in the foreclosing creditor to recognize and protect any Article Two interest of which the creditor is aware. Rather, such a holding reemphasizes the internal consistency of the UCC.

Finally, we find the fact that *Samuels* was a bankruptcy proceeding to be an important distinction. This is crucial because the *Samuels* Court treated the reclamation right there as an unperfected security interest. Under bankruptcy law, an unperfected security interest is cut short by the trustee's status as a hypothetical lien creditor against all assets in the debtor's estate from the date the petition is filed. In the instant case, bankruptcy was not pending; therefore, there is no hypothetical lien creditor to cut short O'Sullivan's interest, and none of TEMI's general creditors have attained that status.

The Right to Proceeds

The issue whether a right of reclamation extends to proceeds has not been squarely addressed in Texas. For the reasons set out below, we hold that a seller's right of reclamation under § 2.702, if properly exercised, extends to traceable proceeds from the sale of goods where all prior interests in those goods have been fully satisfied. To hold otherwise would in many instances render the statutory remedy a nullity. In most instances, a buyer such as TEMI has granted a security interest in his after acquired property to at least one of his financing creditors. The seller is already second in priority to that lender. Furthermore, the right to reclaim goods does not arise unless the buyer is insolvent, a condition that makes foreclosure by the prior lender more than likely. Often there will be very little, if any, money left after the priority debts are paid. To hold that such a foreclosure terminates a reclaiming seller's rights to any remaining proceeds would in most cases emasculate the reclamation remedy. We recognize that Article Nine provides a means by which a seller can defeat prior liens, however, we are not faced with such a situation here. In enacting § 2.702 we believe that the Texas Legislature intended to provide an entirely separate remedy, outside the complexities of Article Nine. It is a remedy which enables a seller to maintain a priority status against the buyer's *unsecured* creditors in a situation such as this. We find support for this position in many contexts.

PRIORITY UNDER THE UCC

Turning first to the language of the statute, the seller's right is made subject to the rights of "a buyer in the ordinary course or other good faith purchaser or lien creditor under this chapter (Section 2.403)." Texas UCC § 2.702(c). Comment 3 to that section lists precisely those interests to which the seller's rights are made subject. Conspicuously missing are the buyer's general unsecured creditors. Quite the contrary, the comment expressly states that "this section constitutes preferential treatment as against the buyer's other creditors."

The Ninth Circuit has held that the Texas right of reclamation survives bankruptcy; thus the right of the trustee as a hypothetical lien creditor cannot supercede the right of the seller to reclaim despite the words of the statute. *Matter of Daylin,* 596 F.2d 853, 855–56 (9th Cir.1979). Citing *In re Telemart Enterprises, Inc.,* 524 F.2d 761 (9th Cir.1975), as authority, the *Daylin* Court further held that:

> Section 2.702 authorizes the exact equivalent of the common law remedy of rescission, and therefore sales described by that section result in a transfer of only voidable title. Consequently, the seller's right can only be cut off by a good faith purchaser for value.

Daylin, supra, 596 F.2d at 856 (citation omitted).

The District Court reasoned that O'Sullivan's right of reclamation was completely terminated when the SBA, as a prior lienholder, foreclosed. However, under the UCC system, the prior lienholder has several duties upon foreclosure of its lien that are designed to protect both the interests of the buyer and those of the buyer's other creditors. Texas UCC § 9.501 *et seq.* The SBA was charged with these duties when it became subrogated to Westside's position. Texas UCC § 9.504(e).

For example, a secured party's right to dispose of collateral is "subject to the chapter on sales (Chapter 2)," therefore, a seller's reclamation right, which is created under Chapter Two, is implicitly recognized as a limitation on the seller's ability to dispose of a debtor's assets. Texas UCC § 9.504(a). Furthermore, § 9.504(a) provides that after the lienholder satisfies its own claim, the proceeds of the sale must be applied to the satisfaction of any junior security interests if written demand is received. The record here clearly reveals that O'Sullivan made written demand on Westside, advising Westside of its § 2.702 claim prior to the foreclosure on TEMI's assets.

After junior interests are satisfied, the secured party must account to the debtor. "[W]here the secured party knows the collateral is owned by a person who is not the debtor, the owner of the collateral and not the debtor is entitled to any surplus." Texas UCC § 9.504(b), Comment 2.

If the nature of a seller's right of reclamation in Texas is that of an unperfected security interest, *see Matter of Samuels, supra,* 526 F.2d at 1244–46, then it seems clear that O'Sullivan was entitled to second priority status with regard to the proceeds after making demand. * * *

However, if O'Sullivan's interest is classified as the "equivalent" of a right to rescind, thereby enabling it to void the buyer's title, *Daylin, supra,* 596 F.2d at 856, then Westside was on notice that the goods in fact were owned by someone other than the debtor, and should have accounted to O'Sullivan for the proceeds. Finally, both the SBA and Westside implicitly recognized that O'Sullivan had retained an interest in the goods by giving O'Sullivan notice of the time and place of the foreclosure sale.

Bankruptcy Reform Act of 1978

While no bankruptcy petition was filed in the instant case, the treatment of a seller's right of reclamation under the new bankruptcy code provides a useful analogy. It is generally recognized that the UCC and the bankruptcy code were intended to provide a comprehensive and interrelated scheme for recognizing different property rights. Hence, the priority scheme of the UCC is incorporated into the bankruptcy code. The new code contains an express provision for dealing with the state UCC created right of reclamation in 11 U.S.C. § 546(c). The legislative history of that section makes clear that "the purpose of the provision is to recognize, in part, the validity of § 2–702 of the Uniform Commercial Code, which has generated much litigation, confusion, and divergent decisions in different circuits." House Judiciary Report No. 95–595 to accompany House Report 8200, 95th Cong., 1st Sess. (1977) pp. 371–72, U.S.Code Cong. & Admin.News 1978, pp. 5787, 6328.

While § 546(c) does not reverse the holding of *Samuels,* it does provide that the trustee's status as a hypothetical lien creditor is *subordinate* to the seller's right of reclamation. Furthermore, if the Court utilizes its power to deny the seller's right of reclamation, it must adequately protect the seller's interest by granting the seller's claim priority as an administrative expense or securing the claim with a lien. 11 U.S.C. § 546(c)(2). Thus, the post-*Samuels,* new bankruptcy code deals with a seller's right of reclamation as equivalent to a perfected security interest under Article Nine. *See* 11 U.S.C. § 363. Finally, the House Report indicates that Congress intended to extend the right of reclamation to proceeds:

> The right is subject however, to the power of the court to deny reclamation and protect the seller by granting him *a priority as an administrative expense for his claim arising out of the sale of the goods.*

House Report, *supra,* at 372, U.S.Code Cong. & Admin.News 1978, p. 6328. (emphasis added). Hence, we see that § 546(c) was intended to allow the reclaiming seller a priority claim against the *proceeds* from the sale of the goods when the Court chooses not to return the goods themselves. Clearly this constitutes "preferential treatment against the buyer's general unsecured creditors." *See* Texas UCC § 2.702 comment 3.

Conclusion

On the basis of all the foregoing, we hold that where a seller of goods has diligently asserted its right of reclamation and otherwise met the requirements of § 2.702, and where all prior lienholders have been fully satisfied, that seller's claim will be afforded priority status as against the buyer's general unsecured creditors. Furthermore, we hold that such a seller's priority will extend to proceeds that are traceable to the goods. We therefore reverse the District Court's holding as to this last point. * * * However, the District Court was clearly correct in granting Westside first priority to the interpleaded fund.

Affirmed in part, reversed in part and remanded.

[Some footnotes omitted.]

Notes

Is it obvious that a secured creditor's claim to after-acquired property is superior to the seller's rights under UCC 2–702?

Problem 7–5

Ronald's Steel Service Center sold steel to Regulation Manufacturing, a builder of truck bodies. Some steel it delivered on March 1, other it delivered on April 10, and still another shipment was shipped on April 8 and arrived at the buyer's loading dock on April 12. On April 17, Regulation filed in Chapter 11. Subsequently it developed that Regulation had been circulating inaccurate balance sheets that showed its finances to be much healthier than they were. It appears that Regulation's liabilities exceeded its assets about a month after its December balance sheet was circulated.

1. Ronald now asks whether it will be able to recover any of the steel from the trustee in bankruptcy. (You may assume that Ronald has taken no step to recover; that it is now April 24 and that there is no claim by a secured creditor.)

2. Contrary to the facts given above, assume that one of the competitors is a secured creditor who had a security interest in all of Regulation's inventory, including after-acquired property. If the secured creditor is not perfected, does that change the analysis?

SECTION 5. PERSONAL PROPERTY SECURITY INTERESTS IN REAL ESTATE TRANSACTIONS

Read UCC 9–102(3), Comment 4 to UCC 9–102 and section 9–104(j). If you now see the potential conflict and confusion among these three provisions you enjoy the beginning of wisdom. If you also realize that this conflict and confusion is compounded because the transactions to which the rules apply are so numerous and varied then you will have taken another major step forward. Consider some of the possibilities: a customer (a real estate mortgagee) might come to the bank seeking a loan and offering as security his debtor's mortgage and note. This is the case contemplated by Comment 4 to UCC 9–102. (It is also possible that the mortgagee might be a financial institution and might offer a bushelbasket full of notes and mortgages.) Still another debtor might, as a vendor, or as an assignee of a vendor, offer as security a vendor's interest under a real estate installment sale contract. In each of these cases one could argue that some part of the transaction is governed by Article 9. In almost all such cases, one could make a plausible argument that our bank should disregard Article 9 and should instead execute a document under the local real estate law and record something in the local real estate records.

In 1978 some of these problems were solved while still others were compounded by enactment of section 541(d) of the Bankruptcy Code. That section reads as follows:

> Property in which the debtor holds, as of the commencement of the case, only legal title and not an equitable interest, such as a mortgage secured by real property, or an interest in such a mortgage, sold by the debtor but as to which the debtor retains legal title to service or supervise the servicing of such mortgage or interest, becomes property of the estate under subsection (a)(1) or (2) of this section only to the extent of the debtor's legal title to such property, but not to the extent of any equitable interest in such property that the debtor does not hold.

Clearly this subsection was designed to cover the case in which the originator of mortgages (for example, a Savings and Loan) sells the interests in those mortgages to another party, but continues to service them. In effect, Congress is telling the trustee to keep his hands off such a transaction and to permit the purchaser of the mortgages to keep them in preference to the trustee's claims.

But here too lurk the seeds of controversy. Note that § 541(d) applies only to mortgages "sold." Does that mean that when one takes an interest in a mortgage that would be characterized not as a purchase or sale of the mortgage, but as a loan against it, § 541(d) does not apply? Observe also that although § 541(d) presumably subordinates the trustee (even his claim under § 544 when it is applicable), it does nothing to determine the priorities among purchaser or lender and other creditors not represented by the trustee.

One plausible way to approach the cases is to view the mortgagee's interest (and the vendor's interest and the lessor's interest) as essentially an interest in personal property, mostly an interest in a stream of promised payments. So viewed, such an interest, as security, would be collateral subject to Article 9 and other personal property rules. At the same time, use of the possessory interest as security—that of the mortgagor (and the lessee and the vendee) would be subject to the rules governing security in real estate. One wishing to take a security interest in the possessory end of things would have to comply with applicable real estate law and do a real estate recording. How should the cases set out below be analyzed and classified?

IN RE KENNEDY MORTGAGE CO.

United States Bankruptcy Court, District, New Jersey, 1982.
17 B.R. 957.

OPINION

WILLIAM LIPKIN, BANKRUPTCY JUDGE.

On March 9, 1981, an involuntary Petition for Relief was filed against the above named Debtor, Kennedy Mortgage Company (Debtor) and on the same day the Debtor consented to the Order for Relief under the provisions of the Bankruptcy Code, 11 U.S.C. 101 sequi.

Generally stated—the Debtor's principal activity was to process applications submitted to it for mortgages on real estate and for the advancement of the funds to the mortgage applicants necessary for completion of settlement. To that end, in addition to lending its own money, the Debtor entered into agreements with various banks and lending institutions for lines of credit whereby the Debtor was to be supplied with funds to carry out the mortgage settlements. The activity of the Debtor with such banks and lending institutions involved many mortgages totaling over forty (40) millions of dollars, as stated to me by the parties.

The banks with whom the Debtor established lines of credit are located in other States as well as New Jersey.

More specifically stated, as to the procedure followed between the Debtor and a lending bank, with whom the Debtor had an agreement establishing a line of credit, whereby the Debtor was put into actual receipt of funds, the transactions giving rise to the Complaint herein of the First National Bank of Boston (FNBB) are generally illustrative.

On August 19, 1980, FNBB and the Debtor entered into a Letter Agreement whereby FNBB agreed to extend to the Debtor a direct revolving warehousing line of credit not to exceed $10,000,000.00 and on that same date the Debtor executed its Demand Promissory Note in the principal sum of $10,000,000.00 with interest to float at the FNBB "Bank Rate". In conjunction therewith the Debtor executed a Letter of Credit and Security Agreement to the FNBB whereby the Debtor granted to FNBB a security interest in the mortgage notes and proceeds thereof to be pledged to FNBB to secure the Debtor's borrowings from FNBB pursuant to the Letter Agreement and the Demand Promissory note.

On February 13, 1981, the Debtor delivered to FNBB four (4) notes totaling the sum of $189,950.00 and on February 18, 1981, it delivered to FNBB a note for $44,150.00, a total of $234,100.00, upon which FNBB advanced to the Debtor the sum of $215,428.18 under the Letter Agreement and Note to it. Thus, the supplier of the funds, FNBB was given possession of the Notes executed by the five mortgagors arising out of the mortgage settlements.

At the time of the settlements the Debtor executed assignments of the mortgages to FNBB which were also delivered along with the original notes. The original mortgages were not delivered to FNBB because the Debtor delivered them to the proper office for recording. The Debtor also delivered various other papers as FNBB may have requested.

The assignments of the mortgages to FNBB were not recorded.

A bit of history is now in order as to the usual course of conduct of such financing by the lending banks. The financing by the so called "mortgage company", or mortgage broker, such as Kennedy, the Debtor, in this case, whereby the lending banks put up money to finance the mortgages is called "warehousing". The lenders have extended a line of credit to the mortgage company and within such limits lend money to the broker and then upon receipt of the note and unrecorded assignment of the mortgage "warehouse" the instruments for a period of time and then possibly sells them to investors in mortgages or transfers them into a pool of mortgages purchased by the Government National Mortgage Association known as "GNMA" or similar entities.

Consistent with such practice and procedures FNBB was in possession on March 9, 1981, the date of the commencement of proceedings in this Court, of the five notes and unrecorded assignments of mortgages as set forth above.

Thereafter, FNBB was advised by the Trustee that the notes were to be sold by the Trustee and become part of GNMA pool being formed by the North Carolina National Bank Mortgage Company (NCNB).[1] FNBB did transmit the

1. Purchase of notes and mortgages by GNMA is not on an individual basis. GNMA purchases such notes and mortgages in very large total numbers and sums and banks or mortgage brokers combine such instruments to make a "pool" of the required amount. In this instance the pool was three million ($3,000,000.00) dollars.

instruments to NCNB in trust and upon sale of the pool the lien claimed by FNBB was to be transferred to the proceeds of sale, with the proceeds to be deposited in an escrow account. Consistent therewith I entered an Order dated March 19, 1981, and the notes and mortgages were sold to GNMA and the proceeds of the sale were deposited in an escrow account with the Fidelity Union Trust Company located in the State of New Jersey.

The sum on deposit associated with the 5 notes and mortgages is $222,395.00.

The parties in this estate, in the interest of preservation of the assets and administration of the Estate, had entered into a stipulation dated the same day, March 19, 1981, dealing with such matters, as in the present issue, whereby it was agreed in paragraph 11

> "There shall be paid to FNBB, IVB and Heritage the funds in their respective escrow accounts upon establishment of the validity and priority of their respective liens, but not more than the amount secured by such established liens."

The Order, to which I have referred, further provided, inter alia, that—

> "Interest on the Escrow accounts shall be payable as the interests of the parties shall appear as determined by the Court."

FNBB now seeks to have me determine that it had a valid lien upon the notes and mortgages and has a right to payment of $222,395.00 plus interest from the escrow account deposited with the National State Bank of Elizabeth.

Basically therefore this Complaint seeks a determination of its alleged lien upon the Escrow Fund to the extent of the 5 notes and mortgages which it sold into the GNMA pool. * * *

* * * On October 5, 1981, the FNBB filed a Motion for a Summary Judgment under the provisions of Bankruptcy Rule 756 (F.R.C.P. 56), supported by a brief and affidavits, alleging,

> "There is no genuine issue as to any material fact and that FNBB is entitled to judgment as a matter of law (i) determining that FNBB has a validly perfected lien with respect to the five transactions at issue (and which became a part of a GNMA pool pursuant to a Stipulation and Order of this Court dated March 19, 1981, a copy of which is attached as Exhibit "A" to the Memorandum in support of this Motion,) and (ii) directing that Robert W. Larson, Trustee, pay to FNBB $222,395.00 from the Escrow Account established pursuant to said Stipulation and Order which contains the proceeds of sale of the notes subject to FNBB's lien, plus interest which has accrued on said escrow account and directing further that Robert W. Larson, Trustee, pay to FNBB an additional amount representing its attorneys fees, costs and per diem interest in excess of the amount in said escrow account."

At first blush, because of the indoctrination that is prevalent today in the commercial world where a creditor has not recorded its lien, pursuant to the requirements of the Uniform Commercial Code, it would appear that FNBB would not have rights superior to other creditors, and in this case superior to the Trustee of the Debtor Estate, who stands in the position of a judgment creditor holding a levy and lien on the Debtors assets. That would appear to be the fact in this case where FNBB obtained possession of a note payable by the mortgagor to the Debtor which note is only a promise to pay or acknowledgment of the debt in written form. The debt to the Debtor, represented by a note was secured by a mortgage, duly recorded, which protected the *Debtor* mortgagee, against any creditors of the *mortgagor.*

A mortgage instrument, though manifesting a lien on real estate, is, actually personal property as to the mortgagee, and in order to be effective in favor of the *mortgagee* as against other *creditors of the mortgagor* must be recorded in the proper office where the real estate is located. The rights of the creditors of the mortgagor are inferior to the rights of the mortgagee.

In this case the plaintiff received possession of the note which evidenced the debt and an assignment of the mortgage which it did not record.

The question therefore is—does the Trustee as a judgment creditor of the debtor, *mortgagee,* holding a lien and levy, have a superior right to the mortgages (and now their proceeds) over FNBB because the assignments to it were not recorded.

Great stress has been made of the fact that a decision which would deny FNBB a security interest in the mortgages would be upsetting to the commercial world.

It was disclosed that mortgage brokers arrange for placing of mortgages throughout the entire United States in the hundreds of millions of dollars and they obtain funds for such purposes from banks and other lending institutions and only surrender possession of the notes and deliver unrecorded assignments of the mortgages upon completion of the mortgage settlement. The bank and lending institutions warehouse the loans and sell them to investors or to GNMA or governmental agencies in blocks of millions of dollars. The method now used for financing of the mortgages would be seriously affected if every assignment had to be recorded. It would require searches of title and delay in transfers as well as involve considerable expense for recording and the recording of assignments. The easy access that mortgage brokers now have for a source of funds would be disrupted and reduce the availability of funds in the mortgage market. However, I cannot let that business practice be the sole and dominant factor in my decision in upholding the right of FNBB to the proceeds of a mortgage under an unrecorded assignment thereof, if the provisions of the Uniform Commercial Code and the Bankruptcy Code clearly dictate a different conclusion. If the Uniform Commercial Code or Bankruptcy Code or State Statutes dictated with certainty that an assignment of a mortgage on real estate be recorded in order to render the lien effective against creditors of the assignor then lending institutions would be obliged to record such assignments regardless of the cost and inconvenience. To hold otherwise would constitute judicial legislation on my part.

However, in determining the interpretation to be made of the pertinent statute, consistent with the limitations imposed upon a Court in determining the rights of litigants which flow from statutes, whereby the Court does not engage in judicial legislation, I am also mindful that the interpretation of such statutes does and should be considered in the light of modern business practices as stated in *Bristol Associates,* 505 F.2d 1056, 1062 (3 Cir.1974). Therein the Court held

> "While a uniform trade practice does not constitute proof that the legal consequences of the practice are what those in the field take them to be, neither can it be assumed that a legislature which passed the Code and

which has considered and passed amendments to it on several occasions would let stand practices or beliefs which it disapproved. * * *

Where language is susceptible of two reasonable meanings, a court, in the commercial field, should choose that interpretation which comports with current universal practices in the business world."

Consistent therewith, I am of the opinion that it is not necessary under the Uniform Commercial Code or the Bankruptcy Code or State Statutes for an assignee of a mortgage to record the assignment of the mortgage in order to have a secured status.

In interpreting and construing the applicable law the provision of the Uniform Commercial Code dealing with General Provisions must be observed wherein it is provided:

12 A:1–102

(1) This Act shall be liberally construed and applied to promote its underlying purposes and policies.

(2) Underlying purposes and policies of this Act are

(a) to simplify, clarify and modernize the law governing commercial transactions;

(b) to permit the continued expansion of commercial practices through custom, usage and agreement of the parties;

(c) to make uniform the law among the various jurisdictions.

More particularly as to the Uniform Commercial Code sections which apply to this case dealing with Secured Transactions I observe the following provisions of 12A:9;—Policy and Scope of Chapter,

"102. Policy and Scope of Chapter [quoting] * * *

"Section 104—Transactions Excluded from Chapter.

This Chapter does not apply

(j) except to the extent that provision is made for fixtures in 12A:9–313, to the creation or transfer of an interest in or lien on real estate, including a lease or rents thereunder; (underlining added)

"Section 302. When Filing Is Required to Perfect Security Interest; Security Interests to Which Filing Provisions of This Chapter *Do Not Apply.*

(1) A financing statement must be filed to perfect all security interest *except* the following:

(a) a security interest in collateral in possession of the secured party under 12A:9–305;" (underlining added)

"304—A Security interest in chattel paper or negotiable documents may be perfected by filing. A security interest in instruments (other than instruments which constitute part of chattel paper) can be perfected only by the secured party's taking possession, except as provided in subsections (4) and (5)." (Underlining added)

"Section 305—*When Possession* by Secured Party Perfects Security Interest Without Filing.

A security interest in letters of credit and advices of credit * * * goods, instruments, negotiable documents or chattel paper may be perfected by the secured party's taking possession of the collateral. * * * A security interest is perfected by possession from the time possession is taken without relation back and continues only so long as possession is retained, unless otherwise specified in this Chapter."

The foregoing sections require a bifurcation in treatment of the note and the unrecorded assignment of the mortgage.

Clearly as to the note executed by the mortgagor to the Debtor the plaintiff, FNBB has a possessory lien thereon. No creditor including the Trustee of the Debtor Estate could claim a right to the obligation represented by the tangible note in the possession of FNBB.

In the *Matter of Bristol Associates, Inc.,* 505 F.2d 1056, 1061 (3 Cir.1974) the court clearly resolved the question whether a promissory note falls within the scope of Article 9 by virtue of its status as an instrument. As stated therein possession of such an instrument creates a perfected lien in favor of the FNBB.

Under the provisions of Sections 302(1)(a) and 304(1) and 305, FNBB perfected its lien on the notes as security for the debt by reason of possession of the notes.

Does the U.C.C. require recording the assignment of the mortgage associated with the note? Can a creditor of the Debtor issue an execution upon the asset represented by the mortgage of record standing in the name of the Debtor as mortgagee? He can do so but the rights that would flow to such execution creditors would be limited by intervening rights of other parties such as the rights of FNBB arising out of the assignment of the mortgage even though the assignment was unrecorded. This conclusion is fortified by the expression of the Supreme Court of New Jersey in *Burke v. Hoffman,* 28 N.J. 467, 475, 147 A.2d 44 (1958) wherein the Court stated

> "A mortgage debt, although a chose in action is yet, where the subject of the security is land, 'an interest in land,' and priorities are governed by the rules applicable to interests in land, and not by the rules which govern interest in personalty.
>
> Pomeroy Ibid., ¶ 697. See also ¶ 712."

See also *Garnick v. Serewitch,* 39 N.J.Super. 486, 496, 121 A.2d 423 (Ch. 1956) wherein it was stated

> "A mortgage is a lien or an interest in realty." * * *

The application for the reasons expressed in *Bristol Associates,* supra, dealing with subsection (j) of Section 12A:9–104 which relates to transactions to be excluded from Chapter 9, and subsection (3) of 12A:9–102 as interpreted by the comment 4 associated with subsection (3), which relates to an obligation secured by a transaction, are indicated in this case. Specifically dealing with 12A:9–102(3) as it relates to mortgages on real estate associated with notes which have been assigned the comment 4 reads as follows:

> "An illustration of subsection (3) is as follows:
>
> The owner of Blackacre borrows $10,000 from his neighbor, and secures his note by a mortgage on Blackacre. This Article is not applicable to the creation of the real estate mortgage. Nor is it applicable to a sale of the note by the mortgagee even though the mortgage continues to secure the note. However, when the mortgagee pledges the note to secure his own obligation to X, this Article applies to the security interest thus created, which is a security interest in an instrument even though the instrument is secured by a real estate mortgage. This Article leaves to other law the question of the effect on rights under the mortgage of delivery or non-

delivery of the mortgage or of recording or non-recording of an assignment of the mortgagee's interest. See Section 9–104(j). But under Section 3–304(5) recording of the assignment does not of itself prevent X from holding the note in due course." (Underlining added)

In dealing with "*other law*"the law of the State of New Jersey is stated in *Rose v. Rein,* 116 N.J.Eq. 70, 73, 172 A. 510 (E & A 1934) which is in accord with *Leonard v. Leonia Heights Land Company,* 81 N.J.Eq. 489, 87 A. 645 (E & A 1913) wherein the court held that an unrecorded assignment of a mortgage is not void as against subsequent judgment creditors. The references to the various statutes in these two decisions may now be found in N.J.S.A. 46:16–1, which provides all deeds or instruments enumerated therein, which included mortgages and assignment of mortgages affecting real estate may be recorded in the office of the county recording offices wherein the real estate is situate.

The effect of recording instruments described in 46:16–1 is found in 46:21–1 wherein it is stated that such filing of record shall be notice to all subsequent creditors, purchasers and mortgagees of the execution of the deed or instrument so recorded and the contents thereof. In addition, 46:17–1 provides for the Registration of Mortgages in the office of the courts recording officer of the county in which the real estate is situate. Finally, as it concerns the issues before me, the provisions of N.J.S.A. 46:18–3 and 4 provide for an indexing record of assignment of mortgages and entry in books of records of assignments of mortgages.

The fact that assignments of mortgages may be recorded does not affect the validity of an assignment of a mortgage which has not been recorded. *Leonard v. Leonia Heights Land Company,* supra; *Clift v. Scheuts,* 83 N.J.Eq. 442 (Ch. 1914) 91 A. 815. The purposes of recording is to establish priorities and rights of individuals who are affected by chain of title or encumbrances on the real estate such as grantees of real estate from record title holders thereof or innocent mortgagors who are obligated to make payment on their mortgages.

As stated hereinabove, the nature of the property involved, namely a mortgage, though personal property of itself, represents an interest in real estate and therefore it is to be included as one of the included items covered by the Uniform Commercial Code under the provisions of Section 9–104(j) which, repeating, reads

> "This Chapter does not apply * * * (j) * * * to the creation of an interest in or lien on real estate * * *"

This construction given to this subsection is a commercially reasonable interpretation. *Bristol Associates,* supra 1063; *In re Middle Atlantic Stud Welding Co.,* 503 F.2d 1133 (3d Cir.1974).

The philosophy of all recording acts, be it as to personalty or realty, is to give notice to possible later purchasers, grantees, creditors and assignees of the status of title or prior interest of any entity in the property involved. In the instant case there was a valid recorded mortgage supported by a note evidencing an indebtedness by the owner of the property, the mortgagor, to the creditor, Debtor, Kennedy.

Any one seeking to buy the property or further encumber the property or obtain an assignment of the mortgage was on notice of a mortgage to Kennedy. They would be obliged to inquire of the owner by a declaration of no-setoff as to the amount admitted due and recognition by the mortgagor that no defense was claimed and that the lien was still in existence; an inquiry would be necessary of the mortgagee as to the amount outstanding on the indebtedness. Should an assignment of the mortgage not be of record then payment to the mortgagee in satisfaction of the mortgage by any one without knowledge of the assignment would be effective against the holder of the unrecorded assigned mortgage. However, the purposes of the recording statutes are being served, and under *Rose v. Rein,* supra and *Leonard v. Leonia Heights,* it is not necessary to record an assignment of the mortgage. Moreover, one important facet must now be recognized—a mortgage is security for a debt. Without the manifestation of the debt, usually evidenced by a note or bond, the mortgage instrument itself is subject to attack. The lien of a mortgage is regarded as no greater than the actual debt secured.

> "The mortgage is regarded primarily as a security; the debt is the principal fact, and the mortgage is collateral thereto."

Grennon v. Kramer, 111 N.J.Eq. 337, 340, 162 A. 758 (E & A 1932) 55 Am.Jur.2d 133. The existence of an obligation to be secured is an essential element of a mortgage.

* * *

> As stated in Am.Jur.2d 133, "The existence of an obligation to be secured is an essential element of a mortgage. The mortgage has no efficacy if unaccompanied by a debt or obligation, either preexisting, created at the time, or contracted to be created. Accordingly, where the obligation secured fails, the mortgage is likewise commonly considered to be a nullity, and a mortgage or deed of trust in the nature of a mortgage given to secure an obligation void by positive prohibition of laws is of no force." [4]

In this case, the FNBB is the owner of the note, secured by the mortgage. Anyone interested in acquiring an interest in the mortgage would be obliged to obtain an interest in the debt. The Trustee in this case could not realize upon a mortgage if he did not own the obligation represented by the note. The failure to record the assignment of the mortgage would not be fatal to the right of FNBB to realize upon the mortgage as against parties such as judgment creditors of the Debtor because FNBB has a perfected lien on the note and the mortgage is only collateral to the note. The mortgage without the debt is of no effect.

For the foregoing findings of fact and conclusion of law, I find that FNBB has a perfected security interest in the five notes and mortgages and that the Trustee herein has no interest in the mortgages given to secure the notes. The notes and mortgages having been sold to GNMA through a pool, the plaintiff, FNBB has a lien upon the proceeds of such sale including the interest which has accrued thereon.

[Some footnotes omitted.]

4. I am not herein concerned with the question whether there is personal liability for the debt in the event of a deficiency between the value of the property and the amount due on the obligation after foreclosure. See 55 Am.Jr. 134, 135.

I emphasize that the question of equitable rights of mortgagors who make payments to the original mortgagee or to assignees with recorded assignments and who have no knowledge of the unrecorded assignment of the mortgage, or the rights of other assignees of the mortgage who also obtain the indicia of the debt and record their assignments are not involved in this case. The issue in this case relates only to the rights of FNBB as against the Trustee who stands in the shoes of a judgment creditor possibly holding a lien and levy on the assets of the Debtor.

IN RE MARYVILLE SAVINGS & LOAN CORP.

United States Court of Appeals, Sixth Circuit, 1984.
743 F.2d 413.

WELLFORD, CIRCUIT JUDGE.

Defendant trustee appeals the district court's determination that plaintiff bank had a perfected security interest in certain promissory notes and the deeds of trust that secured those notes. 31 B.R. 597. We Affirm in part and Reverse in part. Peoples Bank of Polk County, the plaintiff, is a bank organized under the laws of Tennessee. Prior to a name change, Peoples Bank of Polk County was known as Southern United Bank of Polk County. Maryville Savings and Loan Corporation, the debtor, is a corporation organized under the laws of Tennessee. Defendant McDonald is the trustee in bankruptcy of the debtor.

Debtor, through its duly authorized officers, executed a "Promissory Note, Security Agreement and Disclosure Statement" on June 10, 1981. The document provided for the payment, upon demand, by debtor to plaintiff of the principal sum of $75,000, together with interest from the date of execution until the date of payment at the rate of 18% per annum. As collateral for the loan, debtor assigned to plaintiff all rights in certain promissory notes and deeds of trust encumbering real property located in Blount County, Tennessee. This assignment was accomplished by debtor's execution of a "General Assignment of Promissory Note and Trust Deeds." This assignment was duly recorded with the Register of Deeds of Blount County, Tennessee, on June 15, 1981, the usual manner for recordation in Tennessee of interests in real estate.

After the initial borrowing, debtor made certain payments on the principal amount and interest due under the note, bringing the balance due down to approximately $55,000. During January of 1982, debtor secured the advance of an additional $20,000 from plaintiff without the execution of another promissory note, and executed another "General Assignment of Promissory Notes and Trust Deeds," assigning all of its rights in additional notes and deeds of trust on real property to plaintiff. This document was also recorded with the Register of Deeds of Blount County, Tennessee, on January 28, 1982.

Typically, the deeds of trust provided that, among other things, "this conveyance shall secure the above described debt (the loan evidenced by a promissory note), and the interest thereon, or renewals . . . thereof." The "deed of trust notes" recited that payment was due at the Maryville Savings and Loan Corporation. Each "Promissory Note, Security Agreement and Disclosure Statement" granted plaintiff a "security interest" in the underlying property or collateral, including "real or personal property," and the agreements were to be "interpreted according to the laws of the State of Tennessee, except where preempted by Federal law." The general assignments were "to establish a line of credit for Maryville Savings & Loan Corporation."

On March 18, 1982, debtor filed a Chapter 11 bankruptcy petition owing $75,000 plus interest on the note from plaintiff. Plaintiff initiated an adversary proceeding seeking a ruling that its security interest in the promissory notes and deeds of trust was perfected and that it therefore should recover the notes and the deeds of trust despite debtor's filing in bankruptcy. Defendant asserted that plaintiff's failure to take actual possession of the notes and deeds of trust prevented perfection of plaintiff's security interest under Uniform Commercial Code § 9–304(1), Tenn.Code Ann. § 47–9–304(1). Plaintiff argued that the transaction here was not covered by article nine of the U.C.C. because it involved a real estate transaction; as support, plaintiff cited U.C.C. § 9–104, Tenn.Code Ann. § 47–9–104, which provides:

> *Transactions excluded from chapter.*—This chapter does not apply:
>
> * * *
>
> (j) except to the extent that provision is made for fixtures in § 47–9–313, to the creation or transfer of an interest in or a lien on real estate * * *.

Defendant, on the other hand, relies upon U.C.C. § 9–102, Tenn.Code Ann. § 47–9–102, which provides:

> (1) Except as otherwise provided in § 47–9–103 on multiple state transactions and in § 47–9–104 on excluded transactions, this chapter applies so far as concerns any personal property and fixtures within the jurisdiction of this state:
>
> (a) to any transaction (regardless of its form) which is intended to create a security interest in personal property or fixtures including goods, documents, instruments, general intangibles, chattel paper, accounts or contract rights; and
>
> (b) to any sale of accounts, contract rights or chattel paper.
>
> * * *
>
> (3) The application of this chapter to a security interest in a secured obligation is not affected by the fact that the obligation is itself secured by a transaction or interest to which this chapter does not apply.

The bankruptcy court, 27 B.R. 701, held that plaintiff failed to perfect its security interest in the notes and deeds of trust, but the district court reversed, holding that the recordation accomplished, although not in compliance with the U.C.C. as applicable in Tennessee, was sufficient.

In keeping with the parties' approach to this case, both the bankruptcy court and the district court assumed that article nine perfection requirements applied either to the entirety of this transaction or not at all—that is, it applied either to both the notes and the deeds or to neither. We conclude that this approach fails to give meaningful scope, depending on the result reached, either to § 9–102 or to § 9–104(j). Comment four to Tenn.Code Ann. § 47–9–102 illustrates the necessity in cases such as this to analyze the security interest created in the promissory note separately from the interest created in the deed of trust. That illustration reads, [quoting the "Blackacre"]

* * *

We are persuaded that §§ 9–102(3) and 9–104(j) may be reconciled by holding in this case that article nine be applied in regard to the promissory notes but *not* in regard to the deeds of trust.

This conclusion is bolstered by the Third Circuit's careful opinion in *In re Bristol Assoc., Inc.,* 505 F.2d 1056 (3d Cir.1974). In *Bristol,* a case involving Pennsylvania law, the court noted that amendments to the comments to U.C.C. § 9–102 made clear the drafters' intention that "only that portion of the package unrelated to the real property" be governed by article nine when "a promissory note and mortgage together become the subject of a security interest." 505 F.2d at 1061. *See also First Nat'l Bank of Boston v. Larson (In re Kennedy Mortgage Co.),* 17 B.R. 957, 963–65 (Bankr.D.N.J.1982). The Tennessee case law cited by plaintiff does not direct a contrary result.

The Tennessee Supreme Court in *May,** however, did hold that "the U.C.C. does not supercede the law in this state with respect to *liens upon real estate.*" 503 S.W.2d at 117 (emphasis added). Some authority has discussed whether a note pledged by a real estate mortgage given as security for a loan thereby becomes "realty paper" within the purview of article nine of the U.C.C. Our attention has been called to no Tennessee case, however, that even discusses, much less adopts, this concept. We are not prepared to hold that in Tennessee the character of a note as personalty is transformed into a real estate interest merely because it is secured by a mortgage or deed of trust, or assigned as security together with a mortgage or deed of trust. Although the assignments in question did involve "transfers of interests in real property" because they involved deeds of trust, we cannot agree with the district court that the notes themselves constituted "liens upon real estate" nor adopted the character of real property. Both Tenn.Code Ann. § 47–9–102 and Tenn.Code Ann. § 47–9–104 purport to apply only to personal property and fixtures or to security interests in personal property.

In this case, then, we conclude that article nine applies to the plaintiff's security interest but only in the promissory notes themselves. Since plaintiff did not take possession of the notes, plaintiff's security interest in the notes was not perfected. *See* Tenn.Code Ann. § 47–9–304(1). On the other hand, we conclude that article nine does not apply to plaintiff's security interest in the deeds of trust. While defendant argues in his reply brief that plaintiff's security interest in the deeds of trust was not perfected even if article nine were held not to apply, he admits that he did not raise that issue below; plaintiff's security interest in the deeds of trust is therefore deemed to be a perfected interest. Accordingly, the judgment of the district court is Affirmed in part and Reversed in part.

Notes

1. Despite the Sixth Circuit's protestations to the contrary, its decision is in conflict with *In re Kennedy Mortgage Co.,* not so?

2. If you read the last paragraph in the opinion in *Maryville Savings,* consider how you would determine the priorities if you were the judge to whom the case was remanded. On a motion to reconsider, the court held that the notes, although arising from a real estate mortgage were subject to Article 9 and were, therefore, unperfected. In re Maryville Savings & Loan Corp., 760 F.2d 119 (6th Cir.1985).

Problem 7–6

1. Maltese was in the business of building and remodeling commercial and residential properties. It financed its operations by giving Bank a security interest in all of its present and future accounts, contract rights, general intangibles, chattel paper and their proceeds. Bank filed a financing statement at the Secretary of State's office in a jurisdiction that had the second alternative to 9–401. On Maltese's bankruptcy the trustee asserted that Bank did not have a perfected security interest on a series of payments totalling several hundred-thousand dollars that were due to Maltese from buyers of houses and condominiums on land-sale contracts. Does the Bank have a security interest and, if so, is it perfected?

2. Bohemian Savings and Loan Association of Cedar Rapids entered into a "loan participation and service agreement" of a bankrupt company, Columbia Pacific Mortgage. Columbia Pacific financed the construction and purchase of single family

* Commerce Union Bank v. May, 503 S.W.2d 112 (Tenn.1973).

residences and then sold "participations" in its store of mortgages to such persons as Bohemian Savings. Bohemian had an 80 percent interest in a package of 49 mortgage loans in a total amount of $960,078. The trustee asserts that he has a right to the mortgage payments to be made and also to the amount in his possession of $200,000 that was collected on foreclosure of several of the mortgages. He claims under 544(a)(3) of the Bankruptcy Code and asserts that Bohemian is nothing more than an unsecured creditor or, at best, an unperfected secured creditor. Assume that Bohemian made no filing, either in the real estate or in the personal property records. Who wins? Assume, however, that Columbia Pacific recorded the mortgages it received from the account debtors who owned the land. Who wins?

3. Bristol Associates was the lessor of certain store premises for a period of ten years. Early in the lease and in consideration for the loan, it gave Girard Bank and Trust a security interest in the lease. Girard did not record the security interest in the real estate records nor did it file any financing statement under Article 9. Ultimately Bristol went into bankruptcy and the trustee asserts that he has a right to the lease payments. Girard argues that 9–104(j) frees it from any obligation to record or to comply with the personal property laws. What do you think?

SECTION 6. PRIORITY OF BANK'S RIGHT OF "SETOFF"

Setoff is usually exercised by a bank, to set one debt off against another. In the most common circumstance debtor will owe bank a certain amount based on a loan and the debtor's deposit will itself be a loan by the bank back to the depositor. The setoff is merely the netting of the debt owed by the depositor to the bank against the bank's debt owed back to the depositor. The common law of setoff has a number of rules that we need not be concerned with here. For example, it requires that the debts on each side be mutual, i.e., that the same parties be on both sides on both debts, and that the amounts be unliquidated. Here we will assume that there is a right of setoff and we will take no time to examine the common law intricacies. Our concern is only with the question: To what extent does Article 9 govern setoff? Does it require some compliance with the Article 9 filing rules? Does Article 9 determine priority between a bank's setoff right and a secured creditor's security interest?

The starting point for analysis is UCC 9–104(i), which seems to exclude any consideration of the right of setoff from Article 9. That conclusion would seem to be supported by UCC 9–104(*l*), for it perhaps suggests that a security interest in a deposit account, a potential competitor with a setoff, is also outside of Article 9. This analysis would be too simple. One's certainty begins to crumble a bit when he looks at UCC 9–105(1)(e) that provides that accounts evidenced by a certificate of deposit are not deposit accounts. Presumably, therefore, security interests in certificates of deposit are governed by Article 9. Moreover section 9–306 reveals that in certain cases bank accounts constitute proceeds and will often be governed by Article 9.

BROWN & WILLIAMSON TOBACCO CORP. v. FIRST NATIONAL BANK OF BLUE ISLAND

United States Court of Appeals, Seventh Circuit, 1974.
504 F.2d 998.

CLARK, ASSOCIATE JUSTICE.

This appeal, involving Sections 9–205 and 9–306(2) of the Uniform Commercial Code, arises from a judgment entered in favor of appellee, Brown and

Williamson Tobacco Corporation (B & W), for $70,724 and against appellant, First National Bank of Blue Island (Blue Island). We outline the facts here.

F.W. Koenecke & Sons, Inc. (Koenecke, Inc.), a tobacco wholesaler, was controlled by Robert Koenecke and his wife, Imogene. It bought tobacco products from various suppliers, including B & W, R.J. Reynolds Tobacco Corporation (RJR) and others. Its purchases from B & W were covered by a security agreement dated October 22, 1968, which, inter alia, assigned and granted to B & W a continuing security interest in all of Koenecke, Inc. current and future inventory of B & W products, accounts receivable arising from the sale of such products and all products and proceeds of the foregoing, all of which was referred to as "collateral". It further provided " * * * except for the sale of B & W cigarettes and other tobacco products in the ordinary course of business (Koenecke, Inc.) will not sell, assign or create or permit to exist any lien on or security interest in any collateral to or in favor of anyone other than B & W".

Koenecke, Inc. maintained a general checking account at Blue Island (No. 0–072–8) in which it deposited receipts from sales of tobacco products handled by it. Blue Island made loans both to Koenecke, Inc. and to Robert Koenecke and his wife personally. The first of these personal loans to the Koeneckes was on June 6, 1967, for $20,000 and paid on July 6, 1967, by Koenecke, Inc. On February 5, 1968, the Koeneckes borrowed $100,000 which was paid by Mr. Koenecke on April 9, 1968. On June 20, Koenecke, Inc. borrowed $82,000 which was paid by the company on September 17, 1968. On October 23, 1968, the Koeneckes borrowed $67,000 which was paid by the company on December 21, 1968. And on January 9, 1969, the Koeneckes borrowed $108,000, which was paid by the company on January 13, 1969. The proceeds of all of these loans were ultimately deposited in the bank account of Koenecke, Inc., No. 0–072–8.

Throughout the Fall of 1968 and continuing into 1969, Koenecke, Inc. suffered severe adverse publicity—especially through the press in Chicago—the gist of which was that its licensing arrangements were unlawful; its sales of cigarettes bore no Illinois revenue stamps; and some of its licenses were obtained through forgery. This had an adverse effect upon its sales.

On October 29, 1968, a $250,000 loan to Robert Koenecke and his wife was made by Blue Island on their personal, unsecured note. The proceeds of this loan were placed in the Koenecke, Inc. checking account No. 0–072–8, but the company did not sign, guarantee or endorse the same. The note was renewed on December 28, 1968 for 60 days. On February 10, 1969, Blue Island, becoming disturbed over Koenecke, Inc.'s finances, stopped honoring checks of Koenecke, Inc. that were drawn on uncollected funds deposited in checking account No. 0–072–8. Koenecke, Inc. was not notified of this action and, when it found out, it withheld making any further deposits in the account. At this time, there were several hundred thousand dollars in checks drawn against its general account, No. 0–072–8, which Koenecke, Inc. had issued to its suppliers, among whom were B & W and RJR. On February 17, 1969 representatives of RJR appeared in person at the bank, seeking collection of several previously dishonored checks. On that day there was a balance in the Koenecke, Inc. checking account No. 0–072–8 of $713,586.52, of which $113,911 was attributable to sales by Koenecke, Inc. of B & W products which were covered by the security agreement.

On this same day—February 17th—the President and the Vice President of Blue Island spoke by telephone with Robert Koenecke and requested payment of the $250,000 note, although it was not due until February 26, 1969. Mr. Koenecke told Blue Island officers to pay the note from the corporate checking account of Koenecke, Inc., No. 0–072–8 and this was done by a debit memo of the bank on the next day. On February 18th he also directed Blue Island to debit Koenecke, Inc.'s account $40,000 and to issue a cashier's check in that amount to him. He endorsed the cashier's check to RJR.

On the 18th of February, upon the opening of Blue Island, there was a balance of $498,055.85 in the checking account No. 0–072–8 of Koenecke, Inc. and of this amount $70,724 was attributable to the proceeds of the sales of B & W products. Also on February 18th three representatives of B & W called personally on Blue Island to pay several checks drawn on Koenecke, Inc. account No. 0–072–8, but the bank refused because of a reported insufficiency of funds. During that same morning, representatives of RJR conferred with Blue Island officials and Robert Koenecke at the bank's offices in an attempt to collect an additional sum of several hundred thousand dollars for recent sales of its products to Koenecke, Inc. During a coffee break within the RJR meeting, Blue Island officers procured the signature of Robert Koenecke to the debit memo authorizing the payment of the Koeneckes' $250,000 note, but B & W was not advised thereof, although its representatives were in the bank. At the end of that day the checking account of Koenecke, Inc., No. 0–072–8 had a balance of only $3,317.49.

Koenecke, Inc. closed operations on February 24, 1969 and on March 13th a petition was filed to adjudicate Koenecke, Inc. bankrupt. On April 28, 1969, at a hearing on the bankruptcy matter, Vice President Mansfield of Blue Island, with some evasion, testified that at the direction of Mr. Koenecke, he had taken $252,567.70 from checking account No. 0–072–8 of Koenecke, Inc. and paid off with interest the personal note of Robert Koenecke and his wife due Blue Island on February 26, 1969. B & W elected not to participate in the bankruptcy, having decided to stand on its security. The Trustee in bankruptcy of Koenecke, Inc. sued Blue Island for some $530,000 covering several transfers of cash from Koenecke, Inc. to the bank. That suit was settled on November 23, 1970, for $100,000.

The bank raises four issues: (1) Did B & W lose its security interest by permitting the proceeds from the sale of its products to be commingled with other funds in the corporate account of Koenecke, Inc.; (2) Did B & W "cover" or trace its proceeds into the hands of the bank either as to depository or the ultimate transferee; (3) Did an action for conversion lie; (4) Was the transfer of the $252,567.70 to Blue Island from the account of Koenecke, Inc. a fraudulent one.

We decide the first two questions against the bank and affirm. The bank admits that "it sought and obtained preferred treatment for the payment of its $250,000 loan" but insists that its action constituted neither a conversion of B & W property nor a fraudulent transfer thereof. We find it unnecessary to pass on these issues since B & W had a perfected security interest in its "collateral" which was deposited in the Koenecke, Inc. checking account No. 0–072–8 and which it traced to the bank.

I. B & W DID NOT LOSE ITS SECURITY INTEREST:

Blue Island relies primarily upon the argument that B & W gave up its ability to identify its collateral when it permitted Koenecke, Inc. to commingle that collateral with other funds deposited in the latter's account No. 0–072–8. We find both the Uniform Commercial Code and the decided cases to the contrary. Section 9–205 of the Code specifically provides: "a security interest is not invalid * * * by reason of liberty in the debtor to use, commingle, or dispose of all or part of the collateral * * * or * * * of proceeds." And Section 9–306(2) adds: The security "also continues in any identifiable proceeds including collections received by the debtor."

Thus the Code "is explicit in preserving the priority of the secured party to the proceeds notwithstanding his consent to the sale of the primary collateral and further notwithstanding his consent to the debtor's unrestricted use and disposition of these proceeds so long as they remain identifiable." In re Mid State Wood Products Company, 323 F.Supp. 853, 857 (N.D.Ill.1971).

Blue Island urges us to follow a statement by Professor Grant Gilmore that proceeds cease to be identifiable when deposited in a bank account, so that the security interest is lost when such commingling occurs. *See* 2 G. Gilmore, Security Interests in Personal Property, § 27.4 at 735–36 (1965). Since Professor Gilmore was the principal draftsman and Reporter for Article 9 of the Code, his interpretation, though subsequently voiced, commands attention. Nevertheless, examining the language of the Code, in the light of its purpose, we conclude that the more reasonable implication is that the proceeds may be identifiable, and the security interest therein survive, even though commingled.

* * *

Universal C.I.T. Credit Corp. v. Farmers Bank of Portageville, 358 F.Supp. 317 (E.D.Mo.1973), upheld a security interest in cash from the sale of automobiles which had been deposited in the automobile dealer's general bank account. The court held that "proceeds are 'identifiable' if they can be traced in accordance with the state law. * * * The mere fact that the proceeds from the sales of the six automobiles were commingled with other funds * * * does not render the proceeds unidentifiable. * * * " 358 F.Supp. at 323–324. *See also* Associates Discount Corp. v. Fidelity Union Trust Co., 111 N.J.Super. 353, 268 A.2d 330 (1970); Girard Trust Corn Exchange Bank v. Lepley Ford, Inc., 25 Pa.D. & C.2d 395 (Pa.Ct.Comm.P.1958). In Howarth v. Universal C.I.T. Credit Corporation, 203 F.Supp. 279, 282 (W.D.Pa.1962), the court at least assumed that if proceeds of collateral could be traced into a bank account, such proceeds would be deemed identifiable, and subject to the security interest. We are not persuaded by the contrary authority of Morrison Steel Co. v. Gurtman, 113 N.J.Super. 474, 274 A.2d 306 (1971).

Looking to Illinois law, it is clear in the different, but probably analogous, case of a fund impressed with a trust, such fund may be traced into a fund of commingled money, People v. Bates, 351 Ill. 439, 184 N.E. 597, 598 (1933), and it is conclusively presumed in equity that a trustee dissipates or spends his own funds first, before encroaching upon a trust fund. People v. People's Bank and Trust of Rockford, 353 Ill. 479, 187 N.E. 522, 525 (1933).

II. B & W Traced its Collateral to Blue Island:

But Blue Island says that B & W did not trace or "cover" collateral into the hands of the bank. However a reading of the agreed stipulation of facts and of paragraph 3 of B & W's complaint which Blue Island admits to be true, shows the contrary.

There is no difficulty in tracing $70,724 of proceeds in which B & W had a security interest into the money in the checking account February 18, 1969. Blue Island has stipulated that Koenecke, Inc.'s checking account No. 0–072–8 had $498,055.85 in it on February 18 and that $70,724 thereof represented proceeds of sales of B & W products covered by the security agreement, calculated "through the application of generally accepted auditing and accounting principles."

Blue Island has stipulated further on that same day it transferred to itself, out of that same account, $252,567.70 in payment of Robert and Imogene Koenecke's personal note, not yet due. There were other transfers during the day amounting to $247,170.66 and at the close of business the balance was $3,317.49. The bank contends that the $70,724 has not been sufficiently identified as part of the $252,567.70 the bank transferred to itself, and it therefore must not be deemed to have had constructive notice of B & W's security interest therein.

Whether rationalized in terms of identifiability or of fairness in holding the bank to constructive notice, we think that the matter turns upon whether the transfer to Blue Island was a transfer in the ordinary course of business. Official Comment 2(c) to § 9–306 of the Code says as follows:

> Where cash proceeds are covered into the debtor's checking account and *paid out in the operation of the debtor's business,* recipients of the funds of course take free of any claim which the secured party may have in them as proceeds. What has been said relates to payments and transfers in ordinary course. The law of fraudulent conveyances would no doubt in appropriate cases support recovery of proceeds by a secured party from a transferee out of ordinary course or otherwise in collusion with the debtor to defraud the secured party. [Uniform Commercial Code Comment to Smith-Hurd Ill.Rev. Stat. ch. 26 § 9–306, p. 403 (emphasis added).]

Examination of the circumstances of the transfer persuades us that the transfer was clearly outside the ordinary course of business. At the beginning of the day, representatives of B & W appeared at the bank and sought the honoring of checks drawn to B & W on the Koenecke account, payment having been previously refused. Blue Island represented that the account did not contain adequate funds. Bank officers also met with RJR, also seeking payment for goods sold to Koenecke, Inc. During a coffee break in this meeting, Blue Island obtained a debit memorandum from Mr. Koenecke, authorizing the transfer to it. B & W representatives, still at the bank, were not informed.

There is no stipulation nor proof of the nature of the other transfers out of the account during the day nor the order in which they occurred. It seems likely, from the general situation, and we think fair to assume in the absence of proof, that they represented payment of checks which had been issued in the ordinary course of the business of Koenecke, Inc.

Therefore, we conclude that the funds subject to the B & W security interest were identifiable and the security interest continued in the money transferred to Blue Island. It seems fair and equitable to charge a party receiving a transfer from a general bank account outside the ordinary course of business with constructive notice of a security interest in funds therein.

[Footnotes omitted.]

Note

Section 9–306(2) provides for a security interest only in "identifiable proceeds." Did the drafters intend the amounts in a commingled bank account to be "identifiable"?

Problem 7–7

Spock Enterprises develops, produces, and markets children's toys. Spock has a $150,000 line of secured credit from Federation Bank and Trust. Federation has a security interest in Spock's inventory, accounts, equipment, general intangibles, and proceeds. On July 1, 1985 Spock opened an account at Vulcan Savings and Loan with $10,000. Assume that the $10,000 are identifiable proceeds subject to Federation's security interest. Vulcan lent Spock $5,000 without taking security. On August 1, 1985 a judgment creditor of Spock levied on the total balance in the Vulcan's account. During July, Spock's account with Vulcan showed the following activity:

Date	Transaction	Balance
7/1	Opening deposit	$10,000
7/9	Payment of monthly bills due 7/10	6,500
7/11	Deposit (sole stockholder's personal funds)	8,500
7/12	Deposit of Federation proceeds	10,500
7/13	Repayment to Vulcan of $5,000 loan	5,500
7/13	Deposit (sole stockholder's personal funds)	10,000
8/1	Judgment creditor levy (reduces account to	0

Federation sued the judgment creditor for conversion. How much, if anything, should Federation win? Can Federation successfully recover anything from Vulcan?

CITIZENS NATIONAL BANK OF ORLANDO v. BORNSTEIN

Supreme Court of Florida, 1979.
374 So.2d 6.

HATCHETT, JUSTICE.

We have before us certified questions from the United States Court of Appeals for the Fifth Circuit, concerning the set-off rights and defenses available to an obligor against the assignee of a non-negotiable certificate of deposit. *Bornstein v. Citizens National Bank of Orlando,* 564 F.2d 721 (5th Cir.1977). This proceeding is authorized by section 25.081, Florida Statutes (1977) and Fla. R.App.P. 9.510. We conclude: (1) that the transfer of the certificate of deposit as security for the purchase of a bond was the assignment of a non-negotiable instrument entitled to secured transaction treatment under article 9 of the Florida Uniform Commercial Code, sections 679.101 et seq., Florida Statutes (1973); (2) that neither the provisions of section 679.104(9) nor section 679.104(11) exclude the transfer from coverage under article 9; (3) that section 679.318(4) does not invalidate the prohibitions against assignment; and (4) that the obligor, "Bank," is not an "account debtor" entitled to any article 9 defenses under section 679.318(1). We do not reach certified question III.

The facts, as presented by the Court of Appeals for the Fifth Circuit, are as follows:

> On November 30, 1973, Milford Mechanical Corporation (Milford), through its president, Frank Iadarola, purchased a $13,000 certificate of deposit from Citizens National Bank of Orlando (Bank). At the time of the

purchase, Milford was indebted to the Bank. The front of the form of the certificate of deposit states, in relevant part:

> Payable to the registered owner upon presentation and surrender of the certificate * * *.
>
> * * *
>
> This certificate is assignable only with the consent of and on the books of the Citizens National Bank of Orlando.

On the reverse side, the following printed language appears:

> ASSIGNMENT
>
> (Effective only when recorded on the books of the bank)

The certificate of deposit was not negotiable.

At the same time, a signature card relating to the deposit represented by the certificate of deposit was executed by Iadarola on behalf of Milford. Immediately above the signature line on the form is printed:

> This bank is authorized to apply this account, whether savings or certificate of deposit, toward the payment of any indebtedness due this bank from the depositor or depositors, or either of them, whether the debt is several and this account is joint, or the debt is joint and the account is several.

On December 18, 1973, Iadarola signed the assignment on the reverse side of the certificate of deposit on behalf of Milford and filled in National Indemnity Company of Omaha (National Indemnity) as the assignee. This was done to provide collateral for a bond Milford was purchasing from National Indemnity. National Indemnity later typed and executed a similar assignment form on the reverse side of the certificate of deposit and, for National Indemnity's benefit, assigned the certificate of deposit to Barbara Bornstein, as trustee of National Indemnity.

The Bank's records were never changed to show any assignment or transfer of the certificate of deposit and there is no evidence that the Bank was either notified of either assignment or consented to them. In March 1974, the Bank drew a check payable to Milford for the interest earned on the certificate of deposit. This check was endorsed and deposited by Milford.

Milford had borrowed $250,000 from the bank, evidenced by a series of promissory notes, at the time it purchased the certificate of deposit. The last note in the series was an unsecured, consolidated renewal note for $250,000 dated February 21, 1974, and due thirty-two days from that date.

The Bank received the certificate of deposit with a letter requesting payment to Bornstein on April 22, 1974. This was the Bank's first notice of the assignments. On April 29, 1974, the Bank set-off the funds represented by the certificate of deposit against the $250,000 debt owed it by Milford and refused to pay the funds to Bornstein. The next day, the Bank sent a letter to Milford and the co-endorsers informing them of the set-off and demanding that the balance of the debt be paid by May 7, 1974.

From the date of the purchase, November 30, 1973, through April 30, 1974, the Bank did not change its position in reliance upon the certificate of deposit. The Bank, however, did not exercise its right of set-off until April 29, 1974.

564 F.2d 721, 722–3.

It appearing that there were determinative issues involved with no clear controlling precedent in the decisions of this court, the Court of Appeals for the Fifth Circuit certified to us a number of questions which we address in the order outlined by that court.

I. Article Nine Coverage

A. Is the Assignment Entitled to Article Nine Treatment?

We answer in the affirmative. Under section 679.102(1)(a), article 9 is said to apply:

> To any transaction (regardless of its form) which is *intended to create a security interest* in personal property or fixtures including goods, documents, instruments, general intangibles, chattel paper, accounts or contract rights; * * * [Emphasis added.]

Both parties recognize that the assignment by Milford of the certificate of deposit was intended as security for the purchase of a bond from National Indemnity, the assignee. National Indemnity, then, was the clear beneficiary of a security interest in the certificate for its sale of the bond to Milford. Therefore, provided the certificate of deposit properly falls within one of the "personal property" classifications named in section 679.102(1)(a), the assignment is a transfer entitled to secured transaction treatment under article 9. The parties agree that the certificate falls under the "personal property" designation of section 679.102(1)(a), but disagree as to its precise classification—the appellant calling it either a "general intangible" or "contract right" as defined in section 679.106, the appellee insisting that it is best described as an "instrument" under section 679.105(1)(g). In either event, the transaction would fall under article 9's coverage.

We agree with the appellee that the certificate of deposit here is best characterized as an "instrument" under section 679.105(1)(g). As defined in that section, an "instrument" is:

> a negotiable instrument (defined in s. 673.104), or a security (defined in s. 678.102) *or any other writing which evidences a right to the payment of money and is not itself a security agreement or lease and is of a type which is in ordinary course of business transferred by delivery with any necessary endorsement or assignment.* [Emphasis added.]

We believe the emphasized portion of the above definition to be an accurate description of the certificate of deposit here. Although it was later assigned by Milford as security for a bond, the certificate as purchased from the Bank simply evidenced the right to payment and was clearly not an agreement creating or providing for a "security interest" as that term is defined in section 671.201(37). While admitting that most authorities define certificates of deposit as "instruments," the Bank argues that the restrictions on transfer here remove the certificate from coverage under section 679.105(1)(g). (The Bank cites cases dealing with the negotiability of instruments under section 673.104(1) in support of its position.) We disagree. If the code drafters had intended to exclude non-negotiable instruments from coverage under section 679.105(1)(g), they would not have added the [italicized] language in the definition, but would have limited it to include only "negotiable instruments" as was done in article 3.

We find persuasive the reasoning of the Texas Civil Appellate Court in *First National Bank in Grand Prairie v. Lone Star Life Insurance Co.,* 524 S.W.2d 525

(Tex.Civ.App.1975). There, the court held a certificate of deposit payable to the depositor only, with the restrictive legend, "Non-Negotiable," to be an "instrument" under the article 9 definition. The court stated:

> Simplicity and clarity in such transactions is better achieved by holding as a matter of law that a non-negotiable certificate of deposit is an "instrument" as defined by § 9.105(a)(9). [§ 679.105(1)(g), Fla.Stat. (1973).] Unquestionably, it satisfies the requirement in this definition of a "writing which evidences the right to the payment of money." We conclude that it also is "of a type which is in ordinary course of business transferred by delivery with any necessary indorsement or assignment." The word "type" may be interpreted either narrowly or broadly. In the light of the general purpose of the Code, we do not construe it narrowly to refer only to writings of exactly the same character, such as, in this case, other non-negotiable certificates of deposit. Instead, we construe it broadly to include any writing which, like a stock certificate or negotiable instrument, is treated as a token of the rights it represents and, therefore, is normally delivered to any person to whom the rights are transferred. The certificate in question resembles such instruments more than it resembles ordinary deposit accounts * * *. It is a writing which the holder must keep and present as evidence of its right, as its language expressly provides. It may easily be delivered by one party to another in the course of a commercial transaction.

First National Bank in Grand Prairie v. Lone Star Life Insurance Co., 524 S.W.2d 525, 533–4.

We agree that the emphasized language in section 679.105(1)(g) should be interpreted broadly to encompass non-negotiable certificates of deposit. We do not consider the restrictions on assignability requiring consent of and recorded transfer by the Bank to exempt this certificate from the broad coverage of section 679.105(1)(g). We conclude that the certificate of deposit here is an "instrument" as described in the emphasized portion of section 679.105(1)(g) and that the assignment is therefore entitled to secured transaction treatment under article 9.

B. Is the Transfer Excluded From Article Nine Coverage by The Provisions of Section 679.104(9) or Section 679.104(11), Florida Statutes (1973)?

We do not agree with the *Grand Prairie* court that the seller of the certificate, the Bank here, is necessarily prevented from asserting any set-off against the assignee, where the assignee has already perfected the non-negotiable instrument by taking possession under section 679.304(1). The Bank asserts its claim not as a secured party, but as a debtor under the certificate whose claim to the funds represented thereby arises solely by virtue of its asserted right of set-off.[2] We do not interpret the set-off exclusion from article 9 coverage under section 679.104(9) to prevent the bank from asserting any rights to set-off it may have against a secured party with a perfected security interest under article 9. To the contrary, we construe this section to mean that the claimant of a right to set-off need not comply with article 9 security and filing requirements in order to assert whatever set-off rights he may aptly demonstrate. The section

2. See, G. Gilmore, Security Interests in Personal Property § 10.7 at 315–16 (1965), where the distinction between a right to set-off and a security interest led the writer to question the purpose of the set-off exclusion: "This exclusion is an apt example of the absurdities which result when draftsmen attempt to appease critics by putting into a statute something that is not in any sense wicked but is hopelessly irrelevant. Of course a right of set-off is not a security interest and has never been confused with one. The statute might as appropriately exclude fan dancing."

means simply that a right of set-off may exist in a creditor who does not have a security interest. It does not effectuate the exclusion of this transfer from article 9 coverage. *Associates Discount Corp. v. Fidelity Union Trust Co.*, 111 N.J.Super. 353, 263 A.2d 330 (Law Div.1970).

Because we do not construe "deposit account" to include an account evidenced by a certificate of deposit we are equally confident that the transfer in question is not excluded from coverage under article 9 by the section 679.104(11) provision excepting the chapter's application "To a transfer * * * of any deposit, savings, passbook, or like account." See, U.C.C. § 9–105(1)(e) (1972 revision).

II. If Article 9 of the Florida Uniform Commercial Code Covers This Transaction, Are the Restrictions on Assignment Invalidated or the Bank's Asserted Right to Set-Off Established by Sections 679.318(1), (4), Florida Statutes (1973)?

The defenses outlined in section 679.318(1) are available to an "account debtor" as defined in section 679.105(1)(a). Under that section, an account debtor "means the person who is obligated on an account, chattel paper, contract right or general intangible."

* * *

We conclude that the certificate of deposit is not properly classified as an account, chattel paper, contract right, or general intangible. The Bank is, therefore, not an "account debtor" as defined in section 679.105(1)(a). Accordingly, it may not avail itself of the article 9 defenses delineated in section 679.318(1). By the same token, since the transaction does not amount to a "contract between an account debtor and an assignor," section 679.318(4) does not operate to invalidate the restrictions on assignment here.

The Bank finally argues that even if the section 679.318(1) defenses are not expressly available to an obligor against an assignee of a non-negotiable instrument, the Code ought to be liberally construed to permit the Bank to utilize the article 3 "simple contract defense" of section 673.306. Under the Bank's analysis, the simple contract defenses of this section incorporate the set-off rights which are otherwise available to an account debtor on a simple contract under section 679.318. In reaching this conclusion, the Bank presents the following incorporation argument:

(1) No article 9 defenses are available to an obligor when sued by an assignee of an "instrument" as defined in section 679.105(1)(g). (The Bank perceives this to be a "gap" in the Code.)

(2) The assignment rules in sections 673.305, 306, and section 678.202 partially fill this gap in providing defenses for obligors of "negotiable instruments" and "securities."

(3) On the other hand, obligor defenses against assignees of article 9 "non-negotiable instruments" do not appear to be recognized under any Code provision. (Article 3 defines "instrument" only as a "negotiable instrument" in section 673.102(1)(e).)

(4) One exception, however, to the rule that the article 3 term "instrument" means only "negotiable instrument" is found in section 673.805 which provides:

> This chapter applies to any instrument whose terms do not preclude transfer and which is otherwise negotiable within this chapter but which is not payable to order or to bearer, except that there can be no holder in due course of such an instrument.

The official ALI comments to this section state that:

> This section covers the "*non-negotiable instrument*" * * * *It refers to a particular type of instrument which meets all requirements as to form of a negotiable instrument except that it is not payable to order or to bearer.* * * * * Since it lacks words of negotiability there can be no holder in due course of such an instrument, and any provision of any section of this Article peculiar to a holder in due course cannot apply to it. With this exception such instruments are covered by all sections of this Article. [Emphasis added.]

(5) Section 673.306 sets forth the defenses of an obligor against one *not a holder in due course.* Because this section is "not peculiar to a holder in due course," the type of non-negotiable instruments discussed in section 673.805 are covered by it.

(6) Therefore, if the certificate of deposit in this case is the type of "non-negotiable instrument" discussed in section 673.805, the Bank is the beneficiary of the defenses set forth in section 673.306.

(7) Section 673.306(2) provides that a non-holder in due course, the assignee here, takes the instrument subject to "All defenses of any party which would be available in an action on a simple contract."

(8) The "simple contract" language of section 673.306(2) incorporates the article 9 defenses by reference, since the defenses in section 679.318 are available to an account debtor on a *simple contract.*

(9) The article 9, section 679.318 defenses having been made applicable, the rights of the assignee here are subject to "All the terms of the contract between the account debtor [bank] and assignor and any defense or claim arising therefrom." (Section 679.318(1)(a).)

(10) Finally, in the event the court does not feel that the instrument here qualifies as a section 673.805 "non-negotiable instrument," the Bank argues that a liberal construction of the act should be taken to apply every section of article 8 to all "non-negotiable instruments" unless the context of the section otherwise requires. In this event, the section 673.306 defenses would apply to the Bank here.

While the Bank's argument is an appealing one, its incorporation analysis does not withstand close scrutiny. The certificates of deposit in this case are *not* within the category of non-negotiable instruments addressed in section 673.805. That section draws into article 8 coverage any instrument, the terms of which do not preclude transfer and which, *but for the fact that it is not payable to order or to bearer, is otherwise negotiable under the article 8 definition.* The cases cited by the Bank which have used the 3–805 definition in order to extend the 3–306 defenses to obligors on non-negotiable instruments, recognize that the certificates "must meet all the requirements of negotiability" except the "payable to order or to bearer" criterion in order to be covered by section 3–806. *See, D. Nelsen & Sons, Inc. v. General American Development Corp.,* 6 Ill.App.3d 6, 284 N.E.2d 478 (1972). Section 673.104(1)(b) provides that to be negotiable an instrument must, in addition to being payable to order or to bearer, "Contain an unconditional promise or order to pay a sum certain in money." Here, in the event of assignment, the promise to pay is conditioned upon consent of the Bank and reflection of the assignment on the books of the Bank. Because the instrument does not contain an unconditional promise to pay, it does not meet the other "requirements" for negotiability under section 673.104(1). Therefore, the certificate of deposit is not of the non-negotiable variety to which section 673.805 refers, and the Bank's analysis breaks down at point six above.

Even if the court were to adopt a liberal construction of the chapter to apply section 673.306 defenses to all non-negotiable instruments without submitting them to the "otherwise negotiable" test of section 673.805, the "simple contract" defense of section 673.306(2) by no means incorporates the section 679.318 defenses as the Bank suggests. First, the Bank concedes that if the certificate in question was classified as a "contract right" or an "account," section 679.318(4) would invalidate all attempts to prohibit assignments, including the restrictions on alienability here. *See, Florida First National Bank v. Fryd Construction Corp.*, 245 So.2d 883 (Fla. 3d Dist.Ct.App.1971). Second, and more important, section 679.318(1) addresses defenses available to "account debtors." We have earlier determined that the Bank is not an account debtor as defined in section 679.105(1)(a). If it were, the Bank would clearly be entitled to section 679.318 defenses and we would have had no need to pursue this incorporation analysis. The framers apparently intended that the article 9 defenses provided in section 679.318 would not be available to the obligor of an "instrument" since "account debtor" does not include a debtor on an instrument. It is logically inconsistent for the framers of the Code to extend certain defenses only to account debtors under article 9, while permitting these same defenses to be used by obligors of non-negotiable instruments via other provisions of the Code. Accordingly, we reject the Bank's incorporation argument and conclude that it may not utilize section 673.306 to incorporate the article 9 defenses for use against the assignee here.

Because we agree with both parties that the transfer is not excluded from coverage under article 9, we do not reach certified question III.

Summarizing our answers to the questions certified, we find that the assignment by Milford of the certificate of deposit as security for the payment of a bond purchased from National Indemnity was the assignment of a non-negotiable instrument entitled to secured transaction treatment under article 9; that neither the provisions of section 679.104(9) nor section 679.104(11) exclude the transfer from coverage under article 9; that section 679.318(4) does not invalidate the restrictions on assignment since the transaction is not a "contract between an account debtor and an assignor;" and that neither by incorporation through section 673.306 nor by the express terms of article 9 is the Bank's asserted right to set-off established under section 679.318(1).

[Some footnotes omitted.]

Notes

1. After this case, how would you advise the bank issuing the CD? Is a bank adequately protected by a disclaimer on the face of the certificate of deposit?

2. Review the *Citicorp* case, Chapter Four, Section 9, supra.

TRUST COMPANY OF COLUMBUS v. UNITED STATES

United States Court of Appeals, Eleventh Circuit, 1984.
735 F.2d 447.

HENDERSON, CIRCUIT JUDGE:

This is an appeal from the judgment of the United States District Court for the Middle District of Georgia awarding the proceeds of two disputed bank accounts to the appellee, Trust Company of Columbus (Trust Company). The district court determined that a taxpayer's execution of several promissory notes, each containing a clause securing its bank accounts as collateral for loans, created a valid security interest in the funds remaining in the accounts that was superior to a later-imposed, federal tax lien. Finding no error, we affirm.

The taxpayer, Spain & Associates (Spain), maintained two general deposit accounts at the Trust Company. From September of 1980 until February of 1982, the Trust Company made four separate loans to Spain totaling approximately $112,000.00. Each loan was secured by a promissory note which provided in pertinent part:

> The term "Collateral" * * * shall mean the following property which has been or is hereby delivered, pledged, assigned, conveyed and transferred to the holder * * * together with all other property of every kind and description including accounts, monies and deposits now or hereafter in possession or control of [the bank] * * *.
>
> The [debtor] agrees that [the bank] shall have a lien upon, security title to and a security interest in the Collateral to secure payment of this Note * * *.

Record at 17–20.

By November of 1982, Spain had defaulted on all four notes, leaving an unpaid balance of over $95,000.00. Spain also was in arrears to the government on certain back taxes totaling over $50,000.00. Consequently, on November 8, 1982, the Internal Revenue Service (IRS) served a Notice of Levy on the bank and then filed tax liens in Muscogee County, the county in which both Spain and the Trust Company were located.

In response to the notice of levy, the Trust Company forwarded two checks to the IRS totaling approximately $22,000.00, the aggregate amount of Spain's two bank accounts. Subsequently, asserting a prior claim to the funds, the Trust Company wrote to the IRS requesting the return of the money. After receiving no reply, the bank filed this suit for wrongful levy. 26 U.S.C. § 7426.

The cause was submitted to the court on stipulated facts and cross motions for summary judgment. The district court held that the promissory notes created a valid, superior security interest in the bank and ordered the IRS to return the funds. After entry of the judgment, the government filed this appeal contending that the bank did not have a security interest in the deposits but only an equitable right of set-off which is inferior to a federal tax levy.

The only remedy available to a taxpayer who possesses an interest in property upon which the government has levied is a civil suit to regain the property. 26 U.S.C. § 7426(a)(1). A levy is wrongful if it "will or does effectively destroy * * * [an] interest in the property which is *senior* to the federal tax lien." IRC Reg. § 301.7426–1–(b)(iv)(d) (emphasis added). A security interest that arose prior to the filing of notice of a tax lien is senior to that lien. 26 U.S.C. § 6323(a). Therefore, if the bank had a senior security interest in the funds, it would prevail over the government's levy.

The Code defines a security interest as:

> any interest in property acquired by contract for the purpose of securing payment or performance of an obligation or indemnifying against loss or liability. A security interest exists at any time (A) if, at such time, the property is in existence and the interest has become protected under local law against a subsequent judgment lien arising out of an unsecured obliga-

tion, and (B) to the extent that, at such time, the holder has parted with money or money's worth.

26 U.S.C. § 6323(h)(1).

The district court found that the execution of the promissory notes here fell within this statutory definition since the bank parted with money and received the notes as security for the loan. Because we agree with this conclusion, the only question remaining for resolution is whether the interest created by the notes was protected under local law. Consequently, we look to Georgia law for the answer.

Under Georgia law, when money is deposited in a bank, title to the funds passes to the bank and the money becomes a chose in action in favor of the depositor. *See Macon National Bank v. Smith,* 170 Ga. 332, 153 S.E. 4 (1930). The cases make clear that such choses in action are readily assignable to the bank as security for a debt. *See Georgia Bank & Trust Co. v. Hadarits,* 221 Ga. 125, 143 S.E.2d 627 (1965); *Macon National Bank v. Smith,* 170 Ga. 332, 153 S.E. 4 (1930); *Copeland v. Peachtree Bank & Trust Co.,* 150 Ga.App. 262, 257 S.E.2d 353 (1979). Upon such an assignment, the bank obtains a preference to or lien on the account which vests upon the signing of the note. *See Macon National Bank v. Smith,* 170 Ga. at 338, 153 S.E. at 7.

The facts are clear that Spain signed the promissory notes well in advance of the government's notice of a tax levy. Accordingly, the promissory notes created a valid and senior security interest in the bank which was wrongfully defeated by the government tax levy.

As a final matter, we note the government's misplaced reliance on the decision in *United States v. Citizens & Southern National Bank,* 538 F.2d 1101 (5th Cir.1976),[1] *cert. denied,* 430 U.S. 945, 97 S.Ct. 1579, 51 L.Ed.2d 792 (1977).

* * *

In reaching its decision, the court in *Citizens & Southern* reiterated the position taken under Georgia law that depositors retain property rights in their bank accounts. *Id.* at 1107. Where some "rights to property remained in the depositors * * * the issue between the parties is one of priority of liens." *Id.* at 1106. Because a prior lien is not a defense to a federal tax levy, *id.,* the proper procedure in contesting a levy is to surrender the funds and then litigate the priority of liens. *Id.* This is precisely what the Trust Company did here. Therefore, its actions were procedurally correct. Because, as stated before, a valid lien arose at the time the promissory notes were executed and the execution date was prior to the government's notice of levy, the bank's lien was first in time and superior to that of the government.

The judgment of the district court is affirmed.

PEOPLES NATIONAL BANK OF WASHINGTON v. UNITED STATES

United States Court of Appeals, Ninth Circuit, 1985.
777 F.2d 459.

SCHROEDER, CIRCUIT JUDGE.

Peoples National Bank of Washington brought this action against the United States, asking the district court to declare that the United States' tax

1. In *Bonner v. City of Prichard,* 661 F.2d 1206 (11th Cir.1981) (*en banc*), this court adopted as precedent all decisions of the former Fifth Circuit decided prior to October 1, 1981.

levy against a depositor's account was invalid. The district court dismissed the action on the ground that the bank had no interest in the account superior to that of the government. In this appeal, the bank argues that its rights in the account are superior by virtue of either its common law right of setoff or a "security agreement," which the depositor executed before the government provided notice of the tax lien. We hold that neither the right of setoff, which was unexercised, nor the "security agreement," which transferred no control over the account to the bank, created any interest superior to that of the government. We therefore affirm.

The facts are not in dispute. The Internal Revenue Service assessed income taxes against Jerry and Susan Redwine in 1981. The Redwines failed to pay the assessment after notice and demand. By operation of law, this created a lien on all of their property, including after acquired property. 26 U.S.C. § 6321.

Two years later, the Redwines borrowed approximately $194,000 from Peoples National Bank and executed, in addition to a promissory note, a security agreement purporting to grant Peoples a security interest in the Redwines' property, including funds deposited with the bank.

Within three weeks after the loan was made, the IRS issued notice to the bank that it was levying on the Redwines' account in the amount of approximately $5,000. As of the time that Peoples received the notice, it had taken no action to set off the funds in the Redwines' account against any claims it had against the Redwines; nor had it otherwise restricted the Redwines' ability to withdraw funds from their account.

After receiving the notice, Peoples filed this action and delivered a check to the clerk of the district court in an amount which would satisfy the levy. The district court dismissed the action, holding that the bank had no rights in the depositors' account which would defeat the government's levy.

* * *

Authority from other jurisdictions strongly supports the position that an unexercised right of setoff does not terminate the depositor's property rights in an account. * * * We therefore find no basis for holding that, under Washington law, a depositor loses all property rights in his account simply because the bank has a right to set off funds in the account against an indebtedness owed to the bank.

Peoples next argues that its interest in the deposit account is a "security interest" as defined in 26 U.S.C. § 6323(h)(1), and has priority over the IRS lien because it existed prior to the giving of notice of the tax lien. 26 U.S.C. § 6323(a).

A "security interest" is defined in 26 U.S.C. § 6323(h)(1). That statute requires that the interest must be "protected under local law against a subsequent judgment lien arising out of an unsecured obligation." Washington has adopted the Uniform Commercial Code, but its provisions for perfection of security interests do not apply to interests in deposit accounts. Wash.Rev.Code 62A.9–104(1). It is therefore necessary to look to the common law to determine whether the bank's interest in the Redwines' account can defeat a subsequent judgment lien. See 1G. Gilmore, Security Interests in Personal Property § 10.8, at 316 (1965).

Under the common law, a creditor may protect its interest in a deposit account by means of a pledge or an assignment. See Zubrow, Integration of Deposit Account Financing into Article 9 of the Uniform Commercial Code: A

Proposal for Legislative Reform, 68 Minn.L.Rev. 899, 901, 936 (1984). A pledge of a deposit account is effective only upon the transfer from pledgor to pledgee of an indispensable instrument (i.e., one such as a passbook that is necessary to control of the account). * * * Because no such transfer took place in this case, a common-law pledge cannot be said to have occurred.

Similarly, the Redwines did not assign their account to the bank. A security agreement at common law constitutes a valid assignment only if it transfers title from the depositor to the bank. See Zubrow, supra, at 937. Here, the security agreement transferred to the bank no more control over, or interest in, the account to the bank than the bank would have had if there had been no "agreement."

Peoples relies upon Trust Company of Columbus v. United States, 735 F.2d 447 (11th Cir.1984), which held, under Georgia law, that a bank account had been successfully assigned to the bank, and that therefore the bank's interest defeated a tax lien. Under the agreement in Trust Company, however, the collateral was "delivered, pledged, assigned, conveyed and transferred" to the Trust Company. Id. at 448. The depositor thus renounced rights to the account and transferred them to the bank. There was no similar agreement in this case.

Peoples' final argument is that its common-law right of setoff against the Redwines' account should be sufficient, as a matter of law, to defeat the government's tax lien. This circuit, however, has three times rejected the argument that an *unexercised* right of setoff defeats a tax lien. * * *

Affirmed.

Notes

1. The Ninth Circuit is trampling on the grave of *Trust Co. of Columbus v. United States,* is it not?

2. Which of the two decisions is correct?

3. If you were a lawyer in Washington, could you draft a term for Peoples Bank's deposit agreement that would protect their right in these circumstances as against the Internal Revenue Service?

SECTION 7. FEDERAL LAW

A. United States as a Lender

Section 9–104(a) excludes from Article 9's coverage "a security interest subject to any statute of the United States, *to the extent that* such statute governs the rights of parties to and third parties affected by transactions, in particular types of properties * * *". (Italics supplied.) Comment 1 to 9–104 identifies the Ship Mortgage Act of 1920 and, to a limited extent, the Federal Aviation Act of 1958.

Even in the situations where the federal statutes have pre-empted Article 9's filing requirements, many courts have held that Article 9 governs some rights and liabilities because the federal statutes typically are not comprehensive. Although one perfects a security interest in an aircraft by a filing with the FAA in Oklahoma City, the courts generally hold that the mode of repossession and resale is governed by Article 9. To the extent that petitioners can move the Congress to fiddle with subjects governed by Article 9 rules, federal law will displace Article 9. The recent federal override of UCC 9–307 with respect to farm products is a case in point, see supra at p. 201.

An important intrusion of federal law into Article 9's domain occurs when the federal government contracts to lend. Although the Supreme Court has held that such contracts are governed by the federal common law (or by federal statutory or federal regulation where those are available), in 1979, in United States v. Kimbell Foods, Inc., 440 U.S. 715, 99 S.Ct. 1448, 59 L.Ed.2d 711 (1979), the Supreme Court held that a federal agency should normally be subject to state-law rules including Article 9's rules of perfection. Indeed, the Court explicitly adopted the Uniform Commercial Code as the federal common law. *In dictum* the Supreme Court recognized that some federal programs call for uniform law throughout the country, programs which variant state law "might frustrate."

The federal government is a lender in many settings. Thus, among other lender roles, it serves (1) as the Small Business Association, where it typically is a guarantor; (2) as a principal lender to farmers; (3) as a purchaser from and thus a financer of defense contractors. The government has been more successful at establishing its right to a special set of rules in its role as a defense purchaser than it has as a farm or small business lender.

IN RE AMERICAN POUCH FOODS, INC.

United States Court of Appeals, Seventh Circuit, 1985.
769 F.2d 1190, *cert. denied* ___ U.S. ___, 106 S.Ct. 1459, 89 L.Ed.2d 716 (1986).

FAIRCHILD, SENIOR CIRCUIT JUDGE:

In a reorganization proceeding under Chapter 11 of the Bankruptcy Code the district court decided, in response to a complaint by the United States, that the United States held absolute title (and right to possession) to certain goods in the possession of the Debtor, American Pouch Foods, Inc. (Pouch). The court abstained from hearing Pouch's counterclaim. *In Re American Pouch Foods, Inc.,* 30 B.R. 1015 (D.C.N.D.Ill.1983). Pouch appeals. We affirm.

In January 1979, Pouch entered into a procurement contract with the United States Defense Logistics Agency (Government). The contract called for Pouch to produce combat rations, known as "Meals, Ready to Eat" (Food Pouches), for use by branches of the Armed Services. The contract gave Pouch the right to progress payments upon request, not more often than bi-weekly. The payments were limited to 90% of Pouch's cost incurred to the date of payment. The so-called title vesting clause of the progress payment part of the contract provided that title to all parts, materials, inventories, work in process and various other categories immediately vested in the Government.[1] Other provisions gave the Government the right to terminate for default (or for convenience of the Government) and to require delivery to it of completed supplies and manufacturing materials. The contract also provided that if, after

1. The title vesting clause in the contract provided, in pertinent part:

(d) *Title.* Immediately, upon the date of this contract, title to all parts; materials; inventories; work in progress; * * * theretofore acquired or produced by the Contractor and allocable or properly chargeable to this contract under sound and generally accepted accounting principles and shall forthwith vest in the Government; and title to all like property thereafter acquired or produced by the Contractor and allocable or properly chargeable to this contract as aforesaid shall forthwith vest in the Government upon said acquisition, production or allocation. Notwithstanding that title to property is in the Government through the operation of this clause, the handling and disposition of such property shall be determined by applicable provisions of this contract such as: the Default clause and paragraph (h) of this clause; Termination for Convenience of the Government clause; and the Special Tooling clause. * * *

notice of termination for default, it was determined that Pouch was not in default or that default was excusable, the rights and obligations of the parties would be the same as if the notice of termination had been for convenience of the Government.

After making approximately $13 million in progress payments the Government terminated the contract for default. The Government claimed that Pouch had not complied with required production schedules. On November 10, 1980, three days after the contract was terminated, Pouch filed a petition for reorganization under Chapter 11 of the Bankruptcy Code, 11 U.S.C. § 101 *et seq.* The Government claimed ownership and possession of all the property allocable to the contract in Pouch's possession or stored at warehouse facilities on its behalf. On December 5, 1980 the Government filed an adversary complaint in bankruptcy court to obtain possession.

Pouch filed an answer principally alleging wrongful termination of the contract and that the Government's title was a security interest not perfected as required by law and subordinate to the rights of the debtor and creditors. Pouch filed a counterclaim seeking damages arising from wrongful termination of the contract.

On February 9, 1981, the bankruptcy court held that, as a matter of law, the Government had absolute title to the property in question and was entitled to repossess it.

While the appeals were pending the bankruptcy court held that it had jurisdiction to hear Pouch's counterclaim even though the Armed Services Board of Contract Appeals had concurrent jurisdiction over the claim.

After the district court decided that questions of fact must be determined and remanded to the bankruptcy court, the Government filed a motion for reconsideration. In 1983, before that motion was decided, Pouch filed a motion in the district court to withdraw from the bankruptcy court the reference of the Government's adversary proceeding. That motion was granted.

Upon reconsideration the district court held that, as a matter of law, the Government had absolute title to all of the property covered by the title vesting clause. *In Re American Pouch Foods, Inc.,* 30 B.R. at 1023. The court also noted that if the Government only took a lien on the allocable property, to secure its progress payments, the lien would be paramount to any other liens. *Id.* The court decided to abstain from hearing Pouch's counterclaim because the issue was better brought before the Armed Services Board of Contract Appeals. *Id.* at 1024.

I

Pouch is a debtor in possession in a reorganization proceeding and as such claims, under 11 U.S.C. § 544(a)(1), the rights and powers of a creditor with a judicial lien. Pouch argues that the title vesting clause in the contract only gave the Government a security interest (lien) in the contract property and that Pouch's hypothetical lien has priority because the Government's lien was not perfected in compliance with the Illinois Commercial Code.

Pouch relies on *United States v. Kimbell Foods, Inc.,* 440 U.S. 715, 99 S.Ct. 1448, 59 L.Ed.2d 711 (1979). There the Supreme Court was confronted with the issue of "whether contractual liens arising from certain federal loan programs take precedence over private liens, in the absence of a federal statute setting priorities." 440 U.S. at 718, 99 S.Ct. at 1453 (footnote omitted). The loan programs involved were those of the Small Business Administration and Farmers Home Administration. The Court found it clear that priority of liens stemming from federal lending programs must be determined with reference to federal law. 440 U.S. at 726, 99 S.Ct. at 1457. After analysis of the character and purposes of the lending programs, the Court found it prudent in determining priority "to adopt the ready made body of state law as the federal rule of decision until Congress strikes a different accommodation." 440 U.S. at 740, 99 S.Ct. at 1464 (footnote omitted).

Pouch first contends that the title vesting clause in the Pouch contract creates only a security interest in the Government such as was clearly the case in *Kimbell Foods* and secondly that the principles applied in *Kimbell Foods* require application of the Illinois Commercial Code to determine priority here. It would follow that Pouch's statutory lien as debtor in possession would be superior to the lien of the Government.

We first consider whether the Government has title such that there is no question of priority of liens. The clear and precise language of the contract between Pouch and the Government granted the Government title. Pouch argues that, notwithstanding the language of the contract, given the intent of the parties, the many incidents and risks of ownership retained by Pouch under the contract, and modern theory in the law of secured transactions, the title vesting clause should not be interpreted literally as grant of title to the Government.

We acknowledge, generally, that contract language which purports to place title to goods in a party not in possession of them may well create only a security interest in that party. *See, e.g.,* Commercial Code provisions, Ill.Rev.Stat. ch. 26, §§ 1–201(37) (Supp.1985), 9–102 and 9–202 (1974). The terms of this contract left Pouch with many of the incidents and risks of ownership.

Thus there would be considerable reason to treat provisions like these, if found in a private contract, as creating a security interest. On the other hand, this is a contract for the procurement of materials for national defense, with its terms spelled out in the regulations of the Defense Department, 32 C.F.R. § 163.79, and a history suggesting a substantial reason for very literal interpretation of the title vesting language. * * *

[The court reviewed the history of the authorization for and characterization of advance payments under government contracts. The conclusion was that Congress intended to authorize progress payments in exchange for title rather than a lien or security interest. Furthermore, early judicial decisions supported a literal interpretation of the title vesting language.]

In *Marine Midland Bank v. United States,* 687 F.2d 395, 231 Ct.Cl. 496 (1982), the court read the title vesting clause as creating security for repayment (out of amounts due the contractor at final performance) of the progress payments, which the court deemed loans, rather than partial purchases. Having decided that the Government had only a security interest (as Pouch contends here) the court declined to apply the state U.C.C. as the federal rule of decision governing priority. Emphasizing the need for standardization and uniformity in Government procurement, as distinguished from the federal loan programs which were the subject of *Kimbell Foods, supra,* the court chose a rule that "the government's security interest under its title vesting procedures [is] paramount to the liens of general creditors." *Id.* 687 F.2d at 404. We would agree with the latter holding if the Government's interest were only a lien.

We acknowledge the reasonableness of the *Marine Midland* view if we were considering the title vesting provisions on a clean slate. We do not agree, however, that because the 1958 enactment of express authority to make progress payments removed the original motive for using a title vesting clause, the construction of the clause should change at the time of that enactment. *See* 687 F.2d at 401. Notwithstanding Judge Bennett's meticulous explication, we see no reason for departure from the consistent holdings before and after 1958 that the title vesting clause is to be taken literally.

We note, however, that application of the *Marine Midland* rule to the present case would produce the same result we reach, awarding possession to the Government. Pouch does not argue, nor does the record suggest, that the value of the goods exceeds the total of progress payments. *Cf.* 687 F.2d at 405.

In *United States v. Lennox Metal Manufacturing Co.,* 225 F.2d 302 (2nd Cir. 1955) the court considered a contract providing for progress payments (there called partial payments) and containing a title vesting clause. The Government terminated the contract for default and sued the contractor to recover possession of the property and damages. The district court had found with adequate support that the contractor was not in default, and that foreclosed recovery of damages. The district court also denied recovery of possession.

Judge Frank wrote the opinion, stating his individual view in Part I. Part II, 225 F.2d beginning at 317, was agreed to by all three judges. The Government contended that upon failure to prove default by the contractor, it had nevertheless brought about a termination for convenience. The contract so provided. The court affirmed the denial of possession, holding in Part II that the Government's refusal to make larger progress payments had been inequitable and such conduct had disentitled it to equitable relief, *i.e.,* "the enforcement of an equitable lien on the [contractor's] property." 225 F.2d at 317. Evidently, although without explanation, the court interpreted the title vesting clause as creating only an equitable lien.

We do not agree. Our interpretation of the contract is that upon termination, whether for default or convenience, the Government becomes entitled to possession of the property to which it has title. The ultimate rights to pecuniary adjustment between the parties will depend upon the type of termination, but the Government is entitled to possession under either type. The Fifth Circuit has held that:

> [I]n cases involving termination of Government contracts, where the product is part of the national defense effort, the jurisdiction of the district courts does not embrace any issue beyond that of title, so long as the Government represents in its complaint that the contract had been terminated. To hold otherwise would permit a contractor to plead and litigate factual issues surrounding the termination, and delay delivery of vitally-needed defense products.

United States v. Digital Products Corp., 624 F.2d 690, 692 (5th Cir.1980); *accord In Re Greenstreet, Inc.,* 209 F.2d 660, 667 (7th Cir.1954).

Lennox has not been followed, and has been criticized. Even if a court would apply equitable principles against the Government in a case where extreme unfairness were shown, circumstances of that type have not been suggested here.

* * *

The judgment appealed from is affirmed.

SWYGERT, SENIOR CIRCUIT JUDGE, dissenting.

Because this case concerns the rights of the United States arising under a nationwide federal program, there is no question that federal law governs. *United States v. Kimbell Foods, Inc.,* 440 U.S. 715, 726–27, 99 S.Ct. 1448, 1457–58, 59 L.Ed.2d 711 (1979). Yet, in defining the rule of decision that gives content to that federal common law, this court must often resort to State law, particularly where there is no express congressional directive to the contrary and where any other rule would disrupt commercial relations predicated on State law. *See id.* at 728–29, 740, 99 S.Ct. at 1458–59, 1464. I would apply Illinois' Uniform Commercial Code as the rule of decision and would hold that the United States owned only an unperfected security interest in the seized assets.

In *Kimbell,* 440 U.S. at 728–29, 740, 99 S.Ct. at 1458–59, 1464, the Supreme Court held that State law should apply as the rule of decision in a commercial dispute involving a nationwide federal program if (1) there is no congressional directive to the contrary, (2) the federal program in question need not be uniform in character nationwide, (3) the application of State law would not frustrate specific objectives of the program, and (4) the application of a federal rule would disrupt commercial relationships predicated on State law. The majority holds, under two alternative theories, that the first criterion was not satisfied in the case at bar.

First, the majority holds that by passing legislation in 1958 expressly authorizing "progress payments," *see* 10 U.S.C. § 2307(a)(1) (1982), Congress necessarily incorporated as binding federal law the past practices that defined the term. Because the United States had always purported to take absolute title—rather than a security interest—in the parts, work in process, and inventories of government contractors in return for progress payments, Congress must have intended to incorporate this practice into the law. *See ante* at 1193–96.

Yet, as the majority's thorough historical review demonstrates, *ante* at 1193–1194, the 1958 statute simply marked the culmination of Congress' long retreat from its former prohibition of advances of public money to government contractors in excess of the value of services already rendered or goods already delivered. It was Congress' intent to legalize the practice of advance payments in general. The statute and legislative history are silent on the question of whether the title-vesting clause that traditionally accompanied progress payments should be interpreted literally or as a *de facto* security interest. The only relevant concern of Congress was that the federal government be permitted to pay money in advance of contract performance; the specifics of defining the effect and ramifications of various contractual alternatives, such as progress payments, were left open.[1]

Congressional silence on such issues should not be interpreted as an invitation to the courts to fashion a uniform federal common law. The "guiding principle" in deciding whether to fashion rules of federal common law or to incorporate State law is that a "significant conflict between some federal policy or interest and the use of state law in the premises must first be specifically shown." *Wallis v. Pan American Petroleum Corp.,* 384 U.S. 63, 68, 86 S.Ct. 1301, 1304, 16 L.Ed.2d 369 (1966). It is not enough that Congress *could* have readily

1. Thus, in explaining its legalization of advance payments, the Senate Report simply cited the need for a "modernized code of procurement procedures." S.Rep. No. 2201, 85th Cong., 2d Sess., *reprinted in* 1958 U.S.Code Cong. & Ad.News 4021, 4024. Congress approved the principle of advance payments as consistent with modern commercial practice, but left to others the task of defining the specific rules governing advance payments.

enacted a complete code of law governing these commercial transactions better than the available State law; the "latent federal power * * * to displace state law is primarily a decision for Congress," and Congress must explicitly indicate its intent to exercise this power. *See id.*

The second theory advanced by the majority, *see ante* at 1196, is that assuming the Government's interest should be defined as a security interest, pursuant to well-established principles of State commercial law, Congress has already provided by statute the governing law of priority. In authorizing liens to secure "advance" payments, Congress required that such liens be "paramount to any other lien." 10 U.S.C. § 2307(c) (1982). Despite the historical differences between "advance" and "progress" payments, Congress must have used the term "advance payments" in the generic sense to include all kinds of payments in advance of full contract performance. "[W]e can think of no reason why Congress could have intended less protection for the Government when making progress payments than when making advance payments." *Ante* at 1194.

I agree. Because Congress has expressly provided that government liens be paramount, this directive must be incorporated as a rule of priority. But one rule of priority does not make a commercial code. Congress provided no direction on a myriad of issues that must be decided in this case and in other commercial cases. There are no guidelines as to how to judge the validity of a government lien, when it attaches, or what prerequisites—such as perfection—must be met before a particular government lien can be enforced as a paramount lien. I would hold that State law provides the rule of decision in determining the creation, validity, and perfection of government liens.

It is not incongruous to hold that different sources of law govern various, but related, aspects of a single commercial transaction. *Kimbell* does not require that a commercial transaction be governed entirely by federal common law or entirely by State law. Indeed, the Supreme Court has stressed that "[e]ven where there is related federal legislation in an area * * * it must be remembered that 'Congress acts * * * against the background of the total *corpus juris* of the states.'" *Wallis,* 384 U.S. at 68, 86 S.Ct. at 1304 (quoting Hart & Wechsler, *The Federal Courts and the Federal System* 435 (1953)). In *Wallis* the Court adopted the kind of hybrid law I propose in the case at bar. The Court held that while federal law governs the ability of private parties to assign oil and gas leases, State law governs the validity of a particular transfer between two parties. Similarly, this court in *United States v. Meadors,* 753 F.2d 590, 592 (7th Cir.1985), selectively applied State law to only a few of the specific issues of commercial law presented in that case. Such hybrid law is consistent with our conception of federal regulation as often "interstitial in nature, enacted against a background of state law and building on state law relationships." Comment, *Adopting State Law as the Federal Rule of Decision: A Proposed Test,* 43 U.Chi. L.Rev., 823, 829 (1976); *accord* Mishkin, *The Variousness of "Federal Law": Competence and Discretion in the Choice of National and State Rules for Decision,* 105 U.Penn.L.Rev. 797, 804–05 (1957) ("Most pervasive, perhaps, is the principle that a decision to apply state law as a matter of federal judicial incorporation may frequently be made as to a single issue at a time.").

The first prong of *Kimbell* is therefore satisfied: there has been no congressional directive regarding what law should govern the creation, validity, and perfection of a government lien. Turning to the second prong, I would follow the Tenth Circuit's holding that the government's interest in a uniform federal law for military procurement would not be compromised by the incorporation of the

Uniform Commercial Code ("UCC") as the rule of decision. *In re Murdock Machine & Engineering Co. of Utah,* 620 F.2d 767, 772–73 (10th Cir.1980). The need for uniformity is already satisfied by State law itself, inasmuch as every State except Louisiana has enacted the UCC. *See* J. White & R. Summers, *Handbook of the Law Under the Uniform Commercial Code* § 1 at 1 & n. 1 (2d ed. 1980). Here, as in *Kimbell,* 440 U.S. at 732–33 & n. 28, 99 S.Ct. at 1460–61 & n. 28, there is no evidence that the "minor variations" in Article 9 of the UCC from State to State would hinder the government's national program. That the government program here involves national defense does not alter this conclusion. I fail to see how the trivial inconveniences attending compliance with the essentially uniform recording requirements of the States somehow threaten national security. *Accord Murdock,* 620 F.2d at 772–73.

As for the third prong of *Kimbell,* it can be argued that destroying the priority of federal liens by subjecting the federal government to State recording requirements would frustrate a specific objective of the federal procurement effort: to ensure that federal liens are paramount to all others. It is true that incorporating State law as the rule of decision in the case at bar may effectively destroy the value of the Government's claim to the seized assets. Yet, if *noncompliance* with State recording laws would effectively defeat the Federal government's ability to claim a paramount lien, certainly *compliance* would not.[2] The Government's assertion at oral argument that incorporating the UCC into federal law would destroy the value of billions of dollars of government liens is an argument against retroactive application of such a rule, not an argument that the government would be unable to protect its interests under the UCC in the future.

There is no question that the fourth prong of *Kimbell* is satisfied. The application of a federal rule would disrupt commercial relationships predicated on State law. With an annual budget that will soon exceed $300 billion, *see* Boyd, *Leaders Report Budget Accord with President,* N.Y. Times, July 10, 1985, at 11, col. 5, the Defense Department has an enormous, brooding presence in the marketplace. Yet, it is not always obvious that the military is involved in a particular transaction. There is nothing inherent in the purchase of such pedestrian goods as food in the case at bar or steel in *Murdock* that alerts the seller to the military's presence. Thus, allowing the military to hold enormous secret liens wreaks havoc with the expectations of the business community. "Mindful of the burdens of time and expense such investigations [of the possibility of the military's interest in a transaction] would impose on our nation's commerce, and the injustice which would result by dealing government 'wild cards' to businessmen at random," I am "not inclined to create a special commercial law for the government's benefit." *Murdock,* 620 F.2d at 772.

I would therefore hold that State law provides the rule of decision governing the creation and perfection of the Government's security interest. As the majority apparently agrees, *see ante* at 1193, there can be little doubt that the title-vesting clause created a security interest. Illinois' UCC defines a secured transaction to include "any transaction (regardless of its form) which is intended to create a security interest in personal property or fixtures." Ill.Ann.Stat. ch. 26, § 9–102(1)(a) (Smith-Hurd 1974) ("Ill. UCC"). Thus, the Government's characterization of its interest as one of absolute title is irrelevant; it is the intent of

2. I would therefore hold that if the government executes a proper security agreement and if its lien attaches and is perfected, then the government holds a paramount lien—superior in priority even to the perfected security interests of other creditors.

the parties, not the form of the transaction, that is dispositive. Here, the many incidents of ownership conferred on Pouch combined with the federal contract officer's testimony that the purpose of the title-vesting clause was to secure performance, *see* Appellant's Brief at 26–27 (quoting Transcript), compel the conclusion that the parties intend the Government to take only a security interest.

It is undisputed that the Government failed to file a financing statement pursuant to Ill. UCC §§ 9–103, 9–302, 9–401–03. The Government therefore held only an unperfected security interest in the seized assets. *Id.* at § 9–303. To be sure, this did not render the security agreement invalid or unenforceable. And it can be argued that as long as the Government's security interest is valid under State law, the federal rule of priority should apply to render the Government's lien paramount. Yet, the federal statute is so sparse as to what prerequisites should be met to create a valid and enforceable paramount lien that I would define the State perfection requirement as such a prerequisite. Only in this way can federal legislation that is interstitial in nature be brought into harmony with the broad body of State law that remains in force and effect until expressly replaced with more comprehensive federal legislation. *See supra* at 1200.

I would hold then, that before the Government seized Pouch's assets, it held an unperfected security interest. As such, its rights were subordinate to those of a variety of other creditors, including the debtor-in-possession. *See* Ill. UCC §§ 9–301(1), (3).

It should be noted, however, that once the Government came into possession of the collateral, no creditor, regardless of its superior claim of right, could compel repossession. Such repossession would be inconsistent with the sovereignty of the United States. Rather, the remedy for those who held superior claims to the collateral is to sue for their proper share of the proceeds, because in destroying the value of their claims, the Government took their property without just compensation. *See* U.S. Const. amend. V; *Armstrong v. United States,* 364 U.S. 40, 80 S.Ct. 1563, 4 L.Ed.2d 1554 (1960); *United States v. Ansonia Brass & Copper Co.,* 218 U.S. 452, 471, 31 S.Ct. 49, 54, 54 L.Ed. 1107 (1910); *Marine Midland Bank v. United States,* 687 F.2d 395, 397–98, 231 Ct.Cl. 496 (1982), *cert. denied,* 460 U.S. 1037, 103 S.Ct. 1427, 75 L.Ed.2d 788 (1983).

I would therefore reverse and remand for further proceedings.

Note

Judge Swygert is right, is he not?

Problem 7–8

Welco Industries agreed to furnish electric motors and compressors to Wedj. Wedj was producing air conditioners under a government contract for the United States Army. Under an agreement between the parties entered in the presence of the government's administrative officer the contracting officer had "agreed to approve government progress payments to Wedj Inc. for Welco material immediately on receipt at Wedj Inc." The parallel provision gave Wedj's promise to pay the full invoice price within 10 days of receipt. When Welco filed a writ of replevin in the state court in Pennsylvania, the federal government intervened to assert its rights, and had the case transferred to the federal court. Welco argued that under the Memorandum of Understanding, shipments to Wedj were subject to a "retention of title" until full payment had been made. The government contract with Wedj on the other hand provided that "immediately upon the date of this contract, title to all parts; materials, inventory; [and] work in progress * * * acquired or produced by the contractor and allocated or properly charged under this contract under sound and generally accepted accounting principles shall forthwith vest in the government." The government argued that the foregoing contract language applied and that the language transferred title to the compressors and other materials to the government.

1. If the federal government were not involved, would this merely be a case of an unperfected secured creditor who would lose to a subsequent purchaser? What sections would be particularly relevant under Article 9?

2. Assume that Welco had perfected its purchase money security interest and had given whatever notice that might be required under UCC 9–312(3). Would the federal government's claim then be subordinate?

B. The Federal Tax Lien

The federal tax lien (Internal Revenue Code sections 6321 through 6323) is unique for many purposes. Unlike many liens, it carries its own priority schedule.

The student should first understand when and how a tax lien is likely to arise. In a typical income tax case, the tax lien does not arise until after the tax has been "assessed," demand for its payment has been made, and that demand has not been satisfied. Typically, assessment cannot occur until the taxpayer has reported income due and not made payment of it, or until there has been an audit and an ascertainment of tax to be due by the Internal Revenue Service. The threat that brings the taxpayer to the tax court is the threat of "assessment" of the tax. Thus, in the usual proceeding before the tax court and on appeal, there has not yet been an "assessment" and therefore a tax lien cannot exist. The tax lien that a creditors' rights lawyer is most likely to see is not one that arose out of nonpayment of income taxes on the revenue of the debtor, but rather it is a lien arising because of the debtor's failure to withhold and pay over taxes on the salaries of employees.

When such a lien arises under 6321 and 6322, it attaches to all the debtor's property, wherever located, without the necessity for a filing. Under the basic priority rules, 6323(a), the federal tax lien is subordinate to "any purchaser, holder of a security interest, mechanics lienor, or judgment lien creditor until notice thereof" has been filed. Thus, at least in general, the federal tax lien conforms to the first-in-time first-in-right rule. A starting point for one's analysis is to ask whether the federal government has filed notice of the tax lien as provided in 6323(f). If that event has not yet occurred at the time a judgment lien arises or a security interest perfected, etc., a competing claimant typically will be victorious against the tax lien. Although there may be some difficulty and confusion about exactly where the IRS will file its notice, the general rule is not hard to understand or to apply.

A difficulty arises when the competing creditor is asserting a security interest in after-acquired property or a security interest based on an advance made after the filing of the notice of a tax lien or after the creditor's knowledge of the existence of a tax lien. In such cases, UCC 9–312 would grant priority to the first to file over a subsequent creditor despite the fact the security interest was in after-acquired property or that it depended upon a subsequent advance. But the same is true as against a federal tax lien only to a limited extent. That limited extent is spelled out most extensively in 6323(c) and 6323(d). These sections are quite complex, but the student should at least have a general idea about where and how they will apply. Consider the following problem.

Problem 7-9

1. Secured creditor takes and perfects a security interest in debtor's caterpillar tractor on March 1, 1988. On March 5, notice of a tax lien is filed. Who enjoys priority?

2. Bank has a perfected security interest in all of debtor's inventory and accounts receivable, including after-acquired accounts and inventory. Several years after the financing statement was filed and the security agreement was executed and at a time when the debtor had $2,000,000 of accounts and inventory and when $1,500,000 of the loan was outstanding, the federal government filed the notice of tax lien.

a. Who has priority at that point?

b. Assume that secured creditor makes two subsequent advances of $100,000 each. The first is made 20 days after the notice of tax lien is filed, and the second is made 60 days after. Which of the following statements is accurate:

(1) Neither of these advances will be protected under 6323(d).

(2) The first but not the second will be protected under 6323(c).

(3) Both will be protected under 6323(c) or 6323(a)

c. What if the Bank knew of the tax lien but not of the filing at the time it made both advances?

d. If Bank and the IRS both claim inventory and accounts that had been acquired by the debtor 90 days after the filing of the notice of tax lien, who would have priority?

RICE INVESTMENT COMPANY v. UNITED STATES

United States Court of Appeals, Fifth Circuit, 1980.
625 F.2d 565.

RANDALL, CIRCUIT JUDGE:

In October, 1973, Rice Investment Company ("Rice") loaned Handy Stop, Inc. (the "Debtor") $67,583.20. In connection with the loan, the Debtor executed and delivered to Rice a security agreement pursuant to which the Debtor granted to Rice a security interest in all of the Debtor's inventory then owned or thereafter acquired. A financing statement was filed in the office of the Secretary of State of the State of Texas on October 29, 1973. The Debtor made payments on its indebtedness to Rice from time to time. In March, 1975, $46,317.54 remained owing from the Debtor to Rice.

The Debtor incurred liabilities for withholding and FICA taxes for the third and fourth quarters of 1973 and the first quarter of 1974 in the total amount of $11,853.19. Assessments of the taxes were made during March, 1974. Thereafter, a notice of a federal tax lien in the amount of $8,521.51 was filed on April 26, 1974, for the third and fourth quarters of 1973, and a further notice of a federal tax lien in the amount of $4,587.59 was filed on August 5, 1974, for the first quarter of 1974. The Internal Revenue Service levied upon the Debtor's inventory on August 18, 1974. The outstanding tax liability of the Debtor, including interest, at that time was $13,514.18. The perishable inventory was sold by the United States on August 28, 1974 for $750, and the nonperishable items were sold on November 14, 1974 for $3,500.

In September, 1974, Rice brought suit against the United States under 26 U.S.C. § 7426 (1976) seeking recovery from the United States of the proceeds

($4,250) received by the United States from the sale of the Debtor's inventory. Rice's second amended complaint asserts that the lien of the United States under 26 U.S.C. § 6321 (1976) in the inventory of the Debtor was junior to the lien of Rice under 26 U.S.C. § 6323 (1976) (amended 1978; amendment not relevant to this appeal) and that the levy of the United States was therefore unlawful. During the proceedings, in response to interrogatories propounded by the United States, Rice acknowledged that it did not have any information in its possession by which it could determine the exact date on which the Debtor acquired the inventory which was seized by the Internal Revenue Service.[1] Further, Rice admitted, in its motion for summary judgment, that none of the actual inventory on hand in October, 1973, when the security agreement was entered into, was part of the inventory seized and sold on August 28, 1974, and November 14, 1974.

The question presented by this appeal is whether the federal tax lien filed by the United States on April 26, 1974,[2] pursuant to 26 U.S.C. § 6321, primes the security interest held by Rice in the inventory which was seized by the United States on August 18, 1974. We hold that the lien of the United States does prime the security interest of Rice in such inventory, and accordingly, we reverse the summary judgment granted by the district court and remand with instructions to enter summary judgment for the United States.

SOME HISTORY ON THE PROBLEM

* * *

Under 26 U.S.C. § 6321, every federal tax which is not paid on demand becomes a lien "upon all property and rights to property, whether real or personal, belonging to" the taxpayer. After-acquired property, such as the Debtor's property in this case, is reached by the lien. The lien is effective from the date of assessment of the tax and has aptly been described as a secret lien. When the lien was first created in 1866, it prevailed, even though secret, against a bona fide purchaser for value. In 1913, however, Congress extended protection to purchasers, mortgagees and judgment creditors, and in 1939, to pledgees, against federal tax liens of which notice had not been filed in a designated office. Further, recognizing the impracticability of searching for tax liens in some cases, Congress in 1939 provided priority over filed tax liens under certain conditions for purchasers of, and lenders secured by "securities" and in 1964, for purchasers of motor vehicles. However, as against the rest of the world, including the taxpayer himself, the federal tax lien was effective upon assessment without any need for public notice.

The most basic principle employed in the adjudication of the priority of competing liens is "the first in time is the first in right." When a federal tax lien is one of the liens involved, however, the Supreme Court added a gloss on that principle by requiring that in order to be "first in time," the nonfederal lien must first have become "choate," i.e., the identity of the lienor, the property subject to the lien and the amount of the lien must be established beyond any possibility of change or dispute. Further, the determination of whether "a lien has acquired sufficient substance and has become so perfected as to defeat a later-arising or later-filed federal tax lien" is a matter of federal law.

1. The Debtor's business consisted of a drive-in grocery store, and its inventory consisted of the perishable and nonperishable items customarily sold in such a store.

2. Since the amount of gross proceeds from the sale of the inventory ($4,250) is less than the amount of the lien ($8,521.51) as to which notice was filed on April 26, 1974, we concern ourselves here only with the lien filed on that date.

As the federal law on "choateness" developed, few liens prevailed in the battle against federal tax liens.

> Even mortgages and other contractual security interests, despite their specially favored position under the federal statute, were vulnerable before 1966 to subsequently filed federal tax liens to the extent that the security embraced after-acquired property or involved disbursements (whether optional or obligatory) yet to be made, including foreclosure expenses and other outlays for which a mortgagee normally is entitled to a lien with the same priority as the principal debt.

Plumb, *Federal Liens and Priorities—Agenda for the Next Decade,* 77 Yale L.J. 228, 231 (1967) (footnotes omitted).

FEDERAL TAX LIEN ACT OF 1966

Congress enacted the Federal Tax Lien Act of 1966 in an effort to conform the lien provisions of the Internal Revenue Code to the concepts developed in the Uniform Commercial Code. Another primary objective was to provide some limited but specific relief from the harshness of the choateness rule for, among others, commercial lenders whose loans and collateral may change daily.

Section 6323 of the Internal Revenue Code, as amended by the Federal Tax Lien Act of 1966, sets forth certain limitations on the validity and priority of federal tax liens imposed by § 6321 of the Internal Revenue Code as against certain persons, including the holder of a security interest in property which is the subject of such a lien. Subsection (c) of § 6323 is the provision designed to provide a safe haven for the holders of security interests arising in certain commercial financing arrangements. Subsection (c) provides, in relevant part, that

> even though notice of a lien imposed by section 6321 has been filed, such lien shall not be valid with respect to a security interest which came into existence after tax lien filing but which—
>
> (A) is in qualified property covered by the terms of a written agreement entered into before tax lien filing and constituting—
>
> (i) a commercial transactions financing agreement, * * * and
>
> (B) is protected under local law against a judgment lien arising, as of the time of tax lien filing, out of an unsecured obligation.

The balance of subsection (c) and subsection (h) define the terms used in subsection (c). Four of those definitions are relevant for our purposes—the definitions of "commercial transactions financing agreement," "qualified property," "commercial financing security" and "security interest." The term "commercial transactions financing agreement" is defined as

> an agreement (entered into by a person in the course of his trade or business)—
>
> (i) to make loans to the taxpayer to be secured by commercial financial security acquired by the taxpayer in the ordinary course of his trade or business, * * *
>
> but such an agreement shall be treated as coming within the term only to the extent that such loan or purchase is made before the 46th day after the date of tax lien filing or (if earlier) before the lender or purchaser had actual notice or knowledge of such tax lien filing.

The term "qualified property," when used with respect to a commercial transactions financing agreement, is defined to include "only commercial financing security acquired by the taxpayer before the 46th day after the date of tax lien filing." The term "commercial financing security" is defined to mean "(i) paper of a kind ordinarily arising in commercial transactions, (ii) accounts receivable, (iii) mortgages on real property, and (iv) inventory." Finally, subsection (h)(1) of § 6323 defines the term "security interest" as follows:

> The term "security interest" means any interest in property acquired by contract for the purpose of securing payment or performance of an obligation or indemnifying against loss or liability. A security interest exists at any time (A) if, at such time, the property is in existence and the interest has become protected under local law against a subsequent judgment lien arising out of an unsecured obligation, and (B) to the extent that, at such time, the holder has parted with money or money's worth.

Under subsection (c) of § 6323, the holder of a security interest competing for priority with a federal tax lien who is able to demonstrate that such security interest meets the requirements of subsection (c) and the related definition in subsection (h) achieves priority for such security interest over the federal tax lien by virtue of the introductory language of subsection (c) which renders the competing tax lien invalid as against such security interest. It is apparent, simply from reading subsections (c) and (h), that the holder of a security interest seeking to establish priority thereunder over a competing tax lien must clear several complex hurdles under such subsections, and the failure to clear any one of them leaves the holder outside the safe haven of subsection (c). In the case before the court, the United States argues that in view of Rice's admission that it did not have any information in its possession by which it could determine the date on which the Debtor acquired the inventory seized by the United States on August 18, 1974, Rice would be unable to carry its burden under § 6323 of proving that the inventory was "qualified property," i.e., property acquired by the Debtor before June 11, 1974 (the 46th day after the filing of the tax lien on April 26, 1974). We agree, and we hold that the security interest of the United States in the seized inventory is, accordingly, not invalid under § 6323 with respect to the security interest of Rice in such inventory. Our holding is based on the clear language of the statute, and is strongly supported by the equally clear legislative history. At least when the inquiry is solely whether an item of inventory is "qualified property," it is not necessary to resort to notions of "choateness" as a tool for statutory interpretation. In view of our holding, it is also unnecessary to analyze the status of Rice's security interest insofar as the other requirements of § 6323 are concerned, and we express no views with respect thereto.

* * *

Rice urges that we construe the "in existence" language contained in the definition of "security interest" in subsection (h) of § 6323 to cover not only the inventory of the Debtor in existence on the date of the filing of the tax lien, but also any inventory which thereafter replaced such inventory. Rice argues that such a construction is particularly appropriate where, as was the case here, there has been only a single advance by the lender. To accept Rice's argument, however, would be to ignore the clear language of subsection (c) which requires that, wholly apart from the date on which the loan is made (which is itself the subject of certain independent requirements under § 6323 concededly met here), the collateral must be "qualified property." It would also be to ignore the legislative history of the Federal Tax Lien Act of 1966 which evidences a clear intent not to give commercial lenders an infinite priority over the United States, but instead to limit such lenders to property acquired by the taxpayer debtor before the 46th day after the filing of the tax lien. Rice says that a decision in favor of the United States in this case will have the effect of requiring a secured lender to check each day to determine whether a federal tax lien has been filed with respect to each of its borrowers. While this may be something of an exaggeration, it is clear that subsection (c) of § 6323 requires a secured lender regularly to monitor the federal tax lien status of its borrowers because only the prompt ascertainment of the existence of a federal tax lien will put the secured lender in a position to protect its interest in the collateral. As this court noted in *Texas Oil & Gas,* "we realize that this disposition does not afford the protection that commercial lenders who deal with after-acquired property might prefer." 466 F.2d at 1053. But efforts to improve that protection should be directed to Congress and not to the courts.

BACK TO HISTORY

Since the security interest of Rice in the seized inventory is not entitled to priority over the federal tax lien under § 6323, Rice must demonstrate that it is entitled to priority under the federal law developed prior to the enactment of the Federal Tax Lien Act of 1966. However, it is clear that under the federal law on "choateness" described above, the federal tax lien filed by the United States on April 26, 1974, would be entitled to priority over the security interest of Rice in the inventory seized by the United States on August 18, 1974, because Rice, by its own admission, could not prove that the seized property was in existence and owned by the Debtor on the date the tax lien was filed, which would lead to the conclusion that the security interest of Rice in the seized inventory was not sufficiently choate on the date of the tax lien filing to prevail over the tax lien.

Our conclusion that Rice, having failed to secure a safe haven under § 6323, is left with the law on "choateness" and fails under that law is buttressed by this court's similar conclusion in *Texas Oil & Gas.* Having demonstrated, among other things, that the account receivable in that case did not constitute "qualified property" under § 6323, the court turned to a consideration of the status of the account under the federal law on "choateness":

> In the instant case, it is true that the bank had done all it could do under the Uniform Commercial Code to secure its interest in taxpayer-debtor's accounts receivable. However, that conclusion simply does not answer the case law as it has developed in the area of tax liens. However "complete" a lender's perfection may be under state recording laws and however "specific" state law might deem that interest to be, it is federal law that determines the extent to which that state determination will protect a private lien from a federal tax lien. It appears clear from the case law that an account receivable not yet "acquired" at the time of the filing of a tax lien because the final transaction creating the account receivable was not yet in existence cannot be considered choate, save for those accounts receivable now protected by section 6323(c).

Texas Oil & Gas, 466 F.2d at 1051.

In our case, while Rice may well have done all that it could do under the Texas Business & Commerce Code to perfect its security interest in the Debtor's after-acquired inventory, the security interest of Rice in inventory not yet acquired at the time of the filing of the tax lien cannot be considered choate for federal law purposes, and the federal tax lien prevails over such security interest.

Reversed and remanded with instructions to enter summary judgment for the United States.

[Some footnotes omitted.]

Note

Rice comes to you after the decision above and asks what advice you would give to avoid similar outcomes in future cases. What would you suggest?

Note: The "Choateness Doctrine."

Any lawyers who are deeply involved in tax lien litigation will have to wrestle with the "choateness doctrine." One might have hoped that the Federal Tax Lien Act had laid it to rest, but an examination of the *Rice* case and of others like it, shows that it lives on, albeit in a somewhat weakened form. Beware, we have merely opened your eyes to federal tax lien complexities.

CHAPTER 8

THE SECURED CREDITOR IN BANKRUPTCY

SECTION 1. INTRODUCTION

Both the student and the Article 9 lender view the Bankruptcy Code as a frightening and forbidding presence. The student senses that the trustee in bankruptcy has complex rights derived from the Bankruptcy Code that are different from and in some ways much more far-reaching than those of the creditors. Many an Article 9 lender has not merely sensed those things; he has had his nose rubbed in them.

A. *Some History*

In 1978, Congress enacted the Bankruptcy Reform Act, Public Law 95–598, 92 Stat. 2549, which became law on October 1, 1979. This historic legislation repealed the Bankruptcy Act of 1898, as amended, and enshrined the new Bankruptcy Code in Title 11, U.S.C.A. In addition to simplifying and clarifying substantive bankruptcy principles that had evolved over the years, the Code established bankruptcy courts with comprehensive jurisdiction over all cases and civil proceedings arising in, or relating to, cases under the Code and upgraded and clarified the judicial status of the judges of the bankruptcy court. See 28 U.S.C. sections 151–160, 1471–1482.

Since that time, the implementation of the Code has been marked by controversy, complexity, and confusion. The need for further congressional action was made clear by the Supreme Court in Northern Pipe Line Construction Co. v. Marathon Pipe Line Co., 458 U.S. 50 (1982), in which the court held that the broad jurisdiction granted to bankruptcy judges violated Article III of the Constitution. Ultimately, a new and complex jurisdictional system was developed by Congress and enacted into law in 1984 in the Bankruptcy Amendments and Federal Judgeship Act of 1984. Pub.L. No. 98–353, 98 Stat. 333. See King, *Jurisdiction and Procedure Under the Bankruptcy Amendments of 1984,* 38 Vand.L.Rev. 675 (1985). Other corrective amendments, some substantive, were also contained in the 1984 Act, and the process of amendment still continues. One must be aware, therefore, of the latest version of the statute, as well as that version in effect when the case in bankruptcy under study was commenced.

B. *The Effect of Commencing a "Case" In Bankruptcy*

A "case" in bankruptcy is commenced when a petition for relief is filed by or against a debtor with the bankruptcy court. Relief for a business debtor will be either a liquidation under Chapter 7 or a reorganization under Chapter 11. See Code, Chapter 3, Subchapter 1. In Chapter 7 cases, a trustee, who represents the debtor's estate, will be selected. The trustee has numerous responsibilities and powers, including the capacity to sue and to be sued. In Chapter 11, the debtor will become the "debtor in possession" and, as such, exercise the trustee's rights.

When we speak of "the trustee," we mean to include the debtor in possession in a Chapter 11 case.

After a case is commenced, a secured creditor under Article 9 may file a claim against the estate and request a determination, under Section 506, that the claim is secured by property in which the estate has an interest. Two important questions arise at this point: (1) Should the secured claim be allowed? If not (and we will see why this might occur), the claim is unsecured and the creditor, subject to the priorities of Section 507, must share pro rata with other unsecured creditors. (2) If the secured claim is allowed, is the value of the interest in property of the estate less than the amount of the allowed claim? If so, the creditor will be unsecured in the amount of the difference and must pursue that portion of the claim as an unsecured creditor. Valuation questions, therefore, may arise early in the proceedings.

Assume for now that the secured claim is allowed and that the value of the collateral—the property in which the estate has an interest—exceeds the amount of the claim. What are the immediate effects under the Bankruptcy Code of commencing a case? Here are some simple problems that can be answered by reference to the statute.

Problem 8–1

Assume that the Debtor filed a petition for relief under Chapter 7 (liquidation) on July 1, 1987.

1. On July 5, Debtor granted to Secured Party a security interest, enforceable under Article 9, in personal property owned by the Debtor and not previously encumbered. May the trustee avoid the security interest? See Section 549. Is the creation of a security interest a transfer? See Section 101(48).

2. On February 1, Secured Party created and perfected by filing a security interest in Debtor's inventory, existing and after-acquired, and proceeds. On July 5, Debtor acquired rights in inventory subject to the security interest. In addition, Debtor received proceeds from the sale in the ordinary course of business of inventory acquired before July 1. Does Secured Party have a security interest in the after-acquired property? In the proceeds? See Section 552.

3. On June 25, Debtor defaulted under the security agreement. On June 26, Secured Party, acting under Article 9, Part 5, peacefully repossessed all the inventory in Debtor's possession. On July 5, Secured Party sent Debtor a notice under UCC 9–504(3) that it intended to dispose of the inventory by private sale after July 15. Can the trustee block this disposition? See Section 362(a)(5). See also, Sections 541(a)(1) & 542.

4. Debtor's petition for relief in bankruptcy was a default under the security agreement. Can Secured Party thereafter repossess inventory subject to a security interest from Debtor? See Section 362(a)?

C. Importance of Trustee in Bankruptcy

Here we can examine but a small part of the Bankruptcy Code. Mostly we will consider the trustee's so-called avoidance rights (often called avoidance "powers"). Those are the rights that the trustee in bankruptcy can use to "avoid" a security interest or another transfer by the debtor. Although those rights are probably not the most important to be found in the Bankruptcy Code, they may be the most important from the point of view of the secured creditor. Whatever their weight in the bankruptcy scale, the right of the trustee in bankruptcy to avoid or, put another way, to enjoy ultimate priority over Article

9 secured creditors is a far greater source of concern to such creditors than the rights of competing secured creditors, of state-law lien creditors, or of purchasers.

Why are the rights of the trustee in bankruptcy so significant? First, they are significant because the trustee in bankruptcy is ubiquitous. For every competing secured creditor there are even more trustees in bankruptcy. For every competing state-law lien creditor there may even be a hundred trustees in bankruptcy. The competing secured creditor or other creditor arises only occasionally. A trustee in bankruptcy has the potential of arising with respect to every debtor of the Article 9 secured creditor, and springs into being instantly upon the filing of a petition in bankruptcy.

Secondly, the trustee is specially important because he always has rights that are simply not accorded to other competitors. Under section 544 he has the right of a lien creditor arising on the date the petition is filed. For our purposes this is the right granted by UCC 9–301(1)(b) to a state-law lien creditor to defeat an unperfected security interest. The trustee also can void preferences under section 547, can set aside certain perfected security interests under section 522(f) and can set aside a variety of transfers as fraudulent conveyances under section 548 or 544(b). All of these rights arise out of the federal law, but some depend in important respects upon state law. They are rights, however, that go beyond the rights of any individual state-law creditor and are bound in many cases to leave disappointed secured creditors strewn in the wake of their exercise. So the trustee is important not just because he is ubiquitous, but because he has very special rights.

The trustee is important for yet a third reason, namely, that he is not a member of the club. If one secured creditor gets into a dispute with another, it is conceivable, even likely, that they will be able to work out an arrangement that will suit both of them. They may find that they have mutual interests in this case or in another and thus that it is not in the interest of either to litigate. The trustee, on the other hand, is a professional representative of the unsecured creditors. By hypothesis he now deals with a dead, moribund, or badly faltering business, and unlike a solvent debtor or other secured creditor, he may have no long-term interest in working out a deal that is favorable to any given secured creditor. Thus, at least in liquidation, the trustee is willing to go to the mat, to litigate over his rights and to risk losing all against the prospect that he might win all.

Finally the trustee is more important than other competitors because he brings his own court with him. With few exceptions priorities between the trustee in bankruptcy and any secured creditor will be fought out, not in state courts, but in the federal bankruptcy court. They will be heard there by a bankruptcy judge who does nothing but hear such cases. Not only is this judge usually a sophisticated analyst of Article 9 and of the bankruptcy law, he is a judge with a stake in the bankruptcy process. Invariably he will be hostile to any whom he perceives to be at odds with what might be called the bankruptcy system. To the extent that the secured creditor presents himself as one who would rather not submit to the process but would instead prefer to deprive the others of some of the wherewithal (e.g. collateral) to play the bankruptcy game, the bankruptcy judge will not be receptive. Perhaps it is too strong to say that the bankruptcy court is a hostile environment for the secured creditors, but it is appropriate to say that this environment is not dedicated primarily to the secured creditors' interests. The bankruptcy court is clearly a place where the secured creditors' interests can be harmed or compromised in many ways and where secured creditors are unlikely to get their way by trying to fool or intimidate the judge.

We divide this chapter into two parts. In the first we will deal extensively and in depth with the avoidance rights of the trustee, sections 544, 547, 548, and others. In the second part we will deal in a more superficial way with some of the more subtle rights of the bankruptcy trustee. These are not rights to avoid the secured creditors' interests but merely to impede them, to bite at the secureds' heels in the hope of ultimately wearing them down to produce a compromise. These are the rights found in section 362 (the stay), in sections 1129 and 1325 (the cramdown), and in still other sections of the code.

The various forms of bankruptcy are identified by their "chapters." Chapter 7 contains the provisions for liquidation of an individual's or business's assets; Chapter 11 deals with reorganizations and Chapter 13 covers so called wage-earner plans. The students should not only understand this nomenclature, but also understand that many Chapter 11's are in fact merely prolonged liquidations and that a business can sometimes be run even after a Chapter 7 has been filed. In Chapter 13's and Chapter 7's there will always be an independent trustee. In Chapter 11 the debtor becomes the "debtor-in-possession" (sometimes called the "DIP") and himself has and asserts most of the rights of the trustee in bankruptcy. Thus, for the purpose of this course, when one sees a court talking about the rights of the "debtor-in-possession" he should think of that person as the trustee.

SECTION 2. TRUSTEE'S AVOIDANCE RIGHTS ("POWERS")

A. The Basics

It is familiar learning that subsection 544(a) of the Bankruptcy Act is the "strong-arm clause." This clause gives the trustee in bankruptcy the rights of a lien creditor as of the date the petition is filed in a voluntary case. The student should now understand how this section fits hand-in-glove with the lien creditor's rights to strike down unperfected security interests under UCC 9–301(1) and other state law.

Section 544(b) is a more obscure provision. It is a direct descendant of section 70e, the section involved in *In re Plonta* infra at p. 356. By reading *In re Plonta* and applying the Uniform Commercial Code and the Bankruptcy Code of 1978 to it, students should learn why 544(b) is no longer a very significant provision.

The other avoidance section that merits careful and detailed study is section 547 dealing with preferences. It allows a trustee in bankruptcy to recapture certain money and other assets that have been transferred out of the estate prior to the filing of the petition. Two "transfers" that will concern us in this course are the perfection of a security interest and the payment of a debt.

Sections 549, 550, 551 and 552 may be regarded as adjuncts to the more significant avoidance rights of sections 544 and 547. In addition we will consider section 548, a mini-fraudulent conveyance act, and section 558 which gives to the trustee the defenses that would have been available to the debtor.

Finally we will treat subsection 522(f), an avoidance right distinct from all the others. Under 522(f) the debtor may avoid a perfected security interest that could not have been attacked under any of the other provisions in certain circumstances where the debtor has the right to declare the asset as exempt under state law or under 522(d).

To get a grip on the basics the student should examine the lawyer's opinion in the following problem. The lawyer is sometimes, but not always, correct.

Problem 8–2

Assume that Gene Ovelli owns a small lumber mill that has been in financial difficulty for some months. During the current year, Ovelli has engaged in the transactions listed below.

1. January 8: Adams finances Ovelli's purchase of a $1000 piece of equipment from Jones, charges a usurious rate of interest and acquires a security interest duly created and perfected pursuant to Article 9 and which gives Adams a veto power over all of Ovelli's future dealings with others on credit.

2. January 10: First National Bank lent Ovelli $4000, and took Article 9 security in Ovelli's two cement mixers, but because of a slip-up, no financing statement was ever executed or filed.

3. June 11: Holt, who had lent $3000 to Ovelli a year previous pursuant to an unsecured note, became panicky and demanded that Ovelli give him security in a caterpillar that Ovelli owned free and clear. Ovelli and Holt duly executed a valid financing statement that referred to the caterpillar as "collateral" and Holt then duly filed it.

4. June 12: Stein who had lent $4000 to Ovelli pursuant to a secured obligation two years previously, but who had never filed a financing statement, filed a financing statement on June 12.

5. April 19: Brown, who had sold several power saws to Ovelli on unsecured credit, got a judgment against Ovelli and levied on the saws which the sheriff now has in his possession pending a scheduled judicial sale.

6. January 16: Ovelli transferred title to his new and unencumbered Cadillac sedan to his wife. At different times he has described this transfer as a gift out of love and affection for his wife or as a payment for her service without pay at the lumbermill as a bookkeeper. Over the years she has done office work at the mill; she was never paid a formal salary for that work.

7. May 30: Costa, a cousin of Ovelli, lent Ovelli $5000 pursuant to an Article 9 security interest in lumber worth $6000 on Ovelli's premises. Costa did not, however, perfect this interest until June 7. Meanwhile, on June 5, Martin, an unsecured creditor of Ovelli (with a $500 claim) and armed with a judgment, levied on the lumber with knowledge of Costa's interest.

8. June 28: Adams lent Ovelli $5000 pursuant to a valid and contemporaneously perfected security interest in Ovelli's only remaining unencumbered personalty, a compressor worth $7500.

Against the foregoing background, Ovelli went to his lawyer, Drake, stated that his situation seemed hopeless, and that he wanted to "take bankruptcy" and start over.

Ovelli filed a petition in bankruptcy on July 3rd. Let us assume that the trustee in bankruptcy for Ovelli's estate has asked a lawyer, Fraser, to serve as his attorney during the course of the proceeding. The trustee has given Fraser a memorandum recording the eight transactions described above and asked what rights the trustee has, if any, in respect to each. Fraser's comments, gratuitous and otherwise, on some of the transactions follow:

1. *Trustee v. Adams.* Under section 558 the estate has the defenses of the debtor. Among those would be a claim in this case that the contract was usurious and arguably unconscionable.

2. *Trustee v. First National Bank.* This one we will challenge under section 544(a). It is a classic non-perfection-lien creditor situation in which the trustee beats the unperfected secured creditor by asserting the rights of a lien creditor under section 9–301 and section 544.

3. *Trustee v. Holt.* This is a classic section 547 case.

4. *Trustee v. Adams and Stein.* This too is a preference; or did the "transfer" occur before the 90 day term?

5. *Trustee v. Brown.* This one we could have challenged under the old section 67(a) that struck down almost all judicial liens that arose within four months of bankruptcy. I don't see a provision identical to that one in the Bankruptcy Reform Act. There must be one though.

6. *Trustee v. Mrs. Ovelli.* I wonder what we should do here. Certainly we should consider the use of section 548, but we may have difficulty in proving the facts under section 548. I think I will ask my associate if there are other bases upon which we could attack this transfer. What do you think?

7. *Trustee v. Costa and Martin.* We have lots of possibilities here it would seem. First I would think that we could strike Martin's claim down under section 547. Section 547 does not seem to help us against Costa because he perfected within 10 days. What about the possibility of subrogating ourselves to Martin's claim under section 544(b) directly? I wonder if the reference in section 544(b) to subrogation only to a creditor "holding an unsecured claim" deprives us of that right? Conceivably we can reassert Martin's claim under section 551, having struck it down, but does that mean we can unseat Ovelli only to the extent of $500?

8. *Trustee v. Adams and Stein.* I am tired, I will let the students work this one out.

B. Avoidance Rights, Less Basic

Section 544(b) of the Bankruptcy Code provides: "The trustee may avoid any transfer of an interest of the debtor in property or any obligation incurred by the debtor that is voidable under applicable law by a creditor holding an unsecured claim that is allowable under * * * this title. * * *"

IN RE PLONTA

United States Court of Appeals, Sixth Circuit, 1962.
311 F.2d 44.

CECIL, CHIEF JUDGE:

This is an appeal from the United States District Court for the Western District of Michigan, Southern Division. The controversy grows out of the bankruptcy of Eugene (Dean) W. Plonta. Sears, Roebuck and Co., the appellant, claims to be a secured creditor of the bankrupt Plonta. Wadsworth Bissell, trustee in bankruptcy, is the appellee. The parties will be referred to as the Bankrupt, Sears and Trustee, respectively.

The pertinent facts are not in dispute and may be stated as follows: The Bankrupt purchased a 22–foot cabin cruiser from Sears on a conditional sales contract April 30, 1956. The cruiser was in kit form and by agreement between the purchaser and seller, the boat hull, engine, parts and equipment were to be shipped for assembly to North Shore Marina, Incorporated, at Grand Haven, Ottawa County, Michigan. The various parts and equipment arrived at the marina about the middle of May, 1956. The boat was completed and given a trial run on July 3rd or 4th.

After the trial run, the boat remained at the marina for the installation of some additional items of equipment purchased by the Bankrupt and for which he paid the marina. On June 13, 1956, the Bankrupt executed and delivered a promissory note to Sears, for the balance of the purchase price and gave a chattel mortgage to Sears covering the boat and equipment as security for the payment of the note. The chattel mortgage was filed in the office of the Register of Deeds of Muskegon county, Michigan, June 21, 1956. The mortgage was not filed with the Register of Deeds of Ottawa county, the county in which North Shore Marina was located. At all times pertinent to this litigation, the Bankrupt was a resident of Muskegon county.

The installation of the additional equipment was completed about the middle of August. At this time, the Bankrupt took the boat to the Muskegon Yacht Club, in Muskegon county, docked it there one night and then returned it to North Shore Marina, in Grand Haven. It was then taken to a marina in Bear Lake channel, in Muskegon county, and left there two or three nights and again returned to Grand Haven. The Bankrupt traveled back and forth between North Shore Marina and Bear Lake channel until the latter part of August. At this time he was able to rent docking facilities in the channel. The boat remained here until October, when it was returned to the marina in Grand Haven and stored for the winter.

During the following year 1957, although the Bankrupt sometimes used the boat, it was continuously kept at the marina in Grand Haven for repairs and storage. On December 16, 1957, Sears repossessed the boat in foreclosure of its chattel mortgage and paid North Shore Marina its accumulated storage, repair and upkeep charges against the Bankrupt. About two hours after the repossession, the Bankrupt filed his petition in bankruptcy. The time relation between these two events was coincidental and not a race for priority. Subsequent to the repossession, Sears sold the boat for $2300, which was considered to be its fair and reasonable value.

The history of the litigation is as follows: On January 13, 1959, the Trustee filed a petition to require Sears to turn the $2300 over to the bankrupt estate. There was a hearing on this petition and the referee found from the facts above stated that the location of the boat for the purpose of filing a chattel mortgage, under Michigan Statutes Annotated 26.929, M.C.L.A. § 566.140, was Ottawa county, Michigan. He further found that the mortgage was invalid as to the Trustee for failure to file with the Register of Deeds, of Ottawa county, and ordered Sears to turn over $2300 to the estate. There was a petition for review of this order and on review the District Judge adopted the referee's findings of fact and conclusions of law and sustained his order.

Later counsel for Sears moved to set aside this order and for reconsideration of its petition for review. In the meantime, the Supreme Court of Michigan had decided the case of Schueler v. Weintrob, 360 Mich. 621, 105 N.W.2d 42, in which it was held that repossession by a mortgagee prior to the time of filing a petition in bankruptcy was in legal effect equivalent to filing in the county of location (M.S.A. 26.929) and deprived the Trustee in Bankruptcy of any rights under section 70, sub. c of the Bankruptcy Act. (Sec. 110, sub. c, Title 11, U.S.C.A.)

A motion was then filed on behalf of the Trustee for the court to receive additional testimony or remand the matter to the referee to take testimony concerning the extension of credit to the Bankrupt between the date of the execution of the mortgage on June 13, 1956, and the repossession of the property on December 16, 1957. The court sustained the motion and remanded the case to the referee for the purpose of taking further evidence. Upon hearing the referee found that within the interim period involved, Albert B. Doherty extended credit to the Bankrupt in the amount of $10, without knowledge of the mortgage and it was unpaid. The referee concluded that the existence of this interim creditor invalidated the mortgage as a security document pursuant to section 70, sub. e (Sec. 110, sub. e(1), Title 11 U.S.C.A.) of the Bankruptcy Act and that the benefits of the invalidity inured to all the general creditors of the Bankrupt. The turnover order of $2300 was again entered. On petition for review, the District Judge affirmed the order of the referee. In a subsequent order, the motion of Sears to vacate the original order of the court, dated October 20, 1960, was denied.

The first question presented for our consideration is whether, under the law of Michigan, the chattel mortgage should have been filed in Ottawa county, as well as Muskegon county. The Michigan Statute (M.S.A. 26.929) provides: "Every mortgage or conveyance intended to operate as a mortgage of goods and chattels which shall hereafter be made which shall not be accompanied by an immediate delivery and followed by an actual and continued change of possession of the things mortgaged, shall be absolutely void as against the creditors of the mortgagor, and as against subsequent purchasers or mortgagees in good faith, unless the mortgage or a true copy thereof shall be filed in the office of the register of deeds of the county where the goods or chattels are located, and also where the mortgagor resides * * *."

The referee found and concluded, from the facts as stated herein, that Ottawa county was the county of location and under the Michigan statute the mortgage should have been filed there.

* * *

We are bound by the finding of the referee and the District Judge that under the law of Michigan the mortgage was required to be filed in Ottawa county, unless such finding is clearly erroneous. * * *

The conclusion of the referee, affirmed by the trial judge, is amply supported by the evidence. His interpretation of the facts and the inference drawn therefrom as to the location of the boat was warranted and certainly not clearly erroneous.

The mortgage then was invalid, under the Michigan statute (M.S.A. 26.929) as to creditors of the Bankrupt. After the opinion of the court on the question of the necessity of filing the mortgage in Ottawa county, it seemed that Sears' security might be salvaged by the decision of the Supreme Court of Michigan, in Schueler v. Weintrob, 360 Mich. 621, 105 N.W.2d 42, to which reference is heretofore made.

Counsel for the appellant objected to having the case remanded to the referee for further consideration and a determination of the Trustee's rights under section 70, sub. e of the Bankruptcy Act. We find no merit to the appellant's claim that the court erred in remanding the case to the referee for further hearing. It was the duty of the District Judge to see that there was a full and complete discovery of all available evidence pertinent to any issues presented by the facts and law involved.

Section 70, sub. e(1) of the Bankruptcy Act (110, sub. e(1), Title 11, U.S.C.A.) provides: "A transfer made or suffered or obligation incurred by a debtor adjudged a bankrupt under this title which, under any Federal or State law applicable thereto, is fraudulent as against or voidable for any other reason by any creditor of the debtor, having a claim provable under this title, shall be null and void as against the trustee of such debtor."

The following facts, as found by the referee, are substantiated by the evidence: The mortgage was not filed in Ottawa county as required by the Michigan statute. Albert B. Doherty became a creditor in the amount of ten dollars July 20, 1957, when the mortgage was off record and his claim was provable against the Bankrupt under the Bankruptcy Act. The conclusion of the referee, sustained by the District Judge, that the mortgage being invalid under the Michigan statute as to interim creditor Doherty, was null and void as against the Trustee, is a correct application of the law. * * * Moore v. Bay, 284 U.S. 4, 52 S.Ct. 3, 76 L.Ed. 133.

So far as we have been able to ascertain the amount of the credit extended is immaterial and the validity or invalidity of the chattel mortgage is not affected by the size of the creditor's claim. Neither is it material that the debt was not scheduled or that the creditor did not know of the existence of the chattel; nor is it necessary to prove that the creditor would not have extended the credit if he had known of the mortgage. Counsel for the appellant have cited no authorities in support of these claims.

Finding no error in the record the judgment of the District Court is affirmed.

Notes

1. Which of the following is true:

A. If *Plonta* arose in modern day Michigan, which has enacted the 1972 amendments to Article 9, the trustee could prevail under subsection 544(a).

B. The trustee could not prevail under subsection 544(b).

C. The trustee might be successful in using section 547. See subsection 547(e)(2).

2. Note that subsection 544(b) requires the existence of an actual unsecured creditor who could avoid the transfer under applicable state law. In *Plonta,* Mr. Doherty with a $10 claim fulfilled that requirement. Suppose that Debtor, who owed Creditor $5,000, granted Creditor a security interest in collateral worth $100,000 in "consideration of the antecedent debt" and perfected it by filing. The transfer, however, was fraudulent because Debtor actually intended to defraud creditors. To what extent could the trustee, subrogated to Mr. Doherty's rights under subsection 544(b), avoid Debtor's transfer? (Note that a transfer with actual intent to defraud is fraudulent against existing and future creditors. Thus, the trustee—a future creditor—might also be able to avoid the transfer under sections 544(a) or 548.).

SECTION 3. PREFERENCES, SECTION 547

A. *The Basics*

We have touched on section 547 above. Because preferences offer interesting and intricate intellectual problems, they probably command more law school time than they deserve. Nevertheless, manipulating section 547 is fun; let us indulge ourselves.

The principal evil to be cured by the preference provision is that of preventing a debtor from favoring one creditor over others similarly situated through a transaction occurring within a short period prior to bankruptcy. Evidently Congress believed that one who sees bankruptcy on the horizon, and who is already insolvent, should not be free to favor one creditor over another, but should be required to treat all alike. Thus, the classic preference is the simple payment on the eve of bankruptcy of one creditor's debt when comparable payments are not being made to others.

A second common form of preference is to give property to a creditor, not in the form of money but in the form of a grant of a security interest to secure a prior loan on the eve of bankruptcy—"after thought" security. Certainly the granting of a valid security interest would have the same ultimate consequence as the payment of that creditor's debt.

Still different, is a preference given by means of the *perfection* of a previously created security interest within 90 days. One might think that the "transfer" between the creditor and the debtor should be deemed to have occurred at the time the security agreement was executed and the interest conveyed to the creditor. Such a creditor could argue that he was not an "after-thought" creditor, not a person who was particularly abusive, for he had achieved his grant of a security interest well before the 90–day period. Here we are assuming a case in which a security agreement was signed and the loan made long before the 90 days, but in which perfection occurred within 90 days. Section 547 condemns this transaction (though for different reasons) just as much as the one in which the security transfer, and its perfection, occurs after the loan and within the 90 days. True enough, the creditor here is not an after-thought creditor; he bargained for his transfer at a time when bankruptcy was not imminent. This creditor may be guilty of another kind of crime, however, namely that of holding an undisclosed security interest. If we uphold a security agreement that is executed long before the 90 days but perfected by a public filing for the first time on the eve of bankruptcy, we make it substantially easier for the debtor and a cooperating creditor to keep that transfer secret, to mislead other creditors into lending in the belief that the debtor has not granted a security interest, and thus ultimately to distort the distribution in bankruptcy. In this case the preference legislation is justified also as an attack on "secret liens." By putting the creditor at risk for 90 days *after* he perfects, the bankruptcy law renders the granting of such a secret lien much more risky than it would otherwise be.

Finally there are variations on the foregoing themes. They include the case in which the secured creditor's pot is filled by after-acquired property, property acquired for the first time within the 90 days. Before 1978, the secured creditor could argue that such a "transfer" occurred at the time of perfection, prior to the preference period, but that argument is no longer available and thus the trustee will be able to avoid some security interests to the extent that they attach to collateral acquired within 90 days of bankruptcy. A second variation on the earlier theme is the preference that occurs not by an intentional late filing, but by a mistaken late filing. This is the creditor who makes the loan and intends to perfect at once but who only perfects 20 to 30 days later, or conceivably several months later after he discovers, for example, that his first financing statement was not filed in the right place.

The student should now turn to section 547(b) which reads in full as follows:

Except as provided in subsection (c) of this section, the trustee may avoid any transfer of an interest of the debtor in property—

(1) to or for the benefit of a creditor;

(2) for or on account of an antecedent debt owed by the debtor before such transfer was made;

(3) made while the debtor was insolvent;

(4) made—

(A) on or within 90 days before the date of the filing of the petition; or

(B) between ninety days and one year before the date of the filing of the petition, if such creditor at the time of such transfer was an insider;

(5) that enables such creditor to receive more than such creditor would receive if—

(A) the case were a case under chapter 7 of this title;

(B) the transfer had not been made; and

(C) such creditor received payment of such debt to the extent provided by the provisions of this title.

Note that the trustee must satisfy all five of the above tests in order to establish a voidable preference. If he fails on one, the transfer is not voidable. Several will seldom be disputed. First, the debtor is presumed to be insolvent within the 90 days; thus the trustee will invariably succeed under subsection (b)(3). Second, the transfer will almost always be "to or for the benefit of the creditor" and thus subsection (b)(1) will seldom be an issue. The same factors that control subsection (b)(2) are likely to control subsection (b)(4) and vice versa. Thus, for example, if the creditor can convince the court that the transfer occurred outside the 90 days, he may be simultaneously convincing the court that the transfer occurred at the same time as the giving of value and therefore that subsection (b)(2) is not violated. Invariably when a security interest is at stake, the time of the transfer will be critical.

The time of transfer is a technical matter governed for the purposes of section 547 by 547(e). That subsection reads in full as follows:

(e)(1) For the purposes of this section—

(A) a transfer of real property other than fixtures, but including the interest of a seller or purchaser under a contract for the sale of real property, is perfected when a bona fide purchaser of such property from the debtor against whom applicable law permits such transfer to be perfected cannot acquire an interest that is superior to the interest of the transferee; and

(B) a transfer of a fixture or property other than real property is perfected when a creditor on a simple contract cannot acquire a judicial lien that is superior to the interest of the transferee.

(2) For the purposes of this section, except as provided in paragraph (3) of this subsection, a transfer is made—

(A) at the time such transfer takes effect between the transferor and the transferee, if such transfer is perfected at, or within 10 days after, such time;

(B) at the time such transfer is perfected, if such transfer is perfected after such 10 days; or

(C) immediately before the date of the filing of the petition, if such transfer is not perfected at the later of—

(i) the commencement of the case; or

(ii) 10 days after such transfer takes effect between the transferor and the transferee.

(3) For the purposes of this section, a transfer is not made until the debtor has acquired rights in the property transferred.

Generally, the subsection gives a secured creditor a 10 day grace period in which to perfect. If he perfects within that time, the "transfer" is deemed to have occurred at the earlier point when the security agreement was signed or the loan made. The effect of such a relation back is to cause the transfer to occur simultaneously with value and thus for the transfer *not* to be for an antecedent debt. Note that the tests for perfection with respect to real estate and personal property are different.

The final condition, subsection (b)(5), finds its principal importance with respect to payments to secured creditors. The very idea of a preference is that one creditor gets more than he would get by virtue of the transfer than if there had been liquidation immediately prior to the transfer and he had to share with similarly situated creditors. If a creditor has a security interest that is perfected and that gives him a claim to collateral equal to the value of his debt, no payment to him will enable him to receive more money than he would have received under Chapter 7 (i.e., on liquidation) without the transfer. That is because the creditor would take 100 cents on the dollar on liquidation, namely the amount for which his collateral could be sold, and not more. To the extent that he receives a payment prior to liquidation his claim would be reduced and he would be entitled to only 100 cents on the remaining debt. Thus, if one assumes a secured creditor with a $100,000 claim and collateral worth $120,000, he will receive $100,000 on liquidation. A pre-bankruptcy payment up to $100,000 would not improve his position. Even though the payment came out of the estate, the estate would not be diminished because that payment would in turn free $100,000 of collateral for the other creditors. Hence he would not be receiving a preference.

After mastering the substantive provisions in section 547(b), one should turn to the exceptions in subsection 547(c). With the 1984 amendments, the exceptions have become so expansive that they may be more important than subsection (b) itself. Subsection (c)(1) might be looked upon as a loosening of the restraints imposed by subsection (b)(2) and in some sense that is an accurate way to consider it. For example, it would cover the case in which a creditor transferred goods to a debtor, the debtor paid by check, and the check cleared only a week or ten days later. On a strict reading of subsection 547(b) the transaction might constitute a voidable preference because the payment coming ten days later would be regarded as antecedent under (b)(2). Presumably (c)(1) would stretch the antecedency requirement at least this far and would take the transaction described out of section 547.

A more difficult question is whether subsection (c)(1) ever applies to extend the ten-day relation back rule for filing that is embodied in subsection 547(e)(2)(B). It seems doubtful that Congress intended subsection (c)(1) to change a quite specific and rigid requirement of ten days in subsection 547(e).

Many payments both to secured and unsecured creditors that would otherwise be voidable preferences will now be saved by subsection (c)(2). Students should study the subsection to see which payments within the 90–day period might not qualify under subsection (c)(2). Surely it cannot be intended to save all payments. Prior to the 1984 amendments, subsection (c)(2) was of much more limited significance. As it existed prior to 1984, subsection (c)(2) applied only to payments made "not later than 45 days after the debt was incurred." Under that version only short-term obligations such as trade credit or utility obligations could conceivably be covered and payments to commercial lenders rarely fit within the 45–day rule. With removal of the 45–day limit in 1984, it is open season on payments of debt irrespective when the debt was incurred.

Subsection (c)(3) is designed to protect purchase money interests that might otherwise fall afoul of (b), and subsection (c)(4) is to cover the case in which the creditor receives a preference but then makes a subsequent loan. Quaere: what of a case under subsection (c)(4) in which the subsequent loan is secured by the collateral that has been in existence and has secured prior debts? Does such a loan fit within (c)(4) or is it excluded by the "not secured by an unavoidable security interest"?

Subsection (c)(5) is intricate and interesting but of limited significance. The student should read it with care.

Note that subsection (c)(6) is simply an exclusion to make sure that the special rules for statutory liens are not upset by section 547. Subsection (c)(7) is an important exception, added in 1984, that frees a variety of consumer transfers (payments, garnishment of wages) from the reach of the trustee.

Discussion with trustees, judges, and examination of the cases indicate that section 547 on preferences is substantially less significant in practice than a student might imagine. With the expansion of the exceptions in 1984, section 547 will likely become even less significant in practice than formerly.

In summary, the following analysis, in steps, is useful in applying section 547.

First, did the debtor make a transfer "of an interest of the debtor in property?" See subsections 101(48) & 547(b).

Second, if the answer is yes, when was the transfer made? See subsection 547(e). Note that if the transfer was a payment, it was made at the time it took effect between the parties. See subsection 547(e)(2)(A). If, however, the transfer was the grant of a security interest, it may be made later than the time it was effective between the parties. Thus, if a security interest attached on July 1 but was perfected by filing on July 15, the transfer was made—at the earliest—on July 15. Read subsection 547(e) carefully.

Third, was the transfer avoidable because all five conditions in 547(b) were satisfied?

Fourth, if the answer is yes, was the transfer saved by any of the five exceptions in subsection 547(c)? The exceptions to subsection 547(b) found in subsection 547(c) have been called the "safe harbor" provisions.

Please work the following problems.

Problem 8–3

Debtor, a small business, borrowed $10,000 from C1 on July 1 and $20,000 from C2 on July 15. The loans were unsecured. D issued C1 a note payable in six months and issued C2 a note payable on demand. D filed a voluntary case in bankruptcy on December 1 and it is stipulated that Debtor was insolvent from October 15 until December 1.

The trustee has identified the following transfers by Debtor as suspect and asks whether they can be avoided under subsection 547. The trustee asserts that they are all "unfair" grabs within the 90 day period and should be avoided.

1. On September 15, C1 persuaded D to grant a security interest in described collateral in consideration of the existing $10,000 debt. C1 perfected the security interest by filing on September 17. There is no question that the security interest is perfected under Article 9.

2. On October 20, C2 demanded payment of the note. Debtor paid C2 $10,000 by check on October 25.

3. On November 10, C3, another unsecured creditor, obtained a judgment against D and, on November 15, obtained a judicial lien on personal property under applicable state procedures.

Problem 8–4

Suppose, in Problem 8–3 above, that Debtor was insolvent from September 1 until December 1, the date the case was filed. On September 15, Debtor signed a contract to purchase a piece of equipment from Seller for $20,000. Debtor paid Seller $5,000 on September 15 and granted Seller an enforceable security interest in the equipment to secure the $15,000 balance, to be paid in two equal installments over the next six months. The equipment was delivered to Debtor on September 20. Seller perfected the security interest by filing a financing statement on September 28. On November 15, Debtor paid the first installment, some $7,500, to Seller.

The trustee argued that Debtor's grant of a security interest was a preference because it was not perfected until more than 10 days after it became effective between the parties. She cites subsection 547(e)(2)(b). In addition, the trustee claims that the installment payment, made on November 15, was clearly a preference under subsection 547(b).

The attorney for Seller made the following arguments:

1. Even if the transfer—the grant of a security interest—was made on September 28, it was saved from the clutches of subsection 547(b) by subsection 547(c)(3) or (c)(5).

2. Even though the payment—the first installment—was for an antecedent debt, it was saved by subsection 547(c)(2), if not 547(c)(1).

As bankruptcy judge, how would you rule?

B. The "Floating Lien" in Bankruptcy

Recall that Article 9 permits a secured party to create a security interest in existing and after-acquired collateral and proceeds in a single, written security agreement and to perfect that security interest by filing a single financing statement. If the financing statement is filed first, the security interest attaches to and is perfected in the after-acquired collateral when the debtor has "rights in the collateral." UCC 9–203(1) & 9–303(1). Priority against other security interests in the same collateral, however, is determined by the time of filing. UCC 9–312(5)(a). Nevertheless, it is clear that the security interest is effective between the parties at the time of attachment. Thus, under Article 9 at least, the transfer would appear to be for an antecedent debt. Compare UCC 9–108, which attempts to weasle out of this box.

Under the Bankruptcy Act of 1898, the time when a transfer was made for purposes of avoidable preferences was not clearly defined. Section 60 did not say, as does subsection 547(e)(3), that for the "purposes of this section, a transfer is not made until the debtor has acquired rights in the property transferred." The result was a series of judicial opinions which stretched and pulled at the statutory language to preserve the "floating lien" from the preference attack, and an outpouring of literature on both sides of the controversy.

In the early versions of this casebook we included the principal case of *Grain Merchants of Indiana Inc. v. Union Bank and Savings Co.,* 408 F.2d 209 (7th Cir. 1969). That case, decided under the Uniform Commercial Code but prior to the Bankruptcy Reform Act of 1978, held that a secured creditor had an unassailable security interest in after-acquired collateral. In that case the trustee challenged secured creditor's right to after acquired accounts receivable that had arisen within the preference period immediately preceding the debtor's filing. The trustee reasoned that no transfer could occur until the asset transferred came into existence and at that time the creditor was not making contemporaneous loan advances, ergo the after-acquired accounts receivable constituted preferential transfers.

Both in that case and elsewhere, the secured creditor's response to such an argument was that no other creditor had been injured or misled by the "turnover" of collateral, whether that collateral constituted inventory, accounts receivable, or something else. In *Grain Merchants* the secured creditor put forward several arguments. The central argument was that the transfer as defined in section 60, the predecessor to section 547, had occurred at the time the security interest became so far perfected that no lien creditor could have priority over it. Under Article 9 of the UCC the secured creditor maintained that this event occurred upon filing, an act that occurred years prior to the filing of the bankruptcy petition. The court accepted that argument, but this left others uncomfortable. For example, the argument would have validated the acquisition of after-acquired property in circumstances in which the creditor caused the debtor to build up his accounts receivable or inventory immediately prior to bankruptcy and thus arguably to prefer the secured creditor over others. Since the transfer would have been deemed to have occurred when the financing statement was filed, long before the four-month or ninety day period, there would be no preference even in that case. In response to these concerns, Congress passed 547(e)(3), a subsection that destroys the basic creditor argument in *Grain Merchants.* In addition the Congress added subsection 547(c)(5) which validates such after-acquired property clauses in circumstances in which there is no "buildup."

Grain Merchants' opinion also accepted a variety of other creditor arguments to which section 547 has not obviously responded. One argument is that the accounts receivable should themselves be looked at as a "single entity" that is transferred at the outset even though individual accounts come and go. If one regards the "property" as some metaphysical group of accounts and not as single accounts, then subsection 547(e)(3) does not necessarily invalidate such transfer. It seems to us, however, subsection 547(e)(3) should be read to reject this argument. It seems to contemplate the possibility that each item of inventory, each account receivable—commonly recognized as having an individual identity—is to be treated separately for the purpose of bankruptcy. Thus, we believe that 547(e)(3) rejects the "entity" theory.

A third argument appearing in the *Grain Merchants'* decision that probably has continued vitality is the "substitution of collateral doctrine." Presumably no preference occurs when a secured creditor within the preference period agrees to allow his debtor to substitute one asset as the collateral for another. In such case, contemporaneous value is given by the creditor's release of the original collateral in return for acquiring the new collateral. In *Grain Merchants,* the court indicated:

> "As existing accounts receivable were collected by Grain Merchants and deposited to its accounts at the bank, the funds from previously collected accounts were made available to the debtor, enabling it to continue in business and obtain new accounts receivable. * * * Here the newly arising accounts receivable may be considered as having been taken in exchange for the release of rights in the earlier accounts and for present consideration."

408 F.2d at 217.

Nothing in section 547 explicitly rejects the substitution theory and presumably it too has continuing vitality.

Problem 8–5

On July 1, Seller sold Debtor some equipment on credit. Seller created and perfected a security interest in Debtor's "equipment, existing and after-acquired," and Debtor agreed to pay the balance of the contract price on January 2. On September 1, Debtor owed Seller $25,000 and the value of Debtor's equipment was $25,000. On October 1, Debtor sold the equipment to Buyer for $25,000 and used the proceeds to purchase new equipment from another seller. On December 1, the date of bankruptcy, Debtor owed Seller $25,000 and the value of the new equipment was $27,500.

A. Trustee argues that the transfer of the security interest in the new equipment was a preference. Is he correct?

B. If subsection 547(c)(5) does not apply, do any of the other "safe harbor" provisions?

Problem 8–6

On July 1, Debtor signed a security agreement granting Secured Party a security interest in "inventory and accounts, existing and after-acquired." Secured Party filed a proper financing statement on that date. No value was given at this time. On September 15, Secured Party loaned Debtor $20,000 under the security agreement. On that date, the value of the collateral in which Secured Party had a perfected security interest was $15,000. On December 1, the date of bankruptcy, Debtor still owed Secured Party $20,000 and the value of the collateral, which had turned over completely, was $18,000. There was credible evidence that on November 15 the value of the collateral was $5,000 and that Debtor, at the urging of Secured Party, had built up the collateral by purchasing inventory from third parties on credit.

Is there a preference under subsection 547(c)(5)? If so, in what amount?

Problem 8–7

On July 1, Debtor granted Secured Party a written security interest in "inventory, accounts and proceeds, existing and after-acquired." Secured Party made a first advance of $5,000 and agreed to make additional advances over the next 12 months of $95,000, "in its sole discretion." A financing statement was filed on July 1.

On September 1, Debtor owed Secured Party $30,000 and the collateral was valued at $25,000. On December 1, the date of bankruptcy, Debtor owed Secured Party $25,000 and the value of the collateral which had completely turned over, was $23,000. Between September 1 and December 1, Secured Party had advanced an additional $5,000 and Debtor had paid $10,000 under the security agreement.

A. Was the transfer of inventory, clearly a preference under subsection 547(b), saved by subsection 547(c)(5)?

B. Was Debtor's payment of $10,000 a preference? See subsection 547(c)(2). If so, (and Secured Party must return the payment), how should this affect the determination of a preference under subsection 547(c)(5)?

IN RE LACKOW BROTHERS, INC.

United States Court of Appeals, Eleventh Circuit, 1985.
752 F.2d 1529.

HANCOCK, DISTRICT JUDGE:

This case involves an appeal by the Co-Trustees, William R. Roemelmeyer and Jeanette Tavormina (hereinafter referred to as Co-Trustees), of the bankrupt debtor, Lackow Brothers, Inc. (hereinafter referred to as Debtor), from a judgment entered by the bankruptcy court and affirmed by the district court in favor of Walter E. Heller & Company Southeast, Inc. (hereinafter referred to as Creditor). Co-Trustees brought an adversary proceeding in bankruptcy court to avoid a transfer of property made by Debtor to Creditor on the ground that the payments were preferential transfers voidable under 11 U.S.C. § 547(b). We affirm the lower court's determination that the payments were not preferential transfers pursuant to 11 U.S.C. § 547(b) and (c)(5).

Debtor was a manufacturer of moderately priced jewelry with inventory consisting primarily of gold jewelry. In September of 1980 Debtor and Creditor entered into an Inventory Loan Security Agreement and Accounts Financing Security Agreement under which Creditor received a promissory note and agreed to advance Debtor monies in exchange for a security interest in Debtor's inventory, goods, merchandise, accounts receivable, general intangibles and contract rights. On April 1, 1981, Debtor filed a voluntary petition under Chapter 11 of the Bankruptcy Code. After an unsuccessful attempt at reorganization, the case was converted to a Chapter 7 proceeding on August 4, 1981, at which time appellants were appointed Co-Trustees to liquidate Debtor's estate. On February 19, 1982, Co-Trustees filed a complaint alleging that Debtor had made preferential payments in the amount of $365,000 to Creditor within ninety days of the filing of the Chapter 11 petition. In order for the transfer to be avoided under section 547(b), the Co-Trustees had to prove that Creditor received more from these payments than it otherwise would have received in a Chapter 7 liquidation. The Creditor denied the allegations and affirmatively argued that the payments were specifically excluded from the Trustee's avoidance power under section 547(c)(5). In order to fall within this exception to preferential transfers, a creditor must prove that its financial position did not improve within the ninety days prior to bankruptcy.

In bankruptcy court, the Co-Trustees maintained that on the date of the filing of the petition Creditor was undersecured; therefore, according to *Barash v. Public Finance Corp.*, 658 F.2d 504 (7th Cir.1981), the payments made within ninety days of bankruptcy applied first to the unsecured component of Creditor's debt. The Co-Trustees premised this argument on the bankruptcy court's previous determination that the value of the pledged collateral on April 1, 1981 was $922,000. Undisputed evidence showed that on April 1, 1981, Debtor owed Creditor approximately 1.6 million dollars. If the Co-Trustees could get the bankruptcy court to readopt its April 1, 1981 determination of value then Creditor would have a secured claim in the amount of $922,000 and an unsecured claim in the amount of approximately $678,000. Under *Barash, supra,* the $365,000 payment would apply toward the $678,000 unsecured claim and the bankruptcy court would have to avoid the preferential transfer.

Creditor relied on uncontradicted evidence of the "computer value" of the collateral on both the ninetieth day prior to bankruptcy (January 1, 1981) and on the date of bankruptcy (April 1, 1981), both to rebut the allegation of a preferential transfer under section 547(b) and affirmatively to prove the section 547(c)(5) exception. The computer printouts were routine accounting reports sent from Debtor to Creditor, upon which Creditor relied to advance additional funds. These records established that: (1) on January 1, 1981, the pledged collateral was worth approximately 4.7 million dollars while Debtor's obligation was approximately 1.9 million dollars; and (2) on April 1, 1981, the pledged collateral was worth approximately 3.9 million dollars and Debtor's obligation was approximately 1.6 million dollars. These values clearly establish that Creditor was fully secured. Hence, Creditor argued that it received no more than it would have received under Chapter 7 liquidation. Furthermore, since Creditor was fully secured on January 1 and April 1, its position did not improve within the ninety days prior to bankruptcy. Thus, the payments fell within the section 547(c)(5) preferential transfer exception.

Maintaining that the valuation of collateral must be determined on a case-by-case basis, the bankruptcy court refused to adopt its earlier value on April 1, 1981 and held that the proper valuation standard was the "ongoing concern" value of the collateral, as reflected in the routine accounting reports. The bankruptcy court concluded that Creditor did not improve its position by accepting Debtor's payments and therefore the payment was specifically excepted from preference under 11 U.S.C. § 547(c)(5).

On appeal to the district court, the Co-Trustees urged that the bankruptcy court erred in applying the "ongoing concern" value and that the correct standard to be applied was the "liquidation value." In asserting this position, Co-Trustees relied on Creditor's testimony that it had received 1.2 million dollars from the sale of Debtor's inventory and collection of the accounts receivable. Co-Trustees urged the adoption of this valuation standard since under it Creditor would be deemed undersecured and the payments would be preferential transfers pursuant to section 547(b). The district court, however, held that the liquidated value of the collateral, which was sold over six months *after* filing of bankruptcy would not accurately determine whether the Creditor's loan was secured during the ninety-day period *prior* to the filing of the petition; therefore, the "ongoing concern" was the only standard of valuation that could be adopted.

On this appeal the Co-Trustees urge us to find that the only proper standard of valuation in this case is the liquidation value and that payments should be avoided pursuant to section 547(b). The sole issue we must resolve is whether the district court was clearly erroneous in applying the "ongoing concern" value in determining Creditor had not received preferential payments under section 547(b) and in finding that Creditor's position had not improved under section 547(c)(5).

In this case the method used to value the collateral is crucial to determining whether the payments to Creditor in the ninety days prior to bankruptcy are subject to preference attack. Since Creditor had a "floating lien" on Debtor's inventory and accounts receivable, the section 547(c)(5) exception to preferential transfers applies and our inquiry should be whether Creditor's position "improved" relative to what it was preceding bankruptcy. To determine "improvement in position," Creditor's "position" is relevant on two different dates: January 1, 1981, ninety days before the filing of the Chapter 11 petition, and April 1, 1981, the date of the filing of the petition. Thus, the value of the accounts receivable and inventory must be calculated on these two dates. If the "ongoing concern" value is used, no "improvement in position" exists; however, if the liquidation value is used, improvement is apparent and the transfer should be avoided.

Section 506(a) of the Bankruptcy Code provides only general principles we should follow in determining what standard of valuation is proper in calculating the value of a creditor's secured claim: " * * * Such value shall be determined in light of the purpose of the valuation and of the proposed disposition or use of such property, and in conjunction with any hearing on such disposition or use or on a plan affecting such creditor's interest." 11 U.S.C. § 506(a). The legislative comments to this section do not give any further guidance except to reiterate that we are to determine value on a case-by-case basis, taking into account the facts of each case and the competing interests in the case. H.R.Rep. No. 545, 95th Cong., 1st Sess. 356 (1977) *reprinted in* 1978 U.S.Code Cong. & Ad.News 5787, 6312.

In an effort to provide some guidance to the courts in determining what value to use in calculating "improvement in position," Collier on Bankruptcy, a leading treatise in bankruptcy law, suggests that the liquidation value be used in a liquidation case under Chapter 7 and that the going concern value be used in a Chapter 9, 11, or 13 case. This advice is not set in cement, as Collier recognizes that other standards of value may be appropriate in certain cases. 4 Collier on Bankruptcy ¶ 547.41 at 129 (15th ed. 1984). Co-Trustees argue that Collier supports their position that the liquidation value should have been adopted in the bankruptcy and district courts as the value of the collateral on both January 1 and April 1, and therefore, that Creditor's position improved. We are convinced, however, that this case is one in which a standard of value other than the liquidation value is not only more appropriate, but is even mandatory.

The *only* evidence before this court showing what the monetary value of the accounts receivable and inventory was on January 1, 1981, is the value as shown on the computerized accounting reports. Despite Co-Trustees' argument on this appeal that the "computer value" is not credible, we have before us absolutely no evidence indicating that the accounting records were inaccurate or untrustworthy. The Co-Trustees did not challenge the accuracy of those records in the bankruptcy court. Moreover, the bankruptcy court specifically determined that these ongoing concern values were derived from Debtor's own routine accounting reports to Creditor in the regular course of business and that the values were properly admissible. The only evidence in the record of value for the ninetieth day prior to the filing of bankruptcy is the ongoing concern value; therefore, this is the *only* standard of valuation that can be applied to determine if Creditor's position improved between January 1 and April 1, 1981. The fact that Creditor sold Debtor's collateral for 1.2 million dollars six months *after* the Chapter 11 petition was filed does not shed much light on what the collateral was worth nine months earlier on the ninetieth day *before* filing of bankruptcy, especially taking into consideration the nature and type of the collateral. We agree with the district court's holding that the only standard of valuation that could be applied in this case to any degree of accuracy would be the "ongoing concern" standard. See *Matter of Lackow Bros., Inc.,* 19 B.R. 601 (S.D.Fla.1982).

Co-Trustees also rely on *In re Adams,* 2 B.R. 313 (M.D.Fla.1980) and *Matter of Cooper,* 7 B.R. 537 (N.D.Ga.1980) to support their argument that the liquidation value is the *only* proper value to use in this case. Neither of these cases concern the value of inventory or accounts receivable, nor do they involve property values at a point in time *prior* to bankruptcy. We hold that these cases simply do not apply to this appeal.

We conclude that the holdings of the bankruptcy court and the district court were not clearly erroneous in using the ongoing concern value to determine that pursuant to section 547(c)(5) Creditor had not improved his position between the ninetieth day prior to bankruptcy and the actual date the petition was filed. We therefore affirm. [Footnotes omitted.]

Notes

1. Do you agree with the following assertions: (A) The creditor in In re Lackow did not need to rely on subsection 547(c)(5) to avoid the preference—subsection 547(b)(5) would work just as well; (B) In addition to subsection (c)(5), subsection 547(c)(2) would work just as well.

2. Suppose it is clear that payments during the 90 day period were made when the debt exceeded the value of the collateral (the debtor was under-secured) but that the secured party was over-secured at the time of bankruptcy. Are the payments preferential? Or, suppose the payments were made when oversecured but the secured party was undersecured at the time of bankruptcy. What is the critical time for section 547(b), the time of payment or the time of bankruptcy? Cf. Barash v. Public Finance Corp., 658 F.2d 504 (7th Cir.1981), cited in *In re Lackow,* which held, among other things, that where the secured party was under-secured at both critical points, any payments made during the 90 day period should be allocated to the unsecured part of the obligation and were preferences unless saved by subsection 547(c)(1) or (2).

Problem 8–8

Alfred's Building Materials was a seller of air conditioning, air conditioning ducts and equipment. Skilled Trades was a local contractor in the business of installing air conditioning and heating systems. In the summer of 1986 Skilled Trades ordered approximately $8,000 worth of air conditioning equipment and ducting to be installed in the Church of Christ located in Buchanan, Michigan. Alfred's had heard word on the street that Skilled Trades was having difficulty making its payments on its trade debt and told Skilled Trades that it was hesitant to undertake the usual 30 or 90 days credit on such a sale. Accordingly, representatives of Skilled Trades talked to the Board of Trustees of the church who agreed to pay $8,000 when the equipment was delivered. Alfred's maintained that the agreement between it and Skilled Trades was for a "C.O.D. Delivery." In fact, the materials were delivered in three lots to the job site during the last week in October and the first two weeks of November, 1986. The accompanying invoices were marked "C.O.D." Upon delivery, the church, in accordance with its agreement, issued three checks totalling $8,000 to Skilled Trades. On November 17, Skilled Trades issued its check for $7,175.45. Skilled Trades had the check certified on that date, and on that date or the next mailed it to Alfred's. Alfred's in turn deposited the check in its account and the check was paid on November 25, 1986.

Skilled Trades filed a petition in Chapter 7 on December 10, 1986. The trustee has asserted a right to the return of the $7,175.45 on the ground that it constitutes a voidable preference. What result?

Problem 8–9

Albert, a high living bachelor who had entered several disastrous financial transactions, owned a Porsche 928 free and clear. As his creditors closed in upon him he decided to pay off a debt to his brother-in-law by transferring the Porsche to him. He owed his brother-in-law in excess of $50,000, money he had borrowed for an unsuccessful oil and gas partnership. Three weeks before he filed in Chapter 7 he transferred his Porsche to his brother-in-law in full satisfaction of the debt. The brother-in-law promptly resold the car to a local car dealer for $31,000. The brother-in-law then disappeared and has not been seen since. The car dealer has since adopted the car as his personal car and is driving it. The trustee in Albert's Chapter 7 asks whether he can recover the car from the car dealer. What do you think? What if local dealer had not used the car as his own, but had resold it to a local doctor?

C. Proceeds in Bankruptcy

At the date of bankruptcy, a secured party may claim a security interest in identified proceeds from the disposition of the original collateral. This claim, even though supported under UCC 9–306, is subject to the trustee's avoidance powers. Thus, if the security interest in proceeds was not perfected it would be vulnerable under subsection 544(a) and UCC 9–301(1)(b). Or if the security interest in proceeds was perfected but, in combination with other collateral improved the secured party's position under subsection 547(c)(5), it might be avoided as a preference. Subsection 552(b) states, however, that unless otherwise avoidable if the debtor acquired the original collateral before the commencement of the case, the security interest extends to proceeds "acquired by the estate after the commencement of the case to the extent provided by such security agreement and by applicable non-bankruptcy law * * *."

A recurring problem involves attempts to trace proceeds, particularly cash proceeds, see UCC 9–306(1), which have been commingled with other funds in deposit accounts. If state law tracing rules cannot identify the actual asset in which the security interest is claimed, some courts have disallowed the claim. See, e.g., Elliot v. Bumb, 356 F.2d 749 (9th Cir.1966) cert. denied 385 U.S. 829, 87 S.Ct. 67, 17 L.Ed.2d 66 (1966). The "intermediate balance test" has been upheld in bankruptcy. In re Martin, 25 B.R. 25 (Bankr.N.D.Tex.1982). Under this test, proceeds which are traced into a commingled account are presumed to remain there until all funds have been withdrawn. New deposits, however, are presumed not to replenish the proceeds unless they are actually proceeds from the disposition of collateral.

An unresolved controversy has arisen over the application of UCC 9–306(4) in bankruptcy. In this subsection, Article 9 attempts to provide a specific tracing rule for application in insolvency proceedings. Read that subsection carefully.

Problem 8–10

Secured Party created and perfected a security interest in Debtor's "inventory and accounts, existing and after-acquired, and proceeds" on July 1. On September 1, Debtor owed Secured Party $25,000 and the value of the collateral, including proceeds, was $20,000. On December 1, the date of bankruptcy, Debtor still owed Secured Party $25,000. The value of the inventory and accounts was $20,000. In addition, Debtor has a deposit account in which cash proceeds from the sale of inventory have been commingled with other funds.

As of November 21, there was a $100 balance in the account.

On November 22, Debtor deposited $10,000 received from the sale of inventory.

On November 24, Debtor withdrew $10,000 and lost it all in the futures market.

On November 28, Debtor deposited $10,000 received from the sale of factory equipment.

On December 1, Debtor declared bankruptcy.

A. How much can Secured Party claim under the Intermediate Balance Test?

B. How much can Secured Party claim under UCC 9–306(4)?

C. Is the amount claimed under UCC 9–306(4) a preference under section 547 of the Bankruptcy Code? (See the next case).

IN RE GIBSON PRODUCTS OF ARIZONA

United States Court of Appeals, Ninth Circuit, 1976.
543 F.2d 652, cert. denied 430 U.S. 946, 97 S.Ct. 1583, 51 L.Ed.2d 794 (1977).

HUFSTEDLER, CIRCUIT JUDGE:

On this appeal we must referee a collision between the "proceeds" provision of the Uniform Commercial Code (U.C.C. § 9–306(4), A.R.S. § 44–3127(D)) and the bankruptcy trustee's power to avoid preferences under Section 60 of the Bankruptcy Act. The provisions collide under circumstances that place the creditor, asserting a perfected security interest in the debtor's bank account, in the dimmest equitable light: If the creditor prevails, it receives $19,505.27 from the debtor's account on proof that the debtor, within ten days of the insolvency, deposited $10 in the account from the sale of a hair dryer in which the creditor had a perfected security interest. The district court affirmed the bankruptcy judge's order awarding $19,505.27 to the secured creditor. We reverse because we conclude that the operation of U.C.C. section 9–306(4)(d) created a voidable preference by the transfer to the creditor of a perfected security interest in the cash deposited in the debtor's account that exceeded the amount of the creditor's proceeds.

The creditor, Arizona Wholesale Supply Co. ("Wholesale") sold General Electric and Proctor-Silex appliances to the debtor, Gibson Products of Arizona ("Gibson"). Wholesale has a perfected security interest in the appliances. On January 13, 1972, Gibson initiated Chapter XI proceedings. During the ten-day period immediately preceding the institution of these proceedings, Gibson deposited $19,505.27 in its bank account. During the same period, Gibson deposited in the account $10 from the sale of a Proctor-Silex dryer. At the time insolvency proceedings were instituted, Gibson was indebted to Wholesale in the amount of $28,800 for the appliances it had sold to Gibson and for which it has perfected security interests.

* * *

The Code's new twist is extending the creditor's security interest to commingled funds without specifically tracing the creditor's proceeds into the fund, when the debtor has become insolvent. (U.C.C. § 9–306(4)(d).) No collision between the proceeds provision of the Code and the preference sections of the Bankruptcy Act occurs when the creditor's perfected security interest in his collateral is attached to the proceeds from the sale or other disposition of the collateral if (1) his interest was initially perfected in the collateral more than four months before bankruptcy, and (2) he can identify the proceeds to which his security interest has attached. Under these circumstances, the creditor has priority over later creditors when he first perfected his security interest, and his priority relates back to his initial perfection. (Cf. DuBay v. Williams (9th Cir. 1969) 417 F.2d 1277, 1286–87.) The problem arises in the U.C.C. section 9–306(4)(d) situation because that subsection gives the secured creditor a perfected security interest in the entire amount deposited by the debtor within ten days before bankruptcy without limiting the interest to the amount that can be identified as the proceeds from the sale of the creditor's collateral. With respect to the funds that are not the creditor's proceeds, the creditor has no security interest except that conferred by U.C.C. section 9–306(4)(d). His interest in these nonproceeds arises upon the occurrence of two events: (1) insolvency proceedings instituted by or against a debtor, and (2) commingling of some of the proceeds from his collateral with the debtor's cash on hand or with other deposits in his debtor's bank account. His security interest is limited to an "amount not greater than the amount of any cash proceeds received by the debtor within ten days before institution of the insolvency proceedings" and is subject to the additional set-offs in section 9–306(4)(d).

The draftsmen's intent was not to deliver a security bonanza to any secured creditor. As Professor Gilmore observes: "It goes without saying that a provision of state law which purported to give a secured creditor greater rights in the event his debtor's estate was administered in bankruptcy than he would have apart from bankruptcy would be invalid. However, * * * § 9–306(4) does not in the least aim at such a result. Indeed, § 9–306(4) is the reverse of such a statute, since it sharply cuts back the secured party's rights when insolvency proceedings are initiated." (2 G. Gilmore, Security Interests in Personal Property ¶ 45.9, at 1337–38 (1965).) The intent was to eliminate the expense and nuisance of tracing when funds are commingled and to limit the grasp of secured creditors to the amount received during the last ten days before insolvency proceedings, which, the draftsmen assumed, would usually be less than the same creditor could trace if he had a grip on the entire balance deposited over an unlimited time. (Id. at 1340.) On that assumption, awarding a perfected security interest to the secured creditor, good for a short time on the entire balance, gives the secured creditor no windfall to the detriment of general creditors. On our facts, the contrary is true.

When confronted with an analogous situation, the Seventh Circuit limited the secured creditor's interest to those proceeds in the bank account traceable to the sale of the creditor's collateral. The Seventh Circuit's theory was that the term "any cash proceeds" used in section 9–306(4)(d) does not refer to all receipts from any source deposited in the bank account, but, instead, refers to "proceeds" as defined in section 9–306(1), and thus the phrase means "cash proceeds from the sale of collateral in which the creditor had a security interest." (Fitzpatrick v. Philco Finance Corp. (7th Cir.1974) 491 F.2d 1288, 1291–92.)

Although we reach a similar result, we reject the Seventh Circuit's reasoning because, in our view, that construction impermissibly bends the language and structure of section 9–306. The general definition of "proceeds" in section 9–306(1) cannot be transplanted into section 9–306(4) shorn of its statutory freight. The statute divides "proceeds" into two categories, "identifiable" and "commingled," i.e., nonidentifiable proceeds, and alters the reach of a perfected security interest, depending upon whether the proceeds are identifiable or nonidentifiable. (Compare section 9–306(4)(a), (b), (c) with section 9–306(4)(d).) Section 9–306(4)(d) deals only with nonidentifiable cash proceeds. If the cash proceeds could be "identified," i.e., had not been commingled, the secured party would have a perfected security interest in the whole fund under section 9–306(4)(b), just as he did in pre-Code days, without any of the limitations imposed by section 9–306(4)(d). Under the Code scheme, the secured creditor also has a perfected security interest under subsection (d) when he cannot identify his proceeds in the commingled fund, as long as he can show that some of his proceeds were among those in the commingled fund. (See § 9–306, Comment in U.C.C.Rep.Serv., Current Materials, ¶ 9306, at 60 (1968); Gilmore, supra, § 45.9, at 1336–37.)

We leave the language of section 9–306(4) as it was drafted and apply Section 60 of the Bankruptcy Act to resolve the problem. As defined by Section 60a(1), a preference is "[1] a transfer * * * of the property of a debtor [2] to or for the benefit of a creditor [3] for or on account of an antecedent debt, [4] made or suffered by such debtor while insolvent and [5] within four months before the filing * * * [of bankruptcy], [6] the effect of which transfer will be to enable such creditor to obtain a greater percentage of his debt than some other creditor of the same class." Section 60a(2) of the Bankruptcy Act provides that "a transfer of property * * * shall be deemed to have been made or suffered at the time when it became so far perfected that no subsequent lien upon such property obtainable by legal or equitable proceedings on a simple contract could become superior to the rights of the transferee." As we held in DuBay v. Williams, supra, 417 F.2d at 1287:

> " 'Transfer' for the purpose of section 60a(2) is thus equated with the act by which priority over later creditors is achieved and not with the event which attaches the security interest to a specific account."

With respect to Wholesale's security interest in the proceeds from the sale of the collateral, no later creditor could obtain priority over Wholesale from the time its financing statement was filed and further perfected pursuant to section 9–306(3), at least until Wholesale's proceeds were commingled with that of other secured creditors or with cash from other sources deposited in Gibson's bank account. Wholesale's security interest in those proceeds relates back to its initial financing statement. * * * However, Wholesale had no interest in cash other than its own proceeds, and hence no priority over later creditors in such cash, until (1) some part of Wholesale's proceeds were deposited with other cash in Gibson's bank account, (2) within ten days of Gibson's filing its Chapter XI petition. The effect of section 9–306(4) is thus to transfer to Wholesale a security interest in the cash in Gibson's bank account which does not derive from the sale of its collateral. In this situation, the act that gives Wholesale priority and the events that attach the security interest to the questioned asset occur at the same time. The transfer cannot occur earlier than ten days before the institution of bankruptcy. The transfer of the excess, above the wholesaler's proceeds, is a preference unless we can say that the transfer was neither for nor on account of an antecedent debt. We cannot avoid the conclusion that the transfer was on account of an antecedent debt. Wholesale could not qualify for section 9–306(4) treatment absent the antecedent debt; moreover, the transfer does not happen unless the debt owed exceeds the payments made to the creditor during the ten-day period before the bankruptcy petition has been filed.

The result is that Wholesale cannot successfully assert its claim under U.C.C. section 9–306(4)(d) to thwart the trustee's power to set that interest aside as a preference. However, the conclusion does not necessarily also follow that the creditor loses his security interest both in the proceeds from the sale of his collateral and in the nonproceeds in the debtor's bank account. In his contest with the trustee, he only loses his claim to the amounts in excess of his proceeds because only that amount is a preference. His security interest in the whole account, subject to the limitations of U.C.C. section 9–306(4), is valid except that the trustee can avoid it. To the extent that a creditor is able to identify his proceeds to trace their path into the commingled funds, he will be able to defeat *pro tanto* the trustee's assertion of a preference.

By this construction of Section 60 of the Bankruptcy Act and section 9–306(4) of the U.C.C., we do violence neither to statute nor to substantial justice among the parties. The creditor's security interest in the whole account under § 9–306(4) is *prima facie* valid, except as to the trustee, and, as to him, the creditor's security interest is presumptively preferential. The creditor can rebut the presumption by appropriately tracing his proceeds. We think that it is fair to place the burden on the creditor to identify his own proceeds and thus to defeat, in whole or in part, the trustee's claim of preference. The creditor is in a better position than the trustee to trace his proceeds; moreover, if the creditor wants to avoid both the limitations of U.C.C. section 9–306(4)(d) and the burden of proof in a potential contest with the trustee, all he needs to do is to prevent commingling of his proceeds and thus to follow U.C.C. section 9–306(4)(a)–(c).

Reversed and remanded for further proceedings consistent with the views herein expressed. [Footnotes omitted.]

Notes

1. Are you persuaded by Judge Hufstedler's interpretation?

2. What difference in result would occur in *In re Gibson* if the phrase "any cash proceeds" in UCC 9–306(4)(d)(ii) were interpreted to mean "any cash proceeds derived from collateral in which the secured party had a perfected security interest?" How about the result in Problem 8–10, supra?

3. Supporters of UCC 9–306(4) argue that any loss to the estate incurred by denying preferential treatment to security interests in funds in excess of those actually traced will be offset by savings in the cost of tracing and gains from the other deductions from that fund required by UCC 3–306(4)(d)(ii). In short, over time the formula will produce more rather than less for the estate. This is a persuasive argument, is it not? Even so, *In re Gibson* is still alive and well in the Ninth Circuit. See In re Charter First Mortgage, Inc., 56 B.R. 838 (Bkrtcy.D.Or.1985).

4. Some commentators have argued that UCC 9–306(4)(d) in fact fixes a statutory lien on property that first becomes effective on insolvency and should be avoided under Section 545. See Countryman, *Code Security Interests in Bankruptcy,* 4 U.C.C.L.J. 35, 48 (1971) (interpreting the predecessor to section 545). The definition of "statutory lien," however, seems to exclude security interests, even though dependent upon statute. See subsection 101(45).

SECTION 4. FRAUDULENT CONVEYANCES, SECTION 548

In this course we will not discuss the classical fraudulent conveyance, the transfer by one harried family member on the eve of bankruptcy to another family member in return for "love and affection." In the commercial field fraudulent conveyances have taken a more subtle form. In recent years trustees have been quite clever in challenging certain transfers as fraudulent. Commencing with a 1980 case in the Fifth Circuit, *Durrett v. Washington National Insurance,* 621 F.2d 201 (5th Cir.1980), some bankruptcy courts have even found that foreclosures which produce substantially less than the apparent value of the collateral are themselves fraudulent conveyances. Still other courts have indicated that various forms of guaranties, payment of specific debt, and even the incurring of debt in circumstances such as leveraged buyouts might be fraudulent conveyances. In considering the cases and problems that follow, students should ask themselves how far section 548 should be stretched. See, generally, McCoid, *Constructively Fraudulent Conveyances: Transfers for Inadequate Consideration,* 62 Tex.L.Rev. 639 (1983).

IN RE EWING

United States Bankruptcy Court, Western District of Pennsylvania, 1983.
33 B.R. 288.

GERALD K. GIBSON, BANKRUPTCY JUDGE.

The matter presently before the Court is a complaint to avoid a fraudulent transfer, wherein Trustee alleges that secured creditor's involuntary pre-petition sale of stock pledged by Debtor for less than its reasonably equivalent value constitutes a fraudulent transfer under § 548 of the Bankruptcy Code and the Pennsylvania Fraudulent Conveyance Act. Trustee also alleges that the foreclosure sale was not conducted in conformity with reasonable commercial practices as required by the Uniform Commercial Code.

* * *

The facts are briefly as follows. Commencing on or about November 12, 1968, and at various times thereafter, Debtor borrowed sums of money from Pittsburgh National Bank, hereinafter "PNB"; and executed promissory notes and pledge agreements to secure said debt. In September, 1977, Debtor borrowed the sum of $67,000.00 from PNB at which time he pledged 75,000 shares of Class B common stock and 9,500 shares of Class A common stock in Coventry Care, Inc. hereinafter "CCI" to secure the repayment of his indebtedness.

Upon Debtor's default, PNB commenced an involuntary sale of Debtor's shares of CCI. The sale was consummated on April 10, 1980, at which time, CCI purchased the shares for the amount of $72,500.00. Some months later, in August, 1980, Debtor filed a voluntary petition under Chapter 11 of the Bankruptcy Code. The case was subsequently converted to a Chapter 7.

The parties have stipulated that prior to the closed bid sale, PNB advertised the sale in the Wall Street Journal and Pittsburgh Post Gazette. Notice of sale and conditions thereto were sent to those parties who appear on Exhibit D of the Stipulation.

In his brief, Trustee presents the following arguments. A sale of Debtor's equity interest in secured collateral can be interpreted as a fraudulent conveyance pursuant to § 548 of the Bankruptcy Code, which allows the Trustee to avoid any transfer of an interest in debtor's property within one year prior to the filing of the bankruptcy petition while debtor is insolvent for which he receives less than reasonably equivalent consideration. Trustee further argues that the transfer, for purposes of § 548, occurred at the time of sale in April, 1980. Prior thereto, PNB's interest in the stock was limited to that necessary to secure repayment of the loan; and Debtor retained property rights in the remaining value. Finally, Trustee asserts that § 548 is applicable to involuntary foreclosures as well as voluntary transfers by the Debtor.

In its brief in support of its motion to dismiss Trustee's complaint, PNB argues as follows. The transfer which Debtor claims to have been fraudulent within the meaning of § 548 occurred outside the one-year period prior to the filing of the bankruptcy petition and is therefore not vulnerable to attack under § 548. PNB asserts that by virtue of the Uniform Commercial Code, a security interest in instruments is perfected by possession. Since PNB had possession of the securities at all times subsequent to the pledge, its security interest was perfected as against a bona fide purchaser. Therefore, the transfer occurred at the time of the pledge, in September, 1977; or at the latest, upon execution of a new pledge agreement in 1978.

In its brief in support of its motion to dismiss, CCI argues that a sale brought by a secured creditor to enforce its perfected lien in Debtor's property is not a fraudulent conveyance within the meaning of § 548. CCI first asserts that § 548 only pertains to actions taken by the Debtor, and does not include actions taken by a secured creditor in foreclosure upon the collateral. CCI further asserts that since the transfer occurred upon delivery of possession of the pledged stock to PNB in September, 1977, § 548 is inapplicable.

Having summarized the arguments of counsel, the Court now turns to the relevant provisions of the Bankruptcy Code. Section 548(a)(2)(A) provides as follows:

> (a) The trustee may avoid any transfer of an interest of the debtor in property, or any obligation incurred by the debtor, that was made or incurred on or within one year before the date of the filing of the petition, if the debtor—
>
> (2)(A) received less than a reasonably equivalent value in exchange for such transfer or obligation; and
>
> (B)(i) was insolvent on the date that such transfer was made or such obligation was incurred, or became insolvent as a result of such transfer or obligation;

Section 101(40) defines "transfer" as follows:

> (40) "transfer" means every mode, direct or indirect, absolute or conditional, voluntary or involuntary, of disposing of or parting with property or with an interest in property, including retention of title as a security interest.

Section 548(d)(1) further states as follows:

> (d)(1) For the purposes of this section, a transfer is made when such transfer becomes so far perfected that a bona fide purchaser from the debtor against whom such transfer could have been perfected cannot acquire an interest in the property transferred that is superior to the interest in such property of the transferee, but if such transfer is not so perfected before the commencement of the case, such transfer occurs immediately before the date of the filing of the petition.

* * *

Counsel for CCI relies upon the case of *Lovett v. Shuster,* 633 F.2d 98 (8th Cir.1980) decided under the Bankruptcy Act. Therein, the Court considered whether the transfer of collateral for purposes of 67(d) (the fraudulent conveyance provision) took place upon debtor's delivery of stock to the secured party; or upon assignment of title to the secured party. The Court held that for purposes of 67(d)(2), collateral was transferred upon delivery of possession. However, in *Lovett, supra,* the factual situation was significantly different from that at bar for the foreclosure sale took place some months after the filing of the petition in bankruptcy.

Counsel for the defendants cite the case of *In re Alsop,* 14 B.R. 982, 8 B.C.D. 335, 5 C.B.C.2d 797 (Bkrtcy.D.Alaska 1981) in support of their position that a foreclosure sale within one year of bankruptcy does not constitute a transfer within the meaning of § 548. However, other courts have reached different results. In *Durrett v. Washington Nat. Ins. Co.,* 621 F.2d 201 (5th Cir.1980), Debtor-in-Possession under the Bankruptcy Act sought to vacate the transfer of real property nine days prior to filing. The Fifth Circuit affirmed the District Court's holding that a non-judicial sale constituted a transfer within the meaning of § 67(d). The Court further held that the sale price of $115,400 for a parcel valued by the Court at $200,000 was not a fair equivalent and was therefore avoidable under § 67(d).

In *Abramson v. Lakewood Bank and Trust Company,* 647 F.2d 547 (5th Cir. 1981) *cert. denied,* 454 U.S. 1164, 102 S.Ct. 1038, 71 L.Ed.2d 320 (1982), the Fifth Circuit reversed a lower court decision that a nonjudicial foreclosure sale of debtor's land was not a transfer within the meaning of § 67(d). The Court states: "* * * as this transfer occurred within the one-year period, it is subject to being set aside as fraudulent if it was made without fair consideration." (p. 549).

Other courts have reached similar results under the Bankruptcy Code. * * *

While the foregoing cases deal with foreclosure upon real estate, the issue at bar concerns the involuntary sale of securities pledged as collateral. Under Pennsylvania law, upon a contract of pledge, title in the pledged property remains in the pledgor subject to a lien in favor of the pledgee for the amount of the debt. Further, the pledgee is liable for return of the pledged property upon satisfaction of the obligation. *In re Gordon,* 344 Pa. 262, 25 A.2d 304 (1942). Moreover, under the provisions of the Pennsylvania Uniform Commercial Code applicable to the pledge at bar, the secured creditor must account to the debtor for any surplus resulting from the secured creditor's disposition of the collateral upon debtor's default. 13 Pa.C.S.A. § 9504(b).

In the case at bar, PNB was the holder of a properly perfected security interest in the securities pledged as collateral for repayment of Debtor's obligation. However, Debtor retained an interest in the collateral to the extent that its value exceeded PNB's secured debt. It was only upon sale of the collateral to CCI that Debtor's interest therein was extinguished. Therefore, the Court is convinced that the transfer, for purposes of § 548, occurred on April 10, 1980; the date of sale.

Based upon the foregoing, the Court is satisfied that for purposes of § 548, the involuntary sale of stock in the case at bar constituted a transfer within one year of the filing of the petition while Debtor was insolvent, or rendered insolvent thereby. If after further testimony it is determined that the sale was not for reasonably equivalent value, the transfer will be avoided pursuant to § 548.

Notes

1. Was the Bankruptcy Court correct in concluding that the relevant "transfer" occurs at the foreclosure and not at the perfection of the security interest? The District Court held 'no' and reversed. In re Ewing, 36 Bankr. 476 (Bankr.W.D.Pa. 1983). This decision was affirmed, 746 F.2d 1465, 1466 (3d Cir.1984), cert. denied 469 U.S. 1214, 105 S.Ct. 1189, 84 L.Ed.2d 336 (1985). See section 548(d)(1), as amended in 1984.

2. Some might say that a determination that foreclosure under UCC 9–504 is "commercially reasonable" cannot be consistent with a finding that the debtor "received less than a reasonably equivalent value in exchange." What do you think?

In Durrett v. Washington National Insurance Co., 621 F.2d 201 (5th Cir. 1980), debtor-in-possession sought to set aside a foreclosure sale that had occurred pursuant to a deed of trust within the year preceding the filing of the bankruptcy petition. A third party purchased the property at the sale for $115,400. Durrett argued, and the district court found, that the property at that time had a market value of $200,000. Durrett argued that the payment of $115,400 for property worth $200,000 was itself a fraudulent conveyance under section 548's predecessor (subsection 67(d)(1) and (e)(1) of the Bankruptcy Act of 1898). Applying section 67, the court of appeals concluded such a payment was not the "fair equivalent" and thus constituted a fraudulent conveyance. Although there have been thousands of cases in which debtors have challenged foreclosure sales on many theories under state and federal law, this was the first case in which the court held that such a transfer could be a fraudulent conveyance. The issue is of most concern to creditors who lend against real property, because the dollar amounts there are large, and values are often quite uncertain. The *Ewing* case set out above shows that the same ideas may be asserted under Article 9. A critical review of these developments appears in Baird and Jackson, *Fraudulent Conveyance Law and its Proper Domain,* 38 Vand.L.Rev. 829 (1985).

Problem 8–11

You are the general counsel for Bank of Georgia. A loan officer at the Bank has asked you to give some advice on a prospective loan. Two of the Bank's best customers, Bill and Bob Green are principal owners of Greenbrook Carpet Co. They wish to borrow approximately $350,000 to purchase the controlling block of stock in the Lewis Carpet Mills, Inc. The principal asset that the Greens' control are the inventory and accounts receivable of Greenbrook. In order to make the $350,000 loan, the loan officer would like to have a direct claim on those assets. The Greens would prefer not to have personal liability on the loan and that, in turn, makes the loan officer wish to have even more security. The loan officer has suggested several alternatives for your consideration.

1. A loan could be made to the Greens on a non-recourse basis and the Greens could give security in the form of their shares in Greenbrook and in the shares of Lewis to be purchased.

2. A loan could be made to Greenbrook secured by the inventory and accounts receivable of Greenbrook. Greenbrook would be liable on the debt and would then

make a loan to the Green brothers. This loan to the Green brothers would be nonrecourse, but it would be secured by the stock of Lewis.

3. The bank could make the loan directly to the Green brothers and they in turn could cause Greenbrook to put up its inventory and accounts receivable as collateral for the loan.

SECTION 5. AVOIDANCE OF CERTAIN LIENS THAT IMPAIR EXEMPTIONS, SUBSECTION 522(f)

Exemption laws are studied in courses on bankruptcy. For our purposes it suffices to say that the laws of almost every state make certain assets of a debtor exempt from the claims of general creditors. Usually those laws do not apply to perfected security interests, for so to apply them would, in effect, deprive the debtor of a right to give someone else an interest in his property. The Bankruptcy Act contains its own set of exemptions and in a few states an individual debtor is permitted in bankruptcy to keep as exempt from the claims of the trustee and of his general creditors either assets exempt under state law or those provided under subsection 522(d). More than two-thirds of the states have opted out of subsection 522(d) and in those states the debtor can exempt only the property that is exempt under his own state law.

Contrary to the usual rule that security interests cannot be set aside under the exemption rules, subsection 522(f) permits a debtor to set aside even a perfected security interest in property that would otherwise be exempt if certain conditions are met:

> (f) Notwithstanding any waiver of exemptions, the debtor may avoid the fixing of a lien on an interest of the debtor in property to the extent that such lien impairs an exemption to which the debtor would have been entitled under subsection (b) of this section, if such lien is—
>
> (1) a judicial lien; or
>
> (2) a nonpossessory, nonpurchase-money security interest in any—
>
> (A) household furnishings, household goods, wearing apparel, appliances, books, animals, crops, musical instruments, or jewelry that are held primarily for the personal, family, or household use of the debtor or a dependent of the debtor;
>
> (B) implements, professional books, or tools, of the trade of the debtor or the trade of a dependent of the debtor; or
>
> (C) professionally prescribed health aids for the debtor or a dependent of the debtor.

In examining the subsection, one can see a variety of issues that might arise in interpreting 522(f). A crucial and frequently litigated one is the question whether the security interest was a "purchase money security interest" and thus beyond the reach of subsection 522(f).

IN THE MATTER OF RICHARDSON

United States Bankruptcy Court, Western District, Wisconsin, 1985.
47 B.R. 113.

MEMORANDUM DECISION AND ORDER

ROBERT D. MARTIN, BANKRUPTCY JUDGE.

This is an adversary proceeding in a chapter 7 case brought to obtain possession of a 1971 Ford 9000 tractor ("the tractor") in the possession of the defendant/debtor. The plaintiffs ("Johnsons") own a 350 acre farm in Sauk County on which the defendants ("Richardsons") lived and worked for the 1983 crop year. The Johnsons owned the livestock and feed, and the Richardsons grew crops and cared for the livestock. Profits from the farming operations were to be shared 60/40.

On January 19, 1983, the Richardsons made a deposit of $100.00 on the tractor which they hoped to purchase from Simpson's Ford Tractor of Richland Center ("Simpson's"). The purchase was contingent upon the availability of financing. On February 18, 1983, after learning of Ford Motor Credit Company's ("FMCC") acceptance of their credit application, the Richardsons paid Simpson's $500.00 on account for the down payment on the tractor. They paid another $500.00 on account toward the down payment on March 2, 1983. The Richardsons and FMCC apparently entered into a retail installment contract in very early March of 1983. That undated contract provided for a cash down payment of $2,508.00 and a $7,000.00 balance to be financed at 14.5% annual interest.

At some time in early or mid March, the Johnsons and the Richardsons met and agreed to consolidate the Richardsons' loan for the tractor with a loan of additional money to purchase various other farm machinery. On March 17, 1983, Mr. Johnson gave a $900.00 check to Simpson's Ford Tractor which was put on Richardsons' down payment account. A sales invoice was issued to Wayne Richardson on that date, and the Richardsons took possession of the tractor at around the same time. A down payment of $500.00 remained unpaid.

As evidence of their loan agreement with the Johnsons, the Richardsons delivered an Agricultural Universal Note on April 1, 1983, in the amount of $17,100.00, at an annual interest rate of 15%. To secure the debt, the Richardsons delivered an Agricultural Chattel Security Agreement ("the security agreement") granting the Johnsons a security interest in the tractor, as well as in the following items:

1982 Badger Manure Spreader

710 International 5, 18 plow

1240 John Deere plateless corn planter

Ford Manure Loader

After receiving the note and security agreement, the Johnsons gave the Richardsons a check for $1,939.25 on April 4, 1983. Of that sum, $1,200.00 was used to purchase the manure loader which was given as security. Mr. Richardson testified that approximately $725.00 of the remaining money was used to pay his 1982 income taxes. The Johnsons testified that they were unaware of the back tax bill, and believed the money was used towards payment for the tractor. In addition, the Johnsons gave a check of $7,092.45 to FMCC on May 5, 1983, to pay the balance due under Richardsons' contract with FMCC. On July 22, 1983, the Johnsons paid the remaining $500.00 of the cash down payment to Simpson's. The Johnsons perfected the security agreement by filing with the Sauk County Register of Deeds on August 2, 1983.

Monthly payments under the note were made by a milk check assignment. The Johnsons received $500.00 per month from May through October, 1983. Then on November 1, 1983, the Richardsons were evicted from the property. Nonetheless, they gave a $250.00 check to the Johnsons that month. The Richardsons made no further payments to the Johnsons.

The Richardsons filed their bankruptcy petition on December 28, 1983. Their bankruptcy trustee has abandoned all of the property listed on the security agreement.

The Johnsons estimate the fair market value of the tractor to be $7,000.00; the Richardsons estimate a fair market value of $6,000.00. The undisputed fair market value of the other four items of collateral is approximately $5,150.00. The Johnsons are in possession of those four items of collateral, and the Richardsons have possession of the tractor at this time. The Richardsons have listed the tractor on their amended schedule as exempt property under section 522(d)(1) and (5) of the Bankruptcy Code. They contend that the Johnsons' lien impairs their exemption and is therefore avoidable under section 522(f)(2)(B). The Johnsons challenge the avoidance of the lien on the grounds that they possess a purchase money security interest in the tractor and that the tractor does not qualify as a tool of the debtors' trade. Paragraph 2(b) of the security agreement states that "[c]ollateral specifically described above and not now owned by Debtor is being acquired by Debtor with proceeds of a loan from Secured Party." Both parties are in agreement as to the purchase money character of the security interest granted in the four items of collateral listed on the security agreement other than the tractor.

Purchase Money Security Interests

The Richardsons seek to avoid the fixing of a lien on the tractor under section 522(f)(2)(B) of the Bankruptcy Code. That provision states:

> (f) Notwithstanding any waiver of exemptions, the debtor may avoid the fixing of a lien on an interest of the debtor in property to the extent that such lien impairs an exemption to which the debtor would have been entitled under subsection (b) of this section, if such lien is—
>
> * * *
>
> (2) a nonpossessory, nonpurchase money security interest in any—
>
> * * *
>
> (B) implements, professional books, or tools of the trade of the debtor or the trade of a dependent of the debtor.

Thus, in order for the Richardsons to avoid the Johnsons' lien on the tractor it must be a nonpossessory, nonpurchase money lien. The tractor must also qualify as a tool of the Richardsons' trade. * * * [The court concludes that Ford Motor Credit had a purchase money security interest and that when the Johnsons paid money to the Richardsons, who in turn paid Ford Motor Credit, the purchase money status of the security interest was lost. It concluded that the Johnsons' therefore held a non-purchase money security interest in the tractor.]

Lien Avoidance

The Richardsons filed a voluntary joint petition under chapter 7 of the Bankruptcy Code. Section 522 lists the exemptions available to debtors under federal law, and provides that: "[t]his section shall apply separately with respect to each debtor in a joint case." Section 522(m) (amended 1984). Excluding the tractor now in contention, the Richardsons have listed $11,160.00, or $5,580.00 each, in exempt value in property they claim to own jointly and seek to exempt under section 522(d)(1). Section 522(d)(5) (amended 1984) states:

> (d) The following property may be exempted under subsection (b)(1) of this section:

(1) The debtor's aggregate interest, not to exceed $7,500 in value, in real property or personal property that the debtor or a dependent of the debtor uses as a residence. * * *

* * *

(5) The debtor's aggregate interest, not to exceed in value $400 plus any unused amount of the exemption provided under paragraph (1) of the subsection, in any property.

This is the so-called "wild card" provision of section 522 which allows each debtor who does not claim homestead to exempt his aggregate interest in up to $7,900.00 in value in any property. Except as a part of this proceeding the Richardsons' exemptions have not been contested.

The Richardsons scheduled the tractor valued at $5,680.00 as jointly held and exempted under section 522(d)(6) and the "wild card" provision (5) and (1). Section 522(d)(6) provides an exemption for "[t]he debtor's aggregate interest, not to exceed $750 in value, in any implements, professional books, or tools of the trade of the debtor or the trade of a dependent of the debtor."

For purposes of lien avoidance, section 522(f)(2)(B) requires that a nonpossessory, nonpurchase money interest be in an implement of the trade of the debtor or his dependents. The Johnsons admit in their proposed findings of fact and conclusions of law, at number 24, that the tractor is an implement of farming, but propose that it be found not subject to lien avoidance because it has not been used by the Richardsons at any time in 1984. The general rule is that, on the date of the petition the debtor must be engaged in the trade to which the tool belongs, in order to claim the tools as exempt. *In Re Johnson,* 19 B.R. 371, 374 (Bankr.D.Kan.1982). "However, when the debtor has only temporarily ceased the vocation at the time of the petition, the tools of the trade may still be exemptable." 19 B.R. at 374, 375 citing *In Re Hahn,* 5 B.R. 242 (Bankr.S.D.Iowa 1980). * * *

The Richardsons were evicted from the Johnsons' farm on November 1, 1983. Mr. Richardson has testified that he is now employed at Schoepps Ice Cream where he intends to stay, but that he would rather be farming. In 1984 he did put up hay on a custom basis using other tractors which he owns. He testified that he plans to return to farming in the future, first part-time and then full-time. The Richardsons currently own no real estate. As in the *Hahn* and *Pommerer* cases, the circumstances of this case might support a more lenient finding in the Richardsons' favor as their inability to farm at present could be unintentional. A recent opinion of the district court for this district *In Re Nowak,* 48 B.R. 290 (W.D.Wis.1984), displays a more restrictive view of exemptions under section 522(d) for purposes of lien avoidance under section 522(f)(2)(B). While that decision is limited to treatment of automobiles as tools of the trade, that court found it particularly important that the more restrictive interpretation of exemptions under section 522(d) be applied.

Thus, a limited view of the available exemptions is compelled and appropriate where the more expansive treatment would allow a complete avoidance of a nonpossessory, nonpurchase money security interest by virtue of section 522(f). In light of the *Nowak* decision, the *Johnson* analysis appears best suited for determining whether a tractor may qualify as a tool of the trade for purposes of lien avoidance. As the Richardsons have failed to demonstrate any reasonable prospects for re-engaging in farm operations, they may not avoid the Johnsons' lien on the tractor.

Upon the foregoing which constitute my findings of fact and conclusions of law in this case, it is hereby

ORDERED that the plaintiffs may have judgment in accordance with the demand of their complaint for possession of the 1971 Ford 9000 tractor which is the subject of this proceeding.

Notes

1. Section 522(f) is the only place where a trustee is authorized to strike down a fully perfected security interest in circumstances where the secured creditor has done nothing objectionable (such as seek a secret lien, or seek a preference, etc.). What is the justification for such a rule?

2. What if the asset in *Richardson* were an automobile and the Richardsons' claimed that they used the automobile in their business as real estate agents? Would the fact that motor vehicles are explicitly listed in subsection 522(d)(2) lead to the conclusion that no automobile could be a "tool of the trade" under subsection 522(f)(2)(B)?

3. What if the Wisconsin law had provided that the debtor could exempt only "the debtor's interest" in any particular asset, and the creditor had argued that the debt secured by the security interest was greater than the value of the collateral, the debtor had no equity, no "interest" and thus no exemption? The upshot of this, so the argument goes, is that subsection 522(f) does not permit avoidance in such a case because that lien does not "impair" an exemption.

4. Assume, contrary to the fact, that the Wisconsin law exempted tools of the trade, but only to a dollar limit of $1,000 and that the court found the tractor was a tool of the trade. How would subsection 522(f) affect the secured party's security interest in that case?

5. Assume one is in a state that has opted out of the federal exemptions (subsection 522(d)) and has abolished the state exemptions. Debtor now seeks to avoid a perfected nonpurchase-money security interest in his household goods. May he do so?

SECTION 6. LIMITATIONS IMPOSED UPON SECURED CREDITORS IN BANKRUPTCY SHORT OF AVOIDANCE—THE AUTOMATIC STAY, REDEMPTION RIGHTS, CRAMDOWNS

A. The Automatic Stay: Basics

Because they are intricate and their consequences dramatic, the trustee's rights to avoid security interests get extensive coverage in law school courses that deal with secured credit. In the practical arena, however, the less dramatic provisions such as section 362 (the stay), and sections 1322 and 1129 (the cramdown provisions) may well have a greater impact. They are less dramatic for several reasons. First, section 362 simply says that while the action is pending, the creditor may not take any significant action that will improve his position or cause payment to be made. The student should read section 362 and see how expansive it is. Note that it prohibits not only creditor self help and creditor law suits against the "property of the estate," but also against "the debtor." Judicial interpretations of the section so far have not narrowed it.

In effect, upon the filing of the petition the so-called automatic stay (362) says that the secured creditor must wait. He may not have new collateral; he may not perfect; he may not repossess; he may not continue with a foreclosure proceeding already in train under UCC 9–504. If he is particularly aggrieved, he can go to the bankruptcy court and ask that the stay be lifted. His principal ground will be that he has not been "adequately protected" because, for example, his collateral is declining in value. Such an application may produce some relief, but it is far from certain that the secured creditor will get what he wants from the court by such a request. It is entirely possible that he will be informed that he has adequate protection and that he should await the debtor's attempts to work things out. Invariably this "wait" is months long; it may be longer. In the meantime the debtor possesses and perhaps uses the collateral; it is subject to fire, theft, and depreciation, and ultimately to the vagaries of the bankruptcy court and the judgment of the bankruptcy judge. All of these factors doubtless diminish the negotiating leverage of the secured creditor; some elements diminish it altogether.

Of less importance, but still significant, is the right of the debtor in certain circumstances under subsection 1322(b)(2) in Chapter 13 cases and under sections 1123 and 1129 in Chapter 11 to modify–"cramdown"–the rights of the secured creditor despite the creditor's objection to such modifications. Each of those sections contains important limitations that are designed to protect the secured creditor's interests. However, those protections ultimately depend on a finding by the bankruptcy court that the modification of the rights would give the creditor less than he would receive in a liquidation. Again, the creditor finds his fate in the hands of the bankruptcy judge. If the bankruptcy judge concludes that the creditor's collateral is worth significantly less than the creditor believes it to be worth, a plan can be approved over the creditor's objection that gives him substantially less than his own valuation of his collateral.

Because they come into actual play in only a limited number of the cases, these cramdown provisions are much less significant than the stay. Some small percentage, perhaps as small as 10 percent, of Chapter 11 cases produce a confirmed plan under which a court approves the exercise of section 1129 rights. Thus, one might say the cramdown right embodied in sections 1123 and 1129 is unimportant. But this overlooks the impact that those sections have upon the negotiations among the creditors and between the creditors and the debtor in possession. Negotiations take place in the shadow of the cramdown provisions and any competent bankruptcy lawyer representing the debtor in possession is going to use that shadow to his benefit in negotiating a settlement. Even so, the importance of those provisions is surely less than that of the stay which applies in every case from the moment of filing.

A final section of importance is section 722 which applies to consumer bankruptcy. This section in effect modifies the redemption right that would otherwise be provided in UCC 9–506. The student should compare UCC 9–506 with section 722 set out below.

> An individual debtor may, whether or not the debtor has waived the right to redeem under this section, redeem tangible personal property intended primarily for personal, family, or household use, from a lien securing a dischargeable consumer debt, if such property is exempted under section 522 of this title or has been abandoned under section 554 of this title, by paying the holder of such lien the amount of the allowed secured claim of such holder that is secured by such lien.

In a course on Commercial Transactions we can only scratch the surface of the problems associated with these four complicated provisions of the Bankruptcy Reform Act of 1978. But at minimum the student needs to know that such sections exist, and have some sense of how they operate.

B. *The Stay's Fellow Travelers*

To understand the position of the secured creditor once the debtor has filed a petition in Chapter 11 one needs to comprehend not just section 362 but also several other related sections. Section 362's twin, section 361, is the provision that the secured creditor will commonly invoke in asking the court to lift the stay. The stay must be lifted, among other reasons, if the creditor can show that his interest is not "adequately protected." A huge accretion of case law is now building up under section 361. That section may produce more cases in a given year than any other section in the Bankruptcy Code. We will deal with it in connection with section 362.

At least five other related sections significantly affect the rights of the secured creditor in bankruptcy. These are section 363, "Use, Sale or Lease of Property"; section 364 on the obtaining of credit, including secured credit, by the debtor after filing a petition in bankruptcy; section 506(b) on the allowance of interest to the secured creditor pending the disposition of the case; section 549, "Postpetition Transactions"; and section 552, "Postpetition Effect of Security Interest."

Irrespective of the terms of the security agreement, the debtor-in-possession under Chapter 11 and the trustee in certain other chapters can "enter into transactions, including the sale or lease of property of the estate in the ordinary course of business without notice or a hearing, and may use property of the estate in the ordinary course of business * * * ". Thus a debtor-retailer may continue to sell the creditor's collateral to retail purchasers despite the filing of a Chapter 11. Likewise such a debtor may use trucks, equipment, and other collateral, despite the fact such use may cause it to decrease in value. The debtor may ultimately expose it to still other risks as well.

Section 363 bars non-ordinary course use and and disposal unless there is a court approval, and places similar restrictions upon the debtor's use of cash collateral. While the debtor in possession is thus free to continue to operate the business, he is not free to undertake transactions that might be thought to be extraordinary. The secured creditor's principal protection from depreciation or dissipation that might occur under 363 is to be found in section 361, the request for adequate protection. In effect, however, 363 puts the burden on the secured creditor to get the court to act, not vice versa.

One of the important, and at this writing, unresolved issues in commercial bankruptcy law has to do with the right of a secured creditor to recover his opportunity costs, usually lost interest, in bankruptcy. Under Chapter XI of the pre–1978 law, the court was theoretically unable to deal with the property subject to a security interest, and in theory at least, no plan could be proposed or approved to which the secured creditor did not agree. Although the stay was known and authorized by rule, one gathers that the courts were more hesitant to apply it to secured creditors than they are now. Under the current law, collateral subject to a perfected security interest is clearly covered, and the secured creditor's rights are subject to the jurisdiction of the bankruptcy court.

Since the traditional Chapter XI dealt in theory with only the unsecured creditors and the rule was that interest stopped accruing upon the filing of the petition, the drafters of the 1978 act may not have focused as clearly on that issue in the secured creditors' case as they might have. The clearest statement about opportunity costs, the accrual of interest, is to be found in subsection 506(b) which specifically allows interest to the extent that the collateral has a greater value than the amount of the debt. That subsection does not specify the secured creditor's right to interest if he is undersecured (though some might draw an implication from it), nor does it state in so many words the interest rate that should be applied. In the years since 1978 the majority of the courts have read subsection 506(b) to mean that an oversecured creditor draws interest at some rate, usually the agreed rate, but that an undersecured creditor accrues no interest even on that portion of his debt that is secured. At this writing two federal Courts of Appeal have spoken on the issue and have concluded that the section 361 provision for the creditor receiving the "indubitable equivalent" of his claim means that he must be awarded interest at some rate on the value of his collateral if he asks for the stay to be lifted and it is not. A third Court of Appeals has disagreed. Since it is not unknown for Chapter 11's to drag on for one or two years or longer, the issue of accrual and payment of interest in the interim can be a significant one.

IN RE AMERICAN MARINER INDUSTRIES, INC.

United States Court of Appeals, Ninth Circuit 1984.
734 F.2d 426.

JAMESON, SENIOR DISTRICT JUDGE:

Crocker National Bank, a secured creditor, has appealed from a judgment of the bankruptcy court, 10 B.R. 711 (Bkrtcy.C.D.Cal.1981), affirmed by the bankruptcy appellate panel, 27 B.R. 1004 (Bkrtcy. 9th Cir.1983) denying Crocker relief from the automatic stay imposed under 11 U.S.C. § 362(a). We reverse and remand to the bankruptcy court for further findings.

I. ISSUE ON APPEAL

The sole issue is whether an undersecured creditor who is stayed by a bankruptcy petition from repossessing its collateral is entitled, under the concept of "adequate protection", 11 U.S.C. §§ 361, 362, to compensation for the delay in enforcing its rights against the collateral.

II. FACTS AND PROCEEDINGS BELOW

The facts are not disputed. In 1978 Crocker made a loan to American Mariner secured by a perfected security interest in "basically all of the American Mariner's assets." On December 12, 1980, American Mariner filed a petition for reorganization under Chapter 11 of the Bankruptcy Code. 11 U.S.C. §§ 1101–46. At that time American Mariner's debt to Crocker, including accrued interest, was approximately $370,000, secured by collateral worth $110,000. Crocker filed a complaint for relief from or modification of the automatic stay under 11 U.S.C. § 362(d)(1) on February 23, 1981. In its complaint, Crocker claimed *inter alia* that it was entitled to adequate protection under 11 U.S.C. §§ 361 and 362(d)(1) in the form of monthly payments equal to Crocker's prospective return from reinvestment of the liquidation value of the collateral. Crocker argues that state law grants the secured creditor the right, on the debtor's default, to take possession of the collateral, sell it, and loan the money out at interest. To the extent that the automatic stay delays or prohibits the creditor from exercising these rights, Crocker contends, the creditor is denied the present value of its interest in the collateral. Since section 361(3) requires such "adequate protection" as will provide the secured creditor with the "indubitable equivalent" of its interest in the collateral, Crocker concludes that it was entitled to monthly payment as compensation for what it might have earned on the reinvestment of its liquidated interest in the collateral.

The bankruptcy court rejected Crocker's contention that the value of its interest in the collateral was not adequately protected. For the purposes of section 362(d)(2), the court found: (1) the liquidation value of the collateral was $110,000; (2) the collateral was not depreciating[1]; and (3) the collateral was "necessary for an effective reorganization." 10 B.R. at 712. In this appeal, Crocker does not contest the bankruptcy court's appraisal of the collateral nor its finding that the collateral is necessary for effective reorganization. In any case these findings are not clearly erroneous, and must therefore be affirmed. Fed.R.Civ.P. 52(a).

Crocker appealed the adequate protection determination to the Bankruptcy Appellate Panel of the Ninth Circuit. The appellate panel majority similarly rejected Crocker's contentions. The majority recognized, however, that "[i]t is difficult to determine what Congress intended should constitute adequate protection in the context of the stay * * *. Apart from inferences to be sought from the use of the indubitable equivalent language, there is no expression of an intent to compensate the secured party for the delay. * * * " 27 Bankr. at 1009. While Crocker argued that the focus of protection was the value of *its interest* in the collateral, the majority concluded that "[a] construction more consistent with the language and policy to be served would recognize that it is the value of the collateral which is the focus of protection." 27 B.R. at 1010. Since the trial court had protected the collateral against depreciation, the majority affirmed the trial court's judgment as "consistent with the policy and language of § 361(1)."

* * *

V. Statutory Language and Legislative History

A. *Section 361 Protects the Value of the Creditor's Interest in the Collateral*

Crocker's contention that the concept of adequate protection entitles it to interest on the present value of its collateral is principally founded on two sections of the Bankruptcy Code, 11 U.S.C. §§ 361, 362(d). Section 362(d) authorizes "a party in interest" to request relief from the automatic stay "for cause, including lack of adequate protection of an interest in property." Section 361 merely illustrates several means of providing adequate protection, and the methods illustrated are not exclusive. * * * Neither section, apparently by design, defines "adequate protection" or prescribes precisely what is to be protected. * * * Our inquiry beings with these threshold issues and requires us to construe sections 361 and 362.

* * *

The central issue in this case is not how to provide adequate protection but what is to be protected. The bankruptcy court and bankruptcy panel concluded "that it is the value of the collateral which is the focus of protection." 27 B.R. at 1010. Crocker insists that section 361 protects the present value of *its interest* in collateral. * * * Contrary to the conclusion of the bankruptcy court, the * * * language [of section 361] provides for adequate protection of "*an interest of an entity* in property * * * to the extent that the stay * * * results in a

1. The bankruptcy court ordered American Mariner to pay Crocker $1,770 each month to protect against possible depreciation of the collateral. If it is later determined that the payments exceeded depreciation, the excess is to be applied to the principal of Crocker's allowed claim. The court arrived at the $1,770 figure by taking judicial notice that 18%, then the current prime interest rate, on $110,000, the collateral's liquidation value, yielded monthly payments of $1,770.

decrease in *the value of such entity's interest* in such property." (emphasis added). The plain meaning of this language must control unless we can point to convincing evidence that Congress intended something different by the words it chose. See *Watt v. Alaska,* 451 U.S. at 266, 101 S.Ct. at 1678.

We find the legislative history of section 361 conflicting but not without significant support for the plain meaning of the statute. Both the House and Senate Reports clearly express the congressional intention to provide protection for the secured creditor's interest and not merely the value of the collateral:

> The interests of which the court may provide protection in the ways described in this section [361] include equitable as well as legal interests. For example a right to redeem under a pledge or a right to recover property under a consignment are both interests that are entitled to protection.

H.R.Rep. No. 595 at 338, 1978 U.S.Code Cong. & Ad.News at 6294, 6295. Arguably the foregoing examples demonstrate some congressional concern for the safety of the property itself, but that concern does not diminish the general intention to protect a broad range of secured creditors' interests. As the appellate panel observed, the reports do not specifically mention the secured creditor's legal right to take possession of and sell the collateral; nor do the reports mention the creditor's equitable right to reinvest the proceeds of the sale. Unquestionably, however, these are valuable rights of secured creditors, and nothing in the reports suggests they are not among those equitable and legal interests entitled to protection.

The House Report emphasizes the breadth of adequate protection:

> It is not intended to be confined strictly to the constitutional protection required, however. The section, and the concept of adequate protection, is based as much on policy grounds as on constitutional grounds. Secured creditors should not be deprived of the benefit of their bargain. There may be situations in bankruptcy where giving a secured creditor an absolute right to his bargain may be impossible or seriously detrimental to the bankruptcy laws. Thus, this section recognizes the availability of alternate means of protecting a secured creditor's interest. Though the creditor might not receive his bargain in kind, the purpose of the section is to insure that the secured creditor receives in value essentially what he bargained for.

H.R.Rep. No. 595 at 339, 1978 U.S.Code Cong. & Ad.News at 6295. In this case it is clear that Crocker is *not* entitled to the "absolute right to his bargain," which is the right to take possession of and sell the collateral. The bankruptcy court's finding that the collateral is "necessary to an effective reorganization" made this impossible. Nonetheless, Congress seems to have recognized that the secured creditor's rights of repossession and sale are part of its "bargain," which section 361 insures it will receive at least "in value" if not "in kind".

Value is another term intended to have broad scope in the context of providing adequate protection to secured creditors. The House Report stresses that the language of section 361 is directed toward "the value of the protected entity's interest in the property involved."

> The section does not specify how value is to be determined nor does it specify when it is to be determined. These matters are left to case-by-case interpretation and development. It is expected that the courts will apply the concept in light of facts of each case and general equitable principles.

H.R.Rep. No. 595 at 339, 1978 U.S.Code Cong. & Ad.News at 6295. In this case we are engaged in precisely the sort of case-by-case interpretation and development intended by Congress.

We recognize that a congressional directive for "case-by-case interpretation and development" must not be abused. Such judicial interpretation must not overlook the overriding purpose of the automatic stay, namely to give the debtor "a breathing spell from his creditors * * * [to permit] the debtor to attempt a repayment or reorganization plan, or simply to be relieved of the financial pressures that drove him into bankruptcy." H.R.Rep. No. 595 at 340, 1978 U.S. Code Cong. & Ad.News at 6296–97. Nor can we ignore the purposes of business reorganization under Chapter 11 to initially relieve the debtor of its prepetition debts, to free cash flow to meet current operating expenses, and ultimately to permit the debtor "to restructure a business's finances so that it may continue to operate, provide its employees with jobs, pay its creditors, and produce a return for its stockholders." *Id.* at 220, 1978 U.S.Code Cong. & Ad.News at 6179.

At the same time, it seems clear that sections 361 and 362 include exceptional provisions specifically intended by Congress to benefit secured creditors at the expense of the debtor. In addition to the substantive requirement of adequate protection, three procedural provisions of section 362 openly favor the interests of secured creditors over those of the debtor: (1) under 362(e) the stay terminates automatically (leaving the creditor free to proceed against the collateral) if a hearing is not held within 30 days; (2) 362(f) provides creditors with ex parte relief under limited circumstances; and (3) in all proceedings the debtor bears the burden of proving that the creditor's interest is adequately protected. We are convinced, therefore, that the case-by-case development, guided by equitable principles as Congress envisioned, must recognize and protect the *value* of a creditor's interest when, as here, that value is demonstrated to exist and is measurably threatened.

B. Adequate Protection, Compensation, and Indubitable Equivalent

The bankruptcy appellate panel concluded that adequate protection "is intended to provide a measure of protection against, rather than compensate for, risk." 27 B.R. at 1012. We disagree. Whether protection is adequate depends directly on how effectively it compensates the secured creditor for loss of value. Sections 361(1) and (2) by their own terms compensate for "a decrease in the value" of the secured creditor's interest. The compensatory nature of adequate protection is even more apparent from the catch-all alternative of section 361(3) authorizing "such other relief * * * as will result in the realization by such entity of the indubitable equivalent of such entity's interest in such property."

The history of 361(3) with the phrase "indubitable equivalent" lends significant support to the contention that section 361 protects the present value of the secured creditor's interest. Subsection (3) was the product of a compromise between the more restrictive Senate version of 361 and the expansive House version. See 124 Cong.Rec.H. 11092 (daily ed. Sept. 28, 1978) (statement of Representative Edwards of California). The Senate bill had specified two exclusive methods for providing adequate protection, S.Rep. No. 989, 95th Cong.2d Sess. 54, 1978 U.S.Code Cong. & Ad.News 5787, 5840, while the House bill contained four methods including a provision for an administrative expense priority and a general provision similar to the present subsection (3), but without the indubitable equivalent language. The compromise removed the administrative expense priority and added the novel requirement of indubitable equivalence.

Since the original House language provided for "such other relief as will result in the realization by such entity of the value of such entity's interest in such property," we must determine whether Congress intended to change the meaning of the subsection by adding the phrase "indubitable equivalent". After examining the origins of the phrase and its use elsewhere in the Bankruptcy Code, we conclude that it at least encourages if not requires a present value analysis under section 361.

As the bankruptcy court recognized, Congress derived the term "indubitable equivalent" from Judge Learned Hand's opinion in *In re Murel Holding Corp.*, 75 F.2d 941 (2d Cir.1935). In *Murel,* Metropolitan Life Insurance Co. held a mortgage on an apartment house. When the apartment house owners defaulted on the mortgage, Metropolitan attempted to foreclose, but the owners obtained an ex parte stay after filing a petition for reorganization under section 77B of the Bankruptcy Act of 1898 (former 11 U.S.C. § 207). The owners then proposed a plan of reorganization that required Metropolitan to forego amortization payments and extend the due date of the mortgage while the apartment house was renovated. Metropolitan would have received interest in the meantime. Metropolitan rejected the plan and moved to vacate the stay, but its motion was denied.

On appeal Metropolitan argued that its interest was not adequately protected. Judge Hand, for the court, noted that the plan had little hope of success and the ability of the apartment house to satisfy Metropolitan's accruing claims was declining. 75 F.2d at 942. Judge Hand admitted, however, that the court had the power to confirm a plan over the objection of creditors if the plan provided "adequate protection for the realization by them of the full value of their interest, claims, or liens." *Id.* He then explained the concept of adequate protection:

> In construing so vague a grant, we are to remember not only the underlying purposes of the section, but the constitutional limitations to which it must conform. It is plain that "adequate protection" must be completely compensatory; and that payment ten years hence is not generally the equivalent of payment now. Interest is indeed the common measure of the difference, but a creditor who fears the safety of his principal will scarcely be content with that; he wishes to get his money or at least the property. We see no reason to suppose that the statute was intended to deprive him of that in the interest of junior holders, unless by a substitute of the most *indubitable equivalence.*

Id. (emphasis added). The court concluded that the protection offered was inadequate and ordered the stay dissolved.

In its context, Judge Hand's interpretation of adequate protection emphasizes two factors. First, it suggests that to be "completely compensatory" adequate protection must compensate for present value, "that payment ten years hence is not generally the equivalent of payment now." This protection the owners of the apartment house provided in the form of interest. Second, adequate protection must insure the safety of the principal. This the owners failed to do. Judge Hand concluded that the creditor's right "to get his money or at least the property" may be denied under a plan for reorganization only if the debtor provides "a substitute of the most indubitable equivalence." Such a substitute clearly must both compensate for present value and insure the safety of the principal. Significantly, however, Judge Hand added that "[n]o doubt less will be required to hold up the suit for a short time until the debtor shall have a chance to prepare." *Id.* at 943. This qualification, of course, reflects the absence under the former Bankruptcy Code of a statutory requirement for adequate protection during the stay, not to mention the absence of a requirement for an automatic stay.

In the Bankruptcy Reform Act of 1978, "indubitable equivalent" first appeared in the Senate's version of section 1129(b), as part of the so-called cram down provisions similar to those encountered by Judge Hand. But for the use of "indubitable equivalent," it was not clear whether the section required present value compensation. In its final form, however, 11 U.S.C. § 1129(b)(2)(A)(i)(II) clearly requires deferred cash payments under a reorganization plan to equal the present value of the allowed claim. The "indubitable equivalent" requirement appears in section 1129(b)(2)(A)(iii) as an alternative to deferred payments and carries with it, from its original context in *Murel,* the requirement of compensation for present value. See 124 Cong.Rec.H. 1104 (daily ed. Sept. 28, 1978) (statement of Representative Edwards approving present value analysis at H.R. Rep. No. 595 at 414–15, 1978 U.S.Code Cong. & Ad.News at 6370–71); S.Rep. No. 989 at 127, 1978 U.S.Code Cong. & Ad.News at 5913 ("The indubitable equivalent language is intended to follow the strict approach taken by Judge Learned Hand in *In re Murel Holding Corp.,* 75 F.2d 941 (2d Cir.1935)").

Against the foregoing background, we conclude that the use of the term "indubitable equivalent" in section 361 is significant of congressional intent. When the term was first employed by Judge Hand, the Bankruptcy Code did not require adequate protection during a temporary stay. Congress understood the term to represent a "strict approach" to adequate protection in the context of the cram down provisions. Use of the term in section 1129 plainly illustrates that Congress well understood the meaning of the term in its original context and intended to adopt the strict approach that the term represents. That Congress in 1978 should require adequate protection during the automatic stay and then add to that requirement language representing a strict approach to adequate protection convinces us that Congress intended to adopt or at least encourage the same approach to adequate protection in sections 361 and 362.

VI. Cases on Adequate Protection

The early cases, decided before enactment of the Bankruptcy Reform Act of 1978, are of little relevance in construing sections 361 and 362. Among the recent cases construing these sections there is a split of authority. Several courts have relied in part on Judge Hand's opinion in *Murel* to require adequate protection under section 361 of the present value of the secured creditor's interest. * * *

An apparently growing number of bankruptcy courts approve the view, adopted by the bankruptcy appellate panel in this case, extending adequate protection to the value of the collateral alone. * * * The majority of these courts have relied heavily on the detailed, thorough analysis of Judge Mabey in *South Village* [*In re South Village, Inc.,* 25 B.R. 787 (Bkrtcy. Utah 1982)] and *Alyucan* [*In re Alyucan Interstate Corp.,* 12 B.R. 803 (Bkrtcy. Utah 1981).] While we appreciate the care taken in this analysis, we conclude that *South Village* and *Alyucan* accord insufficient weight to the language of the statute and the congressional goal of affording the secured creditor the benefit of its bargain.

VII. Conclusions

The secured creditor's right to take possession of and sell collateral on the debtor's default has substantial, measurable value. The secured creditor bargains for this right when it agrees to extend credit to the debtor and both parties consider the right part of the creditor's bargain. The right constitutes an "interest in property" that is "created and defined by state law," and we are aware of no federal interest that requires this right of the secured creditor to go unprotected "simply because an interested party is involved in a bankruptcy proceeding." See *Butner v. United States,* 440 U.S. 48, 54–55, 99 S.Ct. 914, 917–918, 59 L.Ed.2d 136 (1979). The Court in *Butner* observed that "[u]niform treatment of property interests by both state and federal courts within a State serves * * * to prevent a party from receiving 'a windfall merely by reason of the happenstance of bankruptcy.'" 440 U.S. at 55, 99 S.Ct. at 918 (quoting *Lewis v. Manufacturers National Bank,* 364 U.S. 603, 609, 81 S.Ct. 347, 350, 5 L.Ed.2d 323 (1961)). To the extent that the debtor in bankruptcy can prevent the secured creditor from enforcing its rights against collateral while the debtor benefits from the creditor's money, the debtor and his unsecured creditors receive a windfall at the expense of the secured creditor.

We conclude that sections 361 and 362(d) were drafted to preclude such a windfall and to insure that the secured creditor receives the benefit of its bargain. We are satisfied that our holding in this case will not inhibit successful reorganization but rather will promote among other things the ready availability of affordable credit.

We hold that Crocker National Bank is entitled to compensation for the delay in enforcing its rights during the interim between the petition and confirmation of the plan.[11] Crocker contended that such compensation should take the form of monthly interest payments at the market rate on the liquidation value of the collateral. We agree that this is one method of providing adequate protection but by no means the only method available to the debtor. Consistent with the policies behind sections 361 and 362, the debtor should be permitted maximum flexibility in structuring a proposal for adequate protection. The result, however, should as nearly as possible under the circumstances of the case provide the creditor with the value of his bargained for rights.[12]

Remanded for further findings by the bankruptcy court consistent with this opinion. [Some footnotes omitted.]

11. Since we base our decision on our construction of the statute and its legislative history, we do not reach Crocker's constitutional contentions.

12. There are a few general guidelines that the trial court and debtor should consider. First, to avoid overcompensating the secured creditor, the timing of adequate protection should take account of the usual time and expense involved in repossession and sale of collateral. See *In re South Village, Inc.,* 25 B.R. 987, 996 n. 14 (Bkrtcy.Utah 1982). Second, the market rate of interest is not the only rate that may be applicable under the facts of each case. For example, noting that section 506(b) allows interest to *oversecured* creditors at the *contract* rate, see 3 *Collier on Bankruptcy* ¶ 506.05 (L. King 15th ed. 1983), an undersecured creditor would receive a windfall if the market rate of interest exceeds the contract rate. Compensating the creditor at the contract rate, as noted above, is one method approved in the Senate Report. S.Rep. No. 989 at 54, 1978 U.S.Code Cong. & Ad.News at 5840.

IN RE KELLER

United States Bankruptcy Court, Northern District Iowa 1984.
45 B.R. 469.

WILLIAM W. THINNES, BANKRUPTCY JUDGE.

FINDINGS OF FACT

1. The Debtors-in-Possession, Robert F. Keller and Lois E. Keller, filed their Petition for Relief under Chapter 11 of the Bankruptcy Code on February 15, 1984.

2. The Debtors-in-Possession are farmers in Van Buren County, Iowa, operating approximately 1,931 acres of farm land. The Federal Land Bank of Omaha is the first mortgagee on 1,709 acres of said property. As of the date of filing, the debt owed to Federal Land Bank of Omaha was $1,863,450 with the property being valued by the Debtors-in-Possession's appraiser at $903,000. * * *

7. Testimony was presented on behalf of the Debtors-in-Possession that the real estate will not decrease in value in the upcoming months and the Court so finds notwithstanding the testimony to the contrary provided by the Movant's in-house personnel.

CONCLUSIONS OF LAW

* * *

3. The Debtors-in-Possession have met their burden of proof in showing that the property interest of the Movant, The Federal Land Bank of Omaha, is adequately protected and is not entitled to relief from the automatic stay imposed by 11 U.S.C. § 362(a) or to have the stay conditioned upon the payment of rents by the Debtors-in-Possession.

MEMORANDUM

* * *

Adequate Protection

* * *

FLB asserts that its "interest in collateral" to be protected is the value of the real estate as well as the rights set forth in its mortgage such as the right to have a receiver appointed on default. The Debtors-in-Possession assert that the "interest to be protected" is the value of the real estate and not any intangible contract rights.

* * *

The ninth circuit recently decided [in] *In re American Mariner Industries, Inc.*, 734 F.2d 426 (1984) * * * that "the secured creditor's rights of repossession and sale are part of its 'bargain,' which section 361 insures it will receive at least 'in value' if not 'in kind'." *American Mariner,* 734 F.2d at 431. Having examined the opinion of the ninth circuit in *American Mariner* this Court declines to follow the ninth circuit as to do so would in essence eviscerate the Bankruptcy Code and make Chapter 11 reorganization virtually impossible to accomplish.

In the case at bar, the credible testimony reveals that the real estate will not decline in value in the foreseeable future. Therefore, FLB has been provided adequate protection of its interest.

In the case at bar, forcing the Debtors-in-Possession to pay rents to FLB as adequate protection, thus allowing FLB to receive the "benefit of its bargain," at this point in this bankruptcy would eviscerate the Bankruptcy Code of its protection for the Debtors-in-Possession. The Court in *South Village,* 25 B.R. at 994 n. 8 dealt with the time value of money and concluded that if opportunity costs were to be allowed as a means of adequate protection it would and should have been included in 11 U.S.C. § 361. Opportunity costs as examined in *South Village* are not unlike the "benefit of the bargain" which FLB seeks to have this Court provide. The movant in *South Village* as the Movant in this case was an undersecured creditor. Judge Mabey determined that the movant was not entitled to adequate protection of the benefit of its bargain in the form of opportunity costs.

One final point regarding movant's appealing but unpersuasive argument must be made. Movant relies heavily on *In re Murel,* 75 F.2d 941 (2d Cir.1935) for the proposition that the creditor must be given the "indubitable equivalent" of its bargain. Movant fails to acknowledge that *Murel* was dealing with a plan confirmation hearing. The standard for a "cram down" may well be more rigorous than the adequate protection required by 11 U.S.C. § 362(d)(1). If adequate protection requires the indubitable equivalent of the "benefit of a bargain" such that the creditor is to possess the same rights as it would have enjoyed but for the bankruptcy there would be no reason to have the Bankruptcy Code. This Court declines to follow *American Mariner* and hold that FLB is entitled to the "benefit of its bargain" in the form of rents as the value of the land is not decreasing. To so hold would give a carte blanche to all undersecured mortgagees to enjoy all of their rights as though no bankruptcy had been filed.

* * *

Note: Adequate Protection and Lost Opportunity Costs

It is not uncommon for a Chapter 11 proceeding to drag on for one, two or three years. In such cases secured creditors frequently argue that they are suffering substantial "opportunity costs." But for bankruptcy they would have been able to repossess their collateral, liquidate it, and reinvest the funds to produce a return. The loss of this return is the lost opportunity cost. Thus, creditors argue that they should be granted a return on their investment (value of the collateral), to make them whole for that period. The argument hangs particularly on section 361(3) that adequate protection should provide for "realization * * * of the indubitable equivalent of such entity's interest in such property." The indubitable equivalent language comes from an opinion of Judge Hand written in the 1930s that in fact deals with the time value of money. Opponents of the secured creditor's position have argued first that subsections 361(1) and (2) seem only to contemplate protection of the creditor's principal and not a return for the lost opportunity and thus that subsection (3) should not be read to be in conflict with that. Moreover, the opponents of the secured creditors' position point to subsection 506(b) and 502(b)(2). The former explicitly allows interest to the secured creditor to the extent that the value of the collateral exceeds his debt. The latter explicitly denies post-petition interest to unsecured creditors.

The courts of appeals for four circuits have now addressed this question. The principal case adopting the secured creditor's view of opportunity costs and of subsection 361(3) is In re American Mariner Industries, 734 F.2d 426 (9th Cir.1984). In that case the court essentially adopted the view asserted by the secured creditor that indubitable equivalence demands the protection of opportunity costs. *American Mariner* was followed in Grundy National Bank v. Tandem Mining Corp., 754 F.2d 1436 (4th Cir.1985), and it was rejected in In re Timbers of Inwood Forest Association, 793 F.2d 1380 (5th Cir.1986) on rehearing in the Fifth Circuit. In In re Briggs

Transportation Co., 780 F.2d 1339 (8th Cir.1985), the Eighth Circuit claimed not to reject *American Mariner* but in fact did so.

If *American Mariner* is widely adopted, it probably will have significant impact on Chapter 11; it certainly will pose many new questions. The first question concerns the interest rate that is to be used to award the secured creditor his opportunity costs. Does one adopt some market rate? Does one adopt a rate that could be had on a new investment if the collateral were liquidated? Does one use the interest rate in the security agreement? Must the interest be paid at once or can it be accrued?

If the courts or Congress ultimately require the debtor to pay periodic interest payments, such a holding is likely to have a significant impact on the negotiation and ultimate outcome of Chapter 11 proceedings. By giving an undersecured creditor the power to demand alternatively payments of interest or return of collateral that may be critical to the reorganization, the rule will permit a secured creditor to drive the Chapter 11 in a way that would not otherwise be possible.

In a limited way Congress has already responded to *American Mariner.* Chapter 12 specifically provides that section 361 does not apply in Chapter 12 proceedings. Chapter 12 instead substitutes its own adequate protection provision. The motivation for eliminating 361 from Chapter 12 is to avoid the *American Mariner* outcome. What inference does one draw about Congressional intent in that adoption?

Problem 8–12

Computech Inc. successfully produced and marketed software for various lines of personal computers since the company's organization in 1981. Early in 1984 the company introduced its own personal computer, the Computech 2000. The computer proved a miserable failure. On January 7, 1985, Computech petitioned for bankruptcy in Chapter 11. The bankruptcy court is currently considering several requests for relief from the stay.

1. Saturn Bank holds a mortgage on the Computech manufacturing plant near Los Angeles. The mortgage secured a debt of $600,000 with interest at 2¼ percent plus prime. The current value of Saturn's collateral is stable at $1.2 million. Under *American Mariner,* is Saturn entitled to adequate protection? If so, in what form?

2. Pluto Bank holds a mortgage on a Monrovia office building owned by Computech. The mortgage secures a debt of $500,000 with interest at 1¾ percent plus prime. Computech gambled on a radical building design, hoping to attract innovative, high-tech companies. Unfortunately, only the architect likes the design. The property value has been declining, but now seems to have leveled off at about $260,000. Compuworld, a financially solid concern with hopes of taking over Computech's software business, has offered to guarantee Pluto the recovery of an amount equal to the value of Pluto's collateral plus interest at the contract rate for the duration of bankruptcy proceedings. Is Pluto adequately protected by the arrangement?

3. Assume instead that Computech's current owners hope to continue their software operation after bankruptcy. The owners promise Pluto that their plan will provide Pluto with a present value of payments equal to the value of Pluto's collateral plus interest at the contract rate for the duration of bankruptcy proceedings. The owners point to Computech's prior success in the software industry as evidence of the viability of this plan. Is Pluto adequately protected?

C. Postpetition Claims

The right to payment of prepetition claims of certain critical creditors is also troublesome. Nothing in the Bankruptcy Code explicitly provides for postpetition payment of pre-petition debt (except, of course, as part of a plan or liquidation). Section 549 specifies that payments made after the commencement of the case and not authorized "under this title or by the court" may be avoided by the trustee. Although a few cases allow the payment of pre-petition debt in certain circumstances, the norm is for the debtor-in-possession to be denied the right to make such payment.

That means that after the Chapter 11 has been filed, even a willing debtor-in-possession is prohibited from paying his pre-petition debts. He and his creditor are no longer the masters of their collective fate. All of the hard earned goodwill that may now exist in a debtor's mind for a particular creditor goes for naught.

Finally we turn to section 552. This section will be of interest to every inventory and accounts receivable lender, and indeed to many other secured creditors who have an interest in proceeds or after-acquired property. In general it permits a security interest to continue in proceeds and in analogous forms of property, but prohibits the attachment of a security interest to after-acquired property that does not constitute "proceeds, products, offspring, rents, or profits of such property." If an inventory lender does nothing to protect his interest after a Chapter 11 is filed, it is conceivable that the debtor will sell the collateral in accordance with his rights under section 363, commingle the funds in such a way that the secured creditor's interest cannot be identified as a "proceeds" claim, and either fail to replace the collateral or replace it with money from another source, in which case the secured creditor soon becomes unsecured.

The combination of these sections should cause any Chapter 11 debtor and the debtor's principal secured creditor to negotiate some form of agreement prior to or upon the filing of a petition in Chapter 11. Typically the debtor needs continued financing and typically the secured creditor risks substantial losses because of the sections described above if the secured creditor does not cooperate with the debtor. Because both parties should see that it is in their interests to reach such an agreement, it is common in the early days of a Chapter 11 for a "cash collateral order" to be entered. Such an order may provide for continued financing and for a continued security interest. In it the debtor may give up certain benefits that the debtor would otherwise enjoy under the stay and may promise to operate the business and to make reports.

IN RE AEROSMITH DENTON CORPORATION

Bankruptcy Court, Northern District Texas, 1983.
36 B.R. 116.

MEMORANDUM AND ORDER

BILL H. BRISTER, BANKRUPTCY JUDGE.

Mercantile National Bank at Dallas filed complaint for sanctions against the debtor, alleging that the debtor unlawfully used cash collateral after a Chapter 11 petition was filed without first having obtained consent of the secured party or authorization from the Court. * * *

Aerosmith Denton Corporation filed a voluntary petition for order for relief under Chapter 11 of the Bankruptcy Code on February 25, 1983. On April 15, 1982, and on at least two occasions after that date and prior to the filing of the Chapter 11 petition, the debtor executed notes to Mercantile National Bank at Dallas and secured those notes with a security interest in, among other property, all of the debtor's accounts receivable and contract rights and all cash proceeds thereof. The bank's perfected security interest in the prepetition accounts receivable and proceeds is not challenged.

On April 5, 1983, approximately five weeks after the Chapter 11 petition was filed, the bank filed complaint to terminate stay, to provide adequate protection and for other relief. At the preliminary hearing before Judge Gandy on April 20, 1983, the evidence reflected that in the period since the Chapter 11 petition was filed the debtor had collected $13,444.24 from those prepetition accounts receivable, that it had commingled those cash proceeds in a single debtor-in-possession checking account where there were other monies on deposit, and that the proceeds from the accounts receivable thus lost identity. Judge Gandy enjoined the debtor from further collection of prepetition accounts receivable and ordered the debtor to turn over to the bank all prepetition accounts receivable. The bank seeks a replacement lien on the debtor's postpetition accounts receivable to secure the $13,444.24 in cash proceeds which it contends were unlawfully used by the debtor, an administrative priority claim under § 507(b) of the Code and imposition of civil or criminal penalties upon the debtor and counsel for the debtor.

The debtor opposes all of the requested relief. First it contends that it did not use "cash collateral" of the bank and supports that argument with the contention that the definition of "cash collateral" [1] in § 363(a) of the Code does not include accounts receivable. Further, debtor argues that § 9.306(d)(4) of the Tex.Bus. & Comm.Code, is nonbankruptcy law which limits any potential recovery by the bank to proceeds generated *prior* to the filing of the bankruptcy petition.

In defining cash collateral the drafters of the Code adopted the Senate version rather than the broader House concept of "soft collateral" which would have included also inventory, accounts, contract rights, general intangibles, and chattel paper. By adoption of the Senate version the Code effectively removed limitations that were placed on the use, sale, or lease of those excluded items. 124 Cong.Rec. 11,093 (Sept. 28, 1978); S 17,409 (Oct. 6, 1978). Thus, if one looked no further, it might appear that a trustee or a debtor-in-possession would be authorized, pursuant to § 363(c)(1), to use or sell accounts receivable in the ordinary course of business without notice and hearing.

However, § 552 of the Code also must be considered for its impact on the issue of the existence of a security interest on proceeds which a debtor receives postpetition. Section 552(a) provides, as a general rule, that "after acquired" property of the estate is not subject to any lien resulting from any security agreement entered into by the debtor before the commencement of the case in bankruptcy. That general rule is subject to the exceptions set forth in § 552(b) which provides, in relevant part:

> (b) * * * [I]f the debtor and a secured party enter into a security agreement before the commencement of the case and if the security interest created by such agreement extends to property of the debtor acquired before commencement of the case and to proceeds * * * of such property, then such security interest extends to such proceeds * * * acquired by the estate after the commencement of the case *to the extent provided by such*

1. § 363(a) of the Code defines "cash collateral" as follows:

> (a) In this section, "cash collateral" means cash, negotiable instruments, documents of title, securities, deposit accounts, or other cash equivalents in which the estate and an entity other than the estate have an interest.

security agreement and by applicable nonbankruptcy law, except to the extent that the Court, after notice and hearing and based on the equities of the case, orders otherwise." (emphasis added).

In these proceedings the security devices specifically included "proceeds." However, debtor contends that relevant nonbankruptcy law limits the bank's lien in proceeds generated by the prepetition accounts receivable to cash collected or received by the debtor within ten days before institution of the bankruptcy proceedings. Specifically, debtor relies on § 9.306(d)(4), Tex.Bus. & Comm.Code, which becomes operative on the institution of bankruptcy proceedings by or against the debtor:

"(d) In the event of insolvency proceedings * * *, a secured party with a perfected security interest in proceeds has a perfected security interest only in the following proceeds:

* * *

(4) in all cash and deposit accounts of the debtor in which proceeds have been commingled with other funds, but the perfected security interest under this Subdivision (4) is

(A) subject to any right of setoff; and (B) limited to an amount not greater than the amount of any cash proceeds *received by the debtor within ten days before the institution of the insolvency proceedings* less the sum of (1) the payments to the secured party on account of cash proceeds received by the debtor during such period to which the secured party is entitled under Subdivision (1) through (3) of this subsection (d)." (emphasis added).

Debtor insists that since the monies against which the bank claims a security interest were commingled with other "proceeds" upon their deposit in the debtor-in-possession checking account, the operation of § 9.306(d)(4) is triggered. Since the subject proceeds were received *after* the filing of the Chapter 11 petition, and not within the ten days next preceding the petition, the debtor argues that the bank is left with no security interest in proceeds.

Debtor's argument, while imaginative, is rejected. Acceptance of that theory would have a chaotic effect upon existing liens on property of the type customarily taken by lenders to operating businesses. The drafters of the Code most certainly had other objectives in mind. *See,* e.g. 4 *Collier on Bankruptcy* § 552.02, pp. 552–4 and 552–5, (15th ed. 1982), including also footnote 2, where the author suggests that the phrase "to the extent provided by such agreement and by nonbankruptcy law" was inserted in § 552(b) primarily to insure that the secured party retain his lien in proceeds which are acquired after commencement of the case. While § 9.306(d)(4) of the Tex.Bus. & Comm.Code can be construed to speak in terms of the date the petition is filed, § 552(b) of the Code operates to continue the claim of the secured creditor to proceeds generated postpetition from collateral such as accounts receivable. *See* White and Summers, *Uniform Commercial Code,* p. 1017 (West Publishing Co.), 2nd edition 1980.

Therefore I have concluded that the debtor's use of $13,444.24 in proceeds collected postpetition from prepetition receivables constituted use of "cash collateral" without the requisite consent of the creditor bank or authorization of the court after notice and hearing.

Next debtor argues that even if determination is made that he has used "cash collateral" without complying with the provisions of § 363(c)(1) there are no sanctions which may be applied, because Title 11 is silent regarding a remedy for such failure to comply. It contends that the provisions of 364 which govern the obtaining of credit or incurring of debt and establishing priorities for a creditor has no application because the debtor neither incurred a debt nor obtained credit.

It is true that there are no apparent provisions of the Code which specifically provide sanctions for the failure of the debtor to comply with "cash collateral" requirements. However § 105(a) of the Code gives to the Bankruptcy Court the power to issue any order, process, or judgment that is necessary or appropriate to carry out the provisions of this title. Regardless of debtor's argument that § 105 was not intended to confer the power to create lien rights the Court does have an obligation to carry out the intent of Congress in its enactment of the Bankruptcy Code. As mentioned above the continuation of lending transactions between the business community on the one hand and lending institutions on the other require that liens negotiated in good faith and for which full consideration has been given must be protected. Adoption of the theory advanced by the debtor that there are no applicable sanctions, so that a valid lien of a creditor is recognized by the Court but both the Court and the creditor are powerless to preserve and protect that lien after bankruptcy has been initiated, will result in anarchy. That cannot be the result intended by Congress. Therefore I have interpreted § 105(a) of the Code as giving to the Court the power and the duty to do those things which are reasonably required to protect the Court's jurisdiction and to carry out the intent of Title 11. Specifically, I have interpreted that section as giving to the Court the power to grant to Mercantile National Bank a replacement lien against postpetition accounts receivable to secure the sum of $13,444.24 in proceeds against which the bank had a lien, but which were unlawfully used by the debtor after the Chapter 11 case was filed. To the extent, if any, that the replacement lien does not fully protect the bank for the $13,444.24 obligation, the bank also shall have a priority administrative claim.

* * *

Notes

In some circumstances parties who are only partially secured at the date the petition was filed have agreed to continue lending money to a Chapter 11 debtor in return for an agreement, sometimes obvious and sometimes more subtle, under which the creditor's entire debt, both post- and pre-petition, would be secured by post-petition assets. If a Chapter 11 company were successful in enlarging the assets covered, the effect of such a security interest would be to prefer that creditor over the others. Although section 364 clearly authorizes the granting of preferences over other creditors to those who make post-petition loans (*as to those loans*) in limited circumstances, section 364 does not mention pre-petition loans. How would you respond to the problem that follows in that setting?

Problem 8–13

Hazelwood Hardware is a retail hardware store that filed for Chapter 11 protection on October 12, 1983. Sycamore Savings Bank is the firm's primary source of financing.

Sycamore holds a perfected security interest in the inventory, accounts, and proceeds of Hazelwood. As of October 12, 1983, the book value of Hazelwood's inventory was $800,000 and the book value of its accounts receivables was $225,000. This collateral secured a loan with a balance of $875,000 as of October 12, 1983.

If forced to liquidate Hazelwood's accounts and inventory, Sycamore estimates it will receive a maximum of $500,000. Faced with a $375,000 deficiency, Sycamore decides to negotiate with Hazelwood in hopes of becoming Hazelwood's financier during bankruptcy. Sycamore and Hazelwood agree on the following terms for a $250,000 line of credit, to be applied primarily to the purchase of new inventory.

(1) Interest at prime plus 4½ percent.

(2) Turnover of existing accounts to Sycamore for collection and application of proceeds to Hazelwood's prepetition obligations;

(3) Daily remittance of the cash proceeds of existing and after-acquired inventory and of accounts receivable to Sycamore for application to the prepetition obligations of Hazelwood and after satisfaction of these, to the postpetition obligations;

(4) Superpriority for all Hazelwood's obligations to Sycamore as provided by section 364 of the Bankruptcy Code.

Other creditors of Hazelwood object to the plan. As Judge, should you approve the agreement?

D. The Cramdown, Sections 1322, 1123, 1129

Under subsection 1322(b) the Chapter 13 plan (adjustment of debts of an individual's regular income) can "modify the rights of holder of secured claims * * *". A debtor's counsel first coming upon this section may think he has arrived in Valhalla; but such is not so. The principal limitation upon the debtor's right to affect the secured creditor's rights is subsection 1325(a)(5). That subsection states that a secured creditor who has not accepted the plan must either receive his property back or receive property to be distributed under the plan of the value not less than the amount of his claim. Assume a secured creditor is owed a debt of $100,000 secured by collateral worth $50,000. If, upon liquidation, the unsecured creditors would receive 1 cent on the dollar, any Chapter 13 plan must give our secured creditor present value equal to $50,000 plus $500 (.01 × $50,000). Similar but somewhat more intricate provisions are to be found in Chapter 11, section 1129. A comparable but much more limited section in the consumer liquidation area is section 722, set out above.

Problem 8–14

1. Assume that secured creditor GMAC is owed $10,000 by Consumer. The debt is secured by a properly perfected purchase money security interest in the debtor's 1983 Chevrolet. The car currently has a retail value of $7,000, a wholesale value of $6,500, and it is probably worth in excess of $8,000 to the debtor because of his knowledge of its operation and his idiosyncratic attachment to it. If GMAC opposes each of the following proposals, which ones can be approved despite GMAC's opposition?

a. Assume that debtor is in Chapter 7 and proposes the purchase of the car for $6,500 in cash under section 722.

b. Assume the debtor is in Chapter 13 and proposes the purchase of the car in the Plan by a payment of $194.44 per month over 36 months.

c. Debtor in Chapter 7 proposes the payment of $6,500 in monthly installments over two years under section 722.

Suppose the debtor proposed simply to continue his payments and to keep the car. He tells GMAC that he would agree to reaffirm his debt after the bankruptcy. Can GMAC enter into such a transaction? (See section 524(c).)

2. Assume that Bank has a loan of $1,700,000 outstanding to Retail Debtor. The loan is secured by $1,300,000 worth of equipment and inventory. Debtor goes into Chapter 11 and proposes the following alternatives. If Bank opposes, which can it successfully forestall and which can be approved over Bank's opposition?

a. Payment of $1,300,000 in cash together with a payment of a percentage of the remaining $400,000 of debt of 10 percent (the liquidation value).

b. A continuation of a security interest and a payment of $1,300,000 over six years on the same schedule as was originally set out for the $1,700,000 loan (together with a payment of the unsecured portion at the liquidation percentage):

(1) without any interest;

(2) with interest at the contract rate of 12 percent;

(3) with interest at the current market rate of 14 percent.

BOOK TWO

SALES

PART ONE

INTRODUCTORY MATERIALS

CHAPTER NINE

NATURE AND SCOPE OF ARTICLE 2 ON SALES

SECTION 1. WHY DO SALES AND CONTRACTS FOR SALE TAKE PLACE?

Sales law evolved in response to disputes between private parties over agreements to transfer the ownership of personal property, usually goods, for a price. As in all areas of private law, the transaction, whether a sale or a contract to sell, came first and the law of sales followed. Indeed, it is probable that the various bodies of specialized commercial law, such as negotiable instruments, developed in response to the particular needs of the parties before the need for a general law of contracts occurred to anyone. See G. Gilmore, The Death of Contract 11–12 (1974).

If not compelled by law, why do sales occur? One answer is that in an exchange economy sales have to take place. To put this abstractly, a productive unit in a modern economy specializes in making one or but a few types of goods. Such a unit does not make enough of everything to satisfy all its own needs. It is not self sufficient and must engage in exchanges with other productive units.

But why such specialization in the first place? First, since men and organizations have different capacities and abilities, it becomes economical to match capacities and abilities with productive tasks for which they are best suited. Second, since different regions differ in natural resources and climate it becomes economical to put regions to work on productive activities for which they are best suited. Third, even if capacities, abilities, resources and climates were undifferentiated, it would still be advantageous to have specialization and therefore to have an exchange economy, whether the advantage comes from a greater quantity of production, time saved or improved quality through concentration of effort. See A. Smith, The Wealth of Nations 7–9 (Mod.Lib.Ed.1937).

A variety of factors, then, begets specialization and specialization begets exchanges—sales. According to Ian Macneil, four conditions should exist for an economy based upon exchange to flourish: (1) Specialization of labor and exchange; (2) A sense by individuals of their capacity for choice and the consequences of its exercise; (3) An awareness of the continuum between past, present, and future; and (4) A social matrix which reinforces the exercise of choices made with an eye to the future. Macneil, *The Many Futures of Contracts,* 47 S.Cal.L.Rev. 691, 696–712 (1974).

But the sale, a completed exchange, is one thing and a contract to sell in the future quite another. One might imagine a very simple society in which sales of goods took place but never pursuant to prior contracts to sell. In a complex industrialized society such as ours, however, contracts to sell and to buy goods are essential to planned economic activity. A manufacturer, for example, must have raw materials, and he must be able to rely on receiving them at designated times and places if he is to operate efficiently. For such reason he will make agreements to purchase raw materials, and recognition of these agreements, frequently of long duration, will make it more certain that his business will function as planned.

Another factor is required for a market directed economy to flourish: The legal system must permit and facilitate the acquisition, use and transfer of private property. Article 2 of the UCC is, with a minimum of regulation, devoted to this support function.

SECTION 2. A ROADMAP TO THE SALES ARTICLE OF THE UCC

As part of his essential background, the user of Article Two needs a basic roadmap to the 104 provisions involved. The presentation here will be in terms of stages of the modern mercantile sales deal, which is typically for future delivery of goods on credit, and therefore a deal that progresses from initial agreement through performance to discharge. The discrete stages along the way are typically these: agreement; post-agreement—pre-shipment; the stage of getting the goods (or documents therefor) to the buyer; receipt and inspection, and payment. The overwhelming majority of deals progress all the way through to payment without incident. But a significant proportion do not, and these break down at different stages, in different ways, and for different reasons. Thus, what follows here will be "pathologically oriented" in the respect that, at each stage, the focus will be on the *kinds* of things that can go wrong.

One caveat: Because the discussion in this section is by way of prelude, it is necessarily general and to some extent oversimplified. Also, it is not comprehensive. In each of these respects, so, too, a roadmap.

A. The Agreement Stage

Perhaps the most drastic of all things that can go wrong is for the parties to assume that they have made a binding contract only to find that in law they have not. This is much less of a risk, however, under Article 2 than it is in general contract law. This is so for two reasons. First, Article 2 makes contract formation easier than it is in the general law. Formalities are delimited. See, UCC 2–201 and 2–203. The consideration doctrine is modified with a bias toward contract formation. See UCC 2–205, and 2–209(1). The requirement that an acceptance must be precisely within the terms of an offer to constitute an acceptance is abolished. See UCC 2–207, and 2–206(1)(a). A non-conforming shipment of goods in response to a unilateral offer is, under certain circumstances, nonetheless an acceptance. UCC 2–206(1)(b). Contracts can be formed by mere conduct alone, even though the precise moment of making is undetermined. UCC 2–204(1) and (2).

Second, Article 2 includes a general provision to the effect that a contract for sale does not fail for indefiniteness if the parties have intended to make a contract and there is a reasonably certain basis for giving an appropriate remedy. UCC 2–204(3). Further to this, the Article includes many "gap-filler" provisions which come into play to fill gaps in agreements that might otherwise fail under general contract law for indefiniteness. See UCC 2–204(3), 2–305, 2–306, 2–307, 2–308, 2–309, 2–310, 2–311, 2–503, 2–504, 2–507, and 2–511.

In addition to failures of contract formation, disputes may arise over (1) whether a term is or is not a part of the contract and (2) whether a given term is to be interpreted in one way rather than another. These kinds of disputes can arise at any stage, but it is appropriate to allude to them here. On whether a term is or is not a part of the contract, the parol evidence rule of UCC 2–202 governs. Under Article 2, lawyers and judges will resolve problems of interpretation and construction in part by reference to UCC 1–102 on rules of construction, UCC 1–205 on course of dealing and usage of trade, and UCC 2–208 and 2–207(3) on course of performance or practical construction.

The alert, careful lawyer should, through draftsmanship and advice, be able to reduce if not eliminate altogether any risks that the parties will fail to make a binding contract or even that significant disputes over interpretation will arise.

B. The Post-Agreement—Pre-Shipment Stage

A seller will either have the goods on hand, or have to manufacture them or acquire them elsewhere. In any of these events, there is often a time lapse between the date when the contract is made and the time when the goods are sent to the buyer. During this period, the buyer may repudiate, or the seller may repudiate, or it may become clear that one of the parties will not later be able to perform.

UCC 2–610 and 2–611 deal with repudiation. Assume it is the buyer who repudiates. The seller can call off the deal. See UCC 2–610(b) and 2–703(f). Or he can also seek damages under UCC 2–706 or 2–708 as appropriate. Can he choose to go forward with the transaction and force the goods on the buyer? Yes, under limited circumstances. See UCC 2–704(1)(a) and 2–709(1)(b).

UCC 2–704(2) gives the *manufacturing* seller flexibility in the event of repudiation.

Now let us assume that the seller repudiates at this stage. What are the buyer's rights? Again, the buyer, too, may call off the deal, UCC 2–610(b), 2–711(1), or he may also have damages. UCC 2–711(1), 2–712, 2–713. Can he choose to go forward with the transaction and force the goods out of the seller? See UCC 2–610(b) and 2–711(2)(a) and (b). As with most "goods oriented" remedies, this alternative may put the buyer in conflict with creditors of and purchasers from the seller. If the buyer has a prior perfected Article 9 security interest, he would prevail over most such third parties. Otherwise, the buyer must rely on his right, if any, to specific performance or replevin as specified in UCC 2–716, and this right is generally subject to third party interests.

A closer look at the parties' damages remedy is in order. Can it be combined with other remedies? Yes. The Code does not favor "election" doctrines. (Even cancellation does not extinguish a right to damages. See UCC 2–720). Are there any significant parallels between the seller's damages remedy and that of the buyer? Yes. Both can go into the market and "fix" damages against the other party, so to speak. See UCC 2–706(1) and 2–712(1) and (2). Yet neither is *required* to do this. Both can simply sue for damages for repudiation and get the full market-contract-price differential rather than the differential between contract or market and a substitute transaction consummated by the "reselling" seller or "covering" buyer. See UCC 2–708(1) and 2–713. Can the parties get consequential damages? It is clear that the buyer can. See UCC 2–715.

The rights of a party to call off the deal, to get damages, or to go forward with the deal, are the basic remedial options. They are carefully analyzed in detail in Peters, *Remedies for Breach of Contracts Relating to the Sale of Goods Under the Uniform Commercial Code: A Roadmap for Article Two,* 73 Yale L.J. 199 (1963).

After the agreement and prior to shipment, other things can go wrong besides repudiation. It may emerge that one of the parties will not, later, at the appointed time, be *able* to perform. In such circumstances, UCC 2–609 allows the aggrieved party to demand adequate assurances of performance. Failure to provide such assurances within a reasonable time is classed as a "repudiation." Prospective inability to perform will, when it exists, entitle the aggrieved party to pursue the same general remedial options as may be available upon repudiation.

Insolvency should be mentioned as a special form of prospective inability to perform which inherently introduces third parties. When opposing third party interests are in the picture, "going forward" with the deal becomes less desirable to the seller where the buyer is insolvent, and less freely available to the buyer where the seller is insolvent. Compare UCC 2–702(1) and 2–502(1).

Casualty to goods identified to the contract is another kind of event that can occur after contract and prior to shipment. In some circumstances, it will excuse the seller. See UCC 2–613. The topic of casualty and attendant risk of loss problems will be considered in the next section.

C. *The Stage of Getting the Goods or Documents Therefor to the Buyer*

Many commercial contracts call for the seller to deliver the goods to the buyer at the buyer's town or place of business. For the time, manner and place of delivery, *absent* such contractual stipulation, see UCC 2–309, 2–307, 2–308, 2–503 and 2–507.

Here the primary focus is on seller's performance. Several basic things can go wrong with it at this stage. The seller may deliver late, or at the wrong place, or in improper manner.

Also, the seller who is required or authorized to send the goods to the buyer must, unless otherwise agreed, make a "proper contract" of carriage and notify the buyer of shipment. See UCC 2–504. The seller may simply fail to do this, thereby incurring liability to the buyer. Of course, the rights of the buyer upon default at this stage vary with the nature of the default. Can the buyer always call the deal off? No. See e.g., the last paragraph of UCC 2–504, 2–612, 2–614, and 2–615. But he will generally be entitled to damages. See UCC 2–711.

The carrier may fail to perform *its* obligations. The duties of such a carrier will be specified in the contract of carriage (bill of lading) and in Article 7 of the Code, where the deal is intrastate. If interstate, the Federal Bill of Lading Act governs. The carrier will be liable for damages caused by improper loading for which it is responsible. See UCC 7–301(4). The carrier may negligently cause damage to the goods for which liability lies under UCC 7–309. Or the carrier may simply fail to follow instructions thereby causing loss. For example, the seller may have a right to stop the goods in transit under UCC 2–705 and the carrier may fail to honor stoppage instructions. Here, though, the seller rather than the buyer would be the aggrieved party.

The goods in transit may be lost or damaged (with or without the carrier's fault). The carrier's insurance will often cover most of the loss. But "risk of loss" problems can arise. Generally, risk passes upon tender at destination when the contract calls for delivery at the buyer's city. See UCC 2–509(1)(b). Hence, as between seller and buyer, seller would be responsible for loss occurring during carriage in such a deal. It should be noted that UCC 2–510 says, among other things, that a seller cannot pass the risk of loss *re* non-conforming goods.

If, before risk passes to the buyer, the goods "suffer" total casualty, without fault of either party, then under UCC 2–613 the seller will be excused from the contract if the contract was one which required for its performance goods identified when the contract was made.

The foregoing discussion has centered on deals for goods only. What if the contract calls for delivery of a document of title to the buyer in exchange for the buyer's cash payment on the spot or his signature to a time draft? See UCC 2–503(5). Most of the main kinds of things that can go wrong in procuring and transmitting documents can be readily inventoried. As procured, the document may fail to describe the goods properly. See UCC 7–301. Or it may not be in correct form. See UCC 2–503(5)(a). The document may be lost or stolen. See UCC 7–601. Or it may get into the wrong hands, and, if negotiable, and the transferee takes by due negotiation, then the transferee will generally get title to the document and to the goods. See UCC 7–501 and UCC 7–502. But see UCC 7–503. Or the document may be altered. See UCC 7–306.

D. The Receipt-Inspection Stage

This, in commercial deals, is, to seller and buyer alike, the crucial stage. Here the seller will typically lose any control he has over the goods. Here the buyer will, usually for the first time, inspect and decide whether to accept or reject. Naturally, the buyer will generally prefer to inspect before paying. Blind payment puts him at a disadvantage: when the goods turn out not to be conforming, he finds himself a potential plaintiff, whereas, if there is to be litigation at all, it is generally better to be a potential defendant who has first inspected and then rejected the goods for nonconformity. The blindly paying buyer is also at a disadvantage in the respect that he, as plaintiff, must assume the risk of the seller's insolvency in regard to satisfaction of any judgment he gets against a defaulting seller. Further, the buyer who pays blindly may find that he has assumed control over and therefore responsibility for the goods. See generally, Honnold, *The Buyer's Right of Rejection,* 97 U.Pa.L.Rev. 457 (1949).

Contracts often specifically provide for a right of the buyer to inspect before payment or acceptance. But what if the contract is silent? UCC 2–513 says that the buyer has a right to inspect before payment or acceptance unless he has contracted it away. One way the buyer can give up this right is by agreeing to pay "against documents" covering the goods. UCC 2–513(3)(b), 2–512, 2–310.

What are the ways a seller can fail to perform at this stage (other than "failures of delivery" already considered)? In the main, the seller may fail to tender goods to which he has title, or fail to tender goods that are of the right quantity or of the right quality. These latter two kinds of breaches are not uncommon, as breaches go. And they both may take a variety of forms, depending on the nature of the goods. Similarly, the seller may tender non-conforming *documents* covering goods.

What is the general standard of performance to which the seller is held? The contract is the first touchstone. But, in general contract law, it is familiar that under the doctrine of substantial performance, some departures from the contract are permitted with the result that the non-performing party can still recover "on the contract." Is it the same under the Code? Generally, no. UCC 2–601 seemingly requires "perfect tender." As to quality, the warranty provisions of Article 2 (UCC 2–312—2–315) determine the relevant standard of performance as to quality to the extent the contract is silent. The perfect tender doctrine is, however, modified by UCC 2–508, 2–612, and other provisions.

Assuming the seller has failed to make perfect tender, and that he cannot rely on the doctrine of substantial performance, what are the buyer's rights? His basic damages remedy has already been outlined. See UCC 2–712 and 2–713. The emphasis here should be on the buyer's "goods-oriented" options. If the buyer wishes, he may reject. UCC 2–601. To do so, he has to jump through the right hoops. UCC 2–602, 2–605. If he is a merchant, he may have duties in regard to care and disposition of the goods. UCC 2–603, 2–604. The buyer may, however, want the seller to perform—to send goods that do conform. He *may* be entitled to specific performance or replevin under UCC 2–716.

What if the buyer has accepted the goods (UCC 2–606) and has later discovered a defect, or has accepted the goods with seller's assurances that non-conformities would be corrected, but such has not occurred? Has the buyer forever lost his right to throw the goods back at the seller? No. See UCC 2–608. But the buyer, again, must jump through the right hoops. See UCC 2–608(2) and 2–607(3)(a).

Such revocation of acceptance, along with rejection, leaves the buyer free, too, to pursue damages. See UCC 2–608(3), 2–711(1), and 2–714.

Finally, the buyer may choose to retain non-conforming goods and recover damages. See UCC 2–714(1) and (2). But, if he is to take this avenue, he must give notice of the breach under UCC 2–714(1). In commercial cases, this avenue is more common than in consumer cases where the defect in the goods often makes them of no value at all, and the buyer's main concern is to get damages for breach of warranty, often consequential damages of a personal injury or property damage character. See 2–715(2)(b). Most of Article 2 litigation is warranty of quality litigation, consumer and non-consumer. The Code's basic warranty provisions, to be treated intensively later, are UCC 2–313, 2–314, 2–315, 2–316, 2–317, and 2–318.

To turn, now, to non-performance by the *buyer* at the receipt-inspection stage. He may fail to provide proper facilities for presentation of the goods for inspection. See UCC 2–503(1). He may make a wrongful demand for inspection. See UCC 2–513(3)(b). He may fail to follow contractual or statutorily prescribed procedures for inspection. See UCC 2–513(1). He may "impose" unagreed upon standards of conformity. He may deny the seller's right to cure. UCC 2–508. He may deny any right of the seller to supply less than perfectly conforming goods. UCC 2–612(2). He may mistakenly think the goods do not conform. He may fail to jump through prescribed rejection hoops. UCC 2–602. He may fail to take over the goods and care for or dispose of them as required under UCC 2–603 and UCC 2–604. Perhaps most significant in the usual run of cases, he may refuse, for some reason, to pay at this time as agreed or as required in the absence of agreement. See UCC 2–507(1).

The appropriate maneuver for the seller will vary with the nature of the buyer's breach and the course of action the buyer takes. Often the seller will want and will be entitled to damages, a general remedy already outlined at the post-agreement stage. See UCC 2–703. Here the focus will be on (1) the seller's "goods oriented" remedies assuming the buyer is retaining the goods, and (2) the seller's right to the price, whether or not the buyer retains the goods.

Generally, if the buyer is refusing payment, and payment is due at this stage, the seller will be entitled to replevy the goods from the buyer under UCC 2–507(2) and 2–511. As with most goods-oriented remedies, third parties may enter the picture and defeat the aggrieved party. As against creditors, UCC 2–702 controls. As against buyers from the buyer, UCC 2–403 must be consulted. And, of course, as in all situations, any relevant cases. But the seller could retain a security interest in the goods of high priority entitling him to defeat almost all third parties except "buyers in ordinary course of business." See UCC 9–107, 9–201, 9–307(1).

And when is the seller entitled to the price against a buyer in breach at this stage? If the buyer has accepted the goods (UCC 2–606) and has not properly rejected them or justifiably revoked his acceptance of them, then the seller may have the price. UCC 2–709. The seller may also get the price in two other, more restricted, situations under UCC 2–709(1).

E. The Payment Stage

The overwhelming majority of transactions pass on through the payment stage without incident. But some hang up at this stage, too. Payment due on delivery has already been treated. But in the overwhelming majority of commercial deals, and in a substantial proportion of consumer deals, payment is strung out over some period *after* the buyer comes into possession of the goods. Breakdowns in the payment process in deals of this nature will now be considered.

If the deal is silent on payment, then payment is due on tender of delivery. UCC 2–507. C.O.D. deals and transactions calling for payment of a draft upon presentation of documents may be thought of as assimilations of cash deals.

Credit must be agreed upon. Terms vary. Extension of credit may be *secured* under Article 9. Also, a buyer may be required to sign a time draft, thus giving the seller or his transferee the advantages of having a signed negotiable instrument to sue on. See UCC 3–305.

A buyer may fail to pay because of insolvency. In this situation, the seller will, again, be interested in goods-oriented remedies. His right to recover the goods from the buyer under Article 2 is quite limited. UCC 2–702(2). What is more, this right is itself "subject to" the claims of certain parties under UCC 2–702(3).

The buyer may undertake to pay by drawing a check to seller's order. A check is a negotiable instrument if in proper form (UCC 3–104). A check orders the drawer's bank to pay the payee or to the payee's order or to bearer. The buyer-drawer's bank may refuse to honor the check, for any one of a variety of reasons but most commonly because the check over-draws the buyer's account.

Assume the check is dishonored. What action could the seller take? He could sue the buyer on the underlying obligation. See UCC 3–802(1)(b). But he could not recover from the bank, for a check is not an assignment (UCC 3–409) and a party is not liable on an instrument unless his signature appears thereon. UCC 3–401. Nor is the seller recognized as a third party beneficiary of the contract of deposit between buyer's bank and buyer. It is possible, on the right facts, that bank would be liable to seller on a tort theory. See UCC 3–419.

If the buyer was not the drawer of the check, but simply was indorsing over a check made to him to seller, seller might be a holder in due course under UCC 3–302 and, in an action against the drawer, immune from most ordinary defenses (e.g., failure of consideration, fraud) that a drawer might have against someone suing him on the instrument. See UCC 3–413 and 3–305. Similarly, the seller might be a holder in due course against an indorser and immune from such defenses. See UCC 3–414 and 3–305. To hold such a drawer or indorser liable, though, the seller would have to give notice of dishonor etc. as required by UCC 3–413(2), 3–414, and Part 5 of Article 3. There is the further possibility that the seller will be entitled to recover from a transferor of the instrument on a "warranty" theory. See UCC 3–417(2).

To recapitulate: Upon dishonor of a check given in payment for goods, the seller might have recovery against the buyer on the underlying obligation, or against the buyer and possibly other parties "on the instrument," or possibly against a transferor on a "warranty" theory.

So much for how things might go upon dishonor. What if the buyer's bank does not dishonor the check, but rather, fails to pay the proper party, i.e., the seller, or fails to pay the proper amount? Such events can occur in a variety of ways. We shall at this juncture consider only two situations. Assume the buyer draws a check to seller, but is interrupted and does not sign it as drawer. A thief steals the check, forges buyer's signature, and then takes the check to X who cashes it, giving thief the money. X presents the check to buyer's bank and buyer's bank honors it. Later, the forgery is discovered. Buyer's bank is not entitled to charge drawer's account. UCC 4–401. But drawer-buyer is not, of course, discharged from liability to seller and still must pay. Can the bank retrieve its loss from X? See UCC 3–418.

The seller may be a wrongdoer. What if the seller alters the amount of the check upward and the bank pays? Again, drawer-buyer's account is not chargeable as to the excess unless he negligently contributed to the alteration. UCC 4–401, 3–406. The seller, if he can be found, can be prosecuted. And the bank can recover against seller.

So much for a *sample* of the kinds of things that can go wrong in the payment process where a check is used.

An intermediary bank or carrier may fail to perform its obligations in the payment process. The carrier in a C.O.D. deal may fail to pick up the cash. The bank in a documentary deal may (a) fail to secure proper payment from the buyer upon tender of the documents, or (b) fail to procure buyer's signature to a time draft as agreed. See UCC 4–501, 4–502, and 4–503. The moral for the seller is dual: utilize reliable intermediaries and deal with sound buyers.

What is the plight of a buyer who puts a check in the process of payment or signs a draft or pays cash on a sight draft and thereafter immediately discovers that the goods fail to conform? Is there anything he can do, through prompt action, to "undo" what he has done? These questions will be treated in the context of specific cases.

Conclusion

This concludes what is intended only to be a *general outline* of the main stages of the unfolding sale transaction, of the *kinds* of things that can go wrong at each stage, and of the generally relevant law bearing thereon. The remaining chapters of Book Two on Sales are generally presented according to the foregoing "stage" scheme of organization. Every problem and principle considered in this chapter will be treated again, usually in depth. What the student should now have is: (1) a general overview of the modern commercial sales transaction on credit as it progresses from the agreement stage thrugh performance and aymmeent, (2) some sense of the nature of the things that can go wrong at each stage, (3) a *functionally* useful roadmap through the structure of Article 2, and (4) some idea of how Articles 3, 4, 7, and 9 may bear on sales transactions. Obviously, this section of this chapter should be studied and reviewed. Properly digested, it can equip the student to appreciate more fully what lies ahead. The ultra-conscientious student who wishes to sample other versions of the "big picture" of Article 2 might consult Peters, *Remedies for Breach of Contracts Relating to the Sale of Goods under the Uniform Commercial Code: A Roadmap for Article Two,* 73 Yale L.J. 199 (1963); Braucher, *Sale of Goods in the Uniform Commercial Code,* 26 La.L.Rev. 192 (1966); and Corman, *The Law of Sales under the Uniform Commercial Code,* 17 Rutgers L.Rev. 14 (1962).

SECTION 3. THE SCOPE OF ARTICLE 2

To what disputes does Article 2 apply, either directly or by analogy? Section 2–102 provides that "unless the context otherwise requires, this Article applies to transactions in goods * * *." Article 2, however, "does not apply to any transaction which although in the form of an unconditional contract to sell or present sale is intended to operate only as a security transaction * * *." See UCC 2–102.

Section 2–102 raises more questions than its text answers.

What, for example, are goods? Under UCC 2–105(1) and 2–107 goods are defined as "things * * * which are movable at the time of identification to the contract for sale" and excludes "money in which the price is to be paid, investment securities * * * and things in action." Thus, in a contract for sale, a stereo is goods but an account receivable is not. Compare UCC 9–102(1)(b) & 9–105(1)(h).

When are goods identified to the contract? The question is answered in UCC 2–501. What difference does it make whether goods are identified? Goods must be "existing and identified before any interest in them" can pass to a buyer, UCC 2–105(2), whether that interest be title, UCC 2–401, or a "special" property interest, UCC 2–501(1). The importance of these property interests will be explored later. Note that an attempt to sell "future" goods, i.e., goods that are neither existing nor identified, operates as a "contract to sell."

What is a "transaction" in goods? Section 2–106(1) provides that "In this Article unless the context otherwise requires 'contract' and 'agreement' are limited to those relating to the present or future sale of goods." Thus, where those words are used in Article 2, the transaction is a sale or a contract to sell goods. But the word "transaction" is not clearly defined. Could it include a lease or a bailment? What about a gift?

When does the context "otherwise" require? For example, if the "transaction" is other than a contract for sale, should the context be invoked to broaden or narrow the scope of Article 2? If the use of context broadens scope, should all or part of Article 2 be applied?

Finally, if Article 2 does not directly apply, can it be extended by analogy to the dispute before the court? The comments if not the text of the UCC support this extension, see Comment 1, UCC 1–102, but the question remains when it is proper for a court to apply legislation to a dispute concededly beyond the scope intended by the legislature. See, generally, D. Murray, *Under the Spreading Analogy of Article 2 of the Uniform Commercial Code,* 39 Fordham L.Rev. 447 (1971).

In approaching these questions, remember that there are two kinds of Code limitations on the seemingly unlimited scope of the word "transactions." First, there are other Articles, e.g., Article 7, on bailments for storage or carriage, which may supercede the specific provisions of Article 2. Secondly, many of the specific provisions of Article 2 are themselves cast in terms of "seller" and "buyer" or limited to "contracts for sale." It would thus appear that some provisions of Article 2 might apply to a non-sales situation, e.g., UCC 2–202, 2–206, 2–207, 2–210, 2–302, & 2–316, while other provisions are, seemingly, limited to sales, e.g., UCC 2–205, 2–312, 2–313, 2–314 & 2–315.

Here are some problems and cases. As you study them, ask "What difference does it make whether Article 2 applies?"

Problem 9–1

(1) F orally agreed to sell B his wheat crop yet to be planted for $3 a bushel. Bad weather sharpened the demand for wheat. Before the crop was planted, F repudiated the agreement with B and sold the crop to C for $4 a bushel. B sued F for damages. F defended, invoking the statute of frauds. UCC 2–201. B argued that UCC 2–201 does not apply. What result? See UCC 2–102, 2–105 and 2–201.

(2) S agreed to sell B timber standing on S's land to be severed by S. S severed half of the timber but before B could haul it away, all timber, standing or severed, that B agreed to buy was destroyed by fire. B argued that the Code's risk of loss provisions applied. See UCC 2–102, 2–107(1) and 2–509. Is B correct? What change did the 1972 Official Text make in UCC 2–107?

(3) S owned a building which he contracted to sell to B who was to remove it from its concrete foundation, put it on skids, and drag it away. Before removal, S repudiated. Does Article 2 govern B's remedial rights? See UCC 2–107(1), 2–711 and 2–713. (In Foster v. Colorado Radio Corporation, 381 F.2d 222 (10th Cir.1967), the court applied the Code's remedial provisions only to the goods involved in a combined real estate and personal property sale.)

BARCO AUTO LEASING CORP. v. PSI COSMETICS, INC.

Civil Court of the City of New York, 1984.
125 Misc.2d 68, 478 N.Y.S.2d 505.

EDWARD H. LEHNER, JUDGE.

The issue in this case is whether a lessor's disclaimer of all warranties in an automobile lease is enforceable where a vehicle to be used for business purposes failed to operate properly within a short period after delivery.

This action is against the corporate lessee and the individual grantors (officers of the corporate defendant) for breach of an automobile lease, seeking to recover the accelerated unpaid rental for the remainder of the lease term plus attorneys' fees. Defendants' answer sets forth a general denial and a counterclaim for loss of business resulting from an inability to attend certain business meetings due to the defective nature of the vehicle. Before the court is plaintiff's motion for summary judgment.

On September 27, 1982 defendant PSI Cosmetics, Inc. entered into an automobile lease agreement with plaintiff for the rental of a 1982 Renault. Defendants assert in their papers that: on November 28, 1982 the engine began to smoke and the car was towed to a nearby authorized Renault dealership where it took over three months to repair what was said to be a burned out motor; during this period defendants continued to make all rental payments despite being deprived of the use of the vehicle; upon picking up the vehicle from the repair shop Mr. Golumbia was informed that after driving the vehicle an additional 300 to 600 miles, he should have it retorqued; three days after this work was done the engine again began to burn, and the automobile was rendered inoperative and towed to plaintiff's lot. As a result of this experience Golumbia allegedly missed an important business meeting, resulting in the cancellation of a $40,000 contract, thereby providing the basis for the counterclaim.

The agreement, printed on plaintiff's standardized form without any typed or handwritten riders, contains myriad procedural safeguards by which the lessor seeks to insulate itself. The lease provides that the lessor retains title and a security interest in the vehicle. There is no option to purchase granted to the lessee, who waives "counterclaim, set off, reduction, abatement, deferment or any other kind of defense because of * * * unsatisfactory performance of the vehicle or for any reason whatever. * * *" Repairs and replacement of parts are made the responsibility of the lessee. Further insulation is provided for the lessor by a disclaimer of any warranties, except for the manufacturer's standard warranty. The implied warranties of merchantability and of fitness for a particular use are conspicuously disclaimed (UCC §§ 2–316(2); 1–201(10)).

Although not raised in their answer, defendants contend in their papers that both the warranty disclaimer and the waiver of counterclaims are unconscionable and that, as to the action for the unpaid balance, plaintiff has failed to mitigate its damages in that it failed to sell the automobile.

* * *

The first issue that must be decided is whether Article 2 of the Uniform Commercial Code and the implied warranties which it provides apply to the automobile lease herein. If so, what remains to be resolved is whether the warranty disclaimer is unconscionable.

Several cases in this jurisdiction have applied UCC Article 2 to the leasing of chattels * * *.

Judicial approaches to the applicability of Article 2 to leases has been "placed along a spectrum measuring willingness to depart from the sale construct." Note, Disengaging Sale Law from the Sale Construct: A Proposal to Extend the Scope of Article 2 of the UCC, 96 Harv.L.Rev. 470, 475 (1982).

The "exclusionary" view requires strict adherence to the premise that Article 2 applies only to paradigmatic sales, thereby excluding lease transactions as well as hybrid sales-plus-services contracts from coverage.

The "analogy" approach advocates that Article 2 be applied to transactions held not to be paradigmatic sales, but only when the transactions closely resemble such sales. Murray, Under the Spreading Analogy of Article 2 of the Uniform Commercial Code, 39 Ford.L.Rev. 447, 451 (1971). This has been the approach of the courts in this state. See: *Uniflex, Inc. v. Olivetti Corp. of America*, 86 A.D.2d 538, 445 N.Y.S.2d 993 (1st Dept.1982) (leases); *Aguiar v. Harper & Row Publishers Inc.*, 114 Misc.2d 828, 832, 452 N.Y.S.2d 519 (Civ.Ct. N.Y.Co.1982) (sales-plus-services). Thus, Article 2 is said to be "attended by a penumbra or umbrella of influence in areas of contract law not specifically within the literal definition of sales under section 2–102", Lupiano, J., dissenting in *Leasco Data Processing Equipment Corp. v. Starline Overseas Corp.,* 74 Misc.2d 898, 903, 346 N.Y.S.2d 288 (App.T. 1st Dept.1973), aff'd 45 A.D.2d 992, 360 N.Y.S. 2d 199, mot. for lv. to appeal dismissed, 35 N.Y.2d 963, 365 N.Y.S.2d 179, 324 N.E.2d 557 (1974). See also Restatement, Contracts Second, § 208 (1981), Comment *a.*

Related to the analogy approach is the "policy" approach which further departs from a rigid adherence to the sales model by the selective application of particular provisions of Article 2 whenever the policies underlying such provisions are appropriate to the transaction in issue. Note, The Uniform Commercial Code as a Premise for Judicial Reasoning, 65 Colum.L.Rev. 880 (1965). See, e.g. *Dillman and Associates Inc. v. Capitol Leasing Co.,* 110 Ill.App.3d 335, 66 Ill. Dec. 39, 442 N.E.2d 311, 316 (1982); *Walter E. Heller & Co. v. Convalescent Home of the First Church of Deliverance,* 49 Ill.App.3d 213, 8 Ill.Dec. 823, 365 N.E.2d 1285 (1977).

The most inclusive approach is a more complete departure from the sales construct, focusing on the Article 2 scope provision in § 2–102 ("transactions in goods"). Although the article is replete with terms such as "sale", "seller", and "buyer" [See: Lousin, Leases, Sales and the Scope of Article 2 of the U.C.C. in Illinois, 67 Ill.B.J. 468, 470 n. 20 (1979)], such language is nowhere to be found in § 2–102. An argument for such approach, as applied to lease transactions, is that it recognizes the modern economic realities of less-than-full-title property interests, rejecting the use of location of title as a basis for resolving issues. In eschewing the prevailing analysis of the analogy approach, it is said to avoid ad hoc determinations and the intellectually questionable pigeonholding of facts so that the transaction will more closely resemble a sale. Note, 96 Harv.L.Rev. 470; Murray, supra. Thus, unlike the analogy approach, it does not perpetuate the use of the "covert tools" in decision-making which the draftspersons of the UCC had hoped to avoid. See: UCC § 2–302, Official Comment 1; Llewelyn, The Common Law Tradition 365 (1960); Ackerman, Reconstructing American Law 22 (1984).

Though eloquently advocated, Note, 96 Harv.L.Rev. 470; Murray, supra, the inclusive approach has not been accepted. While it has been noted that "transactions in goods" encompasses a far wider area of activity than a "sale", e.g. *Hertz Commercial Leasing Corp. v. Transportation Credit Clearing House,* supra, 59 Misc.2d 226, at 230, 298 N.Y.S.2d 392, this has been more in the way of judicial lip service. The cases in New York have not specifically relied on the language of the Article 2 scope provision alone, most preferring instead to analyze the underlying facts of the transaction in issue in order to determine whether it sufficiently approximates a sale. See: Annotation, What Constitutes a Transaction, a Contract for Sale, or a Sale Within the Scope of UCC Article 2, 4 A.L.R. 4th 85, 109–118 (1981).

Therefore, much as this court might prefer to indulge in the flexible and inclusive approach in determining whether the lease transaction herein is subject to the provisions of Article 2, the inquiry will be limited to an analysis of the transaction in order to determine whether or not it is analogous to a sale.

The agreement provides for rental payments over a four year period totalling $9153.12. No information has been submitted as to the fair market value of the car at the time that the lease was entered into, nor as to what portion of the price represents finance charges. The lessee is responsible for insurance coverage, repairs and replacement of parts; it bears the risk of damage or loss of the vehicle; and it agrees to indemnify the lessor for any claims. Lessor retains title to the vehicle and a security interest. The agreement is denominated "an agreement of lease only." Finally, there is no option to purchase although the agreement states that such option may be provided by a purchase rider.

In determining the answer to the similar problem of whether a lease of personal property is intended to be a security interest the UCC has adopted a simple test: "Whether a lease is intended as security is to be determined by the facts of each case; however * * * an agreement that upon compliance with the terms of the lease the lessee shall become or has the option to become the owner of the property for no additional consideration or for a nominal consideration does make the lease one intended for security." (UCC § 1–201(37)). The absence of a purchase option does not foreclose the inquiry as to whether a particular transaction is a lease or a security interest; the court merely goes on to consider any other relevant factors in order to make its determination.

The same reasoning applies in determining whether a particular lease transaction is governed by Article 2. Thus, in *Uniflex, Inc. v. Olivetti Corp. of America,* supra, where there was no option to purchase, no provision for a renewal term at a nominal rental, and lessee was required to return the equipment at the end of the initial term, the First Department held that an issue of fact existed as to the nature of the lease since the price for the rental was far in excess of the cost of the equipment. Defendant's affirmative defense based on the four year statute of limitations for the sale of goods (UCC § 2–725) rather than the six year period for contracts (CPLR § 213 subd. 2) was therefore reinstated.

Although the court lacks information as to the value of the car, the relationship of consideration to actual value, while an important factor, is not the only one. While the lessor retains title and a security interest, the fact that the lessee is saddled with both the risks and headaches of ownership suggests that there is no significant economic difference between full title ownership and the instant lease. Therefore the court concludes that the transaction at bar is governed by the provisions of Article 2 of the UCC, and that the lease is subject to the implied warranties of merchantability and of fitness for a particular purpose (UCC §§ 2–314, 2–315) unless they have been effectively disclaimed.

The form of the disclaimer of warranties herein complies with the requirements of UCC § 2–316(2). The question remains as to whether or not such disclaimer is unconscionable, since it is nonetheless subject to judicial scrutiny under UCC § 2–302. * * * See: White and Summers, Uniform Commercial Code 475–481 (2d ed. 1980).

* * *

Since it cannot be determined whether or not this agreement is enforceable without affording both sides the "opportunity to present evidence as to its commercial setting, purpose and effect" (UCC § 2–302 subd. 2), plaintiff's motion for summary judgment on the issue of liability under the agreement is denied.

UCC § 2–302 gives the court the power to refuse to enforce an unconscionable agreement. It does not, however, provide damages to a party who enters into such agreement. *Pearson v. National Budgeting Systems Inc.,* 31 A.D.2d 792, 297 N.Y.S.2d 59 (1st Dept.1969); *Vom Lehn v. Astor Art Galleries Ltd.,* 86 Misc.2d 1, 11, 380 N.Y.S.2d 532 (Sup.Ct. Suffolk Co.1976). Accordingly, defendants' counterclaim for damages is dismissed.

Note: Leases and Article 2

Because of tax advantages, among other things, many manufacturers prefer to lease rather than to sell goods to prospective purchasers. In a variation called leveraged leasing, the manufacturer sells the goods to a bank or other enterprise who will then lease them to the prospective purchaser. There is reason to believe that leasing is the dominant transaction where equipment for use in commercial activity is involved. Thus, an article in the New York Times estimated that the amount of new leases for 1985 would approach $88 billion and concluded that "lease financing has expanded to the point where it is the most important single source of funds to support business expenditures for capital equipment." "The Boom in Lease Financing," New York Times, Business Page, March 13, 1985.

Under a "true" lease, the lessor retains title, the lessee has a possessory interest defined by the lease and the lessor has a "reversionary" interest in the goods at the conclusion of the lease. In theory, at least, the lessor under a "true" lease does not retain a security interest subject to Article 9. A leading case is In re Marhoefer Packing Co., 674 F.2d 1139 (7th Cir.1982), reprinted in Chapter 7, Section 1. Furthermore, disputes over whether the lessor makes warranties and the effect of disclaimers and remedy limitations appear to be outside of the scope of Article 2. The warranty provisions are limited to sellers and buyers in contracts for sale, see UCC 2–313, 2–314 and 2–315, although the controls upon disclaimers and agreed remedies are more open ended. See UCC 2–302, 2–316 and 2–719.

The line between a "true" lease and an installment contract for the sale of goods is frequently difficult to draw. The cases are legion. Note, however, that the line may be more important in defining the scope of Article 9 rather than the scope of Article 2. As BARCO indicates, whether the transaction is a "true" lease or a sale, most courts will find some way to apply Article 2 to resolve disputes over warranties, disclaimers and agreed remedies. Another example is Briscoe's Foodland, Inc. v. Capital Associates, Inc., 42 UCC Rep.Serv. 1234 (Miss.1986). In this limited area, at least, there is no substantial difference in outcome, whether Article 2 applies or not.

The question under Article 9, however, is whether the transaction was "intended to create a security interest" in the goods leased. UCC 9–102(1). If so, retention of "title" is, in effect, the retention of a security interest, UCC 1–201(37), which must be perfected by filing to prevail over the trustee in bankruptcy. If not, the transaction is beyond the scope of Article 9, although a lessor under a "true" lease may file a financing statement to hedge its bets. UCC 9–408.

Given the uncertainty in determining whether a "true" lease was created, this precaution is justified. As you may recall from Chapter 7, some of the relevant questions include: (1) If the "lease" contains an option to purchase the goods, is the option price nominal in relation to the market value of the goods when exercised; (2) Does the total "rent" charged exceed the original cash price of the goods; (3) Does the "lessee" bear most or all of the responsibilities of ownership; and (4) Does the "lessee" have an equity in the goods before the option is exercised? If the answer to all four questions is yes, the essence of the transaction is, in all probability, an installment sale on credit rather than a "true" lease and Article 9 applies. See UCC 1–201(37); In re Rowe, 43 B.R. 157 (E.D.Mo.1984); In re Mitchell, 44 B.R. 485 (N.D. Ala.1984).

The tax advantages, i.e., investment tax credits, accelerated depreciation and, in leveraged leasing, the deduction of interest, suggest that a careful lessor will both structure the transaction to avoid Article 9 and make the optional filing under UCC 9–408 just in case. To what extent, then, should Article 2 be extended to govern disputes arising under the "true" lease? Should the distinction between a sale and a lease be maintained and, if so, why? The issues and solutions, whether they involve a separate "uniform" personal property leasing act, currently being prepared as a proposed Article 2A to the UCC, or an amendment of Article 2 to specifically include leases are complex and beyond the scope of this book. For an excellent, preliminary analysis, see Boss, *Panacea or Nightmare? Leases in Article 2,* 64 B.U.L.Rev. 39 (1984).

COAKLEY & WILLIAMS, INC. v. SHATTERPROOF GLASS CORP.

United States Court of Appeals, Fourth Circuit, 1983.
706 F.2d 456.

MURNAGHAN, CIRCUIT JUDGE:

The strategy of experienced trial lawyers is to avoid, in all but the clearest case, a defense on the basis of a Federal Rules of Civil Procedure 12(b)(6) motion contending that there has been a "failure to state a claim upon which relief can be granted." At so early a stage, all factual inferences must be made in favor of the plaintiff; the facts must be viewed as the plaintiff most strongly can plead them.

Hence, the issues presented to the district court, the foundation underlying much of the law which may govern at subsequent stages of the case, will be addressed in circumstances which may well prove unduly favorable to the plaintiff. With little or no chance of prevailing, the defendant, in filing a 12(b)(6) motion, risks educating the plaintiff to aspects of the case which might otherwise be overlooked or at least not arise in circumstances so predispositive to the plaintiff's side of things.

The present case illustrates the proposition. On an appeal from a dismissal under 12(b)(6) the accepted rule is "that a complaint should not be dismissed for failure to state a claim unless it appears beyond doubt that the plaintiff can prove no set of facts in support of his claim which would entitle him to relief." *Conley v. Gibson,* 355 U.S. 41, 45–46, 78 S.Ct. 99, 101–102, 2 L.Ed.2d 80 (1957). Liberal construction in favor of the plaintiff is mandated. *Jenkins v. McKeithen,* 395 U.S. 411, 421, 89 S.Ct. 1843, 1848, 23 L.Ed.2d 404 (1969). We state as "facts" the allegations and inferences most favorable to the plaintiff.

Washington Plate Glass Company had a contract "to furnish and install aluminum and glass curtain wall and store front work" [3] on a building located in Lanham, Maryland being built by Coakley & Williams, Inc., the plaintiff. To accomplish its contractual undertaking, Washington purchased the glass spandrel required from the defendant, Shatterproof Glass Corp. Still other materials needed for the project, predominantly aluminum, it appears were acquired in part at least elsewhere.

The contract price under the Coakley and Washington agreement amounted to $262,500, subsequently increased by amendment to $271,350.[4] The glass

3. The contract referred to "Spandrel glass to be ¼" gold reflective glass with 1" rigid insulation fastened to curtain wall members approximately 1-½" behind glass spandrel." In addition the agreement called on Washington to provide, *inter alia*: a Texas Aluminum 400 series wall system, vision glass, aluminum objects of several kinds, steel anchor clips, field fasteners, and porcelain enamel panels.

4. Of that increase of $8,850, the bulk ($8,000) reflected specification of ASG Reflectoview Tru-Therm, 1 lite coated with 20 GI Gold and temperal monolithic spandrel ¼" 20 GI Gold to match. The remaining $850 increase was due to a change in the corner configuration from aluminum panel to ¼" Gold Reflectiveview glass.

purchased by Washington from Shatterproof cost $87,715.00,[5] with the proviso that units were "to be properly marked for field installation."

The work progressed and the contract for the aluminum and glass curtain wall and storefront work was completed in March of 1974. Discoloration of the glass ensued, and Coakley complained. To remedy the situation, Washington agreed to replace the glass at no cost to Coakley, and did in fact replace a substantial portion of the glass. Shatterproof supplied the replacement glass and reimbursed Washington for the cost of re-installation, accomplished in April of 1977.

By December of 1977, the glass had again discolored, and complaints began to flow from Coakley to Washington and Shatterproof in or about December 1978. Shatterproof declined to replace a second time. On January 14, 1981, Coakley filed suit against Shatterproof in the Circuit Court for Montgomery County, Maryland alleging breach of implied warranties of merchantability and fitness for a particular purpose. Reliance was placed on certain provisions of the Maryland Uniform Commercial Code, Annotated Code of Maryland, § 1–101 et seq. Removal to the United States District Court for the District of Maryland followed, and Shatterproof sought dismissal under Fed.R.Civ.P. 12(b)(6).

A hearing on the 12(b)(6) motion followed at which Shatterproof contended (1) that the U.C.C. was inapplicable, (2) that lack of privity was fatal to the claim, and (3) that the statute of limitations had run prior to commencement of the action. We now have the case before us on appeal from an order granting the 12(b)(6) motion and dismissing the case solely on the grounds that the U.C.C. was not applicable.

Whether the U.C.C. applies turns on a question as to whether the contract between Washington and Coakley involved principally a sale of goods, on the one hand, or a provision of services, on the other. U.C.C. § 2–314 creates an implied warranty "that the *goods* shall be merchantable" to be "implied in a contract for their sale." Section 2–315 establishes an implied warranty "that the *goods* shall be fit" for a particular purpose, "[w]here the seller at the time of contracting has reason to know [the] particular purpose." (Emphasis added.)

Consequently, unless there has been a buyer of goods, the U.C.C. warranties of merchantability and of fitness for a particular use do not apply. Furthermore, unless there has been a buyer of goods,[9] the elimination of a requirement of privity would not have been achieved.[10] Accordingly, both questions (1) as to the availability of the warranties and (2) as to the amenability of Shatterproof,

5. The complaint is silent as to dollar amounts assignable to the additional materials. Obviously, the more they cost, the less the amount of the contract price attributable to services. We are not inclined to rely on statements of counsel at the time of argument in lieu of well-pleaded allegations. Counsel for Coakley asserted that the evidence would show that the cost of materials was substantially in excess of the cost of installation, *i.e.* more than $130,000. Even without counsel's arguments as a basis, it is still appropriate to recognize that such a possibility is in no way foreclosed by the allegations in the complaint. The plaintiff, at the early 12(b)(6) stage, is entitled to the benefit of the doubt.

9. Under U.C.C. § 2–103(1)(a), the term "buyer" is defined, in unexceptional terms, as "a person who buys or contracts to buy goods."

10. *See* U.C.C. § 2–314(1)(b): "Any previous requirement of privity is abolished as between the *buyer* and the seller in any action brought by the *buyer.*" (Emphasis added.) Absent compliance with § 2–314(1)(b), the lack of privity would have been fatal to Coakley's maintenance of the cause of action. *E.g., Vaccarino v. Cozzubo,* 181 Md. 614, 31 A.2d 316 (1943).

If the transaction was one for goods, Coakley was self-evidently the buyer. Shatterproof was the seller of goods in a transaction in which the intermediary, Washington, not Coakley, was the buyer. However, Washington's purpose in buying was to apply the items purchased to uses benefitting Coakley.

who was not in privity with Coakley, to suit by Coakley, come down to whether the transactions between Washington and Coakley was a sale of goods or the provision of services.

To resolve that question, we must address ourselves to a welter of cases reaching varying results depending on the considerations deemed to predominate in each particular case.[11] It should not pass unnoticed that all were decided at

11. *E.g., Bonebrake v. Cox,* 499 F.2d 951, 960 (8th Cir.1974) (The appeal was from an adjudication on the merits, following a full trial, and reached the conclusion that a contract to supply and install bowling equipment dealt predominantly with goods, even though the amount of services involved was substantial. "The test for inclusion or exclusion [in or from the provisions of the U.C.C.] is not whether they are mixed, but, granting that they are mixed, whether their predominant factor, their thrust, their purpose, reasonably stated, is the rendition of service, with goods incidentally involved (*e.g.,* contract with artist for painting) or is a transaction of sale, with labor incidentally involved (*e.g.,* installation of a water heater in a bathroom). The contract before us, construed in accordance with the applicable standards of the Code, is not excluded therefrom because it is 'mixed,' * * * "); *Burton v. Artery Co., Inc.,* 279 Md. 94, 96, 114–15, 367 A.2d 935, 936, 946 (1977) (In a case where entry of summary judgment was reversed, a standard form construction contract covering "all the work and services" to complete landscaping and sodding was, bearing in mind the canon of construction opposing narrow quibbling or falsely technical construction, held to be predominantly a transaction in goods rather than services); *Ranger Construction Co. v. Dixie Floor Co.,* 433 F.Supp. 442, 444–45 (D.S.C.1977) (On summary judgment, without any contention that pertinent facts were in dispute, the court characterized the agreement for furnishing all labor and materials necessary to install resilient flooring as predominantly a service contract, made by a service corporation in customary construction contract language); *United States v. Akron Mechanical Contractors, Inc.,* 308 F.Supp. 496 (D.Md.1970) (Here the case proceeded to the summary judgment stage. The facts were stipulated, eliminating any possibility of elaboration or resolution of conflicts of fact. The case concerned a building subcontract for plumbing, heating, ventilating and air conditioning work. It was agreed by the parties that the contract covered installation of complete systems and not merely the sale of the constituent materials. The furnishing of materials being incidental to the construction activities, the then applicable Uniform Sales Act was deemed not to apply to the transactions. The real point in the case was whether title was retained or passed, and title was found to have passed. Such a conclusion would be consistent with a contract either for goods or for services, so the decision is not relevant to the problem we confront); *Snyder v. Herbert Greenbaum and Associates, Inc.,* 38 Md.App. 144, 147–48, 380 A.2d 618, 621 (1977) (Here the appeal followed a full trial on the merits. The contract was to supply and install carpeting and the underlying carpet pad in a large group of apartments. The court held: "Despite this difference in the facts which tend to favor the service purpose of the contract, application of the *Bonebrake* test leads us to conclude that the primary thrust of this contract is the *sale,* rather than the installation, of the carpet. Therefore, the Sales Title [of the Uniform Commercial Code] applies to this contract." (emphasis in original)); *Pittsburgh-Des Moines Steel Co. v. Brookhaven Manor Water Co.,* 532 F.2d 572, 580 (7th Cir.1976) (A designer, fabricator and engineer undertook to construct a one-million gallon water tank. In holding the transaction to be a sale of goods, not services, the court had this to say: "We find ample support in the cases arising under the UCC itself that the scope of coverage of 'goods' is not to be given a narrow construction but instead should be viewed as being broad in scope so as to carry out the underlying purpose of the Code of achieving uniformity in commercial transactions. * * * In the words of the UCC this was a 'movable' 'thing' 'specially manufactured.' That which PDM agreed to sell and Brookhaven agreed to buy was not services but goods as defined in the UCC." The decision came following a full trial, and affirmed an award of a judgment n.o.v.); *Van Sistine v. Tollard,* 95 Wisc.2d 678, 681–85, 291 N.W.2d 636, 638–39 (1980) (After a full exploration, in a trial, of pertinent facts, the contract was deemed to be predominantly for supply of services, not of goods, relying on the supplier's self-description as a contractor, the fact that over half of the monetary value was attributable to labor, with some materials furnished by the buyer. The decision was influenced by the court's disenchantment with a U.C.C. provision making a check in payment marked "paid in full" insufficient to its stated purpose where the payee cashed the instrument with an "under protest and without prejudice" endorsement); *Meyers v. Henderson Construction Co.,* 147 N.J.Super. 77, 82–83, 370 A.2d 547, 550 (1977) (A contract to furnish labor, materials (including glass purchased and mounted), tools and equipment for installation of overhead doors was, following a hearing on summary judgment, found to be predominantly for goods, not services, and so covered by the U.C.C.); *Air Heaters, Inc. v. Johnson Electric,*

summary judgment or beyond. No case involving the issue appears to have been disposed of at the Rule 12(b)(6) or demurrer stage. They emphasize, in particular, three aspects which may, or may not, constitute indicia of the nature of the contract: (1) the language of the contract,[12] (2) the nature of the business of the supplier,[13] and (3) the intrinsic worth of the materials involved.[14]

A distillation of the cases outlined in the foregoing notes 11–14 produces an inescapable conclusion that, on the facts in their present pro-plaintiff posture,[15] a reasonable viewing of them would permit a factfinder to conclude that the contract between Washington and Coakley predominantly concerned a sale of goods, and consequently was governed by the U.C.C. A Rule 12(b)(6) motion simply cannot serve to dispose of the case.

As to the first of the emphasized aspects, the contract between Washington and Coakley speaks in terms of furnishing and installing a wall and performing storefront work. Clearly, at the very outset of performance Washington had the responsibility to bring to the affected premises the materials which ultimately would form the glass curtain wall and store front. The U.C.C. in § 2–105 defines "goods" as "*all* things (including specially manufactured goods) which are movable at the time of identification to the contract for sale other than the money in which the price is to be paid, investment securities (Title 8) and things in action." (Emphasis added.) That at least creates an uncertainty to be resolved only by a full factual presentation to determine whether the nature of the Washington business was predominantly the provision of goods or the furnishing of services. The fact that Coakley was a building contractor specializing in construction is not sufficient to provide a completely definitive answer.

Inc., 258 N.W.2d 649, 652 (N.D.1977) (On the basis of facts established in a full scale trial on the merits, a contract to design, manufacture, and install a complete electrical distribution system was scrutinized to determine whether it was predominantly for goods or predominantly for services. The court concluded that the plaintiff, the party on whom the burden lay to establish that the agreement was predominantly for a sale of goods simply failed to meet the burden at trial. "In this case we are not able to determine from the record whether the predominant factor and thrust of this contract is the rendition of services, or a transaction of sale. The record does not include enough factual data concerning this particular contract for us to make that determination." The import of the decision was largely eradicated by a conclusion that, even outside the U.C.C., North Dakota law afforded a right to recover for breach of an implied warranty of fitness. Hence the outcome of the case was unaffected by the "goods or services" discussion); *Cork Plumbing Co., Inc. v. Martin Bloom Associates, Inc.*, 573 S.W.2d 947, 950, 958 (Mo.App.1978) (A judgment in the trial court, entered following a full-scale trial, was affirmed. Contracts were held to be predominantly for services which called for (a) completion of plumbing and sewer work in 176 apartment units and (b) plumbing work to be done on a clubhouse in the apartment complex. The character of the agreements as "construction contracts" appears to have influenced the decision.)

12. *Bonebrake v. Cox, supra,* 499 F.2d at 958 ("The language thus employed is that peculiar to goods, not services. It speaks of 'equipment,' and of lanes free from 'defects in workmanship and materials.' The rendition of services does not comport with such terminology."); *Ranger Construction Co. v. Dixie Floor Co., supra,* 433 F.Supp. at 445 ("It is interesting to note that throughout the contract the defendant, Dixie Floor Co., Inc., is not referred to as a materialman but rather as a subcontractor.").

13. *Ranger Construction Co. v. Dixie Floor Co., supra,* 433 F.Supp. at 445 ("The defendant's responses to interrogatories indicated that the defendant was essentially a service corporation engaged in the installation and construction of flooring.").

14. *Snyder v. Herbert Greenbaum & Associates, Inc., supra,* 38 Md.App. at 156–59, 380 A.2d at 626–27 (The case recognizes that the U.C.C. contemplated as a seller of goods one who obtains the component parts for special assembly, yet who, upon breach of the other party, is restricted to realization of junk value. It reached its decision that a sale of goods, not a provision of services, was involved though neither party "in any sense proved the amount of the resale proceeds of the carpet.").

15. We, of course, have no way of knowing what will actually be developed when the parties are put to their respective proofs.

While often, and perhaps customarily, a contractor is engaged in the provision of services, the scope of a contractor's work is not necessarily monolithic and, in the present circumstances, it becomes a question of unresolved fact whether Coakley, for the purposes of the single relationship to which we are restricted, was a buyer of goods.

In this connection, it is not irrelevant that Coakley has alleged that the purchases by Washington from Shatterproof included anchor clips and field fasteners. At the early stage at which we find ourselves, the allegation requires us to indulge the inference urged by counsel for Coakley that putting the glass in place was a simple snap-on process requiring little expenditure of time or labor. One can readily imagine, without the advantage of specificity deriving from a full trial on the merits, that the contract largely contemplated the provision of precast panels as goods, without the installation being nearly so extensive or significant as the supplying of the glass itself.

The fact that the contract does not follow a standard, routine or regularized form, coupled with the plaintiff's contention that standard form contracts are virtually universal for construction (i.e., generally, service) contracts, operates to leave open the possibility of a finding that the contract is more one for goods than would be the customary construction contract.

Turning to the second point, the nature of Washington's business, the fact that Washington was a dealer and not a manufacturer does not have any particularly dispositive significance. Many retailers of goods function in the role of middleman. Shatterproof sold Washington materials in a transaction which unquestionably, on the sparse record before us at the preliminary stage at which we find ourselves, was a sale of goods, and the question comes down essentially to whether those materials or the services which Washington also provided under its contract with Coakley predominated. Without full consideration of as yet unascertained facts that question is simply not ripe for resolution. It is one of fact, not law; at least it is at this early stage.

Third, the complaint affords no realistic, and certainly no dispositive, information as to the value of the spandrels et al. in case of breakup into the component parts of the glass curtain wall and store front work. That can only be determined by further development of the record, and is, in all events, but one of several factors which must be evaluated in conjunction with all the others in resolving the ultimate factual issue: did Washington and Coakley deal primarily with goods or services?

Accordingly, Coakley has alleged enough to survive a motion to dismiss under Fed.R.Civ.P. 12(b)(6). Nor, at the other extreme, has it alleged too much, permitting sure ascertainment that services, not goods, were the gravamen of the transaction. Coakley should, therefore, be permitted to show, unless the statute of limitations bars recovery, that it was a buyer of goods and, therefore, entitled to proceed under the U.C.C. provisions.[17]

17. Following argument on January 13, 1983 of the instant case, the Maryland Court of Appeals, on January 25, 1983, handed down its decision in *Anthony Pools, a Division of Anthony Industries, Inc. v. Sheehan,* 295 Md. 285, 455 A.2d 434 (1983). That case involves the somewhat different, although related, question of whether, in the case of a hybrid goods and services transaction, a disclaimer of an implied warranty of merchantability was unenforceable, as to the goods component of a contract predominantly for services, because such disclaimers are not legally permitted where there is a sale of consumer goods. U.C.C. § 2–316.1. The disclaimer was held unenforceable on the grounds that consumer goods retained their status as goods despite the fact that the contract was predominantly for services. The all or nothing contention that, the contract being predominantly one for services, none of the items covered by it should be treated as goods was rejected.

* * *

[The court held that the claim was not barred under the statute of limitations, UCC 2–725.]

Accordingly, the judgment is reversed and the case remanded for further proceedings not inconsistent with this opinion.

Reversed and remanded.

[Some footnotes omitted.]

Notes

1. Suppose, after trial, that the court determined that services rather than goods predominated in the transaction. Suppose, also, that the glass supplied by the defendant was unmerchantable, i.e., unfit for the "ordinary purposes for which such goods are used." UCC 2–314(2)(c). Should the plaintiff be entitled to claim breach of the implied warranty of merchantability imposed by UCC 2–314? Or is the plaintiff relegated to the law of service contracts outside of the UCC, where negligence rather than breach of warranty is the exclusive theory of liability?

2. The either-or effect of the "predominate purpose" test was rejected in Anthony Pools v. Sheehan, 295 Md. 285, 455 A.2d 434 (1983), cited by the principal case in footnote 17. Where services predominate, if the goods supplied (a diving board) were unmerchantable and caused loss (personal injuries), Article 2 could be applied both to impose an implied warranty of merchantability and to determine whether a clause purporting to disclaim the implied warranty of merchantability was enforceable. The court stressed that the goods had to be supplied under a commercial transaction, rather than a contract for professional services, and must "retain their character * * * after completion of the performance promised * * *" Note, however, that the goods were supplied to a consumer who suffered personal injuries. Should that make a difference in the analysis?

3. Is a contract to supply a computer software system a contract for the sale of goods or a contract for services? In RRX Industries, Inc. v. Lab-Con, Inc., 772 F.2d 543 (9th Cir.1985), Lab-Con agreed to supply RRX with a software system for use in its medical laboratories and to correct any malfunctions or "bugs" that arose in the system. "Bugs" appeared soon after installation and Lab-Con, even after upgrading the system, was unable to remove them. RRX claimed consequential damages under the UCC and Lab-Con argued that because the contract was for services the UCC did not apply. The court disagreed:

> In determining whether a contract is one of sale or to provide services we look to the essence of the agreement. * * * When a sale predominates, incidental services provided do not alter the basic transaction. * * * Because software packages vary depending on the needs of the individual consumer, we apply a case-by-case analysis. * * *

Here, the sales aspect of the transaction predominates. The employee training, repair services, and system upgrading were incidental to sale of the software package and did not defeat characterization of the system as a good. 772 F.2d at 546.

Problem 9–2

A Law Reform Commission, considering possible amendments to Article 2 of the UCC, has proposed the following revision in the scope of Article 2. What do you

The Maryland Court of Appeals expressly reserved judgment as to whether U.C.C. § 2–316.1's ban on implied warranty disclaimers would also extend to consumer goods used up in the course of rendering the consumer service. At the very least, the result in *Anthony Pools* does nothing to question the soundness of the conclusion we have reached.

think about it at this early stage of the course? See Note, *Disengaging Sales Law From the Sale Construct: A Proposal to Extend the Scope of Article 2 of the UCC,* 96 Harv.L.Rev. 470 (1982) (title passage is an inadequate tool for resolving sales disputes).

Section 2–102. Scope; Certain Security and Other Transactions Excluded From This Article; Extension by Analogy.

1. This Act applies to every contract for the sale of goods.

2. This Act does not apply to any transaction that is intended to operate only as a secured transaction, whether or not it is in the form of an unconditional contract for sale.

3. Whether or not a contract in the form of a lease of goods, bailment, consignment or otherwise is a contract for sale depends on the intention of the parties, the substantial effect of the contract and all the other surrounding circumstances.

4. Any of the provisions of this Act, if relevant in principle and appropriate in the circumstances, may be applied by analogy to a transaction respecting goods other than a contract of sale, such as a lease of goods or a contract for the supply of labor and materials.

SECTION 4. SOME BASIC CONCEPTS IN ARTICLE 2

A. *Introduction*

The present form of Article 2, Sales, emerged from a careful and critical review of the 1952 Official Text by the New York Law Revision Commission in 1953–54, and was promulgated in the 1958 Official Text of the Uniform Commercial Code. The principal draftsperson in the early drafts of Article 2 and its predecessor (the Revised Uniform Sales Act), and its most effective champion until his death in 1962, was Professor Karl N. Llewellyn. (The drafts of Llewellyn's efforts from 1940–44 to revise the Uniform Sales Act are reproduced in E. Kelly, Uniform Commercial Code Drafts (1984), Vols. I and II. Work under the joint auspices of the National Conference of Commissioners on Uniform State Laws and the American Law Institute began on January 1, 1945. See Schnader, *A Short History of the Preparation and Enactment of the Uniform Commercial Code,* 22 U.Miami L.Rev. 1, 5 (1967).) In a real sense, Article 2 is "Karl's Kode:" His ideas and approach to commercial law, even though imperfectly achieved, tended to dominate the final product. For useful discussion, see W. Twining, Karl Llewellyn and the Realist Movement (1973). See also Wiseman, *The Limits of Vision: Karl Llewellyn and the Merchant Rules,* 100 Harv.L.Rev. 465 (1987). Compare Casebeer, *Escape from Liberalism: Fact and Value in Karl Llewellyn,* 1977 Duke L.J. 671 with Danzig, *A Comment on the Jurisprudence of the Uniform Commercial Code,* 27 Stan.L.Rev. 621 (1975). See also, Williams, *Book Review,* 97 Harv.L.Rev. 1495 (1984).

According to Richard Danzig, Llewellyn did not regard law as a "body of deduced rules, or as an instrument chosen by social planners from among a universe of alternatives." Rather, he "saw law as an articulation and regularization * * * of a generally recognized and almost indisputably right rule . . . inherent in, but very possibly obscured by, existing patterns of relationships." For him, law was "immanent" or "imbedded" in any situation and it was the task of the law authority, usually a judge, to discover it. Under this view, the task of the legislature is to prescribe standards, such as commercial reasonableness, on how to find the law and leave the task of particularization, i.e., finding the "situation sense," to the court. *Danzig,* supra, at 624–27. In the rejection of rules and the search for standards which responded to the behavior patterns of the disputants in context, Llewellyn was clearly in step with Arthur L. Corbin and other so-called "Realists." See Speidel, *Restatement Second: Omitted Terms and Contract Method,* 67 Cornell L.Rev. 785, 786–92 (1982).

Article 2 was also influenced by the nature of the problems and actors with which it deals. According to Danzig: "Commercial law is at the margin of public law. It deals with a subcommunity ('merchants'), whose members occupy a status position distinct from society at large, whose disputes are often resolved by informal negotiation or in private forums, whose relationships tend to continue over time rather than ending with the culmination of single transactions, and whose primary rules derive from a sense of fairness wide-spread—if imprecisely defined—within the commercial community. *Danzig,* supra, at 622–23.

B. Agreement, Not Promise, as the Foundation Stone

Students of commercial law have already learned a great deal about the concept of promise in the first year course in contracts. The Restatement (Second) of Contracts even defines a contract as "a promise or a set of promises for the breach of which the law provides a remedy, or the performance of which the law in some way recognizes as a duty." It is true that the analysis of commercial arrangements in terms of the concept of promise fits the facts of many contracts, including many involving the sale of goods. But the analysis fails to fit many other contracts, very felicitously, including some for the sale of goods, thus suggesting that there must be a more fundamental concept. That concept, as we will see, is the concept of agreement, and it is this that is the true foundation stone of Article Two.

Here we will offer some illustrative examples of features of consensual arrangements for the sale of goods that are more felicitously analyzable in terms of agreement rather than the exchange of promises as such. First, in the law of sales many express warranties arise by virtue of the seller's "affirmations of fact," not promises as such. UCC 2–312 expressly so states. Second, many other obligations in the law of sales arise in particular cases by virtue of tacit assumptions, custom, trade usage, course of dealing and course of performance. In such instances, there is rarely anything resembling an express promise, and the concept of an implied in fact promise seldom fits the facts more than fictionally. Third, many sale of goods transactions are not discrete, "one-shot," affairs but occur over time within longer term relationships. Many features of these relationships are not the subject of express promises (or even implied ones) yet they generate important obligations, obligations themselves shored up by the code doctrine of good faith and fair dealing to which we will soon turn. The broad structures of such relationships often pre-exist so that when the parties enter into a particular relation general obligations attendant upon such a relation attach. Finally, countless discrete, "one-shot," exchanges take place each day in which no promises are made on either side yet the law imposes obligations on both parties. "Over the counter" sales and supermarket sales are only the most familiar of these. In all of the foregoing examples, the most fundamental concept at work is that of agreement, not promise (and even agreement does not account for everything). The Code itself recognizes the primacy of agreement. In Article One, agreement and contract are defined in these terms:

1–201 General Definitions

(3) "Agreement" means the bargain of the parties in fact as found in their language or by implication from other circumstances including course of dealing or usage of trade or course of performance as provided in this Act (Sections 1–205 and 2–208). Whether an agreement has legal consequences is determined by the provisions of this Act, if applicable; otherwise by the law of contracts (Section 1–103). (Compare "Contract").

(11) "Contract" means the total legal obligation which results from the parties' agreement as affected by this Act and any other applicable rules of law. (Compare "Agreement.")

C. The Article Two "Merchant" Concept

Article Two includes fourteen provisions in which the term "merchant" appears. UCC 2–104(1) defines merchant to mean:

> A person who deals in goods of the kind or otherwise by his occupation holds himself out as having knowledge or skill peculiar to the practices or goods involved in the transaction or to whom such knowledge or skill may be attributed by his employment of an agent or broker or other intermediary who by his occupation holds himself out as having such knowledge or skill.

The fourteen sections which employ the term "Merchant" are: 2–103(1)(b) (good faith); 2–201(2) (statute of frauds); 2–205 (firm offer); 2–207 ("battle of the forms"); 2–209(2) (modification, rescission and waiver); 2–312(3) (warranty of title); 2–314(1) (implied warranty of merchantability); 2–327(1)(c) (sale on approval); 2–402(2) (rights of creditors of sellers); 2–403(2) (entrusting); 2–509(3) (risk of loss); 2–603(1) (rightful rejection); 2–605(1)(b) (waiver of buyer's objections); and 2–609(2) (adequate assurance of performance).

Section 2–314 imposing an implied warranty of merchantability on merchants, and section 2–201 on the statute of frauds seem to have generated the most litigation over who qualifies as a merchant.

LOEB & COMPANY, INC. v. SCHREINER

Supreme Court of Alabama, 1975.
294 Ala. 722, 321 So.2d 199.

ALMON, JUSTICE.

This is an appeal from a judgment of the Circuit Court of Lowndes County. The court decreed that the plaintiff and the defendant entered into an oral contract for the purchase and sale of one hundred fifty bales of cotton but that the contract was unenforceable under the Alabama Uniform Commercial Code because the defendant was not a "merchant" as that term is used and defined.

The plaintiff-appellant, Loeb and Company, Inc., is engaged in the marketing of raw cotton. James L. Loeb of Montgomery is President of the company and has bought cotton from the defendant-appellee, Charles Schreiner, for the past four or five years. Charles Schreiner is a cotton farmer and has been engaged in the farming of cotton and other crops since 1963.

Following a conversation on the 18th or 20th of April, 1973, with regard to the price paid by appellant company to Marlowe Reese, a neighbor of appellee, appellee telephoned appellant on April 23 and asked if the price paid Reese was available to him. He received from the president of appellant company a statement that he would pay appellee the same price. Appellant maintained at trial that appellee orally contracted with him during the telephone conversation to sell appellant company one hundred fifty bales of cotton. Appellee admitted that there were negotiations but maintained that he never agreed to sell the one hundred fifty bales.

The date, parties, terms and conditions of the alleged contract to sell were confirmed in the records of appellant company on April 23, 1973, and two copies of a confirming statement were mailed to appellee. Appellee received the confirming statement but neither signed it nor returned it, nor in any manner took exception to it until four months later when appellant telephoned him inquiring the whereabouts of the statement. In the meanwhile the price of raw cotton had risen from the price in the alleged contract of 37¼ cents to the middle 80 cents.

When appellant company telephoned appellee and inquired about the confirming statement, appellee said that he did not intend to sign and return it and told appellant to discuss the matter with his attorney.

The trial court found that there was an oral contract but that the contract was unenforceable under the Alabama Uniform Commercial Code because the appellee was not a merchant as that term is used in Tit. 7A, §§ 2–104 and 2–201, Code of Alabama, 1940, Recompiled 1958.

Tit. 7A, § 2–201 is the section which sets out the statute of frauds for Article 2 of the Uniform Commercial Code. It governs all contracts for the sale of "goods." Cotton is included within the definition of "goods" as defined by the Code. *Cox v. Cox,* 292 Ala. 106, 289 So.2d 609 (1974). § 2–201 provides in pertinent part as follows:

> "Except as otherwise provided in this section a contract for the sale of goods for the price of $500 or more is not enforceable by way of action or defense unless there is some writing sufficient to indicate that a contract for sale has been made between the parties and signed by the party against whom enforcement is sought or by his authorized agent or broker. A writing is not insufficient because it omits or incorrectly states a term agreed upon but the contract is not enforceable under this paragraph beyond the quantity of goods shown in such writing.
>
> "(2) *Between merchants* if within a reasonable time a writing in confirmation of the contract and sufficient against the sender is received and the party receiving it has reason to know its contents, it satisfies the requirements of subsection (1) against such party unless written notice of objection to its contents is given within ten days after it is received." (Emphasis added).

Appellant contends that the trial court erred in finding that the appellee cotton farmer was not a merchant and that § 2–201(2) was not applicable. If appellee is not a "merchant," § 2–201 would act as a bar to the enforcement of the contract in question. However, if appellee is a "merchant," he would be liable on the contract because he did not within ten days give notice of objection to appellant's confirming statement. Tit. 7A, § 2–104(1) defines "merchant" as follows:

> "(1) 'Merchant' means a person who deals in goods of the kind or otherwise by his occupation holds himself out as having knowledge or skill peculiar to the practices or goods involved in the transaction or to whom such knowledge or skill may be attributed by his employment of an agent or

broker or other intermediary who by his occupation holds himself out as having such knowledge or skill."

Only a few courts have considered the question of whether a farmer is a "merchant." In *Cook Grains v. Fallis,* 239 Ark. 962, 395 S.W.2d 555 (1965), the Arkansas Supreme Court held that a soybean farmer was not a merchant when he was merely trying to sell the commodities he had raised. The court stated that there was not

> "* * * a scintilla of evidence in the record, or proffered as evidence, that appellee is a dealer in goods of the kind or by his occupation holds himself out as having knowledge or a skill peculiar to the practices of goods involved in the transaction, and no such knowledge or skill can be attributed to him." 239 Ark. at 964, 395 S.W.2d at 556.

In *Oloffson v. Coomer,* 11 Ill.App.3d 918, 296 N.E.2d 871 (1973), the Third Division of the Appellate Court of Illinois stated in dictum that a farmer in the business of growing grain was not a "merchant" with respect to the merchandising of grain. However, in *Campbell v. Yokel,* 20 Ill.App.3d 702, 313 N.E.2d 628 (1974), the Fifth District of the Appellate Court of Illinois dealt with a case that involved an action against some soybean farmers on an alleged breach of an oral contract for the sale of soybeans. The court held that the soybean farmers, who had grown and sold soybeans for several years were "merchants" when selling crops and were therefore barred by § 2–201(2) from asserting the statute of frauds as a defense.

One court has suggested that whether or not a farmer is a "merchant" within the meaning of § 2–104 should turn upon whether or not he has engaged in a particular type of sale in the past. In *Fear Ranches, Inc. v. Berry,* 470 F.2d 905 (10th Cir.1972), a breach of warranty case, the court held that where the defendant cattle farmers made a sale to a non-meatpacker for resale when they had previously sold all of their cattle to meatpackers, they were not "merchants" with respect to the sale to the non-meatpacker. The court felt that the sale of cattle for resale was a sale of a different type of goods and made up a different type of business than the sale of cattle to meat-packers.

We hold that in the instant case the appellee was not a "merchant" within the meaning of § 2–104. We do not think the framers of the Uniform Commercial Code contemplated that a farmer should be included among those considered to be "merchants."

In order for a farmer to be included within the § 2–104 definition of "merchants," he must do one of the following:

1. deal in goods of the kind;
2. *by his occupation* hold himself out as having knowledge or skill peculiar to the practices or goods involved in the transaction; or
3. employ an agent or broker or other intermediary who by his occupation holds himself out as having such knowledge or skill.

Since the farmer in the instant case did not qualify as a merchant under 3 above, he would have to qualify under 1 or 2. It is not sufficient under 2 that one hold himself out as having knowledge or skill peculiar to the practices or goods involved, he must *by his occupation* so hold himself out. Accordingly, a person cannot be considered a "merchant" simply because he is a braggart or has a high opinion of his knowledge in a particular area. We conclude that a farmer does not solely *by his occupation* hold himself out as being a professional cotton merchant.

The remaining thing which a farmer might do to be considered a merchant is to become a dealer in goods. Although there was evidence which indicated that the appellee here had a good deal of knowledge, this is not the test. There is not one shred of evidence that appellee ever sold anyone's cotton but his own. He was nothing more than an astute farmer selling his own product. We do not think this was sufficient to make him a dealer in goods.

The official comment to § 2–104 states in part as follows:

> "This Article assumes that transactions between *professionals* in a given field require special and clear rules which may not apply to a *casual or inexperienced seller or buyer.* It thus adopts a policy of expressly stating rules applicable 'between merchants' and 'as against a merchant', wherever they are needed instead of making them depend upon the circumstances of each case as in the statutes cited above. This section lays the foundation of this policy by defining those who are to be regarded as professionals or 'merchants' and by stating when a transaction is deemed to be 'between merchants'." (Emphasis added).

Although a farmer might sell his cotton every year, we do not think that this should take him out of the category of a "casual seller" and place him in the category with "professionals."

If indeed the statute of frauds has, as claimed, permitted an injustice, it is a matter which addresses itself to the legislature.

The judgment is due to be and is hereby

Affirmed.

HEFLIN, C.J., and MERRILL, MADDOX, FAULKNER, JONES, SHORES and EMBRY, JJ., concur.

HILLINGER, THE ARTICLE TWO MERCHANT RULES: KARL LLEWELLYN'S ATTEMPT TO ACHIEVE THE GOOD, THE TRUE, THE BEAUTIFUL IN COMMERCIAL LAW 73 Geo.L.J. 1141, 1146–1148, 1174, 1175, 1176–1180 (1985).

We are experiencing a merchant muddle that stems from a fundamental misunderstanding about the nature and purpose of the Article 2 merchant rules. They are not what we thought they were. Their intended purpose and function suggest a different approach both to the merchant rules themselves and to their application to nonmerchants.

This article demonstrates that the Article 2 merchant rules were never intended to codify merchant custom and trade usage. Llewellyn, the principal draftsman of Article 2, invented the merchant rules. The necessity that mothered his invention was his passionate desire to make "commercial law and practice clear, sane, *and safe.*" The merchant rules are statutory expressions of Llewellyn's drafting creed that "[s]impler, clearer, and better adjusted rules, built to make sense and to protect good faith, make for more foreseeable and more satisfactory results both in court and out." Llewellyn sculpted the merchant rules to bring "the beautiful" to commercial law and commercial practice.[28] To Llewellyn's eye, legal beauty lay in functional rules—rules that could guide businessmen in conducting their business affairs, rules that could assist them in their "trouble shooting, trouble evasion and forward planning." Llewellyn drafted the merchant rules to apprise businessmen, attorneys, and courts of the peculiar obligations of businessmen. Their clarity, rationality and certainty in application would protect decent businessmen and promote sound, reasonable, and decent business practices.

The idea of separate merchant rules for businessmen sprang from Llewellyn's pragmatism. Llewellyn believed businessmen needed rules on which they could rely, rules that would produce predictable results. The existence of predictable rules would make commercial activity more rational and would thereby encourage its expansion. Moreover, Llewellyn believed the policies and considerations involved in a mercantile situation differed from those in a nonmercantile situation, and that a unitary approach to sales rules would inevitably muddle policies and rationales. This result would jeopardize the predictability he so wanted to create for businessmen. Under a single rule, governing both businessmen and nonbusinessmen, a court trying to protect Aunt Tilly might manipulate, distort, or misconstrue the rule, making uncertain its later interpretation or application to Tilly, Inc. Rules fashioned specifically for a commercial setting, and insulated from nonmercantile considerations, would thus protect the rules' predictability for businessmen. One set of sales rules for businessmen and another for Aunt Tilly would eliminate the possibility of undermining the commercial rule to do justice to Aunt Tilly.

Yet Llewellyn did not intend to preclude judicial application of the merchant rules to nonmerchants in every instance. If application to a nonmerchant would not jeopardize the rule's certainty and predictability, Llewellyn wanted the courts to apply the merchant rule to nonmerchants. Indeed, a provision in the 1949 draft expressly so provided.

* * *

In concluding that good commercial law and practice required special commercial rules, Llewellyn was not concluding that the commercial rules could have no application to a noncommercial context. Section 1–102(3) of the 1949 draft makes that clear: "A provision of this Act which is stated to be applicable 'between merchants' or otherwise to be of limited application need not be so limited when the circumstances and underlying reasons justify extending its application."

* * *

Had the 1949 provision authorizing liberal application of the merchant rules to nonmerchants survived and been enacted, the question of merchant status would not have assumed its current importance. Courts could have sidestepped many status questions by concluding that merchant status was ultimately irrelevant, and the reasons underlying the merchant rule—reasonableness, soundness, and decency—would justify its application to the nonmerchant. Unfortunately, the drafters finally bowed to merchant critics and eliminated section 1–102(3), apparently as a political concession to save the embattled Article 2 merchant distinction itself.

* * *

The farmer cases involving statute of frauds defenses all involve a similar plot. Farmer periodically calls Grain Elevator Company to check on current grain prices. During one call Farmer likes what he hears and the parties conclude a contract on the phone, the grain to be delivered some months later. Shortly after the oral deal, Grain Elevator Company prepares and sends a written confirmation of the phone deal to farmer. Farmer does not respond. Grain Elevator Company then contracts to sell Farmer's grain to a third party. At the time scheduled for delivery, the price of grain has skyrocketed, and not surprisingly, Farmer no longer likes the contract price. He sells his grain to someone else at the higher market price. Farmer's breach forces Grain Elevator Company to cover at the current market price to meet its contractual obligations. It ultimately sues Farmer to recover its loss.

Farmer appears in court outfitted in bib overalls and cowboy boots that cast off a faint perfume of manure. Farmer inevitably makes two responses to Grain Elevator Company's contract action: (1) "We never made a contract" and, (2) "Even if we did, I am a farmer, not a merchant, and therefore, the contract is unenforceable because I never signed anything." Grain Elevator Company always responds that Farmer is a merchant and the statute is therefore satisfied because Farmer never responded to its confirmation letter. As Article 2 is presently understood, the result of the litigation turns on the issue of the farmer's status.

In treating this question, some courts have concluded that the terms "farmer" and "merchant" are mutually exclusive: farmers are "tillers of the soil," while merchants are "traders in goods." The evidence indicates Llewellyn did not consider most farmers to be merchants for purposes of the statute of frauds. In a comment to an early draft, Llewellyn discussed the apple farmer who marketed three to six hundred bushels a year. Although such a farmer would give the implied warranty of merchantability (because he would qualify as a "goods" merchant), he would not be subject to section 2–207's rule that additional minor terms stated in a confirmation became part of the parties' contract (a "practices" merchant provision), because invocation of section 2–207(2)

> depends upon the established practice of regular merchants to attend and reply promptly to correspondence. No such practice exists among small farmers * * * his occupation does not hold him out as familiar with any practice "of the kind involved" or as having the general knowledge or skill in that aspect of a person in trade.

In defending the inapplicability of the statute of frauds to transactions under five hundred dollars, Llewellyn discussed farmers and merchants separately, noting that

> in regard to such transactions, a merchant is protected by his normal procedure of reducing transactions to written sales slip or confirmation; a farmer is protected by his standing in the community.

In some of his articles, Llewellyn distinguished the horse and haystack from "wares-in-commerce," arguing the commercial sales rules that had evolved from horse and haystack deals were unsuited for the new world of modern commerce. One may surmise that Llewellyn intended to leave farmers with their haystack law and to give businessmen new "wares-in-commerce" law. This theory would explain why Llewellyn repeatedly distinguished merchants from farmers and housewives in his testimony before the New York Law Revision hearings.

Although Llewellyn probably would have agreed that a farmer is not an Article 2 "practices" merchant, he would have been upset with the consequences that flow from this conclusion. Courts that have held the farmer not to be a merchant have applied section 2–201(1) (the nonmerchant rule) and refused to enforce the contract. Llewellyn would have wanted the courts to apply section 2–201(2)'s confirmation letter exception despite the farmer's nonmerchant status, because the purpose and policies behind the merchant exception would justify such application. Llewellyn designed section 2–201(2) to accommodate oral deals that the decent businessman confirmed promptly in accordance with sound business practice. He intended section 2–201(2) to serve as a bulwark against one party's indecent speculation at the expense of the other. Here, Farmer's questionable conduct as contrasted with Grain Elevator Company's sound and good business practice of sending out a confirmation letter would justify the application of section 2–201(2). No harm could come to the merchant rule by invoking it in that situation and its application would produce a just and satisfactory result.

Other courts, confronted with the farmer situation, have concluded the farmer is a merchant; one court emphasized that the statutory definition, rather than common sense, controlled. Although these courts have interpreted the merchant definition to include those whom Llewellyn probably did not intend to include, their "misconstruction" enabled them to achieve the result Llewellyn would have wanted, through application of the merchant rule. In short, had 1–102(3) been enacted, courts could have dismissed many "Who is a merchant?" questions with a glib "Who cares?" If the policy fits, the merchant rule should govern. Given the merchant rules' inherent reasonableness, the policy would fit more often than not.

The loss of section 1–102(3) and a basic misunderstanding about the underlying purpose of the Article 2 merchant rules have created a flaw in Article 2's bifurcated system. Courts assume the existence of an Article 2 barrier, which precludes application of the merchant rules to situations involving only one merchant or only nonmerchants. Courts either respect the barrier, often reaching poor results, or surmount it by various means to reach the proper results. Those who are unquestionably nonmerchants suffer most. They can never find refuge in the Article 2 merchant rules This situation is especially ridiculous because there does not appear to be anything intrinsically commercial about most of the Article 2 merchant rules. The merchant rules for firm offers, the statute of frauds, risk of loss, and so on, are edicts issuing forth from the temple of reason, not the marketplace. The merchant rules embody good sense, not just good commercial sense.

Compared with the nonmerchant rules, the merchant rules seem enlightened. The merchant rules impose only the mildest, most modest of responsibilities, such as the duty to open one's mail and respond to it promptly. The merchant's failure to abide by these duties often results in equally innocuous consequences. For example, the businessman who fails to reply to a confirmation letter simply loses his statute of frauds defense against contract enforcement. The businessman who fails to read or respond to the offeree's letter of acceptance is bound by *minor* additional contract terms contained in the acceptance. These are rules which, in most instances, could apply to the common man with little fear of judicial distortion or doctrinal confusion. In fact, it may be said that what's good for businessmen in Article 2 is good for the rest of us. Reprinted from Volume 73 of the Georgetown Law Journal by permission of Professor Ingrid M. Hillinger, © 1985.

D. Power to Contract Out of Article Two

It is one thing for a lawyer and his client to find themselves properly within Article Two of the Code. It is quite another for the relevant Code provisions therein to be controlling in the face of contrary agreement of the parties. For many are not. Article Two, like prior law, grants broad freedom of contract. Scope for the lawyer's role as planner is therefore very great. And, as Llewellyn once stressed:

"[I]n the normal modern case the first measure of the parties' rights is * * * the contract * * *, only an analysis which stresses the contract first and hammers on the necessity of keeping it in mind as the framework of all that follows, is adequate to teaching * * * only by emphasis, from the beginning, on the contract, can one bring to due honor the problem of draftsmanship * * *." Llewellyn, Cases and Materials on Sales xiv–xv (1931).

It should be noted that the "contract" to which Llewellyn refers may be one of three basic kinds. First, it may be fully negotiated between the parties and its terms reduced to writing. This is the least common form. Second, the contract may take the form of a signed standardized printed agreement. This is a very common form. Third, because the parties agree only on the barest essentials of goods and price, the contract may consist largely of "terms" supplied by statute. This is the most common form. Much of Article Two can be viewed as a statutorily standardized contract which comes into play to the extent the agreement of the parties is silent.

Regardless of the form of the contract, the lawyer will need to know his freedom of contract: that is, what Article Two allows, does not allow, and supplies absent contrary agreement. And the good commercial lawyer who is in a position to structure things in advance for his client will be especially alert to the kinds of things that might go wrong with his client's deal as it progresses from stage to stage.

To the lawyer, perhaps the most fundamental distinction here is that between planning and drafting the affirmative business content of a deal, and planning and drafting, *prophylactically* as it were, for things that can go wrong. With regard to the former, the businessman is dominant, though the lawyer contributes as draftsman. *Re* the latter, the lawyer is at the fore. The businessman supplies "business" specifications, e.g., nature, quality and quantity of goods, payment terms and the like, and the lawyer drafts in these, but his most distinctive contributions are frequently not here; rather, they are to try to envision the unfolding transaction as it progresses from stage to stage, to identify the kinds of things that can go wrong at each stage, and then to bring his preventive and remedial sophistication to bear on these possible eventualities *in advance at the agreement stage.*

But while the *contract is,* by virtue of the broad freedom granted in UCC 1–102(3), *primary,* and Article Two secondary, it does not, of course, follow that just any clause the lawyer drafts will stand up under Article Two, (and even if it will stand up under Article Two, other, non-Code law, may sometimes be invoked to strike it down). So far as *Code* limitations on freedom of contract are concerned, it is useful to differentiate four kinds applicable within Article 2. First, there is the type of *specific* Article Two provision that is itself not variable by agreement. Second, Article 2, in UCC 2–302, generally invalidates unconscionable contracts and unconscionable contract clauses. Third, UCC 1–203 imposes an "obligation of good faith" in the performance or enforcement of every contract or duty within the Act. Fourth, UCC 1–103 provides that certain equitable principles shall be controlling. The first kind of limitation will be considered in a general way in the present section, the second, third, and fourth in subsequent sections of this chapter.

The provisions of Article Two fall into three categories: (1) those which themselves explicitly state that they can be varied by agreement, (2) those which themselves *explicitly* state that they can not be varied by agreement, and (3) those which are not thus flagged one way or the other at all. The first kind poses no problems for the draftsman of a sales contract. The second kind he must identify and keep in mind. See, e.g., UCC 2–616(3), 2–718(1), 2–209(3), 2–318, 2–725(1), and 1–204(1). But provisions of the third type (unflagged either way) pose a real problem, for it is *clear* that some of these provisions cannot be varied by agreement, despite the general green light in UCC 1–102(3). Examples are UCC 2–201 on the Statute of Frauds, UCC 2–719(3) protecting "underdogs", and such third party protection provisions as UCC 2–702, 2–502, and 2–403. Yet within this same broad category of unflagged provisions are some that clearly can be varied by agreement. See, for example, the Code provisions on recoverable damages for breach, UCC 2–713, 2–714 and 2–718. The problem, then, is this: If, as is plainly the case, our third category of unflagged provisions includes some which can be varied by agreement and some which cannot, by what criteria are we to determine which is which?

Problem 9–3

Consider the validity of the following clauses which purport to vary the effect of the sections cited.

(1) "Pursuant to this basic agreement, the parties shall make subsequent agreements for the purchase and sale of lumber, each such subsequent agreement to constitute a binding contract only when and if the parties have fully agreed to all material terms." See UCC 2–204(2), (3), and various gap-filler provisions in Part 3 of Article 2.

(2) "In the event that buyer discovers a nonconformity upon delivery of said goods, buyer shall not be required to notify seller thereof, provided that buyer commences any legal proceedings therefor against seller within two years of discovery of said breach." See UCC 2–607(3)(a) and 1–102(3).

(3) "In the event buyer defaults hereunder, seller shall be entitled to recover the agreed price for said goods whether or not Article Two of the Uniform Commercial Code so provides." See UCC 2–709.

E. Legal Controls on Article Two Contractual Behavior: Unconscionability and Good Faith

Below we discuss and consider UCC 2–302, providing that unconscionable contract clauses are invalid, and UCC 1–203, imposing a general obligation of good faith. You have already met both of those sections in your first year course in contracts. It is sometimes said that the unconscionability limitation on freedom of contract applies at the formation stage whereas the good faith limitation applies only to the performance or enforcement stage. Yet that good faith may have some bearing on issues normally resolved at the formation stage is quite evident, as with section 2–305(2) which provides that "A price to be fixed by the seller or by the buyer means a price for him to fix in good faith." Indeed, good faith may even have a bearing on liability for acts or omissions of one party as early as the negotiation stage. Of course, this would have to be via UCC 1–103 on supplemental general principles, for UCC 1–203 itself only imposes an obligation of good faith in the "performance" and "enforcement" of the contract. Similarly, the student will do well to entertain the possibility that unconscionability may have a bearing at *post* formation stages:

ZAPATHA v. DAIRY MART, INC.

Supreme Judicial Court of Massachusetts.
381 Mass. 284, 408 N.E.2d 1370 (1980).

WILKINS, JUSTICE.

We are concerned here with the question whether Dairy Mart, Inc. (Dairy Mart), lawfully undertook to terminate a franchise agreement under which the Zapathas operated a Dairy Mart store on Wilbraham Road in Springfield. The Zapathas brought this action seeking to enjoin the termination of the agreement, alleging that the contract provision purporting to authorize the termination of the franchise agreement without cause was unconscionable and that Dairy Mart's conduct was an unfair and deceptive act or practice in violation of G.L. c. 93A. The judge ruled that Dairy Mart did not act in good faith, that the termination provision was unconscionable, and that Dairy Mart's termination of the agreement without cause was an unfair and deceptive act. We granted Dairy Mart's application for direct appellate review of a judgment that stated that Dairy Mart could terminate the agreement only for good cause and that the attempted termination was null and void. We reverse the judgments.

Mr. Zapatha is a high school graduate who had attended college for one year and had also taken college evening courses in business administration and business law. From 1952 to May, 1973, he was employed by a company engaged in the business of electroplating. He rose through the ranks to foreman and then to the position of operations manager, at one time being in charge of all metal finishing in the plant with 150 people working under him. In May, 1973, he was discharged and began looking for other opportunities, in particular a business of his own. Several months later he met with a representative of Dairy Mart. Dairy Mart operates a chain of franchised "convenience" stores. The Dairy Mart representative told Mr. Zapatha that working for Dairy Mart was being in business for one's self and that such a business was very stable and secure. Mr. Zapatha signed an application to be considered for a franchise. In addition, he was presented with a brochure entitled "Here's a Chance," which made certain representations concerning the status of a franchise holder.[1]

Dairy Mart approved Mr. Zapatha's application and offered him a store in Agawam. On November 8, 1973, a representative of Dairy Mart showed him a form of franchise agreement, entitled Limited Franchise and License Agreement, asked him to read it, and explained that his wife would have to sign the agreement as well.

Under the terms of the agreement, Dairy Mart would license the Zapathas to operate a Dairy Mart store, using the Dairy Mart trademark and associated insignia, and utilizing Dairy Mart's "confidential" merchandising methods. Dairy Mart would furnish the store and the equipment and would pay rent and gas and electric bills as well as certain other costs of doing business. In return Dairy Mart would receive a franchise fee, computed as a percentage of the store's gross sales. The Zapathas would have to pay for the starting inventory, and maintain a minimum stock of saleable merchandise thereafter. They were also

1. It included the following statements: " * * * you'll have the opportunity to own and run your own business * * * "; "We want to be sure we're hooking up with the right person. A person who sees the opportunity in owning his own business * * * who requires the security that a multi-million dollar parent company can offer him * * * who has the good judgment and business sense to take advantage of the unique independence that Dairy Mart offers its franchisees * * * We're looking for a partner * * * who can take the tools we offer and build a life of security and comfort * * *"

responsible for wages of employees, related taxes, and any sales taxes. The termination provision, which is set forth in full in the margin,[2] allowed either party, after twelve months, to terminate the agreement without cause on ninety days' written notice. In the event of termination initiated by it without cause, Dairy Mart agreed to repurchase the saleable merchandise inventory at retail prices, less 20%.

The Dairy Mart representative read and explained the termination provision to Mr. Zapatha. Mr. Zapatha later testified that, while he understood every word in the provision, he had interpreted it to mean that Dairy Mart could terminate the agreement only for cause. The Dairy Mart representative advised Mr. Zapatha to take the agreement to an attorney and said "I would prefer that you did." However, he also told Mr. Zapatha that the terms of the contract were not negotiable. The Zapathas signed the agreement without consulting an attorney. When the Zapathas took charge of the Agawam store, a representative of Dairy Mart worked with them to train them in Dairy Mart's methods of operation.

In 1974, another store became available on Wilbraham Road in Springfield, and the Zapathas elected to surrender the Agawam store. They executed a new franchise agreement, on an identical printed form, relating to the new location.

In November, 1977, Dairy Mart presented a new and more detailed form of "Independent Operator's Agreement" to the Zapathas for execution. Some of the terms were less favorable to the store operator than those of the earlier form of agreement.[3] Mr. Zapatha told representatives of Dairy Mart that he was content with the existing contract and had decided not to sign the new agreement. On January 20, 1978, Dairy Mart gave written notice to the Zapathas that their contract was being terminated effective in ninety days. The termination notice stated that Dairy Mart "remains available to enter into discussions with you with respect to entering into a new Independent Operator's Agreement; however, there is no assurance that Dairy Mart will enter into a new Agreement with you, or even if entered into, what terms such Agreement will contain." The notice also indicated that Dairy Mart was prepared to purchase the Zapathas' saleable inventory.

The judge found that Dairy Mart terminated the agreement solely because the Zapathas refused to sign the new agreement. He further found that, but for this one act, Dairy Mart did not behave in an unconscionable manner, in bad faith, or in disregard of its representations. There is no evidence that the

2. "(9) The term of this Limited Franchise and License Agreement shall be for a period of Twelve (12) months from date hereof, and shall continue uninterrupted thereafter. If DEALER desires to terminate after 12 months from date hereof, he shall do so by giving COMPANY a ninety (90) day written notice by Registered Mail of his intention to terminate. If COMPANY desires to terminate, it likewise shall give a ninety (90) day notice, except for the following reasons which shall not require any written notice and shall terminate the Franchise immediately:

"(a) Failure to pay bills to suppliers for inventory or other products when due.

"(b) Failure to pay Franchise Fees to COMPANY.

"(c) Failure to pay city, state or federal taxes as said taxes shall become due and payable.

"(d) Breach of any condition of this Agreement."

3. In his testimony, Mr. Zapatha said that he objected to a new provision under which Dairy Mart reserved the option to relocate an operator to a new location and to a requirement that the store be open from 7 A.M. to 11 P.M. every day. Previously the Zapathas' store had been open from 8 A.M. to 10 P.M.

There were other provisions, such as an obligation to pay future increases in the cost of heat and electricity, that were more burdensome to a franchisee. A few changes may have been to the advantage of the franchisee.

Zapathas undertook to discuss a compromise of the differences that led to the notice of termination.

On these basic facts, the judge ruled that the franchise agreement was subject to the sales article of the Uniform Commercial Code (G.L. c. 106, art. 2) and, even if it were not, the principles of unconscionability and good faith expressed in that article applied to the franchise agreement by analogy. He further ruled that (1) the termination provision of the agreement was unconscionable because it authorized termination without cause, (2) the termination without cause violated Dairy Mart's obligation of good faith, and (3) the termination constituted "an unfair method of competition and unfair and deceptive act within the meaning of G.L. c. 93A, § 2."

1. We consider first the question whether the franchise agreement involves a "transaction in goods" within the meaning of those words in article two of the Uniform Commercial Code (G.L. c. 106, § 2–103, as appearing in St.1957, c. 765, § 1), and that consequently the provisions of the sales articles of the Uniform Commercial Code govern the relationship between the parties. The Zapathas point specifically to the authority of a court to refuse to enforce "any clause of the contract" that the court finds "to have been unconscionable at the time it was made." G.L. c. 106, § 2–302, as appearing in St.1957, c. 765, § 1.[4] They point additionally to the obligation of good faith in the performance and enforcement of a contract imposed by G.L. c. 106, § 1–203, and to the specialized definition of "good faith" in the sales article as meaning "in the case of a merchant * * * honesty in fact and the observance of reasonable commercial standards of fair dealing in the trade." G.L. c. 106, § 2–103(1)(b), as appearing in St.1957, c. 765, § 1.[5]

We need not pause long over the question whether the franchise agreement and the relationship of the parties involved a transaction in goods. Certainly, the agreement required the plaintiffs to purchase goods from Dairy Mart. "Goods" for the purpose of the sales article means generally "all things * * * which are movable." G.L. c. 106, § 2–105(1), as appearing in St.1957, c. 765, § 1. However, the franchise agreement dealt with many subjects unrelated to the sale of goods by Dairy Mart. About 70% of the goods the plaintiffs sold were not purchased from Dairy Mart. Dairy Mart's profit was intended to come from the franchise fee and not from the sale of items to its franchisees. Thus, the sale of goods by Dairy Mart to the Zapathas was, in a commercial sense, a minor aspect of the entire relationship. We would be disinclined to import automatically all the provisions of the sales article into a relationship involving a variety

4. General Laws c. 106, § 2–302, as appearing in St.1957, c. 765, § 1, reads as follows:

"§ 2–302. Unconscionable Contract or Clause

"(1) If the court as a matter of law finds the contract or any clause of the contract to have been unconscionable at the time it was made the court may refuse to enforce the contract, or it may enforce the remainder of the contract without the unconscionable clause, or it may so limit the application of any unconscionable clause as to avoid any unconscionable result.

"(2) When it is claimed or appears to the court that the contract or any clause thereof may be unconscionable the parties shall be afforded a reasonable opportunity to present evidence as to its commercial setting, purpose, and effect to aid the court in making the determination."

5. Generally throughout the Uniform Commercial Code, "good faith" is defined to mean "honesty in fact in the conduct or transaction concerned." G.L. c. 106, § 1–201(19). The definition of "good faith" in the sales article includes a higher standard of conduct by adding a requirement that "merchants" observe "reasonable commercial standards of fair dealing in the trade." G.L. c. 106, § 2–103(1)(b). There is no doubt that Dairy Mart is a "merchant" as defined under the sales article. See G.L. c. 106, § 2–104.

of subjects other than the sale of goods, merely because the contract dealt in part with the sale of goods. Similarly, we would not be inclined to apply the sales article only to aspects of the agreement that concerned goods. Different principles of law might then govern separate portions of the same agreement with possibly inconsistent and unsatisfactory consequences.

We view the legislative statements of policy concerning good faith and unconscionability as fairly applicable to all aspects of the franchise agreement, not by subjecting the franchise relationship to the provisions of the sales article but rather by applying the stated principles by analogy. * * * This basic common law approach, applied to statutory statements of policy, permits a selective application of those principles expressed in a statute that reasonably should govern situations to which the statute does not apply explicitly. See Note, Article Two of the Uniform Commercial Code and Franchise Distribution Agreements, 1969 Duke L.J. 959, 980–985.

2. We consider first the plaintiffs' argument that the termination clause of the franchise agreement, authorizing Dairy Mart to terminate the agreement without cause, on ninety days' notice, was unconscionable by the standards expressed in G.L. c. 106, § 2–302.[6] The same standards are set forth in Restatement (Second) of Contracts § 234 (Tent.Drafts Nos. 1–7, 1973). The issue is one of law for the court, and the test is to be made as of the time the contract was made. G.L. c. 106, § 2–302(1), and comment 3 of the Official Comments. See *W.L. May, Co. v. Philco-Ford Corp.*, 273 Or. 701, 707, 543 P.2d 283 (1975). In measuring the unconscionability of the termination provision, the fact that the law imposes an obligation of good faith on Dairy Mart in its performance under the agreement should be weighed. See *W.L. May, Co. v. Philco-Ford Corp., supra* at 709, 543 P.2d 283.

The official comment to § 2–302 states that "[t]he basic test is whether, in the light of the general commercial background and the commercial needs of the particular trade or case, the clauses involved are so one-sided as to be unconscionable under the circumstances existing at the time of the making of the contract. * * * The principle is one of prevention of oppression and unfair surprise * * * and not of disturbance of allocation of risks because of superior bargaining power." Official Comment 1 to U.C.C. § 2–302.[7] Unconscionability is not defined in the Code, nor do the views expressed in the official comment provide a precise definition. The annotation prepared by the Massachusetts Advisory Committee on the Code states that "[t]he section appears to be intended to carry equity practice into the sales field." See 1 R. Anderson, Uniform Commercial Code § 2–302:7 (1970) to the same effect. This court has not had occasion to consider in any detail the meaning of the word "unconscionable" in § 2–302. Because there is no clear, all-purpose definition of "unconscionable," nor could there be, unconscionability must be determined on a case by case basis (see *Commonwealth v. Gustafsson*, 370 Mass. 181, 187, 346 N.E.2d 706 [1976]), giving particular attention to whether, at the time of the execution of the agreement, the contract provision could result in unfair surprise and was oppressive to the allegedly disadvantaged party.

6. The agreement permitted immediate termination on the occurrence of certain conditions which are not involved in this case.

7. The comment has been criticized as useless and at best ambiguous (J. White & R. Summers, The Uniform Commercial Code, 116 [1972]), and § 2–302 has been characterized as devoid of any specific content. Leff, Unconscionability and the Code—(The Emperor's New Clause, 115 U.Pa.L.Rev. 485, 487–489 [1967]). On the other hand, it has been said that the strength of the unconscionability concept is its abstraction, permitting judicial creativity. See Ellinghaus, In Defense of Unconscionability, 78 Yale L.J. 757 (1969).

We start with a recognition that the Uniform Commercial Code itself implies that a contract provision allowing termination without cause is not per se unconscionable. See *Corenswet, Inc. v. Amana Refrigeration, Inc.*, 594 F.2d 129, 138 (5th Cir.1979) ("We seriously doubt, however, that public policy frowns on any and all contract clauses permitting termination without cause."); *Division of Triple T Serv., Inc. v. Mobil Oil Corp.*, 60 Misc.2d 720, 730, 304 N.Y.S.2d 191 (1969), aff'd 34 A.D.2d 618, 311 N.Y.S.2d 961 (N.Y.1970). Section 2–309(3) provides that "[t]ermination of a contract by one party except on the happening of an agreed event requires that reasonable notification be received by the other party and an agreement dispensing with notification is invalid if its operation would be unconscionable." G.L. c. 106, § 2–309, as appearing in St.1957, c. 765, § 1. This language implies that termination of a sales contract without agreed "cause" is authorized by the Code, provided reasonable notice is given. * * * There is no suggestion that the ninety days' notice provided in the Dairy Mart franchise agreement was unreasonable.

We find no potential for unfair surprise to the Zapathas in the provision allowing termination without cause. We view the question of unfair surprise as focused on the circumstances under which the agreement was entered into.[8] The termination provision was neither obscurely worded, nor buried in fine print in the contract. Contrast Williams v. Walker-Thomas Furniture Co., 350 F.2d 445, 449 (D.C.Cir.1965). The provision was specifically pointed out to Mr. Zapatha before it was signed; Mr. Zapatha testified that he thought the provision was "straightforward," and he declined the opportunity to take the agreement to a lawyer for advice. The Zapathas had ample opportunity to consider the agreement before they signed it. Significantly, the subject of loss of employment was paramount in Mr. Zapatha's mind. He testified that he had held responsible jobs in one company from 1952 to 1973, that he had lost his employment, and that he "was looking for something that had a certain amount of security; something that was stable and something I could call my own." We conclude that a person of Mr. Zapatha's business experience and education should not have been surprised by the termination provision and, if in fact he was, there was no element of unfairness in the inclusion of that provision in the agreement. * * *

We further conclude that there was no oppression in the inclusion of a termination clause in the franchise agreement. We view the question of oppression as directed to the substantive fairness to the parties of permitting the termination provisions to operate as written. The Zapathas took over a going business on premises provided by Dairy Mart, using equipment furnished by Dairy Mart. As an investment, the Zapathas had only to purchase the inventory of goods to be sold but, as Dairy Mart concedes, on termination by it without cause Dairy Mart was obliged to repurchase all the Zapathas' saleable merchandise inventory, including items not purchased from Dairy Mart, at 80% of its retail value. There was no potential for forfeiture or loss of investment. There is no question here of a need for a reasonable time to recoup the franchisees'

8. As we shall note subsequently, the concept of oppression deals with the substantive unfairness of the contract term. This two-part test for unconscionability involves determining whether there was "an absence of meaningful choice on the part of one of the parties, together with contract terms which are unreasonably favorable to the other party." *Williams v. Walker-Thomas Furniture Co.*, 350 F.2d 445, 449 (D.C.Cir.1965). See *Corenswet, Inc. v. Amana Refrigeration, Inc.*, 594 F.2d 129, 139 (5th Cir.1979). The inquiry involves a search for components of "procedural" and "substantive" unconscionability. See generally Leff, Unconscionability and the Code—The Emperor's New Clause, 115 Pa.L. Rev. 485 (1967). * * *

initial investment. See * * * Gellhorn, Limitations on Contract Termination Rights—Franchise Cancellations, 1967 Duke L.J. 465, 479–481. The Zapathas were entitled to their net profits through the entire term of the agreement. They failed to sustain their burden of showing that the agreement allocated the risks and benefits connected with termination in an unreasonably disproportionate way and that the termination provision was not reasonably related to legitimate commercial needs of Dairy Mart. * * * To find the termination clause oppressive merely because it did not require cause for termination would be to establish an unwarranted barrier to the use of termination at will clauses in contracts in this Commonwealth, where each party received the anticipated and bargained for consideration during the full term of the agreement.

3. We see no basis on the record for concluding that Dairy Mart did not act in good faith, as that term is defined in the sales article ("honesty in fact and the observance of reasonable commercial standards of fair dealing in the trade"). G.L. c. 106, § 2–103(1)(b). There was no evidence that Dairy Mart failed to observe reasonable commercial standards of fair dealing in the trade in terminating the agreement. If there were such standards, there was no evidence of what they were.

The question then is whether there was evidence warranting a finding that Dairy Mart was not honest "in fact." The judge concluded that the absence of any commercial purpose for the termination other than the Zapathas' refusal to sign a new franchise agreement violated Dairy Mart's obligation of good faith. Dairy Mart's right to terminate was clear, and it exercised that right for a reason it openly disclosed. The sole test of "honesty in fact" is whether the person was honest. * * * We think that, whether or not termination according to the terms of the franchise agreement may have been arbitrary, it was not dishonest.[9]

The judge concluded that bad faith was also manifested by Dairy Mart's introductory brochure, which made representations of "security, comfort, and independence." Although this brochure and Mr. Zapatha's mistaken understanding that Dairy Mart could terminate the agreement only for cause could not be relied on to vary the clear terms of the agreement, the introductory brochure is relevant to the question of good faith. However, although the brochure misstated a franchisee's status as the owner of his own business, it shows no lack of honesty in fact relating to the right of Dairy Mart to terminate the agreement. Furthermore, by the time the Zapathas executed the second agreement, and even the first agreement, they knew that they would operate the franchise, but that they would not own the assets used in the business (except the goods to be sold); that the franchise agreement could be terminated by them and, at least in some circumstances, by Dairy Mart; and that in fact the major investment of funds would be made by Dairy Mart. We conclude that the use of the brochure did not warrant a finding of an absence of "honesty in fact." See *Corenswet, Inc. v. Amana Refrigeration, Inc.*, 594 F.2d 129, 138 (5th Cir.1979); *Mason v. Farmers Ins. Cos.*, 281 N.W.2d 344, 347 (Minn.1979).[10]

9. Under G.L. c. 106, § 1–203, "[e]very contract * * * imposes an obligation of good faith *in its performance or enforcement*" (emphasis supplied). We shall assume that an act of termination falls within the "performance" of the agreement. See Baker v. Ratzlaff, 1 Kan.App.2d 285, 288, 564 P.2d 153 (1977). But see Summers, "Good Faith" in General Contract Law and the Sales Provisions of the Uniform Commercial Code, 54 Va.L.Rev. 195, 252 (1968).

10. It has been suggested that, despite the limited definition of good faith in the Code, in some contexts the general obligation of good faith in § 1–203 can be used to import an objective standard of "decency, fairness or reasonableness in performance or enforcement"

4. Although what we have said disposes of arguments based on application by analogy of provisions of the sales article of the Uniform Commercial Code, there remains the question whether the judge's conclusions may be supported by some general principle of law. The provisions of the Uniform Commercial Code with which we have dealt by analogy in this opinion may not have sufficient breadth to provide protection from conduct that has produced an unfair and burdensome result, contrary to the spirit of the bargain, against which the law reasonably should provide protection. See Restatement (Second) of Contracts § 231 (Tent.Drafts Nos. 1–7 1973); Corbin, Contracts § 654A (C.K. Kaufman 1980 Supp.).[11]

The law of the Commonwealth recognizes that under some circumstances a party to a contract is not free to terminate it according to its terms. In *Fortune v. National Cash Register Co.,* 373 Mass. 96, 104–105, 364 N.E.2d 1251 (1977), we held that where an employer terminated an at will employment contract in order to deprive its employee of a portion of a commission due to him, the employer acted in bad faith. There, the employer correctly argued that termination of the employee was expressly permitted by the contract, and that all amounts payable under the terms of the contract at the time of termination had been paid. We concluded, however, that the law imposed an obligation of good faith on the employer and that the employer violated that obligation in terminating the relationship in order to avoid the payment of amounts earned, but not yet payable. The Legislature has limited the right of certain franchisors to terminate franchise agreements without cause.[12] On the other hand, the Legis-

into a contract to which it applies. Farnsworth, Good Faith Performance and Commercial Reasonableness Under the Uniform Commercial Code, 30 U.Chi.L.Rev. 666, 668 (1963). Good faith in this sense can be regarded as an "excluder," barring varied forms of unreasonable conduct in different circumstances. See Summers, "Good Faith" in General Contract Law and the Sales Provisions of the Uniform Commercial Code, 54 Va.L.Rev. 195, 196 (1968). Rather than stretch the Code definition of good faith beyond the plain meaning of the words used to define good faith, we prefer, as we are about to do, to analyze the question of fairness and reasonableness independently of the Code.

11. The unconscionability provision of G.L. c. 106, § 2–302, concerns circumstances determined at the time of the making of the agreement and relates only to the unconscionability of a term or terms of the contract. The "good faith" obligation of G.L. c. 106, § 1–203, deals with "honesty in fact," a question of the state of mind of the merchant or of his adherence to whatever reasonable commercial standards there may be in his trade. A merchant's conduct might not be dishonest and might adhere to reasonable standards, if any, in his trade and thus might be in good faith under § 1–203, and yet be unfair and unreasonably burdensome.

12. See G.L. c. 93B, § 4(3)(e), (4) concerning the cancellation or nonrenewal of a motor vehicle dealer's franchise and requiring good cause for manufacturer's or distributor's action; G.L. c. 93E, §§ 5, 5A, requiring cause for a supplier's termination or nonrenewal of a gasoline station dealer's agreement and imposing an obligation on the supplier to repurchase merchantable products sold to the dealer.

New Jersey has a Franchise Practices Act of general applicability that "prohibits a franchisor from terminating, cancelling or failing to renew a franchise without good cause which is defined as the failure by the franchisee to substantially comply with the requirements imposed on him by the franchise. N.J.S.A. 56:10–5." *Shell Oil Co. v. Marinello,* 63 N.J. 402, 409, 307 A.2d 598, 602 (1973), cert. denied, 415 U.S. 920, 94 S.Ct. 1421, 39 L.Ed.2d 475 (1974). Although the act applied only prospectively (N.J.S.A. 56:10–8), in the *Marinello* case the New Jersey Supreme Court applied the expressed public policy to bar termination of a service station operator's franchise in the absence of good cause, as so defined.

The special status of service station operators has prompted some courts to adopt common law rules requiring good cause for termination in spite of contract language that seemed to allow termination without cause. See *Arnott v. American Oil Co.,* 609 F.2d 873, 880–884 (8th Cir.1979), cert. denied, ___ U.S. ___, 100 S.Ct. 1852, 64 L.Ed.2d 272; *Atlantic Richfield Co. v. Razumic,* 480 Pa. 366, 390 A.2d 736 (1978); *Ashland Oil, Inc. v. Donahue,* 223 S.E.2d 433 (W.Va.1976).

lature has not adopted limitations on the right to terminate all franchise agreements in general, and its failure to do so is understandable because of the varied nature of franchise arrangements, where such varying factors exist as the relative bargaining power of the parties, the extent of investment by franchisees, and the degree to which the franchisee's goodwill, as opposed to that of the franchisor, is involved in the business operation. Further, in recognition of a general duty of good faith and fair dealing in business transactions under the law of the Commonwealth, c. 93A of the General Laws imposes on any person who engages in the conduct of any trade or commerce an obligation not to use any "unfair or deceptive acts or practices," as defined in G.L. c. 93A, § 2(a), as appearing in St.1967, c. 813, § 1, in dealing with another person who engages in any trade or commerce. G.L. c. 93A, § 11, as amended through St.1979, c. 72, § 2.

We thus analyze the case before us in terms of whether in terminating the agreement Dairy Mart failed to act in good faith in a broader sense than the term is used in G.L. c. 106, § 1–203, or dealt unfairly with the Zapathas, and whether Dairy Mart engaged in any unfair or deceptive act or practice. Much of what we said in discussing unconscionability and bad faith in terms of the Uniform Commercial Code applies here and need not be repeated. There is no showing that Dairy Mart usurped funds to which the Zapathas were reasonably entitled. Certainly Dairy Mart did not deprive the Zapathas of income that they had fairly earned, as the employer attempted to do in the *Fortune* case. We know nothing of any goodwill that the Zapathas had developed in their own name. There was no showing that, by their special efforts, the Zapathas built up the business at the Springfield store. As far as the record shows, they would lose no financial investment on termination and would not be left with unsaleable inventory or special purpose supplies and equipment. * * *

We are most concerned, as was the judge below, with the introductory circular that Dairy Mart furnished Mr. Zapatha. The judge ruled that the introductory circular contained misleading information concerning the Zapathas' status as franchisees. However, we cannot find in that document any deception or unfairness that has a bearing on the right of Dairy Mart to terminate the agreement as it did. A representative read the termination clause to Mr. Zapatha before the Zapathas signed the agreement. Mr. Zapatha declined an invitation to take the agreement to a lawyer. He understood individually every word of the termination clause. Moreover, when Dairy Mart terminated the agreement, it offered to negotiate further, and the Zapathas did not take the opportunity to do so.

Unless we were to take the position that termination without cause of a franchise agreement of the character involved here is prohibited invariably by the law of the Commonwealth, a position we decline to adopt * * *, Dairy Mart lawfully terminated the agreement because there was no showing that in terminating it Dairy Mart engaged in any unfair, deceptive, or bad faith conduct.

Judgments reversed.

[Some footnotes omitted. Those retained have been renumbered. Eds.]

SUMMERS, "GOOD FAITH" IN GENERAL CONTRACT LAW AND THE SALES PROVISIONS OF THE UNIFORM COMMERCIAL CODE, 54 Va.L.Rev. 195, 199–202 (1968).

What is the best way to determine a judge's meaning when he uses the phrase "good faith"? In the case law taken as a whole, does the term have a single general meaning of its own, or perhaps several such meanings? (The answers to these questions are closely linked.) Sometimes what a judge means by good faith will be instantly obvious, but frequently it will not be. When not, it may be that he is using the phrase loosely. But even if he is using it with care, there may still be unclarity. He might indicate only that, in a given context, parties are to act in good faith or that a party did or did not act in good faith, without elaborating at all. Or he might elaborate without communicating in any specific way—for example, by laying down some very general definition of good faith, such as acting "honestly" or "being faithful to one's duty or obligation." The analyst of such an opinion is likely to inquire: What is the meaning of good faith itself? He seems to assume that the phrase has some general meaning or meanings, one of which the judge presumably intends.

One of the principal theses of this Article is that in cases of doubt, a lawyer will determine more accurately what the judge means by using the phrase "good faith" if he does not ask what good faith itself means, but rather asks: What, in the actual or hypothetical situation, does the judge intend to rule out by his use of this phrase? Once the relevant form of bad faith is thus identified, the lawyer can, if he wishes, assign a specific meaning to good faith by formulating an "opposite" for the species of bad faith being ruled out. For example, a judge may say: "A public authority must act in good faith in letting bids." And from the facts or the language of the opinion it may appear that the judge is, in effect, saying: "The defendant acted in bad faith because he let bids only as a pretense to conceal his purpose to award the contract to a favored bidder." It can then be said that "acting in good faith" here simply means: letting bids without a preconceived design to award the contract to a favored bidder.

If good faith had a general meaning or meanings of its own—that is, if it were either univocal or ambiguous—there would seldom be occasion to derive a meaning for it from an opposite; its specific uses would almost always be readily and immediately understood. But good faith is not that kind of doctrine. In contract law, taken as a whole, good faith is an "excluder." It is a phrase without general meaning (or meanings) of its own and serves to exclude a wide range of heterogeneous forms of bad faith. In a particular context the phrase takes on specific meaning, but usually this is only by way of contrast with the specific form of bad faith actually or hypothetically ruled out. Aristotle was one of the first to recognize that the function of some words and phrases is not to convey general, "extractable" meanings of their own, but rather is to exclude one or more of a variety of things. He thought "voluntary" was such a word. And the late Professor J.L. Austin of Oxford made much of "excluders."

Note: Good Faith in the Uniform Commercial Code

As we have seen, Uniform Commercial Code section 1–203 generally provides that "[e]very contract or duty within this Act imposes an obligation of good faith in its performance or enforcement." Thirteen sections of Article Two of the Code (on the sale of goods) explicitly require good faith. Nineteen sections of Article Two include comments which also use the phrase. In Article One ("General Provisions") good faith is defined in section 1–201(19) to mean (unless the context otherwise requires) "honesty in fact in the conduct or transaction concerned." However, in Article Two on sales of goods, section 2–103(1)(b) states that "unless the context otherwise requires * * * good faith, in the case of a merchant means honesty in fact and the observance of reasonable commercial standards of fair dealing in the trade."

Problem 9–4

(1) Frank is a book wholesaler in New York City, John a book retailer in a University town where a great law school exists. John has a lot of used copies of a great commercial law casebook about to be superseded by a fourth edition, a fact known to John but not to Frank. John sells a large number of the books to Frank without disclosing the foregoing fact. Later, Frank discovers the fact and seeks to rescind. What result? Assume John's non-disclosure does not constitute "fraud" under tort law. Assume, too, that John has broken no warranty. See UCC 1–203 and 1–201(19). Does UCC 1–203 apply? Is this the only relevant provision? Among other things, what of UCC 1–103? To make effective use of UCC 1–103, what kind of extra-Code case law would you hope to find?

(2) For three years, Ice, Inc., a small ice manufacturer, has been selling roughly 25 tons of ice a month to the Sam McGee Storage, Co., pursuant to a contract one clause of which empowers McGee to order "such ice as it requires." On January 20, McGee, having decided to expand its operations, ordered three hundred tons of ice from Ice, Inc. for February. Ice, Inc., of course, could not supply this amount, and so notified McGee. McGee then declared itself "free to buy all our needs from Prime, Inc., a manufacturer more our size." Ice, Inc. has come to you for advice. What would you advise? Among other things, see UCC 1–203, 1–201(19), 2–306, 2–103(1)(b) and 2–311(1).

(3) Rowan brokered custom-made (new and old) cars, a very special market. Martin, his best customer, wanted a special car for which he was willing to pay dearly $15,000 provided he could get it in time to drive it in the Grand Nationale. Tucker, an always-do-well "consumer" known to Rowan, had such a car which he agreed to sell Rowan for $13,000. Later and just before the Grand Nationale, Tucker, having learned of Rowan's resale price to Martin, insisted that Rowan pay $14,500 "or the deal is off." Rowan finally agreed, got the car, resold it to Martin for $15,000 and then came to you for advice. Does he have any recourse against Tucker? Among other things, see UCC 2–209(1), and relevant comments, 1–203, 1–201(19).

(4) Milk-O-Wheat, Inc. wanted to buy some grain. It had never dealt with seller before, but nonetheless placed a binding order with seller for 100 tons of wheat "delivery no later than August 2, our terminal." One hundred tons of good wheat arrived but not until August 4, due to an unexpected railway disaster. The delay did not slow up Milk-O-Wheat's operations any, but it rejected anyway, since the market had fallen and it was possible to get such wheat much more cheaply elsewhere. You are to assume that in the trade, prompt deliveries are expected, for usually the buyer is relying on such for the efficient conduct of his operations. Seller comes to you for advice. What would you advise? Among other things, see UCC 2–601, 2–508, 2–504, 1–203, 1–201(19), and 2–103(1)(b).

SECTION 5. SUPPLEMENTAL GENERAL PRINCIPLES

Section 1–103 of the Uniform Commercial Code provides:

Unless displaced by the particular provisions of this Act, the principles of law and equity, including the law merchant and the law relative to capacity to contract, principal and agent, estoppel, fraud, misrepresentation, duress, coercion, mistake, bankruptcy, or other validating or invalidating cause shall supplement its provisions.

Equitable principles (not displaced) generally remain intact under the foregoing provision, *even in the face of contrary contractual provisions.* Thus, the parties cannot contract out of the bearing of most equitable notions having to do with estoppel, fraud, misrepresentation, duress, coercion, mistake and the like. See, generally, Summers, *General Equitable Principles Under Section 1–103 of the Uniform Commercial Code,* 72 Nw.U.L.Rev. 906 (1978).

Problem 9–5

(1) Section 2–509(3) of Article Two provides: "In any case not within subsection (1) or (2), the risk of loss passes to the buyer on his receipt of the goods if the seller is a merchant, otherwise the risk passes to the buyer on tender of delivery". Assume the buyer hires the seller to build a boat mast. After the mast is under way, it occurs to the seller that the work should be insured. The buyer represents that insurance he already has covers the work, and, relying on this the seller does not insure. After completion but before delivery, the mast is destroyed by fire and the buyer discovers that his policy does not cover the mast. The seller sues the buyer for the price under section 2–709. The buyer defends by citing section 2–509(3) under which the risk of loss was on the seller, and denies liability. What result? Assume the preamble to the contract between buyer and seller recites that their agreement is the sole controlling law governing the rights of the parties. Would this affect the result? Cf. Mercanti v. Persson, 160 Conn. 468, 280 A.2d 137 (1971).

(2) Seller was in the business of selling lumber to various parties, including Buyer. Buyer knew Seller was operating "close to the margin". Buyer stopped payment of checks issued to pay for the lumber sold and delivered to Buyer and offered to pay only a sum $2000 less than that due under the contract "in full settlement." Seller told Buyer that if Seller failed to get the money, "he would be ruined financially." Buyer told Seller that he, Buyer, had "taken steps to stop payment of money due Seller from other parties too". Seller then agreed to the settlement at $2000 less. Is the settlement valid? Would it make any difference if the settlement recited that the agreement was in all respects a valid and binding contract? Cf. Vyne v. Glenn, 41 Mich. 112, 1 N.W. 997 (undated).

PART TWO

THE AGREEMENT STAGE

CHAPTER TEN

CONTRACT FORMATION

SECTION 1. INTRODUCTION

A classic function of courts and contract law is to determine when parties negotiating for an agreed exchange have concluded an enforceable bargain. At what point have they crossed the line beyond which neither party can withdraw without liability for breach?

Under the Restatement, Second, of Contracts, the answer depends upon concepts with which you should now be familiar. First, contract is defined as a "promise or a set of promises for the breach of which the law gives a remedy. * * *" Section 1. Not all promises, however, are contracts. In bargain transactions, defined in Section 3 of the Restatement, Second as an agreed exchange of promises or performances, there must be a "bargain in which there is a manifestation of mutual assent to the exchange and a consideration." Section 17(1). According to Section 22(1), the manifestation of mutual assent to an exchange "ordinarily takes the form of an offer or proposal by one party followed by an acceptance by the other party or parties. * * *" (An offer is defined as a "manifestation of willingness to enter into a bargain, so made as to justify another person in understanding that his assent to that bargain is invited and will conclude it." Section 24. An acceptance of an offer is defined as a "manifestation of assent to the terms thereof made by the offeree in a manner invited or required by the offer." Section 50(1).)

To constitute consideration, "a performance or a return promise must be bargained for," Section 71(1), i.e., "sought by the promisor in exchange for his promise and * * * given by the promisee in exchange for that promise." Section 71(2).

How does Article 2 conform to the Restatement, Second formula, "Offer plus acceptance plus consideration = contract?"

First, contract "means the total legal obligation which results from the parties' agreement as affected by this Act and any other applicable rules of law." UCC 1–201(11). In contract formation disputes, the relevant provisions of "this Act" are found in Article 2, Part 2, as supplemented by UCC 1–103.

Second, agreement means the "bargain of the parties in fact as found in their language or by implication from other circumstances including course of dealing or usage of trade or course of performance as provided in this Act (Sections 1–205 and 2–208)." Note that the definition of "bargain * * * in fact" does not include a requirement that there be a promise. Further, although the concept of bargain is consistent with an agreed exchange, there is no explicit requirement that the exchange be bargained for. In short, although the agreement may contain promises and the exchange may be bargained for, there is no explicit requirement of either a promise or consideration to satisfy the definition. See Murray, *The Article 2 Prism: The Underlying Philosophy of the Uniform Commercial Code,* 21 Washburn L.J. 1 (1981).

Third, UCC 2–204 is the key formation section in Article 2, Part 2. Read it, please. Note that UCC 2–204(1) and (2) sweep away technical rules on how and when the contract is made: Important evidence will be "conduct by both parties which recognizes the existence of such a contract." Further, UCC 2–204(3) provides a standard to deal with disputes where one party withdraws before all of the material terms have been agreed: "Even though one or more terms are left open a contract for sale does not fail for indefiniteness if the parties have intended to make a contract and there is a reasonably certain basis for giving an appropriate remedy." Thus, there are no rules specifying the quantity of agreement that must be reached before a contract can be formed. Rather, the issue turns on what the parties have "intended" and whether the court can fill the "gaps" with reasonable certainty when giving an appropriate remedy. By "intended," UCC 2–204(3) presumably means an intention to conclude the bargain without further agreement, rather than an intention that the bargain be legally binding. Compare Restatement, Second 21 ("neither real nor apparent intention that a promise be legally binding is essential to the formation of a contract. * * * ").

Read Article 2, Part 2, including the Comments and then work through the following materials.

SECTION 2. OFFER AND ACCEPTANCE—UCC 2–204, 2–205 AND 2–206

In the following problems, first formulate the statutory issues posed and then resolve them as best you can from the Code.

Problem 10–1

S, a retailer, sold personal computers manufactured by M. After preliminary negotiations, B, a corporation, mailed to S a printed form prepared by B inviting S to make an "offer" to sell 10 described personal computers for $25,000. The form contained five paragraphs of printed matter, inserted on a single page between blank lines to be filled in at the top and a signature line at the bottom. The third paragraph above the signature line provided: THIS OFFER WILL BE HELD OPEN FOR 30 DAYS AFTER RECEIPT BY THE OFFEREE. S filled in the blanks as requested by B, signed the form, dating it May 30, 1987, and returned it to B, who received it on June 3, 1987. On June 15, 1987, S notified B by telegram that the offer was revoked: A better deal had been worked out with C for the personal computers. On June 16, 1987, B telegraphed to S an acceptance of the offer, which was received the same day. B insists that there was a contract. Is B correct? Start with UCC 2–205.

Problem 10–2

S, a manufacturer, had a quantity of used computer hardware which it was willing to sell with a limited warranty for $50,000. On June 1, B, a retailer, examined the equipment and discussed terms. An oral agreement was reached on all terms except price. On June 5, B mailed S a signed offer to purchase the equipment for $40,000 and enclosed a $4,000 check as a down payment. S received the offer and check on June 7 and, on June 8, deposited the check in its business account. S did not communicate with B. On June 10, S received an offer from C to purchase the equipment for $50,000 cash. The offer was accepted the same day. On June 11, S informed B that its offer had been rejected and mailed to B a cashier's check for $4,000.

B claims that a contract was formed on June 8 when S deposited the check. B supports his claim with the following arguments: (1) The offer should be construed as inviting an acceptance "in any manner and by any medium reasonable in the circumstances," and depositing the check was a reasonable manner of acceptance, UCC 2–206(1)(a); (2) Depositing the check was a "reasonable mode of acceptance" under UCC 2–206(2); and (3) The sending by B and the deposit by S of the check was "conduct by both parties which recognizes the existence of a contract," UCC 2–204(1), or demonstrated that the "parties have intended to make a contract" under UCC 2–204(3).

Which, if any, of these arguments should the court accept?

Problem 10–3

S, a manufacturer of fertilizer, and B, a farmer, had done business for 10 years. When fertilizer was needed, B would order by telegram a specific quantity and quality and S would fill the order at S's current wholesale price, shipping the goods to B by carrier FOB point of shipment. Frequently, S would ship less or more than what B ordered, but the deviation would never exceed 15%. B invariably accepted and paid for what was actually shipped without objection. On July 10, 1987, a time of price instability in the fertilizer market, B telegraphed to S an order for 500 bags of a specified fertilizer "for prompt shipment." The wholesale price on that date was $18 per bag. On July 12, 1987, S shipped 400 bags of fertilizer to B and mailed an invoice for the wholesale price on that date, $20.00. On July 15, 1987, while the goods were still in transit and the wholesale price was $25.00 per bag, S notified B that the offer had been rejected and diverted the shipment to C, who agreed to pay $26 per bag.

B claimed that there was a contract for the sale of 500 bags of fertilizer on July 12, 1987 at $20.00. B relied upon UCC 2–206(1)(b), asserting that this was precisely the case contemplated in Comment 4. Is B correct?

MID-SOUTH PACKERS v. SHONEY'S, INC.

United States Court of Appeals, Fifth Circuit, 1985.
761 F.2d 1117.

Before WILLIAMS, JOLLY, and HILL, CIRCUIT JUDGES.

PER CURIAM:

This diversity action on a Mississippi contract is before us following the district court's entry of summary judgment in favor of plaintiff Mid-South Packers, Inc., (Mid-South) and against defendant Shoney's, Inc., (Shoney's). We affirm.

I.

The facts, as viewed in the light most favorable to Shoney's, are as follows. In the spring of 1982, Mid-South and Shoney's engaged in negotiations for the sale by Mid-South to Shoney's of various pork products including bacon and ham. A business meeting was held between representatives of the two companies on April 17, 1982, at the offices of Mid-South in Tupelo, Mississippi. The discussion concerned prices and terms at which Mid-South could supply bacon and ham to Shoney's. At this meeting, Mid-South submitted a letter styled "Proposal" that set forth prices and terms at which Mid-South would supply Shoney's with various types of meat. The letter also provided that Shoney's would be informed forty-five days prior to any adjustment in price. The letter contained neither quantity nor durational terms. Shoney's expressed neither assent to nor rejection of the prices outlined in the letter. Shoney's estimated its needs from Mid-South at 80,000 pounds of meat per week. The legal effect of the letter proposal is the center of the controversy.

In July 1982, Shoney's began purchasing goods from Mid-South. The transactions were initiated by Shoney's, either through purchase orders or through telephone calls. On the day following each shipment, Mid-South sent invoices to Shoney's containing additional provisions for payment of both fifteen percent per annum interest on accounts not paid within seven days and reasonable collection costs, including attorney's fees. Shoney's bought vast quantities of bacon from Mid-South until August 12, 1982. On that date, Mid-South informed Shoney's at a meeting of their representatives that the price for future orders of bacon would be raised by $0.10 per pound, due to a previous error in computation by Mid-South. Shoney's objected to the price modification, apparently in reliance on the forty-five day notice provision contained in the disputed letter proposal. After negotiations, Mid-South agreed to increase the price by only $0.07 per pound. Shoney's neither agreed nor refused to purchase at the new price. Mid-South's new proposal was never reduced to writing.

On the first Shoney's purchase order sent after the August 12 meeting, Shoney's requested shipment at the old lower price. When Mid-South received the purchase order its representative, Morris Ates, called Shoney's representative, Ray Harmon, and advised Harmon that Mid-South would only deliver at the new higher price. The uncontradicted testimony of Ates is that Harmon told Ates to ship the bacon and to note the higher price on Shoney's purchase order. The bacon was shipped, and an invoice at the new price followed as did Shoney's payment, also at the new price.

From August 18 until October 5, 1982, Shoney's placed numerous orders for goods, including bacon, with Mid-South. Some if not all of these orders involved telephone conversations between representatives of the two companies, at which time Mid-South again quoted its increased selling price. The telephone conversations were followed by written purchase orders from Shoney's which quoted both the new price from Mid-South and a price computed at the original amount of $0.07 less per pound. In all cases, the orders were filled by Mid-South and invoiced at the new price. These invoices also included the additional terms providing for interest on delinquent accounts and reasonable collection costs. Shoney's paid Mid-South's quoted prices in all instances except the final order. On the final order before Shoney's began purchasing from another supplier, Shoney's offset the amount due on the invoice by $26,208, the amount allegedly overcharged on prior orders as a result of the $0.07 price increase.

Mid-South then brought this action to recover the amount offset plus interest and reasonable collection costs, including attorney's fees, as provided in the invoices. Shoney's admits that it owes $8,064.00 of the offset to Mid-South, inasmuch as this amount is attributable to orders placed after the expiration of the forty-five day notice period which, Shoney's contends, commenced on August 12 when Mid-South asked for the price increase.

II.

Shoney's contends that it accepted the proposal of Mid-South to supply it meat by placing orders with Mid-South, thereby forming a binding contract between the parties. Shoney's characterizes the contract as a "requirements contract" and asserts that the quantity term under the contract was that amount it reasonably and in good faith required. Accordingly, Shoney's argues that the notice provision contained in the letter proposal contractually bound Mid-South to notify Shoney's forty-five days before increasing its prices.

Mid-South asserts that the proposal was at most a "firm offer." Mid-South argues that under Miss.Code Ann. § 75–2–205 (1972), Uniform Commercial Code § 2–205, (hereinafter referred to as U.C.C. or the Code), a firm offer is irrevocable despite a lack of consideration "during the time stated or if no time is stated for a reasonable time; but in no event may such period of irrevocability exceed three (3) months." Thus, Mid-South contends that under any construction of the document, the offer must have expired three months after April 17, 1982, the date of the letter proposal, or on approximately July 17, 1982; therefore, it asserts the right on August 12, 1982, to increase the selling price without notice.

The district court, on consideration of cross summary judgment motions, adopted Mid-South's theory, holding that no long-term requirements contract was created and that each purchase order constituted a separate contract for the amount stated at the price required by Mid-South.

Requirements contracts are recognized in Mississippi and are not void for indefiniteness. Miss.Code Ann. § 75–2–306(1). However, an essential element of a requirements contract is the promise of the buyer to purchase exclusively from the seller either the buyer's entire requirements or up to a specified amount. * * * Absent such a commitment, the requirements contract fails for want of consideration. * * *

Ray Harmon, Shoney's agent in the transaction, maintained that Shoney's at all times had the right to purchase goods from suppliers other than Mid-South, that Shoney's continued to purchase from Mid-South because it was satisfied with its service and the quality of its goods, and that the purchase orders sent by Shoney's to Mid-South beginning in July 1982 "would have been the only commitment (Shoney's) would have made." Mid-South agrees that Shoney's had the right to change suppliers. Thus, by Shoney's own admission, no requirements contract could have arisen from the April 17 letter proposal and the meeting at which it was discussed.

Under the Code, the letter proposal and surrounding negotiations constituted, at most, a "firm offer" which was irrevocable, without consideration, only for a period of three months commencing on April 17 and ending on July 17, 1982. Miss.Code Ann. § 75–2–205.[2] Thus, Mid-South had the right, after July 17, to raise its offered price as it did and the district court was correct in so holding.

The district court was also correct in holding that each purchase order stood on its own as a contract between Shoney's and Mid-South. More specifically, Mid-South's letter proposal was its offer in the sense that it was a promise to sell at the listed prices, justifying Shoney's in understanding that its assent, *i.e.*, its purchase orders or telephone calls, would close the bargain. *Boese-Hilburn Co. v. Dean Machinery Co.*, 616 S.W.2d 520 (Mo.App.1981); *Propane Industrial, Inc.*, 429 F.Supp. at 219; 1 A. Corbin, Contracts § 11 at 25 (1963); 1 S. Williston, Contracts § 24A (3d ed.1957); Restatement (Second) of Contracts § 24 (1981)

2. Section 75–2–205 provides, in part:

An offer by a merchant to buy or sell goods in a signed writing which by its terms gives assurance that it will be held open is not revocable, for lack of consideration, during the time stated or if no time is stated for a reasonable time, but in no event may such period of irrevocability exceed three (3) months.

(offer as promise). Thus, each time Shoney's manifested its assent, in telephone calls or purchase orders to Mid-South, a new and independent contract between the parties was created. *See Coastal Chemical Corporation v. Filtrol Corporation,* 374 F.2d 108, 109 (5th Cir.1967) (Mississippi law); 1A A. Corbin, Contracts § 157 at 40–46 (where the theory here espoused is discussed at length).

Mid-South's offer, held open in its discretion at least after July 17, was properly revoked and replaced by the offer of a seven-cent price increase at the August 12 meeting. *Cf.* 1A A. Corbin § 157 at 46. Shoney's accepted this new offer for the first time on August 18 when Harmon, having been informed by Ates that Mid-South would not sell except at the new price, ordered shipment. Thereafter, Shoney's created separate contracts and obligated itself to pay the new price each time it mailed purchase orders with that price noted on them.[3] Shoney's practice of also noting the old price on the purchase orders had no contractual significance since Harmon admitted that the practice was "a tracking procedure" used by Shoney's internally in order to determine the difference between the old price and the new. Ates' testimony is uncontradicted that Harmon also told him this.

In addition, Harmon admitted that Shoney's ordered at and paid the new price with the intention of causing Mid-South to believe that Shoney's had accepted the new price so that the shipments would continue; and Mid-South attached precisely that significance to Shoney's conduct. Shoney's secretly harbored intent to later deduct the difference between the old and new price could not bind Mid-South. *See, e.g., Hotchkiss v. National City Bank,* 200 Fed. 287, 293 (S.D.N.Y.1911) (Hand, J.), *aff'd* 231 U.S. 50, 34 S.Ct. 20, 58 L.Ed. 115 (1913) (only manifested assent is binding); Restatement (Second) of Contracts §§ 20(2)(a), 201(2)(a) (1981) (same). Conduct may bind a party to a contract if it "show[s] agreement." Miss.Code Ann. § 75–2–204(1); § 75–2–207(3). "Agreement" of the parties must be manifested either in language or conduct in the circumstances. Miss.Code Ann. § 75–1–201(3). The only manifestations Shoney's made were those consistent with assent to Mid-South's new offer. Finally, the parties' "course of performance" is consistent only with Mid-South's expressed offer and Shoney's expressed acceptance of the new price. Miss.Code Ann. § 75–1–205(3)–(4); *Cf.* Miss.Code Ann. § 75–2–202(a).

Shoney's remedy under the circumstances was either to reserve whatever right it might have had to the old price by sending its purchase orders with an "explicit reservation," Miss.Code Ann. § 75–1–207, or to find a supplier who would sell at an acceptable price. No rational theory of the law of contracts could permit Shoney's to manifest acceptance of Mid-South's new offer, thus inducing performance, and then revoke that acceptance and demand compliance with the terms of the prior, withdrawn offer. *See* Miss.Code Ann. § 75–2–606(1)(b); § 75–2–607(1). Hence, the entire $26,208 offset by Shoney's is due and owing Mid-South and the district court's judgment, to this extent, was proper.

* * *

[The Court held that Mid-South's invoices containing additional provisions for payment and attorney fees were "confirmations" under UCC 2–207(1) and that the "additional" terms became part of the agreement under UCC 2–207(2).]

Affirmed. [Some footnotes omitted.]

3. The purchase orders also contained a column entitled "amount" which showed the total purchase price arrived at by multiplying the per unit price by the quantity ordered. On most of the post-August 12 purchase orders, Shoney's used the new higher price in computing the amount total.

Note: Conduct and Mutual Intent to Contract

When does conduct by both parties support a mutual intent to contract, even though material terms have not been agreed? The issue was raised with disputed results in a complex litigation between Bethlehem Steel Corporation and Litton Industries. After extensive negotiations, Litton agreed to construct a newly designed ore vessel for Bethlehem at a fixed price. Thereafter, the parties agreed in writing that Bethlehem should have an option, for a stated period of time, to have Litton construct up to five additional ore vessels of the same design at a stated base price of \$20.4 million. If Bethlehem exercised an option, the base price was subject to escalation to be agreed by the parties for both labor and material costs under stated indices, with the escalation computed to the date a contract was executed. Despite Litton's initial requests, Bethlehem refused to exercise the option or to negotiate over price. After Litton closed its shipyard, however, Bethlehem sought to exercise the option for three additional vessels. Both parties negotiated over the escalated price but, despite apparent good faith efforts, were unable to agree. Bethlehem then sued Litton for \$95,000,000 in damages, claiming that despite the failure to agree on price, the parties intended to contract for the three vessels, see UCC 2–204(3), and that the court should supply a reasonable, escalated price, see UCC 2–305(1).

The trial court treated the intention issue as a question of fact and concluded that, given the importance of the escalation clause to the contract, the complexity of the determinations involved, and the rapid inflation underway, the parties did not intend to contract unless an agreement could be reached on price. This decision was reversed, on appeal, by a three judge panel, Bethlehem Steel Corp. v. Litton Industries, Inc., 35 UCC Rep.Serv. 1091 (Pa.Super.1982). On rehearing, a panel of seven judges reversed the decision of the three judge panel and reinstated the decision of the trial court to the effect that there was no contract. 468 A.2d 748 (Pa. Super.1983). The "panel of seven's" decision was affirmed by an equally divided Supreme Court in Bethlehem Steel Corp. v. Litton Industries, Inc., 507 Pa. 88, 488 A.2d 581 (1985).

The supreme court justices voting to affirm the decision of the trial court stressed: (1) the writings of the parties were ambiguous and many terms were left open; (2) there was competent evidence to support the conclusion that the conduct of the parties was inconsistent with an intent to be bound; (3) there was no reasonably certain basis for giving an appropriate remedy; and (4) the "option" was not supported by consideration.

Justice Zappala, speaking for the justices voting to find a contract concluded, on the other hand, that Litton had acted in bad faith in negotiating over the escalation provision. Despite Bethlehem's willingness to consider a number of price indices, Litton, according to Justice Zappala, "did not intend to develop any language regarding a proposed ship construction contract" and "prevented execution of a ship construction contract by failing to bargain in good faith on the open terms." 488 A.2d at 600. On his view, this was a breach for which Bethlehem was entitled to damages.

SECTION 3. OFFER AND ACCEPTANCE—THE BATTLE OF THE FORMS AND UCC 2–207

Every student knows of the "mirror-image" rule of general contract law: An "acceptance" which varies the terms of an offer is not an acceptance at all, but a counter-offer. This is an old rule, and it makes some sense. But consider its application to the following hypothetical case: Seller sends a written offer to Buyer offering to sell processed rubber at a stated price. Buyer replies by ordering a quantity of rubber from Seller within the terms of Seller's offer, except that Buyer's order form states at the bottom in conspicuous type: "The acceptance of this order you must in any event promptly acknowledge." Seller fails promptly to acknowledge, but ships the rubber. When the rubber arrives, Buyer refuses it, having preferred to buy elsewhere, say because the price has fallen. Seller sues Buyer for breach of contract. Buyer defends claiming that because of his "acknowledgment clause" in his order form, this form was not an acceptance, but was a counter-offer which was never accepted since Seller did not acknowledge promptly. Held: for Buyer, citing the mirror-image rule. Cf. Poel v. Brunswick-Balke-Collender Co., 216 N.Y. 310, 110 N.E. 619 (1915).

There have been such decisions. And they can be traced to the influence of the mirror-image rule. If such decisions are objectionable, then they are peculiarly objectionable in the commercial field, for the scope for such decisions there is great. This is so because of the widespread and long-standing practice whereby many sellers and buyers of goods use their own standard forms in doing business: Seller sends an offer on a form containing printed terms; Buyer "accepts" using his own form with printed terms, or vice versa. Any reasonably close correspondence between the two sets of terms is, in many lines of business, sheerest coincidence. Yet, the parties nonetheless go forward with their transactions. When something goes wrong, in the unusual case, then is there a contract? If so, on what terms—Seller's? Buyer's? Courts applying the mirror-image rule, willy-nilly, might say there is no contract at all, and not even reach the second of these questions. Objections to this solution have been several, as some students once noted:

NOTE, 111 U.Pa.L.Rev. 132, 133 (1962).

"At common law and under the Uniform Sales Act, a purported acceptance which modifies the terms of the offer is a rejection and a counter-offer. Although this rule is supposed to promote certainty in the terms of the agreement, businessmen frequently undertake performance in reliance on the mistaken assumption that such an "acceptance" has created a contract. Moreover, in the context of modern business practice of using standard forms to transmit and acknowledge orders, the rule encourages a "battle of forms"—a constant effort by businessmen to gain an advantage in their transactions by qualifying their obligations by means of forms containing unilaterally beneficial conditions. In addition, the rule provides a loophole for parties wishing to extricate themselves from unfavorable deals which in commercial understanding have been closed." [Footnotes omitted.]

The Official Text of section 2–207 went through still more changes, (including the one reflected in the Roto-Lith case at p. 453 infra), until it took its present form in the 1962 Official Text, which continues to be the form set forth below. (Revisions in the Official Comments were made in 1966.)

§ 2–207. Additional Terms in Acceptance or Confirmation

(1) A definite and seasonable expression of acceptance or a written confirmation which is sent within a reasonable time operates as an acceptance even though it states terms additional to or different from those offered or agreed upon, unless acceptance is expressly made conditional on assent to the additional or different terms.

(2) The additional terms are to be construed as proposals for addition to the contract. Between merchants such terms become part of the contract unless:

(a) the offer expressly limits acceptance to the terms of the offer;

(b) they materially alter it; or

(c) notification of objection to them has already been given or is given within a reasonable time after notice of them is received.

(3) Conduct by both parties which recognizes the existence of a contract is sufficient to establish a contract for sale although the writings of the parties do not otherwise establish a contract. In such case the terms of the particular contract consist of those terms on which the writings of the parties agree, together with any supplementary terms incorporated under any other provisions of this Act.

Problem 10–4

Review the final version of UCC 2–207. It contemplates contract formation by at least three routes. Route A consists of that part of subsection (1) up to the comma. Route B is that which appears after the comma in subsection (1). Route C is found in UCC 2–207(3). Before going farther in this Chapter, answer the following questions.

1. May a contract be formed *via* Route B by conduct? If so, does Route B overlap with Route C?

2. To which of these routes does UCC 2–207(2) relate?

3. Which route is intended to change the "mirror image" rule?

4. Does any route purport, under some circumstances, to preserve the "mirror image" rule? What circumstances?

5. How would you state the general goals of UCC 2–207?

Today, there is a vast body of case law under 2–207. Indeed, almost any law firm with a substantial commercial practice will have at least one "2–207 case" in its office at any given time. One of your co-editors knows of a firm that had five such cases at one time. The section is not only of great practical significance, it tends also to be neglected (or at least not given its due) in most first year courses in contracts. Hence, we provide an opportunity here to plumb some of its depths. We offer only three cases, however. The first, *Roto-Lith, Ltd. v. F.P. Bartlett & Co.,* a 1962 case decided by the Court of Appeals for the first circuit was the first major case under 2–207 and continues to be the one most discussed. It also provides some exceptional object lessons on how 2–207 ought *not* to be interpreted. The second case, *Dorton v. Collins & Aikman Corp.,* decided in 1972, poses a sharp contrast in 2–207 methodology. The court seeks to work hard with the purposes and language of 2–207 (the final official text) and addresses several of the issues in a creditable fashion. It also explores the relationships between the various subsections of 2–207 more satisfactorily than Roto-Lith. The third case, *Daitom, Inc. v. Pennwalt Corp.* is surely one of the most important of the many relatively recent cases on 2–207. It also addresses frontally the question of what happens to "different" terms under 2–207.

ROTO–LITH, LTD. v. F.P. BARTLETT & CO.

United States Court of Appeals, First Circuit, 1962.
297 F.2d 497.

ALDRICH, CIRCUIT JUDGE.

Plaintiff-appellant Roto-Lith, Ltd., is a New York corporation engaged *inter alia* in manufacturing, or "converting," cellophane bags for packaging vegetables. Defendant-appellee is a Massachusetts corporation which makes emulsion for use as a cellophane adhesive. This is a field of some difficulty, and various emulsions are employed, depending upon the intended purpose of the bags. In May and October 1959 plaintiff purchased emulsion from the defendant. Subsequently bags produced with this emulsion failed to adhere, and this action was instituted in the district court for the District of Massachusetts. At the conclusion of the evidence the court directed a verdict for the defendant.[1] This appeal followed.

Defendant asks us to review the October transaction first because of certain special considerations applicable to the May order. The defense in each instance, however, is primarily the same, namely, defendant contends that the sales contract expressly negatived any warranties.[2] We will deal first with the October order.

On October 23, 1959, plaintiff, in New York, mailed a written order to defendant in Massachusetts for a drum of "N-132-C" emulsion, stating "End use: wet pack spinach bags." Defendant on October 26 prepared simultaneously an acknowledgment and an invoice. The printed forms were exactly the same, except that one was headed "Acknowledgment" and the other "Invoice," and the former contemplated insertion of the proposed, and the latter of the actual, shipment date. Defendant testified that in accordance with its regular practice the acknowledgment was prepared and mailed the same day. The plaintiff's principal liability witness testified that he did not know whether this acknowledgment "was received, or what happened to it." On this state of the evidence there is an unrebutted presumption of receipt. Johnston v. Cassidy, 1932, 279 Mass. 593, 181 N.E. 748; cf. Tobin v. Taintor, 1918, 229 Mass. 174, 118 N.E. 247. The goods were shipped to New York on October 27. On the evidence it must be found that the acknowledgment was received at least no later than the goods. The invoice was received presumably a day or two after the goods.

The acknowledgment and the invoice bore in conspicuous type on their face the following legend, "All goods sold without warranties, express or implied, and subject to the terms on reverse side." In somewhat smaller, but still conspicuous, type there were printed on the back certain terms of sale, of which the following are relevant:

> "1. Due to the variable conditions under which these goods may be transported, stored, handled, or used, Seller hereby expressly excludes any and all warranties, guaranties, or representations whatsoever. Buyer assumes risk for results obtained from use of these goods, whether used alone or in combination with other products. Seller's liability hereunder shall be limited to the replacement of any goods that materially differ from the Seller's sample order on the basis of which the order for such goods was made.
>
> "7. This acknowledgment contains all of the terms of this purchase and sale. No one except a duly authorized officer of Seller may execute or modify contracts. Payment may be made only at the offices of the Seller. *If these terms are not acceptable, Buyer must so notify Seller at once."* (Ital. suppl.)

It is conceded that plaintiff did not protest defendant's attempt so to limit its liability, and in due course paid for the emulsion and used it. It is also conceded

1. Also involved was a counter-claim, but this requires no separate discussion.

2. The defendant also contends that the warranties, if any there might have been, were not broken. This is a question of fact with which we are not concerned.

that adequate notice was given of breach of warranty, if there were warranties. The only issue which we will consider is whether all warranties were excluded by defendant's acknowledgment.[3]

The first question is what law the Massachusetts court would look to in order to determine the terms of the contract. Under Massachusetts law this is the place where the last material act occurs. Autographic Register Co. v. Philip Hano Co., 1 Cir., 1952, 198 F.2d 208; Milliken v. Pratt, 1878, 125 Mass. 374. Under the Uniform Commercial Code, Mass.Gen.Laws Ann. (1958) ch. 106, § 2–206, mailing the acknowledgment would clearly have completed the contract in Massachusetts by acceptance had the acknowledgment not sought to introduce new terms. Section 2–207 provides:

> "(1) A definite and seasonable expression of acceptance or a written confirmation which is sent within a reasonable time operates as an acceptance even though it states terms additional to or different from those offered or agreed upon, unless acceptance is expressly made conditional on assent to the additional or different terms.
>
> "(2) The additional terms are to be construed as proposals for addition to the contract. Between merchants such terms become part of the contract unless:
>
> "(a) the offer expressly limits acceptance to the terms of the offer;
>
> "(b) they materially alter it; or
>
> "(c) notification of objection to them has already been given or is given within a reasonable time after notice of them is received."

Plaintiff exaggerates the freedom which this section affords an offeror to ignore a reply from an offeree that does not in terms coincide with the original offer. According to plaintiff defendant's condition that there should be no warranties constituted a proposal which "materially altered" the agreement. As to this we concur. See Uniform Commercial Code comment to this section, Mass.Gen.Laws annotation, supra, paragraph 4. Plaintiff goes on to say that by virtue of the statute the acknowledgment effected a completed agreement without this condition, and that as a further proposal the condition never became part of the agreement because plaintiff did not express assent. We agree that section 2–207 changed the existing law, but not to this extent. Its purpose was to modify the strict principle that a response not precisely in accordance with the offer was a rejection and a counteroffer. Kehlor Flour Mills Co. v. Linden, 1918, 230 Mass. 119, 123, 119 N.E. 698; Saco-Lowell Shops v. Clinton Mills Co., 1 Cir., 1921, 277 F. 349. Now, within stated limits, a response that does not in all respects correspond with the offer constitutes an acceptance of the offer, and a counteroffer only as to the differences. If plaintiff's contention is correct that a reply to an offer stating additional conditions unilaterally burdensome upon the offeror is a binding acceptance of the original offer plus simply a proposal for the additional conditions, the statute would lead to an absurdity. Obviously no offeror will subsequently assent to such conditions.

The statute is not too happily drafted. Perhaps it would be wiser in all cases for an offeree to say in so many words, "I will not accept your offer until you assent to the following: * * *" But businessmen cannot be expected to act by rubric. It would be unrealistic to suppose that when an offeree replies

3. Defendant also relies upon the terms of the invoice in view of the fact that it was admittedly received before plaintiff *used* the goods. Whether an invoice not received until after the goods can modify the contract raises some possible matters which we do not reach.

setting out conditions that would be burdensome only to the offeror he intended to make an unconditional acceptance of the original offer, leaving it simply to the offeror's good nature whether he would assume the additional restrictions. To give the statute a practical construction we must hold that a response which states a condition materially altering the obligation solely to the disadvantage of the offeror is an "acceptance * * * expressly * * * conditional on assent to the additional * * * terms."

Plaintiff accepted the goods with knowledge of the conditions specified in the acknowledgment. It became bound.[4] Garst v. Harris, 1900, 177 Mass. 72, 58 N.E. 174; Doerr v. Woolsey, 1889, 5 N.Y.S. 447 (Com.Pl.Gen.Term); cf. Joseph v. Atlantic Basin Iron Works, Inc., Sup., 1954, 132 N.Y.S.2d 671, aff'd Sup., 143 N.Y.S.2d 601 (App.Div.). Whether the contract was made in Massachusetts or New York, there has been no suggestion that either jurisdiction will not give effect to an appropriate disclaimer of warranties. See Mass.Gen.Laws Ann. c. 106, § 2–316; New York Personal Property Law, McKinney's Consol. Laws, c. 41, § 152. This disposes of the October order.

With respect to the May order a different situation obtains. Here plaintiff ordered a quantity of "N–136–F," which was defendant's code number for a dry-bag emulsion. The order stated as the end use a wet bag. Accordingly, defendant knew, by its own announced standards, that the emulsion ordered was of necessity unfit for the disclosed purpose. In this bald situation plaintiff urges that the defendant cannot be permitted to specify that it made no implied warranty of fitness.

We do not reach this question. In the court below, when plainly asked to state its opposition to the direction of a verdict, plaintiff did not advance the arguments it now makes, and in no way called the court's attention to any distinction between the May and the October orders. An appellant is not normally permitted to have the benefit of a new theory on appeal. It is true that this is not an absolute prohibition. The court in its discretion may relax the rule in exceptional cases in order to prevent a clear miscarriage of justice. Hormel v. Helvering, 1941, 312 U.S. 552, 61 S.Ct. 719, 85 L.Ed. 1037; Bergeron v. Mansour, 1 Cir., 1945, 152 F.2d 27, 32; Palo Blanco Fruit Co. v. Palo Alto Orchards Co., 1 Cir., 1952, 195 F.2d 90. Plaintiff's point, however, is by no means clear-cut. Financially the consequences are not large. Plaintiff was represented by competent counsel, and has had an eight-day trial. We do not think the case one for making an exception to the salutary rule that a party is normally entitled to but one "day" in court.

No question remains as to the counterclaim.

Judgment will be entered affirming the judgment of the District Court.

4. It does not follow that if the acknowledgment had miscarried plaintiff's receipt of the goods would have completed a contract which did not include the terms of the acknowledgment. We are not faced with the question of how the statute may affect the common law under such circumstances.

DORTON v. COLLINS & AIKMAN CORP.

United States Court of Appeals, Sixth Circuit, 1972.
453 F.2d 1161.

Before CELEBREZZE, BROOKS and MILLER, CIRCUIT JUDGES.

CELEBREZZE, CIRCUIT JUDGE.

This is an appeal from the District Court's denial of Defendant-Appellant's motion for a stay pending arbitration, pursuant to Section 3 of the United States Arbitration Act of 1925, 9 U.S.C. § 3. The suit arose after a series of over 55 transactions during 1968, 1969, and 1970 in which Plaintiffs-Appellees [hereinafter The Carpet Mart], carpet retailers in Kingsport, Tennessee, purchased carpets from Defendant-Appellant [hereinafter Collins & Aikman], incorporated under the laws of the State of Delaware, with its principal place of business in New York, New York, and owner of a carpet manufacturing plant [formerly the Painter Carpet Mills, Inc.] located in Dalton, Georgia. The Carpet Mart originally brought this action in a Tennessee state trial court, seeking compensatory and punitive damages in the amount of $450,000 from Collins & Aikman for the latter's alleged fraud, deceit, and misrepresentation in the sale of what were supposedly carpets manufactured from 100% Kodel polyester fiber. The Carpet Mart maintains that in May, 1970, in response to a customer complaint, it learned that not all of the carpets were manufactured from 100% Kodel polyester fiber but rather some were composed of a cheaper and inferior carpet fiber. After the cause was removed to the District Court on the basis of diversity of citizenship, Collins & Aikman moved for a stay pending arbitration, asserting that The Carpet Mart was bound to an arbitration agreement which appeared on the reverse side of Collins & Aikman's printed sales acknowledgment forms. Holding that there existed no binding arbitration agreement between the parties, the District Court denied the stay. For the reasons set forth below, we remand the case to the District Court for further findings.

I

We initially note that the denial of a motion to stay pending arbitration, although interlocutory in nature, is appealable to this Court * * *.

We also find that there is no conflicts of law problem in the present case, the Uniform Commercial Code having been enacted in both Georgia and Tennessee at the time of the disputed transactions. * * *

II

The primary question before us on appeal is whether the District Court, in denying Collins & Aikman's motion for a stay pending arbitration, erred in holding that The Carpet Mart was not bound by the arbitration agreement appearing on the back of Collins & Aikman's acknowledgment forms. In reviewing the District Court's determination, we must look closely at the procedures which were followed in the sales transactions which gave rise to the present dispute over the arbitration agreement.

In each of the more than 55 transactions, one of the partners in The Carpet Mart, or, on some occasions, Collins & Aikman's visiting salesman, telephoned Collins & Aikman's order department in Dalton, Georgia, and ordered certain quantities of carpets listed in Collins & Aikman's catalogue. There is some dispute as to what, if any, agreements were reached through the telephone calls and through the visits by Collins & Aikman's salesman. After each oral order was placed, the price, if any, quoted by the buyer was checked against Collins & Aikman's price list, and the credit department was consulted to determine if The Carpet Mart had paid for all previous shipments. After it was found that everything was in order, Collins & Aikman's order department typed the information concerning the particular order on one of its printed acknowledgment forms. Each acknowledgment form bore one of three legends: "Acknowledgment," "Customer Acknowledgment," or "Sales Contract." The following provision was printed on the face of the forms bearing the "Acknowledgment" legend:

> "The acceptance of your order is subject to all of the terms and conditions on the face and reverse side hereof, including arbitration, all of which are accepted by buyer; it supersedes buyer's order form, if any. It shall become a contract either (a) when signed and delivered by buyer to seller and accepted in writing by seller, or (b) at *Seller's* option, when buyer shall have given to seller specification of assortments, delivery dates, shipping instructions, or instructions to bill and hold as to all or any part of the merchandise herein described, or when buyer has received delivery of the whole or any part thereof, or when buyer has otherwise assented to the terms and conditions hereof."

Similarly, on the face of the forms bearing the "Customer Acknowledgment" or "Sales Contract" legends the following provision appeared:

> "This order is given subject to all of the terms and conditions on the face and reverse side hereof, including the provisions for arbitration and the exclusion of warranties, all of which are accepted by Buyer, supersede Buyer's order form, if any, and constitute the entire contract between Buyer and Seller. This order shall become a contract as to the entire quantity specified either (a) when signed and delivered by Buyer to Seller and accepted in writing by Seller or (b) when Buyer has received and retained this order for ten days without objection, or (c) when Buyer has accepted delivery of any part of the merchandise specified herein or has furnished to Seller specifications or assortments, delivery dates, shipping instructions, or instructions to bill and hold, or when Buyer has otherwise indicated acceptance of the terms hereof."

The small print on the reverse side of the forms provided, among other things, that all claims arising out of the contract would be submitted to arbitration in New York City. Each acknowledgment form was signed by an employee of Collins & Aikman's order department and mailed to The Carpet Mart on the day the telephone order was received or, at the latest, on the following day.[1] The carpets were thereafter shipped to The Carpet Mart, with the interval between the mailing of the acknowledgment form and shipment of the carpets varying from a brief interval to a period of several weeks or months. Absent a delay in the mails, however, The Carpet Mart always received the acknowledgment forms prior to receiving the carpets. In all cases The Carpet Mart took delivery of and

1. The District Court found that "[Collins & Aikman] has not established to this point that the aforementioned acknowledgment forms were received in each instance." The affidavit of J.A. Castle, a partner in The Carpet Mart, however, states that "* * * I would receive a yellow sheet of paper which I believed to be an acknowledgment that my order was being processed and was being sent to me." And at oral arguments before this Court, counsel for The Carpet Mart did not attempt to overcome the presumption that the acknowledgments, having been mailed in each instance according to William T. Hester's affidavit, were received. *See* W.E. Richmond & Co. v. Security National Bank, 16 Tenn.App. 414, 64 S.W.2d 863 (1933); Roto-Lith, Ltd. v. F.P. Bartlett & Co., 297 F.2d 497, 498 (1st Cir. 1962).

paid for the carpets without objecting to any terms contained in the acknowledgment form.

In holding that no binding arbitration agreement was created between the parties through the transactions above, the District Court relied on T.C.A. § 47–2–207 [UCC § 2–207], which provides: [the Court quoted UCC 2–207.]

* * *

The District Court found that Subsection 2–207(3) controlled the instant case, quoting the following passage from 1 W. Hawkland, A Transactional Guide to the Uniform Commercial Code § 1.090303, at 19–20 (1964):

> "If the seller * * * ships the goods and the buyer accepts them, a contract is formed under subsection (3). The terms of this contract are those on which the purchase order and acknowledgment agree, and the additional terms needed for a contract are to be found throughout the U.C.C. * * * [T]he U.C.C. does not impose an arbitration term on the parties where their contract is silent on the matter. Hence, a conflict between an arbitration and a no-arbitration clause would result in the no-arbitration clause becoming effective."

Under this authority alone the District Court concluded that the arbitration clause on the back of Collins & Aikman's sales acknowledgment had not become a binding term in the 50–odd transactions with The Carpet Mart.

In reviewing this determination by the District Court, we are aware of the problems which courts have had in interpreting Section 2–207. This section of the UCC has been described as a "murky bit of prose," Southwest Engineering Co. v. Martin Tractor Co., 205 Kan. 684, 694, 473 P.2d 18, 25 (1970), as "not too happily drafted," Roto-Lith Ltd. v. F.P. Bartlett & Co., 297 F.2d 497, 500 (1st Cir. 1962), and as "one of the most important, subtle, and difficult in the entire Code, and well it may be said that the product as it finally reads is not altogether satisfactory." Duesenberg & King, Sales and Bulk Transfers under the Uniform Commercial Code, (Vol. 3, Bender's Uniform Commercial Code Service) § 3.03, at 3–12 (1969). Despite the lack of clarity in its language, Section 2–207 manifests definite objectives which are significant in the present case.

As Official Comment No. 1 indicates, UCC § 2–207 was intended to apply to two situations:

> "The one is where an agreement has been reached either orally or by informal correspondence between the parties and is followed by one or both of the parties sending formal acknowledgments or memoranda embodying the terms so far as agreed upon and adding terms not discussed. The other situation is one in which a wire or letter expressed and intended as the closing or confirmation of an agreement adds further minor suggestions or proposals such as 'ship by Tuesday,' 'rush,' 'ship draft against bill of lading inspection allowed,' or the like." T.C.A. § 47–2–207 [UCC § 2–207], Official Comment 1.

Although Comment No. 1 is itself somewhat ambiguous, it is clear that Section 2–207, and specifically Subsection 2–207(1), was intended to alter the "ribbon matching" or "*mirror*" rule of common law, under which the terms of an acceptance or confirmation were required to be identical to the terms of the offer or oral agreement, respectively. 1 W. Hawkland, *supra,* at 16; R. Nordstrom, Handbook of the Law of Sales, Sec. 37, at 99–100 (1970). Under the common law, an acceptance or a confirmation which contained terms additional to or different from those of the offer or oral agreement constituted a rejection of the offer or agreement and thus became a counter-offer. The terms of the counter-offer were said to have been accepted by the original offeror when he proceeded to perform under the contract without objecting to the counter-offer. Thus, a buyer was deemed to have accepted the seller's counter-offer if he took receipt of the goods and paid for them without objection.

Under Section 2–207 the result is different. This section of the Code recognizes that in current commercial transactions, the terms of the offer and those of the acceptance will seldom be identical. Rather, under the current "battle of the forms," each party typically has a printed form drafted by his attorney and containing as many terms as could be envisioned to favor that party in his sales transactions. Whereas under common law the disparity between the fine-print terms in the parties' forms would have prevented the consummation of a contract when these forms are exchanged, Section 2–207 recognizes that in many, but not all, cases the parties do not impart such significance to the terms on the printed forms. *See* 1 W. Hawkland, *supra;* § 1.0903, at 14, § 1.090301, at 16. Subsection 2–207(1) therefore provides that "[a] definite and seasonable expression of acceptance or a written confirmation * * * operates as an acceptance even though it states terms additional to or different from those offered or agreed upon, unless acceptance is expressly made conditional on assent to the additional or different terms." Thus, under Subsection (1), a contract is recognized notwithstanding the fact that an acceptance or confirmation contains terms additional to or different from those of the offer or prior agreement, provided that the offeree's intent to accept the offer is definitely expressed, *see* Sections 2–204 and 2–206, and provided that the offeree's acceptance is not expressly conditioned on the offeror's assent to the additional or different terms. When a contract is recognized under Subsection (1), the additional terms are treated as "proposals for addition to the contract" under Subsection (2), which contains special provisions under which such additional terms are deemed to have been accepted when the transaction is between merchants. Conversely, when no contract is recognized under Subsection 2–207(1)—either because no definite expression of acceptance exists or, more specifically, because the offeree's acceptance is expressly conditioned on the offeror's assent to the additional or different terms—the entire transaction aborts at this point. If, however, the subsequent conduct of the parties—particularly, performance by both parties under what they apparently believe to be a contract—recognizes the existence of a contract, under Subsection 2–207(3) such conduct by both parties is sufficient to establish a contract, notwithstanding the fact that no contract would have been recognized on the basis of their writings alone. Subsection 2–207(3) further provides how the terms of contracts recognized thereunder shall be determined.

With the above analysis and purposes of Section 2–207 in mind, we turn to their application in the present case. We initially observe that the affidavits and the acknowledgment forms themselves raise the question of whether Collins & Aikman's forms constituted acceptances or confirmations under Section 2–207. The language of some of the acknowledgment forms ("The acceptance of your order is subject to * * *") and the affidavit of Mr. William T. Hester, Collins & Aikman's marketing operations manager, suggest that the forms were the only acceptances issued in response to The Carpet Mart's oral offers. However, in his affidavit Mr. J.A. Castle, a partner in The Carpet Mart, asserted that when he personally called Collins & Aikman to order carpets, someone from the latter's order department would agree to sell the requested carpets, or, alternatively, when Collins & Aikman's visiting salesman took the order, he would agree to the sale, on some occasions after he had used The Carpet Mart's telephone to call Collins & Aikman's order department. Absent the District Court's determination of whether Collins & Aikman's acknowledgment forms were acceptances or, alternatively, confirmations of prior oral agreements, we will consider the application of section 2–207 to both situations for the guidance of the District Court on remand.

Viewing Collins & Aikman's acknowledgment forms as acceptances under Subsection 2–207(1), we are initially faced with the question of whether the arbitration provision in Collins & Aikman's acknowledgment forms were in fact "additional to or different from" the terms of The Carpet Mart's oral offers. In the typical case under Section 2–207, there exist both a written purchase order and a written acknowledgment, and this determination can be readily made by comparing the two forms. In the present case, where the only written forms were Collins & Aikman's sales acknowledgments, we believe that such a comparison must be made between the oral offers and the written acceptances.[2] Although the District Court apparently assumed that The Carpet Mart's oral orders did not include in their terms the arbitration provision which appeared in Collins & Aikman's acknowledgment forms, we believe that a specific finding on this point will be required on remand.[3]

Assuming, for purposes of analysis, that the arbitration provision was an addition to the terms of The Carpet Mart's oral offers, we must next determine whether or not Collins & Aikman's acceptances were "expressly made conditional on assent to the additional * * * terms" therein, within the proviso of Subsection 2–207(1). As set forth in full above, the provision appearing on the face of Collins & Aikman's acknowledgment forms stated that the acceptances (or orders) were "subject to all of the terms and conditions on the face and reverse side hereof, including arbitration, all of which are accepted by buyer." The provision on the "Acknowledgment" forms further stated that Collins & Aikman's terms would become the basis of the contract between the parties

> "either (a) when signed and delivered by buyer to seller and accepted in writing by seller, or (b) at Seller's option, when buyer shall have given to seller specification of assortments, delivery dates, shipping instructions, or instructions to bill and hold as to all or any part of the merchandise herein described, or when buyer has received delivery of the whole or any part thereof, or when buyer has otherwise assented to the terms and conditions hereof."

Similarly, the provision on the "Customer Acknowledgment" and "Sales Contract" forms stated that the terms therein would become the basis of the contract

> "either (a) when signed and delivered by Buyer to Seller and accepted in writing by Seller or (b) when Buyer has received and retained this order for ten days without objection, or (c) when Buyer has accepted delivery of any part of the merchandise specified herein or has furnished to Seller specifica-

2. In describing the second (offer-acceptance) situation to which Section 2–207 was intended to apply, Official Comment No. 1 describes the acceptance as a "wire or letter" but makes no such reference to a written offer. As in the situation where there is but one written confirmation sent subsequent to an oral agreement—which is expressly referred to in Comment No. 1—we believe the drafters anticipated cases, such as the present one, where a written acceptance would be sent in response to an oral offer.

3. It is not inconceivable that a buyer might request that all claims be submitted to arbitration, *see* Universal Oil Products v. S.C.M. Corp., 313 F.Supp. 905 (D.Conn.1970), or that a buyer might orally submit to the seller's known policy of arbitration in order to facilitate acceptance of the offer.

tions or assortments, delivery dates, shipping instructions to bill and hold, or when Buyer has otherwise indicated acceptance of the terms hereof."

Although Collins & Aikman's use of the words "subject to" suggests that the acceptances were conditional to some extent, we do not believe the acceptances were "expressly made conditional on [the buyer's] assent to the additional or different terms," as specifically required under the Subsection 2–207(1) proviso. In order to fall within this proviso, it is not enough that an acceptance is expressly conditional on additional or different terms; rather, an acceptance must be *expressly* conditional on the offeror's *assent* to those terms. Viewing the Subsection (1) proviso within the context of the rest of that Subsection and within the policies of Section 2–207 itself, we believe that it was intended to apply only to an acceptance which clearly reveals that the offeree is unwilling to proceed with the transaction unless he is assured of the offeror's assent to the additional or different terms therein. *See* 1 W. Hawkland, *supra,* § 1.090303, at 21. That the acceptance is predicated on the offeror's assent must be "directly and distinctly stated or expressed rather than implied or left to inference." Webster's Third International Dictionary (defining "express").

Although the UCC does not provide a definition of "assent," it is significant that Collins & Aikman's printed acknowledgment forms specified at least seven types of action or inaction on the part of the buyer which—sometimes at Collins & Aikman's option—would be deemed to bind the buyer to the terms therein. These ranged from the buyer's signing and delivering the acknowledgment to the seller—which indeed could have been recognized as the buyer's assent to Collins & Aikman's terms—to the buyer's retention of the acknowledgment for ten days without objection—which could never have been recognized as the buyer's assent to the additional or different terms where acceptance is expressly conditional on that assent.[4]

To recognize Collins & Aikman's acceptances as "expressly conditional on [the buyer's] assent to the additional * * * terms" therein, within the proviso of Subsection 2–207(1), would thus require us to ignore the specific language of that provision.[5] Such an interpretation is not justified in view of the fact that Subsection 2–207(1) is clearly designed to give legal recognition to many contracts where the variance between the offer and acceptance would have precluded such recognition at common law.

Because Collins & Aikman's acceptances were not expressly conditional on the buyer's assent to the additional terms within the proviso of Subsection 2–207(1), a contract is recognized under Subsection (1), and the additional terms are treated as "proposals" for addition to the contract under Subsection 2–

4. The common law has never recognized silence or inaction as a mode of acceptance. *See* 1 W. Hawkland, *supra,* § 1.090301, at 17. Under the counter-offer approach which Section 2–207 was designed to modify, the offeror had to take receipt of and pay for the goods without objection before he was deemed to have accepted the terms of the counter-offer. And although Subsection 2–207(2)(c) provides that certain additional terms can be accepted by the offeror's failure to object, nothing in the Code suggests that silence or inaction can be recognized as an offeror's assent in the present context.

5. We are aware that at least two Courts of Appeals have not chosen to read the Subsection 2–207(1) proviso as strictly as we do here. *See* Roto-Lith, Ltd. v. F.P. Bartlett & Co., 297 F.2d 497, 499–500 (1st Cir.1962); Construction Aggregates Corp. v. Hewitt-Robins, Inc., 404 F.2d 505, 509 (5th Cir.1969) (dictum). But see Matter of Doughboy Industries, Inc., and Pantasote Co., 17 A.D.2d 216, 233 N.Y.S.2d 488 (1962). We believe, however, that the approach adopted here is dictated by both the language of the proviso and the purpose of Subsection 2–207(1).

207(2).[6] Since both Collins & Aikman and The Carpet Mart are clearly "merchants" as that term is defined in Subsection 2–104(1), the arbitration provision will be deemed to have been accepted by The Carpet Mart under Subsection 2–207(2) unless it materially altered the terms of The Carpet Mart's oral offers. T.C.A. § 47–2–207(2)(b) [UCC § 2–207(2)(b)].[7] We believe that the question of whether the arbitration provision materially altered the oral offer under Subsection 2–207(2)(b) is one which can be resolved only by the District Court on further findings of fact in the present case.[8] If the arbitration provision did in fact materially alter The Carpet Mart's offer, it could not become a part of the contract "unless expressly agreed to" by The Carpet Mart. T.C.A. § 47–2–207 [UCC § 2–207], Official Comment No. 3.

We therefore conclude that if on remand the District Court finds that Collins & Aikman's acknowledgments were in fact acceptances and that the arbitration provision was additional to the terms of The Carpet Mart's oral orders, contracts will be recognized under Subsection 2–207(1). The arbitration clause will then be viewed as a "proposal" under Subsection 2–207(2) which will be deemed to have been accepted by The Carpet Mart unless it materially altered the oral offers.

If the District Court finds that Collins & Aikman's acknowledgment forms were not acceptances but rather were confirmations of prior oral agreements between the parties, an application of Section 2–207 similar to that above will be required. Subsection 2–207(1) will require an initial determination of whether the arbitration provision in the confirmations was "additional to or different from" the terms orally agreed upon. Assuming that the District Court finds that the arbitration provision was not a term of the oral agreements between the parties, the arbitration clause will be treated as a "proposal" for addition to the contract under Subsection 2–207(2), as was the case when Collins & Aikman's

6. Apparently believing that Collins & Aikman's acknowledgments were acceptances "expressly * * * conditional on assent to the additional or different terms" under the Subsection 2–207(1) proviso, the District Court recognized contracts between the parties under Subsection 2–207(3) since the subsequent performance by both parties clearly recognized the existence of a contract. Absent our conclusion that Collins & Aikman's acknowledgments do not fall within the Subsection 2–207(1) proviso, we believe that the District Court correctly applied Subsection 2–207(3) to Collins & Aikman's "acceptances" notwithstanding the fact that some of the language of that Subsection appears to refer to the typical situation under Section 2–207 where there exist both a written offer and a written acceptance. Although we recognize the value that writings by both parties serve in sales transactions, where Subsection 2–207(3) is otherwise applicable we do not believe the purposes of that Subsection should be abandoned simply because the offeror chose to rely on his oral offer. In such a case, we believe that the District Court's comparison of the terms of the oral offer and the written acceptance under Subsection (3) would have been correct.

7. The parties do not dispute the fact that The Carpet Mart made no objections to the terms embodied in Collins & Aikman's acknowledgments. Therefore, Subsection 2–207(2)(c) is not relevant in the present case. And although it is not inconceivable that an oral offer could "expressly [limit] acceptance to the terms of the offer" under Subsection 2–207(2)(a), The Carpet Mart has never asserted that this was the nature of its offers to Collins & Aikman. We are therefore concerned with only Subsection 2–207(2)(b).

8. While T.C.A. § 47–2–207 [UCC § 2–207]. Official Comment Nos. 4 and 5 provide examples of terms which would and would not materially alter a contract, an arbitration clause is listed under neither. Although we recognize the rule "that the agreement to arbitrate must be direct and the intention made clear, without implication, inveiglement or subtlety," Matter of Doughboy Industries, Inc., and Pantasote Co., 17 A.D.2d 216, 218, 233 N.Y.S.2d 488, 492 (1962) (indicating in dictum that an arbitration clause would materially alter a contract under 2–207(2)(b)), we believe the question of material alteration necessarily rests on the facts of each case. *See* American Parts Co. v. American Arbitration Ass'n, 8 Mich.App. 156, 171, 154 N.W.2d 5, 14 (1967).

acknowledgments were viewed as acceptances above. The provision for arbitration will be deemed to have been accepted by The Carpet Mart unless the District Court finds that it materially altered the prior oral agreements, in which case The Carpet Mart could not become bound thereby absent an express agreement to that effect.

As a result of the above application of Section 2–207 to the limited facts before us in the present case, we find it necessary to remand the case to the District Court for the following findings: (1) whether oral agreements were reached between the parties prior to the sending of Collins & Aikman's acknowledgment forms; if there were no such oral agreements, (2) whether the arbitration provision appearing in Collins & Aikman's "acceptances" was additional to the terms of The Carpet Mart's oral offers; and, if so, (3) whether the arbitration provision materially altered the terms of The Carpet Mart's oral offers. Alternatively, if the District Court does find that oral agreements were reached between the parties before Collins & Aikman's acknowledgment forms were sent in each instance, it will be necessary for the District Court to make the following findings: (1) whether the prior oral agreements embodied the arbitration provision appearing in Collins & Aikman's "confirmations"; and, if not, (2) whether the arbitration provision materially altered the prior oral agreements. Regardless of whether the District Court finds Collins & Aikman's acknowledgment forms to have been acceptances or confirmations, if the arbitration provision was additional to, and a material alteration of, the offers or prior oral agreements, The Carpet Mart will not be bound to that provision absent a finding that it expressly agreed to be bound thereby.

III

If, on remand, the District Court finds that the arbitration provision exists as a term of the contracts recognized under this application of Section 2–207, Collins & Aikman's motion for a stay pending arbitration must be granted despite the fact that this is an action in fraud. In Prima Paint Corp. v. Flood & Conklin Mfg. Co., 388 U.S. 395, 87 S.Ct. 1801, 18 L.Ed.2d 1270 (1967), the Supreme Court held that in passing upon a motion for a stay pending arbitration under 9 U.S.C. § 3, a federal court may not consider claims of fraud in the inducement of the overall contract when the arbitration clause is sufficiently broad to encompass claims of fraud. Rather, in such cases a federal court may consider only claims which relate to the "making" of the arbitration agreement itself. 388 U.S. at 402–404, 87 S.Ct. 1801. In the present case, the language of Collins & Aikman's arbitration clause is virtually identical to that of the arbitration agreement in the *Prima Paint* case.[9] Moreover, although The Carpet Mart challenges the legibility of the fine-print arbitration provision on the reverse side of Collins & Aikman's forms (which was specifically called to the buyer's attention on the face of those forms), The Carpet Mart's claim of fraud relates only to the substitutions for Kodel polyester fibers under the overall contract and not to the arbitration clause itself. Therefore, upon a finding by the District Court that the arbitration clause was a term of the contracts recognized under T.C.A. § 47–2–207 (UCC § 2–207), Collins & Aikman's motion for a stay pending arbitration must be granted.

9. Collins & Aikman's clause reads in pertinent part: "Any controversy arising out of or relating to this contract shall be settled by arbitration. * * *" In comparison, the arbitration agreement in the *Prima Paint* case read in pertinent part: "Any controversy or claim arising out of or relating to this Agreement, or the breach thereof, shall be settled by arbitration. * * *" 388 U.S. at 398, 87 S.Ct. at 1803.

For the reasons set forth above, the case is remanded to the District Court for further findings consistent with this opinion. [Some footnotes omitted.]

J. WHITE AND R. SUMMERS, HANDBOOK OF THE LAW UNDER THE UNIFORM COMMERCIAL CODE 27–31 (2d ed. 1980).

Assume that buyer sends a purchase order which provides that any dispute will be governed by arbitration. Seller responds with an acknowledgement which provides that any dispute will not be resolved by arbitration. If the *bargained* terms on the purchase order and acknowledgement agree, we would find that the seller's document is a definite and seasonable expression of acceptance under 2–207 and that a contract has been formed by the exchange of the documents. We would thus bind the welsher who seeks to get out of the contract before either performs.

Assume that the seller then ships the goods, the buyer receives and pays for them, and the parties fall into dispute about their quality. Does the contract call for arbitration or does it not? * * *

* * * [T]he seller can argue that his acceptance is only an acceptance of the terms on which the two documents agree, and they did not agree on arbitration, nor do Code gap fillers provide for arbitration. This argument finds no explicit support in 2–207, but one of us (White) thinks it finds some support in part of Comment 6. * * *

In the end, how would our hypothetical case come out under the Code? One of us (White) would turn to [Official Comment 6] and find that the two terms cancel one another. On this view the seller's form was only an acceptance of terms in the offer which did not conflict with any terms in the acceptance. Thus the ultimate deal would not include an arbitration clause unless the course of performance (2–208), course of dealing (1–205), or usage of trade (1–205) supplies one. The Code does not expressly authorize this result, but it does not bar it either.

The other of us (Summers) believes that Comment 6 is not applicable. In his view it applies only to variant terms on *confirming* forms, not to variant terms on forms one of which is an offer and the other an acceptance under 2–207(1) (a distinction itself drawn in Comment 1). Thus the buyer's arbitration clause controls, for the seller's no-arbitration clause, as a *different* term embodied in the accepting form, simply falls out; 2–207(2) cannot rescue it since that provision applies only to *additional* terms. White answers that, among other things, this reading gives the sender of the first form (the buyer here) an unearned advantage. Summers does not agree that the "advantage" is entirely unearned. The recipient of the first form at least had an opportunity to object to its contents. Moreover, Summers believes that White's approach is relatively more unfair to the offeror than Summers's approach is to the offeree. According to Summers, the offeror has more (even if only a little more) reason to expect that his clause will control than the offeree has to expect that his will. After all, when the offeree sends his form he will have already received a form from the offeror, and offerees know full well that forms of different parties rarely coincide. But even if the offeror's advantage is to some extent unearned, the text of 2–207, according to Summers, appears more or less plainly to authorize it, and if the drafters intended the White approach, they could have easily drafted the section accordingly.

What if the "different" term comes into being partly by operation of a Code gap filler provision * * * rather than by virtue of a conflict of terms specified in the two forms (as in our hypothetical case)? For example, in Air Products & Chemicals, Inc. v. Fairbanks Morse, Inc.,[12] the seller's accepting form limited consequential damages. The buyer's offering form was silent on this subject but the buyer appears to have urged that the relevant Code gap filler (2–714(3)) "impliedly" provided for full consequential damages, that the seller's term was therefore a "different" term under 2–207(1), and that *it* alone thus fell out, thereby preserving the buyer's Code-provided right to full consequential damages. The Court ultimately reached this result (though not on precisely this reasoning). In light of the text, Summers concurs, though he is concerned that this reading may give the sender of the offering form too much of an overall advantage. (Summers would redraft the statute.)

Consider this further variation. Assume for example that the form offer contains an otherwise valid disclaimer of warranties and that the acceptance contains a conflicting *express* warranty. According to White, neither become part of the contract under 2–207(1) despite the fact that the contract is formed. Likewise neither enters the contract through 2–207(2) because the term in the acceptance is a different, not an additional term. Moreover by its terms 2–207(3) does not apply to this case but applies only to the case where "the writings of the parties do not otherwise establish a contract." Is it possible, nonetheless, that an *implied* warranty enters the contract directly as a gap filler without reference to 2–207(3)? White believes that it does and that indeed most of the gap fillers do not depend upon 2–207 to enter the contract. He says there are many contracts adequately formed by an offer and an acceptance which a gap filler dealing with price or warranty or terms of delivery would enter without any reference to 2–207. On White's view, that seems the proper result in this case. He thinks that the court in Bosway Tube & Steel Corp. v. McKay Machine Co. reached just this result by applying both 2–207(1) and 2–207(3). It seems to him that the court's result is correct (but that it is technically incorrect in finding that 2–207(3) can apply to a case in which the court has already found a 2–207(1) contract).

On White's analysis the foregoing outcome favors neither party. But if the buyer-offeror's argument be accepted, the offeror will almost always get his own terms. If, on the other hand, the *Roto-Lith* decision be followed, and the second document is not an acceptance or is expressly conditional and therefore cannot "operate" as an acceptance, the second party will almost always get his own terms because the second document will constitute a counteroffer accepted by performance. White believes that neither of these results is sound, and would not give either party a term when their documents conflict as to that term. The Code may then provide a term substantially identical to one of those rejected. So be it. At least a term so supplied has the merit of being a term that the draftsmen considered fair.

Summers does not read the cases as does White. More important, Summers believes White misreads 2–207, both in text and in spirit. Summers would, in the foregoing further hypothetical case, uphold the otherwise valid disclaimer as to both express and implied warranties. [Some footnotes omitted.]

12. 58 Wis.2d 193, 206 N.W.2d 414, 12 UCC 794 (1973).

Vermont Law School

South Royalton, Vermont 05068

Telephone: 302/763–8303

September 10, 1980

Professor Robert S. Summers
Cornell University Law School
Ithaca, NY 14853

Dear Professor Summers:

I have meant for a long time to write you and your collaborator, Professor White, to express my admiration for your handbook on the Code. I often consult it and always with profit.

I have most recently been reading your admirable discussion of § 2-207. Let me say at the outset that I thoroughly approve of your decision to let the disagreement between you and White on the proper construction of that abominable section hang out instead of papering it over.

I do think that insufficient attention has been paid to the tangled drafting history of § 2-207. (I am not about to reveal any ''secret history''; I had nothing to do with the drafting of § 2-207 at any stage and I cannot remember ever having discussed it with Karl Llewellyn.) The point is that as late as the 1952 draft of the Code, § 2-207 consisted only of what are now subsections (1) and (2). Subsection (3) was added in response to criticisms of the New York Law Revision Commission (which were probably based on suggestions by John Honnold, who acted as a consultant on Article 2 for the Commission). The 1952 version of § 2-207 was bad enough (particularly in the (2)(b) reference to ''material alteration'') but the addition of subsection (3), without the slightest explanation of how it was supposed to mesh with (1) and (2), turned the section into a complete disaster. To make matters worse, the 1952 Comment (which had presumably been drafted at a much earlier point by Llewellyn) was never adequately revised to take the new subsection (3) into account. (Beginning in 1949 or 1950, Llewellyn refused to have anything to do with the Article 2 Comments, which were thereafter periodically updated by an anonymous hack in the Philadelphia office of the American Law Institute. It might be interesting to check back through earlier drafts of the Code to see how the text and Comment of § 2-207 evolved through 1952.) The later (1966) revisions of the Comment, which you attribute to Braucher, were band-aid jobs.

My principal quarrel with your discussion of § 2-207—and all the other discussions I have read—is that you treat the section much too respectfully—as if it had sprung, all of a piece, like Minerva from the brow of Jove. The truth is that it was a miserable, bungled, patched-up job—both text and Comment—to which various hands—Llewellyn, Honnold,

Braucher and my anonymous hack—contributed at various points, each acting independently of the others (like the blind men and the elephant). It strikes me as ludicrous to pretend that the section can, or should, be construed as an integrated whole in the light of what ''the draftsman'' ''intended.'' (I might note that, when subsection (3) was added, Llewellyn had ceased to have anything to do with the Code project.) One of the chores which we hire courts (and commentators) to perform is to clean up the messes which statutory draftsmen leave behind them. The proper approach to § 2-207, which is arguably the greatest statutory mess of all time, is to take it light-heartedly (or, as Professor Corbin used to say, cheerfully).

Which brings me to the ''infamous'' Rotolith case * * *. On the facts of the case with respect to the October shipment as Judge Aldrich stated them, I think it would have been outrageous to have saddled the seller with warranties which (as the buyer knew) he had expressly (and quite reasonably) disclaimed. I grant you that the opinion does considerable violence to the statutory language, even in the 1952 version * * *. Even so, I find it hard to conceive of a situation in which the commission of statutory mayhem was more justifiable or more necessary. Surely, when the legislature goes mad, the courts can (and should) restore us to sanity.

In the 1950's I used to go around the country peddling the Code. On one occasion I had to explain Article 2 to a group of ''corporate counsel'' in California—they represented airplane manufacturers and similar great enterprises. When I finished with § 2-207, they were, so far as I could tell, appalled. They were not so much concerned with the obvious drafting ambiguities as they were with the (equally obvious) intent to bind contracts at the earliest possible point. They evidently preferred not to be bound (whether their clients were selling or buying) until all the formalities had been accomplished, the last i dotted, the last t crossed. Perhaps, as Stuart Macaulay has suggested, businessmen don't really want binding contracts. Perhaps there was something to be said for the common law rules of offer and acceptance. At all events: Down with § 2-207.

Yours,

Grant Gilmore

Grant Gilmore
Professor of Law

jlm

DAITOM, INC. v. PENNWALT CORP.

United States Court of Appeals, Tenth Circuit, 1984.
741 F.2d 1569.

Before BARRETT, DOYLE and LOGAN, CIRCUIT JUDGES.

WILLIAM E. DOYLE, CIRCUIT JUDGE.

I. STATEMENT OF THE CASE

This is an appeal from the grant of summary judgment against Daitom, Inc. (Daitom), the plaintiff below. The result was dismissal by the United States District Court for the District of Kansas of all three counts of Daitom's complaint.

Daitom had brought this diversity action in federal court on March 7, 1980 against Pennwalt Corporation and its Stokes Vacuum Equipment Division (Pennwalt). Counts I and II of Daitom's complaint alleged breach of various express and implied warranties and Count III alleged negligent design and manufacture by Pennwalt of certain rotary vacuum drying machines sold to and used commercially by Daitom in the production of a vitamin known properly as dextro calcium pantothenate and commonly as Vitamin B-5.

Daitom is a Delaware chartered corporation having its principal place of business in Kansas. It was formed to implement a joint venture between Thompson-Hayward Chemical Company, Inc. of Kansas City, Kansas and Daiichi-Seiyakii Co., Ltd., of Tokyo, Japan. Pennwalt is a Pennsylvania chartered corporation with its principal place of business in Pennsylvania.

Daitom requests a reversal of the district court's grant of summary judgment against Daitom on all counts of its complaint and seeks a remand for a trial on the merits.

We have concluded that there should be a reversal with respect to Counts I and II, together with a remand to the district court for a trial on the merits of those claims. On the other hand, we have concluded that there should be an affirmance of the summary judgment against Daitom on Count III of its complaint.

II. FACTS

The essential facts so far as they pertain to the issues presented in this appeal are as follows.

For the purpose of implementing its joint venture, Daitom planned to construct and operate a manufacturing plant to commercially produce dextro calcium pantothenate. The design of the plant was undertaken and handled on behalf of Daitom by Kintech Services, Inc. (which company will be referred to as Kintech), an engineering design firm located in Cincinnati, Ohio. Kintech had the responsibility not only for designing the plant; it also was responsible for investigating various means of drying the product during the production process, and for negotiating the purchase of certain equipment to be used in the plant. Included in the equipment was automated drying equipment to be used in removing methonol and water from the processed vitamin as part of the purification process.

There were numerous tests made and conducted at Kintech's request by equipment manufacturers. Kintech formulated specifications for the automated drying equipment. (This is referred to as Kintech Specification 342, Record,

Volume I, at 59–65). On behalf of Daitom, Kintech invited various vendors to bid on the needed equipment.

Pennwalt, on September 7, 1976, submitted a proposal for the sale of two rotary vacuum dryers with dust filters and heating systems to dry dextro calcium pantothenate. The typewritten proposal specified the equipment to be sold, the f.o.b. price, and delivery and payment terms. A pre-printed conditions of sale form was also attached to the proposal and explicitly made an integral part of the proposal by the typewritten sheet.

Kintech recommended to Daitom that Pennwalt's proposal be accepted and on October 5, 1976, well within the thirty-day acceptance period specified in the proposal, Daitom issued a purchase order for the Pennwalt equipment. The purchase order consisted of a pre-printed form with the identification of the specific equipment and associated prices typewritten in the appropriate blank spaces on the front together with seventeen lengthy "boilerplate" or "standard" terms and conditions of sale on the back. In addition, on the front of the purchase order in the column marked for a description of the items purchased, Daitom typed the following:

> Rotary vacuum dryers in accordance with Kintech Services, Inc. specification 342 dated August 20, 1976, and in accordance with Stokes proposal dated September 7, 1976.

The two rotary vacuum dryers and the equipment that went along with them were manufactured by Pennwalt and delivered to Daitom's plant in early May 1977. For the reason that there had been no construction of Daitom's plant, the crated equipment was not immediately installed. Instead, it was stored outside in crates. On June 15, 1978, the dryers were finally installed and first operated by Daitom. Daitom notified Pennwalt of serious problems with the operation of the dryers on June 17, 1978.

Daitom's contention was that the dryers suffered from two severe defects: 1) they were delivered with misaligned agitator blades causing a scraping and damaging of the dryer interiors and an uneven distribution of the products being dried; and 2) they were undersized necessitating an overloading of the dryers and a "lumping up" of the product rendering it unsuitable for further use. Pennwalt's repair personnel visited the Daitom plant to investigate the alleged operating difficulties, but Daitom contends the dryers were not repaired and have never performed as required under the specifications and as represented by Pennwalt. This was the basis for the lawsuit.

This suit was brought in federal court on March 7, 1980, after Pennwalt's alleged failure to correct the difficulties with the dryers. On Pennwalt's motion, the district court granted summary judgment against Daitom on all three counts of its complaint. The court dismissed Counts I and II after applying section 2–207 of the Uniform Commercial Code (U.C.C.) and finding that Daitom's breach of warranties claims were barred by the one-year period of limitations specified in Pennwalt's proposal. The court further concluded that alleged damages in Count III for the negligent design and manufacture of the dryers were not available in tort; the sole remedy being in an action for breach of warranties which here was barred by the period of limitations. Consequently, summary judgment was granted against Daitom. Daitom's subsequent motion for reconsideration was denied by the district court on June 3, 1982, and following that, this appeal took place.

III. Discussion

A. The Issues

It is to be noted that the district court granted summary judgment against Daitom on Counts I and II of the complaint, finding the breach of warranties claim barred by the one-year period of limitations which was set forth in Pennwalt's proposal. In ruling against Daitom the court followed a three step analysis. First, it concluded that pursuant to U.C.C. § 2–207(1), a written contract for the sale of the rotary dryers was formed by Pennwalt's September 7, 1976 proposal and Daitom's October 5, 1976 purchase order accepting that proposal. Second, the court found that the one year period of limitations specified in Pennwalt's proposal and shortening the typical four-year period of limitations available under the U.C.C. became part of the contract of sale and governed the claims for breach of warranties. Thus, the court accepted the proposal that was contained in the documents that had been submitted by the defendant-appellee. Third, the court concluded that the one-year period of limitations was not tolled by any conduct of Pennwalt's, so that consequently, Daitom's claims were barred because they were brought after the expiration of the one year limitations period. The view we have of the submission and response is that the approval was initial and general and contemplated further discussion and improvement.

The circumstances surrounding the delivery of this equipment and what occurred thereafter is of high importance. The equipment was delivered in crates and boxes, and at that time Daitom had no plant. Instead of seeking to protect the equipment in some way, Pennwalt simply delivered the boxes and left. The documents which were part of the delivery provided for this one-year period of limitations specified in the Pennwalt proposal. Seemingly, this conduct on the part of Pennwalt in making a quick delivery and quick departure took hold in connection with the motion for summary judgment, the court ruling that more than one year had passed before they were able to try out the machinery and discover the defects. The suggestion is made as to how this machinery could have been utilized or contested because of the conditions that were present. Why, then should the one-year limitations period, created by Pennwalt, be allowed to take effect?

Daitom has challenged the district court's findings as to the terms which became a part of the contract. Daitom argues that its October 5, 1976 purchase order did not constitute an acceptance of Pennwalt's September 7, 1976 proposal. Instead, Daitom claims that its purchase order explicitly made acceptance conditional on Pennwalt's assent to the additional or different terms in the purchase order. As a consequence, Daitom argues, pursuant to U.C.C. § 2–207(1),[1] the exchanged writings of the parties did *not* form a contract, because Pennwalt failed to assent to the additional or different terms in the purchase order. The most relevant additional or different terms Daitom alleges were in *its* purchase order were the terms reserving all warranties and remedies available in law, despite Pennwalt's limitation of warranties and remedies in its

1. The parties, throughout this litigation and through their briefs, agree that the law of Pennsylvania governs their warranty claims. The parties further agree that Pennsylvania has adopted the provisions of the Uniform Commercial Code and that for the purpose of this action the Pennsylvania statute does not modify the U.C.C. provisions. See 13 Pa.C.S. A. § 2207 (Purdon's 1984). Therefore, throughout this memorandum the relevant code sections will be referred to only by the U.C.C. numeral designation.

proposal. In a sense Pennwalt argues it enjoyed an exclusive right to set the conditions.

Daitom argues that on their face the writings failed to create a contract, and, instead, that a contract was to be formed by *the conduct* of both parties, pursuant to § 2–207(3), and the resulting contract consisted of the terms on which the writings agreed, together with "any supplementary terms incorporated under any other provision of [the UCC]." Therefore, Daitom concludes, the resulting contract governing the sale of the rotary dryers incorporated the U.C.C. provisions for express warranties (§ 2–313), implied warranties (§§ 2–314, 2–315), and a four year period of limitations.

As an alternative argument, Daitom contends that even if its October 5, 1976 purchase order did constitute an acceptance of Pennwalt's September 7, 1976 proposal and did form a contract, all conflicting terms between the two writings were "knocked out" and did not become part of the resulting contract, because of their being at odds one with the other. Therefore, Daitom concludes once again that the resulting contract consisted of only those terms in which the writings agreed and any supplementary or "gap-filler" terms incorporated under the provisions of the U.C.C.; specifically §§ 2–313, 2–314, 2–315, 2–725.

Daitom makes a further argument which has some appeal and that is that even if the one-year period of limitations specified in Pennwalt's proposal became a part of the sales contract, it was tolled by Pennwalt's wrongful conduct, which included fraudulent concealment of the equipment's defects and failure of the essential purpose of the limited remedies. Since this court's decision does not rely on the question of the tolling of the limitations period, we will not devote detailed argument to this.

* * *

B. The Applicable Law

The district court found the dispute between Daitom and Pennwalt involved a "transaction in goods," between persons who are "merchants" and, therefore, was governed by Article 2 of the U.C.C. U.C.C. §§ 2–102, 2–104. The district court also stated that the dispute is a classic example of the "battle of the forms."

As previously noted, there has been agreement that the law of Pennsylvania governs these claims for breach of warranty and Pennsylvania has adopted the provisions of the U.C.C. Section 2–207 of the U.C.C. was specifically drafted to deal with the battle of the forms and related problems. U.C.C. § 2–207, Comment 1.

Section 2–207 has been commented on in one case as a "murky bit of prose," (*Southwest Engineering Co., Inc. v. Martin Tractor Co., Inc.*, 205 Kan. 684, 473 P.2d 18, 25 (1970)), and as "one of the most important, subtle, and difficult in the entire code, and well it may be said that the product as it finally reads is not altogether satisfactory." (Duesenberg & King, 3 *Sales and Bulk Transfer Under the Uniform Commercial Code,* § 3.03 at 3–12 (1984)). The Pennsylvania Supreme Court has not addressed the issues presented by this case. In the absence, therefore, of an authoritative pronouncement from the state's highest court, our task is to regard ourselves as sitting in diversity and predicting how the state's highest court would rule. * * * This court must also follow any intermediate state court decision unless other authority convinces us that the state supreme court would decide otherwise. * * * Also, the policies underlying the applicable legal doctrines, the doctrinal trends indicated by these policies, and the decisions of other courts may also inform this court's analysis * * *. With these standards in mind, we proceed to consider and analyze the case.

C. *The Writings and the Contract*

The trial court concluded that the parties' exchanged writings formed a contract. Thus, there was not a formal single document. Pennwalt's September 7, 1976 proposal constituted the offer and Daitom's October 5, 1976 purchase order constituted the acceptance.

It is essentially uncontested that Pennwalt's proposal constituted an offer. The proposal set forth in some detail the equipment to be sold to Daitom, the price, the terms of shipment, and specifically stated that the attached terms and conditions were an integral part of the proposal. One of those attached terms and conditions of sale limited the warranties to repair and replacement of defective parts and limited the period of one year from the date of delivery for any action for breach of warranty.[3]

The proposal was sent to Kintech and forwarded to Daitom with a recommendation to accept the proposal. Daitom sent the October 5, 1976 purchase order to Pennwalt. This purchase order constituted an acceptance of Pennwalt's offer and formed a binding contract for the sale only pursuant to 2–207(1), despite the statement of terms additional to or different from those in the offer.[4] But these terms were not without meaning or consequence. However, the acceptance was not expressly conditioned on Pennwalt accepting these additional or different terms.

There is a provision which Daitom contends made the acceptance expressly conditional on Pennwalt's accepting the additional or different terms which appeared in the pre-printed, standard "boilerplate" provisions on the back of the purchase order. It stated:

3. Paragraph 5 of the terms and conditions of sale stated in full (emphasis added):

6. WARRANTIES:

a. Seller warrants that at the time of delivery of the property to the carrier, it will be, unless otherwise specified, new, free and clear of all lawful liens and security interests or other encumbrances unknown to Buyer. If, within a period of one year from the date of *such delivery* any parts of the property (except property specified to be used property or normal wear parts) fail because of material or workmanship which was defective at the time of such delivery, Seller will repair such parts, or furnish parts to replace them f.o.b. Seller's or its supplier's plant, provided such failure is due solely to such defective material or workmanship and is not contributed to by any other cause, such as improper care or unreasonable use, and provided such defects are brought to Seller's attention for verification when first discovered, and the parts alleged to be so defective are returned, if requested, to Seller's or its supplier's plant. *No action for breach of warranty shall be brought more than one year after the cause of action has accrued*

SELLER MAKES NO OTHER WARRANTY OF ANY KIND, EXPRESS OR IMPLIED, INCLUDING ANY WARRANTY OF FITNESS OF THE PROPERTY FOR ANY PARTICULAR PURPOSE EVEN IF THAT PURPOSE IS KNOWN TO SELLER.

In no event shall Seller be liable for consequential damage.

b. Because of varied interpretations of standards at the local level, Seller cannot warrant that the property meets the requirements of the Occupational Safety and Health Act.

4. The principal additional or different terms referred to the reservation of warranties. Specifically:

(8) WARRANTY. The Seller warrants that the supplies covered by this purchase order will conform to the specifications, drawings, samples, or other descriptions furnished or specified by buyer, and will be fit and sufficient for the purpose intended, merchantable, of good material and workmanship, and free from defect. The warranties and remedies provided for in this paragraph * * * shall be in addition to those implied by or available at law and shall exist not withstanding [sic] the acceptance by Buyer of all or a part of this applies with respect to which such warranties and remedies are applicable.

> Acceptance. Immediate acceptance is required unless otherwise provided herein. It is understood and agreed that the written acceptance by Seller of this purchase order or the commencement of any work performance of any services hereunder by the Seller, (including the commencement of any work or the performance of any service with respect to samples), shall constitute acceptance by Seller of this purchase order and of all the terms and conditions of such acceptance is *expressly limited to such terms and conditions, unless each deviation is mutually recognized therefore in writing.* (Emphasis added.)

This language does not preclude the formation of a contract by the exchanged writings pursuant to § 2–207(1). Nor does it dictate the adoption of a conclusion holding that as a result the acceptance provided the applicable terms of the resulting contract. First, it is well established that a contract for the sale of goods may be made in any manner to show agreement, requiring merely that there be some objective manifestation of mutual assent, but that there must be. There is not a contract until it takes place. See U.C.C. § 2–204; *Ore & Chemical Corporation v. Howard Butcher Trading Corp.*, 455 F.Supp. 1150, 1152 (E.D.Pa. 1978). Here there is such an objective manifestation of agreement on essential terms of equipment specifications, price, and the terms of shipment and payment, all of which took place before the machinery was put to any test. The purchase order explicitly referred to and incorporated on its front Kintech's equipment specifications and Pennwalt's proposal. But we are unwilling to hold such a typewritten reference and incorporation by Daitom brings the matter to a close. The acceptance and warranty terms as provided for by the above excerpted acceptance clause, does manifest a willingness on all essential terms to accept the offer and form a contract. *Cf., Daitom v. Henry Vogt Machine Co.*, No. 80–2081 (D.Kan., unpublished 2/22/82) (In that case the court held that under identical factual circumstances and involving the identical purchase order form language, such typewritten reference and incorporation of the offer constituted a written modification of the purchase order's boilerplate acceptance terms to conform to those in the offer.) This was, of course, before an attempt was made to use the equipment.

Second, the boilerplate provision does not directly address the instant case. The purchase order is drafted principally as an *offer* inviting acceptance. Although this court recognizes that the form may serve a dual condition depending on the circumstances, the imprecision of language that permits such service detracts from Daitom's argument of conditional acceptance.

Third, the courts are split on the application of § 2–207(1) and the meaning of "expressly made conditional on assent to the additional or different terms." *See Boese-Hilburn Co. v. Dean Machinery*, 616 S.W.2d 520 (Mo.App.1981). *Roto-Lith Ltd. v. F.P. Bartlett & Co., Inc.*, 297 F.2d 497 (1st Cir.1962) represents one extreme of the spectrum, that the offeree's response stating a term materially altering the contractual obligations solely to the disadvantage of the offeror constitutes a conditional acceptance. The other extreme of the spectrum is represented by *Dorton v. Collins & Aikman Corporation*, 453 F.2d 1161 (6th Cir. 1972), in which case the court held that the conditional nature of the acceptance should be so clearly expressed in a manner sufficient to notify the offeror that the offeree is unwilling to proceed with the transaction unless the additional or different terms are included in the contract. The middle of the spectrum providing that a response merely "predicating" acceptance on clarification, addition or modification is a conditional acceptance is represented by *Construc-*

tion Aggregates Corp. v. Hewitt-Robins, Inc., 404 F.2d 505 (7th Cir.1968), *cert. denied*, 395 U.S. 921, 89 S.Ct. 1774, 23 L.Ed.2d 238 (1969).

The facts of this case, Daitom asserts, are not of a character that would suggest that there had been an unequivocal acceptance. The defendant-appellee was aware that the machinery had not even been tried. Once it was tried, it broke down in a very short time. It is hard to see a justifiable acceptance, Daitom asserts, when the buyer does not even know whether it works, and, in fact, learns after the fact, that it does not work. This fact alone renders the "contract" to be questionable.

The better view as to the meaning and application of "conditional acceptance," and the view most likely to be adopted by Pennsylvania, is the view in *Dorton* that the offeree must explicitly communicate his or her unwillingness to proceed with the transaction unless the additional or different terms in its response are accepted by the offeror. * * *

Having found an offer and an acceptance which was not made expressly conditional on assent to additional or different terms, we must now decide the effect of those additional or different terms on the resulting contract and what terms became part of it. The district court simply resolved this dispute by focusing solely on the period of limitations specified in Pennwalt's offer of September 7, 1976. Thus, the court held that while the offer explicitly specified a one-year period of limitations in accordance with § 2–725(1) allowing such a reduction, Daitom's acceptance of October 5, 1976 was silent as to the limitations period. Consequently, the court held that § 2–207(2) was inapplicable and the one-year limitations period controlled, effectively barring Daitom's action for breach of warranties.

While the district court's analysis undertook to resolve the issue without considering the question of the application of § 2–207(2) to additional or different terms, we cannot accept its approach or its conclusion. We are unable to ignore the plain implication of Daitom's reservation in its boilerplate warranties provision of all its rights and remedies available at law. Such an explicit reservation impliedly reserves the statutory period of limitations; without such a reservation, all other reservations of actions and remedies are without effect.

The statutory period of limitations under the U.C.C. is four years after the cause of action has accrued. U.C.C. § 2–725(1). Were we to determine that this four-year period became a part of the contract rather than the shorter one-year period, Daitom's actions on breach of warranties were timely brought and summary judgment against Daitom was error.[5]

We realize that our conclusion requires an inference to be drawn from a construction of Daitom's terms; however, such an inference and construction are consistent with the judicial reluctance to grant summary judgment where there is some reasonable doubt over the existence of a genuine material fact. *See Williams v. Borden, Inc.*, 637 F.2d 731, 738 (10th Cir.1980). When taking into account the circumstances surrounding the application of the one-year limitations period, we have little hesitation in adopting the U.C.C.'s four-year limitations reservation, the application of which permits a trial on the merits. Thus,

5. Daitom filed its complaint on March 7, 1980. While the parties dispute when the cause of action accrued and the period of limitations began to run, resolution of the dispute is unnecessary if this court concludes the four-year limitations period controls. Even if it is found the action accrued in May 1977 on delivery of the dryers to Daitom's plant, the four-year period of limitations had not expired on March 7, 1980 when the complaint was filed.

this court must recognize that certain terms in Daitom's acceptance differed from terms in Pennwalt's offer and decide which become part of the contract. The district court certainly erred in refusing to recognize such a conflict.[6]

The difficulty in determining the effect of different terms in the acceptance is the imprecision of drafting evident in § 2–207. The language of the provision is silent on how different terms in the acceptance are to be treated once a contract is formed pursuant to § 2–207(1). That section provides that a contract may be formed by exchanged writings despite the existence of additional or different terms in the acceptance. Therefore, an offeree's response is treated as an acceptance while it may differ substantially from the offer. This section of the provision, then, reformed the mirror-image rule; that common law legal formality that prohibited the formation of a contract if the exchanged writings of offer and acceptance differed in any term.

Once a contract is recognized pursuant to § 2–207(1), § 2–207(2) provides the standard for determining if the additional terms stated in the acceptance become a part of the contract. Between merchants, such *additional* terms become part of the resulting contract *unless* 1) the offer expressly limited acceptance to its terms, 2) the additional terms materially alter the contract obligations, or 3) the offeror gives notice of his or her objection to the additional terms within a reasonable time. Should any one of these three possibilities occur, the *additional* terms are treated merely as proposals for incorporation in the contract and absent assent by the offeror the terms of the offer control. In any event, the existence of the additional terms does not prevent a contract from being formed.

Section 2–207(2) is silent on the treatment of terms stated in the acceptance that are *different,* rather than merely additional, from those stated in the offer. It is unclear whether "different" terms in the acceptance are intended to be included under the aegis of "additional" terms in § 2–207(2) and, therefore, fail to become part of the agreement if they materially alter the contract. Comment 3 suggests just such an inclusion.[7] However, Comment 6 suggests that different terms in exchanged writings must be assumed to constitute mutual objections by each party to the other's conflicting terms and result in a mutual "knockout" of both parties' conflicting terms; the missing terms to be supplied by the U.C.C.'s "gap-filler" provisions.[8] At least one commentator, in support of this view, has suggested that the drafting history of the provision indicates that the word "different" was intentionally deleted from the final draft of § 2–207(2) to

6. There is some indication in its memorandum and order that had the district court considered the effect of the conflicting terms, it would have applied § 2–207(2)(b) and concluded that the terms in Pennwalt's offer controlled because Daitom's conflicting terms would have materially altered the content. Memorandum and Order at 11. Because we hold, *infra,* that conflicting terms should not be analyzed pursuant to § 2–207(2), this conclusion of the district court is also in error.

7. Comment 3 states (emphasis added):

> Whether or not *additional or different* terms will become part of the agreement depends upon the provision of subsection (2).

It must be remembered that even official comments to enacted statutory text do not have the force of law and are only guidance in the interpretation of that text. *In re Bristol Associates, Inc.,* 505 F.2d 1056 (3rd Cir.1974) (while the comments to the Pennsylvania U.C.C. are not binding, the Pennsylvania Supreme Court gives substantial weight to the comments as evidencing application of the Code).

8. Comment 6 states, in part:

> Where clauses on confirming forms sent by both parties conflict each party must be assumed to object to a clause of the other conflicting with one on the confirmation sent by himself * * *. The contract then consists of the terms expressly agreed to, terms on which the confirmations agree, and terms supplied by the Act, including subsection (2).

preclude its treatment under that subsection.[9] The plain language, comments, and drafting history of the provision, therefore, provide little helpful guidance in resolving the disagreement over the treatment of different terms pursuant to § 2–207.

Despite all this, the cases and commentators have suggested three possible approaches. The first of these is to treat "different" terms as included under the aegis of "additional" terms in § 2–207(2). Consequently, different terms in the acceptance would never become part of the contract, because, by definition, they would materially alter the contract (i.e., the offeror's terms). Several courts have adopted this approach. *E.g., Mead Corporation v. McNally-Pittsburg Manufacturing Corporation,* 654 F.2d 1197 (6th Cir.1981) (applying Ohio law); *Steiner v. Mobil Oil Corporation,* 20 Cal.3d 90, 141 Cal.Rptr. 157, 569 P.2d 751 (1977); *Lockheed Electronics Company, Inc. v. Keronix, Inc.,* 114 Cal.App.3d 304, 170 Cal. Rptr. 591 (1981).

The second approach, which leads to the same result as the first, is that the offeror's terms control because the offeree's different terms merely fall out; § 2–207(2) cannot rescue the different terms since that subsection applies only to *additional* terms. Under this approach, Comment 6 (apparently supporting a mutual rather than a single term knockout) is not applicable because it refers only to conflicting terms in confirmation forms following *oral* agreement, not conflicting terms in the *writings* that form the agreement. This approach is supported by Professor Summers. J.J. White & R.S. Summers, *Uniform Commercial Code,* § 1–2, at 29 (2d ed. 1980).

The third, and preferable approach, which is commonly called the "knock-out" rule, is that the conflicting terms cancel one another. Under this view the offeree's form is treated only as an acceptance of the terms in the offeror's form which did not conflict. The ultimate contract, then, includes those non-conflicting terms and any other terms supplied by the U.C.C., including terms incorporated by course of performance (§ 2–208), course of dealing (§ 1–205), usage of trade (§ 1–205), and other "gap fillers" or "off-the-rack" terms (e.g., implied warranty of fitness for particular purpose, § 2–315). As stated previously, this approach finds some support in Comment 6. Professor White supports this approach as the most fair and consistent with the purposes of § 2–207. *White & Summers, supra,* at 29. Further, several courts have adopted or recognized the approach. *E.g., Idaho Power Company v. Westinghouse Electric Corporation,* 596 F.2d 924 (9th Cir.1979) (applying Idaho law, although incorrectly, applying § 2–207(3) after finding a contract under § 2–207(1)); *Owens-Corning Fiberglass Corporation v. Sonic Development Corporation,* 546 F.Supp. 533 (D.Kan.1982) (Judge Saffels applying Kansas law); *Lea Tai Textile Co., Ltd. v. Manning Fabrics, Inc.,* 411 F.Supp. 1404 (S.D.N.Y.1975); *Hartwig Farms, Inc. v. Pacific Gamble Robinson Company,* 28 Wash.App. 539, 625 P.2d 171 (1981); *S.C. Gray, Inc. v. Ford Motor Company,* 92 Mich.App. 789, 286 N.W.2d 34 (1979).

We are of the opinion that this is the more reasonable approach, particularly when dealing with a case such as this where from the beginning the offeror's specified period of limitations would expire before the equipment was even installed. The approaches other than the "knock-out" approach would be inequitable and unjust because they invited the very kind of treatment which the defendant attempted to provide.

9. See D.G. Baird & R. Weisberg, *Rules, Standards, and the Battle of the Forms: A Reassessment of § 2-207,* 68 Va.L.R. 1217, 1240, n. 61.

Thus, we are of the conclusion that if faced with this issue the Pennsylvania Supreme Court would adopt the "knock-out" rule and hold here that the conflicting terms in Pennwalt's offer and Daitom's acceptance regarding the period of limitations and applicable warranties cancel one another out. Consequently, the other provisions of the U.C.C. must be used to provide the missing terms.

This particular approach and result are supported persuasively by the underlying rationale and purpose behind the adoption of § 2–207. As stated previously, that provision was drafted to reform the infamous common law mirror-image rule and associated last-shot doctrine that enshrined the fortuitous positions of senders of forms and accorded undue advantages based on such fortuitous positions. *White & Summers, supra* at 25. To refuse to adopt the "knock-out" rule and instead adopt one of the remaining two approaches would serve to re-enshrine the undue advantages derived solely from the fortuitous positions of when a party sent a form. Cf., 3 Duesenberg & King at 93 (1983 Supp.). This is because either approach other than the knock-out rule for different terms results in the offeror and his or her terms always prevailing solely because he or she sent the first form. Professor Summers argues that this advantage is not wholly unearned, because the offeree has an opportunity to review the offer, identify the conflicting terms and make his or her acceptance conditional. But this joinder misses the fundamental purpose of the U.C.C. in general and § 2–207 in particular, which is to preserve a contract and fill in any gaps if the parties intended to make a contract and there is a reasonable basis for giving an appropriate remedy. U.C.C. § 2–204(3); § 2–207(1); § 2–207(3). Thus, this approach gives the offeree some protection. While it is laudible for business persons to read the fine print and boilerplate provisions in exchanged forms, there is nothing in § 2–207 mandating such careful consideration. The provision seems drafted with a recognition of the reality that merchants seldom review exchanged forms with the scrutiny of lawyers. The "knock-out" rule is therefore the best approach. Even if a term eliminated by operation of the "knock-out" rule is reintroduced by operation of the U.C.C.'s gap-filler provisions, such a result does not indicate a weakness of the approach. On the contrary, at least the reintroduced term has the merit of being a term that the U.C.C. draftpersons regarded as fair.

We now address the question of reverse and remand regarding Counts I and II. The result of this court's holding is that the district court erred in granting summary judgment against Daitom on Counts I and II of its complaint. Operation of the "knock-out" rule to conflicting terms results in the instant case in the conflicting terms in the offer and acceptance regarding the period of limitations and applicable warranties cancelling. In the absence of any evidence of course of performance, course of dealing, or usage of trade providing the missing terms, §§ 2–725(1), 2–313, 2–314, 2–315 may operate to supply a four-year period of limitations, an express warranty,[10] an implied warranty of merchantability, and an implied warranty of fitness for a particular purpose, respectively. The ruling of the district court on Counts I and II does not invite this kind of a broad inquiry, and thus, we must recognize the superiority in terms of justice of the "knock-out" rule. Consequently, the ruling of the district court on Counts I and II must be reversed and the matter remanded for trial consistent with this court's ruling.

10. Daitom alleges that several letters from Pennwalt expressly warrantied the performance of the rotary dryers. *E.g.,* Pretrial Order, Record Volume II at 59, para. 12, 13, 14, 15.

* * *

[The court held that there was no Cause of Action in tort where an allegedly defective product caused only economic loss.]

Accordingly, the district court correctly concluded that Daitom's requested damages are not recoverable in tort. The court's summary judgment ruling against Daitom on Count III, therefore, should be affirmed. As explained above, we reverse the trial court with respect to Counts I and II. The cause is remanded for further proceedings consistent with this opinion.

BARRETT, CIRCUIT JUDGE, dissenting:

I respectfully dissent. Insofar as the issue of contract formation is concerned in this case, we are confronted with a "battle of the forms" case involving the interpretation and application of U.C.C. § 2–207. I would affirm.

Pennwalt's proposal of September 7, 1976, was an "offer." It was submitted to Daitom in response to solicitations initiated by Daitom and it contained specific terms relating to price, delivery dates, etc., and its terms were held "open" for Daitom's acceptance within 30 days. In my view, Daitom accepted the offer with its purchase order. That order repeated the quantity, model number, and price for the items as those terms appeared in the Pennwalt proposal and, by reference, it incorporated four pages of specifications attached to Pennwalt's proposal or "offer." The purchase order did contain some different and additional language from that contained in Pennwalt's proposal. However, the Code has rejected the old mirror image rule. Thus, I agree with the district court's finding/ruling that a contract was formed in the circumstances described.

I also agree with the district court's conclusion that the terms of Pennwalt's proposal constituted the "terms of the contract." I do not agree, as Daitom argues, that its "acceptance" was made "conditional" upon Pennwalt's assent to the additional/different terms set forth in Daitom's purchase order. The court correctly found no such *express* condition in Daitom's acceptance.

The "knock-out" rule should not, in my view, be reached in this case. It can be applied only if, as Daitom argues and the majority agrees, the "conflicting terms" cancel each other out. The "knock-out" rule does have substantial support in the law, but I do not believe it is relevant in this case because the *only* conflicting terms relate to the *scope* of the warranty. In this case, it is not an important consideration because, pursuant to the express time limitations contained in Pennwalt's "offer," Daitom lost its right to assert any warranty claim. There was no term in Daitom's purchase order in conflict with the express one-year limitation within which to bring warranty actions. I agree with the district court's reasoning in rejecting Daitom's contentions that the one-year limitation period should not apply because (1) the term failed of "its essential purpose" of providing Daitom with a limited remedy under U.C.C. § 2–719(2) and (2) the time-limit was tolled due to Pennwalt's alleged fraudulent concealment of the defect. I concur with the trial court's finding that Daitom made no showing that the one-year limitation period was unreasonable because of some act of Pennwalt. As to the fraudulent concealment allegation, the court properly observed that Daitom did not plead this claim with the particularity required and, further, that the alleged fraudulent acts were not independent of the alleged breaches proper.

[Some footnotes omitted.]

Note: Should UCC 2–207 Be Repealed?

The three preceding cases give you a taste of the issues raised in litigation under UCC 2–207. They are but tips of the iceberg of cases and scholarly comment on this legislative attempt to relax the supposed unfairness of the common law "mirror-image" rule.

Let us work with a simple case, based upon the *Bethlehem Steel* litigation, discussed supra. Suppose, after negotiations and agreement on all terms but price, Bethlehem sent Litton a written offer to pay $20.5M for construction of the ship according to the specifications. Litton promptly responded by letter as follows: "We accept your offer to pay $20.5M for construction of the vessel, as specified, plus price escalation to be determined by the attached clause." Bethlehem, claiming that the response was a counteroffer, rejected it and withdrew from the deal. Was there a contract?

At common law the answer was no: The reply was a counteroffer. Under UCC 2–207(1) and Section 59 of the Restatement, Second, of Contracts, however, the answer is yes if Litton's "definite * * * expression of acceptance" was not "expressly made conditional on assent to the additional or different terms." (Section 59 states that a "reply to an offer which purports to accept it but is conditional on the offeror's assent to terms additional or different from those offered is not an acceptance but is a counter-offer.")

But, as the *Diatom* case indicates, a different or additional term which materially alters the bargain does not, alone, constitute an "express" condition: Additional, unequivocal language of condition is required. Thus, Bethlehem, a commercial party, is bound to a contract for $20.5M under UCC 2–207(1) even though Litton wants price escalation and there has been no conduct by both parties which recognizes the existence of a contract. See UCC 2–204(1). Furthermore, Bethlehem is forced to deal with the complex issues in UCC 2–207(2): Is the term automatically part of the bargain or not and, if not, what must Bethlehem do to avoid incorporation? Similarly, suppose Litton's definite acceptance was for a fixed price of $25 million. Should Bethlehem bear the risk that there was a contract under UCC 2–207(1), that the materially different terms cancel each other out and that the price is a "reasonable price at the time for delivery?" UCC 2–305(1).

Between commercial parties where no standard forms are involved, and, therefore, little risk of unfair surprise, the answer to these questions should be no. Whatever the reasons for reversing the presumption of the "mirror image" rule, they make little sense where there is no conduct by both parties supporting an intention to contract and no other evidence of usage or prior dealing to support a conclusion that, in commercial understanding, the deal had been closed. See UCC 2–207, Comment 2. In short, despite Litton's purported acceptance without an express condition, Bethlehem should have the option either to continue negotiations or withdraw on the assumption that no contract has been formed. Surely, the same factors that influenced the Pennsylvania Supreme Court to find no contract where there was a failure to agree on price under UCC 2–204 are relevant to the UCC 2–207 issue. Compare Dataserv Equipment, Inc. v. Technology Finance Leasing Corp., 364 N.W.2d 838 (Minn.1985) (rejection of counteroffer terminates negotiations).

Taking the next step, suppose that Litton responded with a different or additional price term and there was either no "definite * * * acceptance" or there was an express condition. In short, there was no contract under UCC 2–207(1): Litton made a counteroffer which Bethlehem was free to accept, reject or to attempt to negotiate. Suppose, however, that without further explicit agreement on price, there was conduct by both parties which recognized the existence of some contract. What should the price term be if the writings involved do not agree on a price? See UCC 2–207(3).

Again, the choices are similar to those in *Daitom* where there was a contract under UCC 2–207(1) but there were different terms: (1) Bethlehem's price controls; (2) Litton's price controls; or (3) A reasonable price at the time of delivery controls. Assuming that UCC 2–207(3) applies to this dispute, most courts have concluded that unless Bethlehem's conduct was with express awareness of Litton's price term, the "reasonable" price option should be invoked. But, again, how can a commercial party without standard forms not be aware of Litton's price term? If aware (no risk of unfair surprise), then the choice to engage in mutual conduct consistent with the existence of some contract should be sufficient to incorporate Litton's price term into the agreement. There is no reason to protect Bethlehem, who has made an informed choice, from Litton's last proposed price.

The answer, then, to the question posed, "Should UCC 2–207 be Repealed?," is no. But it should be revised to differentiate between transactions where standard forms, and thus the risk of unfair surprise, are included and those where they are not involved. Without the risk of unfair surprise, there is no obvious justification for imposing a contract on Bethlehem, even on its own terms, unless Bethlehem makes an informed choice either to continue negotiations or assent to Litton's terms.

SECTION 4. THE STATUTE OF FRAUDS

A. *History and Purposes*

A statute of frauds imposes additional conditions upon the enforceability of agreements which otherwise qualify as contracts. In general, there must be a writing consistent with the existence of a contract, specifying some if not all of the terms, and signed or authenticated by the party to be charged. The UCC has several such statutes of frauds, see, e.g., UCC 1–206, 8–319 (contract for sale of securities), 9–203(1) (creation of enforceable security interest), including UCC 2–201, which governs contracts for the "sale of goods for the price of $500 or more." UCC 2–201(1).

At least three justifications for the statute of frauds have been asserted. First, the statute avoids fraudulent or perjured claims that some contract was in fact made. Second, the statute avoids fraudulent or perjured claims regarding the terms of a contract admittedly made. Third, the statute serves a useful purpose in so far as it contributes to the business habit of making a writing. See Vold, *The Application of the Statute of Frauds Under the Uniform Sales Act,* 15 Minn.L.Rev. 391, 393–94 (1931).

The first two justifications have long been criticised as anachronistic. The conditions existing in 17th Century England—uncontrolled jury discretion, restrictions upon the competency of witnesses and immature contract doctrine—no longer obtain. See Willis, *The Statute of Frauds—A Legal Anachronism,* 3 Ind. L.J. 427, 429–31 (1928). Attacks of this sort, plus the opportunity provided by the statute for "technical unmeritorious defenses" induced Parliament, in 1954, to repeal the statute of frauds provision in the British Sale of Goods Act. See Grunfield, *Law Reform (Enforcement of Contracts) Act,* 1954, 17 Mod.L.Rev. 451 (1954).

The third justification is more difficult to undercut. According to Professor Vold, the "cases that justify the statute are * * * the thousands of uncontested current transactions where misunderstanding and controversy are avoided by the presence of a writing which the statute at least indirectly aided to procure. * * *" *Vold,* supra. But see Comment, *The Statute of Frauds and the Business Community: A Re-Appraisal in Light of Prevailing Practices,* 66 Yale

L.J. 1038 (1957) (reliance on an oral order rather than the practice of employing writings is prevalent practice). Karl Llewellyn agreed with Vold's assessment, see Llewellyn, *What Price Contract? An Essay in Perspective,* 40 Yale L.J. 704, 746–48 (1931), and his views were influential in the drafting of UCC 2–201.

What justifications exist for UCC 2–201? Should the statute of frauds in Article 2 be repealed? Keep these questions in mind as you work through the following simple problems.

B. *Illustrative Problems and Cases*

The following problems and cases illustrate some of the issues that have arisen over the scope and application of UCC 2–201.

Problem 10–5

On February 1, S, a farmer, entered into an oral contract with B, a grain dealer, to plant his fields in corn and to harvest and deliver the output for $2.30 per bushel by October 1. B immediately resold the corn to C, a cereal producer, for $2.60 per bushel. On April 1, before the fields had been planted, S informed B that he had entered into a written contract with D, another dealer, to sell his output of corn for $3.00 per bushel. B claimed a breach of contract, but S's lawyer stated that the alleged contract was not enforceable because of the statute of frauds. As B's lawyer, identify and assess all arguments that the transaction was not within the scope of UCC 2–201(1).

Problem 10–6

Suppose that on April 1, S had written and signed the following note to B: "The rising corn futures prices makes it necessary for me to cancel our deal. Sorry. Perhaps we can do business again next year." B's lawyer argues that if the oral transaction was within the scope of UCC 2–201(1), that statute was satisfied by the note. B is also prepared to prove that the parties had done business for 10 years and that S had always sold B the output from his land. As S's lawyer, identify and assess all of the arguments to the contrary.

Problem 10–7

Suppose that on February 1, B had written S a signed letter asking whether S would be willing to sell his output of corn "again this year." In response, S had hand written but not signed the following note, which was delivered by a family member: "George. Output is fine, but no deal until we agree on a fair price." On February 5, B (George) visited S on the farm and an oral agreement to sell the output of corn at $2.30 per bushel was reached. On February 7, B mailed the following letter to S, which was received by S on February 9: "Dear Silas. This is to confirm our agreement for the sale of corn at $2.30 per bushel, delivery by October 1. George." S did not respond to the letter. On April 1, S wrote the following signed note to B: "Dear George: We never had a deal. I have sold my output to D. (s) Silas." B's lawyer makes two arguments: (1) The statute of frauds was satisfied by application of UCC 2–201(2); (2) When all of the writings are considered, the statute of frauds has been satisfied. How would you rule?

omit

THOMSON PRINTING MACHINERY CO. v. B.F. GOODRICH CO.

United States Court of Appeals, Seventh Circuit, 1983.
714 F.2d 744.

Before WOOD and CUDAHY, CIRCUIT JUDGES, and GRANT, SENIOR DISTRICT JUDGE.

CUDAHY, CIRCUIT JUDGE.

Appellant Thomson Printing Company ("Thomson Printing") won a jury verdict in its suit for breach of contract against appellee B.F. Goodrich Company ("Goodrich"). The district court concluded, however, that as a matter of law the contract could not be enforced against Goodrich because it was an oral contract, the Statute of Frauds applied and the Statute was not satisfied. Because we conclude that the contract was enforceable on the basis of the "merchants" exception to the Statute of Frauds, we reverse.

INTRODUCTION

Thomson Printing buys and sells used printing machinery. On Tuesday, April 10, 1979, the president of Thomson Printing, James Thomson, went to Goodrich's surplus machinery department in Akron, Ohio to look at some used printing machinery which was for sale. James Thomson discussed the sale terms, including a price of $9,000, with Goodrich's surplus equipment manager, Ingram Meyers. Four days later, on Saturday, April 14, 1979, James Thomson sent to Goodrich in Akron a purchase order for the equipment and a check for $1,000 in part payment.

Thomson Printing sued Goodrich when Goodrich refused to perform. Goodrich asserted by way of defense that no contract had been formed and that in any event the alleged oral contract was unenforceable due to the Statute of Frauds. Thomson Printing argued that a contract had been made and that the "merchants" and "partial performance" exceptions to the Statute of Frauds were applicable and satisfied. The jury found for Thomson Printing, but the district court entered judgment for Goodrich on the grounds that the Statute of Frauds barred enforcement of the contract in Thomson's favor.

HISTORICAL BACKGROUND

In 1671, in Old Marston, Oxfordshire, England, defendant Egbert was sued by plaintiff John over an alleged oral promise by Egbert to sell to John a fighting cock named Fiste. John's friend, Harold, claimed he overheard the "deal" and by that dubious means John won, though in fact there apparently was no deal. In 1676 courts did not allow parties to a lawsuit to testify so Egbert could not testify to rebut Harold's story. Compounding the problem was the fact that courts then could not throw out jury verdicts manifestly contrary to the evidence. So, in response to the plight of the Egberts of this world and to the recurring mischief of the Johns, as well as to combat possible "fraude and perjurie" by the Harolds, Parliament passed in 1677 a "statute of frauds" which required that certain contracts for the sale of goods be in writing to be enforceable.[1]

1. This historical background is based on J. White & R. Summers, Handbook of the Law Under the Uniform Commercial Code 50 (2d ed. 1980) (footnotes omitted). *See generally* E.A. Farnsworth, CONTRACTS ch. 6 (1982).

THE "MERCHANTS" EXCEPTION

A modern exception [2] to the usual writing requirement is the "merchants" exception of the Uniform Commercial Code, OHIO REV.CODE ANN. § 1302.04(B) (Page 1979) (U.C.C. § 2–201(2)), which provides:

> Between merchants if within a reasonable time a writing in confirmation of the contract and sufficient against the sender is received and the party receiving it has reason to know its contents, it satisfies the [writing requirement] against such party unless written notice of objection to its contents is given within 10 days after it is received.

We must emphasize that the only effect of this exception is to take away from a merchant who receives a writing in confirmation of a contract the Statute of Frauds defense if the merchant does not object. The sender must still persuade the trier of fact that a contract was in fact made orally, to which the written confirmation applies.

In the instant case, James Thomson sent a "writing in confirmation" to Goodrich four days after his meeting with Ingram Meyers, a Goodrich employee and agent. The purchase order contained Thomson Printing's name, address, telephone number and certain information about the machinery purchase.[3] The check James Thomson sent to Goodrich with the purchase order also had on it

2. An exception of longstanding, which was also argued here, is the "partial performance" exception. We express no opinion on the application of this exception.

3. Complete Erection Service Miehle Factory Trained Erectors Sales and Service № 8756

THOMSON PRINTING MACHINERY CO.

MAINTENANCE • REPAIRING • REBUILDING

1936 to 1940 Augusta Boulevard • Chicago, Illinois 60622 • Phone 227-8600

BF GOODRICH COMPANY
500 S. MAIN STREET
AKRON, OHIO 44318

Date 4-14-79

Order No.

PURCHASE ORDER

1 # 70 MIEHLE C&C WITH BERRY LIFT

1 # 3/0 MIEHLE TWO COLOR PRINTING PRESS

1 STAUDE MASTER GLUER & ASSORTED PARTS

PACKAGE PRICE		$ 9000.00
	DEPOSIT	$ 1000.00
	BALANCE UPON REMOVAL	$ 8000.00

CERTIFICATE OF INSURANCE BEING MAILED
BY CRITCHELL-MILLER AGENCY

Thomson Printing's name and address, and the check carried notations that connected the check with the purchase order.[4]

Goodrich argues, however, that Thomson's writing in confirmation cannot qualify for the 2–201(2) exception because it was not received by anyone at Goodrich who had reason to know its contents.[5] Goodrich claims that Thomson erred in not specifically designating on the envelope, check or purchase order that the items were intended for Ingram Meyers or the surplus equipment department. Consequently, Goodrich contends, it was unable to "find a home" for the check [6] and purchase order despite attempts to do so, in accordance with its regular procedures, by sending copies of the documents to several of its various divisions. Ingram Meyers testified that he never learned of the purchase order until weeks later when James Thomson called to arrange for removal of the machines. By then, however, the machines had long been sold to someone else.

We think Goodrich misreads the requirements of 2–201(2). First, the literal requirements of 2–201(2), as they apply here, are that a writing "is received" and that Goodrich "has reason to know its contents." There is no dispute that the purchase order and check were received by Goodrich, and there is at least no specific or express requirement that the "receipt" referred to in 2–201(2) be by any Goodrich agent in particular.

> These issues are not resolved by [2–201(2)], but it is probably a reasonable projection that a delivery at either the recipient's principal place of business, a place of business from which negotiations were conducted, or to which the sender may have transmitted previous communications, will be an adequate receipt.

3 R. Duesenberg & L. King, Bender's UCC Service § 2–204[2] at 2–70 (1982).

As for the "reason to know its contents" requirement, this element "is best understood to mean that the confirmation was an instrument which should have been anticipated and therefore should have received the attention of appropriate parties." *Perdue Farms, Inc. v. Motts, Inc.,* 459 F.Supp. 7, 20 (N.D.Miss.1978) (quoting from Bender's UCC Service, *supra,* § 2–204[2] at 2–69). "The receipt of a spurious document would not burden the recipient with a risk of losing the [Statute of Frauds] defense * * *." *Id.* In the case before us there is no doubt that the confirmatory writings were based on actual negotiations (although the legal effect of the negotiations was disputed), and therefore the documents were not "spurious" but could have been anticipated and appropriately handled.

Even if we go beyond the literal requirements of 2–201(2) and read into the "receipt" requirement the "receipt of notice" rule of 1–201(27), we still think Thomson Printing satisfied the "merchants" exception. Section 1–201, the definitional section of the U.C.C., provides that notice received by an organization

4. The notations in the upper left hand corner of the check were "1 70 C & C, 1 3/0 T.C. and 1 STAUDE MASTER GLUER." See PX 1. Compare these notations with the Purchase Order the check accompanied, *supra,* note 3.

5. The district court found that both parties were merchants for the purpose of 2–201(2). We agree. "For purposes of [2–201(2)] almost every person in business would, therefore, be deemed to be a 'merchant' * * * since the practices involved in the transaction are non-specialized business practices such as answering mail." U.C.C. § 2–104, Comment 2.

6. The check itself was deposited pending clarification in a Goodrich "liability" account.

> is effective for a particular transaction * * * from the time when it would have been brought to [the attention of the individual conducting that transaction] if the organization had executed *due diligence.*

U.C.C. § 1–201(27) (emphasis supplied). The Official Comment states:

> reason to know, knowledge, or a notification, although "received" for instance by a clerk in Department A of an organization, is effective for a transaction conducted in Department B only from the time when it was *or should have been* communicated to the individual conducting that transaction.

U.C.C. § 1–201(27), Official Comment (emphasis supplied).

Thus, the question comes down to whether Goodrich's mailroom, given the information it had, should have notified the surplus equipment manager, Ingram Meyers, of Thomson's confirmatory writing. At whatever point Meyers should have been so notified, then at that point Thomson's writing was effective even though Meyers did not see it. *See* 2 A. Squillante & J. Fonseca, WILLISTON ON SALES § 14–8 at 284 (4th ed. 1974) ("the time of receipt will be measured as if the organization involved had used due diligence in getting the document to the appropriate person").

The definitional section of the U.C.C. also sets the general standard for what mailrooms "should do":

> An organization exercises due diligence if it maintains reasonable routines for communicating significant information to the person conducting the transaction and there is reasonable compliance with the routines.

U.C.C. § 1–201(27). One cannot say that Goodrich's mailroom procedures were reasonable as a matter of law: if Goodrich had exercised due diligence in handling Thomson Printing's purchase order and check, these items would have reasonably promptly come to Ingram Meyers' attention. First, the purchase order on its face should have alerted the mailroom that the documents referred to a purchase of used printing equipment. Since Goodrich had only one surplus machinery department, the documents' "home" should not have been difficult to find. Second, even if the mailroom would have had difficulty in immediately identifying the kind of transaction involved, the purchase order had Thomson Printing's phone number printed on it and we think a "reasonable routine" in these particular circumstances would have involved at some point in the process a simple phone call to Thomson Printing. Thus, we think Goodrich's mailroom mishandled the confirmatory writings. This failure should not permit Goodrich to escape liability by pleading non-receipt. *See* WILLISTON ON SALES, *supra,* § 14–8 at 284–85.

We note that the jury verdict for Thomson Printing indicates that the jury found as a fact that the contract had in fact been made and that the Statute of Frauds had been satisfied. Also, Goodrich acknowledges those facts about the handling of the purchase order which we regard as determinative of the "merchants" exception question. We think that there is ample evidence to support the jury findings both of the existence of the contract and of the satisfaction of the Statute.

The district court, in holding as a matter of law that the circumstances failed to satisfy the Statute of Frauds, was impressed by James Thomson's dereliction in failing to specifically direct the purchase order and check to the attention of Ingram Meyers or the surplus equipment department. We agree that Thomson erred in this respect, but, for the reasons we have suggested,

Goodrich was at least equally derelict in failing to find a "home" for the well-identified documents. Goodrich argues that in the "vast majority" of cases it can identify checks within a week without contacting an outside party; in the instant case, therefore, if Goodrich correctly states its experience under its procedures, it should presumably have checked with Thomson Printing promptly after the time it normally identified checks by other means—in this case, by its own calculation, a week at most. Under the particular circumstances of this case, we therefore think it inappropriate to set aside a jury verdict on Statute of Frauds grounds.

The district court's order granting judgment for Goodrich is reversed and the cause is remanded for further proceedings consistent with this opinion.

Reversed and remanded.

QUANEY v. TOBYNE

Supreme Court of Kansas, 1984.
236 Kan. 201, 689 P.2d 844.

PRAGER, JUSTICE:

This is an action brought by the sellers against the buyer to recover damages for breach of an oral contract for the sale and purchase of 285 steers. The plaintiffs are J. Martin Quaney and his sons, William E. Quaney, and James Daniel Quaney, farmers and cattlemen residing in Osage County. The defendant, Lowell Tobyne, is a farmer-rancher and feed lot operator who resides in Washington County, Kansas. In this action, plaintiffs sought to recover the difference between the price which defendant agreed to pay for the cattle and the price received for the cattle when sold by plaintiffs after defendant Tobyne refused to take delivery of the cattle on the agreed delivery date.

* * *

The defendant filed a motion for summary judgment based upon the defense that the statute of frauds (K.S.A. 84–2–201) barred enforcement of the oral agreement, and, furthermore, that the doctrine of promissory estoppel was not applicable in the case. Defendant's motion for summary judgment was denied by the trial court. The case was then tried by a jury which found in its special verdicts that the plaintiffs and defendant had entered into an oral contract for the purchase and sale of the cattle and that the terms of the contract were for the sale of 285 head of cattle (steers) at 65¢ per pound, with no allowance for shrinkage, with an $8,000 down payment and a written contract to be provided by defendant. The cattle were to be picked up on or before October 1, 1982, and the balance was due upon possession of the cattle. The jury also found that the doctrine of promissory estoppel, as explained in the instructions, should be used to enforce the oral agreement of the parties, and that the total amount of damages sustained by the plaintiffs was $16,826.45. Defendant's motion for a new trial was thereafter denied, and he appealed.

The sole point presented in the defendant's brief is stated as follows: Whether the trial court erred in not applying the statute of frauds to bar the claim of the plaintiffs against the defendant where the evidence of the plaintiffs when viewed in a light most favorable to the plaintiffs does not allow the plaintiffs to avail themselves of the exception of promissory estoppel to the bar created by the statute of frauds. As we see it, there are two basic issues of law to be determined on the appeal:

(1) Does the statute of frauds (K.S.A. 84–2–201) bar the plaintiffs from recovery on the oral contract in this case or is the exception set forth in subsection (3)(b) applicable to remove the bar of the statute?

(2) If the exception is not applicable, does the doctrine of promissory estoppel apply so as to enable the plaintiffs to avoid the defense of the statute of frauds?

We first consider the issue whether plaintiffs' action on the oral sales contract is barred by the statute of frauds (K.S.A. 84–2–201) which provides as follows:

* * *

> "(3) *A contract which does not satisfy the requirements of subsection (1) but which is valid in other respects is enforceable*
>
> "(a) if the goods are to be specially manufactured for the buyer and are not suitable for sale to others in the ordinary course of the seller's business and the seller, before notice of repudiation is received and under circumstances which reasonably indicate that the goods are for the buyer, has made either a substantial beginning of their manufacture or commitments for their procurement; or
>
> "(b) *if the party against whom enforcement is sought admits in his pleading, testimony or otherwise in court that a contract for sale was made, but the contract is not enforceable under this provision beyond the quantity of goods admitted;* or
>
> "(c) with respect to goods for which payment has been made and accepted or which have been received and accepted (section 84–2–606)." (Emphasis supplied.)

Under subsection (1) of the statute an oral contract for the sale of goods for the price of $500 or more is not enforceable unless one of the exceptions under subsection (3) is satisfied. It is agreed that the exceptions contained in subsection (3)(a) and (c) are not applicable, and that plaintiffs must rely solely on section (3)(b) in order to avoid the application of the statute. The issue of law presented is whether, on the record before us, the defendant as the party against whom enforcement of the oral contract is sought, admitted in his pleadings, testimony, or otherwise in court that an oral contract for sale was made. This exception was held applicable in *Wendling v. Puls,* 227 Kan. 780, 610 P.2d 580 (1980), which like this case also involved an action for the breach of an oral contract for the purchase and sale of cattle. In *Wendling,* K.S.A. 84–2–201 was discussed and it was noted that all of the parties had frankly and openly admitted the existence of the contract during their oral testimony, with complete agreement on price, quantity of purchase, and date of delivery. In addition, the seller had served a written notice on the buyers containing the provisions of the contract to which the buyers offered neither written nor oral objections. In the case now before us, the plaintiffs/sellers did not serve such a notice on the defendant buyer. So it is necessary that the record establish that the defendant/buyer made the admissions required under K.S.A. 84–2–201(3)(b). It also should be noted that K.S.A. 84–2–201 was set up as a defense to an oral contract in *Miller v. Sirloin Stockade,* 224 Kan. 32, 578 P.2d 247 (1978), which held that the exception provided for in subsection (3)(b) is applicable only if the admission is made by a party to the litigation or by an authorized agent of a party before the termination of his authority. A former employee of a corporation was held to be without authority to bind the corporation by "admissions" made during the course of taking the former employee's deposition.

In the case now before us, we are required to consider the "admissions" made by the defendant, Lowell Tobyne, in the course of the litigation. This requires us to consider any admissions made in his pleadings, testimony, or otherwise in court to the effect that a contract for sale was made. In this case, the only admissions made by defendant were either in his deposition or in his testimony taken at the time of trial. Before taking up defendant's admissions, we should first consider the principles of law involved in the construction and application of K.S.A. 84–2–201. There is an annotation on this subject in 88 A.L.R.3d 416, where cases from various jurisdictions are set forth discussing the purposes of the statute and the question as to what constitutes an admission that the contract for sale was made within the meaning of the statute. In its summary, the annotation indicates that the courts have found three reasons for the adoption of the statutory provision contained in K.S.A. 84–2–201(3)(b) excepting from the operation of the statute of frauds contracts whose existence has been admitted by the party against whom enforcement is sought. It has been stated by the courts that the purposes of the statute are (1) to provide that a party cannot admit the existence of an oral contract for the sale of goods and simultaneously claim the benefit of the statute of frauds, (2) to prevent the statute of frauds from becoming an aid to fraud, and (3) to expand the exceptions to the nonenforceability of oral contracts under the statute of frauds.

In order to come within the terms of the exceptions stated in 84–2–201(3)(b), a statement must in fact constitute an admission, and the courts in several cases have expressly considered what constitutes an admission that a contract for sale was made within the meaning of the statutory exception. A problem has arisen in this regard where a party *admits* the essential terms of the oral contract but denies that a final agreement or meeting of the minds was ever actually consummated. In several cases it has been held that the testimony of the party against whom enforcement of an oral contract for the sale of goods is sought, which, while denying the existence of the oral contract, admits facts which as a matter of law establish the existence of the contract, constitutes an admission within the meaning of the statute.

* * *

We have considered all of these various authorities and the principles of law established thereby and have concluded that the exception to the statute of frauds contained in K.S.A. 84–2–201(3)(b) is satisfied when the party who has denied the existence of an oral contract in reliance on the statute takes the stand and, without admitting explicitly that a contract was made, testifies as to his statements or his actions which establish the terms of the oral contract claimed by the opposing party. It is not necessary that there be an express declaration in which the party admits the making of the oral contract. It is sufficient if his words or admitted conduct reasonably lead to that conclusion.

Turning to the testimony of the buyer, Lowell Tobyne, in the record now before us, the question to be determined is whether there are sufficient admissions as to the existence and terms of the oral contract to satisfy the statutory exception in K.S.A. 84–2–201(3)(b). As noted above, the defendant in one portion of his testimony denied that there had been a final meeting of the minds and further testified that there was to be no binding contract until the contract was reduced to writing. On cross-examination, however, the defendant testified that he telephoned plaintiff Martin Quaney and asked him if he had any cattle for sale, and Quaney replied that he did. He was told that all of the cattle were steers and that Quaney was asking a price of 65¢ per pound. At Quaney's suggestion, he met Quaney at the pasture on August 15, 1982, and drove around and looked at the cattle in the large pasture. He stated that he was satisfied with the quality and type of those cattle. He was told that Quaney had cattle in another pasture and Quaney offered to take him down to the other pasture. He admitted that he did not need to see the other cattle if they were similar to the cattle he had just looked at. He was told by Quaney that they were the same type of cattle that he had just seen. Defendant stated that he *agreed* on a 65¢ per pound price for the cattle on that day. He *agreed* with Quaney that he would load the cattle out around October 1, 1982. He *agreed* that the cattle would be weighed at either St. Marys or Manhattan, Kansas. It was discussed that Mr. Hess would round up the cattle and deliver the same to the defendant for loading. A down payment of $8,000 was agreeable with both parties. He mentioned to Quaney that he was going to put together a written agreement and bring it down to Quaney. From this testimony, it seems clear to us that the defendant admitted in his testimony all of the terms of the agreement for sale and purchase of the cattle as claimed by the plaintiffs. To summarize, in his testimony the defendant testified as to the following terms of the contract:

(1) He was satisfied with the quality and type of cattle—285 steers were to be purchased.

(2) He agreed on a price of 65¢ per pound.

(3) He agreed that the cattle would be weighed at St. Marys or Manhattan to establish their weight.

(4) A loading date for the cattle around October 1, 1982, was agreed upon.

(5) He agreed on a down payment of $8,000.

In addition to this, the defendant testified as to *conduct* which gave recognition to the finality and binding effect of the agreement. After Martin Quaney was injured in the automobile accident on August 19, 1982, the defendant had several telephone conversations with William E. Quaney and James Daniel Quaney. He admitted that in none of these conversations did he state that he was not buying the cattle or indicate that an agreement had not been consummated. As late as September 23, and September 30, 1982, the defendant discussed with Oliver Hess, the manager of the pasture leased to plaintiffs where the cattle were kept, arrangements for the defendant to pick up the cattle. It was agreed that October 2, 1982, was to be the date for the loading of the cattle. On October 1, 1982, the defendant called Martin Quaney and told him that he would not be able to purchase the cattle.

From our analysis of this testimony, we have concluded that, although the defendant did not openly and frankly admit to an oral agreement, his testimony sufficiently establishes that an oral agreement existed. The defendant acknowledged all the principal terms of the agreement. The parties had agreed on a price per pound, type and quality of the cattle, place of loading, place of weighing, and the down payment. Although the defendant never paid the down payment or drew up a written contract as he volunteered to do, we hold that his testimony contained admissions of his statements and actions sufficient to satisfy the requirements of K.S.A. 84–2–201(3)(b).

Since the defendant raised several defenses to the contract, the issues were submitted to the jury and the jury found that the plaintiff and defendant had entered into an oral contract for the purchase and sale of the cattle. There was substantial competent evidence to support that finding. In view of the admissions which the defendant made in his testimony at the trial, the defense of the statute of frauds was removed from the case in accordance with K.S.A. 84–2–201(3)(b).

In view of our holding on this issue, the question as to the applicability of the doctrine of promissory estoppel as a defense to the bar created by the statute of frauds becomes moot. We note, however, the holding of this court in *Decatur Cooperative Association v. Urban,* 219 Kan. 171, 547 P.2d 323. That case involved an action for breach of an oral contract for the sale and purchase of wheat. In that case promissory estoppel was successfully asserted to preclude the statute of frauds as a defense to an oral contract for the sale of goods.

On the basis of the record before us, we find that the issues were properly formulated by court and counsel and submitted to the jury which resolved all issues in favor of the plaintiffs in accordance with established legal principles.

The judgment of the district court is affirmed.

Problem 10–8

IBM and Epprecht entered an oral agreement allegedly for the production by Epprecht of 50,000 print-head assemblies for computers. The assemblies were to conform to particular specifications prepared and furnished by IBM. IBM issued purchase orders for 7,000 assemblies, 4,000 of which were accepted and 3,000 of which were rejected by IBM. IBM paid the price of the assemblies accepted but, claiming quality problems, refused to pay anything for the rejected assemblies and cancelled the agreement. Epprecht, alleging the facts stated above, sued for damages caused by IBM's "wrongful" rejection of 3,000 units. IBM moved for a summary judgment on the basis of UCC 2–201. Epprecht argued that the summary judgment should be denied: Although there was no writing, the statute of frauds was satisfied under UCC 2–201(3)(a) & (c). Epprecht cited Impossible Electronic Techniques, Inc. v. Wackehnut Protective Systems, Inc., 669 F.2d 1026, 1036–37 (5th Cir.1982), where the court stated that the "statute exempts contracts involving 'specially manufactured' goods from the writing requirement because in these cases the very nature of the goods serves as a reliable indication that a contract was indeed formed." Further: "Where the seller has commenced or completed the manufacture of goods that conform to the special needs of a particular buyer and thereby are not suitable for sale to others, not only is the likelihood of a perjured claim of a contract diminished, but denying enforcement to such a contract would impose substantial hardship on the aggrieved party. * * * The unfairness is especially acute where * * * the seller has incurred substantial, unrecoverable expense in reliance on the oral promise of the buyer. * * * The crucial inquiry is whether the manufacturer could sell the goods in the ordinary course of his business to someone other than the original buyer. If with slight alterations the goods could be so sold, then they are not specially manufactured; if, however, essential changes are necessary to render the goods marketable by the seller to others, then the exception does apply." How should the court rule?

LIGE DICKSON CO. v. UNION OIL CO. OF CAL.

Supreme Court of Washington, 1981.
96 Wash.2d 291, 635 P.2d 103.

DORE, JUSTICE.

The Ninth Circuit Court of Appeals certified the following question to us:

> Under the law of the State of Washington, may an oral promise otherwise within the statute of frauds, Wash.Rev.Code § 62A.2–201, nevertheless be enforceable on the basis of promissory estoppel? *See* Restatement

(Second) of Contracts § 217A. *See generally Klinke v. Famous Recipe Fried Chicken, Inc.,* 94 Wash.2d 255, 616 P.2d 644 (1980).

Our answer to this question is "no". Analysis and elaboration follow.

The business relationship between plaintiff Lige Dickson Company (or its predecessor partnership) and defendant Union Oil Company of California is long standing, dating from 1937. Plaintiff was a general contractor and purchased its oil-based products from defendant. In 1964, defendant encouraged and aided plaintiff in entering the asphalt paving business. From 1964 through 1973, with one exception, plaintiff purchased all its liquid asphalt from defendant. In the ordinary course of business, plaintiff telephoned orders to defendant, plaintiff was invoiced, and all bills were paid. Plaintiff and defendant never executed a written contract providing for the sale and purchase of liquid asphalt.

From 1964 until late 1970, the defendant's price for liquid asphalt remained constant. In December 1970, all of the suppliers of liquid asphalt in the Tacoma area raised their prices. Responding to this in May or June of 1971, plaintiff requested, and defendant provided, an oral guarantee against further increases insofar as would affect those contracts which committed the plaintiff to manufacture and sell asphalt paving at fixed, agreed sums. A list was made of the plaintiff's contracts and the parties computed the amount of liquid asphalt needed to fulfill them. At the same time, defendant promised plaintiff that any upward change in price would be applicable only to contracts which plaintiff entered into after the price increase.

At trial, an official of defendant conceded that by November 1973 there was an unwritten custom in the liquid asphalt business in the Tacoma area, well known and acted upon by suppliers, and users, that any increase in price of liquid asphalt would not be applicable to manufacturers' then-existing contracts. From mid–1971 until November 1973, defendant's sales representatives visited plaintiff and ascertained tonnage of liquid asphalt needed for plaintiff to fulfill existing paving contracts and also promised plaintiff that the price for that liquid tonnage would be protected.

Nevertheless, in November 1973 defendant wrote to plaintiff that the price of liquid asphalt was rising by $3 per ton and plaintiff was informed on December 6 and 13, 1973 of further increases. The new prices were to be applicable to all purchases made after December 31, 1973. This was plaintiff's first notification that defendant was abandoning the parties' price protection agreement. In addition, the new prices were on a "verbal, indefinite basis * * * subject to change" with or without notice.

Without a firm supplier, plaintiff was unable to seek new paving contracts during the first part of 1974. What liquid asphalt was available was used by plaintiff to complete existing contracts. Plaintiff incurred a total increased out-of-pocket cost of $39,006.50 in acquiring liquid asphalt to perform existing contracts.

Plaintiff brought suit against defendant in the United States District Court for Western Washington for breach of contract. The trial court found that there was an oral contract between the parties, but the statute of frauds, RCW 62A.2–201 rendered the contract unenforceable. The cause was appealed to the Ninth Circuit which certified the question quoted above to this court.

The facts as outlined above are contained in the District Court's Findings of Facts which were made part of the record before this court. In the Ninth Circuit appeal, defendant has assigned errors to certain of these findings. These contentions, however, are not before us. We do not need certainty in the facts to answer the pure question of law presented for our determination. The Ninth Circuit has retained jurisdiction over all matters but the narrow question of law certified here.

The Restatement (Second) of Contracts § 217A (Tent.Drafts Nos. 1–7, 1973) [3] (hereinafter § 217A) authorizes enforcement of a promise which induced action or forbearance by a promisee notwithstanding the statute of frauds. Adoption of § 217A was before this court in *Klinke v. Famous Recipe Fried Chicken, Inc.*, 94 Wash.2d 255, 616 P.2d 644 (1980).

In *Klinke,* the plaintiff had been induced by defendant to leave his employ in Alaska and to move to Washington to establish a food franchise. Defendant had promised plaintiff that defendant would qualify and register in Washington as a dealer in franchises. After plaintiff's move, defendant failed to secure the proper dealer registration and later abandoned its efforts to do so. The plaintiff claimed $200,000 in lost time and wages and other damages. On summary judgment, the trial court dismissed the case because RCW 19.36.010(1) [4] voids unwritten contracts which cannot be performed in one year. The Court of Appeals reversed the trial court based on two theories. *Klinke v. Famous Recipe Fried Chicken, Inc.*, 24 Wash.App. 202, 600 P.2d 1034 (1979). First, defendant's failure to reduce the agreement with plaintiff to a writing, and plaintiff's reliance on such promise, estopped defendant from asserting the statute of frauds as a defense. Restatement of Contracts, §§ 90, 178, comment f (1932). Second, the Court of Appeals adopted § 217A. On review of that decision, we refused to adopt § 217A but affirmed the court's reversal on its first theory. We stated:

> The unforseen application of section 217A to areas of law outside the scope of the facts of this case convinces us that it would be unwise to adopt that section now unless necessary to effectuate justice. That is not mandated by the facts of this case.

Klinke v. Famous Recipe Fried Chicken, Inc., 94 Wash.2d 255, 262, 616 P.2d 644 (1980).

3. The Restatement (Second) of Contracts § 217A (Tent.Drafts Nos. 1–7, 1973) reads:

"Enforcement by Virtue of Action in Reliance

"(1) A promise which the promisor should reasonably expect to induce action or forbearance on the part of the promisee or a third person and which does induce the action or forbearance is enforceable notwithstanding the Statute of Frauds if injustice can be avoided only by enforcement of the promise. The remedy granted for breach is to be limited as justice requires.

"(2) In determining whether injustice can be avoided only by enforcement of the promise, the following circumstances are significant:

"(a) the availability and adequacy of other remedies, particularly cancellation and restitution;

"(b) the definite and substantial character of the action or forbearance in relation to the remedy sought;

"(c) the extent to which the action or forbearance corroborates evidence of the making and terms of the promise, or the making and terms are otherwise established by clear and convincing evidence;

"(d) the reasonableness of the action or forbearance:

"(e) the extent to which the action or forbearance was foreseeable by the promisor."

[§ 139 in final version. Ed.]

4. RCW 19.36.010 states, in part:

"In the following cases, specified in this section, any agreement, contract and promise shall be void, unless such agreement, contract or promise, or some note or memorandum thereof, be in writing, and signed by the party to be charged therewith, or by some person thereunto by him lawfully authorized, that is to say: (1) Every agreement that by its terms is not to be performed in one year from the making thereof * * *"

Plaintiff in the subject case urges us to now adopt § 217A as being "necessary to effectuate justice". Plaintiff focuses on the parties' long-standing relationship and defendant's responsibility "in great part" for introducing plaintiff into the asphalt paving business. Plaintiff also asserts that defendant's price protection agreement and assurances encouraged (i.e., induced?) plaintiff to make bids and enter into contracts.

Defendant asks this court to distinguish the statute of frauds at issue in *Klinke* from the statute of frauds contained within the Uniform Commercial Code (U.C.C.) at issue here.[5] Such distinction has been recognized.

> The statute of frauds requirements may vary as to the nature of the agreements involved, and a close examination of the subject matter of the oral promise in question is therefore warranted. For example, if the oral promise in question concerned the sale of goods, the attorney would want to be aware of the requirements set out in UCC § 2–201(3) which states the circumstances under which a contract for the sale of goods may be enforceable notwithstanding the statute of frauds * * * It should be pointed out that where there exists, in statute or in case law, clearly established means under which a contract dealing with a particular subject matter may be rendered enforceable notwithstanding the statute of frauds, the courts may be hesitant to apply promissory estoppel in such a manner as to enlarge upon those means of avoiding the statute.

Annotation Comment Note.—Promissory Estoppel as Basis for Avoidance of Statute of Frauds, 56 A.L.R.3d 1037, 1045 (1932). (Footnotes omitted.) The Ninth Circuit Court of Appeals has held, in interpreting and applying California law, that U.C.C. § 2–201 cannot be overcome through the application of the doctrine of promissory estoppel. *C.R. Fedrick, Inc. v. Borg-Warner Corp.,* 552 F.2d 852 (9th Cir.1977). The Kentucky Supreme Court reached the same conclusion based upon the U.C.C.'s internal method of avoiding § 2–201's hardship. *C.G. Campbell & Son, Inc. v. Comdeq. Corp.,* 586 S.W.2d 40 (Ky.App.1979). It reasoned that the statutory avoidance of § 2–201 found in § 2–201(3) was as far as the legislature was willing to go and

> any attempt by the courts to judicially amend this statute which is plain on its face would contravene the separation of powers mandated by the Constitution.

Campbell at page 41.

On the other hand, the Iowa Supreme Court reached the opposite result in *Warder & Lee Elevator, Inc. v. Britten,* 274 N.W.2d 339 (Iowa 1979). That court found that U.C.C. § 1–103[6] provided the authority for the use of promissory estoppel to defeat the statute of frauds. That section provides, *inter alia,* that "unless displaced by the particular provision of this chapter" estoppel and other validating or invalidating doctrines shall supplement the U.C.C. The court reasoned that the exceptions to the statute of frauds found at § 2–201(3)(a)–(c) are "definitional" and were not meant to displace equitable and legal principles otherwise applicable to contract actions.

5. The Uniform Commercial Code as adopted in Washington is found at RCW Title 62A. Reference to U.C.C. § 2–201 and § 1–103 in this opinion are intended to refer to Washington's corresponding sections.

6. Washington's version of § 1–103, found at RCW 62A.1–103, reads:

"Unless displaced by the particular provisions of this Title, the principles of law and equity, including the law merchant and the law relative to capacity to contract, principal and agent, estoppel, fraud, misrepresentation, duress, coercion, mistake, bankruptcy, or other validating or invalidating cause shall supplement its provisions."

> If [2–201] were construed as displacing principles otherwise preserved in [1–103], it would mean that an oral contract coming within its terms would be unenforceable despite fraud, deceit, misrepresentation, dishonesty or any other form of unconscionable conduct by the party relying upon the statute. No court has taken such an extreme position. Nor would we be justified in doing so. Despite differences relating to the availability of an estoppel defense, courts uniformly hold "that the Statute of Frauds, having been enacted for the purpose of preventing fraud, shall not be made the instrument of shielding[,] protecting, or aiding the party who relies upon it in the perpetration of a fraud or in the consummation of a fraudulent scheme." 3 Williston on Contracts § 553A at 796 (Third Ed. Jaeger, 1960).

Warder & Lee Elevator, Inc. v. Britten, supra at page 342.

Defendant asks us to adopt the view of the dissent in *Warder & Lee Elevator, Inc. v. Britten, supra.* The thrust of the dissent is that § 1–103 allows estoppel to supplement the U.C.C. "unless displaced by the particular provisions of this chapter"; and § 2–201 contains its own limiting language in that the statute of frauds applies "except as otherwise provided *in this section.*" (Italics ours.) Further, the dissent noted that a party to an oral contract who has been defrauded has available the equitable remedy of restitution. In such a case, the recovery is based on the wrong, not on a contract.

From the limited record before us in the subject case, it appears that equitable estoppel is not available to the plaintiff. There seems to be neither allegation nor proof of fraud or deceit. Plaintiff's only remedy may be based upon breach of the oral contract. *Nonetheless,* we must hold that promissory estoppel cannot be used to overcome the statute of frauds in a case which involves the sale of goods.

The Uniform Commercial Code was adopted to regulate commercial dealings. Uniformity among different jurisdictions in decisions concerning commerce was a major motivation behind development of the U.C.C. By so doing, it was hoped that this area of the law would become clearer and disputes would be more readily resolved. These policies are enunciated in the U.C.C., in part, as follows:

> 62A.1–102 Purposes; rules of construction; variation by agreement
>
> * * *
>
> (2) Underlying purposes and policies of this Title are
>
> (a) to simplify, clarify and modernize the law governing commercial transactions;
>
> * * *
>
> (c) to make uniform the law among the various jurisdictions.

It was hoped that commercial transactions could take place across state boundaries without the stultifying effect caused by differences in states' laws.

> The Uniform Commercial Code, hammered out by lawyers, judges and law teachers dedicated to clarity and good business sense in commercial law, has brought together into one coherent statement the best laws and practices prevalent in the United States.

American Bar Association, *Uniform Commercial Code Handbook,* "The Uniform Commercial Code," at 1 (1964).

> Because of the federal system, the American lawyer, probably more than any other, has been conscious of the disadvantages of differing laws. Internally he has tried to do something about it.

American Bar Association, *Uniform Commercial Code Handbook,* "The Uniform Commercial Code," at 19 (1964).

If we were to adopt § 217A as applicable in the context of the sale of goods, we would allow parties to circumvent the U.C.C. *See Warder & Lee Elevator, Inc. v. Britten, supra,* (Reynoldson, C.J., dissenting). For example, to prove justifiable reliance (an element of promissory estoppel), the promisee may offer evidence of course of dealing between the parties, as plaintiff did in this case. The Official Comments to RCWA 62A.1–205(4) state that the statute of frauds

> restrict[s] the actions of the parties, and * * * cannot be abrogated by agreement, or by a *usage of trade* * * *

RCWA 62A.1–205 at 71. (Italics ours.)

Notwithstanding our appreciation of plaintiff's dilemma, we cannot help but foresee increased litigation and confusion as being the necessary result of the eroding of the U.C.C. if § 217A is adopted in this case. We join the other courts which limit the doctrine of promissory estoppel from overcoming a valid defense based on the statute of frauds contained within the Uniform Commercial Code. By so doing, we make no comment on the applicability of § 217A to defeat the raising of the statute of frauds as a defense under RCW 19.36.010.

BRACHTENBACH, C.J., and DOLLIVER, WILLIAMS, STAFFORD, DIMMICK and UTTER, JJ., concur.

ROSELLINI, JUSTICE (concurring specially).

I agree with the majority that, in order to preserve the integrity of the Uniform Commercial Code, the question submitted by the Ninth Circuit Court of Appeals must be answered in the negative. It is evident that the legislature gave careful thought to the circumstances which would justify exceptions to the requirement of a written contract, and those exceptions are set forth in the act itself. They do not include circumstances which in other areas of law might invoke the doctrine of promissory estoppel.

While the code makes no provision for relief under the theory of promissory estoppel, it does provide an exception to the requirement of a writing

> if the party against whom enforcement is sought admits in his pleading, testimony or otherwise in court that a contract for sale was made, but the contract is not enforceable under this provision beyond the quantity of goods admitted; * * *

RCW 62A.2–201(3)(b).

There is in the district court's findings some suggestion that there may have been such an admission here. If that were the case, the code itself would provide a remedy.

HICKS, J., concurs.

[Some footnotes omitted.]

CHAPTER ELEVEN

THE POTENTIALLY ADVERSE BEARING OF "PRE-CONTRACT" FACTS AND EVENTS UPON THE AGREEMENT

SECTION 1. INTRODUCTION

Suppose the seller and buyer have concluded a bargain which is enforceable as a contract under Article 2, Part 2. The bargain is reduced to writing and signed by both parties. After performance commences, a dispute erupts over the obligations under the contract. The dispute may involve either the scope of the agreement in fact or the meaning of terms clearly within the scope of agreement. In either case, there is an honest disagreement.

How does Article 2 deal with disputes of this sort? For example, one party, to support his argument about the scope or meaning of the agreement, will undoubtedly seek to introduce evidence beyond the "four corners" of the writing. Can the other party exclude this evidence and, if so, under what circumstances?

The starting place is the definition of agreement in UCC 1–201(3): Agreement means "the bargain of the parties in fact as found in their language or by implication from other circumstances including course of dealing or usage of trade or course of performance as provided in this Act (Sections 1–205 and 2–208.)" Under this expansive definition, agreement may not be limited to the terms in the writing: It may include terms derived from trade usage, a prior course of dealing between the parties or the negotiations leading up to the particular bargain at stake. Thus, as the *Columbia Nitrogen* case, infra at page 498, reveals, one party may seek to supplement a price term contained in the writing by a usage or practice of the trade. See UCC 1–205(2).

If the statutory conditions for admissibility are satisfied, the next question is whether the parties, by agreement, have attempted to limit the scope of their bargain. Have they, for example, attempted to "contract out" of relevant trade usage or the expectations created by a prior course of dealing? If so, should that attempt be recognized by the court? See UCC 1–205(4), where an ordering principle is stated. Similarly, did both parties intend that their writing be a partial or total integration of their agreement, i.e., did they intend to exclude from the writing terms that were in fact agreed prior to or contemporaneously with its adoption? If so, the stage is set for application of the infamous parol evidence rule, UCC 2–202.

Finally, if the scope of agreement is determined, how are disputes over the meaning of terms to which the parties agreed to be resolved? What does the UCC say with regard to contract interpretation disputes and the evidence which is relevant to their resolution?

These questions will occupy our attention in this Chapter.

SECTION 2. PRE-CONTRACT FACTS OR EVENTS WHICH VARY, SUPPLEMENT OR GIVE MEANING TO THE AGREEMENT

COLUMBIA NITROGEN CORP. v. ROYSTER CO.

United States Court of Appeals, Fourth Circuit, 1971.
451 F.2d 3.

BUTZNER, CIRCUIT JUDGE.

Columbia Nitrogen Corp. appeals a judgment in the amount of $750,000 in favor of F.S. Royster Guano Co. for breach of a contract for the sale of phosphate to Columbia by Royster. Columbia defended on the grounds that the contract, construed in light of the usage of the trade and course of dealing, imposed no duty to accept at the quoted prices the minimum quantities stated in the contract. It also asserted an antitrust defense and counterclaim based on Royster's alleged reciprocal trade practices. The district court excluded the evidence about course of dealing and usage of the trade. It submitted the antitrust issues based on coercive reciprocity to the jury, but refused to submit the alternative theory of non-coercive reciprocity. The jury found for Royster on both the contract claim and the anti-trust counterclaim. We hold that Columbia's proffered evidence was improperly excluded and Columbia is entitled to a new trial on the contractual issues. With respect to the antitrust issues, we affirm.

I.

Royster manufactures and markets mixed fertilizers, the principal components of which are nitrogen, phosphate and potash. Columbia is primarily a producer of nitrogen, although it manufactures some mixed fertilizer. For several years Royster had been a major purchaser of Columbia's products, but Columbia had never been a significant customer of Royster. In the fall of 1966, Royster constructed a facility which enabled it to produce more phosphate than it needed in its own operations. After extensive negotiations, the companies executed a contract for Royster's sale of a minimum of 31,000 tons of phosphate each year for three years to Columbia, with an option to extend the term. The contract stated the price per ton, subject to an escalation clause dependent on production costs.

Phosphate prices soon plunged precipitously. Unable to resell the phosphate at a competitive price, Columbia ordered only part of the scheduled tonnage. At Columbia's request, Royster lowered its price for diammonium phosphate on shipments for three months in 1967, but specified that subsequent shipments would be at the original contract price. Even with this concession, Royster's price was still substantially above the market. As a result, Columbia ordered less than a tenth of the phosphate Royster was to ship in the first contract year. When pressed by Royster, Columbia offered to take the phosphate at the current market price and resell it without brokerage fee. Royster, however, insisted on the contract price. When Columbia refused delivery, Royster sold the unaccepted phosphate for Columbia's account at a price substantially below the contract price.

II.

Columbia assigns error to the pretrial ruling of the district court excluding all evidence on usage of the trade and course of dealing between the parties. It offered the testimony of witnesses with long experience in the trade that because of uncertain crop and weather conditions, farming practices, and government agricultural programs, express price and quantity terms in contracts for materials in the mixed fertilizer industry are mere projections to be adjusted according to market forces.*

Columbia also offered proof of its business dealings with Royster over the six-year period preceding the phosphate contract. Since Columbia had not been a significant purchaser of Royster's products, these dealings were almost exclusively nitrogen sales to Royster or exchanges of stock carried in inventory. The pattern which emerges, Columbia claimed, is one of repeated and substantial deviation from the stated amount or price, including four instances where Royster took none of the goods for which it had contracted. Columbia offered proof that the total variance amounted to more than $500,000 in reduced sales. This experience, a Columbia officer offered to testify, formed the basis of an understanding on which he depended in conducting negotiations with Royster.

The district court held that the evidence should be excluded. It ruled that "custom and usage or course of dealing are not admissible to contradict the express, plain, unambiguous language of a valid written contract, which by virtue of its detail negates the proposition that the contract is open to variances in its terms. * * *"

A number of Virginia cases have held that extrinsic evidence may not be received to explain or supplement a written contract unless the court finds the writing is ambiguous. E.g., Mathieson Alkali Works v. Virginia Banner Coal Corp., 147 Va. 125, 136 S.E. 673 (1927). This rule, however, has been changed by the Uniform Commercial Code which Virginia has adopted. The Code expressly states that it "shall be liberally construed and applied to promote its underlying purposes and policies," which include "the expansion of commercial practices through custom, usage and agreement of the parties. * * *" Va.Code Ann. § 8.1–102 (1965). The importance of usage of trade and course of dealing between the parties is shown by § 8.2–202, which authorizes their use to explain

* One witness testified, in part, as follows:

"The contracts generally entered into between buyer and seller of materials has always been, in my opinion, construed to be the buyer's best estimate of his anticipated requirements for a given period of time. It is well known in our industry that weather conditions, farming practices, government farm control programs, change requirements from time to time. And therefore allowances were always made to meet these circumstances as they arose."

"Tonnage requirements fluctuate greatly, and that is one reason that the contracts are not considered as binding as most contracts are, because the buyer normally would buy on historical basis, but his normal average use would be per annum of any given material. Now that can be affected very decidedly by adverse weather conditions such as a drought, or a flood, or maybe governmental programs which we have been faced with for many, many years, seed grain programs. They pay the farmer not to plant. If he doesn't plant, he doesn't use the fertilizer. When the contracts are made, we do not know of all these contingencies and what they are going to be. So the contract is made for what is considered a fair estimate of his requirements. And, the contract is considered binding to the extent, on him morally, that if he uses the tonnage that he will execute the contract in good faith as the buyer. * * *"

"I have never heard of a contract of this type being enforced legally. * * * Well, it undoubtedly sounds ridiculous to people from other industries, but there is a very definite, several very definite reasons why the fertilizer business is always operated under what we call gentlemen's agreements. * * *"

"The custom in the fertilizer industry is that the seller either meets the competitive situation or releases the buyer from it upon proof that he can buy it at that price * * *. [T]hey will either have the option of meeting it or releasing him from taking additional tonnage or holding him to that price. * * *"

And this custom exists "regardless of the contractual provisions."

"[T]he custom was that [these contracts] were not worth the cost of the paper they were printed on." [451 F.2d at 7, n. 3] or supplement a contract. The official comment states this section rejects the old rule that evidence of course of dealing or usage of trade can be introduced only when the contract is ambiguous. And the Virginia commentators, noting that "[t]his section reflects a more liberal approach to the introduction of parol evidence * * * than has been followed in Virginia," express the opinion that Mathieson, supra, and similar Virginia cases no longer should be followed. Va. Code Ann. § 8.2–202, Va.Comment. See also Portsmouth Gas Co. v. Shebar, 209 Va. 250, 253 n. 1, 163 S.E.2d 205, 208 n. 1 (1968) (dictum). We hold, therefore, that a finding of ambiguity is not necessary for the admission of extrinsic evidence about the usage of the trade and the parties' course of dealing.

We turn next to Royster's claim that Columbia's evidence was properly excluded because it was inconsistent with the express terms of their agreement. There can be no doubt that the Uniform Commercial Code restates the well established rule that evidence of usage of trade and course of dealing should be excluded whenever it cannot be reasonably construed as consistent with the terms of the contract. Division of Triple T Service, Inc. v. Mobil Oil Corp., 60 Misc.2d 720, 304 N.Y.S.2d 191, 203 (1969), aff'd mem., 311 N.Y.S.2d 961 (1970). Royster argues that the evidence should be excluded as inconsistent because the contract contains detailed provisions regarding the base price, escalation, minimum tonnage, and delivery schedules. The argument is based on the premise that because a contract appears on its face to be complete, evidence of course of dealing and usage of trade should be excluded. We believe, however, that neither the language nor the policy of the Code supports such a broad exclusionary rule. Section 8.2–202 expressly allows evidence of course of dealing or usage of trade to explain or supplement terms intended by the parties as a final expression of their agreement. When this section is read in light of Va.Code Ann. § 8.1–205(4), it is clear that the test of admissibility is not whether the contract appears on its face to be complete in every detail, but whether the proffered evidence of course of dealing and trade usage reasonably can be construed as consistent with the express terms of the agreement.

The proffered testimony sought to establish that because of changing weather conditions, farming practices, and government agricultural programs, dealers adjusted prices, quantities, and delivery schedules to reflect declining market conditions. For the following reasons it is reasonable to construe this evidence as consistent with the express terms of the contract:

The contract does not expressly state that course of dealing and usage of trade cannot be used to explain or supplement the written contract.

The contract is silent about adjusting prices and quantities to reflect a declining market. It neither permits nor prohibits adjustment, and this neutrality provides a fitting occasion for recourse to usage of trade and prior dealing to supplement the contract and explain its terms.

Minimum tonnages and additional quantities are expressed in terms of "Products Supplied Under Contract." Significantly, they are not expressed as just "Products" or as "Products Purchased Under Contract." The description used by the parties is consistent with the proffered testimony.

Finally, the default clause of the contract refers only to the failure of the buyer to pay for delivered phosphate. During the contract negotiations, Columbia rejected a Royster proposal for liquidated damages of $10 for each ton Columbia declined to accept. On the other hand, Royster rejected a Columbia proposal for a clause that tied the price to the market by obligating Royster to conform its price to offers Columbia received from other phosphate producers.

The parties, having rejected both proposals, failed to state any consequences of Columbia's refusal to take delivery—the kind of default Royster alleges in this case. Royster insists that we span this hiatus by applying the general law of contracts permitting recovery of damages upon the buyer's refusal to take delivery according to the written provisions of the contract. This solution is not what the Uniform Commercial Code prescribes. Before allowing damages, a court must first determine whether the buyer has in fact defaulted. It must do this by supplementing and explaining the agreement with evidence of trade usage and course of dealing that is consistent with the contract's express terms. Va.Code Ann. §§ 8.1–205(4), 8.2–202. Faithful adherence to this mandate reflects the reality of the marketplace and avoids the overly legalistic interpretations which the Code seeks to abolish.

Royster also contends that Columbia's proffered testimony was properly rejected because it dealt with mutual willingness of buyer and seller to adjust contract terms to the market. Columbia, Royster protests, seeks unilateral adjustment. This argument misses the point. What Columbia seeks to show is a practice of mutual adjustments so prevalent in the industry and in prior dealings between the parties that it formed a part of the agreement governing this transaction. It is not insisting on a unilateral right to modify the contract.

Nor can we accept Royster's contention that the testimony should be excluded under the contract clause:

> "No verbal understanding will be recognized by either party hereto; this contract expresses all the terms and conditions of the agreement, shall be signed in duplicate, and shall not become operative until approved in writing by the Seller."

Course of dealing and trade usage are not synonymous with verbal understandings, terms and conditions. Section 8.2–202 draws a distinction between supplementing a written contract by consistent additional terms and supplementing it by course of dealing or usage of trade. Evidence of additional terms must be excluded when "the court finds the writing to have been intended also as a complete and exclusive statement of the terms of the agreement." Significantly, no similar limitation is placed on the introduction of evidence of course of dealing or usage of trade. Indeed the official comment notes that course of dealing and usage of trade, unless carefully negated, are admissible to supplement the terms of any writing, and that contracts are to be read on the assumption that these elements were taken for granted when the document was phrased. Since the Code assigns course of dealing and trade usage unique and important roles, they should not be conclusively rejected by reading them into stereotyped language that makes no specific reference to them. Cf. Provident Tradesmen's Bank & Trust Co. v. Pemberton, 196 Pa.Super. 180, 173 A.2d 780. Indeed, the Code's official commentators urge that overly simplistic and overly legalistic interpretation of a contract should be shunned.

We conclude therefore that Columbia's evidence about course of dealing and usage of trade should have been admitted. Its exclusion requires that the judgment against Columbia must be set aside and the case retried.

* * *

[After affirming the district court's charges to the jury on modification and damage issues and judgment on the anti-trust issue, the court remanded the case for a new trial.]

[Footnotes omitted.]

Notes

1. To achieve the outcome in Columbia Nitrogen, the moving party was required: (1) to prove the existence and scope of the trade usage "as facts", UCC 1–205(2); (2) to prove that both parties were in the trade or, if not, that they were or "should be" aware of the usage, 1–205(3); (3) to persuade the court to admit the usage for a proper purpose, i.e., to "give particular meaning to and supplement or qualify" the terms of the agreement, UCC 1–205(3); (4) to survive a possible claim that the established usage was unreasonable, UCC 1–205, Comment 6; and (5) to persuade the court that the usage can be "construed wherever reasonable as consistent" with any express terms purporting to "contract out" of the usage. UCC 1–205(4). The outcome in the *Columbia Nitrogen* case has been criticized:

> The court's attempt to demonstrate a possible consistent interpretation is a strained exercise in semantic quibbling that * * * boggles the reasonable mind. The opinion reads so poorly because the court did not address the correct issue * * * the inquiry should have examined the relationship of the usage of trade to the facts of the case. That 'contracts' have been treated as 'fair estimates' is not enough: additional facts must be known about the types of contracts so regarded. * * * The * * * opinion, however, did not discuss relevance and only stated some of the facts about the usage of trade. The facts that are detailed in the opinion require further inquiry because they indicate that the disputed contract was unlike the contracts treated as estimates in the trade. Kirst, *Usage of Trade and Course of Dealing: Subversion of the UCC Theory,* 1977 U.Ill.L.F. 811, 844–45 (footnotes omitted).

Do you agree?

2. Shell Oil entered long-term contracts for the supply of Nanakuli's asphalt requirements on the Island of Oahu, Hawaii. Under the 1969 contract, the price was to be Shell's posted price at the time of delivery. In January, 1974, Shell raised the price from $44 to $76 per ton. Nanakuli, however, had previously committed 7,200 tons of asphalt to paving contractors at prices calculated at the $44 per ton price. When Shell charged $76 per ton for the asphalt, Nanakuli refused to pay this price and claimed that it was entitled to "price protection" under a usage of the asphalt paving trade in Hawaii and that this usage was incorporated into the contract. Price protection required that Shell hold the price on all tonnage committed in reliance upon the $44 per ton price prior to the price increase. The jury returned a verdict of $220,000 for Nanakuli on the ground that Shell had breached the contract by failing to protect the $44 price. The federal district judge set aside the verdict and granted Shell's motion for judgment n.o.v. The Ninth Circuit Court of Appeals vacated the district court's decision and reinstated the jury verdict.

In a long, complex opinion, which was clearly sympathetic to the UCC's emphasis on context, the Court held, inter alia, that: (1) the trial judge did not abuse his discretion in defining the applicable trade as the asphalt paving trade, rather than the purchase and sale of asphalt alone; (2) the "price protection" usage in that trade was established and Shell was or should have been aware of it; (3) the usage was reinforced by the conduct of Shell in the performance of the contract with Nanakuli; and (4) the jury could have reasonably construed the price protection usage as consistent with the express price term in the contract and a clause purporting to exclude all prior "oral" agreements from the writing.

The court stated that the agreement must be examined in "light of the close, symbiotic relations between Shell and Nanakuli on the island of Oahu, whereby the expansion of Shell on the island was intimately connected with the business growth of Nanakuli." In addition, the UCC "looks to the actual performance of a contract as the best indication of what the parties intended those terms to mean." Finally, the court concluded that "price protection" was consistent with the express price term "as long as it does not totally negate it." The usage "only came into play at times of price increases and only for work committed prior to those increases on non-escalation contracts." It was, therefore an "exception to, rather than a total negation of, the express price term" which was known to Shell and constituted an "intended part of the agreement, as that term is broadly defined by the Code. * * *" Nanakuli Paving & Rock Co. v. Shell Oil Co., Inc., 664 F.2d 772 (9th Cir. 1980). The Nanakuli court cited and discussed Columbia Nitrogen as a "leading case" in a group of federal decisions that "usually have been lenient in not ruling out consistent additional terms or trade usage for apparent inconsistency with express terms." The court, however, noted Professor Kirst's criticism of *Columbia Nitrogen* for failing to examine the relationship of the trade usage to the facts of the case, but concluded that this objection had been met in *Nanakuli.*

3. It is clear that particular parties can "contract out" of a general usage of trade which otherwise would be part of the agreement. UCC 1–205(4). Draft a one sentence clause which, in your judgment, would be effective to exclude the usages involved in the *Columbia Nitrogen* and *Shell Oil* cases.

ALASKAN NORTHERN DEVELOPMENT, INC. v. ALYESKA PIPELINE SERVICE CO.

Supreme Court of Alaska, 1983.
666 P.2d 33.

James J. White,[*] Ann Arbor, Mich., * * * for appellant.

Before BURKE, C.J., and RABINOWITZ, MATTHEWS and COMPTON, JJ.

OPINION

COMPTON, JUSTICE.

Alaska Northern Development, Inc. ("AND") appeals a judgment in favor of Alyeska Pipeline Service Co. ("Alyeska") in a dispute involving contract formation and interpretation. For the reasons stated below, we affirm.

I. FACTUAL AND PROCEDURAL BACKGROUND

In late October or early November 1976, David Reed, a shareholder and corporate president of AND, initiated discussion with Alyeska personnel in Fairbanks regarding the purchase of surplus parts. The Alyeska employees with whom Reed dealt were Juel Tyson, Clarence Terwilleger and Donald Bruce.

After a series of discussions, Terwilleger indicated that Reed's proposal should be put in writing so it could be submitted to management. With the assistance of AND's legal counsel, Reed prepared a letter of intent dated December 10, 1976. In this letter, AND proposed to purchase "the entire Alyeska inventory of Caterpillar parts." The place for the purchase price was left blank.

Alyeska responded with its own letter of intent dated December 11, 1976. The letter was drafted by Bruce and Tyson in consultation with William Rickett, Alyeska's manager of Contracts and Material Management. Again, the price term was absent. The letter contained the following language, which is the focus of this lawsuit: "Please consider this as said letter of intent, *subject to the final approval of the owner committee.*" (Emphasis added.)

[*] Could this person be one of the editors of this casebook?

Reed was given an unsigned draft of the December 11 letter, which was reviewed by AND's legal counsel. Reed then met with Rickett, and they agreed on sixty-five percent of Alyeska's price as the price term to be filled in the blank on the December 11 letter. Rickett filled in the blank as agreed and signed the letter. In March 1977, the owner committee rejected the proposal embodied in the December 11 letter of intent.

AND contends that the parties understood the subject to approval language to mean that the Alyeska owner committee [1] would review the proposed agreement only to determine whether the price was fair and reasonable. Alyeska contends that Reed was never advised of any such limitation on the authority of the owner committee. In April 1977, AND filed a complaint alleging that there was a contract between AND and Alyeska, which Alyeska breached. The complaint was later amended to include counts for reformation and punitive damages.

Alyeska moved for summary judgment on the punitive damages and breach of contract counts. The superior court granted summary judgment in favor of Alyeska on the punitive damages count. The court initially denied Alyeska's motion for summary judgment on the breach of contract claim; however, based on a review of the case after discovery had closed, the court announced at a hearing on September 26, 1980, that it would reverse its earlier ruling and grant Alyeska's motion. The court confirmed this ruling at a hearing on November 5, 1980, after consideration of AND's Motion for Clarification.

The superior court explained its rationale for granting summary judgment against AND on the breach of contract claim as follows. The court recognized that AND predicated its breach of contract claim on the theory that Reed's letter of December 10th was an offer and that Rickett's letter of December 11th was an acceptance of that offer. Viewed in that light, the court addressed "four theoretical possibilities in analyzing the interplay between the December 11th letter and the December 10th letter." First, the writings could be construed as an offer with a responding promise to pass the offer on to the owner committee, which was responsible for making such determinations. Second, the letters could be construed as an offer and a counter-offer that AND rejected. Third, the letters could be considered as an offer with a responding counter-offer containing, among other things, the unlimited right of the owner committee to review and approve. The court ruled that if the letters were ultimately found to fall into one of these three categories, AND would not prevail, either because the offer embodied in the December 10 letter was never accepted, or because the owner committee never approved the proposal.

The only way in which AND might prevail was on the fourth possibility, i.e., the letters could be construed as an offer followed by a counter-offer limiting the authority of the owner committee to review only the contract price. The court ruled that AND could not establish a breach of contract claim under the fourth construction of the letters because the parol evidence rule barred the admission of extrinsic evidence that might limit the scope of the owner committee's approval power.[2] The only recourse for AND, therefore, was to seek reformation of the December 11 letter that limited the owner committee approval clause.

1. The owner committee is composed of the owner oil companies of Alyeska, a joint venture.

2. AND also predicated its breach of contract claim on the existence of a prior oral agreement. The superior court implicitly rejected this theory in its analysis of the parol evidence rule.

The case proceeded to trial on the reformation claim. After a six-week trial, the superior court concluded that AND had failed to establish that a specific agreement was not properly reduced to writing and therefore rejected its request to reform the December 11 letter. Attorney's fees were awarded to Alyeska.

On appeal, AND does not challenge the superior court's denial of reformation. Instead, it contends that the superior court erred in granting summary judgment on the breach of contract and punitive damages counts, erred in denying a trial by jury on the reformation count, erred in not permitting cross-examination for purposes of impeachment, and erred in awarding attorney's fees to Alyeska.

II. Application of the Parol Evidence Rule

The superior court held that the parol evidence rule of the Uniform Commercial Code, section 2–202, codified as AS 45.02–202,[3] applied to the December 11 letter and therefore no extrinsic evidence could be presented to a jury which limited the owner committee's right of approval. AND contends that the court erred in applying the parol evidence rule. We disagree.

In order to exclude parol evidence concerning the inclusion of additional terms to a writing, a court must make the following determinations. First, the court must determine whether the writing under scrutiny was integrated, i.e., intended by the parties as a final expression of their agreement with respect to some or all of the terms included in the writing. Second, the court must determine whether evidence of a prior or contemporaneous agreement contradicts or is inconsistent with the integrated portion. If the evidence is contradictory or inconsistent, it is inadmissible. If it is consistent, it may nevertheless be excluded if the court concludes that the consistent term would necessarily have been included in the writing by the parties if they had intended it to be part of their agreement. AS 45.02.202; *Braund, Inc. v. White,* 486 P.2d 50, 56 (Alaska 1971); U.C.C. § 2–202 comment 3 (1977).

A. *Was the December 11 Letter a Partial Integration?*

An integrated writing exists where the parties intend that the writing be a final expression of one or more terms of their agreement. *Kupka v. Morey,* 541 P.2d 740, 747 n. 8 (Alaska 1975); Restatement (Second) of Contracts § 209(a) (1979). Whether a writing is integrated is a question of fact to be determined by the court in accordance with all relevant evidence. Restatement (Second) of Contracts § 209 comment c (1979).

In granting summary judgment on the breach of contract claim, the superior court stated that it had carefully considered all relevant evidence, including oral and written records of all facets of the business deal in question, to arrive at its finding that the agreement was partially integrated.[4] After the six-week trial on the reformation issue, the superior court reaffirmed this finding:

3. AS 45.02.202 provides:

Final written expression; parol or extrinsic evidence. Terms with respect to which the confirmatory memoranda of the parties agree, or which are otherwise set out in a writing intended by the parties as a final expression of their agreement with respect to the terms included in the writing, may not be contradicted by evidence of a prior agreement or of a contemporaneous oral agreement, but may be explained or supplemented

(1) by course of dealing or usage of trade (AS 45.01.205) or by course of performance (AS 45.02.208); and

(2) by evidence of consistent additional terms unless the court finds the writing was intended also as a complete and exclusive statement of the terms of the agreement.

4. At the hearing on AND's Motion for Clarification, the superior court stated:

[I]t seems to me absolutely conclusive on this evidence, and I'm making this as a

35. The plaintiff initially contends that the letter of December 11, 1976 (the letter) was not integrated or partially integrated and therefore the court was in error in granting summary judgment in favor of defendant on the contract counts of the plaintiff's complaint on September 26, 1980.

36. After considering the evidence submitted at trial, the court reaffirms its prior conclusion that the letter was integrated as to the Owners Committee's approval clause.

37. The parties intended to write down their discussions in a comprehensive form which allowed Reed to seek financing and allow the primary actors (Tyson, Bruce, Terwilleger, Rickett) to submit the concept embodied by the letter to higher management * * *.

38. There are three subjects upon which plaintiff seeks reformation. * * * As to the first, [limiting the Owner Committee to a consideration of price] which has been plaintiff's primary focus, the court finds that such reference was integrated such that the parole [sic] evidence rule would bar any inconsistent testimony. Testimony that the owners were limited to "price" in their review is inconsistent.

* * *

41. With respect to the Owners Committee's approval clause, according to the plaintiff's contention the owners were entitled to review the transaction, on whatever basis, only one time. This was testified to by both Mr. Reed and argued by plaintiff in closing. * * * It was also conceded in closing that the review by the owners, on whatever standard, would occur prior to any formal contract being negotiated and executed. * * * This is also consistent with the testimony of each of the participants.

42. In addition, Mr. Reed, in consultation with Ed Merdes and Henry Camarot, his attorneys, tendered the letter of March 4, 1977, as a document which could serve as "the contract". * * * The March 4 letter contains no further reference to the Owners Committee's approval function * * *. Therefore, I find that as to the Owners Committee's approval * * * the letter of December 11 constitutes an integration or partial integration * * *. This having been established, the analysis outlined by the court on September 26, 1980, when granting defendant's motion for summary judgment on the contract claims is applicable. [Citations omitted.]

After reviewing the record, we cannot say that this finding of a partial integration was clearly erroneous.

AND contends that the "clearly erroneous" standard used for reviewing findings of fact issued after a trial does not apply because the breach of contract claim was dismissed by summary judgment. Under the circumstances of this case, we believe that the clearly erroneous standard applies rather than the standard of review used in summary judgment cases because the summary judgment ruling was not a final judgment for purposes of appeal.

finding of fact, that this agreement is partially integrated, and I'm not making it by reference only to the four corners of the—of the writings but reference to all the extrinsic evidence that has been proffered to me, read everybody's deposition, considered in detail all the processes of negotiations, everything that was said and done by everybody as related by them up till the time that Rickett included the language in the letter and turned it over to Reed. So we're not here talking about the for [sic] corners or ambiguity or anything like that. We're talking about all the extrinsic evidence, meaning on balance to a conclusion more probable than not that this is a partially integrated agreement.

Rule 54(b) of the Alaska Rules of Civil Procedure provides in relevant part:

> When more than one claim for relief is presented in an action * * * the court may direct the entry of a final judgment as to one * * * of the claims * * * upon an express determination that there is no just reason for delay and upon an express direction for the entry of judgment. In the absence of such determination and direction * * * the order or other form of decision is subject to revision at any time before the entry of judgment adjudicating all the claims and the rights and liabilities of all the parties.

In the pre-trial conference, the superior court indicated that it would make a Rule 54(b) determination if the parties so desired. The parties did not request a Rule 54(b) determination and none was made. During this conference, the court also made it clear that it was willing at the reformation trial to hear all evidence bearing on contract formation, including the negotiations leading up to the letters of intent and the meaning the parties placed on these negotiations and letters. The court emphasized that it was "not cutting out anybody on presenting extrinsic evidence * * * [and] that under Rule 54 the court can, until the end of the case * * * change any decision it's previously reached."

AND contends that the superior court's determination that the only issue at trial concerned reformation "necessarily foreclosed a variety of factual and legal issues on contract formation and interpretation," but does not indicate what evidence it was foreclosed from presenting on these issues. Our review of the record indicates that the integration issue was fully explored by AND during the trial.

After six weeks of testimony, during which time the court had the opportunity to view the demeanor and to judge the credibility of the witnesses, the superior court entered written findings of fact and conclusions of law. As shown in the portion quoted above, these findings reviewed and reaffirmed the findings made in the court's prior summary judgment ruling. Accordingly, the appropriate standard of review is the same as for any other finding of fact, i.e., that the superior court's findings of fact must be upheld unless "clearly erroneous." Alaska R.Civ.P. 52(a). As stated above, the finding of partial integration was not clearly erroneous; therefore, we find no merit in AND's contentions to the contrary.

B. Does the Excluded Evidence Contradict the Integrated Terms?

Having found a partial integration, the next determination is whether the excluded evidence contradicts the integrated portion of the writing. Comment b to section 215 of the Restatement (Second) of Contracts is helpful in resolving this issue.[5] Comment b states:

> An earlier agreement may help the interpretation of a later one, but it may not contradict a binding later integrated agreement. Whether there is a contradiction depends * * * on whether the two are consistent or inconsistent. This is a question which often cannot be determined from the face of the writing; the writing must first be applied to its subject matter and placed in context. The question is then decided by the court as part of a question of interpretation. Where reasonable people could differ as to the credibility of the evidence offered and the evidence if believed could lead a

5. Restatement (Second) of Contracts § 215, which parallels the rule stated in U.C.C. § 2–202, reads: "Except as stated in the preceding Section, where there is a binding agreement, either completely or partially integrated, evidence of prior or contemporaneous agreements or negotiations is not admissible in evidence to contradict a term of the writing."

> reasonable person to interpret the writing as claimed by the proponent of the evidence, the question of credibility and the choice among reasonable inferences should be treated as questions of fact. But the asserted meaning must be one to which the language of the writing, read in context, is reasonably susceptible. If no other meaning is reasonable, the court should rule as a matter of law that the meaning is established.

According to comment b, therefore, a question of interpretation may arise before the contradiction issue can be resolved. If the evidence conflicts, the choice between competing inferences is for the trier of fact to resolve. *Alyeska Pipeline Service Co. v. O'Kelley,* 645 P.2d 767, 771 n. 2 (Alaska 1982). The meaning is determined as a matter of law, however, if "the asserted meaning [is not] one to which the language of the writing, read in context, is reasonably susceptible." Restatement (Second) of Contracts § 215 comment b (1979). See also J. Calamari & J. Perillo, The Law of Contracts §§ 3–12, 3–13 (2d ed. 1977).

AND contends that the superior court erred in granting summary judgment because the evidence conflicted as to the meaning of the owner committee approval clause. It concludes that under *Alyeska* it was entitled to a jury trial on the interpretation issue. Alyeska contends, and the superior court ruled, that a jury trial was inappropriate because, as a matter of law, AND's asserted meaning of the clause at issue was not reasonably susceptible to the language of the writing. The superior court stated:

> The Court is making the * * * ruling that the offer of evidence to show that Rickett's letter really meant to limit owner committee approval to the price term alone * * * is not reasonably susceptible—or the writing is not reasonably susceptible to that purpose. And therefore, that extrinsic evidence operates to contradict the writing, not specific words in the writing, but the words in the context of the totality of the writing and the totality of the extrinsic evidence.

We agree that the words used in the December 11 letter are not reasonably susceptible to the interpretation advanced by AND. Therefore, we find no merit to AND's contention that it was entitled to a jury trial on the interpretation issue.

After rejecting the extrinsic evidence for purposes of interpretation, the superior court found AND's offered testimony, that the owner committee's approval power was limited to approval of the price, to be inconsistent with and contradictory to the language used by the negotiators in the December 11 letter. AND contends that the offered testimony did not contradict, but rather explained or supplemented the writing with consistent additional terms. For this contention, AND relies on the standard articulated in *Hunt Foods & Industries, Inc. v. Doliner,* 26 A.D.2d 41, 270 N.Y.S.2d 937 (N.Y.App.1966). In *Hunt Foods,* the defendant signed an option agreement under which he agreed to sell stock to Hunt Foods at a given price per share. When Hunt Foods attempted to exercise the option, the defendant contended that the option could only be exercised if the defendant had received offers from a third party. The court held that section 2–202 did not bar this evidence from being admitted because it held that the proposed oral condition to the option agreement was not "inconsistent" within the meaning of section 2–202; to be inconsistent, "the term must contradict or negate a term of the writing. A term or condition which has a lesser effect is provable." *Id.* 270 N.Y.S.2d at 940.

The narrow view of consistency expressed in *Hunt Foods* has been criticized. In *Snyder v. Herbert Greenbaum & Associates, Inc.,* 38 Md.App. 144, 380 A.2d 618

(Md.App.1977), the court held that the parol evidence of a contractual right to unilateral rescission was inconsistent with a written agreement for the sale and installation of carpeting. The court defined "inconsistency" as used in section 2–202(b) as "the absence of reasonable harmony in terms of the language *and* respective obligations of the parties." *Id.* 380 A.2d at 623 (emphasis in original) (citing U.C.C. § 1–205(4)). *Accord: Luria Brothers & Co. v. Pielet Brothers Scrap Iron & Metal, Inc.,* 600 F.2d 103, 111 (7th Cir.1979); *Southern Concrete Services, Inc. v. Mableton Contractors, Inc.,* 407 F.Supp. 581 (N.D.Ga.1975), *aff'd mem.,* 569 F.2d 1154 (5th Cir.1978).

We agree with this view of inconsistency and reject the view expressed in *Hunt Foods.*[6] Under this definition of inconsistency, it is clear that the proffered parol evidence limiting the owner committee's right of final approval to price is inconsistent with the integrated term that unconditionally gives the committee the right to approval. Therefore, the superior court was correct in refusing to admit parol evidence on this issue.[7]

* * *

[The court also held that the trial court was correct to deny a jury trial on the reformation issue and to grant a summary judgment against AND on the punitive damage issue.]

Notes

1. In the absence of a "merger" clause, how does the court determine whether the writing was "intended by the parties as a final expression of their agreement" as to some or all of the terms? UCC 2–202. Put differently, how does one evaluate the decision in the *Alaska Northern* case that the writing was intended to be a partial integration with regard to the "approval" clauses? The question is important, for in the absence of any integration, the term limiting the power to reject would be part of the agreement, whether included in the writing or not.

UCC 2–202 and the comments are silent on this question. It may be useful to indulge a presumption, see UCC 1–201(31), that a writing which "reasonably appears to be a complete agreement" is "an integrated agreement unless it is established by other evidence that the writing did not constitute a final expression." Restatement, Second, Contracts 209(3). Since there was no "other" persuasive evidence in the *Alaska Northern* case, the determination that the parties intended a partial integration at least seems sound. What constitutes "other" evidence? According to Comment (c) to Restatement § 209, incompleteness of the writing may be shown by "any relevant evidence, oral or written, that an apparently complete writing never became fully effective, or that it was modified after initial adoption."

2. If the writing is integrated in whole or in part, terms in that writing "may not be contradicted by evidence of any prior agreement or of a contemporaneous oral agreement. * * *" UCC 2–202. Accord: Restatement, Second, Contracts § 215. But if there is a partial integration, as in *Alaska Northern,* the writing may be

6. *Hunt Foods* was implicitly rejected in *Johnson v. Curran,* 633 P.2d 994, 996–97 (Alaska 1981) (parol evidence concerning an early termination right based on nightclub owner's dissatisfaction with the band's performance was inconsistent with parties' written contract specifying definite time without mention of any right of early termination and thus inadmissible).

7. Our affirmance of the superior court's holding that the proposed version is inconsistent with the integrated clause obviates discussion of whether the addition, if consistent, would have been included in the December 11 letter. Furthermore, we decline to reach AND's contentions regarding the applicability of U.C.C. § 2–207 because AND never raised the § 2–207 argument at the superior court level. *See, e.g., Jeffries v. Glacier State Telephone Co.,* 604 P.2d 4, 11 (Alaska 1979).

supplemented "by evidence of consistent additional terms." UCC 2–202(b). Section 216(2) of the Restatement, Second, Contracts puts the matter more affirmatively: "An agreement is not completely integrated if the writing omits a consistent additional term. * * *" We now return to a question that has dominated the trade usage cases: What is a consistent additional term? Is the "absence of reasonable harmony" test applied in *Alaska Northern* the same as the test expressed in Comment 3 to UCC 2–202, i.e., that the term, if agreed upon, "would certainly have been included in the document * * *?" Or, must the "consistent additional agreed term" be one "as in the circumstances might naturally be omitted from the writing?" Section 216(2)(b). For still another application of the "absence of reasonable harmony" test, See ARB. Inc. v. E–Systems, Inc., 663 F.2d 189 (D.C.Cir.1980) (after review of extrinsic evidence, "merger" clause held to express genuine intention of parties).

3. What is the effect of a "merger" clause providing that the writing is the "final and complete agreement of the parties" and that there are "no understandings, agreements, or obligations unless specifically set forth in the writing?" Assuming that the clause is not unconscionable, Seibel v. Layne & Bowler, Inc., 56 Or.App. 387, 641 P.2d 668 (1982) (ordinary consumer unfairly surprised by fine-print merger clause in standard form contract), and assuming that the clause or the contract was not induced by fraud, see UCC 1–103 and Franklin v. Lovitt Equipment Co., 420 So.2d 1370 (Miss.1982), and assuming that there was no other evidence establishing a contrary intention, the UCC answer seems clear: The writing may neither be contradicted by evidence of "any prior agreement or of a contemporaneous agreement" nor "supplemented * * * by evidence of consistent additional terms." UCC 2–202.

May, however, the total integration be "explained or supplemented * * * by course of dealing or usage of trade * * * or by course of performance?" Despite some ambiguity in UCC 2–202, the answer appears to be yes, subject to the limitations imposed by UCC 1–205(4). Thus, evidence of a prior course of dealing has been admitted to explain or supplement the terms of an integrated writing, see e.g., Ralph's Distributing Co. v. AMF, Inc., 667 F.2d 670 (8th Cir.1981), and evidence of trade usage and a prior course of dealing that was thought to "contradict" terms in the writing has been excluded. See, e.g., General Plumbing & Heating, Inc. v. American Air Filter, 696 F.2d 375 (5th Cir.1983). We return, then, full circle to the test of consistency raised in the trade usage cases.

Problem 11–1

Fiber Industries sold fiber to carpet manufacturers for use in the making of carpets. Salem Carpet bought trademark fiber from Fiber Industries on an order-by-order basis. There was no written agreement other than the individual purchase orders. Both Salem's purchase order form and Fiber Industries acknowledgment form contained "merger" clauses, which provided that the form "contains all the terms and conditions of the purchase agreement and shall constitute the complete and exclusive agreement between Seller and Purchaser." In August, 1980 Fiber Industries announced that it was withdrawing from the carpet industry, but that it would supply all customers in an "orderly fashion" until the phase-out was complete. Salem accepted a final order of fiber at a contract price of $407,128.40, but refused to pay the full amount because of losses suffered as a result of Fiber Industries' withdrawal from the market. Salem claimed that there was a "customary practice" in the carpet industry obligating Fiber Industries to fill all orders made by Salem during the projected market life of any carpet style which utilized fiber manufactured by Fiber Industries. Salem was prepared to establish a usage that the "carpet manufacturer will continue to make its branded fiber available for the useful life of the carpet style or for sufficient time to allow the carpet manufacturer to produce and sell sufficient carpet to recoup the large start-up expenses incurred in introducing and marketing a new line of branded carpet."

Assume that both contract forms were silent on the issue. Assume, further, that the usage could be established. Under UCC 1–205(4) and 2–202, should the court admit evidence of the usage as part of the agreement?

FRIGALIMENT IMPORTING CO. v. B.N.S. INTERNATIONAL SALES CORP.

United States District Court, Southern District of New York, 1960.
190 F.Supp. 116.

FRIENDLY, CIRCUIT JUDGE.

The issue is, what is chicken? Plaintiff says "chicken" means a young chicken, suitable for broiling and frying. Defendant says "chicken" means any bird of that genus that meets contract specifications on weight and quality, including what it calls "stewing chicken" and plaintiff pejoratively terms "fowl". Dictionaries give both meanings, as well as some others not relevant here. To support it, plaintiff sends a number of volleys over the net: defendant essays to return them and adds a few serves of its own. Assuming that both parties were acting in good faith, the case nicely illustrates Holmes' remark "that the making of a contract depends not on the agreement of two minds in one intention, but on the agreement of two sets of external signs—not on the parties' having *meant* the same thing but on their having *said* the same thing." The Path of the Law, in Collected Legal Papers, p. 178. I have concluded that plaintiff has not sustained its burden of persuasion that the contract used "chicken" in the narrower sense.

The action is for breach of the warranty that goods sold shall correspond to the description, New York Personal Property Law, McKinney's Consol.Laws, c. 41, § 95. Two contracts are in suit. In the first, dated May 2, 1957, defendant, a New York sales corporation, confirmed the sale to plaintiff, a Swiss corporation, of

"U S Fresh Frozen Chicken, Grade A, Government Inspected, Eviscerated

2½–3 lbs. and 1½–2 lbs. each

all chicken individually wrapped in cryovac, packed in secured fiber cartons or wooden boxes, suitable for export

75,000 lbs. 2½–3 lbs. . . . . at $33.00

25,000 lbs. 1½–2 lbs. . . . . at $36.50

per 100 lbs. FAS New York

scheduled May 10, 1957 pursuant to instructions from Penson & Co., New York."

The second contract, also dated May 2, 1957, was identical save that only 50,000 lbs. of heavier "chicken" were called for, the price of the smaller birds was $37 per 100 lbs., and shipment was scheduled for May 30. The initial shipment under the first contract was short but the balance was shipped on May 17. When the initial shipment arrived in Switzerland, plaintiff found, on May 28, that the 2½–3 lbs. birds were not young chicken suitable for broiling and frying but stewing chicken or "fowl"; indeed, many of the cartons and bags plainly so indicated. Protests ensued. Nevertheless, shipment under the second contract was made on May 29, the 2½–3 lbs. birds again being stewing chicken. Defendant stopped the transportation of these at Rotterdam.

This action followed. Plaintiff says that, notwithstanding that its acceptance was in Switzerland, New York law controls under the principle of Rubin v. Irving Trust Co., 1953, 305 N.Y. 288, 305, 113 N.E.2d 424, 431; defendant does not dispute this, and relies on New York decisions. I shall follow the apparent agreement of the parties as to the applicable law.

[The court first determined that the contract language offered no assistance in determining the meaning of the word, "chicken", which standing alone was ambiguous.]

Plaintiff's next contention is that there was a definite trade usage that "chicken" meant "young chicken." Defendant showed that it was only beginning in the poultry trade in 1957, thereby bringing itself within the principle that "when one of the parties is not a member of the trade or other circle, his acceptance of the standard must be made to appear" by proving either that he had actual knowledge of the usage or that the usage is "so generally known in the community that his actual individual knowledge of it may be inferred." 9 Wigmore, Evidence (3d ed. 1940) § 2464. Here there was no proof of actual knowledge of the alleged usage; indeed, it is quite plain that defendant's belief was to the contrary. In order to meet the alternative requirement, the law of New York demands a showing that "the usage is of so long continuance, so well established, so notorious, so universal and so reasonable in itself, as that the presumption is violent that the parties contracted with reference to it and made it a part of their agreement." Walls v. Bailey, 1872, 49 N.Y. 464, 472–473.

Plaintiff endeavored to establish such a usage by the testimony of three witnesses and certain other evidence. Strasser, resident buyer in New York for a large chain of Swiss cooperatives, testified that "on chicken I would definitely understand a broiler." However, the force of this testimony was considerably weakened by the fact that in his own transactions the witness, a careful businessman, protected himself by using "broiler" when that was what he wanted and "fowl" when he wished older birds. Indeed, there are some indications, dating back to a remark of Lord Mansfield, Edie v. East India Co., 2 Burr. 1216, 1222 (1761), that no credit should be given "witnesses to usage, who could not adduce instances in verification." 7 Wigmore, Evidence (3d ed. 1940), § 1954; see McDonald v. Acker, Merrall & Condit Co., 2d Dept. 1920, 192 App. Div. 123, 126, 182 N.Y.S. 607. While Wigmore thinks this goes too far, a witness' consistent failure to rely on the alleged usage deprives his opinion testimony of much of its effect. Niesielowski, an officer of one of the companies that had furnished the stewing chicken to defendant, testified that "chicken" meant "the male species of the poultry industry. That could be a broiler, a fryer or a roaster", but not a stewing chicken; however, he also testified that upon receiving defendant's inquiry for "chickens", he asked whether the desire was for "fowl or frying chickens" and, in fact, supplied fowl, although taking the precaution of asking defendant, a day or two after plaintiff's acceptance of the contracts in suit, to change its confirmation of its order from "chickens," as defendant had originally prepared it, to "stewing chickens." Dates, an employee of Urner-Barry Company, which publishes a daily market report on the poultry trade, gave it as his view that the trade meaning of "chicken" was "broilers and fryers." In addition to this opinion testimony, plaintiff relied on the fact that the Urner-Barry service, the Journal of Commerce, and Weinberg Bros. & Co. of Chicago, a large supplier of poultry, published quotations in a manner which, in one way or another, distinguish between "chicken," comprising broilers, fryers and certain other categories, and "fowl," which, Bauer acknowledged, included stewing chickens. This material would be impressive if there were nothing to the contrary. However, there was, as will now be seen.

Defendant's witness Weininger, who operates a chicken eviscerating plant in New Jersey, testified "Chicken is everything except a goose, a duck, and a turkey. Everything is a chicken, but then you have to say, you have to specify which category you want or that you are talking about." Its witness Fox said that in the trade "chicken" would encompass all the various classifications. Sadina, who conducts a food inspection service, testified that he would consider any bird coming within the classes of "chicken" in the Department of Agriculture's regulations to be a chicken. The specifications approved by the General Services Administration include fowl as well as broilers and fryers under the classification "chickens." Statistics of the Institute of American Poultry Industries use the phrases "Young chickens" and "Mature chickens," under the general heading "Total chickens," and the Department of Agriculture's daily and weekly price reports avoid use of the word "chicken" without specification.

* * *

[The court next reviewed arguments that the defendant's meaning of the word "chicken" was supported by definitions in Department of Agriculture regulations, by its inability to obtain young chickens at the agreed contract price and by plaintiff's conduct after the first shipment was received.]

When all the evidence is reviewed, it is clear that defendant believed it could comply with the contracts by delivering stewing chicken in the 2½–3 lbs. size. Defendant's subjective intent would not be significant if this did not coincide with an objective meaning of "chicken." Here it did coincide with one of the dictionary meanings, with the definition in the Department of Agriculture Regulations to which the contract made at least oblique reference, with at least some usage in the trade, with the realities of the market, and with what plaintiff's spokesman had said. Plaintiff asserts it to be equally plain that plaintiff's own subjective intent was to obtain broilers and fryers; the only evidence against this is the material as to market prices and this may not have been sufficiently brought home. In any event it is unnecessary to determine that issue. For plaintiff has the burden of showing that "chicken" was used in the narrower rather than in the broader sense, and this it has not sustained.

This opinion constitutes the Court's findings of fact and conclusions of law. Judgment shall be entered dismissing the complaint with costs. [Footnotes omitted.]

Notes

1. Why, you ask, did we include this "old saw?" Here are a few reasons.

First, the case demonstrates that the UCC parol evidence rule has little to do with issues of interpretation. Rather, extrinsic evidence is admissible to assist the trier of fact in determining the meaning of a term which is part of the agreement. See Farnsworth, *Meaning in the Law of Contracts,* 76 Yale L.J. 939 (1967); Corbin, *The Interpretation of Words and the Parol Evidence Rule,* 50 Cornell L.Rev. 161 (1965).

Second, the case supports the attack by the "realists" on the belief that words have a "plain meaning" that can be determined from the four corners of a writing. As Chief Justice Traynor put it, the "* * * test of admissibility of extrinsic evidence to explain the meaning of a written instrument is not whether it appears to the court to be plain and unambiguous on its face, but whether the offered evidence is relevant to prove a meaning to which the language of the instrument is reasonably susceptible." Pacific Gas and Elec. Co. v. G.W. Thomas Drayage & Rigging Co., 69 Cal.2d 33, 69 Cal.Rptr. 561, 442 P.2d 641, 644 (1968). See UCC 2–202, Comment 1(b).

Third, the case illustrates the wide range of facts, including trade usage, that may be relevant to interpretation disputes. It is consistent with the UCC's position that the "meaning of the agreement of the parties is to be determined by the language used by them and by their action, read and interpreted in the light of commercial practices and other circumstances." UCC 1–205, Comment 1. It also illustrates that even with access to evidence from the commercial context, the plaintiff failed to establish that his meaning of "chicken" should prevail. According to the Restatement, in order for the plaintiff to prevail, he would have to establish that either (a) he did not know the different meaning attached by the defendant to "chicken" and the defendant knew the meaning attached by the plaintiff, or (b) the plaintiff had no reason to know of the different meaning attached by the defendant and the defendant had reason to know the meaning attached by the plaintiff. Section 201, Restatement, Second, Contracts. See also, 202–203, 219–223. Does the Restatement test square with the outcome in the "chicken" case? Does the UCC provide any guidance on what the plaintiff must establish to prevail? (We think that the answer is no.)

Fourth, (and finally), the case shows that even though the purpose of the claimed trade usage was proper—to give meaning to the term "chicken"—the plaintiff failed to prove the usage. Review the facts and Judge Friendly's opinion to determine why the proof failed and consider the following note.

Note: Proof of Trade Usage and Other Context Evidence

Trade usage and other context evidence are facts to be established by the moving party, i.e., the party seeking to persuade the court that his interpretation of the scope or meaning of the agreement should prevail. UCC 1–205(2). Since these facts are normally not presumed to exist, see UCC 1–201(31), the plaintiff has the "burden of establishing" them, i.e., he must persuade the "triers of fact that the existence of the fact is more probable than its non-existence." UCC 1–201(8). The moving party, therefore, has both the burden of production and the burden of persuasion. These burdens are normally satisfied, if at all, through expert witnesses and documents, see UCC 1–205(2), in an atmosphere where objections to the expert's qualifications, the authenticity of documents and hearsay and relevance are routine. See, e.g., C. McCormick, Evidence 13 (2d ed. 1972); McElhaney, *Expert Witnesses and the Federal Rules of Evidence,* 28 Mercer L.Rev. 463 (1977). The pitfalls in this process are illustrated by the "Chicken" case.

But there are more problems for the moving party. According to Professors Allen and Hillman, a "comprehensive set of proof rules would establish who must bear the burden of pleading, of persuasion, and of producing evidence, and would define the appropriate contours of judicial comment on the evidence." Allen & Hillman, *Evidentiary Problems In—And Solutions For—the Uniform Commercial Code,* 1984 Duke L.J. 92, 98. They suggest that if the Drafters had stopped with the burden of persuasion rule in UCC 1–201(8) and the burden of production rule in UCC 1–201(31), the "Code's approach to proof problems, if liberally construed, would have been nearly adequate." The Code "could have been interpreted to place on plaintiffs and moving parties the burdens of production and persuasion on all issues—the normal rule—unless it specifically allocated one or the other burden by using the terminology of either section 1–201(8) or 1–201(32)." Further, trial judges "could then have determined pleading requirements and the scope of their authority to comment on the evidence by referring to their jurisdiction's procedural law." Id.

The questions in particular cases, such as proof of trade usage, are (1) whether other Code provisions are inconsistent with these general principles of production and persuasion and, if so, (2) whether the Code contains rules of proof that describe how the burdens should be allocated and provide guidance on pleading or the conditions under which a judge may comment on the evidence. In areas other than proof of trade usage, Professors Allen and Hillman answer the two questions "yes" and "no" and conclude that these failures, as manifested in judicial opinions, have interferred with a basic purpose of the Code to promote clarity and consistency in commercial dealings. Id. at 98–105.

The potential for trouble exists in the trade usage areas as well. Suppose, for example, that a buyer of steel seeks to establish a trade usage that a written contract for goods described as "36 inch steel" is satisfied by steel with a width between 36" and 37". (For such a case, see Decker Steel Co. v. Exchange Nat'l Bank of Chicago, 330 F.2d 82 (7th Cir.1964) and Problem 11–2, infra.) Here are some trouble spots for which the Code has no answers.

(1) At what point in the plaintiff's case does the burden of production shift to the defendant and what proof must the defendant adduce to satisfy that intermediate burden?

(2) Suppose the defendant, by way of affirmative defense, attacks the established usage as unreasonable or unconscionable. Comment 6 to UCC 1–205 states that the "very fact of commercial acceptance makes out a prima facie case that the usage is reasonable, and the burden is no longer on the usage to establish itself as being reasonable." What does this mean for the burdens of production and persuasion?

(3) Finally, suppose the defendant raises express written language purporting to totally integrate the writing, UCC 2–202, or to exclude the usage. Is there a presumption that the writing expresses the intention of both parties? If so, do both the burden of production and the burden of persuasion shift to the plaintiff? How are those burdens satisfied?

In order to clarify the rules governing the proof of facts in a trial under the Code, Professors Allen and Hillman propose the following addition:

"Section 1–210. Rules Governing the Proof of Facts at Trial

(1) Definitions

(a) A burden of production is a requirement that a party produce sufficient evidence on an issue to avoid a directed verdict on that issue. The phrases "to presume" or "prima facie case," and any derivations thereof, shall be interpreted to refer to a burden of production, unless expressly provided otherwise.

(b) A burden of persuasion is a requirement that a party convince the finder of fact to a previously specified level of certainty of the truth of an issue. The phrases "to establish" or "to show" and any derivations thereof shall be interpreted to refer to a burden of persuasion, unless expressly provided otherwise.

(2) General Provisions

(a) Pleading. Unless expressly provided otherwise, all pleading matters shall be governed by the Rule (or Code) of Civil Procedure.

(b) Burden of Production and Persuasion. Unless expressly provided otherwise or unless the interests of justice clearly require otherwise, plaintiffs and moving parties shall bear the burden of production and persuasion on all contested issues. The justification for any judicial exception must be specifically provided by the trial court and is subject to review on appeal. A question of fact upon which allocation of a burden of production or persuasion is conditoned shall be decided by the court for the purpose of allocating the burden of production or persuasion.

(c) Standard of Persuasion. Unless expressly provided otherwise or unless the interests of justice clearly require otherwise, a burden of persuasion is satisfied if the party, bearing it convinces the fact finder that the existence of the fact is more probable than its non-existence, and a burden of production is satisfied if the court determines that a reasonable person could so find. The justification for any judicial exception must be specifically provided by the trial court and is subject to review on appeal.

(d) Peremptory Instruction or Ruling. The trial court may remove an issue from the consideration of the jury if reasonable persons with an understanding of the commercial practices involved would not disagree about the matter.

(e) Order of Proof. The trial court may require the presentation of evidence in the order that it determines would best facilitate the trial process.

(f) Judicial Comment on the Evidence. After the close of the evidence and arguments of counsel, the court may fairly and impartially sum up the evidence or examine the implication of the evidence, or both, for the benefit of the jury. Notice of intended comment shall be provided to counsel, and an opportunity to respond with evidence or argument shall be permitted."

Id. at 105–06.

Problem 11–2

The following excerpt is from the trial transcript in the case of Decker Steel Co. v. Exchange Nat'l Bank of Chicago, 330 F.2d 82 (7th Cir.1964). In that case, Decker Steel, a disappointed buyer, sued its seller and the bank which had issued a letter of credit to its seller. One of the issues was whether the delivered steel had in fact conformed to the contract specifications which called for "prime Thomas quality 36″ X coiled hot rolled steel." Plaintiff alleged that the steel did not conform to the contract because it was 37 inches wide and was not the proper thickness. In the following testimony, the defendant attempted to prove that trade usage accepted 37″ steel under a contract calling for 36″ steel. As you read the transcript, try to visualize how thorny the path to established trade usage can be. What road blocks did the opposing counsel put in the way of proof? Can you think of additional arguments which might have been made for or against the submission of the offered testimony? Would UCC 1–205 help with the problems of proof?

Proceedings Before Hon. Richard B. Austin, June 25, 1963:

Sydney Borenstein, called as a witness on behalf of the defendants, having been first duly sworn, was examined and testified as follows:

Direct Examination

By Mr. Joseph:

Q. Would you state your name and address, please?

A. Sydney Borenstein, 2710 Marl Oak Drive, Highland Park, Illinois.

Q. What is your occupation, Mr. Borenstein?

A. I buy and sell steel and am a warehouser and distributor of steel.

Q. What is the name of your organization?

A. Superior Steel Service.

Q. What is your position with that organization?

A. President.

Q. How many years have you been in the steel business, Mr. Borenstein?

A. About thirteen years.

Q. Among the steel you deal with there, would prime Thomas quality hot rolled steel coils be included?

A. Yes, sir.

Q. And you are acquainted with that kind of steel?

A. Yes, I am.

Q. Mr. Borenstein, are you acquainted with the market conditions for steel at the end of 1959 and the beginning of 1960?

A. Yes, sir.

* * *

Q. Mr. Borenstein, are you acquainted with permissible tolerances in connection with the buying and selling of prime Thomas quality hot rolled steel in coils?

Mr. Marshall: I object, if your Honor please. The documents in the case recite whatever tolerances relate to this transaction.

The Court: The only tolerances that I am aware of in regard to a purchase order is the spread that is permitted in regard to the gauge, and I saw nothing in there in regard to any spreads in regard to the width.

Mr. Joseph: Well, I am prepared to prove, your Honor, that when nothing is said, something else is understood.

* * *

The Court: The objection of this question is overruled. You are each pursuing your own theory of the case.

By Mr. Joseph:

Q. Are you acquainted with permissible tolerances, Mr. Borenstein, in connection with prime Thomas quality hot rolled steel coils?

A. Well, normally in the trade there are references that are made to specifications and when a—

Q. Can you answer the question yes or no? Are you familiar with tolerances?

A. I am familiar with the tolerances and the books from which the specifications can be read.

* * *

Q. Are you acquainted with the American Society for Testing Materials?

A. I am acquainted with that book, and I am also acquainted with the AISI, a copy of which I have with me.

The Court: Which means what, AISI?

The Witness: Well, can I get the book? It is American Iron and Steel Institute.

The Court: This document is what kind of a document of that institute?

The Witness: It is a reference book telling the tolerances, the type tolerances that are permissible and used by the mills in the production of carbon steel sheets.

The Court: And is Thomas steel in that category of prime steel?

The Witness: Yes, sir.

By Mr. Joseph:

Q. Now, can you find in that book—

Mr. Joseph: Let's mark the book as an exhibit—well, let's find the page first.

By Mr. Joseph:

Q. Can you find in this book, Mr. Borenstein, a page which contains a reference to steel of this nature showing the tolerances as to width?

A. I think so.

* * *

Q. What page is it?

A. Page 52.

Q. Is there any part of that page 52 which you have specific reference to?

A. Table 9. Can I read it?

* * *

Q. Is there an item in that column which refers to 36–inch steel?

The Court: Yes or no.

By The Witness:

A. Yes.

By Mr. Joseph:

Q. What is the tolerance indicated for 36–inch steel?

Mr. Marshall: I object, if your Honor please.

The Court: I think maybe the document itself is the best evidence.

Mr. Joseph: All right.

Mr. Marshall: I think that the document, in addition, your Honor, is hearsay.

I have had no opportunity at all to cross examine the author of that document.

I submit to your Honor—It hasn't been marked for identification yet and that is why I have been waiting.

The Court: I think that that page should be at this time, counsel.

Mr. Marshall: But I do object to any reference to the book, and anticipating to some extent that it will be offered in evidence, I will object to it at that time. I think that the book is hearsay.

The Court: I am not aware as to what the American Iron and Steel Institute is. It may be a neighborhood pool hall or a tavern, as far as I know from the evidence.

Mr. Joseph: All right.

Will the reporter please mark this Defendant Exchange National Bank's Exhibit No. 7 for identification.

(Said document marked Defendant's Exhibit 7 for identification.)

By Mr. Joseph:

Q. Mr. Borenstein, what relationship does—what use does this book of which Defendant's Exhibit 7 is a page have in the steel community?

A. Well, the specifications and tolerances as defined by the AISI are the specifications and tolerances used by the mills in the production of their material.

Mr. Marshall: I object. This witness does not know, if your Honor pleases, of his own knowledge what the mills use, and I object to his answer and move to strike it. It must be hearsay.

The Witness: I beg your pardon.

Mr. Joseph: The witness has testified as to what he knows about the document.

The Court: Well, he hasn't testified as to what he knows about what the mills use. I don't know whether he has ever bought any steel in a mill in his life. There is nothing in the record to so indicate it.

By Mr. Joseph:

Q. Mr. Borenstein, what is your business?

A. I buy and sell steel.

Q. From whom do you buy and to whom do you sell?

A. I buy steel from mills. I have imported steel. I buy steel from warehouses. I buy surplus steel.

Q. To whom do you sell?

A. We sell to end users essentially.

Q. What is an end user?

A. A person who takes a piece of raw steel and converts it to a useful purpose.

Q. All right. Are you acquainted with the buying and selling practices of mills and of steel brokers?

A. Yes, I am.

Q. Do you know whether or not the specifications in Defendant's Exhibit 7 for identification are used by the buyers and sellers of steel?

Mr. Marshall: If your Honor please, now the vice of this, and I submit to your Honor that it is immaterial and irrelevant. We have agreements here between these parties. There is no reference in any of the papers to the AISI tolerances book, manual or anything else. The parties to this transaction are available. Mr. Decker is available. He testified in respect to those documents on direct and Mr. Joseph had the opportunity to cross examine him in respect to those documents. The other parties to the transaction, Associated Steel, are available. All of the persons who have signed any of these papers are subject to the processes of this court, and I submit to your Honor that it is not proper by this method to attempt to incorporate these tolerances into some contract between Decker and Associated or some letter of credit between Exchange and Decker and Associated and The First National Bank. There is nothing in the documents if your Honor please, that makes any reference to these tolerances. These parties, when they wanted a tolerance, specified a tolerance and this is true, I might say, not only of the Decker-Associated transaction, but it is also true of the Associated-Brown-Strauss transaction. They specified tolerances as well.

The Court: Which were, as far as I understand it, unknown to either bank other than the 36–inch width, is that right?

Mr. Joseph: That is right.

The Court: There is nothing in either letter of credit that has to do with the gauge.

Mr. Joseph: That is correct, your Honor.

The Court: So we are just talking about width, and I assume that based on the witness' testimony that the stamp of AISI may have the same standing in the trade as AMA does in regard to a medical product or ADS does in regard to Crest toothpaste, and they are an outstanding collection of members of a profession or business who must have some standard to go by so that they can do business with each other, and I am assuming that based upon what has been said here that this is some kind of an understanding that has been drawn up and signed and put down and is the basis for buying and selling of steel.

Mr. Marshall: If your Honor please, there is no reference in the contract, any of the agreements among the various parties to this litigation that makes any reference to this type of tolerance table.

Mr. Joseph: I am not aware, for example, your Honor, that in court that we have mentioned rules of evidence but we live by them just the same because lawyers in court understand, and it is just a matter of our way of proceeding.

Now, sometimes you can have disputes about such things but we all understand that when we have a trial, without saying it, that that is the procedure that we are operating under. If it is the custom and usage in the steel industry to allow for certain tolerances, that is part of the contract because that is the way one steel man talks to another.

Mr. Marshall: That may be true in a general situation, your Honor, but it cannot be true where the parties themselves have specified tolerances. It cannot be.

The Court: Let me see the letter of credit, both letters of credit.

Mr. Joseph: Here is the first—

Mr. Marshall: You have the first one, Judge.

The Court: I have the first here, yes.

Mr. Marshall: I haven't a copy of it.

The Court: No, there is the first one.

Mr. Marshall: I say that I have not got a copy of the Exchange.

The Court: Do you have a copy of the Exchange?

Mr. Joseph: Here, your Honor.

Mr. Marshall: I might also say in respect to the Exchange letter of credit that Mr. Joseph has attempted to lay the foundation to show that other rules in regard to that transaction were all incorporated by reference, a lengthy set of rules. There is nothing in those rules in regard to these tolerances.

I really submit to your Honor that Mr. Joseph by this testimony is seeking to alter the agreements of the parties here.

Mr. Joseph: I am intending to explain the agreements of the parties.

Mr. Marshall: They don't need any explanation. They are not ambiguous on their face. There is no ambiguity on the face of the documents at all and none has been raised by the testimony.

The Court: I know this, I know nothing about the steel business. I don't know whether the First National or Exchange knows anything about it. I am just assuming, because we haven't even got in the evidence what is in Table 9 yet, but had the First—or the Exchange called in recognized authorities in the steel business, and maybe those who belong to the American Iron and Steel Institute all were recognized authorities and had shown them these coils as an additional precaution, which they are not under legal obligation to do, and asked them, "Is this 36–inch steel?"

I assume that these gentlemen would have said that it is 36–inch steel regardless of the fact that it may have been wider than 36 inches as long as it was within the tolerances that have been adopted by those in the trade.

Mr. Joseph: Precisely, your Honor.

Mr. Marshall: If your Honor pleases, though, when the seller of the goods, as is true in the case at bar, Associated Steel Corporation states as it did in the telegram to Mr. Decker that the goods are not 36 inches wide, that is the interpretation that that seller has placed upon the contract and we look to the contract itself to see whether it is ambiguous.

The Court: What do we do in the circumstances—and I am staying with the evidence at this time—where a superior to Mr. Archer in the Associated Corporation assures Exchange National Bank that this should be disregarded, that it is 36–inch steel? Must they accept a telegram from an underling or the verbal assurance of the president of the corporation?

Mr. Marshall: Well, if your Honor pleases, there was one additional fact in regard to the episode of which your Honor refers as Mr. Decker testified: Mr. Fox stated that he didn't know the width of the steel. He didn't know whether it was 36 or 37 inches wide.

Mr. Joseph: That was at the time of the telephone conversation, not at the time—

Mr. Marshall: That was at the time, if your Honor pleases, that the conversations occurred at the bank and Mr. Fox told Mr. Decker to disregard the telegram. Mr. Fox said, "I don't know what the dimensions are," and then Mr. Decker took from him the invoice reciting that it was 36 inches wide. That is a part of my case.

The Court: I understand that.

Let's proceed.

* * *

(The question was read.)

The Court: The objection to that question is overruled.

* * *

By Mr. Joseph:

Q. Is there an item in that table referring to steel of 36 inches—excuse me, strike that and I will start over.

Is there an item in the table which refers to 36–inch steel of the kind that we have been talking about?

A. Yes, there is.

Q. What is the tolerance shown for such steel?

Mr. Marshall: I object, your Honor. The document speaks for itself and I renew my objections.

The Court: Are you offering this page in evidence?

Mr. Joseph: Yes, I am offering this page.

The Court: All right, it may be received and now that it is in evidence he may read from it and you may renew your objection, and if you want to state something for the record, you can; otherwise, it is overruled.

* * *

By Mr. Joseph:

Q. Mr. Borenstein, what is the tolerance shown for steel of 36–inch width in that table?

A. In this table, 36–inch width has a tolerance over and none under of an inch and a quarter.

Q. By that it is meant what?

A. It is meant that the steel, when it comes off the mill, can be wider than 36 inches by 1¼ inches.

The Court: By not more than 1¼ inches.

The Witness: But not more than.

By Mr. Joseph:

Q. And can it be under anything?

A. No, no tolerance under.

* * *

Q. Does it ever occur, Mr. Borenstein, that a buyer of steel would want steel which is precisely 36 inches with no tolerance?

A. Well, there are instances where people want to limit their tolerances. There is no instance where steel is produced exactly to the thousandths. There is a permissible tolerance under all circumstances.

However, if you are interested in getting material as close to 36 as it is possible to get, then you call for coils that are slit, specifically slit to that width so that the specifications that prevail under those terms will apply to the steel.

Q. Would that cost more?

A. Yes.

Q. Mr. Borenstein, do steel brokers ever sell steel one to the other?

A. Yes, they do.

Q. Does it ever happen that you buy steel from one broker and sell it to another broker?

A. Yes, I do.

Q. In connection with purchasing steel from one broker and selling it to another, do you ever arrange to have the bills of lading on which the steel is shipped to you exchanged for other bills of lading from you to your customer?

A. It is a standard procedure in the reshipment of goods when you change title, so to speak, you get new bills issued by surrendering original bills.

Q. What is the purpose of so doing?

* * *

A. Well, in most instances it is a normal transfer of title that occurs. If one broker was buying and selling to another person, in shipping that material he would automatically name the person to whom it was being shipped. That is one of the reasons.

Another reason is that frequently the people who are doing the selling do not wish to divulge their source of steel, so consequently they change—

* * *

A. (Continuing) So it is the practice with such a situation to exchange bills of lading in order to conceal this source.

* * *

Q. Mr. Borenstein, is the width on the outside of a coil necessarily the same as the width on the inside of a coil?

A. If we are talking about inside and outside diameters, they can vary.

The Court: And in 36–inch steel would the variance be more than a quarter of an inch, or if it did, would it take it out of the 36–inch steel category?

The Witness: I will answer the first part. It could vary more than a quarter of an inch.

The Court: I mean an inch and a quarter, let me put it that way.

The Witness: It is possible that it might, your Honor.

The Court: And that portion that measured more than the inch and a quarter above 36 inches would then no longer be 36–inch steel, is that right?

The Witness: Yes, your Honor.

* * *

By Mr. Marshall:

Q. Now, Defendant's Exhibit No. 7, Mr. Borenstein, the page in the American Iron and Steel Institute, this is an American association, is it not?

A. Yes, it is.

Q. And it relates to American production, does it not?

A. It relates to mill practices.

Q. American mill practices?

A. I don't know that it specifically limits it to American mill practices, because for your information a large number of foreign mills are of American manufacture.

Q. Well, does this manual relate to American mills or foreign mills, or both?

A. I would say—

Q. Or do you know, sir?

A. I would say that in the purchase of steel you would use that as the Bible whether you purchased it for domestic or foreign.

Q. Now, I don't think you have answered my question.

* * *

Q. Does the book relate to American specifications or foreign specifications or both?

* * *

The Witness: I don't know.

* * *

Q. Who are members of the American Iron and Steel Institute, Mr. Borenstein?

A. In general? May I—are you asking this in general?

Q. Yes. Do you know what the membership consists of generally?

A. Yes. I would say all the steel mills, all steel producing mills and testing laboratories, people who are especially interested in the resolution of specifications.

Q. And by that you mean the American mills and American testing institutes and so forth, correct?

A. In addition to others, I am sure.

Q. And isn't it a fact, Mr. Borenstein, that the information contained in the book consists of information that has been reported to the American Iron and Steel Institute by its members?

A. Does it say that in there?

Q. Well, I am asking you if you know if that is a fact, sir.

A. I presume that is where they get their information.

* * *

CHAPTER TWELVE

THE EFFECT OF OPEN TERMS AND RESERVED DISCRETION

SECTION 1. INTRODUCTION: THE UCC AS A SOURCE OF SUPPLETIVE TERMS

In the bargain envisioned by the drafters of the First Restatement of Contracts, promulgated in 1931, the transaction was a relatively discrete exchange and the parties were expected to agree on all of the material terms before a contract was formed. Thus, if material terms, such as quantity or price, were left open or to be agreed, the odds were strong that a court would hold that no enforceable contract was created until there was agreement. Examples of this approach include Transamerica Equip. Leasing Corp. v. Union Bank, 426 F.2d 273 (9th Cir.1970); Walker v. Keith, 382 S.W.2d 198 (Ky.1964); Wilhelm Lubrication Co. v. Brattrud, 197 Minn. 626, 268 N.W. 634 (1936).

In the bargain envisioned by the drafters of Article 2, prepared in the years after World War II, the transaction is not limited to a discrete exchange where promises are made. As we have seen, the definition of agreement, UCC 1–201(3), employs a broader theory of relevant behavior: the bargain can be derived from the particular parties' past, present and future conduct, as well as the practices and usages of others engaging in exchange in the same trade or market. In short, Article 2 allows for relational as well as discrete exchange. See Macneil, *Relational Contract: What We Do and Do Not Know,* 1985 Wis.L.Rev. 483, 485–91. Thus, the parties may, by choice or because of complexity, intend to conclude a bargain without agreeing on every material term. Even in a discrete exchange, they may leave an important term, such as the price, open, or to be agreed, or to be fixed by one of the parties. In exchanges of longer duration or where circumstances are expected to change in unanticipated ways, this technique is especially salutary. It obviates the need for complete risk allocation at the time of contracting and puts a premium on negotiation and adjustment in the light of change.

Section 2–204(3) does not require complete agreement on material terms. Rather, it incorporates standards that permit the parties to conclude a contract "even though one or more terms are left open" if they have "intended to make a contract" and there is a "reasonably certain basis for giving an appropriate remedy."

The first question, then, is to decide whether the parties intended to conclude the bargain and, thus, to "make" a contract, when a material term is left open or to be agreed. What factors are relevant to this determination of intent? If the parties did so intend, the second question is whether there is a "reasonably certain basis for giving an appropriate remedy?" Article 2, Part 3, itself, provides many terms to fill "gaps" in the agreement. Study these "off the rack" gap fillers now, for in many cases they will furnish the basis for certainty of remedy.

Another permitted technique is to leave discretion for fixing or defining the terms of performance to one of the parties. Thus, the agreement may provide that the price is to be the price fixed by the seller at the time of delivery, or that the quantity ordered is to be the buyer's requirements. Similarly, the buyer may agree to use "best efforts" to market a product or to purchase described goods "if satisfied" or both parties may agreed to negotiate over an open term in the future. What effect will reserved discretion by one party have on the enforceability of the agreement? Will the illusory character of the deal mean that there was not consideration? If not, what controls should be imposed upon the exercise of that discretion? See UCC 1–203 (good faith duty in performance and enforcement of the contract). For now, work these simple problems, using the provisions of Article 2, Part 3.

Problem 12–1

A. Seller, a dealer in Delaware Cobbler Potatoes, sells existing goods from cold storage. On February 1, Seller agreed, in a writing signed by both parties, to sell Buyer "1,000 sacks of Delaware Cobbler Potatoes." The writing contained no other terms except the following clause: "The parties to this agreement intend to make a contract and consider themselves bound to this writing." On March 15, Seller, without justification and before any potatoes were identified, repudiated the agreement. Buyer promptly "covered," i.e., purchased 1,000 sacks of Delaware Cobblers for $10 a sack on the open market, in full compliance with UCC 2–712. The market price had been $7 per sack on February 1. What damages, if any, can Buyer recover under UCC 2–712?

B. Suppose, in A above, the writing stated that Seller agreed to sell Buyer "Delaware Cobbler Potatoes for $7 per sack with delivery no later than March 15." Seller failed to deliver. On March 15 the market price for Delaware Cobblers was $10 per sack. What damages, if any, can Buyer recover under UCC 2–713?

C. One last problem. Suppose, in A above, that the writing stated that Seller agreed to sell 1,000 sacks of Delaware Cobbler potatoes, delivery by March 15, at a price "to be fixed by the seller." The market price on February 1 was $7 per sack. On March 15, Seller tendered delivery of the goods and fixed a price of $20 per sack. The current market price was $12 and rising. Buyer rejected the tender and "covered" under UCC 2–712 for $13 per sack. Both parties claim that the other breached the contract. Who should prevail?

Note: The Methodology of "Gap" Filling

Article 2 imposes three controls on the power of a court to fill "gaps" in the agreement and, thus, to make a contract for the parties.

First, the issue must arise outside of the scope of the parties' agreement, which includes all express and implicit terms, as fairly interpreted. UCC 1–201(3). Although trade usage may be introduced to supplement terms of the contract, it is not, strictly speaking, a "gap" filler. Rather, it, too, is part of the agreement of the parties.

Second, the parties must intend to conclude the bargain even though some terms have not been agreed. As the Bethlehem Steel litigation, p. 451, indicates, the more important and complex the term, the less likely it is that the requisite intention is present.

Third, even if the parties so intended, the terms to be supplied by the court are defined by the statutory provisions in Article 2, Part 3, which, in turn, are rooted in standards of reasonableness. According to Judge Richard Posner, the judicial power to fill "gaps" reduces the "cost of contract negotiation by supplying contract terms that the parties would probably have adopted explicitly had they negotiated over them." Posner and Rosenfield, *Impossibility and Related Doctrines in Contract Law,* 6 J.Leg.Studies 83, 88–89 (1977).

What are these standards of reasonableness and how should they be elaborated from the surrounding circumstances? Keep these questions in mind as we examine problems dealing, primarily, with quantity and price. Has the UCC gone too far in substituting standards for rules, and in expecting the parties and the court to search for law that is "immanent" in the commercial context? Dean Murray, whose viewpoint follows, would say no. One of your co-authors, however, is more skeptical. He fears that the Code standards have led the courts to the waters of commercial context without instructing them on how to drink. Speidel, *Restatement, Second: Omitted Terms and Contract Method,* 67 Cornell L.Rev. 785 (1982).

SECTION 2. DISPUTES OVER QUANTITY AND PRICE

A. *Introduction*

A problem for the attorney asked to plan a long-term contract for the sale of goods is to draft an agreement which is legally enforceable and preserves flexibility in the areas thought by the client to be the most troublesome or uncertain during performance. The seasoned practitioner may say that the real challenge is to achieve realistic flexibility and risk allocation rather than legal enforceability. This is discussed further in Macneil, *Contracts: Adjustment of Long-term Economic Relations Under Classical, Neoclassical and Relational Contract Law,* 72 Nw.U.L.Rev. 854 (1978) (difficulties in planning long-term supply contract).

The lawyer must understand the client's business needs and risks, assess the probability of changed circumstances, draft appropriate clauses and, in negotiating with the other side, be capable of achieving a mutually satisfactory agreement. This challenge is strikingly posed when problems of quantity and price are involved. Goldberg, *Price Adjustments in Long-Term Contracts,* 1985 Wisconsin L.Rev. 527; Note, *Requirements Contracts: Problems of Drafting and Construction,* 78 Harv.L.Rev. 1212 (1965).

Remember, the statute of frauds, UCC 2–201(1), states that a "contract is not enforceable * * * beyond the quantity of goods shown * * *" in the writing "signed by the party against whom enforcement is sought. * * *" A commitment to supply output or to buy requirements, however, is a quantity term which, because it can be interpreted and limited under UCC 2–306, satisfies the statute of frauds. For effective criticism of the statute of fraud's quantity policy, see Bruckel, *The Weed and the Web: Section 2–201's Corruption of the Code's Substantive Provisions—The Quantity Problem,* 1983 U.Ill.L.F. 811.

B. *Quantity*

Our primary concern in this subsection is with "output" and "requirements" contracts. Here is a "warm-up" problem on the interpretation of UCC 2–306.

Problem 12–2

Seller, a wholesale dealer in plywood, and Buyer, a producer of pine veneer, entered into a five year contract under which Buyer agreed to purchase 50,000 square feet of plywood per year at $1.00 per square foot. Terms on the time and method of shipment and payment were also agreed. The written contract was dated July 1, 1984.

A. On July 1, 1987, the market price of plywood had climbed to $4.00 per square foot. The increase was due, primarily, to sharpened demand for forest products. Buyer was operating at full capacity and Seller could resell all of the plywood obtained from the manufacturers. Seller, however, was unhappy with its arrangement with Buyer. Buyer, no softy, said: "Tough. You assumed the risk!" Is Buyer correct?

B. Assume the same facts except that Buyer agreed to purchase its annual "requirements" of plywood from Seller at $1.00 per square foot. The contract did not explicitly say "all of our requirements exclusively from Seller." Furthermore, the contract did not provide for estimates of quantity or maximum-minimum quantities which Buyer could not exceed. Buyer's annual requirements for the first three years were 25,000, 32,500 and 35,000 square feet. During the fourth year, with the market price at $4.50 per square foot, Buyer requested a total of 60,000 square feet, the capacity of its production facility. Seller objected and Buyer, still no softy, said: "Tough. You assumed the risk!" Seller's lawyer responded by quoting to buyer's lawyer during negotiations from Billings Cottonseed, Inc. v. Albany Oil Mill, Inc., 173 Ga.App. 825, 328 S.E.2d 426, 429, 430 (1985):

> Appellant's argument that a valid requirements contract was established by partial performance on its part is also without merit. Ordinarily, partial performance renders enforceable a contract unenforceable for lack of consideration and mutuality by supplying the lack of mutuality. * * * There can be no partial performance in the context of a requirements contract, however, for it is the promise of exclusivity that provides the consideration to the seller. * * * The promise to buy alone is not sufficient performance, for without exclusivity the purchaser's promise is merely to buy when he wants and the promise of the seller becomes merely an invitation for orders. * * * Thus, the requisite mutuality is not supplied." (Citations omitted.)

What arguments should Buyer make at this point? Should they prevail? See, particularly, Bruckel, *Consideration in Exclusive and Nonexclusive Open Quantity Contracts Under the U.C.C.: A Proposal for a New System of Validation,* 68 Minn.L. Rev. 117 (1983), who rejects the exclusivity requirement.

C. In light of hindsight, what is the best contractual arrangement for an enterprise selling plywood to a producer with a finite capacity, in a period where prices are expected to rise due primarily to increased demand for the product:

(1) Fixed-price plus "requirements," with an upper limit on quantity;

(2) Fixed-price plus an agreement to sell all or a specified part of the seller's "output" of plywood exclusively to the buyer;

(3) An "open" or market price plus either a requirements or an output agreement;

(4) Either separate contracts or short term, i.e., one year, arrangements with fixed prices and fixed quantities;

(5) Other?

ORANGE & ROCKLAND, etc. v. AMERADA HESS CORP.

Supreme Court of New York, Appellate Division, 1977.
59 A.D. 110, 397 N.Y.S.2d 814.

MARGETT, JUSTICE.

This action, for damages as a result of an alleged breach of a requirements contract, raises related but distinctly separate issues as to whether the plaintiff buyer's requirements occurred in good faith and whether those requirements were unreasonably disproportionate to the estimates stated in the contract.

In a fuel oil supply contract executed in early December, 1969, defendant Amerada Hess Corporation (Hess) agreed to supply the requirements of plaintiff Orange and Rockland Utilities, Inc. (O & R) at plaintiff's Lovett generating plant in Tompkins Cove, New York. A fixed price of $2.14 per barrel for No. 6 fuel oil, with a sulphur content of 1% or less, was to continue at least through September 30, 1974, with the price subject to renegotiation at that time. Estimates of the amounts required by plaintiff were included in the contract clause entitled "Quantity". Insofar as those estimates are relevant to the instant controversy, they were as follows:

1970—1,750,000 barrels

1971—1,380,000 barrels

1972—1,500,000 barrels

1973—1,500,000 barrels

The estimates had been prepared by plaintiff on December 30, 1968, as part of a five-year budget projection. The estimates anticipated that gas would be the primary fuel used for generation during the period in question.[1] This was a result of the lower cost of gas and of the fact that gas became readily available for power generation during the warmer months of the year as a result of decreased use by gas customers. Plaintiff expressly reserved its right to burn as much gas as it chose by the inclusion, in the "Quantity" provision of the requirements contract, of a clause to the effect that "[n]othing herein shall preclude the use by Buyer of * * * natural gas in such quantities as may be or become available".

Within five months of the execution of the requirements contract, the price of fuel oil began to ascend rapidly. On April 24, 1970 the market price of the oil supplied to plaintiff stood at between $2.65 and $2.73 per barrel. On May 1, 1970 the price was in excess of $3 per barrel. The rise continued and was in excess of $3.50 per barrel by mid-August, and more than $4 per barrel by the end of October, 1970. By March, 1971 the lowest market price was $4.30 per barrel—more than double the price set forth in the subject contract.

Coincident with the earliest of these increases in the cost of oil, O & R proceeded to notify Hess, on four separate dates, of increases in the fuel oil requirements estimates for the year. By letter dated April 16, 1970, O & R notified Hess that it was expected that over 1,460,000 barrels of oil would be consumed over the period April–December, 1970. Since well over 600,000 barrels of oil had been consumed during the first three months of the year, the total increase anticipated at that time was well in excess of 300,000 barrels over the estimate given in the contract.

Eight days later, by letter dated April 24, 1970, O & R furnished Hess with a revised estimate for the period May through December, 1970. The figure given was nearly 1,580,000 barrels which, when combined with quantities which had already been delivered or were in the process of delivery during the month of April, exceeded the contract estimate by over 700,000 barrels—a 40% increase.

The following month the estimates were again increased—this time to nearly one million barrels above the contract estimate. Hess was so notified by

1. For example, it was projected that in 1970 gas would generate 14,047,545,000,000 BTU while oil would be used to generate 10,810,740,000,000 BTU. The comparable ratios for the following years are: 1971—15/8; 1972—16/9; 1973—9/5.

letter dated May 22, 1970. Finally, a letter dated June 19, 1970 indicates a revised estimate of more than one million barrels in excess of the 1,750,000 barrels mentioned in the contract; an increase of about 63%.

On May 22, 1970, the date of the third of the revised estimates, representatives of the two companies met to discuss the increased demands. At that meeting O & R's president allegedly attributed the increased need for oil to the fact that O & R could make more money *selling* gas than burning it for power generation. Hess refused to meet the revised requirements, but offered to supply the amount of the contract estimate for the year 1970, plus an additional 10 percent.

The June 19, 1970, letter referred to above recited that the Hess position was "wholly unacceptable" to O & R. It attributed the vastly increased estimates to (a) an inability to burn as much natural gas as had been planned and (b) the fact that O & R had been "required" to meet higher electrical demands on its "own system" and to furnish "more electricity to interconnected systems" than had been anticipated.

Thereafter, for the remainder of 1970, Hess continued to supply the amount of the contract estimates plus 10 percent. A proposal by Hess, in October, 1970, to modify the existing contract by setting minimum and maximum quantities, and by setting a price keyed to market prices, was ignored by O & R. Although the proposed modification set a price 65 cents lower than the market price, it was more advantageous for O & R to insist on delivery of the estimated amounts in the December, 1969 contract (at $2.14 per barrel) and to purchase additional amounts required at the full market price.

During the remainder of the contract period Hess continued to deliver quantities approximately equal to the estimates stated in the subject contract. O & R purchased additional oil for its Lovett plant from other suppliers. The contract between Hess and O & R terminated one year prematurely by reason of an environmental regulation which took effect on October 1, 1973 and which necessarily curtailed the use of No. 6 fuel oil with a sulphur content as high as 1%. During the period 1971 through September, 1973 O & R consistently used more than double its contract estimates of oil at Lovett.[2]

This action was commenced in mid–1972. O & R's complaint seeks damages consisting of the difference between its costs for fuel oil during the period in question and the cost it would have incurred had Hess delivered the total amount used by O & R at the fixed contract price of $2.14 per barrel. The trial was conducted in September, 1975 before Mr. Justice Donohoe, sitting without a jury. In an opinion dated March 8, 1976, Trial Term held that plaintiff should be denied any recovery on the ground that its requirements were not incurred in good faith. Specifically, Trial Term found that plaintiff's greatly increased oil consumption was due primarily to (a) increases in sales of electricity to other utilities and (b) a net shift from other fuels, primarily gas, to oil. The former factor was condemned on the premise that "[i]ndirectly, O & R called upon Hess to supply the demands for electricity to the members of the [New York Power] Pool. O & R then shared the savings in the cost of fuel with the other members

2. The Hess contract estimated 1971 usage at 1,380,000 barrels. In fact, 1,301,045 barrels were supplied that year by Hess and 1,844,947 barrels were supplied by other companies, for a total of 3,145,993 barrels. The contract estimate for 1972 was 1,500,000 barrels; a total of 3,325,037 barrels was purchased by O & R. The contract estimate for the first nine months of 1973 was 1,125,000 barrels (75% of the 1,500,000 listed in the contract as an estimate for all of 1973); 2,401,979 barrels were received by O & R during that nine-month period.

of the Pool". The latter factor was not elaborated on to any great degree. Trial Term did, however, infer that O & R seized "the opportunity to release its reserve commitment of gas" and thereby reaped very substantial profits.

Although Trial Term stated in its opinion that one of the questions before it was whether plaintiff's demands were unreasonably disproportionate to the estimates set forth in the contract, it failed to reach this question in the light of its conclusion that plaintiff had failed to act in good faith. Plaintiff contends on this appeal (1) that Trial Term's finding of an absence of good faith is unsupported by the record and (2) that since its requirements for the entire term of the contract were less than twice total contract estimates, its demands were not "unreasonably disproportionate" as a matter of law. We reject both contentions upon the facts of this case and affirm Trial Term's dismissal of the complaint.

It is noted at the outset that the parties agreed, pursuant to their contract, that New Jersey law should apply. The governing statute is section 2–306 (subd. [1]) of the Uniform Commercial Code (UCC), which provides, in relevant part:

> "A term which measures the quantity [to be supplied by a seller to a purchaser of goods] by the * * * requirements of the buyer means such actual * * * requirements as may occur in good faith, except that no quantity unreasonably disproportionate to any stated estimate or in the absence of a stated estimate to any normal or otherwise comparable prior * * * requirements may be * * * demanded" (N.J.Stat.Ann., 12A:2–306, subd. [1], [matter in brackets added]).

There is, as Trial Term observed, a good deal of pre-Code case law on the requirement of "good faith". It is well settled that a buyer in a rising market cannot use a fixed price in a requirements contract for speculation. * * * Nor can a buyer arbitrarily and unilaterally change certain conditions prevailing at the time of the contract so as to take advantage of market conditions at the seller's expense * * *.

There is no judicial precedent with respect to the meaning of the term "unreasonably disproportionate" which appears in subdivision (1) of section 2–306 of the UCC. Obviously this language is not the equivalent of "lack of good faith"—it is an elementary rule of construction that effect must be given, if possible, to every word, clause and sentence of a statute. * * * The phrase is keyed to stated estimates or, if there be none, to "normal or otherwise comparable prior" requirements. While "reasonable elasticity" is contemplated by the section (see Official Comment, par. 2 to UCC § 2–306), an agreed estimate shows a clear limit on the intended elasticity, similar to that found in a contract containing minimum and maximum requirements (see Official Comment, par. 2 to UCC § 2–306). The estimate "is to be regarded as a center around which the parties intend the variation to occur" (supra).

The limitation imposed by the term "unreasonably disproportionate" represents a departure from prior case law, wherein estimates were generally treated as having been made simply for the convenience of the parties and of no operative significance (Note, Requirements Contracts under the Uniform Commercial Code, 102 U.Pa.L.Rev. 654, 660–661; Note, Requirements Contracts: Problems of Drafting and Construction, 78 Harv.L.Rev. 1212, 1218; cf. Shader Contr. v. United States, 276 F.2d 1, 149 Ct.Cl. 535). It is salutary in that it insures that the expectations of the parties will be more fully realized in spite of unexpected and fortuitous market conditions (see Note, Requirements Contracts under the Uniform Commercial Code, 102 U.Pa.L.Rev. 654, 666–667, supra).

Thus, even where one party acts with complete good faith, the section limits the other party's risk in accordance with the reasonable expectations of the parties.

It would be unwise to attempt to define the phrase "unreasonably disproportionate" in terms of rigid quantities. In order that the limitation contemplated by the section take effect, it is not enough that a demand for requirements be disproportionate to the stated estimate; it must be *unreasonably* so in view of the expectation of the parties. A number of factors should be taken into account in the event a buyer's requirements greatly exceed the contract estimate. These include the following: (1) the amount by which the requirements exceed the contract estimate; (2) whether the seller had any reasonable basis on which to forecast or anticipate the requested increase * * *; (3) the amount, if any, by which the market price of the goods in question exceeded the contract price; (4) whether such an increase in market price was itself fortuitous; and (5) the reason for the increase in requirements.

Turning once again to the facts of the instant case, we conclude that, at least as to the year in which this controversy first arose, there was ample evidence to justify a finding of lack of good faith on plaintiff's part. Even through the thicket of divergent and contrasting figures entered into exhibit at trial, the following picture emerges: non-firm sales [3] from plaintiff's Lovett plant, presumably in large part to the New York Power Pool, increased nearly sixfold from 67,867 megawatt hours in 1969 to 390,017 megawatt hours in 1970. The significance of that increase in *non-firm* sales lies in the fact that such sales did not enter into the budget calculations which formed the basis of the estimates included in the contract. Even assuming that a prudent seller of oil could anticipate some additional requirements generated by non-firm sales, an increase of the magnitude which occurred in 1970 is unforeseeable. That increase, of 322,150 megawatt hours, translates into the equivalent of over 500,000 barrels of oil.[4] The conclusion is inescapable that this dramatic change in plaintiff's relationship with the New York Power Pool came about as a result of the subject requirements contract, which insured it a steady flow of cheap oil despite swiftly rising prices.[5] O & R's use of the subject contract to suddenly and dramatically propel itself into the position of a large seller of power to other utilities evidences a lack of good faith dealing.[6]

In addition to this massive increase in sales of power to other utilities, the evidence indicates that at about the time O & R was demanding roughly one million barrels of oil in excess of the 1970 contract estimate, there was an internal O & R proposal to release gas to a supplier which represented the equivalent of 542,000 barrels of oil. An internal O & R memorandum dated May

3. Non-firm sales are to be contrasted with "firm" sales, which are synonymous with predictable sales. Firm sales include predictable sales to O & R's own customers and sales pursuant to contract with other utilities.

4. A figure of 515,400 barrels of oil is arrived at by multiplying the increase in sales of non-firm megawatt hours (322,150) by a very conservative conversion factor of 1.6.

5. Notwithstanding the fact that Hess failed to supply all that was demanded by O & R, it is apparent that even with a mix of Hess and non-Hess oil, plaintiff's costs of producing electricity with oil would have been lower than those of any companies purchasing oil on the open market or with "floating" contracts. This observation is underscored by the fact that O & R found it more advantageous to purchase the balance of its "requirements" on the open market (over and above the contract estimates which Hess was supplying) rather than to renegotiate the contract at a price 65 cents lower than posted market prices.

6. "[A] sudden expansion of the plant by which requirements are to be measured would not be included within the scope of the contract as made but normal expansion undertaken in good faith would be within the scope of this section." (Official Comment, par. 2 to UCC § 2–306.)

26, 1970 (four days after the meeting at which Hess refused to supply the one million additional barrels demanded) recommended that in view of the Hess position, the proposed release be cancelled. Significantly, O & R never did burn as much oil as had been demanded in May and June, 1970. Its total usage for the year was 2,294,845 barrels—471,155 barrels less than its maximum demand. This was explained, by O & R officials, in part, on the ground that their "gas department" had made a "pessimistic estimate" which did not turn out to be quite true.

Thus it appears that in May, 1970 Hess refused an O & R demand of roughly one million barrels in excess of the contract estimate, which demand was occasioned by greatly increased sales to other utilities and a proposed release of gas which might otherwise normally have been burned for power generation.[7] The former factor is tantamount to making the other utilities in the State silent partners to the contract * * *, while the latter factor amounts to a unilateral and arbitrary change in the conditions prevailing at the time of the contract so as to take advantage of market conditions at the seller's expense. Hess was therefore justified in 1970 in refusing to meet plaintiff's demands, by reason of the fact that plaintiff's "requirements" were not incurred in good faith.

With respect to subsequent years however, the record is ambiguous as to the cause of plaintiff's drastically increased requirements. Non-firm sales from Lovett actually declined slightly in 1971 and 1972 although they were still greatly in excess of 1969 sales.[8] If one takes 1969 as a base year, increased non-firm sales from Lovett in 1971 amounted to the equivalent of about one-half million barrels of oil[9], while in 1972 they amounted to the equivalent of just

7. While there was testimony by O & R officials to the effect that this gas, supplied by the Home Gas Company, could not be burned at the Lovett plant because that gas was only transmitted to another geographical sector of O & R's territory, it strains credulity to believe that the interstate pipeline system is so parochial that releases in one sector would not affect operations in another sector. Home Gas Company was, in fact, a subsidiary of the Columbia Gas Transmission Company at the time, and Columbia Gas was burned at the Lovett plant. Furthermore, plaintiff's contention is belied by (a) the May 26, 1970 memo which linked the proposed release to oil deliveries at Lovett and (b) a revised calculation from O & R's gas department, dated May 19, 1970, which allocated Home gas between O & R's two geographical divisions for the purpose of showing gas availability for electrical generation.

8. In 1971 total sales from Lovett amounted to 387,874 MWH; firm sales were 17,294 MWH. Assuming these firm sales were all generated at Lovett, total non-firm sales would have been 370,580 MWH—down slightly from the 390,017 MWH sold on a non-firm basis in 1970. In 1972 total sales from Bowline (a new generating plant), from Lovett, and from gas turbines amounted to 722,329 MWH. Firm sales for the year were 423,734, of which 374,327 MWH were generated at Bowline. Assuming that the remaining 49,407 MWH in firm sales were generated at Lovett (and not by the gas turbines), that plant's non-firm sales for the year would have amounted to 256,320 MWH.

We have focused on non-firm sales in our analysis because the record does not reveal whether firm sales during this period were taken into account in the preparation of the December 30, 1968 budget projection which formed the basis of the contract estimates. If they were, they would be meaningless in attempting to explain the tremendous increase in plaintiff's oil requirements.

While there was evidence that electrical power is "fungible" and that allocation of sales to various plants is an "accounting function", the testimony at trial did establish that the allocation is performed in a sufficiently rational manner. We therefore decline to attribute all O & R sales to the Lovett plant.

9. We choose the increase over 1969 rather than the absolute figure for sales because a certain amount of power pool sales, based on O & R's past experience, would be reasonably foreseeable. In 1971, non-firm sales from Lovett amounted to 370,580 MWH (see n. 8), an increase of 303,007 MWH over the 67,867 MWH sold on a non-firm basis in 1969. If we multiply this increase by the very conservative conversion factor of 1.6, we arrive at a barrel equivalent of 484,811.

over 300,000 barrels.[10] Comparable figures for 1973 are impossible to arrive at with any degree of confidence because sales figures in the record are for the full year, while defendant's obligation to supply oil extended through only three-quarters of the year. In any event, it is apparent that O & R's tremendously expanded use of oil during the period subsequent to 1970 cannot be explained solely by reference to increased sales to other utilities. In 1971 oil use exceeded the contract estimate by over 1,750,000 barrels; the 1972 figure was in excess of 1,825,000 barrels; and for the first nine months of 1973 the increase was more than 1,275,000 barrels.[11]

It appears that a large portion of the difference between actual use and contract estimates during this period can be attributed to a rather large decline in plaintiff's "actual take" of gas as opposed to the estimates of gas availability which were made in 1968 (and which were used in the computation of the December 30, 1968 budget). This decline, with the equivalent figure in barrels of oil,[12] was as follows:

Estimate (Mcf)	Actual Take (Mcf)	Decrease	Equiv. Barrels of Oil
1971—40,615,000	34,518,000	6,097,000	1,016,167
1972—43,661,000	36,274,000	7,387,000	1,231,167
1973 (9 mos) 34,034,700	25,783,000	8,251,700	1,375,283

Even allowing for the fact that O & R's actual system requirements were slightly lower during this period than the estimated system requirements (thus theoretically leaving more gas available for electric generation), it is clear that the decline from the estimates in gas received by O & R was a very major factor in plaintiff's increased use of oil during this period.

The record is unclear as to why this decline came about. Plaintiff introduced into evidence a Public Service Commission memorandum which indicates that gas supplies available to interstate transmission companies had become extremely tight. However plaintiff failed to call one witness who was expert in its gas operations and who could testify as to the link, if any, between this general shortage and plaintiff's operations. While an unfavorable inference may be drawn when a party fails to produce evidence which is within his control and which he is naturally expected to produce, we decline to speculate as to causes of the decline in gas received by plaintiff. In any event, such speculation is not necessary for resolution of this appeal.

We hold that under the circumstances of this case, any demand[13] by plaintiff for more than double its contract estimates, was, as a matter of law, "unreasonably disproportionate" (UCC, § 2–306, subd. [1]) to those estimates.

10. This calculation is made in exactly the same manner as the one for 1971. The increase in sales of non-firm power amounts to 188,453 MWH (256,320 MWH less 67,867 MWH) and application of the conversion factor results in a barrel equivalent of 301,525.

11. This figure is arrived at by subtracting three-quarters of the contract estimate from total oil deliveries during the first nine months of 1973.

12. One barrel of oil is equivalent in heating value to 6 Mcf of gas.

13. There is no indication in the record that O & R continued to supply Hess with updated "requirements" demands after June 19, 1970. In fact, it can be inferred from a fair reading of the record that O & R entered into a contract with another supplier to furnish amounts required in excess of the amounts Hess was willing to supply. Nevertheless, we assume for the sake of argument that there was a continuing "demand" by plaintiff for its total requirements.

We do not adopt the factor of more than double the contract estimates as any sort of an inflexible yardstick.[14] Rather, we apply those standards set forth earlier in this opinion, which are calculated to limit a party's risk in accordance with the reasonable expectations of the parties.

Here, as noted, plaintiff's requirements during the period 1971 through September, 1973, were more than double the contract estimates. Defendant had no reasonable basis on which to forecast or anticipate an increase of this magnitude. Indeed the contract suggests the parties contemplated that any variations from the estimate would be on the downside—else why did plaintiff expressly reserve for itself the right to burn as much as it chose? The market price of the grade of oil supplied had more than doubled by March, 1971. It stayed at or above $4.00 per barrel for the rest of the applicable period and had reached nearly $5.00 per barrel by the end of September, 1973. The record is silent as to whether defendant had any reason to anticipate this enormous increase in oil prices. Finally, the increase in requirements was due in part to plaintiff's increased sales to other utilities and also due to a significant decline in anticipated deliveries of gas, the cause of which was inadequately explained by plaintiff. The quantities of oil utilized by plaintiff during the period subsequent to 1970 were not within the reasonable expectations of the parties when the contract was executed, and accordingly we hold that those "requirements" were unreasonably disproportionate to the contract estimates (see UCC, § 2–306, subd. [1]).

Judgment of the Supreme Court, Rockland County, entered June 4, 1976, affirmed, with costs.

Notes

1. Since 1977, there has been little litigation of significance on the issues decided in Orange & Rockland. See Homestake Mining Co. v. Washington Public Power Supply, 476 F.Supp. 1162, 1167–69 (N.D.Cal.1979) (bad faith for buyer under requirements contract to insist on goods not needed for the particular business activity referred to in contract). For commentary, see White & Summers, Section 3–8; Note, *Requirements Contracts, "More or Less," Under the Uniform Commercial Code,* 33 Rutgers L.Rev. 105 (1980). For discussions of the good faith issue in flexible quantity contracts, see Burton, *Breach of Contract and the Common Law Duty to Perform in Good Faith,* 94 Harv.L.Rev. 369, 381–84, 395–97 (1980); Muris, *Opportunistic Behavior and the Law of Contracts,* 65 Minn.L.Rev. 521, 556–65 (1981).

2. The court in Orange & Rockland used factors existing and events foreseeable at the time of contracting to determine whether the buyer's orders were "unreasonably disproportionate" to the stated estimates. Where the estimates did not apply, however, the court used motives and factors existing at the time the requirements were ordered to determine whether the buyer's conduct was in bad faith. The buyer lost on both counts. Suppose, however, that the amounts ordered were unreasonably disproportionate to the stated estimates but the buyer's actual requirements were in good faith. Which limitation upon the exercise of discretion should prevail under UCC 2–306(1)?

3. Going Out of Business. Suppose the buyer claims that its actual requirements for the goods described in the contract were non-existent or drastically reduced from prior years. Such a decision appears to be justified if made in good faith. UCC 2–306(1). As one court put it, the "seller assumes the risk of all good faith variations

14. Interestingly, plaintiff would have us hold as a matter of law that where an actual requirement varies "only by a factor of two from a stated estimate", it is not unreasonably disproportionate to such estimate.

in the buyer's requirements even to the extent of a determination to liquidate or discontinue the business." It might be said that the buyer's duty to buy is conditioned upon the existence of actual requirements. Further: "The rule is based on a reliance on the self-interest of the buyer, who ordinarily will seek to have the largest possible requirements. Protection against abuse is afforded by penetrating through any device by which the requirement is siphoned off in some other form to the detriment of the seller. The requirement of good faith is the means by which this is enforced and self-interest in its undistorted form is maintained as the standard." HML Corporation v. General Foods Corporation, 365 F.2d 77 (3d Cir.1966) (burden on seller to prove bad faith).

What, then, is bad faith in this setting? What if the decision is not to curtail losses but simply to make more profits on an alternative line of production? Inferences of bad faith abound when the seller has some demand for its output or the buyer still has some requirements and the decision is "merely to curtail losses." UCC 2–306, Comment 2. A leading case is Feld v. Henry S. Levy & Sons, Inc., 37 N.Y.2d 466, 373 N.Y.S.2d 102, 106, 335 N.E.2d 320, 323 (1975), where the court concluded that an "output" seller was justified in a good faith cessation of a single operation rather than entire business "only if its losses from continuance would be more than trivial". A cessation "merely to curtail losses" would be improper. Should the amount of loss from continued performance be the major issue? How much is too much? One of your co-authors believes that the standards derived from the Comments to UCC 2–306 are impossible to apply.

Problem 12–3

A five year "requirements" contract contained an estimate that Buyer would need 20,000 units per year. For the first two years, Buyer ordered 18,750 and 20,500 units. In the third year, Buyer ordered 10,000 units and, shortly thereafter, discontinued that line of its business. It is stipulated that at all times Buyer acted in good faith. Seller, however, argued that Buyer was obligated, despite good faith, to approximate the stated estimates for five years, and that the third year reduction and the discontinuance, because they were unreasonably disproportionate, were breaches of contract. Seller relies on the text of UCC 2–306(1): Actual requirements in good faith is limited by the "except" clause. Buyer points to Comment 2 to UCC 2–306 as permitting "good faith variations from prior requirements * * * even when the variation may be such as to result in discontinuance." R.A. Weaver & Assoc., Inc. v. Asphalt Const., Inc., 587 F.2d 1315, 1321–22 (D.C.Cir.1978) (good faith reduction, though drastic, is permitted even though unreasonably disproportionate). How should this dispute be resolved?

Note: Best Efforts in Exclusive Dealing Relationships

UCC 2–306(2) provides that a "lawful agreement by either the seller or the buyer for exclusive dealing in the kind of goods concerned imposes unless otherwise agreed an obligation by the seller to use best efforts to supply the goods and by the buyer to use best efforts to promote their sale."

An exclusive dealing relationship is a continuing, highly interdependent agency, franchise or contract for distribution. It facilitates the manufacturer's effort to market the goods. It is common for the distributor to agree to order requirements as generated by "best efforts" from and to deal exclusively in some defined territory with the manufacturer. When the agreement to use "best efforts" is coupled with exclusive dealing, there is consideration. Hunt Foods, Inc. v. Phillips, 248 F.2d 23 (9th Cir.1957). There is some risk, however, that the arrangement, because of its restriction upon competition, will run afoul of the antitrust laws. See L. Sullivan, Anti-Trust 163–66 (1977). In any event, the arrangement must be lawful under state and federal law and an agreement by the distributor to make best efforts must exist. See Gerard v. Almouli, 746 F.2d 936 (2d Cir.1984) (no best efforts agreement where condition precedent fails). UCC 2–306(2) presumes that the "best efforts" agreement exists unless the parties have otherwise agreed.

What are "best efforts" when the duty is part of the agreement? Beyond the requirement that the distributor make an honest effort in the particular setting, there is disagreement among the courts. For a leading case and some helpful analysis, see Bloor v. Falstaff Brewing Corp., 601 F.2d 609 (2d Cir.1979) and Goetz & Scott, *Principles of Relational Contracts,* 67 Va.L.Rev. 1089 (1981).

C. The Price Term

In a market directed economy, the sale price is the result of seller costs, buyer demand, information available to and negotiations between the parties and the quality of competition in the relevant market area. Since price is a material term in any sale, the determination of what price was agreed, as well as the method for ascertainment, is important when disputes arise.

Sections 2–204(3) and 2–305 are the key UCC sections. Review them and work through the following materials.

Problem 12–4

During the latter part of 1981, Irving Molever began to entertain the idea of opening a discount house retail business in Wheeling, West Virginia. At that time he came in contact with Ernest Berez, a long-time friend and Vice-President of the Associated Hardware Supply Company, a Pennsylvania corporation and wholesaler of hardware, household goods and other merchandise. Molever incorporated his business in West Virginia under the name of The Big Wheel Distributing Company, and as its representative attempted to negotiate a contract with Associated. Several meetings between the representatives of both corporations were held in the early months of 1982. The primary topic of discussion at these meetings was the method of pricing to be used. Big Wheel insisted that the prices be computed on a cost plus ten percent basis for shipments from Associated's warehouse and cost plus five percent for direct factory shipments. Associated maintained that it could not price goods on this basis because its IBM billing system was geared to discount pricing. Big Wheel alleges that at this time it was told by Associated that the dealer-catalogue less 11% method was equal to the cost plus method it desired. These discussions culminated in an exchange of letters between the parties; the letter from Associated on February 9, 1982, confirmed an offer made at one of these meetings; the reply from Big Wheel on February 24 impliedly agreed to some of the confirmation but explicitly rejected the method of pricing contained therein. (These letters are set out below.)

February 9, 1982

Mr. Irving Molever
400 Carlton House
Pittsburgh, Pa.

Dear Mr. Molever:

We wish to confirm the special offer that we have made to you for the purpose of supplying your new promotional department store, ''The Big Wheel,'' in Wheeling, W.Va.

Specifically, we have agreed to do the following:

We will make available to you on a maximum 48 hour shipment schedule all merchandise from our Pittsburgh warehouse at the same low price that appears in our dealer catalogue. In addition, you will receive 11% beyond these prices as cash discount. Further, we shall make available to you the merchandising services of our organization as they are presently available to all regular dealer accounts. There will be no additional rebates on purchases beyond these discounts. This offer is subject to your purchasing an average of approximately $5,000 per week in carton lot quantities to be delivered at one time from our Pittsburgh warehouse. All merchandise is sold FOB Pittsburgh.

Factory shipments which we make at your direction, are available to you on the basis of our normal dealer cost plus the additional 11% cash discount. Should we be willing to sell an additional operation of this type, this same offer and schedule prices would be available to them providing they meet all other requirements. In return you have agreed to do the following: The initial order of merchandise which we ship at your direction is to be paid less the preferential 11% discount as noted above upon receipt of the merchandise. You have agreed that all invoices from the first through the twenty-fourth of the month will be paid by the 5th of the following month. Invoices from the twenty-fifth through the thirty-first of the month are to be considered as having been shipped as of the next month.

Since we have asked for no financial information on this new corporation, you have agreed to be personally responsible for all credit regardless of amounts that we extend to this corporation.

We further ask that you do not make public the arithmetic of this special offer.

We would appreciate your acknowledging these conditions, and returning a copy for our files.

Very Sincerely Yours,

ASSOCIATED HARDWARE SUPPLY CO.

Agreed: IRVING MOLEVER

/s/ ERNEST S. BEREZ
Ernest S. Berez
Vice President

ESB/o

February 24, 1982

Mr. Ernest S. Berez
Associated Hardware Supply Co.
1020 Saw Mill Run Blvd.
Pittsburgh 26, Pa.

Dear Ernie:

In reply to your letter of February 19 [sic], I cannot possibly sign this and return it.

In the first place, I have talked to some of my other suppliers and, quite frankly, I am still at a loss to understand why you can't set up your bookkeeping and administrative procedures similarly to theirs.

I have discussed this matter thoroughly with Fred, and he is very much concerned that with the inexperienced help we have in your departments much confusion and loss of time will be the results if you bill us at catalogue prices, less an 11% credit memo. You can certainly appreciate his problems. Therefore, if your invoices would come in, similar to Stem Distributing Co., simply at cost, plus 10% it would certainly simplify our pricing procedure at floor level and expedite our getting the merchandise on the floor priced for sale.

Ernie, I can appreciate your problem of the retails already set up on your I.B.M. cards for your dealer accounts—however, it is incomprehensible to me as a C.P.A. to believe that merely handbilling our invoices would result in the necessity of hiring another assistant—especially when you must consider the time consumed in preparing the 11% credit memos on the method you have suggested.

Fred is still so concerned about the confusion which will result in our pricing the goods on the floor that I should like to repeat my statement of the other day; that is, go ahead and bill us on a simple cost plus basis, and if you find it necessary to hire a full-time assistant we will either absorb a pro rated share of her salary, or make some alteration of invoicing to ease your situation.

I might add that Fred is also concerned in view of the Robinson-Pactman [sic] Act that we would not be able to sign your letter without consulting legal counsel.

Since I promised to personally guarantee credit until our current financial statement is finished if you will please send a corrected request I will execute it and return.

IMM:bg

However, either sometime prior to or shortly after sending its letter of February 24, Big Wheel placed an order with Associated for a large quantity of goods which was included in the store's inventory when it opened on March 5. The price paid for the original shipment and for every shipment received thereafter for the next two years was computed on a dealer catalogue less eleven percent basis.

Sales made during this period were not without complaint. As early as August, 1982, Big Wheel began to doubt that the prices it was paying were the equivalent of cost plus 10% on warehouse shipments and cost plus 5% on direct factory shipments. By the following March, at least one of Big Wheel's officers was certain that the prices charged by Associated were considerably higher than cost plus ten percent. These objections were communicated to Associated, which allegedly assured Big Wheel that the prices paid would average out to cost plus 10%.

In spite of its objections to the pricing method, Big Wheel continued to order, receive and pay for merchandise on a dealer catalogue less eleven percent basis until March of 1984. From March through June of 1984, Big Wheel placed orders and received the goods but refused to pay for the merchandise received. Big Wheel, while not denying liability for the goods received, argues that the amount due under the agreement was no more than cost plus 10% and since more than that had been paid on goods previously ordered, it was entitled to an appropriate offset on the goods in dispute.

Is Big Wheel's contention correct under the UCC? Please support your answer with appropriate references to the Code.

IN RE GLOVER CONSTRUCTION CO., INC.

United States Bankruptcy Court, Western District of Kentucky, 1985.
49 B.R. 581.

MERRITT S. DIETZ, BANKRUPTCY JUDGE. Simple contract elements—the offer, acceptance and "meeting of the minds" that bind bargaining parties to their promises—rarely play a part in today's complex bankruptcy litigation. But the outcome of the case at hand depends exactly on the basic question of whether the parties, in the extensive course of their dealings, ever really had an enforceable agreement between them.

In the fall of 1981, the debtors, Glover Construction Company, Inc. and Glover Contracting Company, Inc. (Glover), and the plaintiff, Fleetwash Systems, Inc. (Fleetwash), began negotiating for a contract whereby Fleetwash would furnish Glover with vehicle washing equipment for installation on a construction project at Fort Knox, Kentucky. In February of 1982 the parties executed a "contract" [1] for the purchase of the equipment. The terms of this "purchase order" called for a total price of $370,000 and payments by Glover of "net 30th of month following month in which material is delivered". The purchase order also contained the following language concerning the equipment's price:

Terms: (Options) 10% Down Payment upon approval by owner $37,000.00. 2% Discount on 370,000.00 = $7,400.00 off Final Payment.

25% Down Payment upon approval by Owner $92,500.00. 5% Discount on 370,000.00 = 18,500.00 off Final Payment. 60% Annual Interest Rate.

Immediately after the signing of the purchase order, Glover and Fleetwash began quarreling as to the exact meaning of the above quoted terms. Fleetwash has constantly maintained that the contract called for Glover to make *either* a 10% or 25% down payment before they were to ship the contract materials. Glover, however, has consistently argued that the contract merely granted Glover the *option to earn a discount by making either a 10% or 25% down payment* and that the only mandatory payment terms were those calling for "Net 30th of month following month in which material is delivered". The conduct of the parties following the signing of the purchase order as well as their testimony at the trial showed that neither party intended to be bound by the terms of the purchase order unless the other party agreed to their interpretation of the price/payment provisions.

In September of 1982, Glover offered to make a 25% down payment on the vehicle washing equipment if Fleetwash would provide Glover with releases of liens on the equipment from both Fleetwash and its suppliers. Fleetwash could

1. Although the parties stipulated that they entered into a contract, the facts indicate that a valid contractual relationship never existed. See note 3 infra and accompanying text.

only provide Glover with a release of its own against the equipment, and Glover did not make the down payment.

On November 10, 1982 Glover filed a petition for reorganization under Chapter 11 of the Bankruptcy Code. Robert C. Glover was appointed debtor in possession and Glover continued work on the Fort Knox project. A trustee was appointed by this court for the limited purpose of collecting and disbursing Glover's progress payments.

In February of 1983, one year after the signing of the original purchase order, Fleetwash offered to deliver a portion of Glover's order if Glover would "walk the invoice through [the U.S. Army Corps of Engineers' billing procedures]". The total invoice price of this shipment was $144,200. At the time Fleetwash made this partial shipment, the two parties still had not agreed on the price and payment terms. Glover received the equipment and submitted to the U.S. Army Corps of Engineers a pay request covering the Fleetwash invoice. The Army approved the pay request and issued a check in the net amount of $129,780 [2] to the trustee who still holds these funds. Glover objected to the disbursement of these funds to Fleetwash on a number of grounds, and the present action ensued.

* * *

The initial issue we must address is whether the parties had a valid contract for the sale of the vehicle washing equipment. Although the parties stipulated that they entered into a contract with the signing of the purchase order on February 15, 1982, it is an ancient and unchallenged principle of contract law that for there to be a valid contract there must first be agreement as to the essential terms of that contract.[3] This rule has been modified to some extent by the Uniform Commercial Code (UCC) and its "gap-filler provisions". The provision of Kentucky's [4] version of the UCC which deals with open price terms, KRS 355.2–305, provides that:

> "(1) The parties, if they so intend can conclude a contract for sale *even though the price is not settled.* In such a case the price is a *reasonable price* at the time for delivery if
>
> * * *
>
> "(b) the price is left to be agreed by the parties and they fail to agree
>
> * * *
>
> "(4) *Where, however the parties intend not to be bound unless the price be fixed or agreed and it is not fixed or agreed there is no contract.* In such case the buyer must return any goods already received or if unable so to do must pay their *reasonable value* at the time of delivery" * * * [emphasis added]

In the present case the parties entered into the purchase order without having agreed on the contract's price and payment terms. Kentucky's version of the UCC would ordinarily supply the price terms of the contract, except that the parties to this action clearly intended not to be bound to the terms of the purchase order unless their interpretation of the price terms was accepted by the

2. All payment by the Army Corps of Engineers were subject to a 10% retainage.

3. Smith v. Hilliard, 408 S.W.2d 440 (Ky. 1966); Vidt v. Burgess, 136 S.W.2d 1080 (Ky. 1940); Dean v. Meter, 8 Ky.Opin. 746 (Ky. 1874).

4. As a general rule of law the place of performance of the contract governs the rights of the parties absent a clear showing of contrary intent. Smith v. Stone, 202 F.Supp. 11 (E.D.Ky.1962). In this case the parties intended to have the purchase order "governed and construed according to the laws of the state of Kentucky" since that language was included as a choice of law provision in the order form.

opposing party. Both KRS 355.2–305(4) and pre-UCC case law [5] state that in such a case *there is no contract between the parties.* Due to this finding [6] we need not consider the parties' lengthy, if misplaced, arguments on the issues of breach and damages.[7] Our ruling that no contract existed between Glover and Fleetwash does not preclude payment to Fleetwash for goods delivered to Glover. KRS 355.2–305(4) provides that where there is no contract "the buyer must return any goods already received or if unable so to do must pay their reasonable value at the time of delivery [to the seller]". We therefore must determine the reasonable value of the goods.

Although neither the UCC, applicable case law nor White & Summers define what constitutes "reasonable value", in our opinion the term "reasonable value" as used in this context is merely a codification of the doctrine of restitution [8] as the basis of recovery in cases involving a quasi-contract, or contract implied in law.[9] The term "reasonable value" is not to be considered synonymous with the term "reasonable price", although it is possible—and certainly a commercial ideal—that an item's reasonable value and reasonable price might coincide.

At trial both parties offered extensive evidence as to the value of the equipment. Fleetwash, arguing that the parties intended to contract but merely left open the price and payment terms, placed the reasonable price of the equipment at approximately $137,000. Glover, on the other hand, produced three estimates of value ranging from $32,000 to $34,000.

After carefully reviewing all estimates of the value of the vehicle washing equipment delivered to Glover by Fleetwash, and considering the credibility and reliability of all witnesses as well as the circumstances surrounding their estimates, it is our opinion that the reasonable value of the equipment in question is $43,000. Our basis for this particular figure comes from a letter written by Melvin Wiegand, Vice President of Fleetwash, to the attorney who was representing them in the Chapter 11 reorganization of their predecessor brother-sister corporation, Wiegand Engineering, before a bankruptcy court in Texas. In that letter Fleetwash told its attorney that it would invoice Glover in the net amount of $123,000 for the equipment it sent to be installed at the Fort Knox construction site. The letter went on to say that "This transaction will result in an income of approximately $80,000. * * *" It is our opinion that this letter which indicates the reasonable value to be $43,000 is entitled to more weight by this court than either of the self-serving estimates prepared by

5. Herman v. Jackson, 405 S.W.2d 9 (Ky. 1966); Thompson v. Hunters Ex'r et al., 269 S.W. 266 (Ky.1954); Marshall's Adm'r v. Webster, 155 S.W.2d 13 (Ky.1941).

6. "Whether an agreement has been concluded, in most cases, is a question to be determined by the trier of fact." KRS 355.2–305, Kentucky Commentary (1983). In this case our determination on this issue is clearly factual and is subject to the "clearly erroneous" standard of review. See In re Calhoun, 715 F.2d 1103, 1110 (6th Cir.1983).

7. See White & Summers, Uniform Commercial Code § 3–7, p. 117 (2d ed. 1980).

8. Black's Law Dictionary, (5th ed. 1979) defines restitution as:

"act of restoring; * * * the act of making good or giving equivalent for any loss, damage or injury; * * * restoration of status quo and is amount which would put plaintiff in as good a position as he would have been if *no contract had been made* and restores to plaintiff [the] value of what he parted with in performing [the] contract * * * a person who has been unjustly enriched at the expense of another is required to make restitution to the other. [emphasis added]

9. A contract implied in law or quasi contract indicates a duty imposed by law, "without mutual assent, for the purpose of affording a remedy or right of recovery where money or property or services were received under such circumstances that in equity and good conscience the recipient [must] pay for them." Thompson v. Hunter's Ex'r, 269 S.W.2d at 269.

interested parties in anticipation of litigation *before this court,*[10] or the hopelessly confused estimate presented by the Army Corps of Engineers.[11] This award of $43,000 covers both the 2–wheeled vehicle washing systems as well as the miscellaneous hose station equipment, since from a review of the limited cost data provided by Fleetwash, it is clear that an award of $43,000 for the vehicle washing systems alone would be over-generous. In fact, in making this award we are being extremely generous to Fleetwash by accepting the value estimate contained in their letter to their Texas bankruptcy counsel, instead of placing the reasonable value of the equipment at the figure urged by Glover. This award is in line with the restitutional nature of the "reasonable value" language of KRS 355.2–305(4) since, by Fleetwash's own admission, this amount should place them in as good a position as they would have occupied if they had never made the shipment to Glover.

Therefore it is the opinion of this court that the parties to the purchase order in controversy, Fleetwash and Glover, never agreed as to the meaning of the price and payment terms of the order and did not intend to be bound by the terms of the order unless the other party acquiesced to their interpretation of the price and payment terms. Further the court finds that, in light of the fact that no contract existed between the parties, Fleetwash is entitled to the reasonable value of the goods they delivered to Glover, which we set at $43,000.

An appropriate order reflecting these findings of fact and conclusions of law will be entered by the court.

Notes

1. Consider three questions: (1) What method did the parties adopt to determine the price, see UCC 2–305(1)(b); (2) When that method failed, what evidence persuaded the court that the parties did not intend to be bound unless the price was agreed; and (3) What difference, if any, exists between the price if the parties had intended to be bound, UCC 2–305(1), and the restitution remedy invoked because they did not so intend, UCC 2–305(4)? Review the discussion of the Bethlehem Steel-Litton litigation, supra at 451. See also, Flowers Baking Co. of Lynchburg, Inc., v. R–P Packaging, Inc., 229 Va. 370, 329 S.E.2d 462, 465 (1985), where the court, in concluding that there was no intention to contract, stated: "While it is true that the UCC has greatly modified the rigors of the common-law rules governing the formation of contracts, it remains a prerequisite that the parties' words and conduct must manifest an intention to be bound. Although they may make a contract which deliberately leaves material terms open for future determination, no contract results where their words and conduct demonstrate a lack of intention to contract. * * * Such a lack is not remedied by evidence of custom and usage in the trade * * * or by a written memorandum purporting to confirm oral discussion which did not in themselves amount to an agreement * * * "

2. Under UCC 2–305(1), the same questions are posed if "nothing is said as to price" or the "price is to be fixed in terms of some agreed market or other standard as set or recorded by a third person or agency and it is not so set or recorded:" (1) Did

10. We arrived at a reasonable value of the equipment from this letter by subtracting the expected income from the net invoice amount. For a full text of the letter and the pro forma invoice on the 2 wheeled vehicle wash systems see Appendix A [omitted].

11. The Army Corps of Engineers estimate of the value of the equipment Fleetwash sold Glover, would generally be given much weight by this court. However due to the confused manner in which their evaluation was prepared, the third-hand nature of their representative's testimony at trial and the fact that the Army Corps of Engineers had to "clarify", by unsworn letter, the testimony another representative gave at a deposition on this matter led this court to attach very little weight to their estimate.

the parties intend to "conclude a contract even though the price is not settled;" (2) If not, what remedies are available under UCC 2–305(4); and (3) If so, what is a "reasonable price at the time for delivery?" The pre-Code law is reviewed in Prosser, *Open Price in Contracts For the Sale of Goods,* 16 Minn.L.Rev. 733 (1932); Comment, *UCC Section 2–305(1)(c): Open Price Terms and the Intention of the Parties in Sales Contracts,* 1 Valpo.L.Rev. 381 (1967).

TCP INDUSTRIES, INC. v. UNIROYAL, INC.

United States Court of Appeals, Sixth Circuit, 1981.
661 F.2d 542.

Before ENGEL, KEITH and KENNEDY, CIRCUIT JUDGES.

CORNELIA G. KENNEDY, CIRCUIT JUDGE.

TCP Industries, Inc. (TCP) filed this breach of contract action against Uniroyal, Inc. (Uniroyal) to recover profits lost when Uniroyal refused to purchase butadiene pursuant to an April 1, 1974 contract. Uniroyal counterclaimed seeking damages from TCP and Donald C. Fresne (Fresne), its president and principal shareholder, for fraud, breach of an earlier 1970 contract, and breach of the 1974 contract. The jury returned a verdict for TCP in the amount of $1,045,650 and judgments of no cause of action on Uniroyal's three counterclaims. Uniroyal appeals. The parties agree that the Uniform Commercial Code applies. They did not object to the District Court's application of Michigan law, the law of the forum.

Butadiene is a petrochemical product extracted from gas and oil and principally used in the production of synthetic rubber. TCP does not produce butadiene but has since 1966 acted as a middleman in arranging sales of the product from El Paso Products Company (El Paso), a Texas refinery, to Uniroyal. TCP sold to Uniroyal at the same price it purchased butadiene from El Paso. Historically, its sole profit was limited to a commission or a reseller's discount of two-tenths (2/10) of a cent per pound which El Paso paid TCP out of El Paso's price.

On November 3, 1970, TCP and Uniroyal entered into the 1970 contract. That contract covered the period of April 1, 1971 through March 31, 1974 and provided for the annual sale of 50 million pounds of butadiene at 8.00 to 8.25 cents per pound, depending on place of delivery. The contract restricted any price increase to the third year of the contract and then only to passing on those escalations in El Paso's production costs specifically related to increased labor or natural or butane gas costs which El Paso passed on to TCP. The contract also included a meet or release clause which provided that if Uniroyal received a bona fide offer from another producer to sell it at least 10,000,000 pounds of butadiene at a lower price, then TCP would have to meet that price within 30 days or release Uniroyal from its obligation to purchase such amount under the contract.

El Paso continued to sell butadiene to TCP which resold it to Uniroyal under these conditions until September 1973, six months before the expiration of TCP's contract with Uniroyal, when, unknown to Uniroyal, TCP's three year contract with El Paso expired. El Paso thereupon advised TCP that it would continue to sell it butadiene but that its reseller's discount would be discontinued and TCP should look for its profits solely from its markup to Uniroyal.

In October 1973, TCP increased its price to Uniroyal by .00247 per pound. In February 1973, El Paso increased its price to TCP by 3.5 cents to 11.75 cents per pound. TCP passed this price increase on to Uniroyal along with an additional increase of almost three cents. On March 1, 1974, TCP initiated another one cent per pound increase.[1] Uniroyal continued to accept and pay for butadiene at the increased prices. The parties agree and it is undisputed that except for El Paso's 3.5 cent increase passed along by TCP in February, the remaining increases were contrary to the express provisions of the written contract, and resulted in an overcharge to Uniroyal of $301,679.

During the same period that TCP was raising the price of butadiene under the 1970 contract, the parties were negotiating the terms of the 1974 contract. These negotiations were conducted in an atmosphere described by those in the industry as nothing less than chaotic. Price controls for butadiene expired in early 1974. Because of the shortage of crude oil due to the Arab oil embargo, a greater proportion of the supply of oil was being used to produce fuel oil rather than petrochemicals such as butadiene. Butadiene sellers were refusing to take on new customers. Since Uniroyal could not make synthetic rubber without butadiene, TCP's 50 million pound annual supply was extremely valuable and Uniroyal adopted measures to ensure itself of this dependable supply of butadiene. After several months of bargaining, Uniroyal and TCP entered into a new contract which represented a dramatic departure in form and substance from their previous agreements. This contract did not have a price escalation clause but instead contained the following pricing provision:

> The price for butadiene purchased hereunder shall be $0.1347 per pound F.O.B. point of origin. The price for butadiene is subject to change providing Texas Chemical gives no less than fifteen days notice.

The 1974 contract did not contain a meet or release clause for the first two years of its four year term.

Soon after signing, TCP informed Uniroyal that the price would increase from 13.7 cents on April 1, 1974, to 20.75 cents on July 1, and to 22.55 cents on October 1. By November 1974, the shortage of butadiene had eased and producers were ready to take on new customers. That month Uniroyal took only 489,000 pounds of butadiene as opposed to an average of 3,642,000 pounds in each of the previous seven months. Uniroyal took no butadiene from December 1974 through February 1975, first saying that it needed no butadiene and then explaining that the price was too high. Uniroyal again started to purchase in March 1975 at about 19.0 cents per pound. The parties agreed to reserve their rights against each other under the contract.

* * *

[The court affirmed the jury verdict denying Uniroyal's counterclaim for an alleged breach of the 1970 contract.]

THE 1974 CONTRACT

Uniroyal also argues that the evidence was insufficient to support the jury's finding that TCP was entitled to the price it set under the 1974 contract. The contract contained the following pricing provision:

> The price for butadiene purchased hereunder shall be $0.1347 per pound F.O.B. point origin. The price for butadiene is subject to change providing Texas Chemical gives no less than fifteen days notice.

1. These figures have been taken from the pretrial order. Although there are discrepancies between these figures and those found in the briefs, exhibits and transcripts of the proceedings, the parties do not dispute that the total amount in controversy is $301,679.

The District Court held this language ambiguous and permitted parol evidence. Uniroyal claims that TCP was limited by the parties' prior course of dealing to passing on to Uniroyal changes in the prices charged to TCP by El Paso. Uniroyal contends that if TCP was not limited to passing through El Paso's price, then it failed to set a reasonable price in accordance with M.C.L.A. § 440.2305.

In the usual case, the question of the parties' intentions when a price term is left open is a question for the trier of fact. Official Comment 2, M.C.L.A. § 440.2305. The jury was presented with considerable evidence that the parties vigorously negotiated the 1974 contract. Fresne testified that he told Wills that he wanted the right to unilaterally set the price at the high end of the market. He explained that this was a major reason for the six month negotiation period. TCP negotiated the deletion of the standard meet or release clause during the first two years of the four year contract and refused to include Uniroyal's suggested right to cancel clause if the price charged for butadiene was unacceptable. Also persuasive that the prior course of dealing as to pricing did not govern the 1974 contract was that the pricing language of the 1970 contract was not carried over to, and in fact was changed dramatically in the 1974 contract. The parties intentionally deleted the explicit and elaborate formula for pricing (the escalation clause) found in the 1970 contract and in its place required that TCP give Uniroyal 15 days notice prior to implementing a price increase. If the parties had intended to continue the explicit pricing terms of the 1970 contract, or had intended that only El Paso's increases to TCP would be passed along to Uniroyal, such language could have again been utilized. In fact, that specific language was deleted. The jury was presented with sufficient evidence that the "subject to change" provision of the 1974 contract did not limit TCP's price increases to passing through El Paso's increased costs.

Nor do we accept Uniroyal's alternative argument. M.C.L.A. § 440.2305 governs the open price term of the 1974 contract. The pertinent provisions provide:

> (1) The parties if they so intend can conclude a contract for sale even though the price is not settled. In such a case the price is a reasonable price at the time for delivery if
>
> (a) nothing is said as to price; or
>
> (b) the price is left to be agreed by the parties and they fail to agree; or
>
> (c) the price is to be fixed in terms of some agreed market or other standard as set or recorded by a third person or agency and it is not so set or recorded.
>
> (2) A price to be fixed by the seller or by the buyer means a price for him to fix in good faith.

Official Comment 3, referring to subsection (2), states:

> [D]ealing with the situation where the price is to be fixed by one party rejects the uncommercial idea that an agreement that the seller may fix the price means that he may fix any price he may wish by the express qualification that the price so fixed must be fixed in good faith. Good faith includes observance of reasonable commercial standards of fair dealing in the trade if the party is a merchant. (Section 2–103).

M.C.L.A. § 440.2103(1)(b) defines "good faith" in the case of a merchant as "honesty in fact and the observance of reasonable commercial standards of fair dealing in the trade."

Neither the Code nor the Official Comments to the Code require that a merchant-seller price at fair market value under a contract with an open price term, but specify that prices must be "reasonable" and set pursuant to "reasonable commercial standards of fair dealing in the trade."

> When there is a gap as to price, 2–305 directs the court to determine 'a reasonable price,' provided the parties intended a contract. Note that the section says 'a reasonable price' and not 'fair market value of the goods.' In many instances these two would not be identical. For example, evidence of a prior course of dealing between the parties might show a price below or above market. Without more, a court could justifiably hold in these circumstances that the course of dealing price is the 'reasonable price.'

J. White & R. Summers, *Uniform Commercial Code,* § 3–7, 17 (2d ed. 1980). Similarly, the price might be reasonable although not set pursuant to "reasonable commercial standards of fair dealing." An example would be where the party sets the open price at a reasonable retail price although reasonable commercial standards of fair dealing would require that the price be set at a reasonable wholesale rate. In the instant case the price was set within the wholesale range. The only issue is whether a spot market price within that range was reasonable vis-a-vis the existence of a long term contract price and whether that is a question of fact or of law.

At all times under the 1974 contract TCP sold or offered to sell butadiene to Uniroyal at prices within the range of those reported in the *Chemical Marketing Reporter,* a domestic publication specifically providing information on the butadiene market. The parties stipulated that the following price ranges appeared in the *Chemical Marketing Reporter* for the period April 1, 1974 to March 31, 1976.

April, 1974—June, 1974	12–17 cents
July, 1974—September, 1974	16–25 cents
October, 1974—January, 1975	17½–25 cents
February, 1975—March, 1976	18–22 cents

TCP's prices of 20.75 cents on July 1, 1974, and 22.25 cents on October 1, 1974, while tending toward the high end, were always well within the above range. Although Jesse Owens of El Paso initially testified that 22.25 cents per pound was not a "fair" price for the period of November 1974 through March 1975 he later explained that this conclusion was based on El Paso's long term contracts all of which contained a meet or release clause, the effect of which is to keep prices competitive to within ½ cent per pound. TCP, however, had negotiated with Uniroyal to omit such a clause during the first two years of the contract and include it for the final two years. On the other hand, Ralph Ericsson, president of a company which produces an annual survey of the worldwide butadiene industry, testified that during the last six months of 1974 butadiene prices were rising as high as 28.5 on a straight pass through basis. In his opinion, TCP's price was commercially reasonable under all the circumstances. Thus, there was evidence from which the jury could have reasonably found that TCP's price for butadiene under the 1974 contract was commercially reasonable and set in good faith. Uniroyal too narrowly defines good faith and commercial reasonableness when it contends that as a matter of law TCP met neither because it set its price in accord with total market prices including the spot market rate [rather] than pricing solely on long term contract prices.

While taking testimony on the market price of butadiene the District Court allowed Ralph Ericsson, qualified as an expert in the production and pricing of butadiene, to testify as to the meaning of the pricing clause contained in the 1974 contract. Over objection, Ericsson testified that he had never seen a price clause exactly like that one and that "the way I read this contract, the seller had the right to set the price and the buyer was obligated to accept that price." Following admission of this evidence, the District Court instructed the jury that the testimony was admitted for such value as the jury might wish to give it. Subsequently, Uniroyal's timely motion for new trial on this basis was denied.

Absent any need to clarify or define terms of art, science, or trade, expert opinion testimony to interpret contract language is inadmissible. * * * Here the witness was not testifying about a technical term which needed explaining. Since the witness had never seen a contract without a meet and release clause or cancellation clause where there was an open pricing provision the witness could not testify to the meaning given under such a contract by the trade. The question of what the contract clause meant was a factual one for the jury to determine from the testimony presented. *Loeb v. Hammond,* 407 F.2d 779, 781 (7th Cir.1969).

While we find that the District Court erred in admitting this testimony we note that no error in the admission or exclusion of evidence is ground for reversal or granting a new trial unless refusal to take such action appears to the court to be inconsistent with substantial justice. * * * Considering the entire record we do not find that the District Court's denial of Uniroyal's motion for new trial on the grounds of Ericsson's improper testimony was inconsistent with substantial justice.

* * *

The judgment of the District Court is affirmed.

Note

UCC 2–305(2) provides that a "price to be fixed by the seller or the buyer means a price for him to fix in good faith." In Au Rustproofing Center, Inc. v. Gulf Oil Corp., 755 F.2d 1231 (6th Cir.1985), Au contracted with Gulf to be a Gulf dealer for a period of ten years. Gulf agreed to pay Au a special allowance of two cents per gallon on all gasoline purchased at a "tankwagon" price to be set without contractual restriction by Gulf. After the 1973 oil crisis ruptured the market, Gulf suspended the special discount and charged Au a "tankwagon" price that was not competitive with other suppliers in the relevant market area. As a result, Au's gross margins substantially declined. In the ensuing litigation, the court held, inter alia, that Gulf had no duty to fix competitive gasoline prices for its dealers: "* * * (A)lthough Gulf assumed the implied duty of a party controlling the price to set a reasonable price * * * the record does not establish that the high price Gulf charged to Au was so unreasonable that it negated Gulf's substantial performance of the implied duty. * * * Gulf is required to fix a price in good faith. * * * Good faith includes observance of reasonable commercial standards of fair dealing in the trade or the general range of market prices. * * * Au contends that because its competitors sold gasoline for less than Au could buy it from Gulf, Gulf's prices were unreasonable. * * * In our view, this contention is insufficient to establish that prices set by Gulf contravened reasonable commercial standards in the gasoline market or otherwise constituted bad faith or commercially unreasonable behavior." Id. at 1235–36. But see Nanakuli Paving & Rock Co. v. Shell Oil Co., Inc., 664 F.2d 772 (9th Cir.1981) (Seller with discretion to fix price acted in bad faith in failing to follow "price protection" usage and to give reasonable notice of price increase).

Problem 12–5

B manufactures precious metal products and provides refining services. On July 1, 1979, S delivered 1,600 ounces of sterling silver to B under a contract for sale. B was to process the metal to determine its silver content and fix the price by multiplying the amount of silver by the market price on that day. S understood that B's normal processing time was four to six weeks. Due to B's negligence, however, the silver was misplaced and not found and processed until November 1. During this period, the per ounce price of silver was on the rise: On July 1 it was $17.25, on August 1 it was $18.50, on August 15 it was $20 and on November 1 it was $28. S, citing UCC 2–305(3), claims that it can cancel the contract and recover the silver and sell it on the open market. B argues that the case is governed by UCC 2–305(2): Thus, there was an enforceable contract even if B acted in bad faith and the price should be a reasonable price at the time when B should have completed the processing and fixed the price.

How should the court rule?

V. GOLDBERG, PRICE ADJUSTMENT IN LONG–TERM CONTRACTS, 1985 Wis.L.Rev. 527, 531–34.

* * *

II. THE ECONOMICS OF PRICE ADJUSTMENT

A. The Benefits of Price Adjustment

Business firms have ample incentives to include some form of price adjustment mechanism in their contracts even if both parties are risk neutral. Firms do not generally enter into multi-year contracts because of their concern for the future course of prices. Rather, they enter into the agreements to achieve the benefits of cooperation. Having entered into such an agreement, the parties have to make some decision regarding the course of prices during the life of the agreement. That is, price adjustment will probably be ancillary to the main purposes of the agreement.

Price adjustment can be difficult and costly. Why then bother? Why not simply establish a price or a schedule of prices for the duration of the agreement? I will suggest four reasons that might lead business firms to consider using some form of price adjustment. First, if the contract concerns a complex product that will be continuously redefined during the life of the contract, a price adjustment mechanism can price the "amendments" to the original agreement. Examples include cost-plus pricing of sophisticated defense hardware and complex construction projects. Second, to properly coordinate their behavior, the parties want correct price signals. If the price of an input were below the market price (and if the buyer could not resell at a price greater than the contract price) the buyer would have an incentive to use "too much" of the input. Since this should be anticipated at the formation stage, the costs of poor coordination are borne by both parties. This is a pure "moral hazard" problem akin to an insured person consuming too much health care because the post-insurance price is too low.

Two other reasons are, analytically at least, more interesting: reduction of pre-contract search and post-agreement jockeying. In both these explanations, the success of price adjustment depends upon its ability to reduce the variance of outcomes. The reduced variance is not, however, valued directly. Rather, it enables the parties to curtail mutually harmful behavior, thereby increasing the value of the agreement to both parties.

A contract establishes gains to be divided between the parties; a fixed-price contract determines the distribution of these gains. The parties could attempt to increase their share of the gains before signing the contract by improving their information on the future course of costs and prices. The more they each spend on this search, the smaller the pie. *Ceteris paribus,* the larger the variance of the outcomes, the more resources would be devoted to this effort. The parties, therefore, have an incentive to incorporate into the initial agreement a device that would discourage this wasteful searching. Price adjustment mechanisms can do precisely that by reducing the value of the special information. This argument applies even for standardized commodities sold in thick markets.

If after the firms enter into a long-term agreement the contract price fails to track changing market conditions, the loser will be reluctant to continue performance. It could breach and suffer the legal and reputational consequences, but other, less severe, alternatives to willing compliance exist. A buyer could, for example, insist upon strict compliance with quality standards. The aggrieved party could read the contract literally—"working to the rules" as in labor disputes or in centrally planned economies. This is a variation on the pure moral hazard story. The incorrect price induces the aggrieved party to expend resources in attempting to renegotiate the terms of the agreement. The costs can arise directly from the effort to renegotiate or indirectly through strategic bargaining. That is, the loser might threaten to engage in acts which impose costs upon the other party but do not constitute a legal breach. These costs are a result of the failure to coordinate behavior in the face of changed circumstances. These costs would be unimportant if the parties had easy access to market alternatives; *ceteris paribus,* the more isolated from alternatives the contracting parties are, the more significant are the potential losses from poor coordination. Again, to the extent that the parties can anticipate these problems at the formation stage, the value of the exchange is reduced. If the probability of wasteful behavior increases as the divergence between contract price and the opportunity cost of the aggrieved party widens, price-adjustment rules which narrow the gap become increasingly attractive.

B. The Mechanics of Price Adjustment

The easiest way to adjust the price is to index. But what should the parties be indexing? The overall price level? Input costs? Market price? Ideally the parties would index the market price. The payoff from indexing, after all, is from the reduction in the divergence between the contract price and the market price. However, practical exigencies usually lead parties to index other prices as proxies. Indeed, in a long-term contract there often is no unique external market price. The implications of this fact will become clearer in the discussion of *Alcoa v. Essex* below.

Cost changes will be a reasonably good proxy for changes in the market price if demand does not fluctuate too much or if industry supply is very elastic. However, changes in input prices are not necessarily the same as changes in input costs. If the relative prices of inputs change, the firm has an incentive to alter factor proportions to take advantage of the new price relationships. Also, if factor productivity changes, the connection between input prices and costs deteriorates. Nevertheless, indexing to input prices is common.

While indexing would be the easiest price adjustment mechanism to implement, it has the obvious disadvantage of tracking changing conditions imperfectly. The poorer the correlation between the index and what it is supposed to be tracking, the less attractive it will be. Another relatively simple mechanical rule is permitting one party to solicit outside offers with the other party having the right of first refusal. This allows better tracking of that party's opportunity cost, but it discourages making relation-specific investments. That is, the direct costs of price adjustment would be low, but the indirect costs of discouraging entering into a long-term relationship in the first place might be quite high. Cost-plus pricing tracks cost changes more closely, but is more subject to manipulation; it also gives the seller poorer incentives to control costs, and requires that the parties devote more resources to monitoring performance.

Negotiation is, of course, always an option. Even if the contract explicitly utilizes one of the methods mentioned in the previous paragraph or unambiguously states that the contract is a fixed price agreement, one party could propose that the price be renegotiated. The contract price, the clarity of the legal rule, and the costs of invoking the legal rule provide the background against which the renegotiation might take place.

Renegotiation allows use of accurate, current information in revising the contract; but reopening the contract could result in cost-generating strategic behavior, especially if one of the parties is vulnerable to the threat of nonrenewal. Renegotiation is not a zero-sum affair with one side's gains offset by the other's loss. In exchange for an increased price, for example, a seller could offer a contract extension and the prospect of not working to the letter of the contract. (A threat, after all, is just a promise with the sign reversed.)

The contract could explicitly establish the conditions under which renegotiation is to take place. It could require renegotiation at fixed intervals or have it triggered by specific events (for example, a rise in a price index of more than 20%). Gross inequity clauses call for renegotiation if the contract price is too far out of line, but typically do not spell out the criteria for determining when a gross inequity exists. The parties could agree to renegotiate in good faith and determine what would happen if the negotiations break down. The failure to negotiate a new price could result in continued performance at the current price, termination, mediation or arbitration, and so forth.

There are, in sum, a lot of mechanisms available for adjusting price within a long-term contract. All are imperfect. Their relative costs and benefits will determine which, if any, the parties should choose.

* * *

[Footnotes omitted.]

CHAPTER THIRTEEN

EXCUSE FROM OR ADJUSTMENT OF THE CONTRACT FOR CHANGED CIRCUMSTANCES

SECTION 1. INTRODUCTION

The question, "Who bears what risks arising from changed circumstances in a contract for sale?" is intriguing and eternal. If the "risk events" have been identified in the bargaining process and explicitly allocated in the agreement, the answer is clear: if the agreement is otherwise enforceable, i.e. not unconscionable or avoidable for fraud, and the language, reasonably interpreted, supports a particular risk allocation, then that allocation should prevail. Thus, an agreed fixed price in a contract for sale is thought to allocate the risk for both parties that, during performance, the market price for similar goods will go up or down.

But suppose there is neither an agreed nor a "tacit" risk allocation, yet the person seeking relief has made an unconditional promise. The seller agrees to deliver the goods by December 1 and the agreement says nothing about the risk that a strike may close the seller's major source of supply. When, if ever, should a court grant some relief from changed circumstances? What form should that relief take? The UCC provides a starting point for answers in Sections 2–613 through 2–616. Or, suppose that the parties, in response to changed circumstances, agree to modify or adjust the contract. When should a court enforce an agreed adjustment? The starting point here is UCC 2–209.

These problems have arisen with distressing frequency in the topsy-turvey economy of the last 20 years. We will take a brief look at some of them here. Since many of the cases involve changed circumstances which affect a price mechanism agreed to by the parties, there will be some necessary overlap with the price issues covered in Chapter Twelve. But the excuse issue is distinct and two of us, at least, believe that it deserves separate treatment.

SECTION 2. RELIEF FROM CHANGED CIRCUMSTANCES

Problem 13–1

S, an art dealer, owned a etching by Picasso. B, a collector, examined it at S's gallery and, after negotiations, S agreed to sell it to B for $75,000. Under the written contract for sale, B was to return with a cashier's check the next day and pick up the etching. B returned check in hand but, alas, the Picasso had been destroyed by fire during the night. What are the rights and duties of the parties? See UCC 2–613 and 2–509. Is this a case of changed circumstances?

WICKLIFFE FARMS, INC. v. OWENSBORO GRAIN CO.

Court of Appeals of Kentucky, 1984.
684 S.W.2d 17.

DUNN, JUDGE.

This is an appeal from a summary judgment in favor of appellee, Owensboro Grain Company, entered in the Daviess Circuit Court September 9, 1982, as amended September 29, 1982. The action arises out of a contract to sell No. 2 white corn and the defense of impossibility of performance resulting from a drought.

The appellant, Wickliffe Farms, Inc., in business since 1971, farms several contiguous farms in Muhlenberg County. Of the approximate 1980 acres it farms, the corporation owns about 250 acres, Reynolds Wickliffe, its president and principal shareholder, owns about 1000 acres, and Reynolds' father's estate, the J.W. Wickliffe Estate, owns 730 acres.

The Corporation had done business with the appellee, Owensboro Grain, since 1975, primarily thru Reynolds Wickliffe, representing the corporation, and Julian G. "Sonny" Hayden, employed by Owensboro Grain as a grain merchandiser.

In February, 1980, Wickliffe contacted Hayden by telephone and they orally agreed that the corporation would deliver 35,000 bushels of No. 2 white corn at $3.70 per bushel to Owensboro Grain between December 15, 1980, and January 31, 1981. The agreement was confirmed in a writing executed by Owensboro Grain and signed by Wickliffe on behalf of the corporation. The agreement, prepared by Owensboro Grain, was on its standard "fill in the blanks" form as to quantity, the grain commodity, the price, the routing, and shipment date. It was dated February 29, 1980, and identified the corporation as the accepting party. It contained no additional language of any significance other than the following part of a small print "force majeure" clause unilaterally favoring Owensboro Grain:

> All agreements, undertakings, obligations or liabilities hereunder, made or to be kept and performed by Owensboro Grain Company, are made and shall be kept and performed subject to and contingent upon strikes, embargoes, fires, accidents, war restrictions, acts of God, or other conditions over which Owensboro Grain Company has no control and any inability on its part to keep, perform or satisfy the agreements, undertakings, obligations or liabilities hereunder caused or brought about by reason of any of the foregoing conditions shall, at the option of Owensboro Grain Company, render this contract null and void and the parties hereto shall have no further rights or obligations hereunder * * *

Owensboro Grain's principal business is dealing in the Chicago Board of Trade market area by purchasing grain for future delivery and by arranging an immediate sale of it to consumers or exporters at a margin of profit the market will competitively allow. In reference to his employer's business generally and to the instant transaction specifically, Hayden testified: "* * * my orders from the stockholders are to buy it, sell it, or hedge it. In this case you have to sell it because you can't hedge it."

In keeping with this practice, immediately after the contract was executed for Wickliffe to deliver the No. 2 white corn in the future, Owensboro Grain sold the 35,000 bushels, along with white corn similarly purchased from other farmers, to C.B. Fox, an exporter, at a price that guaranteed a 20 to 25 cent profit.

Unfortunately, in the summer of 1980, Muhlenburg County, together with the rest of western Kentucky, suffered a severe drought. Wickliffe's No. 2 white corn crop was severely damaged as were the crops of the other farmers in the area. Consequently, Wickliffe was unable to produce sufficient No. 2 white corn to fulfill its contract. In January, 1981, it delivered its entire crop, 18,718.57 bushels, to Owensboro Grain and was paid the agreed amount of $3.70 per bushel.

As a result of the short delivery, Owensboro Grain was required to purchase the amount of the shortage at $5.54 per bushel, the then market price, to satisfy its obligation to C.B. Fox entered into as a result of its futures contract with Wickliffe. The total amount spent to make up the bushels' deficit was $29,306.57. This amount was not withheld as a "set off" when it paid Wickliffe for the corn it managed to deliver, but $19,157.07 was withheld from amounts owed Wickliffe for purchase of corn and soybeans in January and February, 1982, by Owensboro Grain.

Wickliffe sued Owensboro Grain in the Daviess Circuit Court for the amount of the sale of the corn and soybeans. Owensboro Grain counterclaimed for its loss resulting from the partial non-delivery of No. 2 white corn in 1981. The trial court entered summary judgment in favor of Owensboro Grain on its counterclaim, later amended to include interest.

On appeal, as well as in the trial court, Wickliffe primarily relies on the defense of impossibility of performance caused by the severe drought, a "force majeure." We agree with the trial court that this defense is not applicable since the contract did not specify the land on which the corn was to be grown. Hence, we affirm.

There is no disagreement that the provisions of § 2–615 of the Uniform Commercial Code (U.C.C.) (1978), adopted as KRS 355.2–615, address the issue before us; also, there is no disagreement that there is no Kentucky law interpreting KRS 355.2–615, particularly with reference to U.C.C. § 2–615 comment 9 (1978), which in pertinent part is as follows:

> The case of a farmer who has contracted to sell crops *to be grown on designated land* may be regarded as falling within * * * this section, and he may be excused, when there is a failure of the specific crop. * * *

We have carefully considered Wickliffe's argument that the contract was one-sided or unconscionable because it contained no specific "force majeure" clause in its favor as it did in favor of Owensboro Grain and conclude the argument is without merit. We reach a like conclusion on Wickliffe's position that an "adhesion contract" resulted from the "fill in the blanks" form of the contract.

Wickliffe's principal argument is that the defense of impossibility provided by KRS 355.2–615 should be available to it due to the fact that it was contemplated by both parties that the No. 2 white corn was to be grown on its 2000 contiguous acres in Muhlenburg County and, that the adverse weather of the 1980 summer was a condition that was unforeseen and unforeseeable by the parties, and which rendered Wickliffe's performance impossible, and, pursuant to the statute, thereby excused his obligation to fully perform.

Nowhere in the contract, however, is there any reference to any specific acreage upon which the crop was to be grown. Wickliffe urges that KRS 355.2–

202 permits contradiction of the written terms of the parties' intention by admission of proof of a contemporaneous oral agreement. This statute provides:

> Terms with respect to which the confirmatory memoranda of the parties agree or which are otherwise set forth in a writing intended by the parties as a final expression of their agreement with respect to such terms as are included therein may not be contradicted by evidence of any prior agreement or of a contemporaneous oral agreement but may be explained or supplemented
>
> (a) by course of dealing or usage of trade (KRS 355.1–205) or by course of performance (KRS 355.2–208); and
>
> (b) by evidence of consistent additional terms unless the court finds the writing to have been intended also as a complete and exclusive statement of the terms of the agreement.

This argument ignores the fact that to be admissible, the proof must come within the provisions of subparagraph (b) of the statute that requires the parol evidence be of additional terms consistent with the written contract. Here there is no consistency between Wickliffe's claim that the corn was to be produced off a particular part of a 2000 acre farm and a contract providing for nothing other than buying and selling 35,000 bushels of No. 2 white corn. There was no proof before the trial court, parol or otherwise, offered or proffered by Wickliffe, to establish that both parties contemplated and agreed upon a contract to sell the corn from any particularly designated acreage.

The undisputed admissible material facts before the trial court prove the ordinary "futures contract" of an agreement to buy and sell a quantity of grain at a given price per bushel, to be delivered at a future date, the purchaser thereafter arranging a "back to back" sale of the commodity. The sellers in such a transaction gamble the market price will not be greater at the time of delivery and the buyers gamble that it will not be lower. All Owensboro Grain was interested in was buying 35,000 bushels of No. 2 white corn from Wickliffe at $3.70 per bushel and nothing more. Its business was not to speculate either in the weather, crop yield or fluctuation of market price. It guaranteed its profit by selling immediately. Wickliffe's only interest was to sell it. It chose to contract to deliver the corn at a given price at a given future date and failed to do so.

Since there exists no issue of material fact and Owensboro Grain is entitled to judgment as a matter of law, the trial court committed no error in granting summary judgment on Owensboro Grain's counterclaims. *Shah v. American Synthetic Rubber Corp.*, Ky., 655 S.W.2d 489 (1983).

The Daviess Circuit Court summary judgment and amended summary judgment are affirmed.

All concur.

Notes

1. Suppose the corn had been planted on the seller's 2,000 acres at the time the contract was signed. Should the result be the same under UCC 2–613? See Bunge Corp. v. Recker, 519 F.2d 449 (8th Cir.1975) (no reference in contract to soybeans planted on particular land). Under either UCC 2–613 or 2–615(a), why must the seller establish an agreement to sell the corn from particularly designated acres?

2. If excuse is granted under UCC 2–613, the contract is avoided if the "loss is total." UCC 2–613(b). If the loss is partial or the goods no longer conform to the

contract, the buyer is given a statutory option either to avoid the contract or to accept the goods with a price adjustment. UCC 2–613(b).

Under UCC 2–615, the adjustment process is more complicated. If delay or non-delivery of the entire performance is excused under UCC 2–615(a), the seller must give the buyer seasonable notification, UCC 2–615(c). The buyer then has the options set forth in UCC 2–616(1), including the right to "terminate and thereby discharge any unexecuted portion of the contract."

In excused cases of delay or non-delivery in "part," however, the seller "must allocate production and deliveries among his customers but may at his option include regular customers not then under contract as well as his own requirements for further manufacture" and this may be done in "any manner which is fair and reasonable." UCC 2–615(b). Note that the seller must now notify the buyer of the delay and the "estimated quota * * * made available for the buyer," UCC 2–615(c).

The buyer's option under UCC 2–616(1) with regard to an allocation "justified" under UCC 2–615(b) is either to terminate the contract or to "modify the contract by agreeing to take his available quota in substitution." But see UCC 2–616(2), imposing a duty on the buyer to act "within a reasonable time not exceeding thirty days." A seller who fails to allocate deliveries in a fair and reasonable manner cannot assert the defense of commercial impracticability under UCC 2–615. Roth Steel Products v. Sharon Steel Corp., 705 F.2d 134 (6th Cir.1983). A buyer who fails to exercise the statutory options within a reasonable time loses the opportunity to preserve an adjusted contract for future performance. See UCC 2–616(2); Federal Pants, Inc. v. Stocking, 762 F.2d 561 (7th Cir.1985) (contract lapses with respect to any deliveries affected).

Note: Failure of Seller's Source of Supply—Herein of the Force Majeure Clause

Section 261 of the Restatement, Second of Contracts provides a test for "discharge" that parallels UCC 2–615(a): "Where, after a contract is made, a party's performance is made impracticable without his fault by the occurrence of an event the non-occurrence of which was a basic assumption on which the contract was made, his duty to render that performance is discharged, unless the language or the circumstances indicate the contrary." This test is particularized for certain distinctive events. Thus, Sections 262 and 263 provide that the death or incapacity of a person whose existence or capacity is required for performance, or the destruction or deterioration of a thing necessary for performance, "makes performance impracticable" and, thus, are events "the non-occurrence of which was a basic assumption on which the contract was made." Compare UCC 2–613.

But what happens when a source of supply deemed necessary by the seller for performance of the seller's contract with the buyer fails? Under the Restatement, this is swept up under the general principle in Section 261 with a corollary that "a party generally assumes the risk of his own inability to perform his duty." Thus: "Even if a party contracts to render a performance that depends on some act by a third party, he is not ordinarily discharged because of a failure by that party because this is also a risk that is commonly understood to be on the obligor." See Section 261, Comment (e); Illustration 13.

An exception to this has been established in cases interpreting UCC 2–615(a). Thus, where a particular supplier is specified in the contract, assumed by the parties to be the exclusive source of supply, and fails to perform, the seller is excused, provided that it: (1) employed all "due measures" to assure that the agreed supplier would perform, and (2) turned over to the buyer any rights against the supplier corresponding to the seller's claim of excuse. UCC 2–615, Comment 5. In Zidell Explorations, Inc. v. Conval International, Ltd., 719 F.2d 1465 (9th Cir.1983), the court held that a failure to tender rights against the seller did not constitute a per se violation of the duty of good faith: Rather, the jury must determine in all the facts and circumstances whether the seller had satisfied its responsibility under Comment 5.

Frequently, a seller will attempt to protect itself against failures in a contemplated source of supply, whether agreed to be exclusive or not, by a force majeure clause. Such clauses vary in scope and content from industry to industry. A common form may look like this:

> "Neither party shall be liable for * * * loss, damage, claims or demands of any nature whatsoever due to delays or defaults in performance caused by impairment in any manner of seller's source of supply by (list causes or events) or by any other event, whether or not similar to the causes specified above * * *, which shall not be reasonably within the control of the party against whom the claim would otherwise be made."

When a force majeure clause is invoked, the following questions must be answered:

(1) Are the events specified and the relief sought within the scope of the clause;

(2) If so, was the event within the control or due to the fault or negligence of the party seeking relief;

(3) If not, did the party seeking relief exercise reasonable efforts after the event occurred to secure performance as agreed from some source, see Nissho-Iwai Co., Ltd. v. Occidental Crude Sales, Inc., 729 F.2d 1530 (5th Cir.1984); and

(4) Is relief under a force majeure clause restricted in any way by UCC 2–615(a)? Put differently, if the parties clearly agree to expand the scope of excuse available under UCC 2–615(a), should the agreement be enforced? In InterPetrol Bermuda Ltd. v. Kaiser Aluminum International Corp., 719 F.2d 992 (9th Cir.1983), the answer was yes, subject to the requirement of conscionability and the good faith duty to seek an alternative source of performance. In addition, the court held that where excuse was based upon the force majeure clause rather than UCC 2–615, there was no requirement that the seller assign its rights against the defaulting source of supply to the buyer:

* * *

> We agree with the district court that comment 5 does not control in this case. Kaiser was not excused under § 2–615 and could not have been. Section 2–615 applies only when the events that made the performance of the contract impracticable were unforeseen at the time the contract was executed. See Taylor-Edwards Warehouse Co. v. Burlington Northern, Inc., 715 F.2d 1330, 1336 (9th Cir.1983). The extensive negotiations over the force majeure clause, discussed above, indicate that the parties not only foresaw the risk that Oxy Crude would default but also bargained over which party would bear the loss in that event. Accordingly, it would violate fundamental principles of contract law, to use § 2–615 of the UCC to rewrite the contract to which the parties agreed. UCC § 2–615, comment 8 (§ 2–615 inapplicable if "contingency in question is * * * included among the business risks which are fairly to be regarded as part of the dickered terms. * * *").
>
> Although there has been some doubt expressed as to whether the Code permits parties to bargain for exemptions broader than those available under § 2–615,[7] at least one circuit has concluded they may. See Eastern Airlines, Inc. v. McDonnell Douglas Corp., 532 F.2d 957, 990 (5th Cir.1976). See also Olson v.

7. See Hawkland, The Energy Crisis and Section 2–615 of the Uniform Commercial Code, 79 Com.L.J. 75 (1974).

Spitzer, 257 N.W.2d 459 (S.D.1977) (exculpatory clause valid for defining events which excuse seller's performance). We agree with the Fifth Circuit. Comment 8 to § 2–615 plainly indicates that parties may "enlarge upon or supplant" § 2–615.[8] While exculpatory clauses phrased in general language should not be construed to expand excuses not provided for by the Code, circumstances surrounding a particular agreement may indicate that the parties intended to accord the seller an exemption broader than is available under the UCC.[9] Eastern Airlines, 532 F.2d at 990–91. We have already decided that the force majeure clause agreed to by Kaiser and InterPetrol was intended to excuse Kaiser prior to shipment of the crude from the Persian Gulf if Kaiser's supplier failed to deliver for any reason. We now hold that it was permissible for them to make such an agreement. Thus, if InterPetrol is to prevail on its claim that it succeeds to Kaiser's rights, it must do so on grounds apart from the Code.

California courts have read into force majeure clauses an implied covenant of good faith. Terry v. Atlantic Richfield Co., 72 Cal.App.3d 962, 964, 140 Cal. Rptr. 510, 511 (1977); see Milton v. Hudson Sales Corp., 152 Cal.App.2d 418, 427, 431, 313 P.2d 936, 942 (1957). This common law covenant of good faith is applicable to force majeure clauses such as the one agreed to by Kaiser and InterPetrol. If the common law requirement of good faith implies a requirement that a seller turn over to its buyer the seller's rights against a defaulting supplier, then the district court erred in granting Kaiser's motion to dismiss.

InterPetrol failed to cite any instance under the common law, under circumstances similar to those of this case, where a buyer succeeded to the rights of the seller against a defaulting supplier.[10] The common law has not provided to a disappointed buyer the rights called for by InterPetrol.

We see no reason to now create a right which has not been recognized by the common law. There is a certain amount of economic wisdom in permitting a seller, consistent with the limiting provisions of the Code,[11] to contract out of liability. In a relatively free and fluid wholesale market, a seller should be entitled to utilize the power of his position to contract to his best advantage. That might include, as here, the extraction of a force majeure clause from a buyer. If the seller's supplier is not able because of market forces to require a similar provision in the agreement between seller and supplier, the result is that the seller is excused but the supplier is not. Yet we see no reason to award the windfall of recovery against the supplier to the buyer, who agreed to excuse the seller, instead of the seller, who was able to insist on better protections. When a

8. Comment 8 to § 2–615 provides that:

"The provisions of this section are made subject to assumption of greater liability by agreement and such agreement is to be found not only in the expressed terms of the contract but in the circumstances surrounding the contracting, in trade usage and the like. Thus the exemptions of this section do not apply when the contingency in question is sufficiently foreshadowed at the time of contracting to be included among the business risks which are fairly to be regarded as part of the dickered terms, either consciously or as a matter of reasonable, commercial interpretation from the circumstances * * *. The exemption otherwise present through usage of trade under the present section may also be expressly negated by the language of the agreement. Generally express agreements as to exemptions designed to enlarge upon or supplant the provisions of this section are to be read in the light of mercantile sense and reason, for this section itself sets up the commercial standard for normal and reasonable interpretation and provides a minimum beyond which agreement may not go."

9. Force majeure clauses are, of course, limited by those sections of the Code prohibiting agreements which are manifestly unreasonable, in bad faith or unconscionable. See §§ 1–102(c), 1–203 and 2–302. See also Eastern Airlines, 532 F.2d at 991 n. 96; Transatlantic Financing Corp. v. United States, 363 F.2d 312, 315 n. 3 (D.C.Cir.1966).

10. InterPetrol did not rely on third-party beneficiary concepts at trial and did not attempt to raise the theory on appeal.

11. See supra note 9.

trader is able to bargain for such favorable conditions, the natural trend will be for traders in the less favorable positions of buyer and supplier to move into the less competitive and therefore more contractually secure part of the market.

We find no reason to transfer the benefit of Kaiser's superior negotiating position to InterPetrol by giving InterPetrol Kaiser's rights against Trako and Oxy Crude. We do find that it serves the forces of natural market adjustments not to transfer Kaiser's rights. We therefore affirm the decision of the district court.[12]

* * *

[719 F.2d at 999–1001]

Note: The ALCOA Case

In Aluminum Company of America v. Essex Group, Inc., 499 F.Supp. 53 (W.D.Pa. 1980), the facts of which are elaborated in the extract from *Goldberg,* infra at 560, the parties entered in 1967 into a 17 year contract under which ALCOA was to process alumina supplied by Essex into molten aluminum to be used by Essex in the manufacture of aluminum wire products. The long-term contract, called a "toll conversion service contract," was to be performed at a plant owned by ALCOA in Indiana. As part of the pricing mechanism, the parties agreed upon an escalation clause, developed by the noted economist Alan Greenspan, which varied with actual production costs at the plant. The clause was developed on the basis of past cost patterns and reflected projected cost variations that would give ALCOA a target profit of $.04 per pound.

In 1973, during the energy crisis, electricity costs at the Indiana plant began to escalate well beyond the projections in the price escalation clause. Even though the contract was profitable up to this time, it was estimated that ALCOA would lose $60 million over the balance of the contract due to a 500% variation between indexed and actual costs. At the same time, Essex was enjoying an apparent windfall gain by reselling converted aluminum for which it paid ALCOA $.364 per pound on the open market for $.733 per pound. When efforts by ALCOA to obtain an agreed price adjustment from Essex failed, ALCOA sued to obtain relief from the escalation clause and a reformation of the contract so that Essex must pay the actual costs incurred at the plant. Essex counterclaimed for breach damages and the issues were joined.

In an unprecedented decision, the court concluded that ALCOA was entitled to "some relief" from the changed circumstances and that the relief should be an equitable reformation of, rather than discharge from, the contract. The court, without the agreement of the parties, devised its own adjustment formula to fill the gap in the agreement. Essex appealed but the parties settled the dispute by agreement before the case could be heard.

Since the contract between ALCOA and Essex was characterized as for services rather than the sale of goods, UCC 2–615 was not directly applicable. The court, however, blended the doctrine of mutual mistake, commercial impracticability and frustration of purpose to achieve a result that, in part, could have been reached under UCC 2–615. The court's analysis was consistent with the four steps required to deal with UCC 2–615's "basic assumption" test:

First, did the seller assume by agreement a greater obligation than the degree of excuse normally available under UCC 2–615? If so, excuse should be denied. ALCOA's answer was no.

12. Our holding is based in part on the fact that Kaiser and InterPetrol were in relatively similar positions in the petroleum market. We have not considered circumstances involving traders from different levels in the hierarchy of the petroleum distribution network. We note too that InterPetrol was not obligated to other buyers to deliver oil it expected to get from Kaiser.

Second, if a greater obligation was not assumed, was the event that materialized a "contingency the non-occurrence of which was a basic assumption on which the contract was made?" If not, excuse should be denied. ALCOA's answer was yes: Both parties assumed at the time of contracting that the escalation clause was reasonable and the changed circumstances were not foreseen as likely to occur.

Third, if so, did the contingency make "performance as agreed * * * impracticable?" If the answer is yes, then the seller is entitled to "some relief." ALCOA's answer was yes: A $60 million loss over the balance of a commercial contract made continued performance "commercially senseless and unjust," particularly where Essex was realizing "windfall" profits.

Fourth, if the seller is entitled to "some relief," what form should that relief take, discharge of the executory contract or preservation of the contract under a court-imposed price adjustment? The Code's answer is not clear. ALCOA's answer was to delete the existing price escalation clause, which had failed its intended purpose, and to impose in the gap a new price term which was thought to respond to the changed circumstances. For more discussion, see Speidel, *Court-Imposed Price Adjustments Under Long-Term Supply Contracts,* 76 Nw.U.L.Rev. 369 (1981).

ALCOA, to date, stands as the high (or low) water mark in disputes under UCC 2–615. Under circumstances comparable to ALCOA, i.e., rising costs of performance or sharply higher prices, other courts have denied any relief to the seller under UCC 2–615(a). See, Iowa Elec. Light and Power Co. v. Atlas Corp., 467 F.Supp. 129, 134 (N.D.Iowa 1978), rev'd on other grounds 603 F.2d 1301 (8th Cir.1979); Louisiana Power & Light v. Allegheny Ludlum Industries, 517 F.Supp. 1319 (E.D.La.1981); Mo. Public Serv. Co. v. Peabody Coal Co., 583 S.W.2d 721 (Mo.App.1979), cert. denied 444 U.S. 865, 100 S.Ct. 135, 62 L.Ed.2d 88 (1979). Under the opposite circumstances, i.e., a sharply reduced demand and, thus, lower prices for the product, buyers have fared no better than sellers. Although the courts, citing Comment 9, concede that UCC 2–615(a) protects buyers, little mercy has been shown to the buyer who, in the light of changed circumstances, has agreed to take goods at a quantity in excess of current needs and pay a price substantially in excess of market. See Northern Illinois Gas Co. v. Energy Cooperative, Inc., 122 Ill.App.3d 940, 78 Ill.Dec. 215, 225, 461 N.E.2d 1049, 1059 (1984), where the court said: "* * * (A)s any trader knows, the only certainty of the market is that prices will change. Changing and shifting markets and prices from multitudinous causes is endemic to the economy in which we live. Market forecasts by supposed experts are sometimes right, often wrong, and usually mixed. If changed prices, standing alone, constitute a frustrating event sufficient to excuse performance of a contract, then the law binding contractual parties to their agreements is no more." Accord: Northern Indiana Public Service Co. v. Carbon County Coal Company, 799 F.2d 265 (7th Cir.1986), where the court, speaking through Judge Posner, stated:

> Since impossibility and related doctrines are devices for shifting risk in accordance with the parties presumed intentions, which are to minimize the costs of contract performance, one of which is the disutility created by risk, they have no place when the contract explicitly assigns a particular risk to one party or the other. As we have already noted, a fixed-price contract is an explicit assignment of the risk of market price increases to the seller and the risk of market price decreases to the buyer, and the assignment of the latter risk to the buyer is even clearer where, as in this case, the contract places a floor under price but allows for escalation. If, as is also the case here, the buyer forecasts the market incorrectly and therefore finds himself locked into a disadvantageous contract, he has only himself to blame and so cannot shift the risk back to the buyer by invoking impossibility or related doctrines. * * * Since 'the very purpose of a fixed price agreement is to place the risk of increased costs on the promisor (and

the risk of decreased costs on the promisee),' the fact that costs decrease steeply * * * cannot allow the buyer to walk away from the contract."

V. GOLDBERG, PRICE ADJUSTMENT IN LONG-TERM CONTRACTS, 1985 Wis.L.Rev. 527, 534–42.

* * *

III. ALCOA V. ESSEX *

A. The Facts

In 1967, Alcoa and Essex entered into a twenty year agreement in which Alcoa agreed to convert Essex's alumina into molten aluminum at Alcoa's Warrick, Indiana plant. Essex purchased its alumina from an Alcoa subsidiary under a second long-term contract. The trial judge insisted that the two contracts were separate and that by design Alcoa's left hand did not know what the right hand was doing. After conversion the molten aluminum would be loaded into crucibles owned by Essex and taken by truck to Essex's nearby fabricating plant built specifically to receive it. The contract was for 50 million pounds per year and included options for three additional blocks of 25 million pounds each. (By 1973, the parties had deleted the last two blocks.) Hence, the contract quantity at the time the litigation arose was 75 million pounds per year.

The initial contract price was 15 cents per pound, composed of a "demand charge" of five cents per pound,[22] and a "production charge". The latter included a fixed component of four cents per pound (which was the "profit" on the plant constructed to fulfill this contract) and three cents each for non-labor (primarily fuel) and labor costs. The former was indexed by the Industrial Component of the Wholesale Price Index and the latter by Alcoa's average hourly labor cost at the Warrick plant. The contract included a ceiling price of 65% of the price of a specified type of aluminum as reported in a trade journal; however, it did not specify a minimum price.

The demand charge was to be paid regardless of whether Essex took any aluminum. In effect, Essex "rented" a portion of Alcoa's Warrick plant at a fixed rate of $7.09 million per year ($4.09 million for the demand charge and $3 million for the fixed charge) and paid a service fee of six cents per pound that was indexed.

Problems arose following the large increase in fuel prices in 1973. In the ensuing years the market price of aluminum and the cost of producing it in Warrick increased far more rapidly than did the contract price. By 1979, Essex received aluminum from Alcoa under the contract at 36 cents per pound and resold some of it in the open market at 73 cents. Non-labor production costs rose from 5.8 cents to 22.7 cents in 1973–78, while the wholesale price index less than doubled. Alcoa attempted to renegotiate the price as early as 1975. In 1978, the dispute went to trial.

The trial court ruled in Alcoa's favor. Indexing non-labor production costs to the Wholesale Price Index was deemed a "mutual mistake" because it tracked those costs so badly. The court also accepted Alcoa's alternative theories of

* Aluminum Co. of America v. Essex Group, Inc., 499 F.Supp. 53 (W.D.Pa.1980).

22. Actually, this price was to be adjusted to cover increased construction costs at the Warrick plant when new blocks of aluminum capacity were ordered. The price of the first block (50 million pounds) was 5.27 cents per pound and the price for the second block was 5.82 cents per pound. These prices would remain constant for the life of the contract.

impracticability and frustration. The court reformed the contract, since rescission would result in a windfall for Alcoa and deprive Essex of the benefits of its long-term supply contract. The court rewrote the price term of the contract to include a minimum price assuring Alcoa a one cent per pound "profit".

The disputed contract represented only a small part of the business of Alcoa and Essex. Alcoa's sales and total assets in 1979 were each almost $5 billion.[23] By the time of trial, Essex had been acquired by United Technologies, another multi-billion dollar firm. Despite its losses on this contract, Alcoa's overall profits in 1979 were around $500 million; its rate of return on equity in 1978 exceeded 14 percent for the first time in 22 years.[24] This is not, clearly, a case in which a bad contract jeopardized the survival of a firm, as in *Westinghouse.* Rather, it is more instructive to view this contract as a poor performer in the firm's much larger portfolio of contracts, a portfolio which was performing very well overall.

B. The $75 Million Misunderstanding

The court placed considerable emphasis on the fact that projected losses from 1977 to 1987 were in the range of $75 million. This is one of those funny numbers that means nothing, but could end up as a fundamental part of the *Alcoa* doctrine, were one to emerge. Alcoa was excused because they stood to lose $75 million; we won't excuse X because it cannot prove that it will lose such a large amount. (As I will note below, the *Alcoa* judge distinguished another case on precisely this ground.) It is, therefore, useful to look at how the court determined the magnitude of the loss.

The "profits" are the revenue minus the actual production costs minus the demand charge (the 5 + cents per pound). The court assumed something (the decision does not make it quite clear what) about future costs and prices for the remaining life of the contract and then added them up. There are three obvious problems with this. First, the future profits are undiscounted. A dollar lost in 1984 is just as important as a dollar lost in 1979. Second, the estimates are based on guesses about the future course of prices; there is nothing wrong with guesses, but time has a way of transforming guesses into facts.[25] But these are quibbles. The most important point is that the estimate, even if done right, is irrelevant.

What does Alcoa lose if it must fulfill the contract? It loses the chance to sell the aluminum to someone else. That is the true measure of the loss, and in this case it is considerably greater than the figure cited by the judge. In the year the suit was brought the loss was over thirty cents per pound, over $20 million. The original cost of construction of the plant is a red herring equivalent to "par value" for a stock, a vestige of the past with no economic content.

The error is important. In an earlier case,[26] the court refused to allow Gulf Oil to escape its obligation to deliver jet fuel under a five-year contract despite the fact that the price index utilized had inadequately tracked the course of oil prices. The court held that the cost data presented were insufficient to ascertain how much it cost Gulf to produce a gallon of jet fuel, and, therefore, Gulf had failed to prove that it had suffered losses on the contract. The *Alcoa* judge

23. *The Fortune Directory,* Fortune, May 5, 1980, pp. 274, 276.

24. *Aluminum's Bosses Are Beaming,* Forbes, Nov. 27, 1978, at 40.

25. In fact, aluminum prices fell sharply in the early 1980's. That price decline undoubtedly facilitated settlement of the dispute.

26. Eastern Air Lines v. Gulf Oil Corp., 415 F.Supp. 429 (S.D.Fla.1975).

applied the "negative accounting profit" test in distinguishing this decision from *Alcoa.*

When faced with a claim of changed circumstances, courts or arbitrators should not look to accounting cost data to determine the merits of the claim. The relevant question is whether the difference between the contract price and the aggrieved party's next best option is large enough to warrant relief. An accounting cost or profit standard is an invitation to produce a lot of information with a low expected value.

C. *Alcoa's Mistake*

In retrospect, of course, Alcoa made a big mistake. However, the mistake singled out by the court to justify reformation of the contract was not the most important one. The failure of the price index to accurately measure the change in fuel prices accounted for only about ten to twelve cents of the difference between the contract price and the market price for aluminum in 1979 (that difference being over 30 cents). The main problem was that the contract did not track changing demand conditions and the demand for aluminum was soaring in the late 1970's.

Moreover, the contract was not designed to adjust to large changes in the overall price level. Sixty percent of the initial contract price (the demand charge plus the fixed "profit") was unadjusted for the life of the contract. A very simple example gives an indication of the type of problem this could cause. Suppose that the price level rises about 7% per year (doubling roughly every ten years); assume that the factors of production remain equally productive and that they continue to be used in the same proportions. The indexed production costs would then rise from six cents per pound to 24 cents per pound in the twentieth year. However, the remaining costs are unindexed, so the final contract price would rise only to (24 + 9 =) 33 cents. To keep the real price of aluminum constant the contract price would have had to increase to 60 cents.

The relevant question is not whether Alcoa made what turned out to be a bad decision. They did. But was it a bad decision at the time they made it? The answer to that is less certain. When I began this project it seemed clear that Alcoa could have, and should have, done better. At a minimum, I thought, they should have indexed the remaining 60% of the costs. However, a more careful look leads me to believe that it is a much closer question.[30]

This long-term contract is in many respects similar to a lease or sale of part of Alcoa's Warrick production capacity to Essex. A fixed rental for long-term leases is not uncommon. Moreover, if one firm sells a durable asset to another, it is the rule rather than the exception, that the price is not to be readjusted after the sale has taken place. It can be argued, then, by analogy, that this component of the long-term contract that looks so much like a lease should also be at a fixed price.

If the contract price of a long-lived asset were to be readjusted to better track the market price, the parties would expend less resources today in pursuit of special information. If this benefit were great; we would expect the parties to incorporate price adjustment arrangements in their sales and leases of assets. However, the benefits will often be very small. Information regarding the future price level, for example, is already incorporated in the term structure of

30. The question of whether Alcoa had made a mistake is unrelated to the court's finding of mutual mistake. I am only trying to determine whether the price adjustment mechanism in this contract was a reasonable one under the circumstances.

interest rates. It is not necessarily *accurate* information, ex post; however, the key question is whether it is *improvable* information, ex ante. Incorporating a general price index, therefore, need not result in reduced information costs.

The lease/sale analogy, however, has difficulties. A pure lease or sale is similar to a contract for a standardized commodity because further coordination between the two parties is unnecessary; the only issue is whether price adjustment reduces the initial price search. However, the more the outcomes depend upon future coordination by the parties, the less likely they will use a fixed price contract.[31] For example, shopping center leases in which the lessor engages in activities which generate business for the tenants will base at least part of the compensation on a percentage of the gross (which automatically provides for some price adjustment). If Alcoa were leasing the plant to Essex and allowing Essex to operate it, the fixed price arrangement would be routine. The fact that operation of the plant was in Alcoa's hands reduced the likelihood that a fixed price would be successful. The increased divergence between the contract price and Alcoa's best alternative would induce Alcoa to engage in strategic behavior, thereby reducing the value of the contract to both parties.

However, it is unlikely that indexing capital costs would result in a more accurate contract price. I would speculate that the pre-1973 experience would confirm that indexing this cost component to the general price level, construction costs, or any other conceivable cost-based measure would have resulted in a poorer fit between the market and contract price.[32]

Instead of using a cost-based price adjustment, the parties could have attempted to track market conditions by, for example, indexing to a particular aluminum price.[33] Using output prices to index is not without problems. First, other goods with published prices that are sufficiently close to the output that we are attempting to index might not exist. Second, the observable external prices are typically list prices, not transaction prices. If these diverge, the index suffers. It is plausible that the two would diverge in a concentrated industry like aluminum since list prices typically change more slowly in such industries.[34] Further, if the contract price were linked to the list price of a type of Alcoa's aluminum, then Alcoa would have an incentive, however modest, to set the list price in excess of the transaction price.

31. This discussion is highly speculative since I am only dimly aware of the adjustment mechanisms actually used in long-term leases. I should note that a common device is to use short-term agreements with fixed prices so that the price can be renegotiated on a regular basis. Such arrangements might also include an expectation, legal or otherwise, of renewal on reasonable terms.

32. Note that this is a different argument than the one accepted by the court. It emphasized how closely the wholesale price index had tracked one component of costs in the pre-contract period. I am claiming that there did not exist an index that would have closely tracked another, and larger, component of costs.

33. Note that in the previous paragraph I treated the capital cost as a historical cost. Alternatively, we could adjust to reflect the value of the fixed plant as it changes during the life of the structure. Thus, the cost of using the plant to fill this contract must include the opportunity cost of using the plant for other purposes (namely supplying aluminum to someone else). If the capital had a wide variety of other uses (for example, retail space or small vans), such an adjustment might be sensible. If, however, the capital was highly idiosyncratic, as in this case, its value would closely track changing market conditions. If these could be indexed accurately it would almost surely be unproductive to index the market value of capital either instead of or in addition to the market price of the output.

34. For example, in 1979 Business Week reported list prices for ingot of 66 cents per pound while the spot price was 75 cents. This is a bit misleading, however, because of the existence of price controls at the time. *Aluminum Wastes No Time Raising Prices,* BUS. WK., Oct. 15, 1979, at 36.

Even if list prices were accurate measures of transaction prices, a more fundamental difficulty remains. The parties do not necessarily confront the same external price. That is, the relevant price to each party is its opportunity cost—the net price it could get from the next best trading partner. In a market for a standardized commodity, the list price and these two opportunity costs would be roughly the same. However, in a long-term contract in which the parties deliberately isolate themselves from the external market, these three prices are more likely to diverge. Generally, the more isolated the contracting parties are from market alternatives, the poorer the relationship between these three prices is likely to be. Thus, while the parties might desire to index their agreement to a published market price, the very nature of a long-term contract makes it likely that the index price would not perform its function adequately. It is, therefore, not at all obvious that indexing the contract to changes in the published price of a particular type of output would be in the interest of the two parties.

In the instant case, Alcoa's opportunity cost is the net price it could receive by using the Warrick capacity to produce ingot for export to other customers. Essex's opportunity cost is the price of delivered aluminum ingot. There is no a priori reason to believe that these will be close to each other. However, for an index to work it is not necessary that the prices be close, only that they move together over time. Whether these two opportunity costs (and the market price for aluminum ingot) move together over time is an empirical question which I intend to explore in a later paper.

Essex chose to incorporate the output price information in the form of a maximum price. Alcoa, however, was not willing to pay (by agreeing to a lower initial contract price) for a price minimum. The failure to do so might well have been a mistake ex ante, but it is at least plausible that a ceiling indexed to published prices would be more valuable to Essex than a similarly indexed floor would have been to Alcoa. Alcoa's superior knowledge of the aluminum industry might make Essex suspicious of the manner in which costs were indexed. A bias in favor of Alcoa, because of Alcoa's superior knowledge, would make a bound on the index relatively more valuable to Essex.

Conceivably, therefore, Alcoa's failure to index plant costs or include a minimum price was not an error ex ante. Looking at the new contract may provide some insight on this issue. We know that the parties rejected the judicially imposed minimum price based on ex ante accounting costs. But we do not know whether that was a reason for rejection and we do not know what replaced it. I would speculate that the new contract includes a minimum and that the minimum depends upon output prices. If so, that would suggest that Alcoa had erred initially.

IV. Resolution of Price Adjustment Disputes

Suppose that contracting parties assign the task of resolving price adjustment disputes to an outsider (a court or an arbitrator). The outsider can be asked to resolve two very different questions: (a) have conditions changed sufficiently to justify relief; and (b) what form should relief take—what will the new price (or price formula) be? Since the parties bear the costs of producing the evidence, they must reckon the expected costs of producing evidence on production costs, accounting profits, market prices, opportunity costs, and so forth, and weigh these against the expected benefits (in terms of reducing the costs arising from the divergence of contract price from market price). These evidentiary costs provide the backdrop for subsequent renegotiation. Thus, for example, if a standard required that one party spend a lot to produce evidence to forestall price revision, its opposite party could use those potential costs as a bargaining chip in renegotiation.

For determining whether relief is justified, accounting cost data of the sort relied upon by the Alcoa judge are largely beside the point. The relevant question is whether the difference between the contract price and the aggrieved party's next best option is large enough to warrant relief. The requisite price differential would vary across contracts. There is no "magic number": if price goes up by at least $X\%$ or losses total at least $\$Y$, adjust the price. A large divergence between the market and contract price for a standardized commodity, for example, would have little adverse effect on the expected value of a contract; it would, therefore, be unlikely that the parties would benefit from revision. Conversely, if a modest price divergence would generate considerable joint costs, revision could be effective. The problem is complicated by the fact that making relief easy to obtain generates additional joint costs as well. Rational parties might easily find that the potential benefits from price revision come at too high a cost.

This is especially true if there is no obvious standard for determining a new contract price. My initial presumption was that if a reasonable measure of the output price were available, the parties would want the arbitrator to use this to guide his decision. Further consideration has led me to conclude that this might not be very helpful. A simple example illustrates the problem. Suppose that when the contract was written Alcoa would have received 10 cents a pound for its aluminum on the open market, Essex would have paid 20 cents per pound, and the contract price was fifteen cents. When the case is litigated, Alcoa could sell at 50 cents and Essex buy at 70, and the contract price is 35 cents. What should the contract price be? Even if this information were costlessly produced and absolutely accurate, are the parties better off putting the decision in the hands of an arbitrator? What decision rule would they want him to apply? When the opportunity costs of the buyer and seller diverge, it is not at all clear what should guide the arbitrator in setting a new price. Thus, the possible divergence not only impairs the value of a published price as an index, but makes it more difficult for the parties to rely upon outsiders (arbitrators and judges) to revise the price. [Some footnotes omitted.]

* * *

INTERNATIONAL MINERALS & CHEMICAL CORP. v. LLANO, INC.

United States Court of Appeals, Tenth Circuit, 1985.
770 F.2d 879.

* * *

[International (IMC) agreed to purchase natural gas from Llano under a ten year contract, scheduled to terminate on June 30, 1982. IMC sought a declaratory judgment that it was excused from its obligation to "take and pay" for an agreed minimum quantity of natural gas during the last eighteen months of the contract, due to more stringent regulation by the New Mexico Environmental Improvement Board of particle emissions from existing combustion evaporators in IMC's plant. Under EIB Regulation 508, IMC was ultimately required to shut down the combustion evaporators, which had consumed approximately 60% of its natural gas requirements. Llano counterclaimed for $3,564,617.12, the amount that it claimed was due under the contract for gas for which IMC should have paid.

The trial court held: (1) UCC 2–615 was not applicable to buyers unless the contract was "conditioned on a definite and specific venture or assumption. * * *"; and (2) The "force majeure" and "adjustment of minimum bill" clauses in the contract, Paragraphs 15 and 16 set out below, did not excuse performance unless it became absolutely impossible or illegal to purchase the minimum amount of gas. On the facts, the trial court denied relief to IMC and concluded that IMC was liable for the contract price for gas it should have taken, even though Llano had been able to sell the gas elsewhere for a higher price.

IMC appealed and the court limited its consideration to whether IMC was excused under either UCC 2–615 or Paragraphs 15 and 16 of the contract.]

BARRETT, CIRCUIT JUDGE.

* * *

The pertinent portions of the contract are as follows:

Now, therefore, in consideration of the premises and of the mutual covenants and agreements hereinafter set forth, the parties do hereby bargain, contract and agree as follows:

1. *SUPPLY OF NATURAL GAS:* Subject to the terms and conditions of this Contract, Seller will sell and deliver to Buyer and Buyer will take, purchase and pay for the entire fuel requirements of Buyer's Plant, provided that Buyer may at its option procure and maintain a supply of standby fuel to be used only to such extent as may be necessary when the gas supply from Seller may be interrupted or curtailed, as hereinafter provided, and in such other amounts as may be necessary from time to time to test such standby facilities and fuel.

* * *

6. *DELIVERY REQUIREMENTS:* During the term of this Contract, unless Seller agrees in writing to the contrary, the minimum daily deliveries that Seller shall make to Buyer and Buyer shall take from Seller shall be 4800 million BTU's per day except as hereafter provided. The maximum daily deliveries that Seller shall be required to make to Buyer shall be 133% of the average daily requirements of Buyer's Plant for the preceding 365 days provided, however, Seller shall at no time be required to deliver in excess of 6400 million BTU's per day unless Seller agrees in writing to the contrary.

Buyer does not contemplate reducing its operations, but on the contrary contemplates the increase thereof from the present daily requirements. In order to meet unanticipated contingencies, it is agreed that in the event Buyer during the term of this Contract reduces its operation by closing a portion of its plant, it shall have the right upon six months notice in writing to reduce the minimum requirements to a figure equal to 70% of the stated minimum of 4800 million BTU's per day. In the event of such reduction in minimum requirements, Seller's price to Buyer then in effect under the terms hereof shall be increased by ½¢ per million BTU's, but not in excess of the highest price for a like quantity of gas then being paid by any potash company in the area.

7. *MINIMUM ANNUAL PURCHASE:* During the term of this Contract, commencing with the first year, Buyer agrees to take from Seller a volume of gas having a BTU content of not less than 355 times the minimum

daily deliveries specified in Section 6 hereof. Buyer agrees to pay Seller for such minimum volume of gas at the price set forth in Section 5 hereof provided that if Buyer fails during any calendar year to take such minimum volume of gas, then the deficiency between the volume actually taken and Buyer's minimum purchase obligation shall be paid at the price in effect during the calendar year in which such deficiency occurs.

Billing for any payment due by reason of a deficiency in Buyer's takings of gas hereunder during a particular calendar year shall be included on the bill rendered to Buyer for gas delivered to Buyer during the month of December in the calendar year in which such deficiency occurred and payment therefore shall be made in the manner provided for monthly bills in Section 11 hereof. Failure on the part of Seller to so bill Buyer for any such deficiency payment shall not constitute a waiver hereof by Seller.

* * *

15. *FORCE MAJEURE:* Either party shall be excused for delay or failure to perform its agreements and undertakings, in whole or in part, when and to the extent that such failure or delay is occasioned by fire, flood, wind, lightning, or other acts of the elements, explosion, act of God, act of the public enemy, or interference of civil and/or military authorities, mobs, labor difficulties, vandalism, sabotage, malicious mischief, usurpation of power, depletion of wells, freezing or accidents to wells, pipelines, permanent closing of Buyer's operations at its Eddy County mine and refinery, after not less than six (6) months notice thereof to Seller, or other casualty or cause beyond the reasonable control of the parties, respectively, which delays or prevents such performance in whole or in part, as the case may be; provided, however, that the party whose performance hereunder is so affected shall immediately notify the other party of all pertinent facts and take all reasonable steps promptly and diligently to prevent such causes if feasible to do so, or to minimize or eliminate the effect without delay. It is understood and agreed that settlement of strikes or other labor disputes shall be at the sole discretion of the party encountering the strike or dispute.

Nothing contained herein, however, shall be construed as preventing the Buyer from discontinuing the operation of the plant for such periods of time as may be required by Buyer to perform necessary overhaul operations on plant properties or to accomplish preventative maintenance operations on such plant properties, which the Buyer may determine as necessary to safeguard its investment in the plant.

16. *ADJUSTMENT OF MINIMUM BILL:* In the event that Seller is unable to deliver or Buyer is unable to receive gas as provided in this Contract for any reason beyond the reasonable control of the parties, or in the event of force majeure as provided in Section 15 hereof, an appropriate adjustment in the minimum purchase requirements specified in Section 7 shall be made.

(Pl.Exh. 3, Def.Exh. C8b).

The contract may be characterized as a requirements contract, with an important limitation: Pursuant to paragraph 6, the buyer (IMC) is obligated to take, at a minimum, a daily average of 4800 million BTU's of gas. Pursuant to paragraph 7, if the buyer does not take this minimum amount, the buyer is obligated to pay for the minimum amount of gas anyway. These provisions are known in the industry as "take or pay" provisions, the purpose of which is to compensate the seller for being ready at all times to deliver the maximum amount of gas to the buyer and to eliminate the risk that the seller would face in a pure requirements contract were the buyer's requirements to drop too low. *See, e.g., Utah International, Inc. v. Colorado—Ute Electric Association,* 425 F.Supp. 1093 (D.Colo.1976) ("take or pay" coal purchase contract); *Mobile Oil Corporation v. Tennessee Valley Authority,* 387 F.Supp. 498 (N.D.Ala.1974) ("take or pay" electricity contract). The harshness of the "take or pay" provisions in this contract are to some extent ameliorated by the "force majeure" provision of paragraph 15 and the "adjustment of minimum bill" provision of paragraph 16; paragraphs 15 and 16 are discussed below.

* * *

On a fundamental level, this case is one of contract construction. Our primary objective, as always, in the construction or interpretation of a contract is to ascertain the intention of the parties. *Schultz & Lindsay Construction Co. v. State,* 93 N.M. 534, 494 P.2d 612, 613 (1972); *Yankee Atomic Electric Company v. New Mexico and Arizona Land Company,* 632 F.2d 855, 858 (10th Cir.1980) (interpreting New Mexico law.) We assume that the parties intended a reasonable interpretation of the language. *Smith v. Tinley,* 100 N.M. 663, 674 P.2d 1123, 1125 (1984). Accordingly, the legal context in which the contract was made will be relevant. As mentioned above, paragraphs 15 and 16 ameliorate the harshness of the "take or pay" provisions in that either party's duty of performance may be excused upon the occurrence of certain contingencies. As we examine the language of paragraphs 15 and 16, an appropriate area to look for guidance is the common law doctrine of impossibility/impracticability, codified at Section 2–615 of New Mexico's Uniform Commercial Code (N.M.Stat.Ann. § 55–2–615 (1978)), which was the law in New Mexico at the time the parties contracted and which remains the law today. While it is a basic premise of both Section 2–615 and the Uniform Commercial Code in general that the parties may allocate risks and penalties between themselves in any manner they choose, N.M.Stat.Ann. §§ 55–1–102 and 55–2–615 (1978), the Code and the common law upon which it is based remain a significant backdrop.

We first consider the effect of paragraph 15, the "force majeure" provision, on IMC's duty of performance under the circumstances of this case. Specifically, Paragraph 15 provides that either party is excused from performance if failure or delay in performance is "occasioned" by such events as fire, flood, act of God, interference of civil and/or military authorities, etc. The party seeking to be excused from performance must provide the other party with immediate notice of all pertinent facts and take all reasonable steps to prevent the occurrence. It also appears that the seller is entitled to six months notice before the buyer can be excused. We agree with the trial court that paragraph 15 does not operate to excuse IMC, although our conclusion is based on a somewhat different rationale. First, IMC's notice to Llano was inadequate in that no reasons were given as to why gas consumption would be decreased. Adequate notice was required to trigger the protections of the provision. Second, even if we assume *arguendo* that Rule 508 prevented IMC from taking the gas, Rule 508 would still pose no obstacle to IMC's ability to pay. Since this is a "take or pay" contract, the buyer can perform in either of two ways. It can either (1) take the minimum purchase obligation of natural gas (and pay) or (2) pay the minimum bill. It is settled law that when a promisor can perform a contract in either of two alternative ways, the impracticability of one alternative does not excuse the promisor if performance by means of the other alternative is still practicable. *Ashland Oil And Refining Co. v. Cities Service Gas Co.,* 462 F.2d 204, 211 (10th Cir.1972); *Glidden Company v. Hellenic Lines, Limited,* 275 F.2d 253, 257 (2d Cir.1960); Restatement (Second) of Contracts § 261, comment f (1981). Paragraph 15 does not compel a different result; it would at most excuse IMC from its duty to "take," not from its duty to "pay."

Paragraph 16, the "minimum bill" provision, however, affords the buyer additional protection. It provides that, in the event the buyer is "*unable* to receive gas as provided in the Contract for any reason *beyond the reasonable control* of the parties * * *" (emphasis added), then "an appropriate adjustment in the minimum purchase requirements specified in Section [paragraph] 7 shall be made." Paragraph 7, in turn, provides for a minimum bill based on the difference between the buyer's minimum purchase obligation and the gas actually taken. It follows that an adjustment of the buyer's minimum purchase requirements made pursuant to paragraph 16 would have the effect of lowering the buyer's minimum bill under paragraph 7. Llano's contention that paragraph 16 provides for a reduction in IMC's minimum purchase obligation but not its minimum bill obligation (Appellee's Brief at 4) is thus quickly disposed of.

The determinative question, then, is: Did the promulgation of Rule 508 constitute an event beyond the reasonable control of IMC that rendered IMC "unable" to receive its minimum amount of gas under the contract?

A simplistic, literal interpretation of the word "unable" would, in our view, be inappropriate and lead to absurd results: IMC could never be "unable" to take Llano's gas; IMC could always take the gas and vent it into the air, even if its facilities were completely destroyed. The word "unable" appears here as a term in a contract, prepared by businessmen and attorneys; thus, it is appropriate to construe the term in light of the common law as it existed in New Mexico when the contract was entered into. For our purposes, then, "unable" is synonymous with "impracticable," as that term is used in the common law and in Section 2–615.

The term "impracticable" has, over the years, acquired a fairly specific meaning. Although earlier cases required that performance be physically impossible before the promisor would be excused, strict impossibility is no longer required. *See* Restatement of Contracts (Second) § 261, comment d (1981). The New Mexico Supreme Court has described the doctrine of impracticability as follows:

> Regarding the meaning of "impossibility" as used in the rules that excuse the non-performance of contracts, it is stated:
>
> "As pointed out in the Restatement of Contracts, the essence of the modern defense of impossibility is that the promised performance was at the making of the contract, or thereafter became, impracticable owing to some extreme or unreasonable difficulty, expense, injury, or loss involved, rather than that it is scientifically impossible. * * * The important question is whether an unanticipated circumstance has made performance of the promise vitally different from what should reasonably have been within the contemplation of both parties when they entered into the contract. If so, the risk should not fairly be thrown upon the promisor." *Wood v. Bartolino*, 48 N.M. 175, 146 P.2d 883, 886, (1944), *quoting* 6 Williston on Contracts, § 1931.

Cf. Gulf Oil Corporation v. Federal Power Commission, 563 F.2d 588, 599 (3d. Cir. 1977), *cert. denied* 434 U.S. 1062, 98 S.Ct. 1235, 55 L.Ed.2d 762 (1978) ("The crucial question in applying that doctrine to any given situation is whether the cost of performance has in fact become so excessive and unreasonable that the failure to excuse performance would result in grave injustice. * * * "); *Mineral Park Land Co. v. Howard,* 172 Cal. 289, 156 P. 458, 460 (1916) ("a thing is impracticable when it can only be done at an excessive and unreasonable cost").

Performance will be excused when made impracticable by having to comply with a supervening governmental regulation. N.M.Stat.Ann. § 55–2–615 (1978); Restatement of Contracts (Second) § 264 (1981). Thus, for example, in the case of *Kansas City, Missouri v. Kansas City, Kansas,* 393 F.Supp. 1 (W.D.Mo.1975), the court held that the defendant city's obligation to accept the plaintiff city's sewage was excused by the enactment of the Federal Water Pollution Control Act Amendments of 1972. The federal act imposed new requirements with regard to the treatment of sewage that was discharged into the Missouri River; the court found that the added expense of such treatment would impose a significant, unreasonable burden on the defendant. *Accord City of Vernon v. City of Los Angeles,* 45 Cal.2d 710, 290 P.2d 841 (1955).

Inasmuch as there was no technically suitable way for IMC to comply with the EIB's Regulation 508 without shutting down the Ozarks and changing to the SOP, with the concomitant decrease in natural gas consumption, we hold that the adjustment provision of paragraph 16 of the contract was triggered. IMC was unable, for reasons beyond its reasonable control, to receive its minimum purchase obligation of natural gas between January 1, 1981 and June 30, 1982; thus, the minimum bill should have been adjusted appropriately. IMC should not be required to pay for any natural gas it did not take under the contract.

Llano contends that there was no supervening legal impracticability in this case because IMC was not required to be in final compliance until December 31, 1984, and that IMC cooperated with the EIB and came into compliance too early. The argument here is that, notwithstanding the interim standards contained in the schedules of compliance, IMC should have stalled in its negotiations with the state regulatory agency, which would have resulted in the pollution of air until the last minute. We must reject this contention on two grounds: First, as a matter of policy, individuals and corporations who cooperate with local regulatory agencies and comply with the letter and spirit of legally proper regulations, environmental or otherwise, are to be encouraged. Stalling tactics are not regarded favorably. Second, as a matter of law, government policy need not be explicitly mandatory to cause impracticability. Thus, for example, in *Eastern Air Lines, Inc. v. McDonnell Douglas Corporation,* 532 F.2d 957 (5th Cir.1976), an aircraft manufacturer was excused from its contractual obligation to deliver commercial jet airliners on certain scheduled dates because it had voluntarily complied with government requests to expedite production of military equipment needed for the war in Vietnam. Similarly, in the maritime context, shipowners have been excused from contractual obligations because they have anticipated governmental intrusion. *The Kronprinzessin Cecilie,* 244 U.S. 12, 37 S.Ct. 490, 61 L.Ed. 960 (1917) (German ship was justified in returning to New York rather than completing a voyage to Great Britain and France on the eve of the outbreak of hostilities in World War I); *The Clavaresk,* 264 F. 276 (2d Cir.1920) (shipowner may anticipate and need not resist government requisition of his ship for wartime service in order to be excused from performance of a charter agreement). There is, we recognize, a limit to the extent to which an individual can seek refuge in the context of a case such as this by cooperating with the government: "any action by the party claiming excuse which causes or colludes in inducing the governmental action preventing his performance would be in breach of good faith and would destroy his exemption." Official Comment 10,

N.M.Stat.Ann. § 55–2–615 (1978). Here, Regulation 508 was promulgated by the EIB as part of New Mexico's State Implementation Plan mandated by the Clean Air Act. Regulation 508's existence and its enforcement mechanism is designed to eliminate pollution of the environment, thus serving the public health and welfare. IMC's recognition of the public benefit goal and its willingness to cooperate in eliminating pollution can hardly be termed improper collusion.

For the reasons described above, the judgment of the trial court in favor of Llano is reversed. The case is remanded with direction that the court enter a declaratory judgment in accordance with this opinion.

Problem 13–2

Softstuff, a coal producer, manufactures coke for steel production. Coke is made by subjecting coal to extreme heat in specially constructed ovens or batteries. Bitum is a steel maker. In May, 1978, the parties began to negotiate over a 10 year coke supply contract. It was agreed that Bitum was to take and pay for 20,000 tons of coke per month. This was, in effect, Softstuff's output from its coke batteries. In addition to agreements on quality, the parties agreed that Bitum was to pay a base price of $42 per ton, subject to escalation based upon externally compiled cost indices. These indices reflected the average costs incurred by coke producers rather than the actual costs of Softstuff's operation.

At the time of negotiation, the demand for coke was strong and the market price per ton was $41. The parties discussed the question of price stability over a ten year period. Softstuff "hoped" that strong demand would continue but Bitum was more pessimistic. Bitum proposed and Softstuff rejected a clause giving Bitum the option to terminate the contract at the end of any year wherein the market price of coke was 30% lower than the adjusted contract price for three or more months. There was no trade usage on price adjustment and the parties had not done business with each other before.

After further negotiations, the parties concluded a contract which, among other things, contained the following clause:

EXCUSE FOR BUYER

1. If because of Buyer's reduced blast furnace production, Buyer's requirements for coke cease or are reduced to a point where it is not practical for Buyer to purchase coke pursuant to this agreement, Buyer shall be released from its future obligations hereunder for the period of such cessation or reduction without any liability whatsoever upon Buyer giving Seller 90 days advance written notice.

2. Buyer's failure to comply or delay in compliance with the terms and conditions of this agreement shall be excused if due to any of the following which render performance commercially impracticable: act of God, fire, flood, strike, work stoppage, labor dispute, accident or mill interruption, complete or partial blast furnace relining, temporary failure of supply of iron ore, pellets or flux, any action by governmental authority, including ecological authorities, or any other cause beyond Buyer's reasonable control.

On January 15, 1979, Softstuff shipped and Bitum accepted and paid for the first 20,000 ton installment of coke at the base contract price. This pattern of performance continued under January 15, 1983, when Bitum notified Softstuff in writing that due to a "collapse in the market for coke and steel products" the contract is "hereby terminated in 90 days." At that time, the escalated contract price for coke was $50 per ton. The market price for comparable coke, however, had dropped to $25 per ton and the demand for Bitum's steel products had dropped 60% since the time of contracting. After an unsuccessful effort to negotiate a modification, Bitum reaffirmed that, after the 90 days period had expired, it would not accept any more coke under the contract.

In August, 1983, Softstuff sued Bitum for breach of contract. The sole question for you is whether Bitum is excused from performance under either paragraph of the EXCUSE FOR BUYER clause.

SECTION 3. ENFORCEABILITY OF AGREED ADJUSTMENTS

The parties to a dispute over contract performance frequently settle the matter by agreement. In one type of settlement, claims are adjusted, payments are made and the contract is discharged. These settlements are sometimes described as an accord and satisfaction. In another type of settlement, contract duties are adjusted in a bargain under which performance is to continue. These settlements are called contract modifications. In both, the enforceability of the settlement may be subsequently attacked on the grounds of fraud, lack of consideration or duress. You have encountered both types in the course on contracts.

In this Section we will focus upon agreed modifications made in response to changed circumstances. The key provision is UCC 2–209.

Problem 13–3

A. Suppose, in Problem 13–2 supra, that before Bitum attempted to terminate the contract under the Excuse clause, Bitum explained the changing market situation and its impact on Bitum to Softstuff and requested Softstuff to consider and to negotiate over a proposed modification of the contract. Bitum suggested that the contract be adjusted in either of two ways for the remaining six years: (1) Keep the pricing structure but permit Bitum to order "requirements;" or (2) Keep the quantity term but permit Bitum to pay the market price of coke at the time of delivery. Bitum argued that S had, at a minimum, a duty to negotiate in good faith over the proposed adjustment, citing UCC 2–209, 1–203, 2–103(1)(b), and Comments 6 & 7 to 2–615. Softstuff declined, contending that unless the contract required it (and it did not), there was no duty to negotiate PERIOD. S cited Missouri Public Serv. Co. v. Peabody Coal Co., 583 S.W.2d 721 (Mo.App.1979), cert. denied 444 U.S. 865, 100 S.Ct. 135, 62 L.Ed.2d 88 (1979), where the court concluded: "Where an enforceable, untainted contract exists, refusing modification of price and seeking specific performance of valid covenants does not constitute bad faith or breach of contract * * *."

How should B respond?

B. Suppose, after negotiations, Softstuff agreed to substitute "market price" for escalated price for the duration of the contract. Thereafter, Softstuff determined that market price would not cover its production costs and claimed that the modification was not enforceable, citing UCC 2–209(1). What result? See the next case.

ROTH STEEL PRODUCTS v. SHARON STEEL CORP.

United States Court of Appeals, Sixth Circuit, 1983.
705 F.2d 134.

[In November, 1972, Roth contracted to purchase 200 tons of "hot rolled" steel per month from Sharon through December, 1973. The price was $148 per ton. Sharon also "indicated" that it could sell "hot rolled" steel on an "open schedule" basis for $140 and discussed the "probability" that Sharon could sell 500 tons of "cold rolled" steel at prices varying with the type ordered. At that time, the steel industry was operating at 70% of capacity, steel prices were "highly competitive" and Sharon's quoted prices to Roth were "substantially lower" than Sharon's book price for steel. In early 1973, market conditions changed dramatically due to the development of an attractive export market and an increased domestic demand for steel. During 1973 and 1974, the steel industry operated at full capacity, steel prices rose and nearly every producer experienced substantial delays in filling orders. In March, 1973, Sharon notified all purchasers, including Roth, that it was discontinuing price concessions given in 1972. After negotiations, the parties agreed that Roth would pay the agreed price until June 30, 1973 and a price somewhere between the agreed price and Sharon's published prices for the balance of 1973. Roth was initially reluctant to agree to this modification, but ultimately agreed "primarily because they were unable to purchase sufficient steel elsewhere to meet their production requirements." Sharon was supplying one-third of Roth's requirements and all other possible suppliers were "operating at full capacity and * * * were fully booked." The parties proceeded under this modification during the balance of 1973, although Sharon experienced difficulties in filling orders on time. During 1974, the parties did business on an entirely different basis. Roth would order steel, Sharon would accept the order at the price "prevailing at the time of shipment." During 1974 and 1975, Sharon's deliveries were chronically late, thereby increasing the price to Roth in a rising market. Roth, however, acquiesced in this pattern because it believed Sharon's assurances that late deliveries resulted from shortages of raw materials and the need for equitable allocation among customers and because there was "no practical alternative source of supply." This acquiescence was jolted in May, 1974 when Roth learned that Sharon was allocating substantial quantities of rolled steel to a subsidiary for sale at premium prices. After several more months of desultory performance on both sides, Roth sued Sharon for breach of contract, with special emphasis upon the modified contract for 1973. Sharon raised several defenses, including impracticability and, in the alternative, the agreed modification. The district court, after a long trial, held, *inter alia,* that Sharon was not excused from the 1973 contract on the grounds of impracticability and that the modification was unenforceable. A judgment for $555,968.46 was entered for Roth.

On appeal, the court of appeals affirmed the district court's decision on the impracticability, modification and other issues, but remanded the case for factual findings on whether Roth gave Sharon timely notice of breach. On the impracticability defense under UCC 2–615(a), the court held that "Sharon's inability to perform was a result of its policy accepting far more orders than it was capable of fulfilling, rather than a result of the existing shortage of raw materials." In refusing to enforce the modification of the 1973 contract, the court had this to say.]

CELEBREZZE, SENIOR CIRCUIT JUDGE.

* * *

C. In March, 1973, Sharon notified its customers that it intended to charge the maximum permissible price for all of its products; accordingly, all price concessions, including those made to the plaintiffs, were to be rescinded effective April 1, 1973. On March 23, 1973, Guerin [Roth's vice pres.] indicated to Metzger [Sharon's sales manager] that the plaintiffs considered the proposed price increase to be a breach of the November, 1972 contract. In an effort to resolve the dispute, Guerin met with representatives of Sharon on March 28, 1973 and asked Sharon to postpone any price increases until June or July, 1973. Several days later, Richard Mecaskey, Guerin's replacement, sent a letter to

Sharon which indicated that the plaintiffs believed that the November, 1972 agreement was enforceable and that the plaintiffs were willing to negotiate a price modification if Sharon's cost increases warranted such an action. As a result of this letter, another meeting was held between Sharon and the plaintiffs. At this meeting, Walter Gregg, Sharon's vice-president and chairman of the board, agreed to continue charging the November, 1972 prices until June 30, 1973 and offered, for the remainder of 1973, to charge prices that were lower than Sharon's published prices but higher than the 1972 prices. Although the plaintiffs initially rejected the terms offered by Sharon for the second half of 1973, Mecaskey reluctantly agreed to Sharon's terms on June 29, 1973.

Before the district court, Sharon asserted that it properly increased prices because the parties had modified the November, 1973 contract to reflect changed market conditions. The district court, however, made several findings which, it believed, indicated that Sharon did not seek a modification to avoid a loss on the contract. The district court also found that the plaintiffs' inventories of rolled steel were "alarmingly deficient" at the time modification was sought and that Sharon had threatened to cease selling steel to the plaintiffs in the second-half of 1973 unless the plaintiffs agreed to the modification. Because Sharon had used its position as the plaintiffs' chief supplier to extract the price modification, the district court concluded that Sharon had acted in bad faith by seeking to modify the contract. In the alternative, the court concluded that the modification agreement was voidable because it was extracted by means of economic duress; the tight steel market prevented the plaintiffs from obtaining steel elsewhere at an affordable price and, consequently, the plaintiffs were forced to agree to the modification in order to assure a continued supply of steel. See e.g. Oskey Gasoline & Oil Co. v. Continental Oil Co., 534 F.2d 1281 (8th Cir.1976). Sharon challenges these conclusions on appeal.

The ability of a party to modify a contract which is subject to Article Two of the Uniform Commercial Code is broader than common law, primarily because the modification needs no consideration to be binding. ORC § 1302.12 (UCC § 2–209(1)). A party's ability to modify an agreement is limited only by Article Two's general obligation of good faith. * * * In determining whether a particular modification was obtained in good faith, a court must make two distinct inquiries: whether the party's conduct is consistent with "reasonable commercial standards of fair dealing in the trade," * * * and whether the parties were in fact motivated to seek modification by an honest desire to compensate for commercial exigencies; * * * ORC § 1302.01(2) (UCC § 2–103). The first inquiry is relatively straightforward; the party asserting the modification must demonstrate that his decision to seek modification was the result of a factor, such as increased costs, which would cause an ordinary merchant to seek a modification of the contract. See Official Comment 2, ORC § 1302.12 (UCC § 2–209) (reasonable commercial standards may require objective reason); J. White & R. Summers, Handbook of Law under the UCC at 41. The second inquiry, regarding the subjective honesty of the parties, is less clearly defined. Essentially, this inquiry requires the party asserting the modification to demonstrate that he was, in fact, motivated by a legitimate commercial reason and that such a reason is not offered merely as a pretext. * * * Moreover, the trier of fact must determine whether the means used to obtain the modification are an impermissible attempt to obtain a modification by extortion or overreaching. * * *

Sharon argues that its decision to seek a modification was consistent with reasonable commercial standards of fair dealing because market exigencies made further performance entail a substantial loss. The district court, however, made three findings which caused it to conclude that economic circumstances were not the reason that Sharon sought a modification: it found that Sharon was partially insulated from raw material price increases, that Sharon bargained for a contract with a slim profit margin and thus implicitly assumed the risk that performance might come to involve a loss, and that Sharon's overall profit in 1973 and its profit on the contract in the first quarter of 1973 were inconsistent with Sharon's position that the modification was sought to avoid a loss. Although all of these findings are marginally related to the question whether Sharon's conduct was consistent with reasonable commercial standards of fair dealing, we do not believe that they are sufficient to support a finding that Sharon did not observe reasonable commercial standards by seeking a modification. In our view, these findings do not support a conclusion that a reasonable merchant, in light of the circumstances, would not have sought a modification in order to avoid a loss. For example, the district court's finding that Sharon's steel slab contract [26] insulated it from industry wide cost increases is correct, so far as it goes. Although Sharon was able to purchase steel slabs at pre-1973 prices, the district court's findings also indicate that it was not able to purchase, at those prices, a sufficient tonnage of steel slabs to meet its production requirements.[27] The district court also found that Sharon experienced substantial cost increases for other raw materials, ranging from 4% to nearly 20%. In light of these facts, the finding regarding the fixed-price contract for slab steel, without more, cannot support an inference that Sharon was unaffected by the market shifts that occurred in 1973. Similarly, the district court's finding that Sharon entered a contract in November, 1972 which would yield only a slim profit does not support a conclusion that Sharon was willing to risk a loss on the contract. Absent a finding that the market shifts and the raw material price increases were foreseeable at the time the contract was formed—a finding which was not made—Sharon's willingness to absorb a loss cannot be inferred from the fact that it contracted for a smaller profit than usual. Finally, the findings regarding Sharon's profits are not sufficient, by themselves, to warrant a conclusion that Sharon was not justified in seeking a modification. Clearly, Sharon's initial profit on the contract [28] is an important consideration; the district court's findings indicate, however, that at the time modification was

26. Sharon was a party to a contract with United States Steel which allowed it to make monthly purchases of slab steel ranging from a minimum of 25,000 tons per month to a maximum of 45,000 tons per month. It was also a party to a contract with Wierton Steel which allowed it to purchase slab steel in amounts varying between 10,000 to 20,000 tons per month. Both of these contracts were entered prior to 1973, at a very attractive price. When the market strengthened in 1973, however, Sharon was unable to obtain the maximum monthly tonnages permitted under these contracts; U.S. Steel delivered only 30,000 tons per month and Wierton 10,000 tons per month.

27. The district court found that Sharon suffered a continuing shortage of slab steel. It found that in 1972 (when Sharon was operating at substantially less than full capacity) it received 602,277 tons of slab steel; that in 1973, it received 506,596 tons of slab steel; and that in 1974 it received 373,898 tons. Thus, the record is clear that Sharon was in a difficult position. As demand for steel increased, and as Sharon's mills began to work at a higher capacity, its supply of slab steel steadily diminished.

28. The district court noted that in the first three months of 1973, Sharon made $3,089.00 on sales to Roth and lost $263.00 on steel sold to Toledo. Although Sharon lost significant sums of money on its contract with the plaintiffs, Sharon enjoyed overall profits in 1973, with net earnings of $11,566,000 on net sales of $338,205,000.

sought substantial future losses were foreseeable.[29] A party who has not actually suffered a loss on the contract may still seek a modification if a future loss on the agreement was reasonably foreseeable. Similarly, the overall profit earned by the party seeking modification is an important factor; this finding, however, does not support a conclusion that the decision to seek a modification was unwarranted. The more relevant inquiry is into the profit obtained through sales of the product line in question. This conclusion is reinforced by the fact that only a few product lines may be affected by market exigencies;[30] the opportunity to seek modification of a contract for the sale of goods of a product line should not be limited solely because some other product line produced a substantial profit.

In the final analysis, the single most important consideration in determining whether the decision to seek a modification is justified in this context is whether, because of changes in the market or other unforeseeable conditions, performance of the contract has come to involve a loss. In this case, the district court found that Sharon suffered substantial losses by performing the contract *as modified*. See note 29, supra. We are convinced that unforeseen economic exigencies existed which would prompt an ordinary merchant to seek a modification to avoid a loss on the contract; thus, we believe that the district court's findings to the contrary are clearly erroneous. * * *

The second part of the analysis, honesty in fact, is pivotal. The district court found that Sharon "threatened not to sell Roth and Toledo any steel if they refused to pay increased prices after July 1, 1973" and, consequently, that Sharon acted wrongfully. Sharon does not dispute the finding that it threatened to stop selling steel to the plaintiffs. Instead, it asserts that such a finding is merely evidence of bad faith and that it has rebutted any inference of bad faith based on that finding. We agree with this analysis; although coercive conduct is evidence that a modification of a contract is sought in bad faith, that prima facie showing may be effectively rebutted by the party seeking to enforce the modification. * * * Although we agree with Sharon's statement of principles, we do not agree that Sharon has rebutted the inference of bad faith that rises from its coercive conduct. Sharon asserts that its decision to unilaterally raise prices was based on language in the November 17, 1972 letter which allowed it to raise prices to the extent of any general industry-wide price increase. Because prices in the steel industry had increased, Sharon concludes that it was justified in raising its prices. Because it was justified in raising the contract price, the plaintiffs were bound by the terms of the contract to pay the increased prices. Consequently, any refusal by the plaintiffs to pay the price increase sought by Sharon must be viewed as a material breach of the November, 1972 contract which would excuse Sharon from any further performance. Thus, Sharon reasons that its refusal to perform absent a price increase was justified under the contract and consistent with good faith.

This argument fails in two respects. First, the contractual language on which Sharon relies only permits, at most, a price increase for cold rolled steel; thus, even if Sharon's position were supported by the evidence, Sharon would not

29. The evidence indicates, and the district court found, that with the exception of hot rolled sheets Sharon absorbed a loss on every rolled steel product which it sold to the defendants in 1973, even though the modified prices were in effect during the third and the fourth quarters.

30. Apparently, Sharon's record overall profit was the result of other operations. It obtained a pre-tax profit of less than one percent on its total sales of rolled steel.

have been justified in refusing to sell the plaintiff's hot rolled steel because of the plaintiffs' refusal to pay higher prices for the product. More importantly, however, the evidence does not indicate that Sharon ever offered this theory as a justification until this matter was tried. Sharon's representatives, in their testimony, did not attempt to justify Sharon's refusal to ship steel at 1972 prices in this fashion. Furthermore, none of the contemporaneous communications contain this justification for Sharon's action. In short, we can find no evidence in the record which indicates that Sharon offered this theory as a justification at the time the modification was sought. Consequently, we believe that the district court's conclusion that Sharon acted in bad faith by using coercive conduct to extract the price modification is not clearly erroneous. Therefore, we hold that Sharon's attempt to modify the November, 1972 contract, in order to compensate for increased costs which made performance come to involve a loss, is ineffective because Sharon did not act in a manner consistent with Article Two's requirement of honesty in fact when it refused to perform its remaining obligations under the contract at 1972 prices.[31]

* * *

Notes

1. Section 89 of the Restatement, Second, of Contracts provides: "A promise modifying a duty under a contract not fully performed on either side is binding (a) if the modification is fair and equitable in view of circumstances not anticipated by the parties when the contract was made; or (b) to the extent provided by statute; or (c) to the extent that justice requires enforcement in view of material change of position in reliance on the promise." Is Roth consistent with the Restatement?

2. Following the logic of UCC 2–209(1) and the comments, Roth invalidated the modification because of Sharon's bad faith rather than because of economic duress. In fact, the court, in note 31, suggested that proof of coercive means will not necessarily invalidate a modification made in good faith. Exactly what is bad faith in the Sixth Circuit?

3. Economic duress may be invoked to invalidate a modification where one party has made a "wrongful" threat to withhold delivery of needed goods, the threatened party can not obtain substitute goods from another source and the ordinary remedy of an action for breach of contract is not adequate. See Austin Instrument, Inc. v. Loral Corp., 29 N.Y.2d 124, 324 N.Y.S.2d 22, 272 N.E.2d 533 (1971). Professor Hillman, for one, favors this approach. See Hillman, *Contract Modification Under the Restatement (Second) of Contracts,* 67 Cornell L.Rev. 680 (1982). Could the modification in Roth be invalidated for economic duress?

Note: Modifications and the Statute of Frauds

Assume that S and B enter an oral contract to sell 10 units of goods for $400. The statute of frauds does not apply because the price is less than $500. UCC 2–201(1). Suppose that the parties, before any performance has occurred, modify the

31. The district court also found, as an alternative ground, that the modification was voidable because the plaintiffs agreed to the modification due to economic duress. See, e.g., Oskey Gasoline & Oil Co. v. Continental Oil, 534 F.2d 1281 (8th Cir.1976). Because we conclude that the modification was ineffective as a result of Sharon's bad faith, we do not reach the issue whether the contract modification was also voidable because of economic duress. We note, however, that proof that coercive means were used is necessary to establish that a contract is voidable because of economic duress. Normally, it cannot be used to void a contract modification which has been sought in good faith; if a contract modification has been found to be in good faith, then presumably no wrongful coercive means have been used to extract the modification.

contract by adding 10 more units of goods for $400. This agreement modifying the contract is clearly enforceable under UCC 2–209(1). But now UCC 2–209(3) comes into play: "The requirements of the statute of frauds * * * (Section 2–201) must be satisfied if the contract as modified is within its provisions." Without question, the "contract as modified" is within UCC 2–201(1), even though neither the original contract nor the modification were for a price of "$500 or more." Thus, it would appear that the modification must meet the requirement of a writing in UCC 2–201(1) or satisfy the exceptions listed in UCC 2–201(3). In addition, the modification should be in writing if it falls within UCC 2–201(1) on its own or if it changes the quantity term of an original contract that fell within UCC 2–201. A literal reading of this somewhat murky provision does not, however, support the conclusion that if the original contract was within UCC 2–201, any modification must also be in writing. See White & Summers 44–45.

The murkiness is not abated as one reads further. UCC 2–209(4) provides: "Although an attempt at modification or rescission does not satisfy the requirements of subsection * * * (3) it can operate as a waiver." A waiver of what, the requirement of UCC 2–201(1) itself? Not likely. And what "operates" as a waiver? Article 2 does not say.

At common law, the concept of waiver was frequently invoked to excuse conditions precedent to a contractual duty to perform. Suppose, for example, that the contract provided that before the buyer had a duty to pay for goods delivered, they must be inspected and certified by a designated third party. In theory, the buyer has no duty to pay until the condition is satisfied. But if, with knowledge that no certificate had been issued, the buyer elected to accept and pay for the goods, the condition was waived. This was waiver by "election." Similarly, if B, before delivery, represented to S that the certificate would not be required and B relied upon that representation, the condition would be excused. This was waiver by estoppel. The former waived conditions which had already failed and the latter waived conditions which had not. See Restatement, Contracts (Second) 84. Although both types of waiver modified or discharged conditions in the contract, they did not affect the right of the waiving party to damages for defective performance:

Only a modification supported by consideration or other valid reasons for enforcement could do that. See National Utility Service, Inc. v. Whirlpool Corp., 325 F.2d 779 (2d Cir.1963).

With this sketchy background, look again at UCC 2–209(2), (4), and (5) and resolve the following problem. (Taken from Wisconsin Knife Works v. National Metal Crafters, 781 F.2d 1280 (7th Cir.1986)).

Problem 13–4

After negotiations, B mailed to S a written order for the purchase of 281,000 "spade bit blanks," for use in the manufacture of spade bits. The goods were to be delivered in installments by the dates stipulated in the purchase order. In addition, the purchase order contained, inter alia, the following "condition" of purchase: "No modification of this contract shall be binding upon Buyer unless made in writing and signed by Buyer's authorized representative. Buyer shall have the right to make changes in the Order by a notice, in writing, to seller." Seller accepted the purchase order in a written acknowledgment and commenced to manufacture the bits.

S was consistently late in tendering delivery. B, however, accepted the late deliveries without declaring a breach or invoking the written modification condition. After accepting 144,000 blanks, however, B, invoking the delivery schedule in the purchase order, cancelled the contract for breach and sued S for damages. (There was some evidence that B cancelled because of a dispute with a sub-purchaser of the completed spade bit rather than S's delays.)

You are clerk to the trial judge. She asks you for a memo on the following questions:

(1) Was the "no modification" condition in the purchase order enforceable against Seller, see UCC 2–209(2);

(2) If so, did B's conduct of accepting S's late deliveries "operate as a waiver" of either the contract delivery schedule or the "no modification" condition, see UCC 2–209(4);

(3) If the conduct did operate as a waiver, how is UCC 2–209(5) relevant to the dispute?

Note: Arbitration of Disputes Arising Under Long-Term Supply Contracts

Arbitration is an informal method of dispute resolution which occurs, in most cases, outside of the judicial process. It depends upon an enforceable agreement between the parties to submit existing or future disputes to arbitration.

The scope of the arbitrator's power to decide is determined by that agreement: It may include "all" disputes between the parties of any kind whatever or be limited to particular disputes, such as the failure to agree upon an adjustment or the excusability of one or both parties due to commercial impracticability.

Arbitration clauses are frequently found in long-term supply contracts, where the incentive of the parties to preserve the relationship while disputes over performance are being resolved is high. Whether an arbitration clause is part of the agreement, however, is frequently disputed in litigation involving the "battle of the forms." See Chapter Ten, Section 3, supra.

Assume that the contract includes a "reopener" clause, which envisions three steps: (1) If changed circumstances not foreseeable as likely to occur substantially affect performance, either party may request the other to agree to an adjustment in the contract; (2) The parties shall negotiate over the requested adjustment in good faith; (3) If the parties fail to agree, the dispute shall be submitted to arbitration where the arbitrator shall determine whether changed circumstances justifying the requested adjustment existed and, if so, what the adjustment should be.

Suppose that the buyer invoked the clause and, after negotiations with the seller, no agreed modification was reached. The buyer then filed a demand for arbitration and the seller refused. In fact, when the buyer refused to pay for goods under the contract until the dispute was resolved, the seller cancelled and sued for breach of contract in a *state court.* What should the buyer do?

In this all too familiar situation, the steps are likely to look like this.

1. The buyer must determine whether state or federal law governs the dispute over arbitration. The issue is less important on matters of substance, i.e. the enforceability of agreements to arbitrate future disputes, since most commercial states have modern, comprehensive arbitration statutes, such as the Uniform Arbitration Act. Uniform Arbitration Act §§ 1–25 (1955) 7 U.L.A. 4 (1978). But the question is crucial in deciding where to sue to compel arbitration and determining what procedures will govern. Let us assume that the dispute is subject to the United States Arbitration Act, 9 U.S.C.A. §§ 1–14 (1982), and that any litigation will be commenced in the United States District Court and be subject to the Federal Rules of Civil Procedure.

2. The buyer should sue in the federal district court to stay the seller's suit for breach of contract and to compel arbitration under the contract. This is the critical early point in the arbitration, for the court must decide such questions as whether the arbitration clause is enforceable and, if so, whether the parties have agreed to

arbitrate the dispute in question. If the answer to either question is no, then the suit to stay and compel is dismissed. If the answer to both questions is yes, then the federal court will issue a preemptive order to the state court to stay the law suit and issue an order to the seller to commence arbitration. The order to compel arbitration is, in effect, a decree of specific performance. See, e.g., Sharon Steel Corporation v. Jewell Coal & Coke Co., 735 F.2d 775 (3d Cir.1984).

3. If the parties have been ordered to arbitrate, the next steps are to select the arbitrators, schedule hearings on the issues to be resolved and conduct the arbitration. Frequently, the American Association of Arbitration (the AAA) will provide material assistance in this process through furnishing lists of potential arbitrators, providing rules and procedures to be followed during the arbitration and facilitating the process from beginning to end. See G. Goldberg, A Lawyer's Guide to Commercial Arbitration, 35–59 (2d ed. 1983).

4. Under American law, an arbitrator's decision on questions of fact and law is binding on the parties, unless judicial review is sought and one of the narrow grounds for overturning an award is satisfied. These grounds go to the honesty of the arbitrators and the integrity of the process rather than to the merits of the dispute. Thus, if the parties agree to arbitrate a clearly defined dispute subject to the rules and procedures of the AAA and one party, thereafter, refuses to arbitrate, the courts will compel arbitration, subject to limited attacks at the threshold upon the arbitrability of the dispute and, thereafter, confirm and enforce the award, subject to attacks upon the honesty of the arbitrators and the integrity of the process.

A standard reference is M. Domke, Domke on Commercial Arbitration (rev. ed by Wilner, 1984).

PART THREE

THE POST-AGREEMENT—PRE-SHIPMENT STAGE

CHAPTER FOURTEEN

BUYER'S BREACH—A SURVEY OF SELLER'S REMEDIES

SECTION ONE. A GENERAL INTRODUCTION TO CODE REMEDIES

Before the time for the seller's performance has arrived, the buyer might repudiate, commit a "total" breach of an installment contract, fail to make an advance payment when due, or the like. In such circumstances, the seller will want to know (1) whether his own performance is excused and (2) to what remedies he may resort.

In Chapter Fourteen, after a preliminary consideration of the nature and significance of the buyer's wrongful conduct, we will survey the various remedies open to the seller. In Chapter Fifteen, we will reverse the position of the parties, and consider the various remedies open to the buyer when the seller repudiates or commits a total breach of an installment contract. These two chapters have been structured to afford the student maximum opportunity to compare seller's remedies and buyer's remedies in comparable situations. Article 2 invites this kind of analysis, for it grants seller and buyer alike a wide range of parallel remedies. Thus, the seller's action for the price (UCC 2–709) is parallel to the buyer's action for specific performance (UCC 2–716). So, too: the respective rights of seller and buyer to damages based on contract-market price differentials (UCC 2–708 and 2–713) and the respective rights of seller and buyer to enter into substitute transactions and measure their losses accordingly (UCC 2–706 and 2–712). A comprehensive analysis appears in Sebert, *Remedies Under Article Two of the Uniform Commercial Code: An Agenda for Review,* 130 U.Pa. L.Rev. 360 (1981). The seminal article is Peters, *Remedies for Breach of Contracts Relating to the Sale of Goods Under the U.C.C.: A Roadmap for Article Two,* 73 Yale L.J. 199 (1963).

Before going further, we should note and respond to the budding heresy (believed by White) that contract and sales remedies are without practical significance. See, generally, White, *Contract Law in Modern Commercial Transactions, An Artifact of Twentieth Century Business Life?,* 22 Washburn L.J. 1 (1982). According to White, the student who knew of the infrequency of suit (businessmen want to preserve relations), the modesty of sums recovered (*Hadley v. Baxendale* and all that) and the increasing resort to alternative forms of dispute resolution (arbitration) might be tempted to include contract and sales remedies among those things one has to study to get through law school but which have little relevance thereafter. In support of this thesis, the studies of

Professor Stewart Macaulay might be cited, e.g., *Non-Contractual Relations in Business: A Preliminary Study,* 28 Am.Sociol.Rev. 55 (1963), which suggest that commercial parties themselves iron out most contract and sales disputes on their own on the basis of common sense and economics.

Even so, Speidel and Summers believe that it hardly follows that the student can ignore the remedial side of the coin. In the first place, not all contract recoveries are inconsequential or piddling. If the contract is a large one which has a long term, even a modest contract-market differential can produce a whopping sum of money. Moreover, a modest relaxation of *Hadley v. Baxendale* and a willingness of the courts to compensate sellers for lost profits and lost volumes could cause an important change in the picture.

More important, however, is the fact that the impact of contract remedy doctrine cannot properly be measured by the frequency of litigation. For surely, the predicted damage and specific performance awards that courts would grant play an important role in the negotiation of every contract dispute which is handled by lawyers. In such cases we bargain at least in part on the basis of the lawyer's judgment about what damages will be awarded at trial. Thus both the lawyer who is going to negotiate a settlement on behalf of an aggrieved client and the lawyer who is going to advise his client how best to extricate himself from a situation in which he or the opposing party has broken a contract need to know the variety of available remedies and the merits and demerits of each.

SECTION 2. IMPAIRING SELLER'S EXPECTATION OF FULL PERFORMANCE: PROSPECTIVE INABILITY; REPUDIATION, AND INSTALLMENT CONTRACTS

A. *Insolvency and Prospective Inability—UCC 2–609*

UCC 2–609(1) provides that a contract for sale "imposes an obligation on each party that the other's expectation of receiving due performance will not be impaired." This obligation is breached when one party gives the other "reasonable grounds for insecurity" with regard to the promised performance. At this point, the aggrieved party "may in writing demand adequate assurance of due performance and until he receives such assurance may if commercially reasonable suspend any performance for which he has not already received the agreed return." Comment 2 to UCC 2–609 stresses that the right to suspend performance includes "any preparation therefor." If the other party, upon receipt of a "justified" demand, fails "to provide within a reasonable time not exceeding thirty days such assurance of due performance as is adequate under the circumstances of the particular case," he has repudiated the contract and the aggrieved party may take appropriate remedial action, including cancellation. Between merchants, the reasonableness of grounds for insecurity and adequacy of any assurance offered "shall be determined according to commercial standards." UCC 2–609(2). Thus, an aggrieved party may suspend his performance even though the other party's conduct is short of breach or repudiation but the aggrieved party cannot cancel the contract until the mandatory communication procedure fails to produce "adequate assurance." In this process, a high incidence of consensual adjustment and continued performance is likely, particularly when the generality of the standards in UCC 2–609 is taken into account. On the other hand, if adjustment does not occur and one party has suspended his performance or cancelled the contract, the other may claim that such action was not justified. Within this framework, courts and lawyers will have to give some content to the phrases "reasonable grounds for insecurity" and "adequate assurance of due performance." For good background discussion, see Wardrop, *Prospective Inability in the Law of Contracts,* 20 Minn.L.Rev. 380 (1936); 6 Corbin, Contracts §§ 1259–1261 (1962); Note, *A Right to Adequate Assurance of Performance in All Transactions; UCC 2–609 Beyond Sales of Goods,* 48 S.Cal.L. Rev. 1358 (1975).

Suppose that under a written contract for the sale of goods the seller is to deliver in a single lot on March 1 and the buyer is to pay the full contract price on April 1. The buyer's basic obligation here is to accept and pay for the goods in accordance with the contract, UCC 2–301, and it is in this regard that grounds for insecurity may arise. Except insofar as the seller has rights under UCC 2–702(2), however, once the buyer has accepted the seller's tender of delivery, the seller can reduce any insecurity he feels about subsequent payment of the price only by exercising rights he may have under an Article 9 security interest—rights he may not have. As a practical matter, UCC 2–609 itself affords little protection to a seller who has fully performed his obligation before the alleged ground for insecurity arises.

Before delivery, however, UCC 2–609 is available and in some cases this availability is spelled out with precision for both seller and buyer alike. See UCC 2–210(5) and UCC 2–611(2). From the seller's point of view, two situations are described which justify protective action. When, in an installment contract, the buyer's default in past due payments is not sufficient to justify a cancellation, the seller may withhold delivery of goods then due until payment for past deliveries is received. UCC 2–612(3), Comment 7. When the seller, in a credit transaction, discovers the buyer to be insolvent (as defined in UCC 1–201(23)), he may "refuse delivery except for cash including payment for all goods theretofore delivered under the contract, and stop delivery" under UCC 2–705. This latter remedy finds firm support in §§ 53(1)(a) and 54(1) of the Uniform Sales Act and in prior case law. See, e.g., Leopold v. Rock-Ola Corporation, 109 F.2d 611 (5th Cir.1940). However, it has been held that insolvency alone does not justify cancellation of the contract. Koppelon v. Ritter Flooring Corp., 97 N.J.L. 200, 116 A. 491 (1922).

Short of the situations noted above, exactly what constitutes either reasonable grounds for insecurity or adequate assurance of due performance is less clear. Resolve the following problem, giving careful attention to the comments to UCC 2–609.

Problem 14–1

S agreed to manufacture special equipment for B. Delivery was to be in installments, with payment for each installment within 15 days of delivery. S commenced performance but, before any deliveries were made, S began to hear unfavorable comments about B's credit. After a quick check, the following facts emerged: (1) Dun & Bradstreet had recently reduced B's credit rating; (2) B's working capital was fully stretched out and some suppliers were experiencing delays in payment; (3) B had recently changed banks, and the "word" was out that B's financial condition was "extended" and that care should be exercised before extending credit; and (4) B's overall financial condition had worsened since the date of the contract.

A. You represent S. On the day before the first delivery was due, S called you for a conference. With the credit information on the table, S stated that unless you could persuade him otherwise, he would refuse to deliver the goods unless B paid cash. What would you recommend? See UCC 1–201(23), 2–702(1), 2–609.

B. Assume that you persuade S to exercise caution and talk to B before taking action. S, therefore, gives B a written demand for "adequate assurance" and temporarily suspends the first delivery. UCC 2–609(1). B, in response, establishes solvency and claims that the current situation is "temporary." B, however, states that long-term viability depends upon getting prompt delivery of the equipment, which is needed in the business, on credit. If there are delays, no assurances can be given.

Does this constitute "adequate assurance" of due performance? What else could S reasonably demand? On this last point, consider the following opinion by Cummings, Circuit Judge, concurring in Pittsburgh-Des Moines Co. v. Brookhaven Manor Water Co., 532 F.2d 572, 583–84 (7th Cir.1976):

"Although I agree with the result reached in the majority opinion, I differ with the reasoning. Reasonable men could certainly conclude that PDM had legitimate grounds to question Brookhaven's ability to pay for the water tank. When the contract was signed, the parties understood that Brookhaven would obtain a loan to help pay for the project. When the loan failed to materialize, a prudent businessman would have 'reasonable grounds for insecurity.' I disagree that there must be a fundamental change in the financial position of the buyer before the seller can invoke the protection of UCC § 2–609. Rather, I believe that the Section was designed to cover instances where an underlying condition of the contract, even if not expressly incorporated into the written document, fails to occur. See Comment 3 to UCC § 2–609. Whether, in a specific case, the breach of the condition gives a party 'reasonable grounds for insecurity' is a question of fact for the jury.

"UCC § 2–609, however, does not give the alarmed party a right to redraft the contract. Whether the party invoking that provision is merely requesting an assurance that performance will be forthcoming or whether he is attempting to alter the contract is a mixed question of law and fact, depending in part upon the court's interpretation of the obligations imposed on the parties. In this case, PDM would have been assured only if significant changes in the contract were made, either by receiving Betke's personal guarantee, by attaining escrow financing or by purchasing an interest in Brookhaven. The district court could probably conclude as a matter of law that these requests by PDM demanded more than a commercially 'adequate assurance of due performance.' "

Note: Scope of Seller's Reclamation Rights

The Code protects a credit seller against specified events within the control of the buyer that occur before delivery. If the buyer commits a breach of contract, the seller may, at a minimum, withhold delivery of the goods involved, UCC 2–703(a), or, in a proper case, stop delivery by a carrier or other bailee to the buyer, UCC 2–705(1). If the buyer becomes insolvent, the seller may "refuse delivery except for cash" under UCC 2–702(1) or "stop delivery" under UCC 2–705(1). Where the buyer gives reasonable grounds for insecurity short of a breach or insolvency, the seller may, if commercially reasonable, "suspend any performance for which he has not already received the agreed return." UCC 2–609(2). The first two cases, at least, illustrate what the common law called a seller's possessory lien and what the Code calls a possessory security interest arising under Article 2. See UCC 1–201(37) & 9–113. So long as the seller retains actual or constructive possession of the goods after default by the credit buyer, it can enforce the security interest in the goods under Article 2, free from, or with priority over, the claims of the buyer's other creditors.

If the goods have been delivered to the buyer, however, the matter becomes more complicated. For now, note the following principles, to which we will return in Chapter 22, Section 4(c).

(1) If the seller retains "title" until payment, the effect is to create a non-possessory security interest, which is within the scope of Article 9. See UCC 1–201(37), 2–401(1), & UCC 9–102(1). Although the security interest is enforceable against the buyer, i.e., the seller could repossess the goods from the buyer, see UCC 9–203(1), 9–501(1) & 9–503, it will be subject to the claims of lien and secured creditors of the buyer unless "perfected" by filing a financing statement and otherwise entitled to priority. See UCC 9–201, 9–301(1), 9–302(1) & 9–312(5).

(2) If the seller does not retain title but the buyer was insolvent at the time of delivery, the seller has a limited claim to reclamation under UCC 2–702(2) & (3). Note that even if all the conditions of subsection (2) are met, the rights of a "buyer in ordinary course or other good faith purchaser" may have intervened.

(3) If the seller did not retain title and the buyer was not insolvent at the time of delivery, the seller has no interest in or claim to the goods upon default by the buyer. The seller has, in effect, only an unsecured claim for the price. UCC 2–709(1).

Problem 14–2

Suppose, in Problem 14–1, above, that on July 1, S shipped a carload of equipment to B by public carrier "FOB the place of shipment." (For what this means, see UCC 2–319(1)(a), 2–503(2) & 2–504). The carrier issued a non-negotiable bill of lading, naming B as "consignee," i.e., the person entitled to the goods under the document. On July 2, while the goods were still in transit, B resold the goods for cash to C, a good faith purchaser for value. On July 3, before receipt of the goods by B, S learned from reliable sources that B was insolvent. The goods were scheduled to arrive by 10 PM on July 3, but could not be picked up until July 5.

A. Can S on July 3 stop delivery of the goods under UCC 2–705?

B. If S can stop delivery against B, under what circumstances, if any, will C, a good faith purchaser for value, nevertheless take free of S's security interest in the goods? See UCC 2–401, 2–403 & 9–307. Is it clear that if S properly stops delivery under UCC 2–705 as against B and before C obtains possession of the goods, C will take subject to S's security interest?

B. Buyer's Repudiation

In the first year course in contracts, considerable attention is usually given to the cognate problems of determining whether a contracting party has repudiated or materially broken an installment contract. Accordingly, our treatment here will be an abbreviated one, emphasizing the relevant Code provisions and the role of the lawyer called upon to advise the seller on what to do in the face of the buyer's conduct. The consequences of an erroneous decision by the lawyer can be catastrophic. The seller's lawyer may advise that the buyer has repudiated or materially broken an installment contract, and that seller is free to cease his own performance and seek damages. If this advice proves incorrect, the seller will turn out to be the wrongdoer, and, accordingly, liable in damages. For such a case, see Teeman v. Jurek, 251 N.W.2d 698 (Minn.1977). In such a case he may just choose another lawyer to defend him. It should be added that the lawyer who renders advice in this context does not always have weeks to do research in the library. His client, the seller, may, be manufacturing the goods, and may want to know *now* what course of action he is free to take in the face of buyer's conduct.

What constitutes a "repudiation"? Although UCC 2–610 uses this word, the Code nowhere defines it. And in real life, it is a lucky and unusual lawyer whose client reports that the other contracting party has repudiated by such unequivocal language as "I repudiate" or "kiss my foot." A more common circumstance finds the other party slowly slipping down that incline into bankruptcy while believing and fully expecting that he will "have the money in just a few days," or that he will "have the goods in just a week." Another common cause for the same lawyer's headache is the chisler—the fellow who asks for more than the contract clearly entitles him to, but not enough more to make his request outrageous. But see Toppert v. Bunge Corp., 60 Ill.App.3d 607, 18 Ill.Dec. 171, 377 N.E.2d 324 (1978) (semi-outrageous conduct).

As we have seen, the client's situation (and therefore his lawyer's) in such a case is greatly eased by UCC 2–609 which gives him the right to demand assurance of performance from the other party and causes failure of assurances to be forthcoming to become a repudiation after "a reasonable time not exceeding thirty days." In some cases clients will be unwilling to twiddle their thumbs for 30 days and the lawyer will be called upon to determine whether a communication from the other party constitutes a repudiation.

The comments to UCC 2–610 give some guidance. Comment 1 reads in part as follows: "* * * anticipatory repudiation centers upon an overt communication of intention or an action which renders performance impossible or demonstrates a clear determination not to continue with performance." Comment 2 continues:

> It is not necessary for repudiation that performance be made literally and utterly impossible. Repudiation can result from action which reasonably indicates a rejection of the continuing obligation. And, a repudiation automatically results under the preceding section on insecurity when a party fails to provide adequate assurance of due future performance within thirty days after a justifiable demand therefor has been made. Under the language of this section, a demand by one or both parties for more than the contract calls for in the way of counter-performance is not in itself a repudiation nor does it invalidate a plain expression of desire for future performance. However, when under a fair reading it amounts to a statement of intention not to perform except on conditions which go beyond the contract, it becomes a repudiation.

Obviously, courts and lawyers will resort to extra-Code case law for guidance in deciding whether or not a given buyer has repudiated. See Restatement, Second, Contracts § 251.

Problem 14–3

In the Spring of 1986, Seller, a lumberyard, contracted to sell a quantity of specially selected hardwood to Buyer, a furniture manufacturer, at a fixed price. The lumber was to be shipped "fob Seller's lumberyard" within 10 days of demand by Buyer. No time for the demand was specified in the agreement. In May, 1986, Seller inquired when the demand would be made and was informed by Buyer "within the next few weeks." At the end of June, Seller, pressed for cash and storage space, requested by letter that Buyer "help us out" by placing the order quickly. When there was no response, Seller telegraphed that "much as we hate to we must ask for some relief" and requested a conference to "straighten the matter out." Buyer replied that it would be glad to have a conference but "if it is in regard to taking any lumber, we would say that we are not in a position, and do not intend to take any lumber this year and probably not until next Fall." Seller telegraphed that the response was "totally unacceptable" and demanded that Buyer take immediate delivery. Two weeks passed without a response. At this time the market price for the hardwoods was over 20% below the contract price.

Your client is furious and wants to cancel the contract, resell the hardwood and "sue those * * * for damages." And he wants action "right now."

A. Has the Buyer repudiated the contract? If you have doubts, what quick steps should be taken to minimize the risk? (Don't overlook the possibility that the Buyer is in breach because a reasonable time for making the demand has expired. See UCC 2–309(1) & 1–204.)

B. If Buyer has repudiated, what remedial options are available? See UCC 2–610, 2–611 & 2–703.

C. Suppose that the date for delivery had been set for December 1 and that the Buyer repudiated on July 3. If the seller cancelled the contract and immediately sued for damages, what would be the measure of damages? See UCC 2–708 & 2–723.

C. Buyer's Substantial Impairment of the Value to the Seller of His Installment Contract With the Buyer

What is an installment contract and what difference does it make to the seller and buyer?

Under UCC 2–612(1), an installment contract "requires or authorizes the delivery of goods in separate lots to be separately accepted, even though the contract contains a clause 'each delivery is a separate contract' or its equivalent." Compare UCC 2–307; Stinnes Interoil, Inc. v. Apex Oil Co., 604 F.Supp. 978 (S.D.N.Y.1985) (whether parties intended installment deliveries or delivery in a single lot is question of fact).

Under an installment contract, payment is due "at the time and place at which the buyer is to receive the goods" unless "otherwise agreed." UCC 2–310(a). Suppose that the buyer fails to pay for an installment when due or repudiates the duty to pay for a single installment? What are the seller's remedies? Can, for example, the seller cancel the contract under UCC 2–703(f), and sue for damages?

Consider, first, a failure to pay a single installment when due. Under UCC 2–703, where the buyer "wrongfully * * * fails to make a payment due on or before delivery * * * then with respect to any goods directly affected and, if the breach is of the whole contract (Section 2–612), then also with respect to the whole undelivered balance, the aggrieved seller may * * * (f) cancel." UCC 2–612(3) provides that there is a "breach of the whole" whenever a "default with respect to one or more installments substantially impairs the value of the whole contract * * *" Thus, the answer is clear: No cancellation unless there is a breach of the "whole" under the substantial impairment standard set in UCC 2–612(3).

Suppose that the buyer fails to pay an installment due after delivery? UCC 2–703 appears to limit the remedy of cancellation to the failure to make payments due "on or before delivery." UCC 2–709(1)(a), however, provides the usual remedy: When the "buyer fails to pay the price as it becomes due the seller may recover * * * the price (a) of goods accepted. * * *" Thus, when the buyer has accepted the goods (and taken possession) and the price then becomes due, the seller is expected to enforce the contract by suing for the price rather than to cancel. Furthermore, UCC 2–709(1) appears to foreclose acceleration of a contract to pay in installments: An action to recover the price is proper when the buyer "fails to pay the price as it becomes due." Thus, if the seller had delivered all the goods in exchange for a promise to pay the price in installments and the buyer failed to pay one or more, the seller's remedy appears to be limited to an action for the price on each installment as the breach occurs.

What about a repudiation by the buyer of an installment not yet due? UCC 2–612(3) is limited to a "default with respect to one or more installments * * *" In common parlance, a repudiation is not a default. Does this mean that the seller can cancel the entire contract? The answer is no. Do you see why? Read UCC 2–610 and 2–703. Unless the repudiation "with respect to a performance not yet due" substantially impairs the value of the contract to the other, the aggrieved party, here the seller, may not resort to the remedies for breach in UCC 2–703.

Here, now, is one of the "great" cases on "material" breach in installment contracts.

PLOTNICK v. PENNSYLVANIA SMELTING & REFINING CO.

United States Court of Appeals, Third Circuit, 1952.
194 F.2d 859.

HASTIE, CIRCUIT JUDGE.

This litigation arises out of an installment contract for the sale of quantities of battery lead by a Canadian seller to a Pennsylvania buyer. The seller sued for the price of a carload of lead delivered but not paid for. The buyer counterclaimed for damages caused by the seller's failure to deliver the remaining installments covered by the contract. The district court sitting without a jury allowed recovery on both claim and counterclaim. This is an appeal by the seller from the judgment against him on the counterclaim. The ultimate question is whether the buyer had committed such a breach of contract as constituted a repudiation justifying rescission by the seller.

Suit was brought in the District Court for the Eastern District of Pennsylvania. Federal jurisdiction is based on diversity of citizenship. Consequently, the conflict of laws rules of the forum, Pennsylvania, are invoked to solve the choice of law problem. Klaxon Co. v. Stentor Electric Mfg. Co., 1941, 313 U.S. 487, 61 S.Ct. 1020, 85 L.Ed. 1477. This involves no difficulty since familiar conflict of laws doctrine accepted generally and in Pennsylvania tells us that legal excuse for the non-performance or avoidance of a contract is to be determined in accordance with the law of the place of performance. Restatement, Conflict of Laws, Pa.Annot. § 358 (1936). Beyond this, the parties agree, and correctly so, that Pennsylvania is the place of performance in this case. Therefore, we apply the substantive law of Pennsylvania, particularly the Uniform Sales Act, to determine the legal consequences of the operative facts.

Uncontested findings of fact show that the contract in question was the last of a series of agreements, several of them installment contracts, entered into by the parties between June and October, 1947. Under these contracts, numerous shipments of lead were made by the seller in Canada to the buyer in Philadelphia. The seller frequently complained, and with justification, that payments were too long delayed. On the other hand, several shipments were not made at the times required by the contracts. However, by the end of March 1948, all contracts other than the one in suit had been fully performed by both parties. In this connection, it was the unchallenged finding of the district court that both parties waived the delays which preceded the buyer's breach involved in this suit. The earlier delays are relevant only insofar as they may reasonably have influenced either party in its interpretation of subsequent conduct of the other party.

The contract in suit was executed October 23, 1947 and called for deliveries aggregating 200 tons of battery lead to be completed not later than December 25, 1947. The agreed price was 8.1 cents per pound, or better if quality warranted. The court found that it was the understanding of the parties that at least 63 percent of the price should be paid shortly after each shipment was delivered and the balance within four weeks after that delivery. This finding is not contested.

Under this contract a first carload was delivered November 7, 1947. About 75 percent of the price was paid six days later. A second carload was received January 8, and about 75 percent of the price was paid 10 days later. Final adjustments and payments of small balances due on these two carloads were completed March 30, and these shipments are not now in dispute. The earliest shipment immediately involved in this litigation, the third under the contract, was a carload of lead received by the buyer on March 23, 1948. This delivery followed a March 12 conference of the parties. They disagree on what transpired at that conference. However, about 290,000 pounds of lead were then still to be delivered under the contract which stated December 25, 1947 as the agreed time for the completion of performance. And shortly after the conference, one carload of 43,000 pounds was delivered. No part of the price of this third carload has been paid. It is not disputed that plaintiff is entitled to the price of this shipment and his recovery on his claim in this suit vindicates that right.

On April 7, the buyer, who had been prodding the seller for more lead for some time, notified the seller that unless the balance of the lead should be delivered within thirty days he would buy in the open market and charge the seller any cost in excess of 8.1 cents per pound. On April 10, the seller replied refusing to ship unless the recently delivered third carload should be paid for. On May 12, buyer's attorney threatened suit unless the undelivered lead should be shipped promptly and at the same time promised to pay on delivery 75 percent of the price of this prospective shipment together with the full price of the third installment already received. Seller's solicitor replied on May 22 that seller regarded the contract as "cancelled" as a result of buyer's failure to pay for lead already delivered. At the same time the letter stated the seller's willingness to deliver at the originally agreed price if the overdue payment should be made by return mail and a letter of credit established to cover the price of the lead not yet shipped. Buyer's attorney replied on May 25 that buyer had withheld the price of the third carload "only as a set-off by reason of the failure of your client to deliver" and that buyer would place the overdue payment in escrow and would accept the remaining lead if shipped to Philadelphia "sight draft attached for the full invoice price of each car". On May 27, seller's solicitors reiterated the position stated in their March 22 letter and on June 2 seller notified buyer that the Canadian government had imposed export control on lead. The district court found, and it is here admitted, that between October 1947 and May 1948 the market price of battery lead increased from 8.1 cents to 11½ cents per pound.

The court concluded that the failure of defendant to make a down payment of at least 63 percent of the price of the third carload constituted a breach of contract but "not such a material breach of the contract as to justify plaintiff in refusing to ship the balance due under the contract within the meaning of section 45 of The Sales Act". This was the decisive conclusion of law which the seller has challenged.

Section 45 of the Sales Act as in force in Pennsylvania provides in relevant part as follows: "Where there is a contract to sell goods to be delivered by stated instalments, which are to be separately paid for, and * * * the buyer neglects or refuses to * * * pay for one or more instalments, it depends in each case on the terms of the contract, and the circumstances of the case, whether the breach of contract is so material as to justify the injured party in refusing to proceed further * * * or whether the breach is severable, giving rise to a claim for compensation, but not to a right to treat the whole contract as broken." Pa.Stat. Ann. Tit. 69, § 255 (Purdon, 1931).

We are dealing, therefore, with a situation in which the controlling statute explicitly makes the circumstances of the particular case determine whether failure to pay the price of one shipment delivered under an installment contract justifies the seller in treating his own obligation with reference to future installments as ended. Our problem is how to determine the legal effect of non-payment in a particular case.

We think the key is to be found in the rational basis of the statute itself. The flexibility of the statute reflects the impossibility of generalization about the consequences of failure to pay promptly for installments as delivered. Yet, the commercial sense of the statute yields two guiding considerations. First, non-payment for a delivered shipment may make it impossible or unreasonably burdensome from a financial point of view for the seller to supply future installments as promised. Second, buyer's breach of his promise to pay for one installment may create such reasonable apprehension in the seller's mind concerning payment for future installments that the seller should not be required to take the risk involved in continuing deliveries. If any such consequence is proved, the seller may rescind. Moreover, the Pennsylvania decisions indicate that these embarrassments and apprehensions are normal consequences of non-payment; but the cases also make it clear that they are not necessary consequences. American Tube & Stamping Co. v. Erie Iron & Steel Co., 1924, 281 Pa. 10, 125 A. 304; G.B. Hurt, Inc., v. Fuller Canneries Co., 1920, 269 Pa. 85, 112 A. 148; Cf., Helgar Corp. v. Warner's Features, Inc., 1918, 222 N.Y. 449, 119 N.E. 113.

In this case there is no evidence that the delay in payment for one carload made it difficult to provide additional lead. To the contrary, seller admits that throughout the period in controversy he had sufficient lead on hand for the full performance of this contract. He could have delivered had he chosen to do so. His excuse, if any, must be found in reasonable apprehension as to the future of the contract engendered by buyer's behavior.

The district court's finding number 16, with which seller takes issue, is a direct negation of the claim of reasonable apprehension upon which seller seeks to establish under Section 45 of the Sales Act his asserted "right to treat the whole contract as broken." It reads as follows: Plaintiff's claim of fear that the defendant would not pay for the balance of battery lead due under Contract No. 5794 at the contract price was without foundation and unreasonable."

In considering the propriety of this finding, it is to be borne in mind that the point here is not the absence of legal justification for the withholding of an overdue payment but rather whether, under the circumstances, that withholding gave the seller reason to believe that there was likelihood of continuing or additional default when and after he should deliver the rest of the lead in accordance with his promise. The substantiality of this alleged apprehension must be judged in the light of the uncontroverted finding that no impairment of buyer's credit had been shown. Moreover, the market was rising and all of the evidence indicates that buyer needed and urgently requested the undelivered lead. Indeed, as early as March 1, before the delivery of the carload for which payment was withheld, the buyer had complained quite urgently of the non-delivery of the entire balance of some 290,000 pounds overdue since December. Thereafter, when the seller shipped 43,000 pounds, about one-seventh of what was due, the buyer insisted that he was withholding payment because of the delay in delivery of the overdue balance. The court's finding that buyer had waived any claim for damages for delay up to that time does not alter this factual picture or its rational implications. In these circumstances, the trial court was justified in concluding that buyer's explanation of his conduct merited belief and that seller had no valid reason to be fearful that payment would not be forthcoming upon full delivery.

The clincher here is provided by the additional evidence concerning the possibility of delivery with sight draft attached. While there is no specific finding on the point, the evidence, including testimony tendered on behalf of seller, shows without dispute that at the beginning of this series of contracts, the seller had the privilege of shipping on sight draft but elected not to do so. And just before the collapse of the efforts of the parties to work out their difficulties amicably, the buyer specifically proposed that the seller assure himself of prompt payment by the use of sight drafts accompanying shipments. It is again important that at this time the market was substantially higher than the contract price and that seller was advised of buyer's urgent need for lead to meet his own commitments. In such circumstances it is incredible that the buyer would refuse to honor sight drafts for the contract price. These facts considered together leave no basis for reasonable apprehension concerning payment.

There is one other relevant and important fact. Throughout the controversial period the seller, with a stock of lead on hand adequate for the full performance of this contract, was using this lead in a rising market for sales to other purchasers at prices higher than agreed in the present contract. The inference was not only allowable but almost inescapable that desire to avoid a bad bargain rather than apprehension that the buyer would not carry out that bargain caused the seller to renounce the agreement and charge the buyer with repudiation. Recission for such cause is not permissible. See Truitt v. Guenther Lumber Co., 1920, 73 Pa.Super. 445, 450.

It follows that the seller has failed to establish justification for recission under Section 45 of the Sales Act and that judgment for the buyer on the counterclaim was proper.

The judgment will be affirmed.

Notes

1. How should Plotnick be analyzed and decided under the UCC?

2. As a law professor, Ellen A. Peters was highly critical of UCC 2–612, especially as it applied to the buyer's remedies upon breach by an installment seller. She called it a "law professor's delight" in that it required "wandering through a maze of inconsistent statutory standards and elliptical cross references." Peters, *Remedies for Breach of Contracts Relating to the Sale of Goods Under the Uniform Commercial Code: A Roadmap for Article Two,* 73 Yale L.J. 199, 223–27 (1963). As a

Justice on the Supreme Court of Connecticut, she had an opportunity to apply UCC 2–612(3) to a default by the buyer in payment.

In Cherwell-Ralli, Inc. v. Rytman Grain Co., Inc., 180 Conn. 714, 433 A.2d 984 (1980), the buyer fell behind in payment for nineteen accepted shipments under an oral installment contract with the seller. Nevertheless, the buyer demanded adequate assurance of due performance, based upon a concern that the seller would close its plant due to product shortages. The seller gave adequate assurances, stating that deliveries would continue if the buyer paid his account. The buyer issued a check for some of the arrearage but then, because of renewed but unfounded concerns about the seller's capacity to perform, stopped payment. The parties reached an impasse in discussions over payment and performance and, ultimately, the seller closed its plant because it could not deliver the goods and cancelled the contract. The seller sued for the price of goods accepted and the buyer counterclaimed for damages caused by the seller's failure to deliver the balance of the installments.

The Supreme Court affirmed the trial court's decision that the buyer, not the seller, had breached the contract. The court, speaking through Justice Peters, reached the following conclusions: (1) On the facts, the improper order to stop payment of the check coupled with the substantial arrearages in payment was a breach which impaired the value of the "whole" contract under UCC 2–612(3); (2) If the breach is of the "whole," the seller may cancel the contract without invoking the adequate assurance provisions of UCC 2–609; (3) The seller did not reinstate the contract by bringing suit to recover the price of past installments: UCC 2–612(3) does not apply where the seller has cancelled and sued for past installments due; (4) The trial court was correct in concluding that the buyer had no "reasonable grounds for insecurity," either before or after the check was issued; and (5) Implicitly, the seller could cancel the contract even though the breach related to payments due after delivery and the buyer did not repudiate its obligation to make future payments.

Note: Cancellation as a Remedy for Breach

As you have seen, the Code gives the seller a number of useful, if not risky, "self-help" remedies. Under UCC 2–609, the seller, if he satisfies the requisite conditions and procedures, may "suspend any performance for which he has not already received the agreed exchange." If the buyer is discovered to be insolvent, the seller may "refuse delivery except for cash * * * and stop delivery under this Article * * *." UCC 2–702(1). Similarly, the seller, under UCC 2–703, may withhold delivery or stop delivery by any bailee of goods "directly affected" by the buyer's breach. These remedies protect the unperformed balance of the seller's obligation but are not inconsistent with the ultimate completion by both parties of the exchange. The disruption may be adjusted and the contract performed.

The remedy of cancellation, however, is more drastic. UCC 2–703(f). Cancellation occurs "when either party puts an end to the contract for breach by the other." UCC 2–106(4). Cf. UCC 2–309 and 2–106(3) (termination occurs when either party "pursuant to a power created by agreement or law puts an end to the contract otherwise than for its breach"). How does an aggrieved party "cancel" a contract? The Code prescribes no procedure and requires no notice to the other party. Thus, if the seller determines that the buyer has breached, decides to cancel rather than to suspend performance or negotiate and takes action inconsistent with continued performance, e.g., resells identified goods, the cancellation is effective. See Mott Equity Elevator v. Svihovec, 236 N.W.2d 900 (N.D.1975). The effect of a cancellation is that the seller "retains any remedy for breach of the whole contract or any unperformed balance." UCC 2–106(4). But see UCC 1–107, where "any claim or right arising out of an alleged breach can be discharged in whole or in part without consideration by a written waiver or renunciation signed and delivered by the aggrieved party." Presumably, a written cancellation without more would not be a renunciation under UCC 1–107. See Goldstein v. Stainless Processing Co., 465 F.2d 392 (7th Cir.1972).

Even if the cancellation is effective, such drastic action must be justified under UCC 2–703. UCC 2–612 imposes one important limitation in installment contracts. And even if the buyer has repudiated, it must be with respect to "a performance not yet due the loss of which will substantially impair the value of the contract to the other. * * *" UCC 2–610. This question figures prominently in the cases. See, e.g., Pillsbury Co. v. Ward, 250 N.W.2d 35 (Iowa 1977) (buyer's unilateral extension of delivery date in rising soybean market substantially impaired the value of the contract to the seller).

Efficient though it may be, there are some limitations upon the remedy of "self help." In Kelly v. Miller, 575 P.2d 1221 (Alaska 1978), the seller, after the buyer had failed to pay the price due on goods delivered, moved in and "repossessed" them. The court, in a dispassionate opinion, found that "in repossessing the tractor without judicial process * * *" the seller had "fashioned his own remedy." Frontier ingenuity notwithstanding, no security interest had been retained under Article 9, there was no right to reclamation under UCC 2–702 and the seller was not entitled to replevin. The consequences? The seller's "failure to seek the remedy provided him under [UCC 2–709] combined with his resort to a remedy not recognized, so far as we have discovered, at either law or equity, precludes him from recovering damages for any loss he may have suffered as a result of [the] breach of contract."

Yet the seller still has the goods! What recourse, if any, is available to the buyer? Cf. UCC 9–507(2).

SECTION 3. SELLER'S ACTION FOR THE PRICE

Read UCC 2–709. Note that when the buyer "fails to pay the price as it becomes due the seller may recover * * * the price (a) of goods accepted. * * *" When goods are accepted is determined under UCC 2–606. See, e.g., Swift & Co. v. Rexton, Inc., 187 Conn. 540, 447 A.2d 9 (1982) (acceptance inferred from buyer's conduct). This is a neat, clean and efficient remedy. The seller gets cash for the goods without the loss of any business volume and the buyer assumes the burden of taking over and disposing of the goods. It is, loosely speaking, like specific performance, although the seller must ultimately proceed in rem, i.e., against the buyer's property. See Schumann v. Levi, 728 F.2d 1141 (8th Cir.1984) (equitable remedy of specific performance and Code's action for the price are "virtually identical").

If, however, the buyer has breached before accepting the goods or incurring the risk of loss, the seller is entitled to recover the price only "if the seller is unable after reasonable effort to resell them at a reasonable price or the circumstances reasonably indicate that such an effort will be unavailing." UCC 2–709(1)(b). Why should the seller have the burdens of possession and dispostion? According to Professor Llewellyn:

> * * * But then decently admeasured damages are all a seller needs, and are just what a seller needs, when the mercantile buyer repudiates. It is, indeed, social wisdom * * * (to require the seller) in most cases which have not involved shipment to a distant point, to dispose of whatever goods may have come into existence or into his warehouse; that is its business, and the buyer's prospective inability has already been evidenced. To force such goods on the buyer, where they are reasonably marketable by the seller, is social waste. * * *

Llewellyn, Through Title to Contract and A Bit Beyond, 25 N.Y.U.L.Q.Rev. 158, 176–177 (1938).

Problem 14–4

Simpka v. Volta: A Continuing Drama

BASIC FACTS:

Simpka manufactured office equipment and has its principal place of business in Ohio. Simpka sells in a 10–state market in the Northeast. The market is competitive and favors low cost and durability rather than style. Volta, a stock broker in New York City, is building a new building to house its expanding operations. It will require a wide assortment of office equipment, both standard and specially manufactured. After defining its needs, Volta negotiated with a number of office equipment firms, including Simpka. Volta decided in favor of Simpka and, on May 1, contracted for the following:

The order is for for two lots: (1) Standard items; 200 desks, 200 chairs, 400 regular chairs, for $120,000, and (2) Custom furniture made to Volta's specifications; 20 desks, 20 desk chairs, 20 tables and 20 easy chairs, for $80,000. Standard goods are to be shipped "fob Ohio" in four equal installments on June 1, July 1, September 1 and October 1. Custom goods are to be shipped in one installment not later than November 1. Payment is due for each installment within 30 days of delivery to the carrier.

Simpka v. Volta: Scene 1

Assume it is now December 1. Volta has accepted all four shipments of standard furniture and has paid for two. Volta has refused to purchase the custom furniture, which Simpka had already manufactured and identified to the contract. Simpka informs you that it could resell the custom furniture in the 10 state market for $40,000 and that it was at least possible that a higher price, not more than $50,000, could be obtained farther West. Simpka, angry at Volta, would like to hold the completed furniture and recover the $80,000 price. Simpka, however, will not pursue this remedy unless you give him an opinion that the odds are at least even that he will win the law suit. A Summer Associate has given you the extract, below, from Foxco Indus., Ltd. v. Fabric World, Inc., 595 F.2d 976, 983–84 (5th Cir.1979). Will you give Simpka such an opinion?

> "UCC § 2–709(1)(b), that portion of § 2–709 which would apply here, provides that an action for the price of goods may be maintained "if the seller is unable after *reasonable* effort to resell them at a *reasonable* price or the circumstances *reasonably* indicate that such effort will be unavailing." Ala.Code tit. 7, § 2–709(1)(b) (1977) (emphasis added). The Official Comment to § 2–709 states, in pertinent part, that:
>
> > "2. The action for the price is now generally limited to those cases where resale of the goods is impracticable * * *
> >
> > "3. This section substitutes an objective test by action for the former 'not readily resalable' standard. An action for the price under subsection (1) (b) can be sustained only after a 'reasonable effort to resell' the goods 'at reasonable price' has actually been made or where the circumstances 'reasonably indicate' that such an effort will be unavailing."
>
> Ala.Code tit. 7, § 7–2–709, Official Comment (1977). As was recognized in Multi-Line Manufacturing, Inc. v. Greenwood Mills, Inc., 123 Ga.App. 372, 180 S.E.2d 917 (1971), a case involving the cancellation of a contract to purchase fabric, the language of § 2–709(1)(b) "clearly evinces legislative intent that these matters

ordinarily should be subject to determination by a jury * * *" Id. at 373, 180 S.E.2d at 918. Thus, we will reverse only if, as a matter of law, there was no way in which the jury could find that Foxco was unable, after reasonable effort, to resell the fabric at a reasonable price or that it was reasonably clear that an effort to resell would have been fruitless.

"The evidence at trial clearly established that all of Foxco's goods were specially manufactured for the customer who ordered them and that it was difficult for Foxco to resell fabric manufactured for one purchaser to another buyer. Further, it was normally very difficult to sell Foxco's spring fabric after the spring buying season had ended; the precipitous decline of the knitted fabric market presented an additional barrier to resale. It was not until the next spring buying season returned that Foxco, in September 1975, finally sold a portion of the goods identified to Fabric World's October 1974 order.

"Fabric World argues that Foxco made no effort whatsoever to resell the goods during the months that intervened (between the contract breach and Foxco's eventual disposition of the fabric in September 1975) despite the presence of some market for the goods in that interim period. Thus Fabric World concludes, the requisites of § 2–709(1)(b) were not satisfied. Under § 2–709(1)(b), however, Foxco was required only to use *reasonable* efforts to resell its goods at a *reasonable* price. From the time of Fabric World's breach to September 1975 there was a 50% decline in the market price of this material. We cannot say that the jury was precluded from finding that Foxco acted reasonably under the circumstances or that there was no reasonable price at which Foxco could sell these goods. Fabric World breached its contract with Foxco, and the jury was entitled to a charge which gave Foxco the full benefit of its original bargain. * * *"

Simpka v. Volta: Scene 2

Suppose that on June 1 Simpka had tendered and Volta had accepted all of the standard items. Volta paid $30,000 on July 1. If Volta fails to pay on August 1, what is Simpka's remedy? Suppose Volta failed to pay and repudiated the contract on September 1. Could Simpka cancel the contract, accelerate the obligation and sue for the price of all goods accepted? See UCC 2–610(b) and 2–709(1).

SECTION 4. SELLER'S RIGHT TO "CONTRACT-MARKET" DAMAGES

If the seller is not entitled to the price under UCC 2–709, what other remedies are available?

One option is to resell the goods under UCC 2–706, whether they were identified to the contract before or after the buyer's breach. See UCC 2–703(c) & 2–704. When the conditions established in UCC 2–706 are satisfied, the seller may recover the "difference between the resale price and the contract price together with any incidental damages * * * but less expenses saved in consequence of the buyer's breach." UCC 2–706(1).

Another option, whether the goods have been resold or not, is to seek damages for "non-acceptance or repudiation" under UCC 2–708. See UCC 2–703. But the measures of damages under UCC 2–708 are strikingly different: Subsection (1), an objective standard, measures loss by the difference between the market price and the contract price while Subsection (2), a subjective standard, allows recovery of the "profit (including reasonable overhead) which the seller would have made from full performance by the buyer. * * *" on the particular contract in dispute.

These options pose two important questions: (1) What limitations, if any, are imposed upon a seller's decision to pursue a particular remedy; and (2) Once a proper remedy has been selected, how are damages to be measured?

Consider, first, UCC 2–708(1). The contract price-market price measure can be fraught with inappropriateness and difficulty. Further, it may either over-or under-compensate the seller. Should it be repealed?

Problem 14–5

Simpka v. Volta: Scene 3

Back to Simpka-Volta. Assume that the contract was for only the standard items and the deal was signed on March 1. The price and delivery schedule are unchanged. Volta repudiated on April 3.

A. On April 5, Simpka accepted Volta's repudiation, cancelled the contract and sued for damages under UCC 2–708(1). See UCC 2–610(b). The case came to trial in the next year and the following evidence was introduced: (1) The aggregate market price on April 5 in Ohio of the four lots was $110,000; (2) Also in Ohio, the market value of the June 1 installment was $24,000, the July 1 installment was $27,000, the September installment was $30,000 and the October installment was $24,000; (3) In New York, the prices are the same except for the October lot, which was $24,000.

Assuming that Simpka has not resold the goods, to what damages is Simpka entitled under UCC 2–708(1)? On the time and place for tender, see UCC 2–503.

B. Assume that, on April 3, Simpka decided to wait to see whether Volta would retract the repudiation. UCC 2–611. Simpka waits until July 15, then cancels the contract and sues for damages under UCC 2–708(1). If Simpka does not resell, will its damages be the same as in A, above?

C. What if Simpka had resold on April 5 for $100,000. Is Simpka bound by this decision? See UCC 2–706. If the UCC 2–708(1) measure was more than $20,000, could Simpka pursue that remedy? See the next case.

TRANS WORLD METALS, INC. v. SOUTHWIRE CO.

United States Court of Appeals, Second Circuit, 1985.
769 F.2d 902.

[In April, 1981 the parties entered into a contract for the sale of 12,000 metric tons of primary aluminum, to be delivered in monthly installments of 1,000 metric tons from January through December, 1982. The contract price was $.77 per pound, or a total price of $20.4 million. Seller shipped 750 metric tons in January, 1982 and the balance of the first installment in early February. Between April, 1981 and March, 1982, the market price of aluminum dropped "dramatically." On March 4, 1982, Buyer, without discussing the late first installment or issuing additional delivery instructions, cancelled the contract because of Seller's default. In Seller's suit for damages, the jury concluded that Buyer had accepted all deliveries and even if late, there was no substantial impairment of the value of either the first installment or the whole contract. Thus, buyer had repudiated the contract. This conclusion was affirmed on appeal.

The jury awarded Seller damages of $7,122,141.84, consisting of $6,702,529 for Buyer's repudiation of the balance of the contract and $419,232.84 for the installment accepted. The district court added prejudgment interest of

$1,304,804.88 and entered a judgment for $8,426,946.72. The propriety of this damage award under the UCC was attacked on appeal.]

NEWMAN, J.

* * *

II.

Southwire complains that the damage award, calculated by the difference between contract and market prices, gave Trans World an unwarranted windfall. Southwire favors an alternative measure of damages based on the rate of profit earned by Trans World on the first month's completed shipments projected over the twelve-month life of the contract. Such a measure, Southwire argues, would better estimate the amount Trans World would have made had the contract been completed. We reject this alternative as contrary to the Uniform Commercial Code.

Seller's damages for repudiation are governed by section 2–708 of the Uniform Commercial Code. Subsection 1 of this section sets forth the general rule that damages are to be calculated by the difference between the contract and market prices:

> (1) Subject to subsection (2) and to the provisions of this Article with respect to proof of market price (Section 2–723), the measure of damages for non-acceptance or repudiation by the buyer is the difference between the market price at the time and place for tender and the unpaid contract price together with any incidental damages provided in this Article (Section 2–710), but less expenses saved in consequence of the buyer's breach.

N.Y.U.C.C. Law § 2–708(1). The drafters of the Uniform Commercial Code recognized that this measure would not adequately compensate certain types of sellers, generally referred to as "lost volume sellers." *See* J. White & R. Summers, Uniform Commercial Code § 7–9, at 274–76 (2d ed. 1980) ("White & Summers"). Therefore, an alternative measure of damages was provided for those sellers who would be *inadequately* compensated by the standard contract/market price differential:

> (2) If the measure of damages provided in subsection (1) is inadequate to put the seller in as good a position as performance would have done then the measure of damages is the profit (including reasonable overhead) which the seller would have made from full performance by the buyer, together with any incidental damages provided in this Article (Section 2–710), due allowance for costs reasonably incurred and due credit for payments or proceeds of resale.

N.Y.U.C.C. Law § 2–708(2). This measure of damages is often preferred by sellers who have not acquired the goods to be sold prior to the buyer's repudiation because such sellers often would be undercompensated by the contract/market price measure of damages.[3]

3. Professors White and Summers refer to such sellers as "jobbers."

> By "jobber" we refer to a seller who satisfies two conditions. First, he is a seller who never acquires the contract goods. Second, his decision not to acquire those goods after learning of the breach is commercially reasonable under 2–704. * * * Since he has no goods on hand to resell, he cannot even resell on the market at the time of tender and so recoup the amount necessary to make him whole by adding such proceeds to his 2–708(1) recovery. Thus the only recovery which grossly approximates the "jobber's" economic loss is a recovery based on lost profits.

White & Summers § 7–10, at 278. In a case involving a commodity like aluminum that fluctuates rapidly in price—as compared to standard-priced goods like cars, *see* 67 Am.Jur.

Southwire argues that the "lost profits" measure should also apply when the seller would be *overcompensated* by section 2–708(1). We disagree. We do not doubt that the contract/market price differential "will seldom be the same as the seller's actual economic loss from breach." White & Summers § 7–7, at 269; *see* Peters, *Remedies for Breach of Contracts Relating to the Sale of Goods Under the Uniform Commercial Code: A Roadmap for Article Two,* 73 Yale L.J. 199, 259 (1963). However, nothing in the language or history of section 2–708(2) suggests that it was intended to apply to cases in which section 2–708(1) might overcompensate the seller. *See* White & Summers § 7–12, at 283. Nor has Southwire cited any New York case that interprets section 2–708(2) as Southwire urges us to interpret it. As a federal court sitting in diversity, we will not extend the application of this state law.

Nor are we convinced that Trans World has been overcompensated. No measure other than the contract/market price differential will award Trans World the "benefit of its bargain," that is, the "amount necessary to put [it] in as good a position as [it] would have been if the defendant had abided by the contract." *Western Geophysical Co. of America, Inc. v. Bolt Associates, Inc.,* 584 F.2d 1164, 1172 (2d Cir.1978) (quoting *Perma Research & Development Co. v. Singer Co.,* 402 F.Supp. 881, 898 (S.D.N.Y.1975), *aff'd,* 542 F.2d 111 (2d Cir.), *cert. denied,* 429 U.S. 987, 97 S.Ct. 507, 50 L.Ed.2d 598 (1976)). The contract at issue in this case is an aluminum supply contract entered into eight months prior to the initial deliveries called for by its terms. The last of the anticipated deliveries of aluminum would not have been completed until a full twenty months after the negotiations took place. It simply could not have escaped these parties that they were betting on which way aluminum prices would move. Trans World took the risk that the price would rise; Southwire took the risk that the price would fall. Under these circumstances, Trans World should not be denied the benefit of its bargain, as reflected by the contract/market price differential.[4] *Cf. Apex Oil Co. v. Vanguard Oil & Service Co.,* 760 F.2d 417 (2d Cir.1985) (defaulting seller obliged to pay damages based on contract/market price differential).

The decision primarily relied upon by Southwire is distinguishable from this case. *Nobs Chemical, U.S.A., Inc. v. Koppers Co., Inc.,* 616 F.2d 212 (5th Cir. 1980), involved a seller acting as a middleman. The seller in Nobs had entered into a second fixed-price contract with its own supplier for purchase of the goods to be sold under the contract sued upon; its "market price" thus had been fixed in advance by contract. Because the seller had contractually protected itself against market price fluctuation, the Fifth Circuit concluded that it would have been unfair to permit the seller to reap a riskless benefit. As that Court noted, "the difference between the fallen market price and the contract price is [not] necessary to compensate the plaintiffs for the breach. Had the transaction been completed, their 'benefit of the bargain' would not have been affected by the fall in the market price. * * *" *Id.* at 215. Whether or not we would have reached the same result in *Nobs,* here the benefit of the bargain under a completed contract would have been affected by the fall in aluminum prices.[5]

2d *Sales* § 1129—the lost profits of a selling jobber may well be adequately reflected by the contract/market price differential.

4. Southwire presented no evidence and made no claim concerning any expenses saved by Trans World as a result of Southwire's breach. Such expenses, if established, would have reduced the recoverable damages. N.Y. U.C.C. Law § 2–708(1); *see Katz Communications, Inc. v. The Evening News Association,* 705 F.2d 20, 26–27 (2d Cir.1983).

5. Although Trans World had available to it about 78,000 tons of aluminum at the time of the breach, Trans World had corresponding

Because Trans World accepted the risk that prices would rise, it is entitled to benefit from their fall.

III.

Southwire raises a number of further points on appeal. The first involves the proper determination of the market price for purposes of calculating the contract/market price differential. The jury relied upon Trans World's damage calculations, which were based on the market price as reflected by bids received on April 26 (and projections discussed below). Southwire argues that because the contract was repudiated on March 4, the market price figure used to calculate damages should be the March 4 price. We do not agree. The measure of damages set forth in section 2–708(1) is "the difference between the market price *at the time and place for tender* and the unpaid contract price." N.Y. U.C.C. Law § 2–708(1) (emphasis added); *cf. id.* § 2–713(1) (*buyer's* damages for repudiation by *seller* measured by contract/market price differential "at the time when the buyer learned of the breach"). Thus, the pertinent market price date is not the date of repudiation but the date for tender.

We would accept Southwire's argument that the date Trans World learned of the repudiation would be the correct date on which to calculate the market price had this action been tried *before* the time for full performance under the contract. *See* N.Y.U.C.C. § 2–723(1) (market price at time aggrieved party learned of repudiation used to calculate damages in action for anticipatory repudiation that "comes to trial before time for performance with respect to some or all of the goods"). However, where damages are awarded *after* the time for full performance, as in this case, the calculation of damages under section 2–708(1) should reflect the actual market price at each successive date when tender was to have been made under the repudiated installment contract. This was the rule prior to enactment of the Uniform Commercial Code. *United States v. Burton Coal Co.,* 273 U.S. 337, 340, 47 S.Ct. 351, 352, 71 L.Ed. 670 (1927) (following repudiation of supply contract, "seller may recover the difference between the contract price and the market value at the times when and the places where deliveries should have been made"); *L.W. Foster Sportswear Co. v. Goldblatt Brothers, Inc.,* 356 F.2d 906, 910 & n. 6 (7th Cir.1966) (recognizing same standard under pre-U.C.C. law and U.C.C. § 2–708); *see* 67A Am.Jur.2d *Sales* § 1115, at 505 n. 19 (2d ed. 1985); *id.* § 1118, at 510 n. 50. New York did not intend to deviate from this measure of damages upon adoption of the Uniform Commercial Code: The Official Comment to section 2–708 indicates that the "prior uniform statutory provision is followed generally in setting the current market price at the time and place for tender as the standard by which damages for non-acceptance are to be determined." N.Y.U.C.C. Law § 2–708 Official Comment 1. The "prior uniform statutory provision" indicated that where " 'there is an available market for the goods * * * [damages should be measured by] the difference between the contract price and the market or current price * * * when the goods ought to have been accepted, or, if no time was fixed for acceptance, then at the time of the refusal to accept.' " *Id.* § 2–708 Practice Commentary (quoting Sales Act § 64 (McKinney's Personal Property Law § 145)).

obligations to deliver about 76,000 tons of aluminum to buyers other than Southwire. Absent any indication that Trans World had "identified" any of this metal to the Southwire contract, *see* N.Y.U.C.C. Law § 2–501(b), we cannot say, as could the court in *Nobs,* that a change in the market price would not affect the seller's "benefit of the bargain."

We therefore conclude that when calculating damages for a buyer's repudiation of an installment contract by the contract/market price differential, "time * * * for tender" under section 2–708(1) is the date for each successive tender of an installment, as specified in the contract. *See* 67A Am.Jur.2d *Sales* § 1118, at 510 ("[W]here the breach is of an installment contract, damages should be measured by the market price at the time of each delivery." (footnote omitted)). In this case the successive dates for tender were the last day of each month in 1982, at which time Trans World was authorized to invoice that month's shipments even if such shipments had not been "released" by Southwire's delivery instructions. A contract/market price differential should have been calculated for each month during 1982.

We recognize that the jury relied upon a damage calculation prepared for Trans World that did not use actual market prices for each month of scheduled tenders. Instead, Trans World's expert took the actual price for April 1982 and projected forward from that date "anticipated" increases of $15 per metric ton for each month thereafter. Though the use of such an estimate was inappropriate because the actual market price for each successive month was known by the date of the trial, Southwire has no basis for complaint. Trans World's projected monthly market prices were closer to the contract price than were the actual market prices. Trans World therefore received less in damages using its expert's projection than it would have received using the correct measure. Furthermore, Southwire did not preserve at trial the factual issue as to the correct market price on each successive date of tender. Southwire did not object to Trans World's use or the accuracy of projected prices nor otherwise raise the issue with the jury, relying instead on its unsuccessful effort to convince the jurors that the contract/market price differential was not an appropriate method for calculating damages. Having failed to preserve the point for appeal, Southwire may not now raise the issue for the first time. *See, e.g., Schmidt v. Polish People's Republic,* 742 F.2d 67, 70 (2d Cir.1984).

* * *

We have considered Southwire's remaining claims and find them to lack merit. The judgment of the District Court is affirmed.

Notes

1. Given the remedial objectives of UCC 1–106(1) and the general duty of good faith in the "enforcement" of the contract, UCC 1–203, was the seller overcompensated under UCC 2–708(1)? Retrace the statutory steps to the seller's victory: UCC 2–610(b), 2–703(e), 2–708(2) (rejected by the court), and 2–708(1). Relying on *Nobs Chemical,* which was distinguished in the principal case, the court in Union Carbide Corporation v. Consumers Power Co., 636 F.Supp. 1498 (E.D.Mich.1986), held that a seller who was a middleman and who did not, under the pricing arrangement, bear the risk of fluctuations in the market price, could not use UCC 2–708(1) when that measure resulted in overcompensation. The court interpreted the word "inadequate" in UCC 2–708(2) to mean "incapable or inadequate to accomplish the stated purpose of the UCC remedies of compensating the aggrieved person but not overcompensating that person or specifically punishing the other person." In short, where the measure of damages in UCC 2–708(1) fails fairly to measure the damages suffered by the plaintiff, that formula is "inadequate" and, to avoid a penalty, UCC 2–708(2) should be applied.

2. Is there any support for the proposition that when the buyer repudiates, the seller's damages should be limited to the difference between the contract price for the entire undelivered balance and the market price determined at a commercially

reasonable time after the repudiation? See UCC 2–610(a). Should this be the law when the seller, under the pricing arrangement, has assumed the risk of movements up or down in market prices?

SECTION 5. SELLER'S RIGHT TO RESELL AND "FIX" DAMAGES

In the *Trans World Metals* case, the seller did not have aluminum conforming or identified to the contract on hand at the time of the breach. Suppose, however, that conforming aluminum in sufficient quantities was within the seller's possession or control. See UCC 2–704(1). If an action for the price is not possible, UCC 2–709(1)(b), the seller should consider the remedy of resale under UCC 2–706, a provision which permits the seller to resell and authoritatively fix his damages based upon the difference between the contract price and what is realized from the resale contract. Lost volume problems aside, this recovery normally places the seller in the position he would have occupied if the buyer had fully performed.

Read UCC 2–706 carefully and work the next problem.

Problem 14–6

Simpka v. Volta: Scene Four

In June, Simpka made the first shipment of standard furniture and received a $30,000 payment from Volta. Volta, however, was dissatisfied with the shipment and a dispute over quality simmered over the summer, with Simpka withholding delivery. On September 14, Volta repudiated the entire contract, including the custom furniture. Assume that Volta's repudiation was a total breach of contract. Simpka has three installments of standard furniture, for which Volta agreed to pay $90,000, and the custom furniture, for which Volta agreed to pay $80,000, on hand and identified to the contract. Simpka would like to resell all of that furniture, either in Ohio or New York, and obtain the maximum damages under UCC 2–706. It is now October 1 and you have the following facts before you:

1. The cost of shipping each installment of standard furniture from Ohio to New York is $6,000. The cost of shipping the custom furniture is $10,000.

2. The market price of the custom furniture in Ohio on September 14 was $75,000. It is expected to remain constant for the balance of the year. The market price of the custom furniture in New York on September 14 was $70,000. It is uncertain how that market will perform in the future.

3. The market price of an installment of standard furniture on September 14 was $30,000 in Ohio and $33,000 in New York. On October 1, the respective prices were $27,000 in Ohio and $30,000 in New York. It is estimated that on November 1, the respective prices will be $22,500 in Ohio and $27,000 in New York and that on December 1 the respective prices will be $18,000 in Ohio and $27,000 in New York.

A. Develop a plan to resell all of the furniture that has the best chance to maximize damages and satisfy UCC 2–706.

B. What remedy, if any, is available if the conditions of UCC 2–706 are not 2-708 satisfied? See Comment 2, UCC 2–706. How should you plan for this contingency? Remember, some courts have held that a seller who acts in bad faith is limited to the damages that should have been recovered under UCC 2–706 if all the conditions had been met. See Note: Seller's Remedial Choices, infra at p. 606.

C. If, upon resale, you satisfy the conditions of UCC 2–706, are you foreclosed from using UCC 2–708(1)? Have you made an election of remedies? See Comment 1, UCC 2–703. YES?

AFRAM EXPORT CORP. v. METALLURGIKI HALYPS, S.A.

United States Court of Appeals, Seventh Circuit, 1985.
772 F.2d 1358.

POSNER, CIRCUIT JUDGE.

The appeal and cross-appeal in this diversity breach of contract suit raise a variety of interesting issues, in particular of personal jurisdiction and contract damages.

Afram Export Corporation, the plaintiff, is a Wisconsin corporation that exports scrap metal. Metallurgiki Halyps, S.A., the defendant, is a Greek corporation that makes steel. In 1979, after a series of trans-Atlantic telephone and telex communications, the parties made a contract through an exchange of telex messages for the purchase by Metallurgiki of 15,000 tons of clean shredded scrap, at $135 per ton, F.O.B. Milwaukee, delivery to be made by the end of April. Metallurgiki apparently intended to use the scrap to make steel for shipment to Egypt, pursuant to a contract with an Egyptian buyer. Afram agreed to pay the expenses of an agent of Metallurgiki—Shields—to inspect the scrap for cleanliness before it was shipped.

The scrap for the contract was prepared, in Milwaukee, by Afram Metal Processing Company. Both Afram Metal Processing and the plaintiff Afram Export are wholly owned subsidiaries of Afram Brothers. All three are Wisconsin corporations, and have the same officers and directors. Unless otherwise indicated, when we say "Afram" we mean "Afram Export."

Shields arrived to inspect the scrap on April 12. He told Afram that the scrap was clean but that Metallurgiki would not accept it, because the price of scrap had fallen. Sure enough, Metallurgiki refused to accept it. Afram brought this suit after selling the scrap to other buyers. Metallurgiki unsuccessfully challenged the court's jurisdiction over it, then filed a counterclaim alleging that Afram had broken the contract and had thereby made it impossible for Metallurgiki to fulfill its contract with the Egyptian purchaser.

After a bench trial, the district judge gave judgment for Afram for $425,149 and dismissed the counterclaim. 592 F.Supp. 446 (D.Wis.1984). Metallurgiki has appealed from the judgment for Afram, and Afram has cross-appealed, contending that the judge should have given it the full damages it sought based on the difference between the contract price and the cover price—$483,750—plus incidental damages of $40,665, prejudgment interest, the costs of a so-called public sale, and attorney's fees for defending against the counterclaim.

* * *

* * * Afram claims that it sold all of the scrap rejected by Metallurgiki at a public sale on June 15, 1979, and that its damages should therefore be based on the price of that sale, which was $102.75 per ton. The district judge disagreed. He found that two-thirds of the scrap had been sold at a substantially higher price to Luria Brothers on June 4 ($118—actually somewhat less, because Afram defrayed some freight costs) and the other third to International Traders on September 15 at a price of $103. Afram points out that the sale on June 4 actually was made by its affiliate, Afram Metal Processing Company, and further argues that since all Afram scrap is sold from the same pile in Milwaukee it is arbitrary to treat the first sale after the breach of contract as

the cover transaction, rather than the sale that Afram designated as that transaction.

We agree with the district judge that the sale on June 4 was a cover transaction, even though the nominal seller was a different corporation from the plaintiff. Not only are both corporations wholly owned subsidiaries of another corporation, not only do all three corporations have the same officers and directors, but the record indicates substantial commingling of assets and operation of the three corporations as a single entity. Shortly after Metallurgiki's rejection, Zeke Afram, an officer of both Afram Export (the party to the contract with Metallurgiki) and Afram Metal Processing (the nominal owner of the scrap sold on June 4), called Luria Brothers and explained that he had extra scrap for sale because of a buyer's breach; apparently he did not bother to indicate which Afram corporation he was calling on behalf of. The June 4 sale followed shortly. The conversation and the timing of the sale are powerful evidence that the breach enabled the sale—that it would not have occurred but for the breach—and hence that the revenue from the sale must be subtracted from the contract price to determine Afram's loss. Cf. *Servbest Foods, Inc. v. Emessee Industries, Inc.,* 82 Ill.App.3d 662, 668–72, 37 Ill.Dec. 945, 951–53, 403 N.E.2d 1, 7–9 (1980).

But this does not dispose completely of the issue of the cover price. If the sale on June 15 was "made in good faith and in a commercially reasonable manner," it fixed Afram's damages on the remaining one-third of the scrap. UCC § 2–706(1), Wis.Stat. § 402.706(1). The question may seem less than earthshaking since the June 15 sale price and the September sale price which the district court used as the cover price for the remaining third were only 25¢ per ton apart. But the bona fides of the June 15 sale casts additional light on the intercorporate relations of the Afram group and hence on the proper interpretation of the sale to Luria Brothers. In any event, the district judge was entitled to find that neither condition in section 2–706(1) was satisfied. Cf. *Coast Trading Co. v. Cudahy Co.,* 592 F.2d 1074, 1080–81 (9th Cir.1979). The June 15 "sale" was about as pure a bookkeeping transaction—as empty of economic significance—as can be imagined. Cf. *Milbrew v. Commissioner of Internal Revenue,* 710 F.2d 1302, 1305 (7th Cir.1983). It consisted of a transfer of the scrap on the books of one affiliated corporation to the books of another. The transferor and transferee were not only under common ownership but were operated as if they were limbs of a single organism. The scrap itself was not moved; it remained on the scrap heap till sold later on. No invoice or check for the sale was produced at trial. The inference that the sale was designed simply to maximize the enterprise's damages, leaving it free to resell the scrap at higher prices later on, is overpowering. The sale of the scrap three months later to International Traders at a (slightly) higher price provided better evidence of what the enterprise actually lost, so far as the scrap not sold to Luria Brothers is concerned, by Metallurgiki's breach of contract.

The next issue relates to incidental damages, which the Uniform Commercial Code allows a seller who is the victim of a breach of contract to recover in addition to the difference between sale price and cover price. UCC § 2–706(1), Wis.Stat. § 402.706(1). Incidental damages are "any commercially reasonable charges, expenses or commissions incurred in stopping delivery, in the transportation, care and custody of goods after buyer's breach, in connection with return or resale of the goods or otherwise resulting from the breach." UCC § 2–710, Wis.Stat. § 402.710. Afram says it borrowed $2.5 million from a bank of which $2.025 million was to finance the purchase of the junked cars that it shredded in order to produce scrap in the form called for by the contract with Metallurgiki. It has calculated the interest (some $40,000) that it paid between the date of breach and the date of cover on the amount of the loan used to finance the cars. But it can recover this interest, if at all, only as incidental damages, and not as consequential damages, for under the Uniform Commercial Code consequential damages are a buyer's not a seller's remedy. See UCC § 2–715, Wis.Stat. § 402.715; *Nobs Chemical, U.S.A., Inc. v. Koppers Co.*, 616 F.2d 212, 216 (5th Cir. 1980).

The line between incidental and consequential damages is rather unclear. It may help in locating it to notice that in many cases of consequential damages, a buyer who is the victim of a seller's breach of contract is seeking damages for consequences that he could have avoided or minimized at lower cost than the contract breaker. *EVRA Corp. v. Swiss Bank Corp.*, 673 F.2d 951, 957 (7th Cir. 1982). In the case that established the common law's position that consequential damages are not recoverable without special notice to the seller, *Hadley v. Baxendale*, 9 Ex. 341, 156 Eng.Rep. 145 (1854), the defendant, a carrier, broke a contract with the plaintiff to deliver the plaintiff's mill shaft to the manufacturer of the shaft for repair. Because the plaintiff had no spare shaft, it was forced to shut down the mill; and it sought the profits that it lost during the period of shut-down caused by the defendant's delay in delivering the shaft. The court refused to award these damages. They could easily have been avoided by the plaintiff's having a spare shaft, which prudence dictated that a mill owner have anyway. This omission could not fairly be charged to the seller. It was not—as the prerequisite for obtaining consequential damages in a contract case has come to be called, see, e.g., Farnsworth, Contracts § 12.14, at p. 876 (1982)—"foreseeable" by him, because a seller is not charged with foreseeing the buyer's imprudence.

This would be the same case, only in the unusual setting of a seller's seeking consequential damages, if Metallurgiki's breach of contract had precipitated Afram into bankruptcy because Afram was paying back-breaking interest on the loan that it had taken out to enable it to fulfill its obligations under the contract. Afram would be responsible for arranging its affairs in such a way as not to be abnormally vulnerable to a breach of contract; excessive leverage would be the counterpart to Hadley's failure to keep a spare shaft on hand. At the other end of the spectrum, reasonable expenses incurred by Afram in putting the scrap in a form where it would be salable to a substitute buyer would be recoverable as incidental damages; virtually by definition, such expenses could not be avoided by greater prudence on the seller's part.

The actual case is somewhere in the middle, but if we had to decide exactly where, we probably would disagree with the district judge, who regarded this as a case of consequential rather than incidental damages. Although knowledge of the details of the seller's financial arrangements is not chargeable to the buyer, it is obvious to the buyer and unavoidable by the seller that the seller will incur an interest cost (explicit or implicit, as we shall see) in the interval between the breach of the contract and the cover sale; and the party who is better able to avoid this expense and who therefore should bear the risk of its occurrence is the contract-breaking buyer, not the seller. The cases therefore allow the seller to recover the additional interest expense as incidental damages. See, e.g., *Bulk Oil (U.S.A.), Inc. v. Sun Oil Trading Co.*, 697 F.2d 481, 482–84 (2d Cir.1983); *Hofmann v. Stoller*, 320 N.W.2d 786, 792–93 (N.D.1982); *Gray v. West*, 608 S.W.2d 771, 781 (Tex.Civ.App.1980).

The district judge also suggested that there was no damage, incidental or consequential: "presumably the interest costs for the money to purchase the junk cars would be recovered when the scrap which they had become was sold to some purchaser," so that Afram would be made "whole as to this cost of raw materials through the award of the difference between the contract price and the resale price." But this implies that the price charged to the substitute buyers, Luria Brothers and International Traders, would be calculated on a cost-plus basis, and thus include the additional interest expense that Afram incurred because of Metallurgiki's breach of contract. Prices in competitive markets are not determined on that basis, however; and so far as the record shows the market for steel scrap is competitive. The prices that Luria Brothers and International Traders were willing to pay for Afram's steel scrap depended on how much these buyers would have had to pay for the product from competing sellers, not on how much extra interest Afram had to pay because of the delay in selling its scrap.

Nevertheless we agree with the district court's conclusion that Metallurgiki is not liable for the interest that Afram seeks. All the record contains is the computation of interest. There is no evidence that Afram would have repaid the loan, or $2.025 million of it, on payment of the contract price by Metallurgiki, had that happy event occurred. The loan agreement was not placed in evidence, and since the loan is for more than the amount used to buy the junked cars, there is no presumption that it would have been paid back as soon as the contract for which the junked cars had been bought was fulfilled. Indeed, we do not even know whether the loan was repaid when Afram resold the scrap to Luria Brothers and International Traders. For purposes of computing prejudgment interest, a separate item of damages is discussed next. Afram kept on calculating interest, at the same rate (prime plus .5 percent) as the interest rate on the loan, right up to the date of trial; this is consistent with Afram's not having repaid the loan when it resold the scrap.

So far as the proof shows, then, Afram is not really complaining about an extra interest expense; it is complaining about losing the use of part of the money it borrowed from the bank, the part that was tied up in the junked cars longer than it would have been had Metallurgiki not broken the contract. This of course is a genuine loss; it is what economists call an "opportunity cost," and courts now understand that an opportunity cost is a real cost. See, e.g., *Simmons v. United States,* 698 F.2d 888, 898 (7th Cir.1983). In this case it would be measured by the interest or profit that Afram could have obtained from investing, or using elsewhere in its business, the money that it would have gotten from Metallurgiki by the end of April if Metallurgiki had not broken the contract, but that as a result of the breach it did not get till June and September.

But a forgone profit from exploiting a valuable opportunity that the breach of contract denied to the victim of the breach fits more comfortably under the heading of consequential damages than of incidental damages. The profits that Afram might have made from using that $2.025 million elsewhere in its business are like the milling profits that Hadley might have made if the carrier had not delayed in delivering the mill shaft for repair. Afram has not tried to establish its lost profits from the temporary loss of the use of the $2.025 million; all it is seeking is the extra interest it had to pay. But its theory is one of opportunity cost, as it makes clear in its brief by stating that it would be entitled to interest as incidental damages even if it had not used borrowed money to pay for the junked cars. Afram is correct that it would incur an opportunity cost whether it used its own money or used money that it had borrowed; in either event it would lose the use of money that it could deploy elsewhere at a profit. But we do not think the law has evolved to the point where every time a buyer breaks a contract, the seller is entitled to the time value of the money tied up in the contract, as incidental damages. All the seller is entitled to is an out-of-pocket interest expense that would not have been incurred but for the breach. We have found no case where (so far as we are able to determine from the statement of facts in the case) the seller was able to recover interest on a general business loan not tied to the subject matter of the sale, but we have found two cases that imply he may not. See *Schiavi Mobile Homes, Inc. v. Gironda,* 463 A.2d 722, 727 (Me.1983); *S.C. Gray, Inc. v. Ford Motor Co.,* 92 Mich.App. 789, 811–12, 286 N.W.2d 34, 43–44 (1979).

* * *

Thus we affirm the judgment of the district court except with respect to the denial of prejudgment interest to Afram, as to which we remand the case for a determination of the amount of prejudgment interest to which Afram is entitled at the statutory rate of five percent. Wis.Stat. § 138.04; *Kilgust Heating Div. v. Kemp,* 70 Wis.2d 544, 550, 235 N.W.2d 292, 295–96 (1975). No costs in this court.

Affirmed in part, reversed in part, and remanded.

Notes

1. Why was the public resale on June 15 at $102.75 per ton improper? Should the September resale price of $103 per ton be used to measure damages under UCC 2–706(1)? UCC 2–708(1)?

2. According to the court, Afram was not a "lost volume" seller—but for the breach, Afram could not have resold the scrap. How, then, are the proceeds from the resale to be treated under UCC 2–706(1)?

3. Exactly how did Judge Posner classify and treat the interest payments made by Afram after the breach on an obligation incurred much earlier? If they are neither incidental nor consequential damages, what are they—fixed or "overhead" costs? In Ernst Steel Corp. v. Horn Construction Division, Halliburton Co., 104 A.D.2d 55, 481 N.Y.S.2d 833 (1984), the court stated: "In an appropriate case a seller is entitled to recover commercially reasonable finance and interest charges incurred as a result of a buyer's breach as a proper item of incidental damages * * * For the most part, however, interest expenses have only been awarded to sellers for indebtedness specifically identified to goods intended for resale to the breaching party and who, as a result of the breaching, cannot repay the loans."

4. Article 2 does not explicitly provide that the seller may recover consequential damages caused by a buyer's breach. Compare UCC 2–715(2). But does it foreclose such a recovery? Suppose that the buyer had promised to pay $100,000 on August 1 for scrap delivered on July 1 and knew that the seller needed prompt payment to renew an advantageous contract with another supplier. Despite assurances that payment would be made, the buyer did not pay and the contract was not renewed. The seller, although making reasonable efforts, was unable to obtain alternative financing. It is clear, is it not, that this is a proper case for a consequential damage claim under general contract law? See UCC 1–103; Restatement, Second, Contracts § 351, Comment (e).

Note: Seller's Remedial Choices—Cumulation or Election?

Comment 1 to UCC 2–703 states that the section "rejects any doctrine of election of remedies as a fundamental policy" and stresses that the "index" is "essentially cumulative in nature" and includes "all of the available remedies for breach." Whether the choice or pursuit of one remedy "bars another depends entirely on the facts of the individual case." Thus, UCC 2–709(3) provides that a seller who pursues an action for the price and is "held not entitled" to it "shall nevertheless be awarded damages for non-acceptance under * * *" UCC 2–708. Similarly, Comment 2 to UCC 2–706 states that a failure to act properly under this section deprives the seller "of damages here provided and relegates him to that provided in Section 2–708." The primary risk of pursuing a particular remedy and failing is, apparently, one of evidence: will the record support a claim for damages under UCC 2–708? A case in point is B & R Textile Corp. v. Paul Rothman Indus., 101 Misc.2d 98, 420 N.Y.S.2d 609, aff'd, 420 N.Y.S.2d 609, 27 UCC Rep.Serv. 994 (N.Y.Sup.Ct.1979), where the buyer argued that the seller's reliance upon the price received in a resale where the required notice was not given constituted an election of remedies. This argument was rejected by a court, which held that the seller's prompt resale generated a price which, when supported by evidence of other sales contemporaneously made by the seller, established the "market price" under UCC 2–708(1). See also, Cole v. Melvin, 441 F.Supp. 193 (D.S.D.1977), where a defective resale left a thin but adequate record from which to establish the market price. The point for the litigator is clear: develop, if possible, the "fall back" evidence necessary to satisfy UCC 2–708(1).

Some policy questions lurk on the fringes. Suppose the seller pursues the resale remedy and complies fully with UCC 2–706. If, thereafter, he sues for higher damages under UCC 2–708(1) will he be limited by UCC 2–706(1)? Or, suppose the seller arguably should have resold under UCC 2–706 but failed to do so. Will a recovery under UCC 2–708(1) be reduced by what he could have obtained on a resale? The answers to these questions may become clearer after we have considered the so-called "lost volume" problem and the application of UCC 2–708(2) in the next section. At least one court, however, has held that if the seller is *not* a "lost volume" seller and has conducted a commercially unreasonable resale under UCC 2–706(1), the recovery under UCC 2–708(1) will be limited by what the seller *should* have received in damages if the resale had been proper. The seller's apparent bad faith in the resale limited the recovery to "actual losses" and precluded any windfall gains permitted under the formula in UCC 2–708(1). See Coast Trading Co. v. Cudahy Co., 592 F.2d 1074 (9th Cir.1978).

SECTION 6. SELLER'S RIGHT TO "PERSONALIZED" DAMAGES—UCC 2–708(2)

In the scheme of things, UCC 2–708(2) appears to be the seller's remedy of last resort. An assumption is that if conforming goods can be identified before or after the breach, the seller will prefer either an action for the price under UCC 2–709 or damages based upon a resale under UCC 2–706. If those remedies fail, the seller can resort to damages under UCC 2–708. But which part of 2–708, subsection (1) with its contract-market price formula, or subsection (2) which awards the "profit (including reasonable overhead) which the seller would have made from full performance by the buyer * * *?"

The Code answer is that UCC 2–708(1) should be applied unless the measure of damages is "inadequate to put the seller in as good a position as performance would have done. * * *" As we have seen, however, if subsection (1) puts the seller in a better position than subsection (2), and does not, when the policy of UCC 1–106(1) is considered, overcompensate, then the buyer cannot limit the seller to the profits that would have been made on their particular contract. This analysis, with its emphasis upon an objective measure of damages, reinforces the residual character of UCC 2–708(2), with its emphasis upon a particularized measure.

Accepting this analysis for the moment, the critical questions for the lawyer and judge are: (1) When should UCC 2–708(2) be used to measure the seller's damages; and (2) When applicable, how should those damages be measured? These questions have generated a continuing flow of law review commentary, much of which attempts to apply rather complex if not sophisticated economic analysis. For a recent example, see Note, *Lost-Profits Damage Awards Under Uniform Commercial Code Section 2–708(2),* 37 Stan.L.Rev. 1109 (1985). For a clear and sensible analysis, see Sebert, *Remedies Under Article Two of the Uniform Commercial Code: An Agenda for Review,* 130 U.Pa.L.Rev. 360, 383–407 (1981).

Problem 14–7

Simpka v. Volta—Scene Five

On July 1, Volta contracted to purchase office furniture, to be manufactured by Simpka, from Dolt, a distributor. The price was $90,000. Dolt then placed an order for the furniture with Simpka for $80,000, with delivery to Volta no later than October 1. On August 15, Volta, without justification, repudiated the contract with Dolt. Dolt promptly cancelled the order with Simpka, who had not started to work on the goods, for a customary cancellation charge of $1,000.

S comes to you for advice. The market price of the furniture at the "time and place for tender", October 1, under UCC 2–708(1) was estimated to be $90,000. S had incurred $2,000 in expenses between July 1 and August 15. S would have paid M $80,000 for the furniture and spent another $1,500 to prepare the goods for delivery if B had not repudiated. These expenditures, however, were not made.

A. Which section should be used to measure S's damages? Why?

B. If UCC 2–708(2) is applicable, how should Dolt's damages be measured?

NATIONAL CONTROLS, INC. v. COMMODORE BUSINESS MACHINES, INC.

Court of Appeal of California, First District, 1985.
163 Cal.App.3d 688, 209 Cal.Rptr. 636.

SCOTT, ASSOCIATE JUSTICE.

Respondent National Controls, Inc. (NCI) brought an action for breach of contract against appellant Commodore Business Machines, Inc. (Commodore). After a court trial, judgment was entered awarding NCI over $280,000 in damages, and Commodore has appealed.

I

NCI manufactures electronic weighing and measuring devices. Among its products is the model 3221 electronic microprocessor technology load cell scale (the 3221), which is designed to interface with a cash register for use at check-out stands. NCI sells the 3221 to cash register manufacturers, also termed original equipment manufacturers, or O.E.M.s. NCI does not maintain an inventory stock of the scales, but builds them to specific order by an O.E.M. The 3221 is a standard unit, which is modified by NCI to meet the specifications of each O.E.M. with respect to cash register compatability, paint, and logo.

In November 1980, Commodore had initial discussions with NCI about the possibility of Commodore becoming an O.E.M. customer. By telephone, Commodore purchased one 3221, which was sent by NCI to Commodore's Texas facility, along with NCI's standard specifications for the 3221 and its standard price schedule. In December 1980, Commodore ordered and paid for four more scales. Again, the orders were made by telephone. NCI did not receive a purchase order from Commodore; instead, Commodore merely gave NCI a Commodore purchase order number over the phone; that number was written on the sales order prepared by NCI and sent to Commodore.

In March 1981, Terry Rogers of Commodore ordered an additional 30 scales. The order was placed by telephone, and once again Commodore did not send NCI a purchase order. Instead, Rogers gave Wiggins of NCI a purchase order number by telephone; that number was entered by Wiggins on NCI's sales order.

On March 31, 1981, in a phone conversation with Wiggins, Rogers placed a firm order for 900 scales: 50 to be delivered in May, 150 in June, 300 in July, and 400 in August. Wiggins and Rogers agreed on quantity, price, and delivery schedule. As in the previous transactions, Rogers gave Wiggins a purchase order number over the telephone, Wiggins then prepared an NCI sales order, entered on it the Commodore purchase order number, and mailed a copy of that sales order to Commodore. NCI also sent a copy of its sales order to its Florida manufacturing facility, which began manufacture of the units.

In a departure from its previous practice, Commodore also mailed its purchase order to NCI. Paragraph 19 of the reverse side of that order contained a provision limiting the damages for which Commodore would be responsible in the event of a breach; in particular, the provision disclaimed liability for any incidental or consequential damages.

Wiggins of NCI testified that he does not recall ever seeing the Commodore purchase order. Both he and Rogers testified that during their phone conversations, there was no discussion of any terms and conditions on that purchase order other than price, quantity, and delivery schedule. According to Commodore's Rogers, the primary purpose of its purchase order was to confirm what had been discussed by telephone and to provide a written copy of the delivery schedule.

Delivery was made to Commodore of the first 200 units, and 300 units were ready to ship in June of 1981. As of that date, the remaining 400 units of the order were nearly complete. However, Commodore accepted only the first 50 scales, and did not accept or pay for the remaining 850 units. Thereafter, all of the 850 units were resold to National Semiconductor, an existing O.E.M. customer. NCI's vice president and general manager in charge of its Florida manufacturing facility testified that in 1980 and 1981, the plant had the production capacity to more than double its output of 3221's.

Among its findings and conclusions, the trial court concluded that the terms of the parties' contract were those established during their telephone discussions prior to and on March 31, 1981, and in the November 1980 letter from NCI to Commodore enclosing a price schedule, as well as "the terms" of NCI's prior sales orders. It then concluded that the provision on limitation of damages in Commodore's purchase order was a proposal for an additional term which did not become part of the contract because it was a material alteration thereof. The court also found that NCI was a "lost volume seller" who was entitled to recover the loss of profit it would have made on the sale of the 850 units to Commodore, notwithstanding its subsequent resale of those units to another customer.

* * *

[The court affirmed the trial court's ruling that Commodore's limitation of damage clause did not become part of the contract.]

III

Commodore also contends that the trial court erred when it relied on section 2708, subdivision (2), to award NCI damages by way of lost profits. In a related argument, Commodore contends that if lost profits were the proper measure of damages, it was entitled under the plain language of section 2708 to credit for the proceeds of NCI's resale of the contract goods to National Semiconductor.

Damages caused by a buyer's breach or repudiation of a sales contract are usually measured by the difference between the resale price of the goods and the contract price, as provided by Uniform Commercial Code section 2–706. When it is not appropriate to use this difference to measure the seller's loss (as when the goods have not been resold in a commercially reasonable manner), the seller's measure of damages is the difference between the market and the contract prices as provided in Uniform Commercial Code section 2–708, subdivision (1). Ordinarily, this measure will result in recovery equal to the value of the seller's bargain. However, under certain circumstances this formula is also not an adequate means to ascertain that value, and the seller may recover his loss of expected profits on the contract under subdivision (2) of Uniform Commercial Code section 2–708. (3 Hawkland, Uniform Commercial Code Series (1982–1984) §§ 2–708—2–708:04.)

Section 2708 provides [the court quoted the statute.]

When buyers have repudiated a fixed price contract to purchase goods, several courts elsewhere have construed subdivision (2) of Uniform Commercial Code section 2–708 or its state counterpart to permit the award of lost profits under the contract to the seller who establishes that he is a "lost volume seller," i.e., one who proves that even though he resold the contract goods, that sale to the third party would have been made regardless of the buyer's breach.[3] (*Neri v. Retail Marine Corporation* (1972) 30 N.Y.2d 393, 334 N.Y.S.2d 165, 168, 285 N.E.2d 311, 314; *Snyder v. Herbert Greenbaum & Assoc., Inc.* (1977) 38 Md.App. 144, 380 A.2d 618, 624–625; *Teradyne, Inc. v. Teledyne Industries, Inc.* (1st Cir. 1982) 676 F.2d 865, 866–868; *Nederlandse, etc. v. Grand Pre-Stressed Corp.* (E.D. N.Y.1979) 466 F.Supp. 846, affd. (2nd Cir.) 614 F.2d 1289.) The lost volume seller must establish that had the breaching buyer performed, the seller would have realized profits from two sales. (See Goetz & Scott, *Measuring Sellers' Damages: The Lost-Profits Puzzle* (1979) 31 Stan.L.Rev. 323, 326.)

In *Neri v. Retail Marine Corporation, supra,* 285 N.E.2d 311, seller contracted to sell a new boat, which it ordered and received from its supplier. The buyer then repudiated the contract. Later, seller sold the boat to another buyer, for the same price. The court relied on Uniform Commercial Code section 2–708, subdivision (2), to award the seller its lost profits under the contract, reasoning that the record established that market damages would be inadequate to put the seller in as good a position as performance would have done. The court drew an analogy to an auto dealer with an inexhaustible supply of cars. A breach of an agreement to buy a car at a standard price would cost that dealer a sale even though he was able to resell the car at the same price. In other words, had the breaching buyer performed, seller would have made two sales instead of one. (*Id.,* at pp. 312–315.)

3. One California court has applied subdivision (2) of section 2708 to hold that a "middleman" is entitled to lost profits. (*Distribu-Dor, Inc. v. Karadanis* (1970) 11 Cal.App.3d 463, 470, 90 Cal.Rptr. 231.) That case is not dispositive here, as it does not involve a lost volume seller.

While the seller in *Neri* was a retailer, the lost volume seller rule is also applicable to manufacturers. (*Nederlandse, etc. v. Grand Pre-Stressed Corp., supra,* 466 F.Supp. 846.) In *Nederlandse,* seller, a manufacturer of steel strand, brought an action against buyer for breach of an agreement to purchase approximately 1,180 metric tons of strand. Defendant had accepted only about 221 tons, and repudiated the remaining 958 tons, of which 317 tons had been already produced by seller. Seller resold the 317 tons to various third party purchasers. (*Id.,* at p. 849.)

The court held that seller was entitled to lost profits under Uniform Commercial Code section 2–708, subdivision (2), and that no set-off would be allowed for profits earned through the sales to third parties. The evidence established that seller had sufficient production capacity to supply not only the 1,180 tons required by the contract, but also the 317 tons sold to third parties. The fact that seller was a manufacturer rather than a retailer, and that he produced only to order rather than maintaining an inventory, was of no significance in determining the applicability of Uniform Commercial Code section 2–708. (*Id.,* at pp. 853–854.)

Commodore accurately points out that the lost volume seller rule has been criticized by some commentators as overly simplistic. (Goetz & Scott, *supra,* 31 Stan.L.Rev. 323, 330–354.) Nevertheless, those courts considering the question have held that Uniform Commercial Code section 2–708 does allow lost profits to a "lost volume seller" and that criticism has not resulted in any revision of the section.

Commodore also contends that if NCI was entitled to lost profits under the contract, Commodore should have received credit for the proceeds of the resale.

The literal language of section 2708, subdivision (2), does provide some support for that contention: "If the measure of damages provided in subdivision (1) is inadequate to put the seller in as good a position as performance would have done then the measure of damages is the profit (including reasonable overhead) which the seller would have made from full performance by the buyer, *together with * * * due credit for payments or proceeds of resale.*" (Emphasis added.) However, courts elsewhere have uniformly held that the underscored language does not apply to a lost volume seller. (See *Neri v. Retail Marine Corporation, supra,* 285 N.E.2d at p. 314, fn. 2; *Famous Knitwear Corporation v. Drug Fair, Inc.* (4th Cir.1974) 493 F.2d 251, 254, fn. 7; *Snyder v. Herbert Greenbaum & Assoc., Inc., supra,* 380 A.2d at pp. 625–626; *Teradyne, Inc. v. Teledyne Industries, Inc., supra,* 676 F.2d 865, 868.)

As the court in *Snyder v. Herbert Greenbaum & Assoc., Inc., supra,* 380 A.2d 618 explained, "Logically, lost volume status, which entitles the seller to the § 2–708(2) formula rather than the formula found in § 2–708(1), is inconsistent with a credit for the proceeds of resale. The whole concept of lost volume status is that the sale of the goods to the resale purchaser could have been made with other goods had there been no breach. In essence, the original sale and the second sale are independent events, becoming related only after breach, as the original sale goods are applied to the second sale. To require a credit for the proceeds of resale is to deny the essential element that entitles the lost volume seller to § 2–708(2) in the first place—the mutual independence of the contract and the resale.

"Practically, if the 'due credit' clause is applied to the lost volume seller, his measure of damages is no different from his recovery under § 2–708(1). Under § 2–708(1) he recovers the contract/market differential and the profit he makes on resale. If the 'due credit' provision is applied, the seller recovers only the profit he makes on resale plus the difference between the resale price and the contract price, an almost identical measure to § 2–708(1). If the 'due credit' clause is applied to the lost volume seller, the damage measure of 'lost profits' is rendered nugatory, and he is not put in as good a position as if there had been performance." (*Id.*, at p. 625.)

In this case, the evidence was undisputed that in 1980 and 1981, NCI's manufacturing plant was operating at approximately 40 percent capacity. The production of the 900 units did not tax that capacity, and the plant could have more than doubled its output of 3221's and still have stayed within its capacity. That evidence was sufficient to support the court's findings that NCI had the capacity to supply both Commodore and National Semiconductor, and that had there been no breach by Commodore, NCI would have had the benefit of both the original contract and the resale contract. Accordingly, the trial court correctly determined that NCI was a lost volume seller, that the usual "contract price minus market price" rule set forth in subdivision (1) of section 2708 was inadequate to put NCI in as good a position as performance would have done, and that NCI was therefore entitled to its lost profits on the contract with Commodore, without any set-off for profits on the resale to National Semiconductor.

Judgment is affirmed.

WHITE, P.J., and BARRY-DEAL, J., concur.

Notes

1. Return to Problem 14–7. Does *Commodore* support a conclusion that Dolt can use UCC 2–708(2) because it was a "lost volume" seller? Professor Sebert concludes that a "jobber" or distributor, i.e., a "middleman whose only role is to procure finished goods and resell them," who decides not to procure the goods after the buyer's repudiation should be able to use UCC 2–708(2). Because the "jobber" does not have finished goods on hand, "UCC 2–708(2) is the only Code damage provision that produces sensible results for such a seller; all of the other damage provisions contemplate the existence of finished goods." Sebert, 130 U.Pa.L.Rev. at 385. Accord: Blair International, Ltd. v. LaBarge, Inc., 675 F.2d 954 (8th Cir.1982) (UCC 2–708(1) not adequate where seller can't resell or does not have goods); Comeq, Inc. v. Mitternight Boiler Works, Inc., 456 So.2d 264 (Ala.1984).

2. The seller, in *Commodore,* was the manufacturer rather than a middleman and actually resold the goods intended for the buyer. What test does the court use to determine whether the plaintiff was a lost volume seller? In measuring damages under UCC 2–708(2), how does the court treat the proceeds of the resale? Does the court do damage to the language of UCC 2–708(2)? Recall in *Afram,* supra, that Judge Posner concluded, correctly we believe, that if the resale could not be made "but for" the breach, the buyer was entitled to credit for the proceeds of resale.

Problem 14–8

Simpka v. Volta—Scene Six

On March 1, Simpka contracted to manufacture custom furniture for Volta for $80,000, delivery f.o.b. Ohio no later than November 1. On May 1, Volta repudiated without justification. Simpka had commenced to manufacture the furniture but no item was completed. The market price of the furniture in Ohio was $60,000. The market price in New York was $55,000. The economy was in a mild recession, and the respective market prices in November were expected to be $40,000 in Ohio and $35,000 in New York.

A. A summer associate has given you the following memo: "It is clear that Simpka could complete the manufacture, UCC 2–704(2), and attempt to resell the custom furniture. See UCC 2–706(2), stating that it is 'not necessary that the goods be in existence or that any or all of them have been identified to the contract before the breach.' If a resale can be made, damages can be recovered under UCC 2–706(1), or, if there is lost volume, under UCC 2–708(2). If a resale cannot be made, Simpka can recover the price from Volta. UCC 2–709(1)(b). I recommend that we advise Simpka to complete the manufacturing process." Do you agree?

B. Suppose, in the exercise of reasonable commercial judgment, Simpka stopped the manufacturing process. UCC 2–704(2). (1) Simpka had components on hand purchased for the contract which cost $20,000. These components were scrapped for $15,000. (2) Simpka had incurred other performance costs ("variable" costs) of $15,000 which could not be salvaged. (3) Because of the breach, Simpka did not have to incur other performance of "variable" costs, estimated to be $25,000. What damages should Simpka recover under UCC 2–708(2)? Who has the burden of establishing that "overhead" is or is not reasonable?

Note: Who Is a Lost Volume Seller?

The assumption underlying the "lost volume" problem is simple to state: If a seller had the capacity to and probably would have made a second sale regardless of the buyer's breach, the goal of UCC 1–106(1) will be frustrated if the profit the seller would have made on the first sale is offset by the proceeds of the second sale. Embracing this assumption, *Commodore* and the authorities cited therein have used UCC 2–708(2) to protect the profit on the first sale without regard to the proceeds of any resale.

In so doing, the courts have adopted a simple test for determining lost volume: If, in the relevant time period, the seller had the capacity to make a second sale and, after the breach, in fact made a resale, the requirement is satisfied. Rejected is the view, advocated by some commentators, that lost volume exists when the seller satisfies three conditions: (1) The buyer who purchased the resold entity would have been solicited by the seller had there been no breach; (2) The solicitation would have been successful; and (3) The seller could have performed the additional contract. Harris, *A Radical Restatement of the Laws of Seller's Damages: Sales Act and Commercial Code Results Compared,* 18 Stan.L.Rev. 66, 80–83 (1965). In refusing to "require proof of a complex economic relationship," one court was satisfied by proof that the seller "would have made the sale to the resale purchaser even if" the buyer had performed, that the seller "resold the parts, and that it had an existing inventory of these parts." Islamic Republic of Iran v. Boeing Co., 771 F.2d 1279, (9th Cir.1985) (Washington law).

In addition, the courts have ignored (if not rejected) the claim by some that even if a second sale could have been made, it would not, in all probability, have been profitable. See Goetz & Scott, *Measuring Seller's Damages: The Lost-Profits Puzzle,* 31 Stan.L.Rev. 323 (1979). Why? The argument is summarized by Professor Sebert:

> One foundation of the Geotz and Scott argument is the accepted proposition that economically efficient entities, whether they be manufacturers or retailers, attempt to operate at a level of output where marginal cost equals marginal revenue. Economic theory also posits that these efficient sellers are likely to be producing at a level where marginal costs are rising as additional units are produced or sold, and that marginal revenue is likely to be falling, or at best remaining constant, because the increased supply caused by additional production or sales will cause the market price to fall. Based upon these traditional economic concepts, Goetz and Scott argue that, even if the seller had the capacity to do so, a seller operating at the level where marginal cost equals marginal

revenue would not have produced the additional goods to sell to buyer 2 if buyer 1 had not breached. In a world of rising marginal costs and static or declining marginal revenue, it would not have been efficient for the seller to produce or obtain additional goods to sell to buyer 2 because the marginal cost of those goods would exceed the marginal revenue received from their sale and the seller would have lost money. Thus, Goetz and Scott suggest that the sale to buyer 2 is a sale that the efficient seller normally would not have made, and therefore the seller is not a lost volume seller.

Sebert at 389–90 *

Professor Sebert rejects Goetz and Scott's presumption that the seller is not a lost volume seller, "even though a seller has the capacity to make an additional sale and even though the resale buyer probably would have bought from the seller had the original buyer not breached" without rejecting the possibility that the resale merely replaces the original sale because of the assumed rising marginal costs. He proposes the following approach: " * * * (O)nce the seller shows that he had the capacity to make an additional sale and that the resale buyer probably would have bought from him anyway, I would place the burden of proof on the breaching buyer to show that the seller would not have made an additional sale because of rising marginal costs." Sebert at 391.

* Another argument by Goetz and Scott, summarized by Sebert, is that a seller normally will not have lost volume because the buyer's breach will cause an increase in demand for the seller's product, offsetting any losses suffered because of the buyer's breach. The assumptions are that the breach indicates that the buyer did not want the goods, and that a sale by the buyer would likely be to someone who otherwise would have bought from the seller. "Because the buyer who breaches can no longer resell the goods, that breach will permit the seller to make an additional sale to a customer who otherwise would have bought from the breaching buyer." Sebert at 392. This argument has been criticized as misrepresenting the problem when the seller is a retailer. Goldberg, *An Economic Analysis of the Lost-Volume Seller,* 57 S.Cal. L.Rev. 283, 288–90 (1984).

CHAPTER FIFTEEN

SELLER'S REPUDIATION AND THE LIKE—A SURVEY OF BUYER'S REMEDIES

SECTION 1. INTRODUCTION

There are three "garden" varieties of breach by a seller; repudiation, failure to deliver and a tender of delivery which does not conform to the contract. This chapter will feature the buyer's remedies which are responsive to the first two varieties, namely, permissible action when the expectation of receiving due performance is impaired, UCC 2–609, claims to goods in the possession of the seller, UCC 2–716 and 2–502, and damages, either after "cover" under UCC 2–712 or under the formula in UCC 2–713. Note that where the seller makes a non-conforming tender and the buyer "rightfully rejects or justifiably revokes acceptance," the buyer may claim damages under UCC 2–712 or 2–713. UCC 2–711(1). The special problems involved in the buyer's remedies of rejection, UCC 2–601, and revocation of acceptance, UCC 2–608, however, prompt us to defer their consideration to Chapter Eighteen. Similarly, we have deferred for more extensive treatment the non-conformity called breach of warranty and the remedies available to a buyer who has accepted defective goods and, for one reason or another, does not revoke acceptance under UCC 2–608. These important remedies include "direct," UCC 2–714(2), "incidental," UCC 2–715(1), and "consequential," UCC 2–715(2) damages. At the same time, we will examine the extent to which a seller can disclaim warranties, UCC 2–316, and the parties can alter by agreement code remedies normally available. UCC 2–719.

It is useful to identify the functional parallels between seller's and buyer's remedies. Compare UCC 2–703 and 2–711. And see UCC 2–702 and 2–502, 2–709 and 2–716, 2–706 and 2–712, 2–708 and 2–713, and 2–710 and 2–715(1). The parallelism is conscious, but there is one important difference from the buyer's perspective. Although the buyer, like the seller, is in business to make a profit (and, undoubtedly, most buyers are also sellers), the purchase contract is designed to obtain goods which will be used in the overall business enterprise. The better the price, the quicker the delivery, and the higher the quality, then the more likely that the overall business will be profitable. Consequently, unless the buyer's plans have changed, an immediate concern upon breach by the seller will be replacement of the goods or inducing the seller to perform. Higher costs and delays in this replacement process both deprive the buyer of the benefit of his bargain and affect overall profitability. Thus, if the goods have not been tendered, the most important remedies will be specific performance, 2–716, or cover, 2–712, and, if delay is involved, recovery of consequential damages under UCC 2–715(2). The "formula" in UCC 2–713(1) is a residual remedy which is used when specific performance is not available and relief for "cover" in UCC 2–712(1) is, for whatever reason, not pursued. Some have urged that UCC 2–713 be repealed. See Childres, *Buyer's Remedies: The Danger of Section 2–713,* 72 Nw.U.L.Rev. 837 (1978). Whatever the value of this "residual" remedy, one thing is clear: since the buyer's contract, unlike the seller's, is not complicated by "lost volume" problems, there is, perhaps, a sounder basis for concluding that a buyer who did cover or should have covered is foreclosed from using UCC 2–713(1) when that would provide a higher recovery. Even if this option is preserved, the buyer cannot recover consequential damages caused by the breach which could have been "reasonably * * * prevented by cover or otherwise." UCC 2–715(2)(a). We will consider these possibilities in the balance of this chapter.

SECTION 2. WHEN HAS SELLER REPUDIATED? COMMITTED A MATERIAL BREACH OF AN INSTALLMENT CONTRACT?

Just as the Code does not define what constitutes a repudiation by a buyer so it does not define what constitutes a repudiation by a seller. The same open-endedness permeates the "adequate assurance" provisions of UCC 2–609, and the impact of breach upon installment contracts, UCC 2–612. In many situations, relevant criteria will be similar for seller and buyer alike. Thus, if either party threatens to cease performance unless the other agrees to a performance not fairly within the scope of the original agreement, a repudiation may have occurred. For illustrations, compare Louis Dreyfus Corp. v. Brown, 709 F.2d 898 (5th Cir.1983), where the court held that a farmer repudiated a contract to deliver grain, with Bill's Coal Co., Inc. v. Board of Public Utilities of Springfield, Mo., 682 F.2d 883 (10th Cir.1982), where the court held that a supplier's bad faith interpretation of the price term was not a repudiation and the buyer's cancellation, therefore, was a breach.

In the *Plotnick* case, supra at 588, the court assessed the significance of the buyer's late payment partly in terms of whether it impaired the seller's capacity to continue performance. A court might ask similar questions about a seller's late delivery. See UCC 2–612(2). But such symmetry will not be found in all cases and there will be borderline situations. For a helpful discussion, see Jackson, *"Anticipatory Repudiation" and the Temporal Element of Contract Law: An Economic Inquiry into Contract Damages in Cases of Prospective Non-Performance,* 31 Stan.L.Rev. 69, 75–101 (1978).

Problem 15–1

The Tivoli Manufacturing Co., a manufacturer of air compressors, contracted with the Ace Supply Co. to furnish at a fixed price a large quantity of specially tooled valves for use in the compressors. Ace agreed to deliver the valves in 6 equal installments at 3 month intervals. Tivoli stated that the installments were geared to a long range production schedule and a projected increase in demand for the compressors. Tivoli furnished design drawings to assist Ace in "tooling up," gave Ace 6 months of lead time, and advanced 25% of the contract price. Two weeks before the first installment was due, Tivoli appeared in your office with the following letter from Ace:

> Gentlemen:
>
> As suggested in our telephone conversation of last week, our engineers misread the design drawings which you furnished us.
>
> We must, therefore, retool our original model value at considerable extra expense and some delay. We regret that we will be unable to meet the first installment, scheduled for delivery in two weeks. We will make every effort to meet the second installment three

> months hence and to deliver the quantity promised in the first installment before the contract delivery schedule is completed.
>
> Yours sincerely,
> Ace Supply Co.

Tivoli states that it would like to cancel the contract and get back the 25% advance. Upon close questioning, you discover: 1) the delay in delivery will "wreak havoc" with Tivoli's production schedule and existing contractual commitments; 2) if the contract were cancelled, Tivoli would purchase 50% of the valves ordered from Ace from another manufacturer who guaranteed full performance in 4 months; 3) Tivoli's estimated demand for the compressors was about 50% too high; 4) in Tivoli's judgment, Ace would "probably" meet the next installment and make up the late deliveries. What is your advice?

SECTION 3. BUYER'S RIGHT TO GET THE GOODS—SPECIFIC PERFORMANCE AND REPLEVIN

Suppose, in Problem 15–1, that Ace repudiated the entire contract with Tivoli because it received an offer to purchase all of the compressor valves on hand and its output of similar valves during the next 12 months at a price that was "too good to refuse." Also, Ace estimated a 35–50% increase in the cost of production over the next year. At the time of repudiation, Ace had on hand 25% of the total quantity ordered by Tivoli. The valves were conforming and identified to the contract. Tivoli needs the valves "yesterday" to meet production orders and estimates that it will take four months and 30% more money to establish a reliable source of supply. In short, Tivoli wants both the valves Ace has on hand and the future output of conforming valves at the agreed price until the quantity ordered has been satisfied.

Problem 15–2

You represent Tivoli in this matter and your client wants results. Which of the following alternatives is best suited to your client's interest and most likely to be successful?

1. Suspend performance and wait under UCC 2–610 and try to negotiate the matter with Ace. Offer more money and couple that with appropriate "non-legal" pressures.

2. Replevin of the valves under UCC 2–716(3). See Tatum v. Richter, 280 Md. 332, 373 A.2d 923 (1977) (replevin of used Ferrari).

3. Seek specific performance of the contract and an order restraining Ace from selling the existing goods and future output to third parties. See UCC 2–716(1); Kaiser Trading Co. v. Associated Metals & Minerals Corp., 321 F.Supp. 923 (N.D.Cal. 1970), appeal dismissed 443 F.2d 1364 (9th Cir.1971).

4. Recover the goods under UCC 2–502.

LACLEDE GAS CO. v. AMOCO OIL CO.

United States Court of Appeals, Eighth Circuit, 1975.
522 F.2d 33.

ROSS, C.J.

The Laclede Gas Company (Laclede), a Missouri corporation, brought this diversity action alleging breach of contract against the Amoco Oil Company (Amoco), a Delaware corporation. It sought relief in the form of a mandatory injunction prohibiting the continuing breach or, in the alternative, damages. The district court held a bench trial on the issues of whether there was a valid, binding contract between the parties and whether, if there was such a contract, Amoco should be enjoined from breaching it. It then ruled that the "contract is invalid due to lack of mutuality" and denied the prayer for injunctive relief. The court made no decision regarding the requested damages. Laclede Gas Co. v. Amoco Oil Co., 385 F.Supp. 1332, 1336 (E.D.Mo.1974). This appeal followed, and we reverse the district court's judgment.

On September 21, 1970, Midwest Missouri Gas Company (now Laclede), and American Oil Company (now Amoco), the predecessors of the parties to this litigation, entered into a written agreement which was designed to provide central propane gas distribution systems to various residential developments in Jefferson County, Missouri, until such time as natural gas mains were extended into these areas. The agreement contemplated that as individual developments were planned the owners or developers would apply to Laclede for central propane gas systems. If Laclede determined that such a system was appropriate in any given development, it could request Amoco to supply the propane to that specific development. This request was made in the form of a supplemental form letter, as provided in the September 21 agreement; and if Amoco decided to supply the propane, it bound itself to do so by signing this supplemental form.

Once this supplemental form was signed the agreement placed certain duties on both Laclede and Amoco. Basically, Amoco was to "[i]nstall, own, maintain and operate * * * storage and vaporization facilities and any other facilities necessary to provide [it] with the capability of delivering to [Laclede] commercial propane gas suitable * * * for delivery by [Laclede] to its customers' facilities." Amoco's facilities were to be "adequate to provide a continuous supply of commerical propane gas at such times and in such volumes commensurate with [Laclede's] requirements for meeting the demands reasonably to be anticipated in each Development while this Agreement is in force." Amoco was deemed to be "the supplier," while Laclede was "the distributing utility."

For its part Laclede agreed to "[i]nstall, own, maintain and operate all distribution facilities" from a "point of delivery" which was defined to be "the outlet of [Amoco] header piping." Laclede also promised to pay Amoco "the Wood River Area Posted Price for propane plus four cents per gallon for all amounts of commercial propane gas delivered" to it under the agreement.

Since it was contemplated that the individual propane systems would eventually be converted to natural gas, one paragraph of the agreement provided that Laclede should give Amoco 30 days written notice of this event, after which the agreement would no longer be binding for the converted development.

Another paragraph gave Laclede the right to cancel the agreement. However, this right was expressed in the following language:

> "This Agreement shall remain in effect for one (1) year following the first delivery of gas by [Amoco] to [Laclede] hereunder. Subject to termination as provided in Paragraph 11 hereof [dealing with conversions to natural gas], this Agreement shall automatically continue in effect for additional periods of one (1) year each unless [Laclede] shall, not less than 30 days prior to the expiration of the initial one (1) year period or any subsequent one (1) year period, give [Amoco] written notice of termination."

There was no provision under which Amoco could cancel the agreement.

For a time the parties operated satisfactorily under this agreement, and some 17 residential subdivisions were brought within it by supplemental letters. However, for various reasons, including conversion to natural gas, the number of developments under the agreement had shrunk to eight by the time of trial. These were all mobile home parks.

During the winter of 1972–73 Amoco experienced a shortage of propane and voluntarily placed all of its customers, including Laclede, on an 80% allocation basis, meaning that Laclede would receive only up to 80% of its previous requirements. Laclede objected to this and pushed Amoco to give it 100% of what the developments needed. Some conflict arose over this before the temporary shortage was alleviated.

Then, on April 3, 1973, Amoco notified Laclede that its Wood River Area Posted Price of propane had been increased by three cents per gallon. Laclede objected to this increase also and demanded a full explanation. None was forthcoming. Instead Amoco merely sent a letter dated May 14, 1973, informing Laclede that it was "terminating" the September 21, 1970, agreement effective May 31, 1973. It claimed it had the right to do this because "the Agreement lacks 'mutuality.'"[1]

The district court felt that the entire controversy turned on whether or not Laclede's right to "arbitrarily cancel the Agreement" without Amoco having a similar right rendered the contract void "for lack of mutuality" and it resolved this question in the affirmative. We disagree with this conclusion and hold that settled principles of contract law require a reversal.

I.

* * *

We conclude that there is mutuality of consideration within the terms of the agreement and hold that there is a valid, binding contract between the parties as to each of the developments for which supplemental letter agreements have been signed.

II.

Since he found that there was no binding contract, the district judge did not have to deal with the question of whether or not to grant the injunction prayed for by Laclede. He simply denied this relief because there was no contract. Laclede Gas Co. v. Amoco Oil Co., supra, 385 F.Supp. at 1336.

Generally the determination of whether or not to order specific performance of a contract lies within the sound discretion of the trial court. Landau v. St. Louis Public Service Co., 364 Mo. 1134, 273 S.W.2d 255, 259 (1954). However, this discretion is, in fact, quite limited; and it is said that when certain equitable rules have been met and the contract is fair and plain "specific performance goes as a matter of right." Miller v. Coffeen, 365 Mo. 204, 280 S.W.2d 100, 102 (1955), quoting, Berberet v. Myers, 240 Mo. 58, 77, 144 S.W. 824, 830 (1912). (Emphasis omitted.)

With this in mind we have carefully reviewed the very complete record on appeal and conclude that the trial court should grant the injunctive relief prayed. We are satisfied that this case falls within that category in which

1. While Amoco sought to repudiate the agreement, it resumed supplying propane to the subdivisions on February 1, 1974, under the mandatory allocation guidelines promulgated by the Federal Energy Administration under the Federal Mandatory Allocation Program for propane. It is agreed that this is now being done under the contract.

specific performance should be ordered as a matter of right. See Miller v. Coffeen, supra, 280 S.W.2d at 102.

Amoco contends that four of the requirements for specific performance have not been met. Its claims are: (1) there is no mutuality of remedy in the contract; (2) the remedy of specific performance would be difficult for the court to administer without constant and long-continued supervision; (3) the contract is indefinite and uncertain; and (4) the remedy at law available to Laclede is adequate. The first three contentions have little or no merit and do not detain us for long.

* * *

[The court, after stressing that the agreement was for the buyer's requirements and was supported by consideration, rejected summarily the notion that "both parties be mutually entitled to * * * specific performance in order that one of them be given that remedy by the court." The defendant's right to performance can be protected by a conditional decree. The argument that specific performance would require excessive supervision was rejected on the ground that the rule invoked was "discretionary" and frequently ignored where the public interest, here providing propane to retail customers, was manifest. Finally, the court concluded that the court could determine the terms of performance with "reasonable certainty." The "requirements" feature offered no problem to enforcement. Nor did the fact that the contract stated no "definite time of duration:" the evidence established that the last subdivision should be converted to natural gas in 10 to 15 years and this set "a reasonable time limit on performance."]

It is axiomatic that specific performance will not be ordered when the party claiming breach of contract has an adequate remedy at law. Jamison Coal & Coke Co. v. Goltra, 143 F.2d 889, 894 (8th Cir.), cert. denied, 323 U.S. 769, 65 S.Ct. 122, 89 L.Ed. 615 (1944). This is especially true when the contract involves personal property as distinguished from real estate.

However, in Missouri, as elsewhere, specific performance may be ordered even though personalty is involved in the "proper circumstances." Mo.Rev.Stat. § 400.2–716(1); Restatement of Contracts, supra, § 361. And a remedy at law adequate to defeat the grant of specific performance "must be as certain, prompt, complete, and efficient to attain the ends of justice as a decree of specific performance." National Marking Mach. Co. v. Triumph Mfg. Co., 13 F.2d 6, 9 (8th Cir.1926). Accord, Snip v. City of Lamar, 239 Mo.App. 824, 201 S.W.2d 790, 798 (1947).

One of the leading Missouri cases allowing specific performance of a contract relating to personalty because the remedy at law was inadequate is Boeving v. Vandover, 240 Mo.App. 117, 218 S.W.2d 175, 178 (1949). In that case the plaintiff sought specific performance of a contract in which the defendant had promised to sell him an automobile. At that time (near the end of and shortly after World War II) new cars were hard to come by, and the court held that specific performance was a proper remedy since a new car "could not be obtained elsewhere except at considerable expense, trouble or loss, which cannot be estimated in advance."

We are satisfied that Laclede has brought itself within this practical approach taken by the Missouri courts. As Amoco points out, Laclede has propane immediately available to it under other contracts with other suppliers. And the evidence indicates that at the present time propane is readily available on the open market. However, this analysis ignores the fact that the contract involved in this lawsuit is for a long-term supply of propane to these subdivisions. The other two contracts under which Laclede obtains the gas will remain in force only until March 31, 1977, and April 1, 1981, respectively; and there is no assurance that Laclede will be able to receive any propane under them after that time. Also it is unclear as to whether or not Laclede can use the propane obtained under these contracts to supply the Jefferson County subdivisions, since they were originally entered into to provide Laclede with propane with which to "shave" its natural gas supply during peak demand periods. Additionally, there was uncontradicted expert testimony that Laclede probably could not find another supplier of propane willing to enter into a long-term contract such as the Amoco agreement, given the uncertain future of worldwide energy supplies. And, even if Laclede could obtain supplies of propane for the affected developments through its present contracts or newly negotiated ones, it would still face considerable expense and trouble which cannot be estimated in advance in making arrangements for its distribution to the subdivisions.

Specific performance is the proper remedy in this situation, and it should be granted by the district court.

CONCLUSION

For the foregoing reasons the judgment of the district court is reversed and the cause is remanded for the fashioning of appropriate injunctive relief in the form of a decree of specific performance as to those developments for which a supplemental agreement form has been signed by the parties. [Some footnotes omitted.]

Notes

1. Laclede Gas is one of the few cases under UCC 2–716(1) which both grants specific performance of a contract to sell goods and attempts to justify the decision on grounds of "other proper circumstances." More recently, specific performance with ancillary injunctive relief in long-term contracts for the supply of natural resources for energy has been granted without discussion. Iowa Elec. Light and Power Co. v. Atlas Corp., 467 F.Supp. 129, 138 (N.D.Iowa 1978), reversed on other grounds 603 F.2d 1301 (8th Cir.1979) (uranium oxide); Missouri Public Serv. Co. v. Peabody Coal Co., 583 S.W.2d 721 (Mo.App.1979), cert. denied 444 U.S. 865, 100 S.Ct. 135, 62 L.Ed. 2d 88 (1979) (bituminous coal). A useful history of UCC 2–716 and a comparison with the Restatement, Second of Contracts, is Greenberg, *Specific Performance Under Section 2–716 of the Uniform Commercial Code: "A More Liberal Attitude" in the "Grand Style,"* 17 N.Eng.L.Rev. 321, 344–53 (1982).

2. Should specific performance rather than damages be the preferred remedy in all cases of breach of contract? Put differently, if it were clear that specific performance (1) best protected the promisee's subjective value in the contract; (2) minimized if not avoided consequential damages; and (3) decreased the overall costs of judicial administration or the parties' post-breach negotiations, what are the arguments for the current rule, i.e., damages are preferred unless they are inadequate? An argument for specific performance "on demand" is made in Ulen, *The Efficiency of Specific Performance: Toward A Unified Theory of Contract Remedies,* 83 Mich.L.Rev. 341 (1984).

Problem 15–3

Suppose, in *Laclede Gas,* supra, that because of unanticipated events, the supplier's cost of production rose dramatically during performance of the contract. The supplier, in good faith, proposed a reasonable prospective modification, which the buyer, without negotiation, rejected. Upon repudiation by the supplier, the buyer sought specific performance plus injunctive relief. In response, the supplier made the following argument:

"May it please the court. We concede that at law our client would not be excused from performance under UCC 2–615 and that the buyer has stated a case for specific performance under UCC 2–716(1). We also concede that the law of this jurisdiction is that the buyer had no duty to negotiate over or agree to our proposed modification, no matter how reasonable. These are harsh outcomes 'at law.'

"Specific performance, however, is an equitable remedy to be granted in the discretion of the court. UCC 2–716(2) provides that a decree of specific performance 'may include such terms and conditions as to payment of the price, damages, or other relief as the court may deem just.' Comment 7 to UCC 2–615, although not directly on point, suggests that good faith may 'justify and even * * * require' a 'good faith inquiry seeking a readjustment of the contract terms to meet the new conditions.' Our proposed modification was fair and equitable in light of the changed circumstances. If the buyer had accepted it, the result would clearly be enforceable under UCC 2–209(1). Thus, your honor, we contend that it would be unjust to grant specific performance in this case without a price adjustment for the balance of the contract. We, therefore, urge the court to condition any decree for specific performance upon the buyer's consent to the reasonable modification which we have proposed."

How should the court rule?

SECTION 4. BUYER'S RIGHT TO "MARKET–CONTRACT" DAMAGES

Note first that UCC 2–713 instructs the court to use the market price "at the time when the buyer learned of the breach," and except in cases of rejection or revocation of acceptance indicates that the place for tender is the place to measure damages. The cognate provision for the seller's damages, UCC 2–708(1), directs the use of the "time and place for tender."

The meaning of the words "when the buyer learned of the breach" is likely to cause trouble only in the anticipatory repudiation situation, as we will see below, Professor Patterson suggested in the New York Law Revision Commission Reports that it was no more than a codification of the New York common law:

PATTERSON, 1 N.Y.LAW REV.COMM.REP. 697–699 (1955) "*Case law on Section UCC 2–713.*

"Since the 'ordinary' measure of damages for non-delivery by the seller (as defined in § 2–711(1)(b)) is the contract price less the market value of the goods, under the Uniform Sales Act enacted in New York in 1911, and even long before that year, we need not multiply New York citations to support that formula. The chief differences between Section 2–713 and the present statute are those relating to the *time when* and the *place where* market value is to be determined. * * *

"*Time when market value determined.*

"The present New York statute (P.P.L., § 148(3)) fixes the market value as of the time when the goods 'ought to have been delivered' or, if no time was fixed for delivery, 'at the time of refusal to deliver.' The proposed statute would make 'the time when the buyer learned of the breach' determine the market price. This is *apparently* a change in New York law; but actually it probably is not a change in the law as applied by New York courts. In at least two New York cases it was held that the market value was to be measured as of the time when the buyer knew of the default.* However, the Court of Appeals' language included 'should have known,' which would be different from the time when the buyer 'learned' of the breach. These cases do not purport to depart from the ordinary rule except where 'special circumstances' justify allowing the buyer a longer time to cover by a second buying in the market. Yet in one case an instruction that damages be measured by the price paid for similar goods bought by the buyer 'within a reasonable time after breach' (to allow him a reasonable time to cover), was held reversible error. In this case it seems that the buyer learned of the breach at once. Ordinarily, it is believed, no significant lag would occur. The purpose of Section 2–713(1), which applies (§ 2–711) only as an alternative to cover (§ 2–712) is presumably to prevent the buyer's getting any more damages by waiting for the market to go down ("speculating at the seller's expense," some courts would say) after he learns of the breach; if the market goes up further, the buyer will have to pay more and yet will recover only the difference (market minus contract price) when he first learns of the breach. The buyer is thus encouraged to 'cover' promptly. However, under Section 2–712 the buyer may cover 'without unreasonable delay' after the *breach* (*not* "learning of the breach"), which means that the buyer could *delay* after (learning of) the breach and *then* fix damages. Then could not a buyer, after learning of the breach on May 1, wait until May 15, when he purchases a larger quantity of the same goods, and then have his option to fix damages on May 1, asserting his purchase on May 15 at a lower price was *not* a 'cover'; or, if the price goes up, to claim that his purchase on May 15 was a 'cover' not unreasonably delayed (§ 2–712) and fix damages at the higher price then prevailing? Should the alternative statement in Section 2–711(1) be tightened to avoid this?"

Problem 15–4

Volta v. Simpka Revisited

Review the facts of *Volta v. Simpka,* Problem 14–4. Suppose that Simpka was to ship the custom furniture in two installments on October 1 and October 15. The first installment, consisting of 60% of the goods, was shipped f.o.b. Ohio on October 1, arrived in New York on October 12 and was rejected by Volta for manufacturing defects on October 15. The second installment was never shipped by Simpka. At trial, the court found that Volta "learned of the breach" on the first installment on October 15 and "learned" of the breach on the second installment on October 20. Assume that the contract price on the first shipment was $48,000 and was $32,000 on the second. Neither side claims that UCC 2–712 governs the case.

The market price for goods comparable to the first installment on October 15 was $60,000 in New York and $50,000 in Ohio. The market price for comparable goods to the second installment on October 20 was $28,000 in Ohio and $40,000 in New York. You may assume that the total cost of shipment from Ohio to New York would have been $4,000, but since the first installment was shipped "for buyer's account," no payment has as yet been made.

* Professor Patterson describes the two New York cases as follows:

Perkins v. Minford, 235 N.Y. 301, 139 N.E. 276 (1923) (action by buyer for breach by seller in shipping at Cuban port (F.O.B.) a quantity of sugar 200,000 lbs. less than seller contracted to ship; buyer did not know of breach until much later, and this is a "special circumstance" under § 148 calling for variation from ordinary damage rule, time of breach); Boyd v. Quinn, 8 Misc. 169, 41 N.Y.Supp. 391 (1896) (contract to ship goods by rail from Peoria, Ill., to New York; buyer didn't know, until he inquired of seller and received seller's refusal, that seller had defaulted).

How much in damages, if any, should the court award to Volta?

Problem 15–5

More Simpka v. Volta

In June, 1986 the *Simpka-Volta* contract was modified to provide that all of the furniture, both standard and custom, was to be shipped in one lot on March 1, 1987. The contract price was increased to $220,000. On July 1, 1986, however, Simpka repudiated the contract in unequivocal terms and no shipments were ever made under the contract. When the case came to trial in February, 1988, Volta made the following argument: "Our damages should be measured on either July 1, 1986, when we learned of the repudiation, or May 1, 1987, when we purchased furniture in substitution (covered) on the open market." The evidence revealed the relevant market prices for comparable goods during this time frame as follows:

July 1–31, 1986	$260,000
August 1–December 31, 1986	200,000
March 1, 1987	220,000
May 1, 1987	280,000

Simpka would like the damages to be measured as of March 1, 1987, the date the goods were to be delivered. You represent Simpka. Develop the strongest arguments you can to support Simpka's position. Then read the next case.

COSDEN OIL v. KARL O. HELM AKTIENGESELLSCHAFT

United States Court of Appeals, Fifth Circuit, 1984.
736 F.2d 1064.

REAVLEY, CIRCUIT JUDGE.

* * *

II. TIME FOR MEASURING BUYER'S DAMAGES

Both parties find fault with the time at which the district court measured Helm's damages for Cosden's anticipatory repudiation of orders 05, 06, and 07. Cosden argues that damages should be measured when Helm learned of the repudiation. Helm contends that market price as of the last day for delivery—or the time of performance—should be used to compute its damages under the contract-market differential. We reject both views, and hold that the district court correctly measured damages at a commercially reasonable point after Cosden informed Helm that it was cancelling the three orders.

Article 2 of the Code has generally been hailed as a success for its comprehensiveness, its deference to mercantile reality, and its clarity. Nevertheless, certain aspects of the Code's overall scheme have proved troublesome in application. The interplay among sections 2.610, 2.711, 2.712, 2.713, and 2.723, Tex.Bus. & Com.Code Ann. (Vernon 1968), represents one of those areas, and has been described as "an impossible legal thicket." J. White & R. Summers, *Uniform Commercial Code* § 6–7 at 242 (2d ed. 1980). The aggrieved buyer seeking damages for seller's anticipatory repudiation presents the most difficult interpretive problem.[6] Section 2.713 describes the buyer's damages remedy:

Buyer's Damages for Non-Delivery or Repudiation

6. The only area of unanimous agreement among those that have studied the Code provisions relevant to this problem is that they are not consistent, present problems in interpretation, and invite amendment.

> (a) Subject to the provisions of this chapter with respect to proof of market price (Section 2.723), the measure of damages for non-delivery or repudiation by the seller is the difference between the market price *at the time when the buyer learned of the breach* and the contract price together with any incidental and consequential damages provided in this chapter (Section 2.715), but less expenses saved in consequence of the seller's breach.

(emphasis added).

Courts and commentators have identified three possible interpretations of the phrase "learned of the breach." If seller anticipatorily repudiates, buyer learns of the breach:

(1) When he learns of the repudiation;

(2) When he learns of the repudiation plus a commercially reasonable time; or

(3) When performance is due under the contract.

See, e.g., First National Bank of Chicago v. Jefferson Mortgage Co., 576 F.2d 479 (3d Cir.1978); *Cargill, Inc. v. Stafford,* 553 F.2d 1222 (10th Cir.1977); J. White & R. Summers § 6–7 at 240–52; Note, *U.C.C. § 2–713: Anticipatory Repudiation and the Measurement of an Aggrieved Buyer's Damages,* 19 Wm. & Mary L.Rev. 253 (1977).

We would not be free to decide the question if there were a Texas case on point, bound as we are by *Erie* to follow state law in diversity cases. We find, however, that no Texas case has addressed the Code question of buyer's damages in an anticipatory repudiation context. Texas, alone in this circuit, does not allow us to certify questions of state law for resolution by its courts. *See United Services Life Insurance Co. v. Delaney,* 396 S.W.2d 855 (Tex.1965).

We do not doubt, and Texas law is clear, that market price at the time buyer learns of the breach is the appropriate measure of section 2.713 damages in cases where buyer learns of the breach at or after the time for performance. This will be the common case, for which section 2.713 was designed. *See* Peters, *Remedies for Breach of Contracts Relating to the Sale of Goods Under the Uniform Commercial Code: A Roadmap for Article Two,* 73 Yale L.J. 199, 264 (1963). In the relatively rare case where seller anticipatorily repudiates and buyer does not cover, * * * the specific provision for anticipatory repudiation cases, section 2.610, authorizes the aggrieved party to await performance for a commercially reasonable time before resorting to his remedies of cover or damages.

In the anticipatory repudiation context, the buyer's specific right to wait for a commercially reasonable time before choosing his remedy must be read together with the general damages provision of section 2.713 to extend the time for measurement beyond when buyer learns of the breach. Comment 1 to section 2.610 states that if an aggrieved party "awaits performance beyond a commercially reasonable time he cannot recover resulting damages which he should have avoided." This suggests that an aggrieved buyer can recover damages where the market rises during the commercially reasonable time he awaits performance. To interpret 2.713's "learned of the breach" language to mean the time at which seller first communicates his anticipatory repudiation would undercut the time that 2.610 gives the aggrieved buyer to await performance.

The buyer's option to wait a commercially reasonable time also interacts with section 2.611, which allows the seller an opportunity to retract his repudiation. Thus, an aggrieved buyer "learns of the breach" a commercially reasonable time after he learns of the seller's anticipatory repudiation. The weight of scholarly commentary supports this interpretation. *See* J. Calamari & J. Perillo, *Contracts* § 14–20 (2d ed. 1977); Sebert, *Remedies Under Article Two of the Uniform Commercial Code: An Agenda for Review,* 130 U.Pa.L.Rev. 360, 372–80 (1981); Wallach, *Anticipatory Repudiation and the UCC,* 13 U.C.C.L.J. 48 (1980); Peters, *supra,* at 263–68.

Typically, our question will arise where parties to an executory contract are in the midst of a rising market. To the extent that market decisions are influenced by a damages rule, measuring market price at the time of seller's repudiation gives seller the ability to fix buyer's damages and may induce seller to repudiate, rather than abide by the contract. By contrast, measuring buyer's damages at the time of performance will tend to dissuade the buyer from covering, in hopes that market price will continue upward until performance time.

Allowing the aggrieved buyer a commercially reasonable time, however, provides him with an opportunity to investigate his cover possibilities in a rising market without fear that, if he is unsuccessful in obtaining cover, he will be relegated to a market-contract damage remedy measured at the time of repudiation. The Code supports this view. While cover is the preferred remedy, the Code clearly provides the option to seek damages. *See* § 2.712(c) & comment 3. If "[t]he buyer is always free to choose between cover and damages for non-delivery," and if 2.712 "is not intended to limit the time necessary for [buyer] to look around and decide as to how he may best effect cover," it would be anomalous, if the buyer chooses to seek damages, to fix his damages at a time before he investigated cover possibilities and before he elected his remedy. *See id.* comment 2 & 3; *Dura-Wood Treating Co. v. Century Forest Industries, Inc.,* 675 F.2d 745, 754 (5th Cir.), *cert. denied,* 459 U.S. 865, 103 S.Ct. 144, 74 L.Ed.2d 122 (1982) ("buyer has some time in which to evaluate the situation"). Moreover, comment 1 to section 2.713 states, "The general baseline adopted in this section uses as a yardstick the market in which the buyer would have obtained cover had he sought that relief." *See* § 2.610 comment 1. When a buyer chooses not to cover, but to seek damages, the market is measured at the time he could have covered—a reasonable time after repudiation. *See* §§ 2.711 & 2.713.

Persuasive arguments exist for interpreting "learned of the breach" to mean "time of performance," consistent with the pre-Code rule. *See* J. White & R. Summers, *supra.* § 6–7; Anderson, *supra.* If this was the intention of the Code's drafters, however, phrases in section 2.610 and 2.712 lose their meaning. If buyer is entitled to market-contract damages measured at the time of performance, it is difficult to explain why the anticipatory repudiation section limits him to a commercially reasonable time to await performance. *See* § 2.610 comment 1. Similarly, in a rising market, no reason would exist for requiring the buyer to act "without unreasonable delay" when he seeks to cover following an anticipatory repudiation. *See* § 2.712(a).

The interplay among the relevant Code sections does not permit, in this context, an interpretation that harmonizes all and leaves no loose ends. We therefore acknowledge that our interpretation fails to explain the language of section 2.723(a) insofar as it relates to aggrieved buyers. We note, however, that the section has limited applicability—cases that come to trial before the time of performance will be rare. Moreover, the comment to section 2.723 states that the "section is not intended to exclude the use of any other reasonable method of determining market price or of measuring damages. * * *" In light of the

Code's persistent theme of commercial reasonableness, the prominence of cover as a remedy, and the time given an aggrieved buyer to await performance and to investigate cover before selecting his remedy, we agree with the district court that "learned of the breach" incorporates section 2.610's commercially reasonable time.[11]

* * *

[Some footnotes omitted.]

ALLIED CANNERS & PACKERS, INC. v. VICTOR PACKING CO.

Court of Appeal of California, First District, 1984.
162 Cal.App.3d 905, 209 Cal.Rptr. 60.

[In early September, 1976, Victor agreed to sell Allied 375,000 pounds of raisins for October, 1976 delivery at 29.75 cents per pound. Victor knew that Allied had contracted to resell the raisins to foreign purchasers. Allied expected to gain a profit of $4,462.50 on the resale transaction. On September 9, 1976, heavy rains severely damaged the region's raisin crop, including that of Victor. When Victor was unable to obtain raisins from other sources, it repudiated the contract with Allied on September 15, 1976. The regulated market for raisins did not reopen until October 18, 1976, at which time the price was 87 cents per pound. In the meantime, Allied's resale buyers had either agreed to rescind their contracts without liability or failed to assert claims for damages by the time of trial.

11. We note that two circuits arrived at a similar conclusion by different routes. In *Cargill, Inc. v. Stafford,* 553 F.2d 1222 (10th Cir.1977), the court began its discussion of damages by embracing the "time of performance" interpretation urged by Professors White and Summers. *Id.* at 1226. Indeed, the court stated that "damages normally should be measured from the time when performance is due and not from the time when the buyer learns of repudiation." *Id.* Nevertheless, the court

> conclude[d] that under § 4–2–713 a buyer may urge continued performance for a reasonable time. At the end of a reasonable period he should cover if substitute goods are readily available. If substitution is readily available and buyer does not cover within a reasonable time, damages should be based on the price at the end of that reasonable time rather than on the price when performance is due.

Id. at 1227. The *Cargill* court would employ the time of performance measure only if buyer had a valid reason for not covering.

In *First Nat'l Bank of Chicago v. Jefferson Mortgage Co.,* 576 F.2d 479 (3d Cir.1978), the court initially quoted with approval legislative history that supports a literal or "plain meaning" interpretation of New Jersey's section 2–713. Nevertheless, the court hedged by interpreting that section "to measure damages within a commercially reasonable time after learning of the repudiation." *Id.* at 492. In light of the unequivocal repudiation and because cover was "easily and immediately * * * available * * * in the well-organized and easily accessible market," *id.* at 493 (quoting *Oloffson v. Coomer,* 11 Ill.App.3d 918, 296 N.E.2d 871 (1973)), a commercially reasonable time did not extend beyond the date of repudiation.

We agree with the *First National* court that "the circumstances of the particular market involved should determine the duration of a 'commercially reasonable time.'" 576 F.2d at 492; *see* Tex.Bus. & Com.Code § 1.204(b). In this case, however, there was no showing that cover was easily and immediately available in an organized and accessible market and that a commercially reasonable time expired on the day of Cosden's cancellation. We recognize that § 2.610's "commercially reasonable time" and § 2.712's "without unreasonable delay" are distinct concepts. Often, however, the two time periods will overlap, since the buyer can investigate cover possibilities while he awaits performance. *See* Sebert, *supra,* at 376–77 & n. 80.

Although the jury in the present case did not fix the exact duration of a commercially reasonable time, we assume that the jury determined market price at a time commercially reasonable under all the circumstances, in light of the absence of objection to the form of the special issue.

Allied sued Victor for damages under UCC 2–713(1), measured by the difference between the contract price, 29.75 cents per pound, and the market price at the time and place for delivery, 87 cents per pound. The trial court concluded that Allied was an exporter rather than a buyer for its own account. Accordingly, Allied could not use UCC 2–713 and was limited to its actual loss on the transaction, $4,462.50. The Court of Appeal, however, held that Allied was a buyer with forward resale contracts and that the buyer's remedies in the Code applied.

The court first reviewed Sections 2–712 through 2–715.

* * *

ROUSE, ASSOCIATE JUSTICE

Sections 2–712 and 2–713 of the Uniform Code are sometimes referred to as "cover" and "hypothetical cover," since the former involves an actual entry into the market by the buyer while the latter does not. (See Childres, *Buyer's Remedies: The Danger of Section 2–713* (1978) 72 Nw.U.L.Rev. 837, 841 [applying those terms] (hereafter cited as *Buyer's Remedies*); Peters, *Remedies for Breach of Contracts Relating to the Sale of Goods Under the Uniform Commercial Code: A Roadmap For Article Two* (1963) 73 Yale L.J. 199, 259 [market under section 2–713 is "purely theoretical"] (hereafter cited as *Remedies for Breach of Contracts*).) It has been recognized that the use of the market price-contract price formula under section 2–713 does not, absent pure accident, result in a damage award reflecting the buyer's actual loss. (*Buyer's Remedies, supra,* at pp. 841–842; *Remedies for Breach of Contracts, supra,* at p. 259; *Market Damages, supra,* 92 Harv.L.Rev. 1395 et seq.; * White & Summers, Uniform Commercial Code, *supra,* at p. 224.)

For example, in this case it is agreed that Allied's actual lost profit on the transaction was $4,462.50, while application of the market-contract price formula would yield damages of approximately $150,000. In *Market Damages, supra,* Simon and Novack describe the courts as divided on the issue of whether market damages, even though in excess of the plaintiff's loss, are appropriate for a supplier's breach of his delivery obligations and observe: "Strangely enough, each view has generally tended to disregard the arguments, and even the existence, of the opposing view. These two rival bodies of law, imposing in appearance, have passed each other like silent ships in the night." (92 Harv.L. Rev. 1395, 1397.) In *Buyer's Remedies, supra,* Professor Childres similarly points out that the courts have generally not undertaken any real analysis of the competing considerations involved in determining the correct measure of damages in such circumstances. (72 Nw.U.L.Rev. 837, 844 et seq.) We will undertake such an analysis.

Professors White and Summers, after noting their belief that "the Code drafters did not by [section 2–713] intend to put the buyer in the same position as performance would have" (White & Summers, Uniform Commercial Code, *supra,* at p. 224), advance two possible explanations for the section. First, they suggest that it is simply a historical anomaly: "Since cover was not a recognized remedy under pre-Code law, it made sense under that law to say that the contract-market formula put buyer in the same position as performance would have *on the assumption that the buyer would purchase substitute goods.* If things worked right, the market price would approximate the cost of the substitute goods and buyer would be put 'in the same position. * * *' But under the Code, 2–712 does this job with greater precision, and 2–713 reigns over only those cases in

* Simon & Novack, *Limiting the Buyer's Market Damages to Lost Profits: A Challenge to the Enforceability of Market Contracts,* 92 Harv.L. Rev. 1395 (1979).

which the buyer does not purchase a substitute. Perhaps the drafters retained 2–713 not out of a belief in its appropriateness, but out of fear that they would be dismissed as iconoclasts had they proposed that the court in noncover cases simply award the buyer any economic loss proximately caused by seller's breach." (*Ibid.*)

They conclude, however, that probably the best explanation for section 2–713 "is that it is a statutory liquidated damage clause, a breach inhibitor the payout of which need bear no close relation to plaintiff's actual loss." (White & Summers, Uniform Commercial Code, *supra,* at p. 225.) They then observe that this explanation conflicts with the policy set forth in section 1–106, which provides in subdivision (1): "The remedies provided by this code shall be liberally administered *to the end that the aggrieved party may be put in as good a position as if the other party had fully performed* but neither consequential or special nor penal damages may be had except as specifically provided in this code or by other rule of law." (Emphasis added.) They find section 2–713 consistent, however, with a belief that plaintiffs recover too little and too infrequently for the law of contracts to be effective, and offer no suggestion for resolution of the conflict. (*Ibid.*)

In her article *Remedies for Breach of Contracts, supra,* then-Professor Peters states: "Perhaps it is misleading to think of the market-contract formula as a device for the measurement of damages. * * * An alternative way of looking at market-contract is to view this differential as a statutory liquidated damages clause, rather than as an effort to calculate actual losses. If it is useful in every case to hold the party in breach to some baseline liability, in order to encourage faithful adherence to contractual obligations, perhaps market fluctuations furnish as good a standard as any." (73 Yale L.J. 199, 259.) She does not discuss the conflict between the market-contract formula and the "only as good a position as performance" policy embodied in section 1–106.

Simon and Novack state: "While it is generally recognized that the automatic invocation of market damages may sometimes overcompensate the plaintiff, a variety of arguments have been employed by commentators and courts to justify this result: the desirability of maintaining a uniform rule and of facilitating settlements; the public interest in encouraging contract performance and the proper functioning of the market; the prevention of defendant's unjust enrichment; the restoration of the very 'value' promised to plaintiff; and the inherent difficulty and complexity of proving actual economic losses not encompassed within the contract terms." (Fns. omitted; *Market Damages supra,* 92 Harv.L.Rev. 1395, 1403.) That a defendant not be unjustly enriched by a bad faith breach is a concern widely shared by commentators and courts. (*Id.,* at p. 1406, fn. 51, and cases there cited.)

Viewing section 2–713 as, in effect, a statutory provision for liquidated damages, it is necessary for us to determine whether a damage award to a buyer who has not covered is ever appropriately limited to the buyer's actual economic loss which is below the damages produced by the market-contract formula, and, if so, whether the present case presents a situation in which the damages should be so limited.

One view is that section 2–713 of the Uniform Code, or a substantively similar statutory provision, establishes the principle that a buyer's resale contract and damage claims made thereunder are irrelevant to an award of damages, and that damages therefore cannot be limited to a plaintiff's actual economic loss. (See 11 Williston, Contracts (3d ed. 1968) § 1388 [Uniform Code];

Coombs and Company of Ogden v. Reed (1956) 5 Utah 2d 419, 303 P.2d 1097 [Uniform Sales Act]; *Brightwater Paper Co. v. Monadnock Paper Mills* (1st Cir. 1947) 161 F.2d 869 [Massachusetts Sales Act then in effect]; *Goldfarb v. Campe Corporation* (1917) 99 Misc. 475, 164 N.Y.S. 583 [New York Sales Act then in effect].) Simon and Novack, while favoring that view, concede that it can be argued that the provision of section 1–106 that an aggrieved party be put " 'in as good a position as if the other party had fully performed' " calls for an opposite conclusion. (*Market Damages, supra,* 92 Harv.L.Rev. 1395, 1412–1413, fn. 71.)

Although we find no cases discussing the interaction of section 1–106 and section 2–713, we note that some pre-Uniform Code cases held that a limitation to actual losses should be placed upon the market price-contract price measure of damages under general contract principles. (See, e.g., *Foss v. Heineman* (1910) 144 Wis. 146 [128 N.W. 881]; *Isaacson v. Crean* (1917) 165 N.Y.S. 218; *Texas Co. v. Pensacola Maritime Corporation* (5th Cir.1922) 279 Fed. 19.) One author on the subject has apparently concluded that such a limitation is appropriate under the Uniform Code when the plaintiff-buyer has a resale contract and the existence of the resale contract is known to the defendant-seller: "It may be supposed * * * that the buyer was bound by a contract made before the breach to deliver to a third person the very goods which the buyer expected to obtain from the seller, and the price under the resale contract may be less than the market price at the time of the breach. If the reason generally given for the rule permitting the recovery of additional damage because of an advantageous resale contract existing and known to the defendant when he contracted be applied, namely, that such consequential damages are allowed because the parties supposedly contract for them, it would follow that in every case the damage that the defendant might normally expect to follow from breach of his contract should be recovered even though the plaintiff actually suffered less damage than the difference between the contract price and the market price." (4 Anderson, Uniform Commercial Code (3d ed. 1983) § 2–711:15, pp. 430–431.)

The only California case directly applying section 2713 is *Gerwin v. Southeastern Cal. Assn. of Seventh Day Adventists* (1971) 14 Cal.App.3d 209, 92 Cal. Rptr. 111. There the plaintiff had contracted to purchase bar and restaurant equipment which he planned to use in a hotel he had recently acquired. The seller failed to deliver the equipment, and plaintiff, who had not covered, was awarded damages of $15,000 as the difference between the contract price and the market price of the equipment. The plaintiff had not covered because substitute items were not available at prices within his financial ability. (*Id.,* at pp. 218–219, 92 Cal.Rptr. 111.) Presumably, after recovering his damage award, the plaintiff in *Gerwin* paid it out to purchase other equipment. That case is inapposite to the present case because the plaintiff there had no resale contract which limited his liability and defined the actual profit he expected to make through the acquisition of the items covered by the sales contract.

We conclude that in the circumstances of this case—in which the seller knew that the buyer had a resale contract (necessarily so because raisins would not be released by RAC unless Allied provided it with the name of the buyer in its forward contract), the buyer has not been able to show that it will be liable in damages to the buyer on its forward contract, and there has been no finding of bad faith on the part of the seller—the policy of section 1106, subdivision (1), that the aggrieved party be put in as good a position as if the other party had performed requires that the award of damages to the buyer be limited to its actual loss, the amount it expected to make on the transaction. We note that in the context of a cover case under section 2712, a Court of Appeal has recently approved the use of section 1106 to limit damages to the amount that would put the plaintiff in as good a position as if the defendant had performed. (*Sun Maid Raisin Growers v. Victor Packing Co.* (1983) 146 Cal.App.3d 787, 792, 194 Cal. Rptr. 612.)

We need not determine in this case what degree of bad faith on the part of a breaching seller might warrant the award of market-contract price damages without limitation, in circumstances otherwise similar to those involved here, in order to prevent unjust enrichment to a seller who deliberately breaches in order to take advantage of a rising market. Although Allied implies that Victor was guilty of bad faith here because after its breach it allowed another packer to acquire reserve raisins to which it was entitled at 36.25 cents per pound, rather than acquiring the raisins and delivering them to Allied, the record is simply not clear on Victor's situation following the rains. It does appear clear, however, that, as the trial court found, the rains caused a severe problem, and Victor made substantial efforts to persuade RAC to release reserve raisins to it in spite of its failure to get its check to RAC before 8:30 a.m. on September 10, 1976. We do not deem this record one to support an inference that windfall damages must be awarded the buyer to prevent unjust enrichment to a deliberately breaching seller. (Compare *Sun Maid Raisin Growers v. Victor Packing Co., supra,* 146 Cal. App.3d 787, 194 Cal.Rptr. 612 [where, in a case coincidentally involving Victor, Victor was expressly found by the trial court to have engaged in bad faith by gambling on the market price of raisins in deciding whether to perform its contracts to sell raisins to Sun Maid].)

The judgment is affirmed. Each party is to bear its own costs on appeal.

KLINE, P.J., and SMITH, J., concur.

Notes

1. Accord: H–W–H Cattle Co., Inc. v. Schroeder, 767 F.2d 437 (8th Cir.1985). But see Apex Oil Co. v. Vanguard Oil & Service Co., Inc., 760 F.2d 417, 424 (2d Cir. 1985), where the court rejected the seller's contention that the buyer, a broker who intended to resell the oil to another customer, could not use the formula in UCC 2–713(1). The court, speaking through Judge Newman, offered the following reasons:

> The formula makes sense when an end user sues the breaching seller because, even if the end user elects not to go into the market and cover, thus demonstrating its out-of-pocket loss, it still has lost the value of having the product. However, in this case, Apex was not an end user, but rather a broker who planned to resell the product to another customer. In the absence of proof that Apex had a customer willing to purchase the oil, it seems fictional to hold that Apex has "lost" the difference between the market price and contract price. However, Vanguard's arguments fail to consider the UCC formula from the perspective of the breaching seller, who always has the option of going into the market and buying products to satisfy its obligation to the buyer. Since Vanguard elected not to cover and thus fix its loss, it saved an amount equal to the difference between the market price and the contract price. The UCC formula reflects a policy judgment that it makes more sense to award the amount of that saving to the buyer than to permit the non-performing and non-covering seller to retain it. Whether that policy decision should be legislatively limited to buyers who demonstrate some prospect of foregone opportunity for profitable resale is not for us to say.

2. A "middleman" or "jobber," other than a consignee, is both a buyer and a seller. Review the treatment of this functionary when seeking damages as a seller. See supra Chapter Fourteen. What conclusions can you draw as to the availability of the standard damages formulas in UCC 2–708(1) and UCC 2–713(1) to the "jobber?"

SECTION 5. BUYER'S RIGHT TO COVER AND "FIX" DAMAGES

Cover, like resale (UCC 2–706), is an important Code innovation. It is an intelligent legal response to the legitimate needs of the ordinary buyer who, when faced with the seller's breach, must look elsewhere for the goods. Under the standard contract-market differential formula, an aggrieved buyer who repurchased to fulfill his needs was taking real pot luck. If, as was likely to be the case, the court measured the market at a time or place other than those at which he purchased, the contract-market paid too much or too little. UCC 2–712 will change all that.

Professor Honnold in the New York Law Revision Commission Reports has described the relation of the cover provision to the prior law in New York as follows:

HONNOLD—1 N.Y.LAW REV.COMM.REP. 569, 570 (1955)

(2) *Effect of "cover" in determining damages under Uniform Sales Act*

Under Section 67(1) and (3) of the Uniform Sales Act (P.P.L., § 148(1)(3)) the basic test for the measurement of damages recoverable by buyer is "the difference between the contract price and the *market or current* price of the goods at the time or times when they ought to have been delivered * * *". The Uniform Sales Act says nothing about "cover," and has no provision which gives binding effect to the price paid by buyer in buying substitute goods.

However, in one situation, at least, some decisions have given controlling effect to buyer's repurchase. If buyer purchases substitute goods for *less* than market price, this repurchase price may be the maximum amount on which damages can be measured. The Code would give a different result, since under Section 2–711(1), buyer is afforded a choice between damages based on "cover" (§ 2–712) and damages based on market price (§ 2–713).

The amount paid by buyer has been held an insufficient basis for proof of his damages if there was a current market for the goods; market price must be proved as the basis for computing damages. This rule has been criticized as unduly harsh to the wronged party, and it has at least one qualification: where the goods in question *are not* readily marketable, the price paid by buyer to secure the goods from another seller will be controlling. Under the Code, as we have seen, a buyer who "covers" need not prove the market price.

The conditions which one must meet to comply with UCC 2–712 are like those of UCC 2–706: at least superficially simple and unspecific.

One must purchase: 1) reasonably and in good faith;
2) without unreasonable delay; and
3) in substitution.

On reflection a few problems appear. The first is the recurring problem: what is the reasonable time and what is a commercially reasonable purchase? If the buyer routinely purchases separate lots of goods and now seeks to allocate one of those routinely purchased lots to this contract's cover, what result? A third problem is the question whether cover, if made, is the exclusive measure of damages. A fourth is, how does one adjust for the difference between cover items and those contracted for—what if the contract calls for AM radios but AM–FM radios are procured as cover?

Problem 15–6

Return again to *Simpka-Volta.* Assume that Simpka missed the first delivery of standard furniture and, on June 15, mailed an unequivocal repudiation of the entire contract. On November 15, Volta replaced, from a supplier in Ann Arbor, the standard furniture for $150,000 and the custom furniture for $100,000. The shipment was f.o.b. New York. Volta claims $50,000 damages under UCC 2–712. Simpka's lawyer has responded with the following arguments:

1. UCC 2–712 is not available, since there was an unreasonable delay in the repurchase. The time starts running from the date of repudiation, not from the date upon which the contract would have been performed.

2. Even so, the $50,000 damages should be reduced by the $5,000 transportation cost which the second seller paid from Ann Arbor. Volta would have had to pay those costs under the repudiated f.o.b. point of shipment contract.

3. In fact, the market for the standard furniture was lower than the contract price. The goods which Volta purchased in New York were Grade A and the contract called for Grade B furniture, merchandise of lesser quality.

What damages?

Problem 15–7

Assume that Simpka fails to perform the contract; a series of negotiations considering possible alternatives are conducted between Volta and Simpka, and these eventually break down in January. At that time Volta purchases nearly identical replacement furniture in the New York market for $188,000. Volta now sues Simpka under UCC 2–713 for the contract-market differential at the time of performance. Assume that the court has ruled in this particular case that the "time when the buyer learned of the breach" was the times of the respective deliveries to be made by Simpka and has further found that the contract market differential at those times is a total of $20,000.

Simpka's counsel has argued that the January purchase constituted a cover and that such cover is the exclusive measure of damages. In support of his argument Simpka's counsel cites comment 5 to UCC 2–713 which reads as follows:

> The present section provides a remedy which is completely alternative to cover under the preceding section and applies only when and to the extent that the buyer has not covered.

Volta has hired Professor (now Justice) Ellen Peters as its counsel, and she makes the following argument in response to the contention that UCC 2–712 is the exclusive remedy.

PETERS, REMEDIES FOR BREACH OF CONTRACTS RELATING TO THE SALE OF GOODS UNDER THE UNIFORM COMMERCIAL CODE: A ROADMAP FOR ARTICLE TWO, 73 Yale L.J. 199, 260–61 (1963).

"Comment 5 is clear enough; but nothing supporting this position can be found in the text of 2–713. However, 2–711, which lists the buyer's rights upon rightful rejection, states its alternatives in a sequence consistent with Comment 5: 'the buyer may * * * "cover" and have damages under the next section [which contains the cover-contract formula] * * *; or * * * recover damages for non-delivery [the market-contract formula].' Section 2–711 is clear that a buyer need not cover unless he so chooses, but seemingly requires damages to be measured by cover if cover has been effectuated. In the case of a seller suing for non-acceptance, there is no parallel limitation, either in comment or text. The only possible explanation for such a difference in the treatment of buyers and sellers would have to be derived from inequalities in the statements of the other half of the option, the market-contract formulae. Perhaps the seller needs a freer hand when he resells than the buyer who covers because the seller's market-contract formula is so erratic a measure of damages.

"But the history of the development of these remedies over the various drafts of the Uniform Commercial Code suggests a quite different explanation. Until the 1957 version, 2–713 on seller's remedies prefaced his right to recover damages for non-acceptance with 'so far as any goods have not been resold.' At that point then, the market-contract formula was equally conditional for both buyers and sellers, the buyer's rights then being identical in text and comment to their present 1962 statement. The 1957 amendment, deleting this language, was promulgated, according to the Report of the 1956 Recommendations of the Editorial Board, at the suggestion of the New York Law Revision Commission 'to make it clear that the aggrieved seller was not required to elect between damages under Section 2–706 and damages under Section 2–708.' This comment is instructive on two counts: it indicates a purpose to safeguard alternative remedies, and, more important, it characterizes the amendment as a clarification rather than as a change. The latter point might be dismissed as mere face-saving on the part of the revision committee but for the fact that changes are called changes in other comments. If the committee's characterization is correct, the reference to resale, even in the old 2–703 on seller's remedies, was addressed not to the existence of a resale but to whether the resale was being relied upon to measure damages. But if this is an accurate reading of the old 2–703, it is equally appropriate to a free choice among the buyer's remedies under 2–711.

"A non-restrictive reading of the various remedies sections to preserve full options to use or to ignore substitute transactions as a measure of damages makes more sense than Comment 5 for a number of reasons. It preserves a parity of remedy for buyers and sellers. It is consistent with a number of other Code sections which frown on premature election of remedies. It is a good deal easier to administer, since it would be most difficult to ferret out from a reluctant complainant information about transactions sufficiently related to the contract in breach to qualify as cover or resale. Finally, preservation of the option encourages recourse to actual market substitutes, since it guarantees to the injured party that he will not lose a remedy in the event of an unusually favorable substitute contract. It is thus consistent with the Code's overall interest in keeping goods moving in commerce as rapidly as possible."

What should Volta receive? For cases permitting recovery under UCC 2–713(1) despite evidence that the buyer had covered, see Ralston Purina Co. v. McFarland, 550 F.2d 967 (4th Cir.1977); Interior Elevator Co. v. Limmeroth, 278 Or. 589, 565 P.2d 1074 (1977).

DURA-WOOD TREATING CO. v. CENTURY FOREST INDUSTRIES, INC.

United States Court of Appeals, Fifth Circuit, 1982.
675 F.2d 745.

[After oral negotiations, Dura-Wood mailed a written order to purchase 20,000 creosote treated hardwood cross-ties from Century Forest at $8.60 each. Both parties were in the business of treating cross-ties. Dura-Wood's order was in partial fulfillment of a preexisting contract to supply ties to a third party, Smith. Century refused to deliver the ties, claiming that no oral agreement existed and, if it did, it was unenforceable under the statute of frauds. After obtaining price quotations from other suppliers, Dura-Wood decided that it could produce the ties "internally at a lower price than it could purchase substitute ties from other manufacturers." Accordingly, Dura-Wood produced the ties, delivered them to Smith and sued Century Forest for damages based upon the difference between the cost to cover and the contract price. The trial court held that the parties had entered an enforceable contract and awarded Dura-Wood damages of $100,000. On appeal, the court of appeals first affirmed that there was an enforceable contract and then turned to the question of damages.]

* * *

JOHNSON, CIRCUIT JUDGE

III. DAMAGES

The district court's damage award will be addressed in three parts. First, there is a question regarding actual damages as they relate to Dura-Wood's "cover." The second part addresses the so-called "potential profits" allegedly lost as a result of Dura-Wood's method of covering. Finally, there is a question regarding profits that Dura-Wood would have received as a result of its contract with Smith Company, but lost because of Century Forest's breach of contract.

A. Cover

When a seller breaches a contract, the buyer "may 'cover' by making in good faith and without unreasonable delay any reasonable purchase of or contract to purchase goods in substitution for those due from the seller." Tex.Bus. & Com. Code Ann. § 2.712(a). "Covering" is an optional remedy for the buyer faced with securing a damage award. *See* Tex.Bus. & Com.Code § 2.711; Tex.Bus. & Com. Code § 2.712; Comment 3, Tex.Bus. & Com.Code § 2.712. If he chooses to cover, "The buyer may recover from the seller as damages the difference between the cost of cover and the contract price together with any incidental or consequential damages." Tex.Bus. & Com.Code § 2.712(b).

In the case *sub judice,* Dura-Wood claims—and the district court found—it engaged in a valid method of cover by manufacturing the necessary ties itself. Century Forest argues this is an invalid mechanism for cover. The basis of Century Forest's argument is that the Tex.Bus. & Com.Code does not contemplate a buyer's covering by purchasing from itself. Century Forest argues the purchase of or contract to purchase goods in substitution of those due from the seller must be made "on the market."

This Court recognizes the language of section 2.712, read literally, appears to contemplate the purchase of cover goods should be from an outside source. However, the Code is to be "liberally construed and applied to promote its underlying purposes and policies." Tex.Bus. & Com.Code § 1.102(a). The Code "is drawn to provide flexibility." Comment 1, Tex.Bus. & Com.Code § 1.102. Consequently, a buyer should be able to cover by manufacturing goods in substitution of those due from the seller, if such a cover otherwise satisfies and promotes the purposes and policies of the Tex.Bus. & Com.Code.

Comment one to section 2.712 states the "section provides the buyer with a remedy aimed at enabling him to obtain the goods he needs thus meeting his essential need." This statement essentially describes two purposes that may be fulfilled by an appropriate cover. First, it puts an aggrieved buyer in the same economic position in which it would have been had the seller actually performed. Second, it allows the buyer to achieve its prime objective, which is acquiring the needed goods. See, White, J. & Summers, R., *Handbook of the Law Under the Uniform Commercial Code* 222 (West 1980).

This Court acknowledges there is some language indicating the purchase of substitute goods should be "on the market." *See Kiser v. Lemco,* 536 S.W.2d 585 (Tex.Civ.App.—Amarillo 1976, no writ). However, this language is explained by the Texas courts' interpretations of section 2.712. As Century Forest itself points out, the Texas courts have noted that one policy behind section 2.712 is a presumption "that the cost of cover will approximate the market price of the undelivered goods." *Jon-T Farms, Inc. v. Good Pasture, Inc.,* 554 S.W.2d 743, 749 (Tex.Civ.App.—Amarillo 1977, writ ref'd n.r.e.). Indeed, an appropriate cover has the effect of setting the market price so that an aggrieved buyer does not have to prove damages through more onerous means. However, actually purchasing the cover goods from another source is not the exclusive means of satisfying the presumption of section 2.712. In an appropriate situation, internally producing the substitute or cover goods can satisfy the recognized underlying presumptions of section 2.712.

Regarding the case *sub judice,* this Court finds no error in the district court's actual damage award based upon Dura-Wood's cover. This Court determines that a buyer, at least in the case *sub judice,* may cover by manufacturing goods internally. The purposes and presumptions of the Tex.Bus. & Com.Code can be, and are, fulfilled in those instances—such as in the instant case—when the buyer is already in the marketplace and can produce the goods at a price approximating or lower than the market price. It would defy reason and the Tex.Bus. & Com.Code's purposes of flexibility and adaptation to reasonable commercial practice to require a buyer to increase losses by covering through the purchase of goods from another seller, if it could produce the goods itself at a lower price. This is particularly true when it is recognized that such a determination would remove the other advantages that section 2.712 contemplates from cover.

As a factual matter, cover by internal manufacturing must be in "good faith." The Tex.Bus. & Com.Code provides workable definitions of good faith in at least two pertinent places. Section 1.201(19) defines good faith as "honesty in fact in the conduct or transaction concerned." Section 2.103(a)(2) expands this basic definition in order to make it specifically applicable to merchants. " 'Good faith' in the case of a merchant means honesty in fact and the observance of reasonable commercial standards of fair dealing in the trade." Tex.Bus. & Com. Code § 2.103(a)(2).

Another factual matter concerns the necessity for the aggrieved buyer to cover without "unreasonable delay" and to make a "reasonable purchase." The Tex.Bus. & Com.Code provides only limited aid for the court attempting to determine whether a cover purchase is reasonable in the appropriate respects. However, there is some aid. Initially, section 1.204(b) provides guidelines for what a reasonable time within which to cover may be. The section states, "What is a reasonable time for taking any action depends on the nature, purpose and circumstances of such action." Additionally, Comment two to section 2.712 dictates, "The test of proper cover is whether at the time and place the buyer acted in good faith and in a reasonable manner, and it is immaterial that hindsight may later prove that the method of cover used was not the cheapest or most effective." At a minimum this "test" suggests a buyer has some time in which to evaluate the situation and attempt to determine what may be the best or most appropriate means to cover. *See* Comment 2, Tex.Bus. & Com.Code § 2.712.

Finally, there is the factual requirement that the goods be "in substitution for those due from the seller." Comment two to section 2.712 points out that "[t]he definition of 'cover' * * * envisages * * * goods not identical with those involved but commercially usable as reasonable substitutes under the circumstances of the particular case."

The record demonstrates good faith on the part of Dura-Wood in choosing to cover by manufacturing the cross-ties internally. Dura-Wood took price quotations and ultimately determined it could produce the ties at a lower price. The district court's finding that Dura-Wood acted in good faith—which is implicit in its determination regarding actual damages—is not clearly erroneous.

Additionally, the district court's finding that Dura-Wood covered within a reasonable time and provided a reasonable substitute was not clearly erroneous. The record reveals Dura-Wood waited to cover in order to evaluate the market for cross-ties. There is evidence demonstrating the cross-tie market is volatile and subject to fluctuations. The price of cross-ties was high during the time Dura-Wood was evaluating the market. Consequently, Dura-Wood's waiting to determine whether a decrease in market price might occur was not unreasonable. In addition, Dura-Wood continued to urge performance, as contemplated by section 2.610 of the Tex.Bus. & Com.Code. The record also demonstrates the internally produced cover goods were commercially usable as reasonable substitutes for those due from Century Forest.

B. Potential Profits

The district court awarded Dura-Wood $42,000 as "potential profits" that it lost "by using its own facilities to produce cross-ties to replace those which the defendant refused to provide." In other words, the district court found that, when Dura-Wood covered by internally manufacturing the cross-ties, it could have been producing cross-ties and selling them to new or different customers instead of producing them in substitution for goods due from Century Forest.

As a general proposition, lost profits are consequential damages as contemplated by Tex.Bus. & Com.Code § 2.715(b). *See General Supply & Equipment Co., Inc. v. Phillips,* 490 S.W.2d 913 (Tex.Civ.App.—Tyler 1973, writ ref'd n.r.e.). Section 2.715 establishes that consequential damages include "any loss resulting from general or particular requirements and needs of which the seller at the time of contracting had reason to know and which could not reasonably be prevented by cover or otherwise." Of course, section 2.712 allows a plaintiff to obtain consequential damages. Tex.Bus. & Com.Code § 2.712.

However, the district court's damage award for "potential profits" does not fall within the contemplation of section 2.715. It is true Dura-Wood, by manufacturing its own cross-ties, covered for less money than if it had purchased ties from some other source. It is also true that, while Dura-Wood was producing its cross-ties, its facilities were tied up and Dura-Wood was unable to manufacture goods for new or different contracts. However, Dura-Wood could have minimized its overall losses. The cost of producing the ties plus the cost of lost profits resulting from Dura-Wood's inability to enter into new or different contracts was greater than the cost of simply purchasing the cover goods from another source. If Dura-Wood had purchased ties from someone else, its facilities would not have been tied up and Dura-Wood would have been able to enter new or different contracts. As a result, Dura-Wood would have had lower overall costs. Century Forest should not be obligated to pay for Dura-Wood's poor choice.

The so-called loss of potential profits could have reasonably been prevented by a different form of cover or otherwise. In the absence of such preventative measures, the district court's award of consequential damages, as it relates to the loss of potential profits, is not authorized by section 2.715.

C. Lost Profits on the Dura-Wood/Smith Contract

The district court also awarded Dura-Wood $13,000 for "lost profits on its contract with the third party [Smith Company]." This amount was computed by determining the amount of profit per tie Dura-Wood would have received from Smith Company had Century Forest performed, and was awarded as consequential damages. However, the award was erroneous since it allows Dura-Wood a double recovery as to the $13,000.

Dura-Wood received an actual damage award that considered the difference between the cost of cover and the contract price. Since Dura-Wood was able to provide Smith Company with cross-ties and received payment, there is no room for the $13,000 award. Stated another way, Dura-Wood already had been compensated for the fact that producing its own cross-ties was more expensive than buying them from Century Forest.

* * *

V. CONCLUSION

This Court affirms the district court's determination that Dura-Wood and Century Forest entered a legally enforceable contract. In addition, it affirms the district court's award of actual damages as expressed in the court's Finding of Fact No. 10. This Court, however, reverses the district court's award of lost profits as expressed in the court's Findings of Fact Nos. 11 and 12.

This case is remanded to the district court for entry of a judgment consistent with this opinion.

Affirmed in part, reversed in part, and remanded.

[Footnotes omitted.]

Notes

1. Accord: Cives Corp. v. Callier Steel Pipe & Tube, Inc., 482 A.2d 852, 858 (Me. 1984), where the court, citing *Dura-Wood Treating,* supra, noted that the buyer did not "resort to in-house cover until after conducting a thorough search for an alternate supplier." The buyer "knew its own capabilities and correctly determined that it could with some extra effort and expense, produce the require steel tubes." Under these circumstances, "resort to in-house cover is a legitimate business decision." See also, Milwaukee Valve Co., Inc. v. Mishawaka Brass Manufacturing, Inc., 107 Wis.2d 164, 319 N.W.2d 885 (App.1982) (diverting existing orders to fill gap caused by seller's breach is a reasonable cover).

2. "Cover" by the buyer through internal production rather than by purchase from a third party raises a series of questions for which there are no easy answers. First, how can the courts get around the language of UCC 2–712(1) which appears to define cover in terms of a "purchase of or contract to purchase goods in substitution for those due from the seller?" Second, by what standard should the seller challenge the buyer's decision to make rather than to buy? Must that decision be "in good faith and without unreasonable delay?" UCC 2–712(1). Third, how does the seller challenge the buyer's claimed "cost of cover" through internal production? For example, must those costs be reasonable? Can the buyer use current market prices rather than historical cost to measure the cost of materials? Fourth, what are "incidental damages" in this setting? See UCC 2–715(1). In *Cives Corp.,* supra, the

buyer claimed as incidental damages certain general overhead expenses allocated to the making of the cover over and above the direct cost of production. The exclusion by the trial court of some of these expenses was upheld on appeal. The court stated: "In order to recover overhead expenses in effecting cover Cives had to establish not only that a portion of its resources was unavailable for other projects for the time when it was effecting cover, but also that it had to forego the performance of other available construction projects. Recoverable proportionate overhead expenses must represent not only an expense, but a loss, i.e., it must be shown that other jobs would have been obtained to absorb such overhead, but had to be given up because of the cover undertaking." 482 A.2d at 860. Fifth, what are "consequential damages" in this setting, see UCC 2–715(2)? Sixth, what are "expenses saved in consequence of the seller's breach?"

SECTION 6. CONSEQUENTIAL DAMAGES FOR BREACH BY DELAY OR NONDELIVERY

A commercial buyer may have different objectives in contracting to buy goods: (1) As a jobber or distributor, to resell goods in the same condition as delivered by the seller; (2) As a manufacturer, to use the goods as part of a product to be manufactured and resold; and (3) As a manufacturer, to use the goods as equipment to maintain or expand its capacity to produce goods for resale. Thus, a jobber would purchase, say, a completed woodstove for resale to consumers while a manufacturer would purchase either steel to be incorporated into a stove to be manufactured or equipment with which to manufacture the stove.

In each case, an unexcused delay or a failure to deliver by the seller results in two potential sources of damages, "direct" damages measured by the contract price and either the market price, UCC 2–713, or the cost to cover, UCC 2–712, and "consequential" damages, measured by the buyer's loss from being unable to use the goods. UCC 2–715(2)(a). Frequently, the buyer claims as consequential damages the net profits that would have been made if the goods had been delivered on time.

There are four traditional limitations upon the recovery of consequential damages. Three limitations are explicit in UCC 2–715(2)(a): (1) The loss must result from or be caused by the breach; (2) The loss must result from "general or particular requirements and needs" of the buyer "of which the seller at the time of contracting had reason to know * * *: and (3) The loss must be one "which could not reasonably be prevented by cover or otherwise." A fourth limitation, applicable to all claims for damages, is that the loss must be proved by the plaintiff with reasonable certainty. To prevail in a claim for consequential damages, the plaintiff must satisfy all four limitations.

For now, consider the following problem and case. We will return to the consequential damages problem in connection with the buyer's claim for damages with regard to accepted goods, infra at Chapter Twenty-One, Section 3.

Problem 15–8

On May 1, F, a farmer, sold B, a dealer, 2,000 bushels of # 1 yellow corn, just planted in F's fields, for $3.00 a bushel. Delivery was promised no later than October 15. On May 15, B resold the corn to C, a cereal manufacturer, for $4.00 a bushel. Due to a drought in other parts of the country, the market price for # 1 yellow at the time of delivery was $5.00 per bushel. F failed to deliver and C demanded delivery from B of 1,000 bushels at $4.00 per bushel.

1. What should B do to maximize damages against F?

2. Suppose, after negotiations, C agreed to release B from the contract upon payment of $500. B paid the $500.

3. Suppose on May 15, B had been able to resell the corn to C for $6.00 a bushel even though the prevailing market price for futures was $4.00. What damages?

HYDRAFORM PRODUCTS CORP. v. AMERICAN STEEL & ALUMINUM CORP.

Supreme Court of New Hampshire, 1985.
127 N.H. 187, 498 A.2d 339.

SOUTER, JUSTICE.

The defendant, American Steel & Aluminum Corporation, appeals from the judgment entered on a jury verdict against it. The plaintiff, Hydraform Products Corporation, brought this action for direct and consequential damages based on claims of negligent misrepresentation and breach of a contract to supply steel to be used in manufacturing woodstoves. American claims that prior to trial, the Superior Court (Nadeau, J.) erroneously held that a limitation of damages clause was ineffective to bar the claim for consequential damages. American further claims, inter alia, that the Trial Court (Dalianis, J.) erred (a) in allowing the jury to calculate lost profits on the basis of a volume of business in excess of what the contract disclosed and for a period beyond the year in which the steel was to be supplied; (b) in allowing the jury to award damages for the diminished value of the woodstove division of Hydraform's business; (c) in failing to direct a verdict for the defendant on the misrepresentation claim; and (d) in allowing Hydraform's president to testify as an expert witness. We hold that the trial court properly refused to enforce the limitation of damages clause, but we sustain the other claims of error and reverse the judgment.

Hydraform was incorporated in 1975 and began manufacturing and selling woodstoves in 1976. During the sales season of 1977–78 it sold 640 stoves. It purchased steel from a number of suppliers until July 1978, when it entered into a "trial run" contract with American for enough steel to manufacture 40 stoves. Upon delivery of the steel, certain of Hydraform's agents and employees signed a delivery receipt prepared by American, containing the following language:

> "Seller will replace or refund the purchase price for any goods which at the time of delivery to buyer were damaged, defective or not in conformance with the buyer's written purchase order, provided that the buyer gives seller written notice by mail of such damage, defect or deviation within 10 days following its receipt of the goods. *In no event shall seller be liable for labor costs expended on such goods or other consequential damages.*"

(Emphasis added.)

When some of the deliveries under this contract were late, Hydraform's president, J.R. Choate, explained to an agent of American that late deliveries of steel during the peak season for manufacturing and selling stoves could ruin Hydraform's business for a year. In response, American's agent stated that if Hydraform placed a further order, American would sheer and stockpile in advance, at its own plant, enough steel for 400 stoves, and would supply further steel on demand. Thereafter Hydraform did submit a purchase order for steel sufficient to manufacture 400 stoves, to be delivered in four equal installments on the first days of September, October, November and December of 1978.

American's acceptance of this offer took the form of deliveries accompanied by receipt forms. The forms included the same language limiting American's liability for damages that had appeared on the receipts used during the trial run agreement. Hydraform's employees signed these receipts as the steel was delivered from time to time, and no one representing Hydraform ever objected to that language.

Other aspects of American's performance under the trial run contract reoccurred as well. Deliveries were late, some of the steel delivered was defective, and replacements of defective steel were tardy. Throughout the fall of 1978 Mr. Choate protested the slow and defective shipments, while American's agent continually reassured him that the deficient performance would be corrected. Late in the fall, Mr. Choate finally concluded that American would never perform as agreed, and attempted to obtain steel from other suppliers. He found, however, that none could supply the steel he required in time to manufacture stoves for the 1978–79 sales season. In the meantime, the delays in manufacturing had led to cancelled orders, and by the end of the season Hydraform had manufactured and sold only 250 stoves. In September, 1979, Hydraform sold its woodstove manufacturing division for $150,000 plus royalties.

In December, 1979, Hydraform brought an action for breach of contract, which provoked a countersuit by American. In January, 1983, American moved to dismiss Hydraform's claims for consequential damages to compensate for lost profits and for loss on the sale of the business. American based the motion on the limitation of damages clause and upon its defense that Hydraform had failed to mitigate its damages by cover or otherwise. In February, 1983, Hydraform's pretrial statement filed under Superior Court Rule 62 disclosed that it claimed $100,000 as damages for lost profits generally and $220,000 as a loss on the sale of the business. Later in February, 1983, the superior court permitted Hydraform to amend its writ by adding further counts, which included claims for fraudulent and negligent misrepresentation. Hydraform did not, however, proceed to trial on the claim of fraud.

In April, 1983, *Nadeau,* J., denied American's motion to dismiss the claims for consequential damages. He relied on the Uniform Commercial Code as adopted in New Hampshire, RSA chapter 382–A, in ruling that the limitation of damages clause was unenforceable on the alternative grounds that the clause would have been a material alteration of the contract, *see* RSA 382–A:2–207(2)(b), or was unconscionable or was a term that had failed of its essential purpose, *see* RSA 382–A:2–719(2) and (3). He further concluded that, under the circumstances of the case, the failure to cover, if proven, would not bar consequential damages.

The case was tried to a jury before *Dalianis,* J. American's exceptions at trial are discussed in detail below. At the close of the evidence, American objected to the use of a verdict form with provision for special findings, and the case was submitted for a general verdict, which the jury returned for Hydraform in the amount of $80,245.12.

* * *

Since the clause was not enforceable, the trial court allowed the jury to consider Hydraform's claims for lost profits in the year of the contract, 1978, and for the two years thereafter, as well as its claim for loss in the value of the stove manufacturing business resulting in a lower sales price for the business in 1979. American argues that the court erred in submitting such claims to the jury, and rests its position on three requirements governing the recovery of consequential damages.

First, under RSA 382–A:2–715(2)(a) consequential damages are limited to compensation for "loss resulting from general or particular requirements and needs of which the seller at the time of contracting had reason to know * * *" This reflection of *Hadley v. Baxendale,* 156 Eng.Rep. 145 (1854) thus limits damages to those reasonably foreseeable at the time of the contract. *See Gerwin v. Southeastern Cal. Ass'n of Seventh Day Adventists,* 14 Cal.App.3d 209, 220, 92 Cal.Rptr. 111, 118 (1971); *Petrie-Clemons v. Butterfield,* 122 N.H. 120, 124, 441 A.2d 1167, 1170 (1982). To satisfy the foreseeability requirement, the injury for which damages are sought "must follow the breach in the natural course of events, or the evidence must specifically show that the breaching party had reason to foresee the injury." *Salem Engineering & Const. Corp. v. Londonderry School Dist.,* 122 N.H. 379, 384, 445 A.2d 1091, 1094 (1982). Thus, peculiar circumstances and particular needs must be made known to the seller if they are to be considered in determining the foreseeability of damages. *Lewis v. Mobil Oil Corporation,* 438 F.2d 500, 510 (8th Cir.1971).

Second, the damages sought must be limited to recompense for the reasonably ascertainable consequences of the breach. *See* RSA 382–A:2–715, comment 4. While proof of damages to the degree of mathematical certainty is not necessary, *Smith v. State,* 125 N.H. 799, 805, 486 A.2d 289, 294 (1984), a claim for lost profits must rest on evidence demonstrating that the profits claimed were "reasonably certain" in the absence of the breach. *Whitehouse v. Rytman,* 122 N.H. 777, 780, 451 A.2d 370, 372 (1982). Speculative losses are not recoverable.

Third, consequential damages such as lost profits are recoverable only if the loss "could not reasonably be prevented by cover or otherwise." § 2–715(2)(a). *See* § 2–712(1) (*i.e.,* by purchase or contract to purchase goods in substitution for those due from seller). In summary, consequential damages must be reasonably foreseeable, ascertainable and unavoidable.

Applying these standards, we look first at the claim for lost profits for the manufacturing season beginning in September, 1978. There is no serious question that loss of profit on sales was foreseeable up to the number of 400 stoves referred to in the contract, and there is a clear evidentiary basis for a finding that Hydraform would have sold at least that number. There was also an evidentiary basis for the trial court's ruling that Hydraform acted reasonably even though it did not attempt to cover until the season was underway and it turned out to be too late. American had led Hydraform on by repeatedly promising to take steps to remedy its failures, and the court could find that Hydraform's reliance on these promises was reasonable up to the time when it finally and unsuccessfully tried to cover.

Lost profits on sales beyond the 400 stoves presents a foreseeability issue, however. Although American's agent had stated that American would supply steel beyond the 400 stove level on demand, there is no evidence that Hydraform indicated that it would be likely to make such a demand to the extent of any reasonably foreseeable amount. Rather, the evidence was that Mr. Choate had told American's agent that the business was seasonal with a busy period of about four months. The contract referred to delivery dates on the first of four separate months and spoke of only 400 stoves. Thus, there appears to be no basis on which American should have foreseen a volume in excess of 400 for the season beginning in 1978. Lost profits for sales beyond that amount therefore were not recoverable, and it was error to allow the jury to consider them.

Nor should the claims for profits lost on sales projected for the two subsequent years have been submitted to the jury. The impediment to recovery of these profits was not total unforeseeability that the breach could have effects in a subsequent year or years, but the inability to calculate any such loss with reasonable certainty. In arguing that a reasonably certain calculation was possible, Hydraform relies heavily on *Van Hooijdonk v. Langley,* 111 N.H. 32, 274 A.2d 798 (1971), a case that arose from a landlord's cancellation of a business lease. The court held that the jury could award damages for profits that a seasonal restaurant anticipated for the three years that lease should have run. It reasoned that the experience of one two-month season provided sufficient data for a reasonably certain opinion about the extent of future profits. The court thus found sufficient certainty where damages were estimated on the basis of one year of operation and profit, as compared with no operation and hence no profit in the later years.

Hydraform's situation, however, presents a variable that distinguishes it from *Van Hooijdonk.* In our case the evidence did not indicate that American's breach had forced Hydraform's stove manufacturing enterprise out of business, and therefore the jury could not assume that there would be no profits in later years. Without that assumption the jury could not come to any reasonably certain conclusion about the anticipated level of sales absent a breach by American. The jury could predict that Hydraform would obtain steel from another source and would be able to manufacture stoves; but it did not have the evidence from which to infer the future volume of manufacturing and sales. Thus, it could not calculate anticipated lost profits with a reasonable degree of certainty.

There is, moreover, a further reason to deny recovery for profits said to have been lost in the later years. Although Hydraform's pretrial statement disclosed that Hydraform claimed $100,000 in lost profits, it did not indicate that the claim related to the seasons beginning in 1979 and 1980. Since the pretrial statement also listed a claim for loss of the value of the business at the time of its sale in 1979, we believe that the statement could reasonably be read as claiming lost profit only for the one year before the business was sold. Therefore the claim for profits in 1979 and 1980 should have been disallowed for failure to disclose the claim as required by Superior Court Rule 62.

We consider next the claim for loss in the value of the business as realized at the time of its sale in 1979. As a general rule, loss in the value of a business as a going concern, or loss in the value of its good will, may be recovered as an element of consequential damages. *See Salem Engineering & Const. Corp. v. Londonderry School Dist.,* 122 N.H. at 384, 445 A.2d at 1094; *Salinger v. Salinger,* 69 N.H. 589, 591–92, 45 A. 558, 559–60 (1899); *see also J. Story, Partnership* § 99, at 169–70 (6th ed.1868).

In this case, however, it was error to submit the claim for diminished value to the jury, for three reasons. First, to the extent that diminished value was thought to reflect anticipated loss of profits in future years, as a capitalization of the loss, it could not be calculated with reasonable certainty for the reasons we have just discussed. Second, even if such profits could have been calculated in this case, allowing the jury to consider both a claim for diminished value resting on lost profits and a claim for the lost profits themselves would have allowed a double recovery. *See Westric Battery Co. v. Standard Electric Co., Inc.,* 522 F.2d 986, 989 (10th Cir.1975). Third, to the extent that diminished value was thought to rest on any other theory, there was no evidence on which it could have been calculated. There was nothing more than Mr. Choate's testimony that he had sold the business in September of 1979 for $150,000 plus minimum royalties, together with his opinion that the sales price was less than the business was worth. This testimony provided the jury with no basis for determining what the business was worth or for calculating the claimed loss, and any award on this theory rested on sheer speculation.

In summary, we hold that the jury should not have been allowed to consider any contract claim for consequential damages for lost profits beyond those lost on the sale of 150 stoves, the difference between the 400 mentioned in the contract and the 250 actually sold. Nor should the trial court have allowed the jury to consider the claim for loss in the value of the business.

* * *

Reversed.

Note: Punitive Damages for Seller's Breach by Repudiation or Non-delivery

Under what circumstances, if any, could Hydraform recover punitive damages for American Steel's breach of contract?

UCC 1–106(1) provides that "penal damages" may not be recovered "except as specifically provided in this Act or by other rule of law." There is nothing in the UCC which "specifically" authorizes punitive damages for any breach of a contract for sale. What about "other" rules of law? Compare UCC 1–103.

In the absence of legislation preempting the UCC, an accepted starting place is Section 355 of the Restatement, Second, of Contracts: "Punitive damages are not recoverable for a breach of contract unless the conduct constituting the breach is also a tort for which punitive damages are recoverable." Thus, if the breach is not "also" a tort, punitives are not recoverable. Even so, the breach which is a tort must, in the view of some courts, be "wilful" and "accompanied by fraud, malice, wantoness or oppression." McIntosh v. Magna Systems, Inc., 539 F.Supp. 1185, 1190 (N.D.Ill.1982). In most cases, this exacting test will not capture a breach that is simply negligent or a breach that is wilful where the objective is to recapture a gain that was foregone in the bargaining at the time of contracting. Moreover, the duty of good faith imposed by general contract law, see Section 205 of the Restatement, Second, Contracts, is classified as a term of the contract. Thus, bad faith in the performance or enforcement of the contract, however defined, is a breach of the bargain for which contract remedies are available. See Sections 5(2), 235(2) and Comment (b). See also, Speidel, *The Borderland of Contract,* 10 N.Ky.L.Rev. 163, 180–81, 188–93 (1983).

A court could, however, decide that a "bad faith" breach was a tort which, if egregious, would support an award of punitive damages. California courts have done so in the context of insurance, and this result has been accepted in many states. Insurance contracts, however, contain elements not normally present in a commercial contract for sale between professional sellers and buyers. See Louderbach & Jurika, *Standards for Limiting the Tort of Bad Faith Breach of Contract,* 16 U.S.F.L. Rev. 187 (1982), who note the existence of a "special" relationship, with elements of unequal capacity, dependence and trust, between the individual insured and a corporate insurer. The absence of these special dimensions in commercial transactions has lead most courts to conclude that tort damages, including punitives, are not appropriate, regardless of the nature or purpose of the breach.

A possible portent of things to come is Seaman's Direct Buying Service, Inc. v. Standard Oil Co., 36 Cal.3d 752, 206 Cal.Rptr. 354, 686 P.2d 1158 (1984), where the Supreme Court of California, in a dispute between commercial parties, stated without clearly holding that a "party to a contract may incur tort remedies when, in addition to breaching the contract, it seeks to shield itself from liability by denying, in bad faith and without probable cause, that the contract exists." 686 P.2d at 1167. *Seaman's,* with its potential for converting all bad faith breaches into torts, has received much critical comment. See, e.g., Comment, *Extending the Bad Faith Tort Doctrine to General Commercial Contracts,* 65 B.U.L.Rev. 355 (1985). Although its future is uncertain, the nose of the punitive damage camel is clearly under the contract tent.

PART FOUR

THE STAGE OF GETTING THE GOODS OR DOCUMENTS TO THE BUYER

CHAPTER SIXTEEN

RISK OF LOSS

SECTION 1. THE BASIC GROUND RULES

There are many slips between the cup and the lip. One is that goods which have been identified to the contract for sale are destroyed or damaged before delivery without the fault or negligence of either party. Which party, seller or buyer, bears the risk of this loss?

The question is important. If the risk of loss has passed, the buyer must, unless insured, absorb the loss and pay the contract price. See UCC 2–709(1)(a). If the buyer has insured them, the insurance company will indemnify the buyer to the extent obligated under the policy and, through equitable or contractual subrogation, assert any claims that the buyer might have against third parties who caused the loss.

If the risk of loss has not passed, the seller, unless insured, must absorb the loss and, unless excused from performance, tender delivery of substitute goods. Again, if the goods are insured, the insurance company will indemnify the seller and, in all probability, assert any claims the seller may have against third parties through subrogation. When is the seller with the risk excused from performance because the goods were lost or damaged? The answer in most cases will be found in UCC 2–613 and 2–615, which you should review at this time.

When does the risk of loss pass? Section 22 of the Uniform Sales Act, which was enacted in 37 states, provided that the goods remained at the seller's risk until the "property" was transferred to the buyer. Thereafter, the risk was on the buyer "whether delivery had been made or not * * *." Section 18, however, provided that the property in "specific or ascertained goods" passed from the seller when the contract intended it to be transferred and Section 19 stated a series of five rules for ascertaining such intention when it was not otherwise made clear.

As the following excerpt reveals, the "property" or "title" approach to risk of loss was thought both to promote confusion and to ignore commercial realities.

LLEWELLYN, 1 HEARINGS BEFORE THE NEW YORK LAW REVISION COMMISSION ON THE UNIFORM COMMERCIAL CODE 96–97, [160–61] (1954).

"May I say one other thing in that connection, and say it without any hesitancy at all for the record? The number of lawyers who have an accurate knowledge of sales law is extremely small in these United States. My brother

Bacon has taught sales law for 28 years. When he says it isn't too difficult to determine where the court will decide the title is or isn't or is going to be or should be, he is speaking a truth within limits for people who have taught sales law for 28 years. I submit to you, sir, that there are not many of them.

"The ordinary lawyer, except for odds and ends of people who have specialized in this field, finds sales law as uncertain and as confused as you yourselves found it, if you are lawyers, when you finished the course in sales and wondered what the deuce you were going to do about an examination in confusion, dealing apparently with confused material and perhaps a confused professor.

"It is a body of law in which we just do not know our way around, and the thing that has been criticized, the elimination of the passing of title or the place where it is to pass, as the vital, focal factor for the courts to think about, is one of the great clarifications that has been offered to the law of these United States over many years.

"The way in which one comes to see that is not by praising the Code. The way in which one comes to see that is to turn to the only body of truly commercial sales law which operates almost entirely without use of the concept of title. There you have a body of sales law which is clean, clear, guidesome, which it is almost impossible to misconstrue, and which practically pays no attention to title at all. That is the law of the C.I.F. contract, and the inspiration of the law of the C.I.F. contract is the inspiration at least to try to bring it home to ordinary sales law, that just doesn't happen to be overseas and confined to a few people; that is what has led to the plan of the Code, working in terms of the facts, what the parties really thought about, and what the issues really are.

"So that, far from giving any excuse on behalf of the drafting staff or the supporting organizations for the elimination of the title concept as the center of the sales chapter, we bring it before you as what we conceive to be a true contribution and a true opportunity to bring a difficult, useful and troubled body of law within the compass of anybody, anytime, anyhow.

"Speaking to you, sir, as one law teacher to another, I suggest that this is going to be a great contribution to the law students of the United States. I think they can really learn their sales, and learn it fast, if you will give them Article 2."

The Code rejected title as the test for determining when the risk of loss has passed: "Each provision of this Article with regard to the rights, obligations and remedies of the seller, the buyer, purchasers or other third parties applies irrespective of title to the goods except where the provision refers to such title." UCC 2–401.

The primary provisions dealing with risk of loss are UCC 2–509 and 2–510. Note that the test is flexible rather than rigid and is keyed to the agreement of the parties and the stage of performance thereunder. More particularly, the risk is tied, in most cases at least, to which party has possession of or control over the goods. Two assumptions appear to underlie this approach: (1) The party in possession or in control is in the "best" position, cost considered, to minimize or avoid loss; and (2) The party in possession or in control is more likely to have insurance against losses that could not be avoided. In short, parties in control of goods are thought to be what economists call the "least cost loss avoiders" and the best insurers against risk. See Note, *Risk of Loss in Commercial Transactions: Efficiency Thrown Into the Breach,* 65 Va.L.Rev. 559

(1979). Thus, the Code sought to minimize the cases where the risk passed to the buyer before the goods changed hands—cases where the risk of loss was not on the party with possession and control and where the one with the risk would often not be insured for the loss. A useful discussion is Howard, *Allocation of Risk of Loss Under the UCC: A Transactional Evaluation of Sections 2–509 and 2–510,* 15 U.C.C.L.J. 334 (1983).

SECTION 2. RISK OF LOSS UNDER THE CODE IN THE ABSENCE OF BREACH

A. Seller Has No Obligation to Ship Goods; Goods in Possession of Bailee

Unless otherwise agreed, the seller has no obligation to ship the goods to the buyer. The place of delivery is the "seller's place of business or if he has none his residence." UCC 2–308(a). What the seller must do to tender delivery to the buyer is spelled out in UCC 2–503(1). If at the time of contracting, identified goods are in the possession "of a bailee and are to be delivered without being moved," what the seller must do to tender delivery is spelled out in UCC 2–503(4). See UCC 2–308(b). For the importance of this, read UCC 2–509(2) & (3) and work through the following materials.

Problem 16–1

Sam purchased a new VCR for $500 in June, 1987. In November, 1987, Sam, pressed for cash, advertised the VCR for sale. On Friday, Bob visited Sam's condo, inspected the unit and, after some negotiations, agreed to buy it for $300, with $150 down and the balance on delivery. Bob asked when he could take the VCR. Sam said he wanted it over the weekend to tape the Bear's game and that he would call Bob at work on Monday to set up a time "after work on Monday." Bob agreed. On Sunday evening, a self-appointed neighborhood "resource reallocator" forcibly entered Sam's condo and "removed" the VCR. When informed, Bob stopped payment on the $150 check. Sam argued that the VCR was Bob's and that he still owed Sam the entire $300. Neither party was insured. Who should prevail?

Problem 16–2

After negotiations and inspection, B agreed in writing to purchase identified, new factory equipment for $15,000. The agreement provided, in part, that the price was due "when goods received by the purchaser" and that delivery was to be to "purchaser's truck within 4 weeks of contract date, seller to give purchaser 7 days notice of delivery." Two weeks later, S notified B in writing that the goods were "in a deliverable state and at your disposal." The notice was received on a Friday. Over the weekend and before B took possession, vandals broke into S's plant and seriously damaged the machinery. B refused to take delivery, claiming that the risk of loss was on S. Neither party was insured. Who prevails?

SILVER v. WYCOMBE, MEYER & CO., INC.

Civil Court of the City of New York, 1984.
124 Misc.2d 717, 477 N.Y.S.2d 288.

DAVID B. SAXE, JUDGE.

This action by an insurance company, as subrogee, to recover proceeds paid to its insured, Martin Silver, was tried before the court on stipulated facts.

Plaintiff, through his agent, Elsie Simpson, an interior decorator, ordered custom furniture from defendant Wycombe, Meyer & Co., Inc. (Wycombe). The furniture was manufactured by codefendant Jackson-Allen Upholstery Corp. (Jackson-Allen), a subsidiary of defendant Wycombe, at its factory in Catasauqua, Pennsylvania. On or about February 23, 1982, Wycombe sent invoices to plaintiff advising that the furniture was ready for shipment. Plaintiff thereupon tendered payment in full and directed Wycombe to ship one room of furniture but to hold the other until instructed further. Accordingly, one room of furniture was shipped to plaintiff. But before any instructions were received as to the second room of furniture, it was destroyed in a fire which was not due to any negligence on the part of defendants. Fireman's Fund Insurance Co. paid plaintiff for the loss and seeks to recover the proceeds from defendants on the theory that the risk of loss never passed to the buyer, its insured.

In the absence of contrary agreement by the parties, risk of loss under the Uniform Commercial Code is determined by the manner in which delivery is to be made (U.C.C. 2–509). The original order, documented by defendant Wycombe's order form, indicates a price of $7053 "+ del'y," and all invoices provide for shipment to plaintiff's home "Truck prepaid." It is clear that the provisions of U.C.C. 2–509 Subdiv. (1) govern the issue of when risk of loss passes to the buyer "where the contract requires or authorizes the seller to ship the goods by carrier * * *" Where the contract requires the seller to deliver the merchandise at a particular location, risk of loss passes upon tender of the goods at that location (U.C.C. 2–509(1)(b)) and where the contract does not require the seller to deliver the goods to a particular destination, it passes upon their delivery to the carrier (par. (a)). Where the contract provides for delivery at the seller's place of business or at the situs of the goods, risk of loss passes upon actual receipt by the buyer, if seller is a merchant, and otherwise upon tender of delivery (U.C.C. 2–509(3)).

Under the facts of the case at bar, the terms of the contract as it regards delivery are not stated. It is apparent, however, that regardless of the particular agreement between buyer and seller, defendants have set forth no facts sufficient to place the risk of loss upon plaintiff under any of the cited U.C.C. provisions. Indeed, the Official Comment 3 to U.C.C. 2–509 makes it clear that "a merchant seller cannot transfer risk of loss and it remains upon him until actual receipt by the buyer, even though full payment has been made and the buyer has been notified that the goods are at his disposal" (Note 3).

Defendants, however, advance the novel theory that, because of plaintiff's request that they hold the furniture subject to further instruction, they became mere bailees of the goods and that the provisions of U.C.C. 2–509(2) should govern this case. They argue that the invoices informing plaintiff that the furniture was ready for shipment constitute acknowledgment of the buyer's right to possession, transferring the risk of loss pursuant to U.C.C. 2–509(2)(b) to the buyer.

This position is entirely without merit. The provisions of U.C.C. 2–509(2) contemplate a situation in which goods are in the physical possession of a third party who will continue to hold them after consummation of the sale. Therefore, this is not a provision appropriately applied to the circumstances at bar which anticipate the passing of title *and* physical possession more or less simultaneously. Furthermore, bailment requires *delivery* of the goods to the bailee (see Black's Law Dictionary, 4th ed., p. 179, 1968). Having concluded that defendants failed to establish delivery of the furniture to plaintiff, by no stretch of the imagination may plaintiff be said to have redelivered it to defendants for safe-keeping.

Defendants cannot transform what is clearly a sale of goods into a bailment simply because they acceded to the buyer's request to postpone delivery. The agreement between buyer and seller clearly contemplates delivery at the buyer's home and, under the Uniform Commercial Code, risk of loss remains upon a merchant seller until he completes his performance with reference to the physical delivery of the goods (U.C.C. 2–401(2); U.C.C. 2–509(3) and Note 3 to U.C.C. 2–509; *Ramos v. Wheel Sports Center,* 96 Misc.2d 646, 409 N.Y.S.2d 505, Civ.Ct., Bx.) It may be that defendant Jackson-Allen is a bailee for defendant Wycombe, but this Court is not required to rule on and makes no determination of this question.

Accordingly, judgment for plaintiff in the amount demanded in the complaint together with costs, disbursements and interest from April 13, 1982.

Notes

1. Under what circumstances, if any, can a merchant seller become a "bailee" for purposes of UCC 2–509(2)?

2. Note that the buyer's insurance company had indemnified the buyer for loss of the goods and sued the seller as a subrogee. Why did the insurer argue that risk of loss had not passed to the buyer? If the risk had passed, upon what theory could the insurer recover from the seller?

JASON'S FOODS, INC. v. PETER ECKRICH & SONS, INC.

United States Court of Appeals, Seventh Circuit, 1985.
774 F.2d 214.

POSNER, CIRCUIT JUDGE.

The jurisdictional question that led us to order a limited remand in *Jason's Foods, Inc. v. Peter Eckrich & Sons, Inc.,* 768 F.2d 189 (7th Cir.1985), has been answered by the district judge: the defendant's principal place of business is Indiana, so there is diversity jurisdiction, and we can proceed to the merits of the appeal. Section 2–509(2) of the Uniform Commercial Code as adopted in Illinois (whose law, the parties agree, governs this diversity suit) provides that where "goods are held by a bailee to be delivered without being moved, the risk of loss passes to the buyer * * * (b) on acknowledgment by the bailee of the buyer's right to possession of the goods." Ill.Rev.Stat. ch. 26, ¶ 2–509(2). We must decide whether acknowledgment to the *seller* complies with the statute. There are no reported cases on the question, either in Illinois or elsewhere. Three commentators have opined that acknowledgment must be to the buyer, but without discussion. See Nordstrom, Handbook of the Law of Sales 404–05 (1970); Howard, *Allocation of Risk of Loss Under the UCC: A Transactional Evaluation of Sections 2–509 and 2–510,* 15 UCC L.J. 334, 347 n. 42 (1983); Comment, *Risk of Loss Under Section 2509 of the California Uniform Commercial Code,* 20 UCLA L.Rev. 1352, 1358 n. 30 (1973). There is a hint of the same position, again without explanation, in Latty, *Sales and Title and the Proposed Code,* 16 Law & Contemp.Prob. 3, 14 (1951); Note, *Risk of Loss Under the Uniform Commercial Code,* 7 Ind.L.Rev. 711, 726 (1974), and Note, *Commercial Transactions: Risk of Loss: What Does the Code Mean by Bailee?,* 21 Okla.L.Rev. 310 (1968). The defendant submitted in the district court an affidavit from a professor of commercial law at Ohio State University (Professor Clovis), who also concluded, also without elaboration, that acknowledgment must be to the buyer. The plaintiff did not question the admissibility of expert testimony on a pure issue of domestic law—though well it might have. See, e.g., *Marx & Co. v. Diners' Club, Inc.,* 550 F.2d 505, 510–11 (2d Cir.1977); *Loeb v. Hammond,* 407 F.2d 779, 781 (7th Cir.1969); *United States v. Zipkin,* 729 F.2d 384, 387 (6th Cir.1984). An alternative procedure would have been for the district judge to invite a disinterested expert on commercial law to submit a brief as *amicus curiae.* See Code of Judicial Conduct for United States Judges, Canon 3(A)(4) and commentary thereto.

On or about December 30, 1982, Jason's Foods contracted to sell 38,000 pounds of "St. Louis style" pork ribs to Peter Eckrich & Sons, delivery to be effected by a transfer of the ribs from Jason's' account in an independent warehouse to Eckrich's account in the same warehouse—which is to say, without the ribs actually being moved. In its confirmation of the deal, Jason's notified Eckrich that the transfer in storage would be made between January 10 and January 14. On January 13 Jason's phoned the warehouse and requested that the ribs be transferred to Eckrich's account. A clerk at the warehouse noted the transfer on its books immediately but did not mail a warehouse receipt until January 17 or January 18, and it was not till Eckrich received the receipt on January 24 that it knew the transfer had taken place. But on January 17 the ribs had been destroyed by a fire at the warehouse. Jason's sued Eckrich for the price. If the risk of loss passed on January 13 when the ribs were transferred to Eckrich's account, or at least before the fire, Jason's is entitled to recover the contract price; otherwise not. The district judge ruled that the risk of loss did not pass by then and therefore granted summary judgment for Eckrich.

Jason's argues that when the warehouse transferred the ribs to Eckrich's account, Jason's lost all rights over the ribs, and it should not bear the risk of loss of goods it did not own or have any right to control. Eckrich owned them and Eckrich's insurance covered any ribs that it owned; Jason's had no insurance and anyway, Jason's argues, it could not insure what it no longer owned. (The warehouse would be liable for the fire damage only if negligent. Cf. *Refrigeration Sales Co. v. Mitchell-Jackson, Inc.,* 770 F.2d 98 (7th Cir.1985).) Finally, Jason's points out that the draftsmen of the Uniform Commercial Code were careful and deliberate. Both subsections (a) and (c) of section 2–509(2)—the subsections that surround the "acknowledgment" provision at issue in this case—provide that the risk of loss passes to the buyer on or after "his receipt" of a document of title (negotiable in (a), nonnegotiable in (c)). If the draftsmen had meant that the acknowledgment of the buyer's right to possession of the goods—the acknowledgment that is subsection (b)'s substitute for a document of title—must be to the buyer, they would have said so.

Eckrich argues with great vigor that it cannot be made to bear the loss of goods that it does not know it owns. But that is not so *outré* a circumstance as it may sound. If you obtain property by inheritance, you are quite likely to own it before you know you own it. And Eckrich's position involves a comparable paradox: that Jason's continued to bear the risk of loss of goods that it knew it no longer owned. So the case cannot be decided by reference to what the parties knew or did not know; and neither can it be decided, despite Jason's' urgings, on the basis of which party could have insured against the loss. Both could have. Jason's had sufficient interest in the ribs until the risk of loss shifted to Eckrich to insure the ribs until then. You do not have to own goods to insure them; it is enough that you will suffer a loss if they are lost or damaged, *Hawkeye-Security Ins. Co. v. Reeg,* 128 Ill.App.3d 352, 83 Ill.Dec. 683, 470 N.E.2d 1103 (1984); *Prince v. Royal Indemnity Co.,* 541 F.2d 646, 649 (7th Cir.1976), as of course

Jason's would if the risk of loss remained on it after it parted with title. See generally Stockton, *An Analysis of Insurable Interest Under Article Two of the Uniform Commercial Code,* 17 Vand.L.Rev. 815, 816–21 (1964). Section 2–509(2) separates title from risk of loss. Title to the ribs passed to Eckrich when the warehouse made the transfer on its books from Jason's' account to Eckrich's, but the risk of loss did not pass until the transfer was "acknowledged."

Thus, as is usually the case, insurability cannot be used to guide the assignment of liability. (The costs of insurance might sometimes be usable for this purpose, as we shall see, but not in this case.) Since whoever will be liable for the loss can insure against it, the court must determine who is liable before knowing who can insure, rather than vice versa. If acknowledgment to the seller is enough to place the risk of loss on the buyer, then Eckrich should have bought insurance against any losses that occurred afterward. If acknowledgment to the buyer is necessary (we need not decide whether acknowledgment to a third party may ever suffice), Jason's should have bought insurance against any losses occurring until then.

The suggestion that the acknowledgment contemplated by subsection (b) can be to the seller seems very strange. What purpose would it serve? When Jason's called up the warehouse and directed that the transfer be made, it did not add: and by the way, acknowledge to me when you make the transfer. Jason's assumed, correctly, that the transfer was being made forthwith; and in fact there is no suggestion that the warehouse clerk ever "acknowledged" the transfer to Jason's. If the draftsmen of subsection (b) had meant the risk of loss to pass when the transfer was made, one would think they would have said so, and not complicated life by requiring "acknowledgment."

A related section of the Uniform Commercial Code, section 2–503(4)(a), makes acknowledgment by the bailee (the warehouse here) a method of tendering goods that are sold without being physically moved; but, like section 2–509(2) (b), it does not indicate to whom acknowledgment must be made. The official comments on this section, however, indicate that it was not intended to change the corresponding section of the Uniform Sales Act, section 43(3). See UCC comment 6 to § 2–503. And section 43(3) had expressly required acknowledgment to the buyer. See, e.g., *Peelle Co. v. Industrial Plant Corp.,* 120 N.J.L. 480, 200 A. 1007 (1938). Rules on tender have, it is true, a different function from rules on risk of loss; they determine at what point the seller has completed the performance of his side of the bargain. He may have completed performance, but if the goods are still in transit the risk of loss does not shift until the buyer receives them, if the seller is a merchant. See UCC § 2–509(3) and UCC comment 3 to section 2–509. In the case of warehouse transfers, however, the draftsmen apparently wanted risk of loss to conform to the rules for tender. For comment 4 to section 2–509 states that "where the agreement provides for delivery of the goods as between the buyer and seller without removal from the physical possession of a bailee, the provisions on manner of tender of delivery apply on the point of transfer of risk." And those provisions as we have said apparently require (in the case where no document of title passes) acknowledgment to the buyer. The acknowledgment need not, by the way, be in writing, so far as we are aware. Jason's could have instructed the warehouse to call Eckrich when the transfer was complete on the warehouse's books. See *Whately v. Tetrault,* 29 Mass.App.Dec. 112, 5 UCC Rep.Serv. (Callaghan) 838 (1964). That is why Jason's' case is not utterly demolished by the fact that the document of title—that is, the warehouse receipt—was not received by Eckrich till after the fire. Acknowledgment in a less formal manner is authorized; indeed, section 509(2)(b) would have no function if the only authorized form of acknowledgment were by document of title, whether negotiable or nonnegotiable.

The second sentence of comment 4 to section 509 is also suggestive: "Due delivery of a negotiable document of title covering the goods or acknowledgment by the bailee that he holds for the buyer completes the 'delivery' and passes the risk." The reference to a document of title is to subsections (a) and (c); and in both of those cases, of course, the tender involves notice to the buyer. It would be surprising if the alternative of acknowledgment did not.

All this may seem a rather dry textual analysis, remote from the purposes of the Uniform Commercial Code, so let us shift now to the plane of policy. The Code sought to create a set of standard contract terms that would reflect in the generality of cases the preferences of contracting parties at the time of contract. One such preference is for assignments of liability—or, what amounts to the same thing, assignments of the risk of loss—that create incentives to minimize the adverse consequences of untoward events such as (in this case) a warehouse fire. There are two ways of minimizing such consequences. One is to make them less painful by insuring against them. Insurance does not prevent a loss—it merely spreads it—but in doing so it reduces (for those who are risk averse) the disutility of the loss. So if one of the contracting parties can insure at lower cost than the other, this is an argument for placing the risk of loss on him, to give him an incentive to do so. But that as we have seen is not a factor in this case; either party could have insured (or have paid the warehouse to assume strict liability for loss or destruction of the goods, in which event the warehouse would have insured them), and so far as the record shows at equal cost.

The other method of minimizing the consequences of an unanticipated loss is through prevention of the loss. If one party is in a better position than the other to prevent it, this is a reason for placing the risk of loss on him, to give him an incentive to prevent it. It would be a reason for placing liability on a seller who still had possession of the goods, even though title had passed. But between the moment of transfer of title by Jason's and the moment of receipt of the warehouse receipt by Eckrich, neither party to the sale had effective control over the ribs. They were in a kind of limbo, until (to continue the Dantesque image) abruptly propelled into a hotter region. With Jason's having relinquished title and Eckrich not yet aware that it had acquired it, neither party had an effective power of control.

But this is not an argument for holding that the risk of loss shifted at the moment of transfer; it is just an argument for regarding the parties' positions as symmetrical from the standpoint of ability either to prevent or to shift losses. In such a case we have little to assist us besides the language of subsection (b) and its surrounding subsections and the UCC comments; but these materials do point pretty clearly to the conclusion that the risk of loss did not pass at the moment of transfer.

When did it pass? Does "acknowledgment" mean receipt, as in the surrounding subsections of 2–509(2), or mailing? Since the evidence was in conflict over whether the acknowledgment was mailed on January 17 (and at what hour), which was the day of the fire, or on January 18, this could be an important question—but in another case. Jason's waived it. The only theory it tendered to the district court, or briefed and argued in this court, was that the risk of loss passed either on January 13, when the transfer of title was made on the books of the warehouse, or at the latest on January 14, because Eckrich knew the ribs would be transferred at the warehouse sometime between January 10 and 14. We have discussed the immateriality of the passage of title on January 13; we add that the alternative argument, that Eckrich knew by January 14 that it owned the ribs, exaggerates what Eckrich knew. By the close of business on January 14 Eckrich had a well-founded expectation that the ribs had been transferred to its account; but considering the many slips that are possible between cup and lips, we do not think that this expectation should fix the point at which the risk shifts. If you were told by an automobile dealer from whom you bought a car that the car would be delivered on January 14, you would not take out insurance effective that day, without waiting for the actual delivery.

Finally, Jason's' argument from trade custom or usage is unavailing. The method of transfer that the parties used was indeed customary but there was no custom or usage on when the risk of loss passed to the buyer.

Affirmed.

Notes

1. At common law, if the goods were identified and in the possession of a bailee, title and, thus, risk of loss, passed at the time of sale even though the buyer was not entitled to take possession. See Tarling v. Baxter, 6 B. & C. 360, 108 Eng.Rep. 484 (KB 1827). Compare UCC 2–401(3). In *Jason's Foods,* the court held that even though title had passed, the risk of loss did not pass until the bailee acknowledged to the buyer the buyer's right to take possession. Do you agree? Compare UCC 2–705(2)(b).

2. The "bailee" in *Jason's Foods* was a warehouseman, i.e., a "person who by a warehouse receipt * * * acknowledges possession of goods and contracts to deliver them." UCC 7–102(1)(a). A warehouse receipt, UCC 1–201(45), is a document of title which "in the regular course of business * * * is treated as adequately evidencing that the person in possession of it is entitled to receive, hold and dispose of the document and the goods it covers." UCC 1–201(15). In *Jason's Foods,* the warehouse receipt issued but not received by the buyer before the fire was not negotiable. See UCC 7–104(1). See UCC 2–509(2)(c) & 2–503(4)(b). Note that the buyer must actually receive the written delivery order and, under UCC 2–503(4)(b), risk of loss remains on the seller "until the buyer has had a reasonable time to present the document or direction * * *." These sections further reinforce Judge Posner's analysis, do they not? Does UCC 2–509(2)(b) even apply to the case where a warehouseman regularly acknowledges a buyer's right to possession by a non-negotiable document of title?

3. The warehouseman's duty of care is stated in UCC 7–204(1).

Problem 16–3

Red Feather, a fine yearling, won her first race. A pleased Owner (much pleased) shipped her back to the stable by common carrier, taking a non-negotiable bill of lading naming O as the consignee. While the horse was in transit, O sold her to B for $10,000. Owner accepted a check for $10,000, handed B the non-negotiable bill of lading and stated "she's all yours." Two hours later, Red Feather was killed in an accident while still in the carrier's possession.

A. B stopped payment on the check and insisted that the risk of loss remained on S. Is B correct?

B. Suppose that, unknown to either party, Red Feather was dead at the time of the contract. What result? See UCC 2–613.

B. *Shipment Contracts*

Probably the most common transaction in which risk of loss disputes will arise involves contracts that require or authorize the seller to ship the goods to the buyer by carrier. It is also likely that the agreement will use certain delivery terms, such as "FOB seller's plant," FAS or CIF. See UCC 2–319 & 2–320. The Code drafters were aware of the common business understanding of these terms and consciously adapted the risk of loss provisions to them. Compare UCC 2–319(1) and 2–509(1). For what the seller must do under these terms to tender delivery, see UCC 2–503 & 2–504.

In most cases, the meaning and consequences of these delivery terms is clear. In an FOB point of origin or shipment contract, the buyer pays the cost of transportation and bears the risk of loss while the goods are in transit. UCC 2–319(1)(a) and 2–509(1)(a). In an FOB point of destination contract, the seller pays the cost of transportation and bears the risk while the goods are in transit. UCC 2–319(1)(b) and 2–509(1)(b). But occasionally there is some confusion.

RAYLO LUMBER COMPANY v. OREGON PACIFIC LUMBER COMPANY

Supreme Court of Oregon, 1960.
222 Or. 257, 352 P.2d 749.

HOLMAN, JUSTICE pro tem.

Plaintiff Raylo Lumber Company brought this action against defendant, Oregon Pacific Lumber Company, for the recovery of the price of a carload of lumber. For the purpose of clarity, this opinion will hereafter refer to the plaintiff, Raylo Lumber Company, as Seller and the defendant, Oregon Pacific Lumber Company, as Buyer.

At its mill in Fortuna, California, Seller received from Buyer a written order for lumber sent from Buyer's place of business in Portland, Oregon. The pertinent parts of the written order were as follows:

> "To Raylo Lbr. Co. Box 575 Fortunia [sic], Calif. Ship to Oregon-Pacific Lumber Co. Council Bluffs, Iowa Rate 1.20 (Show on Bill of Lading) Routing SP UP (via Colby, Kansas) Shipment One week Terms: Regular 2% ADF 10 days Please Show Oregon-Pacific Lumber Co. As Shipper * * * Thoroughly Air Dried White Fir—WCLA Rules No. 15 Constr. & Btr., Allow. 25% standard ALS S4S EE DET—Clean Bright Stock Three (3) Carloads—Approx. 28/30M each. 2 × 4 R/L 70% 16′ 60.00 24.00 84.00".

Seller successfully shipped two carloads about which there is no controversy. The loading of the third car on the siding at Seller's place of business was completed before noon on a particular day and the car was sealed. In the afternoon Seller prepared an invoice to Buyer for the lumber in the car, billing Buyer as follows:

> "Shipped to Oregon—Pacific Lumber Company Council Bluffs, Iowa * * * F.O.B. Delivered $1.20 Rate. * * * 31,152′ White Fir, A.D. 2 × 4 STD. & BTR. S4S, [at] $84.00 Per M—$2,616,77".

Seller also prepared a straight bill of lading naming Buyer both consignor and consignee as instructed, and around 5 o'clock in the afternoon presented it to the railroad at its nearest station at Alton, California, which was some distance from Seller's place of business. The railroad agent signed the bill of lading and Seller immediately deposited both it and the invoice in the mail to

Buyer. Before Buyer received the bill of lading and before the carrier took the car from Seller's siding, fire broke out and the lumber was damaged. The fire was not shown to have been the fault of either party. The damaged lumber was sold with the consent of the parties without prejudice to their rights and the proceeds applied toward the purchase price. This action was brought for the balance, the trial judge tried the case without a jury, and entered findings of fact to the effect that Seller sold and delivered the lumber to Buyer and that the damage to the lumber occurred after the delivery of the lumber to Buyer in accordance with the terms of the agreement. Judgment was rendered for Seller and Buyer appeals.

The rules governing who should sustain the loss in a situation such as this are, of course, those set forth in the Uniform Sales Act which has been adopted by this state. Unless otherwise agreed, risk of loss follows the title to the property in question as the result of ORS 75.220 (Uniform Sales Act § 22), which is as follows:

> "Unless otherwise agreed, the goods remain at the seller's risk until the property therein is transferred to the buyer, the goods are at the buyer's risk whether delivery has been made or not, * * *."

Unless a contrary intention appears, the rules for ascertaining the intention of the parties as to the time title passes are set out in ORS 75.190 (Uniform Sales Act § 19). The pertinent parts of this section are as follows:

> "Unless a different intention appears, the following are rules for ascertaining the intention of the parties as to the time at which the property in the goods is to pass to the buyer:
>
> * * *
>
> "Rule 4. (1) Where there is a contract to sell unascertained or future goods by description, and goods of that description and in a deliverable state are unconditionally appropriated to the contract, * * * the property in the goods thereupon passes to the buyer. * * *
>
> "(2) Where, in pursuance of a contract to sell, the seller delivers the goods to * * * a carrier * * * for the purpose of transmission to * * * the buyer, he is presumed to have unconditionally appropriated the goods to the contract, except in the cases provided for in the next rule. * * *
>
> "Rule 5. If the contract to sell requires the seller to deliver the goods to the buyer, or at a particular place, or to pay the freight or cost of transportation to the buyer, or to a particular place, the property does not pass until the goods have been delivered to the buyer or have reached the place agreed upon."

From the above, it is apparent that where there is a contract to sell unascertained or future goods by description, as was the case here, title passes when the goods are put in a deliverable state and unconditionally appropriated to the contract (Rule 4(1)). Where the Seller delivers the goods to a carrier for delivery to the Buyer, they are presumed to have been unconditionally appropriated to the contract (Rule 4(2)), except that if the contract requires delivery by the Seller to a particular place or to pay the cost of transportation, title does not pass until the goods have reached the place agreed upon. (Rule 5)

Seller claims that the rules set forth under ORS 75.190 do not apply, as by its provisions they are only applicable where no different intention appears; that this is a law case and the trial judge sitting as a jury, by making a finding that there was a sale and a delivery, found that a different intention did appear; that there is sufficient evidence in the record to support the findings and, therefore, they cannot be disturbed.

The question of intention is one of fact. However, if the whole contract of the parties is reduced to writing, or if the facts are so clear as to justify but one conclusion, and generally, if the facts are undisputed from which intention can be determined, the question is determined by the court. See 2 Williston, Sales (Rev.Ed.), p. 10, § 262. In this case, everything was in writing and there are no disputes as to the circumstances involved. This was a determination for the court as such and not one made by the court sitting as a jury.

The findings of the trial court that the lumber was sold, which imputes passage of title, and that there was a delivery is made in the face of Seller's invoice to Buyer which specifies the price as being "F.O.B. Delivered." This required Buyer to pay $84 per thousand for lumber delivered by Seller in Council Bluffs, Iowa. It imputes the passage of title at Council Bluffs and that Seller will pay the freight to that point. The term "F.O.B." has become recognized as having certain definite commercial and legal significance. A text written by Thomas G. Bugan entitled "When Does Title Pass From Shipper to Consignee And Who Has Risk of Loss or Damage in Transportation" (1951) has this to say about the term "F.O.B.": "This term has a certain legal significance of which the courts take judicial notice." After an examination of various judicial and text writers' definitions of the meaning of the term, he states as follows:

> The implication from the above definitions is, that the phrase F.O.B. will ordinarily determine the place where delivery is required and where the title will pass. Likewise, it will usually determine whether the seller or the buyer is to pay the transportation charges.

While recognizing that it may be varied by the other terms of the contract, the Oregon court has recognized the usual significance given the usage of the designation "F.O.B." in the case of Wade v. Johnson, 111 Or. 468, 477, 227 P. 466.

In his chapter entitled "F.O.B. Destination," which we take to be synonymous with the term "F.O.B. Delivered," Mr. Bugan discusses the intention of the parties regarding transfer of title as it affects the usage of the term "F.O.B." and comes to the following conclusion:

> The intent of the parties is the controlling element fixing the time and place of passage of title and risk.
>
> However, in the absence of a definite agreement as to time and place of passage of title, the Uniform Sales Act (or the principles of the common law where the Act does not apply) will prevail to determine the intent. If the words "f.o.b." are employed, they are especially important in solving the intent of the parties, for they have a definite commercial and legal significance of which the courts will take judicial notice.

The meaning of the use of the term has become so well ingrained in commercial and legal parlance that a contrary intention to its usual meaning must be demonstrated with a high degree of probability. The evidence here does not demonstrate such a probability and, therefore, there is no basis upon which to rest the trial court's findings of a sale and delivery.

Seller particularly contends that Buyer's instructions to Seller to ship the lumber showing Buyer as the shipper, shows a sufficient contrary intent. This is overcome, in our opinion, when coupled with an agreement for goods "F.O.B. Delivered." It could also just as logically be claimed that the instruction was for the purpose of not disclosing the identity of Buyer's supplier and customer to each other so they might deal directly without the necessity of a middle man.

The evidence not being sufficient to show a different intent as to the time of the passage of title, Rule 5 of ORS 75.190 is applicable. The Seller having undertaken to deliver the goods to Council Bluffs, Iowa, at the flat price of $84 per thousand and to pay the freight to that point, the property in the lumber had not passed at the time of the fire and risk of loss by virtue of ORS 75.220 was on the Seller.

The judgment of the lower court is reversed.

Notes

1. How would *Raylo* be decided under the Code? See UCC 2–319(1), 2–509(1), 2–503, Comment 5. See also, Pestana v. Karinol Corp., 367 So.2d 1096 (Fla.App.1979); Ninth St. East, Ltd. v. Harrison, 5 Conn.Cir. 597, 259 A.2d 772 (1968) (presumption of shipment rather than a destination contract).

2. In shipment contracts, the risk of loss passes at the time the seller completes or "duly" tenders delivery at the point to which the goods are to be delivered. UCC 2–509(1). In FOB point of shipment contracts, UCC 2–319(1)(a), the critical tender section is UCC 2–504. Although the seller must do a number of things to tender delivery, obtaining insurance for the buyer's account is not one of them. Compare UCC 2–320 (C.I.F. term). For a case holding that the goods were not "duly" tendered where the seller failed to provide prompt notice of shipment in an FOB point of shipment contract, see Rheinberg-Kellerei GMBH v. Vineyard Wine Co., Inc., 53 N.C. App. 560, 281 S.E.2d 425 (1981). Does this position seem sound?

Note: Liability of Overland Carrier for Goods Lost or Damaged in Shipment

As we have seen, in an FOB place of shipment contract, risk of loss passes to the buyer when the seller "duly" tenders the goods to a carrier, whether that carrier be a truck, airplane, railroad or vessel. In addition, under the documents issued by the carrier, the buyer is the person "entitled" to the goods. See UCC 7–102(1)(b) & 7–403(4). Thus, if the goods are lost or damaged in transit, the buyer or its insurance company as subrogee has both the standing and the incentive * to bring suit against the carrier. Kumar Corp. v. Nopal Lines, LTD., 462 So.2d 1178 (Fla.App.1985), holds that plaintiffs with standing to sue the carrier include the party with the risk of loss or his agent and an insurance subrogee.

The common law liability of the overland carrier has been described as follows:

DOBIE, BAILMENTS AND CARRIERS 325 (1914)

"By the common law, the common carrier is, with certain exceptions, an insurer of the goods intrusted to him. According to the very early cases, the only exceptions to the common carrier's liability as an insurer of the safe delivery of the goods were: 1) the act of God; and 2) the public enemy. To these, however, our native justice and the genius of our jurisprudence have added: 3) the act of the shipper; 4) public authority; and 5) the inherent nature of the goods."

* Several things make the carrier an appealing defendant. First, it is likely that it causes or has the potential for causing more loss, destruction and damage than any other party associated with a typical sales transaction. Second, the carrier is almost always solvent. Third, it is easy to prove a case against a carrier. Finally, the carrier, as a public service enterprise, is obliged to deal with all persons and cannot readily use economic pressure of withholding services to forestall a suit. Ed.

The common-law liability of common carriers, however, was subject to contractual limitations and exclusions inserted by carriers in the relevant documents.

The current status of carrier liability is determined under federal and state legislation and international treaties that, in turn, depend upon the type of carrier and the scope of its operation. Thus, the liability of international air carriers is determined by the Warsaw Convention, ratified by the United States in 1934, 49 Stat. 3000 (1934), T.S. No. 876, and the liability of vessels engaged in "foreign trade" is regulated by the Carriage of Goods by Sea Act, enacted by Congress in 1936. 49 Stat. 1207 (1936), 46 U.S.C.A. §§ 1300–15. A general survey appears in Sorkin, *Changing Concepts of Liability,* 17 Forum 710 (1981).

The liability of domestic overland carriers in interstate commerce, i.e., railroads and truckers, is regulated by the 1906 Carmack amendments to the Interstate Commerce Commission Act of 1887, as reenacted in 1980 without substantial change. 49 U.S.C.A. § 11707. The statute is, essentially, a codification of the carrier's insurer liability at common law with the important benefit to the shipper that efforts to exclude or modify the scope of statutory liability by agreement are void. As the statute has been interpreted by the courts, the person entitled under the document states a *prima facie* case against the carrier by showing that the goods were delivered in good condition and arrived in a damaged condition and the amount of damages. To escape liability, the carrier has what is described as a "substantial double burden:" It must show both that it was free from negligence and that the damage to the cargo was due to one of the excepted causes relieving the carrier of liability at common law, i.e., act of God, public enemy, act of shipper himself, act of public authority or an inherent vice in the goods. See Martin Imports v. Courier Newsom Exp., Inc., 580 F.2d 240, 242 (7th Cir.1978), cert. denied 439 U.S. 983, 99 S.Ct. 574, 58 L.Ed.2d 655 (1978). The seminal case in this line is Missouri P.R. Co. v. Elmore & Stahl, 377 U.S. 134, 84 S.Ct. 1142, 12 L.Ed.2d 194 (1964).

The liability of domestic overland carriers in intrastate commerce is determined by Article 7 of the UCC, more particularly, UCC 7–309. See UCC 7–103; Starmakers Pub. Corp. v. Acme Fast Freight, Inc., 615 F.Supp. 787 (S.D.N.Y.1985) (Carmack Act preempts UCC where interstate shipments are concerned). Subsection 7–309(1), which is poorly drafted, starts by imposing a duty of ordinary care on the carrier, but then states that the subsection "does not repeal or change any law or rule of law which imposes liability upon a common carrier for damages not caused by its negligence." Thus, in the many states where the common law liability of a carrier as insurer was recognized, the carrier could be liable even though exercising reasonable care. Subsection 7–309(2) gives limited effect to provisions in the bill of lading limiting liability: The carrier can limit liability to the value of the goods stated in the document but "no such limitation is effective with respect to the carrier's liability for conversion to its own use."

As one might expect, there has been no litigation of significance involving UCC 7–309.

SECTION 3. EFFECT OF BREACH ON RISK OF LOSS—2–510

UCC 2–510 modifies the risk of loss principles established by UCC 2–509 in certain circumstances where one of the parties is in breach. The consequences of this modification are twofold.

First, in some cases the breaching party will have to absorb the loss of or pay for lost, stolen or destroyed goods where, but for the breach, the risk of loss would have been on the other party. Thus, UCC 2–510 reallocates the risk of loss because one party breached the contract and negates the assumptions made ex ante about who was in the best position to insure. This reallocation has been questioned on policy grounds in McCoid, *Allocation of Loss and Property Insurance,* 39 Ind.L.J. 647 (1964).

Second, UCC 2–510 operates, in some circumstances, as an anti-subrogation clause: It places the risk on the non-breaching party's insurance company in circumstances where but for the insurance contract the risk of loss would be on the breaching party. Thus, under UCC 2–510(2), a buyer who, because of the seller's breach, rightfully revokes acceptance may treat the risk of loss as having rested on the seller "to the extent of any deficiency in his effective insurance coverage." Because of the statute, the insurance company must pay if there is no deficiency and, apparently, is precluded from any recovery as a subrogee against the seller. See Comment 3, which states: "This section merely distributes the risk of loss as stated and is not intended to be disturbed by any subrogation of an insurer."

What is the point of all this? One commentator has suggested that UCC 2–510 is of "dubious origin," has little practical impact on the way that insurance companies do business and "serves no practical purpose save the harassment of the legal mind." King, *UCC Section 2–510—A Rule Without Reason,* 77 Com. L.J. 272 (1972). Nothing has emerged since 1972 to cast serious doubt on this conclusion. Professor Howard, in *Allocation of Risk of Loss Under the UCC: A Transactional Evaluation of Sections 2–509 and 2–510,* 15 U.C.C.L.J. 334, 355–68 (1983), questions whether a commercial breach in the absence of bad faith is important enough to undercut the importance of insurance.

Here are some simple problems.

Problem 16–4

On June 1, S contracted to sell B 10 units of described goods for $10,000. S agreed to ship the goods "FOB point of shipment" by June 15 and B agreed to pay in full within 30 days of receipt. S had insurance on the goods until they were delivered to the carrier. B had insurance on the goods when "title" passed to him, i.e., at the "time and place of shipment." UCC 2–401(2)(a). S's insurance covered the current market value of the described goods. B's insurance covered 50% of the current market value of the goods.

A. S delivered the goods to the carrier on June 16 (they were shipped on June 17) and failed to give B any notice of the shipment. Review UCC 2–504. The goods were totally destroyed in transit on June 19. B, citing UCC 2–510, argues that the risk of loss was on S. Consequently, B had no liability for the price. Is B correct? See UCC 2–601 (right of rejection), 2–608 (cure) and 2–606 (acceptance).

B. Suppose, in (A) above, that the goods were not destroyed in transit. Rather, they were tendered by the carrier and accepted by B and taken to its plant. See UCC 2–606. The next day, the goods were destroyed without B's fault or negligence. Who has the risk of loss?

C. Continuing this exercise, suppose in (B) above, that after B accepted the goods, inspection at the plant revealed a latent, substantial defect which justified revocation of acceptance under UCC 2–608(1). B promptly notified S of the revocation. UCC 2–608(2). The next day, before S could send instructions, the goods were destroyed without the fault or negligence of B. Assuming that B, at the time of loss, had no liability for the price, see UCC 2–608(3), who has the risk of loss?

D. In light of these problems, what recommendations would you make for revision of UCC 2–510(1) & (2)? What problems, if any, do you see in the operation of UCC 2–510(3)?

SECTION 4. RISK OF LOSS AND INSURANCE

A. *Some General Principles*

As previously noted, the risk of loss rules in UCC 2–509 were designed, in part, to conform to assumptions about which party, seller or buyer, was in the best position, cost considered, either to prevent or to insure against loss of or damage to the goods. As Judge Posner put it in JASON'S FOODS, supra:

> "The Code sought to create a set of standard contract terms that would reflect in the generality of cases the preferences of contracting parties at the time of contract. One such preference is for assignments of liability—or, what amounts to the same thing, assignments of the risk of loss—that create incentives to minimize the adverse consequences of untoward events such as * * * a warehouse fire. There are two ways of minimizing such consequences. One is to make them less painful by insuring against them. Insurance does not prevent a loss—it merely spreads it—but in doing so it reduces (for those who are risk averse) the disutility of the loss. So if one of the contracting parties can insure at lower cost than the other, this is an argument for placing the risk of loss on him, to give him an incentive to do so. * * * The other method of minimizing the consequences of an unanticipated loss is through prevention of the loss. If one party is in a better position than the other to prevent it, this is a reason for placing the risk of loss on him, to give him an incentive to prevent it. It would be a reason for placing liability on a seller who still had possession of the goods, even though title had passed. * * *" 774 F.2d at 218.

The Code, however, has very little to say about insurance. UCC 2–501 states some but not all the circumstances where the seller and buyer will have an insurable interest in the goods. Thus, the "buyer obtains a special property interest and an insurable interest in goods by identification of existing goods as goods to which the contract refers even though the goods so identified are non-conforming and he has an option to return or reject them * * *," UCC 2–501(1), and the "seller retains an insurable interest in the goods so long as title to or any security interest in the goods remains in him. * * *," UCC 2–501(2). But UCC 2–501(3) provides that "Nothing in this section impairs any insurable interest recognized under any other statute or rule of law." Thus, UCC 2–501 is a one-way ratchet provision: it can expand, but not contract the scope of insurable interest. For the scope of insurable interest in property insurance cases, one may consult Stockton, *An Analysis of Insurable Interest Under Article Two of the Uniform Commercial Code,* 17 Vand.L.Rev. 815 (1964). See also, R. Keeton, Insurance Law 94–119 (1971); Pinzur, *Insurable Interest: A Search for Consistency,* 46 Ins.Counsel J. 109 (1979). Beyond insurable interest and the anti-subrogation rule of UCC 2–510, however, one must look elsewhere when disputes over insurance arise.

To sharpen the issues, read the following fact situation and puzzle over a few questions.

Problem 16–5

Repuenzel contracted to sell 1,000 pistons to Cicero for $10,000, $2,000 of which was paid upon contracting and the balance of which is due 30 days after delivery. Repuenzel created and perfected a security interest in the goods under Article 9 and shipped the goods "FOB place of Shipment," taking a non-negotiable bill of lading naming Cicero as consignee. During transit the goods were totally destroyed by fire. The contract for sale said nothing about risk of loss or insurance.

1. Which party has the risk of loss?

2. Which, if any, party has an insurable interest in the goods while in transit?

3. Standard fire insurance policies, with riders, have limited applicability to goods to be shipped to the buyer under a contract for sale. For the seller, personal property is likely to be defined as "property sold but not removed" from the building. For a buyer, coverage begins for "personal property * * * in cars on tracks when such cars are on the premises or within 100 feet of buildings described; in the open or in vehicles on the premises; on sidewalks, streets, alleys, or detached platforms when within 50 feet of buildings described."

Given these limitations, additional protection must be purchased by sellers and buyers with insurable interests while the goods are in transit. Read through the excerpts from the two types of policies which follow. Is Repuenzel's security interest covered by the Manufacturer's Output Policy? Is Buyer's ownership interest protection under the Transportation—All Risks Form?

MANUFACTURER'S OUTPUT POLICY

1. *Interest and Property Insured:* Except as hereinafter excluded, this policy insures:

(a) The interest of the Insured in all personal property owned by the Insured;

(b) The interest of the Insured in improvements and betterments to buildings not owned by the Insured;

(c) The interest of the Insured in, and legal liability for personal property of others in the actual or constructive custody of the Insured;

(d) Personal property of others

(1) Sold by the Insured which the Insured has agreed prior to loss to insure for the account of the purchaser during course of delivery;

(2) In the custody of the Insured which the Insured has agreed prior to loss to insurer;

(3) Sold by the Insured under an installation agreement whereby the Insured's responsibility continues until the installation is accepted by the purchaser.

2. *Interest and Property Excluded:* This policy does not insure:

(a) Currency, money, notes, securities, growing crops or standing timber;

(b) Property while covered under import or export ocean marine policies;

(c) Animals, aircraft or watercraft;

(d) Property sold by the Insured under conditional sale, trust agreement, installment payment, or other deferred payment plan;

(e) Loss resulting from interruption of business or other consequential loss extending beyond the direct physical loss of or damage to the insured property.

3. *Perils Insured:* This policy insures against all risks of direct physical loss of or damage to the insured property from any external cause (including general coverage and salvage charges on shipments covered while waterborne) except as hereinafter excluded.

* * *

9. *Specific Insurance:* Other insurance in name of and for the benefit of the Insured may be permitted or may be required to be effected applying specifically to any location covered by this policy. Such other insurance is hereinafter

referred to as specific insurance. Where specific insurance has been required by the Company, the Insured agrees to effect and keep in force specific insurance in the specified amount until otherwise agreed to in writing by the Company, and in failure thereof this Company shall not be liable for that part of any loss which would have been recoverable or due thereunder had such specific insurance been in force, whether valid or not and whether collectible or not. With respect to any specific insurance, this policy shall be considered as excess insurance and shall not apply or contribute to the payment of any loss until the amount due from all such specific insurance whether collectible or not shall have been exhausted. Under the policy the Insured is to be reimbursed to the extent of the difference between the amount recoverable or due from any specific insurance whether collectible or not and the amount of loss otherwise recoverable hereunder, not exceeding however, the difference between the limit of liability under this policy at any specified location and the amount of specific insurance at such specified location for loss or damage arising out of the perils insured against by such specific insurance.

10. *Other Insurance:* Except as to specific insurance as defined in Section 9 of this policy, this policy shall not cover to the extent of any other insurance whether prior or subsequent hereto in date, and by whomsoever effected, directly or indirectly covering the same property, and this Company shall be liable for loss or damage only for the excess value beyond the amount due from such other insurance.

The Company agrees to advance to the Insured as a loan the amount which would have been collectible under this policy except for the provisions of this Section, such loan to be repayable only to the extent of and at the time of the Insured's collection from such other insurance.

* * *

15. *Assistance and Cooperation of the Insured:* The Insured shall cooperate with the Company and, upon the Company's request, shall attend hearings and trials and shall assist in effecting settlements, securing and giving evidence, obtaining the attendance of witnesses and in the conduct of suits. Other than as provided in Section 16 of this policy, the Insured shall not, except at his own cost voluntarily make any payment, assume any obligation or incur any expense.

* * *

19. *Carriers or Bailees:* This insurance shall not inure directly or indirectly to the benefit of any carrier, nor without the affirmative consent of the Insured, to the benefit of any other bailee. The Insured may accept without prejudice to this insurance the ordinary bills-of-lading used by common carriers, including released or partially released value bills-of-lading, and the Insured may waive subrogation against railroads under Side Track Agreements, and except as otherwise provided, the Insured shall not enter into any special agreement with carriers otherwise releasing them from their common law or statutory liability. The Company shall not be liable for any loss or damage which, without its consent, has been settled or compromised by the Insured.

20. *Company's Right of Recovery:* In the event of any payment under this policy, the Insured shall execute and deliver instruments and papers and do whatever else is necessary to secure the subrogation rights of the Company. The Insured shall do nothing after loss to prejudice such rights. However, the Company specifically waives its rights of subrogation against all the subsidiary and affiliated companies of the Insured. Any release from liability, other than as provided in Section 19, entered into prior to loss hereunder by the Insured shall not affect this policy or the right of the Insured to recover hereunder. At the option of the Company, the Insured will execute a loan agreement, to the extent of any loss collectible under this policy. Said loan will bear no interest

and will be repayable only in the event and to the extent of the net recovery effected from any party believed to be liable for said loss. Upon payment of any loss or advancement or loan of moneys concerning the loss, the Insured will at the Company's request and expense make claim upon and institute legal proceedings against any party which the Company believes to be liable for such loss, and will use all proper and reasonable means to recover the same, under the exclusive direction and control of the Company.

21. *Company's Options:* In the event of loss hereunder it shall be the option of the Company to take all, or any part, of the property at the agreed or appraised value, and also to repair, rebuild or replace the property destroyed or damaged, with other of like kind and quality, within a reasonable time, on giving notice of its intention so to do within thirty days after the receipt of the Proof of Loss herein required. There can be no abandonment to the Company of any property.

If branded or labeled merchandise covered by this policy is damaged and the Company elects to take all or any part of the property at the agreed or appraised value, the Insured may at his own expense stamp "salvage" on the merchandise or its containers or may remove the brands or labels, if such stamp or removal will not physically damage the merchandise.

TRANSPORTATION—ALL RISKS FORM

ASSURED CICERO CORP.

Loss, if any, payable to assured or order.

On goods and merchandise, including packages, consisting principally of PISTONS shipped by or to the assured at assured's risk within the limits of the Continental United States and Canada (excluding Alaska).

VALUATION: The said goods and merchandise shall be valued at actual invoice cost, including prepaid or advanced freight, if any, together with such costs and charges (including the commission of the assured as selling agent, but excluding duty), as may have accrued and become legally due thereon. In the event of there being no invoice, the valuation of the merchandise insured hereunder shall be the actual cash market value of the property insured at point of destination on the date of disaster.

This policy insures shipments consisting of the property insured for the following amounts in any one loss:

$15,000. while in the custody of any Truckman or Trucking Company,

$15,000. while in the custody of any Railroad or the Railway Express Agency (including while on ferries and/or railroad cars on transfers or lighters),

$1,000.= while in the custody of Air Carriers or Air Express Companies,

$15,000. during transportation to and from conveyances or premises of the above described carriers, in motor trucks or trailers operated by the Assured, (excluding theft, embezzlement, conversion or any wrongful act on the part of the assured, his servants or employees).

In no event shall this Company be liable for more than $30,000. in any one casualty, either in case of partial or total loss, or salvage charges, or any other charges, or expenses, or all combined.

Insurance hereunder attaches when the goods leave factory, store or warehouse at initial point of shipment, and covers continuously thereafter, including while on docks, wharves, piers, bulkheads, in depots, stations and/or on platforms of common carriers, all while in due course of transportation, until same are delivered at factory, store or warehouse at destination.

THIS POLICY INSURES AGAINST

All Risks of loss or damage to the insured property from any external cause (including General Average and/or salvage charges and expenses), except as herein excluded.

THIS POLICY DOES NOT INSURE

(a) Accounts, bills, deeds, evidences of debt, currency, money, coins, bullion, notes, securities, stamps, jewelry, precious stones or fine arts;

(b) Against loss or damage resulting from inadequate packing or improper preparation for shipment or from insecure stowage when not stowed by the carrier;

(c) Against loss or damage by vermin or against loss or damage by leakage, evaporation, shrinkage, breakage, marring, scratching, heat or cold, or by being scented, moulded, rusted, soured, or changed in flavor unless caused by fire, lightning, windstorm, flood, explosion or collision, derailment or overturning of vehicle while on land, or collision or crashing of aircraft while in flight, or by the vessel, craft or lighter being stranded, sunk, burned or in collision while waterborne.

(d) Against loss or damage resulting from delay or loss of market, howsoever caused;

(e) Against loss or damage caused by strikes, locked-out workmen, or persons taking part in labor disturbances, or arising from riot, or civil commotion;

Against loss or damage caused by or resulting from:

(f) (1) hostile or warlike action in time of peace or war, including action in hindering, combating or defending against an actual impending or expected attack, (a) by any government or sovereign power (de jure or de facto), or by any authority maintaining or using military, naval or air forces; or (b) by military, naval or air forces; or (c) by an agent of any such government, power, authority or forces;

(2) any weapon of war employing atomic fission or radioactive force whether in time of peace or war;

(3) insurrection, rebellion, revolution, civil war, usurped power, or action taken by governmental authority in hindering, combating or defending against such an occurrence, seizure or destruction under quarantine or customs regulations, confiscation by order of any government or public authority, or risks of contraband or illegal transportation or trade.

(g) Export shipments laden on board export conveyance or under the protection of marine insurance, whichever first occurs;

(h) Import shipments until fully discharged from import conveyance and then only after marine insurance has ceased to cover;

(i) Shipments by parcel post and/or mail.

Premium Readjustment and Report of Shipments. The premium charged under this policy is based on an estimate of $300,000. value of shipments made during the period insured, and the Assured warrants to report to this Company at the end of ____________________ the actual value of
(Policy year, unless otherwise specified)

all shipments (in accordance with the valuation clause contained in this policy) covered hereunder during the period for which such report is required, and upon the total of all reported shipments exceeding in the aggregate the said estimate of $300,000., the Assured agrees to pay this

Company additional premium at the rate of .05 per $100, such additional premium to become due and payable to this Company immediately upon the furnishing of the aforesaid report or reports; but in the event of the actual shipments falling short of the said estimate of $______ then this Company will return premium at the same rate on the deficiency, but no return premium shall become due or payable until the expiration of this policy; it being understood that by the acceptance of this readjustment clause, the reinstatement clause in the body of this policy is waived.

* * *

Claim Against Carrier. In the event of any loss or damage to the goods and/or merchandise insured hereunder the assured shall immediately make claim in writing against the carrier or carriers involved.

Insurer's Right to Institute Legal Proceedings in Name of Insured. It is expressly agreed that upon payment of any loss or advancement or loan of moneys concerning the same, that the Assured will at the request and expense of the Company, and through such counsel as the Company may designate, make claim upon and institute legal proceedings against any carrier, bailee, or other parties believed to be liable for such loss, and will use all proper and reasonable means to recover the same.

Impairment of Carrier's Liability. Any act or agreement by the Assured, prior or subsequent hereto, whereby any right of the Assured, in the event of loss or damage, to recover the full value of, or amount of damage to, any property insured hereunder, against any carrier, bailee or other party liable therefor, is released, impaired or lost, shall render this policy null and void, but the Insurer's right to retain or recover the premium shall not be affected. It shall, however, be permissible for the Assured, without prejudice to this insurance, to release any carrier to the extent of not less than Fifty Dollars ($50.) per package where the weight of the package does not exceed 100 pounds, or fifty cents per pound, actual weight, where the weight of the shipment exceeds 100 pounds. This Company is not liable for any loss or damage, which without its consent, has been settled or compromised by the Assured.

4. Reread the two insurance policies, reprinted above. To what extent do they confer subrogation rights to "collateral" sources, i.e., contract rights that the seller or buyer may have against each other?

Remember, if a loss occurs within the scope of the policy and all conditions precedent are satisfied, the insurer's liability is for the amount of the actual loss and no more. This principle of indemnification is designed, primarily, to control the insurer's incentive to realize a net gain from the receipt of insurance proceeds. See Keeton, Insurance Law § 3.1(b) (1971). Subrogation often supports the principle of indemnity, since the insurance company, upon paying the insured, steps into the insured's shoes and tries to assert claims of that insured against some other person (the carrier, the other party to the contract, some third party, etc.) for the loss for which it has paid. In theory, at least, subrogation rights and the return from enforcement ought to figure into the calculation by the insurer of the premiums to be charged.

According to conventional doctrine, there are two kinds of subrogation, legal or equitable and contractual. The former arises by operation of law and the latter is created by contract between the insurer and the insured. See Jorski Mill & Elevator Co. v. Farmer's Elevator Mut. Ins. Co., 404 F.2d 143, 147 (10th Cir.1968). The source of subrogation determines the scope of the right. Thus, if B with the risk of loss is insured and the goods are damaged by the negligence of a third party, the insurer, upon paying B, is subrogated by operation of law to any tort claims that B may have against the third party. See, e.g., Home Ins. Co. v. Bishop, 140 Me. 72, 34 A.2d 22

(1943). But what about contract rights that either seller or buyer may have against the other? Here's the rub, for some courts have labeled contract rights as "collateral" sources for subrogation and have required a contract clause specifically granting the right. Put another way, subrogation imposed by operation of law is sometimes held not to reach these collateral rights.

> The difficulty * * * lies in the fact that the problem is basically one of allocation of the burden of loss as between an insurer and an innocent third party. And in the case of "equitable" or "legal" subrogation the equities in favor of the insurer are simply not so decisive as they are when the third party is a tort-feasor.

United States Fidelity & Guar. Co. v. Slifkin, 200 F.Supp. 563, 569 (N.D.Ala.1961).

5. Suppose that Cicero, with the risk of loss, is insured but Repuenzel, with a security interest and an insurable interest, is not insured. If the goods are destroyed without Cicero's fault or negligence and the insurer pays, does Repuenzel have any enforceable claim to the insurance proceeds? Or is the seller now unsecured with a claim only for the unpaid price?

The answers are no and yes, unless (1) The contract for sale required Cicero to obtain insurance for the benefit of Repuenzel and Cicero had complied, or (2) Repuenzel's claim is enforceable under UCC 9–306(1).

In the absence of a contractual obligation to insure, see Royal Zenith Corp. v. Citizens Publications, Inc., 179 N.W.2d 340 (Iowa 1970), casualty insurance is invariably treated as personal to the insured—it is intended to indemnify Cicero's loss (a matter of contract between Cicero and his insurer) not Repuenzel's. See Quigley v. Caron, 247 A.2d 94 (Me.1968). As a matter of planning, therefore, Repuenzel should insist that either Cicero obtain insurance for its benefit or Repuenzel should obtain a policy covering goods sold on a conditional sales contract to the extent of unpaid balances.

What about UCC 9–306(1)? The 1972 Official Text of UCC 9–306(1) provides that "Insurance payable by reason of loss or damage to the collateral is proceeds, except to the extent that it is payable to a person other than a party to the security agreement." This provision overruled decisions under the 1962 Official Text to the contrary, see *Note,* 65 Mich.L.Rev. 1514 (1966), but has some definite limitations: If the proceeds are payable to someone other than Repuenzel or, as cash proceeds, fall into the many pitfalls of maintaining a perfected security in proceeds under UCC 9–306, the security will dissipate.

(6) Suppose Repuenzel, with an insurable interest, is insured to the full value of the goods and Cicero, with the risk of loss, has no insurance. If the goods are destroyed and Repuenzel is paid in full, can Cicero have the benefit of that insurance? Put differently, can Cicero have a credit for the insurance against any price still owed to Repuenzel? If the answer is yes, then Repuenzel's insurer would be denied any right to subrogation to collateral sources granted by contract.

Most courts, after balancing the equities, have answered the question in the negative. See McCoid, *Allocation of Loss and Property Insurance,* 39 Ind.L.J. 647, 669 (1964), who defends the outcome. For a contrary and definitely minority view, see In re Future Mfg. Corp., 165 F.Supp. 111 (N.D.Cal.1958). There have been no recent decisions of significance.

B. Carrier Liable to Insured Party with Risk of Loss: Conflicts Between Insurance Companies

Suppose that Cicero, insured and with the risk of loss, obtains a judgment against the carrier under the Carmack Act, supra, for the value of the goods destroyed. Cicero's insurer, who has paid Cicero, has participated in the litigation as subrogee. What additional problems are posed because the contest is, in essence, between two insurance companies, that of Cicero and that of the carrier?

SORKIN, ALLOCATION OF THE RISK OF LOSS IN THE TRANSPORTATION OF FREIGHT—THE FUNCTION OF INSURANCE, 40 Fordham L.Rev. 67, 85–87 (1971).

* * *

IV. THE ROLE OF INSURANCE IN ALLOCATION OF THE RISK OF LOSS

Although common carriers subject to the Carmack Amendment of the Interstate Commerce Act are held to a high standard of liability, there are some exceptions and limitations to a carrier's liability. Furthermore, the amount of damages sustained is always a potential issue. If the loss or damage is substantial, the carrier will contest the claim, provided it can find a legal basis upon which to do so. Consequently, most commercial shippers are insured against loss or damage to their property during the course of its transportation.

"The shipper's insurance company may be considered as a potential third-party upon whom the ultimate economic burden of the risk of loss or damage should be placed, since the insurance company receives its compensation specifically for assuming the risk of loss or damage, whereas the carrier's compensation is based primarily on the cost of transportation. However, equity and economic burden have usually not been determining factors in allocating the risk of loss between the shipper's insurer and the carrier. The judicial resolution of the problem has historically been based upon the law of contracts and the interpretation of the Interstate Commerce Act.

A. Benefit of Insurance Clauses in Bills of Lading

For over a century the standard form of carrier bill of lading has provided, in effect, that if a shipper of merchandise has purchased insurance against loss or damage to the shipper's goods during the course of their transportation, and if the shipper's goods are lost or damaged, the carrier shall receive the benefit of such insurance. The intended result of such a clause is that the carrier will not be liable for the loss or damage to the extent that the shipper or owner is compensated by his insurance carrier. Judicial recognition of the validity of such benefit of insurance clauses has been established.

An insurer who pays the loss of a shipper is ordinarily subrogated to the shipper's rights. However, if the insured has contracted with the carrier giving the carrier the benefit of any insurance available to the shipper in case of loss or damage, then it has long been held that the insurer loses its right of subrogation. The shipper who insures his goods against loss or damage during their transportation is involved in at least two separate contracts—the contract between the shipper and the common carrier (the bill of lading), and the contract between the shipper and the insurance company (the policy). To counterbalance the benefit of insurance clause in the bill of lading, the insurance companies changed their policies and added a provision which stated that if an insured shipper entered into an agreement giving a carrier the benefit of the shipper's insurance, then the insurance policy issued to the shipper would be void.

The courts, when faced with both the bill of lading provision giving the carrier the benefit of the shipper's insurance and the insurance policy declaring the policy void upon the shipper's acceptance of such a bill of lading provision, conluded that both agreements were effective, i.e., the shipper could agree with the carrier to give the carrier the benefit of the shipper's insurance, but since the insurance was void the carrier received nothing and the shipper could not receive the insurance proceeds. This, of course, was harmful to the shipper and of no benefit to the carrier. The legal draftsmen of the insurance companies were victorious in their word war with the carriers' scriveners.

The bill of lading was then amended to provide that the carrier was to have the benefit of the insurance effected by the shipper 'so far as this shall not avoid the policies or contracts of insurance.' Thus, if the insurance policy stated that the policy would be void if the carrier could get the benefit of insurance, the bill of lading provision stated that in such event the carrier would not get the benefit of the shipper's insurance. The draftsmen for both sides had created a state of equilibrium, except in those cases where an insurance company neglected to provide that the policy would be void if the carrier received the benefit of the shipper's insurance. Thus the determination whether the ultimate burden of loss should be borne by the carrier or the shipper's insurer was made on the basis of interpretation of conflicting contracts without consideration of the economic justification of placing the burden either on the carrier or the insurer and without consideration of its effect upon interstate commerce." [Footnotes omitted]

TOWMOTOR CO. v. FRANK CROSS TRUCKING CO.

Superior Court of Pennsylvania, 1965.
205 Pa.Super. 448, 211 A.2d 38.

[Shipper sued common carrier Towmotor for damages to a vehicle which had been injured while in the possession of the carrier. Defendant responded that plaintiff had been fully insured, had recovered its loss from its insurance company, and under the terms of the bill of lading it was entitled "to the benefit of plaintiff's insurance." The court went on as follows, quoting first from the clause in the bill of lading.]

JACOBS, J.

* * *

> "Any carrier or party liable on account of loss or damage to any of said property shall have the full benefit of any insurance that may have been effected upon or on account of said property so far as this shall not avoid the policies or contracts of insurance: Provided that the carrier reimburse the claimant for the premium paid thereon."

The plaintiff in its reply admits that the above quoted clause was included in the bill of lading. It further admits that the vehicle was insured by Aetna and that Aetna paid it the sum of $3,190.33 but avers that payment was made in the form of a loan rather than in payment of the loss, and asserts in its defense the following quoted condition of the Aetna policy:

> "1. Carrier-Bailee. This insurance shall in no wise inure directly or indirectly to the benefit of any carrier or other bailee, and the Assured agrees that in case any agreement be made or accepted with any carrier or bailee by which it is stipulated that such or any carrier or bailee shall have, in case of any loss for which said carrier or bailee may be liable, the benefit of this insurance or exemption in any manner from responsibility grounded in the fact of this insurance, then and in that event this Company shall be discharged of any liability for such loss hereunder, but this policy in these and all cases of loss or damage by perils insured against shall be liable and

owe actual payment for (only) what cannot be collected from carrier or bailee."

Aetna's policy as well as the release given to Aetna by plaintiff, provide that Aetna shall be subrogated to the rights of the plaintiff to recover for such loss from the persons, firms or corporations who have caused the loss.

If it were not for the benefit of insurance clause in the bill of lading this case would be easily decided. In general a common carrier of goods is regarded as an insurer against all losses. Arabian American Oil Company v. Kirby & Kirby, Inc., 171 Pa.Super. 23, 90 A.2d 410. No exception to the general rule has been averred by the defendant and unless the benefit of insurance clause is sufficient to save it, it is liable for the loss. The benefit of insurance clause in the bill of lading and the clauses referring to such benefit in the insurance policy are the result of the efforts of the insurance companies to shift the common law liability of the carriers on one hand and, on the other hand, to protect against such shifting of liability. We will endeavor to interpret the result of such legal maneuvering.

A benefit of insurance clause such as the one contained in the bill of lading in this case is valid because the carrier itself might have insured against the loss, even though occasioned by its own negligence. Luckenbach v. W.J. McCahan Sugar Refining Co., 248 U.S. 139, 39 S.Ct. 53, 63 L.Ed. 170. The important words in the benefit of insurance clause above quoted are "so far as this shall not avoid the policies or contracts of insurance." Absent those words, should the insurer pay the loss it would lose the benefit of the claim against the carrier to which it would otherwise be subrogated and the carrier would go free. However, when we read the above quoted words in connection with the provisions of the insurance policy we come to another conclusion.

* * *

The benefit of insurance clause not being available to the defendant, it is liable for the loss. Although the plaintiff is the shipper and has been paid for the loss, judgment may properly be entered in its favor. Both the insurance policy and the release given by plaintiff specifically provide that the insurer shall be subrogated to the rights of plaintiff and may sue in plaintiff's name. Any recovery will inure to the benefit of the insurance company.

Judgment affirmed.

FLOOD, J., absent.

Notes

1. In Salon Serv., Inc. v. Pacific & Atlantic Shippers, 24 N.Y.2d 15, 298 N.Y.S.2d 700, 246 N.E.2d 509 (1969), a conflict identical to that in *Towmotor* was manifest in the shipper's bill of lading from the carrier and the insurance policy from its insurer. In affirming the decision of the appellate division, the Court of Appeals, speaking through Judge Burke, held that the "benefit of insurance" clause in the bill of lading was invalid under Section 2 of the Interstate Commerce Act. Enforcing the clause would result in a prohibited rate discrimination because the carrier would, indirectly, receive greater compensation from a shipper who had effected insurance than from one who had not. The court quoted from National Garment Co. v. New York, C. & St.L.R. Co., 173 F.2d 32, 38 (8th Cir.1949):

> "Insurance for the benefit of a carrier is of value to the carrier from the beginning of the transportation and, in the event of transportation without loss, which we assume is the usual case, the carrier has received the compensation forbidden by the Interstate Commerce Act at the expense of the shipper. In the

event of loss the carrier, if it so elects, returns to the shipper the cost of the compensation which it was forbidden by the Act to receive in the first place, avoids its liability as a carrier, and deprives the insurer of its rights under a valid contract." 246 N.E.2d at 511.

Problem 16–6

Seller ships lumber by rail under an FOB destination contract. In the course of shipment the lumber is destroyed by fire. The fire is not caused by an act of God, and the carrier is liable to the seller for the loss. The seller also has insurance which covers this loss. His insurance contract contains the following clauses:

19. *Carrier or Bailees:* "This insurance shall not inure directly or indirectly to the benefit of any carrier, nor without the affirmative consent of the insured, to the benefit of any other bailee. Insured may accept without prejudice to this insurance the ordinary bills of lading used by common carriers, including released or partially released value bills of lading, and the insured may waive subrogation against railroads under sidetrack agreement, and except as otherwise provided, the insured shall not enter into any special agreement with carriers otherwise releasing them from their common law or statutory liability. The companies shall not be liable for any loss or damage which without its consent has been settled or compromised by the insured.

20. *Company's Right of Recovery:* In the event of any payment under this policy, the Insured shall execute and deliver instruments and papers and do whatever else is necessary to secure the subrogation rights of the Company. The Insured shall do nothing after loss to prejudice such rights. However, the Company specifically waives its rights of subrogation against all the subsidiary and affiliated companies of the Insured. Any release from liability, other than as provided in Section 19, entered into prior to loss hereunder by the Insured shall not affect this policy or the right of the Insured to recover hereunder. At the option of the Company, the Insured will execute a loan agreement, to the extent of any loss collectible under this policy. Said loan will bear no interest and will be repayable only in the event and to the extent of the net recovery effected from any party believed to be liable for said loss. Upon payment of any loss or advancement or loan of moneys concerning the loss, the Insured will at the Company's request and expense make claim upon and institute legal proceedings against any party which the Company believes to be liable for such loss, and will use all proper and reasonable means to recover the same, under the exclusive direction and control of the Company."

The bill of lading under which the seller shipped contained the following provision:

> Any carrier or party liable on account of loss of or damage to any of said property shall have the full benefit of any insurance that may have been effected upon or on account of said property, so far as this shall not avoid the policies or contracts of insurance: provided, that the carrier reimburse the claimant for the premium paid thereon.

You are counsel for the insurance company. It would like to pay the seller and be subrogated to his rights against the railroad. Will the insurance company recover from the railroad? What precautions might you suggest to them?

CHAPTER SEVENTEEN

"DOCUMENTARY" AND OTHER SALES INVOLVING DOCUMENTS OF TITLE: POSSIBLE BREAKDOWNS

SECTION 1. INTRODUCTION—DOCUMENTS OF TITLE

When buyers and sellers deal with each other, the goods will often be either (1) as yet unmanufactured, (2) located at the seller's place of business, (3) located at the place of business of the seller's supplier, (4) located in an independent warehouse, or (5) located somewhere else away from the buyer's place of business. Most sellers do not have their own trucking, rail, or waterway facilities. They must, therefore, turn to independent carriers to deliver the goods they sell. When goods are sold while in warehouses, (as is often true in deals made on the commodity exchanges) sellers must also rely on the services of independent warehousemen to make delivery (physically or through "attornment"). These independent third parties—carriers and warehousemen—typically issue "bills of lading" and "warehouse receipts," respectively, covering goods received from shippers and storers. In so doing, these bailees assume certain special obligations both under the terms of such documents and under applicable statutes, as we will see.

In the parlance of commercial lawyers, bills of lading and warehouse receipts (see the forms at pages 674–75) are called "documents of title." UCC 1–201(15) defines document of title as follows:

> (15) "Document of title" includes bill of lading, dock warrant, dock receipt, warehouse receipt or order for the delivery of goods, and also any other document which in the regular course of business or financing is treated as adequately evidencing that the person in possession of it is entitled to receive, hold and dispose of the document and the goods it covers. To be a document of title a document must purport to be issued by or addressed to a bailee and purport to cover goods in the bailee's possession which are either identified or are fungible portions of an identified mass.

As we will see (Section 4 below), documents of title may be "negotiable" or "non-negotiable." It is now pertinent to list the main functions of these pieces of paper issued by carriers and warehousemen. A bill of lading or warehouse receipt serves:

1. As a receipt for the goods received by the bailee from the shipper or storer.

2. As a contract between the bailor and bailee for the transportation and/or storage of the goods.

3. As a kind of legal substitute for the goods themselves when the document is negotiable—the law says that *generally:* "title to the goods moves with title to the negotiable document."

4. As a means whereby the seller may either (a) himself retain a security interest in the goods until they are paid for or (b) readily create a security interest in the goods in favor of his own bank or other lender.

All of these functions of bills of lading and warehouse receipts are quite important. The importance of the function depends on the nature of the transaction involved—on how documents of title are utilized in the transaction. In the next section, one basic transaction pattern will be described.

The "front side" of a typical negotiable bill of lading looks like this:

THIS SHIPPING ORDER must be legibly filled in, in ink, in indelible pencil, or in carbon, and retained by the Agent

FORM 35

7

RECEIVE subject to the classifications and tariffs in effect on the date of the issue of this Shipping Order, the property described below in apparent good order, except as noted contents and condition of contents of packages unknown, marked, consigned and destined as indicated below, which said company [the word company being understood throughout this contract as meaning any person or corporation in possession of the property under the contract agrees to carry to its usual place of delivery of said destination, if on its own road or its own water line, otherwise to deliver to another carrier on the route to said destination. It is mutually agreed, as to each carrier of all or any of said property over all or any portion of said route to destination, and as to each party at any time interested in all or any of the said property, that every service to be performed hereunder shall be subject to all the conditions not prohibited by law, whether printed or written, herein contained, including the conditions on the back hereof, which are hereby agreed to by the shipper and accepted for himself and his assigns. The surrender of the original ORDER Bill of Lading property indorsed shall be required before the delivery of property. Inspection of property covered by this bill of lading will not be permitted unless provided by law or unless permission is indorsed on this original bill of lading or given in writing by the shipper.

131—CHICAGO AND NORTH WESTERN RAILWAY CO.—131	BILL OF LADING DATE	BILL OF LADING NO.	INVOICE NO.	CUSTOMER'S NO.

CAR INITIALS AND NUMBER	KIND	WEIGHT IN TONS			LENGTH OF CAR		MARKED CAPACITY OF CAR		LOAD LIMIT OF CAR
		GROSS	TARE	NET	ORDERED	FURNISHED	ORDERED	FURNISHED	

T TRLR. O INIT.____ F & NO. C	LENGTH	PLAN NO.	DATE	WAYBILL NO.
		TRANSF. TO CAR		

TO NO.	STATION	STATE OR PROV.	STATE CODE	AT NO. ( ) B/A ( )	STATION	STATE OR PROV.	STATE CODE
( )							

ROUTE (Show each Junction and Carrier in route order to destination of waybill)	ROUTE CODE NO.	FULL NAME OF SHIPPER	CODE NO.
131 C & NW			
SHOW "A" IF AGENT'S ROUTING OR "S" IF SHIPPER'S ROUTING			

CONSIGNED TO **ORDER OF**	**ORIGIN AND DATE, ORIGINAL CAR, TRANSFER FREIGHT BILL AND PREVIOUS WAYBILL REFERENCE AND ROUTING WHEN REBILLED.**
Negotiable	

NOTIFY

AT STATE OF COUNTY OF

DESTINATION

SHIPPER'S SPECIAL INSTRUCTIONS

WEIGHED

Received $________ to apply in prepayment of the charges on the property described hereon.

__________ Agent or Cashier.

Per__________ (The signature here acknowledges only the amount prepaid.)

AT________

GROSS________

TARE________

ALLOWANCE________

NET________

IF CHARGES ARE TO BE PREPAID, WRITE OR STAMP HERE "TO BE PREPAID".

WHEN SHIPPER IN THE UNITED STATES EXECUTES THE NO-RECOURSE CLAUSE OF SECTION 7 OF THE BILL OF LADING, INSERT "YES".

*If the shipment moves between two ports by a carrier by water, the law requires that the bill of lading shall state whether it is "carrier's or shipper's weight".

Indicate by symbol in Column provided ★ how weights were obtained for L.C.L. Shipments only. R – Railroad Scale. S – Shipper's Tested Weights. E – Estimated – Weigh and Correct. T – Tariff Classification or Minimum.

NO. PKGS.	DESCRIPTION OF ARTICLES, SPECIAL MARKS AND EXCEPTIONS	COMMODITY CODE NO.	★	*WEIGHT (Subject to Correction)	RATE	FREIGHT	CHARGES ADVANCED	PREPAID

DO NOT USE THIS SPACE

Subject to Section 7 of Conditions, if the shipment is to be delivered to the consignee without recourse on the consignor, the consignor shall sign the following statement The carrier shall not make delivery of this shipment without payment of freight and all other lawful charges

Signature of Consignor

DATE________

Note—Where the rate is dependent upon value, shippers are required to state specifically in writing the agreed or declared value of the property. The agreed or declared value of the property is hereby specifically stated by the shipper to be not exceeding

PER

AGENT________

SHIPPER________ PER________ PER________

The reverse side of both the negotiable and nonnegotiable bill of lading form contains about two acres of fine print called "contract terms and conditions." With the aid of a magnifying glass, these terms can be examined in R. Braucher & R. Riegert, Documents of Title 162–64 (3d ed. 1978).

SECTION 2. "DOCUMENTARY SALES"—THE STANDARD PATTERN

Documents of title may be used in a variety of ways in a sales transaction. In *one* type of transaction called the "documentary sale," the buyer agrees to pay cash in exchange for documents. Besides documents of title (usually bills of lading) this transaction also involves the use of what is called a "sight draft." A sight draft is a draft (see UCC 3–104) drawn up by a seller which orders the buyer to pay so much in cash "at sight" to the party presenting the draft. Below is an illustrative sight draft:

$ 1,000.00 August 7 (1978)

At Sight Pay to

the order of Repeunzel Auto Parts

One thousand and no/100-------------- Dollars

Value received and charge the same to account of

TO Cicero's Automotive, Inc.

) Repeunzel /for

No. 28601) Repeunzel Auto Parts, Inc.

[C3044]

Now, how might the above piece of paper, and a document of title such as a bill of lading actually be put to functional use together in real life transactions? Professor Farnsworth has offered this account of the standard transaction pattern in the so-called "documentary sale":

FARNSWORTH, DOCUMENTARY DRAFTS UNDER THE UNIFORM COMMERCIAL CODE, 22 Bus.Law. 479–487 (1967).

"*Introduction.* The Uniform Commercial Code has as a premise 'that "commercial transactions" is a single subject of the law, notwithstanding its many facets.' * * *

"No better transaction could be chosen to illustrate this recognition than the use of the documentary draft, since it involves the sale of goods, which is dealt with in Article 2 (Sales), a draft, which is dealt with in Article 3 (Commercial Paper), its collection, which is dealt with in Article 4 (Bank Deposits and Collection), and a bill of lading, which is dealt with in Article 7 (Warehouse Receipts, Bills of Lading and Other Documents of Title), in addition to being subject to Article 1 (General Provisions). If a letter of credit were involved, it would also be subject to Article 5 (Letters of Credit) and if the buyer were to finance his purchase by a trust receipt it would also be subject to Article 9 (Secured Transactions: Sales of Accounts, Contract Rights and Chattel Paper). This discussion will not, however, be concerned with either letters of credit or secured transactions.

"Because the documentary draft has long been a feature of both domestic and international sales transactions, the terminology and the rules relating to documentary drafts are relatively well established. * * * This article will be in two parts: first, a description of a typical sales transaction involving a documentary draft with an analysis of the relevant provisions of the code; and second, a discussion of some variations from this standard pattern in the light of the provisions of the Code. Before either, however, a brief discussion of terminology is appropriate.

"*Terminology.* The term 'draft,' used by the Code to replace the older term 'bill of exchange,' in this discussion refers to the order drawn by the seller on the buyer of the goods (UCC 3–104(1)(b), (2)(a)). The term 'documentary draft' is used for a draft, whether negotiable or non-negotiable, with accompanying documents or other papers to be delivered when the draft is honored (UCC 4–104(1)(f)). By 'document' is meant a 'document of title' (UCC 7–102(1)(e)), including a 'bill of lading, dock warrant, dock receipt, warehouse receipt or order for the delivery of goods, and also any other document which in the regular course of business or financing is treated as adequately evidencing that the person in possession of it is entitled to receive, hold and dispose of the document and the goods it covers' (UCC 1–201(15)). The most significant of these for present purposes is the 'bill of lading,' which is defined as 'a document evidencing the receipt of goods for shipment issued by a person engaged in the business of transporting or forwarding goods, and includes an airbill' (UCC 1–201(6)). It may be a negotiable bill if by its terms the goods are to be delivered to bearer or to order or, where recognized in overseas trade, if it runs to a named person or assigns; otherwise it is a non-negotiable bill, the term used by the Code in preference to the traditional synonym 'straight' bill (UCC 7–104). These, then are the essential terms; now to the transaction.

Part I. The Basic Transaction

"*Purpose of the Transaction.* Many domestic and some foreign sales of goods are made on open credit, with payment to be made in 30, 60 or 90 days. But credit must be bargained for and a seller lacking faith in the buyer's credit may refuse to agree to a credit term. In the absence of such an agreement, the Code provides that the buyer must pay when he receives the goods (UCC 2–310(a)). In the simplest case, where the seller and the buyer carry out the exchange face to face, five consequences follow. First, the seller is assured of payment when he gives up control of the goods. Second, the buyer is assured of control of the goods when he pays. Third, the seller finances the transaction only until the goods leave his hands. Fourth, the buyer finances the transaction only after the goods reach his hands. And fifth, the buyer can inspect the goods before he pays (UCC 2–513(1)).

"When the parties are at a distance the situation changes and some means must be found to give each party a measure of the advantages which he enjoys in the simple face-to-face exchange. The traditional method is the documentary exchange, calling for payment by the buyer against a draft with a bill of lading attached. The immediate purpose of this discussion is to inquire into how the Uniform Commercial Code affects such a transaction.

"*The Agreement.* If the buyer's obligation, in the absence of a contrary agreement, is to pay against the delivery of goods, what contract terms suffice to vary this obligation and to oblige him to pay against documents? Since the Code provides no general words of art for this purpose, such conventional formulae as 'sight draft against bill of lading' will continue to suffice. Furthermore, where the goods are sold 'C.I.F.' (cost, insurance and freight), 'C. & F.' (cost and freight),

'F.O.B. vessel' (free on board vessel) or 'F.A.S.' (free along side), 'unless otherwise agreed the buyer must make payment against tender of the required documents and the seller may not tender nor the buyer demand delivery of the goods in substitution for the documents' (UCC 2–319(4), 2–320(4)). The reason is that these terms contemplate shipment to a distant port where the documents will arrive well ahead of the goods, and so a documentary exchange is presumed unless negated by the agreement. The rule does not apply to ordinary 'F.O.B.' (free on board) contracts which do not have these characteristics.

"*Shipment of the Goods.* When the parties have agreed to a documentary exchange, the seller will ordinarily place the goods in the hands of a carrier, obtaining a negotiable bill of lading to his own order. According to the Code, the effect of this 'shipment under reservation' is to reserve in him 'a security interest in the goods' (UCC 2–505(1)(a)). Beyond this, the bill of lading must satisfy the requirements of the sales article, Article 2, of the Code (UCC 7–509). For one example, where the contract contemplates overseas shipment and unless otherwise agreed, under an 'F.O.B. vessel' term, the seller must procure an 'on board' bill of lading, one stating that the goods have actually been loaded, whereas under a 'C.I.F.' or 'C. & F.' term a 'received for shipment' bill of lading, which falls short of stating that the goods have been loaded, is enough (UCC 2–323). For another example, unless otherwise agreed, under an 'F.O.B. point of shipment' contract, the seller must make such a contract for the transportation of the goods as is reasonable in the light of their nature and the other circumstances (UCC 2–504(a)). Although duplicate bills of lading, clearly marked as such, are regularly issued in this country, bills are not issued in sets of multiple originals for domestic trade. The Code expressly prohibits their issuance in sets except where customary in overseas transactions (UCC 7–304(1); see also UCC 7–402).

"The seller, having obtained the negotiable bill of lading to his own order, then attaches it, together with an invoice and any other documents required by the contract, to a sight, or demand, draft for the amount due him drawn by him as drawer upon the buyer as drawee to the seller's own order. The Code allows drafts to be drawn in sets, although their use is in practice confined to foreign trade, where an original may be drawn to go with each of the multiple originals of a bill of lading which has been issued in a set (UCC 3–801). The seller then indorses the draft and bill of lading and takes them to his bank. For the moment, it will be assumed that the bank takes the documentary draft for collection; the situation when it discounts will be discussed presently.

"*Collection of the Draft.* The bank, known as a 'collecting bank' (UCC 4–105(d)) and more specifically as the 'depositary bank' (UCC 4–105(a)), is required to 'present or send the draft and accompanying documents for presentment' (UCC 4–501), which it will normally do by forwarding them through 'customary banking channels' (UCC 2–308(c), 2–503(5)(b)). Most important, it will treat the draft as a 'collection' item rather than a 'cash' item. Checks, the most common items handled by banks, are dealt with in bulk as 'cash' items on the assumption that they will be honored in the overwhelming majority of cases; provisional credits are entered immediately for a check at all stages of the collection process and automatically become final without further action upon payment by the drawee bank (UCC 4–213(2)). Documentary drafts, on the other hand, are handled as 'collection' items and dealt with individually, rather than in bulk, and since no assumption is made that they will be honored, no credits, not even provisional credits, are given until the item has been paid by the buyer.

Ultimately the draft will reach the 'presenting' bank (UCC 4–105(e)), which will undertake to present the documentary draft to the buyer.

"The presenting bank will know the identity and location of the buyer, who will be indicated on the bill of lading as the person to be notified of the arrival of the goods (cf. UCC 7–501(6)) as well as on the draft as the drawee. Unless otherwise instructed, the bank may make presentment to the buyer by sending him a written notice that it holds the item (UCC 4–210(1); see also UCC 2–503(1), (5) and Comment 3 to UCC 2–308). In the event that the buyer does not honor the draft before the close of business on the third banking day after the notice was sent, the bank may treat it as dishonored (UCC 4–210(2)). The buyer may, however, within this time require exhibition of the draft and documents by the bank so that he can determine whether it is properly payable (UCC 4–210, 3–505(1)(a), 3–506(2)). If direct presentment is made to the buyer, instead of presentment by notice, it must be made at the place specified in the draft, or if there be none at his place of business or residence (UCC 3–504(2)(c)), and he then has until the close of business on that day to pay (UCC 3–506(2)). Absent contrary instructions, a collecting bank may have an additional day 'in a good faith effort to secure payment'; it may also be excused for delay caused by circumstances beyond its control (UCC 4–108).

"As already pointed out, under the face-to-face transaction, which the documentary exchange is designed to supplant, the buyer had the right to inspect the goods before paying for them (UCC 2–513(1)). Since the goods will normally travel much more slowly than the documents, they will not ordinarily be available for inspection at the time that the buyer is required to pay under the rules just discussed. Therefore, absent agreement to the contrary, the buyer has no right to inspect the goods before he pays when the contract provides for payment against documents of title, except in the case, to be discussed later, where payment is due only after the goods are to become available for inspection (UCC 2–513(3)(b); see also UCC 2–310(b)). Indeed, the negotiable railway bill of lading typically bears the legend: 'Inspection of property covered by this bill of lading will not be permitted unless provided by law or unless permission is indorsed on this original bill of lading or given in writing by the shipper.' The Code goes on to provide that where, as in the transaction under discussion, the contract calls for payment before inspection, even the nonconformity of the goods does not, with rare exceptions, excuse the buyer from paying (UCC 2–512(1)). But it makes it clear that such payment does not amount to an acceptance of the goods by the buyer and that the buyer retains his right to inspect the goods upon delivery and all of his remedies against the seller for breach of contract (UCC 2–512(2)). He merely loses the opportunity of inspection before payment, an opportunity that gave him advantage of refusing to pay, rather than the disadvantage of having to sue to recover his payment, in the event of a non-conformity.

"Since the draft under discussion is a sight draft, the buyer is called upon to pay, rather than to accept it, before he gets the documents. Only when the draft is payable more than three days after presentment may the presenting bank release the documents against the buyer's acceptance rather than his payment (UCC 2–514, 4–503(a)). Payment may be easily effected if the buyer offers cash or if the presenting bank happens to be one in which the buyer has an account. Short of this, the Code permits the presenting bank to take a cashier's check (a check drawn by a bank on itself), a certified check (a check accepted by the bank on which it has been drawn), or other bank check or obligation [UCC 4–211(1)

(d)]. Should the buyer tender his personal check on another bank, the presenting bank may hold the documents while it gets the check certified. Should it release the documents against his personal check, it will be liable to the seller for any loss caused by the dishonor of the check. The proceeds received from the buyer are then remitted by the presenting bank through banking channels.

"When the buyer honors the draft, he receives the bill of lading. When the goods arrive, he is notified by the carrier and surrenders the bill of lading in return for the goods. At this point the buyer will be able to inspect the goods. Should he find them to be defective, his only recourse will ordinarily be to journey to the seller's jurisdiction and there litigate the issues of breach and damages. Other possible remedies will be discussed presently.

"If the buyer does not pay the draft as outlined earlier, the presenting bank must treat it as dishonored. In this event the presenting bank 'must use diligence and good faith to ascertain the reason for dishonor, must notify its transferor of the dishonor and of the results of its effort to ascertain the reasons therefor and must request instructions' (UCC 4–503(b)). It need not, however, return the draft and documents unless so instructed (UCC 4–202(1)(b)). When the notice gets back to the depositary bank, which first took the draft for collection, it must 'seasonably notify its customer' of the dishonor (UCC 4–501). [The presenting bank] 'is under no obligation with respect to goods represented by the documents except to follow any reasonable instructions seasonably received; it has a right to reimbursement for any expense incurred in following instructions and to payment of or indemnity for such expenses' (UCC 4–503). If it has seasonably requested instructions after dishonor but has not received them in a reasonable time, it may 'store, sell or otherwise deal with the goods in any reasonable manner' (UCC 4–504(1)), and has a lien * * * on the goods or their proceeds for reasonable expenses incurred in doing so (UCC 4–504(2)). If, for example, it was commercially reasonable to put the goods in storage pending receipt of requested instructions, the presenting bank would be protected if it did so even though the requested instructions were later received (Comment to UCC 4–504). The Code seems, however, to make a request for instructions and a failure to receive them within a reasonable time prerequisites to the exercise of initiative by the presenting bank in dealing with the goods.

"In addition to the requirement that notice be given of the dishonor, there may be in some cases the additional requirement of protest. Protest, a formal statement of dishonor executed by a public functionary, such as a notary, is generally required in Continental countries in the case of any dishonor of a negotiable instrument. * * * [See UCC 3–501(3), 3–509 and 4–202(1)(d).]

"This, then, is the standard pattern followed in the documentary exchange where payment is to be made against a sight draft with bill of lading attached. How adequate a substitute for the face-to-face transaction has been achieved can be seen by a comparison with the five consequences noted earlier. First, the seller is still assured of payment when he gives up control of the goods, through surrender of the bill of lading. Second, the buyer is assured of control of the goods when he pays, through possession of the bill of lading. Third, the seller must now finance the transaction *after* the goods leave his hands and until the documentary draft has been paid and the proceeds remitted. Fourth, the buyer must now finance the transaction *before* the goods reach his hands, from the time that he pays the documentary draft until they have arrived. And fifth, the buyer can *not* inspect the goods before he pays. Thus while the first two consequences are unchanged, the third, fourth and fifth are different.

Part II. Some Variations

"*Discount of the Draft.* As to the third consequence, the seller must now finance the transaction for an additional period of time between his delivery of the goods to the carrier and the remission to him of the proceeds after the buyer has paid the draft. The seller may shift this burden of financing to his bank by having that bank discount the draft rather than merely take it for collection. The seller can then receive the face value of the draft, less a discount to cover interest charges, before collection, as soon as he has obtained the bill of lading, and the bank will finance the sale from that point until it receives payment. The bank that does this has a 'security interest' in the draft and in the accompanying documents, and this holds true even if the credit which it gives the seller is not withdrawn, as long as he has the right to withdraw it (UCC 4–208). The bank, however, has the same obligations to the seller with respect to presentment and notification on dishonor as if it were an ordinary collecting bank (UCC 4–501). In case of dishonor of course, the bank can hold the seller ultimately liable on the draft even though it has been discounted. By purchasing the draft it acquires not only its own rights under the draft and bill of lading, but also 'any rights of the seller in the goods including the right to stop delivery and the shipper's right to have the draft honored by the buyer' (UCC 2–506(1), 2–707). The right to stop delivery is a right to order the carrier not to deliver to the buyer goods in the possession of the carrier when the buyer has been discovered to be insolvent (UCC 2–705). If the goods are carload, truckload, planeload or larger shipments, delivery may be stopped in the event of buyer's breach regardless of his solvency. Since the bill of lading is a negotiable document of title, however, the carrier is not obliged to obey a notification to stop until surrender of the document (UCC 2–705(3)(c)).

"Where the depositary bank discounts the draft for the seller, it succeeds to his rights under the sales contract as would an assignee. This suggests the possibility that the discounting bank might also assume the obligations of the seller under the sales contract, and more particularly that it might be liable under the seller's warranties of quality in the event that the goods are defective. The Code makes it clear that this is not the case and that a collecting bank 'known to be entrusted with documents on behalf of another or with collection of a draft or other claim against delivery of documents warrants by such delivery of documents only its own good faith and authority,' and this is true 'even though the intermediary has purchased or made advances against the claim or draft to be collected' (UCC 7–508; compare UCC 7–507).

"This sets the stage for an analysis of the position of the buyer in the rare but not impossible event that he has discovered a breach by the seller after he has paid the draft but before the collecting bank has remitted the proceeds. In the event of the seller's breach, it may be possible for the buyer to get personal jurisdiction over the seller in the buyer's own state. The chances of this have increased with the enactment of 'long arm' statutes. But where personal jurisdiction over the seller cannot be had in the buyer's state, he will ordinarily have to journey to the seller's state and there litigate the issues of breach and damages. He would, of course, prefer to bring his action at home—and may be able to do so if he can attach the proceeds as the basis of jurisdiction in his action. Usually the proceeds will have been remitted well before the arrival of the goods. But in the unusual case where this is not so, the buyer may attach the proceeds as the basis of quasi in rem jurisdiction in an action against the seller, and if successful in the action, have judgment in an amount up to the amount of the proceeds. This, however, assumes that the proceeds are indeed the *seller's* proceeds. Should the draft have been discounted by the depositary bank, then it and not the seller would be entitled to the proceeds, and attachment of the proceeds would not give jurisdiction in an action against the seller. Since the depositary bank, even though it discounts the draft, makes no warranties, there is no possibility of using the proceeds as the jurisdictional basis of an action against the bank. In sum, the buyer's advantage through attachment of the proceeds is not only limited to the rare case where the breach is discovered before the proceeds are remitted, but even then is available only when the draft has not been discounted." [Footnotes omitted.]

Notes

1. What factors motivate some sellers to use the device called the "documentary sale?"

2. What are the functions of the bill of lading and the sight draft in this transaction?

3. The so-called "documentary sale" for cash is not the only type of transaction in which documents of title and/or drafts figure. See White and Summers, pp. 717, 798–809.

SECTION 3. POSSIBLE BREAKDOWNS IN DEALS INVOLVING THE USE OF DOCUMENTS; APPLICABLE LAW

Here we will provide an inventory of the basic ways documentary and similar sales in which bailees hold the goods can break down, and we will identify the relevant sources of law governing these breakdowns. In subsequent sections of this chapter, we will focus on several of these types of breakdowns in more detail.

Below is a list of most of the important types of breakdowns:

(1) The goods may be lost, destroyed or damaged while in the hands of the issuer of the document of title. We have already treated this breakdown earlier in Chapter 16.

(2) The carrier or other bailee may misdeliver the goods to a party other than a party authorized in the document of title. We will take up this breakdown in section 4 below.

(3) Third parties may intervene and claim goods and/or the documents. This will be treated in section 5 below.

(4) One of the parties to the underlying sales transaction may repudiate or become insolvent while the goods are en route. This will be the subject of section 6 below.

(5) The carrier or other bailee may fail, because of non-receipt, misdescription or the like, to deliver what the documents call for. See section 7 below.

(6) The carrier or other bailee may make late delivery. See Chapter 16 supra.

(7) The goods on arrival may fail to conform to warranties and either be rejectable or afford a basis for a breach of warranty action. Breakdowns of this nature will be treated in Chapters 19–22.

In the event of breakdowns such as the above, what law governs? As the Farnsworth extract indicates, most of the strictly sales aspects and commercial paper aspects are governed by Articles 2, 3 and 4 of the Uniform Commercial Code. But what of the rights and liabilities arising specifically from use of bills of lading and warehouse receipts as such?

A. *Law Governing Bills of Lading*

Of course, the language of the bill of lading itself will have important bearing. Otherwise, the rights and liabilities of parties to bills of lading (and related documents) are found principally in three places: Article Seven of the Uniform Commercial Code, the Federal Bills of Lading Act—also called the "Pomerene Act" (Federal Bills of Lading Act of 1916, ch. 415, §§ 1–44, 39 Stat. 538, 49 U.S.C.A. §§ 81–124 (1970)), and the Carmack Amendment to the Interstate Commerce Act (Interstate Commerce Act of 1887, ch. 104, Part I, § 20, 24 Stat. 386, as added, June 29, 1906, ch. 3591, § 7, 34 Stat. 593, as amended, 49 U.S.C.A. § 20(11), (1970)). Article Seven of the Code displaced, in relevant part, the Uniform Bills of Lading Act which had been law in all states. Article Seven also applies to warehouse receipts.

In 1916, Congress enacted the Federal Bills of Lading Act (FBLA) which is substantially identical to the old Uniform Bills of Lading Act. The FBLA includes 44 sections. (We will refer to it as the "FBLA" and will cite it by reference to its United States Code section numbers (49 U.S.C.A. §§ 81–124)). Courts have decided hundreds of cases under the FBLA. Its presence and the presence of the Carmack Amendment on the federal statute books, and the vast case law under both, greatly diminish the significance of Article Seven's provisions on bills of lading. Whenever the FBLA is applicable, it rather than Article Seven controls. The FBLA is applicable to:

> Bills of lading issued by any common carrier for the transportation of goods in any Territory of the United States, or the District of Columbia, or from a place in a State to a place in a foreign country, or from a place in one State to a place in another State, or from a place in one State to a place in the same State through another State or foreign country * * *.

49 U.S.C.A. § 81.

Given the broad scope of the FBLA, what is left for Article Seven to govern? That Article applies mainly to (1) bills of lading issued for the transportation of goods from a place within one state to another place in the same state, provided the goods are not to pass through another state or foreign country *en route,* and (2) bills of lading issued for the transportation of goods from a foreign country into the United States. (A useful general discussion of the latter role of Article Seven is McCune, *Delivery of Cargo Carried Under Straight Bills of Lading,* 17 U.C.C.L.J. 344 (1985)). Even then the scope of Article Seven is cut down to the extent that other federal statutes besides the FBLA apply. Of other federal statutory law in this field the "Carmack Amendment" to the Interstate Commerce Act, 49 U.S.C.A. § 20(11) & (12), is of greatest importance. That amendment codifies the common law liability of interstate carriers for loss, destruction, or damage to goods, imposes this liability on the first of two or more connecting carriers for loss, destruction, or damage caused by any carrier in the chain of carriers transporting an interstate shipment, and proscribes carriers from using certain contract clauses limiting their liability. The Amendment applies to interstate shipments and to export shipments to adjoining countries. The Carmack Amendment covers two full pages in the statute book. The courts have interpreted and applied it in hundreds of cases. There are also various special federal statutes more limited in scope. In 1938, for instance, Congress enacted the Perishable Agricultural Commodities Act. 7 U.S.C.A. §§ 499a–499r. In 1893 and 1936, Congress passed the Harter Act, 46 U.S.C.A. §§ 190–196, and the Carriage of Goods by Sea Act, 46 U.S.C.A. §§ 1300–1315, respectively; both apply to ocean bills of lading.

Besides federal statutes, Article Seven, and relevant case law, the lawyer must often consult regulations and rulings of regulatory bodies, including those of the Interstate Commerce Commission. The I.C.C. has prescribed mandatory forms for bills of lading and has prescribed that "order" bills, which are negotiable because they state "deliver to order or bearer," must be printed on yellow paper and "straight" bills, which are nonnegotiable, on white paper. The I.C.C. has also promulgated numerous rules and regulations that affect the liabilities of interstate carriers.

B. Law Governing Warehouse Receipts

Again, the language of the receipt itself will have important bearing. Generally, Article Seven of the Code will govern, but even though a given state's version of Article Seven applies under relevant conflict of laws principles, some other law may control in the end. This law might be local non-Code state law, or it might be federal law, depending on the facts. Many states have enacted essentially regulatory statutes applicable to the dealings of warehousemen. As to these, UCC 7–103 is quite explicit: "To the extent that any * * * regulatory statute of this state or tariff, classification, or regulation filed or issued pursuant thereto is applicable, the provisions of this article are subject thereto." An illustrative example of a *state* regulatory provision is this California law:

> No warehousemen shall begin to operate any business of a warehouseman, as defined in subdivisions (b) or (c) of Section 239, without first having obtained from the commission a certificate declaring that public convenience and necessity require or will require the transaction of business by such warehouseman.

In addition to state regulatory law, federal law (statute, treaty, judicial decision) may also supersede or supplement Article Seven. The effect of federal law on warehouse receipts is confined mainly to the impact of the United States Warehouse Act, which applies to receipts covering agricultural products stored for interstate or foreign commerce. Most sections of this Act are regulatory, but those sections that specify the content of warehouse receipts and define delivery obligations override Article Seven.

The Code draftsmen intended originally to consolidate the old Uniform Warehouse Receipts Act and Uniform Bills of Lading Act into one unified statute, but the plan could not be fully executed. The result is that the lawyer must usually look in two places. He must look first in the relevant "special provisions" on warehouse receipts and second in the more general provisions covering *both* warehouse receipts and bills of lading. Sometimes the lawyer must search outside of Article Seven in other Articles of the Code, such as Article Nine, which applies to pledges of warehouse receipts.

SECTION 4. MISDELIVERY BY CARRIER OR OTHER BAILEE

As the cases in this section will indicate, "misdelivery" can take a variety of forms. In a misdelivery case, the lawyer must first determine the nature of the transaction involved. Was it a true documentary sale? Or what? Then the lawyer must determine how the case should be decided under *applicable law.* This law is to be found (1) in the terms of the document issued by the carrier or other bailee and (2) in relevant statutory and case law. Be sure to review the terms of any bill of lading. Also, review not only relevant Code provisions (especially UCC 7–403) but also sections 88 and 89 of the Federal Bill of Lading Act below:

§ 88. Duty to deliver goods on Demand; Refusal

A carrier, in the absence of some lawful excuse, is bound to deliver goods upon a demand made either by the consignee named in the bill for the goods or, if the bill is an order bill, by the holder thereof, if such a demand is accompanied by—

(a) An offer in good faith to satisfy the carrier's lawful lien upon the goods;

(b) Possession of the bill of lading and an offer in good faith to surrender, properly indorsed, the bill which was issued for the goods, if the bill is an order bill; and

(c) A readiness and willingness to sign, when the goods are delivered, an acknowledgment that they have been delivered, if such signature is requested by the carrier.

In case the carrier refuses or fails to deliver the goods, in compliance with a demand by the consignee or holder so accompanied, the burden shall be upon the carrier to establish the existence of a lawful excuse for such refusal or failure.

§ 89. Delivery; When Justified

A carrier is justified, subject to the provisions of sections 90–92 of this title, in delivering goods to one who is—

(a) A person lawfully entitled to the possession of the goods, or

(b) The consignee named in a straight bill for the goods, or

(c) A person in possession of an order bill for the goods, by the terms of which the goods are deliverable to his order; or which has been indorsed to him, or in blank by the consignee, or by the mediate or immediate indorsee of the consignee.

REFRIGERATED TRANSPORT CO. v. HERNANDO PACKING CO.

Supreme Court of Tennessee, 1976.
544 S.W.2d 613.

HENRY, JUSTICE.

This controversy between a consignor and a common carrier of property involves the carrier's liability for misdelivery of cargo transported under a straight bill of lading. The trial court found the issues against the carrier and we conclude that he reached the correct conclusion.

I.

On January 3, 1975, Hernando Packing Company, Inc., of Memphis, shipped via Refrigerated Transport Company, Inc., a truck load of frozen meat consigned as follows:

[T]o BROWARD COLD STORAGE (acct. of J & A Trading Co.) 3220 S.W. 2nd Avenue * * * Fort Lauderdale, Florida.

Broward is a public warehouse.

Prior to making this shipment Hernando had received a call from an individual who identified himself as *Al Hark* and held himself out to be a representative of J & A Trading Company. In point of fact he had no connection with J & A Trading Company and that company had gone out of business. Hernando had never done business with Al Hark, but on one prior occasion, had shipped to J & A Trading Company pursuant to a transaction with *Joseph Hark,* its then representative and owner, and father of Al Hark.

It is fairly inferable from the record that this unfamiliarity with Al Hark prompted the precaution of making the shipment to Broward, a public warehouse, for the account of J & A. However, the record is not specific in this regard and the shipment may have been made thusly as a matter of custom in the business or trade.

On January 6, 1975, upon the arrival of Refrigerated's truck in Fort Lauderdale, it was met *across the street from Broward* by Al Hark, but within sight of Broward's manager. Without the knowledge of Hernando or reconsignment or assent of Broward, and after representing himself to Refrigerated's driver as being a representative of J & A, Al Hark caused 84 boxes, or 5,040 pounds of boneless beef to be delivered to another address. Refrigerated's driver did not contact Broward and, insofar as the record shows, delivery was made solely on the basis of the verbal representations of Al Hark.

The next morning Refrigerated's truck came to Broward's dock and was again met by Al Hark. In the sight and presence of the Broward manager, Hark directed that a part of the remaining meat be reloaded on another truck and that the balance be stored with Broward to the account of J & A. Al Hark again represented himself to be a representative of J & A. The record does not show when, to whom, or if the driver surrendered the bill of lading.

By these maneuvers, Al Hark acquired possession of 246 boxes, or 9,520 pounds of meat ranging from ribeyes to oxtails and having a stipulated value of $5,880.86.

On January 7, 1976, Joseph Hark was informed of the arrival of the meat, whereupon he called Hernando and advised that J & A was out of business; that it had placed no order; and that this was not the first time his son, Al Hark, had placed such orders in the name of J & A. Hernando called Broward to direct that the meat not be delivered to Al Hark but was informed that delivery had already been made and without any reconsignment from Broward.

The trial judge, on this set of facts found and decreed:

> That the consignee on the Straight Bill of Lading herein was Broward Cold Storage at 3220 S.W. Second Avenue, Ft. Lauderdale, Florida, and that the Defendant had an absolute duty to deliver the frozen meat involved herein to said consignee and to no other.

II.

This controversy pivots upon the precise provisions of the bill of lading, viz: the consignment to "Broward Cold Storage (account of J & A Trading Co.)." Refrigerated earnestly insists that this, in effect, was a consignment to "J & A Trading Co., care of Broward Cold Storage." While this position is plausible, when consideration is given to the nature and purpose of bills of lading, the duties and obligations arising thereunder, and to the plain terms of the consignment, we cannot embrace this theory of the case.

At the very outset we point out that we are dealing with a "straight" bill of lading which is "[a] bill in which it is stated that the goods are consigned or destined to a specified person", 49 U.S.C. Sec. 82, which is not negotiable and must be so marked (it was in this case), 49 U.S.C. Sec. 86, as opposed to an "order" bill, 49 U.S.C. Sec. 83.[1]

Delivery under a straight bill of lading may only be made to "[a] person lawfully entitled to the possession of the goods, or (b) the consignee named" therein. 49 U.S.C. Sec. 89.

While there are various areas of potential disagreement inherent in this controversy they all boil down to a single question: Who was the consignee under the bill of lading?

In our view, there is no ambiguity. The consignment was to Broward. The parenthetical matter inserted simply advised the warehouse as to the identity of the ultimate receiver of the goods upon Broward's reconsignment. The only address inserted was that of Broward. Al Hark's name does not appear on the bill. It is fairly inferable that the consignment was to Broward as a precautionary measure against an unknown purchaser. Such would have been reasonable and prudent. But we need not speculate since the language was clear. There is no way that this delivery could have been properly made except to Broward and at Broward's address. Most assuredly a street corner delivery to a stranger not named in the bill and not shown by the record to have presented any credentials or authority cannot constitute valid delivery. All the driver ever had to do was to present his bill of lading to an authorized representative of Broward. The failure to do so was a breach of the contract of carriage.

To constitute a valid delivery, absent special circumstances, it is imperative that delivery be made to the right person, at the proper time and place and in a proper manner. This is implicit in the Contract of Carriage.[2]

It is stated in Volume 13, American Jurisprudence, 2nd, Carriers § 416 that "a carrier who delivers to an alleged agent of the consignee does so at its own peril with respect to his status as such." Cited in support of this assertion is our own case of *Dean v. Vaccaro & Co.*, 39 Tenn. 488 (1859), which is fully supportive.

Pertinent to the issue is the North Carolina case of *Griggs v. Stoker Service Co.*, 229 N.C. 572, 50 S.E.2d 914 (1948), wherein the Court said:

> The duty of a common carrier is not merely to carry safely the goods entrusted to him, but also to deliver them to the party designated by the terms of the shipment, or to his order, at the place of destination. 50 S.E.2d at 919.

Another case involving misdelivery of cargo, is *Dickman v. Daniels Motor Freight*, 185 Pa.Super. 374, 138 A.2d 165 (1958), wherein the delivery was made to a business establishment having a similar name and under circumstances suggestive of fraudulent conduct by a "swindler" who placed the order. The bill

1. "Bills of lading issued by any common carrier for the transportation of goods. * * * from a place in one State to a place in another State", among others, are governed by the Federal Bills of Lading Act 49 U.S.C. Sections 81–124.

2. See Vol. 13 Am.Jur.2d, Carriers, Sec. 405 et seq., and particularly Sections 405, 406, 411 and 415.

of lading was directed to a definite company at a definite address. The Court said:

> A common carrier is under an absolute duty to deliver goods to the person designated in the instructions of the shipper. If it fails to follow the express instructions of the shipper in making delivery, it acts at its peril and assumes the risk of wrong delivery. 138 A.2d at 167.

In *Richardson v. Railway Express Agency, Inc.,* 258 Or. 170, 482 P.2d 176 (1971), the Court held that a carrier making a delivery to one other than the named consignee "has the burden of proof to establish the ownership and right of possession of the goods at the time of such delivery." 482 P.2d at 178. The Court indicated the settled rule to be that carriers

> * * * are held strictly to the performance of their duty to make delivery of goods at the place of destination to the person designated to receive them if he presents himself or can be found with reasonable diligence. 482 P.2d at 179.

Refrigerated makes the urgent insistence that delivery to an imposter will discharge the common carrier "if it is to the imposter that the consignor actually intends to ship." We do not fault this as a general rule of law; but, as already pointed out, the shipment, for reasons we think self-evident, was to Broward.

Refrigerated relies upon *Chicago, M., St. P. & P.R. Co. v. Flanders,* 56 F.2d 114 (8th Cir.1932); however, there the imposter held all documentary indicia of ownership and the cattle were consigned to him.

Also relied upon is *Malvern Cold Storage Co. v. American Ry. Exp. Co.,* 206 Iowa 292, 220 N.W. 322 (1938); however, according to Refrigerated's brief filed in this Court, "[t]he circumstances were such that the consignor's actual *intention* was to deliver to [the imposter]." (Emphasis supplied).

Next we are cited to *Fulton Bag & Cotton Mills v. Hudson Navigation Co.,* 157 F. 987 (S.D.N.Y.1907). There no public warehouse was involved; identity of names was involved; due inquiry was made by the carrier prior to delivery; and proper notification was given pursuant to the bill of lading.

Other cases cited by appellee are also distinguishable.

In 54 A.L.R. at 1330, in an annotation relating to delivery to an imposter, it is stated that "the general rule places liability on a carrier for a misdelivery to an imposter of goods placed in the hands of the carrier for shipment". Among the cases cited in support of this proposition is our case of *Sword v. Young,* 89 Tenn. 126, 14 S.W. 481 (1890).

Sword is analogous to the instant case. One Gillenwaters ordered a brick machine under the assumed name of Magrauder, representing Magrauder to be a firm name. Upon arrival of the machine in Knoxville, Gillenwaters presented the bill of lading made in the name of Charles G. Magrauder, paid the freight and took possession of the machine.

The Court recognized the "well settled general rule that the carrier must deliver to the consignee at the place appointed", and thereafter stated:

> It can make no difference that the defendant carrier thought, because Gillenwaters had the bill of lading, that he was Charles G. Magrauder. If he was a stranger, as the proof shows him to be, it was the duty of the carrier to have required him to identify himself as the consignee or his rightfully constituted agent.

* * *

> The consignment was to Charles G. Magrauder. That name was fixed on the machine, and it was a duty to deliver to him only, or, if he could not be discovered, to notify the consignor.
>
> There is no difference between this case and one in which a consignment has been made to an actual person, and the goods delivered by accident, mistake, or carelessless to a cheat who represents himself as the real consignee. It is necessary in both to have proof of identity or authority to receive. 89 Tenn. at 128–29, 14 S.W. at 481.

We hold that Refrigerated breached its duty to deliver the cargo to Broward, the party designated in the bill of lading; that delivery to Al Hark was at Refrigerated's peril; that the burden of validating this delivery by establishing Al Hark's ownership and right to possession was upon Refrigerated and that it failed to carry that burden.

While we make this holding within the context of our view that Broward was the consignee, had we adopted Refrigerated's view that J & A Trading Company was the consignee, with the goods being shipped "in care of" Broward, the result would be the same. This necessarily follows from the facts that J & A was not in existence; that Al Hark had no connection with J & A; and that delivery was made to him without proper inquiry and without notice to Broward, or J & A. Had such inquiry been made and such notice given the driver would have discovered that he was dealing with an imposter.

III.

Refrigerated counter-claimed for the unpaid freight bill in the sum of $675.00 together with interest thereon. The trial court dismissed the counter-claim, without assigning any reason therefor.

We note that the bill of lading contains the entry "FREIGHT TO BE PAID BY: J & A TRADING CO." in Miami. This may have prompted the trial judge.

The record before us is not sufficient to pass upon this portion of the controversy. The bill of lading shows that 498 boxes of meat, weighing 31,068¾ pounds were shipped. The stipulation shows that Al Hark diverted 246 boxes weighing 9,520 pounds. The remaining 252 boxes, containing 21,548 pounds were delivered to Broward.

We have no hesitancy in declaring that Refrigerated, by misdelivery of the diverted meat, breached its contract of carriage and forfeited its right to receive compensation to that extent. Superficially it would appear that Refrigerated would be entitled to recover for the carriage of that portion of the meat ultimately delivered to Broward. However, we make no holding in the latter regard; we merely recognize the considerations involved.

On remand, the trial judge will reconsider the counter-claim and enter such judgment as the facts may indicate and justice may require.

Affirmed in part and remanded.

COOPER, C.J., and FONES, BROCK and HARBISON, JJ., concur.

Notes

1. Why did the court apply section 89 of the FBLA rather than section 7–403 of the UCC? Does it make any difference?

2. Does the result really depend in part on the statute or would it have been enough merely for the court to have invoked the language of the straight bill of lading?

3. In Rountree v. Lydick-Barmann, 150 S.W.2d 173 (Tex.Civ.App.1941), the seller was Lydick-Barmann, the buyer Crone Co., and the carrier Rountree. The carrier issued to Lydick-Barmann a bill which was captioned: "Uniform Motor Carrier Straight Bill of Lading—Original—Not Negotiable—Domestic." The bill also acknowledged receipt of the goods from seller (Lydick-Barmann) at its address in Fort Worth, Texas "Consigned to Lydick-Barmann Company, destination 616 Street, Louisiana City, Little Rock, Ark. State. Notify Crone Company." Seller had no office or agent at the street address in Little Rock given in the bill of lading. The carrier delivered to Crone Company and seller was never paid. Held, for seller, Lydick-Barmann. "Notify Crone Co. was not equivalent to 'Consigned to Crone Co.' When the carrier learned that it could not deliver to Lydick-Barmann at the address given, it should have sought instructions from Lydick-Barmann."

4. In *Refrigerated Transport Co.,* the bill of lading was non-negotiable which is by far the most common case. But a not uncommon transaction is one in which a seller in a foreign country ships goods to the U.S. pursuant to an agreement whereby the carrier issues a negotiable bill of lading to the seller who then sends it and a draft to a bank in the U.S. who acts as collecting agent on behalf of the seller by taking payment from the buyer and endorsing the bill to the buyer who then presents it to the carrier and receives the goods. Such an arrangement breaks down if the carrier delivers the goods to the buyer without insisting on the bill of lading. This is what happened in Koreska v. United Cargo Corp., 23 A.D.2d 37, 258 N.Y.S.2d 432 (1965) and the carrier was held liable to the seller (who did not receive payment from the buyer). The carrier may have a defense in such a case, however, as when the carrier can show that the buyer already had acquired the bill of lading from the collecting agent (without payment) so that the carrier's wrong was not the cause of the loss. Such a defense prevailed in The Pere Marquette Ry. v. J.F. French & Co., 254 U.S. 538, 41 S.Ct. 195, 65 L.Ed. 391 (1921). Still other defenses may be available in such cases. The carrier may be able to show that the seller or the seller's agent waived the requirement of picking up the bill of lading from the buyer. Or the carrier may be able to show that the seller ratified the misdelivery by accepting a partial payment from the buyer subsequently.

5. Sometimes the unpaid seller will find that the collecting agency (often a bank) will be liable. Such a case is Bunge v. First Nat'l Bank, 118 F.2d 427 (3d Cir. 1941) where the bank became liable to the seller for accepting a bad check and handing over the bill of lading duly endorsed to the buyer. The court said the bank became liable "when it received something other than money in payment."

Note: Terminology

The carrier's so-called "absolute liability" for misdelivery can be extracted from the text of sections 88 and 89 of the FBLA, 7–403 of the Code, and the contract of carriage of the parties. But it does not clarify analysis to say that the liability is absolute. After all, the contract between shipper and carrier calls on the carrier to deliver to a given party, and when the carrier fails to do this, a breach of contract occurs. The liability of a carrier for misdelivery is no more and no less absolute than the liability of any party for breach of contract. Ordinarily, it is no defense for the party who breaks his contract to respond that what he did under the circumstances was reasonable, or even that it was his very best effort.

Note: Substitutes for Surrender of "Order" Bills

When one uses a negotiable bill of lading he expects that the carrier will not surrender the goods until the original copy of the bill is presented to him. As we saw, the fine print at the top of such bill provides: "The surrender of this original ORDER BILL OF LADING properly indorsed shall be required before delivery of the property." UCC 7–502 makes plain the idea that this bill of lading embodies the rights to the goods; it specifies that one to whom a document of title has been duly negotiated acquires thereby "title to the document, title to the goods and the direct obligation of the issuer to hold or deliver the goods according to the terms of the document. * * *"

What happens when in the humdrum of real life the mailman fails to get the original of the order bill of lading to the bank and instead returns it with a stamp, "undeliverable," or when the bank loses the bill, or takes two or three days to process the bill and the goods have arrived in the meantime? Of course somebody is going to have to pay a charge to the railroad for holding the goods. And if the goods are melons or peaches or other perishable commodities, it would be intolerable and in no one's interest to have them rot on the siding while everyone hunted for the bill of lading. Shippers and carriers have worked out certain substitutes for surrender of the original bill. These provisions are described in § 3 of Rule 7 of the Uniform Freight Classification and they read as follows:

> **Substitute 1:** cash or its equivalent to the carrier equal to 125% of the invoice value of the property.
>
> **Substitute 2:** a specific bond of indemnity equal to double the invoice value.
>
> **Substitute 3:** a blanket bond of indemnity. This bond can be used repeatedly so long as the bill-of-lading is surrendered within five days of delivery of the freight. If the bill-of-lading does not become available within that time, Substitutes 1 or 2 must be substituted.
>
> **Substitute 4:** an open-end bond. (If an order-notify bill is lost the surety automatically assumes liability for the lading in perpetuity. The open-bond becomes an individual bond, without limit, on each car released.)

If the one for whom delivery is intended under the order bill of lading has not been able to procure the original of the order bill, he can offer any one of the four substitutes and thereby procure the goods. Of course the effect of the substitute is to provide the carrier with a fund out of which he can satisfy his liability for breaching his contract with the shipper.

One way to avoid the problem is this: The shipper can retain control of the goods by using a straight bill of lading if he names himself as the consignee. The following excerpt taken from a letter of the late Mr. J.L. Shissler, Jr., former General Traffic Manager of the Pillsbury Company, explains the Pillsbury Company's use of this method:

> "Under Section 4 of Rule 7 of the Uniform Freight Classification the rail carriers provide for shipments under straight bills-of-lading consigned to one party with provision for notification to a second party with surrender of a written order prior to delivery. Under this system we would simply bill a car to ourselves with the carrier to advise the customer. The bill-of-lading carries the notation 'Do not surrender except upon receipt of written order from The Pillsbury Company.' A delivery order is prepared and accompanies the draft to the bank. When the customer accepts the draft, he receives the delivery order. This in turn he presents to the carrier's destination agent for release of the car.
>
> "In the event the delivery order is lost or delayed the consignee can secure release of the car on the same four substitutes available under the order-notify bill.
>
> "Perhaps, at this point I should point out the difference in the two methods. Under the order bill, once the shipment moves neither the shipper nor the receiver can release the car without surrender of the bill or use of one of the four substitutes. Under the straight-notify bill the receiver must either surrender the delivery order or use one of the four substitutes. The consignor, however,

can release cars by simply notifying the carrier in writing that delivery can be made without surrender of the delivery order."

Observe that in the type of transaction Mr. Shissler describes, the buyer does not pay a sight draft; rather, he "accepts" a time draft as a condition of getting the goods. See UCC 3–410. This device affords seller less protection than does use of a sight draft, yet more protection than sale on open account. Do you see why?

SECTION 5. ASSERTION OF CLAIMS AGAINST SELLER, BUYER OR OWNER BY THIRD PARTIES (Herein of "negotiability")

Third parties (parties other than the seller, the buyer, and the bailee) sometimes assert claims to the goods at some stage of the transaction, and this can cause a breakdown. These parties include: (1) persons who claim to be creditors of the seller or buyer, (2) persons who claim to be purchasers from the seller or buyer, and (3) other persons claiming paramount title (e.g. an alleged prior owner).

Generally, the buyer will be best off in these cases if he has acquired title to the goods by taking (through due negotiation) negotiable documents covering them. Both Article Seven of the Code (UCC 7–104) and the Federal Bill of Lading Act distinguish between negotiable and non-negotiable documents. The relevant sections of the FBLA provide as follows:

82. Straight bill of lading

A bill in which it is stated that the goods are consigned or destined to a specified person is a straight bill. Aug. 29, 1916, c. 415, § 2, 39 Stat. 539.

83. Order bill of lading; negotiability

A bill in which it is stated that the goods are consigned or destined to the order of any person named in such bill is an order bill. Any provision in such a bill or in any notice, contract, rule, regulation, or tariff that it is nonnegotiable shall be null and void and shall not affect its negotiability within the meaning of this chapter unless upon its face and in writing agreed to by the shipper. Aug. 29, 1916, c. 415, § 3, 39 Stat. 539.

The most common type of transaction in which a buyer purchases a *negotiable* bill occurs when a contract between him and his seller calls for him to pay "cash against documents." (See section 2 of this chapter.) Today this type of transaction is not nearly as common in domestic trade as in import-export transactions. As we saw earlier, when a buyer agrees to pay "cash against documents," this ordinarily calls for him to pay a sight draft presented by the seller's agent in exchange for a negotiable bill of lading which entitles the buyer to procure the goods from the carrier and without which the carrier will not deliver them. The seller is not obligated to hand over the bill (and thus control over the goods) until the buyer pays the draft, and the buyer does not have to pay in advance but only simultaneously with acquiring the bill (the means to procure the goods from the carrier when they arrive).

What rights does a good faith purchaser of a negotiable document acquire? First, he generally gets the same rights against the bailee as the bailor had, including the right to have the bailee care for the goods and the right to have the bailee deliver in accordance with the purchaser's instructions. Thus, section 112 of the FBLA provides that the transferee gets "the direct obligation of the carrier to hold possession of the goods for him according to the terms of the bill as fully as if the carrier had contracted directly with him." Section 7–502(1) of Article Seven includes a similar provision. Second, a good faith purchaser of a negotiable bill of lading gets (under section 111 of the FBLA) "such title to the goods as the person negotiating the bill to him had or had ability to convey to a purchaser in good faith for value. * * *" Under section 7–502 of Article Seven, the purchaser gets (subject to UCC 7–503), "title to the document" and "title to the goods." Third, once the bailee issues a negotiable document covering the goods, whatever title to the goods that the document covers can generally be transferred only by appropriate transfer of the document. That is, appropriate transfer of the document is generally the exclusive method of moving title to the goods. Under Article Seven for a purchaser of a negotiable document to acquire rights under UCC 7–502, he must take by "due negotiation." The Article Seven requirements for due negotiation are set forth in UCC 7–501. Under the FBLA, for the purchaser to acquire the rights set forth in section 111, he must "give value therefor in good faith, without notice," and take by indorsement or delivery (as provided in sections 107 and 108).

Problem 17–1

Seller and buyer entered a contract for the purchase of 500 wooden rails. Seller got a negotiable bill of lading from the carrier while the rails were still in seller's yard to be loaded on nearby boxcars. Two days later buyer bought and paid for the bill and took the same by due negotiation. A day later, Ajax, a creditor of seller, levied on the rails while still in seller's yard. As between Ajax and buyer, who prevails? Cf., UCC 7–602, 7–501 and 7–502. See also FBLA section 103.

Problem 17–2

Construct an example in which the holder of a negotiable document received from the seller prevails under the Code over another purchaser of the same goods covered by the bill. Also be sure to note the exception in UCC 7–205.

Problem 17–3

Joe held a negotiable warehouse receipt in "order" form. Art stole the receipt and artfully forged it to John, a good faith purchaser. Joe claims the goods. John claims the goods. To whom must the bailee deliver under the Code? (And where does UCC 7–404 come into play?)

LINEBURGER BROS. v. HODGE

Supreme Court of Mississippi, 1951.
212 Miss. 204, 54 So.2d 268.

ALEXANDER, JUSTICE.

Separate bills were filed against the Federal Compress & Warehouse Company, a corporation, by E.S. Vancleve, J.R. Hodge, and E.A. Bates & Company, a partnership, each praying for a mandatory injunction against the defendant to compel delivery of cotton held by the defendant to them as purchasers and holders of the warehouse receipts covering the number of bales of cotton held respectively by each of the complainants, or in the alternative for the value of the cotton thereby represented. The total number of bales is twenty-four, Vancleve claiming nine, Hodge six, and E.A. Bates & Company nine.

It is adequately shown that all of the cotton was grown and ginned by Lineburger Brothers, B.C. Lineburger, J.G. Outlaw and F.A. Little, and stolen by one J.V. Carr from a gin where the cotton had been processed and tagged. This asportation occurred at night and was conducted with the aid of a truck driver who was not a regular employee of Carr. Early the next morning Carr carried the cotton to the defendant warehouse, and, after weighing, had the receipts issued in three fictitious names and delivered to him. Carr took the receipts to nearby towns and sold the cotton, so identified, to the three complainants in separate lots. The purchasers gave their separate checks to Carr who procured payment by endorsing them respectively in the names of the three fictitious persons. He then disappeared and has not since been located.

As stated, the three buyers filed their separate bills against the warehouse. The gin company was not made a party. Upon application of the planters or owners, they were allowed to intervene and claim the cotton. From a decree dismissing the petition of the intervenors, absolving the warehouse of negligence in the issuance of the receipts, and awarding title to the respective warehouse receipts to the purchasers with full rights to claim the cotton thereby represented, after paying storage charges to the warehouse, the planters, or owners, appeal. A cross-appeal is filed by the complainants which urges that in event of a reversal of the decree, they be awarded a decree against the warehouse for the value of the cotton.

We deal first with the cross-appeal. It is grounded chiefly upon the alleged negligence of the warehouse in issuing the receipts to Carr in the names given by him.

* * *

Regardless of the plausibility of the contention of the appellees, there was an issue of fact in the matter of negligence of the warehouse, and we find no basis for overturning the finding of the chancellor, whose acquittance of the warehouse must of necessity have been upon such absence of negligence.

We approach, then, the rights of the appellants, the planters and owners. As heretofore stated, they had given Carr no authority to take and haul away any of this cotton. Specific instructions, including the time and identity of cotton to be so hauled, were always given, and Carr knew this. It is immaterial whether the warehouse knew of this limitation upon Carr's authority. It is sufficient that this limitation was understood between Carr and appellants. Here there was no dispute, and it is without question that the taking by Carr, under all the circumstances, was larceny, and that the receipts were fraudulently obtained. The next morning Carr was seen and made two different and untrue statements as to where the receipts were. One of these reports was to one of the owners who had discovered that the cotton was missing and was seeking to locate the receipts. There was no one at the gin when the cotton was abstracted, except Carr, his driver, and Mrs. Carr and her small son. The manager of the gin was not present, and he later testified that he had instructions that Carr was not to haul the Lineburger cotton except upon specific instructions. We repeat that the gin is not a party here and the test of the right of the owners must depend on whether this cotton was under any circumstances entrusted to Carr by permission and knowledge of the owners.

We find that the cotton was not so entrusted to Carr, and since the cotton was in fact stolen and the receipts fraudulently obtained, the defense of apparent authority, although available to the warehouse, does not aid the claim of the purchasers of the receipts.

It was held in Unger v. Abbott, 92 Miss. 563, 46 So. 68, that the rule caveat emptor applies against the claim of an innocent purchaser of warehouse receipts who purchased them from the owner's servant who had been sent with cotton to a compress company with instructions to have it weighed and to bring the receipts back to the owner, but who, contrary to his authority and instructions, took the receipts in his own name and sold them.

If it be observed that this case was decided prior to our statutes upon Warehouse Receipts, Chap. 16, Vol. 4, Code 1942, attention is directed to Section 5051, which is as follows: "A negotiable receipt may be negotiated: * * *

> "(b) By any person to whom the possession or custody of the receipt has been entrusted by the owner, if, by the terms of the receipt, the warehouseman undertakes to deliver the goods to the order of the person to whom the possession or custody of the receipt has been entrusted, or if at the time of such entrusting the receipt is in such form that it may be negotiated by delivery."

We look next at Section 5052: "A person to whom a negotiable receipt has been duly negotiated acquires thereby:

> "(a) Such title to the goods as the person negotiating the receipt to him had or had ability to convey to a purchaser in good faith for value, and also such title to the goods as the depositor or person to whose order the goods were to be delivered by the terms of the receipt had or had ability to convey to a purchaser in good faith for value, and * * *."

Section 5058 is also in point. It is as follows: "The validity of the negotiation of a receipt is not impaired by the fact that such negotiation was a breach of duty on the part of the person making the negotiation, or by the fact that the owner of the receipt was induced by fraud, mistake, or duress to entrust the possession or custody of the receipt to such person, if the person to whom the receipt was negotiated, paid or a person to whom the receipt was subsequently negotiated, paid value therefor, without notice of the breach of duty, or fraud, or mistake or duress."

Appellees cite for support Weil Bros., Inc. v. Keenan, 180 Miss. 697, 178 So. 90. Here there was an interpleader suit filed by the warehouse. The testimony disclosed that the receipts had been entrusted to one Spencer by the owner, and were misappropriated by the former. After recognizing that one, especially a trespasser, can not convey a better title than he has, the Court found that the receipts had been entrusted to the thief and an innocent purchaser was protected. To the same effect is Lundy v. Greenville Bank & Tr. Co., 179 Miss. 282, 174 So. 802, and other cases cited by appellees. See also 56 Am.Jur.Warehouses, Sec. 62.

Our statutes do not go so far as those of some other states in protecting a bona fide purchaser of negotiable receipts in cases where the receipts had been stolen. See 56 Am.Jur., Warehouses, Sec. 53. Since such receipts were not negotiable at common law, their negotiability is to be measured by our statutes.

We hold, therefore, that neither the cotton nor the receipts had been entrusted to Carr by the owners and that the latter are not estopped to set up their claim to the cotton as against the several appellees who purchased the receipts.

* * *

The assertion wants no support that the statutes referred to were designed to insure the negotiability of warehouse receipts and to facilitate commerce in the market places where cotton is bought and sold. The innocent purchaser of a negotiable receipt is guaranteed an assurance without which the traffic could not be conducted. Yet, such assurance must take into account the older principle that an owner of cotton may not be divested of title by a trespasser or a thief. In order to strike a just balance between these two concepts the statutes were enacted. The buyer must still beware lest he is buying receipts which have been fraudulently obtained or cotton which has been stolen. We need not analyze the statutes to divine whether the owner, who has voluntarily clothed another with indicia of ownership or entrusted him with possession of receipts, is barred of recovery from an innocent purchaser by principles of estoppel or pursuant to the rule that where two innocent persons must suffer from a fraud, he who reposes confidence in the fraudulent agent must suffer. It is enough that the statute recognizes title in the innocent purchaser who has bought receipts from one to whom they have been entrusted by the owner.

Here, as in all such cases, one of two innocent persons must suffer the loss. The thief has stolen or fraudulently obtained property from someone. We hold that the unlawful act was committed against the owners and that the title to the cotton remains in them. As stated in Unger v. Abbott, supra, "(The appellees) are to be condoled with for their loss by this swindle; but their misfortune can not affect the right of (the appellants) to have (their) cotton. * * * 'Caveat emptor' applies." [92 Miss. 563, 46 So. 68.]

The cause will be reversed and decree awarded to the appellants for the cotton, and the Federal Compress & Warehouse Company is directed to hold the same to the order of appellants, but without storage charges thereon. The cross-appeal is thereby decided adversely.

Reversed and decree here for appellants.

Notes

1. Would this case have been decided the same way under UCC 7–501, 7–502, and 7–503? Explain. What if Carr had been the manager of the gin with power to store?

2. In re Jamestown Farmers Elevator Inc., 49 B.R. 661, 41 UCC Rep Serv. 578 (Bkrtcy.N.D.1985) posed a parallel problem. There, the goods were not stolen and then warehoused and passed to buyers. Rather, Bank had a security interest in the goods, yet allowed debtor to warehouse them and procure a further loan from third party, giving the receipts as security. Held: third party prevails over bank under UCC 7–503.

SECTION 6. A PARTY TO THE SALE REPUDIATES, BECOMES INSOLVENT, OR THE LIKE

A party to the sale may repudiate or become insolvent while the goods (1) are in the hands of a carrier or other bailee and (2) a document of title covering the goods is outstanding. Suppose, for example, that while the goods are en route, the buyer repudiates or becomes insolvent. What may the seller do? May he "stop in transit" under UCC 2–705? May he divert? This depends on (1) the terms of the outstanding document and (2) the applicable statutory and case law. In any event, any new carriage or delivery instructions of the seller will be addressed to the carrier (or other bailee).

It is important to distinguish between the carrier's *right* (without fear of suit) to follow the instructions of a consignor or consignee and its *duty* to do so. In some cases a carrier must follow instructions; in others it may but need not. Likewise one should distinguish a shipper-seller's rights and powers vis-a-vis the carrier from those vis-a-vis his buyer-consignee. The shipper may have the power to halt shipment, but his act may constitute a breach of his sales contract. UCC 2–705(1) gives the seller a right to stop delivery in a case in which "he discovers the buyer to be insolvent" or in the case of the "delivery of carload, truckload, planeload or larger shipments of express or freight when the buyer repudiates or fails to make a payment due before delivery, or if for any other reason the seller has a right to withhold or reclaim the goods." Subsection (3) of UCC 2–705 specifies certain limits on this right to stop. For example, the carrier is not obliged to obey any order to stop a shipment under an order bill until the document has been surrendered.

UCC 7–303(1) gives the carrier the authority but not the obligation to divert a shipment on instructions from:

(a) the holder of a negotiable bill; or

(b) the consignor on a non-negotiable bill notwithstanding contrary instructions from the consignee; or

(c) the consignee on a non-negotiable bill in the absence of contrary instructions from the consignor, if the goods have arrived at the billed destination or if the consignee is in possession of the bill; or

(d) the consignee on a non-negotiable bill if he is entitled as against the consignor to dispose of them.

Note well that the quoted section of the UCC states the law of *intra-state* shipment. Unless the courts adopt it as the federal common law, one must still search for that common law in the federal cases interpreting the Federal Bills of Lading Act in interstate shipments. Because case law is scarce and because the Code represents the current thinking of people who deal with bills of lading, one can hope that the federal courts will adopt the Code rules as the federal common law under the Bills of Lading Act where that Act does not speak explicitly.

CLOCK v. MISSOURI–KANSAS–TEXAS RAILROAD CO. v. CRAWFORD

United States District Court, Eastern District of Missouri, 1976.
407 F.Supp. 448.

OPINION

NANGLE, DISTRICT JUDGE.

Plaintiff Gerald Clock brought this action to recover the cost of goods which were allegedly converted by defendant Missouri-Kansas-Texas Railroad Company. By amended complaint, plaintiff added Stanley L. Crawford as defendant. Plaintiff also alleges that defendant Railroad breached its obligation to deliver the goods. Prior to the filing of plaintiff's amended complaint, defendant Railroad filed a third-party complaint against Crawford, alleging that if the Railroad should be liable to plaintiff, third-party defendant would be liable to the Railroad to the extent of the liability to plaintiff. Crawford now being a defendant in this action, defendant Railroad's complaint is in fact a cross-claim and will be treated as such.

This case was tried before the Court without a jury. The Court having considered the pleadings, the testimony of the witnesses, the documents in evidence, and being otherwise fully advised in the premises, hereby makes the following findings of fact and conclusions of law as required by Rule 52, Federal Rules of Civil Procedure:

Findings of Fact

1. Plaintiff, Gerald Clock, is, and was at all times relevant herein, a citizen of the State of Indiana. Defendant, Missouri-Kansas-Texas Railroad Company ("Railroad") is a corporation incorporated under the laws of the State of Delaware, having its principal place of business in Texas. Defendant Stanley L. Crawford, is, and was at all times relevant herein, a citizen of the State of Oklahoma.

2. On January 14, 1975, Crawford sold two carloads of bulk ammonium nitrate fertilizer to Buford Cunningham and received two checks in payment therefor. On the same date, the goods were placed in the care and custody of defendant Railroad for shipment from Oklahoma to Eaton Agricultural Center in Indiana. Defendant Railroad issued bills of lading to cover the goods. The bills of lading were signed by Crawford. Both bills of lading specify on the top of each that they are

Uniform Straight Bill of Lading

Original—Not Negotiable

3. At the time of sale, Crawford knew that Cunningham was going to sell the goods to a third party. Soon after the sale to Cunningham, Cunningham did sell the goods to plaintiff for $30,195.12. At the time of this sale, plaintiff had no knowledge of any infirmities in title, or right to possession, by Cunningham.

4. On January 23, 1975, the bank notified Crawford that there were insufficient funds in Cunningham's account to cover the checks. Accordingly, they were returned to Crawford.

5. The goods were still in transit at this point. Crawford instructed the Railroad to hold the railroad cars containing the goods until further instructions from him. Defendant Railroad complied.

6. On February 3, 1975, Crawford certified to defendant Railroad that he was the true owner of the goods and he issued a reconsignment order on the goods, instructing that they be sent to Farmers Union Coop, instead of Eaton Agricultural Center. Defendant Railroad complied with these instructions.

7. Plaintiff furnished replacement goods to Eaton Agricultural Center of a like quantity and value, and acquired the right, title and interest of Eaton Agricultural Center to the goods, by reason of an assignment by Eaton Agricultural Center executed on February 10, 1975.

Conclusions of Law

This Court has jurisdiction over the subject matter and of the parties. 28 U.S.C. § 1332.

The bills of lading involved herein are straight bills of lading. 49 U.S.C. §§ 82, 86. It is clear that "[a] straight bill can not be negotiated free from existing equities * * * ". 49 U.S.C. § 109. While not negotiable, straight bills are transferable. The transferee stands in the shoes of the transferor, acquiring no additional rights over those held by the transferor. See *Arizona Feed v. Southern Pacific Transportation Co.,* 21 Ariz.App. 346, 519 P.2d 199 (1974); *Southern Pacific Co. v. Agencia Joffroy, S.A.,* 65 Ariz. 65, 174 P.2d 278 (1946); *Quality Shingle Co. v. Old Oregon Lumber & Shingle Co.,* 110 Wash. 60, 187 P. 705 (1920); § 400.7–104, R.S.Mo. (1969).

A carrier may deliver goods to "[a] person lawfully entitled to the possession of the goods" or to the consignee. 49 U.S.C. § 89. The question for determination therefore is whether Crawford was lawfully entitled to possession of the goods. While it is true that title passes to a buyer when the seller completes his performance under the contract, § 400.2–401, R.S.Mo. (1969), it is equally true that

> where the buyer * * * fails to make a payment due * * * the aggrieved seller may
>
> (a) withhold delivery of such goods;
>
> (b) stop delivery by any bailee * * *;
>
> * * *
>
> (d) resell and recover damages * * *
>
> * * *
>
> (f) cancel. § 400.2–703, R.S.Mo. (1969).

It is the Court's conclusion, therefore, that upon the failure of the checks presented by Cunningham to Crawford, Crawford was "lawfully entitled to the possession of the goods". Plaintiff, as transferee of a straight bill of lading, can not have any greater rights than did Cunningham, and can not have the status of a bona fide purchaser for value. Since Crawford was entitled to possession of the goods, defendant Railroad can not be liable for delivering the goods in accordance with Crawford's instructions. 49 U.S.C. § 89, *Turner Lumber & Investment Co. v. Chicago, R.I. & P. Ry. Co.*, 223 Mo.App. 564, 16 S.W.2d 705 (1929).

The applicable provisions of the Commercial Code provide that

> (1) Unless the bill of lading otherwise provides, the carrier may deliver the goods to a person or destination other than that stated in the bill or may otherwise dispose of the goods on instructions from
>
> (b) the consignor on a nonnegotiable bill notwithstanding contrary instructions from the consignee * * * § 400.7–303, R.S.Mo. (1969).

Under the facts established herein, Crawford was the consignor, as Crawford was "the person from whom the goods have been received for shipment". § 400.7–102(c), R.S.Mo. (1969). Since the bills of lading were nonnegotiable, and defendant Railroad delivered the goods pursuant to the instructions of the consignor, there can be no liability. See Comments, § 400.7–303 and § 400.7–504(3), R.S. Mo. (1969).

Under 49 U.S.C. § 112, the authority of the shipper to stop shipment in transit and redirect it is well established. See *Weyerhaeuser Timber Co. v. First National Bank of Portland,* 150 Or. 172, 38 P.2d 48 (1934); *Cashmere Fruit Growers' Union v. Great Northern Railway Co.,* 149 Wash. 319, 270 P. 1038 (1928), *cert. denied,* 279 U.S. 851, 49 S.Ct. 347, 73 L.Ed. 994; *Quality Shingle Co. v. Old Oregon Lumber & Shingle Co., supra.* The same right is recognized in the Commercial Code. See §§ 400.2–703 and 400.2–705. Accordingly there can be no recovery by plaintiff against Crawford.

Plaintiff has claimed that both the Railroad and Crawford converted the shipments in question to their own use. Conversion has been defined as "* * * an *unauthorized* assumption and exercise of the right of ownership over the personal property of another to the exclusion of the owners' right". *Carson Union May Stern Co. v. Pennsylvania Railroad Co.,* 421 S.W.2d 540 (Mo. App.1967) [emphasis in the original]. Having concluded that Crawford was lawfully entitled to possession of the goods, it is clear that recovery for conversion will not lie.

The cases cited by plaintiff are inapposite as they involve a bona fide purchaser for value. Under the authority of 49 U.S.C. § 81 *et seq.,* there can not be such status where one is a transferee under a straight bill of lading. *North American Van Lines, Inc. v. Heller,* 371 F.2d 629 (5th Cir.1967) is equally unavailing since the Court concludes that Crawford was lawfully entitled to possession.

Accordingly, judgment will be for defendants Railroad and Crawford. Since plaintiff will not recover any damages from defendant Railroad, judgment will be for defendant Crawford on the Railroad's cross-claim.

Problem 17–4

Seller ships under a straight bill of lading and names buyer (in the same state) as consignee. The shipment is a full truckload of leather. On the day the shipment leaves the seller's city, seller receives a "Dun & Bradstreet" on buyer which shows that buyer's fortunes have gone into precipitous decline and that he may have become insolvent.

1. If he instructs truck company not to deliver goods to buyer, will it comply? If it refuses, does he have a cause of action against it? (UCC 7–303, 2–705)

2. If carrier does stop shipment, will seller be in breach of his contract with buyer? (UCC 2–705, 2–609)

3. Would it change your answer if buyer had already received his copy of the bill of lading and had transferred his interest in it and the goods to a third party by an assignment of that bill and had given notice of such transfer to the carrier? (UCC 7–504)

4. Would it make any difference that the shipment was under a negotiable bill of lading and the bill had been negotiated to the third party? (UCC 7–502, 2–705)

5. In this problem does UCC 2–705 enlarge seller's rights against buyer, his control of the goods, neither, or both?

6. If the buyer had not become insolvent and was not otherwise in breach of the contract and if seller ordered the truck company to return the shipment to him, do you think the company would have complied? Would it have had any liability to buyer for doing so?

SECTION 7. BAILEE'S NON-RECEIPT, MISDESCRIPTION OR THE LIKE—EFFECTS ON BUYERS, SELLERS AND FINANCERS

For a variety of reasons the carrier or other bailee may issue documents covering goods that it did not receive, or misdescribe the goods it did receive. As a result buyers or *financers* of buyers (or of sellers for that matter) may rely on the documents to their detriment. The relevant Code sections are UCC 7–203 & 7–301. Relevant sections of the Federal Bill of Lading Act (49 U.S.C.A.) provide:

§ 100. Loading by carrier; counting packages, etc.; contents of bill

When goods are loaded by a carrier, such carrier shall count the packages of goods if package freight, and ascertain the kind and quantity if bulk freight, and such carrier shall not, in such cases, insert in the bill of lading or in any notice, receipt, contract, rule, regulation, or tariff, "Shipper's weight, load, and count," or other words of like purport, indicating that the goods were loaded by the shipper and the description of them made by him, or in case of bulk freight and freight not concealed by packages the description made by him. If so inserted contrary to the provisions of this section, said words shall be treated as null and void and as if not inserted therein.

§ 101. Loading by shipper; contents of bill; ascertainment of kind and quantity on request

When package freight or bulk freight is loaded by a shipper and the goods are described in a bill of lading merely by a statement of marks or labels upon them or upon packages containing them, or by a statement that the goods are said to be goods of a certain kind or quantity or in a certain condition, or it is stated in the bill of lading that packages are said to contain goods of a certain kind or quantity or in a certain condition, or that the contents or condition of the contents of packages are unknown, or words of like purport are contained in the bill of lading, such statements, if true, shall not make liable the carrier issuing the bill of lading, although the goods are not of the kind or quantity or in the condition which the marks or labels upon them indicate, or of the kind or quantity or in the condition they were said to be by the consignor. The carrier may also by inserting in the bill of lading the words "Shipper's weight, load, and count," or other words of like purport, indicate that the goods were loaded by the shipper and the description of them made by him; and if such statement be true, the carrier shall not be liable for damages caused by the improper loading or by the nonreceipt or by the misdescription of the goods described in the bill of lading: *Provided, however,* Where the shipper of bulk freight installs and maintains adequate facilities for weighing such freight, and the same are available to the carrier, then the carrier, upon written request of such shipper and when given a reasonable opportunity so to do, shall ascertain the kind and quantity of bulk freight within a reasonable time after such written request, and the carriers shall not in such cases insert in the bill of lading the words "Shipper's weight," or other words of like purport, and if so inserted contrary to the provisions of this section, said words shall be treated as null and void and as if not inserted therein.

§ 102. Liability for nonreceipt or misdescription of goods

If a bill of lading has been issued by a carrier or on his behalf by an agent or employee the scope of whose actual or apparent authority includes the receiving of goods and issuing bills of lading therefor for transportation in commerce among the several States and with foreign nations, the carrier shall be liable to (a) the owner of goods covered by a straight bill subject to existing right of stoppage in transitu or (b) the holder of an order bill, who has given value in good faith, relying upon the description therein of the goods, or upon the shipment being made upon the date therein shown, for damages caused by the nonreceipt by the carrier of all or part of the goods upon or prior to the date therein shown, or their failure to correspond with the description thereof in the bill at the time of its issue.

G.A.C. COMMERCIAL CORP. v. WILSON

United States District Court, Southern District of New York, 1967.
271 F.Supp. 242.

BRYAN, DISTRICT JUDGE.

Plaintiff G.A.C. Commercial Corporation (G.A.C.), a Delaware corporation, brings this action sounding in fraud against the five individual defendants and in negligence against a New York corporation, Norwood & St. Lawrence Railroad Co. (Norwood), a rail carrier in interstate commerce. Defendant Norwood now moves, pursuant to Rule 12(c), F.R.Civ.P., for judgment on the pleadings dismissing the fourth count of the complaint. Since matters outside the pleadings have been presented and considered the motion will be treated as one for summary judgment under Rule 56, F.R.Civ.P.

The gravamen of the action is spelled out in the first three counts of the complaint, laid solely against the individual defendants. It is alleged that on October 17, 1963, plaintiff G.A.C. entered into an accounts receivable financing agreement with St. Lawrence Pulp & Paper Corp. (St. Lawrence), a New York corporation. Under the terms of the agreement G.A.C. was to make advances to St. Lawrence, which agreed to "pledge, assign and transfer to G.A.C. all the [b]orrower's right, title and interest in and to accounts receivable * * * then owing" to St. Lawrence.

Pursuant to the agreement St. Lawrence forwarded copies of its invoices together with copies of bills of lading to G.A.C., which, upon receipt, advanced the monies to St. Lawrence at the agreed discount. Repayment of the debts due was guaranteed in writing by the defendant Wilson who was a corporate officer of St. Lawrence. G.A.C. ultimately advanced $356,883.57 under the financing agreement, no part of which has been repaid. St. Lawrence is now a bankrupt.

The first claim for relief seeks recovery of the entire amount from the individual guarantor Wilson. The second claim alleges that certain of the accounts receivable forwarded to plaintiff were false and fraudulent, and that in reliance upon these accounts G.A.C. advanced the sum of $254,173.42 which has not been repaid. The individual defendants, who, with the exception of Lalvani, are described as officers and/or directors of St. Lawrence, are charged with knowledge that these accounts were false and fraudulent. The third claim simply adds a conspiracy allegation against the individual defendants describing a scheme to "defraud and deceive the plaintiff" by forwarding false and fraudulent accounts receivable.

This motion is addressed to the fourth claim for relief laid solely against Norwood. That claim alleges that the fraudulent accounts receivable described were "upon the form of bill of lading" of defendant Norwood "and were countersigned by its agent." Norwood is charged with negligence in failing to require any inspection of the quantity of goods shipped before verifying the bills of lading and in permitting a situation to occur in which the fraudulent and nonexistent accounts could be forwarded to G.A.C.

Norwood's answer alleges failure to state a claim on which relief can be granted and contributory negligence. By way of separate defense it denies any knowledge or information as to the falsity of the bills of lading or with respect to the financing agreement between St. Lawrence and G.A.C. The answer also alleges that the bills of lading involved are "uniform straight bill[s] of lading—

not negotiable," as in fact they are, under Section 2 of the Federal Bills of Lading Act. 49 U.S.C.A. § 82.

The controversy here concerns 62 invoices and accompanying straight bills of lading forwarded to G.A.C. by St. Lawrence during 1964. Sixty of these bills concern interstate shipments of paper from St. Lawrence in Norfolk, New York, to Mohegan Converters in Hillside, New Jersey, and involve advances of $245,811.19. Each of the sixty interstate bills was on Norwood's bill of lading, and it is conceded for purposes of this motion, though denied in the answer, that the bills were signed by one of Norwood's agents.

The other two bills involve advances of $8,362.23 on two intrastate shipments from St. Lawrence to Norwood Converting, Inc. in Norfolk, New York, and to Board of Education Depository, Long Island City, New York, respectively. The bills of lading on these shipments were not on Norwood forms and were not signed by Norwood's agents. In fact there is no evidence that Norwood issued these bills or had anything to do with them.

The method by which the alleged fraudulent scheme was carried out appears for purposes of this motion to be as follows: the bankrupt St. Lawrence, as part of its facilities in Norfolk, New York, maintained a railroad siding connected with the lines of defendant carrier which had a freight office approximately 1/8th of a mile from the siding. St. Lawrence was permitted to load freight at its spur track in preparation for shipments on defendant's line. The railroad cars were sealed by St. Lawrence with seals provided by the railroad. St. Lawrence also prepared the bills of lading on blanks furnished in quadruplicate by defendant Norwood. The bills thus prepared were then presented to Norwood's agent who signed the original and one copy without inspecting the contents of the cars. No notation such as "contents of packages unknown" or "shipper's weight, load and count" was written on the bills. The signed copies were returned to St. Lawrence and forwarded with the invoices to G.A.C. which made advances on the goods described, which, as it turned out, had not been shipped.

Since sixty of the bills of lading were issued by a common carrier for the transportation of goods in interstate commerce, the issues as to these bills are controlled by the provisions of the Federal Bills of Lading Act. 49 U.S.C.A. § 81. This statute stands as "a clear expression of the determination of Congress to take the whole subject matter of such bills of lading within its control." 2 Williston, Sales § 406a, at 535 (rev. ed. 1948); see Adams Express Co. v. Croninger, 226 U.S. 491, 33 S.Ct. 148, 57 L.Ed. 314 (1913). As such, it squarely bars the fourth claim asserted against defendant Norwood on the sixty bills representing interstate shipments.

Prior to the passage of the Federal Bills of Lading Act "the United States courts held that a carrier was not liable for the act of its agent in issuing a bill of lading for goods where no goods had in fact been received." Josephy v. Panhandle & S.F. Ry., 235 N.Y. 306, 310, 139 N.E. 277, 278 (1923); see, e.g., Clark v. Clyde S.S. Co., 148 F. 243 (S.D.N.Y.1906). The liability of carriers for acts of their agents was expanded, but not drastically, by the passage of the federal legislation which draws a sharp distinction between order bills of lading and straight bills where in fact the goods are never received for shipment by the carrier. Under § 22 of the Act, 49 U.S.C. § 102, "[i]f a bill of lading has been issued by a carrier or on his behalf by an agent or employee * * *, the carrier shall be liable to * * * the holder of an order bill, who has given value in good faith, relying upon the description therein of the goods, * * * for damages caused by the nonreceipt by the carrier of all or part of the goods upon or prior to the date therein shown." However, the liability of the carrier for nonreceipt extends only to "the owner of goods covered by a straight bill,"[1] provided, of course, he also gives value in good faith in reliance upon the description of goods contained in the bill. See Strohmeyer & Arpe Co. v. American Line S.S. Corp., 97 F.2d 360, 362 (2d Cir.1938).

It is clear that a party in the position of Norwood is not included within the narrow category of those liable on a straight bill under the federal legislation. In the first place there is no question that the straight bills of lading here involved are nonnegotiable. * * * As a consequence plaintiff G.A.C., as apparent transferee of these bills and invoices representing accounts receivable under the agreement with St. Lawrence, upon notification to the carrier of the transfer,[2] could only "become the direct obligee of whatever obligations the carrier owed to the transferor of the bill immediately before the notification." 49 U.S.C.A. § 112; see id. § 109. Norwood obviously owed St. Lawrence nothing because no goods in fact were received. There was therefore no outstanding obligation to G.A.C. * * *

By no stretch of the imagination does G.A.C. qualify as an "owner of goods covered by a straight bill" who can sue the carrier under § 22 of the Federal Bills of Lading Act, 49 U.S.C.A. § 102, for representing that goods in fact had been received. The reason for this is that it is completely illusory to attempt to assign an "owner" to non-existent goods. R. Braucher, Documents of Title 23 (1958); 2 S. Williston, Sales § 419a, at 576–77 (rev. ed. 1948). While the consignee is generally deemed to have title to goods shipped under a straight bill of lading, see George F. Hinrichs, Inc. v. Standard Trust & Sav. Bank, 279 F. 382, 386 (2d Cir.1922), even he cannot sue the carrier for representing in a straight bill that non-existent goods had in fact been received. Martin Jessee Motors v. Reading Co., 87 F.Supp. 318 (E.D.Pa.), aff'd, 181 F.2d 766 (3d Cir.1950). The rationale applied in Martin Jessee Motors—that the consignee can prevail against the carrier "only by proving its title to specific property," 181 F.2d at 767—applies a fortiori to bar the claim of G.A.C. Plaintiff's interest in the "aggregate face value of the accounts receivable pledged as security"[3] under no conceivable reading of the statute can be deemed an "[ownership] of goods covered by a straight bill." G.A.C. is not one of the favored few who can recover under the Federal Bills of Lading Act. * * *

Plaintiff G.A.C. fares no better with respect to the two bills of lading representing intrastate shipments in New York. Of decisive importance, of course, are the facts that these shipments were not on Norwood forms and were not signed by Norwood's agents. Even if they were, the carrier would escape

1. Section 22 of the Act, 49 U.S.C. § 102, in its complete form, reads as follows:

§ 102. Liability for nonreceipt or misdescription of goods

"If a bill of lading has been issued by a carrier or on his behalf by an agent or employee the scope of whose actual or apparent authority includes the receiving of goods and issuing bills of lading therefor for transportation in commerce among the several States and with foreign nations, the carrier shall be liable to (a) the owner of goods covered by a straight bill subject to existing right of stoppage in transitu or (b) the holder of an order bill, who has given value in good faith, relying upon the description therein of the goods, or upon the shipment being made upon the date therein shown, for damages caused by the nonreceipt by the carrier of all or part of the goods upon or prior to the date therein shown, or their failure to correspond with the description thereof in the bill at the time of its issue."

2. The defendant Norwood apparently first received notice from G.A.C. by letter dated February 16, 1965. See Def.Ex.B.

3. Accounts Receivable Agreement Between St. Lawrence and G.A.C., Oct. 17, 1963, ¶ 3.

liability. Although the awkward term "owner" in 49 U.S.C.A. § 102 has been replaced by the word "consignee" in the Uniform Commercial Code § 7–301 and the Uniform Bills of Lading Act § 23, each of which would govern the issues of liability on one of the bills of lading representing an intrastate shipment,[4] the change is immaterial for purposes of this case. Plaintiff, perhaps an assignee, transferee or pledgee of the non-negotiable bills, though it claims not to be, is certainly not a "consignee," which is the only party protected. 2 Anderson, Uniform Commercial Code 261 n. 9 (1961); see R. Braucher, Documents of Title 23–24 (1958). Contrast U.C.C. § 7–203. Thus, as with the sixty interstate bills, G.A.C. cannot successfully sue on the two intrastate bills.

G.A.C. cannot avoid the results dictated by the statute by casting its claim for relief in terms of common law negligence. G.A.C. was sent sixty straight interstate bills of lading by St. Lawrence. The alleged negligence consists of Norwood's permitting a situation to develop in which St. Lawrence could make untrue representations that goods had in fact been shipped under the straight bills. G.A.C. claims that it relied to its detriment upon certain statements contained in the bills. The action is based on the bills not on Norwood's negligence. * * * A holding to the contrary would permit any party to circumvent the restrictions of the Federal Bills of Lading Act through the insertion of a talismanic characterization of its claim as one for "negligence." It is quite plain, however, that the declaration in 49 U.S.C.A. § 81—"bills of lading issued by any common carrier for the transportation of goods" between the states "shall be governed by this chapter"—must be taken to preclude alternative and supplementary liability under state law. * * * The substance of the rule cannot be avoided by the form of the complaint.

* * *

It is true that the result dictated by the federal legislation may lead to some inequities. A straight bill under the Federal Bills of Lading Act is obviously not a good security risk. Casenote, 63 Harv.L.Rev. 1439, 1440 (1950). The fraud of the shipper by failing to deliver goods to the carrier can result, as it did here, in misleading statements on the bills of lading, which operate to the detriment of banks and other commercial financers making advances on the basis of the bills. See Olivier Straw Goods Corp. v. Osaka Shosen Kaisha, 27 F.2d 129, 134 (2d Cir. 1928) (A. Hand, J.). Moreover, the carrier can readily prevent such a situation from arising by inserting "in the bill of lading the words, 'Shipper's weight, load, and count,' or other words of like purport" to "indicate that the goods were loaded by the shipper and the description of them made by him." 49 U.S.C.A. § 101.

But the overriding policy considerations in the Act look the other way on the issue of liability. First, "[t]here is nothing in the statute to indicate that the mere omission of the words 'Shipper's weight, load, and count' in and of itself makes the carrier liable for damages to goods improperly loaded. The omission of the statutory words merely serves to shift upon the carrier the burden of proving that the goods were improperly loaded by the shipper, and that the damage ensued from that cause." Modern Tool Corp. v. Pennsylvania R. Co., 100 F.Supp. 595, 596–597 (D.N.J.1951); see U.C.C. § 7–301(4). According to the allegations the true culprits in this case were the shipper and its agents; there is no reason to saddle defendant Norwood with liability simply because it did not insert the "Shipper's weight, load, and count" language in the bills. In addition,

4. One of the bills is dated September 24, 1964; the other is dated September 28, 1964. In New York the Uniform Commercial Code superseded the Uniform Bills of Lading Act on September 27, 1964.

practicality demands loading arrangements such as those here, where the shipper places his goods aboard and seals the railroad car which the carrier has provided. Section 21 of the Act, 49 U.S.C.A. § 101, anticipates that shippers are expected to do much of the counting and loading on their own sidings or spur tracks. The rapid flow of commerce might well be hindered if the carrier in every instance were charged with ascertaining whether in fact there were goods behind every one of its straight bills.

Moreover, denying security value to a straight bill of lading does not work a hardship upon banks and other commercial institutions. G.A.C., as a knowledgeable lender, is fully aware of the risks inherent in straight bills, and could well have required order bills to protect itself. See Chicago & Northwestern Ry. v. Stevens Nat'l Bank, 75 F.2d 398 (8th Cir.1935). It nevertheless chose to rely upon straight bills to lend money to the now bankrupt St. Lawrence at a profitable rate of interest. Wiser now, G.A.C. seeks to shift its loss to Norwood, an undoubtedly solvent defendant. The Federal Bills of Lading Act protects against this type of hindsight by requiring the lender to accept this kind of security subject to the defenses between the carrier and the shipper.

The motion of defendant Norwood for judgment on the pleadings treated as a motion for summary judgment is granted.

It is so ordered.

Notes

Seller delivered 61 bales of an inferior cotton known as "grabbots" to Carrier for shipment to Buyer. Carriers agent, knowing it to be false, issued a negotiable bill of lading to the Seller's order which described the goods as "61 bales of cotton." In the trade, this description meant "merchantable lint cotton," not "grabbots," an inferior grade. As was customary, Seller indorsed the bill of lading to Buyer, drew a draft on buyer for the purchase price, $3,965, and sent the documents through banking channels to the Buyer. Buyer paid the draft before the goods arrived. After delivery, the goods were stored in a warehouse and, later, destroyed by fire. Buyer sued Carrier for the difference between the amount of the draft paid and the value of the "grabbots", some $2,953, on the theory that the Carrier failed to use ordinary care in issuing the bill of lading. *Held,* for Buyer. The goods were misdescribed and Carrier's agent had notice of this and that the buyer might rely in good faith on that description in paying the sight draft. It was negligence for Carrier to issue the bill of lading without an appropriate qualification under these circumstances. Chicago, R.I. & P.R. Co. v. Cleveland, 61 Okl. 64, 160 P. 328 (1916).

SECTION 8. SALE OF GOODS LOCATED IN A WAREHOUSE—AN ADDENDUM

Sellers not uncommonly sell goods already stored in a warehouse. Since goods in a warehouse are not in motion and are not necessarily the subject of an executory sale transaction, the problems of control over goods in the hands of warehousemen are not as severe as those encountered with goods in the hands of the carrier. UCC 7–403(1) tells us that unless the bailee establishes one of the several defenses there described, the warehouseman is obliged to deliver the goods to "a person entitled under the document." A "person entitled" is defined by subsection (4) as follows: "[The] holder in the case of a negotiable document, or the person to whom delivery is to be made by the terms of or pursuant to written instructions under a non-negotiable document." Moreover UCC 7–403(3) instructs "the bailee [to] cancel the document or conspicuously note the partial delivery thereon or be liable to any person to whom the document is duly negotiated."

Thus the holder of a negotiable document and at least the first possessor-bailor on a non-negotiable document control the goods. The upshot of these rules is that the warehouseman with any sense will demand to see a negotiable warehouse receipt and make a notation on it before he will make any delivery under that warehouse receipt. However he will honor delivery orders signed by the person whom he believes to be the owner of a non-negotiable document without demanding the production of that document. One can easily see the potential for fraud if the owner of a non-negotiable warehouse receipt transfers it to one party and thereafter issues a delivery order to a second party. Presumably each of these acts constitutes "written instructions under a non-negotiable document." In this connection consider the following problem:

Problem 17–5

Repeunzel has 10,000 cans of beans. He puts them in a warehouse and receives a non-negotiable warehouse receipt. On December 1 he transfers his interest in the non-negotiable warehouse receipt together with possession of that receipt to Cicero. On December 3 he signs a non-negotiable delivery order instructing the warehouseman to deliver all of the beans to Leroy. On December 5 Leroy presents his delivery order and takes the beans. On December 10 Cicero comes to you for advice about his rights against the warehouseman. What are his rights? You may assume that everyone except for Repeunzel gave value and acted in good faith. See UCC 7–403, 7–503, 7–504, 7–402, 7–404.

PART FIVE

THE RECEIPT-INSPECTION STAGE

CHAPTER EIGHTEEN

THE BUYER'S RIGHTS TO INSPECT, TO REJECT, OR TO REVOKE ACCEPTANCE OF THE GOODS

SECTION 1. IMPORTANCE TO BUYER OF DISCOVERING NON-CONFORMITY PRIOR TO ACCEPTANCE OR PAYMENT

It is at the "receipt-inspection" stage that the buyer typically has his first opportunity to determine whether the seller's performance conforms to the contract. The seller's failure to perform may take a variety of forms, including breach of delivery obligations (UCC 2–301, 2–307, 2–308, 2–507(1), 2–503, 2–504 & 2–505), failure to perform on time (UCC 2–309), delivery of less than the contract quantity, and, perhaps most important in the usual transaction, non-compliance with contract requirements as to quality of goods sold (UCC 2–313, 314 & 315). Many non-conformities will be readily discoverable ("patent"); others will be harder to discover ("latent"). For non-conformity discovered at the receipt-inspection stage, the buyer *may,* depending upon the circumstances, have a choice between (1) such "goods-oriented" remedies as "rejection" (UCC 2–601) and revocation of acceptance (UCC 2–608), and (2) "damages-oriented" remedies (UCC 2–713 and 2–714). And the buyer may be able, in the circumstances, to combine these remedies, e.g., throw the goods back at the seller and also seek damages. See UCC 2–711(1).

Why might it be important for the buyer to discover non-conformity and reject the goods prior to accepting or paying for them? We will consider sales on credit first, for they are more usual. Although such a buyer need not worry about being out the price before he finds a defect, he may wish to avoid costly unloading and storage of bulky goods. And he should be concerned to identify any non-conformity at least in advance of "acceptance" (UCC 2–606). Absent this, acceptance imposes a duty on the buyer to pay, UCC 2–607(1), and buyers do not want to pay for significantly non-conforming goods. Moreover, acceptance precludes *rejection* of the goods. UCC 2–607(2) and 2–601. But it is true that this does necessarily mean the buyer will be unable rightfully to throw the goods back at the seller. Even after acceptance, should the non-conformity then be discovered, the buyer may be able to revoke his acceptance under UCC 2–608. But we will see that it is harder to throw goods back at a seller under UCC 2–608 than it is under UCC 2–601. Finally, the burden of establishing breach with regard to accepted goods is on the buyer. UCC 2–607(4). Thus it remains true that so far as goods-oriented remedies are concerned the buyer will be best off if he discovers non-conformity prior to acceptance and rejects. But if the buyer either discovers a defect and rejects or later revokes acceptance, the buyer will in both instances escape the bargain (which may in itself be highly advantageous), and also shift any resulting loss due to depreciation back on the seller.

SECTION 2. BUYER'S RIGHT TO "INSPECT" BEFORE ACCEPTANCE OR PAYMENT—GENERAL RULES AND EXCEPTIONS

The general rule is that the buyer has a right to inspect the goods before payment or acceptance, and this is true even in deals in which the seller discharges his delivery obligations at the point of shipment, e.g. "F.O.B. point of origin." UCC 2–513 and 2–310. Note, too, that this rule applies to cash on the barrelhead deals.

What of exceptions? First of all, the buyer can, of course, by contract, agree in so many words to give up the right to inspect prior to acceptance or payment. Second (and this frequently confuses students) the buyer can give up the right of prior inspection before payment by agreeing to a *mode* of payment inconsistent with such a right. For examples see UCC 2–513(3)(a) and (b). For exceptions to this exception, see the "except" clause in UCC 2–513(3)(b) and 2–512(1)(a). Note, too, that payment in a deal calling for payment before inspection does not constitute acceptance. UCC 2–512(2).

A. *The General Right to Inspect*

Problem 18–1

Suppose that student A, who was on the law review and actually attended class, agreed to sell his notes from the course on Commercial Transactions to student B for $100. The agreement was made on January 20 and A was to deliver the notes on February 1 at the law school. On February 1, A and B met to complete the exchange. A had placed the notes in a green canvas bag. Displaying the bag, A said to B: "Here are the notes. May I please have the $100." B refused to pay until he had a chance to inspect the contents of the bag. A refused either to untie the string around or relinquish possession of the bag. When the impasse could not be broken, A stated to B that the "deal was off." Later that afternoon A sold the notes to student C for $150. What is the legal position of A and B under the UCC?

Do you agree with the following analysis?

The basic question is whether B had a duty to accept and pay for the notes at the time when A cancelled the contract. UCC 2–301. At first blush, this seems to turn on whether A has tendered delivery of the goods. If tender has been made, A is entitled to "acceptance of the goods and to payment according to the contract" under UCC 2–507(1) and a tender of payment by B is a condition to A's "duty to tender and complete any delivery." UCC 2–511(1). If the contract requires A to tender delivery at a particular place, i.e., the law school, the tender must meet the standards of UCC 2–503(1). Has it done so here? The answer is that no matter how closely A's conduct matches the language of UCC 2–503(1), B's duty to tender payment or be in breach of the contract has not yet arisen. On the facts of this case, B "has a right before payment or acceptance to inspect" the goods. UCC 2–513(1). By refusing to grant this "right," A has "impaired" his tender of delivery. UCC 2–503, comment 2. Cf. UCC 2–311(3). At the very least, B is excused from any contractual duty to pay the price. See Consolidated Boiler Corp. v. Bogue Electric Co., 141 N.J. Equity 550, 561–64, 58 A.2d 759, 766–68 (1948). In addition, A's unjustified cancellation is a repudiation which entitles B to the appropriate remedies specified in UCC 2–711.

B. *Inspection in Documentary Deals*

Documentary sales were studied in Chapter Seventeen. Here we *focus* on their possible impact on the buyer's inspection rights.

Problem 18–2

Maple Woods, Inc., a manufacturer, agreed to sell 10 dining room sets to Rosen's Furniture, a retail business located 1,000 miles away in the city of Baker.

(1) If the contract said nothing of mode of payment or inspection, but Maple Woods, worried about Rosen's credit, shipped the goods "under reservation" by procuring a non-negotiable bill of lading naming itself as consignee, UCC 2–505(1)(b), would this be a breach of contract? Would it "alter" Rosen's right to inspect? UCC 2–310(b) and 2–513(1) and (3). What if Maple Woods shipped C.O.D.? Would the carrier allow inspection before payment? Are there two contracts here: one between Maple Woods and the carrier, and one between Maple Woods and Rosen's?

(2) If the contract called for Rosen's to pay against a sight draft with bill of lading (negotiable) attached, would Rosen's be entitled to inspect before payment? Would it make any difference that the goods happened to arrive in Baker ahead of the documents? UCC 2–513 and Comment 5.

(3) If the documents were in due form but the goods had been destroyed by fire while in the carrier's possession and Rosen's knew this, could it dishonor the sight draft without breaching the contract?

In Chapter Seventeen we saw that the seller realizes several advantages via use of the "sight draft with negotiable bill of lading" technique. Can he retain any of these and still allow inspection before payment? Buyers can bargain to have seller stamp the bill of lading, even a negotiable one "inspection allowed." Here the carrier would still retain control on behalf of the shipper-seller. Another way the buyer might try to protect himself is via so-called "third-party inspection", which is the subject of the next case.

BARTLETT & CO., GRAIN v. MERCHANTS CO.

United States Court of Appeals, Fifth Circuit, 1963.
323 F.2d 501, 7 A.L.R.3d 541.

WISDOM, CIRCUIT JUDGE.

This action is for breach of contract. The subject of the contract is a barge load of corn which, according to official inspection certificates, was one grade when shipped and two very different grades when it reached its destination. As we see it, the case turns on the construction of a contract which contains two apparently inconsistent provisions. The overall issue is whether the loss should fall on the purchaser or the seller. The district court decided in favor of the buyer. We reverse and remand.

The Merchants Company, and buyer and appellee, is a Mississippi corporation. As the Vicksburg Terminal Division, it is in the business of buying and selling grains. As the Valley Mills Division it manufactures feeds. Bartlett and Company, the seller and appellant, is a Missouri Corporation which maintains grain storage facilities in six mid-western states, including terminal elevators on the Missouri River at Nebraska City, Nebraska. Its general offices are in Kansas City, Missouri.

Merchants contracted through a broker to purchase from Bartlett four barge loads of No. 2 yellow corn. The terms and conditions of sale are found in three documents: (1) a confirmation order from Bartlett to Valley Mills (Merchants); (2) a confirmation order from the broker to both parties; and (3) a confirmation of purchase from Valley Mills (Merchants), signed "accepted" by B.O. Cottier, Bartlett's official secretary in charge of merchandising. The contract called for four barges of No. 2 yellow corn at 5¼ cents under the Chicago July option, F.O.B. the buyer's barges, "*If seller elects to load at Nebraska City 'In Barge' Official Weights & Grades to Govern.*" Merchant's confirmation order, accepted by Bartlett's representative, contained the following clause: "Mark bills of lading 'inspection allowed'. If draft is paid at sight, *we do not waive our right to reject shipment in event quality proves to be below contract grade.*"

Bartlett loaded four double-skin barges, furnished by the buyer, at Nebraska City, Nebraska, on June 19, 1959. The grain in only one of these barges, ABL–2519, is involved in this dispute. That barge was examined at Nebraska City by a federally licensed grain inspector, who, on the date the loading was completed, certified that the barge contained No. 2 yellow corn. Meanwhile, since Merchants had sold four barges of No. 2 yellow corn to O.J. Walls in Guntersville, Alabama, Merchants routed the barges to Guntersville and applied the grain in barge ABL–2519 on the Walls contract. While the barge was in transit from Nebraska City to Guntersville, Merchants paid Bartlett for the grain by draft with the bill of lading attached.

The grain arrived in Guntersville on July 7, Walls first discovered it to be partly "overheating and musty" on July 13. He refused to accept it, since it was below contract grade, and he called for a federal appeal grade inspection. At this inspection, on July 16, 1959, it was certified that approximately 17,000 bushels of the corn in barge ABL–2519 were No. 1 yellow corn and approximately 15,000 bushels were sample grade yellow corn. Walls agreed to handle the barge for Merchants's account and accordingly unloaded, trucked, dried, turned, stored, and again trucked the grain. For these services he charged $7,164.61 and deducted that amount from Merchants's invoice. Both parties to this action agree that these charges were excessive, but Merchants contends that no one else was available to perform the services.

Merchants then sued Bartlett, seeking $7,164.61 for breach of contract and $5,000 in punitive damages. The suit was originally brought in a Mississippi state court as an attachment in chancery (a quasi-in rem action) by attaching Bartlett's deposits in a Mississippi bank. The suit was removed to the United States District Court for the Southern District of Mississippi where it was tried before the court without a jury. The district court found that the grain inspection certificate of June 19, 1959, at Nebraska City "was erroneous and inaccurate"; that it was "not fair * * * and failed to reveal the true condition in this barge on the date of shipment."

The district court found that an inescapable inference from the evidence * * * [is] that barge was loaded in Nebraska City with an excessive amount of molded wheat which contaminated the cargo and accounted for the unsalable condition at Guntersville." The court held that Merchants was not bound by the certificate's recitals, because of the clause in Merchants's purchase confirmation, accepted by Bartlett, giving the buyer the right to reject shipment in the event that the quality proved to be below contract grade. The court awarded damages in the amount of $6,500 with six per cent interest from July 3, 1959, against the funds in the hands of the resident bank. The suit was dismissed as to Bartlett personally for lack of in personam jurisdiction. The court declined to award punitive damages, since the court found no evidence of gross negligence, willfulness, or oppressiveness on the part of the seller.

On appeal, Bartlett makes two major contentions. First, Bartlett contends that there is no evidence the grain in barge ABL–2519 was other than No. 2 yellow corn when it left Nebraska City in the buyer's barge. Second, the official grade certificate at origin should have been conclusive under the terms of the sale agreement, in the absence of gross neglect or willful wrongdoing.

[The Court determined that the law of Missouri governed.]

* * *

I. THE BUYER'S RIGHT TO INSPECT

A buyer dealing with a distant vendor and purchasing goods of a specified quality without first seeing them has a right to inspect them upon receipt. * * * And, in the absence of any contractual provision to the contrary, the buyer may reject an F.O.B. shipment at destination. * * * But the parties may agree instead to abide by the judgment of another, and that judgment, if honestly exercised, is binding on the buyer. * * * The buyer cannot thereafter substitute his own inspection for that conducted by the third party.

* * *

Such an inspection is held to have a conclusive effect even if there is no express provision in the contract that it shall be final. * * *

The contract in question here provides that " 'in barge' official weights & grades" are to govern—if the shipment is made from Nebraska City. But—if the shipment is made from Omaha, although "official in 'in barge' grades" still govern, "*destination official weights*" are to govern. Thus, the contract is drawn to distinguish between an inspection where the grain is loaded and an inspection at its destination. An inspection at the destination is to determine the *weight,* if the grain is loaded at Omaha. That is the only circumstance in which a destination inspection is to control. The terms of the contract therefore required that the transaction be governed by the origin *grades and weights,* since the grain was shipped from Nebraska City.

As we noted, where an inspection by a third party is stipulated, it supersedes the buyer's right to inspect. Merchants, however, seeks to avoid this result by urging that the clause in its printed form contract, which was accepted by Bartlett's agent, gave it the right to inspect at destination and to reject the shipment if the *quality* proved to be below the specified grade at the destination. This interpretation of the contract would nullify the provision for inspection at origin. The obvious purpose of that inspection at origin was to establish a certain, reliable, and objective standard at a fixed place and time to give the transaction certainty. It would serve little use to have this inspection if the buyer were free to accept or reject the shipment after its arrival on the basis of its own inspection at destination. To the extent then that the *printed* clause in the contract may be interpreted to allow Merchants the right, for which it contends, to reject on the basis of its own destination inspection, it is inconsistent with the *typewritten* clause providing for one official inspection at origin. In such case the typed portions prevail. * * *

The contract before us, however, may be construed so as to reconcile the two clauses and thus satisfy the very sensible canon of construction requiring that effect be given to all terms of the contract. The typed clause provides that official grades are to govern, whereas the printed clause, upon which Merchants relies, reserves to it the "right to reject shipment *in event* quality proves to be below contract grade." (Emphasis supplied.) This gives Merchants the right to reject, *if* the quality does not satisfy the contractual requirements; it does not give Merchants the right to determine *whether* the quality measures up to the standard specified. Thus Merchants could reject the grain, if the grade given it by the Nebraska City inspector proved to be lower than that specified in the contract, but the reservation clause does not give it the power to ascertain the grade independently of the origin inspection. Furthermore, this reserved right to reject is expressly conditioned on the draft being paid at sight. Since it is possible that the draft would be paid before receipt of the inspection certificate, this is a reasonable provision. It simply avoids any question that payment of the sight draft might be deemed a waiver of the right to reject the shipment. See Ryder & Brown Co. v. E. Lissberger Co., 1938, 300 Mass. 438, 15 N.E.2d 441, 118 A.L.R. 521, 525–526, in which the court assumed that the right to reject is lost when the title passes to the buyer on payment of a sight draft.

The testimony of Merchants's agent shows that in the customary dealings in the trade lower prices are fixed on condition that there is no right to reject on the basis of a destination inspection when the grain is inspected at origin. Mr. Harriss, Merchants's manager, agreed that Mr. Walls, who received the shipment in Alabama and bought on the same terms as Merchants, had no right to inspect the shipment at Guntersville. Moreover, the broker testified that his confirmation order showed the entire arrangement between the two parties; that it contained no right to reject. We hold, therefore, that Merchants did not have any right to reject the shipment destination on the basis of inspection at destination.

* * *

[The Court reversed the Judgment of the district court and remanded the case for the trial court to ascertain whether there existed fraud, bad faith, or gross mistake amounting to fraud which would warrant setting the inspection certificate aside.]

Notes

1. Considering the legal effect of third-party inspection, what commercial interests of either seller or buyer are protected by establishing such procedures and insuring their finality? Is UCC 2–515 relevant to this problem?

2. If the buyer has paid before inspecting the goods and, after discovering a nonconformity when the goods arrive, brings suit to recover the price and damages for breach of warranty, who has the burden of proving the condition of the goods at the time loaded on the barges, the buyer-plaintiff or the seller-defendant? Suppose the goods have been totally destroyed in transit without the fault of the buyer, who thereafter claims that they did not conform at the time of tender by the seller. Under the UCC, the critical time is at "tender of delivery." UCC 2–725(2), 2–503(2), 2–504, 2–509(1), and UCC 2–510(1). While UCC 2–607(4) provides that the "burden is on the buyer to establish any breach with respect to the goods accepted," there is no specific allocation for other situations. Under the Uniform Sales Act, the principal antecedent of Article Two, the burden was placed upon the party seeking affirmative relief here, the buyer. Glanzer v. J.K. Armsby Co., 100 Misc. 476, 165 N.Y.S. 1006 (S.Ct.1917). This result has been criticized in cases where the goods have been lost in transit: "In the situation where the goods are completely destroyed while in transit, the seller alone will know the facts about conformity. Where the seller delivers the goods which do not conform to the contract and the buyer has not impliedly approved them by acceptance, the seller by virtue of experience in fulfilling the terms of the contract will be better able to sustain the burden of proof in an action for non-

delivery. But where the buyer has refused to accept the goods and has sold them justifiably on behalf of the seller, the facts on conformity are then peculiarly within the knowledge of the buyer." Note, 20 U.Chi.L.Rev. 125, 130 (1952). Do you agree? Should the concern over proper burden of proof allocation be influenced by the feasibility and availability of third-party inspection at the point of shipment as with many agricultural commodities? See S–Creek Ranch, Inc. v. Monier & Co., 509 P.2d 777 (Wyo.1973) (buyer must prove goods defective at time risk of loss was to pass).

C. *Inspection in Overseas Transactions*

This chapter has focused upon the relationship between the buyer's "right" of inspection and his "duty" to accept the goods and pay the contract price. In non-credit domestic transactions under the UCC where a shipment is under an f.o.b. term, the buyer has no right to inspect before payment unless otherwise agreed where the contract calls for payment against documents of title. UCC 2–513(3). The reverse is true in overseas sales where greater shipping distances delay even more the seller's ability to receive payment. Accordingly, the usual practice, reflected in the cases and the Revised American Foreign Trade Definitions of 1941, is that unless otherwise agreed the buyer must pay against documents of title even though the goods are still in the middle of the ocean. See E. Clemens Horst Co. v. Biddel Bros., (1912) A.C. 18. While the buyer must wait until the goods arrive to inspect, he can discount the documents of title or use them as collateral to obtain a loan if the delay puts him under a financial strain. This approach is reflected in the UCC when shipment, whether domestic or overseas, is on a C.I.F. or C & F basis. The UCC seems to rely upon use of the shipping term C.I.F. or C & F to establish the seller's right to payment and does not clearly state whether the usual practice would apply in an overseas sale under a different shipping term. See UCC 2–320(4) and 2–321(3). The Final Act of the United Nations Conference on Contracts for the International Sale of Goods, approved in Vienna in 1980, provides that the buyer is "not bound to pay the price until he has had an opportunity to examine the goods, unless procedures for delivery or payment agreed upon by the parties are inconsistent with his having such an opportunity." Article 58(3). But Article 58(2) states that if the contract involves "carriage of the goods, the seller may dispatch the goods on terms whereby the goods, or documents controlling their disposition, will not be handed over to the buyer except against payment of the price." These and other issues are well treated in J. Honnold, Uniform Law for International Sales 333–39 (1982). The United States Senate ratified the United Nations Convention on Contracts for the International Sale of Goods on December 11, 1986. The treaty becomes effective on January 1, 1988.

A common practice in international sales, however, is for the seller to obtain payment contemporaneously with shipment of the goods. This is accomplished through a letter of credit. In essence, the buyer (customer) obtains from a bank (issuer) a promise for the benefit of the seller (beneficiary) that it will honor a draft drawn on it upon presentation of required documents and compliance with other terms in the letter of credit, which has been sent to the seller. See UCC 5–102(1)(a) and 5–103(1). This is a "documentary" credit which is normally irrevocable. See UCC 5–106(2). Thus, the issuing bank on behalf of the buyer agrees to pay the price against documents presented by the seller shortly after those documents have been issued by the carrier, and usually at the place where the goods have been shipped. While this device does not preclude the buyer's right of inspection when the goods arrive, UCC 5–114(1) provides that the issuing bank cannot dishonor the seller's demand which complies with the credit even though the goods or the documents do not conform with the underlying contract for sale. Compare UCC 2–512. An important case testing the scope of inspection in a transaction using a letter of credit is Banco Espanol de Credito v. State Street Bank & T. Co., 385 F.2d 230 (1st Cir.1967).

SECTION 3. BUYER'S RIGHT TO REJECT THE GOODS

A. *Introduction: Rejection Under Pre-Code Law*

If a promisor's tendered performance conforms in every way to the contract, the buyer must accept and pay for it or break the contract. UCC 2–507(1). Conversely, if the promisor repudiates the contract or fails to tender any performance at all, the promisee is excused from rendering any return performance and, since the promisor's breach is material, may cancel the contract and pursue appropriate remedies. But suppose that the promisor tenders some but not all of the promised performance and then fails to complete the job. Under what circumstances can the promisee seize upon the defective performance as a ground for avoiding any contractual duty to pay for work actually done?

In construction and personal service contracts where, in the absence of agreement to the contrary, the duty to pay is "constructively" conditioned upon completion of all or part of the work, it is usually said that the constructive condition is satisfied by "substantial" performance. See Patterson, *Constructive Conditions in Contracts,* 42 Colum.L.Rev. 903 (1942). Stated another way, if the promisor's defective performance is not material, the promisee must pay for the work at the contract price, adjusted for any damages caused by the breach. Who can forget Judge Cardozo's "sermon" in the classic case of Jacob & Youngs v. Kent, 230 N.Y. 239, 129 N.E. 889 (1921): "The transgressor whose default is unintentional and trivial may hope for mercy if he will offer atonement for his wrong." Since the promisor has rendered an expensive performance which, in many cases, has conferred benefits upon the promisee and is extremely difficult to return, the substantial performance doctrine blunts the rigors of constructive conditions by limiting the promisee's ability to avoid liability under the contract. According to Restatement, Contracts § 275 (1932) and Restatement (Second) of Contracts § 241, whether the promisee can treat the non-performance as material will depend upon several factors: the extent to which the injured party will obtain the substantial benefits which he could reasonably have anticipated; the extent to which the injured party may be adequately compensated in damages for lack of complete performance; the greater or less hardship on the party failing to perform in terminating the contract; the willful, negligent, or innocent behavior of the party failing to perform, and the greater or less uncertainty that the party failing to perform will perform the remainder of the contract. In short, the question is whether the non-performance substantially impairs the value of the bargain to the promisee. If more than substantial performance is desired, the services of an architect or third party expert can be employed. His refusal to issue a certificate or give approval until the specifications are met expressly conditions the promisee's duty to pay and is final and conclusive unless fraudulent or made in bad faith. See Restatement (Second) of Contracts § 227, Ill. No. 5.

In contracts for the sale of goods, however, pre-code law generally held that the doctrine of "substantial" performance is not applicable. See J.W. Anderson & Co., Inc. v. Tomlinson Chair Mfg. Co., Inc., 206 N.C. 42, 172 S.E. 538 (1934); Note, 33 Colum.L.Rev. 1021 (1933). This position can be justified on the following grounds. When a buyer rejects a defective tender by a seller, he does not retain any of the goods without payment. Even though the seller has invested time and expense in obtaining the goods and preparing the tender, upon rejection he still has the goods and may dispose of them elsewhere. Since the element of unjust enrichment present in construction and various other contracts is absent in such a sale of goods case, it makes some sense to put the responsibility for making a perfect tender upon the seller rather than getting involved in a complicated evaluation of objective and subjective factors which underlie the substantial performance doctrine. At the very least if the seller has in fact made a defective tender and the buyer's dissatisfaction is honest and genuine, there seems to be less reason for invoking the doctrine of substantial performance to limit the power to reject.

This justification was reflected, to a large degree, in the Uniform Sales Act, especially where the seller had breached a warranty of quality, USA §§ 12 & 69(1), or had tendered less than the quantity called for by the contract, USA § 44. See Prescott & Co. v. Powles & Co., 113 Wash. 177, 193 P. 680 (1920) (general rule is that the delivery of goods under an executory contract must be of the exact quantity ordered). However, more concern for the interests of the seller was expressed where the non-conformity merely involved delay or the manner of shipment or delivery. See 2 Williston, Sales §§ 452a–453e (rev. ed. 1948). Cf. Continental Grain Co. v. Simpson Feed Co., Inc., 102 F.Supp. 354 (E.D. Ark.1951), affirmed 199 F.2d 284 (8th Cir.1952). This concern was heightened when the delay or defect caused no measurable damage and the facts strongly suggested that the buyer had seized upon the non-conformity as a reason to avoid an unprofitable bargain or to take advantage of a price break. See LeRoy Dyal Co. v. Allen, 161 F.2d 152, 153–56 (4th Cir.1947) (rejection improper under both the common law and the Perishable Agricultural Commodities Act). As a result, there was some criticism of the so-called "perfect tender" rule under pre-Code law. Honnold, *Buyer's Right of Rejection*, 97 U.Pa.L.Rev. 457 (1949). We will now see that the Code cuts back the perfect tender rule rather dramatically.

B. *Scope of Rejection Right Under the Code*

Suppose a buyer, in the exercise of his inspection right, discovers some defect in the seller's tender of delivery—a defect in quality or quantity, delay, an improper tender or documents not in due form. Assume further that this defect is relatively insignificant. May the buyer reject the goods, thus avoiding the contract, or must he accept them with an appropriate adjustment in the contract price? As we have seen, this is an important question. If rejection is effective the goods remain at the seller's risk, UCC 2–510(1), and the buyer may pursue appropriate remedies under UCC 2–711 as if no tender had been made. If rejection would be ineffective and acceptance required, title and risk of loss would upon acceptance pass to the buyer who must pay for the goods at the contract rate, subject to any adjustment for the nonconformity. UCC 2–607(1), 2–714, 2–717. If the buyer improperly rejects, the seller may pursue appropriate remedies under UCC 2–703. See UCC 2–301, 2–602(3).

UCC 2–601 provides that unless the breach is of an installment contract or there is agreement to the contrary, "if the goods or the tender of delivery fail in any respect to conform to the contract, the buyer may (a) reject the whole; or (b) accept the whole; or (c) accept any commercial unit or units and reject the rest." Thus the Code in 2–601 appears to adopt a "perfect tender" rule regardless of the nature of the defect or its impact upon the buyer, subject only to agreement, special rules for installment contracts, UCC 2–612(3) and the buyer's option to accept part or all of the goods. See Moulton Cavity & Mold, Inc. v. Lyn-Flex

Indus., Inc., 396 A.2d 1024 (Me.1979) (trial court erred in charge that UCC 2–601 was satisfied by "substantial performance"). And it is true that the Permanent Editorial Board of the UCC declined to follow a recommendation that the buyer's right to reject be limited to cases of material breach. The Board's reasons were that the buyer should not be required to guess at his peril whether a breach is material and that proof of materiality would sometimes require disclosure of the buyer's private affairs, such as trade secrets and processes. Without more, it might seem that the only other limit upon the rejection remedy is the possibility that a buyer will not discover the non-conformity until after acceptance. In that event, the buyer can revoke his acceptance only if the non-conformity of the lot or unit "substantially impairs its value to him." UCC 2–608(1). But we will now introduce other important limits.

Problem 18–3

The Case of the Lady Dove Tomatoes

Sodfill, Inc., is a grower of vegetables and Blurtaste Co. is a manufacturer of catsup. On April 1, the parties entered into a written contract for the sale of 1,000 bushels of Lady Dove tomatoes at $4.50 per bushel, to be shipped f.o.b. point of shipment on or before July 15 and delivered to Blurtaste in "green" condition, a term having definite meaning in the trade. The goods were to be delivered in a single lot and payment was to be made 30 days after the goods were received. Nothing was said in the agreement about rejection. Assuming that there is no evidence regarding the impact upon the value of the bargain, could Blurtaste properly reject all of the goods in the following circumstances:

1. a timely tender of 990 bushels of "green" Lady Doves;
2. a timely tender of 1,000 bushels of tomatoes, 10 of which did not contain "green" Lady Doves;
3. a tender of 1,000 bushels of "green" Lady Doves which were shipped on July 16;
4. a tender of 1,000 bushels of "green" Lady Doves which were shipped on July 14 but, because of an erroneous delivery instruction by Sodfill, did not arrive until 3 days after the normal time for shipment had expired (see UCC 2–504 & 2–614).
5. Could Blurtaste accept 500 bushels of good tomatoes and reject 500 bushels of bad without incurring liability for the whole? See UCC 2–601, 2–105(6).
6. Suppose Sodfill agreed to ship 500 bushels by July 15 and the balance by August 1, payment to be made by September 1. Could the buyer reject if the first tender was: 10 bushels short; 1% off on quality; shipped 1 day late? See UCC 2–612.
7. If you represented Sodfill, what sort of clause would you draft to limit or eliminate the buyer's rejection right under UCC 2–601? How could you insure that it became part of the contract?

1. Good Faith as a Limit on the Right to Reject

Suppose in the case of Sodfill v. Blurtaste the seller is able to establish that the real reason for the buyer's rejection is a drop in the market price of tomatoes to $3.00 per bushel. If the buyer assigns as a reason for rejection an insubstantial breach by the seller, has he violated the obligation of good faith imposed by UCC 1–203 on the "performance or enforcement" of "every contract or duty within this Act?" It has been suggested that a buyer will "often try to escape from a performance quite within the business understanding of the contract, though not quite the legal, if he finds either that he can purchase the very same goods at a cheaper price on the open market or that his resale market has all but disappeared." The desire to avoid losses or to make greater profits "overcomes the possible desire to be a 'squareshooter' and to shoulder his part of that risk of price fluctuation which any present contract for future delivery carries, both for the seller and for the buyer." Eno, *Price Movement and Unstated Objections to the Defective Performance of Sales Contracts,* 44 Yale L.J. 782, 801 (1935). According to Judge Learned Hand, in this setting "such words as * * * 'good faith' appear to us to obscure the issue. The promisor may in fact be satisfied with the performance, but not with the bargain, in which case, of course, he must pay. * * *" Thompson-Starrett Co. v. La Belle Iron Works, 17 F.2d 536, 541 (2d Cir.1927). But is the conclusion one which a court should reach under the UCC? If so, does this cut down the Code's "perfect tender" rule in 2–601?

NEUMILLER FARMS, INC. v. CORNETT

Supreme Court of Alabama, 1979.
368 So.2d 272.

SHORES, JUSTICE.

Jonah D. Cornett and Ralph Moore, Sellers, were potato farmers in DeKalb County, Alabama. Neumiller Farms, Inc., Buyer, was a corporation engaged in brokering potatoes from the growers to the makers of potato chips. The controversy concerns Buyer's rejection of nine loads of potatoes out of a contract calling for twelve loads. A jury returned a verdict of $17,500 for Sellers based on a breach of contract. Buyer appealed. We affirm.

From the evidence, the jury could have found the following:

On March 3, 1976, the parties signed a written contract whereby Sellers agreed to deliver twelve loads of chipping potatoes to Buyer during July and August, 1976, and Buyer agreed to pay $4.25 per hundredweight. The contract required that the potatoes be United States Grade No. 1 and "chipt [sic] to buyer satisfaction." As the term was used in this contract, a load of potatoes contains 430 hundredweight and is valued at $1,827.50.

Sellers' potato crop yielded twenty to twenty-four loads of potatoes and Buyer accepted three of these loads without objection. At that time, the market price of chipping potatoes was $4.25 per hundredweight. Shortly thereafter, the market price declined to $2.00 per hundredweight.

When Sellers tendered additional loads of potatoes, Buyer refused acceptance, saying the potatoes would not "chip" satisfactorily. Sellers responded by having samples of their crop tested by an expert from the Cooperative Extension Service of Jackson County, Alabama, who reported that the potatoes were suitable in all respects. After receiving a letter demanding performance of the contract, Buyer agreed to "try one more load." Sellers then tendered a load of potatoes which had been purchased from another grower, Roy Hartline. Although Buyer's agent had recently purchased potatoes from Hartline at $2.00 per hundredweight, he claimed dissatisfaction with potatoes from the same fields when tendered by Sellers at $4.25 per hundredweight. Apparently the jury believed this testimony outweighed statements by Buyer's agents that Sellers' potatoes were diseased and unfit for "chipping."

Subsequently, Sellers offered to purchase the remaining nine loads of potatoes from other growers in order to fulfill their contract. Buyer's agent refused this offer, saying "* * * 'I'm not going to accept any more of your potatoes. If you load any more I'll see that they're turned down.' * * * 'I can buy potatoes all day for $2.00.'" No further efforts were made by Sellers to perform the contract.

At the time of Buyer's final refusal, Sellers had between seventeen and twenty-one loads of potatoes unharvested in their fields. Approximately four loads were sold in Chattanooga, Tennessee; Atlanta, Georgia; and local markets in DeKalb County. Sellers' efforts to sell their potato crop to other buyers were hampered by poor market conditions. Considering all of the evidence, the jury could properly have found that Sellers' efforts to sell the potatoes, after Buyer's final refusal to accept delivery, were reasonable and made in good faith.

This case presents three questions: 1) Was Buyer's refusal to accept delivery of Sellers' potatoes a breach of contract? 2) If so, what was the proper measure of Sellers' damages? and 3) Was the $17,500 jury verdict within the amount recoverable by Sellers under the proper measure of damages?

§ 7-2-703, Code of Alabama 1975 (UCC), specifies an aggrieved seller may recover for a breach of contract "Where the buyer *wrongfully* rejects * * * goods * * *" (Emphasis added.) We must determine whether there was evidence from which the jury could find that the Buyer acted wrongfully in rejecting delivery of Sellers' potatoes.

A buyer may reject delivery of goods if either the goods or the tender of delivery fails to conform to the contract. § 7-2-601, Code of Alabama 1975. In the instant case, Buyer did not claim the tender was inadequate. Rather, Buyer asserted the potatoes failed to conform to the requirements of the contract; i.e., the potatoes would not chip to buyer satisfaction.

The law requires such a claim of dissatisfaction to be made in good faith, rather than in an effort to escape a bad bargain. Shelton v. Shelton, 238 Ala. 489, 192 So. 55 (1939); Jones v. Lanier, 198 Ala. 363, 73 So. 535 (1916); Electric Lighting Co. v. Elder Bros., 115 Ala. 138, 21 So. 983 (1896).

Buyer, in the instant case, is a broker who deals in farm products as part of its occupation and, therefore, is a "merchant" with respect to its dealings in such goods. § 7-2-104, Code of Alabama 1975. In testing the good faith of a merchant, § 7-2-103, Code of Alabama 1975, requires "* * * honesty in fact and the observance of reasonable commercial standards of fair dealing in the trade." A claim of dissatisfaction by a merchant-buyer of fungible goods must be evaluated using an objective standard to determine whether the claim is made in good faith. Because there was evidence that the potatoes would "chip" satisfactorily, the jury was not required to accept Buyer's subjective claim to the contrary. A rejection of goods based on a claim of dissatisfaction, which is not made in good faith, is ineffectual and constitutes a breach of contract for which damages are recoverable.

We next consider the proper measure of damages under the UCC. * * * [The court held that the jury verdict on damages was compatible with UCC 2-708(2) and that the judgment should be affirmed.]

* * *

Questions

1. Did the court need to invoke an obligation of good faith or could the court simply have relied on UCC 2–601 and UCC 2–313? What was the relevant contract language?

2. How does the Code define and delineate obligations of good faith?

2. *The Seller's Right to Cure as a Limit on the Right to Reject*

UCC 2–508, in two circumstances, permits the seller to cure a defective tender and thus avoid the buyer's rejection remedy under 2–601. The first circumstance, stated in UCC 2–508(1), is fairly straightforward. If "the time for performance has not yet expired" and the buyer has rejected a non-conforming tender, the seller, "may seasonably notify the buyer of his intention to cure and may then within the contract time make a conforming delivery." Note that if the conditions of UCC 2–508(1) are met, the seller has the right to cure whether the buyer likes it or not. However, the buyer may not compel the seller to cure under any circumstances. If the buyer wants a defect corrected by the seller, his basic recourse is a negotiated agreement. Otherwise, he must reject and cover under UCC 2–712. One scholar has argued that UCC 2–508 should be repealed because it imposes inefficient legal restraints upon post-breach bargaining. Schwartz, *Cure and Revocation for Quality Defects: The Utility of Bargains,* 16 Bost.Coll.Indus. & Com.L.Rev. 543 (1975).

There are some notable variations on this theme. Many manufacturers of complex, expensive goods seek, with the help of retailers, to make a single warranty that the goods are "free from defects in material and workmanship" and to limit the remedy for breach of that warranty to "repair or replacement" of defects. If these efforts are successful, the buyer must permit the seller to cure and may not reject the goods under UCC 2–601 or revoke acceptance under UCC 2–608. See UCC 2–719.

The second circumstance, found in UCC 2–508(2), is undoubtedly explained by the fact that many defective tenders are quite within the business understanding of the contract though not quite the legal. Here, the seller ought to have a chance to cure even though the time for performance has expired. But when does a seller have "reasonable grounds" to believe that his non-conforming tender will be acceptable to the seller?

T.W. OIL, INC. v. CONSOLIDATED EDISON CO. OF NEW YORK, INC.

Court of Appeals of New York, 1982.
57 N.Y.2d 574, 457 N.Y.S.2d 458, 443 N.E.2d 932.

OPINION OF THE COURT

FUCHSBERG, JUDGE.

In the first case to wend its way through our appellate courts on this question, we are asked, in the main, to decide whether a seller who, acting in good faith and without knowledge of any defect, tenders nonconforming goods to a buyer who properly rejects them, may avail itself of the cure provision of subdivision (2) of section 2–508 of the Uniform Commercial Code. We hold that, if seasonable notice be given, such a seller may offer to cure the defect within a reasonable period beyond the time when the contract was to be performed so long as it has acted in good faith and with a reasonable expectation that the original goods would be acceptable to the buyer.

The factual background against which we decide this appeal is based on either undisputed proof or express findings at Trial Term. In January, 1974, midst the fuel shortage produced by the oil embargo, the plaintiff (then known as Joc Oil USA, Inc.) purchased a cargo of fuel oil whose sulfur content was represented to it as no greater than 1%. While the oil was still at sea en route to the United States in the tanker *M T Khamsin*, plaintiff received a certificate from the foreign refinery at which it had been processed informing it that the sulfur content in fact was .52%. Thereafter, on January 24, the plaintiff entered into a written contract with the defendant (Con Ed) for the sale of this oil. The agreement was for delivery to take place between January 24 and January 30, payment being subject to a named independent testing agency's confirmation of quality and quantity. The contract, following a trade custom to round off specifications of sulfur content at, for instance, 1%, .5% or .3%, described that of the *Khamsin* oil as .5%.[1] In the course of the negotiations, the plaintiff learned that Con Ed was then authorized to buy and burn oil with a sulfur content of up to 1% and would even mix oils containing more and less to maintain that figure.

When the vessel arrived, on January 25, its cargo was discharged into Con Ed storage tanks in Bayonne, New Jersey.[2] In due course, the independent testing people reported a sulfur content of .92%. On this basis, acting within a time frame whose reasonableness is not in question, on February 14 Con Ed rejected the shipment. Prompt negotiations to adjust the price failed; by February 20, plaintiff had offered a price reduction roughly responsive to the difference in sulfur reading, but Con Ed, though it could use the oil, rejected this proposition out of hand. It was insistent on paying no more than the latest prevailing price, which, in the volatile market that then existed, was some 25% below the level which prevailed when it agreed to buy the oil.

The very next day, February 21, plaintiff offered to cure the defect with a substitute shipment of conforming oil scheduled to arrive on the *S.S. Appollonian Victory* on February 28. Nevertheless, on February 22, the very day after the cure was proffered, Con Ed, adamant in its intention to avail itself of the intervening drop in prices, summarily rejected this proposal too. The two cargos were subsequently sold to third parties at the best price obtainable, first that of the *Appollonian* and, sometime later, after extraction from the tanks had been accomplished, that of the *Khamsin*.[3]

There ensued this action for breach of contract,[4] which, after a somewhat unconventional trial course, resulted in a nonjury decision for the plaintiff in the sum of $1,385,512.83, essentially the difference between the original contract price of $3,360,667.14 and the amount received by the plaintiff by way of resale of the *Khamsin* oil at what the court found as a matter of fact was a negotiated

1. Confirmatorily, Con Ed's brief describes .92% oil as "nominally" 1% oil.

2. The tanks already contained some other oil, but Con Ed appears to have had no concern over the admixture of the differing sulfur contents. In any event, the efficacy of the independent testing required by the contract was not impaired by the commingling.

3. Most of the *Khamsin* oil was drained from the tanks and sold at $10.75 per barrel. The balance was retained by Con Ed in its mixed form at $10.45 per barrel. The original price in January had been $17.875 per barrel.

4. The plaintiff originally also sought an affirmative injunction to compel Con Ed to accept the *Khamsin* shipment or, alternatively, the *Appollonian* substitute. However, when a preliminary injunction was denied on the ground that the plaintiff had an adequate remedy at law, it amended its complaint to pursue the latter remedy alone.

price which, under all the circumstances,[5] was reasonably procured in the open market. To arrive at this result, the Trial Judge, while ruling against other liability theories advanced by the plaintiff, which, in particular, included one charging the defendant with having failed to act in good faith in the negotiations for a price adjustment on the *Khamsin* oil (Uniform Commercial Code, § 1–203), decided as a matter of law that subdivision (2) of section 2–508 of the Uniform Commercial Code was available to the plaintiff even if it had no prior knowledge of the nonconformity. Finding that in fact plaintiff had no such belief at the time of the delivery, that what turned out to be a .92% sulfur content was "within the range of contemplation of reasonable acceptability" to Con. Ed., and that seasonable notice of an intention to cure was given, the court went on to hold that plaintiff's "reasonable and timely offer to cure" was improperly rejected (*sub nom. Joc Oil USA v. Consolidated Edison Co. of N.Y.*, 107 Misc.2d 376, 390, 434 N.Y.S.2d 623 [Shanley N. Egeth, J.]). The Appellate Division, 84 A.D.2d 970, 447 N.Y.S.2d 572, having unanimously affirmed the judgment entered on this decision, the case is now here by our leave (CPLR 5602, subd. [a], par. 1, cl. [i]).

In support of its quest for reversal, the defendant now asserts that the trial court erred (a) in ruling that the verdict on a special question submitted for determination by a jury was irrelevant to the decision of this case, (b) in failing to interpret subdivision (2) of section 2–508 of the Uniform Commercial Code to limit the availability of the right to cure after date of performance to cases in which the seller knowingly made a nonconforming tender and (c) in calculating damages on the basis of the resale of the nonconforming cargo rather than of the substitute offered to replace it. For the reasons which follow, we find all three unacceptable.

* * *

II

Issue

We turn then to the central issue on this appeal: Fairly interpreted, did subdivision (2) of section 2–508 of the Uniform Commercial Code require Con Ed to accept the substitute shipment plaintiff tendered? In approaching this question, we, of course, must remember that a seller's right to cure a defective tender, as allowed by both subdivisions of section 2–508, was intended to act as a meaningful limitation on the absolutism of the old perfect tender rule, under which, no leeway being allowed for any imperfections, there was, as one court put it, just "no room * * * for the doctrine of substantial performance" of commercial obligations (*Mitsubishi Goshi Kaisha v. Aron & Co.*, 16 F.2d 185, 186 [Learned Hand, J.]; see Note, Uniform Commercial Code, § 2–508; Seller's Right to Cure Non-Conforming Goods, 6 Rutgers—Camden L.J. 387–388).

In contrast, to meet the realities of the more impersonal business world of our day, the code, to avoid sharp dealing, expressly provides for the liberal construction of its remedial provisions (§ 1–102) so that "good faith" and the "observance of reasonable commercial standards of fair dealing" be the rule rather than the exception in trade (see § 2–103, subd. [1], par. [b]), "good faith" being defined as "honesty in fact in the conduct or transaction concerned" (Uniform Commercial Code, § 1–201, subd. [19]). As to section 2–508 in particular, the code's Official Comment advises that its mission is to safeguard the seller "against surprise as a result of sudden technicality on the buyer's part" (Uni-

5. These circumstances included the fact that the preliminary injunction was not denied until April so that, by the time the *Khamsin* oil was sold in May, almost three months had gone by since its rejection.

form Commercial Code, § 2–106, Comment 2; see, also, Peters, Remedies for Breach of Contracts Relating to the Sale of Goods under the Uniform Commercial Code: A Roadmap for Article Two, 73 Yale L.J. 199, 210; 51 N.Y.Jur., Sales, § 101, p. 41).

Section 2–508 may be conveniently divided between provisions for cure offered when "the time for performance has not yet expired" (subd. [1]), a precode concept in this State (*Lowinson v. Newman,* 201 App.Div. 266, 194 N.Y.S. 253), and ones which, by newly introducing the possibility of a seller obtaining "a further reasonable time to substitute a conforming tender" (subd. [2]), also permit cure beyond the date set for performance. In its entirety the section reads as follows:

"(1) Where any tender or delivery by the seller is rejected because non-conforming and the time for performance has not yet expired, the seller may seasonably notify the buyer of his intention to cure and may then within the contract time make a conforming delivery.

"(2) Where the buyer rejects a non-conforming tender which the seller had reasonable grounds to believe would be acceptable with or without money allowance the seller may if he seasonably notifies the buyer have a further reasonable time to substitute a conforming tender."

Since we here confront circumstances in which the conforming tender came after the time of performance, we focus on subdivision (2). On its face, taking its conditions in the order in which they appear, for the statute to apply (1) a buyer must have rejected a nonconforming tender, (2) the seller must have had reasonable grounds to believe this tender would be acceptable (with or without money allowance), and (3) the seller must have "seasonably" notified the buyer of the intention to substitute a conforming tender within a reasonable time.[7]

In the present case, none of these presented a problem. The first one was easily met for it is unquestioned that, at .92%, the sulfur content of the *Khamsin* oil did not conform to the .5% specified in the contract and that it was rejected by Con Ed. The second, the reasonableness of the seller's belief that the original tender would be acceptable, was supported not only by unimpeached proof that the contract's .5% and the refinery certificate's .52% were trade equivalents, but by testimony that, by the time the contract was made, the plaintiff knew Con Ed burned fuel with a content of up to 1%, so that, with appropriate price adjustment, the *Khamsin* oil would have suited its needs even if, at delivery, it was, to the plaintiff's surprise, to test out at .92%. Further, the matter seems to have been put beyond dispute by the defendant's readiness to take the oil at the reduced market price on February 20. Surely, on such a record, the trial court cannot be faulted for having found as a fact that the second condition too had been established.

As to the third, the conforming state of the *Appollonian* oil is undisputed, the offer to tender it took place on February 21, only a day after Con Ed finally had rejected the *Khamsin* delivery and the *Appollonian* substitute then already was en route to the United States, where it was expected in a week and did arrive on March 4, only four days later than expected. Especially since Con Ed pleaded no prejudice (unless the drop in prices could be so regarded), it is almost

7. Essentially a factual matter, "seasonable" is defined in subdivision (3) of section 1–204 of the Uniform Commercial Code as "at or within the time agreed or if no time is agreed at or within a reasonable time". At least equally factual in character, a "reasonable time" is left to depend on the "nature, purpose and circumstances" of any action which is to be taken (Uniform Commercial Code, § 1–204, subd. [2]).

impossible, given the flexibility of the Uniform Commercial Code definitions of "seasonable" and "reasonable" (n. 7, *supra*), to quarrel with the finding that the remaining requirements of the statute also had been met.

Thus lacking the support of the statute's literal language, the defendant nonetheless would have us limit its application to cases in which a seller *knowingly* makes a nonconforming tender which it has reason to believe the buyer will accept. For this proposition, it relies almost entirely on a critique in Nordstrom, Law of Sales (§ 105), which rationalizes that, since a seller who believes its tender is conforming would have no reason to think in terms of a reduction in the price of the goods, to allow such a seller to cure after the time for performance had passed would make the statutory reference to a money allowance redundant.[8] Nordstrom, interestingly enough, finds it useful to buttress this position by the somewhat dire prediction, though backed by no empirical or other confirmation, that, unless the right to cure is confined to those whose nonconforming tenders are knowing ones, the incentive of sellers to timely deliver will be undermined. To this it also adds the somewhat moralistic note that a seller who is mistaken as to the quality of its goods does not merit additional time (Nordstrom, *loc. cit.*). Curiously, recognizing that the few decisions extant on this subject have adopted a position opposed to the one for which it contends, Con Ed seeks to treat these as exceptions rather than exemplars of the rule (e.g., *Wilson v. Scampoli,* 228 A.2d 848 (D.C.App.) [goods obtained by seller from their manufacturer in original carton resold unopened to purchaser; seller held within statute though it had no reason to believe the goods defective]; *Appleton State Bank v. Lee,* 33 Wis.2d 690, 148 N.W.2d 1 [seller mistakenly delivered sewing machine of wrong brand but otherwise identical to one sold; held that seller, though it did not know of its mistake, had a right to cure by substitution]).[9]

That the principle for which these cases stand goes far beyond their particular facts cannot be gainsaid. These holdings demonstrate that, in dealing with the application of subdivision (2) of section 2–508, courts have been concerned with the reasonableness of the seller's belief that the goods would be acceptable rather than with the seller's pretender knowledge or lack of knowledge of the defect (*Wilson v. Scampoli, supra;* compare *Zabriskie Chevrolet v. Smith,* 99 N.J.Super. 441, 240 A.2d 195).

It also is no surprise then that the aforementioned decisional history is a reflection of the mainstream of scholarly commentary on the subject (e.g., 1955 Report of N.Y.Law Rev.Comm., p. 484; White & Summers, Uniform Commercial Code [2d ed.], § 8–4, p. 322; 2 Anderson, Uniform Commercial code [2d ed.], § 2–508:7; Hogan, The Highways and Some of the Byways in the Sales and Bulk

8. The premise for such an argument, which ignores the policy of the code to prevent buyers from using insubstantial remediable or price adjustable defects to free themselves from unprofitable bargains (Hawkland, Sales and Bulk Sales Under the Uniform Commercial Code, pp. 120–122), is that the words "with or without money allowance" apply only to sellers who believe their goods will be acceptable with such an allowance and not to sellers who believe their goods will be acceptable without such an allowance. But, since the words are part of a phrase which speaks of an otherwise unqualified belief that the goods will be acceptable, unless one strains for an opposite interpretation, we find insufficient reason to doubt that it intends to include both those who find a need to offer an allowance and those who do not.

9. The only New York case to deal with this section involved a seller who knowingly tendered a "newer and improved version of the model that was actually ordered" on the contract delivery date. The court held he had reasonable grounds to believe the buyer would accept the newer model (*Bartus v. Riccardi,* 55 Misc.2d 3, 284 N.Y.S.2d 222 [Utica City Ct., Hymes, J.]).

Sales Articles of the Uniform Commercial Code, 48 Cornell L.Q. 1, 12–13; Note, Uniform Commercial Code, § 2–508: Seller's Right to Cure Non-Conforming Goods, 6 Rutgers—Camden L.J. 387, 399; Note, Commercial Law—The Effect of the Seller's Right to Cure on the Buyer's Remedy of Rescission, 28 Ark.L.Rev. 297, 302–303).

White and Summers, for instance, put it well, and bluntly. Stressing that the code intended cure to be "a remedy which should be carefully cultivated and developed by the courts" because it "offers the possibility of conforming the law to reasonable expectations and of thwarting the chiseler who seeks to escape from a bad bargain" (*op. cit.,* at pp. 322–324), the authors conclude, as do we, that a seller should have recourse to the relief afforded by subdivision (2) of section 2–508 of the Uniform Commercial Code as long as it can establish that it had reasonable grounds, tested objectively, for its belief that the goods would be accepted (*ibid.,* at p. 321). It goes without saying that the test of reasonableness, in this context, must encompass the concepts of "good faith" and "commercial standards of fair dealing" which permeate the code (Uniform Commercial Code, § 1–201, subd. [19]; §§ 1–203, 2–103, subd. [1], par. [b]).[10]

As to the damages issue raised by the defendant, we affirm without reaching the merits. At no stage of the proceedings before the trial court did the defendant object to the plaintiff's proposed method for their calculation, and this though the plaintiff gave ample notice of that proposal by means of a preliminary statement and pretrial memorandum filed with the court. So complete was defendant's acquiescence in the theory thus advanced that the plaintiff was permitted to introduce its proof of the *Khamsin* resale alone, and without opposition. Furthermore, in consensually submitting the four jointly framed advisory questions that went to the jury, the language of one of them, which was damages-related, indicates that both parties were acting on the assumption that the *Khamsin* oil was the one with which the court was to be concerned. And, even after the decision at nisi prius revealed that the Judge had acted on such an assumption, so far as the record shows, no motion was ever made to correct it.

It has long been the law that agreement on a theory of damages at trial, even if only implied, must control on appeal (see *Martin v. City of Cohoes,* 37 N.Y.2d 162, 165–166, 371 N.Y.S.2d 687, 332 N.E.2d 867, *supra; Hartshorn v. Chaddock,* 135 N.Y. 116, 123, 31 N.E. 997; 10 Carmody-Wait 2d, N.Y.Prac., § 70:419, p. 690).

For all these reasons, the order of the Appellate Division should be affirmed, with costs.

COOKE, C.J., and JASEN, GABRIELLI, JONES, WACHTLER and MEYER, JJ., concur.

Order affirmed.

10. Except indirectly, on this appeal we do not deal with the equally important protections the code affords buyers. It is as to buyers as well as sellers that the code, to the extent that it displaces traditional principles of law and equity (§ 1–103), seeks to discourage unfair or hypertechnical business conduct bespeaking a dog-eat-dog rather than a live-and-let-live approach to the marketplace (e.g., §§ 2–314, 2–315, 2–513, 2–601, 2–608). Overall, the aim is to encourage parties to amicably resolve their own problems (*Ramirez v. Autosport,* 88 N.J. 277, 285, 440 A.2d 1345; compare Restatement, Contracts 2d, Introductory Note to chapter 10, p. 194 ["the wisest course is ordinarily for the parties to attempt to resolve their differences by negotiations, including clarification of expectations [and] cure of past defaults"]).

ZABRISKIE CHEVROLET, INC. v. SMITH

New Jersey Superior Court, Law Division, 1968.
99 N.J.Super. 441, 240 A.2d 195.

[Defendant purchased a new car from plaintiff, giving a check in full payment. One day later, defendant's wife took delivery of the car. Before she negotiated the 2½ miles home, the car developed transmission trouble and there was no question but that the transmission was defective upon delivery. Defendant stopped payment on the check and informed plaintiff that the sale was cancelled. Plaintiff picked up the car and replaced the transmission. Defendant refused to take the repaired car and commenced negotiations for a new car. However, these negotiations foundered when defendant insisted that the cancellation was effective and plaintiff, denying this, insisted that no credit on a new deal could be given. Plaintiff sued defendant on the check. The court first held that the car was substantially defective upon delivery and that plaintiff's effort to disclaim the implied warranty of merchantability was invalid under UCC 2–316(2). The court next held that defendant did not accept the goods because there was no reasonable opportunity to inspect, UCC 2–606(1)(b) and, even so, the facts supported a revocation of acceptance under UCC 2–608(1)].

* * *

There having been no acceptance, the next issue presented is whether defendant properly rejected under the Code. That he cancelled the sale and rejected the vehicle almost concomitantly with the discovery of the failure of his bargain is clear from the evidence. N.J.S. 12A:2–601, N.J.S.A. delineates the buyer's rights following nonconforming delivery and reads as follows:

> "Subject to the provisions of this Chapter on breach in installment contracts (12A:2–612) and unless otherwise agreed under the sections on contractual limitations of remedy (12A:2–712 and 2–719), if the goods or the tender of delivery *fail in any respect to conform* to the contract, the buyer may
>
> "(a) reject the whole; * * * " (Italics added)

Section 12A:2–602 indicates that one can reject after taking possession. Possession, therefore, does not mean acceptance and the corresponding loss of the right of rejection; nor does the fact that buyer has a security interest along with possession eliminate the right to reject.

> "(1) Rejection of goods must be within a reasonable time after their delivery or tender. It is ineffective unless the buyer seasonably notifies the seller.
>
> "(2) Subject to the provisions of the two following sections on rejected goods (12A:2–603 and 2–604).
>
> "(a) after rejection any exercise of ownership by the buyer with respect to any commercial unit is wrongful as against the seller; and
>
> "(b) if the buyer has before rejection taken *physical possession* of goods in which he does not have a *security* interest under the provisions of this Chapter (subsection (3) of 12A:2–711), he is under a duty after rejection to hold them with reasonable care at the seller's disposition for a time sufficient to permit the seller to remove them; but
>
> "(c) the buyer has no further obligations with regard to goods rightfully rejected." (Italics added)

N.J.S. 12A:2–106, N.J.S.A. defines conforming goods as follows:

> "(2) Goods or conduct including any part of a performance are "conforming" or conform to the contract when they are in accordance with the obligations under the contract."

The Uniform Commercial Code Comment to that section states:

> "2. Subsection (2): It is in general intended to continue the policy of requiring *exact performance* by the seller of his obligations as a condition to his right to require acceptance. However, the seller is in part safeguarded against surprise as a result of sudden technicality on the buyer's part by the provisions of Section 2–508 on seller's cure of improper tender or delivery. Moreover usage of trade frequently permits commercial leeways in performance and the language of the agreement itself must be read in the light of such custom or usage and also, prior course of dealing, and in a long term contract, the course of performance."

There was no evidence at the trial concerning any "custom or usage," although plaintiff in its brief argued that it is the usage of the automobile trade that a buyer accept a new automobile, although containing defects of manufacture, if such defects can be and are seasonably cured by the seller. Perhaps this represents prevailing views in the automobile industry which have, over the years, served to blanket injustices and inequities committed upon buyers who demurred in the light of the unequal positions of strength between the parties. The spirit of the Henningsen opinion, supra, contemplated these conditions which cried out for correction. In the present case we are not dealing with a situation such as was present in Adams v. Tramontin Motor Sales, 42 N.J.Super. 313, 126 A.2d 358 (App.Div.1956). In that case, brought for breach of implied warranty of merchantability, the court held that minor defects, such as adjustment of the motor, tightening of loose elements, fixing of locks and dome light, and a correction of rumbling noise, were not remarkable defects, and therefore there was no breach. Here the breach was substantial. The new car was practically inoperable and endowed with a defective transmission. This was a "remarkable defect" and justified rejection by the buyer.

Lastly, plaintiff urges that under the Code, N.J.S. 12A:2–508, N.J.S.A. it had a right to cure the nonconforming delivery. N.J.S. 12A:2–508, N.J.S.A. states:

> "(1) Where any tender or delivery by the seller is rejected because non-conforming, and the *time for performance has not yet expired,* the seller may seasonably notify the buyer of his intention to cure and may then within the contract time make a conforming delivery.
>
> "(2) Where the buyer rejects a non-conforming tender which the *seller had reasonable grounds to believe would be acceptable* with or without money allowance the seller may if he seasonably notifies the buyer have a further reasonable time to substitute a conforming tender." (Italics added)

The New Jersey Study Comment to 12A:2–508 reads:

> "3. Subsection 2–508(2) has been applauded as a rule aimed at ending 'forced breaches.' See, Hawkland, Sales and Bulk Sales Under the Uniform Commercial Code, 120–122 (1958). * * *
>
> "Section 2–508 prevents the buyer from forcing the seller to breach by making a surprise rejection of the goods because of some minor non-conformity at a time at which the seller cannot cure the deficiency within the time for performance."

The Uniform Commercial Code Comment to 12A:2–508 reads:

> "2. Subsection (2) seeks to avoid injustice to the seller by reason of a surprise rejection by the buyer. However, the seller is not protected unless he had 'reasonable grounds to believe' that the tender would be acceptable."

It is clear that in the instant case there was no "forced breach" on the part of the buyer, for he almost immediately began to negotiate for another automobile. The inquiry is as to what is intended by "cure," as used in the Code. This statute makes no attempt to define or specify what a "cure" shall consist of. It would appear, then, that each case must be controlled by its own facts. The "cure" intended under the cited section of the Code does not, in the court's opinion, contemplate the tender of a new vehicle with a substituted transmission, not from the factory and of unknown lineage from another vehicle in plaintiff's possession. It was not the intention of the Legislature that the right to "cure" is a limitless one to be controlled only by the will of the seller. A "cure" which endeavors by substitution to tender a chattel not within the agreement or contemplation of the parties is invalid.

For a majority of people the purchase of a new car is a major investment, rationalized by the peace of mind that flows from its dependability and safety. Once their faith is shaken, the vehicle loses not only its real value in their eyes, but becomes an instrument whose integrity is substantially impaired and whose operation is fraught with apprehension. The attempted cure in the present case was ineffective.

Accordingly, and pursuant to N.J.S. 12A:2–711, N.J.S.A., judgment is rendered on the main case in favor of defendant. On the counterclaim judgment is rendered in favor of defendant and against plaintiff in the sum of $124, being the amount of the deposit, there being no further proof of damages.

Defendant shall, as part of this judgment, execute for plaintiff, on demand, such documents as are necessary to again vest title to the vehicle in plaintiff.

McKENZIE v. ALLA–OHIO COALS, INC.

United States District Court, District of Columbia, 1979.
29 UCC Rep.Serv. 852, affirmed 610 F.2d 1000.

GASCH, DISTRICT JUDGE. This diversity action for breach of contract is before the court on cross-motions for summary judgment. Plaintiff contends that he is entitled to judgment in his favor because defendant wrongfully rejected coal shipped to it by plaintiff pursuant to their agreement. Plaintiff argues that the only remedy available to defendant was a reduction in the price of the coal, as set forth in a penalty clause contained in the purchase order. Defendant replies that the penalty clause was not the exclusive remedy, and that its timely rejection of the coal was fully justified. Plaintiff brought this action seeking recovery of approximately $7,000 as the difference between what defendant should have paid and what plaintiff received on resale. Plaintiff also seeks approximately $40,000 for the cost of demurrage and transporting the coal. Defendant counterclaimed for $800 in costs for inspecting the coal, and for compensatory and punitive damages for plaintiff's alleged misrepresentations made by plaintiff about delay and the quality of the coal.

BACKGROUND

Defendant Alla-Ohio is a coal broker who agreed to buy coal from plaintiff to resell to certain of its customers. The agreement resulted from oral negotiations over the telephone in June, 1977. During these negotiations, there was no discussion of possible penalties to be applied against deviations in the quality of the coal. On July 5, 1977, defendant sent to plaintiff a purchase order confirming the prior agreement, and specifying the order of 3,000 net tons of coal at an agreed price of $34.00 per net ton F.O.B. car. The letter-purchase order included the specification that the ash content of the coal not exceed 7.5%. The letter also stated: "Should the ash content exceed 7.5% dry, a penalty of $.80 per 1% of ash in excess of 7.5% shall be assessed, fractions in proportion." The letter also stipulated other specifications, including a Free Swelling Index (FSI) of "7 Min."

On or about July 21, 1977, plaintiff shipped 43 railroad cars containing approximately 3,000 tons of coal to Hampton Roads, Virginia for defendant. Plaintiff received defendant's July 5 letter-purchase order on July 25, 1977. The next day, plaintiff sent a reply to defendant, informing defendant that the purchase order did not conform to the oral understanding. Plaintiff also objected to the ash and FSI specifications, claiming 8% and 6, respectively, to be the correct standards. Plaintiff further objected to the penalty provisions, saying, "I consider this order to be incorrect and that all specifications on the coal should be on an as received basis." On July 28, 1977, defendant responded by asserting that the purchase order of July 5 was an accurate embodiment of the oral agreement. Defendant also noted that preliminary test results showed that the ash content of the coal was at least 13.5% and ranged upward. Plaintiff did not respond to the July 28 letter.

On August 15, 1977, defendant rejected the 43 railroad cars of coal, after completing tests of 42 of the cars. Plaintiff demanded that delivery be accepted but defendant refused. Subsequently, plaintiff found a buyer for the coal at a price of $26.74 per ton. The price defendant would have paid pursuant to the penalty clause in the purchase order would have been $29.20 per ton, according to plaintiff's calculation.

This case turns primarily on the issue of whether the penalty clause set out in the purchase order of July 5 was the exclusive remedy for defendant, or whether defendant was entitled to reject coal that did not conform to the specifications. There are, however, other matters which also must be untangled before resolution of the case may be achieved. Therefore, the court will undertake to examine the contentions of the parties roughly in chronological order.

I. The Contract and Its Terms

* * *

Under these circumstances, the court concludes that the contract between the parties contained penalty terms for excess ash content.

II. Limitation of Remedies

Plaintiff argues that the penalty clause was defendant's exclusive remedy in the event that the coal did not conform to the requirements of the contract, and that the parties did not intend to permit the "radical" remedy of rejection. * * * In the absence of an express indication in the writings of the parties, or a course of conduct clearly establishing use of only one kind of remedy, the court cannot conclude that the presumption that remedies be cumulative is overcome.

In addition, the UCC has codified the "perfect tender" rule of the common law,[2] and provides that goods not sold in installments may be rejected if they

2. See Priest, Breach and Remedy for the Tender of Nonconforming Goods under the Uniform Commercial Code: An Economic Approach, 91 Harv.L.Rev. 960 (1978). Although

"fail in any respect to conform to the contract." UCC § 2–601. There is substantial authority, however, that the perfect tender rule has been greatly diminished, and that, where a buyer has suffered no damage, he should not be allowed to reject goods because of an insubstantial nonconformity. See J. White and R. Summers, supra § 8–3 at 256–57, and cases cited therein. Assuming this approach to be the correct one, in this case the nonconformity was substantial. The July 5 purchase order specified that the ash content of the coal was not to exceed 7.5%. The coal delivered to defendant had ash content of at least 13.5% and up to 16%.[3] Moreover, the UCC provides that if the nonconformity will impair the value of the goods to the buyer because of the buyer's particular circumstances, he is entitled to reject the goods even though the seller had no advance knowledge of the circumstances. UCC § 2–608.[4] The coal ordered by defendant here was intended for use as metallugical coal. Metallurgical coal must be high quality coal and may have ash content no greater than 8%, or, for marginal grade metallurgical coal, no greater than 12%. See Defendant's Supplemental Memorandum at 9 n. 4. On the basis of the foregoing facts, the court concludes that the coal tendered by plaintiff did not conform substantially to the requirements of the contract. On that basis, defendant was entitled to reject the nonconforming coal.[5]

A troublesome question, however, is the potential capacity for the seller to cure a nonconforming performance. Under UCC § 2–508, a seller may cure after the time for performance has passed if (1) he had reasonable grounds to believe that a nonconforming tender would be acceptable, (2) he seasonably notifies the buyer of his intention to cure, and (3) he cures within a further reasonable time. Addressing these considerations, the court notes that it is unlikely that a reasonable seller in plaintiff's position would be ignorant of such drastic variances in the quality of the coal. Similarly, no evidence of trade custom in the record indicates that coal with such high ash content would be suitable for use as metallurgical coal, the purpose for which it was purchased. Therefore, the court finds that plaintiff did not have reasonable grounds for believing that a nonconforming tender would be acceptable. Furthermore, although there is evidence that plaintiff offered to take a reduced price for the coal, such attempted cure by price allowance is not one of the methods of cure approved by the UCC. See UCC § 2–508, Comment 4. Under all of these circumstances, then, plaintiff could make no effective cure short of tendering conforming coal. There was never any offer to do so, and defendant was justified in rejecting the high ash coal.

In sum, the contract between plaintiff and defendant did not limit the parties to accepting a price reduction for coal that did not meet the specifications for ash content that were imposed. The coal actually tendered deviated so substantially from the coal promised that defendant was entitled, after inspec-

plaintiff has suggested a novel economic analysis in conformance with the scholarly article cited above, the court declines plaintiff's invitation to undertake that approach on the facts presented.

3. See Letter from Ms. Ursula Mosby to Eugene McKenzie, July 28, 1977.

4. Although UCC § 2–608 governs revocations after acceptance of goods, and not rejection before acceptance, the analysis applicable to both §§ 2–608 and 2–601 is the same. See J. White and R. Summers, supra § 8–3, at 260.

5. A buyer is permitted a reasonable opportunity to inspect goods tendered under a contract, see UCC § 2–606, and may reject nonconforming goods within a reasonable time after inspection reveals the nonconformity, and the buyer must seasonably notify the seller of rejection. UCC § 2–602. Defendant in this case has complied with the above requirements.

tion, to reject the whole. UCC § 2–601. Furthermore, defendant is entitled to recover damages incurred in inspecting the coal. UCC § 2–715(1) provides in part that, "Incidental damages resulting from the seller's breach include expenses reasonably incurred in inspection * * * of goods rightfully rejected * * *" Defendant has by affidavit established that its inspection costs amount to $495.70.

* * *

Accordingly, in view of the foregoing, the court will deny plaintiff's motion for summary judgment, grant defendant's motion for summary judgment on plaintiff's claim, grant defendant's motion for summary judgment on the first count of its counterclaim, and will dismiss without prejudice the second count of defendant's counterclaim.

[Some footnotes omitted.]

C. *Procedural Requirements of Effective Rejection*

Suppose, upon inspection, the buyer finds a non-conformity which would justify rejection of the goods under UCC 2–601. What conditions must be met before the buyer can make an effective rejection? Section 2–602(1) provides that "rejection of goods must be within a reasonable time after their delivery and tender" and that the rejection is "ineffective unless the buyer seasonably notifies the seller." Compare UCC 2–607(3)(a). If the buyer has had a reasonable option under UCC 2–602(1), and fails to act, he has accepted the goods. Section 2–606(1)(b). A second set of problems concerns the content of the notice the buyer is to give the seller. Need it state all, part or none of the defects ascertainable by reasonable inspection as a condition to relying upon them to justify rejection? The UCC answer is provided in UCC 2–605(1). The pre-Code cases are collected and analyzed in Eno, *Price Movement and Unstated Objections to the Defective Performance of Sales Contracts,* 44 Yale L.J. 782 (1935).

Problem 18–4

Suppose that the seller tenders goods at the time specified in the contract. Upon inspection, the buyer finds what he considers to be two defects. Accordingly, he promptly notifies the seller that he is rejecting the goods, thus satisfying UCC 2–602(1). However, his notice of rejection specified only one defect and this later turns out to be an insufficient ground for rejection. The unstated objection, while present in fact, could have been cured by the seller under UCC 2–508(2). Shortly after the notice is received by the seller, the goods are destroyed while in the possession of the buyer but without his fault or negligence. May the seller recover the price of the destroyed goods from the buyer? See UCC 2–602, 2–605, 2–606, and 2–607(1). In Bead Chain Manufacturing Co. v. Saxton Products, Inc., 183 Conn. 266, 439 A.2d 314 (1981) the Supreme Court of Connecticut, Ellen Peters J, remarked that the "consequences of an ineffective rejection is that the buyer is held to have accepted the goods, and thereafter becomes liable for their purchase price." 439 A.2d at 318, n. 2.

INTERVALE STEEL CORP. v. BORG & BECK DIV., BORG–WARNER

United States District Court, Eastern District, Michigan, 1984.
578 F.Supp. 1081.

PRATT, DISTRICT JUDGE. This case involves the application of the Uniform Commercial Code, adopted by Michigan, M.C.L.A. § 440.1101 et seq., to the sale of steel by plaintiff to the defendant. The plaintiff, Intervale Steel Corporation

(Intervale) is the successor to Barry Steel Corporation (Barry) and sold 22 coils of steel to the defendant Borg & Beck (Borg), a division of Borg-Warner Corporation. The latter has refused to remit the purchase price and this suit ensued.

I. Facts

Barry had sold steel to Borg for over 15 years. During most if not all of that period, the defendant's sales representative on the Borg account was Peter Adzema, a metallurgist who was also associated with Barry's quality control department. Adzema visited the Borg plant frequently and was fully aware of Borg's manufacturing processes and procedures. More particularly, Adzema testified he was familiar with Borg's practice regarding the partial fabrication of the parts in question here and the storage of the partially completed parts until customers placed an order, after which the parts would be completed. He was also aware that Borg did not conduct microscopic examinations of ordered steel and did not cut sample pieces from ordered steel and run those samples completely through the fabrication process.

Borg is engaged in the manufacturing or fabrication of parts and components for the automotive industry. In August, 1980, it ordered 98,195 pounds of high carbon cold rolled steel for use in the fabrication of the "Belleville Spring," a component of automobile clutch assemblies. The purchase order set forth the specifications for this steel, which were of critical importance due to the demanding requirements of the "Belleville Spring" and its function in clutch assemblies. The acceptance by plaintiff of the purchase order, of course, resulted in the plaintiff's grant of express and implied warranties of merchantability and fitness for the purpose intended.

Barry obtained the steel originally from Jones and Laughlin Steel in coils. Barry then unrolled the coils, treated the steel, rerolled the coils and on August 26 and 28 of 1980 delivered 22 coils to defendant at the agreed upon price.

Borg, in accordance with its usual practice, checked the steel for dimensional accuracy and chemical content. In August or early September, 1980, Borg began its fabrication process by stamping out "blanks" from strips of the coils and deburring (smoothing) the pieces. It then stored these blanks prior to any further processing pending the receipt of orders from its automotive customers. In late September, Borg removed the pieces from storage and resumed its fabrication process which involved forming by presses, heat treatment, "wheelabrating" (similar to sandblasting), "stroking" (a stress-removal process) and "load-testing" (a quality control measure). During the course of these latter steps, however, it was observed that the springs were cracking and evidencing other failures. Notice was immediately given to Barry and Borg halted production and began extensive testing of the steel. Borg tested for several weeks and communicated to Barry regularly with regard to the testing. Eventually, it was determined that the steel was indeed defective and that the cause was associated with the fact that, contrary to the specifications of that type of steel, it had been annealed[3] once, rather than twice.

Barry admitted the steel was defective and not fit for its intended use and conceded the same at trial. Upon discovering that the entire order had been

3. Annealization is the process of heating and slow cooling in order to toughen the steel and reduce brittleness.

stamped, after providing for some samples for its own testing and demonstrative purposes, Barry authorized Borg to scrap the steel.

The evidence also established that Borg did not conduct metallurgical or microscopic examinations of Barry steel and that Barry was aware of this. It was further established that it is not an industry practice to do so. Moreover, it was also established that "samples" of coil steel are not run through the complete fabrication process due to the high cost of, for example, unrolling the coil, taking samples from representative parts of the coil and tying up the production line for testing purposes.

Intervale, as a successor to Barry, then instituted this suit for $41,612.47, that figure representing the invoice price less credit for the scrap value realized by Borg. It is the position of plaintiff that Borg accepted the steel, is not entitled to revoke that acceptance and is precluded from maintaining an action or asserting the defense of breach of warranty.

II. Acceptance and Revocation

Borg argued that it did not "accept" the goods and should not be held obligated to pay the purchase price of the contract. See M.C.L.A. § 440.2607(1). Borg reasoned that it properly rejected the goods as required under §§ 2–601, 2–602 and 2–606. According to defendant, although it blanked out all the steel, it could reject the steel because defendant acted reasonably and rejected the goods as soon as the breach of warranty could be discovered. Borg supports this position by citing several cases which have found effective rejections by buyers despite their changing or using the goods. It is true that Borg acted reasonably, nonetheless, under the circumstances Borg's action can only be viewed to constitute acceptance of the steel.

First, under the Uniform Commercial Code, Borg's rejection after the steel was entirely stamped out was not effective.[7] Borg did not attempt to reject the steel until after it had received shipment, blanked all the steel, and stored the partially completed parts for over a month. In total, Borg retained the steel for over three months before it notified plaintiff of the problems with the steel. The determination of whether goods have been accepted is governed by § 2–606. That section states:

> "(1) Acceptance of goods occurs when the buyer
>
> "(a) after a reasonable opportunity to inspect the goods signifies to the seller that the goods are conforming or that he will take or retain them in spite of their non-conformity; or
>
> "(b) fails to make an effective rejection (sub-section (1) of Section 2–602), but such acceptance does not occur until the buyer has had a reasonable opportunity to inspect them; or
>
> "(c) does any act inconsistent with the seller's ownership; but if such act is wrongful as against the seller it is an acceptance only if ratified by him.
>
> "(2) Acceptance of a part of any commercial unit is acceptance of that entire unit."

7. A rejection of goods which is wrongful under the Code is deemed ineffective and the items are viewed as accepted. E.g. Blue Sky Forest Products, Inc. v. New Hampshire Doors Co., 663 P.2d 813, 36 UCC Rep. 1179 (Or.App. 1983).

M.C.L.A. § 440.2606. Subsection (1)(b) appears to most appropriately apply in the instant case [8] and would require that Borg's rejection must be both seasonably given and within a reasonable time pursuant to § 2–602.[9]

Borg clearly did not reject the steel within a reasonable time. Not only is three months an over-long period to retain the goods before rejecting them, but Borg's stamping out of all the steel certainly makes its rejection untimely and ineffective. The Code requires that rejection will occur when the goods are tendered and inspected or after the buyer has had a reasonable time for inspection.[12] Timely rejection ensures the goods can be easily restored to the seller so that he can either make them conforming and tender them back to the buyer or simply sell the goods to another. In this way damages will be mitigated and commercial loss curtailed. Rejection is generally not effective after the goods have been manufactured into parts.

Defendant might argue that it did not have "a reasonable opportunity to inspect" the goods as subsection (1)(b) requires, since the defect could not have been reasonably discovered until the steel was processed into parts. This argument is likewise unavailing. The "reasonable opportunity to inspect" provision is to ensure that a buyer's silence, without more, does not automatically impute acceptance until he has had adequate time [14] to inspect the goods. It does not imply that goods which have been drastically changed and used by the buyer can later be rejected and not viewed as accepted, despite the presence of a latent defect. Buyers who receive nonconforming goods with defects that are not easily detected are provided adequate remedies under the Code even though they have accepted the goods.[15] They do not lose the right to recover damages for the seller's breach of warranty by simply having accepted the goods.

8. Plaintiff argues that § 2–606(1)(c) applies to the instant case so that Borg's stamping out of the steel is an act inconsistent with the seller's ownership and means acceptance has occurred. A proper reading of § 2–606 suggests that subsection (1)(c) should only apply when the buyer acts with knowledge of the defect. Once the buyer discovers the defect and acts inconsistently with the seller's rights, then (1)(c) will deem the buyer to have accepted the goods. See M.C.L.A. § 440.2606, comments 3 and 4. In J. White & R. Summers, Uniform Commercial Code § 8–2, at 298–99 (2d Ed 1980) the authors correctly state:

> "We would argue that acts done in ignorance of the defects which buyer could not have discovered are never covered by 2–606(1)(c). The use of the goods and passage of time might constitute an acceptance under 2–606(1)(a) or 2–606(1)(b). But if any use (and all use is theoretically inconsistent with seller's ownership) constitutes an inconsistent act as that term is used in 2–606(1)(c), then there will always be acceptance the minute the buyer uses the goods notwithstanding the fact he had not yet had a 'reasonable opportunity to inspect' under 2–606(1)(a) and still has a 'reasonable time' to reject under 2–602 (and therefore has not accepted under 2–606(1)(b)). The only reading of 2–606(1)(c) which is consistent with the Code policy and which leaves elbow room for the other provisions of 2–606 is to find that use of goods in ignorance of the defective nature of the goods is not 'inconsistent' under 2–606(1)(c)."

(Emphasis supplied.) It should be noted that "any use" language of subsection (1)(c) requires this interpretation in order for the other subsections to have meaning. This does not mean a buyer's use, particularly substantial use, could not deem goods as accepted under (1)(a) or (b).

9. M.C.L.A. § 440.2602(1) states:

> "Rejection of goods must be within a reasonable time after their delivery or tender. It is ineffective unless the buyer seasonably notifies the seller."

12. See generally J. White & R. Summers, supra, note 8, § 8–2, at 296–318.

14. The standard for "adequate" or "reasonable" time is dependent upon the particular circumstances of each case. MCLA § 440.1204(2) ("What is a reasonable time for taking any action depends on the nature, purpose and circumstances of such action.")

15. Section 2–714 provides that a buyer who accepts nonconforming goods can get damages basically for the reduction in value of the goods due to the nonconformity and any incidental or consequential damages the buyer incurs.

This conclusion that Borg's attempt to reject is ineffective is further supported by the relationship the Code establishes between rejection and revocation. The Code provides two methods by which a buyer may act upon nonconforming goods: he may reject them before ever accepting the goods or he may revoke the goods once he has accepted them. The pertinent Code section governing revocation provides:

> "(1) The buyer may revoke his acceptance of a lot or commercial unit whose nonconformity substantially impairs its value to him if he has accepted it
>
> "(a) on the reasonable assumption that its nonconformity would be cured and it has not been seasonably cured; or
>
> "(b) without discovery of such nonconformity if his acceptance was reasonably induced either by the difficulty of discovery before acceptance or by the seller's assurances.
>
> "(2) Revocation of acceptance must occur within a reasonable time after the buyer discovers or should have discovered the ground for it and before any substantial change in condition of the goods which is not caused by their own defects. It is not effective until the buyer notifies the seller of it.
>
> "(3) A buyer who so revokes has the same rights and duties with regard to the goods involved as if he had rejected them."

M.C.L.A. § 440.2608. As the Code suggests, a buyer may more readily reject goods than revoke acceptance since the standard for rejection is more relaxed. A buyer is presented with greater obstacles in order properly to revoke acceptance. For instance, a buyer may reject goods for relatively minor defects. He may not, however, revoke his acceptance unless the "nonconformity substantially impairs" the value of the goods. The difference in standards reflects the degree of prejudice the seller is exposed to in regard to the goods. A buyer's acceptance of the goods will most likely make the seller's ability to cure the nonconformity or resell the goods much more difficult.

Defendant could not avail itself of revocation because a "substantial change in the condition of the goods" was caused by Borg (the steel was stamped into parts) and "not caused by [the goods'] own defect." M.C.L.A. § 440.2608(2). Therefore, it would be a misapplication of the Code to allow defendant's rejection to be effective when it would not be permitted to revoke its acceptance.

Second, the cases defendant cites in support of its argument that it rightfully rejected the steel are not applicable. In each of those cases the contract expressly provided that rejection could occur even after the buyer had changed or used the material. Of course, parties to a contract are free to determine in their agreement when effective rejection can occur. The instant contract, however, cannot be viewed as modifying the Code provisions in regard to the time of rejection and acceptance. It is true that Adzema, Barry's sales representative who was a metallurgist and associated with Barry's quality control department, was familiar with Borg's fabrication schedule—that Borg did not sample test or examine microscopically the steel, and that it stamped, deburred and stored the steel pending customer orders. It is further true that despite his awareness of those procedures he did not object to them, nor suggest any alternatives or modifications. Yet, it is difficult to conclude that Adzema's knowledge of Borg's procedures can be said to imply that the parties' agreement modified the Code to allow Borg to reject the steel even after it had been stamped into parts. Although defendants do not make this contention, Borg could have more reasonably argued that the § 2–608(2) requirement that revocation is not effective if a substantial change in the condition of the goods had occurred was somehow modified by the parties' agreement. But it would be equally difficult to determine that the instant contract intended that modification of the Code also. Thus, Borg's rejection after the steel had been stamped out must be seen as ineffective. Moreover, Borg was likewise not permitted to revoke its acceptance once it had processed all the steel into parts. Defendant is thereby deemed to have accepted and retained the goods.

II. Defendant's Right to Set Off Damages From Its Obligation to Pay Purchase Price

Since defendant accepted the goods under § 2–607(2) defendant became obligated for the purchase price of the steel minus the scrap value of the material which was already turned over to the plaintiff. However, since Borg notified Barry Steel of the breach within a reasonable time, defendant may withhold payment of the purchase price to the extent that it has suffered damages from the seller's breach. See M.C.L.A. § 440.2717.

* * *

In conclusion, defendant is entitled to set off the amount of the purchase price it owes plaintiff with its damages, which is the difference between the scrap value of the steel and the contract price of the material. Thus, plaintiff is not entitled to the $41,612.47 for which it brought this action.

[Some footnotes omitted.]

D. Buyer's Duties Regarding Rejected Goods

BORGES v. MAGIC VALLEY FOODS, INC.

Supreme Court of Idaho, 1980.
101 Idaho 494, 616 P.2d 273.

SHEPARD, J. This is an appeal from a judgment following a jury verdict which awarded plaintiffs-respondents Borges and G & B Land and Cattle Company $12,832.00 for potatoes received by defendant-appellant Magic West pursuant to a contract with respondents. We affirm.

In 1975, respondents grew and harvested approximately 45,000 c.w.t. of potatoes, which were stored in a cellar near Buhl, Idaho. Magic West inspected those potatoes and, although their inspection indicated that some contained a "hollow heart" defect, Magic West agreed to purchase them for $3.80 per c.w.t. "Hollow heart" indicates a vacant space in the middle of the potato. The purchase contract provided that "if internal problems develop making these potatoes unfit for fresh pack shipping, this contract becomes null and void." It was agreed that the cost of transporting the potatoes from the storage cellar to the processing plant would be borne by Magic West. Examination of the potatoes by State inspectors would occur at the plant to determine that the number of potatoes affected by the hollow heart defect did not exceed the limit prescribed for shipping under the fresh pack grade.

The potatoes were transported to the processing plant, where more than 30,000 c.w.t. were processed and shipped under the fresh pack grade. In March, 1976, State inspectors declared the remaining 4,838.77 c.w.t. of potatoes unfit for the fresh pack grade because of the increased incidence of hollow heart condition.[1] On March 31, 1976, the parties met to discuss the problem of the

1. There were also potatoes still in storage which Magic West never paid for due to the hollow heart problems. There is no dispute with regard to those potatoes. Respondents eventually sold them for $3.00 per c.w.t. to be used as french fries. There were also 702 c.w.t. of defective potatoes in transit to the plant on March 31, 1977. The respondents

remaining potatoes and it was apparently agreed that Magic West should attempt to blend them with other potatoes of a higher grade in the hope that such a blend would meet fresh pack grade standards. That experiment failed and Magic West, without notifying the respondents, processed the remaining 4,838.77 c.w.t. of potatoes into flakes and sold them for $1.25 per c.w.t. The evidence in the record disclosed that the remaining potatoes could not be removed from the processing plant without destroying at least one-third of the potatoes.

Respondents demanded the contract price of $3.80 per c.w.t. for the potatoes sold as flakes. Magic West refused, and instead offered to pay $1.25 per c.w.t. This action resulted. The jury returned a general verdict to the respondents of $12,832.00 and the trial court also awarded $6,975.00 as and for attorney fees and costs to the respondents.[2]

Magic West's basic contention is that the 4,838.77 c.w.t. of potatoes were clearly defective and that they were never accepted. It is claimed that when Magic West processed the potatoes into flakes and sold them for $1.25 per c.w.t., they were only following respondents' instructions.

The potatoes in the instant case were clearly movable at the time they were identified in the contract, I.C. § 28–2–105, and, hence, were "goods" within the purview of the Idaho Uniform Commercial Code, I.C. §§ 28–2–101 to –2–725, and the dispute is governed by the provisions of the Uniform Commercial Code.

It is clear and undisputed that Magic West had the responsibility of transporting the potatoes from the storage cellar to the processing plant and that State inspection would occur at the plant. It is also clear that the 4,838.77 c.w.t. of potatoes, unable to make the fresh pack grade, did not conform to the contract and gave Magic West the right of rejection. IC § 28–2–601(a). Also, it is not disputed that when Magic West determined that the potatoes would not meet fresh pack grade, Magic West so notified the respondents and met with them to determine what disposition should be made of the potatoes. The record is unclear as to precisely what was decided at that March 31, 1976 meeting, but respondents apparently approved of Magic West's proposal to blend the defective potatoes with those with higher quality in an attempt to meet the fresh pack grade. However, it is clear that no agreement on price was reached at that meeting.

A buyer must pay the contract rate for any goods accepted. I.C. § 28–2–607(1). Generally, a buyer is deemed to have accepted defective goods when, knowing of the defect, he resells the goods without notifying the seller. See White & Summers, Uniform Commercial Code, § 8–2 (2d ed. 1980); 67 Am Jur2d Sales (1973). A buyer accepts goods whenever he does any act inconsistent with the seller's ownership. I.C. § 28–2–606(1)(c). Respondents assert that Magic West's processing of the remaining potatoes into flakes and the subsequent sale constituted acts inconsistent with the respondents' ownership.

agreed to accept $1.25 per c.w.t. for those potatoes from Magic West.

2. Both parties agreed that the jury had apparently awarded respondents the full contract price of $3.80 per c.w.t. for the potatoes in dispute. If no deductions were made, a jury award of $3.80 per c.w.t. would have resulted in a jury verdict of $18,387.32 [$3.80 × 4838.77]. Obviously, some deductions were made although they are not apparent from the record and were not explained or challenged by counsel. For purposes of this appeal, we assume, as counsel do, that the jury awarded $3.80 per c.w.t. for the potatoes in dispute.

Magic West argues, however, that their processing of the potatoes into flakes and their subsequent sale did not constitute an acceptance, but rather was a permissible resale under the provisions of either I.C. § 28–2–603(1) or I.C. § 28–2–604. I.C. § 28–2–603(1) provides:

> "Subject to any security interest in the buyer * * *, when the seller has no agent or place of business at the market of rejection a merchant buyer is under a duty after rejection of goods in his possession or control to follow any reasonable instructions received from the seller with respect to the goods and in the absence of such instructions to make reasonable efforts to sell them for the seller's account if they are perishable or threaten to decline in value speedily."

I.C. § 28–2–604 provides:

> "Subject to the provisions of the immediately preceding section on perishables if the seller gives no instructions within a reasonable time after notification of rejection the buyer may store the rejected goods for the seller's account or reship them to him or resell them for the seller's account with reimbursement as provided in the preceding section. Such action is not acceptance or conversion."

We note that both I.C. § 28–2–603(1) and I.C. § 28–2–604 were given in their entirety as instructions to the jury. We find it unclear from the record whether the respondents had agents or a place of business at the "market of rejection." Also, the duty to resell under I.C. § 28–2–603(1) is triggered by an absence of instructions from a seller. Here, given the state of the record and its lack of clarity and the conflicting evidence, the jury could have reasonably found that the respondents did instruct Magic West to attempt to blend the potatoes, but did not instruct them to process the potatoes into flakes. While I.C. § 28–2–604 allows a buyer an option to resell rejected goods if the seller gives no instructions within a reasonable time after the notification of rejection, the jury could have reasonably found that respondents' instructions were only to blend the potatoes in hope of accomplishing fresh pack grade and that Magic West's processing of the potatoes into flakes and subsequent resale thereof was a precipitate action taken before the lapse of a reasonable time within which respondents could give further instructions.

In addition, even if a reasonable time had elapsed, thus permitting Magic West to resell the potatoes, the jury properly could have concluded that processing of the potatoes by Magic West was an acceptance rather than a resale. There was no evidence presented either of an attempt to resell the potatoes in the bins to an independent third party, or of the value of the potatoes in the bins, less damage caused by removal, should it have been effected. Absent any evidence that the $1.25 per c.w.t. offered by Magic West was the highest value obtainable for the potatoes, Magic West's use of the potatoes in the ordinary course of its own business (presumably for profit) was an act inconsistent with the seller's ownership, and constituted an acceptance of the goods. I.C. § 28–2–606(1)(c).

The jury was adequately and correctly instructed regarding the provisions of I.C. § 28–2–603(1) and I.C. § 28–2–604, which constituted Magic West's theory of its duty or option of resale because of an absence of instructions from respondents. The jury was at liberty to reject Magic West's theory of defense based on substantial, albeit conflicting, evidence that Magic West's resale of the potatoes after processing them into flakes constituted an acceptance and Magic West was hence liable for the full contract price.

We have examined appellants' remaining assignments of error and find them to be without merit.

Affirmed. Costs to respondents.

DONALDSON, C.J., BAKES, MCFADDEN and BISTLINE, JJ., concur.

Problem 18–5

Suppose in the Sodfill-Blurtaste problem, above, that the bill of lading had permitted inspection and that Blurtaste had discovered the defect in 1, above, while inspecting goods still in the possession of the carrier. Blurtaste did not take possession and promptly notified Sodfill of his decision to reject as required by UCC 2–602. Assume, further, that (1) the weather was quite hot, putting a strain on the refrigeration unit in the railroad car, (2) the tomato market had started a steady decline due to a bumper crop and (3) Sodfill had no local agent at the place of destination. Does Blurtaste have any obligation to Sodfill with regard to the rejected goods? If so, what would you advise Blurtaste to do? See UCC 2–602(2), 2–603 and 2–604.

Note: Perishable Agricultural Commodities

Under section 2(2) of the Perishable Agricultural Commodities Act, 7 U.S.C.A. § 499b, as amended, it is unlawful in interstate transactions "for any dealer to reject or fail to deliver in accordance with the terms of the contract without reasonable cause any perishable agricultural commodity bought or sold or contracted to be bought or sold in interstate * * * commerce by such dealer." The Act was "intended to prevent produce from becoming distress merchandise and to protect sellers who often were at great distance from the buyer." L. Gillarde & Co. v. Joseph Martinelli & Co., 168 F.2d 276, amended 169 F.2d 60, 61 (1st Cir.1948), cert. denied 335 U.S. 885. Remedies include reparation orders for aggrieved shippers and suspension or revocation of licenses. See Chidsey v. Geurin, 443 F.2d 584 (6th Cir. 1971). The Secretary has defined "reject without reasonable cause" to include "refusing or failing without legal justification to accept produce within a reasonable time" and "advising the seller, shipper, or his agent that produce, complying with the contract, will not be accepted." 7 C.F.R. § 46.2(bb) (1986). Reasonable time for rejection is defined with reference to the type of produce and the method of shipment. 7 C.F.R. § 46.2(cc) (1986). A number of commonly used trade terms are crisply defined and, to the extent used by the parties, both preempt state law definitions, e.g., UCC 2–319, and define rights and duties. For example, "rolling acceptance final" means that the buyer "has no recourse against the seller because of any change in condition of the produce in transit" but if the shipment is not rejected the buyer has recourse in damages against the seller for any material breach. 7 C.F.R. § 46.43(t) (1986). The thrust of the definitions is to restrict or prohibit the rejection remedy, especially where the reason for rejection affects the condition or quality of the goods. See Schuman Co. v. Nelson, 219 F.2d 627 (3d Cir.1955) (under earlier regulations, "rolling acceptance final" does not preclude rejection for breach not relating to quality or condition of goods). Since buyers subject to the Act often pay against documents or under a letter of credit arrangement, the need for adequate inspection of the produce at the point of shipment is acute. Federal inspection is available and, in some cases, required under the Act. See 7 U.S.C.A. § 499n; 7 C.F.R. §§ 46.39 & 46.40 (1986); Cove Valley Packers, Inc. v. Pilgrim Fruit Co., 297 F.Supp. 200 (D.Mass.1969).

Note: "Avoidance" of the Contract in International Sales

Professor John Honnold has observed that one of the "thorniest problems" in the law of sales is "when will the breach by one party free the other party of his obligation to perform?" J. Honnold, Uniform Law for International Sales 65 (1982).

This problem has special significance in international sales "because of the cost of transporting goods to a distant buyer and the difficulty of disposing of rejected goods." Ibid.

The 1980 United Nations Convention on Contracts for the International Sale of Goods, which the United States Senate ratified on Dec. 11, 1986 and which becomes effective on Jan. 1, 1988, deals with problems created by the seller's delay in performance or delivery of non-conforming documents or goods in the following manner.

Let us consider only the case of non-conforming goods or documents. Suppose the seller has tendered goods or documents which fail to conform to the contract. The buyer discovers the non-conformity after "examination" of the goods or documents, Article 38, and preserves his rights by giving "notice to the seller specifying the nature of the lack of conformity within a reasonable time after he has discovered it or ought to have discovered it." Article 39(1). What are these "rights"?

First, the buyer may recover damages for breach of contract. Article 74.

Second, the buyer may, in carefully defined situations, compel the seller either to deliver "substitute goods," if the breach is "fundamental," or to "remedy the lack of conformity by repair" if reasonable under all of the circumstances. Article 46. If this remedy is successful, the buyer will owe the price, subject to adjustment for any losses caused by the breach.

Third, the buyer may attempt to "avoid" the contract ("cancel" in UCC parlance)—a remedy that substitutes for "rejection" of the goods. "Avoidance" of the contract requires the buyer to: (a) establish that the non-conformity amounted to a "fundamental" breach, Article 49(1), and (b) give notice to the buyer of the attempt to avoid within a reasonable time after he "knew or ought to have known of the breach." Article 49(2)(b). See Article 26. A breach is "fundamental if it results in such detriment to the other party as substantially to deprive him of what he is entitled to expect under the contract, unless the party in breach did not foresee and a reasonable person of the same kind in the same circumstances would not have foreseen such a result."

Fourth, the "right" to avoid the contract for a fundamental breach, however, is limited by the seller's right to "cure" the defect by replacing or repairing the defective goods, Articles 37 (cure until date of delivery) and 48 (cure after delivery) or conforming the documents. Article 34. See Honnold at 184–85. Thus, if the buyer discovered a "fundamental" breach after delivery, the seller could prevent an "avoidance" of the contract by remedying "at his own expense any failure to perform his obligations, if he can do so without unreasonable delay and without causing the buyer unreasonable inconvenience. * * *" Article 48(1).

Enough has been said to indicate that the 1980 Convention has rejected a "perfect tender" rule for rules that require "fundamental" breach and maximize the seller's opportunity to cure. In short, the 1980 Convention seeks to preserve the contract and to foster adjustments, while protecting the buyer's right to damages for losses caused during the "cure" period. At the same time, one can see that the Convention's solution will not be simple to understand and administer and this problem is complicated by a sometimes murky drafting history. See Speidel, Book Review, 5 Nw.J.Int'l.Law & Bus. 432 (1983). Nevertheless, we believe Professor Honnold's book sheds considerable light on the 1980 Convention and recommend it as the perfect place to start. If your interest is piqued, go next to Rosett, *Critical Reflections on the United Nations Convention on Contracts for the International Sale of Goods,* 45 Ohio S.L.J. 305 (1984).

For now, you may wish to review the UCC's approach to the problem of "rejection" and "cancellation" and compare it with the 1980 Convention.

SECTION 4. NATURE AND CONSEQUENCES OF ACCEPTANCE

So far, we have focused upon the buyer's right to inspect and the remedy of rejection when defects in the seller's tender of delivery are actually discovered. Through both inspection and rejection the buyer seeks to avoid accepting defective goods. Now we will be concerned with three additional but related questions. First, exactly when does a buyer accept tendered goods? The critical section here is UCC 2–606. Second, what is the legal effect of an acceptance? This is particularly important when the goods accepted are actually nonconforming. See UCC 2–510(1) and UCC 2–607. Third, when may the buyer "revoke" his acceptance under UCC 2–608 and what is the effect of a proper revocation of acceptance? Regardless of how the acceptance occurs, a buyer with defective goods on his hands will be in a different and, perhaps, more difficult remedial posture than if the remedy of rejection had properly been invoked. Because the complexity of many goods and the casualness of most inspections naturally contribute to a high incidence of acceptance, a thorough appreciation of this "posture" by the commercial lawyer is required.

PLATEQ CORP. OF NORTH HAVEN v. MACHLETT LABORATORIES, INC.

Supreme Court of Connecticut, 1983.
189 Conn. 433, 456 A.2d 786.

Before SPEZIALE, C.J., and PETERS, ARTHUR H. HEALEY, PARSKEY and GRILLO, JJ.

PETERS, JUDGE.

In this action by a seller of specially manufactured goods to recover their purchase price from a commercial buyer, the principal issue is whether the buyer accepted the goods before it attempted to cancel the contract of sale. The plaintiff, Plateq Corporation of North Haven, sued the defendant, The Machlett Laboratories, Inc., to recover damages, measured by the contract price and incidental damages, arising out of the defendant's allegedly wrongful cancellation of a written contract for the manufacture and sale of two leadcovered steel tanks and appurtenant stands. The defendant denied liability and counterclaimed for damages. After a full hearing, the trial court found for the plaintiff both on its complaint and on the defendant's counterclaim. The defendant has appealed.

The trial court, in its memorandum of decision, found the following facts. On July 9, 1976, the defendant ordered from the plaintiff two leadcovered steel tanks to be constructed by the plaintiff according to specifications supplied by the defendant. The parties understood that the tanks were designed for the special purpose of testing x-ray tubes and were required to be radiation-proof within certain federal standards. Accordingly, the contract provided that the tanks would be tested for radiation leaks after their installation on the defendant's premises. The plaintiff undertook to correct, at its own cost, any deficiencies that this post-installation test might uncover.[1] The plaintiff had not previously constructed such tanks, nor had the defendant previously designed tanks for this purpose. The contract was amended on August 9, 1976, to add

1. The contract incorporated precise specifications in the form of detailed drawings. The drawings for the tank and the tank cover contained specific manufacturing instructions as well as provision 6: "Tank with cover will be tested for radiation leaks after installation. Any deficiencies must be corrected by the vendor."

construction of two metal stands to hold the tanks. All the goods were to be delivered to the defendant at the plaintiff's place of business.[2]

Although the plaintiff encountered difficulties both in performing according to the contract specifications and in completing performance within the time required, the defendant did no more than call these deficiencies to the plaintiff's attention during various inspections in September and early October, 1976. By October 11, 1976, performance was belatedly but substantially completed. On that date, Albert Yannello, the defendant's engineer, noted some remaining deficiencies which the plaintiff promised to remedy by the next day, so that the goods would then be ready for delivery. Yannello gave no indication to the plaintiff that this arrangement was in any way unsatisfactory to the defendant. Not only did Yannello communicate general acquiescence in the plaintiff's proposed tender but he specifically led the plaintiff to believe that the defendant's truck would pick up the tanks and the stands within a day or two. Instead of sending its truck, the defendant sent a notice of total cancellation which the plaintiff received on October 14, 1976. That notice failed to particularize the grounds upon which cancellation was based.[3]

On this factual basis, the trial court, having concluded that the transaction was a contract for the sale of goods falling within the Uniform Commercial Code, General Statutes §§ 42a–2–101 et seq., considered whether the defendant had accepted the goods. The court determined that the defendant had accepted the tanks, primarily by signifying its willingness to take them despite their nonconformities, in accordance with General Statutes § 42a–2–606(1)(a), and secondarily by failing to make an effective rejection, in accordance with General Statutes § 42a–2–606(1)(b). Once the tanks had been accepted, the defendant could rightfully revoke its acceptance under General Statutes § 42a–2–608 only by showing substantial impairment of their value to the defendant. In part because the defendant's conduct had foreclosed any post-installation inspection, the court concluded that such impairment had not been proved. Since the tanks were not readily resaleable on the open market, the plaintiff was entitled, upon the defendant's wrongful revocation of acceptance, to recover their contract price, minus salvage value, plus interest. General Statutes §§ 42a–2–703; 42a–2–709(1)(b). Accordingly, the trial court awarded the plaintiff damages in the amount of $14,837.92.

In its appeal, the defendant raises four principal claims of error. It maintains that the trial court erred: (1) in invoking the "cure" section, General Statutes § 42a–2–508, when there had been no tender by the plaintiff seller; (2) in concluding, in accordance with the acceptance section, General Statutes § 42a–2–606(1), that the defendant had "signified" to the plaintiff its willingness to take the contract goods; (3) in misconstruing the defendant's statutory and contractual rights of inspection; and (4) in refusing to find that the defendant's letter of cancellation was occasioned by the plaintiff's breach. We find no error.

Upon analysis, all of the defendant's claims of error are variations upon one central theme. The defendant claims that on October 11, when its engineer

2. The purchase order sent by the defendant to the plaintiff stipulated that the goods were to be shipped "F.O.B. Origin."

3. The defendant sent the plaintiff a telegram stating: "This order is hereby terminated for your breach, in that you have continuously failed to perform according to your commitment in spite of additional time given you to cure your delinquency. We will hold you liable for all damages incured [sic] by Machlett including excess cost of reprocurement."

Yannello conducted the last examination on the plaintiff's premises, the tanks were so incomplete and unsatisfactory that the defendant was rightfully entitled to conclude that the plaintiff would never make a conforming tender. From this scenario, the defendant argues that it was justified in cancelling the contract of sale. It denies that the seller's conduct was sufficient to warrant a finding of tender, or its own conduct sufficient to warrant a finding of acceptance. The difficulty with this argument is that it is inconsistent with the underlying facts found by the trial court. Although the testimony was in dispute, there was evidence of record to support the trial court's findings to the contrary. The defendant cannot sustain its burden of establishing that a trial court's findings of fact are clearly erroneous; Practice Book § 3060D; *Pandolphe's Auto Parts, Inc. v. Manchester,* 181 Conn. 217, 221–22, 435 A.2d 24 (1980); by the mere recitation in its brief of conflicting testimony entirely unsupported by reference to pages of the transcript. Practice Book § 3060F(b). There is simply no fit between the defendant's claims and the trial court's finding that, by October 11, 1976, performance was in substantial compliance with the terms of the contract. The trial court further found that on that day the defendant was notified that the goods would be ready for tender the following day and that the defendant responded to this notification by promising to send its truck to pick up the tanks in accordance with the contract.

On the trial court's finding of facts, it was warranted in concluding, on two independent grounds, that the defendant had accepted the goods it had ordered from the plaintiff. Under the provisions of the Uniform Commercial Code, General Statutes § 42a–2–606(1) "[a]cceptance of goods occurs when the buyer (a) after a reasonable opportunity to inspect the goods signifies to the seller * * * that he will take * * * them in spite of their nonconformity; or (b) fails to make an effective rejection." [10]

In concluding that the defendant had "signified" to the plaintiff its willingness to "take" the tanks despite possible remaining minor defects, the trial court necessarily found that the defendant had had a reasonable opportunity to inspect the goods. The defendant does not maintain that its engineer, or the other inspectors on previous visits, had inadequate access to the tanks, or inadequate experience to conduct a reasonable examination. It recognizes that inspection of goods when the buyer undertakes to pick up the goods is ordinarily at the seller's place of tender. See General Statutes §§ 42a–2–503, 42a–2–507, 42a–2–513; see also White & Summers, Uniform Commercial Code § 3–5 (2d Ed. 1980). The defendant argues, however, that its contract, in providing for inspection for radiation leaks after installation of the tanks at its premises, necessarily postponed its inspection rights to that time. The trial court considered this argument and rejected it, and so do we. It was reasonable, in the context of this contract for the special manufacture of goods with which neither party had had prior experience, to limit this clause to adjustments to take place after tender and acceptance. After acceptance, a buyer may still, in appropriate cases, revoke its acceptance, General Statutes § 42a–2–608, or recover damages for breach of warranty, General Statutes § 42a–2–714. The trial court reasonably concluded that a post-installation test was intended to safeguard these rights of the defendant as well as to afford the plaintiff a final opportunity to make

10. General Statutes § 42a–2–606(1)(c) provides a third ground, the exercise of dominion, for finding acceptance but that ground was not considered by the trial court, presumably because it has no apparent factual relevance to the circumstances of this case. * * *

needed adjustments. The court was therefore justified in concluding that there had been an acceptance within § 42a–2–606(1)(a). A buyer may be found to have accepted goods despite their known nonconformity and despite the absence of actual delivery to the buyer * * *.

The trial court's alternate ground for concluding that the tanks had been accepted was the defendant's failure to make an effective rejection. Pursuant to General Statutes § 42a–2–606(1)(b), an acceptance occurs when, after a reasonable opportunity to inspect, a buyer has failed to make "an effective rejection as provided by subsection (1) of section 42a–2–602." The latter subsection, in turn, makes a rejection "ineffective unless the buyer seasonably notifies the seller." General Statutes § 42a–2–605(1)(a) goes on to provide that a buyer is precluded from relying, as a basis for rejection, upon unparticularized defects in his notice of rejection, if the defects were such that, with seasonable notice, the seller could have cured by making a substituted, conforming tender. The defendant does not question the trial court's determination that its telegram of cancellation failed to comply with the requirement of particularization contained in § 42a–2–605(1). Instead, the defendant argues that the plaintiff was not entitled to an opportunity to cure, under General Statutes § 42a–2–508, because the plaintiff had never made a tender of the tanks. That argument founders, however, on the trial court's finding that the seller was ready to make a tender on the day following the last inspection by the defendant's engineer and would have done so but for its receipt of the defendant's telegram of cancellation. The trial court furthermore found that the defendant's unparticularized telegram of cancellation wrongfully interfered with the plaintiff's contractual right to cure any remaining post-installation defects. In these circumstances, the telegram of cancellation constituted both a wrongful and an ineffective rejection on the part of the defendant. See *Uchitel v. F.R. Tripler & Co.,* 107 Misc.2d 310, 434 N.Y.S.2d 77, 81–82 (Supreme Court 1980); White & Summers, supra, § 8–3, p. 315.

Once the conclusion is reached that the defendant accepted the tanks, its further rights of cancellation under the contract are limited by the governing provisions of the Uniform Commercial Code. "The buyer's acceptance of goods, despite their alleged nonconformity, is a watershed. After acceptance, the buyer must pay for the goods at the contract rate; General Statutes § 42a–2–607(1); and bears the burden of establishing their nonconformity. General Statutes § 42a–2–607(4)." *Stelco Industries, Inc. v. Cohen,* 182 Conn. 561, 563–64, 438 A.2d 759 (1980). After acceptance, the buyer may only avoid liability for the contract price by invoking the provision which permits revocation of acceptance. That provision, General Statutes § 42a–2–608(1), requires proof that the "nonconformity [of the goods] substantially impairs [their] value to him." * * * On this question which is an issue of fact; * * * the trial court again found against the defendant. Since the defendant has provided no basis for any argument that the trial court was clearly erroneous in finding that the defendant had not met its burden of proof to show that the goods were substantially nonconforming, we can find no error in the conclusion that the defendant's cancellation constituted an unauthorized and hence wrongful revocation of acceptance.

Finally, the defendant in its brief, although not in its statement of the issues presented, challenges the trial court's conclusion about the remedial consequences of its earlier determinations. Although the trial court might have found the plaintiff entitled to recover the contract price because of the defendant's acceptance of the goods; General Statutes §§ 42a-2-703(e) and 42a-2-709(1)(a); the court chose instead to rely on General Statutes § 42a-2-709(1)(b), which permits a price action for contract goods that cannot, after reasonable effort, be resold at a reasonable price.[19] Since the contract goods in this case were concededly specially manufactured for the defendant, the defendant cannot and does not contest the trial court's finding that any effort to resell them on the open market would have been unavailing. In the light of this finding, the defendant can only reiterate its argument, which we have already rejected, that the primary default was that of the plaintiff rather than that of the defendant. The trial court's conclusion to the contrary supports both its award to the plaintiff and its denial of the defendant's counterclaim.

There is no error.

In this opinion the other Judges concurred.

[Footnotes in which court quoted from statute omitted.]

Notes

1. In Zabriskie Chevrolet, Inc. v. Smith, parts of which are reprinted supra at p. 726, the court had this to say about whether the defendant accepted a new car with a defective transmission:

"It is clear that a buyer does not accept goods until he has had a 'reasonable opportunity to inspect.' Defendant sought to purchase a new car. He assumed what every new car buyer has a right to assume and, indeed, has been led to assume by the high powered advertising techniques of the auto industry—that his new car, with the exception of very minor adjustments, would be mechanically new and factory-furnished, operate perfectly, and be free of substantial defects. The vehicle delivered to defendant did not measure up to these representations. Plaintiff contends that defendant had 'reasonable opportunity to inspect' by the privilege to take the car for a typical 'spin around the block' before signing the purchase order. If by this contention plaintiff equates a spin around the block with 'reasonable opportunity to inspect,' the contention is illusory and unrealistic. To the layman, the complicated mechanisms of today's automobiles are a complete mystery. To have the automobile inspected by someone with sufficient expertise to disassemble the vehicle in order to discover latent defects before the contract is signed, is assuredly impossible and highly impractical. Cf. Massari v. Accurate Bushing Co., 8 N.J. 299, 313, 85 A.2d 260. Consequently, the first few miles of driving become even more significant to the excited new car buyer. This is the buyer's first reasonable opportunity to enjoy his new vehicle to see if it conforms to what it was represented to be and whether he is getting what he bargained for. How long the buyer may drive the new car under the guise of inspection of new goods is not an issue in the present case. It is clear that defendant discovered the nonconformity within 7/10 of a mile and minutes after

19. * * * It should be noted that § 42a-2-709(1)(b) is not premised on a buyer's acceptance. Instead, it requires a showing that the goods were, before the buyer's cancellation, "identified to the contract." In the circumstances of this case, that precondition was presumably met by their special manufacture and by the defendant's acquiescence in their imminent tender. See White & Summers, Uniform Commercial Code, § 7-5 (2d Ed. 1980). The defendant has not, on this appeal, argued the absence of identification.

It should further be noted that § 42a-2-709(1)(b), because it is not premised on acceptance, would have afforded the seller the right to recover the contract price even if the trial court had found the conduct of the buyer to be a wrongful rejection (because of the failure to give the seller an opportunity to cure) rather than a wrongful revocation of acceptance.

leaving plaintiff's showroom. Certainly this was well within the ambit of 'reasonable opportunity to inspect.' That the vehicle was grievously defective when it left plaintiff's possession is a compelling conclusion, as is the conclusion that in a legal sense defendant never accepted the vehicle.

"Nor could the dealer under such circumstances require acceptance. Cf. Code Comment 2 (subsection 2) to N.J.S. 12A:2–106, N.J.S.A.:

> 'It is in general intended to continue the policy of requiring exact performance by the seller of his obligations as a condition to his right to require acceptance. * * * ' "

2. Of the many cases involving UCC 2–606, the bulk involve the question whether the buyer, after having a reasonable opportunity to inspect the goods, has failed to "make an effective rejection," UCC 2–606(1)(b), that is, has failed to reject the goods within "a reasonable time after their delivery of tender." UCC 2–602(1). Like words or conduct indicating that the buyer will take the goods, silence for an unreasonable time induces the seller to believe that there is no problem with the tender of delivery. Whether an acceptance by failing to reject has occurred may turn on several factors, e.g., the nature of the defect (latent or patent), agreement on the time in which notice must be given, express warranties or assurances that problems will be corrected by the buyer, effort or lack of it by the buyer to test or inspect the goods, use of the goods by the buyer after the defect was or should have been discovered, special conditions indicating that prompt action is required, and so forth. In most cases, the difficulty will be in applying the legal principles to complicated or controverted facts. More may be at stake than simply losing the right to reject. At some point an unreasonable delay in rejecting may foreclose either a subsequent revocation of acceptance, UCC 2–608(2), or any remedy for the non-conformity, UCC 2–607(3)(a).

3. Under UCC 2–607(2), as well as its predecessor, Uniform Sales Act § 49, the fact of acceptance does not automatically preclude further remedies even though the buyer had a reasonable opportunity to inspect and the defect was "patent." This is an apparent concession to the assumption that the normal buyer's inspection will be less than adequate to deal with the complexities of defective tenders or products. In short, the buyer will not be deprived of any remedy simply because he should have discovered the particular defect complained of. But if acceptance "precludes rejection of the goods accepted," UCC 2–607(2), and the "buyer must pay at the contract rate for any goods accepted," UCC 2–607(1), what remedies remain for the buyer? The choice is between "revoking" the acceptance under UCC 2–608 or seeking damages "for breach in regard to accepted goods" under UCC 2–714. If revocation of acceptance is available and pursued, the buyer "has the same rights and duties with regard to the goods involved as if he had rejected them." UCC 2–608(3). He may, if the breach goes to the entire contract, cancel, recover so much of the price as has been paid and "cover" under UCC 2–712 or recover damages under UCC 2–713. UCC 2–711(1). If UCC 2–608 is not invoked or unavailable, the buyer must pay the contract price reduced by the amount of damages caused by the breach, UCC 2–717, and measured under UCC 2–714 and UCC 2–715.

The distinction between "latent" and "patent" defects, however, does appear in the UCC. UCC 2–607(3)(a) provides that where a tender has been accepted "the buyer must within a reasonable time after he discovers or should have discovered any breach notify the seller of breach or be barred from any remedy." As we shall see, this provision has generated controversy where defects in accepted goods cause damage to person or property. In commercial cases, however, the purpose of notification would seem to be to inform the seller "that the transaction is claimed to involve a breach, and thus [open] the way for normal settlement through negotiation." UCC 2–607, comment 4. Unlike the detail required by UCC 2–605 when goods are rejected, the content of notification under UCC 2–607(3) "need merely be sufficient to let the seller know that the transaction is still troublesome and must be watched." Comment 4. Consider the following problem.

Problem 18–6

The "Red Carpet" Treatment

On October 19, Dr. Miron, a physician who owned some race horses, attended an auction without his trainer. He observed a race horse named "Red Carpet" as he was led into the ring for sale. During a lull in the bidding, the auctioneer recited Red Carpet's "track record" and warranted him to be "sound." Thereafter, bidding picked up and Dr. Miron was the high bidder at $32,000. He took immediate possession and transported Red Carpet by van to his barn at a racetrack some 50 miles away. The next morning, Dr. Miron's trainer inspected Red Carpet and found him to be lame. The left hind leg was swollen and sensitive. X-rays later revealed a broken splint bone. Before noon on October 20, Dr. Miron notified the seller that the horse was not sound as warranted and demanded that the horse be taken back. Seller refused and insisted that the full price be paid.

1. You have been retained to represent Dr. Miron. After some probing, you have accumulated the following evidence:

(a) X-rays showing a broken splint bone in the left hind leg;

(b) Expert testimony that a broken splint bone renders a race horse unsound and, because the symptoms appear quickly, can be discovered by an inspection;

(c) Dr. Miron's affidavit that he was an inexperienced horse buyer, that he attended the auction without a trainer, that he did not examine the horse before the sale and that he did not inspect the horse's legs before transporting him to the barn;

(d) The testimony of other persons who attended the sale that they had examined Red Carpet before the auction and found no symptoms of a broken splint bone;

(e) Testimony of Dr. Miron's trainer that the problem was found and notice given within 24 hours of the sale. However, no blood tests were taken to determine whether the horse had been drugged at the time of sale.

The Seller has agreed to take the horse back if Dr. Miron will pay $20,000. Otherwise, he will sue for the full price under UCC 2–709(1). What would you advise the good doctor to do?

2. Suppose that Dr. Miron could establish that Red Carpet was not sound when the hammer fell. The seller, however, argued that Dr. Miron had accepted the horse and that either revocation of acceptance was barred under UCC 2–608(2) or that the buyer was barred from any remedy under UCC 2–607(3). How would you respond?

3. Suppose that Dr. Miron conceded that he had accepted a lame horse and attempted to revoke that acceptance under UCC 2–608(2). Who has the burden of proof in this situation? Compare UCC 2–607(4). See also, Keck v. Wacker, 413 F.Supp. 1377 (E.D.Ky.1976), another horse case, holding that where an acceptance was revoked the burden was on the seller to show that the horse conformed to the contract. Does this make sense? See UCC 2–515.

[For horse lovers, the case upon which this problem is based is Miron v. Yonkers Raceway, Inc., 400 F.2d 112 (2d Cir.1968).]

SECTION 5. SCOPE OF BUYER'S RIGHT TO REVOKE ACCEPTANCE

One of the consequences of accepting goods is that the buyer loses the rejection remedy provided in UCC 2–601. UCC 2–607(2). He is not necessarily "stuck" with the goods, however, since UCC 2–608 provides a controlled opportunity to "revoke" the acceptance and states that a "buyer who so revokes has the same rights and duties with regard to the goods involved as if he had rejected them." UCC 2–608(3). There is a temptation to equate "revocation of acceptance" with the remedy of rescission given by section 69 of the Uniform Sales Act for breach of warranty with regard to accepted goods. This temptation should be resisted. An effective revocation of acceptance neutralizes the effect of acceptance and enables the buyer to cancel the contract and pursue other available remedies under UCC 2–711. See Welken v. Conley, 252 N.W.2d 311 (N.D.1977). The buyer, however, may wish to keep the contract intact and negotiate for the repair or replacement of the goods involved. In any event, if an effective revocation occurs the remedies available to the buyer are broader and more flexible than under the USA. This is not to say that UCC 2–608 is easy to work with—it is loaded with "weasel" words which must be particularized in each case. Yet the commercial lawyer should spend some time with this section since the frustrated buyer who is unable to get satisfaction from the seller will be likely to seek advice about what to do with non-conforming goods which have been accepted, are still in his possession and may have been paid for in whole or in part.

Note, for example, the conditions attached to the "revocation of acceptance" remedy.

First, what is the effect of accepting the goods under UCC 2–606 without discovering the non-conformity? Or, suppose the buyer knew of the non-conformity and still accepted the goods? In either case, the buyer is protected if the seller made assurances that known defects would be cured or that there were no defects. UCC 2–608(1)(a) & (b). In the former case, the ancient distinction between latent and patent defects seems to be preserved: a buyer is not foreclosed from revocation where the acceptance of non-conforming goods "was reasonably induced * * * by the difficulty of discovery before acceptance. * * *" UCC 2–608(1)(b).

Second, the non-conformity, to justify revocation, must "substantially impair" the value "to him" of the goods accepted. UCC 2–608(1). What does this mean? An emerging view is that the court must make an objective determination that the value of the goods has been substantially impaired but that the determination must be made from the perspective of the particular buyer. Thus, even though leaks and dry rot in a sloop could have been repaired, the defect occurred in a vital part of the boat and "severely undermined" the buyer's confidence in its integrity as a sailing vessel. Its value was "substantially impaired."

Third, revocation of acceptance "must occur within a reasonable time after the buyer discovers or should have discovered the ground for it * * *" UCC 2–608(2). What is prompt action and what is an unreasonable delay are questions of fact.

Fourth, the revocation of acceptance, even if otherwise proper, must occur "before any substantial change in condition of the goods which is not caused by their own defects." This puts a premium on quick action where perishable commodities are involved. It also limits the scope of revocation where the goods were components or other items to be used or consumed in a manufacturing process.

Finally, the revocation is "not effective until the buyer notifies the seller of it." UCC 2–608(2). Is it enough for the buyer to pick up the telephone and say to the seller: "That last delivery was a disaster. We're getting out of this deal?" Apparently not. In Solar Kinetics Corp. v. Joseph T. Ryerson & Son, Inc., 488 F.Supp. 1237 (D.Conn.1980), the court held that the notice, to be adequate, must inform the seller that the buyer has revoked, which goods are involved and the nature of the defect. Cf. UCC 2–607(3).

ATLAN INDUSTRIES, INC. v. O.E.M., INC.

United States District Court, Western District of Oklahoma, 1983.
555 F.Supp. 184.

MEMORANDUM AND ORDER

SAFFELS, DISTRICT JUDGE, Sitting by Designation.

This case involves a complaint for the price of goods sold by plaintiff to defendant. Defendant denies liability for the price of the goods, and contends that the goods contained a latent defect which caused them to be unacceptable and out of conformity with the specifications in the sales contract between plaintiff and defendant.

Plaintiff is a prime supplier of reground plastic and wide specification machinery in the plastics industry. The goods in dispute between defendant and plaintiff are nine hundred thirty-five pounds (935 lbs.) of "Noryl-R-Beige FN 215" at eighty-five cents (85¢) per pound, as described in plaintiff's invoice No. 16886; nine thousand nine hundred fifty pounds (9,950 lbs.) of "Noryl-R-Grey FN 215" at eighty-five cents (85¢) per pound, as described on plaintiff's invoice No. 17114; and seventeen thousand two hundred ninety-five pounds (17,295 lbs.) of "Noryl-R-Grey FN 215" at eighty-five cents (85¢) per pound, as described on plaintiff's invoice No. 17449.

FN 215 is a high density, very hard plastic used primarily in the computer industry for making computer cabinets. There are two types of FN 215 on the market. "Virgin" FN 215 is plastic material which has never been molded and is manufactured only by General Electric. FN 215 "regrind" is plastic which has been molded once or more in its life, has been scrapped and has been ground for use again in a molding process. Defendant is a company which molds plastic into various parts and sells them to the computer industry. Defendant was under contract to a computer company, Magnetic Peripherals, Inc. (hereinafter MPI), to mold a number of computer cabinet parts from FN 215. Plaintiff agreed to supply defendant with raw FN 215 for this molding job. Plaintiff did not know the end use of the FN 215 it was supplying to defendant, and the name of the user was kept secret.

After agreeing to supply defendant with FN 215, plaintiff contacted a supplier about a supply of reground FN 215. Plaintiff tested the FN 215 for contamination and foreign matter, and forwarded a 935-pound sample of the FN 215 to defendant for testing.

In the plastics industry, it is a common practice for a supplier of raw plastic to forward a sample to the molder for testing. The purpose of the test is to see if the plastic material will mold well. No injection molder has facilities to do any other test. The reason for testing regrind material is that some regrind is badly contaminated with metal, which clogs the injection molding equipment and requires the molding machine to be shut down and cleaned. "Regrind" is plastic which has been molded once, and then is ground into pellets to be re-used. The regrinding process sometimes leaves small pieces of metal and metal chips in the plastic.

FN 215 is an expensive plastic which is specially compounded for use in office machines and computers. FN 215 is heat sensitive, but is able to withstand temperatures of at least two hundred five degrees (205°). Because the material is generally used in office machines and computers, it is almost always painted after molding to improve its cosmetic appearance. Defendant does not paint the parts it molds; they forward them to the ultimate user, who paints them.

The particular shipments involved in this lawsuit were molded by defendant and forwarded to their ultimate user, MPI. MPI painted the parts and heated them in an infrared oven to dry the paint. The parts molded from FN 215 "regrind" supplied by plaintiff warped when exposed to the temperature of the infrared heat ovens. The computer parts were warping when exposed to temperatures of between one hundred thirty degrees (130°) and one hundred seventy degrees (170°). Noryl FN 215 will not warp at this temperature range. Defendant molded the entire shipment of Noryl FN 215 into computer parts and tendered them to MPI before the problem surfaced. MPI immediately rejected the goods as defective and non-conforming because of the warping problem. Defendant immediately notified plaintiff that MPI had rejected the goods because of warpage, and that the material supplied by plaintiff was defective and non-conforming.

Defendant was instructed by plaintiff sometime in March, 1982, to return the material to plaintiff. Subsequently, all but four thousand pounds (4,000 lbs.) of the material supplied by plaintiff was returned to plaintiff by defendant in substantially the same condition. Plaintiff was unable to furnish Noryl FN 215 from another source. Due to plaintiff's inability to furnish conforming FN 215, defendant purchased forty thousand pounds (40,000 lbs.) of FN 215 from General Electric at forty-two cents (42¢) per pound higher than plaintiff's price. Defendant invested eighty (80) hours of labor at Ten Dollars ($10) per hour to inspect and regrind the non-conforming FN 215 back to its original state to return to plaintiff. The material was reground because it would therefore be cheaper to ship and easier for plaintiff to resell. In addition, plaintiff agreed that it would be better to regrind the material.

This lawsuit is governed by Article 2 of the Uniform Commercial Code. The court finds that there was a contract for sale of goods between plaintiff and defendant. Plaintiff agreed to sell to defendant a known quantity of Noryl FN 215. It is undisputed that Noryl FN 215 does not warp at one hundred fifty degrees (150°), and it is undisputed that parts made from the Noryl FN 215 supplied by plaintiff did warp when exposed to temperatures of one hundred fifty degrees (150°). Therefore, we find that the goods tendered by plaintiff failed to conform to the contract. Pursuant to Okla.Stat. 12A, § 2–601, if goods fail in any respect to conform to a contract, the buyer may reject all of them or accept all of them.

Acceptance of goods occurs when the buyer, after a reasonable opportunity to inspect them, signifies to the seller that the goods are conforming or that he will take them despite their non-conformity, or where the buyer fails to make an effective rejection, or does any act inconsistent with the seller's ownership. Okla.Stat. 12A, § 2–606(1). A buyer is deemed to have accepted goods when, without making any effort to reject them, he receives the goods, processes them, and sells the finished product to a third-person. *A & G Construction Co., Inc. v. Reid Brothers Logging Co., Inc.,* 547 P.2d 1207 (Alaska 1976). Such actions on the part of the buyer are clearly inconsistent with ownership by the seller. Anderson, *Uniform Commercial Code,* § 2–606:31 (1971). The court finds defendant accepted the goods.

A buyer must pay at the contract rate for any goods he has accepted. Okla. Stat. 12A, § 2–607(1). However, a buyer may revoke his acceptance of goods whose non-conformity substantially impairs their value to him if he has accepted those goods without discovery of the non-conformity where his acceptance was reasonably induced by the difficulty of discovery before acceptance. Okla.Stat. 12A, § 2–608(1)(b). As a condition precedent to revoking acceptance, the buyer must show that the goods are both non-conforming and that the non-conformance substantially impairs the value of the goods to the buyer.

Goods are "conforming" when they are in accordance with the obligations under the contract. Okla.Stat. 12A, § 2–106(2). The Noryl FN 215 in issue in this case was not conforming because it would not tolerate the temperature that Noryl FN 215 is specifically able to tolerate.

The test for whether the non-conformity substantially impairs the value of the goods to the buyer is whether the non-conformity is such as will in fact cause a substantial impairment of the value to the buyer even though the seller had no advance knowledge as to the buyer's particular circumstances. Okla.Stat. 12A, § 2–608, Official Code Comment 2. The court finds that the non-conformity substantially impaired the value of the Noryl FN 215 to the buyer, plaintiff Atlan. FN 215 is primarily used to make computer cabinets and to house office machines. The plastic, when molded, is a dull, off-white or a dull, grey color. It is virtually always painted a more pleasant color before it is sold to its ultimate user. Noryl FN 215 does not have any other reasonable use. The Noryl FN 215 in question, when painted, could not withstand the temperatures in a drying oven. Therefore, the parts could not be painted and dried in the ordinary manner. If the parts could not be painted, they could not be used in the computer and office machinery industry. They were, therefore, substantially without value to the ultimate user and to the molder who had manufactured them. Therefore, the value of this particular Noryl FN 215 was substantially impaired because it did not conform to the characteristics inherent in normal Noryl FN 215.

If the buyer did not know of the non-conformity when he accepted the goods, he must show his acceptance was reasonably induced by the difficulty of discovering the non-conformity before acceptance. The undisputed testimony revealed that in the plastics industry it is common for a molder to test samples only to see whether or not they will mold well. The Noryl FN 215 in question was so tested and did mold well. Plaintiff contends that the defendant was under an additional duty to forward samples he had molded to his customer, MPI, to see whether or not the molded samples would conform to MPI's specifications. While this might be a reasonable provision to place in a contract for sale between plaintiff and defendant, the court finds that the law does not require the buyer to perform any more tests than are common in the industry. Okla.Stat. 12A, § 1–205(2).

Revocation of acceptance must occur within a reasonable time after the buyer discovers the non-conformity. There is no claim in this case that defendant unreasonably delayed notifying plaintiff of the non-conformity, and the court finds that plaintiff was notified within a reasonable time after defendant discovered the warping problem.

A buyer who revokes acceptance has the same rights with regard to the goods involved as if he had rejected them. Okla.Stat. 12A, § 2–608(3). "Rights" includes remedies. Okla.Stat. 12A, § 1–201(36). A buyer who has rightfully rejected goods has no further obligation in regard to those goods, including an obligation to pay their purchase price. Okla.Stat. 12A, § 2–602(2)(c). Therefore, the court finds against plaintiff on his complaint for the purchase price of the Noryl FN 215 involved in this lawsuit, and now turns to the question of defendant's remedies for rejection of non-conforming goods.

* * *

It is by the court therefore ordered that plaintiff take nothing of defendant on plaintiff's complaint. It is further ordered that judgment be entered in favor of defendant and against plaintiff on defendant's counterclaim in the sum of Sixty-Four Thousand Fourteen and 47/100 Dollars ($64,014.47). It is further ordered that costs are assessed against plaintiff.

JOHANNSEN v. MINNESOTA VALLEY FORD TRACTOR CO.

Supreme Court of Minnesota, 1981.
304 N.W.2d 654.

Considered and decided by the court en banc without oral argument.

OPINION

PETERSON, JUSTICE.

The defendants, Ford Motor Co. and Minnesota Valley Ford (dealer), appeal from the judgment entered in favor of the plaintiff, Harvey Johannsen, the buyer of a defective tractor manufactured by Ford and sold to him by the dealer. After a trial in which the jury found that Johannsen had effectively revoked his acceptance of a Ford Model 9700 tractor (9700), the district court entered judgment for the plaintiff in the amount of the purchase price of the tractor less an offset for use and depreciation. Defendants appeal from the order denying post-trial motions for judgment notwithstanding the verdict or a new trial and also appeal from the judgment. We affirm.

The plaintiff revoked his acceptance of the 9700 tractor pursuant to Minn. Stat. § 336.2–608(1)(b) (1980) after he experienced mechanical problems that substantially interfered with its intended use on his 330–acre farm. On July 13, 1977, plaintiff, together with his wife, went to the premises of the dealer to pick up his 1974 Ford Model 9600 tractor (9600), which had been taken to the dealer for repairs. Johannsen had experienced a number of problems with the fourth gear and hydraulic system of his 9600. The tractor had jumped out of fourth gear on a number of occasions while Johannsen was plowing. Johannsen expressed his concern to Brian Gaard, one of the dealer's employees, that the 9600 would again jump out of gear.

Gaard told Johannsen that the transmission of the new 1977 Ford Model 9700 had been redesigned to avoid the transmission defects of the 9600 and that he could solve his tractor transmission problems by purchasing a new 9700 for $26,000. Gaard did not tell Johannsen that Ford had sent a letter to its tractor dealers in May of that year detailing transmission defects in the 9700. Dealers were informed that some 9700's jumped out of fourth and/or eighth gear. They were instructed to check all 9700's in stock for the defect and to sell defective tractors only if they would lose a sale. Johannsen purchased a 9700 from the dealer and traded in his 9600.

The dealer delivered the tractor to Johannsen's farm in late July. The tractor jumped out of fourth gear upon its first use, and at about the same time the frost plugs blew out of the engine, causing a loss of all of the coolant. The dealer sent a repairman to plaintiff's farm on that day who told Johannsen to see the dealer about the transmission defect. On August 3, 1977, the tractor developed a fuel restriction problem and a hydraulic leak, which made it difficult to lower the implements into the soil. The dealer informed Johannsen that it could not fix the hydraulic defect until replacement parts became available in April, 1978. Johannsen told every serviceman who called at his farm that he wanted to return the tractor.

On September 19, 1977, Johannsen, by his attorney, formally notified the dealer in writing of his revocation of acceptance due to transmission, hydraulic and fuel line defects, and he directed the dealer to pick up the tractor immediately.

Johannsen continued to use the tractor after the written revocation and called the dealer on September 28 because the tractor continued to exhibit the same problems. The dealer made service calls on September 28, October 2, and October 9 in response to Johannsen's complaints. Ray Chaik, an employee of the dealer, told Johannsen that he could finish his fall work and bring the tractor in for winter servicing. Johannsen used the tractor for a total of 120 hours but was able to plow or disk only 150 acres of his farm with it. Approximately 90 of those hours were put on the tractor after the revocation letter of September 19. Johannsen put the tractor in storage in late October, 1977.

The defendants contend that the plaintiff did not effectively revoke his acceptance of the 9700 tractor because (1) he did not allow the defendants to attempt to cure the defects, (2) the defects did not substantially impair the value of the tractor, (3) the plaintiff did not revoke his acceptance of the tractor seasonably, and (4) the plaintiff continued to use the tractor after revocation of acceptance.

1. The defendants, although acknowledging that the seller's right to cure pursuant to Minn.Stat. § 336.2–508(2) (1980) is expressly limited by the language of the statute to cases in which the buyer rejects a non-conforming tender, argue that the right to cure should be incorporated into Minn.Stat. § 336.2–608(3) (1980) governing revocation of acceptance.[4] It is our view that any right to cure should be limited to cases in which the defects are minor, and we hold that the seller has no right to cure defects which substantially impair the good's value.

2. We reject defendants' contention that the jury's finding that the defects substantially impaired the value of the tractor to plaintiff is not supported by the evidence. In *Durfee v. Rod Baxter Imports, Inc.*, 262 N.W.2d 349, 353–54 (Minn.1977), we set forth guidelines to establish the substantial impairment requirement of Minn.Stat. § 336.2–608(1):

> [T]wo respected commentators suggest that the test ultimately rests on a commonsense perception of substantial impairment, akin to the determination of a material breach under traditional contract law. White & Sum-

4. Commentators are divided on the issue of whether the seller has a right to cure after the buyer revokes his acceptance. *See e.g.,* J. White & R. Summers, *Uniform Commercial Code,* 293 (1980) (no right to cure); *contra* 3 S. Williston, Williston on Sales 119 (Supp.1980).

> mers, Uniform Commercial Code, § 8–3, p. 257. The cases that involve revocation of acceptance of defective new automobiles are amenable to classification by this practical criterion. Minor defects not substantially interfering with the automobile's operation or with the comfort and security it affords passengers do not constitute grounds for revocation. On the other hand, if the defect substantially interferes with operation of the vehicle or a purpose for which it was purchased, a court may find grounds for revocation. Indeed, substantial impairment has been found even where the defect is curable, if it shakes the faith of the purchaser in the automobile.

Substantial evidence supports the jury's finding that the transmission and hydraulic defects substantially impaired the value of the tractor to plaintiff. He specifically purchased the 9700 to avoid problems with the essential fourth gear which he had experienced with the 9600. As a result of the defects, he was only able to use the tractor on 150 acres of his 330–acre farm. Plaintiff testified that due to the defect it took him two weeks to plow 50 acres of sweet corn ground, a task that should have taken less than 4 hours to complete. Under these circumstances, the jury's finding is supported by the evidence.

3. We likewise reject defendants' contention that plaintiff did not revoke his acceptance within a reasonable time after discovering the defect. The issue of what constitutes a reasonable time within the context of revocation of acceptance is a jury question that depends on the facts and circumstances of the case. We hold that the jury's finding that plaintiff's revocation was timely is supported by the evidence because it could have reasonably concluded that plaintiff gave notice within a reasonable time after discovering through his use of the tractor that it would not adequately perform the tasks for which it was purchased.

4. Defendants additionally contend that plaintiff's use of the tractor after he gave written notice of revocation of acceptance constitutes a second acceptance. Although the revoking buyer's continued use of defective goods may be wrongful under some circumstances,[5] we think that there can be no blanket rule which prohibits such a buyer from continuing to use the goods. A blanket rule prohibiting a revoking buyer from continuing to use the goods would contravene the code's rule of reasonableness and its underlying purpose of modernizing commercial transactions. We agree with those jurisdictions that have so held. *See Minsel v. El Rancho Mobile Home Center, Inc.,* 32 Mich.App. 10, 188 N.W.2d 9 (1971). *Fablok Mills, Inc. v. Cocker Machinery & Foundry Co.,* 125 N.J.Super. 251, 310 A.2d 491 (Super.Ct.App.Div.1973), *cert. denied,* 64 N.J. 317; 315 A.2d 405 (1973).

The reasonableness of the buyer's use of a defective good after revocation is a question of fact for the jury that is to be based on the facts and circumstances of each case. Several factors that the jury may consider include the seller's instructions to the buyer after revocation of acceptance; the degree of economic and other hardship that the buyer would suffer if he discontinued using the defective good; the reasonableness of the buyer's use after revocation as a method of mitigating damages; the degree of prejudice to the seller; and whether the seller acted in bad faith.

5. Minn.Stat. § 336.2–602(2)(a) (1980) provides that any exercise of ownership by a rejecting buyer is wrongful as against the seller. Defendants contend that because section 336–2–608(3) imposes upon revoking buyers the same rights and duties as if they had rejected the goods, that a revoking buyer's continued use of goods is always wrongful.

We hold, limited to the facts and circumstances of this case, that the jury could find that plaintiff's continued use of the 9700 tractor was reasonable and did not constitute a waiver of his revocation of acceptance. The defects in the 9700 tractor were major. Employees of the dealer knew that Johannsen specifically purchased the 9700 to avoid the transmission defect in the 9600, knew of the possibility of the identical defect in the 9700, and yet they led Johannsen to believe that buying the 9700 would solve all of his tractor transmission problems. In addition, evidence in the record tends to show that Johannsen used the tractor only to perform necessary tasks.

We note that the trial court, based upon expert testimony, allowed the defendants a setoff for use and depreciation of the tractor. Allowing the seller to recover for the revoking buyer's use of the tractor best serves the equitable principle incorporated into the code through Minn.Stat. § 336.1–103 (1980)[6] that a party seeking rescission of a contract must return or offer to return that which he had received under it in order to restore the parties to the positions that they occupied prior to the transaction. *See Village of Wells v. Layne-Minnesota Co.*, 240 Minn. 132, 138, 60 N.W.2d 621, 625 (1953).

5. Defendants contend that the trial court improperly excluded for lack of foundation a warranty which limited a buyer's remedies to repair or replacement. Defendants asserted that plaintiff had been given a copy of Ford's standard warranty, but they were unable to produce an executed copy of the warranty. Plaintiff denied that he had executed any such warranty. We conclude that the trial court did not err in the exclusion of the alleged warranty.

The instructions given to the jury by the trial court are in conformity with the law as we have stated it. Defendants' other claims of error on evidentiary matters do not require discussion.

Affirmed.

Problem 18–7

On April 19, 1976, defendant Clarence Miller ordered a 1976 Dodge Royal Monaco station wagon from plaintiff Colonial Dodge which included a heavy-duty trailer package with extra wide tires.

On May 28, 1976, defendant picked up the wagon, drove it a short distance where he met his wife, and exchanged it for her car. Defendant drove that car to work while his wife returned home with the new station wagon. Shortly after arriving home, Mrs. Miller noticed that their new wagon did not have a spare tire. The following morning defendant notified plaintiff that he insisted on having the tire he ordered immediately, but when told there was no spare tire then available, he informed the salesman for plaintiff that he would stop payment on the two checks that were tendered as the purchase price, and that the vehicle could be picked up from in front of his home. Defendant parked the car in front of his home where it remained until the temporary ten-day registration sticker had expired, whereupon the car was towed by the St. Clair police to a St. Clair dealership. Plaintiff had applied for license plates, registration, and title in defendant's name. Defendant refused the license plates when they were delivered to him.

6. Minn.Stat. § 336.1–103 (1978) provides: "Unless displaced by the particular provisions of this Act, the principles of law and equity, including the law merchant and the law relative to capacity to contract, principal and agent, estoppel, fraud, misrepresentation, duress, coercion, mistake, bankruptcy, or other validating or invalidating cause shall supplement its provisions."

According to plaintiff's witness, the spare tire was not included in the delivery of the vehicle due to a nation-wide shortage caused by a labor strike. Some months later, defendant was notified his tire was available.

Plaintiff sued defendant for the purchase price of the car. On January 13, 1981, the trial court entered a judgment for plaintiff finding that defendant wrongfully revoked acceptance of the vehicle. The Court of Appeals decided that defendant never accepted the vehicle. On rehearing, the Court of Appeals, noting the trial court found the parties had agreed that there was a valid acceptance, affirmed the trial court's holding there was not a substantial impairment in value sufficient to authorize defendant to revoke acceptance of the automobile.

How should this case be resolved on appeal to the Supreme Court?

CHAPTER NINETEEN

SELLER'S BREACH OF WARRANTY AS TO THE QUALITY OF GOODS SOLD

SECTION 1. INTRODUCTION

A. *Warranty Theory: Some History*

Disputes over the quality of goods sold frequently end up in court. The buyer's claim is that the goods, because of a condition existing at the time of tender, failed to conform to his expectations regarding basic attributes or suitability. The seller's response may be that the buyer assumed the risk. More particularly, the argument is that since neither party knew of the condition at the time of delivery, i.e., both were equally ignorant, and the buyer could have discovered the condition by inspection or otherwise, there is no sound reason, absent fraud, deceit or mutual mistake, why the seller should bear the risk. Thus, the stage is set, the seller will contend, for application of the doctrine of caveat emptor, the "universal structural characteristic of the law of sales." Rabel, *The Nature of Warranty of Quality,* 24 Tulane L.Rev. 273 (1970). See Hamilton, *The Ancient Maxim of Caveat Emptor,* 49 Yale L.J. 1133 (1931).

One "sound" reason for protecting the buyer's expectations is found in the law of warranty. Warranty is a representational theory of liability. It depends upon the answers to two key questions: (1) What did the seller affirm, represent or promise, expressly or impliedly, about the quality of the goods sold to the buyer; and (2) Was the buyer justified in incorporating the representations into his expectations of quality? The first question poses primarily a question of fact. The second question is primarily a question of law. Clearly, not everything a seller says about the goods will become part of the contract for sale. To the extent that representations of quality become part of the agreement, however, they constitute a standard of quality—a warranty—to which the goods must conform at the time of delivery.

The Anglo-American history of warranty reveals, in commercial transactions at least,* a slow but steady erosion of the doctrine of caveat emptor. The following account, taken from the sources cited below, touches the doctrinal tip of a much larger social iceberg. Hillinger, *The Merchant of Section 2–314: Who Needs Him?,* 34 Hastings L.Rev. 747, 788–807 (1983); Titus, *Restatement (Second) of Torts Section 402A and the Uniform Commercial Code,* 22 Stan.L.Rev. 713, 728–344 (1970); Prosser, *The Implied Warranty of Merchantable Quality,* 27

* There are, in fact, three legal worlds of product liability. The first, with which these Chapters are concerned, concerns disputes over quality between commercial parties where only economic loss is involved. These disputes are governed, in the main, by Article 2. The second involves disputes between individuals and commercial sellers over "defective" products which have caused personal injuries. These disputes are governed by the law of torts, primarily the law of strict products liability. See Section 402A of the Restatement, Second, of Torts. The third involves disputes between individual consumers and commercial sellers over quality where economic loss and, perhaps, property damage has occurred. These are governed in part by Article 2 and in part by a patchwork of federal and supplemental state consumer protection laws. See Rice, *Product Quality Laws and the Economics of Federalism,* 65 B.U.L. Rev. 1 (1985).

Minn.L.Rev. 117 (1943); Llewellyn, *On Warranty of Quality and Society, I*, 36 Colum.L.Rev. 699, 716–31 (1936); Hamilton, *The Ancient Maxim Caveat Emptor*, 40 Yale L.J. 1133, 1163–78 (1931); Williston, *Representation and Warranty in Sales*, 27 Harv.L.Rev. 1 (1913); McClain, *Implied Warranties in Sales*, 7 Harv.L. Rev. 213 (1903).

Warranty disputes involving claims for economic loss first arose between sellers and buyers of goods who were in privity of contract. In the early 17th Century, however, they were asserted in tort as an action on the Case. The buyer had to establish the elements of deceit, i.e., that the seller made an express representation about the nature of the goods knowing it to be false.

By 1790, the action of Deceit, with its requirements of scienter by the representor and reliance by the representee, had developed into a separate writ or action. At about the same time, the English courts first permitted an express warranty claim to be brought in assumpsit, the action in which most contract claims were pursued.

By 1802, it was decided that scienter was not a requirement in Assumpsit for breach of an express warranty, but other limiting formalities, i.e., the representation must be an express term of the contract and intended by the seller to be a warranty, still remained. This early interaction between representations of quality made in exchange transactions and the tort forms of action led Dean Prosser to conclude that warranty was a "freak hybrid born of the illicit intercourse of tort and contract." Prosser, *The Assault Upon the Citadel (Strict Liability to the Consumer)*, 69 Yale L.J. 1099, 1126–27 (1960). The New York Court of Appeals, in a personal injury case, concluded: "Accordingly, for some 400 years the action rested not on an enforcible (sic) promise but on a wrong or tort. In the historical development of the law of warranty, however, as so often happens in law and life in general, accident was evidently confused with essence: from the fact that the cases which arose involved contractual relationships and represented enforcible (sic) promises, the courts seem to have concluded that the contract was the essence of the action. * * * The occasion for the warranty was constituted a necessary condition of it." Randy Knitwear, Inc. v. American Cyanamid Co., 11 N.Y.2d 5, 226 N.Y.S.2d 363, 181 N.E.2d 399, 401 n. 2 (1962).

During the 19th Century, warranty theory developed into the tripartite form which we know today, an express warranty, an implied warranty of fitness for particular purpose and an implied warranty of merchantability (fitness for "ordinary" purposes). The implied warranties emerged, inferentially, at the point where the seller's express representations about or description of the goods failed to cover the exact issue in dispute. All three were captured, in the late 19th Century, by the British Sale of Goods Act and, later, in the American Uniform Sales Act. They appear as Sections 2–313, 2–314 and 2–315 of the Uniform Commercial Code. We will return to examine each and all in more detail.

Before looking at warranty theory under the UCC, a few general questions should be kept in mind.

First, warranties, arising as they do from contracts for sale, have been treated as terms of the contract. Two consequences flow from this treatment: (1) A breach of warranty is a breach of contract, entitling the seller to recover direct and consequential economic loss measured by the expectation interest; (2) Privity of contract has usually been required between the seller and buyer, especially where the buyer claims only economic loss. Are these consequences inevitable? For example, should a plaintiff injured in person by a defective product be permitted to recover under a warranty theory? Or, should a buyer who suffers only economic loss caused by an unmerchantable product manufactured by a remote seller be permitted to recover on a warranty theory without privity of contract?

Second, the tort of misrepresentation has developed apart from warranty theory. In general, the misrepresentation must be material and negligently made. In addition, the plaintiff must justifiably rely upon it and is limited, in many cases, to the recovery of out-of-pocket economic loss. But when the misrepresentation concerns goods sold, there is an obvious overlap with the theory of express warranty. Which should prevail in these cases, express warranties under the UCC or tort theory?

Third, in the last 25 years a special body of law has developed to protect individual consumers who purchase goods for personal, family or household purposes and suffer economic loss. Uneven though this development has been, it reflects a conclusion that there is usually an imbalance of capacity between the individual and the enterprise and that this imbalance creates a risk of exploitation in bargaining or unprovable fraud by the enterprise. The legal response includes the federal Magnuson-Moss Warranty Act and state legislation, such as the "lemon" laws. Is this development justified? If so, how much government regulation is necessary to correct the imbalance, whether it be in bargaining power, information or capacity for choice, and should that regulation be included in the UCC?

Fourth, defective and dangerous products manufactured by sellers frequently cause damage to the person or property of purchasers and other foreseeable users or consumers. Since the great case of *McPherson v. Buick Motor Company,* decided in 1920, injured parties have been able, privity or not, to sue the manufacturer in negligence. Since the 1960s, with the promulgation of Section 402A of the Restatement, Second, Torts, injured parties have been permitted to sue under the theory of strict products liability. Although negligence theory has not been preempted, it has been eclipsed by strict liability.

Given these developments in the law of products liability, to what extent does the UCC preempt tort law where the seller has breached a warranty and the buyer has suffered personal injuries or property loss? Should the buyer with both a claim in warranty and a claim in strict tort be able to choose which to pursue? And what about products that cause only economic loss or cause damage only to the goods sold? Should these claims be limited to warranty theory under the UCC or may they also be pursued under negligence or strict tort theory? What difference does it make? In the materials to follow, we will try to provide some answers to these questions.

B. Warranties Under the Code: An Introduction

According to Comment 4 to UCC 2–313, the basic purpose of warranty law is to determine "what it is that the seller has in essence agreed to sell." As you are now fully aware, agreement means the "bargain in fact as found in their language or by implication from other circumstances." UCC 1–201(3). Thus, whether the buyer's understanding of quality is consistent with the agreement may depend, among other things, upon the description, what the seller has said, common uses in the trade, the price paid and the extent to which the buyer has communicated particular needs to the seller. Interestingly enough, the more detailed the agreement on quality and the allocation of risks, the less room there is for legitimate dispute over conformity of the goods to the contract and the less likely it is that the warranty label will be applied to the controversy.

The UCC draftsmen, however, have selected an approach which yields warranties of different kinds, including express warranties, UCC 2–313, implied warranties of merchantability, UCC 2–314, and implied warranties of fitness for particular purpose, UCC 2–315—a tripartite approach. (The implied warranty of title, UCC 2–312, will be treated later.) In so doing, the draftsmen rejected the unitary approach suggested by the theory of contract and, at the same time, preserved the close tie between warranty and the contract. The initial question, therefore, will be whether the Code's tripartite approach to the problem supports any breach of warranty claim at all. The answer to this question will also be affected by the possible application of exclusionary rules, i.e., disclaimers or rules of interpretation, which neutralize facts which otherwise would support a warranty claim. See UCC 2–316, 2–317 & 2–202. These rules proceed on the assumption that what is rooted in contract can, under controlled circumstances, be taken away or altered by contract.

A second question is when did the buyer discover the alleged breach of warranty? This has immense practical importance. If the defect is discovered before acceptance, the remedy of rejection, UCC 2–601 through 2–605, and the remedial options in UCC 2–711(1) are available. The remedial problems become more complicated after acceptance, and the degree of complication is closely related to how soon thereafter the defect was discovered. The risks of delay are pinpointed in UCC 2–725(2), 2–608(2) and 2–607(3)(a). Other problems flowing from acceptance have to do with revoking acceptance, UCC 2–608(1), burden of proof, UCC 2–607(4), uncertainty in the measure of "direct" damage, UCC 2–714(2), and the increased risk that consequential damages will be involved. UCC 2–715(2). As a general rule, the earlier the breach is discovered and the quicker remedial options are exercised, the better off the buyer will be.

Another question is the extent to which the seller has validly altered by contract the normal remedies available to the buyer upon breach of warranty. Relevant Code sections include UCC 2–316, 2–718, 2–719 & 2–302. A final question is, of course, whether a warranty made by the seller has in fact been breached.

The problem and case that follow introduce the relevant Code warranty sections.

Problem 19–1

The Case of the Hot Casserole

Sam Sweeney owns and operates a supermarket which specializes in produce from many lands. The produce is displayed in open bins at one end of the store under a large sign which reads "Foods from Many Lands." Above each bin is space for a written description of the produce and a price. On the morning of March 5, Sam received a shipment of pepper beans from Africa. The dried beans, which closely resembled lima beans, were extremely hot to the taste. The beans were displayed in an empty bin but, because of the press of other matters, Sam did not describe the goods or fix a price at that time. Sam did not sell dried lima beans at this store, but they could be purchased at other stores for between $.20 and $.25 per pound. On the morning of March 6, Mrs. Banks, a new resident in the area, entered Sam's store for the first time. She wanted to purchase lima beans for a special casserole to be served that evening at a dinner party for her husband's new boss. Mrs. Banks did not notice the "Foods from Many Lands" sign. After walking around the produce bins, she found what seemed to be plain old garden variety lima beans. She asked a salesman the price and was told "$.23 a pound." Pointing to the unmarked bin, she stated, "I will take two pounds of those." The beans were weighed, put into a sack and paid for. Later that afternoon, Mrs. Banks prepared her special casserole which was served to her guests without the true nature of the beans being discovered. The casserole, of course, was somewhat difficult to eat and the dinner party, while interesting, was something less than a success. The next morning, a furious Mrs. Banks consults her attorney.

1. Does she have any legal recourse against Sam? What advice would you give?

2. Suppose that one of Mrs. Banks' guests had become violently ill after eating the beans. Would the guest have a warranty claim against Sam? See UCC 2–318.

3. At what point would Sam, who had knowledge superior to Mrs. Banks, be impressed with a duty to caution or warn about the special nature of the beans? See Addis v. Bernardin, Inc., 226 Kan. 241, 597 P.2d 250 (1979) (seller knew goods sold would not suit buyer's purposes).

HOBSON CONST. CO., INC. v. HAJOCA CORP.

Court of Appeals of North Carolina, 1976.
28 N.C.App. 684, 222 S.E.2d 709.

Plaintiff [Hobson] brought this action against defendant [Hajoca] for damages resulting from defective equipment purchased from Hajoca. It was alleged that the defects amounted to a breach of warranties. Hajoca denied that the equipment was defective and denied liability.

The case was tried without a jury and plaintiff's evidence tended to establish the following:

Triple Community Water Corporation [Water Corp.], located in Drexel, North Carolina, retained the services of Register & Cummings, Engineers, to prepare plans and specifications for a water treatment and conditioning plant. Hobson entered into a contract with the Water Corporation to construct the plant in accordance with the plans and specifications of the engineers.

The plant was to be built primarily for the purpose of filtering iron and manganese from the water supply. The engineers' specifications provided that "filter equipment shall be similar and equal to Diamond Model Three (3) DMG 84–45 as manufactured by Oshkosh Filter and Softener Company." Further specifications provided that the "plate shall contain a sufficient number of corrosion resistant segmented plastic distributors with stainless steel bolts to provide uniform distribution." It was established that Oshkosh was the only company that manufactured the segmented plastic distributors.

Hobson purchased from Hajoca three Diamond Model Three (3) DMG 84–45 filter tanks which were manufactured by Oshkosh. One of Hajoca's representatives stated to Hobson's president that the filter tanks being sold "should remove the iron and manganese from the water."

Near the bottom of each filter tank was a steel plate with fifty-two threaded holes with nipples screwed into them. A segmented plastic distributor head was attached to each nipple. The distributor heads were plastic with small holes through which the filtered water could pass.

The steel plate and distributor heads were covered with silica sand, and above the silica sand was a layer of "green sand." Raw water flowed into the tank at the top, chemicals were added, and the water was supposed to react with the chemicals and green sand in such a way that the iron and manganese would stick to the particles of green sand leaving the finished water to flow through the silica sand and distributor heads and on out the bottom of the tank.

Difficulties developed after the filter tanks were installed in April of 1971. The finished water contained silica sand and green sand, and not enough iron and manganese was removed to comply with government requirements. There were also other serious difficulties and problems. The distributor heads either ruptured or disintegrated and the silica sand and green sand that remained in the tanks became mixed together.

In December of 1971 plaintiff took out the distributor heads, nipples, silica sand and green sand, and bored 88 new holes into the steel plate. The 52 plastic distributor heads and nipples were replaced with 140 stainless steel ones manufactured by a different company. The water treatment plant worked very well thereafter and produced good water.

The president of Hobson testified that he believed the difficulties with the filter tanks were caused by an insufficient number of distributor heads for the amount of water passing through the tanks, and that the distributor heads broke under the excessive water pressure.

At the conclusion of plaintiff's evidence the trial court granted defendant's motion for involuntary dismissal under Rule 41(b) of the N.C. Rules of Civil Procedure. The court made findings of fact and conclusions of law and held that there was no breach by defendant of any express or implied warranty. Plaintiff appealed to this court.

ARNOLD, JUDGE.

* * *

Plaintiff maintains that the filter tanks were defective and in breach of the implied warranty of merchantability. We find no evidence that the tanks were unmerchantable. Plaintiff asserts that the distributor heads were not "fit for the ordinary purposes for which such goods are used" as required by G.S. 25–2–314(2). The evidence, however, merely establishes that the distributor heads were not fit for use under excessive water pressure as contained by the Water Corp.'s system, which was not the ordinary purpose for which the goods were sold.

In regards to any implied warranty of fitness for a particular purpose the court made the following conclusion: "The plaintiff has failed to present evidence of any implied warranty by Hajoca of the fitness of the system to perform its intended purpose, upon which plaintiff relied." That conclusion is supported by the court's finding that under its contract with the Water Corp. plaintiff was required by the specifications, prepared by the engineers, to use the equipment specified as the 3 Model DMG 84–4 [sic] [84–45] Diamond filter units manufactured by Oshkosh, and that plaintiff purchased "in reliance upon the specifications, and pursuant to its contract, and not in reliance upon any warranty, affirmation, or representation, express or implied, by Hajoca as to the merchantability or the fitness of the system for its intended use." There is no warranty of fitness for a particular purpose unless "the buyer is relying on the seller's skill or judgment to select or furnish suitable goods." G.S. 25–2–315.

G.S. 25–2–313 contains the requirements for express warranties. Any affirmation of fact or promise made by the seller concerning the goods sold is an express warranty if it "becomes part of the basis of the bargain." There was no express warranty in the present case in view of the following finding of fact made by the court: "The statements of Hajoca's manager to plaintiff to the effect that the apparatus 'should' be able to remove iron and manganese from the water did not amount to an affirmation of fact effecting [sic] the bargain between plaintiff and Hajoca."

Plaintiff further argues that notwithstanding any other statements made by Hajoca an express warranty arose from the fact that the tanks were described as "iron removal filters." This argument has no merit. There is no evidence that the tanks were not "iron removal filters." They simply failed to sufficiently filter the water under the system as it was designed by the Water Corp., and from the evidence the defect was in the plans and specifications of the engineers, and not the filter tanks.

The judgment appealed from is affirmed.

Affirmed.

PARKER and HEDRICK, JJ., concur.

Notes

In *Hobson,* the plaintiff lost on all three warranties. What additional facts would have supported a victory on all three claims?

SECTION 2. NON-COMPLIANCE WITH EXPRESS WARRANTIES

A. Liability for Statements Constituting "Core" Descriptions or as to Basic Attributes

Exactly what is an express warranty? Let us first consider what it was (or seemed to have been) before the Code.

CHANDELOR v. LOPUS

Exch. Chamber, 1625.
79 Eng. Rep. 3, Cro.Jac. 4.

Action upon the case. Whereas the defendant being a goldsmith, and having skill in jewels and precious stones, had a stone which he affirmed to Lopus to be a bezar-stone, and sold it to him for one hundred pounds; ubi revera it was not a bezar-stone: the defendant pleaded not guilty, and verdict was given and judgment entered for the plaintiff in the King's Bench.

But error was thereof brought in the Exchequer Chamber; because the declaration contains not matter sufficient to charge the defendant, viz. that he warranted it to be a bezar-stone, or that he knew that it was not a bezar-stone; for it may be, he himself was ignorant whether it were a bezar-stone or not.

And all the Justices and Barons (except Anderson) held, that for this cause it was error: for the bare affirmation that it was a bezar-stone, without warranting it to be so, is no cause of action: and although he knew it to be no bezar-stone it is not material; for every one in selling his wares will affirm that his wares are good, or the horse which he sells is sound; yet if he does not warrant them to be so, it is no cause of action, and the warranty ought to be made at the same time of the sale; as F.N.B. 94, c and 98, b; 5 Hen. 7, pl. 41; 9 Hen. 6, pl. 53; 12 Hen. 4, pl. 1, 42 Ass. 8; 7 Hen. 4, pl. 15. Wherefore, forasmuch as no warranty is alleged, they held the declaration to be ill.

ANDERSON to the contrary; for the deceit in selling it for a bezar, whereas it was not so, is cause of action.

But, notwithstanding, it was adjudged to be no cause, and the judgment reversed.

GILMORE, PRODUCTS LIABILITY: A COMMENTARY, 38 U.Chi.L.Rev. 103, 107–08 (1970).

"In connection with the point that most cases—perhaps all cases—are sensibly, or even 'correctly,' decided as of their own time and place, I will indulge myself in a brief digression on a landmark of the common law * * *—a case called Chandelor v. Lopus, which was decided by the Exchequer Chamber in 1625. A goldsmith had sold for £100 a stone which he affirmed to be a bezoar. The stone turned out not to be a bezoar. The disappointed buyer, who had presumably paid the price for a true bezoar, brought an action to recover damages for, as we should say, breach of warranty. Judgment for the goldsmith-seller: he had merely 'affirmed' that the stone was a bezoar without 'warranting' it to be one—wherefore the buyer's action did not lie. For several hundred years the case has been cited, with approval or with scorn, as illustrative of the extremely narrow scope of liability which seventeenth century law placed on sellers for the quality of the goods they sold.

"The report of the case does not bother to explain what a bezoar was—presumably everybody knew what a bezoar was, just as we all know what a diamond is. It occurred to me one day, in thinking about the case, that I for one had no idea what a bezoar might be. The new Oxford Dictionary proved to be illuminating. A bezoar (or 'bezar') was, descriptively, 'a calculus or concretion found in the stomachs of some animals, chiefly ruminants, formed of concentric layers of animal matter deposited round some foreign substance, which serves as a nucleus.' That explains everything except why a bezoar would have been worth £100 in the early 17th century. The true value of a bezoar, it appears, lay in its magic or, as we should say, medicinal properties: application of the bezoar to a diseased part of the body cured the disease. 'Everything that frees the body of any ailment,' it was said, 'is called the Bezoar of that ailment.' And the East India Company had reported in 1618 that: 'On the island of Borneo, diamonds, bezoar stones and gold might be obtained.'

"Now that we know more about bezoars than we did, we may begin to wonder whether our initial reaction to the holding in Chandelor v. Lopus was, historically, correct—or even relevant to the case. It was generally known that there were true, or magic, bezoars. It must also have been a matter of common knowledge that it was extremely difficult, if not impossible, to tell a true bezoar from a false one. And no doubt the attitude of the user counted for something: if I believed in my bezoar it might indeed preserve me from the plague while the same stone in the hands of a skeptical rationalist would be worthless. Under such circumstances a court might hesitate to impose liability on a seller who had merely said that, to the best of his knowledge, he believed (or affirmed) the stone to be a bezoar, but did not warrant it. It may be that the 17th century concept of liability was not as narrow as we have supposed it to be. This digression, at all events, goes to the point that law cases—and rules of law—are really not abstract propositions, although we like to phrase them, and talk about them, as if they were. The cases and the rules—and indeed the codifying statutes—are merely particular responses to particular states of fact (assumed to be true whether or not they are). The law is, and I dare say always will be, *ad hoc* and *ad hominem* to a fault."

[Footnotes omitted.]

SEIXAS v. WOODS

Supreme Court of New York, 1804.
2 Caines 48, 2 Am.Dec. 215.

Action on the case for selling peachum wood for brazilletto; the former being almost worthless, the latter of considerable value. The defendant received the wood from a house in New Providence, whose agent he was, and the invoice described it as brazilletto. He advertised it as such, had shown the invoice to the plaintiff, and had the bill made out for brazilletto. But it was not pretended that he knew that it was peachum, nor did the plaintiff suspect it to be such, as it was delivered from the vessel, and picked out from other wood by a person on behalf of the plaintiff. In fact, either party was ignorant that the wood was other than brazilletto, nor was any fraud imputed. On discovery of the real quality of the wood, it was tendered back to the defendant, and a return of the purchase money demanded. On his refusal, he having remitted the proceeds to his principal, the present action was brought, and a verdict was given for the plaintiffs, subject to the opinion of the court.

KENT, J.

* * *

In the case of Chandelor v. Lopus, Cro.Jac. 4, it was determined in the exchequer by all the judges except one, that for selling a jewel which as affirmed to be a bezoar stone when it was not, no action lay, unless the defendant knew it was not a bezoar stone or had warranted it to be one. This appears to be a case in point and decisive. * * * The mentioning the wood as brazilletto wood in the bill of parcels and in the advertisement some days previous to the sale, did not amount to a warranty to the plaintiffs. To make an affirmation at the time of the sale a warranty, it must appear by evidence to be so intended; Buller, J., 3 T.R. 57; Carth. 90; Salk. 210; and not to have been a mere matter of judgment and opinion, and of which the defendant had no particular knowledge. Here it is admitted the defendant was equally ignorant with the plaintiffs, and could have had no such intention. * * *

* * *

Notes

1. Did the New York court appropriately rely on *Chandelor v. Lopus?* Or, did the court "confuse accident with essence in an earlier court's decision and thereby stunt the law's growth?"

2. Suppose the seller and buyer are of relatively equal capacity and are equally ignorant about the nature of the goods sold. If the seller affirms or describes the goods (things) as a "bezoar stone" or as "brazilleto," how does one determine whether the seller has made a warranty or merely a statement purporting to be an opinion? For what they are worth, here are a few alternative tests. Which do you prefer?

A. The affirmation must be in writing and use the word "warrant" or "guarantee." This test was rejected in UCC 2–313(2).

B. The seller must intend the affirmation to be a warranty, i.e., state a "fact which is or should be within his own knowledge * * *, intending that the buyer should act on it. * * *" Denning, L.J. in Oscar Chess, Ltd. v. Williams, 1 All Eng.Rep. 325, 328–29 (C.A.1957). See Stoljar, *Conditions, Warranties and Descriptions of Quality in Sale of Goods,* Part I, 15 Mod.L.Rev. 425, 428–29 (1952).

The intention requirement was part of the pre-Code American law of warranty: "Though to constitute a warranty requires no particular form of words, the naked averment of a fact is neither a warranty itself nor evidence of it. In connection with other circumstances, it certainly may be taken into consideration; but the jury must be satisfied, from the whole that the vendor actually, and not constructively, consented to be bound for the truth of his representation." Gibson, C.J. in McFarland v. Newman, 9 Watts 55, 34 Am.Dec. 497 (Pa.1839). Accord: *Seixas v. Woods,* supra (warranty must appear from evidence to be intended); McNeir v. Greer-Hale Chinchilla Ranch, 194 Va. 623, 74 S.E.2d 165 (1953) (representations constituted warranty if seller intended that they should be relied upon and they were in fact relied upon by buyer as an inducement to purchase). But under UCC 2–313(2), the buyer need not have a "specific intention to make a warranty."

C. Regardless of the seller's actual intention, did the affirmation lead a reasonable buyer to believe that such statements had been made to induce the bargain and to make the purchase in reliance on them? See Section 12, Uniform Sales Act; Hansen v. Firestone Tire & Rubber Co., 276 F.2d 254, 257 (6th Cir.1960); Williston, Sales 206 (rev. ed. 1948). But see UCC 2–313(1)(a), where the affirmation or promise must become "part of the basis of the bargain."

D. None of the foregoing tests are appropriate. The question is whether the buyer is entitled to believe what the seller says about the goods. The answer will depend, in each case, upon the presence of certain factors which, in a proper combination, will induce the court to allow the case to reach the jury. These factors include but are not limited to:

a. The seller's statement was plain and unambiguous.

b. The seller's statement concerned a matter of objective importance to the buyer.

c. The attribute or quality involved was not something the buyer could easily ascertain on his own.

d. The seller was more of an expert in the matter than the buyer.

e. The buyer was not making up his own mind to buy entirely without regard to the seller's statements.

f. Nothing in the facts indicated that the seller should not be taken seriously.

g. The seller did not himself say things to the buyer that should have put him "on his guard" so to speak.

h. The remedy that the buyer sought was especially appropriate and would not be unduly harsh on the seller.

i. The price tends to support the buyer's claim.

Problem 19–2

The Case of the Unmarked Vitriol

Saldo is a dealer in dry chemicals, selling at wholesale to a variety of buyers. Saldo purchased 2,000 pounds of a copper sulphate described as "blue vitriol" from the Copco Mfgr. Co. The goods arrived in 20 barrels. The barrels were unmarked but the invoice described the goods as "vitriol." The barrels were offered for sale at a quarterly wholesale auction. One of the barrels was opened for prospective buyers to examine. It contained a bluish crystalline substance which one of the prospective buyers thought "looked strange." The purchasing agent of Barston Chemicals, Inc., a dealer which frequently sold at retail, also inspected the barrel. He stated to the auctioneer that while the substance looked like blue vitriol, it could be "green" vitriol, a less valuable chemical. Upon consultation with Saldo, the auctioneer announced that "the next sale will be a 20–barrel lot of blue vitriol in sound order." After spirited bidding, Barston Chemicals was high bidder at $.15 per pound. The price was paid and the goods were removed to the Barston warehouse, where they were immediately resold to a third party at $.18 per pound. The next day, however, it was discovered that the substance in the open barrel had turned green. Chemical analysis revealed that the substance was in fact "green" vitriol in sound order, worth about $.10 per pound at wholesale and $.13 per pound at retail. All of the other barrels contained "green" vitriol. In order to distinguish "green" from "blue" vitriol, either a chemical analysis must be done or the "green" vitriol allowed to stand in the open air for 10 or more hours. Barston promptly notified Saldo of the situation, revoked its acceptance, and demanded the return of the purchase price paid and damages for breach of warranty. The Barston purchasing agent stated that he was "not sure" what was in the barrel when he first examined it but after the auctioneer announced the sale, bid on the assumption that it was blue vitriol. Saldo claims that its officers honestly believed that the barrels contained blue vitriol, but that no warranty was intended and that Barston, as a professional chemical dealer, assumed the risk that the substance was green vitriol.

1. Did the seller make an express warranty in this case? If so, was it by affirmation or promise, description or sample? See UCC 2–313(1).

2. Suppose that the seller had stated that the goods were "vitriol" yet the buyer had assumed they were "blue" vitriol. What result? Compare UCC 2–313(1)(b) with UCC 2–314(2)(a). Does the description "vitriol" simply identify the goods or does it reveal basic attributes or quality? See Ziegel, *The Seller's Liability for Defective Goods at Common Law,* 12 McGill L.J. 183, 186–87 (1966).

SESSA v. RIEGLE

United States District Court, Eastern District of Pennsylvania, 1977.
427 F.Supp. 760, affirmed without opinion, 568 F.2d 770 (3d Cir.1978).

[Sessa purchased from Riegle a standard bred race horse named Tarport Conaway for $25,000. Before the sale, Sessa's friend Maloney examined the horse and reported that he "liked him." Also, Riegle, in a telephone conversation with Sessa, stated among other things that Sessa would like the horse and that he was a "good one" and "sound." The sale was then completed and, after problems in transportation were resolved, the horse was delivered some days later. Shortly thereafter the horse went lame in his hind legs due to a thrombosis which stopped the flow of blood through the arteries. The experts were unable to identify the cause of the thrombosis and the testimony did not establish that the condition was present before Riegle shipped the horse by carrier. Although the condition improved and Tarport Conaway was able to race, Sessa sued for damages under UCC 2–714(2) to be measured in part by the costs incurred in treating the condition.

The case was tried without a jury and the court, after making findings of fact, issued the following opinion.]

HANNUM, DISTRICT JUDGE.

* * *

II. EXPRESS WARRANTIES

On March 10, 1973, the day of the sale of Tarport Conaway, Sessa and Riegle had a telephone conversation during which the horse was discussed in general terms. Arrangements were made for transportation, and Riegle gave Sessa some instructions for driving Tarport Conaway based on Riegle's experience with him. Sessa contends that certain statements made by Riegle during that conversation constitute express warranties on which Riegle is liable in this action. The most important of these is Riegle's alleged statement that, "the horse is sound," or words to that effect.

In deciding whether statements by a seller constitute express warranties, the court must look to UCC § 2–313 which presents three fundamental issues. First, the court must determine whether the seller's statement constitutes an "affirmation of fact or promise" or "description of the goods" under § 2–313(1)(a) or (b) or whether it is rather "merely the seller's opinion or commendation of the goods" under § 2–313(2). Second, assuming the court finds the language used susceptible to creation of a warranty, it must then be determined whether the statement was "part of the basis of the bargain." If it was, an express warranty exists and, as the third issue, the court must determine whether the warranty was breached.

With respect to the first issue, the court finds that in the circumstances of this case, words to the effect that "The horse is sound" spoken during the telephone conversation between Sessa and Riegle constitute an opinion or commendation rather than express warranty. This determination is a question for the trier of fact. Gillette Dairy, Inc. v. Hydrotex Industries, Inc., 440 F.2d 969 (8th Cir.1971); Brunner v. Jensen, 215 Kan. 416, 524 P.2d 1175 (1974). There is nothing talismanic or thaumaturgic about the use of the word "sound." Whether use of that language constitutes warranty, or mere opinion or commendation depends on the circumstances of the sale and the type of goods sold. While § 2–313 makes it clear that no specific words need be used and no specific intent need be present, not every statement by a seller is an express warranty.

Several older Pennsylvania cases dealing with horse sales show that similar statements as to soundness are not always similarly treated under warranty law. In Wilkinson v. Stettler, 46 Pa.Super. 407 (1911), the statement that a horse "was solid and sound and would work any place" was held not to constitute an express warranty. This result was followed in Walker v. Kirk, 72 Pa.Super. 534 (1919) which considered the statement, "This mare is sound and all right and a good worker double." Walker was decided after the passage of § 12 of the Uniform Sales Act, the precursor of U.C.C. § 2–313 and thus presumably rests on the standard there established. The Official Comments to U.C.C. § 2–313 indicate that no changes in the law of warranties under Uniform Sales Act § 12 were intended.

However, in Flood v. Yeager, 52 Pa.Super. 637 (1912) an express warranty was found where the plaintiff informed the defendant that, "he did not know anything at all about a horse and that he did not want * * * the defendant to make a mean deal with him; whereupon the defendant said that the horse was solid and sound; that he would guarantee him to be solid and sound" 52 Pa. Super. at 638. While all three of these cases are premised partly on the now displaced rule that specific intent to warrant is a necessary concomitant of an express warranty, they do show that statements of the same tenor receive varying treatment depending on the surrounding circumstances.

The results in these cases are all consistent with custom among horse traders as alluded to by Gene Riegle. He testified that it is "not a common thing" to guarantee a horse, that he has never guaranteed a horse unless he had an "understanding" with the buyer and that he did not guarantee Tarport Conaway. In other words, because horses are fragile creatures, susceptible to myriad maladies, detectable and undetectable, only where there is an "understanding" that an ignorant buyer, is relying totally on a knowledgeable seller not "to make a mean deal," are statements as to soundness taken to be anything more than the seller's opinion or commendation.

The facts suggest no special "understanding" between Sessa and Riegle. Sessa was a knowledgeable buyer, having been involved with standardbreds for some years. Also, Sessa sent Maloney, an even more knowledgeable horseman, as his agent to inspect the horse.

Also mitigating against the finding of express warranty is the nature of the conversation between Sessa and Riegle. It seemed largely collateral to the sale rather than an essential part of it. Although Sessa testified that Riegle's "personal guarantee" given during the conversation was the quintessence of the sale, the credible evidence suggests otherwise. While on the telephone, Riegle made statements to the effect that "the horse is a good one" and "you will like him." These bland statements are obviously opinion or commendation, and the statement, "The horse is sound," falling within their penumbra takes on their character as such.

Under all the facts and circumstances of this case, it is clear to the court that Riegle's statements were not of such a character as to give rise to express warranties under § 2–313(1) but were opinion or commendation under § 2–313(2).

Even assuming that Riegle's statements could be express warranties, it is not at all clear that they were "part of the basis of the bargain," the second requisite of § 2–313. This is essentially a reliance requirement and is inextricably intertwined with the initial determination as to whether given language may constitute an express warranty since affirmations, promises and descriptions tend to become part of the basis of the bargain. It was the intention of the drafters of the U.C.C. not to require a strong showing of reliance. In fact, they envisioned that all statements of the seller became part of the basis of the bargain unless clear affirmative proof is shown to the contrary. See Official Comments 3 and 8 to U.C.C. § 2–313, 12A P.S. § 2–313.

It is Sessa's contention that his conversation with Riegle was the principal factor inducing him to enter the bargain. He would have the court believe that Maloney was merely a messenger to deliver the check. The evidence shows, however, that Sessa was relying primarily on Maloney to advise him in connection with the sale. Maloney testified that he had talked to Sessa about the horse on several occasions and expressed the opinion that he was convinced "beyond the shadow of a doubt" that he was a good buy. With respect to his authority to buy the horse he testified

> "Well, Mr. Sessa said he had enough confidence and faith in me and my integrity and honesty that I, what I did say about the horse, I was representing the horse as he is or as he was, and that if the horse, in my estimation, was that type of a horse and at that given price, the fixed price of $25,000 he would buy the horse."

When, at the airport, Maloney protested that he did not want to accept full responsibility to go to Ohio alone, Sessa told him " * * * I take your word. I—I trust your judgment and I trust your—your honesty, that if this horse is right, everything will be all right." In Ohio, Maloney examined the horse, jogged him and reported to Sessa over the telephone that he "liked him."

The court believes that Maloney's opinion was the principal, if not the only, factor which motivated Sessa to purchase the horse. The conversation with Riegle played a negligible role in his decision.

* * *

[The court concluded that even if an express warranty had been made, Sessa had accepted the horse and had failed to prove by a preponderance of the evidence that the horse was not sound at the time of tender.]

[Footnotes omitted.]

KEITH v. BUCHANAN

Court of Appeals of California, Second District, 1985.
173 Cal.App.3d 13, 220 Cal.Rptr. 392.

OCHOA, ASSOCIATE JUSTICE.

This breach of warranty case is before this court after the trial court granted defendants' motion for judgment at the close of plaintiff's case during the trial proceedings. We hold that an express warranty under section 2313 of the California Uniform Commercial Code was created in this matter, and that actual reliance on the seller's factual representation need not be shown by the buyer. The representation is presumed to be part of the basis of the bargain, and the burden is on the seller to prove that the representation was not a consideration inducing the bargain. We affirm all other aspects of the trial court's judgment but reverse in regard to its finding that no express warranty was created and remand for further proceedings consistent with this opinion.

STATEMENT OF FACTS

Plaintiff, Brian Keith, purchased a sailboat from defendants in November 1978 for a total purchase price of $75,610. Even though plaintiff belonged to the Waikiki Yacht Club, had attended a sailing school, had joined the Coast Guard Auxiliary, and had sailed on many yachts in order to ascertain his preferences, he had not previously owned a yacht. He attended a boat show in Long Beach during October 1978 and looked at a number of boats, speaking to sales representatives and obtaining advertising literature. In the literature, the sailboat which is the subject of this action, called an "Island Trader 41," was described as a seaworthy vessel. In one sales brochure, this vessel is described as "a picture of sure-footed seaworthiness." In another, it is called "a carefully well-equipped, and very seaworthy live-aboard vessel." Plaintiff testified he relied on representations in the sales brochures in regard to the purchase. Plaintiff and a sales representative also discussed plaintiff's desire for a boat which was ocean-going and would cruise long distances.

Plaintiff asked his friend, Buddy Ebsen, who was involved in a boat building, enterprise, to inspect the boat. Mr. Ebsen and one of his associates, both of whom had extensive experience with sailboats, observed the boat and advised plaintiff that the vessel would suit his stated needs. A deposit was paid on the boat, a purchase contract was entered into, and optional accessories for the boat were ordered. After delivery of the vessel, a dispute arose in regard to its seaworthiness.

Plaintiff filed the instant lawsuit alleging causes of action in breach of express warranty and breach of implied warranty. The trial court granted defendants' Code of Civil Procedure section 631.8 motion for judgment at the close of plaintiff's case. The court found that no express warranty was established by the evidence because none of the defendants had undertaken in writing to preserve or maintain the utility or performance of the vessel, nor to provide compensation for any failure in utility or performance. It found that the written statements produced at trial were opinions or commendations of the vessel. The court further found that no implied warranty of fitness was created because the plaintiff did not rely on the skill and judgment of defendants to select and furnish a suitable vessel, but had rather relied on his own experts in selecting the vessel.

DISCUSSION

I. Express Warranty

California Uniform Commercial Code section 2313 provides, inter alia, that express warranties are created by (1) any affirmation of fact or promise made by the seller to the buyer which relates to the goods and becomes part of the basis of the bargain, and (2) any description of the goods which is made part of the basis of the bargain. Formal words such as "warranty" or "guarantee" are not required to make a warranty, but the seller's affirmation of the value of the goods or an expression of opinion or commendation of the goods does not create an express warranty.

* * *

California Uniform Commercial Code section 2313, regarding express warranties, was enacted in 1963 and consists of the official text of Uniform Commercial Code section 2–313 without change. In deciding whether a statement made by a seller constitutes an express warranty under this provision, the court must deal with three fundamental issues. First, the court must determine whether the seller's statement constitutes an "affirmation of fact or promise" or "description of the goods" under California Uniform Commercial Code section 2313, subdivision (1)(a) or (b) or whether it is rather "merely the seller's opinion or commendation of the goods" under section 2313, subdivision (2). Second, assuming the court finds the language used susceptible to creation of a warranty, it must then be determined whether the statement was "part of the basis of the bargain." Third, the court must determine whether the warranty was breached. (See *Sessa v. Riegle* (E.D.Pa.1977) 427 F.Supp. 760, 765.)

A warranty relates to the title, character, quality, identity, or condition of the goods. The purpose of the law of warranty is to determine what it is that the seller has in essence agreed to sell. (*A.A. Baxter Corp. v. Colt Industries, Inc.* (1970) 10 Cal.App.3d 144, 153, 88 Cal.Rptr. 842.) "Express warranties are chisels in the hands of buyers and sellers. With these tools, the parties to a sale sculpt a monument representing the goods. Having selected a stone, the buyer and seller may leave it almost bare, allowing considerable play in the qualities that fit its contours. Or the parties may chisel away inexactitudes until a well-defined shape emerges. The seller is bound to deliver, and the buyer to accept, goods that match the sculpted form. [Fn. omitted.]" (*Special Project: Article Two Warranties in Commercial Transactions, Express Warranties—Section 2–313* (1978–79) 64 Cornell L.Rev. 30 (hereafter cited as *Warranties in Commercial Transactions*) at pp. 43–44.)

A. Affirmation of Fact, Promise or Description Versus Statement of Opinion, Commendation or Value

"The determination as to whether a particular statement is an expression of opinion or an affirmation of fact is often difficult, and frequently is dependent upon the facts and circumstances existing at the time the statement is made." (*Willson v. Municipal Bond Co.* (1936) 7 Cal.2d 144, 150, 59 P.2d 974.) Recent decisions have evidenced a trend toward narrowing the scope of representations which are considered opinion, sometimes referred to as "puffing" or "sales talk," resulting in an expansion of the liability that flows from broad statements of manufacturers or retailers as to the quality of their products. Courts have liberally construed affirmations of quality made by sellers in favor of injured consumers. (*Hauter v. Zogarts* (1975) 14 Cal.3d 104, 112, 120 Cal.Rptr. 681, 534 P.2d 377; see also 55 Cal.Jur.3d, Sales, § 74, p. 580.) It has even been suggested "that in an age of consumerism all seller's statements, except the most blatant sales pitch, may give rise to an express warranty." (1 Alderman and Dole, A Transactional Guide to the Uniform Commercial Code (2d ed. 1983) p. 89.)

Courts in other states have struggled in efforts to create a formula for distinguishing between affirmations of fact, promises, or descriptions of goods on the one hand, and value, opinion, or commendation statements on the other. The code comment indicates that the basic question is: "What statements of the seller have in the circumstances and in objective judgment become part of the basis of the bargain?" The commentators indicated that the language of subsection (2) of the code section was included because "common experience discloses that some statements or predictions cannot fairly be viewed as entering into the bargain." (See U.Com.Code com. 8 to Cal.U.Com.Code, § 2313, West's Ann.Com.Code (1964) p. 250.)

Statements made by a seller during the course of negotiation over a contract are presumptively affirmations of fact unless it can be demonstrated that the buyer could only have reasonably considered the statement as a statement of the seller's opinion. Commentators have noted several factors which tend to indicate an opinion statement. These are (1) a lack of specificity in the statement made, (2) a statement that is made in an equivocal manner, or (3) a statement which reveals that the goods are experimental in nature. (See *Warranties in Commercial Transactions, supra,* at pp. 61–65.)

It is clear that statements made by a manufacturer or retailer in an advertising brochure which is disseminated to the consuming public in order to induce sales can create express warranties. * * * In the instant case, the vessel purchased was described in sales brochures as "a picture of sure-footed seaworthiness" and "a carefully well-equipped and very seaworthy vessel." The seller's representative was aware that appellant was looking for a vessel sufficient for long distance ocean-going cruises. The statements in the brochure are specific and unequivocal in asserting that the vessel is seaworthy. Nothing in the negotiation indicates that the vessel is experimental in nature. In fact, one sales brochure assures prospective buyers that production of the vessel was commenced "after years of careful testing." The representations regarding seaworthiness made in sales brochures regarding the Island Trader 41 were affirmations of fact relating to the quality or condition of the vessel.

B. "Part of the Basis of the Bargain" Test

Under former provisions of law, a purchaser was required to prove that he or she acted in reliance upon representations made by the seller. (*Grinnell v. Charles Pfizer & Co.* (1969) 274 Cal.App.2d 424, 440, 79 Cal.Rptr. 369.) California Uniform Commercial Code section 2313 indicates only that the seller's statements must become "part of the basis of the bargain." According to official comment 3 to this Uniform Commercial Code provision, "no particular reliance * * * need be shown in order to weave [the seller's affirmations of fact] into the fabric of the agreement. Rather, any fact which is to take such affirmations, once made, out of the agreement requires clear affirmative proof." (See U.Com. Code com. 3 to Cal.U.Com.Code, § 2313, West's Ann.Com.Code (1964) p. 249.)

The California Supreme Court, in discussing the continued viability of the reliance factor, noted that commentators have disagreed in regard to the impact of this development. Some have indicated that it shifts the burden of proving non-reliance to the seller, and others have indicated that the code eliminates the concept of reliance altogether. (*Hauter v. Zogarts, supra,* 14 Cal.3d at pp. 115–116, 120 Cal.Rptr. 681, 534 P.2d 377.) The court did not resolve this issue, but noted that decisions of other states prior to that time had "ignored the significance of the new standard and have held that consumer reliance still is a vital ingredient for recovery based on express warranty." (*Id.,* at p. 116, fn. 13, 120 Cal.Rptr. 681, 534 P.2d 377; see also *Fogo v. Cutter Laboratories, Inc.* (1977) 68 Cal.App.3d 744, 760, 137 Cal.Rptr. 417.)

The shift in language clearly changes the degree to which it must be shown that the seller's representation affected the buyer's decision to enter into the agreement. A buyer need not show that he would not have entered into the agreement absent the warranty or even that it was a dominant factor inducing the agreement. A warranty statement is deemed to be part of the basis of the bargain and to have been relied upon as one of the inducements for the purchase of the product. In other words, the buyer's demonstration of reliance on an express warranty is "not a prerequisite for breach of warranty, as long as the express warranty involved became part of the bargain. See White & Summers, Uniform Commercial Code (2d ed. 1980) § 9–4. If, however, the resulting bargain does not rest at all on the representations of the seller, those representations cannot be considered as becoming any part of the 'basis of the bargain.' * * *" (*Allied Fidelity Ins. Co. v. Pico* (Nev.S.Ct.1983) 656 P.2d 849, 850.)

The official Uniform Commercial Code comment in regard to section 2–313 "indicates that in actual practice affirmations of fact made by the seller about the goods during a bargain are regarded as part of the description of those goods; hence no particular reliance on such statements need be shown in order to weave them into the fabric of the agreement." (*Young & Cooper, Inc. v. Vestring* (1974) 214 Kan. 311, 521 P.2d 281, 291; *Brunner v. Jensen* (1974) 215 Kan. 416, 524 P.2d 1175, 1185.) It is clear from the new language of this code section that the concept of reliance has been purposefully abandoned. * * *

The change of the language in section 2313 of the California Uniform Commercial Code modifies both the degree of reliance and the burden of proof in express warranties under the code. The representation need only be part of the basis of the bargain, or merely a factor or consideration inducing the buyer to enter into the bargain. A warranty statement made by a seller is presumptively part of the basis of the bargain, and the burden is on the seller to prove that the resulting bargain does not rest at all on the representation.

The buyer's actual knowledge of the true condition of the goods prior to the making of the contract may make it plain that the seller's statement was not relied upon as one of the inducements for the purchase, but the burden is on the seller to demonstrate such knowledge on the part of the buyer. Where the buyer inspects the goods before purchase, he may be deemed to have waived the seller's express warranties. But, an examination or inspection by the buyer of the goods does not necessarily discharge the seller from an express warranty if the defect was not actually discovered and waived. * * *

Appellant's inspection of the boat by his own experts does not constitute a waiver of the express warranty of seaworthiness. Prior to the making of the contract, appellant had experienced boat builders observe the boat, but there was no testing of the vessel in the water.[3] Such a warranty (seaworthiness) necessar-

3. Evidence was presented of examination or inspection of the boat after the making of the contract of sale and prior to delivery and acceptance of the vessel. Such an inspection

ily relates to the time when the vessel has been put to sea (*Werner v. Montana* (1977) 117 N.H. 721, 378 A.2d 1130, 1134–35) and has been shown to be reasonably fit and adequate in materials, construction, and equipment for its intended purposes (*Daly v. General Motors Corp.* (1978) 20 Cal.3d 725, 739, 144 Cal.Rptr. 380, 575 P.2d 1162; *Vittone v. American President Lines* (1964) 228 Cal. App.2d 689, 693–694, 39 Cal.Rptr. 758).

In this case, appellant was aware of the representations regarding seaworthiness by the seller prior to contracting. He also had expressed to the seller's representative his desire for a long distance ocean-going vessel. Although he had other experts inspect the vessel, the inspection was limited and would not have indicated whether or not the vessel was seaworthy. It is clear that the seller has not overcome the presumption that the representations regarding seaworthiness were part of the basis of this bargain.

* * *

[The court upheld the trial court's conclusion that the seller did not make and breach an implied warranty of fitness for particular purpose under UCC 2–315: The buyer did not rely on the seller's skill and judgment in selecting a suitable boat.]

[Some footnotes omitted.]

Notes

1. The court in *Keith* cites with approval the three step "basis of the bargain" test employed in *Sessa* but then reaches the opposite result. Can the cases be reconciled? Should Buddy Ebsen be fired as an expert on seaworthiness?

2. Is the "basis of the bargain" test, in essence, the same as a "reliance" test? The answer in *Sessa* is yes: Basis of the bargain is "essentially a reliance requirement and is inextricably intertwined with the initial determination as to whether given language may constitute an express warranty since affirmations, promises and descriptions tend to become a part of the basis of the bargain." Duesenberg and King agree: "(F)or all practical purposes it is suggested that no great change was wrought by the Code. Whether one speaks of reliance or basis of the bargain, little difference exists between the two. * * * What is really crucial is whether the statement was made as an affirmation of fact, the goods did not live up to the statement, and the defect was not so apparent that the buyer could not be held to have discovered it for himself." Sales and Bulk Transfers 6.01, n. 2 (1980).

3. How do we know initially whether a statement is an affirmation of fact or an opinion? In Royal Business Machines, Inc. v. Lorraine Corp., 633 F.2d 34, 41 (7th Cir.1980), the court stated: "(T)he decisive test for whether a given representation is a warranty or merely an expression of the seller's opinion is whether the seller asserts a fact of which the buyer is ignorant or merely states an opinion or judgment on a matter of which the seller has no special knowledge and on which the buyer may be expected also to have an opinion and to exercise his judgment." Accord: Royal Typewriter Co. v. Xerographic Supplies Corp., 719 F.2d 1092 (11th Cir.1983).

would be irrelevant to any issue of express warranty. Although it deals with implied warranties as opposed to express warranties, the Uniform Commercial Code comment 8 to section 2–316 (Cal.U.Com.Code, § 2316) is instructive: "Under paragraph (b) of subdivision (3) warranties may be excluded or modified by the circumstances where the buyer examines the goods or a sample or model of them *before entering into the contract. 'Examination' as used in this paragraph is not synonymous with inspection before acceptance or at any other time after the contract has been made. It goes rather to the nature of the responsibility assumed by the seller at the time of the making of the contract.*" (See U.Com.Code com. 8 to Cal.U.Com.Code, § 2316, West's Ann.Com. Code (1964) p. 308, emphasis added.)

B. Liability for Statements as to "Special Suitability"

Suppose the buyer wants to buy a racehorse that runs well on a slow track, or an office copier with low maintenance costs or a computer system that will process some rather complicated financial data. In short, the buyer has particular or special needs to be satisfied. Compare UCC 2–315.

It is, of course, quite possible that a properly informed seller will make an express warranty that the goods are fit or suitable for the buyer's particular purposes. Northern States Power Co. v. ITT Meyer Industries, 777 F.2d 405 (8th Cir.1985) (seller's technical specifications became part of basis of buyer's bargain). But, as the next case indicates, establishing such an express warranty may be more difficult than when the seller's statements go to core description or basic attributes.

AXION CORP. v. G.D.C. LEASING CORP.

Supreme Judicial Court of Massachusetts, 1971.
359 Mass. 474, 269 N.E.2d 664.

BRAUCHER, JUSTICE.

These cases arise out of the sale of three valve testing machines. The three machines were delivered and two of them were paid for. The seller brings two actions of contract for failure to pay for the third machine, and the buyer brings an action of contract or tort against the seller for damages for breach of express and implied warranties. The cases were consolidated for trial by jury. At the close of the evidence the judge denied the buyer's motions for directed verdicts in the two cases brought by the seller, and allowed the seller's motions for directed verdicts in all three cases. The cases are here on the buyer's exceptions to these actions.

The following facts are substantially undisputed except as indicated. Negotiations began in late 1963, and included a good deal of correspondence. The buyer's purchase order, "To Design and build" the first machine for $7,500, is dated January 9, 1964. The machine was delivered the following May and was paid for in June, 1964. There were many problems with it, and the parties and the buyer's parent company, Watts Regulator Company (Watts), worked together to solve them. In August, 1964, the seller by letter to the buyer listed twenty-eight "revisions in the next two valve setters to be built." The buyer ordered the second and third machines in October, 1964, for a total price of $14,950; they were delivered in December, 1964, and one of them was paid for in March, 1965. At the time of the second order, the first machine was sent back, modified to conform to the new design, then shipped back to the buyer and put into service.

Development and testing continued. In July, 1965, the buyer by letter told the seller it "would like to negotiate a price [for the third machine] which would take into account the amount of money and time that we have had to expend trying to perfect these devices." In August, 1965, the buyer told the seller that the third machine was useless and that the buyer would not pay for it unless it would meet a "plus or minus five per cent" specification. The seller then agreed to take back the third machine at the buyer's expense and to work on it. In January, 1966, representatives of the buyer went to the seller's plant to conduct a series of tests. The parties do not agree on the meaning of the specification or on what the tests showed. In February, 1966, the buyer notified the seller that it was reserving its rights for recovery of its losses and expenses, and that the third machine was unacceptable and would not be paid for.

* * *

Express warranties. Since the buyer has accepted the goods and has not revoked the acceptance, the seller may recover the unpaid portion of the price. UCC § 2–709(1)(a). But if the goods were nonconforming, the buyer may have an offsetting claim for damages. § 2–714. The buyer claims that there were breaches of express warranties, of an implied warranty of merchantability, and of an implied warranty of fitness for a particular purpose. The burden is on the buyer to establish such breaches. § 2–607(4).

The buyer claims express warranties made in the seller's preliminary correspondence. On October 12, 1963, the seller wrote: "About the valve adjustment, we would shoot for a mean of 125 psi [pounds per square inch] and hit it more closely than an operator can. * * * With the air pressure sensing there is bound to be a gain in accuracy * * *. Probably a better statement is that the tolerance will be better than it is by the present method." Again, on October 19, 1963, the seller wrote: "With few reservations the automatic valve setter would be a turnkey operation. * * * We would set up the unit at your plant, check it out, train the people stated, and make whatever changes are then indicated to meet the specifications. * * * Failing to meet performance specifications under these guidelines you could ship back the unit with no charge other than freight to New Fairfield."

The buyer now asserts that these letters created express warranties by "affirmation of fact" and "promise," UCC § 2–313(1)(a), that the machine would be a turnkey device and would be more accurate than the hand method. We think they savor more of prediction than of promise. The former general manager of the buyer understood a "turn-key device" to be "one which operates 100 per cent from the day you receive it," as distinguished from a prototype needing further development; he considered the first machine a "semi-experimental" prototype. The order for the first machine, dated January 9, 1964, was to design and build the machine "substantially as per" an attached inter-office letter of the buyer; that letter described the "automatic pressure setting procedure," referred to items which were "suggested," and closed with the following: "It is probable that some tolerances on this will have to be established but deviations from our basic specification can be determined when the machine is checked out." There was no "turnkey" warranty, and no warranty that the machine would be more accurate than the hand method.

The buyer also claims a breach of a warranty that the machine would set valves "entirely within the ± 5% range," quoting from the seller's letter of January 6, 1966. There was testimony that the buyer followed such a standard and that it was one of the specifications discussed between the parties and referred to in the letter of October 19, 1963. But the standard was not referred to in either of the purchase orders and was never written down with any precision until after the meeting in August, 1965.

At that meeting the parties seem to have thought they had reached an oral agreement on the five per cent specification, to be used in reëvaluating the third machine after the seller had reworked it, but their subsequent correspondence disclosed two conflicting versions: the seller's version called for the machine "to set within the prescribed 5% range 90% of the valves presented for setting"; the buyer's version allowed the machine to reject no more than ten per cent of the valves capable of being set, but required *all* of the valves set to be within the five per cent range. The seller's letter of January 6, 1966, pointed out the discrepancy, said it believed "that our equipment will satisfy also the new criterion, but subject to these conditions." One of the conditions was that the buyer "define the quantity of valves which may be incorrectly set and passed. * * * We are confident that * * * the machine will set valves entirely within the ± 5% range. Recognizing, however, the possibilities of mechanical aberration and therefore of 'strays,' we recommend as the standard that no more than 2% of the valves set by our machine as being within the ± 5% range may be rejected on the water test."

The buyer's representatives reported on January 12, 1966, that in tests made on January 10, 1966, the machine rejected twenty-four out of 452 valves (5.3%), set twenty-four more than five per cent too high (5.3%), and set eighteen more than five per cent too low (3.98%), a total of forty-two set out of tolerance range (9.3%). There was other testimony that all the valves in the test were set within the five per cent tolerance, and if the seller had agreed to the buyer's version of the five per cent specification, there would have been a question of fact whether the machine met the test. But there was no evidence that the seller agreed to the buyer's version, or that the buyer agreed either to the seller's original version or to its January 6, 1966, recommendation. In these circumstances, it cannot be said that the buyer carried its burden of establishing that its version of the five per cent specification became "part of the basis of the bargain" within UCC § 2–313(1)(a).

* * *

Exceptions overruled. [Footnotes omitted.]

Notes

1. In *Axion,* is it fair to say that the buyer tried and failed to establish that the seller made an express warranty that the goods were fit for buyer's particular purposes? Compare UCC 2–315. In Uganski v. Little Giant Crane & Shovel, Inc., 35 Mich.App. 88, 192 N.W.2d 580 (1971), the court concluded that the manufacturer of a crane—the only one of its kind—especially designed to meet a particular need of the buyer made and breached an express warranty that the crane would be suitable for that need.

2. S, a manufacturer, sold a number of office copying machines to B. The machines were to be leased to B's customers. S represented to B that the machines had a useful life of 10 years and that the "maintenance factor" was ½ cent per copy produced. B sued for damages, claiming, inter alia, that the machines did not conform to the representations. Held, even though the machines were fit for "ordinary" purposes, i.e., they were merchantable, see UCC 2–314(1), the seller may have made and breached an express warranty of special suitability. Royal Typewriter Co. v. Xerographic Supplies Corp., 719 F.2d 1092, 1101–02 (11th Cir.1983). The court stated: "Such an express warranty regarding maintenance costs would be tantamount to a guarantee by Royal that no matter what XSC's wage costs and other expenses might reach during the life of the machine, XSC would spend ½ cent per copy for maintenance. To state the nature of such a statement illustrates the difficulty of its proof. Nevertheless, a guarantee is actionable under (UCC 2–313). * * * As unrealistic as such a guarantee may appear, Royal may have made such an express warranty regarding maintenance costs."

In an earlier case between the same seller and a different buyer, the transaction involved a series of copier sales "between the same parties over approximately an 18-month period and concerned two different machines." The court noted that the knowledge and reliance of the parties "may be expected to change in light of their experience during that time." The court concluded: "Therefore, as to each purchase, Booher's expanding knowledge of the capacities of the copying machines would have to be considered in deciding whether Royal's representations were part of the basis of the bargain. The same representations that could have constituted an express warranty early in the series of transactions might not have qualified as an express warranty in a later transaction if the buyer had acquired independent knowledge as to the fact asserted." Royal Business Machines, Inc. v. Lorraine Corp., 633 F.2d 34, 44 (7th Cir.1980).

DOWNIE v. ABEX CORP.

United States Court of Appeals, Tenth Circuit, 1984.
741 F.2d 1235.

[Plaintiffs, the Downies, sued for personal injuries suffered when an airplane passenger loading bridge (Jetway) manufactured by defendant, Abex, collapsed. The defendant filed a third-party complaint against General Motors, the manufacturer of ball-screw assembly which, allegedly, caused the Jetway to fail. The jury found that GM had made and breached a post-sale express warranty that the ball-screw assembly would not fail. The trial court, however, granted GM's motion for judgment n.o.v. on the express warranty claim. Upon appeal, the ruling of the trial court was reversed and the case remanded.]

* * *

II

A

Abex contends that the trial court erred in granting GM's motion for judgment n.o.v. on the express warranty issue. A trial judge may grant a motion for judgment notwithstanding the verdict only if "the facts and inferences point so strongly and overwhelmingly in favor of one party that the Court believes that reasonable men could not arrive at a contrary verdict." *Boeing Co. v. Shipman,* 411 F.2d 365, 374 (5th Cir.1969). Further, in considering a motion for judgment n.o.v. the trial judge must consider all the evidence and reasonable inferences therefrom in the light most favorable to the party against whom the motion is directed. *Wilkins v. Hogan,* 425 F.2d 1022, 1024 (10th Cir.1970). Section 2–313 of the Uniform Commercial Code governs express warranties. It provides:

> "(1) Express warranties by the seller are created as follows:
>
> (a) Any affirmation of fact or promise made by the seller to the buyer which relates to the goods and becomes part of the basis of the bargain creates an express warranty that the goods shall conform to the affirmation or promise.
>
> (b) Any description of the goods which is made part of the basis of the bargain creates an express warranty that the goods shall conform to the description."

Thus, we must determine whether a rational jury could have concluded that GM made an affirmation of fact or promise concerning the failed ball-screw assembly, and, if so, whether it could find that affirmation of fact or promise became part of the basis of the bargain.

B

The original GM warranty was limited to defects in materials and workmanship and specifically excluded all other express or implied warranties. However, the evidence would permit a reasonable jury to find that on at least three occasions GM represented to Abex that its ball-screw assembly was fail-safe and would prevent a free-fall of the Jetway even if the bearings fell out of the assembly.

First, there was the following testimony concerning an exchange that took place on March 30, 1977, when GM employees John Martuch and Lowell Smith made a sales maintenance call on the Jetway manufacturing facilities in Ogden, Utah:

> "Q. (by Abex's counsel) And at that time did either you or Mr. Smith state to Russ Williams and Bob Saunders that if the balls were lost and the deflectors were in place, that there would be interference and there would be no free-fall?
>
> A. (by Mr. Martuch) That is correct.
>
> Q. And there was discussion about that being a fail-safe feature; isn't that correct?
>
> A. That is correct.
>
> Q. And in that discussion neither you nor Mr. Smith limited that statement to the 3-inch ball screw?
>
> A. We were talking about specifically a 3-inch ball screw.
>
> Q. But no one said 3-inch, did they?
>
> A. They didn't have to. There was a print on the table that we were using as a reference that was a 3-inch ball screw.
>
> Q. But no one said, 'We want to make perfectly certain that we're only talking about that drawing'?
>
> A. We were talking about that assembly.
>
> Q. But you never pointed that out, did you?
>
> The Court: Gentlemen, Let's not talk two at one time. She's got to take everything here.
>
> Q. (by Abex's counsel): You never specifically said that, though, did you?
>
> A. Not that I remember."

R. X, 106-07.

Second, Martuch sent a letter to Abex dated April 7, 1977, which referred specifically to life/load charts for "the 3 inch and 4 inch BCD units you use." Pl. Ex. 8. The letter included ten copies of a document describing the design and operation of the patented yolk deflector system. The document stated, "If all balls should be lost from a ball nut equipped with deflectors, these yolk-type units will then cause the ball not to function as a threaded nut. This is a true fail safe feature." Pl.Ex. 7.

Third, GM invited Kenneth Noall and Russell Williams of Abex's Jetway division to Saginaw, Michigan, in May 1977 to observe a test of the fail-safe features of the ball-screw assembly. The test impressed Williams and he asked for and received the test sample. Noall remarked that the fail-safe feature was "worth its weight in gold to our customers." R. IX, 109.

GM argues that all discussions and representations regarding the safety of the ball-screw assemblies were limited to the three-inch assembly, and that the evidence unequivocally establishes that no one from Abex specifically recalled the use of the words "fail-safe" either during the conversations in Ogden or the testing in Saginaw. However, regardless of whether anyone specifically used the words "fail-safe," the literature on the ball-screw assemblies described the yolk deflector mechanism as a "fail safe feature" and did not distinguish between three- and four-inch assemblies. Pl.Ex. 7.[2] In 1977 the three- and four-inch ball-screw assemblies were the only assemblies with yolk deflectors that Abex used in its passenger loading bridges. GM knew that Abex used three- and four-inch assemblies to elevate the bridge. More important, GM, in an internal memorandum, acknowledged Abex's keen interest in the safety features of both the three- and four-inch assemblies. Lowell Smith, in a consumer contact report, stated, "I was requested by Bob Saunders of Jetway to supply a written communication to verify the deflectors in the 3″ or 4″ BCD ball screws will support the 10 6″ load rating with the balls removed from the ball nut." Pl.Ex. 13. Kenneth Noall testified that he understood that the load compression test in Saginaw applied to all ball-screw assemblies equipped with yolk deflectors, R. IX, 105–06, and Russell Williams declared that GM never stated that its tests or representations were limited only to the three-inch assemblies. *Id.* at 230–31.

GM contends that even if GM salesmen and Abex engineers used the word "fail-safe," the use constituted mere puffing rather than any affirmation of fact or promise giving rise to an express warranty. The line between puffing and warranting is often difficult to draw, but the more specific the statement the more likely it constitutes a warranty. J. White & R. Summers, *Uniform Commercial Code* 329 (1980). On the basis of the evidence in the record and resolving all facts and inferences in the light most favorable to Abex, we conclude that a rational jury could have found that GM made affirmations of fact or promises that both the three- and four-inch ball-screw assemblies equipped with yolk deflectors were fail-safe.

C

We next must determine whether a rational jury could have found that GM's affirmations of fact or promises became part of the basis of the bargain for the sale of the ball-screw assemblies. UCC § 2–313 clearly contemplates that warranties made after the sale may become a basis of the bargain. Official Comment 7 to § 2–313 provides:

> "The precise time when words of description or affirmation are made * * * is not material. The sole question is whether the language * * * [is] fairly to be regarded as a part of the contract. If language is used after the closing of the deal (as when the buyer when taking delivery asks and receives an additional assurance), the warranty becomes a modification, and need not be supported by consideration if it is otherwise reasonable and in order."

2. The full text of Plaintiff's Exhibit 7 is as follows:

> "*Design Considerations for Maximum Reliability* (con't)
>
> *Deflection Yokes vs Pickup Fingers*—There are currently two generally used methods of deflecting the bearing balls from the active circuit to the return tube—yoke deflectors and pickup fingers. The yoke deflectors are a patented innovation of Saginaw designed to provide the utmost reliability. Pickup fingers are simple extensions of the return tube guide and normally provide long trouble free service. However, obstructions in the ball groove, such as ice, and the force of skidding balls can break the finger off. If the outer finger of any circuit is broken, the balls in that circuit could be lost. Breakage of inner fingers result in balls being trapped between circuits and the failure of adjacent circuits can occur. The deflection yoke is a solid insert between circuits and outboard of the outer circuits. They are rugged enough to chip away ice in the ball groove. They also fill the space between circuits, thus eliminating the possibility of balls being trapped between circuits. If all balls should be lost from a ball nut equipped with deflectors, these yoke-type units will then cause the ball nut to function as a threaded nut. This is a true fail safe feature."

In *Bigelow v. Agway, Inc.*, 506 F.2d 551 (2d Cir.1974), the court considered whether a salesman's oral statements constituted a valid post-sale warranty modification. In *Bigelow* a farmer sued the manufacturer and distributor of a chemical used to treat hay before baling. Although most farmers will not bale hay with a moisture level higher than twenty to twenty-five percent, apparently the plaintiff was told that the chemical would safely permit the baling of hay with a higher moisture level. Two months after the sale and use of the chemical, defendant's salesman guaranteed that hay treated with the chemical was safe to bale even though it contained a moisture level of thirty-two to thirty-four percent. The farmer baled the hay, and the level of moisture resulted in a fire that destroyed his entire crop. Rejecting defendant's argument that the salesman's representation was not a basis of the bargain, the Second Circuit noted,

> "Although defendants might conceivably contend that since [the salesman's] representations postdated the delivery of the [treatment] * * * and therefore could not be the 'basis of the bargain' as required for recovery * * *, it is undisputed that the [salesman's] visit * * * was to promote the sale of the product. Thus, they might constitute an actionable modification of the warranty."

Id. at 555 n. 6. Similarly, in the case at bar a rational jury could have found that GM's post-sale representations about the safety of ball-screw assemblies with yolk deflectors were designed to promote future sales. This is especially true since GM sent Abex brochures discussing the safety features for distribution to Abex's customers.

GM argues, citing *Durbano Metals, Inc. v. A & K Railroad Materials, Inc.*, 574 P.2d 1159 (Utah 1978); *Terry v. Moore,* 448 P.2d 601 (Wyo.1968); and *Speed Fastners Inc. v. Newsom,* 382 F.2d 395 (10th Cir.1967), that Abex must prove reliance on the express warranty in order to establish that the warranty was part of the basis of the bargain. Official Comment 3 to UCC § 2–313 states, "in actual practice affirmations of fact made by the seller * * * are regarded as part of the description of those goods; hence no particular reliance on such statements need be shown in order to weave them into the fabric of the agreement * * *." We need not decide whether an express warranty may exist without reliance, *see* J. White & R. Summers, *Uniform Commercial Code* 333 (1980) ("Possibly for lack of any other meaningful standard, courts must employ the test of whether buyer relied on the affirmation of fact or promise * * * "), because Abex presented sufficient evidence for a rational jury to find that Abex did rely on GM's express warranty. Robert Saunders, Director of Research and Development and Technical Marketing for Abex, testified that he was not concerned about making safety modifications on Abex's existing stock of ball-screw assemblies because of GM's representations:

> "Q. (by Abex's counsel) Did you feel it was necessary to either alter your existing stock or the ball screws out in the field with runout threads?
>
> A. (by Mr. Saunders) No.
>
> Q. Why not?
>
> A. Because the design that we had, either the thread runout or—the washer was somewhat less critical because of the existence of the deflector yokes.
>
> Q. All right. In other words, you weren't so concerned about the safety features because of the representations about the yoke deflectors?

A. That's correct."

R. IX, 42.

GM contends that Abex cannot recover for breach of express warranty because there was no mutual agreement to modify the limited written warranty as required by § 2–313. In *Cargill, Inc. v. Stafford,* 553 F.2d 1222, 1225 (10th Cir.1977), we noted that the UCC contains an objective test of mutuality of assent as "manifested by the conduct of the parties." On the basis of the evidence presented in this case, we hold that after resolving all factual inferences in favor of Abex, a rational jury could have found that both parties recognized and assented to a warranty on the absolute safety of ball-screw assemblies equipped with yolk deflectors.

III

GM contends that its breach of the express warranty did not proximately cause Abex damage because the collapse of the Jetway had nothing to do with the failure of the yolk deflectors. However, since Abex presented evidence that the screw free-fell through the nut and that GM warranted that the yolk deflectors would engage the nut, we must resolve any doubts in favor of Abex.

Reversed and remanded for further proceedings consistent with this opinion.

[Some footnotes omitted.]

SECTION 3. NON–COMPLIANCE WITH IMPLIED WARRANTIES

A. *Introduction*

The line between an express warranty and the implied warranties of merchantability, UCC 2–314, and fitness for particular purpose, UCC 2–315, can be very fine. The common ground, of course, is the contract description of the goods. Depending on the facts, the description can create an express warranty, UCC 2–313(1)(b), provide a standard to measure merchantability, UCC 2–314(1)(a), and describe goods which meet the buyer's particular purposes. See UCC 2–315. In fact, the "sale by description" is thought to be the transaction from which implied warranty theory evolved. See, e.g., Gardiner v. Gray, 4 Camb. 144, 171 Eng.Rep. 46 (1815); Prosser, *The Implied Warranty of Merchantable Quality,* 27 Minn.L.Rev. 117, 139–45 (1943); Williston, *Representation and Warranty in Sales—Heilbut v. Buckleton,* 27 Harv.L.Rev. 1, 13 (1913).

But if neither the description of the goods nor the seller's other affirmations or promises cover the buyer's particular expectations of quality, how, if at all, is the gap in the agreement to be filled? See UCC 2–314 & 2–315? Implied warranties are clearly terms of the agreement. Are they implied in fact or imposed by law? If the latter, what justifications support the imposition?

We will consider these questions in this Section.

Problem 19–3

Read UCC 2–314 and 2–315. Make up an abstract list of the basic types of facts a plaintiff would *not* have to prove to show breach of an implied warranty of merchantability but would have to prove to show breach of an implied warranty of fitness for a particular purpose.

B. Merchantability

UCC 2–314(1) provides that "a warranty that the goods shall be merchantable is implied in a contract for their sale if the seller is a merchant with respect to goods of that kind." Subsection (2) provides standards to measure merchantability and Subsection (3) provides that "other implied warranties may arise from course of dealing or usage of trade." But the implied warranty of merchantability may be "excluded or modified" by agreement, the content of which is regulated by UCC 2–316(2).

AGOOS KID CO., INC. v. BLUMENTHAL IMPORT CORP.

Supreme Judicial Court of Massachusetts, 1933.
282 Mass. 1, 184 N.E. 279.

[Blumenthal Import Corporation contracted to sell to Agoos Kid Company four thousand dozen "Bagdad goat skins dry salted." Payment was to be: "Net cash or domestic letter of credit against documents"; Agoos paid without inspecting the skins. Serious defects in the skins showed up for which Agoos sued Blumenthal. Plaintiff got judgment and Blumenthal appealed.]

CROSBY, J.

* * *

Upon the question whether there was an implied warranty of merchantable quality under [Uniform Sales Act 15(2)] the following facts were found: The goods described in the contracts known in the trade as "Bagdad goat skins dry salted" are a well known article of commerce. The defendant maintains an organization in various places in Asia Minor and India for the purpose of collecting dry salted skins for shipment to the United States and at the time of the collection of the skins in question it had a representative in Bagdad. At times such representatives buy from local collectors and butchers skins which have been cured by the dry salting process. This process is efficient in preserving the texture of the skins only when an attempt is not made to dry them too quickly by the hot rays of the sun, which is likely to result in a rotting of the inside of the skin, where it cannot be detected by ocular or manual inspection or in any other practicable way until the skins are put into the process of being made into leather. With reasonable precaution in the care and selection of the skins in the Orient, a certain number of improperly cured and rotted skins is likely to be found in a large lot. Both parties were aware of this fact. In the trade it is considered that a lot is normal if it does not appear that more than one and one half per cent, or at the most three per cent, are improperly cured and therefore worthless. "Certainly a lot containing more than three per cent of rotted skins is abnormal." It was found that so far as defects appeared the defendant was ignorant of their condition, and the same was true of the plaintiff until the defects were shown in the plaintiff's tannery. Beginning with the first pack of skins of the first shipment the plaintiff, on January 14, 1931, began the process of manufacturing them into leather, and at different times thereafter all the other packs were put through the process, and many of them showed that more than three per cent were rotten. The entire first shipment was finally put through the process, and it was found that "the defects in the first shipment were very material and important and extended to nearly half the skins contained in it." Upon the foregoing findings which were warranted by the evidence, the further finding was warranted that the goods delivered by the first shipment were not of merchantable quality.

The contracts in question were for a sale of goods by description and there was an implied warranty that they would correspond with the description. G.L. c. 106, § 16. "The goods are merchantable when they are of the general kind which they are described or supposed to be when bought." Williston on Sales (2d Ed.) § 243. "Where goods of a character commonly known in trade are ordered by description, and there is no inspection, there is an implied warranty that those furnished will be such as are merchantable under the descriptive term used by the parties. The purchaser is entitled to get what he ordered." Leavitt v. Fiberloid Co., 196 Mass. 440, 451, 82 N.E. 682, 687, 15 L.R.A., N.S., 855, and cases cited. See, also, Randall v. Newson, 2 Q.B.D. 102; Bristol Tramways, &c. Carriage Co., Ltd. v. Fiat Motors, Ltd., [1910] 2 K.B. 831, 841; Nichol v. Godts, 10 Ex. 191. The plaintiff did not contract to buy seven thousand dozen goat skins, one half of which were to be rotten and worthless. It agreed to buy that number of skins dry salted, and there was an implied warranty that, with the exception of not more than three per cent thereof, they should be of merchantable quality. Keown & McEvoy, Inc. v. Verlin, 253 Mass. 374, 377, 149 N.E. 115, 41 A.L.R. 1319, Whitty Manuf. Co. v. Clark, 278 Mass. 370, 180 N.E. 315. Although it was found that a lot of dry salted goat skins is deemed of merchantable quality and reasonably fit for the purpose of making it into leather if the defect here existing is limited to not more than three per cent of the lot, it was found that the first shipment was not merchantable throughout "within this definition, and was not reasonably fit throughout within this definition for the purpose of being made into leather." * * * [The court reversed because the trial court had excluded defendant's evidence of a custom in the trade to notify the seller of defective skins before starting to process them.]

Notes

1. In a seminal article, written in 1943, William Prosser, later a principal architect of strict tort liability, suggested three overlapping justifications for the implied warranty of merchantability. The first was that the seller had made a "misrepresentation of fact" upon which the buyer had relied. For Prosser, this was "obviously" a tort theory. The second was that the warranty "has in fact been agreed upon by the parties as an unexpressed term of the contract for sale." The warranty was inferred from language, conduct, circumstances and was "pure" contract. The third was that the warranty was "imposed by law" as a matter of policy. The loss from "defective" goods should be placed upon the seller "because he is best able to bear it and distribute it to the public, and because it is considered that the buyer is entitled to protection at the seller's expense." For the third justification, Prosser had in mind cases where defective food caused personal injuries to buyers and consumers. See Prosser, The Implied Warranty of Merchantable Quality, 27 Minn.L.Rev. 117, 122 (1943). Do you agree with Prosser's classifications?

2. Which justification(s) supports the result in *Agoos Kid Co.*? Can you add to the list?

VALLEY IRON & STEEL CO. v. THORIN

Supreme Court of Oregon, 1977.
278 Or. 103, 562 P.2d 1212.

LENT, J.

Plaintiff brought an action in assumpsit for the reasonable value of goods sold and delivered to the defendant. Defendant pleaded affirmative defenses, alleging breaches of the implied warranties of merchantability and fitness for particular purpose. ORS 72.3140; 72.3150. Following a trial to the court, judgment was entered in favor of plaintiff. Defendant appeals, claiming that the court erred in failing to find breaches of the implied warranties and improperly fixed the amount of damages.

Because of the trial court's general finding in favor of plaintiff, we review the evidence in the light most favorable to its contentions.

Plaintiff is a corporation engaged in the manufacture of cast iron products. In 1974 defendant was establishing a retail store to sell equipment and supplies for tree-planting contractors and workers. In September of that year, defendant's agent, Steven Gibbs, met with Roger Herring, Manager of Valley Iron & Steel. Mr. Gibbs inquired if plaintiff could manufacture castings of hoedad collars. A hoedad is a forestry tool used for planting seedling trees. The collar of a hoedad secures the metal blade to a wooden handle.

Mr. Gibbs showed plaintiff a sample collar casting made by Western Fire Equipment and asked if plaintiff could duplicate the casting. The sample collar was shown with a handle, and Mr. Gibbs explained that the tool was an impact tool used for planting trees and that occasionally rocks are struck during the planting process. Plaintiff's witness, Mr. Herring, testified:

> "* * * Mr. Gibbs came in, spoke to me, told me that he needed this particular type of casting, briefly described its intended use, asked me if we could make them.
>
> "I indicated we could. It was a very brief discussion in regards to the type of material we were going to use, and I indicated that because there was potential chance of hitting rock in this * * * operation * * * that it would have to be made out of somewhat of a durable material."

Mr. Herring suggested that the castings be made of durable iron. The parties agreed upon a price, and after defendant obtained a core box and pattern from the model collar, manufacturing commenced. The collars were delivered to defendant in early October, 1974.

Problems developed with the finished product. Defendant's customers complained that the castings were breaking. Eventually defendant returned up to 80% of the castings to the plaintiff. Another foundry later made satisfactory castings from the same core box and pattern but from mild steel instead of cast iron.

At the conclusion of the trial, the court made the following findings:

> "I am not going to make any specific findings—just some general findings—but I will say that my general findings are based upon two findings, I suppose. One is that Mr. Gibbs' directions to Mr. Herring in this case were not sufficient in the sense that the court believes that he knew enough about what he was doing when he went out there to give directions, and the court does not feel that Mr. Herring did anything that was legally wrong and then didn't comply with what he said he was going to do.
>
> "In other words, the court believes that the one at fault was Mr. Gibbs in this particular case. 'Fault' may not be exactly the correct word, but that it was the legal duty of Mr. Gibbs to do more than he did, rather than Mr. Herring doing more than he did.
>
> "So, the court—then, the general finding is that I am finding for the plaintiff."

Defendant contends on appeal that the court erred in failing to find the existence of an implied warranty of merchantability under ORS 72.3140 and an implied warranty of fitness for a particular purpose under ORS 72.3150. ORS 72.3140 provides that:

> "72.3140. Implied warranty: merchantability; usage of trade. (1) Unless excluded or modified as provided in ORS 72.3160, a warranty that the goods shall be merchantable is implied in a contract for their sale if the seller is a merchant with respect to goods of that kind * * *
>
> "(2) Goods to be merchantable must be at least such as:
>
> * * *
>
> "(c) Are fit for the ordinary purposes for which such goods are used; * * *"

In denying defendant any recovery under this theory, the trial court must have concluded either that plaintiff was not a "merchant with respect to goods of that kind" or that the goods were "fit for the ordinary purposes for which such goods are used." It is undisputed that the products were "goods" [1] and that there was a "contract for their sale." Any implied warranty which existed was not excluded or modified under ORS 72.3160.[2]

"Merchant" is defined by ORS 72.1040 as "a person who deals in goods of the kind or otherwise by his occupation holds himself out as having knowledge or skill peculiar to the practices or goods involved in the transaction * * *." While the evidence shows that plaintiff was unfamiliar with hoedads and had not previously manufactured hoedad collars, plaintiff did hold itself out, by operating a foundry, as having skill in the "practice" of casting iron and presumably in the selection of materials to be used in manufacturing castings. Inasmuch as this transaction involved the selection of the type of metal appropriate for hoedad collars, plaintiff was a merchant.[3]

Likewise, plaintiff, for purposes of ORS 72.3140, was a merchant "with respect to goods of that kind"; i.e., castings. Whether this provision is interpreted broadly (in this case to mean castings) or narrowly (to mean hoedad collars) would depend upon the facts of the case. Only merchants, under the Code, warrant merchantability; and this is so because of their expertise or familiarity with the processes or products involved in the transaction. This skill or knowledge is presumed from previous similar transactions. Plaintiff has in the past assisted buyers in choosing particular types of metals to fulfill various tasks in its manufacture of castings.[4] Where the alleged unfitness under ORS

1. "Specially manufactured goods" are included within the definition of "goods" in ORS 72.1050.

2. We do not conclude that plaintiff, by promising to make the castings out of "durable iron" or saying that it was not performing engineering services, effectively modified or excluded any implied warranties as to the ingredients used in manufacturing the castings under ORS 72.3160. Such language does not "in common understanding call the buyer's attention to the exclusion of warranties and make plain that there is no implied warranty." ORS 72.3160(3)(a).

3. In Blockhead, Inc. v. Plastic Forming Company, Inc., 402 F.Supp. at 1017 (D.Conn. 1975) the court held that: "The term 'practices' indicates that one may be a merchant of goods by virtue of his involvement in the process by which those goods are produced as well as by sale of the finished goods from inventory." (402 F.Supp. at 1025.)

4. Mr. Herring testified that he tried to imply to buyers that no guarantee was made as to the selection of the appropriate material for casting but that any lack of guarantee was not discussed with Mr. Gibbs. In special order situations like the present case, it was customary with plaintiff to use the "best efforts at foundry" as to the choice of the proper alloy.

72.3140 arises from this type of choice, plaintiff should be held to the stricter standard imposed on merchants.[5]

The remaining issue is whether the collars were "fit for the ordinary purposes for which such goods are used." The ordinary purpose of custom-made castings depends upon their designated use. Without such a tag the uses would vary so much that any function could be isolated as "ordinary."

The trial court felt that plaintiff was unaware of the intended use. However, the testimony of Mr. Herring shows the contrary. Plaintiff knew that the castings were to join the handle and blade in tree-planting impact tools which occasionally would strike rock. Since the castings were not fit for this purpose, the warranty was breached.

Similarly, plaintiff breached the warranty of fitness for a particular purpose. ORS 72.3150 provides:

> "Implied warranty: fitness for particular purpose. Where the seller at the time of contracting has reason to know any particular purpose for which the goods are required and that the buyer is relying on the seller's skill or judgment to select or furnish suitable goods, there is unless excluded or modified under ORS 72.3160 an implied warranty that the goods shall be fit for such purpose."

Official Comment 1 to this section states that:

> "Under this section the buyer need not bring home to the seller actual knowledge of the particular purpose for which the goods are intended or of his reliance on the seller's skill and judgment, if the circumstances are such that the seller has reason to realize the purpose intended or that the reliance exists. The buyer, of course, must actually be relying on the seller."

In this case, the undisputed evidence shows that the buyer made known the intended purpose and that the choice of metal to be used was left to the discretion of the seller. From this the seller had "reason to know" that buyer was relying on its judgment. It is also plain that the buyer did so rely. It follows that the warranty existed and evidence existed that it was breached.[6]

The trial court rested its decision upon the "fault" of the defendant in failing to provide additional information on the intended use of the castings. "Fault," as such, is irrelevant when dealing with implied warranties. State ex rel. Western Seed v. Campbell, 250 Or. 262, 266, 442 P.2d 215 (1967). It is true that the existence of a warranty of fitness for a particular purpose depends in part upon the comparative knowledge and skill of the parties. Blockhead, Inc. v. Plastic Forming Company, Inc., 402 F.Supp. 1017, 1024 (D.Conn.1975). Here, however, defendant made known his general requirements and the purpose for

5. Thus in cases where the seller possesses no degree of discretion so as to warrant his or her expertise; e.g., where the product is manufactured strictly in accordance with buyer specifications, there may be no implied warranties. See Official Comments to the U.C.C., § 2-316, Comment 9; School Supply Service Co. v. J.H. Keeney & Co., 410 F.2d 481, 483 (5th Cir.1969); Rust Engineering Co. v. Lawrence Pumps, Inc., 401 F.Supp. 328, 333 (D.Mass.1975).

6. Where goods are specially manufactured goods the ordinary purpose of such goods may be equivalent to their particular purpose for purposes of the warranty enumerated in ORS 72.3150. See, generally, Filler v. Rayex Corp., 435 F.2d 336 (7th Cir.1970); Tennessee Carolina Transp., Inc. v. Strick Corp., 283 N.C. 423, 196 S.E.2d 711 (1973). Contra, Blockhead, Inc. v. Plastic Forming Company, Inc., supra n. 3.

Official Comment 2 to the Code states: "A contract may of course include both a warranty of merchantability and one of fitness for a particular purpose."

which the goods were to be used. We fail to see what more the defendant could have disclosed. Where, as here, the needs of a buyer are disclosed and the seller has reason to know of the buyer's reliance, it is incumbent upon the seller to further inquire as to the buyer's wants before representing that the goods can be provided. Lewis v. Mobil Oil Corp., 438 F.2d 500 (8th Cir.1971). See also, Northern Plumbing Supply, Inc. v. Gates, 196 N.W.2d 70 (N.D.1972).

In this case the trial court found that the reasonable value of each casting was $3.75. She estimated the value of the goods returned to be $27.42. Implicit in this finding is the conclusion that 457 of the 571 pieces were returned to the seller.[7] Because we conclude that defendant rightfully revoked acceptance under ORS 72.6080(1)(b), inasmuch as the goods were unfit, defendant has no further obligation as to the returned goods. ORS 72.6020(2)(c). The defendant, however, is obligated to pay for the remaining 114 castings which it accepted. Accordingly, under our powers as enumerated in the Oregon Constitution, Am Art VII § 3, plaintiff's judgment is reduced to $427.50 (the value of 114 pieces at $3.75 per unit).

Affirmed as modified.

Notes

1. Why should the implied warranty of merchantability be limited to sellers who are merchants "with respect to goods of that kind?" UCC 2–314(1). As the court in *Thorin* recognizes, the merchant requirement for UCC 2–314(1) is narrower than the definition of "merchant" in UCC 2–104(1). Compare UCC 2–201(2) & 2–207(2). How can a seller who had never made or sold a hoedad collar be a merchant "with respect to goods of that kind?" See Fred J. Moore, Inc. v. Schinmann, 40 Wash.App. 705, 700 P.2d 754 (1985) (farmer who made "isolated" sale not a dealer in goods of that kind); Smith v. Stewart, 233 Kan. 904, 667 P.2d 358 (1983) (seller of used yacht does not make an implied warranty of merchantability).

2. Who is a merchant for purposes of UCC 2–314(1) is a mixed question of law and fact that depends upon the circumstances of each case. Ferragamo v. Massachusetts Bay Transportation Authority, 395 Mass. 581, 481 N.E.2d 477 (1985) (upheld jury verdict that MBTA is merchant with respect to sporadic sale of old trolley cars). The question whether a farmer who sells livestock or raises crops grown on his own land is a merchant is frequently litigated with diverse results. In Dotts v. Bennett, 382 N.W.2d 85 (Iowa 1986), however, the court rejected the argument that a farmer who sells only a crop grown annually (hay) was not, as a matter of law, a merchant. The jury verdict that the farmer was a merchant with respect to hay was supported by the following factors: "He had been a lifetime farmer; he had 100 to 150 acres in hay in 1981; he has sold about twenty percent of his hay for fifteen years; he has advertised hay for sale; at one time he sold a large quantity of hay to parties in southern Missouri; he has done some custom hay farming; he considers himself a knowledgeable hay farmer; and he has had continuing education in farming. * * *" 382 N.W.2d at 89. A related case is Vince v. Broome, 443 So.2d 23 (Miss.1983) (farmer held to be merchant with regard to cattle sold, four judges dissenting).

3. Cattle and other livestock are frequently sold at auction. Suppose the farmer-owner is not a merchant under UCC 2–314(1) but the auctioneer clearly is:

7. Testimony at the trial by Mr. Herring was that the individual castings weighed around two pounds apiece and that the scrap value was three cents per pound. If each piece was worth six cents as scrap, an offset of $27.42 equates to 457 returned castings. This is consistent with Mr. Herring's testimony that 60–8 of the castings were returned, as 457 is 80% of the 571 units sold.

He regularly deals in goods of that kind. Does the auctioneer make an implied warranty of merchantability? In Powers v. Coffeyville Livestock Sales Co., Inc., 665 F.2d 311 (10th Cir.1981), the answer was no if the auctioneer had revealed the identity of its principal. Disclosure prevented the auctioneer from being a seller at common law and the court incorporated the common law rule through UCC 1–103 to supplement the definition of seller in UCC 2–103(1)(d), which was ambiguous on the point.

DELANO GROWERS' COOPERATIVE WINERY v. SUPREME WINE CO., INC.

Supreme Judicial Court of Massachusetts, 1985.
393 Mass. 666, 473 N.E.2d 1066.

Before HENNESSEY, C.J., and LIACOS, NOLAN, LYNCH and O'CONNOR, JJ.

NOLAN, JUSTICE.

The plaintiff, Delano Growers' Cooperative Winery (Delano), appeals from a final judgment dismissing its complaint and awarding $160,634, with interest, to the defendant, Supreme Wine Co., Inc. (Supreme), on its counterclaim. Supreme appeals from that portion of the judgment which granted Delano an "offset" of $25,823.25 to Supreme's damages under the counterclaim. For the reasons stated below, we affirm the judgment.

Delano filed a complaint in Suffolk County Superior Court seeking $25,823.25 for wine sold and delivered. Supreme admitted receipt of the wine and filed a counterclaim for breach of contract alleging that earlier shipments of wine for which payment had been made and all of the wine for which no payment had been made had spoiled due to the presence of lactobacillus trichodes (Fresno mold). As a defense, Supreme asserted that it did not owe Delano $25,823.25 because the wine was not merchantable. Supreme also sought incidental and consequential damages alleging that the "sick wine" destroyed its reputation and market thereby forcing the company into liquidation.[1]

* * *

The facts as found by the master and accepted by the judge may be summarized as follows. Supreme operated a wine bottling plant in Boston from 1935 to November, 1978. It purchased finished wine, ready for bottling and

1. Supreme purchased all of its sweet wine and some of its nonsweet wine from Delano. Fresno mold only damaged the sweet wine. Supreme's customers began returning defective Delano wine prior to the shipment for which Delano claims in its complaint that it is owed $25,823.25 (the unpaid shipment). Supreme paid for all prior shipments. Supreme's customers continued to return defective Delano wine after Supreme received and bottled the wine in the unpaid shipment. One-half of the unpaid shipment consisted of sweet wine. The record does not indicate what portion of the unpaid shipment or total shipments consisted of damaged wine. However, we need not resolve this question to affirm the judgment in this case. Supreme proved that 8,000 cases of wine were defective. Supreme normally sold this wine to its retail customers for $13 per case. This per case price included the amount Supreme paid Delano for the wine, Supreme's other costs, and its profits. The judge calculated damages by multiplying the number of cases proved as damaged (8,000) by the per case price ($13). The resultant amount includes all of Supreme's cost for wine including the amount remaining unpaid on the last shipment. The judge then deducted the amount that Supreme had not paid for wine ($25,823.25) and made other adjustments as discussed below. This prevents overcompensating Supreme because the per case price ($13) included Supreme's cost for the wine as if it were actually paid. The $25,823.25 represents a portion of this cost that was not paid. This calculation also factors out any need to determine the amount of undamaged wine Supreme received as damages are based solely on the actual amount of defective wine.

consumption, from California, selling it to retailers after bottling under Supreme's label.

In 1968, Supreme began buying sweet wine from Delano, a California winery. By the spring of 1973, Supreme was purchasing all its sweet wine from Delano. Delano shipped this wine to Supreme's bottling plant in Boston in tank cars. When the wine arrived, Supreme took samples from each compartment of the tank cars. The samples were labeled, dated, sealed, and kept in Supreme's safe. Supreme then pumped the wine into redwood vats in its building. The wine was pumped through a filter into storage tanks from which it was later filtered into bottles for delivery.

Until April or May, 1973, Supreme did not experience any difficulty with Delano wine. Supreme then began receiving widespread returns of certain sweet wine from its customers. The wine was producing sediment, was cloudy, and contained a cottony or hairy substance. Supreme could identify the defective sweet wine as Delano wine because it purchased all its sweet wine from Delano. Supreme also matched the returned defective wine with the samples taken from the Delano wine on delivery. This identification was corroborated somewhat by shipment records, the dates of bottling and the color to which the Delano wine was blended.

Supreme made oral reports and complaints about the problem to Delano. It also sent Delano samples from the Delano shipment. When the help promised by Harold Roland, Delano's manager, did not materialize, Supreme purchased wine from another California grower in June, July, and August, 1973. Supreme bottled and sold that wine and received no complaints or returns on it. Roland, with renewed promises of assistance, induced Supreme to recommence purchasing from Delano in September, 1973.

Delano made four shipments of sweet wine to Supreme between September 28 and December 20, 1973. Each shipment invoice stated that payment was due forty-five days from the invoice date. Supreme paid all but the last invoice, which was in the amount of $25,823.25. It withheld payment for that amount as customers continued to return defective wine which was identified as Delano wine. When oral reports and complaints evoked no tangible help, Vito Bracciale, assistant to Supreme's president, wrote to Roland on April 9, 1974. This letter requested assistance and explained Supreme's crisis caused by the defective wine. The letter also indicated the high number of returns caused by this defective wine.

In response to this letter, Delano sent James Lunt, an assistant winemaker, to Supreme's bottling plant. His microscopic examination of the defective wine and a microscopic examination by Delano's chemist in California showed that the wine contained Fresno mold. Lunt had earlier observed the mold in the samples returned to Delano by Supreme. These were samples from the tank cars taken on arrival at Supreme and samples from wine returned by Supreme's customers.

While Lunt was at Supreme, customers returned a number of cases of Delano wine containing Fresno mold. After examining these returns, Lunt told Supreme to pasteurize, refilter, rebottle, and resell the defective wine. Supreme followed Lunt's directions and reprocessed 8,000 cases of spoiled wine (5,000 cases returned from customers and 3,000 cases still on hand). During this process, 1,000 cases were lost through breakage, spillage, and shrinkage. Supreme sold the remaining cases of reprocessed wine at a reduced rate.

* * *

2. *Delano's breach of the implied warranty of merchantability.* This sale of wine by Delano is governed by the Uniform Commercial Code, G.L. c. 106. Delano impliedly warranted that the goods were of merchantable quality. G.L. c. 106, § 2–314. See *Regina Grape Prods. Co. v. Supreme Wine Co.,* 357 Mass. 631, 635, 260 N.E.2d 219 (1970). This warranty required the wine to "pass without objection in the trade under the contract description" and be reasonably suited for ordinary uses for which goods of that kind are sold. G.L. c. 106, § 2–314(2)(*a*). See *Vincent v. Nicholas E. Tsiknas Co.,* 337 Mass. 726, 729, 151 N.E.2d 263 (1958); *Gilbert & Bennett Mfg. Co. v. Westinghouse Elec. Corp.,* 445 F.Supp. 537, 548 (D.Mass.1977).

The contract in this case required Delano to deliver "finished wine" to Supreme. Delano contends that, when it delivered wine that appeared good and which could be bottled, its obligation was satisfied. In support, Delano argues that all California sweet wine contained Fresno mold. Therefore, the presence of Fresno mold could not cause a wine to be unmerchantable. Furthermore, Delano states that an alleged trade usage required Supreme to add sulfur dioxide to the wine to inhibit further growth of these bacteria. Delano's arguments fail to persuade us.

Delano argues that uncontroverted testimony indicated that all California sweet wine contained Fresno mold. The judge acknowledged this testimony. However, the judge found that Supreme never experienced any trouble with bacteria until the 1973 problem with Delano wine. The sweet wine which Supreme bought from other California growers in 1973 did not present any bacterial problems. None of this wine was returned with Fresno mold. Furthermore, the judge found that the bacterial problem could have been prevented and controlled by Delano. Although Fresno mold may have been present in all California sweet wine, there is no indication that it was allowed to go unchecked and thereby destroy the merchantability of finished wine. Supreme's prior experience with Delano and its experience with other California sweet wine in 1973 indicate that the mold could be controlled. The presence of Fresno mold, as it was in the Delano wines, caused those wines to be unmarketable.

Delano argues that Supreme's failure to follow minimum industry standards prevents it from recovering for the unmerchantable wine. The judge specifically ruled that Delano had failed to meet its burden of establishing such standards as a usage of trade applicable to Supreme. Even if Delano had met its burden, its argument would fail. A course of dealing between parties controls the interpretation of usage of trade. G.L. c. 106, § 1–205(4). In this case, Supreme consistently followed the same procedure in processing Delano wine since 1968. This clearly established a course of dealing between Delano and Supreme. Any usage of trade followed in areas outside of Massachusetts cannot control this long-standing course of dealing between the parties.

Once Supreme initially accepted Delano wine it had the burden of establishing that there was a breach of the warranty of merchantability. *Axion Corp. v. G.D.C. Leasing Corp.,* 359 Mass. 474, 479, 269 N.E.2d 664 (1971). Supreme has met that burden. Supreme identified all the returned wine as Delano wine. Delano's chemist also found traces of Fresno mold in the samples "from the compartments of the tank cars in which Delano wine arrived in Boston and wine from the bottles returned by customers." The wine in its returned state was neither merchantable nor fit for bottling or consumption. Only through extensive reprocessing could Supreme mitigate the loss from this wine. The course of dealing between the parties supports the conclusion that the finished wine shipped by Delano normally was ready for bottling and drinking. Although the Delano sweet wine could be bottled shortly thereafter, it could not be drunk.

Delano was required to anticipate the environment in which it was reasonable for its product to be used. *Back v. Wickes Corp.,* 375 Mass. 633, 640–641, 378 N.E.2d 964 (1978). It was reasonably foreseeable that the unchecked presence of Fresno mold would substantially impair the value of the wine. That result occurred. The Delano wine could not pass in the trade as finished wine without objection, was not fit for the ordinary purposes for which finished wine was used, and therefore, was unmerchantable. See G.L. c. 106, § 2–314.

* * *

Notes

1. The buyer, to prevail, must establish that the goods were unmerchantable at the time the seller tendered delivery. See UCC 2–725(2). In *Delano Growers',* to which standards of merchantability in UCC 2–314(2) did the wine fail to conform? How did the buyer avoid the possible conclusion that there was a normal amount of Fresno mold in the wine at delivery but that it got "out of hand" while the wine was being processed by the buyer?

2. In most disputes over merchantability, the key factual question is whether goods sold under a contract description were "fit for the ordinary purposes for which such goods are used." UCC 2–314(2)(c). The trier of fact must know whether the product "conformed to the standard performance of like products used in the trade * * * (and this determination) depends upon testimony of persons familiar with industry standards and local practices and is a question of fact." Pisano v. American Leasing Co., 146 Cal.App.3d 194, 194 Cal.Rptr. 77, 80 (1983). Without any evidence of relevant trade standards or uses, the merchantability claim may fail. Royal Business Machines, Inc. v. Lorraine Corp., 633 F.2d 34 (7th Cir.1980). Similarly, if, because of the newness or complexity of the product, no average or usual standards for determining performance or quality can be determined, the "ordinary purposes" standard will not help the buyer. See, e.g., Price Brothers Co. v. Philadelphia Gear Corp., 649 F.2d 416 (6th Cir.1981).

Problem 19–4

Fisher's, a retail book store, has an extensive inventory in specialized categories, such as law, business, psychology and investments. A new investment book by Barry Greene, entitled "How to go Short in A Bear Market," was published by Big Red Company and heavily advertised in the trade journals as the "key" to success in selling short in the stock market and selling "Puts" in the option markets. Fisher's purchased 300 copies for resale and the books sold well. Mr. N.O. Vice, an inexperienced investor, purchased a copy of the book for $20 and, following Greene's advice, committed $25,000 of his funds over a three month period. He lost $15,000 of that investment before covering his shorts. About the same time, a scathing review of Greene's book by Malcolm P. Barron appeared in the Wall Street Journal. Barron stated that the advice was seriously flawed and should not be taken seriously. Other experts agreed and sales of the book dropped precipitously. Angered, N.O. Vice retains you as counsel to consider whether a law suit against either Fisher's or Big Red could be maintained on a warranty theory. Greene, who went long while others were going short, is now "long gone." What is your advice? Cf. Cardozo v. True, 342 So.2d 1053 (Fla.App.1977).

INTERNATIONAL PETROLEUM SERVICES, INC. v. S & N WELL SERVICE, INC.

Supreme Court of Kansas, 1982.
230 Kan. 452, 639 P.2d 29.

OMIT

FROMME, JUSTICE:

International Petroleum Services, Inc., plaintiff, brought this action to recover for materials and repairs to three units of oil well servicing equipment. Two of these units had been sold previously by plaintiff to S & N Well Service, Inc., defendant herein. The third unit, which was repaired by plaintiff, was leased by defendant from another individual. Defendant filed an answer and a cross-petition. In the cross-petition defendant claimed breach of implied warranties arising from the sales of the equipment and asked for both ordinary and consequential damages. In addition, defendant sought disallowance of certain amounts claimed by plaintiff because plaintiff's charges were said to be unreasonable.

The case was tried to the court and judgment was entered on the petition in favor of plaintiff and against the defendant in the amount of $17,385.83. On defendant's cross-petition, defendant was given judgment against the plaintiff for $1,042.69. A judgment for the net amount of $16,343.14 was entered in favor of plaintiff and against the defendant. The defendant appealed and the Court of Appeals affirmed, 637 P.2d 496, under Rule No. 7.042(b) and (d) (228 Kan. lii, liii). The case is now before this court on an order granting defendant's Petition for Review.

There are two principal questions to be answered in this appeal. The first is whether the implied warranties mentioned in K.S.A. 84–2–314 and 84–2–315 apply to the sale of used goods. The second question is whether consequential damages resulting from a seller's breach of warranty are recoverable, and, if so, under what circumstances.

The uniform commercial code sections on implied warranties arising from the sale of goods cover merchantability, found in K.S.A. 84–2–314, and fitness for a particular purpose, found in K.S.A. 84–2–315. These sections are as follows:

* * *

Considering the above provisions of 84–2–314 it would be inaccurate to say the code defines merchantability. What this statute does is set minimum standards of merchantability. The statutory language is that "[g]oods to be merchantable must be at *least* such as * * *." Emphasis supplied. Thus more may be required by the parties' agreement, course of dealing, or usage of trade, but the minimum standards assure a buyer that if the goods received do not conform at least to normal commercial expectations, the buyer will have a cause of action by which he or she can secure compensation for losses suffered. Even though the seller may be careful not to make a single assertion of fact or promise about the goods, the ordinary buyer in a normal commercial transaction has a right to expect that the goods which are purchased will not turn out to be completely worthless. The purchaser cannot be expected to purchase goods offered by a merchant for sale and use and then find the goods are suitable only for the junk pile. On the other hand, a buyer who has purchased goods without obtaining an express warranty as to their quality and condition cannot reasonably expect that those goods will be the finest of all possible goods of that kind. Protection of the buyer under the uniform commercial code lies between these two extremes. If an item is used or is second hand, surely less can be expected in the way of quality than if the item is purchased new. See Nordstrom, Law of Sales § 76, pp. 232–238 (1970); and White-Summers, Uniform Commercial Code § 9–6, pp. 343–355 (second edition 1980) for further discussion of this subject.

In addition, we note that for a sale to give rise to the implied warranty *of merchantability* the seller must be a merchant.

* * *

All parties to this action agree that the plaintiff, International Petroleum Services, Inc., does manufacture and deal in well servicing equipment of the kind sold to defendant. We conclude that plaintiff was a merchant within the statutory definition when it sold the two units to the defendant.

In passing we note under K.S.A. 84–2–315, relating to the implied warranty of fitness for a particular purpose, there is no requirement that the seller be a merchant. However, the seller at the time of contracting must have reason to know the goods are being purchased for a particular purpose, and the seller must know further that the buyer is relying on the skill and judgment of the seller to select or furnish suitable goods. In such case an implied warranty that the goods shall be fit for such purpose may arise. Further discussion on the subject will follow later.

After examining the uniform commercial code—sales, we find no provision excluding the sale of used goods from the provisions of the code. K.S.A. 84–2–102 merely states that Article 2 on sales applies "to transactions in goods." K.S.A. 84–2–105(1) states:

> " 'Goods' means all things (including specially manufactured goods) which are movable at the time of identification to the contract for sale other than the money in which the price is to be paid, investment securities (article 8) and things in action."

The commentators generally have agreed that the implied warranties recognized by K.S.A. 84–2–314 and 84–2–315 apply to sales of both new and used goods. Note, *Sales: Extension of Implied Warranty of Merchantability to Used Goods,* 46 Mo.L.Rev. 249, 250 (1981); Stasney, *UCC Implied Warranty of Merchantability and Used Goods,* 26 Baylor L.Rev. 630, 637 (1974); Hunt, *Implied Warranties of Quality on Used Motor Vehicles in Texas,* 9 St. Mary's L.J. 308, 315 (1977); *Article Two Warranties in Commercial Transactions,* 64 Cornell L.Rev. 30, 85 (1978). Texas seems to be the only state which has steadfastly refused to recognize implied warranties in the sale of used goods. The old adage "let the buyer beware" applies to the sale of used goods in Texas.

In *Atlas Industries, Inc. v. National Cash Register Co.,* 216 Kan. 213, 531 P.2d 41 (1975), this court recognized an implied warranty in the sale of a used accounting machine, without discussion as to applicability of these warranties to used goods. The parties in that case did not question whether the uniform commercial code—sales covered sales of used equipment.

We note the following statement which appears in the comments following K.S.A. 84–2–314:

> "3. A specific designation of goods by the buyer does not exclude the seller's obligation that they be fit for the general purposes appropriate to such goods. *A contract for the sale of second-hand goods, however, involves only such obligation as is appropriate to such goods for that is their contract description."* Comment 3. Emphasis supplied.

This comment by the drafters of the statute strongly indicates an intent to include sales of both new and used goods within the statutory provisions.

A few of the decisions from other states which have recognized an implied warranty of merchantability in the sale of used goods are: *Brown v. Hall,* 221 So.2d 454, 457 (Fla.Dist.Ct.App.1969); *Georgia Timberlands, Inc. v. Southern Airway Company,* 125 Ga.App. 404, 405, 188 S.E.2d 108 (1972); *Overland Bond and Inv. Corp. v. Howard,* 9 Ill.App.3d 348, 352, 292 N.E.2d 168 (1972); *Tracy v. Vinton Motors, Inc.,* 130 Vt. 512, 515, 296 A.2d 269 (1972).

We hold that the implied warranties recognized in K.S.A. 84–2–314 and 84–2–315 may arise from sales of both new and used goods.

* * *

It should be noted that the extent of the obligation of a merchant who sells used goods depends on the circumstances of the transaction. In the case of a sale by auction of used restaurant equipment it was held no implied warranty of merchantability attached. See *Regan Purchase & Sales v. Primavera,* 68 Misc.2d 858, 860, 328 N.Y.S.2d 490 (1972), wherein it is stated:

> "The specific question here is whether a breach of warranty is made out by evidence that used restaurant equipment bought at an auction did not function upon delivery, in the absence of any competent evidence establishing the character of the defect. The standard formulated in the Official Comment clearly requires careful attention to the realities of the individual transaction.
>
> "What we are concerned with here are two pieces of restaurant equipment—a dishwasher and an ice-maker—undoubtedly larger and more complex than similar equipment intended for home use—both of which had undergone the heavy wear and tear normal in the operation of a restaurant. The possibility that individual components might be worn out or otherwise defective, requiring replacement or repair, is surely implicit in such a transaction.
>
> "Where such pieces of equipment are purchased for continued commercial use at a significant discount from new equipment of the same kind, more is surely required to establish a breach of the warranty than the bare circumstance that they did not operate upon delivery."

Courts have recognized that any number of things can foul the operation of complex machinery, and in the case of used goods, not all of these problems amount to a breach of the warranty of merchantability. The buyer's knowledge that the goods are used, the extent of their prior use, and whether the goods are significantly discounted may help determine what standards of quality should apply to the transaction.

With the foregoing background we turn now to the specific facts of this case. S & N Well Service, Inc. began business in February, 1977. The president of the corporation, Mr. Smith, had been in this type of business since 1970 and had operated eleven oil well servicing rigs before he started the present company.

In February, 1977, Mr. Smith purchased from plaintiff one of the units now in question. It is referred to as a single drum Franks Unit. He was advised and understood the unit was used. The unit was equipped with a diesel engine, and plaintiff informed the purchaser that the engine had been checked out and approved by Detroit Diesel, a company specializing in the sale and servicing of diesel engines. However, no express warranty was given on the unit and no disclaimer was mentioned or declared by the seller. This particular machine had been built by plaintiff from components of several other used oil well servicing rigs. These had been purchased previously by plaintiff and the components from those machines were assembled in plaintiff's shop to make up Unit No. 1. The working parts such as the draw works and engine were used. Only a few of the components such as the cab and fenders were new. Defendant was advised of these facts. We find nothing in the record as to the price paid for the second-hand unit as compared to the price of a new unit.

Problems developed with Unit No. 1 after it had been used only two days. The fourth gear kept slipping out. A rebuilt differential unit was installed by plaintiff. The oil line to the air compressor was not connected properly when sold and the motor threw a connecting rod. The unit was returned to plaintiff. A new connecting rod was installed and the oil line was properly connected. No charges were made for these repairs. Thereafter, the unit worked fine for 90 days, at which time the engine began to misfire and the heat gauge indicated overheating. Close examination disclosed a head gasket was blown. It was then discovered the engine head was cracked and the pistons were cupped out. In effect, the engine was worn out and needed to be completely rebuilt. The machine was returned to the plaintiff.

The engine was then pulled and rebuilt by Diesel Equipment Company of Wichita. For the rebuilding of the engine and the work in pulling and reinstalling the engine plaintiff submitted a bill on invoice No. 9945 for $6,765.01. After defendant complained of the amount of these charges, the bill was reduced to $4,932.27. The defendant was apparently satisfied with this adjustment for a time but did not make payment. Plaintiff sued for the reduced amount.

Now we turn to the second unit purchased from plaintiff in March, 1977. This will be referred to as Unit No. 2. It was a Cardwell K–200 double drum unit. Before purchasing the unit Mr. Smith, acting for the defendant company, asked that the rig be modified from a dual axle to a single axle unit. The single axle left on the machine was too light and within the first few days of use the front axle bent. The rig was hauled in for repairs and the plaintiff company repaired the machine by exchanging the bent axle for a heavy duty axle. There was testimony by an officer of plaintiff company that they would have known the first single axle was too light if they had "ran the figures through right." In order to accommodate the new heavy axle, it was necessary to add larger rims and tires. The original invoice No. 9944 submitted for these charges totaled $3,982.07. The defendant company complained of the charges and again the bill was reduced, this time to $1,042.69 which equaled the cost of the rims and tires. Plaintiff sued for this amount. The trial court disallowed the amount finding there was a breach of warranty which required plaintiff as seller to make these repairs in order to return the value of the machine to the value it would have had at the time of sale if it had been as warranted.

As to Unit No. 1, the Franks Unit, the trial court considered the fact that this was a sale of used or second-hand goods. The unit was a highly complex machine known to be subject to heavy and sustained wear while in operation. It was made up of component parts of used machines of which neither party had knowledge concerning the extent of their use.

In Comment 7 appearing below K.S.A. 84–2–314, the authors of the UCC point out that in cases of doubt as to what quality is intended, the price at which a merchant closes a sale contract is an excellent index of the nature and scope of his obligation under the section. There was no evidence introduced in this case, however, as to the extent of the discount in the price of this used machinery. It is, therefore, nearly impossible to decide what standards of quality should apply to the transaction. We do know that the plaintiff merchant corrected the initial defects in the rig at its own expense. Plaintiff installed a rebuilt differential unit to repair the fourth gear, it connected the oil line to the air compressor, and it put in a new connecting rod in the engine. Thereafter, the unit worked fine for approximately 90 days before the diesel engine had to be rebuilt.

Under these facts and circumstances, we cannot say the trial court was in error in not allowing further damages for breach of the implied warranty of merchantability on Unit No. 1 (Franks Unit). The unit did operate satisfactorily for 90 days after the initial adjustments and repairs were made without charge. The machine was fit for the ordinary purposes for which such goods are generally used, and even after the diesel engine wore out it still could be and was rebuilt. This oil well servicing equipment was then put back in service. By way of analogy we note that used automobiles generally carry no more than a thirty day guarantee. The plaintiff merchant in the present case made no untrue promises or affirmations as to the condition of this machinery. The trial court found that the plaintiff had the diesel engine checked over by Detroit Diesel and that company had approved the engine as being in working condition.

We now consider Unit No. 2, the Cardwell Unit. As previously pointed out, this machine when sold to defendant was a used or second-hand unit. At the request of defendant it was modified by plaintiff company from a dual axle to a single axle unit. Within the first few days after it was put in use, it became inoperable because of a bent single axle. There was testimony that the plaintiff-merchant knew or should have known the machine could not operate on this single axle. It was not strong enough to support the machine. It appears that the unit was not fit for the ordinary purposes for which the machine was to be used since it became inoperable in the first few days of use.

Using the guidelines previously discussed, we agree with the trial court that plaintiff breached an implied warranty when it sold this used oil well servicing unit in such a condition. It knew or should have known the single axle was not strong enough to accommodate the machine after it was changed from a dual axle to a single axle unit. Therefore, the trial court properly allowed defendant to recover the $1,042.69 required to make it operable.

Note: The Relevance of Price in Disputes Over Merchantability

In *International Petroleum,* the court stated that "whether the goods are significantly discounted may help determine what standards of quality should apply to the transactions." See also, Testo v. Russ Dunmire Oldsmobile, Inc., 16 Wash.App. 39, 554 P.2d 349 (1976); UCC 2–314, Comment 7 (price at which a merchant is willing to sell an item is an "excellent index of the quality warranted and the nature and scope of his obligation"). Put differently, the price charged in context, especially where used goods are involved, will provide some assistance in determining the level of quality the buyer can reasonably expect.

This development is a retreat from Lord Mansfield's celebrated dictum in Stuart v. Wilkins, 99 Eng.Rep. 15, 19 (K.B.1778) that a "sound price" does not warrant a "sound product" but stops short of the conclusion that the price so perfectly communicates product risks that the buyer gets what he paid for. See Geistfeld, *The Price-Quality Relationship Revisited,* 16 J.Consumer Aff. 334 (1984) (factors other than quality of goods affect price and market dispersal).

In light of this, how would you resolve the following problem?

OMIT

Problem 19–5

B, a farmer, purchased a used 1980 Dodge Rambler from S, a dealer, for $5,000. The four-wheel drive vehicle had been driven 80,000 "tough" miles without any serious mechanical problems. Although refusing to make any express warranties, the seller made no attempt to disclaim or exclude warranties at the time of sale.

Thirty days and 10,000 miles later, the engine failed due to a condition existing at the time of sale. B had the engine replaced for $2,500 and sued S for breach of the implied warranty of merchantability. At the trial, B established that the $5,000 purchase price was at the low end of the "blue book" range for 1980 Dodge Ramblers. B's expert testified that a 1980 Dodge Rambler with the particular condition of B's would have a fair market value of $750. On cross-examination, the expert conceded that the particular vehicle would "pass without objection in the trade under the contract description." B introduced no additional evidence. S moved for a directed verdict. What result?

C. *Fitness for Particular Purpose*

VAN WYK v. NORDEN LABORATORIES, INC.

OMIT

Supreme Court of Iowa, 1984.
345 N.W.2d 81.

LARSON, JUSTICE.

A large number of cattle owned by the plaintiffs became sick shortly after injection of a vaccine produced by the defendant Norden Laboratories, Inc. and this suit followed. While several theories of liability were asserted by the plaintiffs, the court submitted only one: the implied warranty of fitness for a particular purpose (Iowa Code section 554.2315). The defendant appeals from a judgment for the plaintiffs, arguing that the court erred in submitting this theory under the facts of the case. It contends the implied warranty of fitness did not fit, so to speak. The plaintiffs cross-appeal, complaining that it was error to exclude certain expert evidence and to refuse submission of their alternative theories of strict liability and implied warranty of merchantability. We reverse on both appeals and remand.

In the fall of 1978, three groups of the plaintiffs' cattle, totaling about 750, were treated with a live-virus vaccine, manufactured by the defendant and called Resbo–3, serial 54. Some of the cattle had been raised by the plaintiffs, and some had been shipped in. Some were treated on the farm and some in a sale barn. The cattle were given other treatments such as worming, castration, and dehorning, simultaneously with the series 54 vaccine, but not all of them received the same combination of treatments. Yet, the incidence of bovine viral diarrhea (BVD) appeared, to a large extent, in all three herds. (BVD is one of the illnesses which the series 54 vaccine was designed to prevent.) Within a week of their injection, most of the cattle were sick. Almost 50 died. Plaintiffs' veterinarian witnesses testified that the sickness had been caused by the vaccine. They testified that before and after this incident they had used serial 54 vaccine without similar problems and that while it is reasonable to expect a few cattle to have an adverse reaction, they had never seen anything like the extent of sickness in this case. In view of this common denominator among the separate herds of cattle—their treatment with series 54 vaccine—a strong circumstantial case is claimed by the plaintiffs that the illness was in fact caused, or at least exacerbated by, the vaccine. No direct evidence of a defect was produced, however.

I. The Implied Warranty of Fitness

The only theory of liability submitted by the court was breach of implied warranty of fitness for a particular purpose, Iowa Code § 554.2315 (Uniform Commercial Code § 2–315). That section provides:

> Where the seller at the time of contracting has reason to know any particular purpose for which the goods are required and that the buyer is relying on the seller's skill or judgment to select or furnish suitable goods, there is unless excluded or modified under the next section an implied warranty that the goods shall be fit for such purpose.

The implied warranty of fitness for a particular purpose under section 554.2315 is perhaps better understood when viewed with the implied warranty of merchantability, or fitness for ordinary purposes. Iowa Code section 554.2314 sets out the latter:

* * *

The official comment to the Uniform Commercial Code illustrates the difference between "ordinary" and "particular" purposes under the respective warranties:

> A "particular purpose" differs from the ordinary purpose for which the goods are used in that it envisages a specific use by the buyer which is peculiar to the nature of his business whereas the ordinary purposes for which goods are used are those envisaged in the concept of merchantability and go to uses which are customarily made of the goods in question. For example, shoes are generally used for the purpose of walking upon ordinary ground, but a seller may know that a particular pair was selected to be used for climbing mountains.

U.C.C. § 2–315, Comment 2, 1 U.L.A. 483 (1976).

The warranty of merchantability, Iowa Code § 554.2314, is based on a purchaser's reasonable expectation that goods purchased from a "merchant with respect to goods of that kind" will be free of significant defects and will perform in the way goods of that kind should perform. It presupposes no special relationship of trust or reliance between the seller and buyer. In contrast, the warranty of fitness for a particular purpose, Iowa Code § 554.2315, is based on a special reliance by the buyer on the seller to provide goods that will perform a specific use envisaged and communicated by the buyer. Thus, any recovery under warranty for a specific purpose is predicated on a showing that (1) the seller had reason to know of the buyer's particular purpose; (2) the seller had reason to know the buyer was relying on the seller's skill or judgment to furnish suitable goods; and (3) the buyer in fact relied on the seller's skill or judgment to furnish suitable goods. *Semler v. Knowling,* 325 N.W.2d 395, 399 (Iowa 1982); J. White and R. Summers, *Handbook of the Law Under the Uniform Commercial Code* § 9–9 at 358 (2d Ed.1980). *See also Farm Bureau Mutual Insurance Co. v. Sandbulte,* 302 N.W.2d 104, 111 (Iowa 1981).

The warranty of fitness under section 554.2315 is said to turn on the "bargain-related" facts as to what the seller had reason to know about the buyer's purpose for the goods and about his reliance on the seller's skill or judgment in selecting them. *Jacobson v. Benson Motors, Inc.,* 216 N.W.2d 396, 404 (Iowa 1974). In this case the vaccine was not purchased by the veterinarians to treat these particular cattle but to keep in stock for their general veterinary practice. The plaintiffs, as owners of the cattle, and the defendant, had no direct dealing with regard to the vaccine. The decision as to what vaccine to use was made by the buyers' veterinarians, not by the defendant. There was no evidence that the seller had reason to know of any purpose for the plaintiffs' use of the vaccine, other than its ordinary use, or that the buyer was relying on the seller's skill and judgment in providing it. The implied warranty of fitness for a particular purpose would appear, therefore, to be inapplicable by its terms. *See* Iowa Code § 554.2315; *Semler v. Knowling,* 325 N.W.2d at 399; *Jacobson v. Benson Motors, Inc.,* 216 N.W.2d at 404.

The plaintiffs argue, however, that if the buyer's particular purpose is the same as its general use, a warranty of fitness arises, especially when the product has a specific and limited use. In that case, the other elements of the fitness warranty, i.e., the knowledge of the buyer's purpose, knowledge of the buyer's reliance, and the buyer's actual reliance, are apparently to be presumed. The plaintiffs cite only one case, *Tennessee Carolina Transportation Inc. v. Strick Corp.,* 283 N.C. 423, 196 S.E.2d 711 (1973), in support of this theory. That case involved the sale of truck trailers which proved to be faulty. There the court held that because the buyer's "specific use" was the same as the "general use" to which trailers are usually put, hauling cargo, the warranty of fitness would apply. It rejected the general rule that a "particular" use must be a use not normally expected to be made of the goods, a rule recognized by our cases, e.g., *Madison Silos v. Wassom,* 215 N.W.2d 494, 499–500 (Iowa 1974); *Peters v. Lyons,* 168 N.W.2d 759, 763 (Iowa 1969), and by the Uniform Commercial Code. *See* U.C.C. § 2–315, Comment 2, 1 U.L.A. 483 (1976).

Cases such as *Tennessee Carolina,* moreover, have been criticized as enlarging the fitness warranty beyond the intent of the drafters of the Uniform Commercial Code. *See* J. White and R. Summers, *supra,* § 9–9 at 357, n. 122.

In this case, written material furnished with the vaccine stated that "[f]or reducing the economic loss associated with these viruses, vaccination of healthy animals is recommended before or upon entering the feedlot or dairy herd. Vaccination of stressed animals should be delayed." Use of the vaccine on healthy, unstressed cattle, in accordance with these instructions, is the "ordinary" use for warranty purposes, according to the defendant, and the plaintiffs' evidence was aimed at showing a use in compliance with the instructions, in other words, an "ordinary" use. While there was contradicting evidence presented by the defendant that the cattle were stressed and perhaps not healthy at the time they were vaccinated, there is no claim by the plaintiffs that this deviation from ordinary use is itself a "particular" use. They merely claim that their use here is an ordinary use which we should consider as a particular use for warranty purposes. For the reasons to be discussed, we decline to do so.

Obviously, in some cases a buyer's particular purpose will be the same as the ordinary purpose for which a product is furnished. In that case, both types of implied warranty may arise. *See Jacobson v. Benson Motors, Inc.,* 216 N.W.2d 396, 404 (Iowa 1974) (sale of motor vehicle); *Madison Silos v. Wassom,* 215 N.W. 2d 494, 499–500 (Iowa 1974) (stave silo); 1 R. Anderson, *Uniform Commercial Code,* § 2–314:60 (1970); Iowa Code § 554.2315, official comment 2. It is quite another matter, however, to impose an implied warranty of fitness solely on the basis of this identity of purpose. A particular purpose of the buyer is only one of the elements of that warranty; it still turns on what the seller had reason to know—both as to the buyer's particular purpose and as to the buyer's reliance on the seller's skill and judgment. *Jacobson,* 216 N.W.2d at 404. There are no bargain-related facts in this case to support a finding of these elements and we will not assume their existence merely on the basis of the limited-use nature of cattle vaccine. We will not assume, as the plaintiffs suggest, that the seller had reason to know of the buyers' particular purpose, and their reliance on the skill and judgment of the seller, merely because cattle vaccine is only usable for one purpose. As the record shows in this case, the vaccine may still be used in different ways, some anticipated by the seller and some not. (The defendant claims it was used in a manner proscribed by the written material accompanying the vaccine.)

The plaintiffs have an alternative theory: They claim that the seller had actual reason to know of the particular purpose for the vaccine and to know of the buyers' reliance on the skill and judgment of the seller so as to come within the literal requirements of the implied warranty of fitness. They rely on evidence that sales representatives of the defendant made regular calls on Dr. Hauser, that they discussed the vaccine, and that "[i]t is reasonable to infer from this fact that the representative was familiar with the vaccination procedures of Dr. Hauser and with the use he made of the vaccine." There is no evidence that the representative had reason to know the proposed use of the vaccine on these specific cattle, or even that it was to be used in circumstances similar to these, that is when other treatments such as worming, castration, and dehorning would accompany the vaccination, or that there would be a possibility the cattle could already be incubating the disease. Any conclusion that the defendant was put on notice of the plaintiffs' particular use is simply too speculative.

It was error to submit the theory of warranty of fitness for a particular purpose.

* * *

COMMENT, MANUFACTURER'S RESPONSIBILITY FOR DEFECTIVE PRODUCTS, 54 Calif.L.Rev. 1681, 1691, n. 48 (1966).

"Communication between buyer, seller, and manufacturer play no small role in determining whether or not a product is being supplied which will meet the particular economic needs of the commercial consumer. For example, in a typical * * * situation of the purchase of a heavy-duty diesel truck, most manufacturers offer dozens of different combinations of vehicle wheelbase, engines, transmissions, axles, suspension systems, air brakes, fifth wheel devices, and other component parts, all of which play a vital role in determining the capacity of a truck to meet various hauling requirements of the purchaser. Normally, the experienced trucker comes to the dealer with a good idea of the purpose for which he will use the truck, and often, based on his previous experience with similar vehicles in similar applications, with a fairly specific notion of the type of major component parts he will require. Dealer and customer go over in detail these needs, correlating them with the particular options which the manufacturer offers, and in effect arrive at some preliminary conclusions about the 'design' of the particular vehicle. Even at this stage the manufacturer may be involved, since a phone call to the factory by the dealer may answer a question like: 'Will an *X* diesel engine, coupled with a *Y* transmission and a *Z* rear axle enable our customer to achieve a road speed of *S* miles per hour under normal conditions?' Beyond this, the manufacturer becomes involved in the selection process when he receives the sales order from the dealer and submits it for review to his engineering department; the engineers may suggest several changes to be incorporated. Ultimately, the customer receives a heavy-duty truck which is reasonably tailored to his specific needs.

"Another method of merchandising commonly used in the trucking industry is for a manufacturer to build a certain number of what are called 'stock' trucks, which are then sold or consigned to the dealer. These are built with no particular customer in mind, or perhaps it should be said with the average customer in mind; these are analogous to an automobile dealer's 'showroom' models in that they incorporate most of the standard, *i.e.,* most popular, combinations of running gear. While not tailored to the specific needs of the customer, they of course do have the advantage of being available for immediate delivery. Normally, when a dealer recognizes that a customer's needs can be reasonably satisfied with a 'stock' truck, he will attempt to locate one within the dealer network which will serve the purpose, perhaps with a modification of a few component parts. Here, too, the manufacturer may become involved in the selling process through conferences concerning the ability of a particular 'stock' truck to meet the customer's needs.

"Thus the customer plays an important role in the selection process which is altogether different than that of the average new-car buyer who 'selects' such items as whitewall tires, radio, and heater. The component parts of a truck chosen by buyer, dealer, and/or manufacturer play an important role in determining whether or not the vehicle will be 'fit for a particular purpose,' * * * and the customer's communication of these economic needs is vital. While no spectacular case can be made out for the use of sales law where a manufacturer sells a truck which is so defective as to be virtually unsuited for any purpose, the requirement that the buyer's needs be communicated to the manufacturer before an implied warranty of fitness for a particular purpose would arise * * * would certainly tend to serve the useful purpose of enabling a court to determine whether or not the product was 'defective' in relation to the reasonable expectations of the buyer."

LEWIS v. MOBIL OIL CORP.

United States Court of Appeals, Eighth Circuit, 1971.
438 F.2d 500.

GIBSON, CIRCUIT JUDGE.

In this diversity case the defendant appeals from a judgment entered on a jury verdict in favor of the plaintiff in the amount of $89,250 for damages alleged to be caused by use of defendant's oil.

Plaintiff Lewis has been doing business as a sawmill operator in Cove, Arkansas, since 1956. In 1963, in order to meet competition, Lewis decided to convert his power equipment to hydraulic equipment. He purchased a hydraulic system in May 1963, from a competitor who was installing a new system. The used system was in good operating condition at the time Lewis purchased it. It was stored at his plant until November 1964, while a new mill building was being built, at which time it was installed. Following the installation, Lewis requested from Frank Rowe, a local Mobil oil dealer, the proper hydraulic fluid to operate his machinery. The prior owner of the hydraulic system had used Pacemaker oil supplied by Cities Service, but plaintiff had been a customer of Mobil's for many years and desired to continue with Mobil. Rowe said he didn't know what the proper lubricant for Lewis' machinery was, but would find out. The only information given to Rowe by Lewis was that the machinery was operated by a gear-type pump; Rowe did not request any further information. He apparently contacted a Mobil representative for a recommendation, though this is not entirely clear, and sold plaintiff a product known as Ambrex 810. This is a straight mineral oil with no chemical additives.

Within a few days after operation of the new equipment commenced, plaintiff began experiencing difficulty with its operation. The oil changed color, foamed over, and got hot. The oil was changed a number of times, with no improvement. By late April 1965, approximately six months after operations with the equipment had begun, the system broke down, and a complete new system was installed. The cause of the breakdown was undetermined, but apparently by this time there was some suspicion of the oil being used. Plaintiff Lewis requested Rowe to be sure he was supplying the right kind of oil. Ambrex 810 continued to be supplied.

From April 1965 until April 1967, plaintiff continued to have trouble with the system, principally with the pumps which supplied the pressure. Six new pumps were required during this period, as they continually broke down. During this period, the kind of pump used was a Commercial pump which was specified by the designer of the hydraulic system. The filtration of oil for this pump was by means of a metal strainer, which was cleaned daily by the plaintiff in accordance with the instruction given with the equipment.

In April 1967, the plaintiff changed the brand of pump from a Commercial to a Tyrone pump. The Tyrone pump, instead of using the metal strainer filtration alone, used a disposable filter element in addition. Ambrex 810 oil was also recommended by Mobil and used with this pump, which completely broke down three weeks later. At this point, plaintiff was visited for the first time by a representative of Mobil Oil Corporation, as well as a representative of the Tyrone pump manufacturer.

On the occasion of this visit, May 9, 1967, plaintiff's system was completely flushed and cleaned, a new Tyrone pump installed, and on the pump manufacturer's and Mobil's representative's recommendation, a new oil was used which contained certain chemical additives, principally a "defoamant." Following these changes, plaintiff's system worked satisfactorily up until the time of trial, some two and one-half years later.

Briefly stated, plaintiff's theory of his case is that Mobil supplied him with an oil which was warranted fit for use in his hydraulic system, that the oil was not suitable for such use because it did not contain certain additives, and that it was the improper oil which caused the mechanical breakdowns, with consequent loss to his business. The defendant contends that there was no warranty of fitness, that the breakdowns were caused not by the oil but by improper filtration, and that in any event there can be no recovery of loss of profits in this case.

I. The Existence of Warranties

Defendant maintains that there was no warranty of fitness in this case, that at most there was only a warranty of merchantability and that there was no proof of breach of this warranty, since there was no proof that Ambrex 810 is unfit for use in hydraulic systems generally. We find it unnecessary to consider whether the warranty of merchantability was breached, although there is some proof in the record to that effect, since we conclude that there was a warranty of fitness.

Plaintiff Lewis testified that he had been a longtime customer of Mobil Oil, and that his only source of contact with the company was through Frank Rowe, Mobil's local dealer, with whom he did almost all his business. It was common knowledge in the community that Lewis was converting his sawmill operation into a hydraulic system. Rowe knew this, and in fact had visited his mill on business matters several times during the course of the changeover. When operations with the new machinery were about to commence, Lewis asked Rowe to get him the proper hydraulic fluid. Rowe asked him what kind of a system he had, and Lewis replied it was a Commercial-pump type. This was all the information asked or given. Neither Lewis nor Rowe knew what the oil requirements for the system were, and Rowe, knew that Lewis knew nothing more specific about his requirements. Lewis also testified that after he began having trouble with his operations, while there were several possible sources of the difficulty the oil was one suspected source, and he several times asked Rowe to be sure he was furnishing him with the right kind.

Rowe's testimony for the most part confirmed Lewis'. It may be noted here that Mobil does not contest Rowe's authority to represent it in this transaction, and therefore whatever warranties may be implied because of the dealings between Rowe and Lewis are attributable to Mobil. Rowe admitted knowing Lewis was converting to a hydraulic system and that Lewis asked him to supply the fluid. He testified that he did not know what should be used and relayed the request to a superior in the Mobil organization, who recommended Ambrex 810. This is what was supplied.

When the first Tyrone pump was installed in April 1967, Rowe referred the request for a proper oil recommendation to Ted Klock, a Mobil engineer. Klock recommended Ambrex 810. When this pump failed a few weeks later, Klock visited the Lewis plant to inspect the equipment. The system was flushed out completely and the oil was changed to DTE–23 and Del Vac Special containing several additives. After this, no further trouble was experienced.

This evidence adequately establishes an implied warranty of fitness. Arkansas has adopted the Uniform Commercial Code's provision for an implied warranty of fitness:

> "Where the seller at the time of contracting has reason to know any particular purpose for which the goods are required and that the buyer is relying on the seller's skill or judgment to select or furnish suitable goods, there is unless excluded or modified under the next section an implied warranty that the goods shall be fit for such purpose." 7C Ark.Stat.Ann. § 85–2–315 (1961).

Under this provision of the Code, there are two requirements for an implied warranty of fitness: (1) that the seller have "reason to know" of the use for which the goods are purchased, and (2) that the buyer relies on the seller's expertise in supplying the proper product. Both of these requirements are amply met by the proof in this case. Lewis' testimony, as confirmed by that of Rowe and Klock, shows that the oil was purchased specifically for his hydraulic system, not for just a hydraulic system in general, and that Mobil certainly knew of this specific purpose. It is also clear that Lewis was relying on Mobil to supply him with the proper oil for the system, since at the time of his purchases, he made clear that he didn't know what kind was necessary.

Mobil contends that there was no warranty of fitness for use in his particular system because he didn't specify that he needed an oil with additives, and alternatively that he didn't give them enough information for them to determine that an additive oil was required. However, it seems that the circumstances of this case come directly within that situation described in the first comment to this provision of the Uniform Commercial Code:

> "1. Whether or not this warranty arises in any individual case is basically a question of fact to be determined by the circumstances of the contracting. Under this section the buyer need not bring home to the seller *actual knowledge of the particular purpose* for which the goods are intended or of his reliance on the seller's skill and judgment, if the circumstances are such that the seller has reason to realize the purpose intended or that the reliance exists." 7C Ark.Stat.Ann. § 85–2–315, Comment 1 (1961) (emphasis added).

Here Lewis made it clear that the oil was purchased for his system, that he didn't know what oil should be used, and that he was relying on Mobil to supply the proper product. If any further information was needed, it was incumbent upon Mobil to get it before making its recommendation. That it could have easily gotten the necessary information is evidenced by the fact that after plaintiff's continuing complaints, Mobil's engineer visited the plant, and, upon inspection, changed the recommendation that had previously been made.

Additionally, Mobil contends that even if there were an implied warranty of fitness, it does not cover the circumstances of this case because of the abnormal features which the plaintiff's system contained, namely an inadequate filtration system and a capacity to entrain excessive air. There are several answers to this contention. First of all, the contention goes essentially to the question of causation—i.e., whether the damage was caused by a breach of warranty or by some other cause—and not to the existence of a warranty of fitness in the first place. Secondly, assuming that certain peculiarities in the plaintiff's system did exist, the whole point of an implied warranty of fitness is that a product be suitable for a specific purpose, and that a seller should not supply a product which is not so suited. Thirdly, there is no evidence in the record that the plaintiff's system was unique or abnormal in these respects. It operated satisfactorily under the prior owner, and the new system has operated satisfactorily after it was adequately cleaned and an additive type oil used.

* * * Thus, Mobil's defense that there was no warranty of fitness because of an "abnormal use" of the oil is not appropriate here.

[The court next held that there was adequate evidence to sustain the jury's verdict that the plaintiff's damage was caused by the breach of warranty and not by variations in the plaintiff's system or inadequate maintenance.]

* * *

Notes

1. Was UCC 2–315 the proper warranty provision for application in *Lewis?* Put another way, could the court have reached the same result under an express warranty or an implied warranty of merchantability?

2. Suppose Mr. Lewis had asked Mr. Rowe to provide him with literature describing "oil that I might use in my new commercial hydraulic equipment." If Rowe had furnished literature describing oil with and oil without chemical additives and Mr. Rowe had thereafter ordered Ambrex 810, would the subsequent sale be with an implied warranty of fitness for particular purpose? To test your judgment, see Axion Corp. v. G.D.C. Leasing Corp., 359 Mass. 474, 269 N.E.2d 664 (1971) (reprinted at p. 775, supra).

3. Assuming that Mr. Lewis relied upon Mobil's skill and judgment, suppose Mobil had established that Ambrex 810 would work satisfactorily in some "commercial pump" hydraulic systems but not work in the particular system owned by Mr. Lewis. Assume further that Mr. Lewis was using his system for ordinary purposes. Should this affect the result in the case?

CHAPTER TWENTY

WARRANTY LITIGATION: BUYER'S PROOF, SELLER'S DEFENSES

SECTION 1. INTRODUCTION

To recover damages for a claimed breach of warranty, the buyer must plead and prove that: (1) the seller made some warranty, express or implied, (2) the warranty was breached, see UCC 2–607(4), and (3) the breach "caused" the damages sought. Compare UCC 2–715(2)(b). Since failure to satisfy any of these three requirements is fatal to the claim, it is important for the buyer's attorney to master the strategies for proof.

In addition, the buyer has a number of possible defenses to the claim.

First, a buyer who has accepted the goods may fail to give the notice required by UCC 2–607(3)(a). If so, the claim is barred.

Second, the seller may claim, by way of an affirmative defense, that the buyer misused the goods or failed to follow directions for use. Similarly, the seller may argue that the buyer should have discovered the non-conformity before use or assumed the risk by using goods with a known non-conformity. If so, the buyer's claim may be barred or, at the very least, the damages reduced.

Third, the seller may assert that the suit is time barred under the statute of limitations, UCC 2–725. This defense has posed some complicated questions for the courts.

Fourth, the seller may argue that the warranty claim is inappropriate and should be dismissed. Suppose there is no privity of contract and the buyer, bypassing the retailer, sues the product manufacturer for breach of warranty. Is lack of privity a defense? Or suppose that there is privity of contract between the parties but the UCC statute of limitations has run on the warranty claim. Can the buyer "escape" the UCC statute of limitations by invoking a tort theory, such as strict liability or negligence?

Note: Warranty as a Theory of Strict but Limited Liability

Why is a seller strictly liable for breach of warranty? According to Professor William Bishop, in Bishop, *The Contract-Tort Boundary and the Economics of Insurance,* 12 J.Legal Stud. 241 (1983), the reason is that warranties, when regarded as information provided by the seller to the buyer, are a form of insurance in a setting where there is imperfect information. At the time of contracting, the seller is in the best position, cost considered, to determine the true condition of the goods or to assess their suitability for use. To use the jargon, the seller is the "least-cost-information-provider." When the seller, without a disclaimer, provides information about the goods to the seller in the form of representations, including the price charged, the buyer should be able to hold the seller strictly liable for accuracy, provided that the scope of liability is limited. The warranty, therefore, is guaranteed but limited information for which the buyer has paid. (Bishop argues that "strict duties with known, limited liabilities are the preferred, albeit second best alternative to perfect information." Id. at 246.

What limitations should be imposed upon this form of strict liability? Two such limitations, derived from insurance, are the need to avoid adverse selection and moral hazard.

Adverse selection refers to the probability that the worst risks in a given population will be the most likely to obtain insurance. The insurer, here the seller, must obtain information about the riskiness of the insured. Otherwise, the insurer may insure a "selection of the population whose average risk is adversely different from the general population." Id. at 245. According to Bishop, this limitation provides the buyer with an incentive to convey information to the seller when the value of the information to the seller is greater than the cost to the buyer of transmitting it.

This limitation works in at least two ways under the Code: (1) the seller's warranty does not reach a buyer's particular purposes for the goods unless "at the time of contracting" the seller "has reason to know of any particular purpose for which the goods are required," UCC 2–315, a limitation which we covered in Chapter 19, Section 3(B), and (2) the seller is not liable for any consequential "loss resulting from general or particular requirements and needs" of which, at the time of contracting, he had no "reason to know." UCC 2–715(2)(a). This problem is treated in Chapter 21.

Moral hazard involves the risk that a buyer will fail, either before or after the loss occurred, to take reasonable action to avoid or to minimize the loss. Even though the risk is "average" or communicated to the seller, the buyer may fail to take precautions whose cost to him is less than their value to the insurer. Economic theory and contract law in general suggest that the buyer should bear those losses which he could have avoided by a reasonable expenditure of time and effort.

As you read the materials in this Chapter and Chapter 21, make a list of the limitations upon warranty liability associated with either adverse selection or moral hazard.

Does Bishop's analysis offer a persuasive explanation of the nature of warranty? Is it a useful analogy to insurance?

SECTION 2. THE EFFECT OF PLAINTIFF'S FAILURE TO GIVE NOTICE REQUIRED BY UCC 2–607(3)

Access to various buyer's remedies is hedged by notice requirements. Thus, an attempt at rejection is "ineffective unless the buyer seasonably notifies the seller," UCC 2–602(1), and a revocation of acceptance is "not effective until the buyer notifies the seller of it." UCC 2–608(2). Similarly, where a tender has been accepted and acceptance has not been revoked under UCC 2–608, the "buyer must within a reasonable time after he discovers or should have discovered any breach notify the seller of breach or be barred from any remedy; * * *" UCC 2–607(3)(a). Note that UCC 2–607(3)(a) says "barred" from any remedy, not that the buyer is simply shunted to a less desirable remedy. Also, the buyer may be "barred" even though the nonconformity was not actually discovered.

A number of continuing questions surround the judicial interpretation of UCC 2–607(3)(a):

(1) What purposes are served by notice in commercial cases?

(2) When "should" the buyer have discovered the breach?

(3) When does a "reasonable time" expire?

(4) At what point does the buyer "notify" the seller?

(5) What should the form and content of the notice be?

Regardless of how these questions are answered from case to case, two things are clear: (1) The buyer must, at the very least, plead and prove that adequate notice was given to state a cause of action for breach of warranty, and (2) The notice condition does not apply to actions grounded in strict products liability, i.e., where a defective product has caused damage to person or property. See Restatement, Torts 402A, Comment m.

Problem 20–1

Bristow, the holder of a McDonalds franchise, contracted with Stiko, Inc. a manufacturer, for 17 dozen pans expressly designed for the preparation of Big Mac sandwiches. A December 1 shipment date was agreed. On November 28, Stiko telephoned Bristow to say that they were having "a bit of trouble" and that the pans "could not be delivered until late January." Bristow replied that timely delivery was important and if the pans were not shipped by December 1, "we will consider that you have breached the contract." The pans were shipped on January 17. Bristow accepted the pans and there was no further communication until Stiko sued for the contract price in May. Bristow claimed an offset from the contract price based upon damages for late delivery. The trial court, relying on UCC 2–607(3), denied the offset and entered judgment for the contract price. In his memorandum opinion, the trial judge held that UCC 2–607(3) required notice after acceptance. Here none was given. Further, even if the answer were treated as a notice, "the delay was unreasonable as a matter of law."

What arguments will you make on appeal?

STANDARD ALLIANCE IND. v. BLACK CLAWSON CO.

United States Court of Appeals, Sixth Circuit, 1978.
587 F.2d 813.

[Defendant sold Plaintiff a 175 ton "horizontal automatic radial forging facility", known as the "green monster." After extensive negotiations where Plaintiff persuaded Defendant to manufacture the machine to meet Plaintiff's special needs, Defendant made a series of express performance warranties and agreed to repair or replace defective parts for one year after acceptance. Implied warranties were disclaimed and consequential damages were excluded in the agreement. There were problems with the machine from the start. For five months, Defendant, with Plaintiff's assistance, attempted to remedy the difficulties. Defendant then ceased working on the machine. Thereafter, efforts by Plaintiff, under new ownership, to resolve the problems were unsuccessful and the machine was dismantled and sold for scrap. Just over eleven months after Defendant ceased efforts to repair the machine, Plaintiff brought suit on various warranty theories, claiming damages in excess of $525,000. After trial, the trial court submitted two questions to the jury: 1) did Defendant breach the negotiated performance warranties; and 2) did Defendant breach the express warranty to repair and replace defective parts? The jury found for Plaintiff on both questions. On appeal, Defendant argued that the claim based upon breach of performance warranties was barred by the statute of limitations. Defendant also argued that the claim based upon breach of the warranty to repair and replace was barred because Plaintiff failed to give notice as required by UCC 2–607(3).]

KEITH, CIRCUIT JUDGE.

* * *

B. Notice and Count II

Standard Alliance's claim against Black Clawson is not ended by our decision on Count I. In Count II, Standard Alliance alleges a cause of action for breach of the express warranty to repair or replace defective parts. This cause of action, which is virtually identical to Count I, was not barred by the statute of limitations. Thus, even if Standard Alliance sued too late on its claim that the machine was defective, it did sue on time on its claim that Black Clawson failed to repair the machine.

Black Clawson concedes that suit on Count II was timely filed, but strongly argues that it had no knowledge that anything was wrong with the machine after it quit work on it and that plaintiff's failure to report the machine's defects barred the suit.

To recapitulate: The machine was installed in October of 1967, and plaintiff's employees attempted to make it operable. A letter was sent to Black Clawson on December 27, 1967, fully outlining the machine's defects. Black Clawson responded by sending a team of employees to try to fix the machine. These employees were at Standard Alliance's plant for over five months. On June 21, 1968, Black Clawson's repairmen left Standard Alliance's plant, never to return. Plaintiff claims that this action constituted knowing abandonment of the unrepaired machine. Black Clawson claims that it thought that the machine was satisfactorily repaired and that it knew nothing about any further problems.

The controlling statute is UCC § 2–607(3)(a) which provides:

> "The buyer must within a reasonable time after he discovers or should have discovered any breach notify the seller of breach or be barred from any remedy."

Whether proper notice was given is a question of fact. * * *

Moreover, inasmuch as § 2–607 operates as a condition precedent to any recovery, the burden of proof is on the plaintiff to show that notice was given within a reasonable time. * * *

The district judge submitted the notice issue to the jury, which found for the plaintiff. The question presented here is whether the district judge erred when he refused to overrule the jury's decision and enter judgment N.O.V. for the defendant.

The standard which defendant must meet is a stiff one. To grant a directed verdict or J.N.O.V., the evidence must be "such that there can be but one reasonable conclusion as to the proper verdict." Wolfel v. Sanborn, 555 F.2d 583, 593 (6th Cir.1977). Ohio's standard is the same. Ohio R.Civ.Pro. 50(A). See O'Day v. Webb, 29 Ohio St.2d 215, 280 N.E.2d 896 (1972). If the evidence is clear, however, a court can rule as a matter of law that a party failed to give proper notice. * * *

The notice requirement of § 2–607 is explained by Official Comment 4:

> "The time of notification is to be determined by applying commercial standards to a merchant buyer. 'A reasonable time' for notification from a retail consumer is to be judged by different standards so that in his case it will be extended, for the rule of requiring notification is designated to defeat commercial bad faith, not to deprive a good faith consumer of his remedy.
>
> "The content of the notification need merely be sufficient to let the seller know that the transaction is still troublesome and must be watched.

There is no reason to require that the notification which saves the buyer's rights under this section must include a clear statement of all the objections that will be relied on by the buyer, as under the section covering statements of defect upon rejection (Section 2–605). Nor is there reason for requiring the notification to be a claim for damages or of any threatened litigation or other resort to a remedy. The notification which saves the buyer's rights under this Article need only be such as informs the seller that the transaction is claimed to involve a breach, and thus opens the way for normal settlement through negotiation."

Some courts and commentators have taken the liberal view that almost any kind of notice of dissatisfaction is sufficient. "Quite clearly the drafters [of the UCC] intended a loose test; a scribbled note on a bit of toilet paper will do." J. White & R. Summers Uniform Commercial Code 347 (1972). See e.g., Lewis v. Mobil Oil Corp., 438 F.2d 500, 509 (8th Cir.1971); Metro Investment Corp. v. Portland Rd. Lumber Yard, Inc., 263 Or. 76, 501 P.2d 312 (1972). Other courts have required more than minimal notice where both parties were merchants engaged in on-going transactions. Eastern Air Lines, Inc. v. McDonnell Douglas Corp., 532 F.2d 957, 970–980 (1976); Kopper Glo Fuel, Inc. v. Island Lake Coal Co., 436 F.Supp. 91, 95–97 (E.D.Tenn.1977). * * *

There is no dispute that Standard Alliance gave timely notice that the machine was not in compliance with the performance warranties and that Black Clawson then spent over five months trying to fix the machine. The dispute concerns whether defendant was properly notified that the repairs were inadequate.

Black Clawson's argument can be conveniently subdivided into two subparts. First, it contends that it understood the machine to be operating properly on June 21, 1968, and that it had no knowledge that the machine was defective after that date. Second, it contends that it had no notice that Standard Alliance considered it to be in breach of the warranty to repair or replace defective parts.

The jury's implicit finding that Black Clawson had knowledge that the machine was defective and improperly repaired is supportable by the evidence. Black Clawson Vice-President Romagano did testify that he thought that the machine was repaired on July 21, 1968, and that he had no idea anything was wrong afterward. The jury, however, could have disbelieved this testimony, relying on a June 24, 1968, memo written by Mr. Romagano which reveals that the machine suffered repeated failures on both June 20, 1968, and June 21, 1968. In addition, the jury could have credited letters written in June, July and August of 1968 from Mr. Romagano to a Black Clawson subcontractor, Reliance Electric Co., complaining about the failings of the machine's electric drive, a critical component. Finally, the jury could have believed expert testimony that the machine was so poorly designed that it could not be made to operate in synchronization nor be repaired to meet any of the express warranties. If so, the jury could have reasonably inferred that defendant was aware that its attempts to repair were an utter failure. Thus, there exists evidence to support a jury finding that Black Clawson had knowledge that it was in breach of the repair or replace warranty.[1]

1. The evidence is not one-sided, however. The record indicates that the machine would operate, but was subject to breakdowns and produced a poor product. Repair efforts at times achieved temporary success or offered the hope of success. For example, in a July 15, 1968 internal memorandum, Standard Alliance's Harold Challman indicated that with two weeks of certain indicated repairs, the machine would be ready to make a production run. There thus exists some basis for Black Clawson's subjective belief that the machine

The critical issue is whether Black Clawson had notice that it was considered to be in breach. Black Clawson emphatically argues that there is no evidence at all that it received notice of breach after it quit repair work on June 21, 1968. Standard Alliance directs us to none, and our independent examination of the record reveals none. Incredible as it may seem, Black Clawson quit repair work on June 21, 1968 and was never told anything was wrong until May 29, 1969, when suit was filed.[2]

Standard Alliance argues that it fully informed Black Clawson of the machine's defects at the beginning and that Black Clawson abandoned the machine knowing that it was defective and unrepaired. Under these circumstances, the question presented is whether it was necessary to give additional notice of the failure of repair efforts.

We think that notice should have been given. Section 2–607 expressly requires notice of "any" breach. Comment 4 says that notice "need only be such as informs the seller that the transaction is claimed to involve a breach." The express language of the statute and the official comment mandate notice regardless whether either or both parties had actual knowledge of breach. * * *

We also note that this same result would take place under § 2–607's predecessor, section 49 of the Uniform Sales Act.[3] Judge Learned Hand's oft-quoted words applying section 49 are equally applicable here:

> "The plaintiff replies that the buyer is not required to give notice of what the seller already knows, but this confuses two quite different things. The notice 'of the breach' required is not of the facts, which the seller presumably knows quite as well as, if not better than, the buyer, but of buyer's claim that they constitute a breach. The purpose of the notice is to

was in compliance with the page twelve warranties. Internal Black Clawson memoranda, notably an October 3, 1968 memo from Vice-President Romagano to President Landegger support this belief.

This confusion further underscores the need to give clear notice; especially in a commercial setting where two companies have interacted at different levels, from President to maintenance worker.

2. Black Clawson pressed this issue at trial. Standard Alliance's President Erwin Schulze admitted that no written notice was sent; he did not know whether oral notice was given. Executive Vice-President William G. Shaw, who at the time was head of Standard Alliance's forging division, knew of no communication between the parties concerning the machine's defects after June 21, 1968. Roy W. Clansky, a Standard Alliance Vice-Chairman of the Board intimately involved in the machine's purchase, testified that Black Clawson never failed to respond when called. He did not recall ever getting in touch with his counterpart at Black Clawson to complain about the machine after January 4, 1968. Russell E. Reum, Standard Alliance's purchasing agent, knew of no notice to Black Clawson indicating dissatisfaction with repair efforts after January of 1968. Black Clawson Executive Alfred Romagano testified that Black Clawson never heard a complaint about the machine after June of 1968.

The evidence in the record concerning the circumstances of Black Clawson's termination of repair efforts on June 21, 1968, shows an amicable parting after months of mutual cooperation. Contacts between the parties after June 21, 1968, were minimal and most had nothing to do with the machine's defects. Standard Alliance invited Black Clawson to a trade association tour of its plant in September, 1968, and discussed settling "backcharge" claims for repairs. In addition, two brief service calls were made. Although the record as to the service calls and backcharge negotiations is sketchy, * * * there is no evidence that the issue of breach of warranty was ever raised directly, and Standard Alliance does not argue that it was.

3. Section 49 provided:

"In the absence of express or implied agreement of the parties, acceptance of the goods by the buyer shall not discharge the seller from liability in damages or other legal remedy for breach of any promise or warranty in the contract to sell or the sale. But, if, after acceptance of the goods, the buyer fails to give notice to the seller of the breach of any promise or warranty within a reasonable time after the buyer knows, or ought to know of such breach, the seller shall not be liable therefor."

advise the seller that he must meet a claim for damages, as to which, rightly or wrongly, the law requires that he shall have early warning."

American Mfg. Co. v. United States Shipping Board E.F. Corp., 7 F.2d 565, 566 (2d Cir.1925), cited with approval in Columbia Axle Co. v. American Automobile Ins. Co., 63 F.2d 206 (6th Cir.1933).

An examination of the policy reasons which underlie 2–607 further support our view. Notice of breach serves two distinct purposes. First, express notice opens the way for settlement through negotiation between the parties. Comment Four, supra; Eckstein v. Cummins, 41 Ohio App.2d 1, 321 N.E.2d 897, 901 (1974). Second, proper notice minimizes the possibility of prejudice to the seller by giving him "ample opportunity to cure the defect, inspect the goods, investigate the claim or do whatever may be necessary to properly defend himself or minimize his damages while the facts are fresh in the minds of the parties." Note, Notice of Breach and the Uniform Commercial Code, 25 U.Fla.L.Rev. 520, 522 (1973). * * * Compare 3 Williston on Sales (4th Ed.), § 22–11 and White & Summers, supra at 344 which identify three policy reasons behind the notice requirement: 1) To enable the seller to make adjustments or replacement or to suggest opportunities for cure; 2) To enable the seller to prepare for negotiation or litigation; and 3) To give the seller peace of mind from stale claims. See Steel & Wire Corp. v. Thyssen, Inc., 20 U.C.C.Rep. 892 (E.D.Mich.1976). See also Mattos, Inc. v. Hash, 279 Md. 371, 368 A.2d 993, 996 (1977) (protection against stale claims is the purpose of the statute of limitations, not the purpose of section 2–607(3)).

We do not know whether this lengthy, acrimonious lawsuit could have been settled beforehand. We do know that Standard Alliance's failure to give notice precluded the possibility of compromise.

More important, the record contains evidence suggesting the kind of prejudice which § 2–607's notice requirement seeks to avoid. After Standard Alliance sold its Forgings Division to "the Wiener Group" on September 30, 1968, Wiener attempted to put the machine into operation. When that failed, the machine lay dormant. On May 28, 1969, the day before suit was filed, Standard Alliance, in cooperation with Wiener, started the machine and filmed its malfunctions. On July 14, 1969, a scant six weeks after suit was filed, Wiener began to dismantle the machine. Although Black Clawson was informed of the machine's sale, it never inspected the machine after terminating repair efforts on June 21, 1968, nor was it aware that the machine was to be destroyed.

Standard Alliance contends that the destruction of the machine by a third party was proper and that Black Clawson was remiss in not seeking to inspect the machine during the six-week period after suit was filed, but before the machine was destroyed. This ignores the realities of the litigation process. Six weeks is an insignificant period of time in a case such as this which has dragged on for over nine years. In addition, it was pure chance that the machine was destroyed when it was; Wiener could have taken the machine apart whenever it wanted. Had Black Clawson gotten even minimal notice that it was being held in breach, it might very well have sought inspection and perhaps even made its own film of the machine.

Measuring the impact of potential prejudice here is, of course, difficult since Black Clawson was unable to have its own experts examine the machine. Standard Alliance emphasizes that Black Clawson designed and built the machine and worked on it for over five months. As the machine's creator, it arguably did not need to inspect it. Also, the evidence that the machine was defective was overwhelming. On the other hand, preparing for litigation is a sui generis task. Black Clawson may have been able to put on a spirited defense, especially as to damages, had it gotten early notice and followed up by inspecting the machine. Whatever the degree of prejudice to Black Clawson, UCC § 2–607's notice requirement is designed to forestall the very difficulties which developed here. While we see no justification for the strong language in defendant's brief charging a conspiracy to hide the facts and destroy the machine, we think that this case demonstrates the wisdom of section 2–607's requirement of prompt notice.

Black Clawson also raises independent objections to the film and the circumstances of the machine's destruction, arguing that it should have had specific advance notice of both the film's production and of the machine's demolition. We need not decide these issues. We do note, however, that this court has never sanctioned the sporting theory of justice. Adherents of the theory among the bar are reminded that a law suit is a serious matter; there is no room for games of hide and seek. Neither the federal rules nor statutory law can anticipate every twist and turn which can take place in litigation. "Legal" moves by ingenious litigants will not be countenanced where injustice would result.

These events further demonstrate the merit in those cases which hold merchants to higher standards of good faith than consumers. * * * Black Clawson and Standard Alliance worked together at all times. Black Clawson responded promptly when informed that the machine was not working properly; commercial good faith mandated that it be told that repair efforts had failed and that it was being held in breach. A new car buyer can be excused for failing, in ignorance and exasperation, to notify a car dealer of an obvious breach after persistent repair efforts have ended in failure. A merchant like Standard Alliance cannot be so excused, it should have met section 2–607's non-rigorous notice requirements.

Standard Alliance points to two cases, Ernst v. General Motors Corp., 482 F.2d 1047 (5th Cir.1973), appeal following remand, 537 F.2d 105 (5th Cir.1976), and Metro Invest. Corp. v. Portland Rd. Lumber Yard, Inc., 263 Or. 76, 501 P.2d 312 (1972), for the proposition that proper notice, once given, is sufficient for all related breaches. Standard Alliance's position is that since it concededly gave proper notice that the machine was defective on December 27, 1967, it did not have to give notice later on that repair efforts to cure the defects had failed.

We reject this argument. In Ernst, supra, the court merely concluded that a letter complaining of delays in the start-up of a construction project could be reasonably construed to encompass problems caused by severe winter working conditions which would not have occurred but for the delay. Also, the court did not think that once initial complaint about delay was made, that additional notice of delay had to be given on a regular basis. In Metro Invest. Corp., supra, the buyer gave prompt notice of a defect. The parties met and agreed to wait and see if the defect improved. The Oregon Supreme Court found that the initial notice was sufficient, even though no complaint was made for two years thereafter.

In the instant case, the two warranties are distinct and notice serves different functions for each. When the machine was found to be in breach of the page twelve performance warranties, notice was necessary so that Black Clawson could come in and try to fix the machine. When repair efforts failed, and Black Clawson was allegedly in breach of its warranty to repair or replace defective parts, notice would alert Black Clawson that Standard Alliance thought that repairs were defective and that perhaps litigation was contemplated. At this point, the parties could have discussed settlement, and Black Clawson could have sought evidentiary support for its position that the machine was indeed repaired. Black Clawson was alerted that the machine was defective, but not alerted that its repair efforts were defective. We cannot allow notice of one breach to be carried over to create notice of a subsequent related, but distinct, breach.

We realize that our holding bars what is apparently a meritorious claim. Standard Alliance's inexplicable failure to give any notice whatsoever that Black Clawson was in breach of its repair/replace warranty is fatal; underlying standards of commercial good faith, codified in UCC § 2–607, mandate this result.

Our ruling makes it unnecessary to consider the numerous other issues raised concerning the liability or the damages trial.

* * *

[Some footnotes omitted. Others renumbered.]

Notes

1. UCC 2–607(3)(a) states that the buyer must "notify the seller of breach or be barred from any remedy." In Comment 4, however, there is an apparent conflict: Is the notice sufficient if it "merely" lets the seller know that the "transaction is still troublesome and must be watched" or must the notice inform the seller that the "transaction is claimed to involve a breach * * *?" The latter interpretation, embraced by *Standard Alliance,* would require notice of the buyer's conclusion both that the goods failed to conform to the warranties and that the non-conformity was considered to be a breach.

If, as White and Summers suggest at p. 421, the principal reason for requiring notice "is to enable the seller to make adjustments or replacements or to suggest opportunities for cure to the end of minimizing the buyer's loss and reducing the seller's own liability to the buyer," is such a strict notice requirement necessary? In Paulson v. Olson Implement Co., Inc., 107 Wis.2d 510, 319 N.W.2d 855 (1982), the court held that a seller who had received a timely notice of nonconformity and was unable to effect a cure was not entitled to a further notice from the buyer before the law suit was filed. Compare K & M Joint Venture v. Smith International, Inc., 669 F.2d 1106 (6th Cir.1982), in which the court held that the buyer's claims was barred because of its failure to give the seller any indication that it was claiming a breach of warranty or that it considered the seller to be liable to it.

2. What amendment to UCC 2–607(3)(a) would you recommend to resolve this issue? Would it be sufficient simply to substitute the word "nonconformity" for breach?

Problem 20–2

Your client entered into a contract to purchase a specified quantity of yarn. The expected quality was spelled out in some detail. As part of the contract, client agreed to the following clauses in the sales contract:

> "2. No claims relating to excessive moisture content, short weight, count variations, twist, quality or shade shall be allowed *if made after weaving, knitting, or processing,* or more than 10 days after receipt of shipment. * * * The buyer shall within 10 days of the receipt of the merchandise by himself or agent examine the merchandise for any and all defects."

"4. This instrument constitutes the entire agreement between the parties, superseding all previous communications, oral or written, and no changes, amendments or additions hereto will be recognized unless in writing signed by both seller and buyer or buyer's agent. It is expressly agreed that no representations or warranties, express or implied, have been or are made by the seller except as stated herein, and the seller makes no warranty, express or implied, as to the fitness for buyer's purposes of yarn purchased hereunder, seller's obligations, except as expressly stated herein, being limited to the *delivery of good merchantable yarn of the description stated herein.*"

The yarn was tendered on March 1 and, after an inspection, accepted by client on March 2. Thereafter the yarn was cut and knitted into sweaters and the finished product was washed. During the washing, which took place on March 15 and 16, it was discovered that the color of the yarn had "shaded," that is, there was a variation in color from piece to piece and within the pieces. This was clearly a defect that made the yarn unmerchantable and could not have been discovered by a reasonable inspection. Client promptly gave notice to the seller of the defect. Since revocation of acceptance was not possible (do you see why?), client asserted a claim for damages under UCC 2–714(2) and 2–715(2). Seller, pointing to the contract, denied any liability.

Client comes to you for advice. Is the clause enforceable? See UCC 1–204, 2–302 & 2–719. After you have completed your analysis, you may wish to compare it with Wilson Trading Corp. v. David Ferguson, Ltd., 23 N.Y.2d 398, 297 N.Y.S.2d 108, 244 N.E.2d 685 (1968).

SECTION 3. PROOF OF BREACH: EFFECT OF LACK OF CAUSATION AND PLAINTIFF'S CONTRIBUTORY BEHAVIOR

In Chapter 19, the primary issue was whether the seller had made a warranty, express or implied, to the buyer. Here we are concerned about what the buyer must prove to establish a breach of that warranty and that the breach caused the loss complained of. The answers turn, in part, upon the type of warranty made and the quantum and quality of proof required to get the case to the jury. In addition, the seller must be alert to possible misuse of the goods by the buyer and other conduct suggesting contributory "fault" or assumption of risk. These issues frequently arise in commercial litigation. See, e.g., Phelan and Falhof, *Proving a Defect in a Commercial Products Liability Case,* 24 Trial Law.Guide 10 (1980).

According to Mr. Phelan, an experienced Chicago trial attorney, the plaintiff maximizes the chances of proving both breach and causation when the facts and inferences from the following sources are cumulated:

1. The allegedly non-conforming product;

2. The circumstances surrounding the "accident;"

3. The life history of the product;

4. Relevant trade usages and practices with regard to products of the same description; and

5. Conduct by the buyer in inspecting, maintaining and using the product, both before and after the "accident."

CHATFIELD v. SHERWIN-WILLIAMS CO.

Supreme Court of Minnesota, 1978.
266 N.W.2d 171.

PER CURIAM.

In this action to recover damages allegedly resulting from breaches of warranty in the sale of red barn paint, the jury found by a special verdict that defendant paint manufacturer breached an express warranty that the paint was "good barn paint" and the implied warranties of merchantability and fitness for a particular purpose. It also found that the breaches were a direct cause of plaintiff's damages; that plaintiff was negligent and his negligence was a direct cause of his consequential damages; that 85 percent of the fault causing such consequential damages was attributable to defendant and 15 percent to plaintiff; and that plaintiff sustained general damages of $1,116 and consequential damages of $13,357. The court ordered judgment for plaintiff for $14,473, the total amount assessed by the jury. Defendant appeals, challenging the sufficiency of the evidence to establish breaches of the warranties and that such breaches were a proximate cause of plaintiff's damages. Defendant also contends that plaintiff is precluded from recovery of damages because he did not follow defendant's directions in using its product. Our review satisfies us that the issues raised were properly submitted to the jury and that the judgment appealed from should be affirmed.

In the winter of 1974, plaintiff, an experienced professional painter of farm buildings, purchased 330 gallons of "Commonwealth Ranch Red" paint from defendant for $4.65 per gallon. Before making the purchase plaintiff asked Wendell Swenson, manager of defendant's Wilmar store, if it would be good paint and if he would have any trouble with it. Swenson told plaintiff that people had used this paint on barns for many years and that it was "tried and true." He added, "Besides, this is Sherwin-Williams, you know. It couldn't have a bad name and be that big." Plaintiff then purchased the paint, used 240 gallons on barns and other buildings at 11 farms, and sold the rest to his father who is also a professional painter.

The label on the paint cans plaintiff purchased contained the following directions:

> "New Wood and Extremely Weathered Surfaces:
>
> Add 1 to 2 quarts of raw linseed oil per gallon to the *first coat.* Brush it well into surface. When spraying follow immediately with thorough brushing to work paint into pores. Second coat should be brushed on at package consistency or thinned with up to a pint of S–W exolvent or turpentine per gallon for spraying."

Plaintiff admitted that he never added as much as 1 to 2 quarts of linseed oil and said that when he used that much the paint wrinkled. He said that when painting dry areas, he added as much linseed oil as he thought necessary, depending on the condition of the wood. He thought a ratio of 20 percent was usually correct. He said that under the eaves and along the upper two-thirds of the buildings the wood is often in better condition than the wood below, the lower 5 or 6 feet of a barn usually requiring linseed oil. Plaintiff did not apply the paint with a brush, claiming that his spraying equipment made the paint penetrate into the surfaces far more thoroughly than brushing could.

Several customers testified that plaintiff spray-painted their buildings with Commonwealth Ranch Red during the summer of 1975. The buildings varied in age (from a barn built in 1906 to one built in 1965) and in their need for paint. The customers said they were well satisfied with plaintiff's work in preparing the surfaces and painting the buildings. Within 1 to 4 months after the jobs were completed, however, the owners noticed that the color was fading on their buildings. Witnesses said the surfaces looked chalky, the color continued to bleach, and the paint was chipping and could be rubbed off. Plaintiff testified that the buildings which his father had painted with the 90 gallons he had obtained from plaintiff also faded. After receiving complaints from his customers, plaintiff in turn made complaints to defendant which were ignored for several months. Finally, in April 1975, defendant sent George Linmark, a chemist employed by defendant, to investigate the matter. Linmark looked at the buildings plaintiff had painted on two farms and told him, plaintiff testified, that the wood had been well prepared and the paint well applied. Plaintiff testified that Linmark could not explain why the fading had occurred. Subsequently, plaintiff received a letter saying that defendant had decided to do nothing about the paint because the fading "was to be expected with that quality of paint."

Plaintiff admitted on cross-examination that he had read the instructions on the paint cans and had not added as much linseed oil as they directed. When plaintiff rested, defendant moved for a directed verdict on the ground that plaintiff's evidence showed no negligence on its part and showed that plaintiff had been negligent in using his judgment instead of the manufacturer's. The court denied the motion.

Defendant then called Linmark, a chemist with experience in formulating Sherwin-Williams paint, as an expert witness. He said that the 330 gallons of paint which plaintiff had bought was from a 3,000–gallon batch and that defendant had received no complaints about the rest of the batch. Although defendant stores a sample from each batch it manufactures, it did not test any sample from the batch which was the source of plaintiff's paint to see if it would fade, apparently because it was not clear at first which batch had been the source of plaintiff's purchase.

Linmark testified that paint has two essential ingredients, pigments and vehicles or binders. In Commonwealth Ranch Red, the pigment which gives the color is iron oxide, comprising 14 percent of the pigment, and most of the rest of the pigment is calcium carbonate, which by itself is a white powder but is colorless when added to the paint. The vehicle or binder holds the pigment and causes the paint to adhere to the surface of a building. The binder in defendant's paint consisted of tall oil alkyd resin, blown fish oil, mineral spirits, and raw linseed oil. In Linmark's opinion the fading was caused by insufficient reinforcement of the paint with more linseed oil. He said that on weathered surfaces some of the binder in the paint soaks into the wood or old paint if the new paint being applied is not reinforced with linseed oil, and that when the remaining binder is eroded by the ultraviolet rays of the sun, the pigment stands loose. Thus, he said, the calcium carbonate in Commonwealth Ranch Red became visible, giving the paint the appearance of fading.

Linmark also testified that paint wrinkles if applied too thickly and that linseed oil in any quantity does not cause wrinkling. He admitted telling plaintiff in April 1975 that he had done a good job and that in Linmark's opinion there was "a fade problem." He looked at only two of the sets of buildings plaintiff had painted and admitted that he did not know whether plaintiff had added enough linseed oil in the various jobs. He also said that the paint plaintiff purchased was "the bottom of the line."

In rebuttal, plaintiff's father, Robert Chatfield, testified that he used some of the 90 gallons he had acquired from plaintiff and that he too received complaints of fading. He added 1 quart of linseed oil to 5 gallons of paint while painting a barn for a customer and found that the paint became too thin and would run. He said he applied some of the paint to part of his own buildings without using any linseed oil and they also faded. He purchased other Commonwealth Ranch Red from defendant's Wilmar store himself and applied it to his buildings without adding linseed oil. He said the areas to which he had applied this paint did not fade.

In submitting the case to the jury, the trial court refused to charge that defendant was not liable if plaintiff's use of the product was abnormal or not in accordance with adequate instructions. He instructed the jury that in determining whether plaintiff was negligent they could consider whether he used the paint in accordance with defendant's directions and submitted questions in response to which, as stated, the jury found plaintiff negligent and attributed 15 percent of the fault causing his consequential damage to that negligence.

1. Although apparently not contesting the existence of the warranties on which plaintiff brought suit, defendant argues that its motions for a directed verdict and for judgment notwithstanding the verdict should have been granted because plaintiff did not adduce sufficient proof that the paint faded prematurely because of an inherent defect and thus did not establish any breach of the warranties. It also argues that plaintiff did not prove that any breach of warranty proximately caused his damages, as is essential to recovery. Heil v. Standard Chemical Mfg. Co., 301 Minn. 315, 323, 223 N.W.2d 37, 41 (1974). Defendant's contentions require an examination of plaintiff's evidence in the light most favorable to the verdict.

At the time defendant moved for a directed verdict, plaintiff had presented testimony that he had done a good workmanlike job, testimony which permitted the jury to infer that poor workmanship did not cause the fading. Plaintiff's proof also showed that some areas he had painted did not need linseed oil and that the paint had faded quite uniformly within 1 to 4 months after application, both in areas where he had used linseed oil and in areas where he had not. He admitted that he never added as much linseed oil as defendant's directions advised he should use with "extremely weathered" surfaces but said he added it in a ratio of 20 percent when he thought it was needed. He further testified that defendant informed him that fading was to be expected with a paint of the quality of Commonwealth Ranch Red. This evidence, although it does not directly establish the cause of the fading, furnishes substantial support for the inference that the paint faded because of an inherent defect.

Defendant urges, however, that plaintiff was required to have the paint analyzed and to present expert testimony about the existence and nature of any alleged defect. Although the importance of expert testimony in products liability actions has been emphasized in several cases, this court has said that there is no hard-and-fast rule requiring plaintiff to introduce such testimony. Peterson v. Crown Zellerbach Corp., 296 Minn. 438, 209 N.W.2d 922 (1973). In several earlier breach-of-warranty cases, chemical analysis of the product was not required to establish the breach of warranty. * * *

In Nelson v. Wilkins Dodge, Inc., Minn., 256 N.W.2d 472, 476 (1977), an action for breach of implied warranties in the sale of a pickup, the court held that a defective condition can be proved by circumstantial evidence, saying:

"Plaintiffs assert that there can be no question that proximate cause has been demonstrated with respect to the paint bubbles, the inverted taillight covers, and the loosened windshield-wiper blade and arm and shift lever. Defendant suggests that the paint bubbles and the loosened windshield wiper, horn bracket, and shift lever just as probably resulted from the continuous and hard use to which plaintiffs put the pickup as from any defect inherent in the vehicle when plaintiffs purchased it. Although liability for breach of warranty attaches only when a defect existing in the goods causes a breakdown in quality, * * * generally no specific defect need be alleged, and a defective condition can be proved by circumstantial evidence * * * No direct evidence was introduced as to the causes of the conditions in question. It is reasonable to suppose, however, that vehicles that are fit for ordinary purposes probably do not display these defects this early, even if they are driven a great deal within a short period of time. Thus, the causes of the faulty paint, windshield wiper, horn bracket, and shift lever were questions that should have been decided by the jury. A fortiori, the cause of the inverted taillight covers was a jury question."

Other courts have also held that circumstantial evidence may be sufficient to show the causal relation between the use of a warranted product and the injury which followed its use. See, 77 C.J.S. Sales, § 367. Thus, in Yormack v. Farmers Co-op. Assn. of N.J., 11 N.J.Super. 416, 78 A.2d 421 (1950), in an action for breach of a statutory implied warranty of quality and fitness in the sale of an insecticide (carbolineum) for use about chicken roosts, the court said (11 N.J. Super. 423, 78 A.2d 424):

"We recognize the absence of any evidence which definitely informed the jury of the particular ingredient or constituent of the carbolineum which would in reasonable probability gravely injure and kill the chickens. Proof of unfitness does not necessarily require that degree of exactness and precision. * * *

"Furthermore it was not necessary for the plaintiff to prove by direct evidence the causal relation between the use of the carbolineum and the injurious result; it could be established by circumstantial evidence."

We conclude that although plaintiff's proof of causation was not direct, if his evidence is viewed in the light most favorable to the verdict, the jury could infer from the fact that the fading was quite uniform that the presence or absence of linseed oil had no effect on the fading. Defendant admitted that there was a "fade problem" and fading within so short a time was to be expected with Commonwealth Ranch Red. From this it could be inferred that it was not "good barn paint," not of merchantable quality, and not suitable for the purpose for which plaintiff bought it. Thus, defendant's motions for a directed verdict and for judgment notwithstanding the verdict were properly denied.

2. Defendant also argues that, assuming the warranties involved here were breached, plaintiff is precluded from recovery of damages because he used the paint contrary to the directions and such "misuse" was beyond the scope of the warranties. Although defendant cites several cases in support of this claim—Chisholm v. J.R. Simplot Co., 94 Idaho 682, 495 P.2d 1113 (1972); Elanco Products Co. v. Akin-Tunnell, 516 S.W.2d 726 (Tex.Civ.App.1974); Iverson Paints, Inc. v. Wirth Corp., 94 Idaho 43, 480 P.2d 889 (1971); Brown v. General

Motors Corp., 355 F.2d 814 (4 Cir.1966)—all are distinguishable from this case. In the Chisholm case, watering the fields within a specified time was essential to activate the weed killer which was alleged to have been defective, and the importance of following that direction should have been obvious to plaintiffs. In Iverson also, the directions for using the machine were very precise, and they were almost completely ignored—neither of which is the fact here. In the Elanco case the manufacturer had stressed the necessity of following directions and had disclaimed any affirmations made about the product unless the directions were followed. The court accordingly treated compliance with the directions as a condition precedent to the existence of the express warranty sued on. Here no comparable stress was laid on the importance of the directions, and they certainly were not specific and precise as to quantity. In Brown, plaintiff did not establish that there had been a breach of warranty, and that his use of a tractor by starting it when it was in gear was abnormal and unpredictable. Plaintiff used the paint here for its intended purpose.

We conclude that the trial court correctly instructed the jury that it could consider whether plaintiff complied with defendant's directions in determining whether he was negligent and whether his negligence was a cause of his consequential damages.

We also find little merit in defendant's argument that, if there was a defect in the paint, plaintiff failed to mitigate his damages by continuing to use the paint after he found it wrinkled when combined with the prescribed amount of linseed oil. Plaintiff did not know the paint would fade because, as he thought, defendant's directions called for too much linseed oil. Defendant's argument also assumes that plaintiff was at all times required to add linseed oil, a conclusion not compelled by the evidence. In any event, the court properly instructed the jury on plaintiff's duty to mitigate damages after learning of the breaches of warranty.

Defendant urges, finally, that the trial court improperly awarded plaintiff all of the consequential damages assessed by the jury and argues that these damages should have been reduced by 15 percent to reflect the proportion of fault which the jury attributed to plaintiff's negligence. Whether a comparative-fault principle should be applied in breach-of-warranty actions has not been determined in this state. Wenner v. Gulf Oil Corp., Minn., 264 N.W.2d 374, filed February 17, 1978. Although reducing a party's consequential damages by an amount reflecting the extent to which his own conduct caused them appears to be equitable, appropriate under Minn.St. 336.2–715(2)(b), and compatible with our approach in a recent products liability action based on strict liability, Busch v. Busch Const. Co., Minn., 262 N.W.2d 377 (1977), we decline to consider this issue since it was not presented to the trial court and has been raised for the first time on appeal. International Union of Operating Eng. v. City of Mpls., 305 Minn. 364, 233 N.W.2d 748 (1975).

Affirmed.

Notes

1. No sample was offered from the batch of paint purchased and applied to the barns. How did the buyer survive the seller's motion for directed verdict? In American Fertilizer Specialists v. Wood, 635 P.2d 592, 595–96 (Okl.1981), the court, in affirming the trial court's decision for the buyer, stated: "Facts may be proved by circumstantial, as well as by positive or direct evidence, and it is not necessary that the proof rise to that degree of certainty which will exclude every other reasonable

conclusion than the one arrived at by the trier of facts. It is only required that it appear more probable that the defendant's poor grass crop was the result of the failure of the fertilizer sold by plaintiff to defendant to nourish and enrich defendant's grass lands than any other possible cause."

2. The buyer, in *Chatfield,* concededly failed to follow the seller's printed directions for use. Why didn't the buyer's failure constitute either a use of the product that was not ordinary, thereby undercutting the claim that an implied warranty of merchantability was breached, or a misuse of a product otherwise fit for ordinary purposes, thereby establishing that breach of warranty did not cause the loss? (In Hutchinson Utilities Commission v. Curtiss-Wright Corp., 775 F.2d 231 (8th Cir.1985), the Eighth Circuit, relying on *Chatfield,* held that an agreed inspection schedule was not a condition precedent to the buyer's claim and that a defect in the goods rather than the failure to inspect was the "proximate" cause of the loss.)

3. Assuming that the plaintiff in *Chatfield* was, to some degree, at "fault" in mixing the paint, what effect should that have on the issues of liability and remedy? Consider these possibilities:

(a) The warranty, although made, was not breached;

(b) Although the warranty was made and breached, the plaintiff's "fault" barred it from recovery;

(c) The plaintiff's "fault", whether misuse or failure to discover, is no per se bar, but it may be considered in determining whether the breach caused the loss complained of; and

(d) The plaintiff's "fault" may be used to reduce damages otherwise proximately caused by the breach.

Which, if any, of these possibilities did *Chatfield* employ?

4. The Minnesota Comparative Negligence Statute, Minn.Stat.Ann. § 604.01(1) (Supp.1987), provides that contributory fault is no bar in an action to "recover damages for fault resulting in death or injury to person or property, if the contributory fault was not greater than the fault of the person against whom recovery is sought, but any damages allowed shall be diminished in proportion to the amount of fault attributable to the person recovering." In 1978, the statute was amended to define "fault" to include "breach of warranty, unreasonable assumption of risk not constituting an express consent, misuse of a product and unreasonable failure to avoid an injury or to mitigate damages." § 604.01(1a). The Supreme Court of Minnesota has since held that, in an action to recover for personal injuries and economic loss allegedly caused by a breach of warranty, it was proper to use the plaintiff's "fault" to reduce consequential damages but not direct damages caused by the breach. Peterson v. Bendix Home Systems, Inc., 318 N.W.2d 50 (Minn.1982). Should these later developments change the outcome in *Chatfield?*

Problem 20-3

The courts and legislatures, in applying concepts of comparative fault to product liability suits, have stopped short of cases where only economic loss is involved: The plaintiff, when suing on a warranty theory, must claim damages to person or property before any "fault" comparison will be made. An example is Fiske v. MacGregor Div. of Brunswick, 464 A.2d 719 (R.I.1983). The issues are discussed in Leff & Pinto, *Comparative Negligence in Strict Products Liability: The Courts Render the Final Judgment,* 89 Dick.L.Rev. 915 (1985); Sobelsohn, *Comparing Fault,* 60 Ind. L.J. 413 (1985); Note, *Use of the Comparative Negligence Doctrine in Warranty Actions,* 45 Ohio St. U.L.J. 763 (1984).

As we shall see in Section 5, infra, Article 2 of the UCC is the exclusive source of law in warranty disputes where only economic loss is involved. How does Article 2 deal with problems of the buyer's fault? With this question in mind, re-read Article 2, Parts Six and Seven. Make a list of the "penalties," if any, that the buyer must pay for failure to take reasonable steps to discover the non-conformity or otherwise to avoid the loss.

SECTION 4. THE STATUTE OF LIMITATIONS

Read UCC 2–725 and work the following problem.

Problem 20–4

On May 1, 1982, Seller and Buyer, a grain dealer, entered a written contract for the sale of three prefabricated metal grain bins, each 30 feet tall, for a total price of $50,000. The bins were to be shipped to Buyer FOB Point of Destination and Seller agreed to erect and install them at Buyer's place of business. The contract provided, inter alia, that "the above described bins will, if properly installed, withstand winds up to 90 MPH."

The bins were shipped on June 1, 1982 and arrived on June 5, 1982. The buyer removed the disassembled parts from the carrier and notified the Seller, who completed the installation by July 1, 1982. On June 15, 1986, a severe storm with winds up to 80 MPH hit the area where Buyer did business. Two of the bins were toppled by the wind, resulting in damage to the bins and the stored grain. An expert will testify that the internal support seams had gradually and imperceptibly deteriorated since installation.

Buyer's attorney has asked you, his associate, whether the statute of limitations has run.

STANDARD ALLIANCE INDUS., INC. v. BLACK CLAWSON CO.

United States Court of Appeals, Sixth Circuit, 1978.
587 F.2d 813.

[The facts and the court's opinion on the notice issue are reprinted, supra at p. 808.]

* * *

A. The Statute of Limitations and Count I

Chronology is important to a precise understanding of the issues. The machine was delivered and assembled at Standard Alliance's plant in the fall of 1967. The machine proved defective, and Standard Alliance wrote Black Clawson on December 27, 1967, delineating exactly what was wrong with the machine and requesting that Black Clawson fix it. Black Clawson worked on the machine until June 21, 1968, when it abandoned repair efforts. This suit was filed on May 29, 1969.

The original contract contained a one-year limitations period; * the minimum allowable under UCC § 2–725(1). UCC § 2–725(1) also provides that the limitations period begins to run when the cause of action accrues. UCC § 2–725(2) explains that a cause of action accrues when a breach occurs. A breach of warranty is deemed to occur upon tender of delivery "except that where a warranty explicitly extends to future performance of the goods and discovery of the breach must await the time of such performance the cause of action accrues

* Based upon information provided by counsel, the editors of the Callaghan Uniform Commercial Code Reporting Service state that the exact language of the "limitation" clause was as follows: "Any action or arbitration proceeding for breach of this agreement must be brought within one year after the cause of action has accrued."

when the breach is or should have been discovered." UCC § 2–725(2). Black Clawson argues that the machine was tendered in the fall of 1967 and that, even granting that the warranty extends to future performance, the cause of action under Count I accrued no later than December 27, 1967, when Standard Alliance wrote its letter claiming that the machine was defective. Standard Alliance makes numerous arguments in reply. Primarily, we must consider the question of when breach occurred. This involves analysis of two separate issues: when tender of delivery was made; whether the warranty extended to future performance. In addition, we must consider various estoppel and policy arguments.

Standard Alliance first contends, with some support in the record, that novel machines like the one here often have long "shakedown" periods before they can be made to function properly. The import of its argument is that "tender" of a defective machine should not be deemed to take place until the machine is made to run properly. Since the machine in the instant case did not function properly when initially installed in October of 1967, Standard Alliance argues, tender of delivery was never really made until June 21, 1968, when Black Clawson halted its efforts to get the machine going. Thus, even assuming that the warranty did not extend to future performance, the earliest a breach could have occurred and a cause of action accrued, on Standard Alliance's theory, was June 21, 1968.

This argument is plausible, but withers upon proper examination of the Uniform Commercial Code. UCC § 2–503(1) defines "tender of delivery" as requiring " * * * that the seller put and hold conforming goods at the buyer's disposition * * * " Comment 1 to UCC § 2–503 explains that at times "tender" means "due tender" meaning " * * * an offer coupled with a present ability to fulfill all the conditions resting on the tendering party [which must be] followed by actual performance if the other party shows himself ready to proceed." "At other times [tender] is used to refer to an offer of goods or documents under a contract as if in fulfillment of its conditions even though there is a defect when measured against the contract obligation." Id. We think that "tender" as used in UCC § 2–725(2) is the latter and not the former. A contrary interpretation would extend the statute of limitations indefinitely into the future since a defect at the time of delivery would prevent proper "due tender" from taking place until it was corrected. Under section 2–725, a cause of action accrues upon initial installation of the product regardless whether it functions properly or not so long as the warranty does not extend to future performance. See Val Decker Packing Co. v. Corn Products Sales Co., 411 F.2d 850 (6th Cir.1969).

Secondly, Standard Alliance argues that the page twelve warranties ** did extend to future performance under section 2–725(2), and that the statute of

** The negotiated performance or "page twelve warranties" provided:

"The following express warranties, which relate to mechanical function only become an adjunct to our contract clause # 1 page 11 and supersede all references to warranties that may be contained in the description of the machine pages 2–7, either expressed or implied.

"Black Clawson warrants that the subject machinery will perform the following mechanical functions:

"1. Press will deliver 1000 ton ram capacity at 150 strokes per minute @ 1/4" from bottom dead center.

"2. Press will have a maximum speed of 250 strokes per minute—with a range of 10 to 250 SPM.

"3. Rams at bottom of stroke will have a parallelism of within .005".

"4. Peel and press will trace template within plus or minus .015".

"5. Feed adjustments will have a range up to 0.375" per second.

"6. Peel rotation will have a range of 5 to 100 RPM and will be designed to lock at the 90° positions.

"7. Peel traverse speed will have a range of 1 ft/minute to 45 ft/minute, and will be designed to lock in position.

limitations thus ran from the date of discovery of the defect. It particularly points to the phrase, "Black Clawson warrants that the subject machinery *will* perform the following mechanical functions." Plaintiff's argument proves too much. Since all contracts contain future promises, words of futurity such as "will" are common. When the contract at issue here was signed, the machine was not yet built; the word "will" was necessarily used. The proper question is whether the statute of limitations is meant to run from the day of delivery or from the day when a defect is found sometime in the future.

Most courts have been very harsh in determining whether a warranty explicitly extends to future performance. Emphasizing the word "explicitly," they have ruled that there must be specific reference to a future time in the warranty. As a result of this harsh construction, most express warranties cannot meet the test and no implied warranties can since, by their very nature, they never "explicitly extend to future performance." * * *

Two rare examples where express warranties were found to explicitly extend to future performance are Rempe v. General Electric Co., 28 Conn.Super. 160, 254 A.2d 577 (1969) (product was to "work properly for a lifetime") and Mittasch v. Seal Lock Burial Vault, Inc., 42 A.D.2d 573, 344 N.Y.S.2d 101 (1973) (warranty that vault "will give satisfactory service at all times").

It is clear that a buyer and a seller can freely negotiate to extend liability into the future; that is why specific allowance was made for warranties "explicitly" extending to future performance. * * * In the absence of explicit agreement, however, UCC § 2–725(2) reflecting the drafters' intention to establish a reasonable period of time, four years,[16] beyond which business persons need not worry about stale warranty claims is applicable. This policy consideration underlying § 2–725 makes it acceptable to bar implied warranty claims brought more than a specified number of years after the sale; otherwise merchants could be forever liable for breach of warranty on any goods which they sold. * * * Similarly, an express warranty which makes no reference at all to any future date should not be allowed to extend past the limitations period. Thus, where a manufacturer warrants that a welder will meet certain performance warranties, but makes no mention of how long the warranties are meant to last; the statute of limitations begins to run at delivery. * * *

Where, however, an express warranty is made which extends for a specific period of time, i.e. one year, the policy reasons behind strict application of the limitations period do not apply. If a seller expressly warrants a product for a specified number of years, it is clear that, by this action alone, he is explicitly warranting the future performance of the goods for that period of time. As J. White & R. Summers Uniform Commercial Code 342 (1972), points out, if an automobile is warranted to last for twenty-four thousand miles or four years, the warranty should extend to future performance. If the car fails within the warranty period, the limitations period should begin to run from the day the defect is or should have been discovered.

"8. The mechanical functions can be programmed to operate in automatic sequence in the specified capacities and accuracies or may be operator interrupted and/or commanded as required.

"The quality and quantity of production is not the responsibility of the seller."

16. We are aware that some states have adopted a limitations period greater than four years, e.g. Wis.Stat. § 402.725 (6 years); Okla. Stat. tit. 12A § 2–725 (5 years). Ohio, however, follows the majority of the states in establishing a four year period. Ohio Rev.Code § 1302.98 [UCC § 2–725]. The parties agree that Ohio law governs this diversity action.

In the case at bar, Black Clawson expressly warranted the machine for a period of one year. Thus, we hold that the warranties explicitly extended to future performance for a period of one year. Therefore, under § 2–725(2) the cause of action accrued when Standard Alliance discovered or should have discovered that the machine was defective, so long as the defect arose within the warranty period.[17]

Unfortunately, this holding does not assist the plaintiff. Under the contractual limitations period, Standard Alliance had one year from the date of discovery of defect to bring suit. Standard Alliance reported the machine's problems to Black Clawson by letter on December 27, 1967. At least as of this date, Standard Alliance had discovered the breach. Since suit was not brought until over a year later, on May 29, 1969, this action is barred by section 2–725(2). See Gemini Typographers v. Mergenthaler Lino Co., 48 A.D.2d 637, 368 N.Y.S.2d 210 (1975).

Plaintiff thirdly argues that Black Clawson should be estopped from asserting the statute of limitations as a defense because it promised to repair the defects and spent over five months attempting to do so. In effect, plaintiff contends that it reasonably relied on the repair efforts, to its detriment. Decisions in other jurisdictions are split. * * *

We must determine what the Ohio courts would do if confronted with this issue. Although we have been unable to find direct case authority, an examination of the statute is illuminative. UCC § 2–725(4), as promulgated by the drafters of the Uniform Commercial Code, states:

> "This section does not alter *the law* on tolling of the statute of limitations nor does it apply to causes of action which have accrued before this Act becomes effective." (Emphasis added)

Ohio's version of UCC § 2–725(4) is codified at Ohio Rev.Code § 1302.98(d). That section provides:

> "This section does not alter *sections 2305.15 and 2305.16 of the [Ohio] Revised Code* on tolling of the statute of limitations nor does it apply to causes of action which have accrued before this Act becomes effective." (Emphasis added)

Thus, when the Ohio legislature adopted the Uniform Commercial Code, it substituted "sections 2305.15 and 2305.16 of the [Ohio] Revised Code" for "the law" in the text of UCC § 2–725(4). This significant change in the UCC's wording requires that we limit our analysis to the two Ohio statutes cited.

An examination of these statutes reveals that the limitation period is tolled if a defendant has removed himself from the state, Ohio Rev.Code § 2305.15, or if a plaintiff has suffered from some type of disability. Ohio Rev.Code § 2305.16. Neither is applicable here.

17. Centennial Ins. Co. v. General Electric Co., [253 N.W.2d 696] and Voth v. Chrysler Motor Corp., [545 P.2d 371], indicated that contractual provisions to repair or replace defective parts for a period of one year were not warranties extending into the future for one year, but remedies to be invoked should something go wrong. We see no conceptual distinction between saying that a product is warranted for one year against defects, the remedy limited to repair or replacement and saying that should a breach be discovered within one year, the seller will repair or replace defective parts. Both are warranties explicitly extending to future performance. We recognize that there may be differences between remedies and warranties, * * * but we do not believe that these distinctions make a difference here.

It is, of course, quite possible that the Ohio courts would apply the doctrine of equitable estoppel in a case where an innocent purchaser has relied to his detriment on a seller's promises to repair. "The principle that '* * * no man may take advantage of his own wrong' prevents a defendant whose actions have induced a plaintiff to delay filing a suit until after the running of the limitation period from asserting the statute of limitations as a defense to the action." Ott v. Midland-Ross Corp., 523 F.2d 1367, 1370 (6th Cir.1975). See Markese v. Ellis, 11 Ohio App.2d 160, 229 N.E.2d 70 (1967). Here, however, we have two corporate behemoths, well able to look out for themselves, and no evidence that one lulled the other into not suing on time. * * *

Standard Alliance's two remaining arguments, unsupported by any authority, merit only brief mention. Standard Alliance argues that this court should toll the running of the limitations period or otherwise find timely filing because the limitations period was contractually reduced from four years to one year. It would also find significant that approximately one-half the one-year limitations period was spent in attempted repairs.

The one-year limitations period is specifically allowed by UCC § 2–725(1). We see nothing unfair about this provision in a negotiated contract between two parties of equal bargaining power. Similarly, we find no prejudice to plaintiff resulted from the lengthy repair time. Standard Alliance still had time to file suit on the original breach of warranty claim even after termination of the repair efforts; it also had a cause of action under Count II for failure to fulfill the repair or replacement warranty.[20]

* * *

[Some footnotes omitted.]

Notes

1. In Dowling v. Southwestern Porcelain, Inc., 237 Kan. 536, 701 P.2d 954 (1985), the court held that where the buyer contracted to purchase a completed silo to be installed by the seller, the statute of limitations began to run when the installation was completed, not when the component parts were delivered.

2. Seller, in furnishing spandrel and visions panels for a building, represented that the goods would be free from defects in material and workmanship for a "period of twenty years." The exclusive remedy for breach was limited to replacement of defective panels. The panels, which were delivered between 1974 and 1976, were defective. The buyer sued for damages in 1981 and the district court granted the seller's motion to dismiss based upon the statute of limitations: The court held that seller had only made replacement commitments, not warranties explicitly extending to future performance. *Held,* reversed. The warranties, by explicitly stating a time beyond delivery when the condition would exist, extended the warranty to "future" performance of the goods, with a limitation of the remedy to replacement in the event of a breach. The buyer filed suit within 4 years of the time the breach was or "should have been discovered." R.W. Murray Co. v. Shatterproof Glass Corp., 697 F.2d 818 (8th Cir.1983).

3. Suppose that S, upon delivery on November 1, 1980, explicitly stated that "this warranty shall last for three years." B "should have" discovered a nonconform-

20. Our disposition of Count I on limitations grounds makes it unnecessary to consider the interesting question whether notice of breach had to be given a second time, after repairs failed. Since the repair or replacement warranty is also a remedy to be invoked if the machine did not meet its performance warranties, there is certainly room to argue that UCC § 2–607(3) requires notice that the repair or replacement remedy has failed "of its essential purpose" under UCC § 2–719(2).

ity on November 1, 1986 and actually discovered the defect on July 1, 1987. B sued S on October 30, 1987. S moved to dismiss on grounds that B failed to give notice under UCC 2–607(3)(a) before filing suit. What result?

4. For samples of literature highly critical of UCC 2–725, see Williams, *The Statute of Limitations, Prospective Warranties, and Problems of Interpretation in Article 2 of the UCC,* 52 G.W.L.Rev. 67 (1983); Note, *UCC Section 2–725: A Statute Uncertain in Application and Effect,* 46 Ohio St. U.L.Rev. 755 (1985).

Problem 20–5

B contracted to purchase factory equipment from S on June 1, 1984. S warranted that the goods were free from defects in material and workmanship for the period of one year after installation and agreed to repair or replace defective parts or work. The equipment was delivered and installed on July 1, 1984. On June 1, 1985, B notified S that the machine had stopped working. S, on June 5, arrived at B's plant and attempted to "cure" the problem. After three weeks of effort, the equipment still did not work. S left the premises on June 26, 1985 insisting that he would repair the machine. "Don't worry," he said. In August, 1985, B notified S that the cure had not worked and that he considered S in breach. Again, S assured B that a cure would be forthcoming. S never returned to the plant and B removed the equipment from the floor and put it in storage. In July, 1989, B consults you, his attorney, about the matter. Has the statute of limitations run on B's claim for breach of warranty?

SECTION 5. THE LIMITATIONS OF WARRANTY THEORY

To summarize, warranty is a theory of strict but limited liability. Warranties arise when the seller makes representations, express or implied, about the quality of goods sold upon which a buyer is entitled to depend. Disputes involving warranties are resolved within Article 2 of the UCC, which has a set of limitations and policies associated primarily with exchange transactions, i.e., contracts for the sale of goods. In addition to limitations associated with concerns about adverse selection and moral hazard, which have been noted, Article 2 also permits the parties by agreement to disclaim or limit warranties and limit remedies for breach, issues which will be treated in Chapter 21.

A number of recurring problems, however, have tested the nature of warranty theory and, perforce, the limitations of Article 2. We will identify some of them here, and follow with a decision where the issues are put to the test.

First, should warranty theory be extended to transactions where personal or professional services predominate and the transfer of goods is incidental? The usual answer is no, unless the defendant has expressly promised or represented that the services, when performed, will achieve a specific result. Without an express commitment to achieve a particular result, the performance of the services is judged under tort standards—negligence—rather than implied warranty. See, e.g., Milau Associates v. North Ave. Development, 42 N.Y.2d 482, 398 N.Y.S.2d 882, 368 N.E.2d 1247 (1977); Greenfield, *Consumer Protection in Service Transactions—Implied Warranties and Strict Liability in Tort,* 1974 Utah L.Rev. 661. (Query whether there is much difference between a tort duty to perform services with reasonable care and an implied warranty that the services will be "reasonably fit" for ordinary purposes.)

Second, suppose a seller sells unmerchantable goods which cause damage to the person or property of a buyer. Suppose, further, that the buyer would be foreclosed from recovery by one or more limitations upon warranty liability found in the Code, e.g., failure to give notice of the breach, lack of contractual privity, an enforceable disclaimer or expiration of the statute of limitations. Does Article 2 preempt the dispute or may the buyer also pursue the claim in strict products liability or negligence, where tort rather than contract limitations apply?

Despite the fact that Article 2 explicitly covers personal injury and property damage claims, see UCC 2–715(2)(b), 2–719(3) and 2–318, Alternatives A and B, the usual answer to the question is no: Neither the drafters of Article 2 nor the state legislatures which enacted it intended to preempt the developing theory of strict liability under Section 402A of the Restatement, Second of Torts. See Phipps v. General Motors Corp., 278 Md. 337, 363 A.2d 955 (1976); Murray, *Products Liability vs. Warranty Claims: Untangling the Web,* 3 J.Law & Commerce 269 (1983); Wade, *Tort Liability for Products Causing Physical Injury and Article 2 of the U.C.C.,* 48 Mo.L.Rev. 1 (1983). For contrary opinions, see Cline v. Prowler Industries of Maryland, 418 A.2d 968 (Del.Super.1980); Shanker, *A Reexamination of Prosser's Products Liability Cross Word Game: The Strict or Stricter Liability of Commercial Code Sales Warranty,* 29 Case Wes.Res.L.Rev. 550 (1979) (Article 2 applies to physical damage claims). The upshot is that a plaintiff who is injured in person or property by a defective product may escape Article 2 for the more favorable law of Tort, if he so elects.

Third, suppose a commercial buyer in privity with the seller suffers damage to property or pure economic loss from a breach of warranty. No personal injuries are involved. May the buyer "escape" from Article 2 into tort by invoking either strict products or negligence theory? To put the matter concretely, suppose that the statute of limitations has run under UCC 2–725(1) but has not run in tort. As *Spring Motors,* infra, reveals, the judicial answer is clear where pure economic loss is involved—UCC 2–725 controls—but is uncertain where damage to personal property has occurred.

Fourth, suppose a commercial buyer has suffered pure economic loss caused by an unmerchantable product but is not in privity of contract with the manufacturer. If the buyer cannot escape the UCC into tort, lack of privity is no defense and warranty theory must be pursued. May the manufacturer, who is a seller, defend on the ground that there was no privity of contract? See the next case.

Finally, suppose the buyer is a consumer, i.e., a person who purchased the goods for personal, family or household purposes, who has suffered only economic loss. How, if at all, should the answers to the third and fourth questions, above, differ? Should the "ordinary" consumer with less overall capacity than the professional seller be entitled to greater protection than a commercial buyer and, if so, what and why? See, e.g., Rice, *Product Quality Laws and the Economics of Federalism,* 65 B.U.L.Rev. 1 (1985); Vogel, *Squeezing Consumers: Lemon Laws, Consumer Warranties, and a Proposal for Reform,* 1985 Ariz.St.L. Rev. 589, and Chapter 21, Section 5.

SPRING MOTORS DISTRIBUTORS, INC. v. FORD MOTOR COMPANY

Supreme Court of New Jersey, 1985.
98 N.J. 555, 489 A.2d 660.

The opinion of the Court was delivered by

POLLOCK, J.

The fundamental issue on this appeal concerns the rights of a commercial buyer to recover for economic loss caused by the purchase of defective goods.

More specifically, the question is whether the buyer should be restricted to its cause of action under the Uniform Commercial Code (hereinafter U.C.C. or the Code) or should be allowed to pursue a cause of action predicated on principles of negligence and strict liability. The difference is important because the buyer in the present case instituted its action beyond the four-year period provided by the U.C.C., *N.J.S.A.* 12A:2–725, but within the six-year period applicable to tort actions, *N.J.S.A.* 2A:14–1.

The defendants are a motor vehicle manufacturer, its dealer, and a supplier of transmissions. The gravamen of the complaint is that defects in the transmissions, which were installed in commercial trucks, caused the buyer to sustain a loss in the benefit of its bargain and consequential damages. Specifically, the buyer sought recovery for repair, towing, and replacement parts, as well as for lost profits and a decrease in the value of the trucks.

The trial court perceived the matter as sounding in contract and found that the plaintiff had not instituted its action within the four-year period provided by the U.C.C. *N.J.S.A.* 12A:2–725. In an unreported decision, the court granted summary judgment for defendants. The Appellate Division reversed on the ground that the action was more appropriately characterized as one in strict liability in tort, not contract, and that the six-year period of limitations applicable for tort actions had not expired. 191 *N.J.Super.* 22, 465 *A.*2d 530 (1983). We granted defendants' petition for certification. 95 *N.J.* 208, 470 *A.*2d 427 (1983).

We hold that a commercial buyer seeking damages for economic loss resulting from the purchase of defective goods may recover from an immediate seller and a remote supplier in a distributive chain for breach of warranty under the U.C.C., but not in strict liability or negligence. We hold also that the buyer need not establish privity with the remote supplier to maintain an action for breach of express or implied warranties. Accordingly, the four-year period of limitations provided by the Code, *N.J.S.A.* 12A:2–275, not the six-year general statute of limitations, *N.J.S.A.* 2A:14–1, determines the time within which an action must be commenced against the immediate seller and remote supplier.

I

Because this matter is presented on defendants' motion for summary judgment, we accept as true plaintiff's version of the facts, according that version the benefit of all favorable inferences. *Pierce v. Ortho Pharmaceutical Corp.,* 84 *N.J.* 58, 61, 417 *A.*2d 505 (1980). Plaintiff, Spring Motors Distributors, Inc. (Spring Motors), which is in the business of selling and leasing trucks, operates a fleet of 300 vehicles. Spring Motors agreed to purchase from defendant Turnpike Ford Truck Sales, Inc. (Turnpike) 14 model LN8000 trucks made by defendant Ford Motor Company (Ford) at a purchase price of $265,029.80. Turnpike is a Ford dealer, and throughout these proceedings the two defendants have been treated as a single entity.

In the agreement, Spring Motors specified that the trucks should be equipped with model 390V transmissions made by Clark Equipment Company (Clark), a supplier to Ford. Spring Motors specified Clark transmissions because of "excellent service and parts availability on past models" and because of Clark's advertisements and brochures.

At the time of the sale to Spring Motors, Ford issued a form warranty with each truck to

> repair or replace any of the following parts that are found to be defective in factory material or workmanship under normal use in the United States or

> Canada on the following basis: * * * any part during the first 12 months or 12,000 miles of operations, whichever is earlier * * * transmission case and all internal transmission parts (including auxiliary transmission) * * * after 12,000 miles and during the first 12 months or 50,000 miles of operation, whichever is earlier, for a charge of 50% of the dealer's regular warranty charge to Ford for parts and labor. * * * For series 850 and higher trucks, any part of the * * * transmission * * * for the first 12 months or 100,000 miles of operation, whichever is earlier * * *.

The warranty also stated: "To the extent allowed by law, this WARRANTY IS IN PLACE OF all other warranties, express or implied, including ANY IMPLIED WARRANTY OF MERCHANTABILITY OR FITNESS." Furthermore, the Ford warranty expressly stated: "Under this warranty, repair or replacement of parts is the only remedy, and loss of use of the vehicle, loss of time, inconvenience, commercial loss or consequential damages are not covered."

The warranty that Clark extended to Ford provided: "WARRANTY. Clark Equipment Company ('Clark') warrants to Buyer that each new Clark axle, transmission, torque converter and drive train product, and components thereof, shall be free from defects and material and workmanship under normal use and maintenance" for 12 months or 12,000 miles for on-highway vehicles used on highways or 2,000 miles for off-highway equipment. At Clark's option, the warranty could be limited to repairs or replacements. The warranty also stated: "THIS WARRANTY IS IN LIEU OF ALL OTHER WARRANTIES (EXCEPT OF TITLE), EXPRESSED OR IMPLIED, AND THERE IS NO IMPLIED WARRANTY OF MERCHANTABILITY OR OF FITNESS FOR A PARTICULAR PURPOSE. IN NO EVENT SHALL CLARK BE LIABLE FOR INCIDENTAL, CONSEQUENTIAL OR SPECIAL DAMAGES."

Spring Motors took delivery of the trucks in November 1976, and leased them to Economic Laboratories, Inc. (Economic), which used the trucks in cities and on highways for their intended purpose of hauling. Spring Motors, which serviced the trucks during the period of the lease, began experiencing problems with the performance of the Clark transmissions as early as February 1977. The problems persisted, and Spring Motors communicated directly with Clark, writing in October 1977 that it had "had nothing but trouble" with the transmissions. Later correspondence, dated January 26, 1978, confirmed that Clark analyzed the transmissions and found that "the failure in these gear boxes was a result of improper angle degree in the way certain gears were cut," resulting "in additional strain on the actual gear and the mating gear and related shafts." Still later, Spring Motors pointed out that the transmission failures had cost it "several thousand dollars in out of pocket expenses plus many additional thousands of dollars in lost revenues, customer ill will, replacement equipment, etc."

Clark provided Spring Motors with replacement parts, but the transmission failures continued. On July 11, 1978, Spring Motors wrote to Clark that in the absence of a satisfactory response by August 1, it would remove and replace the Clark transmissions and "take whatever action is necessary to hold you financially responsible." Thereafter, on November 1, 1979, Spring Motors and Economic terminated the truck lease and, as part of a settlement, Economic purchased the trucks for $247,580.97. Four years and one month after the delivery of the trucks, on December 23, 1980, Spring Motors instituted this action.

In the complaint, which contained three counts, Spring Motors sought judgment against all defendants for consequential damages: the expenses of towing, repairs, and replacement of parts; lost profits; and decrease in market value of the trucks. The first count asserted that the defendants breached certain express and implied warranties; the second count claimed a violation of the Magnuson-Moss Act, 15 *U.S.C.* § 2301 to –2312, a claim that Spring Motors no longer pursues; and the third count sought recovery in strict liability and negligence.

The trial court found that a lack of privity barred the action between Spring Motors and Clark and that the four-year period of limitations under the U.C.C., *N.J.S.A.* 12A:2–725, barred any action against Ford and Turnpike. The Court further found the six-year statute of limitations, *N.J.S.A.* 2A:14–1, pertaining to tort actions for property damage, inapplicable. Consequently, the trial court dismissed the complaint as to all defendants.

The Appellate Division affirmed the dismissal of the breach of warranty claim in the first count, but reversed the dismissal of the tort claims, without discussing the negligence aspect of the third count. That court concluded that Spring Motors, as a commercial buyer, could maintain its strict-liability claim against all defendants. 191 *N.J.Super.* at 41, 465 *A.*2d 530. The court also determined that the six-year limitation period provided by *N.J.S.A.* 2A:14–1 applied and that plaintiff's action was, therefore, timely. *Id.* at 44, 465 *A.*2d 530.

We granted petitions for certification by Ford, Turnpike, and Clark to review that part of the Appellate Division judgment that reversed the dismissal of the tort claims. Spring Motors did not file a cross-petition seeking review of the dismissal of the warranty claims, and that issue is not before us.

II

If the legal relationships among the parties are governed by the U.C.C., then plaintiff's action, which was instituted more than four years after the delivery of the trucks, is time-barred. Hence, one question is whether the Code provides the exclusive remedies available to Spring Motors. In answering that question, we turn to the structure and purpose of the Code, which constitutes a comprehensive system for determining the rights and duties of buyers and sellers with respect to contracts for the sale of goods. *Ramirez v. Autosport,* 88 *N.J.* 277, 285–90, 440 *A.*2d 1345 (1982). Its underlying purpose is to clarify and make uniform throughout the United States the law governing commercial transactions. *N.J.S.A.* 12A:1–102.

The Code provides for express warranties regarding the quality of goods, *N.J.S.A.* 12A:2–313, as well as implied warranties of merchantability, *N.J.S.A.* 12A:2–314, and of fitness for a particular purpose, *N.J.S.A.* 12A:2–315. As is subsequently discussed in greater detail, a seller's warranty, whether express or implied, extends to members of the buyer's family or his household guests, who are viewed as third-party beneficiaries, and a seller may not exclude or limit the extension of those warranties to such persons. *N.J.S.A.* 12A:2–318.

Subject to requirements of good faith, diligence, and reasonableness, parties may vary the terms of the Code. *N.J.S.A.* 12A:1–102. A seller may exclude or modify its liability on warranties, and if in writing, the exclusion or modification must be "conspicuous." *N.J.S.A.* 12A:2–316. Furthermore, a buyer and seller may agree to limit the buyer's remedy to the repair and replacement of parts. *N.J.S.A.* 12A:2–719(1)(a). Similarly, the parties may agree to limit or exclude consequential damages, "unless the limitation or exclusion is unconscionable."

N.J.S.A. 12A:2–719(3). Although a limitation of consequential damages for personal injuries in the case of consumer goods is *prima facie* unconscionable, a limitation of damages for a commercial loss is not. *Id.*

When a seller delivers goods that are not as warranted, the buyer's measure of damage is the difference between the value of the defective goods and the value they would have had if they had been as warranted. *N.J.S.A.* 12A:2–714. In a proper case, a buyer may also recover incidental damages, which include reasonable expenses incidental to the breach, *N.J.S.A.* 12A:2–715; consequential damages, including losses resulting from the buyer's particular needs of which the seller had knowledge, *id.* at (2)(a); and property damage, *id.* at (2)(b).

Economic loss can take the form of either direct or consequential damages. A direct economic loss includes the loss of the benefit of the bargain, *i.e.,* the difference between the value of the product as represented and its value in its defective condition. Consequential economic loss includes such indirect losses as lost profits. J. White & R. Summers, *Handbook of the Law Under the Uniform Commercial Code* §§ 11–4 to 11–6 at 405–10 (2d ed. 1980) [hereinafter cited as White & Summers]; Note, "Economic Loss in Products Liability Jurisprudence," 66 *Colum.L.Rev.* 917, 918 (1966); Note, "Manufacturer's Liability to Remote Purchasers for 'Economic Loss' Damages—Tort or Contract?," 114 *U.Pa.L.Rev.* 539, 542 (1966). Because it presents a claim for economic loss, which is not normally recoverable in a tort action, rather than a claim for physical harm, this case probes the boundary between strict liability and the U.C.C. The delineation of that boundary requires a brief summary of the history and nature of strict liability.

One year before the adoption of the U.C.C. in New Jersey, this Court delivered its landmark opinion in *Henningsen v. Bloomfield Motors, Inc.,* 32 *N.J.* 358, 161 *A.*2d 69 (1960). *Henningsen* involved a defective automobile that crashed and caused property damage to the car and personal injuries to the driver, who was the owner's wife. The Court affirmed a judgment in favor of the plaintiffs on the theory of breach of implied warranty of fitness. Justice Francis wrote in now familiar language: "[U]nder modern marketing conditions, when a manufacturer puts a new automobile in the stream of trade and promotes its purchase by the public, an implied warranty that it is reasonably suitable for use as such accompanies it into the hands of the ultimate purchaser." 32 *N.J.* at 384, 161 *A.*2d 69. By extending a warranty of safety to consumers of all products, not just those intended for human consumption, *Henningsen* removed the notion of privity of contract from all cases involving the sale of defective goods that cause physical injury.

Prosser describes the effect of the *Henningsen* holding as "the most rapid and altogether spectacular overturn of an established rule in the entire history of the law of torts." W. Prosser & W. Page Keeton, *Handbook of the Law of Torts* § 97 at 690 (5th ed. 1984) [hereinafter cited as Prosser & Keeton]. Courts throughout the country followed the lead of New Jersey, *id.,* and the American Law Institute (ALI) included a new section, 402A, captioned "Special Liability of Seller of Product for Physical Harm to User or Consumer," in the *Restatement (Second) of Torts.* The comment to section 402A disavows that the section is governed by the warranty provisions of the U.C.C. or by U.C.C. limitations on the scope and content of the warranties.

Underlying the *Henningsen* decision was the Court's recognition that consumers were in an unequal bargaining position with respect to automobile manufacturers and dealers, who required them to sign standard contracts.

Henningsen, supra, 32 *N.J.* at 389–404, 161 *A.*2d 69. One of the main purposes of strict liability, as declared in *Henningsen,* is the allocation of the risk and distribution of the loss to the better risk-bearer. *Id.* at 379, 161 *A.*2d 69; *Suter v. San Angelo Foundry & Mach. Co.,* 81 *N.J.* 150, 173, 406 *A.*2d 140 (1979). Generally, the manufacturer, who is better able to eliminate defects from its product and who can spread the cost of the risk among all of its customers, is the better risk-bearer. *Restatement, supra,* § 402A comment c. By contrast, the individual consumer is poorly situated to bear the entire risk of loss from injuries caused by a defective product. Through allocation of the risk of loss to the manufacturer, strict liability achieves its objective of protecting the consumer who, because of unequal bargaining power, cannot protect him or herself.

The year after the *Henningsen* decision, 1961, the Legislature adopted the U.C.C., effective January 1, 1963. *L.*1961, *c.* 120. Then in 1965 this Court decided *Santor v. A. & M. Karagheusian, Inc.,* 44 *N.J.* 52, 207 *A.*2d 305, which, like *Henningsen,* involved facts that occurred before the adoption of the U.C.C. In *Santor,* a carpet manufacturer sold a defective carpet to a consumer through its wholly-owned distributor. The Court found that the consumer could recover against the manufacturer, although there was no privity between the parties and the action was for an economic loss.

The action was couched in terms of a breach of implied warranty of merchantability, *id.* at 63, 207 *A.*2d 305, but the Court acknowledged that the action could be described better as one in strict liability. *Id.* at 63–67, 207 *A.*2d 305. In *Santor,* Justice Francis made clear that neither mass advertising by the manufacturer nor personal injuries to the consumer was essential to the invocation of strict liability. *Id.* at 65, 207 *A.*2d 305. Echoing his words in *Henningsen,* he stated that the purpose of a strict-liability action was to shift the risk of loss so that it was borne by "the makers of the products who put them in the channels of trade, rather than by the injured or damaged persons who ordinarily are powerless to protect themselves." *Id.* Like the plaintiff in *Henningsen,* the plaintiff in *Santor* was an individual consumer. Furthermore, the action was for a direct economic loss, and the Court limited recovery to the lost benefit of the bargain, *i.e.,* "the difference between the price paid by the plaintiff and the actual market value of the defective carpeting at the time when plaintiff knew or should have known it was defective * * *." *Id.* at 68–69, 207 *A.*2d 305.

* * *

[The court discussed other New Jersey decisions which held that the tort rather than the UCC statute of limitations governed where a defective product caused damage to person or property.]

As the preceding cases demonstrate, the U.C.C. rules pertaining to the sale of goods overlap the doctrine of strict liability for placing a defective product in the stream of commerce. One reason for the overlap is that strict liability, in this regard, evolved from implied warranties of fitness and merchantability under the U.C.C. and its predecessor, the Uniform Sales Act. Those warranties originated as a matter of social policy to compensate consumers who sustained personal injuries from defective food. Prosser & Keeton, *supra,* § 97 at 690. Neither the ALI, which published the *Restatement (Second) of Torts,* nor the permanent editorial board of the U.C.C., which operates as a joint project of the ALI * * * and the Commissioners on Uniform State Laws, has undertaken to resolve the overlap between strict liability as declared in section 402A and the breach of warranty provisions under the U.C.C. 112 *N.J.L.J.* 700 (1983).

From the perspective of the injured party, strict liability generally provides a more congenial environment than contract principles, which may prevent recovery because of a lack of privity with the manufacturer. In addition to privity, the Code retains two other requirements that may pose considerable obstacles to a buyer. The first requirement is that of notice to a seller of a breach of warranty, *N.J.S.A.* 12A:2–607(3); the second arises from the seller's ability to limit or disclaim liability to an innocent purchaser. *N.J.S.A.* 12A:2–316. A buyer who does not deal directly with a manufacturer cannot negotiate over the terms of a disclaimer and might find it impossible to give the manufacturer notice of the breach of warranty following an injury. Prosser & Keeton, *supra,* § 97 at 691–92. Strict liability, on the other hand, circumvents the technical requirements of the U.C.C. with respect to privity, notice, and limitation of damages. Avoiding those requirements is particularly important for persons outside the distributive chain who sustain physical damage caused by a defective product.

By comparison, the U.C.C. emphasizes the simplification of the law governing commercial transactions and the expansion of commercial practices through agreement. *N.J.S.A.* 12A:1–102. Underlying the U.C.C. policy is the principle that parties should be free to make contracts of their choice, including contracts disclaiming liability for breach of warranty. Once they reach such an agreement, society has an interest in seeing that the agreement is fulfilled. Consequently, the U.C.C. is the more appropriate vehicle for resolving commercial disputes arising out of business transactions between persons in a distributive chain.

The problem is ascertaining where on the spectrum to place a cause of action brought by a commercial entity, or even a consumer, for purely economic loss. One gains perspective by reviewing the decisions of this Court and those of the Supreme Court of California.

As explained earlier, this Court's decision in *Henningsen* was couched in warranty terms. In *Greenman v. Yuba Power Prods:, Inc.*, 59 *Cal.*2d 57, 27 *Cal. Rptr.* 697, 701, 377 *P.*2d 897, 901 (1962), which involved personal injuries sustained by a husband from a defective power saw purchased by his wife, the California court drew on *Henningsen,* but declared that the cause of action could be more appropriately denominated as strict liability in tort.

The cross-pollination between the two jurisdictions continued through our *Santor* decision, which relied on *Greenman.* Five months later, however, when the California court was confronted with an individual's claim for economic loss resulting from the purchase of a defective truck, that court rejected *Santor* and held that the consumer could not recover in strict liability for economic loss. *Seely v. White Motor Co.,* 63 *Cal.*2d 9, 45 *Cal.Rptr.* 17, 403 *P.*2d 145 (1965).

In *Seely,* an individual owner-driver purchased a truck for use in his heavy duty hauling business. From the time the purchaser took possession, the truck bounced violently, but the dealer was unable to correct the defect. Thereafter, a brake failure caused the truck to overturn. The truck sustained property damage, and Seely, who stopped making payments after the accident, sued the dealer and the manufacturer for lost profits and the money paid on the purchase price of the truck.

Chief Justice Traynor, writing for the majority of the court, affirmed a judgment for Seely. The absence of privity did not preclude judgment against the manufacturer for the breach of an express warranty that the truck was "free from defects in material and workmanship under normal use and service

* * *." *Seely, supra,* 63 *Cal.*2d at 13, 45 *Cal.Rptr.* at 20, 403 *P.*2d at 148. After reaching that result, the court rejected plaintiff's alternative contention of strict liability. The court ruled that in the absence of personal injuries or property damage strict liability was inapplicable. Although the truck had been damaged, the court sustained a finding of the trial court that defendant had not created the defect that caused the damage.

While rejecting plaintiff's right to recover in strict liability, Chief Justice Traynor observed that the law of sales has been carefully articulated to govern economic relationships between suppliers and consumers. He stated further that strict liability was not intended to undermine the warranty provisions of the U.C.C., but "to govern the distinct problem of physical injuries." *Seely, supra,* 63 *Cal.*2d at 15, 45 *Cal.Rptr.* at 21, 403 *P.*2d at 149.

In a concurring and dissenting opinion, Justice Peters embraced *Santor,* and stated that an individual consumer should be allowed to recover in strict liability for economic damages such as those sustained by Seely. *Seely, supra,* 63 *Cal.*2d at 20–22, 45 *Cal.Rptr.* at 25–27, 403 *P.*2d at 153–55. According to Justice Peters, the roles played by the parties and the nature of the transaction, not the nature of the damage, were important. *Id.* He also distinguished transactions involving consumers from those "*within* the world of commerce, where parties generally bargain on a somewhat equal plane and may be presumed to be familiar with the legal problems involved when defective goods are purchased." *Seely, supra,* 63 *Cal.*2d at 27, 45 *Cal.Rptr.* at 29, 403 *P.*2d at 157 (emphasis in original).

* * *

[The court reviewed decisions from other states and the views of commentators, the substantial majority of which favored the result in *Seely* rather than that in *Santor.*]

In the present case, which involves an action between commercial parties, we need not reconsider the *Santor* rule that an ultimate consumer may recover in strict liability for direct economic loss. To determine whether a commercial buyer may recover economic loss, however, we must reconsider the policies underlying the doctrine of strict liability and those underlying the U.C.C. Those policy considerations include, among others, the relative bargaining power of the parties and the allocation of the loss to the better risk-bearer in a modern marketing system. As a general rule, the rights and duties of a buyer and seller are determined by the law of sales, which throughout this century has been expressed first in the Uniform Sales Act and more recently in the U.C.C. As indicated, however, strict liability evolved as a judicial response to inadequacies in sales law with respect to consumers who sustained physical injuries from defective goods made or distributed by remote parties in the marketing chain.

The considerations that give rise to strict liability do not obtain between commercial parties with comparable bargaining power. *Iowa Elec. Light & Power Co. v. Allis-Chalmers Mfg. Co., supra,* 360 *F.Supp.* at 32 (stating doctrine of strict liability loses all meaning when plaintiff is a large company suing for commercial loss). Furthermore, perfect parity is not necessary to a determination that parties have substantially equal bargaining positions. *Cf. Moreira Constr. Co., Inc. v. Moretrench Corp.,* 97 *N.J.Super.* 391, 394–95, 235 *A.*2d 211 (App.Div.1967), *aff'd o.b.,* 51 *N.J.* 405, 241 *A.*2d 236 (1968) (refusing to apply rule of *Santor* to suit between corporations even though plaintiff was a small company and defendant was the world's largest well point company). Suffice it to state that Spring Motors had sufficient bargaining power to persuade Ford to install Clark transmissions in the trucks that were the subject of the contract.

Insofar as risk allocation and distribution are concerned, Spring Motors is at least as well situated as the defendants to assess the impact of economic loss. Indeed, a commercial buyer, such as Spring Motors, may be better situated than the manufacturer to factor into its price the risk of economic loss caused by the purchase of a defective product. *See* Note, "Economic Loss in Products Liability Jurisprudence," *supra,* 66 *Colum.L.Rev.* at 952–58.

Presumably the price paid by Spring Motors for the trucks reflected the fact that Ford was liable for repair or replacement of parts only. By seeking to impose the risk of loss on Ford, Spring Motors seeks, in effect, to obtain a better bargain than it made. In such a context, the imposition of the risk of loss on the manufacturer might lead to price increases for all of its customers, including individual consumers. *Id.* at 956–57. As between commercial parties, then, the allocation of risks in accordance with their agreement better serves the public interest than an allocation achieved as a matter of policy without reference to that agreement.

Delineation of the boundary between strict liability and the U.C.C. requires appreciation not only of the policy considerations underlying both sets of principles, but also of the role of the Legislature as a coordinate branch of government. By enacting the U.C.C., the Legislature adopted a carefully-conceived system of rights and remedies to govern commercial transactions. Allowing Spring Motors to recover from Ford under tort principles would dislocate major provisions of the Code. For example, application of tort principles would obviate the statutory requirement that a buyer give notice of a breach of warranty, *N.J.S.A.* 12A:2–607, and would deprive the seller of the ability to exclude or limit its liability, *N.J.S.A.* 12A:2–316. In sum, the U.C.C. represents a comprehensive statutory scheme that satisfies the needs of the world of commerce, and courts should pause before extending judicial doctrines that might dislocate the legislative structure.

By allowing this case to proceed under strict liability principles, the Appellate Division erred, * * * it relied too heavily on *Santor,* which did not consider the effect of the U.C.C. on a commercial transaction.

* * *

For the preceding reasons, we hold that a commercial buyer seeking damages for economic loss only should proceed under the U.C.C. against parties in the chain of distribution. Hence, we reverse that part of the judgment of the Appellate Division that permitted Spring Motors to maintain against the defendants an action in strict liability for economic loss.

III

What we have said about Spring Motors' strict liability claim applies substantially to its negligence claim. Underlying that conclusion is the principle that a seller's duty of care generally stops short of creating a right in a commercial buyer to recover a purely economic loss. Thus viewed, the definition of the seller's duty reflects a policy choice that economic losses inflicted by a seller of goods are better resolved under principles of contract law. In that context, economic interests traditionally have not been entitled to protection against mere negligence.

* * *

Although the nature of the damage may be a useful point of distinction, it also signals more subtle differences in the roles that tort and contract play in our legal system. The differences include judicial evaluation of the status, relationship, and expectations of the parties; the ability of the parties to protect themselves against the risk of loss either by contractual provision or by insurance, and the manner in which the loss occurred. *See Pennsylvania Glass Sand Corp. v. Caterpillar Tractor Co.,* 652 *F.*2d 1165, 1173 (3rd Cir.1981) (allowing recovery for damage to defective machinery resulting from fire caused by defect). This evaluation reflects, among other things, policy choices about the relative roles of contracts and tort law as sources of legal obligations. As among commercial parties in a direct chain of distribution, contract law, expressed here through the U.C.C., provides the more appropriate system for adjudicating disputes arising from frustrated economic expectations.

* * *

It follows from our determination that Spring Motors should be restricted to its U.C.C. remedies as against Ford and Turnpike Ford that the appropriate statute of limitations is the four-year time bar contained in *N.J.S.A.* 12A:2–725. More than four years elapsed between the date of the delivery of the trucks and the institution of this action against Ford and Turnpike Ford. Consequently, Spring Motors' suit against them is time-barred.

We also conclude that Spring Motors should be restricted to its U.C.C. remedies against Clark, which are time-barred because of the expiration of the four-year period of limitations provided by the Code. The trial court dismissed Spring Motors' warranty claim against Clark not because of late filing, but because of lack of privity, and the Appellate Division affirmed the dismissal of the warranty claim. 191 *N.J.Super.* at 48, 465 *A.*2d 530. Spring Motors did not cross-petition for certification on that issue and has not pursued it before us. Nonetheless, as we subsequently explain, we conclude that the better rule is to restrict parties that are part of a single distributive chain to the U.C.C. in a suit for economic loss arising out of a commercial transaction. Prosser & Keeton, *supra,* § 101 at 708.

We conclude that the absence of privity between a remote supplier and an ultimate purchaser should not preclude the extension to the purchaser of the supplier's warranties made to the manufacturer. We reach that conclusion notwithstanding our recognition that the Code generally applies to parties in privity, *Herbstman v. Eastman Kodak Co.,* 68 *N.J.* 1, 9–10, 342 *A.*2d 181 (1975); *Heavner v. Uniroyal, Inc., supra,* 63 *N.J.* at 150, 305 *A.*2d 412, and that no privity exists between Spring Motors and Clark.

Privity, the relationship between two contracting parties, developed as a means of limiting relief on warranties. At this late date, little purpose would be served by a lengthy discussion of the erosion of privity as a defense in modern products liability law. * * *

More recently, strict liability in New Jersey has evolved as a means of permitting a consumer to recover for physical damage and direct economic loss against a remote seller, notwithstanding the absence of privity. Insofar as indirect economic losses arising out of a commercial transaction between business entities are concerned, we believe that the U.C.C., not tort law, provides the more appropriate analytical framework. By recognizing the supervening role of the U.C.C. in that context, we come closer to fulfilling the expectations of the parties and the intent of the Legislature. The intended effect of our decision is to satisfy the combined, if occasionally contending, goals of simplifying the law pertaining to business transactions and providing a system of compensation that responds to the needs of the commercial world.

Fundamental to our decision is the role of privity in modern business law, a role that is often described in terms of vertical and horizontal relationships. A vertical relationship describes one that exists between parties in a distributive chain, *i.e.,* between a manufacturer, wholesaler, retailer, and ultimate buyer. A buyer within this chain that did not buy goods directly from the named defendant would be a "vertical non-privity plaintiff" as to that defendant. 2 Hawkland, *supra,* § 2–318:01 at 419; White & Summers, *supra,* § 11–2 at 399. Here, Spring Motors, which purchased the trucks from Ford, is in vertical privity with the Ford defendants, but not with Clark. Thus, Spring Motors is a vertical non-privity plaintiff as to Clark.

"Horizontal non-privity," on the other hand, describes the relationship between the retailer and someone, other than the buyer, who has used or consumed the goods. For example, in an action against a retailer, a "horizontal non-privity plaintiff" would refer to the buyer's spouse or child, but not to the buyer. White & Summers, *supra,* § 11–2 at 399.

In drafting the U.C.C., the Commissioners on Uniform State Laws acknowledged the decline of horizontal privity as a defense to an action for personal injuries caused by the purchase of defective goods. Consequently, section 318, adopted in New Jersey as *N.J.S.A.* 12A:2–318 and now identified as "Alternative A," extends warranties horizontally to "any natural person who is in the family or household of [the] buyer or who is a guest in his home if it is reasonable to expect that such person may use, consume, or be affected by the goods and who is injured in person by breach of the warranty." With respect to vertical privity, the drafters specifically state that the section is "neutral and is not intended to enlarge or restrict the developing case law on whether the seller's warranties, given to his buyer who resells, extend to other persons in the distributive chain." Official Comment 3, § 2–318.

Courts in some states that have adopted Alternative A, however, have abolished the requirement of horizontal privity and allowed "any person," natural or legal, to sue a party in the distributive chain for breach of warranty. *See, e.g., Salvador v. Atlantic Steel Boiler Co.,* 457 *Pa.* 24, 26, 319 *A.*2d 903, 904 (1974) (lack of horizontal privity may no longer bar the plaintiff from recovering for personal injuries under breach of warranty); *JKT Co., Inc. v. Hardwick,* 274 *S.C.* 413, 416, 265 *S.E.*2d 510, 512 (1980) (no valid reason exists for distinguishing between consumer plaintiffs and corporate plaintiffs on the issue of horizontal privity).

In other states, legislatures have refused to adopt Alternative A. California was the first to criticize the section as "a step backward" and to omit the section from its version of the Code. Permanent Editorial Board note, following Official Comment to section 2–318. Still other states developed variants of section 318. In 1966, to stem the proliferation of non-uniform provisions, the members of the Permanent Editorial Board of the U.C.C. recommended Alternatives B and C. *Id.;* 3 Anderson, *Uniform Commercial Code UCC,* § 2–318:2 at 400 (3rd ed.1983) [hereinafter cited as Anderson]. Respectively, these alternatives provide that:

ALTERNATIVE B

> A seller's warranty whether express or implied extends to any natural person who may reasonably be expected to use, consume or be affected by the goods and who is injured in person by breach of the warranty. A seller may not exclude or limit the operation of this section.

ALTERNATIVE C

A seller's warranty whether express or implied extends to any person who may reasonably be expected to use, consume or be affected by the goods and who is injured by breach of the warranty. A seller may not exclude or limit the operation of this section with respect to injury of the person of an individual to whom the warranty extends.

Alternatives B and C go beyond Alternative A in eroding the privity defense. Alternative C, for example, allows "any person" on the horizontal level, including a corporation, to sue for breach of warranty. *Cf. N.J.S.A.* 12A:1–201(30) (defining person as an individual or an organization) and *N.J.S.A.* 12A:1–201(28) (defining organization as including a corporation). Some treatises declare that Alternative C eliminates the requirement of vertical privity, 2 Hawkland, *supra,* § 2–318:04 at 430; Anderson, *supra,* § 2–318:31 at 417, but another text disagrees, White & Summers, *supra,* §§ 11–5 to –6 at 406–10.

The Permanent Editorial Board's comment on Alternative C states that the section reflects "the trend of more recent decisions as indicated by Restatement of Torts 2d § 402A * * *, extending the rule beyond personal injuries." As previously indicated, in most jurisdictions section 402A precludes claims for economic loss. In New Jersey, however, a consumer may recover direct economic loss in a strict liability action against a remote supplier. *Santor v. A & M Karagheusian, Inc., supra,* 44 *N.J.* 52, 207 *A.*2d 305. Because the Code provides the more appropriate framework for resolving disputes between commercial entities, we eschew permitting recovery by a business entity for economic loss under principles of strict liability. Nonetheless, it is consistent with the principles underlying *Santor* and with the intent of the Code's drafters to recognize a claim under the U.C.C. for economic loss in a breach of warranty action without regard to vertical privity.

Furthermore, a plaintiff in a suit for breach of warranty against a remote seller, like a plaintiff in a strict liability action, need not establish privity with or negligence by the defendant. To this extent, our recognition of a warranty action for economic loss by a commercial buyer parallels our recognition in *Santor* of a similar claim by a consumer. One significant difference, of course, is that the plaintiff in a warranty action need not establish the existence of a defect; the failure of the goods to perform as warranted is sufficient. By bringing the action within the ambit of the Code, we believe we come closer to fulfilling the expectations of the parties and the intention of the Legislature that the Code should govern commercial transactions.

* * *

Eliminating the requirement of vertical privity is particularly appropriate in the present action where Spring Motors read advertisements published by Clark, specifically requested Clark transmissions, expected the transmissions to be incorporated into trucks to be manufactured by Ford, contracted with Ford only, and now seeks to recover its economic loss. Given the nature of the transaction and the expectations of the parties, the absence of a direct contractual relationship should not preclude Spring Motors from asserting a cause of action for breach of express warranty against Clark. Because the Code, not principles of tort law, governs the relationship between Spring Motors and Clark, the appropriate period of limitations is that provided by the Code. As previously indicated, the expiration of this period bars Spring Motors' claim against Clark.

Because any action by Spring Motors against Clark is time-barred, we need not determine the outer limits of a suit by an ultimate purchaser against a remote supplier for economic loss. Therefore, we reserve determination on the effectiveness of a remote manufacturer's disclaimer or limitation on express and implied warranties to an ultimate purchaser that did not have the opportunity to negotiate over the terms of the agreement. *N.J.S.A.* 12A:2–316: *N.J.S.A.* 12A:2–719. White & Summers, *supra,* § 11–6 at 409 (the extent to which a remote seller may disclaim warranties is an unresolved issue). We note, however, that in certain circumstances a buyer may recover incidental and consequential damages. *N.J.S.A.* 12A:2–715. We also leave unreviewed the Code requirement that a purchaser notify the seller about the defective condition of the product. *N.J.S.A.* 12A:2–607(3). Similarly, we do not resolve whether a warranty of fitness for a particular purpose, unlike an implied warranty of merchantability, extends only to parties in privity with the seller. *See Pawelec v. Digitcom, Inc.,* 192 *N.J.Super.* 474, 477–78, 471 *A.*2d 60 (App.Div.1984) (holding that implied warranty of fitness for a particular purpose, unlike implied warranty of merchantability, requires privity). For our purposes, it is sufficient to acknowledge that a commercial buyer in a distributive chain may maintain an action under the U.C.C. for purely economic loss arising out of a breach of warranty by a remote supplier.

Accordingly, we reverse the judgment of the Appellate Division and reinstate the dismissal of the complaint as to all defendants.

* * *

[Justice Handler concurred in the result. He concluded that the Court's ruling on privity was, in essence, dictum because of the interaction between Clark and Spring Motors, both before and after the purchase. In short, the privity ruling was attenuated. In addition, he expressed reservations about whether Spring Motors, a commercial buyer, needed the extra protection, when it was capable of bargaining with the dealer or Ford. Although an imbalance in capacity between even commercial parties might justify a direct suit against the manufacturer, no such imbalance was evident in this case.]

Problem 20–6

Suppose, in *Spring Motors,* that the transmissions manufactured by Clark were unmerchantable, UCC 2–314(2). Furthermore, assume that Spring Motors had purchased the trucks from Ford without knowing whose transmissions would be used and, after the problems arose, Ford not Clark made all efforts to "cure." Finally, assume that Spring Motors suffered substantial direct and consequential economic loss caused by the transmissions.

1. Under the reasoning in Spring Motors, can Spring Motors sue Clark under a warranty theory for economic losses caused by the unmerchantable transmissions? Why?

2. If the privity defense is no bar, which if any of Article 2's limitations upon warranty claims should apply to Spring Motors?

Problem 20–7

B, a commercial fisherman, owns a fishing vessel powered by two diesel engines. B needs extra power to reach distant fishing grounds and to operate gear designed for dragging the bottom. S, a dealer, recently sold and installed a new diesel engine in the boat. The engine was manufactured by M but B dealt only with S, who knew B's particular needs, and relied upon S to obtain a suitable engine. In the contract for sale, however, S limited its liability for any breach of warranty to repair and replacement of defective parts and excluded any liability for consequential damages.

Assume that this limitation is effective between S and B. M, in turn, had limited its liability to S in a similar manner.

Shortly thereafter, when B was on the fishing grounds some 60 miles from port, a loud "crack" was heard and smoke poured from the new engine. The engine was quickly shut down and, although the smoke stopped, the engine would not start. When B returned to port, limping under one engine, S discovered that a defective part, manufactured by C, had disintegrated within, and had caused substantial damage to, the engine. Furthermore, B learned that he had missed a "truly remarkable" run on King Crabs at the spot where the engine malfunctioned.

S informed B that the entire engine should be replaced and that this form of "cure" was beyond the scope of the limited warranty.

1. Assess the strength of B's warranty claims, if any, against M and C.

2. Would B have a tort claim against either or both? What difference would it make?

CHAPTER TWENTY ONE

BUYER'S REMEDIES FOR BREACH OF WARRANTY FOR ACCEPTED GOODS UNDER THE CODE AND PER AGREEMENT (HEREIN, TOO, OF DISCLAIMERS)

SECTION 1. INTRODUCTION

First, some words in summary. If the commercial buyer can establish that a warranty was made and breached, the timing of that discovery will be critical to the available remedy choices. If the breach was discovered before acceptance, then rejection may be a proper remedy. UCC 2–601. If the breach was discovered after acceptance and the buyer acts fast, a revocation of acceptance may be proper under UCC 2–608. In both cases, the goods are "thrown back" at the seller. Unless the seller has a right to cure under UCC 2–508 or under the contract, the seller is basically responsible for disposing of the goods and the buyer may shoot for the remedies contained in UCC 2–711.

But our buyer may never reach this position, either because he wants to accept the goods despite their defects, or because he is unable to reject or revoke acceptance, or because the breach may have rendered the goods worthless. What then? Again, if the buyer has given proper notice under UCC 2–607(3), initiated suit before the statute of limitations expires, UCC 2–725, and established that a warranty was made to him and breached, the remedies for breach with regard to accepted goods are available. See UCC 2–714 & 2–715.

In this Chapter, we will, first, explore the scope of protection under these sections. Next we will consider the extent to which the seller can, by agreement with the buyer, disclaim warranties under UCC 2–316 and alter remedies and exclude consequential damages under UCC 2–719.

SECTION 2. THE DIRECT DAMAGE FORMULA: UCC 2–714

UCC 2–714, entitled "Buyer's Damages for Breach in Regard to Accepted Goods," is a functional counterpart of UCC 2–712 and UCC 2–713. All three sections attempt to preserve the benefit of the buyer's bargain with the seller. See UCC 1–106(1). Under UCC 2–714, however, the buyer still has the goods and is liable for their price, UCC 2–607(1), & 2–719(1)(a), subject to the power, upon notice to the seller, to "deduct all or any part of the damages resulting from any breach of the contract from any part of the price still due under the same contract." UCC 2–717. Furthermore, UCC 2–714 is somewhat open-ended and difficult to apply with precision. For example:

1. UCC 2–714(2) provides the measure of damages for breach of warranty. To what disputes does UCC 2–714(1) apply? How does one determine what losses resulted "in the ordinary course of events from the seller's breach as determined by any manner which is reasonable?"

2. In UCC 2–714(2), how does the buyer prove the "difference at the time and place of acceptance between the value of goods accepted and the value they would have had if they had been as warranted?"

3. In UCC 2–714(2), what "special circumstances" show proximate damages of a different amount?

4. How is the line between "direct" damages under UCC 2–714(2) and "incidental and consequential damages" under UCC 2–715 to be drawn?

Problem 21–1

1. Sunshine Cannery contracted on May 1 to purchase 10,000 bushels of # 1 grade tomatoes for $10 a bushel from Seller, a grower. The market price at that time was $8 a bushel. On August 10, the time for delivery, Seller tendered 10,000 bushels of # 2 grade tomatoes. Caught at the end of the canning season, Sunshine accepted the goods. The market value of the tomatoes accepted was $7 per bushel. The market value of # 1 grade tomatoes was $9 per bushel. Seller claims the contract price of $100,000. What damages may Sunshine deduct under UCC 2–714(2)?

2. Assume, above, that at the time of acceptance # 1 tomatoes had risen in value to $12 per bushel and # 2 tomatoes were worth $9 per bushel. What damages?

3. Suppose, in (1) above, the Seller tendered and Sunshine accepted what passed in the trade as # 1 tomatoes. Upon unpacking, however, the entire lot was found to be decayed and suffering from the notorious Law School Rot. Sunshine salvaged the lot for $1,000 and replaced it from another grower for $13 per bushel. What damages? Should Sunshine recover the difference between the replacement cost and the salvage value?

SOO LINE RAILROAD CO. v. FRUEHAUF CORP.

United States Court of Appeals, Eighth Circuit, 1977.
547 F.2d 1365.

[Fruehauf agreed to manufacture, sell and deliver 500 railroad hopper cars to Soo Line for the approximate price of $9,750,000. After delivery, Soo Line discovered cracks in the structure and weld of many cars. Fruehauf refused to repair, claiming it had no responsibility for the alleged defects, and Soo implemented its own program of repair at a total cost of $506,862.78. Soo Line brought suit on the theories of breach of warranty and negligence. The jury found for Soo Line on the warranty theory and the trial court ruled as a matter of law that certain contract provisions were ineffective to limit Fruehauf's liability. The jury, in a special verdict, awarded Soo Line $975,970 "for the difference between the value of the cars as accepted and their value if built to conform to the contract specifications" and additional amounts for consequential and incidental damages. The verdict on the "difference in value" issue reflected that Soo Line's repairs "did not fully restore the cars to totally acceptable operating condition." Fruehauf appealed. The trial court's judgment was affirmed.]

STEPHENSON, CIRCUIT JUDGE.

* * *

III.

The third issue in this appeal is whether the district court erred in allowing the testimony of T.R. Klingel, an expert witness who testified with respect to the diminution in value of the railroad cars resulting from their structural collapse.

In general, Klingel expressed the opinion that the market value of the railcars as actually constructed was approximately $1,000,000 or $2,000 per car less than the value of the cars had they been built in accordance with the contract.

Klingel, who is executive vice president of Soo Line, testified initially that the market value of the railcars had they been constructed according to the contract would have approximated their purchase price of $19,500 per car. He further expressed the opinion, over Magor's objection, that the fair market value of the cars as actually constructed was at the most $17,500 per car. Klingel's opinion, as to the diminution in fair market value of the railcars, basically derived from his viewpoint that a hypothetical buyer of the cars would be confronted with immediate and substantial expenditures for repair and continuation of financing costs without any concomitant receipt of revenue while the railcars were out of service being repaired, and even after the repairs the buyer would possess rebuilt and patched cars worth less than those properly constructed.

Appellant contends that the trial court erred in allowing Klingel's testimony on damages. In Magor's view, Klingel was not qualified to provide expert opinion on the necessity and cost of repair because he allegedly did not possess sufficient practical or technical knowledge. Magor asserts additionally that Klingel's prediction of future maintenance costs was speculatively improper without proof that such damages are reasonably certain to occur. Finally, Magor claims that Klingel's reliance on financing costs as a basis for damages erroneously resulted in a duplicate consequential damage award for revenue lost while the railcars were being repaired.

The trial court's determination that Klingel possessed adequate qualifications, pursuant to Fed.R.Evid. 702, to testify with respect to the diminished market value of the railcars was not an abuse of discretion or clear error of law. * * * Fed.R.Evid. 702 is not limited to experts in the strictest sense of the word but also encompasses a large group called "skilled" witnesses, such as owners, bankers, and landowners testifying on the value of property. * * *

Klingel's responsibilities as Soo Line's executive vice president included overseeing the operations of all trains and the maintenance of all rolling stock and fixed property. He also was charged with determination of the market value of the railroad's rolling stock. Klingel was directly familiar with the railcars manufactured by Magor, and he collaborated closely with Soo Line's mechanical department and H.D. Hollis concerning the problematic conditions in the Magor-constructed railcars. In some instances, Klingel conducted personal inspections of the railcars. Klingel's knowledge was such that his opinion on valuation most likely assisted the trier of fact in arriving at the truth. * * *

In reviewing the substance of Klingel's testimony on valuation, the measure of damages and the limits of relevancy are set by the substantive law of Minnesota. See Johnson v. Serra, 521 F.2d 1289, 1294 (8th Cir.1975). Under Minnesota law, the measure of damages applicable to breach of contract is the difference between the actual value of the cars at the time of acceptance and the value they would have had if they had been as warranted. Minn.Stat.Ann. § 336.2–714(2). * * * The buyer is not limited to repair costs when repair does not completely restore the goods to the value which they would have had if built in conformity with the contract; remaining diminution in value may also be recovered. * * *

Taking into consideration the structural and welding defects existing in the cars manufactured for Soo Line by Magor, Klingel expressed the opinion that the reasonable market value per car was $17,500 at the most. Klingel further opined that he would probably discount the purchase price of the cars by an additional $1,000 or $2,000, which would result in a fair market value of approximately $15,500 per car.

In formulating the diminution in fair market value of the cars, Klingel properly placed reliance on the necessity for present and future repairs and the fact that even a rebuilt patched railcar would be worth less than a correctly constructed one. * * * The record reflects that approximately $1,000 per car in immediate repair costs was expended by Soo Line and that, even after implementation of the repairs, Soo Line had experienced continued maintenance costs beyond those expended for cars other than those manufactured by Magor.

Klingel also stated that a hypothetical buyer of the railcars would discount the purchase price because the buyer's financing costs would continue while the cars were out of service being repaired with no ability to generate revenue. Klingel testified that approximately $200,000 and $400 per car in interest payments would be lost without concomitant benefit during repairs. This statement, of course, may not be considered as evidence of diminution in value of the Soo Line railcars. Cost of financing is not an element of reduced market value pursuant to Minn.Stat.Ann. § 336.2–714. Nonetheless, we reject appellant's contention that this aspect of Klingel's testimony rendered inadmissible his overall opinion on the diminution in market value of the railcars. An objection that an expert's opinion is based on elements of damage not lawfully recoverable generally relates to the weight rather than the admissibility of the testimony. * * *

In addition, the trial court carefully instructed the jury with respect to this element of damages. It stated in part as follows:

> "The measure of damages is, generally speaking, the difference between the fair market value of the cars as accepted by Soo Line, and the fair market value they would have had if they had not been deficient in the particulars in which you found them deficient. This is called the difference or diminution in value approach.
>
> * * *
>
> "If you find that the repair of the cars restored the cars to substantially the same condition as they would have been in if properly manufactured, the difference or diminution value is the same as the reasonable cost of repairing the cars.
>
> "So, if the repair costs actually restored them then the repair cost would equal the diminution in value. However, if you find that the repair of the cars did not restore them to substantially the same condition as they would have been if properly manufactured, then the difference or diminution in value is the reasonable cost of repair, plus the difference between the fair market value of the covered hopper cars if they had been manufactured without faults or defects, and the fair market value of the repairs.
>
> "The total figure, however, cannot exceed the difference between the fair market value as accepted, and the fair market value in the defective condition you find.
>
> " * * * [The court then gave an illustration.]
>
> "Therefore, if you find that the repairs of the cars placed the cars in a better condition than they would have been at the time of acceptance if they had been properly manufactured, then the difference or diminution in value

recoverable by plaintiffs is the difference between the fair market value of the covered hopper cars as accepted by Soo Line and the fair market value they would have had if Magor had manufactured them properly. So, Soo Line in this situation would not be able to recover the full amount spent for repairs.

"In the course of the charge and the special verdict you will find use of the word value. Value is described as the highest price in terms of money for which a product would have sold on the open market, the seller having a reasonable time within which to sell and being willing to sell but not forced to do so; the buyer being ready, willing and able to buy, but not forced to do so, and a full opportunity to inspect the property in question and to determine its condition, suitability for use, and all things about the property that would naturally and reasonably affect its market value."

Moreover, there is sufficient evidence in the record upon which the jury could have relied in awarding $975,970 or $1,951.94 per car, approximately 10% of their original cost, for diminution in market value of the cars. It cannot be said that the verdict constituted a shocking result. * * *

For similar reasons, we reject appellant's assertion that Klingel's reference to "future maintenance costs" was unduly speculative and erroneous. Klingel merely expressed an opinion on the present value of the railcars at the time of acceptance in light of known risks associated with existing defects. Soo Line had already experienced increased maintenance costs with Magor cars previously repaired. Klingel's testimony overall had sufficient probative value to outweigh the danger that it would lead the jury to assess damages on an improper basis. * * * Magor had adequate opportunity to cross-examine and refute Klingel's testimony on valuation. * * * Under these circumstances, we conclude that the trial court did not commit an abuse of discretion in the admission of Klingel's testimony concerning the diminution in market value of the railroad cars resulting from their structural failure.

* * *

[Footnotes omitted]

CHATLOS SYSTEMS, INC. v. NATIONAL CASH REGISTER CORP.

United States Court of Appeals, Third Circuit, 1982.
479 F.Supp. 738 (D.N.J.1979), *affirmed in part, remanded in part,* 635 F.2d 1081 (3d Cir.1980), *decision of District Court on remand affirmed,* 670 F.2d 1304 (3d Cir. 1982), *motion for rehearing denied,* 33 U.C.C.Rep.Serv. 935.

[In July 1974, National Cash Register Corporation (NCR) sold Chatlos Systems, Inc. (Chatlos) an NCR 399/656 disc computer system (NCR 399). The base price of $46,020 included the computer (hardware) for $40,165 and the software, consisting of 6 computer programs, for $5,855. In addition, Chatlos's paid NCR $5,621 for a service agreement and agreed to finance the purchase through a lease from a third party to whom Chatlos sold the system. Chatlos's total cost, including finance charges, for the system was $75,783.

NCR expressly warranted that the six computer programs, e.g., accounts receivable, payroll, order entry, inventory deletion, state income tax and cash receipts, would meet Chatlos's particular business needs. For breach of warranty, however, NCR limited its obligation to the repair or replacement of defective parts or workmanship and excluded any liability for consequential damages.

The hardware was delivered in December, 1974. Despite the presence of a programmer, sent by NCR, and continuing efforts to "cure" by NCR, only two of the programs, payroll and state taxes, functioned properly. The hardware furnished would not operate the other programs to satisfy Chatlos's needs. For example, the system could not delete selected information on a disc without deleting all of the information stored. Efforts to "cure" were discontinued in September, 1976.

Chatlos sued NCR for damages resulting from a breach of warranty. The district court awarded Chatlos damages of $57,153 under UCC 2–714(2), the difference between the value of the system as warranted, $75,783, and the value of the system delivered, $18,630. In addition, the district court awarded consequential and incidental damages of $63,560 under UCC 2–715, for a total recovery of $120,711.

On remand, the district court, on the basis of the previous record made in the case, fixed the fair market value of the NCR 399 as warranted at the time of acceptance at $207,826.50. It reached that figure by valuing a hypothetical system, i.e., the hardware that should have been supplied, at $131,250 and the software that would have functioned as warranted at $76,575.50, for a total of $207,826.50. The court then determined that the present value of the computer hardware, which Chatlos retained, was $6,000. Putting no value on the accepted payroll program, the court deducted the $6,000 and arrived at an award of $201,826.50 plus prejudgment interest of 8 percent. NCR appealed again to the Court of Appeals.]

PER CURIAM.

[The court stated that the question was whether the district court erred in its determination of damages under UCC 2–714(2), which provides: "The measure of damages for breach of warranty is the difference at the time and place of acceptance between the value of the goods accepted and the value they would have had if they had been as warranted, unless special circumstances show proximate damages of a different amount."]

* * *

Waiving the opportunity to submit additional evidence as to value on the remand which we directed, appellant chose to rely on the record of the original trial and submitted no expert testimony on the market value of a computer which would have performed the functions NCR had warranted. Notwithstanding our previous holding that contract price was not necessarily the same as market value, 635 F.2d at 1088, appellant faults the district judge for rejecting its contention that the contract price for the NCR 399/656 was the only competent record evidence of the value of the system as warranted. The district court relied instead on the testimony of plaintiff-appellee's expert, Dick Brandon, who, without estimating the value of an NCR model 399/656, presented his estimate of the value of a computer system that would perform all of the functions that the NCR 399/656 had been warranted to perform. Brandon did not limit his estimate to equipment of any one manufacturer; he testified regarding manufacturers who could have made systems that would perform the functions that appellant had warranted the NCR 399/656 could perform. He acknowledged that the systems about which he testified were not in the same price range as the NCR 399/656. Appellant likens this testimony to substituting a Rolls Royce for a Ford, and concludes that the district court's recomputed damage award was therefore clearly contrary to the evidence of fair market value—which in NCR's view is the contract price itself.

Appellee did not order, nor was it promised, merely a specific NCR computer model, but an NCR computer system with specified capabilities. The correct measure of damages, under N.J.Stat.Ann. § 12A:2–714(2), is the difference between the fair market value of the goods accepted and the value they would have had if they had been as warranted. Award of that sum is not confined to instances where there has been an increase in value between date of ordering and date of delivery. It may also include the benefit of a contract price which, for whatever reason quoted, was particularly favorable for the customer. Evidence of the contract price may be relevant to the fair market value, but it is not controlling. Mulvaney v. Tri State Truck & Auto Body, Inc., 70 Wis.2d 760, 767, 235 N.W.2d 460, 465 (1975). Appellant limited its fair market value analysis to the contract price of the computer model it actually delivered.[3] Appellee developed evidence of the worth of a computer with the capabilities promised by NCR, and the trial court properly credited the evidence.[4]

Appellee was aided, moreover, by the testimony of Frank Hicks, NCR's programmer, who said that he told his company's officials that the "current software was not sufficient in order to deliver the program that the customer [Chatlos] required. They would have to be rewritten or a different system would have to be given to the customer." Appendix to Brief for Appellee at 2.68. Hicks recommended that Chatlos be given an NCR 8200 but was told, "that will not be done." Id. at 2.69. Gerald Greenstein, another NCR witness, admitted that the 8200 series was two levels above the 399 in sophistication and price. Id. at 14.30. This testimony supported Brandon's statement that the price of the hardware needed to perform Chatlos' requirements would be in the $100,000 to $150,000 range.

Essentially, then, the trial judge was confronted with the conflicting value estimates submitted by the parties. Chatlos' expert's estimates were corroborated to some extent by NCR's supporters. NCR, on the other hand, chose to rely on contract price. Credibility determinations had to be made by the district judge. Although we might have come to a different conclusion on the value of the equipment as warranted had we been sitting as trial judges, we are not free to make our own credibility and factual findings. We may reverse the district court only if its factual determinations were clearly erroneous. Krasnov v. Dinan, 465 F.2d 1298 (3d Cir.1972).[5]

3. At oral argument, counsel for appellant responded to questions from the bench, as follows:

Judge Rosenn: "Your position also is that you agree, number one, that the fair market value is the measure of damages here."

Counsel for Appellant: "Yes, sir."

Judge Rosenn: "The fair market value you say, in the absence of other evidence to the contrary that is relevant, is the contract price. That is the evidence of fair market value."

Counsel: "That's right."

Judge Rosenn: "Now seeing that had the expert or had the plaintiff been able to establish testimony that there were other machines on the market that were similar to your machine—"

Counsel: "Yes."

Judge Rosenn: "That the fair market value of those was $50,000, that would have been relevant evidence but it had to be the same machine—same type machine."

Counsel: "Well, I would say that the measure of damages as indicated by the statute requires the same machine—'the goods'—in an operable position."

4. We find the following analogy, rather than the Rolls Royce-Ford analogy submitted by appellant, to be on point:

Judge Weis: "If you start thinking about a piece of equipment that is warranted to lift a thousand pounds and it will only lift 500 pounds, then the cost of something that will lift a thousand pounds gives you more of an idea and that may be—"

Counsel for Appellee: "That may be a better analogy, yes."

Judge Weis: "Yes."

5. The dissent essentially is based on disagreement with the estimates provided by

Upon reviewing the evidence of record, therefore, we conclude that the computation of damages for breach of warranty was not clearly erroneous. We hold also that the district court acted within its discretion in awarding prejudgment interest, Chatlos Systems, Inc. v. National Cash Register Corp., 635 F.2d at 1088.

The judgment of the district court will be affirmed.

ROSENN, CIRCUIT JUDGE, dissenting. The primary question in this appeal involves the application of Article 2 of the Uniform Commercial Code as adopted by New Jersey in N.J.S.A. 12A:2-101 et seq. (1962) to the measure of damages for breach of warranty in the sale of a computer system. I respectfully dissent because I believe there is no probative evidence to support the district court's award of damages for the breach of warranty in a sum amounting to almost five times the purchase price of the goods. The measure of damages also has been misapplied and this could have a significant effect in the marketplace, especially for the unique and burgeoning computer industry.

* * *

Chatlos contends before this court, as it had before the district court on remand, that under its benefit of the bargain theory the fair market value of the goods as warranted was several times the purchase price of $46,020. As the purchaser, Chatlos had the burden of proving the extent of the loss. Council Brothers, Inc. v. Ray Burner Co., 473 F.2d 400, 408 (5th Cir.1973). In remanding to the district court for a reassessment of the damages, we did not reject the contract price for the goods sold as the proper valuation of the computer as warranted. We merely corrected the district court's misconception that the language of the New Jersey statute precluded consideration of fair market value. We held that "value" in § 2-714(2) must mean fair market value at the time and place of acceptance. We pointed out:

> "*It may be assumed that in many cases* fair market value and contract price are the same, and therefore, if a party wishes to show a difference between the two he should produce evidence to that effect."

Chatlos Systems, Inc. v. National Cash Register Corp., 635 F.2d 1081, 1088 (3d Cir.1980) (emphasis added) on remand, No. 77-2548 (D NJ. filed Mar. 12, 1981). Thus, the sole issue before us now is whether the district court erred in fixing the fair market value of the computer system as warranted at the time of acceptance in August 1975 at $207,826.50.

II.

A.

I believe that the district court committed legal error. The majority conclude that the standard of review of the district court's determination of the fair market value of the goods for the purpose of awarding damages is whether the trial judge's determination of market value is clearly erroneous. I disagree. Had the court merely miscalculated the amount of damages, I might agree with the majority's standard, for then our concern would be with basic facts. Here, however, no evidence was introduced as to the market value of the specific goods purchased and accepted had the system conformed to the warranty. Thus, the matter before us is one of legal error, and our standard of review is plenary. But even under the standard applied by the majority, the district court should be

Chatlos' expert, Brandon. The record reveals that he was well qualified; the weight to be given his testimony is the responsibility of the factfinder, not an appellate court.

reversed because its determination of the market value is not supported by probative evidence.

There are a number of major flaws in the plaintiff's attempt to prove damages in excess of the contract price. I commence with an analysis of plaintiff's basic theory. Chatlos presented its case under a theory that although, as a sophisticated purchaser, it bargained for several months before arriving at a decision on the computer system it required and the price of $46,020, it is entitled, because of the breach of warranty, to damages predicated on a considerably more expensive system. Stated another way, even if it bargained for a cheap system, i.e., one whose low cost reflects its inferior quality, because that system did not perform as bargained for, it is now entitled to damages measured by the value of a system which, although capable of performing the identical functions as the NCR 399, is of far superior quality and accordingly more expensive.

The statutory measure of damages for breach of warranty specifically provides that the measure is the difference at the time and place of acceptance between the value "of the goods accepted" and the "value they would have had if they had been as warranted." The focus of the statute is upon "the goods accepted"—not other hypothetical goods which may perform equivalent functions. "Moreover, the value to be considered is the reasonable market value of the *goods delivered,* not the value of the goods to a particular purchaser or for a particular purpose." KLPR–TV, Inc. v. Visual Electronics Corp., 465 F.2d 1382, 1387 (8th Cir.1972) (emphasis added). The court, however, arrived at value on the basis of a hypothetical construction of a system as of December 1978 by the plaintiff's expert, Brandon. The court reached its value by working backward from Brandon's figures, adjusting for inflation.

In presenting its case Chatlos developed its expert testimony as though it were seeking "cover" damages—the cost for the replacement of the computer system under § 2–712 of the statute. First, "cover" damages are obviously inappropriate here because both the district court and this court in its earlier decision held that the measure of damages is governed by section 2–714(2). Furthermore, Chatlos did not "cover" in this case and, although there was testimony that it would use an IBM Series 1 mini-computer to perform the NCR 399 functions, the president of Chatlos personally testified that the IBM "wasn't purchased with intent to replace the 399 system at the time of purchase." Second, Chatlos gave no evidence as to the cost of the IBM Series 1 computer system. However, under the applicable section of the statute, § 2–714, the measure of damages is specifically confined to "the difference between the value of the *goods accepted* and the value they would have had if they had been as warranted" and does not include "the difference between the cost of *cover* and the contract price" as provided by § 2–712.

Although NCR warranted performance, the failure of its equipment to perform, absent any evidence of the value of any NCR 399 system on which to base fair market value, does not permit a market value based on systems wholly unrelated to the goods sold. Yet, instead of addressing the fair market value of the NCR 399 had it been as warranted, Brandon addressed the fair market value of another system that he concocted by drawing on elements from other major computer systems manufactured by companies such as IBM, Burroughs, and Honeywell, which he considered would perform "functions identical to those contracted for" by Chatlos. He conceded that the systems were "[p]erhaps not within the same range of dollars that the bargain was involved with" and he did not identify specific packages of software. Brandon had no difficulty in arriving at the fair market value of the inoperable NCR equipment but instead of fixing a value on the system had it been operable attempted to fashion a hypothetical system on which he placed a value. The district court, in turn, erroneously adopted that value as the fair market value for an operable NCR 399 system. NCR rightly contends that the "comparable" systems on which Brandon drew were substitute goods of greater technological power and capability and not acceptable in determining damages for breach of warranty under § 2–714. Furthermore, Brandon's hypothetical system did not exist and its valuation was largely speculation.

* * *

III.

The purpose of the N.J.S.A. 12A:2–714 is to put the buyer in the same position he would have been in if there had been no breach. See Uniform Commercial Code § 1–106(1). The remedies for a breach of warranty were intended to compensate the buyer for his loss; they were not intended to give the purchaser a windfall or treasure trove. The buyer may not receive more than it bargained for; it may not obtain the value of a superior computer system which it did not purchase even though such a system can perform all of the functions the inferior system was designed to serve. Thus, in Meyers v. Antone, 227 A.2d 56 (D.C.App.1967), the court held that where the buyers contracted for a properly functioning used oil heating system which proved defective, they were free to substitute a gas system (which they did), change over to forced air heating, or even experiment with a solar heating plant. "They could not, however, recover the cost of such systems. They contracted for a used oil system that would function properly, and can neither receive more than they bargained for nor be put in a better position than they would have been had the contract been fully performed." Id. at 59 (citations omitted).

This court, in directing consideration of fair market value as the starting point in deciding damages noted Chatlos' contention that exclusive use of contract price deprives the dissatisfied buyer of the "benefit of his bargain." We accepted the concept of "benefit of the bargain" and explicated our understanding of the concept as follows:

> "If the value of the goods rises between the time the contract is executed and the time of acceptance, the buyer should not lose the advantage of a favorable contract price because of the seller's breach of warranty. Conversely, if the value drops, the seller is entitled to the resulting lower computation."

Chatlos, supra, 635 F.2d at 1088. Ironically, this example of benefit of the bargain is actually based on contract price. If on the date of acceptance the fair market value of the goods has risen or declined from the contract price, the variation must be taken into account in awarding damages. But here plaintiff's market value figures, accepted by the district court on remand, have no connection whatsoever with the contract price.

Although it may be that the "benefit of the bargain" concept is applicable to situations involving other than periodic fluctuations in market prices, the cases cited by Chatlos stand only for the premise that the proved market value of the goods in question must be accepted. * * *

Even if we were to accept plaintiff's theory that the value of other systems may be used to establish the value of the specific computer system purchased, the cases cited by Chatlos to support its theory are distinguishable. * * *

Because Brandon's testimony does not support Chatlos' grossly extravagant claim of the fair market value of the NCR 399 at the time of its acceptance, the only evidence of the market value at the time is the price negotiated by the parties for the NCR computer system as warranted.

> There are many cases in which the goods will be irreparable or not replaceable and therefore the costs of repair or replacement can not serve as a yardstick of the buyer's damages. * * * When fair market value cannot be easily determined * * * the purchase price may turn out to be strong evidence of the value of the goods as warranted.

J. White & R. Summers, Uniform Commercial Code § 10–2, at 380 (2d ed. 1980) (footnotes omitted).

* * *

Thus, where there is no proof that market value of the goods differs from the contract price, the contract price will govern, * * * and in this case that amounts to $46,020. Chatlos has retained the system hardware and the district court fixed its present value in the open market at $6,000. The court properly deducted this sum from the damages awarded.

* * *

VI.

On this record, therefore, the damages to which plaintiff is entitled are $46,020 less $6,000, the fair market value at time of trial of the retained hardware, and less $1,000, the fair market value of the payroll program, or the net sum of $39,020.

Accordingly, I would reverse the judgment of the district court and direct it to enter judgment for the plaintiff in the sum of $39,020 with interest from the date of entry of the initial judgment at the rate allowed by state law. [some footnotes omitted.]

HILL v. BASF WYANDOTTE CORP.

Supreme Court of South Carolina, 1984.
280 S.C. 174, 311 S.E.2d 734.

LITTLEJOHN, JUSTICE:

This case comes before us as a certified question from the United States District Court, District of South Carolina, pursuant to Supreme Court Rule 46.

The question presented is as follows:

> Given the distinction between (1) actual or direct and (2) consequential damages as set forth in §§ 36–2–714 and 36–2–715 of the South Carolina Code of Laws, 1976, as amended, what is the measure of actual damages in a herbicide failure case where there is a valid limitation of consequential, special or indirect damages?

This is a breach of warranty case involving an alleged herbicide failure which caused crop damage.

Plaintiff Hill (Farmer) purchased a quantity of the herbicide, Basalin, from a retail distributor. Basalin is manufactured by defendant BASF Wyandotte Corporation (BWC).

Among other things, to each can of Basalin there were attached the following statements:

1) "BWC" warrants that this product conforms to the chemical description on the label and is reasonably fit for the purpose referred to in the Directions for Use subject to the inherent risks referred to above.

2) In no case shall "BWC" or the Seller be liable for consequential, special or indirect damages resulting from the use or handling of this product, and

3) Read "CONDITIONS OF SALE AND WARRANTY" before buying or using. If terms are not acceptable, return product at once, unopened.

Farmer alleges that he used Basalin on approximately 1,450 acres of soybeans and another herbicide, Treflan, on approximately 200 acres. He further alleges that although there was a severe drought that year, the Treflan treated crops were significantly better than the Basalin crops both in quality and yield per acre.

Farmer initially brought suit in United States District Court on oral and written warranties for damages. A jury awarded him $207,725.00. BWC appealed and the Fourth Circuit Court of Appeals reversed and remanded the case, holding that only the written warranties on the labels of the product apply and that the limitation of remedies quoted above is valid. *Hill v. BASF Wyandotte Corp.*, 696 F.2d 287 (4th Cir.1982).

In footnote 6 the court stated:

> We express no opinion as to whether under subsections (1) and (2) of § 36–2–714 and on the evidence that may be adduced on retrial the appropriate measure of damages would be the purchase price of the herbicide or some other measure.

This question was certified to us by the trial court after remand.

Ordinarily, *S.C.Code Ann.* § 36–2–714(2) (1976) is controlling as the measure of damages in a breach of warranty case. This section provides:

> (2) The measure of damages for breach of warranty is the difference at the time and place of acceptance between the value of the goods accepted and the value they would have had if they had been as warranted, *unless special circumstances show proximate damages of a different amount.* (Emphasis added.)

We find that the formula in this subsection is inapplicable to a herbicide failure case. This formula is most appropriate where the nonconforming good can be repaired or replaced and value (both as warranted and as accepted) can be defined with certainty.

A herbicide failure is a latent defect in the product. There is no reasonable way a farmer can determine in advance whether a herbicide will perform as warranted. Discovery of the problem must await the development of the crop at which time it is usually too late to correct.

The value of a herbicide as warranted is difficult to define. Price and value are not equivalents. From the farmer's perspective, the value of the herbicide is a healthy crop at maturity. In the manufacturer's viewpoint, the value is its selling price.

The value as accepted is equally uncertain and difficult to define. There is no market for such goods and thus no market price. If anything, it has a negative value.

In our view, the inability of a court to ascertain with certainty the value of goods both as warranted and as accepted creates a special circumstance within the meaning of § 36–2–714(2). It is this special circumstance which removes cases of this type from the § 36–2–714(2) measure of damages into subsection (1).

Subsection (1) provides:

> (1) Where the buyer has accepted goods and given notification (subsection (3) of § 36–2–607) he may recover as damages for any nonconformity of tender the loss resulting in the ordinary course of events from the seller's breach as determined in any manner which is reasonable.

Official Comment 2 to § 36–2–714 indicates that subsection (1) is applicable in breach of warranty cases.

It has consistently been held by this Court that the measure of actual damages, in cases similar to this, is the value the crop would have had if the product had conformed to the warranty less the value of the crop actually produced, less the expense of preparing for market the portion of the probable crop prevented from maturing. *See, McCown Clark Co. v. Muldrow,* 116 S.C. 54, 106 S.E. 771 (1929); *Amerson v. F.C.X. Co-Op Service,* 227 S.C. 520, 88 S.E.2d 605 (1955); *W.R. Grace and Co. v. LaMunion,* 245 S.C. 1, 138 S.E.2d 337 (1964) and *Simmons v. Ciba-Geigy Corp.,* 279 S.C. 26, 302 S.E.2d 17 (1983). *See also, Klein v. Asgrow Seed Co.,* 246 Cal.App.2d 87, 54 Cal.Rptr. 609, 620 (1966). We hold this formula to be appropriate in the present case.

BWC has argued that this formula includes lost profits and that lost profits are a consequential damage barred by the limitation of remedies on the cans of Basalin. We disagree.

In *W.R. Grace and Co., supra,* it was noted that the ". . . destruction or loss of a mature crop, which has a realizable value in excess of the cost of harvesting, processing and marketing, results in a monetary loss to the owner, regardless of whether the farming operation would, otherwise, have been profitable."

If the measure of damages we have adopted includes an element of lost profits, such inclusion is merely coincidental as the measure covers the direct loss resulting in the ordinary course of events from the alleged breach of the warranty. *See,* § 36–2–714(1).

The foregoing is the order of this Court.

LEWIS, C.J., and NESS, GREGORY and HARWELL, JJ., concur.

Notes

1. In Martin v. Joseph Harris Co., Inc., 767 F.2d 296 (6th Cir.1985), the plaintiffs purchased and planted cabbage seed infected with "black leg" fungus from the defendant. When the condition was discovered, plaintiffs took action to minimize the damage but still lost a "large portion" of their cabbage crop. Because of the high demand for cabbage, caused by the "black leg" epidemic, plaintiffs were able to sell the smaller cabbage crop at a profit equal to or higher than in previous years. Defendant argued that there is "no breach of the implied warranty of merchantability where there is no economic loss." Although "black leg" was damaging the plaintiffs' cabbage, the "law of supply and demand was making them * * * whole."

The court of appeals affirmed the district court's conclusion that the defendant's attempt to disclaim warranties and exclude liability for consequential damages was unconscionable. The court also affirmed the district court's decision to uphold a jury verdict of $52,000 for the plaintiffs.

"(W)e are persuaded by the district court's finding that the defendant's sale of diseased seed to these two plaintiffs did not create the increased market price. Similarly, we note that [they] purchased some healthy seed from other companies and some other farmers produced completely healthy crops. To further complicate the problem, there was evidence to the effect that the black leg epidemic was partially caused by the sale of diseased seed by other merchants and, thus, the rise in the market price of cabbage did not result entirely from Harris Seed's breach. Therefore, following the dictates of U.C.C. 1–106(1). * * * in order to put Martin and Rick in the same position as many of their neighboring farmers who purchased healthy seed, we hold that the proper measure of damages as applied by the district court is the difference in value between the cabbage crops actually raised by these plaintiffs and the cabbage crops that they would have raised if their seed had not been diseased." [767 F.2d at 302–03.]

2. In *Chatlos* the court enforced the clause excluding liability for consequential damages and awarded the buyer rather extravagant "direct" damages under UCC 2–714(2). In *Hill,* the court enforced the clause excluding liability for consequential damages and awarded the buyer the net value of the lost crop as "direct" damages under UCC 2–714(1). In *Martin,* the court invalidated the clause excluding liability for consequential damages and awarded damages for the net value of the lost crop, citing UCC 1–106(1) but not UCC 2–714 or 2–715. Assuming that the excluder clauses were not enforceable in all three cases, how should the damages claimed be classified, as "direct" or "consequential?"

SECTION 3. INCIDENTAL AND CONSEQUENTIAL DAMAGES: UCC 2–715

Commercial buyers purchase goods for use, perhaps to resell to customers or to consume in the business. If accepted goods fail to conform to warranties made, the buyer's planned use of the goods may be impaired. Put differently, a result of the breach may be that the buyer is deprived of the use of the goods during the time when they are being repaired or replaced.

Damages resulting from loss of use are called consequential damages and are recoverable under UCC 2–714(3) & 2–715(2). They may be recovered without proof of either "special circumstances" or a "tacit agreement" of the seller to assume them, see R.I. Lampus Co. v. Neville Cement Products Corp., 474 Pa. 199, 378 A.2d 288 (1977), if four conditions are satisfied:

(1) The loss results "from general or particular requirements and needs of which the seller at the time of contracting had reason to know," UCC 2–715(2)(a). Compare UCC 2–315 and the *Chatlos* case.

(2) The buyer has mitigated damages, i.e., the loss "could not reasonably be prevented by cover or otherwise," UCC 2–715(2)(a). The burden is on the seller to prove that the buyer failed to mitigate. Cates v. Morgan Portable Building Corp., 780 F.2d 683 (7th Cir.1985). But see International Petrol. Serv., Inc. v. S & N Well Serv., 230 Kan. 452, 639 P.2d 29, 38 (1982) (burden of proving mitigation on buyer).

(3) The breach was the substantial cause in fact of the loss. Compare UCC 2–715(2)(b). Overstreet v. Norden Laboratories, Inc., 669 F.2d 1286 (6th Cir.1982) (no proof that allegedly defective vaccine caused mares to abort foals).

(4) The type and amount of loss is proved by the buyer with reasonable certainty. Horizons, Inc. v. Avco Corp., 714 F.2d 862 (8th Cir.1983).

The conditions are easy to state. Applying them is another matter.

NEZPERCE STORAGE CO. v. ZENNER

Supreme Court of Idaho, 1983.
105 Idaho 464, 670 P.2d 871.

[In March, 1976, Zenner, a wheat farmer, sold Nezperce 2,000 bushels of "spring" wheat. Nezperce resold a portion of the wheat to eight farmers. Six weeks after planting, it became obvious that some of the wheat was not maturing and that the seed had been a mixture of spring and winter wheat. Since winter wheat requires several weeks of freezing weather to mature, the farmers suffered a crop failure. Nezperce settled the farmer's claims for $84,000 and brought suit against Zenner for indemnification.

Zenner, who grew both winter and spring wheat, had harvested his crop in August, 1975 and, according to his testimony, stored it in different bins over the winter. The Winter of 1975–76 was severe and much of the winter wheat planted in the previous fall was killed. A shortage of spring wheat developed, of which Zenner was aware at the time of the sale to Nezperce. Zenner also knew that Nezperce was purchasing his wheat to meet the shortage of spring wheat in the Camas Prairie area.

Nezperce cleaned and bagged the wheat without mixing it with another variety. Nezperce performed a successful "germination" to determine if the seed would grow but did not conduct other tests, i.e., a "grow out" test or an electrofloresis test, to determine if the seed was in fact spring wheat. The evidence was conflicting as to whether either test was available or practical.

The jury returned a verdict that Zenner had made and breached an express warranty and that Nezperce should recover the amount of the settlement made with the farmers.]

* * *

Although many of the allegations of the Nezperce complaint and the Zenners' counterclaim were disputed at trial, the essential arguments upon this appeal are the Zenners' assertions of error relating to the findings of the jury that Joseph Zenner was aware of the shortage of spring wheat seed in the Camas Prairie area and that he knew or had reason to know that Nezperce was purchasing his wheat for processing into spring wheat seed for resale to its customers; that the award of consequential damages was improper and that Nezperce did not reasonably mitigate its damages by testing the seed.

The propriety of awarding consequential damages in the instant case is governed by I.C. § 28–2–715(2)(a), which provides in pertinent part:

> "(2) Consequential damages resulting from the seller's breach include
>
> (a) Any loss resulting from general or particular requirements and needs of which the seller at the time of contracting had reason to know and which could not reasonably be prevented by cover or otherwise. * * *"

Clearly, Nezperce sustained a "loss" in reimbursing its customers for the damages they suffered by purchasing and planting seed which was not spring wheat. In a breach of warranty action, indemnification for this kind of a loss is proper when a seller such as Nezperce receives a warranty from a supplier such as Zenner and passes that warranty on to customers. * * *

As stated in *Clark v. International Harvester Co.,* 99 Idaho 326, 346, 581 P.2d 784, 804 (1978), "there are certain limitations on the right to recover consequential damages under § 28–2–715(2)(a). First, the losses must have resulted from needs which the seller knew or had reason to know at the time of contracting." Here the special interrogatories returned by the jury indicate that Zenner was aware of the shortage of spring wheat seed in the Camas Prairie area and that Zenner had reason to realize that "Nezperce Storage Company's purpose in purchasing MP–1 wheat was to meet an apparent shortage of spring wheat seed on the Camas Prairie," and that Zenner had reason to know that Nezperce was buying the wheat from Zenner to process it into spring wheat seed for resale. Those findings are supported by substantial, albeit conflicting, evidence, and therefore they will not be disturbed on appeal. I.R.C.P. 52(a); *Ellis v. Northwest Fruit & Produce,* 103 Idaho 821, 654 P.2d 914 (1982); *Jolley v. Clay,* 103 Idaho 171, 646 P.2d 413 (1982); *Rueth v. State,* 103 Idaho 74, 644 P.2d 1333 (1982). Hence, the foreseeability requirement of I.C. § 28–2–715(2)(a) has been satisfied.

The propriety of an award of consequential damages must also satisfy the second condition of I.C. § 28–2–715(2)(a), *i.e.,* that they could not have been *reasonably* prevented by cover or otherwise. As to this condition, the Court in *Clark v. International Harvester Co.,* 99 Idaho 326, 347, 581 P.2d 784, 805 (1978), held that "the plaintiffs were only required to take reasonable efforts to mitigate their damages, [citation] and the burden of proving that the damages could have been minimized was on the defendants". In *S.J. Groves & Sons Co. v. Warner Co.,* 576 F.2d 524, 528 (3rd Cir.1978), it was held that, in an action to recover consequential damages under the same UCC provision, "[t]he requirement of * * * mitigation of damages is not an absolute, unyielding one, but is subject to the circumstances," and "[t]he test for plaintiff's efforts [to mitigate damages] is reasonableness * * *." *Id.,* at n. 5. In the instant case the Zenners presented testimony attempting to convince the jury that Nezperce could have mitigated or avoided its consequential damages by subjecting the seed to tests to determine seed variety prior to the time it resold the seed to its customers. As indicated in *West v. Whitney-Fidalgo Seafoods, Inc.,* 628 P.2d 10 (Alaska 1981), and *AES Technology Systems, Inc. v. Coherent Radiation,* 583 F.2d 933 (7th Cir. 1978), the question of whether Nezperce acted properly to mitigate its damages is a factual matter to be determined by the trier of the fact. Here the jury specifically found:

> "it [was] reasonable for plaintiff Nezperce Storage to sell the seed it manufactured from the Zenner wheat to its customers without doing any more than the facts show it did do to determine whether or not such seed was actually of a spring wheat variety."

That finding is supported by substantial, albeit conflicting, testimony and will not be disturbed on appeal. I.R.C.P. 52(a); *Ellis v. Northwest Fruit & Produce, supra; Jolley v. Clay, supra; Rueth v. State, supra.*

The Zenners argue that the finding of the jury should be disregarded because the jury was not properly instructed as to what a "reasonable man" would have done in that the court failed to give Zenners' submitted instructions regarding negligence per se. We disagree and find no error in the refusal of the trial court to give Zenners' requested instructions. In the instant case we need not decide whether negligence per se can ever be used to limit a party's consequential damages under I.C. § 28–2–715(2)(a). While a court may adopt the requirements of a legislative enactment as the standard of conduct of a reasonable man, *Brizendine v. Nampa Meridian Irrigation Dist.,* 97 Idaho 580, 548 P.2d 80 (1976), that doctrine is ordinarily applied in negligence actions where a plaintiff has suffered injury by a defendant who was in violation of a statute or ordinance. However,

"In order for the violation of a statute to be pertinent in a particular case, the statute must be * * * designed to protect (1) the class of persons in which the plaintiff is included (2) against the type of harm which has in fact occurred as a result of its violation." *Kinney v. Smith,* 95 Idaho 328, 331, 508 P.2d 1234, 1237 (1973); *Anderson v. Blackfoot Livestock Commission Co.,* 85 Idaho 64, 375 P.2d 704 (1962); *Curoe v. Spokane Etc. R.R. Co.,* 32 Idaho 643, 186 P. 1101 (1920); *W. PROSSER, LAW OF TORTS* § 36 (4th ed. 1971).

The statute at issue, I.C. § 22–417(3), imposes penalties upon one who sells seeds which are incorrectly labeled when the person selling the seed "has failed to obtain an invoice or growers declaration giving kind, or kind and variety * * * and to take such other precautions as may be necessary to insure the identity to be that stated." We deem it clear and obvious that, in the instant case, the statute was designed to protect the following class of persons: those customers who purchased the seed from Nezperce. Cases construing similar seed laws, *e.g., Agr. Services Ass'n, Inc. v. Ferry-Morse Seed Co., Inc.,* 551 F.2d 1057 (6th Cir.1977), and *Klein v. Asgrow Seed Co.,* 246 Cal.App.2d 87, 54 Cal. Rptr. 609 (1966), have so held. Equally clearly, the statute was not designed to provide protection to the Zenners, who can best be described as suppliers of mislabeled seed. Hence, we deem the statute and the doctrine of negligence per se in the instant case irrelevant. *See also S.J. Groves & Sons Co. v. Warner, supra,* which states:

"Where both the plaintiff and the defendant have had equal opportunity to reduce the damages by the same act and it is equally reasonable to expect the defendant to minimize damages, the defendant is in no position to contend that the plaintiff failed to mitigate. Nor will the award be reduced on account of damages the defendant could have avoided as easily as the plaintiff." At page 530; *See also Shea—S & M Ball v. Massman—Kiewit—Early,* 606 F.2d 1245 (D.C.Cir.1979).

* * *

The judgment of the district court is affirmed. Costs to respondents. No attorney fees allowed.

Notes

1. Suppose Zenner warranted the wheat to be spring wheat, knew that Nezperce intended to resell it to his customers but was unaware of the shortage of spring wheat seed in the Camas Prairie area. Should that alter the result in this case?

2. Suppose that Zenner sold and delivered grain described as "spring wheat" to Nezperce in the Fall of 1975 at $5.00 per bushel. Nezperce immediately resold 50% to customers for April, 1976 delivery at $6.00 per bushel. All of the Zenner wheat was stored together. In March, after the big chill, the price of spring wheat had risen to $20. Nezperce resold the balance to customers for $22 per bushel. Nezperce then had an electroforesis test performed on a sample of Zenner wheat and discovered that it was mixed substantially with winter wheat. Nezperce promptly purchased replacement spring wheat in the open market for $22 per bushel, which was delivered to customers, and sold the Zenner wheat for $5 per bushel. What damages should Nezperce recover for Zenner's breach of warranty?

3. How does the Code treat expenditures made by the buyer after the breach is discovered? If they are made to repair or replace the non-conforming goods, they may be recoverable as "direct" damages under UCC 2–714(2): Repair or replacement costs are frequently used to measure the value of the goods as warranted. In

addition to *Soo Line,* see Vista St. Clair, Inc. v. Landry's Commercial Furnishings, Inc., 57 Or.App. 254, 643 P.2d 1378 (1982). If they are made to avoid losses or to pursue permissible remedies, they may be "incidental" damages under UCC 2–715(1). Or, they may be "consequential" damages under UCC 2–715(2)(a). How is the line to be drawn between incidental and consequential damages? The question is important, for incidental damages need not satisfy all the conditions for the recovery of consequential damages and will not be covered by clauses in the contract purporting to exclude the seller's liability for consequential damages. See, e.g., Reynolds Metals Co. v. Westinghouse Elec. Corp., 758 F.2d 1073 (5th Cir.1985).

4. The buyer's claim for consequential damages caused by the seller's delay or nondelivery is treated in Chapter Fifteen, Section 6.

LEWIS v. MOBIL OIL CORP.

United States Court of Appeals, Eighth Circuit, 1971.
438 F.2d 500.

[The facts and the decision on the warranty issue in this case are reprinted in Section 3(c) of Chapter 19. We now turn to the damages issues.]

* * *

III. DAMAGES

The question with which we are here confronted is what damages are recoverable by the plaintiff for the defendant's breach of warranty. The applicable statutes are §§ 2–714(2), (3) and 2–715 of the Uniform Commercial Code, 7C Ark.Stats.Ann. §§ 85–2–714(2), (3), 85–2–715 (1961), which provide in pertinent part: [The court quoted UCC 2–714(2) and (3) and UCC 2–715.]

* * *

In the instant case the ordinary measure of damages for breach of warranty is not applicable, since the plaintiff-buyer did not pay a price exceeding the value of the goods delivered. Rather, since the breach was of an implied warranty of fitness for a particular purpose, the "special circumstances" exception is applicable here. The proximate damages in this case consisted of the plaintiff's incidental and consequential damages which may be recoverable. The incidental damages consist of the excessive amounts of oil used in the system and the costs incurred in the repair and replacement of mechanical parts damaged by the oil's failing to function properly. There is no controversy between the parties as to the allowability of these damages. There are two major points of controversy on damages: (1) for what period of time are damages recoverable and (2) whether loss of profits during the time plaintiff was unable to operate at full capacity are recoverable.

[The court first rejected plaintiff's "unique" theory that damages should be recoverable for the period of time after the correct oil was used and the system was operating satisfactorily. Plaintiff had argued that the drain on his financial resources during the period of difficulty had restricted his ability to operate at 100% capacity later on. In the view of the court, the cause of this condition was inadequate capitalization not breach of warranty and the proper remedy was a bank loan at the time not damages in subsequent litigation.]

* * *

A more troublesome question is whether the plaintiff should be allowed to recover damages for the full two and one-half year period during which he was using Ambrex 810. Under § 2–715(2)(a) of the Uniform Commercial Code, only those losses are recoverable "which could not reasonably be prevented by cover or otherwise." 7C Ark.Stat.Ann. § 85–2–715 (1961). The "cover" provision of the Uniform Commercial Code, § 2–712, is not applicable here, since that section applies to the buyer's remedies upon failure of the seller to deliver goods or upon the rightful rejection of goods known to be defective. Hence the question here is whether the plaintiff's damage could otherwise have been reasonably prevented. The applicable doctrine is stated by Professor Williston:

> "* * * [D]amages which the plaintiff might have avoided with reasonable effort without undue risk, expense, or humiliation are either not caused by the defendant's wrong or need not have been, and, therefore, are not to be charged against him.
>
> "The principle has wide application and frequently involves the establishment of a standard of reasonable conduct.
>
> * * *
>
> "Where inferior goods have been furnished under a contract, the buyer cannot recover greater consequential damages caused by using them when he knew of their unfitness, than would have been caused by another possible course, although the seller had sold the goods for that purpose. And the principle is general that there can be no recovery for consequences that reasonably could have been avoided." 11 S. Williston, Contracts § 1353 (Jaeger, 3d ed. 1968) (footnotes omitted). * * *

Defendant's argument on this issue is not precise, but the gist of its complaint is that the plaintiff used Ambrex 810 for a period of two and one-half years, during which time there was at least some suspicion that the oil was not functioning properly, and that plaintiff should have taken steps to solve his problems sooner than he did. It is unclear to us whether or not the defendant is contending that the plaintiff used Ambrex 810 with actual knowledge of its unfitness, so as to preclude at least in part his recovery of damages caused by its use. If such is the claim, it is clearly refuted by the evidence. Neither plaintiff nor the Mobil dealer who sold him Ambrex 810 knew the chemical composition of the oil nor what the exact requirements of plaintiff's equipment were. Plaintiff was relying on Mobil to provide him with the proper oil and it was not discovered during that time that the oil was improper. Indeed, plaintiff changed the brand of pump he was using because of the possibility that the problem was mechanical. It was not until a Mobil engineer visited the mill and changed the type of oil recommended that it was discovered that an improper oil had been supplied.

Neither does the defendant precisely phrase its argument in terms of a failure to give timely notice under Ark.Stat.Ann. § 85–2–607, although it relies on an Arkansas case under this section, Ingle v. Marked Tree Equipment Co., 244 Ark. 1166, 428 S.W.2d 286 (1968). However, it seems that under the circumstances of this case, the reasonable notice required by this section was given by the plaintiff. * * *

* * *

Here there is not the slightest suggestion of bad faith on the part of the plaintiff. Furthermore the evidence shows that soon after using Ambrex 810, plaintiff notified the Mobil dealer, Rowe, that he wasn't sure if a proper oil was being supplied, and was constantly in touch with Rowe about his problems thereafter. Mobil certainly had notice that the "transaction [was] still troublesome and must be watched." Defendant continued to supply Ambrex 810. Therefore we cannot conclude that any damages must be barred under this section. See Boeing Airplane Co. v. O'Malley, 329 F.2d 585, 593–596 (8th Cir.1964). The trial judge properly instructed the jury that the plaintiff must have notified the defendant within a reasonable time after he should have discovered the breach, and we cannot say that the jury's verdict was erroneous in this respect.

The only way in which it would have been possible for plaintiff's damages to have been minimized in this case would have been for him to have brought in an independent expert to assess the cause of his trouble. While such a course might have been desirable, and would probably have saved both plaintiff and defendant considerable expense, we cannot say that failure to do so requires a reduction of damages allowable under § 2–715 of the Uniform Commercial Code as a matter of law. This is essentially a question of the plaintiff's duty to use diligence to minimize his damages, which is ordinarily a question of fact for the jury. The trial judge properly instructed the jury that plaintiff had the duty to use diligence to minimize his damages, that defendant was not liable for any damages which resulted from plaintiff's failure to minimize his damages, and that diligence meant the care of a reasonably careful person under the circumstances of the case. The jury's verdict reflects its finding that the plaintiff had acted reasonably in these circumstances, and again we cannot say that it lacks evidentiary support.

Plaintiff was in continuous contact with both the manufacturer of his equipment and with the defendant in an effort to ascertain the cause of his problems. Various remedies were tried and failed until the oil problem was ultimately identified. Throughout this period, defendant continued to supply plaintiff with Ambrex 810, knowing both of his reliance on it to supply the proper oil and his difficulties in operation. Thus we do not think that defendant can rely on plaintiff's failure to obtain an independent opinion to absolve it of liability for its breach of warranty. "The duty to mitigate damages is not an unlimited one * * *." Steele v. J.I. Case Company, 197 Kan. 554, 419 P.2d 902, 911 (1966). We conclude that defendant should be liable for all of plaintiff's damages during the period he was using Ambrex 810.

The final question to be determined is whether under Arkansas law, loss of profits may be recovered as consequential damages for breach of warranty. Defendant relies on a series of Arkansas cases which stand for the proposition that loss of profits cannot be recovered unless the circumstances of the transaction are such as to make it reasonable to assume that the defendant knew he was to be held responsible for such damages and agreed to such liability. See Hawkins v. Delta Spindle of Blytheville, Inc., 245 Ark. 830, 434 S.W.2d 825 (1968); Lamkins v. International Harvester Co., 207 Ark. 637, 182 S.W.2d 203 (1944); Hooks Smelting Co. v. Planters' Compress Co., 72 Ark. 275, 79 S.W. 1052 (1904). The problem with this argument is that all of these cases are non-Code cases which rely on a rule which is expressly rejected by the Uniform Commercial Code Official Commentary to § 2–715:

> "2. * * * The 'tacit agreement' test for the recovery of consequential damages is rejected. * * *
>
> "3. * * * It is not necessary that there be a conscious acceptance of an insurer's liability on the seller's part, nor is his obligation for consequential damages limited to cases in which he fails to use due effort in good faith.
>
> "Particular needs of the buyer must generally be made known to the seller while general needs must rarely be made known to charge the seller with knowledge.

"Any seller who does not wish to take the risk of consequential damages has available the section on contractual limitation of remedy." 7C Ark.Stat. Ann. § 85–2–715, Comments 2 and 3 (1961).

The question essentially is whether lost profits are damages which the seller had reason to know of at the time the contract was made. With respect to breach of warranty, lost profits are held to be foreseeable if they are proximately caused by and are the natural result of the breach. 5 A. Corbin, Contracts § 1012 (1964); Seely v. White Motor Co., 63 Cal.2d 9, 45 Cal.Rptr. 17, 403 P.2d 145, 148–149 (1965). Cf. Superwood Corp. v. Larson-Stang, Inc., 311 F.2d 735 (8th Cir.1963). Where a seller provides goods to a manufacturing enterprise with knowledge that they are to be used in the manufacturing process, it is reasonable to assume that he should know that defective goods will cause a disruption of production, and loss of profits is a natural consequence of such disruption. Hence, loss of profits should be recoverable under those circumstances. Here, the defendant seller knew that the oil it was supplying to plaintiff was to be used in the operation of the sawmill. It also knew that a defective oil would cause the sawmill equipment to operate improperly. It is a natural consequence of the failure of the equipment to function that production would be curtailed and loss of profits would follow. See 5 A. Corbin, Contracts § 1013, p. 92 (1964). We think these damages are the proximate result of the breach and should be recoverable.

Most jurisdictions which have considered the question of the recoverability of lost profits under the Uniform Commercial Code for a breach of warranty in circumstances similar to those in the instant case seem to have allowed them. * * *

We think Arkansas would follow this rule. * * *

* * *

Defendant also contends there was no proper proof of lost profits in this case, and that the damages were purely speculative. We do not agree. While it is true that the damages were excessive in this case because they were allowed for an improper time period, we do not think that the method utilized was unreasonable under the circumstances of this case. First of all, the plaintiff offered considerable evidence that there was a substantial market for his lumber which he was not able to supply. Evidence was offered of a number of customers who testified they would have bought more of his lumber had it been available. A substantial part of plaintiff's business was done as an exclusive supplier of timbers to a bridge building company. Plaintiff was the only sawmill operator who would furnish these timbers with the close tolerances demanded; he was unable to supply all of that customer's needs.

In addition to this market evidence, there is evidence of the profits made by his business both before and after using Ambrex 810. These were substantial, even in the later period when he was unable to operate at full capacity. During the period he was using Ambrex 810 they were significantly less, due to the lost production and added expenses. Past profits of an established business may be utilized to prove loss of profits as an element of damages. 5 A. Corbin, Contracts § 1023 (1964); 11 S. Williston, Contracts § 1346A (Jaeger, 3d ed. 1968). And under the circumstances of this case, we think the jury was entitled to take account of the profits earned by plaintiff once the business was operating successfully after the breach of warranty. While the lost profits could not be proved with absolute certainty of course, we think a reasonable approximation can be made from the evidence in this case.

To summarize our decision in this case, having reviewed the evidence as a whole and the instructions of the able trial judge, we conclude that there was a warranty of fitness for a particular purpose in this case, that the warranty was breached, and that the defendant was liable for the damages caused by this breach, including loss of profits during the time plaintiff was using Ambrex 810. Defendant is not liable for any loss of profits which may have occurred after plaintiff quit using Ambrex 810. The jury's verdict was in the single amount of $89,250. We are unable to determine from the record what would be a proper amount to award for direct damages plus loss of profits for the appropriate time period. Therefore, the judgment must be reversed and remanded for a new trial on the issue of damages.

On Petitions for Rehearing

The petitions for rehearing of both the appellant and the appellee raise questions as to the issue of damages for loss of profits which merit some further comment. At the outset, we would note that the record and the arguments are not entirely clear as to how this element of damages was submitted in this particular case. While we adhere to our opinion that loss of profits is a proper element of damages in a case of this sort, these damages must of course be proved with a certain degree of specificity. For the purposes of this memorandum we will discuss the damages in this case in round figures approximating those in the record.

Plaintiff's profit records show that for the four years prior to his shift to new equipment and using Ambrex 810, he made a total profit of $32,000. In 1961, his profit was $19,000, in 1962, $7,000, in 1963, $8,000, and in 1964, the year in which he was converting his equipment, he had a loss of $2,000. This works out to an annual rate of profits in the pre-Ambrex period of $8,000, and we are not saying that any particular period of time prior to the period the damage was sustained should be used as the basis for calculation. It appears obvious that the immediate prior year's profit has more relevancy to the issue of what profits might be anticipated in the following years than do the more remote years' profits. Likewise, on the other end of the calculation the immediate succeeding year's profit after the use of Ambrex was discontinued would be of greater relevancy than the succeeding years. But even eliminating the year of conversion, this is an annual rate of $11,000. During the period he was using Ambrex 810, approximately 30 months, he made a total of $12,000, for an annual rate of $4,800. In the post-Ambrex period, a period of 24 months, he made a total of $41,000, for an annual rate of approximately $20,500.

The jury verdict in this case was for $89,250, of which approximately $9250 may be attributed to direct damages, leaving $80,000 as the recovery for loss of profits. As we will shortly demonstrate, such a recovery, if it is interpreted as being limited to loss of profits for only the period in which Ambrex 810 was being used, bears no reasonable relationship to the proof in the record of plaintiff's capacity for making profits, with or without Ambrex 810. We were thus confronted with the problem of determining what the basis of this recovery was. We were led by certain arguments made in plaintiff's brief to the conclusion that this recovery represented a loss of profits during the period Ambrex 810 was used, plus a loss of profits for the period of time after Ambrex 810 was used because of his inability to operate at full capacity. We held that such later profits could not be recovered. Plaintiff now contends that the loss of profits recovery did not extend to the later period and was confined to the period in which he was using Ambrex 810. We accept this interpretation of the damage award and find this award is excessive.

If the $80,000 loss of profits is confined to the 30–month period during which Ambrex 810 was used, to this figure must be added the $12,000 in profits which he actually made. This works out to an annual rate of profits of approximately $37,000. There simply is no proof in the record that plaintiff has ever approached such a profit record. Plaintiff argues that his post-Ambrex profit rate, during which he was operating at 50–60 per cent capacity must be inflated to a 100 per cent capacity rate in order to determine his profit rate during the time he was using Ambrex 810. We cannot agree that such a method of determining loss of profits is acceptable, for this accomplishes much the same result as that we disapproved in our original interpretation of the damage award—i.e., it penalizes the defendant Mobil Oil Company for the plaintiff's capital structure and bears no reasonable relationship to actual damages caused by the use of Ambrex 810.

We further wish to emphasize the fact that nothing said in our prior opinion should be taken to mean that the profit rate made in the post-Ambrex period is the sole measure of damages in the period of the use of Ambrex 810. In view of the immediate proximity in time of these two periods, the significant increase in profits in the post-Ambrex period is highly suggestive of the fact that additional profits could have been made in the period Ambrex was used, and may be used as a guide as to what those profits should have been, at least as to their outer limit. However, there is also proof in the record that the market conditions of the plaintiff's business were not entirely similar, particularly in the fact that the selling price for lumber was fluctuating.

Plaintiff's recovery for a loss of profits must take into account these different market conditions, his actual production capacity, his type of operation, its efficiency and any and all other relevant factors that would have a bearing upon and that would influence the amount of profits during the period that profits are recoverable as well as the years used for comparative purposes. See Frank Sullivan Company v. Midwest Sheet Metal Works, 335 F.2d 33, 41 (8th Cir.1964).

Other questions raised in the petitions for rehearing have been considered and rejected as being without merit. The judgment must still be reversed and remanded for a new trial on the issue of damages.

Both petitions for rehearing are denied.

DELANO GROWER'S CO–OP. v. SUPREME WINE CO.

Supreme Judicial Court of Massachusetts, 1985.
393 Mass. 666, 473 N.E.2d 1066.

[The court's decision on the liability issue is printed supra in chapter 19, § 3.]

* * *

6. *Calculation of damages for lost good will.* Delano argues that there is no basis in the record for the conclusion that it caused injury to Supreme's business reputation. The master found that the primary reason for Supreme's decline in sales after 1973 was the defective Delano wine. This finding was prima facie evidence of the causal connection between Delano's acts and the damage to Supreme's business reputation. At trial, Delano presented the testimony of several former Supreme customers to rebut the evidence of a causal

connection. Supreme presented testimony of its former officers to support the evidence that Delano caused the injury to Supreme's business reputation. This record is hardly one, as Delano argues, that is totally devoid of any basis for finding a causal connection between Delano's acts and Supreme's damages. Rather, it exhibits an instance where the judge was required to weigh the credibility of the evidence before him and to determine whether a causal connection existed. The judge's finding that Supreme had proved a causal connection between its loss of business reputation and Delano's breach is not clearly erroneous.

Delano contends that the record contains scant evidence supporting a valuation of Supreme's good will. However, it did not produce any direct evidence at trial before the judge which rebutted Supreme's evidence of the good will value. At trial, Supreme presented the testimony of an expert in business appraising. This expert had over eight years' experience as a business broker engaged in buying and selling businesses in and around Boston. In this connection he was required to appraise a business's value, including the value of its good will. The judge's acceptance of the expert testimony implies that he found this expert sufficiently qualified to render an opinion. *Commonwealth v. Boyd,* 367 Mass. 169, 183, 326 N.E.2d 320 (1975). A finding that this expert possessed sufficient knowledge, skill, and experience to render an opinion was neither an abuse of discretion nor erroneous as matter of law. *Id.* See P.J. Liacos, Massachusetts Evidence 112 (5th ed. 1981).

The expert valued the business at $593,700, including assets and good will. The assets were valued at $237,092. This valuation was based on the business records introduced in evidence and certain other facts. This was a sufficient basis for his opinion. *Uberto v. Kaufman,* 348 Mass. 171, 173, 202 N.E.2d 822 (1964). Supreme's president and its treasurer testified that Supreme's value was $500,000.

The judge found that Supreme's loss of good will attributable to Delano's breach was $100,000. He based this on the evidence in the record and an examination of valuation methods. He rejected Supreme's theories supporting its valuation as lacking factual grounding. In determining the value of Supreme's good will, the judge was not bound by the expert testimony. P.J. Liacos, *supra* at 117, citing *Dodge v. Sawyer,* 288 Mass. 402, 408, 193 N.E. 15 (1934).

Delano argues that the trial judge relied on extraneous materials, not admitted at trial, in determining good will. Specifically, he discussed certain statistics from Business Week, indicating an increased consumption of wine and a growth in the wine industry. This reference occurred in a lengthy discussion of various methods used in valuing good will. This same discussion specifically refers to evidence introduced at trial which sufficiently supported a valuation of the lost good will. There is no clear indication to what degree, if any, the discussion of the extraneous material influenced the good will valuation. The judge found sufficient grounds to reduce the value from that given by Supreme. Where there was sufficient evidence to warrant a valuation of lost good will and the causal connection of that loss, we will not upset this finding. It was not clearly erroneous and was based on the judge's weighing the credibility of the evidence before him. The weight given this evidence was then used in accepted formulations of good will to determine the damage. We do not require that such damages be proved with mathematical certainty. *Productora e Importadora de Papel, S.A. de C.V. v. Fleming,* 376 Mass. 826, 840, 383 N.E.2d 1129 (1978). The judge did not err in calculating the damages for good will.

Neither party has addressed the issue whether lost good will is a proper consequential damage under G.L. c. 106, § 2–715. This court has stated that prospective profits are recoverable in the appropriate case. *Matsushita Elec. Corp. of America v. Sonus Corp.,* 362 Mass. 246, 264, 284 N.E.2d 880 (1972). In examining whether good will is also recoverable, we note that Pennsylvania, in disallowing such recovery, based its decision on the interpretation of its prior law, which did not allow recovery for good will. *Harry Rubin & Sons v. Consolidated Pipe Co. of America,* 396 Pa. 506, 153 A.2d 472 (1959). Other cases in which recovery for good will has been denied are based on the speculative nature of damages in the particular case or on a failure of proof. 96 A.L.R.3d § 18[b], at 396 (1979). Cf. 96 A.L.R.3d § 18[a], at 395 (1979) (loss of good will held recoverable). Under our law as it was before the enactment of the Uniform Commercial Code, "[l]oss of good will [was] recognized as an element of damages flowing from the use of unfit material received from one who warranted it to be fit." *Royal Paper Box Co. v. Munro & Church Co.,* 284 Mass. 446, 452, 188 N.E. 223 (1933) (interpreting G.L. [Ter.Ed.] c. 106, § 17[1]). Where a seller of goods reasonably knows that substantially impaired goods provided for resale could affect continued operations and established good will, the buyer's loss of good will caused by the seller's breach is properly recoverable as consequential damages unless the loss could have been prevented by cover or otherwise. G.L. c. 106, § 2–715(2)(a). This is not a harsh result as the seller may contractually limit this remedy. Uniform Commercial Code § 2–715, comment 3 1A U.L.A. 446 (1976). In this case, Supreme's loss of good will was found to be a direct consequence of Delano's breach. Once sufficiently ascertained, the award of damages for lost good will was properly allowed.

* * *

[Footnotes omitted.]

SECTION 4. SELLER'S DISCLAIMER OF WARRANTY AND CONTRACTUAL MODIFICATION OF REMEDIES FOR BREACH

MARTIN v. JOSEPH HARRIS CO., INC.

United States Court of Appeals, Sixth Circuit, 1985.
767 F.2d 296.

MILBURN, CIRCUIT JUDGE.

The defendant, Joseph Harris Co., Inc., brings this appeal following the district court's granting the plaintiffs' motion for a judgment not withstanding the verdict and a second trial in plaintiffs' action for damages as a result of defective seeds. Because we hold that the district court was correct in holding that, under the facts of this case, the disclaimer of warranty and limitation of remedy clause used by the defendant was unconscionable under Michigan law, and because we further hold that the district court properly held that the implied warranty of merchantability was breached as a matter of law, we affirm.

I.

Plaintiffs Duane Martin and Robert Rick ("Martin and Rick") were commercial farmers in Michigan. In August of 1972, Martin and Rick placed independent orders for cabbage seed with the defendant, Joseph Harris Co., Inc. ("Harris Seed"), a national producer and distributor of seed. Plaintiffs had been customers of Harris Seed for several years and, as in earlier transactions, the order form supplied by Harris Seed included a clause disclaiming the implied warranty of merchantability and limiting buyers' remedies to the purchase price of the seed.[1] A similar clause was also used by Harris Seed's competitors for the same purpose. Neither of the plaintiffs read the clause nor did the salesman make any attempt either to point it out or to explain its purpose.

Three to four months after placing their orders, plaintiffs received Harris Seed's 1973 Commercial Vegetable Growers Catalog. Included in the lower right-hand corner of one page of the catalog was a notification that Harris Seed would no longer "hot water" treat cabbage seed. Hot water treatment had successfully been used since 1947 to eradicate a fungus known as *phoma lingam* or "black leg," a seed borne disease that causes affected plants to rot before maturing.[2]

Plaintiffs planted their cabbage crop in April and May of 1973, using, among other seed, that supplied by Harris Seed. In mid-July, Harris Seed notified plaintiffs that the seed lot used to fill plaintiffs' order was infected with black leg. Although plaintiffs attempted to minimize the effect of the disease, large portions of their cabbage crops were destroyed. However, in marketing their smaller than usual crop, both plaintiffs made a profit equal to or higher than previous years. This unusual profit margin was due to the rise in market price for cabbage in 1973, which in turn was affected in part by the fact that the 1973 black leg epidemic reduced the amount of available cabbage.

On August 5, 1975, plaintiffs brought this action. After a hearing on the enforceability of the disclaimer of warranty and limitation of liability clause, the district court ruled that the clause was unconscionable and, therefore, unenforceable. A jury was impaneled to try plaintiffs' legal liability theories of negligence and breach of implied warranty. Following a six-day trial the jury returned a verdict against plaintiffs on both theories; however, the district court granted the plaintiffs' motion for a j.n.o.v. on the implied warranty issue. A second jury impaneled to hear the issue of damages returned verdicts in favor of Martin in the amount of Thirty-six Thousand ($36,000.00) Dollars and in favor of Rick in the amount of Sixteen Thousand ($16,000.00) Dollars.

II.

Our review of the district court's rulings in this diversity case is controlled by the State of Michigan's version of the Uniform Commercial Code, Mich.Comp. Laws Ann. § 440.1101 *et seq.* As we have often stated, "[w]hen this court is reviewing a district judge's interpretation of state law, we give 'considerable weight' to the interpretation of the judge." *Bagwell v. Canal Insurance Co.*, 663 F.2d 710, 712 (6th Cir.1981). Accordingly, "if a federal district judge has reached a permissible conclusion upon a question of local law, the Court of Appeals

1. The disclaimer of warranties and exclusion of remedies clause, which was printed in the order form, seed catalogs and on the seed packages, appeared as follows:

NOTICE TO BUYER: Joseph Harris Company, Inc. warrants that seeds and plants it sells conform to the label descriptions as required by Federal and State seed laws. IT MAKES NO OTHER WARRANTIES, EXPRESS OR IMPLIED, OF MERCHANTABILITY, FITNESS FOR PURPOSE, OR OTHERWISE, AND IN ANY EVENT ITS LIABILITY FOR BREACH OF ANY WARRANTY OR CONTRACT WITH RESPECT TO SUCH SEEDS OR PLANTS IS LIMITED TO THE PURCHASE PRICE OF SUCH SEEDS OR PLANTS.

No question has been raised as to whether this clause complies with the requirements of Mich.Comp.Laws Ann. § 440.2316 (U.C.C. § 2–316).

2. According to testimony at trial, the only black leg epidemic between 1947 and 1973 was in 1966, and was traced to cabbage seed imported from Australia. The 1947 and the 1973 black leg was traced to State of Washington produced cabbage seed.

should not reverse even though it may think the law should be otherwise." *Insurance Co. of North America v. Federated Mutual Insurance Co.,* 518 F.2d 101, 106 n. 3 (6th Cir.1975) (quoting *Rudd-Melikian, Inc. v. Merritt,* 282 F.2d 924, 929 (6th Cir.1960)).

A.

The first issue raised by Harris Seed is whether the district court erred in holding the disclaimer and limitation clause unconscionable under U.C.C. § 2–302. The question of the unconscionability of a contract clause is one of law for the court to decide in light of "its commercial setting, purpose and effect." U.C.C. § 2–302. Since the Code does not define unconscionability, the district court reviewed case law to aid it in its resolution of this question.

A threshhold problem in this context is whether under Michigan law warranty disclaimers which comply with U.C.C. § 2–316 are limited by U.C.C. § 2–302. In holding Harris Seed's disclaimer clause unconscionable under the facts of this case, the district court implicitly held that U.C.C. § 2–302 is a limitation on U.C.C. § 2–316. Harris Seed argues that by enacting § 2–316 the Michigan Legislature "unequivocally [authorized the] exclusion or modification of the implied warranty of merchantability by disclaimer." We have been presented with no Michigan cases resolving this issue; however, a number of arguments support the district court's conclusion that § 2–316 is not insulated from review under § 2–302. First, § 2–302 provides that "any clause" of a contract may be found unconscionable. Similarly, "section 2–316 does not state expressly that all disclaimers meeting its requirements are immune from general policing provisions like section 2–302. * * *" J. White & R. Summers, *Handbook of the Law Under the Uniform Commercial Code,* § 12–11, at 476 (2d Ed.1980). Had the drafters of the Uniform Commercial Code or the Michigan Legislature chosen to limit the application of § 2–302, language expressly so stating could easily have been included. Furthermore, as pointed out by Professors White and Summers:

> Comment 1 [to § 2–302] lists and describes ten cases which are presumably intended to illustrate the underlying basis of the section: In seven of those cases disclaimers of warranty were denied full effect. It is difficult to reconcile the intent on the part of the draftsman to immunize disclaimers from the effect of 2–302 with the fact that they used cases in which courts struck down disclaimers to illustrate the concept of unconscionability.

Id. (footnotes omitted). Therefore, because this issue is unsettled under Michigan law and according the district court's conclusion "considerable weight," we hold that the district court correctly relied upon § 2–302 as a limitation on § 2–316.

We next turn to a more troublesome subissue; viz., whether within the special facts of this case the disclaimer and exclusionary clause was unconscionable under Michigan law. As has often been stated, commercial contracts will rarely be found unconscionable, *see, e.g., A & M Produce Co. v. FMC Corp.,* 135 Cal.App.3d 473, 186 Cal.Rptr. 114 (1982), *Stanley A. Klopp, Inc. v. John Deere Co.,* 510 F.Supp. 807, 810 (E.D.Pa.1981), *aff'd,* 676 F.2d 688 (3rd Cir.1982),[4] because in

4. It is unclear whether the contract at issue is a commercial contract. As noted by the district court, some courts have held farmers and ranchers are not merchants. *See, e.g., Fear Ranches, Inc. v. Berry,* 470 F.2d 905 (10th Cir.1972); *Cook Grains, Inc. v. Fallis,* 239 Ark. 962, 395 S.W.2d 555 (1965). Other courts have taken the opposite position and held farmers are merchants. *See, e.g., Campbell v. Yokel,* 20 Ill.App.2d 702, 313 N.E.2d 628 (1974); *Nelson v. Union Equity Co-Operative Exchange,* 548 S.W.2d 352 (Tex.1977). Although these

the commercial setting the relationship is between business parties and is not so one-sided as to give one party the bargaining power to impose unconscionable terms on the other party.

In making its determination of unconscionability, the district court relied upon *Allen v. Michigan Bell Telephone,* 18 Mich.App. 632, 171 N.W.2d 689 (1969).[5] In *Allen* an insurance agent contracted with Michigan Bell Telephone Company to place advertisements in the classified telephone directory. When the advertisements were not included, he brought an action for damages. To defend the action, Michigan Bell Telephone Company relied on a limitation of remedies clause which, if upheld, would have limited the plaintiff's recovery to the contract price. In refusing to uphold the limitation, the Michigan court stated "the principle of freedom to contract does not carry a license to insert any provision in an agreement which a party deems advantageous." *Id.* at 691–92. Rather, the court stated that:

> [i]mplicit in the principle of freedom of contract is the concept that at the time of contracting each party has a realistic alternative to acceptance of the terms offered. Where goods and services can only be obtained from one source (or several sources on non-competitive terms) the choices of one who desires to purchase are limited to acceptance of the terms offered or doing without. Depending on the nature of the goods or services and the purchaser's needs, doing without may or may not be a realistic alternative. Where it is not, one who successfully exacts agreement to an unreasonable term cannot insist on the court's enforcing it on the ground that it was "freely" entered into, when it was not. * * *
>
> There are then two inquiries in a case such as this: (1) what is the relative bargaining power of the parties, their relative economic strength, the alternative sources of supply, in a word, what are their options?: (2) is the challenged term substantively reasonable?

Id. at 692.

With reference to the test announced in *Allen,* Harris Seed argues that the relative bargaining power of the parties is not a proper consideration under § 2–302. This is an issue on which courts and commentators have taken varying approaches. *Compare, e.g., Phillips Machinery Co. v. LeBlond, Inc.,* 494 F.Supp. 318 (N.D.Okla.1980) (no requirement of equality of bargaining power, but rather must be some element of deception or substantive unfairness) *and Majors v. Kalo Laboratories, Inc.,* 407 F.Supp. 20, 23 (M.D.Ala.1975) ("[T]he Official Comment to § 2–302 suggests that [consideration of bargaining power] would be inappropriate.") *with Kerr-McGee Corp. v. Northern Utilities, Inc.,* 673 F.2d 323, 329 (10th Cir.1982) (relative considerations include whether "there was a gross inequality

cases deal with the definition of "merchant" in § 2–104 for purposes of application to § 2–201(2) (the "between merchants" exception to the statute of frauds), the inquiry is relevant here for purposes of determining whether the transaction at issue occurred in a true "commercial setting," where unconscionability is rarely found. However, since we hold that, even if considered a "commercial setting," the clause at issue was unconscionable under the facts of this case, we do not reach the issue.

5. Although it may be, as Harris Seed argues, that the criticisms of *Allen* by courts, *see, e.g., Robinson Insurance & Real Estate, Inc. v. Southwestern Bell,* 366 F.Supp. 307 (W.D.Ark.1973), and commentators, *see* J. White & R. Summers, *Handbook of the Law Under the Uniform Commercial Code,* § 4–9, at 172 (2d Ed.1980) are well founded, the Michigan Appellate Court's holding is nevertheless an appropriate guide to our inquiry in the present case. *Cf. Simpson v. Jefferson Standard Life Insurance Co.,* 465 F.2d 1320, 1323 (6th Cir.1972) ("[d]ecisions of intermediate state courts must be followed by the federal courts unless there is reason to believe they would not be followed by the state's highest court.").

of bargaining power.") *and* J. White & R. Summers, *supra,* § 12–11, at 477 ("[o]ne can argue that when a seller has such a strong bargaining position that he can impose a perfectly drafted disclaimer, which operates to deprive the buyer of virtually all protection that a law would otherwise provide, and he refuses to bargain at all concerning its scope, then that clause has become 'oppressive' and so 'one-sided' as to be unconscionable."). We agree with the district court that relative bargaining power is an appropriate consideration in determining unconscionability under the Michigan Uniform Commercial Code.

Other closely related factors suggested by the Michigan court in *Allen* for determining the presence of procedural unconscionability are the relative economic strength of the parties and the alternative sources of supply. With reference to the relative economic strength of the parties, we note that Harris Seed is a large national producer and distributor of seed, dealing here with independent, relatively small farmers. As to alternative sources of supply, the farmers were faced with a situation where all seed distributors placed disclaimers and exclusionary clauses in their contracts. Thus, this presents a situation where "goods [could] only be obtained from * * * several sources on noncompetitive terms * * * and doing without [was] not a realistic alternative." *Allen, supra,* 171 N.W.2d at 692.

Another pertinent factor considered by the district court in its unconscionability finding was that Harris Seed's salesman did not make Martin and Rick, who were uncounseled laymen, aware of the fact that the clauses in question altered significant statutory rights. Such a disclosure is an important consideration under Michigan law. *Mallory v. Conida Warehouses, Inc.,* 134 Mich.App. 28, 350 N.W.2d 825, 827 (1984); *cf. Johnson v. Mobil Oil Corp.,* 415 F.Supp. 264, 269 (E.D.Mich.1976) ("[b]efore a contracting party with * * * immense bargaining power * * * may limit its liability vis-a-vis an uncounseled layman * * * it has an affirmative duty to obtain the voluntary knowing assent of the other party.").

Furthermore, although the terms of the 1972 sale appeared to be the same as in previous years (unknown to Martin and Rick), Harris Seed decided to discontinue the hot water treatment of its cabbage seed, a standard practice for the previous twenty-six years. This decision by Harris Seed was one which had far-reaching consequences to the purchasers of its cabbage seed. As noted above, hot water treatment had been successful in preventing black leg in Washington State produced cabbage seed since 1947, and although Martin and Rick were unaware of the potential effects of black leg, or indeed even what black leg was, Harris Seed had considerable expertise in such matters.

Another important consideration is the fact that the presence of black leg in cabbage seed creates a *latent* defect. Although in many cases the fact that a latent defect is present seems to be dispositive, see *Majors v. Kalo Laboratories, Inc.,* 407 F.Supp. 20 (M.D.Ala.1975); *Corneli Seed Company v. Ferguson,* 64 So.2d 162 (Fla.1953), we note only that it is important to the disposition of this case.

Significantly, in the present case not only was the defect latent, but it was also one which was within the control of Harris Seed to prevent. Even if Martin and Rick had been apprised of and understood the significance of Harris Seed's decision to discontinue hot water treatment, they would have been unable to detect the presence of the disease in the seed until their crop had developed into young plants. If Harris Seed were permitted to rely on the disclaimer and limitation clause to avoid liability under the facts of this case, the farmers who had no notice of, ability to detect, or control over the presence of the black leg could lose their livelihood. On the other hand, Harris Seed which had the knowledge, expertise and means to prevent the disease would only lose a few hundred dollars. Given the unique facts of this case, and giving "considerable weight" to the district court's decision that Michigan law would not permit the disclaimer and limitation clause to be enforced under such circumstances, we affirm the district court's finding of unconscionability.

* * *

[Some footnotes omitted.]

Notes

1. Did the seller's disclaimer satisfy the requirements of UCC 2–316(2)? How would you describe those requirements?

2. How could the seller have avoided the result in this case?

3. Note that the disclaimer was printed on the order form supplied by the seller. In seed cases, the courts have been even more hostile to disclaimers printed on the package or bag of seeds and not seen by the buyer until after the contract is formed, if at all. See, e.g., Gold Kist, Inc. v. Citizens & Southern National Bank of South Carolina, 286 S.C. 272, 333 S.E.2d 67 (1985) (disclaimer not part of agreement).

4. The United States and many states have enacted laws to protect the purchasers of seeds from falsely labeled products. The laws are backed by criminal sanctions. See 7 U.S.C.A. § 1551 (1985). These seed statutes, however, do not preempt Article 2 of the UCC. Thus, even if the seller complies with the statutory labeling requirements, it may still be liable for breach of warranty under the UCC. See, e.g., Hanson v. Funk Seeds International, 373 N.W.2d 30 (S.D.1985).

Problem 21–2

B, an experienced commercial fisherman, purchased a new diesel engine for his fishing boat from S. The engine was installed by S. Over the next 4 months, however, a number of mechanical problems arose, including the emission of excessive quantities of heavy black smoke. S was unable to correct them and the engine was removed from the boat. Experts will testify that it was unmerchantable.

At the time of contracting, B had signed a purchase order prepared by S. The face of the purchase order contained a number of terms and conditions. In the center of the face, this statement appeared: BOTH THIS ORDER AND ITS ACCEPTANCE ARE SUBJECT TO TERMS AND CONDITIONS STATED IN THIS ORDER. On the reverse side of the order at the top of the page, the following words appeared: TERMS AND CONDITIONS. Under that caption were eleven numbered paragraphs, one of which contained a disclaimer in the following form: THE SELLER HEREBY DISCLAIMS AND EXCLUDES ALL IMPLIED WARRANTIES, INCLUDING THE IMPLIED WARRANTY OF MERCHANTABILITY. B did not nor was he asked to read anything on the back of the purchase order. B received a fully executed copy of the order by mail before the engine was installed.

B sued S for damages resulting from breach of an implied warranty of merchantability. S defended on the ground that the warranty had been effectively disclaimed under UCC 2–316(2). What result?

Problem 21–3

S, a boat dealer, advertised a 42 foot Pearson sailing sloop for sale. The boat was manufactured in 1960 and had a wooden hull. B, an experienced sailor, had never owned a sloop with a wooden hull. Without the assistance of a third party, B examined the boat carefully and could find nothing wrong. She questioned S who, at various times stated: "This beauty was her owner's pride and joy. It's in great shape;" "The boat is sound. It rides the waves like a dream;" "The wood is solid throughout. We will replace any dry rot free of charge."

B agreed to purchase the sloop for $50,000. At the time of contracting, B signed a writing prepared by S which on the front provided, in part, as follows: "WARRANTIES. Buyer is buying the goods AS IS WHERE IS and no representations or statements have been made by seller except as herein stated, so that no warranty, express or implied, arises apart from this writing."

B took delivery of the boat, paid the price and went for a long, wet sail. The boat appeared to leak at the stern. An expert was hired to inspect the area and found extensive dry rot, which had clearly been there at the time of the sale. The estimated cost to repair the boat was $15,000.

B claimed damages for breach of warranty, measured by the cost to repair. S argued that all warranties, express or implied, had been disclaimed, citing UCC 2–316(1) & 2–202, UCC 2–316(3)(a) and UCC 2–316(3)(b). Is S correct?

SINGER CO. v. E.I. du PONT de NEMOURS & CO.

United States Court of Appeals, Eighth Circuit, 1978.
579 F.2d 433.

[Plaintiff, a manufacturer of airconditioners and furnaces, acquired an electrodeposition paint system to paint the metal or ware in the products. Under this system, pre-treated ware is conveyed through an electrically charged paint tank and coated with paint in an electroplating process. Defendant agreed to provide paint for the 22,000 gallon tank. From the beginning, Plaintiff had trouble with the paint. Ware emerging from this system was blotched and streaked and had to be repainted. Defendant, which had supervised the installation of the system, tried unsuccessfully for over six months to correct the problem. Ultimately, the Defendant's paint was removed from the tank and replaced with another brand. Plaintiff sued for damages. The key question was the cause of the defective painting. Plaintiff, arguing that the paint was at fault, claimed that Defendant had breached an express warranty and an implied warranty of fitness for particular purpose. Defendant argued that the paint conformed to any express warranty and that no implied warranties were made. Over Defendant's objection, the trial court instructed the jury on the implied warranty issue but not on express warranty. The jury returned a verdict for Plaintiff in the amount of $108,367. Defendant appealed.]

HANSON, SENIOR DISTRICT JUDGE.

* * *

While disagreeing on whether the trial court should have instructed as to an implied warranty of fitness for a particular purpose, the parties are properly in accord that the Illinois adoption of the Uniform Commercial Code governs the disposition of this case. * * * There is also no dispute that the "all tests" provision of the contract, which specified such set standards as color and texture that the paint was to satisfy upon pretreated laboratory test panels, was an express warranty pursuant to § 2–313(1)(b) of the U.C.C. But Singer claims that the contract further preserved an implied warranty of fitness, a warranty that pursuant to Section 2–315 assured plaintiff the paint supplied would satisfactorily cover its substrate. A paragraph in the contract provided:

> "None of the provisions or remedies herein are in lieu of any claims for damages Buyer may have at law or equity under the Uniform Commercial

Code or otherwise, for the breach of any contracts or warranties with Buyer, which rights are specifically reserved by Buyer."

Du Pont contends that parties who have an express warranty regarding a contracted for item cannot also have an implied warranty of fitness for that same item. The warranty of fitness for a specific purpose is alleged to have been limited by expressly defining it in a set of specifications, and Du Pont claims that to find otherwise would permit Singer to escape the parties' true contractual bargain.

Pertinent sections of the U.C.C., and the comments pursuant thereto, lend inferential support to Singer's position that the implied warranty of fitness was cumulative to and not excluded by the express warranty. Section 2–316(2), with regard to the exclusion or modification of such warranties, states:

> " * * * [T]o exclude or modify any implied warranty of fitness the exclusion must be by a writing *and conspicuous.*" (Emphasis added.)

Comment 9 to that section provides in part:

> "The situation in which *the buyer gives* precise and complete *specifications to the seller* is not explicitly covered in this section, but this is a frequent circumstance by which the *implied warranties may be excluded.* The warranty of fitness for a particular purpose would not normally arise since in such a situation there is usually *no reliance on the seller by the buyer.*" (Emphasis added.)

See also U.C.C. § 2–315, comment 2. Because the evidence in this case fully indicates that it was not the buyer but the seller who in fact recommended and supplied the paint specifications, and remained in control of the paint tank, it would appear that the trial court did not err in its determination that an implied warranty of fitness was at issue. This is especially so in view of the purported exclusion of this warranty, which could be scarcely termed "conspicuous."

A reading of the U.C.C. to suggest that an express warranty and an implied warranty of fitness are not necessarily mutually exclusive, as Singer has argued, receives support from Code authority.

> "The fact that a warranty of fitness for a particular purpose does or does not exist has no bearing on any other warranty or theory of product liability. Conversely, the fact that there may be some other basis for liability of the defendant does not preclude the existence of a warranty for a particular purpose. *Thus the fact that there is a warranty of conformity to sample [an express warranty] does not preclude the existence of a warranty for a particular purpose.*" (Emphasis added.) Anderson, Uniform Commercial Code § 2–315:5 (1970).

See also White and Summers, Uniform Commercial Code § 12–7 (1972); 67 Am. Jr.2d Sales § 501 (1973). Relevant case law, in the balance, further indicates that an express warranty would not control under the circumstances of this case.

Cases can be found prior to the adoption of the U.C.C. to support Du Pont's argument of mutual exclusiveness. This court, without specific adoption of the position, recognized in Hercules Powder Co. v. Rich, 3 F.2d 12 (8th Cir.1924) that there was law to the effect that an implied warranty of fitness could not prevail in the presence of an express warranty on the same item or subject.

> "An express warranty excludes an implied warranty relating to the same subject or of the same general nature, on the theory that no warranty should be implied where the parties with relation to the very same subject

have expressed by words the warranty by which they will be bound." Id. at 18.

There was also case law to the contrary. * * * But while there may have once been a split of authority, we fail to find since the general adoption of the above-quoted sections of the U.C.C. any case holding directly in favor of Du Pont's mutual exclusivity agreement. * * * In fact unless the exclusion of the implied warranty of fitness is specifically and conspicuously excluded, courts, often relying upon § 2–317, have found that such implied and express warranties can be cumulative and co-exist within the same agreement. Multivision Northwest, Inc. v. Jerrold Electronics Corp., 356 F.Supp. 207 (N.D.Ga.1972); Murray v. Kleen Leen, Inc., 41 Ill.App.3d 436, 354 N.E.2d 415 (1976); Water Works & Industrial Supply Co. v. Wilburn, 437 S.W.2d 951 (Ky.1969).

Du Pont, in arguing the law upon appeal, relies principally upon two types of cases that have arisen under the U.C.C.: those in which there has been a showing that the buyer, in possession or control of the item, failed to follow the express warranty specifications; and those where an enforceable disclaimer of an implied warranty has been established. With respect to the first type of case, it is clear that the trial court did not confront a situation where a buyer in possession or control of an item failed to follow seller's specifications used the item in a manner for which it was not intended, lost that for which he had contracted, and then erroneously claimed a breach of an implied warranty for fitness. * * * Here, Du Pont, as the seller, was in control of the disputed item. No one denied that Du Pont was throughout this time in control of Singer's paint tank, directing its operation and determining its contents.

The disclaimer cases are likewise inapplicable. Even without a paragraph in the contract reserving all further warranties under the U.C.C., Du Pont would have difficulty in arguing that an express warranty of the paint effected a disclaimer of any further warranty. It is clear from these cases that disclaimers under the Code are not favored and are limited whenever possible. Admiral Oasis Hotel Corp. v. Home Gas Industries, Inc., 68 Ill.App.2d 297, 216 N.E.2d 282 (1965); Dobias v. Western Farmers Association, 6 Wash.App. 194, 491 P.2d 1346 (1971); Annot., 73 A.L.R.3d 248 (1976).

Du Pont also argues in general that to permit Singer to assert an implied warranty of fitness would be to allow utilization of the U.C.C. in avoidance of the parties' true bargain. The true bargain, though, is less than apparent from the face of the contract. This was not a situation where a buyer ordered according to specifications and then claimed an implied warranty of fitness when the product failed to measure up to expectations. In this instance, the buyer approached the seller describing the results desired and the seller professed to be able to supply it, thereby inducing a reliance that created the possibility of an implied warranty of fitness. Notwithstanding the express warranty contained within the specifications particularly defining and describing the item to be supplied, there may have been a further warranty that an item with those specifications would accomplish certain results or be adequate for the specified purpose. That is, the accomplishment of the purpose might be viewed as the essence of the contractual undertaking, and not the mere furnishing of the specified item. Nothing within this contract, or in writings or statements subsequent to it, indicate whether the end of the agreement was the specified item or the use for which the item was intended. Cf. Construction Aggregates, supra.

Du Pont simply failed to negotiate a contract that clearly delineated and limited allocation of risk. This case would never have arisen had defendant, as a party to and a scrivener of the contract, either inserted a specific disclaimer or demanded that the warranty savings clause be deleted.

Having left the contract ambiguous, the question as to whether use rather than supply of the product was intended to be of the essence, as well as questions regarding buyer's reliance and seller's knowledge of that reliance, are for jury determination. * * *

* * *

The judgment appealed from is affirmed. [Footnotes omitted.]

Problem 21–4

B, a baker, planned to expand its capacity by 30%. Accordingly, on March 1, it ordered a custom made oven from S, a manufacturer, to be delivered not later than September 1. B informed S of its planned expansion and stated that "time was of the essence:" B had developed a new bread for hotels and restaurants and wanted to be in production for the Fall convention season. S and B negotiated over how to deal with the risk of delay in delivery.

1. After discussing B's current profit margin and the probabilities that an expansion would be profitable, S agreed, in a clause labeled LIQUIDATED DAMAGES, to pay B $500 for every day of a non-excusable delay in delivery. S did not deliver the oven until October 1. B claimed liquidated damages in the amount of $30,000. S, however, can establish that the convention business during September was very slow and that, at best, B would have made only $2,500 in net profits if the oven had been delivered on time. Is the agreed damage clause enforceable under UCC 2–718?

2. Suppose that the clause was labeled LIMITATION OF DAMAGES S agreed to pay "not more than $500 for each day of unexcused delay." The oven was delivered on October 1. B is prepared to establish that the convention market boomed during September and that the delay in delivery deprived it of at least $2,500 in net profits per day. B claims that the limitation clause was unreasonable. Is B correct. See UCC 2–718 & 2–719.

CAYUGA HARVESTER, INC. v. ALLIS–CHALMERS CORP.

Supreme Court of New York, Appellate Division, 1983.
95 A.D.2d 5, 465 N.Y.S.2d 606.

HANCOCK, JUSTICE:

Under the Uniform Commercial Code, the parties to a sale may, within certain limitations, allocate the risks of their bargain by limiting the remedy of the buyer (Uniform Commercial Code, § 2–719, subd. 1, par. a). When, however, a limited remedy such as an exclusive repair and replacement warranty fails of its essential purpose, the buyer is relieved of its restrictions and may resort to other remedies as provided in section 2–719 (subd. 2). The Code also permits the parties to agree to exclude consequential damages unless the exclusion is unconscionable (Uniform Commercial Code, § 2–719, subd. 3). Here the contract in issue contains both an exclusive repair and replacement warranty and an exclusion of consequential damages; plaintiff claiming that the limited remedy failed of its essential purpose seeks to recover consequential as well as other damages for breach of warranty. A major question arises from plaintiff's contention that proof of the failure of the limited repair and replacement warranty would free it not only from the restrictions of that clause but also from the clause excluding consequential damages.

The action arises out of the sale of an N–7 harvesting machine manufactured by defendant Allis-Chalmers Corporation ("Allis"). Plaintiff, the operator of an extensive corn-growing business in Cato, New York, purchased the machine for $142,213 from defendant R.C. Church & Sons, Inc. ("Church"), a farm machinery dealer, under a written purchase order containing a limited repair and replacement warranty and an exclusion of consequential damages. The balance of the purchase price, after a down payment of $36,989.80, was financed through defendant Allis-Chalmers Credit Corporation ("Allis Credit"). Plaintiff alleges that the machine did not operate or function properly and that it suffered numerous failures and breakdowns preventing it from making a timely and effective harvest of its 1981 corn crop.

The issues considered concerning various sections of the Uniform Commercial Code are as follows:

I. A. whether the limited repair and replacement warranty failed of its essential purpose (§ 2–719, subd. 2);

B. if so, whether, despite the failure, the consequential damages exclusion remains in effect; and

C. whether the clause excluding consequential damages is unconscionable (§§ 2–719, subd. 3; 2–302, subds. 1, 2).

* * *

I

We consider first the grant of summary judgment dismissing the first two causes of action against Allis alleging breaches of express warranties. In the purchase order under the "Allis-Chalmers New Farm Equipment Warranty", Allis gave an express warranty limited to the repair or replacement of defective parts in the following provisions which we quote in part:

WHAT IS WARRANTED

Allis-Chalmers Corporation ("Company") warrants new farm equipment sold by it to be merchantable and free of defects in workmanship and material at the time of shipment from the Company's factory. THERE ARE NO WARRANTIES WHICH EXTEND BEYOND THOSE EXPRESSLY STATED HEREIN. The warranty is made to the original purchaser or lessee from an authorized Allis-Chalmers Dealer of each item of new Allis-Chalmers farm equipment.

1. *Equipment Warranty.* Parts which are defective in workmanship and material as delivered will be repaired or replaced as follows:

* * *

(There follow several paragraphs detailing the terms and conditions of Allis' obligation to make repairs and replacements and the periods during which the warranty is effective.)

I. Remedies Exclusive

THE COMPANY'S LIABILITY, WHETHER IN CONTRACT OR IN TORT, ARISING OUT OF WARRANTIES, REPRESENTATIONS, INSTRUCTIONS, OR DEFECTS FROM ANY CAUSE SHALL BE LIMITED EXCLUSIVELY TO REPAIRING OR REPLACING PARTS UNDER THE CONDITIONS AS AFORESAID, AND IN NO EVENT WILL THE COMPANY BE LIABLE FOR CONSEQUENTIAL DAMAGES, INCLUDING BUT NOT LIM-

ITED TO LOSS OF CROPS, LOSS OF PROFITS, RENTAL OR SUBSTITUTE EQUIPMENT, OR OTHER COMMERCIAL LOSS.

In granting Allis' motions Special Term held that the provision excluding consequential damages in Paragraph "I", above, was, as a matter of law, not unconscionable under Uniform Commercial Code (§§ 2–719, subd. 3; 2–302, subd. 1) and that it acted as a total bar to plaintiff's express warranty claims. The court did not find it necessary to reach the issues before us concerning the alleged failure of the essential purpose of the repair and replacement warranty under the Uniform Commercial Code (§ 2–719, subd. 2) and the effect of that failure on the exclusion of consequential damages.

A

Ordinarily, whether circumstances have caused a "limited remedy to fail of its essential purpose" (Uniform Commercial Code, § 2–719, subd. 2) is a question of fact for the jury and one necessarily to be resolved upon proof of the circumstances occurring after the contract is formed (see *Johnson v. John Deere Co.,* 306 N.W.2d 231, 237, 238 [S.D.1981]). It should be noted that in order to establish a failure of a limited remedy under section 2–719 (subd. 2) it is not necessary to show that the warrantor's conduct in failing to effect repairs was wilfully dilatory or even negligent. Rather, the section is to apply "whenever an exclusive remedy, which may have appeared fair and reasonable at the inception of the contract, as a result of later circumstances operates to deprive a party of a substantial benefit of the bargain" (*Clark v. International Harvester Co.,* 99 Idaho 326, 340, 581 P.2d 784; see Uniform Commercial Code, § 2–719, Official Comment 1; White & Summers, Handbook of the Law under the Uniform Commercial Code, [2d ed.], § 12–10). The damage to the buyer is the same whether the seller diligently but unsuccessfully attempts to honor his promise or acts negligently or in bad faith (see *Beal v. General Motors Corp.,* 354 F.Supp. 423, 427 [D.C. Del., 1973]). Moreover, a "delay in supplying the remedy can just as effectively deny the purchaser the product he expected as can the total inability to repair. In both instances the buyer loses the substantial benefit of his purchase" (*Chatlos Systems, Inc. v. National Cash Register Corp.,* 635 F.2d 1081, 1085 [CCA 3d, 1980]). Thus, if it is found at trial that plaintiff, because of defendant Allis' failure to repair or replace parts within a reasonable time, has been deprived of a substantial benefit of its bargain, it may prevail even though, as is the case here, there is no claim of bad faith or wilfully dilatory conduct and the record demonstrates that defendant made extensive efforts to comply.

The precise question here is whether plaintiff has made a prima facie showing that the limited remedy failed of its essential purpose. On our review of the record we hold that plaintiff has made such a showing and that Special Term was in error in granting summary judgment dismissing the first two causes of action against Allis in their entirety (C.P.L.R. 3212, subd. b). Mr. Sheckler, plaintiff's president, states in an affidavit "that the N–7 combine purchased by plaintiff suffered over 100 mechanical failures and over 100 parts replacements resulting in over 640 actual hours of machine down-time. Because of the inoperability of the N–7 combine a full eight months were required for plaintiff to complete the process of driving the combine over all the acres of corn." Annexed to plaintiff's affidavits are a detailed log of the numerous machine failures and a lengthy list of warranty claims totaling many thousands of dollars submitted by Church to Allis covering work performed and parts supplied from the delivery of the machine in July of 1981 through February, 1982.

It is settled that a finding that a limited warranty has failed of its essential purpose frees the buyer to pursue his remedies under other provisions of the Uniform Commercial Code as if the clause did not exist (see *S.M. Wilson & Co. v. Smith Intern., Inc.,* 587 F.2d 1363 [CCA 9th, 1978]; *County Asphalt, Inc. v. Lewis Welding & Engineering Corp.,* 323 F.Supp. 1300, 1309 [S.D.N.Y.1970], affd. 444 F.2d 372 [CCA 2d, 1971], cert. den. 404 U.S. 939, 92 S.Ct. 272, 30 L.Ed.2d 252; *Johnson v. John Deere Co.,* 306 N.W.2d 231, 236 [S.D.1981], supra). Plaintiff would, therefore, not be precluded by the exclusive remedy clause from recovering under the usual measure of damages in warranty cases; i.e., "the difference at the time and place of acceptance between the value of the goods accepted and the value they would have had if they had been as warranted" (Uniform Commercial Code, § 2–714, subd. 2) (see *American Elec. Power Co., Inc. v. Westinghouse Elec. Corp.,* 418 F.Supp. 435, 457, 458 [S.D.N.Y.1976]; *County Asphalt, Inc. v. Lewis Welding & Engineering Corp.,* supra, p. 1309; *Johnson v. John Deere Co.,* supra, p. 236).

The order granting summary judgment to defendant Allis should be reversed to the extent that it dismisses the first and second causes of action in their entirety.

B

We come next to the legal question whether the consequential damage exclusion in Paragraph "I" would survive a finding that the limited repair and replacement warranty in that paragraph had failed of its essential purpose. We have found no controlling authority on the point in this state, and the numerous decisions in federal courts and the courts of other states are in conflict.

As we view it, the problem requires a two-step analysis: first, construing Paragraph "I" in its context as one clause in a contract concerning a substantial commercial transaction in order to ascertain the allocation of the risks as intended by the parties; and, second, determining whether that agreed-upon allocation of the risks leaves "at least a fair quantum of remedy for breach of the obligations or duties outlined in the contract" (McKinney's Cons.Laws of N.Y., Book 62½, Part 1, Uniform Commercial Code, § 2–719, Official Comment 1, p. 691). Paragraph "I" states:

> THE COMPANY'S LIABILITY, WHETHER IN CONTRACT OR IN TORT, ARISING OUT OF WARRANTIES, REPRESENTATIONS, INSTRUCTIONS, OR DEFECTS FROM ANY CAUSE SHALL BE LIMITED EXCLUSIVELY TO REPAIRING OR REPLACING PARTS UNDER THE CONDITIONS AS AFORESAID, AND IN NO EVENT WILL THE COMPANY BE LIABLE FOR CONSEQUENTIAL DAMAGES, INCLUDING BUT NOT LIMITED TO LOSS OF CROPS, LOSS OF PROFITS, RENTAL OR SUBSTITUTE EQUIPMENT, OR OTHER COMMERCIAL LOSS.

Preliminarily, it may be helpful to set forth two factors which are material to our analysis and, we think, significant: (1) this is not a case involving bad faith or wilfully dilatory conduct on the part of the defendant (compare, e.g., *Jones & McKnight Corp. v. Birdsboro Corp.,* 320 F.Supp. 39, 43 [D.C. Ill., 1970]; *Adams v. J.I. Case Co.,* 125 Ill.App.2d 388, 402, 261 N.E.2d 1: and (2) plaintiff, if it should succeed in proving that the limited warranty has failed, would, regardless of a contrary ruling on the survivability of the consequential damages exclusion, be permitted to recover damages allowed by Uniform Commercial Code (§ 2–714, subd. 2) (see subpart A, supra).

Plaintiff argues that the promise of defendant to repair and replace defective parts in the first part of Paragraph "I" and the clause exempting defendant from the assessment of consequential damages in the second part are mutually dependent, i.e., that a failure on the part of defendant to perform its obligations under the first, as a matter of law, deprives it of its exemption under the second part and frees plaintiff from its limitations. Defendant, on the other hand, maintains that the two provisions are unrelated and independent.

In our view defendant has the better of the argument. Certainly, no wording in Paragraph "I", itself, indicates that the provisions are interrelated or that the failure of defendant to perform under the repair and replacement warranty deprives it of the protection of the consequential damages exclusion. The purposes of the two clauses are totally discrete: that of the first is to restrict defendant's obligations under the transaction to repairing or replacing defective parts while that of the second is to rule out a specific type of damage. Each clause stands on its own and may be given effect without regard to the other. Thus, the plain meaning of Paragraph "I" appears to favor defendant.

Nor, given the larger context of Paragraph "I" as one term in a transaction involving the sale of an expensive piece of farm machinery to a large commercial grower, would it be reasonable to give it a different construction. Adopting plaintiff's interpretation, defendant's failure to repair and replace defective parts would, despite its good-faith efforts to fulfill its obligations, subject it to a lawsuit for consequential damages and loss of profits which, in view of the size of plaintiff's operation, could result in a recovery many times the value of the N–7 combine. It defies reason to suppose that defendant could have intended to assume such risks. The contrary construction urged by defendant entails a more plausible allocation of the risks and one that the parties could reasonably have had in mind: i.e., that a failure of the repair and replacement warranty, despite defendant's good faith efforts to comply, would permit plaintiff to recover the ordinary breach of warranty damages (Uniform Commercial Code, § 2–714, subd. 2) but not loss of profits or other consequential damages.

We find nothing in the Uniform Commercial Code that rules out defendant's construction. On the contrary, under Uniform Commercial Code (§ 2–719) the "parties are left free to shape their remedies to their particular requirements and reasonable agreements limiting or modifying remedies are to be given effect" (McKinney's Cons.Laws of N.Y., Book 62½, Part 1, Uniform Commercial Code, § 2–719, Official Comment 1, p. 691), provided that the remedy limitations are not unconscionable and that "there be at least a fair quantum of remedy for breach of the obligations or duties outlined in the contract" (McKinney's Cons. Laws of N.Y., Book 62½, Part 1, Uniform Commercial Code, § 2–719, Official Comment 1, p. 691). Moreover, Uniform Commercial Code (§ 2–719, subd. 3) provides specifically that consequential damages "may be limited or excluded unless the limitation or exclusion is unconscionable." In a similar vein, the Official Comment 3 to section 2–719 states: "Subsection (3) recognizes the validity of clauses limiting or excluding consequential damages but makes it clear that they may not operate in an unconscionable manner. Actually such terms are merely an allocation of unknown or undeterminable risks. The seller in all cases is free to disclaim warranties in the manner provided in Section 2–316" (McKinney's Cons.Laws of N.Y., Book 62½, Part 1, Uniform Commercial Code, § 2–719, Official Comment 3, p. 691). In sum, plaintiff has offered no good reason why the consequential damage exclusion clause should not be given effect in these circumstances, where the failure of the repair and replacement warranty is not due to bad faith or willfully dilatory conduct. That the clause be given effect here would be an allocation of the risks which leaves the buyer a fair quantum of remedy as required by the Code and one that the parties to this commercial contract could reasonably have intended. We conclude, therefore, that if plaintiff succeeds in establishing that the repair and replacement warranty failed of its essential purpose (Uniform Commercial Code, § 2–719, subd. 2), the exclusion of consequential damages provided by Paragraph "I" remains in effect.

As stated, the decisions are in conflict but the proper rule, we think, is that set forth in *Chatlos Systems, Inc. v. National Cash Register Corp.,* 635 F.2d 1081, 1086 [CCA 3d, 1980], supra: "The limited remedy of repair and a consequential damages exclusion are two discrete ways of attempting to limit recovery for breach of warranty. (Citations omitted.) The Code, moreover, tests each by a different standard. The former survives unless it fails of its essential purpose, while the latter is valid unless it is unconscionable. We therefore see no reason to hold, as a general proposition, that the failure of the limited remedy provided in the contract, without more, invalidates a wholly distinct term in the agreement excluding consequential damages."

* * *

The leading cases cited as supporting the opposite view are *Jones & McKnight Corp. v. Birdsboro Corp.,* 320 F.Supp. 39 [DC Ill., 1970], supra, and *Adams v. J.I. Case Co.,* 125 Ill.App.2d 388, 261 N.E.2d 1, supra (see also *Koehring Co. v. A.P.I., Inc.,* 369 F.Supp. 882 [DC Mich., 1974]; *Beal v. General Motors Corp.,* 354 F.Supp. 423 [DC Del., 1973], supra; *Clark v. International Harvester Co.,* 99 Idaho 326, 581 P.2d 784, supra; *Ehlers v. Chrysler Motor Corp.,* 88 S.D. 612, 226 N.W.2d 157; *Goddard v. General Motors Corp.,* 60 Ohio St.2d 41, 396 N.E.2d 761; *Murray v. Holiday Rambler, Inc.,* 83 Wis.2d 406, 265 N.W.2d 513).

On analysis, however, neither *Jones & McKnight* nor *Adams* is inconsistent with our holding. Each case involves outright repudiation of the repair and replacement warranty or conduct by the seller that was wilfully dilatory. Thus, in *Jones & McKnight* the court held that the buyer was entitled to assume that the seller "would not be unreasonable or wilfully dilatory in making good their warranty in the event of defects in the machinery and equipment" and refused to allow the defendant "to shelter itself behind one segment of the warranty when it has allegedly repudiated and ignored its very limited obligations under another segment of the same warranty" (*Jones & McKnight Corp. v. Birdsboro Corp.,* supra, p. 43). Similarly, in *Adams* the court, in holding that the repair and replacement warranty and the consequential damages exclusion were "not separable" held that "plaintiff could not have made [its] bargain and purchase with knowledge that defendant [ ] would be unreasonable, or, * * * wilfully dilatory or careless and negligent in making good [its] warranty in the event of its breach" (*Adams v. J.I. Case Co.,* supra, 125 Ill.App.2d at p. 402, 261 N.E.2d 1).

We need not decide whether we would follow *Jones & McKnight* and *Adams* if plaintiff could contend, as did the buyers in those cases, that in agreeing to the consequential damages exclusion it never contemplated that defendant would not make good-faith efforts to effect repairs. That issue is not before us.

While not all of the cases following the *Jones & McKnight* and *Adams* rule involve bad faith or wilful repudiation of the repair and replacement warranty, several arise from non-commercial sales where the purchaser was an individual consumer (see, e.g., *Clark v. International Harvester Co.,* supra; *Ehlers v. Chrysler Motor Corp.,* supra; *Goddard v. General Motors Corp.,* supra; *Murray v.*

Holiday Rambler, Inc., supra). Moreover, in *Clark v. International Harvester Co.* (supra), which entailed a purchase of a tractor by an individual custom farmer, the court points to a factor not present in the case at bar, i.e., that there "was a significant disparity in bargaining power between the parties in this case" (*Clark v. International Harvester Co.,* supra, 99 Idaho at p. 343, 581 P.2d 784).

Although we hold that plaintiff may not recover consequential damages, it will, if successful at trial, be entitled to other damages (Uniform Commercial Code, § 2–714, subd. 2). The order granting summary judgment should, therefore, be modified to a grant of partial summary judgment dismissing only those elements of the first two causes of action against Allis which seek consequential damages.

* * *

Finally, we analyze plaintiff's contentions that Paragraph "I" is unconscionable under sections 2–719 (subd. 3) and 2–302 (subds. 1, 2) of the Code. A determination as to the conscionability of a contract relates to the circumstances existing at the time of its formation (Uniform Commercial Code, § 2–302, subd. 1). As a practical matter, however, the determination is inevitably made after a dispute has arisen. Thus, the agreement must be tested as to conscionability as it is applied to the particular breach which has occurred. Here, there is no claim of bad faith or that the failure to repair was wilfully dilatory, and we have held that the parties did not intend in Paragraph "I" that defendant's good faith but unsuccessful efforts to repair would negate the consequential damages exclusion. We have also held that such an agreed upon allocation of the risks does not offend the Code requirement that there be at least a fair quantum of remedy for breach of defendant's obligations. We must now decide whether this agreed upon allocation of the risks is unconscionable.

* * *

On this record, in view of the nature of plaintiff's business as a large commercial grower, the size of the transaction involved, the fact that plaintiff had available other sources for purchasing similar equipment, the experience of its president and his familiarity with similar damage exclusion clauses, we agree with Special Term that plaintiff was not put in a bargaining position where it lacked a meaningful choice; nor was the agreement allocating the risk of crop loss and other consequential damages to the plaintiff, provided that good faith efforts be made to fulfill the repair warranty, unreasonably favorable to the defendant (see *Matter of State of New York v. Avco Fin. Serv. of N.Y.,* 50 N.Y.2d 383, 429 N.Y.S.2d 181, 406 N.E.2d 1075, supra).

The significant facts germane to the conscionability issue were essentially undisputed and we hold that Special Term correctly determined, as a legal question, that Paragraph "I" was not unconscionable and properly did so on the affidavits and other documents before it without the aid of a hearing (see Uniform Commercial Code, § 2–302).

* * *

[Footnotes omitted.]

Notes

1. *Cayuga Harvester* involved a fairly typical risk allocation package with four parts: (1) A limited warranty, i.e., that the goods were "merchantable and free of defects in material and workmanship at the time of shipment. * * *; (2) A disclaimer of all other warranties, express or implied plus a "merger" clause; (3) An agreed, exclusive limited remedy for breach, i.e., the "repair or replacement" of parts

which are "defective in workmanship and material as delivered" within a stated period of time; and (4) An exclusion in any event of liability for consequential damages for liability, "whether in contract or tort, arising out of any warranties made." These packages vary from industry to industry, but the thrust is essentially the same. See Transamerica Oil Corp. v. Lynes, Inc., 723 F.2d 758 (10th Cir.1983), where the court concluded that a similar limitation was so "pervasive" in the trade that the parties must have contracted with reference to it.

The problem arises when, after a defect is discovered, the seller is unable or unwilling to repair it within the stated time.

> This rosy picture of the limited repair warranty, however, rests upon at least three assumptions: that the warrantor will diligently make repairs, that such repairs will indeed 'cure' the defects, and that consequential loss in the interim will be negligible. So long as these assumptions hold true, the limited remedy appears to operate fairly and * * * will usually withstand contentions of 'unconscionability.' But when one of these assumptions proves false in a particular case, the purchaser may find that the substantial benefit of the bargain has been lost.

Eddy, *On the "Essential" Purposes of Limited Remedies: The Metaphysics of U.C.C. Section 2–719(2)*, 65 Calif.L.Rev. 28, 63 (1977).

When a disappointed buyer attacks the limited remedy, the cases tend to agree on the questions which must be answered and that the answers may vary from case to case. Here is a brief sample.

1. Was the limited remedy "expressly agreed to be exclusive"? UCC 2–719(1)(b). If not, resort to it by the buyer is optional. See, e.g., Leininger v. Sola, 314 N.W.2d 39 (N.D.1981). If so, it is "the sole remedy."

2. Did the "circumstances cause an exclusive or limited remedy to fail of its essential purpose. * * *?" UCC 2–719(2). If not, it is enforceable. If so, "remedy may be had as provided in this Act." The most common "circumstances" are the seller's failure to "cure" the defect within the time stated or a reasonable time. As Judge Aspen put it: A limited remedy of repair and replacement fails of its essential purposes when it is inadequate to provide the buyer with goods which conform to the contract within a reasonable time. * * * It is irrelevant to this standard whether the seller's failure to correct the defect is willful or not." Custom Automated Machinery v. Penda Corp., 537 F.Supp. 77 (N.D.Ill.1982). See also, Rudd Construction Equipment Co., Inc. v. Clark Equipment Co., 735 F.2d 974 (6th Cir.1984) (limited remedy fails essential purpose when defect causes fire which destroyed goods before seller had opportunity to cure).

3. If the limited remedy of repair or replacement failed its essential purpose, what is the effect on the total risk allocation package? More particularly, if the failure enables the buyer to pursue normal remedies for "direct" damages under UCC 2–714, what about the clause excluding consequential damages?

There are three closely related sub-questions. First, did the parties intend the exclusion clause to be an integral part of the risk allocation package? If so, the failure of one part spells the doom of the entire package, with the result that the buyer can pursue consequential damages under UCC 2–715(2). See Waters v. Massey-Ferguson, Inc., 775 F.2d 587 (4th Cir.1985); Milgard Tempering, Inc. v. Selas Corp. of America, 761 F.2d 553 (9th Cir.1985) (whether clause is separable a question of intent). If the exclusion clause was intended to be separate from the risk allocation, was the clause conscionable at the time the contract was made? UCC 2–719(3) & 2–302. See S.M. Wilson & Co. v. Smith Int'l, Inc., 587 F.2d 1363 (9th Cir. 1978). If so, consequential damages are not available. Third, if the exclusion clause was separate and conscionable at the time of contracting, was the seller's failure to "cure" so arbitrary or in such bad faith that it would be unfair to deprive the buyer of the substantial benefit of its bargain? A few courts have, on appropriate facts, taken this position. See, e.g., Fiorito Bros., Inc. v. Fruehauf Corp., 747 F.2d 1309 (9th Cir.1984); Caterpillar Tractor Co. v. Waterson, 13 Ark.App. 77, 679 S.W.2d 814 (1984).

Where does *Cayuga Harvester* fit in this range of possibilities?

Note: Contracting out of Tort Liability

In *Cayuga Harvester,* the seller attempted to exclude or "contract out" of "liability * * * in tort, arising out of warranties, representations, instructions, or defects from any cause," at least to the extent consequential damages were involved. What is the effect of these provisions?

If a defect in the product caused personal injuries, strict products liability would apply and the clause would be unenforceable (against public policy) against the plaintiff. See Note, *Enforcing Waivers in Products Liability,* 69 Va.L.Rev. 1111 (1983).

Between commercial parties ("extraordinary" consumers) where only economic loss is involved, the seller is, in most states, not liable in either strict products liability or negligence. In short, the buyer can pursue a warranty but not a tort theory. Review *Spring Motors,* supra at 828. Thus, the disclaimer would be tested under the Code, not in tort.

But suppose a defect in the product caused both economic loss and damage to the property sold, e.g., a defective part caused extensive damage to a turbine sold to the buyer but to no other property. Does warranty or tort theory apply and, if the latter, is the exclusion clause enforceable outside of the Code?

In this borderland between contract and tort where commercial parties are involved and property damage is confined to the goods sold, many courts have concluded that strict tort liability applies if the nature of the defect, the risk created and the manner in which the accident occurred raised an issue of product safety. The emphasis is upon the nature of the risk created to person and property, not upon the type of damage actually caused.

On the tort side of the line, the UCC does not apply. Nevertheless, commercial parties can agree to exculpate the seller from tort liability or from consequential damages if high standards insuring the quality of bargaining have been met. Thus, in Salt River Project Agr. v. Westinghouse Electric Co., 143 Ariz. 368, 694 P.2d 198 (1984), a turbine case, the court upheld an exculpation clause where the parties dealt in a commercial setting from positions of relatively equal bargaining strength, bargained over the specifications of the product and negotiated concerning the risk of loss from defects in the product. See McNichols, *Who Says That Strict Tort Disclaimers Can Never Be Effective? The Courts Disagree,* 28 Okl.L.Rev. 494 (1975).

SECTION 5. CONSUMER BUYERS, PRODUCT WARRANTIES AND ECONOMIC LOSS

An individual purchases a car, or a stereo or furniture or even a mobile home from a dealer for personal, family or household purposes. In short, they are consumer goods. See UCC 9–109(1). A common assumption is that consumer buyers, as a class, have less capacity than the professional seller to protect themselves in the bargain. They are at a disadvantage in assessing risk, evaluating quality, obtaining adequate information, bargaining over contract provisions and pursuing remedies if problems arise. They are "ordinary" consumers who are more susceptible to exploitation or unprovable fraud by the seller than a commercial or "extraordinary" buyer. (The distinction between "ordinary" and "extraordinary" consumers was advanced by Justice Peters, dissenting in Seely v. White Motor Co., 69 Cal.2d 9, 403 P.2d 145 (1965), to draw the line between warranty and tort in products liability cases. According to Peters, the test should depend upon the "relative roles played by the parties to the purchase contract and the nature of the transaction" rather than the type of loss caused and ask whether, at the time of contracting, the goods were sold to a commercial party or to an "ordinary consumer who is usually unable to protect himself * * *" or a commercial buyer who possessed "more bargaining power than does the usual individual who purchases * * * on the retail level." 403 P.2d at 152–58.)

The conclusion from this, is sometimes disputed, see, e.g., Schwartz & Wilde, *Imperfect Information in Markets for Contract Terms: The Examples of Warranties and Security Interests,* 69 Va.L.Rev. 1387 (1983); compare Kronman, *Paternalism and the Law of Contracts,* 92 Yale L.J. 763, 766–74 (1983) (assessing risk of unprovable fraud by seller), is that consumers need more legal protection than commercial buyers.

When the losses are solely economic, the consumer buyer's legal protection from breach of warranty by the seller is, without more, governed by the UCC. Additional, albeit uneven, protection is provided by the Magnuson-Moss Warranty Act on the federal level and, in some states, consumer protection legislation, including the so-called "lemon" laws.

In this Section, we will see how the consumer buyer of a "big ticket" item, a new car, might fare under this mix of federal and state law against the risk allocation package discussed in Section 4, supra. For general background and more detail, we recommend, Rice, *Product Quality Laws and the Economics of Federalism,* 65 B.U.L.Rev. 1 (1985). See also, Braucher, *An Informal Resolution Model of Consumer Product Warranty Law,* 1985 Wis.L.Rev. 1405; Vogel, *Squeezing Consumers: Lemon Laws, Consumer Warranties, and a Proposal for Reform,* 1985 Ariz.St.L.J. 589; Coffinberger & Samuels, *Legislative Responses to the Plight of New Car Purchasers,* 18 U.C.C.L.J. 168 (1985); Miller & Kanter, *Litigation under Magnuson-Moss,* 13 U.C.C.L.J. 10 (1980).

VENTURA v. FORD MOTOR CORP.

Superior Court of New Jersey, Appellate Division, 1981.
180 N.J.Super. 45, 433 A.2d 801.

[Marino Auto sold Ventura a new 1978 Ford. The car was substantially impaired due to persistent and continual stalling and hesitation. Ventura sued both Marino Auto and Ford, the manufacturer, for damages and Marino Auto cross-claimed against Ford for indemnification. At the conclusion of the non-jury trial, the trial judge concluded that Ford had breached a warranty to Ventura, made through Marino Auto, but that Ventura had not proven damages against Ford. Ventura, however, could recover attorney's fees in the amount of $5,165 from Ford under the Magnuson-Moss Warranty Act, 15 U.S.C.A. § 2310(d)(2). In addition, despite an attempt by the dealer to disclaim all warranties, express or implied, Ventura could revoke its acceptance against and recover the purchase price less an allowance for use, a total of $6,745.59, from Marino Auto. Finally, the trial court entered a judgment in favor of Marino Auto against Ford for $2,910.59 and rejected Ventura's claims for interest, punitive damages and treble damages.

On appeal, the judgment was affirmed. The court assumed that Marino Auto's disclaimer of the implied warranty of merchantability was valid under the UCC, and concluded that the judgment was supported by the Magnuson-Moss Warranty Act.]

* * *

The Magnuson-Moss Warranty-Federal Trade Commission Improvement Act, *supra,* was adopted on January 4, 1975, 88 *Stat.* 2183. Its purpose was to make "warranties on consumer products more readily understandable and enforceable." Note, 7 *Rutgers-Camden L.J.* 379 (1976). The act enhances the consumer's position by allowing recovery under a warranty without regard to privity of contract between the consumer and warrantor, by prohibiting the disclaimer of implied warranties in a written warranty, and by enlarging the remedies available to a consumer for breach of warranty, including the award of attorneys' fees. *Id.* The requirement of privity of contract between the consumer and the warrantor has been removed by assuring consumers a remedy against all warrantors of the product.[3] A consumer is defined in 15 *U.S.C.A.* § 2301(3) as follows:

> (3) The term 'consumer' means a buyer (other than for purposes of resale) of any consumer product, any person to whom such product is transferred during the duration of an implied or written warranty (or service contract) applicable to the product, and any other person who is entitled by the terms of such warranty (or service contract) or under applicable State law to enforce against the warrantor (or service contract) the obligations of the warranty (or service contract).

A "supplier" is defined as any person engaged in the business of making a consumer product directly or indirectly available to consumers, § 2301(4), and a "warrantor" includes any supplier or other person who gives or offers to give a written warranty or who is obligated under an implied warranty. § 2301(5). The term "written warranty" is defined in § 2301(6) to include:

> (A) any written affirmation of fact or written promise made in connection with the sale of a consumer product by a supplier to a buyer which relates to the nature of the material or workmanship and affirms or promises that such material or workmanship is defect free or will meet a specified level of performance over a specified period of time, or
>
> (B) any undertaking in writing in connection with the sale by a supplier of a consumer product to refund, repair, replace or take other remedial action with respect to such product in the event that such product fails to meet the specifications set forth in the undertaking.

The Magnuson-Moss Warranty Act provides for two types of written warranties on consumer products, those described as "full" warranties and those described as "limited" warranties. 15 *U.S.C.A.* § 2303. The nature of the "full" warranty is prescribed by § 2304. It expressly provides in subsection (a)(4) that a consumer must be given the election to receive a refund or replacement without charge of a product or part which is defective or malfunctions after a reasonable number of attempts by the warrantor to correct such condition. For the breach of any warranty, express or implied, or of a service contract (defined in 15 *U.S.C.A.* § 2301(8)), consumers are given the right to sue for damages and "other legal and equitable relief" afforded under state or federal law, 15 *U.S.C.A.* § 2310(d); 15 *U.S.C.A.* § 2311(b)(1).

3. In Miller and Kanter, "Litigation Under Magnuson-Moss: New Opportunities in Private Actions," 13 *U.C.C.L.J.* 10, 21–22 (1980), the authors discuss the broad definition of a consumer and state that "an assumption is now created that no privity restriction exists."

Appellant Ford contends that the trial judge improperly invoked § 2304 of the act as a basis for allowing "rescission" in the case since the warranty given by Ford was a limited warranty and not a full warranty. 15 *U.S.C.A.* § 2303(a)(2) provides that all warranties that do not meet federal minimum standards for warranty contained in § 2304 shall be conspicuously designated a "limited warranty." "Limited" warranties protect consumers by prohibiting disclaimers of implied warranties, § 2308, but are otherwise not described in the act. Note, *supra,* 7 *Rutgers-Camden L.J.* at 381. Clearly, Ford's warranty, which is quoted later in this opinion, was a limited warranty.

15 *U.S.C.A.* § 2308 provides as follows:

> (a) No supplier may disclaim or modify (except as provided in subsection (b) of this section) any implied warranty to a consumer with respect to such consumer product if (1) such supplier makes any written warranty to the consumer with respect to such consumer product, or (2) at the time of sale, or within 90 days thereafter, such supplier enters into a service contract with the consumer which applies to such consumer product.
>
> (b) For purposes of this chapter (other than section 2304(a)(2) of this title), implied warranties may be limited in duration to the duration of a written warranty of reasonable duration, if such limitation is conscionable and is set forth in clear and unmistakable language and prominently displayed on the face of the warranty.
>
> (c) A disclaimer, modification, or limitation made in violation of this section shall be ineffective for purposes of this chapter and State law.

We will first consider the application of this act to the dealer, Marino Auto. As quoted above, paragraph 7 of the purchase order-contract provides that there are no warranties, express or implied, made by the selling dealer or manufacturer except, in the case of a new motor vehicle, "the warranty expressly given to the purchaser upon delivery of such motor vehicle. * * *" This section also provides: "The selling dealer also agrees to promptly perform and fulfill all terms and conditions of the owner service policy." Ford contended in the trial court that Marino Auto had "a duty" to properly diagnose and make repairs, that such duty was "fixed both by the express warranty * * * which they passed on * * * and by the terms of [paragraph 7 of the contract with plaintiff]" by which Marino Auto expressly undertook "to perform its obligations under the owner service policy." See 15 *U.S.C.A.* § 2310(f); 16 *C.F.R.* § 700.4 (1980). The provision in paragraph 7 in these circumstances is a "written warranty" within the meaning of § 2301(6)(B) since it constitutes an undertaking in connection with the sale to take "remedial action with respect to such product in the event that such product fails to meet the specifications set forth in the undertaking. * * *" In our view the specifications of the undertaking include, at the least, the provisions of the limited warranty furnished by Ford, namely:

> *LIMITED WARRANTY (12 MONTHS OR 12,000 MILES/19,312 KILOMETRES) 1978 NEW CAR AND LIGHT TRUCK*
>
> Ford warrants for its 1978 model cars and light trucks that the Selling Dealer will repair or replace free any parts, except tires, found under normal use in the U.S. or Canada to be defective in factory materials or workmanship within the earlier of 12 months or 12,000 miles/19,312 km from either first use or retail delivery. All we require is that you properly operate and maintain your vehicle and that you return for warranty service

to your Selling Dealer or any Ford or Lincoln-Mercury Dealer if you are traveling, have moved a long distance or need emergency repairs. Warranty repairs will be made with Ford Authorized Service or Remanufactured Parts.

THERE IS NO OTHER EXPRESS WARRANTY ON THIS VEHICLE.[4]

The record does not contain a written description of the "owner service policy" which the dealer agreed to perform. Nevertheless, since Ford is the appellant here, we take its contentions at trial and documents in the record to establish the dealer's obligation to Ford and to plaintiff to make the warranty repairs on behalf of Ford (subject to the right of reimbursement or other terms that may be contained in their agreement). For the purpose of this appeal we are satisfied that the dealer's undertaking in paragraph 7 constitutes a written warranty within the meaning of 15 *U.S.C.A.* § 2301(6)(B). Accordingly, having furnished a written warranty to the consumer, the dealer as a supplier may not "disclaim or modify [except to limit in duration] any implied warranty to a consumer. * * *" The result of this analysis is to invalidate the attempted disclaimer by the dealer of the implied warranties of merchantability and fitness.[5] Being bound by those implied warranties arising under state law, *N.J. S.A.* 12A:2–314 and 315, Marino Auto was liable to plaintiff for the breach thereof as found by the trial judge, and plaintiff could timely revoke his acceptance of the automobile and claim a refund of his purchase price. *N.J.S.A.* 12A:2–608 and *N.J.S.A.* 12A:2–711. *Zabriskie Chevrolet, Inc. v. Smith,* 99 *N.J. Super.* 441, 240 *A.*2d 195 (Law Div.1968). In this connection we note that the trial judge found that plaintiff's attempted revocation of acceptance was made in timely fashion, and that finding has adequate support in the evidence.

As the trial judge noted, 15 *U.S.C.A.* § 2310(d)(1) provides that a consumer who is damaged by the failure of a warrantor to comply with any obligation under the act, or under a written warranty or implied warranty or service contract, may bring suit "for damages and other legal and equitable relief. * * *" Although the remedy of refund of the purchase price is expressly provided by the Magnuson-Moss Warranty Act for breach of a full warranty, granting this remedy under state law for breach of a limited warranty is not barred by or inconsistent with the act. 15 *U.S.C.A.* § 2311(b)(1) provides that nothing in the act restricts "any right or remedy of any consumer under State law or other Federal law." See also 15 *U.S.C.A.* § 2311(c)(2). Thus, for breach of the implied warranty of merchantability, plaintiff was entitled to revoke acceptance against Marino Auto, and a judgment for the purchase price less an allowance for the use of the vehicle was properly entered against Marino Auto. *N.J.S.A.* 12A:2–608 and 711. *Cf.* 15 *U.S.C.A.* § 2301(12) which defines "refund"

4. The warranty also provided:

TO THE EXTENT ALLOWED BY LAW:

1. ANY IMPLIED WARRANTY OF MERCHANTABILITY OR FITNESS IS LIMITED TO THE 12 MONTH OR 12,000–MILE/19,312–KM DURATION OF THIS WRITTEN WARRANTY.

2. NEITHER FORD NOR THE SELLING DEALER SHALL HAVE ANY RESPONSIBILITY FOR LOSS OF USE OF THE VEHICLE, LOSS OF TIME, INCONVENIENCE, COMMERCIAL LOSS OR CONSEQUENTIAL DAMAGES.

Some states do not allow limitations on how long an implied warranty lasts or the exclusion or limitation of incidental or consequential damages, so the above limitations may not apply to you.

This warranty gives you specific legal rights, and you also may have other rights which vary from state to state.

5. The same holding would apply if the undertaking by Marino Auto to perform the "owner service policy" is construed as a "service contract." 15 *U.S.C.A.* § 2308(a), *supra.*

as the return of the purchase price "less reasonable depreciation based on actual use where permitted" by regulations.

Plaintiff also could have recovered damages against Ford for Ford's breach of its written limited warranty. Marino Auto was Ford's representative for the purpose of making repairs to plaintiff's vehicle under the warranty. *See Henningsen v. Bloomfield Motors, Inc., supra,* 32 *N.J.* at 374, 161 *A.*2d 69; *cf. Conte v. Dwan Lincoln-Mercury, Inc.,* 172 *Conn.* 112, 122–126, 374 *A.*2d 144, 149–150 (Sup. Ct.Err.1976). The limited warranty expressly required the purchaser to return the vehicle "for warranty service" to the dealer or to any Ford or Lincoln-Mercury dealer if the purchaser is traveling or has moved a long distance or needs emergency repairs. Ford contends that it put purchasers on notice that they should advise Ford's district office if they have problems with their cars that a dealer is unable to fix. The record contains a document listing "frequently asked warranty questions" which states:

> The Dealership where you purchased your vehicle has the responsibility for performing warranty repairs; therefore, take your vehicle to that Dealership. * * * If you encounter a service problem, refer to the service assistance section of your Owner's Guide for suggested action.

We do not read these provisions as requiring notice to Ford as a condition of relief against Ford when Ford's dealer has failed after numerous attempts to correct defects under warranty.

Normally, the measure of damages for a breach of warranty is the difference between the price paid by the purchaser and the market value of the defective product. *Santor v. A & M Karagheusian, Inc., supra,* 44 *N.J.* at 63, 68–69, 207 *A.*2d 305; *see Herbstman v. Eastman Kodak Co., supra,* 68 *N.J.* at 11, 342 *A.*2d 181. However, as Judge Conford said in his concurring opinion in *Herbstman, supra,* 68 *N.J.* at 15–16, 342 *A.*2d 181, under principles of strict liability in tort a purchaser may be entitled to rescind the transaction and receive the return of the purchase price from the manufacturer without privity if the defect causes substantial impairment of value of the product. The strict liability in tort doctrine as developed in this state in the *Santor case, supra,* eliminated the need for privity of contract between the purchaser and the manufacturer as a condition for the purchaser's claim for his loss of bargain caused by a defect in the product. As noted above, the Magnuson-Moss Warranty Act accomplished the same result.

One question posed by this case is whether recovery of the purchase price from the manufacturer was available to plaintiff for breach of the manufacturer's warranty. If the warranty were a full warranty plaintiff would have been entitled to a refund of the purchase price under the Magnuson-Moss Warranty Act. Since Ford's warranty was a limited warranty we must look to state law to determine plaintiff's right to damages or other legal and equitable relief. 15 *U.S.C.A.* § 2310(d)(1). Once privity is removed as an obstacle to relief we see no reason why a purchaser cannot also elect the equitable remedy of returning the goods to the manufacturer who is a warrantor and claiming a refund of the purchase price less an allowance for use of the product. *See Seely v. White Motor Co.,* 63 *Cal.*2d 9, 45 *Cal.Rptr.* 17, 20, 403 *P.*2d 145, 148 (Sup.Ct.1965); *Durfee v. Rod Baxter Imports, Inc., supra,* 262 *N.W.*2d at 357–358, where the Minnesota Supreme Court held as a matter of state law that lack of privity does not bar a purchaser of a foreign car from revoking acceptance and recovering the purchase price from the distributor of such cars as distinguished from the local dealer. The decision was made without regard to the Magnuson-Moss Warranty Act.

We are dealing with the breach of an express contractual obligation. Nothing prevents us from granting an adequate remedy under state law for that breach of contract, including rescission when appropriate. Under state law the right to revoke acceptance for defects substantially impairing the value of the product (*N.J.S.A.* 12A:2–608) and to receive a refund of the purchase price (*N.J.S.A.* 12A:2–711) are rights available to a buyer against a seller in privity. Where the manufacturer gives a warranty to induce the sale it is consistent to allow the same type of remedy as against that manufacturer. *See Durfee v. Rod Baxter Imports, Inc., supra; cf. Seely v. White Motor Co., supra.* Only the privity concept, which is frequently viewed as a relic these days, *Koperski v. Husker Dodge, Inc.*, 208 *Neb.* 29, 45, 302 *N.W.*2d 655, 664 (Sup.Ct.1981); *see Kinlaw v. Long Mfg. N.C., Inc.*, 298 *N.C.* 494, 259 *S.E.*2d 552 (Sup.Ct.1979), has interfered with a rescission-type remedy against the manufacturer of goods not purchased directly from the manufacturer. If we focus on the fact that the warranty creates a direct contractual obligation to the buyer, the reason for allowing the same remedy that is available against a direct seller becomes clear. Although the manufacturer intended to limit the remedy to the repair and replacement of defective parts, the failure of that remedy, *see N.J.S.A.* 12A:2–719(2); *Goddard v. General Motors Corp.*, 60 *Ohio St.*2d 41, 396 *N.E.*2d 761 (Sup.Ct.1979); *Seely v. White Motor Co., supra,* and the consequent breach of the implied warranty of merchantability which accompanied the limited warranty by virtue of the Magnuson-Moss Warranty Act, make a rescission-type remedy appropriate when revocation of acceptance is justified. *Durfee v. Rod Baxter Imports, Inc., supra,* 262 *N.W.*2d at 357.

Lastly, we consider Ford's contention that a counsel fee was improperly granted to plaintiff since no judgment was entered in favor of plaintiff against Ford and Ford contends it was not given adequate notice of the defects in the car. 15 *U.S.C.A.* § 2310(d)(2) provides that a consumer who "prevails in any action brought [in any court] under paragraph (1) of this subsection * * * may be allowed by the court to recover as part of the judgment * * * expenses (including attorney's fees based on the actual time expended). * * *" This section is subject to the provisions contained in § 2310(e). Subsection (e) provides that, with certain exceptions, no action based upon breach of a written or implied warranty or service contract may be prosecuted unless a person obligated under the warranty or service contract "is afforded a reasonable opportunity to cure such failure to comply." Here that opportunity was given to Ford's designated representative to whom the purchaser was required to bring the car. A direct employee of Ford, Bednarz, also met with plaintiff or his wife and was made aware of some difficulty with the car. We are not certain of the extent of Ford's knowledge of those difficulties. However, in our view the opportunities given to Marino Auto to repair the vehicle satisfied the requirements of 15 *U.S.C.A.* § 2310(e) in this case.

As noted, Ford also contends that a counsel fee could not be awarded against Ford because plaintiff did not recover a judgment against Ford. The Magnuson-Moss Warranty Act permits a prevailing consumer to recover attorney's fees "as part of the judgment." The trial judge found that Ford had breached its warranty and that the car's value was substantially impaired. He entered no damage judgment against Ford. However, in the absence of proof of actual damages, plaintiff was entitled to a judgment against Ford for nominal damages. *Ruane Dev. Corp. v. Cullere,* 134 *N.J.Super.* 245, 252, 339 *A.*2d 229 (App.Div. 1975); *Ench v. Bluestein,* 52 *N.J.Super.* 169, 173–174, 145 *A.*2d 44 (App.Div.1958); *Winkler v. Hartford Accident and Indem. Co.,* 66 *N.J.Super.* 22, 29, 168 *A.*2d 418

(App.Div.), certif. den. 34 *N.J.* 581, 170 *A.*2d 544 (1961); *Packard Englewood Motors, Inc. v. Packard Motor Car Co.,* 215 *F.*2d 503, 510 (3 Cir.1954). Ford was not prejudiced by the failure of the trial judge to enter a judgment for nominal damages to which the award of attorney's fees could be attached. *See Nobility Homes, Inc. v. Ballentine,* 386 *So.*2d 727, 730–731 (Sup.Ct.Ala.1980). The award of counsel fees fulfills the intent of the Magnuson-Moss Warranty Act. Without such an award consumers frequently would be unable to vindicate warranty rights accorded by law.

As to the amount of counsel fees allowed by the trial judge, we find no abuse of discretion. The allowance was for actual time spent at an hourly rate of $75. Consideration could properly be given to the fact that plaintiff's attorney undertook this claim on a contingency basis with a relatively small retainer. *DR* 2–106(A)(8). The normal breach of warranty case ought not require four separate appearances before the trial court. To some extent this was not in the control of plaintiff's attorney, and plaintiff might have obtained all the relief required against Ford on the first day of trial. But it did not work out that way. In other cases it may be possible to stipulate damages and simplify the issues, thus limiting the cost of this type of litigation for consumers and suppliers alike. But the issues raised in this case were novel in this State, and no one can be faulted for the difficulty and time consumed in this litigation.

We have stated that in an appropriate case a consumer could recover the purchase price from a manufacturer for breach of a limited warranty causing a substantial impairment of the value of the product. The application of the Magnuson-Moss Warranty Act is one distinction between this case and *Herbstman v. Eastman Kodak Co., supra,* 68 *N.J.* at 9–12, n. 1, 342 *A.*2d 181. However, we need not determine whether plaintiff had the right to such relief in this case. Ordinarily, a purchaser seeking such relief after unsuccessful repairs should be required to give timely notice to the manufacturer of revocation of acceptance of defective goods and of his demand for a refund of the purchase price. *See Durfee v. Rod Baxter Imports, Inc., supra,* 262 *N.W.*2d at 353. Plaintiff's complaint alleges that such notice and demand were given to Ford in this case, but no finding was made by the trial judge on plaintiff's claim against Ford. Having determined that plaintiff was entitled to a judgment for nominal damages and counsel fees against Ford, and that judgments against Marino Auto and for indemnification by Ford were properly entered, it makes no difference in this case whether plaintiff was also entitled to a refund of his purchase price from Ford.

The result in this case differs from that reached in *Edelstein v. Toyota Motors Distributors, supra.* However, the differences in the cases, the absence there of proof of any warranty from defendants, and the apparent failure of the purchaser to rely on the Magnuson-Moss Warranty Act make it unnecessary for us to comment on that holding.

Affirmed.

Notes

Here are some questions about the *Ventura* case.

1. The court assumes that the Dealer had effectively disclaimed all warranties under the Code. How does the Magnuson-Moss Warranty Act support the court's conclusion that, nevertheless, the dealer breached an implied warranty of merchantability?

Note that the dealer failed to "cure" the problem and that the buyer's remedy included revocation of acceptance, UCC 2–608(1), and a refund of the price, UCC 2–711(1), adjusted for the value of buyer's use after the revocation. Consequential damages were not claimed. Compare Bogner v. General Motors Corp., 117 Misc.2d 929, 459 N.Y.S.2d 679 (N.Y.Civ.Ct.1982) (although consequential damages excluded, court awards damages for emotional distress). See also, Ramirez v. Autosport, 88 N.J. 277, 440 A.2d 1345 (1982) (buyer properly rejects camper-van for defects, cancels contract and recovers price); Jacobs v. Rosemount Dodge-Winnebago South, 310 N.W.2d 71 (Minn.1981) (limited remedy fails essential purpose, buyer permitted to revoke acceptance and recover consequential damages).

2. Suppose that the dealer made no "written warranty," see 15 U.S.C.A. § 2301(6), and effectively disclaimed all warranties under UCC 2–316. Would the buyer have any claims against the dealer under either the Magnuson-Moss Act or the UCC?

A few states have passed special consumer legislation to deal with perceived shortcomings in the Code. See, for example, Section 2–316A of the Massachusetts UCC, enacted in 1973:

2–316A. Limitation of Exclusion or Modification of Warranties

The provisions of section 2–316 shall not apply to sales of consumer goods, services or both. Any language, oral or written, used by a seller or manufacturer of consumer goods and services, which attempts to exclude or modify any implied warranties of merchantability and fitness for a particular purpose or to exclude or modify the consumer's remedies for breach of those warranties, shall be unenforceable.

Any language, oral or written, used by a manufacturer of consumer goods, which attempts to limit or modify a consumer's remedies for breach of such manufacturer's express warranties, shall be unenforceable, unless such manufacturer maintains facilities within the commonwealth sufficient to provide reasonable and expeditious performance of the warranty obligations.

The provisions of this section may not be disclaimed or waived by agreement.

3. The manufacturer, Ford Motor Company, made a written, "limited" warranty to Ventura. The express warranty was breached and the dealer failed to "cure." What was the maximum protection, liability and remedy, to which Ventura was entitled against Ford under the Magnuson-Moss Act? Read the entire statute, please. Why was Ventura's recovery limited to the recovery of attorney's fees?

4. Suppose that Ford (or the Dealer) had made a written, "full" warranty to Ventura. To what additional protection would Ventura be entitled? See, particularly, 15 U.S.C.A. § 2304(a). How does this differ from protection available under the UCC when a limited remedy "fails" its essential purpose?

As a matter of practice, few manufacturers or sellers are willing to make "full" written warranties, and there is no penalty imposed for that omission under *Magnuson-Moss.*

Problem 21–5

Assume the same facts as in Ventura v. Ford Motor Company. Assume, also, that the state where the dispute arose had enacted a "New-Car Buyer Protection Act," based upon that enacted in Illinois. Ill.Rev.Stat. Ch. 121½, Par. 1201–08.

What protection does this "Lemon Law" add to that available under the Magnuson-Moss Warranty Act?

How does the "Lemon Law" mesh with the applicable provisions of the UCC?

NEW–CAR BUYER PROTECTION ACT

1201. Short title

§ 1. This Act shall be known and may be cited as the New-Car Buyer Protection Act.

1202. Definitions

§ 2. For the purposes of this Act, the following words have the meanings ascribed to them in this Section.

(a) "Consumer" means an individual who purchases a new car from the seller for the purposes of transporting himself and others, as well as their personal property, for primarily personal, household or family purposes.

(b) "Express warranty" has the same meaning, for the purposes of this Act, as it has for the purposes of the Uniform Commercial Code.

(c) "New car" means a passenger car, as defined in Section 1–157 of The Illinois Vehicle Code, which does not qualify under the definition of a used motor vehicle, as set forth in Section 1–216 of that Code. The term does not include motor homes, mini motor homes or van campers, as defined in Section 1–145.01 of The Illinois Vehicle Code.

(d) "Nonconformity" refers to a new car's failure to conform to all express warranties applicable to such car, which failure substantially impairs the use, market value or safety of that car.

(e) "Seller" means the manufacturer of a new car, that manufacturer's agent or distributor or that manufacturer's authorized dealer.

(f) "Statutory warranty period" means the period of one year or 12,000 miles, whichever occurs first after the date of the delivery of a new car to the consumer who purchased it.

1203. Failure of new car to conform to express warranties—Remedies—Presumption—Allowance for consumer use—Suspension of warranty period

§ 3. (a) If after a reasonable number of attempts the seller is unable to conform the new car to any of its applicable express warranties, the manufacturer shall either provide the consumer with a new car of like model line, if available, or otherwise a comparable motor vehicle as a replacement, or accept the return of the car from the consumer and refund to the consumer the full purchase price of the new car, including all collateral charges, less a reasonable allowance for consumer use of the car.

(b) A presumption that a reasonable number of attempts have been undertaken to conform a new car to its express warranties shall arise where, within the statutory warranty period,

(1) the same nonconformity has been subject to repair by the seller, its agents or authorized dealers during the statutory warranty period, 4 or more times, and such nonconformity continues to exist; or

(2) the car has been out of service by reason of repair of nonconformities for a total of 30 or more business days during the statutory warranty period.

(c) A reasonable allowance for consumer use of a car is that amount directly attributable to the wear and tear incurred by the new car as a result of its having been used prior to the first report of a nonconformity to the seller, and during any subsequent period in which it is not out of service by reason of repair.

(d) The fact that a new car's failure to conform to an express warranty is the result of abuse, neglect or unauthorized modifications or alterations is an affirmative defense to claims brought under this Act.

(e) The statutory warranty period of a new car shall be suspended for any period of time during which repair services are not available to the consumer because of a war, invasion or strike, or a fire, flood or other natural disaster.

(f) Refunds made pursuant to this Act shall be made to the consumer, and lien holder if any exists, as their respective interests appear.

(g) For the purposes of this Act, a manufacturer sells a new car to a consumer when he provides that consumer with a replacement car pursuant to subsection (a).

(h) In no event shall the presumption herein provided apply against a manufacturer, his agent, distributor or dealer unless the manufacturer has received prior direct written notification from or on behalf of the consumer, and has an opportunity to correct the alleged defect.

1204. Informal settlement procedure—Notice

§ 4. (a) The provisions of subsection (a) of Section 3 shall not apply unless the consumer has first resorted to an informal settlement procedure applicable to disputes to which that subsection would apply where

(1) The manufacturer of the new car has established such a procedure;

(2) The procedure conforms:

(i) substantially with the provisions of Title 16, Code of Federal Regulation, Part 703, as from time to time amended, and

(ii) to the requirements of subsection (c); and

(3) The consumer has received from the seller adequate written notice of the existence of the procedure.

Adequate written notice includes but is not limited to the incorporation of the informal dispute settlement procedure into the terms of the written warranty to which the car does not conform.

(b) If the consumer is dissatisfied with the decision reached in an informal dispute settlement procedure or the results of such a decision, he may bring a civil action to enforce his rights under subsection (a) of Section 3. The decision reached in the informal dispute settlement procedure is admissible in such a civil action. The period of limitations for a civil action to enforce a consumer's rights or remedies under subsection (a) of Section 3 shall be extended for a period equal to the number of days the subject matter of the civil action was pending in the informal dispute settlement procedure.

(c) A disclosure of the decision in an informal dispute settlement procedure shall include notice to the consumer of the provisions of subsection (b).

1205. Application of Uniform Commercial Code

§ 5. Persons electing to proceed and settle under this Act shall be barred from a separate cause of action under Chapter 26.

1206. Limitations

§ 6. Any action brought under this Act shall be commenced within eighteen months following the date of original delivery of the motor vehicle to the consumer.

1207. Seller to provide statement of consumer's rights

§ 7. The seller who sells a new car to a consumer, shall, upon delivery of that car to the consumer, provide the consumer with a written statement clearly and conspicuously setting forth in full detail the consumer's rights under subsection (a) of Section 3, and the presumptions created by subsection (b) of that Section.

VOGEL, SQUEEZING CONSUMERS: LEMON LAWS, CONSUMER WARRANTIES, AND A PROPOSAL FOR REFORM, 1985 Ariz.St.L.J. 589, 615, 644–47.

* * *

Acting on consumer complaints, legislatures in 37 states have passed lemon laws to help car owners. Although the laws vary in many important respects, they still have a number of features in common. First, the lemon laws apply only to new cars and generally only to cars purchased for noncommercial purposes. Second, the laws require the manufacturer to conform the vehicle to the terms of the warranty upon receiving notice of the problem from the consumer. If the manufacturer is unable to correct the defect within a stated period of time or after a certain number of attempts, the lemon laws allow purchasers to return defective cars and to receive either a refund of the purchase price or a replacement vehicle. However, the refund or replacement remedy may not be available to a consumer unless he or she gives the manufacturer notice that efforts to repair the car have failed. Finally, a number of lemon laws also restrict the resale of returned vehicles to other purchasers.

* * *

As has been seen, the lemon laws by themselves do not provide consumers with an effective remedy. In many respects, they simply restate the present law. In other respects they are more restrictive than alternative legal remedies. Consequently, if a consumer has a warranty problem, it may be necessary to bring an action under the UCC, the Magnuson-Moss Warranty Act, and the lemon law. Generally, the lemon laws allow for this. With the exception of Arizona, Florida, Illinois, New Mexico, North Dakota, and Tennessee,* all the lemon laws contain a provision which states that the lemon law does not limit rights or remedies under other law.**

* ARIZ.REV.STAT.ANN. § 44–1261 to –1265 (Supp. 1984–85); FLA.STAT.ANN. § 681.10–.108 (West Supp.1985); 1985 N.D.Sess.Laws 1378, § (6); TENN.CODE ANN. § 55–24–108 (Supp. 1984). The Tennessee lemon law specifically forecloses any action under another law if the consumer chooses to sue under the lemon law. Given the deficiencies of the lemon law, this provision is highly undesirable. In Tennessee, a consumer might fare better ignoring the lemon law and suing under the U.C.C. The Illinois and New Mexico lemon laws specifically bar any action under the U.C.C. if the consumer sues under the lemon law. ILL.ANN. STAT. ch. 121, ¶ 1205 § 5 (Smith-Hurd 1984–85); 1985 N.M.Laws 126, § 5.

** ALASKA STAT. ch. 101, § 45.45.340 (Supp. 1984); COLO.REV.STAT. § 42–12–105 (1984); CONN.GEN.STAT.ANN. § 42–179(h) (West Supp. 1985); DEL.CODE ANN. tit. 6 § 5008 (Supp. 1984); 1985 Kan.Sess.Laws 118, § 2; LA.REV. STAT.ANN. § 51:1946 (West Supp.1985); ME. REV.STAT.ANN. tit. 10, § 1162(1) (Supp.1984–85); MD.COM.LAW CODE ANN. § 14–1501(b) (Supp.1984); MASS.GEN.LAWS ANN. ch. 90, § 7N½(5) (West Supp.1985); MINN.STAT.ANN. § 325F.655(8) (West Supp.1985); MO.ANN. STAT. § 407.579 (Vernon Supp.1985); MONT. CODE ANN. § 61–4–506 (1983) and 1985 Mont. Laws 295; NEB.REV.STAT. § 60–2708 (1984); NEV.REV.STAT. § 598.786 (1983); N.H.REV. STAT.ANN. § 357–D:7 (1984); N.J.STAT.ANN. § 56:12–27 (West Supp.1985); N.Y.GEN.BUS. LAW § 198–a(f) (Consol.Supp. 1984–85); OR. REV.STAT. § 646.375 (1983); PA.STAT.ANN. tit. 73, § 1962 (Purdon 1985); R.I.GEN.LAWS § 31–5.2–6 (Supp.1984); TEX.REV.CIV.STAT.ANN. art. 4413(36), § 6.07(f) (Vernon Supp.1985); 1985 Utah Laws 29, §§ 13–21–6(3); VT.STAT.ANN. tit. 9, § 4178 (Supp.1984); VA.CODE § 59.1–207.13(F) (Supp.1984); WASH.REV.CODE ANN. § 19.118.070 (Supp.1984); W.VA.CODE § 46A–6A–9 (Supp.1984); WIS.STAT.ANN. § 218.015(5) (West 1984–85); WYO.STAT. § 40–17–101(e) (Supp.1985). The Mississippi law does not specifically state whether other remedies are allowed. 1985 Miss.Laws 224, §§ 1–9.

If lawmakers wish to provide increased protection to purchasers of automobiles, there are certain modifications which would make the lemon laws more effective: (1) clear rules or standards; (2) presumptions which ease the burden of proof, (3) a minimum of technicalities; and (4) a choice between a refund and other damages or a replacement vehicle. They could also publicize consumers' rights under the improved laws.

For consumers and manufacturers to know their rights under the lemon laws, the laws must contain clear rules or standards specifying when the consumer may return the defective car and seek a refund or a replacement vehicle. The lemon laws make strides in this direction by spelling out the number of repair attempts and the number of days a car must be in the shop for repair before the consumer can invoke the refund and replacement provision. However, the standard is often stricter than that governing failure of essential purpose under the UCC. Consumers need a clear rule that does not grant an unreasonable amount of time to repair the car. There is little reason to require that the consumer give the manufacturer more than one repair attempt or one week in the shop. The consumer should not have to suffer through numerous trips to the dealer or long delays in repair.

Specification of a time for repair can significantly ease the burden of the consumer. The easier it is for the consumer to prove that he or she is entitled to the remedies under the lemon laws, the more likely that the consumer will seek redress and reach an equitable agreement with the manufacturer. A short, but reasonable, statutory period should suffice. If the consumer is able to show that the defect was not repaired within the period (perhaps a week), the presumption would apply. The manufacturer would then have the burden of establishing that more time was necessary and reasonable under the circumstances.

The typical lemon law contains other provisions which are unclear. For example, the laws do not define what constitutes substantial impairment of value, safety, or use. As a result, consumers will often not know what they are entitled to, even if the lemon law applies. These terms can be defined and clarified, as has been done in some cases interpreting UCC section 2–608. Specific provision should be made for taking account of the consumer's individual circumstances, as well as of clusters or groups of defects that substantially impair the value of the car.

Having clear rules and presumptions that ease the burden of proof will not mean much if other technical requirements deprive a consumer of the ability to use the lemon law. The notice requirements are especially troublesome. Consumers rarely know about notice requirements and often fail to comply with them. The only notice requirement the lemon laws should contain is the requirement that the consumer notify the dealer of the problem with the car. As was mentioned, the manufacturer will find out about the problem when the dealer seeks reimbursement for the warranty work. The manufacturer should have the responsibility of seeing to it that the dealer supplies it with this information promptly.

Once the consumer establishes that the car was not or could not be fixed, the lemon laws should provide that the consumer can choose between a refund or a replacement vehicle. If the consumer opts for a replacement vehicle, the manufacturer should be required to supply one of equal value. If the consumer chooses a refund, the lemon law should allow the recovery of the purchase price, collateral charges, and incidental and consequential damages when appropriate. If the manufacturer is allowed an offset for use, it should only cover use before the defects occurred and the manufacturer should have the burden of establishing its right to any offset and its amount.

All such changes will have little effect, however, if consumers do not fully understand them. The usual approach to informing consumers is to require the dealers and the manufacturers to supply a written statement which explains consumers' rights under the lemon law. The experience with the Magnuson-Moss Warranty Act indicates that this approach is ineffective. Consequently, legislators should consider using the broadcast media and newspapers to present information concerning consumer remedies. Public service ads on radio and television could greatly increase awareness of consumer warranty rights. Certainly, there is enough talent and knowledge available to structure such a campaign and the expense of conducting it is not likely to be much more than that of printing forms. A number of state and federal consumer protection agencies already conduct such campaigns, and there is no reason why similar efforts cannot be mounted to inform consumers of their rights under automobile lemon laws.

PART SIX

DISPUTES AMONG CREDITORS OVER POSSESSION OF GOODS SOLD

CHAPTER TWENTY-TWO

RIGHTS OF OWNERS, SELLERS OR BUYERS TO GOODS NOT IN THEIR POSSESSION: CLAIMS OF THIRD PARTIES

SECTION 1. INTRODUCTION

When a person has good title to chattels, our legal system affords him extensive protection against a wide range of claims by third persons to the goods. A sale is a transaction whereby title is passed "from the seller to the buyer for a price * * *." UCC 2–106(1). In an effort to clarify when title passes in a contract for sale, Article 2 prescribes the conditions which must exist before any interest in goods can pass, UCC 2–105(1), makes a careful distinction between present and future sales, UCC 2–106(1), and provides an intricate set of rules to assist in transactions where the parties have not otherwise explicitly agreed. UCC 2–401. To this extent, Article 2 closely follows the Uniform Sales Act.

Here, however, the resemblance ends. UCC 2–401 provides that "each provision of this Article with regard to the rights, obligations and remedies of the seller, the buyer, purchasers or other third parties applies irrespective of title to the goods except where the provision refers to such title." See also UCC 9–202, where the same policy is announced for secured transactions. As stated in the comment to UCC 2–101, the "purpose is to avoid making practical issues between practical men turn on the location of an intangible something, the passing of which no man can prove by evidence and to substitute for such abstractions proof of words and actions of a tangible character." Two such practical issues are risk of loss and the seller's action for the price. Under the USA they turned on which party had title to the goods. Under the UCC they are determined by such considerations as whether the seller has completed his tender of delivery, UCC 2–509, or whether the buyer has accepted the goods, UCC 2–709(1).

It is clear that the rules about title contained in UCC 2–401 may be relevant in resolving controversies beyond the scope of Article 2, e.g., the right of the buyer's creditors to levy on goods still in the seller's possession, the coverage of an insurance policy, the applicability of a state sales tax or the criminal responsibility of a person accused of larceny. However, when the transaction is within the scope of Article 2, title becomes relevant only when the applicable provisions specifically refer to title. Such specific reference is made in UCC 2–

403 and UCC 2–312. The range of problems emanating from these sections and their frequent overlap with Article 9 and the special difficulties posed by "bulk" sales will be the subject of this Chapter.

SECTION 2. RIGHTS OF BUYERS IN GOODS SOLD

A. Claims of "True" Owners

Problem 22–1

Abbie, a widow, owned a 10–carat diamond valued at $60,000. Boscoe, a thief, stole the diamond from Abbie's wall safe and sold it to Casper, a diamond merchant, for $55,000. Casper honestly believed that Boscoe was the true owner. Casper then sold the diamond to Dimwit, a buyer in the ordinary course of business, for $60,000. May Abbie replevy the diamond from Dimwit? See UCC 2–403. Assume that the common law gives Casper only "void title," not "voidable title." Justice v. Fabey, 541 F.Supp. 1019 (E.D.Pa.1982) (yes).

Problem 22–2

Suppose that Abbie delivered the diamond to Casper for the purpose of having the clasp on the necklace in which the stone was set repaired. Casper, with intent to defraud, removed the stone from the necklace and sold it to Dimwit, a buyer in the ordinary course of business. May Abbie replevy the diamond from Dimwit? See UCC 2–403(2), (3), and UCC 1–201(9). Cf. Carlsen v. Rivera, 382 So.2d 825 (Fla.App. 1980) (no).

Problem 22–3

Suppose that Abbie owned several diamonds and was in the habit of lending the stones to her society friends for use on important occasions. She charged a good fee for this service and was, of course, fully insured against loss. Abbie leased the stone worth $60,000 to Bessie to be worn at the Muckraker's Ball. Bessie, who was short of cash, sold the diamond to Casper for $55,000. Casper, who had purchased in good faith, sold the stone to Dimwit, a buyer in the ordinary course of business, for $65,000. May Abbie (or her insurance company claiming by subrogation) replevy the necklace from Dimwit? See UCC 2–403(1), (2). Assume that the common law only gives Bessie, as a lessee, void title.

How should the court deal with the argument made by Dimwit that Bessie in fact had a voidable title under UCC 2–403 because she took in a transaction of "purchase" as that term is defined in UCC 2–403 and 1–201? (Dimwit's argument was rejected in similar circumstances by the Indiana Court of Appeals in McDonald's Chevrolet, Inc. v. Johnson, 176 Ind.App. 399, 376 N.E.2d 106 (1978)).

Problem 22–4

While vacationing in Miami Beach, Abbie was approached by a middle-aged man who asked if the lovely diamond necklace was for sale. He said that his name was Boscoe and offered to pay $90,000. Abbie, who was a bit short of cash, agreed to sell but then balked when Boscoe started to write a check. She wanted cash. Boscoe assured her that he was solvent and stated that he was Mr. Fred C. Boscoe of Grosse Pointe. Abbie excused herself from the room and confirmed by a telephone call to a friend in Detroit that Mr. Fred C. Boscoe owned a large home in Grosse Pointe and was a vice-president of a well-known automobile manufacturer. Abbie returned to the room and informed the man that she would accept a check for the stone. Boscoe then drew a counter check on a Detroit bank and delivered it to Abbie in exchange for the necklace. The check, of course, bounced and Abbie then discovered that her purchaser had no account at that bank and was not Mr. Fred C. Boscoe of Grosse Pointe. Further, before disappearing, the "rogue" had sold the diamond for $91,000 to Dimwit, who purchased the stone in good faith. May Abbie replevy the stone from Dimwit? See UCC 2–403(1)(a).

Problem 22–5

In Problem 22–4 would it make any difference if the transaction and the exchange of check for necklace had been completed by mail?

Problem 22–6

Suppose, in Problem 22–2, above, that Casper and Dimwit had entered into a contract for the sale of the stone, delivery and payment to take place in 10 days. Is Abbie's interest cut off at this point or must payment and delivery first take place? Suppose there has been payment but not delivery? Delivery but no payment? Part payment? See UCC 2–403. Compare UCC 1–201(44).

INMI-ETTI v. ALUISI

Court of Appeals of Maryland, 1985.
63 Md.App. 293, 492 A.2d 917.

[Appellant, a resident of Nigeria, ordered a new Honda Prelude while visiting her sister in the United States. Butler, an acquaintance of her family, offered to assist. Appellant returned to Nigeria, leaving cash with the sister to complete the purchase. The sale was completed and a certificate of title was issued in appellant's name. The car, however, was delivered to Butler, who removed it from the sister without permission. The sister had an arrest warrant issued, but it was later quashed. Butler, claiming that appellant was an absconding debtor, then brought suit against her and filed an application for an attachment on the Honda. When appellant did not answer, Butler was granted a summary judgment. Thereafter, appellee, a deputy sheriff, executed the writ of attachment on the Honda but left it in Butler's possession.

Butler, representing that he was the owner, then contracted to sell the Honda to Pohanka, a dealer, for $7,200. Pohanka paid Butler $2,000 and agreed to pay the balance when Butler obtained a certificate of title. After executing a false affidavit in his application for a certificate of title, Butler was issued a certificate in his own name by the Motor Vehicle Administration. Butler then returned to Pohanka and exchanged the certificate for the balance of the contract price.

Appellant, upon returning to the United States, had Butler's summary judgment set aside. In addition, she sued Butler and Pohanka for conversion and appellee for negligent attachment. In the lower court, appellant obtained a default judgment against Butler. The court, however, granted a summary judgment to Pohanka and appellee. On appeal, the summary judgment in favor of appellee was sustained but the summary judgment in favor of Pohanka was reversed.]

* * *

I.

In order for the appellant to establish her right to summary judgment against Pohanka, we must be convinced that the record before the lower court contained undisputed facts and inferences properly deducible therefrom, demonstrating that Pohanka committed a conversion of the appellant's vehicle as a matter of law. Former Md.Rule 610 (new Md.Rule 2–501). In *Interstate Ins. Co. v. Logan,* 205 Md. 583, 588–89, 109 A.2d 904 (1959), the Court of Appeals summarized the law of conversion:

> [F]orcible dispossession of personal property is not essential to constitute a conversion. A "conversion" is any distinct act of ownership or dominion exerted by one person over the personal property of another in denial of his right or inconsistent with it. *Merchants' National Bank of Baltimore v. Williams,* 110 Md. 334, 72 A. 1114 [(1909)]; Martin v. W.W. Lanahan & Co., 133 Md. 525, 105 A. 777 [(1919)].

* * * In the instant case it is undisputed that Pohanka exerted acts of use or ownership over the automobile in question by selling it on February 1, 1982. Nevertheless, our analysis cannot end here. We explain.

At common law the maxim was: "He who hath not cannot give (nemo dat qui non habet)." Black's Law Dictionary 935 (5th ed. 1979). Although at times the Uniform Commercial Code may seem to the reader as unintelligible as the Latin phrases which preceded it, we find in § 2–403 of the Code a definite modification of the above maxim. That section states: * * *.

Md.Code (1975), § 2–403 of the Commercial Law Article. *See generally* Hawkland UCC Series § 2–403:01 *et seq.* for an enlightening history of the origins of § 2–403.

In short, the answer to the appellant's claim against Pohanka depends on whether Butler had "void" or "voidable" title at the time of the purported sale to Pohanka. If Butler had voidable title, then he had the power to vest good title in Pohanka.[1] If, on the other hand, Butler possessed void title (i.e., no title at all), then Pohanka received no title and is liable in trover for the conversion of the appellant's automobile. Preliminarily, we note that there was no evidence that Butler was a "merchant who deals in goods of that kind" (i.e. automobiles). Md.Code, *supra,* §§ 2–403(2) and 2–104(1). Therefore the entrustment provisions of § 2–403(2)–(3) do not apply.

It has been observed that:

> Under 2–403, voidable title is to be distinguished from void title. A thief, for example, "gets" only void title and without more cannot pass any title to a good faith purchaser. "Voidable title" is a murky concept. The Code does not define the phrase. The comments do not even discuss it. Subsections (1)(a)–(d) of 2–403 clarify the law as to particular transactions which were "troublesome under prior law." Beyond these, we must look to non-Code state law.

J. White & R. Summers, Handbook of the Law Under the Uniform Commercial Code § 3–11 (2d ed. 1980) (footnote omitted). White and Summers further explain that: subsection (a) of § 2–403(1) deals with cases where the purchaser *impersonates* someone else; subsection (b) deals with "rubber checks"; subsection (c) deals with "*cash sales*";[2] and subsection (d) deals with cases of *forged checks* and other acts fraudulent to the seller. *Id.* None of these subsections

1. Inasmuch as we decide this case on the basis of a motion for summary judgment, and the evidence regarding Pohanka's good faith purchaser for value status is disputed, we must assume here that Pohanka was entitled to that status.

2. See *First National Bank of Ariz. v. Carbajal,* 132 Ariz. 263, 645 P.2d 778, 781–82 (1982).

apply to the facts of the present case and we, therefore, must turn to "non-Code state law" to determine whether Butler had voidable title.

Hawkland, *supra,* § 403:04, suggests that "voidable title" may only be obtained when the owner of the goods makes a voluntary transfer of the goods. He reaches that conclusion from the Code definitions of the words "delivery" and "purchase" and summarizes:

> Section 2–403(1)(d) does not create a voidable title in the situation where the goods are wrongfully taken, as contrasted with delivered voluntarily because of the concepts of "delivery" and "purchaser" which are necessary preconditions. "Delivery" is defined by section 1–201(14) "with respect to instruments, documents of title, chattel paper or securities" to mean "voluntary transfer of possession." By analogy, it should be held that goods are not delivered for purposes of section 2–403 unless they are voluntarily transferred. Additionally, section 2–403(1)(d) is limited by the requirement that the goods "have been delivered under a transaction of purchase." "Purchase" is defined by section 1–201(32) to include only voluntary transactions. A thief who wrongfully takes goods is not a purchaser within the meaning of this definition, but a swindler who fraudulently induces the victim to voluntarily deliver them is a purchaser for this purpose. This distinction, reminiscent of the distinction between larceny and larceny by trick made by the common law, is a basic one for the understanding of the meaning of section 2–403(1)(d).

Hawkland later states that the above language applies generally to § 2–403(1) and not merely to subsection (1)(d). *See* Hawkland, *supra,* § 2–403:05. The following cases and, indeed, (a) through (d) of § 2–403(1) seem to support Hawkland's theory that only a voluntary transfer by the owner can vest "voidable title" in a "person."

* * *

Without attempting to specify all the situations which could give rise to a voidable title under § 2–403 of the Uniform Commercial Code, we refer to the above authorities to support our conclusion that voidable title under the Code can only arise from a voluntary transfer or delivery of the goods by the owner. If the goods are stolen or otherwise obtained against the will of the owner, only void title can result.

Under the undisputed facts of the present case Butler possessed void title when Pohanka dealt with him. Although the record simply is not sufficient for us to decide whether Butler actually stole the appellant's vehicle, it is undisputed that the appellant at no time made a voluntary transfer to Butler. Thus, Pohanka obtained no title, and its sale of the vehicle constituted a conversion of the appellant's property. We believe the above analysis sufficient to impose liability upon Pohanka. We will nevertheless answer certain of Pohanka's collateral arguments.

We reject any notion that Butler obtained voidable title to the vehicle as a result of the attachment on original process carried out pursuant to former Maryland District Rules G40–60.

* * *

The only way Butler could have obtained title in the vehicle through those attachment proceedings was if he had purchased it at a judicial sale. That clearly never occurred.

Implicit in all that we have said so far is the fact that Butler did not obtain title (voidable or otherwise) merely from the fact that he was able to convince the Motor Vehicle Administration to issue a certificate of title for the automobile to him. Although "[a] certificate of title issued by the Administration is prima facie evidence of the facts appearing on it," Md.Code (1977, 1984 Repl.Vol.), § 13–107 of the Transportation Article, the erroneous issuance of such a certificate cannot divest the title of the true owner of the automobile. *Metropolitan Auto Sales v. Koneski,* 252 Md. 145, 249 A.2d 141 (1969); *Huettner v. Sav. Bank of Balto.,* 242 Md. 477, 219 A.2d 559 (1966); *Lawrence v. Graham,* 29 Md.App. 422, 349 A.2d 271 (1975).

Likewise, we find unpersuasive Pohanka's argument that since Butler had possession of the automobile and a duly issued certificate of title in his name, Pohanka should be protected as a "good faith purchaser for value" under § 2–403 of the Commercial Law Article, *supra.* Such status under that section of the Uniform Commercial Code is relevant in situations where the seller (transferor) is possessed of voidable title. It does not apply to the situation presented by the instant case where the seller had no title at all. * * *

Finally, whether Pohanka converted the vehicle with innocent intent is immaterial. The Restatement (Second) of Torts § 229 (1979) provides:

> One who receives possession of a chattel from another with the intent to acquire for himself or for a third person a proprietary interest in the chattel which the other has not the power to transfer is subject to liability for conversion to a third person then entitled to the immediate possession of the chattel.

Comment e. to § 299 explains:

> Under the rule stated in this Section, one receiving a chattel from a third person with intent to acquire a proprietary interest in it is liable without a demand for its return by the person entitled to possession, *although he takes possession of the chattel without knowledge or reason to know that the third person has no power to transfer the proprietary interest.* The mere receipt of the possession of the goods under such circumstances is a conversion.

(Emphasis added).

Accordingly, we shall reverse the summary judgment in favor of Pohanka and enter judgment in favor of the appellant against Pohanka for $8,200, an amount representing the agreed fair market value of the appellant's automobile at the time of its conversion, plus interest at 10 percent per annum from February 1, 1982, the date when Pohanka sold the automobile. Md.Rule 1075. * * *

Note: Certificates of Title and the BFP of Motor Vehicles

Almost all states have statutes which require motor vehicles to be "titled." Suppose that Owner, whose certificate of title is in the possession of a secured party, entrusts the motor vehicle to a car dealer for repairs. Suppose, further, that the dealer, without Owner's or secured party's consent, puts the car on the lot and sells it to Cal in the ordinary course of business. Cal pays cash and takes delivery of the car only, without knowledge of Owner's title or the outstanding security interest. Assume owner pays off secured party and seeks return of the car from Cal, certificate of title in hand. May owner replevy the car from Cal, or is Cal entitled to a duly endorsed certificate?

Under the Code the answer would appear to be no: UCC 2–402(3) does not apply. UCC 2–403(2) protects Cal and title has passed under UCC 2–401. But the critical question, then, is whether the particular certificate of title act involved preempts 2–403(2) and, in effect, conditions passage of title upon delivery of the certificate. In some states it does, e.g., Messer v. Averill, 28 Mich.App. 62, 183 N.W.2d 802 (1970) but in most states it doesn't, e.g., Godfrey v. Gilsdorf, 86 Nev. 714, 476 P.2d 3 (1970); Martin v. Nager, 192 N.J.Super. 189, 469 A.2d 519 (1983). Even where the Code controls, however, a buyer may have some responsibility for inquiring after the required certificate. See Mattek v. Malofsky, 42 Wis.2d 16, 165 N.W.2d 406 (1969) (merchant buyer from dealer to whom titled car had been entrusted is "unreasonable as a matter of law" in not obtaining the required certificate); Reliance Insurance Co. v. Market Motors, Inc., 498 A.2d 571 (D.C.App.1985); Ellsworth v. Worthey, 612 S.W.2d 396 (Mo.App.1981).

Assume Owner does not pay off secured party and it is secured party who seeks return of the car from Cal. Similarly, while UCC 9–307(1) may protect the buyer against the perfected security interest, this result is subject to any specific rule of priority contained in a preemptive certificate of title act. Compare Williams v. Western Surety Co., 6 Wash.App. 300, 492 P.2d 596 (1972) (buyer wins under Code) with Security Pacific Nat'l Bank v. Goodman, 24 Cal.App.3d 131, 100 Cal.Rptr. 763 (1972) (buyer loses under California statute.)

These issues are well treated in Kunz, *Motor Vehicle Ownership Disputes Involving Certificate of Title Acts and Article Two of the U.C.C.*, 39 Bus.Law. 1599 (1984).

JOHNSON & JOHNSON PROD. v. DAL INTERN. TRADING

United States Court of Appeals, Third Circuit, 1986.
798 F.2d 100.

OPINION OF THE COURT

STAPLETON, CIRCUIT JUDGE.

This is an appeal from a preliminary injunction restraining appellants from selling, distributing, or otherwise disposing of certain products manufactured by appellees and in appellants' possession. Because we conclude that the district court committed an error of law and that the present record will not support a resolution of the legally relevant issue in appellees' favor, we will vacate the preliminary injunction.

I.

Appellants are Quality King Manufacturing, Inc. and Quality King Distributors, Inc., both New York corporations ("Quality King"). Quality King is an independent distributor of national brand health and beauty aids. Its customers include large wholesalers and retail chains. Quality King participates in the so-called "gray market," where imported products are sold in the United States outside the manufacturer's distribution system, often contrary to the wishes of the manufacturer.

Appellees are Johnson & Johnson Products, Inc. ("J & J"), a New Jersey corporation, Johnson & Johnson, Ltd. ("J & J Ltd."), a corporation organized under the laws of Great Britain, and Johnson & Johnson Baby Products Company, a New Jersey corporation. Appellees are all operating subsidiaries of Johnson & Johnson, Inc., a New Jersey corporation.

Appellees claimed in the district court that J & J Ltd., which has its place of business in Great Britain, was fraudulently induced to sell 80,000 dozen toothbrushes and certain baby products to Dal International Trading Company, an instrumentality of the Polish People's Republic (hereinafter "Dal"). The alleged fraud consisted of an oral misrepresentation by Dal in February of 1985 that it intended to distribute the products in Poland only. But for this fraudulent assurance, say appellees, J & J Ltd. would not have entered the transaction.

In March of 1985, Dal ordered the products from J & J Ltd. No written contract was entered. However, J & J Ltd. did execute, in April of 1985, a written contract related to the Dal transaction with Wendexim Trading Company, Ltd., a British firm. The reason for the inclusion of Wendexim in the Dal transaction was the weakness of Polish currency, which necessitated an intermediate barter trade. This intermediate step involved an agreement under which Dal shipped a quantity of wood to Wendexim in return for Wendexim's transmittal of the payment for the wood to J & J Ltd., in satisfaction of Dal's obligation to pay J & J Ltd. for the toothbrushes and baby products.

At the end of June, 1985, J & J Ltd. delivered the toothbrushes to Dal at a J & J Ltd. factory in West Germany. The baby products were shipped from Great Britain at the beginning of June, 1985. Subsequently, J & J Ltd. learned that some or all of these goods had been diverted from their intended destination of Poland and were en route to the United States.

J & J Ltd. investigators followed the goods to the United States, where they came into the possession of Quality King. The goods were packaged in cartons, some of which bore J & J Ltd. shipping labels. The production codes on these labels corresponded to those of the products designated for Dal.

The route by which the J & J Ltd. products came into Quality King's hands was not fully documented below. In early 1985, a British firm called Cubro Trading Company, Ltd. somehow learned of the availability of the J & J Ltd. products and passed this information to Morris Greenfield, the proprietor of Tereza Merchandise Corporation in New York. Greenfield was not interested in the products but advised Glenn Nussdorf, the vice president of Quality King, of the availability of the goods. Nussdorf prepared a purchase order for 75,000 dozen toothbrushes in February of 1985, about the time when Dal and J & J Ltd. were negotiating the sale of 80,000 dozen toothbrushes. Later, Nussdorf added baby products to this purchase order.

Nussdorf had never done business with Cubro before this transaction, so he used Greenfield as an intermediary. The details of the transaction are unclear due to discrepancies in the record as to the disbursements made by Quality King. What is clear is that Quality King purchased and received the goods.

Before the goods arrived at Quality King's warehouse, the J & J Ltd. shipping labels had been stripped from most of the shipping cartons. Greenfield and Nussdorf testified that this was a common gray market practice designed to obscure the identity of supply sources. The protection of these sources is important to gray market middlemen, Nussdorf and Greenfield testified, because if the sources became known, the middlemen would be bypassed in subsequent transactions.

The J & J Ltd. products were priced by it for the Polish market at a level lower than the wholesale price in the United States for Johnson & Johnson products, and even lower than the wholesale price normally offered in Great Britain by J & J Ltd. By purchasing these products in Europe, Quality King was thus in a position to distribute them in the United States at prices below those being charged by J & J.

II.

The district court granted the preliminary injunction after concluding that appellees were likely to prevail on the merits, that appellees would suffer irreparable harm if the injunction were not granted, that an injunction would not harm any other interested person, and that an injunction would not be contrary to the public interest. * * *

The court predicted that appellees would prevail on the merits because it found that Quality King was not a good faith purchaser under Section 2–403(1) of the Uniform Commercial Code (UCC). Under this provision of the UCC, a seller with voidable title, such as that acquired by common law fraud, can transfer good title to a subsequent good faith purchaser. For merchants like Quality King, the UCC defines good faith as "honesty in fact and the observance of reasonable commercial standards of fair dealing in the trade." UCC § 2–103(1)(b). If the subsequent purchaser lacks good faith, however, he acquires only the seller's voidable title and may be required to surrender the goods to the defrauded party.

While the district court concluded that Quality King had no actual knowledge of the alleged fraud, it found that the gray market transaction was conducted under "suspicious circumstances" that "cried out for inquiry." District Court Opinion at 23–24. In the district court's view, Quality King, as a result, should have made inquiries that would have uncovered the voidable title. In the absence of such inquiries, the court concluded, Quality King could not be said to have been "honest in fact."

The most suspicious circumstance noted by the court was the fact that "the entire trade in which Quality King is engaged is conducted in a manner designed to insulate a purchaser of goods from knowledge of potential illegality." District Court Opinion at 22. That is, the gray market trade practice of purposely obscuring the chain of title suggested to the court a silent conspiracy to avoid the consequences of bad faith purchase by preventing the transmission of actual knowledge of fraud in prior transactions. This practice was illustrated by the fact that the J & J Ltd. shipping labels had been stripped prior to arrival at Quality King's warehouse.

An additional suspicious circumstance, in the district court's view, was the fact that Nussdorf used Greenfield as an intermediary, thereby indicating Nussdorf's mistrust of Cubro. Finally, the price of the goods was so low that "Quality King must have known that * * * [J & J Ltd. would not have knowingly sold] * * * its products in Europe for resale in the United States." District Court Opinion at 24.

III.

The district court was undoubtedly justified in concluding that Quality King had reason to suspect that appellees would not approve of a sale of the toothbrushes and baby products to a U.S. distributor. Further, we believe the district court, having reached this conclusion, could appropriately infer that Quality King, in the minds of its officers and agents, subjectively suspected that appellees would not approve of its purchase of these goods. We believe the legally relevant question, however, is whether Quality King knew that the goods had been obtained from J & J Ltd. by fraud, or suspected as much and closed its eyes to the truth. This is a far different question involving an inquiry as to whether Quality King knew or had some reason to know that Dal orally represented to J & J Ltd. that it would distribute only in Poland and that this representation was made at a time when Dal had an affirmative intent to do otherwise.[2] The district court did not address this legally relevant question, and we believe the present record will not support an affirmative answer to it.

While the district court relied heavily on what it understood to be the nature of the gray goods market, there was very little evidence before it concerning that market and *no* evidence before it on the legitimacy of the means by which goods normally get into the gray goods market. The only substantial testimony concerning the workings of that market was the testimony given by Messrs. Nussbaum and Greenfield. Their testimony indicated only that the gray market exists because prices are often lower overseas than in the United States, and that gray market sellers are reluctant to reveal their supply sources for fear of being bypassed in subsequent transactions. This testimony provided a plausible explanation about why there is a gray goods market and why merchants in that market do not generally inquire about the intermediate sources in the distribution chain. However, it does not provide a basis for an inference that all those involved in importing less expensive gray goods know or suspect that there is a defect in the title of the goods which they purchase. Nor does the fact that Quality King was cautious in its dealings with Cubro, its immediate supplier, add enough to win the day for appellees.

Rather than address the legally relevant question of whether Quality King subjectively knew or suspected that there was a flaw in the title of one of its predecessors, the district court found that the circumstances called for inquiry and that, if Quality King had investigated, it would have learned that it was acquiring a voidable title. It is not as clear to us as to the district court that inquiry in this case would have uncovered the fraud. We consider that unimportant, however, because we believe the court committed an error of law when it held that Quality King had a duty to inquire and charged it with the knowledge that an investigation would have arguably disclosed.

The purpose of the good faith purchaser doctrine, codified in Sections 2–403 and 2–102 of the UCC, is to promote commerce by reducing transaction costs; it allows people safely to engage in the purchase and sale of goods without conducting a costly investigation of the conduct and rights of all previous possessors in the chain of distribution. Gilmore, The Commercial Doctrine of Good Faith Purchase, 63 YALE L.J. 1057, 1057 (1954) (The good faith purchaser "* * * is protected * * * to the end that commercial transactions may be engaged in without elaborate investigation of property rights and in reliance on the possession of property by one who offers it for sale * * *"; Farnsworth, Good Faith Performance and Commercial Reasonableness under the Uniform Commercial Code, 30 U.CHI.L.REV. 666, 671 (1963) ("Authority happens to favor the subjective test [of good faith purchase] in order to promote the circulation of goods and commercial paper."); Hawkland, Curing an Improper Tender of Title to Chattels: Past, Present and Commercial Code, 46 MINN.L.REV. 697, 721 (1962); 3 ANDERSON ON THE UNIFORM COMMERCIAL CODE 569–570 (3d

2. It is important to note that the title of a purchaser from Dal would not have been voidable if all Dal had done was resell the goods in violation of a contract clause prohibiting resale outside Poland. If, at the time of contracting with J & J Ltd., Dal had intended to restrict the distribution of goods to Poland and only later decided to distribute the goods elsewhere, no fraudulent inducement to contract would have existed. J & J Ltd. would then have had a cause of action against Dal for breach of contract but subsequent purchasers from Dal would obtain good title. UCC § 2–403(1).

ed. 1983). The imposition on a purchaser of a duty to investigate is thus fundamentally at odds with the rationale underlying these two sections of the UCC. Accordingly, in the absence of clear and controlling precedent so requiring, we are unwilling to sanction the imposition of such a duty on one in the position of Quality King.

As the district court recognized, we are required to apply the law of New Jersey, the forum state. *Erie R.R. Co. v. Tompkins,* 304 U.S. 64, 58 S.Ct. 817, 82 L.Ed. 1188 (1938). Neither the district court nor the appellees have referred us to any New Jersey case which suggests that its Supreme Court would impose a duty of inquiry upon a purchaser of goods under the circumstances of this case and we believe the New Jersey case law suggests the contrary.

The only case relied on by the appellees is a New York case, *Porter v. Wertz,* 68 A.D.2d 141, 416 N.Y.S.2d 254, 259 (1979), *aff'd on other grounds,* 53 N.Y.2d 696, 439 N.Y.S.2d 105, 421 N.E.2d 500 (1981). In *Porter,* a painting was entrusted to an art merchant who asked Peter Wertz, a delicatessen employee, to find a buyer for the painting. Wertz sold it to an art gallery that was unaware of the circumstances by which Wertz had come into possession of the painting. The lower court ruled that the gallery was not protected by UCC Section 2–403 because Wertz was not an art merchant selling the painting in the ordinary course of business. In addition, the court held that even if Wertz had been an art merchant, the gallery would not have been protected by the good faith purchaser provision of Section 2–403 because of its failure to inquire as to Wertz' source. The New York Court of Appeals affirmed on the first ground and withheld opinion on the second. *Porter,* 439 N.Y.S.2d at 107, 421 N.E.2d at 502. Whether or not a duty of inquiry exists in New York in these circumstances is accordingly unclear.

* * *

[The Court, based upon *Breslin v. New Jersey Investors, Inc.,* 70 N.J. 466, 361 A.2d 1 (1976), predicted that New Jersey would "not impose on Quality King a duty to inquire." Rather, "whether Quality King was honest in fact is to be 'determined by looking to the mind of [Quality King]' and not to 'what the state of mind of a prudent man should have been' as a result of inquiry."]

We also note that by adopting the subjective, "pure heart and * * * empty head" standard of *Lawson v. Weston,* 170 Eng.Rep. 640 (K.B.1801), the New Jersey Supreme Court would be aligning itself with the prevailing view of the good faith purchaser concept. *See Goodman v. Simonds,* 61 U.S. (20 How.) 343, 15 L.Ed. 934 (1857) (adopting subjective standard of *Lawson*); Braucher, The Legislative History of the Uniform Commercial Code, 58 COLUM.L.REV. 798, 812 (1958) ("honesty in fact" standard is subjective); Farnsworth, 30 U.CHI.L.REV. at 671.

As we have previously noted, the district court did not make, and the record will not support, a finding that Quality King suspected that fraud had been committed by a predecessor in interest. Accordingly, we may assume for present purposes that New Jersey would exclude from the good faith purchase category one who, though without actual knowledge, subjectively suspects that the title is flawed and proceeds with the purchase despite his or her suspicions. A purchaser may not be certain of the existence of a flaw and still have knowledge of sufficient facts to keep him from being fairly characterized as having been "honest in fact." Excluding such a person from the good faith purchaser category is not the same, however, as judging a purchaser by the facts he or she might have obtained through an investigation of all prior transfers of the goods.

By adopting the latter approach, the district court in this case imposed a burden on commerce which we believe the UCC did not intend that it should bear.

We hold, therefore, that the district court erred in concluding on this record that Quality King had a duty to inquire into the chain of title of the gray market goods.[4] Since the only inference supported by the record is that Quality King had neither knowledge nor suspicion of a fraud by Dal, appellees did not demonstrate a likelihood of ultimate success and Quality King was improperly enjoined *pendente lite.*

IV.

For the foregoing reasons, we will vacate the preliminary injunction.

[Some footnotes omitted.]

B. *Claims of Secured Parties and Other Lien Holders*

IN RE GARY AIRCRAFT CORP.

United States Court of Appeals, Fifth Circuit, 1982.
681 F.2d 365.

WISDOM, CIRCUIT JUDGE:

I.

This dispute over the ownership of one airplane and of the proceeds of the sale of another requires us to determine the reach of the Federal Aviation Act and its impact on state law. We also explore the protection accorded buyers against secured creditors by state law.

In December 1971, Gary Aircraft Corporation ("Gary"), the plaintiff-appellee, entered into a letter of understanding stating its intention to purchase four airplanes from Frederick B. Ayer & Associates, Inc. ("Ayer"), a dealer in aircraft. Two of these airplanes are the subject of the controversy here. Gary did not complete the purchase, but Arthur Stewart, its president, carried out the transaction in his individual capacity, purchasing the first plane in controversy here, N8222H, on December 22, 1971 for $5,000, and the second, N8221H, on January 4, 1972, also for $5,000. On the date of each sale, the airplane purchased was subject to a security interest held by General Dynamics Corporation ("General Dynamics"), the defendant-appellant. General Dynamics held its interest under a security agreement executed by Ayer on February 20, 1969. Under that agreement, Ayer was authorized to sell the collateral, unless it was in default on its obligations to General Dynamics. In case of default, Ayer could not sell without the written consent of General Dynamics. General Dynamics recorded its security agreement with the Federal Aviation Administration on March 3, 1969. On the dates of the sales to Stewart, Ayer was in default.

Crawford, the vice-president of Gary, requested a title search from the Aircraft Owners and Pilots Association on January 4, 1972. The AOPA reported

4. At oral argument, appellees suggested that the district court's decision may have rested in part on that portion of the definition of good faith that refers to an objective standard: "the observance of reasonable commercial standards of fair dealing in the trade." UCC § 2-103(1)(b). While the court spoke at length about practices in the gray goods market, it did not find that it was the practice in that market to investigate the chain of title. Indeed, the evidence suggested that this was not normally done. When a party relies upon trade practice in a situation of this kind, it bears the burden of producing admissible evidence of that practice. *Brattleboro Auto Sales v. Subaru,* 633 F.2d 649, 651 (2d Cir.1980). Since appellees tendered no evidence of trade practice, this portion of the definition of good faith does not aid them.

the results on January 5, 1972. On August 3, 1972, approximately seven months after the sale, Stewart recorded his bill of sale with the FAA. Over the next four years, Crawford communicated periodically with Ayer, requesting that Ayer take action to secure the release of General Dynamic's security interest.

In March 1974, Stewart sold one of the group of four planes to Gary for $13,275. He transferred the two planes at issue here to Gary on November 7, 1975, apparently without consideration. Gary executed a mortgage on the aircraft in favor of the Victoria Bank and Trust Company, the third party defendant. The Victoria Bank recorded its interest with the FAA. On May 28, 1976, General Dynamics informed Gary that it had learned that the aircraft were registered in Gary's name and that General Dynamics was asserting a security interest in the property.

On October 28, 1976, Gary initiated Chapter XI proceedings under the Bankruptcy Act. It brought this action in the bankruptcy court, seeking to sell Airplane N8222H free and clear of liens. Upon the agreement of all interested parties, the court permitted the sale of the airplane, and the proceeds were deposited with the court. The second airplane remains in the possession of Gary.

The bankruptcy court, affirmed by the district court, held that Gary was entitled to the proceeds of the sale of Airplane N8222H and to the possession of Airplane N8221H, free of any interest asserted by General Dynamics. General Dynamics appeals, presenting three theories. First, it contends that the Federal Aviation Act grants it priority because it recorded its security interest with the Federal Aviation Administration before Stewart purchased the aircraft. Second, even if the FAA does not govern the priority question but instead remits it to Texas law, which protects a buyer in the ordinary course of business against the perfected security interest of his seller's creditor, General Dynamics argues that Stewart could not take free of its interest because, according to General Dynamics, Stewart could not qualify as a buyer in the ordinary course of business. Finally, General Dynamics contends that, even if Stewart did qualify as a buyer in the ordinary course, he could not transfer his status to Gary, and Gary did not qualify in its own right so, in Gary's hands, the aircraft are subject to the interest of General Dynamics. Concluding that the FAA does not govern priorities in interests in aircraft, that Stewart, as a buyer in the ordinary course of business, took free of General Dynamic's interest, and that Gary takes the title of its transferor, we affirm.

* * *

III.

Under the Uniform Commercial Code, enacted as the Texas Business and Commerce Code, a buyer in the ordinary course of business is one who, in good faith and without knowledge that the sale to him is in violation of the ownership rights or security interest of a third party, buys from a person in the business of selling goods of that kind. Tex.Bus. & Com.Code Ann. § 1.201(9) (Vernon Supp. 1982). Such a buyer takes free of a security interest created by his seller, even if that interest is perfected and even if the buyer knows of its existence. *Id.*, § 9.307(a).

Since Gary claims its title through Stewart, it cannot hold the aircraft and the proceeds free of General Dynamic's lien unless Stewart held the aircraft free of the lien, as a buyer in the ordinary course of business under section 9.307(a). General Dynamics offers three arguments that it contends require reversal of the holding that Stewart qualified as a buyer in the ordinary course of business.

First, General Dynamics contends that the bankruptcy court misapplied the burden of proof. The burden on this issue does rest with the party claiming the status of a buyer in the ordinary course of business, as General Dynamics urges. *See International Harvester Co. v. Glendenning,* Tex.Civ.App.—Dallas 1974, 505 S.W.2d 320, 324. Nonetheless, General Dynamics cannot prevail on this argument, for we agree with the district court that an examination of the entire opinion of the bankruptcy court shows that it did not misapply the burden of proof. * * *

Second, General Dynamics contends that, even if the bankruptcy judge acted properly in his assignment of the burden of proof, the holding must be reversed because the bankruptcy court considered Stewart's knowledge on December 22, 1971 and January 4, 1972, the dates of purchase, rather than on August 3, 1972, the date of recordation. The district court found some merit in General Dynamic's argument that Stewart's knowledge was to be evaluated as of August 3 but declined to choose between the dates of purchase and the date of recordation, holding that use of the date of purchase would be harmless error because Stewart did not know of the default by Ayer even on August 3. General Dynamics argues to us that the district court's disposition of this issue was improper because August 3 was the relevant time, but the bankruptcy court had made no finding on the state of Stewart's knowledge in August. We disagree with General Dynamics on both grounds.

We conclude that the dates of purchase were the relevant dates. The rule of § 9.307(a) is designed to protect the innocent buyer against prior security interests in retail goods because he cannot be expected to discover those interests, while the secured party may generally be assumed to have authorized the sale of inventory by a retailer. *See generally, e.g.,* J. White & R. Summers, Uniform Commercial Code § 25–14 at 1070 (2d ed. 1980). But this "protection" leaves the buyer vulnerable if he cannot be certain of it until he records. Were that the rule, a buyer who discovered a violated security agreement after purchasing but before recording could have given consideration, in good faith and without knowledge, and taken possession of the goods but he would take a position subordinate to that of the secured lender. Measuring knowledge at the time of sale or earlier, however, prevents any gap in protection, for a potential buyer who discovers a violated security interest at the time of purchase can always decide not to buy.[13]

In the alternative, we conclude that the bankruptcy judge did find that in August Stewart was without knowledge of any violation of the security agree-

13. We find additional support for our conclusion that the dates of purchase are the relevant dates in the limited nature of the current controversy over when the protection of the buyer in the ordinary course attaches. Although there is some debate as to whether one who qualifies as a buyer in the ordinary course prevails over the secured lender if the lender attempts to foreclose before the buyer takes possession of the goods, no one seems to question that, from the time of delivery, the buyer prevails. *See* T. Quinn, UCC Commentary and Law Digest ¶ 3–307[A][8] (1978); Note, *When Does a Buyer Become a Buyer in Ordinary Course? UCC §§ 1–201(9), 9–307(1): A Test and a Proposal,* 60 Neb.L.Rev. 848, 875 (1981); compare, *e.g., Jones v. One Fifty Foot Gulfstar Motor Sailing Yacht,* 5 Cir.1980, 625 F.2d 44, 47 n. 4 (dictum) (the date of contract marks the beginning of protection, at least where the buyer has made partial payment) *with Martin Marietta Corp. v. New Jersey Nat'l Bank,* 3 Cir.1979, 612 F.2d 745, 749 (assuming, without deciding, that the date of identification of the goods to the contract marks the beginning of protection) *and with Chrysler Corp. v. Adamatic, Inc.,* 1973, 59 Wis. 2d 219, 208 N.W.2d 97, 106–07 (the passage of title marks the beginning of protection). Although one might argue that the buyer's qualification should be determined as of a date earlier than that on which the protection takes effect, surely the qualification should not be determined as of a *later* date.

ment between Ayer and General Dynamics. His opinion stated that Stewart was unaware of the lien until after the time of purchase, "and *even then* the mortgage appeared to authorize Ayer to sell free of any lien. * * * Stewart became *and remained* a buyer in ordinary course of business." Bankruptcy Court Op. at 6 (emphasis added).

Third, General Dynamics challenges the correctness of the holding that Stewart bought in good faith and without knowledge that the sale to him was in violation of the rights of General Dynamics. Our holding above was based on alternative grounds—that the dates of purchase are the dates on which Stewart's knowledge is relevant and that the bankruptcy court found that Stewart acted in good faith and had no knowledge on the date of recordation. In keeping with that alternative holding, we will consider Stewart's knowledge and good faith on both dates, although General Dynamics's argument deals mainly with the date of recordation.

The holding that Stewart had no knowledge that the sale violated the security agreement between Ayer and General Dynamics is not clearly erroneous. There is nothing in the record to show any knowledge on the dates of purchase, for the results of the title search did not arrive until January 5, 1972, the day after the second purchase. Once those results arrived, there is nothing to indicate that Stewart saw the security agreement before August 3, 1972, and, even if he did, that agreement appeared to authorize the sale. The record supports the conclusion that Stewart first learned of the default by Ayer from General Dynamics's letter of May 28, 1976. We cannot re-evaluate Stewart's credibility in denying knowledge; that was a question for the trial judge.

General Dynamics also contends that Stewart did not act in good faith, suggesting that he knowingly bought the planes for less than their value and that, though he was experienced in the sale of aircraft, did not undertake a title search before purchasing.[16] To show that Stewart purchased below market value, General Dynamics relies on the gain on the later sale of one of the planes and on the use of a higher value in the 1975 mortgage agreement between Gary and its bank. Stewart apparently made no profit on the sale of the group of planes, and, indeed, his profit on a sale four years down the line is but weak evidence that he originally paid less than fair value for the planes and even weaker evidence that he was aware that this was a bargain too good to be true. Similarly, the use of a higher value in a mortgage agreement consummated three years later is weak evidence of the 1972 market value.

16. General Dynamics also notes a number of other facts that it views as evidence of Stewart's bad faith: (1) Stewart purchased the planes in his individual capacity, (2) he waited seven months to record his title, (3) he gave two planes to Gary and sold another one to Gary at a large gain, (4) in August 1976, Stewart and Gary obtained an indemnification agreement from Ayer, and (5) Gary's files contained a rough draft of a letter, never sent, that misrepresented the date on which Gary learned of the lien. The first three facts are obviously completely irrelevant to the question of Stewart's good faith. The indemnification agreement, obtained some four and a half years after the purchase, shows little about Stewart's good faith on that date or on the date of recordation; if anything, it tends to establish that he acted in good faith because he saw no need for such an agreement at those times. Finally, we are unmoved by General Dynamics's arguments that the rough draft of the letter establishes bad faith. First, the letter was clearly labelled a draft and was never sent, so, at most, it could establish that Stewart thought about acting in bad faith and decided not to do so. Second, the letter was drafted in 1976, long after Stewart's good or bad faith ceased to be relevant. Third, examination of the letter indicates that the author was uncertain of the date of the discovery of the liens, placed it shortly after Gary's sale of one of the planes and only later filled in that date, suggesting that there was no purposeful misrepresentation of the date of the discovery. Finally, the record does not establish that Stewart drafted the letter, and he denied having done so.

Stewart's failure to undertake a title search presents a question only slightly more troublesome. The Texas courts have repeatedly stated that the test of good faith is not negligence or diligence and that it is immaterial that the buyer was aware of facts that would put a reasonably prudent person on inquiry. To lose his status as a buyer in the ordinary course, the buyer must have actual knowledge of facts or circumstances that amount to bad faith. * * *. Thus, although a reasonably prudent person with Stewart's experience might have conducted a title search with the FAA before purchasing, Stewart's failure to do so does not, without more, establish that he acted in bad faith. * * *. Nor did Stewart have actual knowledge of any circumstances that would put him in bad faith. We decline to overrule the holding that Stewart acted in good faith.

IV.

General Dynamics next argues that, even if Stewart qualifies as a buyer in the ordinary course of business, Gary cannot take good title for one of two reasons—first, the security interest was not created by Gary's seller and, second, Gary gave no consideration for the planes. Neither argument has merit.

The first argument is based on the limitation in section 9.307(a): a buyer in the ordinary course of business takes free of a security interest only if it was created by his seller. *See, e.g., National Shawmut Bank v. Jones,* 1967, 108 N.H. 386, 236 A.2d 484. General Dynamics, noting that the security interest it asserts was not created by Stewart (Gary's seller) but by Ayer, contends that Gary cannot be protected against that interest. This argument misses the mark, for Gary does not claim under section 9.307(a). On the contrary, its position is that Stewart took good title under section 9.307(a), and Gary, as Stewart's transferee, took whatever title Stewart had, under section 2.403(a), the "shelter" provision. It is therefore of no consequence that Gary's seller did not create the security interest. General Dynamics attempts to rebut this reasoning by relying on language in *National Shawmut Bank* stating that section 2–403 of the Uniform Commercial Code cannot provide an escape from the limitations of section 9–307. In *National Shawmut Bank* an individual sold a car, subject to a security interest, to a dealer, who then sold it to a buyer in the ordinary course of business. Since the security interest was not created by his seller, the last buyer in the chain could not take free and clear of the interest under section 9–307 of the UCC. Section 2.403(a) provides that a purchaser of goods acquires all title that his transferor had or had power to transfer, and that a seller with voidable title can transfer good title. If, under that provision, a retailer who bought subject to a security interest was one with voidable title and had the power to transfer good title, the "created by his seller" limitation of section 9.307(a) would be without any effect, so the *National Shawmut Bank* court held that section 2.403(a) does not provide an escape to section 9.307(a). That rule has been approved by the commentators, *see* J. White & R. Summers, Uniform Commercial Code § 25–15 (2d ed. 1980), and we do not question it. But the rule is that section 2.403(a) is not available to save one who buys when the seller's title is subject to a security interest but who does not qualify under section 9.307(a). It certainly does not mean that section 2.403(a) is not available to subsequent transferees from a successful section 9.307(a) buyer, as General Dynamics urges. *See* Skilton, *Buyer in the Ordinary Course of Business under Article 9 of the Uniform Commercial Code,* 1974 Wis.L.Rev. 1, 76 (viewing the point as "obvious"). If General Dynamics were correct, section 9.307(a) would be of scant benefit to the "protected" buyer in the ordinary course, for good title means little if one cannot transfer it. We hold that the lien of General Dynamics was extinguished upon the sale by Ayer to Stewart under section 9.307(a), and the subsequent sale to Gary could not resurrect it.

Finally, General Dynamics contends that Gary cannot take good title under section 2.403(a) because it furnished no consideration, receiving the aircraft as a gift. We disagree. Section 2.403(a) applies to a "purchaser" of goods, and section 1.201 defines a "purchaser" as one who takes by "sale, discount, negotiation, mortgage, pledge, lien, issue or reissue, *gift* or any other voluntary transaction". § 1.201(32), (33) (emphasis added). The language could not be clearer. When the draftsmen of the Code wished to require consideration, they used the terms "buyer", "seller", and "sale", defined in sections 2.106(a) and 2.103(a)(1) to require consideration, instead of "purchaser", "transferor", and "purchase". *See, e.g.*, §§ 2.313, 2.314, 2.315. We cannot imagine applying any rule other than that a donee takes the title that his donor had.

V.

We hold that the FAA does not preempt the provisions of the Texas Business and Commerce Code relating to the priority of interests in aircraft. Therefore, Stewart, as a buyer in the ordinary course of business, took the aircraft free and clear of the lien of General Dynamics. And Gary, as the transferee of Stewart, also took free and clear of the lien. Consequently, Gary is entitled to the possession of the remaining airplane and the proceeds of the airplane that was sold. The case is affirmed.

[Some footnotes omitted.]

EXECUTIVE FINANCIAL SERVICES, INC. v. PAGEL

Supreme Court of Kansas, 1986.
238 Kan. 809, 715 P.2d 381.

[Executive Financial Services (EFS) purchased three tractors from Tri-County Farm Equipment Company (Tri-County), a John Deere dealership. EFS then leased the tractors to Mohr-Loyd Leasing, a partnership between the owners of Tri-County. The "lease" was a financing transaction, subject to Article 9, and EFS perfected its security interest in the tractors by filing. EFS neither took possession of the tractors nor segregated them from other tractors held for sale by Tri-County.

Tri-County sold tractor # 1 to Thompson Implement Company, a merchant engaged in the business of selling farm equipment. Thompson, in turn, sold the tractor to Pagel, a buyer in the ordinary course of business. Pagel granted John Deere a purchase money security interest in the tractor, which Deere perfected by filing a financing statement. Tractor # 2 was sold by Thompson to Allen, who also granted Deere a purchase money security interest which Deere perfected by filing. Tractor # 3 was sold by Thompson to Morse. Deere took a purchase money security interest in the tractor but, because it was not perfected on time, it was subject to a preexisting security interest of PCA on Morse's equipment and machinery.

When Mohr-Loyd defaulted on the leases, EFS brought suit, inter alia, to recover the tractors from Pagel, Allen and Morse. The lower courts granted the defendants a summary judgment on the ground that they took free of EFS's security interest under UCC 2–403(2). The cases were consolidated on appeal and the judgments were affirmed. The Supreme Court first held that the transaction between EFS and Mohr-Loyd Leasing was "essentially a financing transaction whereby EFS acquired a security interest in the three tractors.]

* * *

Having so determined, we turn to the issue of whether the buyers of the tractors took free of EFS's security interest pursuant to K.S.A. 84–9–307(1), which provides:

> "A buyer in ordinary course of business * * * other than a person buying farm products from a person engaged in farming operations takes free of a security interest *created by his seller* even though the security interest is perfected and even though the buyer knows of its existence." (Emphasis added.)

Under this section, if Allen, Riverview Farms, Thompson and Pagel were "buyers in ordinary course of business" they would take free of any security interest created "by the seller," which is Tri-County. However, K.S.A. 84–9–307(1) is inapplicable to the facts in this case because Mohr-Loyd created the security interest in question—not Tri-County. A buyer in ordinary course can only take free of a security interest created "by his seller." Since the seller of the tractors, Tri-County, did not create the security interest, the buyers cannot take free of that interest under 84–9–307(1).

We next consider whether, as a matter of law, EFS entrusted the three tractors to Tri-County and, under K.S.A. 84–2–403(2), thereby lost any interest it had in them.

The entrustment doctrine is codified at K.S.A. 84–2–403(2):

> "Any entrusting of possession of goods to a merchant who deals in goods of that kind gives him power to transfer all rights of the entruster to a buyer in ordinary course of business."

"Entrusting" is defined in K.S.A. 84–2–403(3):

> " 'Entrusting' includes any delivery and any acquiescence in retention of possession regardless of any condition expressed between the parties to the delivery or acquiescence and regardless of whether the procurement of the entrusting or the possessor's disposition of the goods have been such as to be larcenous under the criminal law."

Since this statute has not been considered by the court in an analogous fact situation, some general background regarding its purpose and effect is helpful.

The Kansas Comment 1983 to K.S.A. 84–2–403 briefly describes the purpose of the provisions in question:

> "Subsections (2) and (3) extend prior law in protecting buyers in ordinary course of business from hidden entrusting arrangements with merchant-sellers who deal in goods of the kind. Under these subsections, an owner who entrusts goods to a merchant who deals in goods of the kind may lose his rights as against a buyer in ordinary course of business. Under prior law, such good faith purchasers were protected only under the doctrines of estoppel and the like."

At common law, the mere entrustment of goods to a merchant who dealt in goods of a kind did not estop the owner from recovering them from a bona fide purchaser for value. This common law rule has been reversed by UCC § 2–403(2), which provides that any entrusting of possession of goods to a merchant who deals in goods of that kind accords the merchant power to transfer all the entruster's rights to a buyer in ordinary course of business. Hawkland, UCC Series § 2–403:07, p. 611 (1984).

The entrustment doctrine operates on the assumption that both the entruster and the buyer have been equally harmed by the dishonesty of the merchant-dealer, and resolves the issue in favor of the buyer. This result is explained in Hawkland, UCC Series § 2–403:07, as follows:

"In a broad sense, § 2–402(2) exemplifies one effort to 'modernize the law governing commercial transactions' in keeping with the underlying philosophy of the UCC. Accordingly, when a housewife takes her vacuum cleaner for repairs to a merchant who also is in the business of selling vacuum cleaners new and old, the sale by him to a buyer in the ordinary course of business passes a good title to the latter. In this case, the equities of the housewife and the buyer may be said to be equal. The housewife may not have been prudent in entrusting her goods to the dishonest dealer, but, by the same token, the buyer may not have been prudent in buying from him. On the assumption that both the entruster and buyer have been equally victimized by the dishonesty of the merchant-dealer, § 2–403(2) resolves the issue so as to free the marketplace, rather than protect the original owner's property rights. The rule, however, is an absolute one and does not depend in its operation on any balancing of equities or notions of comparative negligence." p. 612.

Entrusting typically falls into one of four fact patterns. These patterns are illustrated in White and Summers, Uniform Commercial Code § 3–11, p. 143 (2d ed. 1980):

"First, Ernie Entruster turns his car over to Dave Dealer so that Dave can sell it for Ernie. A buyer in ordinary course takes free of Ernie's ownership rights. Second, a wholesaler gives Dealer the goods 'on consignment' or under a 'floor planning' agreement. A buyer in ordinary course from Dealer is not bound by any 'title retention' agreement between Dealer and the wholesaler as to passage of title. Third, George leaves goods to be repaired with Dealer who resells them to a buyer in ordinary course. Finally, Edgar buys goods from Dealer but leaves the goods in Dealer's hands. A buyer in ordinary course cuts off Edgar's interest."

The last example is similar to the fact pattern in the present case. EFS purchased three tractors from Tri-County, but left the tractors on Tri-County's lot. Tri-County later resold the tractors to third parties in ordinary course of business. The situation is made more complicated, however, by the fact that prior to the resale by Tri-County, EFS leased the tractors to Mohr-Loyd Leasing, which operated from the same business premises as Tri-County. Furthermore, EFS obtained a security interest in the tractors from Mohr-Loyd Leasing.

Prior to applying K.S.A. 84–2–403(2) to the facts of the instant case, we must consider its potential conflict with our previous application of 84–9–307(1).

Appellant contends that if a buyer does not qualify for the preferred treatment of K.S.A. 84–9–307(1) because the competing security interest is not created by the seller, the buyer cannot then argue it took free of the security interest under the entrustment theory of 84–2–403(2). This argument has received support among some courts and commentators.

White and Summers argue that priority disputes between secured creditors and subsequent purchasers must be governed exclusively by Article 9 and that a subsequent purchaser who is disappointed under 84–9–307 cannot fall back on 84–2–403 and argue that it renders him superior to a prior security interest. They point to the language of 84–9–306(2) which states:

"Except where *this article* otherwise provides, a security interest continues in collateral notwithstanding sale, exchange or other disposition thereof unless the disposition was authorized by the secured party in the security agreement or otherwise. * * * " (Emphasis added.)

See White and Summers, Uniform Commercial Code § 25–15, pp. 1073–74 (2d ed. 1980).

There is also authority, however, for applying the entrustment theory where a buyer is unable to prevail under 84–9–307(1). In his treatise, The Law of Secured Transactions Under the Uniform Commercial Code ¶ 3.4[3] (1985 Cum. Supp. No. 3), Professor Barkley Clark recognizes that an entrustment theory may be applicable, even when 84–9–307(1) is not applicable:

> "But even if the buyer in ordinary course loses his protection under § 9–307(1) because the security interest was created further up the line, he may be able to prevail on a different theory. This is what happened in In re Woods, where the buyer discovered that a bank had a perfected security interest in the collateral created by a previous owner. The court determined that the ultimate buyer could prevail on an *entrustment* theory under §§ 2–403(2) and 2–403(3). Those subsections provide that a person who 'entrusts' the possession of goods to a dealer loses title to a buyer in ordinary course from the dealer. In the usual case, the outright owner entrusts the goods to the dealer for repair. In this case, it was the bank with its prior perfected security interest which did the entrusting. Certainly there is nothing in the language of § 2–403 that would limit that provision to outright owners as entrusters. The Woods case makes the important point that a prior secured party may do sufficient 'entrusting' so that its security interest is lost, even though the security interest was not created by the dealer to which the goods were entrusted. The court in Woods suggested yet another theory to protect the ordinary course buyer: Insofar as the prior secured party permitted the collateral to be delivered to the dealer, it authorized the sale free of its security interest under § 9–306(2). Finally, under either alternative theory, the ultimate buyer was protected even though it knew of the bank's prior perfected security interest; the court correctly concluded that, in order for the secured party to prevail, it would have to show that the ordinary course buyer knew that the sale was in violation of the prior security interest."

The facts here, as in In re Woods, 25 B.R. 924 (Bkrtcy.Tenn.1982), are distinguishable from the usual case. Typically, the entruster and the holder of the security interest are separate entities with the security holder not involved in the entrustment. In such a case the security interest would continue in the goods because under K.S.A. 84–2–403(2) only the "rights of the entruster" would be transferred. Here, however, the security holder is the entruster and its rights as such are transferred to the buyer.

For K.S.A. 84–2–403(2) to be applicable, three steps are required: (1) An entrustment of goods to (2) a merchant who deals in goods of that kind followed by a sale by such merchant to (3) a buyer in ordinary course of business.

Neither party argues Tri-County is not a "merchant who deals in goods of that kind," but they disagree as to whether EFS entrusted the tractors to Tri-County and whether one of the transferees was a buyer in the ordinary course of business.

The first question for our consideration is whether EFS entrusted the goods to Tri-County. As noted earlier, "entrusting" is defined at K.S.A. 84–2–403(3) and includes "any delivery and any acquiescence in retention of possession."

In support of their theory of entrustment, appellees point out that although EFS purchased the tractors from Tri-County, it did not take possession of them. Nor did EFS segregate the tractors from Tri-County's other inventory, identify the tractors in any way as EFS's property, or otherwise manifest any sign of ownership which would be evidence to a subsequent purchaser. Appellees contend that by its lack of action, EFS acquiesced in Tri-County's retention of possession of the tractors.

On the other hand, EFS argues that the mere fact that EFS did not take possession of the tractors does not justify the conclusion that EFS acquiesced in the retention of possession of the tractors by Tri-County. EFS contends that once it leased the tractors to Mohr-Loyd Leasing with the understanding and representation by Mohr-Loyd that the tractors would be leased out to farmers, it became impossible for EFS to acquiesce in the retention of possession of the tractors by Tri-County.

The reason possession was left with the merchant-seller is immaterial under the Code. 3 Anderson, Uniform Commercial Code § 2–403:42, pp. 592–93. The entrustment definition specifically provides that an entrustment can occur "regardless of any condition expressed between the parties to the delivery or acquiescence. . . ." K.S.A. 84–2–403(3).

Thus, the key factor here is EFS's knowledge that the tractors would remain in the Tri-County lot. The fact that EFS expected Mohr-Loyd to eventually lease the tractors to farmers is immaterial. We conclude the tractors were entrusted to Tri-County by EFS.

EFS next contends that even if an entrustment occurred, the Johnson County District Court improperly applied K.S.A. 84–2–403(2) to the transaction involving Riverview Farms because Riverview Farms was not a buyer in ordinary course of business. There is no dispute that Allen and Thompson Implement were buyers in ordinary course of business.

K.S.A. 84–1–201(9) defines "buyer in ordinary course of business":

> " 'Buyer in ordinary course of business' means a person who in good faith and without knowledge that the sale to him is in violation of the ownership rights or security interest of a third party in the goods buys in ordinary course from a person in the business of selling goods of that kind. * * * 'Buying' may be for cash or by exchange of other property or on secured or unsecured credit and includes receiving goods or documents of title under a preexisting contract for sale but does not include a transfer in bulk or as security [for] or in total or partial satisfaction of a money debt."

"Good faith" is defined at K.S.A. 84–1–201(19); " 'Good faith' means honesty in fact in the conduct or transaction concerned."

First, EFS argues the model No. 8640 tractor was not acquired by Riverview Farms for cash or other valid consideration. Rather, EFS contends the tractor was acquired by utilizing $30,000 of credit owed to Riverview Farms by Tri-County. This contention is based on the fact that in March of 1982, Riverview Farms received two checks from Tri-County totalling nearly $30,000. Ted Morse, one of the partners in Riverview Farms, was unable to explain why the checks were given to Riverview Farms. A few months later in August 1982, Riverview Farms delivered a model No. 8630 tractor to Tri-County to be sold by Tri-County.

Appellees argue Riverview Farms acquired the model No. 8640 tractor in an even exchange for the No. 8630 tractor. They concede Tri-County initially offered to sell the No. 8640 tractor to Riverview Farms for a trade-in of the No. 8630 tractor plus $10,000. Later, however, Tri-County agreed to accept the No. 8630 tractor in an even exchange for the No. 8640 tractor. Appellees explained the $30,000 payment to Riverview Farms as credit received when Tri-County sold a No. 7020 tractor and disc which Riverview Farms had traded to Tri-County.

K.S.A. 84–1–201(9) specifically provides that a transfer in total or partial satisfaction of a money debt does not give the purchaser the status of a "buyer in ordinary course." Thus, if Riverview Farms acquired the No. 8640 tractor as the result of a credit obtained initially for the model No. 8630 tractor and the extinguishment of a money debt, it did not have "buyer in ordinary course" status. However, if Riverview Farms acquired the No. 8640 tractor in an even exchange for the No. 8630, it did have buyer in ordinary course status since 84–1–201(9) includes an exchange within the definition of "buying."

The Johnson County District Court made specific findings that Riverview Farms had no actual notice that Mohr-Loyd Leasing existed, that Mohr-Loyd leased the No. 8640 tractor from EFS, or that EFS claimed any interest in the tractor. We conclude the facts justify the district court's ruling that Riverview Farms, like Thompson, Pagel and Allen, was a buyer in ordinary course of business.

We hold all three tractors were entrusted to Tri-County, a merchant who deals in tractors, by EFS and then sold to Allen, Thompson Implement and Riverview Farms in ordinary course of business.

A final issue presented by this appeal is whether EFS may be estopped from claiming any interest in the tractors. We need not discuss this issue since the case is resolved by our application of the entrustment provisions of K.S.A. 84–2–403(2) and (3).

The judgments of the trial courts are affirmed.

Notes

The *Pagel* case, by using UCC 2–403(2), expands the protection of a buyer in ordinary course of business beyond that granted by UCC 9–307(1). Is this result sound? How does the court deal with UCC 2–403(4), which states that the "rights of other purchasers of goods * * * are governed by the Articles on Secured Transactions (Article 9) * * * "?

Note: Rights of Buyer When Goods in Seller's Possession

In a contest with a secured party with a perfected security interest, at what point does a buyer become a "buyer in the ordinary course of business?" Assuming that the conditions in UCC 1–201(37) are satisfied, including the giving of value, there are three possibilities.

First, the status is not achieved until the goods are delivered by the seller. This was a requirement under the Uniform Trust Receipts Act and it has some support in UCC 9–301(1)(c), where the buyer is other than in the ordinary course, and in the case law. See, e.g., Chrysler Corp. v. Adamatic, Inc., 59 Wis.2d 219, 208 N.W.2d 97 (1973), where the court stated that the "status" of a buyer in ordinary course must be determined "as of the time he actually took possession of the goods." Section 9–307(1), however, does not require that possession be transferred.

Second, the status is achieved when the buyer obtains title to the goods even though possession has not been transferred. Obtaining title before delivery requires that the goods be both existing and identified to the contract, see UCC 2–105(2) & 2–501(1), and that the parties agree that title shall pass before delivery. See UCC 2–401(1). Thus, where a buyer made progress payments to a seller who was manufacturing goods for the buyer and the parties agreed that title to all parts and components and to the goods in process should pass to the buyer when the seller acquired them, Kinetics Technology International Corp. v. Fourth National Bank of Tulsa, 705 F.2d 396 (10th Cir.1983), held that the status was achieved when title passed to the buyer under the agreement. Accord: Puget Sound Nat. Bank v. Honeywell, Inc., 40 Wash.App. 313, 698 P.2d 584, 587 (1985).

Third, the status is achieved when the goods are identified to the contract under UCC 2–501(1), even though neither title nor possession have passed. Support for this position can be found in Martin Marietta Corp. v. New Jersey National Bank, 612 F.2d 745 (3d Cir.1979), and Big Knob Vol. Fire Co. v. Lowe & Moyer Garage, 338 Pa. Super. 257, 487 A.2d 953, 956–58 (1985). Thus, the "special property interest" obtained by identification is sufficient to confirm the status of BIOCB and to support an action by the buyer to replevy the goods or to obtain specific performance. See UCC 2–716. See also Tanbro Fabrics Corp. v. Deering Milliken, Inc., 39 N.Y.2d 632, 385 N.Y.S.2d 260, 350 N.E.2d 590 (1976), where the court apparently held that a buyer with at least as "special property" interest became a BIOCB even though the secured party of his seller had possession of the goods.

If, in each of these cases, the buyer has advanced all or part of the contract price to the seller, which approach makes the most sense? Clearly, if the status of BIOCB depends upon the transfer of possession to the buyer, the presumed problems associated with "ostensible ownership" are resolved. The buyer will not be asserting a property interest of which no public notice has been given to reclaim goods in the seller's possession. Compare Note, *"Bailment for Processing:" Article Nine Security Interest or Title Retention Contract,* 61 Ore.L.Rev. 441 (1982), written by the son of one of your co-authors. But will the buyer's interest be adequately protected before delivery?

The answer is yes if the buyer could create and perfect an Article 9 purchase money security interest in the goods being manufactured by the seller and obtain priority over any existing perfected security interests in the collateral. See UCC 9–107 & 9–312(3). This step, however, is easier to recommend than to implement. In short, there are several practical pitfalls in the path of the "financing buyer" which interfere with the use of Article 9. A full exploration of this step should be postponed until you study the materials on Secured Transactions and, more particularly, Chapter 7. See, generally, Jackson & Kronman, *A Plea for the Financing Buyer,* 85 Yale L.J. 1 (1975) (buyer may be unable to insure that funds advanced to seller are used in fact to obtain materials and components for completed goods).

SECTION 3. SELLER'S WARRANTY OF TITLE

In Section 2, a primary question was when does the buyer of goods get "good" title from a seller whose title is defective or nonexistent? Another was when does the buyer "take free" from a perfected security interest? These questions are often litigated when the "true" owner or secured party asserts claims to goods in the possession of the buyer. If "true" owner wins, the buyer will be deprived of the goods and, of course, the benefit of his bargain. Does the buyer have any recourse against his seller? If so, what remedies are available? If "true" owner loses, the buyer may keep the goods. However, he has been put through the stress and expense of a law suit and may have been temporarily deprived of possession. Does he have any recourse against his seller? In short, we are here concerned with whether the seller has made and breached a warranty of title under UCC 2–312 and what the buyer must and may do to achieve adequate redress.

SUMNER v. FEL-AIR, INC.

Supreme Court of Alaska, 1984.
680 P.2d 1109.

OPINION

RABINOWITZ, JUSTICE.

This appeal arises from a dispute over the sale of a Piper Navajo airplane by William Sumner, an Anchorage commercial aircraft dealer, to Fel-Air, Inc., a Barrow air taxi operator. In March 1976, Sumner and Fel-Air orally agreed to the basic terms of the sale, including the purchase price of $105,000.00. Sumner was to receive a Piper Aztec aircraft valued at $30,000 as a downpayment on the Navajo. Fel-Air was to remit the $75,000 balance of the purchase price in monthly installments of $2,000. Interest on the unpaid balance was to accrue at a rate of 12%. These terms were confirmed in a March 31, 1976, letter from Fel-Air's general manager to Sumner.

The Navajo was delivered to Fel-Air in April 1976. Sumner received the Aztec as a downpayment in accordance with the parties' agreement. The Navajo began to experience mechanical difficulties and was taken to Seattle Flight Service for repairs in the early summer of 1976. Two months later, after paying a repair bill of $20,000, Fel-Air regained use of the airplane.

Fel-Air sent the Navajo back to Seattle for repairs in October 1976. Two months later, while the plane was still in the custody of Seattle Flight Service, the president of Century Aircraft, Inc. informed Fel-Air that title to the Navajo was held by Century rather than by Sumner. Century's president had also told Seattle Flight Service that Century owned the aircraft. Sumner's interest in the Navajo was that of a lessee with an option to purchase. After the discovery that Century was the record owner of the Navajo, Seattle Flight Service filed a mechanic's lien against the Navajo for unpaid repair bills.

Fel-Air asserted that it telephoned Sumner in December 1976 and requested either a conditional sales contract or bill of sale which would provide the Federal Aviation Administration with a record of Fel-Air's authority to operate the Navajo, or a full refund of payments made to date on the Navajo, including return of the Aztec. Fel-Air contended that Sumner assured it that the contract would be prepared within three days. Sumner testified that he did not remember such a conversation.

In May of 1977, Fel-Air ceased making monthly payments on the Navajo. On May 10, 1978, Sumner sent a telegram to Fel-Air demanding satisfaction of the lien Seattle Flight Service had filed and payment of monthly installments then due. Fel-Air did not respond. Sumner discharged the $8,000 lien himself and had the plane flown back to Anchorage.

Sumner arranged to have the Navajo's documents of title held in escrow to assure Fel-Air that it would receive title upon payment of the balance of the purchase price and upon compensation of Sumner for payments made to satisfy the Seattle Flight Service lien. On August 3, 1977, the escrow arrangement was completed. The balance then due on the aircraft, including the payment made to discharge the mechanic's lien, was $64,936.47.

Fel-Air subsequently filed suit against Sumner, alleging Sumner had breached implied warranties of merchantability and title and that he was liable to Fel-Air for fraud and misrepresentation. Sumner denied these claims and alleged that Fel-Air had abandoned the Navajo, requested that consideration paid by Fel-Air be deemed an offset for rent owed to Sumner for use of the Navajo, and filed a counterclaim for the $8,000 he had paid to discharge the lien.

The case was tried to the superior court sitting without a jury. The court rejected Fel-Air's claims for breach of the warranty of merchantability and negligent and intentional misrepresentation. However, it concluded that Sumner had breached a warranty of title to the aircraft and awarded Fel-Air $51,166.82 in damages. This sum represented the value of the Aztec used as a downpayment ($30,000), and $21,700 in monthly payments made by Fel-Air to Sumner, less the $533.18 expense of transporting the plane back to Alaska saved by Fel-Air as a result of the breach. Pre-judgment interest accruing at 8% per annum from February 1, 1977, to May 1, 1980, was also awarded, and totaled $13,300.16. Judgment against Sumner was entered for $64,466.98. Fel-Air was also awarded costs and attorney's fees. This appeal followed.

Breach of Warranty of Title

Title 45 of the Alaska Statutes adopts Article 2 of the Uniform Commercial Code as the applicable law of sales in Alaska. Under A.S. 45.02.312, an implied warranty of title accompanies the sale of goods in Alaska. It may expressly be disclaimed. A focal point of the parties' dispute is whether Sumner excluded or modified by specific language the warranty of title. Sumner does not claim that he had good title to the Navajo, but rather alleges that he informed Fel-Air that he leased, but did not own, the Navajo. Fel-Air denies that it was so informed.

The superior court specifically found that Sumner did not inform Fel-Air prior to the sale that he had neither title to the Navajo nor the right to sell it, and that the circumstances surrounding the transaction did not give Fel-Air any reason to know that Sumner did not claim title to the plane in himself. The court concluded that Sumner had therefore breached the warranty of title imposed by A.S. 45.02.312.

Sumner concedes that the superior court's conclusion that there was no express or implied disclaimer of the A.S. 45.02.312 warranty was a finding of fact which may be reversed only if clearly erroneous. Alaska R.Civ.P. 52(a); *Uchitel Co. v. Telephone Co.,* 646 P.2d 229, 233 (Alaska 1982); *Strack v. Miller,* 645 P.2d 184, 186 (Alaska 1982). In the case at bar, the superior court's factual finding was based upon an assessment of the credibility of conflicting testimonial evidence. We have observed that "[i]t is the trial court's function, and not that of a reviewing court, to judge the credibility of the witnesses and to weigh conflicting evidence. This is especially true where the trial court's decision depends largely upon oral testimony." *Penn v. Ivey,* 615 P.2d 1, 3 (Alaska 1980) (citations omitted). Thus, particular deference must be accorded to the superior court's finding that Sumner did not disclaim the A.S. 45.02.312 warranty of title. After review of the entire record before us, and guided by these principles of appellate review, we conclude that the superior court's finding that an implied warranty of title accompanied the sale of the Navajo must be upheld. The question now becomes whether or not Sumner breached that warranty.[8]

8. Sumner argues that Fel-Air should be held to have had "constructive notice" of Century's interest prior to consummation of the sale, since pertinent documents of title to the Navajo were on file at the Federal Aviation Administration (FAA) at that time. This argument is without merit. It is clear from the wording of A.S. 45.02.312 that only actual knowledge on the part of the buyer of the seller's lack of title, or of circumstances which would reasonably lead the buyer to reach such a conclusion, can defeat the statutory warranty. The official commentary to § 2–312 of the U.C.C. specifically states that "[t]he 'knowledge' referred to in subsection 1(b) is actual

Since Sumner did not have good title to the plane when he purported to convey it to Fel-Air, the answer to this question may seem obvious. Yet both parties agree that Century "entrusted" the plane to Sumner within the meaning of A.S. 45.02.403. Under the UCC a merchant to whom goods have been entrusted may give a buyer a better title than the merchant himself possessed. To quote A.S. 45.02.403(b):

> An entrusting of possession of goods to a merchant who deals in goods of that kind gives him power to transfer all rights of the entruster to a buyer in ordinary course of business.

Because Sumner had possession of the Navajo and was a dealer in airplanes, he had the power to transfer all of Century's rights, including its good title to the airplane. Given the facts as the parties have presented them, Fel-Air could have defeated any attempt by Century to regain possession of the Navajo.

It does not follow from the fact that the parties now agree that Fel-Air's title was good that Sumner did not breach the implied warranty of title. This question has divided the commentators. *Compare* 1 Anderson, Uniform Commercial Code § 2–312:36 (3d ed. 1982) (warranty not breached) with 1 Alderman, A Transactional Guide to the Uniform Commercial Code § 1.53–52 (2d ed. 1983) (warranty breached, seller should have chance to cure). Alderman emphasizes the full text of UCC 2–312(a)(1), which provides:

> (a) Subject to (b) of this section there is in a contract for sale a warranty by the seller that
>
> (1) the title conveyed shall be good, *and its transfer rightful.*

A.S. 45.02.312(a) and (a)(1) (emphasis added). As Alderman states, the entrustee's "wrongfulness (lack of right) in making the conveyance * * * is unquestionable, for the transfer of title [is] not made pursuant to any 'right' ". Alderman, *supra,* at 266–67. Here Sumner's lease-purchase arrangement with Century did not authorize him to transfer title to Fel-Air. The transfer he made to Fel-Air was wrongful, and thus we conclude that the warranty UCC 2–312(a)(1) establishes was breached.

Wright v. Vickaryous, 611 P.2d 20 (Alaska 1980), supports this conclusion. *Wright* suggests that a court attempting to determine whether or not a warranty of title was breached must consider the facts as they appeared to the buyer at the time title was called into question. If a reasonable buyer would conclude that "marketable title" had not been conveyed to him, the seller—assuming that he does not save the transaction by showing that the facts are not what the buyer believes them to be—has breached the warranty of title. A "substantial shadow" on title is enough to justify the buyer's refusal to proceed with his contractual performance.[10] Similarly in the instant case the revelation of Century's interest in the Piper Navajo cast such a shadow on the transaction between Sumner and Fel-Air.

knowledge as distinct from notice." § 2–312 comment 1, 1 U.L.A. 303 (1976).

10. In *Wright* various third parties had taken security interests in the seller's cattle. All of them orally consented to the sale, thus releasing their security interests pursuant to UCC 9–306(2). However, the liens remained on the books, the buyer discovered them, and delivery of the cattle was refused, the seller all this time failing to point out that the security interests had been released. We held that this circumstance put a "substantial shadow" on the title and justified refusing to proceed with the sales contract. *Wright* explicitly recognized that the buyer could successfully have defended himself against any former lienholder's lawsuit, but reasoned that the risk of such a lawsuit was enough to excuse the buyer's refusal to accept delivery.

To dispel a similar shadow, the buyer in *Wright* would have had to call all the people he believed to be lienholders; had he done so, he would have discovered that their liens had been released. To dispel the shadow of Century Aircraft, Fel-Air would have had to become an expert on the UCC and would then have had to determine that Sumner had not stolen or borrowed the Navajo from Century, that Sumner was indeed a "merchant who deals in [airplanes]" as the UCC defines "merchant," and that Fel-Air itself qualified as a "buyer in ordinary course of business." The parties' present agreement on these matters does not mean that these things were obvious at the time the transaction between Sumner and Fel-Air began to break down. Even if we decided to ignore A.S. 45.02.312's intimation that a "wrongful" transfer of title breaches the warranty which that section contains, we would be loath to conclude that a breach did not occur in this case. The superior court correctly decided that Sumner breached the implied warranty of title.

* * *

For the foregoing reasons, the judgment of the superior court is affirmed.

[Some footnotes omitted.]

Note: Fifty Ways to Breach the 2–312 Warranty of Title

Paradoxically, the warranty of title was broken in Sumner v. Fel-Air, although the buyer actually got good title. Is the result supported by any specific language in UCC 2–312? Is such a result justified?

A breach of warranty of title has been held to occur when the seller of a motor vehicle fails to provide his purchaser with adequate proof of ownership because of the reasonable doubts which faulty documentation (number on title certificate did not correspond with number on frame of vehicle) raises as to the validity of the title the buyer acquires. Jefferson v. Jones, 286 Md. 544, 408 A.2d 1036 (1979). Here, because of the faulty documentation, the vehicle was seized by the police and the buyer had to incur legal expenses to resolve the matter favorably, expenses he then successfully sought from the seller.

Beyond full adverse ownership claims, various "clouds" have been held to breach the title warranty. Elias v. Dobrowolski, 120 N.H. 212, 412 A.2d 1035 (1980) (valid filed security interest of which buyer had no actual knowledge); Wright v. Vickaryous, 611 P.2d 20 (Alaska 1980) (security interests the prior discharge of which had not been communicated to buyer who then rejected the cattle); National Crane Corp. v. Ohio Steel Tube Co., 213 Neb. 782, 332 N.W.2d 39 (1983) (tax liens); Catlin Aviation Co. v. Equilease Corp., 626 P.2d 857 (Okl.1981) (repairman's lien); Jeanneret v. Vichey, 693 F.2d 259 (2d Cir.1982) (regulations of foreign country applicable to export of paintings could constitute cloud if not complied with).

Not just any assertion of a claim by a third party will breach the warranty of title. Unfounded claims that are also not colorable will not. C.F. Sales, Inc. v. Amfert, Inc., 344 N.W.2d 543 (Iowa 1983).

Also, whenever the buyer has reason to know that the seller does not claim title to himself or that he is purporting to sell only such right or title as he or a third person may have, there is no warranty of title. UCC 2–312(2). For example, where a buyer of a used car received from the seller a certificate of title listing another person as the seller, the jury could have found that the buyer had such "reason to know." Spoon v. Herndon, 167 Ga.App. 794, 307 S.E.2d 693 (1983). But under 2–312(2), a warranty of title or the like can be "excluded or modified only by specific language." Rockdale Cable T.V. Co. v. Spadora, 97 Ill.App.3d 754, 53 Ill.Dec. 171, 423 N.E.2d 555 (1981) (language in bill of sale purporting to transfer "all Seller's right, title, and interest, of every kind and nature, in and to" held insufficiently specific).

UNIVERSAL C.I.T. CREDIT CORP. v. STATE FARM MUT. AUTO. INS. CO.

Court of Appeals of Missouri, 1973.
493 S.W.2d 385.

WASSERSTROM, JUDGE.

This four-party litigation poses the always difficult question of which one of several innocent parties should bear the loss of stolen goods. The specific factual context in which that question arises here is undisputed.

Kansas City Automobile Auction Company is engaged in a business of conducting sales at auction on behalf of automobile dealers having surplus automobiles. The bidders who attend these weekly auctions are also automobile dealers. On September 24, 1969, one of these auctions was conducted by Auction Company, and the Dodge automobile that is the subject of present controversy was sold to Jack Banning Ford Sales, Inc.

Thereafter, Banning resold this Dodge automobile to Donald L. Sensenich. This purchase was financed by Universal C.I.T. Credit Corporation. The credit transaction was in the form of a security agreement signed by Banning and Sensenich, which was then assigned by Banning to C.I.T. Sensenich also procured collision insurance covering the automobile, with a loss payable clause to C.I.T.

Subsequently, the Dodge automobile in question was demolished in a highway accident. In connection with the investigation accompanying the wreck, it was discovered that the automobile had been stolen prior to the time that it came into the hands of Auction Company, and that therefore, the auction sale on September 24, 1969, did not convey good title.

Upon acquiring the information concerning this insufficiency of title, Sensenich terminated any further payment to C.I.T., and he promptly gave notice to Banning of revocation of his acceptance of the automobile. Banning in turn gave notice to Auction Company and requested that Auction Company satisfy the demands of Sensenich. Auction Company denied liability.

Faced with this impasse, C.I.T. filed suit against Sensenich in Count I on the security agreement, and against the insurance company in Count II on the insurance policy. A settlement (accomplished in some manner not disclosed by the transcript on appeal) was made with the insurance company, and Count II of the C.I.T. petition was dismissed before trial.

Sensenich filed answer to Count I of the C.I.T. petition, and also filed a third-party petition bringing in Banning as a third-party defendant. Sensenich's third-party petition against Banning alleged generally the suit against him by C.I.T. and claimed indemnity from fourth-party petition against Auction Company alleging a right to reimbursement under an implied warranty of title from Auction Company to Banning.

The case was tried without a jury, and the trial court entered judgment for C.I.T. against Sensenich for the balance due under the security agreement, after giving credit for the insurance recovery, and also allowed attorney's fees in favor of C.I.T. of 15% as provided in the security agreement, the total so allowed to C.I.T. being $2,207.78. Judgment was also entered in favor of Sensenich against Banning in the sum of $2,998.50. The exact manner of computation of the latter figure is not disclosed by the abbreviated record filed on this appeal, but Sensenich states in his briefs, and his after-trial motion and the court's ruling thereon support the inference, that the sum awarded to Sensenich did not include any allowance for attorney's fee to him, either in resisting the C.I.T. suit or in pressing the third-party claim against Banning.

The judgment further awarded Banning the sum of $3,523.50 against Auction Company. While the abbreviated transcript on appeal does not show how this figure was computed, the parties in their briefs are in agreement that the award to Banning consisted of the judgment against him in favor of Sensenich plus an allowance of $525.00 as an attorney's fee to Banning in defending against the Sensenich claim. * * * The record indicates that Banning has gone out of business.

Auction Company, on its appeal, presents these points: (1) that there is no legal basis for liability against it, for the reason that an auctioneer acts solely as an agent and cannot be held to have given any implied warranty; and (2) that if it is liable at all, its liability must be confined to the value of the automobile at the time of the auction sale, which was the price paid by Banning of $2,415.00.

The points upon which Sensenich relies on his appeal are: (1) that he should have been awarded attorney's fees both in resisting the C.I.T. claim and also for prosecuting his third-party claim against Banning; and (2) that all judgments should have been as net damages directly against Auction Company for each of the three claimants.

* * *

II

Auction Company's principal argument on this appeal is that as an auctioneer it was a mere agent, and that any implied warranties were those of its principal who was the dealer who had delivered the car for sale at auction. This question has as its starting point the Uniform Commercial Code, § 400.2–312 V.A.M.S., which now codifies the law of implied warranty of title in connection with the sale of chattels. This section provides that there shall be a warranty that the title conveyed is good, except under "circumstances which give the buyer reason to know that the person selling does not claim title in himself * * *"

* * *

[T]he correct recourse for purposes of interpretation must be to the common law of this State, in accordance with the provision of § 400.1–103. * * *

Under the common law of this state, as well as under the law generally, an auctioneer is liable as a seller and is held to the burdens of an implied warranty of title, unless the auctioneer discloses the name of his principal at the time of sale. This principle is stated succinctly in the early case of Schell v. Stephens, 50 Mo. 375, l. c. 379, as follows;

> "The mere fact that defendants were acting as auctioneers is not of itself notice that they were not selling their own goods, and they must be deemed to have been vendors, and responsible as such for title, unless they disclosed at the time the name of the principal."

The same rule has been followed consistently since. * * *

Auction Company argues that it should not be held as a seller, because of some evidence in the record emphasized by it to the effect that Banning should have known that the Dodge automobile in question was being sold by Auction Company merely in its capacity as an auctioneer. That argument proceeds on a mistaken view of the law. As stated in the Schell case quoted above, the mere fact that a defendant is acting as an auctioneer is not in itself sufficient notice to provide immunity from liability. The requirement is that auctioneer disclose the name of its principal, and the record in this case is abundantly clear that this was not done. It is conceded that on the copy of the sales receipt delivered to Banning, the name of Auction Company's principal was purposely blocked out. The evidence by Auction Company itself was that this practice was intentional in order to prevent the buying dealer from "going around" the Auction Company. It was also conceded by Clemmons, Auction Company's general manager, that a bidder was not advised and could not ascertain the name of the selling dealer until after the sale had already been consummated. Under these admitted facts, Auction Company must be held to the obligation of an implied warranty to Banning. Moreover, there is sufficient evidence in the record to support a finding that Banning did not know either actually or constructively whether Auction Company was selling as agent or principal; and under these circumstances, it must be deemed that the trial court did so find. Rule 73.01(b), V.A.M.R.

III

Auction Company's alternative argument is that if liable at all, its liability cannot exceed the value of the automobile, measured by the amount received by it from Banning. In making this argument, Auction Company is relying basically on the general measure of damages for breach of warranty as set forth in § 400.2–714 V.A.M.S.; and it denies that this case comes within the concept of "consequential damages" which is recognized by § 400.2–714(3).

The extent to which consequential damages will be allowed is provided in § 400.2–715(2)(a), where that term is defined as including "any loss resulting from general or particular requirements and needs of which the seller at the time of contracting had reason to know * * *" This statutory definition of allowable consequential damages is essentially the same as the rule at common law. Under the common law, the courts of this State prior to the Uniform Commercial Code in an unbroken line of cases have held that a buyer may collect as consequential damages his expenses including attorney's fees in defending title after having given notice to his seller that a third party is claiming adversely. * * *

This result is especially compelled under the circumstances of this case. Under the evidence here, Auction Company should have known and must have realized that Banning would have loss beyond the wholesale value of the car paid by him, should it turn out that the title to the car was defective. By Auction Company's own argument, it knows that all bidders who attend its auction sales are automobile dealers. Obviously, those dealers are buying automobiles for resale; and also obviously, those dealers will be warranting title in turn to their vendees. Thus, if the title received by the auction bidder, in this case Banning, turned out to be bad, then the bidder-purchaser would stand to lose a good deal more than the bare original auction purchase price. For this reason, it must be concluded that the potential loss within the contemplation of the parties included costs which might be incurred in defending suits by subvendees, as well as lost profit of the resale and incidental expense.

In support of its contention that judgment will not lie against it for the attorney's fees paid by Banning in defense of the Sensenich claim, Auction Company cites 46 Am.Jur., Sales, § 755, p. 884, where it is stated: "* * * it has been held that the measure of damages against the original seller cannot be increased by reason of liability subsequently incurred by the buyer on account of independent warranties of the same property to later purchasers." In support of that statement, the text cites Smith v. Williams, 117 Ga. 782, 45 S.E. 394. An opposite result was reached in Thurston v. Spratt, 52 Me. 202. The Smith case is also out of harmony with the philosophy of the Missouri decisions on this point cited above. No significant distinction can be perceived for present purposes whether the claim made against the buyer is by a subvendee or someone completely outside the chain of transactions initiated by Auction Company. Moreover, the Smith case is readily distinguishable from the present case on the ground that the case at bar involves a sale to a dealer who the seller was bound to know would make a resale of the goods in the ordinary course of his business, whereas there is nothing in the Smith opinion to indicate that this was true in that case.

It follows that there was no error in including in Banning's judgment an allowance for attorney's fee incurred in defense of the Sensenich claim.

* * *

V

Sensenich's next claim of error is stated by him as follows: "The court erred in failing to enter judgment under impleader practice as net damages for each other party (plus all costs on Count 1) against fourth-party defendant". * * * To the extent that Sensenich is attempting to make complaint on behalf of Banning in this regard, no such complaint lies because Banning did get a judgment direct against Auction Company. Therefore, our consideration of this assignment reduces itself to the narrow question of whether Sensenich is entitled to a direct judgment against Auction Company. In this connection, it must be noted that Sensenich did not make Auction Company a party to his third-party petition, he did not attempt to state any cause of action against Auction Company, and he did not pray any relief against Auction Company. More fundamentally, however, he had no right of action against Auction Company as a matter of substantive law.

The law on this subject is that a warranty of title on personal property runs only to the immediate buyer and does not extend to subvendees. For this purpose, a warranty of title does not run with the chattel in the manner that a covenant for title runs with land. As stated in Crocker v. Barron, Mo.App., 234 S.W. 1032, l. c. 1033, a case involving suit for breach of warranty of title on personal property: "Warranties of Chattels are available only between parties to the contract, and not in favor of third parties." The law generally is similarly stated in 77 C.J.S. Sales § 352, p. 1259, as follows: "A subvendee has no right of action for breach of warranty to the original purchaser or against one who sold the goods to the person from whom the purchaser bought."

It is true that the requirement of privity in suits on some warranties has been greatly relaxed in recent years. However, that relaxation has occurred for the most part in cases of personal injury where there exists some element of tort. * * * This case does not come within the rationale of the cases which have, in selected situations, permitted recovery on warranties (usually relating to quality or fitness) without the necessity of privity of contract.

* * *

All motions filed in this court now pending are overruled. The appeal by Banning is dismissed. The judgment of the trial court is affirmed.

All concur.

Notes

1. Why did the court "credit" Sensenich with the proceeds of the insurance policy? Instead, why not subrogate the insurance company to the claims of C.I.T. against Sensenich?

2. Does the holding on privity and the fact that Banning has gone out of business mean that Sensenich will have no recovery?

3. If you were the judge how would you deal with the following argument: Since the true owner has not appeared to assert his interest, the warranty of title issues are essentially irrelevant to this law suit. Sensenich is in exactly the same circumstance as he would have been in had he had good title and destroyed the car. The Auction Company should have to make payment neither to Banning nor to Sensenich because the title it conveyed proved to be good at least for the useful life of this car. Thus even though the warranty of good title was breached, no damage was ever suffered by anybody as a result of that. How do you respond to such an argument if you represent Sensenich or Banning?

MENZEL v. LIST

New York Court of Appeals, 1969.
24 N.Y.2d 91, 298 N.Y.S.2d 979, 246 N.E.2d 742.

BURKE, JUDGE.

In 1932 Mrs. Erna Menzel and her husband purchased a painting by Marc Chagall at an auction in Brussels, Belgium, for 3,800 Belgian francs (then equivalent to about $150). When the Germans invaded Belgium in 1940, the Menzels fled and left their possessions, including the Chagall painting, in their apartment. They returned six years later and found that the painting had been removed by the German authorities and that a receipt for the painting had been left. The location of the painting between the time of its removal by the Germans in 1941 and 1955 is unknown. In 1955 Klaus Perls and his wife, the proprietors of a New York art gallery, purchased the Chagall from a Parisian art gallery for $2,800. The Perls knew nothing of the painting's previous history and made no inquiry concerning it, being content to rely on the reputability of the Paris gallery as to authenticity and title. In October, 1955 the Perls sold the painting to Albert List for $4,000. However, in 1962, Mrs. Menzel noticed a reproduction of the Chagall in an art book accompanied by a statement that the painting was in Albert List's possession. She thereupon demanded the painting from him but he refused to surrender it to her.

Mrs. Menzel then instituted a replevin action against Mr. List and he, in turn, impleaded the Perls, alleging in his third-party complaint that they were liable to him for breach of an implied warranty of title. At the trial, expert testimony was introduced to establish the painting's fair market value at the time of trial. The only evidence of its value at the time it was purchased by List was the price which he paid to the Perls. The trial court charged the jury that, if it found for Mrs. Menzel against List, it was also to "assess the value of said painting at such an amount as you believe from the testimony represents its present value." The jury returned a verdict for Mrs. Menzel and she entered a judgment directing the return of the painting to her or, in the alternative, that List pay to her the value of the painting, which the jury found to be $22,500. (List has, in fact, returned the painting to Mrs. Menzel.) In addition, the jury found for List as against the Perls, on his third-party complaint, in the amount of $22,500, the painting's present value, plus the costs of the Menzel action incurred by List. 49 Misc.2d 300, 267 N.Y.S.2d 804.

The Perls appealed to the Appellate Division, First Department, from that judgment and the judgment was unanimously modified, on the law, by reducing the amount awarded to List to $4,000 (the purchase price he had paid for the painting), with interest from the date of the purchase. In a memorandum, the Appellate Division held that the third-party action was for breach of an implied warranty of *quiet* possession and, accordingly, held that the Statute of Limitations had not run on List's claim since his possession was not disturbed until the judgment for Mrs. Menzel. 28 A.D.2d 516, 279 N.Y.S.2d 608. In addition, the court held that the "applicable measure of damages was the price List paid for the painting at the time of purchase, together with interest", citing three New York cases (Staats v. Executors of Ten Eyck, 3 Caines 111, 113; Armstrong v. Percy, 5 Wend. 535; Case v. Hall & Van Elten, 24 Wend. 102).

List filed a notice of appeal as of right from the unanimous modification insofar as it reduced the amount of his judgment to $4,000, with interest from the date of purchase. The Perls filed a notice of cross appeal from so much of the Appellate Division's order as failed to dismiss the third-party complaint, denied costs and disbursements and fixed the date from which interest was to run on List's judgment. The Perls have now abandoned the cross appeal as to the failure to dismiss the third-party complaint and the denial of costs and disbursements, leaving only the issue as to the date from which interest should run.

List's appeal and the Perls' cross appeal present only questions of law for resolution, the facts having been found by the jury and affirmed by the Appellate Division (its modification was on the law as to the proper measure of damages and the running of interest). The issue on the main appeal is simply what is or should be the proper measure of damages for the breach of an implied warranty of title (or quiet possession) in the sale of personal property. The cases cited by the Appellate Division do not hold that the measure of damages is the purchase price plus interest. The *Staats* case (*supra*) was an action for breach of a real property covenant in which there was dicta to the effect that the rule was the same for personal property. The dicta was compromised one year later by the same jurist (Chief Justice KENT who wrote the opinion in *Staats* in Blasdale v. Babcock, 1 Johns. 517 [1806], where it was held that the buyer was entitled to recover in damages the amount which he had been compelled to pay to the true owner, the actual value of the chattel. In Armstrong v. Percy, 5 Wend. 535, *supra* the buyer recovered the purchase price but only because the chattel, a horse, was found to have depreciated in value below the price paid. In Case v. Hall & Van Elten, 24 Wend. 102, *supra,* there is contained a statement which is pure dicta to the effect that warranty damages are the purchase price (the action was in contract for goods sold and delivered). The parties have cited no New York case which squarely meets the issue and it is, therefore, concluded that, contrary to the counter assertions of the parties, neither "purchase plus interest" (Perls) nor "value at date of dispossession" (List) is presently the law of this State. In fact, there is a marked absence of case law on the issue. One legislative source has described this paucity of case law with the understatement that "[t]he implied warranty of title under the Uniform Sales Act [N.Y. Personal Property Law, Consol.Laws, c. 41, § 94] has seldom been invoked." (1955 Report of N.Y.Law Rev.Comm., Vol. 1, p. 387, n. 68, citing Pinney v. Geraghty, 209 App. Div. 630, 205 N.Y.S. 645, a case dealing with the effect of the vendor's ignoring a vouching-in notice.) Furthermore, the case law in other jurisdictions in this country provides no consistent approach, much less "rule", on this issue and it is difficult even to add up jurisdictions to pinpoint a "majority" and a "minority". One attempt to collect and organize the law in this country on this issue concludes that there are at least four distinct "rules" for measuring the damages flowing from the breach of a personal property warranty of title: purchase price plus interest; "value", without specification as to the time at which value is to be determined; value at the time of dispossession; and value at the time of the sale (Ann., Breach of Warranty of Title—Damages, 13 A.L.R.2d 1369). Interestingly enough, the annotator was able to find New York cases each of which used language which would apparently suggest that a different one of these four "rules" was *the* rule. (Ann., *supra,* p. 1380.) In the face of such unsettled and unconvincing "precedent", the issue is one which is open to resolution as a question which is actually one of first impression.

At the time of the sale to List and at the commencement of the *Menzel* replevin action, there was in effect the New York counterpart to section 13 of the Uniform Sales Act (N.Y.Personal Property Law, § 94 [PPL]) which provided that "In a contract to sell or a sale, unless contrary intention appears, there is

1. An implied warranty on the part of the seller that * * * he has a right to sell the goods * * *

2. An implied warranty that the buyer shall have and enjoy quiet possession of the goods as against any lawful claims existing at the time of the sale".

In addition, section 150 of the PPL provided for remedies for breach of warranty and subdivision 6 provided: "The measure of damages for breach of warranty is the loss directly and naturally resulting, in the ordinary course of events, from the breach of warranty". Subdivision 7 applies, by its terms, only to a breach of warranty of quality and is, therefore, not controlling on the question of damages for breach of warranty of title and quiet enjoyment. (3 Williston, Sales [rev.ed.], § 615, n. 9.) Thus, the Perls' reliance on this subdivision is misplaced. The Perls contend that the only loss directly and naturally resulting, in the ordinary course of events, from their breach was List's loss of the purchase price. List, however, contends that that loss is the present market value of the painting, the value which he would have been able to obtain if the Perls had conveyed good title. The Perls support their position by reference to the damages recoverable for breach of warranty of quiet possession as to real property. However, this analogy has been severely criticized by a leading authority in these terms: "This rule [limiting damages to the purchase price plus interest] virtually confines the buyer to rescission and restitution, a remedy to which the injured buyer is undoubtedly entitled if he so elects, but it is a violation of general principles of contracts to deny him in an action on the contract such damages *as will put him in as good a position as he would have occupied had the contract been kept.*" (11 Williston, Contracts [3d ed.], § 1395A, p. 484 [emphasis added].) Clearly, List can only be put in the same position he would have occupied if the contract had been kept by the Perls if he recovers the value of the painting at the time when, by the judgment in the main action, he was required to surrender the painting to Mrs. Menzel or pay her the present value of the painting. Had the warranty been fulfilled, i.e., had title been as warranted by the Perls, List would still have possession of a painting currently worth $22,500 and he could have realized that price at an auction or private sale. If List recovers only the purchase price plus interest, the effect is to *put* him in the same position he would have occupied *if the sale had never been made.*

Manifestly, an injured buyer is not compensated when he recovers only so much as placed him in *status quo ante* since such a recovery implicitly denies that he had suffered any damage. This rationale has been applied in Massachusetts in a case construing a statute identical in language to section 150 (subd. 6) of the PPL where the buyer was held entitled to the value "which [he] lost by not receiving a title to it as warranted. * * * His loss cannot be measured by the [price] that he paid for the machine. He is entitled to the benefit of his bargain" (Spillane v. Corey, 323 Mass. 673, 675, 84 N.E.2d 5 [1949]; see, also, Pillgrene v. James J. Paulman, Inc., 6 Terry 225, 226, 45 Del. 225–226, 71 A.2d 59 [1950] ["The purpose of compensatory damages is to place the buyer in as good condition as he would have occupied had the title been good."]). This measure of damages reflects what the buyer has actually lost and it awards to him only the loss which has directly and naturally resulted, in the ordinary course of events, from the seller's breach of warranty.

An objection raised by the Perls to this measure of damages is that it exposes the innocent seller to potentially ruinous liability where the article sold has substantially appreciated in value. However, this "potential ruin" is not beyond the control of the seller since he can take steps to ascertain the status of title so as to satisfy himself that he himself is getting good title. (Mr. Perls testified that to question a reputable dealer as to his title would be an "insult." Perhaps, but the sensitivity of the art dealer cannot serve to deprive the injured buyer of compensation for a breach which could have been avoided had the insult been risked.) Should such an inquiry produce no reasonably reliable information as to the status of title, it is not requiring too much to expect that, as a reasonable businessman, the dealer would himself either refuse to buy or, having bought, inform his vendee of the uncertain status of title. Furthermore, under section 94 of the PPL, the seller could modify or exclude the warranties since they arise only "unless contrary intention appears". Had the Perls taken the trouble to inquire as to title, they could have sold to List subject to any existing lawful claims unknown to them at the time of the sale. Accordingly, the "prospects of ruin" forecast as flowing from the rule are not quite as ominous as the argument would indicate. Accordingly, the order of the Appellate Division should be reversed as to the measure of damages and the judgment awarding List the value of the painting at the time of trial of the *Menzel* action should be reinstated.

On the cross appeal by the Perls, the issue is as to the time from which interest should run on the judgment in favor of List against the Perls. The Appellate Division indicated that interest should be recovered from the date of purchase in October, 1955, but it did so only in conjunction with its determination that the measure of damages should be the purchase price paid by List on that date. Manifestly, the present-value measure of damages has no necessary connection with the date of purchase and is, in fact, inconsistent with the running of interest from the date of purchase since List's possession was not disturbed until the judgment directing delivery of the painting to Mrs. Menzel, or, in the alternative, paying her the present value of the painting. Accordingly, List was not damaged until that time and there is no basis upon which to predicate the inclusion of interest from the date of purchase. Accordingly, on the cross appeal, the order of the Appellate Division, insofar as it directed that interest should run from the date of purchase, should be reversed and interest directed to be included from the date on which Mrs. Menzel's judgment was entered, May 10, 1966.

SCILEPPI, BERGAN, BREITEL and JASEN, JJ., concur.

FULD, C.J., and KEATING, J., taking no part.

Order reversed, with costs to third-party plaintiff-appellant-respondent, and case remitted to Supreme Court, New York County, for further proceedings in accordance with the opinion herein.

Notes

1. Would the court reach the same result under UCC 2–312? Is this result sound?

2. Would you, as purchaser of the painting, be able to collect from the dealer reasonable attorney fees for defending against the replevin action and asserting the breach of warranty claim as consequential damages under UCC 2–715(2)? See De La Hoya v. Slim's Gun Shop, 80 Cal.App.3d Supp. 6, 146 Cal.Rptr. 68 (1978); Universal C.I.T. Credit Corp. v. State Farm Mut. Auto. Ins. Co., 493 S.W.2d 385 (Mo.App.1973) (attorney fees incurred in defending against claims are recoverable damages).

Problem 22–7

1. On October 1, Domino Truck Sales, Inc. sold and delivered to Paul's Lines, Inc., a second-hand diesel tractor for $5,000. Paul made a down payment consisting of $1,500 cash and a truck valued at $1,000 and agreed to pay the balance in equal monthly installments commencing on December 1. Domino created and perfected by filing a security interest in the tractor. Paul operated two tractor-trailer rigs (the new purchase was a replacement) out of the town where Domino did business. Over the past five years, Paul's lines has averaged an annual net profit of $75,000 doing 45% of its business in the State of New York.

On October 15, Paul discovered that there was an unpaid fuel tax lien in the amount of $2,000 against the tractor in the State of New York. A New York permit for operation could not be obtained until the lien was paid. He promptly advised the president of Domino who expressed surprise and promised to have it removed. By November 25, nothing had been done. Paul again visited Domino and stated that the truck could not be profitably operated without access to New York and that he would not make any monthly payments until the lien was removed. Domino's president repeated his promise to remove the lien but, on December 10, after Paul had failed to make his first payment, repossessed the tractor. It is now December 15. The New York lien has not been removed and Paul has already lost more than two months of profits that could have been earned by operating in that state. Domino still has the tractor but, in an effort to resell, has received a $4,500 offer from a trucker which does no business in New York.

Assuming that Paul could block the resale and recover the tractor if Domino's repossession was improper, what are the rights of the parties under the UCC? Consider both the questions posed by UCC 2–312 and the remedies available to Paul.

2. Suppose that Domino Truck Sales was unable to pass good title to Paul and that one year after the truck had been delivered the "true" owner had it replevied. The evidence will show that the value of the truck at the time of delivery was $7,500, Paul had spent $2,000 in repairs, the value of the use to Paul over the year was $4,800 and that the truck was worth $5,000 on the date of replevin. Paul claims damages in the amount of $7,500, the difference in value between the truck received and the truck as warranted. UCC 2–714(2). Is this correct? How much should Paul recover against Domino for breach of warranty?

SECTION 4. RIGHTS OF SELLER VERSUS CLAIMS OF THIRD PARTIES TO GOODS IN POSSESSION OF BUYER

A. *Introduction*

In Section 2, we considered the extent to which a good faith buyer of goods for value can obtain better title than his seller or take free from a perfected security interest in the goods created by his seller or another secured party. In Section 5, infra, we will examine how the Bulk Sales Law, Article 6, gives unsecured creditors of the seller power to avoid certain presumptively fraudulent transfers to a buyer. These problems can implicate Articles 2, 6 and 9 of the UCC. In addition, the possibility of a breach of the warranty of title, treated in Section 3, hangs over the entire proceedings.

In this Section, we will treat a more focused variation of the same problem. Suppose a seller has delivered possession of goods sold to the buyer. Suppose, further, that credit has been extended in both transactions. To what extent can the seller recover possession of the goods from the buyer without perfecting a security interest under Article 9? In what circumstances can possession be reclaimed without the conclusion that the parties intended to create a security interest which should have been perfected under Article 9? See UCC 9–102(1).

These problems extend beyond the parties to the transaction. They involve third parties as well—secured parties who have perfected a security interest under Article 9, purchasers from the party in possession, and lien creditors. They also raise issues similar to those posed when possession is sought by bailors, lessors under a "true" lease, and consignors—parties who are not sellers and buyers but whose property interest in the goods frequently resembles a security interest. These problems have been treated extensively in Chapter Seven. See, generally, Baird & Jackson, *Possession and Ownership: An Examination of the Scope of Article 9,* 35 Stan.L.Rev. 175 (1983).

Transactional hair splitting aside, there is a common theme: Whenever a seller asserts a property interest to recover possession of goods who has defaulted in payment, someone, frequently a trustee in bankruptcy, will contend that the interest is, in fact, a security interest that should have been perfected under Article 9. The questions, therefore, involve a proper characterization of the interest, the scope of Article 9, see UCC 1–201(37), 9–102(1), and the extent to which the party seeking possession should, in planning the transaction, create and perfect a security interest under Article 9.

B. *Possession Retained*

In a contract for sale, it is clear that if the goods are existing and indentified, the buyer will obtain, at least, a special property interest and, at most, title. In short, the buyer could be the owner of the goods before they are delivered.

It is also clear that, as between the parties, the seller may withhold delivery of the goods if the buyer has become insolvent, UCC 2–702(1), or otherwise breached the contract, UCC 2–703, even though the time for delivery has arrived. By retaining possession, the seller has, in effect, a security interest arising under Article 2. See UCC 9–113. If the dispute cannot be resolved by agreement, the seller can resort to remedies for breach of contract under UCC 2–703, including resale of the goods under UCC 2–706. Resale is a method of enforcing this possessory security interest arising under Article 2, but, unlike the enforcement of security interests arising under Article 9, the seller has no obligation to account to the buyer for any surplus. Compare UCC 9–504(2) with UCC 2–706(6).

Assuming that possession is retained, the seller's rights in the goods should also be effective against creditors of and purchasers from the buyer. Or should they? Consider the following problem.

Problem 22–8

S agreed to manufacture factory equipment according to B's specifications for $100,000. Under the agreement, title was to pass to B when conforming goods were identified to the contract. In addition, B agreed to pay $50,000 upon delivery and to give S a promissory note, due six months after delivery, for the balance. S completed and identified conforming goods to the contract on July 1. On August 1, the date for delivery, S tendered delivery but B failed to pay the $50,000 due. Shortly thereafter, S was beset with the following claims by third parties who had dealt with B:

1. Bank, who had a perfected security interest in B's equipment, existing and after-acquired. Bank argued that B had "rights in the collateral" on July 1, the security interest attached on that date, see UCC 9–203(1), and that it was perfected with priority over S, citing UCC 9–312(5).

2. Lien creditor, whose judgment against B was executed by levy on July 15.

3. Buyer, who paid B $90,000 for the goods, to be delivered later, on July 20.

Which, if any, of these parties should prevail over S, the party in possession of the goods? See UCC 2–403, 2–702, 2–703, 9–113, 9–301(1) & 9–312(5).

Problem 22–9

In Problem 22–8, above, suppose that S had shipped a carload of goods to B "FOB the point of shipment." This meant that both title, UCC 2–401(1), and risk of loss, UCC 2–509(1)(a), passed to B even though the goods were still in the possession of the carrier. Suppose, further, that the carrier issued a non-negotiable bill of lading, naming B as the person entitled to the goods. Suppose, finally, that B repudiated the contract while the goods were in transit. If S were able to stop delivery of the goods against the carrier under UCC 2–705, would this be effective against the third parties asserting claims to the goods? (See In re Hillcrest Foods, Inc., 40 B.R. 360 (Bkrtcy. Me.1984), where the court held that UCC 9–113 was effective until the buyer obtained lawful possession of the goods from the carrier. The seller had shipped FOB point of shipment and obtained a negotiable bill of lading. When the carrier delivered the goods to the buyer without surrender of the indorsed bill, the buyer did not obtain lawful possession.)

IN RE BLACK & WHITE CATTLE CO.

United States Court of Appeals, Ninth Circuit, 1986.
783 F.2d 1454.

BEEZER, CIRCUIT JUDGE:

This appeal involves the rights of a financing buyer of cattle under California law and the Bankruptcy Code. Granada Cattle Services, Inc., Granada Management Corp., (formerly Premier Angus, Inc.), Granada Corp., and Integrated Cattle Systems IV (collectively "Granada"), appeal a partial summary judgment, granted by the bankruptcy court and affirmed by the district court, in favor of appellee Black & White Cattle Co. ("B & W"). The bankruptcy court held Granada has no interest in certain cattle held by B & W, the debtor and debtor in possession, pursuant to a cattle feeding agreement between the parties. We affirm in part and reverse in part.

FACTS

B & W is a California limited partnership, currently in Chapter 11 bankruptcy proceedings, which operated a calf raising facility and a feed lot facility at two separate California locations. Granada is composed of various Texas corporations and partnerships in the business of buying feeder cattle for their customers, causing them to be fed and raised by third parties until they reach slaughter weight, and then selling them for beef.

In February 1981 Granada and B & W began negotiating a "Cattle Feeding Agreement" (the "Agreement"), which was finally executed on July 17. The Agreement provided that B & W would purchase approximately 6,000 day-old calves "on behalf of" or "for the account of" Granada's customers, which are referred to collectively throughout the Agreement as the "Owner," and that "Owner" would retain title to any cattle that it "placed on the facilities." B & W was obligated to reimburse "Owner" for certain losses suffered from the death of "Owner's animals." The Agreement also provided that the cattle could be commingled with other cattle in the calf yard and feed lot facilities "[a]fter the cattle have been properly tagged and identified. * * *" The Agreement was to last for three years.

Between May 15 and June 16, 1981, while the Agreement was being negotiated, B & W acquired numerous calves from its regular suppliers. Among the undifferentiated, commingled calves acquired at that time were 1,204 that B & W later identified as those covered by the Agreement (and the subject of this action). Granada contends, and the bankruptcy court found, that the 1,204 calves were purchased by B & W pursuant to an oral agreement entered into with Granada on May 14. Granada reimbursed B & W for the cost of the 1,204 calves and paid B & W's various monthly charges for caring for the animals, as required by the Agreement.

Although the Agreement was executed on July 17, it had an effective date of May 15 to cover the "Cattle on hand."

After July 17, B & W continued to care for the calves at its calf yard until they were delivered to the feed lot as each reached the desired weight. The deliveries occurred between August 13 and October 15, 1981. Upon reaching the feed lot, B & W for the first time identified the 1,204 cattle as those covered by the Agreement by placing the animals in a separate pen and by giving each an identifying ear tag. The cattle were branded with a brand registered to one of B & W's general partners.

On April 23, 1982, some months after the last of the cattle were delivered to the feed lot, B & W filed a Chapter 11 bankruptcy petition. B & W subsequently filed an adversary proceeding as debtor and debtor in possession in the Bankruptcy Court for the Central District of California seeking, among other things, an order declaring invalid Granada's claimed interest in the 1,204 head of cattle still on B & W's feed lot.[1]

The bankruptcy court granted partial summary judgment in favor of B & W. The court invalidated Granada's claim of ownership on the ground that Granada

1. Although the Agreement contemplated the purchase of 6,000 head of cattle, when B & W fell into financial difficulties, Granada instructed B & W not to acquire additional cattle pursuant to the Agreement. Therefore, only the 1,204 head of cattle initially acquired are now at issue.

did not comply with California Civil Code § 3440.[2] The court reasoned that § 3440 requires actual delivery to and possession by a buyer to avoid a conclusive presumption of fraud against the seller's creditors. The district court summarily affirmed the bankruptcy court's action. Granada appeals.

ANALYSIS

C. Effect of Cal.Civ.Code § 3440

The Agreement that B & W purchase calves "on behalf of" or "for the account of" Granada was signed on July 17 and made retroactive to the day the first animal was purchased. Granada contends that under the terms of the Agreement the cattle were acquired by B & W as agents for Granada, that Granada had title to the cattle at all times and B & W never had title, and that there was therefore no transfer to be set aside by the operation of § 3440. This argument is without merit.

B & W bought the newborn calves directly from suppliers in its own name. B & W spent its own funds and paid suppliers with checks drawn on B & W's account. B & W took possession of the calves and branded them with a brand registered to a general partner of B & W. B & W agreed to and in fact did bear the risk of loss of the newborn calves. At the time of purchase, moreover, the calves were not identified to B & W's contract with Granada. In short, B & W possessed sufficient indicia of ownership to be called the owner of the calves. Although contracting parties may agree to transfer or divest title retroactively, it would be stretching the fiction to say that B & W never had title. The very purpose of § 3440 demands this conclusion; to allow parties to defeat § 3440 by characterizing their relationship as an agency agreement would emasculate § 3440. The July 17 contract, therefore, constituted a transfer of title.[3]

Granada contends that although it did not have actual possession of the cattle, the tagging and segregation of the animals at the feed yard constituted constructive possession sufficient to satisfy the statute. The only facts relevant to this issue are undisputed, namely, that the cattle were at all times in B & W's actual possession, that after they arrived at the feed lot they were segregated from the other animals and given ear tags identifying them as Granada animals, and that they bore a brand registered to a B & W general partner.

Constructive or symbolic delivery "is not altogether forbidden, since not all species of property are subject to the same kind of possession. But symbolic or constructive delivery is insufficient when the nature of the property and the

2. At the time this action was filed, § 3440 provided in relevant part:

> **Conclusive presumption of fraud.** Every transfer of personal property and every lien on personal property made by a person having at the time the possession or control of the property, and not accompanied by an immediate delivery followed by an actual and continued change of possession of the things transferred, is conclusively presumed fraudulent and void as against the transferor's creditors while he remains in possession and the successors in interest of those creditors, and as against any person on whom the transferor's estate devolves in trust for the benefit of others than the transferor and as against purchasers or encumbrancers in good faith subsequent to the transfer.
>
> * * *
>
> Subdivision (2) of § 2402 of the Commercial Code is not restricted by the provisions of this section.

The several recent amendments to § 3440 are not relevant to this appeal.

3. For other cases utilizing this indicia of ownership approach in dealing with problems of ostensible ownership, see generally, *In re Medomak Canning Co.,* 25 U.C.C.Rep. 437 (Bankr.D.Me.1977) (bailment versus sale), *aff'd,* 588 F.2d 818 (1st Cir.1978); *In re Sitkin Smelting & Refining Inc.,* 639 F.2d 1213 (5th Cir.1981) (same); *see also* D. Baird & T. Jackson, *Security Interests in Personal Property* 1–114 (1984).

situation of the parties render it practicable to make actual physical delivery." * * * The only question is whether, under California law, cattle are the type of property that the statute requires to be actually physically delivered.

If delivery is practicable, segregation and labeling will not satisfy the delivery and possession requirements. * * * On the other hand, where the property is "not property of which manual possession could be taken," labeling has been held to satisfy a similar Washington statute. * * * Although no case has decided directly whether penned cattle are too bulky to make actual delivery impracticable, or whether they may be constructively delivered by tagging or segregation, every case in which penned cattle have been sold but not physically delivered has held the sale void. * * * These cases, along with the prior transfer of the same animals from the calf yard to the feed lot, and the generally ambulatory nature of the healthy living animals, strongly imply that physical delivery of cattle in general and these animals in particular was entirely practicable, with the result that constructive delivery will not satisfy the requirements of § 3440.

Therefore, no genuine issue of material fact regarding the delivery and possession of the animals existed, and the bankruptcy judge correctly ruled that the tagging and segregation of the cattle did not satisfy the statutory possession and delivery requirements.[7]

D. Effect of Cal.Comm.Code § 2402(2)

The foregoing analysis, however, does not end our inquiry into the operation of § 3440. The last paragraph of Cal.Civ.Code § 3440 provides that "[s]ubdivision (2) of Section 2402 of the Commercial Code is not restricted by the provisions of this section." Section 2402(2) provides:

> (2) A creditor of the seller may treat a sale or an identification of goods to a contract for sale as void if as against him a retention of possession by the seller is fraudulent under any rule of law of the state where the goods are situated, except that retention of possession in good faith and current course of trade by a merchant-seller for a commercially reasonable time after a sale or identification is not fraudulent.

The official code comment to § 2402 clarifies its purpose:

> Purposes of Changes and New Matter: To avoid confusion on ordinary issues between current sellers and buyers and issues in the field of preference and hinderance by making it clear that:
>
> * * * 2. The retention of possession of the goods by a merchant seller for a commercially reasonable time after a sale or identification in current course is exempted from attack as fraudulent.

The effect of § 2402(2) on the operation of § 3440 is to eliminate the conclusive presumption of fraud where all the requirements are met. *See Gardner v. Sullivan & Crowe Equipment Co.,* 17 Cal.App.3d 592, 597, 94 Cal.Rptr. 893, 895 (1971).

The bankruptcy court's primary objection to the application of § 2402(2) in the instant case was that B & W's retention of possession of the cattle after the transfer was not for a commercially reasonable time. The court reasoned that

7. A financing buyer may now protect its interest through the filing of a financing statement prior to the date of the intended transfer. *See* Cal.Civ.Code § 3440.1(h)(1); Cal. Comm.Code § 9401.

section [2402(2)] basically restates the rule of § 3440. The rationale of this rule likewise parallels that of § 3440. It seeks to protect creditors against a debtor who gives a deceptive appearance of ownership by retaining possession after title has passed to a third party. Unlike § 3440, this section provides a very limited exception where goods are retained for a commercially reasonable period of time.

The bankruptcy court's reasoning essentially reads the statutory exception out of existence. The legislative history of §§ 3440 and 2402 requires greater respect for the effect of § 2402.

Prior to 1963, California Civil Code §§ 1746 and 3440 governed the rights of buyers of undelivered goods and creditors of sellers.[8] In 1963, the California Legislature expanded the rights of buyers by adopting § 2402(2) along with the remainder of the Uniform Commercial Code. The California Code Comments state that "[s]ubdivision (2) is similar to former Civil Code § 1746 (creditor's rights against sold goods in seller's possession), except that under the Commercial Code there is no fraud if in good faith a merchant-seller retains possession for a reasonable time after the sale in the course of trade." Cal.Comm.Code § 2402 (West 1964). The Legislature expressly repealed § 1746. 1963 Cal.Stat. c. 819, p. 1997, § 2, effective January 1, 1965. The expansion of buyers' rights, therefore, altered the existing law. Section 3440, however, temporarily remained unchanged.

The Legislature recognized the potential conflict between § 3440 and the newly adopted § 2402(2). In 1967, the Legislature amended § 3440 by adding the language that stated that § 3440 would not restrict § 2402(2). 1967 Cal.Stat. c. 799, p. 2200, § 1; *see* California Committee on Continuing Education of the Bar, Review of Selected 1967 Code Legislation 48 (1967). This language limits § 3440, not § 2402(2). To the extent that § 2402(2) provides a buyer of goods with greater rights than does § 3440, such a result is the direct product of a deliberate legislative decision. Contrary to the bankruptcy court's conclusion, § 2402(2) is not equivalent to § 3440; section 2402(2) is a significant departure from prior law. This expansion of buyers' rights is consistent with the broad purpose of the Commercial Code to accommodate commercial practices. *See* Cal. Comm.Code § 1102(2)(b).

Recognition of a buyer's rights under § 2402(2) does not render § 3440 nugatory. Section 3440 applies when § 2402(2) does not. *See Gardner v. Sullivan & Crowe Equipment Co.,* 17 Cal.App.3d at 596, 94 Cal.Rptr. at 895. Section 2402(2) only applies when the seller is a merchant, and he retains possession in good faith, in the current course of trade, and for a commercially reasonable time. If any of these conditions are absent, § 2402(2) will not apply and § 3440 will govern.

The bankruptcy court concluded that B & W's actions were not reasonable because Granada was never to obtain actual possession of the cattle. The court's emphasis on delivery to Granada is misplaced. Commercial contracts frequently require delivery of goods to someone other than the immediate buyer. The proper focus is on the time of retention of possession by the seller, not on the

8. Section 1746 provided:

CREDITOR'S RIGHTS AGAINST SOLD GOODS IN SELLER'S POSSESSION. Where a person having sold goods continues in possession of the goods, or of negotiable documents of title to the goods, and such retention of possession is fraudulent in fact or is deemed fraudulent under any rule of law, a creditor or creditors of the seller may treat the sale as void.

Cal.Civ.Code § 1746, *repealed,* 1963 Cal.Stat. c. 819, p. 1997, § 2, effective January 1, 1965.

identity of the person to whom the goods are to be delivered. Cal.Comm.Code § 2402(2).

The court also expressed concern regarding the indefiniteness of the time of retention of possession by B & W. The agreement between B & W and Granada provided that B & W would deliver the cattle to Granada's customers when the cattle reached slaughter weight. Although this provision did not specify a particular date of delivery, it did specify a definite and identifiable condition precedent to B & W's duty to deliver the cattle. *See e.g., Houghland v. Rothblum Packing Co.,* 99 Cal.App. 631, 279 P. 159 (1929) (contract requiring seller to deliver sheep "after fattening" held enforceable on grounds that industry practice indicated that delivery was within reasonable time). The time of delivery, therefore, was definite.

The evidence offered by Granada in opposition to the motion for summary judgment indicated that Granada and B & W had valid business reasons for delaying delivery. B & W's primary obligation was to raise and feed the cattle for distribution to California customers of Granada. Although delivery to Granada in Texas was possible, such a course of action would have defeated Granada's purpose for hiring a California feed lot operator. Moreover, Granada offered affidavit testimony indicating that such feeding arrangements are common in the cattle industry. This evidence created a genuine issue of material fact regarding the commercial reasonableness of the time of retention of possession of the cattle. Summary judgment, therefore, was improper on this issue.[9]

* * *

CONCLUSION

The bankruptcy court's determination that B & W transfered title to Granada without sufficient change of possession to satisfy Cal.Civ.Code § 3440 is affirmed. The court's determination that Cal.Comm.Code § 2402(2) and the corresponding exception to Cal.Civ.Code § 3440 did not apply is reversed and remanded for resolution of factual disputes. * * *

On remand, the court shall consider the customs and practices of the cattle industry to determine whether B & W's retention of possession was commercially reasonable.

If the court on remand determines that B & W's retention of possession was not commercially reasonable within the meaning of Cal.Comm.Code § 2402(2), then Granada shall be entitled to an award of $432,058.02 plus such interest as

9. The bankruptcy court also noted that since B & W had never before entered into a similar agreement, the retention of possession was not in B & W's current course of trade. The bankruptcy court construed "current course of trade" too narrowly. The uncontested evidence establishing that B & W is in the business of buying, raising, and selling cattle. This is exactly what the agreement with Granada entailed. The fact that B & W's relationship with Granada differed somewhat from B & W's previous practice does not mean that the retention of possession was outside of B & W's current course of trade.

B & W also argues that since § 2402(1) only applies to unsecured creditors with statutory rights not possessed by Granada (i.e., rights under Cal.Comm.Code §§ 2502 & 2716), Granada also has no rights under § 2402(2), which B & W characterizes as an exception to § 2402(1). Section 2402(2) specifically refers to "creditors," however, which the legislature has expressly defined to include "a general creditor, a secured creditor, a lien creditor and * * * a trustee in bankruptcy. * * *" Cal.Comm.Code § 1201(12) (West 1970). The legislature should be presumed to have understood the terms it used in both subsections and expressly defined elsewhere. Section 2402(2) is therefore applicable here if all its requirements are met.

the court finds appropriate. Granada is entitled to costs incurred for this appeal.

Affirmed in part, reversed in part and remanded.

C. *Possession Delivered to Buyer*

1. *Credit Sales*

A seller who delivers possession of goods sold to the buyer on credit may create and perfect a security interest in those goods under Article 9. This would be a "purchase money" security interest, see UCC 9–107, which might have priority over pre-existing security interests if the conditions of UCC 9–312(3) & (4) were met. If the buyer defaulted, i.e., failed to pay the price when due, the seller, as a secured party, could enforce the security interest by repossessing the goods, UCC 9–501(1) & 9–503, selling them in a commercially reasonable manner, UCC 9–504(3), and applying the proceeds to the obligation, UCC 9–504(1).

What about claims of third parties to the goods? Our secured party-seller: (1) would clearly have priority over a subsequent lien creditor, UCC 9–301(1)(b); (2) could have priority over an existing secured party with a perfected security interest in after-acquired property, UCC 9–312(3) & (4); and (3) might lose the security interest to a buyer in the ordinary course of business from B, UCC 9–307(1), but would retain a security interest in the proceeds of the sale. In short, playing the Article 9 game is the route to maximum protection in this situation.

If, however, the seller delivers the goods and retains title until the price is paid, the effect is to create a security interest in the goods which is subject to Article 9. See UCC 9–102(1) & 1–201(37). Unless that security interest is perfected under Article 9 by filing or otherwise, it is vulnerable to creditors of and purchasers from the buyer. The reasons for this become clear when you read UCC 9–301(1).

What happens if the seller delivers the goods in a credit transaction without playing the Article 9 game? Consider the following problem, drawn from In re Samuels & Co., 526 F.2d 1238 (5th Cir.1976), cert. denied *sub nom.,* 429 U.S. 834, 97 S.Ct. 99, 50 L.Ed.2d 99 (1976).

Problem 22–10

Farmer raises cattle for beef. When the cattle are ready, Farmer sells them to Bravo, a meat processor. Bravo agrees to pay the price within 30 days after delivery. On March 1, Farmer delivered 50 head of cattle to Bravo for $35,000. Unknown to Farmer, Bravo was insolvent at that time. UCC 1–201(33).

1. Assume that no third parties are involved. If Farmer discovers the insolvency on March 8, what can he do to reclaim the cattle from Bravo. See UCC 2–702(2). Suppose the cattle have been processed and sold but the proceeds of that sale can be identified. Can Farmer reclaim the proceeds under UCC 2–702(2). Compare UCC 9–306. (The cases disagree. An affirmative answer was given in United States v. West Side Bank, 732 F.2d 1258, 1263 (5th Cir.1984), reprinted in Chapter seven, supra, where the court stated that to "hold otherwise would in many instances render the statutory remedy a nullity.")

2. Suppose that Farmer, on March 8, made an oral demand on Bravo for the cattle, which had not yet been slaughtered. On March 6, however, Eric, a creditor, had obtained a judicial lien on all of Bravo's personal property. Can Farmer reclaim the cattle from Bravo free from Eric's lien? See UCC 2–702(3). Note that the '72

version of UCC 2–702(3) does not mention lien creditors. What does one do next? See UCC 1–103.

3. Suppose that Farmer made an oral demand on March 8. On March 6, however, Bravo had filed a voluntary case in bankruptcy. Could Farmer reclaim the cattle against the trustee? The answer is no. Do you see why? Read UCC 9–301(3) and Sections 544(a) and 546 of the Bankruptcy Code.

4. How would Farmer, who made an oral demand on March 8, fare against a buyer from Bravo who, on March 6, had paid the price and satisfied the conditions of ordinary course of business, UCC 1–201(9), but had not taken possession from Bravo on March 8? See UCC 2–702(3).

5. The last (but not least) variation. Suppose that First Bank had created and perfected an Article 9 security interest in Bravo's "inventory, existing and after-acquired," on February 1. The effect of this is that when Bravo obtains "rights" in the cattle (upon delivery by Farmer), First Bank's security interest attaches to and becomes perfected in the cattle. Assuming that First Bank is unaware of Farmer's claim but has made no new advances between March 1 and March 8, could Farmer effectively reclaim against First Bank? Most courts have held no. Do you see why? See UCC 1–201(32).

Note: The Reclaiming Credit Seller in Bankruptcy

Section 546(c) of the Bankruptcy Code provides that the avoidance powers of the trustee in Sections 544(a), 545, 547 and 549 are "subject to any statutory or common law right of a seller of goods that has sold goods to the debtor, in the ordinary course of such seller's business, to reclaim such goods if the debtor has received such goods while insolvent, but—(1) such a seller may not reclaim any such goods unless such seller demands in writing reclamation of such goods before ten days after receipt of such goods by the debtor * * *." This provision has been criticized as unduly restrictive, in that it (1) narrows the scope of reclamation available under UCC 2–702(2) and (2) is the exclusive avenue of relief for the reclaiming seller under the Bankruptcy Code. See Mann & Phillips, *Section 546(c) of the Bankruptcy Reform Act: An Imperfect Resolution of the Conflict Between the Reclaiming Seller and the Bankruptcy Trustee,* 54 Am.Bankr.L.J. 239 (1980). In short, unless the reclaiming seller satisfies both UCC 2–702(2) and Section 546(c), the reclamation claim will fail against the trustee. Even then, it may still be subject to the claim of a "floating lienor" who qualifies as a good faith "purchaser" under UCC 2–403. See, e.g., Lavonia Manufacturing Co. v. Emery Corp., 52 B.R. 944 (E.D.Pa.1985). See also, McDonnell, *The Floating Lienor as Good Faith Purchaser,* 50 S.Cal.L.Rev. 429 (1977), who explores the equities of that result.

2. *Cash Sales*

HOLIDAY RAMBLER CORP. v. FIRST NATIONAL BANK & TRUST CO. OF GREAT BEND, KANSAS

United States Court of Appeals, Tenth Circuit, 1983.
723 F.2d 1449.

SEYMOUR, CIRCUIT JUDGE.

Holiday Rambler Corporation, a manufacturer of recreational vehicles, brought this diversity action against the First National Bank and Trust Company of Great Bend, Kansas. It alleged that First National had wrongfully diverted funds owed to Holiday Rambler by one of its dealers, Kansas Kamper Center, Inc. The district court granted summary judgment for First National, from which Holiday Rambler now appeals. We affirm.

I.

BACKGROUND

When reviewing a district court's summary judgment, we consider the record in the light most favorable to the party opposing the motion * * * and all ambiguities and disagreements must be resolved in its favor * * *. Viewed in this way, the record reveals the following.

Kansas Kamper engaged in the retail sales and service of recreational vehicles and mobile homes. In June 1978, when John R. Morris purchased control of Kansas Kamper, Holiday Rambler conducted a thorough investigation to determine the dealership's credit-worthiness under the new ownership. As a result of that investigation, Holiday Rambler concluded that the dealership's financial condition was "poor." Nevertheless, Holiday Rambler decided to continue to sell campers to Kansas Kamper on a cash-on-delivery (c.o.d.) basis, even though the manufacturer could have insisted upon the economically-safer "floor-plan" basis.[2] Holiday Rambler further elected to accept as payment Kansas Kamper's company checks rather than insisting upon cash, certified check, or bank money order.

In February and March of 1979, Holiday Rambler delivered four campers to Kansas Kamper, accepting in payment four uncertified company checks drawn on the dealer's checking account at First National. Shortly after each sale, Kansas Kamper went to First National to obtain loans, using the campers as collateral. The bank credited Kansas Kamper's checking account with amounts equal to 90 per cent of the camper's invoice price, in exchange for notes and security agreements covering each of the campers. When Holiday Rambler presented its Kansas Kamper checks for payment, however, the Kansas Kamper account had insufficient funds and the checks were dishonored. Between the time of the loans to Kansas Kamper and Holiday Rambler's presentment of its checks for payment, Kansas Kamper had issued checks to the bank at its request to pay some outstanding obligations that Kansas Kamper owed to the bank, leaving insufficient funds to cover Holiday Rambler's checks.

Rather than immediately attempting to reclaim the campers, or taking steps to perfect its security interests in the vehicles, Holiday Rambler instead chose to rely on representations by Morris that the checks would be made good. The manufacturer ran the checks through the bank a second time, and again the checks were dishonored. In May 1979, Kansas Kamper filed for bankruptcy, by which time it had sold three of the campers to customers in the ordinary course of business. It used the proceeds from those sales to cancel the notes and security agreements previously executed with the bank. The fourth camper

2. There is a considerable difference between a c.o.d. and a "floor plan" method of payment. The difference was explained by Holiday Rambler's Vice President of Dealer Finance:

> "In a c.o.d. dealership, the dealership issues a check directly to Holiday Rambler Corporation or our agent in payment of that unit, at which point the m.s.o.'s [manufacturer's statements of origin] are passed to the dealership upon our receipt of that, in the form of a check or cash, certified funds, et cetera.
>
> "In the case of a floor plan, we contact—approximately one week prior to production we contact the lender, secure an approval from the lender to pay for that unit through the floor plan funds that have been extended to the dealership to reserve x number of dollars for that unit. The certificate of origin and the original invoice copy is sent directly to the lender on the day of invoicing after the unit has been completed. The lender then issues a check to Holiday Rambler Corporation in payment of that unit. They then perfect their own security documents with the dealer, depending on the arrangement with the dealership, whether that be individual trust receipts, et cetera. That is the bank's business."

Rec., vol. VII. at 35–36.

remained in Kansas Kamper's possession at the time of its bankruptcy petition; it was later sold at the bankruptcy court's direction. To date, Holiday Rambler remains unpaid for the four vehicles.

Holiday Rambler brought this action against First National for damages equal to the value of the four dishonored checks, plus incidentals. The issues before the court in the summary judgment proceedings were whether under Article Two of the Kansas Uniform Commercial Code Holiday Rambler maintained a right to reclaim the campers as a cash seller with priority over any interest held by First National, and whether First National's security interests were invalid because they were created fraudulently.

The district court concluded as a matter of law that the bank had valid, perfected security interests in the campers that took priority over Holiday Rambler's asserted claim to the vehicles. The court then rejected plaintiff's remaining fraud claim, concluding that First National had collected a legitimate debt from Kansas Kamper which depleted Kansas Kamper's account to the point that it could not pay Holiday Rambler.

On appeal, Holiday Rambler cites as error the district court's determination that the company had lost its right to reclaim, and the court's resolution of the fraud claim. It also contends that it had a breach of contract claim against First National that should have been addressed.

II.

Cash Seller's Right to Reclaim Goods

Holiday Rambler asserts the district court erred in determining that the company had lost its right to reclaim the campers. In a sale of goods, the buyer's right to retain or dispose of goods is conditional upon the seller's right of reclamation. *See* Kansas Comment 1983 to Kan.U.C.C.Ann. § 84–2–507 (Ensley 1983). As long as Holiday Rambler retained a right to reclaim the vehicles, Kansas Kamper could not give First National enforceable security interests because a security interest cannot attach or become enforceable until the debtor has rights in the collateral. Kan.U.C.C.Ann. § 84–9–203(1)(c).

When a seller discovers that a buyer has received goods on credit while insolvent, the seller may reclaim the goods upon demand made within ten days after the buyer's receipt of the goods. Kan.U.C.C.Ann. § 84–2–702. Although the Code has no specific provision for cash sellers, Kan.U.C.C.Ann. §§ 84–2–507(2), Official Comment 3 to 84–2–507, and 84–2–511(3), when read together, provide a right to reclaim for sellers who accept checks that are subsequently dishonored. *See* Kansas Comment 1983 to § 84–2–507; *see also, e.g., Szabo v. Vinton Motors, Inc.*, 630 F.2d 1, 3 (1st Cir.1980); *In re Helms Veneer Corp.*, 287 F.Supp. 840 (W.D.Va.1968).

Thus, section 84–2–507(2) states:

> "Where payment is due and demanded on the delivery to the buyer of goods * * *, his right as against the seller to retain or dispose of them is conditional upon his making the payment due."

Section 84–2–511(3) states that "payment by check is conditional and is defeated as between the parties by dishonor of the check on due presentment." Taken together, these sections provide that a seller of goods who receives in payment a check that is subsequently dishonored has a right to reclaim the goods from the buyer. As long as the seller retains this right to reclaim, the buyer's right to title in the goods is subject to it. However, a seller does not retain its right to reclaim indefinitely. Official Comment 3 to § 84–2–507 provides:

> "Subsection (2) deals with the effect of a conditional delivery by the seller and in such a situation makes the buyer's 'right as against the seller' conditional upon payment * * *. *Should the seller after making such a conditional delivery fail to follow up his rights, the condition is waived.* The provision of this Article for a ten-day limit within which the seller may reclaim goods delivered on credit to an insolvent buyer is also applicable here." (emphasis supplied.)

If a seller fails to "follow up his rights," he loses his right to reclaim. The sale to the buyer is then no longer conditional, and the buyer can sell or give a security interest in the goods to a subsequent purchaser free of any retained right in the seller to reclaim them. The question in this case is whether Holiday Rambler failed to follow up its rights.

It is undisputed that Holiday Rambler made no effort to repossess the four vehicles for two to three months after delivery. However, Holiday Rambler argues that, under Kansas law, "whether a cash seller of merchandise [has] waived his rights as a cash seller [is] a factual question to be resolved by a jury." Brief of Appellant at 14. First National, on the other hand, argues that a cash seller's right to reclaim is waived as a matter of law if not exercised within ten days of delivery. Cases can be found in various jurisdictions to support both positions. *Compare Szabo,* 630 F.2d at 3; *Helms,* 287 F.Supp. at 846; *Stowers v. Mahon (In re Samuels),* 526 F.2d 1238, 1245 (5th Cir.), *cert. denied,* 429 U.S. 834, 97 S.Ct. 98, 50 L.Ed.2d 99 (1976), *with Burk v. Emmick,* 637 F.2d 1172, 1176 (8th Cir.1980). In determining the applicable law in this diversity case, however, we are bound to follow what we determine to be the law of Kansas.

Holiday Rambler relies heavily on an old Kansas Supreme Court case, *People's State Bank v. Brown,* 80 Kan. 520, 103 P. 102 (1909). *Brown* held that whether a seller has waived his right to reclaim is determined by whether he acted "within a reasonable time" to recover possession of the property. *Id.,* 103 P. at 104. Holiday Rambler further argues that the subsequent adoption of the Uniform Commercial Code in Kansas did not affect the holding in *Brown,* relying primarily upon the fact that the Kansas Comment following § 84–2–511 at one time cited *Brown* with approval. *See* Kan.U.C.C.Ann. § 84–2–511, Kansas Comment (Weeks 1965). Whatever view of the law the Kansas Legislature may have had at the time of those comments, that view apparently has changed. The Kansas Comment 1983 to § 84–2–511 no longer cites *Brown,* but rather refers the reader to its 1983 comments to § 84–2–507 for the law respecting a cash seller's right of reclamation. In this latter comment, the Kansas Legislature declares:

> "Subsection (2) [§ 84–2–507(2)] makes clear that the buyer's rights as against the seller are conditional upon payment. Many courts have fashioned a seller's right of reclamation in bad check cases out of this subsection by reading it together with 84–2–511(3). Most such courts have imposed a 10–day limitation on this right, borrowing from 84–2–702. Official UCC Comment 3 to this section supports this. For illustrative cases, see *In re Helms Veneer Corp.,* 287 F.Supp. 840 (W.D.Va.1968); *Szabo v. Vinton Motors, Inc.,* 630 F.2d 1 (1st Cir.1980)."

Kan.U.C.C.Ann. § 84–2–507, Kansas Comment 1983.

It is thus apparent that Kansas has adopted the ten-day limitation on a cash seller's right to reclaim. We need not decide whether the ten-day period begins to run from the date of delivery or from the day a seller first receives notice that his check has been dishonored, for in this case Holiday Rambler failed to repossess within either period. Holiday Rambler therefore waived its right to reclaim and Kansas Kamper acquired full rights in the goods. Consequently, First National's security interest in the goods must prevail unless there is merit to Holiday Rambler's claim that the security interest was fraudulently obtained.

III.

FRAUD

We agree with the district court that the facts alleged by Holiday Rambler do not constitute fraud under Kansas law. First, no fraudulent representation is alleged to have been made by First National. Second, even though a line of cases exists in Kansas that seems to recognize the possibility of actual fraud even absent an express representation, * * * the acts by First National in this case do not amount to fraud under the theory of those cases. The cases look to all the surrounding facts and circumstances to see if there exists some "artifice, trick [or] design," * * * or "an act of deception or cunning intentionally and effectively used to cheat a person of his rights." * * *.

> "A general rule supported by many cases is that a person engaged in a business transaction with another can commit a legal fraud only by * * * such * * * conduct or artifice * * * as will *mislead the other party or throw him off his guard and thus cause him to omit inquiry or examination which he would otherwise make.*"

37 Am.Jur.2d *Fraud and Deceit,* § 224 (1968) (emphasis supplied).

Holiday Rambler has not alleged that, by act, artifice, trick, or any other fraudulent device, First National induced Holiday Rambler to accept uncertified checks from Kansas Kamper as payment for its campers. Holiday Rambler does not claim that First National caused its failure to exercise its right to reclaim or to perfect its security interests in the campers after it learned its checks had been dishonored. Indeed, Holiday Rambler's fraud allegations amount to nothing more than the assertion that the bank loaned money, reserved a security interest, and accepted Kansas Kamper checks to offset existing debts, *when it knew* the goods upon which the security interests were based had not yet been paid for.

Holiday Rambler cites no authority for the proposition that mere knowledge that goods are unpaid for invalidates an otherwise legitimate security interest. The Code does not inquire into such knowledge on the part of a secured party. See Kan.U.C.C.Ann. § 84–9–203, 84–9–312(5), and Kansas Comment 1983 to 84–9–312, subsection (5) ("The first-to-file-or-perfect rule is based upon the 'pure race' concept: knowledge is irrelevant"). Rather, if properly employed, the Code protects unpaid sellers in a variety of other ways. *See, e.g.,* Kan.U.C.C.Ann. §§ 84–2–507, 84–2–702, 84–9–113, 84–9–201, 84–9–203, 84–9–301, 84–9–302, 84–9–312, 84–9–401, 84–9–501. Holiday Rambler simply failed to avail itself of the protections provided by the Code and by commonly-known commercial practice. Accordingly, we affirm the district court on this issue.

* * *

[Some footnotes omitted.]

Notes

1. Assuming that Holiday Rambler exercised its reclamation right in a timely manner, upon what theory is it entitled to regain possession from the buyer free of the Bank's claimed security interest? Would the same theory apply if a lien creditor had intervened or the buyer had resold the goods before the reclamation right was exercised? Compare Iola State Bank v. Bolan, 235 Kan. 175, 679 P.2d 720 (1984), where the court concluded that the "cash" sale doctrine under which a cash buyer did not receive and could not pass an interest in the goods until payment in full was "abolished by adoption of the UCC." The court held, however, that the "floating lienor," claiming as a purchaser, had not acted in good faith.

2. If a "cash" seller was entitled to reclaim against a lien creditor of the buyer under state law, would that reclamation right hold up against a trustee in bankruptcy? Consider the following argument:

MANN & PHILLIPS, THE RECLAIMING CASH SELLER AND THE BANKRUPTCY CODE 39 S.W.L.J. 603, 651–53 (1985).

A. Summary of Our Position

Although the textual discussion of the matter was equivocal, we believe that UCC section 2–507(2) should apply solely to those cash sales not involving payment by check or draft, and UCC section 2–511(3) should be the lone provision governing check or draft cases. Regardless of which section is applicable, the right to reclaim when payment is not made or the check or draft is dishonored should be regarded as inherent to the section in question and as in no way dependent on UCC section 2–702(2). Moreover, UCC section 2–702(2)'s ten-day demand requirement should have no application to cash sale cases in general, and to bad check cases in particular. Due presentment of the check and a demand for reclamation, however, must be made within a reasonable time after notice of dishonor.

UCC section 2–403 should govern all priority questions involving the competing rights of the UCC cash seller and third parties. UCC section 2–403(1) resolves the previous uncertainty surrounding the conflict between the cash seller and the good faith purchaser by subordinating the former to the latter. Since most article 9 secured parties qualify as good faith purchasers for value, UCC section 2–403(1) also enables these parties to defeat the reclaiming cash seller. Section 2–403, however, enables the cash seller to defeat the lien creditor circuitously by compelling reference to UCC section 1–103, which authorizes the use of pre-UCC state law. Under pre-UCC priority rules the cash seller triumphed over the lien creditor.

When the buyer goes into bankruptcy, the reclaiming cash seller should usually be able to prevail in a clash with the trustee. Section 546(c) of the Bankruptcy Code should have no application in such situations. Although judicial interpretations of the section and the section's legislative history provide some support for a contrary position, they are decidedly outweighed by the section's express language, which clearly and unambiguously excludes the cash seller. As a result, a trustee wishing to defeat the cash seller's reclamation petition must utilize other bankruptcy provisions. The two weapons in the trustee's arsenal best suited for this task, sections 544(a) and 547 of the Bankruptcy Code, are unlikely to prove sufficient. The trustee's success under Bankruptcy Code section 544(a) depends upon whether a hypothetical ideal lien creditor assuming that status on the date of bankruptcy can defeat a reclaiming cash seller. Since the reclaiming cash seller will defeat a lien creditor, the cash seller will also defeat a trustee utilizing Bankruptcy Code section 544(a). For a number of reasons articulated above, the reclaiming cash seller should also overcome a trustee asserting that the reclamation is preferential under Bankruptcy Code section 547. To summarize, a seller who complies with either UCC section 2–507(2) or section 2–511(3) should be able to reclaim from the buyer, lien creditors of the buyer, and the buyer's trustee. Good faith purchasers from the buyer and article 9 secured parties, however, generally have rights in the goods superior to those of the reclaiming cash seller.

This interpretation of the cash seller's reclamation rights is in marked contrast to the results that should obtain when a credit seller attempts to reclaim goods sold to the buyer. Unlike the unpaid cash seller, an unsecured credit seller is ordinarily unable to reclaim the goods upon the buyer's failure to pay. Instead, such a seller is limited to such damages as the UCC makes available. Only when the specific conditions of UCC section 2–702(2) are met can the credit seller reclaim. These conditions impose procedural limitations on the exercise of the credit sale reclamation right that are more restrictive than those we believe should apply to the cash seller. The credit seller may reclaim only if the buyer is insolvent and, in most cases, only if demand has been made within ten days after the receipt of the goods. The cash sale reclamation right, on the other hand, is clearly not premised on the buyer's insolvency, and the ten-day demand limitation should not apply in the cash sale context. In addition, the UCC seems to give the reclaiming cash seller more remedial options than the reclaiming credit seller. UCC section 2–702(3) provides that the seller's reclamation of the goods excludes all other remedies. In contrast, neither UCC section 2–507(2) nor section 2–511(3) contains such a limitation. In a proper case, accordingly, the cash seller may be able to reclaim and still recover various types of damages from the buyer. Recovery of such damages is foreclosed to the credit seller who successfully reclaims the goods under UCC section 2–702.

The reclaiming cash seller should also fare better against third parties than his credit sale counterpart. Here the main difference between the two sellers occurs in the bankruptcy context. Under UCC sections 2–403(1) and 2–702(3) both the cash and credit sellers will be subordinate to a good faith purchaser for value. For that reason, both sellers should also lose to a party with a security interest in the goods. Despite the tremendous confusion on this question, however, both the cash and credit sellers should defeat a lien creditor's competing interest in the goods. In bankruptcy the UCC section 2–702 seller's fate is exclusively controlled by Bankruptcy Code section 546(c), while the cash seller's prospects are determined under other Bankruptcy Code provisions. Because Bankruptcy Code section 546(c)'s ten-day written demand limitation will often pose a major obstacle to reclamation and because no ten-day limitation should apply in most cash sale cases, the credit seller should fare less well in bankruptcy than his cash sale counterpart.

[Footnotes omitted] "Copyright, 1985, by Southern Methodist University. Reprinted with permission from Southwestern Law Journal."

3. Consignments

From the foregoing, it is clear that a seller who delivers goods to a buyer on credit will encounter resistance from creditors of and purchasers from the buyer when it seeks, upon non-payment, to regain possession. Unless the seller has perfected a security interest in the goods, the resistance may escalate to a victory for those third parties. The lesson here is plain: When ownership interests, however described, are separated from possession or control of the goods, the need to give public notice to neutralize the perils of ostensible ownership, i.e., the "secret lien," increases.

Another transaction where this need for public notice is evident is the consignment. Here an owner of goods delivers them to an agent or "factor," who is usually a merchant with regard to goods of that kind, with power to sell them to third parties. The owner retains title and fixes the price and conditions of sale. If the goods are sold, the factor delivers possession to the buyer and the title passes directly from the owner. The factor, after taking a commission, accounts to the owner for the price. If the goods are not sold, they are returned by the factor to the owner, usually without obligation. In the interim between delivery and sale, most consignment agreements permit the owner to recover the goods and obligate the factor to return them on request.

A number of questions shroud this transaction with uncertainty.

1. When is the transaction a "true" consignment and when is it a "consignment intended for security?" See UCC 1–201(37)? A leading case stated that the "easiest way to determine the intention of the parties is to concentrate on the function of the consignment." The court continued:

> (C)onsignments are used in two ways: (1) As a security consignment where the goods go to the merchant who is unwilling to risk finding a market for the goods so the "title" remains in the consignor; and (2) as a price-fixing device. Number (1) is clearly a secured transaction with the reservation of title to goods acting as collateral. Number (2) is designed only to insure resale maintenance and has nothing to do with security.

Columbia International Corp. v. Kempler, 46 Wis.2d 550, 562–63, 175 N.W.2d 465, 470–71 (1970). But see Hawkland, *The Proposed Amendments to Article 9 of the UCC: Consignments and Equipment Leases,* 77 Com.L.J. 108, 109 (1972), who suggests that the distinction between true and false consignments was "never clearly articulated or defined by the common law courts" and this "led to uncertain results and made consignment planning hazardous." (For example, suppose that the function of the transaction was to control resale prices and to require the consignee to pay for all or part of the price, even though there was no sale of the goods.) See also Harrington, *The Law of Consignments: Anti-Trust and Commercial Pitfalls,* 34 Bus. Law. 431, 446 (1979), who claims that "any widespread consignment program aimed at resale price maintenance must be viewed as suspect, particularly if there are any elements of coercion of distributors." In short, the characterization process is uncertain and the anti-trust problem lurks in the background.

2. Even if the transaction is a "true" consignment and not within the scope of Article 9, UCC 1–201(37) provides that "a consignment is in any event subject to the provisions on consignment sales (Section 2–326)." At a minimum, UCC 2–326(3) appears to deal with a transaction that is a "true" consignment and not a "sale or return." See UCC 2–326(2) & 2–327(2). See also, General Electric Co. v. Pettingell Supply Co., 347 Mass. 631, 199 N.E.2d 326 (1964), holding that UCC 2–326(3) applies to a transaction which establishes only a principal-agent relationship.

Read UCC 2–326(3) carefully. Note that if three conditions are satisfied, i.e., (1) the goods are "delivered to a person for sale," (2) the person "maintains a place of business at which he deals in goods of the kind involved"; and (3) the person does business "under a name other than the name of the person making delivery," then with respect to the creditors of the person doing business, the "goods are deemed to be on sale or return." In short, the goods are subject to the claims of the consignee's creditors while in the consignee's possession. See UCC 2–326(2).

How is the consignor to deal with this problem of ostensible ownership? Work the following problems.

Problem 22–11

1. Under a "true" consignment, Consignor intends to deliver goods (textbooks) to a Consignee who operates a university bookstore under its own name. Consignor discovers that a secured party has perfected a security interest in Consignee's "inventory, existing and after-acquired." There is no applicable law "providing for a consignor's interest * * * to be evidenced by a sign," UCC 2–326(3)(a), and there is no certain basis for establishing that Consignee is "generally known by his creditors to be substantially engaged in selling the goods of others." UCC 2–326(3)(b). How can Consignor avoid Secured Party's security interest? See UCC 9–408, & 9–114. Compare UCC 9–312(3). If Consignor files under UCC 9–408 and complies with UCC 9–114, what is the effect against Secured Party? What about a lien creditor? What about a purchaser of the goods from Consignee? See UCC 2–403.

2. Suppose that Consignee did not maintain a place of business where he dealt with textbooks. Rather, Consignee entered into contracts with retail outlets under which Consignee would insure that textbooks were delivered in exchange for a commission on sales. Under the contract with Consignor, the books were delivered directly to the retail outlets: Consignee never had possession or control. Consignee, however, would remit the price for books sold and insure that unsold books were returned. Is this transaction subject to UCC 2–326(3)? In re Mincow Bag Co., 29 A.D.2d 400, 401, 288 N.Y.S.2d 364, 366 (1968), affirmed mem. 24 N.Y.2d 776, 300 N.Y.S.2d 115, 248 N.E.2d 26 (1969) held, over a dissent, that it was not: "The unwary could not have been led into becoming creditors * * * based on any ostensible ownership of the merchandise." But this transaction is neither fish (a consignment covered by UCC 2–326(3)) nor fowl (a sale or return covered by UCC 2–326(2)). Can (should) Consignor make a UCC 9–408, 9–114 filing anyway?

3. Suppose the transaction was a "sale or return" rather than a consignment. How does the seller protect itself against the buyer's creditors? Should it create and perfect a security interest under Article 9 or can it simply comply with UCC 2–326(3)? See American National Bank of Denver v. First National Bank of Glenwood Springs, 28 Colo.App. 486, 476 P.2d 304 (1970), holding that the exceptions in UCC 2–326(3) did not apply to a "sale or return" and the goods were subject to the buyer's creditors. But see Simmons First National Bank v. Wells, 279 Ark. 204, 650 S.W.2d 236 (1983), holding that UCC 2–326(3) may apply to a bailment as well as a consignment.

SECTION 5. ARTICLE 6, THE BULK SALE: ANOTHER LIMITATION ON THE DOCTRINE OF BONA FIDE PURCHASE

Suppose that Sam owns and uses various types of personal property in his business—equipment, fixtures, inventory and intangibles. Sam is in reasonably good financial health. There are no judgment liens outstanding. Sam, however, owes Cal, an unsecured creditor, $50,000, and owes $75,000 to Bank, who has perfected a security interest under Article 9 in Sam's "inventory, existing and after-acquired."

From Cal's perspective, there is a continuing risk that Sam might sell some or all of the assets that would, in the case of a financial disaster, be marshalled to pay the claims of Cal and other unsecured creditors. Where inventory is concerned, Cal is subject to Bank's security interest in any event, whether Bank claims the security interest in inventory or the identifiable proceeds of sales in the ordinary course of business. Where other assets are involved, Cal has no interest in either the assets or the proceeds from any sale unless Sam has practiced some form of fraud. Thus, if Sam made a fraudulent transfer, i.e., a sale while insolvent where no "fair consideration" was received, Cal could avoid the transfer and recover the assets for the estate.

But suppose that Sam received "fair" consideration for a sale of inventory or equipment and did not inform Cal or other unsecured creditors before or after the sale. If financial disaster then strikes or Sam dissipates the proceeds, does Cal have any legal grounds to complain? If so, when and against whom?

Article 6, the Bulk Sales Law, provides some protection to Cal when Sam makes a "bulk" transfer of inventory or a transfer of a "substantial part" of the equipment if made "in connection with a bulk transfer of inventory." UCC 6–102. The operative provision is UCC 6–105 which reads, in part, as follows: "* * * Any bulk transfer subject to this article * * * is ineffective against any creditor of the transferor unless at least ten days before he takes possession of the goods or pays for them, whichever happens first, the transferee gives notice of the transfer in the manner and to the persons hereafter provided." Put differently, unless the notice conditions are satisfied, Cal would have a claim, established by a judicial lien, to the assets in the hands of B, even though the transaction between Sam and B was enforceable between them and otherwise passed good title.

Cal, therefore, is given protection against what the drafter's concluded was "two common forms of commercial fraud, namely: (a) The merchant, owing debts, who sells out his stock in trade to a friend for less than it is worth, pays his creditors less than he owes them, and hopes to come back into the business through the back door some time in the future," and (b) The merchant, owing debts, who sells out his stock in trade to any one for any price, pockets the proceeds, and disappears leaving his creditors unpaid." Comment 2, UCC 6–101.

But what, exactly, is a bulk sale? What enterprises are subject to Article 6? What transfers are "excepted" from the Act? Read UCC 6–102 & 103 and the following case.

OUACHITA ELECTRIC COOPERATIVE CORP. v. EVANS–ST. CLAIR

Court of Appeals of Arkansas, 1984.
12 Ark.App. 171, 672 S.W.2d 660.

CORBIN, JUDGE.

Appellant, Ouachita Electric Cooperative Corporation, sued for the collection of past due electric bills in the amount of $37,676.80 for electricity furnished to St. Clair Rubber Company of Arkansas. Appellant sought to charge appellee, Evans-St. Clair, Inc., the purchaser of certain assets of St. Clair Rubber Company of Arkansas, with this responsibility. Appellant alleged below and here on appeal that the transfer of assets violated the Bulk Sales Act of Arkansas, Ark. Stat.Ann. §§ 85–6–101–109 (Add.1961), and that the transfer was a fraudulent conveyance. The chancellor found to the contrary on both issues, but awarded judgment to appellant in the amount of $37,676.80 against St. Clair Rubber Company of Arkansas. We affirm.

On August 3, 1982, St. Clair Rubber Company of Arkansas ("St. Clair"), St. Clair Rubber Company located in Michigan ("St. Clair-Michigan"), National Acceptance Company of America ("NAC") and Evans-St. Clair, Inc. ("Evans-St. Clair") entered into an agreement whereby St. Clair and St. Clair-Michigan would transfer certain machinery, equipment, tools and other property they owned to Evans-St. Clair. In return for the transfer, Evans-St. Clair paid NAC $200,000.00 in cash and signed a promissory note to NAC in the sum of $500,000.00. NAC had previously made loans to St. Clair and St. Clair-Michigan totaling $2,244,524.21 and had a blanket perfected security interest in all the assets transferred to Evans-St. Clair which was cross-collateralized so that the assets of both St. Clair companies secured the full indebtedness. NAC agreed not to sue St. Clair, St. Clair-Michigan, or Mr. S.S. Livingstone, the prior owner and seller of St. Clair, if Evans-St. Clair defaulted on the $500,000.00 promissory note, and further agreed to release any and all security interest which it had in the remaining assets of St. Clair, St. Clair-Michigan and Mr. Livingstone upon payment of $1,544,524.21, a net reduction of indebtedness by $700,000.00.

No inventory was transferred as part of the asset purchase. Evans-St. Clair did receive an option to purchase the inventory at a price equal to 50% of the St. Clair companies' book value, subject to the right of these companies to sell the inventory to anyone else at any time as part of the transaction. If Evans-St. Clair had not purchased the inventory at the end of one year, the St. Clair companies had the right to demand that Evans-St. Clair purchase the inventory still on hand at its wholesale fair market value. At the date of trial, approximately ⅓ of the inventory had been used on an as-needed basis by Evans-St. Clair. The remaining ⅔'s of the inventory was still located at the Evans-St. Clair plant in East Camden and was identifiable as the St. Clair companies' property. The value paid for the assets purchased was arrived at by Evans-St. Clair in reliance upon appraisals furnished by an appraisal company which had a good reputation and had been relied upon in the past by Evans Industries, the parent company of Evans-St. Clair. The representations of the St. Clair companies' owner, Mr. S.S. Livingstone, were also relied upon in arriving at the amount of consideration to be paid. The machinery and equipment located in Michigan were appraised at a forced liquidation value of $167,787.00; the machinery and equipment in Arkansas were appraised at a forced liquidation value of $497,731.00, with $56,925.00 to be subtracted for the toxological boot equipment which was deleted from the transfer; and the real estate in Michigan conveyed was valued at approximately $100,000.00, based upon a three-year old appraisal. Evans-St. Clair negotiated for these assets as a whole package, and not as separate purchases. The allocation of purchase prices set forth in the Bills of Sale was made at the request of NAC, for its own internal accounting purposes.

Appellant contends that the transfer was in violation of the Bulk Sales Act. Ark.Stat.Ann. § 85–6–102 (Add.1961), defines bulk transfers as follows:

> (1) A 'bulk transfer' is any transfer in bulk and not in the ordinary course of the transferor's business of a major part of the materials, supplies, merchandise or other inventory (Section 9–109 [§ 85–9–109]) of an enterprise subject to this Article [chapter].

(2) A transfer of a substantial part of the equipment (Section 9–109 [§ 85–9–109]) of such an enterprise is a bulk transfer if it is made in connection with a bulk transfer of inventory, but not otherwise.

(3) The enterprises subject to this Article [chapter] are all those whose principal business is the sale of merchandise from stock, including those who manufacture what they sell.

(4) Except as limited by the following section all bulk transfers of goods located within this state are subject to this Article [chapter].

Appellant Ouachita Electric Cooperative Corporation argues that a bulk transfer between appellees took place since a major part of the materials, supplies, merchandise and other inventory was sold as well as a substantial part of the equipment as evidenced by the Bill of Sale. Appellant also contends that the fact that title to the inventory did not pass immediately should not be decisive in a determination of a bulk transfer. Finally, appellant argues that although a transfer to a lien creditor in lieu of foreclosure would be within the provisions set out above, the facts in the instant case do not establish a transfer to NAC. We do not agree.

The provisions of the Bulk Sales Act are primarily for the protection of creditors of the seller and compliance with the Act is not compulsory, insofar as the seller is concerned, unless compliance is required by the buyer. *Herrick v. Robinson,* 267 Ark. 576, 595 S.W.2d 637 (1980). We believe the evidence clearly supports the chancellor's finding that the transaction between appellees was not in violation of the Act. The trial court in the case at bar based its finding on the following evidence: (1) no inventory was transferred by the August 3, 1982, agreement; (2) on the day of trial, approximately ²/₃'s of all the inventory on hand as of the August 3, 1982, agreement to transfer had not been purchased by appellee; (3) the ¹/₃ of the inventory which had been used was purchased by appellee on a daily basis, when needed in its industrial process, but not in bulk; and (4) the transfer was in settlement of a valid security interest, and did not harm the position of any unsecured creditors.

Ark.Stat.Ann. § 85–6–103(3) (Supp.1983), provides in part: "The following transfers are not subject to this Article [chapter]: transfers in settlement of realization of a lien or other security interest." NAC had a perfected security interest in all the assets purchased from St. Clair and St. Clair-Michigan, and the assets of both of the companies stood as collateral for an indebtedness which was undisputedly far in excess of their value. Evans-St. Clair paid $700,000.00 to NAC, and the St. Clair companies transferred the assets to Evans-St. Clair. NAC reduced these companies' obligation to it by $700,000.00, and agreed not to sue or look to the St. Clair companies for payment in the event that Evans-St. Clair defaulted on the $500,000.00 note. The transfer was clearly in satisfaction of NAC's security interest. Appellant in its brief cites *Starman v. John Wolfe, Inc.,* 490 S.W.2d 377 (Mo.App.1973), for the proposition that in order to come within the § 85–6–103(3) exception, the transfer should be made to the holder of the security interest and not to a transferee for the benefit of the security interest holder. We agree with appellee that *Starman, supra,* cannot be properly interpreted for such a broad proposition, since in that case the consideration paid for the transfer was not used entirely to pay the superior lien held by the secured creditor, but rather was used to pay in part other parties for the benefit of the transferor, resulting in a preference to some creditors. Furthermore, in *Starman, supra,* there was no evidence in the record to support the proposition that the alleged secured creditor even had a security interest in the property transferred.

In *American Metal Finishers, Inc. v. Palleschi,* 55 App.Div.2d 499, 391 N.Y.S.2d 170, 20 U.C.C.Rept.Ser. 1283 (1977), the plaintiff complained that the transfer would not qualify under U.C.C. § 6–103(3) because the property transfer was made to a third person who assumed the indebtedness of the transferor with a secured creditor who held a security interest in the property transferred. The New York court disagreed, stating as follows:

> The chief rationale of the Bulk Transfers article is the avoidance of the "major bulk sales risk" of "[t]he merchant, owing debts, who sells out his stock in trade * * *, pockets the proceeds, and disappears leaving his creditors unpaid" (citations omitted). But where the transfer is in settlement of a lien or security interest, there are no cash proceeds with which the seller could abscond. Thus, where the consideration is settlement of an indebtedness with no receipt of cash proceeds, the protective purposes of the Bulk Transfers article do not apply.
>
> We see no reason to read subdivision (3) of § 6–103 of the Uniform Commercial Code so restrictively as to add a requirement that the transferee must be the holder of the security interest, thus ruling out transfer to one who in good faith takes over the position of the security holder. The interposition of such new party is not that of an officious volunteer; it serves a socially beneficial purpose of avoidance of foreclosure with its concomitant hardships to creditors, employees and the commercial community.

Similarly, we cannot say appellant in the instant case was prejudiced by the transaction. If St. Clair had closed its doors, NAC could have replevied the collateral and sold it in satisfaction of its security interest. If appellant had levied upon the collateral, any proceeds from a sale would have been subject to the prior security interest of NAC, which secured an indebtedness of $2,244,524.21. St. Clair could have transferred the property directly to NAC without any conceivable violation of the Bulk Sales Act.

The Bulk Sales Act of Arkansas does not purport to regulate agreements to sell inventory in the future. Here we have an option to purchase agreement for the sale of inventory in the future which is not a transfer of inventory and, therefore, is not subject to the Bulk Sales Act, since Ark.Stat.Ann. § 85–6–102(1) (Add.1961), by its terms applies only to "transfers in bulk." The Bulk Sales Act does not purport to regulate agreements for the sale of inventory as opposed to actual transfers of inventory because until the inventory is actually sold, title to it remains in the seller and is at all times subject to being levied upon by the seller's creditor. An agreement to sell the inventory gives the purchaser no property interest in the inventory, but is merely an executory contractual right. Accordingly, we find no merit to this contention.

Appellant also contends that the trial court erred in finding that the transfer was not a fraudulent conveyance pursuant to Ark.Stat.Ann. § 68–1302 (Repl.1979). This statute provides as follows:

> Every conveyance or assignment, in writing or otherwise, of any estate or interest in lands, or in goods and chattels, or things in action, or of any rents issuing therefrom, and every charge upon lands, goods or things in action, or upon the rents and profits thereof, and every bond, suit, judgment, decree or execution, made or contrived with the intent to hinder, delay or defraud creditors or other persons of their lawful actions, damages, forfeitures, debts

> or demands, as against creditors and purchasers prior and subsequent, shall be void.

Fraud is never presumed, but must be affirmatively proved, and the burden of proving fraud is upon the party who alleges it and relies on it. *Rees v. Craighead Inv. Co., Inc.,* 251 Ark. 336, 472 S.W.2d 92 (1971). In a suit to set aside a fraudulent conveyance, the allegation of fraud must be shown by a preponderance of the evidence. *Killian v. Hayes,* 251 Ark. 121, 470 S.W.2d 939 (1971). It has also been held that while fraud may be established by circumstantial evidence, the circumstances must be so strong and well connected as to clearly show fraud. *Stringer v. Georgia State Savings Assoc. of Savannah,* 218 Ark. 683, 238 S.W.2d 629 (1951). Badges or indicia of fraudulent conveyances include insolvency or indebtedness of the transferor, inadequate or fictitious consideration, retention by the debtor of property, the pendency or threat of litigation, secrecy or concealment, and the fact that disputed transactions were conducted in a manner differing from usual business practices. *Harris v. Shaw,* 224 Ark. 150, 272 S.W.2d 53 (1954).

In the case at bar we cannot say that the finding of the chancellor that the transfer was not fraudulent is against the preponderance of the evidence. The assets transferred were the subject of a perfected security interest in favor of NAC which secured an indebtedness of $2,244,524.21 of St. Clair and St. Clair-Michigan. The assets purchased were negotiated as an entire package and not as separate parcels. While the Bill of Sale for the Arkansas assets showed approximately $440,000.00 of assets being transferred at a stated purchase price of $225,000.00, the Michigan Bill of Sale showed assets having a liquidation value of only $167,787.00 and real property having a value of only $100,000.00 which was purchased from St. Clair-Michigan at a price of $475,000.00. All of the assets of both St. Clair companies were pledged to secure the $2,244,524.21 indebtedness to NAC. The allocation of the monies as reflected on the Bills of Sale was at the suggestion of and for the internal accounting purposes of NAC. Furthermore, appellant offered no evidence at trial which would contradict the appraised values of the property transferred.

The $700,000.00 was paid to the lienholder, NAC, in the form of $200,000.00 cash and a $500,000.00 promissory note. It was not paid to St. Clair. Consideration flowed to St. Clair in that NAC agreed not to look to St. Clair for payment in the event that Evans-St. Clair defaulted under the terms of the $500,000.00 promissory note, and further agreed to release the assets of St. Clair upon payment of $1,544,524.21, which constituted a reduction in St. Clair's liability to NAC by $700,000.00. A conveyance by a debtor to a third party of mortgaged property is supported by adequate consideration if the third party grantee agrees to pay the debts owed by the grantor and which are secured by the property. *First State Bank of Corning v. Gilchrist,* 190 Ark. 356, 79 S.W.2d 281 (1935).

In *Sieb's Hatcheries v. Lindley,* 111 F.Supp. 705 (W.D.Ark.1953), the district court quoted from a prior Arkansas decision as follows:

> The creditor who seeks to set aside a conveyance as fraudulent must show that his debtor has disposed of property that might otherwise have been subjected to the satisfaction of his debt.

Here, the record is barren of any evidence which would demonstrate that the lien of NAC was not perfected, or that the value of the assets transferred exceeded the amount secured by the assets.

The transfer would not have been fraudulent unless an inadequate consideration was established. The preference of one creditor over another does not in itself make the transfer to the preferred creditor void or voidable as a fraudulent conveyance. *Nicklaus v. Peoples Bank & Trust Co., Russellville, Ark.,* 258 F.Supp. 482 (E.D.Ark.1965), *aff'd,* 369 F.2d 683 (8th Cir.1966). The consideration in this case was clearly adequate. Appellant presented no evidence which would indicate that a greater price could have been obtained. In determining fraudulent intent on the part of the parties to a transaction, mere inadequacy of price for consideration is insufficient; it is only when the inadequacy of price is so gross that it shocks the conscience, and furnishes satisfactory and decisive evidence of fraud, that it will be sufficient proof that the purchase is not *bona fide. Fluke v. Sharum,* 118 Ark. 229, 176 S.W. 684 (1915). We find no merit to this point. In conclusion, we cannot say that the chancellor's findings were clearly erroneous (clearly against the preponderance of the evidence), A.R.C.P. Rule 52(a), and we affirm.

Affirmed.

CRACRAFT and GLAZE, JJ., agree.

Notes (with answers!)

1. Was the seller, St. Clair Rubber Company, an "enterprise" subject to Article 6? UCC 6–103(3). (Yes.) Suppose S was a lessor rather than a seller of inventory? (No, if "sale" is read literally.) Suppose the total value of the assets sold was $1,000? (There is no *de minimis* limitation.)

2. If St. Clair Rubber sold "a substantial part" of its equipment not in the ordinary course of business, why wasn't the sale a bulk transfer? (Because no inventory was transferred.) Is Article 6 clear enough about when a transfer occurs in a contract to sell inventory? (No.) When a transfer is "not in the ordinary course of the transferor's business?" When a transfer is a "major part" or a "substantial part" of the assets involved?

3. S, a restaurant, owned equipment valued at $200,000. S also owed unsecured creditors $300,000. Without notice to the creditors, S sold the equipment to B for $190,000, closed the restaurant, gave what was left of its food inventory to charity and left with the cash for the Bahamas. Is this a bulk transfer? (Not under 6–102 in the uniform text, but yes in at least 16 states which have amended the statute).

4. Suppose S, an enterprise within UCC 6–103(3) and heavily laden with unsecured creditors, was advised that the Bulk Sales Act would not apply if it sold all or substantially all of its corporate stock to B, rather than inventory or equipment. Is that advice correct? (Yes.) Should it be? (Not according to Rapson, U.C.C. Article 6: Should it Be Revised or "Deep-Sixed"?, 38 Bus.Law. 1753 (1983) infra p. 956.)

5. True or False: If a present transfer of inventory was "in settlement or realization of a lien or other security interests," 6–103(3), it is unnecessary to consider whether either the seller or the transfer were within the scope of Article 6. (True.)

Problem 22–12

S, a sole proprietorship, owned and operated a used book store in leased premises. The average monthly value of the inventory was $100,000 and the equipment was valued at $15,000. S had several unsecured creditors with claims totalling $20,000. There were no secured creditors or judgment lien creditors. The book store grossed around $200,000 per year.

S, who was ready to retire, reached an agreement to sell all of the inventory and equipment and to assign the lease to B for $125,000 cash. B, who intended to operate the bookstore under a new name, did not wish to assume S's business debts. The agreed price, therefore, was reached on the assumption that S would pay all business creditors.

Assume that the transfer of inventory and equipment is a "bulk" sale under UCC 6–102 by an "enterprise" subject to Article 6. B needs advice on the following questions.

A. Could the transfer be excepted from Article 6 under UCC 6–103? (Subsections 6 and 7 are obvious possibilities.)

B. Assuming that UCC 6–106 has not been enacted in our jurisdiction and the sale is not at auction, UCC 6–108, what must B do to comply with Article 6? See UCC 6–104, 6–105, 6–107 & 6–109. Suppose there are creditors of which B is unaware at the time of transfer?

C. Still assuming that UCC 6–106 does not apply, what happens in the following situation: Notice is not given in time to one creditor with a $1,000 claim who was entitled to it. Other unsecured creditors, with claims totalling $14,000, were given notice. Within 6 months of the transfer, see UCC 6–111, the entire inventory "turned over." Assuming that the creditor brings a timely action, which of the following assertions are correct:

1. All of the unsecured creditors may pursue claims even though only one did not receive notice;

2. Claims may be asserted against books sold by B to its customers;

3. B is liable as a converter of assets in which creditors had an enforceable claim;

4. B is personally liable for the amount of the debt;

5. The creditors entitled to notice may pursue claims against the identifiable proceeds of sale, including books purchased with those proceeds.

D. Suppose the state has enacted UCC 6–106. (16 states have). How, if at all, would UCC 6–106 change the scope of B's obligation and the answers to C, above?

RAPSON, U.C.C. ARTICLE 6: SHOULD IT BE REVISED OR "DEEP-SIXED"? 38 The Business Lawyer 1753, 1762–66 (1983).

This leads us to the next question: If the special classification of coverage of Article 6 is no longer justifiable, should the statute be expanded to cover all businesses, or would it make commercial sense to scrap the entire statute? Article 6, in its present form and under the proposed revision, imposes substantial burdens on bulk purchasers in order to protect sellers' creditors. On balance, does the imposition of that burden serve a commercially useful purpose?

WHAT ARE THE CREDITORS' REMEDIES IF THE PARTIES COMPLY WITH ARTICLE 6?

Assume that seller and buyer have contracted for an all-cash sale (with no down payment) of a business that is clearly covered by Article 6; that the jurisdiction has not enacted section 6–106; that the seller has the secret undisclosed intention of pocketing the proceeds and disappearing without paying his creditors; that seller and buyer fully comply with all the requirements of the present Article 6, with seller furnishing a complete and accurate sworn list of all his creditors; and that, pursuant to section 6–105, "at least 10 days before" the buyer either "takes possession of the goods or pays for them" he "gives notice of the transfer in the manner" provided by section 6–107.[48] Assume further that absent extraordinary circumstances, a creditor cannot acquire a lien against the business assets until he obtains a judgment against the seller; and that (as is usually the case) the jurisdiction's rules of civil procedure require that the creditor first institute a lawsuit and that the seller has twenty days to answer following service of process.[49]

What are the rights and remedies of an unsecured creditor who receives notice of that bulk transfer? Specifically, (1) Does the buyer have any further duties to that creditor? and (2) Does the fact that a bulk sale is about to take place entitle the creditor to any kind of extraordinary relief against the closing of the sale or the assets themselves, such as an injunction, attachment, or the like?

The answer clearly seems to be no to both questions. As stated by the Maryland Court of Appeals: "The sanction for noncompliance, established by the Bulk Transfer Act, is that the transfer is ineffective against the seller's creditors who may levy, attach or garnish the goods transferred to a buyer. § 6–104 and § 6–105; see § 6–111, Official Comment 2. Where there is compliance, however, that sanction is unavailable."[50] According to Chancellor Hawkland: "It is generally held that the liquidation of one's inventory is not, of itself, proof of an intent to defraud creditors. * * *"[51] The conclusion is inescapable. In a jurisdiction that has not enacted section 6–106, if the parties comply with Article 6, the notice given to the creditor affords him little or no practical remedies, absent grounds for extraordinary relief.

If the jurisdiction has enacted section 6–106, the conclusion is quite different. The creditor has significant protection. The buyer must apply the purchase price to the debts owed to the creditors, and, if there is not enough money to go around, then the sales proceeds must be applied pro rata. If the buyer breaches this duty he may end up having to pay twice.[52] Clearly, section 6–106 gives very meaningful protection to the creditors, but only by imposing very substantial burdens upon the purchaser.[53]

Is this logical? The avowed purpose of a bulk sale statute is to protect creditors of businesses against the risk that sellers of those businesses will pocket the proceeds and disappear, leaving the creditors unpaid.[54] Yet, the majority of jurisdictions, by rejecting section 6–106, have a toothless statute that does not effectively serve that purpose when the parties comply.

48. U.C.C. section 6–107(3) 1978 requires that the notice "be delivered personally or sent by registered or certified mail. * * *"

49. If the closing of the sale was scheduled for a Monday, a notice mailed by certified mail on the second preceding Thursday would be "ten days before" and timely. Thus, a creditor receiving notice on the following Monday would have no more than five business (or court) days to take action. *See* Hawkland, *Remedies of Bulk Transfer Creditors Where There Has Been Compliance with Article 6,* 74 Com.L.J. 257, 258 (1969).

50. FICO Inc. v. Ghingher, 287 Md. 150, 411 A.2d 430 (1980) (emphasis added).

51. Hawkland, *supra* note 49, at 258.

52. If noncompliance with U.C.C. section 6–106 results in the buyer becoming personally liable for the debt * * * and the debt is not otherwise satisfied, that would be the result. If the seller goes into bankruptcy, that is also the result. * * *.

53. Suppose the seller takes back a purchase money negotiable note as part of the payment of the purchase price and then discounts it with a party qualifying as a holder in due course (U.C.C. § 3–302)? Whom does the bulk purchaser pay when the note becomes due? The holder in due course or the seller's creditors? The answer may be that he has to pay both. The solution is to make the note nonnegotiable.

54. Official Comment 2(b) to U.C.C. § 6–101 (1978).

Why have most jurisdictions rejected section 6–106 [55] and the opportunity to put teeth into the statute? The answer may well lie in a sense of discomfort with the means by which Article 6 attempts to protect the seller's creditors, especially section 6–106.

The rationale of Article 6 is that the creditors should be protected by imposing substantial burdens and sanctions upon *buyers* of businesses, even though they may have acted in good faith and paid top dollar for the purchase. Is that really fair? Does it make sense to place burdens upon a *buyer* in order to protect creditors of the seller who have taken the risk of extending unsecured credit? Can we support a value judgment that the purchaser should bear the risk that a seller will not pay his creditors? If not, as has happened in most jurisdictions,[56] section 6–106 will be rejected and the purchaser will have no duty to apply the purchase proceeds to the payment of the seller's debts. Compliance with Article 6 will be achieved by notifying the creditors, but the purpose of Article 6 will be frustrated because the creditors will not have practical remedies.

DO THE CONSEQUENCES OF NONCOMPLIANCE WITH ARTICLE 6 MAKE COMMERCIAL SENSE?

By contrast, if the bulk purchaser fails to notify the creditors the sanctions for noncompliance are drastic. The sale is "ineffective" as to the seller's creditors,[57] which means that the creditors can enforce their claims by resorting to the purchased assets, even though the purchaser has paid the purchase price in full.[58]

The consequences of failing to comply with Article 6 *may* be more severe in a jurisdiction which has section 6–106. The authorities are divided whether noncompliance with section 6–106 merely furnishes an additional ground for rendering the transaction ineffective against the seller's creditors, or whether it also results in the buyer being personally liable for the seller's debts.[59]

The proposed revision deals directly with the question. First, it wisely introduces the concept of "omitted" creditor [60] and makes it clear that noncompliance makes the sale ineffective only as to an omitted creditor, and not as to all the creditors including those who receive notice—a theoretical possibility under present Article 6. Second, it would add new sections 6–104(4) and 6–106(5) to provide that the bulk purchaser is not personally liable unless he thereafter

> transfers the property to a purchaser for value in good faith and without notice of any noncompliance * * * in which case the transferee shall be personally liable to the creditors (Section 6–109) in an amount measured by

55. Section 6–106 is presented in the Official Text as an optional provision "bracketed to indicate division of opinion as to whether or not it is a wise provision. * * *" Section 6–106 reflects the pre-U.C.C. minority "Pennsylvania rule." It may be that such bracketing deterred adoption. If section 6–106 (or any other provision) is the better rule, brackets should not be used.

56. * * *.

57. U.C.C. §§ 6–104(1) and 6–105 (1978).

58. As stated in Official Comment 2 to U.C.C. § 6–104 (1978): "Any such creditor or creditors may therefore disregard the transfer and levy on the goods as still belonging to the transferor, or a receiver representing them can take them by whatever procedure the local law provides."

59. * * *.

60. U.C.C. section 6–104(1) would be amended to define an "omitted" creditor as follows:

> An "omitted" creditor is a creditor (Section 6–109) who has not been notified of the bulk transfer as provided by sections 6–105 and 6–107 or who has not had the protection provided by this section [or section 6–106], but a creditor is not omitted after the full payment of his claim has been tendered to him by the transferor or transferee.

the fair market value of the property at the time it was subsequently transferred to the said purchaser.[61]

Thus, the sanction for noncompliance would be identical in all jurisdictions whether or not they had enacted section 6–106. This proposal is questionable. It would remove the compulsion of immediate personal liability for noncompliance with section 6–106. Consequently, it would make the alternative of complete noncompliance with Article 6 more attractive because the parties incur no additional risk by not paying the creditors pursuant to section 6–106. If the buyer is not going to apply the purchase price to the creditors' claims, there is no point in notifying them and stirring them up—and the sanction is no worse.

Logically, if we are to retain Article 6, there is little point in doing so without requiring compliance with section 6–106 and making the bulk purchasers personally liable for noncompliance. Otherwise, the statute is a time-consuming, expensive burden having minimal practical benefits.

The proposed revision would significantly increase the burdens and risks of bulk purchasers. Section 6–104(3) would be amended to place an objective duty of care on the bulk purchaser to make reasonable inquiries concerning the completeness and accuracy of the creditors' list:

> (3) Responsibility for the completeness and accuracy of the list of creditors rests on the transferor, and the transfer is not rendered ineffective by errors or omissions therein unless the fact of such errors or omissions is known or disclosed to or reasonably discoverable by the transferee. Such fact is known to or disclosed to or reasonably discoverable by the transferee if, prior to the giving of notice provided in Section 6–105, it is revealed by the transferor's regular bookkeeping records, its existence is known or in any way made known to the transferee, or it would be discovered by his reasonable inquiry concerning the transferor's creditors.

This revision is designed to reject the controversial decision of the New York Court of Appeals in *Adrian Tabin Corp. v. Climax Boutiques, Inc.*[62] permitting the bulk purchaser to rely upon an "affidavit of no creditors" furnished by the seller of an ongoing business. Under the revision, the purchaser would be required to "make reasonable inquiries concerning the transferor's creditors and examine the books of the transferor."[63]

The change would adopt the pre-Code New York rule[64] and apply to any creditor's list, not just affidavits of no creditors. If one believes that the substantial burdens imposed on purchasers by Article 6 are a justifiable means of protecting sellers' creditors, the revision makes sense because it is consistent with the objective of furnishing meaningful protection to the creditors. However, the added burden and risk may be highly objectionable to purchasers of businesses. One of the motivations for a buyer to enter into an asset sale, as distinguished from a stock sale, is that the buyer does not want to be concerned

61. In essence, the buyer would become "liable for damages as a converter when he conveys the property to a bona fide purchaser and cuts off the creditors' rights to reach that property." Final Report, *Justifications for Changes in § 6–106,* par. 2. Inasmuch as the property is usually inventory held for sale, that is a likely result.

62. Adrian Tabin Corp. v. Climax Boutiques, Inc., 34 N.Y.2d 210, 356 N.Y.S.2d 606, 313 N.E.2d 66 (1974).

63. Final Report, *Justifications for Changes in § 6–104,* par. 2.

64. *See* Adrian Tabin Corp. v. Climax Boutiques, Inc., 34 N.Y.2d at ___, 356 N.Y.S.2d at ___, 313 N.E.2d at ___, (1974).

with the seller's creditors.[65] This would no longer be the case under revised section 6–104(3).

The decision to retain Article 6 requires a value judgment that a commercially useful purpose is served by allocating to the bulk purchaser the risk that the seller will not pay his creditors. *If* such a judgment is sound, the protection afforded creditors should be made meaningful by adopting this revision to section 6–104(3) and by requiring enactment of section 6–106. "Copyright 1983 by the American Bar Association. All rights reserved. Reprinted with the permission of the American Bar Association and its section of Corporation, Banking and Business Law.

IN RE McBEE

United States Court of Appeals, Fifth Circuit, 1983.
714 F.2d 1316.

[Colley owned a Gun Shop. In January, 1979, National Bank created and perfected a security interest in Colley's "inventory, existing and after acquired." In April, 1980, Wholesale Supply sold Colley goods on credit and created and perfected a security interest in "inventory" and everything else in sight. Colley, on May 5, 1980, made a "bulk" transfer to McBee, who agreed to comply with the Texas version of Article 6, but did not. Texas had enacted UCC 6–106. Thereafter, on July 16, 1980, Republic Bank created and perfected a security interest in McBee's inventory, existing and after acquired. McBee filed a petition in bankruptcy on October 22, 1980. The inventory remaining at the time of bankruptcy was auctioned by the trustee, producing some $40,000 in proceeds, and all three secured parties asserted security interests in it.

The Court of Appeals reversed the bankruptcy court's decision that National Bank had an unperfected security interest and, after concluding that the bulk transfer was not "effective" under the Texas version of Article 6, determined priorities as follows: (1) National Bank had priority over Wholesale Supply to the extent of the value of the inventory at the time of the bulk sale, not at the time of bankruptcy; (2) Wholesale Supply had priority in the remainder of that value; and (3) Republic Bank's priority was limited to the "excess value, if any, of the sale proceeds over the value of the inventory which existed when the business was transferred and which was transferred in bulk.]

* * *

65. This is no longer possible in acquisitions of manufacturing businesses in jurisdictions adopting the "product line" approach to successor corporation liability for injuries caused by defective products. As enunciated by the New Jersey Supreme Court in Ramirez v. Amsted Indus., Inc., 86 N.J. 332, 431 A.2d 811 (1981):

> [W]e hold that where one corporation acquires all or substantially all the manufacturing assets of another corporation, even if exclusively for cash, and undertakes essentially the same manufacturing operation as the selling corporation, the purchasing corporation is strictly liable for injuries caused by defects in units of the same product line, even if previously manufactured and distributed by the selling corporation or its predecessor. The social policies underlying strict products liability in New Jersey are best served by extending strict liability to a successor corporation that acquires the business assets and continues to manufacture essentially the same line of products as its predecessor, particularly where the successor corporation benefits from trading its product line on the name of the predecessor and takes advantage from its accumulated good will, business reputation and established customers.

Id. at 358, 431 A.2d at 825. *Accord* Cyr v. B. Offen & Co., Inc., 501 F.2d 1145 (1st Cir.1974); Turner v. Bituminous Casualty Co., 397 Mich. 406, 244 N.W.2d 873 (1976); Ray v. Alad Corp., 19 Cal.3d 22, 136 Cal.Rptr. 574, 560 P.2d 3 (1977); Dawejko v. Jorgensen Steel Co., 290 Pa.Super. 15, 434 A.2d 106 (1981).

2. Priorities

The general rule, of course, is that priorities of perfected security claims are determined in the order of filing. *See* Tex.Bus. & Comm.Code Ann. § 9.312(e) (Vernon 1968 & Supp.1982–1983). *See generally* J. White & R. Summers, *Uniform Commercial Code* 1036–42 (2d ed. 1980). Having found National Bank's interest perfected, the order of priority in accordance with the "first to file" rule is clear: first, National Bank, followed by Wholesale Supply, and then Republic Bank. This determination of general priorities, however, does not end our inquiry.

The collateral at issue here is the gun shop inventory held by *McBee* at the time of bankruptcy. Republic Bank, the last creditor in time to file, clearly held a security interest in *McBee*'s inventory. On the other hand, National Bank and Wholesale Supply, the initial creditors to file, held a security interest in the inventory, including "after-acquired property," of the gun shop when owned by *Colley*. This intervening bulk sale of the gun shop and its inventory from Colley to McBee raises the question of whether, and to what extent, the transferor's creditors, National Bank and Wholesale Supply, retain priority over the transferee's subsequent creditor, here Republic Bank. This question must be analyzed in light of the fact that the bulk sale from Colley to McBee was not made in accordance with the requirements of Article 6 of the U.C.C., dealing with bulk sales.

Article 6 of the U.C.C. defines, in general terms, the rights, liabilities and responsibilities of the parties to a bulk sale. As adopted in Texas, Section 6.105 requires that the transferee give notice to the transferor's creditors, in accordance with Section 6.107, *before* the bulk transfer is made. This before-the-fact notice provision affords the transferor's creditors an opportunity to act before the sale to protect their security interests. Another protection, afforded by Section 6.106,[13] is a requirement upon the transferee to see that the relevant part of the proceeds of the sale finds its way into the hands of the transferor's creditors. Texas is among the minority of jurisdictions which has adopted this optional provision, providing further remedial concern for a transferor's creditors in a bulk sale.[14]

The provisions of Article 6, if complied with, also protect the transferee and his future creditors. Secured creditors of the transferor cannot assert any claims against the transferee or his property after a complying bulk transfer; the transferee will not "pay twice" for property thus freed from prior security interests. Similarly, the transferee obtains clear title to the transferred assets and may obtain credit on the unencumbered property. The transferee's credi-

13. This section provides:

§ 6.106. Application of the Proceeds

In addition to the requirements of the two preceding sections:

(1) Upon every bulk transfer subject to this chapter for which new consideration becomes payable except those made by sale at auction it is the duty of the transferee to assure that such consideration is applied so far as necessary to pay those debts of the transferor which are either shown on the list furnished by the transferor (Section 6.104) or filed in writing in the place stated in the notice (Section 6.107) within thirty days after the mailing of such notice. This duty of the transferee runs to all the holders of such debts, and may be enforced by any of them for the benefit of all.

(2) If any of said debts are in dispute the necessary sum may be withheld from distribution until the dispute is settled or adjudicated.

(3) If the consideration payable is not enough to pay all of the said debts in full distribution shall be made pro rata.

14. White and Summers found that in 1980 eighteen states, including Texas, had enacted this provision. *See* J. White & R. Summers, *Uniform Commercial Code* 758 & n. 12 (2d ed. 1980).

tors also need not be concerned with the possibility that prior creditors, in the chain of title, will assert previously perfected interests in the transferee's property.

If the provisions of Article 6 are not complied with, Sections 6.104 and 6.105 state that the transfer is "ineffective" against the transferor's creditors. Tex. Bus. & Comm.Code Ann. §§ 6.104, 6.105 (Vernon 1968). The term "ineffective" is nowhere explicitly defined in the Code, nor by Texas case law. In the immediate case, it is conceded that the transfer from Colley to McBee did not comply with Article 6, despite the fact that McBee had covenanted to comply with the bulk transfer provisions. The bankruptcy court examined the policies underlying Articles 6 and 9, as well as other specific provisions in both articles, and concluded that the term "ineffective" meant that the creditor's original interest and rights are unaffected by the transfer, and continue in the collateral as they would have if the collateral were still owned by the transferor. The court thus concluded that Colley's perfected creditors retained their interest in the collateral, despite the transfer, and retained priority over transferee McBee's non-purchase money creditors. We agree that these pre-transfer interests retain priority to the extent of the value of the inventory-collateral transferred in the noncomplying bulk sale.

In the absence of a bulk sales law, creditors generally would lose all security interest in collateral once transferred to a new owner; the secured creditor's recourse would lie against the debtor-transferor, including an interest in any proceeds received by the transferor from the bulk sale. In many cases, this would leave the secured creditor without any effective remedy. The value received upon transfer might be far less than that of the transferred collateral, or by the time the creditor learned of the transfer little, if any, of the sales proceeds might be recoverable from the debtor-transferor.

Article 6 of the U.C.C., as adopted by Texas, changes the relative position of the parties affected by a bulk sale. "The Bulk Transfers Act and related predecessors were enacted for the protection of creditors who sell goods and merchandise to others on credit for inventory and resale." *Anderson & Clayton Co. v. Earnest,* 610 S.W.2d 846, 848 (Tex.Civ.App.—Amarillo 1980). As summarized above, Article 6 places certain requirements upon the parties to the bulk sale. These requirements serve to notify the transferor's creditors of the intended sale, thus permitting the creditors to protect their security interests *before* the transfer. They also protect the transferee and his subsequent creditors by bringing to light and terminating all prior security claims to the transferred property.

Had Article 6 been complied with, transferor-Colley's secured creditors—National Bank and Wholesale Supply—would have retained no interest in the gun shop in McBee's hands. There is no evidence, however, of any attempt at compliance, although McBee had contracted to do so in her sale agreement with Colley. As a result, Colley's secured creditors were left without the benefit of Article 6's remedial provisions, most notably those requiring notice to the transferor's creditors. Furthermore, these creditors, National Bank and Wholesale Supply, were unable to avail themselves of the additional remedial provision, Section 6–106, adopted in a minority of jurisdictions including Texas, which requires a transferee to see that the relevant part of the proceeds of the sale finds its way into the hands of the transferor's creditors.

The Code provides that this total noncompliance makes the transfer "ineffective" as to the transferor's creditors. Given the remedial purpose behind

Article 6, particularly as adopted in Texas, it is clear that by "ineffective" the Code drafters intended that the pre-transfer security interests survive the transfer, despite the fact that the collateral is no longer owned by the debtor. Republic Bank argues that this result is untenable, particularly with regard to new property purchased by the transferee and never owned by the transferor. At first glance, this argument is appealing: how can a debtor-transferor give his secured creditors an interest in property he no longer owns and, more significantly, in post-transfer property acquired by the transferee which the transferor never owned?

Upon analysis, however, the facial logical persuasiveness and the equitable underpinning of this argument disappears. The transferor gives his creditors a security interest in *his* property which may, as in the immediate case, cover "after-acquired property." It is Article 6, which provides as a "sanction for non-compliance" that the transfer is ineffective against creditors of the transferor. Tex.Bus. & Comm.Code Ann. § 6.106 official comment 2 (Vernon 1968). If this result were not reached, the remedial purposes behind Article 6 would be severely, if not wholly, undercut. The entire Article could be ignored with impunity; the remedial notice provisions, which serve to awaken unknowing creditors to press their claims before transfer, would be avoided. Clearly, a transferee cannot complain if, by his non-compliance, the transferor's creditors' claims attach to his property as they had prior to sale.

The immediate case proves the importance of the statutory requirement. Transferee McBee cannot complain. She was aware of National Bank's interest in the inventory and after-acquired property of the gun shop, yet she breached her specific covenant to comply with Article 6 in her sale agreement with Colley. Nor can the transferee's creditors be heard to complain of the protections afforded the transferor's creditors. The transferee's creditors should inquire as to a debtor's source of title where circumstances warrant. *See* Tex.Bus. & Comm.Code Ann. § 9.402(g) official comment 8 (Vernon Supp.1982–1983). Where, as in the immediate case, a bulk transfer has recently taken place, a subsequent creditor can and should inquire as to whether the transfer complied with Article 6. We find that the underlying policies of the Code are best supported by an interpretation which favors the unknowing prior creditor over the subsequent potential creditor. It is more equitable to place the burden on the potential subsequent creditor to check Article 6 compliance upon application for credit than to require constant vigilance of a prior creditor who, in the absence of notification, may rightfully assume that no bulk transfer cutting off his security interest has occurred.

We find further support for our conclusion in the statutory pattern. The transferor's creditor is not saved harmless forever in a non-complying bulk transfer. Article 6 limits the period in which a transferor's creditor may assert a security interest to six months after the non-complying bulk transfer, unless there has been concealment of the transfer. Tex.Bus. & Comm.Code Ann. § 6.111 (Vernon 1968). This limitations period evidences a policy that at some point a diligent creditor should realize that a transfer has occurred absent concealment of that fact and despite his lack of notice. If the prior creditor does not exercise such diligence, his security interest in the transferred property is lost. This time limitation was met in this case by National and Wholesale Supply. The time limitation supports our conclusion that Article 6 is a reasonable and balanced provision in preserving the security interests of the transferor's creditors effective against the transferee.

* * *

Republic Bank argues that Section 6.110 protects its interest from those of the transferor's creditors. Section 6.110 provides that:

> When the title of a transferee to property is subject to a defect by reason of his noncompliance with the requirements of this chapter, then:
>
> (1) a purchaser of any of such property from such transferee who pays no value or who takes with notice of such noncompliance takes subject to such defect, but
>
> (2) a purchaser for value in good faith and without such notice takes free of such defect.

Tex.Bus. & Comm.Code Ann. § 6.110 (Vernon 1968). Republic Bank reasons that: (1) there is no finding or evidence that it had notice of McBee's failure to comply with Article 6; (2) the term "purchaser" includes a secured party such as Republic Bank under U.C.C. §§ 1.201(32), (33); and therefore (3) its interest is held free of any prior security interests by operation of Section 6.110(2).

This argument is not persuasive. While it is true under the Code that the general term "purchaser" may include a secured party, we find it clear that the term as used in Section 6.110 was not intended to include secured creditors.

As we find, *supra,* Article 6 clearly contemplates that transferors' creditors retain their security interest in the transferred collateral in the event of total noncompliance. This contemplated result would be frustrated were an extensive reading given to the term "purchaser" in Section 6.110 to cover subsequent creditors. Further we doubt whether a subsequent creditor could assert a claim that it took its interest "without notice." If a prior security interest is perfected, the burden is on the subsequent creditor to search for that claim. His failure to receive actual notice cannot be held as a defense to the priority of the prior perfected lien. Since Article 6 clearly provides that after a non-complying bulk transfer the transferor creditors' security interests remain effective, such interests may not be cut off by a broad reading of Section 6.110 at odds with the specific purpose behind Article 6.

* * *

[Some footnotes omitted.]

Notes

1. *McBee* holds that a perfected security interest survives a bulk transfer that did not comply with Article 6 and has priority over a perfected security interest which attached after the bulk sale, to the extent of the value of the inventory at the time of the transfer. What does the court, say, in dictum, about these questions: (A) Does an unperfected security interest continue in assets after a bulk transfer that fails to comply with Article 6?, and (B) Does a perfected security interest continue with priority in assets after a bulk transfer where the buyer complied with Article 6?

2. Does what *McBee* says about these questions appear to be sound? Professor Harris, in an illuminating article which deals with these questions and more, argues that Articles 9 and 6 deal with related but different kinds of fraud. Article 9 requires public notice by filing or possession to overcome the assumption that creditors of the debtor in possession will be mislead. The failure to perfect means that the "secret lien" will be subordinated to lien creditors and other secured parties but not to unsecured creditors. Article 6 requires notice to certain creditors to give them an opportunity for protection in the "bulk" sale. Failure to give notice means, at a minimum, that the creditors could obtain a judicial lien on the goods sold to and now owned by B. Against this background, Harris concludes, inter alia, that *McBee* was incorrect to the extent that it attempted to employ Article 6 to alter property

rights and priorities determined under Article 9: He suggests that Article 6 should be amended to specify that its protection of good faith purchasers "addresses only the right of aggrieved creditors to reach goods transferred in a noncomplying bulk sale and does not affect property rights that are regulated elsewhere." Harris, *The Interaction of Articles 6 and 9 of the Uniform Commercial Code: A Study in Conveyancing, Priorities, and Code Interpretation,* 39 Vand.L.Rev. 179, 247 (1986).

3. The current version of Article 6 has been criticized. For a sampling of these criticisms and some proposals for reform, see the Rapson extract, supra, and the articles in 38 The Business Lawyer 1397, 1729–1794.

*

BOOK THREE

COMMERCIAL PAPER

PREAMBLE: PAYMENT SYSTEMS, THEIR NATURE AND SCOPE

Twenty years ago this subject would have been known as "bills and notes." It would have dealt with checks, and to a lesser extent with promissory notes. It would have focused on Articles 3 and 4 of the Uniform Commercial Code, then sweeping the country. Bills and notes had been taught for more than 50 years before that in American law schools, though the earlier courses were based on common-law cases and on the statutory predecessor of Article 3, the Negotiable Instruments Law.

Today things are more complicated. Since World War II a series of systems, some in the consumer setting, some in the commercial setting, and some in both, has arisen to challenge the check as the conventional mode of payment. The most widely used of these in the consumer setting is the credit card. Arising originally as a two-party device between the consumer and the merchant, third-party credit cards—those issued by banks to their customers for use to pay third-party merchants—are pervasive. The dollars transferred and the credit granted under credit cards are staggering. Also of staggering volume but largely unseen by the public are the electronic funds transfers among financial institutions and between financial institutions and commercial agencies. A final and as yet relatively small but growing volume consists of electronic funds transfers by consumers. These are the transfers that occur when a consumer uses a debit card to draw cash from his bank account at an automated teller machine. Something analogous to a commercial credit card but aimed typically at a specific transaction is the letter of credit. Letters of credit are normally issued by banks to their customers on behalf of those who deal with their customers. These third parties are labeled "beneficiaries." Article Five of the UCC treats letters of credit.

Each of the modes of transfer described above may be called a "payment system," and one can judge the importance of each by estimating the dollar amount attributable to each. The lawyer will find himself much more frequently involved in some than in others. Some systems pose enormous practical problems in controlling credit and coping with fraud and theft, but present few legal problems. Commercial electronic fund transfer systems are illustrative. Checks, on the other hand, appear to present a mass of legal issues out of proportion to the dollars transferred. Thus, the lawyer's perspective on these transactions is necessarily different from the banker's.

Our focus in the pages that follow will be on Articles 3 and 4, on "bills and notes." There are several reasons for that focus. First the output of appellate cases dealing with Articles 3 and 4 tells us that it continues to be a fertile legal battleground. It is something lawyers are expected to know about; it is a place where their advice and counsel is needed. On the other hand, commercial electronic funds transfer, and consumer electronic funds transfer, systems present far fewer lawyer questions. In the consumer context, that is partly because the law has been codified in great detail by the federal government and because the dollar amounts in any given transaction with a debit card are so small that they are typically resolved without litigation.

At the commercial level, the lack of litigated cases can be attributed to the fact that the law is private; it takes the form of agreements among the actors, who are ordinarily professionals. Presumably, therefore, it is drafted to account for the most common kinds of discombobulations. Presumably, too, the huge sums there involved impress the actors with the necessity to adopt careful procedures against theft and mistake. When there is a problem, all parties understand that it is in their interest to work it out without litigation. In a sense one might regard commercial electronic funds transfer players as members of a club. For the most part they have common interests and understand one anothers' desires.

Letter of credit transactions and check deals are in marked contrast to those between members of the EFT Club. In the former to a limited extent and the latter to a great extent, all manner of people are players. The check is used by the least and by the greatest. It is used to pay not just the janitor, but also the Wall Street lawyer, not just for a broom but also for a multi-million dollar piece of commercial machinery. Unlike the debit and credit cards where only small amounts are involved, check transactions, either individually or over time, often involve tens of thousands and even millions of dollars. Thus the costs of bringing a law suit are often quite small compared to the amount to be gained by such a suit.

To some extent recent letter of credit developments have made that area begin to look like the bills and notes arena and less like the private club of commercial electronic funds transfer. Formerly in the United States, letters of credit were limited mostly to international transactions in which an American buyer or seller would be either the beneficiary or the customer of the letter of credit arrangement, itself being designed to facilitate payment to a seller in an international transaction from a buyer in that transaction. More recently, so-called "standby" letters of credit have been widely used in domestic commerce. Here the letter might operate as a stand-in for a guarantee. For example, one bank might give another bank a letter that promised to pay a certain amount of money on default of the first bank's customer. Moreover, international disruptions of the kind caused when the Iranians withdrew substantially from western international commerce have caused periodic outbursts of cases that tend to strain the fabric of Article 5 of the Uniform Commercial Code (and of the Uniform Customs and Practices).

Thus, in the pages that follow we will deal extensively and primarily with bills and notes. Our emphasis will be on a particular kind of bill, namely, the check—a draft drawn on a bank and payable on demand. We deal initially with the basic contract liabilities on these, move on to the holder in due course and ultimately to the various intricate liabilities of banks for delay or unauthorized behavior in the collection and payment of checks. We will also devote time to the various forms of theft and fraud that can occur in the use of the check. One chapter each deals with letters of credit and electronic funds transfer. While both are important, they are less important than bills and notes for most lawyers.

Commercial electronic funds transfer is particularly interesting from the scholar's point of view because it is the subject of proposed legislation and it is an area where the law is still in flux. A committee of the American Law

Institute, known as the "3–4–8 committee" wrestled for years with a draft proposal that would have amended Articles 3, 4 and 8 to make them into a true "payments Code." The principal motivation for this was to adopt a body of statutory rules to govern electronics funds transfer. At this writing it appears as though that effort is dead. It now appears that the Commissioners on Uniform State Law will make relatively modest amendments to Articles 3 and 4 so that electronic funds transfer can be included in those articles and dealt with there. To some extent the lawyer's role in electronic funds transfer is to determine which of the rules in Articles 3 and 4 should be transported there by analogy. Of course, to the extent that a governing rule is provided by contract, the lawyer's job is lessened, but there will be many cases in which the contracts among the parties will not be determinative, and in which one will look to Articles 3 and 4 by analogy or perhaps to the draft of the payments code. Most who study this book as students will live to see statutory law enacted that will govern electronic funds transfer, but one should not underestimate the difficulty of achieving agreement about such legislation.

The chapters that follow, then, examine "payment systems." But the primary emphasis is on checks. We justify that emphasis as explained above on the ground that the check is really the grist for the lawyers' mill. Despite its defects, and in the face of predictions of its early demise, the check has persisted and its use has grown. The student might ask why that is so: Why does a consumer pay for something with a $1,000 check when he could put it on his credit card, postpone payment for 30 days, and thus enjoy the benefit of the use of the $1,000 for that period? Particularly in the case where there is a 30 day free period, there will be no interest charged on the $1,000 on his credit card. Or why carry around checks and worry about balancing the books, etc., when one could use a debit card at a point-of-sale terminal in a retail store? The predictions that credit and debit cards would expand to obliterate the check in consumer transactions have all proved false. Moreover the check has been remarkably persistent even in commercial transactions and seems likely to remain so. For those and the other reasons described above, we believe the check should be the focus of the student's examination of payment systems. The student should leave this subject with an understanding of the rules associated with theories of liability pertaining to the check, including those arising from contract, tort, warranty and statute.

CHAPTER TWENTY-THREE

CONTRACT: THE BASIC LIABILITIES ON DRAFTS AND NOTES

SECTION 1. INTRODUCTION

Article 3 of the Uniform Commercial Code governs the rights and liabilities of parties to what the code calls "commercial paper." Such "paper" calls for the obligor to pay money rather than deliver goods or perform some service. The ordinary check is not only the most familiar species of commercial paper, it is also by far the most commonly used.

Buyers of goods frequently pay for them by issuing checks. Of course, a buyer will often pay cash for many types of goods. But payment by check frequently involves significant advantages over cash. Extensive use of cash would require that buyers keep large quantities of cash on hand, with attendant inconveniences and risks of loss or theft. Further, it is simpler and safer for a buyer or his agent to send a check through the mail than to send cash. Also, a cancelled check, with the payee's indorsement, affords the buyer both a receipt and a good record for accounting purposes. (The student should consider whether the check offers the seller any advantages). Because of such advantages as the foregoing, buyers use millions upon millions of checks each year in paying for goods either just purchased or upon expiration of a period of credit extended at the time of purchase.

But it must not be assumed that the only kind of check is the kind we all tend to carry around for ordinary use. As we will see, there are other kinds of checks, including "cashiers" checks and "certified" checks. Furthermore, checks are not the only species of commercial paper. In addition to checks, Article 3 of the Code also governs the rights and liabilities of parties to notes, drafts, and certificates of deposit (all of which are defined in UCC 3–104(2)). These other species of commercial paper may also figure in sale of goods transactions (e.g., buyers often sign installment notes), but these, just like the check, frequently figure in many non-sale of goods transactions as well, including sales of services, realty and "straight loans."

The student who takes this and the following chapters seriously should acquire substantial knowledge of the ins and outs of Articles 3 and 4, a grasp of the various theories of liability in this field, the capacity to compare and draw analogies among the various forms of commercial paper, an understanding of "negotiability", other forms of transfer, a sense of the importance of being a holder in due course, an understanding of real and personal defenses, a grasp of some of the underlying transactions, and more.

Knowing the underlying transaction is not a matter of merely incidental importance to the practicing commercial lawyer; it is central. Transactions drive the law, not vice versa, and one who is ignorant of the transactions will ask the wrong questions, and thus apply the law in a crude and erroneous way. Thus, the student should not regard the underlying transaction, revealed in the cases that follow, merely as "background" or "contract."

SECTION 2. THE NATURE AND KINDS OF COMMERCIAL PAPER—CHECKS AND NOTES

A. *Checks and Other Drafts*

The received understanding is that the check is, along with Mansfield opinions and the Benthamite calculus, a legacy of the 18th Century. The word "check" is, it seems, derived from the name of an early record-keeping device used to check forgery or alteration of checks. UCC 3–104(2)(b) defines a check as a "draft drawn on a bank and payable on demand." We will shortly consider the meaning of this language. UCC 3–104(1) specifies requisites that a check must meet if "negotiable." Almost all checks are negotiable, but under Article 3 they are but *one* species of negotiable instrument.

We must first see how a bank gets into the act, and explain the general relationship between the drawer ("creator") of the check, and the bank on which the check is "drawn," ("drawee"), and the person to whom the check is made payable ("payee").

Most fundamentally, it is through the existence of banks that the use of checks as we know them becomes possible, for the drawer of a check orders a *bank* to pay in accordance with the drawer's order. The use of checks thus *presupposes* that banks will behave as ordered. How, in particular instances, do banks become willing, indeed, obligated, to respond to such orders? Typically, the drawer of a check is someone who has deposited funds with the drawee bank, the drawee bank agreeing (1) to set up an account therefor in the name of the depositor, and (2) to process the drawer's checks thereon accordingly. The rights of a drawer-depositor *vis-a-vis* the bank are determined partly by the contract set out on the front and back of the "signature card" (signed when the account is opened), partly by other documents such as monthly statements, stop order forms, and the like which pass between the drawer-depositor and his bank, and partly by the provisions of Articles 3 and 4 of the Uniform Commercial Code and relevant case law.

What kind of a legal relationship is created between the drawer-depositor and the depositary bank? One is tempted to say that of bailor-bailee, for one is inclined to think of himself as having "money in the bank." But in the typical case, all this is wrong, at least in law. Though the UCC does not say so in so many words, the relationship for most purposes is rather of creditor (drawer-depositor) and debtor (drawee-bank). By the contract between the depositor and bank, the bank acknowledges its indebtedness to drawer for the amount in the checking account, and agrees to pay out upon demand sums on presentment of checks for payment. The bank can break this contract in various ways, e.g., by wrongful dishonor, by paying over a forgery, failing to honor a valid "stop order," and so on. We treat these legal problems intensively in the following chapters.

So far, we have not considered the general position of the payee of a check *vis-a-vis* the drawee bank. Students familiar with general contract law will be tempted to think of the payee either as a *third party beneficiary* of the contract between drawer-depositor and drawee-bank, or as an *assignee* of the drawer's contract rights. But again, in the typical case this would be all wrong. The payee is not entitled to sue and prevail against the drawee on either of these theories, even where the drawee is actually breaking its contract with the drawer in refusing to honor a particular check of the drawer. A payee is not a "third party beneficiary" nor is he an "assignee." Indeed, the drawee is not liable on an instrument until it "accepts." See UCC 3–401, 3–409, and 3–410.

But this is not to say that a drawee bank could not become liable on a check to the payee. Thus, a drawee might "certify" a check. See UCC 3–411. Following is a certified check.

Observe that when a bank certifies a check, it, so to speak, "puts its credit behind it." When a bank certifies a check it becomes "primarily liable." See UCC 3–411(1) and 3–413(1). When the drawee certifies, it normally at the same time charges the drawer's account. The rights of the holder of the check are less if he has it certified than if the drawer has it certified. See UCC 3–411(1). A refusal to certify is not a "dishonor" of the check. See UCC 3–411(2), 3–501(1)(a) and 3–507(1)(a). When a bank does certify, how does it do this? See UCC 3–410.

Another kind of check besides the ordinary check and the certified one is the so-called cashier's check, an example of which is set forth below.

The following is a bank draft. How does it differ from a cashier's check?

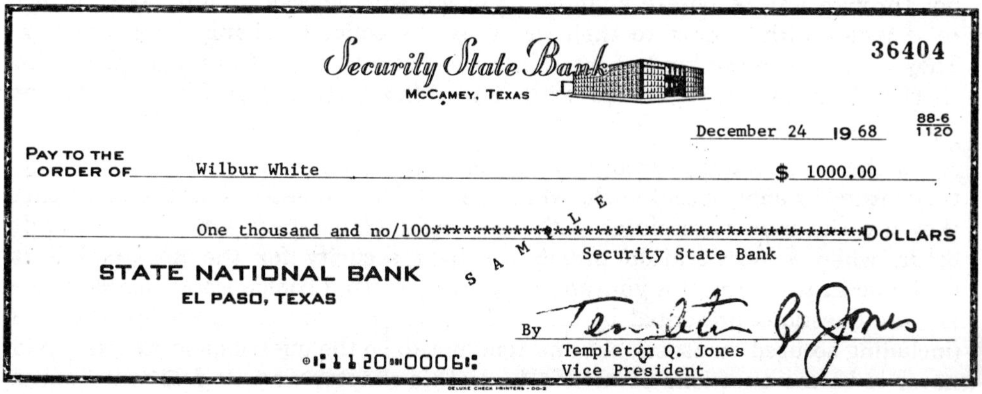

Security State Bank
McCAMEY, TEXAS

36404

December 24 19 68

88-6
1120

PAY TO THE ORDER OF Wilbur White $ 1000.00

One thousand and no/100**************************************DOLLARS

SAMPLE

Security State Bank

STATE NATIONAL BANK
EL PASO, TEXAS

By Templeton Q. Jones
Templeton Q. Jones
Vice President

⑆1120⑈0006⑆

So much for the genesis of checks and the depositor and bank relation, and so much for the main types of checks in use. What of the possible "parties" to checks besides the ones considered so far? As a check passes through various hands, it may or may not be indorsed. If it is indorsed, the indorser may incur liability on the instrument to a subsequent transferee under UCC 3–414 (just as the drawer similarly may incur liability under UCC 3–413). So, too, a transferor, whether or not his name appears on the instrument, may incur warranty liability as a transferor thereof under UCC 3–417 and UCC 4–207. On all of this, more later.

Checks are but one category of draft. Another kind of draft that the student should be able to identify is called a "sight draft." One common kind of sight draft is a draft drawn by a seller ordering a buyer to pay, and payable on presentation to the buyer, i.e., at sight. Of the remaining varieties of commercial paper, the promissory note is by far the most widely used. At page 1026 we set forth an illustrative note and discuss some of its attributes.

B. *Promissory Notes*

The contract of the maker of a note is deceptively similar to the contract of the drawer of a draft. Both are set out in section 3–413. The maker (the primary obligor on a note) is said to be primarily liable because he must pay the sum due without the holder presenting it first to another party. The drawer is said to be only "secondarily" liable because the draft typically must be presented to payor and dishonored before the drawer's liability arises. The apparent similarity of the liabilities is deceiving, however. Checks arise out of transactions that are thought by the parties not to be credit transactions or, at most, to be one or two or three day credit transactions. Also, checks are collected by an elaborate and comprehensive system among banks. The result is that legal issues presented by them are quite different from those presented by notes. With rare exceptions checks are transmitted from bank to bank through the mails by couriers for collection. Typically there are many parties who ultimately have an interest in the transfer and payment of the check from the drawer to the drawee to the collecting bank to the payor. Some notes are also passed from hand to hand but a large share of all notes are not so transferred. Many notes are simply held by the payee and are presented for payment to the maker and not through any elaborate channel as exists with checks. Thus notes do not raise issues with respect to their delay by the collecting bank or payor bank. They do not raise the kind of fraud and theft questions that are associated with checks; legal issues associated with notes tend to be simpler and to present themselves much less frequently.

If the legal issues associated with notes do not have to do with bank delay, theft, fraud, dishonor and such, what are the legal issues? For the most part they are the issues associated with any credit transaction, when does default occur, when is acceleration proper, is there security for the note and is it available in the form of a guarantor's promise? To a considerable degree these are the questions presented by and dealt with in a course on creditors' rights (including secured transactions), and tend not to be the questions of Article 3 and never to be the questions of Article 4. In this chapter we will deal to a limited extent with some of the questions presented on notes. For example, we will address the question when default occurs. We will consider how to characterize a note as a demand note or as some other form of note. Here and elsewhere we will treat holder in due course problems which tend to be the same for notes as for checks. On balance, however, we devote much less time to credit instruments, notes, than to payment instruments, drafts, letters of credit and the like.

Professor Gilmore has described Article 3 as a "collection of antiquities." Most of the sections apply to both checks and notes; only a few are directed explicitly to notes.

Turning to the limited number of sections that deal mostly with notes, consider first section 3–108, the definition of the term "payable on demand." It tells us that a note at which no time of payment is stated is a demand note collectible at any time. Section 3–122(1) indicates that the cause of action accrues on such an instrument at the date stated on it; if there is no date, on the date of issue. Thus, the statute of limitations on a demand note typically begins running with its issuance.

Section 3–402 deals with signatures in an ambiguous capacity and UCC 3–403 deals with signatures by one who claims only to be an agent. Issues about the identity of a maker frequently arise in note cases. Commonly the party who is the defendant in a lawsuit and who has apparently signed the note as the maker in his personal capacity, claims that he was signing as the president of his closely held (but invariably insolvent) corporation. Such issues recur in small business contexts. We deal with them in section 8 below. As the cases there will show, the same issues can arise with respect to checks, but because checks are preprinted, issues of that kind are much less frequent there.

Sections 3–603, 3–604, 3–605 dealing with discharge relate almost exclusively to notes. For the most part the rules there fall within Gilmore's characterization of Article 3 as a collection of antiquities, but there are some important rules as well. Note that under 3–606 one can pay the holder of a negotiable note even in circumstances where another claims rights to the instrument. That issue has obvious importance for a home owner liable on a note in circumstances where two parties claim the right to the note and mortgage, for example. Section 3–604 and 3–605 are more arcane, but they too could be important in certain situations. In section 7 we deal with the rights of accommodation parties. Almost always these persons are co-signers or indorsers of notes. To a considerable degree their rights are governed by UCC 3–606 and to a lesser degree by 3–414 and 3–416. Indorsers on drafts qualify as short-term accommodation parties, but most of the litigation arises out of longer term obligations, that is, the obligations of co-signers and indorsers of notes. We will confront all of these issues later in this chapter.

A final antiquity is section 3–802(1)(b) which states the effect on the underlying obligation when, for example, a payee accepts a time note in return for that obligation. Although UCC 3–802 sometimes applies in check cases its principal application is to notes. The Code section essentially tells us that one who takes a note requiring payment at a later time may not claim payment on the underlying obligation until that later time arrives.

In a sense what we have described in the preceding paragraphs are no more than technical rules dealing with notes. The big issues, some of which we deal with in section Five below, are fundamentally credit issues and they are shared by notes and other credit obligations although many of those obligations arise out of simple contract transactions.

SECTION 3. THE NATURE AND KINDS OF COMMERCIAL PAPER—ANOMALOUS INSTRUMENTS

Not all of the animals in the forest can be as easily classified into species and subspecies under Article 3 as the note and the check. A clever lawyer or a foolish layman can devise documents that defy description. For example, one of your editors was once involved in a lawsuit in which he argued that a document put on letter-sized stationery and titled "Revolving Trust Account" was in fact a promissory note with an acceleration clause. (The "acceleration clause" read: "If client desires his money at any time, so be it.") Apart from thoroughly weird and ambiguous documents that defy description, there are varieties of paper in common use with important commercial functions that do not fit clearly or precisely into Article 3 categories. Most prominent of these is the "money order." A copy of a money order is set out below. One might ask whether the person who "purchases" is a "drawer." It is common for a person who does not have a checking account to go to a bank or other agency and "purchase" a money order. The purchaser then completes the money order and sends it through the mail to the person to whom he owes money. It is possible to argue that the money order is nothing more than a cashier's check and the drawer is in fact the bank or other organization that issues the paper. It is also possible to argue that the "purchaser" is the drawer. How one decides that question determines whether the bank itself has liability on the paper and whether if it chooses to stop payment when the paper is presented, the bank has liability. What do you think?

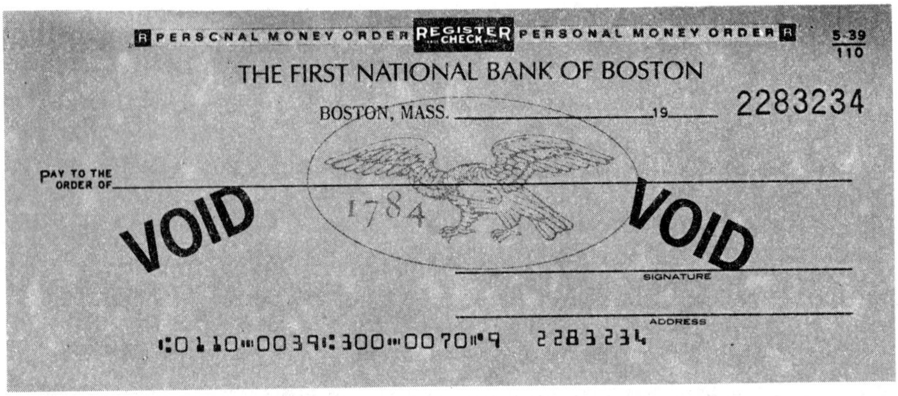
PERSONAL MONEY ORDER REGISTER CHECK PERSONAL MONEY ORDER 5-39/110

THE FIRST NATIONAL BANK OF BOSTON

BOSTON, MASS. ____________ 19____ 2283234

PAY TO THE ORDER OF ____________

VOID VOID

SIGNATURE

ADDRESS

⑆0110⑈0039⑆300⑈0070⑈9 2283234

A second somewhat anomalous but widely used document is a "trade acceptance." Below is a trade acceptance. If Wilbur is selling goods to Linus for $2,000,000 what names and numbers go where?

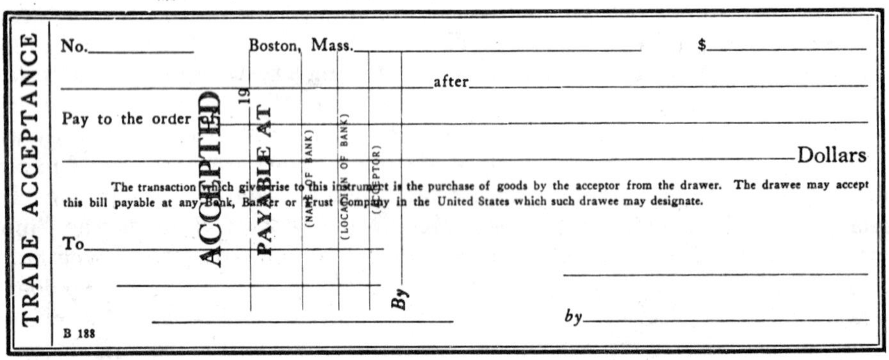
TRADE ACCEPTANCE

No.________ Boston, Mass.________ $________

________ after ________

Pay to the order ________

________ Dollars

The transaction which gives rise to this instrument is the purchase of goods by the acceptor from the drawer. The drawee may accept this bill payable at any Bank, Banker or Trust Company in the United States which such drawee may designate.

To________

ACCEPTED 19__ PAYABLE AT (NAME OF BANK) (LOCATION OF BANK) (ACCEPTOR) By

by________

B 188

Finally, there are papers now commonly in use by credit unions. These papers look like checks, and they are designed for use by credit union members to enable the credit union member in effect to procure goods or services. Ultimately, the paper is presented through bank channels to the credit union and there the manager of the credit union determines whether to "honor" the paper or to send it back. It seems clear that documents like the one set out below are drafts, but who is the drawer?

Maiwurm Credit Union 2-5-73
400 Wiswall, Dearborn

Pay to the Order of Home Appliance $ 750.00
Seven Hundred Fifty and 00/100 Dollars

Pay through
Sue National Bank
Dearborn Branch

Dessaix

The foregoing are only examples of some of the kinds of anomalous commercial paper that a lawyer may see in the course of his practice life. Do not assume that they are exhaustive; they are here only to alert the student to the prospect that he will see some pieces of commercial paper that do not fit the descriptions in Article 3 precisely and to encourage him to be prepared to ask: What is this? How does it fit into Article 3?

The traveler's check is still another example, we will study it at page 994 infra.

SECTION 4. THE RIGHT OF CERTAIN TAKERS OF COMMERCIAL PAPER TO "SUE ON THE INSTRUMENT"—AN INDEPENDENTLY SIGNIFICANT THEORY OF RECOVERY

Negotiable checks, notes and the like are "instruments" in Article 3. In the jargon of this branch of law, the taker may elect to "sue on the instrument" when due, rather than sue for breach of any underlying contract. For example, a seller of goods who receives a check in payment that is not honored upon presentment may choose to sue the buyer "on the check" rather than sue him for breach of his payment obligation embodied in the underlying contract of sale. Such a suit "on the instrument" has long been recognized as an independently significant cause of action different from ordinary breach of contract. In what ways is this cause of action distinctive?

First, in a suit "on a check" or "on a note" (on an instrument), the plaintiff seller (or other person as the case may be) asserts that some party to the instrument is liable "thereon" pursuant to a specific provision of Article 3. In the case of a check, for example, the plaintiff may be asserting that the defendant drawer-buyer is liable under UCC 3–413. Thus in a suit on a check or note acquired in a sale of goods or services or a loan transaction, for example, the *prima facie* liability of the defendant (liability without regard to possible defenses) is defined not by the terms of the underlying contract of sale or service, but by a basic provision of Article 3. We will explore the statutory liabilities of the various "parties" to commercial paper in a later chapter.

Second, in a suit "on a check" or "on a note" the *defenses* that the defendant may set up will often be fewer in number and different in kind from the defenses that the defendant could have set up if the plaintiff had merely sued the defendant not "on the instrument," but "on the underlying obligation." For example, a buyer of goods may defend on grounds of a breach of warranty where the plaintiff sues for breach of the buyer's promise to pay embodied in the underlying contract. But, if the plaintiff is a good faith purchaser of the instrument, he cannot be met with a breach of warranty defense. He will be a "holder in due course" under UCC 3–302 and free of such defenses under UCC 3–305. The student should cast a preliminary glance at UCC 3–302 and 3–305. Just what the various defenses involved may be and the conditions of their assertability will be the subject of chapter 24.

Third, in a suit "on a check" or "on a note," the plaintiff is the beneficiary of certain pleading and proof provisions of Article 3 (see UCC 3–307) which are not similarly available to a plaintiff who merely sues for breach of an underlying promissory obligation embodied in, say, a contract of sale. See Weinberg, *Pleading and Practice in Commercial Paper Cases: Burdens of Proof,* 72 Ky.L.J. 575 (1983–84).

Fourth, for some purposes, the right of a plaintiff to recover in a "suit on the check" or "on a note" supersedes or takes precedence over the plaintiff's right to recover for breach of the underlying obligation. At this juncture, the student may profitably read and mull UCC 3–802(1)(b). The student should then seek to construct a hypothetical case from the sale of goods context that illustrates the application of UCC 3–802(1)(b).

From the preceding discussion, the student might erroneously conclude that the only theories of liability operative in this field are "suits on the instrument" pursuant to such provisions as UCC 3–413 and 3–415, and suits for ordinary breach of contract (breach of the "underlying obligation"). Actually, in this field we will also encounter (1) statutory warranty liability theories, (2) restitutionary theories, and (3) various forms of tort theory including conversion and negligence. These various theories will be introduced at appropriate junctures.

SECTION 5. PRIMA FACIE "CONTRACT" LIABILITY OF DRAWERS, INDORSERS, MAKERS AND ACCEPTORS

In the previous section we distinguished between the liability of a party to commercial paper "on a check" or "on a note" as contrasted with the liability of that very same party on an underlying contractual obligation, such as a promise to pay embodied in a sale of goods contract. We stressed that the "prima facie" liability (liability before assertion of defenses) of a party to commercial paper "on a check" or "on a note" is set forth in Article 3 itself rather than in the terms of any underlying contract. Nonetheless, the drafters of Article 3 chose to call such liability on a check or on a note "contractual." The student should be wary of this use of the same terminology to designate two different sources of liability. This use of contract terminology in the statutory law of commercial paper probably derives partly from the ancient classification of certain checks and notes as "speciality contracts," and partly from the reality that a party signing a check or a note very likely actually intends to incur liabilities very similar if not always identical to those *prima facie* liabilities specified in UCC 3–413 and 3–414. Before we turn to those sections, it is vital to emphasize, in the words of UCC 3–401(1), that "no person is liable on an instrument unless his signature appears thereon."

Section 3–413(1) sets forth the "contract" of the maker and acceptor as follows:

> (1) The maker or acceptor engages that he will pay the instrument according to its tenor at the time of his engagement or as completed pursuant to Section 3–115 on incomplete instruments.

The "maker" is a person familiar to all. He is the student, the businessperson or other debtor who creates ("makes") a note, usually by signing and issuing it. (See the note form at page 1026.) When the note falls due, he must pay.

The "acceptor" may be foreign to the student but there is nothing mysterious about him. A bank that certifies a check is an acceptor; so too the buyer in a commercial transaction who "accepts" a draft drawn on him. (See sight draft at page 674.) An acceptor typically signs across the back of the instrument and so, according to UCC 3–413(1), in effect incurs a maker's obligation, i.e., a direct obligation to pay to the holder the amount specified on the instrument.

Compare this basic liability of the maker of the note with the liability of the drawer on a check. That liability, together with the basic liability of an indorser, is described as follows in 3–413 and 3–414.

Section 3–413

> (2) The drawer engages that upon dishonor of the draft and any necessary notice of dishonor or protest he will pay the amount of the draft to the holder or to any indorser who takes it up. The drawer may disclaim this liability by drawing without recourse.

Section 3–414

> (1) Unless the indorsement otherwise specifies (as by such words as "without recourse") every indorser engages that upon dishonor and any necessary notice of dishonor and protest he will pay the instrument according to its tenor at the time of his indorsement to the holder or to any subsequent indorser who takes it up, even though the indorser who takes it up was not obligated to do so.

Absent acceptance or the drawing of the check on which the drawee is itself the drawer, the drawee has no liability on a check. Section 3–409 makes it clear that a draft is not an assignment of any right owed by the bank to the drawer. Thus, bank has no duty to the third party to recognize that assignment and it remains completely revocable until final payment by the stop order of the drawer. Of course, the bank can accept and thus incur primary liability and as we will see in Chapter 26, the bank who delays too long will incur liability on that basis under the provisions of 4–213 and 4–302.

Normally an acceptance must be "written on the draft" under UCC 3–410. Section 3–411 provides for special certification, and note that the liabilities on a certified check may be determined in part by which party procured the certification. The following problem presents a recurring theme in which one party claims that the drawee bank was liable because of its behavior. Routinely the bank responds that it has no liability unless it has delayed too long or complied with the acceptance ritual. What do you think?

Problem 23–1

Bigger is a farmer and cattle feeder in Biggsville, Illinois. Since 1972, and approximately four times per year, Bigger purchased cattle from Fremont Cattle Company. The dealings between the parties were not unusual until on March 4,

1980, the normal course of dealing was reversed and for the first time Bigger sold 101 calves to Fremont. Bigger received a check for $42,928.56 signed by Keith Mumma. Because he had been dealing with Mumma for so many years, Bigger took no precautions to make sure the check was good before releasing his cattle. Bigger immediately deposited this check at the Bank of Oquawaka. The check was returned by Fremont National Bank for insufficient funds. Bigger had a representative at Oquawaka telephone Fremont National and was assured by an employee in the booking department that if he sent the check back through, it would be "taken care of," and everything "would be all right." The check was returned a second time and Bigger was informed that Fremont Cattle was in Chapter 11 under the Bankruptcy Reform Act. Is Fremont National liable on the check? On what theory?

Problem 23–2

Bank and Debtor had an extended discussion about a loan bank was to make to Debtor and his business partner. It is undisputed that the parties agreed the amount of each of the two notes would be the cost respectively of a particular type of pickup truck and of a used truck. The interest rate was agreed to be the Bank's prevailing rate for similar transactions on the date the loan was made. Before leaving the bank on that day, Debtor signed two notes in blank with the understanding described above. Ultimately the Bank filled in the first note for $15,000 together with an interest rate at 13 percent and the second note for $11,433.00 with an interest rate at 14 percent. These amounts were transmitted by Debtor's secretary to the Bank as the amounts of the purchase price in each case. When the Debtor defaulted on the two notes, Bank sued. Debtor argued that the notes could not be enforced because they were not complete at the time he signed them and, alternatively, the Bank had orally agreed not to enforce the notes without first giving the debtor three months to attempt to refinance them upon any default.

1. Are the notes enforceable despite the fact they were filled in after the Debtor's signature? See UCC 3–115, 3–407.

2. Is parol evidence admissible to show the condition?

All but an insignificant number of "drafts" in circulation on a given day in the United States are checks. These drafts are checks because they are payable on demand and drawn on banks. However, in certain trades, for example payment of insurance proceeds and payment for cattle among cattle dealers, it is commonplace to use drafts that are not checks. Typically an insurance company will draw an instrument of the kind described in the case below on itself and "payable through" its bank. The buyer of cattle might draw a similar document.

By so drawing an instrument, the drawer has transformed his own bank from a payor to a collecting bank. This has serious consequences that we will see in the succeeding chapters. It means, among other things, that the bank should not automatically debit the drawer's account when the instrument is presented, but merely pass it on as though he were another bank. For those who do not understand the legal differences between such documents and checks, there are substantial treacheries. To cite but one example of an important difference, consider the case below under which notice of dishonor was apparently not passed back upstream for nearly 20 days after the draft had been issued. Such a delay on a check by a drawee would almost certainly impose liability on that drawee under Article 4.

GENERAL MOTORS ACCEPTANCE CORP. v. GENERAL ACCIDENT FIRE & LIFE ASSURANCE CORP.

New York Supreme Court, Appellate Division, Fourth Department, 1979.
67 A.D.2d 316, 415 N.Y.S.2d 536.

WITMER, J. On this appeal we examine the legal effect of a draft providing for its payment "through" a designated bank as distinguished from a draft or check drawn on such bank.

One Norek purchased an automobile financed by plaintiff, for which he gave plaintiff a documentary security instrument which was duly filed. He insured the automobile against theft through defendant insurance company. On December 16, 1977 he reported to defendant that the vehicle had been stolen and he filed a claim with defendant for the loss. On January 11, 1978 defendant undertook to honor its apparent obligation under its insurance policy by issuing and delivering to Norek a draft, drawn on itself and payable through the First Pennsylvania Bank, NA of Philadelphia, Pennsylvania, in the amount of $5878.63, payable to Norek, its insured, and also to plaintiff because of the latter's security interest in the insured vehicle. Norek took the draft to plaintiff who had him endorse it and pay the additional sum of $60.01 due on the secured loan, in extinguishment of plaintiff's security interest in the vehicle. Plaintiff thereupon released to Norek its lien on the vehicle and caused documents of title thereto to be delivered to him. Plaintiff also endorsed the draft and deposited it in its account in the Marine Midland Bank, which credited plaintiff's account therewith.

After delivering the draft to Norek defendant learned that the automobile had not been stolen and that Norek's claim for its loss had been fraudulent, and it stopped payment on the draft. Plaintiff was not notified that Norek's claim was fraudulent or of the stop-payment order until January 30, 1978 when its bank, Marine Midland, notified it that First Pennsylvania Bank had dishonored the draft upon its presentment for payment. At that time Marine Midland, in normal course, debited plaintiff's account with the amount of the dishonored draft; and plaintiff demanded of defendant payment of the draft. This action followed defendant's refusal of payment. Special Term found no question of fact in the case and granted summary judgment to plaintiff. We agree.

Because this draft was drawn by defendant on itself, *payable through* the First Pennsylvania Bank, defendant contends that the situation is the same as though it were only the drawee of the draft, and it is not liable thereon because it did not accept it (see UCC, § 3–409(1)) but, instead, stopped payment on the draft; and that Special Term erred in holding it liable thereon.

This draft was not a check because it was not drawn on the drawer's account in the First Pennsylvania Bank as drawee with direction to the bank to pay it (UCC, § 3–104). Instead, it was drawn by the drawer on itself as drawee, *payable through* the drawer's bank, First Pennsylvania. Such an instrument does not call upon that bank, or even authorize that bank, to pay the draft; it merely designates that bank as a collecting bank to present the draft to the drawer-drawee for payment (UCC, § 3–120; * * *). The statute (UCC, § 3–120) recognizes a common practice in certain businesses, including insurance companies. This method of operation permits the drawer of such drafts (who may have authorized many agents to draw them) to take a second look at them to be sure that they are properly drawn before finally approving payment. It also enables the drawer to conduct business in this manner without maintaining idle funds in drawee banks, awaiting presentment of the drafts (see, generally, Murray, Drafts "Payable Through" Banks, 77 Commercial Law Journal 389, Dec 1972).

The drawer of a draft on another party is only secondarily liable upon it (UCC, § 3–413(2); but see also UCC, § 3–502(1) and White and Summers on Uniform Commercial Code, § 13–9, pp. 412–413). He promises to pay if the drawee fails to carry out the order and the holder makes presentment and gives notice of dishonor pursuant to Uniform Commercial Code, § 3–501 (see also UCC, § 3–413(1)). Acceptance of the draft by the drawee (see UCC, § 3–410, Official Comment 4) does not affect the automatic liability of the drawer of the draft, but it interposes the primary independent liability thereon of the drawee (see White and Summers on Uniform Commercial Code, §§ 13–8 and 13–9, pp. 410–411). Upon issuance of the draft the drawer engages that upon its dishonor and appropriate notice and protest, he will pay it, unless he notes thereon that it is drawn without recourse (UCC, § 3–413(2)). The draft in this case was not drawn without recourse and, since there was no drawee (other than defendant itself) who accepted responsibility for it, defendant remains liable thereon (see Taboada v. Bank of Babylon, 95 Misc.2d 1000).

Defendant asserts that because plaintiff was a co-payee of the draft along with Norek, it was not a holder in due course and is subject to defendant's defense against Norek, to wit, that the draft was fraudulently obtained. It is clear that the draft was principally issued to Norek as the insured, and plaintiff's name was added as payee only to protect its duly filed security interest in the insured vehicle. Upon issuance of the draft defendant acknowledged Norek's claim that the vehicle had been stolen, and plaintiff was entitled to rely upon that representation and to accept the draft as a holder in due course in payment and release of its lien on the vehicle. Such action by plaintiff constituted the giving of value for the draft (UCC, §§ 3–302(1), 3–303(b) and (c); Saale v. Interstate Steel Co., 27 A.D.2d 1, 3–5, affd, 19 N.Y.2d 933). After defendant stopped payment on the draft it remained liable on it to plaintiff as a holder in due course (see Official Comment 8, under § 4–403 of Uniform Commercial Code, McKinney's Consolidated Laws of New York, Book 62½, Part 2).

* * *

The judgment should, therefore, be affirmed.

* * *

SIMONS, J.P., HANCOCK, CALLAHAN and MOULE, JJ., concur.

Note

Why would one choose to use a non-check draft as opposed to a check?

In the chapter on the holder in due course we will see the function of an indorsement as the sole method of passing title to certain negotiable instruments. Here we are concerned with the indorsement contract, not with the title passage function. Anyone who has dealt with checks knows that indorsements can be made with a variety of statements and conditions. Common limitations might be those that said "For Deposit Only" or "In Full Settlement of Payee's Claim"; there are countless other clauses that could be added to an indorsement. Here the student should pause a moment to examine the potential legal consequences of various conditions on the indorsement.

WHITE AND SUMMERS, THE UNIFORM COMMERCIAL CODE, 513–15 (2d ed. 1980).

QUALIFIED AND RESTRICTIVE INDORSEMENTS: SECTIONS 3–205, 3–206, 3–419

The clever indorser can subscribe his name under a variety of magic phrases. The Code itself specifies the legal effect of some of these phrases. Some phrases may constitute offers or contract terms of underlying agreements between the parties (for instance, "in full satisfaction of all claims"). Some are only friendly messages ("Kiss my foot"), and more than a few have clouded legal effect.

If an indorser adds the words "without recourse" to his indorsement and so makes a "qualified" indorsement, he does not make the contract embodied in 3–414. That is, he transfers title to the instrument, but he does not promise to pay should the instrument be dishonored upon presentment. (Despite the disclaiming words "without recourse" the indorser makes all the warranties embodied in 3–417 save one.) [90]

Section 3–205 classifies certain indorsements as restrictive:

> An indorsement is restrictive which either
>
> (a) is conditional; or
>
> (b) purports to prohibit further transfer of the instrument; or
>
> (c) includes the words "for collection", "for deposit", "pay any bank", or like terms signifying a purpose of deposit or collection; or
>
> (d) otherwise states that it is for the benefit or use of the indorser or of another person.

The most common restrictive indorsement is the "for deposit" type described in 3–205(c) and only that type will be considered here. Section 3–206(3) explains the effect of this type of indorsement:

> Except for an intermediary bank, any transferee under an indorsement which is conditional or includes the words "for collection", "for deposit", "pay any bank", or like terms (sub-paragraphs (a) and (c) of Section 3–205) must pay or apply any value given by him for or on the security of the instrument consistently with the indorsement and to the extent that he does so he becomes a holder for value. In addition such transferee is a holder in due course if he otherwise complies with the requirements of Section 3–302 on what constitutes a holder in due course.

To see the legal consequences of a "for deposit" indorsement assume that Tom Swift receives a $25 check from his grandparents on his twenty-first birthday. Tom indorses the check with the inscription "for deposit only, Tom Swift," and mails the check to his bank. However, the postman steals Tom's check, adds his name below Tom's indorsement and deposits the check in his account in First National Bank. First National forwards the check to Second National who transfers it to the payor bank, Third National, where the check is finally paid. What right of recovery does Tom have against the various banks? Second National is an intermediary bank [91] and under 3–206(3) has no obligation

90. The "without recourse" language dilutes his warranty in 3–417(2)(d) from one of warranting the absence of defense to warranting only "that he has no knowledge of such a defense". 3–417(3).

91. Section 4–105(c):

"Intermediary bank" means any bank to which an item is transferred in course of collection except the depositary or payor bank.

to respect a restrictive indorsement. It is equally clear under pre-Code law and 3–419 that Tom has a cause of action in conversion against First National, the depositary bank.[92] The only proper indorsement immediately following an indorsement "for deposit" should be that of a bank. What are Tom's rights against Third National, the payor bank? Although 3–206(3) does not expressly except a payor bank from liability for failure to pay consistently with "for deposit" indorsements, a payor who pays the transferee of a thief in such circumstances is not liable for conversion. Section 3–206(2) expressly states that a:

> payor bank which is not the depositary bank, is neither given notice nor otherwise affected by a restrictive indorsement of any person except the bank's immediate transferor or the person presenting for payment.

Might one argue that the draftsmen's failure to exclude payor banks in the specific provision dealing with "for deposit" indorsements, 3–206(3), creates an exception to the general rule stated in 3–206(2)? Any doubts about the effect of 3–206(2) are resolved by 3–419(4) which provides that nondepositary intermediary banks and payor banks are not liable in conversion for paying an instrument inconsistently with a restrictive indorsement made by one other than their immediate transferor.[93] Moreover, 4–205(2) is an almost verbatim restatement of 3–206(2).[94] Intermediary banks and payor banks which are not depositary banks are excepted from 3–206(3) on the ground that the large number of checks they handle makes it impossible for them to scrutinize all prior indorsements.[95]

The sole significant legal consequence, then, of placing "for deposit" above a blank indorsement is to prevent a depositary bank or nonbank taker from a thief from being a holder in due course. Since such depositary bank or other person lacks good title and is not a holder in due course, he is liable in conversion.

SECTION 6. NOTICE OF DISHONOR AND PRESENTMENT

To the extent that there are any significant lawyer questions on contract actions under UCC 3–413 and 3–414, they tend not to be about the contract itself, but about fulfillment of the conditions to the contract; namely, whether dishonor and notice of dishonor have occurred and whether they were timely. These rules are set out in a highly ritualistic and rigid format in part 5 of Article 3.

A quick examination of those rules will reveal a critical assumption that underlies almost all of them. This is the assumption that all of the parties to a check intend that it be passed rapidly from the drawer to final payment by the drawee and that word get back quickly to the earlier parties if there is no payment. The time limits are not only rigid but also short.

92. See Ch. 15 infra (3–419 and conversion liability).

93. Section 3–419(4) provides:

> An intermediary bank or payor bank which is not a depositary bank is not liable in conversion solely by reason of the fact that proceeds of an item indorsed restrictively (Sections 3–205 and 3–206) are not paid or applied consistently with the restrictive indorsement of an indorser other than its immediate transferor.

94. Section 4–205(2) states:

> An intermediary bank, or payor bank which is not a depositary bank is neither given notice nor otherwise affected by a restrictive indorsement of any person except the bank's immediate transferor.

Section 3–603(1) provides in certain cases that payment inconsistent with a restrictive indorsement does not discharge the party making such payment.

95. § 3–206, Comment 3.

Before one looks closely at the specific rules of Part 5, he should consider the effect of failing to comply with those rules. Note how different these are with respect to indorsers on the one hand, and drawers, makers and acceptors on the other.

Section 3–502. Unexcused Delay; Discharge

(1) Where without excuse any necessary presentment or notice of dishonor is delayed beyond the time when it is due

(a) any indorser is discharged; and

(b) any drawer or the acceptor of a draft payable at a bank or the maker of a note payable at a bank who because the drawee or payor bank becomes insolvent during the delay is deprived of funds maintained with the drawee or payor bank to cover the instrument may discharge his liability by written assignment to the holder of his rights against the drawee or payor bank in respect of such funds, but such drawer, acceptor or maker is not otherwise discharged.

(2) Where without excuse a necessary protest is delayed beyond the time when it is due any drawer or indorser is discharged.

One can readily grasp the policy reasons underlying the Code provisions which provide that noncompliance discharges the indorser but does not discharge the drawer (unless the drawee bank has failed). Consider, for example, the position of a drawer who has received goods, services, or cash in return for his promise to pay embodied in his check. After the check's transfer and before it is paid, the drawer is in a net positive position, he has received goods but he has not yet advanced cash from his account. Failure of the payee to make timely presentment injures the drawer only if in the interim the drawee has become insolvent and funds on deposit are lost before they could be applied against the instrument. There the drawer is and ought to be discharged, but if he is otherwise discharged he will get a windfall: he will get goods or services for which he pays nothing.

On the other hand, the ordinary indorser is one who gave up money, goods, or services when he received the instrument. Of course, he received an equivalent amount when he transferred the check but that leaves him in equilibrium with respect to the transaction. If he is excused by the holder's delay (or other noncompliance), he does not receive a windfall. Accordingly the Code requires the holder to act promptly if he hopes to hold the indorser liable.

In the usual check case the drawer's liability and that of the indorser arise only after two conditions occur: dishonor and notice of dishonor. Section 3–507(1) states that dishonor occurs when

(a) a necessary or optional presentment is duly made and due acceptance or payment is refused or cannot be obtained within the prescribed time or in case of bank collections the instrument is seasonably returned by the midnight deadline (Section 4–301); or

(b) presentment is excused and the instrument is not duly accepted or paid.

Upon dishonor the holder has the right to sue the drawer and any indorser, if he complies with the rules of notice of dishonor (discussed below). However, if presentment is not "duly made" there will be no dishonor, thus no recovery and delay may discharge the parties as indicated above under UCC 3–502.

Section 3–504(1) states that presentment is a demand for either payment or acceptance by or on behalf of the holder. Section 3–501 states when and what type of presentment is necessary to charge secondary parties, and section 3–503 governs the time within which presentment must be made. The form it must take is the subject of UCC 3–504(2). Section 3–505(1) allows the party to whom presentment is made to make certain inquiries regarding the presenter's identification and exhibition of the instrument. Note that these rights are exercised without dishonor and if the presenter fails to comply with UCC 3–505, refusal to pay on that ground is not dishonor.

Section 3–501 states the second condition necessary to charge indorsers and drawers, notice of dishonor. Section 3–508 gives the particulars of notice and in certain circumstances UCC 3–511 may excuse untimely notice or presentment.

In the typical check case, the depositary bank will make presentment by sending the check to the drawee bank, through a clearing house, or through the Federal Reserve System. If the depositary bank chooses to do so, it may mail the check directly to the drawee, or, in fact, take the check physically to drawee for payment. Presumably presentment requires the "presentment" of the physical check itself and thus may not be made by a telephonic demand for payment.

The time within which presentment is due is governed by UCC 3–503 and will vary with the type of instrument. If the instrument shows a date payable, presentment is due on that date. In the usual check case, a demand instrument, payment must be made before the passage of a "reasonable time," UCC 3–503(1)(e). In the case of a domestic check, reasonable time will be presumed to be no longer than 30 days with respect to a drawer or 7 days with respect to an indorser. Comments to UCC 3–503 explain the different time limits as follows:

> The time limit provided differs as to drawer and indorser. The drawer, who has himself issued the check and normally expects to have it paid and charged to his account is reasonably required to stand behind it for a longer period, especially in view of the protection now provided by Federal Deposit Insurance. The thirty days specified coincides with the time after which a purchaser has notice that a check has become stale (Section 3–304(3)(c)). The indorser, who has normally merely received the check and passed it on, and does not expect to have to pay it, is entitled to know more promptly whether it is to be dishonored, in order that he may have recourse against the person with whom he has dealt.

Remember that the time limits are only presumptive. They may be extended for any good reason. The 30 day presumption for drawers corresponds to the rule in UCC 3–304(3)(c) that a check is deemed stale and that one is on notice of that fact (and thus not a holder in due course) when the check has been outstanding for more than 30 days.

If all else fails, the party who has failed to comply with the specifics of part 5 of Article 3 can resort to UCC 3–511 on excuse. If a lawyer finds himself representing a client who has missed a step in the ritual outlined above, he should consult UCC 3–511. In many circumstances that section forgives the holder for its delay or failure to comply with the requirements of Part 5, Article 3. As a practical matter UCC 3–511 greatly reduces the harshness of the technical requirements of presentment and notice of dishonor. Not surprisingly it has received the attention of the courts in most of the cases decided under Part 5 of Article 3.

Section 3–511(2) specifies those circumstances which completely excuse presentment or notice of dishonor. The simplest case is one in which the indorser has expressly waived his right to have the instrument presented or to receive notice of dishonor. If the indorser has waived presentment or notice of dishonor, he will have no basis for complaint if there is some defect in the holder's performance of these duties. An express waiver may take any number of forms and might appear on the body of the instrument as well as on the back. Many standard form printed notes contain waivers of notice, protest, and the like. Note that UCC 3–511(5) provides that "[a] waiver of protest is also a waiver of presentment and of notice of dishonor even though protest is not required." An indorser can waive dishonor and notice by implication as well as by express language. Thus in Wiener v. Van Winkle, 273 Cal.App.2d 774, 78 Cal.Rptr. 761 (1969), defendant indorsers were found liable despite plaintiff's failure to make presentment because the indorsers impliedly waived presentment when they requested an extension of time for payment.

Section 3–511(2)(b) says that requirements of presentment and notice are excused when:

> such party has himself dishonored the instrument or has countermanded payment or otherwise has no reason to expect or right to require that the instrument be accepted or paid * * *.

When an indorser has played an active role in causing an instrument to be dishonored, there is little reason to force the holder to go through the formality of presentment and notice of dishonor. A problem arises when the indorser played no active role, but had access to facts from which he could infer that the instrument would not be paid. For instance, does the indorser's knowledge of the maker's insolvency excuse presentment and notice of dishonor? Both pre-Code cases and post-Code cases hold that mere knowledge of insolvency does not excuse presentment and notice of dishonor. For example, in Makel Textiles, Inc. v. Dolly Originals, Inc., 4 UCC Rep.Serv. 95 (N.Y.Sup.Ct.1967), the payee of a corporate promissory note sought payment from the corporation's president and another person, both of whom had signed as individual indorsers. The defendants maintained that they were not liable because plaintiff had not made presentment or given notice of dishonor. The New York Court responded to the corporation president's argument:

> By virtue of his active participation in the affairs of Dolly Originals, Inc., it is obvious that the defendant Nathan Goldberg well knew that the notes could not be and were not paid from corporate funds. Under these circumstances the obligation to serve Goldberg with notice of dishonor and non-payment must be deemed unnecessary, at least impliedly, within the meaning of the Uniform Commercial Code. Plaintiff's failure to present the notes for payment and give the said defendant notice of non-payment could not and did not injure nor prejudice his rights in any way. Formal notice of presentment and dishonor to Mr. Goldberg would be merely a useless gesture of advising him of a fact with which he was most familiar [citing UCC sections 3–511 and 3–507 and several pre-Code cases].

However the other indorser convinced the court that presentment and notice of dishonor were required to hold him liable. The court said:

> As to said defendant Kushner, the record is void of any testimony, or proof of notice of presentment and dishonor as required under the Uniform Commercial Code. Nor is there any evidence of any activity or participation in the affairs of the corporation so as to excuse presentment or notice of dishonor.

The court dismissed the suit against the indorser who did not participate in the corporate affairs and held the corporate president liable.

Under pre-Code law a party's insolvency or bankruptcy did not excuse presentment and notice of dishonor, but UCC 3–511(3) changes that rule:

> Presentment is also entirely excused when
>
> (a) the maker, acceptor or drawee of any instrument except a documentary draft is dead or in insolvency proceedings instituted after the issue of the instrument; or
>
> (b) acceptance or payment is refused but not for want of proper presentment.

Note that an insolvency proceeding, unlike the events described in UCC 3–511(2), does not excuse both presentment and notice of dishonor. Unless the indorser comes under the "or otherwise has no reason to expect" language of UCC 3–511(2)(b), the holder must meet the notice requirements in order to hold the indorser liable. This is understandable, for even if the party primarily liable files bankruptcy, it is not certain that he will lack sufficient assets to pay the instrument. Moreover, undue delay may make it impossible for the indorser to recover from the bankrupt or other prior parties.

The Code requires that the party making presentment or giving notice of dishonor only exercise "reasonable diligence." If by reasonable diligence the presentment or protest cannot be made or the notice given, then the party is entirely excused. Comment 5 to UCC 3–511 explains this section as follows (emphasis added):

> The excuse is established only by proof that reasonable diligence has been exercised without success, *or that reasonable diligence would in any case have been unsuccessful.*

The emphasized language of the comment considerably expands the scope of the subsection. The New York Law Revision Commission expressed approval of the broader version indicated by the comment, but we have found no cases on this point.

Problem 23–3

On January 1, 1988, Massena draws his check payable to the order of Soult for $20,000 to pay for goods received. Massena delivers the check to Soult on January 2, 1988, and Soult deposits the check in his bank account on February 25, 1988. Soult's bank, acting as Soult's agent, presents it for payment on February 26, 1988. The check bounces for want of sufficient funds in Massena's account and is returned to Soult's bank and ultimately to Soult. Soult is out of the country for a year and during that time the check gathers dust in his desk drawer. He has never given notice to Massena of the fact that the check was dishonored.

Upon his return Soult sues Massena on UCC 3–413. His complaint alleges the facts exactly as described above. Massena demurs on the grounds that the complaint:

1. on its face shows a delay in presentment; (see 3–503)

2. fails to allege the giving of notice of dishonor (see, UCC 3–508).

How do you respond to Soult's counsel? See UCC 3–502.

Problem 23–4

Assume in problem 23–3 (above) that Massena had drawn his check payable to the order of Soult for $20,000, that Soult had then passed the check to Desaix in payment of a $20,000 debt and had indorsed it "pay to the order of Desaix, Soult." Assume that the check was presented, that it bounced and was returned to Desaix. Because his bookkeeping system was not very efficient, Desaix failed to make a demand on Soult until 30 days had passed. Soult now denies any liability. If Desaix sues Soult on his indorsement contract, who wins? See UCC 3–502.

CLEMENTS v. CENTRAL BANK OF GEORGIA

Court of Appeals of Georgia 1980.
155 Ga.App. 27, 270 S.E.2d 194.

Before DEEN, C.J., BIRDSONG and SOGNIER, JJ.

BIRDSONG, J. Central Bank was granted a summary judgment against Clements, the indorser of a check which the bank accepted and presented unsuccessfully for collection to the drawee bank in Tennessee. Clements was denied summary judgment against the bank. Clements sought summary judgment on the grounds that the bank had not given Clements timely notice of dishonor and that he was therefore discharged from liability on the check, as a matter of law under Code § 109A–3–502.

The dishonored $30,000 check was drawn on a Tennessee bank by Ridley in Jasper, Tennessee, and made to Clements on September 19, 1978. Clements endorsed the check to Continental Equity Corporation, of which he was a director, on September 25; Continental endorsed the check and deposited it in Central Bank. On that same day, after accepting the check and crediting Continental's account, the bank received notice from the Federal Reserve System that another apparently unrelated check by Ridley was being returned for lack of funds. The vice-president of the bank decided to expedite collection of the $30,000 check endorsed by Clements, and sent it by mail directly to the Tennessee bank, with an attachment instructing: "Check for collection—Return if not paid in three days." On September 29, the bank's branch manager called Bumpus (the Tennessee bank cashier) who informed the bank manager that the check was no good, drawn against uncollected funds, and would more than likely never be paid. The appellee's bank manager gave Bumpus authority to continue holding the check; had he not done so, the Tennessee cashier would have returned the check to the appellee bank. Several other telephone calls concerning the check's collection status were exchanged between the two banks in the following month.

On or about October 24, 1978, the president of the appellee bank, Ham, telephoned Bumpus and Condra, the president of the Tennessee bank. Appellant contends, and Bumpus' and Condra's deposition reveals that both persons informed Ham, president of appellee bank, that the check was no good and would probably not be paid. On October 25, Ham drove to Tennessee and confronted Ridley in person; Ridley told Ham he could not pay the check until he received other money to cover it. Eventually during the meeting, Ham had Ridley execute two deeds of trust in favor of the appellee bank, securing payment of the check. Ham also went to the Tennessee bank offices to discuss the matter with Bumpus and Condra. While at the offices, Ham saw the check, but he did not take it back to Perry, Georgia, when he returned. On October 31, the appellee bank requested that the Tennessee bank return the check; appellee bank received the check on November 3, and on that date appellee bank sent written notice to the indorser Clements that the check was dishonored.

Appellant contends that from the inception, that is from September 25, when appellee's branch manager called Bumpus at the Tennessee bank to inquire about the check, Bumpus and Condra told appellee bank the check was no good. Appellee bank contends, to the contrary, that appellee's officers were informed that representations had been made that funds to cover the check were forthcoming.

The Tennessee bank cashier, Bumpus, by deposition stated that he repeatedly told appellee's officers the check was no good and was drawn on uncollected funds; in his implied opinion, the check was dishonored throughout that time. The Tennessee bank president, Condra, by deposition, stated that he never told appellee's officers the check was good, and that if he had not been advised otherwise by appellee bank, the Tennessee bank would have returned the check to appellee bank within three days. Held:

1. "Every indorser engages that upon *dishonor* and *any necessary notice of dishonor* and protest he will pay the instrument according to its tenor at the time of his indorsement to the holder." (Emphasis supplied.) Code Ann. § 109A–3–414. Appellee, the collecting bank, is at least a holder of the instrument endorsed by Clements and deposited in the appellee bank by Continental Equity. * * * "Unless excused * * * notice of any dishonor is necessary to charge any indorser," Code § 109A–3–501(2). "Any necessary notice must be given by a bank before its midnight deadline * * * after dishonor or receipt of notice of dishonor." Code § 109A–3–508(2). That is, "midnight on its next banking day following the banking day on which it receives the relevant item." Code § 109A–4–104(1)(h). "Where without excuse any necessary * * * notice of dishonor is delayed beyond the time when it is due * * * any indorser is discharged." Code § 109A–3–502(1). * * *

Appellee bank contends the notice of dishonor to Clements on November 3 was timely because it was given within the midnight deadline after appellee bank received the dishonored check from the Tennessee bank, also on November 3. We cannot agree.

Article 3 of the Commercial Code is quite clear that notice of dishonor of an instrument must be given in order to charge any secondary party with liability thereon, within specific time limits of dishonor (see Code §§ 109A–3–414; 109A–3–501(2); 192A–3–508(2); 109A–4–104(1)(h); 109A–3–502(1); Samples, supra). The principal question thus becomes, when was the check dishonored? Code § 109A–3–507 provides that "an instrument is dishonored when (a) * * * in [the] case of bank collections the instrument is *seasonably returned* by the midnight deadline (109A–4–301)." (Emphasis supplied.) Code § 109A–4–301 provides at subsection (3) that "*unless previous notice of dishonor has been sent* an item is dishonored at the time when for purposes of dishonor it is returned or notice sent in accordance with this section." In other words, insofar as the collecting bank is concerned, the check is dishonored when the bank receives it back as having been dishonored, *unless previous notice of dishonor has been sent* (Code § 109A–4–301(3)). Code § 109A–3–508(3), which is expressly applicable (see Code § 109A–4–104(3)) to the Article 4 provision just cited, provides that "notice [of dishonor] may be given in a reasonable manner [and] may be oral or written."

* * *

* * * The Tennessee bank, on September 29, refused to pay the check, and communicated that fact to the appellee. The Tennessee bank did not "accept" the check within the meaning of Code § 109A–3–410 and Code § 109A–3–413(1); if any claim lies against that bank in favor of the appellee bank for any equivocation by the Tennessee bank which might have caused confusion to the appellee, it is not pertinent here. The clear application of Code § 109A–3–506 to this case is that, assuming the check was presented on September 29, the check which was refused payment on September 29, was by law dishonored by the Tennessee bank by September 30, and that although the holder, appellee, could in good faith attempt to obtain acceptance for an additional business day, without dishonor and without discharging the indorser (see also Code § 109A–4–108), after October 1 the indorser was discharged unless necessary notice had been given. The appellee bank was without authority from the indorser (see Code § 109A–3–507(4)) to continue re-presenting the check, and therefore had no legal authority to do so without discharging the indorser in the meantime. (See Code § 109A–3–507(4)).

* * *

What we have distilled here is the specific codal direction of Article 3, with regard to liability of parties (part 4), notice of dishonor (part 5), and discharge (part 6). What is contained in Article 4 (bank deposits and collections), in particular Code § 109A–4–202, is subject to the provisions of Article 3 (Code § 109A–4–102(1)). If Code § 109A–4–202 conflicted with the provisions of Article 3, explained infra, Code § 109A–4–202 would prevail (see Code § 109A–4–102(1)). However, there is no conflict in this legal circumstance. Code § 109A–4–202(1)(b) provides "a collecting bank must use ordinary care in * * * sending notice of dishonor * * * after learning that the item has not been paid or accepted, as the case may be." Code § 109A–4–202(2) provides: "A collecting bank taking proper action before its midnight deadline following receipt of an item, notice or payment acts seasonably; taking proper action within a reasonably longer time may be seasonable but the bank has the burden of so establishing." Article 3 establishes as a matter of law when dishonor occurs, when notice of dishonor must be given to charge the indorser, and under what circumstances it may be excused so as to discharge the indorser. What is "ordinary care" (Code § 109A–4–202(1)), and what is "seasonable" (Code § 109A–4–202(2)) in that context is therefore established as a matter of law by Article 3. The "Draftsmen's Comment" to UCC § 4–202 explains the provision of Code § 109A–4–202(2) by saying, "In the case of time actions, action after the midnight deadline, *but sufficiently in advance of maturity for proper presentation,* is a clear example of a 'reasonably longer time' that is seasonable." This indicates that the leeway provided in Code § 109A–4–202 must still comport with what is required by law, and if it does not then the action is not seasonable under Code § 109A–4–202. Any other interpretation would render most of Article 3, dealing with the circumstances under which liability or discharge of an indorser is determined, utterly meaningless.

Moreover, within Article 4 itself the provisions of Code § 109A–4–108 control the availability of Code § 109A–4–202 in these circumstances. Code § 109A–4–108(1) provides: "Unless otherwise instructed, a collecting bank in a good faith effort to secure payment may * * * waive, modify or extend time limit imposed or permitted by this Act for a period *not in excess of an additional* *banking day without discharge of secondary parties* * * *" (Emphasis supplied.) It is clear that nothing in Article 4 is intended to deprive the indorser, who may ultimately be liable on an instrument if it is unpaid, of the protection of the timely notice of dishonor which is *necessary to charge* (Code § 109A–3–501(2)) him with liability thereon. This clear requirement places no undue burden on the bank, because if it does so, the notice is excused (see Code §§ 109A–3–502, 3–511); indeed in its certainty, it offers protection to both parties.

It was error to grant summary judgment to appellee bank, and error to deny it to Clements on the issue of timely notice of dishonor, subject to the determination of whether notice was excused.

2. Appellee urges that notice of dishonor to Clements was entirely excused under Code § 109A–3–511(2) because Clements had no reason to expect nor right to require that the instrument be accepted or paid. The record shows that both Ridley, the maker, and Clements, the indorser, were members of the board of directors of Continental Equity. According to Ridley, the $30,000 check was given to Clements for Continental Equity as a loan of "front money" to enable Continental to obtain a loan of $650,000 from Calvin Crown in New York. When Ridley first met Crown, Crown was president of the First Bank of Tehran; then president of the First Bank of London; and the third time Ridley went to New York to see Crown, Crown had "gold mining or something" on his office door. The cashier's check[s] which Ridley received from Crown, which were to cover the $30,000 check, were somehow no good. The financial arrangements by which this check was exchanged were obviously complicated and the evidence shows neither that Clements knew the check would not be paid, nor that he "had no inkling" it would not be paid, beyond any issue of material fact. Neither party is entitled to summary judgment on the issue of excused notice under Code § 109A–3–511(2), which remains a question of fact for the jury.

Judgment reversed. DEEN, C.J., and SOGNIER, J., concur.

ON MOTION FOR REHEARING

BIRDSONG, J. On motion for rehearing, the bank argues for the first time the provision at Code Ann. § 109A–4–301(3), that "unless previous notice of dishonor has been *sent* an item is dishonored * * * when * * * it is returned or notice sent in accordance with this section" (emphasis supplied). Bank cites Code Ann. § 109A–1–201(38) as defining "send" to mean deposit in the mail; therefore, oral notice of dishonor from the Tennessee bank to the appellee bank would not trigger the point of dishonor.

The Georgia Commercial Code, at Code Ann. § 109A–3–508(3) specifically provides that notice of dishonor may be given in any reasonable manner, and "may be oral or written." It is neither logical nor credible that the legislature meant to defuse this provision, and to render meaningless the other Article 3 and 4 provisions dealing with discharge of indorser's liability within specific time limits of presentment and nonacceptance (see Code Ann. § 109A–3–506, and this case), by providing that dishonor does not occur until written notice of it is "sent." The terms of Code Ann. § 109A–1–201(38) do not preclude the transmission of oral notice, "if it is received within the time at which it would have arrived if properly sent." Nevertheless, the bank would not prevail, even if we adopted its position that since there was no written notice of dishonor "sent," under Code Ann. § 109A–4–301(3) dishonor should have occurred when the item was returned on November 3. If the item was not returned until November 3, it was because of the appellee bank's entreaty to the Tennessee bank to keep holding it for acceptance. It is undisputed that the Tennessee bank would have returned it within three days of presentment if the appellee bank had not requested otherwise. * * *

In this case, we emphasized that the indisputable fact remains that on September 29, 1978, the appellee bank first received notice of dishonor but the indorser was not notified of this dishonor as required by Code Ann. § 109A–3–508. There was no term in the indorsement on this item allowing a stated time for re-presentment as provided for in Code Ann. § 109A–3–507(4), and the appellee bank had no authority to re-present it without discharging the indorser. The appellee bank in instructing the Tennessee bank to hold the check, and in re-presenting it at a later date, did so at its own peril.

The bank by delaying the giving of notice of dishonor until November 3, 1978, did not give notice before its midnight deadline after receiving notice itself as required by law, and thereby prohibited the appellant from taking whatever action he might deem best to protect himself. The failure to give requisite notice results in the discharge of the indorser, Code Ann. § 109A–3–502(1)(a). There still remains the question of fact as to whether Clements knew or had reason to know that the check ultimately would be dishonored and if so, notice of dishonor would be excused.

Motion for rehearing denied.

Notes

1. The check was sent to the Tennessee Bank with the notation "Check for collection—return if not paid within three days." As we will learn below, the drawee will have only until midnight of the next banking day after receipt to pay a check. If it holds beyond that deadline, typically, it has personal liability on the check. Would the notation sent to the Tennessee Bank in this case have given the bank additional time?

2. Clements indorsed the check to "Continental Equity Corporation." Continental Equity deposited it in its account in Central Bank. Central Bank might have asserted the right to charge back under UCC 4–212. Would it have had a right to do so? Is the case correctly decided or should there be a different rule for indorsers such as Clements who appear to be "in bed with their drawers"?

3. Assume that you represent Central Bank and they do not wish the events described in the case to occur again. What procedures do you suggest to protect them? How should they proceed in a case in which their customer wishes the check to be presented several times or to remain with the payor in the hope that it will be paid and stays there for a period of days?

Problem 23–5

Assume that depositary bank receives oral notice on August 1 that a check was being returned by the clearing house. It failed to receive the check until August 13 and did not notify its indorsers until August 14. The indorsers now argue that they were discharged under UCC 3–501, 3–502, and 3–508. (1) Are they correct, or is the bank's notice on the 14th adequate? (2) Assume that Bank loses its argument. If you were the lawyer for bank, how would you advise them to behave in the future?

Note: The Traveler's Check

One further type of check should be mentioned, the so-called "traveler's check." Very few cases involving dishonor of traveler's checks reach the courts because the issuing companies usually honor the checks even when they feel that they have no legal obligation to do so. The courts which have faced the issue have not produced any consistent results. Thus, traveler's checks have been characterized as "money," Ashford v. Thos. Cook and Sons (Bankers) Ltd., 52 Hawaii 113, 471 P.2d 530 (1970); "certificates of deposit," Williams v. Clark, 202 Misc. 1022, 112 N.Y.S.2d 26 (Sup.Ct. Broome Cty.1952) (but see UCC 3–104(2)); "negotiable instruments," Gray v. American Express Co., 34 N.C.App. 714, 239 S.E.2d 621 (1977); a "security," Peoples Sav. Bank v. American Sur. Co., 15 F.Supp. 911 (W.D.Mich.1936) (but see UCC 8–102); and a "cashier's check," Mellon Nat'l Bank v. Citizens Bank & Trust Co. of Camden, Arkansas, 88 F.2d 128 (8th Cir.1937), cert. denied, 302 U.S. 702, 58 S.Ct. 21, 82 L.Ed. 542 (1937).

The drafters of the Code clearly wished to include traveler's checks within the regulation of Article 3. See UCC 3–104, comment 4. However, they did not indicate how traveler's checks would be classified under UCC 3–104(2). Thus, many questions remain unanswered, such as who is the payee on such an instrument? Is it the person who signs and countersigns the traveler's check or is it the person or entity named in the space following the order or promise to pay? Is a traveler's check without either a signature or countersignature a bearer instrument or is it merely incomplete? See UCC 3–111, 3–115. Similarly, is a signed and countersigned traveler's check in bearer form or is it incomplete when the space following the order or promise to pay is left blank? See UCC 3–111, 3–115, 3–204, Gray v. American Express Co., supra. Is a traveler's check even a negotiable instrument since the issuer's obligation to pay is conditioned upon a countersignature which is identical to the original signature? See UCC 3–104(1)(b), 3–105; Ellinger *Traveller's Cheques and the Law,* 19 U. Toronto L.J. 132, 137–140 (1969). For suggested answers see Hawkland, *American Traveler's Checks,* 84 Banking L.J. 377 (1967).

Most of the problems associated with the characterization of traveler's checks arise from their theft. They can be stolen out of the hands of the issuer or of a bank or other agent of the issuer before they are countersigned, or they can be stolen from the hands of the customer after he has countersigned them. In either case, traveler's checks eventually wind up in the hands of someone who pays value in good faith for them and asserts a right to payment against the issuer. The legal issue in these cases is whether such a right exists or whether the issuer may refuse to pay. *Ashford v. Thomas Cook and Sons,* cited above, illustrates how one court handled that problem by analogizing the traveler's check to money. There the plaintiff had purchased his traveler's checks in Tahiti from some gentlemen who floated up alongside the plaintiff's boat. Earlier that day plaintiff had inquired at a local bank about buying some American currency and had been told that that would be impossible. The floating gentlemen told the plaintiff that they were bank employees and that, although he would not be able to buy currency, he could buy traveler's checks. Presumably much bedazzled by the vagaries of Tahitian banking law and the boat-to-boat service he was receiving, the plaintiff purchased checks having a face value of $8300. Of course it turned out that the floating gentlemen had stolen these very liquid assets before the checks had been signed or countersigned. In this instance the issuer declined to honor the checks and the plaintiff brought suit to recover on them. The court held that it should look to the manner in which traveler's checks were accepted by the public in order to determine their legal status. It explicitly rejected attempting to fit the checks within the provisions of either the Negotiable Instruments Law (N.I.L.) or the UCC. It concluded that the public viewed such checks as substitutes for money and that, therefore, they were money. Thus, it held that the plaintiff should prevail, since "when one in good faith acquires possession of stolen money for valuable consideration, his title is superior to that of the true owner." 471 P.2d at 534. The court went on to uphold the jury's finding that the plaintiff was a bona fide purchaser of the checks.

The *Ashford* case was tried under the N.I.L. However, the court there refused to be bound by any type of statutory scheme, including that of the Code. Such a result can be justified, although it hardly seems expedient to do so. The Code states that one of its underlying purposes and policies is "to permit the continued expansion of commercial practices through custom, usage and agreement of parties." UCC 1–102(2)(b). In addition the Code stipulates that "[u]nless displaced by the particular provisions of this act, the principles of law and equity, including the law merchant * * * shall supplement its provisions." UCC 1–103; see also UCC 1–205(2) and (5). It has been suggested that the treatment of traveler's checks as money is not displaced by any particular provision in the Code and that therefore this result is justified as in accord with current trade usages or customs. See Hawkland, supra at 402–403; Ashford v. Thos. Cook and Son (Bankers) Ltd., supra; Note, *The Legal Nature of Travelers' Checks,* 7 Willamette L.J. 186 (1971).

Of course the analogy to money is hardly perfect. An important feature of traveler's checks is the willingness of the issuer to issue new ones without additional payment to the true owner when his checks are lost or stolen. As Karl Malden makes perfectly clear, that is not an obligation that the United States Treasury undertakes for lost cash. Thus traveler's checks are not identical to money. Professor Hawkland argues that a traveler's check should be considered as a cashier's check. He would characterize the issuer as both the drawer and the drawee and the purchaser as the payee. The customer's countersignature is in effect an indorsement of the instrument. Thus, his original signature represents the designation of the payee made as authorized by the issuer. See UCC 3–115(1). Under this theory, before the purchaser signs the check it should be treated as a blank cashier's check. After the traveler's check is signed it becomes an order instrument, payable after it is countersigned and delivered. See UCC 3–202(1). Hawkland suggests that, after the traveler's check is both signed and countersigned, it is bearer paper since it has been indorsed in blank. When the name of the new payee is filled in, the instrument once again becomes order paper, since there is now a special indorsement by the purchaser. See Hawkland, supra at 391–398, 401, 404, 405–406, 410.

Several consequences arise out of a decision to treat traveler's checks as cashier's checks. The most dramatic of these is that neither the purchaser nor the issuer has the right to stop payment on such checks. Note, *Ability to Prevent Payment on Various Forms of Checks,* 11 Ind.L.Rev. 579, 584–585 (1978); White and Summers, pp. 680–683. One pre-Code case indicated in dicta that this result was correct with respect to traveler's checks. See Rose Check Cash. Serv. v. Chemical Bank N.Y. Trust Co., 43 Misc.2d 679, 252 N.Y.S.2d 100, 102 (App.Term 1964). Under the Code the results derived from this approach closely approximate the manner in which traveler's checks are actually treated by the issuing companies. However, where the purchaser's countersignature is forged the Code analogy to a forged indorsement holds that the issuer need not honor the checks, while currently issuers will usually honor them. Hawkland recommends that this trade usage control in this area. See Hawkland, supra at 410–411.

Unfortunately no case has yet applied the cashier's check theory under the Code. The closest that any court has come is Gray v. American Express Co., 34 N.C.App. 714, 239 S.E.2d 621 (1977). There the plaintiff, a wholesale grocer, received some traveler's checks with a similar signature and countersignature. However, the person countersigning the checks had not filled in either the date or the name of the new payee. The plaintiff attempted to cash the checks. The defendant dishonored them (perhaps because the plaintiff said that he had seen the thief both *sign* and countersign the checks). The court first held that the checks were negotiable instruments under the Code, but did not go any farther in categorizing them. Instead, it pointed out that the name of the payee was an essential element in any negotiable instrument. Since the traveler's checks as indorsed did not contain the name of the new payee, they were incomplete as they stood and, thus were unenforceable since it was unclear if they were payable to order or bearer. See UCC 3–104(1), 3–112. The court did say that the grocer could have completed the checks by inserting his name as payee since the thief had impliedly authorized him to do so, but it held that the grocer's failure to do so was fatal to his cause of action. The *Gray* case does little to advance our knowledge of the legal status of traveler's checks.

SECTION 7. LIABILITIES AND RIGHTS OF ACCOMMODATION PARTIES

"Accommodation party", "surety", "guarantor"—every law student has seen passing reference to these terms in the cases. We suspect that for most students these terms signify a forbidding and mysterious body of law, and one not systematically covered by any law school course at that. The materials that follow are designed to serve as an introduction to suretyship law via several sections of Article 3 on accommodation parties.

We turn first to the Article 3 definitions of "surety", "accommodation party", and "guarantor". Both the student and the lawyer may ascribe far too much legal significance to the differences among those words; for many purposes the words are interchangeable. Section 3–415(1) defines an accommodation party as "one who signs an instrument in any capacity for the purpose of lending his name to another party to it". A guarantor, on the other hand, is one who signs an instrument and adds words such as "collection guaranteed" or "payment guaranteed" to his signature. According to UCC 3–416 the presence of these additional words may limit his liability considerably (as by making him liable only after a judgment is procured against another party) or it may expand his liability (as by making him liable even though he does not get notice of dishonor). Thus a guarantor may for our purposes be considered an accommodation party who has added some words to his name and has thereby altered his "contract". Both the guarantor and the accommodation party are "sureties". Comment 1 to 3–415 puts it as follows:

> Subsection (1) recognizes that an accommodation party is always a surety (which includes a guarantor), and it is his only distinguishing feature. He differs from other sureties only in that his liability is on the instrument and he is a surety for another party to it. * * *

In sum it is probably best for the student to go directly to UCC 3–415(2)–(5), 3–416 and 3–606 and to waste very little initial effort in attempting to determine whether the party with whom she is dealing is a garden variety surety, an accommodation party or a guarantor.

Now we will identify all the actors in the typical suretyship drama. First, there is the principal debtor, i.e., the poor bloke whose promise is not enough alone to get him what he wants. The son who wants to buy a souped-up automobile is a classic example. Secondly, of course is the surety, in our case the accommodation party. This may be a father who co-signs the note with his son so that he can buy the souped-up automobile. Finally, there is the creditor. In our example, this will be the car seller or the finance company, one of whom is the holder of the note and the beneficiary of the accommodation party's promise to pay.

With our imaginary note transaction in mind, we will try to answer four questions: (1) What is the accommodation party's basic liability to the creditor-holder? (2) What defenses are available to the accommodation party against the creditor-holder? (a) Can he assert the defenses of the principal debtor? (b) Does he have some special defenses because of his suretyship status? (UCC 3–606). (3) How does one prove surety or accommodation party status? (4) What rights does the accommodation party have to go against the principal debtor and vice versa? (If son does not pay for the car, can father sue son?)

A. *The Accommodation Party's Basic Liability*

Section 3–415(2) states the accommodation party's liability as follows:

> (2) When the instrument has been taken for value before it is due the accommodation party is liable in the capacity in which he has signed even though the taker knows of the accommodation.

In our car-purchase transaction father might accommodate son in one of two ways. First, he might simply sign the note in the bottom right-hand corner as a *co-maker.* Second he might sign the reverse side as an *indorser.* According to UCC 3–415(2) he will have the liability of a maker (i.e., the capacity in which he signs) in the first case, and that of an indorser in the second. Thus if father signs as a maker, finance company need only to present the note to him for payment and it can insist upon his living up to his maker's contract under UCC 3–413. If he had signed as an indorser, the holder would first have to present the note to the son, give notice of dishonor and then assert liability against the father under UCC 3–414. In the latter case father may hunt for a defense based upon delay, or on failure to give notice, or non-presentment under Part 5 of Article 3, and if the father finds such a defense he may be discharged. If the father has added the words "payment guaranteed" or "collection guaranteed" or "equivalent words" to his signature, he will have thereby altered his liability as provided in UCC 3–416:

> (1) "Payment guaranteed" or equivalent words added to a signature mean that the signer engages that if the instrument is not paid when due he will pay it according to its tenor without resort by the holder to any other party.
>
> (2) "Collection guaranteed" or equivalent words added to a signature mean that the signer engages that if the instrument is not paid when due he will pay it according to its tenor, but only after the holder has reduced his claim against the maker or acceptor to judgment and execution has been returned unsatisfied, or after the maker or acceptor has become insolvent or it is otherwise apparent that it is useless to proceed against him.
>
> (3) Words of guaranty which do not otherwise specify guarantee payment.

Note that "collection guaranteed" considerably restricts the liability of the guarantor, but that "payment guaranteed", if anything, expands it, for under subsection (5) of UCC 3–416 the words of guaranty free the holder from an obligation to make presentment, to give notice of dishonor or to protest.

Problem 23–6

Son wishes to purchase an automobile and father agrees to sign the paper with him. Father signs and son defaults. After son has been in default on his 20th payment for three months, finance company asks father to pay. Does father have a liability in each of the following cases?

1. Assume father signed as co-maker.
2. Assume father signed as indorser with the words "collection guaranteed".

3. Assume father signed on the reverse side with the words "payment assured".

B. The Two Kinds of Defenses Available to the Accommodation Party

Here we consider two kinds of defenses that the accommodation party might wish to assert. Assume in our example that the car which the salesman delivered to son was not merchantable, and that the son would accordingly have had a right to reject it or at minimum the right to set off $1,000 as damages because the car was not merchantable. (See UCC 2–314 and 2–717). Assume that son therefore refuses to pay although he does not make an effective rejection under UCC 2–602. If the car dealer then sues father, may the father raise his son's defenses? Put that simply, the answer would seem to be obviously yes. (But what code sections would you cite?) However, consider the case in which the son takes bankruptcy and so procures a complete defense to car dealer's complaints against him, namely a discharge in bankruptcy. May the father also assert this defense? Is it not equally obvious that the answer here is no; that this is the very eventuality which caused the car dealer to have the father sign? We are thus confronted with the necessity (which did not begin with the Code and will not end with it) of deciding which of the *defenses of the principal debtor* the accommodation party may assert and which he may not assert.

A second less important but more complicated class of defenses that may be available to the father in our example are the so-called suretyship defenses. These defenses are embodied in UCC 3–606 and would let father off the hook in certain circumstances if dealer and son play hanky-panky with one another by altering the terms of the underlying obligation. Thus if car dealer extended the time for payment to son without reserving his rights against father and without telling father, father would be discharged under UCC 3–606 in most circumstances. The justification for such discharge has seemed elusive and unpersuasive to at least one of your editors.

1. Right of Accommodation Party to Assert the Principal's Defenses

An accommodation party's failure to receive dollars in his pocket from the creditor accommodated is not a defense. Time and again sureties respond to a holder's suit by arguing "I am a surety and did not receive consideration *from you* for my contract". This is a losing argument and should be distinguished from the argument "I am a surety and *my principal* did not receive any consideration". Regardless of whether the accommodation party signs gratuitously or receives compensation, his obligation is supported by the consideration which moves from the creditor to the principal debtor (see Comment 2 to UCC 3–415).

There are certain of the principal's defenses which the surety has been traditionally entitled to raise. These include failure of consideration, fraud, and other contract defenses which would totally free the principal debtor from his obligation on the underlying contract. Since the accommodation party is nothing more than a backup for the principal obligor, it is only fair that he not incur liability to the creditor beyond that of the principal obligor.

But there are other defenses which common sense and common business understanding tell us the accommodation party cannot and should not be permitted to raise. These include the defenses of bankruptcy and incapacity because of infancy. Since the implicit, if not explicit, understanding of the parties was that the accommodation party's signature was for the very purpose of protecting against the debtor's bankruptcy or refusal to pay because of his infancy, it is only appropriate to deny the accommodation party those defenses. Except for an occasional case in which an infant principal obligor has returned the goods before reaching majority, courts have routinely denied the defenses of bankruptcy and infant incapacity to the principal obligor.

Under pre-Code law courts differed over the right of the surety to assert those defenses of the principal obligor which were in the nature of set-offs or counterclaims. Assume for example that son finds the car to be defective, but nevertheless accepts it and repairs it thereby acquiring a set-off of $200.00 for breach of warranty under UCC 2–714 and 2–717. Under the pre-Code law some courts allowed the surety to assert that defense; others did not. We find nothing in the Code that addresses this issue. We would allow the surety to assert those defenses.

Because we are interested only in the legal position of those sureties who are also accommodation parties on negotiable instruments, two additional complications arise. First, what is the effect of having a holder in due course sue an accommodation party? Second, what of the Code policy expressed in UCC 3–306(d) that one party may not raise another's defense (so called *jus tertii*)? If the holder who sues the accommodation party is a holder in due course, we believe the accommodation party would have no greater right to raise defenses than would the principal obligor. If, therefore, the defense which the accommodation party wishes to assert is a personal defense, he may not assert it against the holder in due course. If, on the other hand, the defense is one of the real defenses listed in UCC 3–305(2), the accommodation party should be permitted to raise it.

But what if the plaintiff-holder (whether or not a holder in due course) points to the last sentence in UCC 3–306(d) and argues that the accommodation party cannot raise *any* of the defenses of the party accommodated? That sentence reads as follows:

> * * * The claim of any third person to the instrument is not otherwise available as a defense to any party liable thereon unless the third person himself defends the action for such party.

Assuming the principal obligor is out of the picture and not capable of being joined, does the quoted sentence reverse all the well-settled doctrines which authorized the surety to raise his principal's defenses? A crude but appealing answer is simply to say the draftsmen did not contemplate accommodation parties when they drafted UCC 3–306(d) and therefore UCC 1–103 and the common law is applicable. Professor Peters has argued that the accommodation party is in fact asserting his own defense and not that of the principal obligor. See Peters, *Suretyship Under Article 3 of the Uniform Commercial Code,* 77 Yale L.J. 833 (1968). Under this theory the accommodation party would argue that his suretyship obligation was based on an implied condition precedent that the creditor will not act in a manner which substantially increased the surety's risk. And so the argument goes—the creditor's failure to perform increases the accommodation party's risk and gives him his own personal defense. We find no ready answer. We can only hope that courts presented with this issue will follow the traditional doctrine and allow the surety to assert his principal's defenses.

Problem 23–7

Father co-signs note for son for the purchase of a new 1976 model X Ford. Because the Ford burns excessive oil, lacks the appropriate compression in two cylinders and apparently needs a major overhaul after only 500 miles of driving, son stops paying. Ford Dealer, holder of the note, sues father. Assume that son has returned the car to dealer and has asked to get his money back.

1. Father files a counter-claim asserting the warranty defense of son and stating that he is free of any liability because of the breach of warranty by the seller. Ford moves for a summary judgment and argues that the counter-claim is not meritorious and in any event not available to an accommodation party. You are the judge. How do you rule?

2. If the facts are changed slightly so that the plaintiff is not the Ford Dealer but rather First National Bank who claims to be a holder in due course, what outcome?

2. *Defenses Dependent Upon Accommodation Character, UCC 3–606*

Of all the things that students are made to swallow in law school and of all the arguments put forward in classrooms that run contrary to common sense, we suspect that the so-called suretyship defenses rank high. To over-simplify somewhat, the principle of UCC 3–606 is that any substantial modification of the underlying agreement between the creditor and the principal obligor discharges the surety. Thus if the creditor and the principal obligor agree to extend payment of a note from 6 months to a year and the creditor fails explicitly to reserve his rights against the surety, the surety is discharged. So put and so applied we believe the rule makes little sense. However there are circumstances in which the rule makes sense. To put the problem in perspective, consider the following example: Augereau, Inc. is in the rug making business and is expanding its facilities. To finance the expansion it borrows $100,000.00 from bank, giving bank a security interest in the existing plant machinery and getting Lannes, a stock-holder, to co-sign the note. If the bank should later agree to discharge Augereau and to rely exclusively on the promise of Lannes (who had himself expected only to be a backup), it would seem to be an appropriate "punishment" for such underhanded dealing to discharge Lannes. Likewise if the bank failed to perfect its security interest in the machinery, and had to share as a general creditor in the bankruptcy of Augereau, getting only $20,000 instead of the $100,000 it would have received if it had perfected, one can see that Lannes has a legitimate complaint and should be discharged. But it is much less clear that Lannes should be discharged if the bank merely in good faith extended the time for Augereau Inc. to pay. The rationale that supports discharge in such a case is that Lannes's obligation has been increased without his agreement. That is, Lannes arguably calculated the probability that Augereau Inc. would be able to carry on for one year but not for two years and stood ready to pay up if Augereau failed within one year, but did not stand ready to bear a two year risk. Likewise, so the argument goes, Lannes would have had a right of subrogation (to the creditor's claim against the debtor) at the end of one year if there had been no extension, and because of the extension this right was denied him. In actual fact we suspect that the Lanneses of this world usually jump for joy when the creditor accommodated agrees to extend time for payment. In the first place such accommodation parties probably stand to benefit if there is any hope that the principal debtor can pay the obligation. In the second place they commonly have some other connection with the transaction. In our hypothetical case Lannes is not just a guarantor, he is also a stockholder of Augereau. Thus he stands to lose if Augereau goes bankrupt. Perhaps in recognition of the dubiousness of these rules the draftsmen of the Code have authorized creditors and principal obligors to hold accommodation parties by expressly reserving rights against them.

Section 3–606 is applicable not only to accommodation parties of the kind described in UCC 3–415, but also to other sureties such as that class of indorsers who are not technically accommodation parties (because they did not explicitly lend their names to anyone) for it operates to discharge anyone who has "a right of recourse" against the principal obligor (e.g., indorser against maker). Section 3–606(1) reads as follows:

> (1) The holder discharges any party to the instrument to the extent that without such party's consent the holder
>
> (a) without express reservation of rights releases or agrees not to sue any person against whom the party has to the knowledge of the holder a right of recourse or agrees to suspend the right to enforce against such person the instrument or collateral or otherwise discharges such person, except that failure or delay in effecting any required presentment, protest or notice of dishonor with respect to any such person does not discharge any party as to whom presentment, protest or notice of dishonor is effective or unnecessary; or
>
> (b) unjustifiably impairs any collateral for the instrument given by or on behalf of the party or any person against whom he has a right of recourse.

Subsection 3–606(1)(a) enumerates the various changes in the legal relationship between debtor and creditor that discharge the accommodation party. When without his consent the holder, with knowledge of the surety's right of recourse, " * * * releases or agrees not to sue * * * or agrees to suspend the right to enforce * * * the instrument or collateral * * * or otherwise discharges * * * " the principal debtor, the surety is discharged. Although the subsection does not expressly state that granting an extension will discharge the surety, the draftsmen certainly intended that result. The surety can justifiably claim discharge under UCC 3–606 when without his consent and without an "express reservation of rights" a creditor and debtor enter into a binding agreement to extend time for payment. Hence, in the above hypothetical case, if the bank gives Augereau his requested extension, Lannes will be discharged from liability on the note.

Under UCC 3–606(1)(b) the surety is discharged when without his consent the creditor "unjustifiably impairs any collateral for the instrument". Although UCC 3–606(1)(b) does not contain an explicit requirement that the holder have *knowledge* of the surety's existence (as does UCC 3–606(1)(a)), the adverb "unjustifiably" and the standard of care (reasonableness) indicate that knowledge is required. Often the creditor on a guaranteed obligation will have two sources of back-up for the debtor's promise; the surety's promise and a security interest in the debtor's collateral. If the creditor handles the collateral carelessly so that its value is diminished or acts in a way which makes the collateral unavailable to the surety, the surety may claim discharge under UCC 3–606(1)(b). The creditor's conduct with respect to the collateral is measured by the standard of UCC 9–207, i.e., reasonable care (see Comment 5 to UCC 3–606). Thus in our earlier hypothetical the Bank's failure to perfect its security interest in the plant machinery and its consequential loss of priority to the trustee would discharge Lannes' liability on the note.

The creditor can forestall a surety's claims of discharge under UCC 3–606 in either of two ways. First he may procure the surety's express or implied consent to the modification in the relationship with the debtor. Second by adding a sentence to the modification agreement to "expressly reserve" his rights against the surety, he bars discharge.

According to Comment 2 to UCC 3–606 the consent may take many forms and come at any time. That comment reads as follows:

> Consent may be given in advance, and is commonly incorporated in the instrument; or it may be given afterward. It requires no consideration, and operates as a waiver of the consenting party's right to claim his own discharge.

An express statement of consent incorporated in the instrument is effective against the surety, but under UCC 3–118(f) a consent is presumed to be for "a single extension for not longer than the original period, (unless 'otherwise specified')". A sample consent clause found in an instrument reads as follows:

> Extension of the time of payment of all or any part of the amount owing here or any variation, modification, or waiver of any term or condition here of at any time or times shall not affect the liability of any party hereto or co-maker, indorser, guarantor, or surety hereof, it being the intent of all parties to this note that they shall continue jointly and severally absolutely liable for the payment of the aforesaid indebtedness until the same is actually paid in full.

A surety's consent may also take the form of conduct which shows assent to the creditor's action.

If the creditor wishes to release the debtor or grant him an extension of time to make payment, but cannot obtain the surety's consent to such an action, he can preserve his rights against the surety by expressly reserving them (except for his duties under UCC 3–606(1)(b)). Section 3–606(2) reads as follows:

> (2) By express reservation of rights against a party with a right of recourse the holder preserves
>
> (a) all his rights against such party as of the time when the instrument was originally due; and
>
> (b) the right of the party to pay the instrument as of that time; and
>
> (c) all rights of such party to recourse against others.

One might justify the reservation rule on the ground that the surety suffers no injury from the creditor's action because the surety can immediately pay the instrument and exercise his right of recourse against the principal obligor. The problem with this rationale is that the surety will not be able to exercise this option if he does not know that the creditor has released or granted the debtor an extension of time for payment, and UCC 3–606 does not require the creditor to notify the surety of the modification.

Note: A Preliminary Question: Establishing Suretyship Status, 3–415, 3–415(3), (4) Through 3–416.

A necessary condition for one's discharge under any of the suretyship defenses is a finding that one is an accommodation party. Since it will often be in the interest of a person who was never intended to be an accommodation party to argue that he is, and because the labels and other symbolic distinctions between one who has signed as an accommodation party and one who has not are often unclear or entirely missing, the first step in a typical suretyship case is to answer the question: Is this person truly a surety or is he one of the principal obligors. One can divide these questions generally into three groups:

(1) What symbols on the instrument are sufficient to put one on notice that a signer is an accommodation party?

(2) Assuming that the symbols are insufficient to put one on notice, against what kinds of plaintiffs may a defendant prove his suretyship status by parol evidence and so acquire the benefit of the suretyship defenses?

(3) What parol evidence is sufficient to establish suretyship status?

The Code does not answer the first question explicitly. As one might suspect however the position of the surety's signature on the instrument and the words he adds to his signature will be the strongest indicators of his status. The surety who accommodates another party by signing as an indorser will usually disclose his surety status by the relative position of his name on the instrument. Section 3–415(4) of the Code says:

> An indorsement which shows that it is not in the chain of title is notice of its accommodation character.

Normally one indorses an instrument in order to negotiate it to his transferee (UCC 3–202). Section 3–415(4) establishes a statutory presumption that an indorsement which shows that it is not made for the purpose of transfer is made as an accommodation for another party. To see how this provision works in the typical case, assume that Rocky has agreed to become an accommodation party for Bullwinkle's note which is payable to Boris. Bullwinkle executes the note as maker with Boris as payee. Rocky indorses the note *prior* to its delivery to Boris. When Boris negotiates the note to Natasha she has notice under UCC 3–415(4) that Rocky is an accommodation party. Rocky's signature is outside the chain of title because it appears above that of the payee who would normally be the first indorser. Because an indorsement out of the chain shows accommodation status without the need for any words, signature as an indorser is a desirable way for the accommodation party to sign the instrument.

The cases, problems and questions below deal not only with the problem of identifying sureties but also with the suretyship defenses themselves.

COMMERCE UNION BANK v. DAVIS

Court of Appeals of Tennessee, Middle Section, 1978.
581 S.W.2d 142, certiorari denied by Supreme Court, 1979.

Appeal from the Chancery Court, Davidson County.

DROWOTA, JUDGE. This is a suit by Commerce Union Bank for a deficiency following the repossession and sale of an airplane pledged as collateral for a loan. The Chancellor awarded judgment to the Bank in the amount of $12,965.41, and defendant Davis appeals, alleging that the Chancellor erred in failing to find Davis an accommodation party released from liability under T.C.A. § 47–3–606. Defendant Trulson, who did not answer or defend below, is not a party to this appeal.

On January 6, 1975, Gerald Davis executed a note payable to the Bank in the amount of $30,195.60. He also granted the Bank a security interest in his Cessna 337A airplane as collateral for the indebtedness. On January 20, 1976, Davis conveyed his interest in the plane to Clarence T. Trulson. In consideration for the Bank's approval of the transfer, Davis signed a "transfer of equity" agreement wherein he agreed to remain liable on his January 6, 1975, note. Trulson also agreed to be jointly and severally liable with Davis for the remaining balance of $23,965.41. In addition, Trulson executed a security agreement pledging the plane to the Bank as collateral. From the time of the transfer until the date of the suit, however, Trulson made no payments on the note. The Bank gave no notice to Davis of Trulson's defaults on these installments until January 10, 1977, when the Bank filed suit. By the time suit was filed, Trulson had a negative net worth.

The plane was repossessed and sold, and the Chancellor awarded a judgment for the deficiency jointly and severally against Davis and Trulson.

Appellant asserts that the Chancellor's decision was in error because (a) the transfer of equity agreement and the Bank's subsequent conduct "recast" his note to that of an accommodation maker, and (b) the Bank extended the time of payment on the note without Davis's approval, suspended its right of enforcement against Trulson, and permitted Trulson to waste his assets so as to destroy Davis's right of subrogation, thereby releasing Davis from liability by virtue of TCA § 47–3–606. We do not find appellant's arguments persuasive, and must affirm the Chancellor's decision.

T.C.A. § 47–3–415(1) defines an "accommodation party" as "one who signs [an] instrument in any capacity *for the purpose of lending his name to another party to it* * * *" [Emphasis added.] The essential test of an accommodation party's status, then, is the purpose for which he signed the instrument. While an accommodation purpose may be determined by ascertaining a party's subjective intent, a purpose other than accommodation may be inferred by the receipt of any benefit by the party claiming accommodation status, since the "receipt of proceeds from the instrument or other direct benefit" is "generally inconsistent with accommodation status * * *" J. White & R. Summers, Uniform Commercial Code 431 (1972). For decisions in other jurisdictions based on the "benefit" test, see Reigler v. Reigler, 244 Ark. 483, 426 S.W.2d 789 (1968); MacArthur v. Cannon, 4 Conn.Cir. 208, 229 A.2d 372 (1967); J. White & R. Summers, supra, at 431 n 111. Accordingly, the receipt of benefits raises a presumption that a party's purpose is other than mere accommodation, and any person claiming such status must carry the burden of proof.

The appellant has failed to carry this burden. It is clear that the appellant received several benefits from the transfer of the aircraft to Trulson, including a favorable restructuring of his debt to the Bank and the elimination of the cost of maintaining a disabled plane. Indeed, the facts surrounding the transfer indicate that the appellant's motive was not to lend his name to Trulson in order that Trulson's note might be acceptable to the Bank, but to acquire a contract right from Trulson that Trulson would assume appellant's responsibility for making payments on appellant's note. Moreover, it must be observed that appellant's note of January 6, 1975, is the only note involved in the transaction; no cancellation of appellant's liability occurred at the time of the conveyance, nor was a new note executed by Trulson upon which appellant could have signed as accommodation comaker.

Appellant has ignored the "purpose" test outlined by the Code, and has instead relied upon two indices of accommodation status: the Bank's looking only to Trulson for payment of the note and his right of reimbursement against Trulson. While this in and of itself should be fatal to appellant's cause, it must be noted that even were this court to accept appellant's arguments as the proper test of accommodation status, appellant would still not prevail. First, his right of reimbursement from Trulson derives not from the rights of an accommodation party under section 47–3–415(5), but from a contract right for payment for the aircraft conveyed. Second, the Bank, as holder of the appellant's note, was under no obligation to make presentment to appellant upon Trulson's default or to provide appellant any notice of dishonor. T.C.A. §§ 47–3–501, 504(3)(a). As comment 3 to section 47–3–504 states, "[t]he holder is entitled to expect that any one of the named parties will pay or accept, and should not be required to go to the trouble and expense of making separate presentment to a number of them."

Appellant has asserted that even if he were not an accommodation maker, the "surety" defenses of section 47–3–606 would nevertheless be available to him as a comaker, since that code section does not expressly limit its scope to sureties. This, however, is not the law in this State. In Commerce Union Bank v. May, 503 S.W.2d 112, 116 (Tenn. 1973), our Supreme Court stated that "the phrase, 'any party to the instrument,' is used in [section 47–3–606] to embrace parties to the instrument in addition to drawers and endorsers *who are in the position of a known surety.*" [Emphasis in original.] Thus, the defenses of that section are not available to the appellant, and further consideration of his arguments in that regard is unnecessary.

For the reasons stated herein, the decision of the Chancellor is affirmed. Affirmed.

TODD and LEWIS, JJ., concur.

Notes

1. Should UCC 3–606 be interpreted as the Tennessee court has apparently interpreted it? If, for example, A and B are co-makers and neither is a surety in the classic sense (for each we will assume enjoys part of the benefit of the transaction) does each still have an action against the other for contribution upon his payment? Would not such a claim be a "right of recourse" under UCC 3–606(1)(a)? If the answer to that question is yes (two parties have cosigned and the total liability on the note is $10,000), to what extent will UCC 3–606(1)(a) discharge one party if the creditor absolves the other?

2. Although Comment 1 to 3–606 says that having a right of recourse includes "having a right of recourse either on the instrument or dehors it * * *" one can argue persuasively that the right of contribution should not be regarded as a right of recourse. In theory the injury that the creditor does to the guarantor when the creditor discharges the person primarily liable is to destroy the right of subrogation that would otherwise exist for the full amount against the principal obligor. The release of one cosigner, who is not a surety, upon partial payment will not affect the right of contribution. Following that line of thought, creditor has done no injury to the other party, there should be no discharge and thus the other person should not be regarded as having a "right of recourse" as that term is used in UCC 3–606.

HOLCOMB STATE BANK v. ADAMSON

Appellate Court of Illinois, Second District, 1982.
107 Ill.App.3d 908, 63 Ill.Dec. 704, 438 N.E.2d 635.

HOPF, J. Defendant J. Grant Adamson appeals from a judgment in favor of Holcomb State Bank for $13,157.53, the amount of the principal and interest on a note which he co-signed and which was in default. Adamson contends that the extension of the due date of the note without his consent released him from liability. We agree, and reverse.

The evidence adduced at trial reveals that Meinick P. Wick, Adamson's son-in-law, sought a loan of $10,000 from the bank for his mushroom business. The bank would not approve the loan unless Wick found a co-maker approved by the bank. The bank president suggested that Adamson co-sign the note, which he did. On the note was handwritten, "For use in Wick's Mushroom Business" and, at the bottom, "This is Wick's Note & Adamson is co-signer." The bank credited $10,000 to the mushroom company account. Adamson did not receive any of the proceeds from the loan.

The promissory note was dated April 27, 1979. It became due October 27, 1979. Wick paid the interest due on that date but failed to pay any of the principal. On December 15, 1979, the bank and Wick entered into an agreement to extend the due date to March 4, 1980. The interest rate was increased from 10% to 14% per annum. The note was not paid by March 4, 1980, and was in default after that date. The bank president testified that a notice of the extension was mailed to Adamson; however, there is no record that such a notice was sent to Adamson or that Adamson signed an extension form. An officer of the bank testified that he had discussed extending the note with Adamson, but that Adamson had refused to sign an extension of the note. The witness asserted that Adamson expressed the intention to sign a new note but that one was never made. Adamson testified that he learned of the extension two weeks after it had been approved. After the note had become due he talked to an officer of the bank on a number of occasions about getting the note "straightened out." The "hassle" the bank gave him after the note became due was for payment of the overdue interest, not payment of the note, he testified. Adamson testified that he never agreed to extend the note.

After hearing all the evidence, the court found that Adamson was an accommodation party but that an accommodation party was not discharged by an extension of time given by the holder to the principal maker without the accommodating maker's consent. * * *

* * *

Adamson appeals, contending that he signed the note as an accommodation party, and that the extension of the note without his consent and without the express reservation of rights by the bank released him from his obligation under the note.

Section 3–606 of the Uniform Commercial Code states conditions under which a party to an instrument is discharged. The section provides in pertinent part: [quoting]

* * *

The term "any party" as used in this section refers not to co-makers but to persons who "sign ostensibly as makers but who are in fact surety or accommodation makers * * *." (Godfrey State Bank v. Mundy (1980), 90 Ill.App.3d 142, 144, 412 N.E.2d 1131, 1134.) An accommodation party thus is released from his liability on a note when it is extended without his consent or without express reservation of rights by the holder.

Adamson can claim the defense provided by § 3–606 only if he is an accommodation party.

The trial court found Adamson to be an accommodation party, and we agree. An accommodation party is "one who signs the instrument in any capacity for the purpose of lending his name to another party to it." * * * The parties' intention is the significant element in determining whether a party is an accommodation maker. * * * When a party receives no direct benefit from the execution of the note it is likely he will be regarded as an accommodation party. * * * The parties' intention regarding Adamson's status was shown both by the writing on the note and by oral proof, which is permitted by § 3–415(3) (Ill.Rev.Stat. 1979, ch. 26, par. 3–415(3)), against one who is not a holder in due course with [sic; without] notice of the accommodation. The evidence that the bank knew Wick alone sought the loan and that the amount of the loan was credited to Wick's account indicates, contrary to the bank's assertion, that "all the facts and circumstances known to [the bank] at the time" of the making of the note gave the bank reason to know of Adamson's status as accommodation party (Ill.Rev.Stat. 1979, ch. 26, par. 1–201(25)(c)). The bank thus could not be a holder in due course without notice of accommodation, and the use of parol evidence was proper.

That evidence shows that only Wick sought the loan. The bank would not approve the loan unless a co-maker approved by the bank also signed. Adamson signed the note at the bank's suggestion. Adamson was not in business with Wick. The entire amount of the loan was credited to the mushroom company's bank account; Adamson received none of the loan. This evidence, together with the memoranda written on the note, "For use in Wick's Mushroom Business," and "This is Wick's Note & Adamson is co-signer," supports the finding that Adamson was an accommodation party. The fact that Adamson signed the note where makers normally sign does not deny him this status. Godfrey State Bank v. Mundy (1980), 90 Ill.App.3d 142, 412 N.E.2d 1131.

The bank argues, however, that whether or not defendant is an accommodation party he cannot claim the protection of § 3–606 because he consented to the extension. Printed on the back of the note is the following sentence:

> "For Value Received, I hereby guarantee payment at maturity of the within note to the holder thereof, and authorize any extension or extensions the holder may grant the maker, and waive presentment, demand, notice of nonpayment, protest and diligence in collecting the same."

The bank asserts that Adamson is bound by these words, citing section 3–118(f) of the Commercial Code which states in pertinent part,

> "A consent to extension, expressed in the instrument, is binding upon secondary parties and accommodation makers." Ill.Rev.Stat. 1979, ch. 26, par. 3–118(f).

We do not think, however, that the words on the back of this note bind every signer of the instrument. The consent to an extension following the words guaranteeing payment is stated in conjunction with those words of *guaranty*. Only one who guarantees payment of this instrument consents to the rest of the matters contained in the sentence, including consent to the extension of the note. The question to consider next, then, is whether Adamson is a guarantor. Section 3–416 of the Commercial Code concerns the contract of a guarantor and provides, in pertinent part:

> " 'Payment guaranteed' or equivalent words added to a signature mean that the signer engages that if the instrument is not paid when due he will pay it according to its tenor without resort by the holder to any other party." Ill.Rev.Stat. 1979, ch. 26, par. 3–416(1).

The section provides that a contract guaranteeing payment is made by words of guaranty "added to a signature," and we think that these words of guaranty printed in isolation on the reverse side of the note from the parties' signatures are not words added to Adamson's signature so as to bind him to a guaranty of payment of the note. We conclude, therefore, that Adamson was not a guarantor of the note and that the consent to extension and other conditions stated in conjunction with the words of guaranty had no application with regard to him.

The bank also argues that Adamson consented to the extension of the note by his actions. A bank officer testified that he tried unsuccessfully to get Adamson to sign an extension agreement and that Adamson suggested instead renegotiation of the note. Adamson testified he did not learn of the extension until two weeks after it was made. He refused to sign the extension and instead proposed a renegotiation of the note. We do not think Adamson's knowledge about the extension after it was given and his willingness to discuss a new arrangement while flatly refusing to sign an extension constitute a consent to the extension agreement between Wick and the bank.

Finally, an accommodation party, even if he has not consented to an extension, may yet be held bound to an extension if the holder expressly reserved its rights against him. (Ill.Rev.Stat. 1979, ch. 26, par. 3–606(2)(a).) There is no evidence, however, that the bank expressly reserved rights against Adamson.

We conclude therefore that Adamson, an accommodation party who did not consent to the extension of the note and against whom no express reservation of right is alleged, is not bound by the note extended by Wick and the bank. We reverse the judgment of the Ogle County circuit court.

Reversed.

UNVERZAGT and VAN DEUSEN, JJ., concur.

Notes

1. Does Adamson's lawyer deserve a bonus? Must a lawyer be rather clever to make a court conclude that his client is an accommodation party freed from liability from the accommodation party defenses, yet not burdened by a clause intended to bind "guarantors."

2. Would the outcome be different if Adamson merely signed a document that stated that he "agreed to any extensions"? If the extension note had the following sentence on it: "The Bank expressly reserves its rights against Adamson," Adamson would not be discharged.

MAINE NATIONAL BANK v. FONTAINE

Supreme Judicial Court of Maine, 1983.
456 A.2d 1273.

CARTER, J. Following a jury trial in Superior Court, Oxford County, a judgment was entered in favor of the plaintiff, Maine National Bank, against the defendant, Gilbert Fontaine. On appeal, Fontaine contends that the justice erred by refusing to give a jury instruction on Fontaine's status as an accommodation party and on the defenses available to an accommodation party. We vacate the judgment and remand for further proceedings consistent with this opinion.

I. FACTS

The testimony at trial would support the following factual findings. William Porter, a general contractor, hired Gilbert Fontaine as a plumbing and heating subcontractor. As a result of Fontaine's performance of the subcontract, Porter owed Fontaine $36,000. To enable Fontaine to pay his own creditors, Fontaine sought to collect the money that Porter owed him. Because Porter was experiencing financial difficulties, he did not have the money to pay Fontaine. Moreover, due to his financial condition, the Maine National Bank (the Bank) would not lend Porter, on his sole credit, any money to pay off his debt to Fontaine.

Porter and Fontaine went, together, to the Maine National Bank and spoke with Joyce Paulton, the loan officer. Ms. Paulton explained that the Bank would provide Porter with the loan only if Fontaine cosigned the note. Paulton further explained that as a cosignee, Fontaine would be obliged to pay the note if Porter did not pay the note when it was due.

They also discussed the possibility of Porter obtaining a Small Business Administration (SBA) loan. To request such a loan, a borrower must submit an application with financial statements to the Bank. After receiving the completed application, the Bank sends the application to the SBA for approval. Ms. Paulton offered to help Porter prepare the application. The parties agreed that upon approval of the loan by the SBA, Porter would use the proceeds to pay off the loan cosigned by Fontaine.

As a result of these discussions, both Porter and Fontaine, on June 16, 1976, signed a note for $15,000. Porter signed on the line marked borrower and Fontaine signed on the line marked comaker. Fontaine testified at trial that although the Bank requested that Fontaine sign on the line marked "borrower," Fontaine did not sign that line because he did not borrow the money. He further stated that the reason he agreed to cosign the note was that the Bank had assured him that the SBA loan would go through and that the SBA loan proceeds would cover the loan which Fontaine cosigned. However, at the time Fontaine signed the note, he knew that the application had not been submitted to the SBA or approved by the SBA.

Porter subsequently deposited the loan money into his checking account. Immediately thereafter, he wrote a check to Fontaine for the total amount of the note, $15,000. Fontaine questioned the Bank periodically about the progress of the SBA loan application. The Bank told Fontaine that it was in the process of collecting Porter's financial statements. In September or October of 1976, the Bank discovered that Porter's financial statements were inaccurate. As a result, the Bank refused to submit the application to the SBA. Fontaine testified that Ms. Paulton never told him that the Bank had terminated its assistance with Porter's SBA loan application. Ms. Paulton testified, however, that she told Fontaine that the Bank had refused to submit the application to the SBA. On September 14, 1976, December 13, 1976, and June 13, 1977, both Porter and Fontaine signed renewals of the loan. Upon each renewal, the accrued interest was paid.

On March 24, 1978, Porter filed a petition in bankruptcy. The Bank filed a proof of claim in the bankruptcy court for Porter's indebtedness, but the debt received no distribution. As a result of Porter's discharge, the Bank did not obtain any money from him in payment of the loan. On July 21, 1978, the Bank attempted to collect the debt from Fontaine. Fontaine refused to pay. The present suit resulted.

After the presentation of all of the evidence, the jury was instructed to determine whether the loan officer had fraudulently induced Fontaine to sign the note. The defendant requested an instruction on whether Fontaine was an accommodation party and whether prior to Fontaine signing the renewals, the Bank had a duty to disclose to an accommodation party that it had terminated assistance on the SBA loan. The judge refused to give these instructions. The jury rendered a verdict for the plaintiff from which it follows that the jury found that Fontaine had not been improperly induced to cosign the note.

II. DISCUSSION

The defendant argues that because the issue is raised by the facts, he is entitled to a jury instruction on the issue of whether or not he signed the note as an accommodation party. "An accommodation party is one who signs the instrument in any capacity for the purpose of lending his name to another party to it." 11 M.R.S.A. § 3–415(1) (1964). An accommodation party commonly appears on a note as a comaker. See J. White & R. Summers, Uniform Commercial Code, § 13–12 at 516 (2d ed 1980). Although on the face of the instrument it appears that Fontaine signed the note as a comaker, under the circumstances of this case, it may be shown by oral evidence that the defendant signed as an accommodation party. 11 M.R.S.A. § 3–415(3); see also Westbrook Trust Co. v. Timberlake, 121 Me. 64, 65, 115 A. 555, 556 (1921).

In this case, Ms. Paulton testified that Porter would not have received the loan if Fontaine had not signed the note. Moreover, she testified that she had told Fontaine he would be obliged to pay only if Porter did not pay. Finally, Fontaine testified that he did not want to sign on the line labeled borrower because he did not borrow the money. A jury might properly have concluded from this evidence that the defendant signed the note as an accommodation party. It was within the province of the jury to determine, on all the evidence, whether or not Fontaine signed the note in such capacity. It was improper for the justice to have denied the requested instruction.

The defendant also argues that the justice erred in failing to give an instruction on whether or not, prior to Fontaine cosigning the renewals of the note, the Bank had a duty to disclose to an accommodation party that it refused to submit the SBA loan application. An accommodation party is always a surety. 11 M.R.S.A. § 3–415, comment 1. Title 11 M.R.S.A. § 3–606 (1964) provides suretyship defenses. 11 M.R.S.A. § 3–606, comment 1. Under § 3–606(1)(a), a renewal of a note, an extension of time in the right of enforcement, discharges a surety *who has not consented* to such a renewal. See also Westbrook Trust Co., 121 Me. at 66, 115 A. at 556. Consent implies meaningful or informed consent. Consequently, if at the time the surety consents to the extension of time, a creditor knows of facts which the creditor has reason to believe are unknown to the surety, which materially increase the risk beyond the point that the creditor had reason to believe the surety intended to assume, and which the creditor had a reasonable opportunity to communicate to the surety, failure on the part of the creditor to notify the surety of such facts is a defense to the surety. See Sumitomo Bank of California v. Iwasaki, 70 Cal.2d 81, 88, 447 P.2d 956, 963, 73 Cal.Rptr. 564, 571 (1968); accord First National Bank of Arizona v. Bennett Venture, Ltd., 130 Ariz. 562, 564, 637 P.2d 1065, 1067 (App. 1981); Watkins Products, Inc. v. Stadel, 214 N.W.2d 368, 374–75 (N.D. 1973); First National Bank & Trust of Racine v. Notte, 97 Wis.2d 207, 213, 293 N.W.2d 530, 536 (1980).

There was disputed testimony on the issue of whether Ms. Paulton informed Fontaine of the Bank's refusal to submit Porter's SBA loan application. Ms. Paulton testified that she informed Fontaine that the Bank had refused to submit the application to the SBA prior to Fontaine's renewal of the loan. Fontaine testified, however, that he heard about the termination a year later, after he had renewed the loans in September and December of 1976 and in June of 1977. The defendant contends that if he had been supplied this information, he would not have renewed the loans.

It was within the province of the jury to determine, under appropriate legal instructions, whether or not on the evidence the Bank had a duty to inform Fontaine that the Bank had refused to submit Porter's SBA loan application. Additionally, if this issue were properly submitted, the jury might be required to decide as a factual matter whether Ms. Paulton, as the Bank's agent, performed that duty by advising Fontaine that the SBA application had not been submitted. If the jury found in favor of Fontaine on these issues, Fontaine could have been discharged of any obligation under the note. To refuse to permit the jury to consider these issues, therefore, severely prejudiced the defendant.

The entry is

Judgment vacated.

Remanded to the Superior Court for further proceedings consistent with this opinion.

Note

What evidence can be marshalled on either side of the question of Fontaine's suretyship status? Identify specifically.

Problem 23–8

Assume that Bank made two loans to a business, each of $100,000 and each secured by accounts receivable worth $80,000. Husband and wife, owners of the business, were accommodation makers on the first note but not the second. When the business failed, the bank satisfied the second note out of the accounts receivable and then sued husband and wife on the first note for the full $100,000. Husband and wife argued that they were discharged because the acts of the bank constituted an impairment of their collateral under 3–606. Will they win? Could the Bank be forced to use the accounts as to the first loan under a doctrine of marshalling?

Problem 23–9

Assume that Bank agreed to make a $500,000 loan to a partnership, but insisted that each of the partners indorse the note. After the deal had been negotiated the partnership offered to grant the bank security in return for a reduction of the interest rate on the note of ½ of 1 percent. The Bank agreed and the partnership made an appropriate security interest. The Bank failed to perfect its security interest and in the suit against the partners is confronted with 3–606(1)(b). Who will win? If you assume that the partners would win, would the outcome have been different if the partners had executed a general "waiver of suretyship defenses" as part of the indorsement of the note?

One who reads cases on accommodation parties and examines the rules is faced with a handful of lawyer and policy questions. The first and most obvious lawyer question from the cases is why does one still find tens of reported cases (and presumably hundreds or thousands of unreported cases that go only through the trial level) in which the bank loses because it fails to insert a simple paragraph in its loan document "reserving its rights"? Prior to 3–606, in many cases, the bank would need the surety's consent for an extension in order to hold a surety. The Code explicitly rejected that idea and authorizes one to hold the guarantor by simply reserving one's rights against him. Despite that simple solution from the bank's point of view, one sees a multitude of reported cases.

A more interesting question is why we have the suretyship rules at all and whether they merit respect. The comments above and the current status of 3–606 show that the drafters found little to commend the guarantor's arguments, otherwise they would not have allowed the creditor to override the guarantor's defenses merely by "reserving his rights."

Elsewhere White and Summers have argued that that was a correct decision. We have maintained that the guarantor's argument, made after the fact, that had he been given the opportunity at the time the note was due, he would gladly have paid it in order not to have undertaken a longer liability, is not believable. One should understand the guarantor's unpleasant choices at the time the original note is due when the original debtor will not pay. If there is no mechanism by which the creditor can keep the guarantor on the hook, the creditor will be motivated not to extend the loan and simply to sue the debtor and the guarantor at that point. Given that choice, most guarantors would gladly consent to an extension of the original loan. When there is extension without a "reservation of rights" or consultation with the guarantors, the guarantors are not likely to be candid about their true motivation and one should accept their assertions at that point with skepticism.

Given the high transaction costs of resorting to court upon a debtor's first default, and the apparent belief of many creditors and debtors that extrajudicial workouts with extensions and other adjustments are far preferable to a law suit, should the law also favor "workouts"? If so, should one normally enforce waivers and other agreements by guarantors?

To some extent this entire analysis runs contrary to the American common law. Guarantors are sometimes described as fools with pens. Some of them, principally spouses and parents, have signed documents out of love and affection, ignorant of the underlying transaction and in complete reliance upon the assertions of a husband, wife, son or daughter. All of this causes the courts to search for ways out and to be wary of assertions frequently made: "The loan officer assured me that I would never have to pay."

SECTION 8. THE IDENTITY OF THE PARTY LIABLE ON COMMERCIAL PAPER, HEREIN QUESTIONS OF AGENCY, AMONG OTHERS

In the current corporate world in which check writing among other responsibilities must be delegated to a variety of corporate employees, several agency questions inevitably arise: (1) Under what circumstances does one have real or apparent authority to sign commercial paper for another? (2) If the one making the signature is authorized to bind a principal, what kind of inscription must he make on the paper in order for his principal to be bound on the instrument? (3) When is the purported agent personally bound?

Examination of the first question must be left to courses on agency. Section 3–403(1) specifies that a signature may be made by an agent "and his authority to make it may be established as in other cases of representation. No particular form of appointment is necessary to establish such authority." This statement together with the second paragraph of Comment 1 to UCC 3–403 makes clear the drafters' intention to incorporate other statutory and common law rules into the commercial paper sphere on the question of proof of real or apparent authority.

Since "no person is liable on an instrument unless his signature appears thereon," (UCC 3–401(1)) and since even an authorized agent's own signature is not coextensive with that of his principal, it is necessary to determine what additional mark is needed to bind the principal under UCC 3–401: Assume, for example, Repeunzel *has authority* as a Vice President to deposit and cash checks payable to Leroy's order. He indorses a check "Repeunzel" and absconds with the proceeds. Assume that the check was payable to the order of Leroy's Liquor Stores Inc. If payment is stopped on the check, depositary bank will not have a right to sue on Leroy's indorsement. His agent's name alone is insufficient to bind the principal. The New York Supreme Court has stated the rule in such cases as follows:

"* * * Finally, it is alleged that Sullivan, in endorsing the notes, acted as agent for and nominee of the moving third-party defendant Satenstein. The matter is argued solely upon the question whether the movant is liable upon the instruments through the claimed agency of Sullivan. Uniform Commercial Code, section 3–401, provides that 'no person is liable on an instrument unless his signature appears thereon.' Section 3–403 provides that a 'signature may be made by an agent or other representative, and his authority to make it may be established as in other cases of representation. No particular form of appointment is necessary to establish such authority.' Sullivan's signature appearing on the notes, without any description or designation on the face of the notes, cannot bind one alleged to be his principal. The signature of one claiming himself to be an agent, which appears on the face of a note, without more, obligates the agent personally and does not bind the principal. And parole evidence is not admissible to disprove the agent's liability or to establish the liability of the principal. Accordingly, the motion must be and is granted. Settle order providing for severance." First Nat'l Bank of Jersey City v. Maidman, 2 UCC Rep.Serv. 1048, 1048–49 (N.Y.Sup.Ct., N.Y. County 1965).

If Repeunzel had taken care to identify Leroy either by signing the check "Leroy's Liquor Stores, Inc.—Repeunzel" or "Leroy's Liquor Stores, Inc.—Repeunzel, President," then the liquor store would have been liable on the check as indorser (assuming Repeunzel was an agent).

The third question—when is the agent personally liable—probably occurs most commonly in cases of modestly capitalized business associations in which the agent's personal net worth may be greater than that of the corporation or other association. Invariably such cases arise on notes, not on checks. In such instances the note may serve as a device for reaching the agent's assets held outside the corporation. If, for example, the agent does not name the corporation and does not state that he is acting as an agent, section 3–403(2)(a) makes the agent personally liable on the note. If he does one or the other, that is, names his principal or does not name his principal but shows that he is acting as an agent then UCC 3–403(2)(b) gives him an opportunity, as against "immediate parties," to prove by parole evidence that he was acting as an agent and if he can so prove such fact, it relieves him of personal liability. Of course if Repeunzel dots his i's and crosses his t's by revealing both his agency and signing his principal's name (e.g., "Leroy's Liquor Stores, Inc., by Repeunzel, Vice President"), Liquor Stores, Inc. will be liable but Repeunzel will not be personally liable.

It should be clear therefore that if the agent signs the principal's name and is authorized to do so, the principal is liable. In the absence of such authority or of the principal's signature, the principal is not liable. If the agent is authorized, signs his own name, either signs the principal's name or identifies himself as an agent, the agent will not be personally liable to "immediate parties" if he can prove that he was acting in an agency capacity. In such cases of revelation of one but not both of the facts of principal's identity and agency, the agent is personally liable to non-immediate parties and to immediate parties if his proof of agency is unconvincing.

The student should understand why these issues are more likely to be presented by signatures as makers on notes, less frequently by indorsers of checks, and least frequently of all with regard to drawers' signatures on checks. Rarely is one misled by a drawer's signature on a check because the check itself is a pre-printed form identified by its MICR numbers and by the name of the drawer printed on the check. In such case a drawer's agent who does nothing but sign his own name does not mislead the payee. Thus we would expect the courts to find that the numerals and letters printed on the instrument reveal both the agency and the name of the principal in such cases and thus free the agent from liability.

LEGG v. KELLY

Supreme Court of Alabama, 1982.
412 So.2d 1202.

ADAMS, JUSTICE.

These consolidated appeals arise out of grants of summary judgment in favor of Edward Kelly, Jr., Mel Lucas, and Cliff Ellis (defendants). Joseph S. Legg (plaintiff) brought suit against corporate and individual defendants in the Circuit Court for Mobile County. Plaintiff's suit is based upon a contract in which defendant Athletic World Sporting Goods, Inc., (not a party to this appeal) agreed to purchase plaintiff's sporting goods store and assume responsibility for a debt owed by him. Individual defendants were stockholders and officers in the defendant corporation. Plaintiff alleged various theories of recovery against the defendants. After granting summary judgment in favor of Lucas, Ellis, and Kelly, the trial court entered final judgment as to these defendants pursuant to Rule 54(b), Alabama Rules of Civil Procedure. Plaintiff appealed.

By our review of the trial court's action, we conclude that with the exception of three counts of plaintiff's complaint concerning Kelly, it erred by granting summary judgment in favor of defendants. We, therefore, affirm in part, reverse in part, and remand this case. We will consider separately each count of plaintiff's complaint as it pertains to the defendants in reviewing the trial court's action.

* * *

Plaintiff's first count alleges, in pertinent part, that Kelly is personally liable on a promissory note that he signed. The note is part of the agreement by which plaintiff sold his sporting goods business. Athletic World assumed payment of an obligation owed by plaintiff. A default occurred and plaintiff seeks to hold Kelly personally liable for $57,513.71, the amount plaintiff alleges he ultimately paid under his prior obligation. Plaintiff maintains that Kelly agreed to assume personal liability, and signed the note in a like manner. Kelly disputes that and insists his signature on the note was made in a representative capacity for Athletic World. Kelly's signature appears on the note in the following manner:

ATHLETIC WORLD SPORTING GOODS, INC. (L.S.)
(Debtor)

BY: /s/Edward Kelly Jr. (L.S.)
(Debtor)

Kelly contends that the trial court properly entered summary judgment in his favor and urges us to adopt the reasoning of *Southeastern Financial Corporation v. Smith,* 397 F.Supp. 649 (D.Ala.1975), *rev'd on other grounds,* 542 F.2d 278 (5th Cir.1976) (*Smith*). *Smith* held that an individual who signed a check, drawn on a corporation's account, with "by" preceding his signature, signed in a representative capacity which thereby prevented his being held personally liable. We need not decide whether to adopt the reasoning of *Smith.* That case is factually distinguishable from the present one. Although "by" preceded Kelly's signature, the signature line bore the designation of "debtor" and thereby, at least, the instant case is distinguishable from *Smith.* Code 1975, § 7-3-403, addresses the problem of an agent incurring personal liability when signing a note on behalf of his principal. Interpreting that section, this court has observed:

> The purpose of Code 1975, § 7-3-403 is to encourage certainty and definiteness in the law of commercial paper. *See Rotuba Extruders, Inc. v. Ceppos,* 46 N.Y.2d 223, 413 N.Y.S.2d 141, 385 N.E.2d 1068 (1978). The taker of a negotiable instrument should be able "to tell at a glance whose obligation they hold."

Wurzburg Brothers, Inc. v. Coleman, 404 So.2d 334 (Ala.1981) (citation omitted).

Viewed in that light, we cannot agree with Kelly that Athletic World is the only debtor and that he executed the note on its behalf. Kelly's interpretation of the note flies in the face of the "certainty and definiteness" sought by § 7-3-403. His signature on a line designated for a debtor, absent an indication of his purported representative capacity, is consistent with the signature of an individual assuming personal liability on the instrument.

We also are unable to accept Kelly's argument that he is not personally liable under the note because he did not sign as a guarantor on the reverse of the instrument. That argument presupposes Kelly had not personally obligated himself when he signed as a debtor.

Lastly, on this count, Kelly argues that his testimony at deposition was sufficient to justify the entry of summary judgment. Kelly testified that he signed the note in a representative capacity. In view of our holding above, we cannot accept Kelly's argument. His testimony denying personal liability was insufficient to eliminate the issue of fact as to the capacity in which he signed the note. Kelly's testimony merely creates an issue of fact. Accordingly, we hold that the trial court erred by entering summary judgment in Kelly's favor. We note that any issue of parol evidence offered to negate Kelly's personal liability must be resolved in harmony with *Wurzburg Brothers, Inc. v. Coleman, supra.* However, because that problem is not before us, we make no further comment thereon.

* * *

In the appeal involving Lucas and Ellis, the trial court's grant of summary judgment on counts two through five is reversed. In the appeal involving Kelly, the trial court's grant of summary judgment in his favor on counts two, three, and four, is affirmed. However, the grant of summary judgment in Kelly's favor on count one and count five is reversed, and the cause is remanded for further proceedings consistent with this opinion.

* * *

TORBERT, CHIEF JUSTICE (dissenting).

I cannot agree with the majority's decision that Edward Kelly, Jr., signed this note as an individual, thus assuming personal liability. The trial court was correct in granting summary judgment in favor of the defendant.

The majority is correct when it decides that Code 1975, § 7–3–403 applies. However, it is not clear which part of § 7–3–403 results in the personal liability for Kelly.

Section 7–3–403 provides:

"(1) A signature may be made by an agent or other representative, and his authority to make it may be established as in other cases of representation. No particular form of appointment is necessary to establish such authority.

"(2) An authorized representative who signs his own name to an instrument:

"(a) Is personally obligated if the instrument neither names the person represented nor shows that the representative signed in a representative capacity;

"(b) Except as otherwise established between the immediate parties, is personally obligated if the instrument names the person represented but does not show that the representative signed in a representative capacity, or if the instrument does not name the person represented but does show that the representative signed in a representative capacity.

"(3) Except as otherwise established the name of an organization preceded or followed by the name and office of an authorized individual is a signature made in a representative capacity."

I believe the note in this case falls under subsection (3) of § 7–3–403, which provides that a signature is made in a representative capacity when the name of an organization is preceded or followed by the name and office of an authorized individual.

A similar situation can be found in *Southeastern Financial Corp. v. Smith,* 397 F.Supp. 649 (N.D.Ala.1975), *rev'd on other grounds,* 542 F.2d 278 (5th Cir. 1976). The instrument in that case was signed as follows:

"CARRIAGE HOUSE MOBILE HOMES, INC.

"General Account

"By Woody Lacy /s/

Authorized Signature

"By John Smith /s/

Authorized Signature"

In that case, Senior District Judge Lynne stated:

"Plaintiff relies on 3–403(2)(b) as establishing Mr. Smith's liability. That reliance is misplaced, however, since 3–403(3) more closely reflects the facts of this case. Concededly, the signatures of Messrs. Smith and Woody [Lacy] are not followed by any designation of their offices, so that subsection 3 is not precisely applicable. Since 3–403(2) imposes liability on an agent

> only where 'the instrument' fails to reveal his representative capacity, however, we are free to look at the entire instrument for evidence of the capacity of the signer. The facts that the check indicates that it is drawn against the 'General Account' of the corporation and that the signatures are each preceded by the word 'By' are sufficient to remove any possible confusion as to whether Smith and Woody [Lacy] were signing as agents of the corporation. It is improbable that anyone dealing with these checks would be led to believe that Smith and Woody [Lacy] were signing as joint obligors with the corporation."

397 F.Supp. at 653 (citations omitted).

Paraphrasing a portion of that opinion and relating it to this case expresses my belief as follows:

> "Plaintiff relies on 3–403(2)(b) as establishing Mr. Kelly's liability. That reliance is misplaced, however, since 3–403(3) more closely reflects the facts of this case. Concededly the signature of Edward Kelly, Jr., is not followed by any designation of his office, so that subsection (3) is not precisely applicable. Since 7–3–402(2) imposes liability on an agent only where 'the instrument' fails to reveal his representative capacity, however, we are free to look at the entire instrument for evidence of the capacity of the signor. The facts that the note indicates Athletic World Sporting Goods, Inc., was a party to the note and that the signature of Kelly is preceded by the word 'By,' are sufficient to remove any possible confusion as to whether Kelly was signing as agent of the corporation. It is improbable that anyone dealing with the note would be led to believe that Kelly was signing as a joint obligor with the corporation."

It is recognized that in *Giacalone v. Bernstein,* 348 So.2d 679 (Fla.Dist.Ct. App.1977), the Florida court held that just the word "By" preceding a signature without more on the face of the note fails to show that the note was signed in a representative capacity. In that case, however, the name of the corporation did not appear anywhere on the face of the note. In this case, however, more is shown, because the name of the corporation, Athletic World Sporting Goods, Inc., precedes the signature of Kelly.

In an Alabama pre-UCC case, *Little v. Peoples Bank of Mobile,* 209 Ala. 620, 96 So. 763 (1923), a note was signed "Denton Livestock Company 'By J.R. Little.'" No descriptive abbreviation or word designating his office of vice president followed J.R. Little's signature. This Court said in that case:

"So far as the face of the note is concerned, the preposition (*by*) affirmatively restricted J.R. Little's relation to the note to the service of agency thereby unequivocally imported; Little's signature on the face of the note being given in that capacity only." 209 Ala. at 622, 96 So. 763.

This Court held, in *Little,* that the corporation was the principal, the single maker, and J.R. Little was only the agent of the Denton Livestock Company and was not individually bound thereby as a maker or as a comaker of the note with the corporation.

The majority express their view that the face of the instrument involved does not put a person on notice as to who is liable on the instrument. I believe the instrument does give notice of liability. The majority incorrectly expands the scope of *Wurzburg Brothers, Inc. v. Coleman,* 404 So.2d 334 (Ala.1981). I concurred in *Wurzburg* because an examination of the instrument involved indicated that personal liability of the agent was intended when the instrument was signed. The situation in this case is quite different. In *Wurzburg* the name of the corporation did not appear at the bottom of the note where it was signed. I would affirm the summary judgment in favor of Kelly.

MADDOX, SHORES and BEATTY, JJ., concur.

Notes

1. If you represented Kelly and wanted to make it absolutely clear that he had no personal liability, what would you do? If you represented the payee and wanted to make it absolutely clear that Kelly had personal liability, how would you do it?

2. Would it be malpractice for a lawyer to permit a client, who did not intend to be personally liable, to sign an instrument in the way Kelly signed the instrument above after the Supreme Court of Alabama had handed down the decision in 1982? If so, what damages would the lawyer be liable for?

POLLIN v. MINDY MFG. CO., INC.

Superior Court of Pennsylvania, 1967.
211 Pa.Super. 87, 236 A.2d 542.

MONTGOMERY, JUDGE.

This appeal by Robert L. Apfelbaum, one of the defendants, is from a judgment entered against both defendants on the pleadings in an action of assumpsit. The corporate defendant did not appeal.

The complaint sets forth in Count No. 1 that plaintiffs are in the business of cashing checks, that on September 23, 1966 Mindy Mfg. Co., Inc. issued and distributed payroll checks to its employes payable to their orders [1] and drawn on the Continental Bank and Trust Company in payment for wages earned by said employes; that plaintiffs cashed these checks for a small fee on the endorsement and delivery of same by the payees, and in turn endorsed same and deposited them in their account at the Provident National Bank of Philadelphia, which in turn presented them to the Continental Bank and Trust Company, which institution refused payment because Mindy Mfg. Co. did not have sufficient funds on deposit then to cover them; and that thereafter demand was made on Mindy Mfg. Co. for payment, but it was refused; and

In Count No. 2, after incorporating by reference the foregoing allegations it stated that Robert L. Apfelbaum, an individual, signed all of the aforementioned checks, with but one exception, which signature was "absolute and unqualified" but that he has refused to pay those which he signed which total $2,252.09.

The checks are in evidence and are boldly imprinted at the top, Mindy Mfg. Co., Inc., 26th & Reed Streets, Philadelphia, Penna. 19146—Payroll Check No. _______, and also Mindy Mfg. Co., Inc., is imprinted above two blank lines appearing at the lower right hand corner; also on the lower left hand corner appears Continental Bank and Trust Company, Norristown, Pa., in type. Under the imprinted name of the corporate defendant, on the first line, appears the signature of defendant Robert L. Apfelbaum without any designation of office or capacity on all of the checks before us in this appeal; the name of Estelle Apfelbaum appears on the other check mentioned in Count No. 1 which was in the amount of $81, but she was not made a party to the action.

* * *

1. Thirty-six checks are involved, each payable to a different individual in various amounts totaling $2,333.19.

In answer to the other allegations of the second count appellant averred that he signed the checks as president of Mindy Mfg. Co., Inc., and not in his individual capacity.

Summary judgment against appellant was entered by the lower court on the authority of Section 3–403 of the Uniform Commercial Code, the Act of April 6, 1953, P.L. 3, § 3–403, 12A P.S. § 3–403, which provides, "An authorized representative who signs his [own] name to an instrument. * * * (b) except as otherwise established between the immediate parties, is personally obligated if the instrument names the person represented but does not show that the representative signed in a representative capacity * * *". * * *

The issue before us, therefore, is whether a third party to the original transaction, the endorsee in the present case, may recover against one who affixes his name to a check in the place where a maker usually signs without indicating he is signing in a representative capacity, without giving consideration to other parts of the instrument or extrinsic evidence. This appears to be a novel question under the Uniform Commercial Code.

If this were an action brought by the payee parol evidence would be permitted to establish the capacity of the person affixing his signature under Section 3–403(b) previously recited * * *.

However, since this is an action brought by a third party our initial inquiry must be for the purpose of determining whether the instrument indicates the capacity of appellant as a signer. Admittedly, the instrument fails to show the office held by appellant. However, we do not think this is a complete answer to our problem, since the Code imposes liability on the individual only " * * * if the instrument * * * does not show that the representative signed in a representative capacity * * *" This implies that the instrument must be considered in its entirety.

Although Section 3–401(2) of the Uniform Commercial Code provides that "A signature is made by use of any name, including any trade or assumed name, upon an instrument, or by any word or mark used in lieu of a written signature," which would be broad enough to include the printed name of a corporation, we do not believe that a check showing two lines under the imprinted corporate name indicating the signature of one or more corporate officers would be accepted by any reasonably prudent person as a fully executed check of the corporation. It is common to expect that a corporate name placed upon a negotiable instrument in order to bind the corporation as a maker, especially when printed on the instrument, will be accompanied by the signatures of officers authorized by the by-laws to sign the instrument. Norman v. Beling, 33 N.J. 237, 163 A.2d 129, 82 A.L.R.2d 417 (1960), and cases therein cited. While we do not rule out the possibility of a printed name being established as an acceptable signature, we hold that such a situation is uncommon, and in the present case the two lines under the printed name dictate against a valid corporate signature. Corporations act through officers. Whitemarsh Township Authority v. Finelli Brothers, Inc., 408 Pa. 373, 184 A.2d 512 (1962); Lebowitz v. Keystone Insurance Agency, Inc., 198 Pa.Super. 495, 182 A.2d 289 (1962).

Next we must give consideration to the distinction between a check and a note. A check is an order of a depositor on a bank in the nature of a draft drawn on the bank and payable on demand. It is revokable until paid or accepted for payment. A note is an irrevocable promise to pay on the part of the maker. The maker of a check impliedly engages not only that it will be paid, but that he will have sufficient funds in the bank to meet it. First National

Bank of Warren v. J.A. Cadwallader, 10 Sadler 534, 14 A. 410 (1888); Champion v. Gordon, 70 Pa. 474 (1872). In the present instance the checks clearly showed that they were payable from a special account set up by the corporate defendant for the purpose of paying its employes. This information disclosed by the instrument of itself would refute any contention that the appellant intended to make the instrument his own order on the named bank to pay money to the payee. The money was payable from the account of the corporation defendant over which appellant as an individual had no control.

Considering the instrument as a whole we conclude that it sufficiently discloses that appellant signed it in a representative capacity.

If further support for our conclusion is necessary it may be found in the action of appellee who accepted the instrument as that of the corporate defendant. In its complaint it so avers. On that basis it proceeded against the corporate defendant and secured a judgment. That judgment was predicated on a proper execution of the instrument by that defendant which required the signature of its representative. Therefore it accepted appellant's signature as that representative. In fact, in his complaint against appellant he avers the checks were those of the corporation.

Having secured a judgment on that basis against the corporate defendant, we are at a loss to see how he may now contend that appellant's signature was on his individual behalf and not in a representative capacity. It must be one or the other. It cannot be both.

Judgment reversed and entered for appellant-defendant.

WATKINS, J., dissents.

Notes

The two foregoing cases arrive at opposite conclusions concerning the individual liability of a signer. Which of the following statements is correct:

1. Pollin is right but Legg is wrong.
2. Legg is right but Pollin is wrong.
3. Both are right.
4. Both are wrong.
5. Other.

CHAPTER TWENTY-FOUR

HOLDER IN DUE COURSE

SECTION 1. INTRODUCTION

A holder in due course today is a bit like the deposed queen of a much diminished empire. In the heyday of private law, rules about bills and notes were surely among the most important for a student to learn. Chief among those rules was the proposition that one could become a "holder in due course" of a negotiable instrument and thus take free of most defenses that prior parties might set up.

Surely in bygone days the rule had important economic consequences as well. A midwestern farmer might procure credit by giving a negotiable note to his bank who in turn would sell the note to a regional or nationwide lender. The subsequent party, it was thought, would take the note only because it was negotiable and because its negotiability freed him from everything but the credit risk. If there was fraud in the underlying transaction, if the combine purchased with the loan was defective, if there was a breach of contract, none of those need bother the big bank who purchased the note. The bank was insulated from those claims by its status as a holder in due course.

Whether holder in due course status was ever essential to such transactions, it is not any longer. Today there are many other, and more sophisticated, modes of transferring eastern credit to midwestern farmers without relying upon the cumbersome transfers of a note from the farmer to the eastern bank. At least in the case of consumers, the law has almost abolished the status of holder in due course. Thus the idea of holder in due course, once so central to a bread and butter subject, now has lost much of its legal, and, one suspects, much of its economic, significance.

Let us hasten to add that this does not mean that the holder in due course doctrine is unimportant today. The student should understand merely that the doctrine's significance has declined and is likely to be far less important to the student than one might suspect. At the outset one should understand when the doctrine is important and when it is clearly not important. If the obligor on a note or a check has no defenses, the holder in due course status of the one asserting the claim is almost certainly irrelevant. It is only at the third level that holder in due course status becomes important. At level one we must determine that there is a cause of action by the holder against the obligor. At level two we must determine that the obligor has some defense that could be raised in a common-law contract action. Only then, at level three, do we address the question whether that defense is cut off because of the status of the plaintiff. Too often students and courts jump directly to level three without a careful determination whether rights of the kind described in Chapter 23 exist. That is a mistake.

Taking free of defenses is by far the most important advantage of being a holder in due course. There are a few others. For example, section 3–418, which we will consider in detail below, gives specific rights to holders in due course. Section 5–114, which we will study in Chapter 29, gives similar rights to holders in due course. So it is important for reasons other than taking free of defenses, occasionally to know whether one is a holder in due course.

Note, too, that certain parties who are not holders in due course nevertheless have rights as though they were. These are transferees from holders in due course (see 3–201) and takers of certain instruments such as cashier's checks, when the issuing bank tries to escape its obligation. We will discuss the latter question in section 8 below.

Not only does the holder in due course take free of defenses, he also takes the instrument free from all adverse claims of title (3–305(1)). The holder in due course is not liable in conversion to the true owner of a stolen instrument, nor is he subject to adverse title claims that may arise from security interests, garnishments and the like.

One who reads many holder in due course cases will soon discover that the usual issue is not about the legal rights of a holder in due course, but about the question whether this plaintiff is a holder in due course. Seldom is there serious quarrel about the legal consequences if the plaintiff can establish his status as a holder in due course.

The question whether one is a holder in due course tends to present itself in quite different forms depending upon the context in which the problem arises. First are consumer cases. Those are now largely governed by the Federal Trade Commission rule discussed in section 7 below. Most consumer paper now contains the FTC legend; because that legend makes the obligation of the maker conditional, the paper is not negotiable. If the suit is one in which the plaintiff (depositary bank) is charging the drawer on a check, the issue is likely to be whether the bank gave "value" by crediting its depositor's account. Further, if a plaintiff is suing on a stolen instrument, the question will often be whether the plaintiff is a holder and so qualifies as a holder in due course. If the stolen instrument was an "order instrument" at the time of theft, the plaintiff will fail to be a holder and, *a fortiori* fail to be a holder in due course.

Thus, the holder in due course cases tend to involve arguments not about the legal rights of a holder in due course but about the status of the plaintiff, and those arguments in turn fall into three or four separate categories depending upon the context. One may set up five separate conditions that must be met for one to be a holder in due course. They are the following: (1) that the party is a holder; (2) that the document is an instrument; (3) that he gives value; (4) that he takes in good faith; (5) that he takes without notice of any defense or claim. One examining 3–302(1) can easily overlook the first two conditions, holder and instrument. The other conditions are fairly obvious, although it is sometimes difficult to determine where good faith leaves off and notice takes over. These rules are set out in 3–302 as follows:

(1) A holder in due course is a holder who takes the instrument

(a) for value; and

(b) in good faith; and

(c) without notice that it is overdue or has been dishonored or of any defense against or claim to it on the part of any person.

* * *

Of course the holder in due course enjoys all of the procedural benefits that accrue to any holder of a negotiable instrument. Those benefits are embodied principally in section 3–307. Note first that the signature appearing on the document itself is deemed to be the signature that it purports to be unless the defendant specifically challenges it. Even when it is challenged, the signature is presumed to be genuine or authorized unless the "purported signer" has died or become incompetent.

Under UCC 3–307(2) a properly signed instrument effectively makes the plaintiff's entire case. Compare the burden of the plaintiff who is suing on a contract composed of telephone calls, purchase orders and acknowledgments, with the burden of a plaintiff who is relying upon a negotiable note. The former has a much heavier burden to bear than the latter.

Note that when UCC 3–302 refers to an "instrument"; under 3–102(1)(e), "instrument" means a negotiable instrument. A negotiable instrument is defined in turn in 3–104 as follows:

(1) Any writing to be a negotiable instrument within this Article must

(a) be signed by the maker or drawer; and

(b) contain an unconditional promise or order to pay a sum certain in money and no other promise, order, obligation or power given by the maker or drawer except as authorized by this Article; and

(c) be payable on demand or at a definite time; and

(d) be payable to order or to bearer.

(2) A writing which complies with the requirements of this section is

(a) a "draft" ("bill of exchange") if it is an order;

(b) a "check" if it is a draft drawn on a bank and payable on demand;

(c) a "certificate of deposit" if it is an acknowledgment by a bank of receipt of money with an engagement to repay it;

(d) a "note" if it is a promise other than a certificate of deposit.

* * *

The most common negotiable instrument, of course, is a check, a form of draft. Also prevalent and well known to most are notes and certificates of deposit. Beyond those there are a variety of documents that call for the payment of money, contracts of various sorts, that are not negotiable. For the most part these contracts are not negotiable because they contain conditional, rather than unconditional (3–104(1)(b)) promises to pay. In addition, they fail to be negotiable because they are not payable to order or bearer and some may be construed to be not payable at a definite time.

Why, one might ask, should the law of commercial paper have such rigid rules? Why give the attributes of negotiability only to a small and rigidly controlled group of documents? We do not have certain answers to those questions. A common answer is that one must know for sure when he is dealing with an instrument that has these attributes. He must know this because he may be undertaking an obligation to pay even in circumstances where he has a good defense against the initial payee. On the other side of the transaction, the purchaser of the document (the New York banker) wants to be sure that he is taking the credit risk and nothing more. He may be willing to take the risk that the maker will not pay, but he knows nothing of the underlying transaction. He does not wish to be deprived of payment on the ground that there was a breach of warranty by a seller whose reputation is unknown to him. In theory, therefore, the rigid and highly specific requirements of negotiability signal to the various parties the obligations they are undertaking, the rights they are forego-ing and the rights they enjoy. If one believes that a negotiable instrument is frequently used as a device to transfer credit from one who makes a loan locally to another who knows nothing of it, then these rules make sense. If, on the other hand, one is skeptical about the importance of such transactions in a modern society, one should have a corresponding skepticism about the need for such rigid rules.

Whatever the need, the rules exist. Thus, the laborers in the vineyard must be prepared to examine documents and to pass on the question whether they are negotiable and to draft documents that meet the tests of UCC 3–104. As we have indicated above, the most common problem for the lawyer is likely to be the bank that wants to have its cake and eat it too. The bank wants a security agreement together with lots of other provisions and conditions on its promissory note form, yet it wants that form to be "negotiable." Sections 3–105 and 3–120 give the bank some reason for hope, but they do not open the door as widely as the bank might like.

SECTION 2. WHAT IS A NEGOTIABLE INSTRUMENT?

Perhaps the most subtle but important requirements of holder in due course status are first, that a party be a holder and second, the holder of an "instrument." We turn to the latter here.

PROMISSORY NOTE No. 813283
NATIONAL DIRECT STUDENT LOAN PROGRAM
STUDENT ID NUMBER ______________

____
LAST NAME FIRST MIDDLE

APPROVED BY ______________ HOME ADDRESS STREET ______________

DATE ________ TERM ________ CITY ______________
STATE ZIP

TRANS. CODE ________ FUND NO. ________ C/O OR FOREIGN ______________

$________ AMOUNT FINANCED ______________ DOLLARS COLLEGE ______ CLASS ______ SEX ______

DUE DATE OF NOTE ______ INST. TYPE ______ AMT. OF INSTALL. ______ INTEREST (ANNUAL PERCENTAGE RATE) ______ %M.S.____ F.C.____ F.I.____ DATE OF NOTE ______

I, ______________, hereinafter called the Maker, promise to pay to The Regents of The University of Michigan, hereinafter called the Institution located at Ann Arbor, Michigan, the sum of $________ (AMOUNT FINANCED) with interest (FINANCE CHARGE) at an ANNUAL PERCENTAGE RATE OF ________%, together with all attorney's fees and related costs and charges not to exceed 25% of the unpaid AMOUNT FINANCED and FINANCE CHARGE, incurred in the collection of any amount not paid when due according to the terms of this note.

The Maker further understands and agrees, and it is understood between the parties that:

I. All sums advanced pursuant to this Note are drawn from a Fund created under Part E of Title IV of the Higher Education Act of 1965, as amended, hereinafter called the Act. Such terms of the Note as are subject to interpretation shall be construed in the light of such Act and the Federal Regulations pertaining to such Act, copies of which shall be kept by the Institution.

II. Repayment of the AMOUNT FINANCED, together with the accrued FINANCE CHARGE, shall be made over a period commencing 6 months after the date on which the Maker ceases to carry at least one-half the normal full-time academic workload, and ending 10 years and 6 months after such date. The stated academic workload must be carried at an institution of higher education, or at a comparable institution outside the United States approved for this purpose by the U.S. Secretary of Education, hereinafter called the Secretary. The FINANCE CHARGE shall be accrued at the ANNUAL PERCENTAGE RATE from the beginning of such repayment period. If the Maker qualifies as a low-income individual during the repayment period, determined by using criteria of poverty established by the Bureau of the Census, the Maker may request an extension of the repayment period for up to an additional 10 years or an adjustment of the repayment schedule to reflect income, or both.

In the event that more than one loan is made to the Maker from the National Direct Student Loan Fund at the institution, the sum of the amounts advanced to the Maker shall, for repayment purposes, be combined into and regarded as the total loan made to the Maker, representing his/her total indebtedness to the Fund. The FINANCE CHARGE shall be computed on the unpaid balance of the total AMOUNT FINANCED. Hereafter, AMOUNT FINANCED and FINANCE CHARGE shall refer to the Maker's total loan. Each payment made by the Maker to the Institution shall be applied first to the FINANCE CHARGE which has accrued, then to the AMOUNT FINANCED. Repayment shall be made in equal monthly installments, with possible exception of the final installment which shall be for the remaining balance.

A schedule of monthly payments, detailing the number, amount, and due dates of such payments, the Total of Payments, AMOUNT FINANCED, and FINANCE CHARGE will be made available to the Maker by the Institution after the Maker ceases to carry at least a half-time academic load.

III. This Note is subject also to the following conditions:

A. The Maker may, at his/her option and without penalty, prepay all, or any part of the AMOUNT FINANCED plus accrued FINANCE CHARGE at any time. The FINANCE CHARGE shall cease to accrue on any prepayment of the AMOUNT FINANCED, and the Total of Payments shall be reduced accordingly.

B. (1) In the event of a failure to meet a scheduled payment of any of the installments due on this note, or the failure to file cancellation or deferment forms with the institution on time, the entire sum of unpaid AMOUNT FINANCED and accrued FINANCE CHARGE shall, at the option of the institution, become immediately due and payable. If the Maker defaults on the loan repayments the lending institution may disclose that the Maker has defaulted along with other relevant information, to credit bureau organizations. Further, if the Maker defaults on the loan repayments and the loan is sent to the Secretary for collection, the Secretary may disclose that the Maker has defaulted along with other relevant information to credit bureau organizations. (2) In the event of a failure to make timely payment of all or any part of a scheduled installment due on this note, or the failure to file cancellation or deferment forms with the institution on time a $1 penalty charge will be assessed for the first month or part of a month by which the installment or evidence is late, and $2 for each month or part of a month thereafter. If the lending institution elects to add the assessed charge to the outstanding principal of the loan, it must so inform the Maker before the due date of the next installment.

C. The FINANCE CHARGE shall not accrue, and installments need not be paid during any period: (1) during which the Maker is carrying, at an institution of higher education or at a comparable institution outside the United States approved for this purpose by the Secretary, at least one-half the normal full-time academic workload; or (2) not in excess of 3 years during which the Maker (a) is on full-time active duty as a member of the Armed Forces (Army, Navy, Air Force, Marine Corps, or Coast Guard) of the United States; or (b) is in service as a volunteer under the Peace Corps Act; or (c) is in service as a volunteer under Title 1 of the Domestic Volunteer Service Act of 1973 (ACTION); or (d) is a full-time volunteer in services which the Secretary has determined under the regulations to be comparable to service in the Peace Corps or under the Domestic Volunteer Service Act of 1973 (ACTION); or (e) is temporarily totally disabled as established by affidavit of a qualified physician, or unable to secure employment due to providing care required by a spouse who is so disabled; or (f) is an officer on full-time active duty in the commissioned corps of the U.S. Public Health Service; or (3) not in excess of 2 years during which the Maker is serving an internship required for professional recognition which is in turn required to begin professional practice or service.

No repayment of the AMOUNT FINANCED or the FINANCE CHARGE will be required until 6 months after the completion of any deferment period described in (1) or (2): or (3). Any such period in (1) (2) or (3) shall not be included in determining the 10 year period during which repayment must be completed as specified in Paragraph II.

D. For each complete academic year of service as detailed below, the Maker, upon application to the Student Loan Records Office at the Institution, is eligible to have his/her loan reduced at the following rates: 15 percent of the total AMOUNT FINANCED plus accrued FINANCE CHARGE for the first and second year of such service; 20 percent of the total AMOUNT FINANCED plus accrued FINANCE CHARGE for the third and fourth year of such service, and 30 percent of the total AMOUNT FINANCED plus accrued FINANCE CHARGE for the fifth year of such service.

Qualifying service is: (1) as a full-time teacher in a public or other non-profit private elementary or secondary school which is in a school district of a local educational agency which is eligible in such year for assistance pursuant to Title 1 of the Elementary and Secondary Education Act of 1965, and which for the purposes of this clause and for that year has been designated by the Secretary in accordance with the provisions of Section 465(A)(2) of the Act as a school with a high enrollment of students from low-income families; or (2) as a full-time teacher of handicapped children (including mentally retarded, hard of hearing, deaf, speech impaired, visually handicapped, seriously emotionally disturbed, orthopedically impaired, or other health impaired children, or children with specific learning disabilities who by reason thereof require special education and related services) in public or other non-profit elementary or secondary school system.

E. The AMOUNT FINANCED shall be reduced at the rate of 15 percent of the total AMOUNT FINANCED plus accrued FINANCE CHARGE for each complete academic year of service which the Maker is employed as a full-time staff member in a preschool program carried on Under Section 222(a)(1) of the Economic Opportunity Act of 1964 (HEAD START) up to a maximum of 100% of the AMOUNT FINANCED plus accrued FINANCE CHARGE. The program must operate for a period which is comparable to a full school year in the locality, and the salary of the Maker must not be more than the salary of a comparable employee of the local educational agency.

F. The AMOUNT FINANCED shall be reduced at the rate of 12½ percent of the total AMOUNT FINANCED plus accrued FINANCE CHARGE, up to a total of 50 percent of the AMOUNT FINANCED, for each complete year of service as a member of the Armed Forces of the United States in an area of hostilities that qualifies for special pay under Section 310 of Title 37, United States Code.

G. If the Maker should die or become permanently and totally disabled, the entire AMOUNT FINANCED plus the FINANCE CHARGE thereon shall be cancelled.

H. The Maker is responsible for informing the Institution of any name, social security number or address changes and must write to the Student Loan Records Office at the Institution to do so.

I. The Maker is obligated under Michigan Law for the payment of the note even though the Maker may be under eighteen (18) years of age. No delay on the part of the Institution in exercising any of its options, powers or rights or partial or single exercise thereof, shall constitute a waiver of any such options, powers or rights.

J. Notwithstanding the repayment schedule otherwise calculable to paragraph II, the Maker shall repay the total principal amount of this loan at the rate of not less than $30.00 per month. In the event the Maker receives or has received other National Direct Loans from other Funds authorized by the Act at one or more other lending institutions, he/she shall repay this Note at a monthly rate equal to not less than the amount by which $30.00 exceeds the total monthly rate of principal repayment on all such other loans, where only the Institution exercised the $30.00 option, and shall repay this Note and such other loans by dividing among the institutions the minimum repayment in proportion to the amount of principal advanced by each institution, where each institution exercises the $30.00 minimum option.

IV. This Note shall not be assigned by the institution except, (1) to the United States or an institution approved by the Secretary or, (2) to an institution the Maker has transferred to, if that institution is participating in the program (or, if not so participating, is eligible to do so and is approved by the Secretary for such purpose). The provisions of this Note that relate to the institution shall where appropriate relate to an assignee.

V. The Maker agrees to attend a scheduled group Exit Interview during the final term of enrollment at the Institution, or to contact the Student Loan Collections Office at the Institution in the event a scheduled interview cannot be attended.

VI. The Maker hereby certifies that he/she has listed below all National Direct Student Loans or National Defense Student Loans he/she has obtained at other Institutions.

SCHEDULE OF NATIONAL DIRECT STUDENT LOANS AND NATIONAL DEFENSE STUDENT LOANS AT OTHER INSITITUTIONS

AMOUNT	DATE	INSTITUTION	SIGNATURE OF MAKER
$			
$			

By signature below, the Maker acknowledges that he/she (1) has, prior to consummating this loan transaction, read and understand the above completely filled Promissory Note, including all of the consumer credit disclosures required by law, (2) has received a copy of such Note, and (3) agrees to be bound by the terms and conditions of such Note.

(Signature of Maker) Date

CAVEAT — This note shall be executed without security and without endorsement, except that, if the Maker is a minor and this note would not, under State Law, create a binding obligation, either security or endorsement may be required.

[E1119]

Note

Is the foregoing document negotiable under 3–104? When completed, it should be signed by the maker, but is the promise unconditional? It would be payable at a specific time, but where are the magic words "Pay to the Order of"? Consider some of the ways in which this note could be changed to draw its negotiability into question. For example, it might provide for a variable interest rate month by month, depending upon the interest rate on Treasury Bills. That might deprive it of its status as an order to pay a sum certain under 3–104(1)(b) because the sum would vary from period to period. If the note were only to pay to the University instead of pay to the order of University, that too would deprive it of its status as a negotiable instrument even though 3–805 would cause most of the provisions of Article 3 to apply to it. If, on the other hand, the note were simply, Pay to "One Keg of Nails," curiously that would not render it nonnegotiable. Do you see why?

The requisites of negotiability and the rationales therefor are set forth at page 1023. Even a quick reading of UCC 3–104(1) discloses that not every written promise to pay will constitute a negotiable instrument. Two of the easiest ways in which a writing can fail to be an instrument are by containing additional or conditional promises and so violating subsection (1)(b), or by failing to be payable "to order or to bearer" and so violating subsection (1)(d). The careful lawyer is aware that UCC 3–105 and 3–112 contain a variety of amplifications and limitations upon UCC 3–104(1). For example, UCC 3–112(1)(c) permits the maker to promise to maintain or protect collateral without thereby rendering the instrument non-negotiable under UCC 3–104. Thus one faced with the question whether a document is a negotiable instrument must study UCC 3–104, 3–105 and 3–112 with care. Whether an instrument is negotiable can arise in real life in a variety of circumstances. The transferee of a contract may find it in his interest to argue that the contract is negotiable. Likewise one who has taken an instrument that essentially "grew up out of the ground" (i.e., was drafted by a client), may argue that the instrument is negotiable and that he so qualifies as a holder in due course.

Problem 24–1

1. The following "collateral" note is used in secured transactions where the debtor "pledges" stock certificates or other tangibles to the bank. Is it negotiable?

SBIR NON–PURPOSE "STOCK" COLLATERAL DEMAND LOAN

Boston, Massachusetts ______ 19__ $______ ON DEMAND, the undersigned (jointly and severally if more than one) promise(s) to pay to the order of

THE FIRST NATIONAL BANK OF BOSTON (the "Bank")

at said Bank ______ Dollars ______________________________

with interest, payable monthly in arrears prior to maturity at a rate per annum calculated on the basis of a 365–day year for the actual number of days elapsed, which shall at all times be ______% above the Bank's 1978 Small Business Index Rate, as such rate is determined by the Bank from time to time; *provided that,* if (a) the undersigned ceases to qualify for the Bank's 1978 Small Business Index Rate, or (b) the Bank shall reduce its Base Rate to 9¼% or lower, or (c) the Bank, at its discretion, shall terminate the 1978 Small Business Index Rate, then, in each such case, upon notice from the Bank, interest shall be payable at a rate per annum which shall at all times be ______% above the Bank's Base Rate. The Base Rate shall mean the lowest general rate being charged from time to time by the Bank for new 90–day unsecured loans to substantial commercial borrowers. Interest after maturity will be payable on demand at 12% per annum or, if higher, at a rate per annum which shall at all times be 4% above the Base Rate. As collateral for the payment and performance of all Obligations, the following property has been deposited with the Bank:

____

____

Should the holder at any time deem itself insecure, the undersigned shall deliver to the holder, forthwith upon demand, additional collateral in an amount and of a character satisfactory to the holder.

Upon the occurrence of any of the following events of default: (a) default in the payment or performance of any of the Obligations; (b) loss, theft, substantial damage, sale or encumbrance to or of any property constituting collateral hereunder or the making of any levy, seizure or attachment thereof or thereon or the failure to pay when due any tax thereon or, with respect to any insurance policy, any premium therefor; (c) default under any instrument constituting collateral hereunder; (d) death, dissolution, termination of existence, insolvency, business failure, appointment of a receiver of any part of the property of, assignment for the benefit of creditors by, or the commencement of any proceedings under any bankruptcy or insolvency laws by or against any Obligor; thereupon or at any time thereafter (such default not having been previously cured) at the option of the holder, all Obligations of the maker shall become immediately due and payable without notice or demand and the holder shall then have in any jurisdiction where enforcement hereof is sought, in addition to all other rights and remedies, the rights and remedies of a secured party under the Uniform Commercial Code of Massachusetts.

Any sums credited by or due from the holder to any Obligor and any property of any Obligor in which the holder has any security interest or which may be in the possession of the holder may at any time be treated or held as collateral for the payment or performance of the Obligations of such Obligor. Regardless of the adequacy of collateral, the holder may apply such sums or property or realizations upon any such security interest against said Obligations at any time in the case of a primary Obligor but only against matured Obligations in the case of a secondary Obligor.

The holder may at its option, whether or not this note is due, demand, sue for, collect or make any compromise or settlement it deems desirable with reference to collateral held hereunder. Right is expressly granted to the holder at its option to transfer at any time to itself or to its nominee any securities or documents pledged hereunder and to receive the income thereon and hold the same as security herefor, or apply it on the principal or interest due hereon or due on any liability secured hereby. The holder shall have no duty as to the collection or protection of collateral held hereunder or any income thereon, and shall not be bound to take any steps necessary to preserve any rights in collateral against prior parties.

No delay or omission on the part of the holder in exercising any right hereunder shall operate as a waiver of such right or of any other right under this note. No waiver of any right shall be effective unless in writing and signed by the holder nor shall a waiver on one occasion be construed as a bar to or waiver of any such right on any future occasion.

Each Obligor waives presentment, demand, notice, protest, and all other demands and notices in connection with the delivery, acceptance, performance, default or enforcement of this note or of any collateral hereunder, and assents to any extension or postponement of the time of payment or any other indulgence under this note or such collateral, to any substitution, exchange or release of collateral, and to the addition or release of any other party or person primarily or secondarily liable.

The undersigned will pay on demand all costs of collection and attorneys' fees paid or incurred by the holder in enforcing this note on default.

As herein used, "Obligor" means any person primarily or secondarily liable hereunder or in respect hereto; "Obligation" means any Obligation hereunder or otherwise of any Obligor to the holder whether direct or indirect, absolute or contingent, due or to become due, now existing or hereafter arising; and "holder" means the payee or any endorser of this note who is in possession of it, or the bearer hereof if this note is at the time payable to the bearer.

Address ______________________ *Signed* ______________________

only ______________________ *by* ______________________

______________________ ______________________

Problem 24–2

Pascoe has just signed a contract to sell a valuable painting to the Mueller Charitable Foundation for display in its gallery. Under the contract, Pascoe agreed to have the painting cleaned and delivered within six months from the date of the contract and Mueller agreed to make and issue a negotiable promissory note for the price within two weeks from the date of the contract. You represent Pascoe. He tells you that he expects to negotiate the note immediately to a bank and asks you to draft a note that will be negotiable under the Code. The transaction is not secured. He also hands to you a list of items that both he and Mueller would like to have on the face of the note:

the date of the note should be two weeks after the contract for sale, which was dated January 15, 1981;

the note should be made payable to Philpot P. Pascoe or bearer; the purchase price of $150,000 should be stated as payable in three equal installments of $50,000 at 14% interest;

the obligation should be limited to payment from funds of the Mueller Charitable Foundation;

the note should state that Mueller's promise to pay is conditioned upon Pascoe's delivery of the painting on time;

equal payments are due on January 29, 1982, 1983, and 1984, subject to acceleration rights stated in the contract for sale;

if Mueller defaults, the holder may confess judgment against the maker and recover, in addition to the principal amount, reasonable attorney fees and collection costs.

Your job is to draft a negotiable promissory note which accomplishes, to the extent possible, the objectives of both parties. Be prepared to recommend alternatives or improvements. Consult UCC 3–104(1), 3–105, 3–112.

FARMERS PRODUCTION CREDIT ASSOCIATION v. FRANK ARENA

Supreme Court of Vermont, 1984.
145 Vt. 20, 481 A.2d 1064.

GIBSON, JUSTICE.

Defendant appeals a judgment entered against him following trial by court. The parties submitted the matter to the lower court on an agreed statement of facts. We affirm.

Plaintiff brought suit on a promissory note seeking to collect the overdue balance thereon. When the note was executed in 1973, defendant signed as a co-endorser with one Charles Michelson in order to obtain funds for their corporation. A & M Westminster Farm, Inc., to purchase and equip a dairy farm. At that time, defendant was president and 50% owner of the corporation. He signed the note both as president of the corporation and in his individual capacity. The note was secured by a second mortgage on the real property and a security interest in all the farm machinery, all crops and some 450 head of cattle. The corporation also obtained financing from the Federal Land Bank of Springfield, which was given a first mortgage on the real estate.

Defendant managed the farm until 1976 when the other stockholder became dissatisfied with the manner in which the farm was being operated. The dispute was resolved by bringing in Michelson's brother as manager and making him an equal one-third owner with the other two.

In August 1977 defendant learned that most of the herd was gone from the farm and only 37 cattle remained. At that time the corporation's loan payments were also in arrears. When defendant notified plaintiff that the cattle were gone, plaintiff took an assignment of the first mortgage, foreclosed on the property and sold the real estate. Plaintiff also exercised its right to sell the remaining cattle, crops and equipment. Plaintiff then brought this lawsuit to recover the balance due.

In his defense, defendant claims (1) that he is entitled to a discharge from liability under 9A V.S.A. § 3–606 because plaintiff, by making no attempt to locate the missing cattle or assign rights to defendant so he could pursue them, unjustifiably impaired any collateral value the cattle might have had, and (2) that plaintiff is estopped by its actions from seeking recovery from defendant.

9A V.S.A. § 3–606 provides as follows:

> (1) The holder discharges any party to the instrument to the extent that without such party's consent the holder
>
> * * *
>
> (b) unjustifiably impairs any collateral for the instrument given by or on behalf of the party or any person against whom he has a right of recourse.

As used in 9A V.S.A. Article 3, "instrument" is defined to mean "a negotiable instrument." *Id.* § 3–102(1)(e). In order to be "negotiable," an instrument must fulfill certain conditions, including the requirement that it "contain an unconditional promise or order to pay a *sum certain.*" *Id.* § 3–104(1)(b) (emphasis added). The "sum certain" requirement is fulfilled when the holder of an instrument is able to determine the amount then payable from the instrument itself, with any necessary computation. *Id.* § 3–106, comment 1. The computation must be one that can be made from the instrument itself without reference to any outside source; the statute "does not make negotiable a note payable with interest 'at the current rate.' " *Id.*

In this case, the instrument executed by the parties allowed for "future advances" to be made by plaintiff from time to time and also provided for a variable interest rate. As found by the trial court, plaintiff did advance additional funds from time to time, the last advance having been made in June 1975. It is thus impossible to determine from the instrument itself what the principal outstanding balance might be at any particular time or what rate of interest might be in effect. Thus, the instrument was nonnegotiable, and defendant is not entitled to be discharged from liability under 9A V.S.A. § 3–606. * * *

* * * Defendant has not sustained his burden of proof as to either equitable estoppel or estoppel by waiver.

Affirmed.

Notes

1. Often a third party will not know the amount due on a note for there may have been partial payments. If that fact does not deny the note negotiability, why did the future advance clause do so?

2. Surely the court could have applied UCC 3–606 by analogy. For discussion of the problems under UCC 3–606 see p. 1001 supra.

Section 3–104(1)(b) states that a negotiable instrument must have a promise or order to pay a "sum certain in money." The phrase "sum certain" is further defined by 3–106. That section states, for example, that an instrument does not fail the "sum certain" test simply because it provides for an exchange rate with a foreign currency or because there are different stated rates of interest before and after default. In referring to the term that permits a stated discount or addition for early or late payments, Comment 1 states that such a term does not deprive the note of negotiability but "the computation must be one which can be made from the instrument itself without reference to any outside source, and this section does not make negotiable a note payable with interest 'at the current rate'."

Do any or all of the following notes flunk the "sum certain" test?

1. Assume a note that provides for interest "4 points above prime." In determining that such a note did not violate the Louisiana law which calls for a interest rate to be "fixed in writing," the court held as follows:

> "Furthermore, variable interest rates keyed to the prime rate are commonplace in business loans. This court, in the absence of any case authority or logical reason, will not torture the words of the statute to invalidate thousands or perhaps tens of thousands of loans." *In re Jules LeBlanc, III,* 622 F.2d 872, 878–79 (5th Cir.1980).

2. What if the note provided it would bear interest at "ten percent provided such rate shall be adjusted annually to the amount of annual increase or decrease in the one-year United States Treasury Note issued annually on the anniversary of this note."

If some of these notes are not negotiable, should the law be changed? Surely such notes are now prevalent and their use is increasing as banks and other lenders endeavor to match their interest revenue to their own cost of funds.

Problem 24–3

American Surety issued a bond that provided that it would guarantee the repayment of a loan of $60,000 to creditor Getty Grafton (the creditor) who had been made to Omnibus (the debtor). It developed that Getty Grafton never made the loan but that in fact the loan was made by Cobb Bank and Trust to whom the surety bond was assigned. Upon default of Omnibus, Cobb made a demand for payment on the surety. The surety in turn stated that a condition of its making the loan was that there be a default in payments to Getty Grafton. Since the defaults were in payments to Cobb, the condition to their performance under the bond had not been met. The bank responded that the surety bond was itself a negotiable instrument. It argued therefore that it was a holder in due course of the instrument and took free of any such defense. A young lawyer in your office has suggested the following reasons why the bond should not be regarded as a negotiable instrument. Evaluate each of them.

1. The amount is uncertain because the obligation would be to pay not $60,000 (the maximum), but only the amount in default.

2. The bond is payable to "Getty Grafton, payee" and therefore the instrument is not payable to order or bearer.

3. Because of the condition of default on the underlying note and loan, the document is itself conditional and therefore not negotiable.

4. The form itself of the document being labeled "Guarantee" and being signed by a party as "Surety" and set out in the form of a letter means that it cannot be a negotiable instrument.

Which of these arguments is the best, the worst?

IN RE ESTATE OF BALKUS

Court of Appeals of Wisconsin, 1985.
128 Wis.2d 246, 381 N.W.2d 593.

Appeal from the circuit court for Sheboygan county. Before SCOTT, C.J., BROWN, P.J., and NETTESHEIM, J.

NETTESHEIM, J. Ann Vesely appeals from a judgment denying her claims against the estate of her brother, James T. Balkus. Vesely claims that she is entitled to payment on deposit slips and promissory notes found amongst Balkus's possessions because, as a holder in due course, she takes them free from the defenses asserted by the personal representative of the estate. We conclude the deposit slips are not negotiable instruments and, therefore, Vesely is not a holder in due course. We also conclude that the promissory notes are subject to the personal representative's defense of nondelivery because Vesely is not a holder in due course. Finally, we reject Vesely's claim of constructive delivery.

James T. Balkus died intestate on December 4, 1983. Shortly after his death, Vesely examined Balkus's personal property and discovered six deposit slips from a savings account maintained by Balkus. On each slip was a handwritten notation:

> Payable to Ann Balkus Vesely on P.O.D. The full amount and other deposits.[1]

Each slip was dated and signed by Balkus. Both parties treated "P.O.D." as meaning "payable on death." Vesely also found two promissory notes, both of which were made payable to her order. Each note was in the amount of $6000 and provided for five percent interest.[2] One note was dated March 23, 1961 and the other was dated July 10, 1963.

Vesely filed claims against Balkus's estate requesting payment on the deposit slips and the promissory notes. The circuit court disallowed Vesely's claims.

On appeal, Vesely argues that both the deposit slips and the promissory notes are negotiable instruments under Wisconsin's Uniform Commercial Code (UCC), chs. 401–409, Stats. Vesely further argues that under the UCC she is a holder in due course of the instruments and therefore takes the instruments free

1. Some of the deposit slips contained a slightly different notation:

"Payable to Ann Balkus Vesely on P.O.D. The full amts. & other succeeding deposits."

2. Vesely apparently loaned Balkus $12,000 in the early 1960's.

from the defenses asserted by the personal representative. We reject these arguments. * * *

Deposit Slips

We first address Vesely's contention that the endorsed deposit slips are negotiable instruments. Section 403.104(1), Stats., defines a negotiable instrument: [quoting] * * *

We conclude that the endorsed deposit slips are not negotiable instruments because they fail to meet the requirement that the writing be payable at a definite time. Section 403.109(2), Stats., states that an instrument which is "payable upon an act or event uncertain as to time of occurrence is not payable at a definite time." The 1961 Report of the Wisconsin Legislative Council indicates that § 403.109(2) "[m]akes post obituary notes non-negotiable, even after the death has occurred." See Wis.Stats.Ann. § 403.109 (West 1964) * * *[3]

Because the "payable on death" term of the deposit slips makes the instrument payable upon an event uncertain as to the time of occurrence, i.e., the date of Balkus's death, the endorsed deposit slips are not payable at a definite time and are therefore not negotiable instruments. In order to qualify as holder in due course, Vesely must hold a negotiable instrument. See § 403.302 and § 403.305, Stats. Vesely, thus, is not a holder in due course.

Promissory Notes

Holder in Due Course

We now turn to Vesely's arguments concerning the promissory notes she found in Balkus's possessions after his death. Vesely claims the notes are negotiable instruments and she is a holder in due course, taking the notes free from the defense of nondelivery asserted by the personal representative.

A holder in due course is a holder who takes an instrument for value, in good faith, and *without notice* that the instrument is overdue or has been dishonored or *of any defense against or claim to it* on the part of any person. Sec. 403.302(1), Stats. As payee of the notes, Vesely can be a holder in due course. See § 403.302(2). A payee who acquires the status of a holder in due course is, however, the exception rather than the rule. Saka v. Sahara-Nevada Corp., 558 P.2d 535, 536 [20 UCC Rep 958] (Nev.1976). "Where the payee is an immediate party to the underlying transaction, under normal circumstances he cannot claim this status [holder in due course] because he necessarily knows of any defenses to the contract." Id. * * *

Here, as payee of the notes, Vesely necessarily had notice and knowledge of the personal representative's defense of nondelivery because the notes were never delivered to her. Vesely's claim as a holder in due course therefore fails.

Constructive Delivery

Since Vesely is not a holder in due course of the notes and thus takes the notes subject to the defenses asserted by the personal representative, see § 403.306, Stats., we now look to the defense of nondelivery asserted by the

3. Vesely cites Sheldon v. Blackman, 188 Wis. 4, 205 N.W. 486 (1925), in support of her contention that "payment on death" represents a definite time and therefore the deposit slips are negotiable instruments. Sheldon, however, was decided before Wisconsin adopted the UCC. Both the Legislative Council's report and the Official UCC Comments indicate that the UCC changed prior law in which instruments payable upon death were considered negotiable. See Wis.Stats.Ann. § 403.109 (West 1964).

personal representative. It is undisputed that Balkus did not physically deliver the notes to Vesely. She argues, however, that a letter she received from Balkus in August 1974 constituted constructive delivery of the notes. The letter, in pertinent part, stated:

> "Also you will get & shall I say I will bequeath to you all my other junk in my apt. such as tools, radios, TV sets, clothing, clothes and also the money I owe you. I have $6000 in govt. bonds made out in your name & the banker told me, nobody could take it away from you. I also have 2 judgment notes made out to you for the amt. of money I borrowed from you in 1961 & 1962. That should take care of the interest I was supposed to pay you but I didn't."

We reject Vesely's claim that this letter constituted constructive delivery of the notes.

The trial court found that Balkus retained dominion and control of the notes and that he "simply never gave up ownership." These findings are not clearly erroneous. See § 805.17(2), Stats.

The general rule is that a promissory note has no effect unless it is delivered. * * * The UCC defines delivery of an instrument as the "voluntary transfer of possession." Sec. 401.201(14), Stats. A constructive delivery may be sufficient. * * * A constructive delivery occurs only when the maker indicates an intention to make the instrument an enforceable obligation against him or her by surrendering control over it and intentionally placing it under the power of the payee or a third person. * * *

Balkus never surrendered control nor transferred possession of the notes. It is undisputed that the notes were found in Balkus's possessions after his death. The notes were never placed under the control of Vesely or any other third party. We therefore reject Vesely's argument that the letter served as constructive delivery of the notes.

Assuming Holder in Due Course Status

Alternatively, even assuming Vesely is a holder in due course, we reject her argument that she takes the notes free from all defenses. Section 403.305, Stats., outlines the rights of a holder in due course:

> "To the extent that a holder is a holder in due course he takes the instrument free from:
>
> (1) All claims to it on the part of any person; and
>
> (2) *All defenses of any party to the instrument with whom the holder has not dealt except* * * *." [Emphasis added.]

A holder in due course, therefore, does not take an instrument free from the defenses of any party to the instrument with whom the holder has dealt. See, e.g., Bucci v. Paulick, 419 A.2d 1255, 1258 [28 UCC Rep 1391] (Pa.Super.Ct.1980). Balkus, as maker of the notes, was a party to the instrument and the personal representative stands in his place. See generally § 857.01 and § 857.03, Stats.

Here, Vesely dealt with Balkus. She loaned him $12,000. He wrote a letter to her indicating that he had notes in his possession which would pay her back. There were no other parties involved in making the notes nor any transfer of the notes to a third party. Under § 403.305, Stats., therefore, Vesely cannot take the notes free from the personal representative's defense of nondelivery because she dealt with Balkus.

By the Court.—Judgment affirmed.

[Some footnotes omitted.]

Notes

1. Even if the court had determined that the deposit slips were payable at a certain time, they would not have been negotiable. Do you see why?

2. What exactly is the defense that the defendant is asserting in *Balkus?*

3. If you represented Ms. Vesely in a subsequent transaction with a resurrected brother, how would you frame the transaction to insure her repayment out of his estate?

SECTION 3. WHO IS A HOLDER?

Once one has decided that the document with which he is dealing is a negotiable instrument (and in many cases it will take only ten seconds to make that decision as in the case of a routine check), he must determine whether the plaintiff is a holder. This question will most commonly arise when the instrument has been stolen or when there is some other irregularity in the chain of title and one or more of the prior owners' indorsements are missing. Assume for example that Desaix gives his check to Lannes made "payable to the order of Lannes." The check is stolen from Lannes by a thief, and the thief indorses Lannes's signature and passes it on to one who takes it for value and in good faith. When the one in possession sues Desaix, assume Desaix defends on the ground that the plaintiff lacks good title to the instrument, for he traces his title through a thief. *If* the plaintiff is a holder in due course he will have good title, and Desaix's defense will be unavailing. Observe, then, that even if all of the other requirements of holding in due course have been met (the instrument is a negotiable instrument and plaintiff gave value without notice and in good faith), we must still ask: Is the plaintiff a holder? Section 1–201(2) defines holder as follows:

> "Holder" means a person who is in possession of a document of title or an instrument or an investment security drawn, issued or indorsed to him or to his order or to bearer or in blank.

In our hypothetical case the plaintiff indeed has possession, but the question is whether the instrument was "drawn, issued or indorsed to him or to his order or to bearer or in blank." Since the check in question is not and has not ever been "bearer paper" (see UCC 3–111), we must find that the check was "indorsed" to the order of our particular plaintiff. That in turn requires a definition of indorsement, and the only section that comes close to a definition of indorsement is UCC 3–202(2) which reads as follows:

> (2) An indorsement must be written by or on behalf of the holder and on the instrument or on a paper so firmly affixed thereto as to become a part thereof.

Was the indorsement in our case "written by or on behalf of the holder"? The thief of the order instrument was not a holder because the instrument was neither payable to him nor indorsed to his order. Since he was not a holder he did not have the power to make an "indorsement" as that term is defined under UCC 3–202, for that power is reserved only to holders. The thief's transferee is not a holder because the instrument was not "indorsed" to him under UCC 1–201(2) by the thief and he as a non-holder in turn lacks the power under UCC 3–202(2) to indorse to another.

If the instrument was "bearer paper" at the time of its theft, the result is quite the opposite. While it may be open to question whether a thief of the bearer instrument is a holder (we believe that he is), there is no question that by delivering the bearer instrument to a third party he has "negotiated" it (see UCC 3–202) and so made the third party a holder within the language of UCC 3–202(1) and 1–201(20).

To summarize: If an "order" instrument is stolen by a thief no one who claims through the thief will ever be a holder or a holder in due course of that instrument. (For what an "order" instrument is, see UCC 3–110). Conversely such a subsequent taker of a bearer instrument can and likely will be a holder and a holder in due course.

Problem 24–4

Murat is the owner of two checks. Both are drawn by Lannes. One is made payable "to the order of Murat" and the other payable to the order of cash. Thief steals both of the checks and he passes them to McDonald by signing on the reverse side in each case "pay to the order of McDonald, Murat." After the checks are dishonored McDonald sues Lannes on his drawer's contract (3–413(2)). Lannes defends on the ground that McDonald has no title to the checks. McDonald counters that he is a holder in due course and so has good title. To that Lannes responds that one of the checks was always an order instrument and that the other was made into an order instrument by the signature of the thief, thus, so his argument goes, McDonald was a holder in due course of neither check. You are the judge. Who wins?

Note: Indorsement as an Exclusive Method of Passing Title

In the preceding and subsequent chapters, we deal with the contractual liability of the indorser and with his unique status as a surety. One should understand that the indorsement not only creates a contractual liability, but is also the symbolic act that transfers title to the instrument by one party to another. Indeed, as the problem immediately above discloses, indorsement is the exclusive method by which one can transfer the best title to order instruments (ones payable to order of a named person or indorsed so payable). No other attempted transfers of title give rise to holder in due course status. Note that UCC 3–305 refers in subsection 1 to "all claims" and subsection 2 to "all defenses." Subsection 1 thus refers to assertions of paramount title that are cut off by holder in due course status. As the student works through the succeeding chapters, he should be aware of the fact that there are not only contract claims but also title claims (claims often asserted by way of conversion actions), but the title of the defendant or plaintiff will often depend upon the kinds of indorsements through which he traces his own title claim.

SECTION 4. TAKING FOR VALUE

Note that the word "value" means one thing in most of the Code (UCC 1–201(44)) and another thing in Articles 3 and 4 (UCC 3–303 and 4–209). As you deal with the problems and cases that follow, consider why the drafters used a more restrictive definition of value for the purposes of commercial paper than they used elsewhere.

Problem 24–5

Client is a midwestern investor willing to take substantial risks with the possibility of high returns. Client would like to purchase $1,000,000 of bonds of a moderate size oil company that had been offered to him for $230,000. The bonds were originally issued as part of a leveraged buyout and are clearly negotiable. There have been rumors in the trade about some securities violation by the maker.

The cash flow of the maker is not strong and because of the low price of oil (late 1986) the debt instruments of no small size oil companies are selling at a premium. Client wants your written assurance that giving $230,000 for a $1,000,000 obligation will be giving value. Will you give it to him? Are there any other potential difficulties to the client achieving the status of a holder in due course here?

A common route for a check to travel during its lifetime is from the hands of the payee to the hands of the payee's bank (depositary bank—UCC 4–105), thence back to the drawee bank (the drawer's bank) also called the payor bank (UCC 4–105). If a disruption occurs while the check is en route, it is likely to be in the hands of a bank, and it is sometimes important to know whether this "collecting bank" is a holder in due course. The following cases deal with the status of such a bank.

PEORIA SAVINGS AND LOAN v. JEFFERSON TRUST

Supreme Court of Illinois, 1980.
81 Ill.2d 461, 43 Ill.Dec. 712, 410 N.E.2d 845.

Appeal from the Circuit Court of Peoria County.

RYAN, J. The defendant, Jefferson Trust and Savings Bank of Peoria (Jefferson), appeals a judgment entered in the circuit court of Peoria County for the plaintiff, Peoria Savings and Loan Association (Peoria Savings). The appellate court affirmed the judgment and we granted leave to appeal. Broadly stated, the issue is whether Jefferson became a holder in due course of a $70,000 check drawn by Peoria Savings under section 3–303(b) of the Uniform Commercial Code (Ill.Rev.Stat. 1975, ch. 26, par. 3–303(b)) (taking an instrument in payment of an antecedent claim).

On January 30, 1975, Owen D. Cassidy, a Peoria businessman, maintained two accounts with Jefferson. One was a personal account in the name of "Owen D. Cassidy"; the other was an account in the name of "Cassidy Company."

On January 30, 1975, Cassidy deposited a check for $70,000 in his personal account with Jefferson and was given provisional credit for that amount. The check, designating Cassidy as payee, was drawn on a Cassidy Company account at the Harris Trust and Savings Bank in Chicago (the Harris check). Between January 30, 1975, and February 5, 1975, $61,039.30 was withdrawn against the provisional credit given to the Cassidy account for the Harris check, leaving in his account at Jefferson on February 5, 1975, only $8,960.78.

On the morning of February 5, 1975, a Jefferson return teller received a telephone call from the Continental Illinois Bank and Trust Company of Chicago, which was Jefferson's intermediary bank in that city, advising that the Harris check for $70,000 had been dishonored for insufficient funds and was being returned. The Jefferson account at the Continental Bank was charged $70,000 for the dishonor. The teller informed Ned Middendorf, a vice-president of Jefferson, of the dishonor. At approximately 3 p.m. Middendorf informed Cassidy by telephone of the dishonor and advised him that the overdraft would have to be covered that day. Cassidy replied that he would take care of it.

Approximately one-half hour after receiving the demand from Jefferson, Cassidy arrived at Peoria Savings. He informed Barbara Horn, the savings manager, that he desired to open a $10,000 savings account with Peoria Savings. She took Cassidy to meet with the president of Peoria Savings to discuss interest rates. Within a few minutes Cassidy returned to Mrs. Horn and gave her an

$80,000 check payable to Cassidy drawn on a Cassidy Company account at the Northern Trust Company of Chicago (the Northern Trust check). Without verifying the check, Mrs. Horn used $10,000 of the check to open a savings account in Cassidy's name, and gave him a check for $70,000 to cover the difference (the Peoria Savings check). This check was payable to Cassidy and was drawn upon a checking account Peoria Savings maintained at Jefferson. This check was given to Cassidy at approximately 4 p.m.

The buildings housing Peoria Savings and Jefferson were adjacent to each other. At the trial, Middendorf testified he returned to his desk at approximately 4 p.m. after a short absence and discovered the Peoria Savings' check, which had been endorsed by Cassidy, lying on his desk. It was accompanied by a deposit ticket for Cassidy's personal account, the same account in which the dishonored $70,000 Harris check had been deposited.

Middendorf delivered the $70,000 check and deposit ticket to a teller, but before the teller processed the check, he retrieved both documents. Next, Middendorf called Jim Berry, a vice-president at Peoria Savings, and inquired as to the circumstances of the $70,000 Peoria Savings check and if Berry was familiar with transactions involving Cassidy and large checks. Middendorf testified that during prior business relationships Cassidy had mentioned transferring substantial deposits from Chicago banks to Jefferson and that the Peoria Savings check caused him to wonder if the large funds promised to Jefferson had been deposited with Peoria Savings. Berry stated that he knew nothing about the matter, but would inquire and call Middendorf back. After his conversation with Middendorf, Berry talked to Mrs. Horn and learned of the transaction involving Peoria Savings and Cassidy. He then requested that she call the Northern Trust to verify the Cassidy Company account. Mrs. Horn telephoned Northern Trust and was advised that the Cassidy Company account contained sufficient funds to cover an $80,000 check. Horn relayed this information to Berry, and they discussed the matter with Peoria Savings' president, Mr. McFarland. He directed Mrs. Horn to call Northern Trust and request that they place a hold on the funds necessary to pay the $80,000 check. When Mrs. Horn made her request to the Northern Trust she was informed that there were sufficient funds to cover an $8,000 check but not an $80,000 check and that the Northern Trust employee had misunderstood her on the first call. At trial it was established that the balance in the Cassidy Company account at Northern Trust was $8,700.80 on February 5, 1975.

Mrs. Horn related this information to Berry and McFarland. At approximately 4:30 or 4:40 p.m., Berry walked over to the Jefferson and informed Middendorf that Peoria Savings had been advised by Northern Trust that there were insufficient funds to cover the $80,000 drawn on Northern Trust. Middendorf was advised that the $80,000 Northern check was the consideration for Peoria Savings issuing its $70,000 check to Cassidy. There is a dispute as to whether Berry placed a verbal stop order on the Peoria Savings check at this time; however, Middendorf testified he told Berry a written stop order would be prepared and ready for Berry's signature the next morning. After Berry left Jefferson, Middendorf placed the $70,000 Peoria Savings check and the accompanying deposit ticket in the bank vault.

The next morning, February 6, Berry arrived at Middendorf's office about 10 a.m. and signed the stop order that Middendorf had prepared. Middendorf still had the Peoria Savings check and the deposit slip in his possession; they were unprocessed. Later that day he turned them over to George Kirkpatrick, a senior vice-president at Jefferson, who retained possession of the documents. At approximately 4 p.m. on February 7, Kirkpatrick took the Peoria Savings check and deposit slip to the Jefferson proof department, the documents were processed, and Cassidy's account was credited $70,000. Kirkpatrick testified that he did not present the written stop-payment order to the proof department with the check and deposit ticket because Jefferson considered it to be a wrongful order. Consequently, on February 10, the Peoria Savings account at Jefferson was debited $70,000 and Kirkpatrick testified the debit was a setoff for what was considered to be a wrongful stop-payment order. Peoria Savings was notified of the debit on February 11.

Subsequently, as a result of various transactions involving Cassidy's personal and business accounts with Jefferson, the business account was closed, and on March 19, 1975, $13,133.08, the balance remaining in the personal account, was credited to the Peoria Savings account.

On February 4, 1976, Peoria Savings brought this action against Jefferson to recover the amount of $56,866.92, the difference between the $70,000 check and the $13,133.08 credit given to Peoria Savings by Jefferson. On November 3, 1978, after a bench trial, the trial court entered judgment for Peoria Savings for $56,866.92. Jefferson appealed, and the appellate court affirmed the judgment of the trial court. 76 Ill.App.3d 915 [395 N.E.2d 739].

Jefferson argues that it became a holder in due course as soon as Cassidy placed the Peoria Savings check on Middendorf's desk at 4 p.m. on February 5, 1975, and that, as a result, Jefferson took the check free from all defenses except those real defenses enumerated in § 3–305(2) of the Uniform Commercial Code (Ill.Rev.Stat. 1975, ch. 26, par. 3–305(2)). We agree.

This case is controlled by the Uniform Commercial Code, which has been adopted in Illinois. (Ill.Rev.Stat. 1975, ch. 26, par. 1–101 et seq.). Section 3–302(1) (Ill.Rev.Stat. 1975, ch. 26, par. 3–302(1)) provides that a holder in due course is a holder who takes the instrument (a) for value, and (b) in good faith, and (c) without notice that it is overdue or has been dishonored or of any defense against or claim to it on the part of any person.

Under § 3–303(b) (Ill.Rev.Stat. 1975, ch. 26, par. 3–303(b)), a holder takes an instrument for value when he takes the instrument in payment of or as security for an antecedent claim against any person whether or not the claim is due. It is a basic rule of statutory construction that the words of a statute should be given their plain, ordinary and accepted meaning, unless to do so would defeat the legislative intent. (Department of Public Work & Buildings v. Wishnevsky (1972), 51 Ill.2d 550, 552; Droste v. Kerner (1966), 34 Ill.2d 495, 503.) The word "take" means " 'to get into one's possession or power; to acquire; to obtain; to procure.' " (Kimbell Trust & Savings Bank v. Hartford Accident & Indemnity Co. (1928), 333 Ill. 318, 320.) Based upon the plain meanings of the words, it is apparent that Jefferson took the Peoria Savings check at 4 p.m. on February 5, 1975, when it was placed on Middendorf's desk. However, the plaintiff would have us read into the applicable legislative language a requirement that a bookkeeping entry must be made before the holder of the instrument taken in payment of an antecedent claim, or debt, can be said to have taken for value. Under the plain language of § 3–303(b) the holder takes for value when he takes an instrument in payment of an antecedent claim, not when he makes a bookkeeping entry.

Under the facts of this case, Jefferson had a claim against Cassidy before the Peoria Savings check was ever passed. Cassidy was the endorser of the dishonored Harris check and, under the Code, Jefferson did not have to make a bookkeeping entry in Cassidy's account before the claim against him came into existence. (Ill.Rev.Stat. 1975, ch. 26, par. 3–122(3).) In pertinent part, § 3–122(3) provides:

> "(3) A cause of action against * * * an indorser of any instrument accrues upon demand following dishonor of the instrument. Notice of dishonor is a demand."

Thus, a cause of action against Cassidy arose when Cassidy was notified of the dishonor and a demand was made on him to cover this dishonor. The oral notification (Ill.Rev.Stat. 1975, ch. 26, par. 3–508(3)) of dishonor by Middendorf to Cassidy on February 5, 1975, was effective to produce a cause of action running to Jefferson. (Ill.Rev.Stat. 1975, ch. 26, par. 3–414.) It is clearly manifested that Jefferson had a claim or cause of action against Cassidy after Middendorf called Cassidy and demanded that he make good the Harris check.

Peoria Savings argues that Jefferson could not have been a holder in due course at 4 p.m. on February 5, 1975, of the $70,000 Peoria Savings check because Jefferson did not know how much of an overdraft was created in the Cassidy account as a result of the dishonored Harris check. From the facts it is clear Cassidy owed Jefferson a debt upon receiving notice of the overdraft on February 5. The size of the claim has no bearing on the issue of whether Jefferson took the Peoria Savings check for value, but only on the "extent" that Jefferson took for value.

The evidence in this case clearly indicated that the Peoria Savings check, coupled with the deposit slip, left on Middendorf's desk was delivered and taken in payment of Cassidy's antecedent debt to Jefferson. A short review of the facts bears this out. Middendorf testified that he contacted Cassidy by telephone at approximately 3 p.m., informed him of the dishonor of the $70,000 Harris check, and advised him that the overdraft created by the dishonor would have to be covered that day. Cassidy replied that he would take care of it and one hour later delivered the $70,000 Peoria Savings check to Jefferson. Thus it is clear that Cassidy intended the $70,000 Peoria Savings check to cover the antecedent debt he owed to Jefferson.

It has been held that the use of the legislature of certain language in some provisions of a statute, and wholly different language in other provisions, indicates that different results were intended. * * * Had the legislature intended under § 3–303(b) that a holder could not take an instrument for value until the instrument was "posted" to or "applied" to an account, it would have expressly so provided as it did in §§ 4–213(1)(c) and 4–213(4) (Ill.Rev.Stat. 1975, ch. 26, pars. 4–213(1)(c), 4–213(4)). Since the legislature did not so provide, a requirement of "posting" or "applying" it should not be read into § 3–303(b).

Peoria Savings and the appellate court relied heavily on out-of-State cases to read a bookkeeping requirement into § 3–303(b). We find that reliance on these cases was misplaced. In none of the decisions relied on by the appellate court was the issue raised by this case squarely presented. * * *

Peoria Savings' next contention is that Jefferson was not a holder in due course because it took the check with notice that Peoria Savings had a defense. We find no merit to this contention. As noted in the record, when Jefferson took the check from Cassidy at 4 p.m. on February 5, 1975, Peoria Savings did not know it had a defense to the check. It was not until Jefferson contacted Berry, asking about the check, that anyone finally learned that there was a defense. Section 1–201(25) (Ill.Rev.Stat.1975, ch. 26, par. 1–201(25)) of the Code provides that a person has "notice" of a fact when: "(a) he has actual knowledge of it; or (b) he has received a notice or notification of it; or (c) from all the facts and circumstances known to him at the time in question he has reason to know that it exists."

It is true that Middendorf retrieved the Peoria Savings check from the teller and called Berry at Peoria Savings to inquire about Cassidy. Middendorf testified that he was concerned that Cassidy may have made substantial deposits in Peoria Savings which he felt had been promised to Jefferson by Cassidy. Middendorf's actions only show that his suspicions were aroused concerning Cassidy's dealings. These suspicions were not tantamount to a reason for Middendorf to know that Peoria Savings had a defense to its check. Facts and circumstances calculated to merely arouse or excite suspicion cannot be equated with knowledge, or a reason to know. Kavanagh v. Bank of America (1909), 238 Ill. 404, 408.

Jefferson also knew of the dishonor of the Harris check, but this again did not cause it to know, or have reason to know, that Peoria Savings had a defense to its check. The knowledge that one of Cassidy's checks had been dishonored would not, when considered with the other facts, give Middendorf knowledge, or a reason to know, that a defense existed to the Peoria Savings check. Cassidy's credit with Jefferson was good, he had two small notes with Jefferson that were in good standing, and he did not have a history of writing checks which had been dishonored. This was Jefferson's first experience of a dishonored check with Cassidy. Jefferson had seen financial statements showing that Cassidy had substantial income and knew he was from a prominent local family. Considering all of the pertinent evidence in the record, and the applicable authorities, it is clear that Jefferson did not take the Peoria Savings check with notice that Peoria Savings had a defense to the check.

* * *

For these reasons we reverse the judgments of the appellate court and the circuit court of Peoria County.

Notes

1. Exactly when did Jefferson give value? What Code section says so?

2. Section 3–302 says that one must "take" an instrument for value and without notice. Assume, for example, that Jacob takes a check from Esau. Jacob promises to deliver a $100,000 combine to Esau for the check. Before he delivers, Jacob discovers that there is a defense. Since his mere promise to deliver is not value, he has not given value at the time he acquires notice, although he "took" without notice. If an uninformed subordinate of Jacob delivers the combine to Esau, can Jacob later claim holder in due course status?

3. Assume that Cassidy had not just bounced a few checks, but had been involved in a large-scale kiting scheme. Assume further that Middendorf and his colleagues had concluded that such a kiting scheme had existed by a careful examination of the account's history on the evening before they received the check in question. Would that knowledge have deprived them of holder in due course status?

Problem 24–6

On day 1 Augereau gives his check to Bernadotte for $10,000. Bernadotte deposits the check in his bank, First National Bank. On day 2 Augereau orders his bank to stop payment; on day 3 the check is presented to the payor bank and is returned to Bernadotte's bank with a notice of non-payment. On day 4 Bernadotte withdraws the entire $10,000 and leaves his account with only $5,000, the amount that was in his account on day 1. The depositary bank now sues Augereau and claims status as a holder in due course and thus freedom from the good defense which Augereau has against Bernadotte. Who prevails?

CITIZENS NATIONAL BANK OF ENGLEWOOD v. FORT LEE SAVINGS AND LOAN ASSOCIATION

Superior Court of New Jersey, Law Division, Bergen County, 1965.
89 N.J.Super. 43, 213 A.2d 315.

BOTTER, J.S.C.

Citizens National Bank of Englewood has moved for summary judgment to recover monies advanced against a check which was deposited with the bank for collection but was later dishonored. The issue is whether the bank should be protected for advances made to its depositor before the check cleared. The summary judgment is sought against the drawer and payee-indorser who stopped payment on the check.

On August 27, 1963, George P. Winter agreed to sell a house in Fort Lee, New Jersey to defendant Jean Amoroso and her husband. On the same day Amoroso requested her bank, Fort Lee Savings and Loan Association (Fort Lee Savings), to issue the bank's check to her order for $3,100 to be used as a deposit on the contract for sale. Fort Lee Savings complied by drawing the check against its account with the Fort Lee Trust Company. Later that day Amoroso indorsed and delivered the check to Winter, and he deposited the check in his account at the plaintiff bank. At that time he had a balance of $225.33. After the $3,100 check was deposited the bank cashed a $1,000 check for him against his account. In addition, on August 27 or August 28, the bank cleared and charged Winter's account with four other checks totaling $291.76.

The next day Amoroso discovered that Winter had previously sold the property to a third party by agreement which had been recorded in the Bergen County Clerk's Office. Amoroso immediately asked Winter to return her money. She claims that he admitted the fraud and agreed to return the deposit. But when Mrs. Amoroso and her husband reached Winter's office they learned that he had attempted suicide. He died shortly thereafter.

Upon making this discovery, in the afternoon of August 28, the Amorosos went to Fort Lee Savings to advise it of the fraud and request it to stop payment on the check. The bank issued a written stop payment order which was received by the Fort Lee Trust Company, the drawee, on the following day, August 29. In the meantime the $3,100 check was sent by plaintiff through the Bergen County Clearing House to the Fort Lee Trust Company. By then the stop payment order had been received. Notice of nonpayment was thereafter transmitted to plaintiff.

Plaintiff contends that, under the Uniform Commercial Code, N.J.S.A. 12A:1–101 et seq., it is a holder in due course to the extent of the advances made on Winter's account and is entitled to recover these moneys from the drawer and payee-indorser of the check. Plaintiff's claim against the drawee, Fort Lee Trust Company, was voluntarily dismissed by plaintiff at the pretrial conference.

The central issue is whether plaintiff bank is a holder in due course, since a holder in due course will prevail against those liable on the instrument in the absence of a real defense. Of course, it must first be determined that plaintiff is a "holder" if plaintiff is to be declared a holder in due course. Amoroso contends that plaintiff bank does not own the check because it is only an agent of its depositor Winter for collection purposes and, consequently, plaintiff is not a "holder." It is true that a collecting bank is presumed to be an agent of the owner of the item unless a contrary intention appears, or until final settlement. N.J.S.A. 12A:4–201(1). Assuming that the bank was at all times an agent in this case, it does not follow that the bank cannot also be a holder. On the contrary, a collecting bank may be a holder whether or not it owns the item. * * * The definition of "holder" includes a person who is in possession of an instrument indorsed to his order or in blank. N.J.S.A. 12A:1–201(20). It is clear that the bank is a holder of the check notwithstanding that it may have taken the check solely for collection and with the right to charge back against the depositor's account in the event the check is later dishonored. * * *

To be a holder in due course one must take a negotiable instrument for value, in good faith and without notice of any defect or defense. N.J.S.A. 12A:3–302(1). Amoroso contends that plaintiff did not act in good faith or is chargeable with notice because it allowed Winter to draw against uncollected funds at a time when his account was either very low or overdrawn. Winter's account was low in funds. However, this fact, or the fact that Winter's account was overdrawn, currently or in the past, if true, would not constitute notice to the collecting bank of an infirmity in the underlying transaction or instrument and is not evidence of bad faith chargeable to the bank at the time it allowed withdrawal against the deposited check. N.J.S.A. 12A:1–201(19) and (25); N.J.S.A. 12A:3–304. * * * As stated in First Nat'l Bank of Springfield v. DiTaranto, 9 N.J.Super. 246, 253, 75 A.2d 907, 911 (App.Div.1950):

> "Evidence of fraud, not merely suspicious circumstances, must have been brought home to the Bank as a holder for value whose rights had accrued before maturity, in order to defeat its recovery upon the ground of fraud in the inception of the negotiable note or between the parties to it. Hudson County Nat. Bank v. Alexander Furs, Inc., supra. To constitute notice to the Bank of the alleged infirmity in the note or defect in the title of Tidey who negotiated it, the Bank must have had actual knowledge of the infirmity or defect or knowledge of such facts that the action amounted to bad faith."

Moreover, a depositary bank may properly charge an account by honoring a check drawn by a depositor even though it creates an overdraft. N.J.S.A. 12A:4–401(1). It would be anomalous for a bank to lose its status as a holder in due course merely because it has notice that the account of its depositor is overdrawn.

Lacking bad faith or notice of a defect or defense, plaintiff will be deemed a holder in due course if one additional element is satisfied, namely, the giving of value for the instrument. Prior to the adoption of the Uniform Commercial Code the general rule was that a bank does give value and is a holder in due course to the extent that it allows a depositor to draw against a check given for collection notwithstanding that the check is later dishonored. * * * this rule applies even though the item is received for collection only under an agreement with the bank that gives the bank the right to charge back against the depositor's account the amount of any item which is not collected. It is sometimes said that the contract of conditional credit is changed when the bank honors the deposit by allowing a withdrawal, and the bank then becomes the owner of or holder of a lien on the item to the extent of value given. * * *

This result is continued by provisions of the Uniform Commercial Code which give plaintiff a security interest in the check and the monies represented by the check to the extent that credit given for the check has been withdrawn or applied. N.J.S.A. 12A:4–208 and 209. See also N.J.S.A. 12A:4–201 and UCC Comment 5 thereunder. * * * [quoting UCC 4–207 and 4–209]

The New Jersey Study Comment under N.J.S.A. 12A:4–209 includes the following:

> "Because the bank is a holder of the item in most cases, it is possible for it to be a holder in due course if it otherwise qualifies by its good faith taking, prior to maturity, for value. See, UCC sec. 3–302; NIL sec. 52 (N.J.S.A. 7:2–52). It is important for a bank to be a holder in due course when the depositor fails, for this status enables it to prevail over the obligor (drawer or maker) of the instrument even though the obligor has some personal defense against the payee (depositor)."

It would hinder commercial transactions if depositary banks refused to permit withdrawal prior to clearance of checks. Apparently banking practice is to the contrary. It is clear that the Uniform Commercial Code was intended to permit the continuation of this practice and to protect banks who have given credit on deposited items prior to notice of a stop payment order or other notice of dishonor. * * *

It is also contended that liability on the check is excused because N.J.S.A. 12A:4–403 gives Fort Lee Savings the right to order Fort Lee Trust Company to stop payment on the check. However, UCC Comment 8 under this section makes it clear that the stop payment order cannot avoid liability to a holder in due course. "The payment can be stopped but the drawer remains liable on the instrument to the holder in due course * * *." See Carhart v. Second Nat'l Bank, 98 N.J.L. 373, 120 A. 636 (Sup.Ct.1923).

Finally, Amoroso attempts to raise the fraud perpetrated by Winter against Amoroso as a defense to plaintiff's claim. Plaintiff's status as a holder in due course insulates it from all personal defenses of any party to the instrument with whom it has not dealt, although real defenses may still be asserted. N.J. S.A. 12A:3–305. The defense raised here is fraud in inducing Amoroso to enter into the contract. There is no suggestion that either defendant signed the check without knowledge of "its character or its essential terms." N.J.S.A. 12A:3–305(2)(c). Therefore the fraud is a personal defense available only against Winter and cannot be asserted against plaintiff. See Bancredit, Inc. v. Bethea, 65 N.J.Super. 538, 168 A.2d 250 (App.Div.1961); Meadow Brook Nat'l Bank v. Rogers, 44 Misc.2d 250, 253 N.Y.S.2d 501 (Dist.Ct.1964).

Accordingly both Fort Lee Savings as drawer and Amoroso as indorser of the check are liable to plaintiff. N.J.S.A. 12A:3–413(2) and N.J.S.A. 12A:3–414(1), defining the liability of a drawer and indorser of a negotiable instrument to a holder in due course.

The motion for summary judgment will be granted in the sum of $1,066.43, plus interest. The amount of the judgment represents advances made on Winter's account before notice of dishonor, $1,291.76, less the existing balance of $225.33 in Winter's account. This opinion will not deal with the disposition of claims between Amoroso and Fort Lee Savings. By reason of the stop payment order Fort Lee Savings has on hand sufficient funds which were charged against Amoroso's account to meet plaintiff's judgment, and part of these funds, representing the difference between the potential judgment and the $3,100 retained, has been refunded to Amoroso pursuant to the pretrial order.

Problem 24–7

1. Augereau, payee on a $100,000 check, deposits it in his account. He makes the deposit over the counter on Monday, April 2. In which of the following cases has Bernadotte Bank, the depositary bank, given value?

a. Bank has done nothing on the evening of April 2 except to credit the account.

b. Bank credits the account and ten days pass.

c. Bank credits the account and thus changes it from $80,000 overdrawn to a positive balance of $20,000.

d. A provisional credit of $100,000 is given in the account for the uncollected funds and Augereau draws $70,000 out in the form of a cashier's check the next day.

e. On April 2 Augereau gets a provisional credit and on April 3 the Bank makes a loan to Augereau of $50,000.

Can all of the problems above be answered in some way by reference to UCC 4–208? The student should not forget UCC 4–213(4) nor 3–303 and the comments to it.

SECTION 5. IN GOOD FAITH AND WITHOUT NOTICE

Note that a transferee is "in good faith" under UCC 1–201(19) if he takes honestly "in fact in the conduct or transaction concerned." Thus a transferee takes in good faith if he takes honestly albeit imprudently. The statutory history suggests that it is of no consequence that a reasonable, prudent man would not have taken the instrument or would have demanded better identification. The current Code section is a change from a section which contained the following words in 1952: "* * * in good faith *including observance of the reasonable commercial standards of any business in which the holder may be engaged.*" Supplement # 1 to the 1952 Official Draft deleted the italicized words and gave the following reason for change: "The change consists of striking out the reference to reasonable commercial standards * * *. The omission is intended to make clear that the doctrine of an objective standard of good faith * * * is not intended to be incorporated in Article 3." In light of this history, is it still possible that one's lack of diligence may keep him from being a holder in due course?

One should note that a payee may be a holder in due course (UCC 3–302(2)) if he meets the requirements of UCC 3–302(1). In the normal run of circumstances a payee's status as an HIDC is irrelevant because UCC 3–305(2) permits one to take free only of the personal defenses of a "party to the instrument with whom the holder has not dealt." Most payees will have "dealt" with the maker or drawer even if they are technically holders in due course. Thus a payee-holder in due course will not be able to enjoy the most significant benefit normally accorded one in his shoes. This is not to say that a payee will always be subject to the drawer's or maker's defenses; Comment 2 to UCC 3–302 presents a series of hypothetical circumstances in which the payee does not deal with the drawer or maker and would, therefore, take free of any personal defenses.

Satisfying the requirements of UCC 3–202(1) is the most common method of securing the rights of a holder in due course, but there is yet another means of securing that same end, UCC 3–201. According to UCC 3–201 a transferor vests in a transferee such rights as he had in the instrument. Thus although a transferee, X, has notice of a fraud perpetrated in the original transaction (but was not himself a party to the fraud) and, therefore, could not qualify as a holder in due course under UCC 3–302(1), if his transferor, Y, was a holder in due course (ignorant of the fraud), X would succeed to Y's rights and become one with the rights of a holder in due course himself. This is called the "shelter principle." Does the way in which one obtains holder in due course status, through the use of UCC 3–302(1) or 3–201, make any significant difference? Consider the following problem:

Problem 24–8

Desaix gives Augereau a check for $50,000 in return for an extensive manuscript. The check is dated 1–2–75. On 1–5 Augereau transfers the check for value to Lannes who deposits it in his bank on 2–10–75. In the meantime Desaix has discovered that the book is not what was promised and has stopped payment on the check. If Augereau and Lannes disappear, may the bank recover from Desaix notwithstanding his defense of failure of consideration? What is the bank's cause of action?

INDYK v. HABIB BANK LIMITED

United States Court of Appeals, Second Circuit, 1982.
694 F.2d 54.

CARDAMONE, CIRCUIT JUDGE:

* * * The first [issue] is whether a party to whom a bank's postdated cashier's check is delivered takes the check as a holder in due course; we hold that under New York law it may. * * *

On February 4, 1980 plaintiffs Evelyn and Leo Indyk contracted to sell to Dome Investment Company (Dome) 100 percent of the shares of Monroe Contract Corporation (Monroe), a Pennsylvania coal mining firm, for one million dollars. The closing occurred on February 6, 1980 in the offices of Equibank in White Oak, Pennsylvania. Prior to that date Dome had made a down payment to the Indyks of $157,765. At the closing plaintiffs received, as payment on the balance of the purchase price, a cashier's check in the amount of $842,243.83 drawn on defendant Habib Bank Limited (Habib or Bank). The cashier's check was postdated June 4, 1980 and signed by Habib Assistant Vice President S. Hassan Ahmed. When plaintiffs presented the cashier's check on June 4, 1980 at Habib's New York City office, the Bank refused to pay claiming that the check was issued without either authority or consideration.

After Habib's dishonor of the check, plaintiffs entered into a second agreement with the purchasers (Dome and its principals David James and Leslie Ray Smith) who agreed to pay the Indyks the unpaid balance of the purchase price plus interest. In exchange for this promise the Indyks permitted Dome to continue operating Monroe and agreed to transfer the Monroe stock to Dome upon completion of the monthly payments. Under this second agreement the Indyks had received payments from Dome which by September 1980 amounted to $171,067. At that point Dome defaulted and Monroe went bankrupt. The Indyks subsequently brought a diversity action in the United States District Court for the Southern District of New York against Habib on the dishonored cashier's check.

Following a bench trial before Judge Thomas P. Griesa, the court below held that Ahmed's signature on the check was authorized since he was an agent with apparent authority, and that the Indyks were "holders in due course" of the Habib check and took it free of Habib's asserted defense of lack of consideration. Judgment was entered in favor of the Indyks against Habib in the amount of $671,176 plus prejudgment interest and costs. The $671,176 represented the difference between the amount of the check, $842,243, and the installment payments of $171,067 received by the Indyks from Dome which the trial court credited to the Bank as an offset against the amount it owed.

Both parties appeal. Habib claims that the trial court erred in holding that the Indyks were holders in due course who took the postdated check free of Habib's defense of lack of consideration. The Indyks cross-appeal from that portion of the trial court's judgment which allowed Habib to offset the $171,067 received by the Indyks from Dome after Habib's dishonor of the check.

I

We turn first to the issue involving the postdated cashier's check. The Uniform Commercial Code, N.Y.U.C.C. § 3–302(1) [quoting] * * *

Conceding that the Indyks took the cashier's check for value and in good faith, Habib asserts that the Indyks were not holders in due course because they took the postdated cashier's check with notice that defenses against the check existed. Specifically, Habib claims that the Indyks had notice because: they were aware that the cashier's check was postdated; their representative at Equibank, Mrs. Zell, expressed concern over the postdating and telephoned Mr. Ahmed at Habib to verify that the check was proper; banks normally do not use postdated cashier's checks; and the Indyks knew that Dome could not raise the necessary cash for the purchase of Dome's stock until June 4, 1980 and, therefore, at least impliedly knew that Dome did not give any consideration for the cashier's check. We find Habib's contention that the Indyks took the check with notice unpersuasive.

Under New York law notice of defenses means actual, subjective knowledge of defenses. * * * There is no evidence in the record before us that the Indyks had actual, subjective knowledge that the Habib check was issued without consideration or subject to any defenses. The Indyks testified that they had never dealt with or even heard of Habib prior to the closing on February 6, 1980. The check, on its face, was conceded to be a regular Habib Bank cashier's check properly made out and signed by the Assistant Vice President in charge of the bank department that issued cashier's checks. The postdating of the check did cause the Indyks' banker some concern, which prompted her to telephone Mr. Ahmed at the Habib bank. Mrs. Zell was advised that the check had been properly issued and authorized. She reported this information to the plaintiffs. Moreover, the postdating of the check alone was not legally sufficient to give the Indyks notice of a defense. *See* N.Y.U.C.C. § 3–304(4)(a) (McKinney 1964). While postdated cashier's checks are not normally used by banks, the Indyks did not know and had no reason to know of this specific banking practice. The fact that the Indyks might have been aware of Dome's lack of funds does not necessarily demonstrate that they subjectively knew that Dome had not given consideration to Habib for the cashier's check. Dome might well have paid for Habib's check with a note or some other non-cash consideration.

* * * Absent any evidence that the Indyks had actual notice, the district court's conclusion that they were holders in due course entitled to judgment for

the face amount of the check should be upheld. * * * The Habib Bank must pay the full amount of its cashier's check, or $842,243.83. The judgment of the district court is modified accordingly.

Notes

1. Do ideas of efficiency call for an expansive or a restrictive idea of notice? For example, one could argue that people in the position of the Indyks are the least cost risk avoiders, namely that by a modest amount of investigation they could have uncovered the difficulty and thus that the loss should be placed on them. How would you respond to such an argument?

2. How does one escape the conclusion that the Indyks "dealt with" Habib and thus cannot take free of Habib's defenses?

3. Assume that drawer gives a post-dated personal check to payee and tells payee that he does not have enough money in the account at the present time but that he hopes to have the check covered by the time the date on it arrives. Payee transfers the check to a friend with the same statement. When the friend seeks to collect the check it bounces. Is friend a holder in due course who can recover from the drawer despite the fact that the instrument was given in return for some pigs who were not merchantable because they have the bloody scours? UCC 3–304.

Problem 24–9

Greenlane Inc. had contracted with Comfort Cooling for the installation of a large air conditioning system in Greenlane's business location. Shortly after the work commenced, Greenlane executed three notes for a total amount of $100,000 payable to the order of Comfort Cooling. Greenlane now claims that there was an express oral agreement that the notes would not be discounted "but would merely be exhibited for the purpose of obtaining supplies in order to complete the contract." The notes were negotiable and were negotiated to Factors and Note Buyers Inc. sometime between May 20 and May 24. Learning of Comfort Cooling's intention to discount the notes despite the agreement not to do so, Mr. Gottesman of Greenlane telephoned Alexander Mathias, Vice President of Factors and Note Buyers, advised him of Greenlane's position and "emphatically requested that the notes not be discounted." Comfort Cooling failed to complete performance; it went bankrupt and Factors and Note Buyers has sued Greenlane on the notes.

Assuming, for the sake of argument, that the telephone call was made to Mr. Mathias before the notes were transferred, Factors and Note Buyers argues, nevertheless, that it is a holder in due course. In support of its position it quotes the following comment from UCC 3–304: "Mere notice of the existence of an executory promise or a separate agreement does not prevent the holder from taking in due course, and such notice may even appear on the instrument itself. If the purchaser has notice of any default on the promise or agreement which gives rise to a defense or claim *against the instrument,* he is on notice to the same extent as in the case of any other information as to the existence of a defense or claim." (Emphasis added.)

In addition the plaintiffs cite the following statement from a local decision that a duty of inquiry arises "only to the extent that the failure to make inquiry indicates 'a deliberate desire on his part to evade knowledge because of a belief or fear that investigation would disclose a vice in the transaction.'"

(1) If you were the lawyer for Greenlane, how would you respond?

(2) If you were the judge presented with this case, how would you decide?

HATTON v. MONEY LENDERS & ASSOCIATES, LTD.

Court of Appeals of Illinois 1984.
127 Ill.App.3d 577, 82 Ill.Dec. 826, 469 N.E.2d 360.

JIGANTI, J. This action challenges the propriety of an order of summary judgment in which the trial court found that the defendant, Associates Finance, Inc. (Associates), was the holder in due course of a promissory note. The note was initially executed by the plaintiffs, Kenneth and Barbara Hatton, and Money Lenders & Associates, Ltd. (Money Lenders), on December 24, 1979. The terms of the note provided that the plaintiffs would repay a total of $78,000 in 120 monthly payments of $650 each to Money Lenders. This sum included $30,000 in principal and annual interest in excess of 24%. The note was secured by a trust deed on a rental apartment owned by the plaintiffs. At the time the note was executed, the plaintiffs also completed two affidavits in which they swore under oath that the money would be used solely for business purposes.

Associates purchased the promissory note from Money Lenders on January 12, 1980. After making 14 monthly payments to Associates the plaintiffs filed suit against both Money Lenders and Associates, alleging that the note was usurious and that it had been procured by misrepresentation and fraud. A default judgment was entered against Money Lenders. Money Lenders is not a party to this appeal. The trial court granted Associates' motion for summary judgment, finding that Associates was a holder in due course and took the note free from all of the claims and defenses of the plaintiffs. The plaintiffs now appeal from this order of summary judgment.

The plaintiffs maintain on appeal that there were sufficient facts of record to indicate that Associates had notice of the plaintiffs' alleged defense of usury at the time Associates purchased the note from Money Lenders. Consequently, the plaintiffs argue that a genuine issue of material fact was before the trial court and that the court therefore improperly entered summary judgment in favor of Associates. The plaintiffs further contend that holder-in-due-course status is a question of fact which in any event would foreclose the trial court from entering an order of summary judgment on that issue.

Before reaching the merits of the parties' legal arguments, we believe a more detailed recitation of the facts of the case is in order. When Associates purchased the note from Money Lenders, it received copies of the plaintiffs' 1977 and 1978 tax returns and the two affidavits which had been completed by the plaintiffs. The tax returns disclosed that the plaintiffs were engaged in both a snow removal business and a security alarm partnership at certain times over the course of the two years in question. The plaintiff Kenneth Hatton was also employed full-time as a movie projectionist, an occupation which provided approximately 95% of the plaintiffs' income in 1977 and 1978. In the first of the two affidavits sworn to by the plaintiffs, there is a provision that the loan would be used for the "snow removal" business and "that the purpose of the loan applied for by me is solely for the purposes of carrying on such business and proceeds will be used for such purpose and for no other." The second affidavit states that the loan would be used for the "security business" and also contains the above-quoted language.

The plaintiffs and Associates discussed the loan in the course of eight different telephone conversations between January 21, 1980, when Associates verified the loan balance with the plaintiffs following Associates' purchase of the note, and January 9, 1981. At no time during these telephone conversations did the plaintiffs ever inform Associates of any purported claim or defense in connection with the loan. Associates first learned of the plaintiffs' alleged defense when it was served with the plaintiffs' complaint in this action.

In the trial court, the plaintiffs argued that they had borrowed the money to invest in the commodities market and that they had advised Money Lenders that the money would be used for that purpose. At their depositions, the plaintiffs stated that they knew the affidavits were false when they signed them but that they were told by Money Lenders that the signing of the affidavits was a "mere formality." The plaintiffs thus contended that the note was usurious because it was intended for personal rather than business purposes and consequently did not fall under the business loan exception to the Illinois usury statute. See Ill. Rev.Stat.1979, ch. 74, par. 4(1)(c).

Both at trial and now on appeal, the plaintiffs have maintained that Associates had notice of the plaintiffs' alleged usury defense and therefore could not obtain the status of a holder in due course. In support of this contention, the plaintiffs argue that there was no stated interest rate on the note; that there is a discrepancy on the face of the note as to the dollar amount due from the plaintiffs; that the affidavits contradict each other on their face; that the plaintiffs' tax returns indicate that only 5% of their income was received from the snow removal and security businesses; that the note was secured by real estate owned by the plaintiffs; and that the note was purportedly purchased from Money Lenders by Associates at a large discount. Because of these alleged discrepancies, the plaintiffs now maintain that Associates had notice that the loan would be used for nonbusiness purposes and that therefore, Associates had notice that the plaintiffs possessed a defense to the note under the usury statute. The plaintiffs do not maintain that Associates had actual notice of this alleged defense but that, rather, the note and other documents received by Associates from Money Lenders were irregular on their face, thus providing Associates with constructive notice of the alleged defense.

* * *

Section 1–201(25) of the Code defines "notice" and provides:

"(25) A person has 'notice' of a fact when

"(a) he has actual knowledge of it; or

"(b) he has received a notice or notification of it; or

"(c) from all the facts and circumstances known to him at the time in question he has reason to know that it exists." (Ill.Rev.Stat.1983, ch. 26, par. 1–201(25).)

"A purchaser of a negotiable instrument has notice of a claim or defense if:

"(a) The instrument is so incomplete, bears such visible evidence of forgery or alteration, or is otherwise so irregular as to call into question its validity, terms or ownership or to create an ambiguity as to the party to pay; or

"(b) the purchaser has notice that the obligation of any party is voidable in whole or in part, or that all parties have been discharged." (Ill.Rev.Stat.1983, ch. 26, par. 3–304.)"

The crucial time in determining whether a holder has notice of a claim or defense is the time of negotiation of the instrument. * * * Notice received subsequent to the purchase of a loan does not operate to impair holder-in-due-course status. * * *.

In the case at bar, we do not believe that there were any facts of record which demonstrate that Associates had notice of the plaintiffs' alleged defense.

First of all, there is no legal requirement that a negotiable instrument include a stated rate of interest. The fact that the note at issue here did not include such a term was therefore insufficient to put Associates on notice. Second, the record discloses that the plaintiffs' assertion that the note is mathematically incorrect is totally without merit. The note provides that 120 monthly installments of $650 must be paid by the plaintiffs, for a total repayment of $78,000. In fact, the plaintiffs stated during oral arguments that this second contention was erroneous.

The plaintiffs further maintain that because the businesses referred to in their affidavits comprised only a small part of their total income, Associates should have been wary that the loan might be used for nonbusiness purposes. We think, however, Associates correctly points out that there is no requirement that a business enterprise must be of a certain size or produce a certain profit before a business loan can be made to it. Fourth, the plaintiffs also argue that the fact that the note was secured by real estate should have put Associates on notice because, "Any individual who owns a piece of real estate can secure a loan at two or three points over the prime rate from most banks." However, there is absolutely no evidence in the record concerning prevailing interest rates, the credit-worthiness of the plaintiffs, or typical business practices in regard to such loans. This court cannot make the unsupported assumptions urged by the plaintiffs absent any support in the record.

We also find no merit in the plaintiffs' allegations that Associates should have been put on notice because the two affidavits that were executed by the plaintiffs referred to two separate businesses. The two affidavits were executed at the same time and specifically referred to the businesses that the plaintiffs had listed in their Federal income tax returns. The fact that a preprinted portion of the affidavits stated that the loans "will be used for such purpose and for no other," we believe, was utterly insufficient to put Associates on notice that the loan would be used for other than business purposes.

Finally, the plaintiffs maintain that Associates should have been put on notice because the note was sold by Money Lenders to Associates at a large discount. In support of this proposition, the plaintiffs cite Winter & Hirsch, Inc. v. Passarelli (1970), 122 Ill.App.2d 372, 259 N.E.2d 312, wherein the court stated in dicta that a party purchasing negotiable paper at a great discount has a duty to inquire further into the initial transaction to determine if the borrower has a defense to the note. However, in Passarelli, the court found that the holder of the note had intentionally kept itself in ignorance of certain facts which, if known, would have destroyed its holder-in-due-course status. In the case at bar, Associates examined the plaintiffs' income tax returns and their affidavits of business purpose. As we have stated, nothing in those documents would have put Associates on notice regarding the plaintiffs' alleged defense. Furthermore, Associates talked with the plaintiffs on the telephone on eight occasions to verify and discuss the loan. The plaintiffs never mentioned their purported defense. Therefore, even if we accept the language in Passarelli as persuasive support for imposing upon Associates a greater duty of inquiry, we think that Associates in the case at bar satisfied such a duty by going beyond the requirements of the Code to pursue a more comprehensive inquiry than that legally required. Accordingly, we do not believe that any of the alleged "irregularities" cited by the plaintiffs were sufficient to put Associates on notice that the loan would be used for other than business purposes.

While the plaintiffs agree that there is little or no legal support for each of their above contentions, they nonetheless argue that all of their alleged "irregularities" taken together were sufficient to put Associates on notice concerning their purported defense. We disagree. That negotiable paper is freely transferable in the business community is perhaps its greatest attribute. To require a party who wishes to purchase negotiable paper to pursue a lengthy inquiry not required by the Commercial Code would unduly burden such transactions and impede the free exchange of negotiable paper. In the case at bar, Associates even went so far as to talk on the telephone with the plaintiffs on at least eight occasions concerning their loan. The plaintiffs never once mentioned their purported defense. Taken as a whole, we cannot find that Associates possessed any information sufficient to put it on notice of the plaintiffs' alleged defense. Accordingly, we believe the trial court properly found that Associates was a holder in due course and granted summary judgment in favor of Associates.

* * *

For the foregoing reasons, the order of summary judgment entered in favor of Associates is affirmed.

Notes

1. Did Associates deal with the Hattons? If so, there is a problem. See UCC 3–305(2). There is an irony in reducing one's rights because he took greater care than another.

2. Assume that the note was changed so that either there was an explicit expression of an interest percentage on the face of the note or that there were separate amounts stated as principal and interest payments. If those amounts stated a usurious rate of interest, would they deprive Associates of holder in due course status? If so, could the defendants raise not only the usury defense, but also any underlying fraud defenses?

3. Assume that Associates was a subsidiary of Money Lenders and that it had many officers and employees in common. That relationship might deprive Associates of its holder in due course status because of the so called "close connectedness" rule. If the connection is too close courts will find the two corporations to be a single entity.

4. Do you see why the usury issue will seldom be raised in the holder in due course context? This is so because most usury limits apply only to consumer transactions, and, because of the FTC rule, holders of consumer notes are seldom holders in due course.

Problem 24–10

Faithless Employee forged the signature of her employer. She drew a $10,000 check payable to the order of the bank where the employer kept its principal account. She then took the check to the bank and cashed it. Some portion of the funds she received in cash, others were deposited in her own account and she purchased a cashier's check with yet other funds. Apparently the teller was accustomed to depositors dealing with their own funds by drawing checks payable to the bank's order and failed to distinguish this case (where an employee was dealing with her employer's account) from the case in which a depositor was dealing with her own account.

Ultimately the employer sued the bank on alternative grounds of restitution and conversion. The bank defended on the ground that it was a holder in due course. If you represent the plaintiff, how might you attack the bank's argument?

SECTION 6. EGREGIOUS DEFAULT—HOLDER IN DUE COURSE AND REAL DEFENSES

In the foregoing situations we were concerned with the question whether a party who had given a negotiable instrument in payment could raise defenses, to a suit on the instrument, based on the payee's failure of performance. As a general proposition, a party can raise such defenses if the plaintiff is not a holder in due course, but he cannot raise them against a holder in due course. However certain misconduct on the part of the initial transferee (in our case usually the seller) has long been recognized to be so flagrant as to merit no protection by the holder in due course doctrine. These exceptions are commonly called "real defenses" and are listed as follows in UCC 3–305(2):

(a) infancy, to the extent that it is a defense to a simple contract; and

(b) such other incapacity, or duress, or illegality of the transaction, as renders the obligation of the party a nullity; and

(c) such misrepresentation as has induced the party to sign the instrument with neither knowledge nor reasonable opportunity to obtain knowledge of its character or its essential terms; and

(d) discharge in insolvency proceedings; and

(e) any other discharge of which the holder has notice when he takes the instrument.

None of these is likely to be a common occurrence in the businessman's life, but the fraud dealt with in UCC 3–305(2)(c) seems to be the most frequently raised "real defense."

Problem 24–11

Mary made and issued a promissory note in the amount of $1,000 to her friend Barbara in exchange for a loan. The negotiable note was dated July 1, 1981 and was due on January 1, 1982. On December 20, 1981, Mary, who was in law school in another city, mailed a money order to Barbara for the full amount of the loan plus interest. On the enclosed card she requested that the note be "returned as soon as convenient." Barbara, however, had other plans. She applied the proceeds of the money order to her tuition in graduate school (she was in economics, of course) and, on Christmas day, she negotiated Mary's note to Marvin, the young man with whom she lived, in payment for obligations incurred under their agreement to share expenses. On January 1, 1982, Marvin called on Mary to wish her Happy New Year and to present the note for payment. Mary, who had just taken a course in "Bills and Notes," argued that her payment to Barbara discharged the note and, of course, her. She refused to pay Marvin. Is she correct?

BANKERS TRUST CO. v. LITTON SYSTEMS, INC.

United States Court of Appeals, Second Circuit, 1979.
599 F.2d 488.

[Litton decided to purchase photocopiers for use in one of its divisions. A sales agent for Royal, a division of Litton, recommended that Litton lease the goods from Regent. This was done. A clause in the leases permitted assignment and provided that the assignee's rights would be independent of any claims or offsets of Litton against Regent. Unknown to Litton, the agent for Royal was receiving "service fees" or "bribes" from Regent to promote Regent equipment leases to Litton and others. In fact, Regent had purchased from Royal the photocopiers which had been leased to Litton. In order to finance the purchase from Royal, Regent borrowed from Bankers Trust and assigned the Litton leases to them as security. Litton defaulted and in the complex litigation which followed Bankers Trust sued Litton and filed a motion for summary judgment, which was granted by the district court. Upon appeal, the Court of Appeals affirmed the district court's findings that, under the law of New York, the agreement not to assert defenses was valid, Bankers Trust took the leases in good faith and without notice of the "bribes" and there was no cancellation clause in the lease. The court then turned to Litton's argument that the service payments were illegal and that Banker's Trust was subject to that defense under UCC 3–305(2).]

MOORE, CIRCUIT JUDGE:

* * *

The court carefully analyzed the New York cases on the subject and concluded that whereas "such payments could constitute a defense as against Regent * * * the making of such payments could not be asserted against a holder in due course * * *" Accordingly, it granted the banks' motions for summary judgment.

In coming to the conclusion that the Buquicchio payments "could constitute a defense as against Regent" the court relied on McConnell v. Commonwealth Pictures Corp., 7 N.Y.2d 465, 199 N.Y.S.2d 483, 166 N.E.2d 494 (1960) and denied Regent's motion for summary judgment.

However, as to the banks, the court reached a different result. The court concluded that

> "[I]n using the term 'nullity' the Legislature intended to provide a defense against a holder in due course only in cases where the obligation sued upon is void on its face (e.g. a wagering contract or a contract to perform an illegal act), and was not intended to provide a defense against such a holder where one of the parties to the original contract might have an option to declare it void because of some illegal conduct in which the other party may have engaged in the course of the negotiations which gave rise to the contract."

There is a distinction here which should be preserved: the lease contracts for photocopiers were not themselves illegal; the contract to bribe a person in connection with those contracts was illegal. Although the contract being sued upon is not itself illegal, under McConnell v. Commonwealth Pictures Corp., 7 N.Y.2d 465, 199 N.Y.S.2d 483, 166 N.E.2d 494 (1960), and Sirkin v. Fourteenth Street Store, 124 App.Div. 384, 108 N.Y.S. 830 (1st Dept. 1908), a contract would be unenforceable in a suit brought by the wrongdoer if there were a direct connection between the illegal bribe and the obligation sued upon, in this case, the lease. Assuming that Regent, the wrongdoer, cannot enforce the lease contracts, the question which remains is whether a holder in due course may enforce lease contracts not enforceable by the holder's assignor because the contracts were induced by commercial bribery committed by the assignor.

The illegality defense under N.Y.U.C.C. § 3–305(2)(b) is available only if under the applicable state law the effect of the illegality is to make the obligation entirely null and void; the defense is ineffective against a holder in due course if the illegality causes the contract to be merely voidable. Official Comment 6, N.Y.U.C.C. § 3–305. An examination of the language in the New York decisions on the enforceability of bribery-induced contracts suggests that New York holds such contracts to be "void". * * * Nonetheless, upon further analysis, we conclude that under New York law a holder in due course may treat a contract induced by illegal bribery as merely voidable.

The problems and consequences of using the terms "void" and "voidable" were recognized by the Restatement of Contracts:

> "Confusion in the use of the words 'void' and 'voidable' is common, chiefly because it frequently makes no difference whether a contract is void or voidable. In either event the injured party can usually escape liability, and in most cases that is the only question involved. The difference becomes important, however, where property is transferred and subsequently passes to a bona fide purchaser for value. If the original transfer is *voidable* the innocent purchaser acquires an indefeasible title. A similar consequence follows the negotiation of a negotiable instrument that is *voidable.* Furthermore, a contract which is *voidable* may be ratified while a *void* transaction cannot be." Restatement of Contracts § 475, Comment b (1932) (emphasis added).

Since the New York cases on illegal contracts induced by commercial bribery do not involve holders in due course, one could reasonably assume that the authors of those opinions were using the term "void" loosely, without regard to its importance when a holder in due course enters the picture. However, one portion of Sirkin v. Fourteenth Street Store, supra, suggests that the court meant the contract to be truly void. The opinion states that the contract procured by illegal bribery at issue in that case could not be ratified, as could an ordinary contract induced by fraud. 124 App.Div. at 391, 108 N.Y.S. at 835. In light of the Comment to § 475 of the Restatement quoted above, the court apparently was applying to the contract a characteristic of true voidness. Thus, if *Sirkin* is accepted at face value, the plaintiffs' claims would be unenforceable.

It is necessary, however, to consider the basic policy supporting the New York cases, including *McConnell* and *Sirkin.* Once more, the Restatement of Contracts offers a concise explanation. Comment (a) to § 598 states that when a plaintiff sues to recover on an illegal bargain, courts deny relief because the *plaintiff* is a wrongdoer, not because they favor the defendant. Courts will not aid a person "who founds his cause of action upon his own immoral or illegal act." Restatement of Contracts § 598, Comment (a) (1932); see also Restatement (Second) of Contracts, Tent.Dr.No.23, Introductory Note to Ch. 14, p. 46 (1977); 14 Williston on Contracts § 1630A (3d ed. 1972). This rationale is precisely the policy articulated in the New York decisions. In *McConnell* the court said that the court's concern is not with the position of the defendant; instead, the question is whether the plaintiff should be denied a recovery for the sake of public interests. 7 N.Y.2d at 469, 166 N.E.2d at 496, 199 N.Y.S.2d at 485. The well-known maxim that no one shall be permitted to profit by his own fraud summarizes the policy. * * *

Where an innocent third party, such as a holder in due course, is suing upon an illegal contract, the policy argument is inapplicable because the plaintiff has done no wrong for which it should be penalized. Moreover, insofar as it is enforcing the rights of an innocent party, the court does not blacken its name or participate in a wrong when it enforces an illegal contract. See Havighurst, Book Review, 61 Yale L.J. 1138, 1145 (1952).

One New York court has enforced the rights of a holder in due course of a note in the face of the defense that the note had been given as an unlawful preference by a bankrupt to one of his creditors. New Howard Mfg. Co. v. Cohen, 207 App.Div. 588, 202 N.Y.S. 449 (1st Dept.1924).[3] In addition, the New

3. In *New Howard,* the court said:

York Court of Appeals has recognized a general rule that a holder in due course of a negotiable instrument is unaffected by the fact that it originated in an illegal consideration. Sabine v. Paine, 223 N.Y. 401, 119 N.E. 849 (1918).[4]

Bribery which induces the making of a contract is much like a fraud which has the same result. The bribery of a contracting party's agent or employee is, in effect, a fraud on that party. See Restatement of Contracts § 577, Illustrations 4 & 11 (1932). Inasmuch as the New York Uniform Commercial Code allows a holder in due course to enforce a contract induced by fraud, § 3–305(2), the same treatment should be given to a contract induced by bribery. The result ought not be changed by the additional fact that commercial bribery is a criminal offense in New York.

Finally, it would be poor policy for courts to transform banks and other finance companies into policing agents charged with the responsibility of searching out commercial bribery committed by their assignors. We doubt that denying recovery to holders in due course would have an appreciable effect on the frequency of commercial bribery. Moreover, the holder in due course concept embodies important policies which must be weighed against the policy of holding void contracts induced by bribery. To paraphrase Professor Gilmore, the holder in due course is protected not because of his praiseworthy character, but to the end that commercial transactions may be engaged in without elaborate investigation of the process leading up to the contract or instrument and in reliance on the contract rights of one who offers them for sale or to secure a loan. Gilmore, The Commercial Doctrine of Good Faith Purchase, 63 Yale L.J. 1057 (1954); * * *. Abrogation of the rights of a holder in due course is not warranted in this case.

The appellant's other arguments are without merit and were adequately answered by the district court. For the reasons stated above, the decision of the district court is affirmed. [Some footnotes omitted.]

"This case is an authority so strong as to be controlling, that, where the statute itself does not make a contract void but simply prohibits the act, or where the contract is only void as a matter of public policy, the usages of trade and the necessity for protection to negotiable instruments require that the contract should be enforced. To hold that a contract not made void by statutory declaration could be defended as against a *bona fide* purchaser, either because of statutory illegality, or because of illegality by reason of fraud or other offenses *mala in se,* would be a serious embarrassment to the use of these instruments as they are commonly used in trade, as representing actual money.

* * *

"In order to make contracts, whether *mala in se,* or *mala prohibita* void *ab initio,* a statutory declaration to that effect is necessary; and, without that statutory declaration, which does not here exist, the note is good in the hands of a *bona fide* purchaser." 207 App. Div. at 591–2, 202 N.Y.S. at 452.

See also 14 Williston on Contracts § 1676 (3d ed. 1972).

4. In the words of the Court of Appeals:

"The rule [making a usurious contract null and void *ab initio*] is an exception to the general principle that a negotiable instrument, in the hands of an innocent holder, who had received it in good faith in the ordinary course of business, for value, and without notice of a defense, is not invalid and is enforceable by the holder. The general principle has been stated: 'The *bona fide* holder for value who has received the paper in the usual course of business is unaffected by the fact that it originated in an illegal consideration, without any distinction between cases of illegality founded in moral crime or turpitude, which are termed *mala in se* and those founded in positive statutory prohibition which are termed *mala prohibita.* The law extends this peculiar protection to negotiable instruments, because it would seriously embarrass mercantile transactions to expose the trader to the consequences of having the bill or note passed to him impeached for some covert defect.' (1 Daniel on Negotiable Instruments [6th ed.], section 197)." 223 N.Y. at 403–4, 119 N.E. at 850.

SECTION 7. THE HOLDER IN DUE COURSE DOCTRINE IN CONSUMER TRANSACTIONS

The holder in due course doctrine was at one time thought to be the central tentpole upon which the entire tent of consumer credit was draped. Routinely, those dealing with consumers sold goods and services to them, took back negotiable notes, and sold those notes to banks and other financial intermediaries. Periodically, commencing in the late 1950s and with increasing vigor during the 1960s, consumers argued that this process encouraged and protected fly-by-night operators who sold shoddy goods, transferred the paper to a holder in due course and moved on. They maintained that the elimination of the holder in due course status would force the financial intermediaries to winnow out the shoddy sellers and to police the process. The creditors maintained that the abolition of the holder in due course doctrine would drive not just the shoddy sellers but many others as well out of the market. They maintained that such sellers would find it difficult to get credit and therefore that the price of goods and services would rise.

While the foregoing debate continued in the academic journals and elsewhere, the courts and later the legislatures confronted this problem in many ways. In courts, consumer debtors attacked the holder in due course arguments on the various grounds described above. In addition, consumer debtors were occasionally successful in maintaining that the original payee and the assignee were so "closely connected" as to be one, and therefore the putative holder in due course was on notice of the defense, had dealt with the debtor and in either event did not enjoy the rights of a holder in due course. See, e.g., Unico v. Owen, 50 N.J. 101, 232 A.2d 405 (1967).

The legislatures of a few states took tentative steps toward outlawing holder in due course status in consumer transactions by enacting variants of the Uniform Consumer Credit Code. Variants of that Code were enacted in Colorado, Idaho, Indiana, Iowa, Kansas, Maine, Oklahoma, South Carolina, Utah, and Wyoming. In all variations it restricted the holder in due course right and in some it nearly eliminated it.

Moreover it recognized the fact that it was not enough simply to outlaw the holder in due course. It would also be necessary to outlaw "waiver of defense clauses" and somehow to deal with the case in which the seller of goods "dragged the body." These were cases in which a used car dealer, for example, would negotiate the sale with a consumer and would then take the consumer directly to the lender in order to have the lender write the loan between the consumer and the lender and without the intervention of the dealer. Even if the holder in due course doctrine were eliminated, the consumer could not assert his defenses against the creditor who was the payee on the note in such cases. The payee was merely a lender of money, not the assignee of someone else and therefore did not take the note subject to such defenses even if it were not negotiable. In the early 1970s the consumer wave crested. Its status is accurately reflected in the report of National Commission on Consumer Finance.

REPORT OF THE NATIONAL COMMISSION ON CONSUMER FINANCE, CONSUMER CREDIT IN THE UNITED STATES 34–37 (1972).

HOLDER IN DUE COURSE DOCTRINE—WAIVER OF DEFENSE—CLOSELY-CONNECTED LOANS

"Recently, both courts and legislatures have begun to reassess and scrutinize the validity and the impact of the HIDC doctrine and waiver of defense clauses in consumer credit transactions. A number of courts have denied HIDC status to lenders in "too close connection" with sellers of consumer goods. A number of state legislatures have prohibited use of negotiable instruments, and, therefore HIDC status, in retail instalment sales of 'service.' Waiver of defense clauses in consumer sales contracts have also been held void as against public policy by a number of courts and prohibited by several legislatures.

* * *

"Responses to the Commission's *Survey* disclosed that very few creditors engaged in purchasing consumer credit notes and contracts thought that the HIDC doctrine or waiver of defense clauses were among the legal tools most essential to collection activities; but they did indicate reliance on these collection devices to a significant extent in legal actions to collect defaulted obligations.

"The cross-state econometric model indicates that in those states which have prohibited both HIDC and waiver of defense clauses there has been an observable reduction in the availability of other consumer goods credit in two areas: consumer finance companies purchased less other consumer goods paper, and the total amount of other consumer goods credit made available in the retail market declined. Traditionally, finance companies have served the greatest proportion of retailers dealing with high risk credit customers, although banks, too, serve that market. The reductions in availability of other consumer goods credit from finance companies, in all likelihood, would have the greatest impact on consumers who are marginal credit risks and on those businesses which serve or may potentially serve such consumers.

"The cross-state econometric model results also suggest that if finance companies cannot take other consumer goods paper free from claims and defenses to quality of the goods and services, the reduction in credit availability in the other consumer goods retail market would probably be greater than that of the finance company component of the market. Finance companies could reduce their activity in the market by quality credit rationing—rejecting higher risk customers to reduce costs and offset additional potential credit losses. This, in turn, would probably force out of the market many retailers serving marginal risk consumers unable to obtain credit from general market retailers. Because many of these marginal retailers are undercapitalized and tend to be basically inefficient they depend on finance company purchase of paper to restock their inventories. These same limitations would prevent other potential small retailers from entering the market in the absence of finance company financing of other consumer goods credit.

"At the time of the *Survey,* all states allowed either HIDC or waiver of defense clauses or some other equally effective cut-off device in the indirect automobile market. For this reason comparable data were not available to test the effect of prohibiting HIDC and waiver of defense clauses on availability of indirect automobile credit. However, no evidence is available to show that the effect of such prohibitions in the auto indirect market would have any less impact than in the other consumer goods market.

"In recommending abolition of HIDC and waiver of defense clauses in consumer credit transactions, the Commission recognizes that it is placing the burden of policing consumer transactions on the financial institutions which purchase consumer paper. The Commission believes those financial institutions are in a much better position to control credit practices of retail suppliers of consumer goods and services than are consumers. They can choose the retailers and suppliers with whom they will do business. If a financial institution is subject to consumers' defenses against payment, such as failure of consideration, nondelivery, etc., it will discontinue purchase of paper from those merchants who cause trouble thereby forcing the many merchants who desire to stay in business but need financial institutions to buy their consumer credit paper to 'now react responsibly to consumer complaints in order to keep the avenue of credit open.'

* * *

"With abolition of cutoff devices, it is only logical to assume that the financing institutions would probably protect themselves by increasing the dealer reserve (the percentage of each contract price retained by the financial institution as a fund against which to charge bad debts and other credit losses of that particular dealer) or by decreasing the dealer's participation (the dealer's share of the finance charge) in each consumer credit transaction. In either case, the ultimate burden of increased costs to dealers would likely be passed on to the consumer in the form of higher cash prices for the goods or services or in the form of higher finance charges, or both.

"The Commission believes spreading the costs of abolishing third party cutoff devices to all consumers in the marketplace would be more than counterbalanced by the protections which the consuming public will receive in the form of better goods and services. Moreover, the repercussions will probably not be as significant as some have suggested. The Commission agrees with Professor Kripke, when he states:

> 'In a reputable milieu—reputable merchants, reputable products, reputable financers—the freedom from defense rule is statistically unnecessary * * *. Its time has run out.'

* * *

[Recommendations.]

"Notes executed in connection with consumer credit transactions should not be 'negotiable instruments;' that is, any holder of such a note should be subject to all the claims and defenses of the maker (the consumer-debtor). However, the holder's liability should not exceed the original amount financed. Each such note should be required to have the legend 'Consumer Note—Not Negotiable' clearly and conspicuously printed on its face.

"Holders of contracts and other evidences of debt which are executed in connection with consumer credit transactions other than notes should similarly be subject to all claims and defenses of the consumer-debtor arising out of the transaction notwithstanding any agreement to the contrary. However, the holder's liability should not exceed the original amount financed.

* * *

"Growing discontent with cut-off devices in consumer transactions, now apparent in legislatures, courts, and administrative agencies, has led many dealers and financing institutions to devise a new and effective method for the lender to cut off any defenses the buyer might have against the seller. The seller merely suggests that the buyer borrow money for the purchase by direct loan from a cash lender and directs the buyer to a financing institution willing to make the loan. Theoretically, at least, the loan is an independent transaction with no relation to the purchase of the goods. As a result, the obligation to repay the debt would not be subject to defenses arising out of the purchase transaction even in states limiting the HIDC doctrine and use of waiver of defense clauses. The Commission believes routine referral by a seller to a lender or group of lenders should not be permitted to subvert the policy behind a rule restricting or prohibiting use of negotiable promissory notes or waiver of defense clauses. However, drafting legislation barring routine referrals but not inhibiting direct lending for consumer purchases by institutions totally independent of sellers is a difficult task.

* * *

"The Commission's recommendation regarding connected loans is intended to prohibit financing institutions and sellers and suppliers of goods and services from circumventing restrictions on cutoff devices by resorting to direct loan financing arrangements. Making a connected lender subject to the claims and defenses of consumers arising in the underlying transaction will deter interlocking loan arrangements between sellers and financing institutions intended to afford the financing institutions the same cutoff devices available with purchased paper. Lenders will receive no protection where the seller and lender have a continuing business relationship in which the seller directs or otherwise refers the consumer to a particular lender for a purchase money loan. The recommendation is intended to close the umbrella of protection which direct loan financing offers connected lenders.

"The Commission has not attempted to define a connected lender. It has, instead, listed those factors and incidents of dealing which it deems relevant to any determination of a continuing relationship between a vendor and a lender sufficient to establish the connection.

"For this purpose it should be ascertained whether:

"1. The lender supplied forms to the seller, lessor or supplier of services which the consumer used in obtaining the loan.

"2. The seller, lessor or supplier prepared or assisted in preparation of documents used to evidence the loan.

"3. The lender is related to or affiliated with the seller, lessor, or supplier of services.

"a. With regard to individuals, 'related to' refers to any familial relationship;

"b. With regard to corporations, firms, partnerships, trusts, and other organizations, 'affiliated with' refers to (1) direct or indirect control of or by any such organization, (2) interlocking directorates or other form of joint or common management of two or more organizations, or (3) familial relationship with an officer, director, owner, partner, trustee, or similar official of an organization.

"4. The lender directly or indirectly pays the seller, lessor, or supplier of services, any commissions, fees, or other consideration measured by or based in any way on the consumer loan.

"5. The lender has knowledge—including knowledge from dealing with other customers of the seller, lessor or supplier of services or knowledge from records or notices of complaints by other such customers—that the seller, lessor, or supplier of service failed to perform agreements with customers or fails to remedy valid complaints.

"6. The lender has repeatedly and regularly made loans in a 1-year period to finance purchases of goods or services from the seller, lessor, or supplier of services, or persons related to or organizations affiliated with the seller, lessor, or supplier of services, and the lender was recommended to the consumer for the loans in question.

"The Commission believes holding connected lenders liable for consumer claims and defenses stemming from underlying transactions is necessary to the goal of preserving consumer defenses by abolishing cutoff devices in purchased paper transactions. The abolition of cutoff devices should also be extended to credit card transactions. Where the lender is the issuer of a credit card which may be used by the consumer in a sale, lease, or service transaction with the seller, lessor, or supplier of services, the lender-issuer should be subject to the customer's claims and defenses, *except* in those transactions where the credit card is merely a substitute for cash (e.g. transactions up to $50).

* * *

[Recommendations.]

"A creditor in a consumer loan transaction should be subject to all of the claims and defenses of the borrower arising from the purchase of goods or services purchased with the proceeds of the loan, if the borrower was referred or otherwise directed to the lender by the vendor of those goods or services and the lender extended the credit pursuant to a continuing business relationship with the vendor. In such cases, the lender's liability should not exceed the lesser of the amount financed or the sales price of the goods or services purchased with the proceeds of the loan."

In 1975 the Federal Trade Commission issued a new rule that essentially appropriated the field from the states. It provides that every covered consumer note must contain one of the two following legends.

NOTICE

ANY HOLDER OF THIS CONSUMER CREDIT CONTRACT IS SUBJECT TO ALL CLAIMS AND DEFENSES WHICH THE DEBTOR COULD ASSERT AGAINST THE SELLER OF GOODS OR SERVICES OBTAINED PURSUANT HERETO OR WITH THE PROCEEDS HEREOF. RECOVERY HEREUNDER BY THE DEBTOR SHALL NOT EXCEED AMOUNTS PAID BY THE DEBTOR HEREUNDER.

NOTICE

ANY HOLDER OF THIS CONSUMER CREDIT CONTRACT IS SUBJECT TO ALL CLAIMS AND DEFENSES WHICH THE DEBTOR COULD ASSERT AGAINST THE SELLER OF GOODS OR SERVICE OBTAINED WITH THE PROCEEDS HEREOF. RECOVERY HEREUNDER BY THE DEBTOR SHALL NOT EXCEED AMOUNTS PAID BY THE DEBTOR HEREUNDER.

It may seem strange that Federal Trade Commission made no attempt to outlaw the holder in due course doctrine or ostensibly to change the state law at all. For a federal administrative agency openly to have abolished such a sacred private law right would have offended even those with little respect for the state legislatures. Do you see what the FTC did? In a most clever way it left the doctrine nominally intact, but required (under pain of commission of an unfair trade practice) the inclusion of a term on every note that rendered the note non-negotiable. Because any note containing the legend is now explicitly conditional, it is no longer negotiable under 3–104 and no taker of it can be a holder in due course.

Thus, after years of tussling in the courts and lobbying in the state legislatures, the Federal Trade Commission did what no state legislature could do alone, what the Congress would have been afraid to do and what the courts could do only in piecemeal fashion over a great period of time. It effectively abolished the holder in due course doctrine in consumer transactions.

Those who predicted cataclysmic consequences from the abolition of the doctrine were proven wrong. Any marginal increase in cost of consumer credit or restriction in the supply of credit was so small as to be obscured by other factors in the market. That market continued without obvious change. Thus, the big issues are dead. However the FTC rules has left us with a few niggling lawyer questions. We turn to those.

The student should now examine the Federal Trade Commission holder in due course regulation, Title 16, Commercial Practices, Part 433.1, .2, and .3. (These are set out in commonly available selected commercial statutes books.)

Problem 24–12

1. Bank does floor plan lending for Local Chevrolet dealer. Debtor goes to Bank, seeks to borrow $10,000 to buy a new Chevrolet and ultimately executes a note and a security agreement. The proceeds of the loan are given to the Debtor in the form of a check which he takes to Local Chevrolet and transfers to them in return for the automobile. Assume that the note consumer signs does not contain either legend, that Debtor pays $3,000 in installments to the Bank, and then Debtor suffers a serious injury in the automobile that later is determined to be attributable to a defect:

a. Can Debtor refuse to make further payment to the Bank?

b. Has either the Bank or the car dealer violated the Federal Trade Commission rule?

2. Assume that Debtor purchases a car from Local Chevrolet and that the note he signs contains one of the legends set out above. After he has paid $2,000, the $12,000 car is destroyed by a defect in the automobile. Assume there is no insurance.

a. It is now clear, is it not, that Debtor need not make further payments to Bank?

b. In addition, can Debtor recover the $2,000 paid to the Bank?

c. What about the remaining $10,000 that is unpaid and about the $1,000 that was paid to auto dealer as a downpayment? Can he recover any or all of that from Bank?

3. Local Bank, having been through the two cases described above and willing to take the credit risk but no other in such transactions, asks how it should arrange its affairs in order to minimize its liability. Among other things, it has heard from other bankers some suggestions. What is your view of those?

a. Having the original dealer execute a disclaimer of warranty and the disclaimer, if effective, presumably would free the bank from liability, true?

b. Ignoring the whole matter on the ground that it is not subject to the Federal Trade Commission supervision.

c. Other?

Despite the presence of the FTC rule, it would appear that the close-connectedness doctrine is not yet dead. Consider the case that follows.

ST. JAMES v. DIVERSIFIED COMMERCIAL FINANCE CORPORATION

Supreme Court of Nevada, 1986.
714 P.2d 179.

YOUNG, JUSTICE.

On February 22, 1982, Denise E.B. St. James and Timothy T.B. St. James, dba Las Vegas Chiropractic Center (appellants), purchased a debt collection service from National Revenue Corporation (NRC). John Walker, an NRC employee, sold the service to appellants and had them sign two promissory notes payable to respondent Diversified Commercial Finance Corporation (Diversified) to finance the purchase.

Diversified acknowledges that it provides financing for NRC and facilitates that financing by supplying NRC with preprinted promissory notes for NRC's customers to sign. The promissory notes contained the following preprinted provision:

> Borrower recognizes and acknowledges that all funds borrowed on this Promissory Note will be paid to National Revenue Corporation (NRC). Borrower authorizes NRC to pay to Lender [Diversified] any credits or refunds that may become due Borrower to the extent of any outstanding principal amount and interest due under this Promissory Note, with any remaining balance from said credit or refund going to Borrower.

Appellants stopped making payments on the notes after several months because NRC allegedly was not providing the services promised. Diversified filed a complaint seeking the balance due on the notes ($3,940.00) plus interest, costs and attorney's fees. Appellants answered, setting forth as an affirmative defense failure of consideration, i.e., NRC's failure to provide the services promised in the service agreement. The district court granted Diversified's motion for summary judgment on February 1, 1985. The court concluded that Diversified was a holder in due course of the notes and therefore immune from the defenses available against the seller, NRC.

A holder in due course of an instrument is one who takes the instrument (1) for value, (2) in good faith and (3) without notice that it is overdue or has been dishonored or of any defenses or claims to it. *See* NRS 104.3302(1). Payees may be holders in due course. NRS 104.3302(2). Holder in due course status operates to insulate the holder from certain defenses to the instrument of any party with whom the holder has not dealt. NRS 104.3305 (hereafter referred to as "§ 3–305"). However, § 3–305 makes the holder subject to all defenses of a party with whom the holder has dealt.

Appellants contend that they may assert the defense of failure of consideration against Diversified because they are a party with whom the holder—Diversified—has dealt. Under traditional analysis, however, appellants' argument fails because Diversified did fulfill its obligation on the contract: It paid NRC for the services NRC was to provide to appellants. There was no failure of consideration with respect to the transaction because Diversified was not obligated to perform the collection service but only to pay NRC. The failure of consideration allegedly arose in the transaction between appellants and NRC.

Many jurisdictions have broken with this traditional analysis of the holder in due course rule and have limited its application either by statutory enactment or judicial adoption of the close connection doctrine. *See, e.g., Commercial Credit*

Co. v. Childs, 199 Ark. 1073, 137 S.W.2d 260 (1940) (consumer transaction for purchase of automobile; closely-connected assignee of note not a good faith holder in due course because for "all intents and purposes [it was] a party to the agreement and instrument from the beginning"); *Commercial Credit Corp. v. Orange County Mach. Wks.,* 34 Cal.2d 766, 214 P.2d 819 (1950) (sale of mechanical press; finance company not in good faith where it actively participated in transaction by supplying forms to seller); *Unico v. Owen,* 50 N.J. 101, 232 A.2d 405 (1967) (consumer sale of stereo and record album package; financier not holder in due course because not a good faith purchaser where it participated in the underlying transaction); *Westfield Investment Co. v. Fellers,* 74 N.J.Super. 575, 181 A.2d 809 (Ct.Law Div.1962) (door-to-door sale of food plan and freezer; finance company subject to defenses against seller because inextricably linked to seller by supplying preprinted promissory notes and otherwise participating in the transaction). The close connection doctrine holds lenders subject to the defenses that a buyer has against his seller where the lender and seller are closely connected. The Uniform Consumer Credit Code (U3C) and Federal Trade Commission (FTC) rules both contain provisions which make not only assignees of consumer credit paper but also direct lenders in consumer transactions subject to the consumer's claims and defenses against the seller. *See* U3C §§ 3.404, 3.405; FTC Holder in Due Course Regulations, 16 C.F.R. § 433.2 (1978).

The FTC rule would have easily disposed of the case at bar had it involved a consumer transaction. We can discern no reason to limit the doctrine to consumer transactions; we therefore adopt the close connection doctrine with respect to all transactions where the buyer can demonstrate a close connection between the seller and lender.

Whether a lender and seller are closely connected will necessarily depend upon the facts of each case. We adopt the test articulated by the New Jersey Supreme Court in *Unico v. Owen,* 50 N.J. 101, 232 A.2d 405 (1967) for determining whether such a connection exists:

> [W]hen it appears from the totality of the arrangements between [seller] and financer that the financer has had a substantial voice in setting standards for the underlying transaction, or has approved the standards established by the [seller], and has agreed to take all or a predetermined or substantial quantity of the negotiable paper which is backed by such standards, the financer should be considered a participant in the original transaction and therefore not entitled to holder in due course status.

Unico, 232 A.2d at 417.

We conclude that the district court erred in granting summary judgment to Diversified.

MOWBRAY, C.J., and SPRINGER, GUNDERSON, and STEFFEN, JJ., concur.

Notes

1. Do you agree with the court's adoption of the close connectedness rule in the non-consumer context? How might one frame the argument for and against the efficiency of such a rule?

2. Two commentators have argued that the abolition of the holder in due course doctrine in consumer transactions has probably had an inefficient and negative impact upon inventiveness and product availability. Professors Lawrence and Minan in, *The Effect of Abrogating Holder In Due Course Doctrine from the Commercialization of Innovative Consumer Products,* 64 Boston U.L.Rev. 325 (1984), suggest, for

example, that the market for solar energy devices has been insufficiently developed because creditors have been unwilling to buy consumer paper that bears both the consumer credit risk and the risk of warranty violation or other default by the seller. The authors suggest that the same might be true in other consumer products sold by sellers of limited capitalization whose capacity to perform their contracts cannot be readily known by lender.

SECTION 8. RIGHTS OF THOSE WHO ARE NOT HOLDERS IN DUE COURSE

The rights of non-holders are set out in Section 3–306. For most purposes such parties are like contract assignees; in the words of § 3–306 they take the instrument subject to "all valid claims to and on the part of any person" and "all defenses of any party which would be available and an action of a simple contract * * *." So far, so good. The trouble comes however when one asks whether a party to an instrument may defend the suit on the instrument by raising a defense or a claim of the third party, a problem that passes in law school under the rubric of *jus tertii.* Section 3–306(d) deals with that question:

§ 3–306. Rights of One Not Holder in Due Course

Unless he has the rights of a holder in due course any person takes the instrument subject to * * *

> (d) the defense that he or a person through whom he holds the instrument acquired it by theft, or that payment or satisfaction to such holder would be inconsistent with the terms of a restrictive indorsement. The claim of any third person to the instrument is not otherwise available as a defense to any party liable thereon unless the third person himself defends the action for such party.

Note that § 3–306 refers in some parts to "claims" and other places to "defenses." First one wonders whether there is a distinction to be made between the two and, if so, the basis for the distinction. The *jus tertii* question has been presented most frequently and forcefully by the various forms of instruments on which banks are liable—certified, cashiers and bank checks. If a good customer purchases a cashier's check and, disappointed over the deal that he has made, asks the bank to refuse to pay the check when it is presented, the bank may refuse to pay. At minimum the bank will like to know whether it can assert defenses that its customer may have on the underlying transaction. Such cases come in varied forms; in some situations the bank refuses to pay and attempts to assert the customer's defense, a straight *jus tertii* issue. In other cases the bank refuses to stop payment and is sued by its customer for failing to do so. In still others the bank simply brings its customer and the holder of the instrument to court and tenders the money. Keeping § 3–306 in mind consider the following case.

MOON OVER THE MOUNTAIN, LTD. v. MARINE MIDLAND BANK

Civil Court of New York, Special Term, New York County, 1976.
87 Misc.2d 918, 386 N.Y.S.2d 974.

SHEA, JUDGE.

In this motion for summary judgment in lieu of complaint pursuant to CPLR § 3213, plaintiff is the transferee of an official check in the amount of $559.00, signed by an officer of defendant bank, dated February 10, 1976 and made payable to plaintiff's agent, The Patchworks. The check was endorsed by the payee to the plaintiff, deposited into plaintiff's account on February 12, 1976, and thereafter was returned to plaintiff by its bank marked "Payment Stopped." The check was in partial payment for goods received from plaintiff by Lawrence Reinhard III, purchaser of the check.

On the same day that the check issued, Reinhard advised the bank that the check had been lost and requested defendant to stop payment. Subsequently, Reinhard executed a standard bank Affidavit and Indemnity Agreement in which he swore that the check had been "accidentally lost" and that he had not "sold, given, transferred, assigned, [or] delivered * * *" it. The Affidavit and Indemnity Agreement is annexed to defendant's answering papers in support of its contention that it incurred no liability in relying on its customer's stop payment order, and that a triable issue of fact exists as to whether or not the check was lost. Defendant argues that additional issues of fact are present with regard to plaintiff's interest in the check, and as to whether plaintiff took the check with knowledge of alleged but unspecified infirmities. Defendant argues further that Reinhard, as purchaser, and The Patchworks, as payee, are necessary parties to this action. Defendant advises the court that a separate action is pending between Reinhard and plaintiff in which Reinhard claims defects in the goods received and seeks the return of money allegedly paid to plaintiff. Finally, defendant urges that the check herein is not "an instrument for the sum of money" within the terms of CPLR § 3213.

The check which is the subject of this action is an official or cashier's check. It has the name of defendant bank printed on it, the date of issuance, the amount, the payee's name, the words "Official Check", an illegible signature, and under the signature, the printed words "Authorized Signature". The name of the purchaser, Reinhard, does not appear on the check, nor are there any blank spaces.

A cashier's check has been described as "an instrument drawn by a commercial bank on itself, representing an unconditional promise to pay the face value to the payee named thereon * * *" Personal Money Orders and Teller's Checks: Mavericks Under the UCC, 67 Colum.L.Rev. 524, 525 n. 5. A cashier's check establishes a debtor-creditor relationship between the issuing bank and the payee. * * * Unlike an ordinary check drawn on a specific deposit balance, a cashier's check is an obligation of the bank which issues it and a promise to draw the amount of the check from its own resources. The bank becomes both drawer and drawee of a cashier's check and its issuance constitutes an acceptance. * * *

The New York Uniform Commercial Code (UCC) does not cover explicitly the liability of a drawer bank that stops payment of an official or cashier's check. UCC § 4–303(1) provides that a bank is not required to stop payment on a certified check and has been interpreted to mean that there is no right to stop payment after certification. Official Comment 5 to UCC § 4–403, McKinney's Cons.Laws of N.Y., Book 62½ at 611 (1964). UCC § 3–411 provides that certification of a check is acceptance. Although the UCC does not indicate when a cashier's check is deemed accepted, UCC § 3–802 provides for the discharge of the underlying obligation whenever a bank is "drawer, maker or acceptor" of the instrument given in payment. Since under UCC § 3–802 the payee loses its right against the purchaser when it accepts the bank instrument in payment of the underlying debt, the bank cannot be free to refuse payment. Since acceptance is a bank's own engagement to pay (5A N.Y.Jur., Banks and Trust

Companies § 418), it follows that a cashier's check is accepted in advance by the act of issuance and that the issuing bank remains liable, after a stop payment order, even where there is a failure of consideration in the underlying transaction for which the check was given. UCC § 3–401(1), which provides that no person is liable on an instrument unless his signature appears thereon is consistent with this result.

The policy considerations which underlie the UCC support the rule that a bank must remain liable on its official check even after a stop payment order by its customer. To hold otherwise could be a serious impediment to public reliance on our banking system. "[T]he Uniform Commercial Code * * * was enacted to protect persons engaged in business transactions involving instruments for the payment of money * * *" Malphrus v. Home Savings Bank, 44 Misc.2d 705, 707, 254 N.Y.S.2d 980, 983.

* * *

Malphrus * * * was a case factually similar to the case at bar where the purchaser of an automobile stopped payment on a teller's check. The court, in holding the bank liable to the plaintiff-payee, stated:

> "By issuing a teller's check the defendant Savings Bank gave to its depositor an instrument upon which the plaintiff relied in making the sale and delivery of an automobile. The plaintiff did not rely on [the purchaser's] credit but in good faith accepted the check of a savings bank * * * The plaintiff accepted a bank check as in the nature of cash * * * a procedure that is widely followed in business transactions of many varieties * * * A teller's check has generally been treated as 'cash'. Here * * * there is no basis upon which to make a determination that the plaintiff should have considered the teller's check in any different light than he would have considered a certified check. This was a bank obligation which he received as consideration when he delivered his merchandise." 44 Misc. 2d at 706, 254 N.Y.S.2d at 982.

* * *

A teller's check is a check drawn by one bank (usually a savings bank) on another. Unlike a cashier's check, which is accepted at issuance, a teller's check is accepted by the drawee bank when the instrument is presented by the payee. However, a teller's check is similar to a cashier's check in that it is signed by a bank official and is a primary obligation of the issuing bank. The reasoning of the Malphrus, International Firearms Co. and Meckler cases should apply *a fortiori* to a cashier's check.

Garden Check Cashing Service, Inc. v. First National City Bank, 18 N.Y.2d 941, 277 N.Y.S.2d 141, 223 N.E.2d 566, relied upon by defendant, is inapposite. In that case, the Appellate Division, First Department, in an opinion affirmed by the Court of Appeals, considered the effect of a stop payment order on a personal money order. The court concluded that the purchaser of a personal money order, like the maker of a personal check, retains the right to stop payment until acceptance upon presentment, and concomitantly, that bank has no liability until acceptance. However, a cashier's check differs from a personal money order in material ways, and most significantly in that a cashier's check bears the signature of the bank, and not that of the purchaser. As the court said in *Garden Check Cashing,* "Any attempt to analogize the [personal money order] herein with a cashier's or traveler's check fails." Id. 25 A.D.2d 137, 140, 267 N.Y.S.2d 698, 701.

* * *

Defendant's contention that issues of fact exist with regard to plaintiff's interest in the check is similarly without merit. The affidavits of the payee's treasurer and plaintiff's president establish that the payee was plaintiff's agent and that the endorsement on the check was authorized and without restriction. A check drawn in favor of a particular payee may be payable either to the actual payee or, upon his endorsement, to his endorsee.

* * *

In the light of the detailed affidavits submitted for plaintiff by the treasurer of The Patchworks, who received the check, and the president of plaintiff Moon Over the Mountain, Ltd., who was present when the check was delivered by Reinhard, it cannot be said that an issue of fact exists as to whether or not the check was delivered. Defendant submits a hearsay affidavit by a bank officer who alleges that he talked to Reinhard on the telephone and was advised that the check was lost. The only additional evidence submitted by defendant is a copy of the form indemnity agreement executed by Reinhard on February 13, 1976, in confirmation of his oral stop payment order. Defendant offers no explanation for its failure to ascertain how the alleged loss occurred.

A bank issues its own checks in furtherance of its business and wishes the public to accept its checks without question. Sound business practice would suggest that the bank's dishonor of its own check be justified by more than a standard form indemnity agreement with a checkmark next to a printed statement that the check was lost. In any case, if loss by the customer is to be relied upon to defeat a motion for summary judgment, the bank must determine and present to the court the claimed evidentiary facts surrounding the alleged loss. This is particularly true where, as here, the named payee actually had possession of the check, and thus, presumptively received that possession by delivery. UCC § 3–307; Official Comment 4 to UCC § 3–306, McKinney's Cons.Laws of N.Y., Book 62½ at 201 (1964). In this case, the need for documentation is underscored by the customer's independent suit against plaintiff on the underlying transaction. Reinhard, the customer who is alleged to have lost the check is suing for the return of payment given to plaintiff on the ground of claimed defects in the goods delivered. To prevent summary judgment, it is incumbent upon defendant to submit a factual affidavit from Reinhard, or at the least, to offer an explanation for its failure to do so.

The court concludes that plaintiff has established that defendant's check was delivered. Thus, there is no need to consider what effect the loss or non-delivery of the check may have had on the rights of the parties. The court also finds that the issuance and delivery of its cashier's check preclude the bank from raising any defenses Reinhard may have against the payee or against plaintiff.

Accordingly, plaintiff's motion for summary judgment is granted.

Notes

The bank in *Moon Over the Mountain* was a bit infirm on its theory. The court rejected the proposition that the bank could assert the defense of its customer. Is that decision correct under § 3–306? (Note that the courts are not unanimous on this point and that some courts would disagree with the court in *Moon Over the Mountain.*)

Unfortunately many courts use imprecise terminology when they are dealing with cashier's and bank checks. Although they often speak of the "right to stop payment," it is clear to us that the customer who buys a cashier's check has no "right" to stop payment. If the customer procures a court order and gives an indemnity under § 3–603, he may be able to stop a bank from paying, but short of such measures he has no "right." The real issue in these cases is whether the bank, having decided for various reasons not to pay, may subsequently raise either its own defenses or those of its customer. Study Sections 3–306, 3–603 and 3–802 and then answer the following problems.

Problem 24–13

1. Bank issues a cashier's check in return for the purchaser's personal check. The personal check bounces. Now the bank wishes to refuse payment not on the ground that its customer has a defense in the transaction but that it has a defense. May it do so? See UCC 3–306.

2. Customer uses the cashier's check to purchase a new car which proves (in the first three hours of its use) to be a lemon. Bank chooses to refuse payment of the cashier's check and wonders whether it will be free to raise the defenses of the customer against the automobile dealer. See UCC 3–306.

3. In the first case assume customer had drawn a personal check to pay for the cashier's check on another branch of the same bank that issued the cashier's check. Bank now has a potential setoff against the cashier's check and has dealt with the plaintiff in the case. Does that change the outcome?

4. Bank has now been through the case above and your list of hypotheticals; it comes forward with a practical and pragmatic question: In the common case in which our customer buys a cashier's check, purchases a piece of large equipment and then finds that it wishes the check not to be paid, how should we proceed? On the one hand, we do not wish the cashier's checks to lose their utility as cash substitutes, however in many transactions we are much more likely to be interested in retaining our customer and thus in following his wishes. If we follow his wishes and refuse to pay, what steps should we take to protect our interests and what risks will we be undertaking?

5. Finally, what is a cashier's check? Is it the equivalent of a note or is it rather like a draft on which there has been a bank acceptance? Is it something else?

The answers to some of the problems above may follow from one's conclusion about the status of cashier's checks.

CHAPTER TWENTY-FIVE

THEFT BY CHECK

SECTION 1. INTRODUCTION

Sometimes, civil liability is the residue left when the criminal has drained the cup. Such a residue is the substance of this chapter. One who has read the cases or who has worked as an executive or a lawyer for a financial institution for a long period of time will be able to classify various thieves with considerable precision. Perhaps most common and most interesting is the embezzler. The embezzler is a competent, efficient, and apparently honest employee of the ultimate plaintiff or defendant. The classic embezzler steals from the bank account of his employer by causing the employer to sign checks to fictitious parties, by forging the employer's signature and, occasionally, by stealing incoming checks payable to the order of the employer and forging the indorsement. Almost every lawsuit left after the embezzler is in jail will involve sections 3–405 and 4–406. These are sections which in certain circumstances allocate the loss to the employer on the grounds that it was his responsibility not that of the bank to insure that a trusted employee was honest.

A second and less frequent thief is one, not an employee, who steals a check from the mail and procures cash by forging an indorsement. This case will present some but not all of the issues typically present in the embezzler situation. Finally, there is the professional criminal, one with the guile, but not the redeeming virtues, of the embezzler, who forges the drawer's signature or who poses as a drawer. This person we see in the *Perini* and *Altman* cases below.

Lest the student disappear without a trace into the murky forest of UCC 3–418, 4–207, 3–406, 4–406, etc., the student should first view civil liability here from a distance. In general, the Uniform Commercial Code and the law that preceded it allocate the loss occasioned by the passage of an instrument with a forged indorsement or the passage of an altered instrument to the person who took it from the thief. In modern economic parlance that person normally can be regarded as the least cost risk avoider. Because this person dealt with the thief, use of more careful identification procedures might have averted the loss. Thus this person should bear the cost. In the usual case, when a thief alters an instrument or forges an indorsement and passes it to a depositary bank, ultimately the depositary bank should wind up with the loss. (Often those rules are subject to change in a specific case where it is proved that the alteration or forgery was facilitated by the employer's or owner's negligence.) If, in an alteration or a forged indorsement case, Articles 3 and 4 appear to point elsewhere, the student should reexamine his analysis and ask why the taker from the thief is not the ultimate loser.

For reasons that are no longer persuasive, the rule of liability is different with respect to a check bearing a forged drawer's signature. In general the loss on such a check rests on the payor bank (the "drawee"), not on the one who took it from the thief and not typically on the drawer. This is the famous rule of

Price v. Neal. As applied to checks, it is founded on the assumption that the payor bank knows its depositor's signature and is at fault for its failure to dishonor a check signed by one other than its depositor. With the almost complete automation of check payment systems, it has become more difficult to justify the rule of *Price v. Neal* on the ground that the payor bank should have recognized its customer's signature.

The need to distinguish between these two cases, the forged drawer's signature on the one hand and the forged indorsement on the other, has introduced troublesome complexity in Articles 3 and 4. Among other things it calls upon the courts to decide which rule to apply when there are two forged signatures. As we will see, the need for separate rules has made the warranty rules in 3–417 and 4–207 grostesquely complex.

It is hard to learn the rules of liability in this chapter by increments. Each case seems to thrust all of the theories of liability and all of the defenses upon the reader. Nevertheless we have endeavored to divide the issues by selecting appropriate cases and by presenting them in an organized fashion. Doubtless the student will not think our efforts successful, but we have tried.

Before digging into the cases the student should be aware of the six independent theories of liability on a stolen check and three pertinent defenses. First are two claims on the check that we will not discuss in this chapter. One is found in section 3–804. That section allows an "owner" to sue on a lost or stolen instrument. Typically it is useful in the case in which the payee of a check has lost the check and in which the drawer for some reason refuses to replace it. If the drawer has paid a holder he has discharged his liability under UCC 3–804 and on the check itself and thus has no liability. However if the check has been destroyed by the thief or has been paid to one who is not a holder, the owner can sue the drawer under 3–804. The second section with which we do not deal here, is section 4–401. That section authorizes the bank to charge a customer's account on items that are "properly payable." The implication from that authorization is that a bank cannot charge items not properly payable. Among those not properly payable are items bearing forged indorsements and forged signatures.

The cases in section 2 of this chapter are organized insofar as possible to present four theories of recovery in order. Which theory of recovery is appropriate depends in part upon whether the theft was caused by a forged drawer's signature, a forged indorsement or by alteration. It also depends upon the thief's place in the chain.

In many cases a check carrying a forged indorsement will have been paid by the payor bank. If the payor decides to recredit the depositor's account (because of its responsibility under contract and UCC 4–401), it will commonly seek to sue back upstream on the warranties that were given it by depositary banks and others who dealt with the check after the thief but before the payor. These cases will be litigated under sections 4–207 or 3–417, the nearly identical warranty provisions in Articles 4 and 3.

Less frequently the check will have been stolen from an owner-payee, or, even less frequently, from the drawer who will seek to use UCC 3–419 and the theory of conversion to sue someone downstream, someone who has dealt with his stolen asset after its theft. The classic 3–419 case would be one in which a payee sues the payor bank on the theory that the payment over a forged indorsement to a thief or his agent constituted conversion. Section 3–419 was not well drafted. It has left many unanswered questions for the courts, and subsection 3–419(3) has established a rule of law that the courts have been reluctant to accept. We take up those problems below.

The third cause of action that might be brought, and one apparently not contemplated by the drafters of the Code and not recognized in all states, would be an affirmative cause of action in negligence. In section 3 of the chapter we will see how the drafters intended negligence of one or other parties to influence outcomes via the notion of estoppel. It is unlikely that the drafters intended the negligent behavior of any party to give rise to the *affirmative* claim by the owner of a check against such a party, but in California and some other states, courts have ruled otherwise.

The final cause of action with which we will deal is unjust enrichment, i.e., restitution. Surprisingly the drafters have left common law restitution as the principal mode of recovery for checks bearing a forged drawer's signature, and, as we will see in the next chapter, for NSF (non sufficient funds) checks.

In section 3 we deal with the most common defenses of one who would otherwise be liable for paying over a forgery or dealing with an altered item. These are the two negligence defenses, UCC 3–406 and 4–406, and their first cousin, section 3–405 (which may be thought of as a rule of conclusively presumed negligence).

Of course the cases do not divide up as neatly as one would like. All of our "liability" cases present more than one theory of recovery and all our "liability" cases also deal with defenses.

SECTION 2. THEORIES OF RECOVERY

As we have indicated above, it may be hard to wring the correct answer out of the Code, yet it is easy to state and to understand the general rule with respect to forged indorsements and altered instruments. The rule is that the loss so occasioned will normally come to rest on the first solvent party who dealt with the instrument after the thief. The logic in this rule is as follows: it will encourage those who take checks to be careful, to demand identification, and to examine the checks which they take (of course it may cause check-identification overkill and thus inhibit the transfer of checks).

The Code sections that achieve the rule described above are chiefly UCC 4–207(1)(a) and 3–419. Under the former section a person passing the check down the chain of collection gives the implied warranty that he has "good title to the item or is authorized to obtain payment or acceptance on behalf of one who has good title." Note the warranties to the payor under subsection 1 of UCC 4–207 are significantly different from those contained in subsection 2 that go not to the payor but to intermediaries.

The warranty of "good title" means many things, but at minimum it means "this check bears no forged indorsements." Thus, one who takes a check from a thief over a forged indorsement and passes it on has breached the warranty and can be expected to make good on his warranty against a payor that has unwittingly paid it. In most cases this is a proper allocation of the loss because there is no way for the payor to determine that an indorsement was invalid, but proper procedures at the liquor store or the depositary bank, wherever the thief appeared, might have prevented the forgery. The complexity in section 4–207 does not arise from this simple case. It arises from the fact that the drafters had to fashion this simple rule (placing liability on a person after the thief) and to distinguish it from the different rule (placing liability in many cases on the payor) for the case of the forged drawer's signature.

Section 3–419 reads in part as follows:

(1) An instrument is converted when * * *

(c) it is paid on a forged indorsement.

* * *

A cursory reading of this section leaves one with several questions. First, who is the appropriate party plaintiff in a suit contemplated by UCC 3–419? Surely the "payee-owner" who has had a check stolen can sue, but what about a drawer who has prepared a check that has been stolen from his hands before delivery to a payee? Second, who are the appropriate defendants? It is clear that the drawee (payor bank) is an appropriate defendant, but what is the effect of subsection 3 and in what circumstances would the collecting bank be an appropriate defendant? Finally, does the section completely codify the law of conversion of negotiable instruments or is there some residue of common-law conversion? What, for example, of the person who steals a bearer check and passes it? Surely he is liable for conversion, yet 3–419 does not speak of that person.

The leading decision denying the drawer a cause of action in conversion is Stone & Webster Engineering Corp. v. First Nat'l Bank & Trust Co., 345 Mass. 1, 184 N.E.2d 358 (1962). There the Massachusetts Supreme Judicial Court held that a drawer had no cause of action against a collecting bank which had cashed and passed on a check stolen from the drawer's hands. The court gave both a doctrinal reason for its holding and a more pragmatic one. In the first place it found that the drawer of an undelivered check has no "valuable rights" in such a check. Since the drawer does not have the right of a payee or subsequent holder to present it to the drawee for payment the "value of its rights was limited to the physical paper on which [the check] was written * * *" The court went on to point out that the drawer's recovery in conversion against the collecting bank which had paid over the forged indorsement would violate the draftsmen's apparent intent to require the drawer to go against his own bank (UCC 4–401(1)).

In this type of case, if one believes that the drawer has been guilty of negligence, it makes sense to require that he go against his own bank, the drawee, and not the depositary bank. The drawee has sent out the statements and cancelled checks, and can readily prove when the checks were sent to the drawer and when the drawer first gave notice of the forgery. Likewise the drawee is likely to have a greater capacity to know of or to find out about the drawer's business procedures than is some bank that has had no prior dealings with the drawer. If a court allows the drawer to begin his suit directly against a depositary bank with whom he has not previously dealt, that bank is put at a considerable disadvantage in proving the defense of negligence. (See UCC 3–406 and 4–406.) The bank will have no knowledge of when the cancelled checks were sent to the drawer, nor will it know when the drawer communicated his discovery of the forgery to the drawee, and it will have had no previous contact with the drawer to form the basis for conclusions about the drawer's business behavior.

One may also ask why a drawer would sue a depositary bank rather than follow the procedure of insisting that his own bank recredit his account (assuming the forgery is provable). The simple answer may be the drawer's fear that his own negligence can be more readily uncovered by his own bank than by a depositary bank, an event which he obviously does not want to occur. If this is true (and there does not appear to be a way of knowing whether it is or not) then we agree with the court in *Stone and Webster Engineering* that the drawer should base his cause of action on UCC 4–401 as against the drawee bank, and not against the depositary bank on a theory of UCC 3–419 conversion.

The second question here is this: Who are the proper defendants in a conversion suit? If one assumes that a check is stolen from the payee and is then "cashed" at a depositary bank, passed through the hands of various collecting banks and ultimately paid by the drawee, there are several potential defendants. The first is the thief, a notoriously unrewarding and unavailable defendant. Second there is the drawee bank. The drawee bank is clearly an appropriate defendant under the given facts; UCC 3–419(1)(c) makes the drawee liable. The fighting issue in the cases is: Under what circumstances will a depositary bank be liable in conversion? Subsection (3) of UCC 3–419 deals with the problem as follows:

> "Subject to the provisions of this Act concerning restrictive indorsements a representative, including a depositary or collecting bank, who has in good faith and in accordance with the reasonable commercial standards applicable to the business of such representative dealt with an instrument or its proceeds on behalf of one who was not the true owner is not liable in conversion or otherwise to the true owner beyond the amount of any proceeds remaining in his hands."

Read literally this section will render the depositary bank liable under three sets of circumstances. First, the depositary bank is liable unless it cashed in good faith and "in accordance with the reasonable commercial standards applicable to the business." Thus if the bank failed to demand identification in a circumstance in which reasonable commercial standards would have called upon it to demand such identification, it is liable in conversion under section 3–419. Secondly, the depositary bank will have liability in the case where "proceeds" remain in its hands. When the thief does not cash the check but deposits it in his own account and never withdraws the money, there are proceeds. To the extent that the bank pays cash over the counter to the thief it has no proceeds, the *Dauphin Trust* case to the contrary notwithstanding. The third circumstance in which a depositary bank may have liability is if the check was indorsed "for deposit only" and the depositary bank then cashed it over such an indorsement (see UCC 3–419(4), 3–419(3) and 3–206(3)).

The policy then of UCC 3–419(3) was to place substantial limits upon the liability of depositary and other collecting banks. The New York Law Revision Commission criticized these restrictions because they caused circuity of action and provided in many circumstances a very inconvenient defendant for the aggrieved owner (the payee). However for reasons not too clear, UCC 3–419(3) weathered the storm intact.

In *Knesz* (infra page 1080 the New Jersey court has been more respectful of UCC 3–419(3) than have some other courts. Under a variety of rationales a number of courts have evaded the apparent intention of the drafters as expressed in UCC 3–419(3). The student should consider those questions in reading the *Knesz* case.

Sun'n Sand (infra page 1089 is representative of the limited number of cases that recognize negligence as an affirmative basis for recovery under Articles 3 and 4. The student should compare that case with the statutory reference to negligence found in UCC 3–406 and 4–406, sections that we consider extensively in section 3 of this chapter.

Under the pre-Code law a payor that paid over a forged indorsement or paid a check bearing a forged drawer's signature would in some jurisdictions have sued in restitution for money paid by mistake. Sections 35 and 37 of the Restatement of Restitution set out those rights.

Section 35. Forged Indorsement

A person whose claim of title to a bill of exchange or promissory note depends upon a forged or unauthorized indorsement and who has received payment thereof from a person who was liable upon the instrument as a party to it prior to such indorsement and who pays without notice of the invalidity of the indorsement, is under a duty to restore to the payor the amount received, unless he has already satisfied the owner of the instrument.

Section 37. Payment by One Not a Party to the Instrument

A person who has paid for the honor of a party to a negotiable instrument, or in accordance with an agreement with such party, has the same rights of restitution as the person for whom he paid would have had upon payment in accordance with the rules stated in sections 29–36, and in addition he is entitled to restitution from the person for whose honor he makes payment, to the extent that he thereby relieves such person from a duty.

The drafters of the Code chose to supplant section 35 with the warranties in UCC 4–207(1)(a). They did not grant a similar warranty claim when the payor paid over a forged drawer's signature. To allow the liability to rest with the payor bank (in accordance with the rule of *Price v. Neal*), the drafters apparently believe they could not grant a warranty claim, at least in certain circumstances. Nevertheless they did nothing to abolish a restitution claim that would have existed in some circumstances at common law. Here the student should read UCC 3–418. This is the section which in effect states the rule of *Price v. Neal* and states when restitution will *not* be allowed.

As we will see in *Altman* (infra page 1095) restitution was in certain circumstances allowed by a payor against a person who took a check bearing a forged drawer's signature. If, for example, that person had not changed his position in reliance on payment and was not a holder in due course, section 3–418 permits the payor to proceed with his common-law restitution action. Thus we add yet a fourth and confusing affirmative right to go along with the rights of conversion, warranty, and negligence.

MENTHOR, S.A. v. SWISS BANK CORP.

United States District Court, Southern District of New York, 1982.
549 F.Supp. 1125.

LASKER, DISTRICT JUDGE. This action, which raises a number of complicated and technical questions of banking law, concerns a dispute between Manufacturers Hanover Trust Co., Swiss Bank Corp., Chemical Bank, Banco di Napoli and Banco Popular de Puerto Rico as to who is liable for the loss of seven checks totalling $52,059.72, which disappeared somewhere in the international banking system. The facts are as follows: [1]

1. The statement of facts is taken from the Stipulated Facts included in the parties' Pre-trial Order, signed by counsel for all parties on June 25, 1981.

In late December, 1977, Walter N. Rojas, an employee of Menthor, S.A. ("Menthor"), received from Exprinter Casa Bancaria ("Exprinter") seven checks drawn on Exprinter's account at Manufacturers Hanover Trust Co. ("MHT"). The checks were payable to various payees and all of the checks were endorsed in blank by the payees. At the time, Menthor maintained an account at Swiss Bank Corp. ("Swiss"), with whom Rojas transacted business on behalf of Menthor, using the name Herman R. Gfeller. Rojas restrictively endorsed each of the checks by stamping them "Only for deposit" in the account number assigned to Menthor, and signing the name Herman R. Gfeller. On December 23, 1977, Rojas sent the checks to Swiss by registered mail.

On January 18, 1978, Menthor sent a telex to Swiss inquiring as to the status of the checks. On January 23, 1978, Swiss telexed Menthor that the checks had been credited to its account as of January 20, 1978. In fact, the checks were not credited to Menthor's account then or at any other time.

In the meantime, four of the checks showed up at the New York City branch of Banco di Napoli ("BDN"). They were deposited in an account in the name of Alberto Enrique Esteban. At the time of the deposit, the checks were altered in that the stamp affixed by Rojas had been covered with black ink and the checks bore the signature "Esteban." BDN presented the checks through Chemical Bank ("Chemical") to MHT, which paid the checks and transmitted the proceeds through Chemical to BDN. The other three checks were deposited in Banco Popular de Puerto Rico, ("BPPR") also in an account in the name of Alberto Enrique Esteban. The three BPPR checks had been altered in the same manner as the BDN checks. BPPR presented the checks directly to MHT, and they were also paid by MHT without dispute. "Esteban" later withdrew the entire proceeds of all seven checks from both BDN and BPPR.

Menthor brings this action against MHT on grounds of wrongful conversion, pursuant to § 3–419 of the Uniform Commercial Code, NY Uniform Commercial Code (McKinney 1964) ("UCC"), and against Swiss for breach of contract to repay monies deposited. MHT has brought a third-party action against BDN, BPPR and Chemical for breach of warranties.

On the basis of the facts stipulated in the Joint Pre-Trial Order, motions for summary judgment pursuant to Fed.R.Civ.Pr. 56 have been made by Menthor against MHT and Swiss, and by MHT against BDN, BPPR and Chemical. Swiss has cross-moved for summary judgment against Menthor, and BDN has cross-moved for summary judgment against MHT.

(1) MENTHOR V. MHT

MHT does not dispute Menthor's contention that MHT paid on checks bearing forged endorsements, and that, under UCC § 3–419, the owner or holder of a check is entitled to recover from the drawee bank for conversion if the bank pays on a check bearing a forged endorsement. However, MHT contends that Menthor is no longer the holder of the checks and therefore does not have standing to bring an action against MHT. MHT argues that Menthor negotiated the checks to Swiss by delivery to Swiss with the necessary endorsement, and that, upon negotiation, Swiss, the transferee, became the holder. UCC § 3–202.

In response, Menthor and Swiss argue that Swiss was not the holder [2] of the checks, but merely Menthor's agent for their collection until Swiss received

2. Menthor is sometimes referred to as the "holder" of the checks, and other times as their "owner." We attempt to adhere to the distinctions made by the parties. However, we note that the concept of the "holder" is a creation of Article 3, while ownership is a

"settlement" or payment on the checks from the drawee bank, MHT, which never occurred.

Section 4–201(1) of the UCC provides that:

"prior to the time that a settlement of an item is or becomes final * * * the bank is an agent or subagent of the owner and any settlement given for the item is provisional."

Section 4–213(3) specifies that the provisional credit referred to in § 4–201(1) "becomes final" "[*i*]f a collecting bank receives a settlement for an item." (emphasis added).

The Official Comment to § 4–213 explains:

"If previously [the collecting bank] gave to its customer a provisional credit * * * its receipt of final settlement for the item 'firms up' this provisional credit and makes it final. When this credit given by it so becomes final * * * its agency status terminates * * *"

Thus, it appears that Menthor was at all times holder of the checks and Swiss was merely its agent for collection because Swiss never received a "final settlement" for the checks from MHT.

MHT argues that the agency relationship terminated when Swiss sent the telex to Menthor advising it that the checks had been received. However, MHT cites no authority for this argument, and we are unable to find any. To the contrary, it appears that under § 4–213(3), the question whether agency status has terminated depends on what transpired between the collecting bank and the drawee bank, not on transactions between the collecting bank and its customer.

It is arguable that the Article 4 sections of the Code relied on by Menthor are inconsistent with the Article 3 sections concerning negotiations relied on by MHT. However, the possible conflict presents no difficulty, because the Code explicitly provides that in case of conflict between Article 4, which governs bank deposits and collections, and Article 3, which states the general law of commercial paper, the provisions of Article 4 control. See UCC § 4–102 ("In the event of conflict, the provisions of this Article govern those of Article 3.").

* * *

Accordingly, Menthor, as the owner of the checks, has standing to sue MHT for conversion under UCC § 3–419. There being no other defenses raised to Menthor's conversion claim, Menthor's motion for summary judgment against MHT is granted.

(2) MHT v. BDN

MHT's claim against BDN is based on UCC § 4–207(1)(a) and (c), the statutory warranties of transfer or presentment. They read:

"Each * * * collecting bank who obtains payment or acceptance of an item * * * warrants to the payor bank * * * that

"(a) he has good title to the item or is authorized to obtain payment or acceptance on behalf of one who has a good title; and * * *

"(c) the item has not been materially altered * * *"

An alteration is material, under UCC § 3–407, if it alters either "the number or relations of the parties" or "the writing as signed, by adding to it or by removing any part of it." MHT contends that it is entitled to summary judgment against

concept of Article 4. The drafters of the Code recognized that the two articles may be inconsistent in some respects, and provided that, in such an event, the provisions of Article 4 control. See UCC § 4–102.

BDN on the basis of a showing that (a) BDN presented the checks to MHT for payment and MHT paid on them and (b) that the checks were materially altered. The former point has been stipulated, while the latter, MHT argues, is undeniable in view of the presence of the large black mark on the back of the checks which covers the words "only for deposit."

BDN raises a number of defenses to MHT's motion for summary judgment, which are discussed and decided seriatim below:

(a) Section 3–406:

Section 3–406 provides:

> "Any person who by his negligence substantially contributes to a material alteration of the instrument * * * is precluded from asserting the alteration or lack of authority against a holder in due course or against a drawee or other payor * * *"

BDN contends that Menthor, through the actions of its agent Rojas, was negligent in two respects. First, Rojas signed the name Gfeller underneath the "only for deposit" stamp, although the signature was not necessary for the deposit of the checks. BDN contends that had the signature not been present, its tellers might have noticed the black mark on the checks. Second, BDN contends, Rojas signed the checks "in blank," making them freely negotiable.

The argument borders on the frivolous. Although it may not have been necessary for the checks to have been signed, it was not negligent for Rojas to have signed them—he could hardly have expected to have imagined that someone would obliterate the stamped words "only for deposit." As for the contention that the checks were signed "in blank," it is simply inaccurate. One can see through the black mark that the signature follows the words "only for deposit." There is absolutely no evidence that his signature diverted—or could reasonably be believed to have diverted—the attention of BDN's tellers from the bold black line which obliterated the restrictive endorsement "Only for Deposit."

(b) Section 4–406(1) and (2):

Section 4–406 provides that when a bank sends its customer a statement accompanied by items paid, the customer must use reasonable care to examine the statement and items paid, and that if he fails to do so, he may not assert against the bank any losses due to alterations or unauthorized signatures. BDN asserts that Menthor was negligent in failing to timely examine its statements. The purported negligence is that Menthor did not inquire of Swiss as to the status of the checks after Swiss sent the confirming telex, January 23, 1978, until March 16, 1978. Esteban had withdrawn the proceeds of the checks from BDN by the end of March.

As Menthor persuasively responds, § 4–406 is inapplicable because Menthor was not a customer of MHT, and consequently was not sent any MHT statements. The checks in question were drawn on the account to Exprinter and it was to Exprinter that MHT sent statements. Although, as BDN points out, Menthor is a wholly-owned subsidiary of Exprinter, no showing has been made that there is any basis for piercing the corporate veil so as to attribute any negligence of Exprinter (if there was any negligence) to Menthor.

BDN argues further that even if Menthor cannot be held accountable for Exprinter's failure to check its MHT statements, Menthor can be held responsible for its failure to check its own statements from Swiss. However true that may be, § 4–406 provides that the defense of failure to examine bank statements is a defense of the bank that sent the statements, which, in this case, is Swiss, not BDN.

(c) Section 4–406(5):

Section 4–406(5) provides that if the payor bank has a valid defense against its customer and waives that defense, it may not assert a claim against the collecting bank. BDN contends that MHT has waived the defenses against Menthor which BDN is attempting to assert by this motion.

Section 4–406(5), by its terms, applies only to the 4–406 defenses. See Girard Bank v. Mount Holly State Bank, 474 F.Supp. 1225, 1236 (D.N.J. 1979). The only 4–406 defenses which BDN asserts to be applicable to this action are 4–406(1) and (2), which, as explained in the previous section, are not valid defenses. Accordingly, MHT has not waived any valid defenses, and may assert its claim against BDN.

(d) Commercial Reasonableness:

BDN asserts that it acted in a commercially reasonable manner in accepting the checks from Esteban, because there are circumstances in which it is appropriate to accept checks which contain strike-outs.

MHT responds that commercial reasonableness is not a defense to a claim on a warranty of presentment, because liability for a breach of a warranty of presentment is absolute.

Neither party submits any authority on the question whether liability on a warranty of representment is absolute, and we have been unable to find any. However, MHT's position appears to be the more acceptable.

The subsection of the Code which provides for warranties of presentment with respect to alterations, § 4–207(1)(c), simply provides that the collecting bank "warrants" that there have been no material alterations. By contrast, under the immediately preceding subsection, § 4–207(1)(b), the collecting bank warrants that it "*has no knowledge* that the signature of the maker or drawer is unauthorized." (emphasis added) The difference between subsections (b) and (c) suggests that the collecting bank's knowledge or lack of knowledge as to whether there have been material alterations is irrelevant.

Moreover, if commercial reasonableness were a proper defense to a warranty of presentment, one would expect to find some mention of that fact, as well as a discussion of what constitutes commercial reasonableness, in the commentaries on § 4–207. However, neither the Official Comment to the section nor White and Summers' treatise on the Uniform Commercial Code gives any indication that liability on a warranty of presentment for a material alteration is to be other than absolute. See J. White & R. Summers, Handbook of the Law Under the Uniform Commercial Code § 15–5, 597–606 (2d ed. 1980). See also 9 N.Y. Juris. 2d, Banks & Financial Institutions § 419 at 665–666 ("Therefore, if a bank pays a check which is materially altered, it may recover from the * * * collecting bank to whom it paid the check damages for breach of warranty against material alteration.") In fact, White and Summers mention only one defense to a claim of material alteration: untimely assertion of the alteration. Id. at 603–606.

Moreover, the purpose behind the establishment of warranties of presentment appears to be to speed the check collection process by requiring only one bank, the bank which took in the item, to validate endorsements. If a defense of commercial reasonableness were to be read into the statute, that purpose would be in large part defeated, because banks later in the collection process would bear the risk that they might be liable for the loss if the material alteration or forgery was so carefully performed that the bank which received the item had not noticed it despite the use of commercially reasonable standards. Thus, if a commercial reasonableness defense were accepted, it would seem that the better the forgery, the more likely the drawee bank would be the one to pay for the loss. This result would run counter to the purpose of § 4–207, which is to put the burden on the *first* bank in the sequence to assure that all endorsements are proper.

* * *

We conclude that commercial reasonableness is not a defense to a breach of warranty claim under § 4–207(1)(c). In addition, it should be noted that the checks in question have been submitted to the court by Menthor. While the question whether a bank's conduct has been commercially reasonable would ordinarily not be a subject for summary judgment, we have examined the checks, and note that one can read "only for deposit in the account 0–452–704148–00" underneath the black marks on the backs of most of them. Under the circumstances, we find that it was not commercially reasonable for BDN to have accepted the checks. * * *

For the reasons stated above, BDN's defenses to MHT's claim are without merit. MHT's motion for summary judgment against BDN is granted; BDN's cross-motion for summary judgment against MHT is denied.

* * *

It is so ordered.

[Footnotes omitted.]

Notes

1. The foregoing case is terribly complicated, for it involves a simultaneous consideration of several different issues. One of your authors has found it easier to understand such cases by drawing charts such as the one that follows:

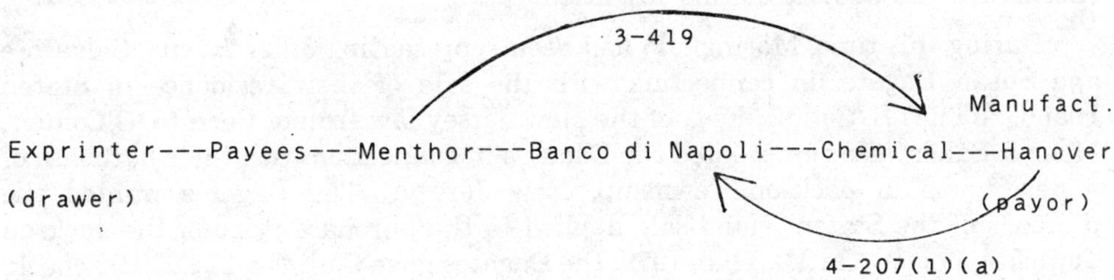

2. Menthor can have only one satisfaction. If it only wins a judgment against the Swiss Bank, who between the Swiss Bank and Banco di Napoli (a stand-in for Manufacturers Hanover) ultimately pays?

3. The case contains an interesting discussion of 4–406(5). Read that section and think about its significance. A bank's good relations with a customer, its fear of losing the customer if it asserts liability against it, may lead the bank to overlook the most obvious defendant (the customer) and seek recovery against a third party. That might have been happening in this case, but 4–406(5) did not technically apply because the drawer was the parent Esprinter, and the plaintiff in the lawsuit was Menthor, the subsidiary. Because the subsidiary was not the drawer, it did not receive the check and did not have the duties spelled out in 4–406.

KNESZ v. CENTRAL JERSEY BANK & TRUST CO. OF FREEHOLD

Supreme Court of New Jersey, 1984.
97 N.J. 1, 477 A.2d 806.

HANDLER, J. Plaintiff, Steve Knesz, a Pennsylvania resident, owned a cooperative apartment in New York City. He engaged Thomas G. Moringiello, a since-disbarred New York attorney, to act as his agent for the purpose of collecting rent from the occupant of the apartment and making disbursements for expenses, including taxes, mortgage amortization, and maintenance costs associated with the apartment. Apparently, Moringiello did not regularly transmit rental proceeds to Knesz because the rents did not exceed these expenses.

On or about March 16, 1979, without plaintiff's knowledge or consent, Moringiello sold the apartment to one Lois Gartlir for $32,651.00. Ms. Gartlir remitted the purchase price to Moringiello by five checks. One was a cashier's check in the amount of $16,974.24, dated March 14, 1979, drawn by Citibank, N.A., at the request of Lois Gartlir, payable to Steve Knesz. Three checks, each dated March 13, 1979, were drawn by Hofheimer, Gartlir, Gottlieb & Gross on Morgan Guaranty Trust Company of New York, payable to Lois Gartlir in the amount of $10,000.00, $5,000.00, and $500.00 respectively. The fifth check was drawn on Banker's Trust in the amount of $177.30, payable to Lois Gartlir. Gartlir specially endorsed the three Morgan Guaranty checks and the Banker's Trust check, all under the legend "pay [or 'payable'] to the order of Steve Knesz." Moringiello forged plaintiff's endorsement on all five instruments. The forger's own signature and the notation "For deposit only," appeared to have been placed under plaintiff's forged endorsement on the back of three of the checks, the $10,000.00 and $500.00 Morgan Guaranty checks and the $177.30 Banker's Trust check totaling $10,677.30. These three checks were collected in due course and credited to Moringiello's account. The two remaining instruments—the $16,974.24 Citibank check and the $5,000.00 Morgan Guaranty check—are the subject of this litigation.

During this time, Moringiello had been representing other clients, Salvatore and Susan Dagate, in connection with the sale of their residence in Staten Island. James E. Collins, Esq., of the New Jersey law firm of Cerrato, O'Connor, Mehr & Saker, also represented the Dagates in connection with their purchase of a new home in Jackson Township, New Jersey. The Dagates wanted the proceeds of the Staten Island sale applied to the purchase price of the Jackson Township home. On March 5, 1979, the Dagates gave Collins a $24,000.00 check, payable to Collins, drawn by Moringiello on his special attorney's account with Central State Bank of New York. The Dagates advised Collins that the check represented the proceeds of the sale of their Staten Island property. After confirming this with Moringiello, Collins endorsed the $24,000.00 check and deposited it into his law firm's trust account with defendant, Central Jersey Bank and Trust Company of Freehold ("Central Jersey").

Moringiello's check bounced. Collins telephoned Moringiello, who apologized for the oversight and promised to deliver immediately replacement checks covering the Dagates' $24,000.00 deposit. On March 14, 1979, Moringiello delivered to Collins three checks totalling $24,000.00: the $16,974.24 Citibank check, the $5,000.00 Morgan Guaranty check, and a personal check from Moringiello's Citibank account in the sum of $2,025.76. Moringiello placed the notation "Pay to the order of James E. Collins" below Knesz's forged signature on the $16,974.24 check.

Collins promptly endorsed and deposited the checks into his firm's trust account with Central Jersey on March 15, 1979. Central Jersey forwarded the checks for payment pursuant to the bank's regular collection process and all three checks were paid in due course by the appropriate payor banks. Subsequently, the Cerrato law firm issued checks against the proceeds of the $24,000.00 on deposit with Central Jersey. Eventually, the entire $24,000.00 was depleted by these disbursements.

Over nine months later, in January 1980, plaintiff first discovered that Moringiello had sold his apartment. Knesz chose to ratify the sale and recover the proceeds. He obtained copies of the five checks bearing his forged endorsement, executed the requisite affidavits of forgery for each, and had them forwarded to the appropriate banks for collection. These items and photocopies of the $16,947.24 Citibank check and the $5,000.00 Morgan Guaranty check were mailed to Central Jersey on August 28 and September 5, 1980. Citibank subsequently paid Knesz $10,677.30, the full amount of the three checks that Moringiello had illicitly deposited there. Central Jersey, however, refused payment on the remaining $16,974.24 and $5,000.00 checks.

On December 17, 1980, Knesz filed a two-count complaint against Central Jersey to recover $21,974.24 for the two unpaid checks. Defendant, Central Jersey, filed an answer and a third-party complaint on April 15, 1981 against Cerrato, O'Connor, Mehr & Saker, asserting that the law firm, as depositor, had warranted the instruments and was therefore liable to the bank. The firm denied its liability, raising the defenses of contributory negligence and intervening causation.

On cross-motions for summary judgment, the trial court ruled that the bank was not liable under the Uniform Commercial Code (UCC), N.J.S.A. 12A:3–419(3), which furnishes a broad immunity to certain banks in their handling of forged checks. The Appellate Division reversed the summary judgment order and remanded the case to the trial court for further proceedings. 188 N.J.Super. 391, 410 (1982). We granted defendant's petition for certification, 93 N.J. 293 (1983), to consider the interpretation and application of the terms of N.J.S.A. 12A:3–419(3) of the UCC.

I

N.J.S.A. 12A:3–419(3) by its general terms purports to provide that a depository or collecting bank that acts in a representative capacity in the negotiation of a forged check, doing so in good faith and in conformity to applicable commercial standards, is not liable to the instrument's true owner except to the extent of any proceeds still remaining with it. Specifically, subsection (3) of N.J.S.A. 12A:3–419 states that these banks may be insulated from liability to the payee or true owner of a forged check when the following circumstances converge: (1) the bank was acting as a "representative"; (2) it honored the forged check in good faith and in accordance with the applicable reasonable commercial standards; and (3) it retained no "proceeds" of the check.

This section of the UCC purports sharply to restrict the causes of action available to the true owner or payee of a check whose endorsement has been forged. Under N.J.S.A. 12A:3–419(1)(c), the owner-payee may bring an action against a drawee or payor bank that transmits final payment on the forged indorsement, the payor bank being defined as "a bank by which an item is payable as drawn or accepted," N.J.S.A. 12A:4–105(b). However, the UCC by the application of the terms § 3–419(3) does not extend this liability to a "depositary" or "collecting" bank that in the chain of collection has handled the check with the forged endorsement, a depositary bank being "the first bank to which an item is transferred for collection" (N.J.S.A. 12A:4–105(a)), and a collecting bank being "any bank handling the item for collection except the payor bank" (N.J.S.A. 12A:4–105(d)).

In concluding that defendant, Central Jersey, was liable to the plaintiff and not entitled to the immunity accorded by § 3–419(3), the Appellate Division did not base its determination on any asserted failure on the part of the bank to adhere to the standards of good faith and commercial reasonableness applicable to such transactions. N.J.S.A. 12A:3–419(3). Conduct falling short of the standards of good faith and commercial reasonableness includes such matters as the failure to make inquiries about facial irregularities on a check or into the endorsing agent's authority. See, e.g., Salsman v. National Community Bank of Rutherford, 102 N.J.Super. 482 [5 UCC Rep 779] (Law.Div. 1968), affd ob, 105 N.J.Super. 164 (App.Div. 1969) (bank was negligent in failure to pay in accordance with terms of restrictive indorsement and to inquire into agent's authority); accord Slavin v. Passaic Nat'l Bank & Trust Co., 114 N.J.L. 341 (E & A 1935) (common law imposed duty on depositary bank to inquire into agent's authority to endorse check payable to designated payee-principal corporation). See generally Comment, "Forged Indorsements, Depositary Banks, and the Defense of Section 3–419(3) of the Uniform Commercial Code," 18 Houston L.Rev. 173, 185–88 (1980).

Here, the trial court expressly found, and the Appellate Division concurred, that Central Jersey acted in a reasonable manner in accepting the instrument with a forged endorsement, having not dealt with the forger, but with its regular customer, James E. Collins, Esq., an attorney whose law firm maintained an account with the bank. There is no question that Collins had authority to endorse a check payable to the law firm and to deposit this into the firm's special account. Both checks were endorsed by Collins and also were stamped with the law firm's restrictive endorsement. Further, affixed to the Citibank check was the restrictive endorsement "Pay to the order of James E. Collins," indicating a proper chain of title from Knesz-to-Collins-to-Cerrato, O'Connor, Mehr & Saker, Esqs. The only arguable irregularity in the instrument was the absence of a similar restrictive endorsement to Collins on the Morgan Guaranty check, but no one contends that such a restrictive endorsement was required or that this slight difference was sufficient to raise any suspicions.

We agree with both courts below that a claim based on lack of good faith or a departure from commercially reasonable practice under § 12A:3–419(3) is unavailable to the plaintiff under these facts.

II

The immunity of § 3–419(3) is expressly granted to "a representative * * * who has * * * dealt with an instrument or its proceeds on behalf of one who was not the true owner * * *." The section explicitly and unmistakably provides that "a representative" shall include "a depositary or collecting bank." Yet, despite the specific designation of depositary or collecting banks as a "representative," the Appellate Division ruled that the term "representative" in § 3–419(3) does not include a depositary bank that accepts for collection a check with a forged indorsement. 188 N.J.Super. 408–10.

The Appellate Division equated the bank's "representative" status under § 3–419(3) with that of a bank acting as an agent of the owner of an item submitted for collection under N.J.S.A. 12A:4–201. Id. This statute reads in pertinent part:

> "Unless a contrary intent clearly appears and prior to the time that a settlement given by a collecting bank for an item is or becomes final . . . the bank is an agent or sub-agent of the owner of the item and any settlement given for the item is provisional."

The Appellate Division reasoned that since the forger can never pass good title if an instrument requires endorsement by the owner, the bank cannot be an agent for the owner when it accepts the check for collection from the forger or his transferee. 188 N.J.Super. at 409. Consequently, the bank cannot qualify for the immunity provided for § 3–419(3) since it has not achieved representative or agent status.

We conclude that the Appellate Division's definition of "representative" is unjustifiably restrictive. The bank's agency status under § 4–201 is based upon its acceptance of a check from "an owner," who by definition cannot be the forger or his transferee. However, § 3–419(3) protects a "representative, including a depositary or collecting bank, who has * * * dealt with an instrument or its proceeds *on behalf of one who was not the true owner* * * *." (Emphasis added). Consequently, "representation" under § 3–419(3) contemplates dealing with a party who is not the true owner of an instrument, whereas "agency" under § 4–201 envisages actions on behalf of a true owner. Thus, the Appellate Division interpretation unreasonably removes the protection of § 3–419(3) from the check-collection process, which, arguably, would provide the most likely occasion for a bank to honor a check with a forged endorsement.

The Appellate Division also stressed that if "agency status" were intended to apply to a bank's handling of a forged check, other language would have accomplished this, "such as use of the word 'customer,' defined by § 4–104(e) to include any person for whom a bank has agreed to collect an item." 188 N.J.Super. at 409. However, New Jersey Study Comment 1 to § 4–201, which the Appellate Division relies on, expressly refers to the depositary bank as the agent of "the *customer* initiating collection," (emphasis added), which could be either the owner-payee or the forger or his transferee.

The Appellate Division further observed that agency status provided under § 4–201 was intended to deal with bank insolvency during the collection process, citing New Jersey Study Comment 1 to N.J.S.A. 12A:4–201. Id. This purpose, however, implies that the definition of "representative" under § 3–419(3) is more appropriately related to the broad definition of representative under N.J.S.A. 12A:1–201(35). This section of the UCC provides an expansive definition of the term "representative," namely, "an agent, an officer of a corporation or association, and a trustee, executor or administrator of an estate, or any other person empowered to act for another." The depositary bank must in some sense be "empowered to act for" the third party who presents the check bearing the payee's forged indorsement. Under § 1–201(35), a depositary or collecting bank acts as its customer's representative in the entire check-collection process. In this process the instrument is accepted and presented to the drawee bank and funds are collected and credited to the customer, whether that customer be the owner-payee or the forger or his transferee. As such, the bank meets the requirement for immunity by acting in a representative capacity "on behalf of one who was not the true owner" under § 3–419(3).

The strongest argument advanced in favor of the non-representative status of depositary or collecting banks in check collection—the argument that was adopted by the Appellate Division—is extrapolated from the UCC's historical background. The Appellate Division stressed that the singular advantage of the pre-UCC common-law rule of strict and direct liability of a depositary or collecting bank to the owner-payee of a forged check that the bank had honored was the avoidance of prolonged, complicated, and circuitous litigation that would otherwise be set in motion in the absence of such liability. 188 N.J.Super. at 398–99. A literal application of § 3–419(3), blocking a direct action against the depositary-collecting bank, would result in a chain of litigation. First, the owner of a check may bring an action against the drawer for fulfillment of the underlying obligation in satisfaction of which the check was originally written, under N.J.S.A. 12A:3–804 (providing recovery for check that has been lost, destroyed, or stolen), or, alternatively, sue the drawee bank for conversion under § 3–419(1)(c). The drawer will sue the drawee or payor bank for wrongfully debiting his or her account for payment to the forger under § 4–401. The drawee or payor bank will be required to proceed against its transferor. Suit will proceed successively up the collection stream on the basis of strict warranties of presentment and transfer under the UCC until the depositary bank, ultimately liable for honoring the forged instrument, is reached.

The Appellate Division agreed—as does the overwhelming body of decisional and scholarly authority—that the policy of a single direct action against the depositary or collecting bank by the owner-payee, and the avoidance of lengthy, circuitous, or chain litigation served by the common-law rule is a powerful reason against the imputation of an intent by the drafters of the Code to abrogate the common-law rule by the enactment of § 3–419(3). In support of its position, the court below pointed to the New Jersey Study Comment 5 on that section indicating that the provisions are new and not founded on past state law, as well as to Official Comment 5 to N.J.S.A. 12A:3–419, which stated:

> "Subsection (3), which is new, *is intended to adopt the rule of decisions* which has held that a representative, such as a broker or depositary bank, who deals with a negotiable instrument for his principal in good faith is not liable to the true owner for conversion of the instrument or otherwise, except that he may be compelled to turn over to the true owner the instrument itself or any proceeds of the instrument remaining in his hands. * * *" [UCC Comment 5 to § 3–419 (emphasis added).]

The irony of the emphasized reference in Comment 5, however, is that the common law "rule of decisions" governing the liability of such banks is almost diametrically opposite to what is stated by the plain language of § 3–419(3), which provides a near-absolute immunity to these banks in handling forged checks. The common-law decisional rule was that a party that honored a check bearing a forged indorsement was liable—not immune—to the payee who was the instrument's "true owner." * * * The common-law rule of liability was imposed strictly, even when the depositary bank was unaware of the unauthorized indorsement and not in privity with the rightful payee; a bank paying on such a check "did so at its peril and became liable to the payee * * * for the proceeds." Teas, supra, 125 N.J.Eq. at 228.

The Appellate Division did not believe that the Code drafters intended to abrogate this well-settled common-law doctrine, at least in the absence of an express announcement of such a purpose. The court emphasized, as we noted earlier, that the New Jersey Study Comment mentioned that § 3–419(3) and § 3–

419(4) " 'are new provisions on which no New Jersey law has been found,' " 188 N.J.Super. at 404–05. It therefore surmised that "the section impacted upon some other legal principle or problem which had not been theretofore addressed in this jurisdiction." Id. at 405. The court determined that this new legal principle adopting the rule of decisions related to "the liability of persons acting as brokers in negotiating the sale of securities," as distinguished from granting a new immunity to banks in the collection process. Id. Because brokers dealing in negotiable instruments were immune from liability in conversion at common law, the court concluded that § 3–419(3) was intended to codify this immunity for brokers, including banks acting as brokers, but was not intended to extend such immunity to depositary or collecting banks engaged in routine check collection. Id. at 406–07.

We disagree with the conclusion of the court below, while acknowledging, as we must, respectable decisional and scholarly support for its result. See, e.g., Tubin v. Rabin, 389 F.Supp 787, 789–90 (N.D.Tex. 1974), affd, 533 F.2d 255 (5th Cir. 1976); Cooper v. Union Bank, 9 Cal.3d 371, 507 P.2d 609, 107 Cal.Rptr. 1 (1973); Grieshaber v. Michigan Nat'l Bank of Detroit, 1255–56 (Mich.Ct.Comm.Pl. 1976); Ervin v. Dauphin Deposit Trust Co., 38 Pa.D. & C.2d 473, (Pa.Ct. of Comm.Pl. 1965); see also Comment, "Payee v. Depositary Bank: What Is the UCC Defense to Handling Checks Bearing Forged Indorsements?" 45 U.Colo.L.Rev 281, 308–10 (1974); Comment, "Cooper v. Union Bank: California Protects the True Owner Against a Forged Indorsement Despite Uniform Commercial Code Section 3–419(3)," 25 Hastings L.J. 715, 736–38 (1974). We are persuaded by other cases and authority that have recognized that § 3–419(3) is phrased in clear and plain language, that applying this provision in accordance with its unambiguous meaning constitutes a reasonable—not an absurd—policy choice by the Legislature, and further, that there is some historical extrinsic support evidencing an underlying intent on the part of the drafters that is consistent with this application of the provision.

Denn v. First State Bank of Spring Lake Park, 316 N.W.2d 532 (Minn. 1982), confirmed and applied the plain language of UCC § 3–419(3) in holding that a depositary collecting bank was immune from liability to the owner-payee of a forged check that it handled for collection. The court recognized that the critical question was whether banks engaged in the routine collection process were intended to be "representatives" insulated from liability in conversion to payees under § 3–419(3). Relying on a historical analysis of § 3–419(3) and its comments, the Denn court noted that the original "representative exception," first included in the May 1949 draft of the UCC, apparently codified the limited exception exempting from liability only those brokers who had been exempt at common law. Id. at 535. Further, noting that in 1951 the drafters inserted the phrase "including a depositary or collecting bank" in § 3–419(3), the Denn court observed that "[t]he fact that this crucial phrase was added to the Code and was not part of the original version supports the idea that the 1951 drafters intended specifically to exempt depositary and collecting banks from liability." Id. Since one year later, in 1952, the drafters added Comment 5, which explicitly included a depositary bank with a "representative such as a broker," the court concluded that the controversial "rule of decisions" exempting such representatives from liability for conversion to true owners was intended to reach depositary and collecting banks. Id.

The Denn court also emphasized the fact that Comment 6 to § 3–419 expressly acknowledges the immunity of a collecting bank to the owner of an instrument in a direct action in the context of the warranties of presentment and transfer under § 34–17 ("a collecting bank might be liable to a drawee bank which had been subject to liability under this section, even though the collecting bank might not be liable directly to the owner of the instrument"). Id. Thus, Comment 6 points to warranties of presentment and transfer (§ 3–417) as the statutory alternative to the common-law direct action, clarifying the fact that circuitous litigation deplored by the commentators and courts alike indeed was anticipated by and within the contemplation of the drafters. This further substantiates the drafters' intent, without confirming their wisdom, to offer new defenses to a depositary or collecting bank that accepted a check with a forged endorsement.

We are in consequence not persuaded that the underlying policy served by the common law—the recognition of a single direct action by an owner-payee against the depositary or collecting bank and the avoidance of circuitous or chain litigation—overrides the plain terms of § 3–419(3). That policy was undoubtedly known to the drafters of the Code. It was presumably within their contemplation when § 3–419(3) was inserted granting immunity to these banks. We are constrained to adhere to the choice made by the Legislature in its enactment. It has not been shown that this choice leads to intolerable or absurd results, a factor that would have given us pause in applying § 3–419(3) in accordance with its terms.[5]

Accordingly, we conclude that N.J.S.A. 12A:3–419(3) recognizes that a depositary or collecting bank handling a forged check in the routine process of check collection acts in a representative capacity on behalf of its customer, who may be one other than the check's true owner or payee. Consequently, such a bank will not be disqualified from claiming, as a "representative," immunity against the owner-payee under N.J.S.A. 12A:3–419(3).

III

A further argument against granting immunity is drawn from the provision of § 3–419(3) that a depositary bank dealing with a check bearing a forged endorsement can be liable to the true owner "beyond the amount of any proceeds remaining in [its] hands." It can be contended that the proceeds of the checks should be considered as still in the control of Central Jersey, thus rendering the bank liable.

This theory of retained proceeds was first advanced in Ervin v. Dauphin Deposit Trust Co., supra, 3 UCC Rep 311. The Pennsylvania court rendered judgment to the plaintiff-payee, finding the defense of § 3–419(3) unavailing to

5. It is possible that the burdensome circuitous litigation deplored by many commentators may be mitigated today. The "circuity argument" has been criticized as being exaggerated and inconsequential in the modern era of long-arm jurisdiction, negotiated settlements, and liberal rules of impleader. See J. White and R. Summers, Handbook of the Law Under the Uniform Commercial Code, § 15–4 at 590–91 (1980). In addition, foreclosing a direct suit against a depositary bank and, instead, forcing the payee to sue his drawer or the drawee bank preserves in some instances the timely presentation of appropriate defenses that would have been unavailable to a depositary bank, such as that of the drawer's negligence in causing or detecting the forgery. See "Recent Developments—Section 3–419(3) of the UCC Does Not Limit the Liability of a Depositary Bank to the True Owner of a Check Paid on a Forged Indorsement," 74 Colum.L.Rev. 104, 114 (1974); Comment, 5 Rut-Cam.L.J. 319, 332 (1974). But see Hinchey, "An Analysis of Bank Defenses to Check Forgery and Alteration Claims under Uniform Commercial Code Articles 3 and 4: Claimants' Negligence and Failure to Give Notice," 10 Pepperdine L.Rev. 1, 5–6 (1982); Note, "Depositary Bank Liability under § 3–419(3) of the Uniform Commercial Code," 31 Wash. & Lee L.Rev. 676, 696 n. 107 (1974).

the depositary bank. One ground of its decision was that although the bank had already paid over the full amount of the checks to the forger, it nonetheless still retained the "proceeds" in its hands, having in effect purchased with its own funds the forged checks drawn on other banks. As a result, the proceeds remained in its hands as money obtained from the drawee bank that belonged to the true owner. 3 UCC Rep at 319.

In Cooper v. Union Bank, supra, 507 P.2d at 613, the court noted that the trial court had held the defendant depositary banks immune under § 3–419(3). It reversed, although offsetting the aggregate recovery to reflect the plaintiff's own contributory negligence. Id. at 620. As partial support for this result, the court, relying on pre-UCC theory, observed that the bank still held the entire "proceeds" of the forged instruments, notwithstanding the fact that the forger's personal account with the bank in which the forged checks had been deposited was depleted. The court reasoned that the bank perpetually retains the proceeds of the forged instrument in trust for the true owner, unless the bank's own assets dwindle below the amount of the check. Id. at 615.

The "retained proceeds" position of Ervin and Cooper has generated considerable academic debate. * * * The Appellate Division rejected the theory of perpetually retained proceeds * * *.

We concur.

"Proceeds" is that amount received from the drawee-payor bank in return for the check of its drawer. See Comment, 5 Rut-Cam.L.J., 319, 323 (1974); Comment, 45 U.Colo.L.Rev., supra, at 293. Remaining proceeds as used in § 3–419(3), we believe, connotes the amount, if any, the bank actually has left in its control as a consequence of dealing with the forged check. Thus, a bank could give the customer a provisional credit, which prevents the customer from withdrawing or obtaining actual credit for the instrument until the bank has effected collection. In that case, the bank would be liable under § 3–419(3) to the owner of the check for the amount, whether full or partial, of the check that remains on deposit in the account of the forger or his transferee. See Farnsworth and Leary, "UCC Brief No. 10: Forgery and Alteration of Checks," 14 Prac.Law. No. 3 at 75, 79–80 (1968); see also Comment, 45 U.Colo.L.Rev., supra, at 304 n 89; Comment, supra, 74 Colum.L.Rev., supra, at 113; Denn, supra, 316 N.W.2d at 537.

In this case, plaintiff has not shown that any funds attributable to the forged instruments are still available in the customer's account. The checks were deposited in the account of the Cerrato law firm, the bank's customer and the transferee of the forger. In due course, the forged checks were transmitted for collection and the proceeds remitted. The funds or proceeds referable to these checks reflected in the customer's account were eventually withdrawn and the account ultimately depleted accordingly. Consequently, no proceeds remain for which this bank can be liable under § 3–419(3).

IV

In conclusion, we are satisfied that the court may not disregard the plain language of N.J.S.A. 12A:3–419(3). The terms of this provision clearly and unmistakably designate a depositary or collecting bank as a representative in the collection of a forged check. We are mindful of the objections to that interpretation. Nevertheless, we must infer that these objections were not ultimately important or persuasive to the Legislature. We rule therefore that generally a depositary or collecting bank handling a forged check in the routine collection process may claim immunity against the true owner or payee under N.J.S.A. 12A:3–419(3). That immunity may be lost, however, under certain circumstances. A depositary or collecting bank may become directly liable to an owner-payee in conversion of a forged check where it (1) acted in bad faith; (2) failed to adhere to reasonable commercial standards of the banking profession applicable to such transactions; or (3) had given a provisional credit to the forger or his transferee and had not yet disbursed the entire amount of the collected proceeds.

None of these enumerated circumstances is present in the instant case. Accordingly, the judgment of the Appellate Division is reversed and summary judgment for the defendant reinstated.

Notes

1. One can assume that Knesz' next step is to sue Morgan Guaranty as the drawee of the $5,000 and Citibank as the drawee of the $16,974.24 checks respectively. His theory will be conversion. Can Knesz recover?

2. If Knesz does recover, what recourse will Citibank and Morgan Guaranty have? Considering only the Citibank check, who will ultimately bear the liability—Knesz, Collins, Central Jersey, or the Dagates? The case might ultimately present an interesting question of New Jersey trust law.

Problem 25–1

Repeunzel draws a check in the amount of $1,000 "payable to the order of cash." He transfers the check in payment of a debt to Cicero; thief steals the check, cleverly raises it to $10,000 and cashes it at Federal Savings Bank. Federal Savings procures payment from the drawee, Malpurgis. Drawee sues to recover its $10,000 from Federal Savings. What result? UCC 4–207.

Problem 25–2

If in the foregoing problem Federal Savings, arguing that it was a "subsequent holder in due course," had joined Repeunzel as a third party defendant and sought the $10,000 from him, what would have been the outcome? UCC 1–201(20), 3–407, 3–413.

Problem 25–3

Repeunzel draws a check in the amount of $5,000 and payable to the order of Cicero. Out of habit Cicero turns the check over and signs "Cicero" on the reverse side. The check is stolen by a thief, raised to $6,000, and then deposited as the initial deposit in the opening of a checking account in Fillansby State Bank. The alteration is so well done that no teller would be put on notice by looking at the face of the check. According to a time-honored filching process thief returns to Fillansby Bank later the same day and withdraws $3,000 of the amount "deposited" in the newly opened checking account. Fillansby ultimately presents the check to Malpurgis who dishonors because Repeunzel in the meantime has stopped payment. Fillansby then withdraws the remaining $3,000 credit in the thief's account. Thereupon a flurry of lawsuits commences:

1. Cicero sues Repeunzel for $5,000 under 3–804. Repeunzel defends on the ground that he has been discharged by UCC 3–407(2) and that in any event there is no cause of action any longer under UCC 3–804 since the check is in the hands of a third party who purports to be a holder.

2. Fillansby sues Repeunzel for $5,000 on his drawer's contract under UCC 3–413. Repeunzel again argues that he was discharged under the provisions of UCC 3–407(2).

3. Cicero sues Fillansby Bank in conversion for $5,000. (Assume that the court has adopted the *Dauphin Trust* theory, namely that UCC 3–419(3) does not prohibit suit against the collecting bank.)

What result in the three cases? See UCC 1–201(20), 3–110, 3–111, 3–204(2), 3–419, 3–407, 3–802, 3–804.

SUN 'N SAND INC. v. UNITED CALIFORNIA BANK

Supreme Court of California, 1978.
21 Cal.3d 671, 148 Cal.Rptr. 329, 582 P.2d 920.

Appeal from the Superior Court, Los Angeles County.

MOSK, J. We address here a variation on the recurring theme (see, e.g., Cooper v. Union Bank (1973) 9 Cal.3d 371) of the rights of an employer to recover funds embezzled by a faithless employee through the manipulation of company checks.

The appeal arises from a judgment (order of dismissal) entered after a general demurrer to plaintiffs' second amended complaint was sustained; prior to the ruling plaintiffs conceded they were unable to amend further.

The material facts alleged are as follows: Plaintiffs are sister corporations (hereinafter collectively referred to as Sun 'n Sand) having the same shareholders and doing business from the same premises. As a duty of her employment with Sun 'n Sand, Eloise Morales prepared checks for signature by a corporate officer. Over a three-year period she made nine of such checks payable to United California Bank (UCB), each for a different, small account. She obtained authorized signatures on these checks from a Sun 'n Sand officer who believed they represented small sums his company owed to UCB. No such debts were in fact owed. Morales then altered the checks, increasing the amount in each case to several thousand dollars, and presented them to UCB. Although UCB was the named payee, it "caused or permitted" the proceeds of the checks to be deposited in a personal account maintained by Morales at UCB.

Sun 'n Sand had its company account with Union Bank. UCB presented each of these checks to Union Bank, which paid them and charged Sun 'n Sand's account for their face amounts. Morales concealed her actions by destroying some and manipulating other company records; [1] as a result, Sun 'n Sand did not discover her fraudulent activity until June 23, 1973, some three months after the last altered check transaction.[2]

Sun 'n Sand instituted this action by filing its original complaint on March 4, 1974. Although the complaints named UCB and Union Bank as codefendants, the present appeal involves Sun 'n Sand's rights against UCB alone. The

1. Although it was not alleged in the complaint that Sun 'n Sand received any statements of account from Union Bank, the trial court judicially noticed that it is the custom of commercial banks to send each of its depositors a monthly statement together with cancelled checks drawn on the depositor's account. (Evid.Code, § 452, subds (g), (h).)

2. The nine altered checks were negotiated on the following dates and in the amounts indicated:

February 6, 1970:	$ 5,767.85
October 2, 1970:	3,545.48
January 13, 1971:	4,143.53
July 19, 1971:	4,011.28
December 2, 1971:	2,952.00
February 22, 1972:	5,231.57
May 10, 1972:	3,585.65
October 16, 1972:	3,227.16
March 15, 1973:	2,293.41
	$34,757.93

amended complaints sought to recover the total amount of the checks in question (fn 2, ante) on six alternative theories: one each based on mistake, fraudulent misrepresentation, negligence, and warranty against material alteration, and two based on title warranties.

UCB demurred on the grounds (1) that each of the six counts fails to state facts sufficient to constitute a cause of action, and (2) that various statutes of limitation bar some or all of the causes of action alleged. The court sustained the demurrer on the grounds stated, "and in particular and in addition, because United California Bank, as payee, owed no duty to plaintiffs which was breached." The court ordered the case dismissed as against UCB, and Sun 'n Sand appealed. (Code Civ.Proc. § 581, subd 3.)

I

In three of the counts it asserts, Sun 'n Sand relies on certain warranty obligations imposed by §§ 3417 and 4207 of the California Uniform Commercial Code. These are parallel provisions, as recognized in the California code comments that explain their effect on California law: "Section 4207 fixes the same warranties for the collection of items through the banking system that Commercial Code § 3417 establishes for the transfer of commercial paper not collected through the banking system." (§ 4207, com 1.) Sun 'n Sand seeks to utilize both sections because of UCB's dual role in the events alleged herein: the complaint predicates liability under § 3417 on the bank's status as payee on the nine checks and under § 4207 on its activity as a collecting bank in the check collection process.

A. Sun 'n Sand's Right to Maintain an Action Based on the Warranties of Sections 3417 and 4207

The first issue we confront is whether Sun 'n Sand, as the drawer of the checks in question, may rely on the warranty provisions it seeks to invoke.

Prior to the development of the UCC, courts split sharply over the right of a drawer to proceed directly against a collecting bank for losses resulting from the bank's negotiation of a check on a forged indorsement. After noting the " 'hopeless conflict' in the authorities" in Cal. Mill Supply Corp. v. Bank of America (1950) 36 Cal.2d 334, 341, we held that the drawer had "no right of direct action against the collecting bank for its loss on checks bearing forged endorsements." Adoption of this view did not relieve collecting banks of ultimate liability, however; the drawer could proceed against the drawee bank for violation of its contractual obligation to pay monies out of the drawer's account only according to his order, and the drawee bank in turn had a remedy against the collecting bank based on the latter's implied warranty of the validity of the indorsement. Placing the loss on the collecting bank by means of this circuitous route was thought to be necessary because the conceptual basis for that bank's liability was an implied contractual warranty and no contractual relationship existed between it and the drawer. (Id. at pp 338–339.)

The rule of California Mill Supply, of course, sharply conflicts with the objective of avoiding multiple suits; we therefore reexamine that rule in light of § 4207, which shifts the basis for imposing liability on the collecting bank from an implied contractual warranty to an explicit statutory warranty. In determining whether the drawer of a check is among those to whom the statutory warranties of § 4207 were intended to be extended, we are guided by our observation in Cooper v. Union Bank (1973) supra, 9 Cal.3d 371, 381–382: "Requiring cumbersome and uneconomical circuity of action to achieve an identical result would obviously run contra the code's explicit underlying purposes "to simplify, clarify and modernize the law governing commercial transactions.' (§ 1102, subd (2)(a).)."

In Allied Concord etc. Corp. v. Bank of America (1969) 275 Cal.App.2d 1, 3–4, the court determined that with the enactment of the California Uniform Commercial Code California Mill Supply was effectively overruled, as the Code authorizes direct suit by a drawer against both depositary and collecting banks. The court found support for its holding in principles of contract law relating to third party beneficiaries. While we agree that direct suit is authorized by the California Uniform Commercial Code, we find it unnecessary to rely on third party beneficiary principles in reaching this conclusion.

Section 4207, subdivision (1), provides that its warranties extend to "the payor bank or other payor who in good faith pays or accepts the item." To receive the benefit of these warranties, then, the drawer of a check must qualify as an "other payor who * * pays." At least one court has held, although without offering any explanatory rationale, that a drawer whose account was debited by his bank is a payor entitled to claim the benefit of these warranties. (Insurance Company of No. Amer. v. Atlas Supply Co. (Ga.App. 1970) 172 S.E.2d 632, 636.) We find this broad construction of the payor concept justified by inferences that can be drawn from the structure of § 4207 and language in the official comments to the UCC.

The warranties provided for in subdivisions (1)(b) and (1)(c) of § 4207 are expressly made subject to certain exceptions which operate in favor of a holder in due course who acts in good faith. These warranties are not extended to a number of parties, including a drawer "whether or not the drawer is also the drawee." (§ 4207, subds (1)(b)(ii) & (1)(c)(ii).) By negative implication, the warranties are given by a collecting bank to a drawer who is not also the drawee (payor) bank—at least when the collecting bank is not a holder in due course or does not act in good faith. Section 4207 is quite clear in excepting drawers under subdivisions (1)(b)(ii) and (1)(c)(ii); accordingly, we may infer that drawers are among those to whom the warranty of § 4207, subdivision (1)(a), extends, as no comparable exceptions are there made.

The inferences thus compelled by the structure of § 4207 indicate the Code contemplates that the drawer of a check is an "other payor" for purposes of that section who may, unless specifically excepted, claim the benefits of the warranties therein created. Although the term "payor" is more commonly used in reference to the drawee than the drawer, it is not defined anywhere in the Code and hence should not be regarded as a term of art used in a narrow, technical sense; when a check is negotiated, it is the drawer who ultimately "pays" when his account is charged in the amount of the check. This is implicitly recognized in the official comments to the UCC: "Similarly, under subparagraph (ii) a drawer of a draft is presumed to know his own signature and if he fails to detect a forgery of his signature and *pays a draft* he may not recover that payment from a holder in due course acting in good faith." (Italics added.) (UCC, § 3417, com 4.)

We therefore hold that the drawer of a check whose account is charged is a payor within the meaning of § 4207 and may maintain an action against a collecting bank based on that section's warranties. For the foregoing reasons, we further hold that the drawer of a check is "a person who in good faith pays" within the meaning of § 3417 and may maintain an action against the payee of a check based on the § 3417 warranties.

Courts in other jurisdictions that have denied to drawers a direct right of action have apparently been concerned that collecting banks would not always be able to assert defenses available to drawee banks. They have assumed that direct suits by drawers would not merely avoid circuity of action, but would alter substantive rights. (See, e.g., Stone & Webster Eng. Corp. v. First National B. & T. Co. (Mass. 1962) 184 N.E.2d 358, 362–363; Life Insurance Company of Virginia v. Snyder (N.J.Dist.Ct. 1976), 358 A.2d 859, 862.) We find nothing to prevent collecting banks (and payees) from asserting the same defenses as drawee banks.

The most important defenses in this context are particularized in §§ 3406 and 4406 of the Code. These provisions, discussed infra, would under certain circumstances preclude parties, including drawers, from asserting the alteration of an instrument or the making of an unauthorized signature.

Section 3406 operates in favor of a holder in due course or "a drawee or other payor who pays the instrument in good faith and in accordance with the reasonable commercial standards of the drawee's or payor's business." Once again we recognize that the term "payor" is not used in a technical sense; it must be read in light of the provision in which it appears and the structure of the Code as a whole. We have determined that the statutory warranties of §§ 3417 and 4207 are given to the drawer of a check; those sections clearly contemplate that a drawer has a direct right of action, and this result is consonant with the Code's important underlying policy of simplifying and modernizing the law governing commercial transactions. Finding nothing in the Code to suggest that all defenses applicable in a suit by the drawer against the drawee bank are not likewise applicable in a direct suit against the collecting bank, we hold that a collecting bank is an "other payor" for purposes of § 3406.

The preclusions of § 4406 may also be invoked by the collecting bank in a direct suit by a drawer. Subdivision (5) of that section provides: "If under this section a payor bank has a valid defense against a claim of a customer upon or resulting from payment of an item and waives or fails upon request to assert the defense the bank may not assert against any collecting bank or other prior party presenting or transferring the item a claim based upon the unauthorized signature or alteration giving rise to the customer's claim." As the court recognized in Allied Concord etc. Corp. v. Bank of America (1969) supra, 275 Cal.App.2d 1, 6, this subdivision implies that § 4406 defenses, available to a drawee bank against claims of its depositors, are also available to a collecting bank in a direct action by the depositor.

Having concluded that Sun 'n Sand, as drawer of the checks in question, may rely on the warranty provisions of §§ 3417 and 4207, we must determine whether it has alleged facts which, if established at trial, would constitute a breach of the warranties it asserts.

* * *

[Here the court concludes that the warranties of good title under 3–417 and 4–207 have not been breached. The court points out that those warranties do not cover the case of a forged drawer's signature or of alteration or of a case such as the present one in which all of the signatures were in fact valid.]

II

Sun 'n Sand proceeds in its fifth cause of action on a theory of negligence, asserting that UCB breached its duty of care in permitting checks on which the bank was named as payee to be deposited in the personal account of Sun 'n

Sand's employee. UCB challenges the sufficiency of this count in a number of respects.

UCB's principal contention is that it had no duty to investigate or make any inquiries under the facts alleged. It first argues that its failure to inquire was nonfeasance rather than misfeasance, and therefore it was not responsible for the acts of a third person—the dishonest conduct of Sun 'n Sand's employee—absent a special relationship with the injured party.

We need not consider whether a special relationship exists between a collecting bank and the drawer of a check, because UCB's "nonfeasance" characterization does not withstand analysis. It is UCB's *conduct* in crediting the embezzler's account with checks drawn payable to UCB that forms the basis for relief herein. Sun 'n Sand contends these circumstances created sufficient doubt as to the authority of its employee to negotiate the checks for her own benefit that UCB should not have acted without making inquiries to confirm the employee's authority. Such inquiries, it asserts, would have revealed the fraud being perpetrated and prevented Sun 'n Sand's loss. The asserted wrong, therefore, is not that UCB failed to intervene beneficially (nonfeasance) but rather that it affirmatively engaged in risk-creating conduct (misfeasance). (Weirum v. RKO General, Inc. (1975) 15 Cal.3d 40, 49.) We must decide, however, whether the circumstances alleged were sufficiently suspicious, and the risks thus sufficiently apparent, that a duty to make reasonable inquiries arose.

* * *

UCB raises other defenses which would partially or completely preclude Sun 'n Sand from asserting breach of the duty recognized herein as a basis for recovery. It suggests that the Code does not permit Sun 'n Sand to proceed by means of a common law action for negligence. Section 1103 declares that the Code is supplemented by "the principles of law and equity," but only if such principles are not "displaced by the particular provisions" of the Code. UCB apparently reasons that § 3405 (fn 13, ante) articulates a loss distributive scheme that applies to fact patterns such as alleged herein and therefore displaces common law negligence actions.

As we noted in discussing the good title warranties, the California and official UCC comments to § 3405 contemplate that losses resulting from certain fraudulent employee behavior—i.e., causing the issuance of checks to payees intended to have no interest therein—should be risks of the employer's business and not of the banking community. This conclusion derives from the premise that the employer/drawer is better able to prevent the success of such frauds than the bank; the former may exercise care in selecting and supervising its employees, while the latter is typically presented with checks bearing indorsements forged in a manner that may be difficult if not practically impossible to detect. The comments assume, however, that such checks will never be delivered to the named payees, whether or not such payees are real persons or entities. We perceive this supposition to be critical to the loss allocative function of § 3405. While it may be less difficult for the employer to prevent the issuance of such checks than for the bank to detect that an indorsement is forged, this is not the relevant comparison when the bank is presented with checks naming it as payee. In the latter circumstance the bank is confronted with an obvious irregularity when the drawer's dishonest employee attempts to negotiate such checks for his own benefit. The bank does not have to be especially vigilant; its agent need only read what appears on the face of the check to be warned that a fraud may be in progress. It is clear therefore that the balance struck under § 3405 has no application in the present context and does not bar Sun 'n Sand from pursuing its remedies in tort.

* * *

III

In its first cause of action, Sun 'n Sand would base liability on a theory of mistake of fact: it alleges that it issued the checks in the mistaken belief that it owed UCB the amounts for which the checks were drawn. Section 1577 of the Civil Code, however, defines a "mistake of fact" as a mistake "not caused by the neglect of a legal duty on the part of the person making the mistake." As might be expected, UCB asserts this qualification as a bar to the first count, claiming that Sun 'n Sand's mistake was caused by its neglect of legal duties imposed by § 4406, subdivision (1), and § 3405.

UCB correctly observes that § 4406, subdivision (1), imposes a duty on bank customers to examine their bank statements and returned checks for alterations and forgeries. It does not follow, however, that breach of this duty by failure to exercise reasonable care in discharging it constitutes the "neglect of a legal duty" such that a cause of action for mistake of fact must be barred. In National Bank of California v. Miner (1914) 167 Cal. 532, 537, we set forth the standard of liability for mistake: " 'It is now settled * * * that money paid under a mistake of fact may be recovered back, however negligent the party paying may have been in making the mistake, unless the payment has caused such a change in the position of the other party that it would be unjust to require him to refund.' " We have since recognized on a number of occasions that "ordinary negligence does not constitute the neglect of a legal duty as that term is used in section 1577 of the Civil Code," (Van Meter v. Bent Construction Co. (1956) 46 Cal.2d 588, 595; see also Elsinore Union etc. Sch. Dist. v. Kastorff (1960) 54 Cal.2d 380, 386–388; M.F. Kemper Const. Co. v. City of L.A. (1951) 37 Cal.2d 696, 702.) The rule developed in these cases reflects a determination that the "neglect of a legal duty" qualification derives content from equitable considerations and principles, and that it would be inequitable to bar relief for mistake because of the breach of a duty of care when the party from whom recovery is sought suffers no loss. That Sun 'n Sand may have failed to exercise care in examining its bank statements is thus not a sufficient basis for denying it equitable relief for mistake.

We need not decide whether § 3405 imposes a duty to supervise employees in the preparation of checks, as UCB contends; for the reasons stated relief for mistake of fact would not be barred even assuming such a duty and Sun 'n Sand's failure to exercise reasonable care in discharging it. * * *

V

In sum, we reach these conclusions:

The first count states a cause of action for mistake of fact; recovery for checks one through three is barred by the limitations period of Code of Civil Procedure § 338, subdivision 4, but Sun 'n Sand may seek to recover the full amount of checks four through nine. * * *

The second, third, and fourth counts fail to state facts sufficient to constitute a cause of action.

The fifth count states a cause of action for negligence; recovery for checks one through three is barred by the limitations period of Code of Civil Procedure § 338, subdivision 3, but Sun 'n Sand may seek to recover the full amount of checks four through nine.

The sixth count states a cause of action for breach of the warranty against material alteration; recovery for checks one through eight is barred by the preclusion of § 4406, subdivision (4), but Sun 'n Sand may seek to recover the difference between the raised amount at which check number nine was negotiated and the original amount in which it was issued.

The judgment (order of dismissal) is reversed as to the first, fifth, and sixth counts, and affirmed as to the second, third, and fourth counts.

TOBRINER, J., concurred.

[Some footnotes omitted]

Notes

1. Is *Sun 'n Sand* in direct conflict with *Knesz?*

2. It is easy to be critical of the California Supreme Court for recognizing an affirmative claim in negligence where none may have been intended and for reading the warranty provisions to extend beyond the payor back around the circle to drawer. In the court's defense one should note that the case is *sui generis;* it is not a straightforward forged indorsement case like *Knesz,* nor a forged drawer case like *First National City Bank v. Altman* below, nor a double forgery case like *Perini,* nor even an imposture or padded payroll case like *J. Gordon Neely.*

Rather, the case involves a theft, repeated in many circumstances, in which the thief cleverly disguises her transaction as a legitimate transaction well known to the teller. Because the teller is harried, marginally trained and perhaps poorly educated, the teller is incapable of distinguishing between this case and the "payable to order of bank therefore deposit in depositor's account" case. It is a case, therefore, that does not fit under any section of the Code. On the one hand, the depositary bank was clearly at fault, in effect paying the check to the order of one who presented it and not to its own order. On the other hand, drawer was at fault in drawing the check in the first place and failing to supervise the key employee.

Reconsider the case. If you were Judge Mosk, wished to do the smallest amount of injury to the general principles under the Code and yet hoped to decide the case fairly, what would your opinion say?

3. There are four exceptions to liability under 4–207(1)(c). One of them may apply to UCB in the case. What is the common characteristic of those who do *not* receive the warranty because of the exceptions to 4–207(1)(c)?

FIRST NAT'L CITY BANK v. ALTMAN

Supreme Court of New York, New York County, 1966.
3 UCC Reporter 815, affirmed 277 N.Y.S.2d 813 (App.Div.1967).

TIERNEY, J.

This is a motion by defendant Altman for summary judgment and a cross-motion by defendant Trade Bank and Trust Company for leave to pay the sum of $23,900.75 into court, and for related relief.

The facts are as follows:

This action was brought to recover the proceeds of two checks, in the respective sum of $22,300.80 and $23,900.75, drawn on the account of J.W. Mays, Inc., a depositor in plaintiff bank, deposited in Altman's account in the Trade Bank and Trust Company, collected by said bank, and credited to Altman's account, on the ground that the signature of the drawer had been forged and the checks were not issued or drawn by J.W. Mays, Inc. nor with its authority or consent; and that payment was made by mistake, in good faith, in reliance on the endorsements of both defendants, without notice or knowledge of any defect in the instruments or in defendants' title thereto, and in the belief that the instruments had been drawn by the depositor, J.W. Mays, Inc.

Defendant Altman interposed an answer consisting of a general denial, an affirmative defense and counterclaim that plaintiff was negligent in failing to discover the forgery before making payment and that its negligence caused him to part with merchandise of the value of the checks, and an additional affirmative defense of estoppel as a result of such negligence. The answer of the Trade Bank and Trust Company consists of a general denial.

Defendant Altman is a wholesale diamond dealer. A Mr. Nieman presented himself at Altman's place of business and introduced himself as a buyer for J.W. Mays, Inc. Nieman selected a number of unset diamonds which Altman placed inside an envelope and sealed. Altman kept the diamonds. A few days later, Nieman sent a letter, on his own stationery, confirming the sale. He also enclosed a check drawn on plaintiff bank against the account of J.W. Mays, Inc., in the sum of $22,300.80, as full payment for the diamonds. Altman deposited the check in his account. Nieman then revisited Altman's place of business and selected more diamonds. The same procedure was followed, and Nieman's letter confirming the sale arrived with a check for $23,900.75, in full payment of the second group of diamonds. Altman, immediately upon receipt, deposited each check into his account at the Trade Bank. When Nieman requested delivery of the first envelope of diamonds, Altman communicated with the Trade Bank and determined that the first check had been paid defendant bank by the drawee, prior to turning over the diamonds. He turned over the second selection of diamonds several days later, but did not first ascertain that the second check had been paid, although in fact plaintiff had made payment; that same afternoon the Trade Bank notified him that plaintiff bank had given notice that both checks had been forged and that payment had been made by mistake.

Payment or acceptance of any instrument is final in favor of "a person who has in good faith changed his position in reliance on the payment" (UCC § 3–418). This legal principle was long ago enunciated in Price v. Neal, 3 Burr. 1354 (1762) where it was held that a drawee who pays an instrument on which the signature of the drawer is forged is bound on his acceptance and cannot recover back his payment from a holder in due course, or a person who has in good faith changed his position in reliance on the payment.

In moving for dismissal of the complaint defendant Altman contends that the doctrine of Price v. Neal is a bar to a recovery by plaintiff on either of the two forged checks herein.

The facts are clear that with respect to the first packet of diamonds, defendant Altman did not make delivery thereof until he had first ascertained that the check by which payment therefor had been made had been paid by plaintiff. Accordingly, defendant Altman, the payee of the check, does qualify as a person who changed his position in reliance on the drawee's payment. However, in all of the circumstances, the court is of the view that the issue of his good faith presents a triable issue of fact which precludes summary dismissal of the action based on the first check (see Banca C.I. Trust Co. v. Clarkson, 274 N.Y. 69). It has been held that the negligence of the purchaser, at the time he acquired title to the instrument, in not making inquiries which, if made, might reveal the fact of forgery, releases the drawee from the rule of Price v. Neal, and enables the drawee to recover from the purchaser the amount paid to him on the instrument (Whitney, The Law of Modern Commercial Practices, 2d ed, section 338, p. 504 [1965]).

Inasmuch as defendant Altman did not determine that the second check had been paid by plaintiff prior to delivery of the second packet of diamonds, said defendant is not in a position to claim the status of "a person who has * * * changed his position in reliance on the payment." Therefore, the proscription against the drawee stated in the rule of Price v. Neal loses its impact and all the issues relative to plaintiff's right to recover the proceeds of the second check remain in issue.

Accordingly, the motion for summary judgment dismissing the complaint is denied.

There is no real opposition to the cross-motion by defendant Trade Bank and Trust Company to deposit the proceeds of the second check into court. Therefore, the cross-motion is granted to the extent of directing said defendant to turn over the sum of $23,900.75 to the proper authorities. Otherwise the cross-motion is denied. Any taxable costs or disbursements shall be chargeable to the unsuccessful party at the conclusion of this litigation.

Settle order.

Notes

1. Even if Altman had not changed his position in reliance, could he not still claim the defense of UCC 3–418?

2. If Altman were found negligent in failing to demand identification, would that be a defense? UCC 3–418, Comment 4.

3. Assume that a Payor Bank argues that the rule of Price v. Neal was founded upon the theory that the payor in such cases was inevitably negligent. It offers to prove that the common commercial practice in present day is not to compare drawers' signatures with signature cards and argues that a bank which does not check such signatures can no longer be regarded as negligent. On that theory it concludes that UCC 3–418 should no longer be followed. If you represented Altman, how would you respond? If negligence is not the theory upon which the rule in UCC 3–418 is predicated, what is the theory and what policy justifies it? See White and Summers § 16–2.

Problem 25–4

Thief steals Repeunzel's checkbook, signs Repeunzel's name to a check payable to "cash," and cashes the check at Depositary Bank. Depositary transfers the check to Malpurgis, the drawee, and Malpurgis makes final payment. Later Malpurgis sues collecting bank and alleges the breach of two warranties under UCC 4–207:

1. That Depositary Bank breached the warranty embodied in UCC 4–207(1)(a) because it did not have good title to the item.

2. That Depositary Bank breached the warranty in UCC 4–207(2)(b) because the drawer's signature was "not genuine."

You have just graduated from law school where some fool has assured you that upon final payment in such circumstances drawee bank could not throw the loss back on the collecting bank. How do you square that thought with the plaintiff's arguments on the plain language of UCC 4–207?

Problem 25–5

What prevents a collecting bank which presents a check bearing a forged indorsement from successfully arguing that the finality doctrine embodied in UCC 3–418 cuts off payor's warranty recovery?

Problem 25–6

Leroy is a statewide liquor dealer with more than 100 retail liquor outlets. The economics of his business require him to accept personal and other checks of his customers. However liquor stores seem to be a favorite target of forgers and burglars. He tells you that others of his friends in the business are now refusing to take third party checks (that is checks upon which the customer is the payee or indorsee) and are willing to cash only checks on which the customer is the drawer. He asks whether there are any reasons in law for such a rule and asks what additional or alternative steps you would suggest in order to maximize his protection against theft and fraud losses. What do you advise?

KWITNY, THE PERINI CAPER, HOW STRANGER CASHED $1.1 MILLION IN CHECKS AT SMALL–TOWN BANK, Wall Street Journal, Sept. 10, 1975, pp. 1, 29.

Boston, with its patrician financial institutions and its North End underworld, right out of a George V. Higgins novel, where shadowy FBI informants double-cross flashy gangsters who bar-hop in chauffeured limousines, hand out thick packets of fresh banknotes and die in real shootouts.

And Cornelia, in the Georgia hill country of the novel and movie, "Deliverance," where small-town bankers, who didn't go to Harvard, command the modest deposits of small farmers and townsfolk for whom the principal law enforcement officer is the local game ranger or the federal whisky revenuer.

Somehow, in 1971, more than 1.1 million patrician dollars from Boston made their way to one of Cornelia's backcountry bankers. The money then went to a fellow who called himself Jesse D. Quisenberry. People noticed that Jesse D. Quisenberry was a little odd. For one thing, he had trouble keeping his Fu Manchu mustache in place. For another, he used a cloth bag to lug away down Cornelia's main street, in broad daylight, huge bundles of small-denomination bills especially trucked up from the Federal Reserve Bank in Atlanta to cash his checks.

* * *

Since 1971, no positive trace of the main character, Jesse D. Quisenberry, has been found. Some people think he successfully pulled off, with a few accomplices, one of the slickest thefts in history and now is living quite well somewhere.

* * *

One thing is sure. The stolen $1.1 million still is missing. And Aetna Casualty & Surety Co., which bonded the financial institutions there, is slugging it out in court with Lumbermens Mutual Casualty Co., which bonded the country bank here. The insurance dispute is being fought in the U.S. District Court in Atlanta. The outcome will determine who has to make up the cash that Jesse D. Quisenberry took.

It is not the kind of case that hits the federal courts every day.

* * *

It begins on Oct. 20, 1971, in the office of Roderick A. Munroe, financial vice president of Perini Corp; the big construction firm based in the Boston suburb of Framingham. The telephone rings. It is Brown Brothers, Harriman & Co., the private bankers, reporting that Perini's checking account is substantially overdrawn. Never before in his 25 years at Perini has Mr. Munroe heard of such a thing.

For several months, Mr. Munroe had been suffering from a nervous condition that, later forced him to take a prolonged leave of absence. His condition isn't helped on Oct. 20 when his secretary, Jill Valle, follows up the phone call. She can't reconcile the latest banking statement from Brown Brothers, which has been lying around since it arrived Oct. 7. Canceled checks accounting for more than $750,000 in charges against Perini's account seem to be missing from the envelope containing the statement.

Mr. Munroe and Mrs. Valle are still trying to figure this out the next day when a call comes from Perini's other blueblood bankers, Morgan Guaranty Trust Co. This Perini account, too, is substantially overdrawn.

Mrs. Valle reminds Mr. Munroe that the entire Morgan statement—checks and all—disappeared from her filing cabinet not long after it arrived Oct. 7. She remembers the date very well because the next morning, Oct. 8, she arrived at work to find that her office had been firebombed, along with much of the rest of the Perini financial department's office.

* * *

Later, after the check swindle was discovered, investigators theorized that, the firebombs weren't intended to cause much damage, but were planted to disguise the theft of canceled checks, vouchers and other documents. Though many documents were missing afterward, few in the office were found burned.

On Oct. 21, Mr. Munroe asked Morgan Guaranty and Brown Brothers for an accounting of the missing checks. The banks found photocopies and reported back that 17 checks, totaling $1,129,232.29, bore preprinted numbers that were out of sequence with the numbers on the rest of the Perini checks that the banks cleared in September.

On hearing this, Mr. Munroe and his second in command, chief accountant Roland A. Kinsley, made their way to the storeroom where Perini kept its supply of unused checks. Getting there was easy enough. The checks were kept in the same unlocked room where Perini stocked styrofoam coffee cups. Every clerk and secretary was used to walking right in. A quick inventory by Messrs. Munroe and Kinsley showed that someone also had walked right out again carrying one box of prenumbered checks on the Morgan Guaranty account and one box of prenumbered checks on the Brown Brothers account. The numbers on the missing checks matched the numbers of the out-of-sequence checks cashed by the banks.

A complete accounting showed that the cashed checks were almost evenly divided between the two banks and carried dates between Sept. 3 and Sept. 22. Because Perini kept larger bank balances, it took almost a month of additional check writing before the accounts ran into the red. The checks were made payable to two construction firms Perini had never done business with, and were endorsed by one Jesse D. Quisenberry, of whom no one at Perini admitted knowledge. They were cashed at First National Bank of Habersham County, Ga.

The checks appeared to have been written on the financial department's checkwriting machine, which automatically signed Mr. Munroe's name to spare him writer's cramp every month. The banks had been told to accept the machine signature. A manager for Burroughs Corp., which makes the machine, testified that "We tout it as the ultimate in check protection and control. Its sole purpose in a customer's office is to afford the highest degree of protection against check fraud."

Despite warnings from its corporate auditors, Arthur Andersen & Co., Perini had found it inconvenient to use certain control procedures. For example: The machine dumped signed checks into a box that was supposed to be locked; the key was supposed to be kept by an employee of a different department. No such employee was assigned, however, and the box was unlocked. Nor did anyone pay any attention to the machine's counter, which kept track of the number of checks written so that the number on any day could be compared with the number of vouchers authorized for payment that day.

* * *

All this, Mr. Kinsley said later in a deposition, was "too much trouble."

To make the unauthorized checks look legitimate, whoever prepared them typed on them numbers similar to real voucher numbers Perini used at the time. This suggested that the schemers had inside knowledge of company accounting procedures. Whoever prepared the checks, too, apparently knew that Perini's balances at a third bank were temporarily low. No checks were drawn on this account.

* * *

Meanwhile, another question was in everyone's mind at Perini: What, and where, was the First National Bank of Habersham County, Georgia?

Across from the First National Bank of Habersham County, dominating the main intersection of Cornelia, Ga., is a 20–foot statue of an apple, painted bright red. Habersham County calls itself "The Home of the Big Red Apple." Founded in 1909, the bank was taken over in 1928 by the late E.M. Reeves. His son, Lewis, dropped out of the 10th grade to become a janitor at the bank. Eventually, Lewis Reeves laid aside his mop and journeyed up Highway 23 to Clarksville, the county seat, and with his brother opened a hardware store. Reeves Hardware—now really a variety store—has become the Macy's of Clarksville.

In 1964, when he was 87, E.M. Reeves decided he needed an understudy to succeed him as banker. So son Lewis left the store, became vice president of the bank and, a year later, when his father retired, took over as president. His sister, Elizabeth Reeves Kimzey, who had joined the bank in 1930, remained vice president and cashier.

At the beginning of 1971, the bank's total resources had reached $18 million.

Mr. Reeves and Mrs. Kimzey have sworn in depositions that the first time they ever saw or heard of Jesse D. Quisenberry was on Sept. 7, 1971, when he walked in unannounced and asked to see the president about opening an account. For the next 24 days, he was a customer of the bank.

Mr. Quisenberry cut quite a figure among the overalled farmers of Cornelia with his mod suits, loud ties, chrome-rimmed glasses, high-heeled shoes, long hair and Fu Manchu mustache. Mr. Reeves said he paid little attention to the Fu Manchu because "I don't believe in mustaches." But to Billy Ray Loudermilk, the bank's collections manager, the mustache clearly was phony.

"I looked down, you know, and I noticed you could see like a Band-Aid looking tape right around the edge of one side." Mr. Loudermilk later said, "And I laughed to myself, 'Well, that son of a gun * * * I would like to buy me some sideburns (like that) because I can't grow them.' I know he knew I noticed it because I bugged my eyes out at him."

Mr. Quisenberry's accent also drew wide notice. "He doesn't talk Southern like I do," Mr. Loudermilk said. To Mr. Reeves, "He didn't have our ole Southern drawl * * * but it wasn't a Boston accent as we hear the Kennedys and those boys talk."

Somehow, Mr. Quisenberry and Mr. Reeves hit it off.

Bank employees and others gossiped about Mr. Quisenberry's peculiar appearance. Mr. Reeves ignored the talk. To speak to Mr. Reeves about Mr. Quisenberry was "sort of like * * * talking to a wall," one vice president testified. When Mr. Loudermilk and another employee were laughing about the mustache, Mr. Reeves walked up, according to Mr. Loudermilk, and asked, "What the hell's so funny?" When he was told, he walked icily off.

Mr. Reeves said that in 10 or 15 minutes on his first visit to the bank, Mr. Quisenberry asked to open an account, filled out application cards and deposited three checks from Perini Corp., drawn on its Brown Brothers account, payable to Quisenberry Contracting Co. The checks, dated Sept. 3, came to $195,861.12. Mr. Quisenberry's personalized checks for his new account were printed on the spot, and he left with them.

Mr. Reeves said he didn't ask his new customer many questions, and Mr. Quisenberry didn't provide much information; he didn't state his business, and he offered no identification. Months later, when the FBI looked up the Atlanta address that Mr. Quisenberry had given the bank, agents found a vacant lot.

On Sept. 10, Mr. Quisenberry deposited two checks dated Sept. 7. On Sept. 15, he deposited three checks dated Sept. 9. By all accounts nobody ever asked why Perini would issue him several checks for varying amounts on the same date.

Mrs. Kimzey testified that in her 40 years at the bank, perhaps five customers had accounts of more than $250,000. But she routinely, without question, submitted Mr. Quisenberry's first half-million dollars of checks to Fulton National Bank in Atlanta, First National's city correspondent, for payment. They were cleared through Brown Brothers.

On Sept. 16, after the first three had cleared, Mr. Quisenberry withdrew $195,707.90 in cash. As the later checks were cleared, he kept on withdrawing. On Sept. 18, he opened a new account for Southern Contracting Co. with Perini checks drawn on Morgan Guaranty.

He dealt only with Mr. Reeves and his sister, Mrs. Kimzey. They said they assumed that Mr. Quisenberry was proprietor of the companies whose checks he deposited. "I asked him if it (one of the companies) was a corporation," Mrs. Kimzey said "and he told me it was a plain company * * * That's the reason I used the plain (application) card."

Other hands at the bank were used to deferring to the management methods of Mr. Reeves and Mrs. Kimzey. George Pierce Short Jr., a retired Army colonel, had gone to work for the bank as a vice president in 1970 and tried to establish standard account handling procedures like those used by bigger banks. But in a deposition last year he said, "It became obvious to me that Mr. Reeves or Mrs. Kimzey had no desire, no intention to allow any paper or guide * * * to change those methods of operation * * * which in most cases were known only to themselves." Shortly after the deposition, Col. Short was fired.

Claud Surface, another vice president, asked for a credit check on Mr. Quisenberry on Sept. 17 from the Fulton National Bank. Three days later, the Atlanta bank phoned that it could find no record of Mr. Quisenberry or his companies. Mr. Surface passed the news on to Mr. Reeves, but the bank continued cashing its new customer's checks.

Curious, Col. Short and Mr. Loudermilk buttonholed Mr. Quisenberry in the bank lobby on occasion but found him uncommunicative. Col. Short recalls: "I got the impression that Quisenberry * * * possibly was interested in constructing a motel" near Cornelia. "I think that our conversation was more about the weather and the climate here in the north Georgia area, perhaps, as opposed to that in Florida; I think. I don't remember that Mr. Quisenberry had very much to say."

Mrs. Kimzey, according to depositions, was always ready with Mr. Quisenberry's enormous currency needs when he came to cash his checks, although sometimes it would take her 15 minutes or so to count out the small bills. Sometimes, before or after his visits, she had to phone the Federal Reserve Bank in Atlanta to rush hundreds of thousands of dollars to Cornelia by armored car. At least once, his check cashing reduced the bank's cash reserve below the legal minimum.

Lynn Jordan, a teller, remembered that once when Mrs. Kimzey didn't have as many $20 bills in the bank vault as Mr. Quisenberry wanted, she borrowed some from the tellers.

Mr. Quisenberry usually hauled off his loot in a black briefcase. But once it wouldn't fit and he had to borrow a cloth bag to carry it, too.

The last week in September, First National mailed Mr. Quisenberry his monthly statement. It came back from the Atlanta post office marked "No known addressee." Mrs. Kimzey said that she told Mr. Quisenberry about it on his next visit and that he said he would pick up his statements in person. On Oct. 1, he cashed a final check for $220,000, leaving $1,156.30 in his two accounts, and told Mrs. Kimzey he wouldn't be back. He wasn't. She later said she asked no questions.

Afterward, she and Mr. Reeves did find a use for some of the Perini money Mr. Quisenberry had left behind. They charged the balance of the accounts $500 for the trouble he had caused by making it necessary for money to be trucked in from the Fed., and another $16 to cover the one imposed on the little bank for letting its cash reserve get too low.

PERINI CORP. v. FIRST NAT'L BANK OF HABERSHAM COUNTY, GEORGIA

United States Court of Appeals, Fifth Circuit, 1977.
553 F.2d 398, rehearing denied, 557 F.2d 823 (5th Cir.1977).

[Perini maintained checking accounts with two New York banks, Brown Brothers and Morgan Guaranty Trust. To draw against these accounts, Perini used a facsimile signature machine. Pre-printed checks were run through the machine and emerged with an appropriate corporate "facsimile" signature. Perini had filed a facsimile specimen with both banks and, in effect, agreed to hold them harmless if checks "bearing or purporting to bear the single facsimile signature of R.A. Munroe" were honored. Alas, disaster struck. Someone obtained 17 pre-printed checks and, apparently, ran them through the machine. Eight checks, totalling $533,707.90, were drawn on Brown Brothers to the order of Quisenberry Contracting Company, probably a fictitious firm. Nine checks, totalling $593,156.30, were drawn on Morgan to the order of Southern Contracting Company, another fictitious firm. Between September 7 and October 1, 1971, a man calling himself Jesse D. Quisenberry opened two accounts in the names of the fictitious payees in the First National Bank of Habersham County, Georgia, deposited the checks in these accounts and, after they were presented through Fulton National Bank of Atlanta to and paid by the drawees, withdrew almost all of the credit in both accounts. Quisenberry endorsed the checks in his *personal capacity*! First National Bank offered no resistance to Quisenberry's requests. By the time Perini learned that its accounts with Brown and Morgan were overdrawn and discovered the fraud, the man called "Quisenberry" was gone and could not be found.

Perini, with losses totalling $1,125,000, sued Morgan, Fulton and Habersham. The district court granted summary judgment in favor of Morgan and Fulton on all counts and, except for claims based upon negligence and breach of warranty, a summary judgment in favor of Habersham. Perini appealed.]

GOLDBERG, CIRCUIT JUDGE.

* * *

II. THE UNIFORM COMMERCIAL CODE AND FORGERY LOSSES

This case illustrates the unwisdom of the belief that codification provides the yellow brick road to juridical certainty. Unimaginable circumstantial concatenations and scientific innovation very often outrun the fixity of a codified consensus. Such is emphatically the situation this court faces today.

The case at bar presents an unusual, fortuitous combination of circumstances: checks bearing undisputedly forged drawer's signatures accompanied by indorsements that may be legally defective because made in a personal capacity without indication of authority to indorse for the named payee businesses, indorsements that may or may not also have been forged, i.e., falsely written. This unique juxtaposition of factors creates numerous and vexing questions relating to the Uniform Commercial Code allocation of forgery losses among the various parties to checks and the check collection process.

One answer is clear, however. Perini has no recourse on the unauthorized signature of R.A. Munroe against Morgan or Brown Brothers. Perini's resolution authorizing the drawees' payment of checks bearing signatures resembling the machine-embossed facsimile signature precludes that course of action.

Perini makes no contrary contention. Rather, it offers claims on this appeal that rest in one way or another on asserted defects in the indorsements signed by Quisenberry. The checks were made payable to "Quisenberry Contracting Co." or "Southern Contracting Co."; each was indorsed simply "Jesse D. Quisenberry." As will be seen, if liability may be rested on these indorsements, none of the appellee banks were entitled to summary judgment. If not, the trial court's action was proper.

* * *

A. The Code Framework

Perpetuating a distinction introduced into the legal annals by Lord Mansfield in the eighteenth century, the Code accords separate treatment to forged drawer signatures (hereinafter "forged checks") and forged indorsements. In general, the drawee bank is strictly liable to its customer drawer for payment of either a forged check or a check containing a forged indorsement. In the case of a forged indorsement, the drawee generally may pass liability back through the collection chain to the party who took from the forger and, of course, to the forger himself is available. In the case of a forged check, however, liability generally rests with the drawee. * * *

1. Forged Indorsements

A check bearing a forged indorsement, included in the § 1–201(43) definition of unauthorized signatures, is not "properly payable". J. White and R. Summers, Uniform Commercial Code 559 (1972).[1] Regardless of the care exercised, a drawee bank is with few exceptions liable to its drawer customer for payment of such a check. See § 4–401.

Upon recrediting the drawer's account after payment over a forged indorsement, the drawee will seek redress against prior parties in the collection chain through an action for breach of the statutory warranty of good title. * * *

Additionally, payment of a check bearing a forged indorsement constitutes conversion under § 3–419(1)(c). * * *

The danger created by forged indorsements is that the party designated by the instrument as entitled to its proceeds will appear with a claim to those proceeds after payment has been made to the malefactor. The statutory actions for improper payment, conversion, and breach of warranty of good title combine, however inartfully, to safeguard the drawer against double liability and to assure the payee of payment. The loss falls on the party who took the check from the forger, or on the forger himself.

2. Forged Checks

As opposed to diverting an intended payment to someone other than the intended recipient, forged checks present the problem of depleting the ostensible drawer's funds when he had intended no payment. * * * The forgery does not operate as the ostensible drawer's signature. See § 3–404(1). Payment consequently is not to the ostensible drawer's order and violates the drawee bank's strict duty to charge its customer's account only for properly payable items. See § 4–401(1).

* * * The drawee's payment of a forged check is final in favor of a holder in due course or one who has relied on the payment in good faith. § 3–418. This final payment rule codifies and attempts to clarify the rule of Price v. Neal, 3 Burr. 1354 (K.B.1762). * * * [See] § 3–418, Comment 1. Prior parties in the collection chain who meet the prerequisites set out in § 3–418 will be immunized by its final payment rule from any liability for negligence in dealing with the forged check.

1. A check drawn to the order of the payee, i.e., an order instrument, may not be negotiated without the payee's indorsement. See § 3–202(1). * * * Negotiation is necessary to confer holder status on a check's transferee. Id. Accordingly, the transferee of a forged indorsement check does not become a holder. Only a holder or the holder's agent may properly present the check for payment. See § 3–504(1). Thus the UCC reaffirms the general pre-Code rule that a drawee may not charge its drawer customer's accounts for payment of an order instrument bearing a forged indorsement. See White and Summers, supra, at 559.

It may be assumed for purposes of this introductory sketch that the analysis described for forged indorsement checks equally applies to checks drawn to a principal and indorsed by an ostensible agent with no showing of representative capacity. * * *

The above scheme allocating forgery losses among the various parties to the check collection process operates without regard to fault. The drawee's duty to charge its customer's account only for "properly payable" items and the warranty of title given by prior parties in the chain of transfer impose standards of strict liability.

Fault does occupy a secondary role in the UCC treatment of forgery losses. * * * [See] § 3–406. * * * The complaining party's negligence will not, however, bar otherwise available recovery against a party, including a drawee, who is also negligent. Id. Additionally, while nothing in the Code precludes a bank and its customer from modifying the forgery loss rules by contract, the bank cannot enforce an agreement permitting it to act in violation of reasonable commercial standards. § 4–103(1).

B. The Code Policy: Incompletely Greasing the Commercial Wheels

In sum, the Code, while allowing for some modification on the basis of fault or agreement, sets up a system of strict liability rules allocating loss according to the type of forgery. The system uneasily rests on two policy bases. First, it incorporates an at least partially outmoded notion of the relative positions of drawee banks and prior parties in the collection chain with respect to detecting different types of forgeries. Second, it incompletely serves the notion that commerce will be facilitated by bringing to the swiftest practicable conclusion the processing of a check transaction.

* * * Price v. Neal * * * left forged check liability on the drawee on the view that, as against other parties in the line of transfer, the drawee stood in the best position to recognize the signature of the drawer, its customer. The corollary principle for forged indorsements is that the person who takes the check from the forger—frequently, as here, the depositary bank—is in the best position to detect the bogus indorsement.

Reaffirming Price v. Neal in the final payment rule of § 3–418, the Code drafters recognized that the case's appraisal of relative opportunity to scrutinize drawer signatures was somewhat unrealistic in a nation where banks may handle some 60 million checks daily.[2] The contemporary pace of commerce has eroded the five senses used by bankers in the face-to-face era of Price versus Neal; little remains save the sensory activity of punching keys. While the drafters thus concluded that Price v. Neal had been drained of all its personality, they nevertheless insisted that its conclusion survives. The drafters noted that modern groundwork for the final payment rule could be found in the

> less fictional rationalization * * * that it is highly desirable to end the transaction on an instrument when it is paid rather than reopen and upset a series of commercial transactions at a later date when the forgery is discovered.

2. For a discussion of the volume of checks processed and the resultant interplay between the law of forgery losses and bankers' perceptions of the forgery problem, see Murray, Price v. Neal in the Electronic Age: An Empirical Survey, 87 Banking L.J. 686 (1970). We note the commentator's interesting observation that many banks do not record separately losses from forged checks and forged indorsements, contrary to the implicit assumption in the final payment rule that the two types of losses represent security breakdowns in different functions of a bank—accepting checks for deposit to its customers' accounts and paying checks drawn by its customers—which might call for different protective measures.

* * * The possibility remains that the separate allocation of strict liability for forged check and forged indorsement losses may act as some incentive for the development of those precautionary measures that consistent with the press of business will most effectively reduce the risk of loss from either type of forgery.

§ 3–418, Comment 1. In recognition of the frenetic commerce of our time, the thrust of the UCC here and elsewhere is for speed and facility at some expense to exact checks and balances.

Leaving forged check liability on the drawee may serve well this finality policy. That policy, however, does not itself justify separate treatment for forged checks and indorsements. * * * See White and Summers, supra, at 522–23; Comment, *Allocation of Losses From Check Forgeries Under the Law of Negotiable Instruments and the Uniform Commercial Code,* 62 Yale L.J. 417, 459–60 (1953).

While finality viewed alone calls for equal treatment of forged checks and forged indorsements, one might still maintain that forged indorsements merit separate rules. The modern demands of commerce have as the drafters recognized, deprived drawees of any superior opportunity to detect forged drawer's signatures. Only a concern for finality therefore justifies placing forged check losses on drawee banks.

Such simple expedients as requiring identification, however, may still permit transferees of checks to provide a significant protection against forged indorsements that drawees cannot. To insure such protective measures are taken, it may be sensible to override the finality policy and to place forged indorsement losses on the depositary bank or other party who takes from the forger. It should be immediately noted, however, that whatever force this approach has in the usual forged indorsement case is diminished where, as here, the suspect indorsement appears on a check that is itself forged. Someone forging a check will likely draw the check to a payee whose identity he can readily assume, such as himself or a fictitious person. In such circumstances the party who first takes the check may well have no particular opportunity to detect any impropriety in the indorsement.

* * * It suffices to note that the Code bases its separate treatment of forged checks and forged indorsements on a finality policy that itself calls for no such distinction. Of course we have no mandate to ignore the codified distinction. The significance for this court today of the slash between the drafters' rule and the drafters' policy lies elsewhere.

Put simply, when we consider the arguments that these forged checks also contain unauthorized indorsements, we must keep in mind the Code's commitment to finality. We cannot call forged indorsements by any other name in order to serve our own interpretations of the balance between the UCC finality policy and relative opportunity to flush out forged indorsements. On the other hand, as we assess whether the highly unusual circumstances before us call for the label of forged check or forged indorsement, or how to operate if we are in the ill-defined and rarely encountered region in which both labels are applicable, we need not prostrate ourselves blindly before the formalisms of title on an assumption that depositary banks should be held accountable in every instance of improper indorsement. Without a uniform commercial blueprint for every possible fraud and forgery, our calling is to interstitial interpretation. In its pursuit we must recognize two considerations—the UCC's concern for finality and the probability that depositary banks, whatever their position in the usual forged indorsement case, have no unique opportunity to detect improper indorsements on checks that are themselves forged.

C. Placing Perini Within the Framework

We may now see how Perini's allegations and claims of error fit into the UCC scheme. Assume Quisenberry had included in his indorsements that he was signing "for" Quisenberry Contracting Co. or Southern Contracting Co. The case would become one involving only forged checks. Accordingly, the drawee banks would be liable to the ostensible drawer, Perini, for improper payment. Perini would be precluded from asserting that liability, however, by its resolution authorizing payment of checks bearing the facsimile signature embossed by the machine or sufficiently similar signatures. Blocked from recourse against the drawees, Perini could reach back up the collection chain only against parties who had taken the checks in bad faith and therefore could not claim the protection of the § 3–418 codification of the Price v. Neal rule.

The court below, after concluding in effect that the indorsements were valid, reached just this result. Under the orders on appeal, Perini is essentially left with a trial on the issue of Habersham's bad faith in handling Perini's checks. Habersham will be able to assert Perini's alleged negligence as a defense, and Perini may press allegations of Habersham's negligence in response.

Perini claims, however, that Quisenberry's failure to indorse in a representative capacity makes the case one of unauthorized indorsements and should entitle the company to recover from any of the three defendant banks on a strict liability basis. * * *

Perini vociferously urges that a "parade of horribles" will follow if this court affirms the trial court's disposition * * * It must be recognized and emphasized, however, that any such dire predictions relate necessarily to the highly questionable manner in which Quisenberry was able to obtain and deposit these checks. The alleged inadequacy of the indorsement bears no relation to those suspicious circumstances. Had the indorsements been letter perfect, Perini would have been limited in equally suspicious circumstances to asserting Habersham's bad faith.

The Code does generally provide an ostensible drawer greater protection in such circumstances. For its own commercial reasons, however, Perini chose to employ a facsimile signature machine and agreed to forfeit its otherwise absolute right to have its drawees recredit its accounts for any payments of forged checks. Perini's inability to recover from the drawees on the basis of the forged drawer's signature cannot fuel in the slightest its arguments regarding the indorsements. Those arguments must stand or fall on their own.

In short, this case does not present the possibility of lowering one whit the UCC protection offered bank customers against losses from forged checks; it presents only the effect on a forged check case of a malefactor's failure to make an indorsement proper in form.

* * *

III. Perini's Claims on the Indorsements

Perini maintains that defects in the indorsements directly give rise to liability under three distinct causes of action. First, the company argues that drawee Morgan Guaranty should be held strictly liable for paying items not "properly payable", in violation of its duties under § 4–401. Second, Perini claims that the defective indorsements resulted in a breach by Habersham and Fulton of the warranty of title imposed by §§ 3–417(1)(a) and 4–207(1)(a). Finally, the appellant would hold all three banks liable in conversion, § 3–419(1)(c), on the basis of the indorsements.

In the circumstances of this case, all three actions rise or fall on the same alleged improprieties in the indorsements and may be treated as one.[3] That one claim raises two possible bases of liability on the indorsements. First, Perini suggests the indorsements were invalid because they were forged, that is, made by someone who only pretended to be Jesse Quisenberry and to represent the payee businesses. Second, Perini argues that the indorsements were invalid because they were not made in a representative capacity. More specifically, Perini claims that the district court erred in disposing of both these questions by summary judgment.

A. *What if Quisenberry Wasn't Quisenberry?*

In analyzing Perini's first contention, we may treat the indorsements as if they had been proper in form. In other words, we here assume that the checks had been drawn to "Jesse D. Quisenberry" and indorsed in that form or that they had been drawn as they were and indorsed in a representative capacity. The claim is that the suspicious circumstances surrounding the checks create sufficient uncertainty regarding the authenticity of any such indorsements that the trial court should have assumed they were forged in assessing defendants' motions for summary judgment.

The Code creates a presumption that signatures on an item are genuine. § 3–307(1)(b).

* * *

Thus the burden of putting in issue the authenticity of Quisenberry's indorsements lay squarely with Perini. Given * * * the many other unusual circumstances developed in the record, however, the court below should have assumed for summary judgment purposes that "Jesse D. Quisenberry" and the two payee contracting companies were nothing other than the products of dark imagination. Whether anything in the record obliged the court also to assume that Perini would prove that the wrongdoers had used the names of a real person and real businesses is less clear. Little in the record suggests that there ever existed a "Jesse Quisenberry", a "Quisenberry Contracting Co.", or a "Southern Contracting Co." Much suggests all were fictitious.

Whether the names were fictitious or not, however, any lack of authenticity does not alter the result reached by the district court.

In either case the Code clearly indicates that lack of authenticity would not render the indorsements ineffective.

3. We note that there exist substantial questions whether the drawer of a check is a proper plaintiff in a conversion action and whether anyone other than the drawee bank that pays the check is a proper defendant to such an action. [citing Stone & Webster Engineering Corp. v. First National Bank & Trust Co., 345 Mass. 1, 184 N.E.2d 358 (1962)] * * * [w]e have recently affirmed a plaintiff's judgment in a conversion action brought by the remitter of a cashier's check against the collecting bank. See Tubin v. Rabin, 533 F.2d 255 (5th Cir.1976). This case was governed by Texas law, but involved the UCC conversion provision, § 3–419(1)(c), adopted by Texas and Georgia without modification.

We do not find a direct answer to those questions in the Georgia cases. The questions need not detain us, however, in the case at bar. In forged indorsement cases, Georgia does permit a drawer to sue directly intermediary and depositary banks for breach of the statutory warranty of title. See Insurance Co. of North America v. Atlas Supply Co., 121 Ga. App. 1, 172 S.E.2d 632 (1970). Perini's claims that Habersham and Fulton became liable by taking and transferring checks with Quisenberry's personal indorsement are not different whether labelled warranty or conversion claims. Georgia law permits Perini to raise those claims under the warranty label, which suffices to take this court to the merits. See White and Summers, supra, at 504–05, n. 25.

The authenticity question is answered by § 3–405(1). * * * Assuming the indorsements were inauthentic, it is clear that whoever drew them intended the named payees, fictitious or real, to have no interest in the checks.[4] Either situation falls squarely within § 3–405(1)(b).[5] Accordingly, § 3–405 eliminates any suggestion that the indorsements in the case at bar were ineffective because they were not genuine. Any ineffectiveness in these indorsements stems from the fact that Quisenberry failed to indorse in a representative capacity.

B. Failure to Indorse in a Representative Capacity

The checks in question name as payee either "Quisenberry Contracting Co." or "Southern Contracting Co." Each is indorsed simply "Jesse D. Quisenberry". Without requiring that the indorsements evidence authority to sign for the named payees, Habersham and Fulton forwarded these checks for payment, and Morgan Guaranty paid them.[6] Perini insists that by doing so each incurred liability.

We agree with the trial court that these indorsements were "arguably ineffective." The argument is that a signature, even by an authorized agent, does not bind the principal unless the signature incorporates in some manner the principal's name. See § 3–401, Comment 1; White and Summers, supra, at 401.[7] A check drawn to the principal requires his signature for negotiation. If, as here, the check does not bear the principal's indorsement, any transferee may be unable to satisfy the statutory warranty of good title, and payment of such a check may not accord with the order of the drawer.

4. The only remaining possibility is that one "bad guy" forged the drawer's signature and made the checks payable to the named businesses actually intending to pay those businesses, and that a second "bad guy" stole the checks and forged the indorsements. Nothing in the record makes the slightest suggestion that such a sequence of events transpired. Accordingly, the legal consequences of such a situation need not concern us. We note, however, that such a situation would present the true "double forgery" problem. See O'Malley, Common Check Frauds and the Uniform Commercial Code, 23 Rutgers L.Rev. 189, 247 n. 368 (1969). Our understanding of the proper disposition of double forgery cases is set out at Part III.B. * * *

5. * * * Section 3–405(1)(b) deals with the standard "fictitious payee" case, in which a disloyal agent draws a check on behalf of the principal to the order of a fictitious payee or to someone whom the agent intends to have no interest. On the assumption that the principal is in the best position to protect against such a situation, the law does not allow him to recover from the paying bank on the basis of the indorsement.

That situation is the same whether the agent employs a fictitious payee or a real payee he intends to have nothing to do with the check. In order to eliminate a problem arising under the predecessor provision, § 9(3) of the Uniform Negotiable Instruments Law, UCC § 3–405 makes clear that the test is "not whether the named payee is 'fictitious', but whether the signer intends that he shall have no interest in the instrument." § 3–405, Comment 3.

Nothing in § 3–405(1)(b) limits its application to cases in which the drawer's signature is authorized. The provision has also been applied in forged check cases. See Aetna Life and Casualty Co. v. Hampton State Bank, 497 S.W.2d 80 (Tex.Civ.App.1973). The rationale underlying such an application will be more thoroughly developed at Part III.B.3.b. infra.

6. Brown Brothers also paid some of the checks. By virtue of agreement with Perini, however, the bank is now aligned as a plaintiff-appellant.

7. Because the Code allows a signature to be made "by use of any name, including any trade or assumed name", or "by any word or mark", § 3–401, one might suggest that a principal could adopt an agent's personal signature as his own. Recognition of such an unlikely arrangement, however, would require proof of such an undertaking by the principal, proof that cannot be said to exist in this record in a manner justifying summary judgment against Perini. Nor could that proof be supplied by the Code's presumption that signatures are genuine. Extension of the presumption to this "agent as principal's signature" theory would run counter to the drafters' recognition of the traditional rule that "a principal whose name does not appear on an instrument signed by his agent is not liable." § 3–401, Comment 1.

Courts have visited liability on collecting and paying banks in cases of indorsements lacking evidence of representative capacity and in analogous cases involving the missing indorsements of a joint payee. It is equally clear, however, that parties in the collection chain are not held strictly accountable for every loss that might have been prevented by refusal to collect or honor checks bearing such defective indorsements. We now turn to the arguments of the appellee banks that the peculiar circumstances of the case at bar preclude shifting Perini's $1.1 million forged check loss on the basis of Quisenberry's failure to indorse in a representative capacity.

1. Sole Proprietor of Named Payee Businesses

The banks first claim that the indorsements were effective because Jesse Quisenberry was the sole proprietor of the named payees. Under Georgia law, a person operating a business under a trade name may indorse personally checks drawn to him under his trade name. See McCrackin v. Hayes, 118 Ga.App. 267, 163 S.E.2d 246 (1968). [and UCC 3–203]

In the case at bar, however, the argument runs factually aground. As in *McCrackin,* supra, the faces of the checks suggest that the payees are corporations. * * * The cards mean little, however, as the district court recognized that it was doubtful whether anyone at Habersham had actually determined that the businesses were sole proprietorships or corporations.

Given this factual uncertainty and the apparent discrepancy between payee and indorser, the district court would have courted severe difficulties had it attempted to rest a grant of summary judgment for defendants on the assumption that the checks were drawn to Quisenberry under trade names. The judge below did not rely on this assumption, and we likewise decline the invitation.

2. Bank Stamp Substitute for Indorsement

The district court did place importance on the fact that Habersham impressed on the back of ten of the checks the following stamp:

> CREDIT TO THE ACCOUNT OF THE Within Named Payee in Accordance with Payee's Instructions Absence of Endorsement Guaranteed.

The court below determined this stamp sufficient to remove any question of the efficacy of Quisenberry's personal indorsement of these ten checks. We cannot agree.

The stamps draw whatever power they have from § 4–205(1). * * *

This Code section, * * * permits banks to speed the collection process "by eliminating any necessity to return to a non-bank depositor any items he may have failed to indorse." § 4–205, Comment 1. The First Circuit has noted that the provision is one of several in Article 4 that recognize the common contemporary practice of accepting unindorsed checks for deposit. See Bowling Green, Inc. v. State Street Bank and Trust Co., 425 F.2d 81 (1st Cir.1970).

* * * § 4–205 allows the bank to forward an indorsed check for collection subject to the same potential warranty liability it faces whenever it transfers a check with a facially regular indorsement. Whether a check bears such an indorsement or a § 4–205 stamp, the collecting banks remain liable for breach of title warranty and the drawee for improper payment if the purported payee proves to have been the thief from, or an unauthorized agent of, the true payee who never received the proceeds of the check.

It may be emphasized here, however, that we are not concerned with whether Quisenberry was in fact the authorized agent of the contracting companies. Like the authenticity of Quisenberry's signatures, this question is answered by § 3–405. Given the fact that the drawer intended those companies, fictitious or real, to have no interest in the checks, anyone could have effectively indorsed them in the name of the payee companies regardless of authorization.

We are concerned rather with the fact that the indorser here omitted the names of the payee companies he appeared to represent. It might be argued that, with questions of authenticity and authorization removed, the stamp could suffice to remedy such an omission. Courts that have dealt with these and analogous omissions, however, have rested their determinations on an assessment of the relationship between the defect in the indorsement and the loss complained of. A § 4–205 stamp, designed to facilitate check collections but not to abrogate the warranty and proper payment obligations imposed by the Code, cannot immunize the appellee banks from scrutiny of the consequences of Quisenberry's defective indorsement.

3. Scope of Liability for Accepting Incomplete Indorsements

Numerous cases under the Code and earlier law recognize that a party who transfers or pays a check bearing an incomplete indorsement incurs no liability if the proceeds of the check reach the intended payee. * * * Emerging from these cases is the notion that in accepting for deposit or in paying a check with an incomplete indorsement, a bank does not become accountable for every loss that would not have occurred had the bank returned the check for a proper indorsement. Rather, the bank becomes accountable for any manifestation of the danger evidenced by an incomplete indorsement; i.e., that some person with a superior claim to the rights created by the instrument will surface and demand payment.

That danger has not manifested itself in the case at bar. There is not the slightest hint in the record that entities named "Southern Contracting Co." and "Quisenberry Contracting Co." or their transferees are loitering in the lobbies with a claim to these checks. As far as this litigation is concerned, the proceeds of the checks went to the payees designated on the face of the instruments.

We need not, however, accept fully the proposition that one dealing with an incomplete indorsement risks only the possibility that he is dealing with someone other than the check's true owner. Rather we may limit our holding to the unusual instances in which a defective indorsement accompanies a forged drawer's signature. We do so with reference to the body of "double forgery" cases, in which the majority of courts have long assessed liability as if the drawer's signature alone were forged. In line with those cases, we conclude that as a matter of law Perini's loss is a forged check loss, not an indorsement loss. Accordingly, no liability can be assessed against the appellee banks on the basis of Quisenberry's indorsements.

a. No Claim to Payment Asserted on Behalf of the Designated Payee

* * * [H]andling a check bearing an incomplete indorsement creates no liability so long as the proceeds reach the payee designated by the instrument. * * *

* * *

Other cases follow this approach. We shall draw on only one for some explication of the undergirding rationale. Decided under the Negotiable Instruments Law, Gilbert v. Chase National Bank, 108 F.Supp. 229 (S.D.N.Y.1962), involved an indorsement very similar to those at issue here. A check drawn to "Snowden Oil & Gas Co., Ltd." was indorsed only in the names of Clark and

Hemby, a limited partner and another party with an interest in the payee. The depositary bank had credited the proceeds to the Snowden account. Then-District Judge Kaufman refused to allow the drawer's claim of improper payment against the drawee.

The court stated baldly that there is no sacred relationship between an indorsement and the legal payment of a check. More specific meaning may be gleaned from the court's quotation from Osborn v. Gheen, 16 D.C. 189, 194 (Sup. Ct.D.C.1886), aff'd, 136 U.S. 646, 10 S.Ct. 1072, 34 L.Ed. 552 (1889):

> But [an indorsement] is not necessary * * * to give validity to a payment. The bank makes the payment of course, at its peril, if the payee shall afterwards challenge the payment and say that the money was not paid to him, but to somebody else.

Gilbert, supra, 108 F.Supp. at 231. The drawee bank in *Gilbert* had complied with the drawer's order. Although the bank might have returned the check for a proper indorsement, its failure to do so did not render it liable for the drawer's loss on the transaction underlying the check.

The Code definition of negotiation and the warranties it imposes may imply a more strict relationship between indorsement and title than that recognized in *Gilbert.* Interpretation of the Code, however, need not be wholly formalistic. Where missing or formally incomplete indorsements are concerned, it is consistent both with the drafters' emphasis on speeding the collection process and with ample customer protection to limit the liability of paying and collecting parties to the situation in which the intended payee did not receive the proceeds of the check.

Cases decided under the Code * * * suggest that such a delimitation of liability is appropriate. It is true, as Perini points out, that in all the cases discussed the drawer did intend to make some payment to the party who eventually received payment. Forcing a bank to reimburse the drawer because of the incomplete indorsement would have resulted in a windfall to the drawer. As the court below noted, however, the cases rest equally on the observation that the losses claimed by the drawers were not related to the improper indorsements. Implicit in that observation is a limitation of liability to claims raised in the name of the true payee.

That limitation bars Perini's indorsement claims. Upon this record, there is no possibility that a true payee will demand payment and subject the appellant company to dual liability. Perini argues that if someone in the collection process had returned the check for proper indorsement, something might have happened in the interim to prevent the loss it did suffer. The argument is of no avail. It could have applied to drawers in all the missing or incomplete indorsement cases discussed above.

Perini has not encountered the peril created by missing or incomplete indorsements. The Code does not compel, and its policies do not counsel, that this court shift the loss Perini did incur to the appellee banks on the basis of Quisenberry's failure to add to his indorsement words of agency.

b. The Presence of Forged Drawer Signatures

* * * [W]e hold only that such a limitation of liability is appropriate when the missing or incomplete indorsement is on a forged check. The ostensible drawer's loss in such a situation can generally, as here, be related to the defective indorsement in only the most speculative fashion. No sound basis exists for

extending liability for handling the indorsement beyond the unlikely event of a claim of superior right to payment under the instrument.[8]

Our holding receives support from the "double forgery" cases in which courts have grappled with claims that forged checks also bear forged or improper indorsements on which liability might be predicated. Prior to the Code, the majority of jurisdictions treated double forgery cases as if they involved forged drawer's signatures alone. See Comment, supra, 62 Yale L.J. at 455. Thus the loss rested with the drawee, who had to recredit the account of the ostensible drawer but could not recover from prior collecting banks under the rule of Price v. Neal.[9]

* * *

Commentators have suggested with remorse that the Code warranties of title overturned this analysis and required treating double forgery cases under the rules of forged indorsement liability. See Comment, supra, 62 Yale L.J. at 455.[10] At least one recent case, however, suggests that the title warranty does not mandate shifting the loss to collecting banks in a double forgery case.

In Aetna Life and Casualty Co. v. Hampton State Bank, 497 S.W.2d 80 (Tex. Civ.App.1973, writ ref'd n.r.e.), the court had to determine whether a forged indorsement rendered a depositary bank liable in circumstances similar to the case at bar. Someone had stolen company checks and forged the drawer's signature. He made the checks payable to a fictitious "Pizza Inn # 32" and indorsed them in that manner. The depositary bank credited an account he had opened in the name of "Pizza Inn # 32."

The court rejected the argument that the forged indorsement deprived the depositary bank of title and gave rise to warranty liability:

> A warranty of title is nothing more than an assurance that no one has better title to the check than the warrantor, and therefore, that no one is in a position to claim title as against the warrantee, as the payee or other owner of a genuine check could do if his endorsement were forged.
>
> On payment of the check to Hampton, Northwest's loss could not be said to have resulted from any breach of Hampton's warranty of title because no person whose name appeared to be endorsed on the check has asserted any claim of title based on lack of a genuine endorsement. Northwest's loss was rather the result of paying out its money on a check to which its own depositor's name was forged.

497 S.W.2d at 84 (citations omitted). The loss in the instant case is equally the result of the drawees' paying checks to which Perini's name was forged, rather

8. This unlikely event would occur only if the forging drawer intended payment to the named payee, the check was subsequently stolen, and the indorsement forged. Even there, however, the named payee would have no right to demand payment from the account of the ostensible drawer whose signature was forged. See O'Malley, supra, 23 Rutgers L.Rev. at 247, n. 368.

9. Perini's corporate resolution regarding the facsimile signatures prevents it from demanding that the drawees recredit its account. We cannot see how this fact could alter any duties of the prior collecting banks from which liability might arise. Those banks had no indication of the drawer-drawee agreement and therefore no reason to treat these checks differently than all others.

10. The authors of this comment, like the great majority of these who have addressed the subject of double forgery, regarded any shift away from the pre-Code analysis as an unwarranted and undesirable departure from the finality principle of Price v. Neal. See Comment, supra, 62 Yale L.J. at 460; O'Malley, supra, 23 Rutgers L.Rev. at 245–47; Palazzi, *Forgeries and Double Forgeries Under Articles 3 and 4 of the UCC,* 42 So.Cal.L.Rev. 659, 678 (1962); O'Malley, *The Code and Double Forgeries,* 19 Syracuse L.Rev. 36, 42–44 (1967).

than any claim of title raised by "Southern Contracting Co." or "Quisenberry Contracting Co." That Perini's facsimile signature resolution precludes it from placing the forged check loss on the drawees does not make it any the less a forged check loss.

It is true that the indorsements in *Aetna* were in the name of the named payee. The case thus fell squarely under § 3–405(1)(b), the "fictitious payee" provision we earlier encountered. Quisenberry's failure to indorse in the name of the contracting companies does remove the case from the coverage of that provision.

Nonetheless we find that the *Aetna* court's definition of title warranty and characterization of a double forgery loss extends persuasively to the case at bar. Others have explained why no warranty liability should arise even in the "true" double forgery situation not covered by § 3–405(1)(b):

> Since the drawer whose signature is forged is not meeting an obligation to the payee and the payee is not entitled to payment in the first place, the drawee bank could not be compelled to pay again. Thus, the drawee bank's loss [here Perini's loss as the estopped drawer] results not from making payment to the wrong person because of a forged indorsement, but from making any payment at all on the basis of a forged drawer's signature.

O'Malley, *The Code and Double Forgeries,* 19 Syracuse L.Rev. 36, 43–44 (1967).[11] The appellee banks did pass along and pay checks with a discrepancy between payee and indorsement. They credited the proceeds, however, to accounts in the names of the designated payees. In such a situation courts dealing with valid checks generally limit indorsement-related liability to the claims of the true payee. We find such a limitation particularly appropriate where the defective indorsement occurs on a forged check, in which case no true payee can demand payment. Accordingly, we hold that the indorser's failure to sign a forged check in a representative capacity provides no basis for imposition of improper payment, warranty, or conversion liability.[12] On this basis we affirm the judgment in favor of appellees on these claims, as well as the claims of common law conversion and breach of an implied deposit contract.[13]

11. The "true" double forgery would occur when a forger drew a check intending payment to the named payee, the check was subsequently stolen, and the thief forged the indorsement.

12. On remand, Perini will be free to raise Habersham's handling of the indorsements in questioning whether it can meet the good faith and absence of notice requirements necessary for the depositary bank to invoke the protections of the final payment rule against claims on the forged drawer's signatures. * * *

13. [C]ases cited by Perini on the double forgery question merit brief comment. In Travco Corp. v. Citizens Federal Savings & Loan Association of Port Huron, 42 Mich.App. 291, 201 N.W.2d 675 (1972), the court shifted a double forgery loss back to the savings and loan association that cashed the checks. The indorsements were in a personal capacity only, though the checks were drawn to fictitious companies. The court found § 3–405(1)(b) [actually § 3–405(1)(c)] inapplicable because the indorsements were not in the names of the named payees. We note that in *Travco* the savings and loan association did not accept a deposit and credit the named payee's account as did Habersham. Rather, it paid out cash immediately to the purported agent. In any case, we are unpersuaded by the terse opinion in *Travco* that Perini's loss should be treated as an unauthorized indorsement loss.

Second, Georgia did follow the minority pre-Code rule in double forgery cases and allow recovery against the collecting banks. See Cairo Banking Co. v. West, 187 Ga. 666, 2 S.E.2d 91 (1939). However, the courts based their approach on the negligence of the collecting parties. When Georgia adopted the Code's final payment rule, which renders negligence of the prior collecting parties irrelevant in a forged check case, the proper approach to double forgery cases became an open question in that state. * * *

IV. PERINI'S FORGED CHECK CLAIMS

* * *

Nothing in the Code provides Perini an action against the collecting banks on the basis of the forged drawer's signature. The UCC, however, displaces common law causes of action only to the extent they are inconsistent with the provisions of the Code. *See* § 1–103. Perini brought negligence and restitutionary causes of action against Habersham and Fulton in connection with the banks' handling of the forged checks. Those actions would allow Perini to recover without demonstrating, as it must under the district court's disposition, that Habersham acted in bad faith or had notice of defenses to the checks. The actions, however, are barred if the banks are entitled to the protections of the final payment rule. See § 3–418, Comment 4; White and Summers, *supra,* at 521–22. We conclude that rule does apply to Perini's claims as ostensible drawer, regardless of the incomplete indorsements.

A. § 3–418 Applies to Suits by a "Drawer"

Perini maintains that the final payment rule protects holders in due course and persons who have relied on the payment in good faith only against the subsequent claims of a drawee or other payor. Perini's argument lacks authority and is completely contrary to the finality policy incorporated in the rule.

The only cases cited by appellant in which a drawer has been permitted to sue directly a depositary or collecting bank involved forged or incomplete indorsements, not forged checks. See Prudential Insurance Company of America v. Marine National Exchange Bank, 315 F.Supp. 520 (E.D.Wis.1970); Insurance Co. of North America v. Atlas Supply Co., 121 Ga.App. 1, 172 S.E.2d 632 (1970). The final payment rule expressly provides that it is subject to warranty claims occasioned by such indorsements. These cases provide no basis for permitting a drawer's forged check suit against a depositary or collecting bank.

No authoritative basis could be supplied for such a suit, for it would completely undermine the finality policy incorporated in § 3–418. That provision allows one who meets its prerequisites to transfer a check secure in the knowledge that payment by the drawee ends the transaction with respect to claims that the drawer's signature is forged. See § 3–418, Comment 1. To allow the drawer, who as a regular customer of the drawee might be tempted to shift the loss away from that bank, the option of reopening the transaction would frustrate the expectations created by the Code. If Habersham and Fulton meet the final payment rule's prerequisites, they are entitled to assert its protection against Perini.

B. "Holders" of Forged Checks Bearing Incomplete Indorsements

The rights of Habersham and Fulton to the sanctuary of Price v. Neal rest on whether those banks may claim holder in due course status. Specifically, we need address only the question whether the incomplete indorsements prevented the banks from becoming holders. Habersham's good faith and lack of notice of defenses to the check, the other relevant requisites to holder in due course status, remain properly set for further proceedings under the orders of the court below. We agree with that court that Perini has failed to raise any issue as to Fulton's good faith and lack of notice.

The Code defines "holder" as a person who is in possession of an instrument "drawn, issued, or indorsed to him or to his order or to bearer or in blank." § 1–201(20). Perini's contention is that Quisenberry's failure to indorse in a representative capacity precluded Habersham from claiming the checks were indorsed to it. In this concatenation of circumstances that appears to have outstripped the imaginations of those who would call themselves learned in the ways of negotiable instruments, we conclude that "holder" need not be construed so narrowly. If a depositary or collecting bank in this situation can satisfy the other requirements of § 3–418, allowing it over the "holder" hurdle is consistent with the Code's separate treatment of forged check and indorsement losses, the ample customer protections provided by that bifurcated scheme, and the drafters' recognition of the fact that banks today frequently do not return checks missing or bearing incomplete indorsements.

First, we note that application of the § 4–205 stamp guaranteeing the absence of indorsements sufficed to make Habersham and Fulton "holders" of the checks bearing those stamps. The court in Bowling Green, Inc. v. State Street Bank & Trust Co., 425 F.2d 81 (1st Cir.1970), recognized that missing indorsements may be supplied by such stamps. See also White and Summers, *supra,* at 459. The stamps should equally operate to remedy the omission of representative capacity.[14]

We also find that, in the highly unusual circumstances presented, the banks may be properly treated as holders of those checks that Habersham failed to stamp. As in *Bowling Green,* supra, where the depositary bank was accorded holder status despite the complete absence of either indorsement or § 4–205 stamp, we have some doubt "whether the bank's status should turn on proof of whether a clerk employed the appropriate stamp." 425 F.2d at 84.

The instant case involves checks that *anyone* could effectively indorse. This is so because the named payees were either fictitious or not intended to receive payment. See § 3–405(1)(b). Thus while in some sense Quisenberry was not necessarily in possession of checks drawn "to him", he or anyone else in possession of the checks did have the capacity to negotiate them. In effect these are checks on which anyone could occupy the position of payee. Where there has been absolutely no indication that the payee contracting companies existed and that Quisenberry was not their authorized agent, his failure to indorse in a representative capacity does not require us to find that Habersham dealt with someone other than the payee.

Under § 3–302(2), a payee may be treated as a holder, despite his taking the instrument directly from the obligor. The shelter provision of § 3–201 conveys to the transferee of an instrument all rights held in the instrument by the transferor, regardless of any lack of indorsement. Given checks which anyone could effectively indorse, the insistence of Habersham on some indorsement, though incomplete, and the fact that Habersham credited accounts of the named payees, the dubious status of "holder" of forged checks may be bestowed upon Habersham and Fulton through "payee" Quisenberry.

True it is that holder in due course status is not to be lightly implied. Moreover, the drafters of the "fictitious payee" provision, § 3–405(1)(b), did suggest in making any one's indorsement effective that takers of such checks require "what purports to be a regular chain of indorsements." § 3–405, Comment 1. Perhaps a different result would obtain had Quisenberry supplied

14. This conclusion is not inconsistent with the observation earlier that the stamps cannot eliminate warranty of title liability. All holders in due course are subject to such potential liability. The § 4–205 stamp merely allows the depositary bank to forward the check secure that the final payment rule will protect it against forged check claims. It remains liable for the risk that it is not dealing with the true payee.

no indorsement or had Habersham failed to credit accounts held in the names of the contracting companies. By crediting a check with an incomplete indorsement to the account of the named payee, however, a depositary bank generally restricts its liability to claims of the true payee. The hole opened by § 3–405(1)(b) to achieving holder status on forged checks is not so narrow that it will shift a forged check loss to a depositary bank which credits the named payee's account and meets the other requirements of holding in due course. Accordingly, Habersham was a holder of these forged checks and by its indorsements transferred that status to Fulton.

Concluding that Habersham and Fulton were holders will not enable banks to treat indorsements any less carefully. A depositary bank of course cannot disregard indorsements on the assumption that checks will prove forged. If we may take any position with confidence in this bog of conundrums it is that such riddles do not occur daily.

Our conferral of holder status rather serves the finality policy which the drafters' recognized as the only valid modern basis for the rule of Price v. Neal. It does so by refusing to turn an impropriety which itself provides no predicate for unauthorized indorsement liability into a device for shifting forged check liability back to collecting parties who may be holders in due course in every respect save that improper indorsement. The Code has given us the bifurcated remedy scheme of Price v. Neal. Treating Habersham and Fulton as holders is the conclusion most consistent with that scheme and its modern policy basis. Accordingly, we affirm the summary judgment in favor of Fulton on the restitutionary and common law negligence claims. We affirm also the conclusion of the district courts that Habersham's position as a holder in due course is to rest on the questions of good faith and notice.[15]

* * *

CONCLUSION

Perini suffered what is unmistakably a forged check loss. For its own commercial reasons it had largely assumed the risk of such loss. We have found no reason to seize upon the caprice of a malefactor's failure to indorse with words of agency and convert the forged check loss into an unauthorized indorsement loss, in derogation of the finality policy incorporated in the modern

15. Citizens & Southern National Bank v. American Surety Co., 347 F.2d 18 (5th Cir. 1965), does not require that Perini be permitted restitutionary recovery from Habersham or Fulton. In *Citizens & Southern* the malefactor stole a company check prepared to the order of Higgins but not yet signed. The thief forged the drawer's and Higgins's signatures. The depositary bank credited the account maintained by the real Higgins, forwarded the check to the drawee bank, and subsequently allowed the thief to draw the funds out of Higgins's account by forging his signature.

This court held that the depositary bank paid the second check, drawn on Higgins's account at the bank, out of its own funds because it was then acting as a drawee bank which is bound to know its customer's signature and pay to his order. Therefore the proceeds of the first forgery were deemed to have remained in Higgins's account, so that Higgins was entitled to them. The court allowed the plaintiff bonding company restitution as assignee of Higgins and the drawee of the first check.

In the case at bar Habersham cannot be charged with having paid funds out of the contracting companies' accounts contrary to the order of its depositors. There is no indication of a true Southern Contracting Co. or Quisenberry Contracting Co. which, like Higgins, could claim a loss or be subjected to liability in the transactions before us. Accordingly, Perini cannot claim that its funds are still in the hands of the collecting banks.

We recognize that the pre-Code decision in *Citizens & Southern* noted that the Code would "arguably" place double forgery liability on collecting banks rather than the drawee. 347 F.2d at 22, n. 4. We have explained earlier our understanding that such predictions of the Code's effect on double forgery problems have proved vulnerable. * * *

incarnation of Price v. Neal. Therefore we relegate Perini to trying the issue it has raised regarding Habersham's good faith and notice of defenses to the checks.

Much of Perini's arguments are in the nature of pleas not to overlook the relative fault of parties to these transactions. While the Code accords fault a limited role in remedying forgery problems, the contest to which Perini and Habersham are now remanded appears precisely designed to ferret out and redress any serious wrongdoing by a party to this litigation. Perini can ask no more. With the possible exception of Habersham, whose good faith remains to be tried, it would be a sham to fasten liability on the defendant banks, which operate in a world of electronic impulses and encoded integers, on the basis of the eyeball to eyeball mercantile confrontations of halcyon days. Minute examination of checks for forgeries is an old banker's tale; two hundred years after Price v. Neal, bankers do not purport to be graphologists.

The long course chartered by Perini has come full circle. Our musings en route have been an attempt to explicate, not obfuscate the orders of the able district court which we readily affirm.

[Some footnotes omitted. Others renumbered.]

Notes

Despite that argument on behalf of the payor bank, one looking at the two foregoing cases might raise questions about the sense of changing the rule. *Altman* did exactly what one might expect of him by holding the diamonds until the check "cleared." If he were to have liability notwithstanding his wait, presumably we would be saying to him that he, better than the payor bank, could have protected against the loss and we would be saying to the backwoods folks at the Bank of Habersham, that they better than the New York banks could have prevented the loss. In the *Perini* case and even under a changed rule, there would be a strong argument that Perini should bear the loss because of its negligence. It is unclear that a change in the rule would cause substantially changed behavior on behalf of somebody such as Altman. If you were in his shoes and you knew that you would bear the loss in case of a forged drawer's signature, how would you change your behavior? (Of course, one possibility is that you would not change it at all because the likelihood of a forged drawer's signature is so small as to be insignificant.)

SECTION 3. THE DEFENSES, 3–406, 4–406, 3–405

The cases in the preceding section show that virtually every claim based on a forged signature or an alteration leads to a counter argument that the plaintiff is himself at fault for having permitted the forgery or alteration or for having failed to discover earlier peccadillos of the thief. Note that these acts of negligence under UCC 3–405, 3–406 and 4–406 do not give rise to a cause of action, rather they "preclude," they estop, the person at fault from asserting the claim that he would otherwise have. At least with respect to UCC 3–406 and 4–406, this preclusion does not apply if, on the one hand, the other party failed to use "reasonable commercial standards" or, on the other, was itself guilty of "lack of ordinary care."

The universe of possible negligence under UCC 3–406 is unlimited. The cases in this chapter will give many and varied examples; life is full of many others. Sections 4–406 and 3–405 govern a more limited set of cases. The student's first responsibility here is to understand the kinds of behavior that might fit within UCC 3–405, 3–406, and 4–406, and to understand which fact patterns will fit which of the sections. There is often, but not always, overlap among the sections. For example, 3–405 assumes for its operation a check that has been signed by one with authority to do so. Section 3–406 might apply equally to a forged signature and to a forged indorsement.

The sections provide other and intricate statutory questions as well. For example, UCC 3–406 seems to apply only to one who asserts rights as a holder in due course or a "drawer" or other payor; yet cases like *O. and K. Construction,* infra page 1123, would apply it in other situations.

J. GORDON NEELY ENTERPRISES, INC. v. AMERICAN NATIONAL BANK OF HUNTSVILLE

Supreme Court of Alabama, 1981.
403 So.2d 887.

ADAMS, JUSTICE. This is an appeal from a judgment of the Circuit Court of Madison County, entered after a nonjury trial, finding that American National Bank of Huntsville (American National), defendant below, was not liable in conversion to J. Gordon Neely Enterprises, d/b/a Midas Muffler (Neely), plaintiff below. The conversion count was based upon a total of 21 checks drawn by Neely, 19 made payable to American National and two made payable to B. Louise Bradshaw. The amount on each of twelve checks was raised and nine checks were unaltered, and all were illegally cashed or deposited by Bradshaw, a former part-time bookkeeper for Neely. The lower court found that American National acted within commercially reasonable standards when it cashed or deposited these checks for Bradshaw, and that Neely's negligence substantially contributed to the material alterations. Furthermore, American National properly paid out on the unaltered checks, since they were bearer paper and were validly negotiated upon delivery. Accordingly, it held in favor of American National. We affirm.

Mr. and Mrs. Neely, the owners and operators of J. Gordon Neely Enterprises, became acquainted with Bradshaw in 1976 when, as a Kelly Girl, she was hired by the company's stockholder accountant to assist him with their account. Mrs. Neely became friendly with Bradshaw and hired her part-time to teach her how to keep the corporate books. Since 1960, Mrs. Neely had performed all of the in-house bookkeeping duties by herself.

The corporate bank account was maintained at First Alabama Bank of Huntsville, N.A. (First Alabama), but Neely accepted Bradshaw's recommendation that the company open a second checking account at American National for personal expenditures and for the corporate payroll. She explained that checks could be drawn on the First Alabama account to fund the second account at American National. Bradshaw also kept her personal checking account at American National. Mr. and Mrs. Neely signed the bank signature card and the corporate resolution, which stated, among other things, that American National was authorized to pay out funds, on either bearer or order paper, to any of the signatories. Bradshaw was entrusted with these documents to return them to the bank, and without the knowledge or authorization of the Neelys, signed the signature card and added her name in a noticeably different type.

The following incidents complained of took place between February 25, 1977, and January 27, 1978. Bradshaw filled out checks drawn on the First Alabama account, except for two drawn on the American National account, made payable to American National and with a large space to the left of the amount written on the designated lines. Mrs. Neely signed these checks being fully aware of these large gaps. She admitted that she never left spaces like that on her personal or corporate checks because it could facilitate alterations, but Mrs. Neely never questioned Bradshaw's practice of doing so because she yielded to Bradshaw's superior knowledge.

Bradshaw altered the checks either by adding a digit or two to the left of the original amount, or by raising the first digit after using liquid erasure. She then made a split deposit by depositing the original amount into Neely's American National payroll account, and depositing to her account the difference between the original and altered amounts. On some occasions she took the difference in cash without depositing it to her account. On those checks that were not raised, she either cashed them and kept the money, or deposited them to her account, or deposited part of the check into the Neely account and kept the rest.

Prior to Bradshaw's employment, Neely's bank statements were mailed to it. But afterwards, Bradshaw arranged with both banks to allow her to pick them up. After a while, Mrs. Neely complained to the banks about this, and eventually the statements were mailed. After Bradshaw picked up the monthly statements and items, she realtered them to reflect the original amounts by using liquid erasure. Together, the two women reconciled the statements with Mrs. Neely calling out the information from her journal entry and with Bradshaw responding from the bank statements and items. Consequently, Mrs. Neely never saw the altered checks or the statements. Even when the statements were mailed, Mrs. Neely never opened them and she never reconciled the statements without Bradshaw. A new accountant hired in the latter part of 1977 discovered the defalcations, totalling $17,005.18.

Neely filed a complaint against Bradshaw and American National for conversion, and the trial court severed the claims. A consent judgment was entered against Bradshaw for $8,000.00. Neely withdrew its jury demand, and the allegations against American National were heard without a jury. The trial court entered a judgment in favor of American National from which Neely appeals.

The issue is whether the lower court erred in holding American National not liable in conversion to Neely when it paid out proceeds to one not named as a payee and when it remitted proceeds on altered checks.

First, Neely contends that the bank converted its funds because it paid out proceeds to Bradshaw when she was not named as payee. We disagree. The checks at issue were made payable to the order of American National as opposed to being drawn to J. Gordon Neely Enterprises, and none of them was endorsed restrictively "For Deposit Only" into Neely's specially designated and numbered account. The bank's expert witnesses testified that a check drawn payable to the order of a bank is recognized in the banking profession as equivalent to a check made payable to the order of cash. Legally, therefore, the instrument becomes bearer paper, Code 1975, § 7–3–111, and is properly negotiated by delivery alone, Code 1975, § 7–3–202(1). Since these checks were bearer paper and were validly negotiated when Bradshaw delivered them for presentment, American National is not liable for paying to her the proceeds even though she was not named as payee.

Neely also relies heavily upon the proposition that

> "It is generally held that a check or draft drawn to the order of a bank precludes the diversion of the proceeds of it to a use other than that of the drawer, and that such diversion can be justified only by proof of authority from drawer." 10 Am Jur 2d Banks § 560 (1963).

However, overlooked by Neely, cited within the same paragraph from which it quotes, is the following:

> "[B]ut * * * if the drawer has clothed his agent with apparent authority to receive the proceeds of such check, the bank is not negligent in, and is not liable to the drawer for, paying, in reliance upon such apparent authority, the proceeds of such check to such agent contrary to his actual authority, if the agent should misappropriate such proceeds." 10 Am Jur 2d Banks § 560 (1963).

The record in this case amply supports the finding that Bradshaw was apparently, if not actually, authorized to receive the money; therefore, the proceeds were not diverted to a use inconsistent with the drawer's intentions.

Neely clothed her with the authority to act on its behalf by entrusting her to pick up and to return the documents necessary to open the American National checking account. Additionally, from the bank's perspective, Bradshaw was actually authorized to withdraw and to receive the corporate funds because the corporate documents on file at the bank explicitly granted her the authority to do so. Although her typewritten name on these forms was different in type from Mr. and Mrs. Neely's, there was testimony at trial upon which the trial court could conclude that the bank's actions were commercially reasonable in this regard.

Bradshaw also received ostensible authority to act for the company when it allowed her to make bank deposits and when it permitted her, albeit reluctantly, to pick up the monthly statements. Moreover, aside from the authority granted by Neely's corporate resolution, it was shown to be customary in the community for a bank to pay cash to an employee out of the corporate account or to make a split deposit into the employee's account out of the corporate check. Often, the employee is sent to get the money for the office petty cash box out of the corporate account. The employee's deposit into the personal account out of the business account may very well represent the employee's pay.

In sum, the lower court did not err in not holding American National liable, because the bank paid the proceeds out on properly negotiated bearer paper and because it did not unlawfully divert those funds beyond the drawer's intentions inasmuch as the facts indicate that Bradshaw was apparently authorized to receive the money.

Next, Neely alleges that American National is liable for paying out on altered instruments. Both parties rely upon Code 1975, § 7–3–406, stating:

> "Any person who by his negligence substantially contributes to a material alteration of the instrument or to the making of an unauthorized signature is precluded from asserting the alteration or lack of authority against a holder in due course or against a drawee or other payor who pays the instrument in good faith and in accordance with the reasonable commercial standards of the drawee's or payor's business."

Neely argues that American National did not pay the instruments according to commercially reasonable standards because the checks allegedly bore visible marks of alteration. American National contends that Neely is precluded from asserting the material alterations as a basis for liability because Neely's negligence substantially contributed to the alterations by leaving large spaces to the left of the amount designation, and by entrusting the same employee with writing the checks and reconciling the bank statements without the protection of internal corporate controls.

We must first resolve whether American National acted in a commercially reasonable manner, because if the bank acted reasonably it cannot assert the defense that Neely's negligence substantially contributed to the alterations. * * *

American National produced expert witnesses testifying that although some of the words and numbers on the amount designation lines were slightly misaligned, and although a few checks visibly contained liquid erasure, the bank did not violate reasonable commercial standards when it paid out on these particular checks to Bradshaw. It was stated that the decision of whether to pay a particular check that may have appeared to be somewhat irregular on its face was based entirely upon a judgment call under the particular circumstances of that check. Based upon the judgment call surrounding the decision to pay each check, and after examining the checks exhibited, the trial court concluded that American National had acted in a commercially reasonable fashion under the circumstances. Inasmuch as this fact issue was found in favor of American National, the nonjury finding will stand on appeal because it was not plainly and palpably erroneous. Stagg v. Van Sant, 390 So 2d 620 (Ala.1980).

After resolving the threshold question of the commercial reasonableness of the bank's actions, we must next determine whether Neely, by its negligence, substantially contributed to the facilitation of the alterations. The Uniform Commercial Code does not define the negligence which will support the defense of § 7–3–406, and instructs that it is an issue strictly left to the factfinder on a case by case approach. Code 1975, § 7–3–406, Comment 3. The official comment does advise, however, that "[n]egligence usually has been found where spaces are left in the body of the instrument in which words or figures may be inserted." * * * It is undisputed that Mrs. Neely signed the checks fully aware of the large gaps in front of the amount.

Similarly, two other examples of negligence are supported by the record: no inquiry was made into Bradshaw's veracity, although it was rumored that previously she had been in trouble with embezzlement in Tennessee, see Commercial Credit Equipment v. First Alabama Bank, supra; and Neely failed to maintain internal controls so that the employee writing the checks was not also the principal person reconciling the bank statements, * * *.

Although each state defines it separately, Alabama construes the phrase "substantially contributes," Code 1975, § 7–3–406, to mean that the drawer's negligence must proximately cause the making of the alteration. * * * Particularly pertinent to this case is the following description of proximate cause:

> "When a person by his negligence produces a dangerous condition of things, which does not become active for mischief until another person has operated upon it by the commission of another negligent act, which might not unreasonably be anticipated to occur, the original act of negligence is then regarded as the proximate cause of the injury which finally results."

Goodwyn v. Gibson, 235 Ala. 19, 21, 177 So. 140, 142 (1937), * * *.

Based upon a thorough and sifting review of the record, we conclude that the accumulation of Mrs. Neely's negligent conduct set in motion an unfortunate chain of events which proximately culminated in the alterations, thus establishing Neely's substantial contribution.

We will not disturb these findings that Neely's negligence substantially contributed to Bradshaw's alterations, because they are not clearly and patently erroneous. Therefore, because American National acted in a commercially reasonable manner and Neely's negligence substantially contributed to the material alteration resulting in the bank's payment to Bradshaw, Neely cannot recover from American National.

Based upon the foregoing analysis and conclusions, the judgment of the trial court is due to be, and is hereby, affirmed.

Affirmed.

TORBERT, C.J., FAULKNER, ALMON and EMBRY, JJ., concur.

GRESHAM STATE BANK v. O AND K CONSTRUCTION CO.

Supreme Court of Oregon, 1962.
231 Or. 106, 370 P.2d 726, opinion clarified on denial of rehearing, 372 P.2d 187 (1962).

O'CONNELL, JUSTICE.

This suit was instituted by the Gresham State Bank, interpleading O and K Construction Company and Ada Zimmerman, dba Zimmerman's Twelve Mile Store, to determine the rights of the defendants to $5,622.98 which was tendered into court by plaintiff bank. This sum represented the amount of money credited to defendant Zimmerman's account in the plaintiff bank upon Zimmerman's deposit of various checks made payable to defendant O and K Construction Company. Zimmerman's Store had cashed the checks upon presentment by F.C. McKenna, a bookkeeper employed by the defendant construction company. McKenna was not authorized to endorse or receive the proceeds of the checks. O and K Construction Company filed a cross-complaint alleging that the checks in question did not bear a valid endorsement of the construction company and sought recovery for conversion of the checks.

The trial court entered an order discharging plaintiff of all liability upon the condition that plaintiff pay into court the sum of $5,622.98, which condition plaintiff met. The court also decreed that plaintiff should receive $500 attorneys fees and its costs incurred in the suit, the amount to be paid out of the money tendered into court.

The court then proceeded to determine the claims of the defendant O and K Construction Company and the defendant Zimmerman to the fund deposited in court by plaintiff. The court entered a judgment for defendant Zimmerman. The judgment also provided that plaintiff and defendant Zimmerman recover their costs and disbursements from defendant O and K Construction Company. Defendant Zimmerman filed a statement of disbursements including $549 previously paid to plaintiff out of the interpleaded funds. Upon objection made by defendant O and K Construction Company the court disallowed the claim for $549. From the order disallowing the claim defendant Zimmerman cross-appeals.

On or about December 15, 1956, the O and K Construction Company employed Francis McKenna to work in its office located at Twelve Mile Corner near Gresham, Oregon. McKenna's principal duties were to keep the books of the company and to perform other office duties in connection with the business, including answering the telephone, opening the mail, receiving payments made to the company by check or in cash and to give receipts for such payments, and various other duties which we shall describe in more detail below. Although McKenna was required to be at the office of the company during the regular working hours from Monday to Saturday, he was permitted to carry on his own private bookkeeping service for others. Osburn and Kniefel, the officers of the company, were seldom present at the office, their work requiring them to be elsewhere in connection with the operation of the contracting business; consequently they exercised very little supervision over the details of McKenna's work for the company.

From time to time McKenna, in the course of his employment, received checks made payable to the construction company. He was authorized to deposit these checks in the First National Bank of Gresham, which was located about a mile from the company's office. To facilitate the making of these deposits McKenna was furnished a rubber stamp bearing the inscription "For deposit only at the First National Bank." The office supplies also included another rubber stamp with the inscription "O & K Construction Co., Route 1, Gresham, Oregon," which was intended to be used in marking statements, invoices, sales books and other similar items.

During the years 1957, 1958 and 1959 McKenna endorsed 30 checks which had been made payable to the company and cashed them at Zimmerman's Twelve Mile Store, which was also located at Twelve Mile Corner about one half block from the office of the O and K Construction Company. The unauthorized endorsement was made by using the stamp "O & K Construction Co., Route 1, Gresham, Oregon" under which McKenna signed his name, followed by the designation "Office Manager" in some instances and "Bkpr" in others. These checks were cashed at Zimmerman's Store. The store maintained a special check cashing counter at which was maintained a "Regis-Scope" machine by which the check and the person cashing it could be photographed. No inquiry concerning McKenna's right to endorse and cash the checks was made of the officers of the O and K Construction Company. After the checks were cashed, the Zimmerman Store endorsed them and deposited them to its account at the plaintiff bank. The checks were sent through the regular banking channels and paid by the drawee banks. In May, 1959, McKenna's defalcations were discovered, whereupon the O and K Construction Company obtained the cancelled checks from the various makers and made a formal demand upon the drawee banks for the face amount of the checks. The drawee banks in turn made demand upon the plaintiff bank. As these demands were made upon the plaintiff bank, it withdrew from the account of Zimmerman's Store an amount equal to the check and placed it in a suspense account. After the last check had been presented the bank filed this suit in interpleader.

The defendant O and K Construction Company relies upon the rule that one who makes payment upon an unauthorized endorsement of the payee's name is liable to the payee for conversion.

Defendant Zimmerman contends that the loss falls upon the defendant construction company on the basis of any one of the following rounds: (1) that McKenna had implied or apparent authority to endorse the checks and to present them to Zimmerman's for payment on behalf of the construction company; (2) the construction company is precluded from recovery by its negligence; (3) where one of two innocent parties must suffer the loss should fall upon the one whose acts made the loss possible.

The third contention adds nothing to the first two. There is no legal principle which places the loss upon one of two innocent parties merely because one acted and the other did not. The law makes the choice upon the basis of fault or some other consideration warranting the preference. In the present case we must decide upon some such rational ground which of the two defendants should be favored.

We begin with the well established rule that one who obtains possession of a check through the unauthorized endorsement of the payee's name acquires no title to it and is liable to the payee for the amount of the check unless the payee is precluded from setting up the want of authority.

The evidence is clear that McKenna had neither the express nor implied authority to endorse the checks other than for deposit. Defendant Zimmerman contends that if there was not an implied authority the facts disclose that McKenna was clothed with apparent authority. To support this contention Zimmerman points to various instances where, it is alleged, the conduct of Osburn and Kniefel constituted indicia of authority in McKenna to make the endorsements.

It is argued that in supplying McKenna with a rubber stamp bearing the name and address of the construction company, he was provided with the means of endorsing paper and thus representing that he had authority to do so. This does not constitute the creation of an appearance of authority. Whatever appearance of authority arose from the use of the stamp was not created by the O and K Construction Company; it was created by McKenna himself. Certainly the mere furnishing of a name and address stamp by the company for use in its office did not create an ostensible authority to endorse checks and receive payment for them. Stamps of this character are used in most offices; the supplying of them signals nothing with respect to the authority of those employed to use them. Where there are other facts from which third persons might reasonably infer that authority was granted the principal may be held liable.

Other facts are relied upon by Zimmerman as a basis for the alleged appearance of authority. It is pointed out that McKenna had authority to receive checks and cash in payment of accounts owing to the construction company; that he was in charge of the office without supervision approximately 85% of the time; that he dealt with people who came to the office; that he used the company's charge account at Zimmerman's Store; that he was permitted to use money out of the petty cash fund; that Osburn and Kniefel were frequently in Zimmerman's Store with McKenna; that Zimmerman's employees who cashed the checks in question relied upon the fact that McKenna was the office manager of the construction company. We fail to see how these and the other facts recited by Zimmerman create an appearance of authority to endorse checks and to receive the cash for them. The mere fact that an employee has charge of a company's office does not entitle third persons dealing with the employee to assume that he has the authority to execute or endorse the company's negotiable paper. We find no evidence to support a finding that McKenna was clothed with apparent authority.

The contention that defendant O and K Construction Company was precluded from recovery because of its negligence presents a more difficult legal problem. There was evidence to support a finding that Osburn and Kniefel were negligent in failing to scrutinize the records of the company over the three-year period during which the defalcation occurred. They made little individual effort to examine their books during that period and no audit was made. Neither of them knew much about bookkeeping and, largely because of that fact, McKenna was able to maneuver the records in such a way as to conceal the misappropriation of the company's funds. Osburn and Kniefel could have discovered the diversion of these funds by checking the bank statements against the company's records showing receipt of payment from various customers. But this was not done and the falsification by McKenna of office records and accounts served to deceive Osburn and Kniefel on the few occasions when they superficially checked the records. During the period in question the company's account was overdrawn on several occasions which, it is argued, should have alerted the officers of the company to the possibility of a misappropriation of their funds. However, apparently it was not uncommon for the company to have overdrafts even when all of its funds found their way to the bank.

It is our conclusion that, although under the circumstances it does not appear that Osburn and Kniefel were seriously at fault in not discovering McKenna's deception, their conduct can be regarded as constituting negligence. To so conclude does not, however, solve the problem in this case. The conduct of both defendant Zimmerman and defendant O and K Construction Company contributed to the successful forgery—Zimmerman in failing to make inquiry as to McKenna's authority to endorse the checks in question, and O and K Construction Company in failing to examine its records. The question is: Who should bear the loss under these circumstances?

In a considerable number of cases it has been held that the negligence of an employer in detecting the dishonest conduct of his employee does not preclude recovery against the payor of an instrument forged by the employee. In some cases this conclusion is reached on the theory that the employer's negligence is not the proximate cause of the loss; the payor's failure to inform himself as to the employee's authority being regarded as the sole cause of the loss.

On the other hand, a substantial number of cases recognize that the payor's duty to ascertain the authority of the employee-endorser is not absolute and that the employer's negligence may bar his recovery against the payor.

It seems evident that the O and K Construction Company's negligence was a causal factor contributing to the forgery. Each of the parties had a duty to exercise due care in connection with the checks in question. Each failed to perform its duty. The question is how to allocate the loss under such circumstances. The conduct of each could be described in terms of negligence. Applying the accepted rule in other negligence cases, the defendant construction company would be barred from recovery because of its contributory negligence. But, it is not necessary or desirable to extend the doctrine of contributory negligence beyond its present scope and there are special reasons why we should not do so in the law of commercial paper.

The pattern for decision in cases such as the one before us is found in § 3–406 of the Uniform Commercial Code which was adopted by the enactment of Oregon Laws 1961, Ch. 726, § 73.4060, to be effective on September 1, 1963. That section (Ore.Laws 1961, Ch. 726, § 73.4060; UCC § 3–406) provides as follows:

> "Any person who by his negligence substantially contributes to a material alteration of the instrument or to the making of an unauthorized signature is precluded from asserting the alteration or lack of authority against a holder in due course or against a drawee or other payor who pays the instrument in good faith and in accordance with the reasonable commercial standards of the drawee's or payor's business."

Although this section is not operative until September 1, 1963, it expresses the legislative view as of the time of its enactment. There is no existing Oregon statute or adjudicated case which announces a contrary principle. As we have already indicated the cases in other jurisdictions are in conflict. We are, therefore, free to adopt the principle which, in our opinion, will comport with the needs of the business community in dealing with commercial paper under circumstances such as we have here. We believe that Section 3–406 of the Uniform Commercial Code expresses the appropriate principle. We therefore adopt it. We believe that it is particularly appropriate to do so because it conforms to the view taken, at least tentatively, by the 1961 Legislative Assembly in adopting Oregon Laws 1961, Ch. 726 with a postponed effective date.

It is apparent that this section requires a weighing process in choosing between the owner of the forged instrument and the payor in allocating the loss. Translating the section in terms of the factual situation before us, the O and K Construction Company is not precluded from asserting McKenna's lack of authority unless two conditions exist: (1) that O and K Construction Company's negligence "substantially contributes" to the making of the unauthorized signature and, (2) that Zimmerman made payment on the instrument in good faith "and in accordance with the reasonable commercial standards of the * * * payor's business."

The requirement that the negligence "substantially contributes" to the making of the unauthorized signature is necessary to satisfy the test of factual causation; it is the equivalent of the "substantial factor" test applied in the law of negligence generally. See Restatement, Torts § 433, p. 733 (Supp.1948); Prosser on Torts, § 44, pp. 218–223 (2d ed. 1955).

There was sufficient evidence to establish the negligence of the O and K Construction Company in failing to check its records and that this negligence substantially contributed to the making of the unauthorized signatures (at least with respect to those checks which were cashed after there was sufficient time for the company to examine its records and discover the depletion of its funds).

This leaves for our consideration the conduct of Zimmerman in cashing the checks. Defendant O and K Construction Company is not precluded from recovery unless Zimmerman's conduct was "in accordance with the reasonable commercial standards" of its business.

Ordinarily the customary practices of a business must be established by evidence. However, it has been judicially recognized in many adjudicated cases that one who cashes a check endorsed by an agent has the duty to inquire as to the agent's authority to make the endorsement. We can, therefore, take judicial notice of this duty to make inquiry as a part of the "reasonable commercial standards" of a business. As we have already indicated, the duty to inquire is not absolute; the payor may rely upon the apparent authority of the agent or may assert an estoppel against the principal upon some other ground. We have already stated that there was not sufficient evidence to establish apparent authority. Zimmerman attempts to establish such authority by evidence that McKenna frequently was in the company of Osburn or Kniefel in Zimmerman's Store; that McKenna had authority to purchase for the construction company items in the store which were charged to the construction company's account; that he had authority to disperse [sic] funds from the petty cash account; that he was in charge of the office approximately 85% of the time, and that he had authority to receive payments on debts owed to the company, as well as to deal generally with people who called at the office. This conduct would not entitle a reasonable man to assume that McKenna had the authority to endorse the construction company's commercial paper. It seems quite evident that Zimmerman's employees cashed these checks not because they relied upon any appearance of McKenna's authority but because they lulled themselves into a false inference, i.e., they apparently assumed that, because McKenna was entrusted with some authority to handle the construction company's business, he had the authority to endorse checks. The cases establish that this is not a reasonable inference.

In testing Zimmerman's conduct by the standard of ordinary commercial practice, it is to be noted that the checks were not cashed by McKenna in connection with any purchase of items in the store on behalf of the construction company. McKenna received the whole amount of the check. Moreover, the amounts paid to him were substantial, including several checks for $300 or more.

Ordinarily, it is the usual practice for a company to deposit checks received by it and to pay for its expenditures by checks drawn on its own account. There was nothing about the character of the O and K Construction Company to warrant an assumption by Zimmerman or his employees that these large amounts of cash were needed to carry on the construction company's business. Had Zimmerman's exercised the degree of prudence customary in their business McKenna's unusual practice of calling for cash would have indicated to Zimmerman that something may have been wrong in McKenna's management of the company's financial affairs.

It is argued that, since no complaint was made by the construction company after the checks were cashed, Zimmerman was led to believe that McKenna's practice was authorized. Under the circumstances, it would have been more reasonable to infer that McKenna had devised a scheme to cover his defalcations.

We hold that, as a matter of law, Zimmerman did not make payment of the checks in accordance with the reasonable commercial standards of his business.

We have accepted the statement in Oregon Laws 1961, Ch. 726, § 73.4060 as the guiding principle in disposing of this issue in the case. However, ample support for the position we take may be found in cases which reach a similar conclusion without benefit of an expression of legislative policy. Where the payor's negligence consists of his failure to ascertain the authority of the agent who forges the endorsement of his principal, the great weight of authority holds that the principal's negligence does not bar him from recovery. The leading case on the subject, California Stucco Co. of Washington v. Marine Nat. Bank, 148 Wash. 341, 268 P. 891, 67 A.L.R. 1531 (1928), holds that, in the absence of actual or apparent authority, the negligence of the principal in failing to supervise his employees, resulting in the forgery, is not a defense to an action against the payor. The court, quoting from Standard Steam Specialty Co. v. Corn Exchange Bank, 220 N.Y. 478, 116 N.E. 386, L.R.A.1918B, 575 (1917), said that " '[t]he stringent rules of agency and the arbitrary rules of the law of negotiable paper alike protect the principal from such unauthorized acts.' " More frequently the rationale is in terms of proximate cause; the principal's negligence in supervising his dishonest employee is not regarded as the proximate cause of a loss arising out of the payor's failure to ascertain the agent's authority.

In some of the cases it is explained that the negligence of the principal, to be a causative factor, must relate to the creation of an appearance of authority in the agent. It would seem more accurate to say that, although the principal's negligence is a causal factor contributing to the loss (reasonable care in supervising his dishonest employee would have prevented it), the payor's negligence outweighs that of the principal in the usual case and he should, therefore, be required to bear the loss. This analysis, recognizing the negligence of both parties as causative factors, would bar the principal in an action against the payor, if the doctrine of contributory negligence were applied. We have indicated above that we would not extend the contributory negligence doctrine to this type of case. It is apparent that Oregon Laws 1961, Ch. 726, § 73.4060 is based upon the same assumption because it permits a negligent principal to recover against a payor who fails to make payment of the instrument in accordance with the reasonable commercial standards of the payor's business.

In the ordinary case it seems proper that the negligent payor, rather than the negligent principal, should bear the loss caused by an agent's unauthorized endorsement of his principal's check. An important factor supporting this conclusion is the relative ease with which the payor, having knowledge of the agency, can ascertain the agent's authority, as compared with the difficulty with which an employee's dishonesty may be detected by his employer. The employer must overcome the obstacles which the employee devises for the very purpose of making it difficult to detect the defalcations. Certainly under the circumstances of the present case, it was more reasonable for the officers of the O and K Construction Company to assume that their employee was honest than it was for Zimmerman to assume that he had the authority to endorse checks and receive payment in cash for no ostensible corporate purpose.

We hold that, because of defendant Zimmerman's negligent failure to act in accordance with the reasonable commercial standards of its business, the defendant O and K Construction Company, although negligent, is not precluded from recovering upon the forged checks. Oregon Laws 1961, Ch. 726, § 73.4060 indicates that the payor's failure to act in accordance with reasonable commercial standards might bar him from setting up the owner's negligence no matter how gross it might be. It is not necessary for us to decide whether the statute will be so interpreted. In the present case the negligence of the O and K Construction Company was clearly outweighed by that of Zimmerman.

We hold that, under these circumstances, Zimmerman cannot rely upon the construction company's negligence to bar the latter's recovery. We reach this conclusion upon a de novo examination of the record, this being a proceeding in equity. The same conclusion would be permissible had this been an action at law because, as we have indicated, Zimmerman's failure to act in accordance with reasonable commercial standards can be declared as a matter of law.

* * *

Reversed and remanded. [Footnotes omitted.]

Notes

1. Under UCC 3–406 who is to benefit from a showing of negligence?

2. How would you have decided these two cases?

3. Assume that Alabama or Oregon passed a statute that generally indorsed comparative negligence in cases where negligence is relevant. Assume the statute made no reference to check cases and that it was stimulated principally by automobile accident and product liability cases. Could and should such a statute be interpreted to modify outcomes under UCC 3–406 and 4–406?

Section 4–406 deals with the customer's behavior after the fact; i.e., customer failure to examine and report "his" unauthorized signature or any alteration. The same preclusion applies, but it applies mainly in circumstances in which the discovery of an early forgery or alteration would have sent the thief to jail and thus avoided the subsequent forgery or alteration. Note too that there is a limitation period and note finally that the limitation period in UCC 4–406(4) applies not just to forged signatures and alterations, but also to "any unauthorized indorsement."

WINKIE, INC. v. HERITAGE BANK OF WHITEFISH BAY

Supreme Court of Wisconsin, 1981.
99 Wis.2d 616, 299 N.W.2d 829.

HEFFERNAN, JUSTICE.

This review stems from a trial court action in which Winkie, Inc., sued its bank, the Heritage Bank of Whitefish Bay, for paying checks not properly payable. It was stipulated that, during the period from 1965 to 1973, Heritage had paid forged checks drawn on the Winkie account in the amount of $148,171.30. On each of these checks, Doris Britton, an employee of Winkie, forged the signature of W.J. Winkie, Jr., the company president. Checks totaling $55,724.19 were single forgeries, in that only the signature of the maker, W.J. Winkie, Jr., was forged. These forged checks generally named Doris Britton as payee, and she passed them by signing her own name as indorser.[1] Checks totaling $92,447.11 were double forgeries, in the sense that the maker's signature was forged and the checks were transferred by Doris Britton's forged indorsement of the named payee.[2] At least one forged check was paid by Heritage without indorsement. None of these checks were issued in payment for goods or services provided to Winkie, Inc.; and Winkie, Inc., neither intended payment nor received benefit of any kind by the issuance of these particular checks. Doris Britton was the sole beneficiary, directly or indirectly, of the proceeds of all the forged checks. Two checks, on which the Heritage Bank itself was the payee, were used by her to pay her personal obligations to the bank.

On May 10, 1973, after eight years of repeated forgeries, irregular procedures employed by Doris Britton were called to the attention of W.J. Winkie, Jr., by another secretarial employee. He immediately investigated, discovered a forged check, and notified the bank; and this led to the discovery of the series of forgeries dating back over a period of eight years. Hundreds of checks were found to have been forged.

Although the Heritage Bank each month sent a statement of account to Winkie, Inc., together with the paid items, W.J. Winkie, Jr., whose signature, false or otherwise, appeared on all the checks, did not examine the statements or the checks and did not reconcile the checking account balance with the balances shown on the bank statements.

At trial, the procedure used in issuing checks and reviewing paid checks was thoroughly explored. One of Doris Britton's principal duties was the preparation of checks on the basis of suppliers' invoices. She apparently verified the invoices and prepared the checks which were to be paid to Winkie suppliers.

The record shows that, whenever accounts were to be paid, bona fide checks were submitted by Doris Britton to W.J. Winkie, Jr., for his signature. His

1. Some, however, named other persons or institutions as payee and were properly indorsed thereby. Nonetheless, even the proceeds of those checks indirectly inured to Doris Britton's benefit.

2. Most of these "double-forged" checks also have an additional indorsement in Doris' own name, following the forged indorsement of the named payee.

signing was perfunctory in nature. He did not check invoices or the sequence of check numbers. He merely determined that the checks on their face appeared to be proper in form and that the numerical figures agreed with the typewritten face value of the checks.

Doris Britton, two or three times a month on the average, using numbered Winkie, Inc., checks and the Winkie checkwriter, forged W.J. Winkie's signature on checks naming herself as payee, or on checks to payees who were not intended to receive the proceeds of the checks.[3] This latter category of checks was transferred by Doris Britton by forging the indorsements of the named payees and, in most cases, adding her own name as indorsee.

The trial court in its opinion exhaustively reviewed the internal operating procedures of Winkie, Inc. The only internal control of the check issuing and the reconciliation procedure was left to Lyle Britton, Doris' husband. However, Winkie never instructed Lyle Britton to reconcile the bank statements nor in the proper means of doing so; and, as far as the record shows, Lyle Britton never reconciled the balance shown on the statement with the office checkbook records or compared the cancelled checks with the numerical sequence of checks issued or with the office's carbon duplicates of the original checks. His job was to post the checks in the books. It is not clear whether this duty encompassed the posting of checks only after they were paid by the bank or whether he was responsible for some record in respect to the checks as they were prepared prior to delivery to the payees.

The forgeries of Winkie's signature were reasonable facsimiles. Winkie indicated that, from the signatures alone, he would not in all cases know that the signatures were not his. The evidence was uncontradicted that a bank, in the exercise of ordinary care, would not have detected the forgeries.

Although a firm of certified public accountants performed some services for Winkie, Inc., the contract under which it was hired did not provide for bank statement reconciliation or item examination. The record shows that no one in the Winkie organization was instructed to examine bank statements or the cancelled items when they were returned. Winkie testified that he assumed that an accountant, earlier employed, had fully instructed Lyle Britton in his duties. To the extent that the returned checks and bank statements were given any review, such review was by Lyle Britton, who was uninstructed and unsupervised in respect to the reconciliation of the checking account and examination of the paid items.

It should be noted that, despite the husband-wife relationship between the forger and the only person charged with any duties with respect to the cancelled checks, there is no claim that Lyle Britton was implicated in the fraudulent scheme.

The trial court found that Winkie, Inc., was negligent for its failure to examine the cancelled checks and the statements returned by the bank and was negligent in failing to make any kind of examination that could have led to the detection of the forgeries or check alterations. It additionally found that the Heritage Bank was not negligent in respect to paying any of the checks, and that the bank had exercised reasonable care and prudence in the processing and payment of the Winkie checks. It concluded that the Heritage Bank was not liable for any of the forged or altered items charged against the Winkie account.

3. A number of checks in this latter category bore, in addition, alterations to, or erasures of, the named payee.

Although the testimony revealed that the Heritage Bank, as a matter of policy, did not check indorsements on checks with a face value of less than $1,000, the trial court found that the bank was not negligent in failing to do so. Judgment, accordingly, was entered dismissing Winkie's complaint.

The Court of Appeals [4] affirmed the judgment of the trial court. In so doing, it sustained the trial court's finding of fact that Winkie, Inc., was negligent because of its failure to examine the cancelled checks drawn on the bank account. It further sustained the trial court's finding that Winkie, Inc., was negligent in failing to establish a reasonable procedure of control after the checks were returned.

We do not reexamine these determinations of the Court of Appeals that the trial court's findings were founded upon sufficient evidence. The Court of Appeals had full access to the record, and this court will not reexamine Court of Appeals' determinations where a question of law is not specifically implicated. We ordinarily would not take a case on review which involved only the question of sufficiency of the evidence. We reserve for further discussion in this opinion the effect of the bank's failure to examine indorsements on checks bearing a face value of less than $1,000. In respect to that issue, the petitioner's contention is that the bank was negligent as a matter of law.

The Court of Appeals also held that Heritage was not negligent in failing to inquire about the issuance of several checks in which Heritage itself was the payee and the proceeds were applied to Doris Britton's personal indebtedness. It correctly concluded that the rule of *Schneider Fuel v. West Allis State Bank,* 70 Wis.2d 1041, 236 N.W.2d 266 (1975), was inappropriate, because Doris Britton was not a "fiduciary" in the sense that term was used in the *Schneider* case.

[The court finds that drawee banks must bear the loss for items "not properly payable" (4–401) unless the drawer, because of its own negligence, is precluded from asserting the bank's liability. Sec. 3–406 provides one such preclusion, but the court finds 3–406 inapplicable here.]

* * *

A second preclusion was found applicable. That preclusion appears in sec. 404.406(1) and (2), Stats. Unlike the preclusion first referred to, this section estops the maker of a check from asserting its claim when it has failed in its duty to discover forgeries or alterations *after* the return of the bank statement and the paid items.

It was undisputed that the Heritage Bank sent Winkie, Inc., a monthly statement of account accompanied by the cancelled checks. Under sec. 404.406(1), Stats., Winkie, Inc., was obligated to "exercise reasonable care and promptness to examine the statement and items to discover his unauthorized signature or any alteration on an item * * *." There is no contention that Winkie, Inc., exercised reasonable care and promptness, nor could there be, for the undisputed facts show that, beyond the minimal steps apparently taken by Lyle Britton and discussed above, there had been no examination of the statements and returned items for at least eight years.

Thus, irrespective of the presumptive liability of the bank for its payment of checks not properly payable, Winkie, Inc., was precluded by the provisions of sec. 404.406(2)(a), Stats., from asserting any claim in respect to unauthorized signatures or alterations if the bank established also that it suffered a loss by reason

4. *Winkie, Inc. v. Heritage Bank of Whitefish Bay,* 92 Wis.2d 784, 285 N.W.2d 899 (Ct. App.1979).

of the customer's failure. For this preclusion to apply, the bank itself must be free of negligence. Sec. 404.406(3). As stated above, the bank, in a technical sense sufficient to satisfy the Uniform Commercial Code, "suffers a loss" whenever it pays a check or other item not properly payable because it cannot charge the item to the customer. Furthermore, a bank could prove that it suffered a loss because a delay by the drawer in failing to report forgeries or altered checks makes it impossible for the bank to promptly proceed against the wrongdoer to recover the losses. In the case before the court, Doris Britton's forgeries went unreported for eight years. The record shows that, when the forgeries and alterations were reported, she was insolvent and uncollectible. Had the customer acted promptly in 1965, the collection prospects of the bank against Doris Britton would have been immeasurably improved. *See* Hawkland, *A Transactional Guide to the Uniform Commercial Code* 407 (1964).

However, in the absence of whatever preclusions may be appropriate in the instant case, the Heritage Bank would sustain the loss in respect to all checks which were altered or which bore unauthorized signatures.

Sec. 404.406(2)(b), Stats., establishes a specific preclusion where the forgeries and alterations are made by the same wrongdoer. That section provides for a preclusion: [quoting]

Hawkland states that sec. 404.406(2)(b), Stats.:

> "* * * conclusively assumes that forgeries and alterations committed by the same wrongdoer are made possible by the customer's failure to discover and report earlier mischief, and the customer is precluded from asserting these subsequent alterations and forgeries even if the bank cannot prove that it suffered a loss by reason of this failure." *Hawkland, supra*, at 407.[6]

The preclusion of sec. 404.406(1) and (2), Stats., does not apply if the bank is negligent. However, the trial court's finding, sustained by the Court of Appeals, was that the bank was not negligent in respect to the unauthorized maker's signatures or alterations by Doris Britton. Because the bank was not negligent, and because the same wrongdoer was responsible for each of the items not properly payable, and because no notification was given to the bank within fourteen days after the first forged item was returned to Winkie, Inc., Winkie is precluded from any claim against Heritage Bank for checks forged or altered by Doris Britton.

* * *

We conclude that the customer, Winkie, Inc., was not entitled to recover on any of the checks. Decision affirmed. [Some footnotes omitted.]

Notes

1. Assume that you represent a bank that "truncates checks," that is, the checks are copied and then destroyed by a collecting bank and are not returned to the payor. Accordingly no check is ever made available to customer. The customer

6. *See also* Official Comment 3 to U.C.C. sec. 4–406 (rule of customer's preclusion under sub. (2)(b) "follows substantial case law that payment of an additional item or items bearing an unauthorized signature or alteration by the same wrongdoer *is a loss suffered by the bank traceable to the customer's failure to exercise reasonable care in examining his statement and notifying the bank of objections to it.*" (Emphasis supplied) The rule is designed to keep down losses caused by the opportunity for a wrongdoer to repeat his misdeeds; "to avoid dispute a specific time limit for action by the customer is designated, namely fourteen calendar days"). *See also* Bailey, *Brady on Bank Checks*, sec. 26.13, p. 26–7 (5th ed. 1979).

simply gets a monthly printout showing the date of the transaction and the amount of the check. Does that foreclose the bank's use of 4–406?

2. Examine 4–406 for the various interpretive difficulties that lie in it. The *Winkie* case demonstrates some of those. Can you see others?

Problem 25–7

Ney was a twenty-year trusted employee of a small church in Tennessee. Ney wrote checks, kept the books and accounts. Late in life, Ney developed a curious passion for dog-track betting, and since financial secretaries of small churches don't make much money, he decided to borrow a bit from the church. Over a year he wrote about 50 checks on the church account to himself as payee and indorsed them to the nearby dog track. Since the checks required two signatures, he forged a trustee's signature. Payor bank paid the checks and church sued Payor. What arguments can be made by both sides? UCC 3–406, 4–401, 4–406.

Like UCC 3–406 and 4–406, section 3–405 is an exception to the general rule that forged indorsements are ineffective to pass title or to authorize a drawee's payment. In effect 3–405 codifies the proposition that certain behavior is negligent and thus renders signatures resulting from that behavior effective against the negligent party. It takes the position that the drawer should bear the loss that results from his being foolish enough to write a check to an impostor. One should also supervise his payroll and other accounts payable clerk and should not be permitted to put that loss on the bank who almost certainly is not the least cost-risk avoider.

A potential problem under UCC 3–405 inheres in the definition of "impostor." Comment 2 states that:

> "Impostor" refers to impersonation, and does not extend to a false representation that the party is the authorized agent of the payee. The maker or drawer who takes the precaution of making the instrument payable to the principal is entitled to have his indorsement.

Thus UCC 3–405(1)(a) does not cover one who represents himself as an agent of General Motors and procures a check payable to the order of General Motors; but it does apply if the party appears on behalf of a third party who is also an impostor and procures the check in the name of that third person.

Comment 3 to UCC 3–405 illustrates the application of UCC 3–405(1)(b) as follows:

> * * * The test stated is not whether the named payee is "fictitious," but whether the signer intends that he shall have no interest in the instrument. The following situations illustrate the application of the subsection.
>
> a. The drawer of a check, for his own reason, makes it payable to P knowing that P does not exist.
>
> b. The drawer makes the check payable in the name of P. A person named P exists, but the drawer does not know it.
>
> c. The drawer makes the check payable to P, an existing person whom he knows, intending to receive the money himself and that P shall have no interest in the check.
>
> d. The treasurer of a corporation draws its check payable to P, who to the knowledge of the treasurer does not exist.

e. The treasurer of a corporation draws its check payable to P. P exists but the treasurer has fraudulently added his name to the payroll intending that he shall not receive the check.

f. The president and the treasurer of a corporation both sign its check payable to P. P does not exist. The treasurer knows it but the president does not.

g. The same facts as f, except that P exists and the treasurer knows it, but intends that P shall have no interest in the check.

In all the cases stated an indorsement by any person in the name of P is effective.

Section 3–405(1)(c) deals with padded payroll cases. The major difficulty with the section concerns its scope. Section 3–405(1)(c) applies only to "agent[s] or employee[s]" of the employer who has "supplied him with the name of the payee intending the latter to have no such interest." The intention of UCC 3–405(1)(c) is to impose on drawers the losses traceable to acts of employees uniquely in a position to steal from the corporation by causing checks to be issued on the corporation.

SNUG HARBOR REALTY CO. v. FIRST NAT'L BANK OF TOMS RIVER, N.J.

Superior Court of New Jersey, Appellate Division, 1969.
105 N.J.Super. 572, 253 A.2d 581, *affirmed by Supreme Court of New Jersey on opinion below,* 54 N.J. 95, 253 A.2d 545 (1969).

LEWIS, J.A.D.

In a suit by plaintiff Snug Harbor Realty Co. against defendants the First National Bank of Toms River, N.J., and The Trust Company of Ocean County, the trial court, at the close of plaintiff's case and, after noting that plaintiff voluntarily abandoned its direct cause of action against the trust company, granted the motion of defendant First National and entered judgment in its favor against plaintiff. The latter appeals.

The matter is before us on an "Agreed Statement in Lieu of Record" which reveals the following basic facts:

Snug Harbor, a construction company, maintained a system under which parties asserting claims against it would submit invoices which were then given to its superintendent, Joseph Magee, for investigation. It was Magee's responsibility to make the necessary inspection and, upon being satisfied that the alleged work was done or materials furnished, to initial the invoices and forward them to the company's bookkeeper for verification of the contract obligations and the preparation of checks payable to the claimants. Checks drawn on First National were then signed by the company's authorized official. Certain checks were picked up by Magee for delivery to the respective payees who authorized the "pick-up." Between January 10, 1964 and August 13, 1965, Magee converted to his own personal use 132 checks, totaling $27,516.27, by forging the indorsements of the payees and cashing the checks.

The trial court found as a matter of law that a provision of the Uniform Commercial Code was "dispositive" and accordingly, that the bank should be relieved of any liability to plaintiff. The pertinent section of the Code, N.J.S. 12A:3–405(1)(c), provides:

"(1) An indorsement by any person in the name of a named payee is effective if * * *

"(c) an agent or employee of the maker or drawer has supplied him with the name of the payee intending the latter to have no such interest."

We find, in the circumstances here presented, that plaintiff proved a prima facie case and that the cited Code provision is inapplicable.

Magee, an unfaithful employee of the construction company, did not supply to his employer "the name of the payee intending the latter to have no such interest." To the contrary, the payees were bona fide creditors of the company who had respectively submitted their invoices for work performed or materials furnished.

It is thus plain that judgment was improvidently entered. The matter should proceed to a plenary hearing for a judicial determination of the merits of plaintiff's complaint in light of any defenses appropriately raised by the defendant bank.

* * *

Reversed and remanded for new trial.

Problem 25–8

On March 25, 1963 First National Bank received in the mail a "Credit Application for Property Improvement Loan" containing the purported signatures of Eva and William Soult. The bank had no physical or personal contact with William Soult. After a brief credit investigation by the bank, it sent a promissory note in the amount of $2,493.92 to William Soult. The note was returned by mail containing the purported signatures of William and Eva Soult. The bank then forwarded its check for $2,493.92 by mail to William and Eva Soult; that check was promptly cashed. The bank received 36 monthly installments of $41.57. Subsequently the bank approved a second and third "Credit Application" in the same fashion. The proceeds check from the third credit application was presented to Central Federal for deposit to the account of Mrs. Joan Bernadotte, daughter of the Soults. The check bore the purported indorsements of William and Eva Soult; it was accepted for deposit and the proceeds credited to Mrs. Bernadotte's account. First National Bank paid the check. After First National received five installments on the third loan, Eva Soult died. William denied any knowledge of the loans and stated that all of the signatures in his name were forgeries. Who are the possible defendants in a suit by First National Bank and what are the arguments in each case? UCC 3–417, 3–404, 3–405.

Problem 25–9

1. Soult, a trusted employee who makes up the payroll every Friday afternoon, adds the name of a fictitious person to the payroll. The treasurer is a busy person and signs fifty or sixty checks (or they are signed automatically) and the check eventually comes back to Soult. Soult signs the name of the fictitious payee as an indorsement and the bank pays. Drawer insists that bank recredit the account. Who wins? UCC 3–405(1)(c).

2. Suppose in 1. above instead of a fictitious name, Soult supplied the name of a real person. What then?

3. Suppose the fictitious name was supplied instead by a clerk in the accounts payable department who submits the name of a fictitious supplier to the accounts payable clerk who then adds the name to a list of checks to be drawn and causes it to

be drawn by a third clerk. Drawer sues to have his account recredited. What result?

What purpose does UCC 3–405 serve? It makes people more careful and places the risk where it belongs. In impostor cases the drawer can and should require identification before he gives a check. In padded payroll cases, the comment says, in effect, that the loss should fall upon the employer as a risk of his business enterprise rather than upon the subsequent holder or drawee. The employer is in a better position to prevent such forgeries by reasonable care in the selection and supervision of employees. If the employer cannot prevent the forgeries it can at least insure, and such fidelity insurance is a proper expense of the business. Can you make an argument for the opposite conclusion, for the proposition that it might be more efficient to put the loss on the bank?

PRUDENTIAL INSURANCE CO. OF AMERICA v. MARINE NAT'L EXCHANGE BANK OF MILWAUKEE

United States District Court, Eastern District Wisconsin, 1974.
371 F.Supp. 1002.

GORDON, DISTRICT JUDGE. This matter is before me on the defendant's motion for summary judgment. No issue exists as to any material fact.

The plaintiff, the Prudential Insurance Company of America (Prudential) issued a check in the amount of $20,000 payable to one of its policy owners, a Hilda Nissen. Through a fraudulent scheme, a Prudential employee and agent, James Williamson, had supplied Mrs. Nissen's name, intending that she have no interest in the instrument. Prudential seeks to recover from the defendant, Marine National Exchange Bank, the sum of $20,000 which that bank paid to Mr. Williamson's alleged bookie, a Mr. Plotkin, over Mrs. Nissen's forged blank endorsement. I conclude that the defendant's motion for summary judgment should be granted.

Section 403.405(1)(c), Wis.Stats., is applicable to "padded payroll" factual situations. That section of the Uniform Commercial Code (UCC) provides that:

> "(1) An indorsement by any person in the name of a named payee is effective if:
>
> "* * *
>
> "(c) An agent or employee of the maker or drawer has supplied him with the name of the payee intending the latter to have no such interest."

To the extent that a cashing bank is subject to the "good faith" requirement of § 401.203, its defense under § 403.405(1)(c) is, of course, not absolute. However, the plaintiff has not alleged or argued that the defendant cashed the check in bad faith or that it was not a holder in due course; these questions are not before this court.

I believe that Prudential's position, that Marine is barred from raising the defense under § 403.405(1)(c) by its alleged negligence in paying over the forged endorsement, is without merit for at least two reasons. First, comment 4 to § 3–405 of the Uniform Commercial Code, now § 403.405, Wis.Stats., flatly states that, in a "padded payroll" case like the one presented here, the loss should fall upon the employer of an unfaithful employee; no qualification for the negligence of the payor bank is indicated. The fact that the draftsmen of the UCC consciously allocated the loss incurred in this type of situation to the employer, suggests the irrelevancy of the bank's alleged negligence.

Secondly, conspicuous by its absence in § 403.405 is a requirement that the paying or collecting bank exercise ordinary care. Compare, e.g., §§ 403.406 and 404.406, Wis.Stats. It is clear that where the draftsmen of the UCC used a particular phrase in certain instances, or omitted that phrase in another, they had a different result in mind. See In re Hardin, 458 F.2d 938 (7th Cir. 1972). Under these circumstances, I conclude that a determination as to the bank's alleged negligence is not relevant; absent a showing of bad faith on the part of the defendant, the plaintiff cannot avoid the defense provided in § 403.405(1)(c), Wis.Stats.

Therefore, It is ordered that the defendant's motion for summary judgment be and hereby is granted.

It is also ordered that the instant action be and hereby is dismissed.

McCONNICO v. THIRD NAT'L BANK IN NASHVILLE

Supreme Court of Tennessee, 1973.
499 S.W.2d 874.

Appeal from Chancery Court, Davidson County.

HUMPHREYS, JUSTICE. This is a suit by the trustee in bankruptcy of W.T. Hardison & Company against the defendant bank which cashed or received for deposit ten checks drawn by W.T. Hardison & Company or payable to that Company. The complainant contends that Tom Hardison, Jr., also referred to as W.T. Hardison and W.T. Hardison, IV, misappropriated the funds of W.T. Hardison & Company by converting the checks in question or their proceeds to his own use, and that the defendant bank participated in said conversion by cashing or receiving the checks for deposit in Hardison's personal account and then permitting him to withdraw the proceeds so deposited. The transactions complained of occurred over a period of three years from February 24, 1967 to August 15, 1969.

Nine of the ten checks upon which the complainant based his claim were checks issued by W.T. Hardison & Company drawn on its account at the First American Bank and signed by W.T. Hardison as president of that Company. The other check involved was issued by Merrill Lynch, Pierce, Fenner & Smith, payable to the order of W.T. Hardison and Company.

The transactions involving the checks can be divided into four separate categories.

(1) A check in the amount of $15,000.00 of W.T. Hardison and Company payable to Cash and deposited by Tom Hardison, Jr., in his personal checking account in the defendant bank.

(2) Two checks of W.T. Hardison and Company payable to Cash and negotiated for cash at the defendant bank by B & B Liquor Store, a transferee of Tom Hardison, Jr.

(3) A check issued by Merrill Lynch, Pierce, Fenner & Smith to W.T. Hardison & Company endorsed for the company by W.T. Hardison and deposited in his personal checking account at the defendant bank.

(4) Checks issued by W.T. Hardison and Company payable to the order of Clear Creek Coal Company, signed by W.T. Hardison and endorsed by him in the name of Clear Creek Coal Company, not delivered to Clear Creek Coal Company but deposited by Hardison in his personal checking account in the defendant bank.

The cause came to be heard before the Chancellor on the pleading, depositions and oral testimony of witnesses, stipulations of the parties, documentary evidence, briefs, and arguments of counsel resulting in a judgment for the plaintiff in the full amount of the ten checks and interest totaling $116,333.73. The Court of Appeals sustained the Chancellor as to the checks payable to the Clear Creek Coal Company, but reversed and remanded as to the two checks cashed for B & B Liquor Store, the $15,000.00 check payable to Cash and deposited by Hardison in his personal account with the defendant bank, and the check of Merrill Lynch, Pierce, Fenner and Smith payable to W.T. Hardison and Company, endorsed by Hardison and deposited by him in his personal account with the defendant.

* * *

The facts in this case are not in dispute; however, the parties do not agree on the inferences and conclusions to be drawn from those facts and the conduct of the parties. In view of the stipulations however, it will be unnecessary to enter into a lengthy discussion of testimony, there being no material determinative facts seriously in dispute, and those stipulations accurately representing the controversy. Those stipulations are as follows:

* * *

(8) That the checks, Exhibit 2 to the stipulation, were drawn on the account of W.T. Hardison & Co. at First American National Bank of Nashville and executed by W.T. Hardison as President of W.T. Hardison & Co., payable to Clear Creek Coal Company of Monterey, Tennessee, and such checks were not delivered to said Coal Company but were endorsed by Tom Hardison, Jr., with the words "Clear Creek Coal Co." and deposited to the account of Tom Hardison, Jr. in the Third National Bank, and

(9) That each of these checks, payable to Clear Creek Coal Company, had written thereon, "For Deposit Only 39–07–906–6" and was paid by the First American National Bank to the Third National Bank and all proceeds were withdrawn from Third National Bank by Tom Hardison, Jr.

* * *

(13) That the First American National Bank of Nashville was the bank upon which each check payable to Clear Creek Coal Company was drawn and upon which the two checks bearing the endorsement of B & B Liquor Store and the checks referred to in paragraph 10 hereof were drawn, and the defendant, Third National Bank, endorsed each of the aforesaid checks, prior endorsements guaranteed, transmitted them through the clearing house to the drawee bank for payment and received payment therefor.

* * *

It is important to note at this point that there is no claim of fraud or dishonesty on the part of the defendant bank in the transactions herein involved. The trustee merely contends that the defendant bank is liable on said checks because it cashed or received them for deposit to Hardison's personal account and permitted him to withdraw the proceeds for his personal use contrary to accepted banking practices. Further, its liability stems from its negligent failure to investigate the transactions in question which were out of the ordinary and conducted in such a manner so as to put the defendant bank on notice of such irregularities.

The defendant bank asserts the following defenses in denying liability:

(1) At the time of each transaction the defendant had no knowledge of any fraud, misappropriation of funds or other wrongdoing by Hardison;

(2) Those checks which defendant cashed or accepted as deposits were received in good faith, in reliance on the validity of the maker's signature and the legal effectiveness of the endorsements, and insists that it was the holder in due course in good faith and for value;

(3) That as to the defendant, the endorsements by Hardison of the payee's name on the checks payable to Clear Creek Coal Company were effective endorsements, since those checks were signed by Hardison on behalf of W.T. Hardison & Company, intending that the payee have no interest in such checks;

(4) That the defendant received the check of Merrill Lynch, Pierce, Fenner & Smith, which was payable to the order of W.T. Hardison & Company and endorsed by Tom Hardison for his Company (with authority to do so) and for deposit to his personal account with the defendant as a holder in due course, without any knowledge of fraud, misappropriation or bad faith;

(5) That the acts of Tom Hardison, Jr. in connection with said checks, were the acts of W.T. Hardison & Company since he acted within the scope of his authority in signing, endorsing and transferring said checks;

(6) That all of the said checks drawn on the W.T. Hardison & Company account at the First American National Bank were paid by the drawee bank to which defendant guaranteed prior endorsements and such payment is final in favor of defendant as a holder in due course;

(7) That Tom Hardison, Jr., the sole stockholder of W.T. Hardison & Company, its President, chief executive and financial officer, so controlled and dominated the corporation that it merged into his individuality and became a mere instrument of his will so that his acts were the acts of the corporation and were authorized by the said corporation with the consent of its shareholders.

* * *

The last category involves six checks in the aggregate amount of $68,048.45 drawn on the account of W.T. Hardison & Company signed by W.T. Hardison, Jr., payable to the Clear Creek Coal Company, endorsed by Hardison in the name of the Clear Creek Coal Company, and deposited to his personal account in the defendant bank.

As to these checks, the defendant bank asserts two primary defenses. First, the defendant contends that since Hardison was authorized to withdraw corporate funds payable to himself, he had no fraudulent intent in endorsing these checks in the name of the payee as he was merely accomplishing, in an unusual manner, that which he was authorized to do. Second, the defendant contends that the endorsements were sufficient to pass title to the defendant as a holder in due course because Hardison, the drawer, intended the payee to have no interest in the check. See, T.C.A. § 47–3–405(1)(b). The Court of Appeals held that the endorsements were outright forgeries not effective to pass title to the defendant, that there was nothing in the record that evidenced an intent by the agents who prepared the checks that the said Coal Company should not have an interest in them, that the defendant bank was negligent in cashing said checks, that the Coal Company was damaged and sustained a loss by the transactions, that a bank receiving and collecting a check upon a forged or unauthorized endorsement is liable to the payee for the proceeds, that where the payee is a bona fide creditor of the drawer, the bank is not relieved of liability to the drawer on the theory that it was not intended that payee have an interest in the instrument, and that the Trustee, standing in the shoes of a bankrupt corporation, can recover on behalf of the corporation and its creditors.

We agree with the Court of Appeals that these endorsements were outright forgeries. T.C.A. § 39–1701 provides that "[F]orgery is the fraudulent making or alteration of any writing to the prejudice of another's rights." The president of the Coal Company testified that W.T. Hardison & Company had been a customer of his company for some five years prior to the time the Hardison Company went into bankruptcy and that the current balance due was "about $33,000.00 or $34,000.00". Further, the records of the bankrupt reflect that the checks in question were credited against the indebtedness of the bankrupt to the Coal Company. Under these facts, it is clear that the Clear Creek Coal Company was damaged and did sustain a loss by the unauthorized cashing of these checks. This is particularly true in view of the fact that the indebtedness was credited on the Hardison Company books. As such, the unauthorized endorsements fall within our statutory definition of forgery.

However, that is not to say that the unauthorized endorsements could not have been effective to pass title as inferred by the Court of Appeals. T.C.A. § 47–3–405(1)(b) specifically provides that "an endorsement by any person in the name of a named payee is effective if a person signing as or on behalf of a maker or drawer intends the payee to have no interest in the instrument." Paragraph 3c of the Official Code Comment to that section states as an example:

> "3. Subsection (1)(b) restates the substance of the original Subsection 9(3). The test stated is not whether the named payee is 'fictitious,' but whether the signer intends that he shall have no interest in the instrument. The following situations illustrate the application of the subsection. * * *
>
> c. The drawer makes the check payable to P, an existing person whom he knows, intending to receive the money himself and that P shall have no interest in the check."

Further, it is clear that the statute is to be applied to unauthorized or forged signatures as subsection (2) provides: "Nothing in this section shall affect the criminal or civil liability of the person so endorsing."

The situation then is precisely the situation mentioned in paragraph 3c of the Official Code Comments to T.C.A. § 47–3–405. The only element which could possibly be in doubt is the intent of the drawer. While intent cannot be presumed, the circumstantial evidence establishes the necessary intent. Hardison signed and endorsed in the name of the payee six checks which he deposited to his personal account. This was a consistent pattern of conduct over fourteen months. Absent some showing to the contrary, the only inference to be drawn is that he intended to use the proceeds himself and intended the payee to have no interest therein. It follows then that the endorsement was effective to pass title to the defendant.

Having established that title passed to the defendant bank, its status as a holder in due course then comes into question. Value and good faith again not being in question, only notice of claim or defense will be discussed. See T.C.A. § 47–3–302. As stated previously in the discussion of notice, negligence goes to the notice requirement of T.C.A. § 47–3–302(1) as defined by 47–3–304 and 47–1–201(25). T.C.A. § 47–3–304(1)(a) provides as follows:

> "1. The purchaser has notice of a claim or defense if
>
> "(a) the instrument is so incomplete, bears such visible evidence of forgery or alteration, *or is otherwise so irregular as to call into question its validity,* terms or ownership or to create an ambiguity as to the party to pay; or * * *."
> (Emphasis added).

In the instant case, there were six checks of W.T. Hardison & Company signed by the president, W.T. Hardison, payable to the Clear Creek Coal Company with the purported endorsement of that company and the following restrictive endorsement: "For Deposit Only 39–07–906–6." From the face of the instrument, it could be determined that the Clear Creek Coal Company, designated payee, was depositing checks in the personal account of the president of the drawer corporation who had himself signed the checks as drawer. Such transactions are highly irregular and call into question their validity. Additional factual circumstances bearing on the question of notice in the instant case are the deposition of Mr. Warren Gray, one of the defendant bank's executive officers who stated the transactions were unusual and should have caused further inquiry, the fact that the defendant bank failed to communicate at any time with the Coal Company regarding these unusual transactions, and the Teller's Manual of the defendant bank which provides: "Checks payable to corporations cannot be cashed. These must be deposited." Presumably this means that such checks must be deposited in the account of the payee, not the personal account of the drawer.

While facially these latter transactions may appear the same as the previous ones, particularly the check from Merrill Lynch to W.T. Hardison & Company, endorsed by Hardison and deposited to his personal account, that is simply not the case. In that instance and the others heretofore cited, the defendant simply did not have actual knowledge or notice from the face of the instrument that a fiduciary was negotiating the instruments for his own benefit and in violation of his duty. As previously pointed out, had the defendant bank checked further, they would have discovered that Hardison was authorized to do what he did. In the case of the checks payable to the Coal Company, however, the defendant bank received notice from the face of the instruments that the transactions were highly irregular thereby calling into question their validity. Had the bank then checked further, they certainly would have discovered that Hardison was not authorized to endorse checks in the name of the Clear Creek Company. It results, therefore, that the defendant bank had notice of an irregularity on the face of instruments payable to the Clear Creek Coal Company, that such notice precludes them from holder in due course status, that their breach of duty resulted in serious detriment to the corporation's creditors, and that they are liable to the Trustee in Bankruptcy on these instruments.

* * *

It results, therefore, having considered the assignments of error of both parties, that the judgment of the Court of Appeals disallowing recovery for the first three categories of checks and allowing recovery for the fourth category involving the forged endorsement of the Clear Creek Coal Company is affirmed, that the trustee has the right to maintain the action, that he may recover the entire amount involved in the fraudulent transactions involving the forged endorsement of the Coal Company, and that recovery is for the benefit of all creditors having claims provable under the act. The cause is remanded for such other and further orders and decrees as may be necessary or proper in conformity with this opinion.

DYER, C.J., CHATTIN and MCCANLESS, JJ., and WILSON, SPECIAL JUSTICE, concur.

Note

Prudential and *McConnico* are apparently in conflict. Can you reconcile the outcomes?

CHAPTER TWENTY-SIX

BANK LIABILITY FOR DELAY IN HANDLING CHECKS

SECTION 1. INTRODUCTION

The cases in this chapter, and many other cases in our courts each year deal with an inevitable consequence of the archaic mode by which we transfer wealth in the United States. Despite the fact that the large industrial and financial corporations have long gone to electronic (non-paper) transfer of money and that such transfers have made inroads via debit cards and credit cards on consumer transactions, a large share of all transactions continues to be by check.

The persistence of checks in the face of apparently more efficient modes of transfer can be explained by several factors. Many transferors have no access to electronic means. Transfer by check is probably easier than an arrangement for a special wire transfer through a bank even for a large commercial company who is seeking to pay an infrequent customer. When consumers are paying merchants who do not take credit cards or merchants who are not close at hand, it will often be easier to use a check than another mode of transfer. So in some settings the use of a check is more efficient.

There may also be some dark or less honorable explanations. One is the use of the "float." Float arises when the payee takes the check in at least provisional settlement for a debt at a time when the bank upon which it is drawn has not yet debited the account. Thus, in effect, the depositor doubles his money. The bank treats him as though he has his money in the bank and the merchant treats him as though he has paid. In "aggressive cash management" of the kind that got E.F. Hutton in trouble in 1985, and of the kind practiced by many corporations, one sees manipulation of the float and a doubling of one's money carried to a refined and arguably illegal extreme. In any event, many commercial actors in our society from the lowly consumer who expects his paycheck to be deposited in his account day after tomorrow, to the most sophisticated commercial company understand the virtue of, and seek to use, the benefits of float. Any system that reduces the delay diminishes this possibility. So we find not just E.F. Hutton, but presumably the consumer, hostile to ideas that will remove the possibility of float.

To minimize the inefficiencies that inhere in the transfer of funds by paper, Articles 3 and 4 prescribe a rigid, explicit and generally short time for action on the part of each of the participants in the check transfer and payment process. In Chapter Twenty-Three we studied Article 3 provisions on the time one has to decide whether to pay a note, the necessity for notice after dishonor and other provisions on timely action.

Here the student will see the complicated set of rules that govern the payor bank's activity and the less precise rules that govern the collecting bank's obligations. Most of the cases in this chapter arise in one way or another out one party's inability to pay a debt. Most of the cases here involve a check drawn on insufficient funds. Generally they may be regarded as "NSF" liability cases.

With some exceptions the persons here are not out-and-out thieves; at worst they are kiters, persons once thought to be of good character who have gradually slipped into irreversible debt.

In Section 2 we provide an exposition of the check collection process. The student must understand how checks are transferred among banks and how banks deal with checks in the counting rooms, or the student has no hope of understanding the cases and legal issues that follow.

Section 3 deals with the obligations of the payor bank. These are doubtless the most important, for most of the losses here fall at the doorstep of the payor. In the fourth section we deal with the collecting bank. Usually the collecting bank is in the position of a Pontius Pilate who can push the liability up or downstream. In section 5, we will deal with documentary drafts. These are drafts, sometimes written on check forms, that are always accompanied by some additional document, a stock certificate, a bill of sale, a certificate of title to a vehicle. Finally we deal with a handful of tangential problems.

Before the students set off to study the payor and collecting banks' responsibility, they should ask themselves what system might eliminate these problems and why they arise in the system as it exists? Why do we not have an electronic funds network that will transfer cash from one's bank account to a merchant without the necessity of an intervening piece of paper? The technology is available and comparatively inexpensive, yet it has made only modest inroads in many areas of consumer and commercial transactions. Is it merely the users' attachment to float that precludes such a system? At the other extreme it is conceivable that we could run a revenue exchange system without such short and rigid rules. What would be the consequence of that?

SECTION 2. CHECK COLLECTION—A NECESSARY DIGRESSION

The student should read the material in this section to get an understanding of the cases that follow. However, only after one has read a few of those cases will the relevance of this material become fully clear. Because certain features of the underlying system varies from place to place and changes from day to day, not all of the materials that follow, which were written over a period of twenty years, will be accurate and none will accurately describe the situation at any particular time in every place in the United States. Thus, the student should understand that what follows are general descriptions, still accurate in most ways. They should not be regarded as describing a day's operating practices at any particular place.

BUNN, BANK COLLECTIONS UNDER THE UNIFORM COMMERCIAL CODE, 1964 Wis.L.Rev. 278, 278–282.

"I. THE DEPOSITOR AND HIS BANK

* * *

"* * * John Depositor has just received a check, $250.00, from a distant city, being a month's rent on some property he owns there. He proposes to deposit it in his checking account in Hometown Bank. How will he go about it?

"* * * [John will deposit it by mail or in person at Hometown Bank.]

* * *

"[T]he $250 credit which Hometown Bank has added to John's account 'is provisional' [UCC 4–201(1)], and if the *item* (the check) bounces the Bank may (and will 'charge back the amount of any credit given for the item to its customer's account or obtain refund from its customer' (that's John). [UCC 4–

212(1).] Only when the settlement for the item received by Hometown Bank 'is or becomes final' does the credit it has given John 'firm up'. [UCC 4–212 and 4–213(3).] That will happen, in most cases, upon *final payment* of the item by the Payor Bank. [UCC 4–213(2); See also 4–211. * * *] And when Hometown Bank has received a final settlement and 'has had a reasonable time to learn that the settlement is final' then (and not until then) John has a right to draw against the credit. [UCC 4–213(4)(a).] If he draws before that the Bank *may* honor his check, although it is not bound to. Then, if the item bounces, he will owe the Bank some money. [UCC 4–401, 4–212(1).]

"May I try to say this very simply, even if not quite accurately: When John deposited his check, his Bank did not become his debtor, yet. First it became his agent, to collect it. When it did collect it (since this was a *deposit,* not simply a collection) it would become his debtor.

"In the meantime, since neither his Bank nor he has any way of knowing that the check will *certainly* be paid, the credit that they gave him is provisional. If the check bounces, the Bank will take the credit back, and if in the meantime they have paid his checks against it, he will owe them money. But since a very high proportion (well over 99%) of all checks drawn in the United States are paid on presentation, he and his Bank proceed on the assumption that this one too will very probably be paid. That is why it is appropriate to give him *any* credit right away, on his deposit. That credit will cease to be provisional and the Bank will *really* be his debtor, when the Bank gets payment for the check. Until that happens they are Agent for collection; the check is his, not theirs; and if it bounces it will bounce right back to him.

"All this is straight and clear. But now you must put with it something else, which to some people, on the first time over, seems inconsistent with it.

"Hometown Bank, at once on John's making his deposit, is Holder of the check. (Remember, he *indorsed* it, whether restrictively or not.) [UCC 1–201(20).] That means that Hometown Bank may transfer it (to another Bank, as subagent for collection), surrender it on payment, or enforce payment (by suit) in its own name. (The last it is not likely to do: if the check bounces to it, it will bounce it on to John. But it does have that power, if needed). [UCC 3–301. Note that all this is stated to be true 'whether or not (the Holder) is the owner.'] In other words, an agent for collection is very often Holder, and when it is, may present, collect, give good receipts, bring suit if needed, or transfer to a subagent, all without departing from its status and duty as an agent. If this is not clear, stop and think it over: the Bank collection law cannot be understood until this combination, Agent and Holder both, at the same time, seems natural and right. (Remember that a law firm also often has both power and duty, as an agent, to collect a client's claim. That doesn't mean it owns the claim.)

"Generally, while the check is in process of collection, the Depositary Bank will be an agent merely, and will have no property interest at all in the check. But if it permits Depositor to draw out part or all of the provisional credit created by the deposit of the check it gets rights *in the check,* a security interest to the extent of the amount withdrawn. [UCC 4–208(1)(a).] Then, if the check ultimately bounces, and Depositor cannot make it good, the Bank has in its own right a claim against the Drawer [UCC 3–413(2)], and is probably, to that extent, a holder in due course [UCC 4–209, 3–302(4).]

II. PRESENTMENT: SENDING

"Assume that we are the staff of Hometown Bank, charged with the duty of collecting not only the check that John Depositor deposited this morning but all the checks that were deposited up to twelve-noon today. How will we go about it?

"We know that our employer is subject to a duty of good faith and ordinary care [UCC 4–103(1), 4–202(1)(a)], and must use a 'reasonably prompt method' to send items out for presentation to Payors. [UCC 4–204(1).] We also know that most checks are paid without dispute on presentation. So we don't expect much trouble. Obviously, what is a 'reasonably prompt method' to get the check from us to the Drawee depends on geography and on institutional arrangements.

"There are several possibilities:

"(1) Hometown Bank may itself be the Drawee and Payor. In that case we don't need any more presentment: the Holder presented it himself when he deposited it this morning. It is now up to Hometown Bank to decide whether it is good and should be paid. For making that decision it has the balance of today and all tomorrow. [UCC 4–301(1) and (2), 4–104(1)(h).] What we should do is pass the check on, now, to the person or department in charge of such decision. [For what that person or department will do, see III, below.]

"(2) The Drawee (Payor Bank) may be across the street, in a town where no clearing house exists. In that case we will make a bundle of all the checks we hold, drawn on that bank, and one of us will walk across the street, at the agreed or customary time, and present them all at once.

"(3) The Drawee and Hometown may both be members of a City Clearing House. In that case Clearing House Rules will be our guide. [UCC 4–103(2) and (3).] Under them, no doubt, before we quit tonight we will bundle all the checks that Hometown holds for presentation to other Member Banks, one bundle for each other Bank, with an adding machine tape and a total for each bundle; at clearing time tomorrow (maybe 9 a.m.) Hometown's representative will take the bundles to the Clearings; there under the eye of the manager of Clearings he will exchange bundles with the representatives of each one of the other Member Banks, and will determine, for each other Bank, which way the balance runs and its amount (this is the *apparent* balance, on the assumption that all checks in both bundles will be found good and paid). On its representative's return from Clearings, Hometown will pay or receive payment of these Balances in accordance with the rules. [These may say, i.e., 'Balances shall be settled by twelve-noon on the day of Clearing by transfer of credits in the Federal Reserve Bank.'] Meanwhile the checks brought back by Hometown's representative from Clearings (those in which Hometown is Drawee and apparently Payor) will be sorted, and the Bookkeeping Department, or whatever it is called, will go to work to determine which checks are good and which are not. For that purpose they have a limited time; checks unpaid must be returned to the Presenting Bank no later than the rules provide (maybe 3:30 p.m. on the day *after* the Clearing). Through all this, until the deadline for returns has passed, the payments made by the settlement of balances remain provisional; checks returned within the time permitted by the Rules must be refunded by the Presenting Bank. [UCC 4–301.] And so, by quitting time on the day following the Clearings, all checks included in the Clearings of the day before, and not returned, have been settled for by set off and by payments of the balances; the Rules will very likely say they are 'considered paid.'

"(4) The Drawee-Payor Bank may be in another city, but it and Hometown may have special relations with each other—i.e. both are branches of the same statewide Bank, both are owned (their shares, that is) by the same Bank Holding Company, or they simply have much business with each other and know each other well. In that case Hometown will very likely mail the check directly to the Drawee [See UCC 4–204(2)(a)] and ask for payment either by credit to an account or by one of the approved methods of remittance in such cases. [UCC 4–211.]

"(5) The Payor may be in another city and have no special relation with Hometown. In that case Hometown will be quite likely to employ the efficient and inexpensive collection and clearing system of the Federal Reserve Banks. [See Fed.Res.Bd.Reg.J.] It will send the check to the Reserve Bank of its district for collection and credit; that Bank will send it to the Reserve Bank of the Payor's district; the latter will send it direct to the Payor for payment, charging the payor's account accordingly. This charge, and the charges and credits all along the line, are provisional at first [UCC 4–201, 4–212] but all will become final upon *final payment* of the item by the Payor Bank. [UCC 4–213(2) and (3).]

"Other methods of Sending and Presentment will be appropriate in other cases. Note that under all of them the original Depositary Bank and all other Collecting Banks are agents or subagents of the owner of the check, and all the credits and the charges are provisional. [UCC 4–201.] This status will continue, generally, until the item bounces, or some Bank makes itself responsible by mailing its own Draft or by exceeding its time limit, or until the Payor Bank makes final payment of the item. The latter is what happens in the majority of cases. * * * "

The process by which the drawee—as payor bank—handles the check once it arrives at its doorstep is almost as occult as the transfer process up to that time. The passages that follow clarify matters.

JORDAN, ENDING THE FLOATING CHECK GAME: THE POLICY ARGUMENTS FOR DELAYED AVAILABILITY REFORM, 36 Hastings L.J. 515, 521–531 (1985).

Each year approximately thirty-five billion checks are processed for collection. The process begins at the bank of deposit and, if the check is paid, ends at the bank on which the check has been drawn. The procedures and legal rules governing the handling of checks pending collection are a blend of banking industry custom, the requirements of the U.C.C., and Federal Reserve regulations. A brief description of the way in which checks are collected sets the stage for assessing the possibilities for delayed availability reform.

THE INITIAL COLLECTION OF A CHECK

A check that has been accepted for deposit falls in one of three categories: the on-us item, the clearinghouse item, and the transit item. A description of each of these follows.

* * *

Clearinghouse and Transit Items

A clearinghouse is an arrangement between banks in the same city or region to exchange checks at a regular, predetermined time. Depositary and collecting banks present checks for payment to other collecting or payor banks at these clearinghouse exchanges. The Federal Reserve is a major clearinghouse, although private clearinghouses are also common.

The exchange of checks within citywide clearinghouses is still done the old-fashioned way. In New York City, for instance, the New York Clearing House, an association of twelve banks, serves as the location for messengers representing clearinghouse member banks to meet and exchange checks that have been cashed or accepted for deposit during the previous day. This face-to-face exchange of bundles of checks, which have been sorted according to the bank on which the item is drawn, is completed within a matter of minutes. The net position of each bank at the end of the exchange is determined by a computerized calculation. Each bank is credited for checks and items it has presented for payment and debited for items presented by other banks for payment. Settlement—an accounting between banks for items exchanged—is executed by virtue of a net credit or debit to each bank's Federal Reserve account balance.

The operation of the clearinghouse is determined by clearinghouse rules. These rules are essentially a contract among the member banks. Unlike ordinary contracts, however, the clearinghouse rules are binding on *depositors,* even though the depositors have neither read them, nor know of their existence. Section 4–103(2) of the U.C.C. gives such rules the "effect of agreements * * *, whether or not specifically assented to by all parties interested in items handled."

Checks drawn on banks in a different region, city, state, or outside the United States, are called transit items. These items are handled in very much the same way as clearinghouse checks, although longer periods of time are required for forwarding these items because they must move through several regions before reaching their destination at a payor bank.

The depositary bank has several options for how it forwards the transit item for collection. * * *

[These items were described above in the Bunn excerpt.]

THE FEDERAL RESERVE SYSTEM

The Role of the Federal Reserve in the Check Collection Process

As previously noted, the Federal Reserve (the Fed) is a major clearinghouse, processing approximately forty percent of all checks written in the United States. The overall speed and safety of the American check clearing system is largely attributable to the reliable national network made available for check clearing by the Fed. Federal Reserve check clearing services are now available to all banks, whether or not they are members of the system.

When the Federal Reserve system was inaugurated, banking was beset by many unsound practices. Chief among these was the practice of circuitous routing. To alleviate these abuses, an efficient nationwide check clearing system was designed based on processing within geographical zones. Today, the Federal Reserve processes checks through a highly automated network of forty-eight regional processing centers. The geographical organization of the Federal Reserve check clearing system creates some economies of scale because most of the checks processed by a regional processing center are drawn on banks within the same region. The use of state-of-the-art banking technology also enhances efficiency. The centers are connected by chartered air couriers and wire services dedicated exclusively to the Federal Reserve check clearing business. High-speed check sorting is accomplished by using machine-readable magnetic encoding (Magnetic Ink Character Recognition, MICR) on checks. This technique automatically identifies the amount of the check and the Federal Reserve zone in which the payor bank is located. Modern technology also speeds the handling of bundles of checks accompanied by cash letters.

From its inception, the Fed was designed to encourage banks to use the Federal Reserve system rather than the private clearinghouses or correspondent banks. Several incentives were used to make the Fed a more attractive clearinghouse. These incentives included immediate provisional credit on all eligible collection items cleared through the Fed. The decision to give immediate provisional credit was justified by the assumption that the majority of collection items would be honored and that very few would be charged back because of dishonor. Initially, as a precaution, immediate credit was not counted as a part of the bank's reserve requirement and was not available for withdrawal until the item actually was paid. Later, withdrawals against uncollected funds were permitted before confirmation of payment, and credit was made available for withdrawal according to a schedule based upon the customary times for receiving notice of dishonor from any given geographic point. On the basis of this schedule, banks clearing through the Federal Reserve were permitted to count these deposits toward their reserve requirements after the fixed period identified in the schedule had elapsed.

Today, immediate credit is available for intra-city and intra-regional checks. Credit on all other checks is available within one to two days. Until July 1983, two days was the maximum period for deferred credit to banks when the items were cleared through the Federal Reserve. In July 1983, the Board of Governors of the Federal Reserve adopted a system of fractional availability in which the cost of float is reflected in the schedule of availability for each item. Now, part of an institution's credit for a deposit is deferred an additional day. The fraction is determined so as to set the average float for the institution at zero.

Settlement: The Role of the Reserve Account

Settlement for items cleared through Federal Reserve channels occurs through reserve accounts with the Federal Reserve bank in the geographic region. Banks that use the Federal Reserve clearing services are required to maintain running reserve accounts. These accounts serve as the master accounting device for keeping track of the deposits and credits owed to each bank. At any given moment, every bank is both a depositary or collecting bank for some items and a payor bank for others. Therefore, credits are given daily to depositing banks for items for which they are entitled to immediate availability and for all items to which deferred availability applies. Debits are entered for the total amount of checks presented for collection. At the end of the day a status report is compiled reflecting the net position of each institution. Adjustments include returned checks, arithmetic errors, and disputed items. The Federal Reserve provides banks with a fixed schedule of availability, which is not dependent upon *actual* collection time.

The credit given to the reserve account for items that have not actually been collected is in essence an interest-free loan, an advance provided to depositing institutions by the Federal Reserve. When the depositing bank has received a credit, although the paying bank has not yet been debited, Federal Reserve float is created. The daily dollar value of this discrepancy has been valued at 3.2 billion.

The amount of float outstanding in the Federal Reserve check clearing system can have an important impact on the national economy. This is so largely because controlling reserve accounts is the principal way that the Federal Reserve monitors and restricts the growth of the money supply. Uncontrolled increases in the amount of float may undercut the desired level of control of the money supply. In addition, the loss of revenue to the federal treasury attributable to float contributes to the federal deficit. By one estimate, the average amount of float in a single year was equal to approximately one eighth of the total reserve account balances then outstanding.

The Federal Reserve check clearing system also plays a dominant role in the soundness and efficiency of the banking system itself. The extent to which immediate credit should be available to collecting banks from either the Fed or a correspondent has always been a matter of substantial controversy. During the early history of this country, the willingness of some clearinghouses to grant immediate availability and to permit member banks to treat these uncollected credits as cash was the source of instability. Even after the Federal Reserve clearing system was in place, many private competitors continued to permit remittance by draft rather than cash for items in collection. In addition, because correspondent banks typically give immediate ledger credit for cash letters received, nonmember banks are often able to meet a substantial proportion of state reserve requirements with uncollected funds and with compensating balances maintained with correspondents for other purposes. Even though immediate ledger credit may be given for cash letters, depositing banks are not free to draw on these funds until they are collected. The most important reason many banks continue to use the services of correspondents is the availability of immediate credit.

The Federal Reserve check clearing service is so vital to the banking industry that it has virtually controlled the terms and standards for check clearing since its inception in 1916. This position has been maintained because the Fed has been able to offer quick, reliable, nationwide clearing at rates that were subsidized by taxpayers. [Footnotes omitted.]

The ultimate objective of the Federal Reserve is to eliminate payment by check through such devices as the Automated Clearing House (ACH) and other forms of electronic transfers. In the electronic age, not quite upon us, debits and credits could be made instantly. Gone would be the billions of checks which clog the system and the "float," estimated on an average daily basis to be $6 billion, between issuance of the check and final payment. See Hamilton, *An Update on the Automated Clearinghouse,* 65 Fed.Res.Bull. 525 (1979). An intermediate objective is to achieve an overnight settlement on most credit items drawn on member banks. Regional Check Processing Centers (RCPCs) and a routing system better aligned to the flow of payment transactions have been developed to improve the existing payment foundation upon which the electronic system of the future can be built. Some progress has been made on all fronts.

Check truncation has been one method of achieving progress toward these objectives. Check truncation is the elimination of the physical handling of paper checks at some point of the check collection process. The data necessary to process the check is obtained through MICR technology. The ACHs use this data to transmit credits or debits to the correct accounts. Currently, banks seldom use check truncation in consumer transactions; however, credit unions normally truncate their consumer's share drafts which are check-like equivalents. At the end of the collection process credit unions do not return processed share drafts to the account holders. The actual paper drafts have been copied then destroyed. Although copies of drafts may be obtained upon request from the credit unions, at the end of the collection process members receive a statement which lists only share draft numbers processed during the month.

Active participation by banks in the check truncation process would reduce the processing costs associated with check collection. Because check truncation expedites the collection process, the time period between the issuance of a check and the final payment would be shortened, decreasing the "float," and shortening the holding period necessary for banks to determine whether a check will ultimately be honored. This would allow payees quicker access to newly deposited funds and eliminate postage and clerical expenses of returning checks.

Notes

There are tensions—practical, political, and legal—inherent in these efforts. Suppose that Corporation A on the west coast owes $250,000 to Corporation C, on the east coast. The yield in the short-term money market is 14 percent and the estimated time (or "float") between issuance and presentment for payment is 10 days. A issues the check against a balance in payor bank. Payor bank has instructions to notify A as soon as the check is presented and funds to cover it will be made available. Ten days of interest are thus saved through this "money management technique." Is there anything illegal about this practice? Suppose the Federal Reserve promulgated a rule (or developed a practice) for "flagging" random large checks for the purpose of wiring a member payor bank with instructions to debit the drawer's account, "check to follow." Could the Fed require member banks to comply? Would such a wire be a good presentment? The question, virtually unanswerable, continues as the various interest groups seek to reform the system.

The discussion about the check collection process can be made more understandable by taking a trip through the processing of a single check.

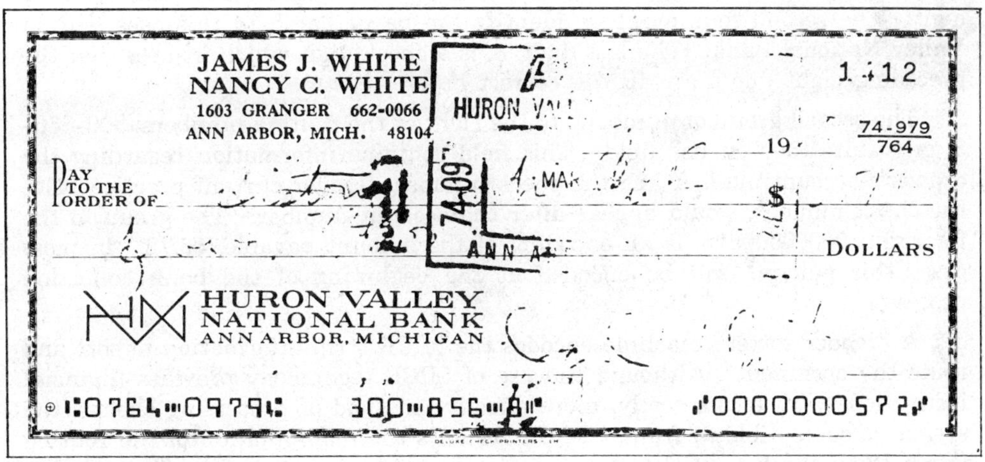

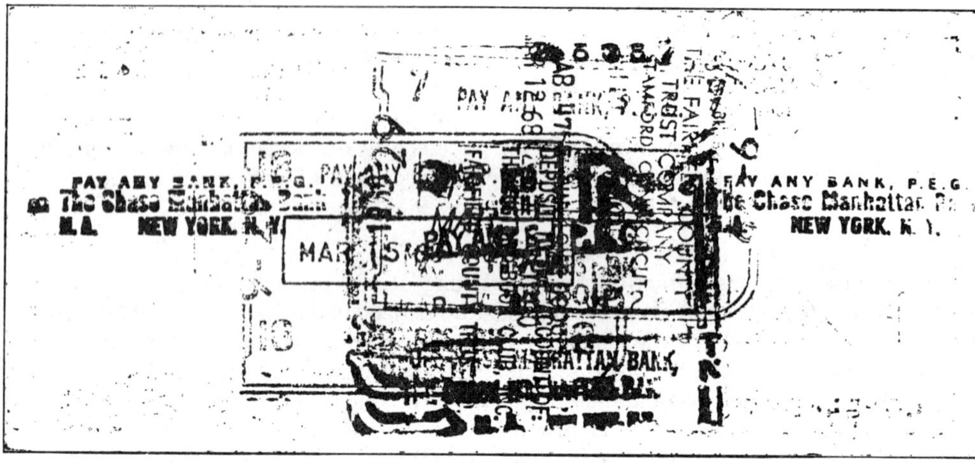

The numerals and symbols printed in the three groups across the bottom of the check are magnetic ink character recognition numbers (MICR). The numbers 0764–0979–8 are the transit or routing symbols. The first four numbers identify the Federal Reserve Bank of the drawee bank. The first digit, 7, indicates that the check was drawn on the Federal Reserve Bank located in the seventh Federal Reserve District, Chicago. The second digit, 6, normally indicates the branch of the Federal Reserve serving the territory in which the drawee bank is located. Each Federal Reserve District assigns its own meaning to the final digit. The second four numbers identify the payor bank, in this case, Huron Valley National Bank. The last digit, 8, is a check digit which insures that the preceding eight digits are in the correct order.

The second group of numbers, to the right of the routing numbers, 300–856–8, constitute the "on us" field. This field contains information regarding the drawer's account number and the check number. Under current practice 1412, the check number, would appear after the account number. The group to the far right, 00000000572, is an encoding of the amount payable, $5.72. In most cases this amount will be encoded at the beginning of the bank collection process.

A "reader sorter" machine encodes the MICR strip information to sort and route the document. Although the use of MICR technology provides financial institutions with a less costly, more effective method of processing checks, the system is susceptible to fraud. MICR fraud is the manipulation of the routing numbers on the face of the check purposely to increase the check's processing period beyond the bank's normal holding period. Because the check collection process operates on a "no news is good news" presumption, a longer time period for routing a check than the bank's holding period may allow the perpetrator of fraud to withdraw funds which it believes will be covered by the drawer. See *United States Fidelity & Guaranty Co. v. Federal Reserve Bank of New York,* infra at 1203.

The physical odyssey of this check was as follows: from Ann Arbor, Michigan via mail to the History Book Club in Stamford, Connecticut. The History Book Club deposited the check in its bank, the Fairfield Trust; the Fairfield

Trust sent the check to Chase Manhattan (Chase) who sent it back to the Federal Reserve in Detroit, who sent it to the computing center at Manufacturer's National Bank (Manufacturers), who sent it to Huron Valley National Bank. At the end of the month, the check was returned to the Whites by Huron Valley Bank. It is likely that the check made the trip to the History Book Club by airmail and that it returned from Chase to the Federal Reserve in Detroit by airmail together with many other checks. It probably traveled from the Fairfield Trust to Chase and from the Federal Reserve to the computing center to Huron Valley by special carrier whose only business is the transfer of checks among banks.

We can only guess at the accounting transactions which went on in the payment process. Fairfield County Trust credited the History Book Club's account with $5.72 when it processed the check. At Chase, Fairfield would have received a credit in its account with Chase for the $5.72. Because Chase handles such a large volume of checks, it sends its checks directly to the Federal Reserve banks outside its area and thus did so with this check. The Federal Reserve in Detroit debited the account which Huron Valley maintains with it and credited the New York Federal Reserve Bank's account for the benefit of Chase.

Since Huron Valley contracts with Manufacturers in Detroit to do its computer work, Manufacturers intercepts the checks prior to their actual receipt at Huron Valley. This process of interception of checks cuts as much as a day off the time it takes for payment. Through the computer at Manufacturers, the Whites' account maintained on the computer memory was debited for $5.72. At 9:00 a.m. on March 20 the computer print-out which is set out below, together with the check, was presented at Huron Valley Bank.

When the print-out arrived at Huron Valley, one of the bank's clerks examined it to see that the Whites' account and the others listed were not overdrawn and to assure that there was no stop order or other hold on any of the accounts on which payments had been made. Another employee examined the check to determine that it had been signed (but not necessarily that the signature was genuine), that it contained at least the payee's indorsement (but not necessarily that all indorsements were in the proper order and appropriate) and checked the date to insure that it was not a "stale" check. Then the Whites' check was photographed, stamped "PAID," and filed with the rest of Whites' checks. At the end of the month, Huron Valley sent the check to the Whites with the rest of their checks drawn during that month.

MANUFACTURERS NATIONAL BANK

DAILY JOURNAL

DATE: 03198

ABA NO. 0764-0979

ACCOUNT NUMBER			YESTERDAY'S BALANCE	DATE LAST DEPOSIT	AMOUNT OF LAST DEPOSIT	DATE LAST TRANS	COLLECTED BALANCE	CURRENT BALANCE
0003008487			453930	312	281426	318	44	446434
0003008509			12303	315	19000	318	1	10939
0003008525			28323	116	42000	304	2	28323
0003008568			34991	229	60712	318	2	27945
0003008576			48000	305	8000	311	4	48000
0003008584			38671	315	32174	318	3	34754
0003008592			17931	318	15000	318	1	17931
0003008614			19282					
0003008614				312	7805	318	1	15713
0003008622			44990	313	46948	315	4	40485
0003008630			113915	304	38601	304	11	113915
0003008657			83051	318	26644	318	8	83051
0003008673			1692-					
0003008673				318	6500	318		3226-
0003008681			14-	307	16418	318		514-
0003008746			729	311	4000	315		729
0003008762			22863	315	13800	318	2	20631
0003008770			86061	318	10000	318	8	83604
0003008797			21830	319	29000	313	5	50030
0003008800			39225	314	2310	318	3	37715
0003008819			3729-					
0003008819				306	34277	318		8334-
0003008835			19849	119	19428	213	1	19849

TRIAL BALANCE

			3				20	
TR Code	AMOUNT	TR CODE	AMOUNT	TR CODE	AMOUNT	TR CODE	AMOUNT	
90	1066	90	4200	90	930	90	1300	
90	864	90	500					
90	3000	90	2000	90	1474	90	572	
90	1792	90	2125					
90	1100	90	239	90	715	90	1140	
90	375							
90	3000	90	1505					
40	2100	52	300	90	700	90	1100	
90	534	90	1000					5
90	500							5
90	545	90	1687					
90	1557	90	900					
20	29000	90	800					
90	1510							
40	1576	40	1806	52	600	90	900	
90	697	90	1695	90	4095			5

The consequence of this process is that the History Book Club's account is $5.72 richer and the Whites' account is $5.72 poorer. In addition of course the transaction has increased the aggregate deposits of the Fairfield County Trust Co. and reduced the aggregate deposits of the Huron Valley.

Now consider the print-out which was received on the morning of the 20th by the Huron Valley. Note that the accounts are numbered serially and that the fourth entry from the top of the page is the one which shows the activity in the Whites' account. It shows that four checks were paid in the computer run on the evening of the 19th and that the balance has been reduced from $349.91 to $279.45 by the payments made that evening.

Note the activity in account number 300–867–3. The minus sign following the amount listed as "yesterday's balance" and "current balance" indicates that the account is overdrawn. Since the Manufacturers-Huron Valley computer is programmed to pay all checks including those which are overdrawn, Huron Valley must return those which it wishes to bounce to the Federal Reserve and then send a communication to the computer on the next evening instructing it to reverse the debit entries made on the previous evening on bounced checks. The code for an account debit is 90; the code for a credit when an amount is added back to the account after the bank has made the decision not to pay is 40. It is likely that the $21.00 check in 300–867–3 was paid by the computer on the evening of the 18th; but the bank officers decided not to cover the overdraft but to bounce the check, and have now instructed the computer to add the $21.00 back to the account. It is also likely that some of the amounts paid out of this account by the computer on the 19th will also appear on the 20th run as reversals since the account is still overdrawn. The symbol 52 indicates a charge to the account for bounced checks.

The fact that an account has been overdrawn does not necessarily mean that the bank will choose not to pay the check. Several courses of action are open to the bank. First it can simply bounce the check by attaching a sticker to the check indicating that there are insufficient funds and sending the check back to the Federal Reserve in Detroit:

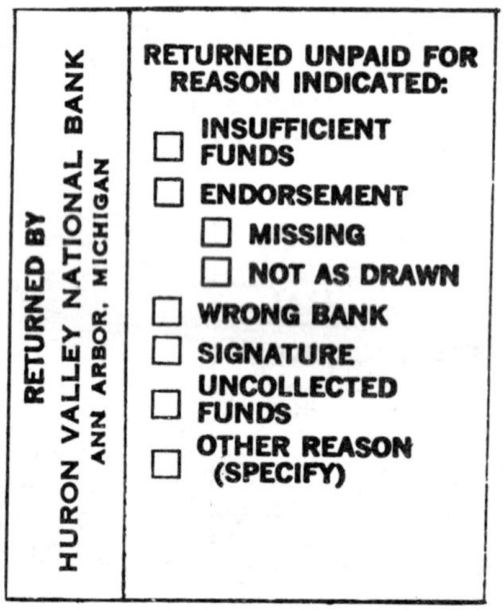
RETURNED BY
HURON VALLEY NATIONAL BANK
ANN ARBOR, MICHIGAN

RETURNED UNPAID FOR REASON INDICATED:

- ☐ INSUFFICIENT FUNDS
- ☐ ENDORSEMENT
  - ☐ MISSING
  - ☐ NOT AS DRAWN
- ☐ WRONG BANK
- ☐ SIGNATURE
- ☐ UNCOLLECTED FUNDS
- ☐ OTHER REASON (SPECIFY)

[C3049]

Second it can decide at once that it is going to pay the check, in which case it need take no action and the check will have been irrevocably paid not later than two or three business days after it was received at Huron Valley (UCC 4–213(1)(c) and (d)). The other alternative is to call the drawer, inform him that his account is overdrawn, and ask him to deposit additional funds or make other arrangements. If he makes satisfactory arrangements, the check will be paid; if not the check can be sent back until the two-or three-day deadline has passed.

The form set out below is an example of a second print-out which the bank receives from Manufacturers on overdrawn accounts. It states the amount of the overdraft, date of the overdraft, whether or not the account has had a number of overdrafts recently (if not, the word "new" will appear), and how many overdrafts this account has previously had.

HURON VALLEY OVERDRAFT LISTING

ANK	BR	TY	ACCOUNT NO	CD	DATE	NEW	NSF	AMOUNT
05	00	2	0002000156	B1	7/16/8	NEW	88	[illegible]742.30-
05	00	2	0002003376	B1	7/16/8		32	237.11-
05	00	2	0002004771	B1	6/29/8			.67-
05	00	2	0002006456	B1	7/16/8		52	2,578.28-
05	00	2	0002007002	B1	7/16/8	NEW	03	[illegible]
05	00	2	0002007231	B1	7/16/8		58	4.71
05	00	2	0002007436	B1	6/29/8		04	26.68-
05	00	2	0002007967	B1	7/16/8	NEW	27	52.28-
05	00	2	0002008149	B1	7/16/8		01	549.99-
05	00	2	0002008556	B1	7/16/8	NEW		[illegible]
05	00	2	0002008602	B1	6/29/8			.11-
05	00	2	0002008750	B1	6/29/8			.58-
05	00	2	0002008815	B1	7/16/8		03	9.67-
05	00	2	0002009323	B1	6/29/8		03	.44-
05	00	2	0002009382	B1	6/29/8			2.84-
05	00	2	0002009390	B1	7/16/8	NEW	42	[illegible]55.39
05	00	2	0002009439	B1	7/16/8		31	28.99-
05	00	2	0002009587	B1	6/29/8			1.81-
05	00	2	0002010712	B1	6/29/8			.25-
05	00	2	0002011263	B1	7/09/8		01	1.45-
05	00	2	0002011832	B1	6/29/8			.74-
05	00	2	0002011921	B1	7/16/8		10	[illegible]
05	00	2	0002012006	B1	7/16/8			512.48-
05	00	2	0002012014	B1	7/16/8	NEW	03	59.70-
05	00	2	0002012359	B1	7/03/8			2.52-
05	00	2	0002012537	B1	6/29/8			2.18-
05	00	2	0002012551	B1	6/29/8			1.40-
								13,242.13-*

Some systems are programmed automatically to reject NSF checks; the Huron Valley-Manufacturers system is programmed to pay them. Under many systems stop orders must be handled manually. That is to say a clerk must examine the payments on each account as to which there is a stop order or other hold. The clerk then must determine whether the check upon which a stop order is given is one of those which has been presented for payment. Some computers are programmed to identify all accounts on the print-out as to which there is a stop order or other hold. However under some systems the computer is not able to single out and actually stop payment on individual checks, for the check number is not encoded and the computer cannot read it. The computer normally reads only the routing and transit numbers, the account and the amount. If check numbers are encoded on checks themselves, it will be possible for the computer itself to stop payment.

SECTION 3. LIABILITY OF THE PAYOR BANK

Students should start by examining UCC 4–104, 4–106, 4–107, 4–109 and sections 4–213, 4–301 and 4–302. These sections, together with UCC 3–418 in Article 3 outline the scope of the payor bank's liability. Perhaps one should start with section 4–213. That section defines a series of events as final payment and states that a payor bank is "accountable" after it has made final payment. With certain exceptions, that means that a payor bank who makes final payment on a check for which there are insufficient funds will bear that loss.

Note what constitutes final payment: paying in cash, settling without reserving a right to revoke (what could that be?), completing the process of posting, making a provisional settlement and failing to revoke the settlement. Starting at the back end first, one should read UCC 4–301 and 4–302 together with UCC 4–213(1)(d) and 4–104(1)(h). The combination of those rules tells one that a payor bank normally must act by midnight of the next banking day after it receives a check or be held to have made final payment. If you cannot get that conclusion out of the sections, read them again.

What constituted the "process of posting" was obvious and simple in the nineteenth century. It was the act of a clerk wearing a green eyeshade and holding a quill pen. The clerk had a check in one hand and before him was the account of the depositor. He compared the signature with the signature of his depositor and determined whether there were enough funds in the account to pay the check. If there were, he marked an appropriate notation with his pen, thus reducing the amount in the account, and stamped or marked the check in his other hand, "paid." Once the clerk had done these things the process of posting was done and the check had been finally paid; the process could not normally be reversed.

Now the man with the green eyeshade is gone. The check comes to the bank in the middle of the night in a sack, it is run through a machine in the basement that reads the microencoding line (the line at the bottom of the check that includes the bank number, the check number, the account number, and the dollar amount) so debits the customer's account and then goes through another machine for photographing and stamping. It is untouched by human hands, and until the next morning, no human being at the bank will have an opportunity to interfere with that process. On that day someone is likely to look at a printout produced by the computer that shows which accounts are overdrawn and which are not. If there is nothing apparently wrong with the account, it will not necessarily be flagged on a special printout for overdrawn or large items or for other reasons. Has the process of posting been completed? If so, when?

The trouble with UCC 4–213(1)(c) is that the "process of posting" is a dead metaphor. It had meaning when accounts were posted manually. It has no explicit meaning in the computer age, and the courts have had difficulty deciding how to interpret it in that age.

Settling for an item without reserving the right to revoke is an unusual event. One might imagine that it has occurred when a bank has given a cashier's check in return for a check drawn on it. Undoubtedly there are other examples, but they are few and far between.

Payment in cash would seem to be a simple matter, but, as we will see in the case below, even that has its complexity for it is not always possible to determine whether the customer deposited the check and withdrew some money or whether the customer received final payment in cash and then deposited some money.

Finally, we must consider the right of restitution and the relationship between UCC 4–213 and 3–418. Prior to the enactment of the Code a payor bank who paid "by mistake" had a right of restitution under the common law of certain states against the one to whom payment had been made. Everywhere this right was cut off if final payment had been made to a holder in due course or to one who had changed his position in reliance on payments (a la 3–418). Rules varied under the law of various states about when the right existed. Had the drafters intended such an important right to continue, one would have thought that they would have codified it. They did not codify it, yet most courts believe that the right of restitution in check cases lives. As we will see, however, the courts are not in agreement on the question when there is a right of restitution nor on the question whether UCC 4–213 itself cuts off that right in favor of one who does not qualify as either a holder in due course or one who has changed his position in reliance.

Final pieces of quasi statutory law are the federal regulations and the federal operating letters. The relevant sections are set out in the Appendix. Specifically the regulation now calls for the payor bank to give wire notice when it dishonors a check of more than $2,500 that has been received through the Federal Reserve System. With the 1985 amendments to the Regulation, this section now fits more comfortably with Article 4, however, the fit is not always certain.

KIRBY v. FIRST & MERCHANTS NAT'L BANK

Virginia Supreme Court of Appeals, 1969.
210 Va. 88, 168 S.E.2d 273.

GORDON, J.

On December 30, 1966, defendant Margaret Kirby handed the following check to a teller at a branch of plaintiff First & Merchants National Bank:

NEUSE ENG. AND DREDGING CO. Check Number ______

68–728
514

12–29–1966

Pay to the order of William J. Kirby & Margaret Kirby $ 2,500.00

Twenty-Five Hundred -------------------- Dollars

FIRST & MERCHANTS
NATIONAL BANK
Virginia Beach, Virginia
. . . 0514. . . 0728

NEUSE ENG. & DREDGING CO.
/s/ W. R. Wood

[C4551]

The back of the check bore the signatures of the payees, Mr. and Mrs. Kirby.

Mrs. Kirby, who also had an account with the Bank, gave the teller the following deposit ticket.[1]

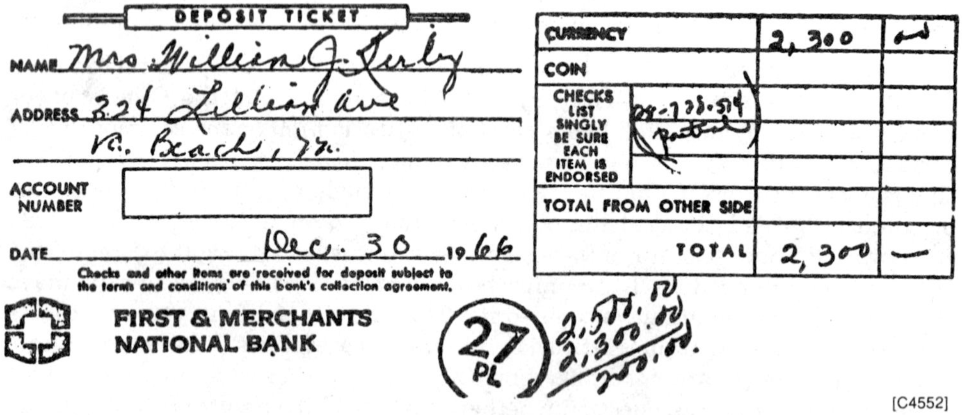

DEPOSIT TICKET

NAME Mrs William J. Kirby

ADDRESS 324 Lillian Ave

Va. Beach, Va.

ACCOUNT NUMBER

DATE Dec. 30 1966

Checks and other items are received for deposit subject to the terms and conditions of this bank's collection agreement.

FIRST & MERCHANTS NATIONAL BANK

27 PL

2,500.00 2,300.00 200.00

CURRENCY		2,300	00
COIN			
CHECKS LIST SINGLY BE SURE EACH ITEM IS ENDORSED	68-728-514 partial		
TOTAL FROM OTHER SIDE			
	TOTAL	2,300	—

[C4552]

The teller handed $200 in cash to Mrs. Kirby, and the Bank credited her account with $2,300 on the next business day, January 3, 1967. The teller or another Bank employee made the notation "Cash for Dep." under Mr. and Mrs. Kirby's signatures on the back of the Neuse check.

On January 4 the Bank discovered that the Neuse check was drawn against insufficient funds. Instead of giving written notice, a Bank officer called Mr. and Mrs. Kirby on January 5 to advise that the Bank had dishonored the check and to request reimbursement. Mr. and Mrs. Kirby said they would come to the Bank to cover the check, but they did not. On January 10 the Bank charged Mrs. Kirby's account with $2,500, creating an overdraft of $543.47.

On January 18 the Bank instituted this action to recover $543.47 from Mr. and Mrs. Kirby. At the trial a Bank officer, the only witness in the case, testified:

> "Q. Did you cash the check [the Neuse check for $2,500] before you credited this deposit [the deposit of $2,300 to Mrs. Kirby's account]?
>
> "A. Yes, sir.
>
> "Q. So the bank, in effect, cashed the check for $2,500.00 and then gave the defendant a credit of $2,300.00 to their [sic] account and gave them [sic] $200.00 in cash?
>
> "A. Correct.
>
> " * * *
>
> "Q. So you cashed the check for $2,500.00?
>
> "A. Yes, sir."

The trial court, sitting without a jury, entered judgment for the plaintiff First & Merchants, and the defendants Mr. and Mrs. Kirby appeal. The question is whether the Bank had the right to charge Mrs. Kirby's account with $2,500 on January 10 and to recover from Mr. and Mrs. Kirby the overdraft created by that charge ($543.47).

1. The handwriting in the upper-left portion of the deposit ticket corresponds with Mrs. Kirby's handwriting on the back of the check. The record does not indicate what persons added the other handwritten information on the ticket.

The symbol "68–728–514" designates a check drawn on First & Merchants by a depositor who has an account with a branch of that Bank in the Norfolk-Virginia Beach area. The word following the symbol is "partial."

UCC § 4–213 [2] provides:

"(1) An item [3] is finally paid by a payor bank when the bank has done any of the following, whichever happens first:

"(a) paid the item in cash;".

So if First & Merchants paid the Neuse check in cash on December 30, it then made final payment and could not sue Mr. or Mrs. Kirby on the check except for breach of warranty.[4]

When Mrs. Kirby presented the $2,500 Neuse check to the Bank on December 30, the Bank paid her $200 in cash and accepted a deposit of $2,300. The Bank officer said that the Bank cashed the check for $2,500, which could mean only that Mrs. Kirby deposited $2,300 in cash.

And the documentary evidence shows that cash was deposited. The deposit of cash is evidenced by the word "currency" before "2,300.00" on the deposit ticket and by the words "Cash for Dep." on the back of the check.[5] The Bank's ledger, which shows a credit of $2,300 to Mrs. Kirby's account rather than a credit of $2,500 and a debit of $200, is consistent with a cashing of the Neuse check and a depositing of part of the proceeds. We must conclude that First & Merchants paid the Neuse check in cash on December 30 and, therefore, had no right thereafter to charge Mrs. Kirby's account with the amount of the check.

The trial court apparently decided that Mr. and Mrs. Kirby were liable to the Bank because they had indorsed the Neuse check. But under UCC § 3–414(1) an indorser contracts to pay an instrument only if the instrument is dishonored. And, as we have pointed out, the Bank did not dishonor the Neuse check, but paid the check in cash when Mrs. Kirby presented it.

As a practical matter, the contract of an indorser under UCC § 3–414(1) does not run to a drawee bank. That contract can be enforced by a drawee bank only if it dishonors a check; and if the bank dishonors the check, it has suffered no loss.

The warranties that are applicable in this case are set forth in UCC §§ 3–417(1) and 4–207(1): warranties made to a drawee bank by a presenter and prior

2. The Uniform Commercial Code ("UCC") has been codified as Titles 8.1 through 8.10 of the Code of Virginia. References to the UCC are to that Code as adopted in Virginia, but citations will omit the title number 8. E.g., UCC § 4–213 means Va.Code Ann. § 8.4–213.

3. The Uniform Commercial Code gives "item" its generally accepted meaning:

"'Item' means any instrument for the payment of money even though it is not negotiable but does not include money." UCC § 4–104(g).

4. As shown by the quotation in the text, UCC § 4–213, which deals with bank deposits and collections, provides without qualification that a payor bank's payment of an item in cash is final. The Code recognizes, however, that a bank may recover a payment when a presenter's warranty is breached, e.g., when an indorsement is forged. UCC §§ 3–417(1), 4–207(1). And under the established law before adoption of the Uniform Commercial Code, a bank could also recover a payment in case of fraud or bad faith on the part of the person receiving the payment. 3 Paton's Digest of Legal Opinions, Overdrafts § 4:1 (1944). In this case there is no evidence of breach of a presenter's warranties or of fraud or bad faith.

Unlike UCC § 4–213, UCC § 3–418, which deals with commercial paper generally, implies that payment of an instrument is final only in favor of a holder in due course or a person who has changed his position in reliance on the payment. First & Merchants neither relied on UCC § 3–418, nor based its right to recover on an assertion that Mr. and Mrs. Kirby were not holders in due course and did not change their position. See UCC § 3–307 and comment. Moreover, insofar as UCC §§ 3–418 and 4–213 conflict, UCC § 4–213 prevails. UCC § 4–102(1).

5. Since no dollar amount was inserted after "checks" on the deposit ticket, the notation "68–728–514 partial" was apparently inserted to identify the source of the currency being deposited. See n. 1 supra.

transferors of a check. Those warranties are applicable because Mrs. Kirby presented the Neuse check to the Bank for payment. UCC § 3–504(1); Bunn, Snead & Speidel, An Introduction to the Uniform Commercial Code § 3.4(B) (1964). And those warranties do not include a warranty that the drawer of a check has sufficient funds on deposit to cover the check.

The rule that a drawee who mistakenly pays a check has recourse only against the drawer was firmly established before adoption of the Uniform Commercial Code:

> "The drawer of a check, and not the holder who receives payment, is primarily responsible for the drawing out of funds from a bank. An overdraft is an act by reason of which the drawer and not the holder obtains money from the bank on his check. The holder therefore in the absence of fraud or express understanding for repayment, has no concern with the question whether the drawer has funds in the bank to meet the check. The bank is estopped, as against him, from claiming that by its acceptance an overdraft occurred. A mere mistake is not sufficient to enable it to recover from him. Banks cannot always guard against fraud, but can guard against mistakes.
>
> "It is therefore the general rule, sustained by almost universal authority, that a payment in the ordinary course of business of a check by a bank on which it is drawn under the mistaken belief that the drawer has funds in the bank subject to check is not such a payment under a mistake of fact as will permit the bank to recover the money so paid from the recipient of such payment. To permit the bank to repudiate the payment would destroy the certainty which must pertain to commercial transactions if they are to remain useful to the business public. Otherwise no one would ever know when he can safely receive payment of a check."

7 Zollman, The Law of Banks and Banking § 5062 (1936). See generally 3 Paton's Digest of Legal Opinions, Overdrafts § 4 (1944).

Virginia followed the same rule. * * *

Nevertheless, First & Merchants contends that under the terms of its deposit contract with Mrs. Kirby, the settlement was provisional and therefore subject to revocation whether or not the Neuse check was paid in cash on December 30.[6] It contends that in this regard the deposit contract changes the

6. The depositor's contract provides:

"Items received for deposit or collection are accepted on the following terms and conditions. *This bank acts only as depositor's collecting agent and assumes no responsibility beyond its exercise of due care. All items are credited subject to final payment and to receipt of proceeds of final payment in cash or solvent credits by this bank at its own office.* This bank may forward items to correspondents and shall not be liable for default or negligence of correspondents selected with due care nor for losses in transit, and each correspondent shall not be liable except for its own negligence. Items and their proceeds may be handled by any Federal Reserve bank in accordance with applicable Federal Reserve rules, and by this bank or any correspondent, in accordance with any common bank usage, with any practice or procedure that a Federal Reserve bank may use or permit another bank to use, or with any other lawful means. *This bank may charge back, at any time prior to midnight on its business day next following the day of receipt, any item drawn on this bank which is ascertained to be drawn against insufficient funds or otherwise not good or payable. An item received after this bank's regular afternoon closing hour shall be deemed received the next business day.*

"This bank reserves the right to post all deposits, including deposits of cash and of items drawn on it, not later than midnight of its next business day after their receipt at this office during regular banking hours, and shall not be liable for damages for nonpayment of any presented item resulting from the exercise of this right.

rule set forth in the Uniform Commercial Code. But in providing that "all items are credited subject to final payment," the contract recognizes that settlement for an item is provisional only until the item is finally paid. Since the deposit contract does not change the applicable rule as set forth in the Uniform Commercial Code, we do not decide whether a bank can provide by deposit contract that payment of a check in cash is provisional.

Even if the Bank's settlement for the Neuse check had been provisional, the Bank had the right to charge that item back to Mrs. Kirby's account only if it complied with UCC §§ 4–212(3) and 4–301. Those sections authorize the revocation of a settlement if, before the "midnight deadline," [7] the bank

> "(a) returns the item; or
>
> "(b) sends written notice of dishonor or nonpayment if the item is held for protest or is otherwise unavailable for return." UCC § 4–301.

The Bank concedes that it neither sent written notice of dishonor nor returned the Neuse check before the "midnight deadline." So the Bank had no right to charge the item back to Mrs. Kirby's account.

For the reasons set forth, the trial court erred in entering judgment for First & Merchants against Mr. and Mrs. Kirby.

Reversed and final judgment.

* * *

[The dissent of Justice Harrison is omitted. Justice Srkal, sitting by extra-special designation (courtesy of the Red Baron) filed the following opinion.]

SRKAL, JUSTICE, legt hierzu folgendes Minderheitsvotum vor:

Das Mehrheitsvotum belegt, in welch traurigem Zustand sich die Juristerei im Staate Virginia befindet. Ein jeder Narr erkennt, dass es im vorliegenden Rechtsstreit nicht um eine, sondern um zwei Banken geht: zum einen um die Filiale der First & Merchants National Bank in Virginia Beach und zum anderen um jene in Norfolk.

Die Tatsache, dass der Scheck auf eine Zweigstelle der Bank gezogen war und bei einer anderen Zweigstelle der selben Bank zum Inkasso eingereicht wurde, bedeutet nie und nimmer, dass die Filiale, die den Scheck entgegen genommen hat, endgültig erfüllt hat. Sie hätte mit dem Scheck alles mögliche machen können: ihn stempeln, darauf herumtrampeln oder bar auszahlen. Nichts von alledem hätte aber Erfüllung bedeutet. Das folgt daraus, dass sie die Inkassobank und nicht die bezogene Bank ist. Ex definitione kann nur die bezogene Bank Erfüllung erbringen. Das Mehrheitsvotum übersieht § 4–106 UCC, der bestimmt, dass in Fällen wie dem vorliegenden, mehrere Zweigstellen einer Bank jeweils wie einzelne, eigenständige Banken anzusehen sind. Mehrere Filialenals eine einzige Bank zu behandeln würde eigenartige und ungewollte Ergebnisse zeitigen.

Im herrschenden Bankensystem von Virginia ist es praktisch unmöglich, dass ein Scheck in anderthalb Tagen vom einen Ende des Staates zum anderen und wieder zurück kommt. Wenn aber Einreichung eines Schecks bei einer Filiale einer Bank, der auf eine andere Filiale dieser selben Bank am entgegengesetzten Ende des Staates gezogen ist, Einreichung bei der bezogenen Bank bedeutet, dann müsste das ganze Geschäft innerhalb von anderthalb Tagen

(Italicized language is quoted in First & Merchants' brief.)

7. "Midnight deadline" is defined in UCC § 4–104(h). See also the Bank's deposit contract, supra n. 6.

abgewickelt sein. Der Gesetzgeber hat dieses Resultat sicher nicht gewollt, denn § 4–106 UCC sollte solche Ergebnisse ja gerade beseitigen.

Entscheidet man sich dafür, dass die Bank, bei der Frau Kirby den Scheck einreichte, eine Inkassobank war, so muss man zu dem Ergebnis kommen, dass die Bank anderthalb Tage hatte, den Scheck zur bezogenen Bank zu schicken, und nochmals anderthalb Tage, um Frau Kirby zu benachrichtigen, dass der Scheck als ungedeckt zurückgekommen sei.

Ausserdem muss festgestellt werden, dass die Bank nur nach § 4–202 UCC haftet, also nur für von ihr fahrlässig verursachten Schaden. Aber selbst wenn man einmal unterstellt, es habe Fahrlässigkeit vorgelegen, kommt man zu dem Ergebnis, dass kein Schaden entstanden ist, weil der Scheck aller Wahrscheinlichkeit nach von Anfang an ungedeckt war und deswegen zwischenzeitlich gar nicht hätte kassiert werden können. Im vorliegenden Fall ist ein fahrlässiges Handeln der Bank aber nicht ersichtlich, womit jegliche Haftung entfällt. Anders als eine bezogene Bank muss eine Inkassobank nämlich keine schriftliche Nachricht erteilen, wenn ein Scheck platzt. Selbst wenn die Umstände des Einzelfalles eine Nachricht erfordern, hat eine Inkassobank mehr Zeit dafür als eine bezogene Bank.

Aus alledem folgt, dass das Mehrheitsvotum schlichtweg irrig ist. Die Entscheidungsgründe der Mehrheit dieses Gerichts zeigen, dass sie unfähig ist, den Uniform Commercial Code zu lesen, geschweige denn, die relevanten Bestimmungen aufzufinden.

Notes

1. If the branch on which the check was drawn is not the same as the one where it was deposited by Mrs. Kirby, was there no final payment by reason of passage of time?

2. How might you instruct the teller in the future to insure that transactions of the kind described in the Kirby case at the teller's window would not themselves constitute final payment?

Problem 26–1

Wesley Prouty, doing business as Foxy Acres, drew and delivered a $30,000 check payable to the order of Idah-Best on October 31, 1975. The check was drawn on the Haley branch of First Security Bank of Idaho. Also on October 31, payee deposited the check in the Twin Falls Bank & Trust Co. Nothing further happened on November 1 and 2, when the Twin Falls Bank was closed as provided by law in Idaho. However, on Monday, November 3, Twin Falls, acting as the payee's agent for collection, mailed the check along with others to the Boise branch of First Security for deposit in Twin Falls Bank & Trusts' commercial account there. The check arrived in Boise on November 4, Twin Falls was given a provisional credit in its account, the amount of the check was encoded and it was run through the data processing center—all in the afternoon and evening of November 4. Also that night the computer in Boise communicated with First Security's main computer in Salt Lake City, and discovered the check was drawn on insufficient funds. All the checks drawn on the Haley branch were then assembled according to account number and were sent to Haley by Bankers' Dispatch on Wednesday, November 5. The check arrived in Haley during the afternoon of the 5th and was examined that night and the next day. On November 6, the branch manager decided to refuse payment of the check, stamped it "refer to maker" and on Thursday, sent it from the Haley branch bank to Boise, where it arrived November 7. On Monday, November 10, Boise debited Twin Falls' account for $30,000 and dispatched the check back to Twin Falls, where it arrived on Wednesday, November 12 (the 11th was Veteran's Day and the banks did not operate). On November 13, Twin Falls sent notice to the payee, who received it on November 14.

The payee has come storming into your office. He points out that he deposited the check initially more than two weeks ago, and that he long since believed the check had been finally paid. He wonders if you can do anything toward recovering from his own bank or preferably from First Security. What do you think?

If you represented First Security, what argument can you put forward to support your position? You may want to read the *Capital City* case, below, before you answer.

CAPITAL CITY FIRST NATIONAL BANK v. LEWIS STATE BANK

District Court of Appeal of Florida, 1977.
341 So.2d 1025.

SMITH, J. Between June 19 and 25, 1974, two checks drawn by the distressed Commonwealth Corporation on uncollected funds were, as one witness put it, "floating around Tallahassee looking for a home." Both checks, totaling $150,000, were drawn by Commonwealth to the order of Commonwealth on its account at Florida State Bank of Tallahassee. Commonwealth deposited the first check, for $10,000, in its account at appellant Capital City First National Bank on June 19, and received credit which Commonwealth immediately used. The second check, for $140,000, was similarly deposited at Capital City the next day, June 20. Florida State, the payor bank, dishonored the two checks and gave notice of dishonor following an intervening weekend, on June 24 and 25. Between their deposit and subsequent dishonor, the checks were handled by appellee Lewis State Bank, which accepted Florida State's dishonor of the checks, rescinded its prior charges to Florida State's account at Lewis, and sued Capital City, the depositary bank which refused to recognize Florida State's dishonor of the checks.

The issue is whether the loss properly falls on Capital City, as held by the circuit court, or on Lewis. Resolution of that issue is controlled by whether Florida State timely dishonored the checks before midnight of the banking day following "presentment" to Florida State. That determination in turn depends on whether delivery of the checks to Lewis and Lewis' handling of them in its proof and transit department on June 20 and 21 was in effect presentment to Florida State, commencing the period for payment or dishonor and rendering tardy Florida State's notices of dishonor on June 24 and 25. The trial court held that presentment to Florida State did not occur when Lewis received the checks and that Lewis' handling of the checks in its proof and transit department on June 20 and 21 was only as an "intermediary collecting bank," not as Florida State's agent to receive presentment. Capital City appeals from the adverse judgment on the principal matter in issue and Lewis cross-assigns error in the trial court's refusal to award interest.

Some of the pertinent statutes are § 673.504, F.S. 1973, "How presentment made":

> "(1) Presentment is a demand for acceptance or payment made upon the * * * payor by or on behalf of the holder.
>
> "(2) Presentment may be made:

"(a) By mail, in which event the time of presentment is determined by the time of receipt of the mail; or

"(b) Through a clearinghouse; or

"(c) At the place of acceptance or payment specified in the instrument * * *

"(3) [Presentment] may be made:

"* * *

"(b) To any person who has authority to make or refuse the acceptance or payment."

Sec 673.506, F.S. 1973, "Time allowed for acceptance or payment":

"(1) Acceptance may be deferred without dishonor until the close of the next business day following presentment * * *"

Sec 673.508(2), F.S. 1973, "Notice of dishonor":

"Any necessary notice [of dishonor] must be given by a bank before its midnight deadline [the next banking day, § 674.104(h)] * * *."

Sec 674.107, F.S. 1973, "Time of receipt of items":

"(1) For the purpose of allowing time to process items, prove balances and make the necessary entries on its books to determine its position for the day, a bank may fix an afternoon hour of two p.m. or later as a cut-off hour for the handling of money and items and the making of entries on its books.

"(2) Any item * * * received on any day after a cut-off hour so fixed or after the close of the banking day may be treated as being received at the opening of the next banking day."

Sec 674.202(2), F.S. 1973, "Responsibility for collection; when action seasonable":

"A collecting bank taking proper action before its midnight deadline [the next banking day, § 674.104(h)] following receipt of an item * * * acts seasonably * * *"

Sec 674.204, F.S. 1973 "Methods of sending and presenting; sending direct to payor bank":

"(2) A collecting bank may send:

"(a) Any item direct to the payor bank;

"* * *

"(3) Presentment may be made by a presenting bank at a place where the payor bank has requested that presentment be made."

The odyssey of the second or $140,000 check deposited to Commonwealth's account at Capital on June 20 was at every stage a banking day later, but otherwise identical to, that of the first or $10,000 check deposited Wednesday, June 19. The issues in the case may conveniently be discussed in terms of the first check. As the depositary bank, Capital had initial control of the manner of presentment of that check to the payor bank, Florida State. Capital might have physically delivered the check for presentment over the counter at Florida State; it might have mailed the check to Florida State for presentment; or it might have included the check in the sack of other checks delivered the night of June 19 to the Federal Reserve Bank of Jacksonville, which would have granted Capital City provisional credit on the morning of June 20 and made presentment to Florida State that morning. If by either of those methods Capital City had forwarded the check for ultimate presentment, and presentment had occurred on Thursday, June 20, Florida State's deadline to dishonor the check would have been midnight of the following day, Friday, June 21, and the check would by law then be deemed finally paid and not subject to dishonor by Florida State on the following banking day, Monday, June 24. Capital City did not so route the check, but sent it the morning of Thursday, June 20, together with other checks held on Tallahassee banks, for handling in the local clearinghouse which Tallahassee banks employ to exchange and provisionally credit items requiring presentment in Tallahassee.

The heart of Capital City's position in this case is the assertion, well documented in this record, that a depositary bank which holds and has granted a depositor credit for a check drawn on another bank has as its primary purpose speedy presentment for payment by the payor. But, the record likewise demonstrates, that purpose may be overridden in favor of a slower method when distance or collection expense are substantial factors. It would not do to mail a check directly for presentment to a New York bank payor, for example, because the mails would delay use of the funds by the depositary bank, which may obtain them provisionally by negotiating the check to a nearby intermediary collecting bank. While a check thus negotiated goes its slower way to New York, the bank of deposit may enjoy use of the provisional credit granted by the collecting bank. The bank of deposit might hasten both provisional and final credit by dispatching an airborne courier to New York with the check, but collection costs would soar.

To serve common objectives of obtaining speedy provisional and final credit, at low collection cost, Tallahassee banks before 1928 instituted a clearing arrangement for locally destined checks. It replaced check-bearing couriers criss-crossing the town bent on presentment and obviated unsporting delays accomplished by banks which paid their local obligations with checks on accounts at distant banks. Four Tallahassee banks thenceforth adhered to a local clearinghouse arrangement whereby each day, at sites rotating among the participants, representatives of the four would meet, provisionally exchange and balance their mutual obligations, and give or receive net payments.

In time a solution was found for the cumbersome assembly of representatives of a growing number of participant banks and for delays in obtaining provisional credit caused by settling daily clearings with checks which themselves required collection. In 1968 the bank which is now Barnett Bank of Tallahassee undertook, for a fee, to collect accumulated checks from banks twice daily, to prepare a settlement sheet and to communicate to each participant bank the amount of its net provisional credit or obligation. Acting as the clearinghouse, Barnett Bank of Tallahassee by telephone caused provisional charges and credits to be made in the accounts of participating banks at Barnett Bank of Jacksonville. That was done following the morning clearing—we are not here concerned with the afternoon clearing—by noon or 12:30 each day. The clearinghouse then delivered the checks in batches to appropriate payor banks.

The recent advent of sophisticated computerized banking services both simplified and, as this case testifies, complicated the Tallahassee clearinghouse arrangement. The computer's speed and economy in sorting items, proving balances, identifying individual accounts and posting charges and credits made it desirable for all Tallahassee banks with which we are concerned to engage computer services; but, while Capital City and Lewis among others invested in the hardware and human skills necessary for computerized banking, others, including the relatively new Florida State Bank, did not. Those that did sold their computer services to those that didn't. Thus, Lewis sold services to Florida

State, and undertook by contract with Florida State to receive and process Florida State checks, including checks endorsed and forwarded for collection by the Federal Reserve Bank of Jacksonville, checks presented over the counter at Florida State and checks delivered through the Tallahassee clearinghouse by other local banks for presentment to Florida State. Florida State furnished Lewis records of its customer accounts and Lewis assimilated them in its computer system.

To gain rapid computer access to Florida State checks processed through the local clearinghouse, Florida State through Lewis directed Barnett, manager of the Tallahassee clearinghouse, to deliver Florida State checks to Lewis and to regard them as drawn on Lewis for purposes of calculating provisional charges and credits in daily settlements among participant banks. Lewis made a similar request for Gulf National Bank checks. Thus, Lewis received from the morning clearing not only its own checks but also those drawn on Florida State or Gulf National. By similar arrangements not directly pertinent here, Capital City received from the morning clearing checks drawn on Industrial National Bank, Capital City Second National Bank and City National Bank, as well as its own.

The morning of June 20, the day after Commonwealth deposited its ill-fated check on Florida State with Capital City, Capital City readied that check and approximately 250 others drawn on Lewis, Florida State and Gulf National for pickup by the clearinghouse courier. They were batched together, without differentiation among the three payor banks, under a machine tape showing the dollar total of the batch. Other batches, destined for clearing to other participant banks, were similarly prepared. The clearinghouse courier made his morning rounds, Barnett prepared the usual settlement sheet account for all items processed in batches that morning, the courier delivered copies of the settlement sheet and the appropriate batches of checks to the participant banks or those banks designated by other banks to receive their checks, and Barnett Bank of Jacksonville adjusted accounts to effectuate net provisional settlements.

Thus, between noon and 12:30 on Thursday, June 20, the Commonwealth check was delivered in an undifferentiated batch, with other batches from clearing, to Lewis. Lewis received them not at its downtown banking house but rather at the Lewis State Bank Data Processing Center, 13 blocks away. That building housed Lewis' computer hardware and operators and, insofar as here pertinent, two separate departments whose heads reported through different channels in Lewis' hierarchy: the proof and transit department and the data processing department. The relevant function of proof and transit was to receive and sign for incoming deliveries both from local clearings and from the Federal Reserve Bank of Jacksonville; to sort the batches into groups of checks drawn on Lewis, Florida State and Gulf National; to prove the dollar amount of items received against the machine tape totals claimed by local originating banks and carried forward in aggregate on Barnett's settlement sheet; to provisionally charge against accounts maintained at Lewis by Florida State and Gulf National the dollar total of checks drawn against them—thus recouping for Lewis the provisional charges made against its Jacksonville account for Florida State and Gulf National checks cleared to Lewis; to microfilm the checks; to endorse them with Lewis' stamp; and to deliver them to the data processing department.

The essential function of the data processing department, housed in the same building as proof and transit, was to receive checks from proof and transit; to post charges to customer accounts of Florida State, Gulf National and Lewis;

and to make ready for pickup by Florida State and Gulf National, in early morning of the next banking day, the checks drawn on those banks, with appropriate records of their handling by Lewis.

Lewis' proof and transit department sorted the checks received by it from the morning clearing of June 20, proved the totals, otherwise normally processed nearly all the checks drawn on Florida State and delivered them before 2:00 p.m. to data processing. But the Commonwealth check on Florida State was not among those delivered because its routing numbers had been improperly encoded on the face of the check, through no fault of Capital City, and the computer sorter employed by proof and transit could not identify the check as being drawn on Florida State. The check therefore missed the routine delivery to data processing and required individual handling by proof and transit which was not complete by 2:00 on June 20.

Although Capital City invariably completed on the day of receipt all processing of checks cleared to it for Industrial National, Capital City Second and City National, other arrangements had been made between Lewis and Florida State. Florida State ended its banking day at 2:00 p.m. and was accustomed to adjusting its reserves each day in reliance on notification at 2:00 p.m. of the amount of the gross provisional charge made to Florida State's account at Lewis by Lewis' proof and transit department. In 1973, Florida State had been embarrassed in the daily adjustment of its reserves by Lewis' addition of slower moving charges to Florida State's account after the 2:00 p.m. notification. Florida State had therefore requested that charges processed after the 2:00 p.m. notification be "held over and charged to our account the following business day." Lewis agreed, but did not notify Capital City or other Tallahassee depositary banks whose final payment of Florida State checks sent through the clearinghouse were to be so delayed.

The Commonwealth check deposited at Capital City on June 19 and cleared to Lewis on June 20 was ready for delivery by Lewis' proof and transit department to Lewis' data processing department after 2:00 p.m. on June 20, and was held over for delivery with Florida State checks to be received and processed before 2:00 p.m. the next day. On June 21, Lewis' proof and transit charged Florida State for the check; and data processing received the check and posted a charge to the Florida State record of Commonwealth's account. The check was physically delivered by Lewis to Florida State early Monday, June 24.

On Monday morning, Florida State's president, who on Friday afternoon had placed "hold orders" on all six Commonwealth checking accounts and had dispatched a messenger to notify Lewis' data processing department, dishonored the Commonwealth check and notified both Capital City and Lewis that the check was being returned. In a telephone conversation with Capital City's president, Florida State's president verbally acquiesced in or agreed to Capital City's assertion that the Commonwealth check had been presented to Florida State for payment on Thursday, June 20, not on Friday, June 21, and that Florida State's refusal of the check on Monday, June 24, was a day late. Although that verbal exchange produced an admission by Florida State of the untimeliness of its dishonor, it was not regarded by the trial court as estopping Florida State, not a party to this action, or Lewis. Capital City took no action in reliance on the verbal concession by Florida State.

Capital City refused to accept back the Commonwealth check from Florida State and refused to reverse the tentative settlement in favor of Capital City which had been made on account of that check in the clearings on June 20.

Although the Tallahassee banking custom was one of "direct return" of dishonored items to the bank of deposit, Florida State returned the check to Lewis, which accepted it as timely dishonored and credited the amount of it back to Florida State's account at Lewis.

As stated above, the second Commonwealth check in the amount of $140,000 was identically treated: it was deposited by Commonwealth to its Capital City account on June 20; sent by Capital City to the clearinghouse on the morning of June 21 and cleared to Lewis around noon on that day; rejected by the computer sorter operated by Lewis' proof and transit department because the routing numbers on its face did not correctly identify the payor bank; held over by proof and transit at 2:00 p.m. on June 21 for delivery on the next banking day, June 24, to Lewis' data processing department; posted by data processing to Commonwealth's Florida State account on the 24th; physically delivered to Florida State on the morning of the 25th; and dishonored by Florida State on the 25th.

The central issue in Lewis' claim is whether, as to each check—again, we will speak only of the first—Florida State timely dishonored it. Granting Florida State until midnight of the banking day following presentment to give notice of dishonor, §§ 673.506–.508(2), F.S. 1973, supra, the question becomes whether presentment was made to Florida State on Thursday, June 20, when the check was processed by Lewis' proof and transit department, or on Friday, June 21, when it was processed by Lewis' data processing department. Lewis concedes for purposes of argument that presentment was made to Florida State at Lewis' data processing department on Friday, June 21. Capital City contends that presentment to Florida State was accomplished by the check's delivery to Lewis from clearing on Thursday, June 20, or by its handling by Lewis' proof and transit on that date; or, alternatively, that Lewis defaulted in a duty to make speedy presentment of the check within Lewis' own building on June 21, or defaulted in a duty to advise Capital City the 2:00 p.m. deadline on charges by Lewis to Florida State would delay presentment. The issue was narrowed in pretrial conferences to one question: was Lewis an "intermediary collecting bank" in its relationship to Capital City and Florida State, so that delivery of the check to Lewis from clearings on June 20 imposed only the obligation to present the check the following day, § 674.202(2), F.S. 1973, supra; or was Lewis, by reason of authority received and exercised under its data processing contract with Florida State, Florida State's agent to receive presentment, in which case Florida State through Lewis received presentment on Thursday, June 20, and had only until midnight Friday to dishonor?

The trial court found, as a matter of mixed law and fact, that Lewis "was performing the functions of an intermediary collecting bank with respect to the two checks sued upon," and consequently that presentment did not occur when Lewis received and processed the checks in its proof and transit department. Thus, the trial court held Florida State's notices of dishonor were timely and that Lewis is entitled to recover the amount of the checks from Capital City.[1] The trial court refused to award Lewis interest on the debt on grounds Lewis' complaint demanded interest at "the average daily Federal funds rate" but Lewis introduced no evidence identifying that rate. The court ruled that Lewis, having failed to prove the special interest rate it alleged the parties contracted

1. Sec 674.212(2), F.S. 1973, in relevant part states: "Within the time and manner prescribed * * *, an intermediary or payor bank, as the case may be, may return an unpaid item directly to the depositary bank and may send for collection a draft on the depositary bank and obtain reimbursement."

for, was not entitled to interest at the statutory legal rate of six percent. Sec 55.03, F.S. 1973.

At the end of the trial, in which witnesses repeatedly emphasized the bankers' desire to obtain provisional and final credit for items in transit as quickly and directly as possible, the trial judge adjourned to consider his decision and instructed counsel, who had offered to send a copy of any controlling precedent that might be discovered:

> "THE COURT: I would dearly love for you to send me a case. And don't send it by any slow method. Send it by the fastest most direct method."

At the conclusion of two hours' oral argument of this appeal, we shared that yearning.

It is appropriate to recognize that the trial court was obliged, as are we, to decide this case without the influence of arguments that might naturally have been advanced by the payor bank, had it become embroiled in the litigation. In resolving this private controversy between Lewis and Capital City, it is not for us to dwell unduly on Lewis' possible reasons for reversing, with such alacrity, its charges to Florida State. But recognizing that our decision may be regarded as precedent for the resolution of other bankers' disputes, or for adjustment of their affairs by contract, we cannot entirely ignore the potential arguments, as we are able to discern them, of the payor bank. One such argument suggests a reason for Florida State's absence from this litigation—a reason more significant than Lewis' presumed desire not to offend its substantial depositor and data processing customer—and brings into sharp focus Lewis' basic premise that presentment could not occur until Florida State or Lewis, acting for Florida State, possessed at the same time and place both the check and sufficient information, not available at its proof and transit department, to decide to pay or not.

Florida State's notice of dishonor was effective against Lewis on Monday morning, June 24, regardless of whether presentment is considered to have occurred on Friday, June 21, when the Commonwealth check was posted to Commonwealth's account at Florida State on Lewis' data processing records, or on Monday, June 24, when the check was first delivered to Florida State. In either event, Florida State acted to dishonor the check before its midnight deadline on the banking day following presentment. But, had Florida State not been removed from the controversy by Lewis, Florida State surely might have contended at least alternatively that it could not receive presentment until it received the check itself, so to verify the signature and complete the statutory "process of posting" which Florida State was entitled to accomplish as an element of final payment. Secs. 674.213(1)(c)–.109, F.S. 1973.

Such an argument, though entirely plausible under the Code, was more than Florida State needed to prevail against Lewis; but if made, that argument could seriously jeopardize Lewis' case against Capital City. For it would show Lewis as a collecting bank—Lewis' own characterization of itself—which received the check June 20 but did not perform its statutory duty to present or send the check for presentment "before its midnight deadline following receipt of an item," i.e., by midnight June 21. Secs. 674.202–.204, F.S. 1973. Hence, Lewis "concedes," for purposes of this case, that presentment to Florida State occurred in the Lewis State Bank Data Processing Center on June 21, when data processing posted a charge to Commonwealth's account. That was before any officer of Florida State had seen the check or knew of it.

A thread of ambiguity therefore runs through the testimony and through Lewis' basic premise that presentment could not occur at proof and transit, but only at data processing, where sufficient information existed for a decision to pay or not. Lewis' manager of data processing, where presentment "concededly" occurred, testified:

"Q. Now at your Department do you make any determination to pay or not to pay?

"A. We do not.

"Q. Who makes that determination?

"A. Florida State Bank."

But Florida State's president described his understanding of presentment and response this way:

> "I understand they would come in a mixed batch; that is, with other checks that Lewis State Bank was performing a similar function on, and would be separated, provisional settlement would be made against Florida State Bank['s] account with Lewis State Bank, they would be microfilmed, *and then they would be presented for payment to the Lewis State Bank Data Processing Center.*"
>
> * * *
>
> "So when they go to Data Processing and are presented for payment, *then we make a determination of whether we will pay, return, or what we'll do* " (emphasis added).

Florida State's president did not explain how, at Lewis' data processing department, "we," meaning Florida State, "make a determination of whether we will pay, return, or what we'll do."

Lewis' position is therefore quite discreet: (1) Lewis denies that presentment to Florida State occurred on June 20 in Lewis' proof and transit department; (2) Lewis does not deny that presentment occurred on June 21 in its data processing department; and (3) Lewis does not deny, because the matter is not here in issue, that presentment occurred on June 24 when the check was physically sent to Florida State.

The controversy cannot properly be resolved by forcing the facts into syllogisms that beg the main question of whether Lewis' proof and transit department was the "place" or "person" designated by Florida State to receive presentment of its checks. Section 673.504(3)(b), [674].204(3), F.S. 1973. It is unavailing for Capital City to urge presentment at Lewis' proof and transit department must have occurred June 20, since no prudent depositary bank would knowingly choose a collection method which delayed presentment until June 21 in preference to collection through Federal Reserve Bank of Jacksonville, which would have made presentment June 20. As depositary bank and the original collection bank, Capital City was obliged by the law of self-interest, but by no other law or practice, to select the most appropriate collection method. It was obliged to know, for example, that Florida State could lawfully fix 2:00 p.m. "as a cut-off hour for the handling of money and items and the making of entries on its books," § 674.107(1), F.S. 1973, and that Florida State had done so. Capital City was obliged to inform itself of potential delays in alternative collection processes available, and to choose wisely.

Nor is the question entirely answered by Lewis' reasoning that, since it was an "intermediary" and "collecting" bank in the statutory sense of any bank handling an item for collection except the depositary or the payor bank, § 674.105(3), (4), F.S. 1973, its proof and transit department could not also be the place or person designated by Florida State for receipt of presentment. Sections 673.504(3)(b), [674].204(3), F.S. 1973. In the latter section, the Uniform Commercial Code specifically recognizes that computerized banking may make it appropriate for a payor to designate a computer center as the place of presentment. See Comment 4 to § 4–204, UCC, 19B F.S.A. § 674.4–204 at 379 (1966). If a nonbank commercial data processing center is designated by the payor bank as the place of presentment, presentment there is effective notwithstanding that the intake department performs the sorting, proving, microfilming, and notification functions here performed by Lewis' proof and transit department. Similarly, if a bank operates a data processing service for other payor banks within or without its banking house, designation of the data processing bank as the place of presentment is not made ineffective by the simple fact the bank "handles" the item for collection and is, therefore, a "collecting bank." Section 674.105(4), F.S. 1973. We accept as true the trial court's finding that Lewis was an "intermediary collecting bank," but we do not draw the legal implication urged by Lewis, that it (more precisely, its proof and transit department) was thereby disqualified as the place for presentment. With that erroneous implication falls Lewis' argument that, since proof and transit gave Capital City provisional credit,[2] made a provisional charge against and so notified Florida State, and microfilmed and endorsed the Commonwealth checks, it could not be the place for presentment.

Neither can we accept Lewis' argument that the personnel of its proof and transit department had no more authority than the guard at the door "to make or refuse the acceptance or payment," § 673.504(3)(b), F.S. 1973, and therefore cannot have been the persons or place designated for presentment. Section 673.504(2)(a), F.S. 1973, also makes presentment by mail effective at "the time of receipt of the mail," and it matters not that the person who receives and opens the mail is a clerk ignorant of information essential to the decision to pay or refuse. Moreover, Lewis' argument that presentment cannot be made except to one having both information and authority to pay or dishonor proves too much. For the previously-quoted testimony of both Lewis' manager of data processing and Florida State's president proved, if nothing else, that only Florida State had authority to pay or refuse. Thus by Lewis' reasoning presentment would be delayed, in the face of Lewis' "concession" and its expert testimony,[3] until the

2. Part of Lewis' demonstration that its proof and transit department acted separately from data processing as a collecting bank was its expert's opinion that proof and transit "granted" Capital City provisional credit and "proved" the sum of the items against the sum claimed in the machine tapes and settlement sheet. But Lewis "granted" Capital City provisional credit only by its standing order to Barnett Bank of Jacksonville to honor instructions by the clearinghouse, Barnett Bank of Tallahassee, for provisional settlements of the items cleared. There is evidence Lewis' proof and transit department "proved" the balances on the settlement sheet sent by the clearinghouse, but no evidence that proof and transit, acting separately or as an integral Lewis department, had anything to do with "granting" Capital City provisional credit for the checks cleared to Lewis.

3. Lewis' banking expert acknowledged that presentment may be designated to occur, and may occur, somewhere other than the place where both the necessary information and the ultimate authority to pay coalesce. He testified: "And then they [proof and transit] had to forward the items to someone who had the information and authority *to begin the process* of making a determination of whether or not an item should be paid or returned. And I believe that * * * data processing basically *begins that process* " (emphasis added). Presumably the witness adverted to circumstances in which the computer had nearly all the information and all but the ultimate authority to return a check drawn on a nonexistent, closed or overdrawn account, or to pay an apparently regular check drawn on an account shown by computer information to be adequate. This record does not inform us whether Lewis' computer could inform anyone at data processing on June 21 that the Commonwealth check was drawn on "uncollected funds."

Commonwealth check reached Florida State on Monday, June 24. When § 673.504(3)(b) speaks of presentment "to any person" with authority to pay or refuse, it speaks not only of individuals but also of organizations, and the term "organization" does not differentiate between departments of a single corporate entity. Sec. 671.201(28), (30), F.S. 1973.

This case combines significant circumstances—presentment through a clearinghouse and a payor bank's use of offsite computer processing—which were separately considered in Geibe v. Chicago Lake State Bank, 160 Minn. 89, 199 N.W. 514 (1924) and Farmers and Merchants Bank of Long Beach v. Bank of America, 20 Cal.App.3d 939, 98 Cal.Rptr. 381 (1971). In Geibe, under Negotiable Instruments Law provisions similar to those of the Commercial Code now applicable in Florida, the Minnesota Supreme Court held that the payor bank is entitled to presentment at its banking house; but that, if the payor bank designates a local clearinghouse member to receive its checks from clearings, presentment "at and through" the clearinghouse is presentment to the payor bank. In Farmers and Merchants Bank, the California court held presentment of a check to the Harbor-Orangewood branch of Bank of America—a bank separate from Bank of America under California law—occurred when a messenger delivered the check for processing for Harbor-Orangewood at Bank of America's Montebello computer center, located apart from the involved banking houses. Because it was unnecessary to the decision, the court assumed without deciding the trial court correctly ruled presentment had not previously occurred at Bank of America's separate Southwest Erma computer center, where the check was first taken in a batch for sorting. The court found the Montebello computer center performed functions antecedent to final payment or dishonor which previously were manually performed on presentment by employees at the payor's banking house. Consequently—to use the characterization by Lewis' expert witness of similar functions in Lewis' data processing department—the Montebello computer center received presentment because it began the process of determining whether to pay or dishonor Harbor-Orangewood's check.

In the circumstances of this case, the Commonwealth check delivered by the Tallahassee clearinghouse to Lewis State Bank Data Processing Center on June 20 was thereby presented to Florida State for payment. Presentment was not there delayed by the need for sorting the check from mixed batches of checks drawn on Florida State, Lewis and Gulf National. Put another way, we reject as a matter of law the distinction urged by Lewis between its proof and transit and data processing departments at the processing center. Three considerations lead us to this result:

First, the data processing contract between Florida State and Lewis contemplated Florida State would deliver its checks and other "input data" to Lewis at Lewis' "banking house," without distinguishing between Lewis' separate buildings or between separate departments within the same building. Although the contract did not employ the term "presentment," it was pursuant to that contract that Lewis concedes and the evidence shows presentment did occur when the check began final processing for payment or dishonor. The contract required Florida State to deliver input items, including checks, in orderly batches. That requirement was not fulfilled, for Florida State's checks were not segregated from those of Lewis and Gulf National by Capital City, which was not requested to do so, nor by the clearinghouse or Florida State. Sorting was therefore necessary at Lewis' processing center, and Lewis by contract retained the option of providing such extra services to make Florida State's items "machine processable" at extra expense to Florida State. The necessity for sorting—at Lewis' choice, done in its proof and transit rather than its data processing department—did not modify or divide the contract's singular purpose: the performance by Lewis, for a fee, of functions which in law constitute presentment of Florida State's checks.

Second, though we need not decide whether presentment occurs at the receiving and sorting facility of an agent for presentment which must forward items to its remote data processing center for presentment functions, as in Farmers and Merchants Bank, we cannot accept Lewis' distinction between separate departments within its single computer center. Granting that a payor bank may reserve entirely to itself the selection of a place for presentment other than its banking house, § 674.204(3), F.S. 1973, Florida State's contract for data processing services and its vicarious participation in the clearinghouse arrangement constituted designation of Lewis State Bank as the place for presentment of Florida State checks processed through the clearinghouse. It explicitly designated "Lewis State Bank Data Processing Center" as the place for presentment of checks in process of collection through Federal Reserve Bank of Jacksonville. In neither its Federal Reserve contract nor its instructions to the clearinghouse did Florida State specify presentment to Lewis' data processing department, as contrasted with its proof and transit department.

And third, Lewis' attempted distinction between its departments at the center would cancel the Code's provision for presentment "[t]hrough a clearinghouse," § 673.504(2)(b), F.S. 1973, and the consistent purpose of the Tallahassee clearinghouse since before 1928. Though not a signatory to the clearinghouse agreement, Florida State elected to participate through Lewis and so became privy to it. Geibe, supra, 160 Minn. at 94, 199 N.W. at 516.[4] Presentment was the immediate, not the remote, object of that arrangement. In earlier days, when Tallahassee bankers met and exchanged checks across a table, that was considered presentment; when later they designated Barnett Bank of Tallahassee to receive, provisionally settle and deliver checks to payor banks, proper delivery of checks was considered presentment; and now, when the clearinghouse has been asked by nonsignatory banks to provisionally settle their checks and deliver them for processing to participant banks having computer capacity, that delivery too is presentment. If Lewis' arrangements with multiple payor banks make sorting necessary by depositary banks, by the clearinghouse, or by Lewis at the place for presentment, that is a matter for the banks to regulate by custom or agreement; but delivery of Florida State's checks to Lewis is nevertheless presentment at the place designated by Florida State.

We therefore hold as a matter of law that delivery of the first Commonwealth check by the clearinghouse to Lewis on June 20 constituted presentment to Florida State; that delivery of the second Commonwealth check on June 21 likewise constituted presentment, and that, regardless of the number or complexity of steps taken by Lewis to make Florida State's checks machine processable for the decision to pay or dishonor, Florida State was obliged by §§ 674.212(2), 674.213 and 674.301, F.S. 1973, to dishonor the checks before midnight of the banking day following presentment or be held "accountable for the amount of the item." Section 674.213(1)(d), F.S. 1973. Florida State having failed to dishonor the Commonwealth checks within the time allowed after presentment,

4. "When, by arrangement with a member bank, an outside bank gains admission to the clearing house, the member bank becomes its agent, and its rights and liabilities should be determined by applying the principles of the law of agency."

its attempt thereafter to dishonor was ineffective as to Capital City, which therefore is not liable to Lewis.

The case will be remanded for entry of judgment for Capital City.

Reversed.

MILLS, ACTING CHIEF JUDGE, and MELVIN, WOODROW M., ASSOCIATE JUDGE, concur.

Notes

1. Consider the learning that the *Lewis* case demanded of the lawyers. It, and many other cases like it, fundamentally depend upon an intimate knowledge of the complex workings in the basement of the bank.

2. If you represented a bank either in a multi-branch system such as that in Idaho, or in a remote processing system such as that in Florida, how would you advise your bank in order to avoid liability? Assume that your bank client suggested the following changes, what do you think of them?

a. To modify the agreement between the data processing bank and the payor bank to provide that presentment shall not be deemed to have occurred until the item physically reaches the payor.

b. Modification of the Clearing House rules to provide a similar result.

c. Modification of the internal rules of the bank to provide that no check shall be deemed finally paid until the process of posting is completed and that the process of posting shall not have occurred until the representatives of the branch on which it is drawn have seen the instrument.

If none of these work, what do you suggest?

3. If cases like *Capital City* continue to hold that a check presented to the processing center is presented for payment, how can a bank that wishes to do so verify that the check presented is in fact one drawn by its customer? Normally this is done by an examination of the signature of the customer. If the check remains in Boise and the signature card is in Haley, that cannot be done. Do you have any suggestions?

H. SCHULTZ & SONS, INC. v. BANK OF SUFFOLK COUNTY

United States District Court, Eastern District New York, 1977.
439 F.Supp. 1137.

PRATT, DISTRICT JUDGE. Plaintiff H. Schultz & Sons, Inc. is incorporated and maintains its principal place of business in New Jersey. Defendant Suffolk County Bank is incorporated and maintains its principal place of business in New York. Plaintiff brought this diversity action to obtain the $40,000 face value of a check which was drawn to plaintiff by Unishops, Inc. on an account maintained by Unishops at the defendant bank, and which plaintiff alleges was wrongfully dishonored after the bank learned of Unishops' bankruptcy. Jurisdiction therefore lies under 28 U.S.C. § 1332.

* * * For the reasons set forth below, plaintiff's motion [for summary judgment] is granted, and defendant's is denied.

FACTS

There is no dispute over the essential facts. For purposes of these motions the parties have agreed that the following facts are true:

1. The $40,000 check was dated November 26, 1973 and drawn by Unishops on its account at defendant's bank, payable to the order of plaintiff.

2. Plaintiff deposited the check for collection on November 27, 1973 in its account at Fidelity Union Trust Co. of Newark, New Jersey.

3. Fidelity forwarded the check to the Federal Reserve Bank of New York, which in turn forwarded the check to defendant. Id.

4. Defendant received the check on November 29, 1973.

5. On the same day, November 29, 1973, the check was photographed, "proven", and debited to Unishops' account by defendant.

6. Defendant learned of Unishops' bankruptcy on November 30, 1973 and on that same day gave telephone notice of dishonor of the check to the Federal Reserve Bank.

7. If defendant had not subsequently learned of Unishops' bankruptcy, no additional processing of the check would have taken place prior to the sending out of Unishops' monthly statement.

8. Defendant never honored the check.

9. Plaintiff was never a depositor with defendant.

CLAIMS

Initially, plaintiff sought judgment on two theories: (1) that since defendant failed to return the check by its "midnight deadline", it was obligated to pay the check to plaintiff, and (2) since defendant had "finally paid" the check it could not thereafter refuse payment based on its subsequent receipt of notice of Unishops' bankruptcy. Prior to and at the time of argument plaintiff withdrew the first ground for relief, urging only that final payment had been made so that subsequent notice of bankruptcy was ineffective to prevent plaintiff's recovery of the proceeds. Defendant seeks summary judgment on the ground that final payment had not occurred and could not occur until expiration of the maximum time permitted for return of the check, here, midnight on the day following receipt of the check or midnight of November 30, 1973.

As to most of the applicable law the parties are in agreement:

1. If under the circumstances of this case a "final payment" had been made, then defendant bank is accountable to plaintiff for the $40,000 proceeds of the check. N.Y.U.C.C. § 4–213(1).

2. Final payment did occur if the bank had "completed the process of posting" the check to Unishops' account. N.Y.U.C.C. § 4–213(1)(c).

3. If the bank had "completed the process of posting", the notice of Unishops' bankruptcy came too late to affect defendant's accountability to plaintiff. N.Y.U.C.C. § 4–303(1)(d).

The parties disagree on whether the bank's "process of posting" was completed here, and this squarely raises a question of law, the proper interpretation of § 4–109 of New York's Uniform Commercial Code. N.Y.U.C.C. § 4–109 defines the "Process of posting" as

> "The usual procedure followed by a payor bank in determining to pay an item and in recording the payment including one or more of the following or other steps as determined by the bank;

"(a) verification of any signature;

"(b) ascertaining that sufficient funds are available;

"(c) affixing a 'paid' or other stamp;

"(d) entering a charge or entry to a customer's account;

"(e) *correcting or reversing an entry or erroneous action* with respect to the item." (Emphasis supplied.)

The first four steps listed were completed by the defendant. As to the fifth step defendant argues that, because of the language of subparagraph (e) of § 4–109, it retained discretion, and indeed had the duty under the Bankruptcy Law, to reverse the entry, and it could properly do so anytime up until the "midnight deadline" even though all other steps in the process of posting had been completed. The "midnight deadline" is defined as midnight on the next banking day [following the banking day] on which the bank receives the relevant item. N.Y.U.C.C. § 4–104(1)(h). Under the deferred posting practice employed by defendant and authorized by N.Y.U.C.C. § 4–301 the latest possible time for defendant to have returned the subject check unpaid was the midnight deadline.

The Official Comments to this uniform act also aid in its interpretation, and their failure to support defendant's position argues strongly against its validity.

Under defendant's interpretation of the statute, however, the only time the process of posting could be completed would be upon expiration of the midnight deadline. This would mean that the draftsmen's specification of the other steps in the process of posting, aimed at the subjective decision of whether to pay the check and the mechanical process of recording the payment, become meaningless.

Plaintiff's interpretation of subparagraph (e) would permit the "correcting or reversing of any entry or erroneous action" only in the event that an error had been made, whether in decision making or in mechanical recording. It does not, according to plaintiff, authorize correcting or reversing an entry merely upon the receipt of additional information or notice which was not brought to the bank's attention prior to completion of the other elements in the process of posting.

Discussion

The question presented here was considered by the Supreme Court of Wisconsin in West Side Bank v. Marine National Exchange Bank, 37 Wis.2d 661, 155 N.W.2d 587 (1968) and decided in favor of the bank. There, the Wisconsin court read the words "reversing an entry" in subsection (e) to authorize the bank to do precisely that—reverse an entry—without restriction as to the reason for the reversal. The court adopted what it viewed to be the plain meaning of the statute, even though it acknowledged that the legislature's intent was probably to the contrary.

The same problem has been reviewed in depth in a law review note entitled "Bank Procedures and the UCC—When is a Check Finally Paid?", 9 Boston College Industrial and Commercial L.Rev. 1957 (1968). The importance of the concept of "final payment" in the banking sections of the UCC is highlighted by the following paragraph from that article:

> "The concept of final payment is central to the scheme of Article 4 because the time of final payment of a check or similar item is the starting point for determining the rights and obligations of a number of parties in relation to an item. When final payment occurs, the payor bank is deemed to be accountable to the presenting party for the amount of the item. At the same time the drawer

of the instrument is relieved of liability to the holder because the amount is deemed to have been paid. Also, if the payor bank becomes insolvent and suspends payment once final payment has occurred, the owner of an item will have a preferred claim against the payor bank for the amount. Final payment, furthermore, is one of the occurrences which can prevent the 'four legals'—notice, stop-order, legal process and setoff—from being effective to prevent actual payment of the item. Provisional settlement, the credit given by the payor bank to the party presenting an item for collection, becomes final when final payment is made, as does credit for the item between the presenting bank, other collecting banks and the customer seeking payment for the item. Final payment, moreover, marks the end of the collection process and the beginning of the remitting process, whereby the amount of the item is returned to the party demanding payment."

[Id. at 957–58] [Footnotes omitted]

Discussing the Wisconsin case, the author rejects the Wisconsin court's analysis, and suggests an alternative design to accommodate both the language of § 4–109 and the policies underlying its adoption: The author's suggestion would apply subsection (e) only to that part of the process of posting relating to the "recording the payment" and not to the second part relating to "determining to pay". While this reasoning has some appeal, it does not fully solve the problem since an error made in the "determining to pay" part of the process of posting should be just as capable of correction prior to the midnight deadline as would be a typographical or mechanical error in "recording the payment".

Sounder analysis seems to require that the legislature's intent be honored. As described in the excerpt from the law review article quoted above, the process of posting was viewed by the draftsmen as encompassing two parts, the mechanical steps of "recording the payment" and the judgmental steps of "determining to pay". Whatever elements a bank injects into those two parts, and, in whatever sequence they may be performed, once all steps have been taken the "process of posting" is then deemed by the statute to be complete. Moreover, the bank's right to return the check unpaid is subject to two conditions: (1) that it has not "made final payment", i.e. "completed the process of posting", and (2) that the midnight deadline has not passed. The failure of either condition would defeat the bank's right to return the check.

(a) Examples 1 and 2 of the Official Comment to UCC § 4–109 contemplate that the process of posting is completed when both the decision to pay has been made and the payment has been recorded, regardless of the order in which those events occur. No mention in those examples is made of an automatic, universal extension of time to the midnight deadline; on the contrary, discussion of the examples given would be unnecessary if, indeed, the draftsmen had intended to make the midnight deadline the only temporal measure of final payment.

(b) Paragraphs 3 and 5 of the Official Comment to UCC § 4–213 indicate the policies sought to be accomplished by the final payment concept. In neither is it suggested that all there is to final payment is the mere expiration of the midnight deadline.

Nor is the language of § 4–109(e) as plain and unambiguous as the Wisconsin court described. If the language as the Wisconsin court viewed it read merely "reversing an entry", there might be substance to the plain meaning argument for rejecting an otherwise clear legislative intent. However, the statute does not read "reversing an entry". Those words appear in a larger phrase: "correcting or reversing an entry or erroneous action". In the context of this larger phrase, the legislature could have contemplated several different meanings. Following a principle of parallel grammatical construction, it could have meant "correcting an entry or reversing an erroneous action", thereby permitting the first verb to operate on the first direct object, and the second verb to operate on the second direct object. Under this interpretation both phrases involve elements of righting an error. "Correcting an entry" would remedy mechanical or recording errors; "reversing an erroneous action" would permit correction of more complex actions such as judgments over a correct signature or determination of whether sufficient funds were available.

Another possible reading of subsection (e) would present four possible combinations of the two verbs and two direct objects: "correcting an entry", "correcting erroneous action", "reversing an entry", and "reversing erroneous action". Under this view of the language, three of the four involve concepts of "correcting" or "erroneous". Only one of them, "reversing an entry", omits any specific reference to a prior mistake. Thus, five out of these six possible readings of subsection (e) focus upon errors, either mechanical or judgmental.

Under these circumstances the statute cannot reasonably be read as having a plain meaning and unambiguously providing that "error" was not the determinative factor. When the underlying policies and intent of the bank collection sections of the UCC are so clearly demonstrated by its history, see Bank Procedures of the UCC—When is a Check Finally Paid?, supra, and by the Official Comments, the court should not adopt an aberrational interpretation of § 4–109(e) such as urged by the defendant here and adopted by the Wisconsin Supreme Court. This is particularly so when the interpretation urged by defendant would render meaningless the remaining four subsections of § 4–109. Furthermore, on a policy level, an enormous legislative effort would be required to substitute in the states' separate enactments of this uniform law language which would unambiguously state the clear legislative purpose.

The underlying policy being clear, the legislative intent being bolstered by the Official Comments, and the language of subsection (e) strongly implying merely a device to rectify mistakes, the court concludes that subsection (e) of § 4–109 does not permit a payor bank, without regard to its reason or purpose, to reverse an entry at any time up to the midnight deadline. Instead, subsection (e) permits corrective action to be taken only in those cases where an error of some type has been made by the bank in completing its process of posting.

Applied to the facts of this case, defendant had made no error and it had, indeed, completed its process of posting. Thereafter, when notice of the bankruptcy was received, it was too late to reverse the entry. Once the process of posting was complete, payment was final, and defendant became accountable to plaintiff for the proceeds, unaffected by the notice of bankruptcy or any other knowledge, notice, stop order, or legal process thereafter received.

Accordingly, plaintiff's motion for summary judgment is granted and defendant's motion is denied.

Notes

1. The court suggests that the process of posting has been completed no sooner than the time when payor bank has taken "the mechanical steps 'of recording payment' and the judgmental steps of 'determining to pay'." In many cases the check will be run through the machines in the basement, the printout will come to an officer's desk showing all of the payments of the night before, but there will never be any "individual determination" with respect to a check unless the account on which

it is drawn has insufficient funds. Once the bank officer has gone through the checks that are overdrawn, has he made the "determination" to pay?

To focus on this question, consider a kiting case in which the officer looks at a series of checks on Monday morning that were brought to the bank some time over the weekend. He sees nothing out of the ordinary and makes no decision to dishonor any of the checks in question. On Tuesday morning and before the midnight deadline (which we assume will occur at Tuesday midnight), the bank decides that the checks drawn against uncollected funds are part of a kite. It wishes to return the checks. Can it do so? If it cannot, that suggests something that every lawyer involved in the aftermath of a kite should be interested in.

Note that 4–109 states the process of posting consists of the "usual procedure followed by the payor bank." Assume that the payor adopted the following policy: "For the purpose of payment at this bank, posting has not been completed on any check until the midnight deadline has run on that check." Would the court interpret the "process of posting" consistent with such a policy on the ground that that was an expression of the "usual procedure" of the bank?

2. Apparently the defendant bank conceded liability if the court found it had finally paid. Could the bank have asserted a right of restitution?

On this question, see the cases that follow.

NATIONAL SAVINGS & TRUST CO. v. PARK CORP.

United States Court of Appeals, Sixth Circuit, 1983.
722 F.2d 1303, cert. denied, 466 U.S. 939, 104 S.Ct. 1916, 80 L.Ed.2d 464 (1984).

MARTIN, CIRCUIT JUDGE. In this diversity action, National Savings and Trust challenges the summary denial of its claim for restitution of $74,737.25 it mistakenly paid to Park Corporation on a bad check.

On January 8, 1980, Park Corporation contracted to sell some used mining equipment to DAI International Investment Corporation. The sales agent for the transaction was Garland Caribbean Corporation. As part of its down payment, DAI gave Garland a check for $75,000 drawn on its account with the plaintiff, National Savings and Trust Company. On January 16, Garland called National Savings to determine if DAI had sufficient funds in its account to cover this check. The bank said DAI did not. That same day, Garland endorsed the check over to Park Corporation. Park Corporation then sent the check to National Savings "for collection."

On January 22, Garland once again called the bank to determine if DAI had sufficient funds in its account to cover the check. Once again, the bank said DAI did not.[1] Moreover, on this occasion, the banking employee who received the inquiry went to the bank's "platform officer" and notified him not to accept any DAI checks drawn on insufficient funds. Unfortunately for the bank, the platform officer only saw checks arriving through normal banking channels and not those coming in "for collection."

DAI's check arrived at the bank that same day. However, the employee who normally processed "for collection" checks was scheduled to work in another department that day. Prior to her departure, she did manage to open the incoming mail, including the DAI check. Her supervisor then volunteered to help out by taking the DAI check to the wire room for payment. Neither employee followed the bank's standard procedure and checked DAI's account to

1. There is no evidence Park was ever aware of Garland's phone conversations with the bank.

ensure that it held sufficient funds to cover the check. Each assumed that the other had done so. As a result, the check was paid even though DAI had only $263.75 in its account.

On January 28, 1980, after discovering its mistake, National Savings asked Park Corporation to return the $75,000. Park refused and National Savings subsequently brought this lawsuit. On motion for summary judgment by the defendant, the court found for Park on the grounds that National Savings had made an improvident extension of credit and that the bank was in a better position to know the true facts and to guard against mistakes. We disagree.

The basic law of restitution in Ohio, the state whose law controls, is summarized in Firestone Rubber & Tire Co. v. Central Nat'l Bank of Cleveland, 159 Ohio St. 423, 112 N.E.2d 636 (1953). The Firestone case held that money paid to another by mistake is recoverable unless the other person has changed his position in reliance on the payment. This rule applies even if the mistake was the result of negligence.

Park Corporation attempts to circumvent the holding in Firestone by arguing that banks are not protected by normal restitutionary principles when they pay an insufficient funds (NSF) check. There is some support for this position. See, e.g., Spokane & Eastern Trust Co. v. Huff, 63 Wash. 225, 115 P. 80 (1911); 7 Zollman, The Law of Banks and Banking § 5062 (1936). * * * Park has not cited, nor have we been able to find, any Ohio cases adopting this rule. Moreover, it is questionable whether such a doctrine, if ever in existence, would survive the subsequent enactment of the Uniform Commercial Code in Ohio and the particular provisions applicable to the facts of the present case.

Park Corporation next argues that Firestone does not control because National Savings' payment was not a mistake but rather a knowing extension of credit. Park relies heavily on the New Jersey case of Demos v. Lyons, 151 N.J.Super. 489, 376 A.2d 1352 (Law.Div. 1977). The factual circumstances of Demos, however, are quite distinct from the present case. In Demos, the bank actually examined the customer's account, realized the customer had insufficient funds to cover the check, yet paid the check anyway. The bank did not want to embarrass its customer and it hoped that he had made a late deposit to cover the check which would appear on the next day's balance sheet. No such deposit was ever made. In our case, National Savings never intended to make good on an NSF check. The platform officer had been notified not to pay out on DAI's check. The "for collection" employees were operating under standing orders to check balances before paying a check and never to pay on an NSF check. Despite all these precautions, the check was paid. At no time, however, did the employees making the payment decision know that DAI's account had insufficient funds to cover the check.

Park's next contention is that the Uniform Commercial Code as adopted in Ohio bars restitutionary recovery for banks that pay NSF checks. This argument focuses on an apparent conflict between two provisions of the UCC, § 3–418 and § 4–213. Section 3–418 of the Code (O.R.C. § 1303.54), which applies to all transactions involving negotiable instruments, states that "payment or acceptance of any instrument is final in favor of a holder in due course, or a person who has in good faith changed his position in reliance on the payment." [2] Because a holder in due course is simply a special type of detrimental relier, this section is basically a codification of restitutionary principles established in

2. Section 3–418 also has special exceptions not applicable here which allow banks and other acceptors and payors to recover where a check has a forged endorsement.

Firestone. Official Comment 3 to this section makes clear that if there is no detrimental reliance by the payee, then recovery of payment is permitted.

Park Corporation argues that another provision of the UCC, § 4–213, establishes a special non-recovery rule for banks which mistakenly pay on a bad check. Section 4–213(1) (O.R.C. § 1304.19(A)) states that "[a]n item is finally paid by a payor bank when the bank has done any of the following, which ever happens first: (a) paid the item in cash. * * *" Park contends that "finally paid" as used in this section has the same meaning as the "payment is final" language in § 3–418, namely restitutionary recovery is no longer possible. Moreover, because § 4–213 does not have the restrictive provisions which limit coverage to holders in due course or those who detrimentally rely, Park argues that § 4–213 makes a bank strictly liable as soon as it pays on an NSF check.[3] Furthermore, UCC § 4–102 provides that, in case of conflict between Articles 3 and 4, the provisions of Article 4 are to govern. Thus, Park argues, National Savings is barred from recovering the $75,000.

At first glance, Park's argument has a certain appeal. That is not surprising because it is based in large part on the work of White & Summers, whose treatise, Uniform Commercial Code (2d ed. 1980), is generally considered the leading authority on commercial transactions. Id. at 613–617. Several courts have also reached the same conclusion. See, e.g., Ashford Bank v. Capital Preservation Fund, Inc., 544 F.Supp. 26, 28–29 (D.Mont. 1982); Kirby v. First & Merchants Nat'l Bank, 210 Va. 88, 168 S.E.2d 273, 275 n. 4 (1969). Confer Bartlett v. Bank of Carroll, 218 Va. 240, 237 S.E.2d 115, 119 (1977).

Nonetheless, opinion on the matter is by no means uniform. Other writers, see H. Bailey, Brady on Bank Checks § 14.20 at 14–32 (5th ed. Supp. 1983); B. Clark, The Law of Check Deposits § 5.3[3] (2d ed. 1981), and other courts, see Demos v. Lyons, 151 N.J.Super. 489, 376 A.2d 1352 (Law.Div. 1977); Blake v. Woodford Bank & Trust Co., 555 S.W.2d 589, 601–02 (Ky.App. 1977), have argued that banks retain their restitutionary rights with respect to mistaken payment of NSF checks. Our own analysis of the Code convinces us that the latter group is correct and that § 4–213 does not expand the final payment doctrine to bar recovery by payor banks from payees who have not detrimentally relied. In our analysis, we rely heavily on the official Comments to §§ 3–418 and 4–213. While these comments to the Code are not part of enacted law, they are a very helpful guide to construing the meaning of Code provisions. See In re Augustin Bros. Co., 460 F.2d 376, 380 (8th Cir. 1972).

An examination of the comments to § 3–418 makes clear both that this section was intended to apply to "the payment of overdrafts, or any other payment made in error as to the state of the drawer's account," Comment 2, and that restitutionary recovery was to be denied only when the payee had relied on the payment. "If no value has been given for the instrument, the holder loses nothing by the recovery of the payment, * * * and it is not entitled to profit at the expense of the drawee. * * *" Comment 3.

The only mention of § 4–213 occurs in Comment 5, where the Code drafters point out that the provisions of § 3–418 do not apply until payment is final as defined in § 4–213. This comment suggests a method for resolving the apparent conflict between § 3–418 and § 4–213. As the court in Demos v. Lyons put it, § 4–213 "is oriented toward time of payment, not legal effect of payment." 376

3. Park agrees with White & Summers, Uniform Commercial Code 617 (2d ed 1980), that there must be a "good faith" requirement read into § 4–213 so that payors acting fraudulently do not benefit.

A.2d at 1356. The purpose of § 4–213 is "to determine *when* settlement for an item or other action with respect to it constitutes final payment." Comment 1, § 4–213 (emphasis added). Section 4–213 determines *when* the final payment rule of § 3–418 comes into effect, not *what* that rule is supposed to mean. Further support for this position comes from the remaining comments to § 4–213. Comment 1 states "final payment is important" because it helps determine "priorities between items and notices, stop orders, legal process and setoffs, [because it] is the 'end of the line' in the collection process, [and because it] is the point at which many provisional settlements become final." The remaining comments discuss such arcane banking matters as posting, provisional settlements, and midnight deadlines. At no point does any comment to § 4–213 mention the effect this section is supposed to have on the restitutionary rights of banks. Thus, it seems evident that the drafters of the Code never intended for § 4–213 to supersede § 3–418, and we can see no reason to adopt a position contrary to that intent.

As further support for our decision, we feel obliged to note that White & Summers, the authorities most relied on for the contrary proposition, now appear to have changed their minds. Professor White, in a note written for a colleague's textbook, has recanted and now supports the view that § 4–213 makes no substantive change in the law of restitution as applied to banks. See D. Epstein & J. Martin, Basic Uniform Commercial Code 514 (2d ed. 1983). Presumably the next edition of his treatise will reflect this change in thinking.

Park Corporation next contends that, even if § 3–418 controls, it is both a holder in due course and one who has changed its position in reliance on National Savings' payment and therefore should be allowed to retain the $75,000. We find no support in the record for either proposition. On the holder in due course issue, Park does not qualify because it did not give value for the check. It was still in possession of the machinery it had contracted to sell to DAI. Although it had promised to deliver the equipment to DAI, such an executory promise does not constitute value. UCC § 3–303, Comment 3. Park Corporation is, of course, no longer required to carry out its promise because DAI has breached its agreement to pay.

As for detrimental reliance, Park contends that it paid $37,500 as a commission to Garland Corporation on the assumption that DAI's check was good. However, Park did not pay Garland until February 13, 1980, two weeks after National Savings had informed Park that it had paid the DAI check by mistake and that it wanted Park to return the money. Section 3–418 only makes payment by the bank final in favor of someone who has "*in good faith* changed his position in reliance on the payment." Once aware of the insufficiency in funds, Park could not have "in good faith" paid Garland $37,500 in reliance on that check. Park also alleges it paid rent for storing the equipment and painted the equipment in reliance on the payment. There is no evidence to support these allegations.

Accordingly, the decision of the district court is reversed.

Notes

1. The court distinguishes *Demos v. Lyons,* the New Jersey case, on the ground that the bank there made a knowing decision to pay despite the absence of adequate funds. How would the court deal with the case that falls between this case and *Demos?*

2. Assume a case in which the bank's computer is programmed routinely to pay checks on uncollected funds. Final payment is so made; no officer looks at the account, and after payment is discovered, the payor asks for restitution? The payee responds that the bank did not pay by mistake and is not entitled to restitution under conventional restitution rules. What do you think?

TOWN & COUNTRY STATE BANK OF NEWPORT v. FIRST STATE BANK OF ST. PAUL

Supreme Court of Minnesota, 1984.
358 N.W.2d 387.

SIMONETT, J. This case concerns the application of provisions of the Uniform Commercial Code to three banks which found themselves involved in a customer's check kiting scheme.

Richard G. Freitag engaged in a check kiting operation involving personal and corporate checking accounts maintained at five banks. First State Bank of St. Paul, Freitag's main bank, was the center of the kite. Freitag transferred checks back and forth between First State and each of four other banks, but did not transfer checks among the four "periphery" banks. The kite collapsed on March 14, 1980, when First State refused to honor checks drawn on its Freitag accounts. Two of the periphery banks—a bank in Stillwater and one in Pine City—managed to extricate themselves before the kite collapsed. Town & Country State Bank of Newport, however, was left with an overdraft of $71,304.43. First State was left with an overdraft of $690,491.21. Heritage State Bank, on the other hand, attempted to avoid a significant overdraft by returning 30 checks to First State after the kite collapsed. Sixteen of these checks, however, were not timely returned.

Plaintiff-appellant Town & Country commenced this action against defendant First State to recover the $71,304.43 overdraft on the theory that First State Bank, having prior knowledge of the kite, improperly used that knowledge to shift more of the overdraft exposure from itself to Town & Country. Defendant First State counterclaimed for $59,892, the amount of three kited checks drawn on Town & Country which Town & Country had returned to First State unpaid on March 17, 1980, after the expiration of its "midnight deadline." In addition, First State served a third-party complaint against Heritage State Bank for $320,000 for Heritage's belated return of the 16 checks. On Heritage's motion, the third-party claim against it was severed for separate trial. The Town & Country case was tried to a jury, which found First State had acted in bad faith; that the bad faith was not the cause of Town & Country's overdraft; but that the bad faith was the cause of Town & Country's late return of the three checks totaling $59,892, on which First State's counterclaim was based. The result was that neither party recovered. Town & Country had to absorb its $71,304.43 overdraft loss, and First State was denied its counterclaim. Town & Country appeals from a denial of its post-trial motions for judgment notwithstanding the verdict or a new trial. First State does not appeal the denial of its counterclaim.

Following the Town & Country jury trial, the third party action by First State against Heritage was tried before Judge Summers, who had also presided at the jury trial. The parties waived a jury and stipulated that the judge decide the case on the record made in the Town & Country trial and certain prior hearing testimony, supplemented with the testimony of a Heritage State Bank official. On March 1, 1983, the trial court issued its decision in favor of First

State Bank for $320,878 plus prejudgment interest. Heritage appeals from the order denying its post-trial motions and from the judgment. We have consolidated the two appeals.

I.

The first issue, common to both appeals, may be broadly stated as follows: Did First State, in the manner and at the time it chose to collapse the check kite, act in such bad faith that it, rather than the other two banks, should bear the overdraft losses? Appellant Town & Country does not so much dispute the jury's verdict of no causal bad faith, but rather claims that the jury was incorrectly instructed and that it is entitled to recover on the bad faith issue as a matter of law. Appellant Heritage makes essentially the same legal arguments and further contends the trial court's findings on lack of bad faith are clearly erroneous. We affirm the trial court's rulings.

Banks normally allow customers to write checks on "uncollected funds" in their checking accounts. An uncollected funds balance represents funds posted to the account for deposited checks drawn on another bank, but which have not yet been finally paid by that other bank. A check accepted by the depositary bank is forwarded to its clearinghouse, then on to the payor/drawee bank, which decides whether to pay or dishonor the check. This check collection process usually takes about 2 days. It may occur to a customer who is short of funds that he can obtain a "loan" from the banks by taking advantage of the 2 days it takes for the checks to clear. He proceeds to write a series of checks for deposit and withdrawal on his uncollected fund balances in different banks, each check deposited providing the credit for the preceding check. Thus a kite is born. The kite continues until cash is actually deposited to cover the uncollected funds or until one of the banks refuses to honor a check. When the kite comes to a halt, an overdraft results in accounts consisting solely of uncollected funds.

A.

Freitag owned a real estate brokerage company and a real estate development company, and, since the early 1970's, banked with First State. He maintained three corporate checking accounts with First State and acquired corporate and personal loans from the bank. He later opened checking accounts with four other banks, including Town & Country and Heritage. At least by early 1979, Freitag's accounts with First State were "problem" accounts. Freitag had a history of overdrafts; his accounts had uncollected fund balances, at times quite substantial; and his company was unprofitable and had a negative net worth. Four months before the kite collapsed, the bank loaned Freitag $40,000 on an unsecured basis. In January 1980, 2 months before the kite collapsed, bank examiners classified $208,000 of First State's loans to Freitag's corporation as substandard.

In February 1980, the First National Bank of Pine City (Pine City) noticed signs of a kite in its Freitag checking account,[2] and, at least by February 29, the bank president conveyed his concern to First State. On Friday, March 7, First State learned that Pine City had bounced checks, totaling some $250,000, which had been deposited at First State. This prompted Robert Jensen, vice president

2. Warning signs of a kite may include overdrafts on checking accounts, deposits primarily from accounts at other banks owned or controlled by the same party, deposits in approximately the same amount, and continued uncollected fund balances. Customers who might be described as "kite suspects" are those in a poor financial situation with a poor cash flow. It should be noted that these are merely signs of a check kite, not conclusive proof of its existence.

and second officer of First State, to call in Freitag for a talk that same day. Later that same Friday, Freitag brought in a cashier's check from Pine City for $249,135.[3] Jensen gave Freitag until Monday, March 10, to rectify the situation, then subsequently extended the deadline to Wednesday, March 12. As the daily uncollected funds report for Wednesday was not available until the next morning, Jensen did not contact Freitag until Thursday, March 13, at which time Freitag was told his progress in reaching a collected funds status was unsatisfactory. Freitag responded with a request for a $350,000 loan, saying he could borrow the remaining balance from a friend. Freitag was told to come in Friday morning, March 14, for the bank's answer, but the bank official testified they decided on Thursday, after the meeting with Freitag, that the loan request would be denied. On Friday morning, March 14, Freitag was told his request for a loan was denied. He asked to have until 3 p.m. to obtain the money. Sometime after 3 p.m. on March 14, First State started returning checks drawn on its Freitag accounts. At the same time, First State stopped presenting for collection Freitag checks drawn on accounts at Town & Country and Heritage. And so the kite collapsed.

First State's officers admitted that they first suspected a check kite on March 7. Given, however, that Freitag was a customer of long standing who had come through on overdrafts before, they felt they should give consideration to Freitag's assurance that he could correct the situation if afforded some time. During this week, from Friday, March 7, through Friday, March 14, Jensen closely monitored the Freitag accounts. He observed continuing signs of a kite, but chose to give continued credence to Freitag's assurances that he could correct the situation if granted some time. During the week of March 7, apparently, the bank at Stillwater started bouncing checks, thus extricating itself from the kite. First State did not relay its suspicion of a kite to either Town & Country or Heritage, and they continued to honor checks; their first notice was the telephone call from the clearinghouse late Friday afternoon, March 14, advising that First State was dishonoring checks drawn on its accounts.

On March 14, before midnight, First State timely returned four checks which had been deposited at Town & Country on March 12. On Monday, March 17, First State timely returned two more checks that had been deposited at Town & Country on March 13. Town & Country, however, did not return any checks drawn on its accounts until Monday, March 17. On Monday it returned eight checks to First State, five within the midnight deadline[4] and three, totaling $59,892, late. The net result for Town & Country was an overdraft of $71,304.43.

As for Heritage, at 3:50 p.m., Friday, March 14, it learned from the clearinghouse that First State was dishonoring checks, totaling $238,664, which had been presented for payment by Heritage. At this time, Heritage had 30

3. Town & Country observes that the cashier's check did not represent "real" money. Pine City's bank president testified that he agreed to accept the checks deposited with his bank only after First State promised that those checks, which had been drawn on First State's accounts, would be honored by First State. Thus the cashier's check simply represented Pine City deposits consisting of checks drawn against uncollected funds in Freitag's accounts at First State.

4. Minn.Stat. § 336.4–302 (1982) provides that in the absence of a valid defense a payor bank is accountable for a demand item received by it when the bank, "where it is not also the depositary bank, retains the item beyond midnight of the banking day of receipt without settling for it or, regardless of whether it is also the depositary bank, does not pay or return the item or send notice of dishonor until after its midnight deadline."

checks drawn on its accounts and presented for payment by First State, all of which it returned to First State on Friday, March 14, or Monday, March 17. Heritage timely returned 14 checks, totaling $384,926, drawn on its Freitag corporate account, by the appropriate midnight deadline, and these checks are not in issue. But Heritage did not timely return six checks, totaling $79,627, drawn on Freitag's personal account, by the midnight deadline. The midnight deadline for these checks was March 14, and Heritage returned them on March 17. It also did not timely return 10 corporate and personal checks totaling $241,251. The midnight deadline for these checks was either March 12 or March 13, and the bank did not return them until March 17. It is these 16 checks, totaling $320,878, which are in issue and for which First State seeks recovery from Heritage.

B.

Minn.Stat. § 336.1–203 (1982) provides: "Every contract or duty within this chapter imposes an obligation of good faith in its performance or enforcement." The parties and the trial court agreed, therefore, that First State had a duty to act in good faith towards Town & Country and Heritage in its handling of the Freitag kite operation, and it was on this fact issue that both cases were tried.

The Town & Country jury, as already noted, by answers to special interrogatories, found that First State had acted in bad faith but that the bad faith was not a cause of Town & Country's overdraft, although it was a cause of Town & Country's payment of the three checks totaling $59,892. Town & Country says the jury must have determined that First State did not begin to act in bad faith until Thursday, March 13, when its officers decided to deny Freitag's loan request.

On appeal, Town & Country seems to concede there was evidence, under the court's instructions, to sustain the jury's verdict that First State did not act in bad faith on the $71,304.43 overdraft. Town & Country contends, however, that the trial court incorrectly instructed the jury on what constitutes good faith. It argues that actual knowledge of a check kite by a presenting bank is bad faith, and it claims that its requested instruction to that effect was erroneously denied by the trial court. Town & Country's argument here is that the evidence overwhelmingly shows that First State knew of the check kite, surely by March 7 when alerted by Pine City, and, therefore, as a matter of law, First State acted in bad faith to Town & Country's detriment. We disagree.

The trial court instructed the Town & Country jury that good faith "is honesty in fact or put another way, honesty in intent." This was a correct statement of the law. Section 336.1–201(19) (1982) defines good faith as "honesty in fact in the conduct or transaction concerned." This is a subjective test, requiring "honesty of intent rather than absence of circumstances which would put an ordinarily prudent holder on inquiry." Eldon's Super Fresh Stores, Inc. v. Merrill Lynch, etc., 296 Minn. 130, 136, 207 N.W.2d 282, 287 (1973). The trial court applied the same legal standard in the Heritage bench trial.

First State's subjective good faith towards the two payor banks was an issue for the trier of fact and we affirm those findings. The trier of fact chose to believe that First State's officers, even though aware of the ominous danger signals of a kite and, indeed, strongly suspecting a kite, nevertheless believed that giving Freitag a week's time to work out his problem was warranted and that in extending this time, First Bank's officers had no dishonest intent to shift the kite loss to the other banks. Town & Country's theory seems inconsistent with the fact that on March 10, for example, First State's overdraft liability was only about

$90,000 and that the further extension of time greatly increased First State's own overdraft exposure. Then too, at the same time First State began returning checks drawn on its accounts, it also stopped presenting checks for collection on the other banks. As the trial court's memorandum for the Heritage bench trial decision states: "[N]othing in First State's experience with Freitag indicates that it thought him a crook, or that it knowingly participated in his kiting scheme. The court believes that Freitag's long-established banking relationship with First State makes it more, rather than less, reasonable for First State to 'carry' him for awhile to see if he could work out his cash flow problem."

Signs of a check kite may be only that—just signs—and, in any event, even if a kite is known to exist, the best remedy is an infusion of cash, if it can be obtained. The proper course of action is not always easy to determine. The difficulty is illustrated not only by First State's conduct, but by that of Town & Country and of Heritage. All three banks knew of Freitag's precarious finances. All three banks had substantial uncollected fund balances in their Freitag accounts. Town & Country argues it did not suspect a kite because its officers did not look at their bank's daily uncollected funds balance—not an especially persuasive argument. The Pine City bank, having noticed the kite signs, took positive action on its own as early as March 7, followed by the Stillwater bank. At Heritage State Bank, the average uncollected fund balance in Freitag's corporate checking account during the month of February 1980 was $208,924 compared with an average of $7,000 in "real money." Yet on March 7, knowing this, Heritage chose to do nothing more than write an innocuous letter to Freitag stating, "If it is possible for you to delay writing checks for one day the problem can be alleviated. I will appreciate your efforts in remedying the situation." Thereafter, Heritage did nothing until First State acted.

We hold that the trial court applied the proper standard for good faith. The trial court's findings of no bad faith in the bench trial are not clearly erroneous and are affirmed. In the jury trial, respondent First State is not challenging the jury's verdict as to its bad faith, and to the extent Town & Country is claiming that First State's bad faith as a matter of law caused the $71,304.43 overdraft, we rule that claim is without merit.

II.

Appellants urge another theory, however, on which liability for the kite losses should rest solely with First State. They contend that, even in the absence of bad faith by a presenting bank (such as First State), and even though a payor bank (such as themselves) has made final payment, a payor bank is relieved of liability if the presenting bank is not a holder in due course or a person who has in good faith changed his position in reliance on such payment. We decline to subscribe to this theory.

For an understanding of the issue, we must look to provisions of the Uniform Commercial Code. Article 4 deals with bank deposits and collections. Minn.Stat. § 336.4–213 describes when an item is deemed "finally paid" by a payor bank, and then concludes, "Upon a *final payment* under subparagraph (b), (c) or (d) the payor bank *shall be accountable* for the amount of the item." (Emphasis added.)[5] To the same effect is Minn.Stat. § 336.4–302 (1982).[6]

5. Minn.Stat. § 336.4–213(1) (1982) reads in its entirety as follows:

"(1) An item is finally paid by a payor bank when the bank has done any of the following, whichever happens first:

6. See note 6 on page 1190.

Here both Town & Country and Heritage made "final payment" on checks presented to them. Town & Country charged the checks presented to it by First State against its Freitag accounts. Heritage failed to dishonor the checks presented to it within the midnight deadline. Consequently, First State argues that under § 4–213, the two payor banks are "accountable for the amount of the item[s]." UCC Comment 7 to § 4–213 defines "accountable" as "imposing a duty to account, which duty is met if and when a settlement for the item satisfactorily clears." The comment goes on to say, the "determination of the time of final payment is based exclusively on the action of the payor bank." Therefore, argues First State, both Town & Country and Heritage are accountable, i.e., Town & Country has no right to recover its final payment of $71,000, whether or not properly payable, and neither may Heritage refuse to pay the checks totaling $320,000 which it failed to timely dishonor. There is considerable support for this position. See Ashford Bank v. Capital Preservation Fund, Inc., 544 F.Supp. 26 (D.Mont. 1982); Northwestern National Insurance Co. v. Midland National Bank, 96 Wis.2d 155, 292 N.W.2d 591 (1980); Kirby v. First and Merchants National Bank, 210 Va. 88, 91 n. 4, 168 S.E.2d 273, 275 n. 4 (1969); J. White and R. Summers, Handbook of the Law under the Uniform Commercial Code, § 16–2 at 613–18 (2d ed. 1980);[7] B. Clark, The Law of Bank Deposits, Collections and Credit Cards, § 3.6[3] at 3–38 to 3–40 (1981).

On the other hand, appellants argue that "final payment" under § 4–213 only fixes the *time* at which final payment occurs, i.e., when notice, stop payment orders, legal process and set-off will not prevent the payment of an instrument. Appellants argue that one must look to Article 3 of the Code, specifically § 3–418, to determine the *effect* of final payment. They rely, therefore, on Minn.Stat. § 336.3–418 (1982), which reads:

(a) Paid the item in cash; or

(b) Settled for the item without reserving a right to revoke the settlement and without having such right under statute, clearinghouse rule or agreement; or

(c) Completed the process of posting the item to the indicated account of the drawer, maker or other person to be charged therewith; or

(d) Made a provisional settlement for the item and failed to revoke the settlement in the time and manner permitted by statute, clearinghouse rule or agreement.

"Upon a final payment under subparagraphs (b), (c) or (d) the payor bank shall be accountable for the amount of the item."

6. Minn.Stat. § 336.4–302 (1982) provides:

"In the absence of a valid defense such as breach of a presentment warranty (subsection (1) of section 336.4–207), settlement effected or the like, if an item is presented on and received by a payor bank the bank is accountable for the amount of

"(a) a demand item other than a documentary draft whether properly payable or not if the bank, in any case where it is not also the depositary bank, retains the item beyond midnight of the banking day of receipt without settling for it or, regardless of whether it is also the depositary bank, does not pay or return the item or send notice of dishonor until after its midnight deadline."

7. Professor White appears to have since partially changed his analysis. Responding to a criticism of his position in a student note, Commercial Paper and Forgery: Broader Liability for Banks? 1980 U.Ill.L.F. 813 (1980), Professor White now seems to advocate interpreting the word "accountable" in § 4–213 to mean only that a bank must settle for an item. Final payment under this section thus cuts off a bank's unqualified right to revoke a provisional credit but does not bar restitution. But he also states that § 4–302 "accountability," which operates whether an instrument is "properly payable or not," would continue to bar restitution where the bank holds the instrument beyond the midnight deadline without settling for it. Professor White's new position appears in an informal comment to teaching materials on the relationship between §§ 3–418 and 4–213. D. Epstein and J. Martin, Basic Uniform Commercial Code Teaching Materials 514 (2d ed. 1983), cited in National Savings and Trust Co. v. Park Corp., 722 F.2d 1303, 1306 (6th Cir. 1983), cert. denied, 104 S.Ct. 1916 (1984). We do not think, however, the drafters intended the essentially identical language on accountability which appears in both §§ 4–213 and 4–302 to have different consequences.

"Except for recovery of bank payments as provided in the article on bank deposits and collections (article 4) and except for liability for breach of warranty on presentment under the preceding section, payment or acceptance of any instrument is final in favor of a holder in due course, or a person who has in good faith changed his position in reliance on the payment."

Appellants argue that this statutory language means payment is only final, in the sense that it cannot be reversed or recovered by the payor bank, when the payment has been made to a holder in due course or a person who has changed his position in reliance on the payments. Conversely, payments made to one who is not a holder in due course or who has not changed position may be recovered. Appellants argue that the introductory clause of § 3–418, which says, "Except for recovery of bank payments as provided in * * * (article 4)," merely intends to preserve a payor bank's right to revoke a payment or settlement before its midnight deadline, even though the person receiving payment is a holder in due course. Therefore, so goes appellants' argument, Town & Country can seek reimbursement of the $71,000 it paid First State, and Heritage, notwithstanding its untimely dishonor, can refuse to pay First State on the Freitag checks for $320,000 presented to it. If First State is neither a holder in due course nor a person who has changed his position in reliance on payment, then the payor banks can impose liability for the kited checks on First State by showing they were induced to act as they did by fraud or mistake.[8] There is also support for this position. See, e.g., Demos v. Lyons, 151 N.J.Super. 489, 376 A.2d 1352 (1977); National Savings & Trust Co. v. Park Corp., 722 F.2d 1303 (6th Cir. 1983), cert. denied, 104 S.Ct. 1916 (1984); Blake v. Woodford Bank & Trust Co., 555 S.W.2d 589, 601 (Ky.App. 1977); Note, Commercial Paper and Forgery: Broader Liability for Banks? 1980 U.Ill.L.F. 813, 830 (1980).

Admittedly, the code provisions and comments are unclear, but to say that the final payment provisions of Article 4 are only given effect under the dictates of section 3–418 would render those sections of Article 4 virtually meaningless. Furthermore, a finality rule has the advantage of simplicity, obviating the need for courts to be "forever wrestling with fine fact questions involving reliance, negligence, notice, damages, and the concept of holder in due course." B. Clark, supra, § 3.6[3] at 3–40. The finality rule is also most consistent with the policies underlying the final payment provisions. The present banking system under which an enormous number of checks are processed daily could not function effectively if banks were not required to make prompt and effective decisions on

8. Even if the appellant payor banks were able to persuade us that Article 3 affords them an avenue of recovery, they would still have two other hurdles to overcome. First, to show that First State was not a holder in due course, they would have to show that First State had "notice" of a defense against presentment of the checks. Minn.Stat. § 336.3–302(1) (1982). Even though the triers of fact found no subjective bad faith, appellants argue that "notice," in the context of a holder in due course, involves an objective test of what the holder knows or has reason to know. See Minn.Stat. § 336.1–201(25) (1982) (definition of "notice"); Eldon's Super Fresh Stores, Inc. v. Merrill Lynch, etc., 296 Minn. 130, 136, 207 N.W.2d 282, 287–88 (1973).

If appellants were able to establish that First State was not a holder in due course, they would still have to establish their right to recovery from First State on some theory of restitution. See, e.g., Demos v. Lyons, 151 N.J.Super. 489, 376 A.2d 1352 (1977). Appellants suggest either fraud or mistake. But the trial court at the Town & Country trial dismissed plaintiff's fraud claim, in part at least, because he found no fiduciary relationship between the banks, and this ruling has not been appealed. As for mistake, Town & Country says in its brief that it paid the checks "in the mistaken belief that Anderson-Freitag, Inc. had good funds in the T & C account," while First State argues this is not the kind of mistake that will support restitution.

whether to pay or dishonor checks. See Bank Leumi Trust Co. v. Bank of Mid-Jersey, 499 F.Supp. 1022, 1026 (D.N.J. 1980). See also Van Senus Auto Parts, Inc. v. Michigan National Bank—Wyoming, 116 Mich.App. 342, 348–49, 323 N.W.2d 391, 394 (1982). Lastly, appellants' interpretation creates an inevitable and direct conflict between the requirements of Articles 3 and 4, and the Code requires that the provisions of Article 4 prevail in the event of a conflict with Article 3. See Minn.Stat. § 336.4–102(1) (1982).

We hold, therefore, that the final payment provisions of Minn.Stat. §§ 336.4–213 and 336.4–302 are not limited by the holder in due course and reliance requirements of § 336.3–418.[9]

* * *

B.

At the Town & Country trial, the trial court ruled as a matter of law that First State had not breached any of its warranties of presentment on the checks presented by First State to Town & Country. We affirm this ruling.

Under Minn.Stat. § 336.4–207 (1982) a presenting bank warrants to the payor bank that it "has no knowledge that the signature of the maker or drawer is unauthorized." An unauthorized signature is "one made without actual, implied or apparent authority and includes forgery." Minn.Stat. § 336.1–201(43) (1982). Town & Country argues that "fraud can never be authorized" and therefore the check signatures were not authorized. There is no merit to this claim. The checks were signed by Freitag and Donald England, persons authorized to sign checks on behalf of the companies involved. Whatever may have been wrong with the checks, it was not with the signatures.

Finally, Heritage claims it was excused from sending a notice of dishonor within the midnight deadline because Minn.Stat. § 336.3–511 (2)(b) excuses "presentment or notice or protest if such party * * * has no reason to expect or right to require" that an item be paid. Here again appellant seeks to insinuate an Article 3 provision into the check collection process established by Article 4. Article 4 already provides a defense to the duty to account if there is delay in dishonoring—namely, if the delay is due to circumstances beyond the bank's control. Article 3 would, therefore, conflict with Article 4, and this is not permitted. Moreover, § 336.3–511(2)(b) clearly refers to "such party"—i.e., "the party to be charged," which normally is the drawer or endorser who would be liable on the instrument itself. * * * The trial court correctly ruled that § 336.3–511 does not excuse Heritage's failure to timely dishonor the checks.

Affirmed.

[Footnote omitted.]

Notes

1. If you are having difficulty understanding how 3–418 interacts with 4–213, you have good company.

2. Even if one adopted the position of the Sixth Circuit in the *Park* case, the Minnesota case should come out as it did. Why is that?

9. The interpretation of the Article 4 final payment provisions adopted by this court significantly limits the scope of § 3–418. The holder in due course and good faith reliance exceptions to final payment will presumably apply to notes and other instruments presented outside the bank collection system. J. White and R. Summers, supra, § 16.2 at 617. For instance, § 4–213 would not apply to payment of a draft by a buyer-drawee because the buyer would not be a payor bank.

3. If you were to commence with a *tabula rasa,* how would you write the law? Would you leave the payor bank liable for the amount of items finally paid irrespective of the status of the recipient of the money as a holder in due course or one who had changed his position in reliance? Or would you conform the law to the Sixth Circuit view—with the right of restitution against all but holders in due course and those who change their position in reliance upon payment?

Note: Check Kiting–Criminal Liability

Check kiting is "a process where checks written on one account are continually covered with deposits of checks written on another account, thereby creating positive *statement* balances and preventing overdrafts but resulting in a steadily increasing deficit in the *collected* balance in most of the accounts." North Carolina National Bank v. South Carolina National Bank, 449 F.Supp. 616, 617 (D.S.C.1976). In its simplest form the scheme is carried out by a kiter with two bank accounts. A check is drawn on account A which exceeds the funds in that account and is deposited in account B. A check sufficient to cover the overdraft in account A is immediately drawn on account B and deposited in account A. Thus when the check drawn on account A is presented for payment the kiter appears to have sufficient funds to cover the check. Of course, account B is once again overdrawn and before this check arrives for payment another check drawn on account A must arrive to provide a sufficient credit balance, and so on. Because these checks must be of sufficient size to cover all previous transactions and leave the kiter with a positive balance, the amounts involved grow increasingly larger.

The success of the kiting scheme depends upon two things. First, the banks involved must allow the kiter immediate credit for any deposits he makes. If one bank refuses to allow the kiter to draw against deposited checks until they are finally paid, checks will bounce and the scheme will be discovered. Second, the banks must not notice the rapid pattern of deposits and withdrawals. If one bank stops payment on a check the scheme will collapse. However, stopping the kiter depends on detection of the kiting operation which may be difficult in sophisticated schemes involving many accounts and many banks.

Under state law a kiter may be guilty of a crime under bad-check statutes or for obtaining property by false pretenses. Almost every state has enacted a criminal "bad check" statute to deal with certain no-account and NSF checks. Although statutes differ as to the required elements of a violation, (1) most do not require property to be obtained from the victim by the giving of a bad check, (2) many statutes require that the drawer have both knowledge of the insufficient funds and an intent to defraud (some require only the knowledge element), (3) many allow a presumption of the required state of mind when the drawer had no account with the drawee or when there are insufficient funds at the time the check is given and again when it is presented for payment. See generally LaFave & Scott, Handbook on Criminal Law, 680–81 (1972).

Consider the following provisions of the New York bad check statute (N.Y.Penal Law §§ 190.00–190.15 McKinney 1975) and its operation with respect to the kiting schemes described below.

190.05 Issuing a bad check

A person is guilty of issuing a bad check when:

1. (a) As a drawer or representative drawer, he utters a check knowing that he or his principal, as the case may be, does not then have sufficient funds with the drawee to cover it, and (b) he intends or believes at the time of utterance that payment will be refused by the drawee upon presentation, and (c) payment is refused by the drawee upon presentation; or

2. (a) He passes a check knowing that the drawer thereof does not then have sufficient funds with the drawee to cover it, and (b) he intends or believes at the time the check is passed that payment will be refused by the drawee upon presentation, and (c) payment is refused by the drawee upon presentation.

190.10 Issuing a Bad Check; Presumptions

1. When the drawer of a check has insufficient funds with the drawee to cover it at the time of utterance, the subscribing drawer or representative drawer, as the case may be, is presumed to know of such insufficiency.

2. A subscribing drawer or representative drawer, as the case may be, of an ultimately dishonored check is presumed to have intended or believed that the check would be dishonored upon presentation when:

(a) The drawer had no account with the drawee at the time of utterance; or

(b)(i) The drawer had insufficient funds with the drawee at the time of utterance, and (ii) the check was presented to the drawee for payment not more than thirty days after the date of utterance, and (iii) the drawer had insufficient funds with the drawee at the time of presentation.

* * *

190.15 Issuing a Bad Check; Defenses

In any prosecution for issuing a bad check, it is an affirmative defense that:

1. The defendant or a person acting in his behalf made full satisfaction of the amount of the check within ten days after dishonor by the drawee * * *.

Bradley Bank v. Hartford Acc. and Indem. Co., 557 F.Supp. 243 (W.D.Wis.1983) involved a classic check-kiting operation. The plaintiff, a bank in Tomahawk, Wisconsin, sued an insurance corporation for losses incurred by the checking activity of its customer Donald Schnabel. Schnabel operated two automobile dealerships in Tomahawk: "Midway Chrysler-Dodge, Inc." and "Don Schnabel Chevrolet-Olds." A bank account in the Midway dealership's name was maintained at the plaintiff bank and an account in the name of the Chevrolet-Olds dealership was held at the Lincoln County Bank in Merrill, Wisconsin, 22 miles from Tomahawk.

On July 2, 1981, Schnabel drew a check on the account of Don Schnabel Chevrolet-Olds at the Lincoln County Bank in the sum of $19,727.41 payable to Midway. This check was deposited personally or by agent on the premises of plaintiff bank into the Midway account of July 3, 1981.

A second check on the Lincoln County Bank account was drawn on July 3, 1981 for $17,114.28 payable to Midway. This check was also deposited into the Midway account on July 3, 1981 by Schnabel or an agent on the premises of plaintiff bank.

A third check on the Lincoln County Bank account was drawn on July 4, 1981 for $16,891.09 payable to Midway. This check was deposited into the Midway account on July 6, 1981 by Schnabel or an agent on the premises of plaintiff bank.

On July 9, 1981, the Lincoln County Bank returned to the Federal Reserve Bank in Minneapolis the aforementioned three checks, stamped "Returned Not Paid-Uncollected Funds—7–9–81."

On July 1, 1981, Schnabel drew a check on the Midway account at plaintiff bank in the amount of $16,891.09 payable to Don Schnabel Chevrolet-Olds. The check was deposited in the Lincoln County Bank account on the same day.

A second check was drawn on the Midway account at plaintiff bank, and payable to Don Schnabel Chevrolet-Olds, for $14,487.50, on July 2, 1981. The check was deposited on the same day.

A third check was drawn on the Midway account at plaintiff bank, and payable to Don Schnabel Chevrolet-Olds, for $20,813.34 on July 3, 1981. The check was deposited in the Lincoln County Bank on the same day.

A fourth check was drawn on the Midway account at plaintiff bank, and payable to Don Schnabel Chevrolet-Olds, for $22,170.44, on July 4, 1981. The check was deposited in the Lincoln County Bank on the same day in its night depository. The check was credited on July 6, 1981.

The total of uncollected funds checks deposited in the plaintiff bank by Schnabel from the Lincoln County Bank account of Don Schnabel Chevrolet-Olds was $53,732.78. Plaintiff bank claims it was damaged in the amount of $45,270.72, the difference apparently representing the positive balance in the Midway account immediately before the account was debited for the uncollected funds deposits, in August, 1981.

[Id. at 245]

An interesting variation of a kiting scheme is presented in United States v. Payne, 602 F.2d 1215 (5th Cir.1979). Payne operated the South Georgia Auto Auction, Inc., a dealer's used car auction in Valdosta, Georgia. He kept the company's business account at the Toney Brothers Bank in Doerun, Georgia. Booker T. Fountain, the co-conspirator, operated a used car dealership in Berrien County, Georgia and kept the business account at the Bank of Alapaha. The banks of both businessmen allowed immediate credit for checks deposited.

The two agreed to exchange checks. Fountain would sell an automobile to himself through Payne's company, South Georgia Auto Auction, Inc., and as the buyer pay for it with a check to the company. South Georgia Auction would then issue a corresponding company check to Fountain as the seller of the automobile after deducting $40 as an auction fee.

The sales Fountain made to himself through Payne's company were fictitious. The automobiles did not exist. Indeed, during December 1977 and January 1978 Fountain sold to himself the same non-existent automobile seven or eight times a week. These fictitious sales were all recorded on the books of South Georgia Auto Auction and, of course, Payne knew that the sales were fictitious. After an exchange of checks, each would deposit in his bank the other's check. Fountain put the South Georgia Auto Auction checks into his account at the Bank of Alapaha. Payne would deposit Fountain's checks in the South Georgia Auto Auction account at the Toney Brothers Bank.

The scheme operated successfully from October 1, 1977 through January 1978. Fountain used the immediate credit he received from the Bank of Alapaha to operate his business. Payne used the funds from the kite to operate his business. In some instances Payne gave Fountain checks drawn on the account of South Georgia Auction when the account was overdrawn $40,000 to $50,000; on one occasion, by $100,000. When a Georgia State bank examiner spotted the kite and put an end to the scheme, the Bank of Alapaha was left with $178,000 in worthless checks.

[Id. at 1217]

Note that in applying the New York bad check statute to kiting no property need be obtained. Also, if the kiter covers his checks one day before the scheme is discovered, there would be no violation because payment has not been refused. If the kiter covers his checks within 10 days of dishonor, an affirmative defense is established, but, a bank need not wait 10 days before prosecuting. Finally, some bad check statutes say checks may not be drawn on insufficient funds *or credit.*

Bad check statutes are most commonly applied to simple NSF checks. The usual defendant has obtained some property through the bad check or has been a habitual bad check giver. Obviously, the law student who bounces a check, even on a great hornbook in commercial law, will rarely be prosecuted because such checks are usually covered and the costs of prosecution to the would be plaintiff are prohibitive.

Should it make a difference for finding a violation that the check was presented before its post date? Before some date the check giver stated he would require to cover the check? The cases say these factors exhibit good faith intent and thus preclude violation. Similarly, reasonable belief (as opposed to mere hope) that funds will be available to cover issued checks and even extreme intoxication have been held to preclude violation.

The second way states often reach no-account, kiting, and NSF checking in general is through the crime of obtaining property by false pretenses. "False pretense" is generally established when property is obtained by a false representation of material past or present fact by one who knows his representation is false and intends thereby to defraud. Most jurisdictions find the giving of the check is an implied representation that the account holds sufficient funds. See generally LaFave & Scott, *id.* at 655. States that have required that property be obtained as an element of a bad check charge may rely solely on the bad check statute for prosecution of checking crimes or allow the prosecutor discretion as to which statute to apply. False pretense (or theft by deception, larceny by deception, etc.) carries heavier penalties than the issuing of a bad check and is therefore usually reserved for more culpable behavior than NSF checks of small amounts. In New York, obtaining a car by bad check, and the kite described above would be prosecuted as larceny, the intentional and wrongful taking of property.

In 1982 the federal government began prosecuting check-kiting as mail fraud under 18 U.S.C.A. § 1341 (1982). In Williams v. United States, 458 U.S. 279, 102 S.Ct. 3088, 73 L.Ed.2d 767 (1982), the Supreme Court reversed a line of cases applying 18 U.S.C.A. § 1014 (1982) (illegally influencing the giving of loans, advances, security, etc.) to a bank president's personal check kiting scheme. The court held that issuing a check does not amount to a false statement, as required by the statute. Technically speaking a check is not a factual assertion and so cannot be considered true or false. The court also noted that the proposed construction would make every bounced check a section 1014 violation.

The mail fraud statute (and the related crime of wire fraud, 18 U.S.C.A. § 1341 (1972), does not require that a false statement be made. It provides in pertinent part:

> § 1341, Frauds and Swindles
>
> Whoever, having devised or intending to devise any scheme or artifice to defraud * * * for the purpose of executing such scheme or artifice * * * places in any post office or authorized depository for mail any matter or thing whatever to be sent or delivered by the Postal Service * * * or knowingly causes to be delivered by mail * * * any such matter or thing, shall be fined not more than $1,000 or imprisoned not more than five years, or both.

A use of the mails is found either in the sending of checks and statements to the kiter which are considered necessary to monitor the kite, or in the mailing between banks in the collection process. To claims that section 1341 applies to any fraudulent checking activity, the Eighth Circuit in affirming a mail fraud conviction for check kiting recently responded that "the government must prove beyond a reasonable doubt that the defendant intentionally devised a fraudulent scheme and caused the use of the mails for the purpose of carrying out the scheme. We trust that these requirements will serve as a restraint on whatever tendency the government might have to prosecute anyone who ever bounced a check." United States v. Freitag, 768 F.2d 240, 244 (8th Cir.1985).

It should also be noted that some checking crimes may violate the federal bank robbery statute, 18 U.S.C.A. § 2113(a) and (b). The circuit courts are divided as to whether a taking by false pretenses is contemplated by the act, but at least two recent cases specifically found check kiting to be a violation. See United States v. Frye, 738 F.2d 196 (7th Cir.1984), and United States v. Pick, 724 F.2d 297 (2d Cir. 1983).

A final interesting issue involving check kiting is: At what point, if ever, does aggressive money management become a crime? The issue is well presented by E.F. Hutton's celebrated checking activity between 1980 and 1982. Spurred apparently by pressure from above to increase interest income, certain Hutton branch managers began kiting checks between branches in effect availing themselves of short-term interest free loans. These loans may have averaged as much as $17,000,000 a day for over a twenty-month period (Am.Banker, May 23, 1985). On May 2, 1985, Hutton pleaded guilty of 2,000 counts of mail and wire fraud resulting from the kiting which involved more than 400 banks and over $4 billion.

Note, however, that Hutton's transgressions were not classical kiting. In almost all criminal prosecutions someone has lost something more than interest on the funds used. Typically one bank or the other is out tens or hundreds of thousands of dollars. That was not the case in Hutton. Based on the facts made public thus far, Hutton would not be in violation of the New York bad check statute set out above because no payment was ever "refused by the drawee on presentation." Until all of the facts in the Hutton case are made public it will be unclear whether Hutton clearly violated the federal law or whether they merely agreed to plead in order to avoid the cost and difficulty of a long and public trial.

The story that follows is a description of a large-scale swindle involving highly sophisticated banks. Can you understand how banks get into the situation described? One suspects that kiters who ultimately pay the money back (as did Heller and Madden) are rarely convicted. Why is that?

THE WALL STREET JOURNAL

Monday, August 11, 1986.
Vol. LXVII No. 210.

By Ed Cony and Stanley Penn.
Staff Reporters of The Wall Street Journal.

New York—Enter the combatants: Marine Midland Bank and giant Citibank, with assets between them of $111 billion, versus Edward "Biff" Halloran and Harold Madden, principals of a pair of local ready-mix-concrete firms.

The companies were called Transit Mix Concrete and Water Tunnel Associates. Water Tunnel wasn't even an active business. But the firms had accounts at the big banks, and the accounts were active indeed.

For over a year, starting in March 1983, Messrs. Halloran and Madden operated a hoary old scam. It was check-kiting: the art of repeatedly taking checks written on one account and quickly depositing them into another, and vice versa, staying a step ahead of the clearing system and thus creating a false impression of the balances in the accounts.

And what a kite it was. The two men sent some 15,000 checks, with a face value of $9.2 billion, flowing back and forth between Transit Mix's account at Citibank and Water Tunnel's at Marine Midland. In terms of the dollar amount of checks written, says a banking expert in New York, it was probably bigger than any other check-overdrafting scheme in U.S. history, including the 1980–82 E.F. Hutton operation involving an estimated $4 billion.

Once false balances have been created, a kiter can take out money against them, and that is just what Messrs. Halloran and Madden did. In all, they helped themselves to $23 million of bank cash—while the kite was flying.

In March of 1984, it came crashing down. The banks demanded restitution, and prosecutors demanded punishment. This is the story of how for 13 months, and with thousands of checks, a pair of businessmen outwitted the financial controls of two major New York banks. They were men who had much but who, trial arguments suggest, wanted much more. And just as striking as their scam's size is the brazen way they justified it, with a stance the trial prosecutor, Brian Rosner, angrily assails as "almost exclusively a rich man's defense."

The end came for the giant check-kite on March 29, 1984. That morning John Dickey, a partner in the law firm of Sullivan & Cromwell, got a call from Marine Midland saying the bank had "a big problem." Citibank had discovered what was going on and closed the Transit Mix Concrete account. As Mr. Dickey later testified at a trial in New York State Supreme Court, "Marine Midland was left with a negative figure of approximately $23 million with no funds [in the Water Tunnel account] to cover it. So if the music stops at that point, Marine Midland would be out $23 million."

It didn't stop there, though. In one of the unusual turns marking this case, when a Marine Midland officer called Mr. Madden about the evident check-kite and expressed fear that it would cost him his own job, Mr. Madden simply told him "not to worry."

Five days later, Messrs. Halloran and Madden admitted they had run the kite. They promised to make the bank whole, securing the promise with real estate. And six months later, after Mr. Halloran sold his interest in two hotels, they paid back the entire $23 million.

That hardly satisfied the Manhattan district attorney, Robert Morgenthau, though. New York criminal law doesn't specifically bar check-kiting, but the two men soon found themselves indicted for the felony of grand larceny and the misdemeanor of scheming to defraud. And because larceny requires an intent to deprive an owner of his property permanently, the defendants' repayment—as well as their ability to repay—promised to loom large in the defense.

It is a situation that irks Mr. Rosner, the prosecutor at the trial. "That's the defense raised in big economic crimes," he says. "The rich guy with money—it's always a temporary borrowing, never intending to deprive permanently. * * * The kid who snatches a wallet, he says he was just borrowing it, but nobody believes him."

Neither Mr. Halloran nor Mr. Madden would talk to this newspaper. But the two men's trial, which recently ended, revealed much about their methods, not to mention their motives. At times it resembled a morality play.

Mr. Halloran came from a well-to-do Philadelphia family whose construction company, with annual sales Mr. Halloran said sometimes hit $100 million, laid the foundation for, among other buildings, the New York City police headquarters in lower Manhattan. But having worked at the family firm since college, he left in the mid–1970's. "I wanted to go out and see if I could make it on my own," he said.

This he certainly did. Within 10 years of moving to New York, Mr. Halloran, now 45, had acquired interests in about 20 companies, including, besides the concrete firms, the Lobster Shanty restaurant chain in Florida and New Jersey, a New York restaurant called La Maganette, a couple of Holiday Inns, a Sheraton hotel and two Manhattan hostelries, the Taft and the Halloran House.

In contrast, Mr. Madden was a poor boy. Under the questioning of his lawyer, John Wing, a sympathetic portrait emerged: His father deserted his mother when Harold was eight, the boy got an after-school job, and he has been working ever since. He joined Transit Mix Concrete as a clerk, went to St. John's University at night and graduated 10th in his class.

Mr. Wing had difficulty suppressing his enthusiasm for his client, now 57. "He is not like a latter-day Willie Sutton, the famous bank robber," the defense lawyer told the jury. "When Mr. Sutton went into a bank and took money at the point of a gun, he intended to keep it. He never intended to give any of it back. Harold Madden is not Willie Sutton."

Prosecutor Rosner took a rather different view. "This is a man who wants more," he told the jury. "Here is a man who just for money, for money, he is going to tell lies. It is not like the man does not have food, or he does not have shelter or does not have clothes, or he does not even have a summer home."

The reference to a summer house was far from casual. Mr. Rosner had told the court that Mr. Madden had taken $217,000 from the Water Tunnel account and put it in his personal account during a period when he was spending about $200,000 on a grandiose expansion of his Catskill Mountains summer home. Mr. Madden testified that he added two stone fireplaces and 11 bedrooms, enlarged the kitchen to seat 45 and put in 13 bathrooms.

On the Stand

The defendants didn't deny kiting checks on a huge scale and pulling millions of dollars out of the accounts. They simply insisted they had no intention of keeping the money—so that what they were doing didn't qualify as larceny. When the wealthy Mr. Halloran took the stand, Mr. Rosner asked him whether he believed that because he was rich he was entitled to take $200,000 from Marine Midland Bank on May 9, 1983.

"Correct," replied Mr. Halloran.

"Correct?" asked the prosecutor. Yes, said Mr. Halloran, he believed he was entitled to the $200,000 as a loan.

At another point, as Mr. Rosner questioned Mr. Halloran about checks drawn on the Water Tunnel account at Marine Midland, this exchange took place:

Mr. Rosner: "You knew Water Tunnel did not have good funds?"

Mr. Halloran: "That's correct."

Mr. Rosner: "And you knew the check-kite would trick the bank into honoring the Water Tunnel checks?"

Mr. Halloran: "That's correct."

Mr. Rosner: "And during March 1983 to March 1984, you engaged in a yearlong course of conduct to trick both banks, right?"

Mr. Halloran: "That's correct."

Mr. Rosner continued: "You knew that if the deceit ended, you would no longer be permitted to take the bank's money, correct?"

To this Mr. Halloran replied: "I don't think I took the bank's money. I believe at worst it was an unauthorized loan."

Mr. Halloran also conceded, in response to a question from the prosecutor, that he got some of his employees to lie to Citibank to keep the kite from being discovered. "Part of the deceit, Mr. Rosner," Mr. Halloran said.

The prosecutor offered the jury a quotation that in his view summed up the case. When Theodore Roosevelt was New York police commissioner a century ago, Mr. Rosner said, the future president remarked, "A man who has never gone to school may steal from a freight car, but you give that man a university education and he will steal the whole railroad."

How it Worked

With the defendants not disputing that an elaborate check-kite existed, the trial didn't offer many details of how it worked. But earlier, Justice Carol Berkman, in refusing to dismiss the indictment, summarized what the grand jury had been told: that thousands of checks were drawn on the Marine Midland account, almost all signed by Mr. Madden, and thousands more deposited in it, all drawn on the Citibank account and almost all signed by Mr. Halloran. The numbers of checks and deposits steadily rose, and the deposits were made at different bank branches and to different tellers.

"The rapid exchange of checks between Citibank and Marine Midland created a 'float,' that is, the appearance of a positive balance in each account," the justice said, in recounting what the grand jury heard. "The truth * * * was that the balance in each account was negative. In March 1983, the Water Tunnel bank balance [at Marine Midland] appeared to be approximately $52,000. One year later, the apparent balance was $23 million."

The illusory balances arose, she added, because deposited checks were quickly credited to the account but checks that were written took a couple of days to clear. Mr. Rosner, in opposing dismissal of the indictment, explained that "Marine Midland and Citibank permitted customers to draw on checks one day after the deposit. [But] for one day after the funds were available, the deposited item could still be returned unpaid by the bank on which the check was drawn."

When an overdraft arose, the new checks steadily arriving in rising amounts would appear to cover it. Justice Berkman's summary of grand-jury testimony noted that Mr. Halloran subscribed to a computer hookup called "Marine Lines" that gave him instant access to data about the Marine Midland accounts of Water Tunnel and other enterprises of his.

Each day a Transit Mix employee "directed the bookkeepers to make up checks in random amounts so as to come up with the required total," according to her summary, and the employee "then brought these checks—possibly hundreds in one day—to Halloran for signature. Indeed, Halloran also sometimes signed large numbers of checks in blank."

Mr. Rosner said Transit Mix accounting employees told the grand jury that "by the final months of the kite, the mechanics of operating the fraud—the calculation of amounts to be deposited and drawn, the physical writing of and depositing of the checks themselves—was their main employment activity."

END OF THE GAME

In February 1984 a Citibank computer analysis finally showed bank officers what was happening. After meetings in March with Mr. Madden, says Justice Berkman's account of grand-jury testimony, Citibank "closed the Transit Mix account, leaving Marine Midland holding the bag for a loss in excess of $23 million. * * *"

The bank, of course, did get the $23 million back. A spokesman for Marine Midland says the whole affair was an "isolated incident" and adds: "It was just an aberration. We feel [our controls] are more than adequate."

Citibank has declined to comment on the incidents.

Testimony at the trial indicated the defendants had been caught in a cash bind. Yet they were trying to show they had intended all along to repay. So to prove they weren't too strapped to do so, the defense focused on Mr. Halloran's resources.

Defense lawyer Frederick Hafetz gave the jury this portrait of Mr. Halloran: "He sits here in New York * * * with his wife and two children, operating his business. Makes no effort to flee to Brazil. He sits right there as big as life, with his over $150 million in total assets. * * * His net realizable value—assets over liabilities—is a startling figure of $48 million."

That Mr. Halloran had assets like that and stayed put, his lawyer argued, was "eloquent testimony to Biff Halloran's intent not to do the banks out of money."

The jurors apparently agreed. On July 25, they found the defendants innocent of the felony charge of grand larceny, which carries a possible seven-year prison sentence. They convicted the two men only of the misdemeanor count of scheming to defraud, for which the maximum sentence is one year. The defendants intend to appeal the conviction.

"The judge indicated it would be larceny if they didn't intend to return the money in a reasonable amount of time," says the jury foreman, Paul Bernstein, a political-science professor at Bloomfield College in New Jersey. "Ability to pay was a factor. We felt [Mr. Halloran] had ability to repay, given the nature of his assets and despite the fact they were not liquid."

Says another juror, Robin Markowitz, an ad-agency media buyer: "It seemed to us they were trying feverishly to sell the hotels, to convert to cash, to take down the kite."

CASES TO COME

Mr. Halloran still faces other legal problems. An indictment obtained by U.S. Attorney Rudolph Giuliani accuses him and others of taking part in a "massive scheme" to defraud developers in Manhattan by rigging bids for concrete work on high-rise buildings. The federal indictment describes the defendants as either members or, in Mr. Halloran's case, an "associate" of an organized-crime family headed by Anthony ("Fat Tony") Salerno. Mr. Halloran and the others have pleaded innocent.

In addition, Transit Mix Concrete and another firm in which Mr. Halloran is a principal, Marine Pollution Service, are defendants in civil antitrust suits filed by the New York state attorney general. One charges restraint of trade in ready-mix concrete in New York City, and the other accuses Mr. Halloran and the two companies of rigging bids on projects including the city's new Jacob Javits convention center. He and the companies deny the charges.

The check-kiting case, meanwhile, may have had some legal effect. Before the trial, the prosecutor, Mr. Rosner, cited the case in urging the New York legislature to stiffen penalties for white-collar crime. It has acted, and as of Nov. 1, a scheming-to-defraud charge such as the one of which Messrs. Halloran and Madden were convicted will be a felony.

And Justice Berkman suggested in court that some legislative attention also is due for what she called the modern problem of check-kiting. In reviewing and rejecting the motion to dismiss the larceny indictment, she commented: "When behavior looks, feels, smells and sounds so thoroughly larcenous as does this elaborate, protracted and enormous scheme of check-kiting, there should be no need even to stop and reflect whether that behavior is indeed against the law."

SECTION 4. COLLECTING BANK'S RESPONSIBILITY

Invariably a bank would prefer to be regarded as a collecting rather than a payor bank. That is both because its responsibility is less onerous and its liability for breach of that responsibility is less severe. Section 4–212 gives a right of chargeback or refund. This may be regarded as simply an elaboration upon basic responsibility for collection under UCC 4–202. Unlike the payor, who must act by the midnight deadline absent unusual circumstances, the midnight deadline is merely a "safe harbor" for the collecting bank who may act at that time or under any longer time provided it acts with ordinary care.

Equally significant is UCC 4–103(5):

> "The measure of damages for failure to exercise ordinary care in handling an item is the amount of the item reduced by an amount which could not have been realized by the use of ordinary care, and where there is bad faith it includes other damages, if any, suffered by the part as a proximate consequence."

Do you see why the collecting bank's liability under UCC 4–103(5) will almost always be smaller than a payor bank's liability under UCC 4–302?

It should come as no surprise that there are a fairly limited number of cases involving collecting banks and a large number of cases involving payors. The fruits of victory for the plaintiff are much greater against a payor and presumably the potential for injury on the part of a payor is greater, the judgment and decisions more significant than those of the collecting bank who merely passes the check along.

As we shall see, occasionally a bank gets stuck in the middle. That has been particularly true in recent cases in which depositors have committed fraud by doing fancy things with the micro-encoding, with the routing numbers in the upper right-hand corner of the check or with the title on the face of the check itself. If one can deposit a large check in his account and make it behave "like the man who never returns" on the MTA, he can likely withdraw that money from the depositary bank because the depositary bank determines when final payment has been made merely by the passage of time. Think about it for a moment. The system is dependent upon a "no news is good news" rule. A payee or depositary bank learns of final payment in a typical case by *not* learning of dishonor. If, therefore, one can deposit a check in a bank and insure, by playing with the micro-numbers that it will travel from coast to coast, the passage of time may lead his bank to believe the check has been finally paid and may allow him to withdraw the money. The case that follows is just such a case.

UNITED STATES FIDELITY & GUARANTY CO. v. FEDERAL RESERVE BANK OF NEW YORK

United States District Court, Southern District New York, 1984.
590 F.Supp. 486.

HAIGHT, DISTRICT JUDGE. Plaintiff Union Trust Company of Maryland ("Union Trust") is the victim of a cleverly executed check fraud. Claiming that the Federal Reserve Bank of New York ("New York Fed") is at least partially responsible for the success of the scheme, it seeks to hold New York Fed liable for the loss. Defendant moves to dismiss the action for failure to state a claim under Rule 12(b)(6), Fed.R.Civ.P.

I.

On May 6, 1980, one Marvin Goldstein, the perpetrator of the fraud, deposited a check for some $880,000 in a Union Trust Account. In hindsight, it is obvious that the check was designed to defraud the bank, for its counterfeit numerals served to turn the mechanized efficiency of the banking system against itself. Explaining its success will require a digression into modern techniques of check processing.

It is common experience that banks "hold" checks deposited for collection for a short period of time after deposit. For that period of time the banks grant only a provisional credit in the depositor's account and do not allow withdrawals of funds against the deposited checks. The purpose of the hold is to permit the depository bank to assure itself that there are sufficient funds in the account on which the check is drawn to permit its payment. Because of the tremendous volume of checks routed through the processing system, however, it is impractical for payor banks, those which hold the account on which the check is drawn, affirmatively to notify depository banks that a particular check has been paid. * * *

* * *

* * * On the face of the check Goldstein deposited at Union Trust were specified not one but two payor banks. The name of one payor bank, First Pennsylvania Bank of Philadelphia ("First Penn") was printed in letters in the lower left-hand corner of the check. The other payor bank, the State Bank of Albany ("Albany State"), was not specified by name; rather, it was specified by the Routing Number printed in the upper right-hand corner. Although this number ordinarily corresponds to the MICR number along the bottom of the check, the MICR number of this check was effectively nonsense in that it identified no known bank. In any event, the check bore two inconsistent destinations. The result of this, as is described in more detail below, was that the check was routed through five banks over the course of nearly two weeks. Although every bank handling the check met its midnight deadline, ten days expired before the Union Trust was notified that neither Albany State nor First Penn would honor the check. The day before, however, Union Trust, having taken the silence as an indication that the check had been paid, had permitted Goldstein to withdraw $755,000 against the check. Because his remaining balance amounted to only about $1,000.00, Union Trust was out $754,035.00. Its insurer absorbed all but $100,000 of this loss.

To understand the alleged basis for liability of the New York Fed, it is necessary to trace the check on its ten-day travels across the Northeast. On the day of deposit, May 6, 1980, Union Trust forwarded the check for collection to

Philadelphia National Bank ("PNB"), a Pennsylvania bank which must not be confused with the previously-mentioned First Penn.[5] PNB apparently selected Albany State as the correct payor bank and routed the check to New York Fed on May 7 in anticipation of its being forwarded by New York Fed to Albany State for collection. New York Fed did forward the check, but Albany State returned it on May 9 stamped "Sent in Error." Intending either that the check be returned to PNB as dishonored or that it be forwarded to First Penn for collection, New York Fed sent the check on May 12 to the Federal Reserve Bank of Philadelphia ("Philadelphia Fed").[8] The Philadelphia Fed apparently selected the latter course and forwarded the check to First Penn on May 14. Early on May 16, First Penn, apparently having located no account on which the check could be drawn, notified PNB by telephone of the dishonor. PNB promptly passed the word to Union Trust, but the notice came too late to prevent the bank's loss.

Union Trust claims that in its handling of the check New York Fed breached its UCC-imposed duty to "use ordinary care in sending notice of dishonor or non-payment or returning an item * * * after learning that the item has not been paid or accepted." N.Y.U.C.C. § 4–202(1)(a) and (b) (McKinney 1964). Plaintiff contends that New York Fed failed to exercise ordinary care by 1) failing to notify it of Albany State's return of the check, 2) sending the check to Philadelphia Fed rather than PNB, 3) failing to notify it of the delay caused by the routing to Albany State, and 4) failing to "wire advice" of Albany State's nonpayment. Any one of these actions would likely have prevented Union Trust's loss. New York Fed challenges each of these claims individually. It also asserts the defense of statute of limitations and argues that public policy and Federal Reserve regulations bar suits such as this.

II.

N.Y.U.C.C. § 4–202(1) requires a bank in the collection chain, such as New York Fed, to "use ordinary care in the exercise of its basic collection tasks. * * * If [the bank] forwards the item to be presented [§ 4–202(1)] requires ordinary care with respect to routing * * * and also in the selection of intermediary banks or other agents." Official Comments 1. & 2., N.Y.U.C.C. § 4–202 (McKinney 1964).[10] See also N.Y.U.C.C. § 4–103(1) (McKinney 1964) (duty of ordinary care may not be waived). The phrase "ordinary care" in Article 4 of the UCC is not intended to refer to a standard of care unique to the banking world. Instead, it is "used with its normal tort meaning." Official Comment 4., N.Y.U.C.C. § 4–103 (McKinney 1964). Nor is it exhaustively defined by the Code, although "action or non-action approved by [Article 4] or pursuant to Federal Reserve regulations or operating letters constitutes the exercise of ordinary care." Id. * * * If a UCC or Federal Reserve regulation

5. Although the parties do not so state, the check was apparently forwarded to PNB because PNB was Union Trust's "correspondent bank"—the bank to which Union Trust sent all of its out-of-state checks for collection. The circumstances surrounding this initial forwarding are currently unknown. Apparently the check was not machine processed since the MICR number specifies no known bank, making machine processing impossible. It is likely, then, that the check was read by hand and forwarded to PNB on the basis of either the Routing Number of Albany State or the written indication of First Penn.

8. Because a week-end intervened, the lapse of time from May 9 to May 12 did not exceed the New York Fed's midnight deadline.

10. New York Fed has abandoned the argument that it was not a collecting bank. See supra, note 9. Federal Reserve regulations recognize by implication that the New York Fed is subject to this duty of ordinary care. 12 C.F.R. § 210.6(a) (1979).

is applicable, however, it provides a safe harbor, and a bank may conclusively demonstrate ordinary care by proving compliance with it.

III.

Plaintiffs first contend that in handling the check New York Fed failed to follow one of its own regulations governing handling of returned checks. Since the particular regulation is paragraph 20 of Federal Reserve Bank of New York Operating Circular No. 4, as revised September 18, 1979,[11] the claim sounds in breach of contract rather than tort, for Operating Circulars are treated as contracts binding on parties having an interest in items handled by the Reserve Bank in question. N.Y.U.C.C. §§ 4–103(1) and 4–103(2).

Paragraph 20 of Operating Circular No. 4 is one of a group of four paragraphs collected under the heading "Uniform instructions regarding protest and advice of nonpayment." It reads in relevant part:

> "20. Except as provided in paragraph 21 hereof [a paragraph all agree to be irrelevant here], all Federal Reserve Banks will receive, handle, and forward cash items [such as checks] subject to the following uniform instructions regarding * * * wire advice of nonpayment * * *:
>
> * * *
>
> "(c) WIRE ADVICE of nonpayment of any item of $2,500 or over * * * unless it bears on its face the legend, 'DO NOT WIRE ADVICE OF NONPAYMENT,' of a Federal Reserve Bank or of a preceding bank endorser * * *.
>
> "(d) DO NOT WIRE ADVICE of nonpayment of: * * *
>
> "(ii) any item of $2,500 or over unless such advice is required by subparagraph (c)." [footnote omitted].

Because the check in question was over $2,500, the relatively straight-forward language of paragraph 20 would appear to have required the New York Fed to wire advice[12] of the check's nonpayment by Albany State.

New York Fed responds by pointing to paragraph 23 of the same operating circular, which is also included under the "Uniform instructions regarding protest and advice of nonpayment" heading. Paragraph 23 reads in relevant part:

> "This Bank shall have no responsibility for determining whether any other bank has * * * (b) given any wire advice of nonpayment required under the provisions hereof, nor shall this Bank have any responsibility for giving wire advice of nonpayment unless a wire advice of nonpayment required hereunder is received from the paying bank or any other bank."

New York Fed argues that unless it received wire advice of nonpayment from Albany State, paragraph 23 absolves it of any duty to wire advice of nonpayment back down the collection chain. Because receipt of such wire advice by New York Fed has not been pleaded, defendant urges dismissal of this ground for recovery.

11. Operating circulars are issued by individual Federal Reserve Banks in order to implement various Federal Reserve System regulations. Although the circular at issue here has been superseded, it was still effective at the time of the events in question. It implemented 12 C.F.R. § 210, otherwise known as Regulation J, governing collection of checks. This operating circular will be referred to throughout as "Operating Circular No. 4," it being understood that this refers to the superseded circular in effect in 1980, not the currently-effective circular designated "No. 4."

12. "Wire advice of nonpayment" refers to the sending of notice of the fact of nonpayment by means of electronic communications to a bank down the collection stream.

Although the duties imposed by the operating circular are by no means clear, I am constrained to agree with New York Fed. It is true, as plaintiffs point out, that the language of paragraph 20 is absolute in requiring wire advice. Because it expressly provides for the one exception of paragraph 21, and only one exception, it arguably includes by implication the checks otherwise excepted by paragraph 23. Indeed, this is a relatively strong argument in support of plaintiffs' position, but it is the only one. Several other factors persuade me to the contrary.

First, to read paragraph 20 as plaintiffs urge would entirely nullify paragraph 23. On the other hand, New York Fed's reading would give effect to both paragraphs: New York Fed would have a duty to wire advice either if it received wire advice of nonpayment or if the nonpayment originated with it. The familiar rule of contract construction that a contract should if possible be read so as to give effect to all of its terms holds true whether the contract is drafted by private parties or by a Federal Reserve Bank. New York Fed's reading permits this; plaintiffs' does not.

Second, other publications clarify the meaning of Operating Circular No. 4 and reinforce the impression that it intends to impose the duty of sending wire advice only when wire advice is received. Administrative Procedure No. 15 of the Bank Operations Conference of the New York Clearing House Association [13] states that "[e]ffective July 1, 1977 all Federal Reserve offices implemented a uniform procedure under which they will not provide advice of nonpayment for cash items in amounts of $2,500 or over * * * unless such advice of nonpayment has been received from the paying bank." From this I infer that the interpretation urged by the New York Fed was accepted by the local banking community. Nor were other New York Fed publications entirely silent on the issue. Operating Circular No. 4 expressly refers to Federal Reserve Bank of New York Operating Circular No. 6, as revised September 18, 1979,[14] as the complement of Operating Circular No. 4. No. 4, entitled "Collection of Cash Items," describes the duties of New York Fed in handling cash items while No. 6, entitled "Instructions to Collecting Banks and Paying Banks," describes the duties of collecting banks and paying banks when dealing with New York Fed in the handling of cash items. Operating Circular No. 6 contains paragraphs numbered 20 and 23 which are identical to those numbered 20 and 23 in Circular No. 4. Although this admittedly makes the two circulars somewhat confusing when read together, the inclusion of paragraphs 20 and 23 in No. 6 has two significant effects. First, it places the burden on collecting and paying banks to wire advice in the first instance, since in paragraph 20 the command to "WIRE ADVICE" is addressed to the collecting and paying banks rather than to New York Fed. In addition, including paragraph 23 in No. 6 has the effect of warning the paying and collecting banks that unless they wire advice to New York Fed it will not pass the advice back down the collection chain. Operating Circular No. 6 thus convinces me that New York Fed attempted to communicate to the banking community the policy it now urges, while the Clearing House publication mentioned above convinces me that the community understood the message.

13. Such rules have the status of an agreement between parties having any interest in items handled by New York banks. N.Y.U.C.C. § 4–103(2).

14. This operating circular, like No. 4 cited above, supra note 11, has also been superseded by an unrelated publication. Again, references to "Operating Circular No. 6" refer to the No. 6 effective in May, 1980.

Finally, practical policy supports the defendant's view. By requiring paying banks to wire advice, the Federal Reserve Banks place the burden for initiating wire advice of nonpayment on the bank in the chain which is first and most certain to recognize that the check will not be paid. The paying bank is at once the most convenient, most trustworthy, and earliest point in the collection chain at which to initiate advice of nonpayment. It thus is the most appropriate.[15]

This claim is thus dismissed. * * *

IV.

The plaintiff's second contention is that N.Y.U.C.C. § 4–202(1)(e) required New York Fed to notify Union Trust of the delay caused by the routing of the check through Albany State. This UCC provision requires a bank to send notice of a "delay in transit." Defendant argues that § 4–202(1)(e) refers to delays in passing a check from one bank to another rather than delays caused by complex routing.

Following a scholarly analysis of the legislative history of UCC § 4–202(1)(e), Judge Knapp concluded in Northpark National Bank v. Banker's Trust Co., 572 F.Supp. 524 (S.D.N.Y. 1983) (hereafter "Northpark"), which involved a check fraud somewhat similar to that alleged here, that § 4–202(1)(e) was intended to apply only to delays occasioned by "mishaps in the mails," not to problems caused by misrouting. 572 F.Supp. at 531. * * *

Plaintiffs argue, however, that Judge Knapp ignored a crucial amendment. Between the time of the 1948 Notes and Comments relied on by Judge Knapp and the 1964 enactment of N.Y.U.C.C. § 4–202(1)(e), plaintiffs point out, the drafting committee changed § 4–202(1)(e) from requiring notice of "loss or delay in transit" to notice of "any loss or delay in transit." Plaintiffs theorize that this addition expanded the scope of the subsection to include the delay at hand.

The phrase "delay in transit" does not clearly reach this situation. "Delay in transit" connotes some impediment to physical transportation of the item in question. Accepting that plaintiffs' interpretation is plausible, however, makes resort to the legislative history appropriate to resolve the uncertainty. Judge Knapp's research discloses that defendants' interpretation was indeed the intended meaning of the phrase. Northpark, supra, 572 F.Supp. at 531. Plaintiffs present no evidence that the addition of the word "any" was intended to change this meaning. The most likely explanation for the amendment is that it was intended to preclude judicial interpolation of some other adjective such as "material." In other words, the drafting committee probably intended to make clear that banks should provide notice of all delays in transit rather than only those delays which the banks or the courts adjudged significant. The word itself gives no hint that its addition was intended to change the substantive meaning of the phrase. Therefore, I adopt Judge Knapp's careful analysis and dismiss this ground for recovery.

V.

Plaintiffs' final two theories of recovery may be considered together. Unlike the previous two claims, neither theory points to a specific statutorily prescribed procedure which New York Fed failed to follow. Rather, plaintiffs propose two alternative courses of conduct which, it is alleged, New York Fed in the exercise of ordinary care should have followed to prevent Union Trust's loss. They thus

15. Whether in these circumstances Operating Circular No. 6 created a duty in Albany State to wire advice of nonpayment is a question I need not reach, since Albany State is not a party to this action.

suggest ways in which New York Fed failed to live up to the duty of ordinary care imposed by N.Y.U.C.C. § 4–202(1).

A.

Upon receiving the check stamped "Sent in Error" from Albany State, New York Fed routed it to the Philadelphia Fed. Plaintiffs argue that at this point New York Fed should instead either have notified Union Trust or PNB of Albany State's nonpayment before sending the check to Philadelphia Fed or have returned the check directly to PNB, which presumably would have timely notified Union Trust of the return. Underlying both of the arguments is the theory that New York Fed's legal duties required it to examine the check, recognize the possibility either that the check was fraudulent or that routing to Philadelphia Fed could cause excess delay, and take some affirmative action to alert Union Trust to the problem. The failure to recognize and alert downstream banks to the possibility of delayed or nonexistent payment is alleged to represent a failure of ordinary care. Whether this failure was in fact negligent is, as was noted above, a question to be determined from all the facts and circumstances which cannot be resolved on a motion to dismiss. New York Fed responds, however, that for various reasons it had no duty to take the actions which plaintiffs urge were proper.

B.

New York Fed first argues that under § 4–202(1) it was required only to send notice of dishonor or to return the unpaid check to its transferor and that its sending the check to Philadelphia Fed satisfied the latter requirement. This position critically misstates the obligation imposed by N.Y.U.C.C. § 4–202(1)(b). That subsection reads in relevant part:

> "(1) A collecting bank must use ordinary care in * * *
>
> "(b) sending notice of dishonor or non-payment or returning an item * * * to the bank's transferor or directly to the depository bank * * * after learning that the item has not been paid or accepted, as the case may be * * *."

The statute does not state that a bank must send notice or return an item upon learning of dishonor. Rather, it requires a bank to use ordinary care in sending notice or returning a dishonored item. The difference is significant, for the former interpretation renders the statute pointless. A paying or collecting bank has little choice upon learning of dishonor than to send notice or return the check. The message of § 4–202(1)(b) is that not only is a collecting bank to notify downstream banks of dishonor but it is to exercise ordinary care in doing so. This includes the duty to use ordinary care both in routing the check and in selecting intermediary banks. Official Comments 1. & 2., N.Y.U.C.C. § 4–202 (McKinney 1964).

C.

Contrary to the provisions of N.Y.U.C.C. § 4–202(1)(b), New York Fed did not return the check to its actual transferor, PNB. Instead it sent the check to the Federal Reserve Bank of which PNB was a member, Philadelphia Fed. Defendant argues that this course was proper under 12 CFR § 210.4, a Federal Reserve regulation designed to speed the processing of checks which must travel between Federal Reserve districts for collection.

A brief explanation is in order. Commercial banks maintain no formal commercial relations with Federal Reserve Banks outside their own district. In order to collect a check drawn on a bank outside their own Federal Reserve district, this structure requires them to send the check to their own Federal Reserve Bank, which then forwards the check to the Federal Reserve Bank in the district of the bank on which the check is drawn. It is this latter Reserve Bank which forwards the check to the payor bank. Beckhart, supra note 7, at 69. Recognizing that this is a rather cumbersome process, the Federal Reserve System has established an internal bookkeeping system which permits Reserve Banks to accept for collection checks sent by commercial banks outside their district. The object is to permit the banks to bypass their own Federal Reserve Banks and send out-of-district checks directly to the Federal Reserve Bank in the district of the payor bank. By eliminating one bank from the chain of collection, this significantly speeds check processing. It is primarily the larger banks which avail themselves of this convenience. Id. The "direct send" process is authorized by § 210.4(a), which in 1980 read in relevant part:

> "* * * as permitted or required by [a bank's own] Federal Reserve Bank, [any] sender may send direct to any other Federal Reserve Bank any cash item * * * payable within the district of such other Federal Reserve Bank."

PNB took advantage of § 210.4(a) in sending this check to New York Fed, the Federal Reserve Bank in the district of Albany State.

It is 12 CFR § 210.4(b) on which New York Fed relies to justify its returning the check to Philadelphia Fed rather than PNB, its actual transferor. Section 210.4(b) is part of the regulation authorizing "direct send" transfers. It states that whenever a bank takes advantage of § 210.4(a) by sending a check directly to a Federal Reserve Bank of which it is not a member,

> "the relationships and the rights and liabilities existing between the sender, the Federal Reserve Bank of its district and the Federal Reserve Bank to which the item is sent will be the same, and the provisions of this Subpart will apply, as though the sender had sent such item to the Federal Reserve Bank of its district and such Federal Reserve had forwarded the item to the other Federal Reserve Bank." 12 CFR § 210.4(b) (1979).

New York Fed draws on § 210.4(b) to make two arguments. First, it argues that the regulation effectively deemed Philadelphia Fed its transferor for the purposes of N.Y.U.C.C. § 4–202(1)(b). As a consequence, when New York Fed sent the check to Philadelphia Fed it was returning the check to its de jure transferor and committed no per se violation of § 4–202(1)(b) by failing to return the check to its "transferor." I accept this argument. The language is quite plain that when an item is "direct sent" under § 210.4(a) "the relationships * * * existing between the sender, the Federal Reserve Bank of its district, and the Federal Reserve Bank to which the item is sent will be the same * * * as though the sender had [first] sent the item to the Federal Reserve Bank of its district." 12 CFR § 210.4(b) (1979). If PNB had first sent the bogus check to its own Reserve Bank, it would have sent it to Philadelphia Fed, and the relationship between Philadelphia Fed and New York Fed would have been one of transferor-transferee. Section 210.4(b) thus authorized New York Fed to deem Philadelphia Fed its transferor and return the check to it in pursuance of N.Y.U.C.C. § 4–202(1)(b).

New York Fed's second argument involving § 210.4(b) goes one step further. It is that not only did § 210.4(b) authorize the return of the check to Philadelphia Fed, it required it. The result is that according to Official Comment 4. of N.Y.U.C.C. § 4–103, New York Fed would prove ordinary care as a matter of law through compliance with an applicable Federal Reserve regulation.

Nothing in the language of § 210.4(b) requires that Federal Reserve banks return directly sent checks through Federal Reserve banks. The regulation simply says that the banks involved will act as though the check had not been directly sent. This certainly permitted New York Fed to return the check, but it is not clear that it required such action. New York Fed has produced no regulation which requires it to return a check to another Federal Reserve Bank when direct send is not used. Another Reserve regulation, 12 CFR § 210.6(a) recognizes that Federal Reserve banks will be liable for a failure to exercise ordinary care. I would be loath to accept an interpretation of the very general language of § 210.4(b) which would require Reserve Banks to avoid "direct return" even though to do so exposes another bank to an unreasonable risk of loss. In any event, I find it unnecessary to decide. Assuming that New York Fed chose to construe § 210.4(b) as it claims, it was then under a duty, as discussed below, to send notice in some other manner so as to prevent foreseeable loss.

D.

It is not a foregone conclusion, however, that New York Fed's forwarding the check to Philadelphia Fed was in any way negligent. It is interesting to note in this connection that although the defendant contends that it "returned" the check to Philadelphia Fed, it is impossible to determine on the information in the pleadings, and perhaps it will ultimately be impossible to determine at all, whether New York Fed sent the check to Philadelphia Fed intending that it be returned or that it be forwarded for collection to First Penn. Because both PNB, to which the check would be returned, and First Penn, to which it would be forwarded for collection, are in the Philadelphia Reserve District, New York Fed's action in sending the check to Philadelphia Fed was consistent with either intention. As discussed above, only in extraordinary circumstances does a Federal Reserve bank send an item for either return or collection to a bank other than a Federal Reserve Bank in another district.

This ambiguity is relevant to the difficulties in plaintiffs' theory of liability. Regardless of New York Fed's intention in sending the check to Philadelphia Fed, if the Philadelphia Fed had then returned the check to PNB the loss would not have occurred, for Union Trust would presumably have received notice of Albany State's dishonor on May 14, the day before it released funds to Goldstein. The forwarding to Philadelphia Fed thus was not in and of itself negligent, nor was it necessarily a cause of Union Trust's loss. The only risk which arguably made New York Fed's action negligent was the risk which materialized: that Philadelphia Fed would not recognize the fraudulent nature of the check and would forward it to First Penn for collection. Of course, there is no guarantee that sending the check to PNB would have avoided this risk. PNB could have sent the check to First Penn as easily as Philadelphia Fed, and the total handling time would have been no shorter.

Whether New York Fed's behavior constituted a lapse in ordinary care thus revolves around three factors: the foreseeability of Philadelphia Fed's failure to return the check, the foreseeability of loss resulting from that action, and the feasibility, given modern banking procedures, of New York Fed's detecting the fraud, discerning the risk, and taking curative action. Section 4–202(1)(b) of the UCC, which requires ordinary care in notifying downstream banks of dishonor, is best interpreted as requiring a bank to send notice of dishonor reasonably calculated to reach the depository bank in time to prevent a withdrawal against a dishonored check. Ordinarily, the seasonable return of a dishonored check is such notice, justifying the express mention of check return in § 4–202. However, as noted in Official Comment 2 to N.Y.U.C.C. § 4–202, the duty of a bank in presenting a check, and by logical implication returning one, goes beyond acting in a timely manner; a bank must also use ordinary care in choosing the route which a check will take. The check which New York Fed forwarded to Philadelphia Fed bore two inconsistent payor bank designations, a nonsensical MICR number, and a stamp reading "Sent in Error" which demonstrated nonpayment by one of the designated payor banks. If it was reasonably foreseeable that Philadelphia Fed would forward such a check to First Penn for collection rather than return it to PNB, that it would be dishonored by First Penn, and that Union Trust would release funds against the check before receiving timely notice of dishonor from First Penn, then New York Fed failed to use ordinary care in routing the check to Philadelphia Fed without taking some precaution to avoid the foreseeable risks. Because it apparently sent no other notice of dishonor to Union Trust, it would have failed in its duty of ordinary care under § 4–202. Cf. Northpark, 572 F.Supp. at 533–535.

E.

The concept of "reasonably foreseeable" in this context must be elaborated. As Judge Knapp noted in Northpark, 572 F.Supp. at 534, ordinary care must be determined with regard to "sound banking practice." In other words, although Official Comment 4 of UCC § 4–103 requires that "ordinary care" be "used with its normal tort meaning," the realities of the modern banking system cannot be ignored in evaluating a bank's negligence. These realities are, after all, some of the "circumstances" which tort law commands us to consider in determining reasonableness.

To the outsider, modern check processing resembles a high stakes game of hot potato. Banks pass checks from hand-to-hand in order to avoid being caught with the check at the expiration of their midnight deadline. The system appears to work amazingly well in the ordinary course of business. It seems wholly unfair to impose liability on New York Fed if detection of this sophisticated fraud was wholly inconsistent with participation in the system.[22] If efforts by all banks to detect this type of fraud would bring check processing to a screeching halt, New York Fed cannot be faulted for not making those efforts. Consequently, before liability can be imposed on New York Fed more questions must be asked than those framed in section V(D) above.

Initially, it must be determined whether this type of fraud is so common that New York Fed in the exercise of ordinary care should have taken exceptional precautions to detect it. Whether the fraud was so common as to warrant such measures is a question of fact to be resolved at trial, but it appears that this type of scheme is rather new and as yet uncommon. See Northpark, supra, 572 F.Supp. at 533; but see id., at 534 n. 24.

If it is determined that special precautions were unwarranted, it must then be determined whether standard banking procedures should have led to detection of the problem and anticipation of Union Trust's loss. This involves two separate questions. The first is whether it is reasonably foreseeable that a check

22. The UCC recognizes that in some circumstances the practical realities of modern check processing make strict adherence to traditional law of negotiable instruments impossible. See, e.g., N.Y.U.C.C. § 3–206(2), Official Comment 3. (McKinney 1964) (permitting intermediary and payor banks to regard [sic] check indorsements because such banks handle checks in bulk and "have no practicable opportunity to consider the effect of restrictive indorsements").

bearing inconsistent routing designations will be rejected by the second payor bank to which it is sent. It may well be that ordinarily such inconsistencies result from innocent printers' errors which do not justify alarm. See Northpark, supra, 572 F.Supp. at 534. If the latter is true, it must then be asked whether the individual characteristics of this particular check were such as to differentiate it from checks which result from printers' errors. In other words, New York Fed may yet be held liable if a bank exercising ordinary care in the standard processing of returned checks would have recognized this to be a bogus check.

F.

In sum, I cannot say as a matter of law that New York Fed was not required to take any affirmative action to prevent Union Trust's loss other than the forwarding of the check to Philadelphia Fed. If New York Fed in the exercise of ordinary care, as described in section V(E) above, should have reasonably foreseen the possibility of Philadelphia Fed's forwarding the check to First Penn and First Penn's nonpayment, it had a duty to take other steps to prevent Union Trust's loss.

VI.

New York Fed asserts two final defenses. First, it argues that public policy, as embodied in footnote 3 of 12 CFR § 210.6(a) (1979), requires that it be excepted from liability in these circumstances. Footnote 3 is found at the end of a sentence which reads, "[a] Federal Reserve Bank shall not have * * * any liability to the sender * * * except for its own lack of good faith or failure to exercise ordinary care.[3]" 12 CFR § 210.6(a) (1979). The footnote reads:

"[3] No Federal Reserve Bank shall be responsible to the sender of any cash item, or any other owner or holder thereof, for any delay resulting from the action taken by the Federal Reserve Bank in presenting, sending, or forwarding the item on the basis of (a) any A.B.A. transit number or routing symbol appearing thereon at the time of its receipt by the Federal Reserve Bank, whether inscribed by magnetic ink or by any other means, and whether or not such transit or routing symbol is consistent with each other form of designation of a paying bank (or nonbank payor) then appearing thereon, or (b) any other form of designation of a paying bank (or nonbank payor) then appearing thereon, whether or not consistent with A.B.A. transit number or routing symbol then appearing thereon."

The textual sentence and the footnote must be read together. The text explicitly acknowledges that Federal Reserve Banks accept responsibility for their own negligence. The footnote should be regarded as a gloss on this acknowledgment: that it is not to be regarded as negligence for a Reserve Bank to forward a check based on its numerical routing symbols, regardless of whether those signals are correct or internally consistent. It appears that this would provide a complete defense to any alleged liability accruing from New York Fed's initial forwarding of the check to Albany State, an act clearly taken in reliance on the routing number printed in the upper right-hand corner, but this act is not alleged as a basis of liability. There are several reasons why footnote 3 does not reach the later sending to Philadelphia Fed. Defendant has consistently maintained that its sending the check to Philadelphia Fed was a return, not a forwarding for collection. Assuming that as true, the routing was based not on the routing symbols but on the endorsement of PNB, the transferor of the check to which it was to be returned. Even if the forwarding to Philadelphia Fed was intended as an act of presentment, the forwarding itself would have been based on the written designation of First Penn as payor, not on any numerical routing symbol. More important, it is not the forwarding per se which constitutes the alleged negligence. Rather, it was the failure to take steps to avoid a foreseeable risk of harm to Union Trust. Footnote 3 seems intended to guard against liability based on misrouting in adherence to an undetected printer's error, not against the more substantial negligence alleged here. * * *

Nor do I find persuasive the defendant's argument that Union Trust, as the bank which accepted the check, should be held solely responsible. It is true that Union Trust was able to observe the depositor and might have had the best chance to examine the check. It is not clear—certainly as a matter of law—that in these circumstances its failure to recognize the fraudulent nature of the check constituted negligence so gross as to bar this action.

Defendant's last argument urges the adoption of a uniform nationwide statute of limitations of two years for actions against Federal Reserve Banks over their handling of checks. Plaintiff urges reference to the UCC provision stating that actions against banks are governed by the law of the place where the bank is located. N.Y.U.C.C. § 4–102(2). Since New York actions for negligence are governed by the three-year period of N.Y.C.P.L.R. § 214(4), plaintiffs' action is timely under their theory, untimely under defendants'.

Under the presumption which has prevailed throughout this opinion that state law applies, N.Y.U.C.C. § 4–102(2) controls. Only if federal common law properly applies and dictates a statute of limitations different from that of New York state law would defendant's theory prevail. I find, however, that even if federal common law did apply it would not dictate a different statute of limitations. * * *

* * * [The Federal Reserve's] plea for uniformity is a frivolous attempt to avoid a decision on the merits.

VII.

Plaintiffs' attempts to find in paragraph 20 of Operating Circular No. 4 (1979) and in N.Y.U.C.C. § 4–202(1)(e) a provision which required New York Fed to notify Union Trust of Albany State's dishonor are unavailing. Plaintiffs may, nevertheless, be able to demonstrate that the failure to notify breached the defendant's general duty of ordinary care. For that reason, as described above, the motion to dismiss is denied.

The parties are directed to proceed with discovery in accordance with the provisions of the separate order filed along with this opinion.

It is so ordered. [Some footnotes omitted.]

Notes

1. The court rejected the Federal Reserve's argument that (a) Union Bank (the depositary bank) was the least cost-risk avoider and (b) therefore should have born the loss. If you were to rewrite the Code, on whom would you place the loss in a case such as this? Who, at the least cost, could avoid it?

2. To some extent the Federal Reserve has the capacity to change the rules of the game by causing the Federal Reserve Board to issue new regulations which might absolve it of liability or restrict its liability. Could the Fed do so in this case?

3. Assume that you are a drafter of regulations for the Federal Reserve. You wish to impose regulations that would not necessarily absolve the federal reserve banks from liability, but which would stimulate banks, including the federal reserve, to take action to minimize the likelihood of such cases. What would you propose?

Problem 26–2

Assume that Congress or your local legislature has passed a law that explicitly requires depositary banks to allow depositors to withdraw funds no later than seven days after checks are deposited. After a case like *United States Fidelity,* how do you advise the bank to avoid losses in circumstances where thieves devise clever ways to make checks float throughout the system for more than seven days?

WELLS FARGO BANK v. HARTFORD NAT'L BANK & TRUST CO.

United States District Court, District of Connecticut, 1980.
484 F.Supp. 817.

BLUMENFELD, SENIOR DISTRICT JUDGE.

RULING ON CROSS-MOTIONS FOR SUMMARY JUDGMENT

This is a suit commenced by Wells Fargo Bank, National Association ("Wells Fargo") to recover $25,000 from Hartford National Bank and Trust Company ("HNBT"). Wells Fargo is seeking to reverse the credit it gave to HNBT in the course of handling a check which it had received for collection on which it was later unable to collect. HNBT, in turn, seeks indemnification from the depositary bank, Lincoln First Bank-Central, National Association ("Lincoln"). Each of the parties have filed for summary judgment on the grounds that no material facts are in dispute, and each claim that Articles 3 and 4 of the U.C.C. entitle them to relief.

Unlike many bank collection cases, this case does not involve the liability of the payor bank, First National Bank of Nevada ("Nevada"), which has not been sued, nor does it involve the liability of the now-bankrupt drawer of the check. The sole question presented by this action is which of these three banks in the chain of collection will have to absorb the loss occasioned by the "bad" check. This court has jurisdiction under 28 U.S.C. § 1332 and there is no dispute as to jurisdiction or venue.

FACTS

The convoluted facts giving rise to this action are not in dispute, and summary judgment is therefore appropriate. However, before setting forth a detailed description of the intricacies of the bank collection process involved in this case, an overview of the transaction may be useful. On November 22, 1971, the check now in dispute was deposited with Lincoln. Since the check was drawn on the Nevada bank, Lincoln forwarded the check to Nevada via HNBT and Wells Fargo. On December 10, 1971, Nevada received the check and discovered that it was drawn on insufficient funds. Consequently Nevada decided to dishonor the item and sent the check back to Lincoln via Wells Fargo and HNBT. Lincoln received notice of the dishonor in late December of 1971, but it had already allowed the depositor of the check to withdraw funds from his account making it impossible to charge back the amount of the dishonored item. Claiming that the notice of dishonor came too late, Lincoln refused to accept the return of the check and instead sent it back again to Nevada via HNBT and Wells Fargo. When Wells Fargo received the item, however, it conditionally accepted responsibility for the loss and sought to collect from the drawer instead of delivering the check to Nevada. These efforts were unsuccessful and Wells Fargo, who now holds the dishonored item, commenced this action.

A. *From Lincoln to Nevada*

On November 22, 1971, John D. Porter as agent for Great Western Industries, Inc. ("Great Western") opened a checking account with Lincoln by depositing a check for $25,000 payable to the order of Lincoln. The check was drawn on the Great Western account with the Reno branch of the Nevada bank. After it received the check and opened the account for Great Western, Lincoln forwarded the check on for collection.

Instead of utilizing the Federal Reserve Bank clearing house system, Lincoln chose instead to use private collection channels, which promised an earlier availability of funds. In this particular case, Lincoln indorsed the check and sent it to HNBT with the understanding that HNBT would promptly forward the check on for collection.

HNBT received the check on November 22, the same day on which it had initially been deposited. After crediting Lincoln's account for $25,000, HNBT indorsed the check and mailed it to its California correspondent bank, Wells Fargo. On November 23, Wells Fargo received and indorsed the check, credited HNBT's account, and then mailed the check to the Las Vegas branch of the Nevada bank.

During this last transfer a substantial delay was encountered. According to the Las Vegas branch bank records, the check inexplicably was not received in the mail until December 8, 1971, 15 days after Wells Fargo sent it. Moreover, an additional one day delay followed because the check was not drawn on the Las Vegas branch but rather on the Reno branch of the Nevada bank. Since Las Vegas records did not reflect the extent of funds in Great Western's Reno account, it was necessary for the Las Vegas branch to forward the check to the Reno branch before the Nevada bank could establish whether there were sufficient funds to cover the check. When the check finally arrived at Reno, the Nevada bank promptly discovered that there were insufficient funds in Great Western's account.

B. *From Nevada to Lincoln*

At 4:45 p.m. on December 10, 1971, Nevada bank personnel sought to inform Wells Fargo by telephone that the check had been dishonored. The call was made to a bank officer in Wells Fargo's San Francisco branch, but it was apparently "rejected" because it was not accompanied by sufficient identifying information. The Nevada bank made a second call, this time to Wells Fargo's Los Angeles branch. At 5:30 p.m. this call was "accepted."

Since December 10, 1971 was a Friday, the next banking day was Monday, December 13, 1971. On Monday, the Nevada bank posted the dishonored check to Wells Fargo, which did not receive it until Friday, December 17. Nevada also reversed the credit which it had given to Wells Fargo.

Upon receiving the check, Wells Fargo immediately wired notice of the dishonor to HNBT. On the same day, Wells Fargo also returned the dishonored item by mail to HNBT and reversed the credit it had previously given. HNBT claims not to have received the telegram on the 17th but admits that it received the check in the mail on Monday, December 21. On that same day, HNBT notified Lincoln by telegram that the check had been dishonored. This notice, however, did not indicate the name of the drawer of the check and therefore failed to give Lincoln effective notice. Lincoln's first opportunity accurately to identify the dishonored item came when it received the check on December 27,

1971. HNBT had mailed the check to Lincoln on December 21 and had at the same time reversed the credit it had given earlier.

C. From Lincoln to Nevada Again

For the purpose of ruling on these motions it is not necessary to detail the remaining transfers of the check. Suffice it to say that on December 28, 1971, Lincoln declined to accept the check, claiming that the notice of dishonor had arrived too late. The item was sent back through the chain of collection and ultimately Wells Fargo ended up with both the check and the $25,000 loss. After several unsuccessful efforts at working out repayment from Great Western, Wells Fargo commenced this action.

Wells Fargo now moves for summary judgment against HNBT on three separate counts. It claims a right to proceed on HNBT's indorsement pursuant to U.C.C. § 3–414(1), a right to proceed on HNBT's breach of an implied warranty pursuant to U.C.C. § 4–207(2), and a right to "charge back" to HNBT pursuant to U.C.C. § 4–212(1). As a necessary prerequisite to recovery under any of these theories, Wells Fargo must first establish that it gave HNBT timely notice of Nevada's dishonor of the check. If Wells Fargo, with all the disputed facts resolved in its favor, cannot establish that it gave a notice of dishonor when due, HNBT and Lincoln are entitled to prevail on their cross-motions for summary judgment. * * *

THE LAW

U.C.C. § 3–508(2) provides that "[a]ny necessary notice must be given by a bank before its midnight deadline." "Midnight deadline," in turn, is defined as "midnight on [the bank's] next banking day following the banking day on which it receives the relevant item or notice * * *" U.C.C. § 4–104(1)(h). Thus, in order to determine whether Wells Fargo gave HNBT a timely notice of Nevada's dishonor, it is first necessary to establish "the banking day on which [Wells Fargo received] the relevant item or notice * * *."

As indicated above, Wells Fargo received a notice of Nevada's dishonor by telephone on Friday afternoon, December 10, 1971. It sent no notice to HNBT before the midnight deadline on its next banking day, Monday, December 13. Wells Fargo first received written notice from Nevada on Friday, December 17, when the dishonored check arrived in the mail. Notice of dishonor was then sent to HNBT prior to midnight on Monday, December 21, the next banking day following receipt of the *written* notice. Therefore, the first question this court must decide is whether oral notice from the payor bank, Nevada, can trigger the obligation of the collecting bank, Wells Fargo, to give notice to its customer, HNBT.

At first reading, section 3–508(3) would seem to resolve this question. That section provides, "Notice may be given in any reasonable manner. It may be oral or written * * *." By virtue of section 4–102(1), § 3–508(3) applies to bank collections unless it conflicts with a specific provision of Article 4. In such a case, the Article 4 provision governs the transaction.

Wells Fargo argues that section 4–301 supersedes § 3–508 with respect to notice from payor banks and that therefore only written notice from such banks triggers the presenting bank's obligation to pass the notice of dishonor down through the chain of collection.[1] This position appears to be meritorious and has

1. U.C.C. § 4–301, which discusses notice of dishonor by payor banks, provides only for written notice. Moreover, the use of the word "sent" in section 4–301(3) further suggests that only written notice from a payor bank constitutes dishonor. See U.C.C. § 1–201(38).

been adopted by several courts.[2] This court, however, need not rule on the specific question.

* * *

Lincoln has raised an issue which dispenses with the need to determine whether oral or written notification is required by the terms of the statute itself. In an introductory section to Article 4, the U.C.C. provides:

> "The effect of the provisions of this article may be varied by agreement except that no agreement can disclaim a bank's responsibility for its own lack of good faith or failure to exercise ordinary care or can limit the measure of damages for such lack or failure; but the parties may by agreement determine the standards by which such responsibility is to be measured if such standards are not manifestly unreasonable.
>
> "Federal reserve regulations and operating letters, clearing house rules, and the like, have the effect of agreements under subsection (1), whether or not specifically assented to by all parties interested in items handled." U.C.C. § 4–103(1), (2).

In its affidavits, Lincoln established that the transaction in question was governed by the terms of the Federal Reserve Operating Circular No. 6.[3] At the time of the transaction this operating circular provided that payor banks can—in

Since "an item is dishonored at the time * * * it is returned or notice sent in accordance with [§ 4–301]," Wells Fargo argues that only the written notice from Nevada triggered its obligation to give HNBT notice of dishonor.

2. Valley Bank & Trust Co. v. First Security Bank of Utah, N.A., 538 P.2d 298, 300 (Utah, 1975); Available Iron & Metal Co. v. First Nat'l Bank, 56 Ill.App.3d 516, 522–24, 13 Ill.Dec. 940, 945–946, 371 N.E.2d 1032, 1037–38 (1977). Contra, Security Trust Co. v. First Nat'l Bank, 79 Misc.2d 523, 358 N.Y.S.2d 943 (Sup.Ct.1974).

3. The affidavit of David M. Stratton, Vice President of Operations for Lincoln, makes clear that the terms of the circular governed this transaction. Although the transaction did not involve the Federal Reserve Bank, Mr. Stratton attests that: "It is now and was in November-December, 1971, the practice in commercial banking to follow Federal Reserve procedures for giving notice of dishonor, regardless of whether the item is sent through the Federal Reserve System or, as in this case, through a correspondent collecting bank." Affidavit of David M. Stratton, ¶ 10, November 8, 1979.

Thus, the terms of the Operating Circular supersede the statutory provisions of article 4 in two distinct ways. The regulations are applicable as agreements "whether or not specifically assented to by all parties" under section 4–103(2). See Security Bank and Trust Co. v. Federal National Bank and Trust Co., 554 P.2d 119 (Okl.App.1976) (Federal Reserve operating letter requiring notice by wire supersedes section 4–301, which requires written notice from payor banks). Alternatively, the conduct of the parties can be said to have evinced an "agreement" under section 4–103(1). As the official comments to this section make clear, the word "agreement" is intended to incorporate the statutory definition set forth in U.C.C. § 1–201(3), which includes those agreements implied from commercial practice. Cf. Delbrueck & Co. v. Manufacturers Hanover Trust Co., 609 F.2d 1047, 1051, (2d Cir.1979) ("The practices associated with banking transactions can be conclusive evidence of the legal effect of those transactions").

While "commercial practice" may not generally be considered an appropriate basis for summary judgment, in this case Lincoln and HNBT have met their burden of establishing that there remains no genuine issue of material fact. On the point here in question, Mr. Stratton's affidavit is uncontroverted. In spite of several opportunities, none of the parties have seen fit to file an opposing document. In fact, all three parties concur that there is no genuine issue of fact in the case. As the Second Circuit has noted: "A party opposing a motion for summary judgment simply cannot make a secret of his evidence until the trial, for in doing so he risks the possibility that there will be no trial. A summary judgment motion is intended to 'smoke out the facts so that the judge can decide if anything remains to be tried.'" Donnelly v. Guion, 467 F.2d 290, 293 (2d Cir.1972).

In the absence of any opposition to Mr. Stratton's affidavit, the only reasonable conclusion this court can draw is that all parties concede it was the regular commercial practice to have Federal Reserve procedures govern private correspondent collecting banks.

fact, must—give notice by "wire" when they dishonor items with values in excess of $1,000.[4] "Wire" is expressly defined to include "telephonic" notices.[5] Thus, since this operating circular governed the transaction here in dispute, it is clear that Nevada's telephonic notice was an adequate notice of dishonor, and Wells Fargo was not entitled to wait for written notice.

As is indicated above, Wells Fargo's failure to give timely notice essentially precludes it from prevailing under any of the three counts in its complaint. Nonetheless, it has argued that it is entitled to relief under § 4–103(5), which provides in pertinent part:

> "The measure of damages * * * is the amount of the item reduced by an amount which could not have been realized by the use of ordinary care * * *."

Wells Fargo argues that even if it had exercised "ordinary care" it would not have been able to protect Lincoln from a loss on the bad check. Lincoln had allowed Great Western to withdraw $23,000 of the $25,000 initially deposited by Mr. Porter within four banking days after the deposit. Wells Fargo argues that this is an unreasonably short time and that no amount of "care" on its part could have avoided the loss. In fact, even as of the first time that Wells Fargo received oral notice from Nevada—December 10, 1971—the funds had already been long since withdrawn from Lincoln's account. Thus, under § 4–103(5), Wells Fargo argues that it should not be saddled with the loss.

This argument misconceives the nature of the statute. By its terms, the statute is only applicable to "[t]he measure of damages for failure to exercise ordinary care in handling an item * * *" In other words, the statute is designed to act as a shield in the hands of a negligent defendant. No cases have been cited to this court nor have any been found where the statute was allowed to act as a sword in the hands of a plaintiff. Consequently, in this case, where no one has filed a complaint against Wells Fargo alleging a lack of ordinary care, the statute is inapplicable.

An example may help to illuminate this distinction. If a collecting bank has failed to use ordinary care in handling an item but nonetheless is entitled to charge back to its customer,[6] its customer can bring a suit under section 4–202(1) for damages arising out of the collecting bank's negligence. In such a case the collecting bank would then be entitled to diminish the extent of its liability pursuant to section 4–103(5). By contrast, the case before this court centers on the right of the collecting bank to charge back in the first instance. No countersuit for negligence has been filed, and consequently the question of damages for negligence is irrelevant.

4. Federal Reserve Operating Circular No. 6, ¶ 17(c) (September 1, 1967) provides:

"WIRE ADVICE of nonpayment of any item of $1,000 or over, unless it has not been paid because of a missing, irregular, or unsatisfactory endorsement or unless it bears on its face the legend, 'DO NOT WIRE NONPAYMENT,' of a Federal Reserve Bank or of a preceding bank endorser. Include in the advice of nonpayment, the amount of the item, the reason for nonpayment, the date of our cash letter, the name of the drawer or maker, and the names of the two endorsers immediately preceding the Federal Reserve Bank or their ABA transit numbers, if any."

5. "For the purposes of this operating circular, the term 'wire' includes telephone, telegraph, and cable." Id. ¶ 17 n. 4.

6. "Thus charge-back is permitted even where nonpayment results from the depositary bank's own negligence." U.C.C. § 4–212, comment 5.

CONCLUSION

For the foregoing reasons, Wells Fargo's motion for summary judgment against HNBT and HNBT's motion for summary judgment against Lincoln are denied. HNBT's motion for summary judgment against Wells Fargo and Lincoln's motion for summary judgment against HNBT are granted.

So ordered. [Some footnotes have been omitted and those retained have been renumbered.]

Notes

1. If the other party had been left with the credit instead of the debit, would the case have come out differently? If so, does this draw the rule in the *Hartford* case in question?

2. Students should compare UCC 4–202 and 4–212. In a quick reading the two seem to conflict. They do not conflict if one concludes that 4–202 determines the ultimate liability and 4–212 merely grants the bank the right to hold the money pending settlement of the dispute (by virtue of a chargeback or setoff).

SECTION 5. DOCUMENTARY DRAFTS

Section 4–104(1)(f) defines documentary draft to mean "any negotiable or non-negotiable draft with accompanying documents, securities or other papers to be delivered against honor of the draft". In certain parts of the country documentary drafts are widely used in connection with the sale of used cars, with the transfer of cattle, and with sale of various other commodities. The practice in the automobile trade is so well defined that the draft itself is often printed on an envelope which contains the certificate of title for the automobile for which the draft is used in payment. The idea in all such cases, of course, is that the one presenting the draft will insist upon payment before it gives up the certificate of title contained in the envelope, or the bill of sale for the cattle or the other documents.

Because these drafts are not subject to the rigid control and standardization of the banking industry in the way checks are, they present a variety of issues to the courts about their meaning and effect. Presumably the most common documentary draft is one in which the buyer is the payor and the bank is merely a collecting bank whose responsibility is defined in sections 4–501 through 4–504.

It seems plausible that the banks behind the drafting of Article 4 did not envision the possibility that they could frequently be the payors of documentary drafts. For that reason there is scant reference in Article 4 to the explicit responsibility of the bank-payor. The most critical section for such a bank-payor is UCC 4–302(b) on late return.

In fact the banks underestimated the imagination of car and cattle dealers, sellers and buyers of airplanes and of parties to commodity transactions. In one case, the parties produced documentary drafts in which the bank became the payor by the simple expedient of clipping the document to a preprinted check. In other cases homegrown documents have proved so uncertain that the courts themselves have disagreed about the identity of the payor and in at least one case have come to the startling conclusion that the parties were "joint payors" of a draft.

Because the life of these documentary drafts are so much shaped by and dependent upon the underlying transactions which they serve, the drafters did not set down specific and certain time limits of the kind found with checks.

Section 4–302(b) provides only that the bank must pay a documentary draft or return it "within the time allowed." Section 4–501 states that a collecting bank must "present or send" and, upon learning that a draft has not been paid or accepted in due course, "must seasonably notify."

The midnight deadline rule with respect to checks is rigid, firm and nearly invariable; the rule for documentary drafts is the opposite. The timeliness of a collecting bank's or payor bank's behavior will be directly influenced by several matters. First are the instructions given by the one seeking collection. Section 4–302(b) specifically refers to such instructions by its reference to the "time allowed." The references to "seasonable" and "in due course" in UCC 4–501 mean that one must listen to the instructions from the transferor. Unfortunately such instructions are themselves sometimes contradictory or ambiguous. For example, the stamp on the back of an instrument may read "for immediate remittance," but the invariable practice with respect to such an instrument in a particular area may be in direct conflict with such instructions. In any event a second factor to be considered is the practice in the trade concerning the holding and return of such items. Indeed, the specific practice between a particular bank and a person who repeatedly seeks collection through that bank may be the most relevant of all.

The student should read part 5 of Article 4 and UCC 4–302(b). Careful reading of UCC 4–302(b) will show that even a payor's obligation on a documentary draft is not the same as a payor's obligation on a check. Presumably the collecting bank's responsibilities are in general similar to those under UCC 4–202 except as explicitly defined in part 5 and except for the fact that negligence is much more difficult to define in the documentary draft context than in the check setting.

MEMPHIS AERO CORP. v. FIRST AMERICAN NATIONAL BANK

Supreme Court of Tennessee, 1983.
647 S.W.2d 219.

HARBISON, J. This case arises under the Uniform Commercial Code. It involves a claim against a commercial bank for late return of a documentary draft which it had received by mail. The Chancellor and the Court of Appeals held that the bank was liable for the amount of the draft. We reverse and dismiss.

There were some disputed factual issues at the trial. However, the following material facts either were undisputed or have been resolved by the courts below.

Appellant, First American National Bank in Nashville (American), received from Trust Company of Georgia on November 14, 1974 the following instrument which is the subject of this suit.

PAY AT SIGHT AT PAR
OTHER CHARGES TO BE PAID BY YOUR CUSTOMER (WHEN PAYABLE) ATLANTA, GA., November 12 19 74

PAY TO THE ORDER OF Piper Finance Corporation $ 30,664.00

Thirty thousand six hundred sixty-four dollars and no/100 DOLLARS

Enclosures: Bill of Sale, Application for Registration, and Release of Lien on N57338

VALUE RECEIVED AND CHARGE TO ACCOUNT OF Mid-South Aviation, Inc.

TO First American National Bank
326 Union Street
Nashville, Tennessee 37237
Attention: Tim Comin

Piper Finance Corporation
(DRAWER)
Regional Manager

1980 MAR 25 PM 3:54
FILED

The documents referred to as "Enclosures" accompanied the draft. Stamped on the back of the instrument was the following:

FOR COLLECTION AND
IMMEDIATE REMITTANCE
All Prior Endorsements Guaranteed
PAY TO THE ORDER OF
ANY BANK OR BANKER
C NOV 12 1974 D
EXECUTIVE PARK OFFICE
TRUST COMPANY OF GEORGIA
64-10 ATLANTA, GEORGIA 64-10

Mr. Tim Comin, an officer of American, received the draft and the other documents. He immediately notified an official of Mid-South Aviation with whom he had dealt on numerous occasions for more than a year. This official had previously advised Mr. Comin that he had authorized the draft. When the instrument arrived, however, Mid-South Aviation did not have sufficient funds to pay it. Although repeated promises were made to Mr. Comin that funds would be made available, this was never done.

The underlying commercial transaction involved the purchase of a Piper aircraft by Mid-South, a local retailer, from a regional Piper dealer, Memphis Aero Corporation. The latter had acquired it from the manufacturer, whose subsidiary, Piper Finance Corporation, retained a security interest. When the local dealer, Mid-South, sold the plane it advised Memphis Aero to draw a draft on First American.[1] Memphis Aero actually had this done by Piper Finance. It and Piper supplied the necessary accompanying title documents to be delivered by American to Mid-South upon payment of the draft. Piper sent the draft and other papers through its own bank, Trust Company of Georgia. The record does not show whether or not that bank gave provisional credit therefor to Piper.

Mid-South, a relatively new but high-volume Piper retail dealer in Nashville, was a customer of First American. It maintained a checking account at that bank through which it passed large sums in connection with the purchase and sale of aircraft. The account was not under the control of any officer or official of American, was never frozen for any purpose, nor did American have authority to pay documentary drafts therefrom without approval from the depositor. American had made commercial loans to Mid-South from time to

1. Validity of this sale, when Mid-South was not the registered owner of the plane, is not involved here. Memphis Aero later repossessed the plane but released it on advice of counsel.

time, some collateralized and some not. It never at any time attempted to set off the customer's checking account against those loans. Only officials of Mid-South had authority to draw checks against the account. American had made no previous agreements with Mid-South or with Piper and Memphis Aero to finance the purchase of the aircraft in question by Mid-South or to carry overdrafts of the latter. It had on some prior occasions made loans to enable Mid-South to purchase planes, but the latter dealt with numerous other banks and also obtained financing from Memphis Aero.

Mr. Comin, the bank officer who handled the documentary draft upon its receipt, had little experience with such instruments. However he immediately notified Mid-South of its arrival and was advised that the latter would acquire sufficient funds to cover the draft but that such funds were not available on the day of presentment. Although he was in communication with both Piper and Memphis Aero by telephone no later than November 26 and advised them of the situation, Mr. Comin did not notify their agent Trust Company of Georgia of the dishonor of the draft, nor did he return it and the title documents until about December 20.

There were several questions presented in the courts below, but as the case comes here the only issue is whether appellant, a "payor bank" under the Code,[2] is strictly liable for the amount of the draft under T.C.A. § 47–4–302(b)[3] or whether its liability is limited to damages proximately caused by its negligence under the general provisions of T.C.A. § 47–4–103(5). If the latter measure is applied, no recovery is warranted because the bank customer, which owed the debt out of which the transaction arose, never had sufficient assets to pay the draft, and the item was essentially worthless at all relevant times. The Court of Appeals correctly held that

> "there is no evidence that, if First American had given timely notice of dishonor and made timely return of the draft and documents, Memphis Aero could have collected the amount due from Mid-South. That is, there is no evidence that Memphis Aero lost any amount as a proximate result of the action or inaction of First American."

On the other hand, the strict liability imposed under T.C.A. § 47–4–302(b) is applicable only if the documentary draft was a "properly payable" item as contemplated in the Code, including the requirement stated in T.C.A. § 47–4–104(i) of "availability of funds for payment at the time of decision to pay or dishonor."

Both the trial court and the Court of Appeals held that appellant, as a payor bank, was strictly liable under T.C.A. § 47–4–302(b), but the Court of Appeals did not address the issue of whether the draft was "properly payable." The Chancellor resolved this issue by holding that the payor bank was also a "joint drawee" of the documentary draft with its customer. The bank was, in fact, solvent and, therefore, had sufficient funds *of its own* to pay the draft. This was deemed to render it strictly liable under T.C.A. § 47–4–302(b) as a *payor bank* — although, as we understand it, liability under that section is not liability *on the document itself* but is liability for the mishandling (delay in giving notice or return) of the item. Making no distinction between liability of a drawee *on the instrument* and liability for mishandling by a *"payor bank,"* the Chancellor,

2. T.C.A. § 47–4–105(b).

3. With some exceptions not material here, a "payor bank" is liable for the amount of certain items not involved in this case and "(b) any other properly payable item unless within the time allowed for acceptance or payment of that item the bank either accepts or pays the item or returns it and accompanying documents."

following the insistence of appellee, virtually eliminated from the Code the requirement that before a payor bank can be held strictly liable for mishandling, a documentary draft must be "properly payable."

Appellee insists that the Code provision that "properly payable includes the availability of funds for payment at the time of decision to pay or dishonor" (T.C.A. § 47–4–104(i)) means sufficient funds of the *payor bank* as well as sufficient funds of the *debtor* in the commercial transaction. Very little authority exists for this proposition. Some of the cases most relied upon by appellee and by the courts below arose and were decided under the equivalent of T.C.A. § 47–4–302(a)—strict liability for not handling demand items by the banking "midnight deadline." Liability is imposed under that provision of the Code, however, for mishandling items *"other than a documentary draft"* and *"whether properly payable or not."* There is a distinct difference between liability under subsection (a) and that under (b) of this Code section.

In other cases cited by appellee where liability has been imposed upon a payor bank under subsection (b), there was no question that the debtor had on deposit with or made available to the payor bank sufficient funds to pay the draft. In still others, the issue was never discussed. One federal case, cited by appellee as a "leading case," merely stated that a payor bank is liable under subsection (b) if it does not pay or return an "item" within a reasonable time and made no reference to the "properly payable" requirement of that statute. This decision was followed by another from the same circuit, holding that the payor bank was obligated to pay late-returned drafts even though there were insufficient funds made available by the debtor and even though the payment would have created an overdraft.

In the present case the debtor at no time had or made available to the payor bank, appellant here, sufficient funds for payment of the draft, which was timely presented. In our opinion the draft was not a "properly payable" item under T.C.A. § 47–4–302(b) so as to render the payor bank strictly liable for its late return. Liability, therefore, is governed by T.C.A. § 47–4–103(5), and the action fails for insufficient proof for damages.

The Court of Appeals at several points drew an analogy between the liability of the drawee of a check and that of a payor bank respecting a documentary draft. There is a significant difference. Checks are usually referred to as "cash" or "demand" items, and the drawee must handle these under its midnight deadline, "whether properly payable or not." T.C.A. § 47–4–302(a). Sight drafts, unaccompanied by title documents, may also fall within that provision. Farmers Cooperative Livestock Market v. Second National Bank, 427 S.W.2d 247 (Ky. 1968). Both the Chancellor and the Court of Appeals correctly held in the present case, however, despite the contention of appellee to the contrary, that the instrument involved here was a "documentary draft" as defined in the UCC. It was described by some witnesses as an "envelope draft." As shown on its face, it was accompanied by a bill of sale to an airplane, a release of lien on the same, and an application for registration of title in the name of the vendee (the debtor in the transaction). The accompanying "advice" or "collection letter" from the transmitting bank called it a "Draft on Mid-South Aviation, Inc., N573 38" [the serial number of the plane], and instructed the appellant to *"Deliver documents only on payment."* Clearly it was contemplated that the title papers were to be "delivered against honor of the draft," T.C.A. § 47–4–104(1)(f), and the draft was a "documentary draft," not a check or a simple sight draft which had to be processed under T.C.A. § 47–4–302(a) "whether properly payable or not."

Further, there is no contention in this case that appellant had agreed that it would pay the draft out of its own funds, that it would lend funds to the purchaser of the airplane or "floor plan" the craft, or that it had obligated itself to the sellers (the drawer and payee) so as to render it liable *on the instrument* for not immediately accepting or paying the draft. It was instructed to present the draft to the purchaser of the plane and to deliver the title papers to the latter only upon payment. It did timely present the draft. It did not timely return the documents to the transferor bank or notify the latter that the purchaser had insufficient funds to meet its obligation. Therein it was negligent. Had this negligence caused loss to the creditor, liability would follow, but there is no evidence that this occurred. Eight business days elapsed between receipt of the draft by appellant and telephone communication between it and the creditor that the draft had been dishonored upon presentment. There is conflicting evidence as to whether this was or was not a reasonable time, but we accept the findings of the courts below that the appellant was negligent in this respect and in not notifying the transmitting bank, agent of the creditors. In that regard, however, we note that the creditors (Memphis Aero and its financing company Piper Finance) by-passed their own agent, Trust Company of Georgia, the transmitting bank, and dealt directly with appellant, the payor bank. While appellant held the draft for a total of thirty-six days, the fact that it was holding the dishonored draft was known to the creditors upon the eighth business day (the twelfth calendar day), at the latest. They thereafter tried to deal directly with the debtor, Mid-South Aviation, to repossess the aircraft and to arrange new financing for the debtor. Only after these efforts failed did they demand that appellant return the draft. It did so immediately.

It will be recalled that under T.C.A. § 47–4–302(b) a payor bank becomes liable for a properly payable item "unless within the time allowed for acceptance or payment" of that item the bank either accepts, pays or returns it.

No specific time is provided under this section of the UCC for the acceptance or payment of a documentary draft. Under special provisions of the Code dealing with the collection of documentary drafts, a collecting bank must "reasonably" notify "its customer" of dishonor. T.C.A. § 47–4–501. Unless otherwise instructed, a bank presenting a documentary draft must deliver the documents "to the drawee" on acceptance of the draft if payable more than three days after presentment or, otherwise, only on payment. T.C.A. § 47–4–503(a). Upon dishonor the presenting bank

> " * * * must use diligence and good faith to ascertain the reason for dishonor, must notify its transferor of the dishonor and of the results of its effort to ascertain the reasons therefor and must request instructions." T.C.A. § 47–4–503(b).

A non-payor bank, that is one which is merely a collecting or presenting bank, is liable for damages proximately caused by its negligence in failing to carry out these duties. T.C.A. §§ 47–4–103(5), –105(d), –105(e). A "payor bank" becomes liable for the amount of the instrument if it fails to carry out its duties and if it is a "properly payable item." T.C.A. § 47–4–302(b).

It is clear that the "midnight deadline" applicable to the handling of checks and other demand items is not applicable to the handling of documentary drafts. Banking institutions are permitted a reasonable or "seasonable" time within which to present, remit or return.

* * *

As noted by the Supreme Court of Virginia, and as abundantly illustrated by the testimony in the present record,

> "The custom followed by banks in handling documentary drafts is not uniform. And the time permitted for their payment or return varies. What is seasonable time, and what is due diligence and good faith, must necessarily depend upon the facts and circumstances of each case. The cashier of Citizens and Marine testified that while the policy of his bank was ten days without specific instructions, under certain circumstances, depending on the customer, an unpaid draft would be retained for a month before being returned." Suttle Motor Corp. v. Citizens Bank of Poquoson, 221 S.E.2d 784, 786 (Va. 1976).

A number of expert witnesses testified in the present case, representing banking institutions from different parts of this state. Others having knowledge of the subject testified to practices of banking institutions in New York, Atlanta and other parts of the United States. The time for holding a documentary draft, according to these witnesses, varies from two days to as much as ten days or longer. Witnesses from American testified that they customarily hold such drafts for about ten days.

We have already stated that we concur in the findings of the courts below that the holding period in the present case was unreasonable under all of the circumstances, although, in view of the direct communication between the creditors and the payor bank, it was not nearly so long or nearly so unreasonable as indicated by the courts below.

If, during the period while American was holding the draft, it had become "properly payable" and the bank had failed to pay or return, an entirely different case would be presented. That was the situation in Suttle Motor Corp., supra. There, while the bank was holding the drafts, funds came into its hands which should have been applied directly to the payment of those specific drafts. The title documents attached to the drafts should have been detached, delivered to customers who had made loans from the bank to purchase their automobiles, and the drafts paid out of the proceeds. Instead the bank applied those proceeds to other debts owed to it by the drawer of the drafts. It served its own interests, proximately and directly damaging the payee of the drafts who had caused them to be sent to the bank for collection. In one instance a bank customer named Harrell borrowed funds from the bank to finance the purchase of a car, and those loan proceeds were credited directly to the drawer of a draft which the bank was holding. The title papers attached to the draft were not delivered to the borrower, and the Supreme Court of Virginia said:

> "Clearly the proceeds from the loan to Harrell should have been applied in payment of the Suttle draft, thereby enabling Harrell to obtain good title to her automobile." 221 S.E.2d at 787.

The court further said:

> "We do not have here a mere delay in the return of a draft. There was delay and inaction at a critical time when Poquoson was making a tremendous effort in its own behalf to reduce the losses which it obviously faced on the Batts and Hockaday account." 221 S.E.2d at 788.

These facts differ drastically from those presented in the present case. While the debtor, Mid-South Aviation, was indebted to American, the latter did not at any time divert funds or assets of Mid-South to the payment of its own claims when these should have been used to pay the draft which the bank was holding. This, indeed, is a case involving nothing more than "a mere delay in the return of a draft," and there is no evidence of any dereliction of duty or neglect other than failure of the bank official to give notice to the transferor bank or to give more prompt notice than he did to the creditors who undertook to deal directly with him.

No question was made in the Suttle Motor Corp. case, supra, but that liability was fixed under § 4–302(b) of the Uniform Commercial Code. The drafts in that case clearly were or became "properly payable" while the bank was holding them, because sufficient funds of the debtor did come into the possession of the bank to pay the drafts—a situation entirely different from that involved here.

We concur in the conclusions of the courts below that American was a "payor bank" and that it was negligent, but since we do not find that the item was "properly payable," in our opinion liability should not have been imposed under T.C.A. § 47–4–302(b).

The judgments of the courts below are reversed and the suit is dismissed at the cost of appellee. The cause will be remanded to the trial court for collection of all costs accrued there.

FONES, C.J., COOPER, BROCK and DROWOTA, JJ., concur. [Some footnotes omitted.]

Notes

1. The lower court concluded that First American National Bank was the payor. That issue was not in contention before the Supreme Court of Tennessee. Was the lower court correct?

2. If First American were not a payor, but only a collecting bank, how would that have changed its potential liability?

Problem 26–3

Assume that seller of cottonseed oil submitted drafts to Southern Bank as collecting agent to collect from the buyer. No specific instructions were given, and Bank made periodic attempts to collect over a three week period. Finally, at the end of 40 days, and despairing of any success at collection, it returned the $50,000 draft to the Southern Cotton Oil Company. Given those facts and nothing more, does Southern Cotton Oil have a cause of action against Southern Bank?

When reviewing the foregoing transaction with your client, assume now that your client, the bank, says that they routinely hold items for periods up to six weeks. In fact he indicates that in identical transactions between Southern Cotton Oil and the buyer in this case, they have in the past held drafts for as long as 60 days before procuring payment. In no case did the seller complain about the delay, and the seller always gladly accepted the money. If that can be proven at the trial, would the bank be free of liability?

Problem 26–4

Suttle received a documentary draft from Batts drawn on Citizens Bank of Poquoson for $6,800, representing the purchase by Batts of a 1972 Cadillac automobile. This draft, with title attached, was deposited by Suttle to its account at Citizens and Marine and was received for collection on October 30, 1972, by Poquoson from State Planters Bank. The draft was written on an envelope and inside the envelope was a certificate of title for a 1972 Cadillac that had been sold by Suttle to Batts. Shortly thereafter Puquoson financed the sale of the Cadillac by Batts (a used car dealer) to purchaser Jones. The proceeds of that financing were credited to Batts' account, the title was never transferred to Jones and remained in an envelope at the bank together with the draft. A number of other transactions of a similar kind went on in October and November.

Early in December the bank depleted Batts' account to zero by setting off a debt of more than $200,000 owed by Batts to the bank. Upon setting off that account it returned the drafts together with a number of others to Suttle Motors. Upon discovery of these facts, Suttle has come to you and asks whether it has a good claim against the bank. You may assume that Suttle still has the certificate of title, that Batts is insolvent, and that the car is in the possession of Jones.

SECTION 6. MISCELLANEOUS TIMING ISSUES

When a collecting or depositary bank deals with a check or a documentary draft within the confines of Article 4, the rules are complex but relatively straightforward. However there are instruments that operate like checks which are not governed by Article 4 and there are checks transmitted outside the system or in ways which give notice that the parties obviously do not intend for them to be treated as ordinary checks. These items pose special questions.

Here we consider some problems dealing with three of those questions. First, consider a draft drawn on a non-bank but transmitted within the system. If the non-bank fails to act, what is the consequence? Second, consider double presentment. It is not uncommon for a depositary bank to present a dishonored instrument a second time. When that happens the question arises whether a payor must comply with a midnight deadline or whether having once done so and having put the depositary bank on notice, it is now relieved from the duty of acting. Finally, suppose that a check is presented "for collection" or with some other notation that indicates it is not to be treated as an ordinary check, i.e., not to be considered a "cash item."

Problem 26–5

Local Ford is a high volume automobile dealer. Ford deals with Local Bank and also with Associated Credit Company. Associated does its floor planning and finances many but not all of the consumer purchases at Local Ford. Over a period of time the following practice has built up: Local Ford sells a car to a customer and, based upon a final or tentative assurance that Associated will buy the loan, Local Ford prepares a draft drawn on Associated as the payor and payable to itself. According to the practice Local Ford then deposits this draft in its own bank (Local Bank) who in turn presents the draft to Associated Credit and ultimately procures payment.

In the waning days of Local Ford's existence the following transactions occurred. Local Ford sold ten cars for a total value of $95,000. In each case it prepared a draft payable to itself and drawn on Associated. It then deposited these drafts in its account at Local Bank and Local Bank gave possession of them to Associated Credit. Ten days passed without any action by Associated Credit. On the eighth day, $90,000 of Local Ford's checks cleared against the $95,000 credit in the account. On the ninth day, Local Ford closed its doors. Except for the provisional credit granted in Local Ford's account by the bank as a result of the deposit of these $95,000 of drafts, there is only $2,000 in the account. Local Bank asks whether it can recover the $95,000 from Associated who has now returned the drafts to the bank and has stated that it does not intend to pay any of them.

If Associated were a "payor bank," would it clearly have liability under UCC 4–213 and 4–302? But Associated correctly points out that it holds no bank charter, is not a member of and has no relation with the Federal Reserve or with any state banking agency. It does not maintain deposit accounts or engage in many of the other transactions that are common for banks. It claims it is "merely a commercial finance company" and as such has no responsibilities of the kinds specified in Article 4. It maintains, furthermore, that its acts constitute a dishonor under Article 3 and therefore that it has no liability on the instrument or because of its acts with respect to the instrument to Local Bank or to anyone else. As Local Bank's counsel how do you analyze this argument?

Problem 26–6

Collecting Bank submitted a $50,000 check to the payor for payment early in January, 1988. Payor returned the check within its midnight deadline with an indication that there were insufficient funds. On January 15 Collecting Bank again presented it for payment. By a mistake this time, payor held the check for two full days and beyond its midnight deadline. It is conceded by all that the payor held the check the second time beyond the midnight deadline and conceded furthermore that there was never enough money in the depositer's account to pay the check. Collecting bank's case is simple and straightforward, namely, that the payor violated its obligation under UCC 4–301 and therefore is liable on the instrument under UCC 4–302.

Payor responds first, that the collecting bank should not be permitted repeatedly to test the payor's procedures in order to attempt to catch them. Secondly, it argues that the collecting bank was already put on notice by the first dishonor and thus has suffered no injury by the second delay. Finally it maintains that it is freed from any obligation to respond by section 3–511(4). How do you respond to those arguments?

DAVID GRAUBART, INC. v. BANK LEUMI TRUST CO. OF NEW YORK

Court of Appeals of New York, 1979.
48 N.Y.2d 554, 423 N.Y.S.2d 899, 399 N.E.2d 930.

FUCHSBERG, J. On this appeal, here on a question certified by the Appellate Division pursuant to C.P.L.R. § 5602(b)(1), we are called upon to determine the role played by article 4 of the Uniform Commercial Code in fixing rights and obligations arising out of a second presentment of a check previously returned for insufficient funds. The heart issue is whether a payor bank is relieved of liability for retaining such an instrument beyond its "midnight deadline" (see N.Y.U.C.C. § 4–302) when it does so by an agreement concordant with a practice among banks for a payor to hold a previously dishonored item long enough to provide an opportunity for sufficient funds to be deposited by the drawer to meet the check.

The operative facts are uncomplicated. Plaintiff David Graubart, Inc. (payee) was issued a check for $13,000 drawn by the Prins Diamond Company on the latter's account with the defendant Bank Leumi Trust Company (payor bank). Graubart then deposited the check in its own account with the National Bank of North America (depositary bank), which, pursuing normal collection channels, routed it to the payor bank via the New York Clearing House. When the payor bank found that the Prins account had been overdrawn, it marked the item "insufficient funds" and promptly returned it to the depositary bank, again through clearing house channels. When the payee was notified of the dishonor, it redeposited the check with its bank, which this time apparently chose to forward it directly to Leumi on a collection basis, thus bypassing the clearing house (see N.Y.U.C.C. § 4–204, subd. 2, par. [a]). The item was accompanied by an "advice to customer" slip—a copy of which was also delivered to Graubart—

indicating, as with collection items generally, that credit would only be given on payment. In addition, in a space bearing the printed legend "Special Instruction: (Return immediately if not paid unless otherwise instructed)," the slip contained a typed direction that the payor bank was to "remit [its] cashiers' [sic] check when paid") cf. N.Y.U.C.C. § 4–211, subd. 1, par. [b]). But when, after no more than seven banking days, the drawer's account remained bare of funds to permit the check to clear, Leumi again returned the check to the depositary bank. Sometime during the course of these transactions the drawer made an assignment for the benefit of creditors.

The gravamen of the fourth cause of action in the suit the payee thereafter commenced against Leumi, as well as of its subsequent motion for summary judgment, was that the latter's failure to return the resubmitted check to the depositary bank before its "midnight deadline"—defined as midnight of the next banking day following that on which the item was received (N.Y.U.C.C. § 4–104, subd 1, par. [h])—without more, rendered it liable to the payee for the face amount of the check under UCC § 4–302 (subd [a]). This section, with seeming finality, provides, in pertinent part, that "if an item is presented on and received by a payor bank the bank is accountable for the amount of * * * a demand item * * * if the bank * * * retains the item beyond midnight of the bank day of receipt without settling for it or * * * does not pay or return the item or send notice of dishonor until after its midnight deadline."

In opposition, and in support of its own cross motion, the payor bank submitted an affidavit by its assistant vice president, who, after setting out his knowledge of banking practice, asserted that the "advice to customer" slip constituted a memorandum of an agreement requiring it to process the instrument in question in accordance with a common banking practice whereunder previously dishonored checks were to be held for such time as is reasonable under all the circumstances, even beyond the midnight deadline if necessary, to enable funds from which to pay them to come into the account. To this, the payee's only reply was in the form of counsel's affirmation. Aside from a bald assertion, for which no foundation was supplied, challenging the existence of the custom, the affirmation merely interjected, for the first time, unsupported allegations of bad faith and collusion on Leumi's part. Though it stated that the drawer was indebted to Leumi at the time of the assignment for the benefit of creditors, it made no showing of any unfair conduct on the part of the payor bank whatsoever.

Special Term denied both motions, holding that triable issues existed, and the Appellate Division, over a vigorous dissent by Mr. Justice Joseph P. Sullivan, has since affirmed. In thereafter granting leave to appeal to this court, it posed the very broad question: "Was the order of the Supreme Court, as affirmed by this Court, properly made?" For the reasons that follow, we conclude a negative response is mandated.

The payor bank's assault on the conclusion of the courts below is grounded on the contention that there were no factual issues precluding summary judgment and that, on the undisputed facts, its actions were proper as a matter of law for two reasons: (1) on the authority of Leaderbrand v. Central State Bank (202 Kan. 450) [450 P.2d 1,] it need not have given the payee notice of dishonor upon representment of the previously dishonored item, and (2) its conduct in varying the Code's midnight deadline pursuant to a valid agreement which accords with custom and usage in the banking community relieves it of the effect of the provisions of article 4 (citing, inter alia, N.Y.U.C.C. § 4–103).

The preliminary dispute as to the existence of unresolved questions of fact need not detain us. The date of the contested transactions and the non-adherence to the midnight deadline, if applicable, were conceded for the purposes of the motion. The payor bank's officer established the custom as to collection of previously dishonored checks, and the payee's own submission of the "advice to customer" slip confirmed that the agreement had been made in contemplation of the custom. * * *

* * *

Though its Leaderbrand point is, therefore, without merit, Leumi's argument that its retention of the check beyond its midnight deadline was consonant with its agreement with the depositary bank is another matter. In this connection, initially we note that § 4–301 of the Code, which establishes the procedural rules enforced by § 4–302, nowhere suggests that the deadline does not apply to previously dishonored items. But, it is well-recognized that the Code's requirements can be modified by agreement to conform them with commercial usage, in or out of banking circles, so that parties may advantage themselves of the "wisdom born of accumulated experience" (Bankers Trust Co. v. J.V. Dowler & Co., 47 N.Y.2d 128, 134). Thus, § 4–103 provides in part:

> "(1) The effect of the provisions of this Article may be varied by agreement except that no agreement can disclaim a bank's responsibility for its own lack of good faith or failure to exercise ordinary care * * *.
>
> * * *
>
> "(4) The specification or approval of certain procedures by this Article does not constitute disapproval of other procedures which may be reasonable under the circumstances."

Though the concept of an "agreement" under the Code is, as with contract law generally, broad enough to permit the written terms of a memorandum to be supplemented and clarified by reference to customs and usages in the commercial milieu in which it is to be performed (e.g., N.Y.U.C.C. §§ 1–201, subd. 3, 1–205; 3 Corbin, Contracts [1960 ed.], § 556; Walls v. Bailey, 49 N.Y. 464), the bare fact that the payor bank acted in accordance with its agreement with the depositary bank does not, in and by itself, relieve the former of liability (Official Comment, McKinney's Cons.Laws of N.Y., Book 62½, part 2, UCC § 4–203, p. 555). Section 4–103 demands that every party sought to be bound—here the payee—have assented to the agreement's terms (Official Comment 2, op. cit., UCC § 4–103, pp. 519–520). However, we hold that here there was such consent.

Under § 4–201 of the Code, a payee's presentment of an item to a depositary bank for collection creates a principal-agent relationship between the two, a status that persists until final settlement (see Official Comment 4, op. cit., UCC § 4–201, pp. 544–545). Graubart's voluntary establishment of its bank's authority constitutes an assent to the latter's dealing with the check in the manner customary in the banking industry (see Restatement [2d], Agency, § 36). To the extent that a payee deems itself aggrieved by a depositary bank's ignoring of limitations on its authority, of which none are claimed here, the law provides recourse against it, but not against a third party who relies on the agent's apparent authority (see Walsh v. Hartford Fire Ins. Co., 73 N.Y. 5; Wen Kroy Realty Co. v. Public Nat. Bank & Trust Co., 260 N.Y. 84).

All this is not to say that any act by a depositary bank as an agent will relieve the payor bank of liability or that a payee may be deemed to have consented to any manner of agreement, no matter how unfair. Limitations remain; in addition to the duties of good faith and ordinary care, the requirement that the agreement be a reasonable one stands undiminished (see N.Y.U.C.C. § 4–103, subd. 4).

As to good faith and ordinary care, neither of these is a serious obstacle in the circumstances of this case. The payee's complaint alleges no bad faith or favoritism on the part of the payor bank, and the mere fact that the drawer was indebted to Leumi when it assigned for the benefit of creditors does not permit us to presume collusion in the absence of specific evidence. Moreover, beyond the superficial sense in which ordinary care is relevant to virtually every step in the collection process (see N.Y.U.C.C. § 4–202, subd. 1), this standard was not intended to prohibit banking procedures that themselves are reasonable and carried out with care (see Leary, Check Handling Under Article Four of the Uniform Commercial Code, 49 Marq.L.Rev. 331, 342; see, also, Sunshine v. Bankers Trust Co., 34 N.Y.2d 404, 410; N.Y.U.C.C. § 4–213, subd. 1, pars. [b], [d] [permitting time of "final payment" of an item to be set by agreement]). Indeed, § 4–103 (subd. 3) goes a long way toward equating "general banking usage," relied upon by Leumi here, with ordinary care.

Further, in this case the reasonableness of the suspension of the midnight deadline is demonstrated by an examination of the underlying purpose of the rule. Far from merely encouraging banks to process deposited instruments promptly, the deadline plays the central role in "firming up" the provisional credit received by each transferor in the payee-depositary bank-intermediary bank chain. Under § 4–213 of the Code, provisional credits become final as soon as the payor bank settles for the item and the time for revocation under the midnight deadline passes. This point is particularly critical for banks that funnel hundreds or thousands of checks per day into the collection stream because it enables them to assume that payment has been effectuated after a certain period of time unless there is a prompt return. (See, generally, Blake v. Woodford Bank & Trust Co., 555 S.W.2d 589, 600–601; Official Comments 7–11, op. cit., UCC § 4–213, pp. 591–593).

These concerns, however, are irrelevant to any evaluation of the custom followed under the agreement between the banks here. It creates no provisional credits that must be firmed up, and the payee can only collect when the payor bank remits its cashier's check, thus signifying that the drawer's account received sufficient funds to cover the check. By its nature, the procedure singles out the item as an exceptional one; no transferor will assume it has been paid until specific notice is received.

Moreover, the concept of a midnight deadline is not compatible with any approach under which the payor bank seeks to wait for the deposit of funds in the drawer's account. The reasonableness of such a banking custom must, therefore, be measured on its own terms. We conclude that this criterion is met when a depositary bank takes a possibly worthless instrument and directs the payor bank to adopt a technique that may provide the only chance for collection.

There is nothing unfair about this procedure. It is calculated to produce satisfied obligations in many instances where legal recourse, with all its attendant expense, inconvenience and uncertainty, would otherwise be necessary. Furthermore, the payee here cannot claim it was injured by its reliance on the payor bank's silence after receipt of the item; the prior dishonor provided adequate warning of the questionable safety of the instrument. In any event, the payee's right to sue the drawer on the underlying obligation was revived upon the first dishonor, and representment in no way cut short that prerogative

(N.Y.U.C.C. §§ 3–802, subd. 1, par. [b], 4–301, subd. 3; Blake v. Woodford Bank & Trust Co., supra, pp. 598–599).

We therefore hold that the payor bank's adherence to the depositary bank's instructions for processing the drawer's check does not render it liable to the payee under § 4–302. Accordingly, the certified question must be answered in the negative, the order of the Appellate Division reversed, and summary judgment granted in the defendant's favor on the fourth cause of action.

Order reversed, with costs, and summary judgment granted in favor of defendant dismissing the fourth cause of action. Question certified answered in the negative. All concur. [Footnotes omitted.]

Notes

1. Assume that you were a depositor in the position of the depositor in Graubart. Could you sue your own bank on the ground that it improperly granted additional time to a payor without your authority to do so? Could you sue the payor on that ground?

2. Through the mail, a bank receives a $500,000 check drawn on it. It does not come through the Federal Reserve or other regular collection channels and it is marked merely "for collection." Your client, the bank officer, asks whether she can safely hold the check for more than a day and one-half. What do you advise? If the instructions in that case make you nervous, what instructions would be adequate before you would tell her for sure she could hold it more than a day and one-half?

FEDERAL RESERVE SYSTEM

PART 210—COLLECTION OF CHECKS AND OTHER ITEMS AND TRANSFERS OF FUNDS

(12 C.F.R. §§ 210.1–210.15 (1986)

Subpart A—Collection of Checks and Other Items

Sec.

210.1 Authority purpose, and scope.
210.2 Definitions.
210.3 General provisions.
210.4 Sending items to Reserve banks.
210.5 Sender's agreement; recovery by Reserve Bank.
210.6 Status, warranties, and liability of Reserve Bank.
210.7 Presenting items for payment.
210.8 Presenting noncash items for acceptance.
210.9 Payment.
210.10 Time schedule and availability of credits for cash items.
210.11 Availability of proceeds of noncash items; time schedule
210.12 Return of cash items.
210.13 Chargeback of unpaid items.
210.14 Extension of time limits.
210.15 Direct presentment of certain warrants.

Subpart B—Wire Transfers of Funds

210.25 Authority, purpose, and scope.
210.26 Definitions.
210.27 General provisions.

AUTHORITY: Federal Reserve Act, sec. 13, (12 U.S.C. 342); sec. 11(i), 12 U.S.C. 248(i); sec. 16, (12 U.S.C. 248(*o*) and 360); and sec. 19, (12 U.S.C. 464), et seq.

SOURCE: 45 FR 68634, Oct. 16, 1980, unless otherwise noted.

Subpart A—Collection of Checks and Other Items

§ 210.1 Authority, purpose, and scope.

The Board of Governors of the Federal Reserve System ("Board") has issued this subpart pursuant to the Federal Reserve Act, section 13 (12 U.S.C. 342), section 16 (12 U.S.C. 248(*o*), 360), section 11(i) (12 U.S.C. 248(i)), and other laws. This subpart governs the collection of checks and other cash and noncash items by Federal Reserve Banks ("Reserve Banks"). Its purpose is to provide rules for collecting items and settling balances.

§ 210.2 Definitions.

As used in this subpart, unless the context otherwise requires:

(a) "Actually and finally collected funds" means cash or any other form of payment that is, or has become, final and irrevocable.

(b) "Bank" includes a depository institution as defined in section 19 of the Federal Reserve Act (12 U.S.C. 461(b)).

(c) "Bank draft" means a check drawn by one bank on another bank.

(d) "Banking day" means a day during which a bank is open to the public for carrying on substantially all its banking functions.

(e) "Cash item" means:

(1) A check other than one classified as a noncash item under this section; or

(2) Any other item payable on demand and collectible at par that the Reserve Bank of the District in which the item is payable is willing to accept as a cash item.

(f) "Check" means a draft, as defined in the Uniform Commercial Code, that is drawn on a bank and payable on demand.

(g) "Item" means an instrument for the payment of money, whether negotiable or not, that is:

(1) Payable in a Federal Reserve District [1] ("District");

(2) Sent by a sender to a Reserve Bank for handling under this subpart; and

1. For purposes of this subpart, the Virgin Islands and Puerto Rico are deemed to be in the Second District, and Guam and American Samoa in the Twelfth District.

(3) Collectible in funds acceptable to the Reserve Bank of the District in which the instrument is payable.

Unless otherwise indicated, "item" includes both cash and noncash items. "Item" does not include a check that cannot be collected at par,[2] or an "item" as defined in § 210.26 that is handled under Subpart B.

(h) "Nonbank payor" means a payor of an item, other than a bank.

(i) "Noncash item" means an item that a receiving Reserve Bank classifies in its operating circulars as requiring special handling. The term also means an item normally received as a cash item if a Reserve Bank decides that special conditions require that it handle the item as a noncash item.

(j) "Paying bank" means:

(1) The bank by which an item is payable, unless the item is payable or collectible through another bank and is sent to the other bank for payment or collection; or

(2) The bank through which an item is payable or collectible and to which it is sent for payment or collection.

(k) "Sender" means any of the following that sends an item to a Reserve Bank: a depository institution, a clearing institution, another Reserve Bank, an international organization, a foreign correspondent, or a branch or agency of a foreign bank maintaining reserves under section 7 of the International Banking Act of 1978 (12 U.S.C. 347d, 3105).

(1) "Depository institution" means a depository institution as defined in section 19(b) of the Federal Reserve Act. (12 U.S.C. 461(b))

(2) "Clearing institution" means:

(i) An institution that is not a depository institution, but maintains with a Reserve Bank the balance referred to in the first paragraph of section 13 of the Federal Reserve Act (12 U.S.C. 342); or

(ii) A corporation that maintains an account with a Reserve Bank in conformity with § 211.4 of this chapter (Regulation K).

(3) "International Organization" means an international organization for which a Reserve Bank is empowered to act as depository or fiscal agent and maintains an account.

(4) "Foreign correspondent" means any of the following for which a Reserve Bank maintains an account: a foreign bank or banker, a foreign state as defined in section 25(b) of the Federal Reserve Act (12 U.S.C. 632), or a foreign correspondent or agency referred to in section 14(e) of that Act (12 U.S.C. 358).

(*l*) "State" means a State of the United States, the District of Columbia, Puerto Rico, or a territory, possession, or dependency of the United States.

[45 FR 68634, Oct. 16, 1980, as amended at 46 FR 42059, Aug. 19, 1981]

§ 210.3 General provisions.

(a) *General.* Each Reserve Bank shall receive and handle items in accordance with this subpart, and shall issue operating circulars governing the details of its handling of items and other matters deemed appropriate by the Reserve Bank. The circulars may, among other things, classify cash items and noncash

2. The Board publishes a "Memorandum on Exchange Charges," listing the banks that would impose exchange charges on cash items and other checks forwarded by Reserve Banks and therefore would not pay at par.

items, require separate sorts and letters, and provide different closing times for the receipt of different classes or types of items.

(b) *Binding effect.* This subpart and the operating circulars of the Reserve Banks are binding on the sender of an item, on each collecting bank, paying bank, and nonbank payor, to which a Reserve Bank (or a subsequent collecting bank) presents or sends an item, and on other parties interested in the item, including the owner.

(c) *Government items.* As depositaries and fiscal agents of the United States, Reserve Banks handle certain items payable by the United States or certain Federal agencies as cash or noncash items. To the extent provided by regulations issued by, and arrangements made with, the United States Treasury Department and other Government departments and agencies, the handling of such items is governed by this subpart. The Reserve Banks shall include in their operating circulars such information regarding these regulations and arrangements as the Reserve Banks deem appropriate.

(d) *Government senders.* Except as otherwise provided by statutes of the United States, or regulations issued or arrangements made thereunder, this subpart and the operating circulars of the Reserve Banks apply to the following when acting as a sender: a department, agency, instrumentality, independent establishment, or office of the United States, or a wholly owned or controlled Government corporation, that maintains or uses an account with a Reserve Bank.

§ 210.4 Sending items to Reserve Banks.

(a) A sender may send any item to the Reserve Bank with which it maintains or uses an account, but that Reserve Bank may permit or require the sender to send direct to another Reserve Bank an item payable within the other Reserve Bank's District.

(b) With respect to an item sent direct, the relationships and the rights and liabilities between the sender, the Reserve Bank of its District, and the Reserve Bank to which the item is sent are the same as if the sender had sent the item to the Reserve Bank of its District and that Reserve Bank had sent the item to the other Reserve Bank.

(c) The Reserve Banks shall receive cash items and other checks at par.

§ 210.5 Sender's agreement; recovery by Reserve Bank.

(a) *Sender's agreement.* By sending an item to a Reserve Bank, the sender:

(1) Authorizes the receiving Reserve Bank (and any other Reserve Bank or collecting bank to which the item is sent) to handle the item subject to this subpart and to the Reserve Bank's operating circulars, and warrants its authority to give this authorization;

(2) Warrants to each Reserve Bank handling the item that: (i) The sender has good title to the item or is authorized to obtain payment on behalf of one who has good title (whether or not this warranty is evidenced by the sender's express guaranty of prior indorsements on the item); and (ii) to the extent prescribed by State law applicable to a Reserve Bank or subsequent collecting bank handling the item, the item has not been materially altered; but paragraph (a)(2) of this section does not limit any warranty by a sender arising under State law; and

(3) Agrees to indemnify each Reserve Bank for any loss of expense sustained (including attorneys' fees and expenses of litigation) resulting from (i) the sender's lack of authority to make the warranty in paragraph (a)(1) of this section; (ii) any action taken by the Reserve Bank within the scope of its authority in handling the item; or (iii) any warranty made by the Reserve Bank under § 210.6(b) of this subpart.

(b) *Recovery by Reserve Bank.* If an action or proceeding is brought against a Reserve Bank that has handled an item, based on:

(1) The alleged failure of the sender to have the authority to make the warranty and agreement in paragraph (a)(1) of this section;

(2) Any action by the Reserve Bank within the scope of its authority in handling the item; or

(3) Any warranty made by the Reserve Bank under § 210.6(b) of this subpart,

the Reserve Bank may, upon the entry of a final judgment or decree, recover from the sender the amount of attorneys' fees and other expenses of litigation incurred, as well as any amount the Reserve Bank is required to pay under the judgment or decree, together with interest thereon.

(c) *Methods of recovery.* The Reserve Bank may recover the amount stated in paragraph (b) of this section by charging any account on its books that is maintained or used by the sender (or if the sender is another Reserve Bank, by entering a charge against the other Reserve Bank through the Interdistrict Settlement Fund), if:

(1) The Reserve Bank made seasonable written demand on the sender to assume defense of the action or proceeding; and

(2) The sender has not made any other arrangement for payment that is acceptable to the Reserve Bank.

A Reserve Bank that has been charged through the Interdistrict Settlement Fund may recover from its sender in the manner and under the circumstances set forth in this paragraph. A Reserve Bank's failure to avail itself of the remedy provided in this paragraph does not prejudice its enforcement in any other manner of the indemnity agreement referred to in paragraph (a)(3) of this section.

§ 210.6 Status, warranties, and liability of Reserve Bank.

(a)(1) *Status and liability.* A Reserve Bank shall act only as the sender's agent in respect of an item. This agency terminates not later than the time the Reserve Bank receives payment for the item in actually and finally collected funds and makes the proceeds available for use by the sender. A Reserve Bank shall not act as agent or subagent of an owner or holder of an item other than the sender. A Reserve Bank shall not have or assume any liability to the sender in respect of an item or its proceeds except for the Reserve Bank's own lack of good faith or failure to exercise ordinary care.

(2) *Reliance on routing designation appearing on item.* A Reserve Bank may present or send an item based on the routing number or other designation of a paying bank or nonbank payor appearing in any form on the item when the Reserve Bank receives it. A Reserve Bank shall not be responsible for any delay resulting from its acting on any designation, whether inscribed by magnetic ink

or by other means, and whether or not the designation acted on is consistent with any other designation appearing on the item.

(b) *Warranties and liability.* By presenting or sending an item, a Reserve Bank warrants to a subsequent collecting bank and to the paying bank and any other payor:

(1) That the Reserve Bank has good title to the item (or is authorized to obtain payment on behalf of one who either (i) has good title or (ii) is authorized to obtain payment on behalf of one who has good title), whether or not this warranty is evidenced by the Reserve Bank's express guaranty of prior indorsements on the item; and

(2) That the item has not been materially altered to the extent prescribed by State law applicable to a Reserve Bank or subsequent collecting bank holding the item.

The Reserve Bank shall not have or assume any other liability to the paying bank or other payor, except for the Reserve Bank's own lack of good faith or failure to exercise ordinary care.

§ 210.7 Presenting items for payment.

(a) *Presenting or sending.* As provided under State law or as otherwise permitted by this section: (1) a Reserve Bank or a subsequent collecting bank may present an item for payment or send the item for presentment and payment; and

(2) A Reserve Bank may send an item to a subsequent collecting bank with authority to present it for payment or to send it for presentment and payment.

(b) *Place of presentment.* A Reserve Bank or subsequent collecting bank may present an item:

(1) At a place requested by the paying bank;

(2) At a place requested by the nonbank payor, if the item is payable by a nonbank payor other than through a paying bank;

(3) Under a special collection agreement consistent with this subpart; or

(4) Through a clearing house and subject to its rules and practices.

(c) *Presenting or sending direct.* A Reserve Bank or subsequent collecting bank may, with respect to an item payable in the Reserve Bank's District:

(1) Present or send the item direct to the paying bank, or to a place requested by the paying bank; or

(2) If the item is payable by a nonbank payor other than through a paying bank, present it direct to the nonbank payor. Documents, securities, or other papers accompanying a noncash item shall not be delivered to the nonbank payor before the item is paid unless the sender specifically authorizes delivery.

(d) *Item payable in another district.* A Reserve Bank receiving an item payable in another District ordinarily sends the item to the Reserve Bank of the other District, but with the agreement of the other Reserve Bank, may present or send the item as if it were payable in its own District.

§ 210.8 Presenting noncash Items for Acceptance.

A Reserve Bank or a subsequent collecting bank may, if instructed by the sender, present a noncash item for acceptance in any manner authorized by law if: (a) The item provides that it must be presented for acceptance; (b) the item is payable elsewhere than at the residence or place of business of the payor; or (c) the date of payment of the item depends on presentment for acceptance. Documents accompanying a noncash item shall not be delivered to the payor upon acceptance of the item unless the sender specifically authorizes delivery. A Reserve Bank shall not have or assume any other obligation to present or to send for presentment for acceptance any noncash item.

§ 210.9 Payment.

(a) *Cash items.* (1) A paying bank becomes accountable for the amount of a cash item received directly or indirectly from a Reserve Bank, at the close of the paying bank's banking day on which it receives [3] the item if it retains the item after the close of that banking day, unless, prior to that time, it pays for the item by:

(i) Debit to an account on the Reserve Bank's books;

(ii) Cash; or

(iii) In the discretion of the Reserve Bank, any other form of payment.

(2) The proceeds of any payment shall be available to the Reserve Bank by the close of the Reserve Bank's banking day on the banking day of receipt of the item by the paying bank. If the banking day of receipt is not a banking day for the Reserve Bank, payment shall be made on the next day that is a banking day for the Reserve Bank by the close of the Reserve Bank's banking day. A paying bank that closes regularly on a weekday which is a banking day for the Reserve Bank shall either pay on that day by the close of the Reserve Bank's banking day for cash items that the Reserve Bank makes available to the paying bank on that day, or compensate the Reserve Bank for the value of the float associated with the items in accordance with procedures provided in its Reserve Bank's operating circular; in such circumstances, the paying bank is not considered to receive the item until its next banking day.

(b) *Noncash items.* A Reserve Bank may require the paying or collecting bank to which it has presented or sent a noncash item to pay for the item in cash, but the Reserve Bank may permit payment by a debit to an account on the Reserve Bank's books or by any of the following that is in a form acceptable to the Reserve Bank: bank draft, transfer of funds or bank credit, or any other form of payment authorized by State law.

(c) *Nonbank payor.* A Reserve Bank may require a nonbank payor to which it has presented an item to pay for it in cash, but the Reserve Bank may permit payment in any of the following that is in a form acceptable to the Reserve Bank: cashier's check, certified check, or other bank draft or obligation.

(d) *Handling of payment.* A Reserve Bank may handle a bank draft or other form of payment it receives in payment of a cash item as a cash item. A Reserve Bank may handle a bank draft or other form of payment it receives in payment of a noncash item as either a cash item or a noncash item.

(e) *Liability of Reserve Bank.* A Reserve Bank shall not be liable for the failure of a collecting bank, paying bank, or nonbank payor to pay for an item, or

3. A paying bank is deemed to receive a cash item on its next banking day if it receives the item:

(1) On a day other than a banking day for it; or

(2) On a banking day for it, but

(i) After its regular banking hours;

(ii) After a "cut-off hour" established by it in accordance with State law; or

(iii) During afternoon or evening periods when it is open for limited functions only.

for any loss resulting from the Reserve Bank's acceptance of any form of payment other than cash authorized in paragraphs (a), (b), and (c) of this section. A Reserve Bank that acts in good faith and exercises ordinary care shall not be liable for the nonpayment of, or failure to realize upon, a bank draft or other form of payment that it accepts under paragraphs (a), (b), and (c).

[45 FR 68634, Oct. 16, 1980, as amended at 49 FR 4200, Feb. 3, 1984]

§ 210.10 Time schedule and availability of credits for cash items.

(a) Each Reserve Bank shall include in its operating circulars a time schedule for each of its offices indicating when the amount of any cash item received by it (or sent direct to another Reserve office for the account of that Reserve Bank) is counted as reserve for purposes of Part 204 of this chapter (Regulation D) and becomes available for use by the sender. The Reserve Bank shall give either immediate or deferred credit in accordance with its time schedule to a sender other than a foreign correspondent. A Reserve Bank ordinarily gives credit to a foreign correspondent only when the Reserve Bank receives payment for the item in actually and finally collected funds, but, in its discretion, a Reserve Bank may give immediate or deferred credit in accordance with its time schedule.

(b) Notwithstanding its time schedule, a Reserve Bank may refuse at any time to permit the use of credit given for any cash item for which the Reserve Bank has not yet received payment in actually and finally collected funds.

§ 210.11 Availability of proceeds of noncash items; time schedule.

(a) *Availability of credit.* A Reserve Bank shall give credit to the sender for the proceeds of a noncash item when it receives payment in actually and finally collected funds (or advice from another Reserve Bank of such payment to it). The amount of the item is counted as reserve for purposes of Part 204 of this chapter (Regulation D) and becomes available for use by the sender when the Reserve Bank receives the payment or advice, except as provided in paragraph (b) of this section.

(b) *Time schedule.* A Reserve Bank may give credit for the proceeds of a noncash item subject to payment in actually and finally collected funds in accordance with a time schedule included in its operating circulars. The time schedule shall indicate when the proceeds of the noncash item will be counted as reserve for purposes of Part 204 of this chapter (Regulation D) and become available for use by the sender. A Reserve Bank may, however, refuse at any time to permit the use of credit given for a noncash item for which the Reserve Bank has not yet received payment in actually and finally collected funds.

(c) *Handling of payment.* If a Reserve Bank receives, in payment for a noncash item, a bank draft or other form of payment that it elects to handle as a noncash item, the Reserve Bank shall neither count the proceeds as reserve for purposes of Part 204 of this chapter (Regulation D) nor make the proceeds available for use until it receives payment in actually and finally collected funds.

§ 210.12 Return of cash items.

(a) *Recovery of payment.* A paying bank that receives a cash item directly or indirectly from a Reserve Bank, other than for immediate payment over the counter, and that pays for the item as provided in § 210.9(a) of this subpart, may recover the payment if, before it has finally paid the item, it:

(1) Returns the item before midnight of its next banking day following the banking day of receipt; or

(2) Takes any other action to recover the payment within the times and by the means provided by State law.

The rules or practices of a clearinghouse through which the item was presented, or a special collection agreement under which the item was presented, may not extend these return times, but may provide for a shorter return time.

(b) *Paying bank's warranties and agreement.* A paying bank that obtains a credit or refund for the amount of a payment it has made for a cash item:

(1) Warrants to the Reserve Bank (and to a subsequent collecting bank, and to the sender and all prior parties) that it took all action necessary to entitle it to recover its payment within the time limits of: (i) This subpart; (ii) State law, unless a longer time is afforded by this subpart; (iii) the rules or practices of any clearing house through which the item was presented; and (iv) any special collection agreement under which the item was presented; and

(2) Agrees to indemnify the Reserve Bank for any loss or expense sustained (including attorneys' fees and expenses of litigation) resulting from the Reserve Bank's giving the credit or refund to the paying bank, or charging, or obtaining a refund from, the sender.

(c) *Notification of Nonpayment.* (1) A paying bank that receives a cash item in the amount of $2500 or more directly or indirectly from a Reserve Bank and determines not to pay it shall provide notice to the first bank to which the item was transferred for collection ("depositary bank") that the paying bank is returning the item unpaid. If the depositary bank is not located in a state, the paying bank shall provide the notice to the bank located in a state that first handled the item for collection.

(2) The paying bank shall provide the notice such that it is received as specified by the operating circular of the paying bank's Reserve Bank by the depositary bank by midnight of the second banking day of the paying bank following the deadline for return of the item as specified in paragraph (a) of this section. If the day the paying bank is required to provide notice to the depositary bank is not a banking day for the depositary bank, receipt of notice on the depositary bank's next banking day shall constitute timely notice under this paragraph. Notice may be provided through any means, including return of the cash item so long as the cash item is received by the depositary bank within the time limits specified in this subparagraph.

(3) The information contained in the notice shall include the name of the paying bank, the name of the payee, the amount of the item, the reason for return, the date of the indorsement of the depositary bank, the account number of the depositor, the branch at which the item was first deposited, and the trace number on the item of the depositary bank, and should otherwise be in accordance with uniform standards and procedures specified by the operating circular of the paying bank's Reserve Bank. A paying bank is not required to provide any information in the notice that it, after exercising ordinary care and acting in good faith, is not able to determine with reasonable certainty from the item itself.

(4) A paying bank is not required to, but may voluntarily, provide notice to the department of the depositary bank or other entity specified by the depositary bank to receive the notice.

(5) If a paying bank provides a notice pursuant to subparagraph (1) of this paragraph and subsequently determines to pay the item, the paying bank shall provide to the depositary bank a second notice as soon as reasonably possible. This second notice should indicate that it is a second notice that is cancelling a previous notice and should contain sufficient information to enable the depositary bank to match the second notice with the previous notice.

(6) A paying bank that fails to exercise ordinary care in meeting the requirements of this paragraph shall be liable to the depositary bank for losses incurred by the depositary bank, up to the amount of the item, reduced by the amount of the loss that the depositary bank would have incurred even if the paying bank had used ordinary care. A paying bank that fails to act in good faith in meeting the requirements of this paragraph may be liable for other damages, if any, suffered by the depositary bank as a proximate consequence. If the paying bank or the depositary bank prevails in litigation involving the requirements of this paragraph, it may recover its court costs and reasonable attorneys' fees. A paying bank shall not be liable for mistake, neglect, negligence, misconduct, insolvency or default of any other bank or other person in connection with providing notice under this paragraph.

(7) Notwithstanding the provisions of section 210.6 of this subpart, a Reserve Bank that fails to exercise ordinary care in undertaking to provide the notice required in this paragraph on a paying bank's behalf shall be liable to the depositary bank for losses incurred by the depositary bank, up to the amount of the item, reduced by the amount of the loss that the depositary bank would have incurred even if the Reserve Bank had used ordinary care. A Reserve Bank that fails to act in good faith in undertaking to provide the notice required in this paragraph on a paying bank's behalf may be liable for other damages, if any, suffered by the depositary bank as a proximate consequence. If the Reserve Bank or the depositary bank prevails in litigation involving the requirements of this paragraph, it may recover its court costs and reasonable attorneys' fees. A Reserve Bank shall not be liable for mistake, neglect, negligence, misconduct, insolvency or default of any other bank or other person, including the paying bank in connection with providing notice under this paragraph.

(8) Notwithstanding the provisions of § 210.6 of this subpart, a Reserve Bank that undertakes to provide the notice required in this paragraph on a paying bank's behalf shall indemnify the paying bank for any claim brought against it by the depositary bank that results from the Reserve Bank's failure to exercise ordinary care or failure to act in good faith in providing the notice. The paying bank shall indemnify a Reserve Bank that undertakes to provide the notice required in this paragraph on the paying bank's behalf for any claim brought against the Reserve Bank by the depositary bank that results from the paying bank's failure to exercise ordinary care or failure to act in good faith in connection with the provision of the notice.

(9) This paragraph does not apply to an item drawn on the account of the U.S. Treasury or to an item indorsed by, or for credit to, the U.S. Treasury.

(10) The following days shall not be considered banking days for purposes of the deadline for notice of nonpayment: Saturdays and Sundays, January 1, the third Monday in January, the third Monday in February, the last Monday in May, July 4, the first Monday in September, the second Monday in October, November 11, the fourth Thursday in November, and December 25. If January 1, July 4, November 11, or December 25 fall on a Saturday, the previous Friday shall not be considered a banking day for purposes of this subsection. If January

1, July 4, November 11, or December 25 fall on a Sunday, the next following Monday shall not be considered a banking day for purposes of this subsection.

(d) A Reserve Bank shall not have or assume any responsibility for determining whether the action taken by a paying bank was timely.

[45 FR 68634, Oct. 16, 1980, as amended at 50 FR 5740, Feb. 12, 1985; 50 FR 41336, Oct. 10, 1985]

§ 210.13 Chargeback of unpaid items.

(a) *Right of chargeback.* If a Reserve Bank does not receive payment in actually and finally collected funds for an item for which the Reserve Bank gave credit subject to payment in actually and finally collected funds, the Reserve Bank shall charge back the amount of the item to the sender, whether or not the item itself can be returned. In the event of chargeback, neither the owner or holder of the item nor the sender shall have any interest in any reserve balance or other funds of the paying bank or a collecting bank in the Reserve Bank's possession.

(b) *Suspension or closing of bank.* A Reserve Bank shall not pay or act on a draft, authorization to charge, or other order on a reserve balance or other funds in its possession after it receives notice of suspension or closing of the bank making the payment for that bank's own or another's account.

§ 210.14 Extension of time limits.

If, because of interruption of communication facilities, suspension of payments by a bank or nonbank payor, war, emergency conditions or other circumstances beyond its control, a bank (including a Reserve Bank) or nonbank payor is delayed in acting on an item beyond applicable time limits, its time for acting is extended for the time necessary to complete the action, if it exercises such diligence as the circumstances require.

§ 210.15 Direct presentment of certain warrants.

If a Reserve Bank elects to present direct to the payor a bill, note, or warrant that is issued and payable by a State or a political subdivision and that is a cash item not payable or collectible through a bank: (a) Sections 210.9, 210.12, and 210.13 and the operating circulars of the Reserve Banks apply to the payor as if it were a paying bank; (b) § 210.14 applies to the payor as if it were a bank; and (c) under § 210.9 each day on which the payor is open for the regular conduct of its affairs or the accommodation of the public is considered a banking day.

CHAPTER TWENTY-SEVEN

THE RELATIONSHIP OF THE BANK AND ITS DEPOSITOR

SECTION 1. INTRODUCTION

The rights of the customer and the bank are determined partly by the contract set out on the signature card and corporate resolution, and partly by the documents such as the monthly statements, stop order forms and saving books which may pass between the depositor and his bank.

These rights are fleshed out by the provisions of UCC 4–401 and following. The Code does not set forth the rights and liabilities between the customer and his bank as fully as it set forth those among the various parties to the check. For example it is well settled that (barring contributory negligence on the part of the depositor) the bank may not charge the account of the depositor for a check paid over a forged indorsement. The Code, however, does not explicitly so state.

Some problems between the depositor and his bank have analogues in Article 3, and some do not. The bank's liability to its customer for inadvertent payment over a stop order is a unique customer-bank problem. Liability of drawee to customer-drawer on lost, stolen and altered checks is similar to the liabilities discussed in Chapter 23 among the various parties to a check. To a certain extent this chapter will review and tie together topics treated in the preceding chapters of Book Three.

SECTION 2. THE DEPOSIT CONTRACT

The foundation of the relationship between bank and customer is the bank's agreement to pay out the customer's money according to his order. The signature card is the basic contract which sets up that relationship. The signature card is drafted by the bank, and at least the usual retail customer is unable to change any of its terms. In effect, the signature card is a "take it or leave it" offer. The bank's superior bargaining position is a result of its greater economic power, knowledge and experience; the signature card may properly be characterized as an adhesion contract.

Questions arise concerning the bank's power to limit its liability through provisions on its signature card. UCC 4–103(1) provides that the provisions of Article 4 "may be varied by agreement except that no agreement can disclaim a bank's responsibility for its own lack of good faith or failure to exercise ordinary care." This provision, for example, stops a bank from disclaiming liability for wrongful dishonor. Since the bank and customer relationship is created via an adhesion contract, some agreements, although not exculpating a bank for bad faith or negligence, may be void for other reasons.

PERDUE v. CROCKER NATIONAL BANK

Supreme Court of California, 1985.
38 Cal.3d 913, 216 Cal.Rptr. 345, 702 P.2d 503.

BROUSSARD, JUSTICE.

Plaintiff filed this class action to challenge the validity of charges imposed by defendant Crocker National Bank for the processing of checks drawn on accounts without sufficient funds. (The parties refer to such checks as NSF checks and to the handling charge as an NSF charge.) He appeals from a judgment of the trial court entered after that court sustained defendant's general demurrer without leave to amend.

On July 3, 1978, plaintiff filed suit on behalf of all persons with checking accounts at defendant bank and a subclass of customers who have paid NSF charges to the bank. The complaint first alleges a contract under which the bank furnishes checking service in return for a maintenance charge.[2] It then asserts that "It is the practice of defendants to impose and collect a unilaterally set charge for processing checks presented against plaintiffs' accounts when such accounts do not contain sufficient funds to cover the amount of the check." "Defendants have at various times unilaterally increased the NSF charge to an amount the defendants deemed appropriate, without reference to any criteria, and defendants imposed and collected the said increased amount without any explanation or justification by defendants to plaintiffs." At the time of filing of the suit, the charge was $6 for each NSF check, whether the check was honored or returned unpaid, even though "the actual cost incurred by the defendants in processing an NSF check is approximately $0.30."

The bank requires each depositor to sign a signature card which it uses "to determine and verify the authenticity of endorsements on checks". In extremely small (6 point) type, the signature card states that the undersigned depositors "agree with Crocker National Bank and with each other that * * * this account and all deposits therein shall be * * * subject to all applicable laws, to the Bank's present and future rules, regulations, practices and charges, and to its right of setoff for the obligations of any of us." The card does not identify the amount of the charge for NSF checks, and the bank does not furnish the depositor with a copy of the applicable bank rules and regulations.[3]

On the basis of these allegations, plaintiff asserts five causes of action: (1) for a judicial declaration that the bank's signature card is not a contract authorizing NSF charges; (2) for a judicial declaration that such charges are oppressive and unconscionable; (3) to recover damages for unjust enrichment derived from the bank's collection of illegal NSF charges; (4) to enjoin alleged unfair and deceptive practices—the bank's failure to inform customers of the contractual nature of the signature card, and its practice of waiving NSF charges as to certain preferred customers; and (5) to recover the difference between the NSF charges and defendant's actual expenses in processing NSF checks on the

2. Paragraph 7 states: "Defendants offer said checking services in exchange for a promise by plaintiffs to pay a predetermined charge set by defendants [hereafter called the maintenance charge.] Plaintiffs, at the commencement of the checking account agreed to pay said maintenance charge, or to maintain a minimum balance in their checking account or some similar arrangement, unless such charge was waived. * * *"

3. Financial Code section 865.2, effective July 1, 1977, requires banks to make information about bank charges available to the public in an area of the bank open to the public. The complaint does not state whether defendant complied with this section.

theory that the charges represent an unreasonable attempt to fix liquidated damages.

Defendant filed general and special demurrers to each of the asserted causes of action. The superior court sustained the general demurrers and, taking notice of the fact that plaintiff had filed three previous complaints in another action raising similar issues, denied leave to amend. Plaintiff appeals from judgment for defendant.

* * *

II. *Plaintiff's Second Cause of Action: Whether the Bank's NSF Charges Are Oppressive, Unreasonable, or Unconscionable*

Plaintiff's second cause of action alleges that the signature card is drafted by defendant bank which enjoys a superior bargaining position by reason of its greater economic power, knowledge, experience and resources. Depositors have no alternative but to acquiesce in the relationship as offered by defendant or to accept a similar arrangement with another bank.[7] The complaint alleges that the card is vague and uncertain, that it is unclear whether it is intended as an identification card or a contract, that it imposes no obligation upon the bank, and permits the bank to alter or terminate the relationship at any time.[8] It then asserts that "The disparity between the actual cost to defendants and the amount charged by defendants for processing an NSF check unreasonably and oppressively imposes excessive and unfair liability upon plaintiffs." Plaintiff seeks a declaratory judgment to determine the rights and duties of the parties.

Plaintiff's allegations point to the conclusion that the signature card, if it is a contract, is one of adhesion. The term contract of adhesion "signifies a standardized contract, which, imposed and drafted by the party of superior bargaining strength, relegates to the subscribing party only the opportunity to adhere to the contract or reject it." (*Neal v. State Farm Ins. Co.* (1961) 188 Cal. App.2d 690, 694, 10 Cal.Rptr. 781 * * *. The signature card, drafted by the bank and offered to the customer without negotiation, is a classic example of a contract of adhesion; the bank concedes as much.

In *Graham v. Scissor-Tail, Inc., supra,* 28 Cal.3d 807, 171 Cal.Rptr. 604, 623 P.2d 165, we observed that "To describe a contract as adhesive in character is not to indicate its legal effect. * * * [A] contract of adhesion is fully enforceable according to its terms [citations] unless certain other factors are present which, under established legal rules—legislative or judicial—operate to render it otherwise." (Pp. 819–820, 171 Cal.Rptr. 604, 623 P.2d 165, fn. omitted.) "Generally speaking," we explained, "there are two judicially imposed limitations on the enforcement of adhesion contracts or provisions thereof. The first is that such a contract or provision which does not fall within the reasonable expectations of the weaker or 'adhering' party will not be enforced against him. [Citations.] The second—a principle of equity applicable to all contracts generally—is that a contract or provision, even if consistent with the reasonable expectations of the parties, will be denied enforcement if, considered in its context, it is unduly oppressive or 'unconscionable.'" (P. 820, 171 Cal.Rptr. 604, 623 P.2d 165, fns. omitted.)

7. Defendant and other banks now offer some depositors an arrangement under which, for a fee, the bank will treat NSF checks up to a certain amount as credit card transactions, and honor such checks. We do not know whether such arrangements were available when plaintiff filed his complaint.

8. The depositor also has the right to terminate the relationship at any time, but lacks the right asserted by the bank to alter the relationship without terminating it.

In 1979, the Legislature enacted Civil Code section 1670.5, which codified the established doctrine that a court can refuse to enforce an unconscionable provision in a contract.[10] Section 1670.5 reads as follows: "(a) If the court as a matter of law finds the contract or any clause of the contract to have been unconscionable at the time it was made the court may refuse to enforce the contract, or it may enforce the remainder of the contract without the unconscionable clause, or it may so limit the application of any unconscionable clause as to avoid any unconscionable result. [¶] (b) When it is claimed or appears to the court that the contract or any clause thereof may be unconscionable the parties shall be afforded a reasonable opportunity to present evidence as to its commercial setting, purpose, and effect to aid the court in making the determination."

In construing this section, we cannot go so far as plaintiff, who contends that even a conclusory allegation of unconscionability requires an evidentiary hearing. We do view the section, however, as legislative recognition that a claim of unconscionability often cannot be determined merely by examining the face of the contract, but will require inquiry into its setting, purpose, and effect.

Plaintiff bases his claim of unconscionability on the alleged 2,000 percent differential between the NSF charge of $6 and the alleged cost to the bank of $0.30.[11] The parties have cited numerous cases on whether the price of an item can be so excessive as to be unconscionable. The cited cases are from other jurisdictions, often from trial courts or intermediate appellate courts, and none is truly authoritative on the issue. Taken together, however, they provide a useful guide to analysis of the claim that a price is so excessive as to be unconscionable.

To begin with, it is clear that the price term, like any other term in a contract, may be unconscionable. * * * Allegations that the price exceeds cost or fair value, standing alone, do not state a cause of action. * * * Instead, plaintiff's case will turn upon further allegations and proof setting forth the circumstances of the transaction.

The courts look to the basis and justification for the price (cf. *A & M Produce Co. v. FMC Corp., supra,* 135 Cal.App.3d 473, 487, 186 Cal.Rptr. 114), including "the price actually being paid by * * * other similarly situated consumers in a similar transaction." (*Bennett v. Behring Corp., supra,* 466 F.Supp. 689, 697, italics omitted.) The cases, however, do not support defendant's contention that a price equal to the market price cannot be held unconscionable. While it is unlikely that a court would find a price set by a freely competitive market to be unconscionable * * * the market price set by an oligopoly should not be immune from scrutiny. Thus courts consider not only the market price, but also the cost of the goods or services to the seller * * *.

* * *

In addition to the price justification, decisions examine what Justice Weiner in *A & M Produce* called the "procedural aspects" of unconscionability. * * * Cases may turn on the absence of meaningful choice (*Patterson v. Walker-*

10. Section 1670.5 is based upon Uniform Commercial Code section 2–302, but expands coverage to include noncommercial contracts.

11. The bank's briefs claim the alleged $0.30 cost is too low and plaintiff's briefs admit that a higher figure, but still $1 or less, might be more accurate. We do not, however, find in plaintiff's briefs a sufficiently clear concession to enable us to depart from the general principle that, in reviewing a judgment after the sustaining of a general demurrer without leave to amend, we must assume the truth of all material factual allegations in the complaint. (*Alcorn v. Anbro Engineering, Inc., supra,* 2 Cal.3d 493, 496, 86 Cal.Rptr. 88, 468 P.2d 216.)

Thomas Furniture Co., supra, 277 A.2d 111, 113 and cases there cited), the lack of sophistication of the buyer (compare *Geldermann & Co., Inc. v. Lane Processing, Inc.* (8th Cir.1975) 527 F.2d 571, 576 [relief denied to sophisticated investor]) with *Frostifresh Corporation v. Reynoso, supra,* 274 N.Y.S.2d 757 [relief granted to unsophisticated buyers]) and the presence of deceptive practices by the seller (*ibid.; Vom Lehn v. Astor Art Galleries, Ltd., supra,* 380 N.Y.S.2d 532).

Applying this analysis to our review of the complaint at hand, we cannot endorse defendant's argument that the $6 charge is so obviously reasonable that no inquiry into its basis or justification is necessary.[12] In 1978 $6 for processing NSF checks may not seem exorbitant, but price alone is not a reliable guide. Small charges applied to a large volume of transactions may yield a sizeable sum. The complaint asserts that the cost of processing NSF checks is only $0.30 per check, which means that a $6 charge would produce a 2,000 percent profit; even at the higher cost estimate of $1 a check mentioned in plaintiff's petition for hearing, the profit is 600 percent. Such profit percentages may not be automatically unconscionable, but they indicate the need for further inquiry.

Other aspects of the transaction confirm plaintiff's right to a factual hearing. Defendant presents the depositor with a document which serves at least in part as a handwriting exemplar, and whose contractual character is not obvious. The contractual language appears in print so small that many could not read it. State law may impose obligations on the bank (e.g., the duty to honor a check when the account has sufficient funds (*Allen v. Bank of America, supra,* 58 Cal. App.2d 124, 127, 136 P.2d 345)), but so far as the signature card drafted by the bank is concerned, the bank has all the rights and the depositor all the duties. The signature card provides that the depositor will be bound by the bank's rules, regulations, practices and charges, but the bank does not furnish the depositor with a copy of the relevant documents. The bank reserves the power to change its practices and fees at any time, subject only to the notice requirements of state law.

In short, the bank structured a totally one-sided transaction. The absence of equality of bargaining power, open negotiation, full disclosure, and a contract which fairly sets out the rights and duties of each party demonstrates that the transaction lacks those checks and balances which would inhibit the charging of unconscionable fees. In such a setting, plaintiff's charge that the bank's NSF fee is exorbitant, yielding a profit far in excess of cost, cannot be dismissed on demurrer. Under Civil Code section 1670.5, the parties should be afforded a reasonable opportunity to present evidence as to the commercial setting, purpose, and effect of the signature card and the NSF charge in order to determine whether that charge is unconscionable. * * *

12. In *Jacobs v. Citibank,* N.A. (1984) 61 N.Y.2d 869, 474 N.Y.S.2d 464, 462 N.E.2d 1182, the New York Court of Appeals upheld a summary judgment for defendant bank in a suit attacking NSF check charges. In rejecting the claim that such charges were unconscionable, the court said that "[p]laintiffs have failed to show that they were deprived of a meaningful choice of banks with which they could do business and that the terms of these agreements with defendant were unreasonably favorable to the bank." (P. 872, 474 N.Y.S.2d 464, 462 N.E.2d 1182.)

While the New York court ruled on a motion for summary judgment, we rule upon a demurrer, and look only to plaintiff's allegations, not to the proof he had advanced to support those allegations. Plaintiff here has alleged that the charges imposed by defendant bank were excessive, and that similar arrangements would be imposed by other banks. Such allegations, which we must assume to be true, distinguish the New York decision.

The judgment is reversed, and the cause remanded to the superior court for further proceedings consistent with this opinion.

BIRD, C.J., MOSK and REYNOSO, JJ., and WHITE, BREINER and SAVITT, JJ., Pro Tem.,* concur.

[Some footnotes omitted.]

Notes

1. Just prior to the argument in the *Perdue* case, Controller of the Currency promulgated a new regulation that said in part as follows: [12 CFR § 7.8000 (1986)]

> "(b) Establishment of deposit account service charges, and the amounts thereof, is a business decision to be made by each bank according to sound banking judgment and federal standards of safety and soundness. In establishing deposit account service charges, the bank may consider, but is not limited to considering:
>
> (1) Costs incurred by the bank, plus a profit margin, in providing the service;
>
> (2) The deterrence of misuse by customers of banking services;
>
> (3) The enhancement of the competitive position of the bank in accord with the bank's marketing strategy;
>
> (4) Maintenance of the safety and soundness of the institution.
>
> "(c) A national bank may establish any deposit account service charge pursuant to paragraphs (a) and (b) of this section notwithstanding any state laws which prohibit the charge assessed or limit or restrict the amount of that charge. Such state laws are preempted by the comprehensive federal statutory scheme governing the deposit-taking function of national banks."

The plaintiffs argued that the regulation was promulgated to influence the decision of the California Supreme Court and at the behest of the banks. The banks argued that the regulation preempted state law and foreclosed the California court from finding compliance with it to be a violation of California state law. The court found that the federal regulations are not binding upon it because if an interpretive regulation, it was not a reasonable interpretation of the controlling statute and if a legislative regulation, it had not been properly adopted. The court concluded "such legislation cannot be enacted in the guise of statutory interpretation." It then concluded that application of state law did not create an actual conflict with federal law in a way that would make it impossible for a party to comply with both.

Why do you suppose the Controller of the Currency adopted the regulation described above? Was it adopted merely out loyalty to its subjects, the national banks?

2. What remedy is plaintiff seeking: Can the court award damages or restitution upon a finding that a contract is unconscionable?

3. When the case goes back for trial, what evidence would you introduce on behalf of the banks? Consider the following suggestions that might be made by someone in your office.

(a) We will show that the cost consists not just in running the computer with respect to a single check but also in all of the officer and employee time in dealing with irate calls of payees who have received NSF checks and time spent by officers determining whether or not to advance funds (pay NFS checks).

(b) "Costs" include those based upon the theory that bouncing checks is antisocial behavior, injurious not only to the banks but also to the payees and that it is fair, therefore, for the bank to charge a penalty to inhibit such behavior.

(c) The fees are permissible because that is "what the market will bear" and banks recently forced to pay interest on demand deposits must have higher profits from other sources in order to continue in a "safe and sound position."

(d) Can you think of others?

4. Can the entire problem be avoided (1) by having the contract in legible form spell out the rights in specific detail and (2) by modifying those rights only by a document sent to all parties with an appropriate opportunity for the parties to remove their funds if they do not like the modification?

5. The *Perdue* court believes that it is important for the customer to have a "meaningful choice." Will such meaningful choice be found where two banks are charging different prices for the same service? Where the same price is charged but that price is quite low?

BEST v. UNITED STATES NATIONAL BANK OF OREGON

Court of Appeals of Oregon, 1986.
78 Or.App. 1, 714 P.2d 1049.

Before RICHARDSON, P.J., and WARDEN and ROSSMAN, JJ.

RICHARDSON, PRESIDING JUDGE.

This is a class action challenging the validity of defendant bank's service charge for processing checks drawn against nonsufficient funds (NSF charge). Plaintiffs brought this action on behalf of themselves and other persons similarly situated. They alleged six claims for relief. On their second (breach of good faith) and fourth (penalty) claims, the trial court certified a class comprised of natural persons who were Oregon residents, had nonbusiness checking accounts with the bank between May 31, 1973, and May 30, 1979, and had paid NSF charges during that period. On their third claim (unconscionability), it certified a subclass consisting of class members who had opened their checking accounts on or after July 1, 1968. The other three claims were peculiar to the named plaintiffs. Only the claims of the class and the subclass are involved in this appeal. Those claims are: (1) the NSF charges were an unlawful penalty for breach of contract; (2) the charges were unconscionable; and (3) the bank breached its implied covenant of good faith by setting the charges at unreasonably high amounts. Plaintiffs sought relief totalling $30 million on those claims. The trial court granted the bank's motion for summary judgment against those claims. Plaintiffs appeal and the bank cross-appeals. We affirm in part and reverse in part.

Our scope of review is to determine whether there are any genuine issues of material fact and whether the bank is entitled to judgment as a matter of law.

* * *

An initial issue is whether various federal statutes and agency regulations preempt state regulation of bank charges and therefore defeat plaintiffs' claims. Plaintiffs contend that the bank did not properly raise that defense in the trial court. We will assume for the sake of argument that it did. The bank asserts essentially the identical preemption argument rejected in *Perdue v. Crocker Nat. Bank*, 38 Cal.3d 913, ___ - ___, 216 Cal.Rptr. 345, 702 P.2d 503 (1985), another class action challenging the validity of NSF charges. *Perdue* contains a thorough, well-reasoned analysis of the preemption issue, and we agree with it. In contrast, *Jacobs v. Citibank, N.A.*, 61 N.Y.2d 869, 474 N.Y.S.2d 464, 462 N.E.2d 1182 (1984), on which the bank relies, contains only two sentences concerning preemption, and we decline to follow it on that issue. Assuming that the issue is properly before us, federal law does not preempt plaintiffs' claims.

The common gravamen of plaintiffs' claims is that the bank's NSF charges were unreasonably high. Plaintiffs introduced evidence, for example, that in 1979, although the bank's cost of processing an NSF check was $1.08, its charge was $5.00.

Plaintiffs' "penalty" claim was based on the theory that they breached their deposit agreement with the bank when they wrote NSF checks and that the NSF charges constituted unreasonably high liquidated damages for that breach and hence were void as a penalty. * * *

Returning to this case, an implied promise in a written contract can arise only when the written terms of the contract reveal that the promise was within the contemplation of the parties when they made the contract or when it is necessary to carry the parties' intention into effect. *Card v. Stirnweis,* 232 Or. 123, 134–35, 374 P.2d 472 (1962). The facts on which plaintiffs rely are not sufficient to establish an implied promise not to write NSF checks. Indeed, plaintiffs' evidence is weaker than that found insufficient to establish such a promise in *Shapiro v. United California Bank, supra.* Plaintiffs' agreement that their accounts would be subject to the bank's service charges does not necessarily include a promise not to write NSF checks. A more reasonable interpretation of the agreement between the parties is that, although the bank discouraged the writing of NSF checks and its customers normally did not intend to write such checks, the writing of NSF checks was not a breach of the deposit agreement. Instead, it was an event contemplated by the parties. The bank knew that its customers would either intentionally or inadvertently write NSF checks, and it therefore provided the service of processing those checks for a fee. Bank customers are generally aware that they will be required to pay a fee if they write NSF checks, and the NSF charge, rather than being a penalty for breach of contract, is simply a fee for processing NSF checks. The deposit agreement in question did not contain an implied promise not to write NSF checks. There is no genuine issue of material fact, and the bank is entitled to judgment on this claim as a matter of law.

We next consider plaintiffs' unconscionability claim. They allege that the NSF charge was unconscionable, because it greatly exceeded the bank's cost of processing NSF checks. They sought restitution of the NSF charges they had paid. The trial court ruled that, under *Rosboro Lumber Co. v. EBI,* 65 Or.App. 679, 672 P.2d 1336 (1983), *rev'd on other grounds,* 297 Or. 81, 680 P.2d 386 (1984), the doctrine of unconscionability is not a basis for affirmative relief.

Plaintiffs cite Uniform Commercial Code § 2–302 (ORS 72.3020) and Restatement (Second) Contracts, § 208 (1979), as the bases of their claim. They contend that the result will be the same whether their claim is analyzed under the UCC or the Restatement. Whether or not that is true, UCC § 2–302 does not apply in this case, because UCC Article 2 is limited to transactions in goods. UCC § 2–102 (ORS 72.1020). However, because the Restatement follows UCC § 2–302, *see* Reporter's Note to § 208, and UCC § 2–302 has been influential in nonsales cases, *see* Comment *a* to § 208, cases decided under that section are helpful in analyzing plaintiffs' claim.

In *Rosboro Lumber,* the plaintiff sought restitution of workers' compensation insurance premiums it had paid to the defendant, on the basis, *inter alia,* that the defendant had engaged in unconscionable conduct. We analyzed that claim under the Restatement and held that, "although unconscionability may be a defense to the enforceability of a contract, it is not a basis for affirmative relief." We affirmed the dismissal of the plaintiff's unconscionability claim. 65 Or.App. at 682, 672 P.2d 1336.

Rosboro Lumber is clearly on point and adverse to plaintiffs' claim. They offer a number of suggestions to avoid its holding. First, they point out that the emphasized portion of the following passage from Dobbs on Remedies 707 (West Ed.1973), which we quoted in *Rosboro Lumber,* 65 Or.App. at 682, 672 P.2d 1336, supports their claim for restitution:

> "* * * [T]he remedy [for unconscionability] remains essentially defensive, for the plaintiff does not recover damages; he will only be relieved of the contractual obligation, *or, possibly, if he has already paid an unconscionable sum, will be allowed restitution to the limits of conscionability.*" (Emphasis supplied.)

Dobbs, however, cites no authority for that assertion and, as discussed below, we have found none. Furthermore, the *holding* of *Rosboro Lumber* is that the doctrine of unconscionability is not a basis for restitution.

Second, plaintiffs cite *Zemp v. Rowland,* 31 Or.App. 1105, 572 P.2d 637 (1977), *rev. den.* 282 Or. 537 (1978), for the proposition that unconscionability is a basis for restitution. There, the plaintiffs brought an action against their landlord to recover a nonrefundable fee that they had paid under a provision of their lease. They alleged that the provision was unconscionable under the Oregon Residential Landlord and Tenant Act. We held that the provision was not unconscionable. We did not hold that restitution would have been available had we found the provision unconscionable. *Zemp* is inapposite.

Finally, plaintiffs urge us to overrule *Rosboro Lumber.* We decline to do that. We have found no authority anywhere that the doctrine of unconscionability is a basis for restitutionary relief. * * * Because the doctrine of unconscionability is not a basis for affirmative relief, the trial court was correct in granting the bank's motion for summary judgment against the unconscionability claim.

Finally, we address plaintiffs' good faith claim. They allege that the bank breached its implied obligation of good faith in using its authority to set the NSF charge by setting the amount of the charge greatly in excess of the costs of processing NSF checks. The trial court evidently ruled that the doctrine of good faith, like the doctrine of unconscionability, is not a basis for affirmative relief.

Every contract contains an implied covenant of good faith and fair dealing. * * * The trial court erred in ruling that plaintiffs had no basis for relief on their good faith claim.

Whether a party has breached the covenant of good faith and fair dealing is a question of fact. Under the deposit agreement in question the bank had the power to set its NSF charges. That power was not unlimited; the bank was required to exercise it in good faith. Plaintiffs introduced evidence that the bank's NSF charges greatly exceeded its costs of processing NSF checks and that the profit derived from NSF check fees exceeded its normal profit margin. That evidence raises a genuine issue of material fact as to whether the bank breached its implied obligation of good faith by setting its NSF charges at unreasonably high rates. The trial court erred in granting the bank's motion for summary judgment on plaintiffs' good faith claim.

Judgment on second claim for relief reversed and remanded; otherwise affirmed.

[Footnotes omitted.]

RAPP v. DIME SAVINGS BANK OF NEW YORK

Supreme Court of New York, Appellate Division, 1978.
64 A.D.2d 964, 408 N.Y.S.2d 540, *affirmed,* 48 N.Y.2d 658, 421 N.Y.S.2d 347, 396 N.E.2d 740 (1979).

MEMORANDUM BY THE COURT

In an action *inter alia* to declare that the defendant bank's time restrictions on when the proceeds of a deposit consisting of checks are available to the depositor for withdrawal are illegal, the parties cross appeal from an order of the Supreme Court, Kings County, dated January 19, 1978, which, *inter alia,* (1) granted defendant's cross motion for summary judgment to the extent of dismissing the fifth through eighth causes of action and denied the cross motion as to the first through fourth causes of action, and (2) granted the plaintiffs' motion for class action status pursuant to C.P.L.R. 902 as to the first four causes of action. The appeals bring up for review so much of an order of the same court, dated March 2, 1978, as, upon reargument, adhered to the original determination.

* * *

Defendant is awarded one bill of $50 costs and disbursements.

The plaintiffs maintain savings and checking accounts with the defendant, The Dime Savings Bank of New York (hereinafter The Dime). Like most other banks, The Dime has imposed certain time restrictions on when withdrawals may be made against deposits into a patron's checking account. These restrictions essentially provide that the proceeds of a deposit consisting of checks are not available to the depositor for (1) 6 business days for local checks and (2) 15 business days for nonlocal checks. The plaintiffs' complaint alleges, in eight separate causes of action, that the imposition of these time restrictions violates various statutes and common-law doctrines.

It is emphasized that it is not alleged that the proceeds of any particular deposit were ever unreasonably withheld from the plaintiffs. On the contrary, the record unequivocally shows that the proceeds of deposits have always been immediately available to the plaintiffs. This resulted from The Dime's policy of allowing immediate withdrawal when: (1) the deposited check does not exceed $50; or (2) the deposited check is equal to or exceeds $50, but the prior checking balance or savings account balance equals or exceeds the amount of the deposited check. If the savings account balance is relied upon an amount equal to the deposited check is held against withdrawal, but continues to draw interest. Nor is it alleged that time restrictions on the availability of checking account deposits made by check are illegal per se. Rather, the gravamen of the complaint is that the particular time restrictions imposed by The Dime are illegal.

Special Term granted The Dime's application for summary judgment dismissing the fifth through eighth causes of action, but denied summary judgment as to the first four causes of action, essentially on the ground that there were questions of fact which required a trial. In addition, Special Term granted the plaintiffs' application for class action certification as to the surviving claims (see C.P.L.R. 902).

The first and second causes of action basically allege that The Dime's time restrictions are in violation of article 4 of the Uniform Commercial Code. Citing sections 4–204 and 4–213 of the Uniform Commercial Code, Special Term determined that dispositive of the first and second causes of action was the issue of the reasonableness of the time restrictions and that since reasonableness is a question of fact, summary judgment did not lie. However, in the circumstances of this case, the dispositive issue is more properly framed in the context of whether the time restrictions comport with the exercise of ordinary care gauged by general banking usage, as long as such standard is not manifestly unreasonable (see Uniform Commercial Code, § 4–103). From this perspective the record unquestionably shows that The Dime has exercised ordinary care in imposing the subject time restrictions and is, therefore, entitled to summary judgment declaring the legality of the said restrictions * * *.

The third and fourth causes of action essentially allege that The Dime engaged in false advertising and fraudulent concealment by advertising that it offered free checking accounts without also advertising its policy of restricting withdrawals for a period of time on deposits made by check.

* * *

The Dime has engaged in neither false advertising nor fraudulent concealment.

* * *

Central to the plaintiffs' complaint is the assertion that the subject time restrictions (6 days on local checks and 15 days on nonlocal checks) are unreasonable. However, it is undisputed that the vast majority of all banks impose some type of time restrictions on when the proceeds of a deposit are available. The basic purpose of such time restrictions is to protect the bank and, indirectly, the bank's depositors, against making payments, via withdrawals, on deposited checks which prove to be uncollectible. Thus, the time restrictions are imposed to give the deposited check time to clear. There is, however, no definite means of determining in advance when a check will clear. Rather, the collecting bank will usually learn that final payment has been made "merely by not learning the opposite within a reasonable time. How much time is 'reasonable' for these purposes will of course depend on the distance the item has to travel and the number of banks through which it must pass * * * and other pertinent facts" (Official Comment, Purpose 10, McKinney's Cons.Laws of N.Y., Book 62½, Part 2, Uniform Commercial Code, § 4–213, p. 593). Certainly, the specific time that final payment is made on a particular check will vary. But the complaint here is not that payment was unreasonably delayed on a particular check. Rather, the complaint is directed at the general time restrictions which are designed to best secure the bank against making payments on uncollectible checks.

The Dime is a "thrift" institution which is not directly associated with either the Federal Reserve Bank or the New York Clearing House Association. For the most part, these organizations will directly deal only with commercial banks. Since a check may be cleared only through these organizations, it is necessary that The Dime, like most other savings banks, clear its checks through the auspices of a commercial bank.

As described by The Dime's fairly detailed papers, the process for the clearance of a local check is as follows: day one, The Dime forwards the check to a commercial bank; days two through five, the commercial bank routes the check; day six, the checks which have not cleared are returned to The Dime. The four-day routing process is beyond the control of The Dime and may involve several different banks. The routing process for nonlocal checks is more complex, typically involving more intermediary banks, and is consequently lengthier. The Dime has substantiated its position by including photostatic copies of local checks which were returned on the sixth business day as uncollectible.

Rather than disputing by competent evidence The Dime's persuasive showing of the reasonableness of its time restrictions, the plaintiffs have done little more than urge that the restrictions are too long and, therefore, are not reasonable. However, in the circumstances of this case, such conclusory claims are insufficient to raise a substantial question of fact. Furthermore, Special Term erred by relying upon sections 4–204 and 4–213 of the Uniform Commercial Code for the proposition that the abstract question of reasonableness is dispositive of the case at bar. Neither of those sections is controlling.

Subdivision (1) of section 4–204 of the Uniform Commercial Code provides:

> "A collecting bank must send items by reasonably prompt method taking into consideration any relevant instructions, the nature of the item, the number of such items on hand, and the cost of collection involved and the method generally used by it or others to present such items."

That subdivision concerns the presentment of items between banks and "prescribes the general standards applicable to proper sending or forwarding of items" (Official Comment, Purpose 1, McKinney's Cons.Laws of N.Y., Book 62½, Part 2, Uniform Commercial Code, § 4–204, p. 557). Other, more specific prescriptions have been promulgated to insure that banking institutions make settlements as quickly as possible. The Dime is subject to these various deadlines, but they are relevant only insofar as they require The Dime to promptly forward checks for clearance. The existence of the 6– to 15–day time restrictions do not bespeak a failure to comply with the applicable regulations. Nor have the plaintiffs made any evidentiary showing which even casts doubt upon The Dime's full compliance with the various regulations governing the timely presentment of items for settlement.

More relevant, though not determinative, is section 4–213 of the Uniform Commercial Code which provides, in part:

> "(4) Subject to any right of the bank to apply the credit to an obligation of the customer, credit given by a bank for an item in an account with its customer becomes available for withdrawal as of right
>
> "(a) in any case where the bank has received a provisional settlement for the item,—when such settlement becomes final and *the bank has had a reasonable time to learn that the settlement is final*". (Emphasis supplied.)

The potential factual issue of whether the 6– to 15–day time restrictions represent a "reasonable time to learn that the settlement is final" has been obviated by operation of section 4–103 of the Uniform Commercial Code, which provides, in pertinent part:

> "(1) *The effect of the provisions of this Article may be varied by agreement* except that no agreement can disclaim a bank's responsibility for its own lack of good faith or failure to exercise ordinary care or can limit the measure of damages for such lack or failure; *but the parties may by agreement determine the standards by which such responsibility is to be measured if such standards are not manifestly unreasonable.*

> "(2) Federal Reserve regulations and operating letters, clearing house rules, and the like, have the effect of agreements under subsection (1), whether or not specifically assented to by all parties interested in items handled.
>
> "(3) Action or non-action approved by this Article or pursuant to Federal Reserve regulations or operating letters constitutes the exercise of ordinary care and, in the absence of special instructions, *action or non-action consistent with* clearing house rules and the like or with a *general banking usage not disapproved by this Article, prima facie constitutes the exercise of ordinary care.*" (Emphasis supplied.)

This section essentially allows the parties to vary any of the provisions of article 4 of the Uniform Commercial Code. As applied to this case, the effect of this section is to functionally define "reasonable time to learn that the settlement is final" in terms of the 6– to 15–day time restrictions. Pursuant to section 4–103, the instant time restrictions must be upheld if they have been agreed to and if they are not manifestly unreasonable (see Official Comment, Purpose 2, McKinney's Cons.Laws of N.Y., Book 62½, Part 2, Uniform Commercial Code, § 4–103, pp. 519–520).

The term "agreement" is given an extremely broad definition in section 1–201 (subd. [3]) of the Uniform Commercial Code, and applies to both direct and indirect agreements. An agreement is merely "the bargain of the parties in fact as found in their language or by implication from other circumstances including course of dealing or usage of trade or course of performance".

In the instant action the applicable agreement concerning time restrictions is evinced by the following "Collection Agreement":

> "Deposits made in cash, including partial deposits of cash, are available on the date received.
>
> "The proceeds of a deposit consisting of checks is *not* available on the date received. Checks should not be issued against this deposit until 6 business days clearance time has elapsed for a local check and/or 15 business days on all other checks." (Emphasis in original.)

This Collection Agreement is printed on the reverse side of each of The Dime's checking account deposit slips, the face of which states: "See Over for Collection Agreement". The Collection Agreement is also prominently posted in each of its branch offices that offers checking accounts. In addition, the terms of the Collection Agreement are explained to each patron when a checking account is opened. It is noted that the plaintiffs have not denied being so advised and plaintiff Julius Rapp admitted in a deposition that he was aware of the terms of the Collection Agreement.

The Official Comment to section 4–103 of the Uniform Commercial Code (Purpose 2) specifically recognizes that "[l]egends on deposit tickets, collection letters and acknowledgments of items, coupled with action by the affected party constituting acceptance, adoption, ratification, estoppel or the like, are agreements if they meet the tests of the definition of 'agreement' " (McKinney's Cons. Laws of N.Y., Book 62½, Part 2, p. 520).

The above-quoted Collection Agreement essentially constitutes a term and condition of maintaining a checking account at The Dime. By voluntarily opening a checking account with The Dime, the plaintiffs implicitly agreed to the terms thereof. This agreement was further ratified each time the plaintiffs voluntarily deposited checks into their account. Thus, the 6– to 15–day time restrictions satisfy the requirements of an agreement and effectively preempt the more ambiguous language of section 4–213 of the Uniform Commercial Code. The terms of the Collection Agreement must be upheld unless the plaintiffs can demonstrate that the time restrictions are manifestly unreasonable or otherwise inconsistent with the exercise of ordinary care (see Uniform Commercial Code, § 4–103, subd. [1]). However, the plaintiffs have failed to make any evidentiary showing which raises a material question of fact as to whether the 6– to 15–day time restrictions depart from the exercise of ordinary care.

As relevant to this case, ordinary care can be measured by the general standards of banking usage (see Uniform Commercial Code, § 4–103, subd. [3]). The relationship between "general banking usage" and "ordinary care" is elucidated, in part, in Official Comment, Purpose 4, to section 4–103 of the Uniform Commercial Code, as follows:

> "Subsection (3) further provides that, absent special instructions, action or non-action consistent with clearing house rules and the like or with a general banking usage not disapproved by the Article, prima facie constitutes the exercise of ordinary care * * * The term 'general banking usage' is not defined but should be taken to mean a general usage common to banks in the area concerned. See Section 1–205(2). Where the adjective 'general' is used, the intention is to require a usage broader than a mere practice between two or three banks but it is not intended to require anything as broad as a country-wide usage. A usage followed generally throughout a state, a substantial portion of a state, a metropolitan area or the like would certainly be sufficient * * * The *prima facie* rule does, however, impose on the party contesting the standards to establish that they are unreasonable, arbitrary or unfair." (McKinney's Cons.Laws of N.Y., Book 62½, Part 2, pp. 522–523).

In support of their general position that the time restrictions are unreasonable, the plaintiffs have compared the time restrictions imposed by The Dime to corresponding restrictions imposed by various commercial banking institutions. It is generally agreed that commercial banks tend to restrict withdrawals against deposits of local checks to 3 business days and impose longer time restrictions (generally 5–10 days) on deposits of nonlocal checks. However, the practices of commercial banking institutions have little bearing on the reasonable practices of a savings bank "thrift" institution in the conduct of its checking accounts. The more appropriate analogy is to the practices of other savings banks, which, like The Dime, must collect checks through commercial banks which are members of the New York Clearing House Association or Federal Reserve Bank.

As part of its extensive evidentiary record made in support of its cross motion for summary judgment, The Dime introduced a table showing the check clearing policies of other local savings banks which offer free checking. The time restrictions for local checks ranged from 5–8 days and the restrictions on nonlocal checks ranged from 8–21 days (with an average of 15 days). This comparison with the practices of other New York City savings banks is undisputed and conclusively establishes that The Dime's time restrictions are fully in accord with general banking usage and therefore comport with the exercise of ordinary care.

In opposition to defendant's cross motion, the plaintiffs have failed to raise even the spectre of a material issue of fact which would preclude summary judgment. Instead, the record conclusively establishes that the 6– to 15–day time restrictions are a term and condition of maintaining a checking account with The Dime and that such restrictions constitute an agreement within the context of section 4–103 of the Uniform Commercial Code. In addition, the record demonstrates that the time restrictions are reasonable and substantially related to the actual time period in which The Dime may expect to be notified that a check is uncollectible. That other banks may have somewhat shorter time restrictions does not mean that their checks clear any faster. Rather, it means only that those institutions are willing to accept the risk of loss at an earlier date. That The Dime's policies may be somewhat more conservative does not suggest that they are unreasonable. Having voluntarily agreed to such practices, if the plaintiffs now feel that the practices are too restrictive, their remedy is simply to deal with another bank.

The third and fourth causes of action complain that The Dime's advertisements of free checking with no minimum balance required, fraudulently conceal the practice of restricting withdrawals on deposits made by checks and are false because a minimum balance is in fact required. The vitality of these allegations is largely dependent upon the resolution of the first and second causes of action. Having determined that The Dime is entitled to summary judgment as to those causes of action, it is also entitled to judgment as to the third and fourth causes of action. In addition, the plaintiffs have failed to submit any evidentiary matter supporting the specific allegations contained in the third and fourth causes of action. Rather, these assertions are patently without merit.

The record clearly shows that no charge is imposed for maintaining a checking account at The Dime. Nor is any minimum balance required to keep the checking account active. This is all that the advertising may fairly be claimed as representing. Furthermore, the time restrictions are well posted and are fully explained to the prospective depositor before the checking account is opened. Thus, nothing is concealed.

Nor may it be inferred that The Dime prospers from the imposition of the time restrictions, except indirectly by protecting itself against making payments on uncollectible checks. Conversely, the plaintiffs have failed to demonstrate how they have been injured. Indeed, even if money in a savings account is held, that money continues to earn interest. Nor may it be claimed that the depositor has lost the use of his money, because there is in actuality no "money" until there has been final payment. Until there is final payment, the collecting bank has a security interest in any payment it may have made (Uniform Commercial Code, § 4–208).

The subject advertising is consistent with that of other banks, each of which imposes some period of restriction on withdrawals. The existence of such restrictions is wholly incidental to whether the checking account is free and, therefore, it must be concluded that the third and fourth causes of action are of no merit.

Accordingly, the defendant is entitled to summary judgment as to the first through fourth causes of action as well as the fifth through eighth causes of action.

Notes

1. Which is the plaintiff's best argument in the preceding three cases?

2. Which court, the one in New York, in California, or in Oregon best analyzes the problem?

3. To what extent should the court regard bank depositor contracts as suspect and in need of general policing? If you find that such need exists, how do you explain it in the face of existing and increasing competition among banks and other deposit institutions for consumers' deposits?

4. Does the court correctly interpret Article 4? If you represented a customer who desired earlier availability for his funds, or represented a bank whose customers were clamoring for earlier availability, how would you handle it in the absence of legislation?

The following are deposit agreements which purport to limit the customer's rights and the bank's liability in several areas. Refer to the deposit agreement when answering Problem 27–1.

STATE BANK AND TRUST COMPANY

FINANCIAL SERVICES BOOKLET AND DEPOSIT AGREEMENT (In Plain English)

Part I—General Provisions

1. *Legal Effect of Provisions in this Booklet.* We have tried to write this Financial Services Booklet and Deposit Agreement in plain English so that you can understand its terms as clearly as possible. When you open a deposit account with the State Bank and Trust Company by signing a Signature Card, and receive a copy of this Booklet, you are agreeing to the terms of this Booklet. It is a legally binding contract. Throughout, State Bank and Trust Company will be called "the Bank" and the depositor will be called "you." Please note that the contract can only be modified as provided in this Booklet; it cannot be modified by any oral agreement. Please READ this Booklet carefully. RETAIN IT so that you can refer to it whenever you have a question about your account with the Bank. If the Booklet does not answer any question you have, feel free to contact a customer representative at the Bank. The Bank's address is ______. The telephone number is ______.

3. *Effect of State and Federal Laws and Regulations.* The deposit relationship between you and the Bank is primarily governed by this Booklet. But it is also governed by the laws of the State of ______ and other applicable states; the laws of the United States; the rules and regulations of the Federal Reserve Board and various Federal Reserve Banks; and the rules and regulations of organizations such as the Greater ______ Clearing House Association and the State Payment Exchange. If any terms of this Booklet come into conflict with applicable law, those terms will be nullified to the extent that they are inconsistent with the law, and the applicable law will govern.

4. *Customer's Waiver of Notice.* By signing the Signature Card, you have waived any notice of non-payment, dishonor or protest regarding any items credited to or against your deposit account. For example, if a check which you deposited is dishonored and returned to the Bank, the Bank does not need to notify you of the dishonor.

5. *Waiver of Rights by the Bank.* The Bank reserves the right to waive the enforcement of any of the terms of this Booklet with you with respect to any transaction or series of transactions. Any such waiver will not affect the right of the Bank to enforce any of its rights with respect to other customers, or to enforce any of its rights with respect to later transactions with you. The fact that the Bank on any given occasion may enforce or waive its rights does not obligate it to enforce or waive similar rights in the future, nor will this be sufficient to modify the terms and conditions of this Booklet.

6. *Modification of Contract by the Bank.* The Bank reserves the right to modify the contract terms in this Booklet at any time by mailing to you, in your statement or to your statement mailing address, a written notice of the modification. Such a modification will be effective upon the date specified in the written notice, but that date will be at least ten days after the date of the mailing unless you specifically consent to an earlier date.

7. *Termination of Contract.* This contract between you and the Bank, as it relates to the covered deposit accounts, can be terminated by either you or the Bank at any time by a notice in writing. Such a termination will not release you from any fees you incur before the termination, or those you incur in the process of closing out your account.

Part II—Ownership of Accounts

1. *Individual Accounts.* If you open an account and place only your own name on it when you sign the Signature Card, the Bank will treat you as the sole owner. You may designate another person to write checks by granting them a limited power of attorney on a form acceptable to the Bank without granting them any ownership interest in your account. Otherwise, you will be the only person authorized to use the account.

2. *Joint Accounts.* If you open a joint account with one or more persons, the Bank will treat you as joint tenants with right of survivorship and not as tenants in common. This means that if one of you dies, the surviving owner has the right to all the funds in the account, subject to all applicable laws regarding death taxes and subject to the Bank's right of setoff and security interest in the account. In part IV of this Booklet are described some of the other special rules which govern joint accounts.

Part III—Types of Accounts

7. *Overdraft Protection and Line of Credit.* If the Bank approves your application for overdraft protection on the accounts you specify, you will have a revolving line of credit with the Bank, and the Bank will credit to your protected account the funds necessary to cover certain overdrafts. This credit line is immediately accessible by writing a personal check. Repayment can be made on a monthly basis or immediately in full, if you wish to save on finance charges. The maximum amount of this overdraft protection is shown on your QUIK DRAW application. You are not required to purchase any insurance for your use of QUIK DRAW protection.

Your use of this overdraft protection is governed by the following provisions:

(a) A protected account will be credited with funds in $100 increments whenever the Bank determines that an advance is necessary to maintain a credit balance in that account. The Bank is not obligated to advance funds in excess of the maximum credit agreed on although it may, in its discretion, make such an advance. If the Bank chooses not to make such an advance, the insufficient funds procedures outlined in Part IV apply.

(b) A finance charge, at the rate set forth in the disclosure statement you receive when your QUIK DRAW application is approved, will be imposed on the daily unpaid principal balance outstanding, but no other fee will be charged for this service. The Bank may change the rate of the finance charge by notifying you in writing, but this notice will be sent at least 30 days before the effective date of the new rate.

Part IV—General Rules Governing Deposit Accounts

1. *Collection of Items.* All items received after the Bank's business day cutoff hour (2:00 p.m.) are deemed received the next business day. In receiving items for deposit or collection, the Bank acts as your collection agent and assumes no responsibility beyond exercise of due care. All items are credited subject to final payment

and receipt of proceeds by the Bank. The Bank will not be liable for default or negligence of its correspondents or for loss in transit, and each correspondent will not be liable except for its own negligence. Items and their proceeds may be handled in accordance with applicable Federal Reserve and clearinghouse rules. Without prior notice to you, the Bank may charge back any item at any time before final payment, whether returned or not, and may also charge back any item drawn on it if, within the normal handling period for such item, the item cannot be honored against the drawer's account. The Bank is authorized to pursue collection of previously dishonored items, and to this end it may permit the payor bank to hold an item beyond the midnight deadline.

2. *"Holds" on Uncollected Funds.* The Bank's policy is to provide to you the earliest availability of funds on deposited items, but it reserves the right to place a "hold" on your account for the amount of checks you deposit until it has finally collected those funds. While the "hold" is in effect, you may not withdraw those funds. The Bank may exercise its "hold" rights at any time, but is more likely to do so when: (a) an account is new, and the Bank has not yet developed enough of a history to know you as a depositor; (b) a check is deposited for an unusually large amount: (c) a deposited check is drawn on another bank or financial institution; or (d) a deposited check or other negotiable instrument is issued by a person or organization whose reliability is not known to the Bank. Notice of a "hold" is not required. Normally "holds" will last no more than four business days on checks drawn on banks located within the metropolitan ______ area, and no more than ten business days on checks drawn on other domestic banks.

3. *Stop Payment Orders.* You have the right to stop payment of a check if it has not already been paid. An oral stop order is effective for only 14 calendar days and *must be confirmed in writing* within that period; a written stop order is effective for six months but renewals in writing may may be made from time to time. A written stop order, renewal or revocation will be valid upon delivery to the Bank. You must inform the Bank of the *exact amount* of the item, the number of the check and the number of the account; otherwise, the computer may not pick up the stop order. If the information given to the Bank is not correct, or if you fail to give it any other reasonable information requested regarding the item, the Bank will not be responsible if it is unable to stop payment. The Bank is entitled to a reasonable period of time after you give a stop order to notify its employees. If it recredits your account after paying a check over a valid and timely stop order, you agree to do two things: you will transfer to the Bank all of your rights against the payee or other holder of the check, and you will help the Bank if it takes legal action against that person later on. If you buy a cashier's check from the Bank you do not have the right to stop payment to a third party.

4. *Post-Dated and Stale Checks.* It is not recommended that you issue a post-dated check as a means of withdrawal. The Bank is not responsible if it charges an otherwise properly payable but post-dated check against your account before the indicated date, unless you notify it in writing that you have issued a post-dated check. If someone presents a "stale" check, i.e., more than six months old, the Bank has the option of either paying the item or dishonoring it.

5. *Insufficient Funds.* If there are not sufficient funds in your account to cover a check or other withdrawal, and if you have not signed up for Overdraft Protection, a service fee will be imposed against your account according to the schedule of service fees given to you. The bank will not be required to honor the check or other withdrawal and may return it. The Bank is not required to send you prior notice if it returns a check for insufficient funds. If your account is overdrawn, you agree to deposit sufficient funds to cover the overdraft and any service fees as soon as you receive notice of the overdraft.

6. *A Special Word About Joint Accounts.* If you have opened a joint account, each joint owner may withdraw, by any means the Bank makes available, any or all of the funds on deposits, close the account, enter into special agreements regarding the account, and stop payment on any check drawn on the account. Each joint owner guarantees the signatures of the other joint owners and authorizes the others to indorse checks for deposit if they are payable to any of the joint owners. Each joint owner also authorizes the Bank to exercise setoff and enforce its security interest in the entire joint account, even though only one of the joint owners is the debtor; this right exists irrespective of who contributed funds to the joint account. Similarly, the Bank can enforce overdraft liability in the joint account against any joint owner individually.

7. *Statements.* The Bank is authorized to mail statements to the last address you have given in writing. You should carefully examine the statement when you receive it. If you feel there is an error on the statement, or that some unauthorized person has withdrawn funds from the account, you should notify the Bank immediately. The Bank will consider the statement to be correct unless it hears from you promptly after any error is discovered. Moreover, because the depositor is in the best position to discover an unauthorized signature, an unauthorized indorsement, or a material alteration, you agree that the Bank will not be liable for paying such items if (a) you did not exercise reasonable care in examining the statement or you have not reported forgeries or alterations to the Bank within 30 days of the mailing date of the earliest statement containing these items, or (b) these items were forged so cleverly (as by unauthorized use of a facsimile machine or otherwise) that the forgery or alteration could not be detected by a reasonable bank employee.

8. *Setoff and Security Interest.* If you ever owe the Bank money as a borrower, guarantor or otherwise, and it becomes due, the Bank has a right under the law (called "setoff") and under this agreement (by which you grant the Bank a security interest in your deposit account) to use the money from your account to pay the debt. The Bank can use the money to pay the debt even if withdrawal results in an interest penalty or dishonor of subsequent checks. If this is a partnership or joint account, each partner or joint owner agrees that the Bank may use the money in the account to satisfy any one of their individual obligations. This right of setoff and security interest do not apply to this account if: (a) it is an IRA or a tax-deferred Keogh retirement account; (b) the debt is created by a consumer credit transaction under a credit card plan; or (c) the debtor's right of withdrawal arises only in a representative capacity.

10. *Transfer of Ownership.* Although checks drawn on your account are negotiable, the account itself is not. Nor is your account transferable except on the Bank's books and records. To transfer title or pledge the account as collateral for a loan from someone other than the Bank, you must provide a written request in a form the Bank approves. If ownership is to be transferred, the Bank may require that the account be closed and re-established, using a new account number. Any pledge of the account to a third party remains subject to the Bank's right of setoff and security interest.

11. *Service Fees.* You agree to pay any service fees that apply to your account including fees for such services as check-writing, stop payment orders, cashier's checks, and insufficient funds checks. These fees, which the Bank will always make reasonable in amount, help the Bank to cover the cost of transactions in your account. Any fees may be deducted from your account without prior notice to you. The Bank will not be liable for dishonoring checks or other withdrawal orders because of insufficient funds resulting from proper deduction of such fees. A schedule of the Bank's current fees will be given to you when you open an account, and is available at State Bank's banking offices. Service fees are subject to change, and any changes will be posted at the Bank or sent to you at the address shown on

the Bank's records. Notice of any changes will be given a reasonable period of time before they become effective.

12. *Authorized Signature.* Your signature on the Signature Card is your authorized signature. For the payment of funds and for other purposes relating to any deposit account you have with the Bank, the Bank is authorized to recognize your signature, but it will not be liable to you for refusing to honor your checks or other signed instructions if it has a bona fide doubt that the signature appearing on such checks or instructions is genuine.

13. *Garnishment of Account.* If any of your accounts is garnished or otherwise subject to levy by lawful legal action, the Bank will not be liable to you for any sums it may be required to pay because of such a garnishment. If the Bank incurs any expenses in responding to a garnishment which are not otherwise reimbursed, it may charge such expenses to your account. Any garnishment or other levy against your account is subject to the Bank's security interest.

14. *Disclosure of Information.* Information about your accounts or any transactions between you and the Bank will not be disclosed to third parties except in strict accordance with law.

Problem 27–1

1. Fred Plevin has overdraft protection for his checking account with State Bank. According to the deposit agreement, Fred's account will be credited with funds of up to $100 whenever such an advance is necessary to maintain a credit balance in his account. In an oral agreement with Fred, however, the president of State Bank agrees to advance funds of up to $1000 whenever necessary to maintain a credit balance. Several times the bank pays checks drawn on Fred's account by advancing funds in excess of the maximum credit agreed on in the deposit agreement per the president's instructions. Will the bank be obligated to honor the next check drawn on Fred's account which overdraws his account by $750?

2. Fred deposits a check in his account which is drawn on National Bank. After a provisional settlement is made, National Bank returns the check to State Bank for insufficient funds. State Bank never notifies Fred that the check was dishonored. Subsequently, Fred overdraws his account on the assumption that the deposited check was honored. Is State Bank liable for damages suffered by Fred if it refuses to pay the overdrawn check? [Assume for the purpose of questions 2 through 5 that Fred does not have overdraft protection.]

3. Fred deposits a check for $500 drawn on a bank in Los Angeles at State Bank (which is located in New York City). Without notifying Fred, State Bank places a hold on the check for ten days. State Bank receives final settlement from the bank in Los Angeles five days later. On the 7th day Fred overdraws his account assuming that he has the $500 check available. Is State Bank liable if it dishonors Fred's check?

4. Fred orally informs State Bank that he would like to stop payment on a $1200 check. This stop order is never confirmed in writing. Seven days after the conversation, State Bank pays the check. Is State Bank liable to Fred for charging his account?

5. Fred's wallet is stolen by a pick pocket while Fred was going to work. In the wallet is a blank check and his signed driver's license. The thief, who is also an accomplished handwriting expert, forges Fred's name and cashes the check. The forged signature is, for all practical purposes, identical with Fred's own. State Bank pays the item. Is the bank liable?

Problem 27–2

Mike McGahey has a checking account with the First National Bank of Waddington. Some of Mike's checks were stolen from his apartment while he was out of town. The thief wrote several checks after forging Mike's name. On October 1, 1984 the bank sends Mike a statement showing two checks written by the thief totalling $1200. The statement reaches Mike's house by October 3. Mike does not get back to Waddington until October 7. Because much mail has accumulated in his absence, Mike doesn't open up the Bank's letter until October 10. Finally, on October 22, Mike notifies the Bank of the forged checks. The Bank's signature card states that all objections to an item not made on or before 15 days after the Bank makes a statement available to the customer are barred.

1. The bank asserts that it is completely absolved from any liability since Mike did not notify the bank of the forged checks until 19 days after the statement reached his house. As Mike McGahey's attorney, what arguments can you make?

2. What kind of evidence must be presented to show the bank's negligence?

A current issue before the state legislatures and the Congress deals with the depositary bank's obligation to allow the depositor to call on uncollected funds, funds represented by checks drawn on other banks that are given to the depositary bank for collection and addition to the depositor's account.

Note: Delayed Funds Availability to Bank Customers

(The following is based substantially upon two articles, Wechsler, *Delayed Funds Availability,* 35 Syracuse L.Rev. 1117 (1984) and Jordan, *Ending the Floating Check Game: The Policy Arguments for Delayed Availability Reform,* 36 Hastings L.J. 514 (1985).)

Approximately two-thirds of one percent of all checks processed are dishonored and returned to the first depositary bank. Although the number of returned checks is relatively small, the potential loss to depositary banks in the dishonor of even a small number of large checks is very high. Therefore, financial institutions have instituted delayed funds availability (DFA) policies to protect themselves against the potential losses from the return of dishonored checks.

The typical DFA policy disallows withdrawal of uncollected funds for a specified period of time. The length of the delay in funds availability to the customer is a function of the time estimated for the return trip of a dishonored check from the drawee to the first depositary institution. This could range from two to 45 days depending on the location of the payor bank and the origin of the check collection process.

Financial institutions justify the need for DFA on two grounds. First, banks experience great difficulty in recovering from bank customers funds withdrawn after a check has been dishonored. Admittedly alternatives to DFA exist which would permit recovery of banks against its depositors. For example, because the credit granted to a customer is provisional, a depositary bank has a right to charge back the item against the customer's account. Moreover, under UCC 3–414(1) the depositary bank may recover in contract against its customer pursuant to the customer's contract of indorsement. However, these alternative remedies available against a depositor are costly and in some instances, fruitless.

The primary reason for the use of DFA policies is the lengthy, inefficient process of returning dishonored checks to the depositary institution. Because the check collection process runs on a no news is good news presumption, depositary banks are unsure whether an item is finally paid or whether an item is to be returned dishonored. Thus, by deferring the availability a bank withholds funds for a period of time that it believes will at least equal the time for the return trip of a check.

The decreased risks achieved by the bank's institution of DFA policies are not without costs to the customer, or the economy. The costs to the depositary customers whose funds are received before the bank's deadline are obvious. The costs to the economy are not so obvious. Because a bank may receive provisional credit for an item after deposit and before final payment, the bank may use the customer's funds interest free, or nearly interest free, during the hold period specified in the DFA policy. It is estimated that one day of such float for the whole banking industry can produce up to one billion dollars in revenue annually.

Two states, New York and California, have enacted legislation to deal with the problems of DFA. Consider the New York Banking Law section 14(d) which provides that retail banking customers must be allowed to draw against items deposited in New York banks within a reasonable time after deposit. The statute authorizes the State Banking Board to promulgate regulations which specify "reasonable times." Some cases are not covered by the reasonable time rule. For example a bank must accord "one business day" availability to funds from commercial banks and savings institutions on all items under $100, on government checks and on those drawn on a New York depositary bank. Depositary banks may apply their own DFA policies and without regard to the reasonable time rule to the following: checks written for over $2,500; checks deposited by new customers for the first 30 days after opening an account; checks of customers who are repeatedly overdrawn; deposits where the bank has a good faith doubt about their collectibility; checks drawn on banks outside of the United States; and those circumstances where a bank and its customer agree that a longer time than specified may be necessary because of unusual circumstances.

The New York scheme applies only to consumer bank accounts; it excludes small businesses. Moreover, federally chartered banks have refused to comply with the New York legislation.

Inherent in any state scheme of regulation is the fundamental problem that a given state cannot deal with the inefficiency of a check process which affects the entire nation.

To see the difficulty one must first understand the source of the problem, namely, the check return process. The process begins when the check deposited is dishonored at the payor bank, the provisional credit is revoked and the check is returned to the original depositary institution. This process sounds simple; however it is full of difficulties. The only incentive to the payor bank is to return the check before its midnight deadline. Professor Jordan states the practices as follows:

> "The treatment of check returns is dramatically different from that of check collections. When a check is forwarded for collection, it receives the benefit of jet couriers and expedited high speed processing. In sharp contrast, items that have been returned, for whatever reason, are handled manually. Each returned item is read and sorted separately without the benefit of the MICR strip, which permits high speed sorting during the initial trip to the payor. Because this is a labor-intensive process, it is slower and more prone to human error. Highly skilled clerical staff are needed to decipher incomplete, missing, and partially obliterated indorsements, adding to the cost of processing.
>
> "Each item is then forwarded to the next prior collecting bank, rather than directly to the original depositary bank. Because of the relatively small volume involved, most dishonored checks are returned to the payor bank using the postal service, further increasing the risk of error. The result is a highly inefficient method for returning items in which the risk of loss and delay increases

exponentially with each mailing to the next prior collecting bank." Jordan, *Delayed Availability Reform,* 36 Hastings L.J. 514, 531–532 (March 1985).

Professor Wechsler has proposed the following solution. What do you think of it?

"This proposal envisions three major elements, that, taken together, provide a workable solution. Each of these is discussed in detail below.

"a. Direct Returns Through the Federal Reserve System

A key component of the solution to the slowness of check returns and the DFA problem * * *: with limited exceptions, all returned checks (whether originally collected by a Federal Reserve Bank or not) would be handled by the Federal Reserve System, bypassing most other banks that had participated in the forward collection process. An exception to the new procedure would be made for those checks that had been processed by local city clearinghouses and that could be returned faster by avoiding the Federal Reserve System. * * * The new return system would be put into effect by the issuance of Federal Reserve operating circulars, which have the effect of a binding and uniform change to the Uniform Commercial Code. Leaving local clearing house items aside, drawees would return checks to their local Federal Reserve Bank office via the Federal Reserve's courier system, which already reaches a great many financial institutions on a daily basis. The Federal Reserve, still using its own couriers, would return the check to the bank-of-first deposit, avoiding most intermediate banks. * * * [W]hen checks were returned across district lines, they would pass through one additional Federal Reserve Bank office. * * * Provisional credits previously given would be allowed to become final; the Federal Reserve would perform the settlement function by crediting the drawee and charging the depositary for the amount of the returned items.

"This proposal of semidirect returns through the Federal Reserve System would have a number of salutary effects. The number of handlings required for each returned check will be significantly reduced by bypassing most intermediate banks. This will both speed returns and reduce the costs associated with them. At the same time, costs could be allocated more fairly and recovered from those who caused them. The substitution of the Federal Reserve courier in place of the presently used U.S. mail will remove one of the primary causes of the slowness of returns and will significantly speed them up. Finally, the return-settlement function can be efficiently handled by the Federal Reserve System without the problems arising under pure direct return.

"Although the possibility of amending the Uniform Commercial Code to allow for this semidirect return procedure should be explored, the use of the Federal Reserve System's power to alter the Code by operating circular has certain advantages. The new proposal could be put into effect quickly, without the need for legislation in fifty-one jurisdictions. Uniformity would be assured and the midnight deadline rule would be met, thus protecting drawees. Finally, the use of a regulation, rather than a statute, would allow for flexibility and responsiveness to any technical difficulties that might be encountered.

b. Machine-Readable Identification of Depositary Bank

"One of the principal causes of slowness in the check return process is the necessity for each bank in the return stream to process returned checks manually. Each check must be examined by a trained clerk, whose task is to determine the identification of the next transferee by deciphering the endorsements stamped on the bank. The ANSI standard attempts to alleviate this problem by reserving certain spaces on the back of the check for the various parties' endorsements, thus preventing the difficulties associated with the overstamping of one endorsement on top of another. The ANSI standard, however, does not call for a machine-readable endorsement and thus is only a partial solution to this aspect of the problem. What is needed is the equivalent of the method used in forward check processing: a machine-readable endorsement that would allow the use of high-speed check-processing equipment and obviate the need for a manual examination of each check. Since this proposal calls for direct returns through the Federal Reserve System, bypassing most intermediate banks, only the depositary's identification would need to be machine-readable.

"A machine-readable identification of the depositary might be achieved either by that bank placing its machine-readable identification number on the check before forwarding it for collection or by the drawee encoding it at the time of return. The former alternative has the advantage that no manual process is required at all; the depositary merely inscribes its routing number on every 'on-others' check as it endorses the item. However, assuming that currently available technology will be used, this procedure may not be feasible at present because there is no space on standard checks for the depositary to imprint an additional MICR line. Other technologies, such as OCR or bar coding, should be considered. If this problem cannot be readily solved, an alternative is to require the depositary to comply with the ANSI endorsement standard (to preserve the readability of its identification) and to have the drawee bank manually read that endorsement and then encode the depositary's routing number and the amount of the check onto an external processing vehicle, such as a secure carrier envelope. Carrier envelopes are universally available, readily adaptable, inexpensive, and can be designed to be recognizable as being intended only for returns. The use of this method does require one manual process, but it has two advantages: it does not require the delay that would be encountered in attempting to redesign the standard check now being used, and only those checks actually being returned would receive this extra attention, rather than the much larger population of all checks.

"Although the adoption of a machine-readable identification of the depositary bank necessarily involves some complex technical considerations, there are numerous benefits to be derived from such a procedure. Machine-readable identification of the depositary bank would allow the use of high-speed check-processing equipment and eliminate or significantly reduce the manual work currently associated with returns. The speed of the return trip would be significantly increased and the high per-item cost now incurred would be reduced. Depending on the technology adopted, it is possible that equipment presently in use in the banking industry could be utilized, thus keeping new investment to a minimum. Machine-readable identification of the depositary, coupled with direct returns through the Federal Reserve System, would have a significant impact on the speed with which checks are returned and thus would allow improved DFA schedules without increased risk to banks.

c. New DFA Hold Schedules

"Since the principal purpose of the steps outlined above for speeding up the return of checks is to benefit bank customers, a key element of this proposal is that banks be required to abide by a new maximum DFA hold schedule. These new hold periods would be mandated by Federal Reserve Board regulation and would be keyed to the new, reduced return times. Although the exact reduction in return times to be gained by automated returns through the Federal Reserve is difficult to predict, it is sure to be a significant amount. The Federal Reserve System has the capability to estimate return times by the use of models and samples and to test those estimates based on its early experience. The new DFA hold schedules should be just long enough to protect banks from risk under the new return system. The reduced number of handlings, the use of Federal

Reserve couriers instead of the U.S. mail, and the use of high-speed check-processing equipment could conceivably reduce a fifteen day round trip to as little as five days, with corresponding reductions in DFA hold periods. This would be a significant improvement for depositors. The new DFA schedule should apply to all bank customers, not just consumers.

"In addition to a basic DFA schedule aligned with the new return times, certain special provisions should be made for the benefit of customers and banks. As under the New York regulations, checks for relatively small amounts should be given availability even more quickly than provided for in the basic schedule. Allowing one-day availability on checks of $100 or less would be very useful to many customers, and would expose banks to a very limited risk of loss. Indeed, it might be desirable to consider raising the low-dollar check amount to $200 or $250. In addition, those checks that are unlikely to be returned for NSF or other causes against which DFA holds protect, such as government checks, cashier's checks, and certified checks, should also be given availability more quickly than provided for in the base schedule. There is little risk for banks on these checks, and giving them rapid availability will be useful to many customers, particularly the elderly (who depend on social-security checks) and those who sell a home and receive a cashier's or certified check to take to their new location.

"At the same time that these exceptions are made for the convenience of customers, some exceptions to the new schedule should be made for the protection of banks. Even though the new schedule will be keyed to the new return-time experience, some checks will take longer than expected. Banks should therefore be given some protection against items that may carry a particular risk. The New York regulations enumerate a number of check categories that deserve special attention as high-risk items. Even with speeded-up returns, the new required release schedule should not apply to depositors with new accounts, to accounts that have previously had bad experience, to high-value checks, or to checks about which the depositary has some specific good-faith doubt. In addition, checks drawn on banks outside the United States and "payable through" drafts should be excluded from the operation of the new schedule. In constructing the new DFA schedule, a differentiation between thrift institutions and commercial banks should be made. Because of their practice of clearing checks through correspondent commercial banks, thrifts might need an extra day or two of protection.

"Once new DFA schedules have been established, banks should be required to fully disclose [sic] them to their customers as clearly as possible so that depositors can receive the benefits of the new schedules. Disclosure should be required to be made to all current account holders, as well as upon the opening of a new account. Appropriate signs could be required in each branch and at automated-teller locations. In addition, customers might be given specific notice of check holds by the bank teller at the time of deposit. For the sake of simplicity, the total number of different categories of checks receiving differing treatment should probably be kept to a minimum. Nevertheless, even a fairly complex set of rules such as New York's can be expressed quite clearly, as early disclosure documents show.

"The new DFA schedule would serve the needs of depositors and allow them access to the funds deposited in their accounts within a reasonable time. In combination with the new methods of handling returned checks that have been proposed, it would also protect banks from increased losses and might even reduce losses below their current levels." (footnotes omitted) Wechsler, *Delayed Funds Availability,* 35 Syracuse L.Rev. 1117, 1205–1214 (1984).

Consider the difficulties with Professor Wechsler's proposal. What interests will favor it? Oppose it? What position should the Federal Reserve take on all this?

SECTION 3. WHEN BANK MAY CHARGE CUSTOMER'S ACCOUNT

Section 4–401(1) authorizes the drawee bank to charge to its customer's account items "properly payable" and by implication, denies the drawee bank the right to charge amounts *not* properly payable. Whether an item is properly payable is the crucial question in a variety of conflicts between customer and bank.

By implication, section 4–401(2) also makes it improper for a bank to charge altered items against a customer's account except to the extent of the original tenor. Moreover, a bank may not charge the tenor of a completed item where the bank knows that such completion was improper.

A. Post-Dated Checks

A payor bank which pays a postdated check before its date may not properly charge its customer's account. Since many banks make the decision to pay a check based on the information contained on the MICR line, the bank will usually not know that it is paying the postdated check prematurely. Postdated checks, like stop payment orders require special handling if the customer's order is to be carried out. In order to rectify this problem, Kansas has added the following to section 4–401:

> (3) No bank shall be liable for charging against its customer's account a postdated check, otherwise properly payable from such account, before the date stated thereon unless the customer has given written notice to the bank that the check is post dated. Such notice shall include the name of the payee, the date, the number and the amount of the check.

Problem 27–3

1. On July 1, Desaix, who has $150,000 in his account, writes a $200,000 check payable to Berthier. The check is post-dated August 25. The bank pays the check on August 1. Assuming that the check will not be cashed until August 25, Desaix writes a check for $100,000 which is presented on August 15 and dishonored for nonsufficient funds. Desaix sues Bank for wrongful dishonor; who wins and why? UCC 4–401, 4–402.

2. Suppose that Desaix issues a stop order on the first check on August 15, only to learn that the bank paid the check on August 1. May Desaix recover in a suit for improper payment? What if Desaix issued the stop order on August 27?

B. Lost, Stolen and Altered Instruments

Pre-Code law concerning the liability of the drawee bank to the drawer for its payment of forged or altered instruments was clear. Courts reasoned that the bank was obliged to pay according to the customer's order; that when it paid over a forged indorsement it had not paid according to such an order and could not therefore charge customer's account. By a similar line of reasoning it was clear that the bank could not charge the customer's account for raised amounts and of course that it could not charge his account on checks which he had not signed or otherwise authorized. Of course all of these rules were and are subject to the caveat that the customer could be estopped from asserting the forgery or alteration if his negligence substantially contributed to it.

Most have assumed that these pre-Code rules survived the enactment of the Code intact. The rules are not explicitly stated in part 4 of Article 4, but many of them are implicit. The pre-Code rules concerning payment over forged indorsements have probably been incorporated in the Code by the words in UCC 4–401(1) which authorize the bank to charge the account for items which are "properly payable." One might infer a similar rule from UCC 4–406 and 4–407 whose principal application would seem to come in cases in which the bank had paid over a forged indorsement and would have an obligation to recredit the account.

The requirement of a proper signature rests on the assumption that the drawee bank is the party in the best position to detect forgery. New practices and possibilities may make that assumption invalid. Once the check enters the banking system by deposit in the depositary bank, further movement of the check itself is no longer needed for the payment process. After the depositary bank has encoded the amount of the check on the MICR line, generally, the check can be paid or dishonored solely on the basis of the information on the MICR line. Rather than physically delivering the check to the payor bank, the information can be transmitted more quickly and more economically by electronic means.

Under radical truncation, which is not currently in use, the depositary bank would keep the check and the payor bank would receive only the MICR encoded information. Since the vast majority of checks are not now examined to verify signatures, this may not cause an insurmountable problem. Radical truncation could be the rule, with an exception for checks exceeding a certain dollar amount. However, sometimes the signature will be of no help in detecting forgery, see Perini v. First National Bank of Habersham County Georgia, supra at 1102.

In view of the facts of *Perini v. First National Bank of Habersham County,* set out above at page 1102, all the checks in that case were drawn by use of a "fascimile signature machine." Perini had filed a facsimile specimen with payor banks, Brown Brothers and Morgan Guaranty, and agreed to hold them harmless if "checks bearing or purporting to bear the single facsimile signature of R.A. Monroe were honored." Since the thief used the machine that is exactly what happened. Surely there is no reason why the court should not recognize the parties' right to allocate the loss by contract in such setting. What do you think of the following provision that might be put in a standard signature card with the regular depositor.

> "Bank shall be free to pay all items, even though the items do not contain the authorized signature of depositor in the following circumstances:
>
> "(1) When the item is truncated and only the micro encoding information is reported to bank.
>
> "(2) When the signature appearing on the item is so similar to the authorized signature that no clerk using reasonable care would be able to distinguish them."

C. Alteration

The drafters dealt somewhat more fully with the problem of alteration. UCC 4–401(2) specifies the rules in such cases as follows:

> (2) A bank which in good faith makes payment to a holder may charge the indicated account of its customer according to

(a) the original tenor of his altered item; or

(b) the tenor of his completed item, even though the bank knows the item has been completed unless the bank has notice that the completion was improper.

Problem 27–4

Lannes wrote a check for $1,000,000.00 to Desaix, Inc. to pay for a private jet. Desaix, Inc. made excellent jets but had a very loose organization. Bertheir, a Desaix, Inc. clerk, got hold of the check, forged the signature of Desaix's treasurer and made it payable to himself and raised the amount to $2,000,000. Bertheir deposited the check in his own account with First National Bank. The check was sent through the usual banking channels and Local Bank paid it. Lannes found out about the skullduggery and demanded that Local Bank recredit his account. Must Local Bank recredit Lannes' account?

SECTION 4. STOP ORDERS

Section 4–403, set out below and entitled "Customer's Right to Stop Payment," gives the customer the right to stop payment on a check provided he gives the bank "a reasonable opportunity" to act on his order.

(1) A customer may by order to his bank stop payment of any item payable for his account but the order must be received at such time and in such manner as to afford the bank a reasonable opportunity to act on it prior to any action by the bank with respect to the item described in Section 4–303.

(2) An oral order is binding upon the bank only for fourteen calendar days unless confirmed in writing within that period. A written order is effective for only six months unless renewed in writing.

(3) The burden of establishing the fact and amount of loss resulting from the payment of an item contrary to a binding stop payment order is on the customer.

Subsection (1) is couched in "may" terms, but both the caption and the language of subsection (2) make it clear that the bank is obliged to follow a stop order and does not have discretion to refuse to do so. Comment 2 to UCC 4–403 states the policy behind that section:

> The position taken by this section is that stopping payment is a service which depositors expect and are entitled to receive from banks notwithstanding its difficulty, inconvenience and expense. The inevitable occasional losses through failure to stop should be borne by the banks as a cost of the business of banking.

If the payor bank fails to stop payment after receiving a proper stop order, it should, and probably will, recredit the customer's account. Questions can arise as to whether the stop order is indeed "proper." Section 4–403(2) explicitly states that an oral stop order is binding on a bank for fourteen days. Some jurisdictions, have varied section 4–403 by requiring a written stop order. Even in those jurisdictions, however, a bank may waive the benefit of the writing requirement. Such occurred in Stamford State Bank v. Miles, 186 S.W.2d 749 (Tex.Civ.App.1945) where the bank accepted the customer's stop order request over the telephone and informed the customer that the stop order would be effective.

Erroneous information in the stop order can make that order improper. It is generally believed that the order must identify the check with reasonable accuracy. The account should be identified either by the drawer's name or account number, and the identity of the check should be shown either by number, by name of the payee or by such information combined with the date and amount of the check. Consequently, a stop order which misstates the name of the payee and the date of the check would probably be invalid. Is a check reasonably identified if a stop order misstates its amount only nominally? Perhaps the answer to that question should depend upon the method of a bank's search.

PARR v. SECURITY NATIONAL BANK

Court of Appeals of Oklahoma, 1984
680 P.2d 648.

REYNOLDS, JUDGE.

We are called upon to decide whether Security National Bank had a reasonable opportunity to stop payment on a check when the description received was exact in all respects except for a single digit error in the check amount. This issue has not been decided by an Oklahoma court.

Parr wrote check number 949 to Champlin Oil. She dated and mailed it September 14, 1981. The amount of the check was $972.96. On September 15, 1981, Parr ordered payment stopped by telephone. Parr gave the bank her account number, the check number, the date, the payee and the amount of the check. A 50 cent error was made in identifying the amount of the check. Parr went to the bank on September 16th or 17th and executed a written stop order dated September 15, 1981. The written stop order was also in error. Security National paid check number 949 on September 17, 1981.

Parr brought suit against Security National seeking recovery for the amount of the check, 12% interest on that amount, reasonable attorney's fees and costs. Security National defended by showing their computers were programed to stop payment only if the reported amount of the check were correct. They argued Parr's 50 cent error relieved them of liability. Timeliness of notice was not at issue.

Section 4–403(1) of the Uniform Commercial Code, 12A O.S.1981 § 4–403(1), contains the applicable law on stop payment orders: [quoting]

* * *

It is appropriate to examine the purpose of this section before construing it.[1] The policy underlying § 4–403 is found in Comment 2 following the section:

> The position taken by this section is that stopping payment is a service which depositors expect and are entitled to receive from banks notwithstanding its difficulty, inconvenience and expense. The inevitable occasional losses through failure to stop should be borne by the banks as a cost of the business of banking.

1. 12A O.S.1981 § 1–102(1): "This Act shall be liberally construed and applied to promote its underlying purposes and policies." Comment 1 following § 1–102 states:

> The Act should be construed in accordance with its underlying purposes and policies. The text of each section should be read in the light of the purpose and policy of the rule or principle in question, as also of the Act as a whole, and the application of the language should be construed narrowly or broadly, as the case may be, in conformity with the purposes and policies involved.

Security National contends that whether a stop payment order has been received "in such manner as to afford the bank a reasonable opportunity to act" should be determined *after* examining how the defendant bank handles stop orders. This interpretation has found favor among highly respected legal authorities,[2] but not among the majority of courts that have addressed this issue.

Both groups acknowledge § 4–403(1) has not changed the common law rule that a stop payment order must identify the check with "reasonable accuracy." It is from this premise that courts have determined whether the description is reasonably accurate without consideration of the defendant/bank's computer program. In *Elsie Rodriguez Fashions, Inc. v. Chase Manhattan Bank,* 23 UCC Rep. 133 (N.Y.Sup.Ct.1978), the customer gave the bank the correct payee, check number and date but made a 10 cent error in the amount of the check. The court determined the check had been described with sufficient accuracy to allow the bank to stop payment. The opinion makes no mention of the bank's computer program. * * * A different result was reached by a New York court where the customer was told by the bank the stop order would not be effective unless she provided the *exact* amount of the check. * * * Security National does not contend they gave notice to Parr that any discrepancy in the check amount would prevent compliance with her stop payment order.

In *Delano v. Putnam Trust Co.,* 33 UCC Rep. 635 (Conn.Super.Ct.1981), a single digit error in the amount of $100.00 did not prevent recovery where customer supplied bank with the correct check number, date, payee, and account number of the check. The bank's computer program required an exact match of check amount before it would stop payment. Court held bank had received sufficient information to allow it a "reasonable opportunity to act" on the stop payment order. Court stated the bank had a duty to inform its customer of the need for precision in reporting the amount before it could rely on customer's error to relieve it of liability.

The Supreme Court of Alabama denied customer's recovery in *Sherrill v. Frank Morris Pontiac-Buick-GMC, Inc.,* 366 So.2d 251 (Ala.1979). Customer gave bank three descriptive elements of the check: check amount, payee and date. The check was not numbered. Two of the three pieces of information were incorrect. Court determined the check was not described with reasonable accuracy, therefore the bank was not afforded a "reasonable opportunity to act" on the stop payment order.

In *FJS Electronics, Inc. v. Fidelity Bank,* 288 Pa.Super. 138, 431 A.2d 326 (1981), Court allowed customer to prevail even though its 50 cent error in check amount prevented bank's computer from acting on stop payment order. The bank asserted § 4–403 "should be read to require compliance with the procedures of a particular bank, regardless of what they are and regardless of whether the customer has been made aware of them." *Id.* 431 A.2d at 328. Court determined that the drafter's policy stated in Comment 2 to § 4–403 precluded such an interpretation. They reasoned:

> Fidelity made a choice when it elected to employ a technique which searched for stopped checks by amount alone. It evidently found benefits to this technique which outweighed the risk that an item might be inaccurately

2. White & Summers, Handbook of the Law Under the Uniform Commercial Code § 17–5, at 679–80 (2nd ed. 1980); Hawkland, Stop Payment Orders Under the Uniform Commercial Code, 3 UCC L.J. 103, 117–18 (1970); Roberts and Mann, A Proposal for Regulating Banks' Use of Exculpatory Clauses in Stop Payment Orders, 84 Com.L.J. 183, 187–88 (1979).

described in a stop order. This is precisely the type of inevitable loss which was contemplated by the code drafters and addressed by the comment quoted above. The focus of § 4–403 is the service which may be expected by the *customer,* and a customer may expect a check to be stopped after the bank is given reasonable notice. A bank's decision to reduce operating costs by using a system which increases the risk that checks as to which there is an outstanding stop payment order will be paid invites liability when such items are paid.

We find this analysis, as well as that in *Delano, supra,* persuasive. We hold Parr described her check with reasonable accuracy, and Security National had a reasonable opportunity to act on the stop payment order.

We are aware of the burden this may place on Oklahoma banks. However, the industry has two alternatives to avoid liability if banking procedures necessitate an exact description of an item: (1) notify the customer at the time a stop order is given, or (2) seek a legislative amendment to § 4–403.

We recognize Parr received the benefit of having her debt paid to Champlin Oil and will recover from Security National for failure to stop payment. To avoid this possibility of unjust enrichment, § 4–407(b) subrogates the payor bank [Security National] to the rights of the payee [Champlin] against the maker [Parr]. In such a suit, an award of attorney's fees and costs to Security National would be proper under 12 O.S.1981 § 936, as Champlin would have been suing Parr on an open account if Security National had stopped payment on the check.

Trial court is reversed and this cause remanded for award of $972.96 plus reasonable attorney's fees and costs consistent with this opinion.

Reversed and remanded.

[Some footnotes omitted.]

Notes

1. Several states have amended section 4–403(1) to require some specificity when a customer issues a stop payment order. California and a few other states require that the check be described with "certainty." Utah provides that the order must "be in writing specifically describing the check ordered stopped." The District of Columbia requires that the drawer state "the amount, date and payee" of the check.

2. The State Bank & Trust Company deposit agreement supra page 1258 contains the following terms regarding stop payment orders:

> "A written stop order * * * will be valid upon delivery to the Bank. You must inform the Bank of the exact amount of the item, the number of the check and the number of the account; otherwise the computer may not pick up the stop order. If the information given to the Bank is not correct, or if you fail to give it any other reasonable information requested regarding the item, the Bank will not be responsible if it is unable to stop payment."

Would this provision be binding on the Bank's customers?

3. Under radical truncation, as discussed earlier, the check is destroyed by the depositary bank and only MICR information is passed on to the payor bank. Under that system, the payor bank could only look for the amount and number of checks which its customers order stopped. The name of the payee and the date of the check would not be passed on to the payor bank. Should a payor bank be obligated to check more than the MICR information in such cases? If so, how could a radical

truncation system be modified to insure that customers' stop orders are actually carried out?

4. Suppose a bank allows a customer to check a certain box on the deposit contract if that customer wishes the bank to search for the name of the payee as well as the check amount. May the bank raise the fee for stopping a check to all of its customers for the added expense it will incur for customers using that option?

Problem 27–5

After writing a check in the amount of $800, Bittner has second thoughts and contacts Town Bank about the possibility of stopping payment. A Bank employee informs Bittner that a stop payment cannot be submitted until the Bank opens the following morning. Bittner then discusses with the employee the possibility of deliberately withdrawing enough money so that there will not be sufficient funds to cover the check in question. After the employee indicates that in those circumstances the check would not be paid, Bittner draws his account down to $200. If Town Bank pays the check anyway, may it sue Bittner to recover the amount of the overdraft?

Even if a stop order is proper, the bank may refuse to recredit and argue that the customer has not established a loss resulting from the payment of the item under UCC 4–403(3). The bank may also defend on the ground that it is subrogated to the rights of a party on the check against the drawer (see UCC 4–407). To a certain extent UCC 4–403(3) and 4–407 fulfill the same function. If there is no causal connection between the bank's failure to follow a stop order and the customer's injury, either of those sections will protect the bank from liability to its customer. As the following case discloses, the exact meaning of UCC 4–403(3) and its relationship to UCC 4–407 is unclear.

THOMAS v. MARINE MIDLAND TINKERS NATIONAL BANK

New York Supreme Court, New York County, 1976.
86 Misc.2d 284, 381 N.Y.S.2d 797.

EGETH, J.

Plaintiff has commenced this action to recover the sum of $2,500 from the defendant bank, claiming that defendant wrongfully paid a check drawn against his account after receiving a proper and timely stop payment order.

FACTS PROVEN ON TRIAL

The following material facts have been proven upon trial:

On Dec. 8, 1973, plaintiff entered into agreement to purchase two rugs from one Ralph Gallo for a price of $10,500. A $2,500 deposit was given by delivery of a postdated check, No. 221, dated Dec. 10, 1973, and drawn upon plaintiff's account at the defendant bank's 140 Broadway, N.Y.C. branch. Plaintiff agreed to pay the balance of the purchase price, to wit: $8,000, by Dec. 30, 1973, and took the smaller rug home that day. At opening, on Dec. 10, 1973, plaintiff went to the branch of defendant bank where his account was maintained, spoke to an officer, Kenneth Hurley, with whom he had prior business relations, and directed that payment be stopped upon the subject check. All required information was correctly given, (except the check was described as No. 222 rather than No. 221, the correct number), and a stop payment memo was issued by the bank. On the afternoon of the next day, Dec. 11, 1973, the check was presented for payment at the very same branch, and it was cashed. Thereafter, plaintiff's account was debited the $2,500 paid on the check. The same day, without knowledge that the check had been cashed, plaintiff telephoned Gallo, told him the contract was rescinded, and asked him to pick up his rug. Two or three days later, the rug was picked up at plaintiff's apartment. Plaintiff had no knowledge that the check had been cashed until he received his January bank statement. He called Gallo demanding return of the $2,500. The request was refused with an indication that Gallo might seek to enforce the purchase agreement. The defendant bank rejected plaintiff's request to restore the $2,500 to his account. At present plaintiff has no rug in his possession nor does he have his $2,500.

During his cross-examination, plaintiff acknowledged the accuracy of the following question and answer in the transcript of his pretrial deposition: "Q. Mr. Thomas, from what you have told us, I believe you testified that you breached your agreement with Mr. Gallo, based upon information which Mr. Meli had given you, is that true? A. This is essentially correct." This question and answer was admitted into evidence over objection solely for impeachment or potential impeachment purposes. It was not received as evidence in chief proving plaintiff's breach of the Gallo purchase agreement. This court does not consider this question which calls for a legal conclusion from a lay witness to be any probative proof of the fact of such breach, or proof of non loss.

Propriety of Stop Order & Payment

UCC § 4–403(1) explicitly provides:

> "A customer may by order to his bank stop payment of any item payable for his account but the order must be received at such time and in such manner as to afford the bank a reasonable opportunity to act on it prior to any action by the bank with respect to the item described in Section 4–303."

It is undisputed that a detailed direction was given to the defendant to stop payment on the check in question (except for a single digit mistake on the check number), the order was confirmed in writing early in the morning, and the subject check was paid at the very same branch in the afternoon of the following day. Under these circumstances, I find that adequate notice and a reasonable opportunity was given to the bank, and that it must be held accountable for its act in making payment of the check in contravention of the stop payment order. A day and one half is more than reasonable notice to enforce a stop order on a check presented at the very same branch, and payment of the item by the bank thereafter constitutes a breach of its obligations to honor the stop order. The normal problem of reasonable computer lag when dealing with a great number of other branches of a large bank has no relevancy to the facts at bar, where all transactions occurred in a single branch. The single digital mistake in describing the check in the stop order is deemed trivial, and insignificant. Enough information was supplied to the bank to reasonably provide it with sufficient information to comply with the stop payment order. The bank is therefore held responsible for its act of improperly making payment upon the check.

Bank's Contentions

Defendant bank has virtually rested on plaintiff's case, in that no affirmative defense has been asserted or proved and no real evidence has been adduced by said defendant. The defendant contends that plaintiff has failed to prove a prima facie case in that no evidence was introduced in his case to negate the ultimate right of the payee of the stopped check to retain the proceeds thereof, or to exclude any right of set-off based upon the value of the rug returned to Gallo.

LEGAL ISSUE RAISED

The bank's trial strategy and its contentions raise legal questions not thus far clearly judicially determined under the Uniform Commercial Code as to the minimal requisites of a prima facie case in an action by a customer against his bank which failed to comply with a timely stop payment order. This issue appears to be complicated by apparent ambiguities and inconsistencies within and between § 4–403(1) and (3) and § 4–407 of the Uniform Commercial Code (Law Revision Commission Reports, 1954 Report, pp 320, 444–5; 1955 Report, Vol 2, pp 1238, 1555, 1560; 1956 Report, p 44).

PRE CODE LAW

Prior to the enactment of the Code, the case law was clear that a plaintiff customer was not required to prove any actual loss as part of his prima facie case against a bank which failed to comply with a timely stop payment order. He merely had to adduce facts proving wrongful payment over a proper stop order, and the amount taken from the account plus an absence of ratification by plaintiff. The defendant, however, was not precluded from proving in such action that plaintiff sustained no loss and thereby was being unjustly enriched as a means of defeating recovery but plaintiff was not compelled to litigate against a third party (payee) against his will as a precondition to the right to assert such an action against a malfeasant bank

QUESTIONS CREATED BY CODE PROVISIONS

In attempting to codify prior case law and make some changes, the current provisions of the Uniform Commercial Code create ambiguity, inconsistency, conflict and confusion. As a result no clear cut judicial determination has yet been made to harmonize the provisions, the statutory design and the realities of the practical commercial world.

The burden imposed upon the customer by UCC § 4–403(3) to establish the fact and amount of loss, which in literal terms might compel him to litigate the merits of his position in the underlying transaction between himself and the payee prior to seeking enforcement of his rights against the bank, would appear to be inconsistent with the overall policy expressed in subdivision (1) of this section of the Code that the depositor's right to stop payment is a service to which he is entitled without regard to any inconvenience or occasional loss to the bank, and such right need not be predicated on proof of sound legal grounds.

Furthermore, while in concept the thrust of the intent of UCC §§ 4–403(2) and 4–407 may appear to be consistent, there is a fundamental conflict on burden of proof. Whenever a bank debits its customer's account having improperly paid over a valid stop payment order, a question can arise as to whether the depositor sustained a real loss. This issue can arise by reason of the fact that the customer's liability on the item continues because the payee is a holder in due course or because the payee or holder has certain contractual rights on the underlying transaction which the bank can assert as a set-off to the claim of the customer. The conflict between these two provisions is whether the customer must establish as part of his prima facie case that he has a good defense against the payee or holder or whether the bank must prove the absence of true loss on the part of the customer by way of defense or counterclaim in the action (Law Revision Commission Reports, 1954 Report, pp 320, 444–5).

Post Code Decisions

Two post Code cases shed light upon the problem of what constitutes a prima facie case in an action such as the one at bar. In Cicci v. Lincoln National Bank (46 Misc2d 465 1965) a judge in the City Court of Syracuse had to deal with the problem without the benefit of the Court of Appeals' 1974 opinion in Sunshine v. Bankers Trust Co. (34 NY2d 404), which first raised the possibility of a distinction between establishing the fact and amount of loss and the duty or burden upon a defendant bank to come forward and adduce evidence showing non loss.

This distinction provides the means of a judicial construction of the statute which harmonizes the conflicts, ambiguities and apparently inconsistent purposes hereinabove referred to.

In Cicci the defendant interposed an affirmative defense of the nonexistence of any loss. The Cicci court examined the statute and its pre-enactment history, applied the facts submitted upon the motion for summary judgment before it, and determined that a trial was required on the issue of no loss raised by the answer. In so doing, the court relied upon the commentators and secondary authorities in support of its hypothesis that unless plaintiff was required to prove something beyond the amount debited from his account, UCC § 4–403[3], relating to the "burden of establishing" by plaintiff, would be rendered meaningless. That court however did not indicate what additional proof or quantum of proof it would require of a plaintiff to prove a prima facie case, nor did it discuss whether in seeking a construction to avoid a negation of meaning as to UCC § 4–403(3) it was in effect thereby rendering the premise of UCC § 4–403(1) meaningless.

With the benefit of the opinion of Judge Wachtler in Sunshine (supra), I follow a different route and come to a different conclusion than that reached by the Cicci court. I need not dwell upon the factual and procedural distinctions between Cicci and the case at bar by asserting in the instant case, unlike Cicci, we have a completed trial in which the defendant adduced no proof of any kind rather than the Cicci situation of a summary judgment motion in a case where the defendant's pleading claims the right to prove the absence of loss as an affirmative defense.

The Court of Appeals in Sunshine clearly states that a defendant bank exercising its subrogation rights created by UCC § 4–407 has the burden of coming forward and presenting evidence which would show an absence of actual loss sustained by a plaintiff depositor suing it for damages arising from an improper payment over a stop payment order. In so stating, the Court of Appeals has not negated plaintiff's ultimate burden of proof upon the issue of loss if the defendant comes forward with proof. The Court of Appeals has thereby provided a means of harmoniously construing §§ 4–403(1), 4–403(3) and 4–407 of the Uniform Commercial Code to effectuate the statutory intent and design.

This distinction between burden of proof and burden of coming forward is not uncommon. The immediate parallel which comes to mind is the shifting burden in a bailment case where the mechanism of proof is quite similar. To restate the principle as applied to the case at bar, if the bank fails to meet its burden with legally sufficient proof of non loss, the customer has proven a prima facie case and is entitled to judgment. Where the burden of going forward is met by the bank, the customer must sustain the ultimate burden of proof on the issue of loss.

It should be noted parenthetically, that the holding in Sunshine radically departs from the long established common law requirement of payment as a condition precedent to the acquisition and exercise of subrogation rights. At bar, this would have permitted defendant, notwithstanding the absence of the mechanical act of crediting plaintiff's account (payment), to assert any rights of Gallo, the payee of the check, as a subrogee pursuant to UCC § 4–407. Such subrogated rights could have been appropriately asserted by the bank to establish non loss or lesser loss.

Conclusion at Bar

In this case, the defendant bank chose to try its case against the plaintiff alone without asserting any affirmative defense as to non loss, or adducing any evidence to negate the claimed loss at trial. No attempt was made to implead any other party from whom the defendant might acquire subrogated rights, to vouch any such party into the action, or to commence its own action against such party and thereafter move for a single consolidated trial. The defendant bank chose rather to maintain a position that plaintiff was required to come forward with evidence as to the underlying transaction to negate any inference of non loss or lesser loss in order to prove plaintiff's prima facie case.

As previously stated the bank's position in this regard is in error under the law existing before and after the enactment of the Code. Therefore plaintiff has proven his prima facie case and defendants' motion to dismiss on that ground must be denied. Plaintiff has not defeated defendant's subrogation rights which still remain viable notwithstanding any disposition herein. The merits of any outstanding dispute arising out of the contract between payee Gallo and plaintiff has not been determined in this case inasmuch as no proof has been adduced by any party on this issue. Therefore, the doctrine of collateral estoppel would not bar assertion of a future claim based thereon.

Plaintiff's good faith act of surrendering possession of the rug to the payee after giving defendant a stop payment order, and his assumption of compliance therewith by the defendant, is understandable and reasonable. Unless done without good faith, such surrender certainly may not defeat defendant's statutory accountability under UCC § 4–403(1) for failure to comply with a proper stop order. The existence of defendant's subrogation right to stand in the shoes of the payee (UCC § 4–407[b]) does not negate the obligation of the subrogee bank to come forward with some evidence in support of any such claimed right. In this case defendant chose not to do so. Defendant therefore failed to produce any evidence to negate plaintiff's prima facie case.

Under such circumstances, there are no issues of fact to be determined regarding plaintiff's failure to meet his burden of establishing the fact and amount of loss under UCC § 4–403(3) because of the defendant's failure to come forward with anything which controverts plaintiff's prima facie showing of loss.

Decision

Accordingly, defendant's motions are denied and plaintiff is granted judgment against the defendant in the sum of $2,500 together with interest, costs, and disbursements as demanded in the complaint.

This constitutes the decision of the court pursuant to C.P.L.R. 4213(b).

Notes

1. Is the decision in *Thomas* consistent with the actual language of section 4–403(3)? What possible meanings can be given to that provision?

2. Assume you are counsel for a bank that has paid over a proper stop order of one of its customers. What kind of evidence would you have to present to a court to satisfy the burden of production required by *Thomas?*

Problem 27–6

Upon discovering that it has paid over a valid stop order of Feldman, its customer, Regional Bank refuses to recredit and argues that the check was properly payable and that it was subrogated to the payee's rights against Feldman. During the ensuing litigation assume that Feldman loses $1,000 interest that he would have earned if the funds had been recredited. If Feldman ultimately wins, can he recover the $1,000 for the use of the money in the interim?

SECTION 5. WRONGFUL DISHONOR

Section 4–402 sets out the payor bank's liability for its wrongful dishonor of checks. That section reads as follows:

> A payor bank is liable to its customer for damages proximately caused by the wrongful dishonor of an item. When the dishonor occurs through mistake liability is limited to actual damages proved. If so proximately caused and proved damages may include damages for an arrest or prosecution of the customer or other consequential damages. Whether any consequential damages are proximately caused by the wrongful dishonor is a question of fact to be determined in each case.

The bank's liability for wrongful dishonor is the converse of the bank's liability for paying checks not properly payable. Comment 2 to UCC 4–402 explains in part:

> "Wrongful dishonor" excludes any permitted or justified dishonor, as where the drawer has no credit extended by the drawee, or where the draft lacks a necessary indorsement or is not properly presented.

Typically wrongful dishonor occurs as the result of bookkeeping errors, a computer error, a charge to the wrong account or the like. It may also occur when the bank improperly exercises a set-off against the customer's account, recognizes third party claims or fails to follow an agreement to pay overdrafts.

Identification of the type and amount of damages the plaintiff may recover in a UCC 4–402 case is a most difficult problem. Under pre-Code law a "trader" (businessman) could recover substantial compensation without proof of actual damage. In theory the bouncing of a check might cause considerable doubt about the financial integrity of a businessman and cause him to lose substantial good will, and yet he might be unable to prove the amount of his loss with any degree of certainty. Because of this difficulty of proof and the public policy of deterring banks from improper dishonor of checks, traders were theoretically allowed liberal recoveries without proof of actual damage. Comment 3 to UCC 4–402 states that the section "rejects" the trader rule but it is perhaps more accurate to say that the section narrows the rule. See White and Summers pp. 670–74.

What kinds of damages can one suffer as a result of a wrongful dishonor? In Loucks v. Albuquerque Nat'l Bank, 76 N.M. 735, 418 P.2d 191 (1966), the bank improperly set off $402.00 on a note and proceeded to bounce ten checks written by Loucks and Martinez. Because their checks bounced, the following happened: their supplier would deal only in cash; people who had previously accepted their checks now refused to do so; credit previously extended was denied; a salesman who had sold them a map for one of the checks that bounced ripped the map off their wall; and Loucks complained of an ulcer and had to miss work. Other cases show customers that complain of three years' lost profits, lost wages, illness, harassment, embarrassment, inconvenience and even jail sentences for passing bad checks. All of the above occurrences may be "proximately caused by the wrongful dishonor" and are subject to proof by the complaining customer.

Comment 5 tells us that the fourth sentence of UCC 4–402 rejects "decisions holding that as a matter of law the dishonor of a check is not the 'proximate cause' of the arrest and prosecution of the customer * * *" Presumably a customer whose check bounces is now entitled to recover any damages that he can convince the court or jury were proximately caused by wrongful dishonor of his checks, including emotional distress. In most cases, however, the plaintiff must prove "oppression, fraud or malice" or "evil motive" on the part of the bank to recover punitive damages. See White and Summers section 17–4. Who can recover under UCC 4–402? "Customers" of the bank, who may include shareholders and officers of an undercapitalized corporation which had issued no stock and where the officers were guarantors on obligations of the corporation owed to the bank. Kendall Yacht Corp. v. United California Bank, 50 Cal.App. 3d 949, 123 Cal.Rptr. 848 (1975). See UCC 4–104(1)(e); 1–201(28).

ANDREWS v. CITIZENS BANK

Court of Appeals of Georgia, 1976.
139 Ga.App. 763, 229 S.E.2d 501, rehearing denied October 4, 1976.

McMURRAY, JUDGE.

On or about Friday, November 1, 1974, Joe B. Andrews deposited approximately $1,600 in a joint checking account he still maintained with his ex-wife, Cynthia Andrews, in The Citizens Bank, Fort Valley, Georgia. Shortly before this he advised Gassett, a vice president of the bank, his intention to make this deposit and to immediately write a check on the account in the sum of $1,617.93 to the Farmers Mutual Exchange of Fort Valley. The sole purpose of making the deposit was to have sufficient funds ($1,693.46) to pay Farmers Mutual $1,617.93. On November 1, 1974, Cynthia Andrews, the former wife of Joe B. Andrews and the joint depositor in the checking account in question, learned by telephone that there were funds in the bank. The inference is that this occurred after Joe B. Andrews made his deposit.

On Monday, November 4, 1974, Cynthia Andrews entered The Citizens Bank and tendered two $600 checks to the teller for the purpose of obtaining cash. These checks were drawn on the joint checking account in question. There were sufficient funds in the account to pay the checks at the time they were tendered, but the $1,617.93 check had arrived by night depository which was opened on Monday, November 4, 1974, and credited to the Farmers Mutual Exchange account, but was not then posted against Joe B. Andrews' account.

The teller to whom Cynthia Andrews tendered the checks did not accept the checks but directed Cynthia Andrews to Mr. Gassett. There is conflicting evidence as to the conversation between the ex-Mrs. Andrews and Mr. Gassett, but she left the bank without the checks having been paid. However, the facts show that Mr. Gassett did tell her that if she would get Mr. Andrews to agree, he would cash the checks.

The following day Cynthia Andrews returned to the bank to again attempt to cash the checks, only to learn that the account then contained less than $100. The account had been reduced by the payment of the check to the Farmers Mutual Exchange drawn on the account by Joe B. Andrews. This check had been in the night depository over the weekend but was not posted to the Andrews' account until the night of November 4, 1974. Gassett contends he acted in reliance on his prior commitment to honor the Farmers Mutual check, and that he so advised Mrs. Andrews, even though he was not aware that the check had arrived at that time.

Cynthia Andrews sued the bank and certain of its employees, individually and as its agents, including Gassett. Plaintiff alleges defendants' failure to pay the check was a wrongful dishonor as defined by Code Ann § 109A–4–402 (Ga.L. 1962, pp. 156, 303), and she seeks to receive the $1,200 represented by the value of the checks and other damages.

Both parties moved for summary judgment. Plaintiff's motion was for summary judgment on the issue of liability and for the sum of $1,200 as the amount of funds wrongfully withheld by failure to cash the checks. Defendants moved for summary judgment as to all issues.

The court denied plaintiff's motion for summary judgment, determined that as a matter of law plaintiff is not entitled to recover the $1,200 represented by the checks, but otherwise denied defendants' motion. Plaintiff appeals from the order granting in part a summary judgment in favor of defendants and from the denial of her motion for summary judgment. Defendants cross appeal from the order granting only a partial summary judgment in favor of the defendants. Held:

1. Generally, in the absence of statute or an express agreement to the contrary, withdrawals from a joint deposit in a bank require the authority of all the depositors. A joint deposit has been recently defined as follows: "When a deposit has been made or hereafter shall be made in a bank in the names of two persons, payable to either, or to either survivor, such deposit or any part thereof, and interest or dividend thereon may be paid to either of said persons or to their order, and the receipt or order of the party so paid shall be valid and sufficient release to discharge the bank from liability for payment. The foregoing right to pay either party shall not be terminated by the death or incompetency of the other party." Clearly, from the evidence here, the Andrews had a joint checking account with the defendant bank, payable to either.

2. As against its customer a bank may charge against his account any item which is otherwise properly payable from the account, even though the charge creates an overdraft. Code Ann. § 109A–4–401 (Ga.L. 1962, pp. 156, 303).

3. The party to whom presentment is made may without dishonor require exhibition of the instrument and reasonable identification of the person making presentment. See Code Ann. § 109A–3–503(1) (Ga.L. 1962, pp. 156, 270).

4. Acceptance may be deferred without dishonor until the close of the next business day following presentment, but the holder may in a good faith effort to obtain acceptance and without dishonor of the instrument, allow postponement of the acceptance for an additional business day. Code Ann. § 109A–3–506(1) (Ga.L. 1962, pp. 156, 271).

5. Payment of an instrument may also be deferred without dishonor pending reasonable examination to determine whether it is properly payable, but payment must be made in any event before the close of business on the day of presentment. Code Ann. § 109A–3–506(2), supra.

6. Generally, under a bank's liability to a customer, plaintiff would be entitled to recover proximate damages caused by defendants' wrongful dishonor of her checks. See Code Ann. § 109A–4–402 (Ga.L. 1962, pp. 156, 303). Plaintiff argues that she was deprived of the $1,200, represented by the two checks, by defendants' wrongful dishonor of those checks and that she should therefore receive judgment for $1,200. Plaintiff was not deprived of this $1,200, as the $1,200 represented by the two checks was paid on a check drawn by plaintiff's joint depositor. This extinguished the obligation of the bank in regard to this sum. Items may be accepted, paid, certified or charged to the indicated account of a bank's customer in any order convenient to the bank. See Code Ann. § 109A–4–303 (Ga.L. 1962, pp. 156, 302).

The evidence here presented on summary judgment simply disclosed a joint checking account of a former husband and wife, and that a prior commitment had been made by the bank to accept a check payable to the Farmers Mutual Exchange of Fort Valley in the amount of $1,617.93. The vice-president of the bank arranged with the depositor, Joe B. Andrews, for the deposit of sufficient funds to create a balance of $1,693.46 to pay this check. This occurred on Friday, November 1, 1974. On Monday, November 4, 1974, this check had been deposited for collection, and the bank was authorized to accept this check in payment before paying the checks drawn by the plaintiff, Mrs. Cynthia Andrews. The court did not err in granting summary judgment in favor of the defendants with respect to the $1,200 sought by the plaintiff and represented by the two checks which the bank refused to pay on the 4th and dishonored for insufficient funds on November 5, 1974.

7. Under the uncontested evidence submitted, as well as the law set forth above, no claim for damages is shown by reason of the bank accepting the check for $1,617.93 drawn in favor of the Farmers Mutual Exchange of Fort Valley prior to dishonor of the two $600 checks submitted by the plaintiff. The account contained insufficient funds when these checks were accepted on November 5, 1974, and were dishonored for insufficient funds. The court erred in refusing to grant summary judgment in favor of the defendants, granting in lieu thereof merely a partial summary judgment.

Judgment affirmed in case No. 52426 and reversed in case No. 52427. MARSHALL and SMITH, JJ., concur.

Notes

1. Was Cynthia Andrews simply trying to pull a fast one on her former husband or did her husband and the bank conspire to deprive her of her rightful claim? Might this depend upon one's judgment about Farmers' Mutual's claim to the original deposit? Does the court hold that the husband's check was orally "accepted"?

2. To pose the question more starkly, assume that Joe Andrews had had the conversation described in the case with the bank officer and then deposited the check in his account. It had been finally paid and the funds had remained in the account for five days. If Cynthia had come to the bank during these five days and demanded the funds, would the bank have had to pay her?

NORTHSHORE BANK v. PALMER

Texas Court of Civil Appeals, 1975.
525 S.W.2d 718.

BROWN, J. James T. Palmer (Palmer or appellee) brought suit against Northshore Bank (Bank or appellant) for the wrongful dishonor of several checks. Trial was to a jury which answered special issues paraphrased as follows: (1) That someone other than Palmer endorsed his name on a $275 check; (2) That thereafter, Bank intentionally refused payment of checks written by Palmer; (3) That the bank attempted to collect an overdraft resulting from the chargeback against the account of the $275 check and insufficient check fund charges resulting from its dishonor of Palmer's checks after it knew or should have known that the endorsement was a forgery; (4) That Palmer had suffered actual damages of $2,000; (5) That Palmer was entitled to punitive damages of $3,500; and (6) That the dishonor of the checks was not a result of a mistake. A Tex.R.Civ.P. 301 motion for judgment notwithstanding the verdict or in the alternative to disregard the answer to special issues four and five was filed by the Bank. The trial court overruled this motion and entered judgment for Palmer for $5,500.

Liability for the wrongful dishonor of an item is governed by Tex.Bus. & Com. Code § 4.402 (UCC 1968) which provides:

> "A payor bank is liable to its customer for damages proximately caused by the wrongful dishonor of an item. When the dishonor occurs through mistake liability is limited to actual damages proved. If so proximately caused and proved damages may include damages for an arrest or prosecution of the customer or other consequential damages. Whether any consequential damages are proximately caused by the wrongful dishonor is a question of fact to be determined in each case."

Appellant attacks the submission and answers to the special issues on damages. Its attack on the actual damages contends that the trial court erred in overruling its Rule 301 motion. The answer to special issue number four is attacked on a factual sufficiency basis as well. In connection with this issue the jury was instructed as follows:

> "In connection with this issue you are instructed that you may take into consideration for finding actual damages the sum of money, if any, not repaid to James T. Palmer by Northshore Bank after Northshore Bank charged the check, payable in the amount of $275.00, dated October 18, 1971, marked as Pltf's. Ex. 1 against his account, the damage to the credit and reputation of James T. Palmer, if any, mental anguish suffered by James T. Palmer, if any, the time lost by James T. Palmer from his employment and schooling, if any, on the occasion or occasions in question."

Appellant did not object to the instruction. Tex.R.Civ.P. 274. The gist of its argument with regard to the 301 motion is that the "actual damages" were established conclusively as to two of the elements: (1) the sum of money not repaid to Palmer after the charge-back and (2) the loss of time from employment and schooling. The Bank claims there was no evidence as to mental anguish or damage to credit and reputation. Given the lack of objection to the instruction in this case, loss of credit and mental anguish were properly considered here as "consequential" damages.

There was testimony by Palmer that he had lost approximately one week of time from school and work. At the time the Bank dishonored the checks,

Palmer was in the process of becoming certified as a pipe welder. There was oral and documentary evidence as to the approximate salary he was making at that time. There was also testimony by an officer of the bank as well as bank records to show that in addition to the charge-back of the $275 forged instrument, Palmer was charged $15 for checks drawn on insufficient funds. This was supplemented by evidence of humiliation, embarrassment and of having been turned down for credit for the first time in his life. Given this evidence, the trial court did not err in overruling the Rule 301 motion. Further, after reviewing the entire record under appropriate standards, we believe that there was factually sufficient evidence to support the jury's finding on actual damages.

Appellant cites State Nat. Bank of Iowa Park, Tex. v. Rogers, 89 S.W.2d 825 (Tex.Civ.App—Fort Worth 1935, no writ), as authority for the proposition that a depositor may not recover exemplary damages for wrongful dishonor. This case was decided before the enactment of § 4.402, supra, and is not applicable. The authors of the code did not attempt to specify whether the bank's liability sounds in contract or tort. See Comment 2 to § 4.402, supra. We think that the liability is "statutory" and more in the nature of tort than contract. The jury did not find that the dishonors were the result of a "mistake" which would have limited appellee to recovery of his *actual* damages only. In the instant case, unlike State Nat. Bank of Iowa Park, Tex. v. Rogers, supra, actual damages were established. Gustason v. Northeast National Bank, 486 S.W.2d 596 (Tex.Civ.App—Fort Worth 1972, no writ), seems to be the only Texas case decided since the Legislature enacted § 4.402, supra. Although mental anguish and exemplary damages were not involved in the case, the court by way of dicta cited 8 Tex.Jur.2d Banks § 261 to the effect that:

> "[d]amages may be recovered for loss of time, money, and credit, provided a foundation for such recovery is laid by the pleadings, but not otherwise. But exemplary damages based on malice or damages for mental suffering are not recoverable."

In addition to this statement being dicta, the case is distinguishable on at least two grounds. First, the court did not consider the full impact of § 4.402 since the court merely sustained an attack on a summary judgment in favor of the bank and the allowable elements of damages were not before it. Second, all of appellant's attacks here are based upon claimed evidentiary deficiencies and not upon any improper elements being submitted to the jury. No objections to the issues were made on the basis that the issues submitted elements of damages which were not recoverable under the statute. The jury found, and appellant does not attack the finding, that the acts of dishonoring the checks were done intentionally. While there was no issue regarding a lack of good faith, appellant did not object to the lack of submission of such an issue. Tex.R.Civ.P. 274. The jury was instructed with regard to exemplary damages as follows:

> "In connection with this issue you are instructed that punitive damages may be recovered only where there has been oppressive conduct or a reckless or malicious disregard of the rights of another. Punitive damages are intended as a warning and an example to prevent the defendant and others from the commission of like offenses and wrongs. In a legal sense an unlawful act done willfully and purposely is, as against that person, malicious."

The issue of malice or reckless disregard of Palmer's rights, if supported in the evidence, must be deemed found in his favor. Tex.R.Civ.P. 279.

A forger had secured a number of printed checks of one Marvel Fikes and proceeded to include Palmer as one of his victims. A person showed up at the

Bank seeking to cash the $275 check payable to Palmer. The teller ascertained that Palmer had an account with the Bank and paid out the money. She could not testify as to whether this person was or was not Palmer. Some four or five days later, the check was returned by the bank on which it was drawn because the signature was not like the signature of Fikes which it had on file. The checks written by Palmer, which are in question here, had already been paid by the Bank, when the situation with respect to the forgery became known to it. The officer in charge immediately charged Palmer's account with the forged check despite his protestations that his endorsement was a forgery. When he went to see the Bank officer to deny endorsement and receipt of the proceeds of the forged check, the officer called over a uniformed guard. Even though the checks had been cleared for payment and were covered by sufficient funds when presented, the Bank recalled them and returned them marked "paid in error" or "account closed." Palmer immediately reported the forgery to the police, contacted the bank on which the forged Fikes check was drawn, and contacted Mr. and Mrs. Fikes. He then underwent the embarrassment of calling on each of the payees of the dishonored checks. The Bank never relented. They charged appellee $5 for each check they considered drawn on "insufficient funds". Additionally, after all of the claims of Palmer were known to the Bank officer having charge of the matter, the Bank placed the claimed balance due in the hands of a collection agency, where it rests today. The Bank never has paid Palmer the $275 which under the jury's findings is wrongfully charged to his account. Under the Bank's own evidence, each step it took was deliberate and intentional and done with a knowledge of Palmer's claim of right. The exemplary damages found by the jury are reasonably related to the amount of actual damages found and are fully justified under the evidence. We overrule appellant's points attacking special issue number five and the answer of the jury thereto.

The case is affirmed.

Problem 27–8

Markey has been a customer of National Bank for 10 years. Since Markey is well known at the Bank and has an excellent reputation in the business community, National has always paid Markey's overdrafts. In the past two years, the Bank has covered such checks on 18 occasions. Without notice that its policy had changed, National bounced one of Markey's checks. Will Markey be successful in a suit for wrongful dishonor?

Problem 27–9

Windsurfing Club Sales & Service Inc. (WCSS) operated the business on land owned by Windsurfing Club Inc., a different corporation, although similarly named. WCSS maintains a checking account with State Bank. On May 11, 1984, at a time when there was $5,000 in the WCSS account, State Bank is served with a sheriff's notice and writ of execution which names Windsurfing Club, Inc. as the judgment debtor. That same day State Bank puts a hold on WCSS's account pending clarification that WCSS is the entity named in the writ. WCSS is not notified of the hold on its account. On May 20, 1984, WCSS deposits $15,000 into the account. On May 21, 1984, WCSS draws a series of checks on its account totalling $12,000. Since WCSS's account is on hold, State Bank bounces the checks. On May 28, 1984, the hold is removed when the bank learns that Windsurfing Club, Inc. and WCSS, Inc. are two separate entities. WCSS then brings an action for wrongful dishonor seeking compensatory and punitive damages. What result?

SECTION 6. THE JOINT ACCOUNT

Because of its peculiar characteristics, the joint account poses special problems involving the bank-customer relationship. Absent language in the deposit contract to the contrary, any party to a joint account has the right to withdraw the entire amount. This is true even if the money in the account was initially owned by only one of the parties. In Michigan there is a presumption that a joint account is owned in equal percentage by the joint depositors. Nevertheless, each party still has the power to liquidate the entire fund. Thus, the joint account brings with it apparently inconsistent rights.

While the UCC does not specifically deal with joint accounts, Arizona, California, Florida and Nevada have amended section 4–403(1) to address this subject. The California provision states:

> "(1) A customer, or any customer if there is more than one, or any person authorized to sign checks or make withdrawals thereon may stop payment of any item payable for or drawn against such customer's or customers' account but the bank may disregard the same unless the order is in writing, is signed by such customer or authorized person, decribes with certainty the item on which payment is to be stopped, and is received by the bank in such time and in such manner as to afford the bank a reasonable opportunity to act on it prior to the happening of the events described in section 4303."

In other states one must look to the common law to deal with such problems. In Williams v. Cullen Center Bank & Trust, 685 S.W.2d 311 (Tex.1985), the court held that absent a provision in the deposit agreement to the contrary, a joint signer of an account will not be held liable for an overdraft solely on the basis of that person's signature on the account card. Where the nonsigner benefited from the overdraft, participated in creating the overdraft or ratified the transaction, however, the nonsigner may be liable. See also United States Trust Co. of New York v. McSweeney, 91 A.D.2d 7, 457 N.Y.S.2d 276 (1982); Cambridge Trust Co. v. Carney, 115 N.H. 94, 333 A.2d 442 (1975).

Problem 27–10

Aaron and Kathy O'Donnell have a joint checking account with Midland Savings Bank. At the time the account was opened, each signed a signature card giving each the power to draw checks on the account.

1. Aaron writes a $6,000 check for a new car, but Kathy decides they don't need the car and stops payment on the check. Must the bank follow her order?

2. Kathy writes a $1,000 check to give to her exhusband Kelly for his birthday. Aaron neither knows nor would approve of such a gift. The O'Donnells only have $200 in their account at that time, but the bank pays. Is Aaron jointly and severally liable for the overdraft?

3. Assume the same facts as in 2. except that the check Kathy writes is for new living room furniture.

4. Would your answers to 2. or 3. be different if Kathy had been the only one writing checks on the account since it opened?

Joint accounts can also create difficulties with respect to a bank's right of setoff. The act of setoff occurs when a deposit owed by the bank to a depositor is netted against the debt owed by the depositor to the bank. One can argue that when the bank owes a debt to several parties on a joint account, and only one of these parties owes a debt to the bank, lack of "mutuality" prevents the bank from setting off. Mutuality is the requirement that the coexisting claims must be between the same parties. Assuming that the mutuality problem does not prevent setoff entirely, what part of the account can be setoff? Since the debtor could have withdrawn the entire amount, one could argue that the entire fund can be properly setoff. On the other hand, one can also argue that a presumption about ownership of the account should be applied.

To avoid the above problems, a bank may want to draft a deposit contract for joint accounts quite carefully. But may the bank draft these contracts with the purpose of increasing its right of setoff?

CHICKERNEO v. SOCIETY NATIONAL BANK OF CLEVELAND

Supreme Court of Ohio, 1979.
58 Ohio St.2d 315, 390 N.E.2d 1183.

PAUL W. BROWN, JUSTICE. The nature of a bank's right to setoff was described by this court in Bank v. Brewing Co. (1893), 50 Ohio St. 151, at pages 158–159, 33 N.E. 1054 at page 1055, as follows:

> It is said to be a well-settled rule of the law merchant that a bank has a general lien on all the funds of a depositor in its possession for any balance due on general account, or other indebtedness contracted in the course of their dealings, and may appropriate the funds to the payment of such indebtedness. The right to make such appropriation, it is held, grows out of the relation of the parties, as debtor and creditor, and rests upon the principle that, 'as the depositor is indebted to the bank upon a demand which is due, the funds in its possession may properly and justly be applied in payment of such debt, and it has therefore a right to retain such funds until payment is actually made.' Falkland v. Bank, 84 N.Y. 145. Though this right is called a 'lien', strictly it is not, when applied to a general deposit, for a person cannot have a lien upon his own property, but only on that of another; and, as we have seen, the funds of general deposit in a bank are the property of the bank. Properly speaking, the right, in such case, is that of setoff, arising from the existence of mutual demands. The practical effect, however, is the same. The cross demands are satisfied, so far as they are equal, leaving whatever balance that may be due on either as the true amount of the indebtedness from the one party to the other.

* * *

Essential, then, to the validity of a setoff is that there be mutuality of obligation. Thus, in Nichols v. Metropolitan Life Ins. Co. (1941), 137 Ohio St. 542, 31 N.E.2d 224, this court stated in the syllabus that:

> A joint and survivorship account in a closed bank, in the absence of some special equity, may not be setoff against an indebtedness to the bank owed by one only of the payees of the joint account.

Only one of the payees (depositors) to the joint and survivorship account in *Nichols* was indebted to the bank, the same payee who sought the setoff. The account money had been furnished not by the indebted payee, but by the co-payee. Mutuality of obligation was therefore lacking and a setoff would have been improper.

Appellant contends that *Nichols* is dispositive of this action. His contention is essentially that the realities of ownership were such that appellant owned all the funds in the account; that the only obligations owed the bank were those of John A. Chickerneo, not of appellant; and that therefore mutual obligations between the bank and appellant or the bank and John A. Chickerneo necessary to justify a setoff were nonexistent.

We would be inclined to agree with appellant, were it not for the fact that at the time the account was created, and at the time of the setoff, the bank had rules and regulations in effect governing accounts like appellant's. These rules and regulations must be considered in conjunction with the case law.

Appellee's rules and regulations relevant to this action provide as follows:

> 1. As used herein, the term 'bank' shall mean Society National Bank of Cleveland; the term 'depositor' shall mean the person or persons in whose name the account is carried on the books of the bank and shall include the masculine, feminine and neuter genders and the plural as well as the singular wherever the context so admits.
>
> * * *
>
> 15. Any indebtedness now or hereafter owing to the bank by a depositor, either individually or jointly, may be charged to any deposit account in the name of such depositor or in the name of such depositor and another or others.

The creation of a joint and survivorship account is a contractual arrangement. Rules and regulations adopted by the bank are, or become a part of, the contract between the bank and its depositors. The question thus presented is whether these particular rules and regulations allow the bank to do what it otherwise could not do under prior case authority, *i.e.*, to setoff John A. Chickerneo's obligations with the funds supplied solely by the appellant in the joint and survivorship account.

The rules and regulations are not difficult to understand. "Depositor" is defined as a person "in whose name an account is carried on the books." Since the joint and survivorship account in issue was carried in the name of appellant and John A. Chickerneo, both were "depositors." The rules and regulations provide further that any indebtedness owed the bank by a "depositor" "may be charged" to an account "in the name of such depositor and another." Here the bank charged the account of the debtor-depositor, John A. Chickerneo, "and another," the appellant. Accordingly, the bank's actions were in conformity with the adopted rules and regulations, and thus lawful under the terms of the contract unless the rules and regulations were in conflict with the public policy of this state.

Public policy is a legal principle which declares that no one can lawfully do that which has a tendency to be injurious to the public welfare. The principle must be applied with caution and limited to those circumstances patently within the reasons upon which the doctrine rests.

Appellant has not persuaded this court that the circumstances before us are such that the public welfare will suffer if we allow these regulations to stand. The record shows that the appellant voluntarily opened an account with the bank and voluntarily selected a joint and survivorship account with John A. Chickerneo as a co-depositor. Other accounts were available at the bank which would not have subjected the appellant to a right of setoff. Under these circumstances, we will not interfere with the contract freely entered into by the parties.

For the foregoing reasons, this court holds, in agreement with the well-reasoned opinion of the Court of Appeals, that where a bank provides by rule, which rules becomes contractually binding on depositors, for the right to setoff funds in a joint and survivorship account against debts owed the bank by a party to the account, the bank may lawfully setoff such funds without violating the public policy of this state, although the funds in the account are supplied exclusively by a non-debtor depositor.

Accordingly, the judgment of the Court of Appeals is affirmed.

Judgment affirmed.

HERBERT, WILLIAM B. BROWN, SWEENEY and HOLMES, J.J., concur.

CELEBREZZE, C.J. and LOCHER, J., dissent.

CELEBREZZE, CHIEF JUSTICE, dissenting. R.C. 1101.06, which expresses the various purposes underlying the Chapters of the Revised Code which deal with banks and building and loan associations, clearly indicates that those statutory provisions seek to safeguard, among others, the interests of a depositor such as Andrew Chickerneo. For example, division (B) of that statute declares that one of the purposes of the referenced legislation is "[t]o provide for the protection of the interests of depositors, creditors, shareholders, and the general public in banks doing business in this state."

As the majority has noted in footnote No. 3 of its opinion, R.C. 1107.06, which deals with the subject of "deposits," specifies, in division (E), that by the acceptance of a "passbook the depositor acknowledges the receipt of and assents to the rules and regulations and any amendments thereto, adopted by the bank, governing such deposits." However, division (B) of the same statute also indicates that in handling funds such as those of the appellant, a bank is nevertheless required to "secure such deposits in the manner and to the extent provided or authorized by law * * *."

Furthermore, although a bank may promulgate various rules and regulations to govern a contractual relationship with its depositors, there are necessary limits to its rulemaking authority. In the second paragraph of the syllabus in Fourth & Central Trust Co. v. Rowe (1930), 122 Ohio St. 1, 170 N.E. 439, this court delineated the permissible scope of those rules and regulations by establishing the following caveat:

> The reasonable rules and regulations adopted by a savings bank and printed in its pass book, signed and agreed to by a depositor, form a contract between the bank and the depositor, and each is bound thereby, unless such rules and regulations are contrary to some positive rule of law or are against public policy.

The relevant inquiry, therefore, is not only whether those rules and regulations are contrary to public policy, as the majority has acknowledged, but whether they also conflict with "some positive rules of law." I agree that appellee's rules must be considered in conjunction with applicable case law and, as a result of that analysis, I find their application, in the record before us, contrary to established precedent encompassing the subject of joint and survivorship accounts. Accordingly, I must respectfully disagree with the conclusion that the mere existence of Rules 1 and 15 automatically authorizes appellee to do that which it could not do under prior case authority.

In Union Properties v. Cleveland Trust Co. (1949), 152 Ohio St. 430, 89 N.E.2d 638, this court held that in controversies concerning joint and survivorship accounts, which arise during the joint lives of the depositors, the "form of the deposit" is not determinative as to the respective interests of the joint depositors. The court indicated the following, at pages 434–435, 89 N.E.2d at page 641:

> In our opinion, in controversies like the present one involving the deposit and arising during the joint lives of the depositors, the form of the deposit should not be treated as conclusive on the subject of joint ownership and the door should be opened to evidence that the deposit was in truth made and maintained on a different basis. In other words, the "realities of ownership" may be shown.

See, also, Fecteau v. Cleveland Trust Co. (1960), 171 Ohio St. 121, 167 N.E.2d 890; Vetter v. Hampton (1978), 54 Ohio St.2d 227, 375 N.E.2d 804.

In *Union Properties, supra,* the facts revealed a joint account established in the names of both a husband and wife. The court concluded, however, that a creditor of the husband could not appropriate the funds in the account where the evidence established that the money was, in reality, the sole property of the wife. Or, as it has been paraphrased elsewhere, such a joint account is not subject to claims against the noncontributing party even though created with his consent. Hershey v. Bowers (1966), 7 Ohio St.2d 4, 6, 218 N.E.2d 455. Similarly, the funds in a joint and survivorship account cannot be used as a setoff against an indebtedness to the bank owed by only one of two depositors where the money was furnished solely by the other, non-debtor depositor and mutuality of obligation is lacking. Nichols v. Metropolitan Life Ins. Co. (1941), 137 Ohio St. 542, 31 N.E.2d 224.

The continued relevance of these legal principles is further evidenced by the previously mentioned obligation of R.C. 1107.06(B) that a financial institution "secure such deposits in the manner and to the extent provided or authorized by law * * *."

Thus, a perusal of the foregoing indicates that a depositor in a joint and survivorship account cannot be precluded, by rule or regulation, from establishing, by probative evidence, corresponding degrees of ownership in such an account before any summary seizure of its funds. Moreover, in light of *Union Properties, supra,* and *Nichols, supra,* it follows logically that a claim on that joint account can only be satisfied to the extent of a debtor-depositor's true or proven interest therein and only where there exists the requisite mutuality of obligation. *See, also,* People's Bank of Denton v. Turner (1936), 169 Md. 430, 182 A. 314.

The record in the present appeal describes the limited extent of John A. Chickerneo's participation in the joint account with his father as the placing of his name on the account and securing his signature on the required signature card. The passbooks that have been issued since the creation of the account on September 30, 1965, have, at all times, been kept in the exclusive control and possession of appellant, Andrew Chickerneo. Furthermore, the fifth paragraph of the stipulations of facts filed in the lower court clearly establishes the "realities of ownership" in this particular account:

> All of the funds deposited and/or withdrawn from the inception of the savings account until it was closed on August 8, 1973, belong solely to Andrew Chickerneo, and said John A. Chickerneo had no separate interest in and to said funds outside of any legal or equitable interest which may have been created by the nature of the account. (Emphasis added.)

It is the opinion of this writer that, to the extent that a construction and application of appellee's rules permit an automatic setoff from a joint account of a non-debtor depositor, simply because the debtor has been classified as a "depositor" by having his name placed on the account and the execution of a signature card, regardless of evidence unequivocally indicating the latter's total lack of ownership in those funds, they are contrary to established precedent, R.C. 1107.06(B), and thus proscribed by Fourth & Central Trust Co., *supra* (122 Ohio St. 1, 170 N.E. 439). Therefore, appellee would be precluded from asserting that appellant had previously bound himself to abide by the setoff because the rules permitting that action are contrary to law.

* * *

In light of the foregoing, I am not convinced that an application of the doctrine of "freedom of contract" is either dispositive of the issues presented on this appeal or brings about an equitable result. Accordingly, I must respectfully dissent from the judgment rendered herein.

LOCHER, J., concurs in the foregoing dissenting opinion.

Notes

1. In *Chickerneo* the court made it clear that absent the special contract rule, setoff would not have been allowed because of the absence of mutuality. Some courts find "mutuality" between individual debts and joint account obligations. In Burgess v. First National Bank of Salida, 31 Colo.App. 67, 497 P.2d 1035 (1972), the court allowed setoff on the basis of a statute and without regard for the respective ownership interests of the joint depositors. In *Burgess* the plaintiff was a joint depositor with one John Alle. The joint deposit account was created to be used as security for the plaintiff in a separate transaction between plaintiff and Allee. The defendant bank setoff to satisfy a loan made only to Allee and the plaintiff challenged the setoff. The court upheld the setoff under C.R.S. 1963, 14–3–6, which in connection with joint deposits, provides in part as follows:

> * * * [S]uch deposit shall be deemed, so far as the rights and liabilities of the bank are concerned, to be owned by said persons in joint tenancy with the right of survivorship, provided, the bank shall have the right of setoff against such deposit to the extent thereof to collect a debt owed to the bank by any joint depositor. * * *

2. The dissent in *Chickerneo* found that the form of deposit should not necessarily be determinative of whether setoff is to be allowed, but rather the "realities of ownership" may be shown. However, this raises the question how the "realities of ownership" are to be determined. Would it be proper for the court to look only to the percentage of the deposit account balance the debtor/depositor has furnished? For instance, if a working husband furnished all of the funds for joint account deposit, can he really be considered the sole owner of the deposit account to the exclusion of his home-making wife who has reared the children? In some states there is a presumption that a joint account is owned in equal percentage by the joint depositors. However, this presumption can be rebutted by evidence of different ownership intentions of the parties. *See* American National Bank and Trust v. Modderman, 37 Mich.App. 639, 195 N.W.2d 342 (1972).

3. As a matter of policy what right should a creditor of one joint depositor have against the deposit account? Because that depositor could himself withdraw the entire amount should the creditor be able to reach it? Should the courts look exclusively to the person who put the money in the account? Should the courts permit testimony by the joint depositor about their private understandings concerning the ownership of the account?

4. The State Bank and Trust Company deposit agreement contains the following provisions concerning joint accounts:

> "Each joint owner also authorizes the Bank to exercise setoff and enforce its security interest in the entire joint account, even though only one of the joint owners is the debtor; this right exists irrespective of who contributed funds to the joint account. Similarly, the Bank can enforce overdraft liability in the joint account against any joint owner individually."

Would this provision be valid when read in conjunction with *Chickerneo?* With *Williams v. Cullen Center Bank & Trust*?

CHAPTER TWENTY-EIGHT

THE CASHLESS SOCIETY: ELECTRONIC FUNDS TRANSFER

SECTION 1. INTRODUCTION

The volume of checks has grown by leaps and bounds—at an average rate of 7 percent annually. In 1945 the annual check volume was 5.3 million; by 1970 it had grown to 22.5 billion, and by 1980 to 45 billion. Government writes only 7 percent of all checks in the United States; business and consumers write the remaining 93 percent. More than half of these are written by the consuming public. Although checks written for more than $10,000 represent 80 percent of the dollar value of funds transferred by check, they constitute only 1 percent of all checks written annually. More than 50 percent of all written checks are for amounts of less than $50, a fact that contributes to the high cost of processing checks.

The cost of operating our present checking system grows daily. It costs an average of 20 cents to process each check. It is estimated that the total bill for handling all the checks in the United States exceeds $11 billion annually. Banks have managed to handle the current demand only by extensive use of computers, and unless some change occurs the additional demands which will be made on the system in the next decade will only increase the delays and aggravate the other flaws of the present system. Of course the possibilities for mis-sorting and losing checks or sending them to the wrong bank or having them stolen, forged and altered should be obvious from reading the foregoing chapters.

If it can be done, why should we not replace not only the collection process but the whole process of payment by check with a series of electronic impulses passed among computers which would read and process the orders and transfer the funds from bank to bank and from drawer to payee? Payment would be virtually instantaneous; the paper whirligig could be entirely dismantled, and banks could be left free to devote their time to other and presumably more fruitful ends.

The checkless society could take many forms, and there are probably some halfway points between our present system and the checkless society which would substantially alleviate the paper burden on the banks. For example, we might free the bank from its obligation to return cancelled checks to the drawer. This practice has existed in the United States for less than a century and is not followed in many banks abroad. Credit unions in the United States, who have offered checks only during the last decade, have never returned cancelled checks.

After several false starts we may now be moving toward the checkless society. Electronic Funds Transfer System (EFTS) is the umbrella term used to cover a multitude of systems and devices to transfer money. The systems service two markets: the high-volume, low-dollar consumer market and the low-volume, high-dollar commercial market.

SECTION 2. CONSUMER EFTS

A. *Point of Sale System*

A point of sale (POS) system is exactly what the name implies, an electronic system that is initiated at the place of a retailer making a sale of goods or services to an individual consumer. Retailers use POS terminology to describe internal computer systems hooked into "smart cash registers." Such systems may be used for inventory control, accounting systems, and marketing analysis. Such systems relate only to the transfer of information from the individual cash register to larger computer processing.

The POS system transfers funds at the time of consumer purchase from the consumer's bank account to the retailer's bank account. In the simplest version the consumer and merchant operate out of the same bank. At the time of purchase the consumer presents his plastic POS card to a computer terminal run by the merchant. If the sponsoring bank also operates automatic teller machines, it is likely the same card will operate both systems. The consumer types in a secret Personal Identification Number (PIN). At the same time the merchant types in the relevant cost information on the item to be purchased. The computer is linked to a computer at the bank, which checks the accuracy of the number and the status of the consumer's account. If all is in order, the bank debits the consumer's account, credits the retailer's account and sends a confirming message back to the terminal in the retail store. This is all done within seconds, completely by computer. The retailer's terminal prints a receipt for the consumer and the purchase is completed and paid for without checks, credit or cash.

By adding an independent switching center between the bank and the merchant, POS systems can be modified to include multiple merchants and various banks and so become accessible to a wider base of consumers.

Problem 28–1

While POS systems can result in a significant cost savings to banks, increased cash flow to merchants and convenience to consumers, acceptance of such systems has been very slow. Can you think of reasons each of these parties in a POS transaction might be hostile to adopting such a system?

If you were designing such a system, how might you address some of these concerns?

Problem 28–2

Boris walks into Rocky's Department Store and picks out a $3,000 computer. He gives the clerk his POS card and furnishes a PIN number. The bank signals the number is okay and Boris leaves with his purchase. The number turns out to be that of the wealthy attorney, Natasha, who never heard of Boris. Who bears the loss?

B. *Automatic Teller Machines*

Automatic teller machines (ATMs) are specially adapted computer terminals that perform many of the routine functions of bank tellers, such as taking deposits, granting withdrawals, making transfers among accounts and answering balance inquiries. Such machines are the most visible sign of the growth of electronics funds transfer systems. They can be found outside of banks, within the premises of retail merchants, and even in their own computer-locked structures.

The machines are activated by the consumer's inserting a plastic card into the ATM. The consumer then types on the ATM keyboard a personal identification number (PIN). After this, or some similar security measure is completed, the computer screen (similar to a television screen) asks the consumer what type of transaction he wishes to accomplish. The terminal is equipped with keys for putting in the PIN and dollar amounts involved in the transaction. ATMs are also outfitted with cash dispensers and a printer for receipts.

The terminal itself can either be on-line (hooked into the bank's main computer to debit or credit the consumer's account automatically) or off-line (where transactions are recorded on a computer tape and fed into the main computer at the end of the business day). On-line systems have the advantage that each account can be checked for overdrafts before dispensing cash on a withdrawal, but such systems are more costly to implement.

Although ATMs with their twenty-four hour service and multiple locations can be more convenient, there is still some consumer hostility to their impersonality. Consumers sense (quite correctly) that the main reason banks provide ATMs is to reduce transaction costs for the bank. One large New York bank discovered the extent of consumer hostility when it forced its small depositers to deal only with ATMs. The bank adopted a rule that all customers with accounts below a given dollar amount were not allowed to use human teller service for routine transactions. A competitor began to advertise its more human (humane?) services, and the policy was soon rescinded.

Banks have tried a variety of ways to humanize the machines and increase consumer acceptance. Direct phone links to the bank are often provided near the machines so the consumer can talk to a "real person" to report a malfunction. The ATM systems are also given names to make the computer seem less forbidding. Examples include Harvey Wallbanger, William Teller, the Wizard of Ease and even Jim.

The advent of EFTS technology brings with it new variations on old funds transfer problems. First, while computers may not make mistakes, the people around them do. Cash machines can record deposits or withdrawals when none are made. Without the written instrument to fall back on, proof problems compound the issue. If the bank computer says that a customer withdrew $100 from a certain machine on a certain date, how can a customer prove otherwise?

Problems need not be inadvertent. The same customer may deny making a withdrawal that he actually made. How can a bank distinguish among the customers who (1) made no withdrawal, or (2) made a withdrawal but forgot (3) made a withdrawal and are lying?

The thief need not be a customer. Who bears the loss if a bank card is stolen? Does the answer depend on how the thief got the PIN number? What about how long it takes the customer to realize the card is gone?

In the fall of 1978, Congress enacted Title IX of the Consumer Credit Protection Act, the Electronic Funds Transfer Act, which deals extensively with consumer electronic funds transfers. As a preliminary matter, one should be aware that the Act contains a substantial list of exclusions and that it does not govern the large dollar volume electronic funds transfers that occur between banks, and among banks and large business organizations.

Moreover, the federal act will override state law only to the extent that it is "inconsistent." It provides: "a state law is not inconsistent with this title if the protection such law affords any consumer is greater than the protection afforded by this title." Further to complicate the federal-state conflict, the federal law provides that states may be exempted from the federal rules if the Federal Reserve Board determines that the law of the state is substantially similar to the federal act. In any state which has enacted an electronic funds transfer law, lawyers will have to be careful to determine whether and to what extent the federal law has preempted that state law. Because the federal law explicitly defers in cases in which the state law is more generous to consumers, it is likely that any state with a comprehensive electronic funds transfer law will find that some of the federal rules apply to its transactions and some of the state rules apply. The extent to which a consumer will be able to pick parts of the federal and parts of the state law remains to be seen. The extent to which the Federal Reserve Board will defer to a state that has comprehensive electronic funds transfer law is equally uncertain.

Section 1693g sets out the basic rules of "consumer liability for unauthorized transfers." The student should read it with care. To see how the statute might govern in actual cases, consider the case that follows.

Question

One concern with the use of ATMs is losses by theft and fraud. One large system requires customers to insert their card, type in their PIN and then reinsert the card before any withdrawal can take place. Can you think of any way a thief could beat this system? The following cases demonstrate one; there are surely others.

OGNIBENE v. CITIBANK, N.A.

Civil Court of the City of New York New York County, 1981.
112 Misc.2d 219, 446 N.Y.S.2d 845.

MARA T. THORPE, JUDGE:

Plaintiff seeks to recover $400.00 withdrawn from his account at the defendant bank by an unauthorized person using an automated teller machine. The court has concluded that plaintiff was the victim of a scam which defendant has been aware of for some time.

Defendant's witness, an assistant manager of one of its branches, described how the scam works: A customer enters the automated teller machine (ATM) area for the purpose of using a machine for the transaction of business with the bank. At the time that he enters, a person is using the customer service telephone located between the two automated teller machines and appears to be telling customer service that one of the machines is malfunctioning. This person is the perpetrator of the scam and his conversation with customer service is only simulated. He observes the customer press his personal identification code into one of the two machines. Having learned the code, the perpetrator then tells the customer that customer service has advised him to ask the customer to insert his Citicard into the allegedly malfunctioning machine to check whether it will work with a card other than the perpetrator's. When a good samaritan customer accedes to the request, the other machine is activated. The perpetrator then presses a code into the machine, which the customer does not realize is his own code which the perpetrator has just observed. After continuing the simulated conversation on the telephone, the perpetrator advises the customer that customer service has asked if he would try his Citicard in the allegedly malfunctioning machine once more. A second insertion of the cards permits cash to be released by the machine, and if the customer does as requested, the thief has effectuated a cash withdrawal from the unwary customer's account.

Plaintiff testified that on August 16, 1981, he went to the ATM area at one of defendant's branches and activated one of the machines with his Citibank card, pressed in his personal identification code and withdrew $20.00. While he did this a person who was using the telephone between plaintiff's machine and the adjoining machine said into the telephone, "I'll see if his card works in my machine." Thereupon he asked plaintiff if he could use his card to see if the other machine was working. Plaintiff handed it to him and saw him insert it into the adjoining machine at least two times while stating into the telephone, "Yes, it seems to be working."

Defendant's computer records in evidence show that two withdrawals of $200.00 each from plaintiff's account were made on August 16, 1981, on the machine adjoining the one plaintiff used for his $20.00 withdrawal. The two $200.00 withdrawals were made at 5:42 p.m. and 5:43 p.m. respectively; plaintiff's own $20.00 withdrawal was made at 5:41 p.m. At the time, plaintiff was unaware that any withdrawals from his account were being made on the adjoining machine.

The only fair and reasonable inferences to be drawn from all of the evidence are that the person who appeared to be conversing on the telephone observed the plaintiff enter his personal identification code into the machine from which he withdrew $20.00 and that he entered it into the adjoining machine while simulating a conversation with customer service about that machine's malfunctioning. It is conceded in the testimony of defendant's assistant branch manager that it would have been possible for a person who was positioned so as to appear to be speaking on the telephone physically to observe the code being entered into the machine by plaintiff. Although plaintiff is not certain that his card was inserted in the adjoining machine more than twice, the circumstances indicate that it was inserted four times. No issue of fraud by plaintiff or anyone acting in concert with him has been raised by defendant. Having observed plaintiff's demeanor, the court found him to be a credible witness and is of the opinion that no such issues exist in this case.

The basic rights, liabilities and responsibilities of the banks which offer electronic money transfer services and the consumers who use them have been established by the federal legislation contained in 15 U.S.C.A. 1693 et seq., commonly called the Electronic Fund Transfers Act (EFT). Although the EFT Act preempts state law only to the extent of any inconsistency (15 U.S.C.A. 1693q), to date New York State has not enacted legislation which governs the resolution of the issues herein. Therefore, the EFT Act is applicable.

The EFT Act places various limits on a consumer's liability for electronic fund transfers from his account if they are "unauthorized." Insofar as is relevant here, a transfer is "unauthorized" if 1) it is initiated by a person other than the consumer and without actual authority to initiate such transfer, 2) the consumer receives no benefit from it, and 3) the consumer did not furnish such person "with the card, code or other means of access" to his account. 15 U.S.C.A. 1693a(11).

In an action involving a consumer's liability for an electronic fund transfer, such as the one at bar, the burden of going forward to show an "unauthorized" transfer from his account is on the consumer. The EFT Act places upon the bank, however, the burden of proof of any consumer liability for the transfer. 15 U.S.C.A. 1693g(b). To establish full liability on the part of the consumer, the bank must prove that the transfer was authorized. To be entitled to even the limited liability imposed by the statute on the consumer, the bank must prove that certain conditions of consumer liability, set forth in 15 U.S.C.A. 1693g(a) have been met and that certain disclosures mandated by 15 U.S.C.A. 1693c(a)(1) and (2) have been made. *Id.*

Plaintiff herein met his burden of going forward. He did not initiate the withdrawals in question, did not authorize the person in the ATM area to make them, and did not benefit from them.

However, defendant's position is, in essence, that although plaintiff was duped, the bank's burden of proof on the issue of authorization has been met by plaintiff's testimony that he permitted his card to be used in the adjoining machine by the other person. The court does not agree.

The EFT Act requires that the consumer have furnished to a person initiating the transfer the "card, code, or other means of access" to his account to be ineligible for the limitations on liability afforded by the Act when transfers are "unauthorized." The evidence establishes that in order to obtain access to an account via an automated teller machine, both the card and the personal identification code must be used. Thus, by merely giving his card to the person initiating the transfer, a consumer does not furnish the "means of access" to his account. To do so, he would have to furnish the personal identification code as well. See 12 C.F.R. 205.2(a)(1), the regulation promulgated under the EFT Act which defines "access device" as "a card, code or other means of access to [an] * * * account or any combination thereof" (emphasis added).

The court finds that plaintiff did not furnish his personal identification code to the person initiating the $400.00 transfer within the meaning of the EFT Act. There is no evidence that he deliberately or even negligently did so. On the contrary, the unauthorized person was able to obtain the code because of defendant's own negligence. Since the bank had knowledge of the scam and its operational details (including the central role of the customer service telephone), it was negligent in failing to provide plaintiff-customer with information sufficient to alert him to the danger when he found himself in the position of a potential victim. Although in June, 1981, after the scam came to defendant's attention, it posted signs in its ATM areas containing a red circle approximately 2½ inches in diameter in which is written "Do Not Let Your Citicard Be Used For Any Transaction But Your Own", the court finds that this printed admonition is not a sufficient security measure since it fails to state the reason why one should not do so. Since a customer of defendant's electronic fund transfer service must employ both the card and the personal identification code in order to withdraw money from his account, the danger of loaning his card briefly for the purpose of checking the functioning of an adjoining automated teller machine would not be immediately apparent to one who has not divulged his personal identification number and who is unaware that it has been revealed merely by virtue of his own transaction with the machine.

Since the bank established the electronic fund transfer service and has the ability to tighten its security characteristics, the responsibility for the fact that plaintiff's code, one of the two necessary components of the "access device" or "means of access" to his account, was observed and utilized as it was must rest with the bank.

For the foregoing reasons and in view of the fact that the primary purpose of the EFT Act and the regulation promulgated thereunder is the protection of individual consumers (12 C.F.R. 205.1(b)), the court concludes that plaintiff did not furnish his code to anyone within the meaning of the Act. Accordingly, since the person who obtained it did not have actual authority to initiate the transfer, the transfer qualifies as an "unauthorized" one under 15 U.S.C.A. 1693a(11) and the bank cannot hold plaintiff fully liable for the $400.00 withdrawal.

To avail itself of the limited liability imposed by the Act upon a consumer in the event of an "unauthorized" transfer, the bank must demonstrate 1) that the means of access utilized for the transfer was "accepted" and 2) that the bank has provided a way which the user of the means of access can be identified as the person authorized to use it. 15 U.S.C.A. 1693g(a) and (b). One definition of "accepted" under the Act is that the consumer has used the means of access. 15 U.S.C.A. 1693a(1). Both of the foregoing conditions of liability have been met here since plaintiff used the means of access to his account to withdraw the $20.00 and had been given a personal identification code.

Additionally, the bank must prove that it disclosed to the consumer his liability for unauthorized electronic fund transfers and certain information pertaining to notification of the bank in the event the consumer believes that an unauthorized transfer has been or may be effected. 15 U.S.C.A. 1693c(a)(1) and (2) and 1693g(b). Defendant did not establish that it made such disclosures to plaintiff. Accordingly, it is not entitled to avail itself of the benefit of the limited liability for unauthorized transfers imposed upon consumers by the Act.

For the foregoing reasons, judgment shall be for plaintiff in the sum of $400.00.

Notes

As a result of the position that it took in the case above and in the following case, namely that it had no liability to consumer who had been duped at one of its terminals, Citibank drew the attention of the Attorney General and received a good deal of bad publicity.

Is it the lawyer's responsibility to warn Citibank about the consequences of such litigation or to advise them about the wisdom of such unfavorable publicity?

Citibank is one of the most sophisticated banks in the country; it is currently the largest. Surely it did not decide to pursue these cases without thoughts about the consequences. Were you the executive at Citibank who made that decision, what factors would influence your decision and what specific information would you like to have from your lawyer to enable you to make it?

Problem 28–3

Cecil Consumer is very careful with the Bank Card and PIN for his account at First National Bank. He keeps the card in his wallet and the PIN he memorized and destroyed any written copies. His son, Benny, takes the card while dad is in the shower and withdraws $100.

1. Would it be an "unauthorized electronic funds transfer" if Benny learned the PIN as follows:

a) By watching Cecil withdraw money;

b) He was told the PIN by Cecil, who also said he was never to use the card.

c) He was told the PIN by Cecil who told him that it was only to be used in emergencies. Benny used the money to buy a skateboard. Would it matter if Benny's old skateboard had broken and Benny felt it was a "real emergency."

2. What if Benny didn't know the PIN but pressed in the letters of the name of their pet hamster, Ben? Cecil had been allowed to pick his own number and had picked the numbers corresponding to Ben's name to make it easier to remember.

3. If Dishonest John, Benny's friend took the card from Cecil is the case different?

Federal Reserve Regulation section 205.2(l) was promulgated to clear up ambiguities in the federal statute. Reconsider the problem in light of this Regulation.

> 12 CFR 205.2(l): "Unauthorized electronic fund transfer" means an electronic fund transfer from a consumer's account initiated by a person other than the consumer without actual authority to initiate the transfer and from which the consumer receives no benefit. The term does not include any electronic fund transfer (1) initiated by a person who was furnished with the access device to the consumer's account by the consumer, unless the consumer has notified the financial institution involved that transfers by that person are no longer authorized, (2) initiated with fraudulent intent by the consumer or any person acting in concert with the consumer, or (3) that is initiated by the financial institution or its employee.

Problem 28–4

Section 1693f deals with error resolution. Use it as an aid in answering the following problem:

1. Ishmel receives his bank statement on May 26, 1986. On June 24 he calls Seaman's Bank to complain that his statement shows five withdrawals of $75.00 each that he did not make. The clerk at the bank takes down all of the information from Ishmel and files it. The clerk also asks Ishmel to send a letter confirming his problem. Ishmel forgets to send a letter until January 13, 1987. When is Seaman's Bank responsible to report to Ishmel? Must it recredit his account? What are Ishmel's damages if Bank fails to act?

2. Suppose Bank promptly sent Ishmel a report showing the computer records that Ishmel withdrew the funds from an ATM in Nantucket. Ishmel doesn't believe the report. In fact, on the dates in question Ishmel was on a fishing trip in the Pacific. What can he do?

3. What if he was in Nantucket at the time, but still claims he did not make the withdrawals?

PORTER v. CITIBANK, N.A.

Civil Court of the City of New York, New York County, 1984.
123 Misc.2d 28, 472 N.Y.S.2d 582.

DECISION

EDWARD H. LEHNER, JUDGE:

To withdraw funds from your Citibank account at any time all you need do is place your card in their machine, enter your secret code, and then push a button. So the advertisement goes. But, complains the plaintiff, on two occasions this was done, no money was received, and yet his account was charged. Thus the Court is faced with another type of dispute between man and machine, for which no precedent has been found.

Plaintiff testified that on August 23, 1983 he sought to withdraw $100 from his checking account. When no money was dispensed from the machine after the necessary buttons were pushed, he reported the fact to a bank official who stated that the matter would be investigated. A few weeks later, on September

5, plaintiff took the requisite steps to make a $200 withdrawal. When no money appeared, he then repeated the process with the same result, which he thereupon reported to management. As a result of the foregoing plaintiff's account showed one withdrawal of $100 and two of $200 (for a total of $500), which amount he seeks to recover in this action.

The witnesses employed in the branch of the bank where the machine involved was located testified that in examining it on the day after the first of the two occurrences they found the account in balance, while on the latter date there was a cash overage of $90. They further indicated that, on the average, the cash machines were out of balance once or twice per week, but never for a sum in excess of $100.

Although no reported decision has been found dealing with this type of situation, *McEvans v. Citibank, N.A.*, 96 Misc.2d 142, 408 N.Y.S.2d 870 (Civil Ct., N.Y.Co., 1978) involved a somewhat analogous problem. There, a customer, who admitted failing to supply the bank with a deposit slip, claimed to have made a deposit by placing cash in an envelope in the cash machine. However, she received no credit because the bank denied receipt. The Court ruled in favor of the customer, but only because it found the bank negligent in failing to follow its own publicized procedures of having one person open the deposit envelopes, with a second employee observing the opening.

In *Employers Insurance of Wausau v. Chemical Bank,* 117 Misc.2d 601, 459 N.Y.S.2d 238 (Civil Ct., N.Y.Co., 1983), the undersigned was confronted with a situation where the plaintiff claimed to have made a deposit in the night depository for which the bank had no record. Believing the testimony of the plaintiff's witness, judgment was rendered in its favor through application of the rules of bailment. See also: *Judd v. Citibank,* 107 Misc.2d 526, 435 N.Y.S.2d 210 (Civil Ct., Queens Co., 1980) and *Ognibene v. Citibank,* 112 Misc.2d 219, 446 N.Y.S.2d 845 (Civil Ct., N.Y.Co., 1981); where bank customers who were tricked into permitting others to use their bank cards were granted recovery.

As indicated in the discussion in *Employers Insurance of Wausau v. Chemical Bank,* supra, a minority of the few courts in the nation that have considered the question have declined to grant a recovery against a bank solely on the testimony of a customer that a deposit was made. This reluctance is based on the fear of fraudulent suits against these public institutions. The policy underlying this view is illustrated by the dicta in *Roscoe v. Central National Bank of Canajoharie,* 96 Misc.2d 517, 521, 409 N.Y.S.2d 189 (Sup.Ct., Schenectady Co. 1978), where it was said that it would be "sheer folly" to "permit unrestrained and unlimited suits against banks simply on the bare assertion of an individual that he made a deposit. Without subsequent discovery, there would be no way of actually knowing whether the claimed deposit was in fact made, and in such a situation, fraught with limitless opportunities for fraud, banks should not be held answerable or liable."

However, the preferable majority view is to permit recovery where the Court is convinced that the deposit was in fact made and the bank could not explain its absence. Although the bailment presumptions applicable to night deposit cases cannot be said to be applicable to the opposite situation at bar where the claim is that the withdrawal was not received, the cases are pertinent in their holdings that a Court may give credence to testimony of an undocumented deposit. Similar to the night depository customer, who is not in a position to produce any documentary evidence to establish that he made the deposit, the cash machine customer can produce nothing to show that the money was not dispensed to him.

Here we are dealing with machines which defendant's witnesses acknowledged were out of balance one or two nights a week (although not to the extent involved in this case). Such witnesses also stated their belief that at times a subsequent machine customer received money properly belonging to the prior user of the machine. Plaintiff was a rather credible witness who had no record of banking problems although he had used the machines numerous times.

Under the circumstances, the Court holds that plaintiff established by a fair preponderance of the evidence that he did not receive the money for which he was charged as a result of the abovementioned transactions. Therefore, he is entitled to judgment for $500, plus interest from September 5, 1983.

In so deciding the Court is not unmindful of the possibility of fraudulent suits. However, this fear exists in many areas of the law and the history of jurisprudence has not indicated that Courts have been unable to competently (although certainly not perfectly) deal with such challenges.

Notes

1. If a statute such as the one set out below were passed, how would it affect the outcome in a case such as *Porter v. Citibank?*

Proof of Transaction

Any receipt required to be made available by Section 507 or any periodic statement required to be mailed or delivered by Section 500 shall be admissible as evidence of any transaction therein recorded and shall give rise to a presumption that such transaction occurred as recorded.

2. What if the same thing happened to Robert Porter again? If you were on a jury, would you believe him?

Problem 28–5

Lucy put her card into an ATM and attempted to withdraw $20. She received her $20 but the machine started spouting out $20 bills one after the other. All together Lucy grabbed $720. If the Bank could trace the withdrawal to Lucy's transaction, how could it recover the money? What sort of proof could it use? Does *Porter v. Citibank* help or hurt the bank in this case?

Problem 28–6

Deacon Saintly receives a statement from his bank showing debits for POS transaction with Sam's City of Sextoys totaling $2400. Saintly tells the bank he never heard of Sextoys. The bank produces computer recordings of the transaction. Who is liable? What sort of proof may Saintly offer against the bank's records?

As the following report from a Washington D.C. newspaper shows, machines and programmers are fallible:

"* * * A computer glitch let a man get away with $140,000 in $10 and $20 bills during a run on 16 automatic teller machines in the nation's capital and its Virginia suburbs, the Secret Service said Wednesday.

"Michael Caputo, 31, of Fairfax Station, Va., admitted in federal court Tuesday that he used a stolen Visa credit card to make more than 400 withdrawals last October.

"The case represents the largest fraud committed against Visa with an automatic teller machine, officials said.

"Why didn't someone else in line notice it?" asked John Magaw, a Secret Service agent. "It's very bizarre. All of a sudden this guy realized how good he had it. His pockets just weren't big enough. The machines just weren't programmed to stop."

"Caputo was photographed by monitors at the 16 mechanized tellers receiving $300 during each transaction—at times smiling, at other times holding bags of money.

"Normally, you can't take more than $200 at a time, and [most machines] will not allow you on nights and weekends to go beyond a certain limit," Magaw said. "Somehow, the safeguards broke down."

Caputo was apprehended by a District of Columbia officer after his photo went up in police stations. At sentencing April 29 he faces up to 10 years in prison and a $280,000 fine."

SECTION 3. COMMERCIAL EFTS

A. Automatic Clearing House

The basic replacement for the cumbersome process of transferring actual checks from depositary bank to collecting banks to payor bank is the Automated Clearing House (ACH). Banks in geographic groupings have banded together to form these ACH organizations. Rather than transfer information by paper (checks themselves) an ACH transfers information by magnetic computer-readable tape or by electronic wire message.

In the case of the magnetic tape, a sending bank groups its payment messages on tape and delivers the tape to a clearing facility. By agreement these facilities are almost universally the local Federal Reserve bank. The clearing facility processes the tapes (and tapes of other sending banks) and then regroups the information into tapes organized by receiving banks. Each of these new tapes contains all the instructions of the various sending banks pertinent to one receiving bank. The tapes are then sent to the individual receiving banks (in all likelihood by the same courier carrying the checks processed by the Fed).

While magnetic tape allows for easier processing, it still retains many of the disadvantages of the traditional check clearing system. As system computers can be linked to a clearing computer by telephone wire, the clearing computer can adjust the Federal Reserve accounts at the affected banks upon receiving a message and can inform the affected bank of the transaction (to allow it to adjust the appropriate customer's balance). All of this could be accomplished by computers "talking" to each other on regular phone lines.

How is such a system used? Direct deposit payments (such as that used by the Social Security system and many employers) rely on ACH transfer. An individual employer gives its bank a magnetic tape of employees with the amount to be credited to each. The bank sorts out the employees with accounts at that bank (often the system will require that employees keep an account at one bank to facilitate direct deposit). The remaining employee information is put onto a new tape and sent to the ACH facility at the local fed. There the messages of accounts held outside the local Federal Reserve District are separated and sent on to other ACH facilities. The remaining messages are sorted by receiving bank and sent out. The local banks have had their Federal Reserve accounts credited for the various amounts and they in turn credit their customers, the employees. The original payor bank has its account at the Fed debited to cover the payment. The drawer corporation has its account at the payor bank debited to cover the whole transaction. The whole system can work in the opposite direction with automatic bill payments. Such payments are offered at many banks for recurring bills such as mortgage payments, utility bills and insurance premiums.

More recently corporations have begun to use ACH facilities to make payments to each other. These corporate trade payments contain other invoice information necessary to corporate bookkeeping. The extra information is transmitted by the bank to allow an automated payment system to become attractive to large-scale business that could take advantage of the lower costs of an ACH, but still require a flow of other information. At the start of 1984 the National Automated Clearing House Association (NACHA) began a pilot program testing such a system.

ACH systems already in place can be further adapted to facilitate other types of EFT such as POS transactions, and ATMs that represent a network of banks. It is important to remember, however, that ACHs are only processors of information and do not themselves make actual payments.

For those who like flow charts, the following shows the flow of information in an ACH transaction.

EXHIBIT 3–1.
Operation of Automated Clearing House System

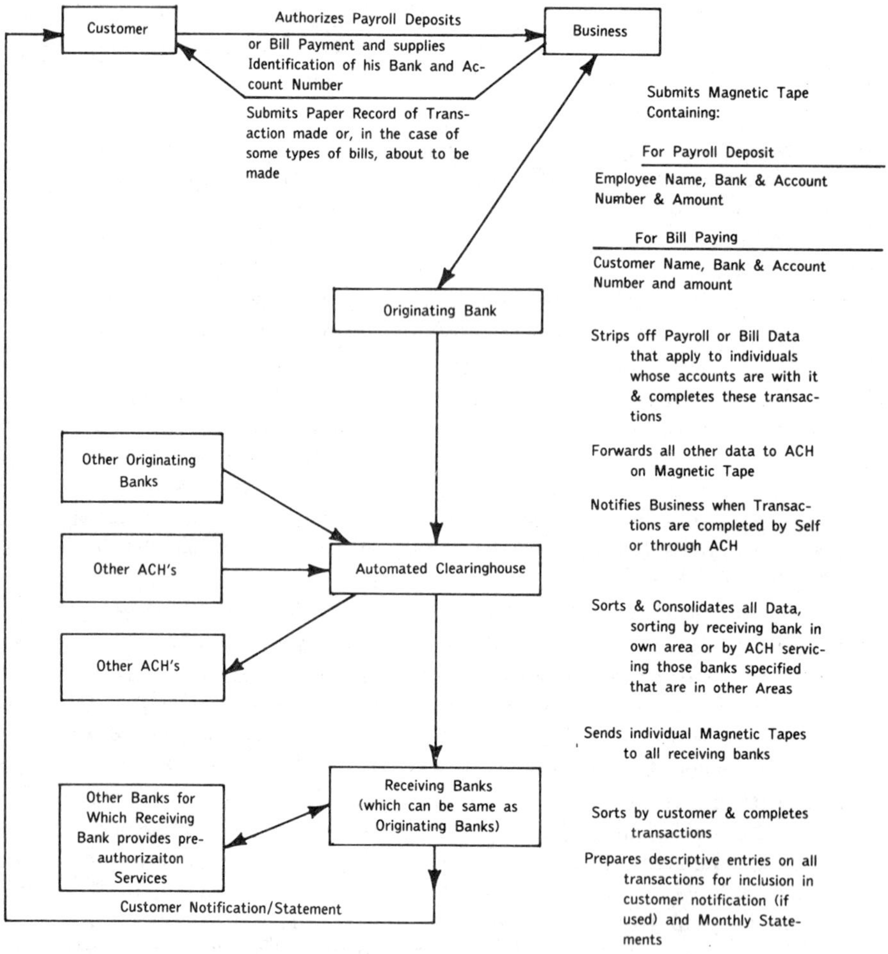

SOURCE: Prepared by Arthur D. Little, Inc., from *The Consequences of EFT* (1975), at 99.

Note: This diagram does not cover the operation of "Bill-Check," which requires a minor modification in the notification/individual approval process.

The diagram does not show the mechanism by which banks receive notice of the fact that a customer has pre-authorized deposit of income and/or payment of bills. This mechanism is apt to vary on a local basis and may even be different for different individual institutions. In all cases, however, the banks will have to receive what they regard as adequate record of authorization.

Beyond ACH's, other information networks are also used by banks to speed the flow of funds. *Contemporary Cash Management* by P. Beehler describes three of these systems: Fed Wire, Bank Wire and Bank Wire II.

> Fed Wire
>
> While ACHs represent a new method of funds transfer, the Fed wire represents an established means of moving funds from one bank to another and is an integral part of the EFTS environment. The Federal Reserve wire system is a communication network used to move funds from one Federal Reserve members account to another, as well as to send administrative messages. The settlement of funds takes place daily at the Federal Reserves so funds are immediately available. The Federal Reserve wire system interconnects the 12 Federal Reserve districts through a communication network switch located in Culpepper, Virginia. The Fed wire, as it is called, handles the largest dollar volume of domestic funds transfer. It is estimated that over $31 trillion were transferred in 1975 representing 17 million transactions. The objective of the Fed wire is to reduce float on large dollar transactions while providing a Federal Reserve communication link. For transfers of $1000 or greater, the Fed has not charged for the service, which has created competitive problems for the Bank Wire service. Fed wire settlements are effected daily on a net basis between the Federal Reserve Bank's member accounts.
>
> Bank Wire
>
> The Payment and Telecommunications Corporation is a communication utility developed by cooperating banks to provide a media for information exchange essentially through administrative messages. The original Bank Wire system was operated under contract by Western Union and moved approximately 24,000 messages per day in early 1977. Fund movement transactions occur through this use of correspondent banks' balances. Consequently, bank A will notify via Bank Wire bank B to transfer bank A funds from their account for credit to a receiving corporate account in bank B. No funds settlement takes place in this service. Approximately 215 banks are members of the Bank Wire system, which processes an estimated 500,000 messages per month.
>
> Bank Wire II
>
> Because of volume, cost, and quality limitations of the Bank Wire service, the development of bank wire II was initiated. The objectives of this expanded service are to:
>
> — Provide flexibility to meet increasing transactions volume with constant or decreasing costs
>
> — Provide for expanded administrative message traffic
>
> — Provide for batch communications
>
> — Exploit technical advances recently developed
>
> Compared to the current Bank Wire system, Bank Wire II is designed to handle 65,000 messages per day and 50% of these are projected to be funds transfer information. The Bank Wire II system is scheduled to participate more fully in EFT function by:

— Transferring funds to provide immediate availability

— Providing net settlements between members on a daily basis

— Providing for processing future dated (value dated) transactions

— Providing ability for debit transfers

Settlement under Bank Wire II would take place through the Federal Reserve.

B. Clearing House Interbank Payment System

Although ACHs handle high-volume, low-dollar transactions, large international interbank payments have become so commonplace that a system was needed to handle high-volume, high-dollar transactions. Because of the concentration of large money center banks, and the routing of foreign exchange payments through these banks, New York City has developed as the center for these transactions. To facilitate the smooth flow of these international payments the New York Clearing House Association developed the Clearing House Interbank Payment System known commonly as CHIPS.

The center of this network is a Burroughs B 6700 computer in the New York Clearing House. Direct-link terminals are located in the offices of the twelve member banks (large New York money center banks) and in a multitude of associate member banks (New York offices of United States and foreign banks).

Before CHIPS, transactions for foreign banks came into a New York correspondent by cable. Any needed processing had to be done manually. Any interbank payments needed a bank check, which was physically delivered through the banking system as part of the large-check processing system already in place.

Penney and Baker, in their book *The Law of Electronic Fund Transfer Systems,* explain the way a payment cable is handled through CHIPS.

> Now, after the cable is received and authenticated, information from the cable is entered by the correspondent's CHIPS computer terminal operator: the names of the European correspondent, the payee, the amount (always in U.S. dollars), the code for the payee's clearinghouse bank, and sometimes other information. The central computer looks up names, addresses, and other information, which it transmits back to the terminal; it retains appropriate entries in its own files, along with the message and waits for an order to release it. The typed form is reviewed and approved. It is then inserted in a "forms handler," which, with additional entries by the operator, is used to order the central computer to release the message either immediately or on some value date. At the time of release, a terminal in the receiving (payee's) bank types up the message and enters the information in the terminal computer's memory without the necessity of operator assistance.
>
> The system relies heavily on codes and on a common name and address file for approximately 10,000 domestic and international accounts, all of which is stored in the central computer's disk file. The system also has a "store and forward" capability and a file organization and constant update procedure that permits account officers to monitor constantly the amount being stored for later release to their banks.
>
> At the end of a business day, the system nets all debits, and credits, and prepares a report showing the position of all participants. Until recently

that report was delivered by the clearing house to the New York Fed the next day, for purposes of making appropriate adjustment to the participant's accounts on the Fed's books. Balances of associate members, largely Edge Act subsidiaries and foreign institutions, are adjusted through the balance of each of their designated members of the New York Clearing House Association. * * *

CHIPS began settling transactions the same day they occur on October 1, 1981. The Federal Reserve Bank of New York has set up an escrow account in which settlement payments are accumulated and disbursed. At the end of each business day, from 5:30 to 5:45 p.m., participants settle with one another on the basis of a net settlement report prepared by the CHIPS computer, which becomes binding on participants at 5:30 p.m., by making transfers through the account using Fed wire. All participants in a debit position must have remitted to the clearing house by 5:45 p.m. before disbursements are made to participants owed funds. The Federal Reserve Board has stated that its facilitation of the settlement process involves no responsibility of the Fed to financially assure completion of the settlement process. It was also announced that the Fed will allow non-New York parents of Edge Act subsidiaries [bank branches operating out of the local state set up for international transactions] that are settling participants in CHIPS to directly transfer to and receive from the New York Fed the net credit and debit positions of their New York Edge Act subsidiaries. There has been increased displeasure on the part of large U.S. banks outside the New York Clearing House membership with respect to access to CHIPS. This concern for more direct participation erupted in the debate over exempting International Banking Facilities (IBFs) from reserve and rate regulations by the Fed. The "outsiders" linked their support for the IBF proposals to easier access to CHIPS. A somewhat related aspect to the same day settlement agreement was to give parents of Edge Act banks outside of New York direct access through manned computer terminals located in New York. Of course, the "outsider" parent banks such as Wells Fargo and Mellon wanted to link their computers in San Francisco and Pittsburgh directly to the CHIPS computer in New York. While there may be a temporary armistice in this battle, the matter does not seem to be completely resolved.

N. Penney and D. Baker, The Law of Electronic Fund Transfer Systems, at 9–12 (1980 & Supp.1984) [Par. 2, 3, 4, Supp. par. 1, exp, of Edge Act 20.1.]

C. S. W. I. F. T.

The importance of CHIPS to international payments is difficult to overestimate. As of 1981 the average daily volume of CHIPS was 60,000 transactions worth about $180 billion. CHIPS in turn mates with an international network for foreign transactions:

CHIPS handles information and settlement for most dollar denominated international payments. Foreign exchange still requires a system for multiple currency transactions. Although there is no automatic clearing equivalent, there is a cooperative society designed to ease the flow of information. Organized under Belgian Law, the Society for Worldwide International Financial Telecommunication (S.W.I.F.T.) began operation with 340 member banks in 15 countries. Membership has been expanding since then.

Because of the technologies available in the various members' actions, S.W.I.F.T. does not use standard technology. Rather the messages themselves are put in a standardized format with a limited number of characters. The computers have their own cables (frequently part of the local country's postal or telephone system) "dedicated" to S.W.I.F.T. use. Thus, banks can send international payment messages with relatively low variable cost, at a high speed and in standardized form. Once the receiving bank gets a S.W. I.F.T. message, the bank must still utilize the local payment mechanism; in the United States this generally means CHIPS.

Fedwire, Bankwire, Bankwire II, See P. Beehler, Contemporary Cash Management, at 276–277 (1978).

D. *Finality, Delay*

The problems that we have seen in the foregoing chapter concerning fraud, negligence, finality of payment and delay are not necessarily remedied by faster communication systems. Rather the same problems emerge in new ways. In reading the *Delbrueck* case and the *Securities Fund Services* case, consider how they might be decided by analogy to a check case. *Delbrueck* is nothing more than a "final payment" case in new clothing, not so? What is the best analogy for the *Securities Fund Services* case?

DELBRUECK & CO. v. MANUFACTURERS HANOVER TRUST COMPANY

United States Court of Appeals, Second Circuit, 1979.
609 F.2d 1047.

MOORE, CIRCUIT JUDGE:

Delbrueck & Company ("Delbrueck") appeals from the dismissal of its complaint after a bench trial held in the United States District Court for the Southern District of New York (Honorable Vincent L. Broderick, *District Judge*). The complaint charged Manufacturers Hanover Trust Company ("Manufacturers") with negligence and breach of contract in failing to revoke two transfers to the Chase Manhattan Bank ("Chase") for the account of Bankhaus I.D. Herstatt, K.G.a.A. ("Herstatt") totaling $12.5 million. The transfers were made via an electronic funds transfer system established by the New York Clearing House Association ("Clearing House") called the Clearing House Interbank Payments System and known as CHIPS.[1] Although the facts are more fully presented in

1. We reproduce in full Judge Broderick's discussion of the CHIPS system, 464 F.Supp. 989 at 992 n. 5:

"The mechanics of effecting an interbank payment under the CHIPS system are as follows: When the paying or sending bank (Manufacturers) receives a telex from one of its customers (Delbrueck) instructing it to make a payment to a receiving bank (Chase), another member of the CHIPS system, for the account of one of the receiving bank's customers (Herstatt), the paying bank (Manufacturers) first tests and verifies the telex. Thereafter, the tested and verified telex is sent to one of the CHIPS computer terminal operators and the payment order contained in the telex is programmed into the terminal by typing into the computer the relevant information—*i.e.*, the identifying codes for the party originating the transfer (Delbrueck), the remitting bank (Manufacturers), the receiving bank (Chase), the party for whom the receiving bank is receiving the transfer (Herstatt) and the amount of the transfer ($10 million and $2.5 million). This information is then transmitted to the central computer located at the Clearing House, which, based upon the identifying codes searches out all the necessary clerical information, stores the message and causes a sending form to be automatically typed at the sending bank. In this case, this step was effected on June 25, 1974.

Once the programming of the computer has been completed, the send form is sent to the appropriate area at the sending bank

Judge Broderick's opinion below (464 F.Supp. 989), a brief statement of those facts is necessary for this discussion of the appeal.

Delbrueck is a German banking house and performs functions as a commercial bank, a brokerage house and an investment bank. In connection with its banking business in 1974, Delbrueck was involved in buying and selling large quantities of foreign currency. Delbrueck maintained an account with Manufacturers, a New York banking corporation, and authorized Manufacturers to make payments out of the account. These authorizations consisted of telex messages which were customarily sent the day before the transfer was to be made.

Delbrueck had entered into three foreign exchange contracts with Herstatt which are of importance for this appeal: one for $2.5 million and one for $10 million, both due on June 26, 1974, and one for $10 million due on June 27, 1974. In accordance with the authorization procedure, Delbrueck sent a telex message to Manufacturers on June 25, 1974 ordering Manufacturers to transfer, on June 26, a total of $12.5 million to Chase for the account of Herstatt. In addition, early on the morning of June 26, Delbrueck authorized the payment of the $10 million due on June 27.

Then the problems began. Herstatt was closed by the German banking authorities around 10:30 a.m. (all times referred to are Eastern Standard Time) on June 26. Chase heard of the closing and immediately froze payments out of Herstatt's account but continued to accept incoming transfers. Delbrueck sent a telex message to Manufacturers at 11:30 a.m. requesting that the $10 million transfer to be made on June 27 be stopped. On June 26 Manufacturers transferred to Chase via the CHIPS system the payments which had been ordered to be made that day, namely, $10 million transferred at 11:36 a.m. and $2.5 million at 11:37 a.m. Delbrueck called Manufacturers at around 12:00 noon and later sent a telex message, trying to stop or recall the $12.5 million in payments which had already been made. That afternoon phone calls were made to Chase by Manufacturers and Delbrueck. These calls were directed at having the funds returned, but were unsuccessful. At around 9:00 p.m. the evening of June 26, Chase formally credited Herstatt's account with the $12.5 million.

Delbrueck maintains that the transfers were revocable until 9:00 p.m. and that by failing to revoke the transfers, Manufacturers was negligent and had breached its implied creditor-depositor contract with Delbrueck. *Stella Flour & Feed Corp. v. National City Bank,* 285 A.D. 182, 136 N.Y.S.2d 139, 142–43 (1st

for approval. When a determination is made at the sending bank (Manufacturers) to make the payment, the form is returned to one of the computer terminal operators, reinserted in the computer and the release key is depressed. At that moment, the central computer at the Clearing House causes a credit ticket to be printed automatically at the terminal of the receiving bank (Chase) and a debit ticket to be printed at the terminal of the sending bank (Manufacturers). Further, the central computer automatically makes a permanent record of the transaction and debits the Clearing House account of the sending bank and credits the Clearing House account of the receiving bank. In this case, this step was effected at 11:36 and 11:37 for the $10 million and $2.5 million payment, respectively, from Manufacturers for Delbrueck to Chase for Herstatt.

The funds received by a receiving bank (*e.g.,* Chase) for the account of one of its customers (*e.g.,* Herstatt) via the receipt of a CHIPS credit message are made available to the customer and can be drawn upon by the customer in the discharge of its obligations that same day, as soon as the receiving bank is aware of the fact that the funds have been received. This running tabulation by the receiving bank is generally referred to as a 'shadow balance.'

At the end of the day, the central computer correlates all of the day's transactions, nets out the debits and credits, and prints out reports showing which banks owe money and which have money due them. That information is delivered to the New York Federal Reserve Bank the next business day and adjustments are made on the appropriate books of account."

Dept.1954), *aff'd,* 308 N.Y. 1023, 127 N.E.2d 864 (1955). Thus, the crucial issue on this appeal is whether the transfers of funds via CHIPS at 11:36 and 11:37 a.m. were final.[2] We hold those transfers were irrevocable and affirm the dismissal of the complaint.

First, the form of the transactions and the manner in which the banks viewed the transactions lead to the conclusion that the 11:36 and 11:37 a.m. transfers were final. The CHIPS system was specifically created to replace cashier's checks as a means of interbank payments of large amounts. As is stated in the CHIPS manual, "CHIPS completely eliminates checks for interbank payment transfers". (App. 377). It is not disputed that cashier's checks are irrevocable when transferred to the payee bank.

In addition, the Clearing House changed its rules after the Herstatt failure to allow revocation of transfers. Although the Clearing House previously had no specific rule concerning the finality of CHIPS transfers, all member banks must have believed that once transfers were released, they were final, except for adjustments made for clerical errors. Delbrueck's conduct supports this fact, because it initially requested stop payment only on the $10 million to be paid on June 27, apparently believing that the June 26 transfers had been made and were irrevocable.

As a direct result of the Herstatt failure, this new procedure was announced on July 1, 1974. The change was necessitated by a backlog in releasing orders created by uncertainties in the financial markets due to the Herstatt failure. Orders were not being released until the transferor was certain that funds were available to cover the transfer. The new procedure outlined in the July 1 announcement allowed members to release payments but still have a right to recall them until 10:00 a.m. of the morning after the transfer. The change would not have been required if the transfers were considered revocable by member banks. And subsequently, on November 4, 1974, the CHIPS system reverted to the tacitly accepted procedure used before July 1, which was that the transfers were irrevocable.

The fact that final settling of the accounts was not done until 9:00 p.m. is irrelevant. That was a mere bookkeeping entry. As Manufacturers asserts, a cash payment or a cashier's check would not have been formally entered on Chase's books until 9:00 p.m. and even Delbrueck agrees that cash or a cashier's check would be irrevocable when transferred.

The practices associated with banking transactions can be conclusive evidence of the legal effect of those transactions. * * * Based on the nature of the CHIPS system, and the fact that the member banks viewed the transactions as irrevocable (as evidenced by the short term change instituted after the Herstatt failure) we hold that the CHIPS transfers were irrevocable when made.

2. Liability for alleged failure to revoke the $12.5 million credit transfers was essentially dependent upon the answer to the question posed by Delbrueck (Delbrueck Br., p. 11) "That issue [breach of contract] inescapably requires consideration of the question, when did the credit transfers to Herstatt become irrevocable?"

The breach of contract issue is characterized by Delbrueck as "the central issue on this appeal". Manufacturers' alleged failure to revoke was "in breach of contract [because it] did not do so". Delbrueck concedes that: "If the credit transfers were irrevocable this appeal must fail, for the contract between Manufacturers and Delbrueck requires that any stop order issued by Delbrueck be received by Manufacturers at a time when Manufacturers still had power to revoke the transfers". (Delbrueck Br., p. 3).

We address the issues 1 and 2 presented for review by Delbrueck and refer to Judge Broderick's opinion, which we endorse, as to the other issues stated. (Delbrueck Br., pp. 1, 2).

The Uniform Commercial Code ("UCC") is not applicable to this case because the UCC does not specifically address the problems of electronic funds transfer. However, analogous use of concepts such as the finality of checks once "accepted" (§§ 3–410, 4–303) would support the irrevocability of these transfers.

The common law supports the view that these transfers were irrevocable. Delbrueck's deposits with Manufacturers were choses in action and as such were assignable. *Miller v. Wells Fargo Bank International Corp.,* 406 F.Supp. 452 (S.D.N.Y.1975), *affirmed,* 540 F.2d 548 (2d Cir.1976). * * *

In order for there to be a valid assignment of a chose in action, there must be a specific direction to transfer by the assignor and notice to the assignee. As the *Miller* court stated:

> "In sum, an assignment requires an agreement whereby the assignor agrees to transfer presently all right, title and control over the subject matter of the assignment to the assignee. Such an agreement may be manifested by conduct, writing or parol, and in particular it exists where the assignor instructs his obligor to pay the specific fund owing to him to the assignee, and the assignor either delivers that order to the assignee or notifies him of it." *Miller, supra,* 406 F.Supp. 452 at 474.

The required notice to the assignee may also be given by the obligor.

> "An order by the creditor [Delbrueck] given directly to the debtor [Manufacturers] requesting him to pay a third person [Chase or Herstatt] does not in the absence of notice to that person make him an assignee of the claim." 3 Williston, *Contracts* § 406 at 156 (3d ed. 1960). *See also Schreiber v. Keller Engraving Co.,* 57 Misc. 644, 108 N.Y.S. 658 (Sup.Ct.1908).

Delbrueck had given Manufacturers a clear direction to transfer these funds in its telex message of June 25. However, Delbrueck argues that the transfers were revocable until the necessary notice was given to the assignee. But notice was given in this case before Delbrueck sought to revoke the transfer.

Chase was the assignee. Delbrueck's direction in the telex message was to pay

> To CHASE BANK N Y
>
> ACCT BANKHAUS ID HERSTATT KGAA
>
> (App. 358).

When Manufacturers transferred the money to Chase, Chase received a written credit slip at its computer terminal. That was notice to Chase of the assignment.

Even if one assumes that Herstatt, not Chase, was the assignee, notice to Chase will be imputed to Herstatt. Chase was the paying and receiving agent of Herstatt, and notice to an agent is imputed to the principal. *Farr v. Newman,* 14 N.Y.2d 183, 187, 250 N.Y.S.2d 272, 199 N.E.2d 369 (1964). *See also Nolan v. Williamson Music, Inc.,* 300 F.Supp. 1311, 1316 (S.D.N.Y.1960); *Ford v. Grand Union Co.,* 268 N.Y. 243, 252, 197 N.E. 266 (1935).

Delbrueck's argument that Chase was not Herstatt's agent after the declared bankruptcy will not stand. Herstatt had directed Chase to "take whatever action [Chase] felt advisable as a result of this information [i.e. the closing of Herstatt]." (App. 68). Thus, Chase's freezing of payments out of Herstatt's account was only Chase continuing to act within the scope of its agency relationship with Herstatt.

Furthermore, the Restatement (Second) of Agency states:

> "The bankruptcy * * * of the principal, of which the agent has notice, terminates his authority as to transactions which he should infer the principal no longer consents to have conducted for him." (§ 114).

Thus, where an agent has a specific contract which is vitiated by the principal's bankruptcy, the agency is terminated. *Lewis Sagal & Co. v. Smith,* 35 F.2d 182, 183 (3d Cir.1929). However, Chase (the agent) could infer in this case that Herstatt (the principal) would consent to Chase gathering payments for Herstatt's account. Indeed, no inference is required because Herstatt specifically requested Chase to "take whatever action * * * advisable". Chase's authority to act as agent for Herstatt in receiving funds was not terminated by the bankruptcy.

Sokoloff v. National City Bank, 250 N.Y. 69, 164 N.E. 745 (1928) is inapposite to this situation. That case dealt with whether or not an intermediary bank can be agent for both the transferor and the transferee. Here, Chase is agent for Herstatt and Manufacturers is agent for Delbrueck. Chase's knowledge of the transfers is imputed to Herstatt, and the assignment was effective.

The other points raised by Delbrueck on appeal were adequately addressed in the well-considered opinion of the court below. We are in agreement with that decision in all respects and hold that the CHIPS payments from Manufacturers to Chase were irrevocable at 11:36 and 11:37 a.m., the times of the transfers.

The dismissal of the complaint is affirmed.

[Some footnotes omitted.]

Note

Analyze *Delbrueck* as though the electronic impulse were an item under the UCC. Under that standard would final payment have been made? See UCC 4–213.

Note: The Proposed Payments Code

The Editorial Board of the Uniform Commercial Code created a committee titled "3–4–8 Committee" in the late 1970s to determine, among other things, whether Articles 3 and 4 should be significantly amended or replaced. This committee, jointly sponsored by the National Conference of Commissioners on Uniform State Laws and the American Law Institute, is composed of representatives of banks, consumer groups, Federal Reserve and others. Ultimately the 3–4–8 Committee drafted a document now called the "New Payments Code." The principal motivation for such a new code was to have a body of statutory law that would govern commercial electronic funds transfer in the way that Articles 3 and 4 govern paper transfers and the way in which the federal law now governs some of the aspects of consumer electronic fund transfer transactions. There was considerable and predictable skepticism about the merits of such a proposal and at this writing it seems unlikely that Articles 3 and 4 will be repealed and will be replaced by a comprehensive code. Rather, it seems more likely that Articles 3 and 4 will be amended in some limited way to deal with certain aspects of commercial electronic funds transfers.

Nevertheless a draft of the "NPC" exists and in many cases it will serve as a useful analogue and as a basis for lawyers' analysis about how Article 4 or the common law ought to respond to a particular electronic funds transfer question. The following excerpt from a paper by Ms. Prutzman, general counsel for the New York Clearing House Association, outlines some of the history and suggests some of the problems.

To get some understanding of the provisions that are contained in the draft of the New Payments Code, we ask the student to consider the problems that follow and to analyze them under the sections of the NPC that are set out after the problem.

PRUTZMAN, CHIPS AND THE PROPOSED UNIFORM NEW PAYMENTS CODE, 10 Rutgers Computer & Tech. L.J. 1, at 3–13 (1984).

I. BACKGROUND OF THE NPC

The initial charge to the 3–4–8 Committee with respect to Articles 3 and 4 was "to evaluate whether there was a serious problem in our legal system insofar as the UCC did not apply to electronic funds transfer transactions." After spending most of its initial period on Article 8, the 3–4–8 Committee turned to Articles 3 and 4 in 1977 and apparently focused almost immediately on the desirability of developing a uniform law for all payment systems.

On February 8, 1978, the Reporter to the 3–4–8 Committee submitted a 254-page document (the "1978 Report") that discusses, among other things, (1) whether Articles 3 and 4 should be amended to regulate electronic funds transfer transactions and (2) whether to draft a new statute that would treat issues common to all payment systems "in a consistent and integrated fashion." While the 1978 Report contains no critical analysis addressing the second issue, it appears to reflect two underlying assumptions:

1. a comprehensive code may be necessary "to eliminate artificial, legally imposed advantages of one payment system over another," and

2. "difficulties in defining the boundaries of legislation offer a strong reason for a comprehensive payment code."

The concern with uniformity apparently led the 3–4–8 Committee to focus almost exclusively on *retail* as opposed to *wholesale* electronic fund transfer issues. This was almost certainly not the original intent of the Committee, as an "interim report" on the NPC illustrates. The interim report resulted from an April 1978, ALI–ABA Invitational Conference on Electronic Fund Transfer Systems and the UCC in Williamsburg, Virginia. The report was prepared by Robert Haydock, Jr., the Chairman of the 3–4–8 Committee, and states:

> It was evident that many participants shared a substantial doubt as to the feasibility and the need for such a code. Concern was expressed on whether such a code should cover all payment systems * * * [and on] whether such a code should deal only with EFT, on the theory that a functional reorganization of Articles 3 and 4 would create as many problems as it would solve; * * *
>
> *At the same time, there was a strong interest in having the 3–4–8 Committee proceed with the project. It was suggested that for Bankwire and related special systems involving a few large banks, a statutory "safety net"—a law that would establish rules where none presently exist either in legislation or in contractual agreements—would serve a useful purpose* and would not hamper the operation of such systems because, with very few exceptions, the rules would be subject to change by agreement.

As a result of the inability to form a consensus in favor of a NPC at the 1978 Williamsburg Conference, Mr. Haydock reported the decision of the 3–4–8 Committee to continue with the NPC on a *qualified* basis, calling for the preparation of the code in two steps, first to draft an outline, and second to draft the statute itself.

An outline was never circulated. In fact, the second step, the drafting and redrafting of the statute itself, was undertaken without soliciting any further public discussion of the NPC's conceptual underpinnings or impact on wholesale wire payments. Remarkably, on May 18–19, 1982, the 3–4–8 Committee recommended to the PEB that a draft of the proposed code be submitted for a "first reading" before the NCC. This recommendation was accepted, but after recognizing the inadequacies of the draft, the 3–4–8 Committee confined its presentation before the NCC to a discussion of certain issues raised by the NPC.

At the same time, the introduction, but not the text, of the latest draft was distributed on August 9, 1982 to certain lawyers attending the ABA's annual meeting in San Francisco. Soon afterwards, the text was made available to interested parties through the offices of the PEB in Philadelphia.

Shortly thereafter, however, a new text, Discussion Draft No. 8, dated October 7, 1982, which contained numerous and substantive revisions, received a limited distribution. Discussion Draft No. 8 was superseded by PEB Draft No. 3, dated June 2, 1983, which adds several lengthy new provisions as well as numerous revisions to previously existing sections.

Scant explanation is given as to why changes were made. Revisions to the commentary appear to be incomplete, in some cases inconsistent, and, in any event, not underscored. Nonetheless, this draft was rushed to a first reading before the NCC during July, 1983, only weeks after publication.

The lack of opportunity for, or solicitation of, wide-scale public discussion of the NPC's various drafts no doubt accounts for its failure to reflect the significant differences between wholesale wire transfers and other payment mechanisms. Even the relatively minor amount of time spent on wholesale wire issues at the Williamsburg Conference this fall served to highlight several of these differences. The NPC was extensively criticized at that conference by a number of participants, including those interested in wholesale wire payments.

Following the conference, the fate of the NPC remains uncertain. By some accounts the NPC is now "dead," less a victim of the NYCH's criticisms than of the failure of consumer and other groups to agree on any point of debarkation from the current status of consumer protections. If other accounts are to be credited, the NPC is likely to be restructured and continued in some manner, perhaps by dropping consumer provisions perceived as "controversial" by the 3–4–8 Committee. If the NPC is to continue in any form, its impact on the payment systems it purports to govern should be clearly understood. One such system is CHIPS.

II. CHIPS TODAY

Transactions over CHIPS are currently governed by the Rules Governing the Clearing House Interbank Payments System ("CHIPS Rules") and the Administrative Procedures of the Clearing House Interbank Payments System ("CHIPS Administrative Procedures") which are incorporated into the CHIPS Rules. The CHIPS Rules and CHIPS Administrative Procedures are adopted by the twelve member banks of the NYCH, which own CHIPS. In general, the CHIPS Administrative Procedures are more technical in scope than the CHIPS Rules. As a consequence, they may be adopted or amended by the Steering Committee of the NYCH, while only the Clearing House Committee, the NYCH's most senior committee, may adopt or amend the CHIPS Rules. In brief, the CHIPS Rules provide that each CHIPS participant may send payment messages through CHIPS to other participants. Once sent, or "released" from storage, a payment message "constitutes the unconditional obligation of such participant to make payment. * * *" However, payment messages may be returned to storage by the Clearing House Committee (but *not* by an individual participant) in certain limited circumstances.

At the present time the dollar amount that a participant may transfer over CHIPS to another participant is unlimited. But this will soon change. In the fall of 1982, the NYCH began to restrict unlimited transfers through the adoption of "bilateral limits" on a trial basis. A "bilateral limit" is a limit set by a receiving participant on the aggregate net dollar amount of payment messages it is willing to receive from a particular sending participant. Thus, a participant wishing to send a payment message may be precluded from doing so by the intended recipient of the payment message.

Bilateral limits will be tested on CHIPS for a limited period, commencing from about March 1984 and ending about October 1984. Assuming satisfactory results, they will be finally adopted thereafter.

The ability to send payment messages may be further constricted by the adoption by the NYCH of limits on the aggregate net dollar amount of payment messages which a participant may send over CHIPS to all other participants. On November 23, 1983, the Clearing House Committee approved the concept of such limits, called "caps," but deferred any final action pending further experience with bilateral limits and the determination of appropriate cap levels.

The adoption of bilateral limits and consideration of caps reflect attempts by the banking industry and bank regulators to reduce risks perceived to exist in large dollar transfer systems such as CHIPS. These risks largely arise from the significant number of banks which during the course of a day incur payment obligations on both Fedwire and CHIPS that exceed, or represent a substantial portion of, their capital. Such substantial obligations, in turn, raise the possibility that a bank will be unable to make settlement in a timely fashion for all the payment messages it has sent.

The industry shares these concerns and, in fact, a recent study prepared by a task force of the Association of Reserve City Bankers recommends three actions to reduce risk, the first of which is to "establish credit limits in two forms: caps and bilateral limits." The report states:

> Credit risk is present to various degrees in Fedwire, CashWire, and CHIPS. * * * Since the extent of any losses realized through use of the payment systems will likely not be known until settlement is completed or until all errors are identified, the goal of any strategy to contain risk should be to allow a reasonably close monitoring of a participant's intraday position across the payment systems for two purposes:
>
> Minimize the possibility that any participant will be unable to settle its position.
>
> Measure the degree of credit risk assumed by participants so that if a participant does fail, losses may be controlled.

This reflects concern that wholesale wire payments may be treated as "good funds" by banks and their customers prior to ultimate settlement. For example, upon receiving a CHIPS payment message, a customer may instruct its bank to make a subsequent payment to a third party, although settlement for the original payment message will not occur until later in the day.

Settlement involves the following procedures: At the end of the CHIPS processing day all payment messages sent over CHIPS are netted and an individual participant's overall debit or credit position with all other participants is calculated. This is called the participant's "net net balance." Each participant is legally obligated to settle its net net balance. Only certain participants, called settling participants, actually exchange funds.

A settling participant may settle either for itself only or for other participants as well. At the end of the day a further netting occurs to determine the aggregate position of each settling participant for itself and all participants for which it settles. Settling participants having a net debit position are obligated to "finally and irrevocably" transfer funds to a special deposit account at the Federal Reserve Bank of New York (the "Settlement Account"). Thus, unlike a transfer of cash or the use of Fedwire where funds are "immediately" available, funds are not transferred in settlement of CHIPS payment messages until the end of the day.

In the event a settling participant is unwilling or unable to make settlement, certain contingency procedures may be implemented. CHIPS Rule 13 provides several options to the NYCH. First, the NYCH may delete from the settlement the payment messages released and received by the participant whose net net position will not be settled and attempt a settlement on the basis of the revision. This is called a "Rule 13 deletion." A deletion does not relieve the deleted participant of its legal obligation to settle for its payment messages, but only removes the NYCH as the vehicle through which such payment would flow. Second, the NYCH may return payment messages to storage. This is called a "Rule 13 unwind." Third, the NYCH can take any other action the Clearing House Committee "deems appropriate" so long as it does not "impose upon any participant any liability in excess of that otherwise provided in [the] Rules."

To the extent the CHIPS Rules and CHIPS Administrative Procedures fail to address an issue arising in connection with a CHIPS transfer, the common law would apply. There are relatively few cases which specifically address wholesale wire transfers. Several are discussed in the text, *infra.*

Problem 28–7

Answer the following under the NPC sections set out below.

1. Henry writes a check drawn on London Bank. Edward, the payee, deposits the check in Nottingham Bank. The check, passed to London, is returned within one day marked NSF. Henry assures Edward that it was all a mistake. The check is resubmitted. In the meantime Henry leaves the country. Six days later the check is returned again. Who is stuck under NPC? Does this differ from the UCC?

2. Tower Corporation sent a wire payment of $10,000,000 to Nottingham Bank to credit the account of Elizabeth. Unfortunately the clerk who sent the order forgot to mark it and an identical second order was sent that same day. Nottingham credited Elizabeth's account with $20,000,000. She promptly left the country and set up residence at a South American beach resort. Three days later, the clerk discovered the error and sent an adjustment and new order for the single payment. Who is stuck?

3. Jill buys a car from Jack and uses a POS card to wire funds from Jill's bank, First National, directly to Jack's bank, American First. Two days later the car explodes in Jill's driveway. Jill directs reverse payment. Where will the loss fall?

4. If final payment can be easily overridden, does it mean anything under the NPC?

NEW PAYMENTS CODE
(Selected Sections)

10: Order

(1) An order is a complete and unconditional direction by a person to pay

(a) a sum certain in money;

(b) from an account which may be accessed to pay a person other than the drawer or the drawee;

(c) to take place immediately or at a definite time;

(d) to or for the benefit of a specific payee, which may be the drawer, or bearer;

(e) with no other direction by the drawer except as otherwise provided in this Code; and

(f) identifying the drawer and, if it is a written draw order, signed by the drawer.

(2) An order must be more than an authorization or request and must identify the drawee with reasonable certainty. It may be addressed to one or more such drawees jointly or in the alternative but not in succession.

(3) An order is complete after the transmission of all information specified by subsection (1) immediately followed by a period or other accepted symbol or means of termination.

(4) A pay order may be implemented by one or more draw orders. Any execution of a pay order by an account institution, by subsequent written or electronic communication, not constituting a draw order, is auxiliary action taken to transmit the order as drawn and does not create additional order(s) if the amount and payee of the order as drawn remain unchanged.

(5) Promissory notes, including certificates of deposit, are not included within the term order. Neither an order accepted by the drawee nor an order drawn by the drawer on itself is a promissory note.

(6) Money itself is not an order.

51: Definitions—Types of Orders

In this Code unless the context otherwise requires,

(1) A *draw order* is an order initiated by the drawer and transmitted to the payee, if any, or initiated on behalf of the drawer by the payee and transmitted to an account institution directing the drawee to pay the payee or the bearer or to accept and includes an order to pay to the drawer or the person authorized to draw on its behalf.

(2) A *pay order* is an order initiated and transmitted by the drawer to the drawee directing the drawee to pay or to effect payment to the payee either directly or through transmitting or settling account institutions, and includes a "wire transfer."

* * *

PAYMENT OF ORDERS—PART III

420: Final Payment of Orders; When Provisional Debits and Credits Become Final

(1) A draw order is finally paid by a payor account institution or other drawee when it has done any of the following, whichever happens first:

(a) paid the order in cash; or

(b) given value for a draw order without reserving a right to revoke the value given and without having such right under statute, regulation, clearing house rule or agreement; or

(c) given value for a draw order and failed to revoke in the time and manner provided in Section 422 or in a manner permitted by statute, regulation, clearing house rule or agreement, but in no event may such revocation occur later than the midnight deadline, except that in the case of a written draw order which has been resubmitted for payment after once being dishonored and returned, such revocation may not occur later than seven (7) business days after the midnight deadline.

(2) A pay order is finally paid by a payor account institution or transmitting account institution when it has done any of the following, whichever happens first:

(a) transmitted an order, or given advice that the order will be transmitted to the payee or to the account institution receiving payment on its behalf, without the reservation of a right to revoke the order communicated to or known by the payee or the account institution receiving payment on its behalf; or

(b) transmitted an order, or given advice that the order will be transmitted to the payee or to the account institution receiving payment on its behalf, without revoking the order by the end of the business day on which the order was transmitted or the advice given; or

(c) agreed to be liable for the order under statute, regulation, clearing house rule or agreement.

(3) In the absence of a valid cause of action such as one based on transmission liability under Section 204, payment effected or the like, upon a final payment under subsection (1)(b), (c), or subsection (2) the payor account institution shall be liable for the amount of the order to the funds claimant, subject to subsection (4) of Section 425 and subsection (5) of this Section.

(4) If provisional payment for a draw order by an account institution is made to the last transmitting account institution through a clearing house or by debits or credits in an account between them, then to the extent that provisional debits or credits for the order are entered in accounts between the last transmitting and payor account institutions or between the transmitting and successive prior transmitting account institutions seriatim, they become final upon final payment of the order by the payor account institution.

(5) Notwithstanding subsection (1), if through a mistake a drawer or payee, other than a consumer drawer or consumer payee, or transmitting account institution has initiated or transmitted erroneous or duplicating orders, as to which payment has become final, such drawer, payee or transmitting account institution may initiate adjustment orders reversing such orders and such

adjustment orders must be acted upon in accordance with their terms by the account institution of the original payees of the erroneous orders, if

(a) the original payees are notified in advance of the adjustment order;

(b) the adjustment orders are received by any account institution which gave value on or for the original orders to persons other than transmitting account institutions within five (5) days of final payment or the settlement date, if specified on the original erroneous or duplicating orders, whichever is later;

(c) new correct orders are transmitted at the same time as the adjustment orders; and

(d) the adjustment orders are transmitted within 24 hours of the discovery of the duplication or error.

Any person initiating adjustment orders pursuant to this subsection shall indemnify all transmittees of such adjustment orders against any loss, including attorneys fees and costs, proximately caused by the collection or payment of such orders. Any transmittee of such adjustment orders, other than the original payee, may require reasonable indemnity, in a form deemed adequate by it, before the adjustment order is acted upon.

421: Account Institution Liability and Customer Right of Withdrawal

(1) Unless otherwise agreed, an account institution is liable to its customer for the actual amount of

(a) a draw order received from its customer at the time it receives final payment for the order;

(b) a pay order received for its customer at the time the customer has the right under subsection (2)(c) to withdraw credit given on the order.

(2) Subject to any right of an account institution to apply the credit to an obligation of the customer, credit given by an account institution on or for an order becomes available for withdrawal as of right

(a) in any case where the account institution has received a provisional payment for a draw order, when such payment becomes final and the account institution has had a reasonable time to learn that payment is final but, in the case of an order drawn by a consumer drawer, in no event sooner than three business days from the time of final payment as provided by Section 420(1)(c);

(b) in any case where the account institution is both a depositary and payor account institution of a draw order, at the opening of the account institution's next business day following the business day of receipt of the order, but in the case of an order drawn by a consumer drawer, in no event sooner than three business days from the time of final payment as provided by Section 420(1)(c); and

(c) in any case where the account institution becomes a funds transferee on a pay order for its customer, at the opening of the account institution's next business day following the business day on which it becomes a funds transferee but, in the case of an order drawn by a consumer drawer, in no event sooner than three business days from the time of final payment as provided by Section 420(1)(d).

(3) Subject to any right of an account institution to apply a deposit of money to an obligation of the customer, the deposit of money becomes available for

withdrawal as of right at the opening of the account institution's next business day following verification by the account institution that the deposit has been made, but in no event later than two business days after the date of the deposit.

(4) An account institution is liable to its customer for all actual damages including consequential damages, proximately caused by its failure to meet its obligations under this Section and such damages may include damage to credit and damages for arrest and prosecution, but may only include punitive damages when the account institution has acted in bad faith.

422: Deferred Posting; Recovery of Payment by Return of Orders; Time of Dishonor

(1) Where an authorized provisional payment for a draw order payable on demand received by a payor account institution otherwise than for immediate payment over the counter has been made before midnight of the business day of receipt, the payor account institution may revoke the provisional payment and recover any credit given if before it has made final payment (subsection (1) of Section 420) and before its midnight or other applicable deadline it

(a) returns the order; or

(b) gives written or electronic notice of dishonor.

(2) If a draw order payable on demand is received by a payor account institution for credit on its books it may return such order or give notice of dishonor and may revoke any credit given or recover the amount thereof withdrawn by its customer, if it acts within the time limit and in the manner specified in subsection (1).

(3) Unless previous notice of dishonor has been given an order is dishonored at the time when for the purposes of dishonor it is returned or notice given in accordance with this Section.

(4) As to written draw orders, an order is returned:

(a) as to an order received through a clearing house, when it is delivered to the presenting or last prior transmitting account institution or to the clearing house or is transmitted or delivered in accordance with its rules; or

(b) in all other cases, when it is transmitted or delivered to the account institution's customer or last prior transmitting account institution or pursuant to its instructions.

(5) If an account institution revokes payment under subsection (1), or otherwise dishonors a draw order by electronic notice of dishonor, it must send a written notice of dishonor confirming the previous dishonor or return the order within one (1) business day of the dishonor.

(6) If an account institution revokes payment under subsection (1) of a draw order over $2,500, or otherwise dishonors a draw order over $2,500, it shall, and if the draw order is $2,500 or less it may, by one business day after its midnight deadline, give electronic notice of such revocation or dishonor and return the order to the first depositary account institution which has transmitted the order, if such account institution can be readily identified from the order as received. Such notice shall include any of the following information which has been transmitted to the account institution in readily decipherable form: the amount of the order; the calendar date the order was transmitted by the depositary account institution; the name of the depositor; the branch or office of the

depositary account institution at which the order was deposited; and an identification of the account institution which transmitted the order to it. If such notice is given it will also constitute notice of dishonor under subsection (1) and Section 416, and no other notice need be given under subsection (1) of this Section.

(7) Any account institution receiving a notice under subsection (6) must, within its midnight deadline, pay to the account institution supplying the notice (notifying account institution) the amount of the order, together with interest, at the average daily Federal Funds rate as published by the Federal Reserve Bank of New York, from the date the order was received by the notifying account institution, as stated in the notice, to the date payment is made. Payment must be by a method which a transmitting account institution may take under Section 428(1).

425: Customer's Right to Stop Payment or Reverse an Order

(1) Any drawer, including a payor account institution which draws an order to a payee in payment of its own underlying obligation, may orally or in writing, stop payment on an order. Stop payment orders must be received at such time and in such manner as to afford the account institution a reasonable opportunity to act on them prior to any action by the account institution with respect to the order described in Section 426.

(2) A consumer drawer has the right to direct a payor account institution, orally or in writing, to reverse payment on an order in the amount of $50 or more until three (3) business days after that order has been finally paid under Section 420(1), and to receive a recredit to the account on which such order was drawn unless

(a) such order is for cash withdrawal; or

(b) is a written draw order transmitted for payment to the payor account institution; or

(c) the person or persons establishing the account have elected in writing, after the disclosure required by Section 701(4), to waive such right.

(3) An oral order is only binding upon the account institution for fourteen (14) calendar days unless confirmed in writing within that period. A written order is only binding for six (6) months unless renewed in writing. Any written order shall be signed by the person exercising the right to stop or reverse payment.

(4) An account institution acting on the direction to reverse payment of an order shall be deemed to be dishonoring the order. It shall have no further liability under Section 420(2) on the order and shall have the right to recover any credit given to its customer, a prior transmittor, or subsequent transmittee. All credits and debits as between transmittors relating to such order may be revoked seriatim along the line.

(5) The burden of establishing the fact and amount of loss resulting from the payment of an order contrary to a binding stop order or order to reverse is on the drawer, but such burden shall not affect the right of the drawer to have its account recredited by a payor account institution when a binding stop order or order to reverse has been issued by the customer.

(6) The right of a drawer to stop or reverse payment as provided herein may be exercised with respect to any order by any person authorized to initiate orders on the account against which such order was drawn, provided that any person

other than the drawer who exercises such right as to any order thereby assumes the obligation of the drawer as provided in Section 100 with respect to such order.

(7) Except as provided in subsection (8), any individual shall have the same right to stop or reverse payment on a draw order drawn on the individual's behalf or accepted by an account institution as would a consumer drawer if the consumer drawer had drawn the order. Such right shall be exercised by a direction to the account institution which has drawn or accepted the order within the time limits specified by subsections (1) and (2). If such account institution has drawn the order on another account institution, it shall before midnight of the business day on which it receives the direction to stop or reverse direct such payor account institution, in accordance with the direction it has received and shall recredit the individual's account for the amount of the order or return to the person any consideration, up to the amount of the order, it received for drawing the order. No drawee or payor account institution on an order so stopped or reversed by such person shall have any further obligation to any funds claimant. Any individual who stops or reverses an order under this subsection assumes the obligation of the drawer on the order, and the individual's underlying obligation, if discharged under Section 801 when the order was transmitted, is reinstated.

(8) Neither an account institution nor any other person may stop or reverse payment on a draw order which,

(a) an account institution has reduced to writing and on which it has assumed the obligations of the drawer or on which an account institution is an accommodation party or acceptor;

(b) is issued in tangible form by the account institution to the person from whom it receives consideration for the order, or is endorsed or accepted in tangible form by the account institution; and

(c) bears prominently on its face the legend that the order is not subject to stop or reversal and should be treated as cash,

for any reason other than loss or a claim that the order is unauthorized. Any party so requesting an account institution to stop or reverse such an order shall either provide indemnity reasonably acceptable to the account institution or enjoin payment of the order by judgment of a court of competent jurisdiction in an action in which the account institution is a party.

(9) Any direction to an account institution to stop or reverse payment of an order must at least accurately identify,

(a) the account number on which such order is drawn;

(b) the dollar amount (not cents) of the order except where a draw order is prearranged;

(c) the payee of the order;

(d) the drawer or person on whose behalf the stop or reversal is directed; and

(e) the date, within one (1) calendar week, of initiation of the order.

(10) A stop payment of an order may be revoked or cancelled only by a writing signed by the person directing the original stop payment.

(11) Any direction to an account institution to stop or reverse payment must be telephoned or delivered to the telephone number or address, as the case may be, specified by the account institution in its disclosure under §§ 501(2)(e) or

701(3) or, in the absence of such disclosure, to any telephone number or address of the branch or office of the account institution where the account is maintained.

(12) An order is for cash withdrawal, within the meaning of this Section, if a drawer receives cash for an order from an account institution, as where cash is withdrawn over-the-counter or from a machine, or in exchange for draw orders payable to cash, drawer or bearer.

(13) An account institution may require any person directing it to stop or reverse an order to pay any fees or charges for such service which it reasonably believes are necessary to cover the cost of providing the service.

411: Responsibility for Transmittal; When Action Seasonable

(1) A transmittor must act in accordance with the reasonable commercial standards of its business in

(a) receiving, processing, presenting or transmitting an order, adjustment order or returned order whether for debit or credit, provided that this Section shall not be the basis for a claim that a transmittor is liable for an unauthorized order; and

(b) notifying its transmittor of any loss or delay in transit within a reasonable time after discovery thereof.

(2) A transmitting account institution must act in accordance with the reasonable commercial standards of its business in

(a) transmitting notice of dishonor or non-payment or returning a draw order to the account institution's transferor or directly to the depositary account institution under subsection (6) of Section 422, after learning that the order has not been paid or accepted as the case may be;

(b) giving value on an order when the account institution receives final payment; and

(c) making or providing for any necessary protest.

(3) A transmitting account institution observes reasonable commercial standards as to timely action if it completes action before its midnight deadline following receipt of the order, returned order or adjustment order, or before the time established under applicable Federal Reserve regulations or operating letters, clearing house rules, association agreements and the like, whichever time is earlier. A transmitting account institution may act in accordance with reasonable commercial standards if it takes proper action within a reasonably longer time, but it has the burden of so establishing.

(4) A transmittor is deemed to have failed to act in accordance with reasonable commercial standards if it fails to honor a specific representation to its customer with regard to any action described in subsection (1), but only the customer can enforce such representation.

(5) Subject to subsections (1)(a) and (b) and Section 429, a transmittor of a draw order is not liable for the insolvency, neglect, misconduct, mistake or default of another institution or person or for loss or destruction of any order in transit or in the possession of others.

(6) No transmitting account institution is required to transmit a pay order before it has become a funds transferee on such order.

(7) The measure of damages under this Section for failure to act in accordance with reasonable commercial standards does not include consequential

damages and shall not exceed the amount of the order reduced by an amount which could not have been realized by acting in accordance with reasonable commercial standards, plus interest, calculated on the basis of the average daily Federal Funds rate, as published by the Federal Reserve Bank of New York, except damages may include all actual damages proximately caused by a party which has acted in bad faith.

E. FRAUD

The same problems that we have seen with fraud in Articles 3 and 4 reappear in the context of EFTS. When dealing with wire transfer, the forgery or alteration of code numbers replaces the forgery of signatures on checks. Is wire transfer more, or less, secure?

SECURITIES FUND SERVICES, INC. v. AMERICAN NATIONAL BANK AND TRUST COMPANY OF CHICAGO

United States District Court, Northern District Illinois, 1982.
542 F.Supp. 323.

MEMORANDUM

LEIGHTON, DISTRICT JUDGE.

I

This is a civil diversity action for damages arising out of a wire transfer transaction. New England Merchants National Bank of Boston (NEMB), at the direction of plaintiff Security Fund Services (SFS), requested, by wire, a transfer of funds disbursed by SFS to an account purportedly in the American National Bank and Trust Company of Chicago (ANB), the defendant. The dispute arises from questions now being raised concerning crediting of the funds by ANB.

The complaint is in nine counts. Count I alleges that defendant engaged in reckless, willful and wanton misconduct constituting gross negligence. Count II alleges a failure to act in accordance with reasonable commercial standards. Count III alleges that defendant acted negligently and failed to exercise ordinary care. These three counts (I–III) will be collectively referred to as the negligence claims. Count IV alleges a breach by the defendant of its duties as an agent of NEMB and SFS. Count VIII alleges a breach of defendant's obligation as agent to act in strict accordance with its instructions. Counts IV and VIII will be referred to as the agency claims. Count V alleges defendant breached its duties as a bailee. Count VI alleges that the plaintiff is a third-party beneficiary to the contract that the defendant breached in failing to properly deliver the funds as directed by NEMB. Count IX alleges that defendant is estopped to deny the existence of a deposit contract and that it breached its duties under that contract. The cause is before the court on defendant's motion to dismiss all nine counts. For the following reasons, Counts I–IV and VII–VIII are allowed to stand, while Counts V, VI and IX are dismissed.

In deciding a motion to dismiss, the court accepts the well-pleaded allegations of fact as true, and reads them in the light most favorable to the plaintiff. *Lundell v. Massey-Fergusen Services,* 277 F.Supp. 940, 941 (N.D.Iowa 1967); *Murphy v. Wheaton,* 381 F.Supp. 1252, 1258 (N.D.Ill.1974); *Jung v. K & D Mining Co.,* 260 F.2d 607, 608 (7th Cir.1958). Accordingly, the following are accepted facts.

II

SFS is the Shareholder Service Agent for Templeton Growth Fund Ltd. (Templeton). SFS processes and records the purchases and redemptions of Templeton shares. In October, 1980, one of Templeton's shareholders was Mr. John Bushman, acting as a trustee for approximately 260,000 shares valued at more than $2 million. On or about October 14, 1980, SFS received instructions, bearing Bushman's signature, requesting that his shares be redeemed and the proceeds be wired to his account at ANB. The account number was said to be 204471. SFS processed the redemption, and directed NEMB, custodian of Templeton's funds, to make the requested wire transfer. NEMB did so and directed the amount of the redemption, the sum of $2,017,867.50, credited to the account of "John Bushman, Trustee // 204471." The transferred funds and accompanying written instructions were received by ANB on or about October 15, 1980. However, the true facts were that ANB had no account in the name of John Bushman, either individually or as trustee. Account 204471 was registered to Gerald S. Haberkorn, Inc. Notwithstanding this discrepancy, ANB credited the funds to Haberkorn's account without addressing any inquiry to either NEMB, SFS, or Templeton. On or about November 4, 1980, SFS learned that the redemption instructions had been forged and that the real John Bushman had no knowledge of the redemption and had no account or relationship with ANB. And, on inquiry, SFS learned from ANB that the funds were credited to Haberkorn's account. Haberkorn had previously agreed to sell approximately $2 million worth of diamonds and jewels to two individuals who promised to pay by wiring the funds into Haberkorn's account at ANB.

After the transfer of funds, Haberkorn delivered the merchandise to the two individuals. Neither the funds transferred into Haberkorn's account nor the jewels purchased with those funds have been recovered. SFS, upon discovery of the forgery, reissued the redeemed shares to the real John Bushman, Trustee, pursuant to an agreement between it and Templeton. The shares were paid for in cash by SFS. In having made whole Templeton and John Bushman, Trustee, SFS brings this suit, contending that it has succeeded to their interests in all claims and rights arising out of these events. In Counts IV and VIII of the complaint, it alleges that ANB, by accepting the transfer of the funds from NEMB with instructions to credit the account of John Bushman, Trustee, became an agent for NEMB, the company which was its agent. Further, SFS claims that ANB's subsequent actions constituted a breach of its duty to act in strict accordance with the instructions it had received, and to inform its principal of all material facts concerning the transaction. Thus, SFS contends that ANB acted as its agent in this transaction.

III

An agency relation may be implied from the facts of the particular case and need not be express. "The existence of an agency relationship and its nature and extent may be shown by reference to the situation of the parties, the property and the acts of the parties." *Kalman v. Bertacchi,* 57 Ill.App.3d 542, 15 Ill.Dec. 204, 373 N.E.2d 550, 556 (1st Dist.1978). This rule of Illinois law is well known. Judge Roszkowski of this court had occasion to apply and follow it in *Evra Corp. v. Swiss Bank Corp.,* 522 F.Supp. 820 (N.D.Ill.1981), *reversed on other grounds,* 673 F.2d 951 (7th Cir.1982). It is helpful for this case to analyze this recent decision.

In *Evra Corp.,* plaintiff entered into a standard form time charter contract with the Pandora Shipping Company for lease of an ocean transport ship. The contract called for monthly payments "in advance" to an account with the Banque de Paris in Switzerland (Swiss Bank). The charter provided for the right of termination by Pandora if the payments were not timely made. As to the particular payment in question, the plaintiff initiated a wire transfer through Continental Bank of Chicago. Continental used the Swiss bank as its correspondent for most of these wire transfer transactions; it performed these services for Continental since the latter did not have direct access to bank operations in Switzerland. Continental in Chicago forwarded the request for transfer to its branch in London and then debited plaintiff's account. After the telex operator in London failed to reach Swiss Bank through its general telex number, Continental diverted the telex message to Swiss Bank's Foreign Exchange Department, a number used by Continental in the past. The facts amply showed that Swiss Bank received the message before the deadline for payment of the charter; however, the payment was never recorded and the transfer was not completed. Swiss Bank had no procedure in its Foreign Exchange Department for transferring telex messages destined for other departments. The court found that Swiss Bank failed to record the message due to either a loss of the message or a failure to keep paper in the machine (there was no automatic shutoff on the machine when the paper ran out). Due to Swiss Bank's negligence in not recording the message, the plaintiff lost its charter contract and suffered damages.

Judge Roszkowski concluded that Swiss Bank breached the duty of care that it owed Evra Corp. By analogy, he reasoned that since there was a contract between plaintiff and Continental, Continental owed plaintiff a duty of care, and Swiss Bank, as Continental's correspondent bank, owed plaintiff that same duty. Citing *Delbrueck v. Manufacturers Hanover Trust Co.,* 609 F.2d 1047 (2d Cir. 1979), which analogized the conceptual use of the finality of checks once accepted to irrevocable wire transfers, he found a similarity between a "collecting bank" as defined in Art. IV of the U.C.C., Ill.Rev.Stat. ch. 26, § 4–105(d) (1979), and Swiss Bank's role as "corresponding bank." This U.C.C. provision states that a collecting bank is "any bank handling the item for collection except the payor bank," U.C.C. 4–105(d).

A corresponding bank is one which "regularly performs services for another in a place or market to which the other does not have direct access." *Black's Law Dictionary* (1979). Under U.C.C. 4–201(1), "[u]nless a contrary intent clearly appears * * * the [collecting] bank is an agent or subagent of the owner of the item." Thus, as Judge Roszkowski held in *Evra,* a correspondent bank in a wire transfer may be presumed to be an agent of the initiator of the transaction until such time as the transaction is completed. Swiss Bank was held to be the agent of Evra Corp. with the same duty of care owed to it by Continental.

In the present case, SFS (like Evra) is the initiator of the wire transfer. NEMB (like Continental Bank) is the custodial bank for funds disbursed by SFS. ANB, as the receiver of the wire transfer, is in the same position as Swiss Bank. In light of the holding in *Evra,* this court concludes that under the facts alleged, an agency relation existed between SFS and ANB. Accordingly, ANB owed SFS a duty of care which its actions in handling the transfer may have breached. Thus, the motion to dismiss Counts IV and VIII is denied.

The first three counts of SFS's complaint allege negligent conduct by ANB in failing to inform NEMB, Templeton, or SFS that the name and account number of the wire transfer did not coincide. ANB questions the existence of a duty owed by it to SFS. Both the plaintiff and the defendant consolidate these three counts into one general issue of negligence. The question, then, is the principle of law to be applied.

Under Illinois law, negligence must be proved by the existence of a duty owed to plaintiff by defendant, a breach of that duty, and an injury proximately resulting from that breach. The existence of such a duty is a question of law. *Evra Corp.,* 522 F.Supp. at 828, citing *Cunis v. Brennan,* 56 Ill.2d 372, 308 N.E.2d 617 (1974). For a legal duty to exist, the occurrence must not be simply foreseeable but "reasonably foreseeable." *Evra Corp., Id.* at 959. The plaintiff in *Evra* contended that the defendant Swiss Bank owed plaintiff a duty to transmit the wire transfer accurately and timely. The court found that Swiss Bank owed a duty of care to Evra to maintain a system of receiving and disposing of telex messages upon which plaintiff could rely, and that Swiss Bank breached that duty. The court stated that the facts indicated "an appalling lack of regard on the part of Swiss Bank for the more than reasonably foreseeable possibility that the negligent maintenance of its foreign exchange telex machines could result in substantial damage to one of its *customers.*" *Id.* at 829 (emphasis added). Thus, Evra, as one of Swiss Bank's "customers," could anticipate due care to be exercised by Swiss Bank in the handling of the wire transfer. In its opinion reversing the lower court, the Seventh Circuit held that this type of "general foreseeability" is insufficient to support an award of consequential damages. *Evra Corp.,* 673 F.2d 951, at 959 (7th Cir.1982). However, the circuit court noted that a different case was presented where, as here, direct damages are sought. *Id.* at 955.

In this case, SFS can likewise be deemed to be a "customer" of ANB. Section 4–104(e) of the U.C.C. defines a customer as "any person having an account with a bank or for whom a bank has agreed to collect items and includes a bank carrying an account with another bank." Through the agency relation discussed, ANB was acting essentially as a collecting bank for NEMB which in turn was the custodial agent of the funds disbursed by SFS. Furthermore, the official comment to U.C.C. 4–203, dealing with the effect of instructions given to a collecting bank by the transferor, states that the collecting bank is liable for failure to exercise good faith or ordinary care. Thus, reading the complaint in the light most favorable to SFS, it was a "customer" of ANB which owed it a duty to use due care in handling the wire transfer. Further, the loss of the transferred funds is the reasonably foreseeable result of a deposit made where the name on the transfer instructions differs from the name on the account into which the funds are deposited. Thus, plaintiff has stated a claim in negligence, therefore, the motion to dismiss Counts I–III is denied.

Count V alleges that ANB was the bailee of the funds transferred for delivery to the account of John Bushman, Trustee, and that ANB breached its duty as bailee by misdelivering; that is, crediting the funds to the wrong account. The defendant contends that the wire transfer of the funds disbursed by SFS did not establish a bailment.

In a depositor-bank relation, there is a well established distinction between a general and a special deposit. In a general deposit situation, the bank merely becomes the debtor of the depositor to the extent of the deposit, and the title to the money passes to the bank. *People ex rel. Russell v. Farmers State & Savings Bank of Grant Park,* 338 Ill. 134, 170 N.E. 236 (1930). The deposit is a general one even when it is evidenced by a certificate of deposit. *Mutual Acc. Ass'n of the Northwest v. Jacobs,* 141 Ill. 261, 31 N.E. 414 (1892). A special deposit, however, is the delivery of either money or chattel to a bank under a special agreement or under circumstances sufficient to create a trust. *Baiar v. O'Connell,* 284 Ill.App. 331, 1 N.E.2d 805 (1936), *aff'd,* 365 Ill. 208, 6 N.E.2d 140 (1936). A special deposit is for a specific purpose, or for safekeeping, and the depositor is entitled to the identical thing or money deposited. This special deposit creates a bailment instead of a debtor-creditor relation, with the depositor's right to demand return of the exact chattel or specific money deposited. *Mid-City National Bank of Chicago v. Mar Building Corporation,* 33 Ill.App.3d 1083, 339 N.E.2d 497, 503 (1975).

In the case at bar, ANB received the wire transfer for deposit to an account, not for any special circumstance, safekeeping or subsequent return to the depositor intact. The wire transfer contemplated a credit to an account and not a safekeeping arrangement. No distinctive feature of a "special deposit" or "bailment" was present here. Thus, ANB's motion to dismiss Count V of the complaint must be granted.

Count VI in SFS' complaint alleges that ANB's failure to transfer the funds to the account of John Bushman, Trustee, or failure to return them to NEMB, constituted actionable conversion. ANB correctly denies the applicability of the conversion claim to this fact situation. One of the legal elements of a conversion, is not present here. The traditional action of trover does not operate on chattels generally, but specifically on property capable of identification as being the actual property or thing wrongfully taken and converted. *Kerwin v. Balhatchett,* 147 Ill.App. 561, 566 (1909). The question remains whether the wire transfer involved specific property.

In *In re Oxford Marketing, United States v. Kallen,* 444 F.Supp. 399 (N.D.Ill. 1978), the court stated that a bank deposit is a chose in action or debt. It is an intangible right and not specific property owned by the depositor or the successor trustee. The court then cited *Kerwin v. Balhatchett,* 147 Ill.App. 561 (1909); *Siegal v. Trac-Ler Karenola Radio & Television Corp.,* 333 Ill.App. 158, 76 N.E.2d 802 (1948) (abstract opinion); and *Janes v. First Federal Savings and Loan Ass'n,* 11 Ill.App.3d 631, 297 N.E.2d 255 (1973), *aff'd in part, rev'd in part on other grounds,* 57 Ill.2d 398, 312 N.E.2d 605 (1974). In the latter case, the court held that Illinois follows the common law rule which does not recognize an action for conversion of intangible rights. Thus, the wire transfer, like a bank deposit, can be considered intangible property. And since it is intangible, an action for conversion cannot be sustained. Furthermore, *Burge v. Englwood,* 213 Ill.App. 357, 363 (1919) stands for the principle that conversion cannot be maintained if the loss resulted from active or passive negligence or breach of contract. *See Janes v. First Federal Savings and Loan Ass'n,* 11 App.3d 631 at 260, 297 N.E.2d 255. Thus, the motion to dismiss Count VI is granted.

Count VII alleges that ANB entered into a contract with NEMB to deliver funds to the account of John Bushman, Trustee, in connection with redemption of Mr. Bushman's Templeton shares. SFS alleges it is a third party beneficiary and has the right to sue ANB for breach of that contract via the improper delivery for the funds. ANB counters that nothing in the complaint supports the legal conclusion that SFS was or could have been a third-party beneficiary in this situation.

The general rule regarding a third party's right to sue for breach of a contract between two other parties was announced in *Carson Pirie Scott & Co. v. Parrett,* 346 Ill. 252, 178 N.E. 498 (1931). There, the Illinois Supreme Court stated that if a contract is made for the direct benefit of a third person not a party to the contract, that third person may sue for a breach thereof. The test to be applied is whether the benefit to the third person is direct to him or is only an incidental benefit. If the benefit is direct, then he may sue; if incidental, then there is no right of recovery. This test is to be determined within the language of the contract. *Id.* at 257–258, 178 N.E. 498. *Accord, People ex rel. Resnik v. Curtis & Davis, Architects & Planners, Inc.,* 78 Ill.2d 381, 36 Ill.Dec. 338, 400 N.E.2d 918 (1980). Furthermore, it is not necessary for the third party who is benefitted by the contract to be named therein if he is otherwise sufficiently described or designated. *Candlewick Lake Utilities Co. v. Quinones,* 82 Ill.App.3d 98, 37 Ill.Dec. 479, 402 N.E.2d 369 (1980); *Gothberg v. Nemerovski,* 58 Ill.App.2d 372, 208 N.E.2d 12 (1965). The question whether the benefit to a third party is direct or incidental depends on the intent of the parties, and must be determined case-by-case. *Midwest Concrete Products Co. v. LaSalle National Bank,* 94 Ill.App.3d 394, 49 Ill.Dec. 968, 418 N.E.2d 988, 990 (1981); *Kravitz v. Lake County,* 62 Ill.App.3d 101, 19 Ill.Dec. 611, 379 N.E.2d 126, 128 (1978).

Under the alleged facts, SFS has adequately pleaded its status as third-party beneficiary. The direct or substantial benefit to SFS is the interest in properly transferring the funds so as to avoid any loss by its customer or SFS itself. Also, SFS did not need to be named within the contract since it is evident that SFS falls within the group designated to benefit from the contract; *i.e.,* Templeton, SFS, and John Bushman, Trustee. Thus, the motion to dismiss Count VII is denied.

SFS' Count IX alleges that ANB acted as though a depositor account in the name of John Bushman, Trustee, actually existed. This purportedly occurred because ANB failed to inquire or give notice to NEMB or SFS of the discrepancy between the name and account number. SFS' reliance on ANB's silence or inaction fostered a belief that an account for John Bushman, Trustee, actually existed, and thus prevented SFS from acting to avoid the loss of the funds. Thus, SFS alleges that ANB is estopped to deny the existence of a deposit contract between ANB and John Bushman. Plaintiff further alleges that by virtue of having reimbursed Bushman and Templeton through its reissuance of the redeemed shares, it has succeeded to their interests and can sue on the deposit contract. The problem with these allegations is that there is no contract between ANB and Bushman. It is undisputed that Bushman did not have an account with ANB and in fact had no relationship with ANB. Rather, Bushman was the beneficiary of a contract for deposit based on the wire transfer between ANB and NEMB. Thus, the contract which SFS seeks to estop ANB from denying does not exist and Count IX should be dismissed.

Accordingly, and for these reasons, the motion to dismiss is granted as to Counts IV, V and IX and denied as to the other counts.

So ordered.

Note

If it were applied, how could UCC 3–405 change the outcome of this case? See also NPC section 202.

SECTION 4. PROSPECTS FOR LEGISLATIVE REFORM

Currently the Commissioners on Uniform State Laws are considering a new statute that would cover liabilities of customers and banks who engage in wire transfers. It is likely that this legislation will take the form of Article 4A to be added to Article 4. Reporters for this project are Professors Warren and Jordan of the UCLA Law School. Much of what follows is taken from their memorandum presented to the Commissioners in the spring of 1986.

The first issue for legislation is the question, what transaction should be covered? Should a statute cover merely "wholesale transactions" and, if so, how does one define those? To the extent that consumer electronic funds transfers are dealt with in the federal law, states have no power to act except insofar as that law specifically permits state options. If a state adopted a statute covering all "wire transfers," what of the case in which a business sent instructions to its bank in writing and the instruction was carried out by an electronic funds transfer among the banks? Would that be a "wire transfer"? These and a variety of other questions will have to be answered in any statute that is enacted.

The second general question for drafters is the extent to which liability for fraud and negligence on the part of customer of one of the banks in the chain should alter the allocation of loss. These are analogous to the questions now dealt with in UCC 3–405, 3–406, 4–406. Presumably any code enacted will have provisions analogous to those. Indeed where the bank's only mode of identification of the customer is the use of a code number or word, there may be even greater reason to impose the loss on a negligent customer than in the typical paper transaction.

How do you think the two following cases should be answered?

Problem 28–8

1. A former employee of customer has access to customer's codes because he knows how and where they are stored and he has access to the storage place. He procures the code and causes $500,000 to be transmitted to his Swiss bank account, withdraws the funds, and disappears. Customer now argues this was an unauthorized transfer (surely it was), and therefore that his account should be recredited. Must the bank do so?

2. What if bank's employee, knowing customer's secret number, has the money wired to the Swiss account and disappears with it? In this case, must customer's account be recredited?

3. In the second case assume that there were a series of ten withdrawals, one per month over ten months, a written statement was transmitted monthly to the customer that showed these withdrawals, and customer failed to examine the statement closely enough to discover the shortage. Should the customer now bear the losses after month one?

Part 3 of the preceding problem raises the issue how and to what extent can or should one replicate UCC 4–406 in an electronics fund environment. One may have a clear picture of a monthly bank account statement that is produced in a typical checkwriting system, but what paper record or documentation will a customer receive as a result of an electronics funds transfer? The law needs to be flexible enough to accommodate various sorts of reports. It seems likely that there is no uniformity about the timing and form of reporting in electronic funds cases.

What of cases in which there is payment by mistake, in which the customer is fooled and the bank perhaps should have known? Consider the following:

Problem 28–9

A clever thief posing as a patron of customer instructs customer (the owner of a mutual fund) to sell a specific number of shares and to deposit the proceeds in his account at Central National Bank. The customer's name is Richard Stein, and the account number is 40546. Bank's customer sells the shares and instructs the bank to make the deposit to Richard Stein's account, 40546. The receiving bank has no account by that name, although it has one by that number. Nevertheless it accepts the funds and puts them in that account where they ultimately are withdrawn by the thief who disappears.

In that case the customer may well have been at fault, but it was the thief, not its own patron who gave the original order. On the other hand, the receiving bank could have been at fault in depositing the money in an account that has the proper number, but the wrong name. On whom should the liability fall and how should it be characterized?

The statute will probably deal as well with the question of consequential damages presented in the case of Evra Corp. v. Swiss Bank Corp., 673 F.2d 951 (7th Cir.1982), in which the customer claimed that he lost a ship charter worth $2.1 million because of the failure of one of the banks in the chain to comply with a $27,000 wire notice. There will also have to be rules about the time within which the bank must act in force majeure. All of these problems are familiar to one who understands Article 4.

At a more fundamental level is the question, how should wire transfers be characterized? The answer to that question will shape the rules concerning "final payment" and its consequences. Professors Warren and Jordan have presented the issues in their March 25, 1986 memorandum as follows:

W. WARREN AND R. JORDAN, MEMORANDUM ON PROPOSED ARTICLE 4A TO COMMISSIONERS ON UNIFORM STATE LAWS (1986)

* * *

11. Theory of Wire Transfer, Risk of Insolvency, and Responsibility for Bank Error

At present the legal system has not developed a theory of wire transfer. The wire transfer system can be described in terms of how it works mechanically, but it is not clear how legal relationships are changed during the various steps in the transfer. Since the purpose of a wire transfer is to pay an obligation or to otherwise transfer funds, the central requirement of the wire transfer statute must be to define when the obligation has been paid or when the funds have been transferred. In essence the task is to define what "funds" means.

In the discussion that follows we explore two concepts of when "funds" have been transferred. Under the first, Debtor pays its debt to Creditor when Creditor is given the benefit of a bank obligation to pay the amount of the transfer. We can refer to this first concept as a cashier's check theory of funds transfer. Under the second concept, Debtor pays its debt to Creditor when Creditor is given the benefit of an obligation that is the equivalent of money. That obligation would normally be an obligation of a Federal Reserve Bank which is an instrumentality of the United States. We can refer to this second concept as a good funds theory of funds transfer.

The two concepts can be illustrated by a simple case. Debtor wants to transfer $1,000,000 to Creditor. It does so by ordering its bank, Sending Bank, to pay $1,000,000 to the account of Creditor in Creditor's bank, Receiving Bank. Sending Bank executes Debtor's order by ordering Receiving Bank to pay $1,000,000 to Creditor's account. If we follow the existing convention of treating an order to pay as imposing on the giver of that order an obligation to pay the amount of the order, the result is that Sending Bank is obligated to pay $1,000,000 to Receiving Bank for the benefit of Creditor. Under the cashier's check theory of funds transfer, payment has been made to Creditor when Receiving Bank, as the authorized agent of Creditor, accepts Sending Bank's order. Under the good funds theory of funds transfer payment to Creditor does not occur until Sending Bank's obligation to pay has been finally settled. If $1,000,000 were the only wire transfer between the two banks, settlement between Sending Bank and Receiving Bank would usually be done by making a $1,000,000 debit to Sending Bank's Federal Reserve account and making a corresponding credit to Receiving Bank's Federal Reserve account. Under both theories of wire transfer Creditor is paid by giving to its authorized agent, Receiving Bank, a claim against another bank. Under the first theory the claim is against Sending Bank. Under the second theory the claim is against a Federal Reserve Bank.

We are presenting two alternative "statutory solutions" for discussion. Solution # 1 incorporates the cashier's check theory of wire transfer and adopts receiver finality. Solution # 2 incorporates the good funds theory of wire transfer and, at least in part, rejects receiver finality.

We also address an entirely different problem in the two alternative statutory solutions. That problem concerns responsibility for error by banks in executing a wire payment order. The issue is whether a bank should be responsible only for its own error or whether it can also be held responsible for the error of another bank in executing the order. Solution # 1 incorporates a rule similar to the New York rule for collection of checks. Solution # 2 incorporates a rule similar to the Massachusetts rule for collection of checks. There is no necessary relationship between either the cashier's check or good funds theory on the one hand and either the New York or Massachusetts rules on the other. For example, Solution # 1, which incorporates the cashier's check theory, could just as well adopt the Massachusetts rule instead of the New York rule. We have made the Solution # 1 pairing because that pairing is most beneficial to the sending customer. We have chosen the pairing in Solution # 2 because that pairing is least beneficial to the sending customer. Thus, the two solutions represent extreme positions.

The two suggested solutions are not the only solutions that could be chosen. Numerous variations are possible. We have presented only two solutions in order to focus discussion. We believe that other alternative solutions or modifications can be raised in the context of the solutions presented.

Statutory Solutions

Sending Customer orders Sending Bank to pay money to the account of Receiving Customer in Receiving Bank. The order is executed by a series of orders as indicated in the diagram.

Sending Customer → Sending Bank → Intermediary Bank → Receiving Bank

Although the diagram shows one intermediary bank there may be several intermediary banks.

Solution # 1

This statutory solution might be characterized as a system approach. It is based on the theory that costs resulting from bank insolvency and from bank error should be borne by the banks that make up the wire payment system rather than by users of the system. At the January meeting Geoff Hazard recommended that we look at an approach that would internalize costs within the payments system. This solution is an attempt at carrying out that objective. The statute will contain provisions that produce the following rules:

Rule # 1. When Sending Bank accepts the order of Sending Customer it warrants to Sending Customer (a) that Receiving Bank will accept an order to pay in compliance with the order of Sending Customer, and (b) that Sending Customer's order will be carried out with due care by Sending Bank and any other bank that takes action in execution of Sending Customer's order.

Rule # 2. Upon acceptance of the order by Sending Bank, Sending Customer is liable to Sending Bank to pay the amount of the order. Sending Customer has no other liability on its payment order.

Rule # 3. When Intermediary Bank accepts the order of Sending Bank it warrants to Sending Bank and Sending Customer (a) that Receiving Bank will accept an order to pay in compliance with the order of Sending Bank and (b) that Sending Bank's order will be carried out with due care by Intermediary Bank and any other bank that takes action in execution of Sending Bank's order. If there are several intermediary banks, each subsequent intermediary bank makes similar warranties to preceding banks in the chain as well as to Sending Customer.

Rule # 4. Upon acceptance of the order by Intermediary Bank, Sending Bank is liable to Intermediary Bank to pay the amount of the order. Sending Bank has no other liability on its payment order.

Rule # 5. When Receiving Bank accepts the order of Intermediary Bank it (a) warrants to Sending Customer and all preceding banks in the chain that it will exercise due care in execution of the order, and (b) is liable to Receiving Customer for the amount of the order.

Rule # 6. Upon acceptance of the order by Receiving Bank, Intermediary Bank is liable to Receiving Bank to pay the amount of the order.

Rule # 7. With respect to the underlying transaction pursuant to which Sending Customer made its payment order, payment by Sending Customer to Receiving Customer occurs when Receiving Bank accepts an order of Intermediary Bank that complies with the order of Sending Customer if the wire transfer was authorized by Receiving Customer.

We will apply these statutory rules to three cases: a failure to settle a payment order obligation because of insolvency, a delay in transmission of a payment order, and a payment to someone other than the receiving customer designated in the sending customer's order.

Failure to Settle, Insolvency and Payment of the Underlying Obligation

Suppose Intermediary Bank accepts the payment order of Sending Bank and transmits its payment order to Receiving Bank before receiving settlement from Sending Bank. Sending Bank fails to settle with Intermediary Bank and that failure was caused by the insolvency of Sending Bank. In this case the loss caused by Sending Bank's insolvency will fall on Intermediary Bank. Intermediary Bank is liable to Receiving Bank on the order given to that bank. Rule # 6.

Thus, if Intermediary Bank is not itself insolvent Receiving Bank will receive payment and will suffer no loss. Because of Rule # 5(b) Receiving Customer has the payment obligation of Receiving Bank so it suffers no loss. Sending Customer's obligation has been paid so it suffers no loss. Rule # 7.

Payment orders are frequently accepted even though the giver of the order has not first provided the funds to pay the order. All of the wire transfer networks adopt the principle of sender finality, i.e., that a sending bank may not revoke its payment order after it has been accepted and that the sending bank has an absolute obligation to provide to the accepting bank the funds covered by the order. Thus, the acceptance of a payment order before settlement is a credit transaction. Nobody disputes the fact that Sending Bank in our hypothetical must take the risk of nonpayment by Sending Customer if it executed Sending Customer's order before receiving payment. That risk is inherent in granting credit. We believe that the same principle should apply to Intermediary Bank. Intermediary Bank had no obligation to accept the payment order from Sending Bank. When it did so it assumed an obligation to carry out the order which involved the granting of credit to Sending Bank. If the bank that grants the credit is made to bear the loss it is more likely that that bank will be more prudent in granting credit and that the banking system will adopt measures to prevent improvident granting of credit. The result should be that less creditworthy banks will be unable to run up excessive debit positions.

It has been argued that the risk of insolvency in a case of this kind should rest on users of the system rather than the banks that extended credit to the failed bank. Solution # 2, which will be discussed later, is designed to carry out that view. Shifting the risk to users of the system is rationalized on various grounds. Users of the system are the primary beneficiaries of wire transfers. If the loss is placed on the banks that accepted payment orders there is a danger that the loss could threaten the solvency of receiving banks as well if they had very large credit positions with the failed sending bank. If the loss is placed on users of the system the loss is spread widely rather than falling on a few receiving banks with large credit positions. We are not persuaded by these arguments.

Another argument against placing the credit risk on accepting banks is that it may cause inefficiencies in the system. Banks that are asked to accept transfers can be expected to limit the size of their credit positions with sending banks in order to reduce the amount of the risk. This is accomplished by refusing to accept payment orders from a particular sending bank so long as acceptance of an order would cause the debit position of the sending bank to exceed a certain limit. In some cases barriers of this kind could cause inefficiencies and delays in the transmittal of funds. For example, a sending bank might have a large debit position with respect to one receiving bank but an overall credit position with respect to all banks in the system. In spite of its overall credit position the sending bank might not be able to send a payment order directly to the receiving bank with which it has a debit position because of a bilateral limitation fixed by the receiving bank. The transfer could be made to the receiving bank only by routing it through other banks with respect to which there were no credit barriers or by use of some other wire payment system.

Another argument is directed at the competitive effect of bilateral credit limits. The onus of those limits is more likely to fall on smaller, less well known sending banks because their creditworthiness may be less certain. If this is so there may be a tendency to concentrate wire transfer business among large banks. Putting the credit risk on banks may also affect pricing. The price charged for wire transfers is currently quite low. If the risk of insolvency of a sending bank is placed on the banking system rather than on users of the system the price to users will probably rise. We cannot confidently evaluate the force of these arguments, but are inclined to believe that there is little hard evidence on the economic effects of bilateral credit limits. We think that it is true that bilateral credit limits are likely to be encouraged by a rule that places the credit risk on the bank that gives the credit, but we look upon that result as positive rather than negative.

The arguments in favor of imposing obligations based on acceptance of a payment order by a sending or intermediary bank apply equally to the destination receiving bank. Upon acceptance of an order a sending or intermediary bank assumes an obligation to act on the order by transmitting a payment order which is in effect a promise to pay the amount of the order. This is the rule currently in effect in all the wire payment systems. When the destination receiving bank accepts a payment order it too should assume an obligation to pay the order. Thus, Rule # 5(b) provides that Receiving Bank when it accepts the order of Intermediary Bank, is liable to pay Receiving Customer regardless of whether Intermediary Bank makes settlement.

Our analysis assumes that all banks in the system accept the payment order that was received. Suppose that a bank that does not want to take a credit risk refuses to accept. If Intermediary Bank decides that Sending Bank is not creditworthy and refuses to accept, Sending Bank would have to seek other avenues for getting the order to Receiving Bank. In the unlikely case that it cannot execute the order, Sending Bank has breached its Rule # 1 warranty because the order has not been transmitted to Receiving Bank. If Sending Customer has not yet paid Sending Bank, it is not required to pay. If it has paid it is entitled to repayment. The case is simply one of a failed attempt at payment. Suppose it is Receiving Bank that refuses to accept the payment order of Intermediary Bank. In that case both Sending Bank and Intermediary Bank have breached their Rule # 1 warranties. Sending Bank is not required to settle with Intermediary Bank because of the breach of warranty by Intermediary Bank. The result is similar to that in which Sending Bank is unable to execute the order.

It is possible, however, that the payment order of Sending Bank was accepted late on Day # 1 so that Intermediary Bank did not have time to act on the order that day. In that case Sending Bank may have settled with Intermediary Bank at the end of Day # 1. If Intermediary Bank does not transmit an order to Receiving Bank on Day # 2 because Intermediary Bank failed on that day Sending Bank will suffer the loss. It cannot charge Sending Customer's account and is left with a claim for repayment against the insolvent Intermediary Bank. One could argue that Sending Bank should not have to take this loss in this case if it did not have any choice about dealing with Intermediary Bank. For example, Intermediary Bank may be the only correspondent of Receiving Bank. If that is so, it can be argued that the loss should fall on Receiving Bank because its agent received payment. The statute could accomplish this result by defining Receiving Bank to include its correspondent bank. We do not favor this approach because it may be difficult or impossible to determine whether an Intermediary Bank was chosen by the Sending Bank or was designated by the Receiving Bank. In our example, Intermediary Bank is likely to be a large money center bank and it may be unrealistic to assume that Sending Bank did not freely choose to deal with it or would not otherwise have dealt with it. In any event, this is an issue that is common to both Solution # 1 and to Solution # 2 which we will consider later.

Solution # 1 is based on several principles. It adopts the principle that a sending customer makes payment to the receiving customer by providing to that customer an ordinary bank obligation rather than by providing "collected funds." It endorses the reasoning of the *Delbrueck* case that assimilates a wire transfer to a cashier's check. We are moving away from a paper-based payment system to a system of very rapid electronic transfers of credits or obligations of banks. The commercial world has long operated on the basis of payment by bank obligations. Cashier's checks and letters of credit are routinely taken as the equivalent of payment in cash. A creditor that has agreed to payment by wire transfer should be treated like a creditor who has agreed to payment by cashier's check. In the latter case UCC § 3–802 provides that the taking of the cashier's check satisfies the obligation. A similar rule should apply to wire transfers. Wire transfers are favored by creditors because they get the funds sooner than is the case of payment by other means. In most cases wire transfers are made at the request or demand of the creditor. We would favor a statutory provision to the effect that payment by wire transfer is deemed to be authorized unless the agreement of the parties provides to the contrary. Our guess is that payment in that manner will become the norm in the future and the statute should reflect that fact.

Solution # 1 also adopts the principle of receiver finality. The event that determines liabilities is acceptance of the payment order rather than settlement of the payment obligation. Whether banks within the wire payments system decide to give credit to each other should be of no concern to users of the system who have no control over that credit and who normally would be unaware of it. Whether obligations between banks are settled or not should be a concern of the banks involved and of the banking system, but should not in any way affect the rights of users.

Delay in Transmission and Payment to Wrong Person

Case # 1. Sending Customer is making payment to Receiving Customer in order to exercise a favorable option to purchase property. Because of negligence by either Sending Bank or Intermediary Bank transmittal of an order to pay in compliance with Sending Customer's order is delayed and not received by Receiving Bank until after expiration of the option. Receiving Customer refused to accept the late payment as an exercise of the option and returned the money to Sending Customer. As a result Sending Customer suffered a substantial loss of profit. Who is liable for the loss?

Sending Bank is liable for its own negligence and also for the negligence of Intermediary Bank. Rule # 1(b). If Intermediary Bank is negligent it is liable to Sending Bank and to Sending Customer. Rule # 3(b). Normally Sending Customer would seek relief against Sending Bank. It will frequently happen that Intermediary Bank is located in a distant place. In the *Evra* case the offending bank was located in a foreign country. Sending Bank normally is in a better position to get relief from Intermediary Bank than is Sending Customer. Considerations of commercial convenience are served if Sending Customer can obtain relief from the bank with which it dealt.

The countervailing argument is that it is unfair to impose on Sending Bank liability for another bank's negligence. This argument is buttressed by the fact that Sending Bank may not have access to information that would allow it to determine whether Intermediary Bank was in fact negligent. If Sending Bank is sued by Sending Customer, Sending Bank may not be able to implead Intermediary Bank because it is not subject to process in the jurisdiction. But a similar argument can be made on behalf of Sending Customer. It may not know which bank acted negligently and there may be several intermediary banks involved. Sending Bank is normally in a better position to discover the facts than is Sending Customer. But commercial convenience may not justify imposing liability on Sending Bank if the liability may be very large and Sending Bank cannot conveniently obtain relief from the culpable bank. Elsewhere we have suggested that the statute should provide for no punitive or consequential damages in a case of this kind except for the rare case of bad faith or reckless conduct. If that principle is adopted the liability in a delay case would be limited to interest for loss of use of funds and incidental expenses. Thus, the burden on the sending bank is small.

Case # 2. Sending Customer ordered payment to Receiving Customer to pay a debt. Intermediary Bank ordered Receiving Bank to pay the wrong account. The funds were withdrawn and cannot be recovered. Who takes the loss?

The outcome in this case is the same as in Case # 1. Sending Bank guaranteed that Receiving Bank would receive an order in compliance with Sending Customer's order. Rule # 1(a). It is liable for the act of Intermediary Bank. In this case, however, there would normally be less uncertainty about the question of liability of the culpable bank. It is normally easy to determine whether a payment order did or did not name the correct receiving customer or account. The extent of liability, however, may be far greater. Sending Bank, because of its breach of warranty, will have to recredit the account of Sending Customer. Sending Bank has a right of recourse against Intermediary Bank. Rule # 3(a). In the case under consideration, Sending Bank dealt directly with Intermediary Bank. It should be relatively easy for Sending Bank to recover from Intermediary Bank because the two banks are likely to have a continuing business relationship. In cases in which there are several intermediary banks and the error is made by a remote intermediary bank, Sending Bank can obtain reimbursement from the intermediary bank with which it dealt because each intermediary bank is responsible for the act of the next intermediary bank in the chain. Thus, there is a chain of liability down to the culpable bank. Rule # 3.

We believe that a rule that makes Sending Bank liable for the errors of Intermediary Bank can be justified on the basis of commercial convenience, but we recognize that there are strong arguments to the contrary, particularly if Sending Bank is a small bank. Solution # 2, which will be discussed later, incorporates rules under which the various banks in the payment chain are responsible only for their own acts and do not guarantee performance by other banks.

It should be emphasized that the rules in Solution # 1 regarding risk of loss for failure to settle and the rules regarding responsibility for negligence are not interdependent. It is possible, for example, to adopt the insolvency risk rules of Solution # 1 and to reject its rules for responsibility for negligence in favor of those set forth in Solution # 2.

Case # 3. Same facts as Case # 2 except that the error in payment was made by Receiving Bank. There is a breach of the warranty of due care by Receiving Bank (Rule # 5(a)) but there is no cause of action by Sending

Customer because it has not suffered any loss. Its obligation to Receiving Customer was satisfied when Receiving Bank accepted the payment order of Intermediary Bank. Rule # 7. Receiving Customer has suffered no loss because Receiving Bank remains liable to pay the amount of Intermediary Bank's order to Receiving Customer. Sending Bank and Intermediary Bank have suffered no loss because they have no liability for Receiving Bank's error in this case. Thus, Receiving Bank is entitled to settlement from Intermediary Bank. Rule # 6. If Receiving Bank is unable to recover from the person to whom payment was mistakenly made Receiving Bank will take the loss.

It should be noted that Solution # 1 does not distinguish between intermediary banks that are chosen by a sending bank and those that are designated by a receiving bank. We believe that in many cases it may be difficult or impossible to determine whether a particular bank falls into one category or the other. To insert this distinction into the statute is to invite wasteful litigation and uncertainty into a commercial context in which certainty is a high priority goal. The statutory technique used is not based on agency concepts. Rather, it is based on commercial convenience which allows the sending customer to get relief from the sending bank with which the customer dealt and to provide for the passing on of the loss through the chain of banks to the culpable bank.

Solution # 1 also allows the sending customer to proceed directly against any bank in the chain because each bank makes a warranty to the sending customer. Rules # 3 and # 5. In most cases this alternative would not be used because normally the sending bank is a more convenient obligor. But since the obligation of each bank in the chain is for the ultimate benefit of the sending customer, there is no reason why direct suit should not be permitted.

Solution # 2

Solution # 1 is based on a theory of wire transfer that incorporates receiver finality. When Receiving Bank accepts the payment order for the transfer of funds to Receiving Customer's account, Receiving Customer has been paid, whether or not settlement is eventually made between Intermediary Bank and Receiving Bank. Under Solution # 1 the critical act is the acceptance by a bank of a payment order and not the eventual settlement of that payment order. Under this solution settlement is a matter for system rules or for agreement between the banks involved. This solution places the risk of insolvency of a transmitting bank on the bank that accepts the payment order, or on the banking system to the extent that system rules provide for the sharing of insolvency losses. With respect to negligence or miscarriage of the sending customer's order Solution # 1 imposes on the bank that accepted that order responsibility for the arrival of a complying payment order to the receiving bank. Thus banks that accept payment orders assume liability not only for their own negligence but also for the negligence of subsequent banks that act on the order.

Solution # 2 rejects receiver finality and provides that a sending customer makes payment to a receiving customer only by providing "good funds" to the receiving bank for the account of the receiving customer. Mere acceptance of the payment order by the receiving bank is not payment to the receiving customer; settlement must occur. Under this solution the risk of insolvency of a transmitting bank falls on the sending customer and not on the bank that accepts the payment order. With respect to negligence or miscarriage of the sending customer's order Solution # 2 provides that banks are responsible only for their own acts or omissions. The burden is placed on the sending customer to recover from the culpable bank.

Our analysis of these two solutions reveals that a characteristic of receiver finality under Solution # 1 is simplicity. A characteristic of the "good funds" rule under Solution # 2 is complexity.

Under Solution # 2 the statute will contain provisions that produce the following rules:

Rule # 1. When Sending Bank accepts the order of Sending Customer it warrants to Sending Customer (a) that it will exercise due care in carrying out the order by transmitting a complying payment order and (b) that it will pay its order. Sending Bank is not responsible for the negligence or insolvency of any other bank that takes action in execution of Sending Customer's order.

Rule # 2. Upon acceptance of the order by Sending Bank, Sending Customer is liable to Sending Bank to pay the amount of the order.

Rule # 3. When Intermediary Bank accepts the order of Sending Bank it warrants to Sending Customer (a) that it will exercise due care in carrying out Sending Bank's order by transmitting a complying payment order and (b) that it will pay its order. Intermediary Bank is not responsible for the negligence or insolvency of any other bank that takes action in execution of Sending Bank's order.

Rule # 4. Upon acceptance of the order by Intermediary Bank, Sending Bank is liable to Intermediary Bank to pay the amount of the order.

Rule # 5. When Receiving Bank accepts the order of Intermediary Bank it warrants to Sending Customer that it will exercise due care in execution of the order.

Rule # 6. When Receiving Bank receives final settlement of Intermediary Bank's obligation to pay its payment order, Receiving Bank is liable to Receiving Customer for the amount of the order.

Rule # 7. Upon acceptance of the order by Receiving Bank, Intermediary Bank is liable to Receiving Bank to pay the amount of the order.

Rule # 8. With respect to the underlying transaction pursuant to which Sending Customer made its payment order, payment by Sending Customer to Receiving Customer of the amount of the order occurs when Receiving Bank receives final settlement of an order of Intermediary Bank that complies with Sending Customer's order, or when Receiving Customer receives final payment from Receiving Bank, whichever occurs first.

Failure to Settle, Insolvency and Payment of the Underlying Obligation

Case # 1. Suppose Receiving Bank accepts the payment order of Intermediary Bank before receiving final settlement and that Intermediary Bank fails to settle because of insolvency. Who takes the loss? If Intermediary Bank fails to settle, Receiving Bank is not obligated to pay Receiving Customer (Rule # 6) and if final payment has not been made the underlying obligation on account of which the wire transfer was made has not been satisfied. Rule # 8. If Receiving Bank has not paid any money to Receiving Customer Receiving Bank has suffered no loss by the failure to settle. Neither has Receiving Customer because its pre-transfer contractual relationship with Sending Customer has not been altered. At most Receiving Customer has lost an expectancy of payment as a result of the failed settlement, but its rights have not been changed in any way.

In Case # 1 the loss falls on Sending Customer because it is obligated to pay Sending Bank which has met the warranty that it made under Rule # 1 by paying its order. Sending Customer has only a claim against insolvent Intermediary Bank for breach of its Rule # 3(b) warranty.

If Receiving Bank has not made any payment to Receiving Customer it is anomalous for the statute to provide that Receiving Bank has a right to enforce the payment order of Intermediary Bank because acceptance of it imposes no monetary obligation on Receiving Bank. Solution # 2 is internally inconsistent with respect to how failure to settle is treated. In the case of Sending Bank and Intermediary Bank acceptance of the payment order imposes a liability on the acceptor (its liability on the payment order which it is required to transmit) which is not excused by a failure to receive settlement on the order that it accepted. Acceptance means that the accepting bank is required to make a promise to pay in the form of a payment order. For that reason the accepting bank must be given a right to enforce the payment order that it accepted. But in the case of Receiving Bank the result is different. Acceptance of the payment order of Intermediary Bank imposes no obligation to pay on Receiving Bank until it receives settlement. Solution # 1, in adopting the principle of receiver finality, treats all banks equally.

Case # 2. What happens if Receiving Bank has already paid Receiving Customer when Intermediary Bank fails to settle? Although Receiving Bank was not obligated to pay Receiving Customer, if the payment was made unconditionally the result is that Receiving Customer has received final payment and Sending Customer has paid its debt. Rule # 8. Since the money was received by Receiving Customer in payment of the debt of Sending Customer there is no basis for a restitution claim by Receiving Bank. There was no payment by mistake, nor was there any unjust enrichment. Receiving Bank simply assumed the risk of nonpayment by Intermediary Bank. Thus Receiving Bank has a loss. It has two causes of action to recoup the loss. It has a claim against insolvent Intermediary Bank, and it should also have a claim against Sending Customer by subrogation. Under a good funds approach Sending Customer is not entitled to have its debt to Receiving Customer satisfied until good funds are received by Receiving Bank. That debt was satisfied in this case but with funds of Receiving Bank rather than funds provided by Sending Customer. Since Receiving Bank has conferred a benefit on Sending Customer it should be subrogated to the rights against Sending Customer that Receiving Customer had on the underlying contract at the time payment was made. The Rules set forth under Solution # 2 do not specifically provide for a subrogation right. If Solution # 2 is adopted the statute should contain a provision that explicitly recognizes the right. If Sending Customer pays Receiving Bank it will have recourse against insolvent Intermediary Bank for breach of its Rule # 3(b) warranty.

Thus, the result in Case # 2 is similar to the result in Case # 1. The ultimate risk of loss falls on Sending Customer.

Case # 3. A similar analysis applies if Sending Bank is the bank that becomes insolvent and fails to settle with Intermediary Bank. Intermediary Bank is liable to Receiving Bank on the payment order given to that bank and failure to receive settlement from Sending Bank does not excuse performance by Intermediary Bank. If Intermediary Bank is not itself insolvent Receiving Bank will receive settlement. When it receives settlement it is liable to Receiving

Customer and the obligation of Sending Customer has been paid. Thus, it is Intermediary Bank that has suffered a loss. But when Intermediary Bank has settled with Receiving Bank it caused Sending Customer's debt to Receiving Customer to be paid. Payment was made with funds of Intermediary Bank rather than funds provided by Sending Customer. To the same extent that Receiving Bank is subrogated to the rights of Receiving Customer on the underlying transaction in Case # 2, Intermediary Bank should be subrogated to those rights in Case # 3. If Sending Customer pays Intermediary Bank it will have a claim against insolvent Sending Bank for breach of its Rule # 1(b) warranty.

There are major practical difficulties with Solution # 2 that are not apparent in the analysis just made. Case # 2 and Case # 3 are basically similar in that they both involve situations in which a bank has made payment under a payment order and then has failed to receive settlement from the bank that made the order. In both cases we state that the paying bank has a claim based on subrogation against the sending customer. But we don't state how the amount of that subrogation claim is calculated. Unless this issue is addressed one can be misled about what will happen in the event of the insolvency of a bank in the payment chain.

Suppose the amount of the wire transfer from Sending Customer to Receiving Customer was $1,000,000. Receiving Bank allowed the $1,000,000 to be withdrawn by Receiving Customer immediately after Receiving Bank accepted the order of Intermediary Bank. At the end of the day Intermediary Bank refused to settle and ceased business because insolvent. This is Case # 2 if the withdrawal was made unconditionally. Does Receiving Bank have a subrogation right of $1,000,000 against Sending Customer? Or, suppose Receiving Bank allowed withdrawal of the $1,000,000 subject to the condition that settlement is received from Intermediary Bank. Does Receiving Bank have a right to recover $1,000,000 from Receiving Customer? The answer to either of the questions is not clear because it is not clear what it means to say that the right of recovery is dependent upon a failure to receive settlement.

Suppose that during the day in question Receiving Bank accepted 800 payment orders totalling $90,000,000 from Intermediary Bank and Intermediary Bank accepted 700 payment orders totalling $50,000,000 from Receiving Bank. Suppose that with respect to the 800 payment orders accepted by Receiving Bank that bank (acting as an intermediary bank) made payment orders to other banks with respect to 400, and that bank (acting as a destination receiving bank) made conditional payments to customers with respect to 200, made unconditional payments to customers with respect to 50 and made no payment at all with respect to 150.

With respect to the 400 orders on which Receiving Bank made payment orders to other banks the failure to receive settlement does not excuse performance by Receiving Bank on its payment orders, but Receiving Bank has subrogation rights against the various sending customers. With respect to the 200 orders on which Receiving Bank made conditional payment Receiving Bank has claims against the various receiving customers. With respect to the 50 orders on which final payment was made Receiving Bank has subrogation rights against the various sending customers. With respect to the 150 orders on which no payment was made Receiving Bank has no claim against anybody because it has suffered no loss. Is it correct to say that Receiving Bank has not received settlement on any of the 900 orders that it accepted? If Receiving Bank has received partial settlement how do we distribute the settlement received among the various orders?

To simplify the analysis assume that Intermediary Bank did not transmit or receive any payment orders to or from any bank other than Receiving Bank. Also assume that it made conditional payment to its own receiving customers on all of the 700 orders that it accepted from Receiving Bank. Does Intermediary Bank (acting as a receiving bank) have a claim against these customers to recover the payments on the ground that it had not received settlement? Were the underlying debts of the sending customers with respect to which the payments were made satisfied because Intermediary Bank had received good funds? We think that the answer to the first question is "NO" and the answer to the second question is "YES," but we are not sure.

The answer to these questions depends upon what effect is given to the fact that settlement is done on a net basis. In the case under discussion if Intermediary Bank had been able to settle it would have done so by paying Receiving Bank the $40,000,000 net amount that it owed. But in the case of insolvency no actual settlement will occur at the end of the day. If Receiving Bank is allowed to treat the $90,000,000 and $50,000,000 debts as mutual debts that can be set off the mutual debts are reduced to a net debt of $40,000,000 owing by Intermediary Bank to Receiving Bank. Setoff is a netting out concept which treats the many obligations of each party as though they were one debt. We don't know in all cases which of the obligations have been satisfied. We might conclude that some were satisfied and others not, or that all were satisfied in part to the extent of the setoff distributed pro rata. In the normal setoff situation this problem is not presented because only the rights of the mutual debtor-creditors are involved. But if payment or nonpayment of any individual obligations affects the rights of third parties it becomes necessary to determine the effect of setoff on each of the obligations involved.

But the difficulty of assigning the setoff to various obligations relates only to the obligations owed to the net creditor. We can say that all of the obligations owed to the net debtor have been satisfied. Thus, in the case under discussion if no money is owed by Receiving Bank (the net creditor) we would conclude that Intermediary Bank (the net debtor) has received settlement from Receiving Bank and that it has received good funds on all of the payment orders it accepted.

If the foregoing analysis is correct then it would follow that Receiving Bank has also received settlement and good funds to the extent of its setoff. If that is true it is necessary to decide which, or what part of, the payment orders accepted by Receiving Bank have been settled. We don't know how to unscramble this omelette, but a statutory solution that results in many hundreds of claims that cannot be readily determined leaves something to be desired. For example, if a rule of proration were adopted it would mean that some underlying debts were satisfied in part, that some conditional payments could be recovered in part, and that Receiving Bank had subrogation rights in part. But the determinations necessary would require litigation that might be protracted. The difficulty is inherent in a good funds theory. There is no certainty about when, or the extent to which, the underlying obligation for which a payment order is transmitted is satisfied. We believe that the uncertainty and complexity of Solution # 2 is the strongest argument against it. We might also point out that this problem may exist under the present system. It is very common for receiving banks to pay receiving customers subject to settlement. It is difficult to know how this might be treated in the courts if an insolvency of the type under discussion ever occurred because under the present system it is not clear when payment of underlying obligations is made in a wire transfer.

Under the current system receiving banks apparently take the view that by making a conditional payment to a receiving customer they are simply making a "loan" to the customer that is discharged when the bank gets settlement and can be called if settlement is not received. But they apparently treat the right as imposing no obligation to prorate the settlement loss among all the orders accepted. Thus, they assume that they can assert the right against any customer to the full extent of the conditional payment and to the extent that the bank has a loss. We are not at all sure whether the courts would allow a bank to discriminate among customers in this way. The issue has never arisen. Our statute could explicitly allow a receiving bank to recover its loss in this manner, but we think that solution is unacceptable as a matter of policy.

If a setoff approach is not appropriate the only other solution that we see is to provide for a complete unwind of all transfers to and from the insolvent bank. But, this we think would lead to chaos. The commercial world relies on the funds received, whether the receipt is conditional or not. The money is often spent or committed before it is received. The receiving customer doesn't expect that repayment will ever be required. We consider any rule of law that contemplates the undoing of very large numbers of transactions to be unsound.

Delay in Transmission and Payment to Wrong Person

Case # 1. Sending Customer is making payment to Receiving Customer to exercise a favorable option to purchase property. Because of negligence by Intermediary Bank transmittal of an order to pay is delayed and not received by Receiving Bank until after expiration of the option. Receiving Customer refused to accept the late payment as an exercise of the option and returned the money to Sending Customer. As a result Sending Customer suffered a substantial loss of profit. Who is liable for the loss?

Sending Bank has no liability in this case because there is no breach of its Rule # 1 warranty. Sending Bank is not liable for the negligence of Intermediary Bank. Sending Customer has a cause of action only against Intermediary Bank for breach of its Rule 3(a) warranty. Solution # 1, by giving Sending Customer a cause of action against either Sending Bank or Intermediary Bank, allows Sending Customer to sue the most convenient defendant. Solution # 2 denies this advantage to Sending Customer.

Case # 2. Sending Customer ordered payment to Receiving Customer to pay a debt. Intermediary Bank ordered Receiving Bank to pay the wrong account. The funds were withdrawn and cannot be recovered. Who takes the loss?

Receiving Bank suffers no loss because it is entitled to settlement from Intermediary Bank. The debt to Receiving Customer has not been satisfied because the order of Intermediary Bank did not comply with Sending Customer's order. Rule # 8. Thus, Sending Customer has suffered a loss. Sending Customer's only cause of action is against Intermediary Bank for breach of its Rule # 3(a) warranty. The result in this case is the same as in Case # 1.

Case # 3. Same facts as in Case # 2 except that the error in paying the wrong account was made by Receiving Bank. In this case Sending Customer has suffered no loss because the obligation to Receiving Customer was paid when Intermediary Bank made final settlement of its accurate payment order. Rule # 8. Although Receiving Bank is in breach of its Rule # 5 warranty there are no damages. Receiving Customer is entitled to recover the amount of the order from Receiving Bank. Rule # 6. Thus, Receiving Bank takes the loss.

In all of these cases the only difference between Solution # 1 and Solution # 2 is in the responsibility of banks other than the negligent bank for the miscarriage of the payment order.

CHAPTER TWENTY-NINE

LETTER OF CREDIT

SECTION 1. INTRODUCTION

To most students the letter of credit will be a completely foreign item. In the United States the use of such letters originated in foreign trade, and they still find their most frequent use there. In the last two decades they have been used much more frequently in domestic transactions, both trade and non-trade.

A. Traditional Letters of Credit

To understand the names of the players in this drama and their general responsibilities consider a case in which a Danish seller is going to sell goods to a Newark, New Jersey buyer. If the parties have dealt with one another over a long period of time, the seller might be willing to ship to the buyer on open credit and to rely upon the buyer's willingness and ability to make payment upon receipt of the goods. If the seller has not dealt with the buyer, he would be foolish to make such an arrangement without doing extensive investigation about the buyer's creditworthiness and reliability. Conversely, the buyer could prepay for the goods, but then he would be taking the entire risk of default. He would be forced to pay without any assurance that the goods had been manufactured, much less manufactured correctly. The letter of credit represents an intermediate position between the two suggested. In such a setting the Newark buyer might procure a letter of credit from his bank; that letter would promise (i.e., put the bank's credit behind the agreement) to pay the purchase price to the seller upon presentation of certain documents. Usually these documents would consist at least of an invoice and bills of lading that showed shipment. They may also include an inspection certificate or a certificate of insurance or other documents.

Note that the American bank officer will make payment at his or her desk. The officer will look at the documents presented and only at those documents. The condition of the goods—that they are marred and scarred, defective or out of style—will be not just irrelevant, but unknown, to the bank officer. In this setting the bank is labeled the "issuer," the American buyer is the "customer," and the Danish seller is the "beneficiary." The bank should look at the transaction as though it were a loan to its "customer," i.e., the person with whom it deals in Newark. If it is unwilling to make that loan, it probably should not write the letter of credit. The bank is essentially relying upon its customer in this transaction, and it will likely have no knowledge of the seller or of the seller's capabilities. The seller, on the other hand, is relying upon the bank. It assumes, correctly, that the bank is less likely to go bankrupt than is a random buyer, that the bank is less likely to withhold some or all of the payment on a trumped up ground and, if the bank is a large international bank, the bank's reputation may itself be known to the Danish seller.

By entering into a letter of credit transaction, how have the parties altered the risks and responsibilities that would otherwise be present in a conventional sales transaction? First, and most obvious, the transaction has, in effect, substituted the credit of the American bank for the credit of its customer. If the customer goes into bankruptcy, that will be no defense to the bank's payment. The risk of the customer's bankruptcy has thus been shifted from the seller (in a credit transaction) to the buyer's bank. Secondly, the debt obligation of the buyer has likely become more liquid. Assume, for example, that shipment is to occur 90 days after the agreement is signed. If the obligation to pay is backed by a letter of credit by a well-known American bank, it is likely that the Danish seller will be able to borrow against that obligation much more readily than if it were simply peddling the obligation of the Newark buyer.

Third, the transaction has shifted the litigation cost and probably shifted the forum in any subsequent dispute. If the buyer later claims that the goods were defective, the buyer will now be made into a plaintiff instead of a defendant because of the letter of credit transaction. This is because the bank will have paid the Danish seller and the burden will be upon the American buyer to find the seller and bring suit against him. If the buyer had not paid, he could simply set off and thus force the seller to come to him. Usually this means not only that the American buyer will be the plaintiff, but also that he will have to go to Denmark to sue. With the expansion of the long-arm statutes and such, and with the more expansive view of doing business, it will now be more likely than formerly that the American buyer could get jurisdiction in the American court over the Danish seller, but that will not invariably be true. So the third and fourth functions of the letter of credit are to shift the burden of bringing suit and in many cases to shift the forum from the hometown of one party to the hometown of the other.

Finally, the letter of credit reduces costs by comparison with other insurance and security devices such as bonds and surety agreements. That is so because the bank presumably already knows its "customer" and need not do an extensive credit search to determine whether to issue the letter of credit. It can call upon its pre-existing knowledge to decide that it will issue a letter and that knowledge, gained from other transactions, will enable it to make an accurate estimation of the credit risk.

Problem 29–1

Examine the document set out below. It is a letter of credit. By referring to it answer the questions that follow.

No. G.C. 58954 irrevocable $97,460.00

THE FIRST NATIONAL BANK OF CHICAGO
CHICAGO 90, ILLINOIS

November 29, 1979

Associated Steel Corporation,
176 West Adams Street
Chicago, Illinois
or Assigns

This letter of credit is Assignable and divisible

GENTLEMEN:

WE HEREBY AUTHORIZE YOU TO DRAW AT ______ SIGHT ON ______ FOR ANY SUM OR SUMS NOT EXCEEDING IN ALL Ninety Seven Thousand Four Hundred Sixty U.S. Dollars FOR ACCOUNT OF Decker Steel Co., Grand Rapids, Michigan.

Drafts are to be accompanied by the following documents:

Commercial invoices showing approximately 500 tons prime Thomas quality 36 inch by coil hot rolled steel.

Railroad or truck clean bill of lading issued to order of shipper blank endorsed notify Decker Steel Company, 1620 Turner Avenue, N.W., Grand Rapids 4, Michigan, and showing shipment from New York, New York to Grand Rapids, Michigan.

This credit will remain in force until February 29, 1980 and drafts must be negotiated on or before that date.

WE HEREBY AGREE WITH DRAWERS, ENDORSERS AND BONA FIDE HOLDERS OF DRAFTS NEGOTIATED UNDER AND IN COMPLIANCE WITH THE TERMS OF THIS CREDIT THAT THE SAME SHALL BE DULY HONORED UPON PRESENTATION AT THE COUNTER OF The First National Bank of Chicago. EACH AMOUNT DRAWN MUST BE ENDORSED ON THE REVERSE HEREOF BY THE NEGOTIATING BANK.

INSURANCE ______

DRAFTS UNDER THIS CREDIT MUST BEAR UPON THEIR FACE THE WORDS:

''DRAWN UNDER THE FIRST NATIONAL BANK OF CHICAGO''

CREDIT NO. G.C. 58954 DATED November 19, 1979

RESPECTFULLY YOURS,

THE FIRST NATIONAL BANK OF CHICAGO

Assistant Vice President

Assistant Cashier

Questions

1. Who is the customer, who the beneficiary, and who the issuer?

2. Assume that Associated Steel and First National Bank of Chicago decided to cancel the letter of credit:

a. After it had been mailed but before it had been delivered to Associated Steel.

b. After it had been delivered to Associated Steel but before Associated had taken any action in reliance upon it.

Could they do so?

3. The letter specifically states that it is assignable. In view of the statement in UCC 5–116(3), how does the fact that this document is "assignable" give the beneficiary greater rights that he would have even if it were not assignable?

B. Standby Letter of Credit

In the past twenty years a pattern of transactions quite unrelated to international trade or, indeed, to the sale of goods of any sort, has grown up in the United States. This is the issuance of "standby" letters of credit. To the dismay of federal regulators and to the concern of accountants, much of this growth has occurred off the balance sheet, and sometimes, one suspects, without careful consideration of the exposure that a large body of standby letters of credit presents to the issuer of those credits. First, what is a standby letter of credit? Basically, it is one in which the issuer promises to make payment to a beneficiary on the occurrence of a default by the customer other than a default in the shipment of goods. For example, a bank might issue a letter of credit to an owner that promises to make payment to the owner in the event that a builder defaults in constructing a home or a building. A bank might grant a letter of credit to a football player (beneficiary) to secure the payment of a multi-year salary by a shaky football team in a new league. It is even conceivable that a letter of credit could be issued on behalf of a seller, as customer, to a buyer to agree to pay the buyer a certain amount of money in case the seller did not deliver goods.

In general the same rules of law apply to the liabilities under standby letters of credit as under those for the sale of goods. One might wish to distinguish the two, first, because standbys present somewhat different risks to the issuer than do traditional letters of credit and, secondly, because they present somewhat different practical issues in connection with the obligations of payment and responsibilities for performance by the beneficiary and the issuer.

If the buyer fails to pay for the goods in our Denmark/Newark transaction, the bank at least will have a security interest (assuming it has executed the proper documents; see UCC 9–304) in the goods and will be able to recoup some of its loss by resale of those goods. In a traditional case, therefore, its exposure is somewhat limited. Compare that with the traditional standby case in which it promises to pay a city $500,000 upon certification that the curb and gutter contractor has defaulted. If the curb and gutter contractor is now in bankruptcy, the payment of the $500,000 to the municipality may be a dead loss for the bank. Thus, the bank's exposure tends to be larger because of the absence of any obvious security growing out of the transaction in the standby case.

Even more significant, in your editor's view, is a distinction in the obligation which the bank secures between the two different kinds of letters. In the traditional letter of credit the bank is making a bet upon its customer's ability to pay money. That is grist for a banker's mill: determining whether a customer can pay money. In a standby case, a bank is making a bet on its customer's ability and willingness to do something that may be much more complex—to build gutters, to drill a well, to construct a development of houses, etc. Here one suspects some bankers are over their heads and are less likely to make an accurate prediction than in the former case. For all of those reasons the federal bank regulators cluck nervously, but ineffectually, as they watch their chicks write a larger and larger volume of standby letters of credits.

C. Documents

What then are the documents that compose the usual letter of credit transaction and what are the basic legal liabilities? In the usual transaction there will be at least three separate documents. First there will be the underlying contract between the beneficiary and the customer. This is the contract of sale between the Danish seller and the Newark buyer; in a standby case it is the contract for the construction of the curbs and gutters by the local contractor and the municipality. Second is the letter of credit itself. As one will see from the letter quoted below, it is addressed to the beneficiary and signed by the issuer. A wise lawyer will call it a letter of credit, not a contract, not a guarantee, not a bond. The third contract is between the issuer and the customer. Examination of this contract shows the guts of the letter of credit transaction, namely, a potential loan to the customer. In it the customer will promise to pay the bank (usually before the bank has to pay the beneficiary), it will grant the bank a security interest to secure any payments that must be made under the letter, and it will make still other promises to the bank. Many bank officers and their lawyers have rued the day when they issued a letter of credit without first having secured the customer's signature on the contract, or having secured that signature on a contract without all of the proper terms.

How does one characterize the legal relation established by the execution of these various documents? The characterizations that come to mind and the analogies that one most easily draws are all flawed in important ways. The bank is not really a guarantor. Nor is its obligation on the letter of credit exclusively a contractual one. Moreover, strictly speaking, the "beneficiary" is not really a beneficiary of the underlying agreement between the bank and the customer. Finally, the bank's issuance of the money to the beneficiary might be regarded as a loan to the customer, but most would not so characterize it. Perhaps the writing of the letter itself should be regarded as a commitment to make a loan to the customer, not so?

Advice for the beneficiary - Avis pour le bénéficiaire

NOM DE LA BANQUE ÉMETTRICE - NAME OF ISSUING BANK

Issuing Bank Limited International Division
23, High Street
London S.W. 25

Lieu et date d'émission - Place and date of issue
London
13 October 1984

Irrevocable documentary credit
Crédit documentaire irrévocable

Number - Numero: 16358

Date and place of expiry - Date et lieu de validité: 30 November 1984 at counters of advising bank

Applicant - Donneur d'ordre:
Joan's Boutique
14 Charlotte Street
London W.C.36

Beneficiary - Bénéficiaire:
The Eastern Trading Company
29, London Road
Hong Kong

Advising Bank - Banque notificatrice — Ref. nr. - No. Ref.:
Bank "X"
35 Kings Road North
Hong Kong

Amount - Montant: HK$ 10,000 (Hong Kong Dollars ten thousand)

Partial shipments / Expéditions partielles: [ ] allowed / autorisées [X] not allowed / non autorisées

Transhipment / Transbordement: [ ] allowed / autorisées [X] not allowed / non autorisées

Shipment/dispatch/taking in charge from/at / Embarquement/expédition/prise en charge de/à: Hong Kong

for transportation to: / à destination de: Heathrow Airport, London

Credit available with - Crédit utilisable chez

[ ] by sight payment / par paiement à vue [X] by acceptance / par acceptation [ ] by negotiation / par négociation

[ ] by deferred payment at / par paiement différé à

against the documents detailed herein / contre les documents précisés ci-après

[X] and beneficiary's draft at / et la traite du bénéficiaire au: 90 days sight

on / sur: Bank "X", 35 Kings Road North, Hong Kong

SIGNED INVOICE IN THREE COPIES certifying that the goods are in accordance with Joan's Boutique Order Number 35 dated 14.8.1984.

AIR CONSIGNMENT NOTE evidencing goods dispatched to Joan's Boutique, 14 Charlotte Street, London W.C. 36 marked "Freight Paid".

PACKING LIST IN TRIPLICATE

We are informed that insurance is being arranged by our principals.

covering Ladies Dresses
C and F Heathrow Airport, London

Documents to be presented within / Documents à présenter dans les [7] days after the date of issuance of the transport document(s) but within the validity of the credit / jours après la date d'émission du/des document(s) de transport mais dans la période de validité du crédit

We hereby issue the Documentary Credit in your favour. It is subject to the Uniform Customs and Practice for Documentary Credits (1983 Revision, International Chamber of Commerce, Paris, France, Publication No. 400) and engages us in accordance with the terms thereof. The number and the date of the credit and the name of our bank must be quoted on all drafts required. If the credit is available by negotiation, each presentation must be noted on the reverse of this advice by the bank where the credit is available.

Nous émettons par la présente ce crédit documentaire en votre faveur. Il est soumis aux Règles et Usances Uniformes relatives aux Crédits Documentaire (Révision 1983, Publication No. 400 de la Chambre de Commerce Internationale, Paris, France) et nous engage selon leurs termes. Le numéro et la date du crédit ainsi que le nom de notre banque devront être mentionnés sur toute traite requise. Si le crédit est utilisable par négociation chaque présentation devra être inscrite au verso de cet avis par la banque où le crédit est utilisable.

Issuing Bank Limited International Division
23, High Street
London S.W. 25

This document consists of / Ce document consiste en [1] signed page(s) / page(s) signée(s)

Notes

1. Would the bank pay on the following draft?

Pay to the order of Eastern Trading Company $1,000 H.K.

—One thousand dollars Hong Kong—

To: Issuing Bank Ltd.
25 High Street
London S.W. 25

A.R. Rogers
Eastern Trading Co.

2. What if the invoices presented appeared to have a stamp on the signature line or a printed inscription? Should the bank pay against those?

3. If the letter of credit set out above were changed to a standby letter of credit, what would the conditions of performance say?

INVOICE FACTURE FACTURA RECHNUNG FACTUUR

Seller (Name, Address, VAT Reg. No.)
Clearchem PLC
Riverside Works, Warren Road
Banbury
Oxfordshire
United Kingdom

Sheet No. 1

Invoice No. & Date (Tax Point): RT 67244 8 Nov 84

Seller's Reference: SPEX/548/789/DEM

Buyer's Reference: Order ARB-548771

Other Reference

Consignee
General Trading Company Limited
Suite 18/88, Eastern House
3487 Soleiman Jamshid Mojdeh
Riyadh
Saudi Arabia

Buyer (if not Consignee)

Country of Origin of Goods: UK (EEC)

Country of Destination: Saudi Arabia

Import licence 892E-44319

Terms of Delivery and Payment
CIF Jeddah
Confirmed Irrevocable Letter of
Credit payable at sight
Payment should be made through:
British Bank Limited
88 Waterloo Place, London SW1
Account no. 120 7532 68

Vessel/Aircraft etc.: Orient Adventurer

Port of Loading: Liverpool

Port of Discharge: Jeddah

Marks and Numbers and Container No.	Number and Kind of Packages; Description of Goods	TT Code No.	Total Gross Wt (Kg)	Total Cube (m³)
G.T.C. ARB-548771 Riyadh via Jeddah 1-80	1 x 20ft Container Chemical products in drums		kg 2141.8	20.620

Total Net Wt (Kg): 2000.0

Item/pkges	Gross/Net/Cube	Description	Quantity	Unit Price	Selling Price
1)	816.8 750.0 7.620	Product D101/5877 Hydrofluoric Acid Solution 50% w/w	30 drums	17.26 /25kg	517.80
2)	1325.0 1250.0 13.000	Product D100/6755 Antimony Trichloride	50 drums	20.47 /25kg	1023.50

					1541.30
		Freight			180.55
		Insurance			39.70

Invoice Total: GBP £ 1761.55

We hereby guarantee that this is a true and correct invoice and that the goods referred to are of the origin, manufacture and production of the United Kingdom.

Name of Signatory: AC Smith, Director

Place and Date of Issue: Banbury 8 NOV 1984

Signature: AC Smith

Notes

Assume that the letter of credit described the commodity as 816.8 Product D101/5857; 750.0 Hydrofluoric Acid; 7.620 Solution 50% w/w.

1. Under which of the following descriptions would you reject the invoice as improper if you were an employee of the issuing bank?

a. "816.8 Product D101/5877."

b. Description as set out in the invoice printed above, but listing 29 or alternatively 32 drums.

c. "750.0 Hydrofluoric Acid."

2. What if the invoice was not that of Clearchem, but an invoice with a proper description of Ambercamp, a related company also located in Banbury? See UPC Article 41.

3. Assume that the invoice contained the precise description, but that an insurance certification was included that described the product merely as "Approximately 30 drums, more or less, hydrofluoric acid."

4. What if the invoice or bill of lading came to the bank not through the mail but by a computer connection from the carrier or shipper, between the sender's computer and bank, which when properly stimulated printed out the above invoice? Would such a document be acceptable? See Article 22. How would you authenticate a document in such case?

D. Sources of Law

There are two significant sources of law in addition to the cases. The first is Article 5 of the Uniform Commercial Code. As section 5–102 will disclose, that Article covers not just documentary credits issued by a bank, but also credits issued by nonbanks. Subsection (3) contains a curious disclaimer:

> This Article deals with some but not all of the rules and concepts of letters of credit as such rules or concepts have developed prior to this act or may hereafter develop. The fact that this Article states a rule does not by itself require, imply or negate application of the same or a converse rule to a situation not provided for or to a person not specified by this Article.

At the conclusion of this chapter the student should have some familiarity with each of the seventeen sections in Article 5.

The second important source of non-case law is a document entitled the Uniform Customs and Practices for Documentary Credits. This is a document issued by the International Chamber of Commerce and, by agreement, it governs a large share of all letters of credit written in international transactions. A current copy is set out beginning at p. 1419. A comparison of Article 5 with the rules in the Uniform Customs and Practices shows that they are by no means identical, but it would be mistake to believe that they contain significantly different rules of law; they do not. The basic rules are the same under either. Because of long experience and because it is devoted explicitly to the international trade arena, the Uniform Customs and Practices will have many detailed provisions that deal explicitly with the sale of goods. For example, Article 14 contains a series of specific rules on the kinds of documents that are appropriate, the kinds of descriptions that are necessary, etc. These rules can be determinative in a case governed by the UCP; they can be persuasive in one governed by the Uniform Commercial Code. At the behest of its banks, New York added the following non-uniform amendment to 5–102. In New York 5–102(4) reads as follows:

> Unless otherwise agreed, this Article 5 does not apply to a letter of credit or a credit if by its terms or by agreement, course of dealing or usage of trade such letter of credit or credit is subject in whole or in part to the Uniform Customs and Practice for Commercial Documentary Credits fixed by the 13th or by any subsequent Congress of the International Chamber of Commerce.

In an earlier version of this book we accused Henry Harfield, then a partner in Sherman and Sterling, and America's preeminent expert on letters of credit, of leading the New York lawyers in an attack on the UCC out of a neurotic attachment to the Uniform Customs and Practices. Mr. Harfield responded to that charge as follows:

> "Dear Professor White:
>
> "* * * As regards the matter discussed and the material referred to in the second paragraph of your letter, I gladly waive any rights I may have and am content that this letter constitutes my release of any liability you may have to me for defamation. On the other hand, you will understand that I cannot and do not undertake to indemnify you against liability to others arising out of the inaccuracy of your statements. The New York Bar was far from uniform in its reaction to the Uniform Commercial Code in general and to Article 5 in particular. I can well imagine that those outstanding members of the Bar who supported the Code with apostolic zeal (and there are many of them) might feel justifiably aggrieved at their unwarranted inclusion with a group of intellectual muckers. At the other end of the spectrum, there is good ground for umbrage by those outstanding members of the New York Bar (and there are many of them) who then were and still are persuaded that the Code is the most mischievous piece of contrivance since the Communist Manifesto. Each of these groups may regard as actionable, your proposed assertion that I was their leader.
>
> "That statement is simply not supported by the record. The facts are that the New York Bar was divided, perhaps even fragmented, and the proceedings before the Law Revision Commission resembled a Donnybrook rather than a knightly tournament. There was a significant group who supported Article 5 in all its aspects and they had their leaders who were devout and dedicated men. There was a group which regarded Article 5, in every aspect, as anathema and they had their leaders who were devout and dedicated men; but I was not a leader of either group. My recollection is that my approach was singular, objective, statesmanlike, and always reasonable. For this I deserve no credit; it is just my nature. * * *"
>
> "Faithfully yours,
>
> "Henry Harfield."

Because of the provision in the New York law and because a large share of all international letters of credit are written in New York by New York banks, many letter of credit transactions in the United States will not be governed by the Uniform Commercial Code, but by the UCP. It is important, therefore, that the student know the UCP, not just as a basis for analogy in Code cases, but as the governing law in many transactions.

Almost all of the cases, an incredibly complex array, arise out of a single problem. Nearly all ask the question: Was the bank which was presented with certain documents required to pay? The basic rule is that if there is compliance with the documentary requirements of the letter, the bank must pay, even though there is a breach of the underlying contract, even though its own customer has gone bankrupt, even though the world is about to come to an end. However, beginning with the *Sztejn* case, infra 1388, the courts and now the Uniform Commercial Code have recognized at least one exception to the bank's obligation to pay on presentation of complying documents, the so-called fraud exception. Many of the cases that now come to the court call upon it to draw the line between fraud on the one hand (where payment is excused) and cases of mere breach of the underlying contract (where payment is not excused).

Many other cases deal in tedious detail with the form of documents that are necessary to comply with the credits. When the bank wishes not to pay, it will of course examine the documents microscopically and will seize on any small detail as a basis for its refusal to pay and as an excuse. Usually the defect in the documents is not the true reason the bank has chosen not to pay. It probably has chosen not to pay because its customer has asked it not to pay, because its customer has gone bankrupt, or because, for some other reason, it believes it or its customer will not be reimbursed. Each time the bank is freed from payment by a court, a little chip is taken out of the solid rock of letter of credit law and practice. Each time the courts grant an injunction against payment, in the words of Henry Harfield: "I fear that the sacred cow of equity may trample the tender vines of letter of credit law." Harfield, *Code, Custom, and Conscience in Letter of Credit Law,* 4 UCC L.J. 7, 11 (1971). Thus, many of the cases are bitterly fought wars over words with nary a mention of the true motivation of the bank and of the other party.

A final set of cases involves the right of a bank who has paid to be repaid out of the assets of its customer, to be subrogated to its customer's or beneficiary's rights or otherwise to protect itself by taking and selling the underlying assets.

SECTION 2. THE ISSUER'S DUTY TO PAY, UCC 5–109, 5–114, THE BASIC RULE

The issuer's duty to its customer is to examine the documents presented and to refuse to pay if the documents are not correct. That duty is set out under UCC 5–109. The issuer's duty to the beneficiary, on the other hand, is the duty to honor on proper presentation and that duty is specified as follows in UCC 5–114(1):

> An issuer must honor a draft or demand for payment which complies with the terms of the relevant credit regardless of whether the goods or documents conform to the underlying contract for sale or other contract between the customer and the beneficiary. The issuer is not excused from honor of such a draft or demand by reason of an additional general term that all documents must be satisfactory to the issuer, but an issuer may require that specified documents must be satisfactory to it.

In the next section we will concern ourselves with exceptions to the duty to honor based upon fraud in the underlying transaction. Those are covered by UCC 5–114(2). To understand UCC 5–114(1) and the cases in this section, imagine a letter of credit department in a large bank. Here are many clerical workers, sophisticated clerical workers, but clerical workers nevertheless. On the one hand they have a stack of letters of credit that call for certain kinds of bills of lading, invoices, insurance certificates, certificates of inspection, certifications of default, etc. The letters have dates of expiration and call for specific kinds of drafts signed by particular persons. The bank officers sitting with these documents look from one to the other and ultimately decide whether the conditions have been met.

The job is the same on the bitterest winter day as it is at the height of summer. It is uninfluenced by the destruction of the goods in the most violent storm of the century, by the bankruptcy of the buyer or the seller, or, theoretically, by any other set of events going on outside the room where our hypothetical bank officers are sitting. The issue is plain and simple in every instance: do these documents meet the conditions of this letter?

Sometimes even that is not an easy question to answer. We will see in the cases that follow that reasonable people could differ and reasonable judges have differed about the exact standards that should be applied in determining whether or not the conditions have been met. Moreover, there will be cases in which the true party in interest, the customer, wants to waive certain conditions of the letter, and others in which the bank's behavior may estop it from claiming that the conditions were not met. Finally there are mysterious provisions in the Code on indemnity (5–113) and on the warranties to be given by the beneficiary (5–111) that may influence the bank's responsibility in ways that are not too clear. Nor should one assume that the job of this bank employee is easy at times when the bank's best customer has spoken to the president of the bank who in turn has spoken to the bank officer, and when all of them would rather not see the customer's $500,000 go out in payment, for example, to an Iranian national company never to be seen again. The question then becomes very difficult: to whom does the bank owe its allegiance—to its best customer or to this abstract image of the letter of credit and to its sanctity and utility? More often than a cynic might expect, the sanctity of the letter of credit prevails over the customer's wishes.

BANCO ESPANOL de CREDITO v. STATE STREET BANK AND TRUST CO.

United States Circuit Court, Third Circuit, 1967.
385 F.2d 230, cert. denied 390 U.S. 1013, 88 S.Ct. 1263, 20 L.Ed.2d 163 (1968), appeal after remand 409 F.2d 711 (1969).

Before ALDRICH, CHIEF JUDGE, MCENTEE and COFFIN, CIRCUIT JUDGES.

COFFIN, CIRCUIT JUDGE. This suit began as a claim by appellant, a Spanish bank (Banco Espanol), against appellee, a domestic bank (State Street), for the latter's allegedly wrongful refusal to accept and pay two drafts drawn upon it pursuant to two irrevocable commercial letters of credit. Each letter was issued by State Street at the behest of its customer, Robert Lawrence, Inc. (Lawrence), a Boston clothing concern. Banco Espanol was designated the advising bank and two Spanish suppliers (Alcides and Longuer) were named as beneficiaries. The cases were consolidated for trial in the district court sitting without a jury and, following judgment for State Street, appellant took these appeals.

The issue is whether State Street, whose letters of credit, as amended, called for the presentation of an inspection certificate by a named firm stipulating "that the goods are in conformity with the order", was justified in refusing to honor the drafts of Banco Espanol on the ground that the inspection certificate did not meet the terms of the letters of credit.

The transaction was initiated by Lawrence to finance the purchase of raincoats, beach jackets, knit shirts, and cardigans from Alcides and Longuer. Based upon preliminary arrangements apparently worked out by an intermediary, of which more later, Lawrence obtained two irrevocable letters of credit from State Street. One letter covered Lawrence orders Nos. 101, 102, and 103 for beach jackets, outer coats and cotton garments in the revised final amount of $105,630, and the other covered Lawrence order No. 100 for wool knit shirts and cardigans in the revised final amount of $13,320. Both letters constituted Banco Espanol the correspondent bank, and required signed invoices, customs invoices, inspection certificates, and full sets of clean on board ocean bills of lading dated not later than March 31, 1963.

At the time of issuance of the letters of credit, State Street called to the attention of its customer, Lawrence, that the requirement of an inspection certificate without a named inspector left a hazardous gap in the documents. Lawrence replied that the letters would be later amended to include the name of an inspection agent.

The next three and one half months were significantly devoted to continuing efforts to resolve this problem. On November 22, 1962 one of the Spanish manufacturers (Alcides) wrote Lawrence's representative that it agreed with the idea of naming an inspection agent and suggested that Lawrence put forward a name. Lawrence's man replied shortly that since he would be in Barcelona near the time of delivery, he would be the inspector. Accordingly, State Street sought to amend the letters in January. Foreseeably, this was not acceptable to the beneficiary as Lawrence learned in early February. Lawrence then wrote State Street (notwithstanding the hiatus in the letters of credit which State Street had noted) that it should not make payment unless inspection certificates were signed by a party acceptable to it. It further agreed to indemnify State Street for any damages resulting from carrying out these instructions, coupling this with a threat to refuse reimbursement if payment were made.

After a meeting between Lawrence and State Street, the object of which was to decide what to do about the inspection issue, a representative of Lawrence went to Spain. This trip resulted in an amendment to the letters of credit, cabled to Alcides on March 1, 1963, which required the inspection certificate to be issued by Supervigilancia Sociedad General de Control S.A. (Supervigilancia) certifying that "the goods are in conformity with the order". While it is not clear on whose initiative this firm was selected, it was apparently well regarded by the State Street official who had been closely associated with this transaction.

Identification of the underlying orders to which the letters of credit referred is not an easy task. In the first place, the record before us contains no document purporting to be an order for the shirts and cardigans (No. 100—the Longuer order). As to the Alcides order, we face two sets of somewhat inconsistent documents, both of which Lawrence sent to the manufacturer: two unnumbered papers dated November 5 and 6, 1962, labelled "order placed by Cavendish Co."—apparently an intermediary for Lawrence; and three papers dated November 13, 1962, labelled "stock sheet", and bearing numbers 101, 102, and 103. Though the earlier set is the only one bearing the label "order" there is evidence both external and internal that it was superseded by the latter: a reference in a letter from Lawrence's representative that he had to create orders to match the numbers in the letter of credit; a reference in another letter to asterisks in the orders—which are found only in the "stock sheets", not in the "orders"; additional documentary requirements in the "stock sheets", not found in the "orders"; and a major change in half the sizes specified in one "order", from "small" to "medium". We cite such minutiae because of the difficulty of interpretation created by Lawrence and because of the assertion of appellee's counsel at trial that the inspecting agency could not determine what the orders were. Leaving aside consideration of what might be the legal effect of a buyer-created impossibility of clear identification of orders where a letter of credit required a certificate of conformity to order, we simply observe here that close scrutiny of the two sets of papers reveals that the "stock sheets" supplanted the earlier "orders".

In any event the most important notation found on the "stock sheets"—and not on the "orders"—was "Coats [and jackets] to be as sample inspected in Spain. Letter of credit to be cashed by presentation of bill of lading and signature of superintendent or local inspection (buyers preference) (will confirm)."

The amendment to the letters of credit—appointing Supervigilancia the inspecting agent—was accepted by the major manufacturer involved—Alcides (and presumably Longuer)—on March 12, 1963 on which date both manufacturers requested Supervigilancia to begin inspection. State Street notified Lawrence on March 13.

Then began a barrage of cabled messages from Lawrence to both Supervigilancia and the manufacturers, which was to endure for two weeks. On March 13 Supervigilancia was asked, without explanation, to delay inspection until further instructions from Lawrence. On March 14, it was told that Lawrence had cabled the manufacturers to postpone shipment to permit Supervigilancia to inspect according to samples "they air mailing you directly". On the same day another cable was sent to Supervigilancia saying that Lawrence was airmailing "our approved samples per order and instructions". On the next day Supervigilancia was told to obtain three complete sets of samples properly marked from each concern, send two to Lawrence, and await instructions. On March 18 this message was repeated.

After these two conflicting sets of instructions, Supervigilancia, on March 23, cabled Lawrence, saying in effect that it was going ahead, acting "according your own indications on credits and orders". To this Lawrence replied on March 25 that Supervigilancia should "withhold certificate until after arrival and inspection of goods by your New York correspondent * * *." This, if we read it aright, is a third position taken by Lawrence. At this point in time the latest date for completion of the bills of lading was five days away, March 31, with no alternative shipping date available within that period.

Supervigilancia, on March 26, executed its two certificates of inspection. It divided each certificate into two parts. The first part tended to the matter at hand saying that (1) it had carried out its inspection

> "* * * basing ourselves on the details shown in the orders or Stock-sheets Nos. [100], 101, 102 and 103 * * * and in the samples that were handed to us by the Requirer [Alcides and Longuer], that corresponded, according to his sayings ratified in presence of a Public Notary, to the samples seen and approved by the Delegate of Firm ROBERT LAWRENCE INC., during his stay in Barcelona, and with [sic] are mentioned in the notes appearing in orders Stocksheets Nos. [100], 101, 102 and 103, where there is a note reading:
>
> 'COATS or JACKETS [Germents (sic)] TO BE AS SAMPLE INSPECTED IN SPAIN' ";

that (2) the letters of credit required it to certify "THAT THE GOODS ARE IN CONFORMITY WITH THE ORDER"; that (3) a ten per cent random sample had been taken; and that (4) the "whole * * * [was] found conforming to the conditions estipulated [sic] on the Order-Stock-sheets."

The second part of each certificate contained a chronological account of the cabled messages we have summarized, followed by this language: "Requirer * * * is formally requiring us for delivering this certificate what we are doing today under reserves, not as far as the goods are concerned, which correspond to the samples seen and produced referred to at the beginning of this certificate, but to the existing difference between both interested parties as per the quoted cables."

All documents were presented to Banco Espanol, which honored them and made payment or the equivalent on March 28 and 29. On April 3 State Street cabled its refusal to accept the drafts on it "because accompanying inspection certificates nonconforming with terms of credits which require certificates certifying goods are in conformity with the orders". A later letter amplified its position by specifying that the certificates merely indicated conformity to samples alleged by the seller to "correspond" to other samples allegedly approved by the buyer and that the certificates were issued "under reserves".

The district court sustained this position, referring to the requirement that documents strictly conform to letter of credit provisions, and pointing out that each certificate failed in three respects: (1) that it merely certified that the goods conformed to "conditions"—which left it unclear if the conformity was to the whole of the order or only part; (2) that there was a doubt whether the "order-stock-sheet" was different from the order; and (3) that the certificate was confined to samples handed to the inspecting agency by a representative of the manufacturer. The court concluded that " * * * this was not the unqualified certificate required by the letter of credit and defendant bank was justified in its refusal to accept it."

We do not agree. Since, in our view, the third alleged defect noted by the court presents the most difficult problem, we shall deal with it first.

We note, at the outset, that an issuing bank's duty to honor a demand for payment is, to some extent, determined by statute. The Uniform Commercial Code, M.G.L.A. (Mass.) c. 106 § 5–114(1) (1958), provides, in relevant part, that "An issuer must honor a draft or demand for payment which complies with the terms of the relevant credit regardless of whether the goods or documents conform to the underlying contract for sale or other contract between the customer and the beneficiary." [1] This Code provision, however, simply codifies long-standing decisional law and does not assist us here in determining whether the inspection certificate submitted by Supervigilancia complied with the terms of the credit.

We take as a starting point the substantial body of case law which establishes and supports the general rule that documents submitted incident to a letter of credit are to be strictly construed. This is because international financial transactions rest upon the accuracy of documents rather than on the condition of the goods they represent. But we note some leaven in the loaf of

1. The district court noted that

"Both parties appear to agree that the case is governed by the Uniform Commercial Code as enacted in Massachusetts. Plaintiff [appellant] also relies upon the Uniform Customs and Practice for Documentary Credits issued by the International Chamber of Commerce, particularly Article 8 thereof. This, however, in substance states only what is contained in the Uniform Commercial Code."

strict construction. Not only does *haec verba* not control absolutely, see, e.g., O'Meara v. National Park Bank, 239 N.Y. 386, 146 N.E. 636, 39 A.L.R. 747 (1925), but some courts now cast their eyes on a wider scene than a single document. We are mindful, also, of the admonition of several legal scholars that the integrity of international transactions (i.e., rigid adherence to material matters) must somehow strike a balance with the requirement of their fluidity (i.e., a reasonable flexibility as to ancillary matters) if the objective of increased dealings to the mutual satisfaction of all interested parties is to be enhanced. See, e.g., Mentschicoff, How to Handle Letters of Credit, 19 Bus.Lawyer 107, 111 (1963). Finally, we recognize that this is not a litigation about the nomenclature of goods. Consequently, we are not measurably helped by such cases as those cited in the margin which turn on discrepancies between the actual terms of invoices or bills of lading and requirements of a letter of credit.

What we face here is a matter of procedure which can, in the first instance, be structured by the purchasing party. How may a buyer in the international market place be assured before payment that his purchase as delivered is of the quality agreed upon by the parties? As buyers become more concerned about quality, this issue is likely to become more important. That there are so few cases or comments addressed to the issue of reasonable precautions to assure quality is indicative of the relatively novel status of the problem, at least so far as courts have dealt with it. We are mindful of the testimony in this case that an official of appellee, a busy bank, engaged in passing upon the issuance of 1,500 to 2,000 letters of credit a year for several decades, has encountered in this case his first experience with a letter of credit calling for a certificate of conformity to the order.

What are the realities of such a requirement on the part of the buyer? It is not enough that he receive the quantity of goods he ordered, nor that he receive goods capable of standard measure or grade. He must also, in such a case as this, receive them cut, tailored, sewn according to a style he has in mind. He must therefore rely on a sample he has seen and liked. Being in a distant part of the globe, the buyer must usually elect one of two alternatives. He may be present during the inspection process to verify the sample or he may select, with his seller's acquiescence, a person or firm in whom he has confidence to represent him. Unless he elects to be present, he is acting on faith—faith that the representative is capable and honest, and faith that the representative has the right samples or criteria to serve as a standard. Even if he mails an approved sample direct to the representative, he must rely on the integrity of the mails.

This act of faith—or its converse, the risk that merchandise will not turn out as hoped—is that of the buyer. As one contemporary student has written,

> "* * * there is one risk against which protection is required and which is less easy to guard against. That is the risk that the goods shipped may not comply with the terms of the sales contract as to quality. This is a risk which normally the buyer will have to bear * * * but * * * [he] can guard against the risk by requiring in his letter of request to the bankers that, in addition to the usual shipping documents, the vendor shall deliver a certificate of quality showing the goods to be as specified in the contract, signed by some responsible person at the place of shipment. The only risk then left to the buyer is that the person nominated to give the certificate may fail in his duty. But an entire absence of risk would mean an absence

of business." A.G. Davis, The Law Relating to Commercial Letters of Credit, 3d ed., London, Sir Isaac Pitman & Sons Ltd., 1963, p. 19.

Or, in the words of other scholars,

> "The requirement of such other documents, and particularly certificates of analysis, quality, weight, and the like, is a reasonable precaution for a prudent buyer to take, since he may in this way obtain some measure of assurance that the merchandise is as ordered * * *. The bank is under no obligation and bears no responsibility for the accuracy of any such representations and certificates. Nevertheless, through selection of a reputable third party, the buyer does have a degree of assurance that the merchandise is as represented." Ward and Harfield, Bank Credits and Acceptances, 4th ed., Ronald Press, 1958, p. 45.

These observations go to the heart of this case. For the buyer here—Lawrence—was striving to assure the delivery of quality goods. To be sure, it deliberately postponed the problem when it caused the letters of credit to be issued without resolving the question of the inspecting agent. Then it naively sought to have the sellers accept one of its own representatives. It had long since sewn the seeds of dispute by sending to the sellers both "stock sheets" which were really orders and "orders" which were merely preliminary papers. When it finally reached agreement with the seller as to an inspecting agency, it neglected to specify precisely how it would conduct the inspection operation, leaving only the bland instruction that the goods must conform to orders. And, so far as the inspecting agency was concerned, the orders merely referred to samples that might very well have been inspected in Spain at some past time.

Consequently when faced on the eve of the shipping deadline both with a barrage of contradictory telegrams from the buyer and with samples which the sellers under oath stated "corresponded" with samples approved earlier by the buyer's representative in Barcelona, Supervigilancia had to act to the dissatisfaction of one of the parties to the basic contract. That it took the word, under oath, of the seller as to the appropriateness of the sample is no more than any inspector must ordinarily do. Unless the buyer is physically present (and Lawrence presumably could have arranged this during the frenetic two week period of cable traffic), the inspector must take someone's word that he is judging by the proper samples.

Even in the well known case of O'Meara v. National Park Bank, 239 N.Y. 386, 146 N.E. 636, 39 A.L.R. 747, (1925), a letter of credit calling for newsprint to "test 11/12–32 pounds" was held to be satisfied by an affidavit that annexed samples "stated [by the affiant] to be representative of the shipment" met the prescribed test. We fail to see how this is any more reliable than the affidavit of "correspondence" in the instant case.

In Basse & Selve v. Bank of Australasia, 90 L.T.R. (n.s.) 618 (K.B.1904), the letter of credit covering a purchase of cobalt ore called for a certificate of analysis of a local chemist showing at least five per cent protoxide. The shipper (bent on delivering worthless ore) gave the chemist a packet of ore for analysis. The chemist furnished a certificate that the ore he examined contained the requisite amount of protoxide. But the negotiating bank refused to pay since there was nothing to indicate that the ore examined was that described in the bill of lading. The unscrupulous shipper then gave the chemist a packet of ore marked as was the bill of lading, "P.M. 2680 bags representing 100 tons". The chemist then referred in his certificate to "The sample of cobalt ore marked 'P.M. 2680 bags representing 100 tons' received from you * * *." The bank paid the shipper and prevailed in a suit against it by its customer to recover the sum so paid. The court said:

> "It is said that [the certificate] professes to show merely the test of the contents of a sample packet with a mark upon it, and does not purport to show a test of the bill of lading of 100 tons of ore. This, I think, is a fanciful objection. Large quantities of produce are necessarily tested by means of samples. Such samples are drawn either by the servants of the owner of the goods or (as it seems) by the servants of the analyst, and if the samples are carefully and skilfully drawn they generally fairly represent the bulk. But in this case it would be no part of the bank's duty to see to the sampling or to ascertain that it was fairly done." 90 L.T.R. (n.s.) at 620.

So we say in this case that, while the sample may be just as misleading as the ore sample in Basse & Selve, the advising bank was equally justified in paying on the strength of the documents.

We see no significant difference in Supervigilancia being told by the manufacturers that the samples were those approved by the buyer and being told that they "corresponded" to such samples. Webster's Dictionary (3d Int'l ed.) gives such meanings of "correspond" as "in agreement", "conformity", "equivalent", "match", "equal". In the context and considering the language difficulty, we think these meanings apply more than the looser ones like "analogous", "parallel", or "similar". In effect, Lawrence in this case, by providing as a referent to the letter of credit requirement of conformity to orders merely the early cryptic description on the stock sheets ("Coats * * * to be as samples inspected in Spain"), procured no more reliable assurance of authenticity than the credit termination clause in Fair Pavilions, Inc. v. First Nat. City Bank, 24 A.D.2d 109, 264 N.Y.S.2d 255 (1965), which was to be triggered " * * * if our Travelers Letter of Credit Department receives * * * from an officer (or one describing himself therein as an officer) of [bank's customer] an affidavit that one or more * * * events * * * has occurred." 264 N.Y.S.2d at 256.

Moreover, if there be ambiguity surrounding the words "correspond" or "sample approved in Spain" we would, like the court in *Fair Pavilions,* " * * * take the words as strongly against the issuer as a reasonable reading will justify. * * *." Supra at 258.

To hold otherwise—that a buyer could frustrate an international transaction on the eve of fulfillment by a challenge to authenticity of sample—would make vulnerable many such arrangements where third parties are vested by buyers with inspection responsibilities but where, apart from their own competence and integrity, there is no iron-clad guarantee of the sample itself.

As for the argument that Supervigilancia's finding that the goods conform "to the conditions estipulated on the Order-Stock-sheets" is a meaningful variance from the terms of the letters of credit, we confess to semantic myopia. "The conditions" mean, as we read the certificates, all the conditions, hence the order itself. As for the dual use by the agency of the words "Order-Stock-sheets", we have already indicated both the nature and cause of the confusion and conclude that Supervigilancia acted solomonically in borrowing the substance of the stock sheets and the label of the "orders". We do not see how it could have done otherwise.

The remaining contention that "under reserves" has some mysterious meaning which infects the entire certificate is not borne out by the inapposite cases cited to us and is directly refuted by the limiting language immediately following—"not as far as the goods are concerned". Further reading of the document indicates clearly that the phrase was directed to the underlying dispute between buyer and seller, which could not be the concern of the advising bank.

We hold, therefore, that the inspection certificate in this case conformed in all significant respects to the requirements of the letter of credit.

Appellee has urged that, in the event we might reverse the district court's judgment, the case should be remanded for a new trial or at least further findings, since the district court did not find it necessary to reach additional defenses. Appellant urges otherwise. It is not clear to us which is correct. We reverse the judgment of the District Court and remand for such further proceedings, consistent with this opinion, as the court feels appropriate. We do say that these additional defenses were not argued before us, nor directly passed upon, but whether this is chargeable to appellee, so that judgment should be entered for appellant forthwith, we leave to the district judge before whom this case was originally heard. [Footnotes omitted.]

COURTAULDS NORTH AMERICA, INC. v. NORTH CAROLINA NATIONAL BANK

United States Court of Appeals, Fourth Circuit, 1975.
528 F.2d 802.

BRYAN, SENIOR CIRCUIT JUDGE. A letter of credit with the date of March 21, 1973 was issued by the North Carolina National Bank at the request of and for the account of its customer, Adastra Knitting Mills, Inc. It made available upon the drafts of Courtaulds North America, Inc. "up to" $135,000.00 (later increased by $135,000.00) at "60 days date" to cover Adastra's purchases of acrylic yarn from Courtaulds. The life of the credit was extended in June to allow the drafts to be "drawn and negotiated on or before August 15, 1973." Bank refused to honor a draft for $67,346.77 dated August 13, 1973 for yarn sold and delivered to Adastra. Courtaulds brought this action to recover this sum from Bank.

The defendant denied liability chiefly on the assertion that the draft did not agree with the letter's conditions, viz., that the draft be accompanied by a "Commercial invoice in triplicate stating [inter alia] that it covers * * * 100% acrylic yarn"; instead, the accompanying invoices stated that the goods were "Imported Acrylic Yarn."

Upon cross motions for summary judgment on affidavits and a stipulation of facts, the District Court held defendant Bank liable to Courtaulds for the amount of the draft, interest and costs. It concluded that the draft complied with the letter of credit when each invoice is read together with the packing lists stapled to it, for the lists stated on their faces: "Cartons marked:—100% Acrylic." After considering the insistent rigidity of the law and usage of bank credits and acceptances, we must differ with the District Judge and uphold Bank's position.

The letter of credit prescribed the terms of the drafts as follows:

"Drafts to be dated same as Bills of Lading. Draft(s) to be accompanied by:

"1. Commercial invoice in triplicate stating that it covers 100,000 lbs. 100% Acrylic Yarn, Package Dyed at $1.35 per lb., FOB Buyers Plant, Greensboro, North Carolina Land Duty Paid.

"2. Certificate stating goods will be delivered to buyers plant land duty paid.

> "3. Inland Bill of Lading consigned to Adastra Knitting Mills, Inc. evidencing shipment from East Coast Port to Adastra Knitting Mills, Inc., Greensboro, North Carolina."

The shipment (the last) with which this case is concerned was made on or about August 8, 1973. On direction of Courtaulds bills of lading of that date were prepared for the consignment to Adastra from a bonded warehouse by motor carrier. The yarn was packaged in cartons and a packing list referring to its bill of lading accompanied each carton. After the yarn was delivered to the carrier, each bill of lading with the packing list was sent to Courtaulds. There invoices for the sales were made out, and the invoices and packing lists stapled together. At the same time, Courtaulds wrote up the certificate, credit memorandum and draft called for in the letter of credit. The draft was dated August 13, 1973 and drawn on Bank by Courtaulds payable to itself.

All of these documents—the draft, the invoices and the packing lists—were sent by Courtaulds to its correspondent in Mobile for presentation to Bank and collection of the draft which for the purpose had been endorsed to the correspondent.

This was the procedure pursued on each of the prior drafts and always the draft had been honored by Bank save in the present instance. Here the draft, endorsed to Bank, and the other papers were sent to Bank on August 14. Bank received them on Thursday, August 16. Upon processing, Bank found these discrepancies between the drafts with accompanying documents and the letter of credit: (1) that the invoice did not state "100% Acrylic Yarn" but described it as "Imported Acrylic Yarn," and (2) "Draft not drawn as per terms of [letter of credit], Date [August 13] not same as Bill of Lading [August 8] and not drawn 60 days after date" [but 60 days from Bill of Lading date 8/8/73]. Finding of fact 24. Since decision of this controversy is put on the first discrepancy we do not discuss the others.

On Monday, August 20, Bank called Adastra and asked if it would waive the discrepancies and thus allow Bank to honor the draft. In response, the president of Adastra informed Bank that it could not waive any discrepancies because a trustee in bankruptcy had been appointed for Adastra and Adastra could not do so alone. Upon word of these circumstances, Courtaulds on August 27 sent amended invoices to Bank which were received by Bank on August 27. They referred to the consignment as "100% Acrylic Yarn", and thus would have conformed to the letter of credit had it not expired. On August 29 Bank wired Courtaulds that the draft remained unaccepted because of the expiration of the letter of credit on August 15. Consequently the draft with all the original documents was returned by Bank.

During the life of the letter of credit some drafts had not been of even dates with the bills of lading, and among the large number of invoices transmitted during this period, several did not describe the goods as "100% Acrylic Yarn." As to all of these deficiencies Bank called Adastra for and received approval before paying the drafts. Every draft save the one in suit was accepted.

Conclusion of Law

The factual outline related is not in dispute, and the issue becomes one of law. It is well phrased by the District Judge in his "Discussion" in this way:

> "The only issue presented by the facts of this case is whether the documents tendered by the beneficiary to the issuer were in conformity with the terms of the letter of credit."

The letter of credit provided:

"Except as otherwise expressly stated herein, this credit is subject to the 'Uniform Customs and Practice for Documentary Credits (1962 revision), the International Chamber of Commerce, Brochure No. 222'." Finding of fact 6.

Of particular pertinence, with accents added, are these injunctions of the Uniform Customs:

"Article 7.—Banks must examine all documents with reasonable care to ascertain that they *appear on their face* to be in accordance with the terms and conditions of the credit."

"Article 8.—In documentary credit operations all parties concerned deal in documents and not in goods.

* * *

"If, upon receipt of the documents, the issuing bank considers that they *appear on their face* not to be in accordance with the terms and conditions of the credit, that bank must determine, on the basis of the documents alone, whether to claim that payment, acceptance or negotiation was not effected in accordance with the terms and conditions of the credit."

* * *

"Article 9.—Banks * * * do [not] assume any liability or responsibility *for the description,* * * * quality, * * * of the goods represented thereby * * *"

* * *

"The description of the goods in the commercial *invoice* must correspond with the description in the credit. *In the remaining documents the goods may be described in general terms.*"

Also to be looked to are the North Carolina statutes, because in a diversity action, the Federal courts apply the same law as would the courts of the State of adjudication. Here applied would be the Uniform Commercial Code—Letters of Credit, Chap. 25 G.S.N.C. Especially to be noticed are these sections:

"§ 25–5–109. Issuer's obligation to its customer.—

"(1) An issuer's obligation to its customer includes good faith and observance of any general banking usage but unless otherwise agreed does not include liability or responsibility

"(a) for performance of the underlying contract for sale or other transaction between the customer and the beneficiary; or

* * *

"(c) based on knowledge or lack of knowledge of any usage of any particular trade.

"(2) An issuer must examine documents with care so as to ascertain that on their face they appear to comply with the terms of the credit but unless otherwise agreed assumes no liability or responsibility for the genuineness, falsification or effect of any document which appears on such examination to be regular on its face."

In utilizing the rules of construction embodied in the letter of credit—the Uniform Customs and state statute—one must constantly recall that the drawee bank is not to be embroiled in disputes between the buyer and the seller, the beneficiary of the credit. The drawee is involved only with documents, not with merchandise. Its involvement is altogether separate and apart from the transaction between the buyer and seller; its duties and liability are governed exclusively by the terms of the letter, not the terms of the parties' contract with each other. Moreover, as the predominant authorities unequivocally declare, the beneficiary must meet the terms of the credit—and precisely—if it is to exact performance of the issuer. Failing such compliance there can be no recovery from the drawee. That is the specific failure of Courtaulds here.

Free of ineptness in wording the letter of credit dictated that each invoice express on its face that it covered 100% acrylic yarn. Nothing less is shown to be tolerated in the trade. No substitution and no equivalent, through interpretation or logic, will serve. Harfield, Bank Credits and Acceptances (5th Ed. 1974), at p. 73, commends and quotes aptly from an English case: "There is no room for documents which are almost the same, or which will do just as well." Equitable Trust Co. of N.Y. v. Dawson Partners, Ltd., 27 Lloyd's List Law Rpts. 49, 52 (1926). Although no pertinent North Carolina decision has been laid before us, in many cases elsewhere, especially in New York, we find the tenet of Harfield to be unshaken.

At trial Courtaulds prevailed on the contention that the invoices in actuality met the specifications of the letter of credit in that the packing lists attached to the invoices disclosed on their faces that the packages contained "cartons marked:—100% acrylic". On this premise it was urged that the lists were a part of the invoice since they were appended to it, and the invoices should be read as one with the lists, allowing the lists to detail the invoices. But this argument cannot be accepted. In this connection it is well to revert to the distinction made in Uniform Customs, supra, between the "invoice" and the "remaining documents", emphasizing that in the latter the description may be in general terms while in the invoice the goods must be described in conformity with the credit letter.

The District Judge's pat statement adeptly puts an end to this contention of Courtaulds:

> "In dealing with letters of credit, it is a custom and practice of the banking trade for a bank to only treat a document as an invoice which clearly is marked on its face as 'invoice' ". Finding of fact 46.

This is not a pharisaical or doctrinaire persistence in the principle, but is altogether realistic in the environs of this case; it is plainly the fair and equitable measure. (The defect in description was not superficial but occurred in the statement of the *quality* of the yarn, not a frivolous concern.) The obligation of the drawee bank was graven in the credit. Indeed, there could be no departure from its words. Bank was not expected to scrutinize the collateral papers, such as the packing lists. Nor was it permitted to read into the instrument the contemplation or intention of the seller and buyer. Adherence to this rule was not only legally commanded, but it was factually ordered also, as will immediately appear.

Had Bank deviated from the stipulation of the letter and honored the draft, then at once it might have been confronted with the not improbable risk of the bankruptcy trustee's charge of liability for unwarrantably paying the draft moneys to the seller, Courtaulds, and refusal to reimburse Bank for the outlay. Contrarily, it might face a Courtaulds claim that since it had depended upon Bank's assurance of credit in shipping yarn to Adastra, Bank was responsible for the loss. In this situation Bank cannot be condemned for sticking to the letter of the letter.

Nor is this conclusion affected by the amended or substituted invoices which Courtaulds sent to Bank after the refusal of the draft. No precedent is cited to justify retroactive amendment of the invoices or extension of the credit beyond the August 15 expiry of the letter.

Finally, the trial court found that although in its prior practices Bank had pursued a strict-constructionist attitude, it had nevertheless on occasion honored drafts not within the verbatim terms of the credit letter. But it also found that in each of these instances Bank had first procured the authorization of Adastra to overlook the deficiencies. This truth is verified by the District Court in its Findings of Fact:

> "42. It is a standard practice and procedure of the banking industry and trade for a bank to attempt to obtain a waiver of discrepancies from its customer in a letter of credit transaction. This custom and practice was followed by NCNB in connection with the draft and documents received from Courtaulds.
>
> "43. Following this practice, NCNB had checked all previous discrepancies it discovered in Courtaulds' documents with its customer Adastra to see if Adastra would waive those discrepancies noted by NCNB. Except for the transaction in question, Adastra waived all discrepancies noted by NCNB.
>
> "44. It is not normal or customary for NCNB, nor is it the custom and practice in the banking trade, for a bank to notify a beneficiary or the presenter of the documents that there were any deficiencies in the draft or documents if they are waived by the customer."

This endeavor had been fruitless on the last draft because of the inability of Adastra to give its consent. Obviously, the previous acceptances of truant invoices cannot be construed as a waiver in the present incident.

For these reasons, we must vacate the decision of the trial court, despite the evident close reasoning and research of the District Judge, Courtaulds North America, Inc. v. North Carolina N.B., 387 F.Supp. 92 (M.D.N.C. 1975). Entry of judgment in favor of the appellant Bank on its summary motion is necessary.

Reversed and remanded for final judgment.

Notes

1. The two cases set out above are commonly cited as being in conflict. Applying the Uniform Customs and Practices (appendix to this chapter) to the two of them, can their holdings be read as consistent?

2. Assuming that their holdings are inconsistent and that Judge Coffin is truly espousing a less strict standard of interpretation, who is right and what policies are at issue?

The doctrines of estoppel and waiver found in the common law and those of indemnity and warranties set out in Article 5 offer, in the words of Judge Coffin, some "leaven" for the loaf. On the one hand they accommodate the practical necessity of paying in certain circumstances against documents that are not adequate. On the other hand they give some room for a court's requiring or approving deviation from the strict standards.

MARINO INDUSTRIES CORP. v. CHASE MANHATTAN BANK, N.A.

United States Court of Appeals, Second Circuit, 1982.
686 F.2d 112.

FRIEDMAN, CHIEF JUDGE, UNITED STATES COURT OF CLAIMS. This is an appeal from a judgment of the United States District Court for the Eastern District of New York entered upon the opinion of United States Magistrate John L. Caden dismissing, after trial, a suit seeking recovery under two letters of credit that the defendant, Chase Manhattan Bank ("Chase"), issued to the plaintiff, Marino Industries Corp. ("Marino"). The magistrate held that Chase justifiably refused to pay under the letters because Marino had not complied with the requirements in the letters for obtaining payment. We affirm in part, reverse in part, and remand for further proceedings.

I.

The dispute grew out of a contract under which Marino, a manufacturer of construction materials, agreed with Bautechnik GmbH, a German company, to ship material to a job site in Kassim, Saudi Arabia. At Bautechnik's request, the Berliner Bank in West Germany issued two similar irrevocable letters of credit in favor of Marino. Chase confirmed the letters. One letter was for $212,456.48, and the other was for $489,956.41. Both letters explicitly were subject to the Uniform Customs and Practice for Documentary Credits (1974 Revision), International Chamber of Commerce Publication No. 290, which, under New York laws, supersedes the Uniform Commercial Code. N.Y.U.C.C.L. § 5–102(4) (McKinney 1964).

Each letter was to be paid in two installments: 40 percent when the goods were shipped and 60 percent when they were received. The letters contained detailed requirements that Marino was required to follow to obtain payment. Marino shipped all the goods to Saudi Arabia. After Bautechnik went bankrupt in late November or early December 1980, Chase refused to pay three of Marino's drafts under the letters, on the ground that Marino had not complied with the requirements for payment.

The complaint, filed in the district court after the suit had been transferred from the New York State Supreme Court where it originally had been filed, contains two counts. Count I seeks recovery of $99,083.80 for Chase's refusal to pay the plaintiff's draft for that amount under the first letter of credit. Count II seeks $270,779.84 for Chase's refusal to make payments of $46,388.00 and $224,391.84 under the second letter. Both parties agreed to a trial before a United States Magistrate.

After trial, the magistrate dismissed the complaint. He held that with respect to each of the three payments Chase refused to make, Marino had not complied with the requirements for payment in the letter. The magistrate rendered a comprehensive opinion discussing in detail the various respects in which he found that Marino had not complied, and made findings of fact and conclusions of law. Marino has appealed from the judgment dismissing the complaint, and Chase has cross-appealed from the magistrate's resolution of one subsidiary issue against Chase.

* * *

III.

Chase refused to pay three different drafts on the two letters that Marino presented. Since each refusal was made for different reasons, we discuss each claim separately. In determining whether Chase's refusal to pay was justified, we are guided by and apply the general principles governing letters of credit just summarized.

A. THE $99,000 CLAIM

The first claim was for $99,083.80. It was made under the 60 percent portion of the first letter of credit, i.e., Marino sought payment from Chase after the goods had been received in Saudi Arabia.

To obtain payment Marino was required to submit a certificate that the goods had been inspected prior to shipment and a certificate that the goods had been received. The letters specified precisely what these certificates were required to state. As extended, the letter of credit expired on Monday, December 1, 1980. This meant that to obtain payment Marino was required to submit by that date certificates that conformed to the requirements in the letter.

1. Marino submitted the inspection certificates on October 15, 1980. On October 17, a Chase employee prepared a discrepancy sheet covering the certificates, which noted various respects in which they did not comply with the requirements in the letter. One of the defects noted was that the certificates did not include copies of the invoices for the shipped goods. The discrepancy sheet contains handwritten comments based upon phone conversations with Marino. The record does not show when these comments were written or which of the deficiencies Chase called to Marino's attention.

On December 2, 1980, the day after the letter had expired, Chase returned the inspection certificates to Marino because the bank was "not able to utilize" them. An accompanying memorandum stated that Chase had "contacted Miss Cinthya [apparently a Marino employee] on the phone several times." It requested Marino: "Please complete requirement of L/C and send documents to us complete." On December 8, Marino resubmitted the inspection certificates to Chase.

2. The letter of credit required the certificates of receipt to be "signed by [a] Midica [sic] [Mdica was the joint venture in Saudi Arabia] representative confirming the arrival of the material on job site Kassim." An amendment to the letter of credit provided that in lieu of a Mdica signature, the notarized signature of the freight forwarder, Zuest & Bachmeier Ag., would be accepted. Berliner Bank had sent to Chase three signature samples of Mdica representatives acceptable to it. Chase never told Marino that only those three signatures would be acceptable or that other signatures would be acceptable if they identified the signer as a Mdica representative (as a Chase representative testified at trial).

On Wednesday, November 26, 1980, a Marino representative, Mr. DeWeil, delivered the certificates of receipt to Pacifico Bautista in Chase's Letter of Credit Department. According to the magistrate, "Mr. Bautista refused to accept the certificates of receipt because they did not contain an authorized signature. * * * In order to rectify the absence of an authorized signature, Mr. Bautista told Mr. DeWeil to have the certificates of receipt countersigned by an officer of the international freight forwarding company, Zust Bachmeier." Mr. DeWeil had the certificates countersigned about 5 p.m., that day, but because it was then too late to return them to the bank, he took the certificates to Marino's office on Long Island.

Mr. Pagano, Marino's vice president in charge of exporting, testified that on Monday, December 1 (the date on which the letter expired), he told Mr. Bautista on the telephone that he had six countersigned certificates of receipt and asked Mr. Bautista when he should bring them in. According to Mr. Pagano, Mr. Bautista "decided that I could send them the following day and hopefully that we would get paid as soon as possible." On cross-examination Mr. Pagano stated that the expiration date of the letter had not been mentioned. Mr. Pagano mailed the certificates of receipt the following day (December 2).

On December 8, Chase informed Marino that it would not make payment because proper certificates had not been timely presented. On December 10 and

12, Chase, with Marino's approval, cabled the Berliner Bank, stated that payment had not been made "due to late presentation" and asked, "May we pay [?]" Berliner Bank cabled back "Do not pay * * * as presented too late." Berliner Bank also rejected a third cabled request from Chase for permission to pay.

3. The magistrate held that Marino had not made a timely presentation of the necessary documents and that Chase had not waived the requirement of timely presentation. He apparently accepted Chase's evidence that bringing documents to the bank and taking them back to have them countersigned, as happened on November 26, "is not a presentation of documents." The magistrate stated that documentary evidence showed that "a full set of documents was not received by Chase until December 8, 1980—eight days after the expiration of the letter of credit on November 30, 1980" and that "[i]n the face of such documentary proof, it is unrealistic to give credence to plaintiff's assertion that there was a timely presentation of conforming documents."

In holding that Chase had not waived the timely presentation requirement, the magistrate pointed to Pagano's admission that neither in his telephone conversation of December 1, 1980, with Mr. Bautista nor in a subsequent meeting with Ms. Soula Stephanides of Chase, at which Marino contended Chase also had waived timely presentation, was it mentioned that the letter had expired. The magistrate further ruled that Chase's cabled requests to the Berliner Bank to make late payment were not waivers but merely were "a courtesy to plaintiff."

4. As we have noted, an important corollary of the strict compliance rule is that the letter of credit must specify precisely and clearly the requirements for payment and that ambiguities in the letter are to be resolved against the bank. Nothing in the letter in this case indicated that the requirement that the certificates of receipt be "signed by [a] Mdica representative" could be satisfied only if one of the three acceptable signatures that Berliner Bank had submitted to Chase was affixed. If that was a condition of payment, Chase was required so to inform Marino. Sun Bank, 609 F.2d at 833; 34 N.Y.Jur. Letters of Credit § 13 at 431 (1964). Similarly, if Chase would accept signatures of other Mdica representatives provided they were expressly identified as such, as Chase's representative testified at trial, Chase also was required to inform Marino of that condition of payment.

The magistrate did not determine whether the signature on the certificates was that of a Mdica representative. On the remand that we order, the magistrate should determine that fact. If the answer is affirmative, Marino made a timely presentation of the certificates of receipt (on November 26) that complied with the requirements in the letter.

Even if Marino had not made a timely presentation on November 26, there is the question whether Chase waived the time limit when, according to Mr. Pagano, Mr. Bautista, on December 1, 1980, authorized Mr. Pagano to submit the documents after that date. The fact that neither Pagano nor Bautista referred to the expiration date of the bill in that conversation is not necessarily dispositive of the question, although it is significant. The magistrate did not determine whether Mr. Bautista had authority to make such a commitment. It would seem, however, that Mr. Bautista had at least apparent authority to do so, upon which Marino's representative was justified in relying.

5. If Marino made a timely presentation of proper certificates of receipt or if Chase waived the time limit, Marino still was not entitled to payment unless it also timely presented certificates of inspection. As noted, Marino supplied those

certificates to Chase on October 15, well in advance of the expiration date of the letter.

Chase's initial inspection of those certificates revealed what Chase believed to be various defects, including the failure to include with the certificates copies of the invoices for the goods. The record does not show, however, whether at that time Chase called these alleged deficiencies to Marino's attention. When Chase finally returned the invoices to Marino for correction on December 2, 1980, the letter had expired.

The letter of credit required Marino to submit

> "[c]lean inspection certificate, 4 copies, issued by superintendent-company acting in conformity with the regulations of S.G.S. (Societe Generale de Surveillance) stating the full compliance of the quantities and qualities of the goods with the specifications, the commercial invoice and the instructions given by Dietrich Garski Bautechnik KG, Berlin."

This is somewhat ambiguous. It is unclear whether Marino was required to submit a single inspection certificate stating that the goods complied with the three conditions, or to submit separately the certificates, the invoices and the instructions. In light of the obvious purpose of the requirement to insure that the goods shipped were as ordered, the most reasonable reading of the provision is that Marino was required to submit a single certificate stating that the "quantities and qualities of the goods" complied with "[i] the specifications, [ii] the commercial invoices, and [iii] the instructions given by" Bautechnik (the purchaser). The magistrate did not determine whether the certificates Marino submitted complied with this requirement.

A further problem with respect to the certificates of inspection is presented by the fact that Chase waited a month-and-a-half before returning them to Marino for correction. Under article 8(d) of the Uniform Customs & Practice for Documentary Credits, Chase had "a reasonable time" within which to examine the documentation. See N.Y.U.C.C. § 5–112(1)(a) (giving banks three banking days). If Chase had returned the certificates promptly, Marino would have had ample time to correct any deficiencies. By not returning the certificates until after the letter had expired, Chase made it impossible for Marino to correct any deficiencies and still make timely presentation. Cf. Barclays Bank D.C.O. v. Mercantile National Bank, 481 F.2d 1224, 1236 (5th Cir. 1973), cert dismissed, 414 U.S. 1139 (1974) (when bank says documents conform, it cannot then deny conformity after expiration). There is a question, therefore, whether Chase is estopped from relying upon defects in the certificates of inspection as a justification for refusing payment.

6. We therefore conclude that we cannot affirm the magistrate's dismissal of the $99,000 claim. The portion of the judgment that dismissed that claim is reversed, and this portion of the case is remanded to the magistrate for further proceedings in accordance with this opinion.

* * *

CONCLUSION

The judgment of the United States District Court for the Eastern District of New York is affirmed in part and reversed in part, and the case is remanded to it for further proceedings before the magistrate on the $99,000 claim in accordance with this opinion.

Problem 29–2

Chase was the beneficiary of a letter of credit issued by Equibank in Pittsburgh. The letter provided that Chase (the "take out" lender on a construction contract) had a right to draw upon Equibank if the underlying debtor failed to complete the loan transaction. Equibank was the interim lender to the developer. The developer failed to carry out the construction on time and on April 30 Chase sent (1) a certification "that [developer] has defaulted and the default has not been cured" and (2) a demand for payment of $108,000.

The letter of credit expired on April 30, 1973. In the afternoon of April 30 a representative of Chase had a phone conversation with a representative of Equibank. The Chase employee stated that the Equibank employee agreed that the document could be forwarded through "domestic collections." Because such collections take several days, the demand did not arrive in Pittsburgh until late in the first week of May when it was rejected on the ground the letter of credit had expired on April 30.

1. Can Chase win on the ground of estoppel?

2. Can it win on the ground of waiver?

3. Would it matter that only three hours intervened between the expiration of the letter on April 30 and the phone conversation?

4. On behalf of Chase can you use UCC 2–209?

DIXON, IRMAOS & CIA v. CHASE MANHATTAN Bank

United States Court of Appeals, Second Circuit, 1944.
144 F.2d 759.

SWAN, CIRCUIT JUDGE.

This appeal raises interesting and important questions as to letters of credit covering C.I.F. shipments abroad. The plaintiff, an exporter of cotton in Sao Paulo, Brazil, contracted to sell cotton to a purchaser in Belgium. A Belgian bank requested the Chase Bank to issue in favor of the plaintiff two irrevocable letters of credit for $7,000 and $3,500 respectively to finance such sales. Chase Bank did so and mailed them to Sao Paulo, where they were received by the plaintiff on May 2, 1940. They bound Chase Bank to honor 90 day drafts drawn under the credits, if presented at its office on or before May 15, 1940 and accompanied by specified documents, including a "full set of bills of lading" evidencing shipment of a stated quantity and quality of cotton "C.I.F. Ghent/ Antwerp." One of the letters of credit (both being the same in form) is set out in the margin.[1] The plaintiff duly shipped the cotton to its Belgian customer in

1. "The Chase National Bank of The City of New York

"April 8, 1940.

"Confirmed Irrevocable Straight Credit

"Dixon Irmaos and Cia Ltda.,

"Sao Paulo, Brazil

"Gentlemen:

"We are instructed by Banque de Bruxelles, S.A., Brussels, Belgium to advise you that they have opened their irrevocable credit in your favor for account of by order of Georgie Alost under their credit Number 40466 for a sum or sums not exceeding a total of About $7000.00 (Seven Thousand Dollars) U.S. Currency available by your drafts on us at 90 days sight, in duplicate to be accompanied by

"Commercial invoice in triplicate, or invoice copy

"Insurance certificate which must cover land and sea risks into the mills, and showing merchandise covered onboard the steamer named and/or other steamer or steamers

"Full set bills of lading. Port or custody bills of lading acceptable evidencing shipment of 22 tons Bresilian Sao Paulo Cotton type MINI shipped during April 1940, CIF Ghent/ Antwerp

"All documents in name of La Georgie.

two lots, receiving for each shipment two originals of the bills of lading. Instead of prepaying freight the plaintiff shipped the goods freight collect and deducted the freight charges from the invoice price. Through the Guaranty Trust Company of New York, the plaintiff's representative, drafts and documents were presented to Chase Bank on May 15, 1940, but only one of the set of two bills of lading was delivered. In lieu of the other, which was in the mail and not yet arrived in New York, an indemnity agreement or guaranty against loss resulting from its absence was tendered by the Guaranty Trust Company.[2] Chase Bank had no objection to the form of the guaranty or to the responsibility of the guarantor, but it refused the drafts on two grounds: (1) Absence of a full set of the bills of lading and (2) failure to prepay the freight. The plaintiff then brought the present action to recover the amount of its drafts, $5,587.15 under the larger letter of credit and $2,757.49 under the smaller. The case was tried without a jury. At the conclusion of the evidence each side moved for judgment. Decision being reserved, the district judge thereafter rendered an opinion and filed findings of fact and law. He gave judgment for the defendant on the ground that the tender of less than a full set of bills of lading did not comply with the terms of the letters of credit.

Assuming for the moment that a C.I.F. shipment does not require the shipper to prepay freight if the freight charges are credited against the invoice price, the Guaranty Trust Company's tender to Chase Bank of drafts and documents fully met the requirements of the letters of credit, except for the fact that one original bill of lading out of each set of two was missing. The plaintiff contends that this fact did not defeat the adequacy of its tender because the evidence established the existence of a custom among New York banks issuing letters of credit to finance a shipment from outside the United States and calling for a "full set of bills of lading", to accept in lieu of a missing part of the set a guaranty by a responsible New York bank against any loss resulting from the absence of the missing part. On this subject the trial judge made the following findings of fact:

"12. The letters of guaranty of the Guaranty Trust Company tendered to the defendant are in the usual form of guaranties tendered by and accepted by leading New York Banks issuing commercial credits, when less than all bills of lading are presented under credits calling for a full set of bills of lading.

"All drafts so drawn must be marked 'Drawn under Chase National Bank Credit No. E71582'

"The above mentioned correspondent engages with you that all drafts drawn under and in compliance with the terms of this credit will be duly honored on delivery of documents as specified if presented at this office on or before May 15, 1940; we confirm the credit and thereby undertake that all drafts drawn and presented as above specified will be duly honored by us.

"Unless otherwise expressly stated, this credit is subject to the uniform customs and practice for commercial documentary credits fixed by the Seventh Congress of the International Chamber of Commerce and certain guiding provisions.

"Yours very truly,

"C.F.Wellman
Assistant Manager

"F.N. Powelson
Assistant Cashier"

2. The Guaranty Trust Company's indemnity agreement stated:

"In consideration of your accepting the above described draft, we hereby agree to hold you harmless from any and all consequences which might arise due to the following discrepancy:

"Only 1 copy presented out of a set of 2 bills of lading issued.

"It is understood that this guarantee will remain in force until such time as you may obtain a release from your clients.

"We shall thank you to take the necessary steps to obtain this release as soon as possible and inform us promptly when it has been obtained."

"12A. The Guaranty Trust Company was and is a prime and leading New York bank with sound financial standing.

"12B. The defendant raised no objection to the form of the guaranties tendered by the Guaranty Trust Company nor with the financial responsibility of the Guaranty Trust Company.

"13. On May 15, 1940, and for some time prior thereto, there existed a general and uniform custom among New York banks, exporters and importers to the effect that in lieu of a missing bill or missing bills of lading presented under credits calling for a full set of bills of lading, that the bank issuing the credits would accept in lieu of the missing bill or bills of lading, a guaranty of a leading New York bank, if it determined the guaranty to be satisfactory in form and if it was satisfied as to the responsibility of the bank issuing the guaranty. The bank issuing the credit was, however, free to exercise its own discretion and make its own determination as to whether it would accept a guaranty in lieu of a missing bill of lading."

We are not entirely clear as to the meaning of the final sentence of finding 13. If it means that the issuer of credit is free to reject the tendered guaranty if doubts are entertained regarding the guarantor's financial responsibility or the sufficiency of the form of the document, it is not inconsistent with the custom stated in the first sentence and may be disregarded; in these respects Chase Bank was satisfied with the guaranty tendered by Guaranty Trust Company. But if it means that even when so satisfied the bank issuing the credit may reject the tendered guaranty and refuse to accept the draft, it is inconsistent with the stated custom and is unsupported by the evidence. Numerous witnesses, experts in the fields of banking and of commerce, testified to the existence of the custom; not one testified to a single instance where a tender such as was here made had been rejected and the draft dishonored solely on the ground that the set of bills of lading was incomplete. Indeed, it is clear that the Chase Bank would in this very case have honored the drafts, had they been presented before the German invasion of Belgium. One of its witnesses naively said that before May 15, 1940 it was the custom to accept such a guaranty as was tendered, but not on that date or thereafter—as though the determining moment were not at the latest when the plaintiff acted upon the letters of credit. In short, the existence of the custom was established beyond dispute.

It is true, as the defendant argues, that the law requires strict compliance with the terms of a letter of credit. International Banking Corp. v. Irving Nat. Bank, 2 Cir., 283 F. 103. It is likewise true that numerous cases, several of which are cited by the defendant, declare that evidence of a custom is not admissible to contradict the unambiguous terms of a written contract.

* * *

* * * But it is also well settled "that parties who contract on a subject-matter concerning which known usages prevail, incorporate such usages by implication into their agreements, if nothing is said to the contrary." Hostetter v. Park, 137 U.S. 30, 40, 11 S.Ct. 1, 4, 34 L.Ed. 568. * * *

Williston, Contracts, rev. ed. §§ 650, 652, 1081A. In our opinion the custom under consideration explains the meaning of the technical phrase "full set of bills of lading" and is incorporated by implication into the terms of the defendant's letters of credit. No authority on the precise point has come to our attention. The statement of Bankes, L.J. in Scott & Co., Ltd. v. Barclay's Bank, Ltd., [1923] 2 K.B. 1, 11, upon which the defendant relies, is inapposite because no custom such as the court found here was there proved or attempted to be proved. Finally, the defendant urges that the reference in the concluding paragraph of the letters of credit to the uniform customs and practice for commercial documentary credits fixed by the Seventh Congress of the International Chamber of Commerce excludes incorporation into the contracts of any other custom. We do not think so. Those customs do not deal with the meaning of a "full set of bills of lading." Hence the problem whether the New York custom gives meaning to those words is unaffected by the reference to those other customs. The reasonableness and utility of the local New York custom is obvious. It is absolutely essential to the expeditious doing of business in overseas transactions in these days when one part of the bill of lading goes by air and another by water. Unless an indemnity can be substituted for the delayed part, not only does quick clearance of such transactions become impossible but also the universal practice of issuing bills of ladings in sets and sending the different parts by separate mails loses much of its purpose. We conclude therefore that the defendant's first ground for dishonor of the drafts was not a valid reason.

The second ground for dishonor was that while the credits specified a C.I.F. shipment, the plaintiff deducted freight charges from the invoices and shipped the goods freight collect. On this subject the court made the following findings:

"15. The ordinary and accepted meaning of a C.I.F. contract is that the contract price includes the cost of the goods, the cost of insurance and the cost of freight to the point of destination. The term does not imply the time when or the place where the freight is to be paid and there was no uniform practice in New York on May 15, 1940 or prior thereto of prepaying freight to the point of destination under a C.I.F. shipment. The practice was that it was sometimes prepaid and sometimes deducted from the invoice.

"16. The 'American Foreign Trade Definitions' are incorporated by reference in the letters of credit and such definitions, including the definition of a C.I.F. contract, is a part of the credit. Under the definition of a C.I.F. contract as defined in 'American and Foreign Trade Definitions' there is no requirement that a shipper must prepay freight.

* * *

"18. The tender of documents showing a deduction of freight from the invoices was not a deviation from the requirement of defendant's credits calling for C.I.F. shipment."

We agree with this conclusion. In the case of a sight draft, it is wholly immaterial to the buyer whether freight is prepaid or credit given on the invoice price. In the case of a time draft, it is true that the buyer may be deprived of the credit period as to part of the purchase price, that is, so much of it as the freight amounts to. In the case at bar the freight was $1359.14. The measure of any possible loss to the buyer is the interest upon this sum for the period between arrival of the goods and the date the drafts would fall due and the possible inconvenience of being called upon for early payment in cash of this portion of the price. The bills of lading were endorsed "on board" on May 5th and, if we assume the voyage would take 30 days, the buyer would not be called upon for the freight until June 5th. The draft if accepted on May 15th would have been due 90 days later, that is, the buyer would have had to pay freight about 70 days earlier than he would otherwise have paid such sum. Interest at 6% would amount to about $17. On a transaction involving about $9,700 such a sum is insignificant. The law has not cut so fine. The point of possible inconvenience is taken care of by ancient usage. The seller has so long had the option of shipping either freight collect or freight prepaid that the cases recognize the option as part of the standard meaning of the term C.I.F., making no distinction between prepayment or shipping freight collect and crediting it on the invoice irrespective of whether the draft be time or sight. * * * As the court pointed out in finding 16 the American and Foreign Trade definitions provide that under a C.I.F. contract the seller must pay the freight but make no mention of prepayment. Furthermore, if the buyer sells the documents before arrival of the goods, as frequently happens in C.I.F. transactions, whether freight was prepaid will be wholly immaterial to him.

The judgment for the defendant is reversed and judgment directed in favor of the plaintiff.

Notes

1. What was the real reason Chase and its customer did not want to pay in this case?

2. Can you formulate a general rule that would tell you when custom may be used to repair an apparently defective presentation of documents and when custom would not achieve this?

FIRST ARLINGTON NATIONAL BANK v. STATHIS

Court of Appeals of Illinois, 1983.
115 Ill.App.3d 402, 71 Ill.Dec. 195, 450 N.E.2d 833.

SULLIVAN, J. This appeal is from the entry of summary judgment for Gus Stathis (defendant) in an action for declaratory judgment brought to determine the rights and obligations of the parties under a letter of credit issued by the plaintiff bank. Plaintiff contends that the trial court erred in ruling that (1) none of the exceptions contained in § 5–114(2) of the Uniform Commercial Code (the Code) (Ill.Rev.Stat. 1979, ch. 26, par. 5–114(2)) excused plaintiff's duty to honor the letter of credit; (2) defendant did not breach any warranties made by him pursuant to § 5–111(1) of the Code (Ill.Rev.Stat. 1979, ch. 26, par. 5–111(1)); (3) none of the other warranty sections of the Code were applicable to the transaction in question; and (4) defendant was entitled to prejudgment interest pursuant to § 2 of "An Act in relation to the rate of interest and other charges in connection with sales on credit and the lending of money" (the Interest Act) (Ill.Rev.Stat. 1979, ch. 74, par. 2) [1] from the date of his demand for payment. In his cross-appeal, defendant maintains that the trial court erred in limiting its award of prejudgment interest to 5%.

In a prior appeal in this case, First Arlington National Bank v. Stathis (1980), 90 Ill.App.3d 802, 413 N.E.2d 1288, we reversed the trial court's entry of summary judgment for plaintiff and remanded for further consideration of defendant's cross-motion for summary judgment. The facts of the transaction in question are set forth in detail in that opinion, and the parties presented no additional evidence after remand; therefore, we shall repeat only such facts as are relevant to the issues herein.

In 1973, defendant agreed to sell certain real estate to Ralph Edgar, Denis Rintz, and Phillip Grandinetti, Jr., and as partial consideration therefor received a promissory note dated March 30, 1973 (the March note), executed by the three

1. Now codified at Ill.Rev.Stat. 1981, ch. 17, par. 6402.

purchasers and their wives in the principal amount of $575,000 with an interest rate of 8% on the outstanding principal. The debt was to be secured by a letter of credit in the amount of $575,000 which was to be replaced each year at least 30 days before its expiration date. If the letter of credit was not renewed, or if the purchasers defaulted in the payment of either interest or principal, the balance due was immediately payable without notice.

Plaintiff issued the required letter of credit, to expire May 5, 1974, in exchange for a note executed by Rintz, Edgar, and Grandinetti in the principal amount of $575,000 at 10% interest, secured by certain property, and the pledge of collateral, i.e., a certificate of deposit in the amount of $187,000 owned by Grandinetti and real estate owned by Rintz and Edgar. The letter of credit guaranteed payment of $575,000 to defendant upon default of the March note, provided that his demand was accompanied by the March note, endorsed by him without recourse to the order of plaintiff; any documents securing the note; defendant's notarized statement that the note was due by reason of acceleration and a detailed statement of the nature of the default; defendant's notarized statement that demand had been made on the makers, and the demand was not complied with for a period of at least 10 days following the demand; and copies of the demand letters.

The makers defaulted on the first payment of interest, due on March 30, 1974, and failed to provide a timely renewal of the letter of credit. On April 23, 1974, Grandinetti, desirous of avoiding litigation concerning the interest due, entered into an agreement with defendant (the Grandinetti agreement). Pursuant thereto, Grandinetti executed a note for one-third of the first interest installment, due June 5, 1974, and a second note for the remaining two-thirds, payable on demand. Defendant agreed to attempt to collect the remaining two-thirds of the interest from the Edgars and Rintzes (Grandinetti's wife was not mentioned) and, if successful, cancel the second note.[2]

On April 25, 1974, defendant sought payment on the letter of credit and presented to plaintiff the documents required by the terms thereof. Plaintiff refused to pay, claiming that, among other defects, the March note did not comply with the letter of credit in that the Grandinetti agreement effectively released Grandinetti's wife from liability on the March note and, as a result, released the other comakers as well by application of § 3–606 of the Code. (Ill.Rev.Stat. 1979, ch. 26, par. 3–606.) It filed a complaint for declaratory judgment and, in granting plaintiff's motion for summary judgment therein and denying defendant's cross-motion, the trial court ruled that plaintiff was not required to honor the letter of credit as a result of the Grandinetti agreement. On appeal, we held that plaintiff could not look beyond the documents presented to the underlying agreement in determining whether to honor the letter of credit. (First Arlington National Bank v. Stathis (1980), 90 Ill.App.3d 802, 809, 413 N.E.2d 1288, 1295.) Since the documents presented complied on their face with the letter of credit (90 Ill.App.3d 802, 816, 413 N.E.2d 1288, 1299) and there was no fraud arising from the Grandinetti agreement which would justify dishonoring the letter of credit (90 Ill.App.3d 802, 811, 413 N.E.2d 1288, 1295), plaintiff was required to honor the demand pursuant to § 5–114 of the Code (Ill.Rev.Stat. 1979, ch. 26, par. 5–114), and we reversed the order granting summary judgment to plaintiff and denying it to defendant. However, because plaintiff had raised other arguments in opposition to defendant's motion for

2. This unpaid interest was the subject matter of defendant's counterclaim against the Grandinettis, Edgars, and Rintzes, which is not before us in this appeal.

summary judgment which were not considered by the trial court in ruling thereon, we remanded the matter for further consideration.

On remand, the parties agreed that the only remaining issue with regard to defendant's motion for summary judgment was whether he breached any warranties on presentment of his draft for payment under the letter of credit. Plaintiff argued that the Grandinetti agreement, which allegedly released Grandinetti's comakers from liability on the March note, and defendant's failure to deliver to it the personal judgment notes executed by Grandinetti under the agreement, breached warranties made by defendant under §§ 5–111, 3–417, 4–207, 7–507, and 8–306 of the Code. (Ill.Rev.Stat. 1979, ch. 26, pars. 5–111, 3–417, 4–207, 7–507, 8–306.) The trial court concluded that our prior opinion barred any consideration of the Grandinetti agreement as grounds for dishonoring the letter of credit. However, it went on to rule that the only applicable warranty was § 5–111(1), and that defendant warranted thereunder merely that the tendered documents complied on their face with the terms of the letter of credit; that this warranty was not breached; and that, in any event, the Grandinetti agreement did not release any of the comakers, contrary to plaintiff's assertion. It further ruled that defendant was entitled to prejudgment interest from April 25, 1974, the date of his demand for payment, at the rate of 5%, "although a greater rate of interest would be more equitable in the present situation." These cross-appeals followed.

OPINION

Plaintiff first contends that the trial court erred in ruling that none of the exceptions to an issuer's duty to honor a demand which complies on its face with the terms of the letter of credit excused plaintiff's duty to honor. It relies on § 5–114(2)(b) of the Code (Ill.Rev.Stat. 1979, ch. 26, par. 5–114(2)(b)), which provides in relevant part:

> "(2) Unless otherwise agreed when documents appear on their face to comply with the terms of a credit but a required document does not in fact conform to the warranties made on negotiation or transfer of a document of title (Section 7–507) or of a security (Section 8–306) or is forged or fraudulent or there is fraud in the transaction
>
> * * *
>
> "(b) * * * as against its customer, an issuer acting in good faith may honor the draft or demand for payment despite notification from the customer of fraud, forgery or other defect not apparent on the face of the documents but a court of appropriate jurisdiction may enjoin such honor."

The trial court held that the warranties under §§ 7–507 and 8–306 (Ill.Rev.Stat. 1979, ch. 26, pars. 7–507, 8–306) are inapplicable to the transaction in question and that plaintiff could not relitigate the question of fraud in the transaction, which was decided adversely to it in our prior opinion. Plaintiff apparently concedes the inapplicability of §§ 7–507 and 8–306 but maintains that the trial court read § 5–114(2)(b) too restrictively, and that the intent of the drafters was clearly to include not only the warranties arising thereunder but also those arising under §§ 3–417 and 4–207 (Ill.Rev.Stat. 1979, ch. 26, pars. 3–417, 4–207). It further argues that because defendant did not disclose the Grandinetti agreement when making presentment, the fraud contemplated by § 5–114(2)(b) was present.

With regard to its first argument, plaintiff cites as its sole authority the official comment to the Code. (Ill.Ann.Stat., ch. 26, par. 5–114, Uniform Commercial Code Comment, at 600 (Smith-Hurd 1963).) However, a careful reading of that commentary in its entirety discloses no such intention to include warranties other than those specifically mentioned in the statute. Therefore, we must look to the general rules of statutory construction to determine the intention of the drafters. The statutory language itself is the best indicator of that intention

* * * In the instant case, the language used by the legislature is unambiguous and leaves no room for expansion by the interpretation. Two code sections are specifically set forth, and had the legislature wished to include others, it could have done so easily, as it did in § 5–111(1) of the Code (Ill.Rev.Stat. 1979, ch. 26, par. 5–111(1)). Moreover, even if we were to resort to rules of construction, the most pertinent in the instant situation is that the enumeration of certain exceptions in a statute implies the exclusion of all others. (People ex rel. Difanis v. Barr (1980), 83 Ill.2d 191, 414 N.E.2d 731.) Thus, express inclusion of §§ 7–507 and 8–306 here would imply that the legislature intended to exclude all other warranty provisions.

* * * Plaintiff next contends that the trial court erred in ruling that defendant did not breach any warranties made by him under § 5–111(1) of the Code (Ill.Rev.Stat. 1979, ch. 26, par. 5–111(1)). It argues that the trial court construed this warranty too narrowly in holding that defendant warranted thereunder merely that the documents submitted complied on their face with the terms of the credit. Plaintiff theorizes that this warranty provision also "protects both the issuer of a letter of credit and its customers from the harsh and limiting effects of the rule that an issuer must honor a demand for payment if the documents appear on their face to conform to the terms of the credit." Therefore, it posits, § 5–111(1) permits it to do what § 5–114 forbids; that is, look to the underlying contract between defendant and its customers in determining whether it has a duty to honor the letter of credit.

Section 5–111(1) provides in relevant part that " * * * the beneficiary by transferring or presenting a documentary draft or demand for payment warrants to all interested parties that the necessary conditions of the credit have been complied with * * *." (Ill.Rev.Stat. 1979, ch. 26, par. 5–111(1).) The parties have not cited, nor has our own research discovered, any cases delineating the scope of the phrase "the necessary conditions of the credit." Neither the Illinois nor the official commentary to the Code defines the phrase in question. The official comment states that "[t]he purpose of this section is to state the peculiar warranty of performance made by a beneficiary * * *." (Ill.Ann.Stat., ch. 26, par. 5–111, Uniform Commercial Code Comment, at 590 (Smith-Hurd 1963).) The Illinois comment appears to acknowledge an ambiguity in the phrase by stating that "[t]he term 'necessary conditions of credit' is not a defined one. It presumably includes the genuineness of the documents. Beyond that the cases are not clear." (Ill.Ann.Stat., ch. 26, par. 5–111, Illinois Code Comment, at 590 (Smith-Hurd 1963).) However, two recent decisions in other states imply that § 5–111(1) is at least coextensive with § 5–114.

In Werner v. A.L. Grootemaat & Sons (1977), 80 Wis.2d 513, 259 N.W.2d 310, the court stated, in dictum, that an issuer who wrongfully honors may have a remedy against the beneficiary under § 5–111(1). (80 Wis.2d 513, 524–25 n. 22, 259 N.W.2d 310, 315–16 n. 22.) Since an issuer wrongfully honors only when it pays on presentation of documents which do not conform on their face to the terms of the credit, a beneficiary warrants under § 5–111(1) that the documents do conform. Werner further indicates that a customer would have a breach of warranty action under § 5–111(1) if the issuer were to honor a letter of credit despite the existence of one of the exceptions set forth in § 5–114(2)(b), as it is permitted to do under that section without jeopardizing its right to reimbursement. (80 Wis.2d 513, 524, 259 N.W.2d 310, 315.) The latter interpretation is also evident, although unstated, in Boucher & Slack Contractors, Inc. v. McLean (La.App. 1980), 382 So.2d 1030, 1034, and supported by the official commentary to § 5–114, which states in relevant part:

> "When * * * no innocent third parties * * * are involved the issuer is no longer under a duty to honor; but * * * the issuer if he acts in good faith is given the privilege of honoring the draft as against its customer, that is to say, with a right of reimbursement against him. * * * In the event of honor, an action by the customer against the beneficiary will lie by virtue of either the underlying contract or Section 5–111(1) of this Article." Ill.Ann.Stat., ch. 26, par. 5–114, Uniform Commercial Code Comment, at 601 (Smith-Hurd 1963).

It appears, then, that the warranties of § 5–111(1) are at least as broad as the circumstances encompassed by § 5–114. Even this interpretation, however, is too narrow to justify denial of summary judgment for defendant, since we have already determined that the documents in question comply on their face with the terms of the letter of credit, and none of the exceptions set forth in § 5–114 are applicable to this transaction. For this reason plaintiff asserts, as noted above, that the warranties of § 5–111(1) are broader in scope and allow the court to go beyond the face of the documents and consider the facts and circumstances of the underlying contract between defendant and its customers. In effect, plaintiff asserts it is not enough that it is protected by its right of reimbursement under § 5–114(3) if it rightfully honors the letter of credit, and by the beneficiary's warranty under § 5–111(1) if it wrongfully honors. It would have us hold that under § 5–111(1) it may also take advantage of any defenses its customers might have to the underlying contract, even where those defenses fall short of the defenses contemplated by § 5–114(2)(b).

The obvious flaw in plaintiff's position is that, if adopted, it would convert the letter of credit into a contract of guaranty or suretyship, for it destroys the sole distinguishing feature between them. As our supreme court stated in Pastor v. National Republic Bank (1979), 76 Ill.2d 139, 147, 390 N.E.2d 894, 897:

> "Although the use of letters of credit is often referred to as being in the nature of a guaranty or a suretyship arrangement, it does not assume the legal significance of either. Under the letter of credit the issuer is bound in the first instance to pay the beneficiary. It is an individual undertaking of the issuer to pay the beneficiary, and the obligation is not subject to the various defenses available to a guaranty or a surety undertaking."

Thus, under a guaranty, the courts must look to the rights and obligations of the parties to the underlying contract in determining the rights and obligations of the guarantor, for a true guaranty is a secondary obligation (Republic National Bank v. Northwest National Bank (Tex. 1978), 578 S.W.2d 109, 114); whereas, a letter of credit is a primary obligation independent of the underlying transaction (Professional Modular Surface, Inc. v. Uniroyal, Inc. (1982), 108 Ill.App.3d 1046, 440 N.E.2d 117). Therefore, even an agreement among beneficiaries and customers releasing or cancelling the underlying obligation will not affect a beneficiary's right to demand payment on an irrevocable letter of credit. (See Housing Securities, Inc. v. Maine National Bank (Me. 1978), 391 A.2d 311.) If we were to accept plaintiff's argument, the stringent duty to honor contained in § 5–114(1) would be completely abrogated, destroying the basic purpose of a letter of credit "to eliminate the risk to the beneficiary that the customer will refuse or halt payment because of alleged deficiencies in the beneficiary's performance." O'Grady v. First Union National Bank (1978), 296 N.C. 212, 232, 250 S.E.2d 587, 600.

For these reasons, we believe that the basic warranties under § 5–111(1) are that the documents comply on their face with the terms of the letter of credit, and that none of the exceptions set forth in § 5–114(2)(b) are present. The warranty provisions do not authorize the issuer to assert defenses which its customer might have to the underlying contract. We need not determine under the facts before us whether other warranties are encompassed by the provision that "the necessary conditions of the credit have been complied with."

We turn next to defendant's assertion of error in the trial court's ruling that defendant did not breach any other warranties under the Code. Section 5–111(1) provides that the warranties contained therein are "in addition to any warranties arising under Articles 3, 4, 7 and 8." (Ill.Rev.Stat. 1979, ch. 26, par. 5–111(1).) Plaintiff contends that the warranties arising under §§ 3–417 and 4–207 (Ill.Rev.Stat. 1979, ch. 26, pars. 3–417, 4–207) relating to the presentment and transfer of negotiable instruments are applicable to the present situation because defendant was required to transfer the March note to it. It argues that defendant has breached thereunder his warranties that he has good title to the instrument, that the transfer is otherwise rightful, and that no defense of any party is good against him.

Initially, we note that the warranties made under §§ 3–417 and 4–207 are identical in their terms, except that § 3–417 is applicable to one who obtains payment or transfers an instrument and receives consideration therefor, while § 4–207 applies to customers and collecting banks that obtain payment or transfer for consideration. It is unclear to us why plaintiff persists in its argument that both are applicable here, since it admits that the warranties are the same. Nevertheless, it is our view that § 4–207 is obviously inapplicable to the present situation, since defendant is neither a collecting bank as defined in § 4–105(d) of the Code (Ill.Rev.Stat. 1979, ch. 26, par. 4–105(d)) nor a customer as defined in § 4–104(1)(e) (Ill.Rev.Stat. 1979, ch. 26, par. 4–104(1)(e)).

With regard to § 3–417, we note that it is applicable to "[a]ny person who transfers an instrument and receives consideration." (Ill.Rev.Stat. 1979, ch. 26, par. 3–417(2).) It is established that these warranties are not made by one who does not receive consideration. (Oak Park Currency Exchange, Inc. v. Maropoulos (1977), 48 Ill.App.3d 437, 363 N.E.2d 54.) Plaintiff posits that if it were to pay defendant's demand, he would receive consideration for the March note. However, plaintiff's obligation to pay is unrelated to the March note; it is obligated to pay under the letter of credit, and will pay on the draft presented as provided in the letter of credit. If § 3–417 has any application at all in this situation, it is to that draft, not to the underlying note, and plaintiff has not pointed to any warranties breached by defendant's presentment of the draft for payment.

Furthermore, it is our view that plaintiff is not injured in any way by the alleged inability to recover on the March note. Since we have determined that it must honor the letter of credit, plaintiff has a right of reimbursement reinforced by a secured note at 10% interest. Surely that means of recovery is preferable to an unsecured, defaulted note bearing 8% interest. In addition, even assuming arguendo that defendant made the warranty asserted under § 3–417, we do not believe that there are any defenses good against him. Plaintiff argues that defendant's alleged release of Mrs. Grandinetti from liability for the accrued interest released Mrs. Rintz and Mrs. Edgar from liability on the March note pursuant to § 3–606 of the Code. (Ill.Rev.Stat. 1979, ch. 26, par. 3–606.) However, that section provides in relevant part that "[t]he holder discharges any party to the instrument *to the extent that* * * * the holder * * * releases or agrees not to sue any person against whom the party has * * * a right of recourse * * *." (Emphasis added.) The phrase "to the extent that" indicates that a release may be pro tanto, and courts considering the phrase have so held, whether the release was the result of impairment of the right of recourse (Provident Bank v. Gast (1979), 57 Ohio St.2d 102, 386 N.E.2d 1357) or impairment of collateral (Farmers State Bank v. Cooper (1980), 227 Kan. 547, 608 P.2d 929). Thus, it appears that when the person against whom a right of recourse is held is partially discharged, others who are only secondarily liable are also discharged, but only to the extent that their rights have been impaired.

In the instant case, the alleged release of Mrs. Grandinetti arises from the omission of her name from the following paragraph of the Grandinetti agreement:

> "4. That said judgment note for $32,515.11 is being executed and delivered by GRANDINETTI for the purpose of indemnifying STATHIS with regard to the aforesaid balance of interest due him and STATHIS hereby agrees as follows:
>
> (a) That he shall pursue * * * RALPH EDGAR, JUDY EDGAR * * *, DENIS J. RINTZ and MARILYN RINTZ * * * for the collection of said balance of interest in the sum of $32,515.11 * * *."

Such a release, however, would only relieve Mrs. Grandinetti of liability for the $32,515.11 in interest. It follows that the other accommodation makers would be released only to the extent that their right of recourse against Mrs. Grandinetti is impaired; that is, on two-thirds of the first interest installment. Since the paragraph in question does not purport to release Mrs. Grandinetti from liability on the note, it could not release Mrs. Rintz or Mrs. Edgar thereon.

Plaintiff has made herein a number of assertions unsupported by pertinent citations to authority or argument as required by Supreme Court Rule 341(e)(7) (73 Ill.2d R. 341(e)(7)). First, in arguing that it was excused from honoring by virtue of defendant's breach of warranties under § 511(1), plaintiff maintained that defendant was obliged to transfer to it "the whole note," including the accrued interest which was the subject matter of the Grandinetti agreement. It cited four cases in support of its proposition that it, rather than defendant, was entitled to that interest—all of which were totally inapplicable and, if they had any value, supported defendant's position. Moreover, plaintiff failed to cite authority for its contention that the interest was unpaid when it received the March note, although defendant admittedly took two notes as payment of accrued interest *before* transferring the March note to plaintiff. Next, plaintiff states that defendant breached three warranties under § 3–417; i.e., that no defense was good against him, that he had good title to the March note, and that the transfer was otherwise rightful. Despite this assertion, plaintiff has neither cited authority nor presented arguments with regard to the latter two warranties. Finally, plaintiff makes the conclusory statement, unsupported by argument or citation, that the Grandinetti agreement, which concerned solely the payment of accrued interest, constituted an extension of time for payment of the March note. It argues that this alleged extension of time released the accommodation makers under § 3–606, thus breaching defendant's warranties under § 4–317, but apparently expects us to take the underlying premise on faith. It is unnecessary for us to address any of these arguments, since the first is disposed of by our determination that plaintiff may not look to the underlying agreement in deciding whether to honor the letter of credit, and the latter two are irrelevant since we have ruled that § 3–417 is inapplicable to the present transaction. However, even if those arguments were not so disposed of, we would be justified in deeming them waived (Department of Transportation v. Association of Franciscan Fathers (1981), 93 Ill.App.3d 1141, 418 N.E.2d 36) for, as one court aptly stated, "a reviewing court is entitled to have the issues clearly defined with pertinent authority cited and is not simply a depository in which the appealing party may dump the burden of argument and research" (Williamson v. Opsahl (1981), 92 Ill.App.3d 1087, 1089, 416 N.E.2d 783, 784).

* * *

For the foregoing reasons, the orders of the trial court are affirmed.

Affirmed.

WILSON, P.J., and LORENZ, J., concur. [Some footnotes omitted.]

Notes

1. The warranty provision in UCC 5–111 is infrequently cited. Surely the *Stathis* court is correct in concluding that it should not be read to incorporate the idea of compliance with the underlying contract; otherwise, it would completely override the principle that the underlying contract and the contract to pay are separate. Presumably it would give rise to a cause of action for breach of warranty in a case in which there was a forged indorsement. It might have an impact in other cases as well, but case law, at least, does not recognize any significant area for its operation.

2. Can you think of a case where it would clearly apply?

3. Consider its impact in the following situation: Beneficiary presents documents that fail to comply with the terms of the credit in some detail that would have permitted bank to refuse payment. Bank overlooks or ignores the detail and pays only to find that its customer has not reimbursed it and has in fact filed in Chapter 11 that very day. Bank sues Beneficiary for return of its payment citing 5–111.

Problem 29–3

Assume the Bank has asked you whether it must pay in each of the following cases:

1. Letter of credit calls for "clean bill of lading." The bills presented contain the notation "Shippers load and count." Does that make them not clean?

2. What of a bill of lading that says "Carrier not responsible for rust." See Articles 17 and 18 of the UCP.

3. A letter of credit issued to the beneficiary "Danish Furniture Company" calls for invoices specifying certain items. Ultimately a draft is presented together with invoices that correctly describe the goods, but the invoices are those of "Copenhagen Manufacturers," not of "Danish Furniture Company." Beneficiary asserts that the two companies are one and the same. Must Bank pay? (See UCC 5–116.)

Problem 29–4

National Builders agreed to sell two prefabricated houses to Mohammud Sofan, a resident of the Yemen Arab Republic. Sofan procured a letter of credit issued by the Yemen Bank for Reconstruction in favor of National Builders. Irving Bank in New York was the confirming bank and National Builders designated National Bank of

Washington as its collecting bank. National Bank of Washington sent Irving all of the documents required, but there were several discrepancies, among them the fact that the bill of lading listing the party to be notified by the shipping company as "Mohammud Soran." Irving agreed to request authorization from the Yemen Bank to pay the letter of credit despite the discrepancy. No authorization was forthcoming, and Irving refused to pay. National Builders now sues Irving and argues among other things the following:

1. A mistake as to a single letter in a name is insignificant and forms no basis for dishonor.

2. National Bank's promise to indemnify if the name in fact caused confusion on delivery to Yemen and to hold it harmless for any damages suffered because of the presence of the letter "r" instead of "f" required it to honor.

3. Irving was estopped from claiming the discrepancy because it held the documents for several days before it notified National Bank of Washington of the deficiency.

4. In any event the case should not have been decided on summary judgment because there was a legitimate issue of fact on the question whether "Soran" properly identifies "Sofan."

Problem 29–5

1. Bank calls you in with the following problem. It appears that Bank issued a letter of credit on behalf of its customer, a football team in a newly formed professional league to the beneficiary, who was their star quarterback, Lance Bugalowski. At the time the bank issued a letter of credit, it believed that the football team would make a go of it, and it issued the credit despite the fact that the team had no security. The team is now teetering on the verge of bankruptcy. It appears unlikely that the league will operate in the next year. Unfortunately the letter of credit obligation to Bugalowski is for $500,000 each of the next three years. The letter has an expiration date three years hence. It says neither that it is revocable or irrevocable. Is the letter revocable and, if so, can the bank revoke it and thus avoid its obligation to Bugalowski? Assume alternatively that the letter is governed by the Uniform Customs and Practices or by the Uniform Commercial Code.

2. Assume that one year has passed and that the football team has gone into bankruptcy and that Bugalowski is about to make a demand on the letter. From reading the local press you understand that Bugalowski has now signed a contract as the principal quarterback for a west coast NFL team and, according to the papers, will be earning in excess of $750,000 a year. Presumably that gain would be set off as mitigation against any damages that he could claim against the customer. Can the bank use that fact to escape any obligation to pay?

A youngster in your office has suggested the following: Any demand now would breach the warranties under UCC 5–111 because Bugalowski does not meet the conditions, namely, having a good claim against the club. Secondly, the youngster has suggested that the Bank simply refuse to pay, take an assignment of the club's rights against Bugalowski and assert them in a counterclaim when he sues the Bank. Will the trustee in bankruptcy of the Club agree to such an assignment, and if so, will it work? Finally, your colleague has suggested that the automatic stay under 362 as applied in the Club's bankruptcy will bar any suit against the Bank by Bugalowski. What do you suggest?

At this point the student would be wise to read the entire Uniform Customs and Practices. It is hardly useful to attempt to remember everything reported there, but it would be well to know the kinds of things that one might find there and to file away the UCP as a source of information on what terms and documents are acceptable and what ones are not. Note, for example, the rule in Article 34 that in many cases will permit a tolerance of plus or minus three percent. There too one finds a definition of the word "about" or "circa."

SECTION 3. ISSUER'S RIGHT TO DISHONOR BECAUSE OF FRAUD

Section 5–114(2) recognizes the bank's right to refuse to honor where a document is "forged or fraudulent or there is fraud in the transaction * * *". Note, however that UCC 5–114(2) permits an issuer acting in good faith to honor despite allegations of fraud, but the last clause in UCC 5–114(2)(b) suggests that "a court of appropriate jurisdiction may enjoin such honor." The extent to which UCC 5–114(2) and the cases decided under that rule cut back on the independence principle and authorize a bank to refuse payment has been a topic of continuing debate in the courts and in the scholarly literature.

First, how does one distinguish between "fraud" and mere breach of contract? As we will see, the case which spawned the subsection, Sztejn v. J. Henry Schroder Banking Corp., infra page 1388, might have been characterized merely as a case of gross and intentional breach of contract.

The second issue present in UCC 5–114(2) is what standard the court is to apply in determining whether to enjoin payment—the question whether the bank that has not been enjoined may use UCC 5–114(2) to justify a refusal of payment.

Professor Dolan has argued persuasively for a narrow interpretation of UCC 5–114(2). Surely he is right in cautioning the courts against broad interpretation of that subsection. An expansive view of it could undermine the utility of the letter of credit and give every bank under pressure from a powerful customer a colorable excuse for refusal to pay. Also lurking in the subsection is the question, what kind of fraud and by whom? Must the fraud be committed by the beneficiary or is it enough that there be fraud in some transaction one step remote from the beneficiary? What, for example, of the case in which a general partner of an oil well drilling partnership defrauds the bank's customer but causes the letter of credit to be drawn with the general partner's bank as the beneficiary? In such case, the beneficiary bank might be completely innocent of the fraud.

The last decade has seen a great deal of stress applied to UCC 5–114(2) and the principles there expressed. This stress has arisen largely out of letters of credit written by American banks for American customers to Iranian beneficiaries. After the overthrow of the Shah and the rupture of relations between Iran and the United States, the various Iranian beneficiaries of the letters of credit called or threatened to call them. Of course the American customers feared that if payment were made and the money transmitted to Iran, the American customers would never have an opportunity to get a fair trial on their rights on the underlying contract. A customer might concede, for example, that the documents presented met the terms of the credit, but maintain that it had failed to perform the contract because of force majeure or because it was actively prevented from doing so by the Iranian officials who were now seeking payment under the letter. In such cases it is not easy to prove fraud, yet there was enormous political and economic pressure not to pay such letters. Not all of the American courts covered themselves with glory.

J. DOLAN, THE LAW OF LETTERS OF CREDIT: COMMERCIAL AND STANDBY CREDITS 7–45 TO 7–50.

[E] IRANIAN CASES

[i] Strict cases. The analysis of the *Intraworld* and *Dynamics* cases is helpful in explaining several decisions involving standby credit disputes that arose out of the U.S./Iranian political problems of 1979. It is the practice of economically strong buyers, especially government buyers dealing with economically weaker sellers, to insist on performance guaranties when they enter into supply contracts. In the Iranian cases, the American sellers induced Iranian banks to issue those guaranties by having a domestic bank issue a standby credit in favor of the Iranian bank. Generally, the standby credit would call for the Iranian bank's draft and a certificate to the effect that it had been required to honor its guaranty. When the Iranian revolution interrupted commerce between the United States and Iran, sellers became anxious about the standby credits. Political and diplomatic turmoil prevented performance of the underlying agreements, and the Iranian political and financial structure appeared to be in the hands of persons who did not inspire the confidence that their counterparts in Amsterdam or London inspire. The sellers resorted to the courts.

Some of the cases lent themselves to resolution on the grounds that the account parties had not satisfied the equity prerequisites for injunctive relief. In *KMW International v. Chase Manhattan Bank, N.A.,* for example, the account party sought an injunction alleging that the Iranian buyer had breached the contract of sale and that any draw on the credit would be fraudulent. There had been no draw, however, and the court held that no injunction against payment should issue. The plaintiff's claim for damages was too speculative and conjectural to satisfy the rules of equity. The court did, however, order the issuer to give the account party three days' notice before honoring any demand. In *United Technologies Corp. v. Citibank, N.A.,* the account party alleged that it had performed the contract of sale and that any demand under the credit would be wrongful. The court denied the injunction, holding that the account party had an adequate remedy at law in the event a draft was fraudulent. In *American Bell International Inc. v. Islamic Republic of Iran,* the account party claimed that the Iranian buyer had breached the contract of sale, and alleged further that the beneficiary's demand, which the issuer had received, was not timely. The court refused to grant the injunction. In response to the account party's argument that the demand was not timely, the court noted that if, in fact, the issuer honored a late demand, the account party would have an adequate remedy at law—a suit for money damages against the issuer. In *Werner Lehara International, Inc. v. Harris Trust & Savings Bank,* the court held that the plaintiff, who was seeking injunctive relief before the beneficiary made any demand, did not satisfy the equity prerequisites and had not made out a case of fraud.

It is perhaps also significant that in the *Werner Lehara, KMW,* and *American Bell* cases the courts weighed against the account party the fact that an injunction might affect the banking relationships of the issuer adversely. It is clear that the issuers in these cases were nervous about the effect the injunctions would have in general on the reputation of credits issued by American banks and by the implicit threat of retaliation from the Iranian government or Iranian banks. In *United Technologies,* the court explicitly found such eventualities too speculative to be considered.

The *Werner Lehara, KMW,* and *American Bell* cases reject firmly the account party's argument that the demands of the Iranian beneficiaries were or would be fraudulent. Those courts viewed the contests as contract disputes, the risks of which the account parties should have foreseen when they entered into the sales contract. The courts refused to let the account parties shift to the banks or to the letter-of-credit industry in general a contract risk that inheres in international sales, a risk of political upheaval. In *United Technologies,* the court did not consider it necessary to decide that issue.

The conclusion of these cases that there was no fraud in the transaction sufficient to invoke the rule of Section 5–114(2) is consistent with the general rule. It may be that the beneficiaries of the guaranties issued by the Iranian banks were guilty of fraud when those beneficiaries required the Iranian banks to pay under the guaranties. The plaintiff's allegations suggest as much. Fraud in that guaranty transaction is not fraud in the letter-of-credit transaction as the *Sztejn* rule requires. The certificates required in the *KMW* and the *American Bell* cases, moreover, did not invite the courts to look into that related contract as the *NMC* and *O'Grady* cases did. The Iranian certificates recited only that the beneficiary was called upon to pay under the letter of guaranty. These carefully drawn credits do not pierce the barrier that insulates the credit from the underlying transaction and do not force the court to look at that underlying transaction.

While a significant number of courts dealing with standby credits issued to Iranian beneficiaries granted notice injunctions requiring the issuer to delay honoring a credit for a short period of time, the more significant cases are those such as *KMW, American Bell,* and *United Technologies.* The latter demonstrate the obstacles facing an account party once the demand arrives. These cases show a marked willingness to enforce the equity prerequisites and a marked unwillingness to relax the strict fraud rule of *Sztejn* or to reallocate the commercial and political risks that these merchant sellers must now shoulder under letter-of-credit law.

[ii] Less strict cases. The adherence to the strict *Sztejn* rule was not unanimous. In *Itek Corp. v. First National Bank,* the defendant bank issued a standby credit to an Iranian bank which, in turn, issued a guarantee to the Iranian Ministry of War. The account party had agreed to sell optical equipment to the Iranian government, and the sales contract contained a force majeure clause permitting either party to cancel the contract before performance under it was complete. The U.S. Department of State revoked the account party's export license, and the account party notified Iran of its election to terminate the contract under the force majeure clause. Subsequently, the account party obtained a temporary restraining order against the issuer; and when the beneficiary presented a conforming demand under the credit, the court enjoined payment. The *Itek* court held that because the account party's suit against the Iranian government would be futile, irreparable injury was evident. With respect to the fraud question, the court held that Section 5–114(2) establishes an exception to the independence principle, but the court also held that it was not necessary to probe the question of whether the fraud would be in the credit transaction or in the underlying transaction. The *Itek* court found the fraud so "blatant" and "undisputed" that it issued the restraining order.

A similar disposition to find fraud was evident in *Touche Ross & Co. v. Manufacturers Hanover Trust Co.,* where the credit ran to the benefit of an Iranian bank that had issued a letter of guaranty to the Iranian Ministry of

War. The underlying contract contained a force majeure clause and stipulated that upon invocation of the clause all letters of guaranty would terminate. The account party invoked the force majeure clause, and the court concluded, therefore, that there could be no legitimate call on the letter of credit. In short, the *Touche Ross* court resolved the underlying contract questions, concluded that the equities were with the account party, and issued the injunction.

The unlikelihood of recovery under the Iranian court system influenced the court in *Harris Corp. v. National Iranian Radio & Television.* In that case, the court rejected the argument that the account party was attempting to reallocate the risks. The court acknowledged that the purpose of the credit was to permit the Iranian buyer to recover its down payment, but the court refused to accept the view that the account party should bear the risk of a fraudulent demand. To the issuer's argument that the account party could have protected itself by negotiating different terms, the court responded vaguely that such an argument ignores "the realities of the drafting of commercial documents." The *Harris Corp.* case rejects the view that the letter of credit used in Middle Eastern transactions reflects the increased bargaining strength of the Middle Eastern buyer and is a device with a purpose of permitting the buyer to recover its down payment automatically. If the *Harris Corp.* case were accepted as the majority rule, such buyers could avoid its effect in a number of ways. They could refuse to accept credits issued by American banks (as Iranian buyers have apparently done), could refuse to make a down payment, or could insist that the down payment be held by the Middle Eastern bank that issues the guaranty letter. Although the account party in the *Harris Corp.* case might find solace in the result, it is doubtful that American sellers in general will be pleased by these attempts by strong buyers to avoid the *Harris Corp.* rule. [Footnotes omitted.]

SZTEJN v. J. HENRY SCHRODER BANKING CORP.

Supreme Court of New York, Special Term, 1941.
177 Misc. 719, 31 N.Y.S.2d 631.

SHIENTAG, JUSTICE.

This is a motion by the defendant, the Chartered Bank of India, Australia and China, (hereafter referred to as the Chartered Bank), made pursuant to Rule 106(5) of the Rules of Civil Practice to dismiss the supplemental complaint on the ground that it fails to state facts sufficient to constitute a cause of action against the moving defendant. The plaintiff brings this action to restrain the payment or presentment for payment of drafts under a letter of credit issued to secure the purchase price of certain merchandise, bought by the plaintiff and his coadventurer, one Schwarz, who is a party defendant in this action. The plaintiff also seeks a judgment declaring the letter of credit and drafts thereunder null and void. The complaint alleges that the documents accompanying the drafts are fraudulent in that they do not represent actual merchandise but instead cover boxes fraudulently filled with worthless material by the seller of the goods. The moving defendant urges that the complaint fails to state a cause of action against it because the Chartered Bank is only concerned with the documents and on their face these conform to the requirements of the letter of credit.

On January 7, 1941, the plaintiff and his coadventurer contracted to purchase a quantity of bristles from the defendant Transea Traders, Ltd. (hereafter referred to as Transea) a corporation having its place of business in Lucknow, India. In order to pay for the bristles, the plaintiff and Schwarz contracted with the defendant J. Henry Schroder Banking Corporation (hereafter referred to as Schroder), a domestic corporation, for the issuance of an irrevocable letter of credit to Transea which provided that drafts by the latter for a specified portion of the purchase price of the bristles would be paid by Schroder upon shipment of the described merchandise and presentation of an invoice and a bill of lading covering the shipment, made out to the order of Schroder.

The letter of credit was delivered to Transea by Schroder's correspondent bank in India, Transea placed fifty cases of material on board a steamship, procured a bill of lading from the steamship company and obtained the customary invoices. These documents describe the bristles called for by the letter of credit. However, the complaint alleges that in fact Transea filled the fifty crates with cowhair, other worthless material and rubbish with intent to simulate genuine merchandise and defraud the plaintiff and Schwarz. The complaint then alleges that Transea drew a draft under the letter of credit to the order of the Chartered Bank and delivered the draft and the fraudulent documents to the "Chartered Bank at Cawnpore, India, for collection for the account of said defendant Transea". The Chartered Bank has presented the draft along with the documents to Schroder for payment. The plaintiff prays for a judgment declaring the letter of credit and draft thereunder void and for injunctive relief to prevent the payment of the draft.

For the purposes of this motion, the allegations of the complaint must be deemed established and "every intendment and fair inference is in favor of the pleading" Madole v. Gavin, 215 App.Div. 299, at page 300, 213 N.Y.S. 529, at page 530; McClare v. Massachusetts Bonding & Ins. Co., 266 N.Y. 371, 373, 195 N.E. 15. Therefore, it must be assumed that Transea was engaged in a scheme to defraud the plaintiff and Schwarz, that the merchandise shipped by Transea is worthless rubbish and that the Chartered Bank is not an innocent holder of the draft for value but is merely attempting to procure payment of the draft for Transea's account.

It is well established that a letter of credit is independent of the primary contract of sale between the buyer and the seller. The issuing bank agrees to pay upon presentation of documents, not goods. This rule is necessary to preserve the efficiency of the letter of credit as an instrument for the financing of trade. One of the chief purposes of the letter of credit is to furnish the seller with a ready means of obtaining prompt payment for his merchandise. It would be a most unfortunate interference with business transactions if a bank before honoring drafts drawn upon it was obliged or even allowed to go behind the documents, at the request of the buyer and enter into controversies between the buyer and the seller regarding the quality of the merchandise shipped. If the buyer and the seller intended the bank to do this they could have so provided in the letter of credit itself, and in the absence of such a provision, the court will not demand or even permit the bank to delay paying drafts which are proper in form. O'Meara Co. v. National Park Bank of New York, 239 N.Y. 386, 146 N.E. 636, 39 A.L.R. 747. * * * Of course, the application of this doctrine presupposes that the documents accompanying the draft are genuine and conform in terms to the requirements of the letter of credit. Lamborn v. Lake Shore Banking & Trust Co., 196 App.Div. 504, 188 N.Y.S. 162; affirmed 231 N.Y. 616, 132 N.E. 911; Bank of Montreal v. Recknagel, 109 N.Y. 482, 17 N.E. 217; 38 Y.L.J. 111, 112.

However, I believe that a different situation is presented in the instant action. This is not a controversy between the buyer and seller concerning a mere breach of warranty regarding the quality of the merchandise; on the present motion, it must be assumed that the seller has intentionally failed to ship any goods ordered by the buyer. In such a situation, where the seller's fraud has been called to the bank's attention before the drafts and documents have been presented for payment, the principle of the independence of the bank's obligation under the letter of credit should not be extended to protect the unscrupulous seller. It is true that even though the documents are forged or fraudulent, if the issuing bank has already paid the draft before receiving notice of the seller's fraud, it will be protected if it exercised reasonable diligence before making such payment. * * * However, in the instant action Schroder has received notice of Transea's active fraud before it accepted or paid the draft. The Chartered Bank, which under the allegations of the complaint stands in no better position than Transea, should not be heard to complain because Schroder is not forced to pay the draft accompanied by documents covering a transaction which it has reason to believe is fraudulent.

Although our courts have used broad language to the effect that a letter of credit is independent of the primary contract between the buyer and seller, that language was used in cases concerning alleged breaches of warranty; no case has been brought to my attention on this point involving an intentional fraud on the part of the seller which was brought to the bank's notice with the request that it withhold payment of the draft on this account. The distinction between a breach of warranty and active fraud on the part of the seller is supported by authority and reason. As one court has stated: "Obviously, when the issuer of a letter of credit knows that a document, although correct in form, is, in point of fact, false or illegal, he cannot be called upon to recognize such a document as complying with the terms of a letter of credit." Old Colony Trust Co. v. Lawyers' Title & Trust Co., 2 Cir., 297 F. 152 at page 158, certiorari denied 265 U.S. 585, 44 S.Ct. 459, 68 L.Ed. 1192. * * *

No hardship will be caused by permitting the bank to refuse payment where fraud is claimed, where the merchandise is not merely inferior in quality but consists of worthless rubbish, where the draft and the accompanying documents are in the hands of one who stands in the same position as the fraudulent seller, where the bank has been given notice of the fraud before being presented with the drafts and documents for payment, and where the bank itself does not wish to pay pending an adjudication of the rights and obligations of the other parties. While the primary factor in the issuance of the letter of credit is the credit standing of the buyer, the security afforded by the merchandise is also taken into account. In fact, the letter of credit requires a bill of lading made out to the order of the bank and not the buyer. Although the bank is not interested in the exact detailed performance of the sales contract, it is vitally interested in assuring itself that there are some goods represented by the documents. * * *

On this motion only the complaint is before me and I am bound by its allegation that the Chartered Bank is not a holder in due course but is a mere agent for collection for the account of the seller charged with fraud. Therefore, the Chartered Bank's motion to dismiss the complaint must be denied. If it had appeared from the face of the complaint that the bank presenting the draft for payment was a holder in due course, its claim against the bank issuing the letter of credit would not be defeated even though the primary transaction was tainted with fraud. This I believe to be the better rule despite some authority to the contrary. See Old Colony Trust Co. v. Lawyers' Title & Trust Co., 2 Cir., 297 F. 152, certiorari denied 265 U.S. 585, 44 S.Ct. 459, 68 L.Ed. 1192; Thayer,

Irrevocable Credits in International Commerce, 37 C.L.R. 1326, 1344; Campbell, Guaranties & The Suretyship Phases of Letters of Credit, 85 U. of Pa.L.R. 261, 272; but see Finkelstein, Legal Aspects of Commercial Letters of Credit, p. 248; O'Meara Co. v. National Park Bank of New York, 239 N.Y. 386, 401, 146 N.E. 636, 39 A.L.R. 747.

The plaintiff's further claim that the terms of the documents presented with the draft are at substantial variance with the requirements of the letter of credit does not seem to be supported by the documents themselves.

Accordingly, the defendant's motion to dismiss the supplemental complaint is denied.

Problem 29–6

At 1:00 on a lazy Friday afternoon as you are having your second martini at your favorite eating club, you are called to the phone and receive the following frantic message from your best client: He tells you that he has procured the issuance of a letter of credit naming his seller as the beneficiary, that he has it on excellent authority that his seller has sealed several freight cars and procured bills of lading stating that the goods are enclosed in those cars, when in fact they are not. He informs you that these documents are now in the hands of seller's bank in a distant city and will probably be presented for payment on Monday morning to the issuing bank in your city. The letter of credit calls for payment of $100,000 and your client is certain that he will have a difficult if not impossible time getting the money back from the seller once it gets into his hands. If the case is governed by the Uniform Commercial Code, what action will you take?

COLORADO NATIONAL BANK OF DENVER v. BOARD OF COUNTY COMMISSIONERS OF ROUTT COUNTY, COLO.

Supreme Court of Colorado, 1981.
634 P.2d 32.

HODGES, CHIEF JUSTICE.

We granted certiorari to review the court of appeals' decision affirming a district court's judgment holding the petitioner, the Colorado National Bank of Denver (the Bank), liable for the face amounts of three letters of credit it issued to secure the completion of road improvements by its customer, the Woodmoor Corporation (Woodmoor). * * * We reverse the judgment as to letters of credit No. 1156 and No. 1157, and affirm the judgment as to letter of credit No. 1168.

Woodmoor planned to develop a mountain recreation community in Routt County, Colorado (the County), to be known as Stagecoach. Early in 1973, Woodmoor obtained plat approval from the Routt County Board of County Commissioners (the Commissioners) for several Stagecoach subdivisions. Pursuant to section 30–28–137, C.R.S. 1973 (1977 Repl Vol 12), and county subdivision regulations, approval of three of these subdivision plats was conditioned upon Woodmoor's agreement to provide a bond or other undertaking to ensure the completion of roads in accordance with the subdivision design specifications. Accordingly, subdivision improvements agreements were executed between Woodmoor and the county.

At Woodmoor's request, the Bank issued three letters of credit to secure Woodmoor's obligations under the agreements. The first two letters of credit,

No. 1156 and No. 1157, were issued January 23, 1973 in the respective amounts of $158,773 and $77,330 bearing expiry dates of December 31, 1975. The third letter of credit No. 1168 was issued March 7, 1973 in the amount of $113,732 bearing an expiry date of December 31, 1976. The face amounts of the letters of credit were identical to the estimated costs of the road and related improvements in the respective subdivision improvements agreements. The County was authorized by each letter of credit to draw directly on the Bank, for the account of Woodmoor, up to the face amount of each letter of credit. Each letter of credit required the County, in order to draw on the letters of credit, to submit fifteen-day sight drafts accompanied by:

> "A duly-signed statement by the Routt County Board of Commissioners that improvements have not been made in compliance with a Subdivision Improvements Agreement between Routt County and the Woodmoor Corporation dated [either January 9, 1973 or March 7, 1973] and covering the [respective subdivisions] at Stagecoach and that payment is therefore demanded hereunder."

Woodmoor never commenced construction of the roads and related improvements. On December 31, 1975, the expiry date of letters of credit No. 1156 and No. 1157, the County presented two demand drafts to the Bank for the face amounts of $158,773 and $77,330. The demand drafts were accompanied by a resolution of the Commissioners stating that Woodmoor had failed to comply with the terms of the subdivision improvements agreements and demanded payment of the face amounts of the letters of credit. On January 5, 1976, within three banking days of the demand,[1] the Bank dishonored the drafts. The Bank did not specifically object to the County's presentation of demand drafts rather than fifteen-day sight drafts as required by the letters of credit.

On December 22, 1976, the County presented the Bank with a demand draft on letter of credit No. 1168 which was accompanied by the required resolution of the Commissioners. The Bank dishonored this draft because of the County's nonconforming demand, viz., that a demand draft was submitted rather than a fifteen-day sight draft. On December 29, 1976, the County presented a fifteen-day sight draft to the Bank. This draft was not accompanied by the resolution of the Commissioners. On December 31, 1976, the Bank dishonored this draft.

The County sued to recover the face amounts of the three letters of credit plus interest from the dates of the demands. The Bank answered the County's complaints alleging several affirmative defenses. The fundamental premise of the Bank's defenses was the assertion that the County would receive a windfall since it had not expended or committed to spend any funds to complete the road improvements specified in the subdivision improvements agreements.

The County filed a motion in limine seeking a determination by the trial court to exclude evidence concerning matters beyond the four corners of the letters of credit and the demands made on the letters of credit. The Bank replied by filing a cross-motion in limine seeking a ruling that it would not be precluded at trial from offering evidence outside the four corners of the letters of credit. The trial court, after extensive briefing by the parties and a hearing, granted the County's motion to limit the admissibility of evidence to the letters of credit, documents and drafts presented thereunder, the demands on the letters of credit, and the Bank's refusals to honor the County's demands for payment.

1. Under § 4–5–112(1)(a), C.R.S. 1973, a bank called upon to honor drafts under a letter of credit may defer until the close of the third banking day following receipt of the documents.

The remaining issues were whether the County's demands conformed to the letters of credit or, if not, whether the Bank had waived nonconforming demands, and whether interest ought to be awarded. The parties agreed on a stipulated set of facts concerning these remaining issues. The Bank did, however, make an offer of proof as to the rejected affirmative defenses. The Bank would have attempted to prove that the subdivisions in question remained raw, undeveloped mountain property for which there was no viable market and that the County had neither constructed, made commitments to construct, nor planned to construct the roads or other improvements described in the subdivision improvements agreements secured by the letters of credit. These allegations were disputed by the County.

The trial court entered judgment against the Bank for the face amounts of the letters of credit plus accrued interest at the statutory rate from the date of the County's demands. Costs were awarded in favor of the County. The Bank's motion for new trial was denied, and the Bank appealed.

The court of appeals affirmed the judgment of the trial court ruling that standby letters of credit are governed by article 5 of the Uniform Commercial Code, section 4–5–101 et seq. C.R.S. 1973, and that an issuer must honor a draft or demand for payment which complies with the terms of the relevant credit regardless of whether the goods or documents conform to the underlying contract. The court of appeals affirmed the trial court's refusal to consider any evidence regarding the County's alleged windfall. The court of appeals also held that any defects in the form of the County's demands were waived by the Bank.

I.

We first address the question whether the trial court properly limited the evidence to be presented at trial to the letters of credit, the demands by the County, and the Bank's replies to the demands. The Bank has continually asserted during each stage of this action that it ought to be permitted to show that the County will receive a windfall if the County is permitted to recover against the letters of credit. The Bank requested an opportunity to prove that the County will utilize the funds it would receive in a manner other than that specified in the road improvements agreements. Fundamentally, the Bank seeks to litigate the question of the completion of the purpose of the underlying performance agreements between Woodmoor and the County. This the Bank cannot do.

An overview of the history and law concerning letters of credit is useful in the consideration of this issue. The letter of credit arose to facilitate international commercial transactions involving the sale of goods. * * * Today the commercial utility of the letter of credit in both international and domestic sale of goods transactions is unquestioned and closely guarded. * * * Harfield, The Increasing Domestic Use of the Letter of Credit, 4 U.C.C.L.J. 251 (1972); Verkuil, Bank Solvency and Guaranty Letters of Credit, 25 Stan.L.Rev. 716 (1973). In recent years, the use of the letter of credit has expanded to include guaranteeing or securing a bank's customer's promised performance to a third party in a variety of situations. * * * This use is referred to as a standby letter of credit. Article five of the Uniform Commercial Code governs both traditional commercial letters of credit and standby letters of credit. * * *

Three contractual relationships exist in a letter of credit transaction. * * * Justice, Letters of Credit: Expectations and Frustrations, 94 Banking L.J. 424 (1977); Verkuil, Bank Solvency and Guaranty Letters of Credit, supra.

Underlying the letter of credit transaction is the contract between the bank's customer and the beneficiary of the letter of credit, which consists of the business agreement between these parties. Then there is the contractual arrangement between the bank and its customer whereby the bank agrees to issue the letter of credit, and the customer agrees to repay the bank for the amounts paid under the letter of credit. See also § 4–5–114(3), C.R.S. 1973. Finally, there is the contractual relationship between the bank and the beneficiary of the letter of credit created by the letter of credit itself. The bank agrees to honor the beneficiary's drafts or demands for payment which conform to the terms of the letter of credit. See generally §§ 4–5–103(1)(a) and 4–5–114(1), C.R.S. 1973; White and Summers, Uniform Commercial Code § 18–6 (2d ed 1980).

It is fundamental that the letter of credit is separate and independent from the underlying business transaction between the bank's customer and the beneficiary of the letter of credit. * * * Arnold & Bransilver, The Standby Letter of Credit—The Controversy Continues, 10 U.C.C.L.J. 272 (1978); * * * "The letter of credit is essentially a contract between the issuer and the beneficiary and is recognized by [article 5 of the Uniform Commercial Code] as independent of the underlying contract between the customer and the beneficiary. * * * In view of this independent nature of the letter of credit engagement the issuer is under a duty to honor the drafts for payment which in fact conform with the terms of the credit without reference to their compliance with the terms of the underlying contract." Section 4–5–114, Official Comment 1, C.R.S. 1973.

The independence of the letter of credit from the underlying contract has been called the key to the commercial vitality of the letter of credit. * * * The bank must honor drafts or demands for payment under the letter of credit when the documents required by the letter of credit appear on their face to comply with the terms of the credit. Section 4–5–114(2), C.R.S. 1973. An exception to the bank's obligation to honor an apparently conforming draft or demand for payment, see Foreign Venture Ltd. Partnership v. Chemical Bank, 59 App.Div.2d 352, 399 N.Y.S.2d 114 (1977), is when a required document is, inter alia, forged or fraudulent, or there is fraud in the transaction. Section 4–5–114(2). The application of this narrow exception is discussed in detail later in this opinion.

As mentioned above, letters of credit have recently come to be used to secure a bank's customer's performance to a third party. When a letter of credit is used to secure a bank's customer's promised performance to a third party, in whatever capacity that might be, the letter of credit is referred to as a "guaranty letter of credit," see East Bank of Colorado Springs v. Dovenmuehle, supra; Verkuil, Bank Solvency and Guaranty Letters of Credit, supra, or a "standby letter of credit," Arnold & Bransilver, The Standby Letter of Credit—The Controversy Continues, supra, 12 CFR § 7.1160 (1980). Standby letters of credit are closely akin to a suretyship or guaranty contract. The bank promises to pay when there is a default on an obligation by the bank's customer. "If for any reason performance is not made, or is made defectively, the bank is liable without regard to the underlying rights of the contracting parties." Verkuil, Bank Solvency and Guaranty Letters of Credit, supra at 723.

While banks cannot, as a general rule, act as a surety or guarantor of another party's agreed performance, see generally Lord, The No-Guaranty Rule and the Standby Letter of Credit Controversy, 96 Banking L.J. 46 (1979), the legality of standby letters of credit has been uniformly recognized. * * *

What distinguishes a standby letter of credit from a suretyship or guaranty contract is that the bank's liability rests upon the letter of credit contract rather than upon the underlying performance contract between the bank customer and the beneficiary of the letter of credit. * * *

The utilization by banks of standby letters of credit is now widespread, although some commentators suggest that bankers may not appreciate the legal obligations imposed by the standby letter of credit. Where the bank issues a standby letter of credit, the bank naturally expects that the credit will not be drawn on in the normal course of events, i.e., if the customer of the bank fulfills its agreed-upon performance, then the credit will not be drawn upon. This expectation of the bank must be compared to the bank's expectation with respect to a traditional letter of credit issued as a means of financing a sale of goods. In the latter situation, the bank expects that the credit will always be drawn upon. * * * It has been suggested that bankers may be lax in considering the credit of a customer with respect to issuing a standby letter of credit to secure the integrity of its customer to complete an agreed-upon performance since it could be easily assumed by the bank that demand for payment would never be made. * * * One solution suggested by many commentators is that the issuing bank treat a standby letter of credit like an unsecured loan. National Banks issuing standby letters of credit are subject to the lending limits of 12 U.S.C. § 84 (1976).

We now turn to a discussion of the present case, and why the Bank cannot introduce evidence beyond that directly relating to its contract with the County. As discussed above, the letters of credit, and the Bank's obligations thereunder, are separate and independent from the underlying subdivision improvements agreements between Woodmoor and the County. The fact that the letters of credit issued by the Bank are standby letters of credit does not alter this general rule. The Bank is bound by its own contracts with the County.

Each of the letters of credit prepared and issued by the Bank in this case sets forth specifically the condition for payment, i.e., that Woodmoor failed to make the improvements in conformance with the respective subdivision improvements agreements. Had the Bank desired additional conditions for payment, such as the actual completion of the road improvements prior to payment under the letters of credit, it could have incorporated such a condition in the letters of credit. * * * To demand payment under the letters of credit, the County was only required to submit a "duly-signed statement by the [Commissioners] that improvements have not been made in compliance with [the] Subdivision Improvements Agreement[s]. * * *"

The Bank cannot litigate the performance of the underlying performance contracts. "[P]erformance of the underlying contract is irrelevant to the Bank's obligations under the letter of credit." West Virginia Housing Development Fund v. Sroka, supra at 1114 (W.D.Pa. 1976). * * * Likewise, the question of whether the beneficiary of the letter of credit has suffered any damage by the failure of the bank's customer to perform as agreed is of no concern. Mid-States Mortgage Corp. v. National Bank of Southfield, 77 Mich.App. 651, 259 N.W.2d 175 (1977). Further, a bank cannot challenge the utilization of funds paid under a letter of credit. * * *

The Bank argues that it is entitled to dishonor the County's drafts under § 4–5–114(2), C.R.S. 1973. This section provides: [quoting]

Under this section, the issuer of a letter of credit may in good faith honor a draft or demand for payment notwithstanding notice from its customer that documents are forged, or fraudulent, or there is fraud in the transaction. The issuer may, however, be enjoined from honoring such drafts or demands for payment. Impliedly, the issuer may also refuse to honor such drafts or demands for payment when it has been notified by its customer of these defects. Section 4–5–114, Official Comment 2, C.R.S. 1973. * * *

In this case, the Bank has not argued, nor can it reasonably assert, that the documents presented by the County are forged or fraudulent. The Bank has not challenged the authenticity of the drafts and demands for payment by the County or the truthfulness of the statements that the requirements of the underlying subdivision improvements agreements have not been fulfilled. The Bank does assert, however, that there has been fraud in the transaction on the basis that the funds the County would receive would be utilized by the County other than to pay for the completion of the road improvements.

Fundamentally, "fraud in the transaction," as referred to in § 4–5–114(2), must stem from conduct by the beneficiary of the letter of credit as against the customer of the bank. See generally White and Summers, Uniform Commercial Code § 18–6 (2d ed. 1980). It must be of such an egregious nature as to vitiate the entire underlying transaction so that the legitimate purposes of the independence of the bank's obligation would no longer be served. * * * "[I]t is generally thought to include an element of intentional misrepresentation in order to profit from another. * * *" West Virginia Housing Development Fund v. Sroka, supra. This fraud is manifested in the documents themselves, and the statements therein, presented under the letter of credit. * * * One court has gone so far as to say that only some defect in these documents would justify a bank's dishonor. O'Grady v. First Union National Bank of North Carolina, 296 N.C. 212, 250 S.E.2d 587 (1978).

In this case, the Bank has not asserted that there is fraud in the transaction between Woodmoor and the County, nor can it reasonably make such an argument. No facts have been pled to establish fraud which vitiated the entire agreement between the County and Woodmoor. No fraud has been asserted by the Bank's offer of proof which would entitle it to dishonor the County's drafts and demands for payment. * * *

Thus, the trial court properly granted the County's motion in limine excluding all evidence beyond the four corners of the letters of credit, the demands thereunder, and the Bank's replies.

* * *

[Some footnotes omitted.]

Notes

1. If the allegations of the bank are correct, the risk against which the letters of credit were issued, namely that there would be a subdivision built, but that the subdividers would not provide the roads, will never arise. If, in such a case, the bank must pay the money and the county can keep the money, the law is "a ass," not so?

2. Had you advised the bank, how would you have drafted the letter to avoid the problem? (One of your editors is advised that the president of the bank typed out the letter on his very own typewriter without assistance of counsel.)

3. If the promise behind the developer's agreement to provide roads had been a conventional surety bond, how would that have changed the legal obligations?

CROMWELL v. COMMERCE & ENERGY BANK

Supreme Court of Louisiana, 1985.
464 So.2d 721.

DIXON, CHIEF JUSTICE. The plaintiffs in these consolidated cases seek reversal of the Court of Appeal decision in which the court found that plaintiffs were not entitled to enjoin the defendant banks from paying on standby letters of credit issued by the banks. We affirm the court of appeal decision insofar as it denies injunctive relief.

FACTS

The plaintiffs in these five consolidated actions consist of the twenty-eight investors who purchased limited partnership interests in Combined Investments, Limited (C.I., Ltd.), a Louisiana limited partnership. C.I., Ltd. was formed by Combined Equities, Incorporated (C.E., Inc.), a company engaged in the syndication and management of investment partnerships. C.E., Inc. was the general partner of C.I., Ltd.

As security for their capital contribution in C.I., Ltd., the limited partners were required to execute letters of credit in favor of C.I., Ltd. The letters of credit were issued by fourteen Louisiana banks. The issuing banks were sued by the plaintiffs in order to prevent the beneficiary from drawing on the letters of credit. The primary basis of plaintiffs' claim was alleged fraudulent activities on the part of C.E., Inc. and C.I., Ltd.

The final beneficiary of the letters of credit was European American Bank (EAB). EAB became the beneficiary under the letters of credit as security for a ten million dollar line of credit established in favor of C.I., Ltd. EAB intervened in these cases in order to assert its right to draw on the letters of credit.

In addition to EAB, several other parties intervened in these cases to assert their interests. C.E., Inc. and C.I., Ltd. intervened in order to refute the plaintiffs' claim that they defrauded the plaintiff-investors. * * *

The formation of C.I., Ltd. began on June 1, 1981, when C.E., Inc. commenced offering partnership units in C.I., Ltd. C.E., Inc. had been in the business of syndicating partnerships since its formation in 1976. C.E., Inc. and its affiliated companies derived their income from fees charged for a variety of managerial and financial services provided to limited partnerships.

Prior to the creation of C.I., Ltd., the C.E., Inc. staff prepared a Private Placement Memorandum (PPM), a two hundred twenty page document which detailed the proposed structure of C.I., Ltd. and listed the terms of the partnership offering. All of the limited partners received a copy of the PPM prior to their investment in C.I., Ltd. The PPM included financial information and historical data concerning the general partner (C.E., Inc.) as well as a series of closing documents which were to be completed by each investor.

The closing documents were comprised of a series of forms to be completed by the investors. One of the purposes of the closing documents of the PPM was to require each investor to appoint an experienced investment advisor ("offeree representative") to review the PPM and advise him concerning the risks of the offering. The investors were each required to provide detailed information regarding their personal finances. Each investor was required to warrant that he was financially able to bear the risks of an investment in C.I., Ltd.

According to the PPM, the partnership's primary objectives were to acquire, transfer and invest in real estate in order to generate cash flow and to obtain long term capital gains. It was also the intention of C.I., Ltd. to secure significant tax advantages for the limited partners. These tax savings were to be obtained by passing through many of C.I., Ltd.'s losses onto the limited partners.

The PPM also indicated that C.I., Ltd. was a "blind pool" offering, since at the time of the offering the partnership did not own any property nor did it intend to acquire any specific property. The risks of such an offering were described in the PPM:

"RISK OF UNSPECIFIED INVESTMENTS

> "The proceeds of this Offering are intended to be invested in Properties which have not yet been selected. There can be no assurance as to if or when the proceeds from the Offering will be fully invested. Pending investment of Limited Partners' capital contributions, the General Partner is not required to invest Partnership funds in any particular manner and during such period investors will not have the opportunity to earn any return on such contributions. Persons who purchase Units will not have an opportunity to evaluate for themselves the specific Properties in which funds of the Partnership will be invested or the terms of any such investments and, accordingly, the Limited Partners must depend solely upon the General Partner with respect to the selection of investments. * * *" PPM, p 27.

Originally the syndication of C.I., Ltd. was intended solely to be accomplished through the sale of up to one hundred limited partnership interests. The purchase price of each unit was $250,000. In order to pay this sum, each limited partner was required to contribute $20,000 in cash, a two year, non-interest bearing demand note for $30,000, and a demand note for $200,000. Each investor was also required to obtain a $200,000 standby letter of credit, securing the $200,000 note.

The highly leveraged terms of the capital contribution allowed the limited partners to obtain significant tax advantages. The federal tax laws allow limited partnerships to pass through losses to their limited partners, based on the amount of the partner's money "at risk." Under the C.I., Ltd. proposal, each partner had $250,000 at risk in spite of the fact that his initial cash investment was only $20,000. During 1981 the partnership passed along a $76,000 tax loss to each investment unit.

Thirty-nine units in C.I., Ltd. were sold and the partnership officially came into existence on September 23, 1981. By the end of November, 1981 all plaintiffs except one had purchased interests; the last purchase was April 13, 1982.

In accordance with the terms of the capital contribution, each plaintiff secured a $200,000 letter of credit from his bank. The letters of credit were all issued in accordance with a form included in the closing package of the PPM. That form provided:

''(LETTERHEAD OF BANK)

ADDRESS

(Date)

Irrevocable Letter of Credit

Combined Investments, Ltd., a
Louisiana Limited Partnership
5551 Corporate Boulevard
Suite 3-A
Baton Rouge, Louisiana

Dear Sirs:

We hereby open our Irrevocable Letter of Credit in your favor for the account of (Name of Investor) (Address of Investor), for a sum or sums not exceeding in the aggregate the sum of Two Hundred Thousand and No/100 ($200,000.00) Dollars, available by your drafts drawn on (Bank), (Address of Bank), at sight to be accompanied by:

An Affidavit signed by an officer of the holder of this Letter of Credit certifying that a default exists under

(i) any loan of Combined Investments, Ltd., a Louisiana Limited Partnership, due such holder, or

(ii) any indebtedness of (Name of Investor) due such holder,

which this Letter of Credit may secure.

Drafts must be drawn and negotiated on or before July 1, 1982, on which date this Letter of Credit expires. This Letter may be drafted against in full without being accompanied by the Affidavit referred to above from June 1, 1982 until July 1, 1982 if this Letter of Credit is not renewed by June 1, 1982 for a period of one year expiring July 1, 1983 in the face amount of $200,000 and in a form acceptable to the Beneficiary, its transferees or assigns.

The right to draw under this Letter of Credit is, by the holder hereof, absolutely irrevocable and unconditional (except as set forth herein) and is transferable and/or assignable in whole or in part.

Each draft must be marked 'Drawn under (Bank), (Address of Bank), Letter of Credit Number _____, Dated _____, 19__, and the amount of each draft so drawn endorsed by the negotiating bank. The final draft drawn under this Letter of Credit must be accompanied by this Letter of Credit. This credit is subject to the Uniform Customs and Practice for Documentary Credits, 1974 Revision, fixed by the International Chamber of Commerce Brochure No. 290.

We hereby agree with Drawers, Endorsers and Bona Fide Holders of Drafts drawn under and in compliance with the Credit that the same shall be duly honored upon presentation to the Drawee Bank as specified above.

Sincerely,

(NAME OF BANK)

By: ______________________

By: ______________________

(NOTE: NEED SIGNATURES OF TWO (2) BANK OFFICERS)'' PPM Closing Documents, Form 3-A.

The limited partners' letters of credit were intended to be used to secure bank financing for C.I., Ltd. The original letter of credit named C.I., Ltd. as beneficiary. In order to secure financing, the letters of credit were to be transferred to lending banks.

After its formation in September, 1981, C.I., Ltd., acting through its general partner, negotiated loans from Mercantile National Bank of Dallas and First National Bank of Lafayette. The Mercantile loan was for 5.4 million dollars and the First National loan was for 2.4 million dollars. In order to secure the loans, the letters of credit were transferred to the banks along with security interests in the demand notes. As further security for the financing, C.E., Inc. and two of its principal officers, Robert Jackson and E. Hardy Swyers, guaranteed payment of the loans.

The proceeds of the Mercantile and First National loans were used primarily to invest in other limited partnerships which were related to C.E., Inc. These affiliated partnerships generally owned real estate interests such as condominiums, hotels and apartments. Some of these investments were in the form of loans to the other limited partnerships.

C.I., Ltd.'s first contact with EAB took place in September, 1981. Representatives of EAB and C.E., Inc. met to discuss the establishment of a line of credit which would replace the Mercantile and First National loans. Through the consolidation of the prior loans with EAB, C.E., Inc. hoped to obtain a lower interest rate on its outstanding debt.

Subsequent meetings and discussions led to EAB's approval of a 10 million dollar line of credit for C.I., Ltd. The loan agreement was signed on March 15, 1982. Prior to the approval of the line of credit, EAB conducted an investigation into the credit worthiness of C.I., Ltd. and lengthy negotiations took place between EAB and C.I., Ltd.

EAB's primary representative throughout the negotiation process was Dennis Devito, the assistant vice president in charge of partnership lending. Devito first learned of C.E., Inc. on September 2, 1981 when he was contacted by Alan Jacobs, a New York attorney who was representing C.E., Inc. As a result of his discussions with Jacobs, Devito requested that C.E., Inc. forward the PPM of C.I., Ltd. to the bank.

On September 16, 1981 a meeting took place between representatives of EAB and C.I., Ltd. at the offices of EAB in New York. Devito, Jerold Frier, EAB's vice president, and Harvey Horowitz, a member of the partnership lending division, represented EAB at the meeting. C.E., Inc. was represented at the meeting by Alan Jacobs, E. Hardy Swyers, vice chairman of the board, and Gil Guidry, bank financing manager. The structure of C.I., Ltd. and the possibility of a 20 million dollar credit facility were discussed at the meeting.

Subsequent to that meeting, Devito prepared a preliminary loan memorandum and went ahead with the loan approval process.

On September 22, 1981 Devito and Alan Churchill, EAB's vice president of real estate advisory services, made a day long trip to C.E., Inc. headquarters in Baton Rouge. The purpose of the meeting was for Devito and Churchill to familiarize themselves with the operation of C.E., Inc. and to meet its officers. Churchill went along on the trip because of his experience with real estate loans. A file memo written by Devito, which was introduced at trial, indicates that Churchill was satisfied with the operation of C.E., Inc.

Subsequent to the initial meetings, C.I., Ltd. sent a variety of financial data and other information concerning C.I., Ltd. and C.E., Inc. to EAB. One of the documents received by EAB was a portfolio of C.E., Inc., dated September, 1981, which gave specific details concerning the management of C.E., Inc. and its investments. Audited financial statements of C.E., Inc. for the fiscal year ending March 31, 1981 were also sent to EAB.

The bank conducted a credit reference check of C.E., Inc. by contacting five banks and three certified public accountants that had done business with C.E., Inc. The banks, except for Capital Bank & Trust Company, Baton Rouge, indicated that their relationship with C.E., Inc. was very satisfactory. Capital Bank indicated that it had increased its line of credit with C.E., Inc. due to cash flow problems. The accountants contacted by EAB recommended C.E., Inc. as a client.

After reviewing the information furnished by C.I., Ltd. and the credit references, an "internal offering memorandum" was prepared by Devito. This memorandum consisted of a loan proposal for a 10 million dollar credit facility to be secured by letters of credit of the limited partners of C.I., Ltd. The memorandum also included an inhouse appraisal of C.I., Ltd. and its general partner. The final paragraph of the memo set forth a recommendation in favor of approval of the C.I., Ltd. loan. This recommendation was primarily based upon the fact that the loan was to be secured by irrevocable letters of credit naming the bank as beneficiary.

The inter-office memo was approved by the bank on October 30, 1981. The bank's approval of the loan on that date was followed by several months of delay before the actual signing of the loan agreement on March 15, 1982. During that interval, EAB and C.I., Ltd. negotiated with regard to the language of the final loan agreement.

On December 10, 1981 EAB sent a proposed loan agreement to C.E., Inc. for review. On December 11, Robert Jackson, the chairman of C.E., Inc. and Glenn Bodin, the senior vice president of C.E., Inc., had dinner with Churchill and Devito to discuss the terms of the loan agreement.

On December 17, 1981 Churchill sent out an internal memo to Devito which stated that: "As of 2:30 today, no commitment of any kind should be made to Combined Equities prior to my review and approval." Churchill circulated the memo after hearing from a confidential source that C.E., Inc. was slow in its payment of a loan. Devito subsequently met with Churchill and on December 18 Churchill released his hold on the commitment to C.I., Ltd.

In response to Churchill's concerns, Devito contacted Capital Bank in Baton Rouge on December 19 to inquire about the credit worthiness of C.E., Inc. Keith Miller, the vice president of Capital Bank, indicated to Devito that the bank's overall relationship with C.E., Inc. was satisfactory but that C.E., Inc. was experiencing some cash flow difficulties. Miller indicated that these problems were the result of the fast growth of C.E., Inc., the delayed closing of real estate syndications and the fact that the cash of C.E., Inc. was not consolidated at a single bank. He also stated that C.E., Inc. was attempting to address these problems.

On January 25, 1982 EAB received a set of financial statements for C.E., Inc. and its subsidiaries. The most recent statements were for the year ending March 31, 1981. Those statements revealed that C.E., Inc. owned assets of $5,904,708 and that it sustained a net loss of $990,913. Devito attributed this loss to the seasonal nature of the real estate syndication business. He also testified that the March 31, 1981 statements of C.E., Inc. were just one set of many financial statements relied on in approving the credit facility.

EAB sent an amended draft of the loan agreement to C.E., Inc. on February 26, 1982. This amended version incorporated several changes which had been requested by C.E., Inc.

The loan agreement was finally signed on March 15, 1982 in New Orleans. Dwayne Broussard, C.E., Inc.'s legal counsel, and Gil Guidry were present at the signing on behalf of C.I., Ltd. Devito signed on behalf of EAB. Immediately prior to the signing of the agreement, four changes to the loan agreement were "penciled" in at the request of the C.E., Inc. representatives. The plaintiffs attach significance to a change made with regard to the guarantees of Robert Jackson and C.E., Inc. Prior to the change, the last sentence of § 2.06 provided: "The bank will only call on the Guarantees after having drawn under the Letters of Credit." The following phrase was added to that sentence at the time of the signing: "and only upon the failure or inability of the issuing bank to make payment under the terms of the Letters of Credit."

Following the consummation of the loan, the limited partners were contacted by C.I., Ltd. and advised to have new letters of credit issued naming EAB as beneficiary. This reissuance was accomplished by having new letters of credit issued in favor of C.I. Ltd. and then transferring those letters of credit to EAB. EAB contacted Mercantile National Bank of Dallas and First National Bank of Lafayette regarding payment of the prior loans. Those banks were instructed to cancel the letters of credit which they held. Upon the receipt of the new letters of credit, EAB paid off the Mercantile and First National loans with the proceeds of the new credit facility.

EAB placed C.I., Ltd. in default in September, 1982. On November 24, EAB drew drafts on the issuing banks for payment under the letters of credit. The plaintiffs sought and obtained a temporary restraining order which enjoined the issuing banks from honoring the drafts by EAB. A hearing was subsequently held after which the trial judge granted a preliminary injunction preventing honor of the drafts. The court held that the plaintiffs were entitled to injunctive relief under R.S. 10:5–114(2) since there was "fraud in the transaction."

The trial court based its holding of fraud on the acts of C.E., Inc. while acting as the general partner of C.I., Ltd. The court found that C.E., Inc. had disregarded the provisions of the PPM in making investments for C.I., Ltd. Also, the court found that C.E., Inc. did not fulfill its representation in the PPM that it would provide up to 5 million dollars in the event of negative cash flow for C.I., Ltd.

The court found that EAB had knowledge of these facts constituting fraud and therefore knew or should have known of the fraud being perpetrated on the investors. Therefore, the court found that EAB made the loan in bad faith. For these reasons, EAB was prohibited from drafting under the letters of credit.

The Court of Appeal reversed, holding that no fraud occurred within the intendment of R.S. 10:5–114(2). Therefore, injunctive relief was denied. The court found that the trial court erroneously concluded that EAB committed a fraud. The court did not decide whether C.E., Inc. had acted fraudulently since under its interpretation of R.S. 10:5–114, such fraud would not have been grounds for an injunction against the issuing banks.

The plaintiffs sought writs from this court to have the trial court judgment reinstated. They claim that the Court of Appeal erroneously overturned the factual findings of the trial court, misconstrued the meaning of "fraud in the transaction" and erroneously accorded EAB rights greater than those of C.I., Ltd.

Issues

In order to determine whether the issuing banks may be enjoined from paying under the letters of credit, the following issues must be decided:

1. What is the meaning of "fraud in the transaction," in R.S. 10:5–114(2), as applied to standby letters of credit which are used to secure bank financing?

2. Whether such fraud occurred in this case, entitling plaintiffs to the injunctive relief provided for in R.S. 10:5–114(2)(b)?

The right to enforce payment of drafts issued under a letter of credit is governed by R.S. 10:5–114, which provides: [quoting]

* * *

Fraud in the Transaction

The primary issue in this case is the interpretation of "fraud in the transaction" in R.S. 10:5–114. Under that provision, the issuing banks must honor EAB's drafts unless the documents presented by EAB were "* * * forged or fraudulent or there is fraud in the transaction." R.S. 10:5–114(2). The plaintiffs do not dispute the validity of the documents submitted by EAB. Therefore, the only issue is whether there was "fraud in the transaction." If such fraud is found to exist, a court is empowered, under R.S. 10:5–114(2)(b), to enjoin the issuing banks from honoring drafts under the credit.

There is more than one "transaction" involved when letters of credit are issued. The first is the contract between the customer and the issuing bank, present in all cases; the conventional case involves a sale and delivery of goods; the standby case involves a contract or performance, or a loan by the beneficiary bank to a borrower, secured by the customer's letter of credit. If the credit secures a loan by the beneficiary bank, that loan is the underlying transaction.

The plaintiffs maintain that "transaction" should be interpreted in its broadest sense. It is their position that by not qualifying "transaction," the drafters intended it to be given by a very general and expansive interpretation. More specifically, they claim that "if a fraud is practiced that would ultimately cause a loss to the customer, injunction will lie against honor regardless of who perpetrated the fraud."

Furthermore, they contend that "transaction" must be understood to include the underlying transaction between the limited partners and C.I., Ltd. Plaintiffs maintain that by not giving transaction a general meaning, lending banks would be permitted to "launder fraud," thereby damaging the integrity of the judicial system.

The intervenors advocate a restrictive interpretation of "transaction." They claim that an injunction may be properly issued only when fraudulent documents are issued, or when the beneficiary commits active fraud against the investors who obtained the letters of credit.

The UCC was adopted in Louisiana in an effort to harmonize the commercial law of Louisiana with that of the other states.[4] We should, therefore, examine the jurisprudence of other states interpreting R.S. 10:5–114(2).[5]

The most frequently cited case on the "fraud in the transaction" exception to UCC § 5–114(2) is Sztejn v. Henry Schroder Banking Corp., 177 Misc. 719, 31 N.Y.S.2d 631 (Sup.Ct.N.Y. 1941). Although Sztejn arose before the drafting of the UCC, most commentators and courts agree that Sztejn was the impetus for the fraud exception.

* * *

In spite of its decision in favor of the plaintiff, the court was careful to leave the independence principle intact:

> "It is well established that a letter of credit is independent of the primary contract of sale between the buyer and the seller. The issuing bank agrees to pay upon presentation of documents, not goods. This rule is necessary to preserve the efficiency of the letter of credit as an instrument for the financing of trade. One of the chief purposes of the letter of credit is to furnish the seller with a ready means of obtaining prompt payment for his merchandise. It would be a most unfortunate interference with business transactions if a bank before honoring drafts drawn upon it was obliged or even allowed to go behind the documents, at the request of the buyer and enter into controversies between the buyer and the seller regarding the quality of the merchandise shipped. If the buyer and the seller intended the bank to do this they could have so provided in the letter of credit itself, and in the absence of such a provision, the court will not demand or even permit the bank to delay paying drafts which are proper in form. * * * Of course, the application of this doctrine presupposes that the documents accompanying the draft are genuine and conform in terms to the requirements of the letter of credit. * * *" (Citations omitted). 31 N.Y.S.2d at 633–34.

The Sztejn court, in determining whether the customer could stop the issuing bank from honoring the draft, determined that the underlying transaction was fraudulent and that the Chartered Bank (presenting the draft for payment on behalf of Transea) was in no better position than the fraudulent Transea.

Sztejn was a commercial letter of credit case which involved active fraud on the part of the beneficiary. The bank (Chartered) that presented the draft for payment was merely the correspondent for the issuing bank, not a holder in due course, but an agent of the seller-beneficiary charged with fraud. The court refused to allow a seller-beneficiary to profit from its own fraudulent conduct.

The Sztejn holding was applied to standby letters of credit in Shaffer v. Brooklyn Park Garden Apartments, 311 Minn. 452, 250 N.W.2d 172 (1977). In Shaffer, two purchasers of units in a limited partnership had letters of credit issued in favor of the limited partnership as part of their capital contribution.

4. R.S. 10:1–102(2)(c).

5. R.S. 10:5–114 varies in two respects from the uniform version of 5–114. However, the differences are minor and have no bearing on the issues in this case.

In R.S. 10:5–114(1), "for sale or other contract" was omitted as being unnecessary. In R.S. 10:5–114(2), a reference to UCC Articles 7 and 8 was omitted.

The letters of credit provided they could be drawn on only after presentment of a promissory note and a certification by the partnership that the investors had failed "to meet payment of authorized loans which are payable." 250 N.W.2d at 175. The letters of credit were subsequently transferred to Wayzata Bank & Trust Company as security for loans to the partnership.

The partnership experienced financial difficulty and Wayzata Bank & Trust Company attempted to draw on the letters of credit. In compliance with the letter of credit, Wayzata presented notes and certifications by the partnership that the investors had failed "to meet payment of authorized loans which are payable."

The investors sued to enjoin Wayzata from drawing on the letters of credit, claiming that the certifications were false. The court found that an injunction was proper because *plaintiffs sought the injunction on the basis of fraud in the documentation.* The court reasoned that:

> "* * * [W]here injunctive relief is sought, the fraud alleged must be in respect to the documents presented and not as to the underlying transaction. The allegations of fraud made by [the plaintiff-investors] is appropriate for injunctive relief since it concerns the certifications by [the partnership] presented by Wayzata." 250 N.W.2d at 180.

Another standby letter of credit situation was faced in O'Grady v. First Union National Bank, 250 S.E.2d 587 (N.C. 1978). In that case, the attachment of a letter of credit to a note it purported to secure, but which had been substituted for the original note and which omitted the signature of one endorser was interpreted by the court as a case involving "fraudulent documentation" which would give rise to injunctive relief. Plaintiffs before us interpret the case as involving fraud "in the underlying transaction."

* * *

Finally, in Cappaert Enterprises v. Citizens and Southern International Bank of New Orleans, 486 F.Supp. 819 (E.D.La. 1980), plaintiff, Cappaert Enterprises, sued to enjoin a Kuwait bank from collecting under a letter of credit which was issued to secure a loan. The letter of credit was obtained by a joint venture comprised of Cappaert and United Fisheries of Kuwait. A dispute developed between Cappaert and United concerning performance of the joint venture agreement. Cappaert sued to enjoin the Kuwait bank from drawing on the letter of credit, claiming that United had committed a fraud against it.

The district court concluded that Cappaert's claim of "fraud in the transaction" was without merit. The court relied heavily on the principle of independence between the letter of credit and the underlying transaction. According to the court:

> "The accuracy of Cappaert's allegation that United Fisheries acted fraudulently in its role as a joint venturer is immaterial to the resolution of this issue, for impropriety in the underlying agreement is irrelevant to an interpretation of the letter of credit. * * *" 486 F.Supp. at 826.

As illustrated in the foregoing cases the independence principle is a strong influence in the decision of cases throughout the country. Adherence to that basic principle is necessary in order to protect the commercial utility of letters of credit.

Nevertheless, the jurisprudence and literature recognize and illustrate the need to extend the meaning of "fraud in the transaction" at least a step beyond fraudulent documentation. The strongest reason for such an extended interpretation is to deny rewarding fraudulent conduct by letter of credit beneficiaries. One author writes:

> "Notwithstanding dictum to the contrary in some of the cases, *the holding of the court in NMC Enterprises, Inc. v. Columbia Broadcasting System, Inc. that fraud in the underlying transaction is sufficient to justify relief is the better rule.* Since the issuer's obligation on a letter of credit is generally completely independent of the underlying transaction, the customer who obtains a letter of credit assumes the risk that payment may be made when the beneficiary has not properly performed the underlying contract. Moreover, the beneficiary may have required the letter of credit in part to assure that a dispute regarding performance of the underlying contract would not delay payment. By obtaining a letter of credit, however, the customer should not be required to assume the risk of making payment to a beneficiary who has engaged in fraudulent conduct in the underlying transaction. Furthermore, a rule that precludes injunctive relief where the fraud is in the underlying transaction will compensate the beneficiary for wrongful acts in situations where the customer will not have an effective legal remedy for the fraudulent conduct and thus tend to encourage fraud, a policy that should be avoided. As the court said in Dynamics Corp. of America v. Citizens & Southern Nat. Bank, there is as much public interest in discouraging fraud as in encouraging the use of letters of credit.
>
> "*While fraud in the underlying transaction should be sufficient to justify injunctive relief, mere failure to properly perform the underlying contract does not constitute fraud.* * * *" (Emphasis added). Hawkland & Holland, UCC Series § 5–114.09 (Art 5).

In the case before us, the "underlying transaction" is the loan transaction between EAB and C.I., Ltd. If the beneficiary EAB was guilty of fraud with respect to the plaintiffs (investors/customers), it should not be permitted to profit from that fraud.

If the banks want an instrument which will be paid without question upon demand, with no recourse by parties upon whom responsibility lies, other means are available.

Our holding is consistent with the cases cited by the parties as well as those found by our research. In all of the cases where letters of credit have been enjoined, the courts have found that either the documents were defective or the beneficiary was guilty of fraud. For example, in Sztejn, the customer sought to enjoin the payment of a draft, presented by the agent of the fraudulent beneficiary, at a time after the issuing bank had notice of the fraudulent shipment by the beneficiary.

Under the foregoing interpretation of "fraud in the transaction," it must now be decided whether such fraud occurred in this case. In accordance with our interpretation of R.S. 10:5–114(2), our analysis will be limited to the loan transaction and the conduct and knowledge of the beneficiary, EAB.

There is more than one measure of "fraud" in the various jurisdictions in the United States.

Cases and writers have called Sztejn an example of "egregious" fraud, and some have required "egregious" fraud in the transaction before according relief to the customer. (KMW International v. Chase Manhattan Bank, 27 UCC Rep. 203, 606 F.2d 10 (C.A.2 1979); Colorado National Bank of Denver v. Board of County Commissioners of Routt County, supra).

Cases and authorities have distinguished "egregious" fraud from "intentional" fraud, and have advocated "intentional" fraud as the better standard to afford injunctive relief to the customer. Hawkland & Holland UCC Series § 5–114:09 (Art 5).

Civil Code provisions defining fraud and the rights of the fraud victim establish standards for commercial transactions in Louisiana and would seem to require the same results reached in most of the fraud cases involving letters of credit.

> "Fraud is a misrepresentation or a suppression of the truth made with the intention either to obtain an unjust advantage for one party or to cause a loss or inconvenience to the other. Fraud may also result from silence or inaction." C.C. 1953.
>
> "Fraud does not vitiate consent when the party against whom the fraud was directed could have ascertained the truth without difficulty, inconvenience, or special skill.
>
> "The exception does not apply when a relation of confidence has reasonably induced a party to rely on the other's assertions or representations." C.C. 1954.
>
> "Error induced by fraud need not concern the cause of the obligation to vitiate consent, but it must concern a circumstance that has substantially influenced that consent." C.C. 1955.
>
> "Fraud committed by a third person vitiates the consent of a contracting party if the other party knew or should have known of the fraud." C.C. 1956.
>
> "Fraud need only be proved by a preponderance of the evidence and may be established by circumstantial evidence." C.C. 1957.
>
> "The party against whom rescission is granted because of fraud is liable for damages and attorney fees." C.C. 1958.

Plaintiffs maintain that EAB obtained knowledge of fraudulent practices in its investigation of C.E., Inc. and C.I., Ltd. The trial court agreed with plaintiffs and found that the entire letter of credit transaction was permeated with fraud; the court also found that EAB had notice of the fraud. Such findings, if supported by the evidence, would warrant injunctive relief under our interpretation of R.S. 10:5–114.

The trial court relied on several factual findings in reaching its determination that "fraud in the transaction" occurred. The first finding relied on by the trial court was that the principals of C.E., Inc. made oral representations to the plaintiffs that C.I., Ltd. was going to invest directly in real estate. Contrary to these representations, C.I., Ltd. invested primarily in other partnerships. These representations have no relevance to the conduct of EAB since they were not written and it was not shown that EAB knew about them.

Secondly, the trial court found that EAB had knowledge of cash flow problems at C.E., Inc. This finding is supported by the testimony of Devito and the December 17, 1981 memo which placed the loan on hold. In spite of this knowledge, it is undisputed that EAB had received a significant number of positive recommendations concerning C.E., Inc.'s ability to pay its debts. It cannot be said that EAB's knowledge that a cash flow problem had existed constitutes fraud.

According to the trial court, the PPM misrepresented that C.E., Inc. could fund five million dollars of capital to C.I., Ltd. The PPM stated that C.E., Inc. would "* * * fund no more than $5,000,000 of working capital and/or negative cash flow * * *" (PPM, p 24). The plaintiffs argue that the trial court found that EAB knew that C.E., Inc. could not fulfill its funding commitment. They claim that this knowledge constituted fraud.

In addition to the above statement in the PPM regarding a capital commitment, the PPM also specifically described the risk of C.E., Inc. becoming unable to make funds available to C.I., Ltd. This risk is described on page 33 of the PPM as follows:

> "There can be no assurance that the General Partner [C.E., Inc.] shall have funds available to it or shall be able to make funds available to the Partnership [C.I., Ltd.] in either case sufficient in amount to satisfy the obligations of the Partnership."

At best, C.E., Inc.'s funding commitment was equivocal. Therefore, EAB did not obtain knowledge of fraud as a result of its review of the funding provisions in the PPM.

According to the trial court, EAB learned from the first supplement to the PPM that C.I., Ltd. had made investments which did not fall within the primary investment objectives stated in the PPM. The PPM stated that C.I., Ltd. intended to invest "primarily" in "existing Properties, such as apartment buildings and complexes, hotels, motels, office buildings and complexes and similar income producing properties." (PPM, p 18). The PPM qualified the above representation in the following terms:

> "It should be noted that although the Partnership currently intends to invest primarily in real property, the Partnership Agreement does not restrict the Partnership in any way from acquiring or investing in any other type of property or investment." (PPM, p 18).

The supplement to the PPM stated that C.I., Ltd. had made eight investments. The largest investment was the purchase of the Bourbon Orleans Hotel in New Orleans for $12,867,300. The majority of the remaining investments consisted of interests purchased in other partnerships. Contrary to the findings of the trial court, EAB cannot be held to have known that these investments were inconsistent with the representations stated in the PPM. The largest of these investments, the Bourbon Orleans Hotel, fell squarely within the primary investment objectives of the PPM. With regard to the other investments, the PPM clearly stated that no guarantees could be given regarding the types of investments to be made by C.I., Ltd.

The trial court attached significance to the fact that the March, 1981 audit of C.E., Inc. was "qualified" due to the existence of outstanding payables and receivables with its affiliated partnerships. The audit report contained the qualification since the scope of the audit did not extend to the affiliated partnerships. Such a qualification, standing alone, is not evidence of fraud on the part of EAB. Devito testified at trial that most syndicators would not have even provided audited financial statements.

The trial court found that since EAB knew that the proceeds of the EAB loan were to be used to pay off prior partnership loans, EAB had notice of an impropriety. The acknowledged reason for obtaining the EAB financing was to replace the Mercantile and FNB loans with lower interest financing. This purpose was legitimate and it was disclosed to the investors.[7] Therefore, EAB's

7. The investors received letters from C.E., Inc. which stated that:

"In order to obtain substantial savings for Combined Investments, Ltd., the general partner has decided to take advantage of an opportunity to transfer to another bank the loan to which your Letter of Credit is now pledged as collateral. Transfer of this loan (now held by Mercantile National Bank at Dallas) to European American Bank and Trust of New York will enable the partnership to decrease the interest rate on this loan by one and one-half (1½%) percent, and therefore to acquire an annual savings of interest in the approximate amount of $115,692." (Letter to the Anderson and Savoy Partnership).

knowledge of the proposed use of the proceeds was perfectly consistent with the interests of the plaintiff-investors.

* * *

Based on our foregoing analysis of the facts relied on by the trial court, we find that there was no evidence of fraud or knowledge of fraud on the part of EAB. Therefore, the "fraud in the transaction" exception of R.S. 10:5–114(2)(b) is not applicable to this case. The trial court's contrary holding was erroneous. Therefore, the Court of Appeal decision reversing the trial court in this respect must be affirmed.

OTHER DEFENSES

We now address plaintiffs' contention that EAB is subject to all of the defenses which could be asserted against C.I., Ltd., since EAB was a mere assignee of the letters of credit from C.I., Ltd. The trial court rejected this argument and found that EAB was entitled to the protected status accorded by the independence principle. We find that EAB was a beneficiary under the letters of credit in its own right and therefore it was not subject to defenses assertable against prior beneficiaries under different letters of credit.

At the time of the EAB loan, the investors were asked to have new letters of credit issued. The investors knew that the letters of credit were to be used to secure bank financing and that EAB would have the right to draw on the credit in case of default. As the new letters of credit were issued, the issuing banks simultaneously wrote EAB acknowledging that "* * * European American Bank & Trust shall be deemed for all purposes to be the beneficiary of the Letter of Credit."

* * *

[Some footnotes omitted.]

Notes

1. Three cheers for the Louisiana Supreme Court. The customers will ultimately get exactly what they deserve in this case, not so? The moral of the story might be as follows: when a sophisticated investor spends a lot of money to buy a tax deduction, even a hometown court won't bend the law to protect his interests.

2. This case shows a quintessential standby letter of credit. The letter has nothing to do with goods; it serves purely as a guarantee of the investors' promises to pay. With the decline in oil and gas prices and with the failure of a number of banks that had made substantial loans to drillers and others in the oil field (Penn Square in Oklahoma City is the best example) many such letters of credit have been called and many courts have faced the question how to define "fraud in the transaction" in such cases. Invariably in such cases the investors have argued that they (the limited partners) were defrauded by the general partner and that this in turn is enough to upset the letter of credit under UCC 5–114. The Louisiana court rejects that argument and is correct in doing so, not so?

What form of interaction by the beneficiary bank with the underlying partnership would be necessary for a court to find the bank involved in the fraud and thus subject to the defense? For example, in the Penn Square case investors alleged that Penn Square (the beneficiary of the letters from other banks) was itself deeply involved with many of the general partners and had first-hand knowledge that the value of their oil and gas prospects were overstated. Based on such allegations, some courts enjoined payment on those letters.

3. If the court had concluded that there was fraud in the underlying transaction, could EAB have argued successfully under UCC 5–114(2)(a) that it was the

"holder of the draft or demand which has taken the draft or demand under the credit and under circumstances which would make it a holder in due course"? If not, could the transaction have been arranged to give it that protection? It is unclear whether the court is addressing that issue at the end of the opinion, but it seems to be talking more generally about the independence issue.

SECTION 4. RIGHTS AGAINST THE GOODS, THE CUSTOMER, AND OTHERS

At the outset we suggested that the bank should regard a letter of credit as tantamount to a loan to its customer and should realize at minimum that it is extending a line of credit to the customer that may be drawn upon. Recognizing that fact, the bank typically will require the customer to execute a document of the kind set out below. Note that the security agreement gives the bank the right to demand payment before it has to pay the money itself. It gives the bank a security interest in the assets that are subject to the credit and in some cases in other assets. Note that UCC 5–114(3) gives the bank a statutory right of "immediate reimbursement," and to be put "in available funds" no later than the day before maturity. Note that UCC 9–304(5) is specifically designed to give a bank a 21 day perfected security interest in goods or documents that are the subject of a letter of credit transaction.

COMMERCIAL LETTER OF CREDIT APPLICATION AND SECURITY AGREEMENT

(APPLICANT: RETAIN INSIDE COPY FOR YOUR FILES.)

To: NATIONAL BANK OF DETROIT
International Division
Detroit, Michigan 48232

L/C No.

Date

Please issue an irrevocable Letter of Credit as set forth below and forward to Beneficiary or your correspondent by

☐ Airmail ☐ Airmail, with short preliminary cable advice ☐ Full Cable, for delivery to the beneficiary.

For Bank use ONLY unless you designate advising bank	FOR ACCOUNT OF (APPLICANT)
IN FAVOR OF (BENEFICIARY)	AMOUNT
☐ TRANSFERRABLE AND THIRD PARTY SHIPPER ALLOWED	Drafts must be presented for negotiation or presented to drawee on or before (Expiry Date)

Available by drafts at ☐ Sight ☐ _______ Days' After _________ drawn, at your option, on you or your correspondent for ______ ______ % of the Invoice value.

When accompanied by the following documents as checked:

☐ COMMERCIAL INVOICE in _______ copies covering: *(Specify Commodity, omitting details as to Grade, Quality, and the like)*

Terms ☐C & F ☐CIF ☐FOB } Port/Country_________________ ☐Other_________________ *(Please specify)*

☐ SPECIAL U. S. CUSTOMS INVOICE

☐ CERTIFICATE OF ORIGIN

☐ PACKING LIST

☐ INSURANCE POLICY OR CERTIFICATE covering: *(State risks required)* _________________

☐ Insurance effected by ourselves. We agree to keep insured until transaction completed.

☐ SHIPPING DOCUMENTS (Full set required if more than one original has been issued)

☐ On Board Ocean Bills of Lading consigned to the order of National Bank of Detroit

☐ Original signed Air Waybill
☐ Original signed Truck Blading
☐ Other: _________________ } CONSIGNED TO: _________________

"Notify" Party:

Shipment From: To:	Latest Shipping Date	Partial Shipments	☐ Permitted	☐ Prohibited
		Transshipments	☐ Permitted	☐ Prohibited
		Freight	☐ Collect	☐ Prepaid

☐ OTHER DOCUMENTS: _________________

☐ SPECIAL INSTRUCTIONS

☒ You may instruct negotiating bank to forward all documents in a single airmailing.

☐ All banking charges outside of the U.S. are for the beneficiaries account.

☐ Other _________________

ALL DOCUMENTS MUST BE PRESENTED TO NEGOTIATING OR PAYING BANK WITHIN ______ DAYS AFTER THE DATE OF ISSUANCE OF SHIPPING DOCUMENTS BUT WITHIN VALIDITY OF LETTER OF CREDIT.

Any questions concerning this application should be referred to:

____

Phone: (____) _________________

ALL PAYMENTS HEREUNDER TO BE CHARGED TO OUR NBD ACCOUNT NO. _________________

NBD 7329 9/80

This Application is made pursuant to Letter of Credit Security Agreement Terms and Conditions which appear as part of this form and apply to this Application and the credit issued pursuant hereto, receipt of which Terms and Conditions is hereby acknowledged.

____
Applicant Signature/Title

[E1226]

COMMERCIAL LETTER OF CREDIT—REIMBUR.S.EMENT AND SECURITY AGREEMENT TERMS AND CONDITIONS

To: National Bank of Detroit
International Division
Detroit, Michigan 48232

1. OBLIGATION OF BANK TO ISSUE CREDITS

Except for a contrary provision in the application for Letter of Credit ("Credit"), the terms and conditions herein set forth shall apply to issuance of the Credit, provided, until issuance of said Credit, you shall be under no obligation to issue the same.

2. OBLIGATION TO PAY

(a) DRAFTS OR ACCEPTANCES

As to drafts or acceptances drawn or purporting to be drawn under the Credit, we agree: (i) in the case of each sight draft, to reimburse you at your office, on demand, the amount paid on such drafts, or, if so demanded by you, to pay to you at your office in advance the amount required to pay such draft; and (ii) in case of each acceptance, to pay to you, at your office, the amount thereof, on demand, but in no event later than maturity, or, in case the acceptance is not payable at your office, then in time to reach the place of payment at maturity. As to drafts or acceptances which are payable in other than U.S. Currency to pay or reimburse you, on demand, in U.S. Currency the equivalent of the amount paid, or estimated by you to be paid, at your current rate of exchange as of the date of payment or at the date of transmission by you for cable transfers to the place of payment where and in the currency in which draft or acceptance is payable, or if there is no such rate at said time, then at such rate as you may fix.

(b) As to documents presented for payment at sight pursuant to the credit, without drafts, we agree our obligation thereunder shall be the same as though sight drafts had been presented or accompanied such documents.

(c) COMMISSIONS, CHARGES, EXPENSES, FEES AND INTEREST

We agree to pay you on demand such commission based on the amount of the credit as is your then current scheduled charges for the particular credit and all charges and expenses paid or incurred by you including, without limitation, FDIC Assessments and the cost of maintenance of required reserves, if any (including expenses of collection or of exercise of your rights hereunder as to security or otherwise and legal fees) and interest on the amount of any payment made by you under the credit and not reimbursed by us as herein provided (plus interest on commissions, charges and expenses not so reimbursed) at the rate of 3% per annum more than the prime rate announced by you as the prime rate for your commercial loans then in effect (which prime rate may not necessarily be the lowest rate charged by you to any of your customers), but not an amount greater than is allowable under the laws of the State of Michigan.

(d) ADVICE FROM CORRESPONDENTS

Telegraphic or other notice from your correspondent or agents of payment, acceptance, or other action under the Credit shall be presumptive evidence of our liability hereunder to reimburse you.

3. ADMINISTRATION OF CREDIT

(a) "UNIFORM CUSTOMS AND PRACTICES FOR DOCUMENTARY CREDITS"

The "Uniform Customs and Practice for Documentary Credits, 1983 revision, ICC Publication N° 400" of the International Chamber of Commerce (copy of which is available from you at our request) shall govern the rights and liabilities of you and us hereunder to the same effect as if stated word for word herein, and the Credit issued hereunder shall be subject to, and be governed by, the provisions of said uniform customs and practices unless the context of this agreement shall be contrary thereto, or in addition thereto, in which event any contrary or additional obligation or liability of us hereunder shall be as stated herein and your rights, obligation or liability as stated herein shall each govern notwithstanding the provisions of said uniform customs and practices which shall be thereby deemed to be superseded and not applicable to the extent of such contrary or additional provisions of this agreement, but not otherwise.

(b) REGULATIONS AND FOREIGN LAW * * *

(c) RELEASE OF PROPERTY OR DOCUMENTS

If you deliver to us, or upon our order, any of the property, documents or instruments relative to the Credit, or held by you as security hereunder, prior to payment in full of all our obligations secured hereby, we will deliver to you trust receipts thereof, or other security agreements and statements of trust receipt financing, or other financing statements, complying with applicable law and in such form as you may request, and pay all necessary filing fees, it being understood that any such delivery is made in reliance upon this Agreement and that your rights specified herein shall be an addition to your rights under any such applicable law, trust receipt or security agreement. Upon any transfer, sale, delivery or surrender or endorsement of any document or instrument at any time held by you, or for your account by any of your correspondents, relative to the Credit, on trust receipt or otherwise, we will indemnify and hold you and any such correspondents harmless from and against each and every claim, demand, action or suit asserted by reason thereof.

(d) STEAMSHIP GUARANTY—AIR RELEASE * * *

(e) LICENSES—INSURANCE * * *

(f) RESPONSIBILITIES OF YOU AND AGENTS

The users of the Credit shall be deemed our agents and we assume all risks of their acts and omissions. Neither you nor your correspondents shall be responsible: for the description, quantity, weight, quality, condition, packing, delivery, value or existence of the property purporting to be represented by documents; for any difference in character, quality, quantity, condition or value of the property from that expressed in documents; for the form, sufficiency, accuracy, genuineness, falsification or legal effect of any documents, even if such documents should in fact prove to be in any or all respects invalid, insufficient, fraudulent or forged; for the time, place, manner or order in which shipment is made; for partial or incomplete shipment, or failure or omissions to ship any or all of the property referred to in the Credit; for the character, adequacy, validity, or genuineness of any insurance; for the solvency or responsibility of any insurer, or for any other risk connected with insurance; for any deviation from instructions, delay, default or fraud by the shipper or anyone else in connection with the property or the shipping thereof; for the solvency, responsibility or relationship to the property of any party issuing any documents in connection with the property; for delay in arrival or failure to arrive of either the property or any of the documents relating thereto; for delay in giving or failure to give notice of arrival or any other notice; for any breach of contract between the shippers or vendors and ourselves or any of us; for failure of any draft to bear any reference or adequate reference to the Credit, or failure of documents to accompany any draft at negotiation, or failure of any person to note the amount of any draft on the reverse of the Credit, or to surrender or take up the Credit or to send forward documents apart from drafts as required by the terms of the Credit, each of which provisions, if contained in the Credit itself, it is agreed may be waived by you; or for errors, omissions, interruptions or delays in transmission or delivery of any messages, by mail, cable, telegraph, wireless, or otherwise, whether or not they be in cipher; nor shall you be responsible for any errors, neglect, or default of any of your correspondents; and none of the above shall affect, impair, or prevent the vesting of any of your rights or powers hereunder. In furtherance and extension, and not in limitation of, the specific provisions hereinbefore set forth, we agree that any action taken by you or by any correspondent of yours under or in connection with the Credit or the relative drafts, documents or property, if taken in good faith, shall be binding on us and shall not put you or your correspondents under any resulting liability to us; and we make like agreement as to any inaction or omission, unless in breach of good faith. We agree that any objection to action taken by you or any correspondent shall be deemed ratified by us unless within 10 days after receipt of such documents or acquisitions of knowledge thereof objection and notice to you is made by us.

(g) COPIES OF DOCUMENTS * * *

(h) DRAFT LESS THAN CREDIT AMOUNT * * *

4. SECURITY INTERESTS

As security for the prompt payment of all our obligations and liabilities hereunder, and in addition to any other security given to you by separate agreement, you are hereby granted a continuing security interest in and, the right to possession and disposition of, all property shipped, stored or dealt with in connection with the Credit, or the drafts drawn thereunder, and to all drafts, documents or instruments or contracts (including shipping documents or warehouse receipts or policies or certificates of insurance) or inventory or accounts or chattel paper or contract rights or general intangibles, arising from or in connection with this Credit, regardless of whether such property or documents or instruments, or other security herein described, are in your actual or constructive possession, or in transit to you, your agents, or correspondents, and the proceeds thereof, and we hereby further grant you a right of set-off upon all deposits and credits with you until our obligations or liabilities to you have been paid and discharged. We agree that this Agreement may be filed as a financing statement or that we will execute such financing statements or other documents or writings as shall be necessary, in your judgment, to perfect or maintain your security interest, as aforesaid, and to pay all costs of filing. We also agree you may execute on our behalf such financing statement and we do irrevocably appoint you as our attorney in fact for such purpose. You shall have all rights and remedies of a secured party under the Uniform Commercial Code of Michigan and you shall give us five (5) days prior written notice to the time and place of any sale upon exercise of your right to sale, public or private, before or after maturity, unless such security is perishable or threatens to decline speedily in value or is of a type customarily sold on a recognized market. You may discount, settle, compromise or extend any obligation, constituting such security, and sue thereon in your name. You shall not be liable for failure to collect or demand payment of, or protest or give notice of, or nonpayment of, any obligations, included in such security or part thereof, or for any delay, nor shall you be under any obligation to take any action in respect of such security, including any obligation to file, record or maintain or establish the validity, priority, or enforceability of your rights in or to the security. Any property or documents representing security hereunder may be held by you in your name or your nominee's name, all without notice and whether a Default exists, or not. Proceeds of sale or transfer of the security shall be applied, in order, to expenses of retaking, holding, preparing for sale, and the reasonable attorney fees and legal expenses incurred or paid by you, and then, to our obligation hereunder until paid in full.

5. DEFAULT

We shall be in Default under this agreement upon occurrence of any one of the following:

(a) Failure to perform or observe any of the terms and conditions hereof; or

(b) Failure to pay, when due, whether upon your demand or otherwise, any amounts due hereunder; or

(c) Any warranty, representation or statement made to or furnished you is untrue in any material respect; or

(d) The loss, theft, destruction, sale or encumbrance of any part or all of the security for this agreement; or

(e) The death, incapacity, insolvency, dissolution, termination of existence, suspension of business or if a receiver is appointed for any part of our property, or if we make an assignment for the benefit of creditors, or upon the commencement of bankruptcy or insolvency proceedings by or against us, or upon the issuance or service of any levy, lien, writ of attachment or garnishment or execution or similar process against us, or any of our property; or

(f) Failure to pay, when due, any tax; or

(g) If, in your sole opinion, our financial responsibility is impaired; or

(h) Any event occurs which results or could result in the acceleration of the maturity of any of our indebtedness to you or to others under any note, agreement or undertaking, in which event you shall have the right to take possession of the security given herein, set-off against same, or the rights of a secured creditor, with or without process of law, and foreclose, sell or otherwise liquidate the security both as herein provided and as provided in the Uniform Commercial Code of the State of Michigan.

6. MODIFICATION OF CREDIT

All extensions, including extensions of maturity or time for presentation of drafts, acceptances or documents, or renewals of the credit or increase or other modification of the terms hereof, or a temporary advance or acceptance or loan in connection with the credit, with or without further documentation or notice or agreement, shall continue to be governed by this agreement.

7. WAIVER

No delay on your part in the exercise of any of your rights or remedies shall operate as a waiver, nor shall any single or partial waiver, or any right or remedy preclude any other further exercise thereof, or the exercise of any other right or remedy, and no waiver or indulgence by you of any default shall be effective unless in writing and signed by you, nor shall a waiver on any one occasion be construed as a bar, or waiver of, any such right on any future occasion.

8. GOVERNING LAW * * *

9. BINDING EFFECT * * *

10. CONSTRUCTION * * *

11. PARTICIPANT * * *

12. DAMAGES

Your liability, if any, for your negligence, acts of omission or otherwise shall be limited to direct actual damages, but without liability for general, punitive or special damages or other consequential damages resulting therefrom.

Revised 1/8/86 (Commercial)

Problem 29–7

Answer the following questions with respect to the Reimbursement and Security Agreement set out above.

1. Assume that Bank knew that drafts for $500,000 would be presented under the letter on Tuesday. Would it have a right to demand payment by the customer of $500,000 on Monday? If the customer refused to pay, what rights would the Bank have under the Reimbursement and Security Agreement?

2. Assume that Bank made payment and now seeks reimbursement under the $500,000 letter of credit and that customer argues that the invoices were not in proper form because the description was not exactly the same as the description on the letter of credit. How will the Agreement affect that dispute between the Bank and its customer? (See (3)(f).)

3. If the customer fails to pay, the Bank has possession of the invoices and bills of lading. Does it have a perfected security interest? If it cannot liquidate the security within a short period of time, how can it maintain perfection of that security interest if the customer refuses to sign a financing statement? (See (4).)

4. What if the Bank extended the time for the beneficiary to present drafts under the letter by one day and the customer then complained that the Bank had violated their agreement? Does the agreement give the Bank the right to issue such waivers and extensions on behalf of customer?

To what extent can the Bank be subrogated to, and otherwise enjoy, rights of Beneficiary? The case that follows deals with that question.

IN RE ECONOMIC ENTERPRISES, INC.

United States Bankruptcy Court, District Connecticut, 1984.
44 B.R. 230.

ALAN H.W. SHIFF, BANKRUPTCY JUDGE. Merchants Bank & Trust Co. (MBT) brings this motion in two counts. First, for relief from the automatic stay under Code § 362(a) in order to commence foreclosure proceedings against property of Galaxy Associates (Galaxy), a debtor under Chapter 11, and second, to participate "pari passu" with the first mortgagee, Citytrust Company (Citytrust). The parties have agreed that this proceeding should be limited to second count. Accordingly, this Memorandum and Order will be confined to the so-called pari passu issue as it relates to the two above captioned Chapter 11 cases.

BACKGROUND

Economic Enterprises, Inc. (Economic), a land developer, now a Chapter 11 debtor and former owner of the Galaxy property, requested that Citytrust finance the construction of condominium units on premises at Fairview Avenue, in Norwalk, Connecticut. Citytrust conditioned approval of the construction mortgage loan on several terms, including Economic's acquisition of an irrevocable letter of credit on terms satisfactory to Citytrust.

On or about December 23, 1981, MBT issued an irrevocable letter of credit to Economic as "customer" and Citytrust as "beneficiary." [1] On the same day, Economic executed a promissory note and construction mortgage deed in favor of Citytrust.

Subsequently, the condition for payment of the letter of credit, i.e. default by Economic on the note to Citytrust, occurred and Citytrust demanded payment from MBT. It is undisputed that MBT paid the full value of the letter of credit to Citytrust.

MBT now contends that because it paid the full value of the letter of credit, it should be subrogated to the first mortgage rights of Citytrust to the extent of the $400,000.00 it paid to Citytrust.[2]

DISCUSSION

The law of the State of Connecticut, which adopts Article 5 of the Uniform Commercial Code, is clear that an issuer of a letter of credit may not look to the underlying contract between its customer and the beneficiary of the letter of credit in connection with its duty to honor the letter of credit. New York Life Insurance Co. v. Hartford National Bank & Trust Co., 173 Conn. 492 (1977); see Conn.Gen.Stat.Ann. §§ 421–5–109, 42a–5–114, and Official Comments thereto.

MBT argues that the prohibition against utilizing the underlying contract as a defense to payment does not prevent a court of equity from allowing an issuer to be subrogated to the rights of a beneficiary after payment to a beneficiary. The only authority MBT presents in support of that argument is an article written by a member of the Oregon bar, which cites no judicial authority for that proposition. Moreover, the author comments upon the precautions an issuer

1. See Conn.Gen.Stat.Ann. § 42a–5–103 for definitions.

2. MBT used the term "pari passu." While pari passu contemplates that creditors share in assets on an equal basis, MBT specifically requests that it be entitled to share ratably in the first mortgage to the extent of $400,000.

might take at the time a letter of credit is issued if the issuer intends to assert a right of subrogation.

> "Insofar as issuers do not want to rely on the subrogation argument, however, they might want to consider altering the documents required of the beneficiary of a standby letter of credit to include an explicit assignment of the beneficiary's security interest in the customer's assets[, a]lthough courts would not be absolutely bound to recognize this assignment."

The beneficiary here, Citytrust, did not agree to an assignment of part of its first mortgage. Indeed it insisted upon an irrevocable letter of credit, not a mere guaranty, as a condition to the granting of a construction mortgage loan.

MBT further contends, by way of analogy, that the Official Comment to UCC § 5–109 supports its argument. That comment provides in pertinent part:

> "The customer will normally have direct recourse against the beneficiary if performance fails, whereas the issuer will have such recourse only by assignment of or in a proper case subrogation to the rights of the customer."

This court does not agree with the logic of MBT's analogy. Simply because MBT might "in a proper case" be subrogated to the rights of Economic (customer), it does not follow that it should be subrogated to the rights of Citytrust (beneficiary). An issuer may not invade the underlying contract after payment on a letter of credit when the customer has no cause of action against the beneficiary. To allow an issuer an equitable right of subrogation under these circumstances would violate the spirit and intent of the law developing under Article 5 which, as noted, prohibits an issuer from interfering with the underlying contract unless explicit language in the letter of credit so provides.

In Data General Corp. v. Citizens National Bank, 502 F.Supp. 776, 788 (D.Conn. 1980), the court explained:

> "[A]n issuing bank's duty to a beneficiary is unrelated to the relationship between the bank and its customer. If a bank issues a letter of credit without first securing funds from its customer, * * * the beneficiary should not be prejudiced by the bank's deliberate inaction or inadvertence."

* * *

[T]he equities in this case favor the legal result. While Citytrust has the sole security of a first mortgage on the property now owned by Galaxy, MBT has security which includes the personal guaranty of three persons and mortgages on three unrelated properties as well as a second mortgage on the Galaxy property.

ORDER

For the foregoing reasons, Merchants Bank & Trust Company is not entitled to be subrogated to the rights of Citytrust or to otherwise interfere with Citytrust's rights under its first mortgage on the Galaxy property.

It is so ordered.

[Some footnotes omitted.]

Notes

1. What policy reasons do you see for or against the court's outcome in this case?

2. If you represented the issuing bank and sought to avoid this problem, how could you do it?

3. If creditor's obligation had been secured by a conventional guarantee instead of a letter of credit, presumably the guarantor would have been subrogated to the

creditor's claim against the debtor. Can you justify the distinction between that case and the case involving the letter of credit?

How in general can the bank protect itself from the kind of exposure it faced in the *Economic Enterprises* case and in the *Routt County* case when the bank is issuing a classic standby letter and when by hypothesis there will be little or no security arising out of the underlying transaction if it is called upon to pay?

THE UNIFORM CUSTOMS AND PRACTICES FOR DOCUMENTARY CREDITS

As an instrument for conducting business, often on an international level, documentary credits had to have standard definitions and terminology to be fully effective. Principles had to be formulated which were to be applicable to international law and set up in the form of brief concise rules for common usage and practice. These would have to suit all users without causing hindrance or restraint.

The ICC carried out a number of projects in this connection as part of its general activities. Based on a brochure published in 1924 by Union syndicale des banques francaises and reversing rules formulated at ICC Congresses in 1933 and 1951, the results appeared in 1962 as "Brochure No. 222".

Further work, done by the ICC Commission on Banking Technique and Practice, under the chairmanship of Mr. B.S. Wheble, led to a revised version in 1974. This became "Publication No. 290" under the title "Uniform Customs and Practice for Documentary Credits" to which banks in some 156 countries have already adhered.

The latest up-dating is the 1983 Revision (Publication No. 400). It became effective from 1st October, 1984.

It has received the following "blessing" of UNCITRAL.

The United Nations Commission on International Trade Law

Expressing its appreciation to the International Chamber of Commerce for having transmitted to it the revised text of "Uniform Customs and Practice for Documentary Credits", which was approved by the Commission on Banking Technique and Practice of the ICC and adopted by the Council of the ICC on 21 June 1983;

Congratulating the ICC on having made a further contribution to the facilitation of international trade by bringing up to date its rules on documentary credit practice to allow for developments in transport technology and changes in commercial practices;

Having regard to the fact that, in revising the 1974 text of "Uniform Customs and Practice for Documentary Credits", the ICC has taken into account the observations made by Governments and banking and trade institutions of countries not represented within it and transmitted to it through the Commission;

Noting that "Uniform Customs and Practice for Documentary Credits" constitutes a valuable contribution to the facilitation of international trade;

Commends the use of the 1983 revision, as from 1 October 1984, in transactions involving the establishment of a documentary credit.

A. General Provisions and Definitions

Article 1

These articles apply to all documentary credits, including, to the extent to which they may be applicable, standby letters of credit, and are binding on all parties thereto unless otherwise expressly agreed. They shall be incorporated into each documentary credit by wording in the credit indicating that such credit is issued subject to Uniform Customs and Practice for Documentary Credits, 1983 revision, ICC Publication No. 400.

Article 2

For the purposes of these articles, the expressions "documentary credit(s)" and "standby letter(s) of credit" used herein (hereinafter referred to as "credit(s)"), mean any arrangement, however named or described, whereby a bank (the issuing bank), acting at the request and on the instructions of a customer (the applicant for the credit),

i is to make a payment to or to the order of a third party (the beneficiary), or is to pay or accept bills of exchange (drafts) drawn by the beneficiary, or

ii authorizes another bank to effect such payment, or to pay, accept or negotiate such bills of exchange (drafts), against stipulated documents, provided that the terms and conditions of the credit are complied with.

Article 3

Credits, by their nature, are separate transactions from the sales or other contract(s) on which they may be based and banks are in no way concerned with or bound by such contract(s), even if any reference whatsoever to such contract(s) is included in the credit.

Article 4

In credit operations all parties concerned deal in documents, and not in goods, services and/or other performances to which the documents may relate.

Article 5

Instructions for the issuance of credits, the credits themselves, instructions for any amendments thereto and the amendments themselves must be complete and precise.

In order to guard against confusion and misunderstanding, banks should discourage any attempt to include excessive detail in the credit or in any amendment thereto.

Article 6

A beneficiary can in no case avail himself of the contractual relationships existing between the banks or between the applicant for the credit and the issuing bank.

B. Form and Notification of Credits

Article 7

a. Credits may be either

i revocable, or

ii irrevocable.

b. All credits, therefore, should clearly indicate whether they are revocable or irrevocable.

c. In the absence of such indication the credit shall be deemed to be revocable.

ARTICLE 8

A credit may be advised to a beneficiary through another bank (the advising bank) without engagement on the part of the advising bank, but that bank shall take reasonable care to check the apparent authenticity of the credit which it advises.

ARTICLE 9

a. A revocable credit may be amended or cancelled by the issuing bank at any moment and without prior notice to the beneficiary.

b. However, the issuing bank is bound to:

i reimburse a branch or bank with which a revocable credit has been made available for sight payment, acceptance or negotiation, for any payment, acceptance or negotiation made by such branch or bank prior to receipt by it of notice of amendment or cancellation, against documents which appear on their face to be in accordance with the terms and conditions of the credit.

ii reimburse a branch or bank with which a revocable credit has been made available for deferred payment, if such branch or bank has, prior to receipt by it of notice of amendment or cancellation, taken up documents which appear on their face to be in accordance with the terms and conditions of the credit.

ARTICLE 10

a. An irrevocable credit constitutes a definite undertaking of the issuing bank, provided that the stipulated documents are presented and that the terms and conditions of the credit are complied with:

i if the credit provides for sight payment—to pay, or that payment will be made;

ii if the credit provides for deferred payment—to pay, or that payment will be made, on the date(s) determinable in accordance with the stipulations of the credit;

iii if the credit provides for acceptance—to accept drafts drawn by the beneficiary if the credit stipulates that they are to be drawn on the issuing bank, or to be responsible for their acceptance and payment at maturity if the credit stipulates that they are to be drawn on the applicant for the credit or any other drawee stipulated in the credit;

iv if the credit provides for negotiation—to pay without recourse to drawers and/or bona fide holders, draft(s) drawn by the beneficiary, at sight or at a tenor, on the applicant for the credit or on any other drawee stipulated in the credit other than the issuing bank itself, or to provide for negotiation by another bank and to pay, as above, if such negotiation is not effected.

b. When an issuing bank authorizes or requests another bank to confirm its irrevocable credit and the latter has added its confirmation, such confirmation constitutes a definite undertaking of such bank (the confirming bank), in addition to that of the issuing bank, provided that the stipulated documents are presented and that the terms and conditions of the credit are complied with:

i if the credit provides for sight payment—to pay, or that payment will be made;

ii if the credit provides for deferred payment—to pay, or that payment will be made, on the date(s) determinable in accordance with the stipulations of the credit;

iii if the credit provides for acceptance—to accept drafts drawn by the beneficiary if the credit stipulates that they are to be drawn on the confirming bank, or to be responsible for their acceptance and payment at maturity if the credit stipulates that they are to be drawn on the applicant for the credit or any other drawee stipulated in the credit;

iv if the credit provides for negotiation—to negotiate without recourse to drawers and/or bona fide holders, draft(s) drawn by the beneficiary, at sight or at a tenor, on the issuing bank or on the applicant for the credit or on any other drawee stipulated in the credit other than the confirming bank itself.

c. If a bank is authorized or requested by the issuing bank to add its confirmation to a credit but is not prepared to do so, it must so inform the issuing bank without delay. Unless the issuing bank specifies otherwise in its confirmation authorization or request, the advising bank will advise the credit to the beneficiary without adding its confirmation.

d. Such undertakings can neither be amended nor cancelled without the agreement of the issuing bank, the confirming bank (if any), and the beneficiary. Partial acceptance of amendments contained in one and the same advice of amendment is not effective without the agreement of all the above named parties.

Article 11

a. All credits must clearly indicate whether they are available by sight payment, by deferred payment, by acceptance or by negotiation.

b. All credits must nominate the bank (nominated bank) which is authorized to pay (paying bank), or to accept drafts (accepting bank), or to negotiate (negotiating bank), unless the credit allows negotiation by any bank (negotiating bank).

c. Unless the nominated bank is the issuing bank or the confirming bank, its nomination by the issuing bank does not constitute any undertaking by the nominated bank to pay, to accept, or to negotiate.

d. By nominating a bank other than itself, or by allowing for negotiation by any bank, or by authorizing or requesting a bank to add its confirmation, the issuing bank authorizes such bank to pay, accept or negotiate, as the case may be, against documents which appear on their face to be in accordance with the terms and conditions of the credit, and undertakes to reimburse such bank in accordance with the provisions of these articles.

Article 12

a. When an issuing bank instructs a bank (advising bank) by any teletransmission to advise a credit or an amendment to a credit, and intends the mail confirmation to be the operative credit instrument, or the operative amendment, the teletransmission must state "full details to follow" (or words of similar effect), or that the mail confirmation will be the operative credit instrument or the operative amendment. The issuing bank must forward the operative credit instrument or the operative amendment to such advising bank without delay.

b. The teletransmission will be deemed to be the operative credit instrument or the operative amendment, and no mail confirmation should be sent, unless the teletransmission states "full details to follow" (or words of similar effect), or states that the mail confirmation is to be the operative credit instrument or the operative amendment.

c. A teletransmission intended by the issuing bank to be the operative credit instrument should clearly indicate that the credit is issued subject to Uniform Customs and Practice for Documentary Credits, 1983 revision, ICC Publication No. 400.

d. If a bank uses the services of another bank or banks (the advising bank) to have the credit advised to the beneficiary, it must also use the services of the same bank(s) for advising any amendments.

e. Banks shall be responsible for any consequences arising from their failure to follow the procedures set out in the preceding paragraphs.

Article 13

When a bank is instructed to issue, confirm or advise a credit similar in terms to one previously issued, confirmed or advised (similar credit) and the previous credit has been the subject of amendment(s), it shall be understood that the similar credit will not include any such amendment(s) unless the instructions specify clearly the amendment(s) which is/are to apply to the similar credit. Banks should discourage instructions to issue, confirm or advise a credit in this manner.

Article 14

If incomplete or unclear instructions are received to issue, confirm, advise or amend a credit, the bank requested to act on such instructions may give preliminary notification to the beneficiary for information only and without responsibility. The credit will be issued, confirmed, advised or amended only when the necessary information has been received and if the bank is then prepared to act on the instructions. Banks should provide the necessary information without delay.

C. Liabilities and Responsibilities

Article 15

Banks must examine all documents with reasonable care to ascertain that they appear on their face to be in accordance with the terms and conditions of the credit. Documents which appear on their face to be inconsistent with one another will be considered as not appearing on their face to be in accordance with the terms and conditions of the credit.

Article 16

a. If a bank so authorized effects payment, or incurs a deferred payment undertaking, or accepts, or negotiates against documents which appear on their face to be in accordance with the terms and conditions of a credit, the party giving such authority shall be bound to reimburse the bank which has effected payment, or incurred a deferred payment undertaking, or has accepted, or negotiated, and to take up the documents.

b. If, upon receipt of the documents, the issuing bank considers that they appear on their face not to be in accordance with the terms and conditions of the credit, it must determine, on the basis of the documents alone, whether to take up such documents, or to refuse them and claim that they appear on their face not to be in accordance with the terms and conditions of the credit.

c. The issuing bank shall have a reasonable time in which to examine the documents and to determine as above whether to take up or to refuse the documents.

d. If the issuing bank decides to refuse the documents, it must give notice to that effect without delay by telecommunication or, if that is not possible, by other expeditious means, to the bank from which it received the documents (the remitting bank), or to the beneficiary, if it received the documents directly from him. Such notice must state the discrepancies in respect of which the issuing bank refuses the documents and must also state whether it is holding the documents at the disposal of, or is returning them to, the presentor (remitting bank or the beneficiary, as the case may be). The issuing bank shall then be entitled to claim from the remitting bank refund of any reimbursement which may have been made to that bank.

e. If the issuing bank fails to act in accordance with the provisions of paragraphs (c) and (d) of this article and/or fails to hold the documents at the disposal of, or to return them to, the presentor, the issuing bank shall be precluded from claiming that the documents are not in accordance with the terms and conditions of the credit.

f. If the remitting bank draws the attention of the issuing bank to any discrepancies in the documents or advises the issuing bank that it has paid, incurred a deferred payment undertaking, accepted or negotiated under reserve or against an indemnity in respect of such discrepancies, the issuing bank shall not be thereby relieved from any of its obligations under any provision of this article. Such reserve or indemnity concerns only the relations between the remitting bank and the party towards whom the reserve was made, or from whom, or on whose behalf, the indemnity was obtained.

Article 17

Banks assume no liability or responsibility for the form, sufficiency, accuracy, genuineness, falsification or legal effect of any documents, or for the general and/or particular conditions stipulated in the documents or superimposed thereon; nor do they assume any liability or responsibility for the description, quantity, weight, quality, condition, packing, delivery, value or existence of the goods represented by any documents, or for the good faith or acts and/or omissions, solvency, performance or standing of the consignor, the carriers, or the insurers of the goods, or any other person whomsoever.

Article 18

Banks assume no liability or responsibility for the consequences arising out of delay and/or loss in transit of any messages, letters or documents, or for delay, mutilation or other errors arising in the transmission of any telecommunication. Banks assume no liability or responsibility for errors in translation or interpretation of technical terms, and reserve the right to transmit credit terms without translating them.

Article 19

Banks assume no liability or responsibility for consequences arising out of the interruption of their business by Acts of God, riots, civil commotions, insurrections, wars or any other causes beyond their control, or by any strikes or lockouts. Unless specifically authorized, banks will not, upon resumption of their business, incur a deferred payment undertaking, or effect payment, acceptance or negotiation under credits which expired during such interruption of their business.

Article 20

a. Banks utilising the services of another bank or other banks for the purpose of giving effect to the instructions of the applicant for the credit do so for the account and at the risk of such applicant.

b. Banks assume no liability or responsibility should the instructions they transmit not be carried out, even if they have themselves taken the initiative in the choice of such other bank(s).

c. The applicant for the credit shall be bound by and liable to indemnify the banks against all obligations and responsibilities imposed by foreign laws and usages.

Article 21

a. If an issuing bank intends that the reimbursement to which a paying, accepting or negotiating bank is entitled shall be obtained by such bank claiming on another branch or office of the issuing bank or on a third bank (all hereinafter referred to as the reimbursing bank) it shall provide such reimbursing bank in good time with the proper instructions or authorization to honour such reimbursement claims and without making it a condition that the bank entitled to claim reimbursement must certify compliance with the terms and conditions of the credit to the reimbursing bank.

b. An issuing bank will not be relieved from any of its obligations to provide reimbursement itself if and when reimbursement is not effected by the reimbursing bank.

c. The issuing bank will be responsible to the paying, accepting or negotiating bank for any loss of interest if reimbursement is not provided on first demand made to the reimbursing bank, or as otherwise specified in the credit, or mutually agreed, as the case may be.

D. Documents

Article 22

a. All instructions for the issuance of credits and the credits themselves and, where applicable, all instructions for amendments thereto and the amendments themselves, must state precisely the document(s) against which payment, acceptance or negotiation is to be made.

b. Terms such as "first class", "well known", "qualified", "independent", "official", and the like shall not be used to describe the issuers of any documents to be presented under a credit. If such terms are incorporated in the credit terms, banks will accept the relative documents as presented, provided that they appear on their face to be in accordance with the other terms and conditions of the credit.

c. Unless otherwise stipulated in the credit, banks will accept as originals documents produced or appearing to have been produced:

i by reprographic systems;

ii by, or as the result of, automated or computerized systems;

iii as carbon copies,

if marked as originals, always provided that, where necessary, such documents appear to have been authenticated.

Article 23

When documents other than transport documents, insurance documents and commercial invoices are called for, the credit should stipulate by whom such documents are to be issued and their wording or data content. If the credit does not so stipulate, banks will accept such documents as presented, provided that their data content makes it possible to relate the goods and/or services referred to therein to those referred to in the commercial invoice(s) presented, or to those referred to in the credit if the credit does not stipulate presentation of a commercial invoice.

Article 24

Unless otherwise stipulated in the credit, banks will accept a document bearing a date of issuance prior to that of the credit, subject to such document being presented within the time limits set out in the credit and in these articles.

D.1. Transport Documents (Documents Indicating Loading on Board or Dispatch or Taking in Charge)

Article 25

Unless a credit calling for a transport document stipulates as such document a marine bill of lading (ocean bill of lading or a bill of lading covering carriage by sea), or a post receipt or certificate of posting:

a. banks will, unless otherwise stipulated in the credit, accept a transport document which:

i appears on its face to have been issued by a named carrier, or his agent, and

ii indicates dispatch or taking in charge of the goods, or loading on board, as the case may be, and

iii consists of the full set of originals issued to the consignor if issued in more than one original, and

iv meets all other stipulations of the credit.

b. Subject to the above, and unless otherwise stipulated in the credit, banks will not reject a transport document which:

i bears a title such as "Combined transport bill of lading", "Combined transport document", "Combined transport bill of lading or port-to-port bill of lading", or a title or a combination of titles of similar intent and effect, and/or

ii indicates some or all of the conditions of carriage by reference to a source or document other than the transport document itself (short form/blank back transport document), and/or

iii indicates a place of taking in charge different from the port of loading and/or a place of final destination different from the port of discharge, and/or

iv relates to cargoes such as those in containers or on pallets, and the like, and/or

v contains the indication "intended", or similar qualification, in relation to the vessel or other means of transport, and/or the port of loading and/or the port of discharge.

c. Unless otherwise stipulated in the credit in the case of carriage by sea or by more than one mode of transport but including carriage by sea, banks will reject a transport document which:

i indicates that it is subject to a charter party, and/or

ii indicates that the carrying vessel is propelled by sail only.

d. Unless otherwise stipulated in the credit, banks will reject a transport document issued by a freight forwarder unless it is the FIATA Combined Transport Bill of Lading approved by the International Chamber of Commerce or otherwise indicates that it is issued by a freight forwarder acting as a carrier or agent of a named carrier.

ARTICLE 26

If a credit calling for a transport document stipulates as such document a marine bill of lading:

a. banks will, unless otherwise stipulated in the credit, accept a document which:

i appears on its face to have been issued by a named carrier, or his agent, and

ii indicates that the goods have been loaded on board or shipped on a named vessel, and

iii consists of the full set of originals issued to the consignor if issued in more than one original, and

iv meets all other stipulations of the credit.

b. Subject to the above, and unless otherwise stipulated in the credit, banks will not reject a document which:

i bears a title such as "Combined transport bill of lading", "Combined transport document", "Combined transport bill of lading or port-to-port bill of lading", or a title or a combination of titles of similar intent and effect, and/or

ii indicates some or all of the conditions of carriage by reference to a source or document other than the transport document itself (short form/blank back transport document), and/or

iii indicates a place of taking in charge different from the port of loading, and/or a place of final destination different from the port of discharge, and/or

iv relates to cargoes such as those in containers or on pallets, and the like.

c. Unless otherwise stipulated in the credit, banks will reject a document which:

i indicates that it is subject to a charter party, and/or

ii indicates that the carrying vessel is propelled by sail only, and/or

iii contains the indication "intended", or similar qualification in relation to

• the vessel and/or the port of loading—unless such document bears an on board notation in accordance with article 27(b) and also indicates the actual port of loading, and/or

• the port of discharge—unless the place of final destination indicated on the document is other than the port of discharge, and/or

iv is issued by a freight forwarder, unless it indicates that it is issued by such freight forwarder acting as a carrier, or as the agent of a named carrier.

ARTICLE 27

a. Unless a credit specifically calls for an on board transport document, or unless inconsistent with other stipulation(s) in the credit, or with article 26, banks will accept a transport document which indicates that the goods have been taken in charge or received for shipment.

b. Loading on board or shipment on a vessel may be evidenced either by a transport document bearing wording indicating loading on board a named vessel or shipment on a named vessel, or, in the case of a transport document stating "received for shipment", by means of a notation of loading on board on the transport document signed or initialled and dated by the carrier or his agent, and the date of this notation shall be regarded as the date of loading on board the named vessel or shipment on the named vessel.

ARTICLE 28

a. In the case of carriage by sea or by more than one mode of transport but including carriage by sea, banks will refuse a transport document stating that the goods are or will be loaded on deck, unless specifically authorized in the credit.

b. Banks will not refuse a transport document which contains a provision that the goods may be carried on deck, provided it does not specifically state that they are or will be loaded on deck.

ARTICLE 29

a. For the purpose of this article transhipment means a transfer and reloading during the course of carriage from the port of loading or place of dispatch or taking in charge to the port of discharge or place of destination either from one conveyance or vessel to another conveyance or vessel within the same mode of transport or from one mode of transport to another mode of transport.

b. Unless transhipment is prohibited by the terms of the credit, banks will accept transport documents which indicate that the goods will be transhipped, provided the entire carriage is covered by one and the same transport document.

c. Even if transhipment is prohibited by the terms of the credit, banks will accept transport documents which:

i incorporate printed clauses stating that the carrier has the right to tranship, or

ii state or indicate that transhipment will or may take place, when the credit stipulates a combined transport document, or indicates carriage from a place of taking in charge to a place of final destination by different modes of transport including a carriage by sea, provided that the entire carriage is covered by one and the same transport document, or

iii state or indicate that the goods are in a container(s), trailer(s), "LASH" barge(s), and the like and will be carried from the place of taking in charge to the place of final destination in the same container(s), trailer(s), "LASH" barge(s), and the like under one and the same transport document, or

iv state or indicate the place of receipt and/or of final destination as "C.F.S." (container freight station) or "C.Y." (container yard) at, or associated with, the port of loading and/or the port of destination.

ARTICLE 30

If the credit stipulates dispatch of goods by post and calls for a post receipt or certificate of posting, banks will accept such post receipt or certificate of posting if it appears to have been stamped or otherwise authenticated and dated in the place from which the credit stipulates the goods are to be dispatched.

ARTICLE 31

a. Unless otherwise stipulated in the credit, or inconsistent with any of the documents presented under the credit, banks will accept transport documents stating that freight or transportation charges (hereinafter referred to as "freight") have still to be paid.

b. If a credit stipulates that the transport document has to indicate that freight has been paid or prepaid, banks will accept a transport document on which words clearly indicating payment or prepayment of freight appear by stamp or otherwise, or on which payment of freight is indicated by other means.

c. The words "freight prepayable" or "freight to be prepaid" or words of similar effect, if appearing on transport documents, will not be accepted as constituting evidence of the payment of freight.

d. Banks will accept transport documents bearing reference by stamp or otherwise to costs additional to the freight charges, such as costs of, or disbursements incurred in connection with, loading, unloading or similar operations, unless the conditions of the credit specifically prohibit such reference.

ARTICLE 32

Unless otherwise stipulated in the credit, banks will accept transport documents which bear a clause on the face thereof such as "shippers load and count" or "said by shipper to contain" or words of similar effect.

ARTICLE 33

Unless otherwise stipulated in the credit, banks will accept transport documents indicating as the consignor of the goods a party other than the beneficiary of the credit.

ARTICLE 34

a. A clean transport document is one which bears no superimposed clause or notation which expressly declares a defective condition of the goods and/or the packaging.

b. Banks will refuse transport documents bearing such clauses or notations unless the credit expressly stipulates the clauses or notations which may be accepted.

c. Banks will regard a requirement in a credit for a transport document to bear the clause "clean on board" as complied with if such transport document meets the requirements of this article and of article 27(b).

D2. INSURANCE DOCUMENTS

ARTICLE 35

a. Insurance documents must be as stipulated in the credit, and must be issued and/or signed by insurance companies or underwriters, or their agents.

b. Cover notes issued by brokers will not be accepted, unless specifically authorised by the credit.

ARTICLE 36

Unless otherwise stipulated in the credit, or unless it appears from the insurance document(s) that the cover is effective at the latest from the date of loading on board or dispatch or taking in charge of the goods, banks will refuse insurance documents presented which bear a date later than the date of loading on board or dispatch or taking in charge of the goods as indicated by the transport document(s).

ARTICLE 37

a. Unless otherwise stipulated in the credit, the insurance document must be expressed in the same currency as the credit.

b. Unless otherwise stipulated in the credit, the minimum amount for which the insurance document must indicate the insurance cover to have been effected is the CIF (cost insurance and freight * * * "named port of destination") or CIP (freight/carriage and insurance paid to "named point of destination") value of the goods, as the case may be, plus 10%. However, if banks cannot determine the CIF or CIP value, as the case may be, from the documents on their face, they will accept as such minimum amount the amount for which payment, acceptance or negotiation is requested under the credit, or the amount of the commercial invoice, whichever is the greater.

ARTICLE 38

a. Credits should stipulate the type of insurance required and, if any, the additional risks which are to be covered. Imprecise terms such as "usual risks" or "customary risks" should not be used; if they are used, banks will accept insurance documents as presented, without responsibility for any risks not being covered.

b. Failing specific stipulations in the credit, banks will accept insurance documents as presented, without responsibility for any risks not being covered.

ARTICLE 39

Where a credit stipulates "insurance against all risks", banks will accept an insurance document which contains any "all risks" notation or clause, whether or not bearing the heading "all risks", even if indicating that certain risks are excluded, without responsibility for any risk(s) not being covered.

ARTICLE 40

Banks will accept an insurance document which indicates that the cover is subject to a franchise or an excess (deductible), unless it is specifically stipulated in the credit that the insurance must be issued irrespective of percentage.

D3. COMMERCIAL INVOICE

ARTICLE 41

a. Unless otherwise stipulated in the credit, commercial invoices must be made out in the name of the applicant for the credit.

b. Unless otherwise stipulated in the credit, banks may refuse commercial invoices issued for amounts in excess of the amount permitted by the credit. Nevertheless, if a bank authorised to pay, incur a deferred payment undertaking, accept, or negotiate under a credit accepts such invoices, its decision will be binding upon all parties, provided such bank has not paid, incurred a deferred payment undertaking, accepted or effected negotiation for an amount in excess of that permitted by the credit.

c. The description of the goods in the commercial invoice must correspond with the description in the credit. In all other documents, the goods may be described in general terms not inconsistent with the description of the goods in the credit.

D4. Other Documents

Article 42

If a credit calls for an attestation or certification of weight in the case of transport other than by sea, banks will accept a weight stamp or declaration of weight which appears to have been superimposed on the transport document by the carrier or his agent unless the credit specifically stipulates that the attestation or certification of weight must be by means of a separate document.

E. Miscellaneous Provisions

Quantity and Amount

Article 43

a. The words "about", "circa" or similar expressions used in connection with the amount of the credit or the quantity or the unit price stated in the credit are to be construed as allowing a difference not to exceed 10% more or 10% less than the amount or the quantity or the unit price to which they refer.

b. Unless a credit stipulates that the quantity of the goods specified must not be exceeded or reduced, a tolerance of 5% more or 5% less will be permissible, even if partial shipments are not permitted, always provided that the amount of the drawings does not exceed the amount of the credit. This tolerance does not apply when the credit stipulates the quantity in terms of a stated number of packing units or individual items.

Partial Drawings and/or Shipments

Article 44

a. Partial drawings and/or shipments are allowed, unless the credit stipulates otherwise.

b. Shipments by sea, or by more than one mode of transport but including carriage by sea, made on the same vessel and for the same voyage, will not be regarded as partial shipments, even if the transport documents indicating loading on board bear different dates of issuance and/or indicate different ports of loading on board.

c. Shipments made by post will not be regarded as partial shipments if the post receipts or certificates of posting appear to have been stamped or otherwise authenticated in the place from which the credit stipulates the goods are to be dispatched, and on the same date.

d. Shipments made by modes of transport other than those referred to in paragraphs (b) and (c) of this article will not be regarded as partial shipments, provided the transport documents are issued by one and the same carrier or his agent and indicate the same date of issuance, the same place of dispatch or taking in charge of the goods and the same destination.

Drawings and/or Shipments by Instalments

Article 45

If drawings and/or shipments by instalments within given periods are stipulated in the credit and any instalment is not drawn and/or shipped within the period allowed for that instalment, the credit ceases to be available for that and any subsequent instalments, unless otherwise stipulated in the credit.

Expiry Date and Presentation

Article 46

a. All credits must stipulate an expiry date for presentation of documents for payment, acceptance or negotiation.

b. Except as provided in Article 48(a), documents must be presented on or before such expiry date.

c. If an issuing bank states that the credit is to be available "for one month", "for six months" or the like, but does not specify the date from which the time is to run, the date of issuance of the credit by the issuing bank will be deemed to be the first day from which such time is to run. Banks should discourage indication of the expiry date of the credit in this manner.

Article 47

a. In addition to stipulating an expiry date for presentation of documents, every credit which calls for a transport document(s) should also stipulate a specified period of time after the date of issuance of the transport document(s) during which presentation of documents for payment, acceptance or negotiation must be made. If no such period of time is stipulated, banks will refuse documents presented to them later than 21 days after the date of issuance of the transport document(s). In every case, however, documents must be presented not later than the expiry date of the credit.

b. For the purpose of these articles, the date of issuance of a transport document(s) will be deemed to be:

i in the case of a transport document evidencing dispatch, or taking in charge, or receipt of goods for shipment by a mode of transport other than by air—the date of issuance indicated on the transport document or the date of the reception stamp thereon whichever is the later.

ii in the case of a transport document evidencing carriage by air—the date of issuance indicated on the transport document or, if the credit stipulates that the transport document shall indicate an actual flight date, the actual flight date as indicated on the transport document.

iii in the case of a transport document evidencing loading on board a named vessel—the date of issuance of the transport document or, in the case of an on board notation in accordance with article 27(b), the date of such notation.

iv in cases to which Article 44(b) applies, the date determined as above of the latest transport document issued.

Article 48

a. If the expiry date of the credit and/or the last day of the period of time after the date of issuance of the transport document(s) for presentation of documents stipulated by the credit or applicable by virtue of Article 47 falls on a day on which the bank to which presentation has to be made is closed for reasons other than those referred to in Article 19, the stipulated expiry date and/or the last day of the period of time after the date of issuance of the transport document(s) for presentation of documents, as the case may be, shall be extended to the first following business day on which such bank is open.

b. The latest date for loading on board, or dispatch, or taking in charge shall not be extended by reason of the extension of the expiry date and/or the period of time after the date of issuance of the transport document(s) for presentation of document(s) in accordance with this article. If no such latest date for shipment is stipulated in the credit or amendments thereto, banks will reject transport documents indicating a date of issuance later than the expiry date stipulated in the credit or amendments thereto.

c. The bank to which presentation is made on such first following business day must add to the documents its certificate that the documents were presented within the time limits extended in accordance with Article 48(a) of the Uniform Customs and Practice for Documentary Credits, 1983 revision, ICC Publication No. 400.

ARTICLE 49

Banks are under no obligation to accept presentation of documents outside their banking hours.

LOADING ON BOARD, DISPATCH AND TAKING IN CHARGE (SHIPMENT)

ARTICLE 50

a. Unless otherwise stipulated in the credit, the expression "shipment" used in stipulating an earliest and/or a latest shipment date will be understood to include the expressions "loading on board", "dispatch" and "taking in charge".

b. The date of issuance of the transport document determined in accordance with Article 47(b) will be taken to be the date of shipment.

c. Expressions such as "prompt", "immediately", "as soon as possible", and the like should not be used. If they are used, banks will interpret them as a stipulation that shipment is to be made within thirty days from the date of issuance of the credit by the issuing bank.

d. If the expression "on or about" and similar expressions are used, banks will interpret them as a stipulation that shipment is to be made during the period from five days before to five days after the specified date, both end days included.

DATE TERMS

ARTICLE 51

The words "to", "until", "till", "from", and words of similar import applying to any date term in the credit will be understood to include the date mentioned. The word "after" will be understood to exclude the date mentioned.

ARTICLE 52

The terms "first half", "second half" of a month shall be construed respectively as from the 1st to the 15th, and the 16th to the last day of each month, inclusive.

ARTICLE 53

The terms "beginning", "middle", or "end" of a month shall be construed respectively as from the 1st to the 10th, the 11th to the 20th, and the 21st to the last day of each month, inclusive.

F. TRANSFER

ARTICLE 54

a. A transferable credit is a credit under which the beneficiary has the right to request the bank called upon to effect payment or acceptance or any bank entitled to effect negotiation to make the credit available in whole or in part to one or more other parties (second beneficiaries).

b. A credit can be transferred only if it is expressly designated as "transferable" by the issuing bank. Terms such as "divisible", "fractionnable", "assignable", and "transmissible" add nothing to the meaning of the term "transferable" and shall not be used.

c. The bank requested to effect the transfer (transferring bank), whether it has confirmed the credit or not, shall be under no obligation to effect such transfer except to the extent and in the manner expressly consented to by such bank.

d. Bank charges in respect of transfers are payable by the first beneficiary unless otherwise specified. The transferring bank shall be under no obligation to effect the transfer until such charges are paid.

e. A transferable credit can be transferred once only. Fractions of a transferable credit (not exceeding in the aggregate the amount of the credit) can be transferred separately, provided partial shipments are not prohibited, and the aggregate of such transfers will be considered as constituting only one transfer of the credit. The credit can be transferred only on the terms and conditions specified in the original credit, with the exception of the amount of the credit, of any unit prices stated therein, of the period of validity, of the last date for presentation of documents in accordance with Article 47 and the period for shipment, any or all of which may be reduced or curtailed, or the percentage for which insurance cover must be effected, which may be increased in such a way as to provide the amount of cover stipulated in the original credit, or these articles. Additionally, the name of the first beneficiary can be substituted for that of the applicant for the credit, but if the name of the applicant for the credit is specifically required by the original credit to appear in any document other than the invoice, such requirement must be fulfilled.

f. The first beneficiary has the right to substitute his own invoices (and drafts if the credit stipulates that drafts are to be drawn on the applicant for the credit) in exchange for those of the second beneficiary, for amounts not in excess of the original amount stipulated in the credit and for the original unit prices if stipulated in the credit, and upon such substitution of invoices (and drafts) the first beneficiary can draw under the credit for the difference, if any, between his invoices and the second beneficiary's invoices. When a credit has been transferred and the first beneficiary is to supply his own invoices (and drafts) in exchange for the second beneficiary's invoices (and drafts) but fails to do so on first demand, the paying, accepting or negotiating bank has the right to deliver to the issuing bank the documents received under the credit, including the second beneficiary's invoices (and drafts) without further responsibility to the first beneficiary.

g. Unless otherwise stipulated in the credit, the first beneficiary of a transferable credit may request that the credit be transferred to a second beneficiary in the same country, or in another country. Further, unless otherwise stipulated in the credit, the first beneficiary shall have the right to request that payment or negotiation be effected to the second beneficiary at the place to which the credit has been transferred, up to and including the expiry date of the original credit, and without prejudice to the first beneficiary's right subsequently to substitute his own invoices and drafts (if any) for those of the second beneficiary and to claim any difference due to him.

Assignment of Proceeds

Article 55

The fact that a credit is not stated to be transferable shall not affect the beneficiary's right to assign any proceeds to which he may be, or may become, entitled under such credit, in accordance with the provisions of the applicable law.

*

Index

References are to Pages

References are to Pages

References are to Pages

References are to Pages

†